ASPEN PUBLISHERS

The 2011 Pension Answer Book

by Stephen J. Krass

A standard in its field, *The 2011 Pension Answer Book* discusses in detail the full spectrum of pension topics—from qualification requirements to taxation of distributions, from minimum distribution requirements to 401(k) plans. It covers the most up-to-date and significant legislative, regulatory, and case law developments affecting these plans. As a decision-making tool, combining theory and practice-based guidance, *The 2011 Pension Answer Book* offers insight and clarification on the critical issues affecting pension administration and compliance. In short, *The 2011 Pension Answer Book* is the one reference tool that provides subscribers with the most current and comprehensive answers to the issues pension professionals face daily in their practice.

Highlights of the 2011 Edition

The 2011 Pension Answer Book has been fully updated to reflect the changes made by the Pension Relief Act of 2010 (PRA 2010), the Small Business Jobs Act of 2010 (SBJA 2010), the Revenue Rulings, Revenue Procedures, Notices, Announcements, and Private Letter Rulings issued by IRS, Opinion Letters and Interpretive Bulletins issued by DOL, final and proposed regulations issued by both IRS and DOL, and important case decisions. Discussed in *The 2011 Pension Answer Book* are the following:

- Provisions of PRA 2010:
  - Permits a sponsor of a single-employer plan to reduce a plan's minimum required contribution by electing to use an extended alternative shortfall amortization schedule
  - Provides a special amortization rule for certain net investment losses in the case of a multiemployer plan
- Provisions of SBJA 2010:
  - Eligible retirement plan distributions from 401(k) and 403(b) plans made after September 27, 2010 may be rolled over to a designated Roth account within the plan
  - Governmental Section 457 plans may add designated Roth accounts to their plans for taxable years beginning after 2010

Wolters Kluwer
Law & Business

- IRS relief for sponsors of statutory hybrid plans that must amend the interest crediting rate in those plans
- Court ruling that former plan participants may not claim a breach of fiduciary duty solely on the basis of alleged oral misrepresentations that purported to alter plan terms
- IRS final regulations regarding the effect of a prefunding balance and a funding standard carryover balance and the limits on benefits and benefit accruals affecting single-employer defined benefit plans
- New cases on the anti-cutback rule
- Erroneous IRS ruling concerning required minimum distributions (RMDs)
- Anti-killer statutes and designated beneficiaries
- State court reformation of a trust cannot create a designated beneficiary
- IRS advice on user fees
- IRS guidance with respect to correcting the failure of not implementing the automatic enrollment feature in a 401(k) plan
- In lieu of completing and filing Form 5500, Form 5500SF may be used by certain small plans
- PBGC proposed regulations that would make significant changes to its regulations on reportable events and conform the regulations with the funding rules arising from the Pension Protection Act (PPA)
- Department of Labor (DOL) plans to issue proposed regulations to expand the current regulatory definition of "fiduciary"
- New cases concerning breaches of fiduciary duties
- United States Supreme Court decision regarding attorneys' fees and costs
- DOL proposed regulations to update the procedures governing the filing and processing of applications for exemption from the prohibited-transaction provisions
- IRS compliance questionnaires to 401(k) plan sponsors
- Employee stock ownership plans (ESOPs) and S corporation stock
- Multiemployer plan contribution and withdrawal liability issues
- IRS ruling that a transaction engaged in by an IRA was subject to a conflict of interest and could constitute a prohibited transaction

- Claims of creditors and inherited IRAs

- 60-day rollover period and direct rollovers

- Antenuptial agreements and spousal rights

11/10

For questions concerning this shipment, billing, or other customer service matters, call our Customer Service Department at 1-800-234-1660.

For toll-free ordering, please call 1-800-638-8437.

ASPEN PUBLISHERS

The 2011 Pension Answer Book

Revised by: Stephen J. Krass
Krass, Snow & Schmutter, P.C.
New York City

(Original Edition by Krass and Keschner)

Stephen J. Krass

Wolters Kluwer
Law & Business

AUSTIN   BOSTON   CHICAGO   NEW YORK   THE NETHERLANDS

This publication is designed to provide accurate and authoritative information in regard to the subject matter covered. It is sold with the understanding that the publisher is not engaged in rendering legal, accounting, or other professional services. If legal advice or other professional assistance is required, the services of a competent professional person should be sought.

—From a *Declaration of Principles* jointly adopted by
a Committee of the American Bar Association and
a Committee of Publishers and Associations

Printed in the United States of America

1 2 3 4 5 6 7 8 9 0

ISBN 978-0-7355-9124-0

About Wolters Kluwer Law & Business

Wolters Kluwer Law & Business is a leading provider of research information and workflow solutions in key specialty areas. The strengths of the individual brands of Aspen Publishers, CCH, Kluwer Law International and Loislaw are aligned within Wolters Kluwer Law & Business to provide comprehensive, in-depth solutions and expert-authored content for the legal, professional and education markets.

CCH was founded in 1913 and has served more than four generations of business professionals and their clients. The CCH products in the Wolters Kluwer Law & Business group are highly regarded electronic and print resources for legal, securities, antitrust and trade regulation, government contracting, banking, pension, payroll, employment and labor, and healthcare reimbursement and compliance professionals.

Aspen Publishers is a leading information provider for attorneys, business professionals and law students. Written by preeminent authorities, Aspen products offer analytical and practical information in a range of specialty practice areas from securities law and intellectual property to mergers and acquisitions and pension/benefits. Aspen's trusted legal education resources provide professors and students with high-quality, up-to-date and effective resources for successful instruction and study in all areas of the law.

Kluwer Law International supplies the global business community with comprehensive English-language international legal information. Legal practitioners, corporate counsel and business executives around the world rely on the Kluwer Law International journals, loose-leafs, books and electronic products for authoritative information in many areas of international legal practice.

Loislaw is a premier provider of digitized legal content to small law firm practitioners of various specializations. Loislaw provides attorneys with the ability to quickly and efficiently find the necessary legal information they need, when and where they need it, by facilitating access to primary law as well as state-specific law, records, forms and treatises.

Wolters Kluwer Law & Business, a unit of Wolters Kluwer, is headquartered in New York and Riverwoods, Illinois. Wolters Kluwer is a leading multinational publisher and information services company.

ASPEN PUBLISHERS SUBSCRIPTION NOTICE

This Aspen Publishers product is updated on a periodic basis with supplements to reflect important changes in the subject matter. If you purchased this product directly from Aspen Publishers, we have already recorded your subscription for the update service.

If, however, you purchased this product from a bookstore and wish to receive future updates and revised or related volumes billed separately with a 30-day examination review, please contact our Customer Service Department at 1-800-234-1660, or send your name, company name (if applicable), address, and the title of the product to:

ASPEN PUBLISHERS
7201 McKinney Circle
Frederick, MD 21704

Important Aspen Publishers Contact Information

- To order any Aspen Publishers title, go to *www.aspenpublishers.com* or call 1-800-638-8437.

- To reinstate your manual update service, call 1-800-638-8437.

- To contact Customer Care, e-mail *customer.care@aspenpublishers .com*, call 1-800-234-1660, fax 1-800-901-9075, or mail correspondence to Order Department, Aspen Publishers, PO Box 990, Frederick, MD 21705.

- To review your account history or pay an invoice online, visit *www.aspenpublishers.com/payinvoices*.

To my grandson Ben,
Go Bucks!!

Preface

The Pension Relief Act of 2010 (PRA 2010), enacted on June 25, 2010, provides temporary relief for plans that suffered significant losses in asset value due to the steep market decline in 2008. PRA 2010 permits a sponsor of a single-employer plan to reduce a plan's minimum required contribution by electing to use an extended alternative shortfall amortization schedule. In the case of a multiemployer plan, PRA 2010 provides a special amortization rule for certain net investment losses. As Yogi Berra said: "Déjà vu all over again." Congress enacts legislation to strengthen the funding of defined benefit plans, then the economy sours, and then Congress enacts legislation to soften the strengthened funding requirements. This is not the first time this has happened

Under the Small Business Jobs Act of 2010 (SBJA 2010), enacted on September 27, 2010, eligible retirement plan distributions from 401(k) and 403(b) plans made after September 27, 2010 may be rolled over to a designated Roth account within the plan. Any amount required to be included in gross income for the 2010 taxable year is included in income in equal amounts for the 2011 and 2012 taxable years unless the taxpayer elects otherwise. In addition, governmental Section 457 plans may add designated Roth accounts to their plans for taxable years beginning after 2010.

IRS issued guidance on military service benefits enacted under the Heroes Emergency Assistance and Relief Tax Act (HEART Act).

The Tax Increase Prevention and Reconciliation Act of 2005 (TIPRA) imposes an excise tax on any entity manager of a tax-exempt entity, such as a qualified retirement plan or an IRA, who knowingly approves a prohibited tax shelter transaction. IRS issued final regulations that became effective on July 6, 2010. The final regulations generally follow the proposed regulations but revise the definition of "party to a prohibited tax shelter transaction" and make other conforming modifications.

IRS extended the deadline for amending qualified retirement plans to meet a number of requirements added by the Pension Protection Act (PPA) by one year to the last day of the first plan year that begins on or after January 1, 2010. This extension applies to a number of provisions, including the deadline for amending cash balance and other applicable defined benefit plans to meet certain requirements.

IRS also announced relief for sponsors of statutory hybrid plans that must amend the interest crediting rate in those plans. IRS expects to issue final regulations and proposed regulations relating to statutory hybrid plans. The regulations will include rules interpreting the requirement that such plans do not have an interest crediting rate in excess of a market rate of return. The rules in the regulations specifying permissible market rates of return are not expected to go into effect before the first plan year that begins on or after January 1, 2011.

A court allowed a plan sponsor to reform its cash balance plan to correct a scrivener's error that caused a transition factor to be used twice in determining participants' opening account balances.

One court ruled that former plan participants may not claim a breach of fiduciary duty solely on the basis of alleged oral misrepresentations that purported to alter plan terms, because oral promises cannot vary the terms of an ERISA plan.

A plan amendment that provided accelerated pension benefits to younger participants, but had no impact on the benefits received by certain older participants, was held not to violate the Age Discrimination in Employment Act (ADEA), because benefit variations were caused by differences in pension status and not by differential treatment based upon age.

A plan's recoupment from a participant of overpayments of plan benefits did not violate the anti-alienation rule. An arrangement for a plan's recoupment of benefit overpayments is not considered an assignment or alienation. An arrangement, for this purpose, is not limited to an agreement between the parties or a provision in the plan. In this case, a letter to the participant informing him of the recoupment was an arrangement sufficient to exclude the recoupment from the anti-alienation provision.

IRS issued final regulations regarding (1) the effect of a prefunding balance and a funding standard carryover balance under Internal Revenue Code (Code) Section 430(f) and (2) the limits on benefits and benefit accruals effecting single-employer defined benefit plans under Code Section 436.

In addition to IRS providing automatic approval for a number of changes in funding method and interest rate, if certain conditions are satisfied, automatic approval is also provided for any change in funding method resulting from a change in valuation software.

An employer spun off a company and later reacquired the spun-off company. The employer then classified the employees of the spun-off company as rehired, which meant that the employees' retirement benefits would be calculated without taking into account service for years when the spun-off company was not part of the employer. The court concluded that the employer did not wrongfully interfere with the employees' retirement benefits.

A court concluded that changes made to the asset allocation of a plan's investments, first to a more conservative balance of equities and fixed income investments and then to a greater allocation to equity investments, did not constitute plan amendments for purposes of the anti-cutback rule. However, an amendment to a union welfare plan that conditioned the receipt of retiree health care benefits on forgoing a single-sum distribution option under the union's pension plan violated the anti-cutback rule by constructively amending the pension plan to reduce an accrued benefit.

One court concluded that a plan's ERISA Section 204(h) Notice adequately disclosed the effect that the plan's conversion to a cash balance formula had on employees; however, the plan's failure to explain how early retirement benefits were determined under the original plan did violate the notice requirements.

Where a participant in a 401(k) plan rolled over a distribution of his plan benefits to an IRA, upon his death, the IRA beneficiaries, and not his wife, were entitled to the IRA. The automatic survivor rules do not apply to IRAs. Where variable annuity contracts will be issued to defined contribution plans and distributed to terminated participants, IRS ruled that the fact that annuity payments will vary with investment performance does not preclude the payments from being considered payments under a qualified joint and survivor annuity (QJSA), provided that the payments would otherwise be considered as made under a QJSA.

A plan administrator abused its discretion under the terms of the plan when it distributed benefits to a deceased participant's children without first clarifying conflicting information regarding the participant's marital status. A married participant retired and, with the consent of his wife, elected a single life annuity. Thereafter, they divorced and the participant remarried. When the participant died, the court concluded that the second wife was not entitled to the survivor annuity.

An IRA owner died after commencing to receive required minimum distributions (RMDs). The IRA owner designated his wife as the sole beneficiary and did not name any contingent beneficiary. The IRA owner's wife died seven days later without (1) disclaiming the IRA; (2) taking any distributions from the IRA; (3) electing to treat the IRA as her own; or (4) naming any beneficiary. As a result, the right to receive the IRA passed by the deceased wife's will to their two children. IRS ruled that, because the wife died before distributions to her had begun, the RMD rules apply as if she were the IRA owner; and, because she died before her required beginning date (RBD) without having a designated beneficiary, the five-year rule applied. The deceased wife's personal representatives proposed to subdivide the IRA into two sub-IRAs, with each sub-IRA being titled "IRA owner (deceased) for the benefit of a specific beneficiary under the will of the wife (deceased)" and to accomplish the subdivision by trustee-to-trustee transfers. IRS ruled that neither the Code nor the RMD regulations precluded the posthumous division of an IRA into more than one IRA, and that the division did not constitute a transfer for purposes of the income in respect of a decedent rules, a taxable distribution, or a rollover. This ruling appears to be incorrect because the IRA owner died after his RBD. Therefore, the IRA owner's wife is the designated beneficiary and RMDs should be based upon her life expectancy.

The beneficiary of an IRA was convicted in the murder of the IRA owner. Even though, pursuant to state law, the beneficiary was deemed to have predeceased the IRA owner, IRS ruled that the murderer was the designated beneficiary for RMD purposes, notwithstanding that the IRA was eventually paid to the deceased IRA owner's stepdaughter. Because of the trial and various court orders delaying the determination of the recipient of, and the payment of, the IRA, IRS waived the excise tax for failure to make an RMD. A plan participant designated his wife as primary beneficiary and his son as secondary beneficiary of any death benefit payable under the plan. The participant's wife was convicted in the death of her husband, which, under state law, precluded her from receiving the plan death benefit. The distribution of the death benefit to the son was includible in his gross income.

Where a trust was the beneficiary of a decedent's IRA and there was no designated beneficiary at the time of the decedent's death, IRS did not allow a state court reformation of the trust to create a designated beneficiary.

IRS ruled that a qualified retirement plan participant whose retirement plan distributions were reported and taxed for several years without excluding his after-tax plan contributions must use the simplified method to determine the excludable amount for the current tax year. The participant could amend prior years' income tax returns to reflect the correct exclusion amounts for those years' retirement plan distributions for each year an amended return was allowable.

On October 1, 1986, the interest of a participant in a company pension plan became vested, as did the interest of his wife as his designated beneficiary. In 1988, the plan was terminated and, in order to satisfy its obligations to the participants, the plan purchased annuity contracts from an insurance company. The annuity contracts contained a provision permitting the annuitant to change the beneficiary designation. The decedent and his wife divorced in 1994 and entered into a settlement agreement whereby each waived any right to an interest in any pension plans, retirement plans, profit sharing plans, etc. At the time of the decedent's death in 2005, he had remarried but never changed the annuity beneficiary designation. His surviving spouse, as the executor of his estate, commenced an action against the former wife and the insurance company, claiming that the former wife had waived her interest in the annuity and that all payments should be made to the estate. The former wife contended that her rights in the plan vested on the date of the decedent's retirement, at which time she was still his wife and designated beneficiary, and that her interest was therefore non-assignable under ERISA. The estate contended that the annuity was a private contract governed by state law and that, under state law, the former wife had waived her interest in the annuity. The district court ruled in favor of the former wife, but the appellate court noted that ERISA permits the termination of a plan where the employer obligates itself to purchase annuities to provide the benefit the employee would have otherwise enjoyed under the plan. The court then held that the purchase of the annuities terminated the plan, and that termination severed the applicability of ERISA. The dispute was thus to be determined pursuant to state law, and the case was remanded to the district court for adjudication of the estate's claims pursuant to state law.

Where an individual failed to establish that the distributions from his individual retirement annuities satisfied any one of the three calculations to be considered substantially equal periodic payments, the 10 percent penalty tax on early distributions was imposed.

IRS issued the opinion and advisory letters for EGTRRA 2001 pre-approved defined benefit plans on March 31, 2010, or, in some cases, as soon as possible thereafter. Employers using a pre-approved plan document to restate a defined benefit plan for EGTRRA will be required to adopt the EGTRRA approved plan document by April 30, 2012.

IRS advised that the user fees for most employer plans' determination letters will increase on February 1, 2011.

IRS provided additional guidance with respect to correcting the failure of not implementing the automatic enrollment feature in a 401(k) plan. The correction method depends on whether the failure to implement automatic enrollment arose from the erroneous exclusion of an eligible employee or the failure to execute the employee's election.

In lieu of completing and filing Form 5500, Annual Return/Report of Employee Benefit Plan, for 2009, Form 5500-SF, Short Form Annual Return/Report of Small Employee Benefit Plan, may be used by certain small plans. Plans that meet the following eligibility conditions may voluntarily choose to file Form 5500-SF:

1. The plan must have had fewer than 100 participants at the beginning of the plan year;
2. The plan must meet the conditions for being exempt from the requirement to be audited annually by an independent qualified public accountant, but not by virtue of enhanced bonding;
3. At all times during the plan year, the plan must be 100 percent invested in certain secure investments that have a readily determinable fair market value;
4. The plan must not hold any employer securities at any time during the plan year; and
5. The plan must not be a multiemployer plan.

Effective January 2010, with respect to filings for 2009, Form 5500 and Form 5500-SF are required to be filed with DOL under the ERISA Filing Acceptance System 2 (EFAST2), an all-electronic system.

A one-participant plan that is required to file an annual return for 2009 must file a paper Form 5500-EZ. A one-participant plan is defined as a qualified retirement plan that covers only:

1. The owner of a business or both the owner and spouse and the business, whether or not incorporated, is wholly owned by the owner or by both the owner and spouse; or
2. Partners (or the partners and their spouses) in a business partnership.

Prior to 2009, Form 5500-EZ could not be used if the plan sponsor was a member of an affiliated service group, controlled group of corporations, or group of businesses under common control or if it leased employees. In addition, if the plan satisfied the coverage requirements only when combined with another plan, Form 5500-EZ could not be used. Form 5500-EZ can now be used because new characteristic codes have been added to identify these features on Form 5500-EZ.

Foreign plans are not eligible to file Form 5500 regardless of whether the plan was previously required to file an annual return on Form 5500. Every foreign plan that is required to file an annual return for 2009 must instead file a paper Form 5500-EZ. A foreign plan is a retirement plan that is maintained outside the United States primarily for nonresident aliens and is required to file an annual return if the employer who maintains the plan is (1) a domestic employer or (2) a foreign employer with income derived from sources within the United States if contributions to the plan are deducted on its U.S. income tax return.

Schedule SSA (Form 5500), Annual Registration Statement Identifying Separated Participants With Deferred Vested Benefits, has been eliminated for plan years beginning on or after January 1, 2009. Previously, Schedule SSA was used to inform IRS of plan participants who separated from service but were not paid retirement benefits. The prior Schedule SSA is being replaced by Form 8955-SSA, which will be filed directly with IRS. The 2009 filing of Form 8955-SSA may be delayed until the time the 2010 Form 5500 filing is due.

Pension Benefit Guaranty Corporation (PBGC) has issued proposed regulations that would make significant changes to its regulations on reportable events and conform the regulations to the funding rules arising from PPA. The proposed regulations would eliminate most of the automatic waivers and extensions in the existing reportable events regulations. PBGC believes that the current rules are depriving it of early warnings that would enable it to mitigate distress situations. Furthermore, PBGC believes that the increased reporting burden stemming from the elimination of most of the automatic waivers and extensions is justified by PBGC's need for timely information that may contribute to plan continuation or the minimizing of funding shortfalls.

Where a plan document is silent as to the grant of decision-making discretion to the plan administrator, but includes the right of amendment as well as a provision stating that the document will prevail over a conflict with the summary plan description (SPD), a provision in the SPD purporting to grant this discretion to the administrator, but also acknowledging the primacy of the plan document, is ineffective to create the necessary discretion to warrant review of the administrator's benefit decisions under the deferential arbitrary and capricious standard, concluded one court.

The Department of Labor (DOL) announced plans to issue proposed regulations to expand the current regulatory definition of "fiduciary" to include more persons, such as pension consultants, as fiduciaries. As a result of the proposed regulatory change, these persons would become subject to ERISA's fiduciary responsibility rules.

A plan's investment in a registered investment company, such as a mutual fund, does not by itself cause the fund's investment adviser or principal underwriter to be deemed to be a fiduciary or a party in interest, except insofar as such investment company or its investment adviser or principal underwriter acts in connection with an employee benefit plan covering employees of the investment company, the investment adviser, or its principal underwriter. In addition, where a plan invests in a security issued by a registered investment company, the assets of the plan are deemed to include the security but are not, solely by reason of such investment, deemed to include any assets of such investment company. A target-date or lifecycle mutual fund, which automatically rebalances to a more conservative asset allocation as the participant approaches the target retirement date, may consist of shares of affiliated mutual funds. In DOL's view, a mutual fund's investment in the shares of affiliated mutual funds would not, by itself, affect the application of the exclusion of mutual funds from the plan asset rules under ERISA. Accordingly, the fact that a target-date or lifecycle mutual fund's assets consist of shares of affiliated mutual funds does not, on that basis alone, make the assets of the target-date or lifecycle mutual fund plan assets of investing employee benefit plans or make the investment advisers to such mutual funds fiduciaries to the investing plans.

An accounting firm was not subject to equitable remedies under ERISA Section 502(a)(3). The firm successfully argued that services it rendered in designing, utilizing, and administering a client's 401(k) plan and cash balance plan did not make the firm liable as a nonfiduciary for knowingly participating in alleged breaches by the plans' fiduciaries. One court held that a plan participant had standing to sue even though he sought redress for alleged breaches committed before he commenced participation in the plan.

Plan fiduciaries breached their duty of prudence because they failed to adequately investigate alternatives to the retail share classes of the mutual fund or to request an easily obtainable waiver of minimum investment requirements applicable to the institutional class of shares, causing plan participants to incur a significant amount of unnecessary fees.

One court concluded that a breach of fiduciary duty claim under ERISA could not be supported where misrepresentations made by the employer and relied on by an employee related to a non-ERISA plan.

The United States Supreme Court ruled that, in an ERISA action, there is no requirement that a litigant be the prevailing party in order to be awarded attorneys' fees and costs. The court concluded that the claimant was entitled to an award where she had achieved some degree of success on the merits of her case. In another case, an attorney's fee award of $45,000 was upheld, even though the plan benefits recovered by the claimant as a result of the litigation were approximately $650. The plan sponsor's argument that the disproportionate size of the award was punitive and invalid was rejected, and the court ruled that fees need not be proportional to the amount recovered to be reasonable. Similarly, in an action by three multiemployer plans to recover approximately $2,000 of delinquent contributions, an attorney's fee award of approximately $51,000 was approved.

DOL issued proposed regulations that would update the procedures governing the filing and processing of applications for exemptions from the prohibited transaction provisions. The proposed rules would consolidate existing policies, clarify the types of information and documentation required to submit a complete filing, expand the methods for transmitting filings to include electronic submissions, and require a summary statement designed to make complex exemptions more understandable to participants and other interested parties.

Where a participant's election of a lump-sum distribution was a restricted benefit, the distribution arrangement was modified so that the benefit payments did not exceed the restrictions. IRS ruled that the final payment, which will be substantially larger than the other payments and will be made within ten years from the date of the first payment, will be an eligible rollover distribution.

IRS will be sending compliance questionnaires to approximately 1,200 401(k) plan sponsors. Data gathered from the results of this compliance check will help IRS with guidance, compliance, and determining where to focus outreach efforts regarding 401(k) plans. The compliance check can be completed on-line, at IRS's website, after receiving the paper work notice to complete the questionnaire.

Plan fiduciaries did not breach their duties under ERISA by continuing to offer an employer stock fund as a plan investment option despite a significant drop in the value of the stock. The ERISA Section 404(c)–compliant 401(k) plan provided sufficient cautions of the risks involved in investing in employer stock to enable the plan participants to exercise control over their accounts and, thereby, shield plan fiduciaries from liability for losses resulting from the participants' investment decisions. Plan amendments adopting the diversification requirements relating to employer stock do not have to be made until the last day of the first plan year that begins on or after January 1, 2010.

If an employee stock ownership plan (ESOP) owns S corporation stock, the S corporation may not deduct any accrued expenses for any ESOP participant, including plan contributions based on accrued compensation. A taxpayer, including an S corporation, may only deduct an expense in the same tax year that the payment is reported as income by a related party. A related party includes any person who directly or indirectly owns any of the S corporation's stock. Therefore, if an ESOP holds S corporation stock, the participants indirectly own stock in the S corporation. The participants do not include accrued compensation in their income until the year in which they receive it; and, therefore, the S corporation cannot deduct any compensation (including any bonus or vacation pay) accrued to the participants. The S corporation also cannot deduct any plan contributions for the participants that are based on accrued compensation.

IRS did not abuse its discretion by retroactively revoking an ESOP's favorable determination letter after the ESOP was terminated where it was later found that the ESOP had never satisfied the minimum coverage requirements.

An employer was held liable for plan contributions under a collective bargaining agreement (CBA) for the entire period covered by the CBA, even before signing a formal letter of consent, because the employer's course of conduct, making payments in accordance with the CBA, demonstrated the employer's assent to the CBA. The owners of an insolvent corporation were held not to be personally liable for unpaid plan contributions because the plan did not provide satisfactory evidence that the owners had used the corporation to fraudulently avoid paying the plan contributions.

For withdrawal liability purposes, one court concluded that an employer is an entity that is either contractually obligated to contribute to a multiemployer plan or obligated under applicable labor-management relations law. Another court concluded that an agreement by a union to indemnify a contributing employer for its withdrawal liability to a multiemployer plan was enforceable.

PBGC divided a multiemployer plan into two separate plans in an effort to extend the solvency of the plan. PBGC also provided guidance on simplified methods for applying the statutory requirements that multiemployer plans in critical status disregard certain benefit reductions in determining the plan's unfunded vested benefits (UVBs) for purposes of determining an employer's withdrawal liability.

An audit conducted by the Treasury Inspector General for Tax Administration (TIGTA) disclosed that noncompliance with IRA excess contribution rules continues to grow, resulting in significant revenue loss to the federal government.

IRS ruled that a transaction engaged in by an IRA was subject to a conflict of interest and could constitute a prohibited transaction. DOL advised that the grant by an IRA owner to a brokerage firm of a security interest in his non-IRA accounts in order to cover indebtedness of, or arising from, his IRA would be a prohibited transaction, because it was akin to a guarantee by the IRA owner.

Although an IRA may be exempt from claims of creditors, one court ruled that a debtor's inherited IRA is not an exempt asset of the debtor's bankruptcy estate. However, other courts ruled otherwise and held that a debtor's inherited IRA was exempted from the bankruptcy estate.

IRS concluded that the penalty for failing to make the required disclosure of a Roth IRA listed transaction should not be treated as a joint and several liability of the husband and wife who filed a joint return. Consequently, if only one spouse engaged in a listed transaction, it would be reasonable to assess the penalty only against the participating spouse.

IRS clarified the circumstances under which a defined contribution plan had to withhold income tax from a 2009 RMD paid between January 1, 2010 and April 1, 2010. Although RMDs from defined contribution plans were suspended for calendar year 2009, IRS noted that some plans continued to pay RMDs. If a 2009 RMD was distributed between January 1, 2010 and April 1, 2010 (for example, to a participant who turned 70½ in 2009, but delayed taking the 2009 RMD until April 1, 2010), the mandatory 20 percent income tax withholding applied to that distribution unless the RMD was not an eligible rollover distribution for some other reason. If the amount distributed between January 1, 2010 and April 1, 2010 was the first distribution from the plan in 2010, the distribution was first applied to the 2010 RMD. The amount of the distribution up to the 2010 RMD was not an eligible rollover distribution and not subject to mandatory withholding; however, if the distribution was greater than the 2010 RMD, the excess was an eligible rollover distribution subject to mandatory withholding.

Where a participant's election of a lump-sum distribution was a restricted benefit, the distribution arrangement was modified so that the benefit payments did not exceed the restrictions. IRS ruled that the final payment, which will be substantially larger than the other payments and will be made within ten years from the date of the first payment, will be an eligible rollover distribution.

The 60-day rollover period does not apply to a direct rollover if the plan makes out the check to the trustee. IRS ruled that, where the distributee gave the check to the trustee more than 60 days after receipt, the delay did not convert the rollover into a taxable distribution.

IRS announced that it expects to publish a revenue procedure for obtaining an opinion letter that the form of a prototype or other pre-approved plan meets the requirements of Code Section 403(b) and the regulations thereunder. Thereafter, IRS intends to publish a revenue procedure for obtaining an individual determination letter for a 403(b) plan. The IRS announcement provides for a remedial amendment period and reliance for employers that, pursuant to the upcoming revenue procedures, either adopt a pre-approved plan with a favorable opinion letter or apply for an individual determination letter when available.

Some courts have concluded that a waiver in an antenuptial agreement is invalid as it applies to a spouse's survivorship rights, but is valid as it applies to the equitable distribution of a plan benefit as marital property. Thus, in a divorce proceeding, the waiver of rights to plan benefits in an antenuptial agreement is enforceable.

The 2011 Pension Answer Book discusses all of these provisions and their effect on pension practice. In addition, it updates subscribers on the most current and pertinent Internal Revenue Code and ERISA provisions, IRS and DOL Regulations, Revenue Rulings and Procedures, Private Letter Rulings, Notices and Announcements, and case law.

Some special features that make *The 2011 Pension Answer Book* especially useful and accessible are listed below.

Format. The questions-and-answer format, with its breadth of coverage and its plain-language explanations (plus numerous illustrative examples), offers a clear and useful guide to understanding the complex area of qualified pension and profit sharing plans.

Number System. The questions are numbered consecutively within each chapter (e.g., 2:1, 2:2, 2:3).

List of Questions. The detailed List of Questions that follows the Table of Contents helps the reader locate areas of immediate interest.

Glossary. Because the pension area is replete with technical terms that have specific legal meanings, a special glossary of terms is provided. Expressions not defined elsewhere, and abbreviations used throughout the book, are defined in the glossary, which is arranged in alphabetical order.

Tables. In order to facilitate easy access to a particular section of the Internal Revenue Code, Treasury Regulations, ERISA, Department of Labor Regulations, Revenue Rulings, Revenue Procedures, Letter Rulings, Notices and Announcements, and to pertinent legal cases, tables of all of the sections and cases referenced in the text and their appropriate question number have been included.

Index. An index is provided as a further aid to locating specific information. Key words included in the glossary are used in the index as well. All references in the index are to question numbers.

Use of Abbreviations. Because of the breadth of subject area, a number of terms and statutory references are abbreviated throughout *The 2011 Pension Answer Book*. Among the most common of these shorthand references are:

- Code—The Internal Revenue Code of 1986, as amended
- ERISA—The Employee Retirement Income Security Act of 1974, as amended
- IRS—The Internal Revenue Service
- DOL—The U.S. Department of Labor
- PBGC—Pension Benefit Guaranty Corporation

For explanations of other abbreviations, consult the glossary.

The 2011 Pension Answer Book offers subscribers insight and practical expertise covering all areas of pension practice and is more useful than ever.

Stephen J. Krass
October 2010

About the Authors

STEPHEN J. KRASS, ESQ., is a member of the law firm of Krass, Snow & Schmutter, P.C. in New York City. Mr. Krass received his B.S. (Accounting) from The Ohio State University and LL.B. and LL.M. (Taxation) from New York University School of Law. Mr. Krass is a member of the American Bar Association Sections on Taxation and Real Property, Trust and Estate Law and the New York State Bar Association Sections on Trusts and Estates and Taxation and is a Charter Fellow of The American College of Employee Benefits Counsel. He has served as President of the Estate Planning Council of New York City and has also been a member of its Board of Directors. Mr. Krass is a member of the Advisory Boards of the N.Y.U. Institute on Federal Taxation, CCH Financial and Estate Planning Reporter, and Journal of Pension Planning & Compliance, and serves as a member of the Planned Giving Committee of Yeshiva University, the New York Region Planned Giving Professional Advisory Committee of the Anti-Defamation League, The Ohio State University Foundation Planned Giving Committee, and the East Coast Major Gifts Committee of The Ohio State University. Mr. Krass has been a panelist on many programs, including New York State Bar Association, AICPA, New York State Society of CPAs, Practising Law Institute, AALU, Association of the Bar of the City of New York, and New York County Lawyers' Association programs. He has spoken at the N.Y.U. Institute on Federal Taxation; The Ohio State University College of Law; Fordham Law School; New York Law School; Baruch College; Columbus (Ohio) Tax Conference; Purdue University Insurance Marketing Institute; UJA-Federation Annual Tax, Estate and Financial Planning Conference; The American College-CCH National Conference on Financial Planning; Institute of Certified Financial Planners Annual Conference; International Association for Financial Planning; American Academy of Matrimonial Lawyers; Hofstra University-Center for Business Studies; C. W. Post Tax Institute; and Iona College Tax Institute. Mr. Krass has been an instructor in the Long Island University Paralegal Program. He has contributed articles to The Journal of Taxation of Estates and Trusts; Estate Planning; Taxes-The Tax Magazine; Journal of the Institute of Certified Financial Planners; The Pension Actuary; The Practical Accountant; CLU Journal; CCH Financial and Estate Planning Reporter; The Journal of Financial Planning; Journal of Pension Planning & Compliance; Taxation for Accountants; and Taxation for Lawyers. Mr. Krass is a frequent lecturer on estate and retirement planning.

STEVEN SCHMUTTER, ESQ., is a member of the law firm of Krass, Snow & Schmutter, P.C. Mr. Schmutter received his B.S. (magna cum laude) from the State University of New York at Binghamton, his J.D. from St. John's University School of Law, and his LL.M. (Taxation) from New York University School of Law. He has served as President of the Pension Council of Long Island (1999–2000), is a member of the Northeast Pension Liaison Group, the American Society of Pension Professionals & Actuaries, and the New York Employee Benefits Group, and has spoken and written on employee benefit plan topics.

RICHARD L. KESCHNER, ESQ. (1945–1989), was a sole practitioner in New York City. Mr. Keschner received his B.S. from Brooklyn College, his M.B.A. from Baruch College, and his J.D. from Brooklyn Law School.

Acknowledgements

As with prior editions, *The 2011 Pension Answer Book* incorporates the efforts of many people. To my partner, Steven Schmutter, I again express my gratitude and appreciation for his invaluable assistance in the preparation of the manuscript. I also thank our secretaries, Terry Joe and Lisa Lindsey, for their efforts, and to others at Krass, Snow & Schmutter, P.C., including Perrin Tomich and Gary English, for their contributions.

Many thanks, as always, to my wife, Sallie, for her patience and understanding.

Thanks again to my editor, Ellen Ros, Mary Stevenson, and all the people at Aspen Publishers, past and present, without whose efforts *The 2011 Pension Answer Book* would not be possible.

SJK

Contents

Contents

Contents

List of Questions

Chapter 1 Overview

Chapter 2 Types and Choices of Plans

Chapter 3 Highly Compensated Employees

Chapter 4 Requirements for Qualification

Chapter 5 Eligibility and Participation

Chapter 7 Permitted Disparity

Chapter 9 Vesting

Chapter 10 General Distribution Requirements

Chapter 11 Minimum Distribution Requirements

General

RMDs During Lifetime

Death Before RBD

Determination of Designated Beneficiary

RMDs from Defined Contribution Plans

Chapter 12 Tax Deduction Rules

Chapter 13 Taxation of Distributions

Chapter 14 Participant Loans

Chapter 15 Life Insurance and Death Benefits

Chapter 16 10 Percent Tax on Early Distributions

Chapter 17 Saver's Credit

Chapter 18 Determination Letters

Chapter 19 IRS and DOL Correction Programs

Chapter 20 Operating the Plan

Chapter 21   Reporting to Government Agencies

Chapter 22 Summary Plan Descriptions

Chapter 23 Fiduciary Responsibilities

Chapter 24   Prohibited Transactions

Chapter 25 Termination of the Plan

Chapter 26 Top-Heavy Plans

Chapter 27 401(k) Plans

Chapter 28 Employee Stock Ownership Plans

Chapter 29 Multiemployer Plans

List of Questions

Chapter 30 Individual Retirement Plans

List of Questions

Chapter 31 Roth IRAs

Chapter 32 Simplified Employee Pensions

Chapter 33 Savings Incentive Match Plan for Employees

Chapter 34 Rollovers

Chapter 35 403(b) Plans

Chapter 36 Qualified Domestic Relations Orders

Chapter 1

Overview

There is no better way for a company to accumulate a substantial nest egg for its loyal employees—and the working owner—than to establish a tax-favored retirement plan. This chapter examines qualified retirement plans—what they are, their tax advantages, the types of costs involved, and the kinds of benefits that can be provided.

Q 1:1 Why should a company adopt a qualified retirement plan?

A qualified retirement plan is one of the best tax shelters available. The company is allowed a current deduction for its contributions to the plan; the employee pays no tax on money contributed for the employee's benefit until a distribution is made; earnings from investments made with funds in the plan may accumulate tax free; and distributions from the plan may be afforded favorable income tax treatment.

A qualified retirement plan is especially attractive to working owners of closely held corporations and to self-employed individuals. Their long-term service with their companies gives them the best opportunity to accumulate large sums of money through the tax-free build-up of capital. Although benefits must be provided for other employees as well, the owner usually receives a much larger benefit than the other employees.

The nontax reasons for adopting a qualified retirement plan include: (1) attracting employees, (2) reducing employee turnover, (3) increasing employee incentive, and (4) accumulating funds for retirement.

Q 1:2 How do the working owners of a closely held corporation benefit from a qualified retirement plan?

There are two basic ways for a working owner to get money out of a closely held corporation: compensation and dividends.

If a working owner earns a salary or bonus from a closely held corporation, the corporation will get a deduction for the amounts paid to the owner. In turn, the owner is taxed on compensation at ordinary income tax rates. A dividend paid to the working owner is treated differently: it is not deductible by the corporation. The dividend is also taxable to the working owner. Payments of dividends, therefore, are subject to double taxation.

Adoption of a qualified retirement plan provides the corporation with a deduction for the amount it contributes to the plan. The working owner, as a participant in the plan, is not currently taxed on the amounts contributed for the owner's benefit. Further, earnings from investments made by the plan may build up tax-free.

Therefore, adoption of a qualified retirement plan provides the corporation with the same tax benefits as does the payment of current compensation; but the working owner of a closely held corporation is able to defer payment of taxes until benefits are received.

Q 1:3   How can the adoption of a qualified retirement plan increase the wealth of the owner of a closely held corporation?

Dramatic results can be achieved by a qualified retirement plan.

Example. Neal, the owner of a closely held corporation, earns a $50,000 annual salary, and the corporation is able to pay a 15 percent bonus ($7,500) each year. From the additional $7,500 each year, Neal will keep about $5,400 after taxes (assuming a 28 percent bracket). If that $5,400 is invested at 8 percent per year, Neal will earn about 6 percent net after taxes. Over a 25-year period, he will be able to build up about $314,000 after taxes.

If the corporation has a qualified profit sharing plan and, instead of giving Neal a $7,500 bonus, contributes that $7,500 to the plan each year on his behalf, the corporation gets the same $7,500 deduction that it would have received had it paid the bonus.

If the profit sharing trust earns the same 8 percent that Neal would have earned individually, then, because the profit sharing trust pays no income taxes, the total build-up of these annual investments in the trust on Neal's behalf, over the 25-year period, will come to $592,000. (Remember, the full $7,500 per year—not $5,400 after taxes—is accumulating in the trust. Furthermore, it is accumulating at the full 8 percent interest rate.)

The above example is oversimplified, especially in the case of a small or medium-size corporation. To give this type of dramatic build-up to the business owner, other employees must also be covered. This, of course, boosts costs; but there are provisions that may be incorporated into the plan to reduce costs.

Q 1:4   How does the adoption of a qualified retirement plan reduce a corporation's tax liability?

To illustrate how a qualified retirement plan reduces a corporation's tax liability, assume the corporation had taxable income of $45,000 in 2010 and no qualified plan. Its income tax liability would be $6,750. If, however, the owners decided to adopt a qualified retirement plan and make a tax-deductible contribution of $21,000 to the plan, the corporation's taxable income would now be $24,000 ($45,000 – $21,000). Its income tax liability would be reduced to $3,600. By adopting the plan and making the contribution, this corporation would cut its tax liability by almost 50 percent. [I.R.C. § 11(b)]

Q 1:5   What is a qualified retirement plan?

There are two distinct elements embodied in the term "qualified retirement plan." The main element is the term "retirement plan." A retirement plan means any plan or program maintained by an employer or an employee organization (or both) that (1) provides retirement income to employees or (2) results in a deferral of income by employees for periods extending generally to the end of employment or beyond, regardless of how plan contributions or benefits are calculated or how benefits are distributed. [ERISA § 3(2)]

The other element is the term "qualified," which means that the retirement plan is afforded special tax treatment for meeting a host of requirements of the Internal Revenue Code (the Code). Qualified retirement plans fall into two basic categories: defined contribution plans and defined benefit plans. A defined contribution plan provides benefits based on the amount contributed to an employee's individual account, plus any earnings and forfeitures of other employees that are allocated to the account. A defined benefit plan provides a definitely determinable annual benefit; that is, the benefits are determined on the basis of a formula contained in the plan.

A participant in a qualified retirement plan sued to have the plan disqualified because the rate of return on the plan's investments was unfavorable. The court ruled that there is no requirement that a retirement plan's investments grow at a specified rate or that its participants be satisfied with the rate of return. [Sonier, 78 T.C.M. 313 (1999)]

When the term "qualified retirement plan" is used in this book, it refers to both defined contribution and defined benefit plans.

Q 1:6   What are the basic tax advantages of a qualified retirement plan?

A qualified retirement plan is afforded special tax treatment. These tax advantages include the following:

1. The sponsoring company is allowed an immediate tax deduction for the amount contributed to the plan for a particular year. [I.R.C. § 404]

2. Participants pay no current income tax on amounts contributed by the company on their behalf. [I.R.C. §§ 402, 403]

3. Earnings of the plan are tax-exempt—permitting the tax-free accumulation of income and gains on investments. [I.R.C. §§ 401, 501]

4. Income taxes on certain types of distributions may be deferred by rolling over the distribution to an IRA or to another eligible retirement plan. [I.R.C. §§ 401(a)(31), 402(c), 403(a)(4), 403(a)(5)]

5. Income taxes on certain types of distributions to a deceased participant's spouse may be deferred by rolling over the distribution to an IRA or to an eligible retirement plan in which the surviving spouse participates. [I.R.C. § 402(c)(9)]

6. Income taxes on certain types of distributions to a deceased participant's nonspouse beneficiaries may be deferred by transferring the distribution directly to an IRA. [I.R.C. § 402(c)(11)]

7. Installment or annuity payments are taxed only when they are received. [I.R.C. §§ 72, 402(a), 403(a)]

Earnings of the plan may be taxable if the earnings are unrelated business taxable income (UBTI; see Q 30:11). [I.R.C. §§ 511, 512, 513, 514] One court ruled that ERISA did not preempt a California law taxing the UBTI of tax-exempt trusts, including those trusts covered by ERISA. The court held that the state law neither referred to nor had a connection with ERISA plans; and, accordingly, it did not relate to ERISA plans, as described in ERISA's preemption clause. [ERISA § 514(a); Hattem v. Schwarzenegger, 449 F.3d 423 (2d Cir. 2006); *but see In re* McKinsey Master Retirement Plan Trust, 2003 WL 21133964 (N.Y. Tax App. Trib. 2003)]

IRS has ruled that a qualified retirement plan that invests funds in a common trust fund has UBTI from the trust fund to the same extent as it would have had it made the same investment directly. A common trust fund is a fund maintained by a bank or trust company for the collective investment of funds contributed to the fund by the bank in its capacity, for example, as a trustee. A common trust fund is not subject to taxation, but its income is included in the gross income of the participants (e.g., a qualified retirement plan) in the fund. Therefore, if a common trust fund operated an active business, income from that business would be UBTI when passed through to the qualified retirement plan. [I.R.C. § 584; Treas. Reg. § 1.584-2(c)(3); Rev. Rul. 98-41, 1998-2 C.B. 256; Rev. Rul. 67-301, 1967-2 C.B. 146; Priv. Ltr. Rul. 200148074]

Q 1:7 Must a company incorporate to have a qualified retirement plan?

No. The benefits of a qualified retirement plan are available to incorporated and unincorporated businesses alike. Sole proprietorships and partnerships can have retirement plans that are comparable to corporate retirement plans.

A plan covering a self-employed individual (see Q 6:60) must, however, satisfy certain requirements in addition to the normal corporate retirement plan qualification requirements. [I.R.C. §§ 401(c), 401(d)] A self-employed individual is an individual who has income from self-employment for the taxable year.

Q 1:8 What tax advantage does a self-employed individual gain by adopting a qualified retirement plan?

The basic tax advantages of adopting a qualified retirement plan, which are similar to those received by the owner of a closely held corporation, are:

1. The self-employed individual receives a federal income tax deduction, subject to the applicable limitations of the Code, for contributions made to the qualified retirement plan.

2. To the extent the contribution the self-employed individual makes to a qualified retirement plan is tax-deductible, the tax on this income is deferred (it will be taxable when it is ultimately received from the plan).

3. Income earned on contributions to the plan (whether or not tax-deductible when made) will escape tax while in the plan, thereby permitting a greater total compounding of earnings than would otherwise be possible (see Q 1:6).

Q 1:9   Is it worthwhile for a self-employed individual to incorporate?

Although there generally is parity between qualified corporate retirement plans and qualified retirement plans for the self-employed, the incorporated business owner will still have advantages that will be unavailable to the unincorporated business owner. Among the advantages are the following:

1. Plan contributions for the incorporated business owner allocable to life, accident, health, or other insurance are deductible. [I.R.C. § 404(e)]

2. The incorporated business owner can terminate employment for lump-sum distribution purposes. [I.R.C. § 402(e)(4)(A)]

3. Plan contributions on behalf of an incorporated business owner can create or increase a net operating loss. [I.R.C. § 172(d)(4)(D)]

4. The incorporated business owner may receive tax-free group term life insurance benefits. [I.R.C. § 79]

5. The incorporated business owner may receive tax-free benefits under a medical expense reimbursement plan. [I.R.C. §§ 105(b), 105(g)]

Note. An individual who incorporates principally to obtain tax deductions not otherwise available to a self-employed individual should review those circumstances in which IRS may allocate income and deductions of a personal service corporation to an employee-owner (see Qs 5:37–5:42).

Q 1:10   How should an existing qualified retirement plan be handled if a self-employed individual incorporates the business?

The simplest and most practical arrangement may be to have the corporation adopt the qualified retirement plan. If the corporation establishes a new qualified retirement plan, the assets of the prior plan can be merged into the new plan or transferred directly to the trustees of the new plan.

If the qualified retirement plan that covered the self-employed individual (see Q 6:60) is being terminated, IRS should be notified (see Q 25:63).

Another alternative is to freeze the plan. Since the individual is no longer self-employed, the individual can make no further contributions to the plan.

However, amounts in the plan will continue to accumulate on a tax-free basis. Distributions can later be made from the plan in accordance with its provisions. However, if a qualified retirement plan covering a self-employed individual is frozen, the plan must still comply with the requirements of the Code. [Rev. Rul. 89-87, 1989-2 C.B. 81; I.R.C. § 401(a); Treas. Reg. § 1.401(a)(26)-2(b)]

IRS representatives have opined that, although the business must be in existence, there is no requirement for active engagement in business and that a legally constituted dormant entity may sponsor a qualified retirement plan. Therefore, it would be more advisable either to have the corporation adopt the plan or effect a merger or have the self-employed individual terminate the plan rather than freeze the plan. If the self-employed individual is a sole proprietor (i.e., the 100 percent owner of the unincorporated business), the death of the sole proprietor may cause the termination of the business; and, without a plan sponsor, the business can no longer maintain a qualified retirement plan. This, in turn, could require the plan to distribute all of its assets to the sole proprietor's beneficiary and subject the benefits to immediate income taxation. To avoid adverse income tax consequences, IRS has permitted a plan to distribute a nontransferable annuity contract to the beneficiary so that the beneficiary will then include in income only the annuity payments received during the taxable year. [I.R.C. § 72; Priv. Ltr. Rul. 200244023; *see also* Priv. Ltr. Ruls. 200548028, 200548027]

Q 1:11   How does the deductibility of employer contributions differ between qualified and nonqualified plans?

Qualified retirement plans are given favorable tax treatment for meeting special requirements of the Code. There is no special tax treatment for nonqualified retirement plans. The basic difference between a qualified plan and a nonqualified plan is that contributions by the company to the nonqualified plan are not deductible until they are includible in the participant's income. This means the company does not get a current deduction for contributions made to a nonqualified plan. In contrast, contributions to a qualified plan are immediately deductible. [I.R.C. §§ 83, 162, 404] The American Jobs Creation Act of 2004 made significant changes to the rules governing nonqualified plans. [I.R.C. § 409A; IRS Notice 2005-1, 2005-1 C.B. 274]

Q 1:12   How do qualified and nonqualified plans differ with regard to the taxation of employer contributions?

A participant in a qualified plan is not taxed until the benefits are distributed to the participant. This is also true in a nonqualified, unfunded plan. If the nonqualified plan is funded, however, the participant generally is taxed in the first year that the participant's rights are transferable or are not subject to a substantial risk of forfeiture. [I.R.C. §§ 83, 402(b)] The American Jobs Creation Act of 2004 made significant changes to the rules governing nonqualified plans.

[I.R.C. § 409A; IRS Notice 2005-1, 2005-1 C B. 274]

IRS has ruled that a transfer of qualified plan benefits to a nonqualified plan would result in taxable distributions to the qualified plan participants and would adversely affect the qualified status of the qualified plan. [Priv. Ltr. Rul. 199928041]

Q 1:13   How do qualified and nonqualified plans differ with regard to coverage of employees and benefit or contribution limitations?

The nonqualified plan is designed primarily to provide retirement income for essential employees. Such a plan does not have to cover a broad spectrum of employees, as the qualified plan does. Furthermore, there are no limits on benefits or contributions, and there are no reporting or bookkeeping requirements in connection with the nonqualified plan so long as it is not funded. [I.R.C. § 401(a)] The American Jobs Creation Act of 2004 made significant changes to the rules governing nonqualified plans. [I.R.C. § 409A; IRS Notice 2005-1, 2005-1 C.B. 274]

Q 1:14   What is the Employee Retirement Income Security Act?

The Employee Retirement Income Security Act of 1974 (ERISA) became law on September 2, 1974. ERISA completely overhauled the federal pension law after Congress found that:

1. Employees with long years of service were losing anticipated retirement benefits due to the lack of plan provisions relating to the vesting of benefits;

2. Many plans lacked adequate funds to pay employees promised retirement benefits; and

3. Plans were being terminated before enough funds had been accumulated to pay employees and their beneficiaries promised retirement benefits.

To protect the interests of retirement plan participants and their beneficiaries, ERISA (1) established a new set of rules for participation in retirement plans, (2) added mandatory schedules for the vesting of benefits, (3) fixed minimum funding standards, (4) set standards of conduct for administering the plan and handling plan assets, (5) required disclosure of plan information, and (6) established a system for insuring the payment of pension benefits.

Q 1:15   What other Acts have affected retirement plans?

The following Acts have affected retirement plans:

- The Multiemployer Pension Plan Amendments Act of 1980 (MPPAA)
- The Economic Recovery Tax Act of 1981 (ERTA)
- The Tax Equity and Fiscal Responsibility Act of 1982 (TEFRA)
- The Tax Reform Act of 1984 (TRA '84)
- The Retirement Equity Act of 1984 (REA)
- The Single-Employer Pension Plan Amendments Act of 1986 (SEPPAA)
- The Tax Reform Act of 1986 (TRA '86)

- The Omnibus Budget Reconciliation Act of 1986 (OBRA '86)
- The Pension Protection Act (PPA), attached to the Omnibus Budget Reconciliation Act of 1987 (OBRA '87)
- The Technical and Miscellaneous Revenue Act of 1988 (TAMRA)
- The Revenue Reconciliation Act (RRA), Title VII of the Omnibus Budget Reconciliation Act of 1989 (OBRA '89)
- The Omnibus Budget Reconciliation Act of 1990 (OBRA '90)
- The Unemployment Compensation Amendments of 1992 (UC '92)
- The Revenue Reconciliation Act of 1993 (RRA '93)
- The Uniformed Services Employment and Re-employment Rights Act of 1994 (USERRA)
- The Pension Annuitants Protection Act (PPA '94)
- The Retirement Protection Act of 1994 (RPA '94)
- The State Income Taxation of Pension Income Act of 1995
- The Small Business Job Protection Act of 1996 (SBA '96)
- The Health Insurance Portability and Accountability Act of 1996 (HIPAA '96)
- The Taxpayer Relief Act of 1997 (TRA '97)
- The Tax Technical Corrections Act of 1998 (TTC '98)
- The Older Americans Act Amendments of 2000
- The Community Renewal Tax Relief Act of 2000 (CRTRA 2000)
- The Economic Growth and Tax Relief Reconciliation Act of 2001 (EGTRRA 2001)
- The Victims of Terrorism Tax Relief Act of 2001
- The Job Creation and Worker Assistance Act of 2002 (JCWAA 2002)
- The Sarbanes-Oxley Act of 2002
- The Pension Funding Equity Act of 2004
- The Working Families Tax Relief Act of 2004
- The Bankruptcy Abuse Prevention and Consumer Protection Act of 2005
- The Katrina Emergency Tax Relief Act of 2005
- The Gulf Opportunity Zone Act of 2005
- The Deficit Reduction Act of 2005
- The Tax Increase Prevention and Reconciliation Act of 2005 (TIPRA)
- The Heroes Earned Retirement Opportunities Act (HERO)
- The Pension Protection Act of 2006 (PPA)
- The Small Business Tax Act of 2007 (SBTA 2007)
- The Heroes Earnings Assistance and Relief Tax Act of 2008 (HEART Act)
- The Worker, Retiree, and Employer Recovery Act of 2008 (WRERA 2008)
- The Pension Relief Act of 2010 (PRA 2010)
- The Small Business Jobs Act of 2010 (SBJA 2010)

**Q 1:16   What is the Uniformed Services Employment and
Re-employment Rights Act of 1994?**

This Act (USERRA) was signed into law on October 13, 1994. USERRA
prohibits discrimination against employees because of membership in the
uniformed services. USERRA generally became effective for reemployment
initiated more than 60 days after the law was enacted, that is, on or after
December 12, 1994. However, qualified retirement plans had two years, or until
October 13, 1996, to comply.

USERRA provides that an individual who is reemployed following protected
military service must be treated as not having incurred a break in service (see
Q 5:10). Furthermore, upon reemployment, the plan must grant vesting and
benefit credit (see Qs 9:1, 9:2) for the period of time the employee was absent for
military service. Defined contribution plans (see Q 2:2) must credit the employee with any allocations of employer contributions, but not earnings or
forfeitures, to which the employee would have been entitled had there been no
interruption in employment. For this purpose, the employee's compensation is
assumed to be at the rate the employee would have received had there been no
interruption in employment.

USERRA further provides that any qualified retirement plan benefit or
contribution that is contingent upon the making of contributions or deferrals by
the employee is due the reemployed person only if the employee makes up the
missed contributions or deferrals. A make-up of employee contributions or
deferrals may be contributed by the employee over a period of time equal to
three times the period of absence due to military service, but not to exceed five
years. For example, if a participant in a 401(k) plan (see Q 27:1) that provides
employer matching contributions is called to 12 months of active military duty,
the employee would have 36 months after returning to employment to make up
the missed deferrals. As the deferrals are made up, the corresponding employer
matching contributions would be credited to the participant's account under the
plan. However, USERRA contains no amendments to the Code to address
coordination of these catch-up contributions, deferrals, and matching contributions with various limitations (see Qs 6:34, 27:51). In addition, nondiscrimination testing for qualification purposes is not addressed (see Qs 27:11, 27:77).

SBA '96 incorporated the provisions of USERRA into the Code and also
clarified a number of plan qualification issues that had not been addressed by
USERRA.

The requirements of USERRA posed potential problems for employers because the annual limits on contributions and benefits under various provisions
of the Code did not authorize exceptions for make-up contributions by or for
reemployed veterans. In addition, the nondiscrimination, minimum coverage,
minimum participation, and top-heavy rules (see chapters 4, 5, 6, 26) did not
make an exception for contributions for reemployed veterans.

Under SBA '96, make-up contributions by an employer or employee to a
defined contribution plan (including a 403(b) plan, SEP, or qualified salary
reduction arrangement) or contributions by an employee to a defined benefit

plan (see Q 2:3) that provides for employee contributions, on behalf of reemployed veterans that are required by USERRA, are not subject to the generally applicable plan contribution limits or the limits on deductible contributions with respect to the year in which the contributions are made. Moreover, the make-up contributions will not be considered in applying the limits to any other contributions made during the year. However, the make-up contributions (including elective deferrals) may not exceed the aggregate amount of contributions that would have been permitted under the applicable limits for the year for which the contributions are made if the individual had continued to be employed by the employer during the period of military service.

A make-up contribution may not exceed the contribution that would have been allowed under the limits that applied in the year to which the contribution relates. Because the limits are subject to annual adjustments or cost-of-living adjustments, the amount of a make-up contribution may vary. For example, a reemployed veteran could have made an elective deferral under a 401(k) plan of $16,500 for the 2010 plan year. However, the make-up contribution would be limited to $15,500 if the contribution related to the 2008 plan year.

Make-up contributions made on behalf of reemployed veterans also will not cause a plan to violate the nondiscrimination, minimum coverage, minimum participation, and top-heavy rules applicable to qualified retirement plans. In applying these qualification rules, the contributions will not be considered for the year in which they are made *or* the year to which they relate.

Generally, loans from a qualified retirement plan to a plan participant must be repaid within five years. However, a plan may suspend an employee's obligation to repay a plan loan during the period of the employee's military service without risking disqualification or engaging in a prohibited transaction (see Qs 13:27, 24:19).

The above rules became effective as of December 12, 1994. [I.R.C. § 414(u)]

The Department of Labor (DOL) issued final regulations designed to clarify the rights of employees and the attendant responsibilities of employers under USERRA. The regulations, which are structured in a question-and-answer format, address a variety of issues related to USERRA's pension and welfare benefit protections and its anti-discrimination and anti-retaliatory provisions. The regulations clarify an employee's reemployment rights and the type and length of military service that entitle an employee to protection under USERRA and also explain the statutory defenses available to employers against claims for USERRA benefits. [DOL Reg. § 1002] On December 10, 2004, President Bush signed into law the Veterans Benefits Improvement Act of 2004, which, among other things, requires employers to provide a notice informing employees of their rights under USERRA. Employers may provide the notice by posting it where employee notices are customarily placed. However, employers may provide the notice to employees in other ways that will minimize costs while ensuring that the full text of the notice is provided (e.g., by handing or mailing out the notice or distributing the notice via electronic mail). DOL also issued a notice of USERRA rights that had to be posted or otherwise communicated to employees by January 18, 2006.

See Q 1:17 for a discussion of the Soldiers' and Sailors' Civil Relief Act of 1940 and Q 1:35 for a discussion of the HEART Act.

Q 1:17   What is the Soldiers' and Sailors' Civil Relief Act of 1940?

This Act (SSCRA) limits the interest that may be charged on outstanding obligations and liabilities of persons who enter active duty military service. DOL has advised that the SSCRA interest limitation applies to plan loans and indicated that a loan will not fail to be a qualified loan under ERISA solely because the interest rate is capped by SSCRA. Generally, SSCRA imposes a 6 percent limit on the interest rate that may be charged to a service member for obligations or liabilities incurred before active duty began, and interest includes service charges, renewal charges, fees, or any other charges associated with the obligation or liability. Although ERISA preempts state law, ERISA provides that nothing in Title I shall be construed to alter, amend, modify, invalidate, impair, or supersede any law of the United States or any rule or regulation issued under any such law. Thus, since a plan loan is an obligation or liability under SSCRA, SSCRA is not preempted by ERISA and the rules and regulations that normally govern plan loans under Title I of ERISA cannot be interpreted so as to preclude the application of SSCRA. [SSCRA § 526; ERISA § 514]

SSCRA has been amended and renamed the Service Members Civil Relief Act, and the revised Act was signed into law by President Bush on December 19, 2003. The Act retains the 6 percent interest cap and forgives the payment of interest in excess of 6 percent a year for obligations or liabilities incurred by the service member, or jointly by the service member and spouse, before the service member entered military service. In order for the interest rate relief to apply, the service member is required to provide the creditor (e.g., plan administrator) with written notice and a copy of the military order calling the service member to active duty and any orders further extending military service. The notice must be provided within 180 days after the date of the service member's termination or release from military service. Once the written notice and required documentation are received by the creditor, the 6 percent interest cap will apply as of the date that the individual was called to military service.

Plan fiduciaries are authorized to petition a court to retain a rate of interest that is higher than 6 percent for individuals with the ability to pay the greater charge, and the court may do so if it determines that the ability of the service member to pay interest on the loan in excess of 6 percent is not materially affected by the individual's military service.

Q 1:18   What is the Pension Annuitants Protection Act?

The Pension Annuitants Protection Act (PPA '94) was signed into law by President Clinton on October 22, 1994. Under this Act, a qualified retirement plan participant, beneficiary, or fiduciary can bring an action for appropriate relief if the purchase of an insurance contract or annuity in connection with the termination of a person's status as a plan participant would violate fiduciary standards.

The Act requires the posting of security, if necessary, to assure that beneficiaries receive the amounts provided by the annuities. Although interest can also be awarded, the Act does not authorize awards of punitive, extracontractual, or consequential damages.

Q 1:19 What is the State Income Taxation of Pension Income Act of 1995?

On January 10, 1996, the State Income Taxation of Pension Income Act of 1995 was signed into law. This Act prohibits states from taxing the retirement income payments of their former residents, effective for retirement income payments received after December 31, 1995.

The Act exempts all retirement income received from certain plans from taxation by states other than the state of the recipient's residence. Retirement income means any income received from, among others, a qualified retirement plan, a SEP (see Q 32:1), a 403(b) plan (see Q 35:1), and an IRA (see Q 30:1). Nonqualified plan benefits (see Q 1:12) are protected under the Act if (1) the distribution is made from an excess benefit plan and payments are received after termination of employment or (2) the distribution is made from any other type of nonqualified plan and the retirement income is part of a series of substantially equal periodic payments (not less frequently than annually) made for the life or life expectancy of the recipient (or the joint lives or joint life expectancies of the recipient and a designated beneficiary) or for a period of not less than ten years.

H.R. 4019 was signed into law by President Bush on August 3, 2006. The bill clarifies that state taxation of retirement income is limited to the state where the retiree resides and applies whether the retirement payments are made to a retired employee or to a retired partner. States may not, therefore, impose an income tax on nonresident retirement income received under certain nonqualified deferred compensation plans, including written plans, in effect at the time of retirement, providing for payments to a retired partner in recognition of prior service. In addition, the bill clarifies the definition of "substantially equal periodic payments," to permit plan caps on retiree payments and cost-of-living adjustments. The substantially equal periodic payment test will be satisfied if payments include components from both a qualified and nonqualified plan.

Q 1:20 What is the Older Americans Act Amendments of 2000?

This Act, signed into law in 2000, authorizes appropriations to certain agencies to provide benefits counseling and related services to older Americans, including pension counseling programs and a federal pension hotline. Under the Act, the Assistant Secretary for Aging in the Department of Health and Human Services is authorized to award grants to eligible entities to establish and carry out programs to provide older Americans with outreach, information, counseling, referral, and other assistance regarding pensions and other retirement benefits. Eligible entities include state agencies or area agencies on aging and certain nonprofit organizations. In addition, the Assistant Secretary is authorized to enter into agreements with other federal agencies to establish and administer a national telephone hotline to provide information regarding pensions and other retirement benefits and rights related to such benefits.

For years beginning after 2001, EGTRRA 2001 (see Q 1:21) excludes from gross income a fringe benefit relating to qualified retirement planning services—that is, any retirement planning advice or information provided to an employee and/or an employee's spouse by an employer maintaining a qualified retirement plan. [I.R.C. § 132]

Q 1:21   What is the Economic Growth and Tax Relief Reconciliation Act of 2001?

The Economic Growth and Tax Relief Reconciliation Act of 2001 (EGTRRA 2001) was signed into law by President Bush on June 7, 2001. EGTRRA 2001 raised contribution limits on IRAs and qualified retirement plans, liberalized portability and vesting rules, and made a host of changes affecting qualified retirement plans. Set forth below is a summary of the salient provisions of the Act.

IRAs

1. Increase IRA contributions to $3,000 in 2002, $4,000 in 2005, and $5,000 in 2008 and thereafter.
2. Increase the IRA limit by $500 in 2002 and by $1,000 in 2006 and thereafter for individuals age 50 or older.
3. Index for inflation the IRA limit in $500 increments after 2008.
4. Permit taxable IRA amounts to be rolled over to a qualified retirement plan.

Qualified Retirement Plans

1. Increase the compensation limit to $200,000.
2. Increase the annual benefit under a defined benefit plan to $160,000.
3. Increase the annual addition limitation under a defined contribution plan to $40,000 and repeal the 25-percent-of-compensation limitation.
4. Increase elective deferrals under 401(k) plans and 403(b) contracts to $11,000 in 2002, $12,000 in 2003, $13,000 in 2004, $14,000 in 2005, and $15,000 in 2006 and thereafter.
5. Index for inflation the elective deferral limit in $500 increments after 2006.
6. Increase SIMPLE plan elective deferrals to $10,000 over four years in $1,000 increments starting in 2002 and then indexing in $500 increments.
7. Permit individuals age 50 and older to make an additional contribution each year to a 401(k) plan, 403(b) contract, or SIMPLE plan.
8. Increase from 15 percent to 25 percent the deduction limit for profit sharing plans.
9. Include elective deferrals in compensation for deduction purposes.
10. Exclude elective deferrals from the employer contribution deduction limit.

11. Accelerate vesting of employer matching contributions.

12. Repeal the multiple use test.

13. Repeal the current liability full funding limit.

14. Create Roth-style 401(k) plans and 403(b) contracts in 2006.

15. Modify top-heavy rules.

16. Permit participant loans to owner-employees and S corporation shareholders.

17. Permit rollovers from various types of defined contribution arrangements to each other without restriction.

18. Permit voluntary employee contributions to be rolled over.

19. Disregard rollovers for cash-outs.

20. Eliminate the user fee in certain cases.

Q 1:22   What is the Victims of Terrorism Tax Relief Act of 2001?

The Victims of Terrorism Tax Relief Act of 2001 was signed into law by President Bush on January 23, 2002. The Act authorizes IRS, DOL, and Pension Benefit Guaranty Corporation (PBGC) to postpone filing and other deadlines for qualified retirement plans by up to one year for reasons of disasters, terrorism, or other military actions.

Under Section 7508A, IRS may prescribe regulations under which a period of up to 120 days may be disregarded for performing various acts under the Code such as filing tax returns, paying taxes, or filing a claim for credit or refund of tax, for any taxpayer determined to be affected by a Presidentially declared disaster. This Act expands and clarifies the scope of the deadlines and required actions that may be postponed under Section 7508A. IRS may prescribe a period of up to one year that may be disregarded in determining the date by which any action by a qualified retirement plan, or by a plan sponsor, plan administrator, participant, beneficiary, or other person would be required or permitted to be completed. Similar authority is provided to DOL and PBGC with respect to actions within their respective jurisdictions.

Q 1:23   What is the Job Creation and Worker Assistance Act of 2002?

This Act (JCWAA 2002) was signed into law by President Bush on March 9, 2002. The Act contained changes to the funding rules for defined benefit plans and made a number of technical corrections to provisions relating to qualified retirement plans that were enacted by EGTRRA 2001 (see Q 1:21).

Among the changes and technical corrections affecting qualified retirement plans are the following:

Catch-up Contributions

1. Individuals who reach age 50 by the end of the year are eligible to make catch-up contributions as of the beginning of the year.

2. Additional elective deferrals that do not exceed the catch-up contribution limit are excludable from an eligible participant's income.

3. A plan's catch-up contribution limit must be applied on an aggregate basis using the controlled group rules.

SEPs

1. The threshold compensation requirement for individual participation in a SEP is increased from $300 to $450.

2. The error in EGTRRA 2001 that limited an employer's contribution to a SEP to 15 percent, rather than 25 percent, of compensation is corrected.

3. Elective deferrals are not taken into account in applying the SEP deduction limits for employer contributions.

4. Compensation for purposes of determining deduction limits for contributions to SEPs includes salary reduction amounts.

Rollovers

1. Qualified retirement plan distributions that are rolled over are treated as consisting first of taxable amounts.

2. Direct rollovers of after-tax amounts from qualified retirement plans can be made only to defined contribution plans and IRAs.

3. Rollovers may be disregarded in determining the present value of a survivor annuity for cash-out purposes.

Small Employer Tax Credit

1. The small employer plan tax credit applies to plans that are first effective after 2001.

2. Aggregation rules for the small employer tax credit are based on the affiliated service group rules.

Other Provisions

1. The aggregate deduction limit for an employer's defined benefit and defined contribution plans does not apply if the defined contribution plan receives only elective deferrals.

2. Retirement contributions that qualify for the saver's credit must be reduced by nontaxable distributions.

3. Rules applying defined contribution plan limits to 403(b) contracts are clarified.

4. A transitional rule allows defined benefit plans that incorporate by reference the annual retirement benefit limitations to disregard the anti-cutback rule.

5. ESOP dividends reinvested in employer securities must be nonforfeitable.

Q 1:24   What is the Sarbanes-Oxley Act of 2002?

The Sarbanes-Oxley Act of 2002 (the Public Company Accounting Reform and Investor Protection Act of 2002) was signed by President Bush on July 30,

2002. The Act bars company directors and executive officers from trading in employer securities during a blackout period (of at least three consecutive business days) imposed on participants in individual account plans (see Q 2:2) of the employer, requires plan administrators (see Q 20:1) to provide at least 30 days advance notice of blackout periods to participants and beneficiaries under individual account plans, and increases criminal penalties for willful violations of ERISA's requirements. In addition, the Act contains a prohibition on loans to company officers, which may be interpreted as preventing company officers from taking loans from 401(k) plans (see Q 27:1) maintained by the company.

Q 1:25   What is the Pension Funding Equity Act of 2004?

On April 10, 2004, President Bush signed into law the Pension Funding Equity Act of 2004. This Act makes significant changes to the way in which a defined benefit plan (see Q 2:3) computes its funding obligations. Specifically, the Act replaces use of the 30-year Treasury bond interest rate used in determining required plan funding contributions. In its place, defined benefit plans may now use a rate based on long-term investment grade corporate bonds, as specified by IRS.

Record low interest rates in recent years created problems for sponsors of defined benefit plans in that they have had to increase funding obligations, pay higher premiums to PBGC, and pay larger single-sum distributions to terminated employees.

Under the Act, the long-term corporate bond interest rate applies in determining a plan's current liabilities. For plan years beginning in 2004 and 2005, the applicable interest rate is within a permissible range of the weighted average of the rate of interest as determined by IRS on amounts that are conservatively invested in long-term investment grade corporate bonds for the four-year period ending on the last day before the plan year begins. Similarly, for purposes of the PBGC variable rate premium, the interest rate used in determining the amount of unfunded vested benefits is based on the annual rate of interest determined by IRS on amounts conservatively invested in long-term investment grade corporate bonds for the month preceding the month in which the plan year begins.

However, the long-term corporate bond interest rate will not apply to the calculation of single-sum benefit distributions. In such cases, for plan years beginning in 2004 and 2005, a plan is prohibited from using an interest rate that is less than the greater of $5\frac{1}{2}$ percent or the interest rate specified in the plan. Under the Act, employers may still use the 30-year Treasury interest rate in calculating the maximum limit on deductible plan contributions. This means that employers may make larger funding contributions than would be required under the new long-term corporate bond interest rate to maximize their deductible plan contributions.

Multiemployer plans (see Q 29:2) are eligible to defer amortization of up to 80 percent of 2002 net experience losses for two plan years. Such plans must satisfy various criteria, including having a net investment loss of 10 percent or more of the average fair market value of assets for 2002 and a certified deficiency for any plan year beginning after June 30, 2003 and before July 1, 2006.

IRS has published the rates necessary for implementing the new law and the methodology used to determine them. The following indices are designated for use in determining the composite corporate bond rates beginning with September 2000 and continuing until further guidance is issued:

1. Citigroup High Grade Credit Index (AAA/AA, 101 Years);

2. Merrill Lynch US Corporates AA-AAA Rated 101 Years; and

3. Lehman Brothers USA Long Credit.

The composite corporate bond rate for a month is determined using the indices designated above. For each index designated for inclusion in determining the composite corporate bond rate for a month, a monthly rate is determined based on the average of the daily values for the yield to maturity for the bonds that are included in the index, as determined by the financial service firm maintaining the index. The composite corporate bond rate for the month is determined by computing the average of these monthly rates. [IRS Notice 2004-34, 2004-1 C.B. 848]

IRS has also set forth the procedure for electing an alternative deficit reduction contribution as permitted under the Act. [Ann. 2004-38, 2004-1 C.B. 878]

The Pension Protection Act of 2006 (see Q 1:33) has made many changes regarding the funding of defined benefit plans. Among the changes, the long-term corporate bond interest rate used in determining a plan's current liabilities has been extended to plan years beginning in 2006 and 2007. [IRS Notice 2006-75, 2006-2 C.B 366.

Q 1:26   What is the Working Families Tax Relief Act of 2004?

This Act was signed into law by President Bush on October 4, 2004. Among the changes and technical corrections affecting qualified retirement plans, the law:

1. Clarifies that the preexisting rounding rule of Section 415(d)(4)(A), governing benefits under defined benefit plans, applies for purposes of other Code provisions that refer to Section 415 but that do not contain a specific rounding rule.

2. Reflects the modified treatment of elective deferrals for purposes of the employer deduction limits, by removing elective deferrals from consideration in the application of the exception to the 10 percent excise tax on nondeductible contributions.

3. Allows wages paid to domestic workers to be treated as compensation in determining SIMPLE plan contributions, even though such amounts are not subject to income tax withholding.

4. Resolves the statutory oversight by requiring rollovers from qualified annuity plans to adhere to all of the requirements pertaining to rollovers from other qualified retirement plans.

5. Makes the spousal rollover option specifically available for distributions from qualified annuity plans.

Q 1:27 What is the Bankruptcy Abuse Prevention and Consumer Protection Act of 2005?

On April 20, 2005, President Bush signed into law the Bankruptcy Abuse Prevention and Consumer Protection Act of 2005, which contains provisions that will protect the retirement assets of bankruptcy filers. The legislation, which took effect on October 17, 2005, protects all retirement plan assets from creditors during bankruptcy proceedings by exempting those assets from the debtor's bankruptcy estate. An individual's bankruptcy estate will not include retirement funds to the extent that those funds are in a qualified retirement plan, SEP (see Q 32:1), SIMPLE plan (see Q 33:1), 403(b) contract (see Q 35:1), IRA (see Q 30:1), Roth IRA (see Q 31:1), or Section 457 plan. The new federal bankruptcy exemption is available whether or not the debtor's home state has opted out of the federal exemptions under the United States Bankruptcy Code.

To qualify retirement assets for the new federal bankruptcy exemption, the debtor must establish that the fund or account that holds the retirement assets is exempt from taxation. If the retirement assets are in a fund or account that has received a favorable determination letter (see Q 18:1) and that determination is in effect as of the date of the filing of the bankruptcy petition, then those assets will be presumed to be exempt from the debtor's bankruptcy estate. However, if the debtor's retirement assets are in a fund or account that has not received a favorable determination letter, then those retirement assets will be exempt from the debtor's bankruptcy estate if the debtor demonstrates that:

1. No prior unfavorable determination has been made by a court or by IRS, and

2. Either:
   a. The retirement fund or account is in substantial compliance with the applicable Code requirements, or
   b. The retirement fund or account is not in substantial compliance with the applicable Code requirements, but the debtor is not responsible for that failure.

The Act does not condition the exemption for IRA assets to those necessary for the support of the debtor and dependents. However, the amount of IRA assets that is protected during bankruptcy proceedings is limited to $1 million (adjusted for inflation), but amounts attributable to rollovers (see Q 34:1) from protected plans do not count toward the $1 million limit. The $1 million limit may also be increased if the interests of justice so require. The limit applies to traditional and Roth IRAs but not to SEPs or SIMPLE plans. The Act contains an exception from a discharge in bankruptcy for amounts owed by a debtor to a qualified retirement plan under loans permitted by ERISA or subject to the Code (see chapter 14). [Act § 224]

Because of the exemption difference between regular IRAs and rollover IRAs, a rollover IRA should be a discrete account (see Q 34:38). The Act provides that the rollover must be deposited not later than 60 days after the distribution. Although IRS can extend the 60-day rollover period (see Q 34:36), it is unclear at this time if such an extension will then cause a rollover IRA to be treated as a regular IRA with a $1 million limit. The Act provides that any distribution from a qualified retirement plan that qualifies as an eligible rollover distribution (see Q 34:8) does not cease to qualify for exemption by reason of such distribution. Apparently, such an eligible rollover distribution continues to be exempt even if not rolled over to an eligible retirement plan (see Q 34:16).

Since the Act did not become effective until October 17, 2005, its provisions do not apply to bankruptcy cases that commenced before the effective date. With respect to pre-effective date cases, see Qs 4:28, 27:111, 30:52, 34:42, and 35:53.

Q 1:28   What is the Katrina Emergency Tax Relief Act of 2005?

On September 23, 2005, President Bush signed the Katrina Emergency Tax Relief Act of 2005 (KETRA) into law. KETRA modifies existing rules governing retirement plan withdrawals and loans in order to free up additional funds for Hurricane Katrina victims.

Qualified Hurricane Katrina distributions defined

Many of the special tax breaks apply only to qualified Hurricane Katrina distributions, which include distributions made from an eligible retirement plan (see Q 34:16) on or after August 25, 2005, and before January 1, 2007, to an individual whose principal place of abode on August 28, 2005, is located in the Hurricane Katrina disaster area and who has sustained an economic loss by reason of Hurricane Katrina. The total amount of qualified Hurricane Katrina distributions that a person can receive from all plans, annuities, or IRAs is $100,000 (that is, the $100,000 limit is applied to each taxpayer and not to each retirement account).

Victims of Hurricane Katrina may withdraw up to $100,000 from a 401(k) plan, an IRA, or other retirement plan without incurring the 10 percent tax on early distributions (see Q 16:1). This provision applies to distributions made on or after August 25, 2005, and before January 1, 2007.

Three-year income averaging available

Individuals eligible for the penalty waiver for qualified Hurricane Katrina distributions are permitted to pay income tax on such distributions ratably over a three-year period, unless the person elects not to have the three-year ratable inclusion rules apply. Amounts distributed may be recontributed to a qualified retirement plan over the three-year period following the distribution date. Any amounts recontributed receive rollover treatment and are not includible in income.

Recontributions of withdrawals for home purchases cancelled due to Katrina

A distribution received by an individual from a 401(k) plan, a 403(b) contract, or an IRA in order to buy a home in the Hurricane Katrina disaster area may be recontributed to the plan, annuity, or IRA in certain circumstances. This KETRA provision applies to an individual who receives a qualified distribution—a hardship distribution from a 401(k) plan or 403(b) contract (see

Qs 27:14, 35:35), or a qualified first-time homebuyer distribution from an IRA (see Q 16:16) (1) that is received after February 28, 2005, and before August 29, 2005, and (2) that was used to buy or construct a principal residence in the Hurricane Katrina disaster area that could not be purchased or constructed because of Hurricane Katrina.

Under the provision, any part of a qualified distribution may, during the period from August 25, 2005, through February 28, 2006, be recontributed to a plan, annuity, or IRA to which a rollover is permitted. Any amount that is recontributed is treated as a rollover and is not includible in income or subject to the 10 percent tax on early distributions.

Increased plan loan limits

The dollar limitations on loans from qualified retirement plans are doubled for Hurricane Katrina victims (see Q 14:4). Under KETRA, plan loan limits are increased to the lesser of (1) $100,000 reduced by the excess of (a) the highest outstanding balance of all other loans to the participant from all plans maintained by the employer during the prior one-year period ending on the day before the loan is made over (b) the outstanding loan balance on the date the loan is made, or (2) the greater of $10,000 or the participant's accrued benefit under the plan. This provision is effective for loans made on or after September 23, 2005, and before January 1, 2007, and apply for qualified individuals whose principal place of abode on August 28, 2005, is located in the Hurricane Katrina disaster area and who has sustained an economic loss due to Katrina.

Any qualified loan that was outstanding on or after August 25, 2005, with any required payment due date falling between August 25, 2005, and December 31, 2006, will have that required due date deferred for one year. Subsequent repayment schedules will be adjusted accordingly for the five-year and the level payment requirements (see Qs 14:5, 14:6).

Provisions relating to plan amendments

KETRA allows for plan amendments made due to the retirement-related provisions of this law to be effective retroactively. In order for this provision to apply, the plan amendment must be made on or before the last day of the first plan year beginning in 2007. IRS is authorized to extend the deadline for making KETRA-related plan amendments. Governmental plans receive an additional two years to make required plan amendments.

If a plan needs to make an amendment in order to retain its qualified status due to KETRA's retirement provisions (or any regulations under KETRA), the amendment must be made retroactively effective as of the date on which the change became effective with regard to the plan. KETRA also requires that the plan be operated in compliance until the amendment is made. If an amendment is made due to KETRA but is not necessary to retain a plan's qualified status, the amendment may be made retroactively effective as of the first day the plan is operated in accordance with the amendment.

Extended filing deadlines

Qualifying taxpayers now have until February 28, 2006, to file any returns and pay taxes for any period that had not expired by August 25, 2005.

IRS announced that, for participants and employers located in areas in Louisiana, Mississippi, and Alabama that have been declared disaster areas as a result of Hurricane Katrina, 401(k) and similar employer-sponsored retirement plans will be permitted to make loans and hardship distributions under streamlined loan procedures and liberalized hardship distribution rules. The relief authorizes a distribution to redress any hardship of the employee resulting from the hurricane and is not limited to hardships enumerated in the regulations. If plans do not currently have loan or hardship distribution features, they will be allowed to make the loans or distributions before the plan is formally amended, as long as the plans are amended no later than the end of the first plan year beginning after December 31, 2005. Distributions must be made between August 29, 2005, and March 31, 2006. [Ann. 2005-70, 2005-2 C.B. 682]

IRS has provided detailed guidance on the provisions of KETRA. [IRS Notice 2005-92, 2005-2 C.B. 1165] See Q 1:29 for a discussion of the Gulf Opportunity Zone Act of 2005.

Q 1:29 What is the Gulf Opportunity Zone Act of 2005?

On December 21, 2005, President Bush signed into law the Gulf Opportunity Zone Act of 2005 (GO Zone). The Act codifies and expands the pension-related relief provided by KETRA (see Q 1:28) to include victims of Hurricanes Rita and Wilma.

Q 1:30 What is the Deficit Reduction Act of 2005?

This Act was signed into law by President Bush on February 8, 2006.

The Act increases the single-employer flat rate premium to $30 per participant (from the current level of $19; see Q 21:27) and increases the multiemployer plan (see Q 29:2) flat-rate premium to $8 (from the current level of $2.60). The increases are effective for plan years beginning after December 31, 2005. For each plan year beginning in a calendar year after 2006, the flat rate premiums will be indexed to the national average wage index.

The Act also contains a new premium for certain single-employer plans that are terminated (generally, situations where PBGC (see Q 25:10) takes over as trustee of the terminated plan). Such plans are subject to a premium of $1,250 multiplied by the number of participants in the plan immediately before the termination date. This new premium is generally effective for plan years beginning after December 31, 2005. However, the premium will not apply to a single-employer plan that is terminated during the pendency of any bankruptcy reorganization under chapter 11 of the United States Bankruptcy Code (or under any similar law of a state or political subdivision of a state), if the proceeding is pursuant to a bankruptcy filing that occurred before October 18, 2005. In addition, the termination premiums will not apply to plans terminated after December 31, 2010.

The Act also increases the limit on federal deposit insurance available for retirement funds held at banks and credit unions from $100,0000 under current law to $250,000.

Q 1:31   What is the Tax Increase Prevention and Reconciliation Act of 2005?

This Act (TIPRA) was signed into law by President Bush on May 17, 2006, and contains a provision repealing the income limits on conversions of traditional IRAs to Roth IRAs, starting in 2010 (see Q 31:44).

Under current law, to convert a traditional IRA to a Roth IRA, the taxpayer's adjusted gross income (AGI) for the year must not exceed $100,000. The $100,000 limit applies to the combined income of a married couple filing jointly. Under TIPRA, the income limit will be eliminated, effective for taxable years beginning after December 31, 2009. Thus, taxpayers, including married taxpayers filing separate returns, would be permitted to make such conversions without regard to their AGI. Under TIPRA, taxpayers could elect to pay tax on amounts converted in 2010 in equal installments in 2011 and 2012. However, income inclusion would be accelerated if converted amounts were distributed before 2012. Taxpayers who convert their IRAs in or after 2011 would pay the resulting tax in the following year.

TIPRA also imposes an excise tax on any entity manager of a tax-exempt entity who knowingly approves a prohibited tax shelter transaction. The amount of the tax imposed on an entity manager who approves the entity as a party to a prohibited tax shelter transaction is $20,000 for each approval (or other act causing participation). Tax-exempt entity includes a qualified retirement plan, a 403(b) contract (see Q 35:1), an IRA, and a Roth IRA. IRS issued a notice to ensure that retirement plans and other tax-exempt entities and other affected parties are aware of the new excise taxes and disclosure rules that target certain potentially abusive tax shelter transactions to which a tax-exempt entity is a party. [IRS Notice 2006-65, 2006-2 C.B. 102]

IRS issued final, temporary, and proposed regulations providing guidance on prohibited tax shelter transactions for tax-exempt entities, such as qualified retirement plans and IRAs. The guidance defines prohibited tax shelter transactions, sets forth disclosure requirements, and specifies parties subject to the applicable excise taxes and attendant reporting and disclosure requirements.

The regulations provide that entity managers of plan entities who are liable for the applicable excise taxes as entity managers are required to file a return on Form 5330, "Return of Excise Taxes Related to Employee Benefit Plans." The Form 5330 is due on or before the 15th day of the fifth month following the close of the manager's taxable year during which the entity entered into a prohibited tax shelter transaction. The regulations also provided a transition rule that Forms 5330 that were due on or before October 4, 2007 would be deemed timely if the Form 5330 was filed, and the tax paid, before that date. Every tax-exempt entity to which the excise tax applies that is a party to a prohibited tax shelter transaction is required to disclose to IRS (in such form and manner and at such time as determined by IRS) that such entity is a party to the prohibited tax shelter transaction and the identity of any other party to the transaction which is known to the tax-exempt entity. Any taxable party to a prohibited tax shelter transaction is required to disclose by statement to any tax-exempt entity to which the excise tax applies that is a party to such transaction that such transaction is a prohibited tax shelter transaction. IRS provided interim guidance regarding the circumstances under which a tax-exempt entity will be treated as a party to a prohibited tax shelter transaction and regarding the allocation to various periods of net income and proceeds attributable to a prohibited tax shelter transaction, including amounts received prior to the effective date of the excise tax. [I.R.C. §§ 4965, 6011(g), 6033(a)(2); Treas. Reg. § 54.6011-1; Temp. Treas. Reg. §§ 54.6011-1T, 1.6033-5T, 301.6033-5T; 53.6071-1T; Prop. Treas. Reg. §§ 53.4965-1–53.4965-9, 301.6011(g)-(1); preambles to final, temporary, and proposed regulations; IRS Notice 2007-18, 2007-1 C.B. 608]

IRS issued final regulations that became effective on July 6, 2010. The final regulations generally follow the proposed regulations but revise the definition of "party to a prohibited tax shelter transaction" and make other conforming modifications. Generally, a tax-exempt entity that enters into a transaction to reduce or eliminate its own tax liability will not be considered a party to a prohibited tax shelter transaction. However, IRS may identify in published guidance specific transactions or circumstances in which a tax-exempt entity that enters into a transaction to reduce or eliminate its own tax liability will be treated as a party to a prohibited tax shelter transaction. The final regulations also modify the proposed regulations regarding the timing for disclosures by the taxable party to the tax-exempt entity. The taxable party must make the disclosure within 60 days after the later of:

1. The date the person becomes a taxable party to the transaction;
2. The date the taxable party knows or has reason to know that the exempt entity is a party to the transaction; or
3. July 6, 2010

The proposed regulations included an exception for persons who do not know or have reason to know that a tax-exempt entity is a party to the transaction on or before the first date on which the transaction is required to be disclosed by the person. The final regulations retain this exception. [Treas. Reg. §§ 53.4965-1 through 53.4965-9, 54.6011-1, 301.6011(g)-1, 1.6033-5, 301.6033-5, 53.6071-1]

Q 1:32   What is the Heroes Earned Retirement Opportunities Act?

President Bush signed this Act (HERO) into law on May 29, 2006.

Under HERO, for taxable years beginning on or after January 1, 2004, members of the armed forces may treat combat pay as compensation for purposes of the IRA contribution and deduction rules.

Individuals who received excluded combat pay for a taxable year beginning after 2003 and ending before May 29, 2006, have a three-year period in which to make a contribution to an IRA for that tax year and to have the contribution treated as having been made on the last day of that taxable year. The period ends on May 28, 2009.

Q 1:33   What is the Pension Protection Act of 2006?

This Act (PPA) was signed into law by President Bush on August 17, 2006, and is the most comprehensive pension legislation since ERISA (see Q 1:14). Among its many provisions, the changes contained in EGTRRA 2001 (see Q 1:21) have been made permanent. Other changes affect:

Minimum Funding Rules

1. Liability for minimum required contributions to single-employer defined benefit plans.
2. Minimum funding standards for single-employer defined benefit plans.
3. Benefit limitations under single-employer defined benefit plans.
4. Restrictions on funding of nonqualified deferred compensation plans by employers maintaining underfunded or terminated single-employer defined benefit plans.
5. Extension of interest rate used in determining a single-employer defined benefit plan's current liabilities.
6. Changes in minimum funding rules for multiemployer plans.
7. Additional funding rules for significantly underfunded multiemployer plans.
8. Testing insolvency of multiemployer plans.
9. Multiemployer plans withdrawal liability rules.

Reporting and Disclosure

1. Annual funding notices for defined benefit plans.
2. Access to multiemployer plan financial information.
3. Additional annual reporting requirements for defined benefit plans.
4. Electronic display of annual report information.
5. Section 4010 filings with Pension Benefit Guaranty Corporation (PBGC).

PBGC

1. Variable rate premium.
2. Variable rate premiums for plans of small employers.
3. Premium overpayment refunds.
4. Limitation on reduction in PBGC guarantee for shutdown and other benefits.
5. Guaranteed benefits and asset allocations if plan sponsor enters bankruptcy.
6. Rules for substantial owner benefits in terminated plans.
7. PBGC computation of benefits attributable to recoveries from employers.

8. Missing participants.

Investment of Plan Assets, Prohibited Transactions, and Fiduciary Rules

1. Diversification requirements for defined contribution plans.
2. Notice of right of divest employer securities.
3. Periodic benefit statement for participants and beneficiaries in defined contribution plans.
4. Investment advice provided to participants by fiduciary advisers.
5. Amendments relating to prohibited transactions.
6. Increased maximum bond amount for plans holding employer securities.
7. Criminal penalties for coercive interference with protected rights.
8. Treatment of investment of assets where participant fails to exercise investment election.
9. Fiduciary standards clarified for buying annuities used for defined contribution plan distributions.

Plan Contributions and Benefits

1. Increase in deduction limitation for contributions to single-employer defined benefit plans.
2. Increase in deduction limitation for contributions to multiemployer defined benefit plans.
3. Overall limitation on deductions for contributions to combined plans relaxed.
4. Vesting schedule accelerated for employer contributions to defined contribution plans.
5. Determination of average compensation for benefit limitation purposes.
6. Lump-sum calculation for minimum valuation rules.

Plan Distributions

1. Valuation of lump-sum distributions.
2. Modification of rules regarding hardships and unforeseen financial emergencies.
3. Distributions during working or phased retirement.
4. Notice and consent period regarding distributions.
5. Transfer of excess pension assets to multiemployer health plans.

Rollovers

1. Direct rollovers from eligible retirement plans to Roth IRAs.
2. Rollover of after-tax contributions to defined benefit plans and tax-sheltered annuity contracts.
3. Rollovers by nonspouse beneficiaries.
4. Effect of rollover distributions on unemployment compensation.

Plan Qualification

1. Cash balance and pension equity plan conversions.
2. Automatic enrollment in 401(k) plans.
3. Combined defined benefit and 401(k) plans.
4. Regulations on time and order of issuance of domestic relations orders.
5. Additional survivor annuity option.

Plan Administration

1. Reporting simplification for small retirement plans.
2. Employee plans compliance resolution system (EPCRS).
3. Provisions related to plan amendments.

Individual Retirement Plans

1. Inflation adjustments to adjusted gross income limitations applicable to IRAs and Roth IRAs.
2. Tax-free IRA distributions to charities.
3. Direct payment of tax refunds to IRAs.
4. Additional IRA contributions for individuals affected by an employer's bankruptcy.

In general, amendments required to comply with PPA need not be made until the last day of the first plan year beginning on or after January 1, 2009, and any such amendment will not violate the anti-cutback rule (see Q 9:25). [PPA § 1107]

Q 1:34   What is the Small Business Tax Act of 2007?

President Bush signed this Act (SBTA 2007) into law on May 25, 2007. Among its provisions, the following are pension-related:

- Revocation of election relating to treatment as multiemployer plan
- Modification of requirements for qualified transfers
- Extension of alternative deficit reduction contribution rules
- Modification of the interest rate for pension funding rules

Q 1:35   What is the Heroes Earnings Assistance and Relief Tax Act of 2008?

This Act (HEART Act) was signed into law on June 17, 2008.

Under the Act, a differential wage payment is any payment that (1) is made by an employer to an individual with respect to any period during which the individual is performing service in the uniformed services while on active duty for a period of more than 30 days, and (2) represents all or a portion of the wages the individual would have received from the employer if the individual were performing service for the employer. Differential wage payments are treated as compensation for purposes of retirement plans that are subject to the special rules relating to veteran's reemployment rights under USERRA (see Q 1:16). Differential wage payments are also included in compensation for purposes of the annual limitations on contributions to IRAs (see Q 30:1) and Roth IRAs (see Q 31:1). During any period in which the individual is performing military service while on active duty for a period of more than 30 days, the individual is treated as having been severed from employment during this period with respect to elective deferrals under a 401(k) plan (see Q 27:1) and amounts attributable to a salary reduction agreement under a 403(b) plan (see Q 35:1). These provisions generally apply for years beginning after December 31, 2008.

The rules allowing for penalty-free distributions from retirement plans for individuals ordered or called to active duty for more than 179 days are now permanent and apply to reservists ordered or called to active duty on or after December 31, 2007 (see Q 16:3).

An individual who receives a military death gratuity or payment under the Servicemembers' Group Life Insurance (SGLI) program may contribute an amount up to the sum of the gratuity and SGLI payments received to a Roth IRA, notwithstanding the annual contribution limit and the income phase-out of the contribution limit that otherwise apply to contributions to Roth IRAs. The contribution will be considered a qualified rollover contribution if the contribution is made before the end of the one-year period beginning on the date on which the amount is received. This provision generally applies with respect to death from injuries occurring on or after June 17, 2008.

A qualified retirement plan and a 403(b) plan must now provide that the survivors of a participant who dies while performing qualified military service are entitled to any additional benefits provided under the plan had the participant returned and then terminated employment on account of death. For benefit accrual purposes, an employer who sponsors a plan may treat a participant in the plan who dies or becomes disabled while performing qualified military service as if the individual had resumed employment on the day preceding death or disability and terminated employment on the actual date of death or disability. These provisions apply with respect to deaths and disabilities occurring on or after January 1, 2007.

IRS discussed highlights of the HEART Act. [*Retirement News for Employers*, Summer 2008] IRS also issued HEART Act guidance on military service benefits. [IRS Notice 2010-15, 2010-6 I.R.B. 390]

The survivors of a participant who dies while performing qualified military service must be entitled to any additional benefits (other than benefit accruals relating to the period of qualified military service) that would be provided under the plan if the participant had resumed employment and then terminated employment on account of death. Qualified military service with respect to an individual is any service in the uniformed services by an individual entitled to reemployment rights under USERRA. The types of additional benefits include accelerated vesting, ancillary life insurance benefits, and other survivor's benefits provided under a plan that are contingent on a participant's termination of employment on account of death. [I.R.C. § 401(a)(37); IRS Notice 2010-15, § II, Q&A-1, 2010-6 I.R.B. 390] Benefit accruals (see Q 9:2) for the period of qualified military service are specifically excepted from the additional benefits to which survivors must be entitled in the case of a participant who dies while performing such service. Accordingly, benefit accruals (whether benefit accruals under a defined benefit plan (see Q 2:3) or contributions under a defined contribution plan (see Q 2:2)) are not required to be imputed for the period of qualified military service for purposes of determining death benefits that are based on a deceased participant's accrued benefit. [IRS Notice 2010-15, § II, Q&A-2, 2010-6 I.R.B. 390] Each period of an individual's qualified military service is, upon reemployment, deemed to constitute service with the employer for vesting (see Q 9:1) and accrual purposes. Although an exception is provided for benefit accruals for the period of qualified military service, there is no exception for vesting service. Accordingly, even though benefit accruals are not required to be provided for the deceased participant's period of qualified military service, service credit for such period must be provided for vesting purposes. [I.R.C. §§ 401(a)(37), 414(u)(8)(B); IRS Notice 2010-15, § II, Q&A-3, 2010-6 I.R.B. 390] A qualified retirement plan must provide that, in the case of a participant who dies while performing qualified military service, the participant's survivors are entitled to certain death benefits. If a participant would not be entitled to reemployment rights with respect to an employer under USERRA if the participant had applied for reemployment rights immediately before death, this provision does not apply in determining the death benefits to which the participant's survivors are entitled under the employer's plan. [I.R.C. § 414(u)(5); IRS Notice 2010-15, § II, Q&A-4, 2010-6 I.R.B. 390]

Under the HEART Act, an employer sponsoring a qualified retirement plan may, for benefit accrual purposes, treat an individual who dies or becomes disabled while performing qualified military service as if the individual had resumed employment in accordance with the individual's USERRA reemployment rights on the date preceding the death or disability and then terminated employment on the actual date of death or disability. This provision applies only if all individuals performing qualified military service with respect to the employer maintaining the plan who die or become disabled as a result of performing qualified military service prior to reemployment by the employer are credited with service and benefits on reasonably equivalent terms. The amount of employee contributions (see Q 27:74) and the amount of elective deferrals (see Q 27:16) of an individual treated as reemployed are determined on the basis of the individual's average actual employee contributions or elective deferrals for the lesser of (1) the 12-month period of service with the employer immediately prior to qualified military service or (2) the actual length of continuous service with the employer. These provisions apply with respect to deaths and disabilities occurring on or after January 1, 2007. [I.R.C. § 414(u)(9)(C); IRS Notice 2010-15, § II, 2010-6 I.R.B. 390] Because these new provisions are permissive rather than mandatory, they may be applied beginning as of any date on or after January 1, 2007. For nondiscrimination rules regarding the timing of plan amendments, see Q 4:21. [IRS Notice 2010-15, § II, Q&A-5, 2010-6 I.R.B. 390]

If, for benefit accrual purposes, a plan provides for treatment of an individual who dies while performing qualified military service as if the individual had resumed employment, the plan must also provide vesting credit for that service. This vesting credit is taken into account for purposes of determining a participant's vested percentage in accruals earned both during qualified military service and during other periods. [I.R.C. § 414(u)(9)(A); IRS Notice 2010-15, § II, Q&A-6, 2010-6 I.R.B. 390] If, for benefit accrual purposes, a plan provides for treatment of an individual who becomes disabled while performing qualified military service as if the individual had resumed employment, the plan need not also provide vesting credit for that service. However, plans are not prohibited from providing vesting credit for a disabled individual's qualified military service to the extent permitted under other applicable rules, including nondiscrimination rules for crediting imputed service (i.e., service other than actual service with the employer) (see Q 4:21). There must be a legitimate business reason for crediting the imputed service (which is deemed to exist in the case of credit for military service); the plan provision crediting the imputed service to any highly compensated employee (HCE; see Q 3:2) must apply on the same terms to all similarly situated non-highly compensated employees (NHCEs; see Q 3:12); and the plan provision must not by design or in operation discriminate significantly in favor of HCEs. Imputed service for a period of qualified military service that is credited for vesting purposes to an individual who became disabled while performing qualified military service will satisfy these requirements if the plan provision crediting the service to any HCE applies on the same terms to all similarly situated NHCEs. [I.R.C. § 414(u)(9)(A); Treas. Reg. §§ 1.401(a)(4)-1(d), 1.401(a)(4)-11(d)(3); IRS Notice 2010-15, § II Q&A-7, 2010-6 I.R.B. 390]

For purposes of how a plan may determine employer-provided contributions or benefits for an individual treated as reemployed where those contributions or benefits are contingent on the individual's employee contributions or elective deferrals, the HEART Act does not provide for actual employee contributions or elective deferrals. Instead, an individual who dies or becomes disabled while performing qualified military service is deemed to have made employee contributions or elective deferrals for the purpose of determining benefits that are contingent on employee contributions or elective deferrals. For this purpose as discussed above, the individual is deemed to have made employee contributions or elective deferrals in an amount equal to the lesser of the actual average employee contributions or elective deferrals made by the individual under the plan during the 12-month period prior to military service or, if service with the employer is less than 12 months, the average actual employee contributions or elective deferrals for the actual length of continuous service with the employer. However, in the case of a disabled individual who is covered by a plan that permits disabled individuals to make employee contributions or elective deferrals and who is treated as reemployed, the plan is not prohibited from allowing the disabled individual to make employee contributions or elective deferrals with respect to periods of qualified military service in the permitted amounts. In that case, the plan is also not prohibited from determining the disabled individual's employer-sponsored contributions or benefits based on the actual employee contributions or elective deferrals made by the disabled individual. [I.R.C. §§ 414(u)(8)(C), 414(u)(9)(C); IRS Notice 2010-15, § II, Q&A-8, 2010-6 I.R.B. 390]

In the case of employees who are called to active duty, some employers have paid some or all of the compensation that a service member would have received from the employer during the service member's period of active duty had the employee not been called to active duty. Prior to the enactment of the HEART Act, these differential wage payments were not treated as wages for federal employment tax purposes. [IRS Notice 2010-15, § III, 2010-6 I.R.B. 390] Differential wage payments are not required to be treated as compensation for purposes of determining contributions and benefits under a plan. However, such payments are treated as compensation for purposes of applying the Code. Accordingly, these payments must be treated as Section 415 compensation (see Q 6:41). [IRS Notice 2010-15, § III, Q&A-9, 2010-6 I.R.B. 390] A plan's definition of compensation will not fail to satisfy Section 414(s) merely because differential wage payments are excluded from the plan's definition of compensation for purposes of determining benefits and contributions (see Q 6:64). [IRS Notice 2010-15, § III, Q&A-10, 2010-6 I.R.B. 390]

The rule that treats an individual as severed from employment while performing service in the uniformed services is not limited to individuals receiving differential wage payments. The rule applies to all individuals on active duty for a period of more than 30 days, regardless of whether they are receiving differential wage payments. Thus, for purposes of applying rules that permit distributions upon severance from employment from 401(k) plans (see Q 27:14), 403(b) plans (see Q 35:35), and governmental Section 457 plans, an individual is treated as having been severed from employment during any period the individual is performing service in the uniformed services while on active duty for a period of more than 30 days. [I.R.C. § 414(u)(12)(B); IRS Notice 2010-15, § III, Q&A-11, 2010-6 I.R.B. 390] Just as a plan may, but is not required to, provide for distributions from a 401(k), 403(b), or governmental Section 457 plan upon actual severance from employment, a plan may, but is not required to, provide for distributions upon a deemed severance from employment. Thus, for example, a plan that provides for distributions upon severance from employment may, but is not required to, also provide for distributions upon a deemed severance from employment. If a plan provides for a distribution upon a deemed severance from employment, the plan must also provide that an individual receiving the distribution may not make an elective deferral or employee contribution during the six-month period beginning on the date of the distribution. [I.R.C. § 414(u)(12)(B)(ii); IRS Notice 2010-15, § III, Q&A-12, 2010-6 I.R.B. 390]

The deemed severance rule applies only for purposes of 401(k), 403(b), and governmental Section 457 plans that permit distributions on severance from employment. Thus, for example, in the event an individual is treated as severed from employment, the individual may receive a distribution otherwise subject to the distribution restrictions. On the other hand, merely because an individual is treated as severed from employment does not cause such individual to be treated as severed from employment under other sections of the Code. [IRS Notice 2010-15, § III, Q&A-13, 2010-6 I.R.B. 390] The deemed severance rule does not apply to individuals who have an actual severance from employment or who otherwise are eligible to take a distribution of plan benefits. The rule does not affect the status of an individual who is on active duty for a period of more than 30 days and who has, in fact, had a severance from employment. Thus, for example, if such an individual receives a distribution from a 401(k) plan and returns to employment within six months, the rule would not preclude the individual from making elective deferrals or employee contributions to the plan before the end of the six-month period. The rule also does not affect a plan's ability to make other in-service distributions to the extent permitted under other applicable rules and plan terms. Thus, for example, a 401(k) plan may distribute a participant's elective deferrals when the participant attains age 59½, or under other permitted circumstances, and the distribution would not be subject to the six-month restriction on elective deferrals (although a six-month restriction may apply to a distribution from a 401(k) on account of a financial hardship). [I.R.C. §§401(k)(2)(B)(i)(I), 401(k)(2)(B)(i)(IV), 414(u)(12)(B)(ii); IRS Notice 2010-15, § III, Q&A-14, 2010-6 I.R.B. 390]

If an individual receives a distribution that meets the definition of a qualified reservist distribution (see Q 16:3), the distribution will be treated as a qualified reservist distribution even if the distribution would also have been permitted as a result of a deemed severance of employment. For example, if a plan provides for qualified reservist distributions and for distributions on deemed severance, a distribution to an individual that could be either type of distribution will be treated as a qualified reservist distribution. In that case, the distribution would not be subject to the six-month restriction on elective deferrals or to the 10 percent tax on early distributions (see Q 16:1). [I.R.C. § 72(t)(2)(G)(iii); IRS Notice 2010-15, § III, Q&A-15, 2010-6 I.R.B. 390] A distribution made because of a deemed severance is an eligible rollover distribution, except to the extent that an exception (other than the exception for hardship distributions) applies (see Q 34:8). Such a distribution is not treated as a hardship distribution ineligible for rollover. An eligible rollover distribution that is paid to an employee (rather than directly rolled over) is subject to 20 percent mandatory withholding (see Q 20:11). [IRS Notice 2010-15, § III, Q&A-16, 2010-6 I.R.B. 390]

The contributions and benefits provided as a result of differential wage payments may be included in a plan's nondiscrimination testing. A qualified retirement plan is not treated as failing to meet the requirements of any nondiscrimination provision by reason of any contribution or benefit based on a differential wage payment, as long as the differential wage payment and the ability to make contributions based on the differential wage payment are provided on reasonably equivalent terms. Accordingly, the contributions and benefits provided under a plan as a result of differential wage payments need not be included in the plan's nondiscrimination testing. On the other hand, this does not prevent such contributions and benefits from being taken into account, as long as they do not cause the plan to fail the nondiscrimination requirements. If such contributions and benefits are included in the plan's nondiscrimination testing for any employee, they must be taken into account for all employees.

[I.R.C. §§ 414(u)(1)(C), 414(u)(12)(A); IRS Notice 2010-15, § III, Q&A-17, 2010-6 I.R.B. 390]

The 10 percent tax on early distributions does not apply to a qualified reservist distribution. A qualified reservist distribution can be made without regard to otherwise applicable restrictions on in-service distributions of amounts attributable to elective deferrals. In addition, during the two-year period beginning on the day after the end of the individual's active duty service, an individual who receives a qualified reservist distribution may make contributions to an IRA in an amount up to the amount of the qualified reservist distribution, which are not subject to the otherwise applicable limits on IRA contributions and are not deductible. As originally enacted, these special rules for qualified reservist distributions applied to individuals ordered or called to active duty after September 11, 2001 and before December 31, 2007. The reference to December 31, 2007 is deleted, so that the special rules for qualified reservist distributions no longer have an expiration date. [I.R.C. § 72(t)(2)(G)(iii); IRS Notice 2010-15, § IV, 2010-6 I.R.B. 390]

Generally, plan amendments adopting required HEART Act changes must be made on or before the last day of the first plan year beginning on or after January 1, 2010 (January 1, 2012, for governmental plans). [IRS Notice 2010-15, § V, 2010-6 I.R.B. 390; IRS Notice 2010-15, § V, Q&As-18, 19, 2010-6 I.R.B. 390]

A qualified rollover contribution includes the contribution to a Roth IRA of a military death gratuity or SGLI payment if the contribution is made before the end of the one-year period beginning on the date on which the IRA beneficiary receives the military death gratuity or SGLI payment. Thus, the annual limits on Roth IRA contributions (see Qs 31:4, 31:5) and the phaseout based on income (see Q 31:16) do not apply to such a contribution. The amount treated as a qualified rollover contribution to a Roth IRA cannot exceed the total amount of the military death gratuity and SGLI payment received, reduced by any portion of such amount contributed to a Coverdell education savings account or another Roth IRA. For purposes of applying the 10 percent tax on early distributions to a distribution from a Roth IRA, the amount treated as a qualified rollover contribution is treated as investment in the contract (see Q 13:3). This generally applies with respect to deaths from injuries occurring on or after June 17, 2008. However, a contribution was permitted to a Roth IRA of a military death gratuity or an SGLI payment received with respect to a death from injuries occurring before June 17, 2008 (on or after October 7, 2001), if the contribution was made no later than June 17, 2009. [IRS Notice 2010-15, § VI, 2010-6 I.R.B. 390]

Q 1:36   What is the Worker, Retiree, and Employer Recovery Act of 2008?

This Act (WRERA 2008) was signed into law on December 23, 2008. Among its provisions are the following:

- Suspends required minimum distributions for 2009
- Clarifies Roth IRA rollover rules

- Mandates nonspouse beneficiary rollovers
- Provides funding relief for defined benefit plans
- Delays provisions relating to multiemployer plans

Q 1:37   What is the Pension Relief Act of 2010?

Signed into law by President Obama on June 25, 2010, PRA 2010 was part of The Preservation of Access to Care for Medicare Beneficiaries and Pension Relief Act of 2010.

PRA 2010 provides temporary relief for plans that suffered significant losses in asset value due to the steep market decline in 2008. PRA 2010 permits a sponsor of a single-employer plan to reduce a plan's minimum required contribution by electing to use an extended alternative shortfall amortization schedule. In the case of a multiemployer plan, PRA 2010 provides a special amortization rule for certain net investment losses.

Q 1:38   What is the Small Business Jobs Act of 2010?

This Act, SBJA 2010, was signed into law by President Obama on September 27, 2010.

Under SBJA 2010, eligible retirement plan distributions from 401(k) and 403(b) plans made after September 27, 2010 may be rolled over to a designated Roth account within the plan. Any amount required to be included in gross income for the 2010 taxable year is included in income in equal amounts for the 2011 and 2012 taxable years unless the taxpayer elects otherwise. In addition, governmental Section 457 plans may add designated Roth accounts to their plans for taxable years beginning after 2010.

Q 1:39   Does the adoption of a qualified retirement plan by an employer constitute a contractual obligation to maintain the plan?

No. Although a qualified retirement plan must be a permanent plan (see Qs 1:42, 25:1), continuance of the plan is voluntary. It is not a contractual obligation of the company, except in the case of certain collectively bargained plans.

A carefully drafted plan will specifically limit the company's obligation to maintain and fund the plan. In addition, the company should expressly retain the right to reduce, suspend, or discontinue contributions and the right to terminate the plan (see Q 25:2).

Q 1:40   What costs will the company incur in adopting a qualified retirement plan?

Professional fees vary, depending on the type of plan adopted by the company. However, the following types of services are generally required:

1. Legal services for drafting the plan and trust and for submitting those and other required documents to IRS to obtain tax qualification;

2. Accounting services; and

3. Actuarial services to provide cost and benefit computations if a defined benefit plan is adopted.

It is also possible to adopt a master or prototype plan (see Q 2:27) designed by an insurance company, a bank, or other investment-oriented company (a mutual fund, for example). These institutions generally charge less for their services because they expect to profit from the products (e.g., life insurance policies) that the adopting company may be required to purchase.

See Q 12:27 for a discussion of the tax credit for new qualified retirement plan expenses.

Q 1:41   Is there any type of tax-favored qualified retirement plan for the business owner that is easy to adopt and inexpensive to operate?

Yes, a SEP requires only a minimal amount of paperwork and expense to adopt and administer. An employer may also adopt a SIMPLE plan for employees that may require minimal paperwork and expense. For details on SEPs and SIMPLE plans, see chapters 32 and 33.

Q 1:42   Must the company contribute to the plan each year once it adopts a qualified retirement plan?

It depends on the type of plan adopted. IRS says that the adoption of a qualified retirement plan commits the company to maintaining the plan on a permanent basis. For this purpose, permanent means that, from the plan's inception, the company must intend to support the plan over a number of years. The term "plan" implies a permanent, as distinguished from a temporary, program. Thus, although the employer may reserve the right to change or terminate the plan, the abandonment of the plan for any reason other than business necessity within a few years after it has taken effect will be evidence that the plan from its inception was not a bona fide program for the exclusive benefit of employees in general. The permanency of the plan will be indicated by all of the surrounding facts and circumstances, including the likelihood of the employer's ability to continue contributions as provided under the plan. [Treas. Reg. § 1.401-1(b)(2)]

Annual contributions to a pension plan are required. Although there are exceptions to this rule, a company considering the adoption of a pension plan must recognize that it is undertaking a commitment to maintain and fund the plan. For details on funding requirements, see chapter 8.

Annual contributions to a profit sharing plan are not usually required. Further, a company that has not done well in a particular year may decide to make either a minimal contribution or no contribution at all for that year (unless the plan itself mandates a contribution each year). Nevertheless, a profit sharing plan is not permanent unless contributions are "recurring and substantial." [Treas. Reg. § 1.401-1(b)(2)]

Q 1:43 Must a qualified retirement plan include all employees?

No. A company is permitted to exclude certain categories of employees from participation in its qualified retirement plan. These exclusions are optional and apply only if they are specified in the plan. [I.R.C. § 410]

Q 1:44 What are the most common eligibility requirements for participation in a qualified retirement plan?

The most common eligibility requirements are those relating to minimum age and length of service with the company.

A plan may exclude any employee who has not yet reached age 21. Plans of certain educational institutions may exclude employees who are under age 26, provided that the service requirement does not exceed one year and the plan provides full and immediate vesting of benefits after one year of service. [I.R.C. §§ 170(b)(1)(A)(ii), 410(a)(1)(A)(i), 410(a)(1)(B)(ii)]

In most instances, the plan requires an employee to complete a certain period of service before being eligible to participate. This service requirement usually does not exceed one year; otherwise, the plan must provide full and immediate vesting of benefits. Under no circumstances may the service requirement exceed two years. The service requirement for 401(k) plans cannot exceed one year. [I.R.C. §§ 401(k)(2)(D), 410(a)(1)(A)(ii), 410(a)(1)(B)(i)]

Q 1:45 What statutory exclusions from participation in a qualified retirement plan are permitted?

The two most common statutory exclusions from plan participation are minimum age and length of service requirements (see Q 1:43).

Other than these exclusions, the most common statutory exclusion applies to union employees on whose behalf negotiations for retirement benefits have been conducted with the company. The company may exclude union employees from coverage, whether or not they are covered under a separate retirement plan, as long as retirement benefits were the subject of good-faith bargaining. Statutory exclusions for air pilots and nonresident aliens are also available. [I.R.C. § 410(b)(3)]

Q 1:46 What other exclusions from participation in a qualified retirement plan are permitted?

Other exclusions—so-called plan exclusions—usually fall into the following categories: (1) classification by job description, (2) classification by geographic location of employment or by specific division of the company, and (3) classification by method of compensation (e.g., hourly as opposed to salaried).

Bear in mind, however, that regardless of the plan's eligibility provisions, coverage of a sufficient number of employees not excluded by statute (see Q 1:44) is needed to satisfy the minimum coverage requirement of the Code, and a minimum participation requirement may also be applicable (see Qs 5:15, 5:23). [I.R.C. §§ 401(a)(26), 410(b)]

Q 1:47 Can a company establish two qualified retirement plans?

Yes. The Code permits a company to maintain as many qualified retirement plans as it chooses, provided that all the plans meet the Code's requirements, including limitations on benefits and contributions.

Quite often, large companies establish separate plans for individual subsidiaries or divisions. These plans need not be comparable in all cases. Indeed, as explained in chapter 5, not all divisions or subsidiaries of the same company or members of a controlled group must adopt a plan in order for another division, subsidiary, or member to maintain a plan for its employees.

The minimum participation requirement (see Q 5:23) may curtail an employer's ability to maintain separate defined benefit plans (see Q 2:3) for individual subsidiaries or divisions. [I.R.C. § 401(a)(26)]

Q 1:48 What kinds of benefits may be provided under a qualified retirement plan?

Qualified retirement plans are primarily intended to provide retirement benefits. Nevertheless, qualified retirement plans also frequently provide benefits upon death, disability, early retirement, or some other termination of employment. These benefits are usually funded by a trust fund, insurance contracts, or a combination of the two.

A profit sharing plan (see Q 2:6) need not be limited to retirement benefits; it may also provide for hardship distributions, for example. In addition, a profit sharing plan may permit distribution of all or part of a participant's vested interest that has remained in the plan for at least two years prior to the distribution. It may also permit a participant with at least five years of participation in the plan to withdraw all or part of the participant's vested interest, including any amount contributed within the last two years. [Rev. Rul. 68-24, 1968-1 C.B. 150; Rev. Rul. 71-224, 1971-1 C.B. 124; Rev. Rul. 71-295, 1971-2 C.B. 184; Rev. Rul. 73-553, 1973-2 C.B. 130] A 401(k) plan may permit a participant who has attained age 59½ to withdraw elective contributions made by the participant to the plan (see Q 27:14). IRS representatives have opined that, if the plan is amended to require satisfaction of either the two-year or five-year rule in addition to the age requirement, the anti-cutback rule (see Q 9:25) would be violated.

If a money purchase pension plan (see Q 2:4) is merged into, or its assets are transferred to, a profit sharing plan, the merged or transferred assets do not take on the character of the profit sharing plan. Thus, the assets attributable to the money purchase pension plan cannot be subject to the profit sharing plan's early withdrawal provisions (see Qs 10:58, 34:28). [Rev. Rul. 94-76, 1994-2 C.B. 46] IRS has issued model language that profit sharing plans can adopt to comply with the rules relating to transfers from money purchase pension plans to profit sharing plans. [Rev. Proc. 96-55, 1996-2 C.B. 387] See Q 25:4 for additional details.

A 10 percent penalty tax applies to most premature distributions from qualified retirement plans and IRAs. Consequently, a profit sharing plan can provide for in-service distributions of plan benefits after the passage of at least two years or because of hardship, but the distribution may be subject to the 10 percent penalty tax, in addition to ordinary income tax. [I.R.C. § 72(t)] For details, see chapter 16.

Q 1:49   Is a voluntary contribution feature attractive to the business owner?

A business owner can make voluntary nondeductible contributions to a qualified retirement plan, but such contributions are subject to limitations and nondiscrimination tests. These nondiscrimination requirements reduce the attractiveness of allowing voluntary employee contributions. For details regarding the limitations on voluntary contributions, see Qs 6:38 and 27:73–27:95.

Q 1:50   May a qualified retirement plan provide life insurance benefits for participants?

Yes. However, different limits may apply to life insurance policies acquired under defined contribution plans and those acquired under defined benefit plans (see Q 15:4). The following general rules also apply:

1. The policies can be ordinary life, term life, universal life, retirement income, or endowment;

2. The insurance must be incidental to the primary purpose of the plan (i.e., to provide benefits at retirement); and

3. The participant pays tax on the cost of the current life insurance protection that is received each year.

By including life insurance in the plan, the corporate business owner is able to shift a personal expense (not tax-deductible) to the corporation. Just as the corporation's plan contributions are deductible, contributions (within limits) to pay for the life insurance are deductible. The corporate business owner will, however, have to include in gross income the cost of the current life insurance protection received under the plan.

There is a different rule for self-employed individuals (see Q 6:60). Plan contributions made on behalf of a self-employed individual that are allocable to the purchase of pure life insurance (the term element, not the entire premium) are not deductible (see Q 15:3). [I.R.C. §§ 404(a)(8)(C), 404(e); Treas. Reg. § 1.404(e)-1A(g)]

For further details, see chapter 15.

Q 1:51 May a qualified retirement plan provide health insurance?

Yes, although the rules governing how much health insurance can be acquired and for whom vary, depending on whether the plan is a pension plan or a profit sharing plan.

A pension plan may provide health insurance, but only for retired employees and their families. [I.R.C. § 401(h); Treas. Reg. § 1.401-14; Priv. Ltr. Rul. 9652021]

A contribution allocated to an individual medical account under a pension plan is treated as part of the annual addition (see Q 6:34) to a defined contribution plan. [I.R.C. § 415(l)]

A profit sharing plan may provide health insurance benefits for all plan participants and their families. If this insurance is purchased with funds that have been in the plan for more than two years, there is no limit on how much the plan may pay for insurance coverage. If the plan uses other funds to buy the insurance, the amount of the premiums must be incidental; that is, the premiums may not exceed 25 percent of the funds allocated to the participant's account that have not been in the plan for at least two years. [Treas. Reg. § 1.401-1(b)(1)(ii); Rev. Rul. 61-164, 1961-2 C.B. 99] IRS has ruled that the payment of premiums under a benefit intended to assist disabled employees in saving for retirement constituted an incidental accident and health insurance benefit if the premiums paid under the benefit, plus any other incidental insurance benefits, do not exceed the permitted limits on such benefits. The purpose of the benefit was to allow employees who became disabled to continue to save for retirement. The benefit was designed to replace the elective deferrals, matching contributions, and any nonelective contributions that would have been credited to a participant's account under the employer's 401(k) plan (see Q 27:1) had the participant not become disabled. [Priv. Ltr. Rul. 200235043]

A profit sharing plan that allowed a participant to have elective contributions (see Q 27:16) allocated to a separate retiree medical subaccount under the plan also permitted the participant either to receive distributions from the subaccount or to use the subaccount to pay health care premiums. IRS ruled that amounts used to pay premiums would be includible in the participant's gross income in the taxable year so used. [Priv. Ltr. Rul. 9405021] IRS also ruled that a profit sharing plan that provides a medical reimbursement account for each participant from which payments may only be distributed to reimburse the participant for expenses for medical care fails to satisfy the qualification requirements and, thus, is not a qualified retirement plan. [Rev. Rul. 2005-55, 2005-2 C.B. 284] A company proposed to allow participants to pay for long-term care insurance from the company's 401(k) plan (see Q 27:1). IRS concluded that such payments would result in taxable distributions to the participants. The use of accounts for the purpose of paying long-term care insurance premiums was considered a distribution from the plan, and participants would be taxed on the distributions. In addition, the plan would fail to comply with the distribution restrictions (see Q 27:14) applicable to 401(k) plans if it made distributions for insurance premiums to the participants. [Priv. Ltr. Rul. 200806013]

Proposed regulations issued by IRS clarify that a payment from a qualified retirement plan for an accident or health insurance premium generally constitutes a taxable distribution to the distributee in the taxable year in which the premium is paid. The taxable amount generally equals the amount of the premium charged against the participant's benefits under the plan. If a defined contribution plan (see Q 2:2) pays these premiums from a current year contribution or forfeiture that has not been allocated to a participant's account, then the amount of the premium for each participant will be treated as first being allocated to the participant and then charged against the participant's benefits under the plan, so that the amount of the distribution is the same as determined under the preceding sentence. The regulations also provide that a distribution for the payment of the premiums by a qualified retirement plan generally is not excluded from gross income, but such distribution would constitute an amount paid for accident or health insurance. Furthermore, to the extent that the payment of premiums for accident or health insurance has been treated as a taxable distribution, amounts received through the accident or health insurance for personal injuries or sickness are excludable from gross income and are not treated as distributions from the plan. The general rule that accident and health insurance premiums are taxable distributions would not apply to amounts held under an individual medical benefit account (see Q 6:34). Accident or health insurance purchased through such an account does not constitute a taxable distribution. [Prop. Treas. Reg. §§ 1.402(a)-1(a)(1)(ii), 1.402(a)-1(e)]

Example. An employer sponsors a qualified profit sharing plan, and the plan provides solely for non-elective employer contributions. The plan's trustee enters into a contract with a third-party insurance carrier to provide health insurance for certain plan participants, and the insurance policy provides for the payment of medical expenses incurred by those participants. The plan limits the amounts used to provide medical benefits with respect to a participant to 25 percent of the funds held in the participant's account. The trustee makes monthly payments of $1,000 to pay the premiums due for Participant A's health insurance. The trustee also reduces Participant A's account balance by $1,000 at the time of each premium payment. In June of a year, Participant A is admitted to the hospital for covered medical care; and, in July of the same year, the health insurer pays the hospital $5,000 for the medical care provided to Participant A in June.

Each of the trustee's payments of the $1,000 constitutes a taxable distribution to Participant A on the date of each payment, and these distributions constitute payments for medical care. The $5,000 payment to the hospital is excludable from Participant A's gross income and is not treated as a distribution from the plan.

Q 1:52   Is a contribution to a qualified retirement plan adopted on the last day of the taxable year fully deductible?

Yes. If the plan and trust are executed by the end of the year and other procedural requirements established by IRS are met, then contributions made by the due date for filing the company's income tax return for that year (including extensions) are fully deductible. [I.R.C. § 404(a)(6); Rev. Rul. 81-114, 1981-1 C.B. 207]

> **Example.** Sallie Corp., a calendar-year corporation, adopts a pension plan to become effective December 31, 2010. If the documents are executed by December 31, 2010, and the contribution is made by March 15, 2011 (or as late as September 15, 2011, if the company has received an extension until that time for filing its tax return), a full deduction will be allowed for 2010.

Q 1:53   May excess contributions made to a qualified retirement plan be returned to the company?

If the company makes an excess contribution to its qualified retirement plan, that excess may be returned to the company only in the following circumstances:

1. An actuarial error caused the excess funds to remain in the trust after the plan's termination and after the payment of all benefits to participants or their beneficiaries. [Treas. Reg. § 1.401-2]

2. The contribution was conditioned on the initial qualification of the plan, the plan did not qualify, and the plan was submitted to IRS for a determination letter (see Q 18:1) within the remedial amendment period. [ERISA § 403(c)(2)(B); I.R.C. § 401(b)]

3. The contribution was conditioned on its deductibility, and the deduction was denied. [ERISA § 403(c)(2)(C)]

4. The excess contribution was made due to a mistake of fact. [ERISA § 403(c)(2)(A)]

In any event, the plan itself must permit the return of the excess contribution; and, in either of the last two situations, earnings attributable to the excess contribution may not be returned to the company. Losses attributable to the excess contribution will reduce the amount to be returned. Further, returns to the employer must be made within one year of the mistaken contribution, denial of qualification, or denial of the deduction. [Treas. Reg. § 1.401-1(a)(2); Greve v. Gates, No. 96-C-50424 (N.D. Ill. 1997); Rev. Rul. 91-4, 1991-1 C.B. 57; Rev. Rul. 77-200, 1977-1 C.B. 98; Rev. Proc. 90-49, 1990-2 C.B. 620; IRS Notice 89-52, Q&A 16, 1989-1 C.B. 692; Priv. Ltr. Ruls. 200742028, 200652045, 200639003, 200637037, 200637036, 200552020, 200541047]

A 10 percent excise tax is imposed on nondeductible contributions to a qualified retirement plan (see Q 12:9). [I.R.C. § 4972]

Special rules apply to excess contributions made to a 401(k) plan. See chapter 27 for details.

Q 1:54   May the company borrow from its qualified retirement plan to acquire assets needed in its business?

Generally, no. A penalty tax (see below) is imposed on any prohibited transaction (see Q 24:1), which includes the lending of money between a plan and the company. Thus, a company may not borrow from its plan for any purpose. [ERISA § 406; I.R.C. § 4975(c)(1)(B)]

DOL, however, may grant an exemption from the loan restrictions. Generally, an exemption is granted only if it is (1) administratively feasible; (2) in the interests of the plan, its participants, and beneficiaries; and (3) protective of the rights of participants and beneficiaries of the plan. [ERISA § 408; I.R.C. § 4975(c)(2)]

Exemptions for loans from a qualified retirement plan to the company to buy business assets have been approved by DOL. The company must have a good credit rating, the interest rate must be comparable to what a bank would charge, and adequate security must be provided. For examples of when an exemption will be allowed, see Q 24:25.

The penalty tax on a prohibited transaction is imposed at the rate of 15 percent of the amount involved in the transaction for every year (or part of a year). If the 15 percent tax is imposed and the prohibited transaction is not corrected within the taxable period, an additional tax equal to 100 percent of the amount involved in the transaction is imposed.

Both the initial and additional taxes are payable by the individual who participated in the prohibited transaction. The taxable period begins when the prohibited transaction occurs; it ends, if it is not corrected, on the earlier of the date the notice of deficiency with respect to the 15 percent tax is mailed or the date the 15 percent tax is assessed. [I.R.C. §§ 4975(a), 4975(b), 4975(f)]

Q 1:55   May a business owner borrow from the qualified retirement plan?

Yes, if the owner is a participant in the corporation's qualified retirement plan and the plan contains a provision authorizing loans to participants. The general rules for loans also apply to both self-employed individuals (see Q 6:60) and owner-employees (see Q 5:32). [I.R.C. §§ 401(a)(13), 4975(d)]

See chapter 14 for a detailed discussion.

Chapter 2

Types and Choices of Plans

The range of retirement plan alternatives is extensive. There are defined contribution plans and defined benefit plans; there are pension plans and profit sharing plans. Before the employer can evaluate the relative merits of the various types of plans and choose the most appropriate plan, the employer must know what each type of plan offers. This chapter describes the categories of retirement plans, examines the basic choices available to a company, and offers guidelines for choosing the appropriate plan.

Q 2:1 What are the basic choices among qualified retirement plans?

Qualified retirement plans generally fit into one of two categories: defined contribution plans (see Q 2:2) and defined benefit plans (see Q 2:3).

Q 2:2 What is a defined contribution plan?

A defined contribution plan is a retirement plan that provides for an individual account for each participant and for benefits based solely upon the amount contributed to the participant's account, and any income, expenses, gains and losses, and any forfeitures of accounts of other participants which may be allocated to such participant's account. [ERISA § 3(34); I.R.C. § 414(i)]

Defined contribution plans include the following:

- Money purchase pension plans (see Q 2:4)
- Target benefit plans (see Q 2:5)
- Profit sharing plans (see Qs 2:6, 2:7)
- Thrift or savings plans (see Q 2:11)
- 401(k) plans (see Q 2:12)
- Stock bonus plans (see Q 2:13)
- Employee stock ownership plans (ESOPs) (see Q 2:14)
- Simplified employee pensions (SEPs) (see Q 2:15)
- Savings incentive match plans for employees (SIMPLE plans) (see Q 2:16)

Three major consequences result when a retirement plan is classified as a defined contribution plan: (1) plan contributions are determined by formula and not by actuarial requirements (except for target benefit plans); (2) plan earnings and losses are allocated to each participant's account and do not affect the company's retirement plan costs; and (3) plan benefits are not insured by the Pension Benefit Guaranty Corporation (PBGC; see Q 25:12). Defined contribution plans must provide for a valuation of investments held by the plan, at least once a year, on a specified date, in accordance with a method consistently followed and uniformly applied. The fair market value on such date must be used for this purpose, and the respective accounts of participants must be adjusted in accordance with the valuation. A plan provision allowing interim valuations at the plan administrator's (see Q 20:1) discretion in addition to a consistent annual valuation does not disqualify the plan so long as the use of the interim valuations does not result in prohibited discrimination. [Rev. Rul. 80-155, 1980–1 C.B. 84]

Upon retirement, a participant in a defined contribution plan was permitted to direct the plan trustees to liquidate the investments in his plan account but, instead, elected to defer liquidation. Between his date of retirement and the date of liquidation, the investments declined in value and the court ruled that the participant suffered no compensable loss. [Brengettsy v. LTV Steel (Republic) Hourly Pension Plan, No. 00-2204 (7th Cir. 2001)]

See Q 1:16 for the effects of USERRA on defined contribution plans.

Q 2:3   What is a defined benefit plan?

A defined benefit plan is a retirement plan "other than an individual account plan." In other words, a plan that is not a defined contribution plan is classified as a defined benefit plan. Under a defined benefit plan, retirement benefits must be definitely determinable. For example, a plan that entitles a participant to a monthly pension for life equal to 30 percent of monthly compensation is a defined benefit plan. [ERISA § 3(35); I.R.C. § 414(j)] The most common types of defined benefit plans are flat benefit plans (see Q 2:17) and unit benefit plans (see Q 2:18).

If a plan is categorized as a defined benefit plan: (1) plan formulas are geared to retirement benefits and not to contributions (except for cash balance plans—see Q 2:23); (2) the annual contribution is usually actuarially determined; (3) certain benefits may be insured by PBGC (see Qs 25:11, 25:12); (4) early termination of the plan is subject to special rules; and (5) forfeitures reduce the company's cost of providing retirement benefits.

Participants begin to earn (accrue; see Q 9:2) retirement benefits as soon as they become a participant in a defined benefit plan. However, they do not obtain a permanent right to the benefits (become vested; see Q 9:1) until they have worked a minimum period of time, as specified in the plan. The participants will then have a legal right to receive a portion, or all, of the benefits at retirement age, even if they change jobs and go to work for another employer before reaching retirement age. Participants may lose their accrued benefits if they leave employment *before* becoming vested, even if they return to the same employer in later years. For example, a worker who leaves a company after four years of service and returns after a five-year break can lose credit for the first four years (see Qs 5:10, 9:12). Being vested means that a participant covered by a defined benefit plan has completed sufficient years of service and is entitled to receive benefits accrued under the plan, whether or not the participant continues with the company until retirement.

The benefit amount earned in a defined benefit plan is determined by a formula that is spelled out in the plan. Usually, it involves compensation and years of service. The longer someone works under the same defined benefit plan, the larger the retirement benefit. Some plans are integrated with Social Security benefits (see Q 2:41). This means that, in these plans, retirement benefits can be reduced because of Social Security coverage.

Defined benefit plans usually are funded entirely by the employer. Employers generally contribute enough annually to cover the normal cost of the plan—an amount that is at least the value of the benefits that participants in the plan have earned that year. In addition, employers may have to make additional contributions for various reasons, such as to make up for any investment losses by the plan. If an employer fails to make the legally required contributions, the employer can be assessed taxes for each year the deficiency exists. IRS may permit the employer to pay the contribution in future years under a funding waiver arrangement. See chapter 8 for details.

See Q 1:16 for the effects of USERRA on defined benefit plans.

Effective for plan years beginning on or after January 1, 2010, employers with 500 or fewer employees may establish a combined defined benefit/401(k) plan. [I.R.C. § 414(x) (as amended by WRERA 2008 § 109(c)(1)); ERISA § 210(e) (as amended by WRERA 2008 § 109(c)(2))] See Q 27:67 for details.

IRS has become concerned that certain qualified defined benefit plans may include nontraditional benefits that are not subject to the protections relating to accrued benefits (see Q 9:2) and other qualification rules (see Q 4:1). Examples of the types of benefits for which this concern arises include (1) benefits that are payable only upon the involuntary termination of an employee or in other limited circumstances that are unrelated to retirement and (2) benefits that could exceed the amount of the accrued benefit payable under the plan. If these benefits are contingent on future events that are not reasonably and reliably predictable on an actuarial basis, it is difficult to determine compliance with the incidental benefit requirements. In the case of benefits that are contingent on events that are reasonably and reliably predictable on an actuarial basis (e.g., death), the probability that those contingencies will occur is taken into account in determining whether retirement benefits are the primary benefit under the plan (i.e., whether nonretirement benefits provided under the plan are merely incidental). Moreover, there may be a risk that, in effect, if the contingent eventon which the benefit is conditioned occurs, such a benefit could become a substantial or even a primary benefit that plan participants expect to receive. Such benefits also may not be the types of benefits that have been customarily included in qualified pension plans. Benefits payable only upon an employee's involuntary separation from service also raise questions regarding whether the availability of the benefits is based on conditions that are within the employer's control, and whether such benefits circumvent the vesting and anti-backloading protections (see Qs 9:2, 9:4), as well as the definitely determinable benefits requirement. In addition, such benefits may not be among the type of benefits that are intended to receive the tax benefits generally applicable to qualified plan benefits.

IRS believes that guidance to clarify the application of the qualification and accrued benefit requirements to these types of benefits may be appropriate in light of the regulations that were issued in 2005 (see Q 9:33). The definitions of an ancillary benefit, a retirement-type benefit, and a retirement-type subsidy (see Qs 4:20, 9:33, 9:34) depend, in part, on whether a benefit is permitted to be provided in a qualified defined benefit plan. However, current guidance does not directly address whether certain benefits (e.g., benefits that are similar to plant shutdown benefits that do not continue after retirement or benefits payable solely upon involuntary separation) are permitted to be provided in a qualified pension plan. Thus, IRS is considering whether to propose guidance that would clarify the types of benefits that are permitted to be provided in qualified defined benefit plans.

The guidance under consideration may include the following:

1. *Permitted benefits.* The guidance might provide that, in addition to the payment of retirement-type benefits (including retirement-type subsidies), the only benefit payments that are permitted to be provided under a qualified defined benefit plan are the payment of the ancillary benefits specifically identified (see Q 9:33). [Treas. Reg. § 1.411(d)-3(g)(2)]

2. *Plan shutdown benefits and similar ancillary benefits.* With respect to a plant shutdown benefit, the guidance might require that the benefit be payable as a result of an objectively defined plant shutdown event, such as an event that requires notice under the Worker Adjustment and Retraining Notification Act of 1988 (WARN). For benefits that are similar to plant shutdown benefits and that do not continue past retirement age, the guidance might set forth the extent to which there are any such similar benefits that are permitted to be provided in a qualified defined benefit plan. [Treas. Reg. § 1.411(d)-3(g)(2)(vi)]

   The guidance also might clarify (a) that an ancillary plant shutdown benefit is permitted to be provided in a qualified defined benefit plan only if the amount payable in any year prior to retirement does not exceed the amount payable annually under the participant's accrued benefit expressed as an annual benefit commencing at normal retirement age (see Q 10:55) and (b) that the benefit may not be paid in a shorter or longer alternative form of payment. Under such a rule, for example, if a plan participant who is below the plan's normal retirement age of 65 had an accrued benefit payable as a life annuity at age 65 of $1,000 a month, the plan would be permitted to provide an ancillary plant shutdown benefit payable as a temporary annuity in an amount up to $1,000 a month. In such a case, the ancillary plant shutdown benefit would be paid to the plan participant up until the annuity starting date (see Q 10:3) for payment of the participant's accrued benefit under the plan (e.g., age 65 or some earlier age when the participant commences payment of the participant's accrued benefit in the form of a qualified joint and survivor annuity (QJSA; see Q 10:8) or elects an alternative optional form). This illustration of an ancillary plant shutdown benefit is different from a subsidized early retirement benefit payable on the occurrence of a plant shutdown.

3. *Contingent accruals and early retirement benefits.* The guidance might also provide that, except for the payment of the accrued benefit in an optional form, a retirement-type benefit (and thus a retirement-type subsidy) is permitted to be provided in a qualified defined benefit plan only if the amount of the benefit is no greater than the unreduced accrued benefit provided under the plan. The guidance might also clarify the extent to which additional accruals are permitted, taking into account the backloading and vesting rules, if those accruals arise by reason of an event other than attainment of a specified age, performance of service, receipt or derivation of compensation, or the occurrence of death or disability (e.g., if those additional accruals arise upon involuntary termination of employment). The guidance also might clarify the extent to which early retirement benefits (i.e., benefits payable before normal retirement age, but after severance from employment, that are not ancillary benefits) payable as a result of a plant shutdown event, an involuntary termination of employment, or another event similarly under the control of the employer are permitted to be provided in a qualified defined benefit plan.

[IRS Notice 2007-14, 2007-1 C.B. 501]

PBGC (see Q 25:10) has released guidance for defined benefit plans that may have experienced significant investment losses resulting from a customer relationship with Bernard L. Madoff Investment Securities LLC, either directly or through an investment advisor. [*PBGC News Release* (Feb. 9, 2009)]

Q 2:4   What is a money purchase pension plan?

A money purchase pension plan is a defined contribution plan in which the company's contributions are mandatory and are usually based solely on each participant's compensation.

The obligation to fund the plan makes a money purchase pension plan different from most profit sharing plans. In most profit sharing plans, there are generally no unfavorable consequences for the company if it fails to make a contribution. However, if the company maintains a money purchase pension plan, its failure to make a contribution can result in the imposition of a penalty tax (see Q 8:22). Contributions must be made to a money purchase pension plan even if the company has no profits. With the increase in the primary limitation on tax-deductible contributions to a profit sharing plan to 25 percent of total compensation, there is little reason for an employer to adopt or continue to maintain a money purchase pension plan (see Qs 1:48, 12:8, 24:4).

Forfeitures that occur because of employee turnover may reduce future contributions of the company or may be used to increase the benefits of remaining participants.

Retirement benefits are based on the amount in the participant's account at the time of retirement, that is, whatever pension the money can purchase.

The following is an example of a money purchase pension plan formula:

> The company shall contribute each plan year during which the plan is in effect on behalf of each participant an amount equal to 10 percent of compensation.

Under the formula, an equal percentage of compensation is allocated to each participant's account. The age and length of service of the participant are irrelevant for both contribution and allocation purposes, although length of service could be considered. [I.R.C. § 411(b)(2); Treas. Reg. § 1.401-1(b)(1)(i)]

This concept is illustrated in the following example. The allocation in column (d) reflects a contribution formula that does not include permitted disparity. When permitted disparity is considered, differences in compensation become more relevant. See chapter 7 for more details.

Thau Management Corporation
Schedule of Contributions to
Money Purchase Pension Plan
for
Plan Year Ended December 31, 2010

(a)	(b)	(c)	(d)
			Allocation of Company
Participant	*Age*	*Compensation*	*Contributions*
Hal	45	$245,000	$24,500
Dorothy	30	50,000	5,000
Total		$295,000	$29,500

The mere fact that a money purchase pension plan has a zero percent-of-compensation contribution formula does not prevent the plan from being a qualified retirement plan (see Qs 1:5, 1:6). An example of a "zero percent" money purchase pension plan is a plan established solely for the purpose of receiving rollover contributions or transfers from another qualified retirement plan (see Qs 34:1, 34:8). [Internal IRS Mem. from Chief, Employee Plans Technical Branch 2, to District Director, Los Angeles Key District (Aug. 10, 1995)]

The requirements of a zero percent plan are:

1. Zero percent contributions by the employer;
2. A tax-exempt trust (see Q 1:6);
3. Definitely determinable benefits; and

4. Satisfaction of the nondiscrimination requirements (see Q 4:10).

These requirements are satisfied by:

1. Providing that no contribution other than employee, rollover, or transfer contributions from another qualified retirement plan will be accepted;
2. Establishing a trust consisting of transferred or rolled over contributions;
3. Maintaining separate participant rollover accounts that will provide definitely determinable benefits based upon the account balances at retirement or separation from service; and
4. Drafting a plan document that contains the form language needed to satisfy the nondiscrimination requirements and language that permits the acceptance of contributions from all employees, rather than only the highly compensated employees (HCEs; see Q 3:2).

Q 2:5   What is a target benefit plan?

A target benefit plan is a hybrid or cross between a defined benefit plan (see Q 2:3) and a money purchase pension plan (see Q 2:4). It is like a defined benefit plan in that the annual contribution is determined by the amount needed each year to accumulate (at an assumed rate of interest) a fund sufficient to pay a projected retirement benefit (the target benefit) to each participant on reaching retirement age. Thus, if a target benefit plan contains a target formula, such as 40 percent of compensation, that is identical to the benefit formula in a defined benefit plan and is based on identical actuarial assumptions (e.g., interest rates, mortality, employee turnover), the employer's initial contribution for the same group of employees will be the same.

However, this is where the similarity ends. In a defined benefit plan, if the actual experience of the plan differs from the actuarial assumptions used (for example, if the interest earned is higher or lower than the assumptions), then the employer either increases or decreases its future contributions to the extent necessary to provide the promised benefits. In a target benefit plan, however, the contribution, once made, is allocated to separate accounts maintained for each participant. Thus, if the earnings of the fund differ from those assumed, this does not result in any increase or decrease in employer contributions; instead, it increases or decreases the benefits payable to the participant.

In this regard, the target benefit plan operates like a money purchase pension plan. In fact, the only difference between a money purchase pension plan and a target benefit plan is that in a money purchase pension plan contributions are generally determined and allocated as a percentage of current compensation; in a target benefit plan, contributions are determined as if the plan were to provide a fixed benefit. In a money purchase pension plan, contributions for identically compensated employees are the same even though their ages differ; in a target benefit plan, age is one of the factors that determines the size of the contributions. Because older employees have less time in which to have their benefits funded, employer contributions on their behalf are greater, as a percentage of compensation, than for younger employees. Consequently, target benefit plans appeal to employers that desire to benefit older employees. See Qs 2:7 and 2:10 for discussions of age-based profit sharing plans and comparability plans.

Since target benefit plans are defined contribution plans, they are subject to the limit on annual additions to a participant's account (see Q 6:34).

Q 2:6 What is a profit sharing plan?

A profit sharing plan is a defined contribution plan to which the company agrees to make "substantial and recurring," although generally discretionary, contributions (see Q 1:42). Amounts contributed to the plan are invested and accumulate (tax-free) for eventual distribution to participants or their beneficiaries either at retirement, after a fixed number of years, or upon the occurrence of some specified event (e.g., disability, death, or termination of employment) (see Q 1:48).

Unlike contributions to a pension plan, contributions to a profit sharing plan are usually keyed to the existence of profits. However, neither current nor accumulated profits are required for a company to contribute to a profit sharing plan. [I.R.C. § 401(a)(27)] Even if the company has profits, it can generally forgo or limit its contribution for a particular year if the plan contains a discretionary formula. The following is an example of such a formula:

> The company shall contribute each plan year during which the plan is in effect out of its earnings for its taxable year, or out of its accumulated earnings, an amount decided upon by the Board of Directors [or owner, partners, etc., as appropriate]. The contribution shall be allocated among the participants in the proportion that the compensation of each participant bears to the aggregate compensation of all the participants.

Under the allocation formula (the second sentence in the example), each participant receives the same percentage of the contribution as the participant's compensation bears to total compensation. The participant's length of service is irrelevant, although this factor can be considered in the allocation formula if prohibited discrimination does not result. However, note that in a discretionary profit sharing plan, the actual amount to be allocated to each participant cannot be determined until the company decides upon its contribution for the year. A profit sharing plan must provide a definite predetermined formula for allocating the contributions made to the plan among the participants. A formula for allocating the contributions among the participants is definite if, for example, it provides for an allocation in proportion to the compensation of each participant. [Treas. Reg. § 1.401-1(b)(1)(ii)] An employer's retroactive amendment of an allocation formula under its discretionary profit sharing plan that was adopted after the end of the plan year violated the anti-cutback rule (see Q 9:25). The plan participants' rights to allocations became protected at the end of the plan year. Because the amendment reduced the protected allocable contributions of some participants for that year, thereby decreasing the amount of those participants' accrued benefits (see Q 9:2), the amendment was not permitted. [Priv. Ltr. Rul. 9735001]

Although many profit sharing plans adopt a discretionary contribution formula, others adopt a fixed formula. For example, a company may obligate itself to contribute to its profit sharing plan a specified percentage of each participant's compensation if profits exceed a specified level.

As with other defined contribution plans, retirement benefits in profit sharing plans are based on the amount in the participant's account at retirement. Unlike defined benefit plans, forfeitures in profit sharing plans arising from employee turnover may be reallocated among the remaining participants.

See Q 27:4 for a discussion concerning the contribution to a profit sharing plan of the dollar equivalent of unused time paid off.

Q 2:7   What is an age-based profit sharing plan?

An age-based profit sharing plan is a profit sharing plan (see Q 2:6) that uses both age and compensation as a basis for allocating employer contributions among plan participants. This concept is similar to a target benefit plan (see Q 2:5), where age and compensation are factors used to determine the amount of the employer contribution.

All of the basic requirements that apply to regular profit sharing plans also apply to an age-based profit sharing plan. An age-based profit sharing plan can have a discretionary contribution formula and provide the employer with flexibility over the amount of the contribution to be made each year. Because age is a factor, this type of plan favors older employees who have fewer years than younger employees to accumulate sufficient funds for retirement (see Q 2:8). [Treas. Reg. § 1.401(a)(4)-8] For purposes of satisfying the nondiscrimination requirements, an age-based profit sharing plan is tested under the cross-testing rules. See Qs 4:11 and 4:22 for more details.

Q 2:8   How does an age-based profit sharing plan benefit older employees?

The basis for allocating employer contributions under an age-based profit sharing plan is determined by calculating the present value of a straight (i.e., single) life annuity beginning at the testing age (see Q 2:9). A standard interest rate, which may not be less than 7.5 percent or more than 8.5 percent, compounded annually, and a straight life annuity factor that is based on the same or a different standard interest rate and on a standard mortality table must be used. [Treas. Reg. §§ 1.401(a)(4)-8(b)(2), 1.401(a)(4)-12]

The following is an example of an allocation formula under an age-based profit sharing plan:

> The contribution shall be allocated among the participants in the proportion that the allocation factor of each participant bears to the aggregate allocation factors of all the participants. The allocation factor of a participant for the plan year shall be the product of (a) the participant's compensation for the plan year, multiplied by (b) the present value of

$1.00, discounted with interest at 8.5 percent from the testing age to the participant's age as of the last day of the plan year.

The following scenario provides a practical application of this allocation formula:

Example. For 2010, Ess-UU-Kay Corporation adopts an age-based profit sharing plan with a calendar-year plan year. The following six employees are eligible to participate in the plan:

Participant	Age	Compensation
A (owner)	50	$200,000
B	40	50,000
C	35	50,000
D	35	40,000
E	30	35,000
F	25	25,000
Total		$400,000

Ess-UU-Kay contributes $52,000 to the plan. The plan uses a testing age of 65. The contribution is allocated among the participants based on each participant's allocation factor, as follows:

Participant	Present Value (PV) of $1.00	Allocation Factor (PV × Compensation)	Contribution
A	.294	58,800	$40,173
B	.130	6,500	4,441
C	.087	4,350	2,972
D	.087	3,480	2,378
E	.058	2,030	1,387
F	.038	950	649
Total		76,110	$52,000

If the contribution is allocated among the participants in proportion to compensation, A's allocation would be only $26,000 ($200,000/ $400,000 × $52,000). If the allocation formula takes permitted disparity into consideration, A will receive $28,656 (see chapter 7 for details). Because A is the oldest participant, A benefits most under the age-based profit sharing plan.

In the above example, the contribution, as a percentage of compensation, is the same for C and D because their ages are the same; but A and B, who are older, receive a greater percentage, and E and F, who are younger, receive a lesser percentage. The plan can be designed to have B through F all receive the same contribution as a percentage of compensation, with A receiving a much greater percentage. See Q 2:10 for a discussion of a comparability plan and Q 4:22 for a discussion of cross-testing.

Q 2:9   What is the testing age for an age-based profit sharing plan?

The testing age is the age from which present value is calculated. If the testing age is 65, the present value of $1.00 at age 65 will be $1.00 and the present value of $1.00 at any lesser age will be a lesser amount. The standard interest rate currently used must not be less than 7.5 percent or more than 8.5 percent, compounded annually. [Treas. Reg. §§ 1.401(a)(4)-8(b)(2), 1.401(a)(4)-12]

An example of a present value table is set forth below:

Present Value Table 8.5% Interest
Testing Age of 65

Age	Present Value	Age	Present Value
65	1.000	44	.180
64	.922	43	.166
63	.849	42	.153
62	.783	41	.141
61	.722	40	.130
60	.665	39	.120
59	.613	38	.111
58	.565	37	.102
57	.521	36	.094
56	.480	35	.087
55	.442	34	.080
54	.408	33	.073
53	.376	32	.068
52	.346	31	.062
51	.319	30	.058
50	.294	29	.053
49	.271	28	.049
48	.250	27	.045
47	.230	26	.042
46	.212	25	.038
45	.196		

If the testing age is 65, the factor for a 50-year-old participant is .294. The testing age is the participant's normal retirement age (see Q 10:55) under the plan if the plan provides the same uniform normal retirement age for all participants or is age 65 if the plan does not provide a uniform normal retirement age—even if the participant is beyond the testing age. For example, if the uniform normal retirement age under the plan is 65 and Bernard is age 70, the factor used for Bernard is 1.000. [Treas. Reg. §§ 1.401(a)(4)-8(b)(1), 1.401(a)(4)-12] IRS representatives have opined that, if participants have a uniform normal retirement age of 55, the testing age is 55; and, if the uniform normal retirement age is changed to 65, the uniform testing age would change to 65. The representatives cautioned that the change in normal retirement age could violate the anti-cutback rule (see Q 9:25). See Qs 4:11 and 4:22 for more details.

Q 2:10   What is a comparability plan?

A comparability plan is generally a profit sharing plan (see Q 2:6) in which the contribution percentage formula for one category of participants is greater than the contribution percentage formula for other categories of participants. As with an age-based profit sharing plan (see Q 2:7), to satisfy the nondiscrimination requirements, a comparability plan is tested under the cross-testing rules (see Qs 4:11, 4:22). A comparability plan must contain a definite predetermined formula for allocating contributions made to the plan among the participants (see Q 2:6). [Treas. Reg. §§ 1.401-1(b)(1)(i), 1.401-1(b)(1)(ii)]

IRS undertook a review of comparability plans to determine whether it was appropriate in all cases to allow the projected future value of employer contributions made to defined contribution plans (see Q 2:2) to be tested as the equivalent of employer-provided benefits under a defined benefit plan (see Q 2:3). IRS was concerned about whether cross-tested plan designs that provide for built-in disparities in contribution rates between HCEs (see Q 3:2) and non-highly compensated employees (NHCEs; see Q 3:12) could be reconciled with the basic purpose of the nondiscrimination rules. IRS was particularly concerned about whether NHCEs actually have an opportunity to earn the higher allocation rates projected under the cross-testing method. [IRS Notice 2000-14, 2000-1 C.B. 737] IRS has promulgated final regulations regarding the cross-testing rules. See Qs 4:11 and 4:22 through 4:24 for more details.

> **Example.** For 2010, Rachael Corporation adopts a comparability profit sharing plan with a calendar-year plan year. Five employees are eligible to participate in the plan, and Rachael Corporation contributes $39,650 to the plan. The entire contribution is deductible for income tax purposes (see Q 12:8), and the allocation of the contribution, which satisfies the final regulations, is as follows:

Participant	Age	Compensation	Contribution	Contribution as a % of Compensation
A (owner)	61	$ 50,000	$23,646	47.3%
B (owner)	61	25,000	11,823	47.3
C	29	35,000	1,750	5.0
D	27	28,750	1,438	5.0
E	29	19,850	993	5.0
Total		$158,600	$39,650	

Q 2:11 What is a thrift or savings plan?

A thrift or savings plan is a defined contribution plan (see Q 2:2) in which employees are directly involved in contributing toward the ultimate benefits that will be provided. The plan can be in the form of a money purchase pension plan (see Q 2:4) or a profit sharing plan (see Q 2:6).

These plans are contributory in the sense that employer contributions on behalf of a particular employee are geared to mandatory contributions by the employee. Employees can participate in the plan only if they contribute a part of their compensation to the plan.

Employer contributions are made on a matching basis—for example, 50 percent of the contribution made by the employee. The plan may permit the employer, at its discretion, to make additional contributions and may also permit employees to make voluntary contributions (see Qs 1:49, 6:38).

A contributory plan must satisfy a nondiscrimination test that compares the relative contribution percentages of HCEs (see Q 3:2) with those of NHCEs (see Qs 3:12, 6:37).

Q 2:12 What is a 401(k) plan?

A 401(k) plan is a qualified profit sharing or stock bonus plan (see Qs 2:6, 2:13) that offers participants an election to receive company contributions in cash or to have these amounts contributed to the plan. A participant in a 401(k) plan does not have to include in income any company contributions to the plan merely because an election could have been made to receive cash instead. [I.R.C. §§ 401(k)(2), 402(a)(8)]

A 401(k) plan may also be in the form of a salary reduction agreement. Under this type of arrangement, each eligible employee may elect to reduce current compensation or elect to forgo a salary increase and have these amounts contributed to the plan. [Treas. Reg. § 1.401(k)-1(a)(3)(i)]

Benefits attributable to employer contributions to a 401(k) plan generally may not be distributed without penalty until the employee retires, becomes disabled, dies, or reaches age 59½. Contributions made by the employer to the plan at the employee's election are nonforfeitable (i.e., 100 percent vesting is required at all times). For a discussion of 401(k) plans, see chapter 27.

Effective for plan years beginning on or after January 1, 2010, employers with 500 or fewer employees may establish a combined defined benefit/401(k) plan. [I.R.C. § 414(x) (as amended by WRERA 2008 § 109(c)(1)); ERISA § 210(e) (as amended by WRERA 2008 § 109(c)(2))]

Q 2:13   What is a stock bonus plan?

A stock bonus plan is similar to a profit sharing plan (see Q 2:6), except that benefit payments must be made in shares of stock of the company. However, a stock bonus plan may distribute cash to a participant, subject to the participant's right to demand a distribution of employer securities. Further, if the plan permits cash distributions and the employer securities are not readily tradable on an established market, participants must be given the right to require the company to repurchase the shares of stock it distributes to them under a fair valuation formula. [I.R.C. § 401(a)(23); Treas. Reg. §§ 1.401-1(a)(2)(iii), 1.401-1(b)(1)(iii)]

Q 2:14   What is an employee stock ownership plan (ESOP)?

An ESOP is a special type of defined contribution plan (usually profit sharing or stock bonus) that can qualify for favorable tax treatment. For a discussion of ESOPs, see chapter 28.

Q 2:15   What is a simplified employee pension (SEP)?

A SEP is a defined contribution plan that takes the form of an individual retirement account (IRA) but is subject to special rules. A SEP may be adopted by both incorporated and unincorporated businesses. For a discussion of SEPs, see chapter 32.

Q 2:16   What is a savings incentive match plan for employees (SIMPLE)?

A SIMPLE plan may be adopted by small employers who do not maintain another employer-sponsored retirement plan covering the same employees. A SIMPLE plan may be either in the form of an IRA for each employee (in this case, the employer cannot maintain any other qualified retirement plan whether or not covering the same employees) or part of a 401(k) plan (see Q 2:12). If established in an IRA form, a SIMPLE plan will not be subject to the nondiscrimination rules generally applicable to qualified retirement plans (including top-heavy rules), and simplified reporting requirements will apply. A SIMPLE plan may be adopted by both incorporated and unincorporated businesses. For a discussion of SIMPLE plans, see chapter 33.

Q 2:17   What is a flat benefit plan?

Under this type of defined benefit plan (see Q 2:3), the benefit for each participant depends solely on compensation. The following is a typical formula used in a flat benefit plan:

> Each participant shall be entitled to a monthly pension, commencing at normal retirement age and thereafter payable for life, of an amount equal to 30 percent of monthly compensation.

Under this formula, a participant whose monthly compensation is $2,000 would receive a monthly pension of $600; a participant whose monthly compensation is $4,000 would receive a monthly pension of twice as much (i.e., $1,200).

Q 2:18   What is a unit benefit plan?

This type of defined benefit plan (see Q 2:3) recognizes service with the company by providing greater benefits for a long-service employee than for a short-term employee with the same average compensation. The following formula represents a type of unit benefit plan:

> Each participant shall be entitled to a monthly pension, commencing at normal retirement age and thereafter payable for life, of an amount equal to 1 percent of monthly compensation multiplied by the number of years of service with the company.

Under this formula, a participant with a monthly compensation of $2,000 and 30 years of employment at retirement would receive a monthly pension of $600, while a participant with the same monthly compensation but only ten years of employment would receive a monthly pension of $200.

This example and the example in Q 2:17 reflect plan formulas that do not take into consideration permitted disparity. When permitted disparity is considered, differences in compensation become more relevant. See chapter 7 for more details on this issue.

Q 2:19   How is the cost of providing benefits under a defined benefit plan determined?

The cost of funding the plan (other than a fully insured plan; see Q 2:25) is determined actuarially. An actuary (generally one enrolled under the auspices of the Joint Board for the Enrollment of Actuaries) may take into consideration many factors in determining each year's plan contribution needed to fund the benefits the plan is to provide. [I.R.C. § 412(c)] Among the most common actuarial assumptions are the following:

- Interest
- Mortality
- Employee turnover
- Salary scale

Each individual actuarial assumption is required to be reasonable or, if not, the assumptions, in the aggregate, must result in a total contribution equivalent to that which would be determined if each assumption were reasonable. Also, the actuarial assumptions must, in combination, offer the actuary's best estimate of anticipated experience under the plan (see Q 2:3). [I.R.C. § 412(c)(3); Citrus Valley Estates, Inc. v. Comm'r, 49 F.3d 1410 (9th Cir. 1995); Wachtell, Lipton, Rosen & Katz v. Comm'r, 26 F.3d 291 (2d Cir. 1994); Vinson & Elkins v. Comm'r, 7 F.3d 1235 (5th Cir. 1993); Rhoades, McKee & Boer v. United States, 1:91-CV-540 (W.D. Mich. 1995); Jerome Mirza & Assocs. Ltd. v. United States, 882 F.2d 229 (7th Cir. 1989); IRS News Release IR-95-43 (June 7, 1995)]

Q 2:20   Must the actuarial assumptions be set forth in the plan?

The actuarial assumptions used to determine the cost of funding a defined benefit plan (see Q 2:3) need not be set forth in the plan. However, the actuarial assumptions used to determine the value of a benefit (e.g., postretirement interest and mortality) must be set forth in the plan in a manner that precludes employer discretion. In other words, the lump-sum value of a participant's benefit and the present value of the monthly benefit must be the same (i.e., actuarially equivalent). If the postretirement actuarial assumptions are not specified, the benefits under the defined benefit plan are not considered to be definitely determinable. [I.R.C. § 401(a)(25); Bilello v. JPMorgan Chase Retirement Plan, 2009 WL 1108756 (S.D.N.Y. 2009)]

Q 2:21   What is a Keogh plan?

A Keogh, or H.R. 10, plan is a qualified retirement plan maintained by a self-employed individual (see Q 6:60), either a sole proprietor or a partner. The self-employed individual may take a tax deduction for annual contributions to the plan made on behalf of the individual and on behalf of any eligible employees. A Keogh plan may be either a defined contribution plan (see Q 2:2) or a defined benefit plan (see Q 2:3).

For more details, see Qs 6:59 through 6:63.

Q 2:22   What is a floor-offset plan?

A floor-offset plan is a hybrid arrangement in which the employer maintains a defined benefit plan (see Q 2:3) and a defined contribution plan (see Q 2:2), and the benefits provided under the defined benefit plan will be reduced by the value of the participant's account in the defined contribution plan. In essence, the defined benefit plan provides a guaranteed floor benefit, but the amount is offset by the benefit provided under the defined contribution plan. [ERISA § 407(d)(9); Treas. Reg. § 1.401(a)(4)-8(d); Rev. Rul. 76-259, 1976-2 C.B. 111; Lunn v. Montgomery Ward & Co. Ret. Sec. Plan, 1999 WL 27489 (7th Cir. 1999)]

If the value of the participant's account in the defined contribution plan declines, the participant will be insulated from the risk of investment loss because the full amount of pension benefits will be received under the defined benefit plan. Alternatively, if the value of the participant's account exceeds the amount of the benefit under the defined benefit plan, the participant will receive benefits exclusively from the defined contribution plan. In other words, the participant has the best of both worlds: the participant is protected against any risk of adverse investment experience under the defined benefit plan and receives the favorable investment experience under the defined contribution plan. One court ruled that the defined benefit plan could calculate the offset amount for the benefit under the defined contribution plan by using deferred, instead of immediate, annuity rates. [White v. Sundstrand Corp., 256 F.3d 580 (7th Cir. 2001)]

Where the benefit of a participant in a multiemployer defined benefit plan (see Q 29:2) was offset by his benefit in a multiemployer defined contribution plan, his claim that the offset constituted an impermissible forfeiture was disallowed. [Brengettsy v. LTV Steel (Republic) Hourly Pension Plan, No. 98 C 5742 (N.D. Ill. 2000)]

The defined contribution plan component of this type of arrangement may be subject to certain restrictions that are not imposed on a defined contribution plan that is not part of a floor-offset arrangement (see Q 23:84).

Q 2:23   What is a cash balance plan?

A cash balance plan is a defined benefit plan (see Q 2:3), but it exhibits features of both defined benefit and defined contribution plans (see Q 2:2). The most recognizable feature of the cash balance plan is its use of a separate account for each participant. A cash balance account is established for each employee upon the employee's becoming a member of the plan. [Treas. Reg. § 1.401(a)(4)-8(c)(3)]

If the plan is replacing an existing defined benefit plan, employees are credited with an opening balance, typically the actuarial present value of their accrued prior plan benefits. Thereafter, the employee's cash balance account receives additional credits. These are likely to be computed as a flat percentage of the employee's pay, such as 4 percent or 5 percent. In addition, employees' balances grow based on interest credits. The rate varies from year to year and is communicated to employees before the start of the year. As an example, it might be the yield on one-year Treasury bills. The interest rate is not tied to the actual investment performance of the plan's assets and is determined independently, based on specific provisions in the plan document. The plan may also set forth a minimum and/or maximum rate; but the minimum cannot be more than the lowest standard interest rate, and the maximum cannot be less than the highest standard interest rate. [Treas. Reg. §§ 1.401(a)(4)-8(c)(3)(iv)(C), 1.401(a)(4)-12; Priv. Ltr. Rul. 9645031]

A court allowed a plan sponsor to reform its cash balance plan to correct a scrivener's error that caused a transition factor to be used twice in determining participants' opening account balances. [Young v. Verizon's Bell Atlantic Cash Balance Plan, 2010 WL 3122795 (7th Cir. 2010)]

The amounts an employer contributes to the plan are determined actuarially to ensure sufficient funds to provide for the benefits promised by the plan. The minimum funding standards (see Q 8:1) apply to cash balance plans, as is the case with other types of defined benefit plans. [I.R.C. § 412]

From the employee's perspective, one of the cash balance plan's advantages is that investment risks are borne by the employer as in any other defined benefit plan. This differs from a defined contribution plan. Cash balance plans provide higher benefits for younger employees and lower benefits for older employees, in contrast to traditional defined benefit plans. However, the costs of providing these benefits are also correspondingly higher for younger employees and lower for older employees, as compared with traditional defined benefit plans. For a discussion of how the present value of benefits under a cash balance plan is determined, see Qs 10:63 and 10:64.

One court concluded that an employer's conversion of its defined benefit plan to a cash balance plan violated the age-discrimination provisions of ERISA (see Q 9:27). [Cooper v. IBM Personal Pension Plan, 274 F. Supp. 2d 1010 (S.D. Ill. 2003); *but see* Godinez v. CBS Corp., 2003 U.S. App. LEXIS 23923 (9th Cir. 2003); I.R.C. § 411(b)(1)(G); ERISA § 204(b)(1)(G)] After much discussion and controversy, the seventh circuit reversed the district court and held that IBM's cash balance plan did not violate the age-discrimination rules. [Cooper v. IBM Personal Pension Plan, 457 F.3d 636 (7th Cir. 2006)] Other courts have also concluded that a cash balance plan conversion did not violate the age-discrimination rules. [Walker v. Monsanto Co. Pension Plan, 2010 WL 2977304 (7th Cir. 2010); Sunder, III v. U.S. Bank Pension Plan, 2009 WL 3714430 (8th Cir. 2009); Rosenblatt v. United Way of Greater Houston, 2008 WL 5396291 (S.D. Tex. 2008); Hurlic v. Southern California Gas Co., 539 F.3d 1024 (9th Cir. 2008); Hirt v. Equitable Retirement Plan for Employees, Managers and Agents, 533 F.3d 102 (2d Cir. 2008); Bryerton v. Verizon Communications, Inc., 533 F.3d 102 (2d Cir. 2008); George v. Duke Energy Retirement Cash Balance Plan, 2008 WL 2307485 (D. S.C. 2008); Drutis v. Rand McNally & Co., 499 F.3d 608 (6th Cir. 2007); Gillis v. SPX Corp. Individual Retirement Plan, No. 07-1777 (1st Cir. 2007); Finley v. Dun & Bradstreet, 2007 WL 196753 (D. N.J. 2007); Wheeler v. Pension Value Plan for Employees of the Boeing Co., 2007 WL 2608875 (S.D. Ill. 2007); Register v. PNC Financial Services Group, Inc., 477 F.3d 56 (3d Cir. 2007); Laurent v. PriceWaterhouseCoopers, 2006 WL 2546805 (S.D.N.Y. 2006); Tootler v. ARINC, Inc., 2004 WL 1285894 (D. Md. 2004); *but see In re* Citigroup Pension Plan ERISA Litigation, 470 F. Supp. 2d 323 (S.D.N.Y. 2006) and *In re* J.P. Morgan Chase Cash Balance Litigation, 460 F. Supp. 2d 479 (S.D.N.Y. 2006)]

After years of litigation, PPA approved the implementation of cash balance plans and pension equity plans, another form of hybrid plan.

Age discrimination plans in general

Under PPA, a plan is not treated as violating the prohibition on age discrimination if a participant's accrued benefit, as determined as of any date under the terms of the plan, would be equal to or greater than that of any similarly situated, younger individual who is or could be a participant. For this purpose, an individual is similarly situated to a participant if the individual and the participant are (and always have been) identical in every respect (including period of service, compensation, position, date of hire, work history, and any other respect) except for age. Under PPA, the comparison of benefits for older and younger participants applies to all possible participants under all possible dates under the plan.

In addition, in determining a participant's accrued benefit for this purpose, the subsidized portion of any early retirement benefit or any retirement-type subsidy is disregarded. In some cases, the value of an early retirement subsidy may be difficult to determine; it is therefore intended that a reasonable approximation of such value may be used for this purpose. In calculating the accrued benefit, the benefit may, under the terms of the plan, be calculated as an annuity payable at normal retirement age, the balance of a hypothetical account, or the current value of the accumulated percentage of the employee's final average compensation. That is, the age discrimination rules may be applied on the basis of the balance of a hypothetical account or the current value of the accumulated percentage of the employee's final average compensation, but only if the plan terms provide the accrued benefit in such form. This provision is intended to apply to hybrid plans, including pension equity plans.

This provision makes it clear that a plan is not treated as age discriminatory solely because the plan provides offsets of benefits under the plan to the extent such offsets are allowable in applying the non-discrimination requirements.

A plan is not treated as failing to meet the age discrimination requirements solely because the plan provides a disparity in contributions and benefits (see Q 7:1). A plan is not treated as failing to meet the age discrimination requirements solely because the plan provides for indexing of accrued benefits under the plan. Except in the case of any benefit provided in the form of a variable annuity, this rule does not apply with respect to any indexing which results in an accrued benefit less than the accrued benefit determined without regard to such indexing. Indexing for this purpose means, with respect to an accrued benefit, the periodic adjustment of the accrued benefit by means of the application of a recognized investment index or methodology. Under this provision, in no event may indexing be reduced or cease because of age.

Rules for applicable defined benefit plans

In general

Under PPA, an applicable defined benefit plan fails to satisfy the age discrimination rules unless the plan meets certain requirements with respect to interest credits and, in the case of conversion, certain additional requirements. Applicable defined benefit plans must also satisfy certain vesting requirements.

Interest requirement

A plan satisfies the interest requirement if the terms of the plan provide that any interest credit (or equivalent amount) for any plan year is at a rate that is not less than zero and is not greater than a market rate of return. A plan does not fail to meet the interest requirement merely because the plan provides for a reasonable minimum guaranteed rate of return or for a rate of return that is equal to the greater of a fixed or variable rate of return. A plan must provide that an interest credit (or an equivalent amount) of less than zero cannot result in the account balance or similar amount being less than the aggregate amount of contributions credited to the account. IRS may provide rules governing the calculation of a market rate of return and for permissible methods of crediting interest to the account (including fixed or variable interest rates) resulting in effective rates of return that meet the requirements of this provision.

If the interest credit rate (or equivalent amount) is a variable rate, the plan must provide that, upon termination of the plan, the rate of interest used to determine accrued benefits under the plan is equal to the average of the rates of interest used under the plan during the five-year period ending on the termination date.

Conversion rules

Under PPA, special rules apply if an amendment to a defined benefit plan is adopted that would have the effect of converting the plan into an applicable defined benefit plan (applicable plan amendment). If an applicable plan amendment is adopted after June 29, 2005, the plan fails to satisfy the age discrimination rules unless the plan provides that the accrued benefit of any individual who was a participant immediately before the adoption of the amendment is not less than the sum of (1) the participant's accrued benefit for years of service before the effective date of the amendment, determined under the terms of the plan as in effect before the amendment, plus (2) the participant's accrued benefit for years of service after the effective date of the amendment, determined under the terms of the plan as in effect after the terms of the amendment. For purposes of determining the amount in (1), the plan must credit the accumulation account or similar amount with the amount of an early retirement benefit or retirement-type subsidy for the plan year in which the participant retires if, as of such time, the participant has met the age, years of service, and other requirements under the plan for entitlement to such benefit or subsidy.

Vesting rules

An applicable defined benefit plan must provide that each employee who has completed at least three years of service has a nonforfeitable right to 100 percent of the employee's accrued benefit derived from employer contributions. The three-year vesting rule applies on a plan year basis and only to participants with an hour of service after the effective date of the rule applicable to the plan.

Minimum present value rules

PPA provides that an applicable defined benefit plan is not treated as failing to meet the minimum present value rules solely because the present value of the accrued benefit (or any portion thereof) of any participant is, under the terms of the plan, equal to the amount expressed as the balance in the hypothetical account or as an accumulated percentage of the participant's final average compensation.

Rules on plan termination

PPA provides rules for making determinations of benefits upon termination of an applicable defined benefit plan. Such a plan must provide that, upon plan termination, (1) if the interest credit rate (or equivalent amount) under the plan is a variable rate, the rate of interest used to determine accrued benefits under the plan is equal to the average of the rates of interest used under the plan during the five-year period ending on the termination date and (2) the interest rate and mortality table used to determine the amount of any benefit under the plan payable in the form of an annuity payable at normal retirement age is the rate and table specified under the plan for such purposes as of the termination date. For purposes of (2), if the rate of interest is a variable rate, then the rate is the average of such rates during the five-year period ending on the termination date.

Definition of applicable defined benefit plan

An applicable defined benefit plan is a defined benefit plan under which the accrued benefit (or any portion thereof) is calculated as the balance of a hypothetical account maintained for the participant or as an accumulated percentage of the participant's final average compensation. IRS is to provide rules that include in the definition of an applicable defined benefit plan any defined benefit plan (or portion of such a plan) which has an effect similar to an applicable defined benefit plan.

Regulations relating to mergers and acquisitions

IRS is directed to prescribe regulations for the application of the provisions relating to applicable defined benefit plans in cases where the conversion of a plan to a cash balance or similar plan is made with respect to a group of employees who become employees by reason of a merger, acquisition, or similar treatment. The regulations are to be issued no later than August 17, 2007.

Effective dates

In general, the PPA provisions are effective for periods beginning on or after June 29, 2005.

The provision relating to the minimum value rules is effective for distributions after August 17, 2006.

In the case of a plan in existence on June 29, 2005, the interest credit and vesting requirements for an applicable defined benefit plan generally apply to years beginning after December 31, 2007, except that the plan sponsor may elect to have such requirements apply for any period after June 29, 2005, and before the first plan year beginning after December 31, 2007. In the case of a plan maintained pursuant to one or more collective bargaining agreements, a delayed effective date applies with respect to the interest credit and vesting requirements for an applicable defined benefit plan.

The provision relating to conversions of plans applies to plan amendments adopted after and taking effect after June 29, 2005, except that a plan sponsor may elect to have such amendments apply to plan amendments adopted before and taking affect after such date.

The direction to IRS to issue regulations relating to mergers and acquisitions is effective on August 17, 2006.

[ERISA § 203(f); I.R.C. § 411(a)(13)]

IRS has extended the deadline for amending qualified retirement plans to meet a number of requirements added by PPA by one year to the last day of the first plan year that begins on or after January 1, 2010. This extension applies to a number of provisions, including the deadline for amending cash balance and other applicable defined benefit plans to meet certain requirements. [IRS Notice 2009-97, 2009-2 C.B. ___]

IRS has provided transitional guidance with respect to the new PPA rules that relate to statutory hybrid plans and the conversion of a defined benefit plan into a statutory hybrid plan. The transitional guidance applies pending the issuance of further guidance.

A. *Section 411(a)(13)(C): Definition of statutory hybrid plan.*

  1. *In general.* A statutory hybrid plan is a plan that is either a lump-sum based plan or a plan that has a similar effect to a lump-sum based plan. For purposes of the notice, a lump-sum based plan is a defined benefit plan under the terms of which the accumulated benefit of a participant is expressed as the balance of a hypothetical account balance or accumulated percentage. Whether a plan is a lump-sum based plan is determined based on how the accumulated benefit of a participant is expressed under the terms of the plan and does not depend on whether the plan provides for an optional form of benefit (see Q 4:20) in the form of a lump-sum payment.

  2. *Similar effect to a lump-sum based plan.*

    (i) *Treated as having a similar effect.* Except as provided in (ii) below, a plan that is not a lump-sum based plan is treated as having a similar effect to a lump-sum based plan if the plan provides that a participant's accrued benefit (payable at normal retirement age) is expressed as a benefit that includes automatic periodic increases through normal retirement age that results in the payment of a larger amount at normal retirement age to a similarly situated participant who is younger. This includes a plan that provides for indexing of accrued benefits, such as a plan that expresses the accrued benefit as an indexed annuity.

    (ii) *Not treated as having a similar effect.*

      (I) *Plan with post-retirement adjustment.* A plan that solely provides for post-retirement adjustment of the amounts payable to a participant is not treated as having a similar effect to a lump-sum based plan.

      (II) *Variable annuity plan.* A variable annuity plan is not treated as having a similar effect to a lump-sum based plan if it has an assumed interest rate used for purposes of adjustment of amounts payable to a participant that is at least five percent. For this purpose, a variable annuity plan includes any plan that provides that the amount payable is periodically adjusted by reference to the difference between the rate of return of plan assets (or specified market indices) and the assumed interest rate.

B. *Section 411(a)(13): Special rules for the application of Sections 411(a)(2), 411(c), and 417(e).*

1. *In general.* Special rules are provided for applicable defined benefit plans with respect to Sections 411(a)(2), 411(c), and 417(e) for benefits expressed as the balance of a hypothetical account maintained for a participant or as the current value of the accumulated percentage of a participant's final average compensation under a lump-sum based plan. Specifically, with respect to such benefits, a lump-sum based plan is not treated as failing to meet the requirements of Section 411(a)(2), or the requirements of Sections 411(c) and 417(e) with respect to such benefits derived from employer contributions, solely because the present value of such benefits of any participant is, under the terms of the plan, equal to the amount expressed as the balance in the hypothetical account or as the accumulated percentage of the participant's final average compensation. The applicable defined benefit plan rules do not apply to benefits under a statutory hybrid plan that are expressed neither as the balance of a hypothetical account maintained for a participant nor as the current value of the accumulated percentage of a participant's final average compensation.

2. *Effective date.* The applicable defined benefit rules are effective for distributions made after August 17, 2006. IRS expects to issue regulations interpreting the effective date of these rules.

3. *Section 411(d)(6) relief.* In the case of a lump-sum based plan that provides for a single-sum distribution to a participant that exceeds the participant's hypothetical account balance or accumulated percentage of final average compensation, the plan may be amended to eliminate the excess for distributions made after August 17, 2006. If the amendment is adopted on or before the last day of the first plan year beginning on or after January 1, 2009, and the plan is operated as if such amendment were in effect as of the first date the amendment is effective, then the amendment does not violate the anti-cutback rules with respect to distributions made after the later of August 17, 2006, or the effective date of the amendment.

4. *Section 4980F.* In the case of an amendment described in section B(3) above, a Section 204(h) Notice (see Q 9:37) must be provided at least 30 days before the date the amendment is first effective. Thus, if an amendment that significantly reduces the rate of future benefit accrual is adopted retroactively (i.e., is adopted after the effective date of the amendment), then the Section 204(h) Notice must be provided at least 30 days before the earliest date on which the plan is operated in accordance with the amendment.

5. *Vesting.* There is a special three-year vesting schedule for statutory hybrid plans.

C. *Section 411(b)(5)(A)(iv): Scope of rule.* In applying the age-discrimination test, a lump-sum based plan may determine the accumulated benefit of a participant as the balance of a hypothetical account or the current value of the accumulated percentage of the employee's final average compensation even if the plan defines the participant's accrued benefit as an annuity at normal retirement age that is actuarially equivalent to such balance or value.

D. *Section 411(b)(5)(B)(i): Market rate of return.*

1. *Future guidance on market rate of return.* During 2007, IRS expects to issue guidance that addresses the market rate of return rules, including the special rule regarding preservation of capital and the minimum rate of return rules. The guidance is also expected to address the extent to which the anti-cutback relief applies to an amendment to a statutory hybrid plan that changes the plan's interest crediting rate where such amendment is adopted after August 17, 2006.

2. *Safe harbor.* Pending further guidance, a market rate of return includes the rate of interest on long-term investment grade corporate bonds or the rate of interest on 30-year Treasury securities. In addition, a market rate of return includes the sum of any of the standard indices and the associated margin for that index as described in part IV of IRS Notice 96-8.

3. *Certain plan termination requirements.* See Section 411(b)(5)(B)(vi) for required plan terms related to termination of a statutory hybrid plan.

E. *Section 411(b)(5)(B)(ii)-(iv): Special rules for conversion amendments.*

1. *In general.* If a conversion amendment is adopted with respect to a plan after June 29, 2005, the plan is treated as failing to meet the requirements that the rate of benefit accrual under a defined benefit plan cannot be reduced because of the attainment of any age unless the requirements of Section 411(b)(5)(B)(iii) are met with respect to each individual who was a participant in the plan immediately before the adoption of the conversion amendment.

2. *Requirements of Section 411(b)(5)(B)(iii).* Subject to Section 411(b)(5)(B)(iv), Section 411(b)(5)(B)(iii) is satisfied with respect to any participant if the accrued benefit of the participant under the terms of the plan as in effect after the conversion amendment is not less than the sum of:

   (i) The participant's accrued benefit for years of service before the effective date of the conversion amendment, determined under the terms of the plan as in effect before the amendment, and

   (ii) The participant's accrued benefit for years of service after the effective date of the amendment, determined under the terms of the plan as in effect after the amendment.

3. *Requirements of Section 411(b)(5)(B)(iv).* A plan must credit the accumulation account or similar account for purposes of the accrued benefit described in (2)(ii) above with the amount of any early retirement benefit or retirement-type subsidy for the plan year in which the participant retires if, as of such time, the participant has met

the age, years of service, and other requirements under the plan for entitlement to such benefit or subsidy. For this purpose, the date on which a participant retires means the annuity starting date for the participant's benefit.

4. *Effective date.* Section 411(b)(5)(B)(ii) applies to a conversion amendment that is adopted after, and takes effect after, June 29, 2005. However, a plan sponsor may elect to have such amendments apply to plan amendments adopted before, and taking effect after, such date.

F. *Safe harbor for conversions related to mergers and acquisitions.*

1. *Future guidance on conversions related to mergers and acquisitions.* IRS expects to issue regulations not later than August 17, 2007, regarding an amendment to convert a defined benefit plan into a hybrid defined benefit plan with respect to a group of employees who become employees by reason of a merger, acquisition, or similar transaction.

2. *Safe harbor.* Pending further guidance, a plan amendment described in Section E above that is also described in paragraph (1) above is not treated as failing to meet the attainment-of-any-age rule if the benefit of each participant under the plan as amended is not less than the sum of:

   (i) The participant's protected benefit with respect to service before the effective date of the conversion amendment, determined under the terms of the plan as in effect before the amendment, and

   (ii) The participant's protected benefit with respect to service on and after the effective date of the conversion amendment, determined under the terms of the plan as in effect after the amendment.

   For purposes of this Section F(2), the benefits under clause (A) and the benefits under clause (B) must each be determined in the same manner as if they were provided under separate plans that are independent of each other (e.g., without any benefit offsets).

[IRS Notice 2007-6, Part III, 2007-1 C.B. 272]

IRS has issued proposed regulations on hybrid defined benefit plans, such as cash balance plans, incorporating and expanding upon the transitional guidance of Notice 2007-6. See Q 2:24 for details. In addition, an IRS ruling concluded that the anti-backloading rules were not violated by a traditional defined benefit plan that converted to a cash balance formula. See Q 9:3 for details.

The Financial Accounting Standards Board (FASB) advised that it added a limited scope project to its agenda that would lead to an Interpretation of FASB Statement No. 87, "Employers' Accounting for Pensions." FASB said the project would address the measurement of obligations under cash balance plans because current accounting guidance did not specifically address the types of benefit arrangements that exist in many cash balance plans. Subsequently, FASB said that entities would apply the following measurement guidance:

1. For cash balance plans with a fixed interest crediting rate, the obligation would be measured by projecting forward the plan participants' notional account balances at the fixed crediting rate as stipulated in the plan's provisions, and discounting the resulting amount using a discount rate determined in accordance with paragraph 44 of FASB Statement No. 87.

2. For cash balance plans with a market or market-related (variable) interest crediting rate, the obligation would be measured by reference to the plan participants' notional account balances. Entities would not project and discount plan participants' notional account balances. [FASB Action Alert No. 04-10 (Mar. 11, 2004)] Seven months later, FASB decided to expand the scope of its rulemaking project and said that it will develop an amendment of FASB Statement No. 87 for all defined benefit plans with lump-sum features (that is, plans that allow employees to receive an immediate and full payment upon termination of employment), so that the pension obligation recorded would be the greater of (a) the undiscounted lump-sum amount that employees would be entitled to if they terminated employment at the measurement date or (b) the actuarial present value of the pension obligation at the measurement date. [FASB Action Alert No. 04-41 (Oct., 2004); *also see* FASB Statement No. 158, FASB News Rel. (Sept. 29, 2006)]

Q 2:24 Has IRS issued proposed regulations on hybrid defined benefit plans, such as cash balance plans?

On December 31, 2007, IRS issued proposed regulations that:

1. Set forth certain rules that apply to statutory hybrid plans;
2. Describe special rules for certain statutory hybrid plans that determine benefits under a lump sum–based benefit formula;
3. Describe the vesting requirement for statutory hybrid plans;
4. Define important terms; and
5. Contain effective/applicability dates.

[I.R.C. § 411(a)(13); Prop. Treas. Reg. § 1.411(a)(13)-1(a)]

A statutory hybrid plan that determines any portion of a participant's benefits under a lump sum–based benefit formula is not treated as failing to meet the minimum vesting requirements (see Q 9:4), or the requirements with respect to the participant's accrued benefit (see Q 9:2) derived from employer contributions, solely because, with respect to benefits determined under that formula, the present value of those benefits is, under the terms of the plan, equal to the balance of the hypothetical account maintained for the participant or to the current value of the accumulated percentage of the participant's final average compensation under that formula. [I.R.C. §§ 411(a)(2), 411(c), 417(e); Prop. Treas. Reg. § 1.411(a)(13)-1(b)]

If any portion of the participant's accrued benefit under a defined benefit plan is determined under a statutory hybrid benefit formula, the plan is not treated as meeting the minimum vesting requirements unless the plan provides that the participant has a nonforfeitable right to 100 percent of the participant's accrued benefit if the participant has three or more years of service. Thus, this three-year vesting requirement applies with respect to the entire accrued benefit of a participant under a defined benefit plan even if only a portion of the participant's accrued benefit under the plan is determined under a statutory hybrid benefit formula. Similarly, if the participant's accrued benefit under a defined benefit plan is, under the plan's terms, the larger of two (or more) benefit amounts, where each amount is determined under a different benefit formula (including a benefit determined pursuant to an offset among formulas within the plan) and at least one of those formulas is a statutory hybrid benefit formula, the participant's entire accrued benefit under the defined benefit plan is subject to the three-year vesting rule. The rule described in the preceding sentence applies even if the larger benefit is ultimately the benefit determined under a formula that is not a statutory hybrid benefit formula. [I.R.C. § 411(a)(13)(B); Prop. Treas. Reg. § 1.411(a)(13)-1(c)]

> **Example 1.** Employer M sponsors Plan X, pursuant to which each participant's accrued benefit is equal to the sum of the benefit provided under two benefit formulas. The first benefit formula is a statutory hybrid benefit formula, and the second formula is not. Because a portion of each participant's accrued benefit provided under Plan X is determined under a statutory hybrid benefit formula, the three-year vesting requirement applies to each participant's entire accrued benefit.

> **Example 2.** The facts are the same as in Example 1, except that the benefit formulas described in Example 1 only apply to participants for service performed in Division A of Employer M and a different benefit formula applies to participants for service performed in Division B of Employer M. Pursuant to the terms of Plan X, the accrued benefit of a participant attributable to service performed in Division B is equal to the benefit provided by a benefit formula that is not a statutory hybrid benefit formula. Therefore, the three-year vesting requirement does not apply to a participant with an accrued benefit under Plan X if the participant's benefit is solely attributable to service performed in Division B.

A lump sum–based benefit formula is a benefit formula used to determine all or any part of a participant's accumulated benefit under a defined benefit plan under which the benefit provided under the formula is expressed as the balance of a hypothetical account maintained for the participant or as the current value of the accumulated percentage of the participant's final average compensation. Whether a benefit formula is a lump sum–based benefit formula is determined based on how the accumulated benefit of a participant is expressed under the terms of the plan and does not depend on whether the plan provides an optional form of benefit (see Q 4:20) in the form of a single-sum payment. A participant is not treated as having a lump sum–based benefit formula merely because the participant is entitled to a benefit under a defined benefit plan that is equal to the greater of the otherwise applicable benefit formula and the benefit properly attributable to after-tax employee contributions (see Q 9:9). [Prop. Treas. Reg. §§ 1.411(a)(13)-1(d)(2), 1.411(b)(5)-1(e)(3)]

A statutory hybrid benefit formula is a benefit formula that is either a lump sum–based benefit formula or a formula that is not a lump sum–based benefit formula but that has an effect similar to a lump sum–based benefit formula. [Prop. Treas. Reg. § 1.411(a)(13)-1(d)(3)(i)] Except as provided below, a benefit formula under a defined benefit plan that is not a lump sum–based benefit formula has an effect similar to a lump sum–based benefit formula if the formula provides that a participant's accumulated benefit payable at normal retirement age (see Q 10:55) (or benefit commencement, if later) is expressed as a benefit that includes the right to periodic adjustments (including a formula that provides for indexed benefits) that are reasonably expected to result in a larger annual benefit at normal retirement age (or benefit commencement, if later) for the participant than for a similarly situated, younger individual who is or could be a participant in the plan. A benefit formula that does not include periodic adjustments is treated as a formula with an effect similar to a lump sum–based benefit formula if the formula is otherwise described in the preceding sentence and the adjustments are provided pursuant to a pattern of repeated plan amendments (see Q 10:46). A participant's accumulated benefit at any date means the participant's benefit, as expressed under the terms of the plan, accrued to that date. For this purpose, the accumulated benefit of a participant may be expressed under the terms of the plan as either the balance of a hypothetical account or the current value of an accumulated percentage of the participant's final average compensation, even if the plan defines the participant's accrued benefit as an annuity beginning at normal retirement age that is actuarially equivalent to that balance or value. [Prop. Treas. Reg. §§ 1.411(a)(13)-1(d)(3)(ii), 1.411(b)(5)-1(e)(2)]

Post-annuity starting date (see Q 10:3) adjustments of the amounts payable to a participant (such as cost-of-living increases) are disregarded in determining whether a benefit formula under a defined benefit plan has an effect similar to a lump sum–based benefit formula. If the assumed interest rate used for purposes of the adjustment of amounts payable to a participant under a variable annuity benefit formula is at least 5 percent, then the adjustments under the variable annuity benefit formula are not treated as being reasonably expected to result in a larger annual benefit at normal retirement age (or benefit commencement, if later) for the participant than for a similarly situated, younger individual who is or could be a participant in the plan; and, thus, such a variable annuity benefit formula does not have an effect similar to a lump sum–based benefit formula. A benefit formula under a defined benefit plan that provides for a benefit equal to the benefit properly attributable to after-tax employee contributions does not have an effect similar to a lump sum–based benefit formula. A variable annuity benefit formula is any benefit formula under a defined benefit plan that provides that the amount payable is periodically adjusted by reference to the difference between the rate of return of plan assets (or specified market indices) and a specified assumed interest rate. [Prop. Treas. Reg. §§ 1.411(a)(13)-1(d)(3)(iii), 1.411(a)(13)-1(d)(4)]

In general, the special rules for plans computing accrued benefits by reference to hypothetical account balances or equivalent amounts apply for periods beginning on or after June 29, 2005. The calculation of benefits applies to distributions made after August 17, 2006. In the case of a plan that is in existence on June 29, 2005 (regardless of whether the plan is a statutory hybrid plan on that date), the three-year vesting requirement applies to plan years beginning on or after January 1, 2008. However, the plan sponsor of such a plan may elect to have such requirement apply for any period after June 29, 2005, and before the first plan year beginning after December 31, 2007. An employer is permitted to adopt an amendment to make this election as late as the last day of the first plan year that begins on or after January 1, 2009 if the plan operates in accordance with the election. In the case of a plan not in existence on June 29, 2005, the three-year vesting requirement applies for periods beginning on or after June 29, 2005. Special rules apply to collectively bargained plans (see Q 29:2). The proposed regulations apply for plan years beginning on or after January 1, 2009, and may be relied upon before that date. [Prop. Treas. Reg. § 1.411(a)(13)-1(e)]

With regard to the reduction in rate of accrual under the defined benefit plan, the proposed regulations also:

1. Describe certain plan design-based safe harbors (including statutory hybrid plans) that are deemed to satisfy the age-discrimination rules (see Q 9:27);
2. Describe rules relating to statutory hybrid conversion amendments;
3. Describe rules restricting interest credits (or equivalent amounts) under a statutory hybrid plan to a market rate of return;
4. Define important terms; and
5. Contain effective/applicability dates.

[I.R.C. §§ 411(b)(1)(H), 411(b)(5)(A); Prop. Treas. Reg. § 1.411(b)(5)-1(a)]

A plan is not treated as failing to meet the age-discrimination rules if, as of any date, the accumulated benefit of a participant would not be less than the accumulated benefit of any similarly situated, younger participant. This test requires a comparison of the accumulated benefit of each individual who is or could be a participant in the plan with the accumulated benefit of each other similarly situated, younger individual who is or could be a participant in the plan. The comparison is based on:

1. The annuity payable at normal retirement age (or current age, if later) if the accumulated benefit of the participant under the terms of the plan is expressed as an annuity payable at normal retirement age (or current age, if later);
2. The balance of a hypothetical account if the accumulated benefit of the participant under the terms of the plan is expressed as a hypothetical account balance; or
3. The current value of an accumulated percentage of the participant's final average compensation if the accumulated benefit of the participant under

the terms of the plan is expressed as an accumulated percentage of final average compensation.
[I.R.C. § 411(b)(1)(H)(i); Prop. Treas. Reg. § 1.411(b)(5)-1(b)(1)(i)]

The safe harbor provided above does not apply to a plan if the accumulated benefit of a participant under the plan is not described in paragraph 1, 2, or 3 above. In addition, except as provided below, that safe harbor also does not apply to a plan if the comparison required involves comparing accumulated benefits that are described in different paragraphs. Thus, for example, if a plan provides an accumulated benefit that is expressed under the terms of the plan as an annuity payable at normal retirement age (paragraph 1) for participants who are age 55 or over, and the plan provides an accumulated benefit that is expressed as the balance of a hypothetical account (paragraph 2) for participants who are younger than age 55, the safe harbor does not apply to the plan. [I.R.C. § 411(b)(5)(A); Prop. Treas. Reg. § 1.411(b)(5)-1(b)(1)(ii)(A)] If a plan provides that a participant's accumulated benefit is equal to the sum of accumulated benefits that are described in different paragraphs, then the plan is deemed to satisfy the comparison test if the plan satisfies the comparison test separately for each of the different accumulated benefits. Similarly, if a plan provides that a participant's accumulated benefit is equal to the greater of accumulated benefits that are described in different paragraphs, then the plan is deemed to satisfy the comparison test if the plan satisfies the comparison test separately for each of the different accumulated benefits. For this purpose, a similarly situated, younger participant is treated as having an accumulated benefit of zero under a benefit formula if the benefit formula does not apply to the participant. [Prop. Treas. Reg. § 1.411(b)(5)-1(b)(1)(ii)(B)]

Any subsidized portion of any early retirement benefit that is included in a participant's accumulated benefit is disregarded. For this purpose, the subsidized portion of an early retirement benefit is the retirement-type subsidy (see Q 9:33) that is contingent on a participant's severance from employment and commencement of benefits before normal retirement age. [Prop. Treas. Reg. § 1.411(b)(5)-1(b)(1)(iii)]

A defined benefit plan is not treated as failing to meet the age-discrimination rules solely because a benefit formula under the plan (other than a lump sum–based benefit formula) provides for the periodic adjustment of accrued benefits under the plan, but only if the adjustment is by means of the application of a recognized investment index or methodology and the plan satisfies the similarly situated participant test. A statutory hybrid plan that is not treated as failing to satisfy the age-discrimination rules pursuant to the preceding sentence must nevertheless satisfy the qualification requirements otherwise applicable to statutory hybrid plans, including the requirements relating to minimum vesting standards, plan conversion amendments, and market rates of return. [Prop. Treas. Reg. § 1.411(b)(5)-1(b)(2)(i)] An adjustment is made pursuant to a recognized investment index or methodology if it is made pursuant to (1) an eligible cost-of-living index (see Q 11:38); (2) the rate of return on the aggregate assets of the plan; or (3) the rate of return on the annuity contract for the employee issued by an insurance company licensed under the laws of a State. [Prop. Treas. Reg. § 1.411(b)(5)-1(b)(2)(ii)]

A plan satisfies the similarly situated participant test if the aggregate periodic adjustments of each participant's accrued benefit under the plan (determined as a percentage of the unadjusted accrued benefit) would not be less than the aggregate periodic adjustments of any similarly situated, younger participant. This test requires a comparison of the aggregate periodic adjustments of each individual who is or could be a participant in the plan for any specified period with the aggregate periodic adjustments of each other similarly situated, younger individual who is or could be a participant in the plan for the same period. [Prop. Treas. Reg. § 1.411(b)(5)-1(b)(2)(iii)]

The indexing of accrued benefits is not permitted with respect to any indexing that results in an accrued benefit less than the accrued benefit determined without regard to such indexing. This prohibition does not apply in the case of a benefit provided under a variable annuity benefit formula, but only if the adjustments under the variable annuity benefit formula are based on the rate of return on the aggregate assets of the plan or the rate of return on the annuity contract for the employee issued by an insurance company licensed under the laws of a State. [I.R.C. § 411(b)(5)(E); Prop. Treas. Reg. § 1.411(b)(5)-1(b)(2)(iv)]

A plan is not treated as failing to meet the age-discrimination rules solely because the plan provides offsets against benefits under the plan to the extent the offsets are allowable in applying the qualification requirements (see Q 4:1) and the applicable requirements of ERISA and the Age Discrimination in Employment Act. [Prop. Treas. Reg. § 1.411(b)(5)-1(b)(3)] A plan is not treated as failing to meet the rules solely because the plan provides for permitted disparity in contributions or benefits (see chapter 7). [Prop. Treas. Reg. § 1.411(b)(5)-1(b)(4)]

An individual is similarly situated to another individual if the individual is identical to that other individual in every respect that is relevant in determining a participant's benefit under the plan (including period of service, compensation, position, date of hire, work history, and any other respect) except for age. In determining whether an individual is similarly situated to another individual, any characteristic that is relevant for determining benefits under the plan and that is based directly or indirectly on age is disregarded. For example, if a particular benefit formula applies to a participant on account of the participant's age, an individual to whom the benefit formula does not apply and who is identical to the participant in all other respects is similarly situated to the participant. By contrast, an individual is not similarly situated to a participant if a different benefit formula applies to the individual and the application of the different formula is not based directly or indirectly on age. [Prop. Treas. Reg. § 1.411(b)(5)-1(b)(5)]

If there is a conversion amendment with respect to a defined benefit plan, then the plan is treated as failing to meet the age-discrimination rules unless the plan, after the amendment, satisfies the requirements of this paragraph. A statutory hybrid plan satisfies the requirements if the plan provides that, in the case of an individual who was a participant in the plan immediately before the date of adoption of the conversion amendment, the participant's benefit at any subsequent annuity starting date is not less than the sum of: (1) the participant's Section 411(d)(6) protected benefit (see Q 9:33) with respect to service before the effective date of the conversion amendment, determined under the terms of the plan as in effect immediately before the effective date of the amendment, and (2) the participant's Section 411(d)(6) protected benefit with respect to service on and after the effective date of the conversion amendment, determined under the terms of the plan as in effect after the effective date of the amendment. For purposes of this paragraph, except as provided below, the benefits under (1) and (2) must each be determined in the same manner as if they were provided under separate plans that are independent of each other (for example, without any benefit offsets); and, except to the extent permitted, each optional form of payment provided under the terms of the plan with respect to a participant's Section 411(d)(6) protected benefit as in effect before the amendment must be available thereafter to the extent of the plan's benefits for service prior to the effective date of the amendment. [Prop. Treas. Reg. §§ 1.411(b)(5)-1(c)(1), 1.411(b)(5)-1(c)(2)]

A statutory hybrid plan under which an opening hypothetical account balance or opening accumulated percentage of the participant's final average compensation is established as of the effective date of the conversion amendment does not fail to satisfy the requirements of the preceding paragraph merely because benefits attributable to that opening hypothetical account balance or opening accumulated percentage (i.e., benefits that are not described in (2)) are substituted for benefits described in (1). [Prop. Treas. Reg. § 1.411(b)(5)-1(c)(3)(i)] For any optional form of benefit payable at an annuity starting date where there was an optional form of benefit within the same generalized optional form of benefits (see Q 9:33) that would have been available to the participant at that annuity starting date under the terms of the plan as in effect immediately before the effective date of the conversion amendment, the requirements of this paragraph are satisfied only if the plan provides that the amount of the benefit under that optional form of benefit available to the participant under the lump sum–based formula that is attributable to the opening hypothetical account balance or opening accumulated percentage, determined under the terms of the plan as of the annuity starting date (including actuarial conversion factors), is not less than the benefit under that optional form of benefit described in (1) of the preceding paragraph. To satisfy this requirement, if the benefit under an optional form attributable to the opening hypothetical account balance or opening accumulated percentage is less than the benefit described in (1) of the preceding paragraph, then the benefit attributable to the opening hypothetical account balance or opening accumulated percentage must be increased to the extent necessary to provide the minimum benefit described in this paragraph. Thus, if a plan is using the option under this paragraph to satisfy the preceding paragraph with respect to a participant, the participant must receive a benefit equal to not less than the sum of: (1) the greater of the benefit attributable to the opening hypothetical account balance as described in this paragraph and the benefit described in (1) of the preceding paragraph and (2) the benefit described in (2) of the preceding paragraph. [Prop. Treas. Reg. § 1.411(b)(5)-1(c)(3)(ii)(A)]

If an optional form of benefit is available on the annuity starting date with respect to the benefit attributable to the opening hypothetical account balance or opening accumulated percentage, but no optional form within the same generalized optional form of benefit was available at that annuity starting date under the terms of a plan as in effect immediately prior to the effective date of the conversion amendment, then, for these purposes, the plan is treated as if such an optional form of benefit were available immediately prior to the effective date of the conversion amendment. In that event, the preceding paragraph must be applied by taking into account the optional form of benefit that is treated as if it were available on the annuity starting date under the terms of the plan as in effect immediately prior to the effective date of the conversion amendment. Thus, for example, if a single-sum optional form of payment is not available under the plan terms applicable to the accrued benefit, but a single-sum form of payment is available with respect to the benefit attributable to the opening hypothetical account balance or opening accumulated percentage as of the annuity starting date, then, for purposes of the preceding paragraph, the plan is treated as if a single-sum option were available under the terms of the plan as in effect immediately prior to the effective date of the conversion amendment. [Prop. Treas. Reg. § 1.411(b)(5)-1(c)(3)(ii)(B)]

An amendment is a conversion amendment that is subject to these requirements with respect to a participant if (1) the amendment reduces or eliminates the benefits that, but for the amendment, the participant would have accrued after the effective date of the amendment under a benefit formula that is not a statutory hybrid benefit formula (and under which the participant was accruing benefits prior to the amendment), and (2) after the effective date of the amendment, all or a portion of the participant's benefit accruals under the plan are determined under a statutory hybrid benefit formula. [Prop. Treas. Reg. § 1.411(b)(5)-1(c)(4)(i)]

Special rules described below treat certain arrangements as conversion amendments. Those rules apply both separately and in combination. Thus, for example, in certain acquisitions, if the buyer adopts an amendment under which a participant's benefits under the seller's plan that is not a statutory hybrid plan are coordinated with a separate plan of the buyer that is a statutory hybrid plan (e.g., through an offset of the participant's benefit under the buyer's plan by the participant's benefit under the seller's plan), the seller and buyer are treated as a single employer and are treated as having adopted a conversion amendment. However, if there is no coordination between the two plans, there is no conversion amendment. Only amendments that eliminate or reduce accrued benefits or a retirement-type subsidy that would otherwise accrue as a result of future service are treated as amendments described in (1) above. If, under the terms of a plan, a change in the conditions of a participant's employment results in a reduction of the participant's benefits that would have accrued in the future under a benefit formula that is not a statutory hybrid benefit formula, the plan is treated for these purposes as if such plan terms constitute an amendment that reduces the participant's benefits that would have accrued after the effective date of the change under a benefit formula that is not a statutory hybrid benefit formula. Thus, for example, if a participant transfers from an operating division that is covered by a non-statutory hybrid benefit formula to an operating division that is covered by a statutory hybrid benefit formula, there has been a conversion amendment as of the date of the transfer. [Treas. Reg. § 1.410(b)-2(f); Prop. Treas. Reg. § 1.411(b)(5)-1(c)(4)(ii)]

An employer is treated as having adopted a conversion amendment if the employer adopts an amendment under which a participant's benefits under a plan that is not a statutory hybrid plan are coordinated with a separate plan that is a statutory hybrid plan, such as through a reduction (offset) of the benefit under the plan that is not a statutory hybrid plan. [Prop. Treas. Reg. § 1.411(b)(5)-1(c)(4)(iii)] If the employer of an employee changes as a result of certain acquisitions or dispositions, then the two employers are treated as a single employer. [Treas. Reg. § 1.410(b)-2(f); Prop. Treas. Reg. § 1.411(b)(5)-1(c)(4)(iv)] For these purposes, a conversion amendment includes multiple amendments that result in a conversion amendment even if the amendments are not conversion amendments individually. For example, an employer is treated as having adopted a conversion amendment if the employer first adopts an amendment described in (1) above and, at a later date, adopts an amendment that adds a benefit under a statutory hybrid benefit formula as described in (2) above, if they are consolidated. In the case of an amendment to provide a benefit under a statutory hybrid benefit formula that is adopted within three years after adoption of an amendment to reduce non-statutory hybrid benefit formula benefits, those amendments are consolidated in determining whether a conversion amendment has been adopted. Thus, the later adoption of the statutory hybrid benefit formula will cause the earlier amendment to be treated as a conversion amendment. In the case of an amendment to provide a benefit under a statutory hybrid benefit formula that is adopted more than three years after adoption of an amendment to reduce benefits under a non-statutory hybrid benefit formula, there is a presumption that the amendments are not consolidated unless the facts and circumstances indicate that adoption of the amendment to provide a benefit under a statutory hybrid benefit formula was intended at the time of reduction in the non-statutory hybrid benefit formula. If an employer adopts multiple amendments reducing benefits, each amendment is treated as a separate conversion amendment, provided that (2) above is applicable at the time of the amendment (taking into account these conversion amendment rules). [Prop. Treas. Reg. § 1.411(b)(5)-1(c)(4)(v)]

The effective date of a conversion amendment is, with respect to a participant, the date as of which a reduction of the participant's benefits occurs. The date of a reduction of those benefits cannot be earlier than the date of adoption of the conversion amendment. [I.R.C. § 411(d)(6); Prop. Treas. Reg. § 1.411(b)(5)-1(c)(4)(vi)]

The following examples illustrate the special rules for plan conversion amendments.

Example 1. *Facts where a plan does not establish an opening hypothetical account balance for participants and a participant elects life annuity at normal retirement age.* Employer N sponsors Plan E, a defined benefit plan that provides an accumulated benefit, payable as a straight life annuity commencing at age 65 (which is Plan E's normal retirement age), based on a percentage of highest average compensation times the participant's years of service. Plan E permits any participant who has had a severance from employment to elect payment in the following optional forms of benefit (with spousal consent if applicable), with any payment not made in a straight life annuity converted to an equivalent form based on reasonable actuarial assumptions: a straight life annuity, and a 50 percent, 75 percent, or 100 percent joint and survivor annuity. The payment of benefits may commence at any time after attainment of age 55, with an actuarial reduction if the commencement is before normal retirement age. In addition, the plan offers a single-sum payment after attainment of age 55 equal to the present value of the normal retirement benefit using the applicable interest rate and mortality table in effect under the terms of the plan on the annuity starting date.

Facts relating to the conversion amendment. On January 1, 2010, Plan E is amended to eliminate future accruals under the highest average compensation benefit formula and to base future benefit accruals on the hypothetical account balance. For service on or after January 1, 2010, each participant's hypothetical account balance is credited monthly with a pay credit equal to a specified percentage of the participant's compensation during the month and also with interest based on the third segment rate described in Section 430(h)(2)(C)(iii). With respect to benefits under the hypothetical account balance attributable to service on or after January 1, 2010, a participant is permitted to elect (with spousal consent) payment in the same generalized optional forms of benefit (even though different actuarial factors apply) as under the terms of the plan in effect before January 1, 2010, and also as a single-sum distribution. The plan provides for the benefits attributable to service before January 1, 2010 to be determined under the terms of the plan as in effect immediately before the effective date of the amendment, and the benefits attributable to service on and after January 1, 2010 to be determined separately under the terms of the plan as in effect after the effective date of the amendment, with neither benefit offsetting the other in any manner. Thus, each participant's benefits are equal to the sum of the benefits attributable to service before January 1, 2010 (to be determined under the terms of the plan as in effect immediately before the effective date of the amendment), plus the benefits attributable to the participant's hypothetical account balance.

Facts relating to an affected participant. Participant A is age 62 on January 1, 2010; and, on December 31, 2009, A's benefit for years of service before January 1, 2010, payable as a straight life annuity commencing at A's normal retirement age (age 65), which is January 1, 2013, is $1,000 per month.

Participant A has a severance from employment on January 1, 2013; and, on January 1, 2013, the hypothetical account balance, with pay credits and interest from January 1, 2010 to January 1, 2013, has become $11,000. Using the conversion factors under the plan as amended on January 1, 2013, that balance is equivalent to a straight life annuity of $100 per month commencing on January 1, 2013. This benefit is in addition to the benefit attributable to service before January 1, 2010. Participant A elects (with spousal consent) a straight life annuity of $1,100 per month commencing January 1, 2013.

Conclusion. Participant A's benefit satisfies the testing requirement because Participant A's benefit is not less than the sum of Participant A's Section 411(d)(6) protected benefit with respect to service before the effective date of the conversion amendment, determined under the terms of the plan as in effective immediately before the effective date of the amendment and Participant A's Section 411(d)(6) protected benefit with respect to service on and after the effective date of the conversion amendment, determined under the terms of the plan as in effect after the effective date of the amendment.

Example 2. *Facts involving plan's establishment of opening hypothetical account balance and payment of pre-conversion accumulated benefit in life annuity at normal retirement age.* The facts in Example 2 are the same as Example 1.

Facts relating to the conversion amendment. On January 1, 2010, Plan E is amended to eliminate future accruals under the highest average compensation benefit formula and to base future benefit accruals on a hypothetical account balance. An opening hypothetical account balance is established for each participant; and, under the plan's terms, that balance is equal to the present value of the participant's accumulated benefit on December 31, 2009 (payable as a straight life annuity at normal retirement age or immediately, if later), using the applicable interest rate and applicable mortality table on January 1, 2010. Under Plan E, the account based on this opening hypothetical account balance is maintained as a separate account from the account for accruals on or after January 1, 2010. The hypothetical account balance maintained for each participant for accruals on or after January 1, 2010 is credited monthly with a pay credit equal to a specified percentage of the participant's compensation during the month. A participant's hypothetical account balance (including both of the separate accounts) is credited monthly with interest based on the third segment rate.

Facts relating to optional forms of benefit. Following severance from employment and attainment of age 55, a participant is permitted to elect (with spousal consent) payment in the same generalized optional forms of benefit as under the plan in effect prior to January 1, 2010, with the amount payable calculated based on the hypothetical account balance on the annuity starting date and the applicable interest rate and applicable mortality table on the annuity starting date. The single-sum distribution is equal to the hypothetical account balance.

Facts relating to conversion protection. The plan provides that, as of a participant's annuity starting date, the plan will determine whether the benefit attributable to the opening hypothetical account payable in the particular optional form of benefit selected is greater than or equal to the benefit accrued under the plan through the date of conversion and payable in the same generalized optional form of benefit with the same annuity starting date. If the benefit attributable to the opening hypothetical account balance is greater, the plan provides that such benefit is paid in lieu of the pre-conversion benefit, together with the benefit attributable to post-conversion contribution credits. If the benefit attributable to the opening hypothetical account balance is less, the plan provides that such benefit is increased sufficiently to provide the pre-conversion benefit, together with the benefit attributable to post-conversion contribution credits.

Facts relating to an affected participant. On January 1, 2010, the opening hypothetical account balance established for Participant A is $80,000, which is the present value of Participant A's straight life annuity of $1,000 per month commencing at January 1, 2013, using the applicable interest rate and applicable mortality table in effect on January 1, 2010. On January 1, 2010, the applicable interest rate for Participant A is equivalent to a level rate of 5.5 percent. Thereafter, Participant's A's hypothetical account balance for subsequent accruals is credited monthly with a pay credit equal to a specified percentage of the participant's compensation during the month. In addition, Participant A's hypothetical account balance (including both of the separate accounts) is credited monthly with interest based on the third segment rate.

Facts relating to calculation of the participant's benefit. Participant A has a severance from employment on January 1, 2013 at age 65 and elects (with spousal consent) a straight life annuity commencing January 1, 2013. On January 1, 2013, the opening hypothetical account balance, with interest credits from January 1, 2010 to January 1, 2013, has become $95,000, which, using the conversion factors under the plan on January 1, 2013, is equivalent to a straight life annuity of $1,005 per month commencing on January 1, 2013 (which is greater than the $1,000 a month payable at age 65 under the terms of the plan in effect before January 1, 2010). This benefit is in addition to the benefit determined using the hypothetical account balance for service after January 1, 2010.

Conclusion. The benefit satisfies the testing requirement with respect to Participant A because A's benefit is not less than the sum of (1) the greater of Participant A's benefits attributable to the opening hypothetical account balance and A's Section 411(d)(6) protected benefit with respect to service before the effective date of the conversion amendment, determined under the terms of the plan as in effect immediately before the effective date of the amendment, and (2) Participant A's Section 411(d)(6) protected benefit with respect to service on and after the effective date of the conversion amendment, determined under the terms of the plan as in effect after the effective date of the amendment.

Example 3. *Facts involving a subsequent decrease in interest rates.* The facts are the same as in Example 2, except that, because of a decrease in bond rates after January 1, 2010 and before January 1, 2013, the rate of interest credited in that period averages less than 5.5 percent; and, on January 1, 2013, the effective applicable interest rate under the plan's terms is 4.7 percent. As a result, participant A's opening hypothetical account balance plus attributable interest credits has increased to only $87,000 on January 1, 2013 and, using the conversion factors under the plan on January 1, 2013, is equivalent to a straight life annuity commencing on January 1, 2013 of $775 per month. Under the terms of Plan E, the benefit attributable to A's opening account balance is increased so that A's straight life annuity commencing on January 1, 2013 is $1,000 per month. This benefit is in addition to the benefit attributable to the hypothetical account balance for service after January 1, 2010.

Conclusion. The benefit satisfies the testing requirement with respect to Participant A because A's benefit is not less than the sum of (1) the greater of A's benefits attributable to the opening hypothetical account balance and A's Section 411(d)(6) protected benefit with respect to service before the effective date of the conversion amendment, determined under the terms of the plan as in effect immediately before the effective date of the amendment, and (2) A's Section 411(d)(6) protected benefit with respect to service on and after the effective date of the conversion amendment, determined under the terms of the plan as in effect after the effective date of the amendment.

Example 4. *Facts involving payment of a subsidized early retirement benefit.* The facts are the same as in Example 2, except that, under the terms of Plan E on December 31, 2009, a participant who retires before age 65 and after age 55 with 30 years of service has only a 3 percent per year actuarial reduction. Participant A has a severance from employment on January 1, 2011, when A is age 63 and has 30 years of service. On January 1, 2011, A's opening hypothetical account balance, with interest from January 1, 2010, to January 1, 2011, has become $86,000, which, using the conversion factors under the plan (as amended) on January 1, 2011, is equivalent to a straight life annuity commencing on January 1, 2011, of $850 per month.

Facts relating to calculation of the participant's benefit. Under the terms of Plan E on December 31, 2009, Participant A is entitled to a straight life annuity commencing on January 1, 2011 equal to at least $940 per month ($1,000 reduced by 3 percent for each of the two years that A's benefits commence before normal retirement age). Under the terms of Plan E, the benefit attributable to A's opening account balance is increased so that A is entitled to a straight life annuity of $940 per month commencing on January 1, 2013. This benefit is in addition to the benefit determined using the hypothetical account balance for service after January 1, 2010.

Conclusion. The benefit satisfies the testing requirement with respect to Participant A because A's benefit is not less than the sum of (1) the greater of Participant A's benefits attributable to the opening hypothetical account balance increased by attributable interest credits and A's Section 411(d)(6) protected benefit with respect to service before the effective date of the conversion amendment, determined under the terms of the plan as in effect immediately before the effective date of the amendment, and (2) Participant A's Section 411(d)(6) protected benefit with respect to service on and after the effective date of the conversion amendment, determined under the terms of the plan as in effect after the effective date of the amendment.

Example 5. *Facts involving addition of a single-sum payment option.* The facts are the same as in Example 2, except that, before January 1, 2010, Plan E did not offer payment in a single-sum distribution for amounts in excess of $5,000. Plan E, as amended on January 2, 2010, offers payment in any of the available annuity distribution forms commencing at any time following severance from employment as were provided under Plan E before January 1, 2010. In addition, Plan E, as amended on January 1, 2010, offers payment in the form of a single-sum attributable to service before January 1, 2010, which is the greater of the opening hypothetical account balance (increased by attributable interest credits) or a single-sum distribution of the straight life annuity payable at age 65 using the same actuarial factors as are used for mandatory cash-outs for amounts equal to $5,000 or less (see Q 10:61) under the terms of the plan on December 31, 2009. Participant B is age 40 on January 1, 2010, and B's opening hypothetical account balance (increased by attributable interest credits) is $33,000 (which is the present value, using the conversion factors under the plan, as amended, on January 1, 2010, of Participant B's straight life annuity of $1,000 per month commencing at January 1, 2035, which is when B will be age 65). Participant B has a severance from employment on January 1, 2013 and elects (with spousal consent) an immediate single-sum distribution. Participant B's opening hypothetical account balance (increased by attributable interest) on January 1, 2013 is $45,000. The present value, on January 1, 2013, of Participant B's benefit of $1,000 per month, commencing immediately using the actuarial factors for mandatory cash-outs under the terms of the plan on December 31, 2009, would result in a single-sum payment of $44,750. Participant B is paid a single-sum distribution equal to the sum of $45,000 plus an amount equal to B's January 1, 2013 hypothetical account balance for benefit accruals for service after January 1, 2010.

Conclusion. Because, under Plan E, Participant B is entitled to the sum of (1) the greater of the $45,000 opening hypothetical account balance (increased by attributable interest credits) and $44,750 (present value of the benefit with respect to service prior to January 1, 2010, using the actuarial factors for mandatory cash-out distributions under the terms of the plan on December 31, 2009), plus (2) an amount equal to B's hypothetical account balance for benefit accruals for service after January 1, 2010, the benefit satisfies the testing requirement with respect to Participant B. If Participant B's hypothetical account balance under Plan E was, instead, less than $44,750 on January 1, 2013, B would be entitled to a single-sum payment equal to the sum of $44,750 and an amount equal to B's hypothetical account balance for benefit accruals for service after January 1, 2010.

Example 6. *Facts involving the addition of a new annuity optional form of benefit.* The facts are the same as in Example 2, except that, after December 31, 2009 and before January 1, 2013, Plan E is amended to offer payment in a five-, ten-, or 15-year term certain and life annuity, using the same actuarial assumptions that apply for other optional forms of distribution. When Participant A has a severance from employment on January 1, 2013, A elects (with spousal consent) a five-year term certain and life annuity commencing immediately equal to $935 per month. Application of the same actuarial assumptions to Participant A's benefit of $1,000 per month (under Plan E as in effect on December 31, 2009), commencing immediately on January 1, 2013, would result in a five-year term certain and life annuity commencing immediately equal to $955 per month. Under the terms of Plan E, the benefit attributable to A's opening account balance is increased so that, using the conversion factors under the plan (as amended) on January 1, 2013, A's opening hypothetical account balance (increased by attributable credits) produces a five-year term certain and life annuity commencing immediately equal to $955 per month commencing on January 1, 2013. This benefit is in addition to the benefit determined using the January 1, 2013 hypothetical account balance for service after January 1, 2010.

Conclusion. This benefit satisfies the testing requirement with respect to Participant A.

Example 7. *Facts involving the addition of a distribution option before age 55.* The facts are the same as in Example 5, except that Participant B (age 43) elects (with spousal consent) a straight life annuity. Under Plan E, the straight life annuity attributable to Participant B's opening hypothetical account balance at age 43 is $221 per month. Application of the same actuarial assumptions to Participant B's benefit of $1,000 per month (under Plan E as in effect on December 31, 2009), commencing immediately on January 1, 2013, would result in a straight life annuity at age 43 of $219 per month.

Conclusion. Because, under its terms, Plan E provides that Participant B is entitled to an amount not less than the present value (using the same actuarial assumptions as apply on January 1, 2013 in converting the $45,000 hypothetical account balance attributable to the opening hypothetical account balance to the $221 straight life annuity) of Participant B's straight life annuity of $1,000 per month commencing at January 1, 2035 and the $221 straight life annuity is in addition to the benefit accruals for service after January 1, 2010, payment of the $221 monthly annuity would satisfy the testing requirement with respect to Participant B.

Subject to rules applicable to plan terminations discussed below, a statutory hybrid plan satisfies the requirement that the rate of benefit accrual under a defined benefit plan cannot be reduced because of attainment of any age (see Q 9:27) only if, for any plan year, the interest crediting rate under the terms of the plan is no greater than a market rate of return. For these purposes, a plan's interest crediting rate means the rate by which a participant's benefit is increased under the ongoing terms of the plan to the extent the amount of the increase is not conditioned on current service, regardless of how the amount of that increase is calculated. The amount of such an increase is an interest credit. Thus, whether the amount is an interest credit for this purpose is determined without regard to whether the amount is calculated by reference to a rate of interest, a rate of return, an index, or otherwise. Generally, an interest crediting rate is not in excess of a market rate of return only if the plan provides an interest credit for the year at a rate that is equal to one of the following rates that is specified in the terms of the plan: (1) the interest rate on long-term investment grade corporate bonds; (2) an interest rate that is deemed to be not in excess of a market rate of return; or (3) an interest rate that is a reasonable minimum guaranteed rate of return or an equity-based rate. [Prop. Treas. Reg. § 1.411(b)(5)-1(d)(1)(i)-(iii)]

A plan must specify the timing for determining the plan's interest crediting rate that will apply for each plan year (or portion of a plan year) using either of the methods described below and must also specify the frequency of interest crediting under the plan. A plan is permitted to provide daily interest credits using a daily interest crediting rate based on the permitted rates specified above. Alternatively, a plan is permitted to provide an interest credit for a stability period that is based on the interest crediting rate for a specified look-back month with respect to that stability period (see Q 10:62). The stability period and look-back month must satisfy the rules for selecting the stability period and look-back month. Interest credits under a plan must be made on an annual or more frequent periodic basis. If a plan provides for the crediting of interest more frequently than annually (e.g., monthly or quarterly), then the interest credit for that period must be a pro rata portion of the annual interest credit. Thus, for example, if a plan's terms provide for interest to be credited monthly and for the interest crediting rate to be equal to the interest rate on long-term investment grade corporate bonds and that interest rate for a plan year is 6 percent, the accumulated benefits at the beginning of each month would be increased by 0.5 percent per month during the plan year. Interest credits under the terms of a plan are not treated as creating an effective rate of return that is in excess of a market rate of return merely because an otherwise permissible interest crediting rate is compounded more frequently than annually. [Prop. Treas. Reg. § 1.411(b)(5)-1(d)(1)(iv)]

An interest crediting rate is not in excess of a market rate of return if the plan provides an interest crediting rate that, under all circumstances, is always less than one of the rates described above. If a statutory hybrid plan provides for an interest credit that is equal to the interest credits determined under the greater of two or more different interest crediting rates, the effective interest crediting rate is not in excess of a market rate of return only if each of the different rates satisfies certain requirements. [Prop. Treas. Reg. §§ 1.411(b)(5)-1(d)(1)(v), 1.411(b)(5)-1(d)(1)(vi)]

To satisfy the prohibition against the reduction in the rate of benefit accrual because of age, the plan must provide that, as of the participant's annuity starting date, the participant's benefit under the plan is no less than the benefit determined as of that date based on the sum of the hypothetical contributions credited under the plan (or the accumulated percentage of the participant's final average compensation, or the participant's accrued benefits determined without regard to any indexing, as applicable). A hypothetical contribution is any amount credited under a statutory hybrid plan other than an interest credit. Thus, if an opening hypothetical account balance or opening accumulated percentage of the participant's final average compensation is established, that opening hypothetical account balance or opening accumulated percentage as of the date established is treated as a hypothetical contribution and, thus, is taken into account for purposes of this preservation of capital requirement. [I.R.C. § 411(b)(5)(E); Prop. Treas. Reg. § 1.411(b)(5)-1(d)(2)]

Generally, a statutory hybrid plan is treated as meeting the market rate of return requirements only if the terms of the plan provide that, upon termination of the plan, a participant's benefit as of the termination is determined using the interest rate and mortality table otherwise applicable for determining that benefit under the plan (without regard to termination of the plan). A statutory hybrid plan is treated as meeting the market rate of return requirements only if the terms of the plan provide that, upon termination of the plan, any interest rate used to determine a participant's benefits under the plan (including any interest crediting rate and any interest rate used to determine annuity benefits) that is a variable rate is determined as the average of the rates of interest used under the plan for that purpose during the five-year period ending on the termination date. [Prop. Treas. Reg. § 1.411(b)(5)-1(d)(3)]

The rate of interest on long-term investment grade corporate bonds means the third segment rate described in Section 430(h)(2)(C)(iii) (determined with or without regard to the transition rules of Section 430(h)(2)(G)), provided that such rate floats on a periodic basis not less frequently than annually. However, for plan years beginning prior to January 1, 2008, the rate of interest on long-term investment grade corporate bonds means the rate described in Section 412(b)(5)(B)(ii)(II) prior to amendment by PPA (see Q 1:33). [Prop. Treas. Reg. § 1.411(b)(5)-1(d)(4)] An interest crediting rate (safe harbor) is deemed to be not in excess of a market rate of return if the rate is adjusted at least annually and is equal to the sum of any of the following rates of interest for Treasury bonds and the associated margin for that interest rate:

Treasury Bond Interest Rates	*Associated Margin*
The discount rate on 3-month Treasury Bills	175 basis points
The discount rate on 12-month or shorter Treasury Bills	150 basis points
The yield on 1-year Treasury Constant Maturities	100 basis points
The yield on 3-year or shorter Treasury bonds	50 basis points
The yield on 7-year or shorter Treasury bonds	25 basis points
The yield on 30-year or shorter Treasury bonds	0 basis points

An interest crediting rate is deemed to be not in excess of a market rate of return if the rate is adjusted no less frequently than annually and is equal to the rate of increase with respect to an eligible cost-of-living index (see Q 11:38), except that the second eligible cost-of-living index is increased by 300 basis points. IRS may specify additional interest crediting rates that are deemed to be not in excess of a market rate of return. [Prop. Treas. Reg. § 1.411(b)(5)-1(d)(5)]

If a plan provides an interest crediting rate that is equal to the interest credits determined under the greater of two or more different interest crediting rates where each of the different rates satisfies the foregoing requirements, then the interest credits provided by the plan satisfy this paragraph only if one or more of the different interest crediting rates under the plan are adjusted as provided in future IRS rules in order to provide that the effective interest crediting rate resulting from the use of the greater of two or more rates does not exceed a market rate of return. This paragraph provides the exclusive rules that may be used for this purpose; and, therefore, a plan does not satisfy the foregoing requirements if the plan provides for interest credits determined using the greater of two or more interest crediting rates and that combination of interest crediting rates is not specifically permitted by this paragraph. [Prop. Treas. Reg. § 1.411(b)(5)-1(d)(7)]

To the extent that benefits have accrued under the terms of a statutory hybrid plan that entitle the participant to future interest credits, an amendment to the plan to change the interest crediting rate for such interest credits results in a decrease of an accrued benefit if the revised rate under any circumstances could result in a lower interest crediting rate as of any date after the applicable amendment date of the amendment changing the interest crediting rate. An amendment to a statutory hybrid plan to change the interest crediting rate for future periods from a safe harbor interest crediting rate to the interest crediting rate based on long-term investment grade corporate bonds does not constitute a decrease of an accrued benefit. However, such an amendment cannot be effective less than 30 days after adoption; and, on the effective date of the amendment, the new interest crediting rate cannot be less than the interest crediting rate that would have applied in the absence of the amendment. [Prop. Treas. Reg. § 1.411(b)(5)-1(d)(8)]

In general, the special rules relating to age apply for periods beginning on or after June 29, 2005. Special rules apply to a conversion amendment that is adopted after, and takes effect after, June 29, 2005. In the case of a plan that is in existence on June 29, 2005 (regardless of whether the plan is a statutory hybrid plan on that date), the market rate of return requirement applies only to plan years beginning on or after January 1, 2008. However, the plan sponsor of such a plan may elect to have such requirement apply for any period after June 29, 2005 and before the first plan year beginning after December 31, 2007. An employer is permitted to adopt an amendment to make this election as late as the last day of the first plan year that begins on or after January 1, 2009 if the plan operates in accordance with the election. In the case of a plan not in existence on June 29, 2005, the market rate of return requirement applies to the plan on and after the later of June 29, 2005 or the date the plan becomes a statutory hybrid

plan. Special rules apply to collectively bargained plans. The proposed regulations apply for plan years beginning on or after January 1, 2009 and may be
relied upon before that date. [Prop. Treas. Reg. § 1.411(b)(5)-1(f)]

IRS announced relief for sponsors of statutory hybrid plans that must amend
the interest crediting rate in those plans. IRS expects to issue final regulations
and proposed regulations relating to statutory hybrid plans. The regulations will
include rules interpreting the requirement that such plans do not have an
interest crediting rate in excess of a market rate of return. The rules in the
regulations specifying permissible market rates of return are not expected to go
into effect before the first plan year that begins on or after January 1, 2011. In
addition, it is anticipated that IRS will exercise its authority to provide that, once
final regulations regarding the market rate of return requirements are issued, an
amendment to a statutory hybrid plan with an interest crediting rate that is in
excess of a market rate of return under those final regulations that is adopted
prior to the effective date of those final regulations will not violate the anti-
cutback rule (see Q 4:27) merely because it reduces the future interest crediting
rate on participants' account balances to the extent necessary to constitute a
permissible rate under those final regulations. Under this anticipated guidance,
the anti-cutback rule will not operate to bar such an amendment, even if the
amendment is adopted after the last day of the first plan year that begins on or
after January 1, 2009. Finally, it is anticipated that future guidance will include
a special timing rule for providing the Section 204(h) Notice (see Q 9:40) to
participants and other applicable individuals with respect to an amendment that
changes a statutory hybrid plan's interest crediting rate that is adopted by the
last day of the first plan year that begins on or after January 1, 2009 and after
November 10, 2009. Under this special timing rule, any required Section 204(h)
Notice relating to such an amendment will be permitted to be provided as late as
30 days after the effective date of the amendment. It is expected that this relief
will apply to an amendment only if the amendment is effective not later than the
first day of the first plan year that begins on or after January 1, 2010. [Ann.
2009-82, 2009-2 C.B. 720]

Q 2:25   What is an insured qualified retirement plan?

An insured plan is a qualified retirement plan that is funded in whole or in
part through the purchase of life insurance policies. The plan can be either
split-funded or fully insured.

In a split-funded plan, there is partial funding of retirement benefits through
insurance policies, with the balance of the retirement benefit coming from an
investment fund. The portion of the plan's assets accumulated in the investment
fund can be invested as the trustee determines.

In a fully insured plan, all company contributions are directed toward the
purchase of insurance, normally in the form of life policies, retirement income
policies, or annuity contracts, or a combination thereof (see Q 8:11). Among the
advantages of a fully insured defined benefit plan (see Q 2:3) are the following:

1. The use of the insurance company's guaranteed rates creates greater initial, deductible plan contributions.

2. The employer's investment risk (see Q 2:3) is minimized because benefits are guaranteed by the insurance company.

3. The plan is eligible for simplified reporting requirements.

4. The plan is exempt from the minimum funding requirements (see Q 8:10).

5. Quarterly contribution payments are not required (see Q 8:32).

6. The reversionary tax (see Q 25:52) on plan termination is avoided because, by design, the plan cannot be overfunded.

7. Significant life insurance coverage can be acquired by the plan on the participant's life as long as the coverage is incidental to the plan's retirement benefits (see Q 15:4).

[I.R.C. §§ 411(b)(1)(F), 412(e)(3); Treas. Reg. §§ 1.412(i)-1(a), 1.412(i)-1(b), 1.412(i)-1(c)]

To be a fully insured plan (also referred to as an individual insurance contract plan), certain requirements must be satisfied for the plan year. [Treas. Reg. § 1.412(i)-1(b)(1)]

The plan must be funded exclusively by the purchase from an insurance company or companies (licensed under the law of a State or the District of Columbia to do business with the plan) of individual annuity or individual insurance contracts, or a combination thereof. The purchase may be made either directly by the employer or through the use of a custodial account or trust. A plan will not be considered to be funded otherwise than exclusively by the purchase of individual annuity or individual insurance contracts merely because the employer makes a payment necessary to comply with the provisions relating to accrued benefits from employee contributions. [Treas. Reg. § 1.412(i)-1(b)(2)(i)]

The individual annuity or individual insurance contracts issued under the plan must provide for level annual, or more frequent, premium payments to be paid under the plan for the period commencing with the date each individual participating in the plan became a participant and ending not later than the normal retirement age (see Q 10:55) for that individual or, if earlier, the date the individual ceases participation in the plan. Premium payments may be considered to be level even though items such as experience gains and dividends are applied against premiums. In the case of an increase in benefits, the contracts must provide for level annual payments with respect to such increase to be paid for the period commencing at the time the increase becomes effective. If payment commences on the first payment date under the contract occurring after the date an individual becomes a participant or after the effective date of an increase in benefits, these requirements will be satisfied even though payment does not commence on the date on which the individual's participation commenced or on the effective date of the benefit increase, whichever is applicable. If an individual accrues benefits after normal retirement age, these requirements are satisfied if payment is made at the time such benefits accrue. If these provisions are set forth in a separate agreement with the issuer of the individual contracts, they need not be included in the individual contracts. [Treas. Reg. § 1.412(i)-1(b)(2)(ii)]

The separate agreement referred to in the preceding paragraph must be executed between the plan sponsor and the contract issuer at plan inception and amended (or a new separate agreement must be entered into) each time the plan adds a participant or whenever a participant receives a benefit increase. Separate agreements containing the information in Part A below will be considered acceptable by IRS, if the reconciliation record described in Part B below is also maintained by the plan sponsor.

Part A. Required data for each participant whose benefits are funded under contracts to which the separate agreement applies:

1. Participant's name, Social Security number, date of birth, date of hire, and date of participation in the plan.
2. For each contract funding benefits for this participant:
   a. Form number, contract number, and issue date of the contract.
   b. The dollar amount of the level premium, premium frequency (e.g., monthly, annual), premium payment period (e.g., ten years, to normal retirement age), the due date or payment date of the first required premium, and the due date of each subsequent premium (e.g., first day of each month). All requirements of the preceding paragraph concerning premium payment dates must be satisfied.
   c. The projected guaranteed annuity benefits provided by the contract (under the normal form at the participant's normal retirement age), assuming that premiums are paid in accordance with the separate agreement.
   d. A list of all optional forms of payment provided under the contract and the actuarial factors used to derive each optional form at the participant's normal retirement age.

Part B. Required reconciliation.

The plan sponsor must maintain records demonstrating that a plan's projected annuity benefits at normal retirement age under all forms of payment are equal in form and amount to the projected guaranteed annuity benefits at normal retirement age under all forms provided by all contracts that fund a participant's benefits (as shown in all separate agreements relating to an individual participant).

For this purpose, the plan sponsor is allowed to reconcile the dollar amount of the normal form of payment at the participant's normal retirement age under the plan and the contracts, and then to demonstrate that the actuarial factors used to calculate all optional forms are identical under the plan and all contracts used to fund the plan benefits. The reconciliation information itself need not be part of the separate agreements with the insurers.

[*Employee Plans News Special Edition* (Aug. 2007)]

The benefits provided by the plan for each individual participant must be equal to the benefits provided under the individual contracts at normal retirement age under the plan provisions. [Treas. Reg. § 1.412(i)-1(b)(iii)] The benefits provided by the plan for each individual participant must be guaranteed by the life insurance company issuing the individual contracts to the extent premiums have been paid. [Treas. Reg. § 1.412(i)-1(b)(2)(iv)]

Except as provided in the following sentence, all premiums payable for the plan year, and for all prior plan years, under the insurance or annuity contracts must have been paid before lapse. If the lapse has occurred during the plan year, this requirement will be considered to have been met if reinstatement of the insurance policy, under which the individual insurance contracts are issued, occurs during the year of the lapse and before distribution is made or benefits commence to any participant whose benefits are reduced because of the lapse. [Treas. Reg. § 1.412(i)-1(b)(2)(v)]

No rights under the individual contracts may have been subject to a security interest at any time during the plan year. This requirement does not apply to contracts that have been distributed to participants if the security interest is created after the date of distribution. [Treas. Reg. § 1.412(i)-1(b)(2)(vi)] No policy loans, including loans to individual participants, on any of the individual contracts may be outstanding at any time during the plan year. This requirement does not apply to contracts that have been distributed to participants if the loan is made after the date of distribution. An application of funds by the issuer to pay premiums due under the contracts will be deemed not to be a policy loan if the amount of the funds so applied, and interest thereon, is repaid during the plan year in which the funds are applied and before distribution is made or benefits commence to any participant whose benefits are reduced because of such application. [Treas. Reg. § 1.412(i)-1(b)(2)(vii)]

IRS has addressed abuses in the use of insurance funded defined benefit plans. For details, see Q 15:17. For an excellent discussion of fully insured plans, see Landsberg, "Section 412(i) Fully Insured Defined Benefit Plans and the Perils of Unintended Consequences," *Journal of Pension Planning & Compliance*, Vol. 30, No. 3 (Fall 2004). According to one court, ERISA did not preempt state law misrepresentation and negligence claims brought against a nonfiduciary life insurance company and a provider of a fully insured plan (see Q 23:57). [Hausmann v. Union Bank of California, N.A., 2009 WL 1325810 (D.C. Cal. 2009)]

Qualified retirement plans can be attractive vehicles for acquiring life insurance. Premiums indirectly paid by the company in the form of plan contributions are deductible. Each insured participant reports taxable income, as determined under IRS tables, representing the cost of current life insurance protection. For further details, see chapter 15.

Q 2:26   What is a custom-designed retirement plan?

A custom-designed (or individually designed) retirement plan is a plan tailored to meet the needs of the client. The custom-designed plan reflects the company's desires and needs more fully than a master or prototype (see Q 2:27) because the client has a greater variety of available options.

Q 2:27   What are master and prototype retirement plans?

A master plan is a form of retirement plan in which the funding organization (trust, custodial account, or insurer) is specified in the sponsor's application. A prototype plan is a form of retirement plan in which the funding organization is specified in the adoption agreement. [Rev. Proc. 2010-6, § 9.02, 2010-1 I.R.B. 193; Rev. Proc. 2005-16, 2005-1 C.B. 674; Ann. 2004-33, § 4, 2004-1 C.B. 862]

Insurance companies, mutual funds, banks, brokerage firms, and other investment management firms have created IRS-approved master and prototype plans. The client adopts the plans by executing an adoption agreement and electing certain available options. Any change in the preapproved plan provisions causes the plan to lose its master or prototype status. [Rev. Proc. 2000-20, 2000-1 C.B. 553; Rev. Proc. 93-39, 1993-2 C.B. 513] IRS representatives have opined that, if an employer adopts a prototype plan but substitutes the trust document, the substitution will be acceptable *only* if IRS has specifically approved the alternative trusts with that specific prototype plan.

IRS has designed prototype plan language and issued draft guidance on an opinion letter program for 403(b) plans (see Q 35:9).

Q 2:28   What are volume submitter plans?

Under the volume submitter program, a practitioner who qualifies may request IRS to issue an advisory letter regarding a volume submitter specimen plan. A specimen plan is a sample plan of a practitioner (rather than the actual plan of an employer) that contains provisions that are identical or substantially similar to the provisions in plans that such practitioner's clients have adopted or are expected to adopt. A specimen plan may include an adoption agreement. A specimen plan may include blanks or fill-in provisions for the employer to complete only if the plan also includes parameters on these provisions that preclude an employer from completing them in a manner that could violate the qualification requirements. Once IRS has approved the specimen plan, employers who adopt the same plan and meet certain conditions will be able to rely on the advisory letter. In addition, the practitioner will be able to file determination letter requests (see Q 18:1) on behalf of employers adopting substantially similar plans who need a determination letter to have reliance or who otherwise desire a determination letter. [Rev. Proc. 2010-6, § 9.02, 2010-1 I.R.B. 193; Ann. 2004-33, § 13, 2004-1 C.B. 862]

A volume submitter plan is a profit sharing plan (without a CODA; see Qs 2:6, 27:1), a profit sharing plan (with a CODA), a money purchase pension plan (see Q 2:4), or a defined benefit plan (see Q 2:3) that is submitted for volume submitter advisory letters (with respect to the specimen plan) and requests for determination letters (with respect to an employer's adoption of a plan that is substantially similar to an approved specimen plan). IRS will not accept volume submitter requests with respect to ESOPs (see Q 28:1) or other stock bonus plans (see Q 2:13), cash balance or similar defined benefit plans (see Q 2:23), or plans that include so-called fail-safe provisions for the nondiscrimination requirements (see Qs 4:10–4:18) or the average benefit test (see Q 5:17). IRS may decline to accept volume submitter requests for other types of plans not described above. [Rev. Proc. 2005-16, 2005-1 C.B. 674]

Q 2:29   How does a company's cash position affect its choice of a qualified retirement plan?

Because adoption of a pension plan entails a commitment to fund the plan even if the company has no profits, a company experiencing a weak cash position would be ill-advised to establish that type of plan. Generally, it does not make good sense for a company to borrow funds to meet its pension obligations. In this situation, a profit sharing plan (see Qs 2:6, 2:30) would be more appropriate.

Q 2:30   What type of retirement plan should a company adopt if profits fluctuate from year to year?

A profit sharing plan (see Qs 2:6, 2:29) is the only type of plan that can afford a company significant flexibility with respect to the contributions it makes from year to year. The typical profit sharing plan—probably most profit sharing plans maintained by small companies—specifies that the company's contribution will be determined annually by its board of directors (or owners, partners, etc., as appropriate). The amount contributed in any year may vary from zero to 25 percent of the total compensation of all plan participants (see Q 12:8).

Q 2:31   Are profit sharing plans best for small companies?

There is no general answer to this question. The decision about the type of retirement plan best suited for a small company must be made on the basis of all the facts and circumstances, including the owner's goals. Profit sharing plans (see Q 2:6) are usually recommended for recently formed companies because no profit pattern exists (see Q 2:30).

Remember, however, that a company's size is not always a factor in choosing the best plan. In many cases, a small company may decide to maximize its tax-deductible contributions. For example, a company with an older workforce that adopts a defined benefit plan increases the amount of the contribution that must be made each year to fund retirement benefits, and this in turn increases the company's tax deduction (see Q 2:32).

Q 2:32   What type of qualified retirement plan is best for a company whose essential employees have reached an advanced age?

For a company whose essential employees have reached an advanced age, a defined benefit plan (see Q 2:3) is a better choice than a defined contribution plan (see Q 2:2) for the following reasons:

1. A defined contribution plan limits the company's tax-deductible contributions on behalf of each employee regardless of age. Except for a target benefit plan (see Q 2:5), an age-based profit sharing plan (see Q 2:7), and a comparability plan (see Q 2:10), all of which are examples of a cross-tested defined contribution plan (see Q 4:22), age is not a factor in determining the company's contribution or the allocation of the company's contribution to plan participants. Contributions on behalf of older employees are based on the same percentage of compensation as those made on behalf of younger employees. Since contributions are limited, there may not be sufficient time left before retirement to accumulate a desired amount for older employees.

2. A defined benefit plan allows a company with older essential employees to make larger contributions to accumulate sufficient funds for retirement. The limit on contributions under a defined benefit plan is the amount necessary to fund the annual pension, and this may far exceed the allowable contribution to a defined contribution plan (see Q 6:34). [I.R.C. §§ 404(a)(1), 415(b), 415(c)]

Q 2:33 Can the bulk of qualified retirement plan contributions and benefits be set aside for the business owner and other essential employees under the terms of the plan?

Generally, no. A qualified retirement plan may not discriminate in favor of employees who are considered highly compensated. Discrimination in favor of HCEs (see Q 3:2) must be avoided in coverage, contributions, and benefits. [I.R.C. §§ 401(a)(4), 410(b)]

An example of discrimination could be a money purchase pension plan (see Q 2:4) that provides for a contribution equal to 25 percent of compensation for HCEs, but only 10 percent of compensation on behalf of all other employees. Such a plan will not qualify for tax-favored status unless it satisfies cross-testing (see Q 4:22). An important exception applies if the plan takes permitted disparity into account (see Qs 2:41, 7:1).

For details on minimum contribution and benefit requirements that may apply to the plan, see chapter 26.

Q 2:34 May a qualified retirement plan lose its tax-favored status if only the business owner and other essential employees will receive benefits?

Even if the plan is not discriminatory as it is written (see Q 4:1), the operation of the plan can result in discrimination, and the plan may lose its tax-favored status.

A plan covers all employees and provides a schedule for the vesting of benefits that meets the requirements of the Code (see Q 9:4). If the only employees attaining vested benefits are the business's HCEs (because rank-and-file workers leave before they have enough years of service to earn vested benefits, for example), the plan—in actual operation—may discriminate in favor of the HCEs and may lose its tax-favored status. [Rev. Rul. 66–251, 1966-2 C.B. 121]

In one case, IRS denied tax-favored status to a profit sharing plan because the rapid rate of turnover among lower-paid employees caused the bulk of the benefits to go to the business owner and the essential employees. However, IRS was rebuffed by the court. The court found that if there was any discrimination in the operation of the plan, it was in favor of permanent employees and against transient employees, not in favor of the HCEs and against rank-and-file employees. This type of discrimination is not prohibited. [Lansons, Inc., 69 T.C. 773 (1978), *aff'd*, 622 F.2d 774 (5th Cir. 1980)]

On the other hand, if discrimination in benefits results from a pattern of abuse by the business owner—for example, if rank-and-file employees are fired before their benefits become nonforfeitable—the plan is likely to lose its tax-favored status. [I.R.C. § 411(d)(1)(A)]

Q 2:35   How much can a business owner contribute to the qualified retirement plan?

It depends on the type of retirement plan the business owner adopts. If either a single defined contribution plan (see Q 2:2) or a combination of defined contribution plans is adopted, the annual addition (see Q 6:34) to the business owner's account during any year may not exceed the lesser of (1) $40,000 (with adjustments for inflation) or (2) 100 percent of compensation. [I.R.C. § 415(c)]

The maximum annual benefit (see Q 6:11) that may be provided to a participating business owner under a defined benefit plan (see Q 2:3) is the lesser of (1) $160,000 (with adjustments for inflation) or (2) 100 percent of the business owner's average compensation for the highest three consecutive years. [I.R.C. § 415(b)]

Bear in mind that under a defined benefit plan, the limitation is placed on the annual benefit payable, not the annual contribution necessary to fund the benefit. The annual contribution is determined actuarially, based on the business owner's age and anticipated annual benefit, the plan's normal retirement age, the form of benefit payable, and the actuarial assumptions used (see Qs 2:19, 2:39).

For a discussion of the limitations on contributions and benefits, see chapter 6.

Q 2:36   Is there any limit on tax-deductible contributions to a qualified retirement plan by a corporation?

Yes. Compensation paid to any employee is tax-deductible by the corporation only if the amount paid is reasonable. In determining reasonableness, all forms of compensation are considered, including contributions to the corporation's qualified retirement plan. Whether a particular business owner's compensation is reasonable is a question of fact in each case (see Q 12:1). [I.R.C. §§ 162, 404; Treas. Reg. § 1.404(a)-1(b)]

For a discussion of the limits on tax-deductible contributions, see chapter 12.

Q 2:37   What type of qualified retirement plan should the business owner install?

From a business viewpoint, it depends initially on the business owner's objectives. The plan may be used to achieve one or more of the following:

- Building a tax-sheltered retirement fund for the business owner and essential employees
- Recruiting essential employees from competitors
- Reducing employee turnover, and
- Establishing a market for the corporate business owner's shares of stock in a closely held corporation

Another consideration is the ability of the business to support the retirement plan. In choosing a plan, the business owner must decide what contributions the business can afford to make.

From a personal viewpoint, the business owner's objectives must be ascertained. These may include one or more of the following:

- Maximizing retirement benefits
- Maximizing contributions made on the owner's behalf
- Having flexibility with regard to annual contributions

If the business owner wants to maximize retirement benefits (the amount available at retirement), the owner's age may be the key factor in determining what type of plan to adopt. A younger business owner may accumulate the most dollars for retirement using a defined contribution plan (see Q 2:2); older business owners may do better using a defined benefit plan (see Q 2:3).

Similarly, if maximizing contributions is the goal, the older business owner can accomplish that by using a defined benefit plan; the younger business owner might do better using a defined contribution plan, although a defined benefit plan could also accomplish the objective.

If flexibility is the goal, a profit sharing plan (see Qs 2:6, 2:30) should be considered. This type of defined contribution plan gives the business owner control over the amount of annual contributions.

Other factors, however, may influence the business owner's decision. For example, how much will it cost to cover the employees? This will depend on how many of them must be covered, their compensation, and their ages. If the business owner's goals would be achieved using a defined benefit plan, but the cost of funding benefits for employees who are older than the business owner is substantial, it may be necessary to modify the objectives and use a defined contribution plan. But, if the employees are younger than the business owner, a defined benefit plan may be better than a defined contribution plan. In either situation, taking permitted disparity into consideration in designing the plan (see Qs 2:41, 7:1) may cut the cost of covering the business owner's employees and enable the objectives to be accomplished.

The older business owner may both maximize contributions and retain flexibility over the amount of annual contributions by adopting an age-based profit sharing plan (see Q 2:7) or a comparability plan (see Q 2:10).

Q 2:38   What type of qualified retirement plan (or plans) should a business owner use to maximize retirement benefits?

There is no one answer. The age of the business owner and the expected rate of return on the plan's investments, however, are the key factors in determining what type of qualified retirement plan will provide the most at retirement.

In a defined benefit plan (see Q 2:3), the actuary first determines the amount needed at retirement to pay the business owner's annual benefit as set by a formula in the plan. The actuary then determines the amount that must be contributed to the plan each year to reach the amount needed at retirement. The actuary uses various factors to compute the annual contribution, including an interest factor (the rate of return on plan investments). This interest factor is usually conservative, even when market rates are greater (see Qs 2:19, 8:14).

Investment gains and losses affect the amount of each year's contribution. Thus, if the interest assumption is 5 percent and the investment return is 8 percent, the investment gain reduces the business owner's future contributions. If the investment return is only 2 percent, the investment loss increases the subsequent contributions. Whether or not the interest assumption holds true, the annual adjustment in required contributions does not affect the final result—the amount in the plan at retirement. If the business owner's compensation remained constant over the period of participation, the amount available at the end would be known at the beginning.

In a defined contribution plan (see Q 2:2), generally, no actuarial calculations are made and no interest factor is assumed. The annual contribution is generally determined by multiplying the business owner's compensation for the year by the contribution percentage established in the plan. Gains from the investment of plan assets inure to the business owner's benefit, and losses are absorbed to the owner's detriment. Thus, if compensation stays constant, under a money purchase pension plan (see Q 2:4), the business owner will know the annual contribution, but not how much will be available at retirement. That will depend on the investment performance.

Example. Matthew, a business owner who is 45 years old, will retire at age 65 and has $40,000 a year to contribute to the qualified retirement plan. Under a defined contribution plan that provides for a $40,000 annual contribution, Matthew will have at retirement $800,000 plus the actual earnings or minus the actual losses on the plan's investments. Thus, if Matthew thinks the plan can realize a return on its investments greater than the interest assumption, the defined contribution plan may be preferable to the defined benefit plan.

In the example above, the business owner's age had no bearing on the final result. If under the defined contribution plan the maximum contribution is $40,000 and under the defined benefit plan the amount that could be contributed is $60,000, the business owner would have more available at retirement under the defined benefit plan (unless the defined contribution plan's investment return was very high). If the business owner is age 35 at the time the plan is adopted, the extra ten years of compounded earnings—assuming a better-than-average return—may make the defined contribution plan a better choice.

Q 2:39 How can the use of a normal retirement age earlier than 65 benefit the business owner?

In a defined benefit plan (see Q 2:3), using a retirement age earlier than 65 may substantially increase the amount of contributions that must be made each year to fund the retirement benefits, and this, in turn, increases the business owner's tax deduction. This is because there are fewer years in which to fund the retirement benefits.

There are several obstacles that must be overcome to take advantage of this planning opportunity. First, IRS says that a retirement age earlier than 65 can be used as a basis for computing required contributions only if the lower age approximates the age at which company employees customarily retire. [Rev. Rul. 78-331, 1978-2 C.B. 158; Rev. Rul. 78-120, 1978-1 C.B. 117; Priv. Ltr. Ruls. 8610002, 8552001] Second, because the defined benefit plan will require larger contributions, the company will have to produce a higher cash flow to fund the plan. If it cannot meet the increased funding required, it may be subject to a penalty tax (see Q 8:22). Finally, the business owner must be able to show that the total compensation package, salary plus retirement plan contributions made on the business owner's behalf, is reasonable (see Qs 2:36, 12:1).

The IRS position regarding the use of a normal retirement age earlier than 65 is that an actuarial assumption that employees retire at a normal retirement age that ignores the actual incidence of retirement in the workforce could cause the assumptions to be unreasonable and the contributions not to be currently deductible. Assumptions should be monitored and adjusted accordingly to reflect current experience. The analysis for funding purposes is based on an assumption of the age at which retirement is most likely to take place, a determination of probability that is derived from the average retirement age of the group. [Priv. Ltr. Rul. 8808005; Rev. Rul. 78-331, 1978-2 C.B. 158; see also Jerome Mirza & Assocs., Ltd. v. United States, 882 F.2d 229 (7th Cir. 1989)]

Courts, however, have concluded that, since the assumptions used were not substantially unreasonable and represented the actuary's best estimate of anticipated experience under the plans based on actuarial assumptions used by similar plans, IRS was precluded from requiring a retroactive change of assumptions. [Citrus Valley Estates, Inc. v. Comm'r, 49 F.3d 1410 (9th Cir. 1995); Wachtell, Lipton, Rosen & Katz v. Comm'r, 26 F.3d 291 (2d Cir. 1994);

Vinson & Elkins v. Comm'r, 7 F.3d 1235 (5th Cir. 1993); IRS News Release IR-95-43 [S2] (June 7, 1995); *but see* Rhoades, McKee & Boer v. United States, 1:91-CV-540 (W.D. Mich. 1995)] For a discussion of these cases, see Q 8:14.

Q 2:40 How can an ESOP or a stock bonus plan benefit a corporation and its shareholders?

An ESOP (see Q 2:14) or a stock bonus plan (see Q 2:13), like all other qualified retirement plans, must be organized and operated for the exclusive benefit of the employees or their beneficiaries. This does not mean that the company and its shareholders cannot also derive a benefit from the plan. In fact, an ESOP or a stock bonus plan can benefit the company and its shareholders by:

- Providing a market for the owner's closely held shares of stock as a tax-favored alternative to a stock redemption
- Giving the company tax deductions without affecting its cash flow, and
- Keeping company stock in what is generally considered friendly hands in the event of a hostile takeover of the company

See chapter 28 for more details.

Q 2:41 Can the company take Social Security contributions or benefits into consideration in its qualified retirement plan?

Yes. The company can combine (integrate) its qualified retirement plan with Social Security and thereby reduce the cost of maintaining its plan. This is referred to as permitted disparity.

Taking permitted disparity into consideration can help business owners reach what may be their primary goal in setting up a retirement plan: rewarding themselves and their essential employees. By designing the retirement plan with permitted disparity, the business owners can give proportionately greater benefits or make proportionately greater contributions to the plan on their behalf than they do for rank-and-file workers. A qualified retirement plan that covers self-employed individuals (see Q 6:60) may consider permitted disparity in the same way that a corporate qualified retirement plan may.

For details on how permitted disparity works, see chapter 7.

Q 2:42 After an employer has chosen a type of qualified retirement plan, what options are available?

After the employer has determined the most suitable qualified retirement plan, consideration must be given to the actual plan provisions. Among the employer's choices are the following:

- Eligibility requirements (see chapter 5), including:
  — Length of service (Q 5:2)
  — Minimum age (Q 5:2)

- — Exclusion of union employees (Q 5:5)
- — Other classification exclusions (Q 5:5)
- Contributions or benefits (see chapters 2, 6, and 26), including:
  - — Defined contribution plan formula
  - — Defined benefit plan formula
  - — Permitted disparity (i.e., integration with Social Security) (Q 7:1)
  - — Voluntary contributions (Q 6:38)
  - — Mandatory contributions (Q 6:37)
  - — Minimum benefits or contributions (Qs 26:36, 26:42)
  - — 401(k) features (Q 27:1)
- Vesting (see chapter 9), including:
  - — Cliff vesting
  - — Graded vesting
  - — Full and immediate vesting
  - — Top-heavy vesting (Q 26:30)
- Investment provisions (see chapter 23), including:
  - — Participant-directed accounts (Q 23:14)
  - — Insurance benefits (Q 15:2)
- Methods of payment of benefits (see chapters 10 and 13), including:
  - — Lump-sum distributions
  - — Annuities
  - — Installment distributions
  - — Hardship distributions (Qs 1:48, 27:14)
- Miscellaneous provisions, including:
  - — Designation of plan administrator (Q 20:1)
  - — Definition of compensation (Q 6:66)
  - — Choice of plan year
  - — Normal retirement age (Q 10:55)
  - — Rollover provision (Q 34:1)
  - — Death benefits (chapter 15)
  - — Loan provisions (chapter 14)

Chapter 3

Highly Compensated Employees

One of the most important terms in the Code is "highly compensated employee." The definition of this term is incorporated in many of the nondiscrimination requirements applicable to qualified retirement plans and is also incorporated in other Code provisions relating to the qualified retirement plan area. This chapter analyzes which employees are considered to be highly compensated.

Q 3:1 To what qualified retirement plan provisions does the definition of highly compensated employee apply?

The term "highly compensated employee" (HCE; see Q 3:2) is relevant in determining if a plan satisfies the general nondiscrimination requirements that apply to all qualified retirement plans (see Q 4:10), the actual deferral percentage test applicable to 401(k) plans (see Q 27:18), the actual contribution percentage test applicable to employer matching contributions and employee contributions (see Q 27:78), certain requirements applicable to SEPs (see Q 32:3), the minimum coverage requirement (see Qs 5:19, 5:20), and the minimum vesting standards (see Q 9:4). The definition also applies in determining if an organization is a member of an affiliated service group (see Q 5:35) and if a loan is exempt from the tax on prohibited transactions (see Q 14:21). [I.R.C. § 401(a)(4), 401(a)(5), 401(k)(3), 401(m), 408(k), 410(b)(1), 411(d)(1), 414(m), 414(q), 4975(d); Temp. Treas. Reg. § 1.414(q)-1T, Q&A-1(b)(1)]

The definition of HCE is applicable *only* to those qualified retirement plan provisions that incorporate the definition by reference, and the definition does *not* apply to provisions that do not incorporate it. For example, the definition of HCE generally has no application to the limitation on plan contributions and benefits (see chapter 6). [I.R.C. § 415; Temp. Treas. Reg. § 1.414(q)-1T, Q&A-1(a) & (b)(2)]

IRS has ruled that an employer that maintained separate retirement plans for its HCEs and non-highly compensated employees (NHCEs; see Q 3:12) violated the nondiscrimination requirements (see Q 4:21) when it amended the NHCE plan to provide annual benefits for the HCEs. An HCE's years of service were included in the computation of accrued benefits (see Q 9:2) under both plans, and benefits provided by the NHCE plan were not offset by benefits provided by the HCE plan. Thus, there was a duplication of service and benefits that discriminated in favor of the HCEs. [Rev. Rul. 99-51, 1999-2 C.B. 652; Treas. Reg. §§ 1.401(a)(4)-1(c)(2), 1.401(a)(4)-5(a)(1), 1.401(a)(4)-5(a)(2), 1.401(a)(4)-11(d)(2), 1.401(a)(4)-11(d)(3)]

> **Example.** Jason Corporation maintained a defined benefit plan, Plan X, benefiting its HCEs and NHCEs. Under Plan X, each employee's accrued benefit equaled an annual benefit commencing at normal retirement age of 1 percent of average annual compensation for each year of service, and a year of service included all years of service with Jason Corporation.
>
> Plan X was amended effective as of December 31, 2010 (the spin-off date), to become two plans: Plan X-H covering the HCEs and Plan X-N covering the NHCEs. The assets and benefit liabilities under Plan X as of the spin-off date were properly allocated between Plan X-H and Plan X-N. Pursuant to the terms of the amendment, NHCEs were excluded from participation in Plan X-H, and HCEs were excluded from participation in Plan X-N. In addition, the amendment provided that there would be no benefit accruals under Plan X-H after the spin-off date; however, benefit accruals continued under Plan X's original formula for the NHCEs in Plan X-N.
>
> Jason Corporation later amended Plan X-N to include the HCEs and to provide the HCEs with an annual benefit commencing at normal retirement age equal to 1 percent of average annual compensation for each year of service with Jason Corporation. The years of service included in the computation of the HCEs' accrued benefit under Plan X-H were included in the computation of their benefits under Plan X-N as well, and the benefits employees accrued under Plan X-N were not offset by their accrued benefits under Plan X-H. Thus, there is a duplication of service and benefits that impermissively discriminates in favor of the HCEs.

Q 3:2   Who is an HCE?

HCEs are divided into two groups: highly compensated active employees (see Q 3:3) and highly compensated former employees (see Q 3:11). In certain circumstances, highly compensated active employees and highly compensated former employees are considered separately in applying the provisions for which the definition of HCE is applicable (see Q 4:21). [I.R.C. § 414(q); Temp. Treas. Reg. § 1.414(q)-1T, Q&A-2]

Q 3:3   Who is a highly compensated active employee?

To determine if an employee is a highly compensated active employee for the determination year, two calculations are required: the look-back year calculation and the determination year calculation (see Q 3:10).

For the *look-back* year calculation, a highly compensated active employee is an employee who performs services for the employer (see Q 3:9) during the determination year, and who during the look-back year:

1. Was a 5 percent owner of the employer (see Q 3:4), or

2. Received compensation from the employer of more than $80,000 (see Qs 3:7, 3:8) and, if the employer elects, was a member of the top-paid group (see Q 3:5) of employees.

For the *determination* year calculation, an employee is a highly compensated active employee only if, during the determination year, the employee is a 5 percent owner. Consequently, an employee is a highly compensated active employee if the employee comes within the definition for *either* the look-back year or the determination year.

[I.R.C. § 414(q)(1)]

For the first year of an employer, only a 5 percent owner can be an HCE because there is no look-back year.

> **Example 1.** The Ezratty Golfing Group Ltd. was organized on January 5, 2010, and adopted a profit sharing plan for calendar year 2010. Both Marty and Rona earned $120,000 in 2010; but, because neither of them was a 5 percent owner, neither Marty nor Rona was an HCE for calendar year 2010. However, for calendar year 2011, Marty and Rona may be HCEs because, in 2011, 2010 becomes the look-back year.

Depending on employee demographics, an employer's election to use membership in the top-paid group (top-paid group election) may allow an employer to include fewer employees in the HCE group. As a result, employees who earn more than $80,000 (as adjusted) may be in the NHCE (see Q 3:12) group, possibly increasing the plan's chances of passing the nondiscrimination tests. For example, if 30 percent of the employees, including 5 percent owners, earn more than $80,000 (as adjusted), the top-paid group election will limit the HCE group to 20 percent of the employer's employees.

An employer may make a top-paid group election for a determination year, and the effect of the top-paid group election is that an employee (who is not a 5 percent owner at any time during the determination year or the look-back year) with compensation in excess of $80,000 (as adjusted) for the look-back year is an HCE *only* if the employee was in the top-paid group for the look-back year. A top-paid group election, once made, applies for all subsequent determination years *unless* changed by the employer. There is no prescribed procedure for making this election; however, the plan document must reflect the election, and any change in the election must be accomplished through a plan amendment. [IRS Notice 97-45, 1997-2 C.B. 296]

> **Example 2.** During the years specified below, Jack, who commenced employment with the employer in 2007, is not a 5 percent owner and is not a member of the top-paid group. For the purpose of this example, the employer elects each year to use membership in the top-paid group and the $80,000 amount is not increased for inflation. For each of the following years, Jack is included in, or excluded from, the HCE group as specified below:

Year	*Compensation*	*Status*
2007	$ 85,000	Excluded
2008	90,000	Excluded
2009	95,000	Excluded
2010	100,000	Excluded
2011	105,000	Excluded

Even though Jack earns more than $80,000 each year, he is excluded from the HCE group because he is neither a 5 percent owner nor a member of the top-paid group during any year.

Example 3. The facts are the same as those in Example 1, except that the employer does not elect to use membership in the top-paid group for 2008 and 2010. For 2009 and 2011, Jack is an HCE because for the look-back years (2008 and 2010) he earned more than $80,000.

Before the change in the definition of HCE made by SBA '96, an employer could substantiate compliance with the nondiscrimination requirements (see Q 4:10) on the basis of snapshot testing, that is, on the basis of the employer's workforce on a single day during the plan year (the "snapshot day"), provided that day was reasonably representative of the employer's workforce and the plan's coverage throughout the year. The snapshot day selected generally had to be consistent from year to year. IRS had established a simplified method of determining HCEs for purposes of testing for compliance with the nondiscrimination requirements. An employer that used this simplified method could choose also to apply the method on the basis of the employer's workforce as of a snapshot day and use reasonably approximated or projected compensation as part of the simplified method of determining HCEs. [Rev. Proc. 93-42, 1993-2 C.B. 540] IRS provided model language to enable plan sponsors to use the simplified method. The model language contained two options for sponsors electing to use the simplified method of determining HCEs, but neither option permitted the use of reasonably approximated or projected compensation as part of the simplified method of determining HCEs. [Rev. Proc. 95-34, 1995-2 C.B. 385]

IRS advised that the guidance provided under section 4 of Rev. Proc. 93-42 and under Rev. Proc. 95-34 does not apply for years beginning after 1996; however, IRS stated its intention to publish guidance that would make appropriate modifications to these items of guidance. [IRS Notice 97-45, 1997-2 C.B. 296] As of now, the IRS has yet to publish such guidance.

IRS also advised that for a year beginning in 1997, employers could continue to utilize the calendar year calculation election, taking into account the statutory amendments made by SBA '96. In addition, a new calendar year data election that an employer may make for a determination year has been provided by IRS. The effect of the calendar year data election is that the calendar year beginning with or within the look-back year is treated as the employer's look-back year for purposes of determining whether an employee is an HCE on account of the employee's compensation for a look-back year. A calendar year data election, once made, applies for all subsequent determination years *unless* changed by the employer. A calendar year data election made by an employer does not apply in determining whether the employer's employees are HCEs on account of being 5 percent owners. Accordingly, if an employee is a 5 percent owner in either the look-back year or the determination year, then the employee is an HCE, without regard to whether the employee's employer makes a calendar year data election. If a plan has a calendar year as its determination year, then the immediately preceding calendar year is the look-back year for the plan. This is the case whether or not a calendar year data election is made. Thus, a calendar year data election would have no effect on the HCE determination for a calendar year plan. [IRS Notice 97-45, 1997-2 C.B. 296]

Notification or filing with IRS of a top-paid election or a calendar year data election is not required in order for the election to be valid. However, under certain circumstances, plan amendments may be required to reflect the election (see Q 3:13).

In order to be effective, a top-paid group election made by an employer must apply consistently to the determination years of all plans of the employer that begin with or within the same calendar year. Similarly, in order to be effective, a calendar year data election made by an employer must apply consistently to the determination years of all plans of the employer, other than a plan with a calendar year determination year, that begin within the same calendar year. The top-paid group election and the calendar year data election are independent of each other. Thus, an employer making one of the elections is not required also to make the other election. However, if both elections are made, the look-back year in determining the top-paid group must be the calendar year beginning with or within the look-back year. [IRS Notice 97-45, 1997-2 C.B. 296]

Q 3:4   Who is a 5 percent owner?

An employee is a 5 percent owner of the employer for the determination or look-back year (see Q 3:10) if, at any time during the year, the employee is a 5 percent owner for top-heavy plan purposes (see Q 26:26). As noted in Q 26:26, a 5 percent owner in actuality means a more than 5 percent owner. [I.R.C. §§ 414(q)(2), 416(i)(1)(B)(i); IRS Notice 97-45, 1997-2 C.B. 296]

If the employer is not a corporation, the ownership test is applied to the person's capital or profits interest in the employer. In determining ownership percentages, each employer, whether related or unrelated (see Q 5:29), is treated as a separate entity. For example, an individual who is a 5 percent owner of a subsidiary corporation that is part of a controlled group of corporations (see Q 5:31) is treated as a 5 percent owner for purposes of determining which employees are HCEs (see Q 3:2). [Temp. Treas. Reg. § 1.414(q)-1T, Q&A-8]

For purposes of determining ownership, an individual is considered as owning the shares of stock owned by the individual's spouse, children, grandchildren, and parents. In addition, shares of stock owned by a corporation, partnership, estate, or trust can be attributed to the individual, and vice versa. If the employer is not a corporation, similar principles apply. Consequently, an employee who is the spouse, child, parent, or grandparent of an individual who has a 5 percent interest in the employer at any time during the look-back year or the determination year is treated as an HCE. [I.R.C. §§ 318(a), 416(i)(1)(B)(iii); Treas. Reg. §§ 1.318-1 through 1.318-4, 1.416-1, Q T-18; IRS Notice 97-45, 1997-2 C.B. 296]

Q 3:5   What is the top-paid group?

An employee was in the top-paid group of employees for the look-back year (see Q 3:10) if the employee was in the group consisting of the top 20 percent of the employer's employees when ranked on the basis of compensation (see Q 3:7) received from the employer (see Q 3:11) during the look-back year. The identification of the employees who are in the top-paid group for a look-back year involves a two-step procedure:

1. The determination of the number of employees that corresponded to 20 percent of the employer's employees, and
2. The identification of the employees who were among the number of employees who received the most compensation during the look-back year.

Use of the top-paid group determination is elective by the employer (see Q 3:3). [I.R.C. §§ 414(q)(1), 414(q)(3); IRS Notice 97-45, 1997-2 C.B. 296]

For purposes of determining the number of employees in the top-paid group for a year, the following employees are excluded:

1. Employees who have not completed six months of service by the end of the year;
2. Employees who normally work less than 17½ hours per week during the year;
3. Employees who normally work six months or less during any year;
4. Employees who are not age 21 by the end of the year; and
5. Certain nonresident aliens.

Union employees (see Qs 1:45, 5:5) are excluded only if they constitute 90 percent of the employer's workforce and the retirement plan covers only nonunion employees. Including union employees has the effect of expanding the number of employees in the top-paid group. [I.R.C. §§ 414(q)(5), 414(q)(8); Temp. Treas. Reg. § 1.414(q)-1T, Q&A-9(b)(1)]

The employer may elect to reduce the period of service or lower the age specified above, including a zero service or age requirement, provided the election applies to all plans of the employer. [I.R.C. § 414(q)(5); Temp. Treas. Reg. § 1.414(q)-1T, Q&A-9(b)(2)]

Q 3:6   Can an employee be described in more than one HCE category?

Yes. An individual who is a highly compensated active employee (see Q 3:3) for a determination year (see Q 3:10) by reason of being described in another category during the look-back year (see Q 3:10) is not disregarded in determining whether another individual is a highly compensated active employee by reason of being described in another category. An individual who is a highly compensated active employee for a determination year by reason of being a 5 percent owner (see Q 3:4) during that year, and who received compensation in excess of $80,000 (see Qs 3:7, 3:8) during the look-back year, is taken into account in determining the group of employees who are highly compensated active employees for the determination year by reason of (1) receiving more than $80,000 (as adjusted) and (2) if elected by the employer, being in the top-paid group (see Q 3:5) during the look-back year. [Temp. Treas. Reg. § 1.414(q)-1T, Q&A-3(d)]

> **Example.** Elaine is the sole shareholder of The Pearlmans of Wisdom, Inc. and, in 2010, earned $180,000. There were nine other employees, and the two next highly compensated were Fred ($120,000) and Tami ($115,000). In 2011, an election is made to use membership in the top-paid group. Even though Elaine is a highly compensated active employee by reason of being a 5 percent owner, she is not disregarded for purposes of determining the top-paid group. Consequently, Tami is not a highly compensated active employee even though she earned more than $110,000 in 2010 because she was not in the top-paid group.

Q 3:7   How is compensation defined for purposes of determining who is an HCE?

The definition of compensation is the same as is used for purposes of the annual addition limitation applicable to defined contribution plans (see Q 6:41). This means that elective or salary reduction contributions to a 401(k) plan (see Qs 27:16, 33:30), a cafeteria plan, a simplified employee pension (SEP; see Q 32:1), a SIMPLE IRA plan (see Q 33:9), a 403(b) plan (see Q 35:1), or a qualified transportation fringe benefit plan are included. Only compensation received by an employee during the look-back year (see Q 3:10) is considered in determining whether the employee is an HCE (see Q 3:3). Compensation is not annualized for purposes of determining an employee's compensation in the look-back year. [I.R.C. §§ 414(q)(4), 415(c)(3); Temp. Treas. Reg. § 1.414(q)-1T, Q&A-13; IRS Notice 97-45, 1997-2 C.B. 296]

> **Example.** Nancy earns $10,000 a month and is employed for five months during 2010. Nancy's compensation for 2010 is $50,000 and not $120,000 ($10,000 × 12).

Where a corporation (acquiring corporation) purchases all of the shares of stock of another corporation (acquired corporation) and the employees of the acquired corporation commence participation in the acquiring corporation's qualified retirement plan, IRS representatives opined that it would be reasonable to base the HCE (see Q 3:3) determination on the prior year's compensation with the acquired corporation. The representatives also opined that it would be reasonable not to do so if the acquiring corporation purchased the assets, and not the shares of stock, of the other corporation.

Q 3:8   Is the compensation amount for HCEs adjusted for inflation?

Yes. The $80,000 compensation amount (see Q 3:3) is adjusted for inflation at the same time and in the same manner as under Section 415(d) (see Qs 6:11, 6:12). However, an adjustment is made only if it is $5,000 or greater and then is made in multiples of $5,000 (i.e., rounded down to the next lowest multiple of $5,000). For example, an increase in the cost-of-living of $4,999 will result in no adjustment, and an increase of $9,999 will create an upward adjustment of $5,000. [I.R.C. §§ 414(q)(1), 415(d)] For years beginning in 2010, the compensation amount remained at $110,000. [IRS Notice 2009-94, 2009-2 C.B. 848] For the five years beginning prior to 2010, the compensation amount was:

Year Beginning in	Compensation Amount
2009	$110,000
2008	105,000
2007	100,000
2006	100,000
2005	95,000

The applicable dollar amount for a look-back year (see Q 3:10) is the dollar amount for the calendar year in which the look-back year begins. The dollar amount for purposes of determining the highly compensated active employees (see Q 3:3) for a particular look-back year is based on the calendar year in which this look-back year begins, not the calendar year in which the look-back year ends or in which the determination year with respect to that look-back year begins. [Temp. Treas. Reg. § 1.414(q)-1T, Q&A-3(c)(2)]

Thus, for plan years that began in 2009, the look-back year began in the 2008 calendar year, and the compensation limitation for determining HCE status was therefore $105,000. The compensation limitation for determining HCE status is $110,000 for plan years beginning in 2010, based on the look-back year beginning in 2009. However, if a special calendar year data election (see Q 3:3) was made, the calendar year beginning with or within the look-back year was treated as the look-back year for purposes of determining whether an employee was an HCE based on the employee's compensation for a look-back year. This election does not change the look-back year for calendar-year plans. However, making this election does change the applicable compensation limitation used in determining HCE status for plans with non-calendar plan years that began in 2009, because the look-back year for these plans was the 2009 calendar year. Thus, if the calendar year data election was made for a plan with a non-calendar-plan year beginning in 2009, the compensation limitation for determining HCE status was $110,000. [IRS Info. Ltr. (Dec. 9, 1999)]

Q 3:9   Who is the employer for purposes of determining HCEs?

The employer is the entity employing the employees and includes all other entities aggregated with the employing entity under the aggregation rules. The following entities must be treated as a single employer for purposes of determining the employees who are HCEs (see Q 3:2):

1. All corporations that are members of a controlled group of corporations that includes the employing entity (see Q 5:31). [I.R.C. § 414(b)]
2. All trades or businesses (whether or not incorporated) that are under common control that includes the employing entity (see Q 5:29). [I.R.C. § 414(c)]
3. All organizations (whether or not incorporated) that are members of an affiliated service group that includes the employing entity (see Q 5:35). [I.R.C. § 414(m)]
4. Any other entities required to be aggregated with the employing entity pursuant to Section 414(o). [I.R.C. § 414(q)(7); Temp. Treas. Reg. § 1.414(q)-1T, Q&A-6(a)]

The separate lines of business rules (see Q 5:44) do not apply in determining the group of HCEs; an employer with separate lines of business is still treated as a single employer. [I.R.C. § 414(r); Temp. Treas. Reg. § 1.414(q)-1T, Q&A-6(c)]

Q 3:10   What are the determination year and the look-back year?

The determination year is generally the plan year, and the look-back year is the 12-month period immediately preceding the determination year. [Temp. Treas. Reg. § 1.414(q)-1T, Q&A-14; IRS Notice 97-45, 1997-2 C.B. 296]

> **Example.** The Rube Corporation has two qualified retirement plans, Plan R and Plan N. If Plan R has a calendar year plan year and Plan N has a July 1 to June 30 plan year, the determination year calculation and the look-back year calculation for Plan R are made on the basis of the calendar year, and the determination year calculation and the look-back year calculation for Plan N are made on the basis of the July 1 to June 30 year.

Q 3:11   Who is a highly compensated former employee?

A highly compensated former employee for a determination year (see Q 3:10) is a former employee who had a separation year prior to the determination year and was a highly compensated active employee (see Q 3:3) for either (1) the employee's separation year or (2) any determination year ending on or after the employee's 55th birthday. The separation year generally is the determination year during which the employee separates from service with the employer. For example, an employee who is a highly compensated active employee for the employee's separation year is a highly compensated former employee for determination years after the separation year. Under an alternative rule, the employer may elect to include as a highly compensated former employee any former employee who separated from service prior to 1987 and was either a 5 percent owner (see Q 3:4) or received compensation (see Q 3:7) in excess of $50,000 in the year of separation or any determination year ending on or after the employee attained age 55. [I.R.C. § 414(q)(6); Temp. Treas. Reg. § 1.414(q)-1T, Q&A-4(a), Q&A-4(d), Q&A-5]

For purposes of determining status as a highly compensated former employee, whether an employee was a highly compensated active employee for a determination year that ended on or after the employee's 55th birthday, or that was a separation year, is based on the rules applicable to determining HCE status as in effect for that determination year. [IRS Notice 97-45, 1997-2 C.B. 296]

> **Example.** Mary's Taverna Corp. maintains a defined benefit plan with a calendar year plan year. Tony was employed by Mary's Taverna Corp. since 1999 and retired at age 65 in 2010. Tony was an HCE in 2002 under the rules applicable in 2002 but was not an HCE in any other year, including 2010. Because Tony was an HCE for a determination year (2002) ending on or after his 55th birthday, Tony is a highly compensated former employee for determination years beginning after his retirement.

The term "highly compensated former employee" is relevant only if a provision of the Code makes a specific reference to the term (see Q 4:21). [Temp. Treas. Reg. § 1.414(q)-1T, Q&A-4(e)(1)]

Q 3:12 Who is a non-highly compensated employee (NHCE)?

A NHCE is any employee who is not an HCE (see Q 3:2). Therefore, a non-highly compensated active employee is an employee who is not a highly compensated active employee (see Q 3:3), and a non-highly compensated former employee is an employee who is not a highly compensated former employee (see Q 3:11).

Q 3:13 Must plans be amended to reflect the HCE rules?

If an employer makes either a top-paid group or calendar year data election (see Q 3:3) for a determination year (see Q 3:10), a plan that contains the definition of HCE must reflect the election; and, if the employer changes either a top-paid group or calendar year data election, the plan must be amended to reflect the change. However, a plan is not required to add a definition of HCE merely to reflect a top-paid group or calendar year data election. [IRS Notice 97-45, 1997-2 C.B. 296]

Chapter 4

Requirements for Qualification

A company's retirement plan will receive favorable tax treatment only if the plan is qualified. The Code sets out a host of requirements that a retirement plan must meet in order to qualify. This chapter analyzes those requirements.

Q 4:1 What basic requirements must all retirement plans meet to qualify for favorable tax treatment?

The four fundamental requirements for a qualified retirement plan are the following:

1. The plan must be a definite written program.
2. The plan must be communicated to the employees.
3. The plan must be permanent (see Q 1:42).
4. The plan must prohibit the use or diversion of funds for purposes other than the exclusive benefit of employees or their beneficiaries (the exclusive benefit rule).

[I.R.C. §§ 401(a)(1), 401(a)(2); Treas. Reg. §§ 1.401-1, 1.401-2; IRS Notice 98-25, 1998-1 C.B. 979; Borrelli v. IRS, 2005 WL 3150533 (2d Cir. 2005); *see also* Cole v. International Union, United Automobile, Aerospace & Agricultural Implement Workers of America, No. 06-3205 (8th Cir. 2008)]

One court ruled that former plan participants may not claim a breach of fiduciary duty solely on the basis of alleged oral misrepresentations that purported to alter plan terms, because oral promises cannot vary the terms of an ERISA plan. [Ladouceur v. Credit Lyonnais, 584 F.3d 510 (2d Cir. 2009)]

IRS has ruled that the exclusive benefit rule is violated if the sponsorship of a qualified retirement plan is transferred from an employer to an unrelated taxpayer and the transfer of the plan sponsorship is not connected to a transfer of business assets, operations, or employees from the employer to the unrelated taxpayer. The decision effectively prevents the transfer of frozen defined benefit plans (see Q 2:3) from an employer to an unrelated party. [Rev. Rul. 2008-45, 2008-2 C.B. 403] When a retirement plan made 22 unsecured loans, representing 75 percent of plan assets, to the sole shareholder of the employer and the sole trustee of the plan over a two-year period, IRS ruled that the loans violated the exclusive benefit rule. [Priv. Ltr. Rul. 9145006; *see also* Priv. Ltr. Ruls. 9724001, 9713002, 9701001] The exclusive benefit rule was also violated where the plan functioned as a bank for the sole shareholder. [Westchester Plastic Surgical Assocs., P.C., 78 T.C.M. 756 (1999); Ada Orthopedic, Inc., 68 T.C.M. 1392 (1994)] IRS has also ruled that an employee stock ownership plan (ESOP; see Q 28:1) that permits a trustee to consider *nonfinancial* employment-related factors, such as continuing job security and employment opportunities, before acting upon tender offers violates the exclusive benefit rule. [Gen. Couns. Mem. 39,870]

However, IRS ruled that the exclusive benefit rule was not violated when a terminated defined benefit plan made a loan to the employer from excess funds that would revert to the employer after the satisfaction of all plan liabilities (see Q 25:59). The loan, however, was a prohibited transaction (see Q 24:1). [Priv. Ltr. Rul. 9430002] IRS has also ruled that if a union makes loans to its local unions and the locals then contribute the borrowed funds to their multiple-employer defined benefit plan, the plan's qualified status is not jeopardized. [Priv. Ltr. Rul. 200005035] IRS issued this ruling because there is no requirement that contributions be made only by employers and employees and because, in instances where outside sources do make contributions, a plan's qualified status will continue as long as all other requirements are met. [Rev. Rul. 68-223, 1968-1 C.B. 154; Rev. Rul. 63-46, 1963-1 C.B. 85] One court determined that, although a loan from a qualified retirement plan violated the prudent person standard (see Q 23:20), the loan did not violate the exclusive benefit rule and the plan was not disqualified. [Shedco, Inc., 76 T.C.M. 267 (1998)] Another court ruled that the exclusive benefit rule was not violated when an employer conditioned eligibility for plan benefits under a special early retirement program on the employee's execution of a broad waiver covering potential Age Discrimination in Employment Act (ADEA) and other employment-related claims against the employer. [Spink v. Lockheed Corp., 125 F.3d 1257 (9th Cir. 1997); *see also* Lockheed Corp. v. Spink, 517 U.S. 882 (1996)] A plan amendment that provided accelerated pension benefits to younger participants, but had no impact on the benefits received by certain older participants, was held not to violate the ADEA, because benefit variations were caused by differences in pension status and not from differential treatment based upon age. [Schultz v. Windstream Communications, Inc., 2010 WL 1266858 (8th Cir. 2010)] Where a defined benefit plan required employee contributions as a condition of participation (see Q 5:6) and plan assets exceeded the present value of accrued benefits (see Q 9:2) by almost $1 billion, the United States Supreme Court ruled that an amendment changing the benefit formula of a plan with surplus assets funded in part by employee contributions did not violate the exclusive benefit rule because the contributing employees had no interest in the surplus assets. [Hughes Aircraft Co. v. Jacobson, 525 U.S. 432 (1999)]

IRS also ruled that the payment of premiums under a benefit intended to assist disabled employees to continue participation in a 401(k) plan (see Q 27:1) did not violate the exclusive benefit rule and did not adversely affect the plan's qualification. The purpose of the benefit was to allow employees who became disabled to continue to save for retirement. The benefit was designed to replace the elective deferrals, matching contributions, and any nonelective contributions that would have been credited to a participant's account under the employer's 401(k) plan had the participant not become disabled. [Priv. Ltr. Rul. 200235043]

IRS issued guidance providing professional employer organizations (PEOs), also known as employee leasing organizations (see Qs 5:58–5:63), that maintain defined contribution plans (see Q 2:2) for the benefit of their worksite employees with limited relief from plan disqualification due to a potential violation of the exclusive benefit rule. To obtain this relief, a PEO that maintains a defined contribution plan must either convert the plan into a multiple employer plan (see Q 8:9) that benefits worksite employees or terminate the plan. [Rev. Proc. 2003-86, 2003-2 C.B. 1211; Rev. Proc. 2002-21, 2002-1 C.B. 911]

IRS established a special procedure under which employers could make restorative payments to defined contribution plans (see Q 2:2) that invested in guaranteed investment contracts (GICs) or guaranteed annuity contracts (GACs) of insurance companies that became insolvent. Under the procedure, a plan that entered into a closing agreement with IRS that required (1) the employer to make restorative payments to the plan due to such an insolvency and (2) the plan to repay the employer once the insurance company resumed payments under the GIC or GAC would not be considered as violating the exclusive benefit rule or the requirement that plans not discriminate in favor of highly compensated employees (HCEs; see Qs 3:2, 4:10). [Rev. Proc. 95-52, 1995-2 C.B. 439; *see also* Rev. Rul. 2002-45, 2002-2 C.B. 116] For further information on restorative payments, see Qs 6:34 and 12:2.

The following requirements must also be met before a retirement plan qualifies for favorable tax treatment:

1. The plan must satisfy a minimum coverage requirement, and a defined benefit plan must also satisfy a minimum participation requirement. For details, see chapter 5. [I.R.C. §§ 401(a)(3), 401(a)(26)]

2. Contributions or benefits under the plan may not discriminate in favor of HCEs. For details, see Qs 4:10 through 4:26. [I.R.C. § 401(a)(4)]

3. The plan must meet requirements for the vesting of benefits. For details, see chapter 9. [I.R.C. § 401(a)(7)]

4. The plan must provide for required minimum distribution of benefits. For details, see chapter 11. [I.R.C. § 401(a)(9)]

5. Additional requirements apply to top-heavy plans. These additional requirements include minimum vesting rules and, for employees who are not key employees, minimum benefits and/or minimum contributions. A retirement plan can qualify only if it contains provisions satisfying the top-heavy plan requirements that automatically take effect if the plan becomes top-heavy. For details, see chapter 26. [I.R.C. § 401(a)(10)(B)]

6. With few exceptions, plans must provide for the payment of benefits in the form of a joint and survivor lifetime annuity and for death benefits in

the form of a preretirement survivor annuity. For details, see chapter 10. [I.R.C. § 401(a)(11)]

7. The plan must provide that benefits may not be assigned or alienated. For details, see Qs 4:27 through 4:30. [I.R.C. § 401(a)(13)]

8. The plan must comply with rules regarding the commencement of benefit payments. For details, see Q 10:53. [I.R.C. § 401(a)(14)]

9. The plan must limit the contributions that can be made to the plan on behalf of an employee (in the case of a defined contribution plan), or it must limit the benefits that can be paid to an employee (in the case of a defined benefit plan). For details, see chapter 6. [I.R.C. § 401(a)(16)]

10. The plan must impose a $200,000 cap (subject to cost-of-living adjustments) on the amount of compensation that can be taken into account (see Q 6:45). [I.R.C. § 401(a)(17)]

11. A defined benefit plan must specify the actuarial assumptions that are used to determine the value of a benefit (see Q 2:20). [I.R.C. § 401(a)(25)]

12. The plan must permit certain types of distributions to be made by a direct trustee-to-trustee transfer to another eligible retirement plan. For details, see Qs 34:8 through 34:34. [I.R.C. § 401(a)(31)]

13. A defined benefit plan subject to Pension Benefit Guaranty Corporation (PBGC) coverage (see Qs 25:10, 25:11) cannot be amended to increase plan liabilities while the employer is in bankruptcy (see Q 25:23). [I.R.C. § 401(a)(33) (as amended by WRERA 2008 § 101(d)(2)(C)); Priv. Ltr. Ruls. 200838028, 200730029, 200403097]

14. Certain defined contribution plans must satisfy diversification requirements regarding publicly traded employer securities (see Q 28:53). [I.R.C. § 401(a)(35) (as amended by WRERA 2008 § 109(a))]

15. A plan may provide that a distribution may be made to an employee who has attained age 62 and who is not separated from employment at the time of such distribution (see Q 10:59). [I.R.C. § 401(a)(36)]

16. A plan must provide that, in the case of a participant who dies while performing qualified military service, the survivors of the participant are entitled to any additional benefits (other than benefit accruals relating to the period of qualified military service) provided under the plan had the participant resumed and then terminated employment on account of death (see Q 1:35). [I.R.C. § 401(a)(37) (as added by HEART Act § 104(a)); HEART Act § 104(d)(2)]

IRS extended the deadline for amending qualified retirement plans to meet a number of requirements added by PPA (see Q 1:33) by one year to the last day of the first plan year that begins on or after January 1, 2010. [IRS Notice 2009-97, 2009-2 C.B. ___]

With regard to the plan sponsor of a qualified retirement plan, IRS representatives have opined that, although the plan sponsor must be in existence, there

is no requirement for active engagement in business and that a legally constituted dormant entity may sponsor a qualified retirement plan (see Q 1:10).

IRS has issued guidelines to address potentially abusive retirement plan
arrangements referred to as Rollovers as Business Start-ups (ROBS) that are
designed to allow individuals to convert their existing retirement accounts into
seed money for funding new businesses without first paying taxes on the
distributions. See Q 4:2 for details.

Q 4:2   What are ROBS?

IRS has identified tax avoidance transactions using plan assets as start-up
business capital, whereby prospective business owners access tax-deferred
retirement funds and avoid applicable distribution taxes by rolling the funds
over into a new plan that is established to invest in employer stock.

IRS has provided initial guidelines for IRS technical specialists on the
acceptability of arrangements referred to as Rollovers as Business Start-ups
(ROBS), currently being marketed to entrepreneurs. Under a ROBS plan, a
prospective business owner acquires business capital by withdrawing money
from the individual's existing retirement accounts and channels the funds into
a new retirement plan. While not stating that such transactions are noncompli-
ant *per se,* IRS has indicated that it will carefully scrutinize these plans on a
case-by-case basis.

The plan created by a ROBS transaction is typically set up as a defined
contribution plan (see Q 2:2), generally established in the form of a profit
sharing plan coupled with a cash-or-deferred arrangement (CODA; see Q 27:2).
ROBS plans are questionable because they may allow the principal establishing
the business to exchange tax-deferred assets for currently available funds by
using a qualified retirement plan that authorizes investment in employer stock,
thus avoiding otherwise assessable distribution taxes. Because the plans generally benefit only the principal who establishes the business and do not allow
rank-and-file employees to acquire employer stock, they may violate the nondiscrimination requirements (see Q 4:10) and not satisfy the benefits, rights, and
features test (see Q 4:20). Such plans may also create a prohibited transaction
(see Q 24:1) between the plan and its sponsor, due to deficient stock valuations.

The following progressive steps make up a ROBS transaction:

1. An individual establishes a shell corporation sponsoring an associated
   and purportedly qualified retirement plan. At this point, the corporation
   has no employees, assets, or business operations and may not even have
   a contribution to capital to create shareholder equity.

2. The plan document provides that all participants may invest the entirety
   of their account balances in employer stock.

3. The individual becomes the only employee of the shell corporation and
   the only participant in the plan. At this point, there is still no ownership
   or shareholder equity interest.

4. The individual then executes a rollover (see Q 34:1) or direct trustee-to-trustee transfer of available funds from a prior qualified retirement plan or IRA into the newly created qualified retirement plan. These available funds may be any assets previously accumulated under the individual's prior employer's qualified retirement plan or under a conduit IRA (see Q 34:38), which itself was created from these amounts. Note that, at this point, because assets have been moved from one tax-exempt accumulation vehicle to another, all assessable income or excise taxes otherwise applicable to the distribution have been avoided.

5. The sole participant in the plan then directs investment of the individual's account balance into a purchase of employer stock. The employer stock is valued to reflect the amount of plan assets that the individual wishes to access.

6. The individual then uses the transferred funds to purchase a franchise or begin some other form of business enterprise. Note that all otherwise assessable taxes on a distribution from the prior tax-deferred accumulation account are avoided.

7. After the business is established, the plan may be amended to prohibit further investments in employer stock. This amendment may be unnecessary, because all stock is fully allocated. As a result, only the original individual benefits from this investment option. Future employees and plan participants will not be entitled to invest in employer stock.

8. A portion of the proceeds of the stock transaction may be remitted back to the promoter in the form of professional fee. This may be either a direct payment from the plan to the promoter or an indirect payment, where gross proceeds are transferred to the individual and some amount of the individual's gross wealth is then returned to the promoter.

Because ROBS transactions generally benefit only the principal involved in setting up a business and do not enable rank-and-file employees to acquire employer stock, IRS believes that some of these plans violate the anti-discrimination requirements. Furthermore, the plan's benefits, rights, and features must be tested to see if they are nondiscriminatory in effect. Benefits, rights, and features testing considerations can arise in many forms, including, as here, the right to make investments in employer securities.

Even if the ROBS initiator is an HCE (see Q 3:2), in many of the identified cases there are no other employees in the initial year of the transaction or for some number of future years thereafter. Therefore, as no finding regarding discrimination can be made in absence of non-highly compensated employees (NHCEs; see Q 3:12) in the transaction year, the current availability testing standard is satisfied. Given that ROBS arrangements are designed to take advantage of a one-time-only stock offering, the investment feature generally would not satisfy the effectively available benefit requirement. The issue of discrimination arises because the plan is designed in a manner that the benefit, right, or feature will never be available to any NHCEs. For this reason, IRS says that ROBS cases should be evaluated for discrimination issues wherever a given plan covers both HCEs and NHCEs and no extension of the stock investment option is afforded to NHCEs.

In all ROBS arrangements, the individual creates capital stock for the purpose of exchanging it for tax-deferred accumulation assets. The value of the stock is set as the value of the available assets. An appraisal may be created to substantiate this value, but it is often devoid of supportive analysis. This potentially creates prohibited transaction issues. Because the corporation is new, there could be a question of whether it is indeed worth the value of the tax-deferred assets for which it was exchanged.

IRS has specifically considered whether the form of the plan, as presented, is entitled to a favorable determination letter ruling (see Q 18:1). It has concluded that there is no inherent violation in the form of a plan containing a ROBS arrangement that would otherwise prevent a favorable ruling. The issues raised by ROBS plans are inherently operational, and beyond the scope of a determination letter ruling, said IRS. Therefore, determination letter applications for plans with ROBS features can be reviewed and approved as appropriate. However, IRS plans to monitor the volume of approval letters issued to these plans.

[*Treasury/IRS Memorandum of Understanding on Rollovers as Business Start-ups* (Oct. 1, 2008)]

Q 4:3 Does a 401(k) plan qualify for favorable tax treatment?

Yes, provided certain special requirements are met in addition to the regular retirement plan qualification requirements. For details, see chapter 27.

Q 4:4 Can an oral trust created in a state that recognizes its validity be used for a qualified retirement plan?

No. Since a qualified retirement plan must be a definite written program (see Q 4:1), an oral trust, which may be valid under local law, will not meet the Code requirements for favorable tax treatment. [Rev. Rul. 69-231, 1969-1 C.B. 118; Fazi, 102 T.C. 695 (1994); Attardo, 62 T.C.M. 313 (1991); *see also* Guilbert v. Gardner, Jr., No. 04-1003-cv (2d Cir. 2007)]

Q 4:5 Can a trust that is not valid under local law be part of a qualified retirement plan?

No. Contributions to a qualified retirement plan's trust must be made to a trust that is valid under local law. [Rev. Rul. 69-231, 1969-1 C.B. 118; Rev. Rul. 81-114, 1981-1 C.B. 207]

The trust must be created or organized in the United States, and it must be maintained at all times as a domestic trust in the United States. [I.R.C. § 401(a); Treas. Reg. § 1.401-1(a)(3)(i)] Trusts that are parts of qualified retirement plans, IRAs (see Q 30:1), and 403(b) plans (see Q 35:1) may pool their assets in a group trust without affecting the exempt status of the separate trusts. [Rev. Rul. 81-100, 1981-1 C.B. 326; Priv. Ltr. Rul. 200242047] A trust will be treated as a domestic trust if:

1. A court within the United States is able to exercise primary supervision over the administration of the trust (court test), and

2. One or more United States persons have the authority to control all substantial decisions of the trust (control test).

In applying the control test, all individuals with power over substantial decisions, whether acting as a fiduciary (see Q 23:1) or not, are considered. However, a special rule for certain trusts provides that these trusts are deemed to satisfy the control test if control of substantial trust decisions is made only by United States fiduciaries. IRS has added to the categories of trusts that may use the special control test group trusts consisting of qualified retirement plan trusts and IRA trusts that meet the requirements of Rev. Rul. 81-100. [I.R.C. § 7701(a)(30)(E); Treas. Reg. § 301.7701-7(d)(1)(iv)]

Q 4:6 Must all qualified retirement plans have trustees?

No. The most common type of qualified retirement plan that has no trustee is an annuity plan funded solely through contracts issued by an insurance company (see Q 2:25).

Q 4:7 Does a retirement plan have to be submitted to IRS for approval?

A retirement plan may qualify for tax-favored status without first being submitted to IRS. Nevertheless, it is prudent to submit the retirement plan for IRS approval, since this is the most important step that can be taken to preserve a retirement plan's qualified status. If, upon review of the application for a determination letter, IRS finds defects in the retirement plan, the timely filing of the application allows the plan to be corrected retroactively (see Q 4:8). [I.R.C. § 401(b); Treas. Reg. § 1.401(b)-1; Ltr. Rul. 200913053]

There is another reason for applying for a determination letter from IRS with regard to the initial qualification of a retirement plan. If IRS does not approve the retirement plan, the employer may recover its contribution only if the employer made a timely request for the determination (see Q 1:53). In that case, the return of the employer's contribution must be made within one year after receipt of the adverse determination. [ERISA § 403(c)(2)(B); Rev. Rul. 60-276, 1960-2 C.B.150]

The procedure for submitting a retirement plan to IRS is discussed in chapter 18.

Q 4:8 Even if a retirement plan is not submitted to IRS for approval, must it nevertheless be amended periodically?

Yes. A retirement plan must be amended to comply with changes in laws, regulations, and rulings that affect retirement plans in general, or the specific type of retirement plan in particular, even if it is not submitted to IRS for approval. A retirement plan's qualification can be revoked if the employer fails to make required plan amendments timely to comply with changes in law, even if such changes would not affect the operation of the plan. [Ronald R. Pawluk, P.C., 69 T.C.M. 1603 (1995); Fazi, 102 T.C. 695 (1994); Mills, Mitchell & Turner, 65 T.C.M. 2127 (1993); Hamlin Dev. Co., 65 T.C.M. 2071 (1993); Kollipara Rajsheker, M.D., Inc., 64 T.C.M. 1153 (1992); Attardo, 62 T.C.M. 313 (1991); Stark Truss Co., 62 T.C.M. 169 (1991); Basch Eng'g, Inc., 59 T.C.M. 482 (1990); Halligan, 51 T.C.M. 1203 (1986); Bolinger, 77 T.C. 1353 (1981); Tionesta Sand & Gravel, Inc., 73 T.C. 758 (1980); Ltr. Rul. 200913053] For additional information, see Qs 13:22, 34:39.

See chapter 19 for details regarding IRS correction programs in connection with plan document failures.

Q 4:9 May an employee's benefits be reduced after retirement to reflect Social Security benefit increases?

No. A qualified retirement plan must provide that benefits cannot be reduced because of increases in Social Security benefits or wage base levels after (1) benefit payments commence to a participant or beneficiary or (2) a participant who has vested benefits under the plan separates from service. [I.R.C. § 401(a)(15)]

Q 4:10 What is the general nondiscrimination rule that applies to every qualified retirement plan?

A retirement plan is a qualified plan only if the contributions or the benefits provided under the plan do not discriminate in favor of HCEs (see Q 3:2). A plan will satisfy this nondiscrimination rule only if it complies *both* in form and in operation with the requirements promulgated by IRS. [I.R.C. § 401(a)(4); Treas. Reg. § 1.401(a)(4)-1(a)]

There are three requirements a plan must meet to satisfy the nondiscrimination rule. The first requirement is that either the contributions or the benefits provided in the plan must be nondiscriminatory in amount (see Q 4:11). A plan generally is permitted to satisfy this requirement on the basis of either contributions or benefits, regardless of whether the plan is a defined contribution plan (see Q 2:2) or a defined benefit plan (see Q 2:3). Thus, a plan is *not* required to establish nondiscrimination in amount with respect to both the contributions and the benefits provided. [Treas. Reg. § 1.401(a)(4)-1(b)(2)(i)]

The second requirement is that the benefits, rights, and features provided under the plan must be available to participants in a nondiscriminatory manner (see Q 4:20). The benefits, rights, and features subject to this requirement are the optional forms of benefit (e.g., retirement annuities and single-sum payments), ancillary benefits (e.g., disability benefits), and other rights and features (e.g., loans and investment options) available to participants. [Treas. Reg. § 1.401(a)(4)-1(b)(3)]

The third requirement is that the effect of plan amendments, including grants of past service credit, and of plan terminations must be nondiscriminatory (see Q 4:21). [Treas. Reg. § 1.401(a)(4)-1(b)(4)]

For purposes of determining whether a retirement plan satisfies the nondiscrimination requirements, all employees of corporations that are members of a controlled group of corporations (see Q 5:31) are treated as if they were employed by a single employer. A comparable requirement applies to affiliated service groups (see Q 5:35) and to businesses that are under common control (see Q 5:29).

Example 1. There are three corporations—Sophie, Inc., Hannah, Inc., and Emma, Inc.—but only Hannah, Inc. adopts a retirement plan. Sophie and Hannah have sufficient common ownership to be a controlled group, and Hannah and Emma have sufficient common ownership to be a controlled group; but Sophie and Emma are not members of a controlled group. To test Hannah's plan for the nondiscrimination requirements, Sophie and Hannah, as one controlled group, are tested separately, as are Hannah and Emma, as a second controlled group. Sophie, Hannah, and Emma are not tested together as a single controlled group.

IRS has ruled that employees who have not satisfied a plan's eligibility requirements for participation (see Qs 1:43, 5:2), but who are permitted to make rollover contributions (see Q 34:1), need not be taken into account for purposes of the nondiscrimination requirements. [Rev. Rul. 96-48, 1996-2 C.B. 31]

IRS has become aware of certain schemes that effectively limit the amounts payable under a retirement plan to a small number of HCEs by limiting participation under the plan to HCEs and to rank-and-file employees with short periods of service (e.g., periods of a few weeks or even a few days). These plans, in the form of defined contribution plans, defined benefit plans, or combinations of both, attempt to satisfy the requirements of various Code sections by allocating amounts to the sponsor's lowest-paid employees that, while perhaps significant relative to the employees' compensation, are actually small in amount because of the employees' small amount of compensation. Thus, these plans provide little or no actual benefits to these employees. Employers use plan designs and hiring practices that limit the non-highly compensated employees (NHCEs; Q 3:12) who accrue benefits under the plan primarily to employees with very small amounts of compensation. By combining these elements, employers contend that the lowest-paid employees may be treated as benefiting under the plan, thereby satisfying the nondiscrimination rules. These employers further contend that the qualification requirements and the regulations are satisfied even though the dollar amounts actually accrued by the lowest paid employees are nominal and even though these employees may never vest in their benefits.

In a memorandum, IRS opines that these plans may violate the nondiscrimination requirements even though they ostensibly satisfy certain provisions in the nondiscrimination regulations. In addition, arrangements similar to those discussed in the memorandum may, in the case of defined benefit plans, raise related issues concerning the minimum participation requirement (see Q 5:23). [IRS Mem. (Oct. 22, 2004)] In a subsequent memorandum, IRS clarified that the earlier memorandum was not intended to suggest that plan designs that have been consistently and repeatedly approved by IRS are now in question. Instead, the earlier memorandum was intended to point out that this combination of characteristics (lowest-paid employees with the shortest service) has the potential to be abusive. [IRS Mem. (Feb. 4, 2005)]

For example, the nondiscrimination requirement is violated by a plan design that satisfies the nondiscrimination general test by using cross-testing where (1) the plan excludes most or all permanent NHCEs, (2) the plan covers a group of NHCEs who were hired temporarily for short periods of time, (3) the plan allocates a higher percentage of compensation to the accounts of the HCEs than to those of the NHCEs covered by the plan, and (4) the compensation earned by the NHCEs covered by the plan is significantly less than the compensation earned by the NHCEs not covered by the plan. This plan design does not interpret cross-testing in a reasonable manner consistent with the purpose of preventing discrimination in favor of HCEs because the results of the general test are distorted through the use of allocation rates produced by the allocation of small amounts to NHCEs hired temporarily for short periods of time.

Example 2. Playa Lynda Corp., which is 100 percent owned by Lynda Kay, is not part of a controlled group of corporations, is not under common control with another trade or business, is not part of an affiliated service group, and has no leased employees (see Q 5:58).

Playa Lynda Corp. maintains Plan L, a defined contribution plan that is intended to be qualified and is the only plan maintained by the corporation. Under its terms, Plan L provides immediate participation, covers only the HCEs of Playa Lynda Corp. and a group of NHCEs defined by Plan L, and provides that the HCEs receive an annual allocation of 20 percent of compensation and that the other covered employees receive an annual allocation of 5 percent of compensation.

In 2010, Playa Lynda Corp. employed 55 employees. These 55 employees included five HCEs, and the remaining 50 employees included 15 employees who were employed on a permanent basis and whose annual compensation ranged from $20,000 to $50,000. These 15 employees were not included in the group of NHCEs covered by Plan L. The other 35 employees were temporarily hired for short periods of time and were included in the group of NHCEs covered by the plan. None of these 35 employees received compensation in excess of $1,000 in 2009, and they all received allocations under the plan of 5 percent of compensation. Plan L intends to satisfy the nondiscrimination in amount general test by using cross-testing.

Plan L fails the reasonable manner requirement because it satisfies the nondiscrimination test by using cross-testing and covering a group of NHCEs who were hired temporarily for short periods of time and who received small amounts of compensation, while at the same time it excludes all higher-paid, permanent NHCEs and allocates a higher percentage of compensation to the accounts of HCEs than to those of the covered NHCEs. This plan design does not interpret cross-testing in a reasonable manner consistent with the purpose of preventing discrimination in favor of HCEs because the results of the general test are distorted through the use of allocation rates produced by the allocation of small amounts to NHCEs hired temporarily for short periods of time. The conclusion would be the same if the allocation rates were inflated through the use of an entry date for plan participation that occurs shortly before the end of the plan year in conjunction with plan provisions limiting compensation, for allocation purposes, to the period of participation.

Depending on the circumstances, the nondiscrimination requirement may also be violated in cases where one of the enumerated elements is not present. For example, the nondiscrimination rules may be violated even though the same percentage of compensation is allocated to the HCEs and to the NHCEs, where the NHCEs covered by the plan are hired for short periods of time and there is no reasonable business reason for hiring these employees on a short-term basis. In the absences of questionable hiring practices, a violation may also occur where the employer uses a plan design to limit benefits to a select group of HCEs and to the lowest-paid of the NHCEs.

Example 3. Smith Hermanos Corp., which is 100 percent owned by Andy Ess, is not part of a controlled group of corporations, is not under common control with another trade or business, is not part of an affiliated service group, and has no leased employees. Smith Hermanos Corp. maintains Plan A, a defined contribution plan that is intended to be qualified and is the only plan maintained by the corporation. Under its terms, Plan A provides immediate participation but covers only Andy Ess and the "lowest paid group of employees." The "lowest paid group of employees" is defined to include the employees with the lowest compensation for the plan year and is limited to the minimum number of these employees needed to satisfy the minimum coverage requirement (see Q 5:15). Plan A provides that Andy Ess receives an annual allocation of 20 percent of compensation and that the other covered employees receive an annual allocation of 5 percent of compensation.

In 2010, Smith Hermanos Corp. employed 55 employees. These 55 employees included Andy Ess and four other HCEs. Under the terms of Plan A, Andy Ess received an allocation of 20 percent of compensation, and the seven lowest-paid employees of the corporation received an allocation of 5 percent of compensation. Each of the lowest-paid group of employees received an allocation of less than $100. The remaining 43 NHCEs and four HCEs received no allocation under the plan. Plan A intends to satisfy the nondiscrimination in amount general test by using cross-testing.

Plan A fails the reasonable manner requirement because it satisfies the nondiscrimination test by using cross-testing and by (1) covering a group of NHCEs who received small amounts of compensation, (2) excluding all higher-paid NHCEs, and (3) allocating a higher percentage of compensation to the account of the sole shareholder. This plan design does not interpret cross-testing in a reasonable manner consistent with the purpose of preventing discrimination in favor of HCEs because the results of the general test are distorted through the use of allocation rates produced by the allocation of small amounts to the lowest paid group of NHCEs.

The examples provided in the IRS Memorandum are not intended to limit the situations where a plan design may be found to be an unreasonable interpretation of the nondiscrimination regulations. Additional situations with similar facts may also violate the requirement that the regulations must be interpreted in a reasonable manner. Also, additional factors may also be considered in determining whether the plan discriminates in favor of the HCEs.

Q 4:11 What does nondiscrimination in amount of contributions or benefits mean?

The first requirement a retirement plan must satisfy is that either the contributions (see Q 4:12) or the benefits (see Q 4:14) provided under the plan must be nondiscriminatory in amount. [Treas. Reg. §§ 1.401(a)(4)-2, 1.401(a)(4)-3]

A defined contribution plan (see Q 2:2) generally will satisfy the nondiscriminatory amount requirement by showing that the *contributions* provided under the plan are nondiscriminatory in amount. However, a defined contribution plan also is permitted to satisfy the nondiscriminatory amount requirement by showing that the *equivalent benefits* provided under the plan are nondiscriminatory in amount (see Q 4:22). 401(k) plans are deemed to satisfy this requirement because such plans must contain a qualified cash-or-deferred arrangement that incorporates a nondiscriminatory amount requirement; however, plans providing for employee or matching contributions must satisfy special rules (see chapter 27). [Treas. Reg. § 1.401(a)(4)-1(b)(2)(ii)(B)]

A defined benefit plan (see Q 2:3) generally will satisfy the nondiscriminatory amount requirement by showing that the employer-provided *benefits* under the plan are nondiscriminatory in amount. However, a defined benefit plan also is permitted to satisfy the nondiscriminatory amount requirement by showing that the *equivalent contributions* provided under the plan are nondiscriminatory in amount (see Q 4:22).

Plans may use certain alternative methods to demonstrate that contributions or benefits are nondiscriminatory in amount.

Q 4:12 How is the nondiscrimination in amount of contributions requirement satisfied?

To determine whether the contributions provided under a defined contribution plan (see Q 2:2) are nondiscriminatory in amount (see Q 4:11), two safe harbor tests are permitted. [Treas. Reg. § 1.401(a)(4)-2(b)(1)]

The first safe harbor is design based. A defined contribution plan complies with this safe harbor if the plan allocates all employer contributions and forfeitures (see Q 9:18) for the plan year under a single uniform formula that allocates to each participant the same percentage of compensation, the same dollar amount, or the same dollar amount for each uniform unit of service (not to exceed one week) performed by the participant. Differences in allocations attributable to permitted disparity (see chapter 7) do not cause the plan to fail to satisfy this safe harbor. The following is an example of a defined contribution plan formula that satisfies this safe harbor:

The company shall contribute each plan year during which the plan is in effect on behalf of each participant an amount equal to 10 percent of compensation.

[Treas. Reg. § 1.401(a)(4)-2(b)(2)]

The second safe harbor permits a defined contribution plan to have a uniform allocation formula weighted for age or service if the average rate of allocations for HCEs (see Q 3:2) under the plan does not exceed the average rate of allocations for NHCEs (see Q 3:12) under the plan. A single uniform formula weighted for age or service is one that would allocate to each participant the same percentage of compensation or the same dollar amount if every participant was the same age and had the same number of years of service or plan participation. A uniform allocation formula need not grant points for both age and service, but must grant points for at least one of them. If points are granted for years of service, the number of years taken into account may be limited to a maximum number. Plans using this second safe harbor need not grant points for units of compensation; but if the allocation formula takes compensation into account, the plan must provide the same number of points for each unit of compensation, and each unit of compensation must not exceed $200. This type of plan is known as a uniform points plan.

> **Example.** Adam & William Corporation adopts a profit sharing plan that allocates its plan contribution among the participants based on points awarded to each participant. Each participant is awarded one point for each $200 of compensation earned during the plan year and ten points for each year of service with Adam & William. The contributions allocated to HCEs average 8 percent of compensation, and the allocations to the NHCEs average 10 percent of compensation. The second safe harbor is satisfied.

[Treas. Reg. § 1.401(a)(4)-2(b)(3)]

The safe harbors are available even though the plan contains, in addition to other permitted provisions, the following provisions:

1. The plan limits allocations to employees in accordance with Section 415 (see chapter 6).

2. The plan limits allocations otherwise provided under the formula to a maximum dollar amount or a maximum percentage of compensation, or it limits the dollar amount of compensation or the number of years of

service or plan participation taken into account in determining the amount of allocations.

3. The plan provides that an allocation to an employee for the plan year is conditioned on the employee's employment on the last day of the plan year or on the employee's completion of a minimum number of hours of service during the plan year (not to exceed 1,000). (See Qs 5:20, 5:21.)

[Treas. Reg. § 1.401(a)(4)-2(b)(4)]

Plans that do not satisfy either of the safe harbors must satisfy the general test for nondiscrimination in the amount of contributions (see Q 4:13).

Q 4:13   Is there a general test for the nondiscrimination in amount of contributions requirement?

Plans that do not satisfy either of the safe harbors (see Q 4:12) generally comply with this nondiscrimination requirement only if each rate group under the plan satisfies the minimum coverage requirements (see Q 5:15). Each rate group consists of an HCE (see Q 3:2) participating in the plan and all other participants (both highly and non-highly compensated) who have an allocation rate greater than or equal to that HCE's allocation rate. In determining allocation rates, permitted disparity may be taken into account. [Treas. Reg. § 1.401(a)(4)-2(c)(1)]

The allocation rate for an employee equals the sum of the allocations to the employee's account for the plan year expressed either as a percentage of compensation or as a dollar amount. The amounts taken into account in determining allocation rates include all employer contributions and forfeitures that are allocated to the employee's account for the plan year, but exclude allocations of income, expenses, gains, and losses. [Treas. Reg. § 1.401(a)(4)-2(c)(2)]

For purposes of determining whether a rate group satisfies the minimum coverage requirements, the rate group is treated as if it were a separate plan that benefits only the employees included in the rate group for the plan year. Generally, the rules that apply in determining whether a rate group satisfies the minimum coverage requirements are the same as apply in determining whether a plan satisfies those requirements. For example, if the rate group does not satisfy the ratio percentage test (see Q 5:16), the rate group must satisfy the average benefit test (see Q 5:17). [Treas. Reg. §§ 1.401(a)(4)-2(c)(3), 1.401(a)(4)-2(c)(4)]

Example 1. (a) A & L Fleischer Ltd. has only six nonexcludable employees, all of whom benefit under Plan D. The HCEs are H1 and H2, and the NHCEs are N1 through N4. For the 2010 plan year, H1 and N1 through N4 have an allocation rate of 5 percent of plan-year compensation. For the same plan year, H2 has an allocation rate of 7.5 percent of plan-year compensation.

(b) There are two rate groups under Plan D. Rate group 1 consists of H1 and all those employees who have an allocation rate greater than or equal to H1's allocation rate (5 percent). Thus, rate group 1 consists of H1, H2, and N1 through N4. Rate group 2 consists only of H2 because no other employee has an allocation rate greater than or equal to H2's allocation rate (7.5 percent).

(c) The ratio percentage for rate group 2 is zero percent, that is, zero percent (the percentage of all non-highly compensated nonexcludable employees who are in the rate group) divided by 50 percent (the percentage of all highly compensated nonexcludable employees who are in the rate group). Therefore, rate group 2 does not satisfy the ratio percentage test. Rate group 2 also does not satisfy the nondiscriminatory classification test and therefore does not satisfy the minimum coverage requirements. As a result, Plan D does not satisfy the general test even though the ratio percentage for rate group 1 is 100 percent.

Example 2. (a) The facts are the same as those in Example 1, except that N4 has an allocation rate of 8 percent.

(b) There are two rate groups in Plan D. Rate group 1 consists of H1 and all those employees who have an allocation rate greater than or equal to H1's allocation rate (5 percent). Thus rate group 1 consists of H1, H2, and N1 through N4. Rate group 2 consists of H2 and all those employees who have an allocation rate greater than or equal to H2's allocation rate (7.5 percent). Thus, rate group 2 consists of H2 and N4.

(c) Rate group 1 satisfies the ratio percentage test because the ratio percentage of the rate group is 100 percent, that is, 100 percent (the percentage of all non-highly compensated nonexcludable employees who are in the rate group) divided by 100 percent (the percentage of all highly compensated nonexcludable employees who are in the rate group).

(d) Rate group 2 does not satisfy the ratio percentage test because the ratio percentage of the rate group is 50 percent, that is, 25 percent (the percentage of all non-highly compensated nonexcludable employees who are in the rate group) divided by 50 percent (the percentage of all highly compensated nonexcludable employees who are in the rate group).

(e) However, rate group 2 does satisfy the nondiscriminatory classification test because the ratio percentage of the rate group (50 percent) is greater than the safe harbor percentage applicable to the plan (45.5 percent).

(f) If rate group 2 satisfies the average benefit percentage test, then rate group 2 satisfies the minimum coverage requirements. In that case, Plan D satisfies the general test because each rate group under the plan satisfies the minimum coverage requirements.

Q 4:14   How is the nondiscrimination in amount of benefits requirement satisfied?

The basic rules for determining whether a plan is nondiscriminatory with respect to the amount of benefits generally apply to defined benefit plans (see Q 2:3). They may, however, also be applied to defined contribution plans (see Q 2:2) in testing nondiscrimination on the basis of equivalent benefits (see Qs 4:11, 4:22). [Treas. Reg. § 1.401(a)(4)-3(a)]

There are five safe harbors under which a plan is considered nondiscriminatory with respect to the amount of benefits (see Qs 4:15–4:17). Four of the safe harbors are design based and require no determination or comparison of actual benefits under the plan. All of the safe harbors require that the plan have a uniform benefit formula, that each subsidized optional form of benefit (see Q 10:45) be provided on similar terms to substantially all participants, that the plan not require employee contributions, that the plan have a uniform normal retirement age for all employees, and that each employee's benefit be accrued over the same years of service that are taken into account in applying the plan's benefit formula to that employee. Uniform normal retirement age means a single normal retirement age under the plan that does not exceed the maximum age and that is the same for all of the employees in a given group. The maximum age is generally 65. The definition of uniform normal retirement age has been expanded to provide generally that a plan's normal retirement provisions will not fail to be uniform merely because benefits commence on different dates for different employees, provided that each employee's normal retirement date does not differ by more than six months from a uniform normal retirement age. [Treas. Reg. §§ 1.401(a)(4)-3(b)(2), 1.401(a)(4)-12]

Plans that do not satisfy any of the five safe harbors must satisfy the general test for nondiscrimination in the amount of benefits (see Q 4:18).

The safe harbors are available even though the plan contains, in addition to other permitted provisions, the following:

1. The plan provides for benefits that were previously accrued under a formula that does not satisfy any of the safe harbors.

2. The plan limits accruals in accordance with Section 415 (see chapter 6) or provides for increases in accrued benefits based solely on adjustments to the dollar limitation.

3. The plan limits accruals to a maximum dollar amount or a maximum percentage of compensation, or it limits the dollar amount of compensation or the number of years of service or participation taken into account in determining the amount of accruals.

4. The plan takes permitted disparity into account (see chapter 7).

[Treas. Reg. § 1.401(a)(4)-3(b)(6)]

Q 4:15   What safe harbors apply to unit credit plans for the requirement of nondiscrimination in amount of benefits?

The first two safe harbors enable *unit credit plans* (see Q 2:18) to satisfy the nondiscrimination requirement with respect to the amount of benefits on the basis of plan design. A unit credit plan is a defined benefit plan (see Q 2:3) that contains a formula under which all employees accrue a fixed benefit (either as a percentage of compensation or as a dollar amount) for each year of service, and all employees with the same number of years accrue the same benefit. For example, a plan constitutes a unit credit plan for this purpose if it provides a benefit of (1) 1 percent of average compensation times years of service up to 20 and (2) 1.25 percent of average compensation times years of service in excess of 20 but not in excess of 30.

The first safe harbor applies to unit credit plans that accrue benefits under the $133^{1}/_{3}$ percent rule (i.e., the benefit accrued in a plan year does not exceed by more than $133^{1}/_{3}$ percent the benefit accrued in any prior plan year). [I.R.C. § 411(b)(1)(B); Treas. Reg. § 1.401(a)(4)-3(b)(3)(i)]

> **Example.** Plan A provides a specific annual accrual for each employee in the plan payable at normal retirement age. For each of the first five years of service, the annual accrual is 1.5 percent of compensation. For the next five years of service, the annual accrual is 1.75 percent; for each additional year of service, the annual accrual is 2 percent. Plan A satisfies this safe harbor because the benefit accrued in a later year (2 percent) does not exceed the lowest benefit accrual in a prior year (1.5 percent) by more than $133^{1}/_{3}$ percent (2% ÷ 1.5% = $133^{1}/_{3}$%).

The second safe harbor applies to unit credit plans that accrue benefits under the fractional rule; that is, the employee's accrued benefit (see Q 9:2) as of a given year equals the benefit projected as of normal retirement age (see Q 10:55) multiplied by the ratio of the employee's years of service as of that year to the employee's projected years of service as of normal retirement age. [I.R.C. § 411(b)(1)(C)]

A plan under which benefits are calculated under a unit credit formula but accrue under the fractional accrual rule may also satisfy the unit credit safe harbor even though all employees with the same number of years of service may not accrue the same benefit. Such a plan satisfies the safe harbor only if the benefit (expressed as a percentage of compensation or a dollar amount) that any employee may accrue in any year is not more than one-third larger than the benefit that any other employee can accrue (disregarding employees with more than 33 years of projected service under the plan). [Treas. Reg. § 1.401(a)(4)-3(b)(4)(i)(C)(1)]

> **Example.** Plan B provides for a benefit equal to 1.6 percent of compensation times each year of service up to 25. Plan B further provides that the plan benefits accrue under the fractional rule. The greatest benefit that an employee can earn in any one year is 1.6 percent of compensation (this is the case for any employee in the plan who will have 25 or fewer years of projected service at normal retirement age). The lowest benefit that will accrue for an employee in the plan with no more than 33 projected years of service is 1.212 percent (this is the case for any employee in the plan with 33 years of projected service under the formula: 1.6% × 25 ÷ 33). Since 1.6 percent is not more than one-third larger than 1.212 percent, Plan B satisfies this safe harbor.

Q 4:16   What safe harbors apply to flat benefit plans for the requirement of nondiscrimination in amount of benefits?

The third safe harbor is a design-based safe harbor for *flat benefit plans* (see Q 2:17) that satisfy the fractional accrual rule (e.g., a defined benefit plan (see Q 2:3) that provides a benefit of 50 percent of compensation, accrued ratably over all years of service). Such a plan satisfies the safe harbor only if the plan provides that the maximum flat benefit will be accrued over a period of at least 25 years. The 25-year rule reduces the potential differences in the rates at which benefits accrue between those employees who enter the plan at younger ages and those who enter at older ages. In this way, this safe harbor applies nondiscrimination rules to flat benefit plans in a manner that takes into account the rate of benefit accrual.

The 25-year rule does not mean, however, that an employee must participate in a plan for 25 years to accrue the maximum annual retirement benefit (see Q 6:11). Rather, the maximum annual retirement benefit can be accrued in less than 25 years if the plan formula would produce a maximum calculated benefit in 25 years that is higher than the maximum annual retirement benefit permitted. The plan must still limit actual benefits to the maximum amount. For example, assume that an employee is age 55 and earns $224,515 (see Qs 6:45, 6:46) and that the maximum annual retirement benefit permitted is $185,000 (82.4 percent of the employee's compensation). To satisfy the safe harbor while permitting this employee to accrue the maximum annual retirement benefit in ten years, the employer could establish a plan that provides a benefit of 206 percent of compensation at normal retirement age, accrued ratably over all years of service (thereby satisfying the fractional accrual rule). The benefit would be proportionately reduced for years of service less than 25, and the accrued benefit at any time would be limited to the maximum annual retirement benefit. Under this plan, at age 65, the employee would have ten years of service and would therefore accrue a benefit of 10/25 of 206 percent of compensation, or 82.4 percent of compensation. [Treas. Reg. § 1.401(a)(4)-3(b)(4)(i)(C)(2)]

The fourth safe harbor, also for flat benefit plans, requires that the average accrual rate of NHCEs (see Q 3:12) as a group be at least 70 percent of the average accrual rate of HCEs (see Q 3:2) as a group. This safe harbor is applied by taking into account all nonexcludable employees of the employer whether they are covered under the plan or not. [Treas. Reg. § 1.401(a)(4)-3(b)(4)(i)(C)(3)]

Q 4:17   What safe harbor applies to insurance contract plans for the requirement of nondiscrimination in amount of benefits?

The fifth and final safe harbor is for *insurance contract plans* (see Q 8:11). Because these plans are subject to special accrual rules and deliver benefits in the form of insurance contract cash values, they are not designed in a way that accords with any of the four safe harbors discussed above (see Qs 4:15, 4:16). An insurance contract plan generally satisfies this safe harbor if it satisfies a special accrual rule and certain funding requirements, and if the stated benefit formula under the plan would satisfy either the unit credit fractional accrual safe harbor (see Q 4:15) or the flat benefit fractional accrual safe harbor (see Q 4:16) if the stated normal retirement benefit were accrued ratably over each employee's period of plan participation through normal retirement age (see Q 10:55). [Treas. Reg. § 1.401(a)(4)-3(b)(5)]

Q 4:18   Is there a general test for the nondiscrimination in amount of benefits requirement?

Those plans that do not satisfy any of the five safe harbors (see Qs 4:15–4:17) must satisfy the general test for nondiscrimination with respect to the amount of benefits. Under this test, the employer must identify, for each HCE (see Q 3:2) benefiting under the plan, the group of employees consisting of that HCE and all other employees (both HCEs and NHCEs; see Q 3:12) with equal or greater normal and most valuable accrual rates (a rate group). Thus, depending on their accrual rates, employees may be included in more than one rate group. A rate group must be determined for each HCE benefiting under the plan. Each rate group so identified must satisfy the minimum coverage requirements (see Q 5:15) as though it were a separate plan. Generally, the rules that apply in determining whether a rate group satisfies the minimum coverage requirements are the same as apply in determining whether a plan satisfies those requirements. For example, if the rate group does not satisfy the ratio percentage test (see Q 5:16), the rate group must satisfy the average benefit test (see Q 5:17). [Treas. Reg. §§ 1.401(a)(4)-3(c)(1), 1.401(a)(4)-3(c)(2), 1.401(a)(4)-3(c)(4)]

Example 1. (a) BeeAndEll Bernstein, Inc. has 1,100 nonexcludable employees: N1 through N1000 are NHCEs, and H1 through H100 are HCEs. BeeAndEll maintains Plan A, a defined benefit plan that benefits all 1,100 nonexcludable employees. The normal and most valuable accrual rates (determined as a percentage of average annual compensation) for the employees in Plan A for the 2010 plan year are listed in the following table:

Employee	Normal Accrual Rate	Most Valuable Accrual Rate
N1–N100	1.0	1.4
N101–N500	1.5	3.0
N501–N750	2.0	2.65
N751–N1000	2.3	2.8
H1–H50	1.5	2.0
H51–H100	2.0	2.65

(b) There are 100 rate groups in Plan A because there are 100 HCEs in Plan A.

(c) Rate group 1 consists of H1 and all those employees who have a normal accrual rate greater than or equal to H1's normal accrual rate (1.5 percent) and who also have a most valuable accrual rate greater than or equal to H1's most valuable accrual rate (2.0 percent). Thus, rate group 1 consists of H1 through H100 and N101 through N1000.

(d) Rate group 1 satisfies the ratio percentage test because the ratio percentage of the rate group is 90 percent; that is, 90 percent (the percentage of all non-highly compensated nonexcludable employees who are in the rate group) divided by 100 percent (the percentage of all highly compensated nonexcludable employees who are in the rate group).

(e) Because H1 through H50 have the same normal accrual rates and the same most valuable accrual rates, the rate group with respect to each of them is identical. Thus, because rate group 1 satisfies the minimum coverage requirements, rate groups 2 through 50 also satisfy the minimum coverage requirements.

(f) Rate group 51 consists of H51 and all those employees who have a normal accrual rate greater than or equal to H51's normal accrual rate (2.0 percent) and who also have a most valuable accrual rate greater than or equal to H51's most valuable accrual rate (2.65 percent). Thus, rate group 51 consists of H51 through H100 and N501 through N1000. (Even though N101 through N500 have a most valuable accrual rate (3.0 percent) greater than H51's most valuable accrual rate (2.65 percent), they are not included in this rate group because their normal accrual rate (1.5 percent) is less than H51's normal accrual rate (2.0 percent).)

(g) Rate group 51 satisfies the ratio percentage test because the ratio percentage of the rate group is 100 percent; that is, 50 percent (the percentage of all non-highly compensated nonexcludable employees who are in the rate group) divided by 50 percent (the percentage of all highly compensated nonexcludable employees who are in the rate group).

(h) Because H51 through H100 have the same normal accrual rates and the same most valuable accrual rates, the rate group with respect to each of them is identical. Thus, because rate group 51 satisfies the minimum coverage requirements, rate groups 52 through 100 also satisfy the minimum coverage requirements.

(i) The benefits under Plan A are nondiscriminatory in amount because each rate group under the plan satisfies the minimum coverage requirements.

A plan that fails the general test discussed above may demonstrate that, on the basis of all relevant facts and circumstances, the plan is not discriminatory. This demonstration is available only to a plan that fails the general test with respect to 5 percent or less of the HCEs (i.e., the plan could pass the test were it allowed to disregard the participation of not more than 5 percent of the HCEs). For this purpose, 5 percent of the number of HCEs may be determined by rounding to the nearest whole number (e.g., 1.4 rounds to 1 and 1.5 rounds to 2). Among the relevant factors that will be considered in determining nondiscrimination are:

1. The extent to which the plan fails the general test;
2. The extent to which the failure is for reasons other than the design of the plan;
3. Whether the HCEs causing the failure are 5 percent owners (in actuality, more than 5 percent; see Q 3:4) or are among the highest-paid non excludable employees;
4. Whether the failure is attributable to a nonrecurring event (e.g., a plant closing); and
5. The extent to which the failure is attributable to benefits accrued under a prior benefit structure or when a participant was not a highly compensated employee.

[Treas. Reg. §§ 1.401(a)(4)-3(c)(3), 1.401(a)(4)-3(c)(4)]

Example 2. The facts are the same as in Example 1, except that H96 has a most valuable accrual rate of 3.5. Each of the rate groups is the same as in Example 1, except that rate group 96 consists solely of H96 because no other employee has a most valuable accrual rate greater than 3.5. Because the plan would satisfy the general test by disregarding H96 (who constitutes less than 5 percent of the HCEs in the plan), IRS may determine that, on the basis of all of the relevant facts and circumstances, the plan does not discriminate with respect to the amount of benefits.

The normal accrual rate for a plan year is the increase in the employee's accrued benefit (see Q 9:2) during the measurement period (current plan year, current plan year and all prior years, or current plan year and all prior and future years), divided by the employee's testing service (the employee's years of service as defined in the plan for purposes of applying the benefit formula under the plan) during the measurement period, and expressed either as a dollar amount or as a percentage of the employee's average annual compensation. [Treas. Reg. § 1.401(a)(4)-3(d)]

The most valuable accrual rate for a plan year is the increase in the employee's most valuable optional form of payment of the accrued benefit during the measurement period, divided by the employee's testing service during the measurement period, and expressed either as a dollar amount or as a percentage of the employee's average annual compensation. It reflects the value of all benefits accrued or treated as accrued that are payable in any form and at any time under the plan, including early retirement benefits, retirement-type subsidies, early retirement window benefits, and so forth. Alternatively, an employee's most valuable accrual rate for the current plan year may be determined as the employee's highest most valuable accrual rate determined for any prior plan year. This option may be used only if the employee's normal accrual rate has not changed significantly from the normal accrual rate for such prior plan year and there has been no plan amendment in the interim period that affects the determination of the most valuable accrual rate. [Treas. Reg. §§ 1.401(a)(4)-3(d)(1)(ii), 1.401(a)(4)-3(d)(1)(iii), 1.401(a)(4)-3(d)(1)(iv)]

Q 4:19   How is the nondiscrimination in amount requirement affected by an acquisition or disposition?

IRS has opined that, with the integrated approach underlying the nondiscrimination requirement (see Q 4:10) and the minimum coverage requirement (see Q 5:15), any failure to satisfy the nondiscrimination requirement can be viewed as failure to satisfy the minimum coverage requirement. Consequently, failure to meet the nondiscrimination requirement will subject HCEs (see Q 3:2) to special sanctions (see Q 5:28). [Preamble to final regulations (Sept. 19, 1991)]

When there is an acquisition (or disposition) among a controlled group of employers (see Q 5:29), the minimum coverage requirement is treated as having been met during the transition period if the minimum coverage requirement was met before the acquisition and there is no other significant change in coverage. [I.R.C. § 410(b)(6)(C); Treas. Reg. § 1.410(b)-2(f); Priv. Ltr. Rul. 9707022]

IRS issued a ruling concerning the effect of an acquisition or disposition on the nondiscrimination in amount requirement (see Q 4:11). [Rev. Rul. 2004-11, 2004-1 C.B. 480] In the ruling, IRS describes a situation and asks:

1. Will the plans described below be treated as satisfying the requirements relating to nondiscriminatory contributions or benefits and the ADP and ACP tests (see Qs 27:18, 27:77), as well as the minimum coverage requirement, by reason of the special transition rule for certain acquisitions or dispositions?

2. Does a significant change in a plan's coverage during the transition period make a plan ineligible for the transition rule or merely curtail the transition period during which the special rule may be applied to the plan?

In the factual situation, subsidiary S, which is part of X, a controlled group of corporations (see Q 5:30), sponsors a defined benefit plan (see Q 2:3) and a profit sharing plan (see Q 2:6) for its employees. The plan year of each plan is the calendar year, and only employees of S are eligible to participate in the plans. The defined benefit plan would satisfy a nondiscrimination safe harbor (see Q 4:14) but for the fact that the plan provides a subsidized early retirement benefit that is not currently available to substantially all employees (see Q 4:20). For purposes of satisfying the nondiscrimination requirements, the defined benefit plan is therefore restructured into two component plans, one component consisting of all the accruals and other benefits, rights, and features provided to those employees to whom the subsidized early retirement benefit is currently available, and the other component consisting of all the accruals and other benefits, rights, and features provided to those employees to whom the subsidized early retirement benefit is not currently available. [Treas. Reg. § 401(a)(4)-9(c)] Each of the component plans separately satisfies a nondiscrimination safe harbor and the other nondiscrimination requirements and also separately satisfies the minimum coverage requirement by satisfying the ratio-percentage test (see Q 5:16). The profit sharing plan includes only a qualified cash-or-deferred arrangement (CODA; see Q 27:9) and matching contributions that are subject to the nondiscrimination requirements (see Qs 27:75, 27:77).

On June 22, 2005, all of the stock of S is sold to corporation Y. Immediately before the sale, the defined benefit plan maintained by S satisfies the minimum coverage requirement by satisfying the ratio percentage test, and the CODA and the matching contribution portion of the profit sharing plan each satisfy the ratio percentage test. For this purpose, neither plan is aggregated with any other plan, and X does not apply the minimum coverage requirement on the basis of separate lines of business (see Q 5:44). In addition, each of the component plans under the defined benefit plan satisfies the nondiscrimination requirements and the ratio percentage test immediately before the sale.

S continues to maintain the profit sharing plan without change after the sale, and S also continues to maintain the defined benefit plan but amends the plan to significantly change the benefit formula effective April 1, 2006.

The sale of S to Y is an acquisition or disposition, and the defined benefit plan and each of the disaggregated portions of the profit sharing plan satisfy the minimum coverage requirement without regard to the special transition rule immediately before the acquisition or disposition. The sale would affect the data required to be taken into account in applying the minimum coverage requirement to the plans in the absence of the special transition rule.

There is no significant change in the 401(k) plan (see Q 27:1) or the coverage of the 401(k) plan (other than the acquisition or disposition) during the transition period. Likewise, there is no significant change in the 401(m) plan (see Q 27:73) or in the coverage of the 401(m) plan. Therefore, the special transition rule may be applied to each of the disaggregated portions of the profit sharing plan for the transition period starting on the date of sale of S to Y (June 22, 2005) and continuing through December 31, 2006 (that is, the last day of the plan year beginning on January 1, 2006). Accordingly, the profit sharing plan will be treated as satisfying the minimum coverage requirement during the transition period.

The coverage requirement for a CODA requires the group of employees eligible to benefit under the arrangement to satisfy the minimum coverage requirement. Therefore, the special rules for certain acquisitions or dispositions may be applied for purposes of satisfying that requirement. Accordingly, the CODA will be treated as satisfying the minimum coverage requirement during the transition period.

On the other hand, the ADP test and ACP test, respectively, do not refer to the minimum coverage requirement. Rather, these tests require the comparison of the average of the actual deferral ratios and actual contribution ratios of the group of eligible HCEs and the group of eligible NHCEs (see Q 3:12) under the plan. Therefore, the special rule for certain acquisitions or dispositions does not apply for purposes of satisfying the ADP test or the ACP test and thus provides no relief from satisfying these tests using the averages of the actual deferral ratios and actual contribution ratios, respectively, of the eligible employees under the plan. Accordingly, the CODA and the matching contributions under the profit sharing plan must satisfy the ADP test and the ACP test following the sale of S to Y using these ratios.

The benefit formula in the defined benefit plan does not satisfy a nondiscrimination safe harbor because the plan provides a subsidized early retirement benefit that is not currently available to substantially all employees. However, for purposes of satisfying the nondiscrimination requirements, the plan is restructured into two component plans each of which separately satisfies a nondiscrimination safe harbor. Each component plan is required to separately satisfy the minimum coverage and nondiscrimination requirements. The minimum coverage requirement is applied to the component plans taking into account any special rules available (other than the permissive aggregation rules). Thus, for purposes of satisfying the nondiscrimination requirements, the special transition rule may be applied, provided (1) each component plan separately satisfies the nondiscrimination and minimum coverage requirements immediately before the acquisition or disposition and (2) neither the plan nor the coverage under the plan is significantly changed during the transition period (other than by reason of the change in the members of the group) or the plan meets such other requirements as IRS may prescribe.

Each component plan under the defined benefit plan separately satisfies the nondiscrimination and minimum coverage requirements immediately before the sale of S to Y, and there is no significant change in the defined benefit plan or in the coverage under the defined benefit plan (other than the acquisition or disposition) during the period following the sale and prior to April 1, 2006.

The plan amendment significantly changing the benefit formula in the defined benefit plan, effective April 1, 2006, is a significant change in the plan or in the coverage of the plan (other than the acquisition or disposition). For this purpose, a change in the plan means a change in the benefits or in the benefit levels under the plan.

The effect of the special transition rule is to provide time for a plan sponsor to consider what coverage or other plan changes will need to be made for the sponsor's plans to continue to satisfy the minimum coverage requirement following an acquisition or disposition. Thus, the plan sponsor is relieved from having to immediately amend its plans or otherwise effect coverage changes to comply with the minimum coverage requirement. The special transition rule is permissive, so that plan sponsors may choose to satisfy the minimum coverage requirement after an acquisition or disposition either with or without regard to the special transition rule. Furthermore, the transition period is the maximum period allowed to a plan sponsor before the sponsor must take into account the change in the employer resulting from the acquisition or disposition. There is no requirement to apply the transition relief for the whole of the allowable transition period. Thus, the effect of a significant change in a plan or in the coverage of a plan (other than the acquisition or disposition) during the transition period is to curtail the period effective as of the date of the change and not to make the plan retroactively ineligible to apply the special transition rule. Accordingly, the defined benefit plan will be treated as satisfying the nondiscrimination and minimum coverage requirements during the applicable transition period from June 22, 2005, through March 31, 2006.

Starting April 1, 2006, the defined benefit plan must satisfy the nondiscrimination and minimum coverage requirements without regard to the special transition rule. That is, the plan must satisfy these requirements taking into account the employees of Y. The profit sharing plan must satisfy the minimum coverage requirement taking into account the employees of Y starting the first day of the plan year beginning on January 1, 2007. The plan amendment significantly changing the benefit formula in the defined benefit plan does not curtail the profit sharing plan's transition period because the plans satisfy the minimum coverage requirement independently of each other.

In conclusion:

1. Under the facts set forth, the defined benefit plan will be treated as satisfying the nondiscrimination and minimum coverage requirements during the applicable transition period from June 22, 2005, through March 31, 2006. The profit sharing plan will be treated as satisfying the minimum coverage requirement by reason of the special transition rule during the plan's applicable transition period from the date of the sale through December 31, 2006. The CODA will also be treated as satisfying the minimum coverage requirement during this transition period. However, the CODA arrangement and the matching contributions under the profit sharing plan will not, by reason of the special transition rule, be treated as satisfying the ADP or the ACP test; and, therefore, the plan must satisfy these tests for the plan years ending on December 31, 2005, and December 31, 2006.

2. A significant change in a plan or in the coverage of a plan curtails the transition period, so that the special transition rule ceases to apply to the plan as of the date of the change. The change does not make the plan retroactively ineligible to apply the special rule.

Q 4:20   What is the nondiscriminatory availability requirement?

The second nondiscrimination requirement a qualified retirement plan must satisfy is that the benefits, rights, and features provided under the plan must be made both currently and effectively available to the participants in a nondiscriminatory manner. The benefits, rights, and features that must satisfy this requirement are the optional forms of benefits, ancillary benefits, and other rights and features provided under the plan. Each optional form of benefit, each ancillary benefit, and each other right or feature provided under a plan must separately satisfy the nondiscrimination requirements with respect to its availability. Two or more benefits, rights, and features may be permissively aggregated if one of the benefits, rights, or features is inherently of equal or greater value than the other, and if the more valuable benefit, right, or feature, standing alone, satisfies the current and effective availability requirements. [Treas. Reg. §§ 1.401(a)(4)-4(a), 1.401(a)(4)-4(b), 1.401(a)(4)-4(c), 1.401(a)(4)-4(d)(4)]

The term "optional form of benefit" (see Q 10:45) means a distribution alternative that is available under a qualified retirement plan. Different optional forms of benefit exist if the distribution alternative is not payable on substantially the same terms. The relevant terms include all terms affecting the value of the optional form, such as the actuarial assumptions used to determine the amount distributed or the method of benefit calculation (see Q 2:20). Different optional forms of benefit may result from differences in payment schedule, timing, commencement, medium of distribution (e.g., in cash or in kind), election rights, eligibility requirements, or the portion of the benefit to which the distribution alternative applies (see Qs 9:29–9:32). [Treas. Reg. § 1.401(a)(4)-4(e)(1); IRS Notice 96-67, 1996-2 C.B. 235]

> **Example.** Peterelke Greenberg Corporation adopts a defined benefit plan that benefits all employees of Divisions S and T. The plan offers a qualified joint and survivor annuity at normal retirement age, calculated by multiplying an employee's single life annuity payment by a factor. For an employee of Division S whose benefit commences at age 65, the plan provides a factor of 0.90; but for a similarly situated employee of Division T, the plan provides for a factor of 0.85. The qualified joint and survivor annuity is not available to employees of Divisions S and T on substantially the same terms and constitutes two separate optional forms of benefit.

The term "ancillary benefit" includes the following:

- Social Security supplements described in Section 411(a)(9)
- Disability benefits not in excess of a qualified disability benefit described in Section 411(a)(9)
- Ancillary life insurance and health insurance benefits
- Death benefits under a defined contribution plan (see Q 2:2)
- Preretirement death benefits under a defined benefit plan (see Q 2:3)
- Other similar benefits

Different ancillary benefits exist if an ancillary benefit is not available on substantially the same terms as another ancillary benefit. [Treas. Reg. § 1.401(a)(4)-4(e)(2)] IRS is considering issuing guidance that would clarify the types of ancillary benefits that are permitted to be provided in defined benefit plans. See Q 2:3 for details.

The term "other right or feature" means any right or feature applicable to participants, other than a right or feature taken into account as part of an optional form of benefit or ancillary benefit provided under the plan, and other than a right or feature that cannot reasonably be expected to be of meaningful value to an employee (e.g., administrative details). Different rights or features exist if the right or feature is not available on substantially the same terms as another right or feature. Other rights and features include, but are not limited to, the following:

- Plan loan provisions
- The right to direct investments [Priv. Ltr. Rul. 9137001]

- The right to a particular form of investment, including, for example, a particular class or type of employer securities (taking into account any difference in conversion, dividend, voting, liquidation preference, or other rights conferred under the security)
- The right to make rollover contributions and transfers to and from the plan

[Treas. Reg. § 1.401(a)(4)-4(e)(3)]

The benefits of a beneficiary other than a surviving spouse may be transferred directly to an IRA (see Q 34:33). If a plan does offer direct rollovers to nonspouse beneficiaries of some, but not all, participants, such rollovers must be offered on a nondiscriminatory basis because the opportunity to make a direct rollover is a benefit, right, or feature that is subject to the nondiscrimination requirements. [IRS Notice 2007-7, § V, Q&A-14, 2007-1 C.B. 395]

A defined contribution plan permitted participants to direct the investment of their account balances (see Q 9:2). Participants who terminated employment before normal retirement age (see Q 10:55) would receive their vested account balances (see Q 9:1) at normal retirement age unless the participant consented to receive an immediate distribution of the vested account balance (see Q 10:61). However, the plan also provided that upon termination of employment the participant could no longer direct investments and that the participant's account would be automatically invested in a money market fund until distributed. IRS ruled that consent to a distribution is not valid if, based on facts and circumstances, the plan imposes a significant detriment on any participant who does not consent to the distribution. IRS concluded that the loss of the right to direct investments was a significant detriment imposed by the plan on a participant who did not consent to a distribution. As a result, IRS ruled that the plan permitted an immediate distribution without a valid consent and failed to meet the consent requirements. [Rev. Rul. 96-47, 1996-2 C.B. 213]

A company establishes two mirror image defined contribution plans. One plan covers the sole owner, the other plan covers the remaining employees, and the owner is the sole trustee of both plans. The plans follow different investment philosophies, but neither plan permits a participant to direct investments. IRS representatives opined that this arrangement is permissible; however, this arrangement appears to be nothing more than an attempt to permit the owner to direct the investments of the owner's account and to deny that right to the other employees. Similarly, IRS representatives have also opined that, where a plan permitted participants to use an investment manager and only HCEs (see Q 3:2) had sufficient account balances to satisfy the minimum amount established by the investment manager, the nondiscriminatory availability requirement was not violated.

A plan must satisfy the nondiscriminatory availability requirement not only with respect to employees who are currently benefiting under the plan but also with respect to employees with accrued benefits (see Q 9:2) who are not currently benefiting under the plan (i.e., frozen participants). A plan satisfies the availability requirement with respect to this latter group of employees if any of the following requirements is met:

1. The benefit, right, or feature must be one that would satisfy the current and effective availability requirements if it were not available to any employee currently benefiting under the plan.

2. The benefit, right, or feature must be one that would satisfy the current and effective availability requirements if all frozen participants were treated as employees currently benefiting under the plan.

3. No change in the availability of the benefit, right, or feature may have been made that is first effective in the current plan year with respect to a frozen participant.

4. Any change in the availability of the benefit, right, or feature that is first effective in the current plan year with respect to a frozen participant must be made in a nondiscriminatory manner. Thus, any expansion in the availability of the benefit, right, or feature to any highly compensated frozen participant must be applied on a consistent basis to all non-highly compensated frozen participants. Similarly, any contraction in the availability of the benefit, right, or feature that affects any non-highly compensated frozen participant must be applied on a consistent basis to all highly compensated frozen participants.

[Treas. Reg. § 1.401(a)(4)-4(d)(2)]

Certain corrective amendments to the availability of benefits, rights, and features are permitted. Because it is difficult or impossible, in many cases, to make a benefit, right, or feature meaningfully available on a retroactive basis, a corrective amendment increasing availability is required only on a prospective basis. However, in order to take the correction into account for a plan year, the group of employees to whom the benefit, right, or feature is available (after taking the amendment into account) generally must satisfy a nondiscriminatory requirement. In addition, the amendment must remain in effect until the end of the plan year following the year in which the amendment is effective and must not be part of a pattern of amendments used to correct repeated failures of the same benefit, right, or feature. Other rules relating to retroactive correction also apply (e.g., the requirement that the correction be made no later than the 15th day of the tenth month after the close of a plan year).

As an alternative to increasing availability, an employer may make a corrective amendment by the last day of the plan year eliminating the benefit, right, or feature (to the extent permitted under Section 411(d)(6)). In that case, the amendment will be treated as if it were in effect throughout the plan year for purposes of nondiscrimination testing. [Treas. Reg. § 1.401(a)(4)-11(g)]

IRS representatives have opined that permitting an HCE to waive participation in a plan, but not permitting an NHCE (see Q 3:12) to waive participation, does not violate the nondiscriminatory availability requirement (see Q 5:27).

For a discussion of whether life insurance policies acquired by a plan must satisfy the nondiscrimination requirements, see Q 15:16.

Q 4:21   What is the nondiscriminatory requirement for plan amendments?

The third nondiscrimination requirement a qualified retirement plan must satisfy is that the effect or timing of plan amendments must be nondiscriminatory. Under this requirement, plan amendments must not have the effect of discriminating significantly in favor of highly compensated active employees (see Q 3:3) or highly compensated former employees (see Q 3:11). A plan amendment includes the establishment or termination of the plan and any change in the benefits, rights, or features, benefit formulas, or allocation formulas under the plan. Whether a plan meets this requirement depends on the relevant facts and circumstances. [Treas. Reg. § 1.401(a)(4)-5(a)(1)]

One court ruled that an employer is not prohibited from amending a plan to provide enhanced early retirement benefits and limiting those benefits to employees selected by the employer. [McNab v. General Motors Corp., 1998 WL 857853 (7th Cir. 1998); see also Piner v. E.I. DuPont de Nemours & Co., 2000 WL 1699837 (4th Cir. 2000)] IRS has ruled that an employer that maintains separate retirement plans for its HCEs (see Q 3:2) and NHCEs (see Q 3:12) violated the nondiscrimination requirements when it amended the NHCE plan to provide annual benefits for the HCEs. An HCE's years of service were included in the computation of accrued benefits under both plans, and benefits provided by the NHCE plan were not offset by benefits provided by the HCE plan. Thus, there was a duplication of service and benefits that discriminated in favor of the HCEs. [Rev. Rul. 99-51, 1999-2 C.B. 652; Treas. Reg. §§ 1.401(a)(4)-1(c)(2), 1.401(a)(4)-5(a)(1), 1.401(a)(4)-5(a)(2), 1.401(a)(4)-11(d)(2), 1.401(a)(4)-11(d)(3)]

> **Example.** Jennifer Corporation maintained a defined benefit plan, Plan X, benefiting its HCEs and NHCEs. Under Plan X, each employee's accrued benefit equaled an annual benefit commencing at normal retirement age of 1 percent of average annual compensation for each year of service, and a year of service included all years of service with Jennifer Corporation.
>
> Plan X was amended effective as of December 31, 2010 (the spin-off date) to become two plans: Plan X-H covering the HCEs and Plan X-N covering the NHCEs. The assets and benefit liabilities under Plan X as of the spin-off date were properly allocated between Plan X-H and Plan X-N. Pursuant to the terms of the amendment, NHCEs were excluded from participation in Plan X-H, and HCEs were excluded from participation in Plan X-N. In addition, the amendment provided that there would be no benefit accruals under Plan X-H after the spin-off date; however, benefit accruals continued under Plan X's original formula for the NHCEs in Plan X-N.
>
> Jennifer Corporation later amends Plan X-N to include the HCEs and to provide the HCEs with an annual benefit commencing at normal retirement age equal to 1 percent of average annual compensation for each year of service with Jennifer Corporation. The years of service included in the computation of the HCEs' accrued benefit under Plan X-H are included in the computation of their benefits under Plan X-N as well, and the benefits

employees accrued under Plan X-N are not offset by their accrued benefits under Plan X-H. Thus, there is a duplication of service and benefits that impermissively discriminates in favor of the HCEs, and Jennifer Corporation cannot use a series of plan amendments to accomplish what would normally be prohibited if it were attempted through a single amendment.

A plan does not satisfy this requirement if the timing of a plan amendment or series of amendments (including amendments terminating the plan) discriminates significantly in favor of highly compensated active or former employees at the time the amendment first becomes effective. Relevant facts and circumstances include the relative numbers of highly and non-highly compensated active and former employees affected by the plan amendment, the relative accrued benefits (see Q 9:2) of the highly and non-highly compensated active and former employees before and after the effective date of the plan amendment, the relative length of service of the highly and non-highly compensated active and former employees, the length of time the plan or plan provisions have been in effect, and the turnover of employees prior to the plan amendment. [Treas. Reg. §§ 1.401(a)(4)-5(a)(2), 1.401(a)(4)-5(a)(4)]

> **Example.** The Glener Corporation adopted a defined benefit plan many years ago that has covered both HCEs and NHCEs for most of its existence. The Glener Corporation decides to wind up the business. Shortly thereafter, at a time when the plan covers only HCEs, the plan is amended to increase benefits and thereafter is terminated. The plan does not satisfy this requirement because the timing of the amendment increasing benefits discriminates significantly in favor of HCEs.

A plan does not satisfy this requirement if plan provisions that provide past service credit have the effect of discriminating significantly in favor of highly compensated active and former employees. Past service credit includes benefit accruals for an employee's service prior to the time a plan is established, increases in existing accrued benefits resulting from an employee's service prior to the effective date of a plan amendment, and benefit accruals for service with another employer. Relevant facts and circumstances include the amount of benefits that former employees would have received had the plan or benefit increase been in effect throughout the period to which the past service credit applies. In addition, those facts and circumstances that are generally relevant to other plan amendments are taken into account. A safe harbor is provided under which a grant of up to five years of past service credit is deemed to be nondiscriminatory. The existence of this safe harbor does not mean that a grant of past service credit for a longer period violates the nondiscrimination rules. [Rev. Rul. 99-51, 1999-2 C.B. 652; Treas. Reg. §§ 1.401(a)(4)-5(a)(2), 1.401(a)(4)-5(a)(3), 1.401(a)(4)-5(a)(4), 1.401(a)(4)-11(d)(3)]

> **Example 1.** Lyla-Howard Ltd. currently has six employees, two of whom, A and B, are HCEs, and the remaining four of whom, C, D, E, and F, are NHCEs. The ratio of HCEs to highly compensated former employees is significantly higher than the ratio of NHCEs to non-highly compensated former employees. Lyla-Howard Ltd. establishes a defined benefit plan providing a 2 percent benefit for each year of service with the employer, including service

rendered before the plan is established. A and B have 15 years of prior service each, C has nine years of past service, D has five years, E has three years, and F has one year. The plan violates the special effect requirement because the grant of past service discriminates significantly in favor of HCEs.

Example 2. Assume the same facts as those in Example 1, except that the plan limits the past service credit to five years. The grant of past service credit does not discriminate significantly in favor of HCEs and is within the safe harbor.

IRS representatives opined that an amendment adding a specific bonus (paid only to HCEs) to an otherwise nondiscriminatory definition of compensation (see Qs 6:64–6:70) would not violate the nondiscriminatory requirement for plan amendments. Neither would an amendment to the plan of an acquiring employer recognizing preacquisition service with the acquired employer even though the few transferred employees were predominantly HCEs, stated the representatives. In both cases, however, a facts-and-circumstances determination would have to be made.

The requirement that a plan must be nondiscriminatory also covers plan terminations. Existing rules (see Q 25:8) that restrict distributions to highly compensated active and former employees upon termination of a defined benefit plan have been liberalized. These restrictions are inapplicable if the payment is less than 1 percent of plan assets or, after the payment of the benefit, the value of plan assets is at least 110 percent of the plan's current liabilities (see Q 25:8). [Treas. Reg. § 1.401(a)(4)-5(b)]

Q 4:22   What does cross-testing mean?

A qualified retirement plan may not discriminate in favor of HCEs (see Q 3:2) with respect to the amount of contributions or benefits. Whether a defined contribution plan (see Q 2:2) satisfies this requirement is generally determined with respect to the amount of contributions (see Q 4:12). As an alternative, however, a defined contribution plan (other than an ESOP; see Q 28:1) may be tested with respect to the equivalent amount of benefits. Similarly, whether a defined benefit plan (see Q 2:3) satisfies this requirement is generally determined with respect to the amount of benefits (see Q 4:14). As an alternative, however, a defined benefit plan may be tested with respect to the equivalent amount of contributions. [Treas. Reg. § 1.401(a)(4)-8]

Example. On January 1, 2010, The Sal-Lee 62nd Street Corporation adopts a profit sharing plan with a calendar-year plan year. The following six employees are eligible to participate in the plan:

Participant	Age	Compensation
A (owner)	55	$245,000
B	45	85,000
C	40	50,000
D	35	35,000

Participant	Age	Compensation
E	30	25,000
F	25	20,000
Total		$460,000

Sal-Lee contributes $59,750 to the plan. The contribution is allocated among the participants on a cross-tested basis with each participant receiving an allocation of no less than 5 percent of compensation. The contribution allocation is as follows:

Participant	Contribution	Percentage of Compensation	Accrual Rate
A	$49,000	20%	4.50%
B	4,250	5	2.77
C	2,500	5	4.07
D	1,750	5	5.68
E	1,250	5	8.04
F	1,000	5	11.51
Total	$59,750		

The accrual rate for A, the sole HCE, is 4.50 percent, and the average accrual rate for the NHCEs (see Q 3:12) is 6.41 percent. Since the accrual rate for the NHCEs is 70 percent or more of A's accrual rate, the plan does not discriminate in favor of the HCE with regard to the equivalent amount of benefits (see Qs 4:11, 4:13).

In the above example, cross-testing enables A to receive an allocation equal to 20 percent of compensation while providing all other employees with a much lesser allocation percentage. An age-based profit sharing plan (see Qs 2:7–2:9) could also provide A with a greater allocation percentage but would provide differing percentages for all of the other employees.

A defined contribution plan that is cross-tested by using the current plan year as the measurement period under the general test (see Q 4:13) may disregard income, expenses, gains, and losses allocated during the current plan year that are attributable to the allocation for the current plan year. Thus, only contributions and forfeitures allocated during the current plan year are taken into account. [Treas. Reg. §§ 1.401(a)(4)-8(b)(2)(i), 1.401(a)(4)-8(b)(2)(ii)]

See Q 2:10 for another example of a cross-tested plan, and see Qs 4:23 and 4:24 for details on IRS developments concerning cross-tested plan designs.

Q 4:23 Has IRS reexamined the appropriateness of cross-tested plan designs?

IRS issued final regulations affecting cross-tested plan designs that became effective for plan years beginning on or after January 1, 2002. [Treas. Reg. § 1.401(a)(4)-8(b)(1)(i)(B)]

The basic structure of the final regulations permits defined contribution plans (see Q 2:2) with broadly available allocation rates or certain age-based allocation rates to test on a benefits basis (cross-test) in the same manner as under current law (see Q 4:22) and permits other defined contribution plans to cross-test once they pass a gateway that prescribes minimum allocation rates for NHCEs (see Q 3:12). Similarly, the final regulations permit a plan that consists of one or more defined contribution plans and one or more defined benefit plans (DB/DC) to test on a benefits basis in the same manner as under current law if the DB/DC plan either is primarily defined benefit in character or consists of broadly available separate plans. Other DB/DC plans are permitted to test on a benefits basis once they pass a corresponding gateway prescribing minimum aggregate normal allocation rates for NHCEs. See Q 4:24 for details.

The final regulations require that a defined contribution plan that does not provide broadly available allocation rates or certain age-based allocation rates satisfy a gateway in order to be eligible to use the cross-testing rules to meet the nondiscrimination requirements (see Qs 4:10–4:21). A plan satisfies this minimum allocation gateway if each NHCE in the plan has an allocation rate that is at least one-third of the allocation rate of the HCE (see Q 3:2) with the highest allocation rate; however, a plan would be deemed to satisfy this minimum allocation gateway if each NHCE received an allocation of at least 5 percent of the NHCE's compensation (see Q 6:41). An individual who does not otherwise benefit under the plan for the plan year is not an employee for this purpose, hence not an NHCE, and need not be given the minimum required allocation under the gateway.

The final regulations do not change the general rule of prohibiting aggregation of a plan that provides for elective contributions and matching contributions (see Qs 27:16, 27:75) with a plan providing nonelective contributions. Accordingly, matching contributions are not taken into account for purposes of the gateway. Similarly, if a plan benefits employees who have not met the minimum age and service requirements (see Q 5:2), the plan may be treated as two separate plans, one for those otherwise excludable employees and one for the other employees benefiting under the plan. Thus, if the plan is treated as two separate plans in this manner, cross-testing the portion of the plan benefiting the nonexcludable employees will not result in minimum required allocations under the gateway for the employees who have not met the minimum age and service requirements.

The final regulations allow a plan to satisfy the gateway by providing an allocation of at least 5 percent of total compensation, limited to a period otherwise permissible under the timing rules applicable under the definition of plan year compensation. The definition of plan year compensation permits use of amounts paid only during the period of participation within the plan year.

A plan that has broadly available allocation rates does not need to satisfy the minimum allocation gateway and may continue to be tested for nondiscrimination on the basis of benefits as under current law. In order to be broadly available, each allocation rate under the plan must be currently available to a group of employees that satisfies the ratio percentage test (see Qs 5:15, 5:16). Thus, for example, if within one plan an employer provides different allocation rates for nondiscriminatory groups of employees at different locations or different profit centers, the plan does not need to satisfy the minimum allocation gateway in order to use cross-testing.

The final regulations liberalize the determination of whether a plan has broadly available allocation rates. First, the final regulations permit two allocation rates to be aggregated in a manner similar to the rule that permits aggregation of certain benefits, rights, or features. This rule permits excess NHCEs with a higher allocation rate to be used to support a lower allocation rate. For example, under this rule, if under a plan there are two groups of participants, one group that receives an allocation rate of 10 percent and another that receives an allocation rate of 3 percent, and if the group of employees who receive the 10 percent allocation rate satisfies the ratio/percentage test, then the 10 percent rate and the 3 percent rate can be aggregated and treated as a single allocation rate for purposes of determining whether the plan has broadly available allocation rates. In addition, the final regulations provide that, in determining whether a plan provides broadly available allocation rates, differences in allocation rates resulting from any method of permitted disparity (see Q 7:1) are disregarded.

The final regulations permit an employee's allocation to be disregarded, to the extent the employee's allocation is a transition allocation for the plan year. Transition allocations that can be disregarded can be defined benefit replacement allocations, pre-existing replacement allocations, or pre-existing merger and acquisition allocations.

In each case, the transition allocations must be provided to a closed group of employees and must be established under plan provisions. Once the allocations are established under the plan, they cannot be modified, except to reduce allocations for HCEs, or because of *de minimis* changes. A plan also does not violate this requirement because of an amendment that either adds or removes a provision applicable to all employees in the group eligible for the allocations under which each employee who is eligible for a transition allocation receives the greater of the transition allocation or another allocation for which the employee would otherwise be eligible. If the plan provides that all employees who are eligible for the transition allocation receive the greater of the transition allocation or an otherwise available allocation, the otherwise available allocation is considered currently available to all such employees, including employees for whom the transition allocation is greater.

The final regulations set forth basic conditions for defined benefit replacement allocations. These conditions provide a framework that is designed to ensure that these allocations are provided in a manner consistent with the general principles underlying the provisions for broadly available allocation rates under the final regulations. IRS has prescribed specific conditions for defined benefit replacement allocations that relate to the basic conditions set forth in the regulations. The basic conditions that allocations must satisfy in order to be defined benefit replacement allocations are as follows:

1. The allocations are provided to a group of employees who formerly benefited under an established nondiscriminatory defined benefit plan (see Q 2:3) of the employer or of a prior employer that provided age-based equivalent allocation rates;

2. The allocations for each employee are reasonably calculated, in a consistent manner, to replace the retirement benefits that the employee would have been provided under the defined benefit plan if the employee had continued to benefit under the defined benefit plan;

3. No employee who receives the allocation receives any other allocations under the plan for the plan year (except as provided in the final regulations); and

4. The composition of the group of employees who receive the allocations is nondiscriminatory.

The defined benefit plan's benefit formula applicable to the group of employees must be one that generated equivalent normal allocation rates (determined without regard to changes in accrual rates attributable to changes in an employee's years of service) that increased from year to year as employees attained higher ages. Further, if the defined benefit plan was sponsored by the employer, the defined benefit plan satisfied the minimum coverage and nondiscrimination requirements, without aggregating with any other plan, for the plan year which immediately precedes the first plan year for which the allocations are provided. Finally, the defined benefit plan must be one that has been established and maintained without substantial change for at least the five years ending on the date benefit accruals under the defined benefit plan cease (with one year substituted for five years in the case of a defined benefit plan of a former employer).

In order to be defined benefit replacement allocations for the plan year, the allocations for each employee in the group must be reasonably calculated, in a consistent manner, to replace the employee's retirement benefits under the defined benefit plan based on the terms of the defined benefit plan as in effect immediately prior to the date accruals under the defined benefit plan cease. In addition, the group of employees who receive the allocations in a plan year must satisfy the ratio/percentage test. There is more than one way in which the allocations may reasonably be calculated, such as a level percentage of pay for each year or an amount that increases as the employee ages.

The final regulations provide a separate exception from the application of the minimum allocation gateway for certain plans with age-based allocation rates (see Qs 2:7–2:9). This provision expands the exception to include plans that provide for allocation rates based on a uniform target benefit allocation.

A plan has a gradual age or service schedule if the schedule of allocation rates under the plan's formula is available to all employees in the plan and provides for allocation rates that increase smoothly at regular intervals. The rules applicable to the schedule of allocation rates are designed to be sufficiently flexible to accommodate a wide variety of age- or service-based plans (including age-weighted profit sharing plans that provide for allocations resulting in the same equivalent accrual rate for all employees). The final regulations clarify that a plan projecting future age or service may not use imputed disparity in determining whether the allocation rates under the schedule increase smoothly at regular intervals. The final regulations also accommodate smoothly increasing schedules of allocation rates that are based on the sum of age and years of service. In addition, to conform with the rules for computation of service (see Q 4:14), references to service have been changed to years of service.

The requirement that the allocation rates under a schedule increase smoothly at regular intervals provides important protection for employees, because this requirement limits the exception from the minimum allocation gateway to plans in which NHCEs actually receive the benefit of higher rates as they attain higher ages or complete additional years of service. The final regulations provide that a plan's schedule of allocation rates does not fail to increase smoothly at regular intervals merely because a specified minimum uniform allocation rate is provided for all employees or because the minimum benefit (see Q 26:41) is provided for all non-key employees (either because the plan is top-heavy or without regard to whether the plan is top-heavy) if one of two alternative conditions is satisfied. These two alternative conditions are intended to limit the potential use of a minimum allocation to provide a schedule of rates that delivers allocations similar to those under a comparability plan (see Q 2:10) without satisfying the minimum allocation gateway.

A plan satisfies the first alternative condition if the allocation rates under the plan that exceed the specified minimum rate could form part of a schedule of allocation rates that increase smoothly at regular intervals in which the lowest allocation rate is at least 1 percent of plan year compensation. The second alternative condition, available for a plan using an age-based schedule, allows the use of a minimum allocation rate if, for each age band above the minimum allocation rate, the allocation rate applicable for that band is less than or equal to the allocation rate that would yield an equivalent accrual rate at the highest age in the band that is the same as the equivalent accrual rate determined for the oldest hypothetical employee who would receive just the minimum allocation rate. Thus, under this condition, the allocation rates above the minimum allocation rate do not rise more steeply than expected under an age-weighted profit sharing plan generally intended to provide the same accrual rate at all ages.

The exception to the minimum allocation gateway for plans with age-based allocation rates also applies to certain uniform target benefit plans that do not comply with the safe harbor testing method (see Q 4:24). A plan has allocation rates based on a uniform target benefit allocation if it would comply with the requirements for a safe harbor target benefit plan except that the interest rate for determining the actuarial present value of the stated plan benefit and the theoretical reserve is lower than a standard interest rate, the stated benefit is calculated assuming compensation increases, or the plan computes the current year contribution using the actual account balance instead of the theoretical reserve.

[Treas. Reg. § 1.401(a)(4)-8(b)(1); Rev. Rul. 2001-30, 2001-2 C.B. 46]

The following examples illustrate the new rules enunciated in the proposed regulations.

Example 1. On January 1, 2011, the Manhattan Marvins Corporation adopts Plan M, a defined contribution plan without a minimum service requirement, that provides an allocation formula under which allocations are provided to all employees according to the following schedule:

Completed Years of Service	Allocation Rate	Ratio of Allocation Rate for Band to Allocation Rate for Immediately Preceding Band
0–5	3.0%	Not applicable
6–10	4.5%	1.50
11–15	6.5%	1.44
16–20	8.5%	1.31
21–25	10.0%	1.18
26 or more	11.5%	1.15

Because Plan M provides that allocation rates for all employees are determined using a single schedule based solely on service, if the allocation rates under the schedule increase smoothly at regular intervals, then the plan has a gradual age or service schedule.

The schedule of allocation rates under Plan M does not increase by more than 5 percentage points between adjacent bands, and the ratio of the allocation rate for any band to the allocation rate for the immediately preceding band is never more than 2.0 and does not increase. Therefore, the allocation rates increase smoothly. In addition, the bands (other than the highest band) are all five years long, so the increases occur at regular intervals. Thus, the allocation rates under the plan's schedule increase smoothly at regular intervals; and, accordingly, the plan has a gradual age or service schedule.

Plan M satisfies the nondiscrimination in amount requirement on the basis of benefits if it satisfies the general test (see Q 4:13) if an equivalent accrual rate were substituted for each employee's allocation rate in the determination of rate groups, regardless of whether it satisfies the minimum allocation gateway.

Example 2. The facts are the same as in Example 1, except that the 4.5 percent allocation rate applies for all employees with ten years of service or less.

Plan M provides that allocation rates for all employees are determined using a single schedule based solely on service. Therefore, if the allocation rates under the schedule increase smoothly at regular intervals, then the plan has a gradual age or service schedule.

The bands (other than the highest band) in the schedule are not all the same length, since the first band is ten years long while other bands are five years long. Thus, the schedule does not have regular intervals. However, the schedule of allocation rates does not fail to increase smoothly at regular intervals merely because the minimum allocation rate of 4.5 percent results in a first band that is longer than the other bands, if either of the alternative conditions is satisfied.

In this case, the schedule of allocation rates satisfies the first alternative condition because the allocation rates under the plan that are greater than the 4.5 percent minimum allocation rate can be included in the following hypothetical schedule of allocation rates that increases smoothly at regular intervals and has a lowest allocation rate of at least 1 percent of plan year compensation:

Completed Years of Service	Allocation Rate	Ratio of Allocation Rate for Band to Allocation Rate for Immediately Preceding Band
0–5	2.5%	Not applicable
6–10	4.5%	1.80
11–15	6.5%	1.44
16–20	8.5%	1.31
21–25	10.0%	1.18
26 or more	11.5%	1.15

Accordingly, Plan M has a gradual age or service schedule and satisfies the nondiscrimination in amount requirement on the basis of benefits if it satisfies the general test if an equivalent accrual rate were substituted for each employee's allocation rate in the determination of rate groups, regardless of whether it satisfies the minimum allocation gateway.

Example 3. On January 1, 2011, the Stamford Suzanne Corporation adopts Plan S, a defined contribution plan, that provides an allocation formula under which allocations are provided to all employees according to the following schedule:

Age	Allocation Rate	Ratio of Allocation Rate for Band to Allocation Rate for Immediately Preceding Band
Under 25	3.0%	Not applicable
25–34	6.0%	2.00
35–44	9.0%	1.50
45–54	12.0%	1.33
55–64	16.0%	1.33
65 or older	21.0%	1.31

Plan S provides that allocation rates for all employees are determined using a single schedule based solely on age. Therefore, if the allocation rates under the schedule increase smoothly at regular intervals, then the plan has a gradual age or service schedule.

The schedule of allocation rates under Plan S does not increase by more than 5 percentage points between adjacent bands and the ratio of the allocation rate for any band to the allocation rate for the immediately preceding band is never more than 2.0 and does not increase. Therefore, the allocation rates increase smoothly. In addition, the bands are all ten years long (other than the highest band and the first band, which is deemed to be the same length as the other bands because it ends prior to age 25), so the increases occur at regular intervals. Thus, the allocation rates under the plan's schedule increase smoothly at regular intervals; and, accordingly, the plan has a gradual age or service schedule.

Plan S satisfies the nondiscrimination in amount requirement on the basis of benefits if it satisfies the general test if an equivalent accrual rate were substituted for each employee's allocation rate in the determination of rate groups, regardless of whether it satisfies the minimum allocation gateway.

Example 4. Plan SM, a defined contribution plan maintained by Sue-Mort Corporation effective January 1, 2011, provides an allocation formula under which allocations are provided to all employees according to the following schedule:

Age	Allocation Rate	Ratio of Allocation Rate for Band to Allocation Rate for Immediately Preceding Band
Under 40	3%	Not applicable
40–44	6%	2.00
45–49	9%	1.50
50–54	12%	1.33

Age	Allocation Rate	Ratio of Allocation Rate for Band to Allocation Rate for Immediately Preceding Band
55–59	16%	1.33
60–64	20%	1.25
65 or older	25%	1.25

Plan SM provides that allocation rates for all employees are determined using a single schedule based solely on age. Therefore, if the allocation rates under the schedule increase smoothly at regular intervals, then the plan has a gradual age or service schedule.

The bands (other than the highest band) in the schedule are not all the same length, since the first band is treated as 15 years long while other bands are five years long. Thus, the schedule does not have regular intervals. However, the schedule of allocation rates does not fail to increase smoothly at regular intervals merely because the minimum allocation rate of 3 percent results in a first band that is longer than the other bands, if either of the alternative conditions is satisfied.

In this case, in order to define a hypothetical schedule that could include the allocation rates in the actual schedule of allocation rates, each of the bands below age 40 would have to be five years long (or be treated as five years long). Accordingly, the hypothetical schedule would have to provide for a band for employees under age 30, a band for employees in the range 30–34, and a band for employees age 35–39.

The ratio of the allocation rate for the age 40–44 band to the next lower band is 2.0. Accordingly, in order for the applicable allocation rates under this hypothetical schedule to increase smoothly, the ratio of the allocation rate for each band in the hypothetical schedule below age 40 to the allocation rate for the immediately preceding band would have to be 2.0. Thus, the allocation rate for the hypothetical band applicable for employees under age 30 would be .75 percent, the allocation rate for the hypothetical band for employees in the range 30–34 would be 1.5 percent, and the allocation rate for employees in the range 35–39 would be 3 percent.

Because the lowest allocation rate under any possible hypothetical schedule is less than 1 percent of plan year compensation, Plan SM will be treated as satisfying the requirement of increasing smoothly at regular intervals only if the schedule of allocation rates satisfies the steepness condition (i.e., the second alternative condition). In this case, the steepness condition is not satisfied because the equivalent accrual rate for an employee age 39 is 2.81 percent, but there is no hypothetical employee in the band for ages 40–44 with an equal or lower equivalent accrual rate (since the lowest equivalent accrual rate for hypothetical employees within this band is 3.74 percent at age 44).

Since the schedule of allocation rates under the plan does not increase smoothly at regular intervals, Plan SM's schedule of allocation rates is not a gradual age or service schedule. Further, Plan SM does not provide uniform target benefit allocations. Therefore, Plan SM cannot satisfy the nondiscrimination in amount requirement for the plan year on the basis of benefits unless either Plan SM provides for broadly available allocation rates for the plan year (i.e., the allocation rate at each age is provided to a group of employees that satisfies the ratio/percentage test), or Plan SM satisfies the minimum allocation gateway for the plan year.

Example 5. Plan MS is a profit sharing plan maintained by Massachusetts Mort Corporation that covers all of its employees, consisting of two HCEs, Mort and Suzanne, and seven NHCEs. Mort's compensation is $170,000, and Suzanne's compensation is $150,000. The allocation for Mort and Suzanne is $30,000 each, resulting in an allocation rate of 17.65 percent for Mort and 20 percent for Suzanne. Under Plan MS, each NHCE receives an allocation of 5 percent of compensation, measured over a period of time permitted under the definition of plan year compensation.

Because the allocation rate for Mort is not currently available to any NHCE, Plan MS does not have broadly available allocation rates. Furthermore, Plan MS does not provide for age-based allocation rates. Thus, Plan MS can satisfy the nondiscrimination in amount requirement for the plan year on the basis of benefits only if it satisfies the minimum allocation gateway for the plan year.

The highest allocation rate for any HCE under Plan MS is 20 percent. Accordingly, Plan MS would satisfy the minimum allocation gateway if all NHCEs have an allocation rate of at least 6.67 percent or if all NHCEs receive an allocation of at least 5 percent of compensation.

Under Plan MS, each NHCE receives an allocation of 5 percent of compensation. Accordingly, Plan MS satisfies the minimum allocation gateway.

Plan MS satisfies the nondiscrimination in amount requirement on the basis of benefits if it satisfies the general test if an equivalent accrual rate were substituted for each employee's allocation rate in the determination of rate groups.

An employer maintains a profit sharing plan only; the plan contributions do not satisfy any of the gateways; and the plan passes the average benefit percentage test (see Q 5:19) on a benefits (cross-tested) basis but not on a contributions basis (see Q 4:11). IRS representatives have opined that, in applying the general test (see Q 4:13) to the amount of contributions, the rate groups may be tested by comparing their ratio percentages to the midpoint of the safe and unsafe harbors (see Q 5:18). In other words, the plan may use cross-testing in the average benefit percentage test even though it may not use cross-testing in the general test. IRS representatives have also opined that a qualified nonelective contribution (QNEC; see Q 27:17) that is used to satisfy the ADP test (see Q 27:18) or the ACP test (see Q 27:77) cannot also be used to satisfy gateway testing, but can be so used if the plan is a safe harbor 401(k) plan (see Q 27:40).

For the discussion of a memorandum issued by IRS concerning the nondiscrimination requirements and cross-testing, see Q 4:10.

Q 4:24   How do the final regulations affect a DB/DC plan?

A DB/DC plan is a plan that consists of one or more defined contribution plans (see Q 2:2) and one or more defined benefit plans (see Q 2:3). [Treas. Reg. § 1.401(a)(4)-9(a)]

The final regulations prescribe rules for testing defined contribution plans that are aggregated with defined benefit plans for purposes of satisfying the nondiscrimination requirements (see Qs 4:10–4:21) and the minimum coverage requirement (see Q 5:15). These rules apply in situations in which the employer aggregates the plans because one of the plans does not satisfy those requirements standing alone. These rules do not apply to safe harbor floor-offset arrangements (see Q 2:22) or to the situation in which plans are aggregated solely for purposes of satisfying the average benefit percentage test (see Q 5:17).

Under the final regulations, the combination of a defined contribution plan and a defined benefit plan may demonstrate nondiscrimination on the basis of benefits if the combined plan is primarily defined benefit in character, consists of broadly available separate plans, or satisfies a gateway requirement. This minimum aggregate allocation gateway is generally similar to the minimum allocation gateway for defined contribution plans that are not combined with a defined benefit plan (see Q 4:23). To apply this minimum aggregate allocation gateway, the employee's aggregate normal allocation rate is determined by adding the employee's allocation rate under the defined contribution plan to the employee's equivalent allocation rate under the defined benefit plan. The use of aggregation would allow an employer that provides both a defined contribution and a defined benefit plan to the NHCEs (see Q 3:12) to take both plans into account in determining whether the minimum aggregate allocation gateway is met.

Under the gateway, if the aggregate normal allocation rate of the HCE (see Q 3:2) with the highest aggregate normal allocation rate under the plan (HCE rate) is less than 15 percent, the aggregate normal allocation rate for all NHCEs must be at least one-third of the HCE rate. If the HCE rate is between 15 percent and 25 percent, the aggregate normal allocation rate for all NHCEs must be at least 5 percent. If the HCE rate exceeds 25 percent, then the aggregate normal allocation rate for each NHCE must be at least 5 percent plus one percentage point for each 5-percentage-point increment (or portion thereof) by which the HCE rate exceeds 25 percent (e.g., the NHCE minimum is 6 percent for an HCE rate that exceeds 25 percent but not 30 percent, and 7 percent for an HCE rate that exceeds 30 percent but not 35 percent). The final regulations provide that a plan is deemed to satisfy this minimum aggregate allocation gateway if the aggregate normal allocation rate for each NHCE is at least $7\frac{1}{2}$ percent of total compensation (see Q 6:41) determined over a period otherwise permissible under the timing rules applicable under the definition of plan year compensation.

In addition, in determining the equivalent allocation rate for an NHCE under a defined benefit plan, a plan is permitted to treat each NHCE who benefits under the defined benefit plan as having an equivalent allocation rate equal to the average of the equivalent allocation rates under the defined benefit plan for all NHCEs benefiting under that plan. This averaging rule recognizes the grow-in feature inherent in traditional defined benefit plans (i.e., the defined benefit plan provides higher equivalent allocation rates at higher ages). The determination of whether a DB/DC plan is primarily defined benefit in character should be based on the relative size of the defined benefit accruals and the defined contribution allocations for individual employees, as reflected in the actual benefits testing that is being done under the nondiscrimination rules. In particular, the actuarial assumptions used to determine whether a DB/DC plan is primarily defined benefit in character must be the same assumptions that are used to apply the cross-testing rules.

A combined plan that is primarily defined benefit in character would not be subject to the gateway requirement and may continue to be tested for nondiscrimination on the basis of benefits as under current law (see Q 4:14). A combined plan would be primarily defined benefit in character if, for more than 50 percent of the NHCEs benefiting under the plan, the normal accrual rate attributable to benefits provided under defined benefit plans for the NHCE exceeds the equivalent accrual rate attributable to contributions under defined contribution plans for the NHCE. For example, a DB/DC plan would be primarily defined benefit in character where the defined contribution plan covers only salaried employees, the defined benefit plan covers only hourly employees, and more than half of the NHCEs participating in the DB/DC plan are hourly employees participating only in the defined benefit plan.

A combined plan that consists of broadly available separate plans would not be subject to the gateway requirement and may continue to be tested for nondiscrimination on the basis of benefits as under current law. A DB/DC plan consists of broadly available separate plans if the defined contribution plan and the defined benefit plan each would satisfy the minimum coverage requirement and the nondiscrimination in amount requirement if each plan were tested separately, assuming satisfaction of the average benefit percentage test (see Q 5:19). Thus, the defined contribution plan must separately satisfy the nondiscrimination requirements (taking into account the final regulations as applicable), but for this purpose assuming satisfaction of the average benefit percentage test. Similarly, the defined benefit plan must separately satisfy the nondiscrimination requirements, assuming for this purpose satisfaction of the average benefit percentage test. In conducting the required separate testing, all plans of a single type (defined contribution or defined benefit) within the DB/DC plan are aggregated, but those plans are tested without regard to plans of the other type.

This alternative would be useful, for example, where an employer maintains a defined contribution plan that provides a uniform allocation rate for all covered employees at one business unit and a safe harbor defined benefit plan for all covered employees at another unit, and where the group of employees covered by each plan is a group that satisfies the nondiscriminatory classification requirement (see Q 5:18). Because the employer provides broadly available separate plans, it may continue to aggregate the plans and test for nondiscrimination on the basis of benefits, as an alternative to using the qualified separate line of business rules (see Q 5:44) or demonstrating satisfaction of the average benefit percentage test.

Component plans under the restructuring rules cannot be used for the determination of whether a defined contribution plan provides broadly available allocation rates or satisfies the minimum allocation gateway, or the determination of whether a DB/DC plan satisfies the minimum aggregate allocation gateway, is primarily defined benefit in character, or consists of broadly available separate plans.

[Treas. Reg. §§ 1.401(a)(4)-9(b)(2)(v), 1.401(a)(4)-9(c)(3)(ii)]

The following examples illustrate the new rules enunciated in the proposed regulations.

Example 1. Benjamin Corporation maintains Plan M, a defined benefit plan, and Plan N, a defined contribution plan. All HCEs of Benjamin Corporation are covered by Plan M (at a 1 percent accrual rate), but not covered by Plan N. All NHCEs of Benjamin Corporation are covered by Plan N (at a 3 percent allocation rate), but not covered by Plan M. Because Plan M does not satisfy the minimum coverage requirement standing alone, Plans M and N are aggregated for purposes of satisfying the minimum coverage and nondiscrimination requirements.

Because none of the NHCEs participates in the defined benefit plan, the aggregated DB/DC plan is not primarily defined benefit in character nor does it consist of broadly available separate plans. Accordingly, the aggregated Plan M and Plan N must satisfy the minimum aggregate allocation gateway in order to satisfy the nondiscrimination in amount requirement on the basis of benefits.

Example 2. Jason Corporation maintains Plan O, a defined benefit plan, and Plan P, a defined contribution plan. All of the six employees of Jason Corporation are covered under both Plan O and Plan P. Under Plan O, all employees have a uniform normal accrual rate of 1 percent of compensation. Under Plan P, Employees A and B, who are HCEs, receive an allocation rate of 15 percent, and participants C, D, E, and F, who are NHCEs, receive an allocation rate of 3 percent. Jason Corporation aggregates Plans O and P for purposes of satisfying the minimum coverage and nondiscrimination requirements. The equivalent normal allocation and normal accrual rates under Plans O and P are as follows:

Employee	Equivalent Normal Allocation Rates for the 1% Accrual Under Plan O (defined benefit plan)	Equivalent Normal Accrual Rates for the 15%/3% Allocations Under Plan P (defined contribution plan)
HCE A (age 55)	3.93%	3.82%
HCE B (age 50)	2.61%	5.74%
C (age 60)	5.91%	.51%
D (age 45)	1.74%	1.73%
E (age 35)	.77%	3.90%
F (age 25)	.34%	8.82%

Although all of the NHCEs benefit under Plan O (the defined benefit plan), the aggregated DB/DC plan is not primarily defined benefit in character because the normal accrual rate attributable to the defined benefit plan (which is 1 percent for all the NHCEs) is greater than the equivalent accrual rate under the defined contribution plan only for Employee C. In addition, because the 15 percent allocation rate is only available to HCEs, the defined contribution plan cannot satisfy the nondiscrimination in amount of contributions requirement and does not have broadly available allocation rates (see Q 4:23). Further, the defined contribution plan does not satisfy the minimum allocation gateway (3 percent is less than one-third of the 15 percent HCE rate). Therefore, the defined contribution plan within the DB/DC plan cannot separately satisfy the nondiscrimination in amounts requirement and does not constitute a broadly available separate plan. Accordingly, the aggregated plans can satisfy the nondiscrimination in amounts requirement on the basis of benefits only if the aggregated plans satisfy the minimum aggregate allocation gateway.

Employee A has an aggregate normal allocation rate of 18.93 percent under the aggregated plans (3.93 percent from Plan O plus 15 percent from Plan P), which is the highest aggregate normal allocation rate for any HCE under the plans. Employee F has an aggregate normal allocation rate of 3.34 percent under the aggregated plans (.34 percent from Plan O plus 3 percent from Plan P) which is less than the 5 percent aggregate normal allocation rate that Employee F would be required to have to satisfy the minimum aggregate allocation gateway.

However, for purposes of satisfying the minimum aggregate allocation gateway, Jason Corporation is permitted to treat each NHCE who benefits under Plan O (the defined benefit plan) as having an equivalent allocation rate equal to the average of the equivalent allocation rate under Plan O for all NHCEs benefiting under that plan. The average of the equivalent allocation rates for all the NHCEs under Plan O is 2.19 percent [(5.91%+1.74%+.77% +.34%) ÷ 4]. Accordingly, Jason Corporation is permitted to treat all the NHCEs as having an equivalent allocation rate attributable to Plan O equal to 2.19 percent. Thus, all NHCEs can be treated as having an aggregate normal allocation rate of 5.19 percent for this purpose (3 percent from the defined contribution plan and 2.19 percent from the defined benefit plan), and the aggregate DB/DC plan satisfies the minimum aggregate allocation gateway.

Q 4:25 Do special rules apply to target benefit plans?

A target benefit plan (see Q 2:5) is generally subject to the alternative cross-testing method applicable to defined contribution plans (see Qs 4:22–4:24). However, a target benefit plan will be deemed to satisfy the nondiscrimination requirement with respect to the amount of equivalent benefits if each of the following requirements is satisfied:

1. Each employee's stated benefit is determined as the straight life annuity commencing at the employee's normal retirement age (see Q 10:55);

2. The same benefit formula applies to all employees, and the benefit formula provides all employees with an annual benefit payable in the same form commencing at the same uniform normal retirement age (see Q 4:14);

3. The stated benefit under the plan complies with one of the defined benefit plan safe harbors that uses the fractional accrual rule (see Qs 4:15, 4:16);

4. Contributions necessary to fund the stated benefit for an employee are determined under the individual level premium funding method and are based on the employee's theoretical reserve (an employee's theoretical reserve generally consists of prior contributions with interest accumulated at the plan's assumed interest rate used for funding purposes for prior years);

5. Generally, an employee's stated benefit may not take into account service prior to the first plan year that the employee benefited under the plan;

6. Forfeitures under the plan are applied to reduce contributions;

7. Employee contributions are not used to fund the stated benefit; and

8. Stated benefits and contributions after normal retirement age satisfy certain additional requirements.

[Treas. Reg. §§ 1.401(a)(4)-8(a), 1.401(a)(4)-8(b), 1.401(a)(4)-12]

Q 4:26 What happens if a retirement plan fails to satisfy the nondiscrimination requirements?

If a retirement plan fails to satisfy any of the qualification requirements of Section 401(a) (see Q 4:1), including the nondiscrimination requirements (see Q 4:10), the tax-exempt status of plan earnings is revoked, employer deductions for contributions may be deferred or eliminated, and all employees must include the value of their vested plan contributions in income. [I.R.C. § 402(b)(1); Priv. Ltr. Rul. 9502030]

However, if the plan fails to satisfy the minimum coverage requirement (see Q 5:15), each HCE (see Q 3:2) must include in income an amount equal to the employee's entire vested accrued benefit (see Q 9:2) not previously included in income, not just current vested plan contributions. If, however, the plan is not qualified solely because it fails to satisfy the minimum coverage requirement, no adverse tax consequences are imposed on NHCEs (see Q 3:12). [I.R.C. § 402(b)(4); Priv. Ltr. Rul. 9502030]

IRS has opined that, with the integrated approach underlying the nondiscrimination requirement and the minimum coverage requirement, any failure to satisfy the nondiscrimination requirements can be viewed as failure to satisfy the minimum coverage requirement. Consequently, failure to meet the nondiscrimination requirements will subject HCEs to the special sanctions. [Preamble to final Treasury regulations (Sept. 19, 1991)]

IRS has developed programs whereby plan defects can be corrected and plan disqualification avoided. For details, see chapter 19.

Q 4:27   May a participant assign his or her vested interest in a qualified retirement plan?

As a general rule, benefits provided under a qualified retirement plan may not be assigned or alienated, which includes any arrangement (direct or indirect, revocable or irrevocable) whereby a party acquires from a participant a right or interest enforceable against the plan in any part of a plan benefit payment which is, or may become, payable to the participant. [I.R.C. § 401(a)(13)(A); ERISA § 206(d)(1); Treas. Reg. § 1.401(a)-13(c)(1)(ii)] There are, however, exceptions to this rule.

A participant or beneficiary whose benefits are in pay status may assign or alienate the right to future benefit payments provided the following conditions are satisfied: (1) the assignment or alienation is voluntary and revocable; (2) the amount does not exceed 10 percent of any benefit payment; and (3) there is no direct or indirect defraying of plan administration costs. [ERISA § 206(d)(2); I.R.C. § 401(a)(13)(A); Treas. Reg. § 1.401(a)-13(d)(1)]

One court concluded that a plan's recoupment from a participant of overpayments of plan benefits did not violate the anti-alienation rule. An arrangement for a plan's recoupment of benefit overpayments is not considered an assignment or alienation. An arrangement, for this purpose, is not limited to an agreement between the parties or a provision in the plan. In this case, a letter to the participant informing him of the recoupment was an arrangement sufficient to exclude the recoupment from the anti-alienation provision. [Palmer v. Johnson and Johnson Pension Plan, 2009 WL 3029794 (D. N.J. 2009); Treas. Reg. § 1.401(a)-13(c)(2)(iii)]

The anti-alienation rule applies to qualified retirement plan benefits and not to plan assets. [*In re* Schantz, 221 B.R. 653 (Bankr. N.D.N.Y. 1998)] Furthermore, the anti-alienation rule does not apply to IRA benefits. Where a qualified retirement plan participant rolled over his plan benefits to an IRA, one court concluded that the IRA was not protected by ERISA (see Qs 30:52, 34:42). [Hawxhurst v. Hawxhurst, A-1312-97T3 (N.J. Super. Ct. App. Div. 1998)]

The anti-alienation rule was not violated, determined one court, where a participant utilized his qualified retirement plan assets to repay the employer in restitution for theft because the participant was not compelled or forced to allow garnishment of his benefits or to liquidate his benefits. [Greve v. J.H. Patterson Co., No. 96 C 50424 (N.D. Ill. 1999)] Another court ruled that a qualified retirement plan participant who was convicted of embezzlement could not be forced to use his plan benefits to pay restitution to the victims of his crime because the anti-alienation rule would be violated. [State v. Kenyon, No. 98-1421 (Wis. Ct. App. 1999)] Similarly, a court concluded that an individual who embezzled funds from a union pension plan could not be forced to use his own qualified retirement plan undistributed benefits to make restitution because his plan was unrelated to the union plan and to do so would violate the anti-alienation rule. [United States v. Jackson, 229 F.3d 1223 (9th Cir. 2000)] A plan prevailed in a suit brought by a participant for increased benefits and was awarded a judgment for attorney's fees; however, the plan was not permitted to satisfy the judgment from the participant's plan benefits because of the anti-alienation rule. [Martorana v. The Bd. of Trustees of Steamfitters Local Union 420 Health, Welfare and Pension Fund, 404 F.3d 797 (3d Cir. 2005); *see also* Kickham Hanley P.C. v. Kodak Retirement Income Plan, 2009 WL 468266 (2d Cir. 2009)] However, another court ruled that a court order requiring a prisoner to pay restitution did not violate the anti-alienation rule because, when the order was entered, the prisoner had substantial funds available other than his retirement plan assets; and, therefore, the prisoner had not been directly ordered to liquidate his retirement assets. [United States v. Kalani, No. S3 98 CR 1238-06 (S.D.N.Y. 2003)] A state statute provided that a prison warden could garnish up to 90 percent of a prisoner's plan benefits to pay the costs of incarceration. The statute also provided that, if a prisoner did not inform the plan of a change of address and did not request that the plan send benefit payments to a prison account, the warden could notify the plan of the change of address and instruct the plan to send all payments to the prison account. The court ruled that the statute violated the anti-alienation rule; however, the court advised that, once a prisoner received the benefits, the state could place a constructive trust on the funds and that it had not come to a decision with regard to whether or not the state could have compelled the prisoner to send the address change to the plan. [Daimler Chrysler Corp. v. Cox, 447 F.3d 967 (6th Cir. 2006)] See Q 4:29 for a discussion of cases concerning restitution to the federal government.

In a novel ruling, a request for a court order requiring that a prisoner's retirement benefits be deposited into his prison account for the purposes of partially reimbursing the state for the cost of his incarceration was ruled to be a prohibited assignment of benefits because the prisoner's retirement benefits would not be voluntarily deposited into his prison account. [State Treasurer v. Baugh, 986 F. Supp. 1074 (E.D. Mich. 1997)] However, a state court ruled otherwise so that the deposit was not a prohibited assignment. [State Treasurer v. Abbott, 660 N.W.2d 714 (Mich. 2003)] Another court ruled that a state law authorizing a deduction from all funds received by prison inmates from outside sources, including ERISA plan benefits, did not violate the anti-alienation rule because the rule does not apply once benefits have been distributed.

[Wright v. Riveland, 219 F.3d 905 (9th Cir. 2000); ERISA § 206(d)(1); Treas. Reg. § 1.401(a)-13(c)(1)(ii)]

A loan made to a participant or beneficiary is generally not treated as an assignment or alienation if the loan is secured by the participant's vested interest and is not a prohibited transaction (see Qs 1:55, 14:21, 24:8). [I.R.C. §§ 401(a)(13)(A), 4975(d)(1); Treas. Reg. § 1.401(a)-13(d)(2)] Even though a loan may be secured by the participant's vested interest, the secured loan could not be accorded priority status in a bankruptcy proceeding, concluded one court. [In re Scott, No. 91-34119 (Bankr. E.D. Va. 1992)] Similarly, payroll deductions to make mandatory plan contributions or to repay a plan loan cannot be excluded from the participant's bankruptcy estate. Although the participant's interest in the plan is exempt from claims of creditors (see Q 4:28), the exemption does not apply to amounts used for mandatory plan contributions or to amounts owed to repay the loan. [In re Taylor, 243 F.3d 124 (2d Cir. 2001); In re Harshbarger, 66 F.3d 775 (6th Cir. 1995); In re Anes, 1999 WL 974330 (3d Cir. 1999); In re Esquivel, 1999 WL 760651 (Bankr. E.D. Mich. 1999); see also In re Whitaker, No. 06-33109 (N.D. Ohio 2007), In re Clark, No. 05-73673 (N.D. Ohio 2007), and Friedman v. Broach, 220 B.R. 679 (B.A.P. 9th Cir. 1998)] Where an insolvent debtor, who had made a loan from a plan in which he participated, repaid the loan only three weeks before an involuntary bankruptcy petition was filed against him, the court ruled that the bankruptcy trustee could set aside the loan repayment as a voidable preference. [In re Yates, 287 F.3d 521 (6th Cir. 2002)]

If a participant designates a beneficiary to receive benefits under a qualified retirement plan upon the participant's death, a disclaimer of the death benefits by the designated beneficiary does not constitute a prohibited assignment or alienation of benefits. [Gen. Couns. Mem. 39,858] However, one court ruled that the legal representative of a deceased beneficiary's estate could not make a disclaimer. [Nickel v. Estes, 122 F.3d 294 (5th Cir. 1997)] The designation of a beneficiary to receive qualified retirement plan death benefits by an insolvent, deceased plan participant is not a prohibited assignment. [Will of King, N.Y.L.J., June 30, 2003 (Surr. Ct. Broome County, N.Y. 2003)]

If a qualified domestic relations order (QDRO; see Q 36:1) requires the distribution of all or part of a participant's benefits to another individual, even though the participant is still employed, the distribution is not considered an assignment or alienation. [I.R.C. §§ 401(a)(13)(B), 414(p); Treas. Reg. § 1.401(a)-13(g)] The creation of a security interest in a participant's plan benefits did not violate the anti-assignment rule because the order creating the security interest was a QDRO. [Priv. Ltr. Rul. 200252093] Because a postnuptial agreement requiring that a portion of the husband's benefits in a qualified retirement plan be segregated in a separate plan account for the wife was not a QDRO, the segregation violated the anti-assignment rule. [Merchant v. Kelly, Haglund, Garnsey & Kahn, 874 F. Supp. 300 (D. Colo. 1995)] A divorce decree requiring payment of the wife's attorneys' fees from the husband's qualified retirement plan account did not meet the requirements of a QDRO and was not enforced because the payment would have violated the anti-alienation rule. [Johnson v. Johnson, 727 A.2d 473 (N.J. Super. Ct. App. Div. 1999)]

A participant's waiver assigning his defined benefit plan (see Q 2:3) benefits to the employer constituted a prohibited assignment or alienation and resulted in his receipt of a taxable distribution (see Q 13:1). The court ruled that the waived benefits did not represent excess assets reverting to the employer (see Q 25:49). [Gallade, 106 T.C. 355 (1996)] However, another court determined that a waiver of benefits was not a prohibited assignment or alienation because the participant knowingly and voluntarily agreed to waive his retirement benefits. [Rhoades v. Casey, 196 F.3d 592 (5th Cir. 1999)]

Where a union official embezzled funds from the union, the United States Supreme Court ruled that the official's union pension plan benefits could not be used to satisfy the union's judgment against him because such use would violate the prohibition on assignment or alienation of pension benefits. [Guidry v. Sheet Metal Workers Nat'l Pension Fund, 493 U.S. 365 (1990)] A different result was reached where a union official embezzled from the union pension plan, where a trustee made unauthorized withdrawals from the plan (see Q 23:47), and also where a company owner stole funds from the plan. [Parker v. Bain, No. 94-55123 (9th Cir. 1995); United States v. Gaudet, No. 91-3647 (5th Cir. 1992); Friedlander v. Doherty, 851 F. Supp. 515 (N.D.N.Y. 1994)] However, one court ruled that a participant's plan benefits could not be offset for an alleged breach of fiduciary duty because the participant was not a fiduciary. [Cottrill v. Sparrow, Johnson & Ursillo, Inc., 1996 U.S. App. LEXIS 29939 (1st Cir. 1996)]

TRA '97 resolved the conflict among the courts and permits a participant's benefit in a qualified retirement plan to be reduced to satisfy liabilities of the participant to the plan due to (1) the participant's being convicted of committing a crime involving the plan, (2) a civil judgment (or consent order or decree) entered by a court in an action brought in connection with a violation of the fiduciary provisions of ERISA, or (3) a settlement agreement between DOL or PBGC (see Q 25:10) and the participant in connection with a violation of the fiduciary provisions of ERISA. The court order establishing such liability must require that the participant's benefit in the plan be applied to satisfy the liability. If the participant is married at the time the benefit is offset to satisfy the liability, spousal consent (see Q 10:21) to such offset is required unless the spouse is also required to pay an amount to the plan in the judgment, order, decree, or settlement or the judgment, order, decree, or settlement provides a joint and 50 percent survivor annuity for the spouse (see Q 10:8). According to the conference agreement, an offset is includible in income on the date of the offset. [ERISA §§ 206(d)(4), 206(d)(5); I.R.C. §§ 401(a)(13)(C), 401(a)(13)(D); TRA '97 § 1502(c)]

One court ruled that improper plan contributions made by an employer would not be excluded from the employer's bankruptcy estate because the anti-alienation rule did not apply. [Bell & Beckwith v. Society Bank & Trust, 1993 U.S. App. LEXIS 23740 (6th Cir. 1993); *see also* Goldman v. Walder, Sondak & Brogan, P.A., 1997 U.S. Dist. LEXIS 15692 (S.D.N.Y. 1997); *but see In re* Jones Truck Lines, Inc., Nos. 96-3224/3305 (8th Cir. 1997)] An amendment to a qualified retirement plan that provided increased benefits to key employees, but decreased the amount of the plan's surplus assets, violated the Federal Bankruptcy Code because it constituted a fraudulent transfer, determined one court. [*In re* Fruehauf Trailer Corp., 444 F.3d 203 (3d Cir. 2006)]

An employer sponsored a pension plan and an early retirement plan. A participant in the pension plan signed a release releasing the employer from any and all claims arising from his employment in exchange for participation in the early retirement plan. The employer calculated the participant's pension benefits, and the participant claimed that he should have received credit for two years during which he was on a military leave of absence. The court concluded that the anti-alienation rule prevented the release from barring this claim for service credits. [Lynn v. CSX Transp., Inc., No. 95-2240 (7th Cir. 1996)] In another case, a release signed by a plan participant in which the participant agreed not to sue for benefits under the plan barred the participant's subsequent suit to recover plan benefits. [Stadler v. McCullouch, Jr., No. 95-1380 (3d Cir. 1996)]

Q 4:28   Are qualified retirement plan benefits exempt from participants' creditors?

In 1992, the United States Supreme Court held that a participant's interest in a qualified retirement plan is exempt from the claims of creditors in a bankruptcy proceeding. [Patterson v. Shumate, 504 U.S. 753 (1992)] On April 20, 2005, President Bush signed into law the Bankruptcy Abuse Prevention and Consumer Protection Act of 2005, which contains provisions that protect the qualified retirement plan assets of bankruptcy filers. See Q 1:27 for a discussion of the salient provisions of this Act. Consequently, the following discussion may apply only to those cases that arose before the October 17, 2005, effective date of the Act.

ERISA and the Code require every qualified retirement plan to prohibit the assignment or alienation of benefits under the plan (see Q 4:27). [ERISA § 206(d)(1); I.R.C. § 401(a)(13)] Federal Bankruptcy Code Section 541(c)(2) excludes from the bankruptcy estate property of the debtor that is subject to a restriction on transfer enforceable under applicable nonbankruptcy law. The Supreme Court ruled that the anti-alienation provision contained in a qualified retirement plan constitutes a restriction on transfer enforceable under applicable nonbankruptcy law; and, accordingly, a debtor may exclude his interest in such a plan from the property of the bankruptcy estate. [*In re* Kunz, 205 U.S. App. LEXIS 1282 (10th Cir. 2005); Taunt v. General Retirement Sys. of Detroit, 2000 WL 1688949 (6th Cir. 2000); *In re* Bissell, 2000 WL 1733281 (Bankr. E.D. Va. 2000); *In re* Moses, 167 F.3d 470 (9th Cir. 1997); *In re* Winkler, No. 94-1475 (4th Cir. 1995); *In re* Schlein, 8 F.3d 745 (11th Cir. 1993); Arkison v. UPS Thrift Plan, 11 F.3d 850 (9th Cir. 1993)] One court ruled that the exception extends to voluntary contributions (see Q 1:49). [*In re* Conner, 73 F.3d 258 (9th Cir. 1996)]

The Supreme Court referred to an "ERISA qualified" plan, which, one court opined, could have one of three interpretations:

1. A plan subject to ERISA;

2. A plan subject to ERISA that contains an anti-alienation clause; or

3. A plan that is tax-qualified under the Code (see Q 1:5), is subject to ERISA, and has an anti-alienation provision as required by ERISA.

[*In re* Kaplan, 1993 Bankr. LEXIS 1534 (Bankr. E.D. Pa. 1993)]

While some courts have concluded that only the second interpretation is relevant, other courts have concluded that the third interpretation is controlling so that whether or not the plan is tax-qualified is relevant. [*In re* Meinen, 228 B.R. 368 (Bankr. W.D. Pa. 1998); SEC v. Johnson, 1996 U.S. Dist. LEXIS 5074 (E.D. Mich. 1996); *In re* Morten, 188 B.R. 444 (Bankr. M.D. Fla. 1995); *In re* Hanes, 162 B.R. 733 (Bankr. E.D. Va. 1994)] In either case, the common thread is "subject to ERISA." For purposes of Title I of ERISA, the term "employee benefit plan" does not include any plan under which no employees are participants covered under the plan. For example, a plan under which only a sole proprietor or only partners are participants is not covered under Title I. However, a plan under which one or more common-law employees, in addition to the self-employed individuals (see Q 6:60), are participants is covered under Title I. Furthermore, an individual and the individual's spouse are not deemed to be employees with respect to a trade or business, whether incorporated or unincorporated, that is wholly owned by the individual or by the individual and the spouse; and, in a partnership, a partner and the partner's spouse are not deemed to be employees with respect to the partnership. [DOL Reg. § 2510.3-3; Gaudette v. Erricola, No. 99-354-B (D.N.H. 2000); Roberts & Lloyd, Inc. v. Zyblut, No. 94-CV-1215 (D.C. Cir. 1997)]

Where the debtor was the sole shareholder and employee of his corporation and the sole participant in the qualified retirement plan, the creditors successfully challenged the exclusion of the shareholder's interest in the plan on the basis that, as the sole shareholder, he was not an employee and, as such, the plan was not an employee benefit plan under ERISA. [Lowenschuss v. Selnick, 170 F.3d 923 (9th Cir. 1999); *In re* Watson, 161 B.R. 593 (9th Cir. 1998); *In re* Branch, 1994 U.S. App. LEXIS 2870 (7th Cir. 1994); *In re* Witwer, 148 B.R. 930 (Bankr. C.D. Cal. 1992)] In other cases, because the plan covered only the sole shareholder and his wife and, as such, was a plan without employees, courts concluded that the plan was not subject to ERISA and that the bankruptcy exemption was contingent upon qualification under both ERISA and the Code. [*In re* Blais, 1994 Bankr. LEXIS 1427 (Bankr. S.D. Fla. 1994); *In re* Hall, 151 B.R. 412 (Bankr. W.D. Mich. 1993)] Where a partnership maintained two plans, the first covering only partners and the second covering the partners and employees, the court determined that the first plan was not subject to ERISA because a non-ERISA plan is not converted into an ERISA plan merely because the partnership maintained a second plan that was subject to ERISA. [Zeiger v. Zeiger, 1997 U.S. App. LEXIS 33673 (9th Cir. 1997)] The United States Supreme Court concluded that, if the plan covers one or more employees other than the business owner and the business owner's spouse, the business owner is a plan participant, is entitled to ERISA protections, and can protect plan assets under the anti-alienation provision from bankruptcy creditors. [Raymond B. Yates, M.D., P.C. Profit Sharing Plan v. Hendon, 124 S. Ct. 1330 (2004)]

One court concluded that the exclusion of a debtor's interest in an ERISA qualified plan is permissive rather than mandatory and, thus, held that a debtor could enter into an agreement to include in his bankruptcy estate his interest in a qualified retirement plan. [*In re* Rains, 428 F.3d 893 (9th Cir. 2005)]

In one case, the court determined that a plan was not subject to ERISA because the husband was the sole shareholder and sole plan participant. The sole shareholder and his wife were divorced, and the settlement agreement gave to the wife a community interest in the husband's plan benefits and one-half of the shares in the corporation. The court then concluded that the plan became subject to ERISA after the divorce and the ex-wife's interest in the husband's plan benefits were excluded from her bankruptcy estate. [McDonald v. Metz, 225 B.R. 173 (B.A.P. 9th Cir. 1998)]

After the Supreme Court decision, bankruptcy trustees developed a new strategy. Since ERISA may protect only qualified retirement plan benefits, bankruptcy trustees began bringing into question the qualified status of the plan. What was once the domain of IRS (see Q 18:1) could become a territorial dispute with the bankruptcy courts. [*In re* Lawrence, 235 B.R. 498 (Bankr. S.D. Fla. 1999); Dzikowski v. Blau, 220 B.R. 484 (S.D. Fla. 1997)]

Although a qualified retirement plan was not an ERISA-qualified plan because the only participants were owners of the employer, the plan assets could still be exempted from bankruptcy under a state statute *provided* the IRS did not disqualify the plan. Courts have also concluded that they need not step into the shoes of IRS to determine if the plan was still qualified, nor were they required to perform a rigorous analysis of the plan to see whether it remained qualified in order to grant a bankruptcy exemption. [*In re* Baker, No. 09-13144 (11th Cir. 2009); *In re* Sewell, 180 F.3d 707 (5th Cir. 1999); *In re* Moses, 167 F.3d 470 (9th Cir. 1998); *In re* Baker, 114 F.3d 636 (7th Cir. 1997); Youngblood v. FDIC, 29 F.3d 225 (5th Cir. 1994); *In re* Fernandez, 236 B.R. 483 (Bankr. M.D. Fla. 1999); *In re* Craig, 204 B.R. 750 (Bankr. D.N.D. 1997); *In re* Feldman, 1994 Bankr. LEXIS 1377 (Bankr. E.D.N.Y. 1994); *In re* Kaplan, 1993 Bankr. LEXIS 1534 (Bankr. E.D. Pa. 1993)] One court concluded that it was not bound by the IRS determination because (1) the determination had been made years before, (2) the plan had never been audited by IRS, and (3) the debtor had abused plan assets. [In the Matter of Plunk, No. 06-10426 (5th Cir. 2007)] Another court ruled that a debtor unlawfully, deceptively, and purposefully overfunded retirement plans sponsored by his wholly owned corporations. Because of the debtor's behavior, the plans were not designed and used primarily for retirement; and, therefore, the state bankruptcy exemption for retirement plan benefits did not apply. [Cunning v. Lloyd Myles Rucker, 2009 WL 1813248 (9th Cir. 2009)]

In another case, the debtor, a self-employed dentist, sought to exclude from the bankruptcy estate his benefits in two plans. Although there were common-law employees who had satisfied the eligibility requirements, and although the plans were top-heavy (see chapter 26), the debtor had made no contributions to either plan on behalf of the employees. The court determined that the plans were not qualified plans and therefore were includible within the bankruptcy estate.

[Bernstein v. Greenpoint Sav. Bank, 149 B.R. 760 (Bankr. E.D.N.Y. 1993); *see also In re* Harris, 1995 Bankr. LEXIS 1534 (Bankr. M.D. Fla. 1995); Stochastic Decisions, Inc. v. Wagner, 1994 U.S. App. LEXIS 24110 (2d Cir. 1994); Pitrat v. Garlikov, 947 F.2d 419 (9th Cir. 1993); *In re* Lane, Jr., 149 B.R. 760 (Bankr. E.D.N.Y. 1993)]

A bankruptcy trustee cannot reach the plan benefits of a debtor by requiring the debtor to make a loan from the plan to fund the bankruptcy plan. [*In re* Stones, 157 B.R. 669 (Bankr. S.D. Cal. 1993)] Another court ruled that funds loaned by a plan to a participant are not exempt. [Friedman v. Broach, 220 B.R. 679 (B.A.P. 9th Cir. 1998)]; *see also In re* Lasowski, No. 07-6063 (Bankr. App. Panel, 8th Cir. 2008) A bankruptcy court cannot require plan benefits to be distributed. [*In re* McLellan, 99 F.3d 1420 (7th Cir. 1996)]

Courts have ruled that a debtor's interest in a qualified retirement plan is exempt even though, after the commencement of the bankruptcy proceedings, the debtor rolled over the benefits to an IRA (see Q 34:34). [*In re* Parks, 2000 WL 1803281 (Bankr. Vt. 2000); Shadduck v. Odolakis, 221 B.R. 573 (Bankr. D. Mass. 1998)] Similarly, the bankruptcy exemption applied even though the debtor received a distribution of plan benefits, part of which he retained and the balance of which he rolled over to an IRA, soon after he filed for bankruptcy. [*In re* Kim, 2000 WL 33128673 (9th Cir. 2000)] In another case, shortly before a debtor filed a voluntary bankruptcy proceeding, he rolled over an IRA, which was not entirely exempt from attachment by creditors under state law, to a qualified retirement plan, which was entirely exempt. The court determined that the rollover was not a fraudulent conveyance *per se* and further ruled that the plan assets were exempt from attachment by creditors. [*In re* Stern, 2003 U.S. App. LEXIS 1828 (9th Cir. 2003)]

One court concluded that a trustee in bankruptcy could recover funds paid from a qualified retirement plan to the attorneys who had represented both the debtor and the plan. Although the attorneys argued that they had represented the plan before the court determined that the plan was part of the bankruptcy estate, the court held that, since the representation did not benefit the bankruptcy estate, it was improper for the attorneys to be paid from funds that were property of the bankruptcy estate. [*In re* Gaudette v. Thomas, Utell, Van De Water & Raiche, P.A., 2001 WL 1301765 (Bankr. D.N.H. 2001)] A debtor in bankruptcy claimed that $40,000 he received as a wrongful discharge settlement should have been exempted from his bankruptcy estate because that portion of the proceeds represented qualified retirement plan contributions that his former employer would have made if he had not been wrongfully terminated. The court concluded that the proceeds were not exempt from bankruptcy because retirement assets that are never placed in a qualified retirement plan are not protected. [*In re* Weinhoeft, No. 01-2412 (7th Cir. 2001)] Similarly, another court ruled that elective contributions (see Q 27:16) a debtor *intended* to make to a 401(k) plan during the bankruptcy plan had to be used to make payments to creditors. [*In re* Prout, 2002 WL 229878 (Bankr. M.D. Fla. 2002); *see also* Hebbring v. U.S. Trustee, 463 F.3d 902 (9th Cir. 2006)] Amounts contributed by a debtor to a 401(k) plan within the year preceding the bankruptcy filing could not be excluded, under state law, from the bankruptcy estate, concluded one court. [*In re* Bellwoar, No. 03-15455 (E.D. Pa. 2003)]

See Q 36:36 for a discussion of the anti-alienation rule and claims of creditors relating to an alternate payee's interest in plan benefits under a QDRO.

Q 4:29   Can IRS levy against a participant's qualified retirement plan benefits?

The Bankruptcy Abuse Prevention and Consumer Protection Act of 2005 (see Q 1:27) protects the qualified retirement plan assets of bankruptcy filers. Since IRS levies and liens can occur in nonbankruptcy proceedings, the provisions of the Act should not affect the following discussion as it relates to nonbankruptcy matters. With the issuance of the IRS Chief Counsel Notice discussed at the end of this Q 4:29, it appears that the Act will have no effect on IRS liens and levies even where there are bankruptcy proceedings.

Although two courts have ruled that IRS could not levy against a participant's benefits because they were exempt under ERISA [ERISA § 206(d); *In re* Wingfield, 2002 U.S. Dist. LEXIS 15885 (E.D. Va. 2002); *In re* Lewis, No. 90-B-02776 D (Bankr. D. Colo. 1990)], most courts have held that the prohibition against the assignment or alienation of retirement plan benefits does not preclude the enforcement of a federal tax levy or the collection by IRS on a judgment resulting from an unpaid tax assessment. [I.R.C. §§ 6331, 6334; Treas. Reg. §§ 1.401(a)-13(b)(2), 301.6334-1 through 301.6334-4; T.D. 8568; Fusaro, 86 T.C.M. 731 (2003); Morgan v. Comm'r, 02-4138 (8th Cir. 2003); *In re* Piper, 02-12096 (Bankr. D. Mass. 2003); United States v. Northern Trust Co, 2002 U.S. Dist. LEXIS 23630 (N.D. Ill. 2002); *In re* Tudisco, 1999 WL 459370 (2d Cir. 1999); Farr v. United Airlines, Inc, No. 97-35907 (9th Cir. 1998); *In re* Allison, No. 97-12264-7 (Bankr. D. Mont. 1998), *aff'd*, CV-98-181 (D. Mont. 1999); Weiler v. United States, No. 94-56465 (9th Cir. 1996); United States v. Sawaf, 74 F.3d 119 (6th Cir. 1996); Scully v. Fireman's Variable Pension Fund, CIV 98-0121 (D. Ariz. 1998); Gregory v. United States, No. 96-CV-70603 (E.D. Mich. 1996); *In re* Wesche, 95-1224-BKC-3F3 (Bankr. M.D. Fla. 1996); Travelers Ins. Co. v. Rattermann, C-1-94-466 (S.D. Ohio 1996); IBEW Local Union No. 640 v. Forman, CIV 94-2431 (D. Ariz. 1995); Ameritrust Co., N.A. v. Derakhshan, No. 1:92CV0931 (N.D. Ohio 1993); Hyde v. United States, No. 90-1258 (D. Ariz. 1993); *In re* Raihl, 152 B.R. 615 (Bankr. 9th Cir. 1993); Anderson v. United States, 149 B.R. 591 (Bankr. 9th Cir. 1992); *In re* Jacobs, Sr., 147 B.R. 106 (Bankr. W.D. Pa. 1992); United States v. Weintraub, No. C-1-76-0032 (S.D. Ohio 1990)]

One court permitted IRS to levy on plan benefits that were payable under the PBGC insurance program (see Q 25:16). [Shanbaum v. United States, 32 F.3d 180 (5th Cir. 1994)] Some courts have ruled that IRS could not secure a tax lien against the bankruptcy estate of a debtor who filed for bankruptcy protection under Chapter 13 of the Bankruptcy Code because the tax lien was based on the debtor's interest in a qualified retirement plan, which was excludable from the bankruptcy estate. [United States v. Snyder, 343 F.3d 1171 (9th Cir. 2003), Acq.

Ann., 2004-41 I.R.B. (Oct. 12, 2004); *In re* Robinson, No. 02-73381 (Bankr. E.D. Va. 2003); *In re* Grant, No. 09-71090 (Bankr. E.D. Va. 2003); *In re* Keyes, 255 B.R. 819 (Bankr. E.D. Va. 2000); *In re* Wilson, 206 B.R. 808 (Bankr. W.D.N.C. 1996); *In re* Taylor, 1991 Bankr. LEXIS 711 (Bankr. D. Md. 1991)] However, other courts have ruled otherwise. [*In re* Berry, 268 B.R. 819 (Bankr. E.D. Tenn. 2001); *In re* McIver, 255 B.R. 281 (D. Md. 2000); *In re* Jones, 206 B.R. 614 (Bankr. D.D.C. 1997); *In re* Lyons, 148 B.R. 88 (Bankr. D.D.C. 1992); *In re* Perkins, 134 B.R. 408 (Bankr. E.D. Cal. 1991)] One court concluded that plan benefits were not subject to an unfiled IRS tax lien. [*In re* Rich, No. 93-02514-C (Bankr. N.D. Okla. 1996)] An individual's plan account was subject to a federal tax lien despite his bankruptcy discharge. Although the IRS agent had acknowledged that the individual's underlying personal tax liability was properly discharged by the bankruptcy proceeding, the discharge only affected one method of collection, that of bringing an action in personam against the debtor. The bankruptcy discharge, however, did not affect the federal tax lien that automatically arose on his property and was in place at the time he filed a bankruptcy petition. Therefore, IRS was allowed to enforce its lien against the individual's plan account. [Iannone, 122 T.C. 287 (2004)]

In one case, the participant wife died without naming a beneficiary, but under the terms of the plan, the husband was the deemed beneficiary. When the husband then died, the court ruled that the plan benefits were part of his estate and that IRS could execute its tax lien against the husband upon the benefits. [Nordstrom, Inc. v. Fall, No. C97-1667D (W.D. Wash. 1998)] Another court concluded that a participant's community property interest in his plan benefits was subject to a federal tax lien, even though his former wife also had a claim to the benefits, because the lien attached prior to the entry of a QDRO (see Q 36:1) transferring the benefits to her. [Agents Pension Plan of Allstate Ins. Co. v. Weeks, 1999 WL 261700 (N.D. Ill. 1999); *see also In re* McIntyre, 2000 WL 963936 (9th Cir. 2000)] In another case where a plan participant transferred his benefits to an IRA (see Q 30:1) without spousal consent (see Q 10:21), the court stated that IRS could levy against the entire IRA even though the participant's wife had not consented to the transfer. [Kopec v. Kopec, 1999 WL 961244 (E.D.N.Y. 1999)]

Even though the United States Supreme Court has held that a participant's interest in a qualified retirement plan is exempt from the claims of creditors in a bankruptcy proceeding (see Q 4:28), the enforcement of a federal tax levy against, or the collection by IRS of an unpaid tax assessment from, plan benefits appears to be permitted. It remains the position of IRS that such levies are permissible. In fact, IRS has advised that it possesses the authority to levy upon qualified retirement plan benefits even though the participant has no immediate right to receipt of benefits, provided the participant has a vested right to a future distribution from the plan; however, IRS further advised that it is precluded from requesting the plan administrator (see Q 20:1) to immediately distribute any assets pursuant to the IRS levy until the participant obtains an immediate right to receive benefits under the plan. IRS has also concluded that a levy did not reach amounts payable to a plan beneficiary as guaranteed death benefits even though the lien attached to the participant's benefits while he was alive.

[Chief Couns. Adv. 200249001, 200102021, 200041029, 200032004, 199936041, 199930039; *see also* Asbestos Workers Local No. 23 Pension Fund v. United States, Civ. 1:01-CV-2253 (M.D. Pa. 2004)] One court ruled that a tax lien may be secured by property of a debtor that is exempt from levy. A levy involves the immediate seizure of property, while a lien is merely a security interest in property. Thus, a federal tax lien attached to all of the debtor's rights in her pension benefits, including the right to future payments. [*In re* Jeffrey, 2001 Bankr. LEXIS 337 (W.D. Pa. 2001)] One court has ruled that the value of a participant's plan account is not reduced by the potential income taxes incurred because of the execution of the IRS levy (see Qs 13:1, 16:11). [E.B. Leedy, 98-15257 (Bankr.__.D. Va. 1999)]

With regard to the above discussion and the divergent opinions of courts, IRS announced a change in its litigation position concerning the application of Federal Bankruptcy Code Section 506(a) to qualified retirement plans that are excluded from the bankruptcy estate under Federal Bankruptcy Code Section 541(c)(2) (see Q 4:28). Under Section 506(a), a creditor with a lien on property of the bankruptcy estate holds a secured claim to the extent of the value of the creditor's interest in the estate's interest in such property. Section 541(a) provides that, upon the commencement of the bankruptcy case, an estate is created which consists of all legal or equitable interests of the debtor on that date. An exception to this rule is found in Section 541(c)(2), which provides that restrictions on the transfer of a beneficial interest in a trust that is enforceable under applicable nonbankruptcy law is enforceable in a bankruptcy case. IRS will no longer argue that it may include in the value of its secured claim the debtor's interest in a plan that is excluded from property of the bankruptcy estate under Section 541(c)(2). In cases where the debtor's interest in a plan is excluded from property of the estate, IRS will not include the value of the debtor's interest in the plan in its secured claim. However, IRS's lien against the debtor's interest in the plan is not extinguished and will continue to exist outside of the bankruptcy proceeding. The practical effect of this change in position is that IRS will levy against the debtor's plan interest outside of the bankruptcy process. [IRS Chief Couns. Notice CC-2004-033 (Sept. 9, 2004)]

IRS advised that Form 668-W (rather than Form 668-A) should be used by IRS to levy a taxpayer's income from a retirement plan. Form 668-A is used to levy the funds accumulated in a retirement plan. [Chief Couns. Adv. 201022015]

IRS advised that it cannot levy on a retirement plan after the death of a taxpayer in order to collect amounts that the taxpayer could have elected to receive, but had not received, while living. While still alive, a taxpayer had submitted a letter to the taxpayer's retirement plan to request a full withdrawal of funds to be made payable to IRS, but died soon after. IRS determined that the taxpayer's letter to the retirement plan was insufficient to elect a withdrawal of funds from the plan. Therefore, IRS was precluded from levying on funds where there was no pre-death election. [Chief Couns. Adv. 200935026]

A writ of garnishment filed against the defined contribution plan (see Q 2:2) of a participant found guilty of wire fraud and tax evasion did not violate ERISA because qualified retirement plans are not among the U.S. Criminal Code's enumerated exceptions to property subject to garnishment, according to one court. [United States v. Garcia, No. 96-10049-01 (D. Kan. 2003)] IRS has ruled that a federal court seeking to collect a fine in an individual's criminal case would not violate the anti-alienation rule by garnishing his 401(k) plan account (see Q 27:1). [Priv. Ltr. Rul. 200342007; *see also* Priv. Ltr. Rul. 200426027] One court ruled that, pursuant to the Mandatory Victims Restitution Act of 1996 (MVRA), the federal government can garnish the pension benefits of a person who pleaded guilty to a crime. The court stated that the MVRA constituted a statutory exception to ERISA's anti-alienation provision because (1) the MVRA is a specific collection statute designed to provide victims with restitution and (2) Congress provided for restitution orders to be enforced like tax liens, which are enforceable against ERISA pension benefits. [United States v. Novak, 2007 U.S. App. LEXIS 3804 (9th Cir. 2007); *see also* United States v. Irving, No. 04-0971 (2d Cir. 2005)] The United States was allowed to proceed with a civil forfeiture action against sums distributed by a qualified retirement plan and rolled over to an IRA. [United States v. Weiss, 2003 WL 22138504 (2d Cir. 2003)]

One court ruled that, under the doctrine of sovereign immunity, a qualified retirement plan was precluded from suing IRS for a refund of a tax levy on a participant's benefit that the plan claimed was improper. [Operating Eng'rs Pension Trust v. United States, No. CV-92-2730-RSWL (C.D. Cal. 1992)]

With regard to state taxes, one court has held that a state statute that allows tax levies against pension benefits to collect delinquent state income taxes was preempted by ERISA as a violation of the anti-alienation rule and the benefits were protected from attachment. [Retirement Fund Trust of the Plumbing, Heating & Piping Indus. of S. Cal. v. Franchise Tax Bd., Nos. 99-6355, 88-6415 (9th Cir. 1990)]

Q 4:30   May a participant's qualified retirement plan benefits be attached or garnished?

According to IRS, an attachment, garnishment, levy, execution, or other legal or equitable process of or against a participant's qualified retirement plan benefits is not a voluntary assignment or alienation (see Q 4:27) and therefore violates the anti-alienation rule. IRS has also held that a transfer of a participant's plan benefits, which violates the anti-alienation rule, results in the disqualification of the plan. [Treas. Reg. § 1.401(a)-13(d)(1); Priv. Ltr. Ruls. 9011037, 8829009]

However, if benefits have been distributed to the participant, the attachment or assignment of the distributed plan benefits will not violate the anti-alienation provisions. [Hoult v. Hoult, 373 F.3d 47 (1st Cir. 2004); Wright v. Riveland, 219 F.3d 905 (9th Cir. 2000); Taylor v. United States, 2000 WL 556864 (8th Cir. 2000); Greve v. JH Patterson Co., No. 96 C 50424 (N.D. Ill. 1999); Guidry v. Sheet Metal Workers Nat'l Pension Fund, 39 F.3d 1078 (10th Cir. 1994); Trucking Employees of N. Jersey Welfare Fund, Inc. v. Colville, 16 F.3d 52 (3d Cir. 1994); Guidry v. Sheet Metal Workers Int'l Ass'n, Local No. 9, 10 F.3d 700 (10th Cir. 1993); *In re* Collin, 182 B.R. 763 (Bankr. N.D. Ohio 1995); Brosamer

v. Mark, No. 27S02-9011-CV-700 (Ind. 1990)] To the contrary, one court has held that monthly benefit payments, even after receipt by the retired participant, are protected by ERISA. [United States v. Smith, 47 F.3d 681 (4th Cir. 1995)] Another court determined that plan benefits, even after distribution, are protected from criminal forfeiture in favor of the government. [United States v. Norton, 2002 U.S. Dist. LEXIS 17052 (W.D. Va. 2002)] One court concluded that the anti-alienation rule was not violated when a Medicaid recipient's retirement benefits were attributed to his wife for purposes of calculating her minimum asset allowance because, once the benefits are distributed, the alienation of benefits is not prohibited. [Robbins v. DeBuono, 218 F.3d 197 (2d Cir. 2000)]

Although plan benefits are generally no longer protected against claims of creditors once they are distributed to the participant, one court ruled that judgment creditors could not attach plan benefits even though a check to the participant had been drawn because the plan trustee had not yet distributed the check. [Shinehouse v. Guerin, No. 96-1500 (3d Cir. 1997)]

A former participant's argument that his pension plan benefits should not be attachable by creditors for a period of 60 days after receipt, because he could elect to roll over his benefits during that period (see Q 34:35), was rejected. [Nations Bank of N.C. v. Shumate, No. 93-2092 (4th Cir. 1994)]

See Q 1:27 for a discussion of the Bankruptcy Abuse Prevention and Consumer Protection Act of 2005.

Chapter 5

Eligibility and Participation

A company's retirement plan does not qualify for tax-favored status unless certain minimum standards for coverage of employees are met. This chapter examines those standards, describes the problems regarding related companies, and discusses important terms.

Q 5:1 Must a company's qualified retirement plan cover all of its employees?

No. However, a minimum coverage requirement, in terms of a percentage of the company's workforce, must be satisfied (see Q 5:15). In addition, a minimum participation requirement, in terms of a percentage or a number of the company's workforce, may have to be satisfied (see Q 5:23). A retirement plan that meets the minimum coverage requirement and, if applicable, the minimum participation requirement may qualify for favorable tax treatment even though some employees are excluded.

It is important to recognize that the coverage requirement and, if applicable, the participation requirement are minimum standards that must be satisfied by a qualified retirement plan. A company may use more liberal standards than those discussed in this chapter. [I.R.C. §§ 401(a)(26), 410(b)]

In the first instance, a determination must be made as to whether or not an individual is an employee. ERISA Section 3(6) defines an employee as any individual employed by an employer. Concluding that the ERISA definition is completely circular and explains nothing, the United States Supreme Court adopted a common-law test for determining employee status. Under the test, the following should be considered:

- The right of the hiring party to control the manner and means by which the product is accomplished
- The skill required
- The source of the instrumentalities and tools
- The work location
- The duration of the parties' relationship

- Whether the hiring party has the right to assign more projects to the hired party
- The extent to which the hired party may decide when and how long to work
- The payment method
- The role of the hired party in hiring and paying assistants
- Whether the work is part of the hiring party's regular business
- Whether the hiring party is in business
- The provision of employee benefits
- The tax treatment of the hired party

All incidents of the relationship must be taken into account, and no single factor will be decisive. [Nationwide Mut. Ins. Co. v. Darden, 503 U.S. 318 (1992); Bruecher Foundation Services Inc., ____ (5th Cir. 2010); Feaster, T.C.M. 2010-157; Nu-Look Design, Inc. v. Comm'r, 03-2754 (3d Cir. 2004); Kolling v. American Power Conversion Corp., 2003 WL 22350886 (1st Cir. 2003); Joseph M. Grey, Pub. Accountant, P.C. v. Comm'r, 02-4417 (3d Cir. 2003); Mulzet v. R.L. Reppert Inc., 2002 WL 31761696 (3d Cir. 2002); Montesano v. Xerox Corp. Ret. Income Guarantee Plan, 256 F.3d 86 (2d Cir. 2001); Hensley v. Northwest Permanente P.C. Ret. Plan & Trust, 2001 WL 868044 (9th Cir. 2001); Vizcaino v. Microsoft Corp., 1997 U.S. App. LEXIS 18869 (9th Cir. 1997); Trombetta v. Cragin Fed. Bank for Sav. ESOP, 102 F.3d 1435 (7th Cir. 1996); Roth v. American Hosp. Supply Corp., 965 F.2d 862 (10th Cir. 1992); Keleher v. Dominion Insulation, Inc., 1992 U.S. App. LEXIS 25561 (4th Cir. 1992); Kiper v. Novartis Crop Protection, Inc., No. 00-528-B-M3 (M.D. La. 2002); Herr v. McCormick Grain-The Heiman Co., 1993 U.S. Dist. LEXIS 15622 (D. Kan. 1993); Jones, 94 T.C.M. 230 (2007); Levine, 89 T.C.M. 1063 (2005); Kumpel, 86 T.C.M. 358 (2003); Ronald McLean E. Video, 85 T.C.M. 763 (2003); Naughton, 84 T.C.M. 275 (2002); Day, 80 T.C.M. 835 (2000); Pariani, 74 T.C.M. 682 (1997); Lozon, 73 T.C.M. 2914 (1997); Ann. 96-13, 1996-12 I.R.B. 33; SBA '96 § 1122; IRS Pub. 15-A (Employer's Supplemental Tax Guide); Priv. Ltr. Ruls. 200407014, 200234007]

In one case, some of a company's employees were transferred to temporary employment agencies but continued to work for the company. The court chose five factors to consider in deciding whether a temporary employee is a common-law employee of the client company:

1. Whether the company or the agency recruited the worker;
2. The extent of the training that the company provides to the worker;
3. The duration of the worker's relationship with the company;
4. The company's right to assign additional projects to the worker; and
5. Whether the company may influence the relationship between the worker and the agency.

Under these factors, the court determined that the workers were common-law employees of the company both before and after their conversion to temporary personnel. [Vizcaino v. Microsoft Corp., C93-178D (W.D. Wash. 1998)]

Just because an individual is deemed to be an employee does not mean that the individual must be eligible to participate in the employer's retirement plan (see Q 5:5). [Bronk v. Mountain States Tel. & Tel., Inc, 216 F.3d 1086 (10th Cir. 2000); Capital Cities/ABC, Inc. v. Ratcliff, No. 97-3031 (10th Cir. 1998); Moxley v. Texaco, Inc., No. 00-1518 CM (C.D. Cal. 2001)] Employees hired by a company, but paid by a third-party payroll agency, could be excluded from participating in the company's benefit plans ruled one court. [Edes v. Verizon Communications, Inc., 2005 WL 1805123 (1st Cir. 2005); *see also* Curry v. CTB McGraw-Hill, LLC, 2008 WL 4542863 (9th Cir. 2008)] However, a plan was disqualified for failure to satisfy the minimum coverage and minimum participation requirements because the employer improperly characterized employees as independent contractors and did not include them as participants in the plan. [Kenney, 70 T.C.M. 614 (1995); *see also* Ramirez, 94 T.C.M. 493 (2007), Peno Trucking, Inc., 93 T.C.M. 1027 (2007), and Orion Contracting Trust, 92 T.C.M. 309 (2006)] A similar problem could arise if independent contractors are improperly characterized as employees and then participate in the plan. [Belluardo v. Cox Enterprises, Inc., Pension Plan, No. 04-3505 (6th Cir. 2005)] IRS has ruled that the participation of an independent contractor in a company's plan did not disqualify the plan where the contractor had been treated as an employee up until a court decision that he was actually an independent contractor. To prevent plan disqualification, the contractor's participation was canceled retroactively, and the contractor's elective contributions and the earnings thereon were distributed to him. [Priv. Ltr. Rul. 9546018]

One court ruled that the employer did not breach its fiduciary duty by failing to inform an employee that he was required to complete forms to enroll in its plan, where the employer provided the employee with other documents informing him of the enrollment requirements. [Brenner v. Johns Hopkins Univ., 2004 U.S. App. LEXIS 2339 (4th Cir. 2004)]

IRS posted a revised document on its website providing answers to questions that may arise after it determines that an individual is an employee rather than an independent contractor. [Notice 989 (Rev. 7-2009) Commonly Asked Questions When IRS Determines Your Work Status is "Employee"]

For a further discussion of the employer-employee relationship, see Q 35:5.

Q 5:2   What minimum age and service requirements may be set by a qualified retirement plan?

A qualified retirement plan may require an employee to reach age 21 before becoming eligible to participate in the plan. A plan may also require an employee to complete one year of service (see Qs 5:5, 5:8) with the company before becoming eligible to participate. [I.R.C. § 410(a)(1)(A)]

For qualified retirement plans that provide full and immediate vesting (see Q 9:13), an employer may condition participation on completion of more than one year of service. The maximum period for such plans is two years; however, for 401(k) plans, the maximum period is only one year (see Qs 5:4, 27:15). [I.R.C. §§ 410(a)(1)(B), 401(k)(2)(D)]

It may be permissible to amend a qualified retirement plan to increase the service requirement from one year to two years for the purpose of delaying the participation date of a particular employee. [McGath v. Auto-Body N. Shore, Inc., 1993 U.S. App. LEXIS 27198 (7th Cir. 1993)]

One spouse worked for the business owned by the other spouse for ten years on a full-time basis (i.e., at least 1,000 hours of service each year) but did not commence receiving compensation until 2004. IRS representatives opined that the spouse's date of employment commenced when compensation commenced and not when the spouse commenced to work. The author strongly disagrees with this opinion; employment relates to the rendering of services to the business and not to when those services are first compensated in dollars.

Q 5:3 May a qualified retirement plan set a maximum age limit for participation?

No. A qualified retirement plan may not exclude from participation employees who are hired after reaching a specified maximum age. [I.R.C. § 410(a)(2); Prop. Treas. Reg. §§ 1.410(a)-4A, 1.411(b)-2]

Although a plan may not exclude older employees by its terms, an older employee may waive plan participation, provided the waiver is knowingly and voluntarily made. A refusal to allow waivers of participation by older employees would be equivalent to imposing mandatory plan participation on that group of employees. [Finz v. Schlesinger, 957 F.2d 78 (2d Cir. 1992); Laniok v. Advisory Comm. of the Brainerd Mfg. Co. Pension Plan, 935 F.2d 1360 (2d Cir. 1991)]

Q 5:4 May a qualified retirement plan require two consecutive years of service for participation?

Qualified retirement plans that provide for immediate 100 percent vesting and require more than one year of service, but not more than two years of service, to be eligible to participate (see Qs 5:2, 9:13) may provide that years of service preceding a one-year break in service (see Q 5:10) be disregarded if the employee has not yet met the service eligibility criterion. Thus, an employee who completes one year of service and then incurs a one-year break in service starts over again, either the next year or when the employee is rehired. However, the plan cannot require that the two years of service be consecutive. [I.R.C. § 410(a)(5)(B); Temp. Treas. Reg. § 1.410(a)-8T(c)(2)]

Example. CeeKay Corp. established a profit sharing plan in 2006 that operates on a calendar-year basis. The plan provides that an employee must complete two years of service before becoming a participant and that the employee will be 100 percent vested upon completion of the two-year eligibility requirement. The following three employees all became employed by CeeKay on December 31, 2006:

Hours of Service Completed

Plan Year	Stephanie	Caroline	James
2007	1,000	1,000	1,000
2008	1,000	700	500
2009	1,000	1,000	1,000
2010	1,000	1,000	700
2011	1,000	1,000	1,000

Stephanie satisfied the plan's service requirement at the end of 2008; Caroline at the end of 2009 because 2007 may not be disregarded, since she did not have a one-year break in service in 2008; and James will have satisfied the requirement at the end of 2011 because 2007 may be disregarded, since he did have a one-year break in service in 2008.

IRS representatives have opined that a plan requiring two years of service to be eligible to participate cannot disregard an employee's prebreak years of service where the employee satisfied the service requirement but terminated employment before the plan's next entry date (see Q 5:7).

Example. Yvonne began working for Mark Corporation on October 1, 2008. Mark Corporation's qualified retirement plan operates on a calendar-year basis and requires that employees complete two years of service. Employees who satisfy the service eligibility requirement commence participation on the next succeeding January 1 or July 1. Since Yvonne met the plan's eligibility requirements on October 1, 2010, she must start to participate in the plan no later than January 1, 2011. Yvonne terminates employment on November 4, 2010 and is rehired by Mark Corporation on October 7, 2011. Because Yvonne was not employed by Mark Corporation on January 1, 2011, she did not become a participant in the plan. However, when Yvonne is rehired, her prebreak years of service cannot be disregarded, and Yvonne will become a participant on January 1, 2012.

Q 5:5 May conditions other than age and service be set for participation in a qualified retirement plan?

Yes. A qualified retirement plan can impose other conditions for participation, provided that the minimum coverage requirement and, if applicable, the minimum participation requirement are satisfied (see Qs 5:15, 5:23). For example, a plan could require that an employee not be an hourly paid employee or not be employed within a specified job description (e.g., sales representative) to be eligible to participate (see Q 1:46). [Treas. Reg. § 1.410(a)-3(d)] One court held that leased employees (see Qs 5:58, 5:59) could be excluded from participation because they were not considered regular employees. [Bronk v. Mountain States Tel. & Tel., Inc., 216 F.3d 1086 (10th Cir. 2000); *see also* Edes v. Verizon Communications, Inc., 2005 WL 1805123 (1st Cir. 2005)] Another court concluded that an employer could exclude a specific category of employees. [Capital Cities/ABC, Inc. v. Ratcliff, No. 97-3031 (10th Cir. 1998)]

The most common exclusion, other than exclusions based upon age and service, applies to union employees on whose behalf negotiations for retirement benefits have been conducted with the company. The company may exclude union employees from coverage, whether or not they are covered under a separate retirement plan, as long as retirement benefits were the subject of good-faith bargaining. Exclusions for air pilots and nonresident aliens are also permitted. [I.R.C. § 410(b)(3)] Where a child of the business owner works for the business in both union and non-union capacities, receives separate union and non-union compensation, and receives all union benefits, including participation in the union pension plan with respect to the child's union compensation, IRS representatives have opined that the child can also participate in the employer's qualified retirement plan with respect to the non-union compensation.

Plan provisions may be treated as imposing age and service requirements even though the provisions do not specifically refer to age or service. Plan provisions that have the effect of requiring an age or service requirement with the employer will be treated as if they impose an age or service requirement.

Example. Attorney Bill, Inc. adopts a profit sharing plan that requires one year of service (Q 5:8) to be eligible to participate but excludes part-time employees (employees who work less than 40 hours per week). The plan does not qualify because the provision could result in the exclusion by reason of a minimum service requirement of an employee who has completed a year of service. Even assuming that the exclusion from plan participation of part-time employees would not cause the plan to fail the minimum coverage requirement, the exclusion nonetheless imposes an indirect service requirement on plan participation that could exceed one year of service. A plan may not exclude any part-time employee where it is possible for that employee to complete one year of service.

[Treas. Reg. §§ 1.410(a)-3(e)(1), §§ 1.410(a)-3(e)(2); Employee Plans Determinations Quality Assurance Bulletin, FY-2006 No. 3 (Feb. 14, 2006); IRS Field Off. Directive (Nov. 22, 1994); Priv. Ltr. Rul. 9508003]

Q 5:6   May the company require employee contributions as a condition of plan participation?

Yes. A company may adopt a plan—commonly called a thrift or savings plan (see Q 2:11)—that gears employer contributions on behalf of an employee to contributions made by the employee. Other types of plans may also require contributions to be made by the employees (e.g., defined benefit plans). Since participation in these plans is usually limited to those employees who contribute, if required employee contributions are so burdensome that non-highly compensated employees (NHCEs; see Q 3:12) cannot afford to participate, the plan may fail to satisfy the minimum coverage requirement and, if applicable, the minimum participation requirement (see Qs 5:15, 5:23, 6:37).

Q 5:7   When must an employee who meets the plan's eligibility requirements begin to participate?

An employee who meets the minimum age and service requirements of the Code (see Q 5:2), and who is otherwise eligible to participate in the qualified retirement plan, must commence participation no later than the earlier of (1) the first day of the first plan year beginning after the date the employee met the eligibility requirements or (2) the date six months after these requirements were met. [I.R.C. § 410(a)(4)]

> **Example.** Ken began working for Danielle Corporation on October 1, 2009. He was 30 years old at that time. Danielle Corporation's qualified retirement plan operates on a calendar-year basis and requires that employees be at least age 21 and complete one year of service. Since Ken met the plan's eligibility requirements on October 1, 2010, he must start to participate in the plan no later than January 1, 2011. This is because January 1, 2011, the first day of the first plan year beginning after Ken has met the eligibility requirements, is earlier than April 1, 2011, the date six months after he has met these requirements.

Q 5:8   What is a year of service for a plan's service eligibility requirement?

A year of service for eligibility purposes means a calendar year, a plan year, or any other consecutive 12-month period (the eligibility computation period) specified in the qualified retirement plan during which the employee completes at least 1,000 hours of service (see Qs 5:5, 5:9). The initial eligibility computation period starts on the date employment commences and ends 12 months thereafter. [I.R.C. § 410(a)(3)(A)] One spouse worked for the business owned by the other spouse for ten years on a full-time basis (i.e., at least 1,000 hours of service each year) but did not commence receiving compensation until 2004. IRS representatives opined that the spouse's date of employment commenced when compensation commenced and not when the spouse commenced to work. The author strongly disagrees with this opinion; employment relates to the rendering of services to the business and not to when those services are first compensated in dollars.

If the employee does not complete 1,000 hours of service during the initial eligibility computation period, the next period commences on the anniversary date of employment or, if provided in the plan, on the first day of the plan year during which the anniversary date falls. If the plan's service eligibility requirement is two years and the plan provides for the second year to start from the first day of the plan year during which the anniversary date falls, the employee will be credited with two years of service if 1,000 hours of service are completed during both the initial eligibility computation period and the plan year.

> **Example 1.** Doctor Adam, Inc. adopted a calendar-year profit sharing plan on January 1, 2009. The service eligibility requirement is two years, and the second year starts from the first day of the plan year. Caroline became employed on July 15, 2009, completed 1,000 hours of service by July 14, 2010,

and completed 1,000 hours of service during calendar year 2010. Caroline is credited with two years of service and will commence participation in the plan on January 1, 2011.

IRS has ruled that two employees, each of whom works an aggregate of at least 20 hours a week for two employers that share common facilities and each employee's services, are deemed to complete at least 1,000 hours of service during the year for each employer. Whether the employees satisfy a year of service requirement with each employer is not determined by the amount of services rendered to each. The characteristics of an employee do not change when the efforts of the employee are shared by more than one employer. [Rev. Rul. 73-447, 1973-2 C.B. 135]

Example 2. The facts are the same as in Example 1, except that Caroline works 15 hours a week for Doctor Adam, Inc. and 15 hours a week for Doctor Benjamin Jason, Inc., and both employers share common facilities. Caroline will still be credited with two years of service and will commence participation in the Doctor Adam, Inc. profit sharing plan on January 1, 2011.

Q 5:9   What is an hour of service?

An hour of service is any hour for which an employee is paid or is entitled to payment by the employer. An hour of service includes any hour for which payments are made due to an employee's vacation, sickness, holiday, disability, layoff, jury duty, military duty, or leave of absence, even if the employee no longer works for the company. An hour of service also includes any hour for which back pay is awarded. [Keleher v. Dominion Insulation, Inc., 1992 U.S. App. LEXIS 25561 (4th Cir. 1992); DOL Reg. § 2530.200b-2]

The general method of crediting service for an employee is based upon the actual counting of hours of service during the applicable 12-consecutive-month computation period. Under this method, each hour is counted so that an employee who works 50 hours per week will reach 1,000 hours of service sooner than an employee who works 40 hours per week. However, the determination as to whether or not the employee has completed a year of service (see Q 5:8) is still made on the first anniversary of the date of employment and not on the day the employee reaches 1,000 hours of service. In lieu of the general method, an alternative method, the elapsed time method, may be used to credit the service of employees for purposes of determining eligibility to participate, vesting, and benefit accrual. The elapsed time method is designed to lessen the recordkeeping burden. Under the elapsed time method of crediting service, the plan is generally required to take into account the period of time that elapses while the employee is employed with the employer *regardless* of the actual number of hours the employee completes during such period. Under this alternative method of crediting service, hours of service may be computed under any of the following methods:

1. Count 190 hours of service for each month for which the employee is paid or entitled to payment for at least one hour of service;

2. Count 95 hours of service for each semimonthly period for which the employee is paid or entitled to payment for at least one hour of service;

3. Count 45 hours of service for each week for which the employee is paid or entitled to payment for at least one hour of service; or

4. Count 10 hours of service for each day for which the employee is paid or entitled to payment for at least one hour of service.

[Treas. Reg. § 1.410(a)-7; DOL Reg. § 2530.200b-3; Gilley v. Monsanto Co., Inc., 490 F.3d 848 (11th Cir. 2007)]

One court ruled that an employee did not receive credit for a year of service for vesting purposes (see Q 9:10) because she was not credited with 1,000 hours of service under the elapsed time method adopted by the plan even though she had completed 1,000 actual hours of service during the year her employment was terminated. [Johnson v. Buckley, 2004 U.S. App. LEXIS 1252 (9th Cir. 2004)] However, another court ruled that an employee did not receive credit for a year of service for vesting purposes even though he was credited with 1,000 hours of service for the 12-month period under the elapsed time method adopted by the plan because the employee terminated employment before the end of the 12-month period. [Coleman v. Interco Inc. Divs.' Plans, No. 90-2700 (7th Cir. 1991)]

Q 5:10   What is a one-year break in service?

A one-year break in service means a calendar year, a plan year, or any other consecutive 12-month period designated in the plan during which an employee does not complete more than 500 hours of service (see Qs 5:9, 5:14). [I.R.C. §§ 410(a)(5)(C), 411(a)(6)(A); DOL Reg. § 2530.200b-4]

An employee who works more than 500 hours during the designated 12-month period does not incur a one-year break in service. An employee's one-year break in service has significance in terms of eligibility (see Qs 5:4, 5:12) and vesting of benefits (see Q 9:12).

Under USERRA (see Q 1:16), an employee who is reemployed following protected military service is treated as not having incurred a one-year break in service.

Q 5:11   What years of service must be taken into account for eligibility purposes?

In general, all years of service with the employer must be counted. For an exception, see Q 5:12. [I.R.C. § 410(a)(5)]

Service with a predecessor of the employer must be counted if the successor-employer maintains the predecessor's qualified retirement plan. [I.R.C. § 414(a)]

Service with any member of a controlled group of corporations or with a commonly controlled entity (see Q 5:29), whether or not incorporated, must be counted for eligibility purposes. Similarly, service with any member of an affiliated service group (see Q 5:35) must be counted. [I.R.C. §§ 414(b), 414(c), 414(m)]

Q 5:12 May any years of service be disregarded for eligibility purposes?

Yes. Most qualified retirement plans may require up to two years of service as a prerequisite to participation (see Q 5:2). For plans that require two years of service as an eligibility requirement, a year of service (see Q 5:8) preceding a one-year break in service (see Q 5:10) need not be considered in determining whether an employee is eligible to participate (see Q 5:4 and the examples). [I.R.C. §§ 410(a)(1)(B), 410(a)(5)(B)]

Q 5:13 May past service with a former employer be used for eligibility purposes in the qualified retirement plan of the present employer?

If the present employer maintains the qualified retirement plan of a predecessor employer, an employee's service with the predecessor counts as service for the present employer (see Q 5:11). [Priv. Ltr. Rul. 9336046]

A qualified retirement plan may provide that service as an employee with a predecessor business counts for purposes of meeting the service eligibility requirement, even if the predecessor business had no qualified retirement plan (see Q 4:21). Furthermore, service as a partner of a partnership may be counted in meeting the service requirement for participation in the plan of a successor corporation. [Priv. Ltr. Rul. 7742003; Farley Funeral Homes, Inc., 62 T.C. 150 (1974)]

Q 5:14 Is a maternity or paternity period of absence treated as a break in service?

For purposes of determining whether a one-year break in service (see Q 5:10) has occurred for both participation and vesting purposes, an employee who is absent from work due to pregnancy or the birth or adoption of a child is treated as having completed, during the absence, the number of hours that normally would have been credited but for the absence, up to a maximum of 501 hours, so as to prevent a one-year break in service.

The hours of service are credited only in the year in which the absence begins (if necessary to prevent a break in service in that year) or in the following year. [I.R.C. §§ 410(a)(5)(E), 411(a)(6)(E)]

Example. Before taking an approved maternity leave, Susan completed 750 hours of service during the 2010 plan year. Since the credit is not needed in 2010 to prevent a break in service, Susan is entitled to up to 501 hours of credited service in 2011. This is true even if Susan returned to employment in

2010 and then terminated employment in 2011 before being credited with 501 hours of service.

Q 5:15 What coverage requirements must a retirement plan satisfy to qualify for favorable tax treatment?

A retirement plan must satisfy one of two coverage tests in order to qualify for favorable tax treatment:

1. The ratio percentage test (see Q 5:16) or
2. The average benefit test (see Q 5:17).

A plan maintained by an employer that benefits only NHCEs (see Q 3:12) or by an employer that has only highly compensated employees (HCEs; see Q 3:2) will automatically satisfy the coverage requirements. [I.R.C. §§ 410(b)(1), 410(b)(2), 410(b)(6)(F); Treas. Reg. §§ 1.410(b)-2(a), 1.410(b)-2(b); Rev. Proc. 95-34, 1995-2 C.B. 385; Rev. Proc. 93-42, 1993-2 C.B. 540; Ann. 93-130, 1993-31 I.R.B. 46; Ann. 92-81, 1992-22 I.R.B. 56]

When there is an acquisition (or disposition) among a controlled group of employers (see Q 5:29), the minimum coverage requirement is treated as having been met during the transition period if the minimum coverage requirement was met before the acquisition and there is no other significant change in coverage. [I.R.C. § 410(b)(6)(C); Treas. Reg. § 1.410(b)-2(f); Priv. Ltr. Rul. 9707022; Rev. Rul. 2004-11, 2004-1 C.B. 480] For additional details, see Q 4:19.

A separate line of business exception may apply for the minimum coverage requirements (see Q 5:44).

Q 5:16 What is the ratio percentage test for the minimum coverage requirement?

Under the ratio percentage test, the percentage of the NHCEs (see Q 3:12) who benefit under the retirement plan must equal at least 70 percent of the percentage of the HCEs (see Q 3:2) who benefit under the plan. Percentages are rounded to the nearest one-hundredth of 1 percent. [I.R.C. § 410(b)(1); Treas. Reg. §§ 1.410(b)-2(b)(2), 1.410(b)-9; Beals Bros. Mgmt. Corp. v. Comm'r, 300 F.3d 963 (8th Cir. 2002)]

> **Example.** For a plan year, Debi Corporation's defined benefit plan covers 60 percent of its NHCEs and 80 percent of its HCEs. The plan's ratio percentage for the year is 75 percent (60% ÷ 80%) and thus satisfies the ratio percentage test.

> **Example.** For a plan year, Danielle Ltd.'s defined contribution plan covers 40 percent of its NHCEs and 60 percent of its HCEs. The plan fails to satisfy the ratio percentage test because the ratio percentage is only 66.67 percent (40% ÷ 60%).

For purposes of satisfying the minimum coverage requirement, employees who do not meet the plan's minimum age or service requirement (see Qs 5:2,

5:5) are not counted. In addition, nonresident aliens who receive no earned income from sources within the United States and union members whose retirement benefits have been the subject of good-faith bargaining between the employer and the union do not count (see Q 5:5). [I.R.C. §§ 410(b)(3), 410(b)(4); Treas. Reg. §§ 1.410(b)-6(a), 1.410(b)-6(b)(1), 1.410(b)-6(b)(2), 1.410(b)-6(c), 1.410(b)-6(d)] A corporation established a defined benefit plan, effective January 1, 2004, with a two-years-of-service eligibility requirement. The business owner, the only HCE, satisfied the eligibility requirement, but no other employee did; therefore, the business owner was the only participant. IRS representatives opined that the plan satisfied the ratio percentage test for 2004. In 2005, other employees became eligible to participate in the plan; however, all of them terminated employment after completing more than 500 hours of service, but before completing 1,000 hours of service, and did not accrue any benefits. The representatives further opined that the plan failed the ratio percentage test for 2005 (see Q 5:21).

IRS has ruled that employees who have not satisfied a plan's eligibility requirements for participation (see Qs 1:44, 5:2), but who are permitted to make rollover contributions (see Q 34:1), need not be taken into account for purposes of the minimum coverage requirements. [Rev. Rul. 96-48, 1996-2 C.B. 31]

Improperly characterizing employees as independent contractors could result in the failure to satisfy the ratio benefit test and the disqualification of the plan (see Q 5:1). [Kenney, 70 T.C.M. 614 (1995); see also Belluardo v. Cox Enterprises, Inc., Pension Plan, No. 04-3505 (6th Cir. 2005), Ramirez, 94 T.C.M. 493 (2007), Peno Trucking, Inc., 93 T.C.M. 1027 (2007), and Orion Contracting Trust, 92 T.C.M. 309 (2006)] IRS posted a revised document on its website providing answers to questions that may arise after it determines that an individual is an employee rather than an independent contractor. [Notice 989 (Rev. 7-2009) Commonly Asked Questions When IRS Determines Your Work Status is "Employee"]

IRS has ruled that an employee, who works an aggregate of at least 20 hours a week for two employers that share common facilities and the employee's services, is deemed to complete at least 1,000 hours of service (see Q 5:8) during the year for each employer. Whether the employee satisfies a year of service requirement with each employer is not determined by the amount of services rendered to each. The characteristics of an employee do not change when the efforts of the employee are shared by more than one employer. [Rev. Rul. 73-447, 1973-2 C.B. 135]

Example. Kolorado Kathy Corp. established a profit sharing plan for the benefit of its employees who complete one year of service. Kolorado Kathy Corp. employs Kathy, who is its president and sole shareholder and who is also the sole participant in the plan. Samantha has been continuously employed by Kolorado Kathy Corp. for the past two years. Samantha is also employed by Bronco Jerry, Inc., which also employs Jerry, its president and sole shareholder.

The two corporations share the facilities of a suite, but each has its own business, including separate office hours. Except for telephone and supplies, the costs of operating the office are shared equally. Samantha is available to assist either corporation as a particular situation requires. While the amount of assistance provided for each corporation may vary from day to day, Samantha performs services in the aggregate of 30 hours per week for the two corporations.

Samantha is deemed to work more than 1,000 hours a year for each of Kolorado Kathy Corp. and Bronco Jerry, Inc. Thus, Kolorado Kathy Corp.'s plan does not satisfy the ratio percentage test because Samantha is not a participant.

Q 5:17   What is the average benefit test for the minimum coverage requirement?

Under the average benefit test, (1) the plan must benefit such employees as qualify under a classification set up by the employer and found by IRS not to be discriminatory in favor of HCEs (see Q 3:2) and (2) the average benefit percentage for NHCEs (see Q 3:12) of the employer must equal at least 70 percent of the average benefit percentage for HCEs of the employer. [I.R.C. § 410(b)(2); Treas. Reg. §§ 1.410(b)-2(b)(3), 1.410(b)-4, 1.410(b)-5]

The classification test is described in Q 5:18 and the average benefit percentage test in Q 5:19.

Q 5:18   What is the classification test?

The classification test is satisfied if, based on all the facts and circumstances, the classification set up by the employer is reasonable and is established under objective business criteria that identify the category of employees who benefit under the plan. Reasonable classifications generally include specified job categories, nature of compensation (i.e., salaried or hourly), geographic location, and similar bona fide business criteria. An enumeration of employees by name or other specific criteria having substantially the same effect as an enumeration by name is not considered a reasonable classification. In addition, the classification must be found to be nondiscriminatory based on either a safe harbor rule or a facts and circumstances test. The safe harbor rule is satisfied only if the plan's ratio percentage (see Q 5:16) is equal to or greater than the employer's safe harbor percentage. The safe harbor rule looks at the percentage (concentration percentage) of all of the employer's employees who are NHCEs (see Q 3:12) and then creates both a safe harbor percentage and an unsafe harbor percentage. The employer's safe harbor percentage is 50 percent reduced by .75 percent for each whole percentage point by which the concentration percentage exceeds 60 percent, and the unsafe harbor percentage is 40 percent reduced by .75 percent for each whole percentage point by which the concentration percentage exceeds 60 percent (but in no event less than 20 percent). [Treas. Reg. §§ 1.410(b)-4(b), 1.410(b)-4(c)]

The following table illustrates the safe harbor and unsafe harbor percentages at each concentration percentage.

NHCE Concentration Percentage	Safe Harbor Percentage	Unsafe Harbor Percentage
0–60	50.00	40.00
61	49.25	39.25
62	48.50	38.50
63	47.75	37.75
64	47.00	37.00
65	46.25	36.25
66	45.50	35.50
67	44.75	34.75
68	44.00	34.00
69	43.25	33.25
70	42.50	32.50
71	41.75	31.75
72	41.00	31.00
73	40.25	30.25
74	39.50	29.50
75	38.75	28.75
76	38.00	28.00
77	37.25	27.25
78	36.50	26.50
79	35.75	25.75
80	35.00	25.00
81	34.25	24.25
82	33.50	23.50
83	32.75	22.75
84	32.00	22.00
85	31.25	21.25
86	30.50	20.50
87	29.75	20.00
88	29.00	20.00
89	28.25	20.00
90	27.50	20.00
91	26.75	20.00
92	26.00	20.00

NHCE Concentration Percentage	Safe Harbor Percentage	Unsafe Harbor Percentage
93	25.25	20.00
94	24.50	20.00
95	23.75	20.00
96	23.00	20.00
97	22.25	20.00
98	21.50	20.00
99	20.75	20.00

Example 1. Mikey Corp. has 200 employees; 120 are NHCEs and 80 are HCEs. The NHCE concentration percentage is 60 percent (120/200). Mikey Corp. maintains a retirement plan that excludes employees of a specified geographic location. The plan benefits 72 HCEs and 60 NHCEs. The plan's ratio percentage is 55.56 percent [(60/120) ÷ (72/80) = (50% ÷ 90%)]. Since the concentration percentage is 60 percent, the safe harbor percentage is 50 percent and the unsafe harbor percentage is 40 percent. Because the ratio percentage (55.56 percent) is greater than the safe harbor percentage (50 percent), the plan's classification satisfies the safe harbor rule.

Example 2. The facts are the same as in Example 1, except that the plan benefits only 40 NHCEs. The plan's ratio percentage is 37.03 percent [(40/120) ÷ (72/80) = (33.33% ÷ 90%)]. Because the ratio percentage (37.03 percent) is below the unsafe harbor percentage (40 percent), the classification is considered discriminatory and the average benefit test (see Q 5:17) is not satisfied.

Example 3. The facts are the same as in Example 1, except that the plan benefits 45 NHCEs. The plan's ratio percentage is 41.67 percent [(45/120) ÷ (72/80) = (37.50% ÷ 90%)]. Because the ratio percentage (41.67 percent) is below the safe harbor percentage (50 percent), but above the unsafe harbor percentage (40 percent), IRS may determine that the classification is nondiscriminatory based on all the facts and circumstances.

Under the facts and circumstances test, a classification satisfies this test if, based on all the relevant facts and circumstances, IRS finds that the classification is nondiscriminatory. No one particular fact is determinative. Included among the facts and circumstances relevant to determining whether a classification is nondiscriminatory are the following:

- *The underlying business reason for the classification.* The greater the business reason for the classification, the more likely it is that the classification will be nondiscriminatory. Reducing the employer's cost of providing retirement benefits is not a relevant business reason.

- *The percentage of the employer's employees benefiting under the plan.* The higher the percentage, the more likely it is that the classification will be nondiscriminatory.

- *Whether the number of employees benefiting under the plan in each salary range is representative of the number of employees in each salary range of the employer's workforce.* In general, the more representative the percentages of employees benefiting under the plan in each salary range, the more likely it is that the classification will be nondiscriminatory.

- *The difference between the plan's ratio percentage and the employer's safe harbor percentage.* The smaller the difference, the more likely it is that the classification will be nondiscriminatory.

- *The extent to which the plan's average benefit percentage exceeds 70 percent.*

[Treas. Reg. § 1.410(b)-4(c)(3)]

The exclusion from plan participation of a class of part-time employees is not an acceptable classification (see Q 5:5).

Q 5:19   What is the average benefit percentage test?

In order for a qualified retirement plan to satisfy the average benefit percentage test, the benefits provided to NHCEs (see Q 3:12) under all plans of the employer (expressed as a percentage of compensation) must generally be at least 70 percent as great, on average, as the benefits provided to the employer's HCEs (see Q 3:2). [Treas. Reg. § 1.410(b)-5(a)]

Satisfaction of the average benefit percentage test requires that the employer determine an employee benefit percentage for each employee taken into account for testing purposes and then separately average the percentages of all employees in the highly compensated and non-highly compensated groups. Employee benefit percentages may be determined on either a contributions or a benefits basis, and employee contributions and benefits attributable to employee contributions are not taken into account. Generally, the employee benefit percentage for an employee is the rate that would be determined for that employee for purposes of applying the general nondiscrimination tests (see Qs 4:13, 4:18, 4:22). [Treas. Reg. § 1.410(b)-5(b), 1.410(b)-5(c), 1.410(b)-5(d), 1.410(b)-5(e)]

IRS has ruled that employees who have not satisfied a plan's eligibility requirements for participation (see Qs 1:44, 5:2), but who are permitted to make rollover contributions (see Q 34:1), need not be taken into account for purposes of the minimum coverage requirement. [Rev. Rul. 96-48, 1996-2 C.B. 31] IRS representatives have opined that, where an employer has a combined 401(k) plan (see Q 27:67) with no service eligibility requirement to participate in the 401(k) part but a one-year-of-service eligibility requirement to participate in the profit sharing allocation, employees with less than a year of service are included for purposes of the average benefit percentage test. The representatives further opined that, in determining the average benefit percentage test, elective contributions returned due to a failed ADP test (see Q 27:18), matching contributions returned due to a failed ACP test (see Q 27:77), matching contributions forfeited due to a failed ACP test or to association with elective contributions returned due to a failed ADP test, and excess elective deferrals are included, but that other returned excess deferrals are not counted.

Improperly characterizing employees as independent contractors could result in the failure to satisfy the average benefit percentage test and the disqualification of the plan (see Q 5:1). [Kenney, 70 T.C.M. 614 (1995) *see also* Belluardo v. Cox Enterprises, Inc., Pension Plan, No. 04-3505 (6th Cir. 2005), Ramirez, 94 T.C.M. 493 (2007), Peno Trucking, Inc., 93 T.C.M. 1027 (2007), and Orion Contracting Trust, 92 T.C.M. 309 (2006)] IRS posted a revised document on its website providing answers to questions that may arise after it determines that an individual is an employee rather than an independent contractor. [Notice 989 (Rev. 7-2009) Commonly Asked Questions When IRS Determines Your Work Status is "Employee"]

Q 5:20 When does an employee benefit under the qualified retirement plan?

For purposes of the minimum coverage rules, an employee must benefit under the qualified retirement plan to be taken into account for the percentage tests (see Qs 5:16, 5:17). An employee is treated as benefiting under the plan for a plan year:

1. In the case of a defined contribution plan (see Q 2:2), only if the employee receives an allocation of contributions or forfeitures.

2. In the case of a defined benefit plan (see Q 2:3), only if the employee receives a benefit accrual (see Q 9:2).

3. In the case of a 401(k) plan, if the employee is eligible to make an elective contribution (see Q 27:16), whether or not the employee actually does so.

4. If the employee fails to accrue a benefit solely because of the Section 415 limits on benefits and annual additions (see Qs 6:34, 6:37, 6:38), except that, in the case of a defined benefit plan, this exception does not apply if benefits in excess of the Section 415 limits are used to determine accrual rates for the general nondiscrimination test (see Q 4:18).

5. If the employee fails to accrue a benefit solely because of a uniformly applicable benefit limit under the plan.

6. If the current benefit accrual is offset by the contributions or benefits under another plan (see Q 2:22).

7. In the case of a target benefit plan (see Q 2:5), if the employee's theoretical reserve is greater than or equal to the actuarial present value of the fractional rule benefit (see Q 4:24).

8. If the employee has attained normal retirement age (see Q 10:55) under a defined benefit plan and fails to accrue a benefit solely because of the provisions regarding adjustments for delayed retirement.

9. In the case of an insurance contract plan (see Q 8:11), only if a premium is paid on behalf of the employee.

[Treas. Reg. §§ 1.410(b)-3(a)(1), 1.410(b)-3(a)(2)(i) through (iv); Rev. Proc. 93-42, 1993-2 C.B. 540; Ann. 93-130, 1993-31 I.R.B. 46; Ann. 92-81, 1992-22 I.R.B. 56]

In the case of a defined contribution plan, if no employee receives an allocation of contributions or forfeitures, the plan is treated as satisfying the minimum coverage requirement for the plan year because the plan benefits no HCEs (see Q 3:2). Thus, a defined contribution plan for which contributions cease and for which no forfeitures can be allocated satisfies the requirement. In the case of a defined benefit plan, if no employee accrues any additional benefits under the plan, the plan is treated as satisfying the requirement for the plan year because no HCEs benefit under the plan during that plan year. However, this special rule is not available with respect to a top-heavy plan that has required minimum contributions or benefit accruals (see Qs 26:35, 26:41), or to a plan where future compensation increases are taken into account in determining the accrued benefit under the plan.

An employee is treated as benefiting under a defined benefit plan for a plan year only if there is an increase in the employee's accrued benefit (see Q 9:2). Increases in the dollar amount of the accrued benefit merely because of the passage of time or because of a change in indices affecting the accrued benefit do not cause an employee to be treated as benefiting. In certain situations, however, an employee in a defined benefit plan will be treated as benefiting for a plan year even though the employee does not receive an accrual for the plan year. One of these situations is where an employee's accrued benefit would have increased if a previously accrued benefit were disregarded. An increase in covered compensation or a decrease in the employee's compensation for the plan year are other examples of situations where this might occur.

IRS representatives opined that, when an employee was rehired near the end of the plan year, immediately recommenced plan participation, but was not paid until the following year, the employee would be considered ineligible for the plan year of reemployment.

For the treatment of terminated employees, see Q 5:21.

Q 5:21   How are employees who terminated employment during the plan year treated for minimum coverage purposes?

At the option of the employer, an employee is not taken into account for purposes of the minimum coverage tests (see Q 5:15) if:

1. The employee does not benefit (see Q 5:20) under the plan for the plan year;

2. The employee is eligible to participate in the plan;

3. The plan has a minimum hours of service requirement or a requirement that an employee be employed on the last day of the plan year (last-day requirement) in order to accrue a benefit or receive an allocation for the plan year;

4. The employee fails to accrue a benefit or receive an allocation under the plan solely because of the failure to satisfy the minimum hours of service or last-day requirement; and

5. The employee terminates employment during the plan year with not more than 500 hours of service (see Q 5:9), and the employee is not an active employee as of the last day of the plan year. (A plan that uses the elapsed time method (see Q 5:9) of determining years of service may use either 91 consecutive calendar days or three consecutive calendar months instead of 500 hours of service, provided it uses the same rule for all employees during a plan year.)

If the employer elects to use this option with respect to any employee for a plan year, it must be applied to all employees for that plan year. [Treas. Reg. § 1.410(b)-6(f)]

Example. Norman of New Mexico, Inc. has 30 employees who are eligible under its profit sharing plan. The plan requires the employee to complete 1,000 hours of service during the plan year to receive an allocation of contributions or forfeitures. Ten employees do not receive an allocation because of their failure to complete 1,000 hours of service. Three of the ten employees completed less than 501 hours of service and terminated their employment. Two of the employees completed between 501 and 999 hours of service and terminated their employment. The remaining five employees did not terminate employment. The three terminated employees who completed less than 501 hours of service are not taken into account unless the employer elects to do so. The other seven employees who do not receive an allocation are taken into account but are treated as not benefiting under the plan.

An employer maintains a defined contribution plan that contains a last-day requirement. In the year in question, the plan year ends on a Sunday and an employee terminates employment on the previous Friday, the last day of the work week. Whether the employee satisfies the last-day requirement is uncertain; however, the plan must not make an interpretation that discriminates in favor of HCEs (see Q 3:2).

Q 5:22   Must a qualified retirement plan satisfy the minimum coverage rules every day during the plan year?

No. A plan must satisfy the minimum coverage rules (see Q 5:15) for a plan year using one of three testing options. However, the annual testing option must be used in a 401(k) plan (see Q 27:1) or an employer matching or employee contribution plan (see Q 27:77) and in applying the average benefit percentage test (see Q 5:17).

The three testing options are:

1. *Daily Testing Option.* The plan must meet the coverage rules on each day of the plan year, taking into account all individuals who are employees (or former employees) on each day.

2. *Quarterly Testing Option.* The plan must satisfy the coverage rules on at least one day in each quarter of the plan year, taking into account only those individuals who are employees (or former employees) on that day,

unless the four quarterly testing dates do not reasonably represent the plan's coverage over the entire plan year.

3. *Annual Testing Option.* The plan must satisfy the testing rules as of the last day of the plan year, taking into account all individuals who were employees (or former employees) at any time during the year.

[Treas. Reg. § 1.410(b)-8(a)]

In addition, plans may test as of a representative "snapshot" day during the year, and plans that do not experience significant change may test as infrequently as once every three years. [Rev. Proc. 95-34, 1995-2 C.B. 385; Rev. Proc. 93-42, 1993-2 C.B. 540]

Q 5:23   What is the minimum participation requirement?

In addition to the minimum coverage requirement (see Q 5:15), a minimum participation requirement must be met by certain retirement plans of the employer in order to be qualified. For years beginning after 1996, the minimum participation requirement applies *only* to defined benefit plans (see Q 2:3). A defined benefit plan must benefit at least the *lesser* of (1) 50 employees or (2) the *greater* of (a) 40 percent of all employees or (b) *two* employees (or if there is only one employee, that employee). This requirement cannot be satisfied by aggregating different plans of the employer. [I.R.C. § 410(a)(26)(A); Treas. Reg. § 1.401(a)(26)]

> **Example 1.** In 2011, S&C Professional Law Corporation employs two attorneys and no other employees. Each attorney cannot participate in a separate defined benefit plan because each plan must cover both attorneys.

> **Example 2.** In 2011, SC&J Professional Law Corporation has 150 employees. Except for 95 associate attorneys and paralegals, all employees are covered by SC&J's defined benefit plan. The minimum participation requirement is satisfied because the plan covers at least the *lesser* of (1) 50 employees (150 − 95 = 55) or (2) 40 percent of all employees (150 × 40% = 60). Even though this requirement is satisfied, the plan must also satisfy the minimum coverage requirement.

Among the plans that were deemed to meet the minimum participation requirement automatically for years beginning prior to 1997 were the following:

1. A plan that was not a top-heavy plan (see Qs 26:1, 26:3), benefited no HCE (see Q 3:2), and was not aggregated with any other plan to enable such other plan to satisfy the nondiscrimination requirements (see Q 4:10) or the minimum coverage requirements (see Q 5:15) [Treas. Reg. § 1.401(a) (26)-1(b)(1)];

2. Certain multiemployer plans (see Q 29:2) [Treas. Reg. § 1.401(a)(26)-1(b)(2)];

3. Certain underfunded defined benefit plans [Treas. Reg. § 1.401(a)(26)-1(b)(3)];

4. Certain 401(k) plans (see Q 27:1) maintained by employers that included governmental or tax-exempt entities [I.R.C. § 401(k)(4)(B); Treas. Reg. § 1.401(a)(26)-1(b)(4)];

5. Certain plans of an employer involved in an acquisition or disposition [Treas. Reg. § 1.401(a)(26)-1(b)(5)];

6. Defined contribution plans under which no employee received an allocation of either contributions or forfeitures for the plan year [Treas. Reg. § 1.401(a)(26)-2(b)]; and

7. Defined benefit plans under which no employee accrued any additional benefit for a plan year (other than those minimum benefits provided for non-key employees under top-heavy plans) but which satisfied the prior benefit structure requirements (see Qs 5:25, 26:35). [Treas. Reg. § 1.401(a)(26)-2(b)]

Since for years beginning after 1996 the minimum participation requirement applies only to defined benefit plans, some of the above exceptions are no longer relevant.

Generally, an employee is deemed to benefit under the plan if the employee is deemed to benefit under the plan for the minimum coverage tests (see Q 5:20). [Treas. Reg. § 1.401(a)(26)-5] A corporation established a defined benefit plan, effective January 1, 2004, with a two-years-of-service eligibility requirement. The business owner, the only HCE, satisfied the eligibility requirement, but no other employee did; therefore, the business owner was the only participant. IRS representatives opined that the plan satisfied the minimum participation requirement for 2004. In 2005, other employees became eligible to participate in the plan; however, all of them terminated employment after completing more than 500 hours of service, but before completing 1,000 hours of service, and did not accrue any benefits. The representatives further opined that the plan failed the minimum participation requirement for 2005 (see Q 5:21).

Improperly characterizing employees as independent contractors could result in the failure to satisfy the minimum participation test and the disqualification of the plan (see Q 5:1). [Kenney, 70 T.C.M. 614 (1995); *see also* Belluardo v. Cox Enterprises, Inc., Pension Plan, No. 04-3505 (6th Cir. 2005), Ramirez, 94 T.C.M. 493 (2007), Peno Trucking, Inc., 93 T.C.M. 1027 (2007), and Orion Contracting Trust, 92 T.C.M. 309 (2006)] IRS posted a revised document on its website providing answers to questions that may arise after it determines that an individual is an employee rather than an independent contractor. [Notice 989 (Rev. 7-2009) Commonly Asked Questions When IRS Determines Your Work Status is "Employee"]

Q 5:24   Which employees are not counted for the minimum participation requirement?

For purposes of applying the minimum participation test (see Q 5:23), all employees other than excludable employees must be taken into account. Generally, these requirements are applied separately to each defined benefit plan of the employer and must be applied on a uniform and consistent basis. [Treas. Reg. § 1.401(a)(26)-6(a)]

An employee, if covered by one of the following exclusions, is an excludable employee:

1. The employee does not meet the plan's minimum age or service requirement (see Q 5:2).

2. The employee is a nonresident alien who receives no earned income from sources within the United States.

3. The employee is a union member whose retirement benefits have been the subject of good-faith bargaining between the employer and the union (see Q 5:5).

[Treas. Reg. § 1.401(a)(26)-6(b)]

Example 1. Jerry of Lawrence Ltd. maintains a defined benefit plan under which employees who have not completed one year of service are not eligible to participate. Jerry of Lawrence Ltd. has six employees. Two of the employees participate in the plan. The other four employees have not completed one year of service and are not eligible to participate. The four employees who have not completed one year of service are excludable employees and may be disregarded for purposes of applying the minimum participation test. Therefore, the test is satisfied because both of the employees who must be considered are participants in the plan.

Example 2. Busy-as-a-Bea Corporation has 100 employees and maintains two defined benefit plans, Plan A and Plan B. Plan A provides that employees who have not completed one year of service are not eligible to participate. Plan B has no minimum age or service requirement. Twenty of Busy-as-a-Bea's employees do not meet the minimum service requirement under Plan A. Each plan satisfies the ratio percentage test (see Q 5:16). In testing Plan A to determine whether it satisfies the minimum participation requirement, the 20 employees not meeting the minimum age and service requirement under Plan A are treated as excludable employees. In testing Plan B, no employees are treated as excludable employees because Plan B does not have a minimum age or service requirement.

In addition, certain terminated employees may be excluded (see Q 5:21), and a separate line of business exception may apply (see Q 5:44). [Treas. Reg. §§ 1.401(a)(26)-6(b)(7), 1.401(a)(26)-6(b)(8)]

Q 5:25   What is a prior benefit structure?

Defined benefit plans (see Q 2:3) must also satisfy the minimum participation requirement (see Q 5:23) with respect to a prior benefit structure. The prior benefit structure under a defined benefit plan for a plan year includes all benefits accrued to that time; therefore, the plan can have only one prior benefit structure. [Treas. Reg. § 1.401(a)(26)-3(a), 1.401(a)(26)-3(b)]

The prior benefit structure satisfies the minimum participation requirement if the lesser of (1) 50 employees or (2) the greater of (a) 40 percent of the employees or (b) two employees (or if there is only one employee, that employee) currently accrued meaningful benefits (see Q 5:23). Whether a plan is providing meaningful benefits is determined on the basis of all the facts and circumstances. This determination is intended to ensure that a plan functions as an ongoing defined benefit plan providing meaningful benefits to at least the required number of the employer's employees. A plan does not satisfy this requirement if it exists primarily to preserve accrued benefits for a small group of employees and thereby functions more as an individual plan for the small group of employees or for the employer. The relevant factors in making this determination include, but are not limited to, the following:

1. The level of current benefit accruals;
2. The comparative rate of accruals under the current benefit formula compared to prior rates of accrual under the plan;
3. The projected accrued benefits under the current benefit formula compared to accrued benefits as of the close of the immediately preceding plan year;
4. The length of time the current benefit formula had been in effect;
5. The number of employees with accrued benefits under the plan; and
6. The length of time the plan had been in effect.

[Treas. Reg. § 1.401(a)(26)-3(c)]

Q 5:26   May a retirement plan that does not satisfy the minimum participation requirement be retroactively corrected?

To satisfy the minimum participation requirement (see Q 5:23), the defined benefit plan (see Q 2:3) must satisfy the test on each day of the plan year. However, the plan will be treated as satisfying the requirement if it satisfies the test on any single day during the plan year, but only if that day is reasonably representative of the employer's workforce and the plan's coverage. A plan does not have to be tested on the same day each plan year. [Treas. Reg. § 1.401(a)(26)-7(a), 1.401(a)(26)-7(b)]

If a plan fails to satisfy the minimum participation requirement for a plan year, the plan may be amended retroactively to satisfy the requirement by expanding coverage, improving benefits, modifying eligibility conditions under the plan, or merging plans and deeming the merger to be effective retroactively to the first day of the plan year. [Treas. Reg. § 1.401(a)(26)-7(c); IRS Field Off. Directive on Good-Faith Compliance (June 12, 1992)]

Q 5:27 Can an employee's waiver of participation in the employer's qualified retirement plan jeopardize the tax-favored status of the plan?

Yes. For example, an employee who is otherwise eligible to participate in the employer's defined benefit plan that requires mandatory employee contributions as a condition of participation may be unable or unwilling to contribute and would therefore waive participation in the plan (see Qs 5:3, 5:6). That employee is included in determining whether the company's retirement plan satisfies the minimum coverage and minimum participation tests (see Qs 5:15, 5:23). Therefore, the plan may lose its tax-favored status if too many employees waive participation. IRS representatives have opined that permitting an HCE (see Q 3:2) to waive participation in a plan, but not permitting a NHCE (see Q 3:12) to waive participation, does not violate the nondiscriminatory availability requirement (see Q 4:20).

An employee's decision not to make an elective contribution (see Q 27:16) to a 401(k) plan is not a waiver of participation that would jeopardize the tax-favored status of the plan for purposes of the minimum coverage requirement (see Q 5:20). [Treas. Reg. §§ 1.410(b)-3(a)(2)(i), 1.401(a)(26)-5(a)(1)]

Q 5:28 What happens if a retirement plan fails to satisfy the minimum coverage or minimum participation requirement?

If a retirement plan fails to satisfy the qualification requirements of Section 401(a) (see Q 4:1), the tax-exempt status of plan earnings is revoked, employer deductions for contributions may be deferred or eliminated, and all employees must include the value of vested (see Q 9:1) plan contributions in income. [I.R.C. § 402(b)(1); Priv. Ltr. Rul. 9502030; Beals Bros. Mgmt. Corp. v. Comm'r, 300 F.3d 963 (8th Cir. 2002)]

However, if the plan fails to satisfy the minimum coverage or minimum participation requirement (see Qs 5:15, 5:23), each HCE (see Q 3:2) must include in income an amount equal to the employee's entire vested accrued benefit (see Q 9:2) not previously included in income, not just current vested plan contributions. If, however, the plan is not qualified solely because it fails to satisfy either of these requirements, no adverse tax consequences are imposed on NHCEs (see Q 3:12). [I.R.C. § 402(b)(4); Priv. Ltr. Rul. 9502030; Gant, 76 T.C.M. 994 (1998)]

IRS has opined that, with the integrated approach underlying the nondiscrimination requirement (see Q 4:10) and the minimum coverage requirement, any failure to satisfy the nondiscrimination requirement can be viewed as failure to satisfy the minimum coverage requirement. Consequently, failure to meet the nondiscrimination requirement will subject HCEs to the special sanctions. [Preamble to final regulations (Sept. 19, 1991)]

Q 5:29   Do special coverage and participation rules apply to commonly controlled businesses?

For purposes of determining whether a retirement plan covers a sufficient number of employees to meet the minimum coverage requirement (see Q 5:15) and, if applicable, the minimum participation requirement (see Q 5:23), as well as other plan-related requirements, all employees of corporations that are members of a controlled group of corporations (see Q 5:31) are treated as if they were employed by a single employer. A comparable requirement applies to affiliated service groups (see Q 5:35), partnerships, sole proprietorships, and other businesses that are under common control. In addition, a special rule applies to owner-employees (see Qs 5:32, 5:33). [I.R.C. §§ 414(b), 414(c), 414(m); Beals Bros. Mgmt. Corp. v. Comm'r, 300 F.3d 963 (8th Cir. 2002)]

> **Example.** There are three corporations—Turner Duplicate Bridge, Inc., Nancy, Inc., and Steve, Inc.—but only Nancy, Inc. adopts a profit sharing plan. Turner and Nancy have sufficient common ownership to be a controlled group, and Nancy and Steve have sufficient common ownership to be a controlled group, but Turner and Steve are not members of a controlled group. To test Nancy's plan for the minimum coverage requirement, Turner and Nancy, as one controlled group, are tested separately, as are Nancy and Steve, as a second controlled group. Turner, Nancy, and Steve are not tested together as a single controlled group.

However, one court held that the employees of two failing corporations should not be aggregated with the employees of a sole proprietorship, all three of which were commonly controlled, where, under the circumstances, neither corporation was able, in good faith, to adopt a permanent retirement plan. IRS did not acquiesce in this decision. [Sutherland, 78 T.C. 395 (1982), *non acq*, 1986-1 C.B. 1]

Two related tax-exempt organizations do not constitute either a controlled group of corporations or trades or businesses under common control, ruled IRS. Both organizations were nonstock, nonprofit corporations governed by their respective boards of trustees, no individual or entity had an ownership interest in either organization, and no person served as a trustee on both boards. Four of the nine trustees on the second organization's board were employees of the first organization; this did not meet the 80 percent control test (see Q 5:31). [Priv. Ltr. Rul. 9442031]

An employee of a partnership was not eligible to participate in a qualified retirement plan established by one of the partners for the benefit of that partner's sole proprietorship. The employee was not an employee of the sole proprietorship and, therefore, was not an employee of the employer (see Q 5:1). [West v. Clarke Murphy, Jr. Self Employed Pension Plan, No. 95-1745 (4th Cir. 1996)]

A separate line of business exception may apply, for purposes of the minimum coverage and participation requirements, to commonly controlled businesses but not to affiliated service groups (see Q 5:44). [I.R.C. §§ 401(a)(26)(F), 410(b)(5), 414(r)]

Q 5:30   If an individual owns two corporations, each of which has employees, can a qualified retirement plan be adopted by only one of the corporations?

Perhaps. For example, assume that Herman owns all of the stock of Herman Corporation and Mabel Corporation. Herman Corporation maintains a defined benefit plan (see Q 2:3) for its employees; Mabel Corporation does not.

The composition of Herman's employees is as follows:

Employee	Age	Service	Compensation
1	50	10 years	$200,000
2	35	6 years	20,000
3	30	4 years	10,000
4	28	less than 1 year	10,000

The composition of Mabel's employees is as follows:

Employee	Age	Service	Compensation
5	45	2 years	$100,000
6	43	2 years	20,000
7	18	less than 1 year	10,000

Employees 1, 2, 3, 5, and 6 satisfy the plan's eligibility requirements (age 21 and one year of service), and employees 1 and 5 are HCEs (see Q 3:3). Employees 4 and 7 need not be counted for purposes of the minimum participation and minimum coverage tests since they have not satisfied the plan's age and service requirements.

Since the retirement plan covers 60 percent of the employees who satisfy the eligibility requirements (i.e., 3 ÷ 5), the plan satisfies the minimum participation requirement (see Q 5:24). In addition, the plan satisfies the ratio percentage test (see Q 5:16) because the plan's ratio percentage is 70 percent or more (i.e., the coverage percentage of NHCEs, 66.67 percent (2 ÷ 3), divided by the coverage percentage of HCEs, 50 percent (1 ÷ 2)).

Q 5:31   When does common ownership result in a controlled group of corporations or businesses?

A controlled group of corporations exists if there is:

1. A parent-subsidiary group of corporations connected through at least 80 percent stock ownership, or
2. A brother-sister group in which
   a. Five or fewer people own 80 percent or more of the stock value or voting power (controlling interest) of each corporation, and

b. The same five or fewer people together own more than 50 percent of the stock value or voting power (effective control) of each corporation, taking into account the ownership of each person only to the extent such ownership is identical with respect to each organization.

[I.R.C. §§ 414(b), 414(c), 1563(a), 1563(f)(5); United States v. Vogel Fertilizer Co., 455 U.S. 16 (1982)]

Example. SJK Corporation owns 100 percent of the stock of SKH Corporation, 80 percent of the stock of CKL Corporation, and 70 percent of the stock of JMK Corporation. The percentage of stock not owned by SJK Corporation is owned by unrelated persons. SJK, SKH, and CKL are members of a controlled group of corporations. JMK is not a member of the group because SJK's ownership is less than 80 percent.

For a brother-sister group determination, the persons whose ownership is considered for purposes of the controlling-interest requirement in 2a above must be the same persons whose ownership is considered for purposes of the effective-control requirement in 2b above. [Treas. Reg. §§ 1.414(c)-2(c)(1), 1.414(c)-2(c)(2), 1.1563-1(a)(3)(i)]

Example 1. Kenneth Corp. and Robert Corp. are owned by four unrelated shareholders in the following percentages:

Percentage of Ownership

Shareholder	*Kenneth Corp.*	*Robert Corp.*
Stanley	80%	20%
Marjorie	10	50
Kenneth	5	15
Robert	5	15
Total	100%	100%

Although the four shareholders together own 80 percent or more of the stock of each corporation, they do not own more than 50 percent of the stock of each corporation taking into account only the identical ownership as demonstrated below:

Shareholder	*Identical Ownership Percentage*
Stanley	20%
Marjorie	10
Kenneth	5
Robert	5
Total	40%

Consequently, Kenneth Corp. and Robert Corp. do not constitute a controlled group of corporations.

Example 2. Caroline Corp. and Adam Corp. are owned by Ben and Jason, who are unrelated, in the following percentages:

Percentage of Ownership

Shareholder	Caroline Corp.	Adam Corp.
Ben	100%	75%
Jason	0	25
Total	100%	100%

The identical ownership is 75 percent for Ben and 0 percent for Jason. Since the identical ownership is less than 80 percent, the controlling-interest requirement is not satisfied. Thus, the two corporations are not members of a brother-sister controlled group.

Various rules of attribution apply. [I.R.C. §§ 1563(d), 1563(e)] For example, an individual is considered as owning shares of stock in a corporation owned, directly or indirectly, by or for the individual's spouse unless certain conditions are satisfied for the taxable year. [I.R.C. § 1563(e)(5)] In addition, a parent is considered as owning shares of stock owned, directly or indirectly, by or for the parent's children who have not attained age 21, and the minor child is considered as owning the shares of stock owned, directly or indirectly, by or for the child's parents. [I.R.C. § 1563(e)(6)]

Example 1. Stephanie is the 100 percent shareholder of SKH Corporation, and her husband, Bill, is the 100 percent shareholder of WPH Corporation. Because certain conditions are satisfied (e.g., neither Stephanie nor Bill is a director or employee or participates in the management of the corporation owned by the other spouse), Stephanie's ownership is not attributed to Bill, and Bill's ownership is not attributed to Stephanie. Consequently, SKH Corporation and WPH Corporation are not members of a controlled group of corporations.

Example 2. The facts are the same as in Example 1, except that Stephanie and Bill become the parents of Jennifer. Because Jennifer is under age 21, she is deemed to own the shares of stock of each of her parents; and, therefore, since Jennifer is deemed to own 100 percent of the shares of stock of both SKH Corporation and WPH Corporation, the corporations are now members of a controlled group.

Where a corporation (Newco) was formed by the merger of six corporations (Oldcos), the plan adopted by Newco did not have to be aggregated with any plans of the Oldcos because the entities did not constitute a controlled group of corporations. [Priv. Ltr. Rul. 9541041] A corporation and a partnership in which the corporation's wholly owned subsidiary had a 33 percent partnership interest were not under common control. [Priv. Ltr. Rul. 9707028]

With regard to a brother-sister group, the controlling-interest requirement (i.e., the 80 percent test) has been eliminated for purposes of corporate tax brackets, the accumulated earnings credit, and the minimum tax. [I.R.C. §§ 1563(a)(2), 1563(f)(5)]

Q 5:32 Who is an owner-employee?

An owner-employee is a self-employed individual (see Q 6:60) who is either a sole proprietor or, in the case of a partnership, a partner who owns more than 10 percent of either the capital interest or the profits interest in such partnership. [I.R.C. § 401(c)(3); Treas. Reg. § 1.401-10(d)]

IRS has issued proposed amendments to regulations dealing with limited partners and members of limited liability companies. [Treas. Reg. § 1.1402(a)-2]

Q 5:33 Does any special coverage requirement apply if an owner-employee controls another business?

Yes, but only for years beginning before 1997. If an individual was an owner-employee (see Q 5:32) of more than one business and participated in a qualified retirement plan maintained by one of the individual's businesses (Plan X), all employees of any other business controlled by the owner-employee had to be covered by a plan that gave them benefits at least as favorable as those provided for the owner-employee under Plan X. This rule also applied if two or more owner-employees together controlled another business as owner-employees.

Control meant (1) ownership of the entire interest in an unincorporated trade or business or (2) ownership of more than 50 percent of either the capital interest or the profits interest in a partnership.

Example. In 1996, Debi was the sole owner of a music store and was also a 51 percent partner in a hardware store. The hardware store maintained a qualified retirement plan. No contributions to the hardware store's qualified retirement plan could have been made on Debi's behalf unless her music store gave its employees equal benefits under a qualified retirement plan.

This special coverage requirement was one of the few restrictions that applied to qualified retirement plans that covered owner-employees but not to corporate retirement plans. For years beginning after 1996, Debi can participate in the hardware store's plan because the music store and the hardware store are not trades or businesses under common control (see Qs 5:29–5:31). *However,* the qualified retirement plan must provide that contributions on behalf of the owner-employee may be made only with respect to the owner-employee's earned income (see Q 6:61) derived from the trade or business adopting the plan. [I.R.C. § 401(d)]

Q 5:34   What happens if the business owner sets up a management corporation?

If the business owner establishes a second corporation to perform management functions for the owner's other closely held corporation (e.g., a manufacturing corporation) and owns at least 80 percent of the stock of each corporation, both corporations will be considered to be members of a controlled group of corporations (see Qs 5:29–5:31). [I.R.C. §§ 414(b), 1563(a)(2), 1563(f)(5); Beals Bros. Mgmt. Corp. v. Comm'r, 300 F.3d 963 (8th Cir. 2002)]

If the management corporation establishes a qualified retirement plan for the business owner (its only employee) and the manufacturing corporation has no plan for its employees, the plan probably will not be qualified because of inadequate coverage and, if applicable, participation (see Q 5:1).

In addition, even if there is no common ownership, if an organization principally performs management functions for one other organization, both such organizations are considered to be an affiliated service group (see Q 5:35).

Q 5:35   What is an affiliated service group?

An affiliated service group consists of a service organization (FSO) and one or both of the following:

1. A service organization (A-ORG) that is a shareholder or partner in the FSO and that either regularly performs services for the FSO or is regularly associated with the FSO in performing services for third persons.

2. Any other organization (B-ORG) if a significant portion of the business of the B-ORG is the performance of services for the FSO or the A-ORG (or for both) of a type historically performed in the service field of the FSO or the A-ORG by employees and 10 percent or more of the interests in the B-ORG is held by individuals who are HCEs (see Q 3:2) of the FSO or A-ORG.

[I.R.C. § 414(m); Rev. Rul. 81-105, 1981-1 C.B. 256]

Example. Medical partnership P consists of corporate partners A, B, and C. Each partner owns one-third of the partnership. The partnership employs nurses and clerical employees. Corporations A, B, and C have only one employee each, the respective shareholders. The partnership does not maintain a retirement plan. Corporations A, B, and C maintain separate retirement plans.

Partnership P may be designated as the FSO. Since corporations A, B, and C are partners in the FSO and regularly perform services for the FSO, corporations A, B, and C are A-ORGs. Because corporations A, B, and C are A-ORGs for the same FSO, corporations A, B, and C and the FSO constitute an affiliated service group. Consequently, all the employees of corporations A, B, and C and the employees of P are considered as employed by a single employer for purposes of testing the qualification of the three separate retirement plans maintained by corporations A, B, and C.

IRS had issued proposed regulations directed at determining what types of organizational structures would be disregarded in order to prevent the avoidance of employee benefit requirements. These regulations covered affiliated service groups, leased employees (see Q 5:58), and other organizational arrangements. However, in 1993, as part of the Regulatory Burden Reduction Initiative, IRS withdrew those proposed regulations because IRS did not plan to finalize them. [T.D. 8474]

One court ruled that an individual who was employed by a corporation that was a member of an affiliated service group was not entitled to participate in a qualified retirement plan adopted by another member of the group because his employer had not adopted the plan. [Lopriore v. Raleigh Cardiovascular & Thoracic, Inc., 2002 WL 199517 (4th Cir. 2002)] Where a corporation (Newco) was formed by the merger of six corporations (Oldcos), the plan adopted by Newco did not have to be aggregated with any plans of the Oldcos because the entities did not constitute an affiliated service group. [Priv. Ltr. Rul. 9541041]

Affiliated service group status under the Code does not, in and of itself, support a conclusion that a group of two or more trades or businesses is a single employer for purposes of determining if an arrangement is an ERISA multiple employer welfare arrangement because of differences in the definitions. [ERISA § 3(40); DOL Info. Ltr. (May 24, 2004)]

Q 5:36   Will IRS rule on the qualified status of the retirement plan of a member of an affiliated service group?

Yes. IRS has set out procedures for obtaining determination letters on the qualification of a retirement plan established by a member of an affiliated service group, including a management organization (see Q 5:34).

An employer (1) that has adopted a new retirement plan, (2) that has amended an existing retirement plan to satisfy the affiliated service group rules, or (3) whose affiliated service group status has changed may request a determination on whether the retirement plan is qualified, taking into consideration employees of any other organization who must be treated as employees of that employer. Generally, a determination letter issued with respect to the retirement plan will cover the affiliated service group rules only if the employer submits, with the determination letter application, certain information. If IRS considers whether the retirement plan of the employer (or group of employers) satisfies the requirements of the affiliated service group rules, the determination letter issued to the employer(s) will indicate that these questions have been considered and that the retirement plan satisfies qualification requirements relating to the affiliated service group rules. Without this statement, a determination letter does not apply to any qualification issue arising by reason of the affiliated service group rules.

The application for a determination letter must include the following:

1. A description of the nature of the business of the employer, specifically whether it is a service organization or an organization whose principal

business is the performance of management functions for another organization, including the reasons therefore;

2. The identification of other members (or possible members) of the affiliated service group;

3. A description of the business of each member (or possible member) of the affiliated service group, describing the type of organization (corporation, partnership, etc.) and indicating whether the member is a service organization or an organization whose principal business is the performance of management functions for the other group members;

4. The ownership interests between the employer and the members (or possible members) of the affiliated service group;

5. A description of services performed for the employer by the members (or possible members) of the affiliated service group, or vice versa, including financial and other data as to whether the services are a significant portion of the member's business and whether, as of December 13, 1980, it was not unusual for the services to be performed by employees of organizations in that service field;

6. A description of how the employer and the members (or possible members) of the affiliated service group associate in performing services for other parties;

7. In the case of a management organization:

   a. A description of management functions, if any, performed by the employer for the members (or possible members) of the affiliated service group, or received by the employer from any other members (or possible members) of the group (including data explaining whether such management functions are performed on a regular and continuous basis) and whether or not it is unusual for such management functions to be performed by employees of organizations in the employer's business field; and

   b. If management functions are performed by the employer for the members (or possible members) of the affiliated service group, a description of what part of the employer's business constitutes the performance of management functions for the members (or possible members) of the group (including the percentage of gross receipts derived from management activities as compared to the gross receipts from other activities);

8. A brief description of any other retirement plan(s) maintained by the members (or possible members) of the affiliated service group if such other retirement plan(s) is designated as a unit for qualification purposes;

9. A description of how the retirement plan(s) satisfies the coverage requirements (see Q 5:15) if the members (or possible members) of the affiliated service group are considered part of an affiliated service group with the employer; and

10. A copy of any ruling issued by the IRS National Office on whether the employer is an affiliated service group; a copy of any prior determination

letter (see Q 18:1) that considered the effect of affiliated service group status on the employer's retirement plan; and, if known, a copy of any such ruling or determination letter issued to any other member (or possible member) of the same affiliated service group, accompanied by a statement as to whether the facts upon which the ruling or determination letter was based have changed.

[Rev. Proc. 2010-6, § 14, 2010-1 I.R.B. 193; Rev. Proc. 85-43, 1985-2 C.B. 501; Rev. Rul. 83-36, 1983-1 C.B. 763; Rev. Proc. 80-30, 1980-1 C.B. 685]

Q 5:37   What is a personal service corporation?

A personal service corporation is a corporation that provides, as its principal activity, personal services substantially performed by the employee-owners (see Q 5:39). This definition is not limited to incorporated professionals but also applies to incorporated salesmen, consultants, and other service-rendering individuals. [I.R.C. § 269A(b)(1); Prop. Treas. Reg. § 1.269A-1(b)(1)]

Q 5:38   Can the income of a personal service corporation be allocated to the employee-owner?

If substantially all of the services of a personal service corporation (see Q 5:37) are performed for one other organization (see Q 5:40) and the principal purpose for forming the corporation is the avoidance of income tax by reducing the income of, or obtaining the benefit of any deduction for, any employee-owner (see Q 5:39) that would not otherwise be available, IRS may allocate income and deductions between the personal service corporation and its employee-owners. [I.R.C. §§ 269A, 482; Prop. Treas. Reg. §§ 1.269A-1(a), 1.269A-1(f); Haag, 88 T.C. 604 (1987); Foglesong v. Comm'r, 691 F.2d 848 (7th Cir. 1982), rev'g 77 T.C. 1102 (1981); Achiro, 77 T.C. 881 (1981); Keller, 723 F.2d 58 (10th Cir. 1983), aff'g 77 T.C. 1014 (1981)]

Since the personal service corporation must perform services for only one other organization and need not have any ownership interest in such organization, this provision both broadens the affiliated service group rules (see Q 5:35) and applies to other situations.

Now that parity between the amount of retirement benefits and contributions available to the employee-owner under qualified corporate retirement plans and qualified retirement plans covering self-employed individuals (see Q 6:60) has been achieved, IRS should not be able to allocate qualified retirement plan deductions to the incorporated employee-owner, since the employee-owner could then receive the same benefits without incorporating. However, if the incorporated employee-owner uses the corporation to obtain other tax benefits not available to an unincorporated employee-owner, those tax deductions may be lost (see Qs 1:9, 5:42).

Where the individual was *not* self-employed and was initially an employee of one other organization (see Q 5:40), IRS failed in its attempt to tax the individual on contributions made to the qualified retirement plan adopted by the individual's personal service corporation. The individual, a professional hockey player, entered into an employment contract with his personal service corporation, which, in turn, contracted with the hockey club to provide the individual's services. The court ruled that valid contractual relationships existed so IRS could not allocate the plan contributions to the individual as taxable income. [Sargent v. Comm'r, 929 F.2d 1252 (8th Cir. 1991)] However, IRS has successfully argued that the entire amount paid to a professional basketball player's personal service corporation by the basketball team was includible in the player's gross income; the corporate entity was effectively disregarded. [I.R.C. § 482; Leavell, 104 T.C. 140 (1995)]

Q 5:39 Who is an employee-owner?

An employee-owner is an employee who, directly or indirectly, owns more than 10 percent of the stock of the personal service corporation. [I.R.C. § 269A(b)(2); Prop. Treas. Reg. § 1.269A-1(b)(2)]

Q 5:40 What is one other organization for purposes of the personal service corporation rules?

For the potential reallocation of income and deductions between the personal service corporation and the employee-owner (see Q 5:39) to occur, substantially all of the services of the corporation must be performed for one other corporation, partnership, or other entity. [I.R.C. § 269A(a)(1); Prop. Treas. Reg. § 1.269A-1(a)(1)]

All related persons are treated as one other entity. [I.R.C. §§ 144(a)(3), 269A(b)(3); Prop. Treas. Reg. § 1.269A-1(b)(3)]

Q 5:41 Is there a safe harbor for a personal service corporation?

Yes. In general, a personal service corporation (see Q 5:37) will be deemed not to have been formed for the principal purpose of avoiding income tax if the federal income tax liability of no employee-owner (see Q 5:39) is reduced in a 12-month period by more than the lesser of (1) $2,500 or (2) 10 percent of the federal income tax liability of the employee-owner that would have resulted in that 12-month period had the employee-owner performed the personal services in an individual capacity. [Prop. Treas. Reg. § 1.269A-1(c)]

Q 5:42 Is a retirement plan considered in determining whether the principal purpose of a personal service corporation is the avoidance of income taxes?

Generally, the existence of a qualified retirement plan will not be taken into account in determining the presence or absence of a principal purpose of the personal service corporation (see Q 5:37) to avoid income tax for purposes of the safe harbor rule (see Qs 5:38, 5:41). [Sargent v. Comm'r, 929 F.2d 1252 (8th Cir. 1991); Prop. Treas. Reg. § 1.269A-1(d)]

Q 5:43   May a director of a corporation establish a qualified retirement plan based on the director's fees?

An outside director may establish a qualified retirement plan on the basis of such fee income. Since many outside directors are in high income tax brackets, the creation of a qualified retirement plan may be an especially attractive tax-saving device for these individuals. [Rev. Rul. 68-595, 1968-2 C.B. 378]

IRS had issued proposed regulations concerning inside directors. An inside director is an individual who is both an employee and a director of the same corporation. If the inside director maintains a qualified retirement plan apart from any plan maintained by the corporation, then, to the extent that contributions, forfeitures, and benefits under the inside director's individual plan are attributable to services performed for the corporation as a director, the individual is treated as an employee of the corporation and the inside director's interest in the individual plan is treated as though it were provided under both (1) a separate qualified retirement plan maintained by the corporation and covering only the inside director and (2) any actual plan maintained by the corporation in which the director participates. If either of these plans fails to meet the qualification requirements (see chapter 4), any plan actually maintained by the corporation that covers the inside director and the plan maintained by the inside director may be disqualified. In 1993, as part of the Regulatory Burden Reduction Initiative, IRS withdrew the proposed regulations because IRS did not plan to finalize them. [T.D. 8474]

The withdrawal of these proposed regulations does not constitute IRS's imprimatur for inside director plans because proposed regulations regarding leased owners and leased managers were not withdrawn, and IRS could still disqualify both plans.

An individual is a "leased owner" with respect to a recipient (e.g., the corporation) if, during the plan year of a plan maintained by a leasing organization (e.g., the inside director), the individual performs any services for a recipient other than as an employee of the recipient and is, at the time such services are performed, a more-than-5-percent owner (see Q 26:26) of the recipient (see Q 6:62). [Jacobs, 66 T.C.M. 1470 (1993)] The fact that an individual may also perform services as an employee of the recipient does not affect the individual's status as a leased owner. [Prop. Treas. Reg. § 1.414(o)-1(b)]

A "leased manager" is an individual (e.g., the inside director) who during the calendar year performs any services for a recipient (e.g., the corporation) other than as an employee of the recipient, performs a significant amount of management activities or services for the recipient, including management functions performed as an employee of the recipient and in any other capacity, and is credited with at least 1,000 hours of service (see Q 5:9) for the recipient, including services performed as an employee of the recipient and in any other capacity. The fact that an individual may also perform services as an employee of the recipient does not affect the individual's status as a leased manager. [Prop. Treas. Reg. § 1.414(o)-1(c)]

Q 5:44   Is there a separate line of business exception to the minimum coverage and minimum participation requirements?

All employees of a single employer (see Q 5:29) are taken into account for purposes of applying the minimum coverage requirement (see Q 5:15) and, if applicable, the minimum participation requirement (see Q 5:23). However, if an employer is treated as operating qualified separate lines of business (see Q 5:47), the employer is permitted to apply the minimum coverage requirement separately with respect to the employees of each qualified separate line of business. A similar exception (but only with IRS consent) is provided for purposes of applying the minimum participation requirement. The separate line of business exception does not apply to an affiliated service group (see Q 5:35). [I.R.C. §§ 401(a)(26)(F), 410(b)(5), 414(r)] The rule that a line of business must have at least 50 employees (see Q 5:48) does not apply in determining whether a defined benefit plan (see Q 2:3) satisfies the minimum participation requirement on a separate line of business basis. This means that the minimum participation requirement may be separately applied to an employer's line of business that has fewer than 50 employees if it otherwise qualifies as a separate line of business. [I.R.C. §§ 401(a)(26)(A), 401(a)(26)(F)]

If the employer operates qualified separate lines of business, the employer need not satisfy the ratio percentage test (see Q 5:16) or the average benefit percentage test (see Q 5:19) on an employer-wide basis. However, even if an employer is treated as operating qualified separate lines of business, every plan of the employer must satisfy the nondiscriminatory classification test (see Q 5:18) on an employer-wide basis. [I.R.C. § 410(b)(5)(B); Treas. Reg. §§ 1.414(r)-8, 1.414(r)-9]

An employer is treated as operating qualified separate lines of business during any year if the employer operates separate lines of business (see Q 5:46) for bona fide business reasons and satisfies certain other conditions. An employer is treated as operating qualified separate lines of business only if (1) the employer identifies all the property and services it provides to customers and designates the property and services provided by each of its lines of business (see Q 5:45); (2) each line of business is organized and operated separately from the remainder of the employer and is therefore a separate line of business; and (3) each separate line of business meets additional statutory requirements (see Q 5:47) and thus constitutes a qualified separate line of business.

An employer is treated as operating qualified separate lines of business only if all the property and services provided by the employer to its customers are provided exclusively by qualified separate lines of business. Therefore, if an employer is treated as operating qualified separate lines of business, no portion of the employer may remain that is not included in a qualified separate line of business. [Treas. Reg. § 1.414(r)-1]

An IRS representative has opined that the separate line of business exception cannot be used to satisfy the universal availability requirement for catch-up contribution purposes (see Q 27:59).

Q 5:45   What is a line of business?

In order to demonstrate that it maintains qualified separate lines of business (see Q 5:47), an employer must initially determine its lines of business. A line of business is a portion of an employer that is identified by the property or services it provides to customers of the employer. [Treas. Reg. § 1.414(r)-2]

In determining its lines of business, the employer first identifies all the property and services it provides to its customers and then designates the property and services provided by each of its lines of business. Therefore, an employer may use its discretion to determine its lines of business in a manner that conforms to its business operations.

Example 1. Rancho Krevat Corporation is a domestic conglomerate engaged in the manufacture and sale of consumer food and beverage products and the provision of data processing services to private industry. The corporation provides no other property or services to its customers. Rancho Krevat Corporation apportions all the property and services it provides to its customers among three lines of business, one providing all its consumer food products, a second providing all its consumer beverage products, and a third providing all its data processing services. Rancho Krevat Corporation has three lines of business.

Example 2. The facts are the same as in Example 1, except that Rancho Krevat Corporation determines that neither the consumer food products line of business nor the consumer beverage products line of business would satisfy the separateness criteria for recognition as a separate line of business. Accordingly, Rancho Krevat Corporation apportions all the property and services it provides to its customers between only two lines of business, one providing all its consumer food and beverage products and a second providing all its data processing services. Rancho Krevat Corporation has two lines of business.

See Q 5:46 for the rules pertaining to vertically integrated lines of business.

Q 5:46   What is a separate line of business?

In order to demonstrate that it maintains qualified separate lines of business (see Q 5:47), an employer must show that its lines of business (see Q 5:45) are organized and operated separately from one another and therefore are separate lines of business. [Treas. Reg. §§ 1.414(r)-3, 1.414(r)-11(b)(2), 1.414(r)-11(b)(3)]

Whether a line of business is a separate line of business is determined by satisfying each of the following objective criteria:

Separate organizational unit. Each line of business must be formally organized by the employer as a separate organizational unit within the employer (i.e., a corporation, a partnership, a division, or other similar unit).

Separate financial accountability. Each line of business must be a separate profit center within the employer. For this purpose, the employer's books and records must indicate separate revenue and expense information for each profit center comprising the line of business.

Separate workforce. Each line of business must have its own separate workforce. Satisfaction of this test will depend upon the degree to which each line shares personnel with other portions of the employer. A line of business has its own separate workforce if at least 90 percent of the employees of the employer who provide any services to the line of business are substantial-service employees (see Q 5:54) with respect to the line of business and are not substantial-service employees with respect to any other line of business.

Separate management. Each line of business must have its own separate management. A line of business has its own separate management only if at least 80 percent of the top-paid workforce who provide services to the line of business are substantial-service employees with respect to the line of business. The top-paid workforce is the top 10 percent, by compensation, of all employees who provide at least 25 percent of their services to the line of business and who are not substantial-service employees with respect to any other line of business. In addition, in determining the group of top-paid employees, the employer may choose to disregard all employees who provide less than 25 percent of their services to the line of business.

Employees of a line of business (the upstream line) that provides property or services to another line of business of the employer (the downstream line) generally are also considered to be providing services to the downstream line of business. Since this presents difficulties for vertically integrated employers desiring to satisfy the separateness tests, an optional rule permits employers to treat these employees as not necessarily providing services to the downstream line. This rule is available only if certain conditions are satisfied, including a requirement that the upstream line provide at least 25 percent of its total output to outside customers of the employer. The optional rule can now apply in the case of an upstream manufacturer that provides all of its product to a downstream line and has few, if any, outside customers. Under this alternative, the vertical integration rule will also apply if, with respect to the downstream line, the business of the upstream line consists primarily of producing or manufacturing tangible property, and the same type of tangible property is provided to unrelated customers by some entities engaged in a business similar to the upstream line. The alternative would apply also for purposes of satisfying the requirement that a line of business provide property to customers of the employer. [Treas. Reg. §§ 1.414(r)-2(b)(2)(i), 1.414(r)-3(d)]

Example. El Glucko Corporation operates two lines of business, one engaged in upholstery textile manufacturing and the other in furniture manufacturing. The upholstery textile line of business provides its entire output of upholstery textiles to the furniture line of business. The furniture line of business uses the upholstery textiles in the manufacture of upholstered furniture for sale to the customers of El Glucko Corporation. The furniture line of business substantially modifies the upholstery textiles provided to it by the upholstery textile line of business in providing upholstered furniture products to customers of the corporation. In addition, although the upholstery textile line of business does not provide upholstery textiles to customers of the corporation, some entities engaged in upholstery textile manufacturing provide upholstery textiles to customers outside their controlled groups. Under these facts, El Glucko Corporation's two lines of business satisfy the requirements for the optional rule. Thus, the employees of the upholstery textile line of business will be deemed to provide services only to that line of business for purposes of the separate workforce and separate management requirements, the 50-employee requirement (see Q 5:48), and the determination of the employees of each qualified separate line of business (see Q 5:54).

Q 5:47 What is a qualified separate line of business?

To demonstrate that the employer maintains qualified separate lines of business, the following requirements must be satisfied: (1) each separate line of business must have at least 50 employees (see Q 5:48); (2) the employer must notify IRS that it treats itself as operating qualified separate lines of business (see Q 5:49); and (3) the line must satisfy administrative scrutiny (see Q 5:50). [Treas. Reg. § 1.414(r)-1(b)(2)(iv)]

The rule that a line of business must have at least 50 employees does not apply in determining whether a defined benefit plan (see Q 2:3) satisfies the minimum participation requirement on a separate line of business basis. This means that the minimum participation requirement may be separately applied to an employer's line of business that has fewer than 50 employees if it otherwise qualifies as a separate line of business (see Q 5:44). [I.R.C. §§ 401(a)(26)(A), 401(a)(26)(F)]

Q 5:48 What is the 50-employee requirement?

One of the requirements to establish that the employer maintains qualified separate lines of business (see Q 5:47) is that each separate line of business (see Q 5:46) must have 50 or more employees. [I.R.C. § 414(r)(2)(A); Treas. Reg. § 1.414(r)-1(b)(2)(iv)(B)]

The 50-employee requirement must be satisfied on each day of the testing year (see Q 5:55). All employees who provide services exclusively to the separate line of business (see Q 5:54), *including* employees who are covered under a collective bargaining agreement, are counted. However, employees who normally work less than 17½ hours per week, who normally work six months or less during the year, who are under age 21, or who have not completed six months of service are not taken into account. [Treas. Reg. §§ 1.414(r)-4(b), 1.414(q)-1, Q&A-9(g)]

The rule that a line of business must have at least 50 employees does not apply in determining whether a defined benefit plan (see Q 2:3) satisfies the minimum participation requirement on a separate line of business basis. This means that the minimum participation requirement may be separately applied to an employer's line of business that has fewer than 50 employees if it otherwise qualifies as a separate line of business (see Q 5:44). [I.R.C. §§ 401(a)(26)(A), 401(a)(26)(F)]

Q 5:49   What is the notice requirement?

To satisfy the notice requirement, the employer must notify IRS that it treats itself as operating qualified separate lines of business (see Q 5:47). [I.R.C. § 414(r)-(2)(B); Treas. Reg. § 1.414(r)-1(b)(2)(iv)(C)] The notice is given with respect to all the qualified separate lines of business of the employer and with respect to all retirement plans of the employer for plan years beginning in the testing year (see Q 5:55). [Treas. Reg. § 1.414(r)-4(c)]

Notice that the employer wishes to be treated as operating qualified separate lines of business is given by filing Form 5310-A, Notice of Plan Merger or Consolidation, Spinoff, or Transfer of Plan Assets or Liabilities; Notice of Qualified Separate Lines of Business. [Rev. Proc. 93-40, 1993-2 C.B. 535; Priv. Ltr. Rul. 9644076] IRS ruled that an employer's election to utilize the qualified separate lines of business provisions was deemed timely, even though its Form 5310-A was filed a day late. The employer was found to have acted reasonably and in good faith because it used reasonable care to ensure that the filing was timely made, it requested relief before IRS discovered the failure to timely make the election, and it had relied on a qualified tax professional to prepare the election form in a timely manner. [Priv. Ltr. Ruls. 200543062, 200534027, 200414049; *see also* Priv. Ltr. Ruls. 200738018, 200718036, 200709069]

Q 5:50   What is the administrative scrutiny requirement?

To satisfy the administrative scrutiny requirement that the employer maintains qualified separate lines of business (see Q 5:47), a separate line of business (see Q 5:46) must meet either the statutory safe harbor test (see Q 5:51) or one of the administrative safe harbors (see Q 5:52). A separate line of business that does not satisfy any of these safe harbors may still satisfy this requirement if the employer requests and receives from IRS an individual determination that the separate line of business satisfies administrative scrutiny (see Q 5:53). Each separate line of business of an employer must satisfy the administrative scrutiny requirement but need not satisfy this requirement in the same manner as the employer's other separate lines of business. [I.R.C. § 414(r)(2)(C); Treas. Reg. § 1.414(r)-1(b)(2)(iv)(D)]

Q 5:51   What is the statutory safe harbor?

A qualified separate line of business (see Q 5:47) satisfies the statutory safe harbor for administrative scrutiny (see Q 5:50) if the percentage of HCEs (see Q 3:2) of the separate line of business (see Q 5:46) falls within a range that is at least 50 percent but no more than 200 percent of the HCE percentage of the employer as a whole (see Q 5:54). The HCE percentage ratio of a separate line of business is calculated by determining a fraction (expressed as a percentage), the numerator of which is the percentage of the employees of the separate line of business who are HCEs, and the denominator of which is the percentage of all employees of the employer who are HCEs.

Additionally, if at least 10 percent of all HCEs of the employer perform services exclusively for a particular separate line of business, that separate line of business will be deemed to satisfy the 50 percent requirement of the statutory safe harbor. However, a separate line of business that satisfies this special 10 percent rule still must satisfy the 200 percent requirement of the statutory safe harbor. [I.R.C. § 414(r)(3); Treas. Reg. § 1.414(r)-5(b)]

Q 5:52   What are the administrative safe harbors?

There are five administrative safe harbors for the administrative scrutiny requirement (see Q 5:50). To permit the application of the minimum coverage and minimum participation standards (see Qs 5:15, 5:23) on a qualified separate line of business basis, these administrative safe harbors delineate situations that IRS has determined pass administrative scrutiny without the need for an individual determination (see Q 5:53). [I.R.C. § 414(r)(2)(C); Treas. Reg. §§ 1.414(r)-5(c) through 1.414(r)-5(g)]

Industry category safe harbor. This administrative safe harbor is satisfied only if the separate line of business (see Q 5:46) is in a different industry or industries from every other separate line of business of the employer. An employer may disregard foreign operations in determining whether a separate line of business is in a different industry or industries from every other separate line of business of the employer. For purposes of this administrative safe harbor, there are 12 industry categories:

1. *Food and Agriculture.* Food, beverages, tobacco, food stores, and restaurants.
2. *Textiles and Clothing.* Textile mill products, apparel and other finished products made from fabrics and other similar materials (including leather and leather products), and general merchandise stores.
3. *Forest Products.* Pulp, paper, lumber and wood products (including furniture).
4. *Transportation.* Transportation equipment and services.
5. *Finance.* Banking, insurance, and financial industries.
6. *Utilities.* Public utilities and other regulated industries and communications.
7. *Coal and Metals.* Metal industries and coal mining and production.
8. *Machinery and Electronics.* Industrial and commercial machinery; computers and other electronic and electrical equipment and components.
9. *Petroleum and Chemicals.* Oil and gas extraction, production and distribution (including gasoline service stations); petroleum refining and related industries; chemicals and allied products; rubber and miscellaneous plastic products.

10. *Construction and Real Estate.* Construction industry, real estate, stone, clay, and glass products.

11. *Leisure.* Entertainment, sports, hotels.

12. *Printing and Publishing.* Printing, publishing and allied industries.

[Rev. Proc. 91-64, 1991-2 C.B. 866]

Merger and acquisition safe harbor. This second administrative safe harbor is satisfied if (1) the employer designates the acquired business as a line of business; (2) the line of business satisfies the separateness criteria; and (3) there are not any significant changes in the workforce of the acquired separate line of business.

FAS 14 safe harbor. The third administrative safe harbor (the reportable business segments safe harbor) requires that a separate line of business be reported as one or more reportable industry segments in accordance with the Statement of Financial Accounting Standards No. 14, Financial Reporting for Segments of a Business Enterprise (FAS 14).

Average benefits safe harbor. If the HCE percentage ratio (see Q 5:51) of the separate line of business is less than 50 percent, the separate line of business will satisfy this administrative safe harbor if the actual benefit percentage of the NHCEs (see Q 3:12) of the separate line of business is at least equal to the actual benefit percentage of all other NHCEs of the employer (see Q 5:19). Similarly, if the HCE percentage ratio of the separate line of business is greater than 200 percent, the separate line of business will satisfy this safe harbor if the actual benefit percentage of the HCEs (see Q 3:2) of the separate line of business does not exceed the actual benefit percentage of all other HCEs of the employer.

Minimum or maximum benefits safe harbor. The fifth and last administrative safe harbor is the minimum or maximum benefits safe harbor. If the HCE percentage ratio of the separate line of business is less than 50 percent, then, under the minimum benefit requirement, at least 80 percent of the NHCEs (excluding those who do not meet the lowest age and service eligibility requirements of any plan that benefits employees in the separate line of business) in that separate line of business must benefit under a retirement plan, and each of these employees must receive at least a specified minimum benefit. The minimum benefit standard can be satisfied on the basis of the average benefit accruals or allocations provided to NHCEs; but, in contrast to the 80 percent requirement, the averaging must be based on 100 percent of such NHCEs. If the HCE percentage ratio of the separate line of business is more than 200 percent, then, under the maximum benefit requirement, each HCE who benefits under a retirement plan in that separate line of business must receive no more than a specified maximum benefit.

Q 5:53 Can the administrative scrutiny requirement be satisfied if the safe harbors are not?

Yes. A separate line of business (see Q 5:46) that does not satisfy either the statutory safe harbor (see Q 5:51) or any of the administrative safe harbors (see Q 5:52) may still satisfy the administrative scrutiny requirement if the employer requests and receives from IRS an individual determination that the separate line of business satisfies administrative scrutiny. [I.R.C. § 414(r)(2)(C); Treas. Reg. § 1.414(r)-6]

This determination process applies to those situations in which the separate line of business does not satisfy any of the administrative scrutiny safe harbors (see Q 5:52). An employer cannot make a request for a testing year (see Q 5:55) that ended prior to the date of the request.

In determining whether a separate line of business will receive an individual determination, IRS will consider all relevant facts and circumstances. Among the factors that may be considered in analyzing whether separate lines of business exist are the following, no one of which will necessarily be determinative:

- Differences in property or services provided
- Separateness of organization and operation
- Nature of business competition
- History of the separate lines of business
- Geographic area in which the businesses are operated
- Degree to which the separate line of business fails to satisfy the applicable safe harbors
- Size and composition of the separate lines of business
- Allocation method used for residual shared employees (see Q 5:54)
- Level of benefits provided by each separate line of business
- Other separate lines of business
- Whether the separate line of business operates in a regulated industry

[Rev. Proc. 93-41, 1993-2 C.B. 536]

If the separate line of business does not satisfy any of the safe harbors and does not obtain a favorable individual determination, the separate line of business will not satisfy administrative scrutiny.

Q 5:54   Who are the employees of each qualified separate line of business?

For purposes of testing retirement plans (see Qs 4:10, 5:15, 5:23) benefiting employees of a qualified separate line of business (see Qs 5:46, 5:47) and for purposes of applying the statutory safe harbor (see Q 5:51) and the minimum or maximum benefits safe harbor (see Q 5:52), an employer must determine which employees are treated as employees of each qualified separate line of business. [Treas. Reg. § 1.414(r)-7]

All employees must be assigned among the employer's qualified separate lines of business. The employees of a qualified separate line of business consist of all employees who provide substantial services to the qualified separate line of business and all other employees who are allocated to the qualified separate line of business. An employee is a substantial-service employee with respect to a line of business (see Q 5:45) for a testing year (see Q 5:55) if at least 75 percent of the employee's services are provided to that line of business for that testing year. Employers may treat employees who provide between 50 percent and 75 percent of their services to a particular qualified separate line of business as substantial-service employees with respect to that line of business and assign those employees to that qualified separate line of business for all purposes. This option may be exercised by the employer on an employee-by-employee basis; and, if not elected, that employee is treated as a residual shared employee. [Treas. Reg. §§ 1.414(r)-11(b)(2), 1.414(r)-11(b)(4)]

Employees who are not substantial-service employees with respect to any line of business are referred to as residual shared employees. All residual shared employees must be assigned under the same allocation method, and each residual shared employee must be allocated to only one qualified separate line of business.

There are four permissible allocation methods:

Dominant line of business method. Under the first method for allocating residual shared employees, an employer is permitted to allocate all its residual shared employees to its dominant line of business. An employer's dominant line of business is the qualified separate line of business that has an employee assignment percentage of at least 50 percent; however, an employer is permitted to determine if it has a dominant line of business by substituting 25 percent for 50 percent if the qualified separate line of business satisfies one of the following requirements:

1. The line of business accounts for at least 60 percent of the employer's gross revenue;

2. The employee assignment percentage would be at least 60 percent if union employees were considered;

3. Each line of business meets the statutory safe harbor, the average benefits safe harbor, or the minimum or maximum benefits safe harbor; or

4. The employee assignment percentage of the line of business is at least twice the employee assignment percentage of any other line of business.

Pro rata method. The second method permits the employer to allocate residual shared employees among its qualified separate lines of business in proportion to the percentage of all substantial-service employees who provide their services to each qualified separate line of business.

HCE percentage ratio method. The third method of allocation permits the employer to allocate residual shared employees among its qualified separate lines of business in a manner generally consistent with the statutory safe harbor for satisfying administrative scrutiny (see Q 5:51).

Small group method. Under the fourth method, the employer chooses a qualified separate line of business to which each residual shared employee is allocated. The residual shared employees need not all be allocated to the same qualified separate line of business; therefore, the employer has flexibility in selecting the plans under which residual shared employees benefit. In order to prevent this allocation method from being used to provide HCEs (see Q 3:2) with excessive benefits relative to the NHCEs (see Q 3:12), its use is subject to three requirements:

1. The entire group of the employer's residual shared employees cannot exceed 3 percent of the employees taken into account in applying the minimum coverage requirement.

2. The qualified separate line of business to which the employer allocates a residual shared employee must include at least 10 percent of the employer's substantial-service employees and must satisfy the administrative scrutiny safe harbor after the allocation.

3. The allocation of residual shared employees must be reasonable.

Q 5:55   What is the testing year?

For purposes of determining whether an employer operates qualified separate lines of business for bona fide business reasons (see Q 5:44), the employer must apply the requirements (see Qs 5:45–5:54) on the basis of the testing year. The testing year is the calendar year. Similarly, an employer's retirement plans are tested for discrimination (see Q 4:10), minimum coverage (see Q 5:15), and minimum participation (see Q 5:23) separately with respect to the employees of each qualified separate line of business for all plan years that begin in the testing year. [Treas. Reg. §§ 1.414(r)-1(d)(6), 1.414(r)-11(b)(5) through (8); Rev. Proc. 93-42, 1993-2 C.B. 540; Ann. 93-130, 1993-31 I.R.B. 46]

See Q 5:22 for a discussion of testing options and snapshot testing.

Q 5:56   What are the averaging rules for the separate lines of business requirements?

For purposes of determining certain percentages (see Qs 5:46, 5:51) for testing whether lines of business satisfy separate lines of business requirements, the employer is permitted to use up to a five-year moving average, absent large fluctuations. In determining whether specific percentages have been satisfied, this rule permits the employer to average the results for the current testing year (see Q 5:55) with the results for the immediately preceding one, two, three, or four testing years. The purpose of this rule is to provide stability from year to year in the application of the separate lines of business requirements. [Treas. Reg. § 1.414(r)-11(c)]

Q 5:57   Is there a flowchart to show how the qualified separate lines of business requirements work?

Yes. IRS has created the flowchart shown on the following page to illustrate how the major provisions of the qualified separate lines of business requirements (see Qs 5:45–5:54) are applied.

Q 5:58   Who is a leased employee?

A leased employee is an individual who performs services for another person (the recipient) under an arrangement between the recipient and a third person (the leasing organization) who is otherwise treated as the individual's employer. The services performed by an individual for the recipient must be under the primary direction or control of the recipient (see Q 5:59). [I.R.C. §§ 414(n)(1), 414(n)(2); see also Qs 4:1, 5:64]

In 1987, IRS issued proposed regulations relating to leased employees. However, in 1993, as part of the Regulatory Burden Reduction Initiative, IRS withdrew these proposed regulations because IRS did not plan to finalize them. [T.D. 8474]

Q 5:59   Who is the employer of a leased employee?

The leased employee (see Q 5:58) is treated as the recipient's employee if the leased employee has performed services for the recipient pursuant to an agreement with the leasing organization on a substantially full-time basis for a period of at least one year and the services are performed under the primary direction or control of the recipient. [I.R.C. §§ 414(n)(1), 414(n)(2); see also Qs 4:1, 5:64]

Factors that should be considered in determining whether an individual is under the primary direction or control of the service recipient include whether the individual is subject to the direct supervision of the recipient and whether the individual must perform services in the manner dictated by the recipient. A recipient may exercise primary direction or control by directly supervising an individual even if the recipient is not empowered to hire or fire the individual, the individual works for other companies, or another company pays the individual's wages and withholds employment and income taxes. [Bronk v. Mountain States Tel. & Tel., Inc., 216 F.3d 1086 (10th Cir. 2000)]

> **Example.** Tim works as a golf professional for MBCC, Inc. He was trained by Inwood Corporation, which also pays his wages, withholds employment taxes, and retains the authority to terminate him. However, Tim is subject to the direct supervision and day-to-day control of MBCC, Inc. and must perform services in the manner dictated by MBCC, Inc. Because Tim has worked for MBCC, Inc. on a full-time basis for more than one year (see Q 5:60), he is a leased employee of MBCC, Inc.

Q 5:60   When is the leased employee first considered an employee of the recipient?

The leased employee (see Q 5:58) is treated as the recipient's employee after the leased employee has performed services for the recipient for a period of one year. Once this occurs, the leased employee's years of service for the recipient include the entire period for which the leased employee performed services for the recipient. [I.R.C. § 414(n)(4); see also Qs 4:1, 5:64]

Just because a leased employee is treated as the recipient's employee does not mean that the leased employee must be eligible to participate in the recipient's qualified retirement plan. Leased employees can be excluded as long as the minimum coverage requirement (see Q 5:15) and, if applicable, the minimum participation requirement (see Q 5:23) are satisfied. [Wolf v. Coca-Cola Co., 2000 WL 33164 (11th Cir. 2000); Casey v. Atlantic Richfield Co., No. CV 99-06437 (C.D. Cal. 2000); Clark v. E.I. DuPont de Nemours & Co., 105 F.3d 646 (4th Cir. 1997)]

Q 5:61 What happens if the leased employee participates in the leasing organization's qualified retirement plan?

If the leasing organization maintains a qualified retirement plan, contributions or benefits for the leased employee (see Q 5:58) are treated as if provided by the recipient to the extent those contributions or benefits are attributable to services performed by the leased employee for the recipient. [I.R.C. § 414(n)(1)(B); see also Qs 4:1, 5:64]

Q 5:62 When will the leased employee not be treated as an employee of the recipient?

A leased employee (see Q 5:58) will not be treated as the recipient's employee if leased employees do not constitute more than 20 percent of the recipient's non-highly compensated workforce and each leased employee is covered by a qualified money purchase pension plan (see Q 2:4) maintained by the leasing organization that provides the following:

- Immediate participation
- Full and immediate vesting
- A nonintegrated contribution rate of 10 percent of compensation

The immediate participation requirement does not apply to (1) employees who perform substantially all of their services for the leasing organization and (2) employees whose compensation from the leasing organization for each of the four preceding plan years is less than $1,000. A money purchase pension plan meeting these requirements is referred to as a safe harbor plan. The term "non-highly compensated workforce" means the aggregate number of individuals other than HCEs (see Qs 3:2, 3:12) who are employees of the recipient and have performed services for the recipient on a substantially full-time basis for one year or who are leased employees with respect to the recipient. [I.R.C. § 414(n)(5); see also Qs 4:1, 5:64]

Q 5:63 Can an employer utilizing the services of leased employees obtain IRS approval of its qualified retirement plan?

Yes. An employer utilizing one or more leased employees (see Q 5:58) may be able to obtain a favorable determination letter (see Q 18:1) by following the application procedure developed by IRS. [Rev. Proc. 2010-6, § 14, 2010-1 I.R.B. 193; Rev. Proc. 85-43, 1985-2 C.B. 501; see also Qs 4:1, 5:64]

The application for a determination letter must include the following:

1. A description of the nature of the business of the recipient organization (see Q 5:58);
2. A copy of the relevant leasing agreement(s);
3. A description of the function of all leased employees (see Q 5:58) within the trade or business of the recipient organization (including data as to whether all leased employees are performing services on a substantially full-time basis);
4. A description of facts and circumstances relevant to a determination of whether such leased employees' services are performed under primary direction or control by the recipient organization (including whether the leased employees are required to comply with instructions of the recipient about when, where, and how to perform the services, whether the services must be performed by particular persons, whether the leased employees are subject to the supervision of the recipient, and whether the leased employees must perform services in the order or sequence set by the recipient); and
5. If the recipient organization is relying on any qualified retirement plan(s) maintained by the employee leasing organization (see Q 5:61) for purposes of qualification of the recipient organization's plan, a description of such plan(s) (including a description of the contributions or benefits provided for all leased employees that are attributable to services performed for the recipient organization, plan eligibility, and vesting).

Q 5:64   What is a professional employer organization?

IRS issued a revenue procedure describing steps that could be taken to ensure the qualified status of defined contribution plans (see Q 2:2) maintained by professional employer organizations (PEOs) for the benefit of worksite employees. PEOs are also commonly known as employee leasing organizations. Worksite employees are employees who receive amounts from a PEO for providing services to a client organization (CO) pursuant to a service agreement between the PEO and the CO.

The employment relationship between workers and the employer maintaining a plan is fundamental to whether a plan is qualified. The determination of whether an employment relationship exists depends on the facts and circumstances of each particular case (see Q 5:1). If a retirement plan provides benefits for individuals who are not employees of the employer maintaining the plan, the plan does not satisfy the exclusive benefit rule (see Q 4:1) and therefore could be disqualified.

IRS recognized the complexity involved in the determination of whether a worksite employee is the common law employee of the PEO or the CO, as well as the need of the PEO, the CO, worksite employees, and plan administrators (see Q 20:1) for certainty in this area. Accordingly, the revenue procedure provides a framework under which plans sponsored by PEOs will not be treated as violating the exclusive benefit rule solely because they provide benefits to worksite employees. Under the approach provided in the revenue procedure, a PEO that maintains a defined contribution plan may establish a multiple employer retirement plan that benefits worksite employees providing services to COs. For purposes of the revenue procedure, a multiple employer retirement plan means a defined contribution plan, including a plan that contains a cash-or-deferred arrangement (see Q 27:2), under which each CO is treated as an employer. For PEOs that do not wish to establish a multiple employer retirement plan, the revenue procedure provides transition rules under which the existing PEO plan will be treated as a qualified retirement plan if it is terminated by the 120th day after the final day of the plan year beginning on or after January 1, 2003.

[Rev. Proc. 2002-21, 2002-1 C.B. 911]

IRS issued a second revenue procedure amplifying the first. The questions and answers contained in the second revenue procedure provide guidance on certain transitional issues that were raised by practitioners after the publication of the first revenue procedure. [Rev. Proc. 2003-86, 2003-2 C.B. 1211]

One court ruled that an employer whose 401(k) plan (see Q 27:1) was maintained by a PEO could not maintain a breach of fiduciary duty action against the PEO for failing to give notice of the IRS rule discussed above that would have prevented the plan from being disqualified for being top heavy (see Q 26:1). [Tassos Epicurean Cuisine, Inc. v. Triad Business Solutions, Inc. v. Bozadzis, 2007 U.S. Dist. LEXIS 22168 (E.D. Mich. 2007)]

Chapter 6

Benefit and Contribution Limitations

ERISA set limits on the amount that could be allocated to an employee under a defined contribution plan and on the amount of the annual retirement benefit that could be provided to an employee under a defined benefit plan. These limits were subject to cost-of-living increases; and, because of the high rates of inflation in the late 1970s, these limits rose significantly. Congress reduced these limits in TEFRA and again in TRA '86; however, EGTRRA 2001 significantly increased these limits. This chapter examines limitations now in effect for both defined contribution and defined benefit plans. On April 4, 2007, IRS published final regulations relating to the limits on benefits and contributions.

Q 6:1   When are the final Section 415 regulations effective?

The final regulations became effective on April 5, 2007, and generally apply for limitation years (see Q 6:58) beginning on or after July 1, 2007. [Treas. Reg. § 1.415(a)-1(g); preamble to final regulations] Comprehensive regulations regarding Section 415 were last issued in 1981, and the final regulations reflect the numerous statutory changes to Section 415 and related provisions that have been made since 1981. Some of the statutory changes reflected in the regulations are as follows:

- The current statutory limitations applicable for defined benefit and defined contribution plans (see Qs 6:11, 6:34), respectively, as most recently amended by EGTRRA 2001 (see Q 1:21)
- Changes to the rules for age adjustments to the applicable limitations under defined benefit plans, under which the dollar limitation is adjusted for commencement before age 62 or after age 65 (see Qs 6:19, 6:20)
- Changes to the rules, including specification of parameters, for benefit adjustments under defined benefit plans (see Q 6:18)
- The phase-in of the dollar limitation over ten years of participation (see Q 6:22)

- The addition of the limitation on compensation that is permitted to be taken into account in determining plan benefits, and the interaction of this requirement with the Section 415 limitations (see Q 6:45)
- Changes to the aggregation rules under which multiemployer plans (see Q 29:2) are not aggregated with single-employer plans for purposes of applying the compensation-based limitation to a single-employer plan (see Q 6:55)
- The repeal of the combined limitation on participation in a defined benefit plan and a defined contribution plan
- The changes that were made in conjunction with the repeal under EGTRRA 2001 of the exclusion allowance relating to 403(b) plans; see Q 35:1)
- The current rounding and base period terms for annual cost-of-living adjustments, as most recently amended in EGTRRA 2001 and the Working Families Tax Relief Act of 2004 (see Qs 1:26, 6:12, 6:35)
- Changes to Section 415(c) under which certain types of arrangements are no longer subject to the limitations (such as individual retirement accounts other than SEPs; see Qs 30:1, 32:1) and other types of arrangements have become subject to the limitations (such as certain individual medical accounts; see Q 6:34)
- The inclusion in compensation (for purposes of Section 415) of certain salary reduction amounts not included in gross income (see Q 6:41)
- The following modifications to Section 415 that were made by PPA (see Q 1:33): (1) changes to the interest rate assumptions that are used for converting certain forms of benefits to an equivalent straight life annuity and (2) elimination of the active participation requirement in determining a participant's high-three years of service (see Qs 6:13, 6:18)

The final regulations provide specific rules regarding when amounts received following severance from employment are considered compensation for purposes of Section 415, and when such amounts are permitted to be deferred pursuant to Section 401(k) (see Q 27:15). The regulations generally provide that amounts received following severance from employment are not considered to be compensation for purposes of Section 415, but provide exceptions for certain payments made by the later of two and one-half months following severance from employment or the end of the year in which the severance occurs. The regulations include corresponding changes to the regulations under Section 401(k) that provide that amounts payable following severance from employment can be deferred only if those amounts are within these same exceptions (see Qs 6:8, 6:43). [Preamble to final regulations]

The final regulations generally apply to limitation years beginning on or after July 1, 2007. However, the two and one-half-month rule discussed above applies with respect to compensation paid (or that would have been paid but for a cash-or-deferred election; see Q 27:3) in plan years beginning on or after July 1, 2007. The regulations reflect revisions to the effective date provisions of the proposed regulations to expand the benefits that are grandfathered from the application of the final regulations. Under the final regulations, a defined benefit plan is considered to satisfy the limitations on the annual benefit for a participant with respect to benefits accrued or payable under the plan as of the end of the limitation year that is immediately prior to the effective date of the final regulations for the plan pursuant to plan provisions (including plan provisions relating to the plan's limitation year) that were both adopted and in effect before April 5, 2007, but only if such plan provisions meet the requirements of statutory provisions, regulations, and other published guidance in effect immediately before the effective date of the final regulations. For this purpose, plan provisions will not be treated as failing to satisfy the requirements of statutory provisions, regulations, and other published guidance in effect immediately before the effective date of the final regulations merely because the plan has not been amended to reflect changes to Section 415(b) made by the Pension Funding Equity Act of 2004 (PFEA; see Q 1:25) and PPA. In addition, for this purpose, plan provisions will not be treated as failing to satisfy the percentage-of-compensation limitation (see Q 6:11) merely because the plan's definition of compensation for a limitation year that is used for purposes of applying the limitations reflects compensation for a plan year that is in excess of the compensation limitation that applies to that plan year. Thus, plans that were in compliance with the rules of Section 415 as in effect for limitation years prior to the effective date of the final regulations for the plan will not be disqualified based on the benefits that arise pursuant to plan provisions that were both adopted and in effect before April 5, 2007, and that accrue prior to the effective date of the final regulations for the plan, even if those benefits no longer comply with the requirements of Section 415 as set forth under the final regulations. However, such a plan will not be permitted to provide for the accrual of additional benefits for a participant on or after the effective date of the final regulations for the plan unless such additional benefits, together with the participant's other accrued benefits, comply with the regulations (see Q 6:13, Example 3).

Generally, a provision of a plan that results in a failure of the plan to satisfy the final regulations is a disqualifying provision (see Q 6:57). [Treas. Reg. § 1.401(b)-1(b)(3)(i)] Therefore, the remedial amendment period rules apply. For example, in the case of a plan with a calendar plan year and a calendar limitation year that is maintained by an employer with a calendar taxable year, the plan's remedial amendment period with respect to a disqualifying plan provision as a result of the final regulations ends on the date prescribed by law for the filing of the employer's income tax return (including extensions) for the 2008 taxable year. In addition, special timing rules apply in the case of certain plan amendments made pursuant to changes made in Section 415 by PFEA and PPA.

Under PFEA (prior to amendment by PPA), a plan amendment to reflect the 5.5 percent interest rate assumption that is generally required to be used for distributions with annuity starting dates (see Q 10:3) in plan years beginning in years 2004 and 2005 (for determining the actuarially equivalent straight life annuity for a form of benefit that is subject to Section 417(e)) must be made on or before the last day of the first plan year beginning on or after January 1, 2006. PPA modified PFEA by extending the due date for the amendment to on or before the last day of the first plan year beginning on or after January 1, 2008. Thus, in the case of an amendment to a plan with a calendar year plan year to reflect the interest rate assumption specified by PFEA, the plan is treated as having been operated in accordance with its terms, and the amendment does not violate the anti-cutback rule (see Q 9:25) provided that the plan is operated in conformity with the amendment and the amendment is adopted no later than December 31, 2008.

A plan amendment that is made pursuant to PPA (or a regulation issued by IRS under PPA) must be made on or before the last day of the first plan year beginning on or after January 1, 2009. If the plan is amended by such date and the plan is operated in conformity with the amendment, the plan is treated as having been operated in accordance with its terms and the amendment does not cause the plan to fail to satisfy the anti-cutback rule. A plan amendment is treated as an amendment that is made pursuant to a statutory amendment made by PPA (or a regulation issued by IRS under PPA) if the amendment is a plan amendment to reflect the changes to the assumptions that are used for converting certain forms of benefits to an equivalent straight life annuity in a limitation year beginning on or after January 1, 2006. [Preamble to final regulations]

Q 6:2 What general rules apply to the limitations on benefits and contributions?

A retirement plan will not be qualified (see Q 4:1) if any of the following conditions exists:

1. In the case of a defined benefit plan (see Q 2:3), the annual benefit with respect to any participant for any limitation (see Q 6:58) year exceeds certain limitations (see Q 6:11).

2. In the case of a defined contribution plan (see Q 2:2), the annual additions credited with respect to any participant for any limitation year exceed certain limitations (see Q 6:34).

3. The plan has been disqualified (see Q 6:57).

[I.R.C. §§ 415(a)(1)(A), 415(a)(1)(B); Treas. Reg. §§ 1.415(a)-1(a), 1.415 (a)-1(c)]

Q 6:3 Are any plan provisions required?

Although no specific plan provision is required under Section 415 in order for a plan to establish or maintain its qualification, the plan provisions must preclude the possibility that any distribution under a defined benefit plan (see Qs 2:3, 6:11) or annual addition (see Q 6:34) under a defined contribution plan (see Q 2:2) will exceed the limitations applicable to such plans. In addition, a defined benefit plan that is subject to the minimum vesting standards (see Q 9:4) must preclude the possibility that any accrual under the plan will exceed the applicable limitations. A defined benefit plan may include provisions that automatically freeze or reduce the rate of benefit accrual, and a defined contribution plan may include provisions that automatically limit the annual addition to a level necessary to prevent the applicable limitations from being exceeded with respect to any participant. Because the operation of such a provision must preclude discretion by the employer, if two defined benefit plans that are aggregated (see Q 6:51) would otherwise provide for aggregate benefits that might exceed the applicable limits, the plan provisions must specify (without involving employer discretion) how benefits will be limited to prevent a violation of the limit on the amount of the annual benefit. [I.R.C. §§ 415(a)(1)(A), 415(a)(1)(B); Treas. Reg. §§ 1.401(a)-1(b)(iii), 1.415(a)-1(d)(1)]

A provision of a profit sharing or stock bonus plan (see Qs 2:6, 2:13) that automatically freezes or reduces the amount of annual additions to ensure that the applicable limitations will not be exceeded must comply with the requirement that such plans provide a definite predetermined formula for allocating the contributions made to the plan among the participants. If the operation of a provision that automatically freezes or reduces the amount of annual additions to ensure that the limitations are not exceeded does not involve discretionary action on the part of the employer, the definite predetermined allocation formula requirement is not violated by the provision. If the operation of such a provision involves discretionary action on the part of the employer, the definite predetermined allocation formula requirement is violated. For example, if two profit sharing plans of one employer otherwise provide for aggregate contributions that may exceed the limits, the plan provisions must specify (without involving employer discretion) under which plan contributions and allocations will be reduced to prevent an excess annual addition and how the reduction will occur. [Treas. Reg. §§ 1.401-1(b)(1)(ii), 1.401-1(b)(1)(iii), 1.415(a)-1(d)(2)]

Q 6:4 Can the Section 415 limitations be incorporated by reference?

A plan is permitted to incorporate by reference the limitations on benefits and contributions (see Qs 6:11, 6:34) and will not fail to meet the definitely determinable benefit requirement or the definite predetermined allocation formula requirement (see Q 6:3), whichever applies to the plan, merely because it incorporates the limits by reference.

Where a limitation provision is permitted to be applied in more than one manner but will be applied in a specified manner in the absence of contrary plan provisions (in other words, a default rule exists), if a plan incorporates the limitations by reference with respect to that limitation provision and does not specifically vary from the default rule, then the default rule applies. With respect to a limitation provision for which a default rule exists, if the limitations will be applied in a manner other than using the default rule, the plan must specify the manner in which the limitation will be applied in addition to generally incorporating the limitations by reference. For example, if a plan generally incorporates the limitations by reference and does not restrict the accrued benefits (see Q 9:2) to which the amendments to Section 415(b)(2)(E) made in 1994 apply, then the amendments to Section 415(b)(2)(E) made in 1994 apply to all benefits under the plan.

If a limitation may be applied in more than one manner and if there is no governing principle pursuant to which that limitation is applied in the absence of contrary plan provisions, then the plan must specify the manner in which the limitation will be applied in addition to generally incorporating the limitations by reference. For example, if an employer maintains two profit sharing plans and if any participant participates in more than one such plan, then both plans must specify (in a consistent manner) under which of the employer's two profit sharing plans annual additions (see Q 6:34) must be reduced if aggregate annual additions would otherwise exceed the applicable limitations.

A plan is not permitted to incorporate by reference formerly applicable requirements of Section 415 that are no longer in force. [Treas. Reg. § 1.415(a)-1(d)(3)(i)–(iv)]

Q 6:5   Can cost-of-living adjustments be incorporated by reference?

A plan is permitted to incorporate by reference the annual adjustments to the limitations on benefits and contributions (see Qs 6:12, 6:35). Notwithstanding that a plan incorporates the cost-of-living increases to the applicable limits by reference, the accrued benefit (see Q 9:2) of a participant and any amount payable to a participant are not permitted to reflect increases pursuant to the annual increase of the dollar limitation or the compensation limit (see Q 6:46) for any period before the annual increase becomes effective. A plan amendment does not violate the anti-cutback rule (see Q 9:25) merely because it eliminates the incorporation by reference of the increases with respect to increases that have not yet occurred.

If a plan incorporates by reference the annual adjustments to the limitations pursuant to this Q 6:5, the plan will be treated as applying the cost-of-living adjustments to the maximum extent permitted under the safe harbor (see Q 6:12), except to the extent provided in this paragraph. Thus, such a plan is not subject to the requirements providing special rules for determining the annual benefit of an employee in the case of multiple annuity starting dates (see Q 6:14) with respect to benefit increases that result solely from a cost-of-living increase in the limits on the annual benefit. If a plan incorporates by reference the annual adjustments to the limitations pursuant to this Q 6:5, the annual increase of the dollar limitation does not apply with respect to a participant if the increase is effective after the participant's severance from employment (see Q 6:8) with the employer maintaining the plan (or, if earlier, after the annuity starting date in the case of a participant who has commenced receiving benefits; see Q 10:3), unless the plan specifies that this annual increase applies. Similarly, if a plan incorporates by reference the annual adjustments to the limitations, the annual increase of the compensation-based limitation does not apply with respect to a participant for increases that are effective after the participant's severance from employment with the employer maintaining the plan (or, if earlier, after the annuity starting date in the case of a participant who has commenced receiving benefits), unless the plan specifies that this annual increase applies.

In general, the annual increase of the dollar limitation and the compensation limitation is treated as a plan amendment, regardless of whether the plan reflects the increase automatically through operation of plan provisions in accordance with this Q 6:5 or the plan is amended to reflect the increase. However, where a plan reflects the annual increase of the dollar limitation or the compensation limitation automatically through operation of plan provisions pursuant to this Q 6:5, the funding method for the plan is permitted to provide for this annual increase to be treated as an experience loss (see Q 8:18) for purposes of applying Sections 404, 412, and 431. [Treas. Reg. § 1.415(a)-1(d)(3)(v)]

Q 6:6   What are the rules for plans maintained by more than one employer?

Except with respect to the aggregation of multiemployer plans with plans other than multiemployer plans (see Q 6:55), for purposes of applying the limitations on benefits and contributions (see Qs 6:11, 6:34) with respect to a participant in a plan maintained by more than one employer, benefits and contributions attributable to such participant from all of the employers maintaining the plan must be taken into account. Furthermore, in applying the limitations with respect to a participant in such a plan, the total compensation received by the participant from all of the employers maintaining the plan is taken into account under the plan, unless the plan specifies otherwise. [Treas. Reg. § 1.415(a)-1(e)]

Q 6:7   What rules apply to affiliated employers and leased employees?

All employees of corporations that are members of a controlled group of corporations (see Q 5:31) are treated as if they were employed by a single employer. A comparable requirement applies to partnerships, sole proprietorships, and other businesses that are under common control (see Q 5:29). [I.R.C. §§ 414(b), 414(c)] However, a special rule applies to parent-subsidiary relationships for benefit and contribution limitation purposes (see Qs 6:11, 6:34). Under this special rule, a controlled group or commonly controlled group exists if there is a parent-subsidiary group connected through more than 50 percent ownership. [I.R.C. § 415(h)] Thus, any defined benefit plan (see Q 2:3) or defined contribution plan (see Q 2:2) maintained by any member of a controlled group of corporations or by any trade or business (whether or not incorporated) that is part of a group of trades or businesses that are under common control is deemed maintained by all such members or such trades or businesses. [Treas. Reg. § 1.415(a)-1(f)(1)]

Any defined benefit plan or defined contribution plan maintained by any member of an affiliated service group is deemed maintained by all members of that affiliated service group (see Qs 5:35, 5:36). [Treas. Reg. § 1.415(a)-1(f)(2)]

With respect to any person (recipient) for whom a leased employee performs services, the leased employee is treated as an employee of the recipient, but contributions or benefits provided by the leasing organization that are attributable to services performed for the recipient are treated as provided under a plan maintained by the recipient. This does not apply to a leased employee with respect to services performed for a recipient if (1) the leased employee is covered by a plan that is maintained by the leasing organization and that meets certain requirements and (2) leased employees do not constitute more than 20 percent of the recipient's non-highly compensated workforce (see Qs 5:58–5:63). [Treas. Reg. § 1.415(a)-1(f)(3)]

Q 6:8   What does severance from employment mean?

Whether an employee has a severance from employment with the employer that maintains a plan is determined in the same manner as for 401(k) plan purposes (see Q 27:14), except that, for purposes of determining the employer of an employee, the modifications to the employer aggregation rules apply (see Q 6:7). Thus, an employee has a severance from employment where the employee ceases to be an employee of the employer maintaining the plan; and an employee does not have a severance from employment if, in connection with a change of employment, the employee's new employer maintains such plan with respect to the employee. The determination of whether an employee ceases to be an employee of the employer maintaining the plan is based on all of the relevant facts and circumstances. [Treas. Reg. § 1.415(a)-1(f)(5)(i)]

A participant in a multiemployer plan (see Q 29:2) is not treated as having incurred a severance from employment with the employer maintaining the multiemployer plan if the participant continues to be an employee of another employer maintaining the multiemployer plan. [Treas. Reg. § 1.415(a)-1(f)(5)(ii)]

Q 6:9   How is an alternate payee treated?

A benefit provided to an alternate payee (see Q 36:5) of a participant pursuant to a qualified domestic relations order (QDRO; see Q 36:1) is treated as if it were provided to the participant for purposes of applying the limitations on benefits and contributions (see Q 36:29). [Treas. Reg. §§ 1.401(a)-13(g)(4)(iv), 1.415(a)-1(f)(6)]

Q 6:10   What effect does Section 415 have on other plan qualification requirements?

Generally, the application of Section 415 does not relieve a plan of the obligation to satisfy other applicable qualification requirements. Accordingly, the terms of the plan must provide for the plan to satisfy Section 415 as well as all other applicable requirements. For example, if a defined benefit plan (see Q 2:3) has a normal retirement age (see Q 10:55) of 62 and if a participant's benefit remains unchanged between the ages of 62 and 65 because of the application of the dollar limit to the participant's annual benefit (see Q 6:11), the plan satisfies the requirements concerning the nonforfeitability of accrued benefits only if the plan either commences distribution of the participant's benefit at normal retirement age (without regard to severance from employment) or provides for a suspension of benefits at normal retirement age that satisfies certain requirements (see Q 6:25). Similarly, if the increase to the participant's benefit under a defined benefit plan in a year after the participant has attained normal retirement age is less than the actuarial increase in the participant's previously accrued benefit because of the application of the compensation limitation (which is not adjusted for commencement after age 65), the plan satisfies the nonforfeitability requirements only if the plan either commences distribution of the participant's benefit at normal retirement age (without regard to severance from employment) or provides for a suspension of benefits at normal retirement age that satisfies those same requirements. [I.R.C. § 411(a)(3)(B); Treas. Reg. § 1.415(a)-1(f)(7); D.O.L. Reg. § 2530.203-3]

Q 6:11 What is the maximum annual benefit that a defined benefit plan may provide?

A defined benefit plan (see Q 2:3) fails to satisfy the limitation on benefits for a limitation year (see Q 6:58) if, during the limitation year, either the annual benefit (see Q 6:14) accrued by a participant (whether or not the benefit is vested; see Qs 9:1, 9:2) or the annual benefit payable to a participant at any time under the plan exceeds the *lesser* of:

1. $160,000 (the dollar limitation), with cost-of-living adjustments (see Q 6:12), or
2. 100 percent of the participant's average compensation for the period of the participant's high-three years of service (the compensation limitation; see Q 6:13). [I.R.C. §§ 415(a)(1)(A), 415(b)(1); Treas. Reg. § 1.415(b)-1(a)(1); Rev. Rul. 2001-1, 2001-2 C.B. 427, Q&A-1]

For purposes of Section 415, a defined benefit plan is any plan, contract, or account to which Section 415 applies (or any portion thereof) that is not a defined contribution plan (see Q 2:2). [I.R.C. § 415(k); Treas. Reg. § 1.415(b)-1(a)(2)]

In order to satisfy the limitations on benefits, the plan provisions (including the provisions of any annuity) must preclude the possibility that any annual benefit exceeding these limitations will be accrued, distributed, or otherwise payable in any optional form of benefit (including the normal form of benefit) at any time (from the plan, from an annuity contract that will make distributions to the participant on behalf of the plan, or from an annuity contract that has been distributed under the plan). Thus, for example, a plan will fail to satisfy the limitations if the plan does not contain terms that preclude the possibility that any annual benefit exceeding these limitations will be accrued or payable in any optional form of benefit (including the normal form of benefit) at any time, even though no participant has actually accrued a benefit in excess of these limitations. [Treas. Reg. § 1.415(b)-1(a)(3)]

The age-adjusted dollar limit is used in place of the dollar limitation in the case of a benefit with an annual starting date that occurs before the participant attains age 62 or after the participant attains age 65 (see Qs 6:19, 6:20). [Treas. Reg. § 1.415(b)-1(a)(3)]

Q 6:12 Will the dollar and compensation limitations applicable to the annual benefit rise?

The dollar limitation applicable to defined benefit plans (see Q 6:11) is adjusted annually to take into account increases in the cost of living. The adjustment of the dollar limitation is made by multiplying the adjustment factor for the year by $160,000 and rounding the result. [I.R.C. §§ 415(b)(1)(A), 415(d)(1)(A; Treas. Reg. § 1.415(d)-1(a)(1)(i)]

The adjustment factor for a calendar year is equal to a fraction, the numerator of which is the value of the applicable index for the calendar quarter ending September 30 of the preceding calendar year and the denominator of which is the value of such index for the base period. The applicable index is determined consistent with the procedures used to adjust benefit amounts under Social Security. If, however, the value of that fraction is less than 1 for a calendar year, then the adjustment factor for the calendar year is equal to 1. For the purpose of adjusting the dollar limitation, the base period is the calendar quarter beginning July 1, 2001. Any increase in the $160,000 amount that is not a multiple of $5,000 is rounded to the next lowest multiple of $5,000. For example, an increase in the cost of living of $4,999 will result in no adjustment, and an increase of $9,999 will create an upward adjustment of $5,000. [I.R.C. §§ 415(d)(2), 415(d)(3)(A), 415(d)(4)(A); Treas. Reg. §§ 1.415(d)-1(a)(1)(ii), 1.415(d)-1(a)(1)(iii)]

For limitation years (see Q 6:58) ending in 2010, the dollar limitation remained at $195,000. [IRS Notice 2009-94, 2009-2 C.B. 848] For the five limitation years ended prior to 2010, the adjusted dollar limitation was:

Limitation Year Ending in	Adjusted Limit
2009	$195,000
2008	185,000
2007	180,000
2006	175,000
2005	170,000

The applicable dollar limitation is the amount in effect on the last day of the limitation year. [Treas. Reg. § 1.415(d)-1(a)(3)]

Example 1. Assume that the dollar limitation increases from $195,000 in 2010 to $200,000 in 2011. FSB Corp. maintains a defined benefit plan with a plan year beginning on February 1 and ending on January 31. The limitation year is the same as the plan year; and Fred and Sue, who are participants in the plan, both have compensation of $200,000 for the limitation year ended January 31, 2011. The maximum annual benefit for both Fred and Sue for the limitation year ended January 31, 2011 is $200,000 even though the limitation year began in 2010.

With regard to participants who have had a severance from employment (see Q 6:8) with the employer maintaining the plan, the compensation limitation (see Q 6:11) is permitted to be adjusted annually to take into account increases in the cost of living. For any limitation year beginning after the severance occurs, the adjustment of the compensation limitation is made by multiplying the annual adjustment factor by the compensation limitation applicable to the participant in the prior limitation year. The annual adjustment factor is prescribed by IRS. [Treas. Reg. § 1.415(d)-1(a)(2)(i)] The annual adjustment factor for a calendar year is equal to a fraction, the numerator of which is the value of the applicable index for the calendar quarter ending September 30 of the preceding calendar year and the denominator of which is the value of such index for the calendar quarter ending September 30 of the calendar year prior to that preceding calendar year. The applicable index is determined consistent with the procedures used to adjust benefit amounts under Social Security. If the value of the fraction is less than 1 for a calendar year, then the adjustment factor for the calendar year is equal to 1. In such a case, the annual adjustment factor for future calendar years will be determined in accordance with revenue rulings, notices, or other published guidance prescribed by IRS. [Treas. Reg. § 1.415(d)-1(a)(2)(ii)]

If, after having severance from employment with the employer maintaining the plan, an employee is rehired by the employer maintaining the plan, the employee's compensation limit is the greater of:

1. 100 percent of the participant's average compensation for the period of the participant's high-three years of service (see Q 6:13), as determined prior to the employee's severance from employment with the employer maintaining the plan, as adjusted (if the plan so provides), or

2. 100 percent of the participant's average compensation for the period of the participant's high-three years of service, with the period of the participant's high-three years of service determined pursuant to the break-in-service rules (see Q 6:13).

[Treas. Reg. § 1.415(d)-1(a)(2)(iii)]

The adjusted dollar limitation applicable to defined benefit plans and the adjusted compensation limit applicable to a participant are effective as of January 1 of each calendar year and apply with respect to limitation years ending with or within that calendar year. However, benefit payments and accrued benefits (see Q 9:2) for a limitation year cannot exceed the currently applicable dollar limitation or compensation limitation (as in effect before the January 1 adjustment) prior to January 1. Thus, where there is an increase in the limitation, any increase in a participant's benefits associated with the limitation increase is permitted to occur as of a date no earlier than January 1 of the calendar year for which the increase in the limitation is effective and may be applied only for payments due on or after January 1 of such calendar year. For example, assume that a participant in a defined benefit plan is currently receiving a benefit in the form of a straight life annuity, payable monthly, in an amount equal to the dollar limit, and that the defined benefit plan has a limitation year that runs from July 1 to June 30. If the plan is amended to reflect the increase to the dollar limit that is effective as of January 1, 2009, the associated increase in the participant's monthly benefit payments is effective only for payments due on or after January 1, 2009 and the participant's benefit cannot be increased to reflect the increase that is effective January 1, 2009 with respect to any monthly payment due prior to January 1, 2009. [Treas. Reg. § 1.415(d)-1(a)(3)]

An adjustment to the dollar limitation is permitted to be applied to a participant who has not commenced benefits before the date on which the adjustment is effective. Annual adjustments to the compensation limit are permitted to be made for all limitation years that begin after the participant's severance from employment and apply to distributions that commence after the effective dates of such adjustments. However, no adjustment to the compensation limit is made for any limitation year that begins on or before the date of the participant's severance from employment with the employer maintaining the plan. [Treas. Reg. § 1.415(d)-1(a)(4)(ii)]

With respect to a distribution of accrued benefits that commenced before the date on which an adjustment to the dollar limitation is effective, a plan is permitted to apply the adjusted limitations to that distribution, but only to the extent that benefits have not been paid. Thus, for example, a plan cannot provide that the adjusted dollar limitation applies to a participant who has previously received the entire plan benefit in a single-sum distribution. However, a plan can provide for an increase in benefits to a participant who accrues additional benefits under the plan that could have been accrued without regard to the adjustment of the dollar limitation (including benefits that accrue as a result of a plan amendment) on or after the effective date of the adjusted limitation. [Treas. Reg. § 1.415(d)-1(a)(4)(iii)]

If a plan is amended to increase benefits payable under the plan in accordance with the following paragraphs of this Q 6:12 (or the plan is treated as applying the next paragraph of this Q 6:12 because the plan incorporates the cost-of-living adjustments automatically by reference; see Q 6:5) or if benefits payable under the plan are increased pursuant to a form of benefit that is described in Q 6:18, then the distribution as increased will be treated as continuing to satisfy the limitations on benefits. If benefits payable under a plan are increased in a manner other than as described in the preceding sentence, the plan must satisfy the requirements of Q 6:14, treating the commencement of the additional benefit as the commencement of a new distribution that gives rise to a new annuity starting date (see Q 10:3). [Treas. Reg. § 1.415(d)-1(a)(4)(iv)]

An amendment to a plan to incorporate adjustments to the limits that increases a distribution that has previously commenced is described in this paragraph if:

1. The employee has received one or more distributions that satisfy the limits before the date the adjustment to the applicable limits is effective (as determined above);

2. The increased distribution is solely a result of the amendment of the plan to reflect the adjustment to the applicable limits; and

3. The amounts payable to the employee on and after the effective date of the adjustment (as determined above) are not greater than the amounts that would otherwise be payable without regard to the adjustment, multiplied by a fraction determined for the limitation year, the numerator of which is the lesser of the applicable dollar limitation, as adjusted for age at commencement, and the applicable compensation-based limitation in effect with respect to the distribution taking into account the adjustment and the denominator of which is the limitation in effect for the distribution immediately before the adjustment. [Treas. Reg. § 1.415(d)-1(a)(5)]

An amendment to a plan that increases a distribution that has previously commenced is made using the safe harbor methodology of this paragraph if:

1. The employee has received one or more distributions that satisfy the limitations on benefits before the date on which the increase is effective, and

2. The amounts payable to the employee on or after the effective date of the increase are not greater than the amounts that would otherwise be payable without regard to the increase, multiplied by the cumulative adjustment fraction. [Treas. Reg. § 1.415(d)-1(a)(6)(i)]

The cumulative adjustment fraction is equal to the product of all of the fractions described above that would have applied after benefits commence if the plan had been amended each year to incorporate the cost-of-living adjustments to the applicable limits and had otherwise satisfied the safe harbor methodology described above. For purposes of the preceding sentence, if, for the limitation year for which the increase to the dollar limitation pursuant to EGTRRA 2001 (see Q 1:21) is first effective (generally, the first limitation year beginning after December 31, 2001), the dollar limit applicable to a participant is less than the compensation limit for the participant, then the fraction for that limitation year is 1.0. [Treas. Reg. § 1.415(d)-1(a)(6)(ii)]

Example 2. Herman is a participant in a defined benefit plan maintained by his employer, Bursky Tennis Court, Inc. The plan has a calendar year limitation year. Under the terms of the plan, Herman is entitled to a benefit consisting of a straight life annuity equal to 100 percent of his average compensation for the period of his high-three years of service. Herman's average compensation for the period of his high-three years of service is $50,000. Herman incurs a severance from employment with the employer maintaining the plan on October 3, 2010 at age 65 with a nonforfeitable right to the accrued benefit after more than ten years of participation in the plan. Herman begins to receive annual benefit payments (payable monthly) of $50,000, commencing on November 1, 2010. The dollar limitation for the 2010 limitation year (as adjusted) is $195,000. Assume that the dollar limitation for the 2011 limitation year (as adjusted) is $200,000 and the annual adjustment factor for adjusting the compensation limitation for the 2011 limitation year is 1.0334. Effective January 1, 2011, the plan is amended to incorporate these adjustments to the dollar and compensation limitations; and, accordingly, Herman's annual benefit payment is increased, effectivefor payments due on or after January 1, 2011. Prior to the plan amendment incorporating the application of the adjusted dollar and compensation limitations, Herman has received one or more distributions that satisfy the limitations. In addition, the adjustment to Herman's annual benefit payments is solely on account of the plan amendment incorporating the adjusted limitations.

For the limitation year beginning January 1, 2011, the dollar limit applicable to Herman is $200,000, and the compensation limit applicable to Herman is $51,670 ($50,000 multiplied by the annual adjustment factor of 1.0334). Accordingly, the adjustment to Herman's benefit satisfies the safe harbor for cost-of-living adjustments if, after the adjustments, his benefit payable in the 2011 limitation year is no greater than $51,670 ($50,000 × $51,670 [Herman's limitation for 2011] ÷ $50,000 [his limitation for 2010]).

Example 3. The facts are the same as in Example 2, except that Herman's average compensation for the period of his high-three consecutive years of service is $200,000. Consequently, Herman's annual benefit payments commencing on November 1, 2010 are limited to $195,000.

For the limitation year beginning January 1, 2011, the dollar limit applicable to Herman is $200,000, and the compensation limit applicable to Herman is $206,680 ($200,000 multiplied by the annual adjustment factor of 1.0334). Accordingly, the adjustment to Herman's benefit satisfies the safe harbor for cost-of-living adjustments if, after the adjustment, his benefit payable in 2011 is no greater than $200,000 ($195,000 × $200,000 [Herman's limitation for 2011] ÷ $195,000 [his limitation for 2010]).

Example 4. Dolores is a participant in Plan T, a defined benefit plan maintained by her employer, Bursky Golf Club, Inc. In the year 2011, Dolores receives a single-sum distribution of her entire accrued benefit under the plan. At the time that Dolores receives the single-sum distribution, her accrued benefit under Plan T is limited by the age-adjusted dollar limit. Dolores accrues no further benefits under Plan T after she receives the single-sum distribution. In the 2012 limitation year, the dollar limit is increased.

In the 2012 limitation year, Plan T may not provide additional benefits to Dolores on account of the increase in the dollar limit.

Example 5. Sylvia is a participant in Plan T, a defined benefit plan maintained by her employer, Ades 62 Corp. Plan T has a calendar limitation year. In 2011, Sylvia incurs a severance from employment with Ades 62 Corp. and commences receiving distributions from Plan T in the form of a single life annuity in an annual amount of $30,000. At the time that Sylvia commences receiving distributions from Plan T, her accrued benefit under Plan T is limited by the compensation limit. In 2012, the annual adjustment factor is 1.03. Ades 62 Corp. amends Plan T, effective as of January 1, 2012, to increase the annual benefit of all participants who, prior to January 1, 2012, incurred a severance from employment with Ades 62 Corp. and who have commenced receiving benefits from Plan T by a factor of 1.015. Assume that for limitation years prior to 2012, Sylvia's distributions from Plan T satisfy the limitations.

The increase in Sylvia's annual benefit pursuant to the amendment effective January 1, 2012 is within the safe harbor. This is because the amount payable to Sylvia under Plan T for the 2012 limitation year and limitation years thereafter (as increased by the amendment effective January 1, 2012) is not greater than the product of the amount payable to Sylvia under Plan T for such limitation years (as determined without regard to the amendment increasing her benefit effective January 1, 2012) and the cumulative adjustment fraction (which in Sylvia's case is 1.03). Thus, Sylvia's annual benefit, as increased by the amendment, is not determined pursuant to the rules concerning multiple annuity starting dates (see Q 6:14).

Example 6. Al participated in Plan A, maintained by Bentley Inc., for more than ten years. Plan A uses a calendar year limitation year, and Plan A automatically adjusts a participant's compensation limit for limitation years after the limitation year in which the participant incurs a severance from employment. Prior to separating from employment with Bentley Inc. in 2012, Al's average compensation for his period of high-three years while a participant in Plan A is $50,000, based on his compensation for 2009, 2010, and 2011, which was $50,000 for each year. Al's compensation for year 2012 was $45,000. In year 2014, Al is rehired by Bentley Inc. and resumes participation in Plan A. Al's compensation in year 2014 is $45,000 and is $70,000 in year 2015. Assume that the annual adjustment factor for the limitation years 2013 through 2015 is 1.03 for each year. Thus, disregarding Al's rehire by Bentley Inc., his average compensation for his period of high-three years while a participant in Plan A for the 2015 limitation year would be equal to $54,636 (or 1.03 × 1.03 × 1.03 × $50,000). Al's average compensation for his period of high-three years while a participant in Plan A for the 2015 limitation year is $54,636.

A plan is permitted to be amended to reflect the cost-of-living adjustments at any time after those limitations become applicable. Alternatively, a plan is permitted to incorporate by reference the cost-of-living adjustments (see Q 6:5). Because the accrued benefit of a participant can reflect increases in the applicable limitations only after those increases become effective, a pattern of repeated plan amendments (see Q 10:46) increasing annual benefits to reflect the increases in the cost of living is permissible. Thus, a plan does not violate the anti-cutback rule (see Q 9:25) merely because the plan has been amended annually for a number of years to increase annual benefits to reflect the cost-of-living increases and subsequently is not amended to reflect later increases in the cost of living. [Treas. Reg. § 1.415(d)-1(d)]

For purposes of applying the limitations on benefits, all defined benefit plans of an employer (whether or not terminated) are treated as a single plan (see Q 6:51). [I.R.C. § 415(f)(1)(A); Treas. Reg. § 1.415(f)-1(a)(1); Priv. Ltr. Rul. 9325055]

Example 7. Henry's Pharmacy, Inc. adopted a defined benefit plan in 1998 and terminated the plan in 2008. In 2011, Henry's Pharmacy, Inc. adopts a new defined benefit plan. Ilene participated in the terminated plan and will participate in the new plan. Ilene's combined annual benefit from both plans cannot exceed the maximum permissible annual benefit.

Example 8. Judy Corp., Murray Corp., and Jayem Co., Inc. are members of a controlled group of corporations (see Q 5:31). Employees of all members of the controlled group are eligible to participate in a defined benefit plan, Plan A. On April 30, 2011, Jayem terminates membership in the controlled group and immediately establishes a new defined benefit plan, Plan X, for its employees. No transfers of assets and liabilities are made from Plan A to the new Plan X. For the 2011 limitation year and subsequent limitation years, benefits under both defined benefit plans (Plan A and Plan X) must be aggregated for purposes of applying the annual benefit limitations.

Where a corporation (Newco) was formed by the merger of six corporations (Oldcos), the plan adopted by Newco did not have to be aggregated with any plans of the Oldcos for annual benefit limitation purposes. [Priv. Ltr. Rul. 9541041]

For annual benefit limitation purposes, all employees of corporations that are members of a controlled group of corporations are treated as if they were employed by a single employer. A comparable requirement applies to partnerships, sole proprietorships, and other businesses that are under common control (see Q 5:29). [I.R.C. §§ 414(b), 414(c)] However, a special rule applies to parent-subsidiary relationships for annual benefit limitation purposes. Under this special rule, a controlled group or commonly controlled group exists if there is a parent-subsidiary group connected through more than 50 percent ownership (see Q 6:7). [I.R.C. § 415(h)]

Example 9. Sallie is the 100 percent shareholder of Ess-W-Kay Corporation, which corporation is a 70 percent shareholder of Ess-Jay-Kay Corporation. Sallie is employed by both corporations, each corporation maintains a defined benefit plan, and Sallie participates in both plans. For annual benefit limitation purposes only, Sallie is deemed to be employed by a single corporation, and her aggregate annual retirement benefit under both plans cannot exceed the lesser of $160,000 (subject to cost-of-living adjustments) or 100 percent of her average compensation.

IRS representatives have opined that, if an individual is a sole proprietor and also owns 70 percent of the shares of stock of a corporation, the two entities would constitute a brother-sister group, not a parent-subsidiary group, and so the special rule would not apply.

Q 6:13 What does average compensation for the period of high-three years of service mean?

Generally, for purposes of applying the limitation on benefits applicable to defined benefit plans (see Q 6:11), the period of a participant's high-three years of service is the period of three consecutive calendar years (taking into account the break-period rule discussed below) during which the employee had the greatest aggregate compensation (see Q 6:41) from the employer, and the average compensation for the period of a participant's high-three years of service is determined by dividing the aggregate compensation for this period by three. In determining a participant's high-three years of service, the plan may use any 12-month period to determine a year of service instead of the calendar year, provided that it is uniformly and consistently applied in a manner that is specified under the terms of the plan. Because the plan is not permitted to base benefits on compensation in excess of the limitation on annual compensation (see Q 6:45), a plan's definition of compensation for a year that is used for purposes of applying the limitations on benefits is not permitted to reflect compensation for a year that is in excess of the limitation on compensation that applies to that year. [[I.R.C. § 415(b)(3); Treas. Reg. § 1.415(b)-1(a)(5)(i)] See Qs 6:46, 6:47 for rules regarding the effective date of increases in the compensation limitation for a plan year and for a 12-month period other than the plan year.

For a participant who is employed by an employer for less than three consecutive years, the period of the participant's high-three years of service is the actual number of consecutive years of service (including fractions of years, but not less than one year). In such a case, the limitation of 100 percent of the participant's average compensation for the period of the participant's high-three years of service is computed by dividing the participant's compensation during the participant's longest consecutive period of service by the number of years in that period (including fractions of years, but not less than one year). The break-period rule discussed below is used for purposes of determining a participant's consecutive years of service. [Treas. Reg. § 1.415(b)-1 (a)(5)(ii)]

In the case of a participant who has had a severance from employment (see Q 6:8) with an employer that maintains the plan and who is subsequently rehired by the employer, the period of the participant's high-three years of service is calculated by excluding years for which the participant performs no services for and receives no compensation from the employer maintaining the plan (referred to as the break period), and by treating the year of service immediately prior to and the year of service immediately after the break period as if such years of service were consecutive. [Treas. Reg. § 1.415(b)-1(a)(5)(iii)] See Q 6:12 for a special rule for determining a rehired participant's compensation limit in the case of a plan that adjusts the compensation limit for limitation years after the limitation year in which the participant incurs a severance from employment.

For purposes of the following examples, except as otherwise stated, the plan year and the limitation year (see Q 6:58) are the calendar year, and the plan uses the calendar year for purposes of determining the period of high-three years of service. In addition, except as otherwise stated, it is assumed that the plan's normal retirement age (see Q 10:55) is 65 and that all participants discussed in these examples have at least ten years of participation in the plan at issue (see Q 6:22).

Example 1. Plan A, which was established on January 1, 2009, covers Participant M, who was hired on January 1, 1991. Participant M's compensation from the employer maintaining the plan is $140,000 each year for 1991 through 1993, is $120,000 each year for 1994 through 2008, and is $165,000 for 2009 and 2010. Assume that for Plan A's 2009 and 2010 limitation years, the age-adjusted dollar limit for M is $190,000 and $195,000, respectively.

As of the end of the 2009 limitation year, the period of M's high-three consecutive years of service runs from January 1, 1991 through December 31, 1993, and M's average compensation for this period is $140,000 ([$140,000 + $140,000 + $140,000] ÷ 3). Thus, the dollar limitation for the 2009 limitation year is $140,000. As of the end of the 2010 limitation year, the period of M's high-three consecutive years of service runs from January 1, 2008, through December 31, 2010, and M's average compensation for this period is $150,000 ([$120,000 + $165,000 + $165,000] ÷ 3). Thus, the dollar limitation for the 2010 limitation year is $150,000.

Example 2. Participant N is a participant in Plan B. N's compensation for 2008, 2009, and 2010 is $300,000 for each year. N's average compensation for the period of N's high-three years of service (determined before the application of limitation on compensation) is $300,000, based on N's compensation for 2008, 2009, and 2010. For all years before 2008, Participant N's compensation was less than the then-applicable compensation limit. On January 1, 2011, N commences receiving benefits from Plan B at the age of 75, ten years after attaining N's normal retirement age under Plan B, when the age-adjusted dollar limit for benefits commencing at that age is $293,453.

Plan B is not permitted to provide for a definition of compensation that includes compensation for a year that is in excess of the limitation that applies to that year. Accordingly, the 100-percent-of-compensation limitation based on N's average compensation for the period of N's high-three years of service must not reflect compensation for a year that is in excess of the limitation on compensation that applies to that year. Thus, if the limitation on compensation for years beginning in 2008, 2009, and 2010 is $230,000, $245,000, and $245,000, respectively, then the 100-percent-of-compensation limitation based on N's average compensation for the period of N's high-three years of service is $240,000.

Example 3. The facts are the same as in Example 2, except that N commences receiving benefits from Plan B on January 1, 2008, at the age of 75, ten years after attaining N's normal retirement age under Plan B. In addition, N's period of high-three years of service is from January 1, 2003 through December 31, 2005, and N's average compensation for this period is $300,000. The compensation limits for 2003, 2004, and 2005 are $200,000, $205,000, and $210,000, respectively. As of December 31, 2007, pursuant to plan provisions adopted and in effect on January 1, 2007, N's accrued benefit under Plan B, payable in the form of a straight life annuity, actuarially adjusted to reflect commencement ten years after normal retirement age, is $300,000. Plan B has not been amended during 2007; and, as of December 31, 2007, Plan B satisfied all of the limitation requirements with respect to N's accrued benefit, pursuant to statutory provisions, regulations, and other published guidance in effect immediately before the limitation year beginning on January 1, 2008.

Under a grandfather rule for preexisting benefits (see Q 6:1), Plan B is considered to satisfy the compensation limit with respect to N's benefit payable at age 75 of $300,000 (which N accrued prior to January 1, 2008) for limitation years beginning after December 31, 2007. This is because the grandfather rule provides that plan provisions will not be treated as failing to satisfy the 100-percent-of-compensation limitation merely because the plan's definition of compensation that is used for purposes of applying the limitations reflects compensation in excess of the compensation limitation for limitation years beginning before January 1, 2008. N, however, cannot accrue any additional benefits under Plan B for limitation years beginning after December 31, 2007 until N's compensation limit increases above $300,000.

Example 4. Participant O participates in Plan C, maintained by Employer X. Plan C does not adjust a participant's 100-percent-of-compensation limit for limitation years after the limitation year in which the participant incurs a severance from employment. Prior to separating from employment with X in 2010, O's average compensation for O's period of high-three years of service is $50,000, based on O's compensation for 2007, 2008, and 2009, which was $50,000 for each year. O's compensation for 2010 is $45,000. O's compensation is $0 for 2011. In 2012, O is rehired by X and resumes participation in Plan C. O's compensation in 2012 is $45,000 and is $70,000 in 2013.

As of the end of the 2013 limitation year, O's average compensation for O's period of high-three years of service is $53,333, based on O's compensation in 2010, 2012, and 2013 ([$45,000 + $45,000 + $70,000] ÷ 3). 2011 is excluded under the break-period rule.

Example 5. The facts are the same as in Example 4, except that Plan C incorporates by reference the cost-of-living adjustments to a participant's 100-percent-of-compensation limit for limitation years after the limitation year in which the participant incurs a severance from employment. Assume that the annual adjustment factor described for 2011 through 2013 is 1.03 for each year. Thus, disregarding O's rehire by X, O's average compensation for O's period of high-three years of service for the 2013 limitation year is equal to $54,636 ($50,000 × 1.03 × 1.03 × 1.03). O's average compensation for O's period of high-three years of service for the 2013 limitation year is $54,636.

Q 6:14   What does annual benefit mean?

The term "annual benefit" means a benefit that is payable in the form of a straight life annuity, and a "straight life annuity" means an annuity payable in equal installments for the life of the participant that terminates upon the participant's death. Examples of benefits that are not in the form of a straight life annuity include an annuity with a post-retirement death benefit and an annuity providing a guaranteed number of payments. If a benefit is payable in the form of a straight life annuity, no adjustment·is made to the benefit to account for differences in the timing of payments during a year (for example, no adjustment is made on account of the annuity being paid in annual or monthly installments). With respect to a benefit payable in a form other than a straight life annuity, the annual benefit is determined as a straight life annuity payable on the first day of each month that is actuarially equivalent to the benefit payable in such other form (see Q 6:18). [I.R.C. § 415(b)(2)(A); Treas. Reg. § 1.415(b)-1(b)(1)(i)]

The annual benefit does not include the annual benefit attributable to either employee contributions or rollover contributions (see Q 6:15). [I.R.C. § 415(b)(2)(A); Treas. Reg. § 1.415(b)-1(b)(1)(ii)] For the treatment of transferred benefits, see Q 6:16.

If a participant has or will have distributions commencing at more than one annuity starting date (see Q 10:3), then the limitations on the annual benefit (see Q 6:11) must be satisfied as of each of the annuity starting dates, taking into account the benefits that have been or will be provided at all of the annuity starting dates. This will happen, for example, where benefit distributions to a participant have previously commenced under a plan that is aggregated with a plan under which the participant receives current accruals (see Q 6:51). In determining the annual benefit for such a participant as of a particular annuity starting date, the plan must actuarially adjust the past and future distributions with respect to the benefits that commenced at the other annuity starting dates. [Treas. Reg. § 1.415(b)-1(b)(1)(iii)(A)]

The rules regarding multiple annuity starting dates apply for purposes of determining the annual benefit of a participant where a new distribution election is effective during the current limitation year (see Q 6:58) with respect to a distribution that previously commenced. These rules also apply for determining the annual benefit of a participant for purposes of applying the limitations where benefit payments are increased as a result of plan terms or a plan amendment applying a cost-of-living adjustment or similar benefit increase, unless the increase is described in the following paragraph. [Treas. Reg. § 1.415(b)-1(b)(1)(iii)(B)]

An increase to benefit payments as a result of plan terms or a plan amendment applying a cost-of-living adjustment or similar benefit increase is described in this paragraph if the increase:

1. Has previously been accounted for as part of the annual benefit (see Q 6:18);

2. Is not required to be accounted for as part of the annual benefit, pursuant to the exception for certain automatic benefit increase features (see Q 6:18);

3. Is pursuant to a plan provision that automatically incorporates cost-of-living adjustments (see Q 6:5); or

4. Complies with one of the safe harbors for annual and other periodic adjustments to distributions (see Q 6:12). [Treas. Reg. § 1.415(b)-1(b)(1)(iii)(C)]

Q 6:15　How are employee and rollover contributions treated for annual benefit purposes?

The following are not treated as employee contributions:

1. Contributions that are picked up by a governmental employer.
2. Repayment of any loan made to a participant from the plan (see Q 14:1).
3. Repayment of a previously distributed amount (see Qs 9:21, 9:22).
4. Repayment of a withdrawal of employee contributions.
5. Repayments that would have been described in number 3 or 4 except that the plan does not restrict the timing of repayments to the maximum extent permitted. [I.R.C. §§ 411(a)(3)(D), 411(a)(7)(B), 411(a)(7)(C), 414(h)(2); Treas. Reg. §§ 1.415(b)-1(b)(2)(i), 1.415(b)-1(b)(2)(ii)]

In the case of mandatory employee contributions (see Q 6:37), the annual benefit attributable to those contributions is determined by applying the factors applicable to mandatory employee contributions to those contributions to determine the amount of a straight life annuity commencing at the annuity starting date (see Q 9:9). [Treas. Reg. § 1.415(b)-1(b)(2)(iii)] See Q 6:34 for rules regarding treatment of mandatory employee contributions to a defined benefit plan as annual additions under a defined contribution plan.

If voluntary employee contributions (see Q 6:38) are made to the plan, the portion of the plan to which voluntary employee contributions are made is treated as a defined contribution plan (see Q 2:2) and, accordingly, is a defined contribution plan. Thus, the portion of a plan to which voluntary employee contributions are made is not a defined benefit plan (see Q 2:3) and is not taken into account in determining the annual benefit (see Q 6:14) under the portion of the plan that is a defined benefit plan. [I.R.C. § 414(k); Treas. Reg. §§ 1.415(b)-1(b)(2)(iv), 1.415(c)-1(a)(2)(i)]

The annual benefit attributable to rollover contributions from an eligible retirement plan (see Q 34:16)—for example, a contribution received pursuant to a direct rollover (see Q 34:17)—is determined in the same manner as the annual benefit attributable to mandatory employee contributions if the plan provides for a benefit derived from the rollover contribution (other than a benefit derived from a separate account to be maintained with respect to the rollover contribution and actual earnings and losses thereon). Thus, in the case of rollover contributions from a defined contribution plan to a defined benefit plan to provide an annuity distribution, the annual benefit attributable to those rollover contributions is determined by applying the rules applicable to mandatory employee contributions, regardless of the assumptions used to compute the annuity distribution under the plan. Accordingly, in such a case, if the plan uses more favorable factors than those specified in Section 411(c) to determine the amount of annuity payments arising from rollover contributions, the annual benefit under the plan would reflect the excess of those annuity payments over the amounts that would be payable using the factors specified in Section 411(c). [Treas. Reg. § 1.415(b)-2(b)(v)] See Q 6:34 for rules excluding rollover contributions maintained in a separate account that is treated as a defined contribution plan from annual additions to a defined contribution plan.

Q 6:16   How are transferred benefits treated for annual benefit purposes?

Except with respect to elective transfers, where there has been a transfer of benefits from one defined benefit plan (see Q 2:3) to another plan, to the extent the benefits transferred to the transferee plan are otherwise required to be taken into account pursuant to the aggregation rules (see Q 6:51) in determining whether the transferor plan satisfies the benefit limitations (see Q 6:11) for a limitation year (see Q 6:58), the transferred benefits are not treated as being provided under the transferor plan. This will occur, for example, if the employer sponsoring the transferor plan and the employer sponsoring the transferee plan are in the same controlled group (see Q 5:31). [Treas. Reg. § 1.415(b)-1(b)(3)(i)(A)]

In addition, except with respect to elective transfers, where there has been a transfer of benefits from one defined benefit plan to another plan, to the extent the benefits transferred to the transferee plan are not otherwise required to be taken into account pursuant to the aggregation rules in determining whether the transferor plan satisfies the benefit limitations for a limitation year, the transferred benefits are treated by the transferor plan as if such benefits were provided under annuities purchased to provide benefits under a plan that must be aggregated with the transferor plan and that terminated immediately prior to the transfer with sufficient assets to pay all benefit liabilities under the plan (see Q 6:17). This will occur, for example, in the case of a transfer of benefits between defined benefit plans maintained by employers that are not required to be aggregated. [Treas. Reg. § 1.415(b)-1(b)(3)(i)(B)]

Furthermore, except with respect to elective transfers, where there has been a transfer of benefits from one defined benefit plan to another defined benefit plan, the transferee plan must take into account the transferred benefits in determining whether it satisfies the benefit limitations. [Treas. Reg. § 1.415(b)-1(b)(3)(i)(C)]

Where there is an elective transfer of distributable benefits to a defined benefit plan from either a defined contribution plan (see Q 2:2) or a defined benefit plan, the amount transferred is treated as a benefit paid from the transferor plan, and the annual benefit provided by the transferee defined benefit plan does not include the annual benefit attributable to the amount transferred (determined as if the transferred amount were a rollover contribution; see Q 6:15). [Treas. Reg. § 1.415(b)-1(b)(3)(ii)]

Q 6:17   What is the treatment of benefits provided under a terminated plan?

If a defined benefit plan (see Q 2:3) is terminated with sufficient assets for the payment of the benefit liabilities of all plan participants and a participant in the plan has not yet commenced benefits under the plan, for purposes of satisfying the benefit limitations (see Q 6:11) with respect to the participant, all other defined benefit plans maintained by the employer that maintained the terminated plan are required to take into account the benefits provided pursuant to the annuities purchased to provide benefits under the terminated plan at each possible annuity starting date (see Q 10:3). [Treas. Reg. § 1.415(b)-1(b)(5)(i)]

If a defined benefit plan is terminated and there are not sufficient assets for the payment of the benefit liabilities of all plan participants, for purposes of satisfying the benefit limitations with respect to a participant, all other defined benefit plans maintained by the employer that maintained the terminated plan are required to take into account the benefits that are actually provided to the participant under the terminated plan. For example, in the case of a plan that is subject to Title IV of ERISA (see Qs 25:9, 25:11, 25:12) and that terminates with insufficient assets for the payment of the benefit liabilities of all plan participants, all other defined benefit plans maintained by the employer that maintained the terminating plan must take into account benefits that are paid by the Pension Benefit Guaranty Corporation (PBGC; see Q 25:10). [Treas. Reg. § 1.415(b)-1(b)(5)(ii)]

Q 6:18   How is the annual benefit adjusted if it is paid in a form other than a straight life annuity?

This Q 6:18 provides rules for adjusting a form of benefit other than a straight life annuity (see Q 6:14) to an actuarially equivalent straight life annuity beginning at the same time for purposes of determining the annual benefit (see Q 6:14). [I.R.C. § 415(b)(2)(B); Treas. Reg. § 1.415(b)-1(c)(1)]

For a benefit paid in a form to which Section 417(e)(3) (see Q 10:62) does not apply, the actuarially equivalent straight life annuity benefit is the greater of:

1. The annual amount of the straight life annuity (if any) payable to the participant under the plan commencing at the same annuity starting date (see Q 10:3) as the form of benefit payable to the participant, or

2. The annual amount of the straight life annuity commencing at the same annuity starting date that has the same actuarial present value as the form of benefit payable to the participant, computed using a 5 percent interest assumption and the applicable mortality table for that annuity starting date. [I.R.C. § 415(b)(2)(E)(i); Treas. Reg. § 1.415(b)-1(c)(2)]

Generally, for a benefit paid in a form to which Section 417(e)(3) applies, the actuarially equivalent straight life annuity benefit is the greatest of:

1. The annual amount of the straight life annuity commencing at the annuity starting date that has the same actuarial present value as the particular form of benefit payable, computed using the interest rate and mortality table, or tabular factor, specified in the plan for actuarial equivalence;

2. The annual amount of the straight life annuity commencing at the annuity starting date that has the same actuarial present value as the particular

form of benefit payable, computed using a 5.5 percent interest assumption and the applicable mortality table for the distribution; or

3. The annual amount of the straight life annuity commencing at the annuity starting date that has the same actuarial present value as the particular form of benefit payable (computed using the applicable interest rate for the distribution and the applicable mortality table for the distribution), divided by 1.05. [I.R.C. § 415(b)(2)(E)(ii); Treas. Reg. § 1.415(b)-1(c)(3)(i)]

The above provision was added by PPA (see Q 1:33) and applies to distributions made in plan years beginning after December 31, 2005. However, the changes do not apply to a plan with a termination date that was on or before August 17, 2006, the date of enactment of PPA. [PPA §§ 303(a), 303(b); IRS Notice 2007-7, § II, Q&A-1, 2007-1 C.B. 395] A plan does not violate the anti-cutback rule (see Q 9:25) if it is amended retroactively to comply with PPA, provided the amendment is adopted on or before the last day of the first plan year beginning on or after January 1, 2009 and the plan is operated as if such amendment were in effect as of the first date the amendment is effective. [IRS Notice 2007-7, § II, Q&A-2, 2007-1 C.B. 395] For years beginning after December 31, 2008, in the case of a plan maintained by an eligible employer, the interest rate used in adjusting a benefit in a form that is subject to the minimum value rules generally must be not less than the greater of (1) 5.5 percent or (2) the interest rate specified in the plan. "Eligible employer" means an employer that had no more than 100 employees who received at least $5,000 of compensation from the employer for the preceding year. An eligible employer that maintains a defined benefit plan for one or more years and that fails to be an eligible employer in a subsequent year is treated as an eligible employer for the two years following the last year the employer was an eligible employer (provided that the reason for failure to qualify is not due to an acquisition, disposition, or similar transaction involving the eligible employer). Thus, clause 3 above is inapplicable in the case of an eligible employer. [I.R.C. §§ 408(p)(2)(C)(i), 415(b)(2)(E)(vi) (as added by WRERA 2008 § 122)]

Plans with plan years beginning before the enactment of PPA may have overpaid or underpaid lump-sum amounts depending upon the interest rate assumption used; and IRS added that, if a plan made a distribution in a plan year beginning in 2006 that satisfied the limitations on benefits (see Q 6:11) prior to the enactment of PPA, but which was in excess of the limitations on benefits taking into account the amendments made by PPA (Section 303 excess distribution), the distribution violates the limitations. However, IRS provided three methods for correcting a Section 303 excess distribution. First, a special correction method was available for a Section 303 excess distribution made prior to September 1, 2006, provided that the correction was completed by March 15, 2007. Second, if correction is completed by December 31, 2007 (even if the Section 303 excess distribution occurs after September 1, 2006), a plan may correct a Section 303 excess distribution by using the correction method for an excess distribution described in the Employee Plans Compliance Resolution System (EPCRS; see Q 19:32) even if the plan does not meet the requirements specified in EPCRS, including the special requirements for self-correction (see Qs 19:17-19:19). Finally, a plan that meets the requirements of EPCRS may correct Section 303 excess distributions by using the correction method for excess distributions under EPCRS even after December 31, 2007. A plan that is amended retroactively to comply with PPA will not fail to satisfy the requirement that the plan be operated in accordance with the terms of the amendment merely because it made a Section 303 excess distribution, provided the Section 303 excess distribution is corrected using one of these three correction methods. [IRS Notice 2007-7, § II, Q&A-3, Q&A-4, 2007-1 C.B. 395]

For a distribution to which Section 417(e)(3) applies and which has an annuity starting date occurring in plan years beginning in 2004 or 2005, except as provided in PFEA (see Q 1:25), the actuarially equivalent straight life annuity benefit is the greater of:

1. The annual amount of the straight life annuity commencing at the annuity starting date that has the same actuarial present value as the particular form of benefit payable, computed using the interest rate and mortality table, or tabular factor, specified in the plan for actuarial equivalence, or

2. The annual amount of the straight life annuity commencing at the annuity starting date that has the same actuarial present value as the particular form of benefit payable, computed using a 5.5 percent interest assumption and the applicable mortality table for the distribution. [Treas. Reg. § 1.415(b)-1(c)(3)(ii)]

For purposes of the adjustments described in this Q 6:18, the following benefits are not taken into account:

1. Survivor benefits payable to a surviving spouse under a qualified joint and survivor annuity (QJSA; see Q 10:8) to the extent that such benefits would not be payable if the participant's benefit were not paid in the form of a QJSA.

2. Ancillary benefits (see Q 4:20) that are not directly related to retirement benefits, such as preretirement disability benefits not in excess of the qualified disability benefit, preretirement incidental death benefits, including a qualified preretirement survivor annuity (QPSA; see Q 10:9), and post-retirement medical benefits. [Treas. Reg. § 1.415(b)-1(c)(4)(i)]

Although a Social Security supplement may be an ancillary benefit, it is included in determining the annual benefit because it is payable upon retirement and therefore is directly related to retirement income benefits. If benefits are paid partly in the form of a QJSA and partly in some other form (such as a single-sum distribution), the rule under which survivor benefits are not included in determining the annual benefit applies to the survivor annuity payments under the portion of the benefit that is paid in the form of a QJSA. [Treas. Reg. § 1.415(b)-1(c)(4)(ii)]

No adjustment is required to a benefit that is paid in a form that is not a straight life annuity to take into account the inclusion in that form of an automatic benefit increase feature, as described below, if (1) the benefit is paid in a form to which Section 417(e)(3) does not apply and (2) the plan satisfies certain requirements. [Treas. Reg. § 1.415(b)-1(c)(5)(i)]

An automatic benefit increase feature is included in a form of benefit if that form provides for automatic, periodic increases to the benefits paid in that form, such as a form of benefit that automatically increases the benefit paid under that form annually according to a specified percentage or objective index, or a form of benefit that automatically increases the benefit paid in that form to share favorable investment returns on plan assets. [Treas. Reg. § 1.415(b)-1(c)(5)(ii)]

A plan satisfies the requirements with respect to a form of benefit that includes an automatic benefit increase feature if the form of benefit without regard to the automatic benefit increase feature satisfies the benefit limits and the plan provides that in no event will the amount payable to the participant under the form of benefit in any limitation year (see Q 6:58) be greater than the benefit limit applicable at the annuity starting date, as increased in subsequent years for cost-of-living adjustments (see Q 6:12). If the form of benefit without regard to the automatic benefit increase feature is not a straight life annuity, then the preceding sentence is applied by reducing the benefit limit applicable at the annuity starting date to an actuarially equivalent amount that takes into account the death benefits under the form of benefit (other than the survivor portion of a QJSA). [Treas. Reg. § 1.415(b)-1(c)(5)(iii)]

The following examples illustrate the provisions of this Q 6:18. For purposes of these examples, except as otherwise stated, actuarial equivalence under the plan is determined using a 5 percent interest assumption and the mortality table that applies under Section 417(e)(3) as of January 1, 2003. It is assumed for purposes of these examples that the interest rate that applies for relevant time periods is 5.25 percent and that the mortality table that applies for relevant time periods is the mortality table that applies as of January 1, 2003. In addition, it is assumed that all participants discussed in these examples have at least ten years of service with the employer and at least ten years of participation in the plan at issue, all payments other than a payment of a single sum are made monthly on the first day of each calendar month, and each plan's normal retirement age (see Q 10:55) is 65.

Example 1. Plan A provides a single-sum distribution determined as the actuarial present value of the straight life annuity payable at the actual retirement date. Plan A provides that a participant's single sum is determined as the greater of the present value determined using the otherwise applicable actuarial assumptions of the plan and the present value determined using the applicable interest rate and the applicable mortality table for the distribution under Section 417(e)(3). Plan A also provides that the single sum is not less than the actuarial present value of the accrued benefit payable at normal retirement age, determined using the applicable interest rate and the applicable mortality table. Participant M retires at age 65 with a benefit under the plan formula (and before the application of the limitation on benefits) of $152,619 and elects to receive a distribution in the form of a single sum. Under the plan and before the application of the limitation on benefits, the amount of the single sum is $1,800,002 (which is based on the 5 percent interest rate and applicable mortality table as of January 1, 2003, since the present value is greater than the present value that would have been determined using the applicable interest rate (5.25 percent) and the applicable mortality table (the January 1, 2003 table) for the distribution).

The annual benefit is the greatest of the annual amount of the actuarially equivalent straight life annuity commencing at the same age (determined using the plan's actuarial factors), the annual amount of the actuarially equivalent straight life annuity commencing at the same age (determined using a 5.5 percent interest assumption and the applicable mortality table for the distribution), and the annual amount of the actuarially equivalent straight life annuity commencing at the same age (determined using the applicable interest rate and applicable mortality table for the distribution) divided by 1.05. Based on the factors used in the plan to determine the actuarially equivalent lump sum (in this case, an interest rate of 5 percent and the applicable mortality table as of January 1, 2003), $1,800,002 payable as a single sum is actuarially equivalent to an immediate straight life annuity at age 65 of $152,619. A single-sum payment of $1,800,002 is actuarially equivalent to an immediate straight life annuity at age 65 of $159,105, using a 5.5 percent interest assumption and the applicable mortality table. Based on the applicable interest rate and the applicable mortality table for the distribution, $1,800,002 payable as a single sum is actuarially equivalent to an immediate straight life annuity at age 65 of $155,853. $148,432 is the result when this annual amount is divided by 1.05. With respect to the single-sum distribution, M's annual benefit for benefit limitation purposes is equal to the greatest of the three resulting amounts ($152,619, $159,105, and $148,432), or $159,105.

Example 2. The facts are the same as in Example 1, except that participant M elects to receive his benefit in the form of a ten-year certain and life annuity. Applying the plan's actuarial equivalence factors, the benefit payable in this form is $146,100.

Because the form of benefit elected by M is a form of benefit to which Section 417(e)(3) does not apply, the annual benefit is the greater of the annual amount of the plan's straight life annuity commencing at the same age or the annual amount of the actuarially equivalent straight life annuity commencing at the same age, determined using a 5 percent interest rate and the applicable mortality table for that annuity starting date. In this case, the straight life annuity payable under the plan commencing at the same age is $152,619. Because the plan's factors for actuarial equivalence in this case are the same standardized actuarial factors required to be applied to determine the actuarially equivalent straight life annuity using the required standardized factors is also $152,619. With respect to the ten-year certain and life annuity distribution, M's annual benefit is equal to the greater of the two resulting amounts ($152,619 and $152,619), or $152,619.

Example 3. The facts are the same as in Example 1. Participant M retires at age 62 with a benefit under the plan (before the application of the limitation on benefits) of $100,000 (after application of the plan's early retirement factors) and a Social Security supplement of $10,000 per year payable until age 65. N chooses to receive the accrued benefit in the form of a straight life annuity. The plan has no provisions under which the actuarial value of the Social Security supplement can be paid as a level annuity for life.

Because the form of benefit elected by M is a form of benefit to which Section 417(e)(3) does not apply and because the plan does not provide for a straight life annuity beginning at age 62, the annual benefit is the annual amount of the straight life annuity commencing at age 62 that is actuarially equivalent to the distribution stream of $110,000 for three years and $100,000 thereafter, where actuarial equivalence is determined using a 5 percent interest rate and the applicable mortality table for the annuity starting date. In this case, the actuarially equivalent straight life annuity is $102,180. Accordingly, with respect to this distribution stream, N's annual benefit is equal to $102,180. The results are the same without regard to whether the Social Security supplement is a qualified Social Security supplement (QSUPP).

Example 4. Plan B is a defined benefit plan that provides a benefit equal to 100 percent of a participant's average compensation for the period of the participant's high-three years of service, payable as a straight life annuity. For a married participant who does not elect another form of benefit, the benefit is payable in the form of a joint and 100 percent survivor annuity benefit that is a QJSA and that is reduced from the straight life annuity. For purposes of determining the amount of this QJSA, the plan provides that the reduction is only half of the reduction that would normally apply under the actuarial assumptions specified in the plan for determining actuarial equivalence of optional forms. The plan also provides that a married participant can elect to receive the plan benefits as a straight life annuity or in the form of a single-sum distribution that is the actuarial equivalent of the joint and 100 percent survivor annuity determined using the applicable interest rate and the applicable mortality table. Participant O elects, with spousal consent, a single-sum distribution.

The special rule that disregards the value of the survivor portion of a QJSA only applies to a benefit that is payable in the form of a QJSA. Any other form of benefit must be adjusted to a straight life annuity. Accordingly, because the benefit payable under the plan in the form of a single-sum distribution is actuarially equivalent to a straight life annuity that is greater than 100 percent of a participant's average compensation for the period of the participant's high-three years of service, the 100-percent-of-compensation limitation has been exceeded.

Example 5. Plan C is a defined benefit plan that provides an option to receive the benefit in the form of a joint and 100 percent survivor annuity with a ten-year certain feature, where the survivor beneficiary is the participant's spouse.

Because this form of benefit is not subject to Section 417(e)(3), for a participant at age 65, the annual benefit with respect to the joint and 100 percent survivor annuity with a ten-year certain feature is determined as the greater of the annual amount of the straight life annuity payable to the participant under the plan at age 65 (if any) or the annual amount of the straight life annuity commencing at age 65 that has the same actuarial present value as the joint and 100 percent survivor annuity with a ten-year certain feature (but excluding the survivor annuity payments), computed using a 5 percent interest assumption and the applicable mortality table for the annuity starting date. This latter amount is equal to the product of the annual payments under this optional form of benefit and the factor that provides for actuarial equivalence between a straight life annuity and a ten-year certain and life annuity (with no annuity for the survivor) computed using a 5 percent interest rate and the applicable mortality table for the annuity starting date.

Example 6. Plan E provides a benefit at age 65 of a straight life annuity equal to the lesser of 90 percent of the participant's average compensation for the period of the participant's high-three years of service and $148,500. Upon retirement at age 65, the optional forms of benefit available to a participant include payment of a QJSA with annual payments equal to 50 percent of the annual payments under the straight life annuity, along with a single-sum distribution that is actuarially equivalent (determined as the greater of the single sum calculated using a 5 percent interest assumption and the mortality table in effect on January 1, 2003 and the single sum calculated using the applicable interest rate and the applicable mortality table for the distribution) to 50 percent of the annual payments under the straight life annuity. Participant Q retires at age 65. Q's average compensation for the period of Q's high-three years of service is $100,000. Q elects to receive a distribution in the optional form of benefit described above, under which the annual payments under the QJSA are $45,000 and the single-sum distribution is equal to $530,734. Q's spouse is three years younger than Q.

Q's annual benefit under Plan E for benefit limitation purposes is determined as the sum of the annual benefit attributable to the QJSA portion of the distribution and the annual benefit attributable to the single-sum portion of the distribution.

Because survivor benefits are not taken into account in determining the annual benefit attributable to the QJSA portion of the distribution, the annual benefit attributable to the QJSA portion of the distribution is determined as if that distribution were a straight life annuity of $45,000 per year commencing at age 65. Thus, no form adjustment is needed to determine the annual benefit attributable to the QJSA portion of the distribution, and the annual benefit attributable to the QJSA portion of the benefit is $45,000.

The annual benefit attributable to the single-sum portion of the distribution is determined as the greatest of the annual amount of the actuarially equivalent straight life annuity commencing at the same age (determined using the plan's actuarial factors), the annual amount of the actuarially equivalent straight life annuity commencing at the same age (determined using a 5.5 percent interest assumption and the applicable mortality table for the distribution), and the annual amount of the actuarially equivalent straight life annuity commencing at the same age (determined using the applicable interest rate and applicable mortality table for distribution) divided by 1.05. With respect to the single-sum distribution, the annual amount of the actuarially equivalent straight life annuity commencing at the same age determined using the plan's actuarial factors is equal to $45,954. The annual amount of the actuarially equivalent straight life annuity commencing at the same age determined using a 5.5 percent interest assumption and the applicable mortality table for the distribution is $46,912. The actuarially equivalent straight life annuity commencing at the same age determined using the applicable interest rate and the applicable mortality table for the distribution is equal to $45,954. This amount divided by 1.05 is equal to $43,766. Thus, the annual benefit attributable to the single-sum portion of the benefit is $46,912.

Q's annual benefit under the optional form of benefit for benefit limitation purposes is equal to the sum of the annual benefit attributable to the QJSA portion of the distribution and the annual benefit attributable to the single-sum portion of the distribution, or $91,912. Because Q's average compensation for the period of Q's high-three years of service is $100,000, the distribution satisfies the 100-percent-of-compensation limit.

Example 7. Plan D is a defined benefit plan with a normal retirement age of 65. The normal retirement benefit under Plan D (and the only annuity available under Plan D) is a life annuity with a fixed increase of 2 percent per year. The increase applies to the benefit provided in the prior year and is thus compounded. The plan provides that the benefit is limited to the lesser of 84 percent of the participant's average compensation for the period of the participant's high-three years of service or 84 percent of the age-adjusted dollar limit (which is assumed to be $180,000 at age 65). Plan D does not incorporate the cost-of-living adjustments for limitation years following the limitation year in which a participant incurs a severance from employment. Participant P retires at age 65, at which time P's average compensation for the period of P's high-three years of service is $165,000. Under Plan D, P commences receiving benefits in the form of a life annuity of $138,600 with a fixed increase of 2 percent per year.

Because Plan D does not provide for a straight life annuity and the form of benefit is not subject to Section 417(e)(3), P's annual benefit for limitation purposes is the annual amount of the straight life annuity, commencing at age 65, that is actuarially equivalent to the distribution stream of $138,600 with a fixed increase of 2 percent per year, where actuarial equivalence is determined using a 5 percent interest rate and the applicable mortality table for the distribution. In order to satisfy the benefit limitations, this annual benefit must not exceed 100 percent of the average compensation for the period of the participant's high-three years of service, or $165,000. Using a 5 percent interest rate and the applicable mortality table for the distribution, the actuarially equivalent straight life annuity is $165,453, which exceeds $165,000. Accordingly, the plan fails to satisfy the compensation-based limitation.

Example 8. The facts are the same as in Example 7, except that Plan D incorporates by reference the cost-of-living adjustments and provides that the benefit is limited to the applicable limit on benefits. Under Plan D, P commences receiving benefits at age 65 in the form of a life annuity of $138,221 with a fixed increase of 2 percent per year.

Because Plan D does not provide for a straight life annuity and the form of benefit is not subject to Section 417(e)(3), P's annual benefit is the annual amount of the straight life annuity, commencing at age 65, that is actuarially equivalent to the distribution stream of $138,221 with a fixed increase of 2 percent per year, where actuarial equivalence is determined using a 5 percent interest rate and the applicable mortality table for P's annuity starting date. In order to satisfy the benefit limitations, this annual benefit must not exceed 100 percent of P's average compensation for the period of P's high-three years of service, or $165,000. Using a 5 percent interest rate and the applicable mortality table for the distribution, the actuarially equivalent straight life annuity is $165,000, which does not exceed $165,000. Accordingly, the plan satisfies the compensation-based limitation.

In addition to the fixed 2 percent per year automatic increase, P's benefit will be increased in limitation years following the limitation year in which P retires in accordance with the plan provisions that incorporate by reference the cost-of-living adjustments (or, if Plan D did not incorporate by reference the cost-of-living adjustments, P's benefit may be increased pursuant to plan amendments that comply with the safe harbors), and such increases will not cause P's benefit to violate the benefit limitations. For example, if in a later limitation year the applicable dollar limit is increased by 3 percent because of the cost-of-living adjustment, P's benefit payable under Plan D will be increased by both the fixed automatic 2 percent per year increase and the 3 percent cost-of-living adjustment. The effect of the combined increases may result in P's benefits for a year exceeding the then-applicable dollar limit, but the plan will not violate the limitation on benefits.

Example 9. The facts are the same as in Example 7, except that the plan provides that benefits are limited to the lesser of 100 percent of the participant's average compensation for the period of the participant's high-three years of service or 100 percent of the age-adjusted dollar limit. Assume that P retires at age 65 with a benefit in the form of a life annuity of $165,000 per year with a fixed increase of 2 percent per year. Additionally, assume that Plan D incorporates by reference the cost-of-living adjustments and the plan provides that in no event will a benefit payable from the plan, as increased by the fixed increase of 2 percent per year, be greater than the limit on benefits applicable as of the annuity starting date for the benefit (increased by cost-of-living adjustments).

The benefit payable to P at age 65 is not required to be adjusted to take into account the fixed increase of 2 percent per year. This is because the benefit payable to P satisfies the limitation on benefits without regard to the fixed increase of 2 percent per year and the plan provides that the benefit payable to P, as increased by the fixed increase of 2 percent per year, will never be greater than the limit on benefits applicable as of P's annuity starting date (increased in subsequent limitation years by cost-of-living adjustments).

In addition to the fixed 2 percent per year automatic increase, P's benefit will be increased in limitation years following the limitation year in which P retires in accordance with the plan provisions that incorporate by reference the cost-of-living adjustments (or, if Plan D did not incorporate by reference the adjustments, P's benefit may be increased pursuant to plan amendments that comply with the safe harbors; see Q 6:12), and such increases will not cause P's benefit to violate the benefit limitations. However, P's benefit during any limitation year, as increased by the 2 percent per year automatic increase feature and any plan provisions that incorporate by reference the cost-of-living adjustments or any plan amendments that increase P's benefits, cannot exceed the then-applicable limit on benefits (as increased by cost-of-living adjustments).

Example 10. Employer T maintains a defined benefit plan. Under the terms of the plan, all benefits in pay status (other than single-sum payments) are adjusted upward or downward annually depending on an annual comparison of actual return on plan assets and an assumed interest rate of 4 percent. Thus, the plan does not offer a straight life annuity form of benefit, and the plan must determine for purposes of applying the benefit limits the actuarially equivalent straight life annuity for benefits provided under the plan.

Benefits under the plan are paid in a form to which Section 417(e)(3) does not apply. In determining the actuarially equivalent straight life annuity of benefits that are subject to the annual investment performance adjustment, the plan must assume a 5 percent return on plan assets. Therefore, in determining the actuarially equivalent straight life annuity, the plan must assume that the form of benefit payable under the plan will be an annuity that increases annually by a factor equal to 1.05 divided by 1.04. This increasing annuity is then converted to an actuarially equivalent straight life annuity using a 5 percent interest rate and the applicable mortality table for the relevant annuity starting date.

Example 11. R is a participant in a defined benefit plan maintained by R's employer. Under the terms of the plan, R must make contributions to the plan in a stated amount to accrue benefits derived from employer contributions.

R's contributions are mandatory employee contributions; and, thus, the annual benefit attributable to these contributions is not taken into account for purposes of testing the annual benefit derived from employer contributions against the applicable limitation on benefits. However, these contributions are treated as contributions to a defined contribution plan maintained by R's employer (see Q 6:34). Accordingly, with respect to the current limitation year, the limitation on benefits is applicable to the annual benefit attributable to employer contributions to the defined benefit plan, and the limitation on contributions and other additions is applicable to the portion of the plan treated as a defined contribution plan, which consists of R's mandatory contributions. These same limitations would also apply if, instead of providing for mandatory employee contributions, the plan permitted voluntary employee contributions, because the portion of the plan attributable to voluntary employee contributions and earnings thereon is treated as a defined contribution plan maintained by the employer and thus is not subject to the limitations on benefits applicable to defined benefit plans.

Example 12. V is a participant in a defined benefit plan maintained by V's employer. Under the terms of the plan, V must make contributions to the plan in a stated amount to accrue benefits derived from employer contributions. V's contributions are mandatory employee contributions. Thus, the annual benefit attributable to these contributions is not taken into account for purposes of testing the annual benefit derived from employer contributions against the applicable limitation on benefits. V terminates employment and receives a distribution from the plan that includes V's mandatory employee contributions. Subsequently, V resumes employment with the employer maintaining the plan. V recommences participation in the plan and repays the prior distribution from the plan (including the portion of the distribution that included V's prior mandatory employee contributions to the plan) with reasonable interest.

In determining V's annual benefit under the plan for purposes of applying the limitations, no portion of V's repayment of the prior distribution is treated as employee contributions (see Q 6:15). However, V's annual benefit under the plan is determined by excluding the portion of the annual benefit attributable to V's employee contributions to the plan made both prior to the first distribution and during V's subsequent recommencement of plan participation.

Q 6:19 How is the annual benefit adjusted if payment commences before age 62?

For a distribution with an annuity starting date (see Q 10:3) that occurs before the participant attains age 62, the age-adjusted dollar limit (see Q 6:11) generally is determined as the actuarial equivalent of the annual amount of a straight life annuity (see Q 6:14) commencing at the annuity starting date that has the same actuarial present value as a deferred straight life annuity commencing at age 62, where annual payments under the straight life annuity commencing at age 62 are equal to the dollar limitation, as adjusted for cost-of-living increases (see Q 6:12) for the limitation year (see Q 6:58), and where the actuarially equivalent straight life annuity is computed using a 5 percent interest rate and the applicable mortality table that is effective for that annuity starting date (and expressing the participant's age based on completed calendar months as of the annuity starting date). However, if the plan has an immediately commencing straight life annuity payable both at age 62 and the age of benefit commencement, then the age-adjusted dollar limit is equal to the lesser of:

1. The limit as otherwise determined under this paragraph, and
2. The amount determined under the following paragraph. [I.R.C. §§ 415(b)(2)(C), 415(b)(2)(E)(i); Treas. Reg. § 1.415(b)-1(d)(1)(i)]

The amount determined under this paragraph is equal to the dollar limit (as adjusted for the limitation year) multiplied by the ratio of the annual amount of the immediately commencing straight life annuity under the plan to the annual amount of the straight life annuity under the plan commencing at age 62, with both annual amounts determined without applying the benefit limitation rules. [Treas. Reg. § 1.415(b)-1(d)(l)(ii)]

For purposes of determining the actuarially equivalent amount described in the first paragraph, to the extent that a forfeiture does not occur upon the participant's death (see Q 9:23) before the annuity starting date, no adjustment is made to reflect the probability of the participant's death between the annuity starting date and the participant's attainment of age 62, unless the plan provides for such an adjustment. To the extent that a forfeiture occurs upon the participant's death before the annuity starting date, an adjustment must be made to reflect the probability of the participant's death between the annuity starting date and the participant's attainment of age 62. [Treas. Reg. § 1.415(b)-1(d)(2)(i)]

For purposes of the preceding paragraph and Q 6:20, a plan is permitted to treat no forfeiture as occurring upon a participant's death if the plan does not charge participants for providing a QPSA (see Q 10:9) on the participant's death, but only if the plan applies this treatment both for adjustments before age 62 and adjustments after age 65. Thus, in such a case, the plan is permitted to provide that, in computing the adjusted dollar limitation, no adjustment is made to reflect the probability of a participant's death after the annuity starting date and before age 62 or after age 65 and before the annuity starting date. [Treas. Reg. § 1.415(b)-1(d)(2)(ii)]

Notwithstanding any other provision of this Q 6:19, the age-adjusted dollar limit applicable to a participant does not decrease on account of an increase in age or the performance of additional service. [Treas. Reg. § 1.415(b)-1(d)(6)]

The following examples illustrate the application of these rules. For purposes of these examples, it is assumed that the dollar limitation for all relevant years is $180,000, that the normal form of benefit under the plan is a straight life annuity payable beginning at age 65, and that all payments other than a payment of a single sum are made monthly on the first day of each calendar month.

Example 1. Plan A provides that early retirement benefits are determined by reducing the accrued benefit by 4 percent for each year that the early retirement age is less than age 65. Participant M retires at age 60 with exactly 30 years of service with a benefit (prior to the application of the limitation on benefits) in the form of a straight life annuity of $100,000 payable at age 65 and is permitted to elect to commence benefits at any time between M's retirement and M's attainment of age 65. For example, M can elect to commence benefits at age 60 in the amount of $80,000, can wait until age 62 and commence benefits in the amount of $88,000, or can wait until age 65 and commence benefits in the amount of $100,000. Plan A provides a QPSA to all married participants without charge. Plan A provides that, for purposes of adjusting the dollar limitation for commencement before age 62 or after age 65, no forfeiture is treated as occurring upon a participant's death before retirement; and, therefore, in computing the adjusted dollar limitation, no adjustment is made to reflect the probability of a participant's death after the annuity starting date and before age 62 or after age 65 and before the annuity starting date.

The age-adjusted dollar limit that applies for commencement of M's benefit at 60 is the lesser of the dollar limit multiplied by the ratio of the annuity payable at age 60 to the annuity payable at age 62, or the straight life annuity payable at age 60 that is actuarially equivalent, using 5 percent interest and the applicable mortality table effective for that annuity starting date, to the deferred annuity payable at age 62 of $180,000 per year. In this case, the age-adjusted dollar limited at age 60 is $156,229 (the lesser of $163,636 [$180,000 × $80,000/$88,000] and $156,229 [the straight life annuity at age 60 that is actuarially equivalent to a deferred annuity for the period between 60 and 62]).

Example 2. The facts are the same as in Example 1, except that participant M elects to retire at age 60, 6 months, and 21 days.

M is treated as age 60 and 6 months (or, age 60.5). Absent the rule that there is no decrease in the age-adjusted dollar limit on account of age or service, the age-adjusted dollar limit that applies for commencement of M's benefit at age 60.5 is the lesser of the dollar limit multiplied by the ratio of the annuity payable at age 60.5 to the annuity payable at age 62, or the straight life annuity payable at age 60.5 that is actuarially equivalent, using 5 percent interest and the applicable mortality table for that annuity starting date, to the deferred annuity payable at age 62 of $180,000 per year. The age-adjusted dollar limit at age 60.5 is $161,769 (the lesser of $167,727 [$180,000 × $82,000/$88,000] and $161,769 [the straight life annuity at age 60.5 that is actuarially equivalent to a deferred annuity of $180,000 commencing at age 62, determined using 5 percent interest and the applicable mortality table, without a mortality decrement for the period between 60.5 and 62]).

Example 3. The facts are the same as in Example 1, except the plan provides that, if a participant has 30 or more years of service, no reduction applies for benefits commencing at age 62 and later.

Absent the rule that there is no decrease in the age-adjusted dollar limit on account of age or service, the age-adjusted dollar limit that applies for commencement of M's benefit at age 60 is the lesser of the dollar limit multiplied by the ratio of the annuity payable at age 60 to the annuity payable at age 62, or the straight life annuity payable at age 60 that is actuarially equivalent, using 5 percent interest and the applicable mortality table for that annuity starting date, to the deferred annuity payable at age 62 of $180,000 per year. In this case, because M has 30 years of service and would be eligible for the unreduced early retirement benefit at age 62, the age-adjusted dollar limit at age 60 would be $144,000 (the lesser of $144,000 [$180,000 × $80,000/$100,000] and $156,229 [the straight life annuity at age 60 that is actuarially equivalent to a deferred annuity of $180,000 commencing at age

62, determined using 5 percent interest and the applicable mortality table, without a mortality decrement for the period between 60 and 62]).

However, at age $59^{11}/_{12}$ with $29^{11}/_{12}$ years of service, the age-adjusted dollar limit for M is $155,311 (the lesser of $162,955 [$180,000 × $79,667/$88,000] and $155,311 [the straight life annuity at age $59^{11}/_{12}$ that is actuarially equivalent to a deferred annuity of $180,000 commencing at age 62, determined using 5 percent interest and the applicable mortality table, without a mortality decrement for the period between 59 and 62]). Thus, after applying the rule that there is no decrease on account of age or service, the age-adjusted dollar limit that applies for commencement of M's benefit at age 60 is $155,311.

Example 4. The facts are the same as in Example 1, except that the plan provides that, if a participant has 30 or more years of service, then no reduction is made in early retirement benefits if the early retirement age is at least age 62; and, in the case of an early retirement age before age 62, the early retirement benefit is determined by reducing the accrued benefit by 4 percent for each year that the early retirement age is less than age 62.

The age-adjusted dollar limit that applies for commencement of M's benefit at age 60 is the lesser of the dollar limit multiplied by the ratio of the annuity payable at age 60 to the annuity payable at age 62, or the straight life annuity payable at age 60 that is actuarially equivalent, using 5 percent interest and the applicable mortality table for that annuity starting date, to the deferred annuity payable at age 62 of $180,000 per year. In this case, because M has 30 years of service and would be eligible for the unreduced early retirement benefit at age 62, the age-adjusted dollar limit at age 60 is $156,229 (the lesser of $165,600 [$180,000 × $92,000/$100,000] and $156,229 [the straight life annuity at age 60 that is actuarially equivalent to a deferred annuity of $180,000 commencing at age 62, determined using 5 percent interest and the applicable mortality table, without a mortality decrement for the period between 60 and 62]).

Example 5. The facts are the same as in Example 1, except that Participant M chooses to receive benefits in the form of a ten-year certain and life annuity under which payments are 97 percent of the periodic payments that would be made under the immediately commencing straight life annuity. Annual payments to M are 97 percent of $80,000, or $77,600. Additionally, M's average compensation for the period of M's high-three years of service is $120,000. As in Example 1, the age-adjusted dollar limit at age 60 is $156,229.

In the case of a form of benefit to which Section 417(e)(3) does not apply, the annual benefit is the greater of the annual amount of the plan's straight life annuity commencing at the same age or the annual amount of the actuarially equivalent straight life annuity commencing at the same age, determined using a 5 percent interest rate and the applicable mortality table for that annuity starting date. In this case, the straight life annuity payable under the plan commencing at the same age is $80,000. The annual amount of the straight life annuity that is actuarially equivalent to the $77,600 benefit payable as a ten-year certain and life annuity is determined by applying the required standardized factors (a 5 percent interest assumption and the applicable mortality table) and is $79,416. With respect to the ten-year certain and life annuity commencing at age 62, M's annual benefit is equal to the greater of the two resulting amounts ($80,000 and $79,416), or $80,000. Because M's annual benefit is less than the age-adjusted dollar limit and is less than the 100 percent-of-compensation limit, M's benefit satisfies the limitation on benefits.

Q 6:20   How is the annual benefit adjusted if payment commences after age 65?

For a distribution with an annuity starting date (see Q 10:3) that occurs after the participant attains age 65, the age-adjusted dollar limit (see Q 6:11) generally is determined as the actuarial equivalent of the annual amount of a straight life annuity (see Q 6:14) commencing at the annuity starting date that has the same actuarial present value as a straight life annuity commencing at age 65, where annual payments under the straight life annuity commencing at age 65 are equal to the dollar limitation as adjusted for cost-of-living increases (see Q 6:12) for the limitation year (see Q 6:58), and where the actuarially equivalent straight life annuity is computed using a 5 percent interest rate and the applicable mortality table that is effective for that annuity starting date (and expressing the participant's age based on completed calendar months as of the annuity starting date). However, if the plan has an immediately commencing straight life annuity payable as of the annuity starting date and an immediately commencing straight life annuity payable at 65, then the age-adjusted dollar limit is equal to the lesser of:

1. The limit as otherwise determined under this paragraph, and
2. The amount determined under the following paragraph. [I.R.C. §§ 415(b)(1)(D), 415(b)(1)(E)(iii); Treas. Reg. § 1.415(b)-1(e)(1)(i)]

The amount determined under this paragraph is equal to the dollar limit (as adjusted for the limitation year) multiplied by the adjustment ratio described in the following paragraph. [Treas. Reg. § 1.415(b)-1(e)(1)(ii)]

For purposes of applying the rule of the preceding paragraph, the adjustment ratio is equal to the ratio of the annual amount of the adjusted immediately commencing straight life annuity under the plan to the adjusted age 65 straight life annuity described below. [Treas. Reg. § 1.415(b)-1(e)(2)(i)]

The adjusted immediately commencing straight life annuity that is used is the annual amount of the immediately commencing straight life annuity payment to the participant, computed disregarding the participant's accruals after age 65 but including actuarial adjustments even if those actuarial adjustments are applied to offset accruals. For this purpose, the annual amount of the immediately commencing straight life annuity is determined without applying the benefit limitation rules. [Treas. Reg. § 1.415(b)-1(e)(2)(ii)]

The adjusted age 65 straight life annuity that is used is the annual amount of the straight life annuity that would be payable under the plan to a hypothetical participant who is 65 years old and has the same accrued benefit (with no actuarial increases for commencement after age 65) as the participant receiving the distribution (determined disregarding the participant's accruals after age 65 and without applying the benefit limitation rules). [Treas. Reg. § 1.415(b)-1(e)(2)(iii)]

For purposes of determining the actuarial equivalent amount, to the extent that a forfeiture does not occur upon the participant's death (see Q 9:23) before the annuity starting date, no adjustment is made to reflect the probability of the participant's death between the participant's attainment of age 65 and the annuity starting date. To the extent that a forfeiture occurs upon the participant's death before the annuity starting date, an adjustment must be made to reflect the probability of the participant's death between the participant's attainment of age 65 and the annuity starting date. [Treas. Reg. § 1.415(b)-1(e)(3)(i)]

For purposes of the adjustment ratio, a plan is permitted to treat no forfeiture as occurring upon a participant's death if the plan does not charge participants for providing a QPSA (see Q 10:9) on the participant's death, but only if the plan applies this treatment both for adjustments before age 62 and adjustments after age 65. Thus, in such a case, the plan is permitted to provide that, in computing the adjusted dollar limitation, no adjustment is made to reflect the probability of a participant's death after the annuity starting date and before age 62 or after age 65 and before the annuity starting date. [Treas. Reg. § 1.415(b)-1(e)(3)(ii)]

> **Example 1.** Plan A provides that monthly benefits payable upon commencement after normal retirement age (which is age 65) are increased by 0.5 percent for each month of delay in commencement after attainment of normal retirement age. Plan A provides a QPSA to all married participants without charge. Plan A provides that, for purposes of adjusting the dollar limitation for commencement before age 62 or after age 65, no adjustment is made to reflect the probability of a participant's death between the annuity starting date and the participant's attainment of age 62 or between age 65 and the annuity starting date. The normal form of benefit under Plan A is a straight life annuity commencing at age 65. Plan A does not provide additional benefit accruals once a participant is credited with 30 years of service. Participant M was credited with 30 years of service under Plan A when M attained age 65. M retires at age 70 on January 1, 2008, with a benefit (prior to the application of the limitations on benefits) that is payable monthly in the form of a straight life annuity of $195,000, which reflects the actuarial increase of 30 percent applied to the accrued benefit of $150,000. It is assumed that all payments under Plan A, other than a payment of a single sum, are made monthly on the first day of each calendar month. It is also assumed that the dollar limit in 2008 is $185,000.

The age-adjusted dollar limit at age 70 is the lesser of the dollar limit multiplied by the ratio of the adjusted immediately commencing straight life annuity payable at age 70 (computed disregarding the benefit limitation rules and accruals after age 65, but including actuarial adjustments) to the adjusted age 65 straight life annuity (computed disregarding the benefit limitation rules and any accruals after age 65), or the straight life annuity payable at age 70 that is actuarially equivalent, using 5 percent interest and the applicable mortality table for the annuity starting date, to the straight life annuity payable at age 65, where annual payments under the straight life annuity payable at age 65 are equal to the dollar limitation. In this case, the age-adjusted dollar limit at age 70 is \$240,500 (the lesser of \$240,500 [\$185,000 × \$195,000/\$150,000] and \$271,444 (the straight life annuity at age 70 that is actuarially equivalent to an annuity of \$185,000 commencing at age 65, determined using 5 percent interest and the applicable mortality table, without a mortality decrement for the period between 65 and 70]).

Example 2. The facts are the same as in Example 1, except that Plan A does not limit benefit accruals to 30 years of credited service, and thus M accrues benefits between ages 65 and 70. Because M's accruals after attaining age 65 are disregarded for purposes of determining the age-adjusted dollar limit applicable to M at age 70, the result is the same as in Example 1.

Example 3. The facts are the same as in Example 1, except that Plan A does not limit benefit accruals to 30 years of credited service. However, benefit accruals after an employee has reached normal retirement age (age 65) are offset by the actuarial increase that the plan provides for commencement of benefits after normal retirement age.

The result is the same as in Example 1, whether the actuarial increases for post-age 65 benefit commencement provided under Plan A do or do not fully offset M's benefit accruals after attaining age 65. This is because benefit accruals after age 65 are disregarded for purposes of determining the age-adjusted dollar limit applicable to M after age 65.

Q 6:21   Is there a minimum annual benefit?

The annual benefit (without regard to the age at which benefits commence) payable with respect to a participant under any defined benefit plan (see Q 2:3) is not considered to exceed the limitations on benefits (see Q 6:11) if:

1. The benefits payable with respect to the participant under the plan and all other defined benefit plans of the employer do not in the aggregate exceed \$10,000 (as adjusted; see Q 6:22) for the limitation year (see Q 6:58) or for any prior limitation year, and

2. The employer (or predecessor employer; see Q 6:52) has not at any time maintained a defined contribution plan (see Q 2:2) in which the participant participated. [I.R.C. §§ 415(b)(4), 415(b)(5)(B), 415(b)(5)(C); Treas. Reg. § 1.415(b)-1(f)(1)]

For purposes of applying the \$10,000 amount, the benefits payable with respect to the participant under a plan for a limitation year reflect all amounts payable under the plan for the limitation year (other than benefits not taken into account in the computation of the annual benefit) and are not adjusted for form of benefit or commencement date. [Treas. Reg. § 1.415(b)-1)(f)(2)]

The special $10,000 exception applies to a participant in a multiemployer plan (see Q 29:2) without regard to whether that participant ever participated in one or more other plans maintained by an employer who also maintains the multiemployer plan, provided that none of such other plans were maintained as a result of collective bargaining involving the same employee representative as the multiemployer plan. [Treas. Reg. § 1.415(b)-1(f)(3)]

Mandatory employee contributions (see Q 6:15) under a defined benefit plan are not considered a separate defined contribution plan maintained by the employer for purposes of this special dollar limitation; and, thus, this special dollar limitation applies to a contributory defined benefit plan. Similarly, for this purpose, an individual medical account under Section 401(h) or an account for postretirement medical benefits established pursuant to Section 419A(d)(1) is not considered a separate defined contribution plan maintained by the employer (see Q 6:34). [Treas. Reg. § 1.415(b)-1(f) (4)]

For purposes of the following examples, it is assumed that each participant has ten years of participation in the plan and service with the employer (see Q 6:22).

Example 1. B is a participant in a defined benefit plan maintained by X Corporation, which provides for a benefit payable in the form of a straight life annuity beginning at age 65. B's average compensation for the period of B's high-three years of service is $6,000. The plan does not provide for mandatory employee contributions, and at no time has B been a participant in a defined contribution plan maintained by X. With respect to the current limitation year, B's benefit under the plan (before the application of the benefit limitations) is $9,500.

Because annual payments of B's benefit do not exceed $10,000 and because B has at no time participated in a defined contribution plan maintained by X, the benefits payable under the plan are not considered to exceed the limitation on benefits otherwise applicable to B ($6,000). This result would remain the same even if, under the terms of the plan, B's benefit of $9,500 were payable at age 60 or if the plan provided for mandatory employee contributions.

Example 2. The facts are the same as in Example 1, except that the plan provides for a benefit payable in the form of a life annuity with a ten-year certain feature with annual payments of $9,500. Assume that, after adjustment (see Q 6:18), B's actuarially equivalent straight life annuity (which is the annual benefit used for demonstrating compliance with the benefit limitations for the current limitation year) is $10,400.

For purposes of applying the special rule for total benefits not in excess of $10,000, there is no adjustment required if the retirement benefit payable under the plan is not in the form of a straight life annuity. Therefore, because

B's retirement benefit does not exceed $10,000, B may receive the full $9,500 benefit without the otherwise applicable benefit limitations being exceeded.

Example 3. The facts are the same as in Example 1, except that the plan provides for a benefit payable in the form of a single sum and the amount of the single sum that is the actuarial equivalent of the straight life annuity payable to B ($9,500 annually) is $95,000.

Because the amount payable to B for the limitation year would exceed $10,000, this special rule does not provide an exception from the generally applicable limits for the single-sum distribution. Thus, the otherwise applicable limits apply to the single-sum distribution, and a single-sum distribution of $95,000 would not satisfy the benefit limitation requirements. Limiting the single-sum distribution to $60,000 (the present value of the annuity that complies with the compensation-based limitation) in order to satisfy the benefit limitation requirement would be an impermissible forfeiture. Accordingly, the plan should not provide for a single-sum distribution in these circumstances.

Q 6:22   Is there a minimum number of years of participation or service required before a participant in a defined benefit plan qualifies for the maximum annual benefit?

Where a participant has less than ten years of participation in the plan, the dollar limit (see Q 6:11), as adjusted (see Qs 6:12, 6:19, 6:20), is reduced by multiplying the otherwise applicable limitation by a fraction, the numerator of which is the number of years of participation in the plan (or 1, if greater) and the denominator of which is 10. [I.R.C. §§ 415(b)(5)(A), 415(b)(5)(C); Treas. Reg. § 1.415(b)-1(g)(1)(i)]

For purposes of determining a participant's years of participation, a participant is credited with a year of participation (computed to fractional parts of a year) for each accrual computation period for which the participant is credited with at least the number of hours of service (or period of service if the elapsed time method is used for benefit accrual purposes; see Q 5:9) required under the terms of the plan in order to accrue a benefit for the accrual computation period and the participant is included as a plan participant under the eligibility provisions of the plan for at least one day of the accrual computation period. If these two conditions are met, the portion of a year of participation credited to the participant is equal to the amount of benefit accrual service credited to the participant for such accrual computation period. For example, if under the terms of a plan, a participant receives one-tenth of a year of benefit accrual service for an accrual computation period for each 200 hours of service, and the participant is credited with 1,000 hours of service for the period, the participant is credited with one-half of a year of participation. A participant who is permanently and totally disabled for an accrual computation period is credited with a year of participation with respect to that period. For a participant to receive a year of participation (or part thereof) for an accrual computation, the plan must be established no later than the last day of such accrual computation period. No more than one year of participation may be credited for any 12-month period. [I.R.C. §§ 22(e)(3), 415(b)(5)(A), 415(b)(5)(C), 415(c)(3)(C)(i); Treas. Reg. § 1.415(b)-1(g)(1)(ii)]

Where a participant has less than ten years of service with the employer, the compensation limit (see Q 6:11) and the $10,000 amount under the special rule for small annual payments (see Q 6:21) are reduced by multiplying the otherwise applicable limitation by a fraction, the numerator of which is the number of years of service with the employer (or 1, if greater) and the denominator of which is 10. [I.R.C. §§ 415(b)(5)(B), 415(b)(5)(C); Treas. Reg. § 1.415(b)-1(g)(2)(i)]

Years of service must be determined on a reasonable and consistent basis. A plan is considered to be determining years of service on a reasonable and consistent basis for this purpose if, subject to the limits discussed below, a participant is credited with a year of service (computed to fractional parts of a year) for each accrual computation period for which the participant is credited with at least the number of hours of service (or period of service if the elapsed time method is used for benefit accrual purposes) required under the terms of the plan in order to accrue a benefit for the accrual computation period. No more than one year of service may be credited for any 12-month period. In addition, only the participant's service with the employer or a predecessor employer (see Q 6:52) may be taken into account in determining the participant's years of service for this purpose. Thus, if an employer does not maintain a former employer's plan, a participant's service with the former employer may be taken into account in determining the participant's years of service only if the former employer is a predecessor employer with respect to the employer. A plan is permitted to provide that a participant who is permanently and totally disabled for an accrual computation period is credited with service with respect to that period. [I.R.C. §§ 22(e)(3), 415(b)(5)(B), 415(b)(5)(C), 415(c)(3)(C)(i); Treas. Reg. § 1.415(b)-1(g)(2)(ii)]

> **Example 1.** C begins employment with Employer A on January 1, 2005, at the age of 58. Employer A maintains only a non-contributory defined benefit plan that provides for a straight life annuity beginning at age 65 and uses the calendar year for the limitation and plan year. Employer A has never maintained a defined contribution plan. C becomes a participant in Employer A's plan on January 1, 2006, and works through December 31, 2011, when C is age 65. C begins to receive benefits under the plan in 2012, and C's average compensation for the period of C's high-three years of service is $40,000. Furthermore, under the terms of Employer A's plan, for purposes of computing C's nonforfeitable percentage in C's accrued benefit derived from employer contributions, C has only seven years of service with Employer A (2005-2011).
>
> Because C has only seven years of service with Employer A at the time C begins to receive benefits under the plan, the maximum permissible annual benefit payable with respect to C is $28,000 ($40,000 × 7/10).

Example 2. The facts are the same as in Example 1, except that C's average compensation for the period of C's high-three years of service is $8,000. Because C has only seven years of service with Employer A at the time C begins to receive benefits, the maximum benefit payable with respect to C would be reduced to $5,600 ($8,000 × 7/10). However, the special rule for total benefits not in excess of $10,000 (see Q 6:21) is applicable in this case. Accordingly, C may receive an annual benefit of $7,000 ($10,000 × 7/10) without the benefit limitations being exceeded.

Example 3. Employer B maintains a defined benefit plan. Benefits under the plan are computed based on months of service rather than years of service. Accordingly, for purposes of applying the reduction based on years of service less than ten to the benefit limitations, the plan provides that the otherwise applicable limitation is multiplied by a fraction, the numerator of which is the number of completed months of service with the employer (but not less than 12 months) and the denominator of which is 120. The plan further provides that months of service are computed in the same manner for this purpose as for purposes of computing plan benefits. The manner in which the plan applies the reduction based on years of service less than ten to the benefit limitations is permissible.

Example 4. G begins employment with Employer D on January 1, 2004 at the age of 58. Employer D maintains a non-contributory defined benefit plan that provides for a straight life annuity beginning at age 65 and uses the calendar year for the limitation and plan year. G becomes a participant in Employer D's plan on January 1, 2005 and works through December 31, 2010, when G is age 65. G performs sufficient service to be credited with a year of service under the plan for each year during 2004 through 2010 (although G is not credited with a year of service for 2004 because G is not yet a plan participant). G begins to receive benefits under the plan during 2011. The plan's accrual computation period is the plan year. The plan provides that a participant is credited with a year of service (computed to fractional parts of a year) for each plan year for which the participant is credited with sufficient service to accrue a benefit for the plan year. G's average compensation for the period of G's high-three years of service is $200,000. The dollar limitation for limitation years ending in 2011 is $195,000.

G has seven years of service and six years of participation in the plan at the time G begins to receive benefits under the plan. Accordingly, the compensation limitation based on G's average compensation for the period of G's high-three years of service that applies pursuant to the required adjustment is $140,000 ($200,000 × 7/10), and the dollar limitation that applies to G pursuant to the required adjustment is $117,000 ($195,000 × 6/10).

As noted above, years of service may include service with businesses that antedate the formation of a corporation. This applies where the transition to a corporate structure resulted in a mere formal or technical change in the employment relationship and continuity otherwise existed with respect to the substance and administration of the business operations of the previous entity and the corporation. Thus, the period during which a doctor operated his practice as a sole proprietorship prior to the business's incorporation and its sponsorship of a defined benefit plan constituted years of service with the employer. [Lear Eye Clinic, Ltd., 106 T.C. 418 (1996)] However, in a consolidated case [Brody Enterprises, Inc.], an attorney who was the sole shareholder and employee of a corporation that adopted a defined benefit plan in which he participated could not include as years of service with the employer the period during which he conducted a part-time private law practice while working full-time for IRS. The practice was located in a different city, the corporation failed to show that the attorney conducted a private law practice, and the attorney maintained no records of the hours that he spent on the practice. In addition, the attorney could not include the five-year period during which he worked for a law firm that was also located in a different city. There was no indication that he had an ownership interest in the firm. Moreover, the evidence did not establish a relationship between the corporation's business operations and those of the law firm. Last, the plan administrator (see Q 20:1) lacked the discretion to include the disputed years as "years of service with the employer" under the plan.

Q 6:23 If a defined benefit plan is not amended to take into account the EGTRRA 2001 increased limit, how may the benefits of plan participants be affected?

If a defined benefit plan (see Q 2:3) is not amended to take into account the increased annual retirement benefit limitations under EGTRRA 2001 (see Q 1:21), the effect on the benefits of plan participants will depend on the plan's existing provisions for applying the annual retirement benefit limitations and any other relevant plan provisions. In some circumstances, a plan's existing provisions could result in automatic benefit increases for participants as of the effective date of the increased limitations for the plan. For example, the increased limitations could result in automatic benefit increases for participants in defined benefit plans that incorporate the limitations by reference. [Rev. Rul. 2001-51, Q&As-1, -2, 2001-2 C.B. 427]

> **Example.** Ben, a participant in a defined benefit plan (Plan BML) with a limitation year (see Q 6:58) beginning March 1, 2001 and ending February 28, 2002, retires on April 1, 2001 at age 65 (Ben's Social Security retirement age (SSRA); see Q 7:13) and receives a single-sum distribution of his benefit on May 1, 2001. On retirement, Ben's annual benefit in the form of an annuity under the plan formula was $170,000, but Ben's accrued benefit (see Q 9:2) under the plan was limited to $140,000 to satisfy the annual retirement benefit limitations. Ben received the single-sum equivalent of an annual benefit of $140,000. The terms of Plan BML incorporate the limitations by reference. The defined benefit dollar limitation in effect for 2001 ($140,000) was used in the calculation of the single sum distributed on May 1, 2001. The increase in the defined benefit dollar limitation to $160,000 under EGTRRA 2001 is effective for Plan BML for the limitation year beginning March 1, 2001 and ending February 28, 2002. Therefore, the $160,000 dollar limitation

applies to Ben's benefit, and Ben's benefit must increase. Ben must receive an additional lump-sum amount to reflect the higher dollar limitation applicable to Ben's benefit. The additional lump-sum benefit is calculated as the actuarial equivalent of the excess of (1) Ben's accrued benefit in the form of a straight life annuity (see Q 6:14) when the dollar limitation applicable at Ben's retirement age under EGTRRA 2001 is taken into account, over (2) Ben's accrued benefit in the form of a straight life annuity when the pre-EGTRRA 2001 dollar limitation applicable at Ben's retirement age is taken into account.

Q 6:24   How do the increased limitations affect the methodology used for a benefit that is not payable as a straight life annuity?

The determination as to whether such a benefit satisfies the increased limitations under EGTRRA 2001 (see Q 1:21) generally follows the same steps and procedures as those used in Q 6:18. A participant's benefit must not exceed the lesser of the dollar limitation and the compensation limitation applicable to the participant (see Q 6:11).

Effective for limitation years (see Q 6:58) ending after December 31, 2001, the dollar limitation is reduced when a participant's benefit commences prior to age 62, rather than for a benefit that commences prior to a participant's SSRA (see Qs 6:23, 7:13), and there are no age adjustments to the dollar limitation where a participant's benefit commences after age 62 and no later than age 65. Where a participant's benefit commences prior to age 62, the dollar limitation applicable to the participant at the earlier age is the annual benefit payable in the form of a straight life annuity commencing at the earlier age that is actuarially equivalent to the dollar limitation applicable to the participant at age 62, calculated using assumptions that satisfy the interest rate and mortality table requirements.

Effective for limitation years ending after December 31, 2001, the dollar limitation is increased when a participant's benefit commences after age 65, rather than for a benefit that commences after a participant's SSRA. Where a participant's benefit commences after age 65, the dollar limitation applicable to the participant at the later age is the annual benefit payable in the form of a straight life annuity commencing at the later age that is actuarially equivalent to the dollar limitation applicable to the participant at age 65, calculated using assumptions that satisfy the interest rate and mortality table requirements. [Rev. Rul. 2001-51, Q&A-3, 2001-2 C.B. 427]

Q 6:25   What special considerations apply?

In the case of a defined benefit plan (see Q 2:3) with a normal retirement age (see Q 10:55) less than 65, the requirements for nonforfeitability of benefits and actuarial increase for delayed retirement must be coordinated with the annual retirement benefit requirements. If benefits are not paid to a participant after the participant attains the plan's normal retirement age and the plan's terms do not provide for the suspension of the participant's benefits (see Q 10:53), then the participant's benefit must be actuarially increased for late retirement to avoid any forfeiture of the participant's benefit. [I.R.C. § 411(a)(3)(B); D.O.L. Reg. § 2530.203-3] However, the dollar limitation (see Q 6:11) applicable to a participant does not increase between ages 62 and 65 (see Q 6:24). If a participant continues to work past a plan's normal retirement age that is less than 65 and the participant's benefit equals the dollar limitation at an age between 62 and 65, any actuarial increase to the participant's benefit after that age and prior to age 65 would violate the annual retirement benefit limitation. In such a case, the terms of the plan must either provide for the in-service payment of the participant's benefit (where the participant has attained normal retirement age and has a benefit that cannot be actuarially increased without violating the annual retirement benefit limitation) or provide for the suspension of benefits. [Rev. Rul. 2001-51, Q&A-4, 2001-2 C.B. 427]

Q 6:26 How are current or former employees affected by the EGTRRA 2001 increased limits?

A defined benefit plan (see Q 2:3) may provide for benefit increases to reflect the increased EGTRRA 2001 limitations for a current or former employee who has commenced benefits under the plan prior to the effective date, but only if the employee or former employee is a participant in the plan on or after that effective date. For this purpose, an employee or former employee is a participant in the plan on a date if the employee or former employee has an accrued benefit (see Q 9:2; other than an accrued benefit resulting from a benefit increase that arises solely as a result of the increases in the annual retirement benefit limitation) on that date. Thus, benefit increases to reflect the increases in the annual retirement benefit limitation cannot be provided to current or former employees who do not have accrued benefits under the plan on or after the effective date of the limitation increases for the plan. However, if a current or former employee accrues additional benefits under the plan that could have been accrued without regard to the increased limitation (including benefits that accrue as a result of a plan amendment) on or after the effective date of the increased limitation for the plan, then the current or former employee may receive a benefit arising from the increased limitation. [Rev. Rul. 2001-51, Q&A-5, 2001-2 C.B. 427]

For any limitation year (see Q 6:58) beginning on or after the effective date for the plan of the increased limitations, the benefit payable to any current or former employee who has commenced benefits under the plan prior to such effective date in a form not subject to Section 417(e)(3) may be increased to a benefit that is no greater than the benefit that could have been provided had the provisions of EGTRRA 2001 been in effect at the time of the commencement of benefits. Thus, the annual benefit for limitation years beginning on or after the effective date is limited to the benefit limitation for the employee (increased for cost-of-living adjustments, if the plan provides for such adjustments) based on the employee's age at the time of commencement. Benefits attributable to limitation years beginning before the effective date for the plan of the increased benefit limitations cannot reflect benefit increases that could not be paid for those years. In addition, any plan amendment to provide an increase as a result of the increased limitations under EGTRRA 2001 can be effective no earlier than the effective date of the increased limitations under EGTRRA 2001 for the plan. [Rev. Rul. 2001-51, Q&A-6, 2001-2 C.B. 427]

> **Example.** Plan JAL has a calendar year limitation year and provides that retiree benefits are increased as cost-of-living adjustments are made. Jason, a participant of Plan JAL, retired in 2000 at age 60 with 20 years of participation. Jason's SSRA (see Q 6:23) is 66. Jason's annual benefit under the plan formula before limitation was $180,000, and his benefit was limited by the defined benefit dollar limit to $85,252 (the applicable mortality table and 6 percent are used under the plan for early retirement purposes). The defined benefit compensation limitation applicable to Jason was $200,000 and, thus, did not limit Jason's benefit.

> Following the increase in the dollar limit on January 1, 2001 to $140,000, Jason's benefit was increased to $88,409 [$85,252 × ($140,000/$135,000)]. After the increase in the dollar limit under EGTRRA 2001 is applicable to Plan JAL for the limitation year beginning January 1, 2002, Jason's annual benefit may be increased to an amount equal to the annual benefit commencing at age 60 that is actuarially equivalent (calculated using actuarial assumptions that satisfy the early retirement rules) to an annual benefit of $160,000 payable at age 62. In other words, Jason's benefit may be increased to an amount equal to the benefit that a 60-year-old could receive if the defined benefit dollar limit is $160,000 (with no reduction in the dollar limit for benefits that commence before age 65 and on or after age 62, but reduced actuarially for benefits that commence before age 62). Jason's annual benefit may be increased to $134,720. However, Jason may not receive this increased benefit until January 1, 2002.

In the case of a form of benefit that is subject to Section 417(e)(3), the benefit payable for any limitation year beginning on or after the effective date for the plan of the increased limitations may be increased by an amount that is actuarially equivalent to the amount of increase that could have been provided had the benefit been paid in the form of a straight life annuity (see Q 6:14). Benefits attributable to limitation years beginning before the effective date for the plan of the increased limitations cannot reflect benefit increases that could not be paid for those years because of the prior limitations. In addition, any plan amendment to provide an increase as a result of the increased limitations can be effective no earlier than the effective date. [Rev. Rul. 2001-51, Q&A-7, 2001-2 C.B. 427]

> **Example.** Jennifer, a participant in a defined benefit plan (Plan JKH) with a calendar year limitation year and plan year, retires on January 1, 2001, Jennifer's 64th birthday, with 25 years of service and participation. Jennifer's SSRA is 65. The terms of Plan JKH provide for increases in retiree benefits (that are limited) as the limits are increased for cost-of-living adjustments. On retirement, Jennifer's annual benefit in the form of an annuity under the plan formula, before limitation, is $200,000. Jennifer's accrued benefit under the plan in the form of an annuity is limited to $130,667 [($140,000) × (1− (5/9) × (12) × (.01))]

Jennifer's benefit is payable in the form of ten equal annual installments commencing January 1, 2001. For purposes of actuarial equivalence for early commencement and optional forms, the plan provides for the use of the applicable mortality table and the applicable interest rate (assumed to be 6 percent for purposes of this example).

When Jennifer's benefits began, the benefit was calculated as a straight life annuity of $130,667 per year, adjusted for payment as ten annual payments. The annuity benefit of $130,667 was multiplied by an age 64 annuity factor (calculated using the applicable mortality table and the applicable interest rate), and the resulting amount was spread over ten years, using the applicable interest rate. Jennifer has an accrued benefit under Plan JKH when EGTRRA 2001 becomes effective for Plan JKH on January 1, 2002. If Plan JKH is amended to provide for such increases to retired participants, then Jennifer's benefits, if payable in the form of a straight life annuity, could be increased to a straight life annuity of $160,000 in the limitation year beginning January 1, 2002. As of January 1, 2002, Jennifer has nine remaining installment payments. The remaining nine installment payments could be increased by the actuarial equivalent (spread over a period of nine years) of the value of the increase in the straight life annuity that would have been payable beginning January 1, 2002, if Jennifer had elected a straight life annuity on retirement rather than the installment payment option. That is, the maximum increase that Jennifer is permitted to receive in 2002 as a result of the increase under EGTRRA 2001 is the amount equal to the product of $29,333 ($160,000 − $130,667) times an age 65 annuity factor (derived using the applicable mortality table and the applicable interest rate), spread over nine years at an assumed interest rate equal to the applicable interest rate.

Q 6:27   How are multiemployer defined benefit plans affected by EGTRRA 2001?

The 100-percent-of-compensation limitation (see Q 6:11) does not apply to multiemployer defined benefit plans (see Q 29:2) for limitation years (see Q 6:58) beginning after 2001. Additionally, the aggregation rules (see Q 6:55) affecting multiemployer plans were changed to provide that, for limitation years beginning after 2001, a multiemployer plan is not combined or aggregated (1) with a non-multiemployer plan for purposes of applying the compensation limit to the non-multiemployer plan or (2) with any other multiemployer plan for purposes of applying the annual retirement benefit limitations (see Q 6:11). [Rev. Rul. 2001-51, Q&A-9, 2001-2 C.B. 427]

Q 6:28   How will a plan that takes into account the increased limitations as of the first day of the first limitation year for which the increases are effective for the plan satisfy the nondiscrimination in amount of benefits requirement?

A defined contribution (see Q 2:2) or defined benefit (see Q 2:3) plan that uses the safe harbor (see Qs 4:12, 4:14) and takes into account the increased limitations under EGTRRA 2001 as of the first day of the first limitation year (see Q 6:58) for which the increases are effective for the plan will not fail to satisfy the uniformity requirements merely because the increased limitations are taken into account under the plan. [Treas. Reg. §§ 1.401(a)(4)-2(b), 1.401(a)(4)-3(b)(2)]

For purposes of the general test for nondiscrimination in amount of contributions, increased contributions allocated under the terms of a defined contribution plan due to the increased limitations must be taken into account for the plan year for which the increased allocations are made (see Q 4:13). For purposes of the general test for nondiscrimination in amount of benefits, increased benefits provided to an employee under the terms of a defined benefit plan due to the increased limitations must be included as increases in the employee's accrued benefit (see Q 9:2) and the employee's most valuable optional form of payment of the accrued benefit and must be included in the computation of both the normal and most valuable accrual rates for any measurement period that includes the plan year for which the increase occurs (see Q 4:18). If the limitations are taken into account in testing the plan for limitation years for which the increased limitations are effective for the plan, those limitations must reflect the increased limitations. [I.R.C. § 411(a)(7)(A)(i); Treas. Reg. §§ 1.401(a)(4)-2(c)(2)(ii), 1.401(a)(4)-3(d)]

[Rev. Rul. 2001-51, Q&A-11, 2001-2 C.B. 427]

Q 6:29   How are other nondiscriminatory requirements affected by the increased EGTRRA 2001 benefits?

If the benefit increases resulting from the increased limitations under EGTRRA 2001 are provided as of the effective date of the increased limitations for the plan to either (1) all current and former employees who have an accrued benefit (see Q 9:2) under the plan immediately before the effective date of the increased limitations or (2) all employees participating in the plan that have one hour of service after the effective date, through the adoption of a plan amendment, then the timing of such an amendment satisfies the nondiscrimination requirement relating to plan amendments (see Q 4:21) and the nondiscrimination requirements relating to the amount of contributions or benefits of former employees are satisfied. If, as of the effective date of the increased limitations, benefit increases are provided to either of the two groups described in the preceding sentence through the operation of the plan's existing provisions, then these requirements are satisfied. [Treas. Reg. §§ 1.401(a)(4)-5, 1.401(a)(4)-10(b)]

If benefit increases due to the increased limitations are provided only to a certain group of current or former employees not described in the preceding paragraph through the adoption of a plan amendment or if a plan amendment to reflect the increased limitations is effective as of a date later than the effective date of the increased limitations, then the timing of such an amendment (considered in conjunction with the effect of the increased limitations) must satisfy a facts-and-circumstances determination. [Treas. Reg. §§ 1.401(a)(4)-5(a)(2), 1.401(a)(4)-10]

[Rev. Rul. 2001-51, Q&A-12, 2001-2 C.B. 427]

Q 6:30   May a plan be amended to limit the extent to which a participant's benefit would otherwise automatically increase under the terms of the plan as a result of the increased limitations under EGTRRA 2001?

Yes, if the amendment is adopted before the effective date of the increased limitations for the plan. However, see Q 6:31 for certain qualification requirements that may be affected by such an amendment. A plan sponsor may wish to make a plan amendment to preclude a benefit increase that would otherwise occur as a result of the increased limitations under EGTRRA 2001 in order to provide time for the plan sponsor to consider the extent to which a benefit increase relating to the increased limitations should or should not be provided at some later date consistent with all relevant qualification requirements. A plan amendment to limit the extent to which such a benefit increase would otherwise occur that is not both adopted prior to, and effective as of, the first day of the first limitation year (see Q 6:58) for which the increased limitations are effective for the plan may fail to satisfy the anti-cutback rule (see Q 9:25). Therefore, a plan amendment that is intended to limit such a benefit increase should be adopted both prior to, and effective as of, the first day of the first limitation year for which the increased limitations are effective for the plan.

The following is an example of language that could have been used by a plan sponsor, on an interim or permanent basis, in amending a defined benefit plan (see Q 2:3) that would otherwise provide for a benefit increase due to the increased limitations to retain the effect of the pre-EGTRRA 2001 limitations in determining a participant's accrued benefit (see Q 9:2) under the plan (without failing to satisfy the anti-cutback rule):

> Effective as of the first day of the first limitation year for which the increased § 415 limitations under EGTRRA 2001 are effective for the Plan (the "Effective Date"), and notwithstanding any other provision of the Plan, the accrued benefit for any participant shall be determined by applying the terms of the Plan implementing the limitations of § 415 as if the limitations of § 415 continued to include the limitations of § 415 as in effect on the day immediately prior to the Effective Date.

[Rev. Rul. 2001-51, Q&A-13, 2001-2 C.B. 427]

Q 6:31   Are there qualification requirements that may not be satisfied if a plan continues to limit benefits?

There are some qualification requirements that may not be satisfied if a plan continues to limit benefits using the pre-EGTRRA 2001 limitations after the first day of the first limitation year (see Q 6:58) for which the increased limitations are effective for the plan. Any exception from the otherwise applicable qualification rules that is permitted solely in order to satisfy the maximum limitations on contributions or benefits with respect to a participant does not apply if the participant's contributions or benefits are below the limitations. Such an exception is not permitted where a plan limits benefits in a manner that is more restrictive than required. For example, at any time on or after the first day of the first limitation year beginning on or after January 1, 2002, a defined contribution plan (see Q 2:2) could not provide that the rules relating to excess annual additions (see Q 6:34) would be applied to place an amount that does not exceed the annual addition limitations, but that does exceed the pre-EGTRRA 2001 limitations, in an unallocated suspense account as an excess annual addition. Similarly, a qualified cash-or-deferred arrangement (see Q 27:9) could not provide that the rules relating to the distribution of elective deferrals (see Q 27:63) would be applied to permit the distribution of elective deferrals that do not exceed the annual addition limitations, but that exceed the pre-EGTRRA 2001 limitations. [Treas. Reg. § 1.415-6(b)(6)]

The qualification issues described above may arise whenever a lower limitation is applied under a plan in lieu of a statutory limitation on contributions or benefits that applies for the limitation year.

[Rev. Rul. 2001-51, Q&A-14, 2001-2 C.B. 427]

Q 6:32 How may a plan that continues to limit benefits using the pre-EGTRRA 2001 limitations satisfy the nondiscrimination in amount of benefits requirement?

The use of safe harbors by defined contribution plans (see Q 2:2) for nondiscrimination in amount of contributions purposes (see Q 4:12) is not precluded by plan provisions (which must apply uniformly to all employees) that (1) limit allocations otherwise provided under the allocation formula to a maximum dollar amount or a maximum percentage of plan year compensation, (2) limit the dollar amount of plan year compensation taken into account in determining the amount of allocations, or (3) apply the restrictions relating to employee stock ownership plans (see Q 28:47) on the annual addition limitation (see Q 6:34). [Treas. Reg. § 1.401(a)(4)-2(b)(4)(iv)]

The use of safe harbors by defined benefit plans (see Q 2:3) for nondiscrimination in amount of benefits purposes (see Q 4:14) is not precluded by plan provisions (which must apply uniformly to all employees) that (1) limit benefits otherwise provided under the benefit formula or accrual method to a maximum dollar amount or to a maximum percentage of average annual compensation or in accordance with the permitted disparity rules (see Q 7:1), (2) apply the annual retirement benefit limits (see Q 6:11), or (3) limit the dollar amount of compensation taken into account in determining benefits. [Treas. Reg. § 1.401(a)(4)-3(b)(6)(v)]

Because the pre-EGTRRA 2001 limitations uniformly limit allocations or benefits to a maximum dollar amount or percentage of compensation, a plan that continues to apply the pre-EGTRRA 2001 limitations does not fail to satisfy a safe harbor solely because it continues to apply such limitations.

If a plan continues to limit benefits using the pre-EGTRRA 2001 limitations, on or after the first day of the first limitation year (see Q 6:58) for which the increased limitations under EGTRRA 2001 are effective for the plan, the annual additions or accrued benefits (see Q 9:2) that are taken into account in performing the general tests for nondiscrimination in amount of contributions or benefits (see Qs 4:13, 4:18) must reflect the plan provisions that limit benefits in this manner.

[Rev. Rul. 2001-51, Q&A-15, 2001-2 C.B. 427]

Q 6:33 What happens if the employee's accrued benefit under a defined benefit plan exceeded the TRA '86 limitations?

If the defined benefit plan (see Q 2:3) was in existence on May 6, 1986, the employee was a participant as of the first day of the first plan year beginning after 1986, and the employee's accrued benefit (see Q 9:2) as of the end of the plan year beginning before 1987 exceeded the TRA '86 maximum allowable benefit, the higher accrued benefit is preserved. [TRA '86 § 1106(i); Ann. 95-99, 1995-48 I.R.B. 10] This will also be the case if the pre-TRA '86 accrued benefit exceeds the EGTRRA 2001 maximum allowable benefit (see Qs 6:11, 6:12).

Q 6:34 How much may the company contribute to a defined contribution plan on behalf of a participant?

The annual addition credited to the account of a participant in a defined contribution plan (see Q 2:2) for the limitation year (see Q 6:58) must not exceed the lesser of:

1. $40,000, as adjusted for cost-of-living increases (see Q 6:35), or
2. 100 percent of the participant's compensation (see Q 6:41) for the limitation year. [I.R.C. §§ 415(a)(1)(B), 415(c)(1); Treas. Reg. § 1.415(c)-1(a)(1)]

A defined contribution plan includes an annuity plan and a simplified employee pension (SEP; see Q 32:1). [I.R.C. §§ 403(a), 408(k), 415(k)(l); Treas. Reg. § 1.415(c)-1(a)(2)(i)] Contributions to the following arrangements are treated as contributions to a defined contribution plan:

1. Mandatory employee contributions to a defined benefit plan (see Q 6:15).
2. Contributions allocated to any individual medical benefit account that is part of a pension or annuity plan.
3. Amounts attributable to medical benefits allocated to an account established for a key employee (any employee who, at any time during the plan year or any preceding plan year, is or was a key employee; see Q 26:23). [I.R.C. §§ 401(h), 411(c)(2), 415(*l*), 419A(d); Treas. Reg. § 1.415(c)-1(a)(2)(ii); Priv. Ltr. Rul. 200718038]

Annual additions under a 403(b) plan (see Q 35:1) are treated as annual additions under a defined contribution plan. [Treas. Reg. § 1.415(c)-1(a)(2)(iii)]

The term "annual addition" means the sum, credited to a participant's account for any limitation year, of:

1. Employer contributions;
2. Employee contributions; and
3. Forfeitures.

[I.R.C. § 415(c)(2); Treas. Reg. § 1.415(c)-1(b)(1)(i)]

The annual addition limitation is best explained by an example:

Participant's compensation for 2010	$245,000
Employer contribution	45,000
Employee contribution	4,000
Forfeitures allocated to participant's account	2,000
Computation of annual addition	
Employer contribution	$ 45,000
Employee contribution	4,000
Forfeitures	2,000
Annual addition	$ 51,000

The total amount to be allocated to the participant under the defined contribution plan will be $51,000 unless it exceeds the limitation amount, which is the lesser of $40,000 (subject to cost-of-living adjustments) or 100 percent of the participant's compensation. Because the limitation for 2010 is $49,000, the annual addition of $51,000 exceeds the limitation amount. The contributions and other additions to this participant's account, therefore, may not exceed $49,000. If plan contributions allocated to the account of a participant exceed the annual addition limitation, the plan may lose its qualified status (see Qs 1:5, 6:57). [Van Roekel Farms, Inc. v. Comm'r, 2001 U.S. App. LEXIS 14201 (8th Cir. 2001); Howard E. Clendenen, Inc. v. Comm'r, 207 F.3d 1071 (8th Cir. 2000); Roblene, Inc., 77 T.C.M. 1998 (1999)] If a plan is disqualified because contributions allocated to the account of a participant exceeded the annual addition limitation, the disqualification continues until remedial action is taken. [Howard E. Clendenen, Inc., 85 T.C.M. 825 (2003)]

Contributions do not fail to be annual additions merely because they are excess contributions (see Q 27:25) or excess aggregate contributions (see Q 27:82), or merely because excess contributions or excess aggregate contributions are corrected through distribution (see Qs 27:26, 27:83). [Treas. Reg. § 1.415(c)-1(b)(1)(ii)] The direct transfer of a benefit or employee contributions from a qualified retirement plan to a defined contribution plan does not give rise to an annual addition. [Treas. Reg. § 1.415(c)-1(b)(1)(iii)] The reinvestment of dividends on employer securities under an employee stock ownership plan (ESOP; see Qs 28:1, 28:18) does not give rise to an annual addition. [Treas. Reg. § 1.415(c)-1(b)(1)(iv)]

An annual addition includes employer contributions credited to the participant's account for the limitation year and other allocations described below that are made during the limitation year. See Q 6:36 for timing rules applicable to annual additions with respect to employer contributions. [Treas. Reg. § 1.415(c)-1(b)(2)(i)]

The restoration of an employee's accrued benefit by the employer is not considered an annual addition for the limitation year in which the restoration occurs. This treatment of a restoration of an employee's accrued benefit as not giving rise to an annual addition applies regardless of whether the plan restricts the timing of repayments to the maximum extent allowed (see Qs 9:21, 9:22). [I.R.C. §§ 411(a)(3)(D), 411(a)(7)(C); Treas. Reg. § 1.415(c)-1(b)(2)(ii)(A)] A catch-up contribution (see Qs 27:52, 32:11, 33:11, 35:27) does not give rise to an annual addition. [I.R.C. § 414(v)(3)(A); Treas. Reg. § 1.415(c)-1(b)(2)(ii)(B)]

A restorative payment that is allocated to a participant's account does not give rise to an annual addition for any limitation year. For this purpose, restorative payments are payments made to restore losses to a plan resulting from actions by a fiduciary for which there is reasonable risk of liability for breach of a fiduciary duty under Title I of ERISA or under other applicable federal or state law, where plan participants who are similarly situated are treated similarly with respect to the payments. Generally, payments to a defined contribution plan are restorative payments only if the payments are made in order to restore some or all of the plan's losses due to an action (or a failure to act) that creates a reasonable risk of liability for such a breach of fiduciary duty (other than a breach of fiduciary duty arising from failure to remit contributions to the plan). This includes payments to a plan made pursuant to a Department of Labor (DOL) order, DOL's Voluntary Fiduciary Correction Program (see Q 19:36), or a court-approved settlement, to restore losses to a defined contribution plan on account of the breach of fiduciary duty (other than a breach of fiduciary duty arising from failure to remit contributions to the plan). Payments made to a plan to make up for losses due merely to market fluctuations and other payments that are not made on account of a reasonable risk of liability for breach of a fiduciary duty under Title I of ERISA are not restorative payments and generally constitute contributions that give rise to annual additions. [Treas. Reg. § 1.415(c)-1(b)(2)(ii)(C)] A shareholder in his capacity as an employee received a distribution from a qualified retirement plan and contributed the distribution to the plan to partially compensate other participants for losses caused by a trustee's embezzlement. IRS ruled that the contribution was a restorative payment, that the distribution was taxable to the shareholder-employee, and that the shareholder-employee was entitled to deduct the contribution as an ordinary and necessary business expense subject to the 2-percent-of-adjusted gross income floor. [Priv. Ltr. Rul. 200640003] IRS has ruled that a company's payment to a plan for the purpose of restoring to participants' accounts the amount of loss that would result from the imposition of surrender charges on the liquidation of annuity contracts would be treated as an employer contribution subject to the annual addition limitation, not as a restorative payment, because sufficient evidence was not presented to demonstrate a reasonable risk of liability to the company for a breach of fiduciary duty. [Priv. Ltr. Rul.

200317048] Conversely, where surrender charges and fees were improperly imposed under a group annuity contract when the employer elected to transfer all assets held under the contract to another investment medium and the employer sued and recovered the charges and fees, IRS ruled that the employer's contribution of the proceeds of the lawsuit to the plan was a replacement payment with the same consequences as a restorative payment. [Priv. Ltr. Rul. 200337017] For further details, see Q 12:2.

Excess deferrals that are distributed (see Q 27:63) do not give rise to annual additions. [Treas. Reg. § 1.415(c)-1(b)(2)(ii)(D)]

An annual addition includes mandatory employee contributions as well as voluntary contributions (see Q 6:37). However, an annual addition does not include:

1. Rollover contributions (see Q 34:1);
2. Repayments of loans made to a participant from the plan (see Q 14:1);
3. Repayments of distributions (see Q 9:22);
4. Repayments that would have been described in 3., except that the plan does not restrict the timing of repayments to the maximum extent permitted; or
5. Employee contributions to a qualified cost-of-living arrangement. [I.R.C. §§ 411(a)(7)(B), 415(k)(2); Treas. Reg. § 1.415(c)-1(b)(3)]

IRS may in an appropriate case, considering all of the facts and circumstances, treat transactions between the plan and the employer, transactions between the plan and the employee, or certain allocations to participants' accounts as giving rise to annual additions. Further, where an employee or employer transfers assets to a plan in exchange for consideration that is less than the fair market value of the assets transferred to the plan, there is an annual addition in the amount of the difference between the value of the assets transferred and the consideration. Such a transaction may constitute a prohibited transaction (see Q 24:1). [Treas. Reg. § 1.415(c)-1(b)(4)]

A contribution by the employer or employee of property rather than cash is considered to be a contribution in an amount equal to the fair market value of the property on the date the contribution is made. For this purpose, the fair market value is the price at which the property would change hands between a willing buyer and a willing seller, neither being under any compulsion to buy or to sell and both having reasonable knowledge of relevant facts. In addition, such a contribution may constitute a prohibited transaction (see Q 24:19). [Treas. Reg. § 1.415(c)-1(b)(5)]

> **Example 1.** P is a participant in a profit sharing plan maintained by P's employer, ABC Corporation. The limitation year for the plan is the calendar year. P's compensation for the current limitation year is $30,000. Because the compensation limitation applicable to P for the current limitation year is lower than the dollar limitation, the maximum annual addition that can be allocated to P's account for the current limitation year is $30,000 (100% × $30,000).

Example 2. The facts are the same as in Example 1, except that P's compensation for the current limitation year is $140,000. The maximum amount of annual additions that may be allocated to P's account in the current limitation year is the lesser of $140,000 (100 percent of P's compensation) or the dollar limitation as in effect as of January 1 of the calendar year in which the current limitation year ends. If, for example, the dollar limitation in effect as of January 1 of the calendar year in which the current limitation year ends is $49,000, then the maximum annual addition that can be allocated to P's account for the current limitation year is $49,000.

The limit of 100 percent of the participant's compensation for the limitation year does not apply to an individual medical account or a post-retirement medical benefit account for a key employee. [I.R.C. 415(*l*); Treas. Reg. § 1.415(c)-1(e)] For annual addition purposes, special rules apply to ESOPs (see Q 28:26).

All defined contribution plans of an employer are treated as a single plan (see Q 6:51). [I.R.C. § 415(f)(1)(B); Treas. Reg. § 1.415(f)-1(a)(2); Priv. Ltr. Rul. 9325055]

Example 3. In 2010, Mi Linda Amiga Corporation maintains both a 10-percent-of-compensation money purchase pension plan and a 15-percent-of-compensation profit sharing plan. Bob, who is a participant in both plans, earns $245,000. The contribution and other additions to Bob's accounts may not, in the aggregate, exceed $49,000 in the 2010 limitation year.

Where a corporation (Newco) was formed by the merger of six corporations (Oldcos), the plan adopted by Newco did not have to be aggregated with any plans of the Oldcos for contribution limitation purposes. [Priv. Ltr. Rul. 9541041]

Just because the limitation on contributions is satisfied for a limitation year does not mean that the employer's entire contribution to the plan will be deductible (see Q 12:17). However, the employer's tax-deductible contribution can be maximized by adopting a combined 401(k) plan (see Q 27:67).

Example 4. In 2011, Sandy, age 50, is the sole employee of I-Ra-Asher-Man Corporation, and the corporation adopts a profit sharing plan with a CODA (see Q 27:2). In 2011, Sandy has a salary of $116,000 after making an elective contribution (see Q 27:16) of $16,500 (see Q 27:51) and a catch-up contribution (see Q 27:52) of $5,500. Sandy's compensation for the year is $138,000 ($116,000 + $16,500 + $5,500; see Q 6:41), and the corporation makes a contribution to the plan of $32,500 for Sandy's benefit. Because the catch-up contribution is not considered for the annual addition limitation, Sandy's annual addition is $49,000 ($32,500 + $16,500) and does not exceed the limitation of the lesser of $49,000 or 100 percent of compensation. In addition, the entire $54,500 ($32,500 + $16,500 + $5,500) contributed to the plan in 2011 is deductible because elective and catch-up contributions are not considered employer contributions and are not subject to the employer deduction limitation relating to the 25-percent-of-compensation limitation for profit sharing plan contributions (see Q 12:15).

Example 5. The facts are the same as in Example 4, except that the annual addition limitation increases to $51,000 for the 2011 limitation year (see Q 6:35), but the elective and catch-up contributions do not increase for 2011. The corporation can now make a contribution to the plan of $34,500 for Sandy's benefit. Sandy's annual addition is $51,000 ($34,500 + $16,500), and the entire $56,500 ($34,500 + $16,500 + $5,500) is deductible. If the limitation on elective contributions increases to $17,000 in 2011 and Sandy makes an elective contribution of that amount, the corporation's contribution for Sandy's benefit will be limited to $34,000 because her annual addition cannot exceed $51,000 ($34,000 + $17,000).

All employees of corporations that are members of a controlled group of corporations (see Q 5:31) are treated as if they were employed by a single employer. A comparable requirement applies to partnerships, sole proprietorships, and other businesses that are under common control (see Q 5:29). [I.R.C. §§ 414(b), 414(c)] However, a special rule applies to parent-subsidiary relationships for benefit and contribution limitation purposes. Under this special rule, a controlled group or commonly controlled group exists if there is a parent-subsidiary group connected through more than 50 percent ownership (see Q 6:7). [I.R.C. § 415(h)]

Example 6. Steve is the 100 percent shareholder of Ess-Jay-Kay Corporation, which corporation is a 70 percent shareholder of Ess-W-Kay Corporation. Steve is employed by both corporations, each corporation maintains a defined contribution plan, and Steve participates in both plans. For limitation purposes only, Steve is deemed to be employed by a single corporation, and his aggregate annual addition under both plans cannot exceed the lesser of $40,000 (subject to cost-of-living adjustments) or 100 percent of his compensation.

IRS representatives have opined that, if an individual is a sole proprietor and also owns 70 percent of the shares of stock of a corporation, the two entities would constitute a brother-sister group, not a parent-subsidiary group, and so the special rule would not apply.

IRS has instructed its agents to review the following when auditing a defined contribution plan:

1. Determine all defined contribution plans and defined benefit plans (see Q 2:3) that are currently maintained by the employer or have ever been maintained by the employer, along with their effective dates and earliest participation dates.
2. Determine whether the employer is a member of: (a) a controlled group of corporations; (b) trades or businesses (whether or not incorporated) under common control; or (c) an affiliated service group (see Q 5:35).
3. Determine the limitation year for each plan.
4. If the limitation year has been changed and a short limitation year is created, has a prorated dollar limitation been used for the short limitation year, and has compensation earned during the short limitation year been used (see Q 6:58)?

5. Determine whether the limitations on annual additions are tested using the sum of the annual additions for all defined contribution plans of the employer, including features of plans that are treated as defined contribution plans, such as employee contributions under contributory defined benefit plans (see Q 6:15), and all defined contribution plans of any other employer(s) that are treated along with the employer's plan(s) as a single plan.

6. Are contributions allocated to any individual medical account that is part of a pension or annuity plan treated as an annual addition to a defined contribution plan?

7. Are amounts attributable to medical benefits allocated to accounts for postretirement medical benefits provided to key employees treated as an annual addition to a defined contribution plan?

8. Are all employees tested for satisfaction of the limitation on annual additions using the correct definition of compensation (see Q 6:41)?

9. Is a Section 415 definition of compensation (see Q 6:41) used under the plan for purposes of determining whether the limitations have been exceeded?

10. Does the plan specify which definition is used for purposes of determining compensation (see Q 6:41)?

11. Is the employee's compensation from all members of a controlled group (see item 2) taken into account?

12. Does the plan specify the method that will be used when excess annual additions result from the allocation of forfeitures, a reasonable error in estimating a participant's annual compensation, or a reasonable error in determining the amount of elective contributions (see Q 27:16) that may be made?

13. Was the method of correction (see item 12) justified?

14. Where elective or employee contributions are returned to the extent necessary to reduce excess annual additions, does the plan provide for such returns?

[Employee Plans Examination Guidelines Handbook ch. 7]

See Q 6:36 for a discussion of the timing rules.

Q 6:35 Will the dollar limitation on the annual addition rise?

The $40,000 annual addition limit (see Q 6:34) is adjusted annually to take into account increases in the cost of living, and the adjusted dollar limitation is published each year by IRS. [I.R.C. §§ 415(c)(1)(A), 415(d)(1)(C); Treas. Reg. § 1.415(d)-1(b)(1)]

The base period taken into account for purposes of adjusting the dollar limitation is the calendar quarter beginning July 1, 2001. The dollar limitation is adjusted with respect to the calendar year based on the increase in the applicable index for the calendar quarter ending September 30 of the preceding calendar year over such index for the base period. Adjustment procedures similar to the procedures used to adjust Social Security benefits are used. Any increase in the $40,000 amount that is not a multiple of $1,000 is rounded to the next lowest multiple of $1,000. The adjusted dollar limitation applicable to defined contribution plans is effective as of January 1 of each calendar year and applies with respect to limitation years. (see Q 6:58) ending with or within that calendar year. Annual additions for a limitation year cannot exceed the currently applicable dollar limitation (as in effect before the January 1 adjustment) prior to January 1. However, after a January 1 adjustment is made, annual additions for the entire limitation year are permitted to reflect the dollar limitation as adjusted on January 1. [I.R.C. §§ 415(d)(2), 415(d)(3)(D), 415(d)(4); Treas. Reg. § 1.415(d)-1(b)(2)]

For limitation years ending in 2010, the dollar limitation remained at $49,000. [IRS Notice 2009-94, 2009-2 C.B. 848] For the five limitation years ended prior to 2010, the adjusted dollar limitation was:

Limitation Year Ending in	Adjusted Limit
2009	$49,000
2008	46,000
2007	45,000
2006	44,000
2005	42,000

Example. Assume that the dollar limitation increases from $49,000 in 2010 to $51,000 in 2011. Doctor Ric Corporation maintains a 25-percent-of-compensation defined contribution plan with a plan year beginning on February 1 and ending on January 31. The limitation year is the same as the plan year; and Eric and Maria, who are participants in the plan, both have compensation of $245,000 for the limitation year ended January 31, 2011. The maximum annual additional for both Eric and Maria for the limitation year ended January 31, 2011 is $51,000 even though the limitation year began in 2010.

A plan is permitted to be amended to reflect any of the cost-of-living adjustments at any time after those limitations become applicable. Alternatively, a plan is permitted to incorporate by reference any of the adjustments (see Q 6:5). [Treas. Reg. § 1.415(d)-1(d)]

Q 6:36 When is an annual addition deemed credited to a participant's account?

An annual addition (see Q 6:34) is credited to the account of a participant for a particular limitation year (see Q 6:58) if it is allocated to the participant's account under the terms of the plan as of any date within that limitation year.

Similarly, an annual addition that is made pursuant to a corrective amendment (see Q 4:20) is credited to the account of a participant for a particular limitation year if it is allocated to the participant's account under the terms of the corrective amendment as of any date within that limitation year. However, if the allocation of an annual addition is dependent upon the satisfaction of a condition (such as continued employment or the occurrence of an event) that has not been satisfied by the date as of which the annual addition is allocated under the terms of the plan, then the annual addition is considered allocated as of the date the condition is satisfied. [Treas. Reg. § 1.415(c)-1(b)(6)(i)(A)]

Employer contributions are not treated as credited to a participant's account for a particular limitation year unless the contributions are actually made to the plan no later than 30 days after the end of the period during which contributions must be made to be currently deductible (see Q 12:3) with respect to the taxable year with or within which the particular limitation year ends. If, however contributions are made by an employer exempt from federal income tax, the contributions must be made to the plan no later than the 15th day of the tenth calendar month following the end of the calendar year or fiscal year (as applicable, depending on the basis on which the employer keeps its books) with or within which the particular limitation year ends. If contributions are made to a plan after the end of the period during which contributions can be made and treated as credited to a participant's account for a particular limitation year, allocations attributable to those contributions are treated as credited to the participant's account for the limitation year during which those contributions are made. [Treas. Reg. § 1.415(c)-1(b)(6)(i)(B)]

Employee contributions, whether voluntary or mandatory (see Q 6:34), are not treated as credited to a participant's account for a particular limitation year unless the contributions are actually made to the plan no later than 30 days after the close of that limitation year. [Treas. Reg. § 1.415(c)-1(b)(6)(i)] A forfeiture is treated as an annual addition for the limitation year that contains the date as of which it is allocated to a participant's account as a forfeiture. [Treas. Reg. § 1.415(c)-1(b)(6)(i)(D)] The extent to which elective contributions constitute plan assets for purposes of the prohibited transaction provisions is determined in accordance with DOL regulations and rulings (see Q 23:32). [Treas. Reg. § 1.415(c)-1(b)(6)(i)(E)]

If, in a particular limitation year, an employer allocates an amount to a participant's account because of an erroneous forfeiture in a prior limitation year or because of an erroneous failure to allocate amounts in a prior limitation year, the corrective allocation will not be considered an annual addition with respect to the participant for that particular limitation year, but will be considered an annual addition for the prior limitation year to which it relates. An example of a situation in which an employer contribution might occur under the circumstances described in the preceding sentence is a retroactive crediting of service for an employee in accordance with an award of back pay. If the amount so contributed in the particular limitation year takes into account actual investment gains attributable to the period subsequent to the year to which the contribution relates, the portion of the total contribution that consists of such gains is not considered as an annual addition for any limitation year. [Treas. Reg. § 1.415(c)-1(b)(6)(ii)(A)]

In the case of a defined contribution plan to which the minimum funding rules apply (see Q 8:1), a contribution made to reduce an accumulated funding deficiency will be treated as if it were timely made for purposes of determining the limitation year in which the annual additions arising from the contribution are made, but only if the contribution is allocated to those participants who would have received an annual addition if the contribution had been timely made. In the case of a defined contribution plan to which the rules apply and for which there has been a waiver of the minimum funding standards (see Q 8:24) in a prior limitation year, that portion of an employer contribution in a subsequent limitation year which, if not for the waiver, would have otherwise been required in the prior limitation year will be treated as if it were timely made (without regard to the funding waiver) for purposes of determining the limitation year in which the annual additions arising from the contribution are made, but only if the contribution is allocated to those participants who would have received an annual addition if the contribution had been timely made (without regard to the funding waiver). For these purposes, a reasonable amount of interest paid by the employer is disregarded. However, any interest paid by the employer that is in excess of a reasonable amount, as determined by IRS, is taken into account as an annual addition for the limitation year during which the contribution is made. [Treas. Reg. § 1.415(c)-1(b)(6)(ii)(B)]

If, in a particular limitation year, an employer contributes an amount to an employee's account with respect to a prior limitation year and such contribution is required by reason of such employee's rights resulting from qualified military service (see Q 1:16), then such contribution is not considered an annual addition with respect to the employee for that particular limitation year in which the contribution is made, but is considered an annual addition for the limitation year to which the contribution relates. [Treas. Reg. § 1.415(c)-1(b)(6)(ii)(D)]

Example 1. Employer N maintains a profit sharing plan that uses the calendar year as its plan year and its limitation year. N's taxable year is a fiscal year beginning June 1 and ending May 31. Under the terms of the profit sharing plan maintained by N, employer contributions are made to the plan two months after the close of N's taxable year and are allocated as of the last day of the plan year ending within the taxable year (and are not dependent on the satisfaction of a condition). Thus, employer contributions for the 2009 calendar year limitation year are made on July 31, 2010 (the date that is two months after the close of N's taxable year ending May 31, 2010) and are allocated as of December 31, 2009.

Because the employer contributions are actually made to the plan no later than 30 days after the end of the period with respect to N's taxable year ending May 31, 2010, the contributions will be considered annual additions for the 2009 calendar year limitation year.

Example 2. The facts are the same as in Example 1, except that the plan year for the profit sharing plan maintained by N is a 12-month period beginning on

February 1 and ending on January 31. The limitation year continues to be the calendar year. Under the terms of the plan, an employer contribution that is made to the plan on July 31, 2010 is allocated to participants' accounts of January 31, 2010.

Because the last day of the plan year is in the 2010 calendar year limitation year and because, under the terms of the plan, employer contributions are allocated to participants' accounts as of the last day of the plan year, the contributions are considered annual additions for the 2010 calendar year limitation year.

Example 3. XYZ Corporation maintains a profit sharing plan to which a participant may make voluntary employee contributions for any year not to exceed 10 percent of the participant's compensation for the year. The plan permits a participant to make retroactive make-up contributions for any year for which the participant contributed less than 10 percent of compensation. XYZ uses the calendar year as the plan year and the limitation year. Under the terms of the plan, voluntary employee contributions are credited to a participant's account for a particular limitation year if such contributions are allocated to the participant's account as of any date within that limitation year. Participant A makes no voluntary employee contributions during limitation years 2008, 2009, and 2010. On October 1, 2011, participant A makes a contribution of $13,200 (10 percent of A's aggregate compensation for limitation years 2008, 2009, 2010, and 2011 of $132,000). Under the terms of the plan, $3,000 of this 2011 contribution is allocated to A's account as of limitation year 2008; $3,200 is allocated to A's account as of limitation year 2009; $3,400 is allocated to A's account as of limitation year 2010; and $3,600 is allocated to A's account as of limitation year 2011.

Employee contributions will not be considered credited to a participant's account for a particular limitation unless the contributions are actually made to the plan no later than 30 years after the close of that limitation year. Thus, A's voluntary employee contribution of $13,200 made on October 1, 2011 would be considered as credited to A's account only for the 2011 calendar year limitation year, notwithstanding the plan provisions.

Q 6:37 What limits apply to employee contributions required under a qualified retirement plan?

A special nondiscrimination test, the actual contribution percentage (ACP) test, applies to required (i.e., mandatory) employee contributions under all qualified defined contribution plans (see Qs 2:2, 27:73–27:88). If the plan satisfies the special requirements regarding such employee contributions, the plan will not be discriminatory. [Treas. Reg. § 1.401(a)(4)-1(b)(2)(ii)(B)]

Since a defined benefit plan does not separately account for required employee contributions (such contributions are not allocated or credited to separate accounts), the special nondiscrimination test does not apply, but the plan will generally be deemed nondiscriminatory only if such employee contributions are made at the same rate, expressed as a percentage of compensation, by all employees under the plan. [Treas. Reg. § 1.401(a)(4)-6]

If required employee contributions are so burdensome that non-highly compensated employees (NHCEs; see Q 3:12) cannot afford to participate, the plan may fail to satisfy the coverage requirements (see chapter 5) and not be a qualified retirement plan.

Required employee contributions made to a defined contribution plan are considered employee contributions that must satisfy the annual addition limitation (see Qs 6:15, 6:34).

See Q 34:2 relating to rollovers of employee after-tax contributions.

Q 6:38   Is any limit set on the amount that a participant can voluntarily contribute to a qualified retirement plan?

The same special nondiscrimination test (see Q 6:37) applies to employee voluntary contributions. Since employee voluntary contributions under a defined benefit plan (see Q 2:3) will be separately accounted for, there is no limit on the amount of employee voluntary contributions made to either a defined contribution plan (see Q 2:2) or a defined benefit plan as long as the ACP test and other special requirements are satisfied (see Qs 27:73–27:88).

However, under all circumstances, whether the employee voluntary contributions are made to a defined contribution plan or a defined benefit plan, these contributions are considered employee contributions that must satisfy the annual addition limitation (see Q 6:34).

If employee voluntary contributions are withdrawn and then replaced during the same limitation year (see Q 6:58), they are treated as part of the annual addition.

Example. Sallie makes employee voluntary contributions of $3,000 in January 2011 and withdraws $2,000 in June. If she replaces the $2,000 within the same limitation year of the $3,000 contribution, she will be deemed to have made a total of $5,000 of employee voluntary contributions. [Priv. Ltr. Rul. 8622044]

Q 6:39   What tax advantages are gained when a qualified retirement plan permits participants to make voluntary contributions?

Although participants cannot deduct their voluntary contributions to the plan, they do get the advantage of having their contributions build up free of tax under the protection of the qualified retirement plan's tax shelter (see Qs 1:1, 1:6).

See Q 34:2 relating to rollovers of employee after-tax contributions.

Q 6:40   May a qualified retirement plan permit deductible employee contributions?

The law permitting deductible employee contributions was repealed. [TRA '86 § 1101(b)]

Although deductible employee contributions are no longer permitted, separate accounting by the employer or plan administrator (see Q 20:1) is required with respect to any such contributions that were ever made to the plan to ensure that an employee who later receives a distribution from the plan is able to compute the tax due correctly. However, assets purchased by the plan with deductible employee contributions need not be segregated from other plan assets. [IRS Notice 82-13, 1982-1 C.B. 360]

Distributions of deductible employee contributions (including earnings) are taxed as ordinary income in the year received unless they are rolled over (that is, transferred tax free) to an IRA or to another qualified retirement plan. Distributions of deductible employee contributions may also be subject to the early distribution tax (see chapter 16).

See Qs 30:36 and 31:24 relating to deemed IRAs and deemed Roth IRAs.

Q 6:41   What does compensation mean for purposes of the limitations on benefits and contributions?

For purposes of the limitations on the annual benefit (see Q 6:11) and the annual addition (see Q 6:34), compensation is the total compensation received from the employer for the limitation year (see Q 6:58). For a self-employed individual (see Q 6:60), compensation generally means earned income (see Q 6:61). This is commonly referred to as Section 415 compensation. [I.R.C. §§ 415(c)(3)(A), 415(c)(3)(B); Treas. Reg. § 1.415(c)-2(a)]

The term "compensation" means remuneration for services of the following types:

1. The employee's wages, salaries, fees for professional services, and other amounts received (without regard to whether or not an amount is paid in cash) for personal services actually rendered in the course of employment with the employer maintaining the plan, to the extent that the amounts are includible in gross income (or to the extent amounts would have been received and includible in gross income but for an election). These amounts include, but are not limited to, commissions paid to salespersons, compensation for services on the basis of a percentage of profits, commissions on insurance premiums, tips, bonuses, fringe benefits, and reimbursements or other expense allowances under a nonaccountable plan.

2. In the case of a self-employed individual, the employee's earned income, plus amounts deferred at the election of the employee that would be includible in gross income but for an election.

3. Amounts described in Section 104(a)(3), 105(a), or 105(h), but only to the extent that these amounts are includible in the gross income of the employee.

4. Amounts paid or reimbursed by the employer for moving expenses incurred by an employee, but only to the extent that at the time of the payment it is reasonable to believe that these amounts are not deductible by the employee.

5. The value of a nonstatutory option (which is an option other than a statutory option) granted to an employee by the employer, but only to the extent that the value of the option is includible in the gross income of the employee for the taxable year in which granted.

6. The amount includible in the gross income of an employee upon making the election described in Section 83(b).

7. Amounts that are includible in the gross income of an employee under the rules of Section 409A or 457(f)(1)(A) or because the amounts are constructively received by the employee. [I.R.C. § 415(c)(3); Treas. Reg. § 1.415(c)-2(b)]

Compensation does not include:

1. Contributions (other than elective contributions) made by the employer to a plan of deferred compensation (including a SEP (see Q 32:1) or a SIMPLE retirement account (see Q 33:2), and whether or not qualified) to the extent that the contributions are not includible in the gross income of the employee for the taxable year in which contributed. In addition, any distributions from a plan of deferred compensation (whether or not qualified) are not considered as compensation, regardless of whether such amounts are includible in the gross income of the employee when distributed. However, if the plan so provides, any amounts received by an employee pursuant to a nonqualified unfunded deferred compensation plan are permitted to be considered as compensation in the year the amounts are actually received, but only to the extent such amounts are includible in the employee's gross income.

2. Amounts realized from the exercise of a nonstatutory option or when restricted stock or other property held by an employee either becomes freely transferable or is no longer subject to a substantial risk of forfeiture.

3. Amounts realized from the sale, exchange, or other disposition of stock acquired under a statutory stock option.

4. Other amounts that receive special tax benefits, such as premiums for group-term life insurance (but only to the extent that the premiums are not includible in the gross income of the employee and are not salary reduction amounts).

5. Other items of remuneration that are similar to any of the items listed in paragraphs 1. through 4. [Treas. Reg. § 1.415(c)-2(c)]

See Q 6:44 for special rules that apply to the determination of compensation. The annual compensation of an employee taken into account under a qualified retirement plan may not exceed $200,000, with adjustments for inflation. For details, see Qs 6:45 through 6:50.

Q 6:42　Are there safe harbor rules regarding a plan's definition of compensation?

There are safe harbor definitions of compensation that are automatically considered to satisfy Section 415(c)(3) if specified in the plan. IRS may provide additional definitions of compensation that are treated as satisfying Section 415(c)(3). [Treas. Reg. § 1.415(c)-2(d)(1)]

The first safe harbor definition of compensation includes only those items of includible compensation listed in paragraphs 1. and 2. of Q 6:41 and excludes all of the items of excludable compensation listed in Q 6:41. [Treas. Reg. § 1.415(c)-2(d)(2)]

The second safe harbor definition of compensation includes wages within the meaning of Section 3401(a) (for purposes of income tax withholding at the source), plus amounts that would be included in wages but for an election. However, any rules that limit the remuneration included in wages based on the nature or location of the employment or the services performed (such as the exception for agricultural labor in Section 3401(a)(2)) are disregarded for this purpose. [Treas. Reg. § 1.415(c)-2(d)(3)]

The third and last safe harbor includes amounts that are compensation under the second safe harbor definition, plus all other payments of compensation to an employee by the employer (in the course of the employer's trade or business) for which the employer is required to furnish the employee a Form 1099, Form W-2, or a statement regarding payment of wages in the form of group-term life insurance. This safe harbor definition of compensation may be modified to exclude amounts paid or reimbursed by the employer for moving expenses incurred by an employee, but only to the extent that, at the time of the payment, it is reasonable to believe that these amounts are deductible by the employee. [I.R.C. §§ 6041(d), 6051(a)(3), 6052; Treas. Reg. § 1.415(c)-2(d)(4)]

Q 6:43　When must compensation be paid to be taken into account for a limitation year?

In order to be taken into account for a limitation year (see Q 6:58), Section 415 compensation (see Qs 6:41, 6:42) must be actually paid or made available to an employee (or, if earlier, includible in the gross income of the employee) within the limitation year. For this purpose, compensation is treated as paid on a date if it is actually paid on that date or it would have been paid on that date but for an election, such as an election to defer under a 401(k) plan (see Q 27:1). In addition, the compensation must be paid or treated as paid to the employee prior to the employee's severance from employment (see Q 6:8) with the employer maintaining the plan. [Treas. Reg. § 1.415(c)-2(e)(1)]

A plan may provide that compensation for a limitation year includes amounts earned during that limitation year but not paid during that limitation year solely because of the timing of pay periods and pay dates if (1) these amounts are paid during the first few weeks of the next limitation year; (2) the amounts are included on a uniform and consistent basis with respect to all similarly situated employees; and (3) no compensation is included in more than one limitation year. [Treas. Reg. § 1.415(c)-2(e)(2)]

Regular pay after severance from employment does not fail to be Section 415 compensation merely because it is paid after the employee's severance from employment with the employer maintaining the plan, provided the compensation is paid by the later of 2-1/2 months after severance from employment with the employer maintaining the plan or the end of the limitation year that includes the date of severance from employment with the employer maintaining the plan. Such pay is included if the payment is regular compensation for services during the employee's regular working hours, or compensation for services outside the employee's regular working hours (such as overtime or shift differential), commissions, bonuses, or other similar payments, and the payment would have been paid to the employee prior to a severance from employment if the employee had continued in employment with the employer. [Treas. Reg. §§ 1.415(c)-2(e)(3)(i), 1.415(c)-2(e)(3)(ii)]

In addition, with regard to leave cashouts and deferred compensation, the plan may provide that such amounts are included in Section 415 compensation if those amounts are paid by the later of 2-1/2 months after severance from employment with the employer maintaining the plan or the end of the limitation year that includes the date of severance from employment with the employer maintaining the plan, and those amounts would have been included in the definition of compensation if they were paid prior to the employee's severance from employment with the employer maintaining the plan. To be included, such amounts must either be payment for unused accrued bona fide sick, vacation, or other leave, but only if the employee would have been able to use the leave if employment had continued, or received by an employee pursuant to a nonqualified unfunded deferred compensation plan, but only if the payment would have been paid to the employee at the same time if the employee had continued in employment with the employer and only to the extent that the payment is includible in the employee's gross income. [Treas. Reg. §§ 1.415(c)-2(a)(3)(i), 1.415(c)-2(e)(3)(iii)]

Any payment that is not described above is not considered compensation if paid after severance from employment with the employer maintaining the plan, even if it is paid within the above-described time period. Thus, compensation does not include severance pay, or parachute payments, if they are paid after severance from employment with the employer maintaining the plan, and does not include post-severance payments under a nonqualified unfunded deferred compensation plan unless the payments would have been paid at that time without regard to the severance from employment. [Treas. Reg. § 1.415(c)-2(e)(3)(iv)]

The above rules do not apply to payments to an individual who does not currently perform services for the employer by reason of qualified military service (see Q 1:16) to the extent those payments do not exceed the amounts the individual would have received if the individual had continued to perform services for the employer rather than entering qualified military service, but only if the plan so provides. In addition, the rules do not apply to compensation paid to a participant who is permanently and totally disabled if the conditions set forth in Q 6:44 are satisfied (applied by substituting a continuation of compensation for the continuation of contributions), but only if the plan so provides. [Treas. Reg. § 1.415(c)-2(e)(4)]

> **Example 1.** Participant A was a common law employee of Employer X, performing services as a script writer for Employer X from January 1, 2008 to December 31, 2008. Pursuant to a collective bargaining agreement, Employer X, Employer Y, and Employer Z maintain and contribute to Plan T, a multiemployer plan (see Q 29:2) in which Participant A participates. Under the collective bargaining agreement, Participant A is entitled to residual payments whenever television shows that Participant A wrote are reused commercially (these residual payments constitute compensation). In the year 2011, Participant A receives residual payments from Employer X for television programs using the scripts that Participant A wrote in the year 2008 that were rebroadcast in the year 2011. In the years 2009, 2010, and 2011, Participant A was a common law employee of Employer Y and did not perform any services for Employer X.

The residual payments received from Employer X by Participant A in the year 2011 are Section 415 compensation. The payments are not treated as made after severance from employment, because Plan T is a multiemployer plan and Participant A continues to be employed by an employer maintaining Plan T.

> **Example 2.** The facts are the same as in Example 1, except that Participant A ceases employment with Employer Y in the year 2009; subsequently moved away from the area in which A formerly worked; performs no services as an employee for any employer; and commenced receiving distributions under Plan T in March 2009.

Based on facts and circumstances, Participant A has ceased employment with any employer maintaining Plan T. Because compensation must be paid prior to an employee's severance from employment with the employer maintaining the plan, the residual payments received by Participant A in the year 2011 are not Section 415 compensation.

Q 6:44 Are there special rules that apply to the determination of compensation?

In the case of an employee of two or more corporations that are members of a controlled group of corporations (see Q 5:31), compensation for such employee includes compensation from all employers that are members of the group, regardless of whether the employee's particular employer has a qualified retirement plan. This special rule is also applicable to an employee of two or more trades or businesses (whether or not incorporated) that are under common control (see Q 5:29), to an employee of two or more members of an affiliated service group (see Q 5:35), and to an employee of two or more members of any group of employers that must be aggregated and treated as one employer pursuant to Section 414(o). [Treas. Reg. § 1.415(c)-2(g)(2)]

If a 403(b) plan (see Q 35:1) is aggregated with a qualified retirement plan of a controlled employer (see Q 6:51), then, in applying the annual addition limitations (see Q 6:34) in connection with the aggregation of the 403(b) plan with a retirement plan, the total compensation from both employers is permitted to be taken into account. [Treas. Reg. § 1.415(c)-2(g)(3)]

If the conditions set forth in this paragraph are satisfied, then, in the case of a participant in any defined contribution plan (see Q 2:2) who is permanently and totally disabled, the participant's compensation is the compensation the participant would have received for the year if the participant had been paid at the rate of compensation paid immediately before becoming permanently and totally disabled, if such compensation is greater than the participant's compensation determined without regard to this paragraph. This rule applies only if the following conditions are satisfied:

1. Either the participant is not a highly compensation employee (HCE; see Q 3:2) immediately before becoming disabled, or the plan provides for the continuation of contributions on behalf of all participants who are permanently and totally disabled for a fixed or determinable period;

2. The plan provides that the rule treating certain amounts as compensation for a disabled participant applies with respect to the participant; and

3. Contributions made with respect to amounts treated as compensation are nonforfeitable when made. [Treas. Reg. § 1.415(c)-2(g)(4)]

Amounts paid to an individual as compensation for services do not fail to be treated as Section 415 compensation (see Qs 6:41, 6:42) merely because those amounts are not includible in the individual's gross income on account of the location of the services. Similarly, compensation for services does not fail to be treated as Section 415 compensation merely because those amounts are paid by an employer with respect to which all compensation paid to the participant by such employer is excluded from gross income. Thus, for example, the determination of whether an amount is treated as Section 415 compensation is made without regard to the exclusions from gross income under Sections 872, 893, 894, 911, 931, and 933. With respect to a nonresident alien who is not a participant in a plan, the plan may provide that the compensation described in this paragraph is not treated as compensation to the extent the compensation is excludable from gross income and is not effectively connected with the conduct of a trade or business within the United States, but only if the plan applies this rule uniformly to all such employees. [I.R.C. § 7701(b)(1)(B); Treas. Reg. § 1.415(c)-2(g)(5)]

A plan is permitted to provide that deemed Section 125 compensation is Section 415 compensation, but only if the plan applies this rule uniformly to all employees with respect to whom amounts subject to Section 125 (i.e., cafeteria plans) are included in compensation. Deemed Section 125 compensation is an amount that is excludable from the income of the participant under Section 106 and that is not available to the participant in cash in lieu of group health coverage under a Section 125 arrangement solely because that participant is not able to certify that the participant has other health coverage. Under this definition, amounts are deemed Section 125 compensation only if the employer does not otherwise request or collect information regarding the participant's other health coverage as part of the enrollment process for the health plan. [Treas. Reg. § 1.415(c)-2(g)(6)]

Payments awarded by an administrative agency or court or pursuant to a bona fide agreement by an employer to compensate an employee for lost wages are Section 415 compensation for the limitation year to which the back pay relates, but only to the extent such payments represent wages and compensation that would otherwise be included in compensation. [Treas. Reg. § 1.415(c)-2(g)(8)]

See Q 1:16 for special rules regarding compensation of employees who are in qualified military service.

Q 6:45   Is there an annual compensation limit under a qualified retirement plan?

Yes. For each employee who participates in a qualified retirement plan, an annual limit on compensation is required. [I.R.C. § 401(a)(17); Treas. Reg. § 1.401(a)(17)-1]

This limit applies to a qualified retirement plan in two ways. First, a plan may not base allocations, in the case of a defined contribution plan (see Q 6:34), or benefits, in the case of a defined benefit plan (see Q 6:11), on compensation in excess of the annual limit. Second, the amount of an employee's annual compensation that may be taken into account in applying certain specified nondiscrimination rules is subject to the annual limitation. [Treas. Reg. §§ 1.401(a)(17)-1(a)(1), 1.415(c)-2(f)]

The annual compensation limit is $200,000, adjusted for cost-of-living increases (see Q 6:46), for plan years beginning after 2001. [I.R.C. § 401(a)(17)] For plan years beginning after 1993 and before 2002, the annual compensation limit was $150,000, adjusted for cost-of-living increases (see Qs 6:46, 6:50).

Q 6:46   Will the limit on annual compensation rise?

The amount of the annual limit, $200,000 (see Q 6:45), is adjusted for increases in the cost of living. However, an adjustment will be made only if it is $5,000 or greater and then will be made in multiples of $5,000 (i.e., rounded down to the next lowest multiple of $5,000). For example, an increase in the cost of living of $4,999 will result in no adjustment, and an increase of $9,999 will create an upward adjustment of $5,000. [I.R.C. §§ 401(a)(17); Treas. Reg. § 1.401(a)(17)-1(a)(3)]

To calculate the cost-of-living increase for any particular year, the CPI-U must be obtained from DOL for the calendar quarter beginning July 1 of the previous year. The sum of the three indices is then compared to the sum of the indices for the calendar quarter beginning July 1, 2001. The quotient of these sums is rounded to four decimal places. This result is multiplied by the $200,000 limitation. Finally, if this result is an even multiple of $5,000, the result obtained is the new dollar limitation; otherwise, the result is rounded to the next lowest multiple of $5,000 to obtain the new dollar limitation.

For plan years that begin in 2010, the $200,000 compensation cap remained at $245,000. [IRS Notice 2009-94, 2009-2 C.B. 848] For plan years that began in 2001, the $150,000 compensation cap, as adjusted, was $170,000. [IRS Notice 2000-66, 2000-2 C.B. 600] For the five years prior to 2010, the compensation limits were as follows:

Year	Compensation Limit
2009	$245,000
2008	230,000
2007	225,000
2006	220,000
2005	210,000

The adjustment applies to plan years *beginning* in the calendar year in which the adjustment is effective. In addition, except for plan years that began in 2002, any increase in the annual limit applies only to compensation taken into account for the year of the increase and subsequent years and does not apply to compensation for prior years that are used in determining an employee's benefit (see Q 6:50). [Treas. Reg. § 1.401(a)(17)-1(b)]

Example. C & A Corp. maintains a defined contribution plan with a plan year beginning on July 1 and ending on June 30. For the plan year ended June 30, 2011, Caroline's compensation is $260,000. Because the plan year began in 2010, the annual compensation limit in effect on January 1, 2010 ($245,000) applies to the plan for the entire plan year and Caroline's excess compensation of $15,000 ($260,000 − $245,000) has to be disregarded.

Q 6:47 Can a qualified retirement plan use a 12-month period other than the plan year to determine compensation?

Yes. Alternatively, a qualified retirement plan may determine compensation used in computing allocations or benefit accruals for the plan year for all employees on the basis of a 12-consecutive-month period (or periods) ending no later than the last day of the plan year. If compensation is based on these alternative 12-month periods, the annual compensation limit (see Qs 6:45, 6:46) applies to compensation for each of those periods based on the annual compensation limit in effect for the respective calendar year in which each 12-month period begins (see Q 6:50). [Treas. Reg. § 1.401(a)(17)-1(b)(3)(ii)]

If compensation for a period of less than 12 months is used for a plan year, then the otherwise applicable annual compensation limit is reduced in the same proportion as the reduction in the 12-month period. Furthermore, if the period for determining compensation used in calculating an employee's allocation or accrual for a plan year is a short plan year (i.e., shorter than 12 months), the annual compensation limit is an amount equal to the otherwise applicable annual compensation limit multiplied by the fraction, the numerator of which is the number of months in the short plan year and the denominator of which is 12. [Treas. Reg. § 1.401(a)(17)-1(b)(3)(iii)(A)]

> **Example 1.** B & S Corp. adopts a profit sharing plan on October 1, 2010, and the first plan year is the short period of October 1, 2010 to December 31, 2010. Barbra's compensation from B & S Corp. for calendar year 2010 is $245,000. The annual compensation limit for the plan for the short period is $61,250 (3/12 × $245,000), and Barbra's excess compensation of $183,750 ($245,000 − $61,250) is disregarded.

However, no proration is required if the plan formula provides that the allocation or accrual for each employee is based on compensation for the portion of the plan year during which the employee is a participant. [Treas. Reg. § 1.401(a)(17)-1(b)(3)(iii)(B)]

> **Example 2.** S & B Corp. adopts a calendar year profit sharing plan on January 1, 2010. Barbra, whose compensation is $25,000 per month, commences participation in the plan on July 1, 2010. For purposes of allocating employer contributions, only compensation earned after an employee becomes a participant is used. Barbra's entire compensation of $150,000 earned from July 1, 2010 to December 31, 2010 may be used because there is no proration of the annual compensation limit.

Q 6:48 How is the annual compensation limit applied if an employee participates in a qualified retirement plan sponsored by more than one employer?

If the employers are part of a controlled group or an affiliated service group (see Qs 5:29, 5:31, 5:35), the annual compensation limit (see Q 6:45) is applied on an aggregate basis to compensation received from all members of the group; but, if the employers are not related, the annual compensation limit applies separately with respect to the compensation received by an employee from each unrelated employer maintaining the plan rather than to the total compensation from all employers maintaining the plan. [I.R.C. §§ 413(c), 414(b), 414(c), 414(m); Treas. Reg. § 1.401(a)(17)-1(b)(4)]

> **Example.** Maxine Corp., Sooper-Max Inc., and Maxfly Ltd., which are each unrelated to the others, all adopt a single 25-percent-of-compensation profit sharing plan for calendar year 2010. Bob is employed by all three corporations and has compensation from each of $196,000. The plan is permitted to take into account the full $588,000 of Bob's compensation from the three corporations for the plan year without violating the annual compensation limit.

Although compensation need not be aggregated in the above example, for purposes of applying the annual addition limitation (see Q 6:34) and the annual benefit limitation (see Q 6:11), contributions or benefits attributable to the employee from all three corporations must be taken into account. Consequently, under the profit sharing plan in the above example, Bob's annual addition limitation is $49,000 in the aggregate. [Treas. Reg. § 1.415(c)-1(a)(1)] However, if each employer adopted a separate 25-percent-of-compensation profit sharing plan, the employer contribution allocated to Bob under each plan would be $49,000 (25% of $196,000), or $147,000 in the aggregate.

Q 6:49   Does the annual compensation limit affect the Code's nondiscrimination requirements?

The annual compensation limit (see Qs 6:45, 6:46) applies for purposes of applying the nondiscrimination rules under Sections 401(a)(4), 401(a)(5), 401(k)(3), 401(l), 401(m)(2), and 410(b)(2). The limit also applies in determining whether an alternative method of determining compensation impermissibly discriminates in favor of HCEs (see Qs 3:2, 6:64–6:71). [Treas. Reg. § 1.401(a)(17)-1(c)]

Q 6:50   When was the annual compensation limit effective?

A $200,000 annual compensation limit was generally effective for plan years beginning after 1988, and the $150,000 annual compensation limit was generally effective for plan years beginning after 1993. Effective for plan years beginning after 2001, the annual compensation limit again became $200,000 (see Qs 6:45, 6:46).

Benefits accrued (see Q 9:2) under a defined benefit plan (see Q 2:3) for plan years beginning before January 1, 1994 are not subject to the $150,000 annual compensation limit. For example, an employee's benefits accrued prior to the 1994 plan year that are based on compensation in excess of $150,000 are not required to be reduced, and these accruals based on excess compensation are not required to be offset against the employee's benefit accruals in subsequent years. [Treas. Reg. § 1.401(a)(17)-1(d)(5)]

To implement the reduction in the compensation limit, "fresh start" rules are provided for defined benefit plans. The fresh start rules allow benefits accrued before a reduction to be frozen under a formula; there are several available formulas, and each plan must specify the method it uses. Multiple fresh start rules are set forth, so that benefits accrued before the $200,000 limit became effective may be frozen and benefits accrued before the $150,000 limit became effective may also be frozen. [Treas. Reg. §§ 1.401(a)(17)-1(d)(5)(iii), 1.401(a)(17)-1(e)(3)]

Example. On January 1, 1984, Boca Stanley Corp. adopted a calendar year defined benefit plan providing an annual benefit for each year of service equal to 2 percent of compensation averaged over an employee's high-three consecutive calendar years' compensation. As of December 31, 1988, Marjorie had five years of service and earned $250,000 each year. Marjorie's accrued benefit as of December 31, 1988 was $25,000 (2% × 5 × $250,000).

Effective January 1, 1989, the plan was amended to provide that an employee's benefit will equal the sum of the employee's accrued benefit as of December 31, 1988 (determined as though the employee terminated employment on that date and without regard to any amendments after that date) and 2 percent of compensation averaged over an employee's high-three consecutive calendar years' compensation times years of service, taking into account only years of service after December 31, 1988.

Marjorie earned $275,000 in each of 1989 and 1990 and $300,000 in each of 1991, 1992, and 1993. The annual compensation limit was $222,220, $228,860, and $235,840 for plan years beginning January 1, 1991, 1992, and 1993, respectively. The compensation that may be taken into account for plan benefits in 1993 cannot exceed $228,973 (the average of $222,220, $228,860, and $235,840). Therefore, as of December 31, 1993, Marjorie's accrued benefit was $47,897 [$25,000 (Marjorie's December 31, 1988, frozen accrued benefit) + $22,897 (2% × 5 × $228,973)].

As of January 1, 1994, the plan was amended to provide that an employee's benefit will equal the sum of the employee's accrued benefit as of December 31, 1993 (determined as though the employee terminated employment on that date and without regard to any amendments after that date) and 2 percent of compensation averaged over an employee's high three consecutive years' compensation times years of service taking into account only years of service after December 31, 1993.

Assume that Marjorie earns $350,000 in each of the years 1994 through 1999 and that the $160,000 annual compensation limit for plan years beginning on or after January 1, 1998 is adjusted to $170,000 for the plan year beginning on or after January 1, 1999. The compensation that may be taken into account for the 1999 plan year cannot exceed $163,333 (the average of $160,000 for 1997, $160,000 for 1998, and $170,000 for 1999).

Therefore, on December 31, 1999, Marjorie's accrued benefit is $67,497 [$47,897 (Marjorie's December 31, 1993, frozen accrued benefit) + $19,600 (2% × 6 × $163,333)].

IRS has ruled that, if a participant had less than ten years of participation (see Q 6:22) at the fresh start date, the frozen accrued benefit cannot be increased because the participant continues to participate in the defined benefit plan. However, for benefits accrued after the fresh start date, the plan may provide that all years of plan participation will be taken into account. [Priv. Ltr. Rul. 9842062]

EGTRRA 2001 (see Q 1:21) provides that the increase in the annual compensation limit applies to years beginning after 2001. Thus, for purposes of determining benefit accruals or the amount of allocations for plan years beginning on or after January 1, 2002, compensation taken into account may not exceed the $200,000 annual compensation limit. In the case of a plan that uses annual compensation for periods prior to the first plan year beginning on or after January 1, 2002 to determine accruals or allocations for a plan year beginning on or after January 1, 2002, the plan is permitted to provide that the $200,000 annual compensation limit applies to annual compensation for such prior periods in determining such accruals or allocations. [IRS Notice 2001-56, 2001-2 C.B. 277]

The $200,000 annual compensation limit is adjusted for cost-of-living increases as of the beginning of a calendar year. As under prior law, any such increases apply only with respect to annual compensation during the plan year or other 12-month period over which compensation is determined that begins with or within such calendar year and any subsequent calendar year (see Q 6:46). [IRS Notice 2001-56, 2001-2 C.B. 277]

Example. Jennifer is a participant in The Driftwood Drive Corporation defined benefit plan. The plan has a calendar plan year and a benefit formula that provides for an annual benefit at normal retirement age (see Q 10:55) equal to years of service times 1 percent times high-three-year average compensation. For this purpose, high-three-year average compensation is the average of the compensation over the three consecutive plan years for which the average is the highest, and compensation for each year is limited to $150,000, as adjusted for cost-of-living increases. As of December 31, 2001, Jennifer has ten years of service and compensation of $250,000 for each of the three years 1999, 2000, and 2001. Jennifer's high-three-year average compensation of $166,667 is determined as the average of annual compensation of $160,000 for 1999, $170,000 for 2000, and $170,000 for 2001 (see Q 6:46). Jennifer's annual benefit under the plan formula as of December 31, 2001, is $16,667 (10 × 1% × $166,667).

In 2002, the plan is amended (1) to use the $200,000 annual compensation limit for compensation paid in years beginning after December 31, 2001 and (2) to use the $200,000 annual compensation limit for compensation paid in years beginning prior to January 1, 2002 in determining benefit accruals in years beginning after December 31, 2001. Jennifer has annual compensation of $250,000 for 2002. A high-three-year average compensation of $200,000 is determined for Jennifer as of December 31, 2002, as the average of annual compensation of $200,000 for 2000, $200,000 for 2001, and $200,000 for 2002. As of December 31, 2002, Jennifer's annual benefit under the plan formula is $22,000 (11 × 1% × $200,000).

In the above example, the plan is not required to implement the EGTRRA 2001 increase in the annual compensation limit in its benefit formula. The plan could retain the compensation limit in effect prior to EGTRRA 2001 or provide for any other compensation limit that is less than the compensation limit as amended. Accordingly, the plan could be amended to provide that the increased annual compensation limit applies only to annual compensation paid in plan years beginning on or after January 1, 2002. In that case, a high-three-year average compensation of $180,000 would be determined for Jennifer as of December 31, 2002, as the average of annual compensation of $170,000 for

2000, $170,000 for 2001, and $200,000 for 2002. Jennifer's annual benefit as of December 31, 2002 would be $19,800 (11 × 1% × $180,000). [IRS Notice 2001-56, 2001-2 C.B. 277]

IRS has ruled that amendments to defined benefit plans to apply the increased compensation limits under EGTRRA 2001 to all former employees who retain accrued benefits under the plan, effective with the first plan year beginning after December 31, 2001, will satisfy the nondiscrimination rules (see Q 4:21) and minimum coverage requirement (see Q 5:15). [Rev. Rul. 2003-11, 2003-1 C.B. 285; Treas. Reg. §§ 1.401(a)(4)-10(b)(1), 1.410(b)-2(c), 1.410(b)-3(b)]

> **Example.** The Eric Cinco de May Corporation maintains a defined benefit plan with a calendar year plan year and a benefit formula that provides for all participants an annual retirement benefit at normal retirement age equal to the product of: (years of service) × (1 percent) × (high-three-year average compensation). For this purpose, high-three-year average compensation is the average of the compensation over the three consecutive plan years for which the average is the highest, and compensation for each year is limited to $150,000, as adjusted for cost-of-living increases (the pre-EGTRRA 2001 limit). Lynn is a former participant in the plan who retires as of December 31, 2001. As of December 31, 2001, Lynn has ten years of service and compensation of $250,000 for each of the three years 1999, 2000, and 2001. Lynn's high three-year average compensation of $166,667 is determined as the average of annual compensation of $160,000 for 1999, $170,000 for 2000, and $170,000 for 2001 (see Q 6:46). Lynn's annual retirement benefit under the plan formula as of December 31, 2001, is $16,667, calculated as (10) × (.01) × ($166,667). As of December 31, 2001, Lynn is a highly compensated former employee (see Q 3:11).

> In 2002, the plan is amended (1) to use the $200,000 compensation limit for compensation paid in years beginning after December 31, 2001, (2) to use the $200,000 compensation limit for compensation paid in years beginning prior to January 1, 2002 in determining benefit accruals in years beginning after December 31, 2001, and (3) to use the $200,000 compensation limit in determining retirement benefits to be paid after December 31, 2001 to employees who retired on or before December 31, 2001. A high-three-year average compensation of $200,000 is determined for Lynn as of December 31, 2002 as the average of annual compensation of $200,000 for 1999, $200,000 for 2000, and $200,000 for 2001. As of December 31, 2002, Lynn's annual retirement benefit under the plan formula is $20,000, calculated as (10) × (.01) × ($200,000).

> The plan amendment to apply the increased compensation limits satisfies the nondiscrimination rules and the minimum coverage requirements.

Q 6:51 What general rules apply to the aggregation of plans?

Except with respect to multiemployer plans (see Q 6:55), and taking into account the rules regarding (1) the break-up of affiliated employers and affiliated service groups discussed below, (2) predecessor employers (see Q 6:52), and (3) nonduplication (see Q 6:53), for purposes of applying the limitations on benefits (see Q 6:11) and contributions (see Q 6:34) applicable to a participant for a particular limitation year (see Q 6:58):

1. All defined benefit plans (without regard to whether a plan has been terminated) ever maintained by the employer (or a predecessor employer) under which the participant has accrued a benefit are treated as one defined benefit plan;

2. All defined contribution plans (without regard to whether a plan has been terminated) ever maintained by the employer (or a predecessor employer) under which the participant receives annual additions are treated as one defined contribution plan; and

3. All 403(b) plans (see Q 35:1) purchased by an employer (including plans purchased through salary reduction contributions) for the participant are treated as one 403(b) plan.

[I.R.C. § 415(f)(1); Treas. Reg. § 1.415(f)-1(a)]

See Q 6:7 for rules regarding aggregation of employers in the case of affiliated employers and affiliated service groups and for rules regarding the treatment of leased employees. [Treas. Reg. § 1.415(f)-1(b)(1)]

A formerly affiliated plan of an employer is taken into account for purposes of applying the aggregation rules to the employer, but the formerly affiliated plan is treated as if it had terminated immediately prior to the cessation of affiliation with sufficient assets to pay benefit liabilities under the plan and had purchased annuities to provide plan benefits. See Q 6:17 for rules determining annual benefits under a terminated defined benefit plan under which annuities are purchased to provide plan benefits. A formerly affiliated plan of an employer is a plan that, immediately prior to the cessation of affiliation, was actually maintained by one or more of the entities that constitute the employer (as determined under the employer affiliation rules) and, immediately after the cessation of affiliation, is not actually maintained by any of the entities that constitute the employer (as determined under the employer affiliation rules). A cessation of affiliation is the event that causes an entity to no longer be aggregated with one or more other entities as a single employer under the employer affiliation rules (such as the sale of a subsidiary outside the controlled group) or that causes a plan to not actually be maintained by any of the entities that constitute the employer under the employer affiliation rules (such as a transfer of plan sponsorship outside of a controlled group). [Treas. Reg. § 1.415(f)-1(b)(2)]

See Q 6:56 for illustrative examples.

Q 6:52   How are predecessor and successor employers treated for plan aggregation purposes?

A former employer is a predecessor employer with respect to a participant in a plan maintained by an employer if the employer maintains a plan under which the participant had accrued a benefit while performing services for the former employer (for example, the employer assumed sponsorship of the former employer's plan or the employer's plan received a transfer of benefits from the former employer's plan), but only if that benefit is provided under the plan maintained by the employer. In such a case, in applying the limitations to a participant in a plan maintained by the employer, the aggregation rules (see Q 6:51) require the plan to take into account benefits provided to the participant under plans that are maintained by the predecessor employer that are not maintained by the employer. The former affiliated plan rules (see Q 6:51) apply as if the employer and predecessor employer constituted a single employer (see Q 6:7) immediately prior to the cessation of affiliation (and as if they constituted two, unrelated employers under those rules immediately after the cessation of affiliation) and cessation of affiliation was the event that gives rise to the predecessor employer relationship, such as a transfer of benefits or plan sponsorship. [Treas. Reg. § 1.415(f)-1(c)(1)]

With respect to an employer of a participant, a former entity that antedates the employer is a predecessor employer with respect to the participant if, under the facts and circumstances, the employer constitutes a continuation of all or a portion of the trade or business of the former entity. This will occur, for example, where formation of the employer constitutes a mere formal or technical change in the employment relationship and continuity otherwise exists in the substance and administration of the business operations of the former entity and the employer. [Treas. Reg. § 1.415(f)-1(c)(2)]

See Q 6:56 for illustrative examples.

Q 6:53 What special rules apply for plan aggregation purposes?

In applying the limitations on benefits (see Q 6:11) and contributions (see Q 6:34) to a plan maintained by an employer, if the plan is aggregated with another plan pursuant to the aggregation rules (see Q 6:51), a participant's benefits are not counted more than once in determining the participant's aggregate annual benefit or annual additions. For example, if a defined benefit plan is treated as if it terminated immediately prior to a cessation of affiliation (see Q 6:51), the plans maintained by the employer (as determined after the cessation of affiliation) that actually maintains the plan do not double count the annual benefit provided under the plan by aggregating both the participant's annual benefit provided under the plan and the participant's annual benefit under the plan as a formerly affiliated plan. Instead, the plans maintained by the employer include the annual benefit provided to the participant under the actual plan that the employer maintains. Similarly, if a defined benefit plan maintained by an employer (the transferee plan) receives a transfer of benefits from a defined benefit plan maintained by a predecessor employer (the transferor plan) and the transferred benefits are required to be treated by the transferee plan as if the benefits were provided under a plan that must be aggregated with the transferor plan that terminated immediately prior to the transfer (see Q 6:16), the transferee plan does not double count the transferred benefits by taking into account both the actual benefit provided under the transferee plan and the benefit provided under the deemed terminated plan that the predecessor employer is treated as maintaining (and that otherwise would have to be taken into account by the transferee plan under the predecessor employer aggregation rules (see Q 6:52)). Instead, the transferee plan takes into account the transferred benefits that are actually provided under transferee plan (see Q 6:16) and any nontransferred benefits provided under plans maintained by the predecessor employer with respect to a participant whose benefits have been transferred to the transferee plan. [Treas. Reg. § 1.415(f)-1(d)(1)]

If two or more defined benefit plans are aggregated for a particular limitation year (see Q 6:58), in applying the reduction for participation of less than ten years (see Q 6:22) to the dollar limitation (see Q 6:11), time periods that are counted as years of participation under any of the plans are counted in computing the limitation of the aggregated plans. [Treas. Reg. § 1.415(f)-1(d)(2)] If two or more defined benefit plans are aggregated for a particular limitation year, in applying the reduction for service of less than ten years (see Q 6:22) to the compensation limitation (see Q 6:11), time periods that are counted as years of service under any of the plans are counted in computing the limitation of the aggregated plans. [Treas. Reg. § 1.415(f)-1(d)(3)]

If a plan, annuity contract, or arrangement is subject to a special limitation (see Q 35:26) in addition to, or instead of, the regular limitations (see Qs 6:11, 6:34) and is aggregated with a plan that is subject only to the regular limitations, the following rules apply:

1. Each plan, annuity contract, or arrangement that is subject to a special limitation must meet its own applicable limitation, and each plan subject to the regular limitations must meet its applicable limitation.

2. The limitation for the aggregated plans is the larger of the applicable limitations for the separate plans.

[Treas. Reg. § 1.415(f)-1(h)]

See Q 6:56 for illustrative examples.

Q 6:54   What happens if previously unaggregated plans become aggregated?

Two or more defined contribution plans (see Q 2:2) that are not required to be aggregated (see Q 6:51) as of the first day of a limitation year (see Q 6:58) do not fail to satisfy the limitations on contributions (see Q 6:34) with respect to a participant for the limitation year merely because they are aggregated later in that limitation year, provided that no annual additions are credited to the participant's account after the date on which the plans are required to be aggregated. [Treas. Reg. § 1.415(f)-1(e)(2)]

Two or more defined benefit plans (see Q 2:3) that are not required to be aggregated as of the first day of a limitation year do not fail to satisfy the limitations on benefits (see Q 6:11) for the limitation year merely because they are aggregated later in that limitation year, provided that no plan amendments increasing benefits with respect to the participant under either or any plan are made after the occurrence of the event causing the plan to be aggregated. [Treas. Reg. § 1.415(f)-1(e)(3)(i)]

Two or more defined benefit plans that are required to be aggregated during a limitation year subsequent to the limitation year during which the plans were first aggregated do not fail to satisfy the limitations on benefits with respect to a participant for the limitation year merely because they are aggregated if there have been no increases in the participant's accrued benefit derived from employer contributions (including increases as a result of increased compensation or service) under either or any of the plans within the period during which the plans have been aggregated. [Treas. Reg. § 1.415(f)-1(e)(3)(ii)]

See Q 6:56 for illustrative examples.

Q 6:55   How are multiemployer plans treated for plan aggregation purposes?

Multiemployer plans (see Q 29:2) are not aggregated with other multiemployer plans for purposes of applying the limits on benefits (see Q 6:11) and contributions (see Q 6:34). [I.R.C. § 415(f)(2)(B); Treas. Reg. § 1.415(f)-1(g)(1)]

Notwithstanding the rule discussed in Q 6:6, a multiemployer plan is permitted to provide that only the benefits under that multiemployer plan that are provided by an employer are aggregated with benefits under plans maintained by that employer that are not multiemployer plans. If the multiemployer plan so provides, then, where an employer maintains both a plan that is not a multiemployer plan and a multiemployer plan, only the benefits under the multiemployer plan that are provided by the employer are aggregated with benefits under the employer's plans other than multiemployer plans (in lieu of including benefits provided by all employers under the multiemployer plan). [Treas. Reg. § 1.415(f)-1(g)(2)(i)]

A multiemployer plan is not aggregated with any other plan that is not a multiemployer plan for purposes of applying the compensation limit (see Q 6:11). [I.R.C. § 415(f)(3)(A); Treas. Reg. § 1.415(f)-1(g)(2)(ii)]

Q 6:56   Has IRS provided examples illustrating the plan aggregation rules?

The following examples illustrate the aggregation rules (see Qs 6:51-6:55). Except to the extent otherwise stated in an example, each entity is not and has never been affiliated with another entity under the employer affiliation rules (see Q 6:7), each entity has never maintained a qualified retirement plan (other than the plans specifically mentioned in the example), and the limitation year (see Q 6:58) for each qualified plan is the calendar year. [Treas. Reg. § 1.415(f)-1(j)]

Example 1. *Facts.* M was formerly an employee of ABC Corporation and is currently an employee of XYZ corporation. ABC maintains a defined benefit plan (Plan ABC) and a defined contribution plan in which M participates, and XYZ maintains a defined benefit plan (Plan XYZ) and a defined contribution plan in which M participates. ABC Corporation owns 60 percent of XYZ Corporation.

Treatment as a single employer. ABC Corporation and XYZ Corporation are members of a controlled group of corporations (see Q 6:7); and, because ABC Corporation and XYZ Corporation are members of a controlled group of corporations, M is treated as being employed by a single employer.

Plan aggregation. The sum of M's annual benefit under Plan ABC and M's annual benefit under Plan XYZ is not permitted to exceed the limitation on benefits (see Q 6:11), and the sum of the annual additions to M's account under the defined contribution plans maintained by ABC and XYZ may not exceed the limitations on contributions (see Q 6:34). A year of service for either employer is considered as a year of service for the phase-in rules for the compensation limit, and a year of participation under either plan is considered as a year of participation for purposes of the rules for the dollar limit (see Q 6:22).

Example 2. *Facts.* The facts are the same as in Example 1, except that ABC Corporation and XYZ Corporation do not maintain defined contribution plans. In addition, Participant O was formerly an employee of ABC Corporation and is currently an employee of XYZ Corporation. Participant O has an accrued benefit under the ABC Plan, but Participant O has no accrued benefit under the XYZ Plan. Effective January 1, 2011, ABC Corporation sells all of its shares of stock of XYZ Corporation to an unaffiliated entity, LMN Corporation (the 2011 stock sale). After the 2011 stock sale, XYZ corporation continues to maintain plan XYZ. LMN Corporation maintains a defined benefit plan (Plan LMN). After the 2011 stock sale, M begins to accrue benefits under Plan LMN, but O does not participate in Plan LMN.

Affiliated employer status of the corporations. Immediately after the 2011 stock sale, ABC Corporation and XYZ Corporation are no longer members of a controlled group of corporations and, accordingly, are no longer treated as a single employer under the employer affiliation rules. Immediately after the 2011 stock sale, LMN Corporation and XYZ Corporation are members of a controlled group of corporations and, accordingly, are treated as a single employer under the employer affiliation rules.

Treatment of plans maintained by ABC Corporation after the 2011 stock sale. Any plan maintained by any member of a controlled group of corporations is deemed maintained by all members of the controlled group; and, for purposes of applying the limitations on benefits, all defined benefit plans ever maintained by an employer (as determined under the affiliation rules) are treated as one defined benefit plan. Therefore, defined benefit plans maintained by ABC Corporation must take into account the annual benefit of a participant provided under Plan XYZ in applying the limitations on benefits to the participant because Plan XYZ is a plan that had once been maintained by ABC Corporation. However, beginning with the 2011 limitation year, the aggregation of the annual benefit accrued by a participant under Plan XYZ for purposes of testing defined benefit plans maintained by ABC Corporation is limited to the annual benefit accrued by the participant under Plan XYZ immediately prior to the 2011 stock sale. This is because a formerly affiliated plan of an employer is treated as if it had terminated immediately prior to the cessation of affiliation with sufficient assets to pay benefit liabilities under the plan and had purchased annuities to provide plan benefits (see Q 6:51). The 2011 stock sale is a cessation of affiliation because this event caused XYZ Corporation to no longer be affiliated with ABC Corporation under the employer affiliation rules. Immediately after the 2011 stock sale, Plan XYZ is a formerly affiliated plan with respect to ABC Corporation because, immediately prior to the cessation of affiliation, Plan XYZ was actually maintained by XYZ Corporation (which together with ABC Corporation constituted a single employer under the employer affiliation rules); and, immediately after the cessation of affiliation, Plan XYZ is not actually maintained by ABC Corporation or any other entity affiliated with it.

Application of rules to Participants M and O with respect to plans maintained by ABC Corporation after the 2011 stock sale. In applying the limitation on benefits to Participant M for the 2011 limitation year and later limitation years, Plan ABC must take into account the annual benefit provided under Plan ABC to Participant M and the annual benefit provided under Plan XYZ to Participant M, but treating Plan XYZ as if it had terminated immediately prior to the 2011 stock sale with sufficient assets to pay benefit liabilities under the plan and had purchased annuities to provide plan benefits. The aggregation of Plan XYZ with Plan ABC is irrelevant for purposes of Participant O because Participant O does not have any accrued benefit under Plan XYZ (as determined prior to the 2011 stock sale).

Treatment of plans maintained by LMN Corporation and XYZ Corporation after the 2011 stock sale. When applying the limitations on benefits to a participant under Plans LMN and XYZ for the 2011 limitation year and later years, the annual benefit provided to the participant under Plans LMN, XYZ, and ABC must be aggregated. Benefits under Plan ABC must be included in this aggregation because XYZ Corporation is deemed to have once maintained Plan ABC; and, because LMN Corporation and XYZ Corporation constitute a single employer, aggregation is required of all defined benefit plans ever maintained by LMN Corporation and XYZ Corporation. However, in performing this aggregation, a participant's annual benefit under Plan ABC is limited to the annual benefit accrued by the participant immediately prior to the 2011 stock sale. This is because Plan ABC is a formerly affiliated plan of LMN Corporation and XYZ Corporation.

Application of rules to Participants M and O with respect to plans maintained by LMN Corporation and XYZ Corporation after the 2011 stock sale. In applying the limitation on benefits to Participant M for the 2011 limitation year and later limitation years, Plan LMN and Plan XYZ must take into account the annual benefit provided under Plans LMN and XYZ to Participant M and the annual benefit provided under Plan ABC to Participant M as if Plan

ABC had terminated immediately prior to the 2011 stock sale with sufficient assets to pay benefit liabilities under the plan and had purchased annuities to provide plan benefits. Participant O does not have an accrued benefit under Plan LMN or Plan XYZ, so the aggregation of Plan ABC with Plans LMN and XYZ is currently irrelevant with respect to Participant O. However, if Participant O were to ever participate in Plans LMN or XYZ after the 2011 stock sale, Participant O's annual benefit under Plan ABC (determined as if Plan ABC terminated immediately prior to the 2011 stock sale) would have to be aggregated with any annual benefit that Participant O accrues under Plan LMN or Plan XYZ.

Application of nonduplication rule. After the 2011 stock sale, plans maintained by ABC Corporation do not take into account the deemed termination of Plan ABC because ABC Corporation maintains Plan ABC after the cessation of affiliation. Similarly, after the 2011 stock sale, plans maintained by LMN Corporation and XYZ corporation do not take into account the deemed termination of Plan XYZ because XYZ Corporation maintains Plan XYZ after the cessation of affiliation. See Q 6:53 regarding the nonduplication rule.

Example 3. *Facts.* The facts are the same as in Example 2, except that, on January 1, 2010, Plan ABC transfers Participant M's benefit to Plan XYZ.

Treatment of plans maintained by ABC Corporation. M's benefit that is transferred from Plan ABC to Plan XYZ is not treated as being provided under Plan ABC (see Q 6:16) for the limitation year in which the transfer occurs (2010). This is because M's transferred benefit is otherwise required to be taken into account by Plan ABC for the 2010 limitation year because Plan XYZ must be aggregated with Plan ABC. This result does not change for the 2011 limitation year and later limitation years, where Plan XYZ becomes a formerly affiliated plan with respect to ABC Corporation due to the 2011 stock sale. Plan XYZ (the formerly affiliated plan) is treated from the perspective of plans maintained by ABC Corporation (Plan ABC) as if Plan XYZ terminated immediately prior to the 2011 stock sale with sufficient assets to pay benefit liabilities under the plan and had purchased annuities to provide plan benefits. However, the pre-2011 stock sale benefits of Plan XYZ include the January 1, 2010 transfer of Participant M's benefit. Thus, in the 2011 limitation year, M's transferred benefit is still otherwise required to be taken into account by Plan ABC on account of the aggregation of Plan XYZ with Plan ABC; and, therefore, the transferred benefit is not treated as being provided by Plan ABC.

Treatment of plans maintained by LMN Corporation and XYZ Corporation. Participant M's benefit that is transferred to Plan XYZ from Plan ABC must be treated as provided under Plan XYZ for purposes of applying the limitations on benefits to Plan XYZ with respect to Participant M for the limitation year in which the transfer occurs and later years. This result does not change on account of the 2011 stock sale. When applying the limitation on benefits to Plans LMN and XYZ for the 2011 limitation year and later years, Plans LMN and XYZ must aggregate the annual benefit provided to a participant under each plan along with the participant's benefit under Plan ABC. However, for the 2011 limitation year and later years, this aggregation of M's Plan ABC benefit includes only the annual benefit attributable to a participant's accrued benefit under Plan ABC immediately prior to the 2011 stock sale, which (due to the 2010 transfer) is zero.

Example 4. *Facts.* The facts are the same as in Example 2, except that, on January 1, 2012, Plan ABC transfers Participant M's benefit to Plan XYZ.

Treatment of plans maintained by ABC Corporation for the 2012 limitation year and later years. M's benefit that is transferred from Plan ABC to Plan XYZ during the 2012 limitation year is treated by Plan ABC for the 2012 limitation year and later years as if the transferred benefit were provided under a plan that must be aggregated with Plan ABC that terminated immediately prior to the transfer with sufficient assets to pay benefit liabilities under the plan and had purchased annuities to provide plan benefits. This is because M's transferred benefit is not otherwise required to be taken into account by Plan ABC for the 2012 limitation year and later years. While Plan ABC must take into account Participant M's annual benefit under Plan XYZ, Participant M's annual benefit for this purpose is limited to M's accrued benefit under Plan XYZ immediately prior to the 2011 stock sale, and Participant M's pre-2011 stock sale accrued benefit under Plan XYZ excludes the 2012 transfer.

Treatment of plans maintained by LMN Corporation and XYZ Corporation for the 2012 limitation year and later years. Participant M's benefit that is transferred to Plan XYZ from Plan ABC must be treated as provided under Plan XYZ for purposes of applying the limitations on benefits to Plan XYZ with respect to Participant M for the limitation in which the transfer occurs and later years. In applying the limitations on benefits to Plans LMN and XYZ with respect to Participant M for the 2011 limitation year and later years, the annual benefit of Participant M under Plans ABC, LMN, and XYZ must be aggregated; but, for this purpose, Participant M's benefit under Plan ABC is treated as if it were provided under a plan that terminated immediately prior to the cessation of affiliation of ABC Corporation and XYZ Corporation with sufficient assets to pay benefit liabilities under the plan and had purchased an annuity to provide Participant M's benefits. In applying the limitations on benefits to Plans LMN and XYZ with respect to Participant M for the 2012 limitation year and later years, the annual benefit of Participant M under Plans ABC, LMN, and XYZ still must be aggregated. However, beginning with the 2012 limitation year, ABC Corporation is a predecessor employer with respect to LMN Corporation and XYZ Corporation with respect to Participant M on account of the transfer of benefits from Plan ABC to Plan XYZ. Therefore, Plans LMN and XYZ must take into account benefits that Participant M accrued under Plan ABC after the January 1, 2011 cessation of affiliation of ABC Corporation and XYZ Corporation that were not transferred to Plan XYZ on January 1, 2012 (see Qs 6:52, 6:53). Because all of Participant M's benefit in Plan ABC is transferred to Plan XYZ on January 1, 2012, Participant M's annual benefit from Plan ABC for purposes of aggregating Plan ABC with Plans LMN and XYZ is zero.

Example 5. The facts are the same as in Example 2, except that, instead of the 2011 stock sale, XYZ Corporation sells some of its operating assets to LMN Corporation; under the facts and circumstances, the sale does not result in XYZ Corporation constituting a predecessor employer of LMN Corporation (see Q 6:52); and, in connection with the asset sale, LMN Corporation assumes sponsorship of Plan XYZ in place of XYZ Corporation, effective January 1, 2011.

Treatment of plans maintained by ABC Corporation and XYZ Corporation. All defined benefit plans ever maintained by ABC Corporation and XYZ Corporation must be aggregated as a single defined benefit plan for purposes of applying the limitations on benefits. However, for purposes of determining the annual benefit under Plan XYZ for the 2011 limitation year and later years, the aggregation of a participant's benefit under Plan XYZ is limited to the participant's annual benefit accrued immediately prior to the January 1, 2011 transfer of sponsorship of Plan XYZ. This is because a formerly affiliated plan of an employer is treated as if it were a plan that terminated immediately prior to the cessation of affiliation with sufficient assets to pay benefit liabilities under the plan and had purchased annuities to provide plan benefits. The January 1, 2011 transfer of sponsorship of Plan XYZ is a cessation of affiliation because this event causes Plan XYZ to no longer actually be maintained by either ABC Corporation or XYZ Corporation. Effective immediately after the January 1, 2011 transfer of sponsorship, Plan XYZ is a formerly affiliated plan with respect to ABC Corporation and XYZ Corporation because, immediately prior to the cessation of affiliation, Plan XYZ was actually maintained by XYZ Corporation; and, immediately after the cessation of affiliation, Plan XYZ is not actually maintained by either XYZ Corporation or ABC Corporation. Therefore, in applying the limitations on benefits to Participant M for the 2011 limitation year and later limitation years, Plan ABC must take into account the annual benefit provided under Plan ABC to Participant M and the annual benefit provided under Plan XYZ to Participant M as if Plan XYZ had terminated immediately prior to the 2011 stock sale with sufficient assets to pay benefit liabilities under the plan and had purchased annuities to provide plan benefits. The aggregation of Plan XYZ with Plan ABC is irrelevant for purposes of Participant O because Participant O does not have any accrued benefit under Plan XYZ (as determined prior to the 2011 transfer of sponsorship).

Treatment of plans maintained by LMN Corporation. All defined benefit plans ever maintained by LMN Corporation or a predecessor employer must be aggregated as a single plan for purposes of applying the limitations. ABC Corporation and XYZ Corporation constitute a predecessor employer with respect to the participants who participate in Plan XYZ on the date of the transfer of sponsorship of Plan XYZ (the transferred participants) from XYZ Corporation to LMN Corporation, such as Participant M. This is because, effective with the January 1, 2011 transfer of sponsorship, LMN Corporation maintains a plan (Plan XYZ) under which the participants accrued a benefit while performing services for XYZ Corporation (which is in turn affiliated with ABC Corporation), and such benefits are provided under a plan maintained by LMN Corporation. Therefore, for the 2011 limitation year and later years, the annual benefit under Plan ABC of the transferred participants (such as Participant M) must be aggregated with the annual benefit provided to such participants under Plan XYZ and LMN for purposes of determining whether Plan LMN or Plan XYZ satisfies the limitations on benefits. However, the aggregation of the transferred participants' Plan ABC annual benefits is limited to the annual benefit accrued under Plan ABC immediately prior to the January 1, 2011 transfer of sponsorship. This is because Plan ABC is treated from the perspective of plans maintained by LMN Corporation as if Plan ABC had terminated immediately prior to the transfer of sponsorship of Plan ABC to LMN Corporation with sufficient assets to pay benefit liabilities under the plan and had purchased annuities to provide plan benefits. ABC Corporation and XYZ Corporation do not constitute a predecessor employer with respect to Participant O. Thus, if Participant O is a participant in Plan LMN or becomes a participant in Plan XYZ after the 2011 transfer of sponsorship, neither plan aggregates Participant O's Plan ABC benefits for purposes of the limitations. In applying the aggregation rules to a participant, plans maintained by LMN Corporation do not double count the participant's annual benefit (see Q 6:53). Thus, such plans do not aggregate the annual benefit provided under Plan XYZ with the annual benefit from the deemed termination of Plan XYZ that LMN Corporation's predecessor employer (which are ABC and XYZ Corporations) must take into account in applying the aggregation rules and, instead, consider the annual benefit actually provided under Plan XYZ.

Example 6. *Facts.* N is employed by a hospital that purchases a 403(b) contract (see Q 35:1) on N's behalf for the current limitation year. N is in control of the hospital. The hospital also maintains a defined contribution plan during the current limitation year in which N participates.

Conclusion. The hospital, as well as N, is considered to maintain the 403(b) contract. Accordingly, for N, the sum of the annual additions under the defined contribution plan and the 403(b) contract must satisfy the limitations on contributions.

Example 7. *Facts.* The facts are the same as in Example 6, except that, instead of being in control of the hospital, N is the 100 percent owner of a professional corporation, P, that maintains a defined contribution plan in which N participates.

Conclusion. The professional corporation, as well as N, is considered to maintain the 403(b) contract. Accordingly, the sum of the annual additions under the defined contribution plan maintained by professional corporation P and the 403(b) contract must satisfy the limitations on contributions. See the example in Q 6:57 for the treatment of a contribution to a 403(b) contract that exceeds the contribution limits by reason of the required aggregation.

Example 8. *Facts.* J is an employee of two corporations, N and M, each of which has employed J for more than ten years. N and M are not required to be aggregated. Each corporation has a defined benefit plan in which J has participated for more than ten years. Each plan provides a benefit that is equal to 75 percent of a participant's average compensation for the period of the participant's high-three years of service and is payable in the form of a straight life annuity beginning at age 65. J's average compensation for the period of J's high-three years of service from each corporation is $160,000. In July 2010, N Corporation becomes a wholly owned subsidiary of M Corporation.

Plan aggregation analysis. As a result of the acquisition of N Corporation by M Corporation, J is treated as being employed by a single employer. Therefore, because all defined benefit plans of an employer are required to be treated as one defined benefit plan, the two plans must be aggregated for purposes of applying the limitations on benefits. However, because the plans were not aggregated as of the first day of the 2010 limitation year (January 1, 2010), they will not be considered aggregated until the limitation year beginning January 1, 2011, provided that no plan amendment increasing benefits with respect to participant J is made after the acquisition of N by M (see Q 6:54).

Application to Participant J. J has a total benefit under the two plans of $240,000, which, as a result of the plan aggregation, is in excess of the limit on benefits. However, the limitations applicable to J may be exceeded in this situation without plan disqualification so long as J's accrued benefit derived from employer contributions is not increased (that is, J's accrued benefit does not increase on account of increased compensation, service, participation, or other accruals) during the period within which the limitations are being exceeded.

Example 9. *Facts.* A, age 30, owns all of the stock of X Corporation and also owns 10 percent of the stock of Z Corporation. F, A's father, directly owns 75 percent of the stock of Z Corporation. Both corporations have defined contribution plans in which A participates. A's compensation for 2011 is $20,000 from Z Corporation and $150,000 from X Corporation. During the period January 1, 2011 through June 30, 2011, annual additions of $20,000 are credited to A's account under the plan of Z Corporation, while annual additions of $40,000 are credited to A's account under the plan of X Corporation. In both instances, the amount of annual additions represent the maximum allowable. On July 15, 2011, F dies and A inherits all of F's stock in Z in 2011.

Conclusion. As of July 15, 2011, A is considered to be in control of X and Z Corporations, and the two plans must be aggregated for purposes of applying the limitations on contributions. However, even though A's total annual additions for 2011 are $60,000, the limitations are not violated for 2011, provided no annual additions are credited to A's accounts after July 15, 2011 (the date that A is first in control of Z) for the remainder of the 2011 limitation year.

Example 10. *Facts.* P is a key employee (see Q 26:23) of employer XYZ who participates in defined contribution plan (Plan X). P is also provided postretirement medical benefits (see Q 6:34), and XYZ has taken into account a reserve for those benefits. In the 2011 limitation year, P's compensation is $30,000, and P's annual additions under Plan X are $5,000. A separate account for the medical benefits is maintained for P that is credited with an allocation of $32,000 for the 2011 limitation year. It is assumed that the dollar limit for 2011 is $51,000.

Separate testing analysis. Plan X and the individual medical account must separately satisfy the limitations on contributions, taking into account any special limit applicable to the arrangement (see Q 6:53). In this case, the contributions to Plan X separately satisfy the limitations on contributions. While the individual medical account is treated as a defined contribution plan subject to the limitations on contributions, it is not subject to the 100-percent-of-compensation limit, so the contributions to that account satisfy the limitations.

Aggregation analysis. The sum of the annual additions under Plan X and the amounts contributed to the separate account on P's behalf must satisfy the limitations on contributions. The limit applicable to the aggregated plan is equal to the greater of the limits applicable to the separate plans (see Q 6:53). In this case, the limit applicable to the medical account is $51,000 (which is greater than the limit of $30,000 applicable to the qualified plan), so the limit that applies to the aggregated plan is $51,000, and the aggregated plan satisfies the contribution limitations.

Q 6:57 Can a plan be disqualified because of the limitation on benefits and contributions?

With respect to a particular limitation year (see Q 6:58), a plan is disqualified if certain conditions described below occur. The determination of whether a plan or a group of aggregated plans exceeds the limitations imposed on benefits and contributions for a particular limitation year is, except as otherwise provided, made by taking into account the aggregation of plan rules (see Qs 6:51-6:54). [I.R.C. § 415(g); Treas. Reg. § 1.415(g)-1(a)(1)]

A plan is disqualified if annual additions with respect to the account of any participant in a defined contribution plan maintained by the employer exceed the limitations imposed on contributions (see Q 6:34). [Treas. Reg. § 1.415(g)-1(a)(2)] A plan is disqualified if the annual benefit (see Q 6:14) of a participant in a defined benefit plan maintained by the employer exceeds the limitations imposed on benefits (see Q 6:11). [Treas. Reg. § 1.415(g)-1(a)(3)]

If any plan is disqualified for a particular limitation year, then the disqualification is effective as of the first day of the first plan year containing any portion of the particular limitation year. [Treas. Reg. § 1.415(g)-1(b)(1)]

In the case of a single defined benefit plan (determined without regard to the aggregation rules) maintained by the employer that provides an annual benefit in excess of the limitations on benefits for any particular limitation year, such plan is disqualified in that limitation year. Similarly, if the employer maintains only a single defined contribution plan (determined without regard to the aggregation rules) under which annual additions allocated to the account of any participant exceed the limitations on contributions for any particular limitation year, such plan is also disqualified in that limitation year. [Treas. Reg. § 1.415(g)-1(b)(2)]

If the limitations on benefits or contributions are exceeded for a particular limitation year with respect to any participant solely because of the application of the aggregation rules, then one or more of the plans is disqualified in accordance with the ordering rules discussed below until, without regard to annual benefits or annual additions under the disqualified plan or plans, the remaining plans satisfy the applicable limitations. [Treas. Reg. § 1.415(g)-1(b)(3)(i)]

If there are two or more plans that have not been terminated at any time, including the last day of the particular limitation year, and if one or more of these plans is a multiemployer plan (see Q 6:55), then one or more of the plans (as needed to satisfy the limitations on benefits or contributions) that has not been terminated and is not a multiemployer plan is disqualified in that limitation year. For purposes of the preceding sentence, the determination of whether a plan is a multiemployer plan is made as of the last day of the particular limitation year. [Treas. Reg. § 1.415(g)-1(b)(3)(ii)(A)]

If, after the application of the preceding paragraph, there are two or more plans and one or more of the plans has been terminated at any time, including the last day of the particular limitation year, then one or more of the plans (as needed to satisfy the applicable limitations) that has not been so terminated (regardless of whether the plan is a multiemployer plan) is disqualified in that limitation year. [Treas. Reg. § 1.415(g)-1(b)(3)(ii)(B)]

If there are two or more plans of an employer within a group of plans, one or more of which is to be disqualified, the employer may elect, in a manner determined by IRS, which plan or plans are disqualified. If those two or more plans are involved because of the application of the rules regarding affiliated employers (see Q 6:7), the employers involved may elect, in a manner determined by IRS, which plan or plans are disqualified. However, the election described in the preceding sentence is not effective unless made by all of those employers. If the election is not made, then IRS, taking into account all of the facts and circumstances, has the discretion to determine the plan that is disqualified in the particular limitation year. In making this determination, some of the factors that will be taken into account include, but are not limited to, the number of participants in each plan, the amount of benefits provided on an overall basis by each plan, and the extent to which benefits are distributed or retained in each plan. [Treas. Reg. § 1.415(g)-1(b)(3)(iii)]

If there are two or more plans, one or more of which is to be disqualified, and if one of the plans is a SEP (see Q 32:1), then the SEP is not disqualified until all of the other plans have been disqualified. However, if one of the plans has been terminated, then the SEP is disqualified before the terminated plan. In the event that aggregating a medical account and a defined contribution plan other than such a medical account (see Qs 6:34, 6:53) causes the limitations on contributions applicable to a participant to be exceeded for a particular limitation year, the defined contribution plan other than the medical account is disqualified for the limitation year. In the event that aggregating a 403(b) contract (see Q 35:1) and a defined contribution plan causes the limitations on contributions applicable to a participant under the aggregated defined contribution plans to be exceeded for a particular limitation year, the excess of the contributions to the 403(b) contract plus the annual additions to the plan over such limitations is attributed to the 403(b) contract and therefore includible in the gross income of the participant for the taxable year with or within which that limitation year ends. [Treas. Reg. § 1.415(g)-1(b)(3)(iv)]

The following example illustrates the application of the aggregation of a 403(b) contract and defined contribution plan. It is assumed that the dollar limitation that applies for all relevant limitation years is $49,000.

Example. N is employed by a hospital that purchases a 403(b) contract on N's behalf for the current limitation year. N is also the 100 percent owner of a professional corporation, P, that maintains a defined contribution plan during the current limitation year in which N participates (see Example 7 in Q 6:56). N's compensation from the hospital for the current limitation year is $160,000. For the current limitation year, the hospital contributes $30,000 for the 403(b) contract on N's behalf, which is within the limitations applicable to N under the 403(b) contract (specifically, the limit under the 403(b) contract is $49,000). Professional corporation P also contributes $25,000 to the defined contribution plan on N's behalf for the current limitation year (which represents the only annual additions allocated to N's account under the plan for such year), which is within the $49,000 dollar limitation applicable to N under the plan.

The professional corporation, as well as N, is considered to maintain the 403(b) contract. Accordingly, the sum of the annual additions under the defined contribution plan maintained by professional corporation P and the 403(b) contract must satisfy the limitations on contributions.

Because the total aggregate contributions ($55,000) exceed the dollar limitation applicable to N ($49,000), $6,000 of the $30,000 contributed to the 403(b) contract is considered an excess contribution and therefore currently includible in N's gross income. The contract continues to be a 403(b) contract only if, for the current limitation year and all years thereafter, the issuer of the contract maintains separate accounts for each portion attributable to such excess contributions. [Treas. Reg. § 1.415(a)-1(b)(2)]

Q 6:58   What is the limitation year?

Unless the terms of the plan provide otherwise, the limitation year, with respect to any qualified retirement plan maintained by the employer, is the calendar year. [Treas. Reg. § 1.415(j)-1(a)] However, instead of using the calendar year, the terms of a plan may provide for the use of any other consecutive 12-month period as the limitation year. This includes a fiscal year with an annual period varying from 52 to 53 weeks, so long as the fiscal year satisfies certain requirements. A plan may provide only for one limitation year, regardless of the number or identity of the employers maintaining the plan. [I.R.C. § 441(f); Treas. Reg. § 1.415(j)-1(b)]

Where an employer maintains more than one qualified retirement plan, those plans may provide for different limitation years. This rule also applies to a controlled group of corporations or trades or businesses (whether or not incorporated) under common control (see Qs 5:29, 5:31). If the plans of an employer (or a controlled group of employers whose plans are aggregated) have different limitation years, the limitations on contributions and benefits are applied in accordance with the rules discussed below. [Treas. Reg. § 1.415(j)-1(c)(1)]

If a participant is credited with annual additions (see Q 6:34) in only one defined contribution plan (see Q 2:2), in determining whether the limitations are satisfied, only the limitation year applicable to that plan is considered. However, if a participant is credited with annual additions in more than one defined contribution plan, each such plan satisfies the limitations on annual additions only if the limitations are satisfied with respect to amounts that are annual additions for the limitation year with respect to the participant under the plan, plus amounts credited to the participant's account under all other plans required to be aggregated with the plan that would have been considered annual additions for the limitation year under the plan if they had been credited under the plan rather than an aggregated plan (see Q 6:51). [Treas. Reg. § 1.415(j)-1(c)(2)]

If a participant has participated in only one defined benefit plan (see Q 2:3), in determining whether the limitations on the annual benefit (see Q 6:11) are satisfied, only the limitation year applicable to that plan is considered. However, if a participant has participated in more than one defined benefit plan, a plan satisfies the limitations only if the annual benefit under all plans required to be aggregated for the limitation year of that plan with respect to the participant satisfy the applicable limitations. Thus, for example, the dollar limitation applicable to the limitation year for each plan must be applied to annual benefits under all aggregated plans to determine whether the plan satisfies the annual benefit limitations. [Treas. Reg. § 1.415(j)-1(c)(3)]

Once established, the limitation year may be changed only by amending the plan. Any change in the limitation year must be a change to a 12-month period commencing with any day within the current limitation year. The limitations are applied in the normal manner to the new limitation year and are separately applied to a limitation period that begins with the first day of the current limitation year and ends on the day before the first day of the first limitation year for which the change is effective. In the case of a defined contribution plan, the dollar limitation with respect to this limitation period is determined by multiplying (1) the applicable dollar limitation for the calendar year in which the limitation period ends by (2) a fraction, the numerator of which is the number of months (including any fractional part of a month) in the limitation period and the denominator of which is 12. This adjustment of the dollar limitation applies *only* to a defined contribution plan; and, thus, in the case of a defined benefit plan, no adjustment is made to the annual benefit limitations to reflect a short limitation year. If a defined contribution plan is terminated effective as of a date other than the last day of the plan's limitation year, the plan is treated as if the plan was amended to change its limitation year. Thus, these rules apply to the terminating plan's final limitation year. [Treas. Reg. § 1.415(j)-1(d)]

Example 1. Stuart is employed by both Lori Corp. and Dana Corp., each of which maintains a defined contribution plan. Stuart participates in both of these plans. The limitation year for Lori Corp.'s plan is January 1 through December 31, and the limitation year for Dana Corp.'s plan is April 1 through March 31. Dale Corp. owns 100 percent of the stock of both Lori Corp. and Dana Corp., and the two plans in which Stuart participates are required to be aggregated for purposes of applying the limitations to annual additions made with respect to Stuart. Thus, for example, for the limitation year of Lori Corp.'s plan that begins January 1, 2011, annual additions with respect to Stuart that are subject to the limitations include both (1) amounts that are annual additions with respect to Stuart under Lori Corp.'s plan for the period beginning January 1, 2011 and ending December 31, 2011 and (2) amounts contributed to Dana Corp.'s plan with respect to Stuart that would have been considered annual additions for the period beginning January 1, 2011 and ending December 31, 2011 under Lori Corp.'s plan.

Example 2. In 2010, Sil-Fen, Inc., an employer with a profit sharing plan using the calendar year as the limitation year, elects to change the limitation year to a period beginning July 1 and ending June 30. Because of this change, the plan must satisfy the limitations for the limitation period beginning January 1, 2010 and ending June 30, 2010. In applying the limitations to this limitation period, the amount of compensation taken into account may include compensation only for this period. Furthermore, the dollar limitation for this period is $24,500 ($49,000 × 6/12; see Q 6:34).

Q 6:59 Can a self-employed individual set up a qualified retirement plan?

Yes. However, if (1) the self-employed individual (see Q 6:60) is an owner-employee (see Q 5:32) of more than one business, (2) the businesses are not under common control (see Qs 5:29–5:31), and (3) the individual participates in a qualified retirement plan maintained by one of the individual's businesses, the qualified retirement plan must provide that contributions on behalf of the owner-employee may be made only with respect to the owner-employee's earned income (see Q 6:61) derived from the trade or business adopting the plan (see Q 5:33).

A self-employed individual is an individual who has earned income from self-employment for the taxable year. An S corporation (see Q 28:2) shareholder is not a self-employed individual, and S corporation pass-through income is not income from self-employment. Therefore, an S corporation shareholder cannot establish a retirement plan and make deductible contributions thereto based upon the pass-through income. [Rev. Rul. 59-221, 1959-1 C.B. 225; Durando v. United States, 70 F.3d 548 (9th Cir. 1995); Ding, 74 T.C.M. 708 (1997)]

IRS has released the following fact sheet covering retirement plans established by self-employed business owners for themselves and their employees. In particular, the fact sheet explains how self-employed individuals can avoid IRS examinations and additional assessments by preventing incorrect deductions for contributions to retirement plans.

> Retirement plans are not just for big businesses. They are also available for sole proprietorships. If you are a self-employed small business owner, you can set up a qualified retirement plan for yourself and your employees.

> If you are a sole proprietor, you can deduct contributions you make to the plan for yourself. You can also deduct trustee fees if contributions to the plan do not cover them.

> The Internal Revenue Code provides significant tax incentives for employers that establish and maintain retirement plans that comply with the requirements of the Code.

> Generally, contributions that are set aside for retirement may be currently deductible by the employer but are not taxable to the employee until distributed from the plan.

> You must set up and fund a qualified retirement plan. No matter what type of plan for the self-employed you are considering, you must actually make contributions to a qualified and properly maintained retirement plan account. This fact sheet provides a quick look at preventing incorrect deductions for retirement plans.

> **Qualifications to claim deductions**

> If you are self-employed, you may qualify for a tax deduction for contributions you make to a qualified retirement plan. You must have self-employment income to qualify. Self-employment income consists of net profits from Schedule C or Schedule F (see Q 6:61).

> The deduction is the total plan contributions you can subtract from gross income on your federal income tax return. Limits apply to the amount deductible. You can avoid examinations and additional assessments by making sure you qualify for the deduction.

> **The self-employed retirement plan deduction may not be allowable if:**

> - Form 1040, Schedule SE, Section A (if applicable), Line 4, is less than the amount on Form 1040, Line 28.
> - Form 1040, Schedule SE, Section B (if applicable), Line 6, is less than the amount on Form 1040, Line 28.
> - Form W-2 indicates an individual is a Statutory Employee and the amount in Box 1 is less than Form 1040, Line 28.

More information

There are many other factors to consider when choosing a retirement plan that is right for you and for your business. A retirement plan has many benefits, including investing in the future now for financial security when you retire. As a bonus, you may qualify for significant tax advantages and other incentives.

Publication 560, Retirement Plans for Small Business, is a valuable resource for computing self-employment income and determining limitations on retirement contributions and deductions.

[IRS Fact Sheet FS-2008-24 (Oct. 31, 2008)]

Q 6:60 Who is a self-employed individual?

Anyone who carries on a trade or business as a sole proprietor or who is a member of a partnership is self-employed. Although the individual need not carry on regular full-time business activities to be considered self-employed, an individual must have earned income (see Qs 6:61, 6:62). [I.R.C. § 401(c); Treas. Reg. § 1.1402(c)-1] An S corporation (see Q 28:2) shareholder is not a self-employed individual, and S corporation pass-through income is not earned income. [Rev. Rul. 59-221, 1959-1 C.B. 225; Durando v. United States, 70 F.3d 548 (9th Cir. 1995); Ding, 74 T.C.M. 708 (1997)]

Q 6:61 What is earned income?

The criterion for contributions to a qualified retirement plan on behalf of a self-employed individual (see Q 6:60) is earned income. [I.R.C. § 415(c)(3)(B)] This means that contributions by or for a sole proprietor or partner may be made to a qualified retirement plan only if personal services are performed. Thus, for example, inactive owners who derive income solely from investments may not participate in a qualified retirement plan. [Treas. Reg. § 1.401-10(c)(3); Frick, 56 T.C.M. 1368 (1989); Pugh, 49 T.C.M. 748 (1985); Frick, 50 T.C.M. 1334 (1985)] Earned income is defined as the net earnings from self-employment in a trade or business in which personal services of the taxpayer are a material income-producing factor. In effect, earned income is the net profit of the business. The fact that capital is an important aspect of the self-employed individual's business is not significant in determining earned income. [I.R.C. § 401(c)(2); Priv. Ltr. Rul. 9652007; *see also* IRS Pub. 560, Priv. Ltr. Rul. 9750001] An individual who had no earned income from self-employment could not make a deductible contribution to a qualified retirement plan. [Rosetti, 85 T.C.M. 1427 (2003)]

Distributions of income to a limited partner are not considered net earnings from self-employment. However, guaranteed payments made to a limited partner are considered net earnings from self-employment if paid for services rendered to or for the partnership. [I.R.C. § 1402(a)(13); Treas. Reg. § 1.401-11(d)(2)(ii)] Distributions in liquidation of a terminating partner's interest in a partnership are not earned income. [Kellough, 69 T.C.M. 2998 (1995)] IRS has issued proposed amendments to regulations relating to limited partners and members of limited liability companies. [Treas. Reg. § 1.1402(a)-2]

An S corporation (see Q 28:2) shareholder is not a self-employed individual, and S corporation pass-through income is not earned income. Therefore, an S corporation shareholder cannot establish a retirement plan and make deductible contributions thereto based upon the pass-through income. [Rev. Rul. 59-221, 1959-1 C.B. 225; Durando v. United States, 70 F.3d 548 (9th Cir. 1995); Ding, 74 T.C.M. 708 (1997)]

Payments to a former employee under a deferred compensation plan represent compensation for past services and are not considered earned income. [Priv. Ltr. Rul. 8522057]

For purposes of computing the limitations on deductions for contributions to a qualified retirement plan, earned income is computed after taking into account amounts contributed to the plan on behalf of the self-employed individual (i.e., the self-employed individual's earned income is reduced by the deductible contributions to the plan). Furthermore, earned income is computed after the deduction allowed to the self-employed individual for one-half of the individual's self-employment taxes (see Q 6:63). [I.R.C. §§ 164(f), 401(c)(2)(A)(v), 401(c)(2)(A)(vi), 404(a)(8)(D), 1401]

Under SBJA 2010 (see Q 1:38), for taxable years beginning in 2010 *only*, to calculate self-employment taxes, the deduction for health insurance costs of a self-employed individual is taken into account in computing earned income. [I.R.C. § 162(*l*)]

Q 6:62   May an individual be both self-employed and an employee of another employer?

An individual may be an employee of one entity and still be self-employed with regard to another entity. With respect to the same employer, regardless of the form of entity (e.g., sole proprietorship, partnership, or corporation), the classifications as self-employed and employee are normally mutually exclusive; however, it is possible to be an employee of an entity and also be self-employed with regard to that entity. [Reese, 63 T.C.M. 3129 (1992)]

Example. Carol is employed by Billy's Ambulette Corporation as an accountant and also has her own part-time accounting practice. Even though Carol may participate in Billy's Ambulette Corporation's qualified retirement plan, she is also able to establish a qualified retirement plan for her self-employment income. [Treas. Reg. § 1.401-10(b)(3)(ii)]

However, where an individual was the president, the sole shareholder, and a director of a corporation, his compensation was ruled wages and not self-employment income. Consequently, the individual could not establish a qualified retirement plan. [Jacobs, 66 T.C.M. 1470 (1993)]

Q 6:63   How much may be contributed to a qualified retirement plan on behalf of a self-employed individual?

The contribution limits that apply to corporate plans apply to plans covering self-employed individuals (see Q 6:60). Thus, the annual addition limit for defined contribution plans is the lesser of $40,000 (subject to cost-of-living adjustments) or 100 percent of compensation (see Qs 6:34, 6:35). But because the deduction limitation for contributions to a defined contribution plan is 25 percent of earned income and earned income is computed after taking into account amounts contributed to the plan on behalf of the self-employed individual and after the deduction for one-half of the individual's self-employment taxes (see Qs 6:61, 12:17), the effective percentage limit on the contribution is 20 percent of earned income computed after the self-employment tax deduction but before the contribution ($1 \div 1.25 = .80; 1.0 - 80 = .20$).

For 2010, the self-employment tax rate is 15.3 percent (12.4 percent for Social Security and 2.9 percent for Medicare); the Social Security base is $106,800, but the Medicare base is unlimited.

Example 1. James adopted a 10-percent-of-compensation defined contribution plan for 2010. His earned income before the deductions for the plan contribution on his behalf and one-half of his self-employment taxes is $106,800. James's deductible contribution to the plan is $9,023, determined by completing the following steps:

Step 1	Enter the rate $[1.0 - (1 \div 1.10)]$	.090909
Step 2	Enter James's net earnings	$106,800
Step 3	Enter deduction for one-half of James's self-employment taxes	7,545
Step 4	Step 2 less Step 3	99,255
Step 5	Step 1 × Step 4	9,023
Step 6	10% (plan contribution rate) × $245,000 (but not more than $49,000)	24,500
Step 7	Deductible contribution: lesser of Step 5 or Step 6	9,023

Example 2A. Caroline adopted a 15-percent-of-compensation defined contribution plan for 2010. Her earned income before the deductions for the plan contribution on her behalf and one-half of her self-employment taxes is $245,000. Caroline's maximum deductible contribution to the plan is $30,665, determined by completing the following steps:

Step 1	Enter the rate $[1.0 - (1 \div 1.15)]$	.130435
Step 2	Enter Caroline's net earnings	$245,000
Step 3	Enter deduction for one-half of Caroline's self-employment taxes	9,902

Step 4	Step 2 less Step 3	235,098
Step 5	Step 1 × Step 4	30,665
Step 6	15% (plan contribution rate) × $245,000 (but not more than $49,000)	38,100
Step 7	Deductible contribution: lesser of Step 5 or Step 6	30,665

Example 2B. Assume the same facts as in Example 2A, except that Caroline's earned income before the deductions for the plan contribution on her behalf and one-half of her self-employment taxes is $265,000. Caroline's maximum deductible contribution to the plan is $33,239, determined by completing the following steps:

Step 1	Enter the rate [1.0 − (1 ÷ 1.15)]	.130435
Step 2	Enter Caroline's net earnings	$265,000
Step 3	Enter deduction for one-half of Caroline's self-employment taxes	10,170
Step 4	Step 2 less Step 3	254,830
Step 5	Step 1 × Step 4	33,239
Step 6	15% (plan contribution rate) × $245,000 (but not more than $49,000)	38,100
Step 7	Deductible contribution: lesser of Step 5 or Step 6	33,239

Example 3A. Stephanie adopted a 25-percent-of-compensation defined contribution plan for 2010. Her earned income before the deductions for the plan contribution on her behalf and one-half of her self-employment taxes is $245,000. Stephanie's deductible contribution to the plan is $47,020, determined by completing the following steps:

Step 1	Enter the rate [1.0 − (1 ÷ 1.25)]	.20
Step 2	Enter Stephanie's net earnings	$245,000
Step 3	Enter deduction for one-half of Stephanie's self-employment taxes	9,902
Step 4	Step 2 less Step 3	235,098
Step 5	Step 1 × Step 4	47,020
Step 6	25% (plan contribution rate) × $245,000 (but not more than $49,000)	49,000
Step 7	Deductible contribution: lesser of Step 5 or Step 6	47,020

Example 3B. Assume the same facts as in Example 3A, except that Stephanie's earned income before the deductions for the plan contribution on her behalf and one-half of her self-employment taxes is $265,000. Stephanie's deductible contribution to the plan is the maximum of $49,000, determined by completing the following steps:

Step 1	Enter the rate [1.0 − (1 ÷ 1.25)]	.20
Step 2	Enter Stephanie's net earnings	$265,000
Step 3	Enter deduction for one-half of Stephanie's self-employment taxes	10,170
Step 4	Step 2 less Step 3	254,830
Step 5	Step 1 × Step 4	50,966
Step 6	25% (plan contribution rate) × $245,000 (but not more than $49,000)	49,000
Step 7	Deductible contribution: lesser of Step 5 or Step 6	49,000

All of the above examples assume that the self-employed individual did not earn any salary that was subject to Social Security taxes during 2010. If the individual does earn a salary, the self-employment tax deduction will be reduced. Because the Medicare base is unlimited, the self-employment tax deduction must always be computed regardless of the individual's salary income.

Example 4. Assume the same facts as in Example 1, except that James also earned a salary of $106,800 in 2010. James's deductible contribution to the plan is $9,579 determined by completing the following steps:

Step 1	Enter the rate [1.0 − (1 ÷ 1.10)]	.090909
Step 2	Enter James's net earnings	$106,800
Step 3	Enter deduction for one-half of James's self-employment taxes	1,430
Step 4	Step 2 less Step 3	105,370
Step 5	Step 1 × Step 4	9,579
Step 6	10% (plan contribution rate) × $245,000 (but not more than $49,000)	24,500
Step 7	Deductible contribution: lesser of Step 5 or Step 6	9,579

IRS representatives have opined that, if an individual is a sole proprietor, has a 50 percent interest in a partnership, and has earned income of $100,000 from each entity, the deduction for one-half of the individual's self-employment taxes should be reasonably apportioned to each entity and that allocating the entire deduction to one entity would be unreasonable.

The contribution limit to a defined benefit plan is based upon a maximum annual retirement benefit equal to the lesser of $160,000 (subject to cost-of-living adjustments) or 100 percent of compensation (see Qs 6:11, 12:14).

Q 6:64   Can the definition of compensation used in a qualified retirement plan cause prohibited discrimination?

Yes. Section 414(s) provides rules for defining compensation for purposes of applying any provision that specifically refers to Section 414(s). For example, Section 414(s) is explicitly referred to in many of the nondiscrimination provisions applicable to qualified retirement plans. The amount of plan benefits or contributions, expressed as a percentage of compensation (see Qs 6:65–6:71), is generally one of the key factors in determining whether these nondiscrimination provisions are satisfied. [I.R.C. § 414(s); Treas. Reg. § 1.414(s)-1(a); IRS Notice 2001-37, 2001-1 C.B. 1340]

Q 6:65   May different definitions of compensation be used if an employer maintains more than one qualified retirement plan?

An employer may use any definition of compensation that satisfies Section 414(s) to determine if an applicable provision is satisfied with respect to a qualified retirement plan. This rule is designed to permit an employer, whenever possible, to use the definition used under the plan for calculating contributions or benefits to determine if an applicable nondiscrimination provision is satisfied. Consequently, an employer that maintains more than one qualified retirement plan may generally use one definition of compensation that satisfies Section 414(s) in determining whether one of the plans satisfies a particular nondiscrimination requirement (e.g., the general nondiscrimination requirements of Section 401(a)(4)) and use the same or a different definition of compensation in determining whether another plan satisfies the same nondiscrimination requirement. The definition of compensation selected generally must be used consistently to define the compensation of all employees taken into account in determining whether a plan satisfies the nondiscrimination provision. [Treas. Reg. §§ 1.414(s)-1(b)(1), 1.414(s)-1(b)(2)(i), 1.414(s)-1(b)(2)(ii)]

One court ruled that different definitions of compensation used to calculate different benefit formulas under the same plan were acceptable. [Gallo v. Amoco Corp., 1996 U.S. App. LEXIS 33086 (7th Cir. 1996)]

Q 6:66   Are there specific definitions of compensation that will satisfy Section 414(s)?

A definition of compensation that includes all compensation within the meaning of Section 415(c)(3) and excludes all other compensation will automatically satisfy Section 414(s) (see Q 6:41). In addition, Section 414(s) will be satisfied if either of the Section 415(c)(3) safe harbor definitions is used (see Q 6:42). [Treas. Reg. § 1.414(s)-1(c)(2)]

A safe harbor alternative definition of compensation that will automatically satisfy Section 414(s) without further testing is permitted. Under the safe harbor, compensation may be defined as set forth in the preceding paragraph but may be reduced by all of the following items (even if includible in income): (1) reimbursements or other expense allowances; (2) fringe benefits (cash and noncash); (3) moving expenses; (4) deferred compensation; and (5) welfare benefits. [Treas. Reg. § 1.414(s)-1(c)(3)] However, Section 415 compensation now includes elective or salary reduction contributions to a qualified transportation fringe benefit plan. [I.R.C. §§ 414(s)(2), 415(c)(3)(D)(ii); IRS Notice 2001-37, 2001-1 C.B. 1340] One court ruled that excluding from compensation the value of trips awarded to employees was permissible. [Giaquinto, Jr. v. Southern New England Tel. Co., No. 97-7511 (2d Cir. 1997)]

Any of the safe harbor definitions may be modified to permit additional items or amounts of compensation to be excluded from the compensation of HCEs (see Q 3:2), but not from the compensation of any NHCEs (see Q 3:12). HCEs need not be treated consistently. A safe harbor definition will continue to satisfy Section 414(s) automatically even if the definition is modified to exclude any portion of the compensation of some or all of the HCEs. [Treas. Reg. § 1.414(s)-1(c)(5)]

Q 6:67 Are there any alternative definitions of compensation that may satisfy Section 414(s)?

A definition of compensation will satisfy Section 414(s) with respect to employees if the definition of compensation is reasonable, does not by design favor HCEs (see Q 3:2), and satisfies the nondiscrimination requirement (see Q 6:68). Even if the definition is reasonable, it still must not favor the HCEs or be discriminatory. A reasonable definition of compensation is permitted to exclude, on a consistent basis, all or any portion of irregular or additional compensation, including one or more of the following:

1. Any type of additional compensation for employees working outside their regularly scheduled tour of duty (such as overtime pay, premiums for shift differential, and call-in premiums);

2. Bonuses; or

3. Any type of compensation excluded under the safe harbor alternative definition (see Q 6:66).

Whether a type of compensation is irregular or additional is determined based upon all the relevant facts and circumstances. [Treas. Reg. §§ 1.414(s)-1(d)(1), 1.414(s)-1(d)(2)(i), 1.414(s)-1(d)(2)(ii)]

A definition of compensation is not reasonable if the definition includes an item or amount not includible under a safe harbor definition (e.g., business expenses substantiated to the payor under an accountable plan). In addition, a definition is *not* reasonable if it provides that each employee's compensation is a specified portion of the employee's total compensation (such as 90 percent). However, a definition of compensation is not unreasonable merely because it excludes all compensation in excess of a specified dollar amount. [Treas. Reg. § 1.414(s)-1(d)(2)(iii)] One court ruled that excluding from compensation the value of trips awarded to employees was permissible. [Giaquinto, Jr. v. Southern New England Tel. Co., No. 97-7511 (2d Cir. 1997)]

Only compensation paid in the course of employment with the employer maintaining the plan is considered; commissions, bonuses, and management fees paid to an employee as an independent contractor are not included as compensation. [Van Roekel Farms, Inc. v. Comm'r, 2001 U.S. App. LEXIS 14201 (8th Cir. 2001); Howard E. Clendenen, Inc. v. Comm'r, 207 F.3d 1071 (8th Cir. 2000); Roblene, Inc., 77 T.C.M. 1998 (1999)] Workers compensation payments cannot form the basis for additional plan contributions because such payments are not made by the employer. [Campanella v. Mason Tenders District Council Pension Plan, 2005 WL 414844 (2d Cir. 2005)] A participant was entitled to a plan contribution based on compensation he received after resigning from employment, concluded one court. [Tomasko v. Ira H. Weinstock, P.C., 2003 WL 22701470 (3d Cir. 2003)]

Q 6:68 Must an alternative definition of compensation be nondiscriminatory?

Yes. An alternative definition of compensation is nondiscriminatory if the average percentage of total compensation included under the alternative definition for an employer's HCEs (see Q 3:2) as a group does not exceed by more than a *de minimis* amount the average percentage included under the alternative definition for the employer's NHCEs (see Q 3:12) as a group. Self-employed individuals (see Q 6:60) and employees with zero compensation (see Q 6:70) are disregarded for purposes of this nondiscrimination test (see Q 6:71). [Treas. Reg. §§ 1.414(s)-1(d)(3)(i), 1.414(s)-1(d)(3)(iii); Rev. Proc. 95-34, 1995-2 C.B. 385; Rev. Proc. 93-42, 1993-2 C.B. 540; Ann. 93-130, 1993-31 I.R.B. 46; Ann. 92-81, 1992-22 I.R.B. 56]

To calculate the average percentage, total compensation means all compensation within the meaning of Section 415(c)(3) and excludes all other compensation (see Qs 6:41, 6:42). If a portion of the compensation of some HCEs is excluded (see Q 6:66), the total compensation of such affected HCEs is reduced; but, if the exclusion applies consistently to all HCEs, the adjustment is not required. Total compensation taken into account for each employee (including the elective contributions) may not exceed the annual compensation limit (see Qs 6:45, 6:46). [Treas. Reg. § 1.414(s)-1(d)(3)(ii)]

To determine whether the average percentage requirement is satisfied, the employer must calculate individual percentages for each employee in a group and then average the percentages (individual-percentage method). However, the employer may use any other reasonable method to determine the average percentages. Thus, an employer may calculate an aggregate compensation percentage for each group of employees by dividing the aggregate amount of compensation of all employees in that group that is included under the alternative definition by the aggregate amount of total compensation of all employees in that group (aggregate-percentage method). Alternatively, the individual-percentage method may be used for one group, and the aggregate-percentage method may be used for the other group. An alternative method is considered reasonable only if the percentage is not reasonably expected to vary significantly from the average percentage produced using the individual-percentage method because of the extra weight given employees with higher compensation in the relevant group. [Treas. Reg. § 1.414(s)-1(d)(3)(iv)]

The determination of whether the average percentage of total compensation included for the employer's HCEs as a group exceeds by more than a *de minimis* amount the average percentage of total compensation included for the employer's NHCEs as a group is based on the applicable facts and circumstances. The differences between the percentages for prior periods may be considered in determining whether the amount of the difference between the percentages for a given period is more than *de minimis*. In addition, an isolated instance of a more than *de minimis* difference between the compensation percentages that is due to an extraordinary, unforeseeable event (such as overtime payments due to a major hurricane) will be disregarded if the amount of the difference in prior determination periods was *de minimis*. [Treas. Reg. § 1.414(s)-1(d)(3)(v)]

Q 6:69   Can a rate-of-pay definition of compensation be used?

Rate of pay is permitted as an alternative definition of compensation (see Q 6:67). Therefore, compensation may be defined as the amount of each employee's basic or regular compensation using the employee's basic or regular *rate* of compensation rather than using the employee's *actual* basic or regular compensation. For this purpose, the employee's rate of compensation must be determined using an hourly pay scale, weekly salary, or similar unit of basic or regular compensation applicable to the employee. It is permissible to define compensation as (1) including each employee's basic or regular compensation, the amount of which is determined using each employee's basic or regular rate of compensation plus actual amounts of irregular or additional compensation, such as overtime or bonuses, or (2) the greater of the employee's actual compensation or basic or regular compensation using the employee's basic or regular rate of compensation. Of course, the rate-of-pay definition must be nondiscriminatory. [Treas. Reg. § 1.414(s)-1(e)(1)]

A rate-of-pay definition cannot be used to determine if elective contributions (see Q 27:16), matching contributions (see Q 27:75), or employee contributions (see Q 27:74) satisfy, for example, the ADP test (see Q 27:18) or the ACP test (see Q 27:77). [Treas. Reg. § 1.414(s)-1(e)(2)]

The amount of each employee's basic or regular compensation for the determination period must be determined using the employee's basic or regular rate of compensation as of a designated date in the determination period. If the determination period is a calendar year, this requirement would be satisfied if the amount of each employee's basic or regular compensation for the calendar year is determined using the basic or regular rate of compensation as of January 1. Alternatively, the amount of each employee's basic or regular compensation for a determination period can be the sum of the amounts separately determined for shorter specified periods (e.g., weeks or months) within the determination period, provided that the amount of each employee's basic or regular compensation for each specified period is determined using the employee's basic or regular rate of compensation as of a designated date within the specified period. [Treas. Reg. §§ 1.414(s)-1(e)(3)(ii), 1.414(s)-1(h)(2)]

One or more dates may be used to determine employees' rates of compensation for a determination period or specified period provided that, if the same date is not used for all employees, the dates selected are designed to determine the rates of compensation for that period on a consistent basis for all employees taken into account for the determination period. For example, if annual compensation increases are provided to different groups of employees on different dates during the year, it would be consistent to choose a different date for each group in order to include the annual increase in the employees' rates of compensation for the determination period. [Treas. Reg. § 1.414(s)-1(e)(3)(iii)]

An employee's compensation may generally be determined using only the rate of compensation for employment periods during which the employer actually compensates the employee. However, if an employee terminates employment or otherwise stops performing services (e.g., for a leave of absence, layoff, or similar event), either without compensation or with reduced compensation during a determination period, the employer may continue to credit the employee with compensation based on the employee's rate of compensation for a period of up to 31 days after the event, but not beyond the end of the determination period (see Q 6:71). [Treas. Reg. § 1.414(s)-1(e)(3)(iv)]

Q 6:70   Can prior-employer compensation and imputed compensation be used?

Solely for purposes of determining whether a defined benefit plan (see Q 2:3) satisfies certain requirements (see Qs 4:10, 5:15), an alternative definition of compensation that includes prior-employer compensation or imputed compensation may be a reasonable alternative definition (see Q 6:67). Prior-employer compensation is compensation from an employer other than the employer (determined at the time that the compensation is paid) maintaining the defined benefit plan that is credited for periods prior to the employee's employment with the current employer maintaining the plan, and during which periods the employee performed services for the other employer. Imputed compensation is compensation credited for periods after an employee has commenced or recommenced participation in a defined benefit plan while the employee is not compensated by the employer maintaining the plan, or is compensated at a reduced rate by that employer because the employee is not performing services as an employee for the employer (including a period in which the employee performs services for another employer, e.g., a joint venture) or because the employee has a reduced work schedule. [Treas. Reg. §§ 1.414(s)-1(f)(1), 1.414(s)-1(f)(4)]

Crediting prior-employer compensation or imputed compensation must apply on the same terms to all similarly situated employees; there must be a legitimate business purpose, based on all of the relevant facts and circumstances, for crediting such compensation to an employee; and, based on all of the relevant facts and circumstances, crediting such compensation must not by design or in operation discriminate significantly in favor of HCEs (see Q 3:2). Subject to certain requirements, any reasonable method may be used to determine the amount of prior-employer compensation or imputed compensation. [Treas. Reg. §§ 1.414(s)-1(f)(2), 1.414(s)-1(f)(3)]

Q 6:71   Are there any special rules for self-employed individuals?

If an alternative definition of compensation (see Q 6:67) is used, an equivalent alternative compensation amount must be determined for any self-employed individual (see Q 6:60) who is in the group of employees for whom the consistency requirement (see Q 6:65) requires a single definition of compensation to be used. This equivalent alternative compensation amount is determined by multiplying the self-employed individual's total earned income (see Q 6:61) by the percentage of total compensation (see Q 6:68) included under the alternative definition for the employer's common-law NHCEs (see Q 3:12) as a group. For purposes of this determination, common-law HCEs (see Q 3:2) must be disregarded. This equivalent alternative compensation amount will be treated as compensation determined using the alternative definition of compensation. An alternative definition may provide that compensation for some or all self-employed individuals who are HCEs is a specified portion of, rather than equal to, the equivalent compensation amount. [Treas. Reg. §§ 1.414(s)-1(b)(3), 1.414(s)-1(g)(1)(i), 1.414(s)-1(g)(1)(iii), 1.401(a)(17)-1(c)]

Chapter 7

Permitted Disparity

A company can make its qualified retirement plan part of an overall retirement scheme that includes Social Security; this combination is called permitted disparity. This chapter examines how permitted disparity works and the opportunity it affords a company to provide benefits favorable to shareholder-employees and key personnel without running afoul of the prohibition against discrimination.

Q 7:1   What does permitted disparity mean?

Every employer is already paying for a retirement plan for its employees—Social Security. By providing for permitted disparity in its qualified retirement plan (i.e., combining its private retirement plan with Social Security), the employer gets the benefit of its Social Security tax payments. The employer in effect makes its qualified retirement plan part of one overall scheme that combines both Social Security and the employer's private plan.

Technically, a plan that provides for permitted disparity means a qualified retirement plan that is not considered discriminatory merely because the benefits provided under the plan favor highly compensated employees (HCEs; see Q 3:2), as long as the difference in benefits is attributable to what IRS refers to as permitted disparity (i.e., Social Security integration). Permitted disparity may be taken into account to demonstrate that the amount of contributions or benefits does not discriminate in favor of HCEs (see Qs 4:11, 4:12, 4:14).

Permitted disparity can mean a substantial saving for the employer because the cost of the employer's qualified retirement plan can be reduced.

[I.R.C. §§ 401(a)(5), 401(*l*); Treas. Reg. § 1.401(*l*)-1]

Q 7:2   What types of qualified retirement plans can provide for permitted disparity?

Both defined contribution plans (see Q 2:2) and defined benefit plans (see Q 2:3) can provide for permitted disparity.

A defined contribution excess plan is a defined contribution plan under which the rate at which employer contributions (and forfeitures) are allocated to the accounts of participants with respect to compensation above a level specified in the plan (expressed as a percentage of such compensation) is greater than the rate at which employer contributions (and forfeitures) are allocated with respect to compensation at or below such specified level (expressed as a percentage of such compensation). [Treas. Reg. § 1.401(*l*)-1(c)(16)(ii)]

A defined benefit excess plan is a defined benefit plan under which the rate at which employer-provided benefits are determined with respect to average annual compensation (see Q 7:22) above a level specified in the plan (expressed as a percentage of such compensation) is greater than the rate with respect to compensation at or below such specified level (expressed as a percentage of such compensation). [Treas. Reg. § 1.401(*l*)-1(c)(16)(i)]

A defined benefit offset plan is a defined benefit plan that is not a defined benefit excess plan and that provides that each participant's employer-provided benefit is reduced by a specified percentage of the participant's final average compensation (see Q 7:24) up to the offset level under the plan. [Treas. Reg. § 1.401(*l*)-1(c)(25)]

For purposes of the permitted disparity rules, target benefit plans (see Q 2:5) are generally treated like defined benefit plans. [Treas. Reg. § 1.401(*l*)-2(a)(1)]

A qualified retirement plan designated as an employee stock ownership plan (ESOP; see Q 28:1) may not provide for permitted disparity if the plan is established after November 1, 1977. An ESOP providing for permitted disparity before that date can continue to do so, but the plan cannot be amended to increase the integration level or the integration percentage. [Treas. Reg. § 54.4975-11(a)(7)(ii)]

Q 7:3 What general rules apply to a defined contribution excess plan?

A defined contribution excess plan (see Q 7:2) will meet the permitted disparity rules only if the excess contribution percentage (ECP; see Q 7:4) does not exceed the base contribution percentage (BCP; see Q 7:5) by more than the lesser of (1) the BCP or (2) the greater of 5.7 percentage points, or the percentage equal to the rate of tax attributable to the old-age insurance portion of the Old-Age, Survivors, and Disability Insurance (OASDI) as of the beginning of the plan year. [I.R.C. § 401(*l*)(2); IRS Notice 89-70, 1989-1 C.B. 730]

For purposes of the permitted disparity rules, target benefit plans (see Q 2:5) are generally treated like defined benefit plans. [Treas. Reg. § 1.401(*l*)-2(a)(1)]

Q 7:4 What is the excess contribution percentage?

The ECP is the percentage of compensation at which employer contributions (and forfeitures) are allocated to the accounts of participants with respect to compensation of participants above the integration level (see Q 7:6) specified in the defined contribution plan (see Q 2:2) for the plan year. [I.R.C. § 401(l)(2)(B)(i); Treas. Reg. § 1.401(l)-1(c)(15)]

Q 7:5   What is the base contribution percentage?

The BCP is the percentage of compensation at which employer contributions (and forfeitures) are allocated to the accounts of participants with respect to compensation of participants at or below the integration level (see Q 7:6) specified in the defined contribution plan (see Q 2:2) for the plan year. [I.R.C. § 401(l)(2)(B)(ii); Treas. Reg. § 1.401(l)-1(c)(4)]

Q 7:6   What is the integration level?

The integration level is the amount of compensation specified in the defined contribution or defined benefit excess plan (see Q 7:2) at or below which the rate of contributions or benefits provided under the plan is less than the rate with respect to compensation above such level. [I.R.C. § 401(l)(5)(A)(i); Treas. Reg. § 1.401(l)-1(c)(20)]

For defined contribution excess plans, the integration level must meet one of the following requirements:

1. The integration level for each participant is the taxable wage base (TWB; see Q 7:7) in effect as of the beginning of the plan year.
2. The integration level for all employees is a single dollar amount (either specified in the plan or determined under a formula specified in the plan) that does not exceed 20 percent of the TWB in effect as of the beginning of the plan year.
3. The integration level for all employees is a single dollar amount (either specified in the plan or determined under a formula specified in the plan) that is greater than the amount in (2) above and less than the TWB in effect as of the beginning of the plan year, provided the limitation of 5.7 percentage points (see Q 7:3) is reduced. If the integration level is more than 20 percent of the TWB but not more than 80 percent of the TWB, the 5.7 percentage points factor is reduced to 4.3 percentage points. If the integration level is more than 80 percent but less than 100 percent of the TWB, the 5.7 percentage points factor is reduced to 5.4 percentage points.

[Treas. Reg. § 1.401(l)-2(d)]

See Q 7:16 for a discussion of the integration level in defined benefit excess plans.

Q 7:7   What is the taxable wage base?

The TWB is the maximum amount of earnings in any calendar year that may be considered wages for Social Security purposes. For 2010, this amount remains at $106,800.

For the five prior calendar years, the TWB was:

Year	Taxable Wage Base
2009	$106,800
2008	102,000
2007	97,500
2006	94,200
2005	90,000

[Rev. Rul. 2009-40, 2009-52 I.R.B. 942]

Q 7:8   How are the permitted disparity rules applied to contribution formulas under defined contribution excess plans?

The following examples illustrate whether or not a defined contribution excess plan meets the permitted disparity rules (see Qs 7:2, 7:3):

Example 1. J.T. Corporation has a money purchase pension plan with a calendar-year plan year. For the 2010 plan year, the plan provides that each participant will receive a contribution of 5 percent of compensation up to the TWB (see Q 7:7) and 10 percent of compensation in excess of the TWB. The plan meets the permitted disparity rules because the ECP (see Q 7:4), 10 percent, does not exceed the BCP (see Q 7:5), 5 percent, by more than the lesser of 5 percentage points or 5.7 percentage points.

Example 2. Assume the same facts as those in Example 1, except that the plan provides that, with respect to compensation in excess of the TWB, each participant will receive a contribution for the plan year of 10.7 percent of such excess compensation. The plan does not meet the permitted disparity rules because the ECP, 10.7 percent, exceeds the BCP, 5 percent, by more than the lesser of 5 percentage points or 5.7 percentage points.

Example 3. For the 2010 plan year, a profit sharing plan uses an integration level of $22,000, which is less than 80 percent of the TWB of $106,800 but more than $21,360 (20% × $106,800). Consequently, the 5.7 percentage points factor must be replaced by 4.3 percentage points.

If in Example 3 the integration level is reduced by $1,000 to $21,000, the 5.7 percentage points factor will be used. This anomaly occurs because the reduced integration level does not exceed 20 percent of the TWB [$21,360 (20% × $106,800)].

Q 7:9   What general rules apply to a defined benefit excess plan?

A defined benefit excess plan (see Q 7:2) will meet the permitted disparity rules if the excess benefit percentage (EBP; see Q 7:10) does not exceed the base benefit percentage (BBP; see Q 7:11) by more than the maximum excess allowance (MEA; see Q 7:12). Also, benefits must be based on average annual compensation (see Q 7:22).

Furthermore, any optional form of benefit, preretirement benefit, actuarial factor, or other benefit or feature provided with respect to compensation above the integration level (see Q 7:16) must also be provided with respect to compensation below the integration level. Thus, for example, if a lump-sum distribution option, calculated using particular actuarial assumptions, is available for benefits relating to compensation above the integration level, the same lump-sum option must be available on an equivalent basis for benefits based on compensation up to the integration level. [I.R.C. § 401(l)(3); Treas. Reg. § 1.401(l)-3]

For purposes of the permitted disparity rules, target benefit plans (see Q 2:5) are generally treated like defined benefit plans. [Treas. Reg. § 1.401(l)-2(a)(1)]

Q 7:10 What is the excess benefit percentage?

The EBP is the percentage of compensation at which employer-provided benefits are determined with respect to average annual compensation (see Q 7:22) of participants above the integration level (see Q 7:16) specified in the defined benefit plan for the plan year. [I.R.C. § 401(l)(3)(A); Treas. Reg. § 1.401(l)-1(c)(14)]

Q 7:11 What is the base benefit percentage?

The BBP is the percentage of compensation at which employer-provided benefits are determined with respect to average annual compensation (see Q 7:22) of participants at or below the integration level (see Q 7:16) specified in the defined benefit plan for the plan year. [I.R.C. § 401(l)(3)(A); Treas. Reg. § 1.401(l)-1(c)(3)]

Q 7:12 What is the maximum excess allowance?

The MEA for a plan year is the lesser of either the BBP (see Q 7:11) or .75 percentage point. [I.R.C. § 401(l)(4)(A); Treas. Reg. § 1.401(l)-3(b)(2)]

Q 7:13 What is the Social Security retirement age?

Social Security retirement age (SSRA) means the age used as the retirement age under the Social Security Act and depends on the calendar year of birth.

Year of Birth	*SSRA*
Before 1938	65
After 1937 but before 1955	66
After 1954	67

[I.R.C. § 415(b)(8); Social Security Act § 216(1)]

For limitation years (see Q 6:58) ending after 2001, SSRA is no longer relevant for purposes of calculating adjustments to the dollar limitation (see Q 6:11) on benefits payable under a defined benefit plan (see Qs 6:12, 6:13). [I.R.C. §§ 415(b)(2)(C), 415(b)(2)(D)] However, for purposes of calculating certain adjustments with respect to formulas in defined benefit plans using permitted disparity (see Qs 7:15, 7:20), SSRA is still relevant.

Q 7:14 How are the permitted disparity rules applied to benefit formulas under defined benefit excess plans?

The following examples illustrate whether or not a defined benefit excess plan meets the permitted disparity rules (see Qs 7:2, 7:9):

Example 1. M. P. Corporation maintains a defined benefit excess plan. The formula is .5 percent of the participant's average annual compensation (see Q 7:22) up to covered compensation (see Q 7:23) for the plan year plus 1.25 percent of the participant's average annual compensation for the plan year in excess of the participant's covered compensation for the plan year, multiplied by the participant's years of credited service with the company up to a maximum of 35 years. The plan formula provides a benefit that exceeds the MEA (see Q 7:12) because the EBP (see Q 7:10), 1.25 percent, for the plan year exceeds the BBP (see Q 7:11), .5 percent, for the plan year by more than the BBP.

Example 2. If the BBP in Example 1 was .75 percent, the plan would meet the permitted disparity rules because the EBP (1.25 percent) would not exceed the BBP (.75 percent) by more than the MEA (.75 percentage point).

Example 3. Walter-Michele Corporation maintains a defined benefit excess plan. The formula is 1 percent of average annual compensation up to the integration level for each year of service plus 1.85 percent of average annual compensation in excess of the integration level for each of the first ten years of service plus 1.65 percent of average annual compensation in excess of the integration level for each year of service more than ten. The disparity provided under the plan exceeds the MEA because the EBP for each of the first ten years of service (1.85 percent) exceeds the BBP (1 percent) by more than .75 percent.

Example 4. The facts are the same as in Example 3, except that the plan provides an EBP of 1.65 percent of average annual compensation in excess of the integration level for each of the first ten years of service and an EBP of 1.85 percent of average annual compensation in excess of the integration level for each year of service more than ten. The disparity provided under the plan exceeds the MEA because the EBP for each year of service more than ten (1.85 percent) exceeds the BBP (1 percent) by more than .75 percent.

[Treas. Reg. § 1.401(l)-3(b)(5)]

Q 7:15 Can benefits commence prior to or after SSRA in a defined benefit excess plan?

Yes; but, if benefits commence prior to or after the SSRA (see Q 7:13), the .75 percentage point factor (see Q 7:12) is reduced or increased depending on the age at which benefits commence and the participant's SSRA.

The factors in the following table are applicable to benefits that commence in the month the employee attains the specified age. Accordingly, if benefits commence in a month other than the month in which the employee attains the specified age, appropriate adjustments in the .75 percentage point factor in the MEA (see Q 7:12) must be made. For this purpose, adjustments may be based on straight-line interpolation from the factors in the tables or in accordance with other methods of adjustment specified in the regulations.

Age at Which Benefits Commence	SSRA 67	SSRA 66	SSRA 65
70	1.002	1.101	1.209
69	0.908	0.998	1.096
68	0.825	0.907	0.996
67	0.750	0.824	0.905
66	0.700	0.750	0.824
65	0.650	0.700	0.750
64	0.600	0.650	0.700
63	0.550	0.600	0.650
62	0.500	0.550	0.600
61	0.475	0.500	0.550
60	0.450	0.475	0.500
59	0.425	0.450	0.475
58	0.400	0.425	0.450
57	0.375	0.400	0.425
56	0.344	0.375	0.400
55	0.316	0.344	0.375

Example 1. Saul Corp. maintains a defined benefit excess plan. The plan provides that for an employee with an SSRA of 65, the normal retirement benefit is 1.25 percent of average annual compensation up to the integration level (BBP; see Q 7:11), plus 2.0 percent of average annual compensation in excess of the integration level (EBP; see Q 7:10), for each year of service up to 35. For an employee with at least 20 years of service, the plan provides a benefit commencing at age 55 that is equal to the benefit payable at age 65.

For that employee, the disparity provided under the plan at age 55 is .75 percent (2% × 1.25%). Because this disparity exceeds the .375 percent factor provided in the table for a benefit payable at age 55 to an employee with an SSRA of 65, the plan fails to satisfy the requirements with respect to the early retirement benefit.

Example 2. Assume the same facts as in Example 1, except that the BBP is 1.75 percent. Thus, the disparity provided under the plan at age 55 is .25 percent (2% × 1.75%). Because the disparity does not exceed the .375 percent factor provided in the table for a benefit payable at age 55 to an employee with an SSRA of 65, the plan satisfies the requirements with respect to the early retirement benefit.

Since participants will generally have different SSRAs, the following simplified table may be used.

Age at Which Benefits Commence	Simplified Table
70	1.048
69	0.950
68	0.863
67	0.784
66	0.714
65	0.650
64	0.607
63	0.563
62	0.520
61	0.477
60	0.433
59	0.412
58	0.390
57	0.368
56	0.347
55	0.325

Example 3. Assume the same facts as in Example 1, except that the BBP is 1.675 percent and the plan uses the simplified table. Thus, the disparity provided under the plan at age 55 is .325 percent (2% × 1.675%). Because the disparity does not exceed the .325 percent factor provided in the simplified table for a benefit payable at age 55, the plan satisfies the requirements with respect to the early retirement benefit.

[Treas. Reg. § 1.401(*l*)-3(e)]

Q 7:16   What integration levels can be used in a defined benefit excess plan?

For defined benefit excess plans, the integration level must meet one of the following requirements:

1. The integration level for each participant is the participant's covered compensation (see Q 7:23).

2. The integration level for each participant is a uniform percentage (greater than 100 percent) of each participant's covered compensation that does not exceed the TWB (see Q 7:7) in effect for the plan year, and the .75 percent factor is adjusted.

3. The integration level for all participants is a single dollar amount that does not exceed the greater of $10,000 or one-half of the covered compensation of an individual who attains SSRA (see Q 7:13) in the calendar year in which the plan year begins.

4. The integration level for all participants is a single dollar amount that is greater than the amount determined in (3) above, that does not exceed the TWB, and that satisfies special demographic requirements, and the .75 percent factor is adjusted.

5. The integration level for all participants is a single dollar amount described in (4) above, and the .75 percent factor in the MEA (see Q 7:12) is reduced to the lesser of an adjusted factor or 80 percent of the otherwise applicable factor.

[Treas. Reg. § 1.401(l)-3(d)]

Q 7:17   What general rules apply to a defined benefit offset plan?

A defined benefit offset plan (see Q 7:2) will meet the permitted disparity rules if the participant's accrued benefit (see Q 9:2) is not reduced by reason of the offset by more than the maximum offset allowance (MOA; see Q 7:18) and benefits are based on average annual compensation (see Q 7:22). [I.R.C. § 401(l)(3)(B); Treas. Reg. § 1.401(l)-3(b)]

A defined benefit plan may offset a participant's benefit by a percentage of the participant's primary insurance amount under Social Security. [Treas. Reg. § 1.401(l)-3(c)(2)(ix); IRS Notice 92-32, 1992-2 C.B. 362]

For purposes of the permitted disparity rules, target benefit plans (see Q 2:5) are generally treated like defined benefit plans. [Treas. Reg. § 1.401(l)-2(a)(1)]

Q 7:18   What is the maximum offset allowance?

The MOA for a plan year is the lesser of (1) .75 percentage point or (2) one-half of the gross benefit percentage multiplied by a fraction (not to exceed 1), the numerator of which is the participant's average annual compensation (see Q 7:22) and the denominator of which is the participant's final average compensation (see Q 7:24) up to the offset level (see Q 7:21). The gross benefit percentage is the percentage of employer-provided benefits (before application of the offset) with respect to a participant's average annual compensation. [I.R.C. § 401(*l*)(4)(B); Treas. Reg. §§ 1.401(*l*)-1(c)(18), 1.401(*l*)-3(b)(3)]

Q 7:19   How are the permitted disparity rules applied to benefit formulas under defined benefit offset plans?

The following example illustrates whether or not a defined benefit offset plan meets the permitted disparity rules (see Qs 7:2, 7:17):

Example. Jill Corporation maintains a defined benefit offset plan. The formula provides that, for each year of credited service with the company up to a maximum of 35 years, a participant receives a normal retirement benefit equal to 2 percent of the participant's average annual compensation (see Q 7:22), reduced by .75 percent of the participant's final average compensation up to covered compensation (see Qs 7:23, 7:24). The plan meets the permitted disparity rules because the MOA is equal to .75 percent, the lesser of .75 percent or one-half of the gross benefit percentage [1% (1/2 × 2%)].

If the formula in the above example provided for a normal retirement benefit equal to 1 percent of the participant's average annual compensation, the plan would not meet the permitted disparity rules because the MOA would be equal to .5 percent, the lesser of .75 percent or one-half of the gross benefit percentage [.5% (1/2 × 1%)]. [Treas. Reg. § 1.401(*l*)-3(b)(5)]

Q 7:20   Can benefits commence prior to or after SSRA in a defined benefit offset plan?

Yes; but, if benefits commence prior to or after SSRA (see Q 7:13), the .75 percentage point factor (see Q 7:18) is reduced or increased depending on the age at which benefits commence and the participant's SSRA. [Treas. Reg. § 1.401(*l*)-3(e)]

See Q 7:15 for the tables used to adjust the .75 percentage point factor in the MOA.

Q 7:21   What is the offset level?

The offset level is the dollar limit specified in the defined benefit offset plan (see Q 7:2) on the amount of each participant's final average compensation (see Q 7:24) taken into account in determining the offset. [Treas. Reg. § 1.401(*l*)-1(c)(23)]

For defined benefit offset plans, the offset level must meet one of the following requirements:

1. The offset level for each participant is the participant's covered compensation (see Q 7:23).

2. The offset level for each participant is a uniform percentage (greater than 100 percent) of each participant's covered compensation that does not

exceed the participant's final average compensation, and the .75 percent factor is adjusted.

3. The offset level for all participants is a single dollar amount that does not exceed the greater of $10,000 or one-half of the covered compensation of an individual who attains SSRA (see Q 7:13) in the calendar year in which the plan year begins.

4. The offset level for all participants is a single dollar amount that is greater than the amount determined in (3) above, that does not exceed the participant's final average compensation, and that satisfies special demographic requirements, and the .75 percent factor is adjusted.

5. The offset level for all participants is a single dollar amount described in (4) above, and the .75 percent factor in the MOA (see Q 7:18) is reduced to the lesser of an adjusted factor or 80 percent of the otherwise applicable factor.

[Treas. Reg. § 1.401(*l*)-3(d)]

Q 7:22   What is average annual compensation?

Average annual compensation means the participant's highest average annual compensation for (1) any period of at least three consecutive years or (2) if shorter, the participant's full period of service. For this purpose, a participant's compensation history may begin at any time, but must be continuous, be no shorter than the averaging period, and end in the current plan year. [I.R.C. § 401(*l*)(5)(C); Treas. Reg. §§ 1.401(a)(4)-3(e)(2)(i), 1.401 (*l*)-1(c)(2)]

Q 7:23   What does covered compensation mean?

Covered compensation means the average (without indexing) of the TWBs (see Q 7:7) for the 35 calendar years ending with the year an individual attains SSRA (see Q 7:13). A defined benefit plan can provide for permitted disparity on the basis of each individual employee's covered compensation. Covered compensation does not refer to the amount of compensation that the employee actually earned, but reflects the ceiling for Social Security wages (TWBs) over the years.

2010 Covered Compensation Table

Calendar Year of Birth	Year of SSRA	Covered Compensation
1907	1972	$4,488
1908	1973	4,704
1909	1974	5,004
1910	1975	5,316
1911	1976	5,664

2010 Covered Compensation Table (cont'd)

Calendar Year of Birth	Year of SSRA	Covered Compensation
1912	1977	6,060
1913	1978	6,480
1914	1979	7,044
1915	1980	7,692
1916	1981	8,460
1917	1982	9,300
1918	1983	10,236
1919	1984	11,232
1920	1985	12,276
1921	1986	13,368
1922	1987	14,520
1923	1988	15,708
1924	1989	16,968
1925	1990	18,312
1926	1991	19,728
1927	1992	21,192
1928	1993	22,716
1929	1994	24,312
1930	1995	25,920
1931	1996	27,576
1932	1997	29,304
1933	1998	31,128
1934	1999	33,060
1935	2000	35,100
1936	2001	37,212
1937	2002	39,444
1938	2004	43,992
1939	2005	46,344
1940	2006	48,816
1941	2007	51,348
1942	2008	53,952
1943	2009	56,628
1944	2010	59,268
1945	2011	61,884
1946	2012	64,464

2010 Covered Compensation Table (*cont'd*)

Calendar Year of Birth	Year of SSRA	Covered Compensation
1947	2013	67,008
1948	2014	69,408
1949	2015	71,724
1950	2016	73,920
1951	2017	76,044
1952	2018	78,084
1953	2019	80,052
1954	2020	81,972
1955	2022	85,620
1956	2023	87,384
1957	2024	89,064
1958	2025	90,660
1959	2026	92,184
1960	2027	93,648
1961	2028	95,052
1962	2029	96,372
1963	2030	97,680
1964	2031	98,940
1965	2032	100,116
1966	2033	101,220
1967	2034	102,192
1968	2035	103,068
1969	2036	103,824
1970	2037	104,448
1971	2038	105,012
1972	2039	105,552
1973	2040	106,032
1974	2041	106,392
1975	2042	106,656
1976 and later	2043 and after	106,800

Because the TWB is the same for 2010 as it was for 2009, the Covered Compensation Table is also the same for 2009 and 2010.

In lieu of using the table set forth above, defined benefit plans may use the following table that rounds the actual amounts of covered compensation for different years of birth.

2010 Rounded Table

Year of Birth	Covered Compensation
1937	$39,000
1938–1939	45,000
1940	48,000
1941	51,000
1942	54,000
1943	57,000
1944	60,000
1945–1946	63,000
1947	66,000
1948	69,000
1949	72,000
1950–1951	75,000
1952	78,000
1953–1954	81,000
1955–1956	87,000
1957–1958	90,000
1959–1960	93,000
1961–1962	96,000
1963–1965	99,000
1966–1968	102,000
1969–1972	105,000
1973 and later	106,800

A plan may use an amount of covered compensation for a plan year earlier than the current plan year provided that the earlier plan year is the same for all employees and is not earlier than the plan year that begins five years before the current plan year.

Example. In 2004, Michael Corp. adopted a defined benefit excess plan (see Q 7:2) with a calendar plan year. For the 2004 through 2009 plan years, the plan's integration level for each participant, based upon the 2004 covered compensation table, was permissible. However, the integration level must be changed for the 2010 plan year and may be the covered compensation table for the 2005 or any later plan year.

[I.R.C. § 401(*l*)(5)(E); Treas. Reg. § 1.401(*l*)-1(c)(7); Rev. Rul. 2009-40, 2009-52 I.R.B. 942; IRS Notice 89-70, 1989-1 C.B. 730]

An increase in covered compensation will result in a smaller benefit at retirement. However, a participant's accrued benefit may not be reduced because of the increase in covered compensation (see Q 9:25).

Q 7:24   What is final average compensation?

Final average compensation means the average of the participant's annual compensation for (1) the three-consecutive-year period ending with or within the plan year or (2) if shorter, the participant's full period of service; but it does not include compensation for any year in excess of the TWB (see Q 7:7) in effect at the beginning of such year. [I.R.C. § 401(*l*)(5)(D); Treas. Reg. § 1.401(*l*)-1(c)(17)]

Q 7:25   What does compensation mean?

Compensation means compensation as defined under the plan provided that such definition is nondiscriminatory and satisfies Section 414(s) (see Qs 6:66–6:71). An employer may elect not to include as compensation elective deferrals under 401(k) plans (see Q 27:1), 403(b) plans (see Q 35:1), simplified employee pensions (SEPs; see Q 32:1), and cafeteria plans. [I.R.C. §§ 401(*l*)(5)(B), 414(s); Treas. Reg. §§ 1.401(*l*)-1(c)(2), 1.401(*l*)-1(c)(17)]

Q 7:26   What is uniform disparity?

With respect to qualified retirement plans that provide for permitted disparity (see Q 7:2), the disparity for all participants under the same plan must be uniform. [Treas. Reg. §§ 1.401(*l*)-2(a)(4), 1.401(*l*)-3(a)(4)]

The disparity under a defined contribution excess plan is uniform only if the plan uses the same BCP (see Q 7:5) and the same ECP (see Q 7:4) for all participants. However, an exception to this rule applies if the plan provides that, in the case of an employee for whom no FICA taxes are required to be paid, employer contributions allocated to the account of that participant are based on the participant's total plan-year compensation at the ECP. [Treas. Reg. §§ 1.401(*l*)-2(c)(1), 1.401(*l*)-2(c)(2)(iii)]

> **Example.** Sharon Corp. has a money purchase pension plan. For the 2010 calendar plan year, the plan provides that each participant will receive a contribution of 10 percent of compensation up to the TWB (see Q 7:7) and 15.7 percent of compensation in excess of the TWB, but that a "non-FICA" employee will receive an allocation based solely on the ECP. Mindy, a FICA employee, and Jill, a non-FICA employee, earn $120,000 each. The contribution made to Sharon Corp.'s plan on Mindy's behalf is $12,752 [$10,680 (10% × $106,800) + $2,072 (15.7% × $13,200)], and the contribution made on Jill's behalf is $18,840 (15.7% × $120,000). In this case, the disparity is considered uniform even though different BCPs are used.

The disparity provided under a defined benefit excess plan is uniform only if the plan uses the same BBP (see Q 7:11) and the same EBP (see Q 7:10) for all participants with the same number of years of service. The disparity provided under a defined benefit offset plan is uniform only if the plan uses the same gross benefit percentage and the same offset percentage (see Q 7:18) for all participants with the same number of years of service. However, an exception to these rules applies if the plan provides that, in the case of an employee for whom no FICA taxes are required to be paid, employer-provided benefits are determined with respect to the participant's total average annual compensation at the EBP or gross benefit percentage applicable to a participant with the same number of years of service. [Treas. Reg. §§ 1.401(*l*)-3(c)(1), 1.401(*l*)-3(c)(2)(vii)]

Q 7:27 Can the termination of a defined benefit plan affect permitted disparity?

Yes. If a defined benefit plan providing for permitted disparity is terminated and the plan assets exceed the present value of the accrued benefits (see Q 9:2), the use of the excess funds to increase benefits under the plan must not violate the permitted disparity rules. [Rev. Rul. 80-229, 1980-2 C.B. 133] The termination of a qualified retirement plan may not discriminate in favor of HCEs (see Q 3:2). [Treas. Reg. § 1.401(a)(4)-5(a)(1)]

Q 7:28 What special restrictions on permitted disparity apply to top-heavy plans?

A top-heavy defined benefit plan (see Q 26:1) must provide each participant who is a non-key employee (see Q 26:27) with a minimum annual retirement benefit, and a top-heavy defined contribution plan (see Q 26:3) must provide each participant who is a non-key employee with a minimum annual contribution. A top-heavy plan cannot take into account Social Security benefits or contributions to satisfy these minimum requirements (see Qs 26:35, 26:41, 26:45). [I.R.C. § 416(e); Treas. Reg. § 1.416-1, Q M-11]

Chapter 8

Funding Requirements

To ensure that sufficient money will be available to pay promised retirement benefits to employees when they retire, certain qualified retirement plans are subject to minimum funding requirements. Effective after 2007, under PPA, defined benefit plans are subject to new funding rules. This chapter examines the funding requirements—which qualified retirement plans must meet them, how they work, and how they are enforced.

Q 8:1 What are the minimum funding standards?

To ensure that sufficient money will be available to pay promised retirement benefits to employees when they retire, minimum funding standards have been established for defined benefit plans (see Q 2:3), money purchase pension plans (see Q 2:4), and target benefit plans (see Q 2:5). [ERISA §§ 301, 302; 303(a); I.R.C. §§ 412, 430, 431]

Effective for plan years beginning after 2007, employers maintaining single-employer defined benefit plans are subject to new funding rules that will require them to make a minimum contribution to the plan. A plan will be treated as satisfying the minimum funding standard for a plan year if:

1. In the case of a defined benefit plan which is not a multiemployer plan (see Q 29:2), the employer makes contributions to or under the plan for the plan year which, in the aggregate, are not less than the minimum required contribution for the plan for the plan year;

2. In the case of a money purchase pension plan which is not a multiemployer plan, the employer makes contributions to or under the plan for the plan year which are required under the terms of the plan; and

3. In the case of a multiemployer plan, the employers make contributions to or under the plan for any plan year which, in the aggregate, are sufficient to ensure that the plan does not have an accumulated funding deficiency as of the end of the plan year.

[I.R.C. § 412(a)]

Certain qualified retirement plans are not subject to minimum funding standards (see Q 8:10).

Q 8:2 What is the minimum required contribution?

The term "minimum required contribution" means, with respect to any plan year of a defined benefit plan which is not a multiemployer plan:

1. In any case in which the value of assets of the plan (reduced by credit balances) is less than the funding target of the plan for the plan year, the sum of:

   a. The target normal cost of the plan for the plan year;

   b. The shortfall amortization charge (see Q 8:3) if any for the plan for the plan year; and

   c. The waiver amortization charge (see Q 8:4) if any for the plan for the plan year; and

2. In any case in which the value of assets of the plan (reduced by credit balances) equals or exceeds the funding target of the plan for the plan year, the target normal cost of the plan for the plan year reduced (but not below zero) by such excess. [I.R.C. § 430(a)]

The term "funding target" means, the present value of all benefits accrued or earned under the plan as of the beginning of the plan year. [I.R.C. § 430(d)(1)]

The term "target normal cost" means, for any plan year, the excess of:

1. The sum of:

   a. The present value of all benefits that are expected to accrue or to be earned under the plan during the plan year, plus

   b. The amount of plan-related expenses expected to be paid from plan assets during the plan year, over

2. The amount of mandatory employee contributions expected to be made during the plan year.

For purposes of determining target normal cost, if any benefit attributable to services performed in a preceding plan year is increased by reason of any increase in compensation during the current plan year, the increase in such benefit will be treated as having accrued during the current plan year. [I.R.C. § 430(b)]

The interest rate used in determining present value will be based on the performance of corporate bonds as reflected in a segmented yield curve that reflects the age of the employer's workforce. The yield curve consists of different interest rates applicable to benefits payable in three different time periods. The segmented interest rate will be phased in over a three year period for plans in existence before 2008. IRS has issued guidance on the corporate bond yield curve and the segment rates required to compute the funding target. [IRS Notice 2007-81, 2007-2 C.B. 899]

IRS has issued regulations providing mortality tables to determine present value and permitting the use of substitute, plan-specific tables if certain conditions apply. [Treas. Reg. § 1.430(h)(3)] IRS has also issued a Revenue Procedure providing further guidance on the steps needed to request approval for substitute, plan-specific mortality tables and a Notice providing the static mortality tables to be used during calendar years 2009 through 2013. [Rev. Proc. 2008-62, 2008-2 C.B. 935, *updating* Rev. Proc. 2007-37, 2007-1 C.B. 1433; IRS Notice 2008-85, 2008-2 C.B. 905] In granting approval for a group of retirement plans to use substitute mortality tables for up to ten years, IRS considered whether the tables sufficiently reflected the mortality experience of the applicable plan populations. [Priv. Ltr. Rul. 200823024]

See Q 25:36 regarding interest rates and mortality assumptions used for terminating plans.

Plans with more than 500 participants that have a funding target attainment percentage in the preceding year below designated thresholds will be deemed at risk and subject to increased target liability for plan years beginning after 2007. The term "funding target attainment percentage" means, the ratio (expressed as a percentage) that (a) the value of plan assets, bears to (b) the funding target of the plan. [I.R.C. §§ 430(d), 430(i)]

[Prop. Treas. Reg. § 1.430(a)-1]

Effective for plan years beginning before 2008, for defined benefit plans, employers were required each year to fund the retirement benefits earned that year by the employees (the normal cost). In addition, formulas were established for amortizing over stated periods (1) the cost of retirement benefits for employees' services in the past for which funds had not yet been set aside (past service liabilities), (2) the cost of retroactively raising the level of benefits by plan amendments, and (3) the cost of making up experience losses and increases in liabilities attributable to changes in actuarial assumptions. See Qs 8:1 and 8:2 of *The 2008 Pension Answer Book* for details.

For a money purchase pension plan, both before and after 2007, the amount required to be contributed each year is based on the plan's contribution formula. For example, if the employer has a money purchase pension plan with a 10-percent-of-compensation formula and the participants' aggregate compensation for the year totals $80,000, the employer's required contribution is $8,000.

In a target benefit plan, the required contribution is based on the participant's compensation, age, and an assumed interest rate that is specified in the plan document.

Effective for plan years beginning after 2007, multiemployer plans (see Q 29:2) continue to be subject to funding rules similar to those in effect prior to 2008. [I.R.C. § 431] See Q 8:20 regarding the funding standard account.

Q 8:3   What is the shortfall amortization charge?

The shortfall amortization charge for a plan for any plan year is the aggregate total (not less than zero) of the shortfall amortization installments for such plan year with respect to the shortfall amortization bases for such plan year and each of the six preceding plan years.

The shortfall amortization installments are the amounts necessary to amortize the shortfall amortization base of the plan for any plan year in level annual installments over the seven-plan-year period beginning with such plan year. The shortfall amortization installment for any plan year in the seven-plan-year period with respect to any shortfall amortization base is the annual installment determined for that year for that base. The shortfall amortization base of a plan for a plan year is:

1. The funding shortfall of such plan for such plan year, minus
2. The present value of the aggregate total of the shortfall amortization installments and waiver amortization installments (see Q 8:4) that have been determined for such plan year and any succeeding plan year with respect to the shortfall amortization bases and waiver amortization bases of the plan for any plan year preceding such plan year.

The funding shortfall of a plan for any plan year is the excess (if any) of:

1. The funding target (see Q 8:2) of the plan for the plan year, over
2. The value of plan assets of the plan for the plan year that are held by the plan on the valuation date.

In any case in which the value of plan assets of the plan is equal to or greater than the funding target of the plan for the plan year, the shortfall amortization base of the plan for such plan year is zero. A special transition rule makes this exemption available to a plan if its assets are at least 92 percent of the funding target for the 2008 plan year, 94 percent of the funding target for the 2009 plan year, and 96 percent of the funding target for the 2010 plan year. This transition rule is not available to any plan that was subject to the deficit reduction contribution rules in 2007. Additionally, any plan that does not meet the exemption threshold for a year may not take advantage of the transition rule in any subsequent year. [I.R.C. § 430(c); Prop. Treas. Reg. § 1.430(a)-1(c)]

The proposed regulations, when finalized, will not apply to plan years beginning before January 1, 2009. [IRS Notice 2008-21, 2008-1 C.B. 431]

For the 2008, 2009, and 2010 plan years, the applicable exemption threshold will be used to determine whether the plan has a funding shortfall and, if so, to determine the shortfall amount. Additionally, a plan may take advantage of this relief in 2009 and 2010 even if it did not achieve the exemption threshold in a previous year. For example, a plan that is only 90 percent funded in 2008 will determine its shortfall amount based on the 92 percent exemption threshold for 2008 and will still be able to use the 94 percent exemption threshold in 2009 and the 96 percent exemption threshold in 2010. However, a plan that was subject to the deficit reduction contribution rules in 2007 may not take advantage of the transition relief in 2008, 2009, or 2010. [I.R.C. § 430(c)(5)(B)(iii) (as amended by WRERA §§ 101(b)(2)(B), 101(b)(2)(C))]

The Pension Relief Act of 2010 (PRA 2010; see Q 1:37) permits a plan sponsor to reduce a plan's minimum required contribution (see Q 8:2) for certain years by electing to use an extended alternative shortfall amortization schedule. Generally, for eligible plan years, plan sponsors are permitted to elect between two different schedules: a "two plus seven-year" amortization schedule, which provides for interest-only payments for two years after which seven-year amortization would apply, and a 15-year amortization schedule. The eligible plan years for making an election are plan years that begin in 2008, 2009, 2010, or 2011. However, an election may only be made for these years if the due date for the payment of the minimum required contribution for the plan year occurs on or after June 25, 2010, the date of enactment of PRA 2010. [I.R.C. § 430(c)(2)(D) (as added by PRA 2010 § 201(b)(1)); IRS Notice 2010-55, 2010-33 I.R.B. 253]

Q 8:4   What is the waiver amortization charge?

The waiver amortization charge (if any) for a plan for any plan year is the aggregate total of the waiver amortization installments for such plan year with respect to the waiver amortization bases for each of the five preceding plan years. The waiver amortization installments are the amounts necessary to amortize the waiver amortization base of the plan for any plan year in level annual installments over a period of five plan years beginning with the succeeding plan year. The waiver amortization installment for any plan year in the five-year period with respect to any waiver amortization base is the annual installment determined for that year for that base. The waiver amortization base of a plan for a plan year is the amount of the waived funding deficiency (if any) for such plan year under Section 412(c).

In any case in which the funding shortfall of a plan for a plan year is zero, for purposes of determining the waiver amortization charge for such plan year and succeeding plan years, the waiver amortization bases for all preceding plan years (and all waiver amortization installments determined with respect to such bases) are reduced to zero.

[I.R.C. § 430(e); Prop. Treas. Reg. § 1.430(a)-1(d)]

The proposed regulations, when finalized, will not apply to plan years beginning before January 1, 2009. [IRS Notice 2008-21, 2008-1 C.B. 431]

Q 8:5   Can certain funding balances reduce the minimum required contribution?

Certain funding balances referred to as the "prefunding balance" and the "funding standard carryover balance" are permitted to be used to reduce the otherwise applicable minimum required contribution (see Q 8:2) for a plan year. [I.R.C. § 430(f)]

IRS has issued final regulations regarding the effect of a prefunding balance and a funding standard carryover balance under Section 430(f).

A. *In general*

1. *Overview.* The regulations provide rules regarding the application of Section 430(f), relating to the establishment and maintenance of a funding standard carryover balance and a prefunding balance.

2. *Multiple employer plans.* In the case of a multiple employer plan (see Q 8:9), the rules are applied separately for each employer under the plan,

as if each employer maintained a separate plan. Thus, each employer under such a multiple employer plan may have a separate funding standard carryover balance and a separate prefunding balance for the plan.

[Treas. Reg. § 1.430(f)-1(a)]

B. *Maintenance of balances*

1. *Prefunding balance.* A plan sponsor is permitted to elect to maintain a prefunding balance for a plan. A prefunding balance maintained for a plan consists of a beginning balance of zero, increased by the amount of excess contributions to the extent the employer elects to do so. If the plan sponsor of a plan elects to add to the plan's prefunding balance, as of the first day of a plan year following the first effective plan year for the plan, the prefunding balance is increased by the amount so elected. The amount added to the prefunding balance cannot exceed the present value of the excess contributions for the preceding plan year. As of the first day of each plan year, the prefunding balance of a plan is decreased (but not below zero) by the sum of (a) any amount of the prefunding balance that was used to offset the minimum required contribution (see Q 8:2) of the plan for the preceding plan year and (b) any reduction in the prefunding balance for the plan year. The present value of the excess contributions for the preceding year is increased for interest accruing for the period between the valuation date for the preceding plan year and the first day of the current plan year.

2. *Funding standard carryover balance.* A funding standard carryover balance is automatically established for a plan that had a positive balance in the funding standard account as of the end of the pre-effective plan year for the plan. As of the first day of each plan year, the funding standard arryover balance of a plan is decreased (but not below zero) by the sum of (a) any amount of the funding standard carryover balance that was used to offset the minimum required contribution of the plan for the preceding plan year and (b) any reduction in the funding standard carryover balance for the plan year.

[Treas. Reg. § 1.430(f)-1(b)]

C. *Effect of balance on the value of plan assets*

Generally, in the case of any plan with a prefunding balance or a funding standard carryover balance, the amount of those balances is subtracted from the value of plan assets for purposes of Sections 430 and 436.

[Treas. Reg. § 1.430(f)-1(c)]

D. *Election to apply balances against minimum required contributions*

Subject to certain limitations in the case of any plan year with respect to which the plan sponsor elects to use all or a portion of the prefunding balance or the funding standard carryover balance to offset the minimum required contribution for the plan year, the minimum required contribution for the plan year is offset as of the valuation date for the plan year by the amount so used. In general, the amount of prefunding and funding standard carryover balances that may be used to offset the minimum required contribution for a plan year must take into account any decrease in those balances that results from a prior election either to use the prefunding balance or funding standard carryover balance or to reduce those balances. To the extent that a plan has a funding standard carryover balance greater than zero, no amount of the plan's prefunding balance may be used to offset the minimum required contribution. Thus, a plan's funding standard carryover balance must be exhausted before the plan's prefunding balance may be applied. An election to use the prefunding balance or funding standard carryover balance to offset the minimum required contribution is not available for a plan year if the plan's prior plan year funding ratio is less than 80 percent. For this purpose, the term "prior plan year funding ratio" is a fraction (expressed as a percentage), the numerator of which is the value of plan assets on the valuation date for the preceding plan year, reduced by the amount of any prefunding balance, and the denominator of which is the funding target (see Q 8:2) of the plan for the preceding plan year.

[Treas. Reg. § 1.430(f)-1(d)]

E. *Election to reduce balances*

A plan sponsor may make an election for a plan year to reduce any portion of a plan's prefunding and funding standard carryover balances. If such an election is made, the amount of those balances that must be subtracted from the value of plan assets will be smaller and, accordingly, the value of plan assets taken into account for purposes of Sections 430 and 436 will be larger. Thus, the election to reduce a plan's prefunding and funding standard carryover balances is taken into account in determining the value of plan assets for the plan year and applies for all purposes under Sections 430 and 436, including determining the plan's prior plan year funding ratio for the following plan year. To the extent that a plan has a funding standard carryover balance greater than zero, no election is permitted to be made that reduces the plan's prefunding balance. Thus, a plan must exhaust its funding standard carryover balance before it is permitted to make an election with respect to its prefunding balance.

[Treas. Reg. § 1.430(f)-1(e)]

F. *Elections*

1. *Method.* Any election by the plan sponsor must be made by providing written notification of the election to the plan's enrolled actuary (see Q 20:29) and the plan administrator (see Q 20:1). The written notification must set forth the relevant details of the election, including the specific dollar amount involved in the election. A plan sponsor may provide a standing election in writing to the plan's enrolled actuary to use the funding standard carryover balance and the prefunding balance to offset the minimum required contribution for the plan year to the extent needed to avoid an unpaid minimum required contribution.

2. *Timing.* Any election with respect to a plan year must be made no later than the last date for making the minimum required contribution for the plan year. For this purpose, an election to add to the prefunding balance relates to the plan year for which excess contributions were made. For example, an election to add to the prefunding balance as of the first day of

the plan year that began on January 1, 2010 (in an amount not in excess of the present value of the excess contribution as of the valuation date in 2009), had to be made no later than September 15, 2010, even though the election is reported on the 2010 Schedule SB (Form 5500), which is not due until 2011. An election may not be made prior to the first day of the plan year to which the election relates.

[Treas. Reg. § 1.430(f)-1(f)]

Q 8:6   Are there funding-based limits on benefits and benefit accruals?

A single-employer defined benefit plan must meet certain funding-based limits on benefits and benefit accruals in order for the plan to remain qualified. [I.R.C. § 401(a)(29)]

Generally, the restrictions do not apply if a plan's funding target attainment percentage (see Q 8:2) is at least 92 percent in 2008, 94 percent in 2009, 96 percent in 2010, and 100 percent thereafter. Plan participants must be notified within 30 days after the plan has become subject to a restriction. The following limitations are applicable:

- For plans less than 80 percent funded, plan amendments increasing benefits are prohibited
- For plans between 60 percent and 80 percent funded, lump-sum payments are limited to (a) 50 percent of the original amount, or (b) the present value of the maximum PBGC benefit at the participant's age
- For plans less than 60 percent funded, (a) plan accruals are frozen, (b) shutdown benefits may not be triggered unless immediately funded, and (c) lump-sum payouts are prohibited [I.R.C. § 436]

For plan years that began on or after October 1, 2008 and before October 1, 2009, if a plan was not subject to the mandatory freeze in the previous year, it was not subject to this restriction for the 2009 plan year. [I.R.C. § 430(e) (as amended by WRERA § 203)]

IRS has issued final regulations regarding the limits on benefits and benefit accruals under single-employer defined benefit plans.

A. *General rules*

1. *In general.* The regulations set forth the rules that a defined benefit plan, subject to the minimum funding standards (see Q 8:1) and that is not a multiemployer plan (see Q 29:2), must satisfy in order to meet the requirements of Section 436 regarding funding-based limits for qualification.

2. *New plans.* The limitations described in Section 436(b) regarding shutdown benefits and other unpredictable contingent event benefits (see paragraph I below), in Section 436(c) regarding plan amendments increasing liability for benefits, and in Section 436(e) regarding benefit accruals for plans with severe shortfalls do not apply to a plan for the first five years of the plan. For purposes of applying this new plan rule, plan years under a plan are aggregated with plan years under a predecessor plan. Thus, the

only benefit limitation that could apply under a plan that is not a successor plan during the first five years of its existence is the Section 436(d) limitation applicable to accelerated benefit distributions (such as single-sum distributions) except for payments pursuant to a plan termination.

3. *Special rules for certain plans*

   a. *New plans.* With respect to a multiple employer plan (see Q 8:9), the regulations apply separately with respect to each employer under the plan, as if each employer maintained a separate plan. Thus, the benefit limitations could apply differently to participants who are employees of different employers under such a multiple employer plan.

   b. *Plan termination.* The limitations applicable to accelerated payments do not apply to prohibited payments (see paragraph I below) that are made to carry out the termination of a plan in accordance with applicable law. For example, a plan sponsor's purchase of an irrevocable commitment from an insurer to pay benefit liabilities in connection with the standard termination of a plan is not prohibited.

4. *Treatment of plan as of close of prohibited or cessation period.* If a limitation on accelerated benefit payments (such as single-sum distributions) applies to a plan as of a Section 436 measurement date (see paragraph I below), but that limit subsequently ceases to apply to the plan as of a later Section 436 measurement date, then the limitation does not apply to benefits with annuity starting dates (see 10:3) that are on or after that later Section 436 measurement date. With respect to a participant who had an annuity starting date within a period during which the accelerated benefit payment limitation rules applied to the plan, once the limitation ceases to apply, the participant's benefits will continue to be paid in the form previously elected unless the plan permits the participant to be offered a new election that would modify the prior election. A plan is permitted to be amended to provide that any unpredictable contingent event benefits that were limited will be paid or reinstated when the limitation no longer applies.

5. *Deemed election to reduce prefunding and funding standard carryover balances.* If a limitation on accelerated benefit payments would otherwise apply to a plan, the plan sponsor is treated as having made an election to reduce the prefunding balance (see Q 8:5) or funding standard carryover balance (see Q 8:5) by such amount as is necessary for the adjusted funding target attainment percentage (AFTAP; see paragraph I below) to be at or above the applicable threshold (60 or 80 percent, as the case may be) in order for the benefit limitation not to apply to the plan.

   In the case of a plan maintained pursuant to one or more collective bargaining agreements (see Q 29:6) in which a benefit limitation would otherwise apply to the plan, the employer is treated as having made an election to reduce the prefunding balance or funding standard carryover balance by such amount as is necessary for the AFTAP to be at or above the applicable threshold for the benefit limitation not to apply to the plan.

[Treas. Reg. § 1.436-1(a)]

B. *Limitation on plant shutdown and other unpredictable contingent event benefits*

A plan that provides for any unpredictable contingent event benefit must provide that the benefit will not be paid to a plan participant during a plan year if the AFTAP for the plan year is (1) less than 60 percent or (2) 60 percent or more, but would be less than 60 percent if the AFTAP were predetermined applying an actuarial assumption that the likelihood of occurrence of the unpredictable contingent event during the plan year is 100 percent. However, this prohibition on payment of unpredictable contingent event benefits no longer applies for a plan year, effective as of the first day of the plan year, if the employer makes the contribution as described in paragraph F below.

[Treas. Reg. § 1.436-1(b)]

C. *Limitations on plan amendments increasing liability for benefits*

A plan satisfies the limitation on plan amendments increasing liability for benefits only if the plan provides that no amendment to the plan that has the effect of increasing liabilities of the plan by reason of increases in benefits, establishment of new benefits, changing the rate of benefit accrual, or changing the rate at which benefits become nonforfeitable is permitted to take effect if the AFTAP for the plan is (1) less than 80 percent or (2) 80 percent or more, but would be less than 80 percent if the benefits attributable to the amendment were taken into account in determining the AFTAP. However, this prohibition on plan amendments no longer applies for a plan year if the employer makes the contribution as described in paragraph F below. The limitation on amendments increasing liabilities does not apply to any amendment that provides for an increase in benefits under a formula that is not based on a participant's compensation. To the extent that any amendment results in (or is made pursuant to) a mandatory increase in the vesting of benefits, that amendment does not constitute an amendment that changes the rate at which benefits become nonforfeitable.

D. *Limitations on prohibited payments*

  1. *Funding percentage less than 60 percent.* A plan must provide that, if the plan's AFTAP for a plan year is less than 60 percent, the plan will not pay any prohibited payment with an annuity starting date that is on or after the applicable Section 436 measurement date.

  2. *Bankruptcy.* A plan must provide that the plan will not pay any prohibited payment with an annuity starting date that is during any period during a plan year in which the plan sponsor is a debtor in bankruptcy until the date on which the enrolled actuary (see Q 20:29) of the plan certifies that the plan's AFTAP is not less than 100 percent.

  3. *Limited payment if percentage at least 60 percent but less that 80 percent.* A plan must provide that, in any case in which the plan's AFTAP for a plan year is 60 percent or more but is less than 80 percent, the plan will not pay any prohibited payment unless the present value of the portion of the benefit being paid does not exceed the lesser of (a) 50 percent of the

present value of the benefit payable in the optional form or (b) 100 percent of the PBGC maximum benefit guarantee amount (see Q 25:19). If an optional form of benefit that is otherwise available under the terms of the plan is not available as of the annuity starting date because it is a prohibited payment that cannot be paid, then the plan must permit the participant to elect to (a) bifurcate the benefit into unrestricted and restricted portions, (b) commence benefits in another optional form, or (c) defer commencement of the payments (to the extent permitted under applicable qualification requirements).

4. *Exception for certain frozen plans.* The limitations on accelerated benefit distributions will not apply to a plan for any plan year if the terms of the plan, as in effect for the period beginning on September 1, 2005, provided for no benefit accruals with respect to any participants.

[Treas. Reg. § 1.436-1(d)]

E. *Limitation on benefit accruals*

A plan must provide that, in any case in which the plan's AFTAP for a plan year is less than 60 percent, benefit accruals under the plan will cease as of the applicable Section 436 measurement date. If a plan must cease benefit accruals under this limitation, then the plan is also not permitted to be amended in a manner that would increase the liabilities of the plan by reason of an increase in benefits or establishment of new benefits. This prohibition on additional benefit accruals will no longer apply for a plan year if the plan sponsor makes the contribution as described in paragraph F below.

[Treas. Reg. § 1.436-1(e)]

F. *Rules relating to contributions required to avoid benefit limitation*

An employer sponsoring a plan that would otherwise be subject to the limitations can avoid the application of those limits through one of four different techniques: (1) reducing the funding standard carryover balance and prefunding balance; (2) making additional contributions for a prior plan year that are not added to the prefunding balance; (3) making specific contributions; and (4) providing security.

Under the first of the techniques, if a plan sponsor elects to reduce the plan's funding standard carryover balance or the prefunding balance, this will have the effect of increasing the plan assets that are taken into account in determining the plan's funding target attainment percentage (FTAP; see paragraph I below) and AFTAP and, thereby, will raise the AFTAP to a level so that the benefit limitations may no longer apply to the plan.

Alternatively, if the deadline for making prior year contributions has not passed, the plan sponsor could utilize the second technique — that is, making additional contributions for the prior plan year. If these additional contributions are not added to the prefunding balance, then the additional contribution willalso have the effect of increasing the plan's FTAP and AFTAP.

Under the third technique, the plan sponsor makes additional contributions that are specifically designated at the time the contribution is used to avoid the application of the limitations on shutdown and other unpredictable contingent event benefits, plan amendments increasing liability for benefits, and benefit accruals for plans with severe funding shortfalls.

Under the fourth technique, the plan sponsor provides security to avoid the application of the benefit limitations. In such a case, the AFTAP for the plan year is determined by treating as an asset of the plan any security provided by a plan sponsor by the valuation date for the plan year in a form meeting certain specified requirements. However, this security is not taken into account for any other purpose. The only security permitted to be provided by a plan sponsor for this purpose is (1) a bond issued by a corporate surety company or (2) cash or United Stales obligations that mature in three years or less that are held in escrow by a bank or insurance company.

[Treas. Reg. § 1.436-1(f)]

G. *Presumed underfunding for purposes of benefit limitations*

In any case in which a plan was subject to a benefit limitation on the last day of the prior plan year, the first day of the plan year is a Section 436 measurement date and the AFTAP of the plan for the current plan year is presumed to be equal to the preceding year's certified AFTAP until the plan's enrolled actuary certifies the AFTAP of the plan for the current plan year.

If the enrolled actuary of the plan has not certified the AFTAP of the plan for the current plan year by the first day of the fourth month of the plan year and the AFTAP for the preceding year was certified to be at least 60 percent but less than 70 percent or at least 80 percent but less than 90 percent, then the first day of the fourth month of the current plan year is a Section 436 measurement date, and the AFTAP of the plan is presumed to be equal to 10 percentage points less than the AFTAP of the plan for the preceding plan year. This presumption will apply until the earlier of the date the enrolled actuary certifies the AFTAP for the plan year or the first day of the tenth month of the plan year.

In any case in which no certification of the specific AFTAP for the current plan year is made before the first day of the tenth month of such year, that date is a Section 436 measurement date and, as of that date, the plan's AFTAP is conclusively presumed to be less than 60 percent. In such a case, the presumed AFTAP of under 60 percent for the current plan year will continue to apply until such time as the enrolled actuary certifies the AFTAP for either the current plan year or the next plan year.

The enrolled actuary's certification of the AFTAP for a plan year must be made in writing, must be signed and dated, must be provided to the plan administrator (see Q 20:1), and must certify the plan's AFTAP for the plan year. As an alternative to certifying a specific number for the plan's AFTAP, the enrolled actuary is permitted to certify during a plan year that the plan's AFTAP for that plan year either is less than 60 percent, is 60 percent or higher (but is less than 80 percent), is 80 percent or higher, or is 100 percent or higher. If the enrolled actuary has issued such a range certification for a plan year and the enrolled actuary subsequently issues a certification of the specific AFTAP for the plan before the end of that plan year, then the certification of the specific AFTAP is treated as a change in the applicable AFTAP and must be applied for the portion of the plan year beginning on the date of the earlier certification.

The enrolled actuary is generally not permitted to certify the AFTAP based on a value of assets that includes contributions receivable for the prior year that have not actually been made as of the date of the certification.

[Treas. Reg. § 1.436-1(h)]

H. *Rules of operation for periods prior to and after certification*

A plan must provide that, for any period during which a presumption under paragraph G applies to the plan, the limitations under paragraphs B, C, D, and E are applied to the plan as if the AFTAP for the year were the presumed AFTAP.

I. *Definitions*

The "adjusted funding target attainment percentage" (AFTAP) for a plan year is a fraction (expressed as a percentage), the numerator of which is the adjusted plan assets for the plan year and the denominator of which is the adjusted funding target for the plan year.

The "adjusted plan assets" for a plan year is generally determined by subtracting the plan's funding standard carryover balance and prefunding balance as of the valuation date from the value of plan assets for the plan year and increasing the resulting value by the aggregate amount of purchases of annuities for participants and beneficiaries (other than HCEs; see Q 3:2) which were made by the plan during the preceding two plan years.

The "adjusted funding target" equals the funding target (see Q 8:2) for the plan year increased by the aggregate amount of purchases of annuities that were added to assets for purposes of determining the plan's adjusted plan assets.

The "Section 436 measurement date" is (1) the date that stops or starts the application of the limitations on accelerated benefits and benefit accruals for plans with severe funding shortfalls and (2) the date used for calculations with respect to applying the limitations on shutdown and other unpredictable contingent event benefits and plan amendments increasing liability for benefits. In addition, the date of the enrolled actuary's certification of the AFTAP for the plan year is a Section 436 measurement date if it occurs within the first nine months of the plan year.

An "unpredictable contingent event benefit" means any benefit or increase in benefits to the extent the benefit or increase would not be payable but for the occurrence of an unpredictable contingent event, and an "unpredictable contingent event" means a plant shutdown (whether full or partial) or similar event, or an event other than the attainment of any age, performance of any service, receipt or derivation of any compensation, or the occurrence of death or disability.

A "prohibited payment" means:

1. Any payment for a month that is in excess of the monthly amount paid under a single life annuity (plus any Social Security supplements) to a participant or beneficiary whose annuity starting date occurs during any period that a limitation on accelerated benefit payments is in effect;

2. Any payment for the purchase of an irrevocable commitment from an insurer to pay benefits;

3. Any transfer of assets and liabilities to another plan maintained by the same employer that is made in order to avoid or terminate the application of the benefit limitation under Section 436; and

4. Any other payment that is identified as a prohibited payment by IRS.

[Treas. Reg. § 1.436-1(j)]

Q 8:7   Is a funding notice required to be provided annually?

For plan years beginning after 2007 plan administrators (see Q 20:1), for both single-employer and multiemployer defined benefit plans are required to provide an annual funding notice for each plan year. This annual funding notice must be provided to:

a. The PBGC;

b. Each plan participant and beneficiary;

c. Each labor organization representing plan participants and beneficiaries; and

d. Each contributing employer, with respect to multiemployer plans.

In addition to certain identifying information, the annual funding notice must include specific information. This information varies depending on whether the plan is a single-employer plan or a multiemployer plan.

For single-employer plans, the following specific information is required to be included:

a. A statement as to whether the plan's funding target attainment percentage (see Q 8:2) for the plan year and the two prior plan years is at least 100 percent or, if not, the actual percentage;

b. A statement of (i) the total assets and liabilities of the plan for the plan year and the two preceding plan years, and (ii) the value of the plan's assets and liabilities for the plan year;

c. A summary of the rules governing termination of single-employer plans; and

d. If applicable, a statement that the sponsor was required to provide additional information to PBGC (see Q 21:35) for the plan year.

The notice must also include the following:

• The number of participants

- A statement setting forth the plan's funding policy and the plan's asset allocation of investments

- An explanation and effect of any plan amendments, scheduled benefit increases or reductions, or other known event taking effect in the current plan year and having a material effect on plan liabilities or assets for the year

- A general description of the benefits under the plan that are eligible to be guaranteed by PBGC

- A statement that a copy of the plan's annual report (Form 5500) may be obtained upon request

The funding notice must be provided no later than 120 days after the end of the plan year relating to the notice. However, for plans that have 100 or fewer participants, the notice should be provided at the same time the Form 5500 is due. [ERISA § 101(f)]

DOL has provided guidance regarding the annual funding notice requirements and will treat the requirements as being satisfied, if the plan administrator (see Q 20:1) has complied with the guidance and has acted in accordance with a good-faith, reasonable interpretation of those requirements not specifically addressed. DOL has provided two model notices: the model in Appendix A is for single-employer defined benefit plans, and the model in Appendix B is for multiemployer defined benefit plans (see Q 29:2). Use of the models is not mandatory, and plans may use other notice forms to satisfy the annual funding notice content requirements. However, pending further guidance, use of an appropriately completed model notice will satisfy the content requirements. [FAB 2009-01 (Feb. 10, 2009)]

Q 8:8   Are there additional funding rules for multiemployer plans?

Effective for plan years beginning after December 31, 2007, generally, all multiemployer plans (see Q 29:2) are required to obtain an annual actuarial certification regarding their funding status. Special funding and operational requirements apply to plans that are certified to be endangered or critical.

A plan is in endangered status for a plan year if the plan is not in critical status for the plan year and as of the beginning of the plan year, either:

1. The plan's funded percentage for such plan year is less than 80 percent, or

2. The plan has an accumulated funding deficiency (see Q 8:22) for such plan year or is projected to have such an accumulated funding deficiency for any of the six succeeding plan years.

A plan is in critical status for a plan year if as of the beginning of the plan year:

1. The funded percentage of the plan is less than 65 percent and it is significantly underfunded and not projected to improve its funded percentage over the next seven years,

2. It is expected that credits to its funding standard account will not exceed charges to the account for the current plan year or for any of the next three or four years,

3. The plan's normal cost for the current year plus interest exceeds the present value of the reasonably anticipated employer contributions for the current plan year, the present value of the nonforfeitable benefits of inactive participants is greater than the present value of the nonforfeitable benefits of active participants, and the plan has an accumulated funding deficiency for the current plan year, or

4. The current assets and expected contributions over the next five years are not sufficient to satisfy the plan's expected obligations over that period.

A plan in endangered status must adopt and implement a funding improvement plan designed to allow the plan to meet applicable funding improvement benchmarks during a funding improvement period and satisfy certain operational requirements. An employer that fails to timely make a contribution required under an endangered plan's funding improvement plan is subject to an excise tax in the amount of 100 percent of the contribution.

A plan in critical status must adopt and implement a rehabilitation plan designed to enable the plan to emerge from critical status and satisfy certain operational requirements. An employer that fails to timely make a contribution required under a plan's rehabilitation plan is subject to an excise tax in the amount of 100 percent of the contribution. [I.R.C. §§ 432, 4971(g)(2)]

DOL has the authority to assess civil monetary penalties of up to $1,100 per day against plan sponsors that fail to timely adopt funding improvement or rehabilitation plans and against plan sponsors of certain plans in endangered status that fail to meet applicable benchmarks by the end of the funding improvement period. [ERISA § 502(c)(8)]

By the 90th day of each plan year, the actuary of a multiemployer defined benefit plan must certify to IRS and the plan sponsor whether the plan is endangered, critical, or neither for the plan year. [I.R.C. § 432(b)(3)] Under a special rule, for the first plan year that began on or after October 1, 2008, and not later than September 30, 2009, the plan sponsor could have elected that the plan's funding status be the same as its status for the prior year. [I.R.C. § 432(b) (as amended by WRERA § 204)] Furthermore, for multiemployer plans in endangered or critical status for a plan year that began in 2008 or 2009, the plan sponsor could have elected to extend the plan's ten-year funding improvement period or rehabilitation period to 13 years; and, if an election was made for a plan that was in seriously endangered status for a plan year that began in 2008 or 2009, the 15-year funding improvement period was extended to 18 years. [I.R.C. § 432(c) (as amended by WRERA § 205)]

[IRS Notice 2009-31, 2009-1 C.B. 856, *modified by* IRS Notice 2009-42, 2009-1 C.B. 1011]

Q 8:9   Are there special funding rules for multiple employer plans?

Yes. The minimum funding requirements for a multiple employer plan (a plan maintained by more than one employer) established after December 31, 1988, are generally determined by treating each employer as maintaining a separate plan. Multiple employer plans established before that date generally must be funded as if all participants in the plan were employed by a single employer. However, the plan administrator of a pre-1989 multiple employer plan was permitted to elect to have the new rules apply and fund the plan as if each employer maintains a separate plan. The election was required to be attached to Schedule B of Form 5500 (see Q 21:6) for the first plan year beginning after November 10, 1988. If the election was made, the funding requirements for that first plan year and all subsequent plan years are determined in accordance with the new rules. The election may be revoked only with the consent of IRS. [I.R.C. § 413(c)(4); Ann. 90-3, 1990-3 I.R.B. 36]

Q 8:10   Which qualified retirement plans are not subject to the minimum funding standards?

The minimum funding standards do not apply to profit sharing (see Q 2:6), stock bonus (see Q 2:13), 401(k) (see chapter 27), or employee stock ownership plans (ESOPs; see chapter 28). Pension plans funded exclusively by the purchase of certain insurance contracts (insurance contract plans; see Q 8:11) are also exempt from the funding standards. [I.R.C. § 412(e)]

Other retirement plans that are not subject to the minimum funding standards include:

1. Plans that do not provide for employer contributions after September 2, 1974 (such as plans to which only employees contribute);
2. Unfunded nonqualified plans that are maintained by the employer primarily to provide deferred compensation for selected management or highly compensated employees;
3. Supplemental plans that provide benefits in excess of the limits on contributions and benefits under the Code;
4. Governmental plans; and
5. Certain church plans.

[ERISA § 301(a); I.R.C. §§ 412(e), 414(d), 414(e)]

Q 8:11   What is an insurance contract plan?

An insurance contract plan, also referred to as a 412(i) plan, is a pension plan that is funded exclusively by individual insurance contracts and meets the following requirements:

1. The insurance contracts provide for level annual premiums from the time the employee commences plan participation until retirement age.

2. Benefits under the plan are equal to the benefits provided under the contracts.

3. Benefits are guaranteed by an insurance company licensed to do business in the state in which the plan is located.

4. Premiums are paid timely or the contracts have been reinstated.

5. No rights under the contracts were subject to a security interest during the plan year.

6. No policy loans were outstanding during the plan year.

A pension plan that is funded exclusively by group insurance contracts having the same characteristics as those listed above is also considered to be an insurance contract plan. PPA (see Q 1:33) deleted Section 412(i) and replaced it with Section 412(e)(3). For purposes of *The Pension Answer Book*, a fully insured plan will still be referred to as a 412(i) plan. [ERISA § 301(b); I.R.C. § 412(e)]

For details, see Qs 2:25, 15:17.

Q 8:12 Can a pension plan be converted to an insurance contract plan?

Yes. Although the conversion of an existing pension plan to a plan that is funded exclusively by insurance contracts might cause the premium payments to begin after an employee commences participation in the plan (see Q 8:11), the converted plan may be considered to be an insurance contract plan for future years if certain requirements are met. The conversion will be permitted if all future benefits are funded by level annual premium contracts, all benefits previously accrued are guaranteed, there are meaningful continuing benefit accruals for at least three years, and certain other requirements are met. [Rev. Rul. 94-75, 1994-2 C.B. 59]

Where a defined benefit plan (see Q 2:3) was terminated, all benefit accruals ceased, and the trustee purchased annuity contracts to provide plan benefits, IRS concluded that the plan had not been converted to an insurance contract plan because a conversion must provide for continued meaningful level premium accruals. [Priv. Ltr. Rul. 9234004]

Q 8:13 Should the employer contribute more than the amount needed to meet the minimum funding standards?

Only if the additional amount is deductible. If the additional amount is not deductible, a tax is imposed on the employer equal to 10 percent of the nondeductible contributions to the plan (see Qs 12:9, 12:10, 12:17, 12:18). [I.R.C. § 4972]

Q 8:14   Must actuarial assumptions used in determining plan costs be reasonable?

Yes. Effective for plan years beginning after December 31, 2007, in the case of a single-employer defined benefit plan, the determination of any present value or other computation must be made on the basis of actuarial assumptions and methods (1) each of which is reasonable (taking into account the experience of the plan and reasonable expectations) and (2) which, in combination, offer the actuary's best estimate of anticipated experience under the plan. [I.R.C. § 430(h)] IRS has prescribed the interest rate for determining the funding target and the mortality table (see Q 8:2). IRS has issued regulations providing mortality tables to determine present value and guidance on the use of substitute, plan-specific tables if certain conditions apply and a Notice providing the static mortality tables to be used during calendar years 2009 through 2013. [Treas. Reg. § 1.430(h)(3); IRS Notice 2008-85, 2008-2 C.B. 905] IRS has also issued a Revenue Procedure providing guidance on the steps needed to request approval for substitute, plan-specific mortality tables. [Rev. Proc. 2008-62, 2008-2 C.B. 935, *updating* Rev. Proc. 2007-37, 2007-1 C.B. 1433] A plan was granted permission to use a substitute mortality table with respect to the non-disabled male population for five years. The rates sufficiently reflected the mortality experience of the applicable population. [Priv. Ltr. Rul. 200824026] Similarly, in granting approval for a group of retirement plans to use substitute mortality tables for up to ten years, IRS considered whether the tables sufficiently reflected the mortality experience of the applicable plan populations. [Priv. Ltr. Rul. 200823024]

Effective for plan years beginning prior to 2008, and in the case of multiemployer plans (see Q 29:2), all plan costs, liabilities, interest rates, and other factors must be determined on the basis of actuarial assumptions and methods (1) each of which is reasonable (taking into account the experience of the plan and reasonable expectations) or which, when taken together, produce a total contribution that is the same as if each assumption and method were reasonable and (2) which, in combination, offer the actuary's best estimate of anticipated experience under the plan. [I.R.C. § 431(c)(3)]

The actuarial assumptions used to determine the cost of funding a defined benefit plan need not be set forth in the plan (see Q 2:20). However, even if the actuarial assumptions and methods are set forth in the plan, that does not mean they will always be reasonable or acceptable. [Rev. Rul. 78-48, 1978-1 C.B. 115]

Due to the changes in the funding rules under PPA (see Q 8:1), the following discussion applies to plan years beginning prior to January 1, 2008 and may apply to plan years beginning after December 31, 2007.

IRS ruled that with respect to valuations effective for plan years beginning after December 31, 2003, the aggregate entry age normal funding method will not be treated as a reasonable funding method because it produces experience gains or losses, even if all actuarial assumptions are exactly realized. [Rev. Rul. 2003-83, 2003-2 C.B. 128]

In one case, the court agreed with IRS that use of a 5 percent interest rate was not reasonable and that an 8 percent interest rate was appropriate at a time when safe investments were yielding approximately 12 percent or more. The court concluded that "the reasonableness of an actuary's assumption must be evaluated in light of the plan's experience and reasonable expectations." [Jerome Mirza & Assocs., Ltd. v. United States, 882 F.2d 229 (7th Cir. 1989); *see also* Priv. Ltr. Ruls. 9111004, 9031001]

In another case, IRS recalculated a corporation's tax deduction by rejecting the actuarial assumptions contained in its defined benefit plan. IRS concluded that the actuarial assumptions contained in the plan did not reflect current plan experience. IRS determined that a more appropriate interest rate was 8 percent (instead of the plan's assumed 5½ percent rate) and that the normal retirement age for this one-participant plan should have been age 65, rather than age 55 as provided for in the plan. As a result of these modifications by IRS, no deduction for the taxable year involved was allowable. [Priv. Ltr. Rul. 8552001] In a similar case, IRS determined that the plan's normal retirement age of 60 was not reasonable and, based on plan experience and other investments available at the time, the 5 percent preretirement interest rate assumption was too low; therefore, the entire deduction for two years was disallowed. [Priv. Ltr. Rul. 9244006]

In yet another case, IRS disallowed the entire contribution made to a defined benefit plan after recalculation of the plan's liabilities and costs. The assumed 6 percent preretirement interest rate and 6½ percent postretirement interest rate were determined to be unreasonable in the aggregate when the actual investment rate of return over a five-year period exceeded 15 percent. [Priv. Ltr. Rul. 9226001] Similarly, IRS determined in another case that the actuarial assumptions used were not reasonable in the aggregate in view of the experience of the plan. The assumed rate of interest was 7 percent, but the average annual investment return over the prior five plan years was over 12 percent. [Priv. Ltr. Rul. 9226004] In another ruling, IRS determined that a 7.5 percent assumed rate of interest was not reasonable because the plan's investment returns far exceeded 7.5 percent and could reasonably be expected to continue to do so. [Priv. Ltr. Rul. 9250002] IRS, in yet another ruling, determined that the funding method and actuarial assumptions used were unreasonable and therefore disallowed the entire deduction. The actuary failed to explain in any detail the funding method used and did not furnish proper evidence that the owner would likely retire at age 55. [Priv. Ltr. Rul. 9119007] In a different case, although IRS concluded that interest and mortality assumptions were not reasonable, the poor health of the participant justified a normal retirement age of 55. Therefore, only a portion of the contribution was disallowed. [Priv. Ltr. Rul. 9249003]

IRS had expanded its defined benefit plan actuarial examination program and questioned the funding of defined benefit plans if the annual contribution per participant indicated that the actuaries may have exceeded the contribution limits for any of the following reasons:

1. Using an inappropriate funding method;

2. Exceeding the maximum benefit limitation under Section 415;

3. Using an unreasonably low interest rate not supported by the facts and circumstances of the plan; or

4. Employing an unreasonably low retirement age not supported by the facts and circumstances of the plan.

However, IRS's actuarial examination program experienced major setbacks when courts, in a number of cases, ruled in favor of the employers, finding that an interest rate assumption of less than 8 percent and a retirement age assumption of below age 65 were, among other assumptions, reasonable actuarial assumptions. [Citrus Valley Estates, Inc. v. Comm'r, 49 F.3d 1410 (9th Cir. 1995); Wachtell, Lipton, Rosen & Katz v. Comm'r, 26 F.3d 291 (2d Cir. 1994); Vinson & Elkins v. Comm'r, 7 F.3d 1235 (5th Cir. 1993); *but see* Rhoades, McKee & Boer v. United States, 1:91-CV-540 (W.D. Mich. 1995)]

With regard to the interest rate assumption, the courts considered the following:

1. The deference Congress gave to enrolled actuaries under ERISA for defined benefit pension plans;

2. The tendency of actuaries to be conservative in adopting actuarial assumptions;

3. That the plans were designed for a long-term time frame during which available rates of return on plan investments were likely to fluctuate;

4. That the plans' investments were self-directed, which could reduce the rate of return;

5. That the plans, due to their recent adoption, lacked credible experience;

6. The risk that the use of too optimistic an interest rate assumption would create a funding deficit that would require increased contributions in later years;

7. The relatively slight differences between the actuarial experts' suggested ranges for proper interest rate assumptions and the rate used by the plans' actuaries; and

8. That most small defined benefit plans used interest rate assumptions of between 5 percent and 6 percent for the years at issue.

The courts also found that a retirement age earlier than age 65 was justifiable under the circumstances. Most important, the courts concluded that, since the assumptions used were not "substantially unreasonable" and represented the actuary's best estimate of anticipated experience under the plans based on actuarial assumptions used by similar plans, IRS was precluded from requiring a retroactive change of assumptions.

Q 8:15   Must a change in a plan's funding method be approved?

Effective for plan years beginning after December 31, 2007, if the funding method, the valuation date, or a plan year for a plan is changed, the change will take effect only if approved by IRS. [I.R.C. § 412(d)(1)]

However, IRS provides automatic approval for a number of changes in funding method and for changes in the interest rate. For the first plan year beginning on or after January 1, 2008, any changes in funding method that are not inconsistent with the requirements of Section 430 are treated as having been approved and do not require specific prior approval. For plan years beginning in 2009 and 2010, certain changes in funding method (concerning the methodology of allocating liabilities to years, the selection of the valuation date, and the selection of the asset valuation method) and in the selection of interest rates are also automatically approved.

In addition, due to concerns regarding changes in valuation software, further guidance provides that, for plan years beginning on or after January 1, 2009, automatic approval is provided for any change in funding method under Section 430 if the following conditions are satisfied:

1. There has been a change both in the enrolled actuary (see Q 20:29) for the plan and in the business organization providing actuarial services to the plan;

2. The new method is substantially the same as the method used by the prior enrolled actuary and is consistent with the description of the method contained in the prior actuarial valuation report or prior Schedule SB (Form 5500) (see Q 21:6);

3. The funding target and target normal cost as determined for the prior plan year by the new enrolled actuary, are both within 5 percent of those values as determined by the prior enrolled actuary; and

4. For plan years beginning on or after January 1, 2011, the actuarial value of plan assets as determined for the prior plan year by the new enrolled actuary is within 5 percent of the value as determined by the prior enrolled actuary.

For plan years beginning on or after January 1, 2009, automatic approval is provided for any change in funding method under Section 430 resulting from a change in valuation software if the following conditions are satisfied:

1. There has not been a change in both the enrolled actuary for the plan and the business organization providing actuarial services to the plan;

2. Except to the extent automatic approval has been provided for a change in funding method without regard to this guidance, the underlying method is unchanged and is consistent with the information contained in the prior actuarial valuation report and prior Schedule SB (Form 5500);

3. The new valuation software is generally used by the enrolled actuary for the single employer plans to which the enrolled actuary provides actuarial services;

4. The funding target and target normal cost under the new valuation software are each within 2 percent of the respective values under the prior valuation software;

5. For plan years beginning on or after January 1, 2011, the actuarial value of assets for the plan under the new valuation software is within 2 percent

of the value under the prior valuation software (all other factors being held constant); and

6. The modifications to the computations in the valuation software or the use of a different valuation software system are designed to produce results that are no less accurate than the results produced prior to the modifications or change.

[Treas. Reg. § 1.430(d)-1(g)(3); Ann. 2010-3, 2010-4 I.R.B. 333]

For plan years beginning prior to 2008, IRS was required to approve a change in a defined benefit plan's funding method. [I.R.C. § 412(c)(5)(A)] (prior to amendment). Due to the changes in the funding rules under PPA (see Q 8:1), the following discussion applies to plan years beginning prior to January 1, 2008 and may apply to plan years beginning after December 31, 2007. The funding method of a plan includes not only the overall funding method used by the plan but also each specific method of computation used in applying the overall method. Therefore, for example, the funding method of a plan includes the date on which assets and liabilities are valued (the valuation date) and the definition of compensation that is used to determine the plan's normal cost or accrued liability. Furthermore, a change in a particular aspect of a funding method does not change any other aspect of that method. For example, a change in the funding method from unit credit to the level dollar individual entry age normal method does not change the current valuation date or asset valuation method used for the plan. [Treas. Reg. § 1.412(c)(1) (prior to amendment); Rev. Proc. 2000-40, 2000-2 C.B. 357; Rev. Proc. 2000-41, 2000-2 C.B. 371]

Subject to certain restrictions, automatic approval will be granted for a change to one of the following funding methods:

- Unit credit
- Level percent of compensation aggregate
- Level dollar aggregate
- Level percent of compensation individual aggregate
- Level dollar individual aggregate
- Level percent of compensation frozen initial liability
- Level dollar frozen initial liability
- Level percent of compensation individual entry age normal
- Level dollar individual entry age normal

Automatic approval will be granted for a change to one of the following asset valuation methods:

- Fair market value
- Average market value (without phase-in)
- Average market value (with phase-in)
- Smoothed market value (without phase-in)
- Smoothed market value (with phase-in)
- Average value

Also, automatic approval will be granted for a change in the valuation date to the first day of the plan year and for a change in the funding method used for valuing ancillary benefits to the method used for valuing retirement benefits.

Automatic approval will be granted in the following special situations:

- Certain changes to remedy unreasonable allocation of costs
- Change in method for a fully funded terminated plan where certain conditions are met
- Change in method for takeover plans where certain conditions are met
- Change in method that results from a change in valuation software where certain conditions are met
- Change in method in connection with a *de minimis* merger where certain conditions are met
- Change in method in connection with a merger, other than a *de minimis* merger, with same plan year and merger date of first or last day of plan year, where certain conditions are met
- Change in method in connection with a merger, other than a *de minimis* merger, with a transition period no more than 12 months, where certain conditions are met
- Change in method in connection with a merger, other than a *de minimis* merger, with a transition period more than 12 months, where certain conditions are met

Automatic approval is *not* available if:

1. A Schedule B (see Q 21:6) has been filed for the plan year using a different funding method;
2. Agreement to the change is not indicated on the Form 5500 series return/report (see Q 21:1);
3. A minimum funding waiver (see Q 8:24) has been requested or is being amortized;
4. The plan is under examination or has been notified of an impending examination; or
5. The plan is terminated (with certain exceptions).

[Rev. Proc. 2000-40, 2000-2 C.B. 357]

Furthermore, IRS must approve changes in actuarial assumptions, other than interest rate and mortality assumptions (e.g., salary scale, employee turnover), used to determine the current liability for certain defined benefit plans with significant unfunded current liability.

Approval of these changes is required if:

1. The plan is covered by Title IV of ERISA (see Qs 25:9, 25:11);
2. The aggregated unfunded vested benefits exceed $50 million as of the end of the preceding plan year; and

3. The change in assumptions (after taking into account any interest rate and mortality table changes) decreases the plan's unfunded current liability for the current plan year by either (a) more than $50 million or (b) more than $5 million and at least 5 percent of the current liability before the change.

[I.R.C. § 412(c)(5) (prior to amendment)]

Approval was granted for a change in a plan's actuarial assumptions where the employer conducted a study of the plan's experience regarding rates of retirement, disability, and termination and the form of benefit payment, and the proposed rates were consistent with the plan's actual experience during the study period. [Priv. Ltr. Rul. 201035046] In another case, IRS approved a change in retirement rate assumptions so that individual rates at various ages would reflect a higher concentration of expected retirements at later ages. [Priv. Ltr. Rul. 9646035] However, a dual funding method designed to accomplish full funding of plan liabilities that was used by a terminating defined benefit plan was held unreasonable and unacceptable by IRS because it was impermissible to use two funding methods and then select the method that resulted in the lowest cost. [Treas. Reg. § 1.412(c)(3)-1(b)(2) (prior to amendment); Priv. Ltr. Ruls. 9409002, 9409001]

Q 8:16   Is there any penalty for overstatement of pension liabilities?

Yes. A penalty tax is imposed on the underpayment of tax created by a substantial overstatement of pension liabilities. A 20 percent penalty tax is imposed if the actuarial determination of pension liabilities is between 200 percent and 399 percent of the amount determined to be correct; if the actuarial determination is 400 percent or more of the correct amount, the penalty tax is increased to 40 percent. No penalty will be imposed if the underpayment attributable to the substantial overstatement is $1,000 or less. [I.R.C. §§ 6662(a), 6662(f), 6662(h)]

Q 8:17   Can a pension plan's normal retirement age affect the minimum funding standards?

Yes. Each actuarial assumption used to determine pension plan costs should be reasonable and must offer the actuary's best estimate of anticipated experience under the plan. [I.R.C. §§ 430(h), 431(c)(3)] Therefore, an assumption that employees will retire at the normal retirement age specified in the plan, ignoring the fact that employees normally retire at earlier or later ages, would not be reasonable (see Q 8:14).

Q 8:18   Do the pension plan's investment earnings affect the funding requirement?

Yes. The plan's earnings will affect the required minimum contribution (see Q 8:2).

Q 8:19 How are assets valued in a defined benefit plan?

Effective for plan years beginning after December 31, 2007, in general, with respect to single-employer defined benefit plans the valuation date of a plan for any plan year must be the first day of the plan year. However, if, on each day during the preceding plan year, a plan had 100 or fewer participants, the plan may designate any day during the plan year as its valuation date for such plan year and succeeding plan years.

[I.R.C. § 430(g)(2)]

In general, the value of plan assets is the fair market value of the assets. A plan may determine the value of plan assets on the basis of the averaging of fair market values, but only if such method:

1. Is permitted under IRS regulations;

2. Does not provide for averaging of such values over more than the period beginning on the last day of the 25th month preceding the month in which the valuation date occurs and ending on the valuation date (or a similar period in the case of a valuation date which is not the first day of a month); and

3. Does not result in a determination of the value of plan assets which, at any time, is lower than 90 percent or greater than 110 percent of the fair market value of such assets at such time.

Any such averaging shall be adjusted for contributions and distributions. Effective for all plan years beginning on and after January 1, 2008, plans can "smooth" their asset values by adjusting the 24-month average for expected earnings. However, the earnings assumption used may not be greater than the third segment rate used for funding purposes. This is a permanent change to the rules for valuing plan assets.

[I.R.C. § 430(g)(3) (as amended by WRERA § 121(b)); IRS Notice 2009-22, 2009-1 C.B. 741]

Q 8:20 What is the funding standard account?

Effective for plan years beginning after December 31, 2007, with respect to single-employer defined benefit plans, the new funding rules (see Q 8:2) under PPA replace the funding standard account.

The following discussion applies to multiemployer plans (see Q 29:2) and single-employer plans for plan years beginning prior to January 1, 2008. Each pension plan subject to the minimum funding standards (see Q 8:1) must maintain a funding standard account, which is a device used to ease the administration of the funding rules. Each year, the funding standard account is charged with amounts that must be paid to satisfy the minimum funding standards and is credited with the plan contributions made, any decrease in plan liabilities, and experience gains. If the pension plan meets the minimum funding standards (the charges equal the credits) at the end of any plan year, the funding standard account will show a zero balance. If the employer has contributed more than the minimum amount required for any year (the credits exceed the charges), the account will show a positive balance and the employer is credited with interest on the excess. If the employer contributed less than the minimum amount required for any year (the charges exceed the credits), the account will show an accumulated funding deficiency. An excise tax is imposed on that deficiency (see Q 8:22). [I.R.C. § 431(b)]

The following examples illustrate how the funding standard account works.

Example 1. In 2009, MuMu Corporation established a defined benefit plan, with less than 100 participants, that is subject to the minimum funding requirements. For the plan's first year, the normal cost (the cost of benefits earned during the year) was $80,000. Past service costs (the cost of benefits for employees' services before the plan was adopted) are $1,000,000. The actuarially assumed rate of interest is 6 percent. MuMu contributed $148,537 to the plan. The funding standard account is charged with $80,000 of normal cost and with $68,537, which represents amortization of the past service costs of $1,000,000 at 6 percent over 30 years. Since the total charges ($148,537) equal the contribution, the funding standard account has a zero balance.

Example 2. In 2010, MuMu amended its defined benefit plan to increase benefits, so that past service costs rose by $100,000. The plan's normal cost increased to $85,000. In addition, the plan had an experience gain (the plan's actual investment growth was higher than that actuarially estimated) of $5,000. MuMu contributed $170,000 to the plan in 2010. The funding standard account for 2010 is credited with the $170,000 contribution plus $1,120 (representing amortization of the $5,000 experience gain at 6 percent over five years), for a total credit of $171,120. The funding standard account is charged with $85,000 normal cost and $68,537 for amortizing past service costs over 30 years, plus $6,854 for amortizing past service costs resulting from the plan amendment over 30 years, for a total charge of $160,391. Since the account's credits exceed the charges by $10,729 ($171,120 − $160,391), the funding standard account has a positive balance of $10,729. Add to this $644, representing interest on the $10,729 at 6 percent, and the account has a balance of $11,373 to be credited to future years.

The Pension Relief Act of 2010 (PRA 2010; see Q 1:37) provides a special amortization rule for certain net investment losses in the case of a multiemployer plan that meets a solvency test. The special rule applies to the portion of the plan's experience loss or gain attributable to net investment losses (if any) incurred in either or both of the first two plan years ending after August 31, 2008 (an applicable plan year). This portion is amortized over the period beginning with the plan year in which it is first recognized in the actuarial value of assets and ending with the last plan year in the 30-plan-year period beginning with the plan year in which the net investment loss was incurred. [I.R.C. § 431(b)(8)(A) (as added by PRA 2010 § 211(a)(2)); IRS Notice 2010-56, 2010-33 I.R.B. 254]

Q 8:21 Must separate funding standard accounts be maintained for each pension plan established by a controlled group of companies?

Yes. Even though identical, but separate, pension plans are established by members of a controlled group of companies (see Q 5:31), separate funding standard accounts (see Q 8:19) must be maintained for each plan. [ERISA § 302(b)(1); I.R.C. § 412(b)(1); Rev. Rul. 81-137, 1981-1 C.B. 232]

See Q 8:2 regarding the new funding rules effective after 2007 under PPA that replace the funding standard account.

Q 8:22 What happens if the company fails to make the required contribution to its pension plan?

There is an excise tax for failure to comply with the minimum funding standards (see Q 8:1). Effective for plan years beginning after December 31, 2007, the excise tax is equal to:

1. In the case of a single-employer plan, 10 percent of the aggregate unpaid minimum required contributions for all plan years remaining unpaid as of the end of any plan year ending with or within the taxable year, and

2. In the case of a multiemployer plan (see Q 29:2), 5 percent of the accumulated funding deficiency as of the end of any plan year ending with or within the taxable year.

An excise tax equal to 100 percent of the unpaid minimum required contribution (see Q 8:2) or accumulated funding deficiency, whichever is applicable, to the extent not so paid or corrected, is imposed on any unpaid required minimum contribution if such amount remains unpaid as of the close of the taxable period or on any accumulated funding deficiency if the accumulated funding deficiency is not corrected within the taxable period.

[I.R.C. §§ 412(a), 4971]

Prior to 2008, the excise tax for failure to comply with the minimum funding standards was equal to 10 percent (5 percent for multiemployer plans) of the amount of the accumulated funding deficiency. If the accumulated funding deficiency was not corrected, an excise tax equal to 100 percent of such uncorrected amount was imposed. "Accumulated funding deficiency" means the excess of the total charges to the funding standard account for all plan years over the total credits to such account for such years (see Q 8:20). [I.R.C. §§ 412(a) (prior to amendment), 431, 4971 (prior to amendment)]

PPA (see Q 1:33) amended the funding rules and, with respect to single-employer plans, deleted the term "accumulated funding deficiency" (see Q 8:20) with respect to plan years beginning after December 31, 2007. However, PPA retains the excise tax for employers that fail to make required minimum contributions under the new funding rules. Accordingly, although the following discussion may refer to the term "accumulated funding deficiency," the examples apply to multiemployer plans and may still apply to single-employer plans for plan years beginning after December 31, 2007.

Form 5330 (see Q 21:18) is used to report and pay the tax on the failure to meet minimum funding standards. If an accumulated funding deficiency or unpaid liquidity shortfall (see Q 8:32) is disclosed on Form 5330 or in an attached statement, the statute of limitations for collecting the tax expires three years after the filing of Form 5330 in which the deficiency or unpaid liquidity shortfall is disclosed. If an accumulated funding deficiency or unpaid liquidity shortfall is not disclosed on Form 5330 or in a statement attached to Form 5330, the statute of limitations on assessment is six years. If Form 5330 has not been filed for a year in which an accumulated funding deficiency or unpaid liquidity shortfall occurs, the tax may be assessed, or a proceeding in court for the collection of the tax may be begun without assessment, at any time after the date prescribed for filing the return. In each case, the statute of limitations is determined without regard to whether the accumulated funding deficiency or unpaid liquidity shortfall has been disclosed on Form 5500. The filing of Form 5330, not Form 5500, starts the running of the statute of limitations for purposes of the excise tax. [Rev. Rul. 2003-88, 2003-2 C.B. 292]

An accumulated funding deficiency caused by an employer's failure to make timely contributions due to its reliance on the erroneous advice of its plan consultant could not be excused even though the employer had set aside the necessary amount in a segregated checking account. The court ruled that the imposition of the excise tax was mandatory and not subject to an exception that would excuse an employer's unintentional or inadvertent failure to meet the minimum funding requirements. However, the court noted that IRS may waive the 100 percent tax and is also authorized to grant an employer any reasonable period in order to correct the accumulated funding deficiency. [D.J. Lee, M.D., Inc. v. Comm'r, 931 F.2d 418 (6th Cir. 1991)] Similarly, an employer that did not make a timely contribution to its plan was liable for the tax on the accumulated funding deficiency; financial hardship and plan termination did not excuse this mandatory tax. [Lee Eng'g Supply Co., 101 T.C. 189 (1993)] A sole proprietorship that failed to timely satisfy the minimum funding standard for its money purchase pension plan (see Q 2:4) was liable for the mandatory 10 percent tax even though the contribution was made by the extended due date of the taxpayer's income tax return in accordance with the terms of the plan (see Q 8:31). [Hoyez, 80 T.C.M. 198 (2000); Wenger, 79 T.C.M. 1995 (2000)]

In other cases, no excise tax for underfunding was imposed when a bookkeeping error caused contributions to pension and profit sharing plans of the employer to be misallocated between them [Ahlberg v. United States, 780 F. Supp. 625 (D. Minn. 1991)]; and, where a terminated plan had accumulated funding deficiencies for several years and its assets were taken over by PBGC (see Q 25:10), IRS waived the 100 percent tax, but not the 10 percent tax. [Priv. Ltr. Rul. 9623062; *see also* Priv. Ltr. Ruls. 9716027, 9630041, 9626045, 9332046] Similarly, IRS granted waivers of the 100 percent tax where the company had negative net worth and negative working capital, paid the 10 percent tax, filed a distress termination (see Q 25:15), and reached agreement with PBGC regarding the termination, and PBGC was appointed trustee of the plan. [Priv. Ltr. Rul. 200236050] A company that intended to file for a distress termination with PBGC and withdrew its requests for waivers of the minimum funding standards was granted waivers of the 100 percent tax. [Priv. Ltr. Ruls. 200548032, 200548031; *see also* Priv. Ltr. Ruls. 200551030 and 200549016 where the companies sought a distress termination and Priv. Ltr. Rul. 200549013 where a not-for-profit hospital was in the process of an involuntary termination] A conditional waiver of the 100 percent tax was granted where the company agreed to make certain contributions to its terminated plan and pay the 10 percent tax. [Priv. Ltr. Rul. 199918064] Waivers of the 100 percent tax were granted subject to the condition that the plan be terminated within 180 days. The company, a sole proprietorship, had suffered a severe financial hardship and the 10 percent excise taxes had been paid. [Priv. Ltr. Rul. 200738024] IRS also granted conditional waivers of the 100 percent tax for two years where a money purchase pension plan was frozen and converted into a profit sharing plan, and the employer agreed to a payment schedule with allocations to all non-management participants. [Priv. Ltr. Rul. 200204052] IRS denied a request for a waiver of the 10 percent tax, but granted a conditional waiver of the 100 percent tax where a company with negative working capital and net operating losses was in the process of terminating its plan. The waiver was subject to the condition that an agreement satisfactory to PBGC be concluded. [Priv. Ltr. Rul. 9642050; *see also* Priv. Ltr. Rul. 9841048] Where a defined benefit plan was terminated and assets distributed to all participants other than the owner of the company and his spouse, IRS granted a conditional waiver of the 100 percent tax, but not the 10 percent tax. [Priv. Ltr. Rul. 9635046; *see also* Priv. Ltr. Rul. 199917083] IRS granted a one-year conditional waiver of the 100 percent tax in order for the employer to formulate a plan to meet its obligation. [Priv. Ltr. Rul. 9514002] Similarly, the 100 percent tax due to an uncorrected accumulated funding deficiency of a multiemployer pension plan was waived for certain years. [Priv. Ltr. Rul. 9607015]

IRS will waive the 100 percent tax imposed on accumulated funding deficiencies that are *not* corrected under certain circumstances. With respect to a defined benefit plan, the tax is waived for all applicable years if the following conditions are met:

1. The plan is subject to Title IV of ERISA and is terminated in a standard termination (see Q 25:13);

2. The plan participants are not entitled to any portion of residual assets remaining after all plan liabilities to participants and their beneficiaries have been satisfied (see Qs 25:49–25:51);

3. The 10 percent excise tax that has been or could be imposed has been paid for all taxable years, including the taxable year related to the year of plan termination; and

4. All applicable forms in the Form 5500 series (see Q 21:1), including Schedule B, have been filed for all plan years, including the year of plan termination.

[Rev. Proc. 2000-17, 2000-1 C.B. 766]

IRS has delegated the authority to waive all or part of the 100 percent tax to the Director of Employee Plans. [Delegation Order 7-7]

See Q 8:24 for more details on the minimum funding standards waiver.

The United States Supreme Court has ruled that excise taxes imposed by IRS for failure to meet the minimum funding standards are considered penalties (not taxes) and, therefore, do not have priority status under federal bankruptcy law. [United States v. Reorganized CF & I Fabricators of Utah, Inc., 518 U.S. 213 (1996)] IRS has clarified its position that claims for the excise tax related to a bankruptcy estate's post-petition obligations are entitled to administrative expense priority in bankruptcy. [IRS Chief Counsel Notice CC-2006-007 (Dec. 29, 2005)]

The failure to meet minimum funding standards triggers a reportable event IRS Notice requirement to PBGC if the required minimum funding payment is not made by the 30th day after its due date (see Q 21:34). [ERISA § 4043; PBGC Reg. § 4043.25]

In addition, if a quarterly payment (see Q 8:32) or any other payment required by the minimum funding standards is not made, PBGC must be notified within ten days of the due date of the payment if the unpaid balance exceeds $1 million (see Q 21:35). Furthermore, a lien is created in favor of the plan upon all property of the employer if the delinquency exceeds $1 million. [ERISA § 303(k); I.R.C. § 430(k); PBGC Reg. § 4043.81]

Q 8:23   Who is liable for failure to make contributions?

Liability for contributions to a pension plan (other than a multiemployer plan; see Q 29:2) is joint and several among the employer-sponsor and the members of the controlled group (see Q 5:31) of which the employer is a member. General partners who were responsible for making contributions to the partnership's pension plan were jointly and severally liable for excise taxes (see Q 8:22) resulting from the partnership's failure to satisfy the minimum funding standards. [Priv. Ltr. Rul. 9414001] Also, all members of the controlled group are subject to the lien (see Q 8:22) in favor of a pension plan maintained by any member if the contributions are late. [I.R.C. §§ 412(b), 430(k)]

Furthermore, if an employer fails to make a required payment to meet minimum funding requirements or a required quarterly payment (see Qs 8:31, 8:32) within 60 days after it is due, the employer must notify each participant and beneficiary of such failure. This IRS Notice requirement does not apply to multiemployer plans or if the employer has a funding waiver request pending with IRS. This IRS Notice requirement is in addition to the requirement that participants be notified of the filing of an application for a funding waiver (see Q 8:26). [ERISA § 101(d)]

Q 8:24   May IRS waive the minimum funding standards for a particular company?

Yes. IRS may grant a waiver of the minimum funding standards for any year in which the employer or in the case of a multiemployer plan (see Q 29:2), 10 percent or more of the number of employers contributing to or under the plan, are unable to make the necessary contributions without "temporary substantial business hardship" ("substantial business hardship" for multiemployer plans) and if meeting the funding requirement would be adverse to the interests of plan participants in the aggregate. [I.R.C. § 412(c)(1)]

IRS examines several factors in deciding whether to waive the funding standards, including the following:

1. Is the employer operating at a loss?
2. Is there substantial unemployment or underemployment in the industry?
3. Are sales and profits of the industry depressed or declining?
4. Will the pension plan be continued only if the waiver is granted?

[I.R.C. § 412(c)(2)]

These factors are not all-inclusive. Furthermore, IRS must be convinced that the employer's business hardship is temporary. A conditional waiver of the minimum funding standards was granted where a company experienced temporary business hardship due to flood damage but anticipated resumption of full production. [Priv. Ltr. Rul. 9438032; *see also* Priv. Ltr. Ruls. 9808047, 9703037] In one case, a conditional waiver was granted where the company, which conducted substantially all of a city's transit and related operations, suffered a temporary business hardship due to a severe weather event but whose long-term prospects for recovery were good. [Priv. Ltr. Rul. 200847020] IRS has granted a conditional waiver of the minimum funding standards to a company that has experienced net losses, but whose financial situation was improving. [Priv. Ltr. Ruls. 9818064, 9626047, 9610033, 9541033, 9517052, 9514027, 9423035; *see also* Priv. Ltr. Rul. 200451034, where the company's prospects for recovery were excellent] In one case, a company experienced temporary substantial business hardship as evidenced by a declining demand in all product lines, and, additionally, because the company's information system was not compatible with year 2000 (Y2K), it was necessary to spend in excess of $750,000. IRS granted a waiver and determined that the company had taken a number of actions to effect recovery, including increasing its market share and the profitability of a specific line, reducing overhead and employees, lowering material costs through centralized purchasing, introducing lower-cost designs, and implementing less costly manufacturing through improved shop productivity. [Priv. Ltr. Rul. 200001043; *see also* Priv. Ltr. Rul. 199937054]

A conditional funding waiver was granted where a company that was formed by the merger of two hospitals experienced temporary substantial business hardship caused by economic factors impacting hospitals nationwide. Measures taken to increase working capital, effect a turnaround, and increase revenue included enhanced collection procedures, staff reductions, elimination of non-profitable services, outsourcing functions, consolidation of services, inventory control, installation of newer technology, upgrading operating room equipment, adding a family practice clinic, and privatization of a care center. [Priv. Ltr. Rul. 200402025; *see also* Priv. Ltr. Rul. 200342006, where, in order to effect recovery, a hospital reduced staff, recruited new physicians, and negotiated more favorable reimbursement agreements from HMOs and purchasing agreements for supplies, Priv. Ltr. Rul. 200502048, where a health care company negotiated improved payment arrangements with its two largest insurance company payors and anticipated increased payments from Medicare and Medicaid, Priv. Ltr. Rul. 200501024, where a tax-exempt corporation providing services to the elderly became eligible for Medicare funding, Priv. Ltr. Rul. 200829031, where although IRS concluded that a hospital suffered a substantial business hardship due in part to the dissolution of its merger with a national health care organization thus straining the hospital's cash flow, it demonstrated a commitment to funding the pension plan, and Priv. Ltr. Rul. 200921030, where a hospital that suffered financial difficulties due to a disbanded merger with a national health care organization, reduced in-patient admissions, and increased uninsured patients, in order to return to profitability, explored the sale of underutilized property and a unit, sought grant requests, received additional patients due to the closing of a nearby hospital, and became a critical care facility] In another case, where a hospital experienced operating problems related to the high level of bad debt write-offs for uninsured patients, a decrease in grant funding for alcohol and substance abuse programs, an increase in the number of Medicaid and lower-income self-pay patients being treated, and a decline in reimbursements from government and private insurers, IRS concluded the business hardship was temporary and granted a waiver because the hospital cut costs by decreasing its full-time staff, sought state approval to open a cardiac unit, and became certified as a stroke center. [Priv. Ltr. Rul. 200820036] Similarly, a hospital was granted waivers for its three plans where, although the hospital suffered a temporary substantial business hardship due to work stoppages and a conversion to a new Medicaid transaction processor, its financial recovery appeared good because new collective bargaining agreements had been reached. The waivers were granted subject to the conditions that collateral be acceptable to PBGC, quarterly contributions be timely made, contributions to meet the minimum funding standards be made, excess contributions be made if pre-2008 funding waiver amortizations are not carried over, and proof of payment be provided. [Priv. Ltr. Ruls. 200936050, 200936042, 200936041] In yet another case, a hospital that had suffered a business downturn but was in the middle of an acquisition by another local hospital and planned to use the resulting income to fully fund the plan on a termination basis was granted a waiver. [Priv. Ltr. Rul. 200831027]

In one case, IRS granted a conditional waiver where recovery was expected when a parent company was unable to fund its subsidiary's plan because the value of the currency in the country in which the parent was located dropped dramatically and the country went into economic crisis. [Priv. Ltr. Rul. 200049043] In another case, a conditional waiver was granted where the plan sponsor, expecting a return to profitability as a result of cost-cutting programs, had net losses primarily due to nonrecurring events, such as bad debt losses following the bankruptcies of two large customers, closing costs related to the discontinuance of a line of business, pension expenses related to early retirement programs, and extraordinary consulting and legal fees related to a reorganization. [Priv. Ltr. Rul. 200242043] A company was granted a conditional waiver where it took steps to recover from its hardship partially caused by a fire that destroyed its headquarters and main operating facility, a one-time event. [Priv. Ltr. Rul. 200518086] A funding waiver was granted where an accident caused the company's financial hardship as a result of (1) paying claims, (2) incurring costs for new safety measures, and (3) suffering a reduction in revenue due to the shutdown of a portion of its business. [Priv. Ltr. Rul. 200501023] In yet another case, a conditional waiver was granted where the company took steps to effect recovery and the temporary substantial business hardship was caused by (a) problems associated with a new product, including inadequate documentation and training materials, and (b) the new controller's improper use of employees' withheld wages. [Priv. Ltr. Rul. 200351028] A funding waiver was granted where a company regained its major customer that it previously lost and expected operating margins and cash flow to improve. [Priv. Ltr. Rul. 200135042] IRS granted funding waivers to members of a controlled group (see Q 5:29) with insufficient cash flow to meet routine operating expenses such as payroll and contributions to its plans, but that anticipated profitability in the next year. [Priv. Ltr. Ruls. 199914058, 199914057]

IRS granted a conditional funding waiver, although a company had both a very large negative working capital and a negative tangible net worth, when a substantial payment—enough to pay the required pension plan contribution —was expected from the state. [Priv. Ltr. Rul. 9216034] Where foreign competition, general downturn in the industry, and increased pension costs led to a decline in sales and had a negative impact on the company's cash flow, IRS granted a waiver where the company reduced costs by streamlining its manufacturing and operations, restructured its workforce, introduced its product to new foreign markets, expanded its product line, negotiated a new contract with a major corporation, and received $1.7 million of additional equity from its shareholder-owners. [Priv. Ltr. Rul. 200751034] In another case, IRS granted a conditional funding waiver where the employer had taken a number of steps to improve its financial condition, including expansion into new and profitable product lines and markets, consolidation of company functions to streamline operations, and refinancing its debt on longer and more favorable repayment terms. [Priv. Ltr. Rul. 9304032; *see also* Priv. Ltr. Ruls. 200711021, 200301042, 200251023, 200048049] IRS granted a conditional funding waiver where the company took steps to overcome business hardship that was caused by a general decline in its business and a litigation loss. Steps taken to effect recovery included a strict cost containment program, rejuvenating marketing efforts, deferring vendor payments, freezing pension accruals, and increasing employee contributions to a medical plan. [Priv. Ltr. Rul. 9611067; *see also* Priv. Ltr. Rul. 200323043] Similarly, a conditional funding waiver was granted where a company's financial condition improved as a result of staff downsizing and the streamlining of operations after experiencing substantial temporary business hardship due to market decline and workforce reduction. Moreover, the company amended its plan to cease benefit accruals and place a temporary freeze on the payment of lump-sum distributions to terminated vested participants who had not reached normal retirement age. [Priv. Ltr. Rul. 9846047] In another case, a waiver was granted where the company had taken several steps to increase revenues and reduce costs, including the closure of a facility, staff reduction, development of a new product line, and opening negotiations with a foreign company in order to obtain worldwide product distributions. [Priv. Ltr. Rul. 200402023] In yet another case, IRS granted a waiver where, in order to improve its financial condition, a company reduced production, personnel, and expenses, broadened its product mix, instituted new marketing initiatives, widened its customer base, and ceased benefit accruals. [Priv. Ltr. Ruls. 200851042, 200851041] Additionally, a waiver was granted where the company focused on achieving cost reduction through union negotiations, reductions in employee benefit costs, closure of a plant, restructuring of its secured debt, significant expenditure and inventory control, entering into an exit financing facility, and divestiture of its poorly performing foreign investments. [Priv. Ltr. Rul. 200512031]

Conditional waivers were granted where, as part of its recovery efforts, the company took steps such as freezing plan benefits, cancelling wage increases, reducing its workforce, streamlining management, entering into financing programs with vendors to improve liquidity, and restructuring long term debt. [Priv. Ltr. Ruls. 200328041, 200328037; *see also* Priv. Ltr. Ruls. 200453025, 200445028, 200332021] IRS granted a conditional waiver to a company where the business downturn was temporary due to the cyclical nature of the company's business and where the company took steps to effect recovery, including increasing prices of its product and reducing staff. [Priv. Ltr. Ruls. 200137067, 200023053; *see also* Priv. Ltr. Ruls. 200652047, 200652046, and 200652044, where the company closed and consolidated operations and increased prices, Priv. Ltr. Ruls. 200315037 and 200315036, where the company reduced staff and received orders from new customers, Priv. Ltr. Rul. 200301044, where the company reduced staff, improved plan productivity through employee education and increased supervision, and was pursuing an outsourcing strategy to lower manufacturing costs, and Priv. Ltr. Rul. 200418049, where the company reduced costs, including health insurance costs] In another case, a conditional funding waiver was granted where, as a result of business hardship, one plan sponsor made a number of changes to improve its financial situation such as cutting staff, designating new officers, and instituting operational improvements. [Priv. Ltr. Rul. 200123067; *see also* Priv. Ltr. Rul. 200704039, where the company increased prices, eliminated employee positions, shifted sales efforts, reduced rent, and reduced salary of the CEO and majority shareholder, Priv. Ltr. Rul. 200547017, where the company implemented a new budget process, reduced overhead, reduced shareholders' compensation, and sold nonessential assets, Priv. Ltr. Ruls. 200548034 and 200548033, where the company reduced its workforce, froze employee merit increases, and passed on medical premium increases to employees, Priv. Ltr. Rul. 200917047, where the company laid off employees, discontinued unprofitable product lines, initiated discounted bulk purchase programs for slow-moving inventory, reviewed product lines for profitability and supplier costs, extended payment terms with vendors, and worked with its bank for additional funds, and Priv. Ltr. Rul. 200351029, where the company reduced the number of employees, restructured debt, reduced operating expenses, reduced overhead costs, and postponed raises] In other cases, IRS granted conditional funding waivers where the company had negative net earnings or net losses but took significant measures to effect a recovery such as downsizing, closing facilities, hiring outside management, and filing a suit against a competitor. [Priv. Ltr. Ruls. 200148079, 200148076, 200148067, 200148065, 200148061; *see also* Priv. Ltr. Rul. 200809041, where the company ceased benefit accruals, decreased its employees by one-third, reduced inventory by 60 percent, and developed a new marketing plan, Priv. Ltr. Rul. 200649039, where the company adopted new accounting software, changed staffing in a division from full-time to independent consultants, laid off employees, reduced pay, reduced pension accruals, and consolidated offices to one location, Priv. Ltr. Rul. 200511026, where the company reduced its payroll through layoffs, replaced its primary supplier with a new lower cost supplier, initiated an aggressive marketing campaign to expand its customer base, continued to make contributions to the plan, and merged the plan into another plan of the company to reduce administrative expenses and improve the overall funded status of the plans, Priv. Ltr. Rul. 200447043, where efforts to effect a recovery in the company's financial position included freezing accruals in its pension plans, downsizing staff, aggressively reducing overhead, capital expenditures, and discretionary spending, reviewing product lines, receiving federal grant money for employee training programs, reducing production costs, establishing alliances with other producers, ensuring security of lines of credit with its banks, and implementing aggressive energy conservation and productivity programs, Priv. Ltr. Rul. 200443041, where the company reduced wages to clerical, union, salaried, and owner employees, introduced new management, hired an outside consulting firm that specialized in turnaround work, and hired an experienced sales person, and Priv. Ltr. Rul. 201012054, where a not-for-profit corporation established to sponsor a symphony orchestra froze wages, negotiated a shorter season and use of the performance hall rent-free, and hired experienced directors to oversee marketing, artistic programming, and the endowment campaign.

A conditional funding waiver was granted by IRS to a company that incurred net losses and had negative net worth on a consolidated basis, but had disposed of several unprofitable operating subsidiaries and ceased pension accruals. [Priv. Ltr. Rul. 9717038] In another case, IRS granted a conditional funding waiver where, due to the death of the prior company president, the company experienced a substantial business hardship as shown by negative working capital and net losses; but, with new management in place, the company had undertaken numerous cost-cutting measures that resulted in a slight net profit. [Priv. Ltr. Rul. 9632023] Where a nonprofit company experiencing financial difficulties and cash flow shortages implemented changes recommended by a third-party efficiency reviewer with positive results, IRS granted a conditional funding waiver. [Priv. Ltr. Rul. 9839041; *see also* Priv. Ltr. Rul. 200127056] A conditional funding waiver was granted where new owners who were experienced in helping failing companies invested additional funds in the company. [Priv. Ltr. Rul. 9804059] Furthermore, IRS granted conditional funding waivers where the company had initiated many cost-cutting programs, including the reduction of employees and salaries. [Priv. Ltr. Rul. 9413048; *see also* Priv. Ltr. Ruls. 200751035, 200505027, 200321025, 200321026, 200149046, 200103077, 200049042] In another case, IRS granted a funding waiver where the company implemented several cost-cutting measures, including contract negotiations with supply companies, quality improvement projects, and labor negotiations to hold down costs. [Priv. Ltr. Rul. 200001044] Similarly, a funding waiver was granted where the company took steps to improve its cash flow and profitability, such as outsourcing some manufacturing, establishing contacts with foreign raw material sources, negotiating with domestic suppliers, and reducing the plan's benefit formula. [Priv. Ltr. Rul. 200315030] IRS also granted conditional funding waivers where the company was acquired by another company and its net worth and working capital became positive. [Priv. Ltr. Ruls. 9711031, 9711030]

In one case, IRS granted an unconditional funding waiver where the company ceased production in several operational lines in order to concentrate on its business in the remaining areas of operation and enacted measures to effect a recovery, including reducing its workforce and obtaining extension for its bank credit. [Priv. Ltr. Rul. 9642057] Similarly, where salaries were reduced as part of a collective bargaining agreement and the company's debt was renegotiated, a conditional waiver was granted. [Priv. Ltr. Rul. 200402024] In another case, IRS granted conditional funding waivers where the company enacted numerous measures to effect a recovery, including consolidating operations, reducing its workforce, and obtaining extension for its bank credit. IRS granted the conditional waivers because the profitability of the company was still uncertain. [Priv. Ltr. Ruls. 9642058, 9642056; *see also* Priv. Ltr. Ruls. 200030032, 199936051] In one case, IRS granted a multiemployer plan a waiver of the minimum funding standards where at least 10 percent of the participating employers had temporary substantial business hardship. To effect recovery, real estate held in the plan was liquidated due to a drastic downturn in the value of plan assets, benefit accruals were frozen, legal proceedings were initiated against delinquent employers, and employer contribution rates were expected to be increased. [Priv. Ltr. Rul. 200210064]. In another case, IRS granted a waiver to a collectively bargained, multiemployer plan, where the funding problems were due to a downturn in the construction industry, but where the trustees took a number of steps to manage the plan's financial difficulties, including adopting an amendment to reduce benefit accruals, negotiating a contribution rate increase with contributing employers, and pursuing a merger with a financially healthy plan. [Priv. Ltr. Rul. 200810032]

A hospital that filed for bankruptcy primarily caused by a temporary decertification from the Medicare and Medicaid provider was granted a conditional waiver. Although the prospects for recovery were uncertain, denying the request would have precluded a financial recovery and put the plan at risk of termination. [Priv. Ltr. Rul. 200819019]

Modifications of previously granted waivers of the minimum funding standard were approved for three plans, where the modifications were requested in order to comply with final plans of reorganization approved by the Bankruptcy Court. [Priv. Ltr. Ruls. 200821041, 200821040, 200821039] Similarly, IRS approved modifications of previously granted conditional waivers for three plans where the modifications extending the companies' deadlines for emergence from bankruptcy were critical to implement the companies' reorganization plans.

However, IRS has denied requests for waiver of the minimum funding standards to companies whose prospects of recovery were tenuous. [Priv. Ltr. Ruls. 9740036, 9633047, 9609045, 9537029, 9444046, 9349031] In one case, a waiver was denied because the company intended to terminate the plan once it was fully funded; and, accordingly, it was not reasonable to expect the plan to continue as required to determine temporary substantial business hardship. [Priv. Ltr. Rul. 200713026] Where the financial hardship did not appear to be temporary, IRS has similarly denied requests for waivers. [Priv. Ltr. Ruls. 200749021, 200608024, 200603039] IRS denied a request for waivers where the employer had net losses and negative net worth for four years, ceased operations, closed facilities, and had not taken steps to rectify the funding deficiencies or terminate the plans. [Priv. Ltr. Rul. 200246034] A company was denied a funding waiver where it was questionable whether the substantial business hardship was temporary. Due to the loss of a major client and downsizing of staff, losses and debt continued to increase, and there was a possibility that the company would file for bankruptcy. [Priv. Ltr. Rul. 9846049] A request for a waiver was denied where a proposed rescue plan for a collectively bargained, multiemployer plan indicated that accumulated funding deficiencies would be generated in future years even if the waivers were granted. [Priv. Ltr. Rul. 200749022] IRS denied a waiver where it was unreasonable to expect a plan to continue where the sponsor was declaring bankruptcy and selling off its assets. [Priv. Ltr. Rul. 200602048] Similarly, requests for waivers of the minimum funding standards were denied where a company that filed for bankruptcy failed to demonstrate that the business hardship was temporary and PBGC instituted proceedings to terminate the plan. [Priv. Ltr. Ruls. 200434024, 200317054, 200317053, 200317052] In two other rulings, waivers were denied where PBGC informed IRS that the plans were in the process of being terminated and, accordingly, it was not reasonable to expect the plans would continue. [Priv. Ltr. Ruls. 201001029, 201001028] A company that was pursuing a distress termination for both of its plans was denied waivers because IRS concluded the financial hardship was not temporary and noted the company owed excise taxes for prior years. [Priv. Ltr. Rul. 200610024] In another case, a request for a funding waiver was denied where the plan's assets were equal to 81 percent of the plan's benefits, the company filed for reorganization, and the information furnished failed to demonstrate that the hardship was temporary. [Priv. Ltr. Rul. 199950043] A request for a funding waiver was denied where a company had a negative net worth, commenced bankruptcy proceedings, and failed to demonstrate that the hardship was temporary. [Priv. Ltr. Rul. 200135048] IRS denied a waiver of the minimum funding standards where, although the company had net losses, the company's parent had operating income 13 times the amount requested to be waived and the information furnished failed to demonstrate that the controlled group (see Q 8:23) had a temporary substantial business hardship. [Priv. Ltr. Rul. 9649047] In another case, a conditional waiver of the minimum funding standards was denied where the controlled group of which the company was a member did not have a temporary substantial business hardship, had a profit of more than double the amount of the requested waiver, had net worth equal to more than 20 times the amount of the requested waiver, and had cash of more than three times the amount of the requested waiver. [Priv. Ltr. Rul. 200134028] In one ruling, IRS granted waivers for two plans sponsored by a member of a controlled group but denied waivers for two other plans sponsored by another group member. The controlled group, on a consolidated basis, suffered severe business hardship; but one of the subsidiaries, considered alone, had not demonstrated economic hardship and appeared capable of satisfying the minimum funding standards. [Priv. Ltr. Ruls. 9226054, 9219041] In another ruling, IRS denied a request for a waiver where the companies had substantial net worth and were able to satisfy the minimum funding standards without experiencing a substantial temporary business hardship. [Priv. Ltr. Rul. 9423033] In yet another case, the waiver request was denied where the trustees failed to provide sufficient information that at least 10 percent of the multiemployer plan's contributing employers were unable to satisfy the minimum funding standard without experiencing substantial business hardship. [Priv. Ltr. Rul. 201001030] Waiver requests were denied for two plans where it was unreasonable to assume that the plans would continue only if funding waivers were granted since there was a decline in demand for the companies' products, and the companies intended to terminate their plans and sell the assets of their businesses. [Priv. Ltr. Ruls. 200512032, 200512030] Although substantial business hardship existed, a waiver request was denied where the remaining employers would not be able to make periodic payments to cover both the amortization payments on the funding waiver and the future ongoing cost of the retirement plan. Since the plan would be unable to continue whether or not the waiver was granted, there was no point in granting the waiver. [Priv. Ltr. Rul. 200822042]

See Q 8:22 for examples of the waiver of the 100 percent tax.

The legislative history indicates that a waiver should not be granted to an employer if it appears that the employer will not recover sufficiently to make its waived contributions. Chances for a waiver are improved if the plan's assets are greater than the benefits to which the participants are entitled.

As a practical matter, IRS, in its efforts to avert plan terminations, generally approves a hardship waiver request if it can find reasonable grounds for doing so. In one case, where a conditional funding waiver was granted, an additional request for approval of a retroactive plan amendment was granted with respect to contributions due for all the officers of the company, but was denied with respect to all other employees. [Priv. Ltr. Rul. 9416044] In another case, IRS required the owner, as a condition for granting the waiver, to reduce his accrued benefit until plan assets became sufficient to meet plan liabilities. [Priv. Ltr. Rul. 7945047] In yet another case, a conditional funding waiver was granted where the company was to (1) provide a security interest to the plan that was satisfactory to PBGC, (2) contribute certain amounts to the plan pursuant to a schedule, and (3) amend certain plan provisions regarding service and compensation for a special grandfathered benefit. [Priv. Ltr. Rul. 9845031] Two companies that had experienced business difficulties and had implemented corporate reorganizations, but whose prospects for recovery appeared to be good, were granted waivers subject to the conditions that (1) the waiver amounts be secured in a manner acceptable to PBGC and (2) contributions be made to meet the minimum funding requirements for a specified future year. [Priv. Ltr. Ruls. 200438040, 200438039; *see also* Priv. Ltr. Rul. 200934047, where a waiver was granted subject to the conditions that (1) collateral acceptable to PBGC be provided and (2) quarterly payments to the plan be made regularly, and Priv. Ltr. Rul. 200930054, where a company that had taken steps to return to profitability but whose prospects for recovery were uncertain was granted a conditional waiver stipulating that (1) collateral acceptable to PBGC be provided, (2) required quarterly contributions be timely made to the plan, and (3) contributions be made to meet the minimum funding requirements for a specified future year] Similarly, a conditional waiver was granted where even though the company struggled financially, a payment agreement was reached with PBGC, benefit accruals were frozen, and other cost-cutting measures were taken. [Priv. Ltr. Rul. 200202073] Furthermore, IRS granted a conditional waiver of the minimum funding standards subject to the adoption of an amendment ceasing the accrual of benefits for participants who were also shareholders. [Priv. Ltr. Rul. 8847079]

There are other rules with respect to funding waivers. They include:

1. The number of waivers allowed within a 15-year period is three (five for multiemployer plans).
2. With respect to single-employer plans, if the employer applying for a funding waiver is a member of a controlled group, not only must the employer-applicant meet the standards, but the standards must be met as if all members of the controlled group were treated as a single employer.
3. The amortization period of a waived funding deficiency is five years (15 years for multiemployer plans).
4. With respect to single-employer plans, the interest rate used for computing the amortization installment is the segment rates used for determining present value (see Q 8:3). Prior to 2008, the interest rate used was the greater of (a) 150 percent of the federal midterm rate or (b) the plan interest rate.
5. IRS is authorized to require security when outstanding waived amounts are $1 million or more.

[ERISA § 312(c); I.R.C. §§ 412(c), 430(e)]

Q 8:25 What is the procedure for obtaining a waiver of the minimum funding standards?

Although changes in the funding rules were made under PPA (see Q 8:2), many of the rules with respect to waiver of the minimum funding standards were retained; and, accordingly, the following discussion may still apply after 2007.

The request for a waiver of the minimum funding standards must include evidence that (1) the minimum funding standards cannot be satisfied without temporary substantial business hardship and (2) meeting the funding standards would adversely affect the interests of the plan's participants in the aggregate. The request should include the following items:

1. *General facts concerning the employer.* A statement concerning the employer's business, its history, and its ownership, any recent or contemplated changes that might affect its financial condition, and whether the employer is to be aggregated with any other entity (see Q 5:31).

2. *The financial condition of the employer.* The current and preceding two years' financial statements (the balance sheets, profit and loss statements, and notes to the financial statements). Uncertified statements are acceptable if certified statements have not been prepared. If the employer files financial reports with the Securities and Exchange Commission, the most recent ones should be submitted. If neither the statements nor reports are available, copies of federal income tax returns may be submitted.

3. *Executive compensation arrangements (not required for multiemployer plans).* For each person who is an officer or director, a detailed statement concerning all amounts that the employer has paid or will pay to such person during the plan year for which the request is made and the immediately preceding 24 months.

4. *Nature and extent of the business hardship.* A comprehensive discussion of the nature and extent of the business hardship, including a discussion of the underlying reasons that led to the current situation (e.g., declining sales, unexpected losses, labor disputes), financial projections, and statements that (a) discuss the prospects of recovery and why recovery is likely, (b) describe actions taken or planned to effect recovery, and (c) explain when and to what extent it is anticipated that required contributions can reasonably be expected to resume.

5. *Facts concerning the pension plan.* The following information should be included:

   a. The name of the plan and the plan's identification and file folder number;

   b. The date the plan was adopted;

   c. The effective date of the plan;

   d. The classes of employees covered;

   e. The number of employees covered;

   f. A copy of the plan document and summary plan description (see Q 22:1);

   g. A brief description of any plan amendment during the last five years that affects plan costs;

   h. The current and preceding two years' actuarial reports;

   i. A statement of how the plan is funded (e.g., trust fund, insurance policies);

   j. The contribution history for the current plan year and prior two plan years;

   k. The plan year for which the waiver is requested;

   l. The approximate contribution required to meet the minimum funding standards;

    m. A copy of the most recent annual report, Form 5500 series (see Q 21:1), and for defined benefit plans, a copy of Schedule B (see Q 21:6);

    n. A statement as to whether the plan is subject to PBGC jurisdiction (see Q 25:11); and

    o. Information concerning the granting of any prior waivers.

6. *Other plans.* The following information concerning any other plans maintained by the employer:

    a. A brief description of the plan;

    b. The number of employees covered;

    c. The classes of employees covered;

    d. The approximate annual contribution required;

    e. The amount of contributions that have been made, or are intended to be made, for any plan year of such other plan commencing in, or ending in, the plan year for which the waiver is requested; and

    f. A statement as to whether a waiver request is contemplated for the plan.

7. *Other information.* The following additional information should be included:

    a. A description of any other matters pertaining to the plan are currently pending or about to be submitted to IRS, DOL, or PBGC;

    b. Details of any existing arbitration, litigation, or court procedure that involves the plan; and

    c. A statement as to which IRS Area Office maintains files concerning the plan.

Although not required, a digest of certain information from the financial statements will facilitate the processing of the waiver request.

Furthermore, a checklist has been provided for the convenience of the taxpayer submitting the request. The checklist must be completed, signed, and dated by the employer or representative and should be placed on top of the request.

Both defined contribution plans (see Q 2:2) and defined benefit plans (see Q 2:3) must satisfy the above requirements in order to obtain a waiver of the minimum funding standards.

[Rev. Proc. 2004-15, 2004-1 C.B. 490]

In addition to the above, a defined contribution plan subject to the minimum funding standards must adopt an amendment to the plan specifying how the waived contribution will be made up and allocated to the plan participants. [Rev. Rul. 78-223, 1978-1 C.B. 125; Priv. Ltr. Ruls. 200214030, 199949047, 9547030, 9438042, 9331056] In order to provide maximum flexibility in obtaining a waiver for a defined contribution plan, the following three alternative procedures are provided:

1. The request can be for a waiver ruling only, without submission of a plan amendment. This request will require the use of a plan amendment supplied by IRS.

2. The request can be for a waiver ruling only, with the submission of a plan amendment.

3. A request can also be for a waiver ruling and a determination letter (see Q 18:1). This type of request will be treated as a request for technical advice from the Determinations Manager and will require payment of a user fee (see Qs 8:27, 18:2) for both the waiver request and the determination letter request and a completed Form 5300 and all necessary documents, plan amendments, and information required with Form 5300 (see Q 18:12).

Requests for waivers must be submitted no later than the 15th day of the third month following the close of the plan year for which the waiver is requested, and this deadline may not be extended. A request for a waiver with respect to a multiemployer plan (see Q 29:2) generally must be submitted no later than the close of the plan year following the plan year for which the waiver is requested. The application for a waiver with respect to a plan year that has not yet ended generally should not be submitted earlier than 180 days prior to the end of the plan year for which the waiver is requested, because the evidence required to support the request may not be available. [I.R.C. § 412(c)(5); Rev. Proc. 2004-15, 2004-1 C.B. 490; Priv. Ltr. Ruls. 199937056, 9422054, 9310050]

Requests for a waiver only should be addressed to:

Employee Plans

Internal Revenue Service

Commissioner, TE/GE

Attention: SE:T:EP:RA

P.O. Box 27063

McPherson Station

Washington, D.C. 20038

[Rev. Proc. 2004-15, 2004-1 C.B. 490]

Q 8:26 Are there any IRS Notice requirements when a funding waiver request is filed?

Yes. The applicant must give advance IRS Notice of the waiver application to (1) each participant in the plan, (2) each beneficiary under the plan, (3) each alternate payee (see Q 36:5), and (4) each employee organization representing participants in the plan. The IRS Notice must be hand delivered or mailed within 14 days prior to the date of the application and must include a description of the extent to which the plan is funded for benefits that are guaranteed by PBGC and the extent to which the plan is funded for benefit liabilities. IRS has provided a model IRS Notice that the applicant may use. [ERISA § 302(c)(6)(A); I.R.C. § 412(c)(6)(A); Rev. Proc. 2004-15, 2004-1 C.B. 490]

Q 8:27 What additional information and fees are required for the funding waiver request?

IRS charges a user fee for a request for a waiver of the minimum funding standards. The user fee is $14,500 for a waiver of $1 million or more and $10,000 for a waiver of less than $1 million. [Rev. Proc. 2010-8, § 6, 2010-1 C.B. 234]

Additionally, the following procedural requirements must be met:

1. The request must be signed by the employer maintaining the plan or its authorized representative.
2. A statement attesting to the truthfulness of the statements must be included with the request and signed by the employer, not the authorized representative.
3. Since the waiver request is a formal ruling request, it must comply with public disclosure requirements under Section 6110.
4. The request must include a copy of the written IRS Notice (see Q 8:26) regarding the waiver application and state that such IRS Notice was mailed or hand delivered to the appropriate parties.

[Rev. Proc. 2004-15, 2004-1 C.B. 490]

Q 8:28 May a pension plan be amended if a waiver of the funding standards is in effect for a particular year?

Yes, but the funding waiver automatically ends if one of the following types of plan amendments is adopted:

1. An amendment increasing plan benefits;
2. An amendment changing the accrual of benefits if the change would increase the plan's liabilities; or
3. An amendment changing the rate at which benefits become nonforfeitable if the change would increase the plan's liabilities.

These amendments will not cause a funding waiver to cease if (1) DOL decides that the amendment is reasonable and has only a small impact on plan liabilities, (2) the amendment merely repeals a retroactive plan amendment reducing benefits, or (3) the amendment must be made for the plan to remain qualified for tax-favored status. [I.R.C. § 412(c)(7)]

Although the following discussion relates to cases prior to 2008, because PPA retains the rule regarding the restriction on plan amendments if a waiver is in effect, it appears the following may still apply after 2007. IRS ruled that amendments to a defined benefit plan (see Q 2:3) causing an increase of more than 6 percent in the plan's liabilities were not *de minimis*; and, therefore, previously granted waivers were null and void. [Priv. Ltr. Rul. 9719038] In other cases, IRS ruled that amendments increasing benefits were neither reasonable nor *de minimis*; therefore, previously granted waivers no longer applied. [Priv. Ltr. Ruls. 9444045, 9226075, 9224051] IRS has also ruled that an amendment increasing benefits was not reasonable merely because the amendment was agreed to in collective bargaining; and, therefore, the previously granted waivers ceased to apply. [Priv. Ltr. Rul. 9244040] However, in another case, IRS ruled that since a collectively bargained plan amendment that would increase disability benefits, ease retirement requirements, and provide for severance payments was reasonable and resulted in only a *de minimis* increase in plan liabilities, the plan amendment would not affect the funding waiver previously granted. [Priv. Ltr. Rul. 9342050] IRS has ruled that a previously granted funding waiver was still effective where one part of a plan amendment caused an increase in plan liabilities, but the combined effect of the amendment did not increase liabilities. [Priv. Ltr. Rul. 9741048]. A hospital was allowed to amend its defined benefit plan and 401(k) plan resulting in an increased liability even though a waiver of the minimum funding standard was in effect. It was determined that the amendment to the 401(k) plan resulted in a *de minimis* increase in benefits and the amendments to both plans, made as a result of corrections under EPCRS (see Q 19:2), were required as a condition of qualification. [Priv. Ltr. Rul. 200728049] Similarly, a company was allowed to amend its 401(k) plan although a prior conditional waiver of its pension plan noted that any amendment that increased liabilities to any other plan covering employees who were also covered by the pension plan would not be allowed. The proposed amendments were necessary in order to reduce employee turn-over and attract new employees, and the net cost effect of the defined benefit plan freeze and amendments to the 401(k) plan were determined to be *de minimis*. [Priv. Ltr. Rul. 200738026]

In one case, an employer proposed that a plan that had previously been granted a waiver of the minimum funding standards be converted to a 401(k) plan. IRS ruled that, since the contributions under the new plan would represent an impermissible increase in contribution levels, the previously granted funding waiver would be revoked. [Priv. Ltr. Rul. 9036037] However, in another case involving a plan that had previously been granted a waiver, the employer adopted a 401(k) plan, but IRS ruled the waiver would not be revoked because the contributions to the new plan were equal to the waived amount. [Priv. Ltr. Rul. 9036050]

IRS ruled that where a company sponsored three pension plans, two of which were subject to funding waivers, the third plan was not subject to the restrictions regarding plan amendments that increase plan liabilities. IRS noted that the third plan covered employees who were not participants in the company's other two plans. [Priv. Ltr. Rul. 200546050] Where (1) future accruals ceased in a pension plan subject to a funding waiver that resulted in decreased future contributions to that plan and (2) a defined contribution plan was instituted that provided for employer contributions, the combined result was a decrease of costs over the remaining years of the waiver. Accordingly, IRS ruled that because the overall contribution of both plans did not exceed the required contribution of the pension plan prior to the cessation of accruals, there would be no increase in liabilities; and, therefore, these changes had no effect on the prior funding waiver. [Priv. Ltr. Rul. 200539032]

Q 8:29   What alternative is available if IRS will not waive the minimum funding standards?

Although the following discussion relates to cases prior to 2008 and PPA made changes to the funding rules (see Q 8:2), it appears the following may still apply after 2007. To keep the pension plan in compliance with the minimum funding standards, owners of the company may have to waive their benefits irrevocably. In small pension plans, the costs attributable to the owners' benefits are usually a large portion of the required contribution. Thus, if the owners are permitted to waive their contributions or benefits, the amount that has to be contributed to the pension plan to meet the minimum funding standards may be reduced substantially. IRS has ruled that an accumulated funding deficiency could not be corrected by the waiver of a key employee's benefits upon plan termination. [Priv. Ltr. Rul. 9146005]

A plan sponsor may request IRS approval to retroactively reduce accrued benefits (see Qs 9:25, 9:35) if (1) a minimum funding waiver is not available or would be inadequate and (2) such reduction is necessary because of a substantial business hardship. The amendment to retroactively reduce an accrued benefit to a date no earlier than the first day of the plan year to which it applies must be adopted no later than two and a half months after the close of that plan year. In one case, IRS approved a retroactive reduction of a required contribution to a defined contribution plan from 10 percent to 5 percent of each employee's compensation. Despite the employer's steps to economize, including reducing the officer's salary, the financial hardship was not temporary, so a funding waiver would have been inadequate. [Priv. Ltr. Rul. 9644076] A company, owned by five physicians who were the only employees and plan participants, was granted approval by IRS to retroactively amend its money purchase pension plan (see Q 2:4) to reduce accrued benefits. Although the business hardship was substantial, it was not temporary and, therefore, a waiver would have been unavailable or inadequate. [Priv. Ltr. Rul. 9736044] In another case, IRS approved a retroactive reduction of accrued benefits because of substantial business hardship since the plan sponsor had been operating at a loss and may have been unable to continue the plan without the amendments. Furthermore, although a waiver of the minimum funding standards may have been available, it would have been inadequate because the waiver would only reduce the current year's costs, but future contributions would increase. [Priv. Ltr. Rul. 9614004] IRS has denied a request for approval of a retroactive amendment where the amendment was executed subsequent to two and a half months after the plan year end. [Priv. Ltr. Rul. 200049039] In another case, IRS denied a request for approval to retroactively reduce the accrued benefits of participants. The plan, which covered officers and business agents of participating local unions, had terminated, and IRS determined that it would not be reasonable to expect the plan to continue if the reduction in accrued benefits was allowed. [Priv. Ltr. Rul. 200306039] IRS has issued procedures for obtaining approval of plan amendments that retroactively reduce accrued benefits. [I.R.C. §§ 412(d)(2); 412(c)(8) (prior to amendment); Rev. Proc. 94-42, 1994-1 C.B. 717]

Q 8:30 May an employer obtain an extension of an amortization period to help it meet the minimum funding standards?

Effective for plan years beginning after December 31, 2007, if the plan sponsor of a multiemployer plan (see Q 29:2) submits an application to IRS for an extension of the amortization period for any unfunded liability and includes a certification by the plan's actuary, the amortization period will be extended for the period (not in excess of five years) requested in the application. This extension is referred to as an automatic extension. [I.R.C. § 431(d)(1)] In addition, the plan sponsor of a multiemployer plan may submit an application for an extension of the amortization period for an unfunded liability for a period of time not in excess of ten years less the number of years of any automatic extension. This extension is referred to as an alternative extension. [I.R.C. § 431(d)(2)]

For plan years beginning prior to 2008, IRS was authorized to grant an extension for a period not in excess of ten years if the employer showed that the extension would provide adequate protection for participants and their beneficiaries and denial of the extension would (1) risk the continuation of the plan or might cause a curtailment of retirement benefits or employee compensation and (2) be adverse to the interests of the participants. [I.R.C. § 412(e)(l) (prior to amendment)]

With respect to single-employer plans, PPA (see Q 1:33) repealed the provision under which the amortization period could be extended. Effective for plan years beginning after December 31, 2007, there is no provision for single-employer plans to receive an extension of the amortization period for any unfunded liability.

An application to extend an amortization period must meet the following general procedures:

1. *Who may submit.* A request for approval to extend the period of years required to amortize any unfunded liability must be submitted by the plan sponsor or by an authorized representative of the applicant.

2. *Submission.* The application to extend an amortization period must be submitted to:

    Employee Plans
    Internal Revenue Service
    Commissioner, TE/GE
    Attention: SE:T:EP:RA
    P.O. Box 27063
    McPherson Station
    Washington, D.C. 20038

    The appropriate user fee must be sent with such request.

3. *Necessary Procedural Documents.* A request will not be considered unless it (a) contains a penalty of perjury statement and (b) complies with public disclosure requirements under Section 6110.

4. *Notification.* The applicant must provide a copy of a written notification to each employee organization representing employees covered by the plan, to each contributing employer, and to each participant, beneficiary, and alternate payee (see Q 36:5) of the plan, that an application for an extension of the amortization period has been submitted to IRS.

An application for an automatic extension must include the following additional information:

1. The unfunded liability for which an extension of the amortization period is requested.

2. The length of the extension of the amortization period being requested (up to a maximum of five years).

3. Whether a prior application for an amortization extension (automatic or alternative) was submitted, whether an application was granted under Section 412(e) (prior to PPA) with respect to the prior 15 plan years, and whether the plan is in endangered or critical status (see Q 8:8) in the first plan year for which the extension is requested.

4. A certification by the plan's actuary that, based on reasonable assumptions:

   a. Absent the extension for which the plan is applying, the plan would have an accumulated funding deficiency (see Q 8:20) in the current plan year or any of the nine succeeding plan years,

   b. The plan sponsor has devised a plan to improve the plan's funding status,

   c. The plan is projected to have sufficient assets to timely pay expected benefits and anticipated expenditures over the amortization period as extended, and

   d. The required notice has been provided.

Upon receipt of the application with the necessary information, and verification that the criteria stated above have been met, IRS will issue a statement to the applicant providing approval for the requested extension.

In numerous instances, approval was granted for a five-year automatic extension for amortizing a plan's unfunded liabilities. In each instance, the plan showed that, absent the extension, the plan would have an accumulated funding deficiency in the current plan year or any of the nine succeeding plan years, the plan's sponsor had adopted a plan to improve the plan's funding status, the plan was projected to have sufficient assets to timely pay expected benefits and anticipated expenditures over the extended amortization period, and required notice was provided. [Priv. Ltr. Ruls. 201020027 through 201020032, 201019021 through 201019032, 201017068 through 201017075, 201016096, 201016094, 201014074 through 21014076, 201013074, 201013068 through 201013071, 200925050 through 200925055, 200924052 through 200924055, 200924058 through 200924060, 200924063, 200923049 through 200923055, 200923058 through 200923060, 200921031, 200921032, 200921034, 200921035]

An application for an alternative extension must include certain information. The applicant must furnish appropriate evidence that the extension of the amortization period would carry out the purposes of ERISA and PPA and would provide adequate protection for the participants and their beneficiaries, and that the failure to permit the extension would result in a substantial risk to the voluntary continuation of the plan, or a substantial curtailment of benefit levels or employee compensation, and be adverse to the interests of the plan participants in the aggregate. The following information should be provided:

1. General facts concerning the participating employers.
2. The financial condition of the principal employers.
3. Information concerning the extension of the amortization period must include the following:
   a. The unfunded liability for which an extension of the amortization period is requested.
   b. The reasons an extension of the amortization period is needed.
   c. The length of the extension of the amortization period desired (up to a maximum of ten years less any automatic extension).
   d. Information concerning the actions taken by the applicant to reduce the plan's unfunded liability before the request for an extension has been made. Such actions would include the reduction of future plan benefit accruals and increases in employer contribution rates. Also, a description of any benefit reductions, contribution rate increases, or other actions that are intended to be taken in the future.
   e. Projections of (i) funding standard account credit balance/accumulated funding deficiencies, (ii) actuarial value of assets and market value of assets, (iii) current liabilities, and (iv) funding ratios, for the length of the extension of the amortization period requested and for the period ten years afterwards.
   f. The plan year for which the extension is requested.
4. The following information regarding the plan must be supplied:
   a. The name of the plan, the plan's identification number, and file folder number (if any).
   b. The date the plan was adopted.
   c. The effective date of the plan.
   d. The classes of employees covered.
   e. The number of employees covered.
   f. A copy of the current plan document and the most recent summary plan description.
   g. A copy of the most recent determination letter issued to the plan.
   h. A brief description of all plan amendments adopted during the year for which the extension is requested and the previous four years that affect plan costs, including the approximate effect of each amendment on such costs.

    i. The most recent actuarial report plus any available actuarial reports for the preceding two plan years.

    j. A description of how the plan is funded (i.e., trust fund, individual insurance policies, etc.).

    k. A list of the contributions actually paid in each month, from the 24th month prior to the beginning of the plan year for which the extension is requested.

    l. The approximate contribution required to meet the minimum funding standard.

    m. A copy of the most recently completed Annual Return/Report (Form 5500 series, as applicable; see Q 21:1) and, in the case of a defined benefit plan, a copy of the corresponding Actuarial Information schedule (Schedule B of Form 5500 for plan years beginning before 2008, or Schedule MB for plan years beginning after 2007; see Q 21:6).

    n. A copy of each ruling letter that waived the minimum funding standard during the last 15 plan years.

    o. A copy of each ruling letter that granted an extension of time to amortize any unfunded liability which became applicable at any time during the last 15 plan years.

    p. A copy of the certification of whether or not the plan is in critical status or endangered status.

    q. A copy of any funding improvement plan or rehabilitation plan to which the plan is currently subject.

5. Other information that should be provided includes (a) a description of any matters currently pending or are intended to be submitted to IRS, DOL, or PBGC, and (b) details of any existing arbitration, litigation, or court procedure that involves the plan.

A checklist has been provided in Appendix B for the convenience of the applicant submitting the application for an alternative extension. The checklist must be signed and dated by the applicant or authorized representative and placed on top of the request.

All extension requests must be submitted by the last day of the first plan year for which the extension is intended to take effect. IRS will consider applications for extensions submitted after this date only upon a showing of good cause. In seeking an extension of an amortization period with respect to a plan year that has not yet ended, the applicant may have difficulty in furnishing sufficient current evidence in support of the request. For this reason, it is generally advised that a request not be submitted earlier than 90 days prior to the end of the plan year for which the extension is requested. This 90-day period does not apply to applications for an automatic extension.

These procedures are effective for all ruling requests received with respect to plan years beginning after December 31, 2007.

[Rev. Proc. 2008-67, 2008-2 C.B. 1211, *superseding* Rev. Proc. 2004-44, 2004-2 C.B. 134]

See Q 8:30 of *The 2009 Pension Answer Book* for rules prior to 2008.

The following discussion relates to plan years beginning before 2008 and may relate to multiemployer plans after December 31, 2007.

In one case, IRS granted a multiemployer plan's (see Q 29:2) request to extend for four years the time to amortize the unfunded liability. IRS determined that a five-year extension provided rapidly increasing credit balances; a three-year extension provided limited relief; but, a four-year extension provided moderate increases in the credit balance. If the extension was not granted, the plan would have large accumulated deficiencies in subsequent years that could cause employer withdrawal and employees to look for other employment, so IRS concluded that the extension encouraged the voluntary continuation of the plan and was not adverse to the interests of participants in the aggregate. [Priv. Ltr. Rul. 200225043] Similarly, IRS concluded that an extension was not adverse to the participants in the aggregate and granted a conditional approval for an extension for amortizing the unfunded liabilities where the potential increase in employer contribution necessary to avoid funding deficiencies and the possible excise taxes that would result if the deficiencies were not avoided could lead to a loss of jobs for the employees covered by the plan. [Priv. Ltr. Rul. 200641007] Although the plan's funded status had deteriorated as a result of investment losses and decreased employer membership, a request for a ten-year extension was approved because several steps were taken to improve the plan's funding, such as increasing employer contribution and amending the plan to reduce the benefit accrual rate, tightening eligibility for lump-sum death benefits, increasing reduction for early retirement benefits, increasing the age requirement for early retirement benefit, and increasing the hours needed to earn pension credits. [Priv. Ltr. Rul. 200743017] With respect to a multiple employer plan, an extension of seven years to the amortization bases was granted subject to the condition that the contributions required to satisfy the minimum funding standards be timely made. To deal with the funding problem, the rate of future benefit accruals was reduced and the rate of contributions from contributing employers was increased. [Priv. Ltr. Rul. 200547019] In another case, a conditional approval to extend the amortization period to 3.7 years was granted where, due to the plan's negative investment returns, the amount the company would have been required to contribute would have resulted in a substantial risk to the financial viability of the company. [Priv. Ltr. Rul. 200510041] IRS granted conditional approval to extend certain amortization periods where the company experienced a decline in business but instituted cost-cutting measures to effect a recovery. The plan was fully funded with respect to the non-owner participants; and, if extensions were not granted, the company would be forced to substantially curtail pension benefits or employee compensation. Accordingly, extensions were not adverse to the participants in the aggregate. [Priv. Ltr. Rul. 200444040] Where projections indicated that the plan would have a funding deficiency, a ten-year extension was granted because failure to permit the extension would result in a substantial risk to the voluntary continuation of the plan and would be adverse to the participants in the aggregate, but was conditioned that a certain credit balance be maintained in the funding standard account. [Priv. Ltr. Rul. 200724037; *see also* Priv. Ltr. Rul. 200743037] In another case, IRS granted a request for a five-year extension of the time (after denial of a ten-year extension) to amortize the unfunded liability of a multiemployer plan. IRS determined that denial of an extension sufficient to reduce future accumulated funding deficiencies would result in possible termination of the plan and benefit curtailments. Furthermore, the granting of the request was not adverse to the interests of plan participants. [Priv. Ltr. Rul. 9632022] IRS did not revoke this letter ruling where, subsequently, a plan amendment that recognized reciprocal vesting service for participants who shifted between two plans was reasonable and resulted in only a *de minimis* increase in the plan's liabilities. The increase in total plan costs was less than .05 percent and contributions from the new contributing employer exceeded the added costs. [Priv. Ltr. Rul. 9727033] In another case, it was determined that a proposed amendment increasing future benefit accruals in order to sustain participation and promote growth of a plan provided only a *de minimis* increase in plan benefits and was deemed reasonable; therefore, the previously granted extension of the amortization periods would still apply. The financial strengths of the plan had improved on the basis of better investment advice, increased employer contribution rates, and close monitoring of the plan's financial position. [Priv. Ltr. Rul. 200123068]

However, IRS denied a request for a ten-year extension of the time to amortize the unfunded liability of a multiemployer plan where there was no risk of plan termination, no indication that the current benefit level was in jeopardy, and no explanation of how the failure to grant the extension would affect participants. [Priv. Ltr. Rul. 9715029] Also, a request for an extension was denied where projections indicated that the plan would not experience a funding deficiency until 2017, so that failure to grant an extension would not result in either a substantial risk to the voluntary continuation of the plan or a substantial curtailment of pension benefit levels or employee compensation, or be adverse to the interests of plan participants in the aggregate. [Priv. Ltr. Rul. 200751029] Similarly, a request for an extension of the amortization period submitted by a multiemployer plan was denied where the plan was not expected to have a deficiency for several years, the plan's funding status had improved, and denying the extension would not pose a risk to the voluntary continuation of the plan. [Priv. Ltr. Rul. 200738030] In another case, a request for an extension of the amortization period was denied because the continuation of the plan was not substantially at risk in the foreseeable future because the funding deficiency was not projected to occur for another seven years and a substantial curtailment of benefits was not imminent. [Priv. Ltr. Rul. 200706013] IRS also denied a request for a ten-year extension of the time to amortize the unfunded liability of a multiemployer plan where the employers' financial situation was expected to improve and where failure to grant the extension would neither result in a substantial risk to the voluntary continuation of the plan nor result in a substantial curtailment of benefit levels. [Priv. Ltr. Rul. 9808046] In another case, a request for a ten-year extension of the time to amortize the unfunded liability for a pension plan was denied where there was no indication that the hardship was temporary or that there was a fair chance of recovery. [Priv. Ltr. Rul. 9216029]

Q 8:31   May a contribution be timely for the minimum funding standards but not for tax deduction purposes?

Yes. Contributions made after the close of a plan year may relate back to that year if they are made within 8½ months (2½ months for multiemployer plans; see Q 29:2) after the close of the plan year. This special deadline does not extend the time limit for making a contribution for tax deduction purposes; that is, payment by the due date, including extensions, for filing the employer's federal income tax return (see Q 12:4). [ERISA § 303(j); I.R.C. § 430(j)(1), 431(c)(8)]

This special deadline applies only for purposes of minimum funding and the excise tax (see Q 8:21) imposed for failure to meet the funding requirements. Employer contributions to its plan after the due date for filing its federal income tax return (including extensions) but within 8½ months after the close of the plan year are not deductible as contributions for the closed year. Although the minimum funding standards may be met, the tax deduction requirements are not. [Priv. Ltr. Rul. 7949018] Conversely, employer contributions to its plan on or before the due date for filing its federal income tax return (including extensions) but after 8½ months after the close of the plan year are deductible as contributions for the closed year. Although the tax deduction requirements may be met, the minimum funding standards are not. [Hoyez, 80 T.C.M. 198 (2000); Wenger, 79 T.C.M. 1995 (2000)]

> **Example.** Dylan, a sole proprietor, adopts a money purchase pension plan for calendar year 2010. For 2010, Dylan receives an extension to file his federal income tax return allowing him to file his return on October 17, 2011. On October 11, 2011, Dylan makes his required plan contribution. Although the contribution is deductible on Dylan's 2010 return, the contribution is not timely for the minimum funding standards because the contribution is made after September 15, 2011 (more than eight and one-half months after the end of the 2010 plan year).

IRS representatives have opined that when the date for making a plan contribution falls on a weekend or holiday, the extension for filing returns until the next business day does not apply to the deadline for the minimum funding standards.

A multiemployer plan (see Q 29:2) could not use contributions made in the grace period following the end of its plan year for funding purposes for that year because the contributions were for work performed in a different plan year; there must be a causal connection between the event occurring in the plan year and the contribution. [Priv. Ltr. Rul. 200517034]

Q 8:32   Must quarterly contributions be made to a defined benefit plan?

Yes. Effective with respect to plan years beginning after December 31, 2007, quarterly contribution payments are required to be made to a defined benefit plan (other than a multiemployer plan; see Q 29:2) that has a funding shortfall for the preceding plan year. Prior to 2008, the quarterly payments were required to be made to a plan that had a funded current liability percentage of less than 100 percent for the preceding plan year. The quarterly payments are due 15 days after the end of each quarter of the plan year. The percentage of each required quarterly payment is equal to 25 percent of the required annual payment. The required annual payment is the lesser of (1) 90 percent of the amount required to be contributed to the plan for the plan year in order to meet minimum funding or (2) 100 percent of the amount so required for the preceding plan year. Quarterly contributions are not required for the first plan year. [ERISA § 303(j); I.R.C. § 430(j); Prop. Treas. Reg. § 1.430(j)-1; Rev. Rul. 95-31, 1995-1 C.B. 76; IRS Notice 89-52, 1989-1 C.B. 692]

For plan years beginning after 2007, if an employer fails to pay the full amount of a required installment for the plan year, then the amount of interest charged on the underpayment for the period of underpayment is determined by using the plan's effective rate of interest plus 5 percentage points. [I.R.C. § 430(j)(3)]

The required quarterly payments may result in nondeductible contributions (see Q 8:12). IRS has instituted procedures for the return of nondeductible contributions. Generally, before nondeductible contributions may be returned, the contributions must be disallowed by obtaining a ruling letter from IRS, but a formal ruling is not necessary for nondeductible contributions of less than $25,000. [Rev. Proc. 90-49, 1990-2 C.B. 620]

A plan, subject to the quarterly contribution rules, that has more than 100 participants is required to maintain liquid plan assets at an amount approximately equal to three times the total disbursements made from the plan during the 12-month period ending on the last day of each quarter for which the plan has a required quarterly installment. If this requirement is not met, the plan is treated as failing to pay the full amount of any required quarterly contribution and the plan sponsor will be subject to a nondeductible excise tax equal to 10 percent of the liquidity shortfall. The excise tax is increased to 100 percent if the liquidity shortfall remains outstanding after four quarters. IRS may waive all or part of the excise tax if the liquidity shortfall was due to reasonable cause and not willful neglect and reasonable steps have been taken to remedy the liquidity shortfall. [I.R.C. §§ 430(j)(4), 4971(f); Prop. Treas. Reg. § 54.4971(c)-1; Rev. Rul. 95-31, 1995-1 C.B. 76]

Although the following discussion relates to cases prior to 2008, because PPA retains the rule regarding required quarterly contributions, it appears the following may still apply after 2007. In one case, IRS waived the 10 percent tax and concluded that the liquidity shortfalls were due to reasonable cause and not willful neglect. Although the company experienced net losses and severe negative cash flow, the company's president was removed, and state authorities intervened in the company's affairs, the company satisfied the minimum funding requirements. The liquidity shortfalls were the result, in part, of the payment of many small single-sum distributions to terminated employees and were corrected in the next year. [Priv. Ltr. Rul. 199920046] Similarly, waivers of the taxes were granted where a plan was merged to correct the liquidity shortfall that resulted from the payment of many small single-sum distributions after the sale of the company's assets and close of business. [Priv. Ltr. Rul. 199920037] Furthermore, IRS granted a waiver of the 10 percent tax where the company had experienced a liquidity shortfall due, in part, to the payment of a large number of single-sum distributions upon the termination of employees when the plan was acquired by another company. [Priv. Ltr. Rul. 199928038] In another case, IRS waived the 10 percent tax where due to the incorrect calculation of single-sum benefits in prior years, large disbursements were paid in order to correct the miscalculations and the individuals who received the corrected benefits caused the plan to have more than 100 participants. In addition, the company lost a contract with its largest customer but began the process of restructuring its debt and refocusing its marketing efforts. [Priv. Ltr. Rul. 200120038] Also, a waiver of the 10 percent tax was granted where the shortfalls were due to reasonable cause, not willful neglect, the company took reasonable steps to remedy the situation, and a full correction within the prescribed periods would have resulted in a substantial financial hardship on the company. [Priv. Ltr. Rul. 199931050] In another case, the waiver of the 10 percent tax was granted where the plan was being terminated in a distress termination (see Q 25:15) and IRS concluded that reasonable steps were taken to remedy the liquidity shortfalls. [Priv. Ltr. Rul. 200120039] IRS granted a waiver of the 10 percent tax where the company was unaware of the liquidity shortfalls since the consultant did not timely make any calculations and the liquidity requirements had subsequently been satisfied. [Priv. Ltr. Rul. 200219041; *see also* Priv. Ltr. Ruls. 200443042, 200428030, 200401018] Similarly, where, due to turnover in staff at the actuarial firm, the enrolled actuary did not timely inform the company regarding the liquidity shortfall, a waiver was granted because the company contributed the missed amounts soon after the shortfall was discovered. [Priv. Ltr. Rul. 200547018] In another case, IRS granted a waiver of the 10 percent tax where a company that was unaware of the liquidity shortfall made corrections to meet the shortfall once it was recommended and then adopted a policy of maintaining the funding of the plan at no less than 100 percent of current liability. [Priv. Ltr. Rul. 200246033; *see also* Priv. Ltr. Rul. 200406047, where a company implemented a procedure to timely provide asset information to the consulting firm, which would then promptly perform computations regarding the liquidity shortfall]

Q 8:33 Does the minimum funding requirement cease once a pension plan terminates?

Generally, the minimum funding standards apply to a pension plan until the end of the plan year in which the plan terminates and do not apply to the plan in later years. Therefore, prior to 2008, the funding standard account (see Q 8:19) must be maintained through the end of the plan year in which the pension plan terminates, even if the termination occurs before the last day of the plan year. [J.P. Jeter Co., 65 T.C.M. 2783 (1993)] IRS has opined that an actuarial report (formerly known as Schedule B; see Q 21:6) must be filed for the plan year in which a defined benefit plan terminates but need not be filed for the plan year after the year in which the plan terminates (see Q 25:63). [Spec. Rul. (July 27, 1993)]

If plan assets are not distributed as soon as administratively feasible after the date of plan termination, the plan will not be treated as terminated and, therefore, such a plan remains subject to the minimum funding standards (see Q 25:63). [Rev. Rul. 89-87, 1989-2 C.B. 81; Rev. Rul. 79-237, 1979-2 C.B. 190]

A defined benefit plan (see Q 2:3) with a beginning of the year valuation date was merged into another defined benefit plan; and, although the plans as merged were fully funded, a funding deficiency existed with respect to the first plan because a contribution was not made during the eight and one-half months after the close of its plan year (see Q 8:31). IRS ruled that the minimum funding standards apply through the end of the plan year in which the plan ceases to exist (i.e., the year the plan is terminated, the year the merger occurs). [Priv. Ltr. Rul. 200312025]

For details on plan terminations, see chapter 25.

Chapter 9

Vesting

One of the major features of a qualified retirement plan is the requirement that it provide for the vesting of benefits according to one of several schedules set by law. Thus, at a certain point, an employee acquires a nonforfeitable interest in benefits under the plan. This chapter examines what vesting means, the minimum requirements set by law, and how vesting works.

Q 9:1   What does vesting mean?

Vesting represents the nonforfeitable interest of participants in their (1) account balances under a defined contribution plan (see Q 2:2) or (2) accrued benefits under a defined benefit plan (see Q 2:3).

> **Example.** Assume a participant is 40 percent vested (that is, the participant has a nonforfeitable right to 40 percent of the benefit accrued in the plan). In a defined contribution plan, the participant's vested accrued benefit is equal to 40 percent of the balance in the account. In a defined benefit plan, the participant has a nonforfeitable right to 40 percent of the normal retirement benefit that has been accrued. Thus, if the accrued normal retirement benefit is $150 a month, the participant has a nonforfeitable right to $60 a month.

Vesting is directly related to an employee's length of service with the employer or group of employers (see Q 9:4).

USERRA (see Q 1:16) provides that an individual who is reemployed following protected military service must be treated as not having incurred a break in service (see Q 5:10). Furthermore, upon reemployment, the plan must grant vesting credit for the period of time the employee was absent for military service.

Special vesting rules apply to top-heavy plans (see Q 26:30).

Q 9:2   What is an accrued benefit?

A participant's accrued benefit is the benefit that has accumulated up to a particular point in employment. Earning accrued benefits does not mean that a participant has a nonforfeitable (i.e., vested) right to those benefits. The nonforfeitability of an accrued benefit is determined by the retirement plan's vesting schedule.

Defined contribution plans (see Q 2:2) must provide separate accounts with respect to each participant's accrued benefit. This means that a participant's accrued benefit is the balance of the participant's individual account. [I.R.C. § 411(a)(7)(A)(ii)]

Defined benefit plans (other than those funded solely through insurance contracts) are required to include a procedure for determining a participant's accrued benefit that satisfies one of three alternative benefit accrual formulas. Generally, accrued benefits are determined with reference to the benefits that are payable at normal retirement age (see Q 10:55) and that accrue over the period of the employee's participation in the plan or service with the employer. The alternative formulas limit the amount of backloading (providing a higher rate for accrual of benefits for later years of service than for earlier years); however, they do not require the same rate of benefit accrual each year. [Langman v. Laub, 328 F.3d 68 (2d Cir. 2003); *see also* LaFlamme v. Carpenters Local 370 Pension Plan, 2005 WL 414963 (2d Cir. 2005), King v. Pension Trust Fund of the Pension, Hospitalization and Benefit Plan of the Electrical Industry, 2005 WL 414871 (2d Cir. 2005), and Melvin v. U.A. Local 13 Pension Plan, 2005 WL 414850 (2d Cir. 2005)] Frontloading (providing a higher rate for accrual of benefits for earlier years of service than for later years) is permitted, although such front loading also may be limited. One court concluded that a defined benefit plan, which provided for benefit accrual at 2 percent of average monthly earnings for the first 24 years of service but, at 25 years of service, provided for the recalculation of all previous years of service at 2 percent of final average monthly earnings, violated the minimum accrual rules. The plan failed to satisfy the $133\frac{1}{3}$ percent accrual formula because the plan's use of a higher base for computing benefits at the 25th year was determined solely by a participant's increase in service. [I.R.C. § 411(b)(1); Rev. Rul. 85-131, 1985-2 C.B. 138; IRS Notice 87-21, 1987-1 C.B. 458, Q&A-16; IRS Notice 89-45, 1989-1 C.B. 684; Jerome Mirza & Assocs., Ltd. v. United States, 882 F.2d 229 (7th Cir. 1989); Carollo v. Cement & Concrete Workers Dist. Council Pension Plan, No. 96 Cv. 3152 (E.D.N.Y. 1997); DeVito v. Pension Plan of Local 819 IBT Pension Fund, No. 90 Civ. 5299 (S.D.N.Y. 1997)] See Q 9:3 for a discussion of an IRS ruling concerning the three alternative benefit accrual formulas applicable to defined benefit plans.

USERRA (see Qs 1:16, 1:35) provides that an individual who is reemployed following protected military service must be treated as not having incurred a break in service (see Q 5:10). Furthermore, upon reemployment, the plan must grant benefit credit for the period of time the employee was absent for military service. Defined contribution plans must credit the employee with any allocations of employer contributions, but not earnings or forfeitures, to which the employee would have been entitled had there been no interruption in employment. For this purpose, the employee's compensation is assumed to be at the rate the employee would have received had there been no interruption in employment.

One court concluded that a plan had to include the present value of future cost-of-living adjustments in the calculation of single-sum distributions because benefits paid under the plan in the form of annuities provided for such adjustments. There can only be one definition of "accrued benefit" ruled the court; and, because the plan provided for such adjustments in annuity payments, it had to account for such adjustments when benefits were paid in the form of a single-sum distribution. [Laurenzano v. Blue Cross & Blue Shield of Mass., Inc. Ret. Income Trust, 2001 WL 327132 (D. Mass. 2001)] The court also subsequently ruled that, because the COLA adjustments were accrued, they could not be waived. [Laurenzano v. Blue Cross & Blue Shield of Mass., Inc. Ret. Income Trust, No. 99-11751 (D. Mass. 2002)]

For a discussion of vesting and accrued benefits relating to employee contributions, see Q 9:9.

Q 9:3 Has IRS issued a ruling concerning the conversion of a defined benefit plan with a traditional benefit formula to a cash balance formula?

IRS issued a revenue ruling that addresses the application of the accrual rules for defined benefit plans (see Q 9:2). The revenue ruling analyzes a traditional pension plan that was converted into a cash balance pension plan (see Q 2:23) prior to the effective date of the new conversion requirements under PPA (see Q 1:33). The scenario analyzed in the revenue ruling is one in which certain participants had their pensions determined using the greater of (1) the benefit under a continuation of the pre-conversion plan formula for a limited number of years after the conversion date and (2) the benefit under the new cash balance formula. The ruling illustrates how, under the current regulations, the backloading rules apply to this scenario. The ruling provides relief to ensure that plans that have requested or received a determination letter (see Q 18:1) from IRS and certain other plans will not be disqualified for plan years beginning before January 1, 2009 solely because the plan provides benefits based on the greatest of two or more formulas.

FACTS

Plan A is a defined benefit pension plan that (prior to the amendment described below) provided a normal retirement benefit payable in the form of a straight life annuity commencing at the age 65 normal retirement age (see Q 10:55) under the plan equal to the product of 1.1 percent of average compensation for the three consecutive years of service, with the highest such average multiplied by the number of years of service at normal retirement age. Under Plan A, the accrued benefit (prior to the amendment described below) of a participant at any point prior to attainment of normal retirement age is the benefit, payable in the form of a straight life annuity commencing at the age 65 normal retirement age, equal to the product of 1.1 percent of the participant's highest average compensation at such point multiplied by the participant's number of years of service at such point. Plan A provides that an employee commences participation in the plan on the first day of the first month after commencing employment or, if later, the first day of the first month following attainment of age 21.

Plan A was amended in 2001 to change the plan's benefit formula effective for plan years beginning on or after January 1, 2002. The new benefit formula is a lump sum-based benefit formula as further described below. Under the lump sum-based benefit formula, a hypothetical account is created for each participant. For participants who were employees on December 31, 2001, the opening account balance was equal to the actuarial present value of the participant's accrued benefit determined as of that date. Under Plan A, this actuarial present value was determined using the applicable interest rate, post-retirement mortality using the applicable mortality table for 2002, and no pre-retirement mortality. Thereafter, the hypothetical account balance is credited with hypothetical interest at the rate of interest on three-year Treasury Constant Maturities for the month prior to the first day of the plan year plus 25 basis points (for the 2002 plan year, the rate of interest was determined as 3.8 percent, which is 3.62 percent, the yield on three-year Treasury Constant Maturies for December 2001, plus 25 basis points). Additionally, the hypothetical account for each participant is credited at the end of each accrual computation period (which is the plan year) with pay credits that are determined as a percentage of compensation for the participant for the plan year. The percentage is determined, based upon the age of the participant at the beginning of the plan year, in accordance with the following table:

Age at Beginning of Year	Percentage
25 or less	3
26–40	4
41–50	5
51–60	6
61 or more	7

The annual benefit payable at the age 65 normal retirement age under the new benefit formula is determined by converting the hypothetical account balance at the time to a straight life annuity. The plan provides for the conversion to a straight life annuity to be made using the applicable interest rate and applicable mortality table, defined as the 30-year Treasury rate as published by IRS for the month prior to the beginning of the plan year, and the mortality table published by IRS. For 2002, that applicable interest rate was 5.48 percent and that applicable mortality table was the mortality table set forth in Revenue Ruling 2001-62.

The amendment to Plan A also changed how the accrued benefit of a participant is determined under the plan. For participants who were employed on December 31, 2001, had completed 15 years of service, and had attained age

50 as of that date, Plan A provides that the accrued benefit will be the greater of the accrued benefit provided by the hypothetical account balance at the age 65 normal retirement age (determined as described above) and the accrued benefit determined under the pre-conversion formula as in effect on December 31, 2001, taking into account compensation and years of service after December 31, 2001, but not taking into account compensation and years of service after December 31, 2005. Plan A refers to such participants as grandfathered participants. The accrued benefit provided by the hypothetical account balance at the age 65 normal retirement age is equal to the hypothetical account balance at that age (including projected interest credits under the plan to age 65), converted to a straight life annuity commencing at age 65 using the applicable interest rate and applicable mortality table.

For participants who were employed on December 31, 2001, and who either had not completed 15 years of service or had not attained age 50 as of that date (i.e., participants who are not grandfathered participants), Plan A provides that the accrued benefit at any point in time is determined as the greater of (1) the accrued benefit determined under the terms of the plan under the pre-conversion formula immediately before the amendment, but taking into account only service and compensation through December 31, 2001 and (2) the accrued benefit provided by the hypothetical account balance at the age 65 normal retirement age (determined as described above). Accordingly, compensation increases and years of service after December 31, 2001 are not taken into account in determining the accrued benefit under the pre-conversion formula.

For all new participants (i.e., those employees who commenced participation on or after January 1, 2002), the accrued benefit at any point is the accrued benefit provided by the hypothetical account balance at the age 65 normal retirement age (determined as described above).

ANALYSIS

A plan satisfies the accrual rules if, for all participants, the accrued benefit of each participant satisfies one of the three alternative methods (the 3 percent method, the $133\frac{1}{3}$ percent rule, or the fractional rule). In applying each of the three alternative methods to a participant (including, in the case of the $133\frac{1}{3}$ percent rule, anyone who could be a participant), it is required that the benefits under all formulas applicable to the participant be aggregated. Therefore, even if one formula applicable to a participant by itself would produce a benefit that satisfies the $133\frac{1}{3}$ percent rule, and another formula by itself would produce a benefit that satisfies the fractional rule, the total benefit provided by the interaction of the two formulas must accrue in a manner that satisfies at least one of the three alternative methods.

If the benefits of all participants do not satisfy the same accrual rule, the plan is permitted to satisfy one of the accrual rules for some participants and another accrual rule for other participants, but only if the different classification of participants is not structured so as to evade the accrued benefit requirements. This determination of whether the different classification of participants is not structured so as to evade the accrued benefit requirements is made with consideration of which classification of participants is satisfying which of the three accrual rules. Another consideration in this determination is whether the assignment of a participant to a classification will change merely because of the passage of time.

When determining the accrued benefit for purposes of ascertaining whether a plan satisfies the accrued benefit requirements, the accrued benefit as determined is tested regardless of how the accrued benefit may be defined in the plan. Thus, if the plan does not define the accrued benefit as an annual benefit commencing at normal retirement age, the annual benefit commencing at normal retirement age that is the actuarial equivalent of the accrued benefit under the plan is tested to determine whether the plan satisfies the accrued benefit requirements.

Analysis of 133¹/₃ Percent Rule in General

Because the benefits provided by Plan A, both before and after the conversion, accrued over a period of years in excess of 33¹/₃ years, Plan A fails to satisfy the 3 percent method. Accordingly, the analysis starts with the 133¹/₃ percent rule.

Under the 133¹/₃ percent rule, the annual rate at which the retirement benefits payable at normal retirement age accrue under the plan (the annual rate of accrual) must be determined under the terms of the plan for anyone who is or could be a participant in the plan. The annual rate of accrual with respect to a participant is determined for the current plan year and for all future plan years. Then the annual rate of accrual for any future plan year is compared to the annual rate of accrual for any year beginning on or after the current plan year and, before such future plan year, to see whether the ratio of the later annual rate of accrual to the earlier annual rate of accrual exceeds 133¹/₃ percent.

The annual rate of accrual for a plan year is determined by aggregating all benefit formulas. Furthermore, the value of all relevant factors used to determine benefits for the current plan year is kept constant in determining the annual rates of accrual for future years. Thus, for example, for the plan year under consideration, which is 2002, the 3.87 percent interest crediting rate, the 5.48 percent applicable interest rate, and the applicable mortality table are assumed to remain constant in determining the annual rate of accrual for each plan year after 2002.

If a plan has a single benefit formula, the annual rate of accrual for a plan year is generally determined as the increase in the accrued benefit under that benefit formula for the plan year. If a plan has more than one benefit formula applicable to a participant, the annual rate of accrual for the participant for the plan year must be determined using a single methodology, such as the increase in the dollar amount of the accrued benefit or the increase in the dollar amount of the accrued benefit expressed as a percentage of compensation for the plan year. Thus, the annual rate of accrual may be determined as the difference between (1) the dollar amount of the accrued benefit as a percentage of average compensation at the beginning of the plan year and (2) the dollar amount of the accrued benefit as a percentage of average compensation at the end of the plan year. In applying the 133⅓ percent rule for a plan year, whichever methodology is used to determine the annual rate of accrual must be used consistently for all plan years (i.e., the current plan year and all future plan years).

In applying the 133⅓ percent rule, the analysis considers at least three groups of employees: (1) those who became employed after December 31, 2001 (who will accrue benefits solely under the lump sum-based benefit formula); (2) those who were not grandfathered participants, but who were employed on December 31, 2001 (who will accrue some benefits under the lump sum-based benefit formula, but whose benefits were frozen under the pre-conversion formula); and (3) the grandfathered participants (who will accrue benefits for a time under both the pre-conversion formula and the lump sum-based benefit formula).

Analysis of 133⅓ Percent Rule for New Employees

For the group of new employees, the annual rate of accrual for a plan year is most easily determined as the increase in the dollar amount of the accrued benefit payable at the age 65 normal retirement age for a plan year expressed as a percentage of compensation for the plan year. Thus, for any year, the annual rate of accrual is determined by (1) multiplying the compensation of a participant for the plan year by the percentage from the table of pay credit percentages set forth under the facts above, (2) accumulating such result with hypothetical interest to age 65, (3) converting the accumulation at age 65 to a single life annuity, and (4) dividing the result by compensation for the year. Accordingly, the annual rate of accrual for a year will depend on the pay credit for the year, future interest credits, and the conversion factor. For purposes of applying the 133⅓ percent rule to the plan, the interest crediting rate (the current year's value of the three-year Treasury Constant Maturity rate plus 25 basis points) and the conversion factor for future years (using the applicable interest rate and the applicable mortality table) are assumed to be the same for the current plan year.

For 2002, the three-year Treasury Constant Maturity rate is 3.62 percent (which is the rate for December 2001), and the resulting hypothetical interest crediting rate is 3.87 percent. For 2002, the 30-year Treasury rate is 5.48 percent (the rate for December 2001) and the applicable mortality table is the table set forth in Revenue Ruling 2001-62. The following table shows the annual rates of accrual for each age assuming that these values for 2002 remain the same for future plan years:

Age at Beginning of Plan Year	Annual Rate of Accrual
21	1.41%
22	1.35%
23	1.30%
24	1.26%
25	1.21%

Age at Beginning of Plan Year	Annual Rate of Accrual
26	1.55%
27	1.49%
28	1.44%
29	1.38%
30	1.33%
31	1.28%
32	1.24%
33	1.19%
34	1.15%
35	1.10%
36	1.06%
37	1.02%
38	0.98%
39	0.95%
40	0.91%
41	1.10%
42	1.06%
43	1.02%
44	0.98%
45	0.94%
46	0.91%
47	0.87%
48	0.84%
49	0.81%
50	0.78%
51	0.90%
52	0.87%
53	0.84%
54	0.80%
55	0.77%
56	0.75%
57	0.72%
58	0.69%
59	0.66%
60	0.64%
61	0.72%

Age at Beginning of Plan Year	Annual Rate of Accrual
62	0.69%
63	0.67%
64	0.64%

As may be seen by inspection of the table, the annual rate of accrual for any later year is not more than 133⅓ percent of the annual rate of accrual for any earlier year; and, thus, the lump sum-based benefit formula standing alone satisfies the 133⅓ percent rule. For example, in considering a participant who is age 21 in 2002, the highest ratio of any future annual rate of accrual to any future annual rate of accrual to any earlier rate is 128.1 percent (which is less than 133⅓ percent). This occurs at age 26, where the ratio of 1.55 percent (which also happens to be the highest rate of accrual) to the 1.21 percent rate for age 25 (which is the smallest rate between ages 21 and 26) is 128.1 percent.

Analysis of 133⅓ Percent Rule for Participants Who Are Not Grandfathered Participants

For participants who were employed on December 31, 2001, and who were not grandfathered participants, the accrued benefit under the pre-conversion formula does not increase after 2001, and the participants will only accrue benefits under the lump sum-based benefit formula. However, whether there is any increase in the accrued benefit of a participant will depend on the extent to which the new lump sum-based benefit formula provides a benefit that exceeds the benefit that had been accrued under the pre-conversion formula as of December 31, 2001. If, for a period of years, the lump sum-based benefit formula does not provide a greater benefit than the frozen accrued benefit under the pre-conversion formula as of December 31, 2001, then there is a period where the annual rate of accrual is zero. After that period, there will be a period of positive annual rate of accrual as the lump sum-based benefit formula begins to provide a benefit that exceeds the frozen accrued benefit under the pre-conversion formula.

Ordinarily, a period of a zero annual rate of accrual followed by a period of positive annual rates of accrual would result in a plan failing to satisfy the 133⅓ percent rule. However, because there is no ongoing accrual under the pre-conversion formula for these participants for service after the January 1, 2002 effective date of the conversion amendment, the lump sum-based benefit formula is the only formula under the plan (other than the Section 411(d)(6) protected benefit; see Q 10:45), and, pursuant to a special rule, that formula is treated as if it were in effect for all other plan years. Accordingly, the benefits under the lump sum-based benefit formula are the only benefits that need to be considered for purposes of applying the 133⅓ percent rule (and the Section 411(d)(6) protected benefit under the pre-conversion formula accrued through the date of conversion is disregarded in applying the 133⅓ percent rule). As illustrated above, the lump sum-based benefit formula standing alone satisfies the 133¹/₃ percent rule, and Plan A thus satisfies the rule for participants who are not grandfathered participants.

Analysis of 133¹/₃ Percent Rule for Grandfathered Participants
Age 61 and Above

For participants who are grandfathered participants, the pre-conversion formula continues for a period of four years after the effective date of the amendment and thus is not disregarded pursuant to the special rule. For grandfathered participants who are age 61 or above on January 1, 2002, the pre-conversion formula continues at least through normal retirement age (age 65); and, based upon calculations using the 3.87 percent crediting rate and the applicable interest rate and applicable mortality table, such participants have an annual rate of accrual of 1.1 percent, the rate of accrual under the pre-conversion formula (because the lump sum-based benefit formula never provides a higher benefit). Thus, the annual rate of accrual through normal retirement age will continue to be 1.1 percent of highest average compensation, and the plan satisfies the 133¹/₃ percent rule with respect to those participants.

Analysis of 133¹/₃ Percent Rule for Grandfathered Participants Below Age 61
Who Do Not Accrue Additional Benefits Under the Lump Sum-Based Benefit
Formula Before Normal Retirement Age

For grandfathered participants who are at least age 50 and not yet age 61 on January 1, 2002, the pre-conversion formula provides a greater benefit for the next four years after the amendment (assuming that the relevant factors used to compute benefits as of 2002 are held constant in the future). Thereafter, the accrued benefit under the pre-conversion formula does not increase, and the participants will accrue benefits only under the lump sum-based benefit formula. However, whether there is any increase in the accrued benefit of a participant after 2005 and before normal retirement age will depend on the extent to which the new lump sum-based benefit formula provides a benefit that exceeds the benefit that had been accrued as of December 31, 2005. If there is a period of time after December 31, 2005 when the benefit under the pre-conversion formula (taking into account service at least through December 31, 2005) remains larger than the benefit under the lump sum-based formula, then there will be a period of zero annual rates of accrual. Assuming that the relevant factors in effect for the 2002 plan year remain the same for all future plan years, for grandfathered participants who are at least age 55 and not yet age 61 on January 1, 2002, the period of zero annual rates of accrual extends at least through the age 65 normal retirement age, because the benefit payable at age 65 under the plan will be the accrued benefit under the pre-conversion formula as of December 31, 2005. Because the annual rate of accrual for these participants changes from 1.1 percent to zero and then does not increase prior to normal retirement age, Plan A satisfies the 133¹/₃ percent rule with respect to these participants for 2002.

Analysis of 133¹/₃ Percent Rule for Grandfathered Participants Below Age 61
Who Do Accrue Additional Benefits Under the Lump Sum-Based Benefit
Formula Before Normal Retirement Age (Age 50 to 55)

For grandfathered participants who are at least age 50 and not yet age 55 on January 1, 2002, assuming that the relevant factors used to compute benefits as of 2002 remain constant in the future, the period of zero accruals after 2005 will be followed by a period of annual rates of accrual prior to normal retirement age greater than zero. In such a case, the later annual rate of accrual that is greater than zero will exceed 133¹/₃ percent of the zero annual rate of accrual, and thus Plan A does not satisfy the 133¹/₃ percent rule with respect to these participants for 2002.

The effect on grandfathered participants who are at least age 50 and not yet age 55 on January 1, 2002 may be illustrated by a participant who commenced participation at age 35 with compensation of $40,000. Assume that the participant's compensation increased at the rate of 3 percent per year in the years before 2002. The participant on December 31, 2001 was age 50, had 15 years of service, and had highest average compensation of $58,758. Accordingly, the participant's accrued benefit at that date is $9,695 per year (1.1 percent of $58,758 multiplied by 15 years of service), payable at normal retirement age. At age 54, four years after the conversion, assuming the participant's compensation remains constant at the 2001 level, the participant would have an accrued benefit under the pre-conversion formula of $12,645 per year (1.1 percent of $60,504 multiplied by 19 years of service) payable at normal retirement age. The opening account balance at January 1, 2002 is $49,352. Taking into account expected hypothetical contributions to the account in accordance with the table of pay credit percentages above, and assuming that the hypothetical account is credited with interest at 3.87 percent, the cash balance account would provide a benefit of less than $12,645 for the first nine plan years after conversion. Therefore, there would be a period of approximately five plan years (after the four-year period of continued accruals under the pre-conversion formula) for which the participant has no increase in accrued benefit (i.e., effectively an annual rate of accrual of zero). In approximately the tenth plan year after the conversion, the participant would have a small annual rate of accrual, and the participant would have a relatively larger annual rate of accrual in the remaining five plan years until age 65.

Thus, there are some grandfathered participants who are at least age 50 and not yet age 55 with respect to whom Plan A fails to satisfy the 133¹/₃ percent rule for 2002. Accordingly, Plan A cannot satisfy the accrual rules unless it can satisfy the accrual rules through the use of the fractional rule. While the fractional rule cannot effectively be used on a permanent basis for Plan A (for the reasons discussed below), the post-conversion transitional accruals under the pre-conversion formula result in a pattern of accrued benefits that may satisfy the fractional rule on a temporary basis for the grandfathered participants who are at least age 50 and not yet age 55 on January 1, 2002. Therefore, Plan A may be able to satisfy the accrual rules by using the fractional rule for these participants and the 133¹/₃ percent rule for the other participants.

Analysis of Fractional Rule for Grandfathered Participants Age 50 to 55

In order to apply the fractional rule to the grandfathered participants in Plan A who do not satisfy the 133⅓ percent rule, the fractional rule benefit must be determined for each such participant. This benefit is determined under the terms of the plan by assuming that participation continues to normal retirement age and that all relevant factors used to determine benefits are kept constant as of the current year for all years after the current year. The fractional rule benefit for a participant is also determined by reflecting all of the participant's prior compensation and years of participation and by assuming that the participant continues to earn the same rate of compensation in future years that is taken into account under the plan, but taking into account no more than ten years of compensation. For this purpose, the number of years of compensation that would be taken into account under the plan is determined as if the participant had attained normal retirement age on the date the determination is made.

The fractional rule benefit, as so determined, is multiplied by a fraction, the numerator of which is the number of years of participation at each future point and the denominator of which is the number of years of participation the participant will have if participation continues through normal retirement age. If, for the current plan year and each future plan year, the accrued benefit under the plan equals or exceeds the result obtained by multiplying the fractional rule benefit by the applicable fraction for that year, the plan satisfies the fractional rule with respect to that participant for the current plan year.

For grandfathered participants who are at least age 50 and not yet 55 on January 1, 2002, the fractional rule benefit is the greater of the benefit that is projected to be provided by the pre-conversion benefit formula and the benefit that will be provided by the hypothetical account of each participant, based upon the participation and compensation history of the participant. In determining the benefit that will be provided by the hypothetical account, future pay credits are determined by assuming that compensation for each future year is equal to the average of the compensation taken into account under the plan for the immediately preceding ten years of participation (or for all years of participation for employees with less than ten years of participation).

The fractional rule benefit for a participant may be determined at a date as illustrated by the following steps:

1. Assuming that the participant had no additional service, participation, or compensation after the date of determination, determine which benefit formula would provide the benefit payable at normal retirement age under the plan (based on all other relevant factors on such date).

2. For the formula determined in step 1, determine the number of years of service for which compensation is taken into account under that formula as of the determination date. For this purpose, where the lump sum-based benefit formula is the formula in step 1 and the plan provided for the establishment of an opening account balance equal to the present value of the accrued benefit determined under the pre-conversion formula, the number of years of service is the number of years of service taken into

account in determining that balance, plus one year for each year since the initial account balance is determined.

3. Determine the participant's average compensation as of the determination date for the immediately ten preceding years or, if less, the number of years determined in step 2.

4. Assume that the participant's compensation for each future year of participation until attainment of normal retirement age is the average compensation determined in step 3.

5. Determine the participant's fractional rule benefit as the benefit that would be payable upon attainment of normal retirement age under the plan by applying the plan formulas based on future participation using the compensation determined under step 4 and based on the assumption that all other relevant factors remain constant through normal retirement age at the values for the date on which the determination is being made.

Under these facts, where the pattern of accruals results from a transition from a final average pay formula that satisfies the fractional rule to an accumulation formula that satisfies the 133⅓ percent rule by providing the greater of the benefit under the final average pay formula or the benefit under the lump sum-based benefit formula during the transition period, the classification of participants between at least age 50 and not yet age 55 on January 1, 2002 (including the use of the fractional rule with respect to such participants) is not a classification that is structured to evade the accrued benefit requirements. Accordingly, the grandfathered participants in Plan A whose annual rate of accrual fails the 133⅓ percent rule may pass the accrual rules by using the fractional rule.

To illustrate this, consider the grandfathered participant described above who commenced participation at age 35. For the plan year under consideration, which is 2002, this participant had a projected benefit at the age 65 normal retirement age under the pre-conversion 1.1 percent formula (based on service through the end of the grandfathering period and using the compensation determined under steps 1 through 4 above, which is $58,758) equal to $12,281. The projected benefit from the hypothetical account balance at the age 65 normal retirement age (assuming the pay credit percentage under the table above and future compensation of $58,758, and assuming that the 3.87 percent interest crediting rate, the 5.48 percent applicable rate, and the applicable mortality table remain the same for future years) is $13,999. Therefore, the fractional rule benefit is $13,999. As may be seen from the following table, the accrued benefit under the plan (the greater of the $12,281 benefit under the prior 1.1 percent formula and the benefit provided by the hypothetical account balance) is not less than the pro rata portion of the fractional rule benefit at the end of each future year. Accordingly, the benefit with respect to this participant satisfies the fractional rule for 2002.

Age at End of Plan Year	Fraction	Fraction × $13,999	Accrued Benefit at End of Future Plan Year
51	16/30	$ 7,466	$10,341
52	17/30	$ 7,933	$10,998
53	18/30	$ 8,399	$11,634
54	19/30	$ 8,866	$12,281
55	20/30	$ 9,333	$12,281
56	21/30	$ 9,799	$12,281
57	22/30	$10,266	$12,281
58	23/30	$10,733	$12,281
59	24/30	$11,199	$12,281
60	25/30	$11,666	$12,281
61	26/30	$12,132	$12,461
62	27/30	$12,599	$12,867
63	28/30	$13,066	$13,259
64	29/30	$13,532	$13,636
65	30/30	$13,999	$13,999

Because the accrued benefit of this participant at any future point will not be less than the result obtained by multiplying the fractional rule benefit by the ratio of the number of years of participation to that point to the total number of years of participation the participant will have at normal retirement age, Plan A satisfies the fractional rule for this participant for 2002.

If Plan A can make a similar demonstration for all grandfathered participants who are at least age 50 and not yet age 55 on January 1, 2002, then Plan A can satisfy the fractional rule for these participants and the 133¹/₃ percent rule for all other participants. Under the facts presented, it is expected that such a demonstration will show that, for 2002, the fractional rule is satisfied for all participants whose accrual patterns were unable to satisfy the 133¹/₃ percent rule.

It is similarly likely that a demonstration will show that, for 2002, the fractional rule is satisfied for all grandfathered participants age 55 or above on January 1, 2002. Also, the use of the fractional rule with respect to all such participants is not a classification that is so structured as to evade the accrued benefit requirements.

HOLDING

Plan A satisfies the 133¹/₃ percent rule for 2002 for all participants except the grandfathered participants who are at least age 50, but not yet age 55, on January 1, 2002. Under the above facts, the class of grandfathered participants who are at least age 50, but not yet age 55, on January 1, 2002 is not a classification that is structured to evade the accrued benefit requirements so that the fractional rule may be used for these participants. With respect to the grandfathered participants who are at least age 50, but not yet age 55, on January 1, 2002, if the accrued benefits of these participants satisfy the fractional rule as set forth in the revenue ruling, Plan A satisfies the accrual rules for 2002.

Satisfaction of Accrual Rules in Future Years

The analysis and holding in the revenue ruling address only the 2002 plan year. It is possible for a plan described in the facts of the ruling to fail to satisfy the accrual rules for a subsequent year, either due to changes in relevant factors that are treated as constant for any given year or due to changes in facts relating to plan participants. For example, in the facts addressed in the ruling, whether the pattern of increasing pay credits results in an annual rate of accrual that is more than 133⅓ percent of the annual rate of accrual for any earlier year is affected by the rate of interest that is credited under the plan (which is treated as constant for all future years for purposes of applying the accrual rules to any year). In the year 2002, that interest rate is 3.87 percent. If the rate of interest credited under the plan for a later year were to be less than 1.58 percent, Plan A would not satisfy the 133⅓ percent rule for that later year for participants who are not grandfathered participants and thus would need to be amended in order to satisfy the 133⅓ percent rule.

As another example, if the grandfathered participant described above who did not satisfy the 133⅓ percent rule were to continue to have compensation increases in years after 2002 at an annual 3 percent rate, then, by 2013, the fractional rule benefit would be so large that the aggregate accrued benefit of the participant for that year would be less than the result obtained by multiplying that larger fractional rule benefit by the applicable fraction (the number of years of participation to that time to the total number of years of participation the participant will have at normal retirement age). Accordingly, even compensation increases that are regular and predictable can result in the failure of Plan A to satisfy the fractional rule for the grandfathered participants. Moreover, the possible volatility resulting from unpredictable future compensation increases is a major reason why the fractional rule cannot effectively be used on a permanent basis for plans such as Plan A.

If changes to relevant factors (such as a decrease in the interest crediting rate or an increase in future compensation) were to result in a failure to satisfy the accrual rules, the plan's benefit formula would need to change. Some of the types of changes that may be used are outlined below with respect to Plan A. Any change would need to satisfy applicable qualification requirements, including satisfaction of the anti-cutback rules (see Q 9:25) and the requirement that a plan provide benefits that are definitely determinable (see Q 2:3).

In order to bring the plan into compliance in the event of a decrease in the interest crediting rate, Plan A's benefit formula could be changed to increase the hypothetical pay credits at the earlier ages, reduce the hypothetical pay credits at the higher ages, or a combination of an increase at the lower ages and a reduction at the higher ages. The resulting pattern of credits would have to be less steep than before in order for the 133⅓ percent rule to be satisfied using the lower interest crediting rate. Plan A could also provide an interest crediting rate higher than 1.58 percent for that year and all future years for participants for whom the 133⅓ percent rule is not satisfied, but any such minimum rate could not result in a rate of interest that exceeds a market rate of interest (see Q 2:24).

It may be possible that Plan A could be changed to adjust the hypothetical pay credits to ensure compliance with the accrual rules for future years. Such a provision would need to provide that, if the interest crediting rate at the beginning of any plan year is less than 1.58 percent, the hypothetical pay credits are adjusted so that the resulting pattern of pay credits satisfies the 133⅓ percent rule, using the interest crediting rate for the year. Any such possible provision would need to include specific rules on how the adjustment is made, which would typically be dependent on the extent to which the interest crediting rate is less than 1.58 percent. Furthermore, the provision would need to be clear as to what happens in future years should the interest crediting rate again change. It should be noted that it may be difficult to design such provisions and, furthermore, difficult to put them into effect in actual plan operations on a timely basis.

With respect to the possibility that compensation increases for any future year may result in a plan's failure to satisfy the fractional rule for that year, provisions would be necessary either to ensure that the plan could instead satisfy the 133⅓ percent rule for that year (as described in the preceding two paragraphs) or to provide a combination of increases in the accrued benefit for earlier years or decreases in the accruals for future years (but decreases would not be permitted for service before the applicable amendment date) in order to satisfy the fractional rule for that year. However, unlike the discussion above concerning interest crediting rates, it is not clear how a provision to alter accrual rates or accrued benefits could be implemented annually by a plan provision in the absence of relevant participant information such as the compensation history through the plan year. It may be possible to limit the compensation taken into account for any participant by providing that only compensation increases up to some specified percentage are taken into account. However, any such provision would be difficult to design and extremely difficult to put into effect in actual plan operation on a timely basis.

Section 7805(b) Relief

This paragraph provides relief for plans under which a group of employees specified under the plan receives a benefit equal to the greatest of the benefits provided under two or more formulas (an applicable greater-of benefit), provided that each such formula standing alone would satisfy an accrual rule for the years involved. This relief applies to a plan only if (1) as of February 19, 2008, the plan provisions under which the applicable greater-of benefit is provided have been the subject of a favorable determination letter; (2) as of February 19, 2008, a remedial amendment period (see Q 18:6) for the plan provisions under which the applicable greater-of benefit is provided has not expired; or (3) the plan is otherwise a moratorium plan (see Q 2:23). Under the relief set forth in this paragraph, for plan years beginning before January 1, 2009, IRS will not treat a plan described in the preceding sentence as failing to satisfy the accrual rules solely because the plan provides an applicable greater-of benefit, where the separate formulas, standing alone, would satisfy an accrual rule. For this purpose, a plan described in (2) that provides a group of employees specified under the plan an applicable greater-of benefit can be retroactively amended (but not violate the anti-cutback rule) so that each formula, standing alone, would satisfy an accrual rule for the years involved. For example, a moratorium plan that has a determination letter request pending under which the lump sum-based benefit formula, standing alone, fails to satisfy the accrual rules for a plan year beginning before January 1, 2009 (because the interest credits under the plan are insufficient to compensate for the effect of age-based or service-based pay credits) can be retroactively amended so that the lump sum-based benefit formula satisfies an accrual rule for the years involved.

The relief under the prior paragraph does not extend to other issues relating to accrued benefits or vesting. Accordingly, before a favorable determination letter can be issued, the plan must otherwise satisfy the accrued benefit and vesting requirements. Thus, for example, in order to avoid a forfeiture of the accrued benefit under the plan, or to ensure compliance with the accrual rules, the annual benefit payable at normal retirement age attributable to the lump sum-based benefit formula at the end of the current year must not change thereafter, assuming that no change were to occur in any relevant factor used to determine benefits and disregarding any future pay credits (e.g., under the plan, the annual benefit payable at normal retirement age attributable to the lump sum-based benefit formula as of the end of a year cannot increase or decrease after that year due merely to operation of the plan and the passage of time, as opposed to additional pay credits or changes in a relevant factor used to determine benefits).

[Rev. Rul. 2008-7, 2008-1 C.B. 419; Rev. Rul. 2001-62, 2001-2 C.B. 632; I.R.C. §§ 401(a)(7), 401(b), 411(a)(7)(A)(i), 411(b)(1)(A), 411(b)(1)(B), 411(b)(1)(C), 411(d)(6), 7805(b); Treas. Reg. §§ 1.411(a)-7(a)(1), 1.411(b)-1(a)(1), 1.411(b)-1(b)(1)(i), 1.411(b)-1(b)(2), 1.411(b)-1(b)(3); Treas. Dept. News Rel. HP-796 (Feb. 1, 2008)]

A court ruled that a plan's use of a grandfather provision did not violate the anti-backloading provisions and refused to follow Revenue Ruling 2008-7. [Hurlic v. Southern California Gas Co., 2008 WL 3852685 (9th Cir. 2008)]

Subsequent to the publication of Revenue Ruling 2008-7, IRS issued proposed regulations to provide relief from the aggregation rules applying to benefit accruals by defined benefit plans with two or more benefit formulas. The proposed regulations would extend the relief provided in Revenue Ruling 2008-7 to plan years beginning on or after January 1, 2009, and to plans that convert their benefit formula for plan years beginning on or after January 1, 2009. The proposed regulations provide a limited exception under which plans that determine a participant's benefits as the greatest of benefits determined under two or more separate formulas can satisfy the $133\frac{1}{3}$ percent rule by demonstrating that each separate formula satisfies this rule. A plan would be entitled to use this exception only if each formula used a different basis for determining benefits. [Prop. Treas. Reg. § 1.411(b)-1(b)(2)(ii)(G); *see also* Lonecke v. Citigroup Pension Plan, 2009 WL 3335910 (2d Cir. 2009)]

Q 9:4   Are minimum vesting standards set by law?

Yes. Two minimum vesting schedules apply to a participant's accrued benefit (see Q 9:2) derived from employer contributions. [I.R.C. § 411(a)(2); Temp. Treas. Reg. §§ 1.411(a)-3T(b), 1.411(a)-3T(c), 1.411(a)-3T(e)] These schedules, either one of which may be used, are as follows:

Five-Year Vesting

Years of Service	Nonforfeitable Percentage
Less than 5	0%
5 or more	100

Seven-Year Graded Vesting

Years of Service	Nonforfeitable Percentage
Less than 3	0%
3	20
4	40
5	60
6	80
7 or more	100

Example 1. Stanley Corporation's retirement plan provides for plan participation after the completion of one year of service and provides for 100 percent vesting after five years of plan participation rather than service. The plan does not satisfy the minimum vesting standards because, under the plan, an employee becomes 100 percent vested only after completion of more than five years of service. Vesting based upon years of participation is permitted as long as the minimum vesting standards are satisfied. [Ferrara v. Allentown Physician Anesthesia Assocs., Inc., 711 F. Supp. 206 (E.D. Pa. 1989)]

Example 2. Marjorie Corporation's retirement plan contains the following vesting schedule:

Years of Service	Nonforfeitable Percentage
1 or less	0%
2	10

Years of Service	Nonforfeitable Percentage
3	25
4	45
5	65
6	75
7 or more	100

The plan does not satisfy the minimum vesting standards because the nonforfeitable percentage after six years of service (75 percent) is less than the percentage required at that time (80 percent). The fact that the nonforfeitable percentage for years prior to the sixth year of service is greater than the percentage required is immaterial.

Qualified retirement plans that require more than one year of service (see Q 5:8) to be eligible to participate must provide for immediate 100 percent vesting (see Qs 5:2, 5:4, 9:13).

One court concluded that the reduction of defined benefit plan (see Q 2:3) benefits by renewal commissions earned by retired participants is a form of pension integration and does not violate the minimum vesting requirement. [ERISA §§ 203(a), 204(b)(1); Bonovich v. Knights of Columbus, 1998 U.S. App. LEXIS 10230 (2d Cir. 1998); see also Alessi v. Raybestos-Manhattan, Inc., 451 U.S. 504 (1981)]

Faster vesting schedules apply to employer matching contributions (see Q 27:75). Employer matching contributions are required to vest at least as rapidly as under one of the following two alternative minimum vesting schedules. A plan satisfies the first schedule if a participant acquires a nonforfeitable right to 100 percent of employer matching contributions upon the completion of three years of service. A plan satisfies the second schedule if a participant has a nonforfeitable right to 20 percent of employer matching contributions for each year of service beginning with the participant's second year of service and ending with 100 percent after six years of service. The faster vesting schedules are effective for *contributions* for plan years beginning after 2001 but does not apply to any employee until the employee has an hour of service after the effective date. In applying the new vesting schedules, service before the effective date is taken into account. [I.R.C. § 411(a)(12) (repealed by PPA § 904(a)(2), effective for contributions for plan years beginning after December 31, 2006); PPA § 904(c)]

PPA (see Q 1:33) makes a number of changes regarding vesting as discussed below.

The present-law vesting schedule for matching contributions will be applicable to *all* employer contributions to defined contribution plans (see Q 2:2). This accelerated vesting provision does not apply to any employee until the employee has an hour of service after the effective date. In applying the new vesting schedule, service before the effective date is taken into account. The accelerated vesting provision is generally effective for contributions for plan years beginning after December 31, 2006. However, in the case of a plan maintained pursuant to one or more collective bargaining agreements (see Q 29:6), the provision is not effective for contributions (including allocations of forfeitures) for plan years beginning before the earlier of (1) the later of the date on which the last of such collective bargaining agreements terminates (determined without regard to any extension thereof on or after August 17, 2006) or January 1, 2007, or (2) January 1, 2009. Furthermore, in the case of an employeestock ownership plan (ESOP; see Q 28:1) that on September 26, 2005, had outstanding a loan incurred for the purpose of acquiring qualifying employer securities, the provision does not apply to any plan year beginning before the earlier of (1) the date on which the loan is fully repaid or (2) the date on which the loan was, as of September 26, 2005, scheduled to be fully repaid. [I.R.C. §§ 411(a)(2), 411(a)(12) (repealed by PPA § 904(a)(2)); PPA § 904(c); Priv. Ltr. Rul. 200929023]

IRS issued guidance concerning the new vesting requirements for employer contributions to defined contribution plans. [IRS Notice 2007-7, § VII, 2007-1 C.B. 395]

A plan amendment that changes the vesting schedule must satisfy the requirement that certain participants may elect to stay under the old vesting schedule (see Qs 9:7, 9:8). Although this provision would require a participant with at least three years of service to elect to have the nonforfeitable percentage of the accrued benefit determined without regard to the amendment, the plan must ensure that any such election satisfies the new vesting requirements. Thus, such a participant must be provided, at all times, a vesting percentage that is no less than the minimum under a vesting schedule that satisfies the new requirements and the vesting percentage determined under the plan without regard to the amendment. No election need be provided for any participant whose nonforfeitable percentage under the plan, as amended, at any time cannot be less than such percentage determined without regard to such amendment. [IRS Notice 2007-7, § VII, Q&A-28, 2007-1 C.B. 395; Temp. Treas. Reg. § 1.411(a)-8T]

A plan can have a vesting schedule for employer nonelective contributions for plan years beginning after December 31, 2006 and another vesting schedule for other employer nonelective contributions under the plan, provided that the plan separately accounts for the contributions made under the vesting schedule in effect prior to the first day of the first plan year beginning after December 31, 2006 and the vesting schedule for employer nonelective contributions for plan years beginning after December 31, 2006 satisfies the new vesting requirements. [IRS Notice 2007-7, § VII, Q&A-29, 2007-7 C.B. 395] A contribution is for a plan year that begins before January 1, 2007 if it is allocated under the terms of the plan as of a date in that plan year and is not subject to any conditions that have not been satisfied by the end of that plan year. This applies even if the contribution is not made until the next plan year. Thus, for example, if a plan with a calendar-year plan year makes a contribution as of December 31, 2006, based on compensation and service in 2006, and the contribution is not contingent on the occurrence of an event after 2006, then the contribution is treated as made for the 2006 plan year and is not subject to the new vesting requirements, even if it is not contributed until 2007. Forfeitures (see Qs 9:18, 9:19) and ESOP (see Q 28:1) allocations from a suspense account are treated in the same manner for this purpose. [IRS Notice 2007-7, § VII, Q&A-30, 2007-1 C.B. 395]

An applicable defined benefit plan (see Q 2:23) must provide that each employee who has completed at least three years of service has a nonforfeitable right to 100 percent of the employee's accrued benefit derived from employercontributions. In the case of a plan in existence on June 29, 2005, the vesting requirements for an applicable defined benefit plan generally apply to years beginning after December 31, 2007, except that the plan sponsor may elect to have such requirements apply for any period after June 29, 2005, and before the first plan year beginning after December 31, 2007. In the case of a plan maintained pursuant to one or more collective bargaining agreements, a delayed effective date applies with respect to the vesting requirements for an applicable defined benefit plan. [I.R.C. § 411(a)(13)(B)]

With regard to 401(k) plans (see Q 27:1), effective for plan years beginning after December 31, 2007, any matching or other employer contributions taken into account in determining whether the requirements for a qualified automatic enrollment feature (see Q 27:5) are satisfied must vest at least as rapidly as under two-year cliff vesting. That is, employees with at least two years of service must be 100 percent vested with respect to such contributions. [I.R.C. § 401(k)(13)(D)(iii)(I)]

Q 9:5   Do the minimum vesting standards apply to multiemployer plans?

A multiemployer plan (see chapter 29) had been permitted to use a ten-year cliff vesting schedule (that is, an employee with at least ten years of service is 100 percent vested) for participants covered under the plan pursuant to a collective bargaining agreement. [I.R.C. §§ 411(a)(2)(C) (prior to repeal by SBA '96 § 1442(a)), 414(f)(1)(B); Temp. Treas. Reg. §§ 1.411(a)-3T(d), 1.411(a)-3T(e); Smith v. Contini, 205 F.3d 597 (3d Cir. 2000)]

The special vesting rule for multiemployer plans no longer applies, and multiemployer plan participants must have a nonforfeitable right to accrued benefits derived from employer contributions under either the five-year cliff or the seven-year graded vesting schedule (see Q 9:4).

Where the benefit of a participant in a multiemployer defined benefit plan was offset by his benefit in a multiemployer defined contribution plan, his claim that the offset constituted an impermissible forfeiture was disallowed. [Brengettsy v. LTV Steel (Republic) Hourly Pension Plan, No. 98 C 5742 (N.D. Ill. 2000)]

The faster vesting schedules applicable to employer matching contributions (see Q 9:4) also apply to multiemployer plans. However, the effective date was delayed until the plan year that began on the earlier of (1) the later of (a) the date on which the last collective bargaining agreement terminated (determined without regard to extensions) or (b) January 1, 2002; or (2) January 1, 2006. [EGTRRA 2001 § 633(c)] See Q 9:4 for a discussion of the accelerated vesting provisions of PPA.

Q 9:6   Does the adoption of one of the minimum vesting schedules guarantee the retirement plan's qualification?

Unless there has been a pattern of abuse or actual misuse in the operation of a retirement plan, the use of one of the two minimum vesting schedules (see Q 9:4) will satisfy the plan's qualification requirements with regard to vesting. The intentional dismissal of employees to prevent vesting may indicate a pattern of abuse. See chapter 26 for details relating to vesting under a top-heavy plan. [I.R.C. § 411(d)(1); ERISA § 510; Prop. Treas. Reg. § 1.411(d)-1(b); Rev. Proc. 89-29, 1989-1 C.B. 893]

When an employee was discharged by the employer shortly before his qualified retirement plan benefits would have become vested, courts have found that the proximity of the termination date and the vesting date was sufficient to infer that the employer's purpose in discharging the employee was to deprive him of his retirement benefits. [Hazen Paper Co. v. Biggins, 507 U.S. 604 (1993); Olitsky v. Spencer Gifts, Inc., No. 91-1010 (5th Cir. 1992); see also Chailland v. Brown & Root, Inc., No. 93-3543 (5th Cir. 1995)] Another court ruled that, because an employer is prohibited from discharging an employee for the purpose of interfering with the attainment of any right that the employee may become entitled to receive under a plan, this prohibition applied to an employee who was discharged shortly before he became qualified for early retirement, even though he was fully vested in his accrued benefit (see Q 9:2). [Heath v. Varity Corp., 71 F.3d 256 (7th Cir. 1995)] Because employees could show an intent to interfere with their rights to plan benefits and could show a causal connection between the decision to terminate them and their plan benefits, one court ruled in favor of the employees. The employees had been terminated five and six years before the age 65 normal retirement date and, as a result of the termination, lost about half of the benefits they would have received had they worked until age 65. [Pennington v. Western Atlas, Inc., 2000 WL 132673 (6th Cir. 2000)] Employees who were subject to an eight-month no-hire agreement between their parent company and a purchasing company that had the practical effect of cancelling the employees' accrued benefits under their former parent company's defined benefit plans (see Q 2:3) presented sufficient prima facie evidence to support a claim for interference with protected rights, ruled one court. [Eichorn v. AT&T Corp., 248 F.3d 131 (3d Cir. 2001); see also Eichorn v. AT&T Corp., 484 F.3d 644 (3d Cir. 2007)] In another case, the court concluded that an employer did not abuse its discretion or violate former employees' rights when it set their termination date and paid the former employees for their unused vacation time rather than allowing them to continue to work, even though the earlier termination later excluded the former employees from a plan benefit increase. The employer had legitimate and nondiscriminatory reasons for its decisions, and such decisions were permitted under the plain language of the plan. [Shores v. Lucent Techs., Inc., 2000 U.S. App. LEXIS 455 (4th Cir. 2000)] An employer's amendment of a plan to benefit one individual and its refusal to amend the plan to benefit other individuals is not the type of discrimination prohibited by the interference provisions of ERISA. [Coomer v. Bethesda Hosp., Inc., No. 02-3700 (6th Cir. 2004)] In another case, the court ruled that discrimination did not occur where a union laid off an employee to reduce expenses, because there was insufficient evidence to show that the union's decision was centered on its desire to interfere with the employee's right to benefits. [Schweitzer v. Teamsters Local 100, 413 F.3d 533 (6th Cir. 2005)] A company did not interfere with its employees' ability to collect retirement benefits when it terminated their employment and outsourced them to another company where they were not eligible to receive such benefits. [Jakimas v. Hoffman-La Roche, Inc., 485 F.3d 770 (3d Cir. 2007)]

Other courts have ruled that the prevention of further benefit accruals or additional vesting must be a motivating factor in the employer's decision to discharge an employee. [Crawford v. TRW Automotive U.S. LLC, 560 F.3d 607 (6th Cir. 2009); Fischer v. Andersen Corp., No. 06-2273 (8th Cir. 2007); Fletcher v. Lucent Technologies, Inc., No. 05-3604 (3d Cir. 2006); Makenta v. University of Pa., 2004 WL 188332 (3d Cir. 2004); Wright v. Sears, Roebuck & Co., 2003 WL 22701327 (6th Cir. 2003); Szczesny v. General Elec. Co., 2003 WL 21152956 (3d Cir. 2003); Majewski v. Automatic Data Processing, Inc., 2001 WL 1635906 (6th Cir. 2001); Potelicki v. Textron, Inc., 2000 U.S. App. LEXIS 2428 (6th Cir. 2000); Lightfoot v. Union Carbide Corp., 1997 U.S. App. LEXIS 5785 (2d Cir. 1997); Jefferson v. Vickers, No. 95-4205 (8th Cir. 1996); Daughtrey v. Honeywell Inc., No. 92-8221 (11th Cir. 1993); Clark v. Coats & Clark Inc., No. 92-8024 (11th Cir. 1993); Lanahan v. Mutual Life Ins. Co. of N.Y., No. 96 Civ. 5301 (S.D.N.Y. 1998); Cleland v. Arvida Realty Sales, Inc., No. 93-644-CIV-T-17A (M.D. Fla. 1996); see also Almond v. ABB Indus. Sys., Inc., 2003 WL 173640 (6th Cir. 2003); Vasquez v. Zenith Travel, Inc., No. 00-9459 (2d Cir. 2001); Singley v. Illinois & Midland R.R. Inc. (C.D. Ill. 2001); Sager v. Trustmark Ins. Co., No. 98 C 50129 (N.D. Ill. 2000)] Another court concluded that an employee who claimed he was transferred from one plant to another by the employer to avoid paying early retirement benefits could maintain an action against the employer even though the employee had not been discharged or constructively discharged. [Eret v. Continental Holding Inc., 1993 U.S. Dist. LEXIS 10537 (N.D. Ill. 1993)] In a novel case, an employee argued that the employer interfered with her pension rights by giving her a promotion. The court concluded that the employer did not violate ERISA by promoting the employee who was two years from being fully vested in a pension plan to a division that was about to be sold because the employee did not prove that her pension benefits were a motivating factor in the employer's decision. [Petrus v. Lucent Techs., Inc., 2004 U.S. App. LEXIS 13853 (6th Cir. 2004)]

It has also been held that a cause of action by an employee may exist for an employer's retaliation against the employee's collection of plan benefits even where the employee applied for and received all benefits due under the plan

[Kowalski v. L & F Prods, 1996 U.S. App. LEXIS 10090 (3d Cir. 1996); Kimbro v. Atlantic Richfield Co., 889 F.2d 869 (9th Cir. 1989)]; but another court held that an employer's discharge of an employee shortly after he complained about failing to receive matching contributions was not an attempt by the employer to retaliate against the employee where there was sufficient evidence to show that the actual reason for the employee's dismissal was his misconduct. [Grottkau v. Sky Climber, Inc., No. 95-2132 (7th Cir. 1996); *see also* Edwards v. A.H. Cornell and Son, Inc., 2009 WL 2215074 (E.D. Pa. 2009) and Nicolaou v. Horizon Media, 402 F.3d 325 (2d Cir. 2005)] Also, an employer was held not to have interfered with an employee's retirement benefits by terminating the employee one year after he refused to accept early retirement because the employee failed to establish a causal connection between his termination and his refusal to retire. [Montgomery v. John Deere & Co., No. 98-1628 (8th Cir. 1999)] Another court concluded that an employee could not sustain a retaliatory discharge claim against his employer because he had already been discharged when the alleged retaliatory conduct occurred. [Helfrich v. Metal Container Corp, No. 02-0311 (6th Cir. 2002)]

In other cases, one court upheld the plan's vesting schedule even though a significant number of participants never became vested because of the transient nature of their employment [Phillips v. Alaska Hotel & Rest. Employees Pension Fund, Nos. 89-35735, 90-35144 (9th Cir. 1991)], and another court ruled that an employer that terminated an employee as a part of a reduction in its workforce did not unlawfully interfere with the employee's pension rights. [Card v. Hercules Inc., No. 92-4169 (10th Cir. 1993)] A company's outsourcing of some of its functions to subcontractors in order to win a bid on a government contract was not intended to interfere with the pension rights of outsourced employees, concluded another court. [Register v. Honeywell Federal Manufacturing & Technologies, LLC, 397 F.3d 1130 (8th Cir. 2005)]

One court ruled that, where an employer reclassified certain employees as independent contractors without being able to articulate a legitimate nondiscriminatory business reason for doing so, it could possibly be determined that the employer had the specific intent to deprive those employees of the right to accrue future benefits (see Q 5:1). [Gitlitz v. Compagnie Nationale Air France, No. 96-5131 (11th Cir. 1997)] Where a plan participant consented to being reclassified as an independent contractor, the court concluded that she could not claim interference with the attainment of a benefit because her consent negated the required specific intent to deny employee benefits on the employer's part. [Benders v. Bellows and Bellows, Nos. 06-1487, 06-2715 (7th Cir. 2008)] Another court determined that the prohibition against interfering with the rights of plan participants and beneficiaries was not limited to situations involving either an employer or a labor union, but could be applied against an estate where the estate reduced required payments under a prenuptial agreement to the surviving spouse after she received death benefits from a qualified retirement plan in which the deceased spouse participated. [Mattei v. Mattei, 126 F.3d 794 (6th Cir. 1997)] It has also been ruled that a sole proprietor may have discriminated against his former employee in violation of ERISA by requiring that the employee choose between her existing salary with no pension and a lower salary with a contribution to a pension plan. [Garratt v. Walker, 164 F.3d 1249 (10th Cir. 1998)] The United States Supreme Court concluded that the prohibition against interference was not limited to vested rights but also applied to nonvested welfare plan benefits. [Inter-Modal Rail Employees Ass'n v. Atchison, Topeka & Santa Fe Ry., 52 U.S. 510 (1997)]

Where a former employee commenced an action under ERISA alleging that his employment was terminated because he wished to enroll in the employer's 401(k) plan (see Q 27:1), the court ruled that he could not bring an ERISA action because he was not a plan participant. However, since the employee's claim was not preempted by ERISA, the employee could maintain an action based upon state law principles. [Clancy v. Bay Area Bank, 1998 U.S. App. LEXIS 6636 (9th Cir. 1998); Freedman v. Jacques Orthopaedic & Joint Implant Surgery Med. Group, 721 F.2d 654 (9th Cir. 1983); see also Gurecki v. Northeast Med. Assocs., P.C., No. 98-7289 (3d Cir. 1999); but see Shahid v. Ford Motor Co., 76 F.3d 1404 (6th Cir. 1996)] One court ruled that a former participant who claimed that he was discharged in retaliation for his opposition to the employer's termination of the plan had standing to sue even though he had received a distribution of his benefits. [McBride v. PLM Int'l, Inc., 1999 WL 355936 (9th Cir. 1999); see also McGrath v. Lockheed Martin Corp., 2002 WL 31269646 (6th Cir. 2002)] An employer that refused to rehire former employees in order to avoid higher pension costs did not violate ERISA, ruled one court, because ERISA does not cover discrimination in hiring decisions. [Becker v. Mack Trucks, Inc., 281 F.3d 372 (3d Cir. 2002)] An employer spun off a company and later reacquired the spun-off company. The employer then classified the employees of the spun-off company as rehired, which meant that the employees' retirement benefits would be calculated without taking into account service for years when the spun-off company was not part of the employer. The court concluded that the employer did not wrongfully interfere with the employees' retirement benefits. [Ensley v. Ford Motor Co., 2010 WL 816731 (6th Cir. 2010)]

ERISA does not specify a statute of limitations for actions relating to the prevention of vesting. One court concluded that it must apply the limitations period of the state law cause of action most analogous to the federal claim and ruled that a two-year statute of limitations was applicable. [Sandberg v. KPMG Peat Marwick, L.L.P., 1997 U.S. App. LEXIS 7296 (2d Cir. 1997)] Another court concurred and concluded that the statute of limitations began to run when the employer refused to let a temporary employee into its benefit plans and that there was no ongoing violation that would extend the statute of limitations. [Berry v. Allstate Ins. Co., 2004 WL 34807 (5th Cir. 2004)] A six-month limitation in an employment contract for bringing an employment-related action against the employer prevented as untimely an employee's cause of action, ruled another court. [Caimi v. DaimlerChrysler Corp., 2008 WL 619220 (E.D. Mo. 2008)]

Q 9:7   May a qualified retirement plan's vesting schedule be changed?

Yes. Like other provisions in a qualified retirement plan, the vesting schedule may be amended by the employer, even after IRS has approved the plan as initially adopted.

If the vesting schedule is amended, however, each participant in the qualified retirement plan on the date the amendment is adopted or becomes effective (whichever is later) who has completed at least three years of service may elect, during the election period (see Q 9:8), to stay under the old vesting schedule. A participant's failure to make that election means that the participant is subject to the new schedule—provided that the participant was notified of the right to elect. An amendment of the vesting schedule may not cause any participant to forfeit (directly or indirectly) vested benefits regardless of length of service. [I.R.C. § 411(a)(10); Temp. Treas. Reg. § 1.411(a)-8T(b)(1)] The increase in a collectively bargained defined benefit plan's (see Q 2:3) normal retirement date (see Q 10:55), resulting solely from an increase in the federally mandated retirement age due to the enactment of legislation, was not a change by plan amendment in the plan's vesting schedule that would be prohibited with respect to any affected participant. [Priv. Ltr. Rul. 200936045]

A qualified retirement plan may require more than one year of service to be eligible to participate (see Q 9:4).

Example. BML Corporation maintains a calendar-year qualified retirement plan with a two-years-of-service eligibility requirement and semiannual entry dates of January 1 and July 1 (see Q 5:7). Because Ben was hired on August 1, 2009 and will complete two years of service on August 1, 2011, Ben will commence participation in the plan on January 1, 2012, and will be 100 percent vested. On October 1, 2011, the plan is amended, retroactive to January 1, 2011, to reduce the service eligibility requirement to one year and add a seven-year graded vesting schedule (see Q 9:4). With the amendment, Ben commences participation on January 1, 2011.

According to IRS representatives, Ben will be subject to the graded vesting schedule even though he had completed more than one and one-half years of service at the time of the amendment. Since Ben obviously did not have three years of service, the vesting schedule election is not available to him.

A new determination letter should be obtained, particularly if the plan's vesting schedule has been made less liberal (see Q 25:5). See chapter 18 for details.

Q 9:8   What is the period within which a participant may elect to stay under the old vesting schedule?

A participant must have at least 60 days to elect the old vesting schedule. In addition, the election period must begin no later than the date on which the amendment is adopted and end no earlier than 60 days after the latest of the following dates:

1. The date the amendment is adopted;

2. The date the amendment becomes effective; or

3. The date the participant "is issued written notice of the plan amendment by the employer or plan administrator."

[I.R.C. § 411(a)(10)(B); Temp. Treas. Reg. § 1.411(a)-8T(b)(2)]

Q 9:9 What vesting standards apply to an employee's own contributions?

Whether contributions are mandatory or voluntary (see Qs 6:37, 6:38), the employee at all times must have a nonforfeitable right to 100 percent of the benefits derived from the employee's own contributions. [I.R.C. § 411(a)(1); Treas. Reg. §§ 1.411(a)-1(a)(2), 1.411(c)-1] One court held that a qualified retirement plan's noncompetition clause (see Q 9:20) that was used to deny the early distribution of an employee's benefits was not enforceable against vested benefits consisting entirely of *employee* contributions. [Brower v. Comark Merch., Inc., Civ. No. 95-6131 (D.N.J. 1996)]

Since mandatory or voluntary employee contributions under a defined contribution plan (see Q 2:2) and voluntary employee contributions under a defined benefit plan (see Q 2:3) are separately accounted for, determining the accrued benefit (see Q 9:2) derived from the employee's own contributions is not difficult. However, since a defined benefit plan does not separately account for mandatory employee contributions, the determination requires a number of calculations. To determine the employee-derived accrued benefit, IRS has issued proposed regulations. [Prop. Treas. Reg. §§ 1.411(c)-1(c)(1), 1.411(c)-1(c)(2), 1.411(c)-1(c)(3), 1.411(c)-1(c)(5), 1.411(c)-1(c)(6), 1.411(c)-1(d), 1.411(c)-1(g)]

Example 1. Stephanie, an unmarried participant, terminated employment with William Corporation on January 1, 1997, at age 56 with 15 years of service. As of December 31, 1987, Stephanie's total accumulated mandatory employee contributions to the plan, including interest compounded annually at 5 percent for plan years beginning after 1975 and before 1988, equaled $3,021. Stephanie will receive her accrued benefit in the form of a single life annuity commencing at normal retirement age. Stephanie's annuity starting date is January 1, 2006 (the determination date). For purposes of this example, it is assumed that Stephanie's total accrued benefit under the plan in the normal form of benefit commencing at normal retirement age is $2,949 per year. Stephanie's benefit, as of January 1, 2006, would be determined as follows:

1. Determine Stephanie's total accrued benefit in the form of a single life annuity commencing at normal retirement age under the plan's formula ($2,949 per year payable at age 65).

2. Determine Stephanie's accumulated contributions with interest to January 1, 1997. As of December 31, 1987, Stephanie's accumulated contributions with interest under the plan provisions were $3,021. Stephanie's employee contributions are accumulated from December 31,

1987, to January 1, 1997, using 120 percent of the federal midterm rate. One hundred twenty percent of the actual federal midterm rate is used for 1988 through 1995, and it is assumed for purposes of this example that 120 percent of the federal midterm rate is 7 percent for each year between 1996 and 2006 and that the 30-year Treasury rate for December 2005 is 8 percent. Thus, Stephanie's contributions accumulated to January 1, 1997, equal $6,480.

3. Determine Stephanie's accumulated contributions with interest to normal retirement age (January 1, 2006) using, for the 1996 plan year and for years until normal retirement age, 120 percent of the federal midterm rate ($11,913).

4. Determine the accrued annual annuity benefit derived from Stephanie's contributions by dividing Stephanie's accumulated contributions determined in paragraph 3 by the plan's appropriate conversion factor. The plan's appropriate conversion factor at age 65 is 9.196, and the accrued benefit derived from Stephanie's contributions would be $1,295 ($11,913 ÷ 9.196).

5. Determine the accrued benefit derived from employer contributions as the excess, if any, of the employee's accrued benefit under the plan over the accrued benefit derived from employee contributions. Thus, Stephanie's accrued benefit derived from employer contributions is $1,654 ($2,949 − $1,295).

6. Determine the vested percentage of the accrued benefit derived from employer contributions under the plan's vesting schedule (100 percent).

7. Determine the vested accrued benefit derived from employer contributions by multiplying the accrued benefit derived from employer contributions by the vested percentage, $1,654 ($1,654 × 100%).

8. Determine Stephanie's vested accrued benefit in the form of a single life annuity commencing at normal retirement age by adding the accrued benefit derived from employee contributions and the vested accrued benefit derived from employer contributions, the sum of paragraphs 4 and 7, $2,949 ($1,295 + $1,654).

Example 2. Assume the same facts as Example 1, except that Stephanie's total accrued benefit under the plan in the normal form of benefit commencing at normal retirement age is $1,000 per year. Stephanie's benefit, as of January 1, 2006, would be determined as follows:

1. Determine Stephanie's total accrued benefit in the form of a single life annuity commencing at normal retirement age under the plan's formula ($1,000 per year payable at age 65).

2. Determine Stephanie's accumulated contributions with interest to January 1, 1997 ($6,480 from paragraph 2 of Example 1).

3. Determine Stephanie's accumulated contributions with interest to normal retirement age (January 1, 2006) ($11,913 from paragraph 3 of Example 1).

4. Determine the accrued annual annuity benefit derived from Stephanie's contributions by dividing Stephanie's accumulated contributions determined in paragraph 3 of this Example 2 by the plan's appropriate conversion factor ($1,295 from paragraph 4 of Example 1).

5. Determine the accrued benefit derived from employer contributions as the excess, if any, of the employee's accrued benefit under the plan over the accrued benefit derived from employee contributions. Because the accrued benefit derived from employee contributions ($1,295) is greater than the employee's accrued benefit under the plan ($1,000), the accrued benefit derived from employer contributions is zero, and Stephanie's vested accrued benefit in the form of a single life annuity commencing at normal retirement age is $1,295 per year.

Q 9:10   What is a year of service for vesting purposes?

For purposes of determining a participant's vested benefits, a year of service means a 12-consecutive-month period specified in the qualified retirement plan during which the participant completes at least 1,000 hours of service (see Q 5:9). [I.R.C. § 411(a)(5)]

The elapsed time method for counting hours of service may also be utilized for this purpose. One court ruled that an employee did not receive credit for a year of service for vesting purposes because she was not credited with 1,000 hours of service under the elapsed time method adopted by the plan even though she had completed 1,000 actual hours of service during the year her employment was terminated. [Johnson v. Buckley, 2004 U.S. App. LEXIS 1252 (9th Cir. 2004)] However, another court ruled that an employee did not receive credit for a year of service for vesting purposes even though he was credited with 1,000 hours of service for the 12-month period under the elapsed time method adopted by the plan because the employee terminated employment before the end of the 12-month period. [Coleman v. Interco Inc. Divs.' Plans, No. 90-2700 (7th Cir. 1991)]

Q 9:11   What years of service must be taken into account for vesting purposes?

In general, all years of service with the employer must be counted. For the exceptions, see Q 9:12. [I.R.C. § 411(a)(4)]

IRS has ruled that the freezing of accruals under a defined benefit plan (see Qs 2:3, 26:14), so that a partial termination (see Q 25:5) of the plan occurs, does not constitute a plan termination (see Q 25:1) for purposes of determining whether service with the employer after the plan was established may be disregarded toward vesting if accruals resume under the plan. Therefore, all years of service with the employer following the establishment of the previously frozen plan must be taken into account for purposes of vesting. If, instead, the accruals are earned under a new plan maintained by the same employer and the new plan is merged with the frozen plan, then the same conclusion results, so that, after the merger, service after the frozen plan was established must be taken into account for purposes of vesting in any benefit accruals under the new plan. [Rev. Rul. 2003-65, 2003-1 C.B. 1035; Treas. Reg. § 1.411(a)-5(b)(3)(iii)]

> **Example.** Casey Corporation maintains a defined benefit plan under which benefit accruals were frozen as of December 31, 2004. Under the plan's benefit formula prior to January 1, 2005, a participant received a specified percentage of highest average pay multiplied by total years of service. The plan provides that each participant becomes fully vested in the accrued benefit after five years of service. The freezing of accruals under the plan caused a partial termination in 2005, so that all participants in the plan became fully vested in their accrued benefits following the freeze. Casey Corporation subsequently amends the plan to provide that, as of January 1, 2011, participants will begin accruing benefits under a different formula. A participant's accrued benefit under the plan, as amended, will be the sum of the accrued benefit under the old formula and the accrued benefit under the new formula. All of the participant's years of service with Casey Corporation must be considered for vesting purposes.

Service with a predecessor of the employer must be counted if the successor-employer maintains the predecessor's qualified retirement plan. [I.R.C. § 414(a)] A company merged its Plan A and Plan B (the plan created by the merger is referred to as the Merged Plan). Plan A was established after Plan B; and, under Plan A, the accrued benefit (see Q 9:2), as of any given date, is the monthly amount of retirement income that would be payable in the form of a single life annuity that is the actuarial equivalent of the participant's cash balance account (see Q 2:23). Plan A generally provides for five-year vesting (see Q 9:4), and vesting service is generally defined as years, months, and days of active employment with the company after the date Plan A became effective. However, Plan A also provides that vesting service includes, for participants who were covered under Plan B, employment with the company during which such participants were covered under Plan B. Plan B was established through the merger of two frozen defined benefit plans. Subsequently, four additional frozen plans were merged into Plan B. All participants in Plan B are 100 percent vested in their accrued benefits, and Plan B is substantially overfunded. Participants in the Merged Plan who were formerly participants in Plan A will continue to accrue cash balance plan benefits under the Merged Plan. Frozen accrued benefits for participants in the Merged Plan who were formerly partici-pants in Plan B will continue to be frozen. Participants who were formerly participants in both Plans A and B will also continue to accrue cash balance plan benefits under the Merged Plan, and the accrued benefits under Plan B for such participants will continue to remain frozen. IRS ruled that the merger of Plan A and Plan B would require vesting service credit under the Merged Plan with regard to service before the effective date of Plan A for any Plan A participant who had never been a participant in Plan B. [Priv. Ltr. Rul. 200337015, *revoking* Priv. Ltr. Rul. 200315039; Treas. Reg. § 1.411(a)-5(b)(3)(ii)]

IRS has said that, in the case of a predecessor-partnership, service with the partnership could be counted for vesting purposes under the successor corporation's retirement plan, even though the corporation did not continue the partnership's retirement plan. [Priv. Ltr. Rul. 7742003] Service with any member of a controlled group of corporations or with a commonly controlled entity (see Qs 5:29, 5:31), whether or not incorporated, must be counted for vesting purposes. Similarly, service with any member of an affiliated service group (see Q 5:35) must be counted. [I.R.C. §§ 414(b), 414(c), 414(m)]

A multiple-employer defined benefit plan that does not credit vesting service attributable to periods for which an employer does not make required contributions to the plan does not satisfy the minimum vesting requirements. [Rev. Rul. 85-130, 1985-2 C.B. 137]

Q 9:12   May any years of service be disregarded for vesting purposes?

Yes. There are limited exceptions to the general rule that all years of service with an employer must be counted for vesting purposes (see Q 9:11). [I.R.C. § 411(a)(4); Silvernail v. Ameritech Pension Plan, 2006 U.S. App. LEXIS 4926 (7th Cir. 2006)]

The following years of service may be disregarded:

1. Years of service before the employee reached age 18;

2. Years of service before the qualified retirement plan went into effect;

3. Years of service during which the employee declined to make required (mandatory) contributions; and

4. Years of service before a one-year break in service (see Q 5:10) if the number of consecutive one-year breaks in service equals or exceeds the greater of five or the number of prebreak years of service, and the participant did not have any nonforfeitable right to the accrued benefit (see Q 9:16).

Elective contributions (see Q 27:16) to a 401(k) plan (see Q 27:1) are considered as employer, not employee, contributions for vesting purposes (see Q 9:13). Thus, a plan may not disregard years of service for vesting purposes because of the failure to make elective contributions; the exclusion applies only to the failure to make *mandatory* employee contributions. [Treas. Reg. § 1.411(a)-5(b)(2)]

Q 9:13   Is an employee's length of service ever irrelevant in determining the degree of vesting?

Yes. In any of the following circumstances an employee is fully vested (that is, has a nonforfeitable right to 100 percent of the employer-provided account balance or accrued benefit) regardless of how many years of service the employee has completed:

1. The employee reaches normal retirement age under the plan (see Q 10:55). [I.R.C. §§ 411(a), 411(a)(8)]

2. The qualified retirement plan is terminated, a partial termination of the plan has occurred, or plan contributions are completely discontinued (see Qs 25:4, 25:5, 25:58). [I.R.C. § 411(d)(3)]

3. The minimum service requirement for participation is more than one year of service (see Qs 5:4, 27:15). [I.R.C. § 410(a)(1)(B)(i)]

4. The plan is a qualified 401(k) plan and the accrued benefit is derived from employer contributions made pursuant to the employee's election or is a safe harbor contribution. See chapter 27 for details. [I.R.C. §§ 401(k)(2)(C), 401(k)(12)(E)(i)]

Despite the requirement that an employee must become fully vested upon plan termination, one court concluded that the partially vested benefit of a previously terminated participant who had yet to receive a distribution of his vested benefit can be forfeited upon plan termination if the employer is liquidated at the same time. [Borda v. Hardy, Lewis, Pollard & Page, P.C., 138 F.3d 1062 (6th Cir. 1998); *see also* Flanagan v. Inland Empire Elec. Workers' Pension Plan & Trust, 3 F.3d 1246 (9th Cir. 1993)]

The plan may also provide for full vesting under any of these circumstances:

1. The employee reaches the early retirement age set by the qualified retirement plan.

2. The employee becomes disabled.

3. The employee dies.

Q 9:14   What vesting schedule is best for the employer?

It depends on how long employees usually stay with the employer.

Example. Keren Corporation adopted a 5-percent-of-compensation money purchase pension plan on January 1, 2010. Sharon completes a year of service on January 1, 2011, and joins the plan. Sharon earns $20,000 a year. Below is a calculation of Sharon's benefits under the seven-year graded and five-year cliff vesting schedules (see Q 9:4):

	Seven-Year		Five-Year	
Plan Year	Contribution/ Account Balance	Vesting Percentage/ Vested Benefits	Contribution/ Account Balance	Vesting Percentage/ Vested Benefits
1	$\frac{0}{0}$		$\frac{0}{0}$	
2	$\frac{\$1,000}{\$1,000}$	$\frac{0\%}{\$0}$	$\frac{\$1,000}{\$1,000}$	$\frac{0\%}{\$0}$
3	$\frac{\$1,000}{\$2,000}$	$\frac{20\%}{\$400}$	$\frac{\$1,000}{\$2,000}$	$\frac{0\%}{\$0}$

	Seven-Year		Five-Year	
Plan Year	Contribution/ Account Balance	Vesting Percentage/ Vested Benefits	Contribution/ Account Balance	Vesting Percentage/ Vested Benefits
4	$1,000 / $3,000	40% / $1,200	$1,000 / $3,000	0% / $0
5	$1,000 / $4,000	60% / $2,400	$1,000 / $4,000	100% / $4,000
6	$1,000 / $5,000	80% / $4,000	$1,000 / $5,000	100% / $4,000
7	$1,000 / $6,000	100% / $6,000	$1,000 / $6,000	100% / $6,000

In plan years 3 and 4, less vested benefits are provided under the five-year cliff vesting schedule; and, in plan years 5 and 6, less vested benefits are provided under the seven-year graded vesting schedule. Thus, if employees customarily leave before completing five years of service, five-year cliff vesting is more favorable to the employer; but, if they leave after completing five or six years of service, the seven-year graded schedule is more favorable to the employer. After seven years of service, both schedules provide equal benefits.

As an alternative, Keren Corporation could require employees to complete two years of service to become eligible, but then employees must be 100 percent vested immediately (see Qs 9:4, 9:13). With a two-year service requirement and 100 percent immediate vesting, Sharon's benefits would be as follows:

Plan Year	Contribution/ Account Balance	Vesting Percentage/ Vested Benefits
1	0 / 0	
2	0 / 0	
3	$1,000 / $1,000	100% / $1,000
4	$1,000 / $2,000	100% / $2,000
5	$1,000 / $3,000	100% / $3,000

Plan Year	Contribution/ Account Balance	Vesting Percentage/ Vested Benefits
6	$1,000 / $4,000	100% / $4,000
7	$1,000 / $5,000	100% / $5,000

In plan years 3 and 4, the least vested benefits still occur under five-year cliff; in plan year 5, the least vested benefits still occur under seven-year graded; in plan year 6, the most vested benefits are still created under five-year cliff; and, in plan year 7 and in all subsequent plan years, the least vested benefits occur with the two-year service requirement. Therefore, if employees customarily leave after completing seven or more years of service, the two-year service requirement will be most favorable to the employer.

Q 9:15 How does a one-year break in service affect an employee if the qualified retirement plan requires the employee to have more than one year of service in order to be eligible to participate?

Qualified retirement plans that provide for immediate 100 percent vesting but require more than one year of service to be eligible to participate (see Qs 5:12, 9:13) may provide that years of service preceding a one-year break in service (see Q 5:10) be disregarded if the employee has not yet met the service eligibility criterion. Thus, an employee who completes one year of service and then incurs a one-year break in service starts over again when rehired (see Q 5:4). [I.R.C. § 410(a)(5)(B)]

Q 9:16 How does a one-year break in service affect a previously nonvested participant's right to benefits?

A nonvested participant's years of service before any period of consecutive one-year breaks in service (see Q 5:10) may be disregarded for vesting purposes if the number of consecutive one-year breaks in service equals or exceeds the greater of five or the participant's years of service before the break. [I.R.C. § 411(a)(6)(D)]

Example. KSL Corporation's profit sharing plan, which operates on a calendar-year basis, requires an employee to complete one year of service to become a participant. Under the plan's vesting provision, a participant becomes 100 percent vested after five years of service. Lauren began working for KSL on January 1, 2006, separated from service on December 11, 2007, and was rehired on January 13, 2011. Lauren's two years of service before her break in service must be counted because her consecutive one-year breaks in service are less than five.

A participant's prebreak years of service do not have to be taken into account until a year of service is completed after reemployment. [I.R.C. § 411(a)(6)(B)]

Q 9:17   How does a one-year break in service affect a vested participant's right to benefits?

The years of service of a vested participant in a defined contribution plan (see Q 2:2) or a fully insured defined benefit plan (see Q 2:25) completed after a one-year break in service (see Q 5:10) need not be counted for purposes of computing the participant's right to benefits derived from employer contributions accruing before the one-year break in service if the participant has at least five consecutive one-year breaks in service. [I.R.C. § 411(a)(6)(C)]

> **Example.** Jay-Kay Corporation has a profit sharing plan in which James participated. At the time James separated from service, he had a nonforfeitable right to 20 percent of his accrued benefit, but no distribution was made. In 2011, after incurring a one-year break in service, James is rehired and becomes an active participant in the plan once again. The plan is not permitted to disregard James's postbreak service for purposes of computing the vested percentage of his prebreak accrued benefit.

If a participant's prebreak years of service are required to be taken into account, such years of service need not be counted until the participant completes a year of service after resuming employment. [I.R.C. § 411(a)(6)(B)]

Q 9:18   What is a forfeiture of benefits?

If an employee terminates employment before becoming 100 percent vested, the employee may be entitled to some benefits. This will usually depend on the number of years the employee worked for the company. Thus, if, at the time of termination, the employee's account balance in a profit sharing plan is $10,000 and the employee is 60 percent vested, the vested benefit is $6,000 (60% × $10,000). The balance in the account that is not vested at the time of termination generally will be forfeited at the earlier of (1) when the employee receives a distribution or (2) after the employee incurs five consecutive one-year breaks in service (see Q 5:10). [I.R.C. § 411(a)(6)(C)]

One court concluded that an employer's unwritten policy of resetting seniority to zero when an employee voluntarily transferred from one division to another, effectively reducing the contribution the employee could make to a defined contribution plan, did not violate ERISA because the employer's seniority system did not cause any forfeiture of the employee's benefits. [Casillas v. Federal Express Corp, No. 00-3170 D/V (W.D. Tenn. 2001)]

Q 9:19   What happens to amounts forfeited by participants?

Only defined benefit plans (see Q 2:3) are restricted in the application of forfeitures. Forfeitures under a defined benefit plan must be used to reduce future employer contributions and may not be used to provide additional benefits for remaining participants. Defined contribution plans (see Q 2:2) may provide that forfeitures be used either to reduce contributions or to increase benefits provided under the plan. [I.R.C. § 401(a)(8)]

IRS has ruled that a profit sharing plan may provide for the allocation of forfeitures to participants on the basis of their account balances provided such allocation does not discriminate in favor of highly compensated employees (HCEs; see Q 3:2). [Rev. Rul. 81-10, 1981-1 C.B. 172; Treas. Reg. §§ 1.401-4(a)(1)(iii), 1.401(a)(4)-1(c)(10), 1.401(a)(4)-11(c)]

Q 9:20   May a nonforfeitable benefit ever be forfeited?

The courts have differed on whether forfeitures can be imposed because of employee dishonesty (so-called bad boy clauses) or violation of a promise not to compete. Some courts say such forfeitures are not permitted. Other courts have ruled that if the forfeiture provisions do not cause a forfeiture of an amount greater than what would result under the minimum vesting standards (see Q 9:4), the forfeiture is allowed. [Clark v. Lauren Young Tire Ctr. Profit Sharing Trust, 816 F.2d 480 (9th Cir. 1987); Noell v. American Design Inc. Profit Sharing Plan, 764 F.2d 827 (11th Cir. 1985); Westwood Chem. Co. v. Kulick, 570 F. Supp. 1032 (S.D.N.Y. 1983); Montgomery v. Lowe, 507 F. Supp. 618 (E.D. Tex. 1981); Hepple v. Roberts & Dybdahl Inc., 622 F.2d 962 (8th Cir. 1980); Winer v. Edison Bros. Stores Pension Plan, 593 F.2d 307 (8th Cir. 1979); Nedrow v. MacFarlane & Hays Co. Employees' Profit Sharing Plan & Trust, 476 F. Supp. 934 (E.D. Mich. 1979)]

According to IRS, vested benefits in excess of the benefits required to be nonforfeitable under the statutory alternatives (see Q 9:4) may be forfeited because of an employee's misconduct or dishonesty. The qualified retirement plan must provide the specific criteria for application of this bad boy clause, and its use cannot be discriminatory in operation.

> **Example 1.** Nephew Mikey Corporation's retirement plan provides that an employee is fully vested after the completion of three years of service. The plan also provides that, if the employee works for a competitor, the employee's rights in the plan will be forfeited. Such a provision could result in a prohibited forfeiture; but, if the plan limited the forfeiture to employees who completed less than five years of service, the plan would not fail to satisfy the minimum vesting requirements.

> **Example 2.** Aunt Sallie Corporation's retirement plan has a seven-year graded vesting provision and provides for forfeiture of benefits if an employee with less than five years of service terminates employment and works for a competitor. This is permissible because the plan could have had five-year cliff vesting.

[Temp. Treas. Reg. §§ 1.411(a)-4T(a), 1.411(a)-4T(c); Treas. Reg. § 1.411(d)-4, Q&A-6(a); Rev. Rul. 85-31, 1985-1 C.B. 153]

One court concluded that a different rule applies to public employees and upheld the partial forfeiture of a nurse's benefits under a state (New Jersey) qualified plan based on her insurance fraud conviction. The court ruled that the vesting requirements of the Code did not apply to public employees whose employment was terminated as a direct result of a conviction related to the employment, and that New Jersey's forfeiture statute was exempt from the vesting requirements of the Code and ERISA absent termination of the plan by the state. [Debell v. Board of Trustees, Pub. Employees' Ret. Sys., A-1012-01T1 (N.J. Super. Ct. App. Div. 2003)]

Q 9:21   Does a distribution (cash-out) of benefits affect how many years of service must be taken into account?

Yes. Upon termination of the employee's participation in a qualified retirement plan, the plan may disregard service for which the employee has received (1) an involuntary distribution of the present value of the employee's nonforfeitable benefit up to a maximum of $5,000 (see Q 10:61) or (2) a voluntary distribution of the present value of the nonforfeitable benefit. [I.R.C. §§ 411(a)(7)(B), 411(a)(11)(A); Treas. Reg. § 1.411(a)-7(d)(4)]

In order to disregard the prior service of a participant who resumes employment and participation under the qualified retirement plan and who previously received a distribution of less than the present value of the accrued benefit, the plan must provide the participant with the opportunity to repay the entire amount of the distribution (see Q 9:22). [I.R.C. § 411(a)(7)(C); Treas. Reg. § 1.411(a)-7(d)(4)]

For purposes of determining an employee's right to an accrued benefit derived from employer contributions under a plan, the plan may disregard service performed by the employee with respect to which:

1. The employee receives a distribution of the present value of the entire nonforfeitable benefit at the time of the distribution;
2. The requirements relating to the $5,000 cash-out limit and present value determination rules are satisfied at the time of the distribution;
3. The distribution is made due to the termination of the employee's participation in the plan; and
4. The plan has a repayment provision in effect at the time of the distribution.

[Treas. Reg. § 1.411(a)-7(d)(4)(i)]

A distribution is deemed to be made due to the termination of an employee's participation in the plan if it is made no later than the close of the second plan year following the plan year in which such termination occurs or if such distribution would have been made under the plan by the close of such second plan year but for the fact that the present value of the nonforfeitable accrued benefit then exceeded the $5,000 cash-out limit. For purposes of determining the entire nonforfeitable benefit, the plan may disregard service after the distribution. [Treas. Reg. § 1.411(a)-7(d)(4)(vi)]

Q 9:22   How can a reemployed participant restore (buy back) forfeited benefits?

In most situations, upon reemployment, a participant is entitled to repay a prior distribution from the qualified retirement plan and to have any forfeited benefits restored. This buy-back provision must permit the employee to pay back the full amount distributed. The plan can require repayment by the reemployed participant before the earlier of (1) five years after reemployment or (2) when the participant incurs a period of five consecutive one-year breaks in service (see Q 5:10) commencing after the distribution. Thus, the employer is not required to offer this buy-back right to a participant who has five consecutive one-year breaks in service after the distribution. [I.R.C. § 411(a)(7)(C)] IRS representatives have opined that a plan could require the participant to repay the entire amount of the distribution, including 401(k) plan elective contributions (see Q 27:16) and employee voluntary contributions (see Q 6:38).

A defined benefit plan may require that any repayment include interest on the full amount of the distribution. The maximum interest rate that may be charged upon repayment is 120 percent of the federal midterm rate in effect on the first day of the plan year during which repayment occurs. [I.R.C. §§ 411(a)(7)(C), 411(c)(2)(C), 1274; Treas. Reg. § 1.411(a)-7(d)(2)(ii)(B)]

An employee who received a distribution of the nonforfeitable benefit from a plan that is required to provide a repayment opportunity to such employee upon reemployment and who, upon subsequent reemployment, repays the full amount of such distribution must be reinstated in the full array of Section 411(d)(6) protected benefits (see Q 10:45) that existed with respect to such benefit prior to distribution. [Treas. Reg. § 1.411(d)-4, Q&A-2(a)(2)(iii)]

> **Example.** Sallie, a partially vested employee, receives a single-sum distribution of the present value of her entire nonforfeitable benefit on account of separation from service under a defined benefit plan providing for a repayment provision. Upon reemployment with the employer, Sallie makes repayment in the required amount. Sallie may, upon subsequent termination of employment, elect to take such repaid benefits in any optional form provided under the plan as of the time of her initial separation from service. If the plan was amended prior to such repayment to eliminate the single-sum optional form of benefit with respect to benefits accrued after the date of the amendment, Sallie has a protected right to take distribution of the repaid benefit in the form of a single-sum distribution.

Q 9:23   May a qualified retirement plan provide for the forfeiture of vested benefits on the death of an employee?

Yes, with the following exception: the surviving spouse of a participant in a qualified retirement plan subject to the survivor annuity requirements must be paid an annuity based on the participant's vested accrued benefit unless the participant waived the coverage with the spouse's consent (see Qs 10:20, 10:21). [I.R.C. § 401(a)(11)]

A qualified retirement plan may not provide for the forfeiture of vested benefits derived from employee contributions, whether mandatory or voluntary (see Q 9:9). However, a forfeiture does not occur merely because benefits derived from contributions of both the employer and the employee are paid out in the form of an annuity that stops on the employee's death. [Treas. Reg. § 1.411(a)-4(b)(1)]

Q 9:24   May any years of service be disregarded for accrual purposes?

Yes. A qualified retirement plan may impose a limitation on the amount of benefits an employee may accrue or the number of years of service that will be taken into account in determining an employee's accrued benefit (see Q 9:2). Therefore, a qualified retirement plan may disregard an employee's service that occurs after the specified benefit level or the specified number of years of service has been reached. However, a retirement plan may not cease an employee's accrual of benefits (or reduce the rate of accrual) solely because the employee attains a certain age. [I.R.C. § 411(b)(1)(H); Prop. Treas. Reg. § 1.411(b)-2; Greenlagh v. Putnam Sav. Bank, 1998 U.S. App. LEXIS 6482 (2d Cir. 1998); Atkins v. Northwest Airlines Inc., No. 91-3179MN (8th Cir. 1992); American Ass'n of Retired Persons v. Farmers Group Inc., No. 90-55872 (9th Cir. 1991)]

Example. Stephanie Corporation maintains a defined benefit plan under which the participant's normal retirement benefit will be based on the highest annual salary earned by the participant during the time of employment. The plan further provides that each participant will accrue an interest in the benefit at the rate of 4 percent per year of service. The plan does, however, limit the number of years of service that will be taken into account in determining each participant's retirement benefit to 20. Therefore, a participant's normal retirement benefit will be limited to 80 percent of the participant's highest annual salary. This type of accrual scheme is permissible despite the fact that an older participant is more likely to be affected by the plan provision.

See Qs 11:5 and 11:34 for a discussion of the actuarially increased accrued benefit of a participant who has a deferred required beginning date.

Q 9:25   Can a qualified retirement plan be amended to reduce accrued benefits?

Generally, no. A qualified retirement plan may not be amended to eliminate or reduce a Section 411(d)(6) protected benefit (see Q 10:45) that has already accrued (the anti-cutback rule), unless IRS approves a request to amend the plan or the elimination or reduction satisfies certain requirements (see Qs 8:28, 9:28, 9:35). This is the rule even if such elimination or reduction is contingent upon the employee's consent. In addition, an amendment cannot otherwise place greater restrictions or conditions on a participant's rights to protected benefits, even if the amendment merely adds a restriction or condition that is otherwise permitted under the vesting rules. However, a plan may (subject to certain notice requirements) be amended to eliminate or reduce Section 411(d)(6) protected benefits with respect to benefits not yet accrued as of the later of the amendment's adoption date or effective date (see Q 9:36). [I.R.C. §§ 411(d)(6), 412(d)(2); ERISA §§ 204(g), 302(c)(8), 4281; Prop. Treas. Reg. § 1.411(d)-3(a)(3); Treas. Reg. §§ 1.411(d)-3(a)(3), 1.411(d)-4, Q&A-2(a)(1); Smith v. National Credit Union Admin. Bd., 1994 U.S. App. LEXIS 30390 (11th Cir. 1994); Production & Maint. Employees' Local 504 v. Roadmaster Corp., Nos. 89-1464, 90-2698 (7th Cir. 1992); Nichols v. Asbestos Workers Local 24 Pension Plan, 835 F.2d 881 (Fed. Cir. 1987); Rev. Proc. 94-42, 1994-1 C.B. 717; Priv. Ltr. Ruls. 9723048, 9614004, 9346012]

Example 1. Plan A provides an annual benefit of 2 percent of career average pay times years of service commencing at normal retirement age (age 65; see Q 10:55). Plan A is amended on November 1, 2010, effective as of January 1, 2011, to provide for an annual benefit of 1.3 percent of final pay times years of service, with final pay computed as the average of a participant's highest three consecutive years of compensation. As of January 1, 2011, Ed has 16 years of service, his career average pay is $37,500, and the average of his highest three consecutive years of compensation is $67,308. Thus, Ed's accrued benefit (see Q 9:2) as of the applicable amendment date is increased from $12,000 per year at normal retirement age (2% × $37,500 × 16 years of service) to $14,000 per year at normal retirement age (1.3% × $67,308 × 16 years of service). As of January 1, 2011, Barbara has six years of service, her career average pay is $50,000, and the average of her highest three consecutive years of compensation is $51,282. Barbara's accrued benefit as of the applicable amendment date is decreased from $6,000 per year at normal retirement age (2% × $50,000 × 6 years of service) to $4,000 per year at normal retirement age (1.3% × $51,282 × 6 years of service). While the plan amendment increases the accrued benefit of Ed, the plan amendment fails to satisfy the anti-cutback rule because the amendment decreases Barbara's accrued benefit below the level of her accrued benefit immediately before the applicable amendment date.

Example 2. The facts are the same as Example 1, except that Plan A includes a provision under which Barbara's accrued benefit cannot be less than what it was immediately before the applicable amendment date (so that Barbara's accrued benefit could not be less than $6,000 per year at normal retirement age). The amendment does not violate the anti-cutback rule with respect to Ed (whose accrued benefit has been increased) or with respect to Barbara (although Barbara would not accrue any benefits until the point in time at which the new formula amount would exceed the amount payable under the minimum provision, approximately three years after the amendment becomes effective).

Example 3. Tucker Corporation maintains Plan C, a defined benefit plan (see Q 2:3) under which an employee participates upon completion of one year of service and is 100 percent vested in the employer-derived accrued benefit upon completion of five years of service. Plan C provides that a former employee's years of service prior to a break-in-service (see Q 5:10) will be reinstated upon completion of one year of service after being rehired. Plan C has participants who have fewer than five years of service and who are accordingly 0 percent vested in their employer-derived accrued benefits. On December 31, 2010, effective January 1, 2011, Plan C is amended to provide that any nonvested participant who has five consecutive one-year breaks-in-service and whose number of consecutive one-year breaks-in-service exceeds the participant's number of years of service before the breaks will have the pre-break service disregarded in determining vesting under the plan. The plan amendment does not satisfy the anti-cutback rule because the amendment places greater restrictions or conditions on the rights to pro-tected benefits, as of January 1, 2011, for participants who have fewer than five years of service, by restricting the ability of those participants to receive further vesting protections on benefits accrued as of that date.

Example 4. Tucker Corporation also sponsors Plan D, a profit sharing plan (see Q 2:6) under which each employee has a nonforfeitable right to a percentage of the employer-derived accrued benefit based on the following table:

Years of Service	Nonforfeitable Percentage
Less than 3	0%
3	20%
4	40%
5	60%
6	80%
7 or more	100%

In January 2010, Tucker Corporation acquires Baltimore Corp., which maintains Plan E, a profit sharing plan under which each employee who has completed five years of service has a nonforfeitable right to 100 percent of the employer-derived accrued benefit. In 2011, Plan E is merged into Plan D. On the effective date of the merger, Plan D is amended to provide that the vesting schedule for participants of Plan E is the seven-year graded vesting schedule of Plan D. The plan amendment provides that any participant of Plan E who had completed five years of service prior to the amendment is fully vested. In addition, the amendment provides that any participant in Plan E who has at least three years of service prior to the amendment is permitted to make an irrevocable election to have the vesting of the participant's nonforfeitable right to the employer-derived accrued benefit determined under either the five-year cliff vesting schedule or the seven-year graded vesting schedule (see Q 9:7). Eduardo, who has an account balance of $10,000 on the applicable amendment date, is a participant in Plan E with two years of service as of that date. As of the date of the merger, Eduardo's nonforfeitable right to the employer-derived accrued benefit is 0 percent under both the seven-year graded vesting schedule of Plan D and the five-year cliff vesting schedule of Plan E.

The plan amendment does not satisfy the anti-cutback rule because the amendment places greater restrictions or conditions on the rights to protected benefits with respect to Eduardo and any participant who has fewer than seven years of service and who elected (or was made subject to) the new vesting schedule. A method of avoiding a violation with respect to account balances attributable to benefits accrued as of the applicable amendment date and earnings thereon would be for Plan D to provide for the vested percentage of Eduardo and each other participant in Plan E to be no less than the greater of the two vesting schedules (e.g., for Eduardo and each other participant in Plan E to be fully vested if the participant completes five years of service) for those account balances and earnings.

A plan may treat a participant as receiving the entire nonforfeitable accrued benefit (see Q 9:1) under the plan if the participant receives the benefit in an optional form of benefit (see Q 10:45) in an amount determined under the plan that is at least the actuarial equivalent of the employee's nonforfeitable accrued benefit payable at normal retirement age under the plan. This is true even though the participant could have elected to receive an optional form of benefit with a greater actuarial value than the value of the optional form received, such as an optional form including retirement-type subsidies (see Qs 9:33, 9:34), and without regard to whether such other, more valuable optional form could have commenced immediately or could have become available only upon the employee's future satisfaction of specified eligibility conditions. [Treas. Reg. § 1.411(d)-4, Q&A-2(a)(2)(i)]

Except for purposes of the buy-back rule (see Q 9:22), a plan does not violate the anti-cutback rule merely because an employee's election to receive a portion of the nonforfeitable accrued benefit in one optional form of benefit precludes the employee from receiving that portion of the benefit in another optional form of benefit. The employee retains all protected rights with respect to the entire portion of the nonforfeitable accrued benefit for which no distribution election was made. For purposes of this rule, an elective transfer of an otherwise distributable benefit is treated as the selection of an optional form of benefit (see Q 9:32). [Treas. Reg. § 1.411(d)-4, Q&A-2(a)(2)(ii)]

Example 5. The KSS defined benefit plan provides, among its optional forms of benefit, for a subsidized early retirement benefit payable in the form of an annuity and available to employees who terminate from employment on or after their 55th birthdays. In addition, the plan provides for a single-sum distribution available on termination from employment or termination of the plan. The single-sum distribution is determined on the basis of the present value of the accrued normal retirement benefit and does not take the early retirement subsidy into account. The plan is terminated December 31, 2010. Terry, age 47, Gary age 55, and Marsha, age 47, all continue in the service of the employer. Diane, age 47, Lisa, age 55, and Liz, age 47, terminate from employment with the employer during 2010. Terry and Gary elect to take the single-sum optional form of distribution at the time of plan termination. Diane and Lisa elect to take the single-sum distribution on termination from employment with the employer. The elimination of the subsidized early retirement benefit with respect to Terry, Gary, Diane, and Lisa does not result in a violation of the anti-cutback rule. This is the result even though Terry and Diane had not yet satisfied the conditions for the subsidized early retirement benefit. Because Marsha and Liz have not selected an optional form of benefit, they continue to have a protected right to the full array of Section 411(d)(6) protected benefits provided under the plan, including the single-sum distribution form and the subsidized early retirement benefit.

Section 411(d)(6) protected benefits may not be eliminated merely because they are payable with respect to a spouse or other beneficiary. [Treas. Reg. § 1.411(d)-4, Q&A-2(a)(4)]

One court has held that a defined contribution plan (see Q 2:2) could not be retroactively amended to change the plan's valuation date where the effect of the amendment was to reduce the amount of benefits payable to a terminated plan participant. In this case, the value of the terminated participant's account balance in the plan decreased markedly from the prior valuation date. Under the plan in effect on his termination date, the terminated participant was entitled to a distribution of his account balance valued as of the nearest prior valuation date. After the participant's termination, the plan was amended (retroactive to the beginning of the plan year) to provide for interim valuation dates. An interim valuation resulted in a much smaller account balance for the terminated participant. The court held that, in a defined contribution plan, the accrued benefit is the participant's account balance (see Q 9:2). Thus, the participant's account balance could not be reduced by a retroactive plan amendment adopted after the participant terminated employment. [Pratt v. Petroleum Prod. Mgmt., Inc. Employee Sav. Plan & Trust, 920 F.2d 651 (10th Cir. 1990); Wulf v. Quantum Chem. Corp., 1994 U.S. App. LEXIS 14677 (6th Cir. 1994); Boog v. Bradley, Campbell, Carney & Madsen, P.C. Defined Benefit Pension Plan & Trust, No. 96CA0531 (Colo. Ct. App. 1997); *see also* Kay v. Thrift & Profit Sharing Plan for Employees of Boyertown Casket Co., 780 F. Supp. 1447 (E.D. Pa. 1991); *but see* Wininger v. Wilcox Fuel, Inc., 2004 U.S. Dist. LEXIS 591 (D. Conn. 2004)] In a similar vein, IRS ruled that the allocation formula in a profit sharing plan (see Q 2:6) could not be retroactively amended after the end of the plan year for which the contribution was made. [Priv. Ltr. Rul. 9735001] In another case, the court ruled that, under the terms of the plans, the participant was entitled to the distribution of his benefits based upon the interim plan valuation date he requested, rather than upon the plans' preceding annual valuation date or the date he submitted his distribution election forms. [Goldstein v. Assocs. in Gastroenterology of Pittsburgh Amended and Restated Pension Plan, No. 04-2252 (3d Cir. 2005); *see also* Janeiro, Jr. v. Urological Surgery Professional Assn., No. 633-05 (1st Cir. 2006)] Also, one court ruled that two employees who elected to receive enhanced early retirement benefits were entitled to receive those benefits because a subsequent amendment, which affected the two employees by placing limitations on the number of employees who could receive the enhanced benefits, was an impermissible retroactive amendment that affected accrued benefits. [Gould v. GTE N. Inc., No. 1:97-CV-524 (W.D. Mich. 1999)] However, IRS determined that the transfer of participants' account balances from one company's plan that had a hardship provision (see Q 27:14) to another company's plan that did not was not a violation of the anti-cutback rule. [Priv. Ltr. Rul. 9743045]

An employer with an existing defined benefit plan proposed a plan amendment that would add a new cash balance plan (see Q 2:23) with more modest benefits. Under the proposal, long-term employees would remain covered by the original defined benefit plan, but shorter-term employees, and long-term employees who left employment and were subsequently rehired, would be transferred into the new cash balance plan. The court ruled that the employer could not ratify a plan amendment retroactively to the date the amendment was proposed, where doing so would indirectly affect the accrued benefits of a plan participant. Plan amendments that indirectly affect accrued benefits, such as by affecting provisions relating to breaks in service used in determining benefit accrual, are prohibited. Thus, the court further ruled that the employer could not apply the plan amendment to a long-term employee who left employment and was subsequently rehired; therefore, his participation in the older defined benefit plan resumed upon reemployment. [Depenbrock v. CIGNA Corp., No. 03-3575 (3d Cir. 2004)]

One court ruled that the failure of a defined benefit plan (see Q 2:3) to specify the actuarial assumptions (see Q 2:20) used to reduce benefits of former employees who elected to receive plan benefits prior to age 65 did not give rise to an action under ERISA and, in addition, that a retroactive plan amendment that did specify the actuarial assumptions to be used did not constitute a reduction of accrued benefits. [Stamper v. Total Petroleum, Inc. Ret. Plan for Hourly Rated Employees, 1999 WL 674487 (10th Cir. 1999)] Another court concluded that a defined benefit plan amendment that froze the accrual of benefits as of December 31, 1997 and caused a disabled employee's benefits to be recalculated as of the freeze date, rather than his normal retirement date (see Q 10:55), did not violate the anti-cutback rule because the employee's benefits beyond 1997 were not accrued (see Q 9:35). [Arndt v. Security Bank SSB Employees' Pension Plan, 182 F.3d 538 (7th Cir. 1999)] A plan administrator's (see Q 20:1) interpretation of a defined benefit plan provision requiring the use of a mortality table as authorizing a nine-month set forward for calculating benefits for distribution to participants who elected to receive actuarially equivalent forms of benefits was reasonable and did not violate the anti-cutback rule, determined one court. [McDaniel v. Chevron Corp., 203 F.3d 1099 (9th Cir. 2000)] A denial of plan benefits that was based upon a union's executive board's resolutions was improper because the resolutions eliminated accrued service credits and violated the anti-cutback rule. [Craig v. IBEW, No. 98-5318 (3d Cir. 1999)]

Amendments eliminating participants' rights to elect lump-sum distributions or delaying the right to payment of retirement benefits constitute prohibited elimination of or reduction in accrued benefits. [Counts v. Kissack Water & Oil Serv. Inc. Profit Sharing Plan, No. 92-8036 (10th Cir. 1993); Davis v. Burlington Indus., Inc., No. 91-1725 (4th Cir. 1992); Auwarter v. Paper Sales Corp. Defined Benefit Pension Plan, No. 91-3082 (E.D.N.Y. 1992); *but see* Perrecca v. Gluck, 295 F.3d 215 (2d Cir. 2002); Smyth v. Cumberland Farms, Inc., 2002 U.S. Dist.

LEXIS 20053 (E.D. Pa. 2003)] Plan amendments meant to prevent recipients of lump-sum distributions from receiving a windfall due to the use of certain mortality tables and discount rates violated the anti-cutback rule, according to another court. [Call v. Ameritech Mgmt. Pension Plan, 475 F.3d 816 (7th Cir. 2007)] However, one court decided that the spin-off of a member of a controlled group of corporations (see Q 5:31) did not entitle employees of the spun-off corporation to an immediate distribution of assets from the controlled group's plan and did not violate the anti-cutback rule because the spun-off corporation continued to maintain plans for its employees and, thus, the employees did not incur a separation from service. [Hunter v. Caliber Sys., Inc., 220 F.3d 702 (6th Cir. 2000)]

An amendment increasing the interest rate, the effect of which reduced the amount of lump-sum payments, has been held to violate the anti-cutback rule [Costantino v. TRW, Inc., 1993 U.S. App. LEXIS 29479 (6th Cir. 1993); *but see* Ryberczyk v. TRW, Inc., No. 97-4167 (6th Cir. 2000)]; but other courts have held such an amendment not to violate the rule. [Cooke v. Lynn Sand & Stone Co., 1995 U.S. App. LEXIS 33252 (1st Cir. 1995); Dooley v. American Airlines, Inc., 1993 U.S. Dist. LEXIS 15667 (N.D. Ill. 1993); *see also* Mathews v. Sears Pension Plan, 144 F.3d 461 (7th Cir. 1998); Krumme v. WestPoint Stevens, Inc., 143 F.3d 71 (2d Cir. 1998)] For plan years beginning in 2004 or 2005, 5½ percent is substituted for the applicable interest rate for benefits paid in a form other than a straight life annuity (see Q 6:12). IRS has advised that a plan amendment incorporating this change will not violate the anti-cutback rule, provided that the plan is amended on or before the last day of the first plan year beginning on or after January 1, 2006, and the plan is operated as though the amendment were in effect during the period beginning on the date the amendment is effective. [I.R.C. § 415(b)(2)(E)(ii); IRS Notice 2004-78, 2004-2 C.B. 879] IRS's determination that the employer's GUST amendments relating to the change in interest rates did not violate the anti-cutback rule was upheld because the amendments were executed within the GUST remedial amendment period and other safe harbor requirements were met. [Stepnowski v. Comm'r, 2006 WL 2074808 (3d Cir. 2006)]

The elimination of a postretirement cost-of-living adjustment in monthly retirement benefits constitutes a prohibited reduction in accrued benefits [Hickey v. Chicago Truck Drivers, Helpers & Warehouse Workers Union, 980 F.2d 465 (7th Cir. 1992); *see also* Williams v. Rohm and Haas Pension Plan, 2007 WL 2302173 (7th Cir. 2007)], but another court ruled that such an elimination did not violate the anti-cutback rule, because the elimination affected only employees who had retired before the cost-of-living adjustment had been adopted by the plan. [Board of Trustees of the Sheet Metal Worker's Nat'l Pension Fund v. Comm'r, 318 F.3d 599 (4th Cir. 2003); Priv. Ltr. Rul. 9723048] After a participant's retirement, the plan was amended three times to increase benefits for both active and retired participants. Thereafter, a plan amendment rescinded the third benefit increase for participants who had retired prior to the adoption of the third plan amendment. The court concluded that the rescission did not violate the anti-cutback rule because the benefit increase did not create an accrued benefit for those participants who had retired before the benefit increase was adopted. [Thornton v. Graphic Communications Conf. of the International Bhd. of Teamsters Supplemental Retirement and Disability Fund, 566 F.3d 597 (6th Cir. 2009)] Other cases have held that early retirement benefits are not accrued benefits so that a reduction in such benefits does not violate the anti-cutback rule. [Hunger v. A.B., 1993 U.S. App. LEXIS 32743 (8th Cir. 1993); Dade v. North Am. Philips Corp., 68 F.3d 1558 (3d Cir. 1995); *but see* Bellas v. CBS, Inc., 221 F.3d 517 (3d Cir. 2000); Ahng v. Allsteel, Inc., Nos. 95-2721, 95-3734 (7th Cir. 1996)] However, one court determined that a plan amendment that reduced the amount of benefits for service performed before a participant's break-in-service violated the anti-cutback rule where the participant's benefits were considered accrued benefits, and not early retirement benefits [Ryan v. Asbestos Workers Union Local 42 Pension Fund, 2002 WL 90976 (3d Cir. 2002)]; and another court decided that, where an employee who had been receiving early retirement benefits was reemployed, then retired again, his retirement benefits could not be reduced under a plan amendment by the actuarial value of the early retirement benefits he had already received because the amendment violated the anti-cutback rule. [Michael v. Riverside Cement Co. Pension Plan, 2001 WL 1078738 (9th Cir. 2001)] Another court concluded that an employer violated the anti-cutback rule when it amended its plan to provide that continuous service at a former subsidiary would no longer count toward early retirement. [Adams v. Bowater, Inc., 2003 U.S. Dist. LEXIS 9234 (D. Me. 2003), and 2003 U.S. Dist. LEXIS 21729 (D. Me. 2003)] A plan's prospective elimination of a death benefit for its participants did not violate the anti-cutback rule, one court held, because the death benefit was not an accrued benefit or retirement-type subsidy (see Q 9:33) protected from elimination by the anti-cutback rule. [Kerber v. Qwest Pension Plan, 2009 WL 2096221 (10th Cir. 2009)]

One court concluded that a suspension, as opposed to a decrease, elimination, or reduction, did not violate the anti-cutback rule. [Spacek v. Maritime Ass'n, 134 F.3d 283 (5th Cir. 1998); *see also* Whisman v. Robbins, 55 F.3d 1140 (6th Cir. 1995)] However, the United States Supreme Court held that a plan amendment that expanded the types of postretirement employment that required the suspension of early retirement benefit payments when applied to suspend benefit payments to participants who had retired prior to the amendment violated the anti-cutback rule. [Central Laborers' Pension Fund v. Heinz, 541 U.S. 739 (2004)] IRS has released guidance permitting plans to cure potentially disqualifying amendments relating to the United States Supreme Court's decision in *Central Laborers' Pension Fund v. Heinz*. The guidance provides relief from the risk of disqualification from a suspension of benefits amendment that is impermissible under the Court's decision. To be applicable for relief, the plan must be amended and take action to correct the impermissible elimination or reduction of an early retirement benefit, a retirement-type subsidy, or an optional form of benefit. Concurrent with the release of the guidance, IRS published on its website an "Example to Illustrate Heinz Revenue Procedure Compliance," which describes retroactive correction for four participants. [Rev. Proc. 2005-23, 2005-1 C.B. 991] Subsequently, IRS extended the deadline to comply with the relief provisions to January 1, 2007. [Rev. Proc. 2005-76, 2005-2 C.B. 1139] Subsequent to the Supreme Court's decision, one court ruled that the decision required a pension plan to restore a plan participant's wrongfully suspended early retirement benefits to the date of their original suspension, not just to the date of the Supreme Court decision. In addition, the court ruled that the plan could not rely on the relief provisions of Revenue Procedure 2005-23 to do otherwise. [Swede v. Rochester Carpenters Pension Fund, 2006 WL 3000967 (2d Cir. 2006)] See Q 9:33 for later developments concerning the United States Supreme Court decision.

A plan could not offset the hypothetically appreciated value of a participant's prior single-sum distribution against pension benefits for employees who were rehired prior to the issuance of a summary plan description (SPD; see Q 22:1) notifying participants of the use of a "phantom account" in computing offset amounts. Thus, use of the phantom account method violated the anti-cutback rule and could not be used to reduce pension benefits of employees rehired before the plan amendment date. [Frommert v. Conkright, 433 F.3d 254 (2d Cir. 2006); *see also* Miller v. Xerox Corp. Retirement Income Guarantee Plan, 447 F.3d 728 (9th Cir. 2006)] However, the same court ruled that plan participants knowingly and voluntarily waived their pension rights when they signed a release form, and the fact that the amount of the retirement benefits to which the participants were entitled was uncertain did not render the releases unenforceable. [Frommert v. Conkright, 535 F.3d 111 (2d Cir. 2008)] In the continuing saga, the United States Supreme Court reversed the second circuit and held that, with regard to the plan administrator's interpretation of the phantom account as it related to the rehired employees, the plan administrator should have been given a second chance to correct this single honest mistake. In effect, a plan interpretation by the administrator with discretionary authority to interpret the plan should be accorded deference, even though the administrator's prior related interpretation was determined to be invalid. [Conkright v. Frommert, 130 S. Ct. 1640 (2010)] Another court held that a plan that was amended to suspend the retirement benefits of various retirees did not violate the anti-cutback rule because the amended terms consisted of essentially the same rules as applied under the old plan. [Herman v. Central States, Southeast and Southwest Areas Pension Fund, 423 F.3d 684 (7th Cir. 2005)] An employer established a plan that consisted of both an ESOP (see Q 28:1) portion and a 401(k) plan (see Q 27:1) portion. Participants who received employer securities were given a put option (see Q 28:70). The plan was amended and eliminated the put option from the 401(k) portion. The court concluded that the put option was an optional form of benefit and that its elimination violated the anti-cutback rule. [Goodin v. Innovative Technical Solutions, Inc., 2007 U.S. Dist. LEXIS 31320 (D. Hawaii 2007)]

In a case involving the sale of a subsidiary, the court held that the inability of the affected employees to continue to participate in the seller's plan was not an amendment reducing benefits. [Andes v. Ford Motor Co., 70 F.3d 1332 (D.C. Cir. 1995); *see also* McCay v. Siemens Corp., No. 06-12346 (11th Cir. 2007); Richardson v. Pension Plan of Bethlehem Steel Corp., 1997 U.S. App. LEXIS 9860 (9th Cir. 1997)] Another court concluded that changes made to the asset allocation of a plan's investments, first to a more conservative balance of equities and fixed income investments and then to a greater allocation to equity investments, did not constitute plan amendments for purposes of the anti-cutback rule. [Thompson v. Retirement Plan for Employees of S.C. Johnson Sons, Inc., 2009 WL 3245506 (D. Wis. 2009)] However, an amendment to a union welfare plan that conditioned the receipt of retiree health care benefits on forgoing a single-sum distribution option under the union's pension plan violated the anti-cutback rule by constructively amending the pension plan to reduce an accrued benefit. [Battoni, Jr. v. IBEW Local Union No. 102 Employee Pension Plan, 594 F.3d 230 (3d Cir. 2010)] Since the merger of two defined benefit plans was a plan amendment that was subject to the notice requirements (see Q 9:36), the failure to provide notice that an amendment reducing plan benefits was being adopted entitled the affected participants to benefits at a higher accrual rate. [Koenig v. Intercontinental Life Corp., No. 92-5758 (E.D. Pa. 1995)] Another court concluded that the anti-cutback rule was not violated when an employee's pension plan benefits were reduced by workers' compensation benefits. [Huppler v. Oscar Mayer Foods Corp., No. 93-3765 (7th Cir. 1994)]

An employer that amended its defined benefit plan to change the definition of normal retirement age under the plan from age 65 to age 67 did not violate the requirements relating to normal retirement age, benefit accruals, or vesting (see Qs 9:1, 9:2, 9:13). The amended plan, which used age 67 for determining the level of benefits but maintained age 65 for purposes of benefit accruals and vesting satisfied the benefit accrual and vesting requirements and did not violate the anti-cutback rule. [Lindsay v. Thiokol Corp., 1997 U.S. App. LEXIS 7904 (10th Cir. 1997)] A multiemployer plan (see Q 29:2) board of trustees' action to amend the plan definition of "final average earnings" and apply it to plan retirees constituted a breach of fiduciary duty because such an act reduced benefits and impaired the vested right of retirees to receive benefits under the plan. [Walker v. Board of Trustees, Reg'l Transp. Dist. & Amalgamated Transit Union Div. 1001 Pension Fund, No. 02-1173 (10th Cir. 2003)]

In a novel case, the court determined that the employer did not violate the anti-cutback rule by failing to terminate a group of employees who would have received enhanced benefits under the employer's plan had they been terminated by a certain date. [Bodine v. Employers Cas. Co, 352 F.3d 245 (5th Cir. 2003)]

A court has allowed a class action to proceed against PBGC (see Q 25:10). The action is based on PBGC's alleged violations of the anti-cutback rule. The court held that requiring the participants to exhaust their administrative remedies under the plan was not a prerequisite to judicial review where the claim involved a statutory violation of ERISA. [Coleman v. PBGC, 2000 WL 527010 (D.D.C. 2000)]

One court has concluded that the statutory limitation period for claims alleging that plan amendments reduced accrued benefits did not commence until such time as a clear repudiation of the benefits occurred. [Romero v. The Allstate Corp., 404 F.3d 212 (3d Cir. 2005)]

IRS representatives have opined that a profit sharing plan amendment adding a requirement of spousal consent for a single-sum distribution (see Qs 10:6,

10:21) with regard to pre-existing account balances does not violate the anti-cutback rule. IRS has announced its intention to issue proposed regulations that will provide guidance on benefits that are treated as early retirement benefits and retirement-type subsidies for purposes of the anti-cutback rule. [IRS Notice 2003-10, 2003-1 C.B. 369] In an August 7, 2007, letter from the IRS Assistant Secretary for Tax Policy to the ranking member of the House Ways and Means Committee, the position of IRS was stated to be that IRS would not challenge a plan amendment as a prohibited cutback if the amendment has the same applicable effective date as another amendment, and the net effect of the two amendments does not involve a prohibited cutback.

For discussions of new rules relating to the anti-cutback rule, see Qs 6:12, 9:27, 10:62, and 10:64; for a discussion of the effect of the increase of benefit and contribution limits on the anti-cutback rule, see Q 6:32; and, for a discussion of the special rule applicable to an employee stock ownership plan (ESOP) of an S corporation, see Q 28:2.

Q 9:26   Can an accrued benefit decrease because of increasing age or service?

A defined benefit plan see (Q 2:3) will not satisfy the accrued benefit (see Q 9:2) requirements if a participant's accrued benefit is reduced on account of any increase in age or service. This prohibition does not apply to benefits under the plan commencing before entitlement to Social Security benefits if the plan benefits (1) do not exceed the Social Security benefit and (2) terminate when the Social Security benefits commence. [I.R.C. § 411(b)(1)(G); ERISA §§ 204(b)(1)(G), 204(b)(l)(H); Treas. Reg. §§ 1.411(a)-7(c)(4), 1.411(b)-1(d)(3)]

For example, a defined benefit plan provides for an annual retirement benefit equal to 3 percent of average annual compensation (AAC) multiplied by the participant's years of service and the plan defines AAC as the participant's average annual compensation during the three consecutive years during the participant's last ten years of service that produces the highest average. IRS representatives have opined that, if the definition of AAC causes a reduction in a participant's accrued benefit, the prohibition against reduction will be violated. Presumably, this could occur when a participant's highest years of compensation precede, in whole or in part, the last ten years of service.

A court has determined that an employer violated the age discrimination provisions of ERISA when it amended its defined benefit plans by (1) adopting a pension equity plan, under which a participant's accrued benefits were reduced on account of age and the rate of a participant's benefit accruals were reduced because of the attainment of a certain age, and (2) subsequently converting the plan to a cash balance plan (see Qs 2:23, 10:63), under which employees' accrued benefits decreased as the employees became older. [Cooper v. IBM Personal Pension Plan, 274 F. Supp. 2d 1010 (S.D. Ill. 2003); *but see* Godinez v. CBS Corp., 2003 U.S. App. LEXIS 23923 (9th Cir. 2003)] After much discussion and controversy, the seventh circuit reversed the district court and held that IBM's cash balance plan did not violate the age discrimination rules. [Cooper v. IBM Personal Pension Plan, 457 F.3d 636 (7th Cir. 2006)] Other courts have also concluded that a cash balance plan conversion did not violate the age-discrimination rules. [Jensen v. Solvay Chemicals, Inc., 2010 WL 3479245 (10th Cir. 2010); Engers v. AT&T Corp., 2010 WL 2326211 (D. N.J. 2010); Rosenblatt v. United Way of Greater Houston, 2008 WL 5396291 (S.D. Tex. 2008); Drutis v. Rand McNally & Co., 499 F.3d 608 (6th Cir. 2007); Register v. PNC Financial Services Group, Inc.; 477 F.3d 56 (3d Cir. 2007); Tootle v. ARINC, Inc., 2004 WL 1285894 (D. Md. 2004)]

For a discussion of proposed regulations applying the age-discrimination rules to cash balance plans, see Q 9:27.

Q 9:27   How do the age-discrimination rules apply to cash balance plans?

The rate of benefit accrual under a defined benefit plan (see Q 2:3) cannot be reduced because of the attainment of any age (see Qs 2:23, 9:26, 10:63). [I.R.C. § 411(b)(1)(H)] Both ERISA and the Age Discrimination in Employment Act (ADEA) have similar provisions that prohibit discrimination in employee benefit plans on the basis of age. [ERISA § 204(b)(1)(H); ADEA § 4(i)]

See Qs 2:24 and 9:3 for additional discussions of cash balance plans.

Q 9:28   Has IRS made changes to the anti-cutback rule?

A qualified retirement plan is precluded from adopting an amendment that has the effect of eliminating optional forms of benefit (see Q 9:25); however, IRS is authorized to provide exceptions to the anti-cutback rule. [I.R.C. § 411(d)(6)(B)]

IRS has exercised its authority to address a number of concerns in this area. IRS believed that any such relief should take into account the interests of participants and the practical needs of employers in effectively and efficiently providing retirement benefits for their employees, including the need to adapt plans to changing circumstances. IRS recognized that the accumulation of a variety of payment choices under plans may increase the cost and complexity of plan operations. For example, an employer that initially adopted a prototype plan (see Q 2:27) may be using a different prototype plan that offers a different array of distribution forms. The requirement to preserve the preexisting optional forms for benefits accrued up to the date of change in the prototype plan may present significant practical problems in certain cases.

Similar issues arise where employers merge with or acquire other businesses. These employers often face issues of whether to maintain separate plans, terminate one or more of the plans, or merge the plans. If an employer chooses to merge the plans, the resulting plan may accumulate a wide variety of optional forms, some of which may differ in insignificant ways or may entail special administrative costs.

The primary focus of the final regulations issued by IRS is on defined contribution plans (see Q 2:2), and the provisions of the regulations relating to elimination of alternative forms of payment are limited to defined contribution plans. Defined benefit plans (see Q 2:3) have special characteristics, including benefit payment calculation specifications, early retirement benefits, and other retirement-type subsidies (see Qs 9:33, 9:34). Features such as these are not characteristic of defined contribution plans and provide important protections to participants.

The final regulations became effective September 6, 2000, and generally apply to plan amendments adopted and effective on or after September 6, 2000. [Treas. Reg. § 1.411(d)-4, Q&A-2(e)(1)(ii), Q&A-2(e)(4), Q&A-3(c)(1)(ii); Ann. 2000-71, 2000-2 C.B. 456]

For a discussion of the final regulations, see Qs 9:29 through 9:32. Furthermore, a defined contribution plan to which benefits are transferred will not be treated as reducing a participant's or beneficiary's accrued benefit even though it does not provide all of the forms of distribution previously available under the transferor plan if (1) the plan receives from another defined contribution plan a direct transfer of the participant's or beneficiary's benefit accrued under the transferor plan, or the plan results from a merger or other transaction that has the effect of a direct transfer (including consolidations of benefits attributable to different employers within a multiple employer plan), (2) the terms of both the transferor plan and the transferee plan authorize the transfer, (3) the transfer occurs pursuant to a voluntary election by the participant or beneficiary that is made after the participant or beneficiary received a notice describing the consequences of making the election, and (4) the transferee plan allows the participant or beneficiary to receive a distribution of benefits under the transferee plan in the form of a single-sum distribution. The rules relating to survivor annuities (see Q 10:1) are not modified, so that a plan that is a transferee of a plan subject to the joint and survivor rules is also subject to those rules (see Q 10:6). [I.R.C. § 411(d)(6)(D)]

EGTRRA 2001 (see Q 1:21) added a new Code section to provide that a defined contribution plan will not violate the anti-cutback rule merely because of the elimination of a form of distribution previously available if (1) a single-sum payment is available to the participant at the same time or times as the form of distribution being eliminated and (2) such single-sum payment is based on the same or greater portion of the participant's account as the form of distribution being eliminated. [I.R.C. § 411(d)(6)(E)] To implement the EGTRRA 2001 change, IRS has issued final regulations (see Qs 9:29, 9:30). [Treas. Reg. § 1.411(d)-4, Q&A-2(e)]

EGTRRA 2001 also amended Section 411(d)(6)(B) directing IRS to issue regulations providing that subparagraph (B) will not apply to any plan amendment that reduces or eliminates benefits or subsidies that create significant burdens or complexities for the plan and plan participants, unless such amendment adversely affects the rights of any participant in a more than *de minimis* manner. [I.R.C. § 411(d)(6)(B)] IRS requested comments on which optional forms of benefit (including early retirement benefits and retirement-type subsidies) should be permitted to be eliminated and the circumstances under which they should be permitted to be eliminated. [IRS Notice 2002-46, 2002-2 C.B. 96] IRS responded by issuing proposed regulations (see Qs 9:33, 9:34).

Q 9:29 What rule applies if a participant can receive a distribution in cash or in the form of an annuity contract?

The right of a participant to receive a benefit in the form of cash payments from a plan and the right of a participant to receive that benefit in the form of the distribution of an annuity contract that provides for cash payments that are identical in all respects to the cash payments from the plan except with respect to the source of the payments are not separate optional forms of benefit (see Q 10:45). Therefore, for example, if a plan includes an optional form of benefit under which benefits are distributed in the medium of an annuity contract that provides for cash payments, that optional form of benefit may be modified by a plan amendment that substitutes cash payments from the plan for the annuity contract, where those cash payments from the plan are identical to the cash payments payable from the annuity contract in all respects except with respect to the source of the payments (see Q 9:30). The anti-cutback rule (see Q 9:25) may not be avoided by the use of annuity contracts. Thus, protected benefits (see Q 10:45) already accrued may not be eliminated or reduced merely because a plan uses annuity contracts to provide such benefits, without regard to whether the plan, a participant, or a beneficiary of a participant holds the contract or whether such annuity contracts are purchased as a result of the termination of the plan. However, to the extent that an annuity contract constitutes payment of benefits in a particular optional form elected by the participant, the plan does not violate the anti-cutback rule merely because it provides that other optional forms are no longer available with respect to such participant. [Treas. Reg. § 1.411(d)-4, Q&A-2(a)(3)(ii)(A)]

> **Example 1.** A profit sharing plan that is being terminated satisfies the anti-cutback rule only if the plan makes available to participants annuity contracts that provide for all protected benefits under the plan that may not otherwise be reduced or eliminated. Thus, if such a plan provided for a single-sum distribution upon attainment of early retirement age and a provision for payment in the form of ten equal annual installments, the plan would satisfy the anti-cutback rule only if the participants had the opportunity to elect to have their benefits provided under an annuity contract that provided for the same single-sum distribution upon the attainment of the participant's early retirement age and the same ten-year installment optional form of benefit.

> **Example 2.** A defined benefit plan permits each participant who separates from service on or after age 62 to receive a qualified joint and survivor annuity (QJSA; see Q 10:8) or a single life annuity commencing 45 days after termination from employment. For a participant who separates from service before age 62, payments under these optional forms of benefit commence 45 days after the participant's 62nd birthday. Under the plan, a participant is to elect among these optional forms of benefit during the 180-day period preceding the annuity starting date (see Q 10:3). However, during such

period, a participant may defer both benefit commencement and the election of a particular benefit form to any permissible later date. In January 2011, the employer decides to terminate the plan as of July 1, 2011. The plan will fail to satisfy the anti-cutback rule unless the optional forms of benefit provided under the plan are preserved under the annuity contract purchased on plan termination. Thus, such annuity contract must provide a participant the same optional benefit commencement rights that the plan provided. In addition, such contract must provide the same election rights with respect to such benefit options. This is the case even if, for example, in conjunction with the termination, the employer amended the plan to permit participants to elect a QJSA, single life annuity, or single-sum distribution commencing on July 1, 2011.

A defined contribution plan (see Q 2:2) does not violate the anti-cutback rule merely because the plan is amended to eliminate or restrict the ability of a participant to receive payment of accrued benefits under a particular optional form of benefit if, after the plan amendment is effective with respect to the participant, the alternative forms of payment available to the participant include payment in a single-sum distribution form that is otherwise identical to the optional form of benefit that is being eliminated or restricted (see Q 9:30). [Treas. Reg. § 1.411(d)-4, Q&A-2(e)(1)]

Q 9:30 What is an otherwise identical single-sum distribution?

A single-sum distribution form is otherwise identical to an optional form of benefit (see Q 10:45) that is eliminated or restricted only if the single-sum distribution form is identical in all respects to the eliminated or restricted optional form of benefit (or would be identical except that it provides greater rights to the participant) except with respect to the timing of payments after commencement. For example, a single-sum distribution form is not otherwise identical to a specified installment form of benefit if the single-sum distribution form is not available for distribution on the date on which the installment form would have been available for commencement, is not available in the same medium of distribution as the installment form, or imposes any condition of eligibility that did not apply to the installment form. However, an otherwise identical distribution form need not retain rights or features of the optional form of benefit that is eliminated or restricted to the extent that those rights or features would not be protected from elimination or restriction (see Q 9:54). [Treas. Reg. § 1.411(d)-4, Q&A-2(e)(2)]

Example. Jason is a participant in Plan A, a profit sharing plan with a calendar plan year that is invested in mutual funds. The distribution forms available to Jason under Plan A include a distribution of his vested account balance in the form of distribution of various annuity contract forms (including a single life annuity and a joint and survivor annuity). The annuity payments under the annuity contract forms begin as of the first day of the month following Jason's termination of employment or as of the first day of any subsequent month. Jason has not previously elected payment of benefits in the form of a life annuity, and Plan A is not a direct or indirect transferee of any plan that is a defined benefit plan or a defined contribution plan that is subject to the minimum funding standards (see Q 10:6). Plan A provides that distributions on the death of a participant are made to the surviving spouse. On September 2, 2011, Plan A is amended so that, effective for payments that begin on or after November 1, 2011, Jason is no longer entitled to any distribution in the form of the distribution of an annuity contract. However, after the amendment is effective, Jason is entitled to receive a single-sum cash distribution of his vested account balance payable as of the first day of the month following his termination of employment or as of the first day of any subsequent month. Plan A does not violate the anti-cutback rule (see Q 9:25) merely because, as of November 1, 2011, the plan amendment has eliminated Jason's option to receive a distribution in any of the various annuity contract forms previously available.

For the effective date rules, see Q 9:28.

Q 9:31   How are in-kind distributions treated?

If a defined contribution plan (see Q 2:2) includes an optional form of benefit (see Q 10:45) under which benefits are distributed in the form of marketable securities, other than securities of the employer, that optional form of benefit may be modified by a plan amendment that substitutes cash for the marketable securities as the medium of distribution. Marketable securities is defined in Section 731(c)(2), and securities of the employer include securities of a parent or subsidiary corporation of the employer corporation. [I.R.C. § 402(e)(4)(E)(ii); Treas. Reg. § 1.411(d)-4, Q&A-2(b)(2)(iii)(A)]

If a defined contribution plan includes an optional form of benefit under which benefits are distributable to a participant in a medium other than cash, the plan may be amended to limit the types of property in which distributions may be made to the participant to the types of property specified in the amendment. For this purposes, the types of property specified in the amendment must include all types of property (other than marketable securities that are not securities of the employer) that are allocated to the participant's account on the effective date of the amendment and in which the participant would be able to receive a distribution immediately before the effective date of the amendment if a distributable event occurred. In addition, a plan amendment may provide that the participant's right to receive a distribution in the form of specific types of property is limited to the property allocated to the participant's account at the time of distribution that consists of property of those specified types. [Treas. Reg. § 1.411(d)-4, Q&A-2(b)(2)(iii)(B)]

If a plan includes an optional form of benefit under which benefits are distributed in specified property, that optional form of benefit may be modified for distributions after plan termination by substituting cash for the specified property as the medium of distribution to the extent that, on plan termination, an employee has the opportunity to receive the optional form of benefit in the form of the specified property. This exception is not available, however, if the employer that maintains the terminating plan also maintains another plan that provides an optional form of benefit under which benefits are distributed in the specified property. [Treas. Reg. § 1.411(d)-4, Q&A-2(b)(2)(iii)(C)]

Example 1. Jennifer Co., Inc. maintains a profit sharing plan under which participants may direct the investment of their accounts. One investment option available to participants is a fund invested in common stock of the employer. The plan provides that the participant has the right to distribution in the form of cash upon termination of employment. In addition, the plan provides that, to the extent a participant's account is invested in the employer stock fund, the participant may receive an in-kind distribution of employer stock upon termination of employment. On October 8, 2010, the plan is amended, effective on January 1, 2011, to remove the fund invested in employer common stock as an investment option under the plan and to provide the stock held in the fund to be sold. The amendment permits participants to elect how the sale proceeds will be allocated among the remaining investment options and provides for amounts not so reallocated as of January 1, 2011, to be allocated to a specified investment option. The plan does not violate the anti-cutback rule solely on account of the plan amendment relating to the elimination of the employer stock investment option, which is not a protected benefit (see Q 9:54). Moreover, because the plan did not provide for distributions of employer securities except to the extent participants' accounts were invested in the employer stock fund, the plan is not required operationally to offer distributions of employer securities following the amendment. In addition, the plan would not violate the anti-cutback rule on account of a further plan amendment, effective after the plan has ceased to provide for an employer stock fund investment option (and participants' accounts have ceased to be invested in employer securities), to eliminate the right to a distribution in the form of employer stock.

Example 2. Benjamin Corp. maintains a profit sharing plan under which a participant, upon termination of employment, may elect to receive benefits in a single-sum distribution either in cash or in kind. The plan's investments are limited to a fund invested in employer stock, a fund invested in XYZ mutual funds (which are marketable securities), and a fund invested in shares of PQR limited partnership (which are not marketable securities). The following alternative plan amendments would not cause the plan to violate the anti-cutback rule.

1. A plan amendment that limits noncash distributions to a participant on termination of employment to a distribution of employer stock and shares of PQR limited partnership.

2. A plan amendment that limits noncash distributions to a participant on termination of employment to a distribution of employer stock and shares of PQR limited partnership, and that also provides that only participants with employer stock allocated to their accounts as of the effective date of the amendment have the right to distributions in the form of employer stock, and that only participants with shares of PQR limited partnership allocated to their accounts as of the effective date of the amendment have the right to distributions in the form of shares of PQR limited partnership.

To comply with the plan amendment, the plan administrator (see Q 20:1) retains a list of participants with employer stock allocated to their accounts as of the effective date of the amendment and a list of participants with shares of PQR limited partnership allocated to their accounts as of the effective date of the amendment.

3. A plan amendment that limits noncash distributions to a participant on termination of employment to a distribution of employer stock and shares of PQR limited partnership to the extent that those assets are allocated to the participant's account at the time of the distribution.

4. A plan amendment that limits noncash distributions to a participant on termination of employment to a distribution of employer stock and shares of PQR limited partnership, and that provides that only participants with employer stock allocated to their accounts as of the effective date of the amendment have the right to distributions in the form of employer stock, and that only participants with shares of PQR limited partnership allocated to their accounts as of the effective date of the amendment have the right to distributions in the form of shares of PQR limited partnership, and that further provides that the distribution of that stock or those shares is available only to the extent that those assets are allocated to those participants' accounts at the time of the distribution. To comply with the plan amendment, the plan administrator retains a list of participants with employer stock allocated to their accounts as of the effective date of the amendment and a list of participants with shares of PQR limited partnership allocated to their accounts as of the effective date of the amendment.

Example 3. Jason Ltd. maintains a stock bonus plan (see Q 2:13) under which a participant, upon termination of employment, may elect to receive benefits in a single-sum distribution in employer stock. This is the only plan maintained by the employer under which distributions in employer stock are available, and the employer decides to terminate the stock bonus plan. If the plan makes available a single-sum distribution in employer stock on plan termination, the plan will not violate the anti-cutback rule solely because the optional form of benefit providing a single-sum distribution in employer stock on termination of employment is modified to provide that such distribution is available only in cash.

These rules are effective for plan amendments adopted and effective on or after September 6, 2000. [Treas. Reg. § 1.411(d)-4, Q&A-2(e)(4)]

Q 9:32   Does the transfer of benefits between defined benefit plans and defined contribution plans (or similar transactions) violate the anti-cutback rule?

Section 411(d)(6) protected benefits (see Q 10:45) may not be eliminated by reason of transfer or any transaction amending or having the effect of amending a plan or plans to transfer benefits. Thus, for example, generally, an employer who maintains a money purchase pension plan (see Q 2:4) that provides for a single-sum optional form of benefit (see Q 10:45) may not establish another plan that does not provide for this optional form of benefit and transfer participants' account balances to the new plan. [Treas. Reg. § 1.411(d)-4, Q&A-3(a)(1)]

The defined benefit feature of an employee's benefit under a defined benefit plan (see Q 2:3) and the separate account feature of an employee's benefit under a defined contribution plan (see Q 2:2) are Section 411(d)(6) protected benefits. Thus, for example, the elimination of the defined benefit feature of an employee's benefit under a defined benefit plan through transfer of benefits from a defined benefit plan to a defined contribution plan or plans will violate the anti-cutback rule (see Q 9:25). [Treas. Reg. § 1.411(d)-4, Q&A-3(a)(2)]

In general, except as provided below, a participant may not elect to waive Section 411(d)(6) protected benefits. Thus, for example, the elimination of the defined benefit feature of a participant's benefit under a defined benefit plan by reason of a transfer of such benefits to a defined contribution plan pursuant to a participant election, at a time when the benefit is not distributable to the participant, violates the anti-cutback rule. [Treas. Reg. § 1.411(d)-4, Q&A-3(a)(3)]

A direct rollover (see Q 34:17) that is paid to a qualified retirement plan is not a transfer of assets and liabilities (see Q 9:55) and is not a transfer of benefits for purposes of applying the anti-cutback rule. Therefore, for example, if a direct rollover is made to another qualified retirement plan, the receiving plan is not required to provide, with respect to amounts paid to it in a direct rollover, the same optional forms of benefit that were provided under the plan that made the direct rollover. [Treas. Reg. §§ 1.401(a)(31)-1, Q&A-14, 1.411(d)-4, Q&A-3(a)(4)]

Generally, an elective transfer of a participant's entire benefit between qualified defined contribution plans (other than any direct rollover) that results in the elimination or reduction of Section 411(d)(6) protected benefits does not violate the anti-cutback rule if the following requirements are met:

1. The plan from which the benefits are transferred must provide that the transfer is conditioned upon a voluntary, fully-informed election by the participant to transfer the participant's entire benefit to the other qualified defined contribution plan. As an alternative to the transfer, the participant must be offered the opportunity to retain the participant's Section 411(d)(6) protected benefits under the plan (or, if the plan is terminating, to receive any optional form of benefit for which the participant is eligible under the plan).

2. To the extent the benefits are transferred from a money purchase pension plan, the transferee plan must be a money purchase pension plan; to the extent the benefits being transferred are part of a qualified cash-or-deferred arrangement (CODA; see Q 27:2), the benefits must be transferred to a qualified CODA; and to the extent the benefits being transferred are part of an employee stock ownership plan (ESOP; see Q 28:1), the benefits must be transferred to another ESOP. Benefits transferred from a profit sharing plan other than from a qualified CODA, or from a stock

bonus plan other than an ESOP, may be transferred to any type of defined contribution plan.

3. The transfer must be made either in connection with an asset or stock acquisition, merger, or other similar transaction involving a change in employer of the employees of a trade or business (i.e., an acquisition or disposition) or in connection with the participant's change in employment status to an employment status with respect to which the participant is not entitled to additional allocations under the transferor plan.

[Treas. Reg. §§ 1.410(b)-2(f), 1.411(d)-4, Q&A-3(b)(1)]

An elective transfer described above is a transfer of assets or liabilities and, thus, must satisfy the applicable requirements. In addition, elective transfer rules only provide relief for purposes of the anti-cutback rule; thus, a transfer must satisfy all other applicable qualification requirements. For example, if the survivor annuity requirements (see Q 10:1) apply to the plan from which the benefits are transferred, but do not otherwise apply to the receiving plan, the survivor annuity requirements must be met with respect to the transferred benefits under the receiving plan. In addition, the vesting provisions under the receiving plan must satisfy the requirements with respect to the amounts transferred (see Q 9:7). [Treas. Reg. § 1.411(d)-4, Q&A-3(b)(2)]

A right to a transfer of benefits from a plan pursuant to the elective transfer rules is another right or feature, the availability of which is subject to the nondiscrimination requirements (see Q 4:20). However, for purposes of applying the nondiscrimination rules, the following conditions will be disregarded in determining the employees to whom the other right or feature is available:

1. A condition restricting the availability of the transfer to benefits of participants who are transferred to a different employer in connection with a specified asset or stock disposition, merger, or other similar transaction involving a change in employer of the employees of a trade or business, or in connection with any such disposition, merger, or other similar transaction.

2. A condition restricting the availability of the transfer to benefits of participants who have a change in employment status to an employment status with respect to which the participant is not entitled to additional allocations under the transferor plan.

[Treas. Reg. §§ 1.410(b)-2(f), 1.411(d)-4, Q&A-3(b)(3)]

An elective transfer of a participant's benefits between qualified plans that results in the elimination or reduction of Section 411(d)(6) protected benefits does not violate the anti-cutback rules if:

1. The transfer occurs at a time at which the participant's benefits are distributable;

2. For a transfer that occurs on or after January 1, 2002, the transfer occurs at a time at which the participant is not eligible to receive an immediate distribution of the participant's entire nonforfeitable accrued benefit

(see Qs 9:1, 9:2) in a single-sum distribution that would consist entirely of an eligible rollover distribution;

3. The voluntary election requirements are met;

4. The participant is fully vested (see Q 9:1) in the transferred benefit in the transferee plan;

5. In the case of a transfer from a defined contribution plan to a defined benefit plan, the defined benefit plan provides a minimum benefit, for each participant whose benefits are transferred, equal to the benefit, expressed as an annuity payable at normal retirement age (see Q 10:55) that is derived solely on the basis of the amount transferred with respect to such participant; and

6. The amount of the benefit transferred, together with the amount of any contemporaneous direct rollover to the transferee plan, equals the entire nonforfeitable accrued benefit under the transferor plan of the participant whose benefit is being transferred, calculated to be at least the greater of the single-sum distribution provided for under the plan for which the participant is eligible (if any) or the present value of the participant's accrued benefit payable at normal retirement age (recalculated by using interest and mortality assumptions that satisfy the present value requirements (see Q 6:18)).

[Treas. Reg. § 1.411(d)-4, Q&A-3(c)(1)]

An elective transfer of distributable benefits generally is treated as a distribution. For example, the transfer is subject to the cash-out rules (see Q 10:61), the early termination requirements (see Q 25:8), and the survivor annuity requirements. However, such a transfer is not treated as a distribution for purposes of the minimum distribution requirements (see chapter 11). A right to a transfer of benefits from a plan pursuant to these elective transfer rules is an optional form of benefit, the availability of which is subject to the nondiscrimination requirements. [Treas. Reg. § 1.411(d)-4, Q&A-3(c)(2)]

For these elective transfer purposes, a participant's benefits are distributable on a particular date if, on that date, the participant is eligible, under the terms of the plan from which the benefits are transferred, to receive an immediate distribution of these benefits (e.g., in the form of an immediately commencing annuity) from that plan under provisions of the plan. [Treas. Reg. § 1.411(d)-4, Q&A-3(c)(3)]

The elective transfer rules are applicable for transfers made on or after September 6, 2000. [Treas. Reg. § 1.411(d)-4, Q&A-3(d)]

Q 9:33 How are early retirement benefits, retirement-type subsidies, and optional forms of benefit affected by the anti-cutback rule?

IRS has issued final regulations that implement the provisions of EGTRRA 2001 (see Q 1:21) by permitting the elimination of early retirement benefits, retirement-type subsidies, and optional forms of benefit under a plan that create significant burdens or complexities for the plan and its participants, but only if the elimination does not adversely affect the rights of any participant in a more than *de minimis* manner. These rules relating to the permissible elimination of Section 411(d)(6)(B) protected benefits are in addition to the rules permitting elimination of Section 411(d)(6) protected benefits (see Qs 9:28-9:32, 10:45).

The regulations also take into account and respond to certain judicial decisions (see Q 9:25). [Board of Trustees of the Sheet Metal Workers' Nat'l Pension Fund v. Comm'r, 318 F.3d 599 (4th Cir. 2003); Michael v. Riverside Cement Co. Pension Plan, 2001 WL 1078738 (9th Cir. 2001); Bellas v. CBS, Inc., 221 F.3d 517 (3d Cir. 2000)] For example, the regulations provide that the anti-cutback rule (see Q 9:25) applies to a participant's entire accrued benefit (see Q 9:2) without regard to whether any portion of that accrued benefit is accrued before a participant's severance from employment or is included in the accrued benefit of the participant pursuant to a plan amendment adopted after the participant's severance from employment. This is contrary to the analysis in *Board of Trustees of the Sheet Metal Workers' National Pension Fund v. Commissioner*. IRS also issued final regulations reflecting the holding in *Central Laborers' Pension Fund v. Heinz* (see Q 9:25) that address the interaction of the vesting rules with the anti-cutback rules taking into account the United States Supreme Court's decision. The final regulations provide that a plan amendment that decreases accrued benefits, or otherwise places greater restrictions on the right to Section 411(d)(6) protected benefits, is a violation, even if the amendment merely adds a restriction or condition on receipt of Section 411(d)(6) protected benefits that is otherwise permitted under the vesting rules.

The final regulations retain the rules in the former and proposed regulations that provide that, for purposes of determining whether or not any participant's accrued benefit is decreased, all plan amendments affecting, directly or indirectly, the computation of accrued benefits are taken into account, and that, in determining whether a reduction has occurred, all amendments with the same applicable amendment date (the later of the adoption date or the effective date) are treated as one plan amendment, and would provide that these rules apply to Section 411(d)(6)(B) protected benefits as well. Thus, for example, if there are two amendments with the same applicable amendment date, and one amendment increases accrued benefits and the other amendment decreases the early retirement factors that are used to determine the early retirement annuity, the amendments are treated as one amendment and only violate the anti-cutback rule if the net dollar amount of any early retirement annuity, with respect to the accrued benefit of any participant as of the applicable amendment date, is lower on that applicable amendment date than it would have been without the two amendments. This is contrary to the analysis in *Michael v. Riverside Cement Co. Pension Plan*.

With respect to the final regulations, the following definitions are important:

1. *Actuarial present value*: Actuarial present value determined using reasonable actuarial assumptions. [Treas. Reg. §§ 1.401(a)(4)-12, 1.411(d)-3(g)(2)]

2. *Ancillary benefit*: (a) A social security supplement (other than a qualified social security supplement (QSUPP)) under a defined benefit plan (see

Q 2:3); (b) a benefit payable under a defined benefit plan in the event of disability (to the extent that the benefit exceeds the benefit otherwise payable), but only if the total benefit payable in the event of disability does not exceed the maximum qualified disability benefit; (c) a life insurance benefit; (d) a medical benefit; (e) a death benefit under a defined benefit plan other than a death benefit that is a part of an optional form of benefit; or (f) a plant shutdown benefit or other similar benefit in a defined benefit plan that does not continue past retirement age and does not affect the payment of the accrued benefit, but only to the extent that such plant shutdown benefit, or other similar benefit (if any), is permitted in a pension plan. [I.R.C. §§ 401(h), 411(a)(9); Treas. Reg. §§ 1.401-1(b)(1)(i), 1.401(a)(4)-12, 1.411(d)-3(g)(2)]

3. *Annuity commencement date*: The annuity starting date (see Q 10:3), except that, in the case of a retroactive annuity starting date (see Q 10:20), it means the date of the first payment of benefits pursuant to a participant election of a retroactive annuity starting date. [I.R.C. § 417(a)(7); Treas. Reg. §§ 1.411(d)-3(g)(3), 1.417(e)-1(b)(3)(iv)]

4. *Applicable amendment date*: With respect to a plan amendment, the later of the effective date of the amendment or the date the amendment is adopted. [Treas. Reg. § 1.411(d)-3(g)(4)]

5. *Core options*: (a) A straight life annuity generalized optional form under which the participant is entitled to a level life annuity with no benefit payable after the participant's death; (b) a 75 percent joint and contingent annuity generalized optional form under which the participant is entitled to a life annuity with a survivor annuity for any individual designated by the participant (including a nonspousal contingent annuitant) that is 75 percent of the amount payable during the participant's life; (c) a 10-year certain and life annuity generalized optional form under which the participant is entitled to a life annuity with a guarantee that payments will continue to any person designated by the participant for the remainder of a fixed period of ten years if the participant dies before the end of the 10-year period; and (d) the most valuable option for a participant with a short life expectancy. [Treas. Reg. § 1.411(d)-3(g)(5)(i)]

6. *Early retirement benefit*: The right, under the terms of a plan, to commence distribution of a retirement-type benefit at a particular date after severance from employment with the employer and before normal retirement age (see Q 10:55). Different early retirement benefits result from differences in terms relating to timing. [Treas. Reg. § 1.411(d)-3(g)(6)(i)]

7. *Optional form of benefit*: A distribution alternative (including the normal form of benefit) that is available under the plan with respect to benefits described in Section 411(d)(6)(A) or a distribution alternative with respect to a retirement-type benefit (see Q 10:45). [Treas. Reg. § 1.411(d)-3(g)(6)(ii)]

8. *Retirement-type benefit*: (a) The payment of a distribution alternative with respect to an accrued benefit or (b) the payment of any other benefit under a defined benefit plan (including a QSUPP) that is permitted to be

in a pension plan, continues after retirement, and is not an ancillary benefit. [Treas. Reg. § 1.411(d)-3(g)(6)(iii)]

9. *Retirement-type subsidy*: The excess, if any, of the actuarial present value of a retirement-type benefit over the actuarial present value of the accrued benefit commencing at normal retirement age or at actual commencement date, if later, with both such actuarial present values determined as of the date the retirement-type benefit commences. Examples of retirement-type subsidies include a subsidized early retirement benefit and a subsidized qualified joint and survivor annuity (QJSA; see Q 10:8). [Treas. Reg. § 1.411(d)-3(g)(6)(iv)]

10. *Subsidized early retirement benefit or early retirement subsidy*: The right, under the terms of a plan, to commence distribution of a retirement-type benefit at a particular date after severance from employment with the employer and before normal retirement age where the actuarial present value of the optional forms of benefit available to the participant under the plan at that annuity starting date exceeds the actuarial present value of the accrued benefit commencing at normal retirement age (with such actuarial present values determined as of the annuity starting date). Thus, an early retirement subsidy is an early retirement benefit that provides a retirement-type subsidy. [Treas. Reg. § 1.411(d)-3(g)(6)(v)]

11. *Eliminate; elimination; reduce; reduction*: When used in connection with a Section 411(d)(6)(B) protected benefit, to eliminate, or the elimination of, an optional form of benefit or an early retirement benefit and to reduce, or a reduction in, a retirement-type subsidy; and, when used in connection with a retirement-type subsidy, to reduce, or a reduction in, the amount of the subsidy. For these purposes, an elimination includes a reduction and a reduction includes an elimination. [Treas. Reg. § 1.411(d)-3(g)(7)]

12. *Generalized optional form*: A group of optional forms of benefit that are identical except for differences due to the actuarial factors that are used to determine the amount of the distributions under those optional forms of benefit and the annuity starting dates. [Treas. Reg. § 1.411(d)-3(g)(8)]

13. *Maximum QJSA explanation period*: The maximum number of days before an annuity starting date for a QJSA for which a written explanation relating to the QJSA would satisfy the timing requirements (see Qs 10:20, 10:29). [I.R.C. § 417(a)(3); Treas. Reg. §§ 1.411(d)-3(g)(9), 1.417(e)-1(b)(3)(ii); Prop. Treas. Reg. § 1.417(e)-1(b)(3)(ii)]

14. *Other right and feature*: See Q 4:20.

15. *Refund of employee contributions feature*: A feature with respect to an optional form of benefit that provides for employee contributions and interest thereon to be paid in a single sum at the annuity starting date with the remainder to be paid in another form beginning on that date. [Treas. Reg. § 1.411(d)-3(g)(11)]

16. *Retirement; retirement age*: For these purposes, the date of retirement is the annuity starting date. Thus, retirement age is a participant's age at the annuity starting date. [Treas. Reg. § 1.411(d)-3(g)(12)]

17. *Retroactive annuity starting date feature*: A feature with respect to an optional form of benefit under which the annuity starting date for the distribution occurs on or before the date the required written explanation is provided to the participant. [Treas. Reg. § 1.411(d)-3(g)(13)]

18. *Section 411(d)(6) protected benefit*: The accrued benefit of a participant as of the applicable amendment date for purposes of the anti-cutback rule and any Section 411(d)(6)(B) protected benefit. [Treas. Reg. § 1.411(d)-3(g)(14)]

19. *Section 411(d)(6)(B) protected benefit*: The portion of an early retirement benefit, a retirement-type subsidy, or an optional form of benefit attributable to the benefits accrued before the applicable amendment date. [Treas. Reg. § 1.411(d)-3(g)(15)]

20. *Social security leveling feature*: With respect to an optional form of benefit commencing prior to a participant's expected commencement of social security benefits that provides for a temporary period of higher payments that is designed to result in an approximately level amount of income when the participant's estimated benefits from social security are taken into account. [Treas. Reg. § 1.411(d)-3(g)(16)]

An annuity does not fail to be a core option (e.g., a joint and contingent annuity or a ten-year term certain and life annuity) as a result of differences to comply with applicable law, such as limitations on death benefits to comply with the incidental benefit requirement (see Q 11:28) or on account of the spousal consent rules (see Q 10:21). [Treas. Reg. § 1.411(d)-3(g)(5)(ii)]

The most valuable option for a participant with a short life expectancy is, for an annuity starting date, the optional form of benefit that is reasonably expected to result in payments that have the largest actuarial present value in the case of a participant who dies shortly after the annuity starting date, taking into account both payments due to the participant prior to the participant's death and any payments due after the participant's death. For this purpose, a plan is permitted to assume that the spouse of the participant is the same age as the participant. In addition, a plan is permitted to assume that the optional form of benefit that is the most valuable option for a participant with a short life expectancy when the participant is age 70½ also is the most valuable option for a participant with a short life expectancy at all older ages, and that the most valuable option for a participant with a short life expectancy at age 55 is the most valuable option for a participant with a short life expectancy at all younger ages. [Treas. Reg. § 1.411(d)-3(g)(5)(iii)(A)]

A plan is permitted to treat a single-sum distribution option with an actuarial present value that is not less than the actuarial present value of any optional form of benefit eliminated by the plan amendment as the most valuable option for a participant with a short life expectancy for all of a participant's annuity starting dates if such single-sum distribution option is available at all such dates, without regard to whether the option was available before the plan amendment. If a plan, before the amendment, does not offer a single-sum distribution option, the plan is permitted to treat a joint and contingent annuity with a continuation percentage that is at least 75 percent and that is at least as great as the highest continuation percentage available before the amendment as the most valuable option for a participant with a short life expectancy for all of a participant's annuity starting dates if such joint and contingent annuity is available at all such dates, without regard to whether the option was available before the plan amendment. If the plan before the amendment offers neither a single-sum distribution or option nor a joint and contingent annuity with a continuation percentage of at least 75 percent, a plan is permitted to treat a term certain and life annuity with a term certain period of no less than 15 years as the most valuable option for a participant with a short life expectancy for each annuity starting date if such 15-year term certain and life annuity is available at all annuity starting dates, without regard to whether the option was available before the plan amendment. [Treas. Reg. § 1.411(d)-3(g)(5)(iii)(B)]

Different optional forms of benefit exist if a distribution alternative is not payable on substantially the same terms as another distribution alternative. The relevant terms include all terms affecting the value of the optional form, such as the method of benefit calculation and the actuarial factors or assumptions used to determine the amount distributed. Thus, for example, different optional forms of benefit may result from differences in terms relating to the payment schedule, timing, commencement, medium of distribution (e.g., in cash or in kind), election rights, differences in eligibility requirements, or the portion of the benefit to which the distribution alternative applies. Likewise, differences in the normal retirement ages of employees or in the form in which the accrued benefit of employees is payable at normal retirement age under a plan are taken into account in determining whether a distribution alternative constitutes one or more optional forms of benefit. [Treas. Reg. § 1.411(d)-3(g)(6)(ii)(A)]

If a death benefit is payable after the annuity starting date for a specific optional form of benefit and the same death benefit would not be provided if another optional form of benefit were elected by a participant, then that death benefit is part of the specific optional form of benefit and is thus protected under Section 411(d)(6)(B). A death benefit is not treated as part of a specific optional form of benefit merely because the same benefit is not provided to a participant who has received the entire accrued benefit prior to death. For example, a $5,000 death benefit that is payable to all participants except any participant who has received the accrued benefit in a single-sum distribution is not part of a specific optional form of benefit. [Treas. Reg. § 1.411(d)-3(g)(6)(ii)(B)]

Generally, a plan is not a qualified plan (see Q 1:5), and a trust forming a part of such plan is not a qualified trust, if a plan amendment decreases the accrued benefit of any plan participant (the anti-cutback rule). [Treas. Reg. § 1.411(d)-3(a)(1)]

For purposes of determining whether a participant's accrued benefit is decreased, all of the amendments to the provisions of a plan affecting, directly or indirectly, the computation of accrued benefits are taken into account. Plan provisions indirectly affecting the computation of accrued benefits include, for example, provisions relating to years of service and compensation. In determining whether a reduction in a participant's accrued benefit has occurred, all plan amendments with the same applicable amendment date are treated as one amendment. Thus, if two amendments have the same applicable amendment date and one amendment, standing alone, increases participants' accrued benefits and the other amendment, standing alone, decreases participants' accrued benefits, the amendments are treated as one amendment and will only violate the anti-cutback rule if, for any participant, the net effect is to decrease the participant's accrued benefit as of that applicable amendment date. A plan amendment violates this requirement if it is one of a series of plan amendments that, when taken together, have the effect of reducing or eliminating a Section 411(d)(6) protected benefit in a manner that would be prohibited if accomplished through a single amendment. For purposes of applying this rule, generally, only plan amendments adopted within a three-year period are taken into account. [Treas. Reg. § 1.411(d)-3(a)(2)]

Generally, these rules apply to a plan amendment that decreases a participant's accrued benefits, or otherwise places greater restrictions or conditions on a participant's rights to Section 411(d)(6) protected benefits, even if the amendment merely adds a restriction or condition that is permitted under the vesting rules. However, such an amendment does not violate the prohibition against reducing accrued benefits by a plan amendment to the extent it applies with respect to benefits that accrued after the applicable amendment date. A plan amendment that satisfies the DOL rules relating to vesting computation periods does not fail to satisfy these requirements merely because the plan amendment changes the plan's vesting computation period. [Treas. Reg. § 1.411(d)-3(a)(3); DOL Reg. § 2530.203-2(c)]

Except as provided in the final regulations, a plan is treated as decreasing an accrued benefit if it is amended to eliminate or reduce a Section 411(d)(6)(B) protected benefit. This applies to participants who satisfy (either before or after the plan amendment) the preamendment conditions for a Section 411(d)(6)(B) protected benefit even if the condition on which the eligibility for the Section 411(d)(6)(B) protected benefit depends is an unpredictable contingent event (e.g., a plant shutdown). For purposes of determining whether a participant's Section 411(d)(6)(B) protected benefit is eliminated or reduced, the rules apply to Section 411(d)(6)(B) protected benefits in the same manner as they apply to accrued benefits for purposes of the anti-cutback rule. As an example, if there are two amendments with the same applicable amendment date and one amendment increases accrued benefits and the other amendment decreases the early retirement factors that are used to determine the early retirement annuity, the amendments are treated as one amendment and violate the anti-cutback rule only if, after the two amendments, the net dollar amount of any early retirement annuity with respect to the accrued benefit of any participant as of the applicable amendment date is lower than it would have been without the two amendments. As another example, a series of amendments made within a three-year period that, when taken together, have the effect of reducing or eliminating early retirement benefits or retirement-type subsidies in a manner that adversely affects the rights of any participant in a more than *de minimis* manner violates Section 411(d)(6)(B) even if each amendment would otherwise be permissible. [Treas. Reg. § 1.411(d)-3(b)(1)]

A plan is permitted to be amended to eliminate a Section 411(d)(6)(B) protected benefit if the elimination is in accordance with the final regulations or is a permitted elimination of an optional form of benefit (see Qs 9:28-9:32). An amendment is not treated as eliminating an optional form of benefit or eliminating or reducing an early retirement benefit or retirement-type subsidy under the plan, if, effective after the plan amendment, there is another optional form of benefit available to the participant under the plan that is of inherently equal or greater value (see Q 4:20). Thus, for example, a change in the method of calculating a joint and survivor annuity from using a 90 percent adjustment factor on account of the survivorship payment at particular ages for a participant and a spouse to using a 91 percent adjustment factor at the same ages is not treated as an elimination of an optional form of benefit. Similarly, a plan that offers a subsidized QJSA option for married participants under which the amount payable during the participant's lifetime is not less than the amount payable under the plan's straight life annuity is permitted to be amended to eliminate the straight life annuity option for married participants. [Treas. Reg. § 1.411(d)-3(b)(2)]

Section 411(d)(6) does not provide protection for benefits that are ancillary benefits, other rights and features, or any other benefits that are not described in Section 411(d)(6). However, a plan may not be amended to recharacterize a retirement-type benefit as an ancillary benefit. Thus, for example, a plan amendment to recharacterize any portion of an early retirement subsidy as a social security supplement that is an ancillary benefit violates Section 411(d)(6). Section 411(d)(6) protects only benefits that accrue before the applicable amendment date. Thus, a plan is permitted to be amended to eliminate or reduce an early retirement benefit, a retirement-type subsidy, or an optional form of benefit with respect to benefits that accrue after the applicable amendment date without violating Section 411(d)(6). However, notice of an amendment to an applicable pension plan that either provides for a significant reduction in the rate of future benefit accrual or that eliminates or significantly reduces an early retirement benefit or a retirement-type subsidy is required (see Q 9:37). [Treas. Reg. §§ 1.411(d)-3(b)(3), 1.411(d)-4, Q&A-1(d)]

Except with regard to a social security leveling feature or a refund of employee contributions feature, a plan is permitted to be amended to eliminate an optional form of benefit for a participant with respect to benefits accrued before the applicable amendment date if:

1. The optional form of benefit is redundant with respect to a retained optional form of benefit;

2. The plan amendment is not applicable with respect to an optional form of benefit with an annuity commencement date that is earlier than the number of days in the maximum QJSA explanation period (180 days; see Q 10:20) after the date the amendment is adopted; and

3. The burdensome and of *de minimis* value requirements are satisfied in any case in which either (a) the retained optional form of benefit for the participant does not commence on the same annuity commencement date as the optional form of benefit that is being eliminated or (b) as of the

date the amendment is adopted the actuarial present value of the retained optional form of benefit for the participant is less than the actuarial present value of the optional form of benefit that is being eliminated. [Treas. Reg. § 1.411(d)-3(c)(1)].

An optional form of benefit is redundant with respect to a retained optional form of benefit if, after the amendment becomes applicable, (a) there is a retained optional form of benefit available to the participant that is in the same family of optional forms of benefit as the optional form of benefit being eliminated and (b) the participant's rights with respect to the retained optional form of benefit are not subject to materially greater restrictions (such as conditions relating to eligibility, restrictions on a participant's ability to designate the person who is entitled to benefits following the participant's death, or restrictions on a participant's right to receive an in-kind distribution) that applied to the optional form of benefit being eliminated. An optional form of benefit that is a core option may not be eliminated as a redundant benefit unless the retained optional form of benefit and the eliminated core option are identical except for certain differences described below. Thus, for example, a particular ten-year term certain and life annuity may not be eliminated by plan amendment unless the retained optional form of benefit is another ten-year term certain and life annuity. [Treas. Reg. § 1.411(d)-3(c)(2)]

Not every optional form of benefit offered under a plan necessarily fits within a family of optional forms of benefit. Each optional form of benefit that is not included in any particular family of optional forms of benefit is in a separate family of optional forms of benefit that would be identical to that optional form of benefit but for differences that are disregarded. [Treas. Reg. § 1.411(d)-3(c)(3)(i)]

The determination of whether two optional forms of benefit are within a family of optional forms of benefit is made without regard to actuarial factors or annuity starting dates. Thus, any optional forms of benefit that are part of the same generalized optional form are in the same family of optional forms of benefit. For example, if a plan has a single-sum distribution option for some participants that is calculated using a 5 percent interest rate and a specific mortality table (but no less than the minimum present value) and another single-sum distribution option for other participants that is calculated using the applicable interest rate and the applicable mortality table (see Q 10:62), both single-sum distribution options are part of the same generalized optional form and thus in the same family of optional forms of benefit. However, differences in actuarial factors and annuity starting dates are taken into account for purposes of the *de minimis* requirement. [Treas. Reg. § 1.411(d)-3(c)(3)(ii)(A)]

The determination of whether two optional forms of benefit are within a family of optional forms of benefit relating to joint and contingent families is made without regard to the following features:

1. Pop-up provisions (under which payments increase upon the death of the beneficiary or another event that causes the beneficiary not to be entitled to a survivor annuity);

2. Cash refund features (under which payment is provided upon the death of the last annuitant in an amount that is not greater than the excess of the present value of the annuity at the annuity starting date over the total of payments before the death of the last annuitant); or

3. Term-certain provisions for optional forms of benefit within a joint or contingent family.

[Treas. Reg. § 1.411(d)-3(c)(3)(ii)(B)]

The determination of whether two optional forms of benefit are within a family of optional forms of benefit is made without regard to social security leveling features, refund of employee contributions features, or retroactive annuity starting date features. [Treas. Reg. § 1.411(d)-3(c)(3)(ii)(C)]

The following are families of optional forms of benefit:

1. *Joint and contingent options with continuation percentages of 50 percent to 100 percent.* An optional form of benefit is within the 50 percent or more joint and contingent family if it provides a life annuity to the participant and a survivor annuity to an individual that is at least 50 percent and no more than 100 percent of the annuity payable during the joint lives of the participant and the participant's survivor.

2. *Joint and contingent options with continuation percentages less than 50 percent.* An optional form of benefit is within the less than 50 percent joint and contingent family if it provides a life annuity to the participant and a survivor annuity to an individual that is less than 50 percent of the annuity payable during the joint lives of the participant and the participant's survivor.

3. *Term certain and life annuity options with a term of ten years or less.* An optional form of benefit is within the ten years or less term certain and life family if it is a life annuity with a guarantee that payments will continue to the participant's beneficiary for the remainder of a fixed period that is ten years or less if the participant dies before the end of the fixed period.

4. *Term certain and life annuity options with a term longer than ten years.* An optional form of benefit is within the longer than ten years term certain and life family if it is a life annuity with a guarantee that payments will continue to the participant's beneficiary for the remainder of a fixed period that is in excess of ten years if the participant dies after the end of the fixed period.

5. *Level installment payment options over a period of ten years or less.* An optional form of benefit is within the ten years or less installment family if it provides for substantially level payments to the participant for a fixed period of at least two years and not in excess of ten years with a guarantee that payments will continue to the participant's beneficiary for the remainder of the fixed period if the participant dies before the end of the fixed period.

6. *Level installment payment options over a period of more than ten years.* An optional form of benefit is within the more than ten years installment

family if it provides for substantially level payments to the participant for a fixed period that is in excess of ten years with a guarantee that payments will continue to the participant's beneficiary for the remainder of the fixed period if the participant dies before the end of the fixed period. [Treas. Reg. § 1.411(d)-3(c)(4)]

To the extent an optional form of benefit that is being eliminated includes either a social security leveling feature or a refund of employee contributions feature, the retained optional form of benefit must also include that feature; and, to the extent the optional form of benefit that is being eliminated does not include a social security leveling feature or a refund of employee contributions feature, the retained optional form of benefit must not include that feature. To the extent an optional form of benefit that is being eliminated does not include a retroactive annuity starting date feature, the retained optional form of benefit must not include the feature. [Treas. Reg. § 1.411(d)-3(c)(5)]

If a plan permits the participant to make different distribution elections with respect to two or more separate portions of the participant's benefit, the redundancy rules are permitted to be applied separately to each such portion of the participant's benefit as if that portion were the participant's entire benefit. Thus, for example, if one set of distribution elections applies to a portion of the participant's accrued benefit and another set of distribution elections applies to the other portion of the participant's accrued benefit, then, with respect to one portion of the participant's benefit, the determination of whether any optional form of benefit is within a family of optional forms of benefit is permitted to be made disregarding elections that apply to the other portion of the participant's benefit. Similarly, if a participant can elect to receive any portion of the accrued benefit in a single sum and the remainder pursuant to a set of distribution elections, the redundancy rules are permitted to be applied separately to the set of distribution elections that apply to the portion of the participant's accrued benefit that is not payable in a single sum (for example, for the portion of a participant's benefit that is not paid in a single sum, the determination of whether any optional form of benefit is within a family of optional forms of benefit is permitted to be made disregarding the fact that the other portion of the participant's benefit is paid in a single sum). [Treas. Reg. § 1.411(d)-3(c)(6)]

Except as otherwise provided below, a plan is permitted to be amended to eliminate an optional form of benefit for a participant with respect to benefits accrued before the applicable amendment date if:

1. After the amendment becomes applicable, each of the core options is available to the participant with respect to benefits accrued before and after the amendment;

2. The plan amendment is not applicable with respect to an optional form of benefit with an annuity commencement date that is earlier than four years after the date the amendment is adopted; and

3. The burdensome and of *de minimis* value requirements are satisfied in any case in which either (a) one or more of the core options are not available commencing on the same annuity commencement date as the

optional form of benefit that is being eliminated or (b) as of the date the amendment is adopted the actuarial present value of the benefit payable under any core option with the same annuity commencement date is less than the actuarial present value of benefits payable under the optional form of benefit that is being eliminated. [Treas. Reg. § 1.411(d)-3(d)(1)]

For purposes of the permissible elimination of noncore optional forms of benefit, to the extent an optional form of benefit that is being eliminated includes either a social security leveling feature or a refund of employee contributions feature, at least one of the core options must also be available with that feature; to the extent that the optional form of benefit that is being eliminated does not include a social security leveling feature or a refund of employee contributions feature, each of the core options must be available without that feature; and, to the extent an optional form of benefit that is being eliminated does not include a retroactive annuity starting date feature, each of the core options must be available without that feature. If the most valuable option for a participant with a short life expectancy is eliminated, then, after the plan amendment, an optional form of benefit that is identical, except for certain differences, must be available to the participant. However, such a plan amend-ment cannot eliminate a refund of employee contributions feature from the most valuable option for a participant with a short life expectancy. A plan amendment is not treated as satisfying the permissible elimination rule if it eliminates an optional form of benefit that includes a single-sum distribution that applies with respect to at least 25 percent of the participant's accrued benefit as of the date the optional form of benefit is eliminated. If a plan is amended to eliminate an optional form of benefit using this core options rule, then the employer must wait three years after the first annuity commencement date for which the optional form of benefit is no longer available before making any changes to the core options offered under the plan (other than a change that is not treated as an elimination). Thus, for example, if a plan amendment eliminates an optional form of benefit for a participant using the core options rule, with an adoption date of January 1, 2007 and an effective date of January 1, 2011, the plan would not be permitted to be amended to make changes to the core options offered under the plan (and the core options would continue to apply with respect to the participant's accrued benefit) until January 1, 2014. If a plan offers joint and contingent annuities under which a participant is entitled to a life annuity with a survivor annuity for the individual designated by the participant (including a nonspousal contingent annuitant) with continuation percentage options of both 50 percent and 100 percent, the plan is permitted to treat both of these options as core options, in lieu of a 75 percent joint and contingent annuity. Thus, such a plan is permitted to use the core option rule if the plan satisfies all of the other requirements other than the requirement of offering a 75 percent joint and contingent annuity. [Treas. Reg. § 1.411(d)-3(d)(2)]

A plan amendment satisfies the burdensome and of *de minimis* value requirements if (1) the amendment eliminates Section 411(d)(6)(B) protected benefits that create significant burdens or complexities for the plan and (2) the amendment does not adversely affect the rights of any participant in a more than *de minimis* manner. [Treas. Reg. § 1.411(d)-3(e)(1)]

The determination of whether a plan amendment eliminates Section 411(d)(6)(B) protected benefits that create significant burdens or complexities for the plan and its participants is based on facts and circumstances. In the case of an amendment that eliminates an early retirement benefit, relevant factors include whether the annuity starting dates under the plan considered in the aggregate are burdensome or complex (e.g., the number of categories of early retirement benefits, whether the terms and conditions applicable to the plan's early retirement benefits are difficult to summarize in a manner that is concise and readily understandable to the average plan participant, and whether those different early retirement benefits were added to the plan as a result of a plan merger, transfer, or consolidation) and whether the effect of the plan amendment is to reduce the number of categories of early retirement benefits. In the case of a plan amendment eliminating a retirement-type subsidy or changing the actuarial factors used to determine optional forms of benefit, relevant factors include whether the actuarial factors used for determining optional forms of benefit available under the plan considered in the aggregate are burdensome or complex (e.g., the number of different retirement-type subsidies and other actuarial factors available under the plan, whether the terms and conditions applicable to the plan's retirement-type subsidies are difficult to summarize in a manner that is concise and readily understandable to the average plan participant, whether the plan is eliminating one or more generalized optional forms, whether the plan is replacing a complex optional form of benefit that contains a retirement-type subsidy with a simpler form, and whether the different retirement-type subsidies and other actuarial factors were added to the plan as a result of a plan merger, transfer, or consolidation) and whether the effect of the plan amendment is to reduce the number of categories of retirement-type subsidies or other actuarial factors. [Treas. Reg. § 1.411(d)-3(e)(2)(i)]

If the annuity starting dates under the plan considered in the aggregate are burdensome or complex, then elimination of any one of the annuity starting dates is presumed to eliminate Section 411(d)(6)(B) protected benefits that create significant burdens or complexities for the plan and its participants. However, if the effect of a plan amendment with respect to a set of optional forms of benefit is merely to substitute one set of annuity starting dates for another set of annuity starting dates, without any reduction in the number of different annuity starting dates, then the plan amendment does not satisfy the burdensome or complex requirements. If the actuarial factors used for determining benefit distributions available under a generalized optional form considered in the aggregate are burdensome or complex, then replacing some of the actuarial factors for the generalized optional form is presumed to eliminate Section 411(d)(6)(B) protected benefits that create significant burdens or complexities for the plan and its participants. However, if the effect is merely to substitute one set of actuarial factors for another set of actuarial factors, without any reduction in the number of different actuarial factors or the complexity of those factors, then the plan amendment does not satisfy these requirements unless the change of actuarial factors is merely to replace one or more of the plan's actuarial factors for determining optional forms of benefit with new actuarial factors that are more accurate (e.g., reflecting more recent mortality experience or more recent market rates of interest). [Treas. Reg. § 1.411(d)-3(e)(2)(ii)]

In accordance with the multiple amendment rules, a plan amendment does not eliminate a Section 411(d)(6)(B) protected benefit that creates burdens and complexities for a plan and its participants if, less than three years earlier, a plan was previously amended to add another retirement-type subsidy in order to facilitate the elimination of the original retirement-type subsidy, even if the elimination of the other subsidy would not adversely affect the rights of any plan participant in a more than *de minimis* manner. [Treas. Reg. § 1.411(d)-3(e)(2)(iii)]

For purposes of the redundancy rule, the elimination of an optional form of benefit does not adversely affect the rights of any participant in a more than *de minimis* manner if:

1. The retained optional form of benefit described has substantially the same annuity commencement date as the optional form of benefit that is being eliminated, and

2. Either the actuarial present value of the benefit payable in the optional form of benefit that is being eliminated does not exceed the actuarial present value of the benefit payable in the retained optional form of benefit by more than a *de minimis* amount or the amendment satisfies the delayed effective date rule. [Treas. Reg. § 1.411(d)-3(e)(3)(i)]

For purposes of the *de minimis* value requirement, the elimination of an optional form of benefit does not adversely affect the rights of any participant in a more than *de minimis* manner if, with respect to each of the core options:

1. The core option is available after the amendment with substantially the same annuity commencement date as the optional form of benefit that is being eliminated, and

2. Either the actuarial present value of the benefit payable in the optional form of benefit that is being eliminated does not exceed the actuarial present value of the benefit payable under the core option by more than a *de minimis* amount or the amendment satisfies the delayed effective date rule. [Treas. Reg. § 1.411(d)-3(e)(3)(ii)]

Annuity starting dates are considered substantially the same if they occur within six months of each other. [Treas. Reg. § 1.411(d)-3(e)(4)] A difference in actuarial present value between the optional form of benefit being eliminated and the retained optional form of benefit or core option is not more than a *de minimis* amount if, as of the date the amendment is adopted, the difference between the actuarial present value of the eliminated optional form of benefit and the actuarial present value of the retained optional form of benefit or core option is not more than the greater of (1) 2 percent of the present value of the retirement-type subsidy (if any) under the eliminated optional form of benefit prior to the amendment or (2) 1 percent of the greater of the participant's compensation for the prior plan year or the participant's average compensation for the high three years. [Treas. Reg. § 1.411(d)-3(e)(5)]

An amendment that eliminates an optional form of benefit satisfies the delayed effective date requirements if the elimination of the optional form of benefit is not applicable to any annuity commencement date before the end of the expected transition period for that optional form of benefit. The expected transition period for a plan amendment eliminating an optional form of benefit is the period that begins when the amendment is adopted and ends when it is reasonable to expect, with respect to a Section 411(d)(6)(B) protected benefit (i.e., not taking into account benefits that accrue in the future), that the form being eliminated would be subsumed into another optional form of benefit after taking into account expected future benefit accruals. The expected transition period for a plan amendment eliminating an optional form of benefit must be determined in accordance with actuarial assumptions that are reasonable at the time of the amendment and that are conservative (i.e., reasonable actuarial assumptions that are likely to result in the longest period of time until the eliminated optional form of benefit would be subsumed). For this purpose, actuarial assumptions are not treated as conservative unless they include assumptions that a participant's compensation will not increase and that future benefits accruals will not exceed accruals in recent periods. If, during the expected transition period for a plan amendment eliminating an optional form of benefit, the plan is subsequently amended to reduce the rate of future benefit accrual (or otherwise to lengthen the expected transition period), that subsequent plan amendment must provide that the elimination of the optional form of benefit is void or must provide for the effective date for elimination of the optional form of benefit to be further extended to a new expected transition period that satisfies the delayed effective date rule, taking into account the subsequent amendment. An amendment eliminating an optional form of benefit under the delayed effective date rule must be limited to participants who continue to accrue benefits under the plan through the end of the expected transition period. Thus, for example, the plan amendment may not apply to any participant who has a severance from employment during the expected transition period. [Treas. Reg. § 1.411(d)-3(e)(6)]. See Q 9:43 for a special rule regarding the Section 204(h) Notice.

A plan is permitted to be amended to eliminate all of the optional forms of benefit that comprise a generalized optional form for a participant with respect to benefits accrued before the applicable amendment date if:

1. None of the optional forms of benefit being eliminated is a core option;

2. The plan amendment is not applicable with respect to an optional form of benefit with an annuity commencement date that is earlier than the number of days in the maximum QJSA explanation period (180 days) after the date the amendment is adopted; and

3. During the look-back period (a) the generalized optional form has been available to at least the applicable number of participants who are taken into account as determined below and (b) no participant has elected any optional form of benefit that is part of the generalized optional form with

an annuity commencement date that is within the look-back period. [Treas. Reg. § 1.411(d)-3(f)(1)]

The look-back period is the period that includes (a) the portion of the plan year in which such plan amendment is adopted that precedes the date of adoption (the pre-adoption period) and (b) the two plan years immediately preceding the pre-adoption period. In the look-back period, at least one of the plan years must be a 12-month plan year. A plan is permitted to exclude from the look-back period the calendar month in which the amendment is adopted and the preceding one or two calendar months to the extent those preceding months are contained within the pre-adoption period. In order to have a look-back period that satisfies the minimum applicable number of participants require-ment, the look-back period is permitted to be expanded, so as to include the three, four, or five plan years immediately preceding the plan year in which the amendment is adopted. Thus, in determining the look-back period, a plan is permitted to substitute the three, four, or five plan years immediately preceding the pre-adoption period for the two plan years described above. However, if a plan does not satisfy the minimum applicable number of participants require-ment using the pre-adoption period and the immediately preceding five plan years, the plan is not permitted to be amended in accordance with this utilization test. [Treas. Reg. § 1.411(d)-3(f)(2)]

A participant is taken into account only if the participant was eligible to elect to commence payment of an optional form of benefit that is part of the generalized optional form being eliminated with an annuity commencement date that is within the look-back period. However, a participant is not taken into account if the participant:

1. Did not elect any optional form of benefit with an annuity commencement date that was within the look-back period;

2. Elected an optional form of benefit that included a single-sum distribution that applied with respect to at least 25 percent of the participant's accrued benefit;

3. Elected an optional form of benefit that was only available during a limited period of time and that contained a retirement-type subsidy where the subsidy that is part of the generalized optional form being eliminated was not extended to any optional form of benefit with the same annuity commencement date; or

4. Elected an optional form of benefit with an annuity commencement date that was more than ten years before normal retirement age. [Treas. Reg. § 1.411(d)-3(f)(3)]

The applicable number of participants is 50 participants. However, a plan is permitted to take into account any participant who elected an optional form of benefit that included a single-sum distribution that applied with respect to at least 25 percent of the participant's accrued benefit, but only if the appli-cable number of participants is increased to 1,000 participants. [Treas. Reg. § 1.411(d)-3(f)(4)] An election includes the payment of an optional form of benefit that applies in the absence of an affirmative election. [Treas. Reg. § 1.411(d)-3(f)(5)]

Except as otherwise provided in this paragraph, the final regulations apply to amendments adopted on or after August 12, 2005. The unpredictable contingent event provision (e.g., a plant shutdown) applies to amendments adopted after December 31, 2005. With respect to a plan amendment that places greater restrictions or conditions on a participant's rights to Section 411(d)(6) protected benefits by adding or modifying a plan provision relating to suspension of benefit payments during a period of employment or unemployment, the rules in these regulations apply for periods beginning on or after June 7, 2004. However, for a plan amendment that places greater restrictions or conditions on a participant's right to Section 411(d)(6) protected benefits with respect to vesting, other than a plan amendment relating to a suspension of benefit payments, the rules in these regulations apply to plan amendments adopted after August 9, 2006. The change to the regulations permitting a plan to apply the redundancy rules separately to each portion of a participant's benefit to which separate distribution elections apply is applicable for amendments adopted after August 9, 2006. The rules concerning the utilization test are effective for amendments adopted after December 31, 2006. [Treas. Reg. § 1.411(d)-3(j)]

For illustrative examples, see Q 9:34.

Q 9:34 Has IRS provided examples regarding the Section 411(d)(6)(B) protected benefits?

Yes. The following examples illustrate the application of the final regulations (see Q 9:33). [Treas. Reg. § 1.411(d)-3]

Example 1. *Amendments to an early retirement subsidy.* Plan A provides an annual benefit of 2 percent of career average pay times years of service commencing at normal retirement age (age 65; see Q 10:55). Plan A is amended on November 1, 2010, effective as of January 1, 2011, to provide for an annual benefit of 1.3 percent of final pay times years of service, with final pay computed as the average of a participant's highest three consecutive years of compensation. Larry is age 50, he has 16 years of service, his career average pay is $37,500, and the average of his highest three consecutive years of compensation is $67,308. Thus, Larry's accrued benefit as of the effective date of the amendment is increased from $12,000 per year at normal retirement age (2% × $37,500 × 16 years of service) to $14,000 per year at normal retirement age (1.3% × $67,308 × 16 years of service). Before the amendment, Plan A permitted a former employee to commence distribution of benefits as early as age 55 and, for a participant with at least 15 years of service, actuarially reduced the amount payable in the form of a straight life annuity (see Q 9:33) commencing before normal retirement age by 3 percent per year from age 60 to age 65 and by 7 percent per year from age 55 through age 59. Thus, before the amendment, the amount of Larry's early retirement benefit that would be payable for commencement at age 55 was $6,000 per year ($12,000 per year − $1,800 (3% for 5 years) − $4,200 (7% for 5 more years)). The amendment also alters the actuarial reduction factor so that, for a participant with at least 15 years of service, the amount payable in a straight life annuity commencing before normal retirement age is reduced by 6 percent per year. As a result, the amount of Larry's early retirement benefit at age 55 becomes $5,600 per year after the amendment ($14,000 − $8,400 (6% for 10 years)).

The straight life annuity payable under Plan A at age 55 is an optional form of benefit that is an early retirement subsidy (see Qs 9:33, 10:45). The plan amendment fails to satisfy the prohibition against reduction or elimination because the amendment decreases the optional form of benefit payable to Larry below the level that he was entitled to receive immediately before the effective date of the amendment. If instead Plan A had included a provision under which Larry's straight life annuity payable at any age could not be less than what it was immediately before the amendment (so that Larry's straight life annuity payable at age 55 could not be less than $6,000 per year), then the amendment would not fail to satisfy these requirements with respect to Larry's straight life annuity payable at age 55 (although the straight life annuity payable to Larry at age 55 would not increase until the point in time at which the new formula amount with the new actuarial reduction factors exceeds the amount payable under the minimum provision, approximately 14 months after the amendment becomes effective).

Example 2. *Plant shutdown benefits.* Plan B permits participants who have a severance from employment before normal retirement age (age 65) to commence distributions at any time after age 55 with the amount payable to be actuarially reduced using reasonable actuarial assumptions regarding interest and mortality, but provides that the annual reduction for any participant who has at least 20 years of service and who has a severance from employment after age 55 is only 3 percent per year (which is a smaller reduction than would apply under reasonable actuarial reductions). Plan B also provides two plant shutdown benefits to participants who have a severance of employment as a result of a plant shutdown. First, the favorable 3 percent actuarial reduction will apply for commencement of benefits after age 55 and before age 65 for any participant who has at least ten years of service and who has a severance from employment as a result of a plant shutdown. Second, all participants who have at least 20 years of service and who have a severance from employment after age 55 (and before retirement age at age 65) as a result of a plant shutdown will receive supplemental payments. Under the supplemental payments, an additional amount equal to the participant's estimated old-age insurance benefit under the Social Security Act is payable until age 65. The supplemental payments are not a qualified social security supplement (QSupp) because the plan's terms do not state that the supplement is treated as an early retirement benefit that is protected.

The benefits payable with the 3 percent annual reduction are retirement-type benefits (see Q 9:33). The excess of the actuarial present value of the early retirement benefit using the 3 percent annual reduction over the actuarial present value of the normal retirement benefit is a retirement-type subsidy and the right to receive payments of the benefit at age 55 is an early retirement benefit. These conclusions apply not only with respect to the rights that apply to participants who have at least 20 years of service, but also to participants with at least ten years of service who have a severance from employment as a result of a plant shutdown. Thus, the right to receive benefits based on a 3 percent annual reduction for participants with at least ten years of service at the time of a plant shutdown is an early retirement benefit that provides a retirement-type subsidy and is a protected benefit (even though no plant shutdown has occurred). Therefore, a plan amendment cannot eliminate this benefit with respect to benefits accrued before the applicable amendment date (see Q 9:33), even before the occurrence of the plant shutdown. Because the plan provides that the supplement cannot exceed the Social Security benefit, the supplemental payments constitute a social security supplement (but not a QSUPP), which is an ancillary benefit that is not a protected benefit and, accordingly, is not taken into account in determining whether a prohibited reduction has occurred.

Example 3. *Greater restrictions or conditions on protected benefits.* Plan C, a multiemployer defined benefit plan (see Q 29:2), in which participation is limited to electricians in the construction industry, provides that a participant may elect to commence distributions only if the participant is not currently employed by a participating employer and provides that, if the participant has a specified number of years of service and attains a specified age, the distribution is without any actuarial reduction for commencement before normal retirement age. Since the plan's inception, Plan C has provided for suspension of pension benefits during periods of disqualifying employment. Before 2011, the plan defined disqualifying employment to include any job as an electrician in the particular industry and geographic location to which Plan C applies. This definition of disqualifying employment did not cover a job as an electrician supervisor. In 2009, Jorge, having rendered the specified number of years of service and having attained the specified age to retire with a fully subsidized early retirement benefit, retires from his job as an electrician with Elvira Corp. and starts a position with Bay Club Ltd. as an electrician supervisor. Bay Club Ltd. is not a participating employer in Plan C but is an employer in the same industry and geographic location as Elvira Corp. When Jorge left service with Elvira Corp., his position as an electrician supervisor was not disqualifying employment for purposes of Plan C's suspension of pension benefit provision, and Jorge elected to commence benefit payments in 2009. In 2010, effective January 1, 2011, Plan C is amended to expand the definition of disqualifying employment to include any job (including supervisory positions) as an electrician in the same industry and geographic location to which Plan C applies. On January 1, 2011, Jorge's pension benefits are suspended because of his disqualifying employment as an electrician supervisor. (These facts are generally comparable to the facts in *Central Laborers' Pension Fund v. Heinz* (see Q 9:25).)

The 2011 plan amendment violates the anti-cutback rule (see Q 9:25) because the amendment places greater restrictions or conditions on a participant's rights to protected benefits to the extent it applies with respect to benefits that accrued before January 1, 2011. The result would be the same even if the amendment did not apply to former employees and instead applied only to participants who were actively employed at the time of the applicable amendment.

Example 4. *Protected benefits that create significant burdens and complexities.* Plan D is a defined benefit plan (see Q 2:3) under which employees may select a distribution in the form of a straight life annuity, a straight life annuity with cost-of-living increases, a 50 percent qualified joint and survivor annuity (QJSA; see Q 10:8) with a pop-up provision (under which payments increase upon the death of the beneficiary or another event that causes the beneficiary not to be entitled to a survivor annuity), or a ten-year term certain and life annuity. On January 15, 2011, Plan D is amended, effective August 1, 2011, to eliminate the 50 percent QJSA with a pop-up provision and replace it with a 50 percent QJSA without the pop-up provision (and using the same actuarial factor).

Plan D satisfies the burdensome or complex requirements because, based on the relevant facts and circumstances (e.g., the amendment replaces a complex optional form of benefit with a simpler form), the amendment eliminates protected benefits that create significant burdens and complexities. Accordingly, the plan amendment is permitted to eliminate the pop-up provision, provided that the plan amendment satisfies all the other applicable requirements. For example, the plan amendment must not eliminate the most valuable option for a participant with a short life expectancy, and the plan amendment must not adversely affect the rights of any participant in a more than *de minimis* manner, taking into account the actuarial factors for the joint and survivor annuity with the pop-up provision and the joint and survivor annuity without the pop-up provision.

Example 5. *Elimination of optional forms of benefit as redundant.* Plan E is a defined benefit plan under which employees may elect to commence distributions at any time after the later of termination of employment or attainment of age 55. At each potential annuity starting date (see Q 10:3), Plan E permits employees to select, with spousal consent (see Q 10:21) where required, a straight life annuity or any of a number of actuarially equivalent alternative forms of payment, including a straight life annuity with cost-of-living increases and a joint and contingent annuity (see Q 9:33) with the participant having the right to select any beneficiary and any continuation percentage from 1 percent to 100 percent, subject to modification to the extent necessary to satisfy the requirements of the incidental benefit requirement (see Q 11:20). The amount of any alternative payment is determined as the actuarial equivalent of the straight life annuity payable at the same age using reasonable actuarial assumptions. On June 2, 2010, Plan E is amended to delete all continuation percentages for joint and contingent options other than 25 percent, 50 percent, 75 percent, or 100 percent, effective with respect to annuity commencement dates that are on or after January 1, 2011.

The optional forms of benefit described above are members of four families (see Q 9:33): a straight life annuity; a straight life annuity with cost-of-living increases; joint and contingent options with continuation percentages of less than 50 percent, and joint and contingent options with continuation percentages of 50 percent or more. The amendment does not affect either of the first two families but does affect the two families relating to joint and contingent options.

The amendment satisfies the redundant requirement (see Q 9:33). First, the eliminated optional forms of benefit are redundant with respect to the retained optional forms of benefit because each eliminated joint and contingent annuity option with a continuation percentage of less than 50 percent is redundant with respect to the 25 percent continuation option, and each eliminated joint and contingent annuity option with a continuation percent of 50 percent or higher is redundant with respect to any one of the retained 50 percent, 75 percent, or 100 percent continuation options. In addition, to the extent that the optional form of benefit that is being eliminated does not include a social security leveling feature, return of employee contribution feature, or retroactive annuity starting date feature, the retained optional form of benefit does not include that feature. Second, the amendment is not effective with respect to annuity commencement dates before November 29, 2010 (i.e., that are less than 180 days from the date of the amendment). Third, the plan amendment does not eliminate any available core option (see Q 9:33), including the most valuable option for a participant with a short life expectancy, treating a joint and contingent annuity with a 100 percent continuation percentage as this optional form of benefit. Finally, the amendment need not satisfy the burdensome or of *de minimis* value requirement because the retained optional forms of benefit are available on the same annuity commencement dates and have the same actuarial present value as the optional forms of benefit that are being eliminated.

Example 6. *Elimination of optional forms of benefit as redundant if additional restrictions are imposed.* The facts are the same as Example 5, except that the plan amendment also restricts the class of beneficiaries that may be elected under the four retained joint and contingent annuities to the employee's spouse.

The amendment fails to satisfy the redundant requirement because the retained joint and contingent annuities have materially greater restrictions on the beneficiary designation than did the eliminated joint and contingent annuities. Thus, the joint and contingent annuities being eliminated are not redundant with respect to the retained joint and contingent annuities. In addition, the amendment fails to satisfy the requirements of the core option rules because the amendment fails to be limited to annuity commencement dates that are at least four years after the date the amendment is adopted, the amendment fails to include a required core option because the participant does not have the right to designate any beneficiary, and the amendment fails to include another required core option because the plan does not provide a 10-year certain and life annuity.

Example 7. *Elimination of a social security leveling feature and a period certain annuity as redundant.* Plan F is a defined benefit plan under which participants may elect to commence distributions in the following actuarially equivalent forms, with spousal consent if applicable: a straight life annuity; a 50 percent, 75 percent, or 100 percent joint and contingent annuity; a 5-year, 10-year, or a 15-year period certain and life annuity; and an installment refund annuity (i.e., an optional form of benefit that provides a period certain, the duration of which is based on the participant's age), with the participant having the right to select any beneficiary. In addition, each annuity offered under the plan, if payable to a participant who is less than age 65, is available both with and without a social security leveling feature. The social security leveling feature provides for an assumed commencement of social security benefits at any age selected by the participant between ages 62 and 65. Plan F is amended on June 2, 2010, effective as of January 1, 2011, to eliminate the installment refund form of benefit and to restrict the social security leveling feature to an assumed social security commencement age of 65.

The amendment satisfies the redundant requirement. First, the installment refund annuity option is redundant with respect to the 15-year certain and life annuity (except for advanced ages where, because of shorter life expectancies, the installment refund annuity option is redundant with respect to the 5-year certain and life annuity and also redundant with respect to the 10-year certain and life annuity). Second, with respect to restricting the social security leveling feature to an assumed social security commencement age of 65, straight life annuities with social security leveling features that have different social security commencement ages are treated as members of the same family as straight life annuities without social security leveling features (see Q 9:33). To the extent an optional form of benefit that is being eliminated includes a social security leveling feature, the retained optional form of benefit must also include that feature, but it is permitted to have a different assumed age for commencement of social security benefits. Third, to the extent that the optional form of benefit that is being eliminated does not include a social security leveling feature, a return of employee contribution feature, or retroactive annuity starting date feature, the retained optional form of benefit must not include that feature. Fourth, the plan amendment does not eliminate any available core option, including the most valuable option for a participant with a short life expectancy, treating a joint and contingent annuity with a 100 percent continuation percentage as this optional form of benefit. Fifth, the amendment is not effective with respect to annuity commencement dates before November 29, 2010 (i.e., that are less than 180 days from the date the amendment is adopted). The amendment need not satisfy the burdensome or of *de minimis* value requirement because the retained optional forms of benefit are available on the same annuity commencement dates and have the same actuarial present value as the optional forms of benefit that are being eliminated.

Example 8. *Elimination of noncore options.* May Wee Bonnie Corp. sponsors Plan G, a defined benefit plan that permits every participant to elect payment in the following actuarially equivalent optional forms of benefit (Plan G's uniformly available options), with spousal consent if applicable: a straight life annuity; a 50 percent, 75 percent, or 100 percent joint and contingent annuity with no restrictions on designation of beneficiaries; and a 5-year, 10-year, or 15-year period certain and life annuity. In addition, each can be elected in conjunction with a social security leveling feature, with the participant permitted to select a social security commencement age from age 62 to age 67. None of Plan G's uniformly available options includes a single-sum distribution. The plan has been in existence for over 30 years, during which time May Wee Bonnie Corp. has acquired a large number of other businesses, including merging over 20 defined benefit plans of acquired entities into Plan G. Many of the merged plans offered optional forms of benefit that were not among Plan G's uniformly available options, including some plans funded through insurance products, often offering all of the insurance annuities that the insurance carrier offers, and with some of the merged plans offering single-sum distributions. In particular, under the Larry Tennis Court Corp. acquisition that occurred in 1994, the Larry Tennis Court Corp. acquired plan offered a single-sum distribution option that was frozen at the time of the acquisition. On April 1, 2010, each single-sum distribution option applies to less than 25 percent of the Larry Tennis Court Corp. participants' accrued benefits. May Wee Bonnie Corp. has generally, but not uniformly, followed the optional forms of benefit for an acquired unit to an employee's service before the date of the merger, and has uniformly followed this practice with respect to each of the early retirement subsidies in the acquired unit's plan. As a result, as of April 1, 2011, Plan G includes a large number of generalized optional forms of benefit that are not members of families of optional forms of benefit, but there are no participants who are entitled to any early retirement subsidies because any subsidies have been subsumed by the actuarially reduced accrued benefit. Plan G is amended in April of 2011 to eliminate all of the optional forms of benefit that Plan G offers other than Plan G's uniformly available options, except that the amendment does not eliminate any single-sum distribution option except with respect to Larry Tennis Court Corp. participants and permits any commencement date that was permitted under Plan G before the amendment. Plan G also eliminates the single-sum distribution option for Larry Tennis Court Corp. participants. Further, each of Plan G's uniformly available options has an actuarial present value that is not less than the actuarial present value of any optional form of benefit offered before the amendment. The amendment is effective with respect to annuity commencement dates that are on or after May 1, 2015.

The amendment satisfies the requirements concerning the permissible elimination of noncore optional forms of benefit where core options are offered. First, Plan G, as amended, does not eliminate any single-sum distribution option, except for single-sum distribution options that apply to less than 25 percent of a plan participant's accrued benefit as of the date the option is eliminated (May 1, 2015). Second, Plan G, as amended includes each of the core options, including offering the most valuable option for a participant with a short life expectancy (treating the 100 percent joint and contingent annuity as this benefit). The 100 percent joint and contingent annuity option (and not the grandfathered single-sum distribution option) is the most valuable option for a participant with a short life expectancy because the grandfathered single-sum distribution option is not available with respect to a participant's entire accrued benefit. In addition, to the extent an optional form of benefit that is being eliminated includes either a social security leveling feature or a refund of employee contributions feature, at least one of the core options is available with that feature and, to the extent that the optional form of benefit that is being eliminated does not include a social security leveling feature or a refund of employee contributions feature, each of the core options is available without that feature. Third, the amendment is not effective with respect to annuity commencement dates that are less than four years after the date the amendment is adopted. Finally, the amendment need not satisfy the burdensome or of *de minimis* value requirement because the retained optional forms of benefit are available on the same annuity commencement date and have the same actuarial present value as the optional forms of benefit that are being eliminated. The conclusion that the amendment satisfies these requirements assumes that no amendments are made to change the core options before May 1, 2018.

Example 9. *Reductions in actuarial present value.* Plan H is a defined benefit plan providing an accrued benefit of 1 percent of the average of a participant's highest three consecutive years' pay times years of service, payable as a straight life annuity beginning at age 65. Plan H permits employees to elect to commence actuarially reduced distributions at any time after the later of termination of employment or attainment of age 55. At each potential annuity commencement date, Plan H permits employees to select, with spousal consent, either a straight life annuity, a joint and contingent annuity with the participant having the right to select any beneficiary and a continuation percent of 50 percent, 66⅔ percent, 75 percent, or 100 percent, or a 10-year certain and life annuity with the participant having the right to select any beneficiary, subject to modification to the extent necessary to satisfy the incidental benefit requirement. The amount of any joint and contingent annuity and the 10-year certain and life annuity is determined as the actuarial equivalent of the straight life annuity payable at the same age using reasonable actuarial assumptions. The plan covers employees at four divisions, one of which, division X, was acquired on January 1, 2003. The plan provides for distributions before normal retirement age to be actuarially reduced; but, if a participant retires after attainment of age 55 and completion of ten years of service, the applicable early retirement reduction factor is 3 percent per year for the years between ages 65 and 62 and 6 percent per year for the ages from 62 to 55 for all employees at any division, except for employees who were in division X on January 1, 2003, for whom the early retirement reduction factor for retirement after age 55 and ten years of service is 5 percent for each year before age 65. On June 2, 2010, effective January 1, 2011, Plan H is amended to change the early retirement reduction factors for all employees of division X to be the same as for other employees, effective with respect to annuity commencement dates that are on or after January 1, 2012, but only with respect to participants who are employees on or after January 1, 2012, and only if Plan H continues accruals at the current rate through January 1, 2012 (or the effective date of the change in reduction factors is delayed to reflect the change in the accrual rate). For purposes of this example, it is assumed that an actuarially equivalent early retirement factor would have a reduction shown in column 4 of the following table, which compares the reduction factors for division X before and after the amendment:

1	*2*	*3*	*4*	*5*
Age	*Old Division X Factor (as a %)*	*New Factor (as a %)*	*Actually Equivalent Factor (as a %)*	*Column 3 minus Column 2*
65	N/a	N/a	N/a	N/a
64	95	97	91.1	+2
63	90	94	83.2	+4
62	85	91	76.1	+6
61	80	85	69.8	+5
60	75	79	64.1	+4
59	70	73	59.0	+3
58	65	67	54.3	+2
57	60	61	50.1	+1
56	55	55	46.3	0
55	50	49	42.8	−1

On January 1, 2011, the employee with the largest number of years of service is Employee E who is age 54 and has 20 years of service. For 2010, Employee E's compensation is $80,000 and E's highest three consecutive years of pay on January 1, 2011, is $75,000. Employee E's accrued benefit as of the January 1, 2011 effective date of the amendment is a life annuity of $15,000 per year at normal retirement age (1% × $75,000 × 20 years of service), and E's early retirement benefit commencing at age 55 has a present value of $91,397 as of January 1, 2011. It is assumed for purposes of this example that the longest expected transition period for any active employee does not exceed 5 months (20 years and 5 months × 1% × 49% exceeds 20 years × 1% × 50%). Finally, it is assumed for purposes of this example that the amendment reduces optional forms of benefit that are burdensome or complex.

The amendment reducing the early retirement factors has the effect of eliminating the existing optional forms of benefit (where the amount of the benefit is based on preamendment early retirement factors in any case where the new factors result in a smaller amount payable) and adding new optional forms of benefit (where the amount of benefit is based on different early retirement factors). Accordingly, the elimination must satisfy the requirements concerning redundancy or permissible elimination of noncore optional forms of benefit where core options are offered if the amount payable at any date is less than would have been payable under the plan before the amendment.

The amendment satisfies the redundant requirement. First, with respect to each eliminated optional form of benefit (i.e., with respect to each optional form of benefit with the Old Division X Factor), after the amendment there is a retained optional form of benefit that is in the same family of optional forms of benefit (i.e., the optional form of benefit with the New Factor). Second, the amendment is not effective with respect to annuity starting dates that are less than 180 days from the date the amendment is adopted. Third, to the extent that the plan amendment eliminates the most valuable option for a participant with a short life expectancy, the retained optional form of benefit is identical except for differences in actuarial factors.

The plan amendment must satisfy the burdensome or of *de minimis* value requirement because, as of the June 2, 2010 adoption date, the actuarial present value of the early retirement subsidy is less than the actuarial present value of the early retirement subsidy being eliminated. The plan amendment satisfies the burdensome requirement because the amendment eliminates optional forms of benefit that create significant burdens or complexities for the plan and its participants.

The amendment does not satisfy the *de minimis* requirement because the reduction in the actuarial present value is more than a *de minimis* amount. For example, for Employee E, the amount of the joint and contingent annuity payable at age 55 is reduced from $7,500 (50% of $15,000) to $7,350 (49% of $15,000), and the reduction in present value as a result of the amendment is $1,828 ($91,397 − $89,569). In this case, the retirement-type subsidy at age 55 is the excess of the present value of the 50 percent early retirement benefit over the present value of the deferred payment of the accrued benefit, or $13,921 ($97,269 − $83,348), and the present value at age 54 of the retirement-type subsidy is $13,081. The reduction in present value is more than the greater of 2 percent of the present value of the retirement-type subsidy and 1 percent of E's compensation because the reduction in present value exceeds $800 (the greater of $262 (2% of the present value of the retirement-type subsidy for the benefit being eliminated) and $800 (1% of E's compensation of $80,000)).

The amendment satisfies the delayed effective date requirement and, thus, satisfies the *de minimis* requirement. First, as assumed under the facts above, the amendment reduces optional forms of benefit that are burdensome or complex. Second, the plan amendment is not effective for annuity commencement dates before January 1, 2012, and that date is not earlier than the longest expected transition period for any participant in Plan H on the date of the amendment. Third, the amendment does not apply to any participant who has a severance from employment during the transition period. If, however, a later plan amendment reduces accruals under Plan H, the initial amendment will no longer satisfy the delayed effective date requirement (and must be voided) unless, as part of the later amendment, the expected transition period is extended to reflect the reduction in accruals under Plan H.

Example 10. *Elimination of noncore options using utilization test.* Plan I is a calendar-year defined benefit plan under which participants may elect to commence distributions after termination of employment in the following actuarially equivalent forms, with spousal consent, if applicable: a straight life annuity; a 50 percent, 75 percent, or 100 percent joint and contingent annuity; or a 5-year, 10-year, or a 15-year term certain and life annuity. A participant is permitted to elect a single-sum distribution if the present value of the participant's nonforfeitable accrued benefit is not greater than $5,000. The annuities offered under the plan are generally available both with and without a social security leveling feature. The social security leveling feature provides for an assumed commencement of social security benefits at any age selected by the participant between the ages of 62 and 67. Under Plan I, the normal retirement age is defined as age 65.

In 2011, the plan sponsor of Plan I, after reviewing participants' benefit elections, determines that, during the period from January 1, 2009 through June 30, 2011, no participant elected a five-year term certain and life annuity with a social security leveling option. During that period, Plan I has made the five-year term certain and life annuity with a social security leveling option available to 142 participants who were at least age 55 and who elected optional forms of benefit with annuity commencement dates during that period. In addition, during that period, 20 of the 142 participants elected a single-sum distribution and there was no retirement-type subsidy available for a limited period of time. Plan I is amended on July 1, 2011, effective as of January 1, 2012, to eliminate all five-year term certain and life annuities with a social security leveling option for all annuity commencement dates on or after January 1, 2012.

The amendment satisfies the requirements of the utilization test (see Q 9:33). First, the five-year term certain and life annuity with a social security leveling option is not a core option. Second, the plan amendment is not applicable with respect to an optional form of benefit with an annuity commencement date that is earlier than the number of days in the maximum QJSA explanation period after the date the amendment is adopted. Third, the five-year term certain and life annuity with a social security leveling option has been available to at least 50 participants who are taken into account during the look-back period (see Q 9:33). Fourth, during the look-back period, no participant elected any optional form that is part of the generalized optional form being eliminated (i.e., the five-year term and life annuity with a social security leveling option).

Q 9:35   Can accrued benefits be eliminated or reduced?

IRS may provide for the elimination or reduction of Section 411(d)(6) protected benefits (see Q 10:45) that have already accrued only to the extent that such elimination or reduction does not result in the loss to plan participants of either a valuable right or an employer-subsidized optional form of benefit (see Qs 9:33, 9:34, 10:45) where a similar optional form of benefit with a comparable subsidy is not provided or to the extent such elimination or reduction is necessary to permit compliance with other qualification requirements. [Treas. Reg. § 1.411(d)-4, Q&A-2(b)(1)]

It is permissible to eliminate or reduce accrued benefits (see Q 9:2) if any of the following circumstances is present:

1. *Change in statutory requirement.* The amendment constitutes timely compliance with a change in law affecting plan qualification (IRS gives Section 7805(b) relief), and the elimination or reduction is made only to the extent necessary to comply with the plan qualification rules. An amendment will not be treated as necessary if it is possible to satisfy the applicable qualification requirement through other modifications to the plan (e.g., by expanding the availability of an optional form of benefit to additional employees).

2. *Joint and survivor annuity.* A qualified retirement plan that provides a range of three or more actuarially equivalent joint and survivor annuity options may be amended to eliminate any of such options, other than the options with the largest and smallest optional survivor payment percentages. The amendment is permissible even if the effect of such amendment is to change the option that is the QJSA (see Q 10:8).

   Example. A retirement plan provides three joint and survivor annuity options with survivor payments of 50 percent, 75 percent, and 100 percent, respectively. The options are uniform with respect to age and are actuarially equivalent. The employer may eliminate the option with the 75 percent survivor payment, even if this option had been the QJSA under the plan.

3. *In-kind distributions.* For details, see Q 9:31.

4. *Coordination with diversification requirement.* An ESOP (see Q 28:1) may be amended to provide that a distribution is not available in employer securities to the extent that an employee elects to diversify benefits (see Q 28:57).

5. *Involuntary distributions.* For details, see Q 10:42.

6. *Distribution exception for certain profit sharing plans.* If a defined contribution plan that is not subject to the minimum funding standards (see Q 8:1) and does not provide for an annuity option is terminated, the plan may be amended to provide for the distribution of a participant's accrued benefit (see Q 9:1) upon termination in a single-sum optional form without the participant's consent. This exception does not apply if the employer maintains any other defined contribution plan (other than an ESOP).

Example 1. Ironton Nancy Corp. maintains a defined contribution plan that is not subject to the minimum funding standards. The plan provides for distribution in the form of equal installments over five years or equal installments over twenty years, and Ironton Nancy Corp. maintains no other defined contribution plans. Ironton Nancy Corp. terminates its defined contribution plan after amending the plan to provide for the distribution of all participants' accrued benefits in the form of single-sum distributions, without obtaining participant consent. This amendment does not violate the anti-cutback rule.

Example 2. Ironton Nancy Corp. and Steeler Larry Ltd. are members of the Chelsea-Jamie controlled group of employers (see Q 5:31). Both Ironton Nancy Corp. and Steeler Larry Ltd. maintain defined contribution plans. Ironton Nancy Corp.'s plan, which is not subject to the minimum funding standards, covers only employees working for Ironton Nancy Corp.; and Steeler Larry Ltd.'s plan, which is subject to the minimum funding standards, covers only employees working for Steeler Larry Ltd. Ironton Nancy Corp. terminates its defined contribution plan. Because the Chelsea-Jamie controlled group maintains another defined contribution plan, Steeler Larry Ltd.'s plan, Ironton Nancy Corp.'s plan may not provide for the distribution of participants' accrued benefits upon termination without participant consent.

7. *Distribution of benefits on default of loans.* Notwithstanding that the distribution of benefits arising from an execution on an account balance used to secure a loan on which there has been a default is an optional form of benefit, a plan may be amended to eliminate or change a provision for loans, even if such loans would be secured by an employee's account balance (see Q 14:21).

8. *Provisions for transfer of benefits between and among defined contribution plans and defined benefit plans.* For details, see Q 9:32.

9. *De minimis change in the timing of an optional form of benefit.* A plan may be amended to modify an optional form of benefit by changing the timing of the availability of such optional form if, after the change, the optional form is available at a time that is within two months of the time such optional form was available before the amendment. To the extent the optional form of benefit is available prior to termination of employment, six months may be substituted for two months.

10. *Amendment of hardship distribution standards.* A qualified CODA (see Q 27:9) that permits hardship distributions (see Q 27:14) may be amended to specify or modify nondiscriminatory and objective standards for determining the existence of an immediate and heavy financial need, the amount necessary to meet the need, or other conditions relating to eligibility to receive a hardship distribution. For example, a plan will not be treated as violating the anti-cutback rule merely because it is amended to specify or modify the resources an employee must exhaust to qualify for a hardship distribution or to require employees to provide additional statements or representations to establish the existence of a hardship. A qualified CODA may also be amended to eliminate

hardship distributions. This paragraph also applies to profit sharing or stock bonus plans that permit hardship distributions.

11. *Section 415 limitations.* For details, see Q 6:33.

[Treas. Reg. § 1.411(d)-4, Q&A-2(b)(2)]

In addition, other special rules apply to ESOPs (see Q 28:2); and, for other circumstances permitting a reduction of accrued benefits, see Q 8:29.

The required beginning date for a non-5 percent owner is April 1 of the calendar year following the later of the calendar year in which the participant attains age 70½ or retires (see Q 11:5). An amendment that eliminates the right to receive a distribution before retirement (in-service distribution) after age 70½ is precluded if the amendment applies to benefits accrued as of the later of the adoption date or the effective date of the amendment. IRS has issued advice with regard to plan amendments eliminating the option to receive in-service distributions after age 70½. [Ann. 97-24, 1997-11 I.R.B. 24; IRS Notice 96-67, 1996-2 C.B. 235]

Q 9:36   Can a qualified retirement plan be amended to reduce future accruals of benefits?

Yes. A plan may be amended to eliminate or reduce a protected benefit with respect to benefits not yet accrued as of the later of the amendment's adoption date or effective date without violating the anti-cutback rule (see Q 9:25). [Treas. Reg. § 1.411(d)-4, Q&A-2(a)] One court concluded that a defined benefit plan (see Q 2:3) amendment that froze the accrual of benefits as of December 31, 1997 and caused a disabled employee's benefits to be recalculated as of the freeze date, rather than his normal retirement date (see Q 10:55), did not violate the anti-cutback rule because the employee's benefits beyond 1997 were not accrued. [Arndt v. Security Bank SSB Employees' Pension Plan, 182 F.2d 538 (7th Cir. 1999)] Another court determined that an amendment that removed a plan provision under which retired participants would receive the same benefit increases that active employees received was not prohibited, because the amendment eliminated only future benefit accruals and did not reduce existing accrued benefits. [Labrosse v. Trustees of the Asbestos Workers Local 47 Ret. Trust Plan, No. 1:00-CV-582 (W.D. Mich. 2001)] However, an amendment to a qualified retirement plan subject to the minimum funding requirements (see Q 8:1) that provides for a "significant reduction in the rate of future benefit accrual" will not be effective unless the plan administrator (see Q 20:1) provides written notice to all participants, any alternate payee under a QDRO (see Q 36:1), and each employee organization representing participants. That notice, which must set forth the amendment and its effective date, is required to be sent to such parties after adoption of the amendment and at least 15 days prior to its effective date. The reduction may result in either a termination or partial termination of the plan. See chapter 25 for details. [ERISA § 204(h); Treas. Reg. § 1.411(d)-6, Q&As-1 to 4]

One court concluded that it was not necessary to provide defined benefit plan participants with advance notice when the plan was converted to a cash balance plan (see Q 2:23) because the conversion did not result in a significant reduction in the rate of the participants' future benefit accruals. [Engers v. AT&T Corp., 2010 WL 2326211 (D. N.J. 2010); Engers v. AT&T Corp., No. 98-3660 (D. N.J. 2006)] However, another court determined that the conversion of an employer's defined benefit plan to a cash balance plan violated the notice requirements. [Amara v. CIGNA Corp., 348 Fed. Appx. 627 (2d Cir. 2009); *but see* Lonecke v. Citigroup Pension Plan, 2009 WL 3335910 (2d Cir. 2009)]

In a case in which an employer amended its qualified retirement plan to cease benefit accruals retroactively and gave notice of the amendment to its employees before the amendment was adopted and after the amendment's effective date, the court held that the amendment violated the prohibition against reducing accrued benefits and thus was ineffective. [Production & Maint. Employees' Local 504 v. Roadmaster Corp, Nos. 89-1464, 90-2698 (7th Cir. 1992)] In another case, the court ruled that an amendment to the employer's qualified retirement plan that excluded certain income from the plan's definition of compensation, the effect of which was to reduce future benefit accruals, was ineffective because prior written notice was not given to plan participants. [Davidson v. Canteen Corp., 957 F.2d 1404 (7th Cir. 1992)] Another court concluded that a participant was not entitled to notice regarding an amendment that contained a new benefit formula and new methodology for calculating single-sum benefits, because the participant never accrued benefits under the old formula. [Strom v. Shintech, Inc., No. 00-15809 (9th Cir. 2001)]

The written notice is called the Section 204(h) Notice. With regard to the Section 204(h) Notice, IRS has issued regulations effective for amendments adopted on or after December 12, 1998. [Treas. Reg. § 1.411(d)-6, Q&A-17] EGTRRA 2001 added Section 4980F and provisions affecting the Section 204(h) Notice, and IRS has promulgated regulations to reflect the EGTRRA 2001 changes (see Qs 9:37-9:53).

Q 9:37   How does EGTRRA 2001 affect the Section 204(h) Notice?

EGTRRA 2001 (see Q 1:21) added to the Code a requirement that the plan administrator (see Q 20:1) of a defined benefit plan (see Q 2:3) or an individual account plan subject to the minimum funding requirements (see Qs 2:2, 8:1) furnish a written notice concerning a plan amendment that provides for a significant reduction in the rate of future benefit accrual, including any elimination or significant reduction of an early retirement benefit or retirement-type subsidy. The plan administrator is required to provide in this notice, in a manner calculated to be understood by the average plan participant, sufficient information (as defined in regulations) to allow participants to understand the effect of the amendment.

IRS is authorized to provide a simplified notice requirement or an exemption from the notice requirement for plans with less than 100 participants and to allow any required notice to be provided by using new technologies. IRS is also authorized to provide a simplified notice requirement or an exemption from the notice requirement if participants are given the option to choose between benefits under the new plan formula and the old plan formula.

The plan administrator is required to provide this notice to each affected participant, each affected alternate payee (see Q 36:5), and each employee organization representing affected participants. An affected participant or alternate payee is a participant or alternate payee whose rate of future benefit accrual may reasonably be expected to be significantly reduced by the plan amendment. The plan administrator is required to provide the notice within a reasonable time before the effective date of the plan amendment. A plan administrator is permitted to provide any required notice to a person designated in writing by the individual to whom it would otherwise be provided.

There is imposed on a plan administrator which fails to comply with the notice requirement an excise tax equal to $100 per day per omitted participant and alternate payee. No excise tax is imposed during any period during which any person subject to liability for the tax did not know that the failure existed and exercised reasonable diligence to meet the notice requirement. In addition, no excise tax is imposed on any failure if any person subject to liability for the tax exercised reasonable diligence to meet the notice requirement and such person provides the required notice during the 30-day period beginning on the first date such person knew, or exercising reasonable diligence would have known, that the failure existed. Also, if the person subject to liability for the excise tax exercised reasonable diligence to meet the notice requirement, the total excise tax imposed during a taxable year of the employer will not exceed $500,000. Furthermore, in the case of a failure due to reasonable cause and not a willful neglect, IRS is authorized to waive the excise tax to the extent that the payment of the tax would be excessive relative to the failure involved.

In addition, the current ERISA notice requirement regarding significant reductions in normal retirement benefit accrual rates is expanded to include early retirement benefits and retirement-type subsidies (see Q 9:43). [Treas. Reg. § 54.4980F-1(b), Q&A-8(c)]

The above provisions are effective for plan amendments taking effect on or after June 7, 2001 (see Q 9:53).

[I.R.C. § 4980F; ERISA § 204(h)]

It was not necessary to provide defined benefit plan participants with a Section 204(h) Notice when the plan was converted to a cash balance plan (see Q 2:23) because, the conversion did not result in a significant reduction in the rate of the participants' future benefit accruals. [Engers v. AT&T Corp., 2010 WL 2326211 (D. N.J. 2010); Engers v. AT&T Corp., No. 98-3660 (D. N.J. 2006)] However, another court determined that the conversion of an employer's defined benefit plan to a cash balance plan violated the Section 204(h) Notice requirements. [Amara v. CIGNA Corp., 348 Fed. Appx. 627 (2d Cir. 2009); *but see* Lonecke v. Citigroup Pension Plan, 2009 WL 3335910 (2d Cir. 2009)]

IRS has issued final regulations reflecting the EGTRRA 2001 changes (see Qs 9:38-9:53).

Q 9:38   What are the notice requirements of the Code and ERISA?

Section 4980F and ERISA Section 204(h) each generally requires notice of an amendment to an applicable pension plan (see Q 9:39) that either provides for a significant reduction in the rate of future benefit accrual or eliminates or significantly reduces an early retirement benefit or retirement-type subsidy (see Qs 9:33, 9:34, 9:43). The notice is required to be provided to plan participants or alternate payees (see Q 36:5) who are applicable individuals (see Q 9:43), to certain employee organizations, and to contributing employers under a multi-employer plan (see Q 9:45). The plan administrator (see Q 20:1) must generally provide the notice before the effective date of the plan amendment (see Qs 9:44, 9:46, 9:47). This notice is called the Section 204(h) Notice. [I.R.C. § 4980F; Treas. Reg. § 54.4980F-1(b), Q&A-1(a); Priv. Ltr. Rul. 200407021]

Other provisions of law may require that certain parties be notified of a plan amendment. For example, for requirements relating to summary plan descriptions and SMMs, see chapter 22. [Treas. Reg. § 54.4980F-1(b), Q&A-1(b)]

The notice requirements of Section 4980F generally are parallel to the notice requirements of ERISA Section 204(h), as amended by EGTRRA 2001 (see Q 1:21). However, the consequences of the failure to satisfy the requirements of the two provisions differ: Section 4980F imposes an excise tax on a failure to satisfy the notice requirements, while ERISA Section 204(h)(6), as amended by EGTRRA 2001, contains a special rule with respect to an egregious failure to satisfy the notice requirements (see Qs 9:49, 9:50). Except to the extent specifically indicated, the regulations apply both to Section 4980F and to ERISA Section 204(h). [Treas. Reg. § 54.4980F-1(b), Q&A-2]

Q 9:39   What is an applicable pension plan?

For purposes of Section 4980F, an applicable pension plan means a qualified defined benefit plan (see Qs 1:5, 2:3) or an individual account plan that is subject to the minimum funding standards (see Q 8:1). For purposes of ERISA Section 204(h), an applicable pension plan means a defined benefit plan that is subject to part 2 of subtitle B of Title I of ERISA or an individual account plan that is subject to such part 2 and to the minimum funding standards of the Code. Accordingly, individual account plans that are not subject to the minimum funding standards, such as profit sharing and stock bonus plans (see Qs 2:6, 2:13), are not applicable pension plans to which either Section 4980F or ERISA Section 204(h) apply. Similarly, a defined benefit plan that neither is qualified nor is subject to part 2 of subtitle B of Title I of ERISA is not an applicable pension plan. [I.R.C. § 4980F(f)(2); Treas. Reg. § 54.4980F-1(b), Q&A-3(a); Priv. Ltr. Rul. 200407021]

The Section 204(h) Notice is not required for a plan under which no employees are participants covered under the plan (see Q 24:4) and which has fewer than 100 participants. [Treas. Reg. § 54.4980F-1(b), Q&A-3(b); DOL Reg. § 2510.3-3(b)]

Q 9:40   For which amendments is a Section 204(h) Notice required?

The Section 204(h) Notice is a notice that complies with Section 4980F(e), ERISA Section 204(h)(1), and the final regulations. A Section 204(h) Amendment (see Q 9:41) is an amendment for which the Section 204(h) Notice is required. [Treas. Reg. § 54.4980F-1(b), Q&A-4]

The Section 204(h) Notice is required for an amendment to an applicable pension plan (see Q 9:39) that provides for a significant reduction in the rate of future benefit accrual. The Section 204(h) Notice is also required for an amendment to an applicable pension plan that provides for the significant reduction of an early retirement benefit or retirement-type subsidy (see Qs 9:33, 9:34, 9:41). [I.R.C. §§ 4980F(e), 4980F(f)(3); Treas. Reg. § 54.4980F-1(b), Q&A-5 (a), Q&A-5(b); Priv. Ltr. Rul. 200407021]

In addition, for these purposes, the terms "reduce" or "reduction" include "eliminate" or "cease" or "elimination" or "cessation." [Treas. Reg. § 54.4980F-1(b), Q&A-5(c)]

IRS may provide in revenue rulings, notices, or other guidance that the Section 204(h) Notice need not be provided for plan amendments otherwise described above that IRS determines to be necessary or appropriate, as a result of changes in the law, to maintain compliance with the requirements of the Code (including requirements for tax qualification), ERISA, or other applicable federal law. [Treas. Reg. § 54.4980F-1(b), Q&A-5(d)]

It was not necessary to provide defined benefit plan participants with a Section 204(h) Notice when the plan was converted to a cash balance plan (see Q 2:23) because, at the time of the conversion, the conversion was not reasonably expected to result in a significant reduction in the rate of the participants' future benefit accruals. [Charles v. Pepco Holdings, Inc., 2008 WL 4787128 (3d Cir. 2008); *see also* Engers v. AT&T Corp., 2010 WL 2326211 (D. N.J. 2010) and Engers v. AT&T Corp., No. 98-3660 (D. N.J. 2006)] However, another court determined that the conversion of an employer's defined benefit plan to a cash balance plan violated the Section 204(h) Notice requirements. [Amara v. CIGNA Corp., 348 Fed. Appx. 627 (2d Cir. 2009); *but see* Lonecke v. Citigroup Pension Plan, 2009 WL 3335910 (2d Cir. 2009)] One court concluded that a plan's Section 204(h) Notice adequately disclosed the effect that the plan's conversion to a cash balance formula had on employees; however, the plan's failure to explain how early retirement benefits were determined under the original plan did violate the notice requirements. [Jensen v. Solvay Chemicals, Inc., 2010 WL 3472945 (10th Cir. 2010)]

Q 9:41   What is a Section 204(h) Amendment?

A Section 204(h) Notice is required if an amendment reduces the rate of future benefit accrual or reduces an early retirement benefit or retirement-type subsidy (see Qs 9:33, 9:34, 9:43). [Treas. Reg. § 54.4980F-1(b), Q&A-6(a)]

For purposes of Section 4980F and ERISA Section 204(h), an amendment to a defined benefit plan (see Q 2:3) reduces the rate of future benefit accrual only if it is reasonably expected that the amendment will reduce the amount of the future annual benefit commencing at normal retirement age (see Q 10:55), or at actual retirement age if later, for benefits accruing for a year. For this purpose, the annual benefit commencing at normal retirement age is the benefit payable in the form in which the terms of the plan express the accrued benefit (or, in the case of a plan in which the accrued benefit is not expressed in the form of an annual benefit commencing at normal retirement age, the benefit payable in the form of a single life annuity commencing at normal retirement age that is the actuarial equivalent of the accrued benefit expressed under the terms of the plan). [I.R.C. § 411(c)(3); Treas. Reg. § 54.4980F-1(b), Q&A-6(b)(1)] It was not necessary to provide defined benefit plan participants with a Section 204(h) Notice when the plan was converted to a cash balance plan (see Q 2:23) because the conversion did not result in a significant reduction in the rate of the participants' future benefit accruals. [Engers v. AT&T Corp., No. 98-3660 (D. N.J. 2006)] However, another court determined that the conversion of an employer's defined benefit plan to a cash balance plan violated the Section 204(h) Notice requirements. [Amara v. CIGNA Corp., 348 Fed. Appx. 627 (2d Cir. 2009); *but see* Lonecke v. Citigroup Pension Plan, 2009 WL 3335910 (2d Cir. 2009]

For purposes of Section 4980F and ERISA Section 204(h), an amendment to an individual account plan (see Q 9:39) reduces the rate of future benefit accrual only if it is reasonably expected that the amendment will reduce the amount of contributions or forfeitures allocated for any future year. Changes in the investments or investment options under an individual account plan are not taken into account for this purpose. [Treas. Reg. § 54.4980F-1(b), Q&A-6(b)(2); Priv. Ltr. Rul. 200407021]

The rate of future benefit accrual for these purposes is determined without regard to optional forms of benefit (see Qs 4:20, 10:45), other than the annual benefit described above. The rate of future benefit accrual is also determined without regard to ancillary benefits and other rights or features (see Q 4:20). [Treas. Reg. §§ 1.401(a)(4)-4(e), 1.411(d)-4, Q&A-1(b), 54.4980F-1(b), Q&A-6(b)(3)]

For purposes of Section 4980F and ERISA Section 204(h), an amendment reduces an early retirement benefit or retirement-type subsidy only if it is reasonably expected that the amendment will eliminate or reduce an early retirement benefit or retirement-type subsidy (see Qs 9:33, 9:34, 9:43). [Treas. Reg. § 54.4980F-1(b), Q&A-6(c)]

Q 9:42 What plan provisions are considered to determine if an amendment is a Section 204(h) Amendment?

All plan provisions that may affect the rate of future benefit accrual, early retirement benefits, or retirement-type subsidies of participants or alternate payees (see Q 36:5) must be taken into account in determining whether an amendment is a Section 204(h) Amendment (see Q 9:41). For example, plan provisions that may affect the rate of future benefit accrual include:

- The dollar amount or percentage of compensation on which benefit accruals are based
- The definition of service or compensation taken into account in determining an employee's benefit accrual
- The method of determining average compensation for calculating benefit accruals
- The definition of normal retirement age (see Q 10:55) in a defined benefit plan (see Q 2:3)
- The exclusion of current participants from future participation
- Benefit offset provisions
- Minimum benefit provisions
- The formula for determining the amount of contributions and forfeitures allocated to participants' accounts in an individual account plan (see Q 9:39)
- In the case of a plan using permitted disparity, the amount of disparity between the excess benefit percentage or excess contribution percentage and the base benefit percentage or base contribution percentage (see chapter 7)
- The actuarial assumptions used to determine contributions under a target benefit plan (see Q 2:5)

Plan provisions that may affect early retirement benefits or retirement-type subsidies include the right to receive payment of benefits after severance from employment and before normal retirement age and actuarial factors used in determining optional forms for distribution of retirement benefits (see Qs 4:20, 9:33, 9:34, 9:43, 10:45).

[Treas. Reg. § 54.4980F-1(b), Q&A-7(a)(1); Priv. Ltr. Rul. 200407021]

If all or part of a plan's rate of future benefit accrual, or an early retirement benefit or retirement-type subsidy provided under the plan, depends on provisions in another document that are referenced in the plan document, a change in the provisions of the other document is an amendment of the plan.

[Treas. Reg. § 54.4980F-1(b), Q&A-7(a)(2)]

Plan provisions that do not affect the rate of future benefit accrual of participants or alternate payees are not taken into account in determining whether there has been a reduction in the rate of future benefit accrual. Further, any benefit that is not a Section 411(d)(6) protected benefit (see Q 9:54) or that is a Section 411(d)(6) protected benefit that may be eliminated or reduced (see Qs 9:28, 9:35) is not taken into account in determining whether an amendment is a Section 204(h) Amendment. Thus, for example, provisions relating to the right to make after-tax contributions (see Q 27:77) are not taken into account. [Treas. Reg. § 54.4980F-1(b), Q&A-7(b)]

Example 1. A defined benefit plan provides a normal retirement benefit equal to 50 percent of highest five-year average compensation times a fraction (not in excess of one), the numerator of which equals the number of years of participation in the plan and the denominator of which is 20. A plan amendment is adopted that changes the numerator or denominator of that fraction. The plan amendment must be taken into account in determining whether there has been a reduction in the rate of future benefit accrual.

Example 2. Plan C is a multiemployer defined benefit plan (see Q 29:2) subject to several collective bargaining agreements (CBAs). The specific benefit formula under Plan C that applies to an employee depends on the hourly rate of contribution of the employee's employer, which is set forth in the provisions of the CBAs that are referenced in the Plan C document. CBA-1 between Jason Corporation and the union representing its employees is renegotiated to provide that the hourly contribution rate for an employee of Jason Corporation who is subject to CBA-1 will decrease. That decrease will result in a decrease in the rate of future benefit accrual for the employees of Jason Corporation. The change to CBA-1 is a plan amendment that is a Section 204(h) Amendment if the reduction in the rate of future benefit accrual is significant.

Q 9:43 What is the basic principle used in determining whether a reduction is significant?

Whether an amendment reducing the rate of future benefit accrual or eliminating or reducing an early retirement benefit or retirement-type subsidy provides for a reduction that is significant is determined based on reasonable expectations, taking into account the relevant facts and circumstances at the time the amendment is adopted or, if earlier, at the effective date of the amendment. [Treas. Reg. § 54.4980F-1(b), Q&A-8(a)]

For a defined benefit plan (see Q 2:3), the determination of whether an amendment provides for a significant reduction in the rate of future benefit accrual is made by comparing the amount of the annual benefit commencing at normal retirement age (see Q 9:41), or at actual retirement age if later, under the terms of the plan as amended with the amount of the annual benefit commencing at normal retirement age, or at actual retirement age if later, under the terms of the plan prior to amendment. For an individual account plan (see Q 9:39), the determination of whether an amendment provides for a significant reduction in the rate of future benefit accrual is made by comparing the amounts to be allocated in the future to participants' accounts under the terms of the plan as amended with the amounts to be allocated in the future to participants' accounts under the terms of the plan prior to amendment (see Q 9:41). An amendment to convert a money purchase pension plan to a profit sharing or other individual account plan that is not subject to the minimum funding requirements (see Qs 8:1, 25:4) is, in all cases, deemed to be an amendment that provides for a significant reduction in the rate of future benefit accrual. [Treas. Reg. § 54.4980F-1(b), Q&A-8(b); Priv. Ltr. Rul. 200407021]

Because the Section 204(h) Notice is required only for reductions that are significant, the notice is not required for an amendment that reduces an early retirement benefit or retirement-type subsidy if the amendment relates to the elimination or reduction of benefits or subsidies that create significant burdens or complexities for the plan and plan participants unless the amendment adversely affects the rights of any participant in a more than *de minimis* manner. [I.R.C. § 411(d)(6)(B); Treas. Reg. §§ 1.411(d)-3, 54.4980F-1(b), Q&A-8(c)]

If a defined benefit plan offers a distribution to which the minimum present value rules apply and the plan is amended to reflect the changes to the applicable interest rate and mortality table made by PPA (see Q 1:33) (and no change is made in the dates on which the payment will be made), no Section 204(h) Notice is required to be provided. [Treas. Reg. § 54.4980F-1(b), Q&A-8(d)]

Example 1. A defined benefit plan provides a rate of benefit accrual of 1 percent of highest-five years' pay multiplied by years of service, payable annually for life commencing at normal retirement age (or at accrual retirement age, if later). An amendment to the plan is adopted on August 1, 2010, effective January 1, 2011, to provide that any participant who separates from service after December 31, 2010 and before January 1, 2016, will have the same number of years of service the participant would have had if service continued to December 31, 2015. The effective date of the plan amendment is January 1, 2011. While the amendment will result in a reduction in the annual rate of future benefit accrual from 2012 through 2015 (because, under the amendment, benefits based upon an additional five years of service accrue on January 1, 2011, and no additional service is credited after January 1, 2011 until January 1, 2016), the amendment does not result in a reduction that is significant because the amount of the annual benefit commencing at normal retirement age (or at actual retirement age, if later) under the terms of the plan as amended is not under any conditions less than the amount of the annual benefit commencing at normal retirement age (or at actual retirement age, if later) to which any participant would have been entitled under the terms of the plan had the amendment not been made.

Example 2. The facts are the same as in Example 1, except that the 2010 amendment does not alter the plan provisions relating to a participant's number of years of service, but instead amends the plan's provisions relating to early retirement benefits. Before the amendment, the plan provides for distributions before normal retirement age to be actuarially reduced; but, if a participant retires after attainment of age 55 and completion of ten years of service, the applicable early retirement reduction factor is 3 percent per year for the years between ages 65 and 62 and 6 percent per year for the ages from 62 to 55. The amendment changes these provisions so that an actuarial reduction applies in all cases, but provides that no participant's early retirement benefit will be less than the amount provided under the plan as in effect on December 31, 2010, with respect to service before January 1, 2011. For participant X, the reduction is significant. The amendment will result in a reduction in retirement-type subsidy provided under Plan A (i.e., Plan A's early retirement subsidy). The Section 204(h) Notice must be provided to participant X and any other participant for whom the reduction is significant, and the notice must be provided at least 45 days before January 1, 2011, or by such other date as may apply (see Q 9:44).

Example 3. The facts are the same as in Example 2, except that, for participant X, the change does not go into effect for any annuity starting date before January 1, 2012. Participant X continues employment through January 1, 2012. The conclusion is the same as in Example 2. Taking into account the rule that the amendment is treated in the same manner as an amendment that limits the retirement-type subsidy that accrues before the applicable amendment date, the reduction that occurs for participant X on January 1, 2012, is treated as the same reduction that occurs under Example 2. Accordingly, assuming the reduction is significant, the Section 204(h) Notice must be provided to participant X at least 45 days before the January 1, 2011 effective date of the amendment or by such other date as may apply.

Q 9:44   When must the Section 204(h) Notice be provided?

Except as described below, the Section 204(h) Notice must be provided at least 45 days before the effective date of any Section 204(h) Amendment (see Q 9:41). [I.R.C. § 4980F(e)(3); Treas. Reg. § 54.4980F-1(b), Q&A-9(a)]

Except for amendments relating to certain plan transfers described below, in the case of a small plan, the Section 204(h) Notice must be provided at least 15 days before the effective date of any Section 204(h) Amendment. [Priv. Ltr. Rul. 200407021] For this purpose, a small plan is a plan that the plan administrator (see Q 20:1) reasonably expects to have, on the effective date of the Section 204(h) Amendment, fewer than 100 participants who have an accrued benefit (see Q 9:2) under the plan. [Treas. Reg. § 54.4980F-1(b), Q&A-9(b)] The 15-day rule also applies to multiemployer plans (see Q 29:2). [Treas. Reg. § 54.4980F-1(b), Q&A-9(c)] In addition, except for amendments relating to certain plan transfers described below, if a Section 204(h) Amendment is adopted in connection with an acquisition or disposition, the Section 204(h) Notice must be provided at least 15 days before the effective date of the Section 204(h) Amendment. [Treas. Reg. §§ 1.410(b)-2(f), 54.4980F-1(b), Q&A-9(d)(1), 54.4980F-1(b), Q&A-9(d)(3)]

If a Section 204(h) Amendment is adopted with respect to liabilities that are transferred to another plan in connection with a transfer, merger, or consolidation of assets or liabilities, the amendment is adopted in connection with an acquisition or disposition, and the amendment significantly reduces an early retirement benefit or retirement-type subsidy, but does not significantly reduce the rate of future benefit accrual, then the Section 204(h) Notice must be provided no later than 30 days after the effective date of the Section 204(h) Amendment. [I.R.C. § 414(*l*); Treas. Reg. §§ 1.410(b)-2(f), 1.414(*l*)-1, 54.4980F-1(b), Q&A-9(d)(2), 54.4980F-1(b), Q&A-9(d)(3)]

In general, the Section 204(h) Notice of a Section 204(h) Amendment that provides applicable individuals (see Q 9:45) with a choice between the old and the new benefit formulas (see Q 9:47) must be provided in accordance with the applicable time period described above. [Treas. Reg. § 54.4980F-1(b), Q&A-9(e)]

Special rules are provided with respect to a plan amendment that would not violate the anti-cutback rule (see Q 9:25) even if the amendment were to reduce Section 411(d)(6) protected benefits (see Q 10:45), which are limited to accrued benefits that are attributable to service before the applicable amendment date. For example, these special rules apply to amendments that are permitted to be effective retroactively (see Q 8:29). [Treas. Reg. § 54.4980F-1(b), Q&A-9(g)(1)] For an amendment to which these special rules apply, the amendment is effective on the first date on which the plan is operated as if the amendment were in effect. Thus, except as otherwise provided by these special rules, a Section 204(h) Notice that is required for an amendment that is adopted after the effective date of the amendment must be provided, with respect to any applicable individual, at least 45 days (or 15 days, if applicable) before the date the amendment is put into operational effect. [Treas. Reg. § 54.4980F-1(b), Q&A-9(g)(2)]

Notwithstanding the timing requirements of this Q 9:44 and the content requirements (see Q 9:46), if a plan provides one of the following notices in accordance with the applicable timing and content rules for such notice, the plan is treated as timely providing a Section 204(h) Notice with respect to a Section 204(h) Amendment. These notices are as follows:

1. A notice required under any revenue ruling, notice, or other guidance published by IRS to affected parties in connection with a retroactive plan amendment (see Q 8:29);

2. A notice required under ERISA Section 101(j) if an amendment is adopted to comply with the benefit limitation requirements of Section 436 (see Q 8:6);

3. A notice required under ERISA Section 4244A(b) for an amendment that reduces or eliminates accrued benefits attributable to employer contributions with respect to a multiemployer plan in reorganization (see Q 29:12);

4. A notice required under ERISA Section 4245(e), relating to the effects of the insolvency status for a multiemployer plan (see Q 29:12); and

5. A notice required under ERISA Section 4281 for an amendment of a multiemployer plan reducing benefits (see Q 29:50). [Treas. Reg. § 54. 4980F-1(b), Q&A-9(g)(3)]

IRS may provide special rules under Section 4980F in revenue rulings, notices, or other guidance that it determines to be necessary or appropriate with respect to a Section 204(h) Amendment (1) that applies to benefits accrued before the applicable amendment date but that does not violate the anti-cutback rule, or (2) for which there is a required notice relating to a reduction in benefits and such notice has timing and content requirements similar to a Section 204(h) Notice with respect to a significant reduction in the rate of future benefit accruals. [Treas. Reg. § 54.4980F-1(b), Q&A-9(g)(4)]

One court held that the statute of limitations did not begin to run with respect to a claim that an employer had violated the Section 204(h) Notice requirement until the employees knew or should have known that a plan amendment had the effect of significantly reducing benefits. [Romero v. The Allstate Corp., 404 F.3d 212 (3d Cir. 2005)]

Q 9:45   To whom must the Section 204(h) Notice be provided?

The Section 204(h) Notice must be provided to each applicable individual, to each employee organization representing participants who are applicable individuals, and, for plan years beginning after December 31, 2007, to each employer that has an obligation to contribute to a multiemployer plan (see Q 29:2). Applicable individual means each participant in the plan, and any alternate payee (see Q 36:5), whose rate of future benefit accrual under the plan is reasonably expected to be significantly reduced, or for whom an early retirement benefit or retirement-type subsidy under the plan may reasonably be expected to be significantly reduced, by the Section 204(h) Amendment (see Q 9:41). The determination is made with respect to individuals who are reasonably expected to be participants or alternate payees in the plan at the effective date of the Section 204(h) Amendment. [I.R.C. §§ 4980F(e)(1), 4980F(f)(1); ERISA § 4212(a); Treas. Reg. § 54.4980F-1(b), Q&A-10(a) through (c); Priv. Ltr. Rul. 200407021]

The Section 204(h) Notice may be provided to a person designated in writing by an applicable individual or by an employee organization representing participants who are applicable individuals, instead of being provided to that applicable individual or employee organization. Any designation of a representative made through an electronic method that satisfies certain standards (see Q 9:48) satisfies the requirement that a designation be in writing. [I.R.C. § 4980F(e)(4); Treas. Reg. § 54.4980F-1(b), Q&A-10(d)]

Whether a participant or alternate payee is an applicable individual is determined on a typical business day that is reasonably proximate to the time the Section 204(h) Notice is provided (or at the latest date for providing the Section 204(h) Notice, if earlier), based on all relevant facts and circumstances. [Treas. Reg. § 54.4980F-1(b), Q&A-10(e)]

> **Example 1.** A defined benefit plan requires an individual to complete one year of service to become a participant who can accrue benefits, and participants cease to accrue benefits under the plan at severance from employment with the employer. There are no alternate payees, and employees are not represented by an employee organization. On November 18, 2010, the plan is amended effective as of January 1, 2011, to significantly reduce the rate of future benefit accrual. The Section 204(h) Notice is provided on November 1, 2010. The Section 204(h) Notice is required to be provided only to individuals who, based on the facts and circumstances on November 1, 2010, are reasonably expected to have completed at least one year of service and to be employed by the employer on January 1, 2011.

> **Example 2.** The facts are the same as in Example 1, except that the sole effect of the plan amendment is to alter the pre-amendment plan provisions under which benefits payable to an employee who retires after 20 or more years of service are unreduced for commencement before normal retirement age. The amendment requires 30 or more years of service in order for benefits commencing before normal retirement age to be unreduced, but the amendment applies only for future benefit accruals. The Section 204(h) Notice is only required to be provided to individuals who, on January 1, 2010, have

completed at least one year of service but less than 30 years of service, are employed by the employer, have not attained normal retirement age, and will have completed 20 or more years of service before normal retirement age if their employment continues to normal retirement age.

Example 3. A plan is amended to reduce significantly the rate of future benefit accrual of all current employees who are participants in the plan. Based on the facts and circumstances, it is reasonable to expect that the amendment will not reduce the rate of future benefit accrual of former employees who are currently receiving benefits or of former employees who are entitled to deferred vested benefits. The plan administrator is not required to provide the Section 204(h) Notice to any former employees.

Example 4. Assume in Example 3 that the plan also covers two groups of alternate payees. The alternate payees in the first group are entitled to a certain percentage or portion of the former spouse's accrued benefit; and, for this purpose, the accrued benefit is determined at the time the former spouse begins receiving retirement benefits under the plan. The alternate payees in the second group are entitled to a certain percentage or portion of the former spouse's accrued benefit; and, for this purpose, the accrued benefit was determined at the time the QDRO (see Q 36:1) was issued by the court. It is reasonable to expect that the benefits to be received by the second group of alternate payees will not be affected by any reduction in a former spouse's rate of future benefit accrual. Accordingly, the plan administrator is not required to provide the Section 204(h) Notice to the alternate payees in the second group.

Example 5. A plan covers hourly employees and salaried employees. The plan provides the same rate of benefit accrual for both groups. The employer amends the plan to reduce significantly the rate of future benefit accrual of the salaried employees only. At that time, it is reasonable to expect that only a small percentage of hourly employees will become salaried in the future. The plan administrator is not required to provide the Section 204(h) Notice to the participants who are currently hourly employees.

Example 6. A plan covers employees in Division M and employees in Division N. The plan provides the same rate of benefit accrual for both groups. The employer amends the plan to reduce significantly the rate of future benefit accrual of employees in Division M. At that time, it is reasonable to expect that in the future only a small percentage of employees in Division N will be transferred to Division M. The plan administrator is not required to provide the Section 204(h) Notice to the participants who are employees in Division N.

Example 7. Assume the same facts as in Example 6 except that, at the time the amendment is adopted, it is expected that soon thereafter Division N will be merged into Division M in connection with a corporate reorganization and the employees in Division N will become subject to the plan's amended benefit formula applicable to the employees in Division M. In this case, the plan administrator must provide the Section 204(h) Notice to the participants who are employees in Division M and to the participants who are employees in Division N.

Example 8. A plan is amended to reduce significantly the rate of future benefit accrual for all current employees who are participants. The plan amendment will be effective on January 1, 2011, and the plan will provide the notice to applicable individuals on October 31, 2010. In determining which current employees are applicable individuals, the plan administrator determines that October 1, 2010, is a typical business day that is reasonably proximate to the time the Section 204(h) Notice is provided. In this case, October 1, 2010, is considered a typical business day that satisfies the relevant facts and circumstances requirement.

Q 9:46 What information is required to be provided in the Section 204(h) Notice?

The Section 204(h) Notice must include sufficient information to allow applicable individuals (see Q 9:45) to understand the effect of the plan amendment. To satisfy this rule, a plan administrator (see Q 20:1) providing the Section 204(h) Notice must satisfy each of the requirements discussed below. [I.R.C. § 4980F(e)(2); Treas. Reg. § 54.4980F-1(b), Q&A-11(a)(1); Priv. Ltr. Rul. 200407021] The information must be written in a manner calculated to be understood by the average plan participant and to apprise the applicable individual of the significance of the notice. [I.R.C. § 4980F(e)(2); Treas. Reg. § 54.4980F-1(b), Q&A-11(a)(2)]

In the case of an amendment reducing the rate of future benefit accrual, the notice must include a description of the benefit or allocation formula prior to the amendment, a description of the benefit or allocation formula under the plan as amended, and the effective date of the amendment. [Treas. Reg. § 54.4980F-1(b), Q&A-11(a)(3)(i)]

In the case of an amendment that reduces an early retirement benefit or retirement-type subsidy (other than as a result of an amendment reducing the rate of future benefit accrual), the notice must describe how the early retirement benefit or retirement-type subsidy (see Qs 9:33, 9:34, 9:43) is calculated from the accrued benefit before the amendment, how the early retirement benefit or retirement-type subsidy is calculated from the accrued benefit after the amendment, and the effective date of the amendment. For example, if, for a plan with a normal retirement age of 65, the change is from an unreduced normal retirement benefit at age 55 to an unreduced normal retirement benefit at age 60 for benefits accrued in the future, with an actuarial reduction to apply for benefits accrued in the future to the extent that the early retirement benefit begins before age 60, the notice must state the change and specify the factors that apply in calculating the actuarial reduction (e.g., a 5 percent per year reduction applies for early retirement before age 60). [Treas. Reg. § 54.4980F-1(b), Q&A-11(a)(3)(ii)]

The Section 204(h) Notice must include sufficient information for each applicable individual to determine the approximate magnitude of the expected reduction for that individual. In any case in which it is not reasonable to expect that the approximate magnitude of the reduction will be reasonably apparent from the description provided, further information is required. The further information may be provided by furnishing additional narrative information or in other information that satisfies these requirements. [Treas. Reg. § 54.4980F-1(b), Q&A-11(a)(4)(i)(A)] To the extent any expected reduction is not uniformly applicable to all participants, the notice must either identify the general classes of participants to whom the reduction is expected to apply, or by some other method include sufficient information to allow each applicable individual receiving the notice to determine which reductions are expected to apply to that individual. [Treas. Reg. § 54.4980F-1(b), Q&A-11(a)(4)(i)(B)]

The requirement to include sufficient information for each applicable individual to determine the approximate magnitude of the expected reduction for that individual is deemed satisfied if the notice includes one or more illustrative examples showing the approximate magnitude of the reduction in the examples. Illustrative examples are in any event required to be provided for any change from a traditional defined benefit formula (see Qs 2:17, 2:18) to a cash balance formula (see Q 9:27) or a change that results in a period of time during which there are no accruals (or minimal accruals) with regard to normal retirement benefits or an early retirement subsidy (a wear-away period). [Treas. Reg. § 54.4980F-1(b), Q&A-11(a)(4)(ii)(A)]

Where an amendment results in reductions that vary (either among participants, as would occur for an amendment converting a traditional defined benefit formula to a cash balance formula, or over time as to any individual participant, as would occur for an amendment that results in a wear-away period), the illustrative example(s) to be provided must show the approximate range of the reductions. However, any reductions that are likely to occur in only a *de minimis* number of cases are not required to be taken into account in determining the range of the reductions if a narrative statement is included to that effect and examples are provided that show the approximate range of the reductions in other cases. Amendments for which the maximum reduction occurs under identifiable circumstances, with proportionately smaller reductions in other cases, may be illustrated by one example illustrating the maximum reduction, with a statement that smaller reductions also occur. Further, assuming that the reduction varies from small to large depending on service or other factors, two illustrative examples may be provided showing the smallest likely reduction and the largest likely reduction. [Treas. Reg. § 54.4980F-1(b), Q&A-11(a)(4)(ii)(B)]

The examples required are not required to be based on any particular form of payment (such as a life annuity or a single sum), but may be based on whatever form appropriately illustrates the reduction. The examples generally may be based on any reasonable assumptions (e.g., assumptions relating to the representative participant's age, years of service, and compensation, along with any interest rate and mortality table used in the illustrations, as well as salary scale assumptions used in the illustrations for amendments that alter the compensation taken into account under the plan), but the Section 204(h) Notice must identify those assumptions. However, if a plan's benefit provisions include a factor that varies over time (such as a variable interest rate), the determination of whether an amendment is reasonably expected to result in a wear-away period must be based on the value of the factor applicable under the plan at a time that is reasonably close to the date the Section 204(h) Notice is provided, and any wear-away period that is solely a result of a future change in the variable factor may be disregarded. For example, to determine whether a wear-away occurs as a result of a Section 204(h) Amendment (see Q 9:39) that converts a defined benefit plan to a cash balance plan that will credit interest based on a variable interest factor specified in the plan, the future interest credits must be projected based on the interest rate applicable under the variable factor at the time the Section 204(h) Notice is provided. [Treas. Reg. § 54.4980F-1(b), Q&A-11(a)(4)(ii)(C)]

The foregoing requirements may be satisfied by providing a statement to each applicable individual projecting what that individual's future benefits are reasonably expected to be at various future dates and what that individual's future benefits would have been under the terms of the plan as in effect before the Section 204(h) Amendment, provided that the statement includes the same information required for examples, including showing the approximate range of the reductions for the individual if the reductions vary over time and identification of the assumptions used in the projections. [Treas. Reg. § 54.4980F-1(b), Q&A-11(a)(4)(ii)(D)]

A Section 204(h) Notice may not include materially false or misleading information (or omit information so as to cause the information provided to be misleading). [Treas. Reg. § 54.4980F-1(b), Q&A-11(a)(5)]

If an amendment by its terms affects different classes of participants differently (e.g., one new benefit formula will apply to Division A and another to Division B), then these requirements apply separately with respect to each such general class of participants. In addition, the notice must include sufficient information to enable an applicable individual who is a participant to understand of which class the individual is a member. [Treas. Reg. § 54.4980F-1(b), Q&A-11(a)(6)(i)]

If a Section 204(h) Amendment affects different classes of applicable individuals differently, the plan administrator may provide to differently affected classes of applicable individuals a Section 204(h) Notice appropriate to those individuals. Such Section 204(h) Notice may omit information that does not apply to the applicable individuals to whom it is furnished, but must identify the class or classes of applicable individuals to whom it is provided. [Treas. Reg. § 54.4980F-1(b), Q&A-11(a)(6)(ii)]

The following examples illustrate the requirements discussed above. In each example it is assumed that the notice is written in a manner calculated to be understood by the average plan participant and to apprise the applicable individual of the significance of the notice.

Example 1. Plan A provides that a participant is entitled to a normal retirement benefit of 2 percent of the participant's average pay over the three consecutive years for which the average is the highest (highest average pay) multiplied by years of service. Plan A is amended to provide that, effective January 1, 2011, the normal retirement benefit will be 2 percent of the participant's highest average pay multiplied by years of service before the effective date, plus 1 percent of the participant's highest average pay multiplied by years of service after the effective date. The plan administrator provides notice that states:

> Under the Plan's current benefit formula, a participant's normal retirement benefit is 2 percent of the participant's average pay over the three consecutive years for which the average is the highest multiplied by the participant's years of service. This formula is being changed by a plan amendment. Under the Plan as amended, a participant's normal retirement benefit will be the sum of 2 percent of the participant's average pay over the three consecutive years for which the average is the highest multiplied by years of service before the effective date, plus 1 percent of the participant's average pay over the three consecutive years for which the average is the highest multiplied by the participant's years of service after December 31, 2010. This change is effective on January 1, 2011.

The notice does not contain any additional information. The notice satisfies the requirements.

Example 2. Plan B provides that a participant is entitled to a normal retirement benefit at age 64 of 2.2 percent of the participant's career average pay times years of service. Plan B is amended to cease all accruals, effective January 1, 2011. The plan administrator provides notice that includes a description of the old benefit formula, a statement that, after December 31, 2010, no participant will earn any further accruals, and the effective date of the amendment. The notice does not contain any additional information. The notice satisfies the requirements.

Example 3. Plan C provides that a participant is entitled to a normal retirement benefit at age 65 of 2 percent of career average compensation times years of service. Plan C is amended to provide that the normal retirement benefit will be 1 percent of average pay over the three consecutive years for which the average is the highest times years of service. The amendment applies only to accruals for years of service after the amendment, so that each employee's accrued benefit is equal to the sum of the benefit accrued as of the effective date of the amendment plus the accrued benefit equal to the new formula applied to years of service beginning on or after the effective date. The plan administrator provides notice that describes the old and new benefit formulas and also explains that, for an individual whose compensation increases over the individual's career such that the individual's highest three-year average exceeds the individual's career average, the reduction will be less or there may be no reduction. The notice does not contain any additional information. The notice satisfies the requirements.

Example 4. Plan D is a defined benefit plan under which each participant accrues a normal retirement benefit, as a life annuity beginning at the normal retirement age of 65, equal to the participant's number of years of service times 1.5 percent times the participant's average pay over the three consecu- tive years for which the average is the highest. Plan D provides early retirement benefits for former employees beginning at or after age 55 in the form of an early retirement annuity that is actuarially equivalent to the normal retirement benefit, with the reduction for early commencement based on reasonable actuarial assumptions that are specified in Plan D. Plan D provides for the suspension of benefits of participants who continue in employment beyond normal retirement age. The pension of a participant who retires after age 65 is calculated under the same normal retirement benefit formula, but is based on the participant's service credit and highest three-year pay at the time of late retirement with any appropriate actuarial increases.

Plan D is amended, effective July 1, 2011, to change the formula for all future accruals to a cash balance formula under which the opening account balance for each participant on July 1, 2011, is zero, hypothetical pay credits equal to 5 percent of pay are credited to the account thereafter, and hypothetical interest is credited monthly based on the applicable interest rate at the beginning of the quarter. Any participant who terminates employment with vested benefits can receive an actuarially equivalent annuity (based on the same reasonable actuarial assumptions that are specified in Plan D) com- mencing at any time after termination of employment and before the plan's normal retirement age of 65. The benefit resulting from the hypothetical account balance is in addition to the benefit accrued before July 1, 2011 (taking into account only service and highest three-year pay before July 1, 2011), so that it is reasonably expected that no wear-away period will result from the amendment. The plan administrator expects that, as a general rule, depending on future pay increases and future interest rates, the rate of future benefit accrual after the conversion is higher for participants who accrue benefits before approximately age 50 and after approximately age 70, but is lower for participants who accrue benefits between approximately age 50 and age 70.

The plan administrator announces the conversion to a cash balance formula on May 16, 2010. The announcement is delivered to all participants and includes a written notice that describes the old formula, the new formula, and the effective date.

In addition, the notice states that the Plan D formula before the conversion provided a normal retirement benefit equal to the product of a participant's number of years of service times 1.5 percent times the participant's average pay over the three years for which the average is the highest (highest three-year pay). The notice includes an example showing the normal retire- ment benefit that will be accrued after June 30, 2011, for a participant who is age 49 with ten years of service at the time of the conversion. The plan administrator reasonably believes that such a participant is representative of the participants whose rate of future benefit accrual will be reduced as a result of the amendment. The example estimates that, if the participant continues employment to age 65, the participant's normal retirement benefit for service from age 49 to age 65 will be $657 per month for life. The example assumes that the participant's pay is $50,000 at age 49. The example states that the estimated $657 monthly pension accrues over the 16-year period from age 49 to age 65 and that, based on assumed future pay increases, this amount annually would be 9.1 percent of the participant's highest three-year pay at age 65, which over the 16 years from age 49 to age 65 averages 0.57 percent per year times the participant's highest three-year pay. The example also states that the sum of the monthly annuity accrued before the conversion in the ten-year period from age 39 to age 49 plus the $657 monthly annuity estimated to be accrued over the 16-year period from age 49 to age 65 is $1,235 and that, based on, assumed future increases in pay, this would be 17.1 percent of the participant's highest three-year pay at age 65, which over the employee's career from age 39 to age 65 averages 0.66 percent per year times the participant's highest three-year pay. The notice also includes two other examples with similar information, one of which is intended to show the circumstances in which a small reduction may occur and the other of which shows the largest reduction that the plan administrator thinks is likely to occur. The notice states that the estimates are based on the assumption that pay increases annually after June 30, 2011, at a 4 percent rate. The notice also specifies that the applicable interest rate for hypothetical interest credits after June 30, 2011, is assumed to be 6 percent, which is the applicable interest rate under the plan for 2011.

The information in the notice satisfies the requirements with respect to applicable individuals who are participants. The additional requirements are satisfied because the notice describes the old formula and describes the estimated future accruals under the new formula in terms that can be readily compared to the old formula (i.e., the notice states that the estimated $657 monthly pension accrued over the 16-year period from age 49 to age 65 averages 0.57 percent of the participant's highest three-year pay at age 65). The requirement that the examples include sufficient information to be able to determine the approximate magnitude of the reduction would also be satisfied if the notice instead directly stated the amount of the monthly pension that would have accrued over the 16-year period from age 49 to age 65 under the old formula.

Example 5. The facts are the same as in Example 4, except that, under the plan as in effect before the amendment, the early retirement pension for a participant who terminates employment after age 55 with at least 20 years of service is equal to the normal retirement benefit without reduction from age 65 to age 62 and reduced by only 5 percent per year for each year before age 62. As a result, early retirement benefits for such a participant constitute a retirement-type subsidy. The plan as in effect after the amendment provides an early retirement benefit equal to the sum of the early retirement benefit payable under the plan as in effect before the amendment taking into account only service and highest three-year pay before July 1, 2011, plus an early retirement annuity that is actuarially equivalent to the account balance for service after June 30, 2011. The notice provided by the plan administrator describes the old early retirement annuity, the new early retirement annuity, and the effective date. The notice includes an estimate of the early retirement annuity payable to the illustrated participant for service after the conversion if the participant were to retire at age 59 (which the plan administrator believes is a typical early retirement age) and elect to begin receiving an immediate early retirement annuity. The example states that the normal retirement benefit expected to be payable at age 65 as a result of service from age 49 to age 59 is $434 per month for life beginning at age 65 and that the early retirement annuity expected to be payable as a result of service from age 49 to age 59 is $270 per month for life beginning at age 59. The example states that the monthly early retirement annuity of $270 is 38 percent less than the monthly normal retirement benefit of $434, whereas a 15 percent reduction would have applied under the plan as in effect before the amendment. The notice also includes similar information for examples that show the smallest and largest reduction that the plan administrator thinks is likely to occur in the early retirement benefit. The notice also specifies the applicable interest rate, mortality table, and salary scale used in the example to calculate the early retirement reductions.

The information in the notice satisfies the requirements with respect to applicable individuals who are participants. The requirements are satisfied because the notice describes the early retirement subsidy under the old formula and describes the estimated early retirement pension under the new formula in terms that can be readily compared to the old formula (i.e., the notice states that the monthly early retirement pension of $270 is 38 percent less than the monthly normal retirement benefit of $434, whereas a 15 percent reduction would have applied under the plan as in effect before the amendment). The requirements would also be satisfied if the notice instead directly stated the amount of the monthly early retirement pension that would be payable at age 59 under the old formula.

See Q 9:44 for special rules relating to Section 204(h) Notices provided in connection with other written notices.

Q 9:47 What special rules apply if participants can choose between the old and new benefit formulas?

In any case in which an applicable individual (see Q 9:45) can choose between the benefit formula (including any early retirement benefit or retirement-type subsidy) in effect before the Section 204(h) Amendment (see Q 9:41; old formula) or the benefit formula in effect after the Section 204(h) Amendment (new formula), the Section 204(h) Notice has not been provided unless the applicable individual has been provided the required information (see Q 9:46) and has also been provided sufficient information to enable the individual to make an informed choice between the old and new benefit formulas. The information required must be provided by the date otherwise required (see Q 9:44). The information sufficient to enable the individual to make an informed choice must be provided within a period that is reasonably contemporaneous with the date by which the individual is required to make the choice and that allows sufficient advance notice to enable the individual to understand and consider the additional information before making that choice. [Treas. Reg. § 54.4980F-1(b), Q&A-12]

Q 9:48   How may the Section 204(h) Notice be provided?

A plan administrator (see Q 20:1; including a person acting on behalf of the plan administrator, such as the employer or plan trustee) must provide the Section 204(h) Notice through a method that results in actual receipt of the notice, or the plan administrator must take appropriate and necessary measures reasonably calculated to ensure that the method for providing the Section 204(h) Notice results in actual receipt of the notice. The Section 204(h) Notice must be provided either in the form of a paper document or in an electronic form that satisfies the requirements. First-class mail to the last known address of the party is an acceptable delivery method; likewise, hand delivery is acceptable. However, the posting of a notice is not considered provision of the Section 204(h) Notice. The Section 204(h) Notice may be enclosed with or combined with other notice provided by the employer or plan administrator (for example, a notice of intent to terminate; see Q 25:25). Except as provided below, a Section 204(h) Notice is deemed to have been provided on a date if it has been provided by the end of that day. When notice is delivered by first-class mail, the notice is considered provided as of the date of the United States postmark stamped on the cover in which the document is mailed. [Treas. Reg. § 54.4980F-1(b), Q&A-13(a); Priv. Ltr. Rul. 200407021]

> **Example.** Plan A is amended to reduce significantly the rate of future benefit accrual effective January 1, 2011. The Section 204(h) Notice is required to be provided at least 45 days before the effective date of the amendment (see Q 9:44). The plan administrator causes the Section 204(h) Notice to be mailed to all affected participants. The mailing is postmarked November 16, 2010. Because the Section 204(h) Notice is given 45 days before the effective date of the plan amendment, the timing requirement is satisfied.

A Section 204(h) Notice may be provided to an applicable individual (see Q 9:45) through an electronic method (other than an oral communication or a recording of an oral communication), provided that all of the following requirements are satisfied:

1. Either the notice is actually received by the applicable individual, or the plan administrator takes appropriate and necessary measures reasonably calculated to ensure that the method for providing the Section 204(h) Notice results in actual receipt of the notice by the applicable individual.

2. The plan administrator provides the applicable individual with a clear and conspicuous statement, in electronic or non-electronic form, that the applicable individual has a right to request and obtain a paper version of the Section 204(h) Notice without charge; and, if such request is made, the applicable individual is furnished with the paper version without charge.

3. A Section 204(h) Notice provided through an electronic method must be delivered on or before the requirement date (see Q 9:44) and must satisfy the information requirements (see Q 9:46), including the content requirements and the requirements that it be written in a manner calculated to be understood by the average plan participant and to apprise the applicable individual of the significance of the notice. Accordingly, when it is not otherwise reasonably evident, the recipient should be apprised (either in electronic or non-electronic form), at the time the notice is furnished electronically, of the significance of the notice. [I.R.C. § 4980F(g); Treas. Reg. § 54.4980F-1(b), Q&A-13(c)(1)]

Example 1. On July 1, 2011, Mike, a plan administrator of The Host With The Most Corporation's plan, sends notice intended to constitute a Section 204(h) Notice to Marge, an employee of the corporation and a participant in the plan. The notice is sent through e-mail to Marge's e-mail address on the corporation's electronic information system. Accessing the corporation's electronic information system is not an integral part of Marge's duties. Mike sends the e-mail with a request for a computer-generated notification that the message was received and opened. Mike receives notification indicating that the e-mail was received and opened by Marge on July 9, 2011. With respect to Marge, although Mike has failed to take appropriate and necessary measures reasonably calculated to ensure that the method for providing the Section 204(h) Notice results in actual receipt of the notice, Mike satisfies the requirement on July 9, 2011, which is when Marge actually receives the notice.

Example 2. On August 1, 2011, Steve, a plan administrator of The Park Company's plan, sends a notice intended to constitute a Section 204(h) Notice to Hetty, who is an employee of the company and a participant in the plan. The notice is sent through e-mail to Hetty's e-mail address on the company's electronic information system. Hetty has the ability to effectively access electronic documents from Hetty's e-mail address on the company's electronic information system, and accessing the system is an integral part of Hetty's duties. Because access to the system is an integral part of Hetty's duties, Steve has taken appropriate and necessary measures reasonably calculated to ensure that the method for providing the Section 204(h) Notice results in actual receipt of the notice. Thus, regardless of whether Hetty actually accesses her e-mail on that date, Steve satisfies the requirement on August 1, 2011, with respect to Hetty.

This requirement is deemed to be satisfied with respect to an applicable individual if the Section 204(h) Notice is provided electronically to an applicable individual, and

1. The applicable individual has affirmatively consented electronically, or confirmed consent electronically, in a manner that reasonably demonstrates the applicable individual's ability to access the information in the electronic form in which the notice will be provided, to receiving the Section 204(h) Notice electronically and has not withdrawn such consent;

2. The applicable individual has provided, if applicable, in electronic or non-electronic form, an address for the receipt of electronically furnished documents;

3. Prior to consenting, the applicable individual has been provided, in electronic or non-electronic form, a clear and conspicuous statement indicating:

    a. That the consent can be withdrawn at any time without charge;

    b. The procedures for withdrawing consent and for updating the address or other information needed to contact the applicable individual;

    c. Any hardware and software requirements for accessing and retaining the documents; and

    d. The required address information; and

4. After consenting, if a change in hardware or software requirements needed to access or retain electronic records creates a material risk that the applicable individual will be unable to access or retain the Section 204(h) Notice:

    a. The applicable individual is provided with a statement of the revised hardware and software requirements for access to and retention of the Section 204(h) Notice and is given the right to withdraw consent without the imposition of any fees for such withdrawal and without the imposition of any condition or consequence that was not disclosed at the time of the initial consent, and

    b. The consent requirement is again satisfied. [Treas. Reg. § 54.4980F-1(b), Q&A-13(c)(3)]

IRS issued regulations (see Q 20:5) setting forth rules that clarify existing procedures regarding the use of electronic media to provide notices to plan participants and includes the Section 204(h) Notice. [Treas. Reg. § 54.4980F-1(b), Q&A-13(c)(1)(ii)]

Q 9:49 What are the consequences if a plan administrator fails to provide the Section 204(h) Notice?

ERISA provides that, in the case of any egregious failure to meet the notice requirements with respect to any plan amendment, the plan provisions are applied so that all applicable individuals (see Q 9:45) are entitled to the greater of the benefit to which they would have been entitled without regard to the amendment or the benefit under the plan with regard to the amendment. [ERISA § 204(h)(6)(A); Treas. Reg. § 54.4980F-1(b), Q&A-14(a)(1)] For a special rule applicable in the case of a plan termination, see Q 9:52.

There is an egregious failure to meet the notice requirements if a failure to provide required notice is within the control of the plan sponsor and is either an intentional failure or a failure, whether or not intentional, to provide most of the individuals with most of the information they are entitled to receive. For this purpose, an intentional failure includes any failure to promptly provide the required notice or information after the plan administrator (see Q 20:1) discovers an unintentional failure to meet the requirements. A failure to give the Section 204(h) Notice is deemed not to be egregious if the plan administrator reasonably determines, taking into account ERISA Section 204(h), Section 4980F, the final regulations, other administrative pronouncements, and relevant facts and circumstances, that the reduction in the rate of future benefit accrual resulting from an amendment is not significant (see Q 9:43) or that an amendment does not significantly reduce an early retirement benefit or retirement-type subsidy. [Treas. Reg. § 54.4980F-1(b), Q&A-14(a)(2); Brady v. Dow Chemical Co. Retirement Board, 2009 WL 394322 (4th Cir. 2009)]

> **Example.** Plan A is amended to reduce significantly the rate of future benefit accrual effective January 1, 2011. The Section 204(h) Notice is required to be provided 45 days before January 1, 2011 (see Q 9:44). A timely Section 204(h) Notice is provided to all applicable individuals (and to each employee organization representing participants who are applicable individuals), except that the employer intentionally fails to provide the Section 204(h) Notice to certain participants until May 16, 2011. The failure to provide the Section 204(h) Notice is egregious. Accordingly, for the period from January 1, 2011, through June 30, 2011 (which is the date that is 45 days after May 16, 2011), all participants and alternate payees are entitled to the greater of the benefit to which they would have been entitled under Plan A as in effect before the amendment or the benefit under the plan as amended.

If an egregious failure has not occurred, the amendment with respect to which the Section 204(h) Notice is required may become effective with respect to all applicable individuals. However, see ERISA Section 502 for civil enforcement remedies. Thus, where there is a failure, whether or not egregious, to provide the Section 204(h) Notice, individuals may have recourse under ERISA Section 502. [Treas. Reg. § 54.4980F-1(b), Q&A-14(b)]

Excise taxes may apply to a failure to notify applicable individuals of an amendment that provides for a significant reduction in the rate of future benefit accrual or eliminates or significantly reduces an early retirement benefit or retirement-type subsidy, regardless of whether or not the failure is egregious (see Q 9:50). [Treas. Reg. § 54.4980F-1(b), Q&A-14(c)]

Q 9:50 What are some of the rules that apply with respect to the excise tax?

An excise tax is imposed if there is a failure of an applicable pension plan (see Q 9:39) to meet the Section 204(h) Notice requirements with respect to any applicable individual (see Q 9:45). [I.R.C. § 4980F(a)]

The excise tax on any failure with respect to any applicable individual is $100 for each day in the noncompliance period with respect to such failure. The noncompliance period is the period beginning on the date the failure first occurred and ending on the date the notice to which the failure relates is provided or the failure is otherwise corrected. [I.R.C. § 4980F(b)] If the failure is due to reasonable cause and not to willful neglect, IRS may waive all or part of the excise tax to the extent that payment would be excessive or otherwise inequitable relative to the failure involved. [I.R.C. § 4980F(c)(4)] Effective November 7, 2007, IRS delegated to its Managers in Employee Plans Technical the authority to waive all or part of the excise tax, but this authority may not be redelegated. [Delegation Order 7-7]

In the case of a plan other than a multiemployer plan (see Q 29:2), the employer is responsible for reporting and paying the excise tax. In the case of a multiemployer plan, the plan is responsible for reporting and paying the excise tax. [I.R.C. § 4980F(d); Treas. Reg. § 54.4980F-1(b), Q&A-15(a)]

No excise tax is imposed on a failure for any period during which it is established to the satisfaction of IRS that the employer (or other person responsible for the tax) exercised reasonable diligence, but did not know that the failure existed. No excise tax applies to a failure to provide the Section 204(h) Notice if the employer (or other person responsible for the tax) exercised reasonable diligence and corrects the failure within 30 days after the employer (or other person responsible for the tax) first knew, or exercising reasonable diligence would have known, that such failure existed. A person has exercised reasonable diligence, but did not know that the failure existed if and only if:

1. The person exercised reasonable diligence in attempting to deliver the Section 204(h) Notice to applicable individuals by the latest date permitted (see Q 9:44), and

2. At the latest date permitted for delivery of the Section 204(h) Notice, the person reasonably believes that the Section 204(h) Notice was actually delivered to each applicable individual by that date. [I.R.C. §§ 4980F(c)(1), 4980F(c)(2); Treas. Reg. § 54.4980F-1(b), Q&A-15(b)]

Example. Plan A is amended to reduce significantly the rate of future benefit accrual. The employer sends a Section 204(h) Notice to all affected participants and other applicable individuals and to any employee organization representing applicable individuals, including actual delivery by hand to employees at worksites and by first-class mail for any other applicable individual and to any employee organization representing applicable individuals. However, although the employer exercises reasonable diligence in seeking to deliver the notice, the notice is not delivered to any participants at one worksite due to a failure of an overnight delivery service to provide the notice to appropriate personnel at that site for them to timely hand deliver the notice to affected employees. The error is discovered when the employer subsequently inquires to confirm delivery. The appropriate Section 204(h) Notice is then promptly delivered to all affected participants at the worksite. Because the employer exercised reasonable diligence, but did not know that a failure existed, no excise tax applies, assuming that participants at the worksite receive the Section 204(h) Notice within 30 days after the employer first knew, or exercising reasonable diligence would have known, that the failure occurred.

Q 9:51   How do Section 4980F and ERISA Section 204(h) apply when a business is sold?

Whether a Section 204(h) Notice is required in connection with the sale of a business depends on whether a plan amendment is adopted that significantly reduces the rate of future benefit accrual or significantly reduces an early retirement benefit or retirement-type subsidy. [Treas. Reg. § 54.4980F-1(b), Q&A-16(a)]

Example 1. Yasuko Bridge Corporation maintains Plan A, a defined benefit plan that covers all employees of Yasuko Bridge Corporation, including employees in its Division M. Plan A provides that participating employees cease to accrue benefits when they cease to be employees of Yasuko Bridge Corporation. On January 1, 2011, Yasuko Bridge Corporation sells all of the assets of Division M to Harry Corporation. Harry Corporation maintains Plan B, which covers all of the employees of Harry Corporation. Under the sale agreement, employees of Division M become employees of Harry Corporation on the date of the sale (and cease to be employees of Yasuko Bridge Corporation), Yasuko Bridge Corporation continues to maintain Plan A following the sale, and the employees of Division M become participants in Plan B. No Section 204(h) Notice is required because no plan amendment was adopted that reduced the rate of future benefit accrual. The employees of Division M who become employees of Harry Corporation ceased to accrue benefits under Plan A because their employment with Yasuko Bridge Corporation terminated.

Example 2. Rena Corporation is a wholly owned subsidiary of Vic Corporation. Rena Corporation maintains Plan C, a defined benefit plan that covers employees of Rena Corporation. Vic Corporation sells all of the stock Rena Corporation to Benjamin Corporation. At the effective date of the sale of the stock of Rena Corporation, in accordance with the sale agreement between Vic Corporation and Benjamin Corporation, Rena Corporation amends Plan C so that all benefit accruals cease. The Section 204(h) Notice is required to be provided because Rena Corporation adopted a plan amendment that significantly reduced the rate of future benefit accrual in Plan C.

Example 3. As a result of an acquisition, Alan Corporation maintains two plans: Plan D covers employees of Division Sue and Plan E covers the rest of the employees of Alan Corporation. Plan E provides a significantly lower rate of future benefit accrual than Plan D. Plan D is merged with Plan E, and all of the employees of Alan Corporation will accrue benefits under the merged plan in accordance with the benefit formula of former Plan E. The Section 204(h) Notice is required.

Example 4. The facts are the same as in Example 3, except that the rate of future benefit accrual in Plan E is not significantly lower. In addition, Plan D has a retirement-type subsidy that Plan E does not have and the Plan D employees' rights to the subsidy under the merged plan are limited to benefits accrued before the merger. The Section 204(h) Notice is required for any participants or beneficiaries for whom the reduction in the retirement-type subsidy is significant (and for any employee organization representing such participants).

Example 5. Gayle Corporation maintains several plans, including Plan F, which covers employees of the Jennifer Division. Plan F provides that participating employees cease to accrue further benefits under the plan when they cease to be employees of Gayle Corporation. Gayle Corporation sells all of the assets of the Jennifer Division to Paul Corporation, which maintains Plan G for its employees. Plan G provides a significantly lower rate of future benefit accrual than Plan F. Plan F is merged with Plan G as part of the sale, and employees of the Jennifer Division who become employees of Paul Corporation will accrue benefits under the merged plan in accordance with the benefit formula of former Plan G. No Section 204(h) Notice is required because no plan amendment was adopted that reduces the rate of future benefit accrual or significantly reduces an early retirement benefit or retirement-type subsidy. Under the terms of Plan F as in effect prior to the merger, employees of the Jennifer Division cease to accrue any further benefits (including benefits with respect to early retirement benefits and any retirement-type subsidy) under Plan F after the date of the sale because their employment with Gayle Corporation terminated.

Q 9:52 How are amendments to cease accruals and terminate a plan treated?

An amendment providing for the cessation of benefit accruals on a specified future date and for the termination of a plan is subject to Section 4980F and ERISA Section 204(h). [Treas. Reg. § 54.4980F-1(b), Q&A-17(a)(1)]

Example. An employer adopts an amendment that provides for the cessation of benefit accruals under a defined benefit plan on December 31, 2010, and for the termination of the plan as of a proposed termination date that is also December 31, 2010. As part of the notice of intent to terminate (see Q 25:25) in order to terminate the plan, the plan administrator (see Q 20:1) gives the Section 204(h) Notice of the amendment ceasing accruals, which states that benefit accruals will cease on December 31, 2010, whether or not the plan is terminated on that date. However, because all the requirements for a plan termination are not satisfied, the plan cannot be terminated until a date that is later than December 31, 2010.

Nonetheless, because the Section 204(h) Notice was given stating that the plan was amended to cease accruals on December 31, 2010, ERISA Section 204(h) does not prevent the amendment to cease accruals from being effective on December 31, 2010. The result would be the same had the Section 204(h) Notice informed the participants that the plan was amended to provide for a proposed termination date of December 31, 2010, and to provide that benefit accruals will cease on the proposed termination date whether or not the plan is terminated on that date. However, neither Section 4980F nor ERISA Section 204(h) would be satisfied with respect to the

December 31, 2010, effective date if the Section 204(h) Notice had merely stated that benefit accruals would cease on the termination date or on the proposed termination date.

A plan that is terminated in accordance with Title IV of ERISA is deemed to have satisfied Section 4980F and ERISA Section 204(h) not later than the termination date (or date of termination, as applicable) established under ERISA Section 4048. Accordingly, neither Section 4980F nor ERISA Section 204(h) would in any event require that any additional benefits accrue after the effective date of the termination. [Treas. Reg. § 54.4980F-1(b), Q&A-17(b)]

To the extent that an amendment providing for a significant reduction in the rate of future benefit accrual or a significant reduction in an early retirement benefit or retirement-type subsidy has an effective date that is earlier than the termination date (or date of termination, as applicable) established under ERISA Section 4048, that amendment is subject to Section 4980F and ERISA Section 204(h). Accordingly, the plan administrator must provide the Section 204(h) Notice (either separately, with, or as part of the notice of intent to terminate) with respect to such an amendment. [Treas. Reg. § 54.4980F-1(b), Q&A-17(c)]

Q 9:53   What are the effective dates of Section 4980F, ERISA Section 204(h), as amended by EGTRRA 2001, and the final regulations?

Section 4980F and ERISA Section 204(h), as amended by EGTRRA 2001, apply to plan amendments taking effect on or after June 7, 2001 (statutory effective date), which is the date of enactment of EGTRRA 2001. [Treas. Reg. § 54.4980F-1(b), Q&A-18(a)(1)]

For amendments applying after the statutory effective date and prior to the regulatory effective date, the requirements of Section 4980F(e)(2) and (3) and ERISA Section 204(h), as amended by EGTRRA 2001, are treated as satisfied if the plan administrator (see Q 20:1) makes a reasonable, good-faith effort to comply with those requirements. [Treas. Reg. § 54.4980F-1(b), Q&A-18(a)(2)]

The Section 204(h) Notice was not required by Section 4980F(e) or ERISA Section 204(h), as amended by EGTRRA 2001, to be provided prior to September 7, 2001 (the date that was three months after the date of enactment of EGTRRA 2001), and the requirements of Section 4980F and ERISA Section 204(h), as amended by EGTRRA 2001, did not apply to any plan amendment that took effect on or after June 7, 2001, if, before April 25, 2001, notice was provided to participants and beneficiaries adversely affected by the plan amendment (and their representatives) that was reasonably expected to notify them of the nature and effective date of the plan amendment. [Treas. Reg. § 54.4980F-1(b), Q&A-18(a)(3)] The requirement that a Section 204(h) Notice be provided to each employer that has an obligation to contribute to the plan applies to Section 204(h) Amendments adopted in plan years beginning after December 31, 2007. [Treas. Reg. § 54.4980F-1(b), Q&A-18(a)(5)]

The final regulations (see Qs 9:38-9:52) apply to amendments with an effective date that is on or after September 1, 2003; however, the final regulation relating to a change in the provisions of a document that is referenced in the plan document applies to amendments with an effective date that is on or after January 1, 2004 (regulatory effective date). [Treas. Reg. § 54.4980F-1(b), Q&A-18(b)]

With respect to any Section 204(h) Amendment to a lump sum-based benefit formula, the special rules under the regulations relating to an amendment that applies with respect to benefits accrued before the applicable amendment date apply to amendments adopted after December 21, 2006. However, a special 30-day timing rule for providing a Section 204(h) Notice applies to such amendments effective on or after December 21, 2006, and not later than December 31, 2008. [Treas. Reg. § 54.4980F-1(b), Q&A-18(b)(3)(iii)]

Q 9:54   What benefits are not Section 411(d)(6) protected benefits?

The following are examples of benefits that are not Section 411(d)(6) benefits and, therefore, may be reduced or eliminated by an amendment to a qualified retirement plan:

1. Ancillary life insurance protection;

2. Accident or health insurance benefits;

3. Social Security supplements described in Section 411(a)(9) [Cattin v. General Motors Corp., Nos. 90-1016, 90-1051, 90-1052 (6th Cir. 1992)];

4. The availability of loans (other than the distribution of an employee's accrued benefit upon default under a loan);

5. The right to make after-tax employee contributions or elective deferrals;

6. The right to direct investments [Franklin v. First Union Corp., No. 3:99CV344 (E.D. Va. 2000)];

7. The right to a particular form of investment (e.g., investment in employer stock or securities or investment in certain types of securities, commercial paper, or other investment media);

8. The allocation dates for contributions, forfeitures, and earnings, the time for making contributions (but not the conditions for receiving an allocation of contributions or forfeitures for a plan year after such conditions have been satisfied), and the valuation dates for account balances;

9. Administrative procedures for distributing benefits, such as provisions relating to the particular dates on which notices are given and by which elections must be made; and

10. Rights that derive from administrative and operational provisions, such as mechanical procedures for allocating investment experience among accounts in defined contribution plans.

[Treas. Reg. § 1.411(d)-4, Q&A-1(d)]

IRS issued regulations that provide guidance on benefits that will be treated as early retirement benefits and retirement-type subsidies for purposes of the anti-cutback rule (see Qs 9:33, 9:34, 9:43).

Q 9:55 What happens to a participant's benefits if the qualified retirement plan merges with another plan?

In case of a merger or consolidation of qualified retirement plans, or a transfer of assets or liabilities from one qualified retirement plan to another, each participant must be entitled to receive a benefit after the merger that is at least equal to the value of the benefit the participant would have been entitled to receive before the merger. (The before-and-after merger benefits are determined as if the plan had been terminated.) [I.R.C. §§ 401(a)(12), 414(*l*); ERISA §§ 208, 4044(d); Treas. Reg. §§ 1.401(a)-12, 1.414(*l*)-1; Rev. Rul. 2002-42, 2002-2 C.B. 76; Priv. Ltr. Ruls. 200734022, 200009061, 9720037, 9422059] See Q 25:4 for additional details.

One court ruled that participants in a defined benefit plan (see Q 2:3) were not entitled to increased benefits upon the merger of the plan, which had surplus plan assets attributable to employee contributions, with a second defined benefit plan. [Brillinger v. General Elec. Co, 130 F.3d 61 (2d Cir. 1997)] Another court concluded that where two employers merged, the surviving employer was liable for the delinquent plan contributions of the other employer under the general corporate law principle that a surviving employer is liable for the debts of a predecessor employer. [Teamsters Pension Trust Fund of Phila. & Vicinity v. Littlejohn, No. 97-1856 (3d Cir. 1998)]

Generally, the plan sponsor or plan administrator (see Q 20:1) of a merged plan must apprise IRS of the merger by completing Form 5310-A, Notice of Plan Merger or Consolidation, Spinoff, or Transfer of Plan Assets or Liabilities; Notice of Qualified Separate Lines of Business, and filing the form at least 30 days before the event. Form 5310-A should be filed for each plan involved in the merger. Although IRS will not issue a determination letter (see Q 18:1) when a Form 5310-A is filed, an actuarial statement of valuation must be submitted, and, of course, IRS may request additional documentation with regard to any filing.

There is a penalty for late filing; the penalty is $25 a day for each day Form 5310-A is late (up to a maximum of $15,000). For exceptions to the requirement for filing Form 5310-A, see Q 9:56.

Q 9:56 Must Form 5310-A always be filed if there is a merger of qualified retirement plans?

No. Form 5310-A is *not* required to be filed in the following four situations:

1. Two or more defined contribution plans (see Q 2:2) are merged, and all of the following conditions are met:

   a. The sum of the account balances (see Q 9:2) in each plan prior to the merger (including unallocated forfeitures, an unallocated suspense account for excess annual additions, and an unallocated suspense account for an ESOP; see Q 28:7) equals the fair market value of the entire plan assets (e.g., neither plan has an outstanding waiver balance (see Q 8:25)).

   b. The assets of each plan are combined to form the assets of the plan as merged.

   c. Immediately after the merger, each participant in the plan as merged has an account balance equal to the sum of the account balances the participant had in the plans immediately prior to the merger. [Treas. Reg. § 1.414(*l*)-1(d)]

2. There is a spin-off of a defined contribution plan, and all of the following conditions are met:

   a. The sum of the account balances in the plan prior to the spin-off equals the fair market value of the entire plan assets (e.g., the plan has no outstanding waiver balance).

   b. The sum of the account balances for each participant in the resulting plan(s) equals the account balance of each participant in the plan before the spin-off.

   c. The assets in each of the plans immediately after the spin-off equal the sum of the account balances for all participants in that plan (e.g., there is no unallocated suspense account for an ESOP). [Treas. Reg. § 1.414(*l*)-1(m)]

3. Two or more defined benefit plans (see Q 2:3) are merged into one defined benefit plan, and both of the following conditions are met:

   a. The total liabilities (the present value of benefits, whether or not vested; see Q 9:1) that are merged into the larger plan involved in the merger are less than 3 percent of the assets of the larger plan. This condition must be satisfied on at least one day in the larger plan's plan year during which the merger occurs. All previous mergers (including transfers from another plan) occurring in the same plan year are taken into account in determining the percentage of assets. Also, mergers occurring in previous plan years are taken into account in determining the percentage of assets if the series of mergers is, in substance, one transaction with the merger occurring during the current plan year. Aggregating mergers may cause a merger, for which a Form 5310-A was not initially required to be filed, to become reportable as a result of a subsequent merger. In this case, the merger(s) must be reported on the Form 5310-A filed for the subsequent merger.

Example 1. Assume that a merger involving almost 3 percent of the assets of the larger plan occurs in the first month of the larger plan's plan year. In the fourth month of the larger plan's plan year, a second merger occurs involving liabilities equal to 2 percent of the assets of the larger plan. The total of both mergers exceeds 3 percent of the assets of the larger plan. As a result of the second merger, both mergers must be reported on Form 5310-A.

    b. The provisions of the larger plan that allocate assets upon termination must provide that, in the event of a spin-off or termination of the plan within five years following the merger, plan assets will be allocated first for the benefit of the participants in the other plan(s) to the extent of their benefits on a termination basis just prior to the merger. [Treas. Reg. § 1.414(l)-1(h)]

4. There is a spin-off of a defined benefit plan into two or more defined benefit plans, and both of the following conditions are met:

    a. For each plan that results from the spin-off, other than the spun-off plan with the greatest value of plan assets after the spin-off, the value of the assets spun off is not less than the present value of the benefits spun off (whether or not vested).

    b. The value of the assets spun off to all the resulting spun-off plans (other than the spun-off plan with the greatest value of plan assets after the spin-off) plus other assets previously spun off (including transfers to another plan) during the plan year in which the spin-off occurs is less than 3 percent of the assets of the plan before the spin-off as of at least one day in that plan's plan year. Spin-offs occurring in previous or subsequent plan years are taken into account in determining the percentage of assets spun off if such spin-offs are, in substance, one transaction with the spin-off occurring during the current plan year. Aggregating spin-offs may cause a spin-off, for which a Form 5310-A was not initially required to be filed, to become reportable as a result of a subsequent spin-off. In this case, the spin-off(s) must be reported on the Form 5310-A filed for the subsequent spin-off. [Treas. Reg. § 1.414(l)-1(n)(2)]

Example 2. Assume that a spin-off involving almost 3 percent of the assets of the plan occurs in the first month of the plan year. In the fourth month of the plan year, a second spin-off occurs involving liabilities equal to 2 percent of the assets of the plan. The total of both spin-offs exceeds 3 percent of the plan assets. As a result of the second spin-off, Form 5310-A must be filed to report both spin-offs.

A transfer of assets or liabilities is considered a combination of separate plan spin-offs and mergers. Form 5310-A is not filed for the transferor plan in a transfer transaction if the assets transferred satisfy the spin-off conditions in 2 or 4 above, or for the transferee plan in a transfer transaction if the plan liabilities transferred satisfy the merger conditions in 1 or 3 above. Thus, in some situations, the transferor plan may have to file Form 5310-A but not the transferee plan, or the transferee plan may have to file but not the transferor plan.

Example 3. Plans A, B, and C are separate plans. A portion of the assets and liabilities of both Plan B and Plan C will be transferred to Plan A. None of the plans is excluded from filing under the exceptions. In this situation, three Forms 5310-A must be filed.

Example 4. Plans A, B, and C are separate plans. Plans A, B, and C are being merged. Assets and liabilities from each plan will be merged into Plan D, a new plan that was established for the purpose of effecting the merger. None of the plans is excluded from filing under the exceptions. In this situation, four Forms 5310-A must be filed.

Where a defined contribution plan provides that forfeitures under the plan are held in suspense until used to reduce employer contributions (see Q 9:19), IRS representatives opined that (1) the plan can be merged with another defined contribution plan while forfeitures are held in suspense as long as the suspended forfeitures are applied against future employer contributions in the normal course of plan operations and (2) the filing of Form 5310-A would not be necessary.

A transferor plan in a spin-off of a defined contribution plan was required to account for changes in the value of assets between the previously agreed-upon spin-off date and the actual date of transfer. [John Blair Communications, Inc. Profit Sharing Plan v. Telemundo Group, Inc. Profit Sharing Plan, 26 F.3d 360 (2d Cir. 1994)]

A spun-off defined benefit plan was not entitled to a pro rata share of residual plan assets even though the benefits of its participants represented more than 50 percent of all plan benefits. The agreement between the companies divided the residual assets equally between the plans, and the court ruled that the protection accorded to the spun-off participants related to plan benefits and not plan assets. [Systems Council EM-3 v. AT&T Corp., No. 97-7155 (Fed. Cir. 1998); I.R.C. § 414(*l*)(2) (as amended by WRERA 2008 § 101(d)(2)(E))] A qualified plan's split into a defined contribution plan and a defined benefit plan was approved by IRS because the sum of the account balances for each of the participants in the defined contribution plan equaled the account balance of the participants before the spin-off and because the assets of the defined contribution plan equaled the sum of those account balances. Additionally, the defined benefits of all the plan participants were allocated to the defined benefit plan, and the value of its assets was not less than the present value of defined benefits before the spin-off. Further, the no-reduction requirement was satisfied even though the defined contribution portion of the plan was spun off into a separate plan without the allocation of any surplus funds that existed relating to the defined benefit portion of the plan because no allocation was necessary. Moreover, there was no diversion of assets because the participants' aggregate benefits remained unchanged and because the plan's surplus, if any, was allocated to the defined benefit plan. Thus, the spin-off did not constitute a reversion of plan assets to the employer followed by a contribution to the defined contribution plan (see Qs 25:49-25:52). [Priv. Ltr. Rul. 200442037]

Chapter 10

General Distribution Requirements

Numerous rules govern the timing and form of benefit distributions. This chapter examines qualified joint and survivor annuity (QJSA) requirements, qualified preretirement survivor annuity (QPSA) requirements, limits on optional forms of benefit, and related matters.

Q 10:1   Must a qualified retirement plan provide benefits to a participant's surviving spouse?

If a married participant survives until the annuity starting date (see Q 10:3), all vested benefits must, with certain exceptions, be paid in the form of a QJSA (see Q 10:8). If a married participant with vested benefits dies before the annuity starting date, a QPSA (see Q 10:9) must, with certain exceptions, be provided to the participant's surviving spouse. A QPSA must be provided whether or not the participant separated from service before death. The QJSA and the QPSA must be provided by all qualified retirement plans except certain profit sharing plans (see Q 10:6), but may be waived if the applicable notice, election, and spousal consent requirements are satisfied (see Qs 10:20–10:26). Also, the automatic survivor benefit requirements do not apply to a payment of the benefit before the annuity starting date if the present value of the married participant's benefit is $5,000 or less (see Q 10:61). [I.R.C. §§ 401(a)(11), 411(a)(11)(A), 417]

It is possible that one portion of a married participant's benefit may be subject to a QJSA and another portion to a QPSA at the same time. For example, a participant in a money purchase pension plan (see Q 2:4) may have separate accounts for employer contributions and employee contributions. An in-service withdrawal of the employee contribution account would be subject to the QJSA. The QPSA would apply to the employer contribution account if the participant died prior to the annuity starting date. [Treas. Reg. § 1.401(a)-20, Q&A-9]

Where a participant never was divorced from his first wife and purportedly married a second woman, the first wife was entitled to benefits upon the participant's death because the purported marriage to the second woman was void as a matter of state law. [Grabois v. Jones, No. 94 Civ. 2070 (D. Miss. 1997)] If a participant's marriage is not valid under state law (the prior marriage of the participant's spouse was never legally terminated), the participant's designation of his purported spouse as beneficiary is equally invalid for the QJSA and QPSA requirements. [Boyd v. Waterfront Employers ILA Pension Plan, 1999 WL 496265 (4th Cir. 1999)] However, another court reached a contrary conclusion. A plan participant was married; and, when the couple separated, a formal judgment of separation was entered by a state court but no divorce decree was ever obtained. Some years later, after an interim second marriage, the participant married another woman and remained married to her until his death. Both the first and third wives applied for surviving spouse benefits under the plan. The court concluded that state law applied in determining who was the surviving spouse because the plan itself did not include a definition. The law of the participant's domicile at death was deemed controlling, and state law recognized the concept of putative marriage. A putative marriage is one that was entered into in good faith by at least one of the parties but is invalid by reason of an existing impediment on the part of one or both of the parties. Where such a marriage exists, the putative spouse has the same right to property acquired during the relationship as if she were the lawful spouse, and the court ruled in favor of the third wife. [Central States, Southeast & Southwest Areas Pension Fund v. Gray, No. 02 C 8381 (N.D. Ill. 2003)] A decision by the plan administrator (see Q 20:1) to treat a plan participant's second wife, and not his first wife, as his survivor beneficiary under the plan was permissible, where the determination that retirement occurred at the benefit commencement date and not at the date of termination of employment was a reasonable interpretation of the plan's terms. [Sznewajs v. U.S. Bancorp Amended and Restated Supplemental Benefits Plan, 572 F.3d 727 (9th Cir. 2009)]

A terminated participant advises the plan administrator that the participant is not married and receives a distribution of benefits; however, the participant is, in fact, married. IRS representatives opined that the spouse is entitled to a benefit and that the plan administrator can pursue the participant to recover any overpayment. The representatives also advised that an IRS correction program is available (see Q 19:2).

Q 10:2   Must a qualified retirement plan continue to pay benefits to a surviving spouse who remarries?

Yes. The remarriage of a surviving spouse does not affect a qualified retirement plan's obligation to continue to pay benefits to the surviving spouse under the QJSA (see Q 10:8) or QPSA (see Q 10:9). The plan must continue to pay benefits to the surviving spouse as long as the participant and surviving spouse are married on the date of the participant's death with respect to a QPSA, and on the annuity starting date (see Q 10:3) with respect to a QJSA (see Q 10:19). [Treas. Reg. § 1.401(a)-20, Q&A-25(b)]

Q 10:3   What is the annuity starting date?

The annuity starting date is the first day of the first period for which a benefit is payable as an annuity. For benefits payable in any other form, it is the first day on which all events have occurred that entitle the participant to the benefit. For example, if an annuity is scheduled to begin on January 1, 2010, the annuity starting date is January 1, 2010, even though the first payment is not made until July 1, 2010. If the benefit is a deferred annuity, the annuity starting date is the date on which the annuity payments are scheduled to commence, not the date that the deferred annuity is elected or the date the deferred annuity contract is distributed. [I.R.C. § 417(f)(2)(A); Treas. Reg. § 1.401(a)-20, Q&A-10(b); PBGC v. Wilson N. Jones Mem'l Hosp., No. 4:01-CV-94 (E.D. Tex. 2003)]

There is a special rule that applies to disability benefits. The annuity starting date of a disability benefit is the first day of the first period for which the disability benefit becomes payable, unless it is an auxiliary benefit. An auxiliary disability benefit is disregarded in determining the annuity starting date. A disability benefit is considered auxiliary if it is not taken into account in determining the disabled participant's retirement benefit under the plan. [I.R.C. § 417(f)(2)(B); Treas. Reg. § 1.401(a)-20, Q&A-10(c)]

Q 10:4 What is the significance of the annuity starting date for survivor benefit requirements?

The annuity starting date (see Q 10:3) determines whether benefits are payable as a QJSA (see Q 10:8), QPSA (see Q 10:9), or any other selected optional form of benefit. If a participant is living on the annuity starting date, the benefits must be payable as a QJSA. If the participant dies before the annuity starting date, the surviving spouse must receive a QPSA.

The annuity starting date is also relevant in determining when a participant may waive a QJSA and when a spouse may consent to the waiver. Such waivers and consents are effective only if made within 180 days before the annuity starting date (see Q 10:20). Since, under a deferred annuity, the annuity starting date is the date on which the payments are to commence (see Q 10:3), the QJSA cannot be waived until 180 days before such time. [Treas. Reg. § 1.401(a)-20, Q&A-10(a); Prop. Treas. Reg. § 1.401(a)-20, Q&A-10(a)]

Q 10:5 How do the automatic survivor benefit requirements apply to unmarried participants?

A QJSA (see Q 10:8) for an unmarried participant is a life annuity (i.e., payments cease on the participant's death). Thus, an unmarried participant must be provided with a life annuity unless the participant elects another form of benefit.

There is no requirement to provide a QPSA (see Q 10:9) with respect to an unmarried participant who dies before the annuity starting date (see Q 10:3). [Treas. Reg. § 1.401(a)-20, Q&A-25(a)] However, one court concluded that a beneficiary designated by an unmarried participant, who later married, was entitled to the death benefit under the plan because the spousal consent requirement (see Q 10:21) was inapplicable to an unmarried participant and the marriage did not nullify the earlier designation. [Kartiganer v. Bloom, No. 66606 (N.Y. App. Div. 3d Dep't. 1993)]

Q 10:6   Are all qualified retirement plans required to provide automatic survivor benefits?

The automatic survivor benefit requirements (see Q 10:1) apply to defined benefit plans (see Q 2:3) and also to defined contribution plans (see Q 2:2) subject to minimum funding requirements (i.e., money purchase pension and target benefit plans; see Q 8:1).

The automatic survivor benefit requirements also apply to participants in a profit sharing plan (see Q 2:6), stock bonus plan (see Q 2:13), or a 401(k) plan (see Q 2:12) *unless*:

1. The plan provides that, upon the participant's death, the participant's vested benefit (reduced by any security interest held by the plan by reason of a loan outstanding to such participant) is payable in full to the participant's surviving spouse (unless the participant has elected with spousal consent that such benefit be paid instead to a designated beneficiary) (see Q 10:18);

2. The participant does not elect the payment of benefits in the form of a life annuity; and

3. With respect to the participant, the plan is not a direct or indirect transferee plan (see Q 10:13) or a floor-offset arrangement (see Q 10:14).

[I.R.C. § 401(a)(11); Treas. Reg. § 1.401(a)-20, Q&A-3(a); Leckey v. Stefano, 2007 WL 2458540 (3d Cir. 2007); Leckey v. Stefano, 2001 WL 957401 (3d Cir. 2001)]

If a participant elects a life annuity option provided by a plan otherwise exempt from the automatic survivor benefit requirements, the participant's benefits under the plan will be subject to automatic survivor requirements thereafter. Generally, plans eligible to avoid the automatic survivor benefit requirements will offer benefits only in the form of a single-sum distribution or over a fixed period that is less than the participant's life expectancy. [Treas. Reg. § 1.401(a)-20, Q&A-4; Prop. Treas. Reg. § 1.401(a)-20, Q&A-4] Where a participant in a 401(k) plan (see Q 27:1) rolled over a distribution of his plan benefits to an IRA (see Q 34:8), upon his death, the IRA beneficiaries, and not his wife, were entitled to the IRA. The automatic survivor rules do not apply to IRAs (see Q 30:1). [Charles Schwab & Co. v. Dibickero, 2010 WL 200276 (9th Cir. 2010)]

Q 10:7   Are there any other conditions that must be satisfied, with respect to a participant, to be exempt from the automatic survivor rules?

Yes. In order for a participant in a profit sharing plan (or other defined contribution plan not subject to the minimum funding standards; see Q 10:6) to be exempt from the automatic survivor rules:

1. The benefit payable to the participant's surviving spouse must be available within a reasonable period after the participant's death (whether the period is reasonable will be determined on the basis of facts and circumstances; however, 90 days will be deemed to be reasonable); and

2. The benefit must be adjusted for gains or losses occurring after the participant's death in accordance with plan provisions specifying the adjustment of account balances for other plan distributions.

[Treas. Reg. § 1.401(a)-20, Q&A-3(b); Leckey v. Stefano, 2001 WL 957401 (3d Cir. 2001)]

Q 10:8   What is a qualified joint and survivor annuity (QJSA)?

A QJSA is an immediate annuity for the life of the participant, with a survivor annuity for the life of the participant's spouse. The amount of the survivor annuity may not be less than 50 percent, or be more than 100 percent, of the amount of the annuity payable during the time that the participant and spouse are both alive. The QJSA must be at least the actuarial equivalent of an annuity for the life of the participant only. [I.R.C. § 417(b)]

In the case of an unmarried participant, the QJSA may be less valuable than other optional forms of benefit (see Q 10:45) payable under the plan (see Q 10:5). In the case of a married participant, the QJSA must be at least as valuable as any other optional form of benefit payable under the plan at the same time. Thus, if a plan has two joint and survivor annuities that would satisfy the requirements for a QJSA, but one has a greater actuarial value than the other, the more valuable joint and survivor annuity is the QJSA. If there are two or more actuarially equivalent joint and survivor annuities that satisfy the requirements for a QJSA, the plan must designate which one is the QJSA and, therefore, the automatic form of benefit payment. A plan, however, may allow a participant to elect out of such a QJSA, without spousal consent (see Q 10:21), in favor of another actuarially equivalent joint and survivor annuity that satisfies the QJSA conditions. Such an election is not subject to the requirement that it be made within the 180-day period before the annuity starting date (see Q 10:20). For example, if a plan designates a joint and 100 percent survivor annuity as the QJSA and also offers an actuarially equivalent joint and 50 percent survivor annuity that would satisfy the requirements of a QJSA, the participant may elect the joint and 50 percent survivor annuity without spousal consent. The participant, however, does need spousal consent to elect a joint and survivor annuity that was not actuarially equivalent to the automatic QJSA. A plan does not fail to satisfy these requirements merely because the amount payable under an optional form of benefit that is subject to the minimum present value requirements is calculated using the applicable interest rate and, for periods when required, the applicable mortality table (see Q 10:62). [Treas. Reg. § 1.401(a)-20, Q&A-16; Prop. Treas. Reg. § 1.401(a)-20, Q&A-16] Where variable annuity contracts will be issued to defined contribution plans (see Q 2:2) and distributed to terminated participants, IRS ruled that the fact that annuity payments will vary with investment performance does not preclude the payments from being considered payments under a QJSA, provided that the payments would otherwise be considered as made under a QJSA. [Priv. Ltr. Rul. 200951039]

A participant must be allowed to receive a QJSA at the participant's earliest retirement age, which is generally the earliest date on which the participant could receive a distribution from the plan. The participant (but not the participant's spouse) must consent to the distribution in the form of a QJSA before the participant's benefits are immediately distributable. A participant's benefits are immediately distributable at the later of normal retirement age (see Q 10:55) or age 62. Once benefits are immediately distributable, a QJSA may be distributed without the participant's consent (but see Qs 10:37–10:51 on optional forms of benefit). Distributions may not be made at any time in a form other than a QJSA unless the participant so elects and the participant's spouse consents. [Treas. Reg. §§ 1.401(a)-20, Q&A-17, 1.417(e)-1(b), 1.417(e)-1(c); Prop. Treas. Reg. § 1.417(e)-1(b)(3)]

A married participant retired and commenced receiving a QJSA; and, after the death of the participant's wife, he remarried. One court determined that entitlement to a survivor annuity applied only to the individual who was the participant's wife at the time of his retirement, not to the subsequent wife. [Holloman v. Mail-Weil Corp., No. 05-10850 (11th Cir. 2006); *see also* Carmona v. Carmona, 2008 WL 4225547 (9th Cir. 2008)] In another case, a married participant retired and, with the consent of his wife, elected a single life annuity. Thereafter, they divorced and the participant remarried. When the participant died, the court concluded that the second wife was not entitled to the survivor annuity. [Hall v. Kodak Retirement Income Plan, No. 09-1674 (2d Cir. 2010)]

Effective for plan years beginning after December 31, 2007, PPA (see Q 1:33) revises the minimum survivor annuity requirements to require that, at the election of the participant, benefits will be paid in the form of a qualified optional survivor annuity (QOSA). A QOSA means an annuity for the life of the participant with a survivor annuity for the life of the spouse that is equal to the applicable percentage of the amount of the annuity that is (1) payable during the joint lives of the participant and the spouse and (2) the actuarial equivalent of a single annuity for the life of the participant. If the survivor annuity provided by the QJSA under the plan is less than 75 percent of the annuity payable during the joint lives of the participant and spouse, the applicable percentage is 75 percent. If the survivor annuity provided by the QJSA under the plan is greater than or equal to 75 percent of the annuity payable during the joint lives of the participant and spouse, the applicable percentage is 50 percent. Thus, for example, if the survivor annuity provided by the QJSA under the plan is 50 percent, the survivor annuity provided under the qualified optional survivor annuity must be 75 percent. [I.R.C. § 417(g); IRS Notice 2008-30, Q&A-8, 2008-1 C.B. 638] The written explanation required to be provided to participants explaining the terms and conditions of the QJSA must also include the terms and conditions of the QOSA (see Q 10:29).

A plan that is subject to the automatic survivor benefit requirements (see Qs 10:6, 10:7) must provide an optional joint and spouse survivor annuity that (1) is at least actuarially equivalent to the plan's single life annuity form of benefit payable at the same time as the optional joint and spouse survivor annuity and (2) provides a spouse survivor annuity percentage that is equal to the spouse survivor annuity percentage required to be provided under a QOSA. The plan need not be amended so that the optional joint and spouse survivor annuity is designated as a QOSA, and its administrative procedures need not be revised to designate the optional form of benefit as a QOSA. For example, a plan that, both before and after the effective date, provides a QJSA for a married participant that includes a spouse survivor annuity percentage of 50 percent, and also provides an optional joint and spouse survivor annuity that includes a spouse survivor annuity percentage of 75 percent and is at least actuarially equivalent to the plan's single life annuity form of benefit payable at the same time as the optional joint and spouse survivor annuity, complies with PPA without the need for any amendment or other administrative change. [IRS Notice 2008-30, Q&A-9, 2008-1 C.B. 638]

A plan subject to the automatic survivor benefit requirements must provide a QOSA that is at least actuarially equivalent to the plan's form of benefit that is a single life annuity for the life of the participant payable at the same time as the QOSA. The QOSA need not be actuarially equivalent to the plan's QJSA. [IRS Notice 2008-30, Q&A-10, 2008-1 C.B. 638]

In general, spousal consent is required for a participant to waive a plan's QJSA form of distribution and elect an alternative distribution form. However, a participant may elect out of the QJSA, in favor of an actuarially equivalent alternative joint and survivor annuity that satisfies the conditions to be a QJSA, without spousal consent. Because a QOSA, by definition, satisfies the conditions to be a QJSA, no spousal consent is required if a plan participant elects a QOSA that is actuarially equivalent to the plan's QJSA. If the QOSA is not actuarially equivalent to the QJSA, spousal consent is required for the participant to waive the QJSA and elect the QOSA. [IRS Notice 2008-30, Q&A-11, 2008-1 C.B. 638] A plan that is subject to the automatic survivor benefit requirements can satisfy the requirement that it provide to a participant a written explanation of the terms and conditions of the QOSA available to the participant by satisfying the written explanation requirements (see Q 10:31). In satisfying these written explanation requirements, the plan must treat the QOSA as an optional form of benefit presently available to participants under the plan. The written explanation need not designate the optional form of benefit as the plan's QOSA. [IRS Notice 2008-30, Q&A-12, 2008-1 C.B. 638]

A plan that is subject to the automatic survivor benefit requirements must offer participants a QOSA that is an alternative form of distribution to the QJSA. There is no requirement that the plan offer to participants, as an alternative to a QPSA, a preretirement survivor annuity that is based on a QOSA. [IRS Notice 2008-30, Q&A-13, 2008-1 C.B. 638]

A plan amendment made pursuant to PPA generally will not violate the anti-cutback rule (see Q 9:25) if certain requirements are met. Thus, a plan is not treated as having decreased the accrued benefit of a participant solely by reason of the adoption of a plan amendment pursuant to the provision requiring that the plan offer a QOSA. The elimination of a subsidized QJSA (see Q 10:36) is not protected by the anti-cutback provision in PPA unless an equivalent or greater subsidy is retained in one of the forms offered under the plan as amended. For example, if a plan that offers a subsidized 50 percent QJSA is amended to provide an unsubsidized 50 percent QJSA and an unsubsidized 75 percent joint and survivor annuity as its qualified optional survivor annuity, the replacement of the subsidized 50 percent QJSA with the unsubsidized 50 percent QJSA is not protected by the anti-cutback provision in PPA. [PPA § 1107] If a plan is amended to implement a QOSA within the period established in PPA and the plan is operated as if the amendment were in effect during the period from the effective date of the changes made by PPA until the date of the amendment, the plan is treated as being operated in accordance with its terms during such period, and the amendment is treated as being adopted on the effective date of such changes made by PPA. However, an amendment that implements a QOSA is not eligible for any relief from the anti-cutback requirements. Thus, for example, a plan amendment that implements a QOSA may eliminate a distribution form or reduce or eliminate a subsidy with respect to a distribution form only to the extent such reduction or elimination is permitted. [IRS Notice 2008-30, Q&A-14, 2008-1 C.B. 638]

In general, the changes made by PPA apply to distributions from a plan that is subject to the automatic survivor benefit requirements with annuity starting dates (see Q 10:3) in plan years beginning after December 31, 2007. However, in the case of such a plan that is maintained pursuant to one or more collective bargaining agreements (CBAs; see Q 29:2) between employee representatives and one or more employers ratified on or before August 17, 2006, the changes made by PPA apply to distributions with annuity starting dates during plan years beginning on or after the earlier of (1) January 1, 2008 or, if later, the date on which the last CBA related to the plan terminates (determined without regard to any extensions to a CBA made after August 17, 2006), or (2) January 1, 2009. In the event a participant elects a distribution with a retroactive annuity starting date (see Q 10:20) that is before the effective date, the date of the first actual payment of benefits based on the retroactive annuity starting date is substituted for the annuity starting date for purposes of applying the rules of this paragraph. [IRS Notice 2008-30, Q&A-15, 2008-1 C.B. 638]

Q 10:9   What is a qualified preretirement survivor annuity (QPSA)?

A QPSA is an immediate annuity for the life of the surviving spouse of a participant who dies before the annuity starting date (see Q 10:3). Under a QPSA, each payment to the surviving spouse will be the same as (or the actuarial equivalent of) the payment that would have been made to the surviving spouse under the plan's QJSA (see Q 10:8) if:

1. In the case of a participant who dies after attaining the earliest retirement age (see Q 10:8) under the plan, the participant had retired with an immediate QJSA on the day before the participant's death.

2. In the case of a participant who dies upon or before attaining the earliest retirement age under the plan, the participant had: (a) separated from service on the date of death, (b) survived to the earliest retirement age,

(c) retired with an immediate QJSA at the earliest retirement age, and (d) died on the day after the day on which the earliest retirement age would have been attained. (If the participant had separated from service prior to death, the amount of the QPSA is calculated by reference to the actual date of separation from service rather than the date of death to prevent the participant from accruing benefits after separation from service.)

Example. Steve, who is married, participates in a pension plan, and early retirement age under the plan is age 50. The plan must provide automatic survivor coverage in the form of a QJSA and a QPSA. In 2009, Steve reaches age 50 but does not elect early retirement. Although Steve continues to work after age 50, a QPSA must be provided for his wife in the event that he dies before he retires.

The QPSA may be payable from a defined benefit plan (see Q 2:3) to the surviving spouse at any time, but must be available to the surviving spouse no later than the month in which the participant would have reached the earliest retirement age under the plan. A defined benefit plan may provide that the QPSA is forfeited if the surviving spouse does not survive until the QPSA is payable under the plan. Similarly, the plan may provide that the QPSA is forfeited if the surviving spouse elects to defer payment of the QPSA but does not survive until the deferred commencement date. [I.R.C. § 417(c); Treas. Reg. § 1.401(a)-20, Q&A-18, Q&A-19, Q&A-22(a)]

The QPSA provided under a defined contribution plan (see Q 2:2) must be available to the surviving spouse within a reasonable time after the participant's death (see Q 10:7). The QPSA may not be less valuable than 50 percent of the vested account balance of the participant as of the date of the participant's death. A defined contribution plan may *not* provide that the QPSA is forfeited if the surviving spouse does not survive until the QPSA is payable under the plan. [I.R.C. § 417(c)(2); Treas. Reg. § 1.401(a)-20, Q&A-20, Q&A-22(b)]

One court concluded that a divorce decree could not be modified retroactively to give a deceased participant's former spouse a QPSA because the divorce decree was not a qualified domestic relations order (QDRO; see Q 36:1). [Samaroo v. Samaroo, 193 F.3d 185 (3d Cir. 1999); *see also* Dorn v. IBEW, 211 F.3d 938 (5th Cir. 2000); Robson v. Electrical Contractors Ass'n Local 134, 727 N.E.2d 692 (Ill. App. Ct. 1st Dist. 2000); Rich v. Southern Cal. IBEW-NECA Pension Plan, 2d Civil No. B12715 (Cal. Ct. App. 2d App. Dist. 1999); *but see* Patton v. Denver Post Corp., 2003 WL 1919443 (10th Cir. 2003)] The third circuit distinguished its holding in *Samaroo v. Samaroo* and determined that a property settlement agreement entered into prior to the participant's death, and before the entry of a QDRO, conferred plan benefits to the participant's former spouse, because the agreement provided the former spouse with a right to benefits for which the participant had been eligible prior to his death. [Files v. ExxonMobil Pension Plan, 428 F.3d 478 (3d Cir. 2005)] Another court held that the rights of a surviving spouse to a QPSA cannot be divested by the claims of children designated as beneficiaries in a marital dissolution order, because only the surviving spouse, or a former spouse properly designated in a QDRO, may be eligible for a QPSA. Without a QDRO, the children are not in a position to assert claims competing with the widow's rights as a surviving spouse, the court said. Further, the dissolution order did not qualify as a QDRO, because it did not comply with the specificity requirements for a QDRO, concluded the court. [Hamilton v. Washington State Plumbing & Pipefitting Industry Pension Plan, 433 F.3d 1091 (9th Cir. 2006)] To be entitled to a survivor benefit, being married means being legally married where the state does not recognize common law marriage. [Robinson v. New Orleans Employers ILA AFL-CIO Pension Welfare Vacation & Holiday Funds, 2008 WL 687289 (5th Cir. 2008)]

PPA directed DOL to issue regulations to clarify the status of certain DROs. [PPA § 1001] See Q 36:2 for a discussion of the DOL regulations.

Q 10:10 How is a survivor annuity treated for estate tax purposes?

The value of a surviving spouse's interest in a QJSA (see Q 10:8) or QPSA (see Q 10:9) is included in the participant's gross estate for estate tax purposes. The marital deduction is allowable unless the deceased participant's executor elects not to take the deduction (see Q 15:22). [I.R.C. §§ 2039, 2056(b)(7)(C)]

Q 10:11 What is the effect of a loan on the amount of a QJSA or QPSA?

In determining the amount of the QJSA (see Q 10:8) or QPSA (see Q 10:9), the accrued benefit (see Q 9:2) is reduced by any security interest held by the plan by reason of a loan outstanding to the participant if, at the date of death or benefit payment, the security interest is treated as payment of the loan under the plan (see Q 10:12). The plan may offset any loan outstanding at the participant's death that is secured by the participant's account balance against the spousal benefit. [I.R.C. § 417(c)(3); Treas. Reg. § 1.401(a)-20, Q&A-24(d)]

Q 10:12 Is spousal consent necessary for plan loans?

Yes, if the participant's accrued benefit (see Q 9:2) is used as security for the loan (see Q 10:11). Consent is required even if the accrued benefit is not the primary security for the loan. Spousal consent is not required, however, if the total accrued benefit subject to the security is $5,000 or less (see Qs 10:1, 10:61). Spousal consent must be obtained within 90 days of the date that the loan is so secured, and in the same manner as the consent to the waiver of the QJSA (see Q 10:8) or QPSA (see Q 10:9) is obtained (see Q 10:21). For purposes of spousal consent, any renegotiation, extension, renewal, or other revision of a loan is treated as a new loan. [Treas. Reg. § 1.401(a)-20, Q&A-24; Prop. Treas. Reg. § 1.401(a)-20, Q&A-24(a)(1)]

Q 10:13 What is a transferee plan?

Although profit sharing plans, stock bonus plans, and 401(k) plans are generally not subject to the automatic survivor benefit requirements (see Qs 10:1, 10:6), these plans become subject to such requirements to the extent the plan is a transferee plan with respect to any participant. A plan is a transferee plan with respect to a participant if it is a direct or indirect transferee of that participant's benefits held on or after January 1, 1985, by one of the following:

- A defined benefit plan
- A defined contribution plan subject to the minimum funding standards (see Q 8:1), or
- A defined contribution plan that is subject to the automatic survivor benefit requirements with respect to that participant

Neither a transfer made before 1985 nor a rollover contribution (see Q 34:1) made by a participant at any time is treated as a transfer that subjects a plan to the survivor benefit rules with respect to the participant. Even if a plan is a transferee plan with respect to a participant, the automatic survivor benefit requirements apply only to benefits attributable to the transferred assets, as long as there is an acceptable separate accounting between the transferred assets and other plan benefits. If a separate accounting is not maintained for the transferred assets, the survivor benefit requirements apply to all benefits payable with respect to the participant under the plan. [I.R.C. § 401(a)(11)(B)(iii)(III); Treas. Reg. § 1.401(a)-20, Q&A-5; Leckey v. Stefano, 2007 WL 2458540 (3d Cir. 2007)]

Q 10:14   Do the automatic survivor annuity requirements apply to floor-offset plans?

Yes. If benefits of a plan not otherwise subject to the survivor annuity requirements (see Qs 10:1, 10:6) are used to offset benefits that would otherwise accrue under a plan subject to the survivor annuity requirements (e.g., a defined benefit plan), the floor-offset plan (see Q 2:22) will be subject to the survivor annuity requirements. [Treas. Reg. § 1.401(a)-20, Q&A-5]

Q 10:15   Must annuity contracts distributed to a participant or spouse by a plan satisfy the automatic survivor benefit requirements?

Yes. If a plan is required to provide automatic survivor benefits (see Q 10:1), such benefits may not be eliminated or reduced because the plan uses annuity contracts to provide benefits or because such a contract is held by a participant or spouse instead of a plan trustee. [Treas. Reg. § 1.401(a)-20, Q&A-2]

Q 10:16   Must a frozen or terminated plan provide automatic survivor benefits?

Benefits under a plan that is subject to the survivor benefit requirements must be provided in the form of a QJSA (see Q 10:8) or QPSA (see Q 10:9) even if the plan is frozen or terminated. [Treas. Reg. § 1.401(a)-20, Q&A-6]

Q 10:17 Does it make any difference if PBGC is administering the plan?

No. If PBGC (see Q 25:10) is administering a plan, it will pay benefits in the form of a QJSA (see Q 10:8) or QPSA (see Q 10:9). [Treas. Reg. § 1.401(a)-20, Q&A-7]

Q 10:18 To which benefits do the automatic survivor rules apply?

Benefits derived from both employer and employee contributions are subject to the automatic survivor benefit requirements (see Q 10:1).

For defined benefit plans (see Q 2:3), the automatic survivor benefit requirements apply only to benefits in which the participant was vested immediately before death. They do not apply to benefits to which the participant's beneficiary becomes entitled by reason of death or to the proceeds of a life insurance contract maintained by the plan for the participant to the extent such proceeds exceed the present value of the participant's vested benefits existing immediately before death.

For defined contribution plans (see Q 2:2), the survivor annuity requirements apply to all vested benefits, whether vested before or upon death, including the proceeds of insurance contracts. This rule also applies in determining the vested benefits that must be paid to the surviving spouse under a defined contribution plan exempt from the survivor annuity requirements since such a plan is required to pay all death benefits to the surviving spouse (see Q 10:6). [I.R.C. §§ 401(a)(11), 417(f)(1); Treas. Reg. § 1.401(a)-20, Q&A-11, Q&A-12, Q&A-13]

Q 10:19 Can a qualified retirement plan treat married participants as not married under any circumstances?

Yes. A qualified retirement plan is not required to treat a participant as married unless the participant was married throughout the one-year period ending on the earlier of the participant's annuity starting date (see Q 10:3) or date of death. The one-year marriage requirement is optional, and the plan need not contain this one-year provision. However, if the plan contains a one-year marriage requirement and if the participant marries within one year of the annuity starting date and dies after that date, the participant's spouse is still entitled to the QJSA (see Q 10:8), provided the marriage lasted for at least one year. This is true even if the spouse and the participant are not married on the date of the participant's death, except as may be provided in a QDRO (see Q 36:1). [I.R.C. § 417(d); Treas. Reg. § 1.401(a)-20, Q&A-25(b)(2), Q&A-25(b)(3); Overby v. National Assn. of Letter Carriers, 595 F.3d 1290 (D.C. Cir. 2010); Hinkel v. Navistar Int'l Corp., No. 90-3992 (6th Cir. 1992); Bond v. Trustees of the STA-ILA Pension Fund, No. K-95-1338 (D. Md. 1995); Kyrouac v. Northern Ill. Gas Co., No. 91 C 0364 (N.D. Ill. 1991); Enlow v. Fire Protection Sys., Inc., No. 91-04080 (E.D. Mo. Ct. App. 1991)]

Also, a qualified retirement plan can refuse payment of a survivor annuity to a participant's surviving spouse who pleaded guilty to the murder of the participant. [New Orleans Elec. Pension Fund v. Newman, No. 90-1935 (E.D.

La. 1992); Priv. Ltr. Rul. 9008079] However, one court ruled that a husband who had not waived his right to survivor benefits (see Q 10:21) was entitled to benefits upon his wife's death despite a state law under which he would forfeit all rights to his wife's property because of his allegedly adulterous conduct. The court held that the state law was preempted by ERISA. [Moore v. Philip Morris Cos., 1993 U.S. App. LEXIS 26601 (6th Cir. 1993)] Another court concluded that a surviving spouse who was still married to the deceased participant at the time of his death had waived her interest in the death benefit where the family court had previously issued a judicial order relating to a division of marital assets but had never issued a decree of divorce. [Graef v. Retirement Income Plan for Employees of Albemarle Corp, 1998 WL 879687 (4th Cir. 1998)]

Q 10:20　May a participant waive the automatic survivor benefits?

A plan required to provide automatic survivor benefits must also provide the participant with an opportunity to waive the QJSA (see Q 10:8) or the QPSA (see Q 10:9) during the applicable election period. In addition, the participant is permitted to revoke any election during this period. There is no limit on the number of times the participant may waive the QJSA or QPSA or revoke a waiver. [I.R.C. § 417(a)(1); Davenport v. Davenport, 146 F. Supp. 2d 770 (D.N.C. 2001)]

The applicable election period is:

1. In the case of a QJSA, the 180-day period ending on the annuity starting date (see Q 10:3), or

2. In the case of a QPSA, the period beginning on the first day of the plan year in which the participant attains age 35 and ending on the date of the participant's death.

[I.R.C. § 417(a)(6); Treas. Reg. § 1.401(a)-20, Q&A-10, Q&A-33]

A plan must provide participants with a written explanation of the QJSA (see Q 10:29) no less than 30 days and no more than 180 days before the annuity starting date, except with regard to a retroactive annuity starting date. [I.R.C. § 417(a)(6)(A); IRS Notice 2007-7, § VIII, 2007-1 C.B. 395; see Q 10:57 for further details] However, if the participant, after having received the written explanation, affirmatively elects a form of distribution and the spouse consents to that form of distribution (see Q 10:21), a plan will not fail to satisfy the notice requirements merely because the annuity starting date is less than 30 days after the written explanation is provided to the participant, provided that the following requirements are met:

1. The plan administrator (see Q 20:1) provides information to the participant clearly indicating that the participant has a right to at least 30 days to consider whether to waive the QJSA and consent to a form of distribution other than a QJSA.

2. The participant is permitted to revoke an affirmative distribution election at least until the annuity starting date or, if later, at any time prior to the

expiration of the seven-day period that begins the day after the explanation of the QJSA is provided to the participant.

3. The annuity starting date is after the date that the explanation of the QJSA
   is provided to the participant. However, the plan may permit the annuity
   starting date to be before the date that any affirmative distribution
   election is made by the participant and before the date that the distribution is permitted to commence.

4. Distribution in accordance with the affirmative election does not commence before the expiration of the seven-day period that begins the day
   after the explanation of the QJSA is provided to the participant.

[Treas. Reg. § 1.417(e)-1(b)(3)(ii); Prop. Treas. Reg. § 1.417(e)-1(b)(3)(ii)]

A plan is also permitted to provide the written explanation of the QJSA after
the annuity starting date if the distribution begins at least 30 days after the
explanation is provided, subject to the same waiver of the 30-day minimum
waiting period as described above. [I.R.C. § 417(a)(7)(A)]

The plan may permit the annuity starting date to be before the date that any
affirmative distribution election is made by the participant (and before the date
that distribution is permitted to commence as described above), provided that,
except as otherwise provided regarding administrative delay, distributions
commence not more than 180 days after the explanation of the QJSA is provided.
[Treas. Reg. § 1.417(e)-1(b)(3)(iii); Prop. Treas. Reg. § 1.417(e)-1(b)(3)(iii)]

A defined benefit plan (see Q 2:3) is permitted to provide benefits based on
a retroactive annuity starting date if the requirements described below are
satisfied. However, a defined benefit plan is not required to provide for
retroactive annuity starting dates. If a plan does provide for a retroactive annuity
starting date, it may impose conditions on the availability of a retroactive
annuity starting date in addition to those imposed as described below, provided
that imposition of those additional conditions does not violate any of the rules
applicable to qualified retirement plans. For example, a plan that includes a
single-sum payment as a benefit option may limit the election of a retroactive
annuity starting date to those participants who do not elect the single-sum
payment. A defined contribution plan (see Q 2:2) is not permitted to have a
retroactive annuity starting date. [Treas. Reg. § 1.417(e)-1(b)(3)(iv)(A)]

A retroactive annuity starting date is an annuity starting date affirmatively
elected by a participant that occurs on or before the date the written explanation
is provided to the participant. For a plan to treat a participant as having elected
a retroactive annuity starting date, future periodic payments with respect to a
participant who elects a retroactive annuity starting date must be the same as
the future periodic payments, if any, that would have been paid with respect to
the participant had payments actually commenced on the retroactive annuity
starting date. The participant must receive a make-up payment to reflect any
missed payment or payments for the period from the retroactive annuity starting
date to the date of the actual make-up payment (with an appropriate adjustment
for interest from the date the missed payment or payments would have been

made to the date of the actual make-up payment). Thus, the benefit determined as of the retroactive annuity starting date must satisfy the present value requirements (see Q 10:62), if applicable, and the annual retirement benefit limitation (see Q 6:16), with the applicable interest rate and applicable mortality table determined as of that date. Similarly, a participant is not permitted to elect a retroactive annuity starting date that precedes the date upon which the participant could have otherwise started receiving benefits (e.g., in the case of an ongoing plan, the earlier of the participant's termination of employment or the participant's normal retirement age) under the terms of the plan in effect as of the retroactive annuity starting date. A plan does not fail to treat a participant as having elected a retroactive annuity starting date merely because the distributions are adjusted to the extent necessary to satisfy the present value and annual retirement benefit limitation requirements. [Treas. Reg. § 1.417(e)-1(b)(3)(iv)(B)]

If the participant's spouse as of the retroactive annuity starting date would not be the participant's spouse determined as if the date distributions commence was the participant's annuity starting date, consent of that former spouse is not needed to waive the QJSA with respect to the retroactive annuity starting date, unless otherwise provided under a QDRO (see Q 36:1). [Treas. Reg. § 1.417(e)-1(b)(3)(iv)(C)]

A distribution payable pursuant to a retroactive annuity starting date election is treated as excepted from the present value requirements if the distribution form would have been described in Q 10:62 had the distribution actually commenced on a retroactive annuity starting date. Similarly, annuity payments that otherwise satisfy the requirements of a QJSA will not fail to be treated as a QJSA for annual retirement benefit limitation purposes merely because a retroactive annuity starting date is elected and a make-up payment is made. Also, for purposes of the 10 percent penalty tax (see Qs 16:1, 16:7), a distribution that would otherwise be one of a series of substantially equal periodic payments will be treated as one of a series of substantially equal periodic payments notwithstanding the distribution of a make-up payment. [Treas. Reg. § 1.417(e)-1(b)(3)(iv)(D)]

> **Example.** Under the terms of a defined benefit plan, Casey is entitled to a QJSA with a monthly payment of $1,500 beginning as of his annuity starting date. Due to an administrative error, the QJSA explanation is provided to Casey after the annuity starting date. After receiving the QJSA explanation, Casey elects a retroactive annuity starting date. Pursuant to this election, Casey begins to receive a monthly payment of $1,500 and also receives a make-up payment of $10,000. Under these circumstances, the monthly payments may be treated as a QJSA for annual retirement benefit limitation purposes. In addition, the monthly payments of $1,500 and the make-up payment of $10,000 may be treated as part of a series of substantially equal periodic payments for purposes of the 10 percent penalty tax.

A distribution is permitted to have a retroactive annuity starting date with respect to a participant's benefit only if the following requirements are satisfied:

1. The participant's spouse (including an alternate payee (see Q 36:5) who is treated as the spouse under a QDRO), determined as if the date distributions commence were the participant's annuity starting date, consents to the distribution in a manner that would satisfy the spousal consent requirements (see Q 10:21). The spousal consent requirement for retroactive annuity starting date purposes does not apply if the amount of such spouse's survivor annuity payments under the retroactive annuity starting date election is no less than the amount that the survivor payments to such spouse would have been under an optional form of benefit that would satisfy the requirements to be a QJSA and that has an annuity starting date after the date that the explanation was provided.

2. The distribution (including appropriate interest adjustments) provided based on the retroactive annuity starting date would satisfy the annual retirement benefit limitation requirements if the date the distribution commences is substituted for the annuity starting date for all purposes, including for purposes of determining the applicable interest rate and the applicable mortality table. However, in the case of a form of benefit that would have been excepted from the present value requirements if the distribution had actually commenced on the retroactive annuity starting date, the requirement to apply the annual retirement benefit limitation as of the date distribution commences does not apply if the date distribution commences is twelve months or less from the retroactive annuity starting date.

3. In the case of a form of benefit that would have been subject to the present value requirement if distributions had commenced as of the retroactive annuity starting date, the distribution is no less than the benefit produced by applying the applicable interest rate and the applicable mortality table determined as of the date the distribution commences to the annuity form that corresponds to the annuity form that was used to determine the benefit amount as of the retroactive annuity starting date. Thus, for example, if a distribution paid pursuant to an election of a retroactive annuity starting date is a single-sum distribution that is based on the present value of the straight life annuity payable at normal retirement age, then the amount of the distribution must be no less than the present value of the annuity payable at normal retirement age, determined as of the distribution date using the applicable mortality table and applicable interest rate that apply as of the distribution date. Likewise, if a distribution paid pursuant to an election of a retroactive annuity starting date is a single-sum distribution that is based on the present value of the early retirement annuity payable as of the retroactive annuity starting date, then the amount of the distribution must be no less than the present value of the early retirement annuity payable as of the distribution date using the applicable mortality table and applicable interest rate that apply as of the distribution date.

[Treas. Reg. § 1.417(e)-1(b)(3)(v)]

In the case of a retroactive annuity starting date, the date of the first actual payment of benefits based on the retroactive annuity starting date is generally substituted for the annuity starting date for purposes of satisfying the timing requirements for giving consent and providing an explanation of the QJSA. Thus, the written explanation must generally be provided no less than 30 days and no more than 180 days before the date of the first payment of benefits and the election to receive the distribution must be made after the written explanation is provided and on or before the date of the first payment. Similarly, the written explanation may also be provided less than 30 days prior to the first payment of benefits if the notification requirements would be satisfied if the date of the first payment is substituted for the annuity starting date. [I.R.C. § 417(a)(6)(A); Treas. Reg. § 1.417(e)-1(b)(3)(vi); Prop. Treas. Reg. § 1.417(e)-1(b)(3)(vi); IRS Notice 2007-7, § VIII, 2007-1 C.B. 395; see Q 10:57 for further details]

A plan will not fail to satisfy the 180-day timing requirements merely because, due solely to administrative delay, a distribution commences more than 180 days after the written explanation of the QJSA is provided to the participant. [Treas. Reg. § 1.417(e)-1(b)(3)(vii); Prop. Treas. Reg. § 1.417(e)-1(b)(3)(vii)]

> **Example.** Terry, a married participant in a defined benefit plan who has terminated employment, is provided with the explanation of the QJSA on November 28. Terry elects (with spousal consent) on December 2 to waive the QJSA and receive an immediate distribution in the form of a single life annuity. The plan may permit Terry to receive payments with an annuity starting date of December 1, provided that the first payment is made no earlier than December 6 and Terry does not revoke the election before that date. The plan can make the remaining monthly payments on the first day of each month thereafter in accordance with its regular payment schedule. [Treas. Reg. § 1.417(e)-1(b)(3)(iii); Prop. Treas. Reg. § 1.417(e)-1(b)(3)(iii)]

One court has ruled that a participant who retires early may waive the QJSA after his date of actual retirement. [Shields v. Reader's Digest Ass'n, Inc., 331 F.3d 536 (6th Cir. 2003)]

IRS has issued regulations providing guidelines for the proper electronic transmission of certain notices and consent requirements. In providing flexible standards, as opposed to detailed requirements, the regulations permit:

1. Electronic delivery of the notice of distribution options and the right to defer;
2. Participant consent to a distribution to be given electronically; and
3. A plan to provide notices more than 90 days prior to a distribution if the plan provides a summary of the notices within 90 days before the distribution.

In general, an electronic notice must be reasonably designed to give the notice in a manner as understandable to the participant as a written paper document. Although the electronic notice need not be identical in form or content to a corresponding notice provided in paper format, it must contain all required information. For further details, see Q 20:23.

IRS issued regulations (see Q 20:5) setting forth rules that clarify and expand existing procedures regarding the use of electronic media to provide notices to plan participants and to transmit elections or consents relating to retirement plans.

A retirement plan was terminated and made distributions to the plan participants. Thereafter, a plan participant commenced an action; and, pursuant to a settlement, additional funds were to be distributed to the former participants. IRS ruled that new participant waivers and spousal consents (see Q 10:21) had to be obtained, despite waivers and consents having been obtained previously for the earlier distributions. [Priv. Ltr. Rul. 200745022]

Q 10:21   Must the participant's spouse consent to the waiver of the QJSA or QPSA?

Yes. A spouse's consent to the participant's waiver (see Q 10:20) of the QJSA (see Q 10:8) or the QPSA (see Q 10:9) is effective only if:

1. The spouse consents to the waiver in writing;
2. The election designates a beneficiary (or a form of benefit) that may not be changed without spousal consent (unless the consent expressly allows such amended designations);
3. The spouse's consent acknowledges the effect of the election; and
4. The consent is witnessed by a plan representative or notary public. [Howard v. Branham & Baker Coal Co., 968 F.2d 1214 (6th Cir. 1992); Farris v. Farris Chem. Co., No. 91-5530 (6th Cir. 1992)]

One court held that the lack of notarization did not invalidate the spousal consent with regard to profit sharing plan benefits because the spouse admitted that the signature was his; thus, the benefits were payable to the deceased participant's daughter. In the same case, however, the court also held that the pension plan benefits, despite the spousal consent, were payable to the deceased participant's spouse, and not the daughter, because the plan specified that the QPSA was payable to the surviving spouse and not to a nonspouse beneficiary. [Butler v. Encyclopedia Britannica, Inc., 41 F.3d 285 (7th Cir. 1994)] In another case, the court held that the spousal consent was invalid because the consent form did not acknowledge the effect of the election and was not properly witnessed or notarized; in other words, for the consent to be valid, the spouse has to be given sufficient information to understand the choices and alternatives of giving or not giving consent. [Lasche v. George W. Lasche Basic Ret. Plan, 870 F. Supp. 336 (S.D. Fla. 1994); *see also* Strand v. Automotive Machinists Pension Trust, 2007 WL 1039497 (D. Ore. 2007)] On appeal, the appellate court ruled that the waiver failed as a matter of law because the waiver did not satisfy the unambiguous requirement that the consent be witnessed by a plan representative or a notary public. [Lasche v. George W. Lasche Basic Ret. Plan, 1997 U.S. App. LEXIS 9986 (11th Cir. 1997)]; *see also* Alfieri v. Guild Times Pension Plan,

No. 03-5717 (E.D.N.Y. 2006)] One court determined that a former participant's claim for additional retirement benefits was barred by the statute of limitations despite the plan's failure to comply with the requirements for proper notice of its denial and of the participant's right to review of the claim, because the court concluded that the participant had been aware of the plan's denial of his claim for at least 12 years prior to his commencing the action. [Chuck v. Hewlett Packard Co., 455 F.3d 1026 (9th Cir. 2006)] A surviving spouse's claim that her waiver of the QJSA was invalid because she was not properly advised of its effect was denied, and the court also ruled that her claim was time-barred by the statute of limitations. [Redmon v. Sud-Chemie, Inc. Retirement Plan for Union Employees, 2008 WL 4911160 (6th Cir. 2008)] Another court ruled that a husband who was the plan administrator (see Q 20:1) and a trustee of, and a participant in, a profit sharing plan may have breached his fiduciary duty to his wife if he failed to inform her of her spousal rights under the plan prior to obtaining her written consent to waive her spousal benefits. [Neidich v. Estate of Neidich, No. 01 Civ. 7464 (S.D.N.Y. 2002)] A participant executed a waiver of the QJSA, the spouse consented to the waiver, and the participant died 16 months later. The court concluded that the plan representative could have breached her fiduciary duty by knowing that a waiver of the survivor benefits would be beneficial only if the participant was expected to live many more years, which he was not, and by failing to disclose this information despite evidence that the spouse misunderstood the forms she was signing. If the plan representative was found to have breached her fiduciary duty, then the plan could not rely on the waiver to deny the spouse's claim for survivor annuity benefits. [Canestri v. NYSA-ILA Pension Trust Fund & Plan, 2009 WL 799216 (D. N.J. 2009)]

Where a participant changed beneficiaries of his qualified retirement plan from his wife to others without spousal consent, courts have determined that the participant's wife was entitled to his plan benefits. [Estate of Robbins v. Robbins, No. 1-99 CV 303 (N.D. Miss. 2000); Edelman v. Smith Barney, Inc., No. 98-Civ-691 (S.D.N.Y. 1999)] where a participant changed beneficiaries from his wife to his children during divorce proceedings without the required spousal consent, the parties were later divorced, and the participant then changed the beneficiary to a trust for his children, the court ruled that the participant's former wife was not entitled to his plan benefits. Although the first beneficiary change was invalid because of the lack of consent, the second beneficiary change was valid because spousal consent was not required at that time. [Lehman v. University of Hartford Defined Contribution Ret. Plan, 2002 WL 31076080 (D. Conn. 2002)]

The consent must be given within the applicable election period (see Qs 10:20, 10:57). Spousal consent is not required if the participant establishes to the satisfaction of the plan representative that there is no spouse or the spouse cannot be located, or if there is a court order stating that the participant is legally separated or has been abandoned unless a QDRO (see Q 36:1) provides otherwise. [Davenport v. Davenport, 146 F. Supp. 2d 770 (D.N.C. 2001)] A separation agreement is not a legal separation unless there is a court order. [Board of Trustees of the Equity-League Pension Trust Fund v. Royce, 238 F.3d 177 (2d Cir. 2001)] Without a court order, the estrangement of a participant and spouse is *not* sufficient reason to avoid the QPSA requirement. [Merchant v. Corder, No. 98-2128

(4th Cir. 1998)] A participant's notarized letter alleging that his spouse could not be located was not sufficient because the plan administrator (see Q 20:1) should have protected the spouse's rights by further questioning the participant and trying to contact the spouse at her last known address or telephone number. [I.R.C. § 417(a)(2); Treas. Reg. § 1.401(a)-20, Q&A-27; Lefkowitz v. Arcadia Trading Co. Ltd. Benefit Pension Plan, 1993 U.S. App. LEXIS 15138 (2d Cir. 1993); Lester v. Reagan Equip. Co. Profit Sharing Plan & Employee Sav. Plan, 1992 U.S. Dist. LEXIS 12872 (E.D. La. 1992)] Another court concluded that a surviving spouse who was still married to the deceased participant at the time of his death had waived her interest in the death benefit where the family court had previously issued a judicial order relating to a division of marital assets but had never issued a decree of divorce. [Graef v. Retirement Income Plan for Employees of Albemarle Corp., 1998 WL 879687 (4th Cir. 1998)]

If a determination is made that spousal consent is not required, the plan is discharged from liability to the extent of previously made payments. [ERISA § 205(c)(6)] Where a plan mistakenly paid benefits to a participant in the form of a single life annuity because he falsely informed the plan administrator that he was unmarried, the court held that, after the participant's death, the widow was entitled to the payment of survivor benefits after the plan had recovered the amount of the overpayment made to the participant. [Hearn v. Western Conference of Teamsters Pension Trust Fund, 1995 U.S. App. LEXIS 27941 (9th Cir. 1995)] Similarly, where a plan participant forged his wife's signature on a revocation of a joint and survivor annuity election, the court ruled that ERISA provided only a limited safe harbor that saved the plan from incurring a greater liability for the payment of benefits than it would have incurred if the joint and survivor annuity had not been revoked. [Lombardo v. United Techs., Inc., 1997 U.S. Dist. LEXIS 7651 (D. Conn. 1997)] In another case where the participant transferred his benefits to an IRA (see Q 30:1) without spousal consent, the court stated that the plan would still be obligated to provide survivor benefits to the participant's wife if the participant predeceased her. [Kopec v. Kopec, No. 97-CV-3800 (E.D.N.Y. 1999)] A terminated participant advised the plan administrator (see Q 20:1) that the participant was not married and received a distribution of benefits; however, the participant was, in fact, married. IRS representatives opined that the spouse was entitled to a benefit and that the plan administrator could pursue the participant to recover any overpayment. The representatives also advised that an IRS correction program was available (see Q 19:2). A plan administrator abused its discretion under the terms of the plan when it distributed benefits to a deceased participant's children without first clarifying conflicting information regarding the participant's marital status. [Smith v. New Mexico Coal 401(k) Personal Savings Plan, 2009 WL 1598454 (10th Cir. 2009)]

A spouse's consent to the waiver of the QJSA or QPSA is binding only on that spouse; it is not binding on a subsequent spouse of the participant. A plan may preclude a spouse from revoking the consent to the waiver once it has been given, but a plan may also permit a spouse to revoke the consent and render ineffective the participant's prior election to waive the QJSA or QPSA. [Treas. Reg. § 1.401(a)-20, Q&A-29, Q&A-30] Spousal consent is also required for distributions made in the form of a direct trustee-to-trustee transfer from a qualified retirement plan to an eligible retirement plan (see Qs 34:17, 34:28). A married participant retired and, with the consent of his wife, elected a single life annuity. Thereafter, they divorced and the participant remarried. When the participant died, the court concluded that the second wife was not entitled to the survivor annuity. [Hall v. Kodak Retirement Income Plan, No. 09-1674 (2d Cir. 2010)]

A retirement plan was terminated and made distributions to the plan participants. Thereafter, a plan participant commenced an action; and, pursuant to a settlement, additional funds were to be distributed to the former participants. IRS ruled that new participant waivers and spousal consents had to be obtained, despite waivers and consents having been obtained previously for the earlier distributions. [Priv. Ltr. Rul. 200745022] IRS representatives have opined that, if a new benefit accrues after required minimum distributions (RMDs; see Q 11:4) commence, the new benefit is subject to the RMD rules and spousal consent is required only if the new benefit will be paid in a form other than a QJSA.

IRS has provided sample language designed to make it easier for spouses of plan participants to understand their rights to survivor annuities under qualified retirement plans. The sample language can be included in a form used for a spouse to consent to a participant's waiver of a QJSA or QPSA or to a participant's choice of a nonspouse beneficiary in a defined contribution plan not subject to the QJSA and QPSA requirements (see Q 10:6). The language is designed to assist plan administrators in preparing spousal consent forms that meet the statutory requirements. No one is required to use the sample language, and plan administrators that choose to use it are free to incorporate all or any part of it in their spousal consent forms. [IRS Notice 97-10, 1997-1 C.B. 370]

The Appendices to Notice 97-10 contain four sets of sample language:

1. Appendix A contains sample language that can be included in a spouse's consent to a participant's waiver of a QJSA. This language can be used for a defined benefit plan (see Q 2:3) and for a defined contribution plan (see Q 2:2) to the extent that it is subject to the automatic survivor benefit requirements (see Q 10:18).

2. Appendix B contains sample language that can be included in a spouse's consent to a participant's waiver of a QPSA and, if the plan so provides, to the participant's choice of a beneficiary other than the spouse to receive any survivor benefit. This language can be used for a defined benefit plan.

3. Appendix C contains sample language that can be included in a spouse's consent to a participant's waiver of a QPSA and, if the plan so provides, to the participant's choice of a beneficiary other than the spouse to receive any survivor benefit. This language can be used for a defined contribution plan to the extent that it is subject to the automatic survivor benefit requirements.

4. Appendix D contains sample language that can be included in a spouse's consent to a participant's choice of a beneficiary other than the spouse for a participant's account balance. This language can be used for a defined contribution plan to the extent that it is not subject to the automatic survivor benefit requirements.

If the plan administrator chooses to use the sample language provided in one of these Appendices, the sample language should be conformed to the terms of the plan. The plan administrator should read the sample language carefully and select only those portions of the sample language that apply to the particular plan. For example, the sample language in Appendix A refers to certain optional forms of benefits (see Q 10:37) under the plan, including a single-sum payment. If a plan administrator decides to include this sample language in the plan's spousal consent form, the sample language should be compared to the optional forms of benefit payments available under the plan and modified, if necessary, to reflect the plan's optional forms. Further, spousal consent forms for some plans will need additional language discussing issues specific to the plan.

In order for a spouse's consent to be valid, the spousal consent form is *not* required to include the specific language contained in the Appendices. In all cases, however, spousal consent forms should be written clearly to ensure that the spouse both understands and acknowledges the effect of the participant's waiver of rights.

The Appendices provide sample language for incorporation in a spousal consent form only. The Appendices do *not* provide sample language for the explanation of the QJSA or QPSA that is required to be provided to the participant or for the agreement in which the participant waives the QJSA or QPSA (see Qs 10:29, 10:30).

IRS issued regulations (see Q 20:5) setting forth rules that clarify and expand existing procedures regarding the use of electronic media to provide notices to plan participants and to transmit elections or consents relating to retirement plans and includes spousal consents that are required to be witnessed by a plan representative or a notary public.

Q 10:22   Is spousal consent contained in an antenuptial agreement effective?

An agreement entered into *prior* to marriage does not satisfy the consent requirement (see Q 10:21) even if the agreement is executed within the applicable election period (see Q 10:20). [Treas. Reg. § 1.401(a)-20, Q&A-28]

Courts have held the purported waiver to be invalid because the agreement was not signed by the participant's "spouse" since the agreement predated the marriage, another beneficiary was not specified (see Q 10:23), and the agreement did not acknowledge the effect of the waiver (see Q 10:21). [Hagwood v. Newton, Jr., 2002 WL 266824 (4th Cir. 2002); Manning v. Hayes, 212 F.3d 866 (5th Cir. 2000); Pedro Enters., Inc. v. Perdue, 998 F.2d 491 (7th Cir. 1993); Hurwitz v. Sher, 982 F.2d 778 (2d Cir. 1992); Ford Motor Co. v. Ross, 2001 WL

89639 (E.D. Mich. 2001); Richards v. Richards, 232 A.D.2d 303 (1st Dept. N.Y. 1996); Nellis v. Boeing Co., 1992 WL 122773 (D. Kan. 1992)] However, one court ruled otherwise and held that a waiver contained in a valid prenuptial agreement was enforceable because state marital property law overrides federal law. [Critchell v. Critchell, 746 A.2d 282 (Fed. Cir. 2000); *see also* Sabad v. Fessenden, 2003 Pa. Super. 2002, 825 A.2d 682 (2003); *In re* Estate of Hopkins, 574 N.E.2d 230 (Ill. App. Ct. 2d Dist. 1991)] Other courts have concluded that a waiver in an antenuptial agreement is invalid as it applies to a spouse's survivorship rights, but is valid as it applies to the equitable distribution of a plan benefit as marital property. Thus, in a divorce proceeding, the waiver of rights to plan benefits in an antenuptial agreement is enforceable. [Strong v. Dubin, ___ A.D.3d ___ (1st Dept. N.Y. 2010); Savage-Keough v. Keough, 861 A.2d 131 (N.J. Super., App. Div. 2004); Edmonds v. Edmonds, 710 N.Y.S.2d 765 (N.Y. Sup. Ct. 2000)]

One court determined that the surviving spouse would be required to pay plan benefits to the deceased spouse's estate if the surviving spouse had refused to sign a spousal consent form as required by the antenuptial agreement. [Callahan v. Hutsell, Callahan & Buchino P.S.C. Revised Profit Sharing Plan, 14 F.3d 600 (6th Cir. 1993)]

After being divorced, a plan participant remarried; he entered into an antenuptial agreement with his second wife, who purportedly waived her rights to plan benefits, and he never removed his first wife as beneficiary. The court ruled that the second wife was entitled to the QPSA (see Q 10:9) and that the first wife was entitled to the balance of the death benefits. [National Auto. Dealers & Assocs. Ret. Trust v. Arbeitman, 89 F.3d 496 (8th Cir. 1996)]

One court concluded that a postnuptial agreement requiring the surviving spouse to share 50 percent of the deceased participant's benefits with the participant's children was not preempted by ERISA and might be enforced. [Pruchno v. Pruchno, Mich. App. LEXIS 1875 (Mich. Ct. App. Dist. II 2004)]

Q 10:23 Must the waiver of the QJSA or QPSA specify an alternate beneficiary?

Yes. The participant's waiver of a QJSA (see Q 10:8) or QPSA (see Q 10:9), and the spouse's consent, must specify the nonspouse beneficiary (or class of beneficiaries) who will receive the benefit (see Q 10:21). For example, if the spouse consents to the participant's election to have benefits payable upon the participant's death before the annuity starting date (see Q 10:3) paid to the participant's children, the participant may not subsequently change beneficiaries (to someone other than a child) without the consent of the spouse unless the change is back to a QPSA or the spouse gave a general consent (see Q 10:26). If the spouse consents only to the designation of a trust as beneficiary, no further spousal consent to the designation of trust beneficiaries is required. [Treas. Reg. § 1.401(a)-20, Q&A-31(a)]

Q 10:24   Must the waiver of a QJSA specify the optional form of benefit chosen?

Yes. Both the participant's waiver of a QJSA (see Q 10:8) and the spousal consent must specify the particular optional form of benefit (see Q 10:45). A participant who has waived a QJSA with spousal consent in favor of another form of benefit may not subsequently change the optional form of benefit without the spouse's consent unless the change is back to a QJSA or the spouse gave a general consent (see Q 10:26). If the plan so provides, the participant may change the optional form of benefit after the spouse's death or a divorce (other than as provided in a QDRO; see Q 36:1). [Treas. Reg. § 1.401(a)-20, Q&A-31(b)(1)]

Q 10:25   Must the waiver of a QPSA specify the optional form of benefit chosen?

No. A participant's waiver of a QPSA (see Q 10:9) and the spouse's consent need not specify the optional form of any preretirement benefit. A participant may subsequently change the form of the preretirement benefit without obtaining further spousal consent. However, the participant may not change the nonspouse beneficiary without spousal consent unless there was a general consent (see Qs 10:23, 10:26). [Treas. Reg. § 1.401(a)-20, Q&A-31(b)(2); Herrero v. Cummins Mid-Am., Inc., No. WD 51770 (W.D. Mo. Ct. App. 1996)]

Q 10:26   May a plan allow a spouse to give general consent to waive a QJSA or QPSA?

Yes, a plan may permit a spouse to execute a general consent. A general consent will enable the participant to waive a QJSA (see Q 10:8) or QPSA (see Q 10:9) and change the optional form of benefit or a designated beneficiary without further spousal consent. Alternatively, the spouse may give a limited general consent; that is, the spouse consents only to changes with respect to certain beneficiaries or forms of benefits.

A general consent executed after October 21, 1986 will not be valid unless the general consent acknowledges that the spouse (1) has the right to limit consent to a specific beneficiary and a specific optional form of benefit and (2) voluntarily elects to relinquish both such rights. A general consent, including a limited general consent, is effective only if it is made during the applicable election period (see Q 10:20). [Treas. Reg. § 1.401(a)-20, Q&A-31(c)]

Q 10:27   Does the nonparticipant spouse's consent to the waiver of a QJSA or a QPSA by the participant result in a taxable gift?

No. Such consent by the nonparticipant spouse before the participant's death does not result in a taxable transfer for purposes of the gift tax. After the participant's death, the surviving spouse may be able to disclaim the survivor benefit and avoid the gift tax. [I.R.C. §§ 2503(f), 2518]

Q 10:28   Should the plan document specifically set forth the spousal consent rules?

It is highly recommended to ensure that plan representatives obtain valid spousal consents. One court ordered a plan to pay the QPSA (see Q 10:9) to the surviving spouse because the plan "by its own terms" did not require that spousal consent meet the requirements of the Code and ERISA. [Profit-Sharing Plan for Employees of Republic Fin. Servs., Inc. v. MBank Dallas, N.A., 683 F. Supp. 592 (N.D. Tex. 1988)]

Q 10:29   Must participants be notified of the QJSA?

A plan that is required to provide a QJSA (see Qs 10:6, 10:8, 10:20) must give each participant a written explanation of:

1. The terms and conditions of the QJSA;
2. The participant's right to make, and the effect of, an election to waive the QJSA;
3. The rights of the participant's spouse; and
4. The right to make, and the effect of, a revocation of an election.

Participants must also be furnished with a general description of the eligibility conditions and other material features of the optional forms of benefit, as well as sufficient information to explain the relative values of the optional forms of benefit. This explanation must be given to the participant within a reasonable period before the annuity starting date (see Q 10:3). The plan must provide this explanation to both vested and nonvested participants. [I.R.C. § 417(a)(3)(A); Treas. Reg. §§ 1.401(a)-11(c), 1.401(a)-20, Q&A-34, Q&A-36] For plan years beginning after December 31, 2007, the required explanation must also include the terms and conditions of the QOSA (see Q 10:8). [I.R.C. § 417(a)(3)(A)(i); IRS Notice 2008-30, Q&A-12, 2008-1 C.B. 638]

One court has ruled that the failure to inform a plan participant that the election of a QJSA became irrevocable after the participant's retirement may amount to a claim for breach of fiduciary duty under ERISA (see Q 23:1). [Jordan v. Federal Express Corp., 117 F.3d 1005 (3d Cir. 1997)]

IRS finalized regulations regarding the required explanation of the QJSA (see Qs 10:31–10:35).

Q 10:30   Must participants be notified of the QPSA?

A plan that is required to provide a QPSA (see Qs 10:6, 10:9) must give each participant a written explanation of the QPSA similar to the explanation required for the QJSA (see Q 10:29). This explanation must be given to both vested and nonvested participants within whichever of the following applicable periods ends last with respect to a participant:

1. The period beginning with the first day of the plan year in which the participant attains age 32 and ending at the end of the plan year preceding the plan year in which the participant attains age 35;

2. The period beginning one year before and ending one year after the individual becomes a participant;

3. The period beginning one year before and ending one year after the survivor benefit applicable to the participant is no longer subsidized (see Q 10:36);

4. The period beginning one year before and ending one year after the survivor benefit requirements become applicable to the participant; or

5. In the case of a participant who separates from service before age 35, the period beginning one year before and ending one year after the separation.

[I.R.C. § 417(a)(3)(B); Treas. Reg. § 1.401(a)-20, Q&A-35, Q&A-36]

IRS finalized regulations regarding the required explanation of the QPSA (see Qs 10:31-10:35).

Q 10:31   Is there a required explanation of the QJSA and QPSA?

A plan meets the survivor annuity requirements (see Q 10:1) only if the plan meets the requirements regarding the written explanation required to be provided a participant with respect to a QJSA (see Q 10:8) or a QPSA (see Q 10:9). A written explanation required to be provided to a participant with respect to either a QJSA or a QPSA is referred to as a Section 417(a)(3) Explanation. See Q 10:36 for exceptions to the written explanation requirement in the case of a fully subsidized QPSA or QJSA. [Treas. Reg. § 1.417(a)(3)-1(a)(1)] Also see Q 10:20 for rules governing the timing of the QJSA explanation and Q 10:30 for rules governing the timing of the QPSA explanation. [Treas. Reg. § 1.417(a)(3)-1(a)(2)] For plan years beginning after December 31, 2007, the required explanation must also include the terms and conditions of the QOSA (see Q 10:8). [I.R.C. § 417(a)(3)(A)(i); IRS Notice 2008-30, Q&A-12, 2008-1 C.B. 638]

A Section 417(a)(3) Explanation must be a written explanation. First-class mail to the last-known address of the participant is an acceptable delivery method; and, likewise, hand delivery is acceptable. However, the posting of the explanation is not considered provision of the Section 417(a)(3) Explanation. The explanation must be written in a manner calculated to be understood by the average participant. [Treas. Reg. §§ 1.417(a)(3)-1(a)(3), 1.417(a)(3)-1(a)(4)]

With regard to the Section 417(a)(3) Explanation, IRS issued final regulations in 2003 and proposed regulations in 2005 modifying the 2003 regulations. In 2006, IRS finalized the 2005 regulations with various modifications. The effective date rules of the 2003 regulations continue to apply to QPSA explanations. Thus, the Section 417(a)(3) Explanation requirements apply to explanations provided on or after July 1, 2004.

Except as set forth below, the Section 417(a)(3) Explanation requirements apply to a QJSA explanation with respect to any distribution with an annuity starting date (see Q 10:3) that is on or after February 1, 2006.

Except with respect to any portion of a QJSA explanation that is subject to the earlier effective date rule discussed in this paragraph, a reasonable, good faith effort to comply with the regulations will be deemed to satisfy the requirements for QJSA explanations provided before January 1, 2007, with respect to distributions with annuity starting dates that are on or after February 1, 2006. The Section 417(a)(3) Explanation requirements also apply to a QJSA explanation with respect to any distribution with an annuity starting date that is on or after October 1, 2004, and before February 1, 2006, if the actuarial present value of any optional form of benefit that is subject to the present value requirements (see Q 10:62) is less than the actuarial present value of the QJSA. The actuarial present value of an optional form is treated as not less than the actuarial present value of the QJSA if:

1. Using the applicable interest rate and applicable mortality table (see Q 6:18), the actuarial present value of that optional form is not less than the actuarial present value of the QJSA for an unmarried participant, and

2. Using reasonable actuarial assumptions, the actuarial present value of the QJSA for an unmarried participant is not less than the actuarial present value of the QJSA for a married participant.

In the case of a retroactive annuity starting date (see Q 10:20), the date of commencement of the actual payments based on the retroactive annuity starting date is substituted for the annuity starting date.

[Treas. Reg. § 1.417(a)(3)-1(f)]

Q 10:32   Is there a content requirement for the Section 417(a)(3) Explanation?

The QPSA explanation (see Qs 10:9, 10:31) must contain a general description of the QPSA, the circumstances under which it will be paid if elected, the availability of the election of the QPSA, and, except as provided in Q 10:34, a description of the financial effect of the election of the QPSA on the participant's benefits (i.e., an estimate of the reduction to the participant's estimated normal retirement benefit that would result from an election of the QPSA). [Treas. Reg. § 1.417(a)(3)-1(b)(1)]

The QJSA explanation (see Qs 10:8, 10:31) must satisfy either the requirements of Q 10:33 or Q 10:34. The QJSA explanation must contain certain specific information relating to the benefits available under the plan to the particular participant; or, alternatively, the QJSA explanation can contain generally applicable information in lieu of specific participant information, provided that the participant has the right to request additional information regarding the participant's benefits under the plan. [Treas. Reg. § 1.417(a)(3)-1(b)(2)]

Q 10:33   What is the participant-specific information requirement?

Generally, a QJSA explanation (see Qs 10:8, 10:31) satisfies this requirement if it provides, with respect to each of the optional forms of benefit (see Q 10:37) presently available to the participant (i.e., optional forms of benefit for which the QJSA explanation applies that have an annuity starting date (see Q 10:3) after the providing of the QJSA explanation and optional forms of benefit with retroactive annuity starting dates (see Q 10:20) that are available with payments commencing at that same time), a description of:

1. The optional form of benefit;
2. The eligibility conditions for the optional form of benefit;
3. The financial effect of electing the optional form of benefit (i.e., the amounts and timing of payments to the participant under the form of benefit during the participant's lifetime, and the amounts and timing of payments after the death of the participant);
4. In the case of a defined benefit plan (see Q 2:3), the relative value of the optional form of benefit compared to the value of the QJSA, in the manner described in the following paragraph; and
5. Any other material features of the optional form of benefit. [Treas. Reg. § 1.417(a)(3)-1(c)(1)]

The description of the relative value of an optional form of benefit compared to the value of the QJSA must be expressed to the participant in a manner that provides a meaningful comparison of the relative economic values of the two forms of benefit without the participant having to make calculations using interest or mortality assumptions. Thus, in performing the calculations necessary to make this comparison, the benefits under one or both optional forms of benefit must be converted, taking into account the time value of money and life expectancies, so that the values of both optional forms of benefit are expressed in the same form. For example, such a comparison may be expressed to the participant using any of the following techniques:

1. Expressing the actuarial present value of the optional form of benefit as a percentage or factor of the actuarial present value of the QJSA;
2. Stating the amount of the annuity that is the actuarial equivalent of the optional form of benefit and that is payable at the same time and under the same conditions as the QJSA; or
3. Stating the actuarial present value of both the optional form of benefit and the QJSA. [Treas. Reg. § 1.417(a)(3)-1(c)(2)(i)]

In lieu of providing different QJSA explanations for married and unmarried individuals, the plan may provide a QJSA explanation to an individual that does not vary based on the participant's marital status. For a married participant, in lieu of comparing the value of each optional form of benefit presently available to the participant to the value of the QJSA, the plan can compare the value of each optional form of benefit (including the QJSA) to the value of a QJSA for an unmarried participant (i.e., a single life annuity), but only if the same single life annuity is available to that married participant. For an unmarried participant, in lieu of comparing the value of each optional form of benefit presently available to the participant to the value of the QJSA for that individual (which is a single life annuity), the plan can compare the value of each optional form of benefit (including the single life annuity) to the value of the joint and survivor annuity that is the QJSA for a married participant, but only if that same joint and survivor annuity is available to that unmarried participant. [Treas. Reg. § 1.417(a)(3)-1(c)(2)(ii)]

Two or more optional forms of benefit that have approximately the same value may be grouped for purposes of a required numerical comparison described below. For this purpose, two or more optional forms of benefit have approximately the same value if none of those optional forms of benefit vary in relative value in comparison to the value of the QJSA by more than 5 percentage points when the relative value comparison is made by expressing the actuarial present value of each of those optional forms of benefit as a percentage of the actuarial present value of the QJSA. For such a group of optional forms of benefit, the requirement relating to disclosing the relative value of each optional form of benefit compared to the value of the QJSA can be satisfied by disclosing the relative value of any one of the optional forms in the group compared to the value of the QJSA and disclosing that the other optional forms of benefit in the group are of approximately the same value. If a single-sum distribution is included in such a group of optional forms of benefit, the single-sum distribution must be the distribution form that is used for purposes of this comparison. [Treas. Reg. § 1.417(a)(3)-1(c)(2)(iii)(A)]

If, in accordance with the preceding paragraph, two or more optional forms of benefit are grouped, the relative values for all of the optional forms of benefit in the group can be stated using a representative relative value as the approximate relative value for the entire group. For this purpose, a representative relative value is any relative value that is not less than the relative value of the member of the group of optional forms of benefit with the lowest relative value and is not greater than the relative value of the member of that group with the highest relative value when measured on a consistent basis. For example, if three optional forms have relative values of 87.5 percent, 89 percent, and 91 percent of the value of the QJSA, all three optional forms can be treated as having a relative value of approximately 90 percent of the value of the QJSA. As required under the preceding paragraph, if a single-sum distribution is included in the group of optional forms of benefit, the 90 percent relative factor of the value of the QJSA must be disclosed as the approximate relative value of the single sum, and the other forms can be described as having the same approximate value as the single sum. [Treas. Reg. § 1.417(a)(3)-1(c)(2)(iii)(B)]

The relative value of all optional forms of benefit that have an actuarial present value that is at least 95 percent of the actuarial present value of the QJSA and no greater than 105 percent of the actuarial present value of the QJSA is permitted to be described by stating that those optional forms of benefit are approximately equal in value to the QJSA or that all of those forms of benefit and the QJSA are approximately equal in value. [Treas. Reg. § 1.417(a)(3)-1(c)(2)(iii)(C)]

For the purpose of providing a numerical comparison of the value of an optional form of benefit to the value of the immediately commencing QJSA, the following rules apply:

1. If an optional form of benefit is subject to the requirements of Section 417(e)(3) (see Q 10:62), any comparison of the value of the optional form of benefit to the value of the QJSA must be made using the applicable mortality table and the applicable interest rate (see Q 10:62) (or, at the option of the plan, another reasonable interest rate and reasonable mortality table used under the plan to calculate the amount payable under the optional form of benefit), and

2. All other optional forms of benefit payable to the participant must be compared with the QJSA using a single set of interest and mortality assumptions that are reasonable and that are applied uniformly with respect to all such optional forms payable to the participant (regardless of whether those assumptions are actually used under the plan for purposes of determining benefit payments). For this purpose, the reasonableness of interest and mortality assumptions is determined without regard to the circumstances of the individual participant. In addition, the applicable mortality table and the applicable interest rate are considered reasonable actuarial assumptions for this purpose and thus are permitted (but not required) to be used. [Treas. Reg. § 1.417(a)(3)-1(c)(2)(iv)]

The notice must provide an explanation of the concept of relative value, communicating that the relative value comparison is intended to allow the participant to compare the total value of distributions paid in different forms, that the relative value comparison is made by converting the value of the optional forms of benefit presently available to a common form (such as the QJSA or a single-sum distribution), and that this conversion uses interest and life expectancy assumptions. The explanation of relative value must include a general statement that all comparisons provided are based on average life expectancies and that the relative value of payments ultimately made under an annuity optional form of benefit will depend on actual longevity. [Treas. Reg. § 1.417(a)(3)-1(c)(2)(v)(A)]

A required numerical comparison of the value of the optional form of benefit to the value of the QJSA under the plan is required to disclose the interest rate that is used to develop the comparison. If all optional forms of benefit are permitted to be grouped, then this requirement does not apply for any optional form of benefit not subject to the requirements of Section 417(e)(3). [Treas. Reg. § 1.417(a)(3)-1(c)(2)(v)(B)]

If the plan does not disclose the actuarial assumptions used to calculate the required numerical comparison, then the notice must be accompanied by a statement that includes an offer to provide, upon the participant's request, the actuarial assumptions used to calculate the relative value of optional forms of benefit under the plan. [Treas. Reg. § 1.417(a)(3)-1(c)(2)(v)(C)]

For purposes of providing descriptions of the financial effect of the distribution forms available to a participant and the relative value of an optional form of benefit compared to the value of the QJSA for a participant, the plan is permitted to provide reasonable estimates (e.g., estimates based on data as of an earlier date than the annuity starting date, a reasonable assumption for the age of the participant's spouse, or, as in the case of a defined contribution plan (see Q 2:2), reasonable estimates of amounts that would be payable under a purchased annuity contract), including reasonable estimates of the applicable interest rate. [Treas. Reg. § 1.417(a)(3)-1(c)(3)(i)]

If a QJSA notice uses a reasonable estimate, the QJSA explanation must identify the estimate and explain that the plan will, upon the request of the participant, provide a more precise calculation, and the plan must provide the participant with a more precise calculation if so requested. Thus, for example, if a plan provides an estimate of the amount of the QJSA that is based on a reasonable assumption concerning the age of the participant's spouse, the participant can request a calculation that takes into account the actual age of the spouse, as provided by the participant. [Treas. Reg. § 1.417(a)(3)-1(c)(3)(ii)]

If a more precise calculation described in the preceding paragraph materially changes the relative value of an optional form compared to the value of the QJSA, the revised relative value of that optional form must be disclosed, regardless of whether the financial effect of selecting the optional form is affected by the more precise calculation. For example, if a participant provides a plan with the age of the participant's spouse and that information materially changes the relative value of an optional form of benefit (such as a single sum) compared to the value of the QJSA, then the revised relative value of the optional form of benefit and the value of the QJSA must be disclosed, regardless of whether the amount of the payment under that optional form of benefit is affected by the more precise calculation. [Treas. Reg. § 1.417(a)(3)-1(c)(3)(iii)]

For a written explanation provided by a defined contribution plan, a description of financial effect with respect to an annuity form of benefit must include a statement that the annuity will be provided by purchasing an annuity contract from an insurance company with the participant's account balance under the plan. If the description of the financial effect of the optional form of benefit is provided using estimates rather than by assuring that an insurer is able to provide the amount disclosed to the participant, the written explanation must also disclose this fact. [Treas. Reg. § 1.417(a)(3)-1(c)(4)]

Certain simplified presentations of financial effect and relative value of optional forms of benefit to permit more useful presentations of information to be provided to participants in certain cases in which a plan offers a range of optional forms of benefit may be used. Simplified presentations of financial effect and relative value for a plan that offers a significant number of substantially similar optional forms of benefit and for a plan that permits the participant to make separate benefit elections with respect to parts of a benefit may be used. [Treas. Reg. § 1.417(a)(3)-1(c)(5)(i)]

If a plan offers a significant number of substantially similar optional forms of benefit and disclosing the financial effect and relative value of each such optional form of benefit would provide a level of detail that could be overwhelming rather than helpful to participants, then the financial effect and relative value of those optional forms of benefit can be disclosed by disclosing the relative value and financial effect of a representative range of examples of those optional forms of benefit as described below if the requirements (relating to additional information available upon request) are satisfied. [Treas. Reg. § 1.417(a)(3)-1(c)(5)(ii)(A)] Optional forms of benefit are substantially similar if those optional forms of benefit are identical except for a particular feature or features (with associated adjustment factors) and the feature or features vary linearly. For example, if a plan offers joint and survivor annuity options with survivor payments available in every whole number percentage between 50 percent and 100 percent, those joint and survivor annuity options are substantially similar optional forms of benefit. Similarly, if a participant is entitled under the plan to receive a particular form of benefit with an annuity starting date that is the first day of any month beginning three years before commencement of a distribution and ending on the date of commencement of the distribution, those forms of benefit are substantially similar optional forms of benefit. [Treas. Reg. § 1.417(a)(3)-1(c)(5)(ii)(B)]

A range of examples with respect to substantially similar optional forms of benefit is representative only if it includes examples illustrating the financial effect and relative value of the optional forms of benefit that reflect each varying feature at both extremes of its linear range, plus at least one example illustrating the financial effect and relative value of the optional forms of benefit that reflects each varying feature at an intermediate point. However, if one intermediate example is insufficient to illustrate the pattern of variation in relative value with respect to a varying feature, examples sufficient to illustrate such pattern must be provided. Thus, for example, if a plan offers joint and survivor annuity options with survivor payments available in every whole number percentage between 50 percent and 100 percent, and if all such optional forms of benefit would be permitted to be disclosed as approximately equal in value, the plan could satisfy the requirement to disclose the financial effect and relative value of a representative range of examples of those optional forms of benefit by disclosing the financial effect and relative value with respect to the joint and 50 percent survivor annuity, the joint and 75 percent survivor annuity, and the joint and 100 percent survivor annuity. [Treas. Reg. § 1.417(a)(3)-1(c)(5)(ii)(C)] If a QJSA explanation discloses the financial effect and relative value of substantially similar optional forms of benefit by disclosing the financial effect and relative value of a representative range of examples, the QJSA explanation must explain that the plan will, upon the request of the participant, disclose the financial effect and relative value of any particular optional form of benefit from among the substantially similar optional forms of benefit and the plan must provide the participant with the financial effect and relative value of any such optional form of benefit if the participant so requests. [Treas. Reg. § 1.417(a)(3)-1(c)(5)(ii)(D)]

If the plan permits the participant to make separate benefit elections with respect to two or more portions of the participant's benefit, the description of the financial effect and relative values of optional forms of benefit can be made separately for each such portion of the benefit, rather than for each optional form of benefit (i.e., each combination of possible elections). [Treas. Reg. § 1.417(a)(3)-1(c)(5)(iii)]

Q 10:34 Can generally applicable information be substituted for participant information in the Section 417(a)(3) Explanation?

In lieu of providing the required information (see Q 10:33) for each optional form of benefit *presently* available to the participant, the QJSA explanation (see Qs 10:8, 10:31) may contain such information for the QJSA and each other optional form of benefit *generally* available under the plan, along with a reference to where a participant may readily obtain the required information for any other optional form of benefit that is presently available to the participant. [Treas. Reg. § 1.417(a)(3)-1(d)(1)]

In lieu of providing the required statement of the financial effect of electing an optional form of benefit or the required comparison of relative values (see Q 10:33) based on the actual age and benefit of the participant, the QJSA explanation is permitted to include a chart (or other comparable device) showing the financial effect and relative value of optional forms of benefit in a series of examples specifying the amount of the optional form of benefit payable to a hypothetical participant at a representative range of ages and the comparison of relative values at those same representative ages. Each example in this chart must show the financial effect of electing the optional form of benefit and a comparison of the relative value of the optional form of benefit to the value of the QJSA, using reasonable assumptions for the age of the hypothetical participant's spouse and any other variables that affect the financial effect, or relative value, of the optional form of benefit. The requirement to show the financial effect of electing an optional form can be satisfied through the use of other methods (e.g., expressing the amount of the optional form as a percentage or a factor of the amount payable under the normal form of benefit), provided that the method provides sufficient information so that a participant can determine the amount of benefits payable in the optional form. The chart or other comparable device must be accompanied by the disclosures described in Q 10:33 explaining the concept of relative value and disclosing certain interest assumptions. In addition, the chart or other comparable device must be accompanied by a general statement describing the effect of significant variations between the assumed ages or other variables on the financial effect of electing the optional form of benefit and the comparison of the relative value of the optional form of benefit to the value of the QJSA. [Treas. Reg. § 1.417(a)(3)-1(d)(2)(i)]

The generalized notice described in the preceding paragraph will satisfy the content requirements (see Q 10:32) only if the notice includes either the amount payable to the participant under the normal form of benefit or the amount payable to the participant under the normal form of benefit adjusted for immediate commencement. For this purpose, the normal form of benefit is the form under which payments due to the participant under the plan are expressed under the plan, prior to adjustments for form of benefit. For example, assuming that a plan's benefit accrual formula is expressed as a straight life annuity, the generalized notice must provide the amount of either the straight life annuity commencing at normal retirement age or the straight life annuity commencing immediately. Reasonable estimates may be used to determine the amount payable to the participant under the normal form of benefit if the additional requirements are satisfied with respect to those estimates (see Q 10:33). [Treas. Reg. § 1.417(a)(3)-1(d)(2)(ii)]

The generalized notice must be accompanied by a statement that includes an offer to provide, upon the participant's request, a statement of financial effect and a comparison of relative values that is specific to the participant for any presently available optional form of benefit, and a description of how a participant may obtain this additional information (see Q 10:33). [Treas. Reg. § 1.417(a)(3)-1(d)(2)(iii)]

In lieu of providing a specific description of the financial effect of the QPSA election, the QPSA explanation (see Qs 10:9, 10:31) may provide a general description of the financial effect of the election. Thus, for example, the description can be in the form of a chart showing the reduction to a hypothetical participant's normal retirement benefit at a representative range of participant ages as a result of the QPSA election (using a reasonable assumption for the age of the hypothetical participant's spouse relative to the age of the hypothetical participant). In addition, this chart must be accompanied by a statement that includes an offer to provide, upon the participant's request, an estimate of the reduction to the participant's estimated normal retirement benefit and a description of how a participant may obtain this additional information (see Q 10:33). [Treas. Reg. § 1.417(a)(3)-1(d)(3)]

If, as permitted above, the content of a QJSA explanation does not include all the items required to be described (see Q 10:33), then, upon a request from the participant for any of the required information for one or more presently available optional forms (including a request for all optional forms presently available to the participant), the plan must furnish the information required with respect to those optional forms. Thus, with respect to those optional forms of benefit, the participant must receive a QJSA explanation specific to the participant that is based on the participant's actual age and benefit. In addition, the plan must comply with the material change requirements (see Q 10:33). Further, if the plan does not disclose the actuarial assumptions used to calculate the required numerical comparison, then, upon request, the plan must provide the actuarial assumptions used to calculate the relative value of optional forms of benefit under the plan. [Treas. Reg. § 1.417(a)(3)-1(d)(4)(i)]

If, as permitted above, the content of a QPSA explanation does not include all the items required to be described (see Q 10:32), then, upon a request from the participant, the plan must furnish an estimate of the reduction to the participant's estimated normal retirement benefit that would result from a QPSA election. [Treas. Reg. § 1.417(a)(3)-1(d)(4)(ii)]

A QJSA explanation does not fail to satisfy the above requirements merely because it contains an item of participant-specific information in place of the corresponding generally applicable information. [Treas. Reg. § 1.417(a)(3)-1(d)(5)]

Q 10:35   Are there examples illustrating the Section 417(a)(3) Explanation requirements?

Yes. Solely for purposes of these examples, the applicable interest rate that applies to any distribution that is subject to the rules of Section 417(e)(3) is assumed to be 5.5 percent, and the applicable mortality table is assumed to be the table that applies as of January 1, 2003 (see Q 10:62). In addition, solely for purposes of these examples, assume that a plan that determines actuarial equivalence using 6 percent interest and the applicable mortality table that applies as of January 1, 1995 is using reasonable actuarial assumptions.

Example 1. Bluma participates in Plan C, a defined benefit plan (see Q 2:3). Under Plan C, the QJSA (see Q 10:8) is a joint and 100 percent survivor annuity that is actuarially equivalent to the single life annuity determined using 6 percent interest and the applicable mortality table that applies as of January 1, 1995. On October 1, 2004, Bluma will terminate employment at age 55. When she terminates employment, Bluma will be eligible to elect an unreduced early retirement benefit, payable as either a life annuity or the QJSA. Bluma will also be eligible to elect a single-sum distribution equal to the actuarial present value of the single life annuity payable at normal retirement age (age 65), determined using the applicable mortality table and the applicable interest rate.

Bluma is provided with a QJSA explanation that describes the single life annuity, the QJSA, and the single-sum distribution option under the plan, and any eligibility conditions associated with these options. Bluma is married when the explanation is provided. The explanation indicates that, if Bluma commenced benefits at age 55 and had a spouse age 55, the monthly benefit under an immediately commencing single life annuity is $3,000, the monthly benefit under the QJSA is estimated to be 89.96 percent of the monthly benefit under the immediately commencing single life annuity, or $2,699, and the single sum is estimated to be 74.7645 times the monthly benefit under the immediately commencing single life annuity, or $224,293.

The QJSA explanation indicates that the single life annuity and the QJSA are of approximately the same value but that the single-sum option is equivalent in value to a QJSA of $1,215. This amount is 45 percent of the value of the QJSA at age 55 [$1,215 ÷ (89.96% × $3,000)]. The explanation states that the relative value comparison converts the value of the single life annuity and the single-sum options to the value of each if paid in the form of the QJSA and that this conversion uses interest and life expectancy assumptions. The explanation specifies that the calculations relating to the single-sum distribution were prepared using 5.5 percent interest and average life expectancy, that the other calculations were prepared using a 6 percent interest rate, and that the relative value of actual annuity payments for an individual can vary depending on how long the individual and spouse live. The explanation notes that the calculation of the QJSA assumed that the spouse was age 55, that the amount of the QJSA will depend on the actual age of the spouse (for example, annuity payments will be significantly lower if the spouse is significantly younger than the participant), and that the amount of the single-sum payment will depend on the interest rates that apply when the participant actually takes a distribution. The explanation also includes an offer to provide a more precise calculation to the participant taking into account the spouse's actual age.

Bluma requests a more precise calculation of the financial effect of choosing a QJSA, taking into account the actual age of her spouse. Based on the fact that the spouse is age 50, Plan C determines that the monthly payments under the QJSA are 87.62 percent of the monthly payments under the single life annuity, or $2,628.60 per month, and provides this information to Bluma. Plan C is not required to provide an updated calculation of the relative value of the single sum because the value of the single sum continues to be 45 percent of the value of the QJSA.

Example 2. The facts are the same as in Example 1, except that the comparison of the relative values of optional forms of benefit to the value of the QJSA is not expressed as a percentage of the actuarial present value of the QJSA but instead is expressed by disclosing the actuarial present values of the optional forms and the QJSA. In addition, the plan uses the applicable interest rate and the applicable mortality table for all comparison purposes. Accordingly, the QJSA explanation indicates that the QJSA has an actuarial present value of $498,089, while the single-sum payment has an actuarial present value of $224,293 (i.e., the amount of the single sum is $224,293) and that the single life annuity is approximately equal in value to the QJSA. The explanation states that the relative value comparison converts the value of the single life annuity and the QJSA into an amount payable in the form of a single-sum option (even though a single-sum distribution in that amount is not available under the plan) and that this conversion uses interest and life expectancy assumptions. The explanation specifies that the calculations were prepared using 5.5 percent interest and average life expectancy and that the relative value of actual annuity payments for an individual can vary depending on how long the individual and spouse live. The explanation notes that the calculation of the QJSA assumed that the spouse was age 55, that the amount of the QJSA will depend on the actual age of the spouse (for example, annuity payments will be significantly lower if the spouse is significantly younger than the participant), and that the amount of the single-sum payment will depend on the interest rates that apply when the participant actually takes a distribution. The explanation also includes an offer to provide a more precise calculation to the participant taking into account the spouse's actual age.

Example 3. The facts are the same as in Example 1, except that, in lieu of providing information specific to Bluma in the QJSA notice, Plan C satisfies the QJSA explanation requirement providing Bluma with a statement that her monthly benefit under an immediately commencing single life annuity (which is the normal form of benefit under Plan C, adjusted for immediate commencement) is $3,000, along with the following chart. The chart shows the financial effect of electing each optional form of benefit for a hypothetical participant with a $1,000 benefit and a spouse who is the same age as the participant. Instead of showing the relative value of these optional forms of benefit compared to the value of the QJSA, the chart shows the relative value of these optional forms of benefit compared to the value of the single life annuity. Separate charts are provided for ages 55, 60, and 65 as follows:

Optional Form	Amount of Distribution per $1,000 of Immediate Single Life Annuity	Relative Value
Age 55 Commencement:		
Life Annuity	$1,000 per month	N/a
QJSA (joint and 100% survivor annuity)	$900 per month ($900 per month survivor annuity)	Approximately the same value as the life annuity
Lump sum	$74,764	Approximately 45% of the value of the life annuity
Age 60 Commencement:		
Life Annuity	$1,000 per month	N/a
QJSA (joint and 100% survivor annuity)	$878 per month ($878 per month for survivor annuity)	Approximately the same value as the life annuity
Lump sum	$99,792	Approximately 66% of the value of the life annuity
Age 65 Commencement:		
Life Annuity	$1,000 per month	N/a
QJSA (joint and 100% annuity)	$852 per month ($852 per month for survivor annuity)	Approximately the same value as the life annuity
Lump sum	$135,759	Approximately the same value as the life annuity

When Bluma requests specific information regarding the amounts payable under the QJSA, the joint and 100 percent survivor annuity, and the single-sum distribution and provides the age of her spouse, Plan C determines that Bluma's QJSA is $2,628.60 per month and the single-sum distribution is $224,293. The actuarial present value of the QJSA (determined using the 5.5 percent interest and the applicable mortality table) is $498,896 and the actuarial present value of the single life annuity is $497,876.

Accordingly, the specific information discloses that the single-sum distribution has a value that is 45 percent of the value of the single life annuity available to Bluma on October 1, 2004. The QJSA notice provides that the QJSA is of approximately the same value as the single life annuity.

Example 4. The facts are the same as in Example 1, except that, under Plan C, the single-sum distribution is determined as the actuarial present value of the immediately commencing single life annuity. In addition, Plan C provides a joint and 75 percent survivor annuity that is reduced from the single life annuity and that is the QJSA under Plan C. For purposes of determining the amount of the QJSA, if the participant is married, the reduction is only half of the reduction that would normally apply under the actuarial assumptions specified in Plan C for determining actuarial equivalence of optional forms.

In lieu of providing information specific to Bluma in the QJSA notice (see Q 10:33), Plan C satisfies the QJSA explanation requirement (see Q 10:34) by providing Bluma with a statement that her monthly benefit under an immediately commencing single life annuity (which is the normal form of benefit under Plan C, adjusted for immediate commencement) is $3,000, along with the following chart showing the financial effect and the relative value of the optional forms of benefit compared to the QJSA for a hypothetical participant with a $1,000 benefit and a spouse who is three years younger than the participant. For each optional form generally available under the plan, the chart shows the financial effect and the relative value, using the grouping rules (see Q 10:33). Separate charts are provided for ages 55, 60, and 65, as follows:

Optional Form	Amount of Distribution per $1,000 of Immediate Single Life Annuity	Relative Value
Age 55 Commencement:		
Life Annuity	$1,000 per month	Approximately the same value as the QJSA
QJSA (joint and 75% survivor annuity for a participant who is married)	$956 per month $717 per month survivor annuity	N/a
Joint and 100% survivor annuity	$886 per month ($886 per month for survivor annuity)	Approximately the same value as the QJSA
Lump sum	$165,959	Approximately the same value as the QJSA
Age 60 Commencement:		
Life Annuity	$1,000 per month	Approximately 94% of the value of the QJSA

Optional Form	Amount of Distribution per $1,000 of Immediate Single Life Annuity	Relative Value
QJSA (joint and 75% survivor annuity for a participant who is married)	$945 per month ($709 per month for survivor annuity)	N/a
Joint and 100% survivor annuity	$859 per month ($859 per month for survivor annuity)	Approximately 94% of the value of the QJSA
Lump sum	$151,691	Approximately the same value of the QJSA
Age 65 Commencement:		
Life Annuity	$1,000 per month	Approximately 93% of the value of the QJSA
QJSA (joint and 75% survivor annuity for a participant who is married)	$932 per month ($699 per month for survivor annuity)	N/a
Joint and 100% survivor annuity	$828 per month ($828 per month for survivor annuity)	Approximately 93% of the value of the QJSA
Lump sum	$135,759	Approximately 93% of the value of the QJSA

The chart disclosing the financial effect and relative value of the optional forms specifies that the calculations were prepared assuming that the spouse is three years younger than the participant, that the calculations relating to the single-sum distribution were prepared using 5.5 percent interest and average life expectancy, that the other calculations were prepared using a 6 percent interest rate, and that the relative value of actual payments for an individual can vary depending on how long the individual and spouse live. The explanation states that the relative value comparison converts the single life annuity, the joint and 100 percent survivor annuity, and the single-sum options to the value of each if paid in the form of the QJSA and that this conversion uses interest and life expectancy assumptions. The explanation notes that the calculation of the QJSA depends on the actual age of the spouse (for example, annuity payments will be significantly lower if the spouse is significantly younger than the participant) and that the amount of the single-sum payment will depend on the interest rates that apply when the participant actually takes a distribution. The explanation also includes an offer to provide a calculation specific to the participant upon request and an offer to provide mortality tables used in preparing calculations upon request.

Bluma requests information regarding the amounts payable under the QJSA, the joint and 100 percent survivor annuity, and the single sum. Based upon the information about the age of the spouse, Plan C determines that Bluma's QJSA is $2,856.30 per month, the joint and 100 percent survivor annuity is $2,628.60 per month, and the single sum is $497,876. The actuarial present value of the QJSA (determined using the 5.5 percent interest and the applicable mortality table) is $525,091. Accordingly, the value of the single-sum distribution available to Bluma at October 1, 2004 is 94.8 percent of the actuarial present value of the QJSA. In addition, the actuarial present value of the life annuity and the 100 percent joint and survivor annuity are 95 percent of the actuarial present value of the QJSA.

Plan C provides Bluma with a QJSA explanation that incorporates these more precise calculations of the financial effect and relative value of the optional forms for which she requested information.

[Treas. Reg. § 1.417(a)(3)-1(e)]

Q 10:36   What happens if the plan fully subsidizes the cost of the QJSA or QPSA?

If a plan fully subsidizes a QJSA (see Q 10:8) or QPSA (see Q 10:9) and does not permit a participant to waive the benefit or to designate another beneficiary, it need not provide the required written explanation (see Qs 10:29–10:35). If a plan that subsidizes the cost of the QJSA or QPSA offers such election, the plan must satisfy the election, consent, and notice requirements. [I.R.C. § 417(a)(5); Treas. Reg. § 1.401(a)-20, Q&A-37]

A fully subsidized QJSA is one under which no increase in cost or decrease in benefits to the participant could possibly result from the participant's failure to elect another benefit. For example, if a plan provides a joint and survivor annuity and a single-sum option, the plan does not fully subsidize the joint and survivor annuity (even if the actuarial value of the joint and survivor annuity is greater than the amount of the single-sum payment) because, in the event of the participant's early death, the participant would have received less under the annuity than under the single-sum option. Similarly, if a plan provides for a life annuity of $100 per month and a joint and 100 percent survivor benefit of $99 per month, the plan is not fully subsidizing the joint and survivor benefit.

A QPSA is fully subsidized if the participant's benefit is not reduced because of the QPSA coverage and the participant is not charged for the QPSA coverage. Therefore, a QPSA is fully subsidized in a defined contribution plan because the participant's account balance is not reduced by the QPSA coverage and no charge is made against the account for such coverage. [Treas. Reg. § 1.401(a)-20, Q&A-38]

Q 10:37   Can a qualified retirement plan provide optional ways in which to pay benefits?

Yes. However, the optional forms of benefit provided by a qualified retirement plan must comply with IRS guidelines. Generally, each optional form of benefit must (1) be provided in a way that does not discriminate in favor of highly compensated employees (HCEs; see Qs 3:2, 4:10, 4:19, 10:38–10:44) and (2) be available to eligible employees without employer discretion (see Qs 10:45–10:51). [I.R.C. §§ 401(a)(4), 411(d)(6); Treas. Reg. §§ 1.401(a)(4)-4, 1.401(a)-4, 1.411(d)-4]

If a plan offers optional forms of benefit, the different forms must be actuarially equivalent and the plan must specify the actuarial assumptions to be used in calculating the equivalent benefits. [I.R.C. § 401(a)(25); Rev. Rul. 79-90, 1979-1 C.B. 155]

Q 10:38   Can a plan permit optional forms of benefit payment that favor HCEs?

No. A qualified retirement plan must provide benefits that do not discriminate in favor of HCEs (see Qs 3:2, 4:10). If a plan provides for optional forms of benefit payment—for example, different forms of distribution commencing at the same time or the same form of distribution commencing at different times—the availability of each of these optional forms of benefit payment is subject to this nondiscrimination requirement (see Qs 4:20, 11:4). This is true whether or not the particular benefit option is the actuarial equivalent (see Qs 2:19, 2:20) of any other form of benefit under the plan. To meet the nondiscrimination requirement, the optional form of benefit must be both currently available (see Q 10:39) and effectively available (see Q 10:40) in a nondiscriminatory manner. It is not necessary, however, to apply a nondiscriminatory test to the actual receipt of each optional form of benefit. [I.R.C. § 401(a)(4); Treas. Reg. §§ 1.401(a)(4)-4(b), 1.401(a)(4)-4(c), 1.401(a)-4, Q&A-1, Q&A-2]

Q 10:39   How is the determination made as to whether the current availability of an optional form of benefit is nondiscriminatory?

An optional form of benefit must be currently available to a group of employees that satisfies one of the minimum coverage tests (see Q 5:15). Generally, current availability is determined on the basis of current facts and circumstances. However, certain specified conditions on the availability of an optional form of benefit (e.g., minimum age or service, disability, hardship, vesting, family status, or waiver of rights under federal or state law) are disregarded in determining whether a benefit is currently available to an employee.

If an employer eliminates an optional form of benefit with respect to *future* benefit accruals, the current availability test is treated as satisfied for all years after the elimination if the optional form satisfied the nondiscrimination requirement immediately prior to its elimination.

Example. A profit sharing plan that provided for a single-sum distribution available to all employees on termination of employment was amended in 2003 to eliminate the single-sum option with respect to benefits accrued after December 31, 2003. As of December 31, 2003, the single-sum optional form of benefit was available to a group of employees that satisfied the ratio percentage test (see Q 5:16). As of January 1, 2005, all non-highly compensated employees (NHCEs; see Q 3:12) who were entitled to the single-sum optional form of benefit have terminated employment and taken a distribution of their benefits. The only remaining employees who are eligible to take a portion of their benefits in a single sum on termination of employment are HCEs (see Q 3:2). Because the availability of the single-sum optional form of benefit satisfied the current availability test as of December 31, 2003, the availability of such optional form of benefit will be deemed to continue to satisfy the current availability test.

[Treas. Reg. §§ 1.401(a)(4)-4(b), 1.401(a)-4, Q&A-2(a), Q&A-2(b)]

Q 10:40   How is the determination made as to whether the effective availability of an optional form of benefit is nondiscriminatory?

This determination must be based on all the surrounding facts and circumstances of the employer maintaining the plan. A condition with respect to the availability of a particular optional form of benefit payment violates the effective availability test if it substantially favors HCEs (see Q 3:2).

Example. Lee-Lisa Corporation maintains a qualified retirement plan in which all of its eligible employees participate. Under the plan, a participant is entitled to receive a retirement benefit at age 65. Moreover, an employee who terminates employment after age 55 with at least 30 years of service may also receive early retirement benefits. Both of Lee-Lisa Corporation's HCEs, but only two of Lee-Lisa Corporation's eight NHCEs (see Q 3:12), may become eligible to receive early retirement benefits because they were hired before age 35. Even though the early retirement benefit is currently available to all participants, because age and service requirements are disregarded, it does not meet the effective availability test because the availability conditions substantially favor HCEs.

[Treas. Reg. §§ 1.401(a)(4)-4(c), 1.401(a)-4, Q&A-2(a)(3)]

Q 10:41   May a qualified retirement plan deny a participant an optional form of benefit payment for which the participant is otherwise eligible?

No. Even though this type of provision may satisfy the nondiscrimination requirements in certain circumstances, such a provision impermissibly results in the employer or some person other than the participant having discretion as to the optional form of benefit payment (see Qs 10:37, 10:47). [I.R.C. § 411(d)(6)]

Q 10:42   Will a qualified retirement plan be considered discriminatory if it requires that an involuntary distribution be made?

No. A qualified retirement plan will not be treated as discriminatory merely because it provides for an involuntary distribution if the present value of an employee's benefit is $5,000 or less. Thus, a plan may require a single-sum distribution to terminating employees whose benefits have a present value of $5,000 or any lower amount. Also, a plan may be amended to provide for the involuntary distribution of an employee's benefit to the extent such involuntary distribution is permitted. Thus, for example, an involuntary distribution provision may be amended to require that an employee who terminates from employment with the employer receive a single-sum distribution in the event that the present value of the employee's benefit is not more than $5,000 without violating the anti-cutback rule (see Q 9:25). In addition, for example, the employer may amend the plan to reduce the involuntary distribution threshold from $5,000 to any lower amount and to eliminate the involuntary single-sum option for employees with benefits between $5,000 and such lower amount without violating the anti-cutback rule. However, this rule does not permit employer discretion in deciding whether or not to cash out involuntarily a terminating employee and does not apply to distributions after the annuity starting date (see Q 10:3). [I.R.C. §§ 411(a)(11), 417(e); Treas. Reg. §§ 1.401(a)(4)-4(b)(2)(ii)(C), 1.401(a)-4, Q&A-4, 1.411(d)-4, Q&A-2(b)(2)(v)]

For rules relating to the calculation of the present value of an employee's benefit, see Q 10:61.

Q 10:43   Can a qualified retirement plan containing discriminatory optional forms of benefit be amended?

Yes. If the availability of an optional form of benefit in an existing qualified retirement plan is discriminatory, the plan must be amended either to eliminate the optional form or to make the availability of the optional form nondiscriminatory. The availability of an optional form of benefit may be made nondiscriminatory by making the benefit available to a sufficient number of additional NHCEs (see Q 3:12) or by imposing nondiscriminatory objective criteria on its availability so that the group of employees to whom the benefit is available is nondiscriminatory. The plan sponsor may also amend the plan in that manner if the availability of an optional form of benefit may reasonably be expected to discriminate.

Certain corrective amendments to the availability of an optional form of benefit are permitted. Because it is difficult or impossible, in many cases, to make an optional form of benefit meaningfully available on a retroactive basis, a corrective amendment increasing availability is required only on a prospective basis. However, in order to take the correction into account for a plan year, the group of employees to whom the optional form is available (after taking the amendment into account) generally must satisfy a nondiscriminatory requirement. In addition, the amendment must remain in effect until the end of the plan year following the year in which the amendment is effective and must not be part of a pattern of amendments used to correct repeated failures. Other rules relating to retroactive correction also apply (e.g., the requirement that the correction be made no later than the 15th day of the tenth month after the close of a plan year).

As an alternative to increasing availability, an employer may make a corrective amendment by the last day of the plan year eliminating the optional form of benefit (to the extent permitted under Section 411(d)(6)). In that case, the amendment will be treated as if it were in effect throughout the plan year for purposes of nondiscrimination testing.

[Treas. Reg. § 1.401(a)(4)-11(g); IRS Notice 96-67, 1996-2 C.B. 235]

Q 10:44   Should the plan administrator provide any notice that the qualified retirement plan's optional forms of benefit are being modified?

Yes. Although there is no special reporting requirement regarding modification of a qualified retirement plan's optional forms of benefit, a plan administrator (see Q 20:1) is required to furnish to participants a summary of material modifications (SMM) within 210 days after the close of the plan year in which the modification is adopted (see Qs 22:8, 22:9).

However, even before a modification is formally adopted, it is prudent for the plan administrator to give prompt notice of any such modification to participants. Giving prompt notice to participants would reconcile the conflict between ERISA's mandate that the plan be administered in accordance with the terms of its plan documents and IRS's operational requirement that the plan be administered consistent with a conforming plan amendment that has not yet been adopted. [ERISA §§ 104, 404(a)(1)(D); DOL Reg. § 2520.104b-3]

See Qs 9:29 through 9:32 for a discussion of final IRS regulations, and Qs 9:33 and 9:34 for a discussion of proposed regulations, relating to the elimination of optional forms of benefit.

Q 10:45   What are Section 411(d)(6) protected benefits?

Benefits, early retirement benefits, retirement-type subsidies, and optional forms of benefit are Section 411(d)(6) protected benefits to the extent they have accrued and cannot, therefore, be eliminated, reduced, or made subject to employer discretion except to the extent permitted by regulations (see Qs 9:25,10:43). [I.R.C. § 411(d)(6); Treas. Reg. § 1.411(d)-4, Q&A-1(a); Bellas v. CBS, Inc., 221 F.3d 517 (3d Cir. 2000); Ahng v. Allsteel, Inc., Nos. 95-2721, 95-3734 (7th Cir. 1996); Costantino v. TRW Inc., 1993 U.S. App. LEXIS 29479 (6th Cir. 1993); Gillis v. Hoechst Celanese Corp., 1993 U.S. App. LEXIS 22527 (3d Cir. 1993); Counts v. Kissack Water & Oil Serv., Inc., No. 92-8036 (10th Cir. 1993); Davis v. Burlington Indus., Inc., No. 91-1725 (4th Cir. 1992); Auwarter v. Donohue Paper Sales Corp. Defined Benefit Pension Plan, No. 91-3082 (E.D. N.Y. 1992); Rev. Rul. 85-6, 1985-1 C.B. 133; Rev. Proc. 92-10, 1992-1 C.B. 661; IRS Notice 96-67, 1996-2 C.B. 235] In one case, however, the employer was not estopped from following the plan as amended in determining the benefit to be paid to retirees who retired in years after the plan amendment was adopted. [Ryberczyk v. TRW, Inc., No. 97-4167 (6th Cir. 2000)] See Q 9:54 for examples of benefits that are not Section 411(d)(6) protected benefits; note that there appears to be a conflict among various courts.

An optional form of benefit is a distribution form with respect to an employee's benefit that is available under the plan and is identical with respect to all features relating to the distribution form, including the payment schedule, timing, commencement, medium of distribution (e.g., in cash or in-kind; see Q 9:31), the portion of the benefit to which such distribution features apply, and the election rights with respect to such optional forms. To the extent there are any differences in such features, the plan provides separate optional forms of benefit. Differences in amounts of benefits, methods of calculation, or values of distribution forms do not result in optional forms of benefit for purposes of this rule. However, such amounts, methods of calculation, or values may be protected benefits. [Treas. Reg. §§ 1.411(d)-4, Q&A-1(b), 1.401(a)(4)-4(e)(1)]

Example 1. A plan permits each participant to receive a benefit under the plan as a single-sum distribution, a level monthly distribution over 15 years, a single life annuity, a joint and 50 percent survivor annuity, a joint and 75 percent survivor annuity, a joint and 50 percent survivor annuity with a benefit increase for the participant if the beneficiary dies before a specified date, or a joint and 50 percent survivor annuity with a ten-year certain feature. Each of these forms of benefit payment is an optional form of benefit, whether or not their values are actuarially equivalent.

Example 2. A plan permits each participant to receive a benefit under the plan as a single life annuity commencing at termination from employment, a joint and 50 percent survivor annuity commencing at termination from employment, a single-sum distribution that is actuarially equivalent to the single life annuity determined by using a specified interest rate (X percent) for the employees of Division A, and a single-sum distribution that is actuarially equivalent to the single life annuity determined by using an interest rate that is 80 percent of X percent for employees of Division B. This plan provides three optional forms of benefit. While the interest rates used to determine the single-sum distributions available to the employees of Division A and employees of Division B respectively differ, this difference does not result in two single-sum optional forms of benefit.

Example 3. A plan permits each participant who is employed by Division A to receive a benefit in a single-sum distribution payable upon termination from employment and each participant who is employed by Division B to receive a benefit in a single-sum distribution payable upon termination from employment on or after the attainment of age 50. This plan provides two single-sum optional forms of benefit because they begin at different times.

Example 4. A plan provides a single life annuity that begins in the month of termination of employment and a single life annuity that begins after five consecutive one-year breaks in service (see Q 5:10). These are optional benefit forms because they begin at different times.

Example 5. A profit sharing plan permits each participant who is employed by Division A to receive an in-service distribution up to $5,000 and each participant who is employed by Division B to receive an in-service distribution of up to the participant's total benefit. These in-service distribution options differ as to the portion of the accrued benefit (see Q 9:2) that may be distributed in a particular form and are, therefore, two optional forms of benefit.

Example 6. A profit sharing plan provides for a single-sum distribution on termination of employment. The plan is amended in 2001 to eliminate the single-sum optional form of benefit with respect to benefits accrued after the date of amendment. This single-sum optional form of benefit continues to be a single optional form of benefit although, over time, the percentage of various employees' accrued benefits that are potentially payable under this single sum may vary because the form is only available with respect to benefits accrued up to and including the date of the amendment.

Example 7. A profit sharing plan permits loans that are secured by an employee's account balance. In the event of default on such a loan, there is an execution on the account balance. Such execution is a distribution of the employee's accrued benefit under the plan. A distribution of an accrued benefit contingent on default under a plan loan secured by such accrued benefits is an optional form of benefit under the plan.

IRS has ruled that, although a qualified retirement plan's hardship distribution provision (see Q 27:14) is a protected benefit, the plan may be amended to eliminate the provision without risk to the plan's qualified status, and that a protected benefit may be eliminated by a trustee-to-trustee transfer from a plan with a hardship distribution provision to another company's plan without the provision without adversely affecting the qualified status of either plan (see Q 9:29). [Priv. Ltr. Rul. 9743045]

Section 411(d)(6) protected benefits may not be eliminated merely because they are payable with respect to a spouse or other beneficiary. [Treas. Reg. § 1.411(d)-4, Q&A-2(a)(4)]

See Qs 9:29 through 9:32 for a discussion of IRS final regulations relating to the elimination of optional forms of benefit. A defined contribution plan (see Q 2:2) will not violate the anti-cutback rule (see Q 9:25) merely because of the elimination of a form of distribution previously available if (1) a single-sum payment is available to the participant at the same time or times as the form of distribution being eliminated and (2) such single-sum payment is based on the same or greater portion of the participant's account as the form of distribution being eliminated. [I.R.C. § 411(d)(6)(E)]

IRS issued final regulations providing guidance on benefits that are treated as early retirement benefits and retirement-type subsidies for purposes of the anti-cutback rule. See Qs 9:33 and 9:34 for a discussion of the final regulations.

Q 10:46   Can a pattern of plan amendments result in an optional form of benefit?

Yes. Generally, benefits are considered to be provided as an optional form of benefit (see Q 10:45) only if such optional form is provided under the terms of the qualified retirement plan. If, however, an employer establishes a pattern of repeated plan amendments providing for similar benefits in similar situations for substantially consecutive, limited periods of time, those benefits may be treated as provided under the terms of the plan without regard to the limited periods of time. For example, a pattern of repeated plan amendments making single-sum distributions available only to certain participants for a limited period may result in single-sum distributions being treated as provided under the terms of the plan to all participants, without regard to any restrictions provided by the terms of the plan. However, where an employer amended its plan in each of four consecutive plan years to provide an early retirement window benefit, IRS held that the recurrence of the plan amendments did not convert this benefit to a permanent plan feature because the amendments were made in connection with the employer's efforts to reorganize its business, decrease operating costs, and reduce its workforce. [Rev. Rul. 92-66, 1992-2 C.B. 92; Treas. Reg. § 1.411(d)-4, Q&A-1(c)]

A plan amendment that modifies an optional form of benefit with respect to benefits already accrued will be evaluated in light of previous amendments. Thus, for example, amendments made at different times that, when taken together, constitute the elimination or reduction of a valuable right, will be treated as the impermissible elimination or reduction of an optional form of benefit even though each amendment, considered alone, may otherwise be permissible. [Treas. Reg. § 1.411(d)-4, Q&A-2(c)]

See Qs 9:29 through 9:32 for a discussion of IRS final regulations, and Qs 9:33 and 9:34 for a discussion of proposed regulations relating to the elimination of optional forms of benefit.

Q 10:47   Can a plan provide that the employer may, through the exercise of discretion, deny a participant an optional form of benefit?

Generally, no. A qualified retirement plan that permits an employer directly or indirectly (see Q 10:48), through the exercise of discretion, to deny a participant a Section 411(d)(6) protected benefit (see Q 10:45) provided under the plan for which the participant is otherwise eligible (but for the employer's exercise of discretion) violates the anti-cutback rule (see Q 9:25). In other words, to the extent benefits have accrued, the discretionary denial of the optional form of the benefit is not permitted. A plan provision that makes a protected benefit available only to those employees as the employer may designate is within the scope of this prohibition. Thus, for example, a plan provision under which only employees who are designated by the employer are eligible to receive a subsidized early retirement benefit constitutes an impermissible provision. In addition, a pension plan that permits employer discretion to deny the availability of a Section 411(d)(6) protected benefit will fail to satisfy the requirement that all benefits be definitely determinable (see Q 2:3). This is so even if the plan specifically limits the employer's discretion to choose among optional forms of benefit that are actuarially equivalent. However, a plan may permit limited administrative discretion (see Q 10:49). [Treas. Reg. § 1.411(d)-4, Q&A-1(a), 4(a); Johnson v. Allsteel, Inc., 2001 WL 896936 (7th Cir. 2001)]

Q 10:48 When is the exercise of discretion by persons other than the employer treated as employer discretion?

For the purposes of determining impermissible employer discretion (see Q 10:47), the employer is considered to include a plan administrator (see Q 20:1), fiduciary (see Q 23:1), trustee, actuary, independent third party, and other persons. Thus, if a qualified retirement plan permits any person—other than the participant and the participant's spouse—to exercise discretion to limit or deny the availability of an optional form of benefit (see Q 10:45), the plan violates these rules. [I.R.C. §§ 401(a), 411(d)(6); Treas. Reg. § 1.411(d)-4, Q&A-5]

Q 10:49 What is the scope of the administrative discretion exception?

A qualified retirement plan may permit limited discretion (see Qs 10:47, 10:48) with respect to the ministerial or mechanical administration of the plan, including the application of objective plan criteria specifically set forth in the plan. The following are examples of permissible provisions of limited administrative discretion:

1. Commencement of benefit payments as soon as administratively feasible after a stated date or event;

2. Employer authority to determine whether objective criteria specified in the plan (see Q 10:50) have been satisfied; and

3. Employer authority to determine, pursuant to specific guidelines set forth in the plan, whether the participant or spouse is dead or cannot be located.

[Treas. Reg. § 1.411(d)-4, Q&A-4(b)]

Q 10:50 May a plan condition the availability of a Section 411(d)(6) protected benefit on objective criteria that are specifically set forth in the plan?

The availability of a Section 411(d)(6) protected benefit (see Qs 10:37, 10:45) may be limited to employees who satisfy certain objective conditions. The conditions must be ascertainable, clearly set forth in the qualified retirement plan, and not subject to the employer's discretion, except to the extent reasonably necessary to determine whether the objective conditions are met (see Qs 10:47–10:49). In addition, the availability of the Section 411(d)(6) protected benefit must meet the nondiscrimination requirements (see Q 4:20). [Treas. Reg. §§ 1.411(d)-4, Q&A-6, 1.401(a)(4)-4, 1.401(a)-4; IRS Notice 96-67, 1996-2 C.B. 235]

For example, a plan may provide that the single-sum benefit distribution option is not available to participants for whom life insurance is not available at standard rates at the time the single-sum distribution would otherwise be payable. A plan may also provide that an otherwise permissible single-sum distribution option may be available only in the event of extreme financial need, determined under standards specifically set forth in the plan. Another example is a provision making a single-sum distribution available only upon the execution of a covenant not to compete, provided that the plan sets forth objective conditions with respect to employees required to execute a covenant, its terms, and the circumstances requiring execution of the covenant.

On the other hand, a plan may not condition the availability of Section 411(d)(6) protected benefits on factors that are within the employer's control. For example, the availability of an optional form of benefit payment from a defined benefit plan (see Q 2:3) may not be conditioned on the level of the funding of the plan because the amount of plan funding is within the employer's discretion. However, a plan may limit the availability of a Section 411(d)(6) protected benefit (e.g., a single-sum distribution) in an objective manner. For example, a plan may provide that single-sum distributions of $25,000 and less are available without limit, and single-sum distributions in excess of $25,000 are available for a given year only to the extent that the total amount of such distributions for that year does not exceed $5 million. However, the plan must then also provide an objective and nondiscriminatory method for determining which particular single-sum distributions will and will not be distributed because of the $5 million limitation.

Q 10:51 May a plan be amended to add employer discretion or other conditions restricting the availability of a Section 411(d)(6) protected benefit?

No. The addition of employer discretion or restrictive conditions (see Qs 10:47–10:50) with respect to a Section 411(d)(6) protected benefit (see Q 10:45) that has already accrued violates the anti-cutback rule (see Q 9:25). The addition of conditions or the change of any existing conditions, even if they are objective conditions, is impermissible if it results in any further restrictions. However, objective conditions and restrictions may be imposed prospectively to benefits accrued after the later of the adoption or effective date of the amendment. [Treas. Reg. § 1.411(d)-4, Q&A-7; IRS Notice 96-67, 1996-2 C.B. 235]

Q 10:52   May participants choose the way benefits will be paid to them?

Yes, if the qualified retirement plan itself provides alternatives, although the participant's spouse may have to consent (see Q 10:21). Retirement benefits are taxed when paid, not if merely made available to the participant. Thus, a deferral of the receipt of benefits also defers the taxation of the benefits. [I.R.C. § 402(a); Schikore v. Bank Am. Supplemental Ret. Plan, 269 F.3d 956 (9th Cir. 2001)]

Q 10:53   When must benefit payments to a participant begin?

The plan must provide that, unless the participant elects to defer payment, payment of benefits to the participant will begin not later than the 60th day after the close of the plan year in which the latest of the following events occurs:

1. The participant reaches the plan's normal retirement age (see Q 10:55) or age 65, whichever is earlier;

2. The tenth anniversary of the employee's participation in the plan is reached; or

3. The participant terminates service with the employer.

[I.R.C. § 401(a)(14); Treas. Reg. § 1.401(a)-14(a); Rev. Proc. 92-16, 1992-1 C.B. 673; Rev. Proc. 92-10, 1992-1 C.B. 661]

If benefit payments commence after termination of employment and the employee is later reemployed, the plan may, but is not required to, suspend benefit payments. [I.R.C. § 411(a)(3)(B); Militello v. Central States, Southeast and Southwest Areas Pension Fund, No. 02-3058 (7th Cir. 2004)]

See chapter 11 for details on minimum distribution requirements.

Q 10:54   May a participant defer payment of benefits indefinitely?

No. The qualified retirement plan must provide that (1) the entire interest of the participant be distributed to the participant not later than the required beginning date or (2) the participant's interest be paid out in installments that start on or before the required beginning date. The installments must be paid over (1) the life of the participant, (2) the lives of the participant and the participant's designated beneficiary, or (3) a period not extending beyond the life expectancy of the participant or the joint life expectancy of the participant and the participant's designated beneficiary. [I.R.C. § 401(a)(9)(A)]

See chapter 11 for details on minimum distribution requirements.

Q 10:55   What does the term "normal retirement age" mean?

Normal retirement age means the earlier of (1) the time specified in the plan as the normal retirement age or (2) the later of the time a participant attains age 65 or the fifth anniversary of the participant's date of initial plan participation. A qualified retirement plan must provide that an employee's right to benefits is nonforfeitable once the employee reaches the plan's normal retirement age (see Q 9:13). [ERISA § 3(24); I.R.C. §§ 411(a), 411(a)(8)]

Ordinarily, a defined benefit plan (see Q 2:3) uses a normal retirement age of 65. However, a plan will not fail to qualify merely because it provides for a normal retirement age earlier than 65. (Planning aspects relating to the use of a normal retirement age earlier than 65 are discussed in Q 2:38.) [Rev. Rul. 78-120, 1978-1 C.B. 117]

Unlike defined benefit plans, the normal retirement age used by a defined contribution plan (see Q 2:2) other than a target benefit plan (see Q 2:5) does not affect the company's plan contribution. Thus, for example, a profit sharing plan may permit a participant to retire at age 55 and receive full benefits under the plan at that time even if employees in the particular industry involved customarily retire at a later age. [Rev. Rul. 80-276, 1980-2 C.B. 131]

An employer that amended its defined benefit plan to change the definition of normal retirement age under the plan from age 65 to age 67 did not violate the requirements relating to normal retirement age, benefit accruals, or vesting (see Qs 9:1, 9:2, 9:13). The amended plan, which used age 67 for determining the level of benefits but maintained age 65 for purposes of benefit accruals and vesting satisfied the benefit accrual and vesting requirements and did not violate the anti-cutback rule (see Q 9:25). [Lindsay v. Thiokol Corp., 1997 U.S. App. LEXIS 7904 (10th Cir. 1997)]

Q 10:56 May benefits commence earlier than the deadlines required under the law?

Yes. The law and regulations establish only the time by which the plan must begin paying benefits (see Qs 10:53, 10:54). As long as participants are not treated in a discriminatory manner (see Qs 10:38–10:44), benefits may begin earlier.

Generally, defined benefit plans (see Q 2:3) and certain defined contribution plans, including money purchase pension plans (see Q 2:4) and target benefit plans (see Q 2:5), may not make distributions to employees who have not reached normal retirement age (see Q 10:55) or qualified for early retirement benefits (see Q 10:60). However, an employee may receive a distribution if a severance from employment has occurred. A severance from employment occurs during an employer's reorganization (e.g., sale, merger, or liquidation) only if the employee no longer works for an employer sponsoring the plan after the reorganization. An employee who works at the same job for a new employer may receive a distribution from the former employer's plan because the employee's employment has been severed, but the employee may not have had a "separation from service" for the purpose of treating the distribution as a lump-sum distribution (see Qs 13:5, 13:10, 27:14). [Treas. Reg. § 1.401-1(b)(1)(i); Gen. Couns. Mem. 39,824 (July 6, 1990)]

Plan benefits are taxed only when they are paid to the employee or a beneficiary. They are not taxed if they are merely made available (see Q 10:52).

It is not necessary, therefore, to draft a plan so that a participant does not have an absolute, unrestricted right to demand payment of benefits upon satisfying certain plan provisions. [I.R.C. § 402(a)]

See Q 10:59 for a discussion of proposed regulations permitting phased retirement distributions from pension plans.

Q 10:57   What type of election by the participant is required to postpone the commencement of benefits?

A qualified retirement plan that permits an election by a participant to postpone the receipt of benefits beyond the latest of the three dates referred to in Q 10:53 must require that the election be made by submitting to the plan administrator (see Q 20:1) a written statement (signed by the participant) describing the benefit and the date payments will begin. [Treas. Reg. § 1.401(a)-14(b)(2)]

However, an election to postpone the payment of benefits cannot be made if it would cause benefits payable under the plan, with respect to the participant, to begin after the required beginning date or to violate the incidental death benefits rule. [Treas. Reg. § 1.401(a)-14(b)(3)] For details, see chapter 11.

PPA (see Q 1:33) directs IRS to modify the applicable regulations to provide that the description of a participant's right, if any, to defer receipt of a distribution must also describe the consequences of failing to defer such receipt. The modification applies to years beginning after December 31, 2006. In the case of a description of the consequences of a participant's failure to defer receipt of a distribution that is made before the date 90 days after the date on which IRS makes a modification to the applicable regulations, the plan administrator is required to make a reasonable attempt to comply with this requirement. [PPA § 1102(b)]

Pursuant to the above direction, IRS issued guidance. [IRS Notice 2007-7, § VIII, 2007-1 C.B. 395]

The provisions concerning the increase in the notice and consent period from 90 days to 180 days apply to plan years that begin after December 31, 2006. This means that the new rules relating to the content of the notices apply only to notices issued in those plan years, without regard to the annuity starting date (see Q 10:3) for the distributions. Similarly, the 180-day period for distributing notices applies to notices distributed in a plan year that begins after December 31, 2006. This change to the 180-day period also modifies the definition of the maximum QJSA explanation period (see Q 10:20) and is used in applying the timing rules for the effective date of a plan amendment relating to the redundancy rules and utilization test (see Q 9:33) in the case of an amendment that is adopted in a plan year that begins after December 31, 2006. [PPA § 1102; IRS Notice 2007-7, § VIII, Q&A-31, 2007-1 C.B. 395]

A plan administrator is required to revise the notice regarding the right to defer the receipt of benefits pursuant to the modifications made by PPA before the regulations are amended to reflect this requirement and is required to revise the notice provided in plan years beginning after December 31, 2006. However, a plan will not be treated as failing to meet the new requirements if the plan administrator makes a reasonable attempt to comply therewith in the case of a notice that is provided prior to the 90th day after the issuance of regulations reflecting the modifications. [PPA § 1102(b); IRS Notice 2007-7, § VIII, Q&A-32, 2007-1 C.B. 395]

There is a safe harbor available to a plan administrator that would be considered a reasonable attempt to comply with the requirement that a description of a participant's right to defer receipt of a distribution include a description of the consequences of failing to defer. A description that is written in a manner reasonably calculated to be understood by the average participant and that includes the following information is a reasonable attempt to comply with the new requirement:

1. In the case of a defined benefit plan (see Q 2:3), a description of how much larger benefits will be if the commencement of distributions is deferred;

2. In the case of a defined contribution plan (see Q 2:2), a description indicating the investment options available under the plan (including fees) that will be available if distributions are deferred; and

3. The portion of the summary plan description (SPD; see Q 22:1) that contains any special rules that might materially affect a participant's decision to defer.

For purposes of 1., a plan administrator can use a description that includes the financial effect of deferring distributions based solely on the normal form of benefit (see Q 10:34). [PPA §§ 1102(b)(1), 1102(b)(2)(B); IRS Notice 2007-7, § VIII, Q&A-33, 2007-1 C.B. 395]

See Q 10:61 for a discussion of proposed regulations concerning a description of the consequences of failing to defer.

Q 10:58   May a participant receive benefit payments from a pension plan while still employed by the plan sponsor?

Yes, provided the participant has reached the plan's normal or early retirement age. However, a participant who has reached early retirement age cannot receive benefit payments until the earlier of reaching normal retirement age or separating from service (see Q 10:56). [Rev. Rul. 80-276, 1980-2 C.B. 131; Rev. Rul. 74-254, 1974-1 C.B. 91; Rev. Rul. 56-693, 1956-2 C.B. 282; Priv. Ltr. Ruls. 8311071, 8137048]

If a pension plan is merged into a profit sharing plan, this restriction on distributions continues to apply to the transferred pension plan assets. However, if a participant rolls over pension plan benefits to a profit sharing plan (see Q 34:28), this restriction does *not* apply to the rollover amounts and the profit sharing plan distribution rules apply (see Q 1:48). [Rev. Proc. 96-55, 1996-2 C.B. 387; Rev. Rul. 94-76, 1994-2 C.B. 825]

See Q 10:59 for a discussion of proposed regulations permitting phased retirement distributions from pension plans and for the authorization of a phased retirement program contained in PPA.

Q 10:59 What is a phased retirement program?

PPA (see Q 1:33) authorizes a phased retirement program. Under PPA, for purposes of the definition of pension plan under ERISA, a distribution from a plan, fund, or program is not treated as made in a form other than retirement income or as a distribution prior to termination of covered employment solely because the distribution is made to an employee who has attained age 62 and who is not separated from employment at the time of such distribution. [ERISA § 3(2)(A)] In addition, under the Code, a pension plan does not fail to be a qualified retirement plan solely because the plan provides that a distribution may be made to an employee who has attained age 62 and who is not separated from employment at the time of the distribution. [I.R.C. § 401(a)(36)] PPA's phased retirement plan provision is effective for distributions in plan years beginning after December 31, 2006. IRS requested comments concerning the PPA authorized phased retirement program. [IRS Notice 2007-8, 2007-1 C.B.278]

IRS issued final regulations that are generally applicable May 22, 2007. In the case of a plan maintained pursuant to one or more collective bargaining agreements (see Q 29:2) that have been ratified and are in effect on May 22, 2007, the final regulations do not apply before the first plan year that begins after the last of the agreements terminates determined without regard to any extension thereof (or, if earlier, May 22, 2010).

A provision of a plan that results in the failure of the plan to satisfy the final regulations is a disqualifying provision. Therefore, the remedial amendment period rules apply (see Q 18:6). For example, in the case of a plan with a calendar plan year that is maintained by an employer with a calendar taxable year (and the plan is not a governmental plan and is not maintained pursuant to a collective bargaining agreement), the plan's remedial amendment period with respect to the final regulations ends on the date prescribed by law for the filing of the employer's income tax return (including extensions) for the 2007 taxable year.

In the case of a plan amendment that increases the plan's normal retirement age pursuant to the final regulations, the amendment may also eliminate a right to an in-service distribution prior to the normal retirement age under the plan as amended without violating the anti-cutback rule (see Q 9:25) if the amendment is adopted after May 22, 2007, and on or before the last day of the applicable remedial amendment period.

[Treas. Reg. § 1.401(a)-1(b)(4); preamble to final regulations]

In order for a plan to be qualified, the plan must be established and maintained by an employer primarily to provide systematically for the payment of definitely determinable benefits to its employees over a period of years, usually for life, after retirement or attainment of normal retirement age (see Q 10:55). A plan does not fail to satisfy this requirement merely because the plan provides that a distribution may be made from the plan to an employee who has attained age 62 and who is not separated from employment at the time of such distribution. [Treas. Reg. § 1.401(a)-1(b)(1)]

The normal retirement age under a plan must be an age that is not earlier than the earliest age that is reasonably representative of the typical retirement age for the industry in which the covered workforce is employed. A normal retirement age under a plan that is age 62 or later is deemed to satisfy this requirement. In the case of a normal retirement age that is not earlier than age 55 and is earlier than age 62, whether the age satisfies this requirement is based on all of the relevant facts and circumstances. A normal retirement age that is lower than age 55 is presumed not to satisfy this requirement, unless IRS determines that under the facts and circumstances the normal retirement age is not earlier than the earliest age that is reasonably representative of the typical retirement age for the industry in which the covered workforce is employed. A normal retirement age under a plan that is age 50 or later is deemed to satisfy this requirement if substantially all of the participants in the plan are qualified public safety employees. [Treas. Reg. § 1.401(a)-1(b)(2)]

For purposes of the definitely determinable benefits rule, retirement does not include a mere reduction in the number of hours that an employee works. Accordingly, benefits may not be distributed prior to normal retirement age solely due to a reduction in the number of hours that an employee works. [Treas. Reg. § 1.401(a)-1(b)(3)]

There is a transition period during which a plan is permitted to eliminate a right to in-service distributions in connection with an amendment to ensure that the plan's normal retirement age satisfies the final regulations. A plan amendment that changes the normal retirement age under the plan to a later normal retirement age does not violate the anti-cutback rule merely because it eliminates a right to an in-service distribution prior to the amended normal retirement age. However, this transition rule does not provide relief from any other applicable requirements. For example, this relief does not permit the amendment to violate the requirement that the normal retirement benefit not be less than the greater of any early retirement benefit payable under the plan or the benefit under the plan commencing at normal retirement age (see Q 9:33), the requirements concerning amendment changes to the plan's vesting rules (see Qs 9:7, 9:8), the rules relating to Section 411(d)(6) protected benefits (see Q 10:45), or the rules relating to an amendment that reduces the rate of future benefit accrual (see Q 9:37). This transition rule only applies to a plan amendment that is adopted after May 22, 2007, and on or before the last day of the applicable remedial amendment period with respect to the final regulations. [Treas. Reg. § 1.411(d)-4, Q&A-12(a)]

Example. Plan A is a defined benefit plan (see Q 2:3), is maintained by a calendar year taxpayer, and has a normal retirement age that is age 45. For employees who cease employment before normal retirement age with a vested benefit, Plan A permits benefits to commence at any date after the attainment of normal retirement age through attainment of age 70½ and provides for benefits to be actuarially increased to the extent they commence after normal retirement age. For employees who continue employment after attainment of normal retirement age, Plan A provides for benefits to continue to accrue and permits benefits to commence at any time, with an actuarial increase in benefits to apply to the extent benefits do not commence after normal retirement age. Age 45 is an age that is earlier than the earliest age that is reasonably representative of the typical retirement age for the industry in which the covered workforce is employed. On February 18, 2008, Plan A is amended, effective May 22, 2007, to change its normal retirement age to the later of age 65 or the fifth anniversary of participation in the plan. The amendment provides full vesting for any participating employee who is employed on May 21, 2007, and who terminates employment on or after attaining age 45. The amendment provides employees who cease employment before the revised normal retirement age and who are entitled to a vested benefit with the right to be able to commence benefits at any date from age 45 to age 70½. The plan amendment also revises the plan's benefit accrual formula so that the benefit for prior service (payable commencing at the revised normal retirement age or any other age after age 45) is not less than would have applied under the plan's formula before the amendment (also payable commencing at the corresponding dates), based on the benefit accrued on May 21, 2007, and provides for service thereafter to have the same rate of future benefit accrual. Thus, for any participant employed on May 21, 2007, with respect to benefits accrued for service after May 21, 2007, the amount payable under the plan (as amended) at any benefit commencement date after age 45 is the same that would have been payable at that benefit commencement date under the plan prior to amendment. The plan amendment also eliminates the right to an in-service distribution between age 45 and the revised normal retirement age. Plan A has been operated since May 22, 2007, in conformity with the amendment adopted on February 18, 2008.

The plan amendment does not violate the anti-cutback rule. Although the amendment eliminates the right to commence benefits in-service between age 45 and the revised normal retirement age, the amendment is made before the last date of the remedial amendment period applicable to the plan and, therefore, is permitted. Further, the amendment does not result in a reduction in any benefit for service after May 22, 2007. Thus, the amendment does not result in a reduction in any benefit for future service, and advance notice of a significant reduction in the rate of future benefit accrual is not required.

After the promulgation of the final regulations, IRS provided temporary relief, until the first day of the first plan year that begins after June 30, 2008, for certain plans under which the definition of normal retirement age may be required to be changed to comply with the regulations [IRS Notice 2007-69, 2007-2 C.B. 468]

The remedial amendment period with respect to the final regulations is extended to the end of a plan's applicable five-year or six-year remedial amendment cycle (see Qs 18:7, 18:8) that includes the date on which the remedial amendment period would otherwise end, if, by that date, the plan sponsor either adopts a good faith interim amendment to comply with the final regulations or reasonably and in good faith determines that no amendment is required. The filing of a determination letter application (see Q 18:1) within a plan's remedial amendment period tolls the running of the period until the end of 91 days after the determination letter is issued. [Treas. Reg. § 1.401(b)-1(e)(3)]

IRS has provided two forms of relief, as described in A and B below. The relief is available to plans that meet the eligibility requirements in A or B, and that might otherwise be required to be amended to raise the plan's normal retirement age effective before the first day of the first plan year beginning after June 30, 2008, in order to satisfy the 2007 regulations. The relief applies to a plan maintained pursuant to one or more collective bargaining agreements that have been ratified and are in effect on May 22, 2007, if the first plan year beginning after the last of the agreements terminates (determined without regard to any extension thereof) begins before July 1, 2008.

A. Temporary Relief for Plans with Normal Retirement Age Lower Than Age 62.

IRS will not propose to disqualify a plan solely because the plan fails to satisfy the final regulations if the plan satisfies the following conditions:

1. The plan, immediately prior to May 22, 2007, provided a definition of normal retirement age that was earlier than age 62.

2. No possible plan participant hired at age 18 or older could attain the plan's normal retirement age before the age of 40.

3. Unless the plan sponsor reasonably and in good faith determines that no amendment is necessary, the sponsor adopts a good faith interim amendment to comply with the final regulations effective no later than the first day of the first plan year beginning after June 30, 2008, and the plan is operated in compliance with such amendment as of the amendment's effective date.

4. The plan sponsor adopts the interim amendment by the later of (a) the last day of the first plan year beginning after June 30, 2008, or (b) the due date (including extensions) for filing the employer's income tax return for the employer's taxable year that includes the first day of the first plan year beginning after June 30, 2008.

In addition, relief is provided for the rare and unusual circumstance where the plan sponsor has acted in good faith in making a determination that the plan's normal retirement age is not earlier than the typical retirement age for the industry in which the covered workforce is employed, but the plan's normal retirement age actually is earlier than the typical retirement age for the industry in which the covered workforce is employed. In such a case, if the plan sponsor applies for a determination letter within the applicable remedial amendment cycle, IRS will require corrective action to be taken prospectively only from the date of issuance of the determination letter, so that the plan's normal retirement age will not be required to be raised retroactively. For this purpose, the applicable remedial amendment cycle is the plan's remedial amendment cycle that includes the interim amendment deadline determined under condition 4 above. Any plan amendment that is determined to be necessary to comply with the final regulations will not be required to be adopted earlier than the 91st day after the date of the IRS's determination letter. This relief applies only if the plan's normal retirement age is not earlier than age 55.

B. Temporary Presumption of Reasonableness for Plans with Normal Retirement Lower Than Age 55.

Eligible plans with a normal retirement age lower than age 55 will temporarily be accorded the same presumption as plans with a normal retirement age between ages 55 and 62. Thus, for periods prior to the date on which IRS rules on an eligible plan's normal retirement age for the industry in which the covered workforce is employed will generally be given deference, assuming that the determination is reasonable under the facts and circumstances.

A plan is eligible for the relief under B if it satisfies the following conditions:

1. The plan, immediately prior to May 22, 2007, provided a definition of normal retirement age that was earlier than age 55.

2. No possible plan participant hired at age 18 or older could attain the plan's normal retirement age before the age of 40.

3. The plan sponsor submits a request for a letter ruling on whether its definition of normal retirement age satisfies the standard in the final regulations, in accordance with the procedures described below, by June 30, 2008.

If IRS determines during the ruling process that the plan's normal retirement age does not reasonably represent the typical retirement age for the industry in which the covered workforce is employed, IRS will require corrective action to be taken prospectively only from the date of issuance of the ruling letter, so that the plan's normal retirement age will not be required to be raised retroactively. In addition, the letter ruling request will be treated as an application for a determination letter on the qualification of the plan, so that any plan amendment that is determined to be necessary to comply with the final regulations will not be required to be adopted earlier than the 91st day after the date of IRS's ruling.

An application for a letter ruling as to whether a plan's normal retirement age reasonably represents the typical retirement age for the industry in which the covered workforce is employed is to be made in accordance with the procedures governing letter ruling requests. The request must include the user fee for a letter ruling (see Q 18:2).

The statement and analysis of facts of the letter ruling request must:

1. Indicate whether and when a determination letter for the plan with respect to the plan's current remedial amendment cycle has been or will be filed.

2. Describe the industry in which the covered workforce is generally employed.

general distribution requirements

3. Identify the sources and date of compliance of data that was used in determining the typical retirement age for the industry, which may include data concerning employee retirement from the plan sponsor. (It is expected that the data will include the actual ages of termination of employment of career employees, i.e., employees whose principal career has been in the employment of the plan sponsor.)

4. Present and analyze the data the plan sponsor used to determine the typical retirement age.

5. Describe any other relevant information (whether or not used by the plan sponsor in determining the typical retirement age).

IRS reserves the right to request any other information it considers necessary.

IRS representatives opined that, if a normal retirement date earlier than age 62 is used, it must be reasonable within the plan sponsor's industry, even if it is between ages 55 and 62. IRS will give some deference to the employer's statement that a certain retirement age is normal, and probably will give it more weight the closer the normal retirement age gets to age 62. However, the employer's statement of what is standard within the industry is not sufficient; there must be some basis for saying the normal retirement age is reasonable. Care should be taken if the plan sponsor is in an area of potential abuse, such as in-service distributions based on the normal retirement age.

Q 10:60 Can a qualified retirement plan provide early retirement benefits?

Yes. However, if a defined benefit plan (see Q 2:3) permits a participant to receive an early retirement benefit if the participant meets certain age and service requirements (e.g., age 60 and ten years of service), the plan must also permit a former participant who fulfilled the service requirement, but separated from service before meeting the age requirement, to receive benefit payments when the former participant meets the age requirement. [I.R.C. § 401(a)(14); Treas. Reg. § 1.401(a)-14(c)]

> **Example.** The Ruthie Tennis Corporation Defined Benefit Plan provides that a normal retirement benefit will be payable to a participant upon attainment of age 65. The plan also provides that a reduced retirement benefit will be payable, upon application, to any participant who has attained age 60 and completed ten years of service with Ruthie Tennis Corporation. When Stuart is 55 years of age and has completed ten years of service with Ruthie Tennis Corporation, he leaves the company and does not return. The plan must provide that Stuart will be entitled to receive a reduced normal retirement benefit when he attains age 60.

A plan was permitted to pay a more valuable early retirement benefit to participants electing periodic payments than to participants electing single-sum distributions. Those electing single-sum distributions received the benefits they were entitled to, but they did not receive the supplemental payments made to the early retirees who elected to receive periodic payments. [DeNobel v. Vitro

Corp., 885 F.2d 1180 (4th Cir. 1989)] In another case, a court determined that a plan did not violate ERISA by reducing early retirement benefits taken by former employees at 6.75 percent, a discount rate higher than the 3 percent rate for benefits taken by current employees. [McCarthy v. Dun & Bradstreet Corp., 2007 U.S. App. LEXIS 7323 (2d Cir. 2007)]

Q 10:61 Can a qualified retirement plan make immediate distributions without the participant's consent?

A qualified retirement plan may provide for an involuntary, immediate distribution of the present value of the benefits under either a QJSA (see Q 10:8) or a QPSA (see Q 10:9) if the present value does not exceed $5,000. The plan may pay benefits in the form of a QJSA or a QPSA at any time after the benefits are no longer immediately distributable (see Q 10:8), whether or not the present value exceeds $5,000. A surviving spouse can demand that the survivor portion of the QPSA not become payable following the participant's death until such time as the participant would have attained age 62 if the amount of the benefit exceeds $5,000. A plan may provide that a participant may elect a QJSA at any time without spousal consent. [I.R.C. §§ 411(a)(11), 417(e); Treas. Reg. § 1.417(e)-1(b)(1)] If an accrued benefit is immediately distributable, plans are permitted to provide for the distribution of any portion of a participant's nonforfeitable accrued benefit only if the applicable consent requirements are satisfied. [Treas. Reg. § 1.411(a)-11(c)(1)]

If the distribution exceeds $5,000, the participant must consent in writing before a distribution may be made. [Treas. Reg. §§ 1.411(a)-11(c)(3), 1.417(e)-1(b)(2); Myers-Garrison v. Johnson & Johnson, 210 F.3d 425 (5th Cir. 2000); Franklin v. Thornton, 983 F.2d 939 (9th Cir. 1993)] No consent is valid unless the participant has received a general description of the material features of the optional forms of benefit available under the plan. In addition, so long as a benefit is immediately distributable, a participant must be informed of the right, if any, to defer receipt of the distribution (see Q 10:57). Furthermore, consent is not valid if a significant detriment is imposed under the plan on any participant who does not consent to a distribution. Whether or not a significant detriment is imposed will be determined by IRS by examining the particular facts and circumstances. In addition, so long as a benefit is immediately distributable, a participant must be informed of the right, if any, to defer receipt of the distribution and of the consequences of failing to defer such receipt. Written consent of the participant to the distribution must not be made before the participant receives the notice of his or her rights and must not be made more than 180 days before the date the distribution commences. A plan must provide participants with notice of their rights no less than 30 days and no more than 180 days before the date the distribution commences. However, if the participant, after having received this notice, affirmatively elects a distribution, a plan will not fail to satisfy the consent requirement merely because the distribution commences less than 30 days after the notice was provided to the participant, provided that the plan administrator (see Q 20:1) informs the participant that the participant has a right to at least 30 days to consider whether to consent to the distribution (see Q 10:20). [I.R.C. § 417(a)(6)(A); IRS Notice 2007-7, § VIII, 2007-1 C.B. 395; Treas. Reg. §§ 1.411(a)-11(c), 1.417(e)-1(b)(3); Prop. Treas. Reg. §§ 1.411(a)-11(c)(2)(ii), 1.411(a)-11(c)(2)(iii), 1.417(e)-1(b)(3)(i); McCarter v. Retirement Plan for the District Managers of the American Family Ins. Group, 2008 WL 4052905 (7th Cir. 2008)]

A plan must provide a participant with the notice at a time that satisfies the preceding paragraph or if the plan provides the participant with the notice and a summary of the notice within the applicable time period. In addition, if the participant so requests after receiving the summary, the plan must provide the notice to the participant without charge and no less than 30 days before the date the distribution commences, subject to the rules for the participant's waiver of that 30-day period. The summary must advise the participant of the right, if any, to defer receipt of the distribution and of the consequences of failing to defer such receipt, must set forth a summary of the distribution options under the plan, must refer the participant to the most recent version of the notice (and, in the case of a notice provided in any document containing information in addition to the notice, must identify that document and must provide a reasonable indication of where the notice may be found in that document, such as by index reference or by section heading), and must advise the participant that, upon request, a copy of the notice will be provided without charge. [Treas. Reg. § 1.411(a)-11(c)(2)(iii); Prop. Treas. Reg. § 1.411(a)-11(c)(2)(iii)]

A notice that is required to describe the consequences of failing to defer receipt of a distribution until it is no longer immediately distributable must, to the extent applicable under the plan and in a manner designed to be easily understood, provide the participant with the following information and explain why it is relevant to a decision of whether to defer.

1. A description of the following federal tax implications of failing to defer: differences in the timing of inclusion in taxable income of an immediately commencing distribution that is not rolled over (or not eligible to be rolled over; see Q 34:1) and a distribution that is deferred until it is no longer immediately distributable (including, as applicable, differences in the taxation of distributions of designated Roth contributions (see Q 27:96)); application of the 10 percent additional tax on certain distributions before age 59½ (see Q 16:1); and, in the case of a defined contribution plan (see Q 2:2), loss of the opportunity upon immediate commencement for future tax-favored treatment of earnings if the distribution is not rolled over (or not eligible to be rolled over) to an eligible retirement plan.

2. In the case of a defined benefit plan, a statement of the amount payable to the participant under the normal form of benefit both upon immediate commencement and upon commencement when the benefit is no longer immediately distributable (assuming no future benefit accruals). The statement need not vary based on the participant's marital status if the plan is permitted to provide a QJSA explanation that does not vary based on the participant's marital status (see Q 10:33).

3. In the case of a defined contribution plan, a statement that some currently available investment options in the plan may not be generally available on

similar terms outside the plan and contact information for obtaining additional information on the general availability outside the plan of currently available investment options in the plan.

4. In the case of a defined contribution plan, a statement that fees and expenses (including administrative or investment-related fees) outside the plan may be different from fees and expenses that apply to the participant's account and contact information for obtaining additional information on the fees and expenses that apply to the participant's account.

5. An explanation of any provisions of the plan (and provisions of an accident or health plan maintained by the employer) that could reasonably be expected to materially affect a participant's decision of whether to defer receipt of the distribution. Such provisions would include, for example: plan terms under which a participant who fails to defer may lose eligibility for early retirement subsidies or social security supplements; plan terms under which the benefit of a rehired participant who failed to defer may be adversely affected by the decision not to defer; and, in the case of a defined contribution plan, plan terms under which undistributed benefits that otherwise are nonforfeitable become forfeitable upon the participant's death.

In general, the information required to be provided in the notice must appear together (for example, in a list of consequences of failing to defer). However, the notice will not be treated as failing to satisfy these requirements merely because the notice includes a cross-reference to where the required information may be found in notices or other information provided or made available to the participant, as long as the notice of consequences of failing to defer includes a statement of how the referenced information may be obtained without charge and explains why the referenced information is relevant to a decision of whether to defer. [Prop. Treas. Reg. § 1.411(a)-11(c)(2)(vi)]

The provisions that describe the requirement to notify participants of the consequences of failing to defer are effective for notices provided on or after the first day of the first plan year beginning on or after January 1, 2010. [Prop. Treas. Reg. § 1.411(a)11-(h)]

No single-sum distribution may be made after the annuity starting date (see Q 10:3) unless the participant (and spouse or surviving spouse, if applicable) consents in writing to the distribution, whether or not the present value exceeds $5,000. [I.R.C. §§ 411(a)(11), 417(e); Treas. Reg. §§ 1.411(a)-11(c)(3), 1.417(e)-1(b)(2)]

The involuntary cash-out amount was increased from $3,500 to $5,000 for plan years beginning after August 5, 1997. [I.R.C. § 411(a)(11)(A)] IRS has issued regulations relating to the increase from $3,500 to $5,000 of the cash-out limit.

Prior to the increase from $3,500 to $5,000, the written consent of a participant was required before the commencement of the distribution of any portion of the participant's accrued benefit (see Q 9:2) if the present value of the nonforfeitable (see Q 9:1) total accrued benefit was greater than $3,500. If the present value did not exceed $3,500, the consent requirements were deemed satisfied, and the plan could distribute that portion to the participant as a single sum. If the present value determined at the time of a distribution to the participant exceeded $3,500, then the present value at any subsequent time was deemed to exceed $3,500; this was commonly referred to as the look-back rule.

The regulations remove the look-back rule for all distributions. The regulations also provide that, in the case of plans subject to Sections 401(a)(11) and 417, consent is required after the annuity starting date for the immediate distribution of the present value of the accrued benefit being distributed in any form, including a QJSA or a QPSA, regardless of the amount of that present value. Where only a portion of an accrued benefit is being distributed, this provision applies only to that portion (and not the portion with respect to which no distributions are being made). Under this removal of the look-back rule, the present value of a participant's nonforfeitable accrued benefit could be distributed without consent if the present value does not exceed $5,000, even if the present value of the participant's nonforfeitable accrued benefit exceeded $5,000 at the time of a previous distribution. Thus, if the present value of a participant's nonforfeitable accrued benefit previously had been $6,000, but is presently $4,000, the regulations permit the plan to be amended to permit the present value of that participant's nonforfeitable accrued benefit to be distributed without consent (provided that the distribution would not fail to satisfy Section 417(e)(1)). [Treas. Reg. §§ 1.411(a)-11(c)(3)(i), 1.411(a)-11(c)(3)(ii), 1.417(e)-1(b)(2)(i)]

A profit sharing plan offered a broad range of investment choices to current participants. However, the plan also provided that, upon termination of employment, participants who did not consent to an immediate distribution and who chose to leave their account balances with the plan could no longer choose among investment alternatives. Instead, the participants' accounts were automatically invested in a money market fund until distributed. IRS ruled that the loss of the right to choose was tantamount to an immediate distribution without a valid consent. [Rev. Rul. 96-47, 1996-2 C.B. 35]

IRS has ruled that a plan amendment that changes the default method of payment to a direct rollover (see Q 34:17) for involuntary distributions when a distributee fails to affirmatively elect to make a direct rollover or to elect a cash payment does not adversely affect the qualification of the plan. In this case, a defined contribution plan (see Q 2:2) provides that, if a terminated employee's vested account balance is $5,000 or less and the employee does not elect a direct rollover, the vested account balance will be paid in a single-sum cash payment to the employee. The plan is amended to provide that in the absence of an affirmative election on the part of the employee, the default form of payment of any involuntary cash-out from the plan that is between $1,000 and $5,000 will be a direct rollover to an IRA. The plan administrator (see Q 20:1) will establish an IRA (see Q 30:1) with a trustee unrelated to the employer on behalf of an employee who fails to elect the direct rollover or cash payment and will make initial investment decisions for the IRA. [Rev. Rul. 2000-36, 2000-2 C.B. 140]

DOL has issued final regulations and IRS has issued guidance in connection with automatic rollover provisions. For details, see Qs 34:18, 34:19.

The cash-out rule will not be violated if, under the terms of the plan, the present value of the nonforfeitable accrued benefit is determined without regard to the portion of the benefit that is attributable to rollover contributions (see Q 34:1) and earnings allocable thereto. [I.R.C. §§ 411(a)(11)(D), 417(e)(1), 417(e)(2)(A)] For a discussion of the method used to determine present value, see Qs 10:62 and 10:63.

Q 10:62   How is the present value of benefits determined under a defined benefit plan?

A defined benefit plan (see Q 2:3) must provide that the present value of any accrued benefit (see Q 9:2) and the amount of any distribution, including a single sum, must not be less than the amount calculated using the applicable interest rate and the IRS mortality table (see Q 6:18). The present value of any optional form of benefit (see Q 10:37) cannot be less than the present value of the normal retirement benefit determined in accordance with the preceding sentence. The same rules are used to compute the present value of the benefit for purposes of determining whether consent for a distribution is required (see Q 10:61). The applicable interest rate for a month is the constant maturities rate on 30-year Treasury securities as specified by the IRS for that month. [I.R.C. §§ 411(a)(11)(B), 417(e)(3)(A); Treas. Reg. § 1.417(e)-1(d)(1)-(3); Rev. Rul. 2001-62, 2001-2 C.B. 632; Rev. Rul. 95-6, 1995-1 C.B. 452; PBGC v. Wilson N. Jones Mem'l Hosp., No. 4:01-CV-94 (E.D. Tex. 2003); Myers-Garrison v. Johnson & Johnson, 210 F.3d 425 (5th Cir. 2000); Piggly Wiggly S., Inc. v. PBGC, No. 95-6362 (11th Cir. 1996)]

> **Example.** JMK Corporation has a defined benefit plan with a calendar-year plan year. The plan uses the IRS mortality table and provides that the applicable interest rate for the plan is the annual interest rate on 30-year Treasury securities as specified by IRS for the first full calendar month preceding the calendar month that contains the annuity starting date (see Q 10:3). Jamie was age 65 in January 1995, the month that contained his annuity starting date. Jamie had a monthly accrued benefit of $1,000 and elected to receive a distribution in the form of a single sum in January 1995. The annual interest rate on 30-year Treasury securities as published by IRS for December 1994 was 7.87 percent. Based upon the applicable interest rate and the IRS mortality table, Jamie could not receive a single-sum distribution of less than $111,351.

The applicable interest rate to be used for a distribution is the rate for the applicable look-back month. The applicable look-back month for a distribution is the look-back month for the month (or other longer stability period) that contains the annuity starting date for the distribution. The time and method for determining the applicable interest rate for each participant's distribution must be determined in a consistent manner that is applied uniformly to all participants in the plan. A plan must specify the period for which the applicable interest rate remains constant. This stability period may be one calendar month, one plan quarter, one calendar quarter, one plan year, or one calendar year. A plan must also specify the look-back month that is used to determine the applicable interest rate. The look-back month may be the first, second, third, fourth, or fifth full calendar month preceding the first day of the stability period. A plan may use a permitted average interest rate with respect to the plan's stability period instead of the rate for the applicable look-back month for the stability period. For this purpose, a permitted average interest rate with respect to a stability period is an interest rate that is computed by averaging the applicable interest rates for two or more consecutive months from among the first, second, third, fourth, and fifth calendar months preceding the first day of the stability period. For this to apply, a plan must specify the manner in which the permitted average interest rate is computed. [Treas. Reg. § 1.417(e)-1(d)(4); Hampton v. Henry Ford Health System, No. 04-CV-70221 (E.D. Mich. 2005)]

> **Example.** Steph-Will Corporation maintains a defined benefit plan with a calendar-year plan year. Steph-Will wishes to amend the plan so that the applicable interest rate will remain fixed for each plan quarter and so that the applicable interest rate for distributions made during each plan quarter can be determined approximately 80 days before the beginning of the plan quarter. Consequently, the plan is amended to provide that the applicable interest rate is the annual interest rate on 30-year Treasury securities as specified by IRS for the fourth calendar month preceding the first day of the plan quarter during which the annuity starting date occurs.

If a plan provides for use of an interest rate or mortality table other than the applicable interest rate or the IRS mortality table, the plan must provide that a participant's benefit must be at least as great as the benefit produced by using the applicable interest rate and the IRS mortality table. For example, where a plan provides for use of an interest rate of 7 percent and the UP-1984 mortality table in calculating single-sum distributions, the plan must provide that any single-sum distribution is calculated as the greater of the single-sum benefit calculated using this actuarial basis (i.e., 7 percent and the UP-1984 mortality table) and the single-sum benefit calculated using the applicable interest rate and the IRS mortality table. [Treas. Reg. § 1.417(e)-1(d)(5)]

The present value determination rules do not apply to the amount of a distribution paid in the form of an annual benefit that:

1. Does not decrease during the life of the participant or, in the case of a QPSA (see Q 10:9), the life of the participant's spouse, or

2. Decreases during the life of the participant merely because of (a) the death of the survivor annuitant (but only if the reduction is to a level not below 50 percent of the annual benefit payable before the death of the survivor annuitant), or (b) the cessation or reduction of Social Security supplements or qualified disability benefits (see Q 4:20).

[Treas. Reg. § 1.417(e)-1(d)(6)]

Because the accrued benefit under a defined contribution plan (see Qs 2:2, 9:2) equals the account balance, a defined contribution plan is not subject to the present value determination rules. [Treas. Reg. § 1.417(e)-1(d)(7)]

For a discussion of cash balance plans and the interaction of the present value determination rules and the anti-cutback rule, see Qs 10:63 and 10:64.

Effective for plan years beginning after December 31, 2007, PPA (see Q 1:33) changes the interest rate and mortality table used in calculating the minimum value of certain optional forms of benefit, such as single sums.

Minimum value is calculated using the first, second, and third segment rates as applied under the funding rules (see Q 8:3) with certain adjustments, for the month before the date of distribution or such other times as prescribed by IRS regulations. The adjusted first, second, and third segment rates are derived from a corporate bond yield curve prescribed by IRS for such month that reflects the yields on investment grade corporate bonds with varying maturities (rather than a 24-month average, as under the minimum funding rules). Thus, the interest rate that applies depends upon how many years in the future a participant's annuity payment will be made. Typically, a higher interest applies for payments made further out in the future.

A transition rule applies for distributions in 2008 through 2011. For distributions in 2008 through 2011, minimum single-sum values are determined as the weighted average of two values: (1) the value of the single sum determined under the methodology under present law (the old methodology) and (2) the value of the single sum determined using the methodology applicable for 2008 and thereafter (the new methodology). For distributions in 2008, the weighting factor is 80 percent for the single-sum value determined under the old methodology and 20 percent for the single sum determined under the new methodology. For distributions in 2009, the weighting factor is 60 percent for the single-sum value determined under the old methodology and 40 percent for the single sum determined under the new methodology. For distributions in 2010, the weighting factor is 40 percent for the single-sum value determined under the old methodology and 60 percent for the single sum determined under the new methodology. For distributions in 2011, the weighting factor is 20 percent for single-sum value determined under the old methodology and 80 percent for the single sum determined under the new methodology.

The mortality table that must be used for calculating single sums is based on the mortality table required for minimum funding purposes, modified as appropriate by IRS. IRS is also to prescribe gender-neutral tables for use in determining minimum single sums. IRS has released proposed rules providing mortality tables to determine present value, as well as permitting the use of substitute, plan-specific tables, if certain conditions apply. See Q 8:3 for details.

[I.R.C. §§ 417(e)(3), 430]

IRS has issued the guidance required to calculate minimum lump-sum distributions beginning with the 2008 plan year. The revenue ruling contains the 2008 applicable mortality table and information on the applicable interest rates used for determining the present value of plan benefits, which cannot be less than the present value calculated by using the mortality table and the interest rate. The ruling discusses the following three issues:

ISSUES

1. Do the timing rules for the determination of the applicable interest rate continue to apply for distributions with annuity starting dates (see Q 10:3) occurring during plan years beginning on or after January 1, 2008?

2. What mortality table is the applicable mortality table for distributions with annuity starting dates occurring during plan years beginning on or after January 1, 2008?

3. Does an amendment that implements the new interest rates and mortality table violate the anti-cutback rule?

HOLDING

Issue 1. The rules regarding the time for determining the applicable interest rate continue to apply for plan years beginning on or after January 1, 2008, without regard to the change in the basis for determining the applicable interest rate. If the first day of the first plan year beginning on or after January 1, 2008 does not coincide with the first day of a stability period for a plan, the applicable interest rate for distributions with annuity starting dates during the stability period that contains the first day of the plan year will change during that period. For distributions with annuity starting dates within that period that are before the effective date of the PPA statutory change, the applicable interest rate is determined without regard to the statutory change; and, for distributions with annuity starting dates within that period that are on or after the effective date of the statutory change, the applicable interest rate is determined reflecting the statutory change.

Issue 2. The applicable mortality table for 2008 is published in the Appendix to the ruling (2008 Applicable Mortality Table). This mortality table is based upon a fixed blend of 50 percent of the static male combined mortality rates and 50 percent of the static female combined mortality rates published in proposed regulations for valuation dates occurring in 2008. The table shows, for each age, the number living based upon a starting population of one million lives at age $1(lx)$, and the annual rate of mortality (qx). The applicable mortality table for each subsequent year will be published in the future (Subsequent Applicable Mortality Tables). Except as otherwise stated in future guidance, the applicable mortality table for each subsequent year will be determined from the Section 430(h)(3)(A) mortality tables on the same basis as the applicable mortality table for 2008. In general, the applicable mortality table for a year applies to distributions with annuity starting dates that occur during stability periods that begin during the calendar year to which the applicable mortality table applies. However, pursuant to the effective date rules of PPA, the 2008 Applicable Mortality Table does not apply before the first day of the first plan year beginning in 2008. Thus, for example, in the case of a plan with a September 1 to August 31 plan year, and a calendar year stability period, the 2008 Applicable Mortality Table (as well as the applicable interest rates that are based on the segment rates) would not apply to distributions with annuity starting dates prior to September 1, 2008, but would apply to distributions with annuity starting dates beginning on or after September 1, 2008. A reference in a plan to the applicable mortality table will, as of a particular date, be treated as a reference to the table that applies to distributions with annuity starting dates (other than a retroactive annuity starting date) on that date. Such a reference will mean the 2008 Applicable Mortality Table for annuity starting dates to which that mortality table applies, and each Subsequent Applicable Mortality Table for annuity starting dates to which the Subsequent Applicable Mortality Table applies. Such a reference would not have to be amended each year to reflect changes in the applicable mortality table. By contrast, a plan provision that specifically refers to an annual applicable mortality table (such as the 2008 Applicable Mortality Table) would have to be amended each year to reflect Subsequent Applicable Mortality Tables, and such amendments would have to satisfy the anti-cutback rule.

Issue 3. An amendment to determine the applicable interest rate in effect for plan years beginning on or after January 1, 2008 will not violate the anti-cutback rule solely because of the reduction in accrued benefits or a reduction in the amount of any distribution with an annuity starting date occurring during a plan year beginning in 2008 or in a subsequent year if the cause of such reduction is the substitution of the modified segment rates for the 30-year Treasury rate for the same period. However, if the amendment changes the time for determining the interest rate, certain requirements must be satisfied (see Q 10:64). In addition, if the cause of the reduction is an amendment to substitute the modified segment rates for a rate that is not the 30-year Treasury rate, the amendment must satisfy the anti-cutback rule. A plan amendment to incorporate by reference the applicable mortality table that is prescribed by the ruling and by subsequent guidance issued by IRS will not violate the anti-cutback rule solely because of a reduction in accrued benefits or a reduction in the amount of any distribution with an annuity starting date occurring during a plan year beginning in 2008 or in a subsequent year if the cause of such reduction is the substitution of the applicable mortality table for the prior applicable mortality table.

EFFECTIVE DATE

The revenue ruling is effective for plan years that begin on or after January 1, 2008. [Rev. Rul. 2007-67, 2007-2 C.B. 1047]

PBGC (see Q 25:10) issued guidance for plans with termination and final distribution dates that straddle the effective date for the required changes in the interest rate and mortality assumptions for lump-sum valuations. PBGC advised that lump-sum valuations for single-employer plans terminating prior to the January 1, 2008 effective date in standard terminations should use pre-PPA interest rate and mortality assumptions, even when the final distribution occurs after that date. PBGC noted that the minimum lump-sum value of the participant's accrued benefit is calculated using the definitions of applicable interest rate and applicable mortality table in effect on the plan's termination date, but the time for determining the specific assumptions is based on the distribution date. PBGC further noted that plan provisions that incorporate the changes cannot take effect before the first plan year beginning on or after January 1, 2008. Therefore, PBGC reasoned, such plan provisions, whether modified before or after the termination date, are not effective for a plan with a termination date before the beginning of its 2008 plan year, even if the distribution date is after the 2007 plan year. Lastly, PBGC noted that the guidance does not address whether the applicable interest rate and applicable mortality table would be those in effect on the plan's termination date or those in effect on the distribution date, when both dates are subsequent to January 1, 2008. PBGC advised that it intends to address this situation in future guidance. [PBGC Tech. Update 07-3]

IRS issued additional guidance relating to the new applicable mortality table and applicable interest rate. A plan does not fail to satisfy the requirement that the QJSA for a married participant be at least as valuable as any other form of benefit payable under the plan at the same time merely because the amount payable under an optional form of benefit that is subject to the minimum present value requirement is calculated as the more favorable to participants of (1) the amount calculated by using the pre-PPA applicable mortality table and pre-PPA applicable interest rate or (2) the amount calculated by using the post-PPA applicable mortality table and post-PPA applicable interest rate. This special treatment for amounts calculated by using the pre-PPA applicable mortality table and pre-PPA applicable interest rate generally applies only until the last day of the first plan year beginning on or after January 1, 2009. [PPA § 117(b)(2)(A); IRS Notice 2008-30, Q&A-16, 2008-1 C.B. 638]

In general, relief under PPA applies to an amendment that provides the more favorable to participants of an amount calculated by using the pre-PPA applicable mortality table and pre-PPA applicable interest rate or an amount calculated by using the post-PPA applicable mortality table and post-PPA applicable interest rate, even if the pre-PPA applicable interest rate and/or pre-PPA applicable mortality table apply only for a specified period of time (as long as the amendment is timely adopted). For example, if a plan is amended to provide that the amount payable under an optional form of benefit that is subject to the minimum present value requirements is calculated in the manner described in the preceding paragraph (i.e., pursuant to a better-of calculation) for a specified period of time, and thereafter is calculated without reference to the pre-PPA applicable mortality table and pre-PPA applicable interest rate, the plan will not fail to satisfy the anti-cutback requirements by reason of the amendment. However, with respect to a particular plan provision, relief under PPA applies only to the first plan amendment that implements the post-PPA applicable interest rate and/or post-PPA applicable mortality table with respect to the provision, and any subsequent amendment with respect to the provision will not be treated as adopted pursuant to statutory provisions under PPA, as required for relief under PPA. For purposes of determining whether an amendment that implements the post-PPA applicable interest rate and/or post-PPA applicable mortality table with respect to a particular plan provision is the first such amendment, amendments adopted on or before June 30, 2008 are disregarded. Thus, if a plan amendment is adopted that provides that the amount payable under an optional form of benefit that is subject to the minimum present value requirements is calculated in the manner described in the preceding paragraph, and the plan is subsequently amended (during the period established in PPA) so that the amount payable is calculated without reference to the pre-PPA applicable mortality table and pre-PPA applicable interest rate, the relief under PPA will apply with respect to the subsequent amendment only if the initial amendment was adopted on or before June 30, 2008. [PPA § 1107; IRS Notice 2008-30, Q&A-17, 2008-1 C.B. 638]

The relief under PPA applies to an amendment to a plan that is subject to the automatic survivor benefit requirements and that replaces a plan reference to the pre-PPA applicable mortality table and/or pre-PPA applicable interest rate with a reference to the post-PPA applicable mortality table and/or post-PPA applicable interest rate, without regard to whether PPA requires such amendment. For example, if a plan calculates the amount of an optional form of benefit that is not subject to the minimum present value requirements by reference to the pre-PPA applicable mortality table and/or pre-PPA applicable interest rate and the plan is amended, pursuant to an amendment adopted during the period established in PPA, so that it calculates the amount of the optional form of benefit by reference to the post-PPA applicable mortality table and/or post-PPA applicable interest rate, the plan will not fail to satisfy the anti-cutback requirements by reason of the amendment. [PPA § 1107(b)(2)(A); IRS Notice 2008-30, Q&A-18, 2008-1 C.B. 638]

Q 10:63   How is the present value of benefits determined under a cash balance plan?

In general terms, a cash balance plan (see Q 2:23) is a defined benefit plan that defines benefits for each employee by reference to the amount of the employee's hypothetical account balance. An employee's hypothetical account balance is credited with hypothetical allocations and hypothetical earnings determined under a formula set forth in the plan. These hypothetical allocations and hypothetical earnings are designed to mimic the allocations of actual contributions and actual earnings to an employee's account that would occur under a defined contribution plan (see Q 2:2). Cash balance plans often specify that hypothetical earnings (i.e., interest credits) are determined using an interest rate or rate of return under a variable outside index (e.g., the annual yield on one-year Treasury securities). Most cash balance plans also are designed to permit, after termination of employment, a distribution of an employee's entire accrued benefit (see Q 9:2) in the form of a single-sum distribution equal to the employee's hypothetical account balance as of the date of the distribution.

In order to comply with the present value determination rules and the anti-cutback rule in calculating the amount of a single-sum distribution under a cash balance plan (see Q 10:64), the balance of the employee's hypothetical account must be projected to normal retirement age (see Q 10:55) and then the employee must be paid at least the present value, determined in accordance with the present value determination rules, of that projected hypothetical account balance. If a cash balance plan provides interest credits using an interest rate that is higher than the applicable interest rate, payment of a single-sum distribution equal to the hypothetical account balance as a complete distribution of the employee's accrued benefit may result either in a violation of the present value determination rules or in a violation of the anti-cutback rule. This is because, in such a case, the present value of the employee's accrued benefit, determined using the applicable interest rate, will generally exceed the hypothetical account balance. The following example illustrates this potential problem.

> **Example.** A cash balance plan provides for interest credits at a fixed rate of 8 percent per annum that are not conditioned on continued employment and for annuity conversions using the applicable interest rate and IRS mortality table. A fully vested employee with a hypothetical account balance of $45,000 terminates employment at age 45 and elects an immediate single-sum distribution. At the time of the employee's termination, the applicable interest rate is 6.5 percent. The projected balance of the employee's hypothetical account as of normal retirement age is $209,743. If $209,743 is discounted to age 45 at 6.5 percent (the applicable interest rate), the present value equals $59,524. Accordingly, if the plan paid the hypothetical account balance of $45,000, instead of $59,524, the employee would receive $14,524 less than the amount to which the employee is entitled.

Even if a cash balance plan provides interest credits using an interest rate that exceeds the applicable interest rate, the plan can satisfy the present value determination and anti-cutback rules. Such a plan would provide that the amount of any single-sum distribution is equal to the present value of the employee's accrued benefit determined in a manner that satisfies these rules, even if the amount of the single sum exceeds the employee's hypothetical account balance. Thus, in the example above, the plan would satisfy these rules if the employee received a single-sum distribution of $59,524 (the present value of the accrued benefit) rather than $45,000 (the hypothetical account balance).

[IRS Notice 96-8, 1996-1 C.B. 359]

A cash balance plan must incorporate a formula that ensures that a preretirement single-sum distribution in an amount equal to the cash balance account will always equal or exceed the present value of the participant's normal retirement benefit. A terminated employee claimed that the single-sum distribution she received was less than the present value of her normal retirement benefit, resulting in an impermissible forfeiture of benefits. The plan utilized three steps in computing the present value of the employee's normal retirement benefit: first, the current account balance was projected forward at a rate of 4 percent interest to age 65; second, the projected balance was converted to the equivalent of an annuity; and third, the annuity was discounted to present value at an interest rate prescribed by PBGC (see Q 25:10). The employee would then receive the greater of the current account balance or the present value of the benefit under the plan commencing at normal retirement age, as calculated.

The employee contended that, in the first step, the plan should have used at least a 5½ percent interest rate rather than a 4 percent rate to project the current account balance because 5½ percent was the rate used to project the amount payable to her at age 65 and was the minimum interest rate credit payable under the plan. She alleged that the plan's method fixed the outcome so that the final result of the computation would always be less than the current account balance, allowing the plan to systematically underpay participants who elected to take a single-sum distribution. The district court concluded that there was no impermissible forfeiture of benefits because using the 4 percent rate ensured compliance with the rules applicable to cash balance plans since the 4 percent projection rate was less than the applicable PBGC rate used in the third step to discount the converted annuity to present value. However, the appellate court reversed the district court and determined that the plan should have used at least a 5½ percent interest rate to project the current account balance.

[Esden v. Retirement Plan of the First Nat'l Bank of Boston, 229 F.3d 154 (2d Cir. 2000), *rev'g* 1998 U.S. Dist. LEXIS 15536 (D. Vt. 1998); *see also* Thompson v. Retirement Plan for Employees of S.C. Johnson Sons, Inc., 2010 WL 3282666 (D. Wis. 2010), Sunder v. U.S. Bank Pension Plan, 2009 WL 3714430 (8th Cir. 2009), Lyons v. Georgia Pac. Corp. Salaried Employees Ret. Plan, 221 F.3d 1235 (11th Cir. 2000), and Eaton v. Onan Corp., 117 F. Supp. 2d 812 (S.D. Ind. 2000)]

A corporation's conversion of its defined benefit plan to a cash balance plan, and its subsequent inclusion of a provision under which an employee's benefit would not begin to grow until the benefit under the new plan equaled the employee's accrued benefit under the defined benefit plan, did not violate the anti-cutback rule because only the expected, as opposed to accrued, benefit was reduced or eliminated. [Campbell v. Bank Boston, N.A., 327 F.3d 1 (1st Cir. 2003)] Another court concluded that the use of a preretirement mortality discount in a cash balance plan would result in an impermissible forfeiture of benefits. [Berger v. Xerox Ret. Income Guar. Plan, 338 F.3d 755 (7th Cir. 2003)] A cash balance plan's single-sum distribution calculations violated ERISA because the plan failed to use the projection rate established by the plan and the discount rate established by ERISA. [West v. A.K. Steel Corp. Ret. Accumulation Pension Plan, 2007 WL 1159951 (6th Cir. 2007)]

For a discussion of cash balance plans and age discrimination, see Qs 2:23, 2:24, 9:3, 9:27.

Q 10:64 Do the present value determination rules violate the anti-cutback rule?

A plan amendment that changes the interest rate, the time for determining the interest rate, or the mortality assumptions used to determine present value (see Q 10:62) is subject to the anti-cutback rule (see Qs 9:25–9:28). However, a plan amendment that changed the interest rate or the mortality assumptions merely to eliminate use of a specified interest rate or the applicable mortality table with respect to a distribution form to which the present value determination rules do not apply (see Q 10:62) for distributions with annuity starting dates (see Q 10:3) occurring after a specified date that was after the amendment was adopted did not violate the anti-cutback rule if the amendment was adopted on or before the last day of the last plan year that ended before January 1, 2000. [Treas. Reg. § 1.417(e)-1(d)(10)(i)]

If a plan amendment changes the time for determining the applicable interest rate (including an indirect change as a result of a change in plan year), the amendment will not be treated as reducing accrued benefits in violation of the anti-cutback rule merely on account of this change if:

1. For amendments effective on or after the adoption date, any distribution for which the annuity starting date occurs in the one-year period commencing at the time the plan amendment is effective must use the interest rate provided under the plan determined at either the date for determining the interest rate before the amendment or the date for determining the interest rate after the amendment, whichever results in the larger distribution, or

2. For amendments adopted retroactively (i.e., the amendment is effective prior to the adoption date), the plan must use the interest rate determination date resulting in the larger distribution for the period beginning with the effective date and ending one year after the adoption date. [Treas. Reg. § 1.417(e)-1(d)(10)(ii); Myers-Garrison v. Johnson & Johnson, 210 F.3d 425 (5th Cir. 2000)]

A participant's accrued benefit (see Q 9:2) is not considered to be reduced in violation of the anti-cutback rule merely because of a plan amendment that changes any interest rate or mortality assumption used to calculate the present value of a participant's benefit under the plan if:

1. The amendment replaces the PBGC interest rate (or an interest rate or rates based on the PBGC interest rate) as the interest rate used under the plan in determining the present value of a participant's benefit, and

2. After the amendment is effective, the present value of a participant's benefit under the plan cannot be less than the amount calculated using the applicable mortality table and the applicable interest rate for the first full calendar month preceding the calendar month that contains the annuity starting date. [Treas. Reg. § 1.417(e)-1(d)(10)(iii)]

In addition, the anti-cutback rule will not be violated if (1) the condition of item 1 above is satisfied and (2) after the amendment is effective, the present value of a participant's benefit under the plan cannot be less than the amount calculated using the applicable mortality table and the applicable interest rate. For this safe harbor exception to apply, the applicable interest rate must be the annual interest rate on 30-year Treasury securities for the calendar month that contains the date as of which the PBGC interest rate (or an interest rate or rates based on the PBGC interest rate) was determined immediately before the amendment, or for one of the two calendar months immediately preceding such month. [Treas. Reg. § 1.417(e)-1(d)(10)(iv)] IRS did not err in issuing a favorable determination letter (see Q 18:4) in which it found that a defined benefit plan amendment to the plan's lump-sum payment option did not violate the anti-cutback rule, concluded one court. The amendment changed the applicable interest rate used to compute the present value of a lump-sum benefit from one based on the PBGC interest rate to one based on the annual interest rate on 30-year Treasury securities. The replacement of the PBGC interest rate with the 30-year Treasury securities rate fell squarely within the safe harbor, said the court. [Stepnowski v. Comm'r, 2006 WL 2074808 (3d Cir. 2006); Rev. Proc. 2001-55, 2001-2 C.B. 552; Rev. Proc. 99-23, 1999-1 C.B. 920]

Furthermore, the anti-cutback rule will not be violated if (1) the condition of item 1 above is satisfied; (2) after the amendment is effective, the present value of a participant's benefit under the plan cannot be less than the amount calculated using the applicable mortality table and the applicable interest rate; and (3) the plan amendment satisfies either the condition of Treasury Regulations Section 1.417(e)-1(d)(10)(ii) cited above (determined using the interest rate provided under the terms of the plan after the effective date of the amendment) or the special early transition interest rate rule discussed below. [Treas. Reg. § 1.417(e)-1(d)(10)(v)]

A plan amendment is not considered to reduce a participant's accrued benefit even if the plan amendment provides for temporary additional benefits to accommodate a more gradual transition from the plan's old interest rate to the new rules. The anti-cutback rule, however, may be violated if a plan amendment replaces an interest rate other than the PBGC interest rate (or an interest rate or rates based on the PBGC interest rate) with another interest rate to be used under the plan in determining the present value of a participant's benefit. An interest rate is deemed based on the PBGC interest rate if the interest rate is defined as a specified percentage of the PBGC interest rate, the PBGC interest rate minus a specified number of basis points, or an average of such interest rates over a specified period. [Treas. Reg. §§ 1.417(e)-1(d)(10)(vi)(A), 1.417(e)-1(d)(10)(vi)(B)]

A plan amendment satisfies the special early transition interest rate rule if any distribution for which the annuity starting date occurs in the one-year period commencing at the time the plan amendment is effective is determined using whichever of the following two interest rates results in the larger distribution:

1. The interest rate as provided under the terms of the plan after the effective date of the amendment, but determined at a date that is either one month or two months (as specified in the plan) before the date for determining the interest rate used under the terms of the plan before the amendment, or

2. The interest rate as provided under the terms of the plan after the effective date of the amendment, determined at the date for determining the interest rate after the amendment. [Treas. Reg. § 1.417(e)-1(d)(10)(vi)(C)]

Example 1. On December 31, 1994, a defined benefit plan provided that all single-sum distributions were to be calculated using the UP-1984 mortality table and the PBGC interest rate for the date of distribution. On January 4, 1995, and effective on February 1, 1995, the plan was amended to provide that all single-sum distributions are calculated using the applicable mortality table and the annual interest rate on 30-year Treasury securities for the first full calendar month preceding the calendar month that contains the annuity starting date. This amendment is not considered to reduce the accrued benefit of any participant in violation of the anti-cutback rule.

Example 2. On December 31, 1994, a defined benefit plan provided that all single-sum distributions were to be calculated using the UP-1984 mortality table and an interest rate equal to the lesser of the PBGC interest rate for the date of distribution or 6 percent. On January 4, 1995, and effective on February 1, 1995, the plan was amended to provide that all single-sum distributions are calculated using the applicable mortality table and the annual interest rate on 30-year Treasury securities for the second full calendar month preceding the calendar month that contains the annuity starting date. The 6 percent interest rate is not based on the PBGC interest rate. Therefore, the plan must provide that the single-sum distribution payable to any participant must be no less than the single-sum distribution calculated using the UP-1984 mortality table and an interest rate of 6 percent, based on the participant's benefits under the plan accrued through January 31, 1995, and based on the participant's age at the annuity starting date.

Example 3. On December 31, 1994, a calendar-year defined benefit plan provided that all single-sum distributions were to be calculated using the UP-1984 mortality table and the PBGC interest rate for January 1 of the plan year. On March 1, 1995, and effective on July 1, 1995, the plan was amended to provide that all single-sum distributions are calculated using the applicable mortality table and the annual interest rate on 30-year Treasury securities for August of the year before the plan year that contains the annuity starting date. The plan amendment provides that each distribution with an annuity starting date after June 30, 1995, and before July 1, 1996, is calculated using the 30-year Treasury rate for August of the year before the plan year that contains the annuity starting date, or the 30-year Treasury rate for January of the plan year that contains the annuity starting date, whichever produces the larger benefit. This amendment is not considered to have reduced the accrued benefit of any participant in violation of the anti-cutback rule.

Example 4. Car-Ad Corporation maintains a defined benefit plan with a calendar-year plan year. As of December 7, 1994, the plan provided for single-sum distributions to be calculated using the PBGC interest rate as of the annuity starting date for distributions not greater than $25,000, and 120 percent of that interest rate for distributions over $25,000. Car-Ad wishes to delay the effective date of the RPA '94 rules for a year and to provide for an extended transition from the use of the PBGC interest rate to the new applicable interest rate. On December 1, 1995, and effective on January 1, 1996,

Car-Ad amends the plan to provide that single-sum distributions are determined as the sum of:

1. The single-sum distribution calculated using the applicable mortality table and the annual interest rate on 30-year Treasury securities for the first full calendar month preceding the calendar month that contains the annuity starting date, and

2. A transition amount. The transition amount for distributions in the years 1996-1999 is a transition percentage of the excess, if any, of the amount that the single-sum distribution would have been under the plan provisions in effect prior to this amendment over the amount of the single sum described in paragraph 1. The transition percentages are 80 percent for 1996, decreasing to 60 percent for 1997, 40 percent for 1998, and 20 percent for 1999. The amendment also provides that the transition amount is zero for plan years beginning on or after the year 2000. The plan is not considered to have reduced the accrued benefit of any participant in violation of the anti-cutback rule by reason of this plan amendment.

Example 5. On December 31, 1994, a calendar-year defined benefit plan provided that all single-sum distributions were to be calculated using the UP-1984 mortality table and the PBGC interest rate for January 1 of the plan year. On March 1, 1995, and effective on July 1, 1995, the plan was amended to provide that all single-sum distributions are calculated using the applicable mortality table and the annual interest rate on 30-year Treasury securities for August of the year before the plan year that contains the annuity starting date. The plan amendment provides that each distribution with an annuity starting date after June 30, 1995, and before July 1, 1996, is calculated using the 30-year Treasury rate for August of the year before the plan year that contains the annuity starting date, or the 30-year Treasury rate for November of the plan year preceding the plan year that contains the annuity starting date, whichever produces the larger benefit. This amendment is not considered to have reduced the accrued benefit of any participant in violation of the anti-cutback rule.

In November 2002, IRS announced on its website that an amendment to a cash balance plan adopting the new applicable mortality table would not violate the anti-cutback rule and also that a Section 204(h) Notice would not have to be provided (see Qs 9:37–9:53). [Rev. Rul. 2001-62, 2001-2 C.B. 632]

Q 10:65　Does a participant have to formally apply for benefits?

No. However, failure to apply for benefits would result in the participant receiving the benefit in the form of a QJSA (see Q 10:8), if applicable, or in the normal form of benefit under the terms of the plan, rather than an optional form of benefit that the participant might have preferred. If the participant has received notice of the QJSA and optional forms of benefit no less than 30 days and no more than 180 days after the annuity starting date (see Qs 10:3, 10:20), a QJSA can be distributed without the participant's consent after the participant reaches normal retirement age (see Q 10:55), or age 62, if later. I.R.C. § 417(a)(6)(A); Treas. Reg. §§ 1.411(a)-11(c)(2)(ii), 1.411(a)-11(c)(2)(iii); Prop. Treas. Reg. §§ 1.411(a)-11(c)(2)(ii), 1.411(a)-11(c)(2)(iii); IRS Notice 2007-7, § VIII, 2007-1 C.B. 395; see Q 10:57 for further details]

The trustees of a pension plan improperly rejected a participant's application for a pension on the basis that the application had not been timely filed, where neither the plan nor the SPD (see Qs 22:1, 22:5) specified a particular time frame in which participants must apply. [Pepe v. Newspaper and Mail Deliverers'— Publishers' Pension Fund, 2009 WL 647711 (2d Cir. 2009)] A defined benefit plan (see Q 2:3) participant could not be deprived of three months of pension payments, representing the period between his retirement and the date he applied for the pension, because that would be a forfeiture of his benefits, held one court. [Contilli v. Local 705 International Brotherhood of Teamsters Pension Fund, 2009 WL 735961 (7th Cir. 2009)]

One court concluded that a plan's administrative committee abused its discretion when it denied a retired employee's application for a postretirement joint and survivor annuity because the employee failed to make a written election for the annuity at least 30 days prior to his retirement. The court ruled that the committee acted arbitrarily by failing to undertake a full and fair review of the relevant issues before it refused to grant a waiver of the 30-day waiting period, which it was authorized to grant under the plan, and ordered the plan to pay the joint and survivor annuity. [Hussey v. E.I. DuPont de Nemours & Co. Pension & Benefit Plan, No. 6:96-0402 (S.D. W. Va. 1997)] Another court determined that the common law "mailbox rule" should apply to plan benefit claims and held that a plan participant's assertion that she mailed a benefit payment election form before the due date was sufficient to invoke the presumption that the plan received the form. [Schikore v. Bank Am. Supplemental Ret. Plan, 269 F.3d 956 (9th Cir. 2001); *see also* Kuchar v. AT&T Pension Benefit Plan—Midwest Program, 2007 WL 838985 (N.D. Ill. 2007)]

One court ruled that a plan administrator (see Q 20:1) abused its discretion when it rejected a participant's appeal (see Q 10:66) without explanation, basing its denial on a document that had been incorporated into the formal plan document but not into the SPD. [Marolt v. Alliant Techsystems, Inc., No. 97-2817 (8th Cir. 1998)] Where a plan administrator demanded reimbursement from a plan participant for benefit payments allegedly made in error and gave notice to the participant that future benefit payments would be offset, one court concluded that the administrator's interpretation of the plan was not rational because ERISA requires that every plan provide for a claims procedure affording participants adequate notice of an administrator's decision to deny benefits and an opportunity for a review of any decision denying a claim for benefits. [Board of Admin., Canton Drop Forge, Inc. v. Huntsman, No. 98-3766 (6th Cir. 1999)] Another court ordered a plan administrator to make immediate retroactive benefit payments to a participant, without remanding the case to the administrator for further reconsideration of the claim because claim denial was so arbitrary and capricious there was no need to give the administrator a second opportunity to review the claim. [Cooper v. Life Ins. Co. of North America, 486

F.3d 157 (6th Cir. 2007)] A court ruled in favor of a plan participant and awarded him benefits where the participant was held by the plan to a stricter evidentiary standard than other similarly situated participants. [Foley v. IBEW Local Union 98 Pension Fund, No. 98-906 (E.D. Pa. 2000)]

Where a union member, whose employer had not contributed to the union's pension plan on his behalf for a portion of his career, presented detailed evidence that he had been engaged in covered employment during this period, the plan's denial of retirement benefits for this period was arbitrary and capricious, ruled one court. [Glascoe v. Central States, Southeast & Southwest Areas Pension Fund, 2002 WL 486391 (6th Cir. 2002)] A plan's denial of retirement benefits to a participant that was based on the participant's failure to produce additional supporting documentation was improper, because the plan's documentation request was unreasonably vague, concluded another court. [Morgan v. Contractors, Laborers, Teamsters & Eng'rs Pension Plan, No. 01-1839 (8th Cir. 2002)] Another court determined that, while a plan administrator can deny benefits he believes to be the product of an illegitimate attempt to amend a plan, the proper resolution of such a conflict must remain with the courts, without deference to the interpretation of the plan administrator. The rule providing for judicial deference to the determinations of the plan administrator where the plan grants the administrator broad discretion to administer the plan does not extend to such a case. [Johannssen v. District No. 1—Pac. Coast Dist., MEBA Pension Plan, 2002 WL 1012036 (4th Cir. 2002); see also Metropolitan Life Ins. Co. v. Glenn, 554 U.S. 105 (2008) and Firestone v. Bruch, 489 U.S. 101 (1989)]

Although the plan administrator failed to include in its denial an explanation of the appeal procedures, the court found that ensuing communications between the parties were sufficient to ensure that the claimant understood the reasons for the denial and his right to a review of the decision. [Coreno v. Baker Material Handling Corp. Pension Plan, 2000 U.S. App. LEXIS 6482 (6th Cir. 2000)] A participant was permitted to bring a claim for benefits against a qualified retirement plan despite a bankruptcy court order discharging such claims, because the employer had entered into bankruptcy proceedings as a result of which the plan was terminated, but the plan participants were not notified of the proceedings. [Christopher v. Kendavis Holding Co., 2001 WL 409499 (5th Cir. 2001)]

A claim for benefits accrues for ERISA statute of limitations purposes at the time a plan participant knows of the denial of the claim for benefits, even if the participant has not made a formal application for benefits. In 1989, a participant inquired about his retirement benefits and was informed that he was not eligible for benefits. The participant appealed the determination, which was upheld in 1991, and filed a formal application for benefits in 1996, which was denied. When the participant commenced a suit for benefits in 1998, the court dismissed the claim on the basis that it was time-barred by ERISA's six-year statute of limitations applicable to claims for benefits. The participant argued that his claim did not accrue until his formal application for benefits was denied in 1996, but the court held that the claim accrued in 1991 when the participant was advised that the claim for benefits was denied. Thus, a claim brought in 1998 was barred by the ERISA statute of limitations. [Carey v. IBEW Local 363 Pension Plan, No. 99-7059 (2d Cir. 1999); *see also* Muldoon v. C.J. Muldoon & Sons, 2002 WL 88994 (1st Cir. 2002); Henglein v. Colt Indus. Operating Corp., Nos. 00-2529, 00-2746 (3d Cir. 2001); Vail v. Plumbers, Pipefitters & Apprentices Local No. 112 Pension Fund, No. 99-CV-1878 (N.D.N.Y. 2001)] However, another court ruled otherwise holding that the statute of limitations for a plan participant's appeal of the denial of benefits by the plan is based upon the date of the plan's latest denial of benefits, even if every one of the plan's previous and numerous benefits determinations was identical. [Williams v. Ironworkers Local 16 Pension Fund, No. 05-1511 (4th Cir. 2006)]

ERISA requires that every plan establish and maintain reasonable claims procedures, which must be described in the SPD. A claim is a request for a plan benefit by a participant or beneficiary. DOL regulations further provide that a claim is filed when the requirements of a "reasonable claim filing procedure" of a plan have been met. If a reasonable procedure for filing claims has not been established by the plan, a claim is deemed filed when a written or oral communication is made by the claimant or the claimant's authorized representative that is reasonably calculated to bring the claim to the attention of:

1. In the case of a single employer plan, either the organizational unit that has customarily handled employee benefits matters of the employer, or any officer of the employer.

2. In the case of a plan to which more than one unaffiliated employer contributes, or which is established or maintained by an employee organization, either the joint board, association, committee, or other similar group (or any member of any such group) administering the plan, or the person or organizational unit to which claims for benefits under the plan customarily have been referred.

3. In the case of a plan the benefits of which are provided or administered by an insurance company, insurance service, or other similar organization, which is subject to regulation under the insurance laws of one or more states, the person or organizational unit which handles claims for benefits under the plan or any officer of the insurance company, insurance service, or similar organization.

A communication is deemed to have been brought to the attention of an organizational unit if it is received by any person employed in such unit. [DOL Reg. § 2560.503-1] This new DOL claims procedure regulation began to apply to new claims filed on and after January 1, 2002. The claims procedure regulation changes the minimum procedural requirements for the processing of benefit claims for all employee benefit plans covered under ERISA, although the changes are minimal for qualified retirement plans other than those that provide disability benefits. To assist plans in complying with the claims procedure regulation, the Pension and Welfare Benefits Administration (PWBA) has posted questions and answers on its website. [PWBA Web site, Dec. 17, 2001]

Where an employer failed to provide a participant with adequate claims procedure information and the employer's actions in engaging the participant in informal attempts to resolve his benefits dispute caused the participant to fail to exhaust his administrative remedies and extinguished his time to apply for benefits, the court ruled that the participant's claim be remanded to the plan administrator and that the employer be estopped from arguing before the plan administrator that the employee's claim was time-barred. [Bourgeois v. Pension Plan for the Employees of Santa Fe Int'l Corp., 215 F.3d 475 (5th Cir. 2000)] One court ruled that trustees had no reasonable justification for interpreting a plan to bar claimants from retaining their own stenographer to record benefits denial hearings. [Eisenreich v. Minneapolis Meat Cutters & Food Handlers Pension Fund, 2003 U.S. Dist. LEXIS 16421 (D. Minn. 2003)]

DOL representatives have opined that the claims procedure rules do not apply in the case of a domestic relations order (DRO; see Q 36:2) that is determined by the plan administrator not to be a qualified domestic relations order (QDRO; see Q 36:1). The DRO does not constitute a claim for benefits by the alternate payee (see Q 36:5) until the DRO is determined to be a QDRO.

Q 10:66 What are the participant's rights if a claim for benefits is denied?

If the claim for benefits is denied, either in part or in full, the plan administrator (see Q 20:1) must furnish written notice to the participant or beneficiary explaining why the claim was denied within a reasonable period of time; such notice must be written in a manner calculated to be understood by the claimant. Moreover, the plan must afford a reasonable opportunity to the participant or beneficiary to have a full and fair review of that decision. [ERISA § 503; DOL Reg. § 2560.503-1; Redding v. AT&T Corp., No. 96-1394 (10th Cir. 1997); Hussey v. E.I. DuPont de Nemours & Co. Pension & Benefit Plan, No. 6:96-0402 (S.D. W. Va. 1997)] One court concluded that an e-mail notice of benefit denial constitutes an adverse benefit determination. [Maniscalco v. J.A.C. Ams. Comprehensive Healthcare Plan, 2004 U.S. Dist. LEXIS 13347 (S.D.N.Y. 2004)] Another court determined that deference to a plan administrator's denial of a claim for benefits was inappropriate where no final administrative decision had been made, and appeal rights could not be waived without prior adequate notice of those rights. [Strom v. Siegel Fenchel & Peddy P.C. Profit Sharing Plan, No. 06-3104-cv (2d Cir. 2007)] Where a plan required a participant to bear one-half of the cost of arbitrating an appeal from an adverse determination by the trustees, one court ruled that he was deprived of his right to a full and fair review of the decision denying his claim for benefits. [Bond v. Twin Cities Carpenters Pension Fund, 307 F.3d 704 (8th Cir. 2002)]

If notice of the denial of a claim is not furnished within a reasonable period of time, the claim is deemed denied. A period of time is deemed to be unreasonable if it exceeds 90 days after receipt of the claim by the plan, unless special circumstances require an extension of time for processing the claim. If an extension of time for processing is required, written notice of the extension must be furnished to the claimant prior to the termination of the initial 90-day period.

In no event should the extension exceed a period of 90 days from the end of the initial period. The extension notice must indicate the special circumstances requiring an extension of time and the date by which the plan expects to render the final decision. [DOL Reg. § 2560.503-1(e)]

A claimant who is denied a claim for benefits must be provided with written notice setting forth:

1. The specific reason or reasons for denial;

2. Specific reference to pertinent plan provisions on which the denial is based;

3. A description of any additional material or information necessary for the claimant to perfect the claim and an explanation of why such material or information is necessary; and

4. Appropriate information as to the steps to be taken if the participant or beneficiary wishes to submit the claim for review. [DOL Reg. § 2560. 503-1(f)]

Where the denial failed to satisfy the above requirements, the court ruled that the appropriate remedy is to remand the matter to the plan administrator for an out-of-time administrative appeal. [Cromer-Tyler v. Teitel, 2008 WL 4335938 (11th Cir. 2008)] One court held that a plan administrator could articulate a new reason for denying a claim on appeal after the initial benefit determination had been rendered. [Abatie v. Alta Health & Life Ins. Co., 2005 U.S. App. LEXIS 8836 (9th Cir. 2005)] Another court concluded that it was permissible to refer to a closing agreement between a union and an employer when evaluating partici- pants' claims for plan benefits because the closing agreement was a plan document relevant to the plan administrator's decision and could not be ignored. [Wilson v. Moog Auto., Inc. Pension Plan, 1999 WL 800046 (8th Cir. 1999)]

Every plan must establish and maintain a procedure by which a claimant or a duly authorized representative has a reasonable opportunity to appeal a denied claim to an appropriate named fiduciary or to a person designated by the fiduciary, and under which a full and fair review of the claim and its denial may be obtained. The procedure shall include, but not be limited to, provisions that a claimant or the duly authorized representative may:

1. Request a review upon written application to the plan;

2. Review pertinent documents; and

3. Submit issues and comments in writing.

Generally, the appropriate named fiduciary will be the plan administrator or another person designated by the plan, provided that the plan administrator or other person is either named in the plan document or is identified pursuant to a procedure set forth in the plan as the person who reviews and makes decisions on claim denials. A plan may establish a limited period within which a claimant must file any request for review of a denied claim. The time limits must be reasonable and related to the nature of the benefit that is the subject of the claim and to other attendant circumstances. In no event may the period expire less than 60 days after receipt by the claimant of written notification of denial of a claim. [DOL Reg. § 2560.503-1(g); Northlake Reg'l Med. Ctr. v. Waffle House Sys. Employee Benefit Plan, 160 F.3d 1301 (11th Cir. 1998)]

A decision by the appropriate named fiduciary must be made promptly and should not ordinarily be made later than 60 days after the plan's receipt of a request for review, unless special circumstances (such as the need to hold a hearing, if the plan procedure provides for a hearing) require an extension of time for processing, in which case a decision should be rendered as soon as possible, but not later than 120 days after receipt of a request for review. In the case of a plan with a committee or board of trustees designated as the appropriate named fiduciary, which holds regularly scheduled meetings at least quarterly, a decision on review should be made no later than the date of the meeting of the committee or board that immediately follows the plan's receipt of a request for review, unless the request for review is filed within 30 days preceding the date of such meeting. In such case, a decision may be made no later than the date of the second meeting following the plan's receipt of the request for review. [DOL Reg. § 2560.503-1(h); Price v. Xerox Corp., 2006 WL 1007967 (8th Cir. 2006)]

If special circumstances require a further extension of time for processing, a decision should be rendered not later than the third meeting of the committee or board following the plan's receipt of the request for review. If an extension of time for review is required because of special circumstances, written notice of the extension must be furnished to the claimant prior to the commencement of the extension. The decision on review must be in writing and include specific reasons for the decision, written in a manner calculated to be understood by the claimant, as well as specific references to the pertinent plan provisions on which the decision is based. The decision on review must be furnished to the claimant within the appropriate time described above. If the decision on review is not furnished within such time, the claim is deemed denied on review. [DOL Reg. § 2560.503-1(h)] A plan administrator could not claim a deemed denial where the only response during the required period was a letter advising the claimant that the appeal was still pending and was awaiting further review. [Jebian v. Hewlett Packard Co., 2002 WL 31553407 (9th Cir. 2002)]

DOL has issued a new claims procedure regulation designed to expedite the processing of benefit claims. [DOL Reg. § 2560.503-1] This new DOL claims procedure regulation began to apply to new claims filed on and after January 1, 2002. The claims procedure regulation changes the minimum procedural requirements for the processing of benefit claims for all employee benefit plans covered under ERISA, although the changes are minimal for qualified retirement plans other than those that provide disability benefits. To assist plans in complying with the claims procedure regulation, PWBA posted questions and answers on its website. [PWBA Web site, Dec. 17, 2001]

While an employer may have an obligation to issue a foreign-language version of a plan's SPD (see Q 22:14), there is no such duty with respect to benefit denials. Therefore, there was no inadequacy in a benefit denial that excused a non-English-speaking claimant from exhausting a plan's administrative remedies before bringing a suit for benefits. [Diaz v. United Agric. Employee Welfare Benefit Plan & Trust, 50 F.3d 1478 (9th Cir. 1995)]

If the claim is denied after the review, the claimant can commence a court action. However, before starting a lawsuit, the claimant must exhaust the plan's administrative remedies (i.e., file a claim, request a review) unless the claimant can show that doing so would be futile. [Noren v. Jefferson Pilot Financial Ins. Co., 2010 WL 1841892 (9th Cir. 2010); Moyle v. Golden Eagle Ins. Corp., 2007 WL 2436881 (9th Cir. 2007); Galvan v. SBC Pension Benefit Plan, 2006 WL 2460879 (5th Cir. 2006); Wert v. Liberty Life Assurance Co. of Boston, Inc., 2006 U.S. App. LEXIS 12092 (8th Cir. 2006); Boivin v. U.S. Airways, Inc., 2006 U.S. App. LEXIS 10875 (D.C. Cir. 2006); Smith v. Local No. 25 Iron Workers' Pension Plan, 2004 U.S. App. LEXIS 10605 (6th Cir. 2004); McGowin v. Manpower Int'l, Inc., No. 03-41201 (5th Cir. 2004); Borman v. Great Atl. & Pac. Tea Co., 2003 U.S. App. LEXIS 10424 (6th Cir. 2003); Back v. Danka Corp., 2003 U.S. App. LEXIS 14031 (8th Cir. 2003); Benaim v. HSBC Bank USA, 2001 U.S. App. LEXIS 25377 (2d Cir. 2001); Rosser v. U.S. Steel Group, No. 99-2821 (7th Cir. 2000); Burds v. Union Pac. Corp., 223 F.3d 814 (8th Cir. 2000); Rivera-Diaz v. American Airlines, Inc., 2000 WL 1022888 (1st Cir. 2000); Gallegos v. Mt. Sinai Med. Ctr., 2000 WL 490749 (7th Cir. 2000); Perrino v. Southern Bell Tel. & Tel. Co., No. 98-5189 (11th Cir. 2000); Ames v. American Nat'l Can Co., No. 97-4055 (7th Cir. 1999); Lindemann v. Mobil Oil Corp., No. 95-2808 (7th Cir. 1996); Communications Workers of Am. v. American Tel. & Tel. Co., 1994 U.S. App. LEXIS 33043 (Fed Cir. 1994); Conley v. Pitney Bowes, 1994 U.S. App. LEXIS 24798 (8th Cir. 1994); Roitman v. Mt. Sinai Med. Ctr. LTD. Ins. Plan, 2004 U.S. Dist. LEXIS 6635 (N.D. Ill. 2004); Schwab v. Medfirst Health Plans La., No. 99-2695 (E.D. La. 2000); Schultz v. Quaker Oats Co., No. 97 C 6735 (E.D. Ill. 1999); Green v. Graphic Communications Int'l Union Officers, Representatives & Organizers Ret. Fund & Plan, No. 94-2118 (D.D.C. 1996); Stumpf v. Cincinnati, 1994 U.S. Dist. LEXIS 13589 (S.D. Ohio 1994); Kimble v. International Bhd. of Teamsters, Chauffeurs, Warehousemen & Helpers of Am., No. 93-1569 (E.D. Pa. 1993)]

A class action has been allowed to proceed against PBGC (see Q 25:10). The action is based on PBGC's alleged violations of the anti-cutback rule (see Q 9:25). The court held that requiring the participants to exhaust their administrative remedies under the plan was not a prerequisite to judicial review where the claim involved a statutory violation of ERISA. [Coleman v. PBGC, 2000 WL 527010 (D.D.C. 2000)] Another court ruled that the unnamed class members in a class action suit need not exhaust their administrative remedies as a condition to being allowed to be class members. [*In re* Household Int'l Tax Reduction Plan, 441 F.3d 500 (7th Cir. 2006)] According to one court, a former plan participant was not required to exhaust the plan's administrative remedies concerning how her single-sum distribution was determined, because her complaint concerned the legality of the plan's method for determining single sums and was not just a request to recalculate her distribution. [Durand v. The Hanover Insurance Group, Inc., 560 F.3d 436 (6th Cir. 2009); *see also* French v. BP Corp. North America, Inc., 2009 WL 3490428 (D. Ken. 2009)] Former participants were not required to exhaust their administrative remedies before commencing an action for the wrongful denial of benefits because the employer did not represent to the court satisfaction of the requirement that each participant be given notice of the review procedures. [McDowell v. Price, 2009 WL 2044454 (E.D. Ark. 2009)]

An employee was deemed to have exhausted the plan's administrative remedies even though she was given the opportunity to make a second appeal. The court ruled so because the claimant had no additional information to provide. [Hager v. Nations Bank, N.A., 1999 WL 58737 (5th Cir. 1999)] Another court similarly ruled because the plan itself thwarted exhaustion of the claim procedures and deprived the participant of a fair opportunity to get a timely review of his claim. [Lee v. California Butchers' Pension Trust, 1998 WL 569024 (9th Cir. 1998)] Where participants did not exhaust all administrative remedies before commencing an action because the SPD did not require exhaustion, the court determined that they were required to do so because exhaustion of administrative remedies is a judicial requirement that is not governed by plan provisions [Whitehead v. Oklahoma Gas & Elec. Co., No. 97-5233 (10th Cir. 1999)]; however, another court ruled otherwise where the SPD could reasonably be interpreted as not requiring exhaustion. [Watts v. Bell S. Telecomms., Inc., 2003 WL 23394 (11th Cir. 2003)] A plan's argument that a participant's claim against it should be dismissed for failure to exhaust his administrative remedies was waived because the plan failed to raise the exhaustion argument in a timely manner. [McCoy v. Board of Trustees of the Laborers' Int'l Union, Local No. 222 Pension Plan, No. 0-1481 (D.N.J. 2002)] Failure to exhaust administrative remedies is an affirmative defense. If the plan does not raise the defense at the trial court, it cannot do so at the appellate court. [Paese v. Hartford Life and Accident Ins. Co., 2006 U.S. App. LEXIS 13007 (2d Cir. 2006)]

Failure to exhaust administrative remedies may bar the claimant from pursuing judicial relief. When a claim has been denied and the participant fails to request a review within the time limit set forth in the plan, courts have ruled that judicial review of the underlying claim for benefits is precluded. [Davenport v. Harry N. Abrams, Inc., 249 F.3d 130 (2d Cir. 2001); Sasser v. Mosler, Inc., 1997 U.S. App. LEXIS 14919 (6th Cir. 1997); Glisson v. United States Forest Serv., 55 F.3d 1325 (7th Cir. 1995); Petropoulos v. Outbound Marine Corp, 1995 U.S. Dist. LEXIS 10545 (N.D. Ill. 1995); Graham v. Federal Express Corp., 725 F. Supp. 429 (W.D. Ark. 1989); Tiger v. AT&T Techs., 633 F. Supp. 532 (E.D.N.Y. 1986)] This was the result even though the failure to file the appeal was caused by the negligence of the claimant's attorney. [Gayle v. United Parcel Service, Inc., 2005 U.S. App. LEXIS 3935 (4th Cir. 2005)] However, courts have determined that a claim of fiduciary breach of responsibility (see Q 22:16) is not subject to the requirement of exhausting administrative remedies because the adjudication of such a claim rests with the judiciary [Galvan v. SBC Pension Benefit Plan, 2006 WL 2460879 (5th Cir. 2006); Smith v. Sydnor, Jr., 1999 U.S. App. LEXIS 15183 (4th Cir. 1999)]; but another court held that plan participants were required to exhaust their administrative remedies before bringing an action alleging breach of fiduciary duty against the plan because the claim was more properly characterized as one for plan benefits. [D'Amico v. CBS Corp., 297 F.3d 287 (3d Cir. 2002)] One court concluded that a plan participant did not have to exhaust the plan's administrative remedies in order to proceed with his suit for the recovery of benefits because the plan did not institute a claims procedure until after the suit was filed. [Eastman Kodak Co. v. STWB, Inc., 2006 U.S. App. LEXIS 16079 (2d Cir. 2006)] The requirement that a plan participant exhaust administrative remedies before commencing an action against a plan in federal court was not waived where the participant, following denial of an oral claim for benefits, had not followed the plan's procedures for administrative review after a formal denial of his claim. [Bennett v. Prudential Ins. Co., No. 05-5033 (3d Cir. 2006)]

One court ruled that a plan participant who received his benefits after a long delay could bring an action against the plan under ERISA to collect interest on the delayed payment. [ERISA § 502(a)(3)(B); Fotta v. United Mine Workers of Am., 165 F.3d 209 (3d Cir. 1998); *see also* Skretvedt v. E.I. DuPont de Nemours & Co., 2006 U.S. Dist. LEXIS 89411 (D. Del. 2006); Skretvedt v. E.I. DuPont de Nemours & Co., Nos. 02-3620, 02-4283 (3d Cir. 2004); Dunnigan v. Met Life Ins. Co., No. 00-7399 (2d Cir. 2002)] However, other courts have determined that no interest would have to be paid because the delay was caused by the participant. [Twomey v. Delta Airlines Pilots Pension Plan, 328 F.3d 27 (1st Cir. 2003); Jones v. Local 705 Int'l Bhd. of Teamsters Pension Fund, 2003 WL 716582 (7th Cir. 2003)]

Chapter 11

Minimum Distribution Requirements

The primary purpose of a qualified retirement plan is to provide retirement income to employees when they retire from employment. This objective will not be satisfied if employees can defer the receipt of benefits indefinitely. Comprehensive and complex proposed regulations were issued by IRS in July 1987; and, because of this complexity and concerns expressed by practitioners, IRS responded by issuing revised proposed regulations in January 2001. In response to comments submitted by practitioners, IRS promulgated final and temporary regulations in April 2002. The temporary regulations were finalized in June 2004. The final regulations make it much easier for individuals—both plan participants and IRA owners—and plan administrators to understand and apply the minimum distribution rules. This chapter discusses when retirement benefits must be distributed, how much must be distributed each year, and the penalty for failure to satisfy these requirements. It also analyzes in detail the final regulations.

General

Q 11:1   What is the effective date of the final regulations?

The final regulations are applicable for determining required minimum distributions (RMDs) for calendar years beginning on or after January 1, 2003. For determining RMDs for calendar year 2002, taxpayers were permitted to rely on the final and temporary regulations, the 2001 proposed regulations, *or* the 1987 proposed regulations. [Preamble to 2002 final and temporary regulations; Rev. Proc. 2003-10, 2003-1 C.B. 259; Rev. Proc. 2002-29, 2002-1 C.B. 1176]

IRS issued a revenue procedure providing that qualified retirement plans generally must be amended by the end of the first plan year beginning on or after January 1, 2003, to the extent necessary to comply with the final and temporary regulations relating to RMDs. The revenue procedure contains model plan amendments that sponsors of master and prototype (M&P), volume submitter, and individually designed plans may adopt to satisfy this requirement. The first model amendment is for defined contribution plans (see Q 2:2), and the second model amendment is for defined benefit plans (see Q 2:3). A plan sponsor or a sponsor of a pre-approved plan that timely adopts the appropriate model amendment verbatim (or with only minor changes) will have reliance that the form of its plan satisfies the requirements of the final and temporary regulations, and the adoption of the model amendment will not adversely affect the plan sponsor's reliance on a favorable determination, opinion, or advisory letter, or cause a pre-approved plan to be treated as an individually designed plan. For this purpose, changes to either of the model amendments to incorporate the adoption agreement elective provisions into the body of the amendment or to remove the elective provisions in favor of the default rules in the body of the amendment are minor changes.

In general, qualified retirement plans must be amended by the last day of the first plan year beginning on or after January 1, 2003, to the extent necessary to comply with the requirements of the regulations. Whether and the extent to which a particular plan must be amended depends on the plan's current terms. Any plan amendments for the regulations must apply in determining RMDs under the plan for calendar years beginning on or after January 1, 2003.

[Rev. Proc. 2002-29, 2002-1 C.B. 1176]

IRS postponed until the end of the EGTRRA 2001 remedial amendment period (see Q 1:21) the time by which defined benefit plans must be amended to comply with the regulations. [Rev. Proc. 2003-10, 2003-1 C.B. 259] IRS also postponed the time by which defined contribution plans had to be amended until the later of the end of the first plan year that began after January 1, 2003, or the end of the GUST remedial amendment period. [Rev. Proc. 2003-72, 2003-2 C.B. 578] Subsequently, IRS implemented a system that staggered remedial amendment periods for individually designed plans (see Q 2:26). This new system establishes regular five-year cycles for plan amendments and determination letter renewals for individually designed plans. Defined benefit and defined contribution plans are subject to these five-year cycles that are based on employer identification numbers (EINs). On February 1, 2006, IRS began accepting applications for determination letters for individually designed plans that took into account the requirements of EGTRRA 2001 as well as other changes and qualification requirements. [Rev. Proc. 2005-66, 2005-2 C.B.509] See Q 18:7 for details.

Beginning with 2003, all employees and IRA owners must use the final regulations even if distributions began before 2003. If an employee or IRA owner died before 2003, the final regulations apply even if distributions began before 2003. This means that the designated beneficiary (see Q 11:14) and the applicable distribution period (see Qs 11:9, 11:23) must be redetermined for purposes of determining the amount required to be distributed for 2003 and subsequent years. [Treas. Reg. § 1.401(a)(9)-1, Q&A-2(b)(1)]

IRS is directed to issue regulations under which a governmental plan is treated as satisfying the RMD requirements if the plan satisfies a reasonable, good faith interpretation of those requirements. The regulations will apply to years in which the RMD rules apply to the plan. Although this provision is effective on August 17, 2006, the Report of the Joint Committee on Taxation states that the regulation should apply to periods before that date. [PPA § 813; Jt. Comm. on Taxation, Technical Explanation of the Pension Protection Act of 2006 (JCX-38-06)]

In each of calendar years 2006 and 2007, individuals who had attained age 70$\frac{1}{2}$ could direct that up to $100,000 be transferred from their IRAs or Roth IRAs directly to qualified charitable organizations. The individuals did not recognize income on the transfer and were not entitled to a charitable income tax deduction. In addition, the transfer counted towards the individual's RMD for that year. A provision of The Emergency Economic Stabilization Act of 2008 extended this exclusion to calendar years 2008 and 2009. See Q 30:44 for further details. [I.R.C. § 408(d)]

No minimum distribution was required for calendar year 2009 from defined contribution plans, including 403(b) plans (see Q 35:1) and IRAs. Thus, any annual minimum distribution for 2009 from these plans required under current law, otherwise determined by dividing the account balance by a distribution period, was not required to be made. The next RMD is for calendar year 2010. This suspension applied to lifetime distributions to employees and IRA owners and post-death distributions to beneficiaries. [I.R.C. § 401(a)(9)(H) (as added by WRERA 2008 § 201(a); WRERA 2008 § 201(c)(1))]

IRS issued guidance relating to the waiver of 2009 RMDs. IRS understood that, due to the enactment of WRERA 2008 (see Q 1:36) late in 2008, many plan administrators (see Q 20:1) were unable to timely modify procedures relating to 2009 RMDs to accommodate the new rules. Also, prior to the issuance of the guidance, plan sponsors were unsure of the options available to them. A plan will not be treated as failing to satisfy the requirement that it be operated in accordance with its terms merely because, during the period beginning on January 1, 2009, and ending on November 30, 2009, (1) distributions that equal the 2009 RMDs or that are one or more payments in a series of substantially equal periodic distributions (that include the 2009 RMDs) made at least annually and expected to last for the life (or life expectancy) of the participant, the joint lives (or joint life expectancy) of the participant and the participant's designated beneficiary, or for a period of at least ten years were or were not paid; (2) participants and beneficiaries were not given the option of receiving or not receiving distributions that include 2009 RMDs; or (3) a direct rollover option was or was not offered for 2009 RMDs or for other amounts that could be rolled over pursuant to the rollover relief provided in the guidance (Q 34:8). [IRS Notice 2009-82, 2009-41 I.R.B. ___]

To address the concerns of plan sponsors, two alternative sample plan amendments are provided in the Appendix to the IRS guidance that individual plan sponsors and sponsors of pre-approved plans can adopt or use in drafting individualized plan amendments. Both sample amendments provide participants and beneficiaries the choice between receiving and not receiving distributions related to 2009 RMDs, but only if the distributions would otherwise be equal to the 2009 RMDs or be one or more payments in a series of substantially equal periodic distributions (that include the 2009 RMDs) as discussed in the preceding paragraph. All other distributions, including distributions that consist partly of 2009 RMDs, will be made. For example, a 75-year-old retiree's request to have the remaining plan account balance distributed in 2009 in a lump sum, or in five approximately equal annual installments over a period that includes 2009, would not be affected by the sample amendments. The first sample amendment provides that the plan default that applies in the absence of a participant's or beneficiary's election will be to pay out distributions that include 2009 RMDs, and the second sample amendment provides that the plan default that applies in the absence of a participant's or beneficiary's election will be to not pay out distributions that include RMDs.

Both sample amendments also provide direct rollover choices (in addition to ones already provided for in the plan), with the default in each amendment being that the plan will offer a direct rollover option only for pre-WRERA 2008 eligible rollover distributions (i.e., a direct rollover option will not be offered for 2009 RMDs or for amounts that can be rolled over solely due to the transition relief (see Q 34:8). One option provides for the direct rollover of 2009 RMDs and of other amounts that may be rolled over pursuant to the transition relief for plans (the latter amounts referred to as "Extended 2009 RMDs" in the sample amendments). Another option provides for the direct rollover of the entire amount of a distribution, but only where the distribution consists of part or all of a 2009 RMD amount and an additional amount that is an eligible rollover distribution without regard to the suspension of RMDs.

Either plan amendment may be chosen by a plan sponsor, regardless of current plan language. Plan sponsors may have to modify the sample amendment chosen to conform to their plan's terms and administrative procedures.

The amendment must be adopted no later than the last day of the first plan year beginning on or after January 1, 2011, and, except as provided in the transition relief discussed above, must reflect the operation of the plan to either cease or continue distributions that include 2009 RMDs in the absence of a participant's or beneficiary's choice. The timely adoption of the amendment must be evidenced by a written document that is signed and dated by the employer (including an adopting employer of a pre-approved plan).

In either case, the amendment (as modified, if necessary, to conform to the plan's terms and administrative procedures) will not result in the loss of reliance on a favorable opinion, advisory, or determination letter (see Q 18:1). Also, IRS will not treat the adoption of one of the sample plan amendments (as modified, if necessary, to conform to the plan's terms and administrative procedures) as affecting the pre-approved status of a master and prototype (M&P) plan (see Q 2:27) or volume submitter plan (see Q 2:28). That is, such an amendment to an M&P plan that is adopted by an employer will not cause the plan to fail to be an M&P plan. Similarly, such an amendment to a volume submitter plan that is adopted by an employer will not cause the plan to fail to be a volume submitter plan.

The format of the sample plan amendment generally follows the design of pre-approved plans, including all M&P plans, that employ a basic plan document and an adoption agreement. Thus, the sample plan amendment includes language designed for inclusion in a basic plan document and language designed for inclusion in an adoption agreement to allow the employer to select among options related to the application of the basic plan document provided. Sponsors of plans that do not use an adoption agreement should modify the format of the amendment to incorporate the appropriate adoption agreement options in the terms of the amendment. In such case, the notes in the adoption agreement portion of the sample amendment should not be included in the amendment that will be signed and dated by the employer.

[IRS Notice 2009-82, 2009-41 I.R.B.]

Q 11:2   What plans are subject to the minimum distribution requirements?

All qualified retirement plans are subject to the minimum distribution requirements (see Qs 11:3–11:51). [I.R.C. § 401(a)(9); Treas. Reg. § 1.401(a)(9)-1, Q&A-1, Q&A-2]

The RMD rules also apply to IRAs (see Qs 11:56–11:66), SEPs (see Q 32:19), SIMPLE IRAs (see Q 33:15), and 403(b) contracts (see Qs 11:52–11:55). [I.R.C. §§ 403(b)(3), 408(a)(6); Treas. Reg. §§ 1.403(b)-3, Q&A-1 through Q&A-4, 1.408-8, Q&A-1 through Q&A-11] The lifetime RMD rules (see Q 11:4) do *not* apply to Roth IRAs (see Q 31:26). [I.R.C. § 408A(c)(5); Treas. Reg. §§ 1.408A-1, Q&A-2, 1.408A-6, Q&A-14]

Wherever the term "employee" is used in this chapter, it is intended to include not only a participant in a qualified retirement plan but also an IRA owner.

Q 11:3   What provisions must a plan contain in order to satisfy the RMD rules?

A qualified retirement plan must include the provisions reflecting the minimum distribution requirements. First, the plan must generally set forth the statutory rules, including the incidental death benefit requirement (see Q 11:4). Second, the plan must provide that distributions will be made in accordance with the final regulations. The plan document must also provide that these provisions override any distribution options in the plan inconsistent with the minimum distribution requirements. Finally, the plan must include any other provisions as may be prescribed in the future by IRS. [Treas. Reg. § 1.401(a)(9)-1, Q&A-3(a); Rev. Proc. 2003-10, 2003-1 C.B. 259; Rev. Proc. 2002-29, 2002-1 C.B. 1176]

The plan may also include written provisions regarding any optional provisions governing plan distributions that do not conflict with the minimum distribution requirements. [Treas. Reg. § 1.401(a)(9)-1, Q&A-3(b)]

Plan distributions commencing after an employee's death will be required to be made under the default provision for distributions unless the plan document contains optional provisions that override such default provisions (see Q 11:12). Thus, if distributions have not commenced to the employee at the time of death, distributions after death must be made automatically in accordance with the default provisions unless the plan either specifies the method under which distributions will be made or provides for elections by the employee (or beneficiary) and such elections are made by the employee or beneficiary. [Treas. Reg. § 1.401(a)(9)-1, Q&A-3(c)]

RMDs During Lifetime

Q 11:4   How must the employee's benefits be distributed during the employee's lifetime?

To satisfy the minimum distribution requirements, the entire interest of the employee (1) must be distributed to the employee not later than the required beginning date (RBD; see Q 11:5) or (2) must be distributed, in installments, beginning not later than the RBD. The installments must be paid over (1) the life of the employee, (2) the joint lives of the employee and the employee's designated beneficiary (see Q 11:14), or (3) a period not extending beyond the life expectancy (see Qs 11:22, 11:24) of the employee or the joint life expectancy of the employee and the employee's designated beneficiary. [I.R.C. § 401(a)(9)(A); Treas. Reg. § 1.401(a)(9)-2, Q&A-1(a)]

Lifetime distributions must also satisfy the incidental benefit requirements. The amount required to be distributed for each calendar year in order to satisfy the lifetime distribution rules generally depends on whether a distribution is in the form of distributions under a defined contribution plan (see Q 2:2) or annuity payments under a defined benefit plan (see Q 2:3). For the method of determining the RMD from an individual account under a defined contribution plan, see Qs 11:20 through 11:27, 11:36; for the method of determining the RMD in the case of annuity payments from a defined benefit plan or an annuity contract, see Qs 11:28 through 11:40. [I.R.C. § 401(a)(9)(G); Treas. Reg. § 1.401(a)(9)-2, Q&A-1(b), Q&A-1(c)]

Q 11:5   What is the required beginning date (RBD)?

Except with respect to a 5 percent owner, RBD means April 1 of the calendar year following the *later* of the (1) calendar year in which the employee attains age 70½ or (2) the calendar year in which the employee retires from employment with the employer maintaining the plan. In the case of an employee who is a 5 percent owner, RBD means April 1 of the calendar year following the calendar year in which the employee attains age 70½. A 5 percent owner is an employee who is a 5 percent owner with respect to the plan year ending in the calendar year in which the employee attains age 70½. A plan is permitted to provide that the RBD for *all* employees is April 1 of the calendar year following the calendar year in which the employee attained age 70½ regardless of whether the employee is a 5 percent owner. [I.R.C. § 401(a)(9)(C); Treas. Reg. § 1.401(a)(9)-2, Q&A-2; Priv. Ltr. Rul. 200524032]

A 5 percent owner means, if the employer is a corporation, any individual who owns (or is considered as owning) *more* than 5 percent of the outstanding stock of the corporation or stock possessing *more* than 5 percent of the total combined voting power of all stock of the corporation or, if the employer is not a corporation, any individual who owns (or is considered as owning) *more* than 5 percent of the capital or profits interest in the employer. Among the rules of attribution, an individual is considered as owning the stock owned, directly or indirectly, by or for the individual's spouse, children, grandchildren, and parents (see Q 26:26). Once an employee is a 5 percent owner, distributions must continue to the employee even if the employee ceases to be a 5 percent owner in a subsequent year. [I.R.C. §§ 318, 416(i); IRS Notice 97-75, 1997-2 C.B. 337; Priv. Ltr. Rul. 200524032]

RMDs for calendar year 2009 were suspended (see Q 11:1). [I.R.C. § 401(a)(9)(H) (as added by WRERA 2008 § 201(a); WRERA 2008 § 201(c)(1))] If an employee attained age 70½ in 2009, the employee was not required to take an RMD on or before April 1, 2010, because the distribution calendar year was 2009 (see Q 11:20). However, the suspension does not change the employee's RBD for purposes of determining the RMD for calendar years after 2009. Thus, for an employee whose RBD is April 1, 2010, the RMD for 2010 will be required to be made no later than the last day of calendar year 2010, because the distribution calendar year is 2010. If an employee attained age 70½ in 2008, the RMD had to be taken on or before April 1, 2009, because the distribution calendar year was 2008.

Example 1. Marjorie, the sole shareholder of M&S Corporation, participates in its profit sharing plan that has a calendar-year plan year. In 2009, when Marjorie was age 69½, she transferred all of her stock to her husband, Stanley. Even though Marjorie does not retire, her RBD is April 1, 2011 (the

April 1 following the calendar year in which she reaches age 70½), because Stanley's stock ownership is attributed to Marjorie and, hence, she is deemed to be a 5 percent owner.

Example 1A. The facts are the same as in Example 1, except that Marjorie attained age 69½ in 2008, and therefore attained age 70½ in 2009. Without the suspension, Marjorie's RBD would be April 1, 2010. With the suspension, no distribution was required for 2009 and, thus, no distribution was required to be made by April 1, 2010. However, the provision does not change Marjorie's RBD for purposes of determining the RMD for calendar years after 2009. Thus, Marjorie's RMD for 2010 will be required to be made no later than December 31, 2010.

According to IRS guidance, for a plan to determine which distributions made during 2009 were 2009 RMDs, the first distributions in 2009 were any RMDs from prior years that were not yet distributed, followed by 2009 RMDs. [IRS Notice 2009-82, Q&A-8, 2009-41 I.R.B.]

An employee attains age 70½ as of the date six calendar months after the employee's 70th birthday. For example, an employee whose date of birth is June 30, 1941 attains age 70½ on December 30, 2011, and an employee whose date of birth is August 31, 1941 attains age 70½ on February 29, 2012. [Treas. Reg. § 1.401(a)(9)-2, Q&A-3]

Example 2. Arnold, a 5 percent owner, was born on June 30, 1941, and his 70th birthday was June 30, 2011. Arnold becomes 70½ on December 30, 2011, and must begin to take RMDs by his RBD, April 1, 2012. Nina, who is also a 5 percent owner, was born on July 1, 1941, and she becomes age 70½ on January 1, 2012. Nina must begin to take RMDs by her RBD, April 1, 2013.

In the case of a non-5 percent owner who participates in a defined benefit plan (see Q 2:3) and who retires in a calendar year after the calendar year in which such employee attains age 70½, the employee's accrued benefit (see Q 9:2) will be actuarially increased to take into account the period after age 70½ in which the employee was not receiving any benefits under the plan. The actuarial adjustment rule does not apply to defined contribution plans (see Q 2:2). [I.R.C. § 401(a)(9)(C); IRS Notice 97-75, 1997-2 C.B. 337]

Example 3. Jerry, a 5 percent owner, and Linda, a non-5 percent owner, participate in the Ridge-Way Corporation defined benefit plan, and both attain age 70½ in 2010 but continue to work for Ridge-Way Corporation. Jerry must begin receiving distributions by April 1, 2011. However, Linda, a non-5 percent owner, need not commence receiving distributions until April 1 of the calendar year following the calendar year in which she retires. Linda's accrued benefit will be actuarially increased.

See Q 11:34 for details regarding the actuarial increase in the employee's accrued benefit.

A plan will not fail to satisfy the minimum distribution requirements merely because it provides for minimum distributions to commence no later than an employee's RBD of April 1 of the calendar year following the calendar year in which the employee attained age 70½, regardless of whether the employee is a 5 percent owner. [Treas. Reg. § 1.401(a)(9)-2, Q&A-2(e)]

Even if the plan provides for minimum distributions to commence no later than April 1 of the calendar year following the calendar year in which the employee attains age 70½, the employee's RBD for excise tax purposes (see Qs 11:67–11:71) and whether or not a distribution is an eligible rollover distribution are determined in accordance with the Code definition of RBD. [Priv. Ltr. Rul. 200123070] Thus, in the case of an employee who is not a 5 percent owner, no excise tax will apply prior to the calendar year in which the employee retires. However, beginning with that year, the amount that is required to be distributed each year to satisfy the minimum distribution requirements for purposes of the excise tax and rollover rules will be determined using the RBD under the plan. [IRS Notice 97-95, 1997-2 C.B. 337, Q&A-10]

IRS has ruled that an employee who was not a 5 percent owner, who received a distribution from a qualified retirement plan after he attained age 70½ but before retirement, and who rolled over the distribution to an IRA, could delay his first RMD from the IRA until the year following the year of the rollover. [Priv. Ltr. Rul. 200123070]

Example 4. Bill, a 72-year-old non-5 percent owner, is employed by SWJ Corporation and participates in its profit sharing plan. Bill receives a distribution from the plan in January 2010 and rolls it over to his IRA. Bill's first RMD from his IRA must be made on or before December 31, 2011.

IRS representatives have opined that an IRA owner may roll over funds from an IRA to a qualified retirement plan and delay RMDs until retirement if the IRA owner is a non-5 percent owner of the plan sponsor.

Example 5. Stephanie, a 68-year-old non-5 percent owner, is employed by SWJ Corporation and participates in its profit sharing plan. In 2010, Stephanie rolls over her IRA to the plan and continues to work for SWJ Corporation until July 13, 2017, her 75th birthday. Stephanie's first RMD from the plan, including her rollover account, must be made by April 1, 2018, her RBD with regard to her plan benefits. Had Stephanie not rolled over her IRA to the plan, her RBD with respect to her IRA would be April 1, 2014 (April 1 of the calendar year following the calendar year in which Stephanie attained age 70½; that is, January 13, 2013).

A strategy similar to the strategy utilized in Example 5 has been approved by IRS. A participant in a qualified retirement plan sponsored by a company of which the participant was a 5 percent owner rolled over his account balance to another plan in which he participated. The second plan was sponsored by a company in which the participant was a non–5 percent owner. IRS ruled that the participant could delay RMDs from the second plan until retirement. [Priv. Ltr. Ruls. 200453026, 200453015]

Q 11:6   Must distributions made before the RBD satisfy the minimum distribution requirements?

Lifetime distributions made *both* before the employee's RBD (see Q 11:5) and before the employee's first distribution calendar year (see Q 11:20) need *not* satisfy the minimum distribution requirements (see Q 11:4). However, if distributions commence under a particular distribution option, such as in the form of an annuity, before the employee's RBD for the employee's first distribution calendar year, the distribution option will fail to satisfy the minimum distribution requirements when distributions commence if, under the particular distribution option, distributions to be made for the employee's first distribution calendar year or any subsequent distribution calendar year will not satisfy the minimum distribution requirements (see Qs 11:20, 11:28–11:40). [Treas. Reg. § 1.401(a)(9)-2, Q&A-4]

Q 11:7   If distributions have begun before the employee's death, how must distributions be made after death?

If distribution of the employee's benefit has begun (see Q 11:8) and the employee dies before the entire benefit is distributed, the remaining portion of the employee's benefit must be distributed *at least as rapidly* as under the distribution method in effect as of the date of the employee's death. The amount required to be distributed for each distribution calendar year (see Q 11:20) following the calendar year of death generally depends on whether a distribution is in the form of distributions from an individual account under a defined contribution plan (see Q 2:2) or annuity payments under a defined benefit plan (see Q 2:3). For the method of determining the RMD from an individual account, see Q 11:23 for the calculation of the distribution period that applies when an employee dies after the RBD (see Q 11:5). In the case of annuity payments from a defined benefit plan or an annuity contract, see Qs 11:28–11:40. [I.R.C. §§ 401(a)(9)(A)(ii), 401(a)(9)(B)(i); Treas. Reg. § 1.401(a)(9)-2, Q&A-5]

Q 11:8   When are distributions considered to have begun?

Except in the case of annuity payments from a defined benefit plan (see Q 2:3) or an annuity contract (see Qs 11:28–11:40), distributions are not treated as having begun to the employee until the employee's RBD (see Q 11:5) even though payments have been made before that date. [Treas. Reg. § 1.401(a)(9)-2, Q&A-6(a)]

Example 1. Jack retires in 2010 at age 65½ and begins receiving installment distributions from a profit sharing plan over the joint life expectancy of Jack and his wife, Jill, age 50. Distributions will not be treated as having begun until April 1, 2016 (the April 1 following 2015, the calendar year in which Jack attains age 70½). Thus, if Jack dies before April 1, 2016 (his RBD), distributions to Jill must be made in accordance with the rules regarding distributions that begin after death and before the RBD (see Q 11:9). This is the case without regard to whether the plan has distributed the minimum distribution for the first distribution calendar year (see Q 11:20) before Jack's death.

Example 2. Assume the same facts as those in Example 1, except that Jack dies on July 1, 2016, without having received his RMD for 2016. If Jill elects to receive the entire remaining benefit in 2016, she may roll over the entire distribution into her own IRA, except the amount of the 2016 RMD (see Q 34:33). [Priv. Ltr. Rul. 9005071]

If a plan provides that the RBD for all employees is April 1 of the calendar year following the calendar year in which the employee attains age 70½ (see Q 11:5), an employee who dies after the RBD determined under the plan terms is treated as dying after the RBD even though the employee dies before the April 1 following the calendar year in which the employee retires. [Treas. Reg. § 1.401(a)(9)-2, Q&A-6(b)]

Example 3. Juan participates in a profit sharing plan under which the RBD for all employees is April 1 of the calendar year following the calendar year in which the employee attains age 70½. Juan continues to work after the RBD and dies, while still employed, at age 77. Juan is treated as dying after the RBD.

Death Before RBD

Q 11:9   If the employee dies before the RBD, how must the employee's benefit be distributed?

Except in the case of annuity payments from a defined benefit plan (see Q 2:3) or an annuity contract (see Qs 11:28–11:40), if an employee dies before the RBD and, thus, generally before distributions are treated as having begun (see Qs 11:5, 11:8), distributions must be made under one of two methods. The first method (the five-year rule) requires that the entire interest of the employee be distributed within five years of death regardless of to whom or to what entity the distribution is made (see Qs 11:10, 11:12). The second method (the life expectancy rule) requires that any portion of the employee's interest that is payable to a designated beneficiary (see Q 11:14) be distributed, commencing within one year of the employee's death, over the life of such beneficiary or over a period not extending beyond the life expectancy (see Q 11:24) of such beneficiary (see Qs 11:11, 11:12). Special rules apply if the designated beneficiary is the employee's surviving spouse (see Qs 11:11, 11:13, 11:45). [I.R.C. § 401(a)(9)(B)(ii), 401(a)(9)(B)(iii), 401(a)(9)(B)(iv); Treas. Reg. § 1.401(a)(9)-3, Q&A-1(a); Priv. Ltr. Ruls. 200837046, 200644022, 200433019, 200234074, 200211049, 200013041, 199908060]

A retired plan participant, who had not attained her RBD (see Q 11:5), requested a single-sum distribution from the plan and then died before receiving the check, which was made payable to an IRA in the decedent's name. Even though the IRA had not been established prior to her death, IRS allowed the executor to establish the IRA in the decedent's name and perform the rollover. However, IRS noted that the IRA into which the distribution would be rolled over would not have a designated beneficiary (see Q 11:14); and, thus, the distribution period with respect to the rollover IRA would be that applicable to an individual who died prior to having attained her RBD without having designated a beneficiary thereof (i.e., the five-year rule applied). [Priv. Ltr. Rul. 200453022]

Where an employee's child filed a missing person report with the appropriate authorities on November 10, 1997, and a court, on October 5, 1999, declared the employee dead as of November 10, 1997, the employee was deemed to have died on October 5, 1999, for purposes of the minimum distribution requirements. [Priv. Ltr. Rul. 200111055]

For distributions using the life expectancy rule, see Qs 11:14 through 11:19 in order to determine the designated beneficiary. See Qs 11:20 through 11:27 for the rules for determining RMDs under a defined contribution plan, and see Qs 11:28 through 11:35 for RMDs under defined benefit plans.

RMDs for calendar year 2009 were suspended (see Qs 11:1, 11:10, 11:11). [I.R.C. § 401(a)(9)(H) (as added by WRERA 2008 § 201(a); WRERA 2008 § 201(c)(1))]

Q 11:10 By when must the employee's entire interest be distributed in order to satisfy the five-year rule?

If an employee dies before the RBD and, thus, generally before distributions are treated as having begun (see Qs 11:5, 11:8), then, to satisfy the five-year rule, the employee's entire interest must be distributed no later than December 31 of the calendar year that contains the fifth anniversary of the date of the employee's death. For example, if the employee dies at any time during 2010 (whether January 1, December 31, or any other day during the year), the entire interest must be distributed by December 31, 2015. [I.R.C. § 401(a)(9)(B)(ii); Treas. Reg. § 1.401(a)(9)-3, Q&A-2; Priv. Ltr. Rul. 200644022]

RMDs for calendar year 2009 were suspended (see Qs 11:1, 11:9). If the five-year rule applies with respect to a decedent, the five-year period is determined without regard to calendar year 2009. Thus, the suspension affects the interests of employees who died between 2004 and 2009. [IRS Notice 2009-82, Q&A-2, 2009-41 I.R.B.]

> **Example 1.** Zeke died during 2005. Under the five-year rule, Zeke's entire interest must be distributed by December 31, 2010. However, because 2009 is excluded from the five-year rule under the suspension, the last date for distribution becomes December 31, 2011.

> **Example 2.** Zack died during 2009. Under the five-year rule, Zack's entire interest must be distributed by December 31, 2014. Because 2009 is excluded, the last distribution date becomes December 31, 2015, the same date as if Zack had died in 2010.

An IRA owner died after commencing to receive RMDs. The IRA owner designated his wife as the sole beneficiary (see Q 11:14) and did not name any contingent beneficiary. The IRA owner's wife died seven days later without (1) disclaiming the IRA (see Q 11:17); (2) taking any distributions from the IRA; (3)

electing to treat the IRA as her own (see Q 11:60); or (4) naming any beneficiary. As a result, the right to receive the IRA passed by the deceased wife's will to their two children. IRS ruled that, because the wife died before distributions to her had begun, the RMD rules apply as if she were the IRA owner (see Q 11:35); and, because she died before her RBD without having a designated beneficiary (see Q 11:15), the five-year rule applied. [Priv. Ltr. Rul. 200945011] This ruling appears to be incorrect because the IRA owner died after his RBD (see Q 11:7). Therefore, the IRA owner's wife is the designated beneficiary, and RMDs should be based upon her life expectancy (see Q 11:23).

IRS has ruled that where the decedent's brother was not notified that he was the beneficiary until almost four years after the decedent's death, the five-year rule applied and the life expectancy rule (see Q 11:11) was unavailable. [Priv. Ltr. Rul. 9812034] It is uncertain whether this ruling will continue to apply under the final regulations because the life expectancy rule may be required if there is a designated beneficiary (see Q 11:12).

Q 11:11   When are distributions required to commence in order to satisfy the life expectancy rule?

If an employee dies before the RBD and, thus, generally before distributions are treated as having begun (see Qs 11:5, 11:8), then, to satisfy the life expectancy rule, if the designated beneficiary (see Qs 11:14–11:19) is *not* the employee's surviving spouse (see Q 11:45), distributions must commence on or before December 31 of the calendar year immediately following the calendar year in which the employee died. This rule also applies if an individual is designated as a beneficiary in addition to the surviving spouse. See Q 11:43 if the employee's benefit is divided into separate accounts or segregated shares. [I.R.C. § 401(a)(9)(3)(iii); Treas. Reg. § 1.401(a)(9)-3, Q&A-3(a); Priv. Ltr. Ruls. 200837046, 200438044, 200433019, 200211049]

> **Example 1.** Dick, a participant in a qualified retirement plan, dies in 2011 at age 68, having designated his daughter, Jane, as beneficiary. To satisfy the life expectancy rule, distributions to Jane must commence on or before December 31, 2012.

RMDs for calendar year 2009 were suspended (see Qs 11:1, 11:9). In Example 1, if Dick died in 2009, distributions to Jane had to commence on or before December 31, 2010. The suspension for calendar year 2009 did not apply, because the distribution calendar year was 2010 (see Q 11:20). However, had Dick died in 2008, the first distribution to Jane could have been delayed until December 31, 2010, because the distribution calendar year was 2009. [IRS Notice 2009-82, Q&A- 2, 2009-41 I.R.B.] In this latter situation, Jane's age attained in 2010 would determine the applicable distribution period. See Q 11:23 for the determination of the applicable distribution period.

Where an employee's child filed a missing person report with the appropriate authorities on November 10, 1997 and a court, on October 5, 1999, declared the employee dead as of November 10, 1997, the employee was deemed to have died on October 5, 1999 for purposes of the minimum distribution requirements.

[Priv. Ltr. Rul. 200111055] Thus, assuming the employee died before the RBD and the child was the sole designated beneficiary, distributions to the child had to commence on or before December 31, 2000, not December 31, 1998, to satisfy the life expectancy rule.

If the sole designated beneficiary is the surviving spouse, distributions must commence on or before the *later* of (1) December 31 of the calendar year immediately following the calendar year in which the employee died or (2) December 31 of the calendar year in which the employee would have attained age 70½. [I.R.C. § 401(a)(9)(B)(iv); Treas. Reg. § 1.401(a)(9)-3, Q&A-3(b); Priv. Ltr. Ruls. 200936049, 200105058, 200008048]

> **Example 2.** Jill, a participant in a qualified retirement plan, dies in 2011 at age 64½ having designated her husband, Jack, age 72, as beneficiary. Since Jack is the surviving spouse, distributions can be deferred until December 31, 2017, the calendar year in which Jill would have attained age 70½. This is so even though Jack will be age 78 in 2017.

In Example 2, if Jill designated as beneficiary a trust created for Jack's benefit, the deferral would not be permissible if there are beneficiaries of the trust other than Jack. [Priv. Ltr. Rul. 9847022] This may be true even if Jack is the sole lifetime beneficiary of the trust because others will be remainder beneficiaries (see Qs 11:18, 11:25). [Rev. Rul. 2006-26, 2006-1 C.B. 939]

Q 11:12 How is it determined whether the five-year rule or the life expectancy rule applies to a distribution?

If a plan does not adopt an optional provision specifying the method of distribution after the death of an employee, distribution must be made as follows:

1. If the employee has a designated beneficiary (see Qs 11:14–11:19), distributions must be made in accordance with the life expectancy rule (see Q 11:11).

2. If the employee has no designated beneficiary, distributions must be made in accordance with the five-year rule (see Q 11:10).

[Treas. Reg. § 1.401(a)(9)-3, Q&A-4(a)]

> **Example 1.** Harry is a participant in two qualified retirement plans, Plan A and Plan B. Harry dies in 2011 at age 65, and his son, Larry, is the designated beneficiary under both plans. Larry must commence distributions over his life expectancy from both plans by December 31, 2012, because he is the designated beneficiary.

The plan may adopt a provision specifying either that the five-year rule will apply to certain distributions after the death of an employee even if the employee has a designated beneficiary or that distribution in every case will be made in accordance with the five-year rule. Further, a plan need not have the same method of distribution for the benefits of all employees. [Treas. Reg. § 1.401(a)(9)-3, Q&A-4(b)]

Example 2. The facts are the same as in Example 1, except that Plans A and B provide that the five-year rule applies in every case. Distributions from Plans A and B must be made to Larry by December 31, 2016.

A plan may adopt a provision that permits employees (or beneficiaries) to elect on an individual basis whether the five-year rule or the life expectancy rule applies to distributions after the death of an employee who has a designated beneficiary. Such an election must be made no later than the earlier of (1) the end of the calendar year in which distribution would be required to commence in order to satisfy the requirements for the life expectancy rule or (2) the end of the calendar year which contains the fifth anniversary of the date of death of the employee. As of the last date the election may be made, the election must be irrevocable with respect to the beneficiary (and all subsequent beneficiaries) and must apply to all subsequent calendar years. If a plan provides for the election, the plan may also specify the method of distribution that applies if neither the employee nor the beneficiary makes the election. If neither the employee nor the beneficiary elects a method and the plan does not specify which method applies, distribution must be made in accordance with the life expectancy rule if there is a designated beneficiary or in accordance with the five-year rule if there is no designated beneficiary. [Treas. Reg. § 1.401(a)(9)-3, Q&A-4(c)]

Example 3. The facts are the same as in Example 1, except that Plans A and B permit Larry to elect the applicable rule and specify that the five-year rule will apply if Larry fails to make an election. Larry elects the life expectancy rule for Plan A but fails to make an election for Plan B. Distributions to Larry over his life expectancy from Plan A will commence by December 31, 2012, and Harry's entire interest in Plan B must be distributed to Larry by December 31, 2016.

Where a decedent's brother was not notified that he was the designated beneficiary until almost four years after the decedent's death, the five-year rule applied and the life expectancy rule was unavailable. [Priv. Ltr. Rul. 9812034] It is uncertain whether this ruling will continue to apply under the final regulations because the life expectancy rule may be required if there is a designated beneficiary (see Q 11:12).

An IRA owner designated his daughter as beneficiary and died in 2005, prior to his RBD (see Q 11:5). After the IRA owner's death, the IRA was retitled as IRA owner, deceased, for benefit of daughter, beneficiary. Under the terms of the IRA, if the owner died before the RBD, a nonspouse beneficiary would receive RMDs under the life expectancy rule unless the beneficiary elected the five-year rule. The beneficiary did not elect the five-year rule, failed to take RMDs in 2006 and 2007, and took the RMDs for 2006, 2007, and 2008 in the aggregate in 2008. The beneficiary paid the 50 percent excise tax (see Q 11:67) for failure to timely receive the RMDs for 2006 and 2007. IRS ruled that (1) the RMDs for 2006, 2007, 2008, and all subsequent years may be based upon the beneficiary's life expectancy determined in 2006 (and then reduced by one each year thereafter); (2) the failure to take RMDs in 2006 and 2007 did not affect the calculation of RMDs in subsequent years; and (3) the failure to take RMDs in 2006 and 2007 resulted in the imposition of the excise tax for those years. [Priv. Ltr. Rul. 200811028]

Q 11:13 If the employee's surviving spouse is the sole designated beneficiary and dies after the employee, but before distributions have begun to the surviving spouse, how is the employee's interest to be distributed?

Generally, the surviving spouse (see Q 11:45) stands in the shoes of the employee and thus can designate beneficiaries. If the employee dies prior to the RBD (see Q 11:5) and the surviving spouse dies after the employee, but before distributions to the surviving spouse have begun, the five-year rule (see Q 11:10) and the life expectancy rule (see Q 11:11) are applied as if the surviving spouse were the employee. In applying this rule, the date of death of the surviving spouse is substituted for the date of death of the employee. However, in such case, the special deferral rule (see Q 11:11) is not available to the surviving spouse of the deceased employee's surviving spouse. This ensures that the RMDs will not be deferred again. Thus, if the original surviving spouse (surviving spouse 1) remarries and dies before RMDs were to begin, any new surviving spouse (surviving spouse 2) cannot be treated as a "surviving spouse" for purposes of these rules. These rules apply to the relationship between the employee and surviving spouse 1; it is the relationship to the employee, not the relationship to surviving spouse 1, that determines the treatment of any subsequent distribution. [Treas. Reg. § 1.401(a)(9)-3, Q&A-5; Ann. 95–99, 1995-48 I.R.B. 10]

> **Example.** The facts are the same as those in Example 2 in Q 11:11, except that Jack marries Jane in 2013 and dies in 2014, before RMDs were to begin. Jack is permitted to name his new wife, Jane, as his designated beneficiary, but distributions to Jane must begin by December 31, 2015.

Distributions are considered to have begun to the surviving spouse of an employee on the date, determined in accordance with the special deferral rule, on which distributions are required to commence to the surviving spouse, even though payments have actually been made before that date. See Qs 11:28–11:40 for a special rule for annuities. [Treas. Reg. § 1.401(a)(9)-3, Q&A-6] The rules discussed in this Q 11:13 apply even if distributions to the surviving spouse have begun but the surviving spouse dies before the entire interest has been distributed. [EGTRRA 2001 § 634(a)]

An IRA owner died after commencing to receive RMDs. The IRA owner designated his wife as the sole beneficiary (see Q 11:14) and did not name any contingent beneficiary. The IRA owner's wife died seven days later without (1) disclaiming the IRA (see Q 11:17); (2) taking any distributions from the IRA; (3) electing to treat the IRA as her own (see Q 11:60); or (4) naming any beneficiary. As a result, the right to receive the IRA passed by the deceased wife's will to their two children. IRS ruled that, because the wife died before distributions to her had begun, the RMD rules apply as if she were the IRA owner (see Q 11:35); and, because she died before her RBD without having a designated beneficiary (see Q 11:15), the five-year rule applied. [Priv. Ltr. Rul. 200945011] This ruling appears to be incorrect because the IRA owner died after his RBD (see Q 11:7). Therefore, the IRA owner's wife is the designated beneficiary, and RMDs should be based upon her life expectancy (see Q 11:23).

IRS representatives have opined that, if the surviving spouse waits until four years after the employee's death before taking a distribution of the death benefit, the surviving spouse can roll over (see Q 34:6) the benefit into an existing IRA in the deceased spouse's name and defer commencement of distributions until the deceased spouse would have attained age 70½. If the surviving spouse rolled over the benefit into an IRA in the name of the surviving spouse, not the deceased spouse, distributions could be deferred until the surviving spouse's RBD. The IRS representatives also opined that nonspouse beneficiaries could not roll over the deceased employee's death benefit to an IRA in the name of the deceased employee.

If a surviving spouse commences distribution of the deceased spouse's plan benefits or rolls the benefits over to an IRA in the deceased spouse's name and then commences distribution, the 10 percent early withdrawal tax does not apply. However, if the rollover is made to an IRA in the surviving spouse's name, this exception does not apply. See chapter 16 for details.

Determination of Designated Beneficiary

Q 11:14   Who is a designated beneficiary?

A designated beneficiary is an individual who is designated as a beneficiary under the plan. An individual may be designated as a beneficiary under the plan either by the terms of the plan or, if the plan provides, by an affirmative election by the employee (or the employee's surviving spouse; see Qs 11:11, 11:13, 11:45) specifying the beneficiary. A beneficiary designated as such under the plan is an individual who is entitled to a portion of an employee's benefit, contingent on the employee's death or another specified event. For example, if a distribution is in the form of a joint and survivor annuity over the lives of the employee and another individual, the plan does not satisfy the minimum distribution requirements unless such other individual is a designated beneficiary under the plan. A designated beneficiary need not be specified by name in the plan or by the employee to be a designated beneficiary as long as the individual who will be the beneficiary is identifiable under the plan. The members of a class of beneficiaries capable of expansion or contraction (e.g., the employee's children) will be treated as being identifiable if it is possible at the time of determination to identify the class member with the shortest life expectancy (see Qs 11:24, 11:25). The fact that an employee's interest under the plan passes to a certain individual under applicable state law (e.g., laws of intestacy) does not make that individual a designated beneficiary unless the individual is designated as a beneficiary under the plan. [I.R.C. § 401(a)(9)(E); Treas. Reg. § 1.401(a)(9)-4, Q&A-1] A surviving spouse elected to treat her deceased husband's IRA as her own (see Q 11:60), but she died before designating a beneficiary. IRS ruled that their daughter, who was the legal representative of her mother's estate, could not designate herself as beneficiary of that IRA. [Priv. Ltr. Rul. 200126036]

Under the will of an IRA owner, his estate was placed in trust for eight beneficiaries. On the IRA beneficiary form, the decedent's only description was the phrase "as stated in will." IRS ruled that the beneficiary designation was insufficient to identify the beneficiary; and, thus, no beneficiary of the trust qualified as a designated beneficiary. [Priv. Ltr. Ruls. 200849020, 200849019, 200846028]

An employee (or the employee's surviving spouse) need not make an affirmative election specifying a beneficiary for an individual to be a designated beneficiary because a designated beneficiary is an individual who is designated as a beneficiary under the plan whether or not that designation was made by the employee. The choice of beneficiary is subject to the rules relating to the survivor annuity requirements (see Q 10:1) and QDROs (see Q 36:1). [Treas. Reg. § 1.401(a)(9)-4, Q&A-2]

> **Example 1.** Abel, who is married, has children, and participates in a profit sharing plan, fails to designate a beneficiary and dies on January 1, 2011. However, under the terms of the plan, if a participant fails to designate a beneficiary, the participant's spouse is deemed to be the beneficiary or, if there is no spouse, the participant's children are deemed to be the beneficiaries. Even though Abel failed to designate a beneficiary, his spouse is identifiable based upon her relationship to Abel; and, if Abel was not married, his children are identifiable.

> **Example 2.** Cane, who is not married, has children, and participates in a profit sharing plan, fails to designate a beneficiary and dies on January 1, 2011. The plan contains no provision concerning a participant who fails to designate a beneficiary, and Cane's plan benefits pass to his children under the applicable state laws of intestacy. Cane's children are not designated beneficiaries because they are not designated as beneficiaries under the plan.

If an employee (or IRA owner) files a beneficiary designation form with the plan (or IRA custodian), the plan (or IRA custodian) should be asked to acknowledge receipt of the form and return an acknowledged copy to the employee (or IRA owner).

The beneficiary of an IRA was convicted in the murder of the IRA owner. Even though, pursuant to state law, the beneficiary was deemed to have predeceased the IRA owner, IRS ruled that the murderer was the designated beneficiary for RMD purposes, notwithstanding that the IRA was eventually paid to the deceased IRA owner's stepdaughter. [Priv. Ltr. Rul. 201008049]

Q 11:15   May a person other than an individual be a designated beneficiary?

No. Only individuals may be designated beneficiaries (see Q 11:14) for purposes of the minimum distribution requirements. A non-individual, such as the employee's estate or a charitable organization, may not be a designated beneficiary. If a person other than an individual is designated as a beneficiary, the employee will be treated as having no designated beneficiary, even if there are also individuals designated as beneficiaries. [I.R.C. § 401(a)(9)(E); Treas. Reg. § 1.401(a)(9)-4, Q&A-3; Priv. Ltr. Ruls. 201021038, 200742026, 200647030, 200646028] For special rules that apply to trusts, see Qs 11:18 and 11:19; and, for rules that apply to separate accounts or segregated shares, see Q 11:43.

> **Example.** Abel, who is a widower, has a child, and participates in a profit sharing plan, fails to designate a beneficiary and dies on January 1, 2011. Under the terms of the plan, if a participant fails to designate a beneficiary, the participant's estate is deemed to be the beneficiary. Abel is deemed to have no designated beneficiary.

In the above Example, assume that Abel has a will that leaves his entire estate to his only child and the legal representative of Abel's estate assigns the entire plan benefit to Abel's child prior to September 30, 2012 (the determination date; see Q 11:16). Abel's estate will still be deemed to be the beneficiary because Abel's child is not designated as a beneficiary *under the plan,* and the plan benefit passes to his child under applicable state law (see Q 11:14). [Priv. Ltr. Rul. 200742026]

An IRA owner died after commencing to receive RMDs. The IRA owner designated his wife as the sole beneficiary and did not name any contingent beneficiary. The IRA owner's wife died seven days later without (1) disclaiming the IRA (see Q 11:17); (2) taking any distributions from the IRA; (3) electing to treat the IRA as her own (see Q 11:60); or (4) naming any beneficiary. As a result, the right to receive the IRA passed by the deceased wife's will to their two children. IRS ruled that, because the wife died before distributions to her had begun, the RMD rules apply as if she were the IRA owner (see Q 11:35); and, because she died before her RBD (see Q 11:5) without having a designated beneficiary, the five-year rule applied (see Q 11:10). The deceased wife's personal representatives proposed to subdivide the IRA into two sub-IRAs, with each sub-IRA being titled "IRA owner (deceased) for the benefit of a specific beneficiary under the will of the wife (deceased)" and to accomplish the subdivision by trustee-to-trustee transfers. IRS ruled that neither the Code nor the RMD regulations precluded the posthumous division of an IRA into more than one IRA, and that the division did not constitute a transfer for purposes of the income in respect of a decedent rules (see Q 30:47), a taxable distribution (see Q 30:40), or a rollover (see Q 34:6). [Priv. Ltr. Rul. 200945011; IRC §§ 408(d)(1), 408(d)(3), 691(a)(2); Rev. Rul. 92-47, 1992-1 C.B. 198; Rev. Rul. 78-406, 1978-2 C.B. 157] This ruling appears to be incorrect because the IRA owner died after his RBD (see Q 11:7). Therefore, the IRA owner's wife is the designated beneficiary, and RMDs should be based upon her life expectancy (see Q 11:23).

An IRA owner, who died in 2002, designated a trust for his three children as beneficiary of his IRA. At the date of the IRA owner's death, the trust had no assets and was not entitled to receive any assets other than as beneficiary of the IRA. The trust required the trustee to:

1. Pay from the trust assets the expenses of the IRA owner's last illness, the funeral and burial expenses, the probate administration expenses, and estate taxes to the extent that the probate estate was insufficient to cover these items, and

2. Distribute the balance of the trust assets, if any, in equal shares to the owner's three children.

Prior to the determination date of September 30, 2003, the trustee withdrew funds from the IRA to pay estate administration expenses, trust administration expenses, and estate taxes. Additionally, as of September 30, 2003, the trustee withdrew from the IRA funds to cover the estimated income taxes attributable to the IRA withdrawals and funds, then given to the legal representative of the IRA owner's estate, to cover additional probate administration expenses (other than additional estate taxes). After September 30, 2003, only expenses related to the trust, not to the estate, would be paid from the IRA withdrawals; and, if additional estate taxes became due, payment would be made from the other estate assets, and not from the IRA unless all other estate assets were exhausted.

IRS ruled that the IRA owner's estate was not a beneficiary of the IRA, because all estate-related expenses were paid from IRA withdrawals made on or before September 30, 2003. Therefore, on September 30, 2003, the IRA owner's three children were the only trust beneficiaries, and RMDs could be made over the life expectancy of the oldest child (see Q 11:25). IRS also stated that the use of trust assets to pay future trust-related expenses or the possibility, in this particular situation, that trust assets may be required to pay additional estate taxes does not change the conclusion that only the children, and not the estate, were beneficiaries.

[Priv. Ltr. Ruls. 200432029, 200432028, 200432027; *see also* Priv. Ltr. Rul. 200433019]

In another ruling, a decedent designated a trust for the benefit of his grandchildren as beneficiary of his accounts in two qualified retirement plans. The trustee had discretion to use trust assets to pay funeral and burial expenses, estate taxes, and costs of administration. No assets passed under the decedent's will, so his probate estate was insolvent. The trustee filed a petition requesting court approval to pay only a portion of the estate administration expenses and estate taxes, and a bank creditor filed an objection asserting that all debts and expenses of the estate should be paid. Although a state statute exempted plan benefits from claims of creditors (see Q 4:28), the bank argued that the statute did not apply because the estate was insolvent and that the statute's protection ceased once the plan benefits were distributed. The bank's arguments were sustained by the court. Despite the court decision, IRS ruled that the creditors would not be treated as potential beneficiaries so that plan distributions could be made to the trust over the life expectancy of the oldest grandchild. No mention of the determination date was made in the ruling. [Priv. Ltr. Rul. 200440031]

Q 11:16   When is the designated beneficiary determined?

To be a designated beneficiary, an individual (see Q 11:15) must be a beneficiary as of the date of the employee's death. Consequently, a designated beneficiary cannot be added after the employee's death. [Priv. Ltr. Ruls. 200849020, 200849019, 200846028] Except with respect to a surviving spouse (see Q 11:45) as discussed below and except with respect to defined benefit plans (see Qs 11:28–11:40), the employee's designated beneficiary (see Q 11:14) will be determined based on the beneficiaries designated as of the date of death who remain beneficiaries as of September 30 of the calendar year following the calendar year of the employee's death. Consequently, except under defined benefit plans, any person which was a beneficiary as of the date of the employee's death, but is *not* a beneficiary as of that September 30 (e.g., because the person receives the entire benefit to which the person is entitled before that September 30), is not taken into account in determining the employee's designated beneficiary for purposes of determining the distribution period for RMDs after the employee's death. Accordingly, if a person disclaims entitlement to the employee's benefit, pursuant to a qualified disclaimer (see Q 11:17) by that September 30 thereby allowing other beneficiaries to receive the benefit in lieu of that person, the disclaiming person is not taken into account in determining the employee's designated beneficiary. [Treas. Reg. § 1.401(a)(9)-4, Q&A-4(a); Priv. Ltr. Rul. 200837046]

> **Example 1.** Ralph designates as beneficiaries both his daughter and a charitable organization and dies on April 15, 2011. Because Ralph designated a charitable organization as a beneficiary and a charitable organization is not an individual (see Q 11:15), he is treated as having no designated beneficiary. However, if the charitable organization receives its entire share of the benefit before September 30, 2012, and Ralph's daughter is the only remaining beneficiary on September 30, 2012, his daughter is treated as the sole designated beneficiary and may commence distributions over her life expectancy (see Q 11:24). [Priv. Ltr. Rul. 200740018]

As discussed in Q 11:13, if the employee's spouse is the sole designated beneficiary as of the September 30 of the calendar year following the calendar year of the employee's death and the surviving spouse dies after the employee, the surviving spouse will be treated as the employee. Thus, for example, the relevant designated beneficiary for determining the distribution period after the death of the surviving spouse is the designated beneficiary of the surviving spouse. Similarly, such designated beneficiary will be determined as of the date of the surviving spouse's death and who remain beneficiaries as of September 30 of the calendar year following the calendar year of the surviving spouse's death. [Treas. Reg. § 1.401(a)(9)-4, Q&A-4(b)]

> **Example 2.** Ralph designates as beneficiary his daughter, age 40, and his granddaughter, age 10, and dies on April 15, 2011. Both his daughter and granddaughter are designated beneficiaries. Since his daughter has the shorter life expectancy, she will be the designated beneficiary for purposes of determining the distribution period (see Q 11:25).

Example 3. The facts are the same as in Example 2, except that Ralph's daughter receives her entire share of the benefit before September 30, 2012, and his granddaughter is the only remaining beneficiary on September 30, 2012. Ralph's granddaughter is treated as the sole designated beneficiary and may commence distribution over her longer life expectancy.

An individual who is a beneficiary as of the date of the employee's death and dies prior to September 30 of the calendar year following the calendar year of the employee's death without disclaiming (see Q 11:17) continues to be treated as a beneficiary as of that September 30 in determining the employee's designated beneficiary for purposes of determining the distribution period for RMDs after the employee's death, without regard to the identity of any successor beneficiary who may be entitled to distributions as the beneficiary of the deceased beneficiary. The same rule applies in the case of distributions to an employee's surviving spouse so that, if an individual is designated as a beneficiary of the employee's surviving spouse as of the spouse's date of death and dies prior to September 30 of the year following the year of the surviving spouse's death, that individual will continue to be treated as a designated beneficiary of the surviving spouse. [Treas. Reg. § 1.401(a)(9)-4, Q&A-4(c); Priv. Ltr. Rul. 200438044]

Example 4. The facts are the same as in Example 2, except that Ralph designates his daughter as beneficiary if she survives him and designates his granddaughter as contingent beneficiary if his daughter predeceases him. Ralph's daughter survives him but dies on September 15, 2012, prior to September 30, 2012, the date of determination. Even though Ralph's daughter died prior to September 30, 2012, she is considered to be the designated beneficiary for purposes of determining the distribution period for RMDs after Ralph's death.

If one of the beneficiaries is not an individual and such beneficiary does not receive its entire share of the benefit before the date on which the designated beneficiary is to be determined, the employee will be treated as having no designated beneficiary.

Example 5. The facts are the same as in Example 1, except that the charitable organization does not receive its entire share of the benefit before September 30, 2012. Because Ralph is treated as having no designated beneficiary, if death occurred after the RBD (see Qs 11:5, 11:8), the distribution period is limited to Ralph's remaining life expectancy (see Q 11:23). If death occurred before the RBD, the five-year rule applies.

An individual designated a trust as the beneficiary of his IRA (see Q 11:18). Under the terms of the trust, the surviving spouse receives all of the trust income each year; the trustees may distribute trust principal to any one or more of the deceased individual's surviving spouse, children, and grandchildren; and, upon the death of the surviving spouse, 90 percent of the trust assets will be allocated to trusts for the children with the remaining 10 percent to be distributed to one or more charitable organizations. Pursuant to a court order, the trust assets were divided on a pro rata basis between two separate and independent trusts, one with 10 percent of the assets that will all be distributed to charitable organizations upon the surviving spouse's death, and the other with 90 percent of the assets that will remain in trust for the benefit of the children after the surviving spouse's death. IRS ruled that IRA distributions could be made to the 90 percent trust over the surviving spouse's lifetime without regard to the charitable organizations. IRS further ruled that the separate account rule applied (see Q 11:43). [Priv. Ltr. Rul. 200218039] This result cannot be achieved under the final regulations because the separate account rule is not available to beneficiaries of a trust with respect to a trust's interest in an IRA. [Treas. Reg. § 1.401(a)(9)-4,Q&A-5(a)]

Q 11:17 Who is the designated beneficiary if a disclaimer is executed?

If a person makes a qualified disclaimer with respect to any interest in property, the estate, gift, and generation-skipping transfer tax rules apply with respect to such interest as if the interest had never been transferred to such person. [I.R.C. § 2518(a)] The term "qualified disclaimer" means an irrevocable and unqualified refusal by a person to accept an interest in property, but only if:

1. Such refusal is in writing;
2. Such writing is received by the transferor of the interest, the transferor's legal representative, or the holder of the legal title to the property to which the interest related not later than the date which is nine months after the later of (a) the date on which the transfer creating the interest in such person is made or (b) the date on which such person attains age 21;
3. Such person has not accepted the interest or any of its benefits; and
4. As a result of such refusal, the interest passes without any direction on the part of the person making the disclaimer and passes either (a) to the spouse of the decedent or (b) to a person other than the person making the disclaimer. [I.R.C. § 2518(b)]

If an individual dies and a qualified disclaimer is executed by the primary designated beneficiary (see Q 11:16), the designated beneficiary will be the secondary or contingent beneficiary (or, possibly, more remote contingent beneficiaries) for purposes of calculating the distribution period for distributions beginning after death. [Treas. Reg. § 1.401(a)(9)-4, Q&A-4(a); Priv. Ltr. Ruls. 200837046, 200532060, 200521033, 200453023, 200444034, 200444033, 200234074, 200208033]

> **Example 1.** Adam, age 68, designates his wife Eve, age 65, as beneficiary of his plan benefit. Adam also provides that, if Eve does not survive him, his son Abel, age 32, will be the beneficiary. Adam dies on January 15, 2011, and Eve, who survived him, executed a qualified disclaimer on or before October 15, 2011. Because of the qualified disclaimer, Abel becomes the designated beneficiary and distributions to Abel may commence on or before December 31, 2012, and be made to Abel over his life expectancy.

In Example 1, if Eve died before executing the qualified disclaimer, it was unclear whether her legal representative could do so on her behalf for purposes of the RMD rules. However, for other purposes at least, a legal representative can make a qualified disclaimer on behalf of a decedent. [Treas. Reg. § 25.2518-1(b)] IRS has now ruled that the disclaimer of a surviving spouse's interest in her deceased husband's IRA, made by the surviving spouse's daughter in her capacity as personal representative of her mother's estate, was a qualified disclaimer. [Priv. Ltr. Rul. 200616041] For a discussion of who may be the designated beneficiary if Eve did not disclaim but died prior to September 30, 2010, see Q 11:16. The beneficiary of an IRA was convicted in the murder of the IRA owner. Even though, pursuant to state law, the beneficiary was deemed to have predeceased the IRA owner, IRS ruled that the murderer was the designated beneficiary for RMD purposes, notwithstanding that the IRA was eventually paid to the deceased IRA owner's stepdaughter. [Priv. Ltr. Rul. 201008049] Apparently, if the murderer made a qualified disclaimer, the stepdaughter would have become the designated beneficiary for RMD purposes.

> **Example 2.** Alex, age 72 and a non-5 percent owner (see Q 11:5), designated his wife Alexandra, age 65, as beneficiary of his plan benefit. Alex also provided that, if Alexandra did not survive him, his daughter Alexis, age 32, would be the beneficiary. Alex died on December 15, 2006, and Alexandra, who survived him, executed a qualified disclaimer on or before September 15, 2007. Because of the qualified disclaimer, Alexis became the designated beneficiary, and distributions to Alexis could commence on or before December 31, 2007, and be made to her over her life expectancy.

> **Example 3.** The facts are the same as in Example 2, but Alex was a 5 percent owner and did not take his 2006 RMD, which RMD had to be paid on or before December 31, 2006 (see Q 11:22). If the 2006 RMD was paid to Alexandra, it appeared that she could not make a qualified disclaimer because she would have accepted a portion of the plan benefit.

The author noted that, to avoid the result in Example 3, Alexandra could have made a qualified disclaimer by December 31, 2006, so that the 2006 RMD could be timely made to Alexis. Alternatively, the 2006 RMD could be made to Alexis after December 31, 2006, and after Alexandra made a qualified disclaimer. However, Alexis would be subject to the excise tax for failure to take the 2006 RMD timely, but IRS could waive the excise tax (see Qs 11:67, 11:71). IRS took note of this dilemma and ruled that Alexandra could make a qualified disclaimer even though she had taken the 2006 RMD. [Rev. Rul. 2005-36, 2005-1 C.B. 1368; Treas. Reg. §§ 25.2518-3(c), 25.2518-3(d), Examples 17 and 19] Under the facts of the ruling, the decedent died in 2004. At the time of his death, the decedent had an IRA with a fair market value of $2,000, and he had passed his RBD (see Q 11:5) and was receiving RMDs; however, at the time of death, the decedent had not received the 2004 RMD. In the ruling, IRS described three situations, which have been modified to incorporate Example 3 above.

Situation 1: Under the terms of the IRA beneficiary designation, Alexandra is designated as the sole beneficiary of the IRA after Alex's death. Alexis, the child of Alex and Alexandra, is designated as the beneficiary in the event Alexandra predeceases Alex. Three months after Alex's death, the IRA custodian pays

Alexandra $100, the RMD for 2007. No other amounts have been paid from the IRA since Alex's date of death.

Seven months after Alex's death, Alexandra executes a written instrument pursuant to which she disclaims the pecuniary amount of $600 of the IRA account balance plus the income attributable to the $600 amount earned after the date of death. The income earned by the IRA between the date of Alex's death and the date of Alexandra's disclaimer is $40. The disclaimer is valid and effective under applicable state law. Under applicable state law, as a result of the disclaimer, Alexandra is treated as predeceasing Alex with respect to the disclaimed property. As soon as the disclaimer is made, in accordance with the IRA beneficiary designation, Alexis, as successor beneficiary, is paid the $600 amount disclaimed plus that portion of IRA income earned between the date of death and the date of the disclaimer attributable to the $600 amount ($12 [$600 ÷ $2,000 × $40]).

Situation 2: The facts are the same as in Situation 1, except that, instead of disclaiming a pecuniary amount, Alexandra validly disclaims, in the written instrument, 30 percent of her entire interest in the principal and income of the balance of the IRA account remaining after the $100 RMD for 2007 and after reduction for the pre-disclaimer income attributable to the $100 RMD ($2 [$100 ÷ $2,000 × $40]). As soon as the disclaimer is made, in accordance with the beneficiary designation, Alexis is paid 30 percent of the excess of the remaining account balance over $2.

Situation 3: The facts are the same as in Situation 1, except that Alexis is designated as the sole beneficiary of the IRA after Alex's death, Alexandra is designated as the beneficiary in the event Alexis predeceases Alex, and the $100 RMD for 2007 is paid to Alexis three months after Alex's death. Seven months after Alex's death, Alexis disclaims the entire remaining balance of the IRA account except for $2, the income attributable to the $100 RMD paid to Alexis. As soon as the disclaimer is made, in accordance with the IRA beneficiary designation, the balance of the IRA account, less $2, is distributed to Alexandra as successor beneficiary. Alexis receives a total of $102.

In Situations 1, 2, and 3, the beneficiary's receipt of the $100 distribution from the IRA constitutes an acceptance of $100 of corpus, plus the income attributable to that amount. The amount of income attributable to the $100 distribution that the beneficiary is deemed to have accepted, and therefore cannot disclaim, is $2, computed as follows:

$$\frac{\$100 \text{ (distribution)}}{\$2,000 \text{ (date of death value of IRA)}} \times \$40 \text{ (IRA income from date of death to}$$
$$\text{date of disclaimer)}$$

However, the beneficiary's acceptance of these amounts does not preclude the beneficiary from making a qualified disclaimer with respect to all or a portion of the balance of the IRA.

Accordingly, in Situation 1, Alexandra's disclaimer constitutes a qualified disclaimer of the $600 pecuniary amount, plus $12 (the IRA income attributable to the disclaimed amount [$600 ÷ $2,000 × $40])

In Situation 2, Alexandra disclaims an undivided portion (30 percent) of her principal and income interest in the remaining IRA account balance, rather than a pecuniary amount as in Situation 1. However, as in Situation 1, Alexandra's receipt of the $100 distribution also constitutes acceptance of $2 of income deemed attributable to the amount distributed. Alexandra may not disclaim any portion of the $2. Therefore, in Situation 2, Alexandra's disclaimer of 30 percent of her entire interest in the principal and income of the balance of the IRA account remaining after the $100 RMD for 2007 and after reduction for the pre-disclaimer income attributable to that amount ($2) constitutes a qualified disclaimer to the extent of 30 percent of the remaining IRA account balance after reduction for the $2 of income Alexandra is deemed to have accepted (that is, .30 [value of remaining account balance on date of disclaimer − $2])

The results in Situations 1 and 2 would be the same if the amount disclaimed, plus that portion of the post-death IRA income attributable to the disclaimed amount, is not distributed outright to Alexis, but instead is segregated and maintained in a separate IRA account of which she is the beneficiary. Separate accounts for Alexis and Alexandra may be made effective as of the date of Alex's death in 2007, and the 2007 RMD does not have to be allocated among the beneficiaries of the separate accounts for purposes of the separate account rules (see Q 11:43).

In Situation 3, Alexis disclaims her entire principal and income interest in the remaining IRA account balance after the payment of the RMD for 2007, except for $2. As in Situations 1 and 2, Alexis's receipt of the $100 RMD also constitutes an acceptance of the $2 of income that is deemed attributable to the RMD that is distributed. Alexis may not disclaim any portion of the $2. Therefore, in Situation 3, Alexis's disclaimer of the entire principal and income balance of the IRA remaining after the payment of the RMD for 2007, except for $2 (that is, 100% of value of the remaining account balance on the date of the disclaimer, less $2) constitutes a qualified disclaimer.

In addition, any person who was a beneficiary of the employee's benefit as of the date of the employee's death, but is not a beneficiary as of September 30 of the calendar year following the calendar year of the employee's death, is not considered a designated beneficiary. In Situation 3, Alexis both received the RMD and timely disclaimed entitlement of the entire balance of the IRA account on or before September 30, 2008. Accordingly, if Alexis is paid the $2 of income attributable to the RMD amount on or before September 30, 2008, she will be treated as not entitled to any further benefit as of September 30, 2008 and, therefore, will not be considered a designated beneficiary of the IRA.

In conclusion, IRS ruled that a beneficiary's disclaimer of a beneficial interest in a decedent's IRA is a qualified disclaimer (if all of the requirements are met), even though, prior to making the disclaimer, the beneficiary receives the RMD for the year of the decedent's death from the IRA. The beneficiary may make a qualified disclaimer with respect to all or a portion of the balance of the account, other than the income attributable to the RMD that the beneficiary received, provided that, at the time the disclaimer is made, the disclaimed amount and the income attributable to the disclaimed amount are paid to the beneficiary entitled to receive the disclaimed amount or are segregated in a separate account. Further, a person disclaiming the entire remaining interest in an IRA will not be considered a designated beneficiary of the IRA if the qualified disclaimer is made on or before September 30 of the calendar year following the calendar year of the employee's death and if, on or before that September 30, the disclaimant is paid the income attributable to the RMD, so that the disclaimant is not entitled to any further benefit in the IRA after September 30 of the calendar year following the calendar year of the employee's death.

An individual designated his wife as beneficiary of his IRA and also executed a will that provided that his estate would be added to a separate trust agreement that he had previously established. After the individual died, his wife disclaimed a portion of the IRA and the disclaimed portion became payable to his estate. Even though the entire estate would be added to the separate trust agreement, IRS ruled that the estate, and not the trust beneficiaries (see Q 11:19), was the beneficiary and, as a non-individual (see Q 11:15), could not be a designated beneficiary. Because the individual died before his RBD, the five-year rule applied (see Qs 11:10, 11:11). [Priv. Ltr. Rul. 200327059; *see also* Priv. Ltr. Ruls. 200850058 and 200843042]

Q 11:18   Can the beneficiary of a trust be a designated beneficiary?

Only an individual may be a designated beneficiary (see Q 11:14) for purposes of determining the distribution period for RMDs (see Qs 11:22, 11:23). Consequently, a trust cannot be a designated beneficiary, even though the trust is named as a beneficiary. However, if the requirements set forth below are satisfied, the beneficiaries of the trust will be treated as designated beneficiaries of the employee for purposes of determining the distribution period. These requirements are satisfied if, during any period during which RMDs are being determined by treating the beneficiaries of the trust as designated beneficiaries of the employee, the following requirements are met:

1. The trust is a valid trust under state law or would be but for the fact that there is no corpus.

2. The trust is irrevocable or will, by its terms, become irrevocable upon the death of the employee.

3. The beneficiaries of the trust who are beneficiaries with respect to the trust's interest in the employee's benefit are identifiable from the trust instrument (see Q 11:19).

4. Certain documentation (see Q 11:19) has been provided to the plan administrator (see Q 20:1).

[Treas. Reg. § 1.401(a)(9)-4, Q&A-5(a), Q&A-5b); Priv. Ltr. Ruls. 201038019, 200843042, 200809042, 200750019, 200740018, 200708084, 200634070, 200620026, 200610027, 200610026, 200608032]

In the case of payments to a trust having more than one beneficiary, see Q 11:25 for the rules for determining the designated beneficiary whose life expectancy will be used to determine the distribution period and the treatment of trust remainder beneficiaries, and see Q 11:15 for the rules that apply if a non-individual is designated as a beneficiary. Where a trust was the beneficiary of a decedent's IRA and there was no designated beneficiary at the time of the decedent's death (see Q 11:16), IRS did not allow a state court reformation of the trust to create a designated beneficiary. [Priv. Ltr. Rul. 201021038] If the beneficiary of the trust named as beneficiary is another trust, the beneficiaries of the other trust will be treated as having been designated as beneficiaries of the first trust and, thus, having been designated by the employee under the plan for purposes of determining the distribution period, provided that the above requirements are satisfied with respect to such other trust in addition to the trust named as beneficiary. [Treas. Reg. § 1.401(a)(9)-4, Q&A-5(c), Q&A-5(d)]

Under the will of an IRA owner, his estate was placed in trust for eight beneficiaries. On the IRA beneficiary form, the decedent's only description was the phrase "as stated in will." IRS ruled that the beneficiary designation was insufficient to identify the beneficiary; and, thus, no beneficiary of the trust qualified as a designated beneficiary. [Priv. Ltr. Ruls. 200849020, 200849019, 200846028]

IRS ruled that a trust which is designated as the beneficiary of a Roth IRA (see Q 31:1) that holds amounts transferred from a traditional IRA in violation of the income limitation rule (see Q 31:44) may be treated as the beneficiary of the traditional IRA into which the Roth IRA will be transferred to effectuate a recharacterization (see Q 31:9). [Priv. Ltr. Rul. 200234074]

IRS advised that a revocable trust will not fail to be a trust for purposes of the minimum distribution rules merely because the trust elects to be treated as an estate under Section 645, as long as the trust continues to be a trust under state law. [Preamble to 2002 final regulations]

Q 11:19　If a trust is named as beneficiary, what documentation must be provided to the plan administrator?

If an employee designates a trust as the beneficiary of the entire benefit and the employee's spouse is the sole beneficiary of the trust, then, to satisfy the documentation requirement for RMDs commencing *before* the death of an employee so that the spouse can be treated as the sole designated beneficiary (see Q 11:14) of the employee's benefits, the employee must comply with either of the following:

1. The employee provides to the plan administrator (see Q 20:1) a copy of the trust instrument and agrees that, if the trust instrument is amended at any time in the future, the employee will, within a reasonable time, provide to the plan administrator a copy of each such amendment, or
2. The employee—
   a. Provides to the plan administrator a list of all of the beneficiaries of the trust (including contingent and remainder beneficiaries (see Q 11:25) with a description of the conditions on their entitlement);
   b. Certifies that, to the best of the employee's knowledge, this list is correct and complete and that the trust requirements (see Q 11:18) are satisfied;

    c. Agrees that, if the trust instrument is amended at any time in the future, the employee will, within a reasonable time, provide to the plan administrator corrected certifications to the extent that the amendment changes any information previously certified; and

    d. Agrees to provide a copy of the trust instrument to the plan administrator upon demand.

[Treas. Reg. § 1.401(a)(9)-4, Q&A-6(a)]

There is no specified date by which the employee must comply with the foregoing documentation requirements. However, for lifetime distributions to the employee, if the sole beneficiary of the trust is the employee's spouse (see Q 11:25, Example 4) and the spouse is more than ten years younger than the employee (see Q 11:22), then, to use the joint life expectancy of the employee and the employee's spouse, the documentation requirements should be complied with by the later of the RBD (see Q 11:5) or the date the trust is named as beneficiary. [Treas. Reg. § 1.401(a)(9)-4, Q&A-5(a), Q&A-5(b)]

To satisfy the documentation requirement for RMDs *after* the death of the employee (or the death of the employee's spouse, if applicable; see Q 11:13), by October 31 of the calendar year immediately following the calendar year in which the employee died, the trustee of the trust must either:

1. Provide the plan administrator with a final list of all beneficiaries of the trust (including contingent and remainder beneficiaries, with a description of the conditions on their entitlement) as of the September 30 of the calendar year following the calendar year of the employee's death; certify that, to the best of the trustee's knowledge, this list is correct and complete and that the trust requirements are satisfied; and agree to provide a copy of the trust instrument to the plan administrator upon demand, or

2. Provide the plan administrator with a copy of the actual trust document for the trust that is named as a beneficiary of the employee under the plan as of the employee's date of death.

[Treas. Reg. § 1.401(a)(9)-4, Q&A-6(b)]

If RMDs are determined based on the information provided to the plan administrator in certifications or trust instruments, a plan will not fail to satisfy the minimum distribution requirements merely because the actual terms of the trust instrument are inconsistent with the information in those certifications or trust instruments previously provided to the plan administrator, but only if the plan administrator reasonably relied on the information provided and the RMDs for calendar years after the calendar year in which the discrepancy is discovered are determined based on the actual terms of the trust instrument. For purposes of determining the amount of the excise tax (see Qs 11:67-11:71), the RMD is determined for any year based on the actual terms of the trust in effect during the year. [Treas. Reg. § 1.401(a)(9)-4, Q&A-6(c)]

RMDs from Defined Contribution Plans

Q 11:20 If an employee has an individual account in a defined contribution plan, what is the RMD for each calendar year?

If an employee's accrued benefit (see Q 9:2) is in the form of an individual account under a defined contribution plan (see Q 2:2), the minimum amount required to be distributed for each distribution calendar year is equal to the quotient obtained by dividing the account (see Q 11:21) by the applicable distribution period (see Q 11:22). However, the RMD will never exceed the entire account balance on the date of the distribution (see Q 11:26). Further, the *minimum* distribution required to be distributed on or before an employee's RBD (see Q 11:5) is always determined as if the account will be distributed over (1) the life of the employee or the joint lives of the employee and a designated beneficiary (see Q 11:14) or (2) a period not extending beyond the life expectancy of the employee or the joint life expectancy of the employee and a designated beneficiary, whether or not there is in fact a designated beneficiary. [I.R.C. § 401(a)(9)(A)(ii); Treas. Reg. § 1.401(a)(9)-5, Q&A-1(a); Priv. Ltr. Rul. 200951039]

A calendar year for which a minimum distribution is required is a distribution calendar year. If an employee's RBD is April 1 of the calendar year following the calendar year in which the employee attains age 70½, the employee's first distribution calendar year is the year the employee attains age 70½. If an employee's RBD is April 1 of the calendar year following the calendar year in which the employee retires, the employee's first distribution calendar year is the calendar year in which the employee retires. In the case of distributions to be made in accordance with the life expectancy rule, the first distribution calendar year is the calendar year containing the date described in Q 11:11, and the determination of that date depends upon whether or not the surviving spouse is the sole designated beneficiary. [Treas. Reg. § 1.401(a)(9)-5, Q&A-1(b)]

The distribution required to be made on or before the employee's RBD is treated as the distribution required for the employee's first distribution calendar year. The RMD for other distribution calendar years, including the RMD for the distribution calendar year in which the employee's RBD occurs, must be made on or before the end of that distribution calendar year. Thus, if the employee attains age 70½ in 2010 and defers the initial distribution until 2011, two RMDs must occur in 2011. The RMD for 2010 must occur by April 1, 2011, and the RMD for 2011 must occur by December 31, 2011. Taking two RMDs in a single calendar year could place the employee in a higher income tax bracket. [Treas. Reg. § 1.401(a)(9)-5, Q&A-1(c)]

Example 1. Shirley attains age 70½ on December 30, 2010, and has an RBD of April 1, 2011. Shirley's RMD to be made on or before April 1, 2011, is $20,000, and she is paid that amount on June 21, 2010. Even though Shirley is only age 69 on June 21, 2010, the distribution is an RMD.

Example 2. The facts are the same as in Example 1, except that Shirley defers her first RMD to April 1, 2011. Shirley's second RMD must be made on or before December 31, 2011, so that Shirley will have two RMDs in 2011.

RMDs for calendar year 2009 were suspended (see Q 11:1). [I.R.C. § 401(a)(9)(H) (as added by WRERA 2008 § 201(a); WRERA 2008 § 201(c)(1))] If an employee attained age 70½ in 2009, the employee was not required to take an RMD on or before April 1, 2010, because the distribution calendar year was 2009. However, the suspension does not change the employee's RBD for purposes of determining the RMD for calendar years after 2009. Thus, for an employee whose RBD is April 1, 2010, the RMD for 2010 will be required to be made no later than the last day of calendar year 2010, because the distribution calendar year is 2010. If an employee attained age 70½ in 2008, the RMD had to be taken on or before April 1, 2009, because the distribution calendar year was 2008. According to IRS guidance, for a plan to determine which distributions made during 2009 were 2009 RMDs, the first distributions in 2009 were any RMDs from prior years that were not yet distributed, followed by 2009 RMDs. [IRS Notice 2009-82, Q&A-8, 2009-41 I.R.B.]

If distributions are made in accordance with the above rules, the minimum distribution incidental benefit (MDIB) requirement will be satisfied. Further, with respect to the retirement benefits provided by that account balance, to the extent the incidental benefit requirement requires a distribution, that requirement is deemed to be satisfied if distributions satisfy the MDIB requirement. [I.R.C. § 401(a)(9)(G); Treas. Reg. §§ 1.401-1(b)(1)(i), 1.401(a)(9)-5, Q&A-1(d)]

Instead of satisfying the above rules, the RMD requirement may be satisfied by the purchase of an annuity contract from an insurance company (see Q 11:31) with the employee's entire individual account. If such an annuity is purchased after distributions are required to commence, payments under the annuity contract purchased will satisfy the RMD rules for distribution calendar years after the calendar year of the purchase if payments under the annuity contract are made in accordance with the rules applicable to defined benefit plans (see Qs 11:28–11:40). In such a case, payments under the annuity contract will be treated as distributions from the individual account for purposes of determining if the individual account satisfies the RMD rules for the calendar year of the purchase. An employee may also purchase an annuity contract for a portion of the employee's account (see Q 11:43). [Treas. Reg. § 1.401(a)(9)-5, Q&A-1(e)]

The amount distributed in satisfaction of the minimum distribution requirement is determined annually. No credit is given for amounts distributed in previous years that exceeded the required amount (see Q 11:21). [Treas. Reg. § 1.401(a)(9)-5, Q&A-2]

Q 11:21   What is the amount used for determining the employee's RMD in the case of an individual account?

In the case of an individual account, the benefit used in determining the RMD for a distribution calendar year (see Q 11:20) is the account balance as of the last valuation date in the calendar year immediately preceding that distribution calendar year (valuation calendar year), as adjusted. The account balance is *increased* by the amount of any contributions or forfeitures allocated to the account balance as of dates in the valuation calendar year after the valuation date. For this purpose, contributions that are allocated to the account balance as of dates in the valuation calendar year after the valuation date, but that are not actually made during the valuation calendar year, are permitted to be excluded. The account balance is *decreased* by distributions made in the valuation calendar year after the valuation date. [Treas. Reg. § 1.401(a)(9)-5, Q&A-3(a), Q&A-3(b), Q&A-3(c); Priv. Ltr. Rul. 200951039]

If an amount is distributed by one plan and rolled over to another plan (receiving plan), additional rules are provided for determining the benefit and RMD under the receiving plan. If an amount is transferred from one plan (transferor plan) to another plan (transferee plan), additional rules are also provided for determining the amount of the RMD and the benefit under both the transferor and transferee plans. See Q 11:41 for details.

Q 11:22 What is the applicable distribution period for RMDs during an employee's lifetime?

Except where the employee's spouse (see Q 11:45) is the sole designated beneficiary (see Q 11:14), the applicable distribution period for RMDs for distribution calendar years (see Q 11:20) *up to and including* the distribution calendar year that includes the employee's date of death is determined using the Uniform Lifetime Table set forth below for the employee's age as of the employee's birthday in the relevant distribution calendar year. [Treas. Reg. § 1.401(a)(9)-5, Q&A-4(a)]

Uniform Lifetime Table

Age of Employee	Distribution Period	Age of Employee	Distribution Period
70	27.4	82	17.1
71	26.5	83	16.3
72	25.6	84	15.5
73	24.7	85	14.8
74	23.8	86	14.1
75	22.9	87	13.4
76	22.0	88	12.7
77	21.2	89	12.0
78	20.3	90	11.4
79	19.5	91	10.8
80	18.7	92	10.2
81	17.9	93	9.6

Uniform Lifetime Table (*cont'd*)

Age of Employee	Distribution Period	Age of Employee	Distribution Period
94	9.1	105	4.5
95	8.6	106	4.2
96	8.1	107	3.9
97	7.6	108	3.7
98	7.1	109	3.4
99	6.7	110	3.1
100	6.3	111	2.9
101	5.9	112	2.6
102	5.5	113	2.4
103	5.2	114	2.1
104	4.9	115 and older	1.9

[Treas. Reg. § 1.401(a)(9)-9, Q&A-2]

IRS may change the Uniform Lifetime Table. [Treas. Reg. § 1.401(a)(9)-9, Q&A-4]

If an employee dies on or after the RBD (see Q 11:5), the distribution period applicable for calculating the amount that must be distributed during the distribution calendar year that includes the employee's death is determined as if the employee had lived throughout that year. Thus, an RMD, determined as if the employee had lived throughout that year, is required for the year of the employee's death, and that amount must be distributed to a beneficiary to the extent it has not already been distributed to the employee. [Treas. Reg. § 1.401(a)(9)-5, Q&A-4(a)] The RMD for the year of the employee's death will be paid to the employee's estate *only* if the estate has been designated as the beneficiary or if the estate is the default beneficiary.

If the sole designated beneficiary of an employee is the employee's spouse, the applicable distribution period for RMDs during the employee's lifetime is the *longer* of the distribution period determined in accordance with the Uniform Lifetime Table or the joint life expectancy of the employee and the spouse (see Q 11:24) using the employee's and the spouse's attained ages as of their birthdays in the distribution calendar year. This will be relevant only if the spouse is more than ten years younger than the employee. The spouse is the sole designated beneficiary for purposes of determining the applicable distribution period for a distribution calendar year during the employee's lifetime only if the spouse is the sole beneficiary of the employee's entire interest *at all times* during the distribution calendar year. [Treas. Reg. § 1.401(a)(9)-5, Q&A-4(b)(1)]

Example 1. Gerry is a participant in the Chip Off The Old Bloch Corporation profit sharing plan. In 2011, when Gerry is age 77, he designates his estate as beneficiary of his plan benefit. The applicable distribution period for Gerry's 2011 RMD is 21.2.

Example 2. In 2012, when Gerry is age 78, he changes the beneficiary to his four daughters, Susan, Janice, Amy, and Elizabeth. The applicable distribution period for Gerry's 2012 RMD is 20.3. This would be the case even if Gerry kept his estate as beneficiary.

Example 3. On May 30, 2013, when Gerry is age 79, he changes the beneficiary from his four daughters to his wife, Nedra, age 65. The applicable distribution period for Gerry's 2013 RMD is 19.5, even though Nedra, who is more than ten years younger than Gerry, is now the designated beneficiary. This is so because Nedra is not the sole beneficiary at all times during 2013.

Example 4. In 2014, when Gerry is 80 and Nedra is age 66, Gerry does not change the beneficiary. The applicable distribution period for Gerry's 2014 RMD is 21.3, their joint life expectancy, and not 18.7 from the table. This is so because Nedra is the sole beneficiary at all times during 2014, and she is more than ten years younger than Gerry.

If the employee and the employee's spouse are married on January 1 of a distribution calendar year, but do not remain married throughout that year (i.e., the employee or the employee's spouse dies or they become divorced during that year), the employee will not fail to have a spouse as the employee's sole beneficiary for that year merely because they are not married throughout that year. If an employee's spouse predeceases the employee, the spouse will not fail to be the employee's sole beneficiary for the distribution calendar year that includes the date of the spouse's death solely because, for the period remaining in that year after the spouse's death, someone other than the spouse is named as beneficiary. However, the change in beneficiary due to the death or divorce of the spouse will be effective for purposes of determining the applicable distribution period in the distribution calendar year *following* the distribution calendar year that includes the date of the spouse's death or divorce. [Treas. Reg. § 1.401(a)(9)-5, Q&A-4(b)(2)]

An IRS representative has stated, however, that, if a divorce occurs and the employee names a new beneficiary during the year in which the divorce occurs, the change in beneficiary will be effective for purposes of determining the applicable distribution period in the distribution calendar in which the divorce occurs. [IRS Pub. 590]

Example 1. Paul is a participant in a profit sharing plan and designates his wife, Paula, as his sole beneficiary. During 2011, Paul attains age 72 and Paula attains age 57. The applicable distribution period for Paul's 2011 RMD is 29.2.

Example 2. The facts are the same as in Example 1, except that Paul and Paula become divorced in 2011 and Paul does not change his beneficiary. The applicable distribution period remains 29.2.

Example 3. The facts are the same as in Example 2, except that Paul changes his beneficiary to his daughter, Pauline, age 35. The applicable distribution period for Paul's 2011 RMD now becomes 25.6.

Example 4. The facts are the same as in Example 3, except that Paul changes his beneficiary to his new wife, Paulette, age 27. The applicable distribution period for Paul's 2011 RMD would now become 56.3 based upon a literal reading of the IRS representative's statement. However, the applicable distribution period should be 25.6 because Paulette is not the sole beneficiary throughout 2011 and thus Paulette's age cannot be used until 2012 (provided she is the sole beneficiary throughout 2012). [IRS Pub. 590]

For a spouse to be treated as the sole designated beneficiary, the spouse must be the sole beneficiary for the entire year. Therefore, it appears that this condition cannot be satisfied for the year in which the marriage occurs. [Priv. Ltr. Rul. 200250037]

Example 5. Steve, age 72, designates his friend Sallie, age 55, as the sole beneficiary of his profit sharing plan benefits. On May 3, 2011, Steve and Sallie are married. For Steve's 2011 RMD, the applicable distribution period is 25.6 using the Uniform Lifetime Table and not 30.8 using their joint life expectancy, because Steve and Sallie were not married for the entire year even though Sallie was the sole beneficiary for the entire year.

Q 11:23   What is the applicable distribution period for RMDs after an employee's death?

If an employee dies *after* distribution has begun (see Q 11:8), generally after the employee's RBD (see Q 11:5), to satisfy the minimum distribution requirements, the applicable distribution period for distribution calendar years (see Q 11:20) after the distribution calendar year containing the employee's date of death is either:

1. If the employee has a designated beneficiary (see Q 11:14) as of the date of determination (see Q 11:16), the longer of (a) the remaining life expectancy (see Q 11:24) of the employee's *designated beneficiary* and (b) the remaining life expectancy of the *employee,* or

2. If the employee does not have a designated beneficiary as of the date of determination, the remaining life expectancy of the *employee.*

[Treas. Reg. § 1.401(a)(9)-5, Q&A-5(a); Priv. Ltr. Ruls. 200850058, 200742026]

If an employee dies *before* distribution has begun (generally before the employee's RBD) and the employee has a designated beneficiary, to satisfy the minimum distribution requirements and the life expectancy rule (see Qs 11:9, 11:11), the applicable distribution period for distribution calendar years after the distribution calendar year containing the employee's date of death is the remaining life expectancy of the designated beneficiary. [Treas. Reg. § 1.401(a)(9)-5, Q&A-5(b)] See Q 11:12 to determine when the five-year rule applies (e.g., there is no designated beneficiary or the five-year rule is elected or specified by plan provision).

If the employee's surviving spouse (see Q 11:45) is not the employee's *sole* beneficiary, the applicable distribution period measured by the beneficiary's remaining life expectancy is determined using the beneficiary's age as of the beneficiary's birthday in the calendar year immediately following the calendar year of the employee's death. In subsequent calendar years, the applicable distribution period is reduced by one for each calendar year that has elapsed after the calendar year immediately following the calendar year of the employee's death. However, if the surviving spouse of the employee is the employee's *sole* beneficiary, the applicable distribution period is measured by the surviving spouse's life expectancy using the surviving spouse's birthday for each distribution calendar year after the calendar year of the employee's death up through the calendar year of the spouse's death. In other words, the surviving spouse's life expectancy is recalculated for each distribution calendar year. For calendar years after the calendar year of the *spouse's* death, the applicable distribution period is then determined based upon the life expectancy of the spouse using the age of the spouse as of the spouse's birthday in the calendar year of the spouse's death. In subsequent calendar years, the applicable distribution period is reduced by one for each calendar year that has elapsed since the calendar year of the spouse's death. [Treas. Reg. § 1.401(a)(9)-5, Q&A-5(c)(1), Q&A-5(c)(2)]

If the employee dies after the RBD and there is no designated beneficiary, the applicable distribution period is based upon the employee's remaining life expectancy using the age of the employee as of the employee's birthday in the calendar year of death. In subsequent calendar years, the applicable distribution period is reduced by one for each calendar year that has elapsed after the calendar year of death. [Treas. Reg. § 1.401(a)(9)-5, Q&A-5(c)(3); Priv. Ltr. Rul. 200850058]

> **Example 1.** Carl and Carla, twins, attain age 75 on April 30, 2011. Each designates the other as beneficiary, and Carl dies on October 30, 2011. Since Carl has a designated beneficiary, the applicable distribution period is the longer of the remaining life expectancy of Carl and Carla. However, Carl's remaining life expectancy is determined in the year of death, 2011, and is 13.4, whereas Carla's remaining life expectancy is determined in the year following Carl's death, 2012, and is 12.7. Since the first distribution must be made on or before December 31, 2012, and Carl's remaining life expectancy is reduced by one (13.4 − 1.0 = 12.4) for 2012, the author believes that the applicable divisor should be 12.7, Carla's remaining life expectancy in 2012.

> **Example 2.** Willie designates his daughter, Billie, as beneficiary and commences RMDs. In 2011, when Willie is age 77 and Billie is age 41, Willie dies. Distribution will be made to Billie over her remaining life expectancy, determined in 2012, and commencing on or before December 31, 2012. Billie's life expectancy in 2012, at age 42, is 41.7 years. Her first distribution will be the December 31, 2011, account balance divided by 41.7. The divisor, 41.7, will be reduced by one each year thereafter.

> **Example 3.** The facts are the same as in Example 2, except that Willie designated his estate as beneficiary. Because his estate is the beneficiary, the applicable distribution period will be measured by Willie's life expectancy in

2011, the year of death, and reduced by one each year thereafter. Willie's remaining life expectancy at age 77 is 12.1 years. The first distribution to be made on or before December 31, 2012, is the December 31, 2011, account balance divided by 11.1 (12.1 − 1.0).

Example 4. The facts are the same as in Example 2, except that Billie is Willie's wife, not his daughter. The distribution to be made to Billie in 2012, the first year after Willie's death, is calculated in the same manner as in Example 1. However, in 2013 and subsequent years, the RMD to be made to Billie is based upon her *recalculated* life expectancy using her age at her birthday in each such distribution calendar year. Thus, in 2013, the RMD will be the December 31, 2012, account balance divided by 40.7; and, in 2014, the RMD will be the December 31, 2013, account balance divided by 39.8. In this case, Billie's life expectancy is not reduced by one each year.

Example 5. Mack and Jack, twin brothers, attain age 70½ on October 31, 2011, and each designates his respective estate as beneficiary. Mack and Jack each has a RBD of April 1, 2012. Mack dies on March 31, 2012, and Jack dies on April 2, 2012. Since Mack died *before* his RBD and he has no designated beneficiary, his entire interest must be distributed by December 31, 2017 (see Q 11:10). Because Jack died *after* his RBD, his interest can be distributed over his remaining life expectancy even though he, too, has no designated beneficiary.

An IRA owner designated his estate as beneficiary and died after his RBD. The IRA owner's will provided for the outright distribution of his estate to his three children. Because the estate cannot be a designated beneficiary (see Q 11:15), distribution had to be made over the remaining life expectancy of the deceased IRA owner. However, IRS ruled that each child's one-third interest in the IRA could be segregated and held in separate IRAs by means of trustee-to-trustee transfers. Each resulting IRA would be in the name of the deceased IRA owner for the benefit of a different child. [Priv. Ltr. Rul. 200343030; *see also* Priv. Ltr. Ruls. 200850058, 200843024, 200647030, 200646028, 200453023, 200444034, 200444033] An IRA owner died after commencing to receive RMDs. The IRA owner designated his wife as the sole beneficiary (see Q 11:14) and did not name any contingent beneficiary. The IRA owner's wife died seven days later without (1) disclaiming the IRA (see Q 11:17); (2) taking any distributions from the IRA; (3) electing to treat the IRA as her own (see Q 11:60); or (4) naming any beneficiary. As a result, the right to receive the IRA passed by the deceased wife's will to their two children. IRS ruled that, because the wife died before distributions to her had begun, the RMD rules apply as if she were the IRA owner (see Q 11:35); and, because she died before her RBD without having a designated beneficiary, the five-year rule applied (see Q 11:10). The deceased wife's personal representatives proposed to subdivide the IRA into two sub-IRAs, with each sub-IRA being titled "IRA owner (deceased) for the benefit of a specific beneficiary under the will of the wife (deceased)" and to accomplish the subdivision by trusteetotrustee transfers. IRS ruled that neither the Code nor the RMD regulations precluded the posthumous division of an IRA into more than one IRA, and that the division did not constitute a transfer for purposes of the income in respect of a decedent rules (see Q 30:47), a taxable distribution (see Q 30:40), or a rollover (see Q 34:6). [Priv. Ltr. Rul. 200945011; IRC §§ 408(d)(1), 408(d)(3), 691(a)(2); Rev. Rul. 92-47, 1992-1 C.B. 198; Rev. Rul. 78-406, 1978-2 C.B. 157] This ruling appears to be incorrect because the IRA owner died after his RBD. Therefore, the IRA owner's wife is the designated beneficiary, and RMDs should be based upon her life expectancy.

Q 11:24   What life expectancies must be used for purposes of determining RMDs?

Life expectancies for purposes of determining RMDs must be computed by using the Single Life Table or the Joint and Last Survivor Table. [Treas. Reg. § 1.401(a)(9)-5, Q&A-6]

The Single Life Table, used for determining the life expectancy of an individual, is as follows:

Age	Life Expectancy Period	Age	Life Expectancy Period
0	82.4	22	61.1
1	81.6	23	60.1
2	80.6	24	59.1
3	79.7	25	58.2
4	78.7	26	57.2
5	77.7	27	56.2
6	76.7	28	55.3
7	75.8	29	54.3
8	74.8	30	53.3
9	73.8	31	52.4
10	72.8	32	51.4
11	71.8	33	50.4
12	70.8	34	49.4
13	69.9	35	48.5
14	68.9	36	47.5
15	67.9	37	46.5
16	66.9	38	45.6
17	66.0	39	44.6
18	65.0	40	43.6
19	64.0	41	42.7
20	63.0	42	41.7
21	62.1	43	40.7

Age	Life Expectancy Period	Age	Life Expectancy Period
44	39.8	78	11.4
45	38.8	79	10.8
46	37.9	80	10.2
47	37.0	81	9.7
48	36.0	82	9.1
49	35.1	83	8.6
50	34.2	84	8.1
51	33.3	85	7.6
52	32.3	86	7.1
53	31.4	87	6.7
54	30.5	88	6.3
55	29.6	89	5.9
56	28.7	90	5.5
57	27.9	91	5.2
58	27.0	92	4.9
59	26.1	93	4.6
60	25.2	94	4.3
61	24.4	95	4.1
62	23.5	96	3.8
63	22.7	97	3.6
64	21.8	98	3.4
65	21.0	99	3.1
66	20.2	100	2.9
67	19.4	101	2.7
68	18.6	102	2.5
69	17.8	103	2.3
70	17.0	104	2.1
71	16.3	105	1.9
72	15.5	106	1.7
73	14.8	107	1.5
74	14.1	108	1.4
75	13.4	109	1.2
76	12.7	110	1.1
77	12.1	111 and older	1.0

[Treas. Reg. § 1.401(a)(9)-9, Q&A-1]

The Joint and Last Survivor Table (see Appendix A) is used for determining the joint and last survivor life expectancy of two individuals. [Treas. Reg. § 1.401(a)(9)-9, Q&A-3] Apparently, the only time that this table is utilized is in the case of lifetime distributions to an employee whose spouse (see Q 11:45) is the sole beneficiary and who is more than ten years younger than the employee (see Q 11:22).

IRS may change these tables. [Treas. Reg. § 1.401(a)(9)-9, Q&A-4]

Q 11:25   What happens if an employee has more than one designated beneficiary?

If more than one individual is designated as a beneficiary (e.g., the employee's children) as of the applicable date for determining the designated beneficiary (see Qs 11:14, 11:16), the designated beneficiary with the shortest life expectancy (see Q 11:24) will be the designated beneficiary for purposes of determining the distribution period. [Treas. Reg. § 1.401(a)(9)-5, Q&A-7(a)(1); Priv. Ltr. Ruls. 201038019, 200809042, 200750019, 1200740018, 200708084, 200634070, 200620026, 200616040, 200610027, 200610026, 200608032]

See Q 11:15 for rules that apply if a non-individual is designated as a beneficiary, and see Q 11:43 for special rules that apply if an employee's benefit under a plan is divided into separate accounts (or segregated shares in the case of a defined benefit plan; see Q 2:3) and the beneficiaries with respect to a separate account differ from the beneficiaries of another separate account.

If a beneficiary's entitlement to an employee's benefit after the employee's death is a contingent right, such contingent beneficiary is nevertheless considered to be a designated beneficiary for purposes of determining whether a non-individual is designated as a beneficiary (resulting in the employee being treated as having no designated beneficiary) and which designated beneficiary has the shortest life expectancy. [Treas. Reg. § 1.401(a)(9)-5, Q&A-7(b)] A person will not be considered a beneficiary for purposes of determining who is the beneficiary with the shortest life expectancy or whether a beneficiary who is not an individual is a beneficiary merely because the person could become the successor to the interest of one of the employee's beneficiaries after that beneficiary's death. However, the preceding sentence does not apply to a person who has any right (including a contingent right) to an employee's benefit beyond being a mere potential successor to the interest of one of the employee's beneficiaries upon that beneficiary's death. Thus, for example, if the first beneficiary has a right to all income with respect to an employee's individual account during that beneficiary's life and a second beneficiary has a right to the principal but only after the death of the first income beneficiary (any portion of the principal distributed during the life of the first income beneficiary to be held in trust until that first beneficiary's death), both beneficiaries must be taken into account in determining the beneficiary with the shortest life expectancy and whether only individuals are beneficiaries. [Treas. Reg. § 1.401(a) (9)-5, Q&A-7(c)(1); Priv. Ltr. Ruls. 200453023, 200449040, 200444033, 200440031,

200438044, 200432027]. If the individual beneficiary whose life expectancy is being used to calculate the distribution period dies after September 30 of the calendar year following the calendar year of the employee's death, such beneficiary's remaining life expectancy will be used to determine the distribution period without regard to the life expectancy of the subsequent beneficiary. [Treas. Reg. § 1.401(a)(9)-5, Q&A-7(c)(2)]

> **Example 1.** Double D Corporation maintains a defined contribution plan. David, an employee of Double D Corporation, died in 2011 at the age of 55, survived by his spouse, Davida, who was 50 years old. Prior to David's death, Double D Corporation had established an account balance for David in the plan. David's account balance is invested only in productive assets. David named the trustee of a testamentary trust established under David's will as the beneficiary of all amounts payable from David's account in the plan after his death. A copy of the trust and a list of the trust beneficiaries were provided to the plan administrator (see Q 11:19) by October 31 of the calendar year following the calendar year of David's death. As of the date of David's death, the trust was irrevocable and was a valid trust under the laws of the state of David's domicile (see Q 11:18). David's account balance in the plan was includible in his gross estate, and the legal representative of David's estate made a QTIP election for both the account balance and the trust.

Under the terms of the trust, all trust income is payable annually to Davida, and no one has the power to appoint trust principal to any person other than Davida. David's children, who are all younger than Davida, are the sole remainder beneficiaries of the trust. No other person has a beneficial interest in the trust. Under the terms of the trust, Davida has the power, exercisable annually, to compel the trustee to withdraw from David's account balance in the plan an amount equal to the income earned on the assets held in the account during the calendar year and to distribute that amount through the trust to Davida. The plan contains no prohibition on withdrawal from David's account of amounts in excess of the annual RMDs. In accordance with the terms of the plan, the trustee of the trust elects to receive annual RMDs using the life expectancy rule (see Q 11:11) for distributions over a distribution period equal to Davida's life expectancy. If Davida exercises the withdrawal power, the trustee must withdraw from the account under the plan the greater of the amount of income earned in the account during the calendar year or the RMD. However, under the terms of the trust and applicable state law, only the portion of the plan distribution received by the trustee equal to the income earned by the account is required to be distributed to Davida (along with any other trust income).

Because some amounts distributed from David's account to the trust may be accumulated in the trust during Davida's lifetime for the benefit of David's children, as remainder beneficiaries of the trust, even though access to those amounts is delayed until after Davida's death, David's children are beneficiaries of David's account in addition to Davida and Davida is not the sole beneficiary of the account. Thus, the designated beneficiary used to determine the distribution period from David's account is the beneficiary with the shortest life expectancy. Davida's life expectancy is the shortest of all of the potential beneficiaries of the trust's interest in David's account in the plan (including remainder beneficiaries). Thus, the distribution period is Davida's life expectancy. Because Davida is not the sole beneficiary of the trust's interest in David's account, the special deferral rule (see Q 11:11) is not available and the annual RMDs from the account to the trust must begin no later than the end of the calendar year immediately following the calendar year of David's death. [Rev. Rul. 2006-26, 2006-1 C.B. 939]

Example 2. The facts are the same as in Example 1, except that, in addition to David's children, a charitable organization is a remainder beneficiary of the trust. Since only individuals may be designated beneficiaries (see Q 11:15), David is treated as having no designated beneficiary and the five-year rule applies (see Q 11:10). Thus, the distribution period cannot be Davida's life expectancy.

Example 3. The facts are the same as in Example 1, except that the testamentary trust provides that *all* amounts distributed from David's account in the plan to the trustee while Davida is alive will be paid directly to Davida upon receipt by the trustee of the trust. This is known as a conduit or passthrough trust.

In this case, Davida is the *sole* beneficiary of David's account for purposes of determining the designated beneficiary. No amounts distributed from David's account to the trust are accumulated in the trust during Davida's lifetime for the benefit of any other beneficiary. Therefore, the remainder beneficiaries of the trust are mere potential successors to Davida's interest in David's account. Because Davida is the sole beneficiary of the trust's interest in David's account, the RMDs from the account must begin no later than the end of the calendar year in which David would have attained age 70½, rather than the calendar year immediately following the calendar year of David's death. [Priv. Ltr. Ruls. 200252097, 200105058, 199903050] In addition, since Davida is the sole beneficiary, her life expectancy will be recalculated each year after distributions commence (see Q 11:23). This is true also in Example 2 because all of the remainder beneficiaries are being disregarded.

In Example 1 above, the trust is a lifetime trust for Davida with David's children as the remainder beneficiaries. In this situation, both Davida and David's children are designated beneficiaries. However, if the trust is for a term of years and the trust beneficiary is expected to survive the term and receive the trust assets, IRS now believes that remainder beneficiaries should *not* be disregarded. A grandparent designated trusts for her two grandchildren. Each trust provided that the grandchild could withdraw all of the trust assets at age 30; if the grandchild died prior to age 30, the trust assets would be distributed to the other grandchild; and, if both grandchildren died prior to age 30, the trust assets would be distributed to remainder beneficiaries who were older than the grandchildren. IRS ruled that the remainder beneficiaries were designated beneficiaries and that distribution of the IRA had to be based upon the life expectancy of the oldest remainder beneficiary. [Priv. Ltr. Rul. 200228025] In a prior ruling where the grandchild would receive the trust assets at age 21, IRS ruled that distributions could be based upon the grandchild's life expectancy and never discussed contingent beneficiaries of which there had to be at least one. [Priv. Ltr. Rul. 200040035; *see also* Priv. Ltr. Ruls. 199903050, 9846034]

Example 4. Zeke designates a trust for his 11-year-old daughter, Zena, as beneficiary of his IRA. The trust provides that Zena will receive all of the trust assets at age 21 and that, if Zena dies before age 21, the trust assets will be distributed to Zeke's sister, Zelda, age 50, and Zeke's brother, Zane, age 40. Even though Zena has a 71.8 year life expectancy, the shorter life expectancy of Zelda must be used to determine the distribution period.

With regard to the question of possible trust beneficiaries, there are three areas that require clarification. The first relates to where the trust beneficiary is given a power of appointment whereby the trust beneficiary can direct the trustee to make a distribution of trust assets to any one or more other persons. Thus, if the beneficiary can appoint to a charitable organization and the organization is also considered a beneficiary of the trust, then there will not be a designated beneficiary. However, although the author believes that permissible appointees should not be considered because they are not generally considered as beneficiaries of a trust for other purposes, IRS ruled otherwise. [Priv. Ltr. Rul. 201021038] The second concerns whether or not the plan benefits payable to a trust could be used to pay estate taxes, the deceased employee's debts, or estate administration expenses. If the benefits could be so used, then IRS might assert that the estate is a beneficiary under the trust and, thus, there is no designated beneficiary. [Priv. Ltr. Ruls. 200018055, 200010055, 199912041] However, see Q 11:15 for a discussion of more recent and illuminating IRS rulings. The third relates to the treatment of successor remainder beneficiaries of a trust. In Example 2, David is treated as having no designated beneficiary, because a charitable organization is a remainder beneficiary with David's children. If the charitable organization would receive the trust assets only if all of David's children predeceased Davida, it is unclear whether the charitable organization should be considered a remainder beneficiary or disregarded as merely a successor to the children's interest.

A recent IRS ruling may provide the answer to the third area. An IRA owner designated as beneficiary a trust for his son. The trust provided that the final distribution of trust principal would be made to the son at age 40; and, if the son died prior to age 40, the remaining trust principal would be distributed to the son's descendants or, if none, to the IRA owner's heirs at law. When the IRA owner died, his son had no descendants; and, under state law, the surviving spouse was the sole heir at law. IRS ruled that the surviving spouse would at all times through the determination date (see Q 11:16) be the sole heir at law for purposes of determining the remainder beneficiary of the trust. IRS ruled that:

1. The son and the surviving spouse are the only individuals who need be considered for purposes of determining who is the designated beneficiary for purposes of calculating RMDs.

2. The surviving spouse was the designated beneficiary with the shortest life expectancy for purposes of determining the distribution period.

[Priv. Ltr. Rul. 200843042]

Assume that the trust in the ruling provided that, if the son died prior to age 40 without descendants, the remainder beneficiary would be the surviving spouse and, if the surviving spouse was not then living, the remainder beneficiary would be a charitable organization. In this situation, it appears that the ruling would conclude that the charitable organization would be a mere successor in interest to the surviving spouse's interest and, therefore, not considered for purposes of determining if there is a designated beneficiary.

In Example 1, the legal representative of the estate made a QTIP election for both the account balance and the trust. See Q 30:47 for a discussion of the QTIP election and additional examples.

Q 11:26 How does vesting affect RMDs?

If the employee's benefit is in the form of an individual account (e.g., a defined contribution plan; see Q 2:2), the benefit used to determine the RMD for any distribution calendar year (see Q 11:20) will be determined without regard to whether or not any portion of the employee's benefit is vested (see Q 9:1). If any portion of the employee's benefit is not vested, distributions will be treated as being paid from the vested portion of the benefit first. If, as of the end of a distribution calendar year (or as of the employee's RBD (see Q 11:5), in the case of the employee's first distribution calendar year), the total amount of the employee's vested benefit is less than the RMD for the calendar year, only the vested portion, if any, of the employee's benefit is required to be distributed by the end of the calendar year (or, if applicable, by the employee's RBD). However, the RMD for the subsequent distribution calendar year must be increased by the sum of amounts not distributed in prior calendar years because the employee's vested benefit was less than the RMD. [Treas. Reg. § 1.401(a)(9)-5, Q&A-8]

Q 11:27 What distributions are taken into account in determining whether the minimum distribution requirements are satisfied?

Except as provided below, all amounts distributed from an individual account (e.g., a defined contribution plan; see Q 2:2) are distributions that are taken into account in determining whether the minimum distribution requirements are satisfied, regardless of whether the amount is includible in income. Thus, for example, amounts that are excluded from income as recovery of investment in the contract (see Q 13:3) are taken into account for purposes of determining whether the minimum distribution requirements are satisfied for a distribution calendar year (see Q 11:20). Similarly, amounts excluded from income as net unrealized appreciation on employer securities (see Q 13:18) also are amounts distributed for purposes of determining if the requirements are satisfied. [Treas. Reg. § 1.401(a)(9)-5, Q&A-9(a)]

The following amounts are *not* taken into account in determining whether the required minimum amount has been distributed for a calendar year:

1. Elective deferrals and employee contributions that are returned (together with the income allocable thereto) in order to comply with the Section 415 limitations (see Qs 27:63, 27:85).

2. Corrective distributions of excess deferrals together with the income allocable to these distributions (see Q 27:63).

3. Corrective distributions of excess contributions under a qualified CODA (see Q 27:25) and excess aggregate contributions (see Q 27:82), together with the income allocable to these distributions.

4. Loans that are treated as deemed distributions (see chapter 14).

5. Dividends that are paid on employer securities (see Q 27:36). Amounts paid to the plan that are included in the account balance and subsequently distributed from the account lose their character as dividends.

6. The costs of life insurance coverage (see Q 15:6).

7. Similar items designated by IRS.

[Treas. Reg. § 1.401(a)(9)-5, Q&A-9(b)]

RMDs from Defined Benefit Plans

Q 11:28   How must distributions under a defined benefit plan be paid in order to satisfy the RMD rules?

To satisfy the minimum distribution requirements, distributions of the employee's entire interest under a defined benefit plan (see Q 2:3) must be paid in the form of periodic annuity payments for the employee's life (or the joint lives of the employee and beneficiary) or over a period certain that does not exceed the maximum length of the period certain determined as set forth in Q 11:30. The interval between payments for the annuity must be uniform over the entire distribution period and must not exceed one year. Once payments have commenced over a period, the period may only be changed as set forth in Q 11:37. Life (or joint and survivor) annuity payments must satisfy the MDIB requirements (see Q 11:29). Except as otherwise provided (such as permitted increases described in Q 11:38), all payments (whether paid over an employee's life, joint lives, or a period certain) also must be nonincreasing. [I.R.C. §§ 401(a)(9)(A)(ii), 401(a)(9)(B)(iii); Treas. Reg. § 1.401(a)(9)-6, Q&A-1(a); Priv. Ltr. Rul. 200951039] The suspension of RMDs for calendar year 2009 did not apply to defined benefit plans (see Q 11:1). [I.R.C. § 401(a)(9)(H) (as added by WRERA 2008 § 201(a))]

The annuity may be a life annuity (or joint and survivor annuity) with a period certain if the life (or lives, if applicable) and period certain each meet the above requirements. If distribution is permitted to be made over the lives of the employee and the designated beneficiary (see Q 11:14), references to life annuity include a joint and survivor annuity. [Treas. Reg. § 1.401(a)(9)-6, Q&A-1(b)]

Annuity payments must commence on or before the employee's RBD (see Q 11:5). The first payment that must be made on or before the employee's RBD must be the payment that is required for one payment interval. The second payment need not be made until the end of the next payment interval even if that payment interval ends in the next calendar year. Similarly, in the case of distributions commencing after death, the first payment that must be made on or before the date required under the life expectancy rule (see Q 11:11), which date depends upon whether or not the surviving spouse is the sole designated beneficiary, must be the payment that is required for one payment interval. Payment intervals are the periods for which payments are received (e.g., bimonthly, monthly, semiannually, or annually). All benefit accruals as of the last day of the first distribution calendar year (see Q 11:20) must be included in the calculation of the amount of annuity payments for payment intervals ending on or after the employee's RBD. [I.R.C. §§ 401(a)(9)(B)(iii), 401(a)(9)(B)(iv); Treas. Reg. § 1.401(a)(9)-6, Q&A-1(c)(1)]

Example. A defined benefit plan provides monthly annuity payments of $500 for the life of unmarried participants with a ten-year period certain. Leonard, an unmarried participant in the plan, attains age 70$\frac{1}{2}$ in 2011. The first payment of $500 must be made on behalf of Leonard on or before April 1, 2012, and the payments must continue to be made in monthly payments of $500 thereafter for the life and ten-year period certain.

In the case of a single-sum distribution of an employee's entire accrued benefit (see Q 9:2) during a distribution calendar year, the amount that is the RMD for the distribution calendar year (and thus not eligible for rollover) is determined using either of the following rules:

1. The portion of the single-sum distribution that is an RMD is determined by treating the single-sum distribution as a distribution from an individual account plan (e.g., defined contribution plan; see Q 2:2) and treating the amount of the single-sum distribution as the employee's account balance as of the end of the relevant valuation calendar year. If the single-sum distribution is being made in the calendar year containing the RBD and the RMD for the employee's first distribution calendar year has not been distributed, the portion of the single-sum distribution that represents the RMD for the employee's first and second distribution calendar years is not eligible for rollover.

2. The portion of the single-sum distribution that is an RMD is permitted to be determined by expressing the employee's benefit as an annuity that would satisfy these requirements with an annuity starting date (see Q 10:3) as of the first day of the distribution calendar year for which the RMD is being determined, and treating one year of annuity payments as the RMD for that year, and not eligible for rollover. If the single-sum distribution is being made in the calendar year containing the RBD and the RMD for the employee's first distribution calendar year has not been made, the benefit must be expressed as an annuity with an annuity starting date as of the first day of the first distribution calendar year and

the payments for the first two distribution calendar years would be treated as RMDs, and not eligible for rollover.

[Treas. Reg. § 1.401(a)(9)-6, Q&A-1(d)]

The rule prohibiting increasing payments under an annuity applies to payments made upon the death of the employee. However, for these purposes, an ancillary death benefit described below may be disregarded in applying that rule. Such an ancillary death benefit is excluded in determining an employee's entire interest, and the rules prohibiting increasing payments do not apply to such an ancillary death benefit. A death benefit with respect to an employee's benefit is an ancillary death benefit if:

1. It is not paid as part of the employee's accrued benefit or under any optional form of the employee's benefit, and

2. The death benefit, together with any other potential payments with respect to the employee's benefit that may be provided to a survivor, satisfy the incidental benefit requirement (see Q 11:29).

[Treas. Reg. §§ 1.401-1(b)(1)(i), 1.401(a)(9)-6, Q&A-1(e)]

Additional guidance regarding how distributions under a defined benefit plan must be paid in order to satisfy the minimum distribution requirements may issued by IRS. [Treas. Reg. § 1.401(a)(9)-6, Q&A-1(f)]

Q 11:29   How must distributions in the form of an annuity be made to satisfy the MDIB requirement?

If the employee's benefit is payable in the form of a life annuity for the life of the employee satisfying the minimum distribution requirements without regard to the MDIB requirement, the MDIB requirement will be satisfied. [I.R.C. §§ 401(a)(9)(A), 401(a)(9)(G); Treas. Reg. § 1.401(a)(9)-6, Q&A-2(a)]

If the employee's sole beneficiary, as of the annuity starting date (see Q 10:3) for annuity payments, is the employee's spouse (see Q 11:45) and the distributions satisfy the minimum distribution requirements without regard to the MDIB requirement, the distributions to the employee will be deemed to satisfy the MDIB requirement. For example, if an employee's benefit is being distributed in the form of a joint and survivor annuity for the lives of the employee and the employee's spouse and the spouse is the sole beneficiary of the employee, the amount of the periodic payment payable to the spouse would not violate the MDIB request if it was 100 percent of the annuity payment payable to the employee regardless of the difference in the ages between the employee and the employee's spouse. [Treas. Reg. § 1.401(a)(9)-6, Q&A-2(b); Priv. Ltr. Rul. 200951039]

If distributions commence under a distribution option that is in the form of a joint and survivor annuity for the joint lives of the employee and a beneficiary other than the employee's spouse, the MDIB requirement will not be satisfied as of the date distributions commence unless, under the distribution option, the annuity payments to be made to the employee on and after the RBD (see Q 11:5) will satisfy the conditions that are set forth in this paragraph. The periodic annuity payment payable to the survivor must *not* at any time on or after the employee's RBD exceed the applicable percentage of the annuity payment payable to the employee using the table below. The applicable percentage is based on the adjusted employee/beneficiary age difference. The adjusted employee/beneficiary age difference is determined by first calculating the excess of the age of the employee over the age of the beneficiary as of their birthdays in a calendar year. Then, if the employee is younger than age 70, the age difference determined in the previous sentence is reduced by the number of years that the employee is younger than age 70 on the employee's birthday in the calendar year that contains the annuity starting date. In the case of an annuity that provides for increasing payments, the requirement of this paragraph will be satisfied if the increase is determined in the same manner for the employee and the beneficiary. [Treas. Reg. § 1.401(a)(9)-6, Q&A-2(c); Priv. Ltr. Rul. 200951039]

Adjusted Employee/ Beneficiary Age Difference	Applicable Percentage
10 years or less	100
11	96
12	93
13	90
14	87
15	84
16	82
17	79
18	77
19	75
20	73
21	72
22	70
23	68
24	67
25	66
26	64
27	63
28	62
29	61
30	60
31	59
32	59

Adjusted Employee/ Beneficiary Age Difference	Applicable Percentage
33	58
34	57
35	56
36	56
37	55
38	55
39	54
40	54
41	53
42	53
43	53
44 and greater	52

Example. Distributions commence on January 1, 2011 to Shirley, born March 1, 1945, after retirement at age 65. Shirley will attain age 66 in 2011. Shirley's daughter Ellen, born February 5, 1975, is Shirley's beneficiary. Ellen will attain age 36 in 2011. The distributions are in the form of a joint and survivor annuity for the lives of Shirley and Ellen, with payments of $500 a month to Shirley and, upon Shirley's death, of $500 a month to Ellen (that is, the projected monthly payment to Ellen is 100 percent of the monthly amount payable to Shirley). Accordingly, compliance is determined as of the annuity starting date. The adjusted employee/beneficiary age difference is calculated by taking the excess of the employee's age over the beneficiary's age and subtracting the number of years the employee is younger than age 70. In this case, Shirley is 30 years older than Ellen and is commencing benefit payments four years before attaining age 70, so the adjusted employee/ beneficiary age difference is 26 years. Under the table, the applicable percentage for a 26-year adjusted employee/beneficiary age difference is 64 percent. As of January 1, 2011 (the annuity starting date), the plan does not satisfy the MDIB requirement because, as of such date, the distribution option provides that, as of Shirley's RBD, the monthly payment to Ellen upon Shirley's death will exceed 64 percent of Shirley's monthly payment.

If a distribution form includes a life annuity and a period certain, the amount of the annuity payments payable to the beneficiary need not be reduced during the period certain; but, in the case of a joint and survivor annuity with a period certain, the amount of the annuity payments payable to the beneficiary must satisfy this requirement after the expiration of the period certain. [Treas. Reg. § 1.401(a)(9)-6, Q&A-2(d)]

Except in the case of distributions with respect to an employee's benefit that include an ancillary death benefit (see Q 11:28), to the extent the incidental benefit requirement requires a distribution, that requirement is deemed to be satisfied if distributions satisfy the MDIB requirement. If the employee's benefits include an ancillary death benefit, the benefits (including the ancillary death benefit) must be distributed in accordance with the incidental benefit requirement, and the benefits (excluding the ancillary death benefit) must also satisfy the MDIB requirement. [Treas. Reg. §§ 1.401-1(b)(1)(i), 1.401(a)(9)-6, Q&A-2(e)]

Q 11:30   How long is a period certain under a defined benefit plan permitted to extend?

The period certain for any annuity distributions commencing during the life of the employee with an annuity starting date (see Q 10:3) on or after the employee's RBD (see Q 11:5) generally is not permitted to exceed the applicable distribution period for the employee determined in accordance with the Uniform Lifetime Table (see Q 11:22) for the calendar year that contains the annuity starting date. See Q 11:35 for the rule for annuity payments with an annuity starting date before the RBD. However, if the employee's sole beneficiary is the employee's spouse (see Q 11:45), the period certain is permitted to be as long as the joint life and last survivor expectancy of the employee and the employee's spouse (see Appendix A), if longer than the applicable distribution period for the employee, provided the period certain is not provided in conjunction with a life annuity (see Q 11:29). [Treas. Reg. § 1.401(a)(9)-6, Q&A-3(a)]

If annuity distributions commence after the death of the employee under the life expectancy rule (see Q 11:11), the period certain for any distributions commencing after death cannot exceed the applicable distribution period determined under Q 11:23 for the distribution calendar year (see Q 11:20) that contains the annuity starting date. If the annuity starting date is in a calendar year before the first distribution calendar year, the period certain may not exceed the life expectancy of the designated beneficiary (see Q 11:14) using the beneficiary's age in the year that contains the annuity starting date. [Treas. Reg. § 1.401(a)(9)-6, Q&A-3(b)]

Q 11:31   May distributions be made from an annuity contract that is purchased from an insurance company?

A plan will not fail to satisfy the minimum distribution requirements merely because distributions are made from an annuity contract that is purchased with the employee's benefit by the plan from an insurance company, as long as the payments satisfy the requirements applicable to defined benefit plans (see Qs 11:28–11:30, 11:32–11:35). If the annuity contract is purchased after the RBD (see Q 11:5), the first payment interval must begin on or before the purchase date and the payment required for one payment interval must be made no later than the end of such payment interval. If the payments actually made under the annuity contract do not meet the minimum distribution requirements, the plan fails to satisfy such requirements. [Treas. Reg. § 1.401(a)(9)-6, Q&A-4; Priv. Ltr. Rul. 200951039]

The suspension of RMDs for calendar year 2009 did not apply to defined benefit plans (see Q 11:1). [I.R.C. § 401(a)(9)(H) (as added by WRERA 2008 § 201(a))]

Q 11:32   For annuity distributions under a defined benefit plan, how must additional benefits that accrue after the first distribution calendar year be distributed?

In the case of annuity distributions under a defined benefit plan (see Q 2:3), if any additional benefits accrue in a calendar year after the employee's first distribution calendar year (see Q 11:20), distribution of the amount that accrues in a calendar year must commence in accordance with the rules set forth in Q 11:28 beginning with the first payment interval ending in the calendar year immediately following the calendar year in which such amount accrues. [Treas. Reg. § 1.401(a)(9)-6, Q&A-5(a)]

A plan will not fail to satisfy the minimum distribution requirements merely because there is an administrative delay in the commencement of the distribution of the additional benefits accrued in a calendar year, provided that the actual payment of such amount commences as soon as practicable. However, payment must commence no later than the end of the first calendar year following the calendar year in which the additional benefit accrues, and the total amount paid during such first calendar year must be no less than the total amount that was required to be paid during that year under the preceding paragraph. [Treas. Reg. § 1.401(a)(9)-6, Q&A-5(b)]

The suspension of RMDs for calendar year 2009 did not apply to defined benefit plans (see Q 11:1). [I.R.C. § 401(a)(9)(H) (as added by WRERA 2008 § 201(a))]

Q 11:33   If a portion of an employee's benefit is not vested as of December 31 of a distribution calendar year, how is the RMD affected?

In the case of annuity distributions from a defined benefit plan (see Q 2:3), if any portion of the employee's benefit is not vested (see Q 9:1) as of December 31 of a distribution calendar year (see Q 11:20), the portion that is not vested as of such date will be treated as not having accrued for purposes of determining the RMD for that distribution calendar year. When an additional portion of the employee's benefit becomes vested, such portion will be treated as an additional accrual. See Q 11:32 for the rules for distributing benefits that accrue under a defined benefit plan after the employee's first distribution calendar year. [Treas. Reg. § 1.401(a)(9)-6, Q&A-6]

Q 11:34   If an employee (other than a 5 percent owner) retires after age 70½, must the employee's accrued benefit be actuarially increased?

If an employee (other than a 5 percent owner; see Q 11:5) retires after the calendar year in which the employee attains age 70½, to satisfy the actuarial increase requirement, the employee's accrued benefit (see Q 9:2) under a defined benefit plan (see Q 2:3) must be actuarially increased to take into account any period after age 70½ in which the employee was not receiving any benefits under the plan. The required actuarial increase must be provided for the period starting on April 1, following the calendar year in which the employee attains age 70½, or January 1, 1997, if later. The period for which the actuarial increase must be provided ends on the date on which benefits commence after retirement in an amount sufficient to satisfy the minimum distribution requirements. [I.R.C. § 401(a)(9)(C)(iii); Treas. Reg. § 1.401(a)(9)-6, Q&A-7(a), Q&A-7(b)]

If, as permitted, a plan provides that the RBD (see Q 11:5) for *all* employees is April 1 of the calendar year following the calendar year in which the employee attained age 70½ (regardless of whether the employee is a 5 percent owner) and the plan makes distributions in an amount sufficient to satisfy the minimum distribution requirements using that RBD, no actuarial increase is required. [Treas. Reg. § 1.401(a)(9)-6, Q&A-7(c)]

The actuarial increase requirement does not apply to governmental or church plans. [Treas. Reg. § 1.401(a)(9)-6, Q&A-7(d)]

To satisfy the actuarial increase requirement, the retirement benefits payable with respect to an employee as of the end of the period for actuarial increases must be no less than the actuarial equivalent of:

1. The employee's retirement benefits that would have been payable as of the date the actuarial increase must commence if benefits had commenced on that date; plus

2. Any additional benefits accrued after that date; reduced by

3. Any distributions made with respect to the employee's retirement benefits after that date.

Actuarial equivalence is determined using the plan's assumptions (see Q 2:20). [I.R.C. §§ 401(a)(9)(C)(iii), 411(c)(3); Treas. Reg. § 1.401(a)(9)-6, Q&A-8]

For any of an employee's accrued benefit to be nonforfeitable (see Q 9:1), a defined benefit plan must make an actuarial adjustment to an accrued benefit, the payment of which is deferred past normal retirement age (see Qs 9:24, 10:55). The only exception to this rule is that, generally, no actuarial adjustment is required to reflect the period during which a benefit is suspended as permitted under ERISA Section 203(a)(3)(B). The actuarial increase required for minimum distribution purposes is generally the same as, and not in addition to, the actuarial increase required for the same period under Section 411 to reflect any delay in the payment of retirement benefits after normal retirement age.

However, unlike the actuarial increase required under Section 411, the actuarial increase required for minimum distribution purposes must be provided even during the period during which an employee's benefit has been suspended in accordance with ERISA Section 203(a)(3)(B). [I.R.C. §§ 411(b)(1)(G), 411(b)(1)(H); Treas. Reg. § 1.401(a)(9)-6, Q&A-9]

Q 11:35   What rule applies if distributions commence before the RBD and the distribution form is an annuity?

If distributions commence to an employee before the employee's RBD (see Q 11:5) in installments (see Q 11:4) and the distribution form is an annuity (see Qs 11:28, 11:31), the annuity starting date (see Q 10:3) will be treated as the RBD. Thus, for example, the designated beneficiary's (see Q 11:14) distributions will be determined as of the annuity starting date. Similarly, if the employee dies after the annuity starting date but before the RBD, after the employee's death, the remaining portion of the employee's interest must continue to be distributed over the remaining period over which distributions commenced. The rules that apply if an employee dies before the RBD (see Qs 11:9–11:13) do not apply in this case. [I.R.C. § 401(a)(9)(A)(ii); Treas. Reg. § 1.401(a)(9)-6, Q&A-10(a)]

If, as of the employee's birthday in the year that contains the annuity starting date, the age of the employee is under 70, for purposes of applying the rule set forth in the first paragraph of Q 11:30, the applicable distribution period for the employee is the distribution period for age 70, determined in accordance with the Uniform Lifetime Table (see Q 11:22) plus the excess of 70 over the age of the employee as of the employee's birthday in the year that contains the annuity starting date. [Treas. Reg. § 1.401(a)(9)-6, Q&A-10(b)] See Q 11:29 for the determination of the adjusted employee/beneficiary age difference in the case of an employee whose age on the annuity starting date is less than 70.

If distributions commence to the surviving spouse (see Q 11:45) of an employee under the life expectancy rule (see Q 11:11) before the date on which distributions are required to commence and the distribution form is an annuity (see Qs 11:28, 11:31), distributions will be considered to have begun on the actual commencement date. Consequently, in such case, the rule treating the surviving spouse as the employee (see Q 11:13) will not apply upon the death of the surviving spouse. Instead, the annuity distributions must continue to be made over the remaining period over which distributions commenced. [I.R.C. §§ 401(a)(9)(B)(iii)(II), 401(a)(9)(B)(iv)(II); Treas. Reg. § 1.401(a)(9)-6, Q&A-11]

Q 11:36   How are the minimum distribution requirements satisfied for an annuity contract under an individual account plan?

Prior to the date that annuity payments commence under an individual account plan (e.g., defined contribution plan; see Q 2:2) from an annuity contract, the interest of an employee or beneficiary under that contract is treated as an individual account for purposes of the minimum distribution requirements. Thus, the RMD for any year with respect to that interest is determined under the rules applicable to defined contribution plans (see Qs 11:20–11:27). For purposes of applying these rules, the entire interest under the annuity contract as of December 31 of the relevant valuation calendar year (see Q 11:21) is treated as the account balance for the valuation calendar year. The entire interest under an annuity contract is the dollar amount credited to the employee or beneficiary under the contract plus the actuarial value of any additional benefits (such as survivor benefits in excess of the dollar amount credited to the employee or beneficiary) that will be provided under the contract. However, the following paragraph describes certain additional benefits that may be disregarded in determining the employee's entire interest under the annuity contract. The actuarial present value of any additional benefit will be determined using reasonable actuarial assumptions, including reasonable assumptions as to future distributions, and without regard to an individual's health. [Treas. Reg. § 1.401(a)(9)-6, Q&A-12(a), Q&A-12(b)]

The actuarial present value of any additional benefits provided under an annuity contract may be disregarded if the sum of the dollar amount credited to the employee or beneficiary under the contract and the actuarial present value of the additional benefits is no more than 120 percent of the dollar amount credited to the employee or beneficiary under the contract and the contract provides only for the following additional benefits:

1. Additional benefits that, in the case of a distribution, are reduced by an amount sufficient to ensure that the ratio of such sum to the dollar amount credited does not increase as a result of the distribution, and

2. An additional benefit that is the right to receive a final payment upon death that does not exceed the excess of the premiums paid, less the amount of prior distributions.

If the only additional benefit provided under the contract is the additional benefit described in item 2, the additional benefit may be disregarded regardless of its value in relation to the dollar amount credited to the employee or beneficiary under the contract. [Treas. Reg. § 1.401(a)(9)-6, Q&A-12(c)]

The following examples, which use a 5 percent interest rate and the mortality table provided in Revenue Ruling 2001-62 (see Q 6:18), illustrate the application of these rules.

Example 1. Jim is the owner of a variable annuity contract under an individual account plan which has not been annuitized. The contract provides a death benefit until the end of the calendar year in which the owner attains the age of 84 equal to the greater of the current contract notional account value (dollar amount credited to Jim under the contract) and the largest notional account value at any previous policy anniversary reduced proportionally for subsequent partial distributions (high water mark). The contract provides a death benefit in calendar years after the calendar year in which the owner attains age 84 equal to the current notional account value, provides that assets within the contract may be invested in a fixed account at a guaranteed rate of 2 percent, and provides no other additional benefits.

At the end of 2011, when Jim has an attained age of 78 and 9 months, the notional account value of the contract (after the distribution for 2011 of 4.93 percent of the notional account value as of December 31, 2010) is $550,000, and the high water mark, before adjustment for any withdrawals from the contract in 2011, is $1,000,000. Thus, the contract will provide additional benefits (i.e., the death benefits in excess of the notional account value) through 2017, the year Jim turns 84. The actuarial present value of these additional benefits at the end of 2011 is determined to be $84,300 (15 percent of the notional account value). In making this determination, the following assumptions are made: (1) on the average, deaths occur mid-year; (2) the investment return on his notional account value is 2 percent per annum; and (3) RMDs (determined without regard to additional benefits under the contract) are made at the end of each year. The following table summarizes the actuarial methodology used in determining the actuarial present value of the additional benefit.

Year	Death Benefit During Year	End-of-Year Notional Account Before Withdrawal	Average Notional Account	Withdrawal at End of Year	End-of-Year Notional Account After Withdrawal
2011	$1,000,000				$550,000
2012	950,739[1]	$561,002[2]	$555,500[3]	$28,205[4]	532,795
2013	901,983	543,451	538,123	28,492	514,959
2014	853,749	525,258	520,109	29,769	496,490
2015	806,053	506,419	501,454	29,034	477,385
2016	758,916	486,933	482,159	29,287	457,645
2017	712,356	466,798	462,222	29,525	437,273

Year	Survivorship to Start of Year	Interest Discount to End of 2010	Mortality Rate During Year	Discounted Additional Benefits Within Year
2011				
2012	1.00000	.97590	.04426[5]	$17,070
2013	.95574	.92943[6]	.04946	15,987[7]
2014	.90847[8]	.88517	.05519	14,807
2015	.85833	.84302	.06146	13,564
2016	.80558	.80288	.06788	12,150
2017	.75090	.76464	.07477	10,734
				$84,300

---

[1] $1,000,000 death benefit reduced 4.93 percent for withdrawal during 2011.

[2] Notional account value at end of prior year (after distribution) increased by 2 percent return for year.
[3] Average of $550,000 notional account value at end of prior year (after distribution) and $561,000 notional account value at end of current year (before distribution).
[4] December 31, 2011 notional account (before distribution) divided by uniform lifetime table age 79 factor of 19.5 (see Q 11:22).
[5] One-quarter age 78 rate plus three-quarters age 79 rate.
[6] 5 percent discounted 18 months $(1.05^{\wedge}(-1.5))$.
[7] Blended age 79/age 80 mortality rate $(.04946) \times \$363,860$ excess of death benefit over the average notional account value $(\$901,983 - \$538,123) \times .95574$ probability of survivorship to the start of 2013 $\times$ 18 month interest discount of .92943.
[8] Survivorship to start of preceding year $(.95574) \times$ probability of survivorship during prior year $(1 - .04946)$.

Because the contract provides that, in the case of a distribution, the value of the additional death benefit (which is the only additional benefit available under the contract) is reduced by an amount that is at least proportional to the reduction in the notional account value and, at age 78 and 9 months, the sum of the notional account value (dollar amount credited to the employee under the contract) and the actuarial present value of the additional death benefit is no more than 120 percent of the notional account value, the exclusion is applicable for 2012. Therefore, for purposes of applying the rules for RMDs from defined contribution plans, the entire interest under the contract may be determined as the notional account value (i.e., without regard to the additional death benefit).

Example 2. The facts are the same as in Example 1, except that the notional account value is $450,000 at the end of 2011. In this instance, the actuarial present value of the death benefit in excess of the notional account value in 2011 is determined to be $108,669 (24 percent of the notional account value). The following table summarizes the actuarial methodology used in determining the actuarial present value of the additional benefit.

Year	Death Benefit During Year	End-of-Year Notional Account Before Withdrawal	Average Notional Account	Withdrawal at End of Year	End-of-Year Notional Account After Withdrawal
2011	$1,000,000				$450,000
2012	950,739	$459,000	$454,500	$23,077	435,923
2013	901,983	444,642	440,282	23,311	421,330
2014	853,749	429,757	425,543	23,538	406,219
2015	806,053	414,343	410,281	23,755	390,588
2016	758,916	398,399	394,494	23,962	374,437
2017	712,356	381,926	378,181	24,157	357,768

Year	Survivorship to Start of Year	Interest Discount to End of 2010	Mortality Rate During Year	Discounted Additional Benefits Within Year
2011				
2012	1.00000	.97590	.04426	$ 21,432
2013	.95574	.92943	.04946	20,286
2014	.90847	.88517	.05519	19,004
2015	.85833	.84302	.06146	17,601
2016	.80558	.80288	.06788	15,999
2017	.75090	.76464	.07477	14,347
				$108,669

Because the sum of the notional account balance and the actuarial present value of the additional death benefit is more than 120 percent of the notional account value, the exclusion does not apply for 2012. Therefore, for purposes of applying the rules for RMDs from defined contribution plans, the entire interest under the contract must include the actuarial present value of the additional death benefit.

Q 11:37   When can an annuity payment period be changed?

An annuity payment period may be changed in accordance with the provisions set forth in the following paragraph or in association with an annuity payment increase described in Q 11:38. [Treas. Reg. § 1.401(a)(9)-6, Q&A-13(a)]

If, in a stream of annuity payments that otherwise satisfies the minimum distribution requirements, the annuity payment period is changed and the annuity payments are modified in association with that change, this modification will not cause the distributions to fail to satisfy such requirements, provided the conditions set forth in the following paragraph are satisfied, and either:

1. The modification occurs at the time when the employee retires or in connection with a plan termination;

2. The annuity payments prior to modification are annuity payments paid over a period certain without life contingencies; or

3. The annuity payments after modification are paid under a QJSA (see Q 10:8) over the joint lives of the employee and a designated beneficiary (see Q 11:14), the employee's spouse (see Q 11:45) is the sole designated beneficiary, and the modification occurs in connection with the employee becoming married to such spouse.

[Treas. Reg. § 1.401(a)(9)-6, Q&A-13(b)]

In order to modify a stream of annuity payments in accordance with the preceding paragraph, the following conditions must be satisfied:

1. The future payments under the modified stream satisfy the minimum distribution requirements and the rules relating to defined benefit plans (see Qs 11:26–11:36, 11:38–11:40) (determined by treating the date of the change as a new annuity starting date (see Q 10:3) and the actuarial present value of the remaining payments prior to modification as the entire interest of the participant);

2. For purposes of the benefit limitations (see Qs 6:11–6:13) and the survivor annuity requirements (see Q 10:1), the modification is treated as a new annuity starting date;

3. After taking into account the modification, the annuity stream satisfies the benefit limitations (determined at the original annuity starting date, using the interest rates and mortality tables applicable to such date); and

4. The end point of the period certain, if any, for any modified payment period is not later than the end point available under the minimum distribution requirements to the employee at the original annuity starting date.

[Treas. Reg. § 1.401(a)(9)-6, Q&A-13(c)]

For the following examples, assume that the applicable interest rate throughout the period from 2005 through 2008 is 5 percent and throughout 2009 is 4 percent, the applicable mortality table throughout the period from 2005 to 2009 is the table provided in Revenue Ruling 2001-62, and the maximum annual retirement benefit (see Qs 6:11–6:12) in 2005 at age 70 for a straight life annuity is $255,344.

Example 1. James, who has ten years of participation in a frozen defined benefit plan, attains age 70½ in 2005. James is not retired and elects to receive distributions from the plan in the form of a straight life (i.e., level payment) annuity with annual payments of $240,000 per year beginning in 2005 at a date when he has an attained age of 70. The plan offers non-retired employees in pay status the opportunity to modify their annuity payments due to an associated change in the payment period at retirement, and the plan treats the date of the change in payment period as a new annuity starting date. Thus, for example, the plan provides a new QJSA election and obtains spousal consent.

The plan determines modifications of annuity payment amounts at retirement such that the present value of future new annuity payment amounts (taking into account the new associated payment period) is actuarially equivalent to the present value of future pre-modification annuity payments (taking into account the pre-modification annuity payment period). Actuarial equivalency for this purpose is determined using the applicable interest rate and the applicable mortality table as of the date of modification.

James retires in 2009 at the age of 74 and, after receiving four annual payments of $240,000, elects to receive his remaining distributions from the plan in the form of an immediate final single-sum payment (calculated at 4 percent interest) of $2,399,809. Because payment of retirement benefits in the form of an immediate final single-sum payment satisfies (in terms of form) the minimum distribution requirements, the condition described in item 1 on page 11-53 is met. Because the plan treats a modification of an annuity payment stream at retirement as a new annuity starting date, the condition described in item 2 on page 11-53 is met.

After taking into account the modification, the annuity stream determined as of the original annuity starting date consists of annual payments beginning at age 70 of $240,000, $240,000, $240,000, $240,000, and $2,399,809. This benefit stream is actuarially equivalent to a straight life annuity at age 70 of $250,182, an amount less than the maximum annual retirement benefit limit determined at the original annuity starting date, using the interest and mortality rates applicable to such date. Thus, the condition described in item 3 on page 11-53 is met.

Thus, because a stream of annuity payments in the form of a straight life annuity satisfies the minimum distribution requirements and because each of the conditions is satisfied, the modification of annuity payments to James described in this example is permissible.

Example 2. The facts are the same as in Example 1, except that the straight life annuity payments are paid at a rate of $250,000 per year and after James retires the single-sum payment at age 75 is $2,499,801. Thus, after taking into account the modification, the annuity stream determined as of the original annuity starting date consists of annual payments beginning at age 70 of $250,000, $250,000, $250,000, $250,000, and $2,499,801. This benefit stream is actuarially equivalent to a straight life annuity at age 70 of $260,606, an amount greater than the maximum annual retirement benefit limit determined at the original annuity starting date, using the interest and mortality rates applicable to such date. Thus, the single-sum payment to James fails to satisfy the condition described in item 3 on page 11-53 and, therefore, fails to meet the requirements set forth in this Q 11:37 and fails to satisfy the minimum distribution requirements.

Example 3. Jimmy, who has ten years of participation in a frozen defined benefit plan, attains age 70$\frac{1}{2}$ and retires in 2005 at a date when his attained age is 70. Jimmy elects to receive annual distributions from the plan in the form of a 27-year period-certain annuity (i.e., a 27-year annuity payment period without a life contingency) paid at a rate of $37,000 per year beginning in 2005, with future payments increasing at a rate of 4 percent per year (i.e., the 2006 payment will be $38,480, the 2007 payment will be $40,019, and so on). The plan offers participants in pay status whose annuity payments are in the form of a term-certain annuity the opportunity to modify their payment period at any time and treats such modifications as a new annuity starting date. Thus, for example, the plan provides a new QJSA election and obtains spousal consent.

The plan determines modifications of annuity payment amounts such that the present value of future new annuity payment amounts (taking into account the new associated payment period) is actuarially equivalent to the present value of future pre-modification annuity payments (taking into

account the pre-modification annuity payment period). Actuarial equivalency for this purpose is determined using 5 percent and the applicable
mortality table as of the date of modification.

In 2008, Jimmy, after receiving annual payments of $37,000, $38,480, and
$40,019, elects to receive his remaining distributions from the plan in the
form of a straight life annuity paid with annual payments of $92,133 per year.
Because payment of retirement benefits in the form of a straight life annuity
satisfies (in terms of form) the minimum distribution requirements, the
condition described in item 1 on page 11-53 is met. Because the plan treats a
modification of an annuity payment stream at retirement as a new annuity
starting date, the condition described in item 2 on page 11-53 is met.

After taking into account the modification, the annuity stream determined as
of the original annuity starting date consists of annual payments beginning at
age 70 of $37,000, $38,480, and $40,019 and a straight life annuity beginning
at age 73 of $92,133. This benefit stream is equivalent to a straight life
annuity at age 70 of $82,539, an amount less than the maximum annual
retirement benefit limit determined at the original annuity starting date,
using the interest and mortality rates applicable to such date. Thus, the
condition described in item 3 on page 11-53 is met.

Thus, because a stream of annuity payments in the form of a straight life
annuity satisfies the minimum distribution requirements and because each of
the conditions is satisfied, the modification of annuity payments to Jimmy
described in this example is permissible.

Q 11:38   Are annuity payments permitted to increase?

Except as otherwise provided with respect to defined benefit plans (see
Q 2:3), all annuity payments (whether paid over an employee's life, joint lives,
or a period certain) must be nonincreasing or increase only in accordance with
one or more of the following:

1. With an annual percentage increase that does not exceed the percentage
    increase in an eligible cost-of-living index as defined in the following
    paragraph for a 12-month period ending in the year during which the
    increase occurs or in the prior year;

2. With a percentage increase that occurs at specified times (e.g., at specified
    ages) and does not exceed the cumulative total of annual percentage
    increases in an eligible cost-of-living index since the annuity starting date
    (see Q 10:3) or, if later, the date of the most recent percentage increase.
    However, in cases providing such a cumulative increase, an actuarial
    increase may not be provided to reflect the fact that increases were not
    provided in the interim years;

3. To the extent of the reduction in the amount of the employee's payments
    to provide for a survivor benefit, but only if there is no longer a survivor
    benefit because the beneficiary whose life was being used to determine
    the distribution period during lifetime over which payments were being

made dies or is no longer the employee's beneficiary pursuant to a qualified domestic relations order (QDRO; see Q 36:1);

4. To pay increased benefits that result from a plan amendment;

5. To allow a beneficiary to convert the survivor portion of a joint and survivor annuity into a single-sum distribution upon the employee's death; or

6. To the extent increases are permitted in accordance with the following provisions of this Q 11:38.

[Treas. Reg. § 1.401(a)(9)-6, Q&A-14(a)]

An eligible cost-of-living index means:

1. A consumer price index that is based on prices of all items (or all items excluding food and energy) and issued by the Bureau of Labor Statistics, including an index for a specific population (e.g., urban consumers or urban wage earners and clerical workers) and an index for a geographic area or areas (e.g., a given metropolitan area or state).

2. A percentage adjustment based on a cost-of-living index described in item 1 or, if less, a fixed percentage. In any year when the cost-of-living index is lower than the fixed percentage, the fixed percentage may be treated as an increase in an eligible cost-of-living index, provided it does not exceed the sum of (a) the cost-of-living index for that year and (b) the accumulated excess of the annual cost-of-living index from each prior year over the fixed annual percentage used in that year (reduced by any amount previously utilized).

[Treas. Reg. § 1.401(a)(9)-6, Q&A-14(b)]

In the case of annuity payments paid from an annuity contract purchased from an insurance company, if the total future expected payments exceed the total value being annuitized, the payments under the annuity will not fail to satisfy the nonincreasing payments requirement merely because the payments are increased in accordance with one or more of the following:

1. By a constant percentage, applied not less frequently than annually;

2. To provide a final payment upon the death of the employee that does not exceed the excess of the total value being annuitized over the total of payments before the death of the employee;

3. As a result of dividend payments or other payments that result from actuarial gains, but only if actuarial gain is measured no less frequently than annually and the resulting dividend payments or other payments are either paid no later than the year following the year for which the actuarial experience is measured or paid in the same form as the payment of the annuity over the remaining period of the annuity (beginning no later than the year following the year for which the actuarial experience is measured); and

4. An acceleration of payments under the annuity.

[Treas. Reg. § 1.401(a)(9)-6, Q&A-14(c)]

In the case of annuity payments paid under a defined benefit plan (other than annuity payments under an annuity contract purchased from an insurance company), the payments under the annuity will not fail to satisfy the nonincreasing payment requirement merely because the payments are increased in accordance with one of the following:

1. By a constant percentage, applied not less frequently than annually, at a rate that is less than 5 percent per year;

2. To provide a final payment upon the death of the employee that does not exceed the excess of the actuarial present value of the employee's accrued benefit calculated as of the annuity starting date using the applicable interest rate and the applicable mortality table (or, if greater, the total amount of employee contributions) over the total of payments before the death of the employee; or

3. As a result of dividend payments or other payments that result from actuarial gains, but only if:

   a. Actuarial gain is measured no less frequently than annually;

   b. The resulting dividend payments or other payments are either paid no later than the year following the year for which the actuarial experience is measured or paid in the same form as the payment of the annuity over the remaining period of the annuity (beginning no later than the year following the year for which the actuarial experience is measured);

   c. The actuarial gain taken into account is limited to actual gain from investment experience;

   d. The assumed interest used to calculate such actuarial gains is not less than 3 percent; and

   e. The payments are not increasing by a constant percentage.

[Treas. Reg. § 1.401(a)(9)-6, Q&A-14(d)]

For purposes of this Q 11:38, the following definitions apply:

1. Total value being annuitized is:

   a. In the case of annuity payments under a Section 403(a) annuity plan or under a deferred annuity purchased by a qualified retirement plan, the value of the employee's entire interest (see Q 11:36) being annuitized (valued as of the date annuity payments commence);

   b. In the case of annuity payments under an immediate annuity contract purchased by a defined benefit plan, the amount of the premium used to purchase the contract; and

   c. In the case of a defined contribution plan (see Q 2:2), the value of the employee's account balance used to purchase an immediate annuity under the contract.

2. Actuarial gain is the difference between an amount determined using the actuarial assumptions (i.e., investment return, mortality, expense, and other similar assumptions) used to calculate the initial payments before

adjustment for any increases and the amount determined under the actual experience with respect to those factors. Actuarial gain also includes differences between the amount determined using actuarial assumptions when an annuity was purchased or commenced and such amount determined using actuarial assumptions used in calculating payments at the time the actuarial gain is determined.

3. Total future expected payments are the total future payments expected to be made under the annuity contract as of the date of the determination, calculated using the Single Life Table (see Q 11:24) or, if applicable, the Joint and Last Survivor Table (see Appendix A) for annuitants who are still alive, without regard to any increases in annuity payments after the date of determination, and taking into account any remaining period certain.

4. Acceleration of payments is a shortening of the payment period with respect to an annuity or a full or partial commutation of the future annuity payments. An increase in the payment amount will be treated as an acceleration of payments in the annuity only if the total future expected payments under the annuity (including the amount of any payment made as a result of the acceleration) is decreased as a result of the change in payment period.

[Treas. Reg. § 1.401(a)(9)-6, Q&A-14(e)]

Example 1. Mickey, a retired participant in a defined contribution plan maintained by the Miami Beach Todd Organization Corp., attains age 70 on March 5, 2011, and, thus, attains age 70½ in 2011. Mickey elects to purchase an annuity contract from an insurance company in 2011. The contract is a single life annuity contract with a ten-year period certain, and the contract provides for an initial annual payment calculated with an assumed interest rate (AIR) of 3 percent. Subsequent payments are determined by multiplying the prior year's payment by a fraction the numerator of which is one plus the actual return on the separate account assets underlying the contract since the preceding payment and the denominator of which is one plus the AIR during that period. The value of Mickey's account balance in the plan at the time of purchase is $105,000, and the purchase price of the contract is $105,000. The contract provides Mickey with an initial payment of $7,200 at the time of purchase in 2010; and the total future expected payments to Mickey under the contract are $122,400, calculated as the initial payment of $7,200 multiplied by the age 70 life expectancy of 17 years (see Q 11:24). Because the total future expected payments on the purchase date exceed the total value used to purchase the contract and payments may only increase as a result of actuarial gain, with such increases, beginning no later than the next year, paid in the same form as the payment of the annuity over the remaining period of the annuity, distributions received by Mickey from the contract meet the requirements of item 3 on page 11-61.

Example 2. Tim, a retired participant in a defined contribution plan maintained by Villa del Verde Ltd., attains age 70 on May 1, 2011, and, thus, attains age 70½ in 2011. Tim elects to purchase an annuity contract from an insurance company in 2011. The contract is a participating single life annuity contract with a ten-year period certain; and the contract provides for level annual payments with dividends paid in a single sum in the year after the year for which the actuarial experience is measured or paid out levelly beginning in the year after the year for which the actuarial gain is measured over the remaining lifetime and period certain (i.e., the period certain ends at the same time as the original period certain). Dividends are determined annually by the insurance company based upon a comparison of actual actuarial experience to expected actuarial experience in the past year. The value of Tim's account balance in the plan at the time of purchase is $265,000, and the purchase price of the contract is $265,000. The contract provides Tim with an initial payment of $16,000 in 2011, and the total future expected payments to Tim under the contract are calculated by multiplying the annual initial payment of $16,000 by the age 70 life expectancy of 17 years, for a total of $272,000. Because the total future expected payments on the purchase date exceed the total value used to purchase the contract and payments may increase only as a result of actuarial gain, with such increases, beginning no later than the next year, paid in the same form as the payment of the annuity over the remaining period of the annuity, distributions received by Tim from the contract meet the requirements of item 3 on page 11-61.

Example 3. The facts are the same as in Example 2, except that the annuity provides a dividend accumulation option under which Tim may defer receipt of the dividends to a time selected by him. Because the dividend accumulation option permits dividends to be paid later than the end of the year following the year for which the actuarial experience is measured or as a stream of payments that increases only as a result of actuarial gain, with such increases beginning no later than the next year, paid in the same form as the payment of the annuity over the remaining period of the annuity in Example 2, the dividend accumulation option does not meet the requirements of item 3; and neither does the dividend accumulation option fit within any of the other increases described above. Accordingly, the dividend accumulation option causes the contract, and consequently any distributions from the contract, to fail to meet these requirements and thus fail to satisfy the minimum distribution requirements.

Example 4. The facts are the same as in Example 2, except that the annuity provides an option under which actuarial gain under the contract is used to provide additional death benefit protection for Tim. Because this option permits payments as a result of actuarial gain to be paid later than the end of the year following the year for which the actuarial experience is measured or as a stream of payments that increases only as a result of actuarial gain, with such increases beginning no later than the next year, paid in the same form as the payment of the annuity over the remaining period of the annuity in Example 2, the option does not meet the requirements of item 3; and neither does the option fit within any of the other increases described above. Accordingly, the addition of the option causes the contract, and consequently any distributions from the contract, to fail to meet these requirements and thus fail to satisfy the minimum distribution requirements.

Example 5. Pat, a retired participant in a defined contribution plan maintained by Verde Zihua Corp., attains age 70½ in 2011. Pat elects to purchase an annuity contract from an insurance company, and the contract is a life annuity contract 20-year period certain (which does not exceed the maximum permitted period certain) with fixed annual payments increasing 3 percent each year. The value of Pat's account balance in the plan at the time of purchase is $110,000, and the purchase price of the contract is $110,000. The contract provides Pat with an initial payment of $6,000 at the time of purchase in 2011; and the total future expected payments to Pat under the contract are $120,000, calculated by multiplying the initial annual payment of $6,000 by the period certain of 20 years. Because the total future expected payments on the purchase date exceed the total value used to purchase the contract and payments increase only as a constant percentage applied not less frequently than annually, distributions received by Pat from the contract meet the requirements of item 1 on page 11-61.

Example 6. The facts are the same as in Example 5, except that the initial payment is $5,400 and the annual rate of increase is 4 percent. In this example, the total future expected payments are $108,000, calculated by multiplying the initial payment of $5,400 by the period certain of 20 years. Because the total future expected payments are less than the total value of $110,000 used to purchase the contract, distributions received by Pat do not meet these requirements and thus fail to meet the minimum distribution requirements.

Example 7. Orlando, a retired participant in a defined contribution plan maintained by Orlando's Bar, Inc., attains age 78 in 2011. Orlando elects to purchase an annuity contract from an insurance company, and the contract provides for a single life annuity with a ten-year period certain (which does not exceed the maximum period certain permitted) with annual payments. The contract provides that Orlando may cancel it at any time before he attains age 84 and receive, on his next payment due date, a final payment in an amount determined by multiplying the initial payment amount by a factor obtained from Table M of the contract, using Orlando's age as of his birthday in the calendar year of the final payment. The value of Orlando's account balance in the plan at the time of purchase is $450,000, and the purchase price of the contract is $450,000. The contract provides Orlando with an initial payment in 2011 of $40,000. The factors in Table M are as follows:

Age at Final Payment	Factor
79	10.5
80	10.0
81	9.5
82	9.0

Age at Final Payment	Factor
83	8.5
84	8.0

The total future expected payments to Orlando under the contract are $456,000, calculated as the initial payment of $40,000 multiplied by the age 78 life expectancy of 11.4 provided in the Single Life Table. Because the total future expected payments on the purchase date exceed the total value being annuitized (i.e., the $450,000 used to purchase the contract), the permitted increases are available. Furthermore, because the factors in Table M are less than the life expectancy of each of the ages in the Single Life Table, the final payment is always less than the total future expected payments. Thus, the final payment is a permitted acceleration of payments.

As an illustration of the above, if Orlando were to elect to cancel the contract on the day before he was to attain age 84, his contractual final payment would be $320,000. This amount is determined as $40,000 (the annual payment amount due under the contract) multiplied by 8.0 (the factor in Table M for the next payment due date, age 84). The total future expected payments under the contract at age 84 before the final payment is $324,000, calculated as the initial payment amount multiplied by 8.1, the age 84 life expectancy provided in the Single Life Table. Because $320,000 (the total future expected payments under the annuity contract, including the amount of the final payment) is less than $324,000 (the total future expected payments under the annuity contract, determined before the election), the final payment is a permitted acceleration of payments.

Example 8. The facts are the same as in Example 7, except that the annuity provides that Orlando may request, at any time before he attains age 84, an ad hoc payment on his next payment due date, with future payments reduced by an amount equal to the ad hoc payment divided by the factor obtained from Table M (from Example 7) corresponding to Orlando's age at the time of the ad hoc payment. Because, at each age, the factors in Table M are less than the corresponding life expectancies in the Single Life Table, total future expected payments under the contract will decrease after an ad hoc payment. Thus, ad hoc distributions received by Orlando from the contract will satisfy the requirements.

As an illustration, if Orlando were to request, on the day before he was to attain age 84, an ad hoc payment of $100,000 on his next payment due date, his recalculated annual payment amount would be reduced to $27,500. This amount is determined as $40,000 (the amount of Orlando's next annual payment) reduced by $12,500 (his $100,000 ad hoc payment divided by the Table M factor at age 84 of 8.0). Thus Orlando's total future expected payments after the ad hoc payment (and including the ad hoc payment) are equal to $322,750 ($100,000 plus $27,500 multiplied by the Single Life Table value of 8.1). Note that this $322,750 amount is less than the amount of Orlando's total future expected payments before the ad hoc payment

($324,000, determined as $40,000 multiplied by 8.1), and the requirements are satisfied.

Example 9. Sam, a participant in a defined contribution plan maintained by Hollander Tunnel Corp., attains age 70½ in 2011. Sam elects to purchase an annuity contract from an insurance company in 2011 with a premium of $1,000,000. The contract is a single life annuity contract with a 20-year period certain and provides for an initial payment of $200,000, a second payment one year from the time of purchase of $40,000, and 18 succeeding annual payments each increasing at a constant percentage rate of 4.5 percent from the preceding payment.

The contract fails to meet the minimum distribution requirements because the total future expected payments without regard to any increases in the annuity payment, calculated as $200,000 in year one and $40,000 in each of years two through 20, is only $960,000 (i.e., an amount that does not exceed the total value used to purchase the annuity).

The distribution of an annuity contract, in and of itself, is not a distribution for RMD purposes. [Treas. Reg. § 1.401(a)(9)-8, Q&A-10]

Q 11:39   Are there special rules applicable to payments made under a defined benefit plan or annuity contract to a surviving child?

Yes; payments under a defined benefit plan (see Q 2:3) or annuity contract that are made to an employee's child until such child reaches the age of majority (or dies, if earlier) may be treated, for minimum distribution purposes, as if such payments were made to the surviving spouse (see Q 11:41) to the extent they become payable to the surviving spouse upon cessation of the payments to the child. For purposes of the preceding sentence, a child may be treated as having not reached the age of majority if the child has not completed a specified course of education and is under the age of 26. In addition, a child who is disabled (see Q 16:6) when the child reaches the age of majority may be treated as having not reached the age of majority so long as the child continues to be disabled. Thus, when payments become payable to the surviving spouse because the child attains the age of majority, recovers from a disabling illness, dies, or completes a specified course of education, there is not an increase in benefits (see Q 11:28). Likewise, the age of the child receiving such payments is not taken into consideration for purposes of the minimum incidental benefit requirement (see Q 11:29). [I.R.C. § 401(a)(9)(F); Treas. Reg. § 1.401(a)(9)-6, Q&A-15]

Q 11:40   What were the rules for determining RMDs for defined benefit plans and annuity contracts for calendar years 2003, 2004, and 2005?

A distribution from a defined benefit plan (see Q 2:3) or annuity contract for calendar years 2003, 2004, and 2005 did not fail to satisfy the minimum distribution requirements merely because the payments did not satisfy the rules pertaining to such distributions (see Qs 11:28–11:39), provided the payments satisfied the minimum distribution requirements based on a reasonable and good-faith interpretation of the RMD provisions. [Treas. Reg. § 1.401(a)(9)-6, Q&A-17]

Rollovers and Transfers

Q 11:41   How does a rollover or transfer affect the RMD rules?

If an amount distributed by one plan (distributing plan) is rolled over to another plan (receiving plan), the amount distributed is still treated as a distribution by the distributing plan, notwithstanding the rollover. However, an RMD may not be rolled over to another qualified retirement plan or to an IRA. [I.R.C. § 402(c)(4)(B); Treas. Reg. § 1.401(a)(9)-7, Q&A-1] See chapter 34 for a discussion of rollovers. The portion of any distribution that is not included in gross income (e.g., basis; see Q 13:3) can be part of the RMD (see Q 11:27).

> **Example.** Ben attained age 70½ in 2010 and, in the first quarter of 2011, elects to receive a distribution of his voluntary contributions (see Q 1:48) and to make a direct rollover to an IRA of the balance of his profit sharing plan account. The RMDs for 2010 and 2011 are $37,000, and his voluntary contributions were $63,000. Ben satisfies the minimum distribution requirements and receives the distribution of his voluntary contributions income tax free.

If an amount distributed by a distributing plan is rolled over to a receiving plan, the benefit of the employee under the receiving plan is increased by the amount rolled over for purposes of determining the RMD for the calendar year immediately following the calendar year in which the amount rolled over is distributed. If the amount rolled over is received after the last valuation date in the calendar year under the receiving plan, the benefit of the employee as of such valuation date, as adjusted (see Q 11:21), will be increased by the rollover amount valued as of the date of receipt. In addition, if the amount rolled over is received by the receiving plan in a different calendar year from the calendar year in which it is distributed by the distributing plan, the amount rolled over is deemed to have been received by the receiving plan in the calendar year in which it was distributed by the distributing plan. [Treas. Reg. § 1.401(a)(9)-7, Q&A-2]

In the case of a transfer of an amount of an employee's benefit from one plan (transferor plan) to another (transferee plan), the transfer is not treated as a distribution by the transferor plan for RMD purposes. Instead, the benefit of the employee under the transferor plan is decreased by the amount transferred. However, if any portion of an employee's benefit is transferred in a distribution calendar year (see Q 11:20) with respect to that employee, to satisfy the minimum distribution requirements, the transferor plan must determine the amount of the RMD with respect to that employee for the calendar year of the transfer using the employee's benefit under the transferor plan before the transfer. Additionally, if any portion of the employee's benefit is transferred in the employee's second distribution calendar year but on or before the employee's RBD (see Q 11:5), to satisfy the minimum distribution requirements, the transferor plan must determine the amount of the RMD requirement for the employee's first distribution calendar year based on the employee's benefit under the transferor plan before the transfer. The transferor plan may satisfy the RMD for the calendar year of the transfer (and the prior year if applicable) by segregating the amount that must be distributed from the employee's benefit and not transferring that amount. Such amount may be retained by the transferor plan and must be distributed on or before the date required. For purposes of determining any RMD for the calendar year immediately following the calendar year in which the transfer occurs, in the case of a transfer after the last valuation date for the calendar year of the transfer under the transferor plan, the benefit of the employee as of such valuation date, as adjusted, will be decreased by the amount transferred, valued as of the date of the transfer. [Treas. Reg. § 1.401(a)(9)-7, Q&A-3]

In the case of a transfer from a transferor plan to a transferee plan, the benefit of the employee under the transferee plan is increased by the amount transferred in the same manner as if it were a plan receiving a rollover contribution. [Treas. Reg. § 1.401(a)(9)-7, Q&A-4]

For purposes of determining an employee's benefit and RMD, a spinoff, a merger, or a consolidation (see Qs 9:55, 9:56) will be treated as a transfer of the benefits of the employees involved. Consequently, the benefit and RMD of each employee involved under the transferor and transferee plans will be determined in accordance with the two preceding paragraphs. [Treas. Reg. §§ 1.401(a)(9)-7, Q&A-5, 1.414(l)-1]

RMDs from IRAs and defined contribution plans (see Q 2:2) were suspended for calendar year 2009 (see Q 11:1). If all or a portion of a distribution during 2009 was an eligible rollover distribution (see Q 34:8) because it was no longer an RMD, the distribution was not treated as an eligible rollover distribution for purposes of the direct rollover requirement (see Q 34:17) and the notice and written explanation of the direct rollover requirement (see Q 34:29), as well as the mandatory 20 percent income tax withholding for an eligible rollover distribution (see Q 20:10), to the extent the distribution would have been an RMD for 2009 absent this provision. Thus, for example, if a qualified retirement plan distributed an amount to an individual during 2009 that was an eligible rollover distribution but would have been an RMD for 2009, the plan was permitted, but not required, to offer the employee a direct rollover of that amount and to provide the employee with a written explanation of the requirement. If the employee received the distribution, the distribution was not subject to mandatory 20 percent income tax withholding and the employee could have rolled over the distribution by contributing it to an eligible retirement plan (see Q 34:16) within 60 days of the distribution (see Q 34:3). This was effective for calendar years beginning after December 31, 2008. However, the provision did not apply to any RMD for 2008 that was permitted to be made in 2009 by reason of an individual's RBD being April 1, 2009. [I.R.C. § 402(c)(4) (as amended by WRERA 2008 § 201(b); WRERA 2008 § 201(c)(1))]

According to IRS guidance, for a plan to determine which distributions made during 2009 were 2009 RMDs, the first distributions in 2009 were any RMDs from prior years that were not yet distributed, followed by 2009 RMDs. [IRS Notice 2009-82, Q&A-8, 2009-41 I.R.B.] A 2009 RMD that was paid from a plan in 2009 was not treated as an eligible rollover distribution for purposes of the 20 percent mandatory withholding rules. For example, if a plan made a distribution in 2009 to a retiree of the entire account balance under the plan and part of the distribution was a 2009 RMD, the portion of the distribution that was not a 2009 RMD was subject to the 20 percent mandatory withholding rules and the portion of the distribution that was a 2009 RMD was subject to the 10 percent optional withholding rules. On the other hand, if the retiree was receiving monthly distributions from the plan that exceeded the RMDs and that are expected to last for a period of at least ten years, then the whole amount of each distribution was subject to the periodic payment optional withholding rules. This rule applied only to 2009 RMDs paid from a plan in 2009. Withholding for a 2009 RMD that is paid in 2010 (for example, where the employee turns 70½ in 2009 and delays payment until April 1, 2010) is determined without regard to this rule. [IRS Notice 2009-82, Q&A-7, 2009-41 I.R.B.]

RMDs from an IRA to a Canadian citizen who was a nonresident alien were eligible for the 15 percent reduced withholding rate under the Canada–United States income tax treaty. The RMDs distributed to the IRA owner constituted a periodic pension payment for purposes of the treaty. [Priv. Ltr. Rul. 201009012]

Special Rules

Q 11:42 What distribution rules apply if an employee is a participant in more than one plan?

If an employee is a participant in more than one plan, the plans in which the employee participates are not permitted to be aggregated for purposes of testing whether the minimum distribution requirements are met. The distribution of the benefit of the employee under each plan must *separately* meet the requirements. Thus, if the employee is a participant in more than one qualified retirement plan, the employee must receive a minimum distribution from each plan. For this purpose, a plan described in Section 414(k) is treated as two separate plans, a defined contribution plan (see Q 2:2) to the extent benefits are based on an individual account and a defined benefit plan (see Q 2:3) with respect to the remaining benefits. [Treas. Reg. § 1.401(a)(9)-8, Q&A-1]

Example. Beverly, age 71, participates in three separate qualified retirement plans. Plan 1 has an account balance of $300,000; Plan 2, $20,000; and Plan 3, $10,000. The RMD for each Plan is separately calculated. The RMD for Plan 1 is $11,320.75; for Plan 2, $754.72; and for Plan 3, $377.36. Beverly cannot take the aggregated amount of $12,452.83 from any one plan or any combination of the three plans to satisfy her RMDs for the year; the distribution from each plan must separately satisfy the RMD rules.

Q 11:43   What is the separate account or segregated share rule?

Separate accounts in an employee's account are separate portions of an employee's benefit reflecting the separate interests of the employee's beneficiaries under the plan as of the date of the employee's death for which separate accounting is maintained. The separate accounting must allocate all post-death investment gains and losses, contributions, and forfeitures for the period prior to the establishment of the separate accounts on a pro rata basis in a reasonable and consistent manner among the separate accounts. However, once the separate accounts are actually established, the separate accounting can provide for separate investments for each separate account under which gains and losses from the investment of the account are only allocated to that account, or investment gains or losses can continue to be allocated among the separate accounts on a pro rata basis. A separate accounting must allocate any post-death distribution to the separate account of the beneficiary receiving that distribution. [Treas. Reg. § 1.401(a)(9)-8, Q&A-3; Priv. Ltr. Ruls. 200548028, 200548027, 200307095, 200248031, 200248030, 200234074, 200218039, 200208033, 200208030]

Except as otherwise provided below, if an employee's account under a defined contribution plan (see Q 2:2) is divided into separate accounts under the plan, the separate accounts will be aggregated for purposes of satisfying the minimum distribution requirements. Thus, except as otherwise provided below, all separate accounts, including a separate account for voluntary employee contributions (see Q 6:38), will be aggregated for RMD purposes. [Treas. Reg. § 1.401(a)(9)-8, Q&A-2(a)(1)]

If the employee's benefit in a defined contribution plan is divided into separate accounts and the beneficiaries with respect to one separate account differ from the beneficiaries with respect to the other separate accounts of the employee under the plan, for years subsequent to the calendar year containing the date on which the separate accounts were established, or the date of death if later, such separate account under the plan is not aggregated with the other separate accounts under the plan to determine whether the distributions from such separate account under the plan satisfy the minimum distribution requirements. Instead, the RMD rules separately apply to such separate account under the plan. Since the benefits of the separate accounts first apply for the subsequent calendar year, the separate accounts should be established, if possible, during the employee's lifetime or during the year in which the employee's death occurs. Because of the delayed effectiveness of the separate account rule, concerns were raised that, for employees who die late in a calendar year, it is nearly impossible to set up separate accounts by the end of the year so that they can be used to determine RMDs for the year after death. In response to these concerns, IRS modified the regulations to provide that, if separate accounts, determined as of an employee's date of death, are actually established by the end of the calendar year following the year of an employee's death, the separate accounts can be used to determine RMDs for the year following the year of the employee's death. In addition, the applicable distribution period for each such separate account is determined disregarding the other beneficiaries of the employee's benefit *only* if the separate account is established on a date no later than the last day of the year following the calendar year of the employee's death. For example, if, in the case of an installment distribution where the employee dies before the RBD (see Q 11:11), the only beneficiary of a separate account under the plan established on a date no later than the end of the year following the calendar year of the employee's death is the employee's surviving spouse (see Q 11:45) and beneficiaries other than the surviving spouse are designated with respect to the other separate accounts of the employee, distribution of the spouse's separate account need not commence until the deceased spouse would have attained age 70½, even if distribution of the other separate accounts must commence at an earlier date. Similarly, in the case of a distribution after the death of an employee who died prior to the RBD, distribution from a separate account of an employee established on a date no later than the end of the year following the year of the employee's death may be made over a beneficiary's life expectancy even though distributions from other separate accounts under the plan with different beneficiaries are being made in accordance with the five-year rule (see Qs 11:9–11:12). [Treas. Reg. § 1.401(a)(9)-8, Q&A-2(a)(2)]

> **Example 1.** Steve participates in the Essjaykay Enterprises Ltd. profit sharing plan and designates his four grandchildren, Benjamin, Jennifer, Jason, and Casey, as beneficiaries. If Steve dies and his plan account is divided into four separate accounts prior to December 31 of the calendar year following the calendar year in which death occurs and Benjamin becomes beneficiary of one account, Jennifer the second, Jason the third, and Casey the fourth, each account will be considered a separate account for the minimum distribution rules for all calendar years subsequent to the calendar year in which the separate accounts are established. With the modification of the separate account rules, if the separate accounts are established during the calendar year following Steve's death, the separate account rule can be utilized commencing with that calendar year.

The separate account rule is not available to beneficiaries of a trust with respect to the trust's interest in an employee's benefit. [Treas. Reg. § 1.401(a)(9)-4, Q&A-5(c); Priv. Ltr. Ruls. 201038019, 200809042, 200750019, 200740018, 200708084, 200610027, 200608032, 200538034, 200528035, 200453023, 200444033, 200440031, 200432029, 200432028, 200432027, 200410019] Consequently, the beneficiary designation itself should specify each trust that will be treated as the beneficiary of a separate account.

> **Example 2.** The facts are the same as in Example 1, except that Steve designates a trust for his grandchildren as beneficiary, and upon Steve's death the trust is divided into four separate trusts, one for each grandchild. The separate account rule does not apply, and RMDs must be made over the life expectancy of the oldest beneficiary of the trust (see Q 11:25).

> **Example 3.** The facts are the same as in Example 1, except that Steve designates a trust for Benjamin as beneficiary of one-quarter of his plan account, a trust for Jennifer as beneficiary of one-quarter of his plan account, a trust for Jason as beneficiary of one-quarter of his plan account, and a trust for Casey as beneficiary of the remaining one-quarter of his plan account. If

Steve's plan account is divided into four separate accounts prior to December 31 of the calendar year following the calendar year in which death occurs, each account will be considered a separate account for the minimum distribution rules for all calendar years subsequent to the calendar year in which death occurred. The separate trusts for Ben, Jennifer, Jason, and Casey can be created under a single trust agreement established by Steve during his lifetime. [Priv. Ltr. Rul. 200537044]

As a general statement, the separate account rule and the use of trusts may be incompatible unless a conduit or passthrough trust (see Q 11:25, Example 3) is used. This is because contingent trust beneficiaries may be taken into account. Consequently, in Example 3 above, if Steve's three children are contingent beneficiaries, Steve's oldest child may be considered the designated beneficiary for purposes of determining the distribution period with such child's remaining life expectancy (see Q 11:24) being used. Using a conduit or passthrough trust negates this incompatibility. [Priv. Ltr. Rul. 200537044]

A recent IRS ruling may demonstrate that a conduit or passthrough trust will not be needed in certain circumstances. An IRA owner designated as beneficiary a trust for his son. The trust provided that the final distribution of trust principal would be made to the son at age 40; and, if the son died prior to age 40, the remaining trust principal would be distributed to the son's descendants or, if none, to the IRA owner's heirs at law. When the IRA owner died, his son had no descendants; and, under state law, the surviving spouse was the sole heir at law. IRS ruled that the surviving spouse would at all times through the determination date (see Q 11:16) be the sole heir at law for purposes of determining the remainder beneficiary of the trust. IRS ruled that:

1. The son and the surviving spouse are the only individuals who need be considered for purposes of determining who is the designated beneficiary for purposes of calculating RMDs.

2. The surviving spouse was the designated beneficiary with the shortest life expectancy for purposes of determining the distribution period.

[Priv. Ltr. Rul. 200843042]

Assume that, when the IRA owner died, his son had descendants. In this situation, it appears that the ruling would conclude that the surviving spouse would be a mere successor in interest to the descendants' interest and, therefore, not considered for purposes of determining the distribution period.

Even if the separate account rule cannot be used, IRS will permit, as an example, a deceased owner's IRA to be segregated into separate IRAs, each in the name of the deceased IRA owner for the benefit of a different beneficiary, by means of trustee-to-trustee transfers. [Priv. Ltr. Ruls. 200608032, 200538034, 200528035, 200453023, 200444033, 200349009] An IRA owner died after commencing to receive RMDs. The IRA owner designated his wife as the sole beneficiary (see Q 11:14) and did not name any contingent beneficiary. The IRA owner's wife died seven days later without (1) disclaiming the IRA (see Q 11:17); (2) taking any distributions from the IRA; (3) electing to treat the IRA as her own (see Q 11:60); or (4) naming any beneficiary. As a result, the right to receive the IRA passed by the deceased wife's will to their two children. IRS ruled that, because the wife died before distributions to her had begun, the RMD rules apply as if she were the IRA owner (see Q 11:35); and, because she died before her RBD without having a designated beneficiary (see Q 11:15), the five-year rule applied (see Q 11:10). The deceased wife's personal representatives proposed to subdivide the IRA into two sub-IRAs, with each sub-IRA being titled "IRA owner (deceased) for the benefit of a specific beneficiary under the will of the wife (deceased)" and to accomplish the subdivision by trustee-to-trustee transfers. IRS ruled that neither the Code nor the RMD regulations precluded the posthumous division of an IRA into more than one IRA, and that the division did not constitute a transfer for purposes of the income in respect of a decedent rules (see Q 30:47), a taxable distribution (see Q 30:40), or a rollover (see Q 34:6). [Priv. Ltr. Rul. 200945011; IRC §§ 408(d)(1), 408(d)(3), 691(a)(2); Rev. Rul. 92-47, 1992-1 C.B. 198; Rev. Rul. 78-406, 1978-2 C.B. 157] This ruling appears to be incorrect because the IRA owner died after his RBD (see Q 11:7). Therefore, the IRA owner's wife is the designated beneficiary, and RMDs should be based upon her life expectancy (see Q 11:23). However, this error does not affect the ability to subdivide the IRA.

When a deceased IRA owner designated his surviving spouse as beneficiary of 45 percent of his IRA and two other individuals as beneficiaries of the remaining 55 percent, IRS ruled that the spouse's 45 percent share constituted a separate account, of which she was the sole beneficiary. [Priv. Ltr. Rul. 200121073] In this ruling, there was no actual division of the IRA as respects the surviving spouse and the other beneficiaries. It is unclear whether IRS would rule similarly under the final regulations. If IRS would, then the separate accounts would be established immediately upon death without any actual division. However, it will be the wiser course of action to actually establish separate accounts as soon after death as practicable.

A portion of an employee's account balance under a defined contribution plan is permitted to be used to purchase an annuity contract while the remaining portion stays in the account. In that case, to satisfy the minimum distribution requirements, the remaining account under the plan must be distributed in accordance with the rules applicable to defined contribution plans (see Qs 11:20–11:26) and the annuity payments under the annuity contract must satisfy the rules applicable to defined benefit plans (see Qs 11:28–11:35). [Treas. Reg. § 1.401(a)(9)-8, Q&A-2(a)(3)]

The above rules also apply to benefits under a defined benefit plan where the benefits under the plan are separated into separate identifiable components that are separately distributed (segregated shares). [Treas. Reg. § 1.401(a)(9)-8, Q&A-2(b)]

Q 11:44   Must an RMD be made even if there is no consent?

Yes. Employee and spousal consent to certain distributions of plan benefits while such benefits are immediately distributable may be required (see Qs 10:8,

10:21, 10:61). If an employee's normal retirement age (see Qs 10:55, 11:44) is later than the RBD (see Q 11:5) and, therefore, benefits are still immediately distributable, the plan must, nevertheless, distribute plan benefits to the employee (or where applicable, to the spouse) in a manner that satisfies the minimum distribution requirements. These requirements must be satisfied even though the employee (or spouse, where applicable) fails to consent to the distribution. In such a case, the plan may distribute in the form of a QJSA (see Q 10:8) or in the form of a QPSA (see Q 10:9), and the consent requirements are deemed to be satisfied if the plan has made reasonable efforts to obtain consent from the employee (or spouse if applicable) and if the distribution otherwise meets the QJSA or QPSA requirements. If the plan is not required to distribute in the form of a QJSA to an employee or a QPSA to a surviving spouse (see Q 10:6), the plan may distribute the RMD amount at the required time and the consent requirements are deemed to be satisfied if the plan has made reasonable efforts to obtain consent from the employee (or spouse if applicable) and if the distribution otherwise meets the QJSA or QPSA requirements. [I.R.C. §§ 401(a)(11)(B), 411(a)(11), 417(e); Treas. Reg. §§ 1.411(a)-(11)(c)(2), 1.417(e)-1(c), 1.401(a) (9)-8, Q&A-4; Prop. Treas. Reg. §§ 1.411(a)-11(c)(2)(ii), 1.411(a)-11(c)(2)(iii)(A)]

IRS representatives have opined that spousal consent is required only if the benefit will be paid in a form other than a QJSA. If paid as a QJSA, spousal consent is not required. If a new benefit has been accrued after RMDs begin, the new benefit is subject to the RMD rules and spousal consent is required only if it will be in a form other than a QJSA.

No RMD was required for calendar year 2009 from defined contribution plans (see Qs 2:2, 11:1, 11:5). For plans subject to the spousal consent rules, if no new annuity starting date (see Q 10:3) is chosen, spousal consent is not required under most circumstances. If the plan provides that there is a new annuity starting date, spousal consent may be required to suspend distributions that include 2009 RMDs and to restart such distributions in 2010, depending on the form of distribution. [IRS Notice 2009-82, Q&A-5, 2009-41 I.R.B.; IRS Notice 97-75, Q&A-8, 1997-2 C.B. 337]

Q 11:45   Who is an employee's spouse or surviving spouse?

Except in the case of distributions of a portion of an employee's benefit payable to a former spouse pursuant to a QDRO (see Qs 11:46, 36:1), an individual is a spouse or surviving spouse of an employee if such individual is treated as the employee's spouse under applicable state law. In the case of distributions after the death of an employee, for purposes of determining whether, under the life expectancy rule, the special spousal deferral rule (see Q 11:11) applies, the spouse of the employee is determined as of the date of death of the employee. [Treas. Reg. § 1.401(a)(9)-8, Q&A-5]

Q 11:46 Are there any special rules that apply to a distribution to an alternate payee pursuant to a QDRO?

A former spouse to whom all or a portion of the employee's benefit is payable pursuant to a QDRO (see Qs 36:1, 36:12–36:17) will be treated as a spouse (including a surviving spouse) of the employee for RMD purposes, including the MDIB requirement, regardless of whether the QDRO specifically provides that the former spouse is treated as the spouse for purposes of a QJSA or QPSA (see Q 11:44). [Treas. Reg. § 1.401(a)(9)-8, Q&A-6(a)]

If a QDRO provides that an employee's benefit will be divided and a portion will be allocated to an alternate payee (see Q 36:5), such portion will be treated as a separate account (or segregated share (see Q 11:43)) that separately must satisfy the minimum distribution requirements and may not be aggregated with other separate accounts (or segregated shares) of the employee for purposes of satisfying the RMD requirements. Except as otherwise provided below, distribution of such separate account allocated to an alternate payee pursuant to a QDRO must be made in accordance with the minimum distribution requirements. For example, in general, distribution of such account will satisfy the lifetime RMD rules (see Qs 11:20–11:26) if RMDs from such account during the *employee's* lifetime begin not later than the *employee's* RBD (see Q 11:5) and the RMD is determined for each distribution calendar year using either the Uniform Lifetime Table (see Q 11:22) or the joint life expectancy of the employee and a spousal alternate payee if the spousal alternate payee is more than ten years younger than the employee (see Appendix A). The determination of how distribution from such account after the death of the employee to the alternate payee will be made will depend on whether distributions have begun (see Qs 11:7–11:12). For example, if the alternate payee dies before the employee and distribution of the separate account allocated to the alternate payee pursuant to the QDRO will be made to the alternate payee's beneficiary, such beneficiary may be treated as a designated beneficiary (see Q 11:14) for purposes of determining the RMD required from such account after the death of the employee if the beneficiary of the alternate payee is an individual and if such beneficiary is a beneficiary under the plan or specified to or in the plan. Specification in or pursuant to the QDRO will also be treated as specification to the plan. [Treas. Reg. § 1.401(a)(9)-8, Q&A-6(b)(1)]

Distribution of the separate account allocated to an alternate payee pursuant to a QDRO will satisfy the lifetime RMD rules if such account will be distributed, beginning not later than the *employee's* RBD, over the life of the alternate payee (or over a period not extending beyond the life expectancy of the alternate payee). Also, if the plan permits the employee to elect whether distribution upon the death of the employee will be made in accordance with the five-year rule (see Q 11:10) or the life expectancy rule (see Q 11:11), such election can be made only by the alternate payee for purposes of distributing the separate account allocated to the alternate payee pursuant to the QDRO. If the alternate payee dies after distribution of the separate account allocated to the alternate payee pursuant to a QDRO has begun (see Q 11:8) but before the employee dies, distribution of the remaining portion of that portion of the benefit allocated to the alternate payee must be made in accordance with the rules for distributions during the life of the employee. Only after the death of the employee is the amount of the RMD determined in accordance with the rules that apply after the death of the employee. [Treas. Reg. § 1.401(a)(9)-8, Q&A-6(b)(2)]

If a QDRO does not provide that an employee's benefit will be divided but provides that a portion of an employee's benefit (otherwise payable to the employee) will be paid to an alternate payee, such portion will not be treated as a separate account (or segregated share) of the employee. Instead, such portion will be aggregated with any amount distributed to the employee and will be treated as having been distributed to the employee for purposes of determining whether the minimum distribution requirements have been satisfied with respect to that employee. [Treas. Reg. § 1.401(a)(9)-8, Q&A-6(c)]

A plan will not fail to satisfy the minimum distribution requirements merely because it fails to distribute an amount otherwise required to be distributed during the period in which the issue of whether a domestic relations order (see Q 36:2) is a QDRO is being determined, provided that the period does not extend beyond an 18-month period (see Q 36:21). To the extent that a distribution otherwise required is not made during this period, any segregated amounts will be treated as though the amounts are not vested during the period and any distributions with respect to such amounts must be made under the relevant rules for nonvested benefits (see Qs 11:26, 11:33). [Treas. Reg. § 1.401(a)(9)-8, Q&A-7]

Q 11:47 How do state insurer delinquency proceedings affect the RMD rules?

A plan will not fail to satisfy the minimum distribution requirements merely because an individual's distribution from the plan is less than the amount otherwise required to satisfy the minimum distribution requirements because distributions were being paid under an annuity contract issued by a life insurance company (see Q 11:31) in state insurer delinquency proceedings and have been reduced or suspended by reasons of such state proceedings. To the extent that a distribution otherwise required is not made during the state insurer delinquency proceedings, this amount and any additional amount accrued during this period will be treated as though such amounts are not vested during the period and any distributions with respect to such amounts must be made under the relevant rules for nonvested benefits (see Qs 11:26, 11:33). [Treas. Reg. § 1.401(a)(9)-8, Q&A-8]

Q 11:48 What happens if the employee has not attained normal retirement age under the plan?

A plan will not fail to qualify solely because the plan permits distributions to commence to an employee on or after April 1 of the calendar year following the calendar year in which the employee attains age 70½ (see Q 11:5) even though the employee has not retired or attained the plan's normal retirement age (see Q 10:55) as of the date on which such distributions commence. This rule applies without regard to whether or not the employee is a 5 percent owner (see Q 11:5) with respect to the plan year ending in the calendar year in which distributions commence. [Treas. Reg. § 1.401(a)(9)-8, Q&A-9]

Q 11:49   Will a payment by a plan after the death of an employee fail to be treated as an RMD solely because it is made to an estate or a trust?

No. As a result, the estate or trust which receives a payment from a plan after the death of an employee need not distribute the amount of such payment to the beneficiaries of the estate or trust. Since an estate may not be a designated beneficiary (see Q 11:15), distribution to the estate must satisfy the five-year rule (see Q 11:10) if the distribution to the employee had not begun (see Q 11:8) as of the employee's date of death. For provisions under which beneficiaries of a trust with respect to the trust's interest in an employee's benefit are treated as having been designated as beneficiaries of the employee under the plan, see Qs 11:18, 11:19. [Treas. Reg. § 1.401(a)(9)-8, Q&A-11]

Q 11:50   Will a plan violate the anti-cutback rule if it is amended to eliminate benefit options that do not satisfy the RMD rules?

A plan is not permitted to eliminate for all employees a Section 411(d)(6) protected benefit (see Q 10:45) that has already accrued (see Q 9:25). However, a plan must provide that, notwithstanding any other plan provisions, it will not distribute benefits under any option that does not satisfy the minimum distribution requirements (see Q 11:3). [Treas. Reg. § 1.401(a)(9)-8, Q&A-12]

Q 11:51   Can distributions be delayed until after the RBD?

Yes, but only if the employee made a valid election under Section 242(b)(2) of TEFRA before 1984. In that case, the employee can defer distributions until the employee actually retires. A Section 242(b)(2) election is valid only if it designated a distribution method that would not have disqualified the plan under pre-TEFRA law. IRS ruled that elections that deferred distributions until one year prior to the expiration of the electing employee's life expectancy or until ten years after retirement were invalid. Also, elections that did not explicitly set forth the form of payment and beneficiary of death benefits were valid with regard to lifetime distributions to the electing employee but were not applicable with regard to the distribution of death benefits. [Treas. Reg. § 1.401(a)(9)-8, Q&A-13; IRS Notice 83-23, 1983-2 C.B. 418; Priv. Ltr. Ruls. 200510035, 199908060, 9042063] IRS has ruled, however, that an election was not valid where the employee did not specify the beneficiary of the death benefit. [Priv. Ltr. Rul. 9638040]

If the Section 242(b)(2) election is revoked *after* the employee's RBD (see Q 11:5), the total amount of distributions that would have been required by the revocation date must be distributed by the end of the calendar year after the year of revocation and RMDs must continue to be made. [Treas. Reg. § 1.401(a)(9)-8,

Q&A-16; IRS Notice 83-23, 1983-2 C.B. 418] Satisfaction of the spousal consent requirements (see Q 10:21) is not considered a revocation. [Treas. Reg. § 1. 401(a)(9)-8, Q&A-13]

Under a Section 242(b)(2) election, an employee elected to receive a single-sum distribution at the later of age 65 or termination of employment. The employee subsequently modified the election to increase the age from 65 to 70½, and IRS ruled that the modification caused a revocation of the Section 242(b)(2) election. [Priv. Ltr. Rul. 9617048] Where the form of payment chosen in the Section 242(b)(2) election was a single-sum payment and, after the employee's RBD, the employee changed the form of payment to one based on the joint life expectancy of the employee and his spouse, the change constituted a revocation of the election and catch-up distributions were required. [Priv. Ltr. Rul. 9430035] Although any change in the designation will generally be considered a revocation of the designation, IRS has ruled that the mere substitution or addition of another beneficiary (one not named in the designation) under the designation will not be considered a revocation of the designation, so long as the substitution or addition does not alter the period over which distributions will be made under the designation, directly or indirectly (for example, by altering the relevant measuring life). IRS ruled that an employee could take an in-service distribution in accordance with the plan terms without it being considered a revocation. [Priv. Ltr. Ruls. 200124028, 200034031]

In the case in which an amount is transferred from one plan (transferor plan) to another plan (transferee plan), the amount transferred may be distributed in accordance with a Section 242(b)(2) election made under the transferor plan if the employee did not elect to have the amount transferred and if the amount transferred is separately accounted for by the transferee plan. However, only the benefit attributable to the amount transferred, plus earnings thereon, may be distributed in accordance with the Section 242(b)(2) election made under transferor plan. [Priv. Ltr. Rul. 200110034] If the employee elected to have the amount transferred, the transfer will be treated as a distribution and rollover of the amount transferred. In the case in which an amount is transferred from a transferor plan to a transferee plan, the amount transferred may not be distributed in accordance with a Section 242(b)(2) election made under the transferee plan. If a Section 242(b)(2) election was made under the transferee plan, the amount transferred must be separately accounted for under the transferee plan. If the amount transferred is not separately accounted for under the transferee plan, the Section 242(b)(2) election under the transferee plan is revoked. A merger, spinoff, or consolidation (see Qs 9:55, 9:56) will be treated as a transfer for purposes of the Section 242(b)(2) election. [Treas. Reg. § 1.401(a)(9)-8, Q&A-14]

A revocation of a Section 242(b)(2) election does not result from (1) the change in the employer's form of business from a corporation to a partnership or (2) the revocation of the election with respect to another plan within a commingled trust. An employee's Section 242(b)(2) election under a terminated profit sharing plan will not be revoked by the employer's transfer of the employee's account balance, without the employee's consent, to a segregated account in a 401(k) plan sponsored by the employer. The election will continue to apply only to the transferred account and not to the employee's other accounts in the 401(k) plan. When one plan was merged into another plan and the employee had made identical Section 242(b)(2) elections under each plan, the transferee plan could make distributions in accordance with the elections even though the transferee plan did not account separately for the transferred funds. An employee's election was also not revoked when he withdrew a portion of his voluntary contributions (see Q 6:39), because the withdrawal was not inconsistent with the election and the terms of the plan both before and after the election. [Priv. Ltr. Ruls. 9310026, 9215040, 9052058, 9013011, 8938073]

If an amount is distributed by one plan (distributing plan) and rolled over (see Q 34:1) into another plan (receiving plan), the receiving plan must distribute the amount rolled over in accordance with the minimum distribution requirements whether or not the employee made a Section 242(b)(2) election under the distributing plan. Further, if the amount rolled over was not distributed in accordance with the election, the election under the distributing plan is revoked and the minimum distribution requirements will apply to all subsequent distributions by the distributing plan. Finally, if the employee made a Section 242(b)(2) election under the receiving plan and such election is still in effect, the amount rolled over must be separately accounted for under the receiving plan and distributed in accordance with the minimum distribution requirements. If amounts rolled over are not separately accounted for, any Section 242(b)(2) election under the receiving plan is revoked and the minimum distribution requirements will apply to subsequent distributions by the receiving plan. [Treas. Reg. § 1.401(a)(9)-8, Q&A-15]

403(b) Contracts

Q 11:52   Are 403(b) contracts subject to the RMD rules?

Yes. 403(b) contracts (see Q 35:1) are subject to the minimum distribution requirements (see Qs 11:1–11:51). A 403(b) contract means an annuity contract (see Q 35:6), a custodial account (see Q 35:7), or a retirement income account (see Q 35:55). [I.R.C. §§ 403(b)(7), 403(b)(9), 403(b)(10); Treas. Reg. §§ 1.403(b)-6(e)(1), 1.403(b)-6(e)(5)]

For RMD purposes, 403(b) contracts are treated as IRAs (see Qs 11:56–11:66) for purposes of determining RMDs for calendar years beginning on or after January 1, 2003 (see Q 11:1). [Treas. Reg. § 1.403(b)-6(e)(2)] The RBD (see Q 11:5) is April 1 of the calendar year following the later of the calendar year in which the employee attains age 70½ or the calendar year in which the employee retires from employment with the employer maintaining the plan. However, for any 403(b) contract that is not part of a governmental plan or church plan (see Q 35:55), the RBD for a 5 percent owner (see Q 11:5) is April 1 of the calendar year following the calendar year in which the employee attains 70½. [I.R.C. §§ 403(b)(1)(A), 403(b)(10); Treas. Reg. § 1.403(b)-6(e)(3)] Although 403(b) contracts are treated as IRAs, the surviving spouse (see Q 11:45) of an employee is not permitted to treat a 403(b) contract of which the surviving spouse is the sole beneficiary as the surviving spouse's own 403(b) contract (see Q 11:60). [Treas. Reg. § 1.403(b)-6(e)(4)]

Annuity payments provided with respect to retirement income accounts will not fail to satisfy the requirements of Q 11:31 merely because the payments are not made under an annuity contract purchased from an insurance company, provided the relationship between the annuity payments and the retirement income accounts is not inconsistent with any rules prescribed by IRS. [Treas. Reg. § 1.403(b)-6(e)(5)]

RMDs from 403(b) plans for calendar year 2009 were suspended (see Qs 11:1, 11:5, 11:10, 11:11). [I.R.C. § 401(a)(9)(H) (as added by WRERA 2008 § 201(a); WRERA 2008 § 201(c)(1))]

Q 11:53   To what 403(b) contract benefits do the RMD rules apply?

The minimum distribution requirements apply to all 403(b) contract (see Q 35:1) benefits accruing after December 31, 1986 (post-'86 account balance). The RMD rules do *not* apply to the undistributed portion of the account balance under the 403(b) contract valued as of December 31, 1986, exclusive of subsequent earnings (pre-'87 account balance). Consequently, the post-'86 account balance includes earnings after December 31, 1986 on contributions made before January 1, 1987, in addition to the contributions made after December 31, 1986, and earnings thereon. [Treas. Reg. § 1.403(b)-6(e)(6)(i)] The issuer or custodian of the 403(b) contract must keep records that enable it to identify the pre-'87 account balance and subsequent changes as set forth below and provide such information upon request to the relevant employee or beneficiaries with respect to the 403(b) contract. If the issuer or custodian does not keep such records, the entire account balance will be treated as subject to the RMD rules. [Treas. Reg. § 1.403(b)-6(e)(6)(ii)]

In applying the minimum distribution rules, only the post-'86 account balance is used to calculate the RMD for a calendar year. The amount of any distribution from a 403(b) contract will be treated as being paid from the post-'86 account balance to the extent the distribution is required to satisfy the minimum distribution requirement with respect to that contract for a calendar year. Any amount distributed in a calendar year in excess of the RMD for a calendar year with respect to that contract will be treated as paid from the pre-'87 account balance, if any, of that contract. [Treas. Reg. § 1.403(b)-6(e)(6)(iii)]

If an amount is distributed from the pre-'87 account balance and rolled over to another 403(b) contract, the amount will be treated as part of the post-'86 account balance in that second 403(b) contract. However, if the pre-'87 account balance under a 403(b) contract is directly transferred to another 403(b) contract, the amount transferred retains its character as a pre-'87 account balance, provided the issuer of the transferee 403(b) contract satisfies the recordkeeping requirements discussed above. [Treas. Reg. § 1.403(b)-6(e)(6)(iv)]

Prior to the enactment of TRA '86, there was no specific time by which 403(b) contract distributions were required to begin. On an administrative basis, IRS required 403(b) contract distributions to commence by age 75. Thus, with regard to the pre-'87 account balance, distributions need not commence until the employee attains age 75. However, IRS has indicated that distributions need not commence until the *later* of age 75 or April 1 of the calendar year immediately following the calendar year in which the employee retires. This exception applies *only* if records have been maintained to identify the pre-'87 account balance; if not, the entire benefit will be subject to the RMD rules. [Priv. Ltr. Ruls. 9442030, 9345044, 7913129, 7825010; IRS Notice 88-39, 1988-1 C.B. 525; I.R.M. 7.7.1.13.7.3] If the pre-'87 account balance is rolled over to an IRA (see Q 35:42), the delayed distribution date will no longer be available.

A violation of the RMD rules will not occur if distributions are not made because the insurance company that issued the 403(b) contract is in delinquency proceedings (see Q 11:47). [Rev. Proc. 92-16, 1992-1 C.B. 673; Rev. Proc. 92-10, 1992-1 C.B. 661]

The distinction between the pre-'87 account balance and the post-'86 account balance has no relevance for purposes of determining the portion of a distribution that is includible in income. [Treas. Reg. § 1.403(b)-6(e)(6)(v)]

Q 11:54   Must the pre-'87 account balance be distributed in accordance with the incidental benefit requirement?

Yes. Distributions attributable to the pre-'87 account balance are treated as satisfying the incidental benefit requirement if all distributions from the 403(b) contract (see Q 35:1) (including distributions attributable to the post-'86 account balance) satisfy the incidental benefit requirement without regard to the RMD rules, and distributions attributable to the post-'86 account balance satisfy the RMD rules. Distributions attributable to the pre-'87 account balance are treated as satisfying the incidental benefit requirement if all distributions from the 403(b) contract (including distributions attributable to both the pre-'87 account balance and the post-'86 account balance) satisfy the RMD rules. Thus, distributions in accordance with the age 75 rule discussed in Q 11:53 should satisfy the incidental benefit requirement. [Treas. Reg. §§ 1.401-1(b)(1)(i), 1.403(b)-6(e)(6)(vi)]

Q 11:55   Is the RMD from one 403(b) contract permitted to be distributed from another 403(b) contract?

Yes. The RMD must be separately determined for each 403(b) contract (see Q 35:1) of an employee; however, such amounts may then be totaled and the total distribution taken from any one or more of the individual 403(b) contracts. Under this rule, however, only amounts in 403(b) contracts that an individual holds as an employee may be aggregated. Amounts in 403(b) contracts that an individual holds as a beneficiary of the same decedent may be aggregated, but such amounts may not be aggregated with amounts held in 403(b) contracts that the individual holds as an employee or as the beneficiary of another decedent.

Distributions from 403(b) contracts will not satisfy the minimum distribution requirements for IRAs (see Qs 11:56–11:64), nor will distributions from IRAs satisfy the minimum distribution requirements for 403(b) contracts. [Treas. Reg. § 1.403(b)-6(e)(7)]

> **Example.** Stanley, age 71, has three 403(b) contracts. 403(b) contract 1 has an account balance of $300,000; 403(b) contract 2, $20,000; and 403(b) contract 3, $10,000. The RMD for each 403(b) contract is separately calculated. The RMD for 403(b) contract 1 is $11,320.75; for 403(b) contract 2, $754.72; and for 403(b) contract 3, $377.36. Stanley can take the aggregated amount of $12,452.83 from 403(b) contract 1, 403(b) contract 2, or any other combination of the three 403(b) contracts to satisfy his RMDs for the year.

Individual Retirement Plans (IRAs)

Q 11:56   Are IRAs subject to the RMD rules?

Yes. Except as otherwise provided in Qs 11:57 through 11:66, IRAs (see Q 30:1) are subject to the RMD rules provided for qualified retirement plans (see Qs 11:1–11:51) for calendar years beginning on or after January 1, 2003 (see Q 11:1). For example, whether the five-year rule or the life expectancy rule applies to distributions after death occurring before the IRA owner's RBD (see Q 11:5) is determined in accordance with Qs 11:9 through 11:13; the rules set forth in Qs 11:14 through 11:19 apply for purposes of determining an IRA owner's designated beneficiary; the amount of the RMD for each calendar year from an individual retirement account will be determined in accordance with Qs 11:20 through 11:25; and whether annuity payments from an individual retirement annuity satisfy the minimum distribution requirements will be determined in accordance with Qs 11:28 through 11:36. The IRA owner is the individual for whom an IRA is originally established by contributions for the benefit of that individual and that individual's beneficiaries. [I.R.C. §§ 408(a)(6), 408(b)(3); Treas. Reg. § 1.408-8, Q&A-1(a)]

RMDs from IRAs for calendar year 2009 were suspended (see Qs 11:1, 11:5, 11:10, 11:11). [I.R.C. § 401(a)(9)(H) (as added by WRERA 2008 § 201(a); WRERA 2008 § 201(c)(1))]

For purposes of applying the RMD rules relating to qualified retirement plans, the IRA trustee, custodian, or issuer is treated as the plan administrator (see Q 20:1), and the IRA owner is substituted for the employee. [Treas. Reg. § 1.408-8, Q&A-1(b)]

An audit conducted by the Treasury Inspector General for Tax Administration (TIGTA) disclosed that noncompliance with the minimum distribution requirements applicable to IRAs continues to grow, resulting in significant revenue loss to the federal government. [Audit Rept. No. 2010-40-43, TIGTA News Rel., May 2010]

See Q 31:37 for RMD rules that apply to a Roth IRA.

Q 11:57   Are SEPs or SIMPLE IRA plans subject to the RMD rules?

Yes. IRAs that receive employer contributions under a SEP (see Q 32:1) or a SIMPLE IRA plan (see Q 33:2) are treated as IRAs, rather than qualified retirement plans, and are, therefore, subject to the minimum distribution requirements applicable to IRAs. [I.R.C. §§ 408(k), 408(p); Treas. Reg. § 1.408-8, Q&A-2]

RMDs from SEPs and SIMPLE IRAs for calendar year 2009 were suspended (see Q 11:56).

Q 11:58   What does RBD mean for distributions from an IRA?

With respect to distributions from an IRA, RBD means April 1 of the calendar year following the calendar year in which the individual attains 70½. The concept of 5 percent owner has no relevance to IRA owners (see Q 11:5). [Treas. Reg. § 1.408-8; Q&A-3]

Q 11:59   What portion of an IRA distribution is not eligible for rollover as an RMD?

The portion of a distribution that is an RMD from an IRA and thus not eligible for rollover is determined in the same manner as provided for distributions from qualified retirement plans (see Q 34:11). For example, if an RMD is required for a calendar year, an amount distributed during a calendar year from an IRA is treated as an RMD to the extent that the total RMD for the year for that IRA has not been satisfied. This requirement may be satisfied by a distribution from the IRA or from another IRA (see Q 11:64). [Treas. Reg. § 1.408-8, Q&A-4]

Any amount paid before January 1 of the year in which the IRA owner attains age 70½ (see Q 11:5) will not be treated as an RMD and, thus, is an eligible rollover distribution if it otherwise qualifies. Conversely, any amount paid on or after January 1 of the year in which the IRA owner attains age 70½ will be treated as an RMD to the extent of the required amount and, hence, not an eligible rollover distribution. [Treas. Reg. § 1.402(c)-2, Q&A-7(b)]

> **Example.** Shirley attains age 70½ on December 30, 2010, and has an RBD (see Q 11:58) of April 1, 2011. Shirley's RMD to be made on or before April 1, 2011 is $20,000, and she receives a $25,000 distribution from her IRA on June 21, 2010. Even though Shirley is only age 69 on June 21, 2010, $20,000 of the $25,000 distribution is an RMD and, thus, is not an eligible rollover distribution.

RMDs from IRAs for calendar year 2009 are suspended (see Qs 11:41, 11:56).

Q 11:60   Do special rules apply if the beneficiary is the IRA owner's surviving spouse?

The surviving spouse (see Q 11:45) of a deceased IRA owner may elect to treat the surviving spouse's entire interest as a beneficiary in the deceased's IRA (or the remaining part of such interest if distribution thereof has commenced to the surviving spouse) as the surviving spouse's own IRA. [Priv. Ltr. Rul. 200110033] This election is permitted to be made at any time *after* the deceased IRA owner's date of death. To make this election, the surviving spouse must be the sole beneficiary of the IRA and have an unlimited right to withdraw amounts from the IRA. This requirement is not satisfied if a trust is named as beneficiary of the IRA even if the surviving spouse is the sole beneficiary of the trust (see Q 11:18). If the surviving spouse makes the election, the surviving spouse's interest in the IRA is then subject to the minimum distribution requirements applicable to the surviving spouse as the IRA owner rather than those applicable to the surviving spouse as the deceased IRA owner's beneficiary. Thus, the RMD for the calendar year of the election and each subsequent calendar year will be determined under the lifetime distribution rules (see Q 11:4) with the surviving spouse as IRA owner. However, if the election is made in the calendar year containing the IRA owner's death, the surviving spouse is not required to take an RMD as the IRA owner for that calendar year. Instead, the spouse is required to take an RMD for that year, determined with respect to the deceased IRA owner, to the extent such a distribution was not made to the IRA owner before death. [Treas. Reg. § 1.408-8, Q&A-5(a)]

The election is made by the surviving spouse redesignating the account as an account in the name of the surviving spouse as IRA owner rather than as beneficiary. Alternatively, a surviving spouse eligible to make the election is deemed to have made the election if, at any time, either of the following occurs:

1. Any amount in the IRA that would be required to be distributed to the surviving spouse as beneficiary is not distributed within the required time period (see Qs 11:10–11:13), or

2. Any additional amount is contributed to the IRA that is subject, or deemed to be subject, to the lifetime distribution requirements.

[Treas. Reg. § 1.408-8, Q&A-5(b)]

The result of the election is that the surviving spouse is then considered the IRA owner for whose benefit the IRA is maintained for all purposes, including possibly being subject to the 10 percent tax on early distributions (see Q 16:5). [Treas. Reg. § 1.408-8, Q&A-5(c)] A participant in a qualified retirement plan designated his wife as the sole beneficiary. At the time of the participant's death, he did not have an IRA. IRS permitted the wife to (1) establish an IRA in her deceased husband's name designating herself as beneficiary and (2) transfer the husband's plan account directly to the new IRA. In this way, distributions from the IRA to the wife, who had not attained age 59½, would not be subject to the 10 percent penalty tax. [Priv. Ltr. Rul. 200450057; *see also* Priv. Ltr. Rul. 200936049] An IRA owner requested a distribution from his IRA but died before receiving the distribution. The decedent's surviving spouse established a new IRA in the decedent's name and deposited the distribution into the new IRA within 60 days after receipt. IRS ruled that this was a valid rollover. However, IRS also ruled that the surviving spouse could not treat the new IRA as her own; and, thus, she was deemed to be the beneficiary, not the owner, of the new IRA for RMD purposes. [Priv. Ltr. Rul. 200717021]

If the surviving spouse dies before the election is made, the surviving spouse's estate cannot make the election. [Priv. Ltr. Ruls. 9822059, 9704019, 9630034, 9534027, 9237038] Where a surviving spouse elected to treat her deceased husband's IRA as her own, but died before designating a beneficiary, IRS ruled that their daughter, who was the legal representative of her mother's estate, could not designate herself as beneficiary of that IRA. [Priv. Ltr. Rul. 200126036] An IRA owner died after commencing to receive RMDs. The IRA owner designated his wife as the sole beneficiary (see Q 11:14) and did not name any contingent beneficiary. The IRA owner's wife died seven days later without (1) disclaiming the IRA (see Q 11:17); (2) taking any distributions from the IRA; (3) electing to treat the IRA as her own; or (4) naming any beneficiary. As a result, the right to receive the IRA passed by the deceased wife's will to their two children. IRS ruled that, because the wife died before distributions to her had begun, the RMD rules apply as if she were the IRA owner (see Q 11:35); and, because she died before her RBD (see Q 11:5) without having a designated beneficiary (see Q 11:15), the five-year rule applied (see Q 11:10). The deceased wife's personal representatives proposed to subdivide the IRA into two sub-IRAs, with each sub-IRA being titled "IRA owner (deceased) for the benefit of a specific beneficiary under the will of the wife (deceased)" and to accomplish the subdivision by trustee-to-trustee transfers. IRS ruled that neither the Code nor the RMD regulations precluded the posthumous division of an IRA into more than one IRA, and that the division did not constitute a transfer for purposes of the income in respect of a decedent rules (see Q 30:47), a taxable distribution (see Q 30:40), or a rollover (see Q 34:6). [Priv. Ltr. Rul. 200945011; IRC §§ 408(d)(1), 408(d)(3), 691(a)(2); Rev. Rul. 92-47, 1992-1 C.B. 198; Rev. Rul. 78-406, 1978-2 C.B. 157] This ruling appears to be incorrect because the IRA owner died after his RBD (see Q 11:7). Therefore, the IRA owner's wife is the designated beneficiary, and RMDs should be based upon her life expectancy (see Q 11:23).

Instead of electing to treat the deceased's IRA as that of the surviving spouse, the surviving spouse can roll over the deceased's IRA into an IRA in the name of the surviving spouse. [Priv. Ltr. Rul. 200605017] If the surviving spouse makes the election and has passed the RBD, the surviving spouse must take an RMD by December 31 of the calendar year following the calendar year in which occurred the deceased IRA owner's death. If the surviving spouse uses the rollover alternative, a question arises as to whether the surviving spouse may roll over the entire IRA or only the portion of the IRA in excess of that year's RMD. Some commentators opine that the entire IRA may be rolled over to be consistent with the election alternative, while others opine that only the excess may be rolled over because an RMD cannot be rolled over (see Q 11:59). The author agrees with the latter opinion. The next question is whether the RMD is calculated using the Single Life Table (see Q 11:24) or the Uniform Life Table (see Q 11:22). The question is whether the surviving spouse is the IRA beneficiary or the IRA owner. The author believes that the surviving spouse is still the beneficiary of the IRA, so that the RMD would be calculated using the Single Life Table.

Q 11:61   How is the benefit determined for purposes of calculating the RMD from an IRA?

To determine the RMD to be made from an IRA in any calendar year, the account balance of the IRA as of the December 31 of the calendar year immediately preceding the calendar year for which distributions are required to be made is used. This determination is the same as the amount used to determine an employee's RMD in the case of an individual account (see Q 11:21). Except as provided in Qs 11:62 and 11:63, no adjustments are made for contributions or distributions after that date. [Treas. Reg. § 1.408-8, Q&A-6]

Example. Beverly, born October 1, 1939, attains age 70½ in calendar year 2010. Beverly's RBD is April 1, 2011. As of December 31, 2009, the value of Beverly's IRA was $265,000. The applicable distribution period (see Q 11:22) for an individual age 71 is 26.5 years. The RMD for calendar year 2010 is $10,000 ($265,000 ÷ 26.5). That amount is distributed to Beverly on April 1, 2011.

The value of Beverly's IRA as of December 31, 2010, is $274,000. To determine the IRA account balance to be used in calculating the RMD for calendar year 2011, the IRA account balance of $274,000 is *not* reduced by $10,000, the amount of the RMD for calendar year 2010 made on April 1, 2011. Thus, the IRA account balance for purposes of determining the RMD for calendar year 2011 is $274,000. If, instead of $10,000 being distributed to Beverly, $30,000 is distributed on April 1, 2011, the IRA account balance of $274,000 would still not be reduced to determine the benefit to be used in calculating the RMD for calendar year 2011. The amount of the distribution made on April 1, 2011, to meet the RMD for 2010 would still be $10,000. The remaining $20,000 ($30,000 – $10,000) of the distribution is not the RMD for 2010. Instead, the remaining $20,000 of the distribution is more than sufficient to satisfy the RMD requirement with respect to Beverly for calendar year 2011. The amount that is required to be distributed for calendar year 2011 is $10,703 ($274,000 ÷ 25.6, the applicable distribution period for an individual age 72). Consequently, no additional amount is required to be distributed to Beverly in 2011 because $20,000 exceeds $10,703. However, the remaining $9,297 ($20,000 – $10,703) may not be used to satisfy the RMD requirement for calendar year 2012 or any subsequent calendar years (see Q 11:20).

Q 11:62   What rules apply in the case of a rollover to an IRA of an amount distributed by a qualified retirement plan or another IRA?

If the surviving spouse (see Q 11:45) of an employee rolls over a distribution from a qualified retirement plan to an IRA of the deceased spouse, the surviving spouse may elect to treat the IRA as the surviving spouse's own IRA (see Q 11:60). In the event of any other rollover to an IRA of an amount distributed by a qualified retirement plan or another IRA, the rules relating to death before the RBD (see Qs 11:9–11:13) will apply for purposes of determining the account balance for the receiving IRA and the RMD from the receiving IRA. However, because the value of the account balance is determined as of December 31 of the year preceding the year for which the RMD is being determined and not as of a valuation date in the preceding year, the account balance of the receiving IRA is only adjusted if the amount is not received in the calendar year in which the amount rolled over is distributed. In that case, for purposes of determining the RMD for the calendar year in which such amount is actually received, the account balance of the receiving IRA as of December 31 of the preceding year must be adjusted by the amount received (see Q 11:41). [Treas. Reg. § 1.408-8, Q&A-7]

Q 11:63   What rules apply in the case of a transfer from one IRA to another?

In the case of a trustee-to-trustee transfer from one IRA to another IRA that is not a distribution and rollover, the transfer is not treated as a distribution by the transferor IRA for minimum distribution purposes. Accordingly, the minimum distribution requirement with respect to the transferor IRA must still be satisfied. Except as provided below, after the transfer, the IRA owner's account balance and the RMD under the transferee IRA are determined in the same manner as an account balance and RMD are determined under an IRA receiving a rollover contribution (see Q 11:62). [Treas. Reg. § 1.408-8, Q&A-8(a)]

If an amount is contributed to a Roth IRA that is a conversion contribution or failed conversion contribution and that amount (plus net income allocable to that amount) is transferred to another IRA (transferee IRA) in a subsequent year as a recharacterized contribution (see Q 31:9), the recharacterized contribution (plus allocable net income) must be added to the December 31 account balance of the transferee IRA for the year in which the conversion or failed conversion occurred. [Treas. Reg. § 1.408-8, Q&A-8(b)] A recharacterization of a Roth IRA back to a traditional IRA may trigger an RMD from the traditional IRA. However, IRS, in granting an extension to make a recharacterization, allowed an individual until the end of 2003 to take RMDs from the traditional IRA that should have been made for 1999 and later years. It appears that no excise tax was imposed (see Qs 11:67–11:71). [Priv. Ltr. Rul. 200213030]

The minimum distribution for a year is not reduced even if a portion of the IRA assets is transferred to a former spouse pursuant to a divorce decree during the year (see Q 30:51). The RMD is still based on the account balance on December 31 of the year before the transfer. [Priv. Ltr. Rul. 9011031]

Q 11:64   Is the RMD from one IRA permitted to be distributed from another IRA?

Yes. The RMD must be calculated separately for each IRA; however, the separately calculated amounts may then be totaled and the total distribution taken from any one or more of the individual's IRAs. Generally, only amounts in IRAs that an individual holds as the IRA owner may be aggregated. However, amounts in IRAs that an individual holds as a beneficiary of the same decedent and that are being distributed under the life expectancy rule (see Q 11:11) may be aggregated, but such amounts may not be aggregated with amounts held in IRAs that the individual holds as the IRA owner or as the beneficiary of another decedent. Distributions from 403(b) contracts (see Qs 11:55, 35:1) will not satisfy the distribution requirements from IRAs, nor will distributions from IRAs satisfy the distribution requirements from 403(b) contracts. Distributions from Roth IRAs (see Q 31:1) will not satisfy the distribution requirements applicable to IRAs or 403(b) contracts, and distributions from IRAs or 403(b) contracts will not satisfy the distribution requirements from Roth IRAs. [Treas. Reg. § 1.408-8, Q&A-9]

> **Example.** Katie, age 71, has three IRAs. IRA 1 has an account balance of $300,000; IRA 2, $20,000; and IRA 3, $10,000. The RMD for each IRA is separately calculated. The RMD for IRA 1 is $11,320.75; for IRA 2, $754.72; and for IRA 3, $377.36. Katie can take the aggregated amount of $12,452.83 from IRA 1, IRA 2, or any other combination of the three IRAs to satisfy her RMDs for the year.

Q 11:65   Is any reporting required for the minimum amount that is required to be distributed from an IRA?

Yes. The trustee, custodian, or issuer of an IRA is required to report information with respect to the minimum amount required to be distributed from the IRA for each calendar year to individuals or entities, at the time and in the manner prescribed by IRS as well as in applicable federal tax forms and accompanying instructions. [Treas. Reg. § 1.408-8, Q&A-10]

IRA trustees must identify to IRS on Form 5498 each IRA for which a minimum distribution is required to be made to an IRA owner. The IRA trustee does not need to report the amount of the RMD to the IRS; however, the IRA trustee must provide additional information regarding the IRA to the IRA owner required to receive an RMD. The IRA trustee either must report the amount of the RMD for the IRA to the IRA owner or must advise the IRA owner that a minimum distribution with respect to the IRA is required for the year, offer to calculate the amount of the RMD for the IRA owner upon request, and then, if requested, calculate the amount and provide it to the IRA owner. Reporting is only required with respect to IRA owners, and no reporting is required with respect to beneficiaries at this time. [IRS Notice 2002-27, 2002-1 C.B. 814] IRS has announced that IRA trustees can satisfy the minimum distribution reporting requirements with regard to IRA owners by using one or both of the two alternatives and has clarified that an IRA trustee may use both alternatives, so that one may be used for some IRA owners and the other alternative for other IRA owners. IRS also provided that trustees can transmit RMD reporting statements electronically only if the electronic transmission procedures for Form W-2 (Wage and Tax Statement) are satisfied. [IRS Notice 2003-3, 2003-1 C.B. 258]

In the Example in Q 11:64, each IRA trustee, custodian, or issuer must report to Barbara the RMD for that year or advise her that an RMD is required and offer to calculate the amount, even though Barbara may choose to take the aggregate RMD from only IRA 1 or IRA 2.

Q 11:66   What amounts distributed from an IRA are considered for RMD purposes?

Except as provided below, all amounts distributed from an IRA are taken into account in determining whether the minimum distribution rules are satisfied, regardless of whether the amount is includible in income. [Treas. Reg. § 1.408-8, Q&A-11(a)]

The following amounts are not taken into account in determining whether the required minimum amount with respect to an IRA for a calendar year has been distributed:

1. The return of excess contributions, together with the income allocable to these contributions (see Qs 30:9, 31:8);
2. The return of other excess contributions;
3. Corrective distributions of excess SEP contributions, together with the income allocable to these distributions (see Q 32:6); and
4. Similar items designated by IRS.

[I.R.C. §§ 408(d)(4), 408(d)(5), 408(k)(6)(C); Treas. Reg. § 1.408-8, Q&A-11(b)]

Excise Tax

Q 11:67   Is there a penalty for failure to make an RMD?

Yes. If the amount distributed to a payee under any qualified plan for a calendar year is less than the RMD for such year, a nondeductible excise tax is imposed on the payee for the taxable year beginning with or within the calendar year during which the amount is required to be distributed. The tax is equal to 50 percent of the amount by which such RMD exceeds the actual amount distributed during the calendar year. This tax is imposed upon and paid by the payee. The RMD for a calendar year is the RMD amount required to be distributed during the calendar year. See Q 11:70 for a special rule for amounts required to be distributed by an employee's (or individual's) RBD (see Q 11:5). [I.R.C. §§ 4974(a), 4974(b); Treas. Reg. § 54.4974-2, Q&A-1; Priv. Ltr. Rul. 200811028]

For purposes of the excise tax, each of the following is a qualified plan:

1. A qualified retirement plan;
2. An annuity plan described in Section 403(a);
3. A 403(b) contract (see Q 35:1);
4. An IRA (see Q 30:1), including a Roth IRA (see Q 31:1);
5. Any other plan, contract, account, or annuity that, at any time, has been treated as a plan, account, or annuity described above, whether or not such plan, contract, account, or annuity currently satisfies the applicable requirements for such treatment.

[I.R.C. § 4974(c); Treas. Reg. § 54.4974-2, Q&A-2]

Example 1. Shirley should have taken a 2005 RMD of $5,000 by April 1, 2006, a 2006 RMD of $5,040 by December 31, 2006, and a 2007 RMD of $5,500 by December 31, 2007; but Shirley does not take the RMDs for those three years until December 1, 2008. On December 1, 2008, she also takes her 2008 RMD of $5,650. In 2008, Shirley amends her 2006 income tax return to pay the 50 percent excise tax of $5,020 on her 2005 and 2006 RMDs [($5,000 + $5,040) × 50%] and also pays any interest accumulated on that amount. Shirley amends her 2007 income tax return to pay the 50 percent excise tax of $2,750 ($5,500 × 50%) on her 2007 RMD and also pays the interest that has accumulated on that amount. For 2008, Shirley must take the RMDs distributed in 2008 into income ($5,000 + $5,040 + $5,500 + $5,650). Since Shirley has taken her RMD for the 2008 year on a timely basis, the 50 percent excise tax does not apply to that distribution.

Example 2. Ellen is the beneficiary of the profit sharing plan account balance of her aunt Helen, who died in 2003, before reaching her RBD. Ellen did not commence distributions by December 31, 2004, and, therefore, must take out the entire account balance by December 31, 2008. Ellen takes no distributions until March 30, 2009, at which time she takes a distribution of the entire amount. She owes an excise tax equal to 50 percent of the December 31, 2008, account balance for her 2008 tax year (see Q 11:12).

RMDs for calendar year 2009 were suspended (see Qs 11:1, 11:10).

A recharacterization of a Roth IRA back to a traditional IRA may trigger an RMD from the traditional IRA (see Q 31:9). However, IRS, in granting an extension to make a recharacterization, allowed an individual until the end of 2003 to take RMDs from the traditional IRA that should have been made for 1999 and later years. It appears that no excise tax was imposed. [Priv. Ltr. Rul. 200213030]

To avoid plan disqualification, IRS has suggested that plan sponsors consider the Self-Correction Program (SCP; see Q 19:17) and the Voluntary Correction Program (VCP; see Q 19:20) contained in the Employee Plan Compliance Resolution System (EPCRS; see Q 19:2). Plan sponsors may self-correct minimum distribution errors using the SCP. Significant distribution errors must be corrected within two years after the plan year in which the violation occurs. Additionally, IRS has advised plan sponsors that it will waive the 50 percent excise tax if, when they apply for relief through the VCP, the plan sponsors request such a waiver (see Q 11:71). [Retirement News for Employers (Spring 2005)]

Q 11:68   If a payee's interest in a plan is in the form of an individual account, how is the RMD determined?

If a payee's interest under a qualified plan (see Q 11:67) is in the form of an individual account and distribution of such account is not being made under an annuity contract (see Q 11:69), the amount of the RMD for any calendar year for excise tax purposes is the RMD amount required to be distributed for such calendar year in order to satisfy the minimum distribution requirements. For a qualified retirement plan, see Qs 11:4 through 11:51; for a TSA, see Qs 11:52 through 11:55; and, for an IRA, see Qs 11:56 through 11:66. [Treas. Reg. § 54.4974-2, Q&A-3(a)]

Unless otherwise provided under the qualified plan, the default provisions (see Q 11:12) apply in determining the RMD for purposes of the excise tax. [Treas. Reg. § 54.4974-2, Q&A-3(b)] If the five-year rule (see Q 11:10) applies to the distribution to a payee, no amount is required to be distributed for any calendar year to satisfy the RMD requirement until the calendar year that contains the date five years after the date of the employee's death. For the calendar year that contains the date five years after the employee's death, the amount required to be distributed is the payee's entire remaining interest in the qualified plan. [Treas. Reg. § 54.4974-2, Q&A-3(c)]

If there is any remaining benefit with respect to an employee (or IRA owner) *after* the calendar year in which the entire remaining benefit is required to be distributed, the RMD for each calendar year subsequent to such calendar year is the entire remaining benefit. [Treas. Reg. § 54.4974-2, Q&A-5]

RMDs for calendar year 2009 were suspended (see Qs 11:1, 11:5).

Q 11:69   If a payee's interest in a plan is being distributed in the form of an annuity, how is the RMD determined?

If a payee's interest in a qualified plan (see Q 11:67) is being distributed in the form of an annuity either directly from the plan, in the case of a defined benefit plan (see Q 2:3), or under an annuity contract purchased from an insurance company (see Qs 11:28–11:32), the amount of the RMD for excise tax purposes is determined as follows:

1. A *permissible* annuity distribution option is an annuity contract (or, in the case of annuity distributions from a defined benefit plan, a distribution option) that specifically provides for distributions that, if made as provided, would for every calendar year equal or exceed the RMD amount required to be distributed for every calendar year. If the annuity contract (or, in the case of annuity distributions from a defined benefit plan, a distribution option) under which distributions to the payee are being made is a permissible annuity distribution option, the RMD for a given calendar year will equal the amount that the annuity contract (or distribution option) provides be distributed for that calendar year.

2. An *impermissible* annuity distribution option is an annuity contract (or, in the case of annuity distributions from a defined benefit plan, a distribution option) under which distributions to the payee are being made that specifically provides for distributions that, if made as provided, would for any calendar year be *less* than the RMD amount required to be distributed for the year. If the annuity contract (or, in the case of annuity distributions

from a defined benefit plan, the distribution option) under which distributions to the payee are being made is an impermissible annuity distribution option, the RMD for each calendar year will be determined as follows:

a. If the qualified plan under which distributions are being made is a defined benefit plan, the RMD amount required to be distributed each year will be the amount that would have been distributed under the plan if the distribution option under which distributions to the payee were being made was the following permissible annuity distribution option:

   i. In the case of distributions commencing before the death of the employee, if there is a designated beneficiary (see Q 11:14) under the impermissible annuity distribution option, the permissible annuity distribution option is the joint and survivor annuity option under the plan for the lives of the employee and the designated beneficiary that provides for the greatest level amount payable to the employee determined on an annual basis. If the plan does not provide such an option or there is no designated beneficiary under the impermissible distribution option, the permissible annuity distribution option is the life annuity option under the plan payable for the life of the employee in level amounts with no survivor benefit.

   ii. In the case of distributions commencing after the death of the employee, if there is a designated beneficiary under the impermissible annuity distribution option, the permissible annuity distribution option is the life annuity option under the plan payable for the life of the designated beneficiary in level amounts. If there is no designated beneficiary, the five-year rule (see Qs 11:9, 11:10) applies. To determine whether or not there is a designated beneficiary and to determine which designated beneficiary's life will be used in the case of multiple beneficiaries, see Qs 11:14–11:19 and Q 11:25. If the defined benefit plan does not provide for distribution in the form of the applicable permissible distribution option, the RMD for each calendar year will be an amount as determined by IRS.

b. If the qualified plan under which distributions are being made is a defined contribution plan (see Q 2:2) and the impermissible annuity distribution option is an annuity contract purchased from an insurance company, the RMD amount required to be distributed each year will be the amount that would have been distributed in the form of an annuity contract under the permissible annuity distribution option under the plan determined in the same manner as for defined benefit plans. If the defined contribution plan does not provide the applicable permissible annuity distribution option, the RMD for each calendar year will be the amount that would have been distributed under an annuity described below purchased with the employee's or individual's account used to purchase the annuity contract that is the impermissible annuity distribution option.

    i. In the case of distributions commencing before the death of the employee, if there is a designated beneficiary under the impermissible annuity distribution option, the annuity is a joint and survivor annuity for the lives of the employee and the designated beneficiary that provides level annual payments and that would have been a permissible annuity distribution option. However, the amount of the periodic payment that would have been payable to the survivor will be the applicable percentage (see Q 11:29) of the amount of the periodic payment that would have been payable to the employee or individual. If there is no designated beneficiary under the impermissible distribution option, the annuity is a life annuity for the life of the employee with no survivor benefit that provides level annual payments and that would have been a permissible annuity distribution option.

    ii. In the case of a distribution commencing after the death of the employee, if there is a designated beneficiary under the impermissible annuity distribution option, the annuity option is a life annuity for the life of the designated beneficiary that provides level annual payments and that would have been a permissible annuity distribution option. If there is no designated beneficiary, the five-year rule applies. The amount of the payments under the annuity contract will be determined using the interest rate and actuarial tables prescribed under Section 7520 determined using the date of determination (see Q 11:11) when distributions are required to commence and using the age of the beneficiary as of the beneficiary's birthday in the calendar year that contains that date. To determine whether or not there is a designated beneficiary and to determine which designated beneficiary's life will be used in the case of multiple beneficiaries, see Qs 11:14–11:19 and Q 11:25.

c. If the five-year rule applies to the distribution to the payee under the contract (or distribution option), no amount is required to be distributed to satisfy paragraph 1 until the calendar year that contains the date five years after the date of the employee's death. For the calendar year that contains the date five years after the employee's death, the amount required to be distributed is the payee's entire remaining interest in the annuity contract (or under the plan in the case of distributions from a defined benefit plan).

d. If the plan provides that the RBD for all employees is April 1 of the calendar year following the calendar year in which the employee attained age 70½ (see Q 11:5), the RMD for each calendar year for an employee who is not a 5 percent owner will be the lesser of the amount determined based on the RBD as set forth in Q 11:5 or the RBD under the plan. Thus, for example, if an employee dies after attaining age 70½, but before April 1 of the calendar year following the calendar in which the employee retired, and there is no designated beneficiary as of September 30 of the year following the employee's year of death (see Q 11:16), RMDs for calendar years after the calendar year containing the employee's date of death may be based on the applicable distribution period provided under either the five-year rule or the employee's remaining life expectancy (see Q 11:23).

[Treas. Reg. § 54.4974-2, Q&A-4]

If there is any remaining benefit with respect to an employee (or IRA owner) *after* the calendar year in which the entire remaining benefit is required to be distributed, the RMD for each calendar year subsequent to such calendar year is the entire remaining benefit. [Treas. Reg. § 54.4974-2, Q&A-5]

Q 11:70   For which calendar year is the excise tax imposed where the RMD is not distributed by the RBD?

If the first RMD is not paid by April 1 of the calendar year containing the employee's or individual's RBD (see Q 11:5), the unpaid amount is an RMD for the previous calendar year, that is, for the first distribution calendar year (see Q 11:20). However, the excise tax is imposed for the calendar year containing the employee's or individual's RBD (i.e., April 1), even though the preceding calendar year is the calendar year for which the amount is required to be distributed. There is also a separate or second RMD for the calendar year that contains the employee's or individual's RBD. This separate or second distribution is also required to be made during the calendar year that contains the employee's or individual's RBD. However, this distribution must be made on or before December 31 of such calendar year. [Treas. Reg. § 54.4974-2, Q&A-6]

> **Example.**   Jason had an RBD of April 1, 2011. Jason's first RMD was $5,000, but he failed to take the distribution until October 15, 2011. Even though Jason's first distribution calendar year was 2010, the excise tax would be imposed for the 2011 calendar year because that was the calendar year containing Jason's RBD.

RMDs for calendar year 2009 were suspended (see Q 11:1). [I.R.C. § 401(a)(9)(H) (as added by WRERA 2008 § 201(a); WRERA 2008 § 201(c)(1))] In the above example, if Jason attained age 70½ in 2009 and had an RBD of April 1, 2010, he would not have been required to take his RMD for the 2009 distribution calendar year (see Q 11:5).

Q 11:71   Are there any circumstances when the excise tax may be waived?

IRS may waive the excise tax if the payee establishes that the shortfall was due to reasonable error and that steps have been taken, or are being taken, to remedy the shortfall (see Q 19:34). The tax is shown on Form 5329, Additional Taxes on Qualified Plans (Including IRAs) and Other Tax-Favored Accounts, which is attached to the payee's income tax return. IRS advises that, if the individual believes a waiver is appropriate, the individual should file Form 5329 and attach a letter of explanation. [I.R.C. § 4974(d); Treas. Reg. § 54.4974-2, Q&A-7(a); IRS Pub. 590; instructions to Form 5329]

With respect to a failure to take an RMD from a qualified retirement plan, an alternative to applying for a waiver may be the use of IRS's correction methods (see Q 19:31).

The excise tax will be automatically waived, unless IRS determines otherwise, if:

1. The payee is an individual who is the sole beneficiary and whose RMD amount for a calendar year is determined under the life expectancy rule (see Q 11:11) in the case of an employee's or individual's death before the employee's or individual's RBD (see Q 11:5), and

2. The employee's or individual's entire benefit to which that beneficiary is entitled is distributed by the end of the fifth calendar year following the calendar year that contains the employee's or individual's date of death (see Q 11:10). [Treas. Reg. § 54.4974-2, Q&A-7(b)]

Example. George designated his daughter, Georgia, as beneficiary of his IRA and died on May 11, 2010, at age 64. Because George died before his RBD and Georgia is his designated beneficiary (see Qs 11:14, 11:16), Georgia must commence her RMDs by December 31, 2011. Georgia does not receive any distribution during the period of 2011–2014 but receives a distribution of George's entire IRA on December 15, 2015. Because the entire IRA is distributed to Georgia by December 31, 2015, the excise tax will be automatically waived.

RMDs for calendar year 2009 were suspended (see Qs 11:1, 11:10). In the above example, if George had died in 2009, 2009 would be excluded because of the suspension, and Georgia would still have until December 31, 2015 to receive a distribution of George's entire IRA.

The beneficiary of an IRA was convicted in the murder of the IRA owner. Even though, pursuant to state law, the beneficiary was deemed to have predeceased the IRA owner, IRS ruled that the murderer was the designated beneficiary for RMD purposes, notwithstanding that the IRA was eventually paid to the deceased IRA owner's stepdaughter. Because of the trial and various court orders delaying the determination of the recipient of, and the payment of, the IRA, IRS waived the excise tax. [Priv. Ltr. Rul. 201008049]

Chapter 12

Tax Deduction Rules

One of the primary tax advantages of a qualified retirement plan is that a current deduction is allowed for the company's contributions to a plan that provides future benefits. This chapter examines when a contribution must be made in order to be deductible on a current basis and the limits that are set on the amount of a tax-deductible contribution.

Q 12:1 What are the basic requirements for deducting employer contributions to a qualified retirement plan?

For such a contribution to be tax deductible, it must be an "ordinary and necessary" business expense and must be compensation for services actually rendered. Thus, for example, a contribution on behalf of a shareholder may be made only if the shareholder is also an employee actually rendering services to the corporation. [Van Roekel Farms, Inc. v. Comm'r, 2001 U.S. App. LEXIS 14201 (8th Cir. 2001)] Also, the contribution, when considered together with the employee's regular compensation, must be "reasonable in amount" for the services rendered. Reasonable current compensation and the plan contribution may include additional amounts for previously uncompensated prior services. The president of a family corporation received compensation of 400 percent more than his prior year's compensation. The court determined that the increased compensation was reasonable because the president had been underpaid in prior years. [Devine Bros., 85 T.C.M. 768 (2003); see also Multi-Pak Corp., T.C.M. 2010–139] What constitutes reasonable compensation depends upon the facts and circumstances of each particular case. I.R.C. §§ 162, 404; Treas. Reg. § 1.404(a)-1(b); Ann. 98-1, 1998-1 C.B. 282; E.J. Harrison & Sons, Inc., 06-74316 (9th Cir. 2008); Universal Marketing, Inc., 94 T.C.M. 374 (2007); Vitamin Village, Inc., 94 T.C.M. 278 (2007); Wechsler & Co., Inc., 92 T.C.M. 138 (2006); Miller & Sons Drywall, Inc., 89 T.C.M. 1279 (2005); Menard, Inc., 88 T.C.M. 229 (2004); Brewer Quality Homes, Inc., 86 T.C.M. 29 (2003); Normandie Metal Fabricators, Inc. v. Comm'r, No. 00-4169 (2d Cir. 2001); Eberl's Claim Serv., Inc. v. Comm'r, 249 F.3d 994 (10th Cir. 2001); Damron Auto Parts, Inc., 82 T.C.M. 344 (2001); Wagner Constr., Inc., 81 T.C.M. 1869 (2001); Metro Leasing & Dev. Corp., 81 T.C.M. 1644 (2001); Label Graphics, Inc. v. Comm'r, 221 F.3d 1091 (9th Cir. 2000); Alpha Med., Inc. v. Comm'r, 172 F.3d 942 (6th Cir. 1999);

Dexsil Corp., 77 T.C.M. 1973 (1999); Herold Mktg. Assocs., Inc., 77 T.C.M. 1306 (1999); Dexsil Corp.v. Comm'r, 147 F.3d 96 (2d Cir. 1998); H&A Int'l Jewelry, Ltd., 74 T.C.M. 915 (1997); RAPCO, Inc., 85 F.3d 950 (2d Cir. 1996); Donald Palmer Co., No. 95-60381 (5th Cir. 1996); Modernage Developers, Inc., 66 T.C.M. 1575 (1993); Acme Constr. Co., 69 T.C.M. 1596 (1995); BOCA Constr. Inc., 69 T.C.M. 1589 (1995); Comtec Sys. Inc., 69 T.C.M. 1581 (1995); Manohara, M.D., Inc., 68 T.C.M. 142 (1994); Thomas A. Curtis, M.D., Inc., 67 T.C.M. 1958 (1994)]

Some courts have used a five-factor test to determine reasonableness of compensation:

1. The employee's role in the company;
2. A comparison of the compensation paid the employee with that paid to similarly situated employees in similar companies;
3. The character and condition of the company;
4. Whether a conflict of interest exists that might permit the company to disguise dividend payments as deductible compensation; and
5. Whether the compensation was paid under a structured, formal, and consistently applied program. [Beiner, Inc., 88 T.C.M. 297 (2004); Leonard Pipeline Contractors Ltd., 210 F.3d 384 (9th Cir. 2000); Elliots, Inc. v. Comm'r, 716 F.2d 1241 (9th Cir. 1983)]

Other courts have rejected the five-factor test and have utilized an independent investor test to determine reasonable compensation. [Haffner's Serv. Stations, Inc. v. Comm'r, 326 F.3d 1 (1st Cir. 2003); B&D Founds., Inc., 82 T.C.M. 692 (2001); Exacto Spring Corp. v. Comm'r, 196 F.3d 833 (7th Cir. 1999); Dexsil Corp. v. Comm'r, 147 F.3d 96 (2d Cir. 1998)] One court disallowed a portion of the compensation paid to its executives because the compensation was allocated between them in proportion to their stock ownership. The court concluded that the excess compensation was a disguised dividend even though IRS's own expert witness believed that a portion of the disallowed amounts represented reasonable compensation. [OSC & Assocs., Inc. v. Comm'r, 187 F.3d 1116 (9th Cir. 1999)]

A contribution on behalf of a self-employed individual (see Q 6:60) satisfies the ordinary-and-necessary business expense requirement if it does not exceed the individual's earned income (see Q 6:61) for the year determined without regard to the deduction for the contribution (see Q 12:14). [I.R.C. § 404(a)(8); Temp. Treas. Reg. § 1.404(a)(8)-1T; *but see* Gale v. United States, 768 F. Supp. 1305 (N.D. Ill. 1991)]

Q 12:2 How are restorative payments treated?

IRS has ruled that an employer could deduct in full a restorative payment made to its defined contribution plan (see Q 2:2) in response to actual and potential claims for breach of fiduciary duty because the payment was considered an ordinary and necessary business expense and was not limited by the plan deduction limits (see Qs 12:8, 12:17). [Rev. Rul. 2002-45, 2002-2 C.B. 116] In a number of rulings, claims were brought after the plan incurred significant losses attributable to unwise investments. In addition, the restorative payment was not taxable income to the participants, was not subject to the excise tax on nondeductible contributions (see Q 12:9), and was not subject to the annual addition limitation (see Q 6:34). [Priv. Ltr. Ruls. 201007077, 200640003, 200446026, 200317050, 200230044, 200147056, 200137064]

A payment made to a defined contribution plan is not treated as a contribution to the plan if the payment is made to restore losses to the plan resulting from actions by a fiduciary for which there is a reasonable risk of liability for breach of a fiduciary duty under ERISA and plan participants who are similarly situated are treated similarly with respect to the payment. These payments are referred to as restorative payments.

The determination of whether a payment to a defined contribution plan is treated as a restorative payment, rather than as a contribution, is based on all of the relevant facts and circumstances. As a general rule, payments to a defined contribution plan are restorative payments only if the payments are made in order to restore some or all of the plan's losses due to an action (or a failure to act) that creates a reasonable risk of liability for breach of fiduciary duty. In contrast, payments made to a plan to make up for losses due to market fluctuations and that are not attributable to a fiduciary breach are generally treated as contributions and not as restorative payments. In no case will amounts paid in excess of the amount lost (including appropriate adjustments to reflect lost earnings) be considered restorative payments. Furthermore, payments that result in different treatment for similarly situated plan participants are not restorative payments. The failure to allocate a share of the payment to the account of a fiduciary responsible for the losses does not result in different treatment for similarly situated participants.

Payments to a plan made pursuant to a Department of Labor (DOL) order or court-approved settlement to restore losses to a defined contribution plan on account of a breach of fiduciary duty generally are treated as having been made on account of a reasonable risk of liability.

In no event are payments required under a plan or necessary to comply with the requirements of the Code considered restorative payments, even if the payments are delayed or otherwise made in circumstances under which there has been a breach of fiduciary duty. Thus, for example, while the payment of delinquent elective deferrals or employee contributions is part of an acceptable correction under the VFC Program (see Qs 19:36–19:50), such payment is not a restorative payment. Similarly, payments to correct qualification failures (see Q 19:5) are generally considered contributions and do not constitute restorative payments. However, the payment of appropriate adjustments to reflect lost earnings required under EPCRS (see Q 19:2) is generally treated in the same manner as a restorative payment.

Example 1. BJC Corporation maintains a defined contribution plan, and BJC Corporation caused an unreasonably large portion of the plan assets to be invested in a high-risk investment. It is later determined that the investment has become worthless.

A group of plan participants files a suit against BJC Corporation alleging a breach of fiduciary duty in connection with the investment. Following the filing of the suit, the parties agree to a settlement pursuant to which BJC Corporation does not admit that a breach of fiduciary duty occurred but makes a payment to the plan equal to the amount of the losses (including an appropriate adjustment to reflect lost earnings) to the plan from the investment. The settlement also provides that the payment will be allocated among the individual accounts of all of the participants and beneficiaries in proportion to each account's investment over the appropriate period. The court approves the settlement and enters a consent order. BJC Corporation makes the payment to the plan, and the payment is allocated to the appropriate accounts.

In this example, the payment is made pursuant to a court-approved settlement of the suit filed by plan participants and is not in excess of the amount lost (including appropriate adjustments to reflect lost earnings). Therefore, the payment is made based on a reasonable determination that there is a reasonable risk of liability for breach of fiduciary duty and to restore losses to the plan. In addition, the payment is allocated among the individual accounts of the participants and beneficiaries in proportion to each account's investment so that similarly situated participants are not treated differently. Thus, the payment is a restorative payment and, as such, is not a contribution to a qualified retirement plan.

Example 2. The facts are the same as in Example 1, except that no lawsuit is filed against BJC Corporation. However, BJC Corporation becomes aware that plan participants are concerned about the investment and are considering taking legal action. BJC Corporation also learns that lawsuits alleging fiduciary breach have been filed against other companies by those companies' employees over losses to their qualified retirement plans due to that same investment. BJC Corporation decides to make the payment to the plan before a lawsuit is filed after reasonably determining that it has a reasonable risk of liability for breach of fiduciary duty based on all of the relevant facts and circumstances.

In this example, the payment is made after BJC Corporation reasonably determines, based on all of the relevant facts and circumstances, that it has a reasonable risk of liability for breach of fiduciary duty even though no suit has yet been filed. In reaching this determination the following facts are taken into account: (1) the investment was a high-risk investment; (2) a large portion of the plan assets had been invested in the investment; (3) participants expressed concern about the investment; and (4) several lawsuits had been filed against other employers alleging fiduciary breach in connection with that same investment. Therefore, the payment is made based on a reasonable determination that there is a reasonable risk of liability for breach of fiduciary duty and to restore losses to the plan. In addition, the payment is allocated among the individual accounts of the participants and beneficiaries in proportion to each account's investment so that similarly situated participants are not treated differently. Thus, the payment is a restorative payment and, as such, is not a contribution to a qualified retirement plan. [Rev. Rul. 2002-45, 2002-2 C.B. 116]

A payment by a company director to a qualified retirement plan to partially compensate participants for losses caused by the bankruptcy of the company and the subsequent worthlessness of its stock was a restorative payment. [Priv. Ltr. Rul. 200334041] A shareholder in his capacity as an employee received a distribution from a qualified retirement plan and contributed the distribution to the plan to partially compensate other participants for losses caused by a trustee's embezzlement. IRS ruled that the contribution was a restorative payment, that the distribution was taxable to the shareholder-employee, and that the shareholder-employee was entitled to deduct the contribution as an ordinary and necessary business expense subject to the 2-percent-of-adjusted-gross-income floor. [Priv. Ltr. Rul. 200640003] However, an employer's payment to a plan for the purpose of restoring to participants' accounts the amount of loss that would result from the imposition of surrender charges on the liquidation of annuity contracts was treated as an employer contribution, not as a restorative payment, because sufficient evidence was not presented to demonstrate a reasonable risk of liability to the employer for a breach of fiduciary duty. [Priv. Ltr. Rul. 200317048] Conversely, where surrender charges and fees were improperly imposed under a group annuity contract when the employer elected to transfer all assets held under the contract to another investment medium and the employer sued and recovered the charges and fees, IRS ruled that the employer's contribution of the proceeds of the lawsuit to the plan was a replacement payment with the same consequences as a restorative payment. [Priv. Ltr. Rul. 200337017; *see also* Priv. Ltr. Rul. 200404050]

Q 12:3   When must contributions be made to be currently deductible?

Tax-deductible contributions to a qualified retirement plan may be made at any time during the taxable year and even after the end of the taxable year up to the due date (including valid extensions) for the filing of the employer's federal income tax return for the particular year. Timely contributions made after the end of the taxable year are deductible for that taxable year if the plan treats the payment in the same manner it would treat a payment actually received on the last day of the preceding taxable year and if either (1) the employer designates in writing to the plan administrator (see Q 20:1) or trustee that the contribution is for the preceding year or (2) the employer claims the contribution as a deduction on its tax return for the preceding year. Such a designation, once made, is irrevocable. [I.R.C. § 404(a)(6); Rev. Rul. 76-28, 1976-1 C.B. 106; Priv. Ltr. Ruls. 200523033, 199935062] IRS ruled that an employer's plan contribution made after the end of its taxable year could be treated as made in that taxable year even though the employer initially designated the contribution as a contribution for the taxable year in which it was made. [Priv. Ltr. Rul. 200311036]

One court ruled that, although the employer's contributions on which its deductions were based were made prior to the extended due date for filing the tax returns, the contributions were not made on account of the taxable years for which they were claimed. [Airborne Freight Corp v. United States, 1998 WL 511890 (9th Cir. 1998)] Similarly, an employer's contributions to multiemployer plans (see Q 29:2) based on hours worked between the end of the employer's taxable year and the extended due date of its return were not deductible in that taxable year. [Vons Cos. v. United States, 55 Fed. Cl. 709 (2003); American Stores Co. v. Comm'r, 170 F.3d 1267 (10th Cir. 1999); Lucky Stores, Inc. v. Comm'r, 153 F.3d 964 (9th Cir. 1998); Priv. Ltr. Rul. 200242001; Field Serv. Adv. 19991220] See Q 12:15 for additional details.

A contribution is timely if it is made before the income tax return extended due date even if it is made after the return is filed. An employer must obtain a valid extension to file the return in order to extend the time to make a contribution. IRS has ruled that a request for an automatic extension of time to file the employer's tax return was invalid because the employer failed to pay the balance of tax due shown on extension request Form 7004. An application for an extension of time to file is invalid if the employer fails to comply with all requirements of the regulations. [Rev. Rul. 66-144, 1966-1 C.B. 91; I.R.C. § 6081(b); Treas. Reg. § 1.6081-3; Priv. Ltr. Rul. 9033005; *Retirement News for Employers*, Winter 2010]

> **Example.** Jason, a sole proprietor, adopts a qualified retirement plan on December 31, 2010. Jason's 2010 income tax return is due on April 15, 2011, but he receives an extension to file until October 17, 2011. If Jason files his return on August 31, 2011, and makes the required contribution on September 15, 2011, the contribution is deductible on his 2010 return.

The employer's timely mailing of the contribution is adequate. Thus, a contribution mailed and bearing a postage cancellation date no later than the due date of the employer's tax return, including extensions, is timely even if the trust received it after such due date. [Priv. Ltr. Rul. 8536085] Previously, taxpayers could only use the United States Postal Service, but IRS is now authorized to name private delivery services meeting specific criteria that taxpayers may use in lieu of the Postal Service. [I.R.C. § 7502; IRS Notice 2004-83, 2004-2 C.B. 1030; IRS Notice 97-26, 1997-1 C.B. 413; Estate of Cranor, 81 T.C.M. 1111 (2001); Diller v. Comm'r, No. 97-7171 (3d Cir. 1997)]

IRS has added the deadline for qualified retirement plan contributions to the list of tax-related deadlines that may be postponed by reason of a Presidentially declared disaster. IRS is allowed to disregard a period of up to one year in determining whether plan contributions were made within the time prescribed. [I.R.C. § 7508A(b); Treas. Reg. § 301.7508A-1; IRS Notice 2002-27, 2002-1 C.B. 489; IRS Notice 2001-68, 2001-2 C.B. 504; IRS Notice 2001-61, 2001-2 C.B. 305]

The portion of employer contributions to its qualified retirement plan that is used to purchase life insurance on behalf of plan participants is deductible (see Q 15:3). If the employer pays the life insurance premiums directly to the insurance company and reports the premium payments as plan contributions, the payments are deductible as plan contributions because the invoice for the premiums is to the plan, not to the employer, and it is a liability of the plan that is being satisfied by the employer's contribution.

A bookkeeping entry showing that a portion of the employer's certificate of deposit belonged to a qualified retirement plan as of the deadline for tax-deductible contributions is not timely payment of the contribution. [Rollar Homes, Inc., 53 T.C.M. 471 (1987)]

In another case, an employer mistakenly made out and mailed its plan contribution check for the taxable year to Pension Benefit Guaranty Corporation (PBGC; see Q 25:10). The check was returned by PBGC, and the contribution was paid late. IRS ruled that the contribution was not timely made and, therefore, was not deductible for that taxable year. [Priv. Ltr. Rul. 9031033]

Q 12:4   May a contribution be timely for tax deduction purposes but not for the minimum funding standards?

Yes. The rules regarding timeliness for tax deduction purposes are based on the employer's taxable year and are independent of the rules regarding timeliness for purposes of the minimum funding standards (see Q 8:1) that are based on the plan year. Tax-deductible plan contributions may be made after the end of the taxable year if payment is made by the due date (including extensions) for filing the employer's federal income tax return for that taxable year (see Q 12:3). For purposes of the minimum funding standards, contributions made after the end of the plan year may relate back to that year if they are made within eight and one-half months after the end of the plan year. [I.R.C. § 412(c)(10)(A); Rev. Rul. 77-82, 1977-1 C.B. 121; Hoyez, 80 T.C.M. 198 (2000); Wenger, 79 T.C.M. 1995 (2000)]

> **Example.** Zeke, a sole proprietor, adopts a defined contribution plan for calendar year 2010. For 2010, Zeke receives an extension to file his federal income tax return allowing him to file his return on October 17, 2011. On October 7, 2011, Zeke makes his required plan contribution. Although the contribution is deductible on Zeke's 2010 return, the contribution is not timely for the minimum funding standards because the contribution is made after September 15, 2011 (more than eight and one-half months after the end of the 2010 plan year).

IRS has added the deadline for qualified retirement plan contributions to the list of tax-related deadlines that may be postponed by reason of a Presidentially declared disaster. IRS is allowed to disregard a period of up to one year in determining whether plan contributions were made within the time prescribed. [I.R.C. § 7508A(b); Treas. Reg. § 301.7508A-1; IRS Notice 2002-27, 2002-1 C.B. 489; IRS Notice 2001-68, 2001-2 C.B. 504; IRS Notice 2001-61, 2001-2 C.B. 305]

Q 12:5   May an employer deduct the fair market value of property other than money contributed to its qualified retirement plan?

Yes. If property is contributed, the employer may deduct the fair market value of the property at the time of the contribution. However, if the fair market value exceeds the employer's basis in the property, the employer has a taxable gain equal to the excess; but, if the basis exceeds the fair market value, there is no recognizable loss to the employer. [I.R.C. §§ 267, 1001; Rev. Rul. 75-498, 1975-2 C.B. 29; Rev. Rul. 73-583, 1973-2 C.B. 146; Rev. Rul. 73-345, 1973-2 C.B. 11; Priv. Ltr. Rul. 199910057] Where an employer never legally transferred securities to a qualified retirement plan, the employer could not deduct the fair market value of the securities. [Reed Smith Shaw & McClay, 75 T.C.M. 1806 (1998)]

If an employer purchases real estate from its qualified retirement plan for an amount in excess of the real estate's fair market value, such excess is considered a contribution to the plan. [Priv. Ltr. Rul. 8949076]

An employer's contribution of property to or the purchase of property from its qualified retirement plan may be a prohibited transaction (i.e., a transfer, sale, or exchange of assets between a party in interest and the plan) and may subject the employer to penalty taxes (see Qs 24:5, 24:19). [Ann. 98-1, 1998-1 C.B. 282] However, an employer may contribute employer securities to an employee stock ownership plan (ESOP) and deduct the fair market value of the securities at the time of the contribution (see Qs 28:1, 28:8). [J.P. Emco, Inc. v. United States, 90-617T (Fed. Cl. 1996)] IRS ruled that the contribution of stock options granted by the employer to its 401(k) plan (see Q 27:1) was deductible by the employer to the extent of the fair market value of the options granted. [Priv. Ltr. Rul. 9712033] However, IRS announced that it would reexamine its ruling and subsequently revoked it. [Ann. 97-45, 1997-17 I.R.B. 20; Priv. Ltr. Rul. 200401021] No reference was made in the initial ruling concerning potential prohibited transaction issues, but the employer made an application to DOL for an exemption from the prohibited transaction rules (see Qs 24:1, 24:8, 24:20). [Exemption Application No. D-10269 (61 Fed. Reg. 68,794)] However, DOL representatives have opined that a 401(k) plan cannot hold a right to allow any of its participants to purchase employer securities at a fixed price for an entire year. Although the right is an option and the option is an employer security, it is not a qualifying employer security (see Q 23:86), and holding it in the plan constitutes a prohibited transaction.

Q 12:6 May an employer make a timely contribution to the qualified retirement plan by check?

Yes. The contribution will be considered timely even if the plan trustee receives payment after the deadline for a deductible contribution (see Q 12:2) if the employer mails the check to the plan trustee before such deadline, the check is promptly presented for payment, and it is paid in the regular course of business. However, the contribution is not timely if the trustee delays presentation of the check because of the employer's financial problems. Also, the contribution was not considered timely in one case because the employer could not explain why the check was not negotiated until two weeks after the contribution deadline. [Flomac, Inc., 53 T.C.M. 305 (1987); Walt Wilger Tire Co., 38 T.C.M. 287 (1979); Cain-White & Co., 37 T.C.M. 1829 (1978)]

If the check bounces, no contribution is deemed to have been made. [Springfield Prods., Inc., 38 T.C.M. 74 (1979)]

Q 12:7 Is a contribution of the employer's promissory note a deductible payment?

No. The employer must make a timely contribution in cash or its equivalent to obtain a tax deduction for its contribution for the current or preceding taxable year (see Q 12:2). Since the contribution by the employer of its own promissory note is merely a promise to pay, it is not considered a payment of cash or its equivalent. [Don E. Williams Co. v. United States, 429 U.S. 569 (1977); Rev. Rul. 80-140, 1980-1 C.B. 89; Ann. 98-1, 1998-1 C.B. 282]

A contribution of the employer's own promissory note is also a prohibited transaction (see Q 24:1). [Ann. 98-1, 1998-1 C.B. 282]

Q 12:8 What is the primary limitation on tax-deductible contributions to a defined contribution plan?

The primary limitation on tax-deductible contributions to a defined contribution plan (see Q 2:2) is 25 percent of the total compensation (see Q 12:15) paid to all participants during the taxable year. [I.R.C. § 404(a)(3)(A); Treas. Reg. § 1.404(a)-9(c); Priv. Ltr. Rul. 9548036]

With respect to a SIMPLE 401(k) plan (see Q 33:25), the primary limitation is the *greater* of:

1. 25 percent of the total compensation paid to all participants during the taxable year, or
2. The aggregate of the employee elective contributions and required employer matching or nonelective contributions (see Q 33:29).

[I.R.C. § 404(a)(3)(A)(i)(I)]

> **Example.** Ben-Jason-Casey Corp. adopts a defined contribution plan for calendar year 2010, and the total compensation paid to plan participants during 2010 is $750,000. Ben-Jason-Casey Corp. may contribute to the plan and deduct the amount of $187,500 (25% × $750,000).

If an employer maintains more than one defined contribution plan, the deductible limit with respect to the employer's defined contribution plans is determined by aggregating all of the contributions made to the plans and by limiting such aggregate amount to 25 percent of the aggregate compensation of all employees covered by the plans. Consequently, the employer may contribute more than 25 percent of the total compensation of the employees covered by a particular plan. [Treas. Reg. § 1.404(a)-9(b); Priv. Ltr. Ruls. 200436015, 199909060, 9635045]

If the employer makes less than the maximum permissible contribution in a taxable year, it may *not* carry over the unused difference.

Q 12:9 How are excess amounts contributed to a qualified retirement plan treated for tax purposes?

There is an excise tax imposed on the employer equal to 10 percent of the portion of any contribution to any qualified retirement plan that is not deductible (see Qs 12:10–12:14, 12:18, 12:21). [I.R.C. § 4972; Ann. 98-1, 1998-1 C.B. 282]

Amounts contributed in excess of the primary limitation (see Q 12:8) are generally carried forward and may be deducted in later years. However, the total amount deductible in a later taxable year, including the contribution to the defined contribution plan (see Q 2:2) for that year, is limited to 25 percent of the compensation of the participants in the later taxable year. [I.R.C. § 404(a)(3)(A); Treas. Reg. § 1.404(a)-9(e); Rev. Rul. 83-48, 1983-1 C.B. 93; Rev. Rul. 73-608, 1973-2 C.B. 147]

> **Example.** Joel Corporation contributes $30,000 to its profit sharing plan in 2009, $32,000 in 2010, and $36,000 in 2011. If $27,000 is 25 percent of the total compensation paid to all participants in 2009, Joel's deduction for 2009 is limited to $27,000, and $3,000 ($30,000 − $27,000) is carried over to later years. Joel will be subject to an excise tax of $300 (10% × $3,000). If $33,000 is 25 percent of compensation in 2010, Joel's deduction for 2010 is $33,000 ($32,000 + $1,000 carried over from 2009) and the excise tax would be $200 [10% × ($3,000 − $1,000)]. If $38,000 is 25 percent of compensation in 2011, Joel's deduction for 2011 is $38,000 ($36,000 plus the remaining $2,000 carried over from 2009) and there would be no excise tax.

With respect to a SIMPLE 401(k) plan (see Q 33:25), the total amount deductible in a later taxable year, including the contribution to the plan for that year, is limited to the *greater* of:

1. 25 percent of the total compensation paid to all participants in the later taxable year, or
2. The aggregate of the employee elective contributions and required employer matching or nonelective contributions (see Q 33:29).

[I.R.C. § 404(a)(3)(A)]

For purposes of determining the amount of nondeductible contributions, compensation of the plan participants includes certain elective deferrals (see Q 12:15).

A payment by a company director to a qualified retirement plan to partially compensate participants for losses caused by the bankruptcy of the company and the subsequent worthlessness of its stock was a restorative payment (see Q 12:2) and, as such, was not subject to the excise tax on excess contributions. [Priv. Ltr. Rul. 200334041]

Q 12:10 How is the amount of nondeductible contributions computed?

Nondeductible contributions are defined as the sum of (1) amounts contributed by an employer to a qualified retirement plan for a taxable year in excess of the amount allowable as a deduction for that taxable year plus (2) the unapplied amounts from the preceding taxable year.

The unapplied amounts from the preceding taxable year are the amounts subject to the excise tax in the preceding taxable year reduced by the sum of (1) the portion that is returned to the employer during the taxable year plus (2) the portion that is deductible during the current taxable year.

[I.R.C. § 4972(c)]

> **Example.** Nan Corporation makes a nondeductible contribution of $100,000 for its 2009 taxable year. Nan contributes $75,000 in 2010 when its deductible limit is $150,000. In 2011, it contributes $75,000 when its deductible limit is $100,000. Nan must pay an excise tax of $10,000 for 2009 (10% × $100,000) and $2,500 for 2010 [10% × ($100,000 + $75,000 − $150,000)]. It owes no excise tax for 2011 [10% × ($25,000 + $75,000 − $100,000)].

IRS has ruled that the excise tax would not be applied with respect to nondeductible contributions made by an employer seeking to amend its qualified retirement plans to allow employees transferred to a related foreign company to continue to participate in the plans, to the extent that the contributions did not exceed the deductible limit. IRS reasoned that the focus of the excise tax is on the amount allowable as a deduction and not the amount deductible. In other words, if the amount of the contribution does not exceed the deductible limit, the excise tax does not apply. In this case, if the amount of the contributions for the transferred employees does not exceed the deductible limit (assuming deductibility), then the contributions do not exceed the amount allowable as a deduction and the excise tax does not apply. [Priv. Ltr. Rul. 200211050]

Q 12:11   When are nondeductible contributions for a given taxable year determined?

Nondeductible contributions for purposes of the excise tax are determined as of the close of the employer's taxable year. If, however, a nondeductible contribution is returned by the last day on which a deductible contribution could be made for that year (see Qs 1:52, 12:3), the returned amount is not treated as a nondeductible contribution and is not subject to the tax (see Q 12:10). [I.R.C. § 4972(c)(3)]

Q 12:12   What happens if a deduction for plan contributions is subsequently disallowed?

The excise tax applies to contributions for which the deduction is disallowed. [General Explanation of TRA '86, tit. XI, D2, at 748]

Q 12:13   Does the excise tax imposed on nondeductible contributions apply to tax-exempt organizations?

No. The 10 percent excise tax imposed on an employer for making nondeductible plan contributions (see Qs 12:9–12:12) does not apply to an employer that has, *at all times*, been exempt from tax. [I.R.C. §§ 4972(d)(1)(B), 4980(c)(1)(A); Ann. 98-1, 1998-1 C.B. 282; Priv. Ltr. Rul. 200020009]

IRS has ruled, however, that a tax-exempt organization that had been subject to tax on unrelated business taxable income (UBTI) was not subject to the excise tax because the portion of the nondeductible contribution attributable to the UBTI was *de minimis* [Priv. Ltr. Rul. 9304033]; but, where UBTI was more than *de minimis*, the excise tax was imposed. [Priv. Ltr. Rul. 9622037]

In other rulings, IRS concluded that plan contributions made by a tax-exempt organization, which was a member of a controlled group (see Qs 5:29, 5:31) that contained at least one nonexempt employer whose employees were covered under the plan, was subject to the 10 percent excise tax whether or not the organization had UBTI. When one of the controlled group members maintaining the plan is nonexempt, the whole group is considered nonexempt; and, therefore, the exempt organization does not qualify for the exception. [Priv. Ltr. Ruls. 9616003, 9236026]

For more information on UBTI, see Qs 1:6 and 30:11.

Q 12:14 Do any special limitations apply to the deduction for contributions made to a qualified retirement plan on behalf of a self-employed individual?

The criterion for contributions to a qualified retirement plan on behalf of a self-employed individual (see Q 6:60) is earned income (see Q 6:61). For purposes of computing the limitations on deductions for contributions to a qualified retirement plan, earned income is computed after taking into account amounts contributed to the plan on behalf of the self-employed individual (i.e., the self-employed individual's earned income is reduced by the deductible contributions to the plan). Furthermore, earned income is computed after the deduction allowed to the self-employed individual for one-half of the individual's self-employment taxes. [I.R.C. §§ 164(f), 401(c)(2)(A)(v), 401(c)(2)(A)(vi), 404(a)(8)(D), 1401]

The contribution limits that apply to corporate defined contribution plans apply to defined contribution plans covering self-employed individuals. Thus, for a limitation year, the annual addition limit is the lesser of $40,000 (subject to cost-of-living adjustments) or 100 percent of compensation; but the deductible contribution is subject to the 25-percent-of-compensation limitation (see Qs 6:58, 12:17). Because earned income is computed after taking into account amounts contributed to the plan on behalf of the self-employed individual and after the deduction for one-half of the individual's self-employment taxes, the effective percentage limit on the deductible contribution is 20 percent of earned income computed after the self-employment tax deduction but before the contribution $(1 \div 1.25 = .80; 1.0 - .80 = .20)$. See Q 6:63 for examples of defined contribution plans covering self-employed individuals.

However, unlike a corporate defined benefit plan to which an employer can make deductible contributions in excess of an employee's compensation if such contributions are necessary to fund the employee's benefit, an employer's deductible contribution on behalf of a self-employed individual is limited to the self-employed individual's earned income for the year (computed after the deduction for one-half of the individual's self-employment taxes, but without regard to the deduction for employer contributions made on the individual's behalf). [I.R.C. §§ 162, 164(f), 212, 401(c)(2), 404(a)(8)(B), 404(a)(8)(C), 404(a)(8)(D); Temp. Treas. Reg. § 1.404(a)(8)-1T; Ann. 98-1, 1998-1 C.B. 282]

> **Example.** Caroline, a sole proprietor, has net earnings (after the deduction for one-half of her self-employment taxes) of $50,000 from her business. The maximum deductible contribution she can make on her own behalf to her defined benefit plan is $50,000. (Caroline's earned income is $50,000 for deduction purposes.)

Because the annual contribution to a defined benefit plan is actuarially determined (see Qs 2:3, 2:34, 2:38), Caroline, in the above example, may be required to contribute more than $50,000 in order to satisfy the minimum funding standards (see Qs 8:1, 8:23). Even though Caroline contributes more than $50,000 and the contribution in excess of $50,000 is not deductible, the excess contribution is *not* treated as a nondeductible contribution and the 10 percent excise tax will *not* be imposed (see Qs 12:9–12:11). [I.R.C. § 4972(c)(4); Ann. 98-1, 1998-1 C.B. 282]

An S corporation (see Q 28:2) shareholder is not a self-employed individual, and S corporation pass-through income is not earned income. Therefore, an S corporation shareholder cannot establish a retirement plan and make deductible contributions thereto based upon the pass-through income. [Durando v. United States, 70 F.3d 548 (9th Cir. 1995); Rev. Rul. 59-221, 1959-1 C.B. 225; *see also* Ding, 74 T.C.M. 708 (1997); Priv. Ltr. Rul. 9750001]

Q 12:15 What does compensation mean for purposes of the limits on deductible contributions to a defined contribution plan?

Compensation generally includes the total compensation of all plan participants paid or accrued during the taxable year. Even if, for purposes of allocating employer contributions, the plan defines compensation as base salary only, other forms of compensation (e.g., overtime, bonuses, and commissions) are included for purposes of the defined contribution plan deduction limitations (see Qs 6:46–6:50, 6:59–6:61). Elective deferrals (see Q 27:16) to a 401(k) plan (see Q 27:1), SEP, 403(b) plan (see Q 35:1), qualified transportation fringe benefit plan, and cafeteria plan are compensation for purposes of determining the limitation on deductible contributions. [I.R.C. §§ 404(a)(12), 415(c)(3)(D); Treas. Reg. § 1.404(a)-9(b); Rev. Rul. 80-145, 1980-1 C.B. 89; IRS Notice 2001-37, 2001-1 C.B. 1340; Priv. Ltr. Rul. 9225038]

The deduction for contributions to a 401(k) plan that are attributable to services rendered by participants after the end of the employer's taxable year will not be allowed because compensation must be earned before it can be deferred and contributed to the plan. [Rev. Rul. 2002-73, 2002-2 C.B. 805; Rev. Rul. 2002-46, 2002-2 C.B. 117; Rev. Rul. 90-105, 1990-2 C.B. 69; IRS Notice

2002-48, 2002-2 C.B. 130; IRS Coordinated Issue Paper UIL No. 9300.23-00 (Sept. 24, 2004); IRS Coordinated Issue Paper UIL No. 404.11-00 (Oct. 23, 1996); IRS Appeals Settlement Guidelines UIL No. 9300.01-1 (Oct. 1, 2004); Priv. Ltr. Rul. 200110031; Field Serv. Adv. 200107012; Chief Couns. Adv. 200038004]

Example 1. Bea-Bernie Corp. maintains a plan, which consists of a cash-or-deferred arrangement (see Q 27:2) and provides for matching contributions (see Q 27:75). Bea-Bernie Corp.'s taxable year is the fiscal year ending June 30. The plan has a calendar plan year and was amended to provide for Bea-Bernie Corp.'s board of directors to set a minimum contribution for a plan year to be allocated first toward elective deferrals and matching contributions, with any excess to be allocated to participants as of the end of the plan year in proportion to compensation earned during the plan year. Pursuant to this plan amendment, Bea-Bernie Corp.'s board adopted a resolution on June 15, 2010, setting a minimum contribution of $80,000 for the 2010 calendar plan year. By December 31, 2010 (the last day of the plan year), Bea-Bernie Corp. had contributed $80,000 to the plan. These amounts consisted of (1) $38,000 for elective deferrals and matching contributions attributable to compensation earned by the plan participants before the end of Bea-Bernie Corp.'s taxable year ending June 30, 2010 (pre-year-end service contributions), and (2) $42,000 for elective deferrals and matching contributions attributable to compensation earned by plan participants after the end of Bea-Bernie Corp.'s taxable year ending June 30, 2010 (post-year-end service contributions). Bea-Bernie Corp. made each contribution attributable to compensation earned during each pay period contemporaneously with the issuance of wage payments for the pay period.

Bea-Bernie Corp. receives an extension of time to March 15, 2011 to file the income tax return for its taxable year ending June 30, 2010 (2010 taxable year). On the income tax return for its 2010 taxable year, which was timely filed on March 1, 2011, Bea-Bernie Corp. claimed a deduction for the entire $80,000 for elective deferrals and matching contributions made to the plan during the plan's 2010 calendar plan year, relating to both pre-year-end service contributions and post-year-end service contributions. The total amount contributed and claimed by Bea-Bernie Corp. as a deduction did not exceed 25 percent of the total compensation otherwise paid or accrued during Bea-Bernie Corp.'s 2010 taxable year to participants under the plan.

The plan amendment and the board resolution setting a minimum contribution for the plan year established a liability, prior to the end of Bea-Bernie Corp.'s taxable year, to make that contribution. However, Bea-Bernie Corp.'s post-year-end service contributions still are attributable to compensation earned by plan participants after the end of the taxable year. Neither the plan amendment nor the board resolution bears on when that compensation is earned. Thus, for example, the post-year-end service contributions in these circumstances are still on account of that subsequent taxable year rather than on account of Bea-Bernie Corp.'s 2010 taxable year, and so cannot be deemed paid at the end of Bea-Bernie Corp.'s 2010 taxable year. Therefore, Bea-Bernie Corp.'s post-year-end service contributions are not deductible for its

2010 taxable year. This applies regardless of whether the employer's liability to make a minimum contribution is fixed before the close of the taxable year.

Example 2. The facts are the same as in Example 1, but there are two variations, neither of which involves contributions after the end of the taxable year. One variation involves an actual payment to the plan before the end of the taxable year in anticipation of deferrals and matching contributions to occur after the end of the taxable year (but before the end of the overlapping plan year). The other variation involves such a prepayment, combined with a guaranteed minimum contribution. Because these variations involve actual payments before the end of the taxable year, the payments are deductible for Bea-Bernie Corp.'s 2010 taxable year.

IRS has issued regulations that may require individuals, trusts, partnerships and their partners, C corporations, and S corporations and their shareholders to file a statement with their income tax or information returns reporting certain tax avoidance transactions involving contributions to 401(k) plans attributable to compensation earned after the close of the taxable year. IRS has included in tax avoidance transactions those transactions in which taxpayers claim deductions for contributions to a 401(k) plan or matching contributions to a defined contribution plan (see Qs 2:2, 27:77) where the contributions are attributable to compensation earned by plan participants after the end of the taxable year. In general, a separate statement will be required for each reportable transaction for each taxable year in which an individual's or an entity's federal income tax liability is affected by its participation in such a transaction. [Treas. Reg. §§ 1.6011-4, 54.6011-4; Rev. Proc. 2003-25, 2003-1 C.B. 601; IRS Notice 2001-51, 2001-2 C.B. 190] IRS has concluded that the two variations described in Example 2 are not reportable transactions. [IRS Notice 2002-48, 2002-2 C.B. 130]

If a terminated employee does not receive a share of the employer's contribution for the year of termination, such employee's compensation is not included for deduction limitation purposes. [Dallas Dental Labs., 72 T.C. 117 (1979); Rev. Rul. 65-295, 1965-2 C.B. 148] In a defined contribution plan, a disabled participant may be deemed to receive compensation at the rate of compensation paid immediately before becoming disabled, and such "phantom" compensation is included for deduction limitation purposes (see Q 6:41). [I.R.C. §§ 415(c)(3)(C), 404(a)(12)]

For taxable years beginning after 2001, there is a $200,000 per participant compensation cap that applies to the computation of deductions for contributions to all qualified retirement plans. The $200,000 limitation is subject to cost-of-living adjustments (see Q 6:46), but an adjustment will be made only if it is $5,000 or greater and then will be made in multiples of $5,000 (i.e., rounded down to the next lowest multiple of $5,000). For example, an increase in the cost-of-living of $4,999 will result in no adjustment, and an increase of $9,999 will create an upward adjustment of $5,000. Any adjustment will be applied to taxable years *beginning* in the calendar year in which the adjustment becomes effective. [I.R.C. §§ 401(a)(17), 404(*l*)]

For taxable years that begin in 2010, the compensation cap remained at $245,000. [IRS Notice 2009-94, 2009-2 C.B. 848] For the five years prior to 2010, the compensation limits were as follows:

Year	Compensation Limit
2009	$245,000
2008	230,000
2007	225,000
2006	220,000
2005	210,000

In addition to elective deferrals being included in compensation for deduction limitation purposes, these elective deferrals are not considered employer contributions and, therefore, are not subject to the employer deduction limitations relating to the 25 percent of compensation limitation for contributions:

1. To profit sharing plans (see Q 12:8);
2. Where an employer maintains both a defined contribution plan and a defined benefit plan (see Q 12:21); and
3. To a leveraged ESOP (see Q 28:7).

[I.R.C. § 404(n)]

However, the employer's tax deductible contribution can be maximized by adopting a combined 401(k) plan (see Q 27:67).

Example 3. In 2011, Renee, age 50, is the sole employee of ParaSiegel Corporation, and the corporation adopts a profit sharing plan with a CODA (see Q 27:2). In 2011, Renee has a salary of $116,000 after making an elective contribution of $16,500 (see Q 27:51) and a catch-up contribution (see Q 27:52) of $5,500. Renee's compensation for the year is $138,000 ($116,000 + $16,500 + $5,500; see Q 6:41), and the corporation makes a contribution to the plan of $32,500 for Renee's benefit. Since the catch-up contribution is not considered for the annual addition limitation, Renee's annual addition is $49,000 ($32,500 + $16,500) and does not exceed the limitation of the lesser of $49,000 or 100 percent of compensation. In addition, the entire $54,500 ($32,500 + $16,500 + $5,500) contributed to the plan in 2011 is deductible because elective and catch-up contributions are not considered employer contributions and are not subject to the employer deduction limitation relating to the 25-percent-of-compensation limitation for profit sharing plan contributions.

Example 4. The facts are the same as in Example 3, except that the annual addition limitation increases to $51,000 for the 2011 limitation year (see Q 6:12), but the elective and catch-up contribution limits do not increase for 2011. The corporation can now make a contribution to the plan of $34,500 for Renee's benefit. Renee's annual addition is $51,000 ($34,500 + $16,500), and the entire $56,500 ($34,500 + $16,500 + $5,500) is deductible. If the limitation on elective contributions increases to $17,000 in 2011 and Renee makes an elective contribution of that amount, the corporation's contribution for Renee's benefit will be limited to $34,000 because her annual addition cannot exceed $51,000 ($34,000 + $17,000).

Q 12:16 May a company make a deductible contribution to the qualified retirement plan of an affiliated company?

Although contributions to a profit sharing plan are not required to be based on profits (see Q 2:6), a profit sharing plan may require profits in order to make a contribution. If a member of an affiliated group of corporations cannot make a contribution to its profit sharing plan because it has no current or accumulated earnings or profits, another member of the affiliated group may make a contribution for the employees of the unprofitable member. However, the contribution is deductible only if both members participate in the same profit sharing plan, and the contributing corporation has current or accumulated earnings or profits; the contribution is not deductible if they maintain separate plans. [I.R.C. §§ 404(a)(3)(B), 1504; Treas. Reg. § 1.404(a)-10(a)(1)]

This rule does not apply to pension plans. However, when the common parent of an affiliated group and several of its subsidiaries made contributions to the pension plans maintained by another subsidiary of the parent, the recipient subsidiary was allowed to deduct the contributions. Contributions by other subsidiaries of the common parent were treated as distributions to the common parent, followed by contributions of capital to the recipient subsidiary and constructive contributions by the recipient subsidiary to the plans. Contributions to the recipient subsidiary's pension plans by its own subsidiaries were treated as constructive dividends to the recipient subsidiary followed by constructive contributions by the recipient subsidiary to the plans. Contributions by the common parent were treated as constructive contributions of capital to the subsidiary, followed by constructive contributions from the subsidiary to its pension plans. The contributing companies could not deduct the amounts contributed, but such amounts were deductible by the recipient subsidiary as if it had made the contributions directly. [Priv. Ltr. Rul. 9337025; *see also* Priv. Ltr. Rul. 199913003]

Q 12:17 What is the limit on tax-deductible contributions to defined contribution plans?

The deduction for defined contribution plans that are pension plans (e.g., money purchase pension and target benefit plans; see Qs 2:4, 2:5) is the same as profit sharing plans. Thus, subject to IRS regulations, such pension plans are subject to the 25-percent-of-compensation limitation (see Q 12:8). [I.R.C. § 404(a)(3)(A)(v)]

However, in computing the amount deductible for contributions to any type of defined contribution plan (see Q 2:2), if the annual addition (see Q 6:34) of any participant under the plan is more than the amount allowed by law, the excess amount of the company contribution will not be deductible (see Q 12:24). [I.R.C. § 404(j)(1)(B)]

> **Example 1.** Villa del Sandy Corp. established a money purchase pension plan in 2010 for its only employee, Maxine. The plan provided a 25-percent-of-compensation contribution formula. Maxine's compensation was $208,000, and the contribution under the formula was $52,000. The excess portion of Villa del Sandy Corp.'s contribution for 2010 of $3,000 ($52,000 – $49,000) is not deductible. In addition, the nondeductible contribution is subject to a nondeductible 10 percent excise tax penalty (see Qs 12:9–12:11).

> **Example 2.** Mexico Maxine Corp. establishes a money purchase pension plan in 2010. The plan provides for contributions equal to the lesser of $49,000 or 100 percent of compensation. The only two participants are Sandy, who earns $236,000, and Maxine, who earns $12,000. The contribution for Sandy is $49,000 [the lesser of $49,000 or $236,000 (100% × $236,000)], and the contribution for Maxine is $12,000 [the lesser of $49,000 or $12,000 (100% × $12,000)]. The contribution of $61,000 is deductible because it does not exceed $62,000 (25% × $248,000), the 25-percent-of-compensation limitation.

For a discussion of the per participant limitation on compensation for making tax-deductible contributions, see Q 12:15.

Q 12:18　What is the limit on tax-deductible contributions to a defined benefit plan?

In the case of a defined benefit plan (see Q 2:4), an actuarial valuation is performed by an actuary to determine benefits, liabilities, minimum funding requirements, and the maximum tax-deductible contribution, among other things. The maximum deduction is based in part on the benefits provided by the plan and the assumptions employed by the actuary, such as interest, mortality, and turnover (see Qs 8:14, 12:19). [Ann. 98-1, 1998-1 C.B. 282]

The employer's deduction is taken for a taxable year but is determined with reference to a plan year. When the two years are the same, the concurrent plan year controls the taxable year deduction. However, if the two years do not coincide, the deductible limit is determined from one of (1) the plan year that begins in the taxable year, (2) the plan year that ends in the taxable year, or (3) a pro rata share of each year. The linkage that is chosen by the employer cannot be changed unless approved as a change in accounting method. [I.R.C. § 446(e); Treas. Reg. § 1.404(a)-14(c); Ann. 98-1, 1998-1 C.B. 282; Field Serv. Adv. 1999778] Where the plan year was a calendar year and the company's taxable year ended on the last Saturday of January, the deductible limit could include the expected increase in current liability due to benefits accruing during the full plan year commencing within the taxable year; however, the interest adjustment for the determination of expected assets and expected current liability should be calculated to the end of the taxable year. [Priv. Ltr. Rul. 200450058]

No deduction is allowed for any contribution to fund a retirement benefit in excess of any participant's annual benefit limit (see Q 12:25). [I.R.C. § 404(j)(1)(A)] For a discussion of the per participant limitation on compensation for making tax-deductible contributions, see Q 12:15.

In determining the amount of nondeductible contributions (see Qs 12:9–12:11), the employer is permitted to elect not to take into account contributions to a defined benefit plan. An employer making such an election for a year is not permitted to take advantage of the exceptions for certain contributions to defined contribution plans (see Q 12:21). [I.R.C. § 4972(c)(7)]

IRS ruled that an employer's contributions to an account within its defined benefit plan to provide post-retirement medical benefits to certain plan participants would be deductible to the extent the contributions do not exceed the greater of (1) the sum of the level-distribution amount of each employee's remaining unfunded cost of past and current credits distributed over the remaining years of future service or (2) 10 percent of the cost to completely fund the medical benefits. [Treas. Reg. § 1.404(a)-3(f)(2); Priv. Ltr. Rul. 9652021]

In the case of contributions to a single-employer defined benefit plan, the maximum deductible amount is equal to the greater of (1) the excess (if any) of the sum of the plan's funding target, the plan's target normal cost, and a cushion amount for a plan year, over the value of plan assets (as determined under the minimum funding rules), and (2) the minimum required contribution for the plan year.

However, in the case of a plan that is not in at-risk status, the first amount above is not less than the excess (if any) of the sum of the plan's funding target and target normal cost, determined as if the plan was in at-risk status, over the value of the plan assets.

The cushion amount for a plan year is the sum of (1) 50 percent of the plan's funding target for the plan year and (2) the amount by which the plan's funding target would increase if determined by taking into account increases in participant's compensation for future years or, if the plan does not base benefits attributable to past service on compensation, increases in benefits that are expected to occur in succeeding plan years, determined on the basis of average annual benefit increases over the previous six years. For this purpose, the dollar limits on benefits and on compensation apply; but, in the case of a plan that is covered by PBGC (see Q 25:11), increases in the compensation limit (see Q 6:13) that are expected to occur in succeeding plan years may be taken into account. The rules relating to projecting compensation for future years are intended solely to enable employers to reduce volatility in pension contributions; the rules are not intended to create any inference that employees have any protected interest with respect to such projected increases. See Q 8:3 through 8:6 for more details.

[I.R.C. §§ 404(a)(1)(A), 404(a)(1)(B), 404(o) (as amended by WRERA 2008 § 108(a)(1))]

In the case of contributions to a multiemployer defined benefit plan (see Q 29:2), the maximum deductible amount is not less than the excess (if any) of (1) 140 percent of the plan's current liability, over (2) the value of plan assets. [I.R.C. §§ 404(a)(1)(D), 404(a)(1)(D)(i) (as amended by WRERA 2008 § 108(b))]

IRS provided guidance on certain of the changes made by PPA (see Q 1:33) to the rules concerning the deduction for plan contributions. Some of the changes are effective for years beginning after 2005 (the 2006 changes), and others are effective for years beginning after 2007 (the 2008 changes). Guidance is provided with respect to the 2006 changes and one related issue. Future guidance will be provided with respect to the 2008 changes. [IRS Notice 2007-28, 2007-1 C.B. 880]

As previously discussed, if the plan year of the plan and the taxable year of the employer do not coincide, the deductible limit for the taxable year of the employer is permitted to be determined as any one of the following alternatives: (1) the deductible limit determined for the plan year beginning in the taxable year; (2) the deductible limit determined for the plan year ending in the taxable year; or (3) a weighted average of alternatives (1) and (2). A plan year used under any of these alternatives is referred to as an associated plan year. The calculations of the deductible limit for a taxable year are based on the calculations with respect to an associated plan year or years and must reflect the law in effect for the taxable year. For example, with respect to the 2006 calendar taxable year, any associated plan year (i.e., a plan year beginning in 2006 or plan year ending in 2006 that is used to determine the deductible limit for the 2006 taxable year) must reflect the 2006 changes. Thus, if the deductible limit is determined with respect to the plan year ending in 2006 (which begins in 2005), the calculation of the limit with respect to that plan year must reflect the use of an interest rate within the permissible corporate rate range (instead of an interest rate within the permissible 30-year Treasury rate range) that was used for purposes of the minimum funding standards, and must reflect the limitation based upon 150 percent of current liability (in place of the limitation based on 100 percent of current liability). The funding method and other actuarial assumptions that were used for purposes of the minimum funding standards for that plan year must also be used for the calculations of the deductible limit. As another example, in the case of a taxable year that is not the calendar year and that begins in 2005 and ends in 2006, and a plan year that is the calendar year, the deductible limit for any associated plan year must not reflect the 2006 changes. Thus, if the deductible limit for the taxable year beginning July 1, 2005, and ending June 30, 2006, is determined based upon the plan year beginning in the taxable year (the 2006 calendar plan year), the calculations of such limit must not reflect the limitation based on 150 percent of current liability (i.e., must be limited to 100 percent of unfunded current liability) and may use the 30-year Treasury rate in place of the corporate rate. [IRS Notice 2007-28, Q&A-1, Q&A-2, 2007-1 C.B. 880]

In general, PPA amended the deduction rules for contributions to defined benefit plans for years beginning after 2005, to replace the limitation based upon unfunded current liability with a limitation based on 150 percent of current liability (140 percent in the case of a multiemployer plan). In addition, PPA eliminated the option to use any interest rate within 90 percent to 110 percent of the weighted average of the rates of interest on 30-year Treasury securities during the four-year period ending on the last day before the beginning of the plan year (the permissible 30-year Treasury rate range) for purposes of determining current liability in determining the maximum deduction rather than an interest rate within the 90 percent to 100 percent of the weighted average of the rates of interest on amounts invested conservatively in long-term investment grade corporate bonds (the permissible corporate rate range). [IRS Notice 2007-28, Q&A-3, 2007-1 C.B. 880; IRS Notice 90-11, 1990-1 C.B. 319]

The deductible limit is determined as of the valuation date for the plan year and is adjusted for interest to the earlier of the end of the plan year or the end of the taxable year of the employer (the "relevant date"). [IRS Notice 2007-28, Q&A-4, 2007-1 C.B. 880; Treas. Reg. § 1.404(a)-14(f)(3)]

In the case of a plan that has 100 or fewer participants for the plan year, unfunded current liability does not include the liability attributable to benefit increases for highly compensated employees (HCEs; see Q 3:2) resulting from a plan amendment that is made or becomes effective, whichever is later, within the last two years. For this purpose, the adoption of a new plan will not be treated as a plan amendment only if the employer did not maintain a defined benefit plan covering any HCE covered by the new plan during the past two years. Thus, for an employer with a taxable year that is the calendar year, if an HCE was covered by a defined benefit plan of the employer at any time during 2004 or 2005, a new plan established during the 2006 taxable year that covers that HCE would be considered a plan amendment for this purpose. [I.R.C. § 404(a)(1)(D)(ii); IRS Notice 2007-28, Q&A-5, 2007-1 C.B. 880]

Q 12:19   How does a defined benefit plan's funding method affect its tax-deductible contributions?

The amount of deductible contributions cannot exceed the cost based on reasonable funding methods and actuarial assumptions. [I.R.C. § 412(c)(3); Treas. Reg. § 1.404(a)-3(b)]

For example, a contribution calculated on the basis of an assumption that plan assets would earn interest at a rate of 5 percent was unreasonable in view of the availability of investments with a significantly higher interest rate. Further, the calculation under the normal cost method in a plan's first year of existence unreasonably failed to allocate costs between the normal cost of benefits accrued for service during the year of the contribution and the cost of benefits accrued during the year for past service, which must be amortized over no less than ten years (see Q 12:18). [Jerome Mirza & Assocs., Ltd. v. United States, 882 F.2d 229 (7th Cir. 1989); Custom Builders, Inc., 58 T.C.M. 696 (1989); Priv. Ltr. Ruls. 9119007, 9031001]

An assumption that employees will retire at the normal retirement age specified in the plan, ignoring the fact that employees normally retire later, may be unreasonable and result in a nondeductible contribution (see Qs 2:19, 2:39). [Rev. Rul. 78-331, 1978-2 C.B. 158]

In a number of cases, however, courts have concluded that, since the assumptions used were not "substantially unreasonable" and represented the actuary's best estimate of anticipated experience under the plans based on actuarial assumptions used by similar plans, IRS was precluded from requiring a retroactive change of assumptions. [Citrus Valley Estates, Inc. v. Comm'r, 49 F.3d 1410 (9th Cir. 1995); Wachtell, Lipton, Rosen & Katz v. Comm'r, 26 F.3d 291 (2d Cir. 1994); Vinson & Elkins v. Comm'r, 7 F.3d 1235 (5th Cir. 1993); *but see* Rhoades, McKee & Boer v. United States, 1:91-CV-540 (W.D. Mich. 1995)] For a discussion of these cases, see Q 8:14.

An employer cannot rely on uncertified, preliminary information furnished by its actuarial firm (see Q 20:26) to support a tax-deductible contribution to its defined benefit plan. Based upon preliminary advice that utilized a 6 percent interest rate assumption, the employer contributed and deducted $60,000. Subsequently, the actuarial firm increased the interest rate assumption, the effect of which increase was to lower the deductible contribution to $20,000, and the actuarial firm certified Schedule B (see Q 20:6) setting forth this lesser amount and the interest rate change. Upon audit by IRS, a new actuarial firm advised that it would certify a revised Schedule B that would support a contribution of $60,000 based on an interest rate assumption of 6 percent. The court concluded that the employer was not entitled to file an amended Schedule B; once a Schedule B is filed, an amended Schedule B containing a different set of actuarial assumptions cannot be filed unless IRS determines that the actuarial assumptions set forth on the original Schedule B were not reasonable. [Rubin, 103 T.C. 200 (1994); Treas. Reg. § 1.404(a)-3(c)]

Q 12:20 Are excess amounts contributed to a defined benefit plan deductible in later years?

The excess contributions may be carried over and deducted in later years. For example, suppose that for 2010 the maximum deduction is $20,000 and the employer contributes $25,000 to the plan. There is a $5,000 carryover that is tax deductible only in a later year in which a full contribution is not made. So, if in 2011 the maximum deduction is $22,000 and the employer contributes $20,000 to the plan, $2,000 of the $5,000 carryover can be deducted for that year. [I.R.C. § 404(a)(1)(E)]

Excess amounts contributed to a defined benefit plan (or any other qualified retirement plan) may be subject to an excise tax equal to 10 percent of the nondeductible contributions (see Qs 12:9–12:11, 12:18). [I.R.C. § 4972]

Q 12:21 Are there any special limits on tax-deductible contributions if an employer maintains both a defined contribution plan and a defined benefit plan?

If no employee is covered by both plans, the regular deduction limitations apply with respect to each plan. However, if at least one employee is covered by any combination of defined contribution and defined benefit plans (see Qs 2:2, 2:3) maintained by the same employer, a special deduction limitation applies:

the *greater* of (1) 25 percent of the aggregate compensation of all participants or (2) the amount necessary to meet the minimum funding standard for the defined benefit plan (see Q 8:1). This limitation is applied after the regular limitations have been determined for each plan. [I.R.C. §§ 404(a)(7)(A)(as amended by WRERA 2008 §108(a)(2)), 404(a)(7)(C) (as amended by WRERA 2008 § 108(c)); Ann. 98-1, 1998-1 C.B. 282; Priv. Ltr. Ruls. 200612018, 200346024] However, the combined limit applies only in the case of employer contributions to one or more defined contribution plans to the extent that such contributions exceed 6 percent of the compensation otherwise paid or accrued during the taxable year to the beneficiaries under the plan. WRERA 2008 (see Q 1:36) modifies the overall deduction limit for employers that maintain one or more defined contribution plans and one or more defined benefit plans. With the modification, if contributions to defined contribution plans are less than six percent of compensation, the defined benefit plan is not subject to the overall deduction limit. If contributions to defined contribution plans exceed six percent of compensation, only the contributions in excess of six percent are counted toward the overall deduction limit. [I.R.C. § 404(a)(7)(C)(iii) (as amended by WRERA 2008 § 108(c)); IRS Notice 2007-28, Q&A-6, 2007-1 C.B. 880]

> **Example.** Adam Corporation maintains a defined benefit plan and a defined contribution plan on a calendar-year basis. Adam's ten employees participate in both plans. For 2010, Adam must make a contribution equal to 31 percent of the participants' aggregate compensation to fund both plans. The contribution to the defined benefit plan is an amount equal to 25 percent of the participants' aggregate compensation. Because Adam's contribution to the defined contribution plan does not exceed 6 percent of the aggregate compensation, Adam can deduct the full amount of both contributions on its 2010 income tax return; no portion of the contribution is not deductible, and no excise tax will be imposed.

To alleviate the impact of the paired plan deduction limitation and the excise tax on nondeductible contributions, the defined contribution plan may provide that required contributions will be limited to amounts that are deductible. [I.R.C. § 404(a)(7)(A)] However, the paired plan deduction limitation does not apply if no amounts, other than elective deferrals (see Q 27:16), are contributed to any defined contribution plan for the taxable year. [I.R.C. §§ 402(g)(3), 404(a)(7)(C)(ii)] IRS representatives have opined that where an employer adopts a defined benefit plan covering five of its ten employees and a defined contribution plan covering the other five employees, the paired plan deduction limitation does not apply; but, if the defined contribution plan is amended to permit all ten employees to make elective deferrals, the paired plan deduction limitation will become applicable.

Aggregate compensation includes the total compensation paid or accrued during the taxable year of all employees who are participants in either the defined benefit plan or the defined contribution plan, or both (see Q 12:15). [Treas. Reg. § 1.404(a)-13(a)] Elective deferrals are included in compensation for determining the limitation on deductible contributions, and these elective deferrals are no longer considered employer contributions and, therefore, are not subject to the employer deduction limitations relating to the 25-percent-of-compensation limitation (see Q 12:15).

Under PPA (see Q 1:33), in applying the overall deduction limit to contributions to one or more defined benefit plans and one or more defined contribution plans, single-employer defined benefit plans that are covered by PBGC (see Q 25:11) are not taken into account. Thus, the deduction for contributions to a defined benefit plan or a defined contribution plan is not affected by the overall deduction limit merely because employees are covered by both plans if the defined benefit plan is covered by PBGC (i.e., the separate deduction limits for contributions to defined contribution plans and defined benefit plans apply). In addition, in applying the overall deduction limit, the amount necessary to meet the minimum funding requirement with respect to a single-employer defined benefit plan that is not covered by PBGC is treated as not less than the plan's funding shortfall (as determined under the minimum funding rules; see Q 8:1). [I.R.C. §§ 404(a)(7)(A) (as amended by WRERA 2008 § 108(a)(2)), 404(a)(7)(C)(iv)]

In addition, in applying the overall deduction limit to contributions to one or more defined benefit plans and one or more defined contribution plans, multiemployer plans (see Q 29:2) are not taken into account. Thus, the deduction for contributions to a defined benefit plan or a defined contribution plan is not affected by the overall deduction limit merely because employees are covered by both plans if either plan is a multiemployer plan (i.e., the separate deduction limits for contributions to defined contribution plans and defined benefit plans apply). [I.R.C. § 404(a)(7)(C)(v); IRS Notice 2007-28, Q&A-6, 2007-1 C.B. 880]

A plan that contains a qualified cash-or-deferred arrangement (CODA; see Q 27:2) is taken into account for purposes of the combined limit; however, elective deferrals are not taken into account. Thus, matching contributions (see Q 27:75) and nonelective employer contributions (see Q 27:17) are taken into account in applying the deduction limits, including the combined limit. If elective deferrals are the only contributions under a defined contribution plan, then the plan is not taken into account in applying the combined limit. [IRS Notice 2007-28, Q&A-7, 2007-1 C.B. 880]

When employer contributions to defined contribution plans (other than elective deferrals) exceed 6 percent of compensation of participants in those plans, the amount of employer contributions to defined contribution plans to which the combined limit applies is equal to the amount of employer contributions for the plan year less 6 percent of compensation of participants in those plans. Thus, the combined limit (i.e., the greater of 25 percent of compensation or the contributions to the defined benefit plan or plans to the extent such contributions do not exceed the amount necessary to satisfy the minimum funding standard for the defined benefit plans, treating a contribution that does not exceed the unfunded current liability as an amount necessary to satisfy the minimum funding standard for each defined benefit plan) applies to the total of employer contributions to defined benefit plans and employer contributions to defined contribution plans (other than elective deferrals), less 6 percent of compensation of participants in the defined contribution plans. [IRS Notice 2007-28, Q&A-8, 2007-1 C.B. 880]

When employer contributions to defined contribution plans (other than elective deferrals) do not exceed 6 percent of compensation of participants in those plans, the combined limit does not apply to any employer contributions to defined contribution plans. In such a case, the combined limit applies only to contributions to the defined benefit plans. [IRS Notice 2007-28, Q&A-9, 2007-1 C.B. 880]

Q 12:22   Are there any other limitations on the deductibility of employer contributions?

Yes. For certain employers engaged in the production of property or the acquisition of property for resale, the uniform capitalization rules require the capitalization of a portion of contributions to various employee benefit plans, including qualified retirement plans. [I.R.C. § 263A; Treas. Reg. §§ 1.263A-1–1. 263A-15]

Essentially, an employer that is covered by the uniform capitalization rules and maintains a qualified retirement plan must first calculate its otherwise allowable deductible contribution under the generally applicable limits under Section 404 and then allocate that amount between production or inventory costs, which must be capitalized, and other costs, which are deductible. [I.R.C. § 263A(a); Treas. Reg. §§ 1.263A-1 through 1.263A-15; General Explanation of TRA '86, tit. VIII, D, at 513; IRS Notice 88-86, 1988-2 C.B. 401; Ann. 98-1, 1998-1 C.B. 282; Ann. 88-55, 1988-13 I.R.B. 35; Field Serv. Adv. 200137016]

Q 12:23   Will excess assets of an employer's overfunded defined benefit plan that are transferred to a defined contribution plan be considered taxable income to the employer?

Yes. However, the employer may deduct the amount transferred as a contribution to the defined contribution plan, subject to applicable deduction limits (see Qs 12:8, 12:17). [Gen. Couns. Mem. 39,744 (1988)]

Example. SCJ Corporation maintains two qualified retirement plans: a defined benefit plan that is overfunded and a profit sharing plan. SCJ terminates its defined benefit plan; and, after all benefits are paid to plan participants, it transfers the defined benefit plan's excess assets to the profit sharing plan. SCJ deducted all of its contributions to the defined benefit plan when made. SCJ must recognize income upon the transfer from the defined benefit plan to the profit sharing plan. SCJ will be entitled to a deduction for the transferred funds if its contribution to the profit sharing plan during the year of the transfer and the amount of transferred funds are less than or equal to 25 percent of the compensation of plan participants.

A different result will occur if the profit sharing plan is a qualified replacement plan (see Q 25:53).

Q 12:24   Are excess amounts contributed to a combination of plans deductible?

If an amount is contributed by the employer to both a defined benefit plan and a defined contribution plan in excess of the deduction limitation (see Q 12:21), the excess contribution may be deducted in the succeeding taxable years. However, the total deduction in any succeeding year, including the contributions for that year, is limited to 25 percent of the compensation of the participants during that year. [I.R.C. § 404(a)(7)(B); Treas. Reg. § 1.404(a)-13(c); Priv. Ltr. Rul. 9107033]

> **Example.** Assume that, in the Example in Q 12:21, Adam Corporation contributed 10 percent, not 6 percent, of the participants' aggregate compensation to the defined contribution plan and made its contribution to both plans on February 28, 2011. The contributions were timely for 2010 minimum funding standard purposes (see Q 8:1). The amount deductible in 2010 is only 31 percent of aggregate 2010 compensation, but the portion of the contributions not deductible in 2010 (4 percent of aggregate 2010 compensation) may be deductible in 2011.

Excess amounts contributed to any qualified retirement plan (or combination of plans) are subject to an excise tax equal to 10 percent of the nondeductible contributions (see Qs 12:9–12:11, 12:18). [I.R.C. § 4972]

Q 12:25   May an employer deduct contributions to provide benefits to a participant in excess of Section 415 limits?

No. The deductible limit for a contribution to a defined contribution plan (see Q 2:2) is reduced to the extent the contribution produces an annual addition in excess of the Section 415 limit for the year. Similarly, no deduction is allowed for the portion of a contribution to a defined benefit plan (see Q 2:3) to fund a benefit for any participant in excess of the annual benefit limitation for the year. [I.R.C. § 404(j)(1); Van Roekel Farms, Inc. v. Comm'r, 2001 U.S. App. LEXIS 14201 (8th Cir. 2001); Howard E. Clendenen, Inc. v. Comm'r, 207 F.3d 1071 (8th Cir. 2000)] For details on contribution and benefit limits, see chapter 6.

In calculating the contribution to a defined benefit plan, anticipated cost-of-living increases in the allowable annual retirement benefit (see Q 6:11) cannot be taken into account before the year in which the increase first becomes effective. [I.R.C. § 404(j)(2); Feichtinger, 80 T.C. 239 (1983); Ann. 98-1, 1998-1 C.B. 282; Ann. 95-99, 1995-48 I.R.B. 10; *see also* Rev. Rul. 98-1, Q&A-19, Q&A-20, 1998-1 C.B. 249]

> **Example.** Sandi Corporation sponsors a defined benefit plan for its only employee, Steve, who is currently age 52 and has average annual compensation for plan purposes of $245,000. The plan provides an annual retirement benefit of 100 percent of compensation in the form of a straight life annuity at the normal retirement age of 62. Any portion of the company's contribution for the 2010 year that funds the excess benefit of $50,000 ($245,000 − $195,000) will not be deductible and will be subject to a 10 percent excise tax.

That result is not changed by the fact that it is reasonable to project that Steve will be entitled to receive an annual benefit of $245,000 at retirement due to cost-of-living increases in the allowable annual retirement benefit.

Two doctors were the only shareholders of two corporations, which entities constituted a controlled group of corporations (see Q 5:31). Since both corporations adopted defined benefit plans (each plan provided the doctors with the maximum allowable benefit), the doctors were receiving double the permissible benefit. The deduction for the contribution made by one of the corporations was disallowed and substantial penalties were imposed (see Q 8:16). [Anesthesia Consultants, PC v. United States, No. 94-WYO-419 (D. Colo. 1995)]

Q 12:26   Is the employer's payment of plan expenses deductible?

Many qualified retirement plans provide that general administrative expenses may be paid from plan assets unless paid by the employer. If the employer pays the administrative fees (e.g., the fees of trustees and actuaries) directly, or indirectly by reimbursing the trust, the amounts paid are deductible under Section 162 or Section 212 to the extent that they satisfy the requirements of those sections and are not considered plan contributions. [Rev. Rul. 84-146, 1984-2 C.B. 61; Ann. 98-1, 1998-1 C.B. 282; Priv. Ltr. Ruls. 9001002, 8941010, 8941009, 8940014, 8940013] One court ruled that the employer, as plan sponsor, could deduct as business expenses litigation costs incurred on behalf of the plan when it sued the plan's securities investment manager and his firm for various violations. The litigation costs were business expenses deductible under Section 162 and not plan contributions. [Sklar, Greenstein & Scheer, P.C., 113 T.C. 135 (1999)]

However, brokers' commissions incurred in connection with nonrecurring transactions such as the purchase and sale of plan assets, investment manager fees, and wrap fees are not separately deductible under Section 162 or Section 212. Instead, amounts paid by the employer directly to the broker or investment manager, or indirectly by payment to the trust as reimbursement for the brokers' commissions or the investment managers' fees, are treated as plan contributions and used to provide benefits. Consequently, such contributions are deductible, subject to the limits of Section 404. [Rev. Rul. 86-142, 1986-2 C.B. 60; Ann. 98-1, 1998-1 C.B. 282; Priv. Ltr. Ruls. 9124034 (modifying Priv. Ltr. Rul. 8941010), 9124035 (modifying Priv. Ltr. Rul. 8941009), 9124036 (modifying Priv. Ltr. Rul. 8940013), 9124037 (modifying Priv. Ltr. Rul. 8940014)]

See Q 12:27 for a discussion of the tax credit that may be available for plan expenses.

Q 12:27   Is there a tax credit for new qualified retirement plan expenses?

The costs incurred by an employer related to the establishment and maintenance of a retirement plan (e.g., payroll system changes, investment vehicle setup fees, consulting fees) generally are deductible by the employer as ordinary and necessary expenses in carrying on a trade or business.

Small employers will receive a tax credit for some of the costs of establishing new retirement plans. The credit equals 50 percent of the start-up costs incurred to create or maintain a new employee retirement plan; the credit is limited to $500 in any taxable year; and the credit may be claimed for qualified costs incurred in each of the three years beginning with the taxable year in which the plan becomes effective.

An eligible employer plan includes a new qualified retirement plan, a SIMPLE plan (see Q 33:1), or a SEP (see Q 32:1). For the employer to qualify for the tax credit, the plan must cover at least one non-highly compensated employee (see Q 3:12). To qualify for the tax credit as an eligible small employer, the employer must not have employed more than 100 employees who received at least $5,000 of compensation from that employer in the preceding year. Aggregation rules apply in determining the number of an employer's employees, and all eligible employer plans are treated as one eligible employer plan.

The tax credit is available only for new plans. An employer must not have established or maintained a qualified plan during the three taxable year period immediately preceding the first taxable year in which the new plan is effective, and the new plan will not qualify for the credit if the prior plan received contributions or accrued benefits for substantially the same employees as the new plan will cover. Aggregation rules apply to determine whether a prior plan existed, and the employer and any predecessor must not have been a member of a controlled group (see Q 5:29) or a member of an affiliated service group (see Q 5:35) in which a member established or maintained a qualified plan (that received contributions or accrued benefits for the same employees covered by the new plan) during the three taxable year period.

Qualified start-up costs are any ordinary and necessary expenses incurred to establish or administer an eligible plan or to educate employees about retirement planning. The credit is limited to the first $1,000 of qualified costs incurred in the first year the new plan is effective and in each of the following two years. The credit is a general business credit. The 50 percent of qualifying expenses that are effectively offset by the tax credit are not deductible; however, the other 50 percent of the qualifying expenses (and other expenses) are deductible to the extent they are ordinary and necessary business expenses.

At the employer's election, the credit may be claimed in the year immediately preceding the first year in which the new plan is effective, and an eligible employer may also elect not to apply the credit for a taxable year.

[I.R.C. §§ 38(b)(14), 39(d), 45E]

IRS has issued Form 8881 (Credit for Small Employer Pension Plan Startup Costs) for use by employers claiming the credit.

Chapter 13

Taxation of Distributions

The form and time of payment of distributions from a qualified retirement plan depend primarily on the type of plan. Defined benefit plans generally pay benefits in the form of an annuity on the participant's early or normal retirement date. Defined contribution plans generally pay benefits in a single-sum payment upon the participant's termination of employment. Some retirement plans also permit participants to receive distributions prior to their retirement or termination of employment as in-service withdrawals or loans. This chapter discusses the tax treatment of the various forms of distribution.

Q 13:1 In general, how are distributions from qualified retirement plans taxed?

Generally, all distributions from qualified retirement plans are includible in the recipient's gross income when received. If property other than money is distributed, the amount includible in gross income is the fair market value of such property (see Q 15:14). The taxation of certain types of distributions may be postponed through a tax-free rollover to an IRA or another plan; however, if the distribution is not rolled over, it is includible in gross income in the taxable year received, not the taxable year in which the rollover could have been made (see chapter 34 for more details). In some cases, favorable tax treatment may be available for a lump-sum distribution (see Q 13:5). A distribution received from a qualified retirement plan in the form of a loan will not be taxable if certain requirements are met (see Q 13:27). [I.R.C. §§ 72, 402; Treas. Reg. §§ 1.72-16(c)(2)(ii), 1.402(a)-1(a)(1)(iii), 1.402(a)-1(a)(2); IRS Notice 89-25, Q&A-10, 1989-1 C.B. 662; Ann. 95-99, 1995-48 I.R.B. 10] See Q 1:51 for a discussion of proposed regulations issued by IRS that a payment from a qualified retirement plan for an accident or health insurance premium generally constitutes a taxable distribution.

An individual had to include in income the total amount of a distribution he received, despite the fact that an IRS employee who had provided assistance to him with the preparation of his return erroneously reported only 10 percent of the distribution as income. [Bradley, T.C. Summ. Op. 2006-11] The purchase of two variable annuity contracts by the trustee of a qualified retirement plan and the distribution of the contracts to two individuals treated as the designated beneficiaries (see Q 11:17) of a deceased participant did not result in taxable distributions to the beneficiaries. The annuity contract, after distribution to the beneficiary, could not be transferred or assigned and could not be sold, discounted, or pledged as collateral for a loan or be used as security for the performance of an obligation. [I.R.C. § 401(g); Priv. Ltr. Ruls. 200548028, 200548027]

A transfer of funds from a qualified retirement plan to the temporary administrator of a deceased participant's estate is a distribution includible in the estate's gross income in the year of receipt. [Machat, 75 T.C.M. 2194 (1998); Priv. Ltr. Rul. 9320006] Payments from a deceased participant's plan account to his surviving spouse were includible in the surviving spouse's income even though the employer mistakenly used the deceased participant's social security number on documents relating to the plan payments. [Whittaker, 82 T.C.M. 447 (2001)] The transfer of funds from a qualified retirement plan to a nonqualified plan (see Qs 1:11–1:13) will result in taxable distributions to the qualified plan participants and also adversely affect the qualified status of the retirement plan. [Priv. Ltr. Rul. 199928041] However, the transfer of funds from a qualified retirement plan to a successor qualified retirement plan (see Q 9:55) was not a taxable event to any participant in either plan. [Priv. Ltr. Rul. 9438044] A participant's voluntary transfer of funds from his 401(k) plan account to his account in the employer's contributory defined benefit plan to purchase prior or additional service credit for the participant was not a distribution. [Priv. Ltr. Rul. 200335035] IRS has also concluded that a restorative payment made by an employer to its plan did not constitute taxable income to the participants (see Q 6:34).

Where an employee received a single-sum distribution from a qualified retirement plan and, pursuant to a divorce decree, paid a portion of the distribution to the employee's former spouse, it has been ruled that the mere fact that the employee was required to pay over a portion of the distribution to the former spouse did not entitle the employee to exclude those funds from income. Even if the distribution is made by the plan directly to the nonemployee spouse, the distribution will be taxable to the employee unless it is made pursuant to a qualified domestic relations order (QDRO; see Q 36:1). [Dorn, 86 T.C.M. 5 (2003); Burton, 73 T.C.M. 1729 (1997); Rodoni, 105 T.C. 29 (1995); In re Boudreau, 93-9491-8G3 (Bankr. M.D. Fla. 1995); Powell, 101 T.C. 489 (1993); Karem, 100 T.C. 521 (1993); Darby, 97 T.C. 51 (1991); see also Hackenberg, T.C. Summ. Op. 2010–135 and Amarasinghe, No. 08-1226 (4th Cir. 2008)]

At the time of a married couple's divorce, the husband was entitled to receive pension benefits, but he chose to continue working. Under the state community property law, the ex-wife was entitled to one-half of his accrued benefit, and the husband was ordered to pay his ex-wife an amount equal to one-half thereof until he retired. Under the state's community property law, each spouse is taxed on one-half of both spouses' income because the earnings are the property of the community and not of the spouse providing the services that produce the income. Since the income assigned to his ex-wife did not belong to the husband, he was not liable for the taxes thereon, and he therefore was not required to include in his income the amount he paid to his ex-wife. [Dunkin, 124 T.C. 180. (2005)] On appeal, the decision was reversed; the husband had to include in income the amount paid to his ex-wife, and the amount paid was not deductible as alimony. [United States v. Dunkin, 500 F.3d 1065 (9th Cir. 2007)]

In another case, a divorced wife was required to include in income distributions made to her from her ex-husband's pension plan because a divorce decree determined that she was the rightful owner of a portion of the pension funds. [Witcher, 84 T.C.M. 582 (2002)] One court concluded that a transfer of funds from a qualified retirement plan to a holding company was a distribution to the participant who directed the transfer because the participant could not prove that the plan was a partner with the holding company or that the funds were invested on behalf of the plan. [Federated Graphics Cos., 63 T.C.M. 3153 (1992)] An individual who withdrew funds from his profit sharing plan to make a down payment on a home had to include the withdrawal in income. [Grow, 70 T.C.M. 1576 (1995); *see also* Eagan v. United States, 80 F.3d 13 (1st Cir. 1996)]

A plan participant designated his wife as primary beneficiary and his son as secondary beneficiary of any death benefit payable under the plan. The participant's wife was convicted in the death of her husband, which, under state law, precluded her from receiving the plan death benefit. The distribution of the death benefit to the son was includible in his gross income. [D.N. v. United States, 2009 WL 4781902 (D. Ore. 2009)]

A participant's waiver assigning his retirement plan benefits to the employer constituted a prohibited assignment or alienation (see Q 4:27) and resulted in his receipt of a taxable distribution. The court ruled that the waived benefits did not represent excess assets reverting to the employer. [Gallade, 106 T.C. 355 (1996)]

An individual constructively received a distribution from a profit sharing plan upon delivery of the check to his residence, even though he was confined in an alcohol rehabilitation center and immediately thereafter in prison and did not cash the check until the following year. Except for the individual's own inaction while in rehabilitation, the distribution was subject to his will and control in the year of receipt and delivery. [Roberts, 84 T.C.M. 543 (2002)] See Q 34:36 for changes to the rollover rules.

A profit sharing plan that allowed a participant to have elective contributions (see Q 27:16) allocated to a separate retiree medical subaccount permitted the participant, upon retirement, either to receive taxable distributions from the subaccount or to use the subaccount to pay health care premiums. IRS ruled that amounts distributed from a qualified retirement plan that the distributee elects to have applied to pay health insurance premiums under a cafeteria plan are includible in the distributee's gross income and that the same conclusion applies if amounts distributed from the plan are applied directly to reimburse medical care expenses incurred by a participant in the plan. [Rev. Rul. 2003-62, 2003-1 C.B. 1034] IRS has also ruled, however, that the conversion of unused sick leave to an amount that is then contributed to a multiemployer cash balance plan (see Qs 2:23, 29:2) does not create taxable income for the plan participants at the time of contribution to the plan. [Priv. Ltr. Rul. 9840006; I.R.C. § 451(a); Treas. Reg. §§ 1.451-1(a), 1.451-2(a); Rev. Rul. 75-539, 1975-2 C.B. 45]

IRS has ruled that participants in a profit sharing plan who allocated a portion of their elective contributions to purchase long-term disability (LTD) insurance policies through the plan would not be taxed currently with the premium payments. The plan was the purchaser and owner of the LTD policies, and the participants from whose accounts the elective contributions were deducted to purchase the policies did not own the policies. The LTD policies were added as a benefit to provide for the continuation of benefit accumulations that would not occur if a participant became disabled, and benefits under the LTD policy would be paid directly to the plan. IRS concluded that because the purchase of the LTD policies was not a distribution, participants would not be currently taxed on the cost of the premiums, and also ruled that the proceeds, when paid to the plan, would not be taxable to the participants on whose behalf they were paid, because no distribution event under the plan would occur at the time the insurance proceeds were paid. [Priv. Ltr. Rul. 200031060]

IRS has also ruled that a transfer of assets and liabilities from a qualified retirement plan will be treated as a taxable distribution where the transfer is made to either (1) a nonqualified foreign trust or (2) a plan that satisfies the qualification requirements of the Puerto Rico Internal Revenue Code, even if the plan qualifies as an ERISA Section 1022(i)(l) Puerto Rican plan exempt from tax under Section 501(a). [Rev. Rul. 2008-40, 2008-2 C.B. 166]

Qualified retirement plan distributions to a nonresident alien were excludable from income, but distributions received by the individual after he became a resident alien were includible in income. [Priv. Ltr. Rul. 200105005]

In certain instances, penalty taxes may be imposed on distributions that commence too early (see Q 13:26) or too late (see Q 11:67). Distributions to a deceased participant's beneficiaries generally are also included in the deceased participant's estate for federal estate tax purposes (see Q 15:22).

See Q 1:28 for a discussion of the Katrina Emergency Tax Relief Act of 2005 and other developments for their effect on the taxation of distributions and other issues.

Q 13:2   If a plan overpays a participant, how are repayments by the participant treated?

IRS has ruled that, in situations in which an individual's payments from a qualified retirement plan are reduced in one or more taxable years to recoup overpayments made in prior taxable years that were properly included in gross income in such prior years, only the amounts received by the individual after the plan's required reduction to recoup an earlier plan overpayment are includible in the individual's gross income in the taxable year of distribution. Where an individual repays in the current year an overpayment made by a qualified retirement plan in a previous year and the amount actually paid in the previous year was properly included in gross income, the amount of the repayment is deductible. [Rev. Rul. 2002-84, 2002-2 C.B. 953] To illustrate these results, IRS provided three examples.

Example 1. BML Corporation maintains a defined benefit plan (see Q 2:3) that does not provide for employee contributions. At the beginning of 2010, Ben retired and started to receive an annual annuity payment of $36,000 from the plan. Ben included $36,000 in gross income in 2010. In June 2011, it was determined that Ben's annuity benefit had been miscalculated and the annuity payment for 2010 should have been $35,000. Under the administrative procedures of the plan, which are in accordance with the relevant correction procedures of EPCRS (see chapter 19), erroneous payments from the plan can be corrected by recouping the entire excess payment made in 2010 from Ben's remaining benefit payments for 2011. Thus, Ben's annual annuity benefit for 2011 of $35,000 is reduced to $33,940 to reflect the excess benefit amounts (increased by interest) that were paid from the plan to Ben during 2010.

Example 2. JAL Corporation maintains a defined benefit plan that does not provide for employee contributions. Jason retired in 2000 and started to receive an annual annuity of $14,000 from the plan. In November 2010, it was determined that Jason's annuity benefit had been miscalculated and that the annual payment for 2000 through 2009 should have been $13,000. Thus, the plan overpaid Jason by $1,000 per year for ten years and he included these amounts in gross income in the years received. Under the administrative procedures of the plan, erroneous payments from the plan can be recouped by reducing future payments so that the actuarial present value of the reduction is equal to the erroneous overpayments plus interest attributable to the overpayment based on the plan's interest rate factors. The plan's correction method is consistent with the procedures of EPCRS. The plan administrator (see Q 20:1) determines that to recoup the overpayment, future payments should be reduced $900 annually for life commencing in 2010. The plan adjusts Jason's annuity accordingly so that his annual annuity benefit of $13,000 is reduced for 2010 and subsequent years to $12,100 to reflect the excess benefit amounts (increased by interest) that were paid from the plan to Jason.

Example 3. The facts are the same as in Example 1, except that the benefit is paid to Ben in a single-sum distribution in 2010, and he included the entire distribution in gross income in 2010. The amount of the single-sum distribution exceeded the amount that was due Ben by $2,000. In 2011, the plan administrator discovered the overpayment; and, pursuant to the plan's procedures, the plan administrator notified Ben of the overpayment and demanded repayment with appropriate interest. In 2011, Ben repaid $2,120 (the $2,000 overpayments plus $120 interest) to the plan.

Amounts payable under a qualified retirement plan are included in gross income of the participant in the taxable year of distribution. The amounts are taxable to a distributee at the time of receipt, even though the distributee may be later obligated to repay amounts attributable to a plan overpayment in subsequent taxable years, either by direct payment or by payment reduction. Consequently, in the three examples, the amounts attributable to a plan overpayment are taxable distributions. [I.R.C. § 402(a)]

In years after the year of the plan overpayment, under the facts presented in Examples 1 and 2, only the amounts received by the distributee after the plan's required reduction to recoup an earlier plan overpayment are included in the distributee's gross income in the year of distribution. [Rev. Rul. 67-350, 1967-2 C.B. 58; Rev. Rul. 80-9, 1980-1 C.B. 11; Priv. Ltr. Rul. 200452039] Consequently, the qualified retirement plan participants in Examples 1 and 2 who received distributions that included overpayments, and included the full amount of these distributions in gross income in the year of distribution, are in subsequent years only required to treat as taxable distributions amounts distributed by the plan after offset or adjustment to correct for the prior overpayments. Because these participants are not treated as receiving the amounts attributable to the offset or adjustment, these participants cannot take a loss deduction as a result of such offset or adjustment. [Rev. Rul. 80-9, 1980-1 C.B. 11] This tax result is limited to situations in which the amount of the plan overpayment was included in the gross income of the participant for the year the overpayment was distributed to the participant and the qualified retirement plan has demanded the adjustment or offset to recoup the plan overpayment.

In contrast to Examples 1 and 2, in Example 3 the overpayment is not recouped by a reduction in the amount of benefits paid to a participant but instead is repaid by the taxpayer directly in a single-sum payment. For overpayments repaid to a qualified retirement plan in the *same* taxable year as the overpayment, the amount repaid reduces the taxable amount received as a distribution by the participant from the plan in the taxable year. For overpayments repaid in a taxable year or years *subsequent* to the year of the overpayment, a participant would be entitled to a deduction because the amount of the plan overpayment is attributable to compensation for services rendered to the employer. The deduction is allowable in the year that the single-sum payment is paid by the taxpayer, but only if the taxpayer itemizes deductions. A deduction for an individual with losses that are incurred in trade or business is considered a miscellaneous itemized deduction and, thus, is subject to the 2-percent floor established for miscellaneous itemized deductions. [I.R.C. §§ 67(a), 165(a)] If the amount of the distribution had instead exceeded the amount that was due Ben by more than $3,000, the deduction would be determined without regard to the 2-percent floor. [I.R.C. §§ 67(b)(9), 1341]

One court concluded that an injunction sought by former employees as equitable relief to prevent a defined benefit plan's reduction of their monthly benefits was actually a claim for monetary damages and, thus, not available as equitable relief under ERISA. [ERISA § 502(a)(3); Ramsey v. Formica Corp., 398 F.3d 421 (6th Cir. 2005)] Another court ruled that a retirement plan's recoupment of benefits overpaid to retired participants was not prohibited by ERISA because the plan sought contractual, not legal, relief. [Northcutt v. General Motors Hourly-Rate Employees Pension Plan, 467 F.3d 1031 (7th Cir. 2006); *see also* Bocchino v. Trustees of District Council Ironworkers Funds of Northern

New Jersey, 2009 WL 2038645 (3d Cir. 2009) and Verizon v. Adams, 2007 WL 4150928 (W.D. Pa. 2007)] A third court permitted the plan to reduce a former participant's monthly benefit to recoup an overpayment and stated that ERISA is governed by trust rather than contract law. [Johnson v. Retirement Program Plan for Employees of Certain Employers at the U.S. Dept. of Energy Facilities at Oak Ridge, Tenn., No. 3:05-cv-588 (E.D. Tenn. 2007)] A fourth court concluded that a plan's recoupment from a participant of overpayments of plan benefits did not violate the anti-alienation rule (see Q 4:27). An arrangement for a plan's recoupment of benefit overpayments is not considered an assignment or alienation. An arrangement, for this purpose, is not limited to an agreement between the parties or a provision in the plan. In this case, a letter to the participant informing him of the recoupment was an arrangement sufficient to exclude the recoupment from the anti-alienation provision. [Palmer v. Johnson and Johnson Pension Plan, 2009 WL 3029794 (D. N.J. 2009); Treas. Reg. § 1.401(a)-13(c)(2)(iii)]

One court determined that a plan administrator was not authorized to alter a plan's benefit calculation formula based on his determination that the formula had been amended mistakenly as a result of a scrivener's error when the plan was last restated. Therefore, the plan was liable to participants for benefits under the unaltered formula in the plan. [Cross v. Bragg, 2009 WL 2196887 (4th Cir. 2009)]

Q 13:3   Are any distributions from qualified retirement plans income tax free?

Yes, if the participant has an investment in the contract (also known as basis). [I.R.C. §§ 72(b), 72(c), 72(d), 72(e)(5)(E); Burke, T.C. Summ. Op. 2003-77; Roundy v. Comm'r, 122 F.3d 835 (9th Cir. 1997); George v. United States, 90 F.3d 473 (Fed. Cir. 1996); Malbon v. United States, 43 F.3d 466 (9th Cir. 1994); Montgomery v. United States, 18 F.3d 500 (7th Cir. 1994); Guilzon v. Comm'r, 985 F.2d 819 (5th Cir. 1993); Shimota v. United States, 21 Cl. Ct. 510 (1990), aff'd, 943 F.2d 1312 (Fed. Cir. 1991); Gomez, 71 T.C.M. 2942 (1996); Grow, 70 T.C.M. 1576 (1995); Kirkland, 67 T.C.M. 2976 (1994); Parker v. United States, 860 F. Supp. 657 (E.D. Mo. 1994); Simmons, 65 T.C.M. 1887 (1993); Twombly, 62 T.C.M. 597 (1991); Rev. Proc. 92-86, 1992-2 C.B. 495; Priv. Ltr. Rul. 200317045]

A participant's investment in the contract or basis includes:

1. The participant's after-tax contributions to the qualified retirement plan (i.e., voluntary or mandatory contributions; see Qs 6:37, 6:38) [Priv. Ltr. Ruls. 200828037, 200117045, 200117044, 9847032, 9310035],

2. Current insurance protection costs (see Qs 15:6, 15:14) [Priv. Ltr. Rul. 9618028], and

3. Loans from the qualified retirement plan to the participant that were treated as taxable distributions (see Q 13:27) [Priv. Ltr. Rul. 9122059].

IRS has ruled that, in addition to the current insurance protection costs, upon the death of an insured participant, the investment in the contract includes the net death benefit of the policy (i.e., the policy proceeds in excess of the cash surrender value). [Priv. Ltr. Rul. 9618028] A participant's elective contributions to a 401(k) plan (see Q 27:1) do not constitute basis. [Palermino, T.C. Summ. Op. 2003-45] Similarly, an employer's plan contributions based upon an employee's pay and years of service do not constitute employee contributions that later can be claimed as basis. [Lange, 90 T.C.M. 69 (2005)] IRS representatives have opined that, where a self-employed individual (see Q 6:60) made required contributions to a defined benefit plan (see Q 2:3) to satisfy the minimum funding standards (see Q 8:1) that were not deductible (see Q 12:14), the nondeductible contributions did not constitute basis.

In one case, the beneficiary of a friend's qualified retirement plan death benefits had made an oral agreement to pay the friend's debts in return for being named beneficiary. The beneficiary could not deduct the friend's debts from the amount of the taxable distribution; the assumption of the debts did not constitute basis. [Ballard, 63 T.C.M. 2748 (1992)] In another case, an employee who, after receiving a distribution from a qualified retirement plan, made a payment to his former employer could not characterize the payment as an after-tax plan contribution. [Silver, 71 T.C.M. 2057 (1996)] IRS ruled that an individual who brought an action to obtain additional pension benefits could deduct attorney's fees and court costs because the settlement award resolved a claim of unlawful discrimination. [I.R.C. §§ 62(a)(19)[20], 62(e); Priv. Ltr. Rul. 200550004]

Qualified retirement plan benefits paid to a charitable organization or to a charitable remainder trust upon a participant's death are not subject to income tax because the charitable beneficiary is exempt from tax. [I.R.C. §§ 501(a), 664(c); Priv. Ltr. Ruls. 199901023, 9818009, 9634019] IRS has ruled that, when a private foundation received plan death benefits, the foundation was subject to the 2 percent excise tax on net investment income on amounts in excess of the contributions made to the plan on behalf of the deceased participant. [Priv. Ltr. Rul. 9633006] However, in both an earlier and later ruling, IRS reached the opposite conclusion. [Priv. Ltr. Ruls. 9341008, 9838028]

Q 13:4 How are annuity payments from a qualified retirement plan taxed?

Annuity payments from a qualified retirement plan under which the participant has no investment in the contract or basis (see Q 13:3) are taxed as ordinary income in the year received by the participant or beneficiary (see Q 13:1). [I.R.C. §§ 72(m), 402(a)]

If the annuity starting date was *before* November 19, 1996 and a participant had basis, a portion of each distribution is considered a return of the participant's investment in the contract and is therefore not taxable. The following formula applies to determine the part of each payment that is excluded from taxable income:

$$\frac{\text{Investment in the contract}}{\text{Expected return under the annuity}} \times \text{Annual annuity payment}$$

If payments commenced *before* November 19, 1996, the expected return was determined at the time of commencement on the basis of unisex life expectancy tables. The ratio of the participant's investment in the contract to the expected return under the contract was then applied to each annuity payment to derive the nontaxable portion. [I.R.C. §§ 72(b)(1), 72(e)(8); Treas. Reg. § 1.72-9; Roundy v. Comm'r, 122 F.3d 835 (9th Cir. 1997); George v. United States, 90 F.3d 473 (Fed. Cir. 1996); Malbon v. United States, 43 F.3d 466 (9th Cir. 1994); Montgomery v. United States, 18 F.3d 500 (7th Cir. 1994); Guilzon v. Comm'r, 985 F.2d 819 (5th Cir. 1993); Shimota v. United States, 21 Cl. Ct. 510 (1990), *aff'd*, 943 F.2d 1312 (Fed. Cir. 1991); Gomez, 71 T.C.M. 2942 (1996); Green, 68 T.C.M. 167 (1994); Kirkland, 67 T.C.M. 2976 (1994); Parker v. United States, 860 F. Supp. 657 (E.D. Mo. 1994); Simmons, 65 T.C.M. 1887 (1993); Twombly, 62 T.C.M. 597 (1991); Priv. Ltr. Rul. 9618028]

The participant may not exclude from income an amount greater than the participant's investment in the contract. Thus, once the participant recovers the entire basis, all remaining payments are fully taxable. If the participant dies before recovering the entire investment in the contract, the unrecovered basis can be deducted on the participant's last income tax return. [I.R.C. §§ 72(b)(2), 72(b)(3), 72(b)(4)]

> **Example 1.** Able, an individual age 65, had a 20-year life expectancy. Able commenced receiving his monthly pension before November 19, 1996. Able's monthly pension is $1,000, and he has basis of $24,000. The expected return is $240,000 ($1,000 × 12 × 20). The exclusion ratio is 10 percent ($24,000 ÷ $240,000), and $100 of the monthly payment (10% × $1,000) represents recovery of basis and is nontaxable. After 240 payments, 100 percent of each payment will be taxable. If Able dies after 15 years, the unrecovered basis of $6,000 ($24,000 – $18,000) will be deductible on Able's last income tax return.

In addition, if payments commenced *before* November 19, 1996, then, instead of using the unisex life expectancy tables, a simplified safe harbor method could have been used. [IRS Notice 88-118, 1988-2 C.B. 450, *rendered obsolete by* IRS Notice 98-2, 1998-1 C.B. 266] Under the simplified method, the following table was used:

Age of Employee at Annuity Starting Date	Expected Number of Payments
55 and under	300
56–60	260
61–65	240
66–70	170
71 and over	120

> **Example 2.** If Able elected to use the simplified method, he would have the same total payments projection of $240,000 (240 × $1,000), and his exclusion ratio would still be 10 percent ($24,000 ÷ $240,000). However, if

Able were 63, his exclusion ratio under the regular method would have only been 9.3 percent (expected return multiple of 21.6 × $12,000 = $259,200; $24,000 ÷ $259,200 = 9.3%).

If the annuity starting date is *after* November 18, 1996 and *before* January 1, 1998, a different method is adopted to derive the nontaxable portion of each payment. [Priv. Ltr. Rul. 9847032] Under this method, the portion of each payment that is nontaxable is generally equal to the employee's basis as of the date payments commence, divided by the number of anticipated monthly payments. The same expected number of payments applies to an employee whether the employee is receiving a single life annuity or a joint and survivor annuity (see Q 10:8). The expected number of payments is set forth in the table below.

Age of Employee at Annuity Starting Date	Expected Number of Payments
55 and under	360
56–60	310
61–65	260
66–70	210
71 and over	160

For annuity starting dates beginning *after* December 31, 1997, the table used to determine the expected number of payments depends on whether the payments are based on the life of more than one individual. In the case of an annuity payable based on the life of only one individual, the total number of monthly payments expected to be received is based on the individual's age at the annuity starting date. The expected number of payments for an annuity based on the life of one individual is set forth in the table above.

In the case of an annuity payable based on the life of more than one individual, the total number of monthly payments expected to be received is based on the combined age of the annuitants at the annuity starting date. If the annuity is payable to a primary annuitant and more than one survivor annuitant, the combined age of the annuitants is the sum of the age of the primary annuitant and the youngest survivor annuitant. If the annuity is payable to more than one survivor annuitant but there is no primary annuitant, the combined age of the annuitants is the sum of the age of the oldest survivor annuitant and the youngest survivor annuitant. In addition, any survivor annuitant whose entitlement to payments is contingent on an event other than the death of the primary annuitant is disregarded. The expected number of payments is set forth in the table below.

Combined Ages at Annuity Starting Date	Expected Number of Payments
110 and under	410
111–120	360

Combined Ages at Annuity Starting Date	Expected Number of Payments
121–130	310
131–140	260
141 and over	210

If the number of payments is fixed, that number is used rather than the number of anticipated payments listed in the table. These simplified methods do not apply if the individual has attained age 75 on the annuity starting date unless there are fewer than five years of guaranteed payments under the annuity. As under prior law, in no event is the total amount excluded from income as nontaxable return of basis greater than the participant's total investment in the contract.

Under the simplified method, the individual recovers the investment in the contract in level amounts over the expected number of monthly payments determined from the tables set forth above. The portion of each payment that is excluded from gross income for income tax purposes is a level dollar amount determined by dividing the investment in the contract by the set number of annuity payments. The following formula applies to determine the part of each payment that is excluded from taxable income:

$$\frac{\text{Investment in the contract}}{\text{Expected number of monthly payments}} = \begin{array}{c}\text{Tax-free portion of}\\\text{monthly annuity payment}\end{array}$$

The dollar amount determined above, as of the annuity starting date, will be excluded from each monthly annuity payment, even where the amount of the annuity payments changes. For example, the amount to be excluded from each annuity payment determined at the annuity starting date remains constant, even if the amount of the annuity payments increases due to cost-of-living increases, or decreases in the case of a reduced survivor annuity after death of one of the annuitants.

If the amount to be excluded from each payment is greater than the amount of the annuity payment (e.g., because of decreased survivor payments), then each annuity payment will be completely excluded from gross income until the entire investment is recovered.

Where two or more annuitants are receiving payments at the same time, each annuitant will exclude from each annuity payment a pro rata portion of this amount determined according to a ratio, the numerator of which is the amount of the beneficiary's annuity payment, and the denominator of which is the total amount of the monthly annuity payments to all beneficiaries.

In the case where annuity payments are not made on a monthly basis, an adjustment must be made to take into account the period on the basis of which such payments are made. One way to make this adjustment is to determine the number of expected payments by dividing the applicable expected number of months in the applicable table above by the number of months in each period. Another way (the result of which is equivalent to the first way) is to determine the tax-free portion of a monthly payment using the applicable expected number of months from the applicable table above and then multiply the resulting dollar amount per month by the number of months in each period.

The application of the simplified methods is illustrated by the following examples.

Example 1. Upon retirement, Able, age 65, begins receiving retirement benefits in the form of a joint and 50 percent survivor annuity to be paid for the joint lives of Able and his spouse, age 64. Able's annuity starting date is January 1, 1997. Able has basis of $26,000, will receive a monthly retirement benefit of $1,000, and his spouse will receive a monthly survivor benefit of $500 upon Able's death. Because the annuity starting date is prior to January 1, 1998, the expected number of monthly payments for an individual who is age 65 is 260. The tax-free portion of each $1,000 monthly annuity payment to Able is $100, determined by dividing his basis ($26,000) by the expected number of payments (260). Upon Able's death, if he has not recovered the full $26,000 basis, his spouse will also exclude $100 from each $500 monthly annuity payment. Any annuity payments received after the 260 monthly payments have been made will be fully includible in gross income. If Able and his spouse die before 260 monthly payments have been made, a deduction is allowed for the last income tax return in the amount of the unrecovered basis.

Example 2. Upon retirement, Baker, age 65, begins receiving retirement benefits in the form of a joint and 50 percent survivor annuity to be paid for the joint lives of Baker and her spouse, age 64. Baker's annuity starting date is January 1, 1998, and she has basis of $26,000. Baker will receive a monthly retirement benefit of $1,000, and her spouse will receive a monthly survivor benefit of $500 upon Baker's death. The expected number of monthly payments is 310 for two individuals whose combined age is 129. The tax-free portion of each $1,000 monthly annuity payment to Baker is $83.87, determined by dividing her basis ($26,000) by the expected number of payments (310). Upon Baker's death, if she has not recovered the full $26,000 basis, her spouse will also exclude $83.87 from each $500 monthly annuity payment. Any annuity payments received after the 310 monthly payments have been made will be fully includible in gross income. If Baker and her spouse die before 310 monthly payments have been made, a deduction is allowed for the last income tax return in the amount of the unrecovered basis.

Example 3. Upon retirement, Charlie, age 66, begins receiving retirement benefits in the form of a joint and 50 percent survivor annuity to be paid for the joint lives of Charlie and his spouse, age 65. Charlie's annuity starting date is January 1, 1997, and he has basis of $42,000. Charlie will receive a quarterly retirement benefit of $6,000, and his spouse will receive a quarterly survivor benefit of $3,000 upon Charlie's death. Because the annuity starting date is prior to January 1, 1998, the expected number of monthly payments for an individual who is age 66 is 210. Because Charlie's annuity is paid quarterly, the appropriate adjustment is to divide the expected number of payments (210) by the number of months in the period (3), which equals 70. Thus, the tax-free portion of each $6,000 quarterly annuity payment is $600 determined by dividing the basis ($42,000) by the expected number of quarterly payments (70). Alternatively, the appropriate adjustment can be made by dividing $42,000 by 210 and multiplying the resulting $200 per month by the number of months in the period, three, which equals a $600 recovery of basis per quarter.

[I.R.C. § 72(d); IRS Notice 98-2, 1998-1 C.B. 266; Priv. Ltr. Ruls. 200840056, 200450056, 200450053, 200438049, 200009066]

IRS ruled that a qualified retirement plan participant whose retirement plan distributions were reported and taxed for several years without excluding his after-tax plan contributions (see Q 13:3) must use the simplified method to determine the excludable amount for the current tax year. The participant could amend prior years' income tax returns to reflect the correct exclusion amounts for those years' retirement plan distributions for each year an amended return was allowable. [Priv. Ltr. Rul. 201021042]

An individual cannot apply an inflation factor to increase basis for purposes of calculating the nontaxable portion of each annuity payment. [Nordtvedt v. Comm'r, 2001 U.S. App. LEXIS 25027 (9th Cir. 2001)]

The purchase of two variable annuity contracts by the trustee of a qualified retirement plan and the distribution of the contracts to two individuals treated as the designated beneficiaries (see Q 11:17) of a deceased participant did not result in taxable distributions to the beneficiaries. The annuity contract, after distribution to the beneficiary, could not be transferred or assigned and could not be sold, discounted, or pledged as collateral for a loan or be used as security for the performance of an obligation. [I.R.C. § 401(g); Priv. Ltr. Ruls. 200635013, 200548028, 200548027]

Q 13:5   What is a lump-sum distribution?

A lump-sum distribution is a distribution from a qualified retirement plan of the balance to the credit of an employee (see Q 13:6) made within one taxable year of the recipient. The distribution must be made on account of the employee's death, attainment of age 59½, separation from service (except for self-employed individuals; see Q 6:60), or disability (self-employed individuals only). [I.R.C. § 402(e)(4)(D)(i); Clark, 101 T.C. 215 (1993); Acquisto, 62 T.C.M. 44 (1991); Baskovich, 61 T.C.M. 2628 (1991); Priv. Ltr. Ruls. 200634059, 199908060, 9248047] A lump-sum distribution cannot be made from a pension plan simply because the employee has attained age 59½, unless the employee has also attained normal retirement age under the plan (see Q 10:55) or terminated employment. However, a lump-sum distribution can be made from a profit sharing plan if the employee has attained age 59½, even though termination of employment has not occurred. [Priv. Ltr. Ruls. 200050049, 9721036, 8810088, 8805025]

The distribution must be made from a qualified retirement plan (see Q 13:22); a distribution from the employer's general funds is not a lump-sum distribution [Gruber, 68 T.C.M. 923 (1994)], nor is a distribution from a nonqualified plan. [Nordin v. IRS, Civ. A2-95-176 (D.N.D. 1997)]

A distribution will not qualify as a lump-sum distribution unless the employee was a plan participant for at least five of the employee's taxable years prior to the year of distribution, and IRS has ruled that plan participants who have their entire account balances transferred directly from an old plan to a new plan may include years of participation in both plans to satisfy the five-year participation requirement. This five-year participation requirement does not apply to a beneficiary receiving a distribution after the participant's death (see Q 13:14). [Prop. Treas. Reg. § 1.402(e)-2(e)(3); Deisenroth, 58 T.C.M. 838 (1989); Priv. Ltr. Ruls. 9425042, 9423032, 9221045, 9114059, 9114058]

Lump-sum distributions may qualify for favorable income tax treatment (see Q 13:14). Further, the participant (or surviving spouse) may elect to defer payment of taxes by rolling over the distribution into an IRA or another qualified retirement plan. See chapter 34 for details.

One court ruled that a plan participant could rescind his decision to take a lump-sum distribution where the employer had breached its fiduciary duty by failing to notify him that the distribution would be subject to tax. The participant did not have to repay the entire distribution, only the amount he received net of the income taxes he had paid. Thereafter, he would receive monthly annuity payments for life based on the net amount repaid. [Griggs v. E.I. DuPont de Nemours & Co., 385 F.3d 440 (4th Cir.)]

Q 13:6 What does the term "balance to the credit of an employee" mean?

Balance to the credit of an employee means either the vested (nonforfeitable) account balance (see Q 9:2) that will be distributed from a defined contribution plan (see Q 2:2) or the vested (nonforfeitable) accrued benefit (see Qs 9:1, 9:2) that will be distributed from a defined benefit plan (see Q 2:3). [Powell v. Comm'r, 129 F.3d 321 (4th Cir. 1997); Scallion v. United States, Civ. WMN-97-711 (D. Md. 1998); Miller, Civ. WMN-97-709 (D. Md. 1998); Logsdon, 73 T.C.M. 1674 (1997); Emmons, 71 T.C.M. 3159 (1996); Pumphrey, 70 T.C.M. 882 (1995); Humberson, 70 T.C.M. 886 (1995)]

In determining whether a distribution is the balance to the credit of the employee, all qualified profit sharing plans must be aggregated, all qualified stock bonus plans must be aggregated, and all qualified pension plans (defined benefit, money purchase, and target benefit plans) must be aggregated. Because only similar plans of the employer are required to be aggregated, a distribution to the employee from a profit sharing plan may qualify as a lump-sum distribution even though the employee still has an interest in a pension plan maintained by the employer. [I.R.C. § 402(e)(4)(D)(ii); Brown v. Comm'r, No. 95-2174 (4th Cir. 1996); Priv. Ltr. Ruls. 200634059, 200250036]

Only the vested portion of an employee's account balance or accrued benefit is taken into account in determining the balance to the credit. For this purpose, amounts attributable to deductible employee contributions (see Q 13:25) are ignored. Accordingly, a partially vested employee who receives a distribution of the entire vested balance may qualify for lump-sum distribution tax treatment. [I.R.C. § 402(e)(4)(D)(i)]

Two beneficiaries were permitted to elect lump-sum distribution treatment with respect to their deceased mother's qualified retirement plan benefits because the account balance of the mother's predeceased husband was not included in calculating the balance to her credit. The mother's election, as beneficiary of her predeceased husband's benefits, to receive annual distributions after his death, did not preclude her beneficiaries from electing lump-sum distribution treatment with regard to the mother's own account. [Priv. Ltr. Rul. 9541036]

The balance to the credit does not include amounts payable to an alternate payee under a QDRO (see Q 36:30). [I.R.C. § 402(e)(4)(D)(vii)] A distribution from an employee stock ownership plan (ESOP; see Q 28:1) constituted the balance to the credit of the employee for lump-sum distribution purposes, even though in prior years the employee had received dividend distributions from the ESOP (see Q 28:9). [Priv. Ltr. Rul. 199947041; *see also* Priv. Ltr. Rul. 200634059]

To qualify as a lump-sum distribution, the balance to the credit of the employee must be paid within one taxable year of the recipient. Thus, if more than one payment is planned, all the payments must be made within the same calendar year (most individuals are calendar-year taxpayers). However, if an individual receives lump-sum distributions from both a pension plan and a profit sharing plan of the same employer in the same taxable year, the individual must elect forward averaging treatment for both distributions or neither will qualify for forward averaging. The same rule applies if an individual receives lump-sum distributions from qualified retirement plans of different employers in the same taxable year. [I.R.C. §§ 402(e)(4)(D)(i), 402(e)(4)(D)(ii); Sites v. United States, 896 F. Supp. 500 (D. Md. 1995); Middleton v. United States, 822 F. Supp. 1549 (S.D. Ala. 1993); Fowler, 98 T.C. 503 (1992); Blyler, 67 T.C. 878 (1977); Priv. Ltr. Rul. 9003061]

If a portion of a participant's benefits in an existing qualified retirement plan (Plan A) is transferred to a new plan (Plan B), and Plan A is terminated soon thereafter, IRS has ruled that the distribution of the remaining benefits in Plan A does not constitute the balance to the credit of the employee and, therefore, is not a lump-sum distribution. [Rev. Rul. 72-242, 1972-1 C.B. 116; Priv. Ltr. Rul. 9139031]

Q 13:7   How are frozen plan assets treated for the balance to the credit requirement?

In order to determine whether a qualified retirement plan distribution is a lump-sum distribution (see Q 13:5), the employee's balance to the credit (see Q 13:6) in the plan must be determined.

When the distribution of plan assets invested in group annuity contracts was contingent upon their release pursuant to court-authorized proceedings, IRS ruled that a plan participant's balance to the credit may be determined by excluding the portion of the participant's benefit that was attributable to amounts that were not being paid to the plan by the insurance company because of the court-authorized proceedings. [IRS Spec. Rul. (Oct. 3, 1991); Rev. Rul. 83-57, 1983-1 C.B. 92; Priv. Ltr. Rul. 9219042]

However, when complete distribution of plan assets could not be made within one taxable year because a portion of the plan assets was in a frozen real estate fund, IRS ruled that the distribution of all other plan assets would not be a lump-sum distribution. [Priv. Ltr. Ruls. 9316047, 9137046] But, if a qualified retirement plan holds illiquid, nonmarketable assets, IRS has ruled that a distribution of both liquid assets and an interest in the illiquid assets can constitute a lump-sum distribution. An independent, nonqualified trust is established, and the illiquid assets are transferred to the nonqualified trust. Each participant, in addition to receiving a distribution of liquid assets, receives a transferable certificate representing the participant's interest in the nonqualified trust. This total distribution may qualify for favorable income tax treatment (see Q 13:14). [Priv. Ltr. Ruls. 9507032, 9418028, 9226066, 9108049, 9104038]

Q 13:8 Can an employee who received installment payments later receive a lump-sum distribution from the same qualified retirement plan?

No. If an employee separates from service, receives benefits in installment payments, and then takes the balance to the employee's credit under the qualified retirement plan in a subsequent taxable year in lieu of the remaining installment payments, the payout will not qualify as a lump-sum distribution. [Prop. Treas. Reg. § 1.402(e)-2(d)(1)(ii)(C); Priv. Ltr. Ruls. 9137037, 8917020; *see also* Priv. Ltr. Rul. 200634059]

However, if an employee commences receiving distributions while still employed and subsequently terminates employment and receives the balance to the employee's credit under the plan within a single taxable year, IRS has ruled that the final distribution will qualify as a lump-sum distribution. [Priv. Ltr. Ruls. 9143078, 9052058]

Q 13:9 Are the tax benefits of a lump-sum distribution lost when an additional distribution is made in a subsequent taxable year?

Not necessarily. If a distribution constituted the balance to the credit of the employee at the time it was made and all other requirements are satisfied (see Qs 13:5, 13:6), it is treated as a lump-sum distribution even if additional amounts are credited and distributed to the employee in a later taxable year. The additional distribution, however, is not a lump-sum distribution. [Campbell, 64 T.C.M. 1117 (1992); Prop. Treas. Reg. § 1.402(e)-2(d)(1)(ii)(B); Rev. Rul. 69-190, 1969-1 C.B. 131; Rev. Rul. 56-558, 1956-2 C.B. 290; Priv. Ltr. Ruls. 200215032, 9009055, 8952010; *but see* Priv. Ltr. Rul. 9252034]

Q 13:10   What does separation from service mean?

Separation from service and termination of employment are synonymous. Separation from service does not occur when the employee continues on the same job for a different employer as a result of a corporate transaction (e.g., merger or sale) or continues on the same job for the same employer after the sale of a shareholder's shares, or when the individual's status changes from an employee and sole shareholder of a professional corporation to a sole proprietor. Separation from service occurs only upon death, retirement, resignation, or discharge, and not when the employee continues in the same job for a different employer. [Gen. Couns. Mem. 39,824; Vidrine, 66 T.C.M. 123 (1993); Burton, 99 T.C. 622 (1992); Dickson, 59 T.C.M. 314 (1990); Edwards v. Comm'r, 906 F.2d 114 (4th Cir. 1990); United States v. Johnson, 331 F.2d 943 (5th Cir. 1964); Rev. Rul. 81-141, 1981-1 C.B. 204; Rev. Rul. 81-26, 1981-1 C.B. 200; Rev. Rul. 80-129, 1980-1 C.B. 86; Rev. Rul. 79-336, 1979-2 C.B. 187; Priv. Ltr. Ruls. 9706017, 9652025, 9443041, 9243048, 8441071] One court decided that the spin-off of a member of a controlled group of corporations (see Q 5:31) did not entitle employees of the spun-off corporation to an immediate distribution of assets from the controlled group's plan because the spun-off corporation continued to maintain plans for its employees and, thus, the employees did not incur a separation from service. [Hunter v. Caliber Sys., Inc., 220 F.3d 702 (6th Cir. 2000)] However, IRS has ruled that separation from service did occur notwithstanding continued employment with another employer that had assumed certain functions performed previously by the first employer. Both employers were unrelated; ownership of both employers did not change; and the transfer of functions was not incident to an asset transfer, exchange of stock, merger, or consolidation. [Field Serv. Adv. 199931046; Priv. Ltr. Rul. 9325045]

IRS has ruled that separation from service does occur where less than substantially all of an employer's assets are sold to an unrelated entity and most of the seller's employees are hired by the buyer as of the date of sale and continue to perform, without interruption and in the same capacity, the same functions for the buyer that they performed for the seller prior to the sale. [Rev. Rul. 2000-27, 2000-1 C.B. 1016] This ruling was issued in the context of 401(k) plans (see Q 27:14), and it is unclear whether this ruling has applicability to the lump-sum distribution requirement of separation from service.

Distribution need not be made in the year of the employee's termination of employment to be considered made on account of the employee's separation from service. Thus, distributions from qualified retirement plans that permit distributions to be deferred until a specified age or time may qualify as lump-sum distributions. [Priv. Ltr. Ruls. 8949102, 8541094, 8541116] An individual received a distribution from a state retirement system when he elected to transfer the balance of his benefits to the state pension system. The individual retired at about the same time. Even though the distribution was made because of the transfer from one system to the other and not because of the individual's retirement, the court concluded that the distribution was made "on account of" his separation from service. [Adler v. Comm'r, 86 F.3d 378 (4th Cir. 1996); Brown v. Comm'r, No. 95-2174 (4th Cir. 1996)]

A distribution to a self-employed individual (see Q 6:60) cannot qualify as a lump-sum distribution solely by reason of separation from service (see Q 13:5). [I.R.C. § 402(e)(4)(D)(i); Priv. Ltr. Rul. 8945053]

Q 13:11   Can a distribution from a qualified retirement plan to a disabled employee qualify as a lump-sum distribution?

No, unless the employee terminates employment at that time (see Q 13:10). On the other hand, a distribution from a qualified retirement plan to a disabled (see Q 16:6) self-employed individual (see Q 6:60) can be a lump-sum distribution (see Q 13:5). [I.R.C. §§ 72(m)(7), 402(e)(4)(D)(i)]

Although some courts [Burnham, No. 15339-04S (Tax Ct. 2006); Picard v. Comm'r, 165 F.3d 744 (9th Cir. 1999); Berner v. United States, No. 79-1485 (W.D. Pa. 1981); Wood, 590 F.2d 321 (9th Cir. 1979); Masterson v. United States, 478 F. Supp. 454 (N.D. Ill. 1979)] have ruled that amounts paid to a disabled employee under the disability retirement provisions of a qualified retirement plan are tax-free disability payments, IRS and most other courts have ruled that such amounts are taxable. [I.R.C. § 105(c); Rev. Rul. 85-105, 1985-2 C.B. 53; IRS Litig. Guideline Mem. (TL-60); Estate of Hall, Jr. v. Comm'r, 103 F.3d 112 (3d Cir. 1997); Kiourtsis, 72 T.C.M. 1438 (1996); Kelter, 72 T.C.M. 573 (1996); Dorroh, 68 T.C.M. 337 (1994); Burnside, 67 T.C.M. 2557 (1994); Berman v. Comm'r, 925 F.2d 936 (6th Cir. 1991); Beisler v. Comm'r, 787 F.2d 1325 (9th Cir. 1986); Gordon, 88 T.C. 630 (1987); Mabry, 50 T.C.M. 336 (1985); Caplin v. United States, 718 F.2d 544 (2d Cir. 1983); Christensen v. United States, 7 Employee Benefits Cas. (BNA) 1110 (D. Minn. 1986); Gibson v. United States, 643 F. Supp. 181 (W.D. Tenn. 1986); Priv. Ltr. Rul. 9504041]

Q 13:12   How is a lump-sum distribution from a qualified retirement plan to the beneficiary of a deceased participant taxed?

If the beneficiary is the surviving spouse of the deceased participant, the same options that would have been available to the participant (see Q 13:14) are available to the spouse. Other beneficiaries have the same options, except they cannot take advantage of a tax-free rollover (see Q 34:33). [I.R.C. § 402(c)(9)]

The five-year participation requirement for electing forward averaging does not apply to distributions due to death (see Qs 13:5, 13:14).

Q 13:13   Can the beneficiary of a deceased participant who received annuity payments from a qualified retirement plan receive a lump-sum distribution?

Yes. A distribution to an employee before the employee's death, in the form of annuity payments after retirement, will not prevent the employee's beneficiary from receiving a lump-sum distribution. [Prop. Treas. Reg. § 1.402(e)-2(d)(1)(ii)(B); Rev. Rul. 69-495, 1969-2 C.B. 100]

Q 13:14   How is a lump-sum distribution from a qualified retirement plan to an employee taxed?

An employee who has completed at least five years of plan participation prior to the year of distribution (see Q 13:5) may have four income tax options:

1. The ordinary income portion of the distribution (amount attributable to post-1973 plan participation) might qualify for ten-year forward averaging, and the rest of the distribution (amount attributable to pre-1974 plan participation) might qualify as long-term capital gain (see Qs 13:15, 13:19, 13:20). [Murtagh, 74 T.C.M. 75 (1997); Priv. Ltr. Rul. 199908060]

2. The entire distribution may be reported as ordinary income and might qualify for ten-year forward averaging (see Qs 13:15, 13:19).

3. The entire distribution may be reported as ordinary income without electing ten-year forward averaging. [I.R.C. § 402(a)]

4. All or part of the distribution may be rolled over to an IRA or to another plan; no tax is paid on the amount rolled over; and the rest is taxed as ordinary income without the availability of electing ten-year forward averaging (see chapter 34). [I.R.C. § 402(c); Barrett, 64 T.C.M. 1080 (1992)]

For options available when the participant has not satisfied the five-year participation requirement, see Q 13:16.

An individual who receives a lump-sum distribution and who attained age 50 on or before January 1, 1986 is eligible to elect special tax treatment (see Q 13:15).

If more than one lump-sum distribution is received in a single taxable year, all such distributions received that year must be aggregated, and the election to use forward averaging will apply to the aggregate amount. If the employer maintains more than one qualified retirement plan, special rules apply (see Q 13:6). [I.R.C. § 402(e)(4)(D); Hegarty, 63 T.C.M. 2335 (1992)]

Q 13:15   What special rules apply to a lump-sum distribution with regard to an individual who had attained age 50 on or before January 1, 1986?

If an individual who had attained age 50 on or before January 1, 1986, receives a lump-sum distribution, the individual may elect capital gains treatment for the pre-1974 portion of the distribution (see Q 13:20). [Murtagh, 74 T.C.M. 75 (1997); Priv. Ltr. Ruls. 199908060, 9804058, 9221045] For the post-1973 portion of the distribution (see Q 13:20), the individual can elect ten-year averaging at the rates in effect during 1986 (see Q 13:19). If the capital gains election is made, capital gains will be taxed at a flat 20 percent rate (the rate in effect during 1986). Alternatively, the individual can elect ten-year averaging on the entire distribution. [Priv. Ltr. Ruls. 199908060, 9804058, 9648048]

The opportunities to do rollovers of distributions have been significantly increased (see Q 34:1). An individual cannot preserve capital gain and averaging treatment if the individual rolls over a distribution from a qualified retirement plan to a 403(b) plan (see Q 35:1) or to a governmental Section 457 plan and then rolls over the distribution back to a qualified retirement plan. To preserve the special rules, the rollover must first be made to a conduit IRA (see Q 34:38) and then back into a qualified retirement plan. For eligible individuals, the new rollover rules do not eliminate the necessity of using a conduit IRA. A surviving spouse who rolls over a distribution attributable to the deceased spouse to a qualified retirement plan in which the surviving spouse participates will not be eligible to elect the special rules. [EGTRRA 2001 § 641(f)(3)]

Q 13:16 What tax options are available when a participant does not satisfy the five-year participation requirement?

Forward averaging is not an option (see Q 13:5), so only two tax choices are available:

1. A tax-free rollover into an IRA or another plan, or
2. Inclusion of the distribution in gross income for the year of receipt (see Q 13:1).

Q 13:17 What portion of a lump-sum distribution is taxable?

Several adjustments that reduce the taxable amount of a lump-sum distribution (see Q 13:5) are made before any tax is computed. The amount of the employee's investment in the contract (see Q 13:3) is subtracted from the distribution in computing the taxable amount. If any part of the distribution is made in employer securities, special rules apply (see Q 13:18).

If the recipient elects to use forward averaging, a minimum distribution allowance reduces the tax on relatively small distributions. The allowance, which is subtracted in computing the taxable amount of the payout, is the lesser of $10,000 or one-half of the total taxable amount of the payout, reduced by 20 percent of the excess of the total amount over $20,000. In effect, there is no minimum distribution allowance if the total taxable amount is $70,000 or more.

> **Example.** Assume that Sallie receives a lump-sum distribution of $50,000 in cash from a qualified retirement plan, has no basis, and the entire payment is ordinary income (i.e., attributable to post-1973 plan participation). The minimum distribution allowance is the lesser of $10,000 or one-half of the total taxable amount. Because it is less than $25,000 (i.e., one-half of $50,000), the $10,000 figure applies. The $10,000 figure is then reduced by 20 percent of the excess of the taxable amount of the payment over $20,000, or $6,000 (20 percent of $30,000). This makes the minimum distribution allowance $4,000 and the taxable amount of the distribution $46,000.

Q 13:18 What is the tax treatment of a lump-sum distribution that includes employer securities?

Special rules apply to appreciated stock or other securities of the employer that are included in a lump-sum distribution (see Q 13:5). These rules apply to employer securities distributed from an ESOP (see Q 28:1) or from any other type of qualified retirement plan. The gain on the securities while they were held by the qualified retirement plan (the net unrealized appreciation) is not subject to tax until the securities are sold by the recipient, at which time the gain is eligible for capital gains treatment. The basis of the securities (the value when contributed to the plan) is includible in income upon distribution. If the value of the securities at the time of distribution is less than basis, the total value of the securities is taxable in accordance with the general rules applicable to lump-sum distributions. [I.R.C. §§ 402(e)(4), 402(j); Prop. Treas. Reg. § 1.402(a)-1(b)(1); Treas. Reg. § 1.402(a)-1(b)(2); Rev. Rul. 81-122, 1981-1 C.B. 202; Rev. Rul. 75-125, 1975-1 C.B. 254; Rev. Rul. 69-297, 1969-1 C.B. 131; Priv. Ltr. Ruls. 200509032, 200410023, 200138031, 200138030, 199951052, 199931051, 9821055, 9803025, 9643033, 9636031, 9619079; IRS Pub. 575] It is imperative that the distribution of the employer securities be part of a lump-sum distribution. [Priv. Ltr. Rul. 200434022; *see also* Priv. Ltr. Rul. 200433020]

This special rule applies even where the participant receives a distribution of employer securities from an ESOP and immediately exercises the put option to sell the securities to the employer (see Q 28:70). Therefore, even if a participant immediately exchanges the securities for cash, the participant is entitled to exclude the net unrealized appreciation from ordinary income and treat the appreciation as capital gain realized upon the sale of the securities. [Priv. Ltr. Rul. 200841042]

An employee who received a plan distribution on or within three months after the one-year anniversary of his second termination of employment with a wholly owned subsidiary was entitled to net unrealized appreciation treatment with respect to the distribution of the parent company's securities from his participant's ESOP account. Net unrealized appreciation treatment was available to the employee despite the fact that he received a distribution of his participant's deferral and matching accounts after his first separation from service with the subsidiary. However, a second employee who received a distribution of his participant's ESOP account within one tax year was not entitled to net unrealized appreciation treatment. The employee had already received a distribution of his participant's deferral, matching, and profit sharing accounts and would not receive a distribution of his ESOP account until a later date due to the delayed distribution provisions under the plan. A distribution to a third employee from her participant's ESOP account was not entitled to net unrealized appreciation treatment. This employee had received a distribution from her ESOP account in a prior tax year because her plan loan, which was due and payable upon termination of employment, was not repaid and, thus, was defaulted and offset by a portion of her ESOP account (see Q 14:10). [Priv. Ltr. Rul. 200634059]

The common stock of a corporation acquired in a merger was treated as securities of the employer corporation with respect to which net unrealized appreciation could be excluded from gross income upon distribution to a participant or beneficiary. The mere conversion of employer securities into the stock of the employer's merger partner did not change its status as stock of the employer, ruled IRS. [Priv. Ltr. Rul. 200340030; *see also* Rev. Rul. 80-138, 80-1 C.B. 87, Rev. Rul. 73-312, 1973-2 C.B. 142, Rev. Rul. 73-29, 1973-1 C.B. 198, and Priv. Ltr. Ruls. 200935046, 200927040, 200615007, 200537042, 200537041]

An employee who received appreciated employer securities and rolled over to an IRA the balance of his qualified retirement plan account (see Q 34:9) could defer income tax on the net unrealized appreciation on the employer securities. The receipt of the employer securities and the rollover of the balance of his account constituted a lump-sum distribution for this special rule, concluded IRS. [Priv. Ltr. Ruls. 200410023, 200315038, 200302048, 200250036, 200243052, 200215032, 200202078, 200038057, 200038052, 200038050]

> **Example 1.** Randye, a participant in the Kings Highway Corp. profit sharing plan, terminated employment, received employer securities and cash on June 1, 2010, and rolled over the cash to her IRA. Randye may defer income tax on the net unrealized appreciation on the employer securities. The same result would occur if Randye elected a direct rollover (see Q 34:17) of the cash portion of the distribution.

> **Example 2.** The facts are the same as in Example 1, except that Randye rolls over the entire distribution to her IRA. By rolling over the entire distribution, Randye defers all income tax. However, if Randye later receives a distribution from her IRA of the employer securities or the sales proceeds thereof, the entire distribution will be taxed as ordinary income and the benefits of the net unrealized appreciation will have been lost. [Priv. Ltr. Rul. 200442032]

If the recipient transfers the appreciated employer securities to a charitable remainder trust, the recipient will not recognize gain on the net unrealized appreciation. [Priv. Ltr. Ruls. 200215032, 200202078, 200038050] However, the recipient may recognize gain where there is a prearranged plan whereby the charitable remainder trust is under an obligation to enter into transactions involving the donated property that have a benefit to the recipient. [Blake v. Commissioner, 697 F.2d 473 (2d Cir. 1982); Priv. Ltr. Rul. 200038050] Even if an employee receives appreciated employer securities and defers income tax on the net unrealized appreciation, the basis of the securities may be subject to the 10 percent penalty tax on early withdrawals unless an exception applies (see Q 13:26). [Villarroel v. Comm'r, 202 F.3d 271 (6th Cir. 2000)]

Generally, the capital gains tax rate on the sale or exchange of certain assets held for more than 12 months is 15 percent (5 percent in the case of gain that would otherwise be taxed at either 10 percent or 15 percent). The amount of net unrealized appreciation that is not included in the basis of the securities in the hands of the distributee at the time of distribution is considered a gain from the sale or exchange of a capital asset held for more than 12 months to the extent that such appreciation is realized in a subsequent taxable transaction. Accordingly, for a sale or other disposition of employer securities, the actual period that an employer security is held by a qualified retirement plan need not be calculated in order to determine whether, with respect to the net unrealized appreciation, the disposition qualifies for the rate for capital assets held for more than 12 months. However, with respect to any further appreciation in the employer securities after distribution from the plan, the actual holding period in the hands of the distributee determines the capital gains rate that applies.

Example 3. In Example 1, assume that the basis of the employee securities received by Randye on June 1, 2010, was $20,000 and the fair market value was $50,000, and, on January 4, 2011, Randye sold the securities for $60,000. For 2010, Randye must include $20,000 (the basis amount) in gross income as ordinary income. In 2011, Randye has both long-term and short-term capital gain: long-term capital gain of $30,000 ($50,000 − $20,000) because the securities are deemed to be an asset held for more than 12 months, and short-term capital gain on the $10,000 post-distribution appreciation ($60,000 − $50,000) because, after the distribution, Randye held the securities for less than one year.

If employer securities held in a participant's plan account are the subject of a stock split or a stock dividend is received, the basis of the original employer securities is allocated proportionately between the old and new securities.

Example 4. Jennifer is a participant in the JKH Corp. profit sharing plan; 1,000 shares of JKH Corp. stock are in Jennifer's plan account; and the basis of the shares is $10,000 or $10 per share. On October 8, 2011, JKH Corp. splits its stock on a 2-for-1 basis, and an additional 1,000 shares are allocated to Jennifer's plan account. The basis of the 2,000 shares in Jennifer's account remains at $10,000, but the basis per share is reduced from $10 to $5 ($10,000 ÷ 2,000). [Priv. Ltr. Ruls. 200828036, 200828035; *see also* Priv. Ltr. Rul. 200935046]

The recipient of a distribution that includes employer securities may elect to have the net unrealized appreciation included in income at the time the distribution is received rather than taxed as a capital gain at the time the securities are sold. This election is made on the recipient's tax return for the year in which the distribution is received. [I.R.C. § 402(e)(4)(B); IRS Notice 89-25, Q&A-1, 1989-1 C.B. 662]

An employee's novel contention that his receipt of employer securities from an ESOP was not taxable because it represented a mere name change from the ESOP trustee to the employee was rejected. [Stoddard, 66 T.C.M. 585 (1993)]

As a general rule, if the owner of appreciated securities dies, the basis of the securities is increased to the fair market value of the securities at the date of death. However, the step-up in basis rules do not apply to property that constitutes a right to receive an item of income in respect of a decedent, and net unrealized appreciation constitutes a right to receive income in respect of a decedent. Thus, upon the death of the owner of the appreciated employer securities, there is no step-up in basis for the net unrealized appreciation so that there may be a realization of capital gain upon the subsequent sale of the employer securities by the estate or a beneficiary of the estate. [I.R.C. §§ 691, 1014; Rev. Rul. 75-125, 1975-1 C.B. 254]

The amount of taxable income that may be offset by some loss carryovers and recognized built-in losses when a loss corporation experiences a change in ownership is limited. IRS has issued temporary and proposed regulations addressing whether a distribution of shares in a loss corporation by a qualified retirement plan results in a change in ownership and triggers special limitations. Under the regulations, when a qualified retirement plan distributes shares in a loss corporation, the plan participant is treated as having received the shares at the same time and in the same manner as the plan for purposes of testing for a change in ownership. In addition, the distribution itself gives rise to a testing date. The temporary regulations are effective for distributions from qualified retirement plans after June 27, 2003. [I.R.C. § 382; Prop. Treas. Reg. § 1.382-10; Temp. Treas. Reg. § 1.382-10T]

Q 13:19 How is the tax on a lump-sum distribution computed using the ten-year averaging method?

Ten-year forward averaging is available only if the participant had attained age 50 on or before January 1, 1986 (see Q 13:15), and averaging has not been elected for a prior lump-sum distribution made after 1986. Since ten-year forward averaging remains keyed to the 1986 income tax rates, the following schedule (which takes into account the minimum distribution allowance; see Q 13:17) may be used to calculate the tax on a lump-sum distribution for which this averaging method is elected:

If 1/10th of the Adjusted Total Taxable Amount Is		The Ten-Year Averaging Tax Is 10 Times		
Over	But Not Over	This Amount	Plus This %	Of the Excess Over
. . .	$ 1,190	Zero	11	Zero
$ 1,190	2,270	$ 130.90	12	$ 1,190
2,270	4,530	260.50	14	2,270
4,530	6,690	576.90	15	4,530
6,690	9,170	900.90	16	6,690
9,170	11,440	1,297.70	18	9,170
11,440	13,710	1,706.30	20	11,440
13,710	17,160	2,160.30	23	13,710
17,160	22,880	2,953.80	26	17,160
22,880	28,600	4,441.00	30	22,880
28,600	34,320	6,157.00	34	28,600
34,320	42,300	8,101.80	38	34,320
42,300	57,190	11,134.20	42	42,300
57,190	85,790	17,388.00	48	57,190
85,790	. . .	31,116.00	50	85,790

The following schedule (which takes into account the minimum distribution allowance) sets forth the ten-year averaging tax and effective income tax rate for various lump-sum distribution amounts:

Lump-Sum Distribution Amount	Ten-Year Averaging Tax	Effective Income Tax Rate
$ 25,000	$ 1,801	7.2%
50,000	5,874	11.7
75,000	10,305	13.7
100,000	14,471	14.5
125,000	19,183	15.3
150,000	24,570	16.4
175,000	30,422	17.4
200,000	36,922	18.5
225,000	43,422	19.3
250,000	50,770	20.3
275,000	58,270	21.2
300,000	66,330	22.1
350,000	83,602	23.9
400,000	102,602	25.7
450,000	122,682	27.3
500,000	143,682	28.7
550,000	164,682	29.9
600,000	187,368	31.2
650,000	211,368	32.5
700,000	235,368	33.6
750,000	259,368	34.6
800,000	283,368	35.4
850,000	307,368	36.2
900,000	332,210	36.9
950,000	357,210	37.6
1,000,000	382,210	38.2
1,500,000	632,210	42.1
2,000,000	882,210	44.1

Example. Yvette retires on June 1, 2011, at age 77 and receives a lump-sum distribution from the Katz Ltd. profit sharing plan. Yvette is eligible for ten-year forward averaging because she attained age 50 on or before January 1, 1986.

Q 13:20 What portion of a lump-sum distribution from a qualified retirement plan may be eligible for capital gains treatment?

Generally, no portion of a lump-sum distribution from a qualified retirement plan is eligible to be taxed under separate tax rates applicable to capital gains. [I.R.C. § 402(a)(2), *before repeal by* TRA '86 § 1122(b)(1)(A)]

However, an individual who attained age 50 on or before January 1, 1986 may elect to treat the capital gain portion of a lump-sum distribution under the 1986 tax provisions. This means that the capital gain portion will be taxed at a flat 20 percent rate (see Q 13:15). [Murtagh, 74 T.C.M. 75 (1997); Priv. Ltr. Ruls. 199908060, 9804058, 9221045]

An employee (or the employee's beneficiaries) who is able to treat the portion attributable to pre-1974 participation as long-term capital gain may also irrevocably elect to use forward averaging on the entire distribution. This election is significant because, as a capital gain, part of a lump-sum distribution might otherwise be subject to the alternative minimum tax. [I.R.C. § 402(e)(4)(L), *before repeal by* TAMRA § 1011(A)(b)(8)(G); Brown, 93 T.C. 736 (1989)] However the election may affect the determination of the individual's minimum tax credit. [I.R.C. §§ 53, 55; Priv. Ltr. Rul. 200006012]

The allocation between the capital gain portion and the ordinary income portion is made on the basis of the number of months of active participation before 1974 as compared with the total number of months of plan participation (see Q 13:21). The portion of the taxable amount of a distribution that is taxed as long-term capital gain is determined as follows:

$$\text{Taxable amount} \times \frac{\text{Number of months of plan participation before}}{\text{Number of months of plan participation}}$$

[I.R.C. § 402(a)(2) (before repeal by TRA '86 § 1122(b)(1)(A))]

If the qualified retirement plan from which the distribution is made had assets transferred to it from another qualified retirement plan or if the distributee plan was merged into the plan making the distribution, the period of active participation includes both participation in the distributing plan and participation in the distributee plan. Although IRS has ruled that plan participants who have their entire account balances transferred directly from one plan to another may treat pre-1974 participation in the distributee plan as pre-1974 participation in the distributing plan for purposes of determining the capital gain portion of the distribution [Priv. Ltr. Ruls. 9114059, 8934051, 8535116], it later ruled that pre-1974 participation would apply only to the transferred account balances. [Priv. Ltr. Rul. 9425042]

Q 13:21   How is the number of months of plan participation computed?

To compute an employee's number of months of participation (see Q 13:20), any part of a calendar year prior to 1974 in which the employee participated in the qualified retirement plan is counted as 12 months, and any part of a calendar month after 1973 in which the employee participated in the plan is counted as one month. [Prop. Treas. Reg. § 1.402(e)-2(d)(3)(ii)]

If an employee commenced participation in a plan on December 22, 1970, and terminated employment on May 2, 2010, the employee would have 48 (12 × 4) months of pre-1974 participation and 437 [(12 × 36) + 5] months of post-1973 participation, for a total of 485 months of participation. If the total taxable amount of the distribution received by the employee is $970,000, the capital gain portion is $96,000 (48 ÷ 485 × $970,000) and the ordinary income portion is $874,000 (437 ÷ 485 × $970,000).

Q 13:22   How is the distribution taxed if the retirement plan loses its qualified status?

If IRS revokes the favorable determination letter (see Q 18:1) previously issued to the retirement plan, the plan is no longer qualified, and a distribution from the retirement plan will not be eligible for favorable tax treatment (see Q 13:14) or qualify as an eligible rollover distribution. [Treas. Reg. §§ 1.402(a)-1(a)(1)(ii), 1.402(a)-1(a)(1)(v), 1.402(b)-1(b); Meyers v. Comm'r, No. 95-1542 (7th Cir. 1996); Cass v. Comm'r, 774 F.2d 740 (7th Cir. 1985); Baetens v. Comm'r, 777 F.2d 1160 (6th Cir. 1985); Woodson v. Comm'r, 651 F.2d 1094 (5th Cir. 1981); Weddel, 71 T.C.M. 1950 (1996); Fazi, 105 T.C. 436 (1995); Fazi, 102 T.C. 695 (1994); *but see* Greenwald v. Comm'r, 366 F.2d 538 (2d Cir. 1966)]

Q 13:23   How does a recipient elect special forward averaging for a lump-sum distribution?

Form 4972, Tax on Lump-Sum Distributions (From Qualified Retirement Plans of Participants Born Before January 2, 1936), is used for electing ten-year averaging and computing the tax. The form must be attached to the individual's tax return for the year in which the distribution is received. [Prop. Treas. Reg. § 1.402(e)-3(c)(2)]

Plan administrators (see Q 20:1) must issue Form 1099-R (Distributions from Pensions, Annuities, Retirement or Profit-Sharing Plans, IRAs, Insurance Contracts, etc.) to let the recipient know the amount of the distribution and the breakdown between ordinary income and capital gain. This statement must be issued to the recipient by January 31 of the year following the distribution, and a copy must be sent to IRS by the end of February.

Q 13:24   Must all recipients of a single lump-sum distribution elect to use forward averaging?

No. When more than one person receives a payment qualifying as a lump-sum distribution (e.g., if the payments are made to several beneficiaries on the participant's death), any eligible recipient may elect to use forward averaging even if the others do not. Similarly, any recipient may decide to treat amounts attributable to pre-1974 participation as ordinary income instead of capital gain (see Q 13:20). [Technical Information Release-1426 (Dec. 15, 1975); Ann. 76-51, 1976-15 I.R.B. 30]

Form 4972 (see Q 13:23) is used to make the election and compute the tax.

Q 13:25   What is the income tax treatment of distributions of deductible employee contributions made by a participant?

Distributions of deductible employee contributions (see Q 6:40), including earnings, are taxed as ordinary income in the year received. They do not qualify for forward averaging tax treatment as a lump-sum distribution (see Q 13:5). If a distribution is premature (i.e., made before the participant reaches age 59½, dies, or is disabled), a penalty tax equal to 10 percent of the amount distributed may be imposed (see Q 13:26). [I.R.C. §§ 72(o), 72(t)]

Distributions of deductible employee contributions may be rolled over to an IRA or another qualified retirement plan on a tax-free basis. See chapter 34.

Q 13:26   May participants be subject to a penalty for early distribution of benefits?

A distribution from a qualified retirement plan before the participant reaches age 59½, may be subject to a 10 percent penalty tax (i.e., the tax is increased by an amount equal to 10 percent of the amount includible in gross income).

For a complete discussion of the 10 percent penalty tax on early withdrawals and the exceptions that may apply, see chapter 16.

Q 13:27   Can a loan from a qualified retirement plan be a taxable distribution?

Yes. For a complete discussion of participant loans, see chapter 14.

Chapter 14

Participant Loans

Some retirement plans permit participants and beneficiaries to make loans from the plan. Myriad requirements apply to participant loans, and a failure to comply with any one requirement may result in a taxable distribution that may also be subject to the penalty tax on early distributions. In addition, a plan loan may be a prohibited transaction and expose the borrower to excise taxes. This chapter analyzes these requirements and discusses the tax and penalty implications.

Q 14:1   Can a qualified retirement plan make a loan to a participant?

Yes; but loans from qualified retirement plans (see Q 14:2) are subject to a number of limitations and requirements (see Q 14:3).

An amount received by a participant (or beneficiary) as a loan from a qualified retirement plan is treated as having been received as a distribution from the plan (a deemed distribution), unless the loan satisfies the applicable limitations and requirements. A loan made from a contract (e.g., insurance policy) that has been purchased under a plan, including a loan made from a contract that has been distributed to the participant, is considered a loan made under the plan. If a participant assigns or pledges any portion of the participant's interest in a plan as a security for a loan, the portion of the interest assigned or pledged is treated as a loan from the plan. Any assignment or pledge by a participant of any portion of the participant's interest in a contract that has been purchased under a plan is considered an assignment or pledge of an interest in the plan. [Armstrong v. United States, 366 F.3d 622 (8th Cir. 2004)] However, if all or a portion of a participant's interest in a plan is pledged or assigned as security for a loan from the plan to the participant, only the amount of the loan received by the participant, not the amount pledged or assigned, is treated as a loan. [I.R.C. §§ 72(p)(1), 72(p)(5); Treas. Reg. § 1.72(p)-1, Q&A-1; Armstrong v. United States, A4-02-042 (D.N.D. 2003); Geib, 80 T.C.M. 931 (2000); Medina, 112 T.C. 51 (1999)]

IRS has ruled that when a plan participant's account balance is transferred directly from one plan to another and the transfer includes an outstanding loan of the participant, the participant will not be considered to have received a distribution or to have renegotiated or modified the loan. [Priv. Ltr. Ruls. 9617046, 9043018; Rev. Rul. 67-213, 1967-2 C.B. 149] The rules regarding plan loans apply to both direct and indirect loans to a participant. IRS has ruled that bank loans to participants that were contingent upon the plan making deposits of plan funds in the bank equal to the amounts of the loans were indirect participant loans and, consequently, would be treated as if the plan had made the loans directly to the participants. [IRS Spec. Rul. (Aug. 12, 1992)]

One court upheld a plan administrator's (see Q 20:1) determination that a loan program added to the plan by a former trustee was invalid because the loan program was not approved by the employer's board of directors as required by the plan document. [Fenster v. Tepfer & Spitz, Ltd., 2002 WL 1993510 (7th Cir. 2002)]

A loan made to a beneficiary of a deceased participant is subject to the same rules as a loan to a participant. Throughout this chapter, the discussion on loans to participants also relates to loans to beneficiaries of deceased participants.

IRS has alerted plan sponsors, plan administrators, and practitioners to common problems concerning plan loan failures and the deemed distributions that can result and has also provided employers with solutions using the Employee Plans Compliance Resolution System (EPCRS; see Q 19:2). [*Retirement News for Employers* (Summer 2006)] IRS has also advised employers and employees concerning the tax consequences of plan loans. [*Retirement News for Employers* (Summer 2009)]

The Financial Accounting Standards Board (FASB) approved a recommendation that loans to participants by defined contribution plans (see Q 2:2) be classified as notes receivable on such plans' financial statements. [Summary of FASB Decisions, Sept. 16, 2010]

See Q 1:28 for a discussion of the Katrina Emergency Tax Relief Act of 2005 and other developments for their effect on participant loans and other issues.

Q 14:2   What is a qualified retirement plan for purposes of participant loans?

A qualified retirement plan means:

1. A plan or program maintained by an employer or an employee organization (or both) that (a) provides retirement income to employees or (b) results in a deferral of income by employees for periods extending generally to the end of employment or beyond, regardless of how plan contributions or benefits are calculated or how benefits are distributed and (c) is afforded special tax treatment for meeting a host of requirements of the Code (see Q 1:5);

2. An annuity plan described in Section 403(a);

3. A 403(b) plan (see Q 35:1);

4. Any plan, whether or not qualified, established and maintained for its employees by the United States, by a State or political subdivision thereof,

or by an agency or instrumentality of the United States, a State or a political subdivision of a State; or

5. Any plan that was (or was determined to be) described in any of the preceding paragraphs.

[I.R.C. § 72(p)(4); Treas. Reg. § 1.72(p)-1, Q&A-2]

If an individual borrows from an IRA, the IRA is treated as having distributed all its assets to the individual (see Qs 30:3, 30:45, 34:4). However, IRS representatives have opined that an individual may roll over funds from an IRA to a qualified retirement plan (see Q 34:7) and then make a loan from the plan.

Q 14:3 What requirements must be satisfied for a participant loan not to be a deemed distribution?

A loan to a participant from a qualified retirement plan (see Q 14:2) will not be a deemed distribution (see Q 14:1) to the participant if the loan satisfies the repayment term requirement (see Q 14:5), the level amortization requirement (see Q 14:6), and the enforceable agreement requirement (see Q 14:7), but only to the extent the loan satisfies the amount limitations (see Q 14:4). [I.R.C. § 72(p)(2); Treas. Reg. § 1.72(p)-1, Q&A-3(a)]

Q 14:4 Is there a dollar limitation on loans from qualified retirement plans?

A loan from a qualified retirement plan (see Q 14:2) to a participant is not treated as a deemed distribution (see Q 14:1) to the extent the loan (when added to the outstanding balance of all other loans from the plan to the participant) does not exceed the *lesser* of:

1. $50,000 reduced by the excess (if any) of

   a. The highest outstanding balance of loans from the plan during the one-year period ending on the day before the date on which such loan was made, over

   b. The outstanding balance of loans from the plan on the date such loan was made; or

2. The greater of

   a. 50 percent of the present value of the participant's vested benefit (see Q 9:1) under the plan (determined without regard to any deductible employee contributions; see Q 6:40), or

   b. $10,000.

[I.R.C. § 72(p)(2)(A); Medina, 112 T.C. 51 (1999); Prince, 74 T.C.M. 112 (1997)]

For the purpose of applying the loan limits, all qualified retirement plans maintained by the same employer and all qualified retirement plans maintained by a member of a controlled group (see Qs 5:29, 5:31) or an affiliated service group (see Q 5:35) are treated as one plan. [I.R.C. § 72(p)(2)(D)]

Example. On April 2, 2010, Casey borrowed $40,000 from his employer's qualified retirement plan, and he repaid $30,000 on December 3, 2010. On March 5, 2011, Casey's vested interest under the plan is $150,000, and he wishes to make another loan. Until December 2, 2010, Casey can borrow only $10,000 more. Here's why:

Highest outstanding loan balance	$40,000
Balance on March 5, 2011	−10,000
Reduction in maximum loan amount	$30,000
Maximum loan amount	$50,000
Reduction	−30,000
Reduced loan limit	$20,000
Balance on March 5, 2011	−10,000
Maximum loan not a distribution	$10,000

With regard to the 50 percent limitation, IRS representatives have opined that using the participant's vested benefit as of the latest plan valuation date is acceptable.

Example. Johnson Bridge Club, Ltd. maintains a profit sharing plan with a calendar year plan year. Participant accounts are valued once each year on December 31. On December 31, 2010, Jo's vested account balance is $100,000. On April 2, 2011, Jo borrows $50,000 from the plan. Between January 1, 2011, and April 2, 2011, the plan investments suffered losses; if a valuation had been made on April 2, 2011, the date of Jo's loan, her vested account balance would have been only $95,000 and the loan would exceed 50 percent of her then-vested account balance. Because the applicable vested account balance is determined on December 31, 2010, the 50 percent limitation is not violated.

Q 14:5   What is the repayment term requirement?

A loan to a participant from a qualified retirement plan (see Q 14:2) must be required to be repaid within five years, or it is treated as a deemed distribution at the time the loan is made (see Qs 14:1, 14:8). The five-year period commences with the date of the loan. However, the five-year repayment period does not apply to a loan used to acquire any dwelling unit that within a reasonable time will be used (determined at the time the loan is made) as the principal residence of the participant (a principal residence plan loan). [I.R.C. § 72(p)(2)(B); Treas. Reg. § 1.72(p)-1, Q&A-5; Campbell, 81 T.C.M. 1641 (2001); Plotkin, 81 T.C.M. 1395 (2001); Garcia v. Comm'r, 190 F.3d 538 (5th Cir. 1999); Medina, 112 T.C. 51 (1999)]

A principal residence has the same meaning as a principal residence under Section 121. A loan is not required to be secured by the dwelling unit that will within a reasonable time be used as the participant's principal residence in order to satisfy the requirements for a principal residence plan loan. The tracing rules established under Section 163(h)(3)(B) apply in determining whether a loan is treated as for the acquisition of a principal residence in order to qualify as a principal residence plan loan. Generally, a refinancing (see Q 14:14) will not qualify as a principal residence plan loan. However, a loan from a plan used to repay a loan from a third party will qualify as a principal residence plan loan if the plan loan qualifies as a principal residence plan loan without regard to the loan from the third party. [Treas. Reg. § 1.72(p)-1, Q&A-5 through Q&A-8]

> **Example 1.** On July 1, 2011, Steve requests a $50,000 plan loan to be repaid in level monthly installments over 15 years. On August 1, 2011, Steve acquires a principal residence and pays a portion of the purchase price with a $50,000 bank loan. On September 1, 2011, the plan loans $50,000 to Steve, which Steve uses to repay the bank loan. Because the loan satisfies the requirements to qualify as a principal residence plan loan (taking into account the tracing rules), the plan loan qualifies for the exception to the five-year repayment period.

Loans renewed, renegotiated, redefined, or extended may be treated as new loans (see Q 14:14). [TRA '86 § 1134(e); Priv. Ltr. Ruls. 9344001]

Loan repayments may be made by payroll deductions. However, when a participant filed for bankruptcy protection, the employer could no longer make deductions from the participant's paychecks. [*In re* Delnero, 191 B.R. 539 (Bankr. N.D.N.Y. 1996)] The Department of Labor (DOL) has opined that participant loan repayments (whether made to the employer for purposes of being forwarded to the plan or withheld from employee wages by the employer for forwarding to the plan) become plan assets (see Q 23:32) as of the earliest date on which the repayments can reasonably be segregated from the employer's general assets. [DOL Reg. § 2510.3-102; DOL Op. Ltr. 2002-02A] See Q 23:32 concerning DOL's safe harbor regulations for participant loan repayments.

Q 14:6 What is the level amortization requirement?

The loan repayment schedule must provide for level amortization. That is, repayment must be made in substantially equal installments consisting of principal and interest and must be made no less frequently than quarterly over the term of the loan. Accordingly, the participant cannot repay the loan in one balloon payment at the end of the loan term. [I.R.C. § 72(p)(2)(C); Zacky, 87 T.C.M. 1378 (2004); Plotkin, 81 T.C.M. 1395 (2001); Medina, 112 T.C. 51 (1999); Prince, 74 T.C.M. 112 (1997); *see also* Leonard, T.C. Summ. Op. 2004-11] An individual made a loan from his pension plan and signed a note requiring that interest be paid annually with the loan principal being payable on demand. Even though the individual made quarterly interest and principal payments and the loan was repaid over a five-year period, because the note, by its terms, did not require level amortization, the loan was a deemed distribution (see Qs 14:1, 14:8). [Estate of Gray, 70 T.C.M. 556 (1995)]

The level amortization requirement does not apply for a period, not longer than one year (or such longer period as may apply below), during which a participant is on a bona fide leave of absence, either without pay from the employer or at a rate of pay (after applicable employment tax withholdings) that is less than the amount of the installment payments required under the terms of the loan. However, the loan (including interest that accrues during the leave of absence) must be repaid by the latest permissible term of the loan (that is, the suspension of loan payments cannot extend the term of the loan beyond five years in the case of a loan that is not a principal residence plan loan plus any additional period of suspension permitted below; see Q 14:5), and the amount of the installments due after the leave ends must not be less than those required under the terms of the original loan. [Treas. Reg. § 1.72(p)-1, Q&A-9(a), Q&A-9(c)]

> **Example 1.** On July 1, 2011, Sallie borrows $40,000 to be repaid in level monthly installments of $825 each over five years. The loan is not a principal residence plan loan. Sallie makes nine monthly payments and commences an unpaid leave of absence that lasts for 12 months. Sallie was not performing military service during this period. Thereafter, Sallie resumes active employment and resumes making repayments on the loan until the loan is repaid. The amount of each monthly installment is increased to $1,130 in order to repay the loan by June 30, 2016. Because the loan satisfies the plan loan requirements, Sallie does not have a deemed distribution. Alternatively, Sallie could continue to pay the monthly installments in the original amount after resuming active employment and, on June 30, 2016, repay the full balance remaining due.

If a plan suspends the obligation to repay a loan made to an employee from the plan for any part of a period during which the employee is performing service in the uniformed services, whether or not qualified military service, such suspension will not be taken into account for purposes of the plan loan requirements. Thus, if a plan suspends loan repayments for any part of a period during which the employee is performing military service, such suspension does not cause the loan to be deemed distributed even if the suspension exceeds one year and even if the term of the loan is extended. However, the loan will not satisfy the repayment term requirement (see Q 14:5) and the level amortization requirement unless loan repayments resume upon the completion of the period of military service and the loan is repaid thereafter by amortization in substantially level installments over a period that ends not later than the latest permissible term of the loan, plus the period of the military service. [I.R.C. § 414(a); Treas. Reg. § 1.72(p)-1, Q&A-9(b)]

> **Example 2.** The facts are the same as in Example 1, except that Sallie was on a leave of absence performing service in the uniformed services for two years and the rate of interest charged during her period of military service is reduced to 6 percent compounded annually (see Q 1:17). After the military service ends on April 2, 2014, Sallie resumes active employment on April 19, 2014, continues the monthly installments of $825 thereafter, and, on June 30, 2018, repays the full balance remaining due of $6,387. Because the loan satisfies the plan loan requirements and the exception for military service, Sallie does not have a deemed distribution. Alternatively, the requirements would also be satisfied if the amount of each monthly installment after April 19, 2014, is increased to $930 in order to repay the loan by June 30, 2018 (without any balance remaining due then).

For the effective dates of the final regulations relating to participant loans, see Q 14:16. Loans renewed, renegotiated, redefined, or extended may be treated as new loans (see Q 14:14). [TRA '86 § 1134(e); Priv. Ltr. Ruls. 9344001]

Loan repayments may be made by payroll deductions. However, when a participant filed for bankruptcy protection, the employer could no longer make deductions from the participant's paychecks. [*In re* Delnero, 191 B.R. 539 (Bankr. N.D.N.Y. 1996)] DOL has opined that participant loan repayments (whether made to the employer for purposes of being forwarded to the plan or withheld from employee wages by the employer for forwarding to the plan) become plan assets (see Q 23:32) as of the earliest date on which the repayments can reasonably be segregated from the employer's general assets. [DOL Reg. § 2510.3-102; DOL Op. Ltr. 2002-02A] See Q 23:32 concerning DOL's safe harbor regulations for participant loan repayments.

Q 14:7 What is the enforceable agreement requirement?

A loan to a participant from a qualified retirement plan (see Q 14:2) does not satisfy the plan loan requirements (see Qs 14:4–14:6) *unless* the loan is evidenced by a legally enforceable agreement (which may include more than one document) and the terms of the agreement demonstrate compliance with the requirements for plan loans. Thus, the agreement must specify the amount and date of the loan and the repayment schedule. The agreement does not have to be signed if the agreement is enforceable under applicable law without being signed. The agreement must be set forth either:

1. In a written paper document;
2. In an electronic medium that is reasonably accessible to the participant and that is provided under a system that satisfies the following requirements:
    a. The system must be reasonably designed to preclude any individual other than the participant from requesting a loan.
    b. The system must provide the participant with a reasonable opportunity to review and to confirm, modify, or rescind the terms of the loan before the loan is made.
    c. The system must provide the participant, within a reasonable time after the loan is made, a confirmation of the loan terms either through a written paper document or through an electronic medium that is reasonably accessible to the participant and that is provided under a system that is reasonably designed to provide the confirmation in a manner no less understandable to the participant than a written document and, under which, at the time the confirmation is provided, the participant is advised that a written paper document may be requested and received at no charge, and, upon request, that document is provided to the participant at no charge; or
3. In such other form as may be approved by IRS.

[Treas. Reg. § 1.72(p)-1, Q&A-3(b); Patrick v. Comm'r, 181 F.3d 103 (6th Cir. 1999)]

IRS has issued proposed regulations (see Q 20:5) setting forth rules that clarify and expand existing procedures regarding the use of electronic media to provide notices to plan participants and to transmit elections or consents relating to retirement plans and includes participant loans.

Q 14:8   When does a deemed distribution occur?

A deemed distribution (see Q 14:1) occurs at the first time that the requirements for plan loans are not satisfied, in form or in operation (see Qs 14:4–14:7). This may occur at the time the loan is made or at a later date. If the terms of the loan do not require repayments that satisfy the repayment term requirement or the level amortization requirement, or the loan is not evidenced by an enforceable agreement, the entire amount of the loan is a deemed distribution at the time the loan is made. [Zacky, 87 T.C.M. 1378 (2004); Leonard, T.C. Summ. Op. 2004-11; Campbell, 81 T.C.M. 1641 (2001); Plotkin, 81 T.C.M. 1395 (2001); Garcia v. Comm'r, 190 F.3d 538 (5th Cir. 1999); Medina, 112 T.C. 51 (1999); Estate of Gray, 70 T.C.M. 556 (1995)] If the loan satisfies the plan loan requirements except that the amount loaned exceeds the dollar limitation, the amount of the loan in excess of the applicable limitation is a deemed distribution at the time the loan is made. [W.L. Miller, PSC v. Comm'r, No. 93-2432 (6th Cir. 1994)] If the loan initially satisfies the plan loan requirements and the enforceable agreement requirement, but payments are not made in accordance with the terms of the loan, a deemed distribution occurs as a result of the failure to make such payments. [Duncan, 90 T.C.M. 35 (2005); White, No. 1815-04S (Tax Ct. 2005); Molina, 88 T.C.M. 441 (2004); Williams, T.C. Summ. Op. 2004-57]

[Treas. Reg. § 1.72(p)-1, Q&A-4]

Example 1. Caroline has a vested account balance of $200,000 and receives $70,000 as a loan repayable in level quarterly installments over five years. Caroline has a deemed distribution of $20,000 (the excess of $70,000 over $50,000) at the time of the loan because the loan exceeds the $50,000 limit. The remaining $50,000 is not a deemed distribution.

Example 2. James has a vested account balance of $30,000 and borrows $20,000 as a loan repayable in level monthly installments over five years. Because the amount of the loan is $5,000 more than 50 percent of James's vested account balance [$20,000 − (50% × $30,000)], James has a deemed distribution of $5,000 at the time of the loan. The remaining $15,000 is not a deemed distribution. (Note also that, if the loan is secured solely by James's account balance, the loan may be a prohibited transaction; see Q 14:21.)

Example 3. Adam's vested account balance is $100,000, and a $50,000 loan is made to Adam repayable in level quarterly installments over seven years. The loan is not a principal residence loan. Because the repayment period exceeds the maximum five-year period, Adam has a deemed distribution of $50,000 at the time the loan is made.

Example 4. On August 1, 2011, Bill has a vested account balance of $45,000 and borrows $20,000 from the plan to be repaid over five years in level monthly installments due at the end of each month. After making monthly payments through July 2012, Bill fails to make any of the payments due thereafter. As a result of the failure to satisfy the requirement that the loan be repaid in level monthly installments, Bill has a deemed distribution on August 31, 2012, the date of the first missed payment.

Failure to make any installment payment when due in accordance with the terms of the loan results in a deemed distribution at the time of such failure. However, the plan administrator (see Q 20:1) may allow a cure period, and a violation will not occur until the last day of the cure period. A cure period will be given effect only to the extent it does not continue beyond the last day of the calendar quarter following the calendar quarter in which the required installment payment is due. If there is a failure to pay the installment payments required under the terms of the loan (taking into account any cure period allowed), then the amount of the deemed distribution equals the entire outstanding balance of the loan (including accrued interest) at the time of such failure. [Treas. Reg. § 1.72(p)-1, Q&A-10; Leon and Tilley, T.C. Summ. Op. 2008-86; White, No. 1815-04S (Tax Ct. 2005)]

> **Example 5.** Assume the same facts as in Example 4, except that the plan administrator allows a three-month cure period. As a result of the failure to satisfy the requirement that the loan be repaid in level installments, Bill has a deemed distribution on November 30, 2012, which is the last day of the three-month cure period for the August 31, 2012 installment. The amount of the deemed distribution is the outstanding balance on the loan at November 30, 2012. Alternatively, if the plan administrator had allowed a cure period through the end of the next calendar quarter, there would be a deemed distribution on December 31, 2012 equal to the outstanding balance of the loan at December 31, 2012.

For the tax consequences of a deemed distribution, see Q 14:9; and, for the effective date of the final regulations relating to participant loans, see Q 14:16.

IRS representatives have stated that a deemed distribution does not automatically give rise to a prohibited transaction (see Qs 14:21, 23:1).

Q 14:9   What are the tax consequences of a deemed distribution?

A deemed distribution (see Q 14:1) is includible in gross income. However, if the participant has basis (see Qs 13:3, 14:15), all or a portion of the deemed distribution may not be taxable. In addition, a taxable loan to a participant may also be subject to the penalty tax on early distributions (see Q 16:21). [Treas. Reg. § 1.72(p)-1, Q&A-11; Billups, T.C. Summ. Op. 2009-86; Marquez, T.C. Summ. Op. 2009-80; Leon and Tilley, T.C. Summ. Op. 2008-86; White, No. 1815-04S (Tax Ct. 2005); Molina, 88 T.C.M. 441 (2004); Zacky, 87 T.C.M. 1378 (2004); Leonard, T.C. Summ. Op. 2004-11; Campbell, 81 T.C.M. 1641 (2001); Plotkin, 81 T.C.M. 1395 (2001); Patrick v. Comm'r, 181 F.3d 103 (6th Cir. 1999); Chapman, 73 T.C.M. 2405 (1997); Estate of Gray, 70 T.C.M. 556 (1995); Earnshaw, 69 T.C.M. 2353 (1995)]

A deemed distribution is treated as a distribution to the participant only for income tax purposes and is not a distribution of the participant's accrued benefit (see Q 9:2). [Treas. Reg. § 1.72(p)-1, Q&A-13(a)] A deemed distribution is also not treated as an actual distribution for other purposes. For example, if a participant in a money purchase pension plan (see Q 2:4) who is an active employee has a deemed distribution, the plan will not be considered to have made an in-service distribution to the participant in violation of the qualification requirements (see Q 13:5) applicable to money purchase pension plans. Similarly, the deemed distribution is not eligible to be rolled over to an eligible retirement plan and is not considered an impermissible distribution of an amount attributable to elective contributions (see Q 27:16). [Treas. Reg. §§ 1.72(p)-1, Q&A-12, 1.402(c)-2, Q&A-4(d), 1.401(k)-1(d)(5)(ii)]

The amount includible in income as a result of a deemed distribution is required to be reported on Form 1099-R (or any other form prescribed by IRS). [Treas. Reg. § 1.72(p)-1, Q&A-14] Where a participant ceased making loan repayments in 1999, but Form 1099-R reported 2000 as the year of distribution, the court determined that the taxable deemed distribution occurred in 1999. [Molina, 88 T.C.M. 441 (2004)] A bankruptcy court has ruled that it did not have jurisdiction to determine if plan loans were taxable distributions. [*In re* Somma, No. 585-648 (Bankr. N.D. Ohio 1992)]

If there is an express or tacit understanding that a plan loan will not be repaid or, for any reason, the transaction does not create a debtor-creditor relationship or is otherwise not a bona fide loan, then the amount transferred is treated as an actual distribution from the plan, includible in gross income, and is not treated as a loan or as a deemed distribution. [Treas. Reg. § 1.72(p)-1, Q&A-17; Patrick v. Comm'r, 181 F.3d 103 (6th Cir. 1999)]

For a further discussion of the consequences of a deemed distribution, see Qs 14:11, 14:13 through 14:15, 14:19, and 14:20; and, for the effective date of the final regulations relating to participant loans, see Q 14:16.

Q 14:10   How does a reduction (offset) of an account balance to repay a loan differ from a deemed distribution?

A loan to a participant from a qualified retirement plan (see Q 14:2) can give rise to two types of distributions:

1. A deemed distribution (see Qs 14:1, 14:8), and
2. A distribution of a plan loan offset amount.

A deemed distribution occurs when certain requirements are not satisfied but the transaction is not treated as an actual distribution from the plan (see Q 14:9).

A distribution of a plan loan offset amount occurs when, under the terms governing a loan to a participant, the participant's accrued benefit (see Q 9:2) is reduced (offset) in order to repay the loan (including the enforcement of the plan's security interest in the accrued benefit). A distribution of a plan loan offset amount could occur in a variety of circumstances, such as where the terms governing the loan require that, in the event of the participant's request for a distribution, a loan be repaid immediately or treated as a default. A distribution of a plan loan offset amount also occurs when the loan is canceled, accelerated, or treated as if it were in default (e.g., where the plan treats a loan as in default upon an employee's termination of employment or within a specified period thereafter). A distribution of a plan loan offset amount is an actual distribution, not a deemed distribution. [Treas. Reg. §§ 1.72(p)-1, Q&A-13(a), Q&A-13(b), 1.402(c)-2, Q&A-4, Q&A-9(b); Jordan, 91 T.C.M. 1129 (2006); Royal, 91 T.C.M. 1004 (2006); Murtaugh, 74 T.C.M. 75 (1997); Caton, 69 T.C.M. 1937 (1995)] A plan offset amount is an eligible rollover distribution (see Q 14:20). [Priv. Ltr. Rul. 200617037]

However, a plan may be prohibited from making a plan loan offset under provisions prohibiting or limiting distribution to an active participant. [I.R.C. §§ 401(a), 401(k)(2)(B), 403(b)(11) (as amended by PPA § 827(b)(3)); Treas. Reg. §§ 1.72(p)-1, Q&A-13(b), 1.402(c)-2, Q&A-9(c)]

Q 14:11   Do withholding rules apply to participant loans?

To the extent that a loan, when made, is a deemed distribution (see Q 14:1) or an account balance is reduced (offset; see Q 14:10) to repay a loan, the amount includible in income is subject to withholding (see Q 20:10). If a deemed distribution of a loan or a loan repayment by benefit offset results in income at a date after the date the loan is made, withholding is required only if a transfer of cash or property (excluding employer securities) is made to the participant from the plan (see Q 14:2) at the same time. [Treas. Reg. § 1.72(p)-1, Q&A-15]

The maximum amount to be withheld on any designated distribution, that is, a distribution from a qualified retirement plan (including any eligible rollover distribution) must not exceed the sum of the cash and the fair market value of property (excluding employer securities) received in the distribution. The amount of the sum is determined without regard to whether any portion of the cash or property is a designated distribution or an eligible rollover distribution. For purposes of this rule, any plan loan offset amount is treated in the same manner as employer securities (see Q 20:16). Thus, although plan loan offset amounts must be included in the amount that is multiplied by 20 percent, the total amount required to be withheld from an eligible rollover distribution is limited to the sum of the cash and the fair market value of property received by the distributee, excluding any amount of the distribution that is a plan loan offset amount. For example, if the only portion of an eligible rollover distribution that is not paid in a direct rollover (see Q 34:17) consists of a plan loan offset amount, withholding is not required. [Treas. Reg. §§ 31.3405(c)-(1), Q&A-9, Q&A-11, 35.3405-1, Q&A F-4]

> **Example 1.** In 2011, Julie, a participant in Kenneth Corporation's profit sharing plan, has an account balance of $10,000, of which $3,000 is represented by a plan loan secured by her account balance. Upon termination of employment in 2011, Julie elects a distribution of her entire account balance, and the outstanding loan is offset against the account balance on distribution. Julie elects a direct rollover of the distribution, and $7,000 is paid to an eligible retirement plan. When Julie's account balance was offset by the amount of the $3,000 unpaid loan balance, she received an offset amount (equivalent to $3,000) that is an eligible rollover distribution. No withholding

is required on account of the distribution of the $3,000 offset amount because no cash or other property (other than the offset amount) is received by Julie from which to satisfy the withholding.

Example 2. The facts are the same as those in Example 1, except that Julie elects to receive a distribution of her account balance that remains after the $3,000 offset. In this case, the amount of the distribution received by Julie is $10,000, not $3,000. Because the amount of the $3,000 offset attributable to the loan is included in determining the amount that equals 20 percent of the eligible rollover distribution received by Julie, withholding in the amount of $2,000 (20% × $10,000) is required. The $2,000 is required to be withheld from the $7,000 to be distributed to Julie in cash, so that Julie actually receives a check for $5,000.

IRS has ruled that when a plan participant's account balance is transferred directly from one plan to another and the transfer includes an outstanding loan of the participant, no withholding is required. [Priv. Ltr. Ruls. 9617046]

Example 3. The facts are the same as those in Example 1, except that the eligible retirement plan of Julie's new employer accepts the promissory note as part of its direct rollover procedures and Julie elects a direct rollover of both the $7,000 cash and the $3,000 plan loan to the eligible retirement plan. In this case, no withholding is required.

Q 14:12 How are loans made pursuant to a residential mortgage loan program treated?

Residential mortgage loans made by a qualified retirement plan (see Q 14:2) in the ordinary course of an investment program are not subject to the limitations and restrictions on loans to participants if the property acquired with the loans is the primary security for such loans and the amount loaned does not exceed the fair market value of the property. An investment program exists only if the plan has established, in advance of a specific investment under the program, that a certain percentage or amount of plan assets will be invested in residential mortgages available to persons purchasing the property who satisfy commercially customary financial criteria. A loan will not be considered as made under an investment program if:

1. Any of the loans made under the program matures upon a participant's termination from employment;
2. Any of the loans made under the program is an earmarked asset of a participant's individual account in the plan; or
3. The loans made under the program are made available only to participants in the plan.

[Treas. Reg. § 1.72(p)-1, Q&A-18(a)]

Item 3 does not apply to a plan which, on December 20, 1995, and at all times thereafter, has had in effect a loan program under which the loans comply with items 1 and 2 to constitute residential mortgage loans in the ordinary course of an investment program. [Treas. Reg. § 1.72(p)-1, Q&A-18(b)] However, IRS has ruled that mortgages given to plan participants under a qualified retirement plan's residential mortgage investment program would be deemed loans to the plan participants and not plan investments because over 90 percent of the persons eligible for mortgages under the program were plan participants. [Priv. Ltr. Ruls. 9110039]

No loan that benefits an officer, director, or owner of the employer maintaining the plan, or their beneficiaries, will be treated as made under an investment program. [Treas. Reg. § 1.72(p)-1, Q&A-18(c)]

Even though the investment program may satisfy the above requirements, a residential mortgage loan could be a prohibited transaction (see Qs 14:21, 23:1) or not be consistent with the fiduciary standards of ERISA (see Q 23:20). [Treas. Reg. § 1.72(p)-1, Q&A-18(d)]

For the effective date of the final regulations relating to plan loans, see Q 14:16.

Q 14:13   If there is a deemed distribution, is the interest that accrues thereafter an indirect loan for income tax purposes?

Except as provided below, a deemed distribution (see Q 14:1) of a loan is treated as a distribution (see Q 14:9). Therefore, a loan that is deemed to be distributed ceases to be an outstanding loan, and the interest that accrues thereafter on the amount deemed distributed is disregarded for income tax purposes. Even though interest continues to accrue on the outstanding loan (and is taken into account for purposes of determining the tax treatment of any subsequent loan), this additional interest is not treated as an additional loan (and thus does not result in an additional deemed distribution). However, a loan that is deemed distributed is not considered distributed for all purposes of the Code (see Q 14:9). [Treas. Reg. § 1.72(p)-1, Q&A-16, Q&A-19(a)]

A loan that is deemed distributed (including interest accruing thereafter) and that has not been repaid (such as by a plan loan offset; see Q 14:10) is considered outstanding for purposes of determining the maximum amount of any subsequent loan to the participant (see Q 14:4). [Treas. Reg. § 1.72(p)-1, Q&A-19(b)(1)] If a loan is deemed distributed and has not been repaid (such as by a plan loan offset), then no payment made thereafter to the participant is treated as a loan unless the loan otherwise satisfies the plan loan requirements (see Qs 14:4–14:7) and either of the following conditions is satisfied:

1. There is an arrangement among the plan, the participant, and the employer, enforceable under applicable law, under which repayments will be made by payroll withholding. For this purpose, an arrangement will not fail to be enforceable merely because a party has the right to revoke the arrangement prospectively.

2. The plan receives adequate security from the participant that is in addition to the participant's accrued benefit (see Q 9:2) under the plan.

[Treas. Reg. § 1.72(p)-1, Q&A-19(b)(2); Priv. Ltr. Rul. 200601045]

If, following a deemed distribution that has not been repaid, a payment is made to a participant that satisfies the above conditions for treatment as a plan loan and, subsequently, before repayment of the second loan, the above conditions are no longer satisfied with respect to the second loan (for example, if the loan recipient revokes consent to payroll withholding), the amount then outstanding on the second loan is treated as a deemed distribution. [Treas. Reg. § 1.72(p)-1, Q&A-19(b)(3)]

For the effective date of the final regulations relating to plan loans, see Q 14:16.

Q 14:14   May a participant refinance an outstanding loan or have more than one loan outstanding from a plan?

A participant who has an outstanding loan that satisfies the plan loan requirements (see Qs 14:4–14:7) may refinance that loan or borrow additional amounts if, under the facts and circumstances, the loans collectively satisfy the amount limitations (see Q 14:4) and the prior loan and the additional loan each satisfy the repayment term and level amortization requirements (see Qs 14:5, 14:6). For this purpose, a refinancing includes any situation in which one loan replaces another loan.

If a loan that satisfies the plan loan requirements is replaced by a loan (a replacement loan) and the term of the replacement loan ends after the latest permissible term of the loan it replaces (the replaced loan), then the replacement loan and the replaced loan are both treated as outstanding on the date of the transaction. For purposes of the preceding sentence, the latest permissible term of the replaced loan is the latest date permitted (that is, five years from the original date of the replaced loan, assuming that the replaced loan does not qualify as a principal residence plan loan (see Q 14:5) and that no additional period of suspension applied to the replaced loan (see Q 14:6)). Thus, for example, if the term of the replacement loan ends after the latest permissible term of the replaced loan and the sum of the amount of the replacement loan plus the outstanding balance of all other loans on the date of the transaction, including the replaced loan, fails to satisfy the amount limitations, then the replacement loan results in a deemed distribution. This does not apply to a replacement loan if the terms of the replacement loan would satisfy the plan loan requirements determined as if the replacement loan consisted of two separate loans, the replaced loan (amortized in substantially level payments over a period ending no later than the last day of the latest permissible term of the replaced loan) and, to the extent the amount of the replacement loan exceeds the amount of the replaced loan, a new loan that is also amortized in substantially level payments over a period ending not later than the last day of the latest permissible term of the replaced loan.

[Treas. Reg. § 1.72(p)-1, Q&A-20; Billups, T.C. Summ. Op. 2009-86; Marquez, T.C. Summ. Op. 2009-80]

Example 1. Bella, a participant with a vested account balance that exceeds $100,000 borrows $40,000 from a plan on January 1, 2011, to be repaid in 20 quarterly installments of $2,491 each. Thus, the term of the loan ends on December 31, 2015. On January 1, 2012, when the outstanding balance on the loan is $33,322, the loan is refinanced and is replaced by a new $40,000 loan from the plan to be repaid in 20 quarterly installments. Under the terms of the refinanced loan, the loan will be repaid in level quarterly installments (of $2,491 each) over the next 20 quarters. Thus, the term of the new loan ends on December 31, 2016.

The amount of the new loan, when added to the outstanding balance of all other loans from the plan, must not exceed $50,000 reduced by the excess of the highest outstanding balance of loans from the plan during the one year period ending on December 31, 2011, over the outstanding balance of loans from the plan on January 1, 2012, with such outstanding balance to be determined immediately prior to the new $40,000 loan. Because the term of the new loan ends later than the term of the loan it replaces, both the new loan and the loan it replaces must be taken into account for purposes of applying the plan loan requirements, including the amount limitations. The amount of the new loan is $40,000, the outstanding balance on January 1, 2012, of the loan it replaces is $33,322, and the highest outstanding balance of loans from the plan during 2011 was $40,000. Accordingly, the sum of the new loan and the outstanding balance on January 1, 2012, of the loan it replaces must not exceed $50,000 reduced by $6,678 (the excess of the $40,000 maximum outstanding loan balance during 2011 over the $33,322 outstanding balance on January 1, 2012, determined immediately prior to the new loan) and thus must not exceed $43,322. The sum of the new loan ($40,000) and the outstanding balance on January 1, 2012, of the loan it replaces ($33,322) is $73,322. Since $73,322 exceeds the $43,322 limit by $30,000, there is a deemed distribution of $30,000 on January 1, 2012.

However, no deemed distribution would occur if, under the terms of the refinanced loan, the amount of the first 16 installments on the refinanced loan were equal to $2,907, which is the sum of the $2,491 originally scheduled quarterly installment payment amount under the first loan, plus $416 (which is the amount required to repay, in level quarterly installments over five years beginning on January 1, 2012, the excess of the refinanced loan over the January 1, 2012, balance of the first loan ($40,000 − $33,322 = $6,678)), and the amount of the four remaining installments were equal to $416. The refinancing would satisfy the exception for replacement loans because the terms of the new loan would satisfy the plan loan requirements (including the substantially level amortization requirements) determined as if the new loan consisted of two loans, one of which is in the amount of the first loan ($33,322) and is amortized in substantially level payments over a period ending December 31, 2015 (the last day of the term of the first loan) and the other of which is in the additional amount ($6,678) borrowed under the new loan. Similarly, the transaction also would not result in a deemed distribution if the terms of the refinanced loan provided for repayments to be made in level quarterly installments (of $2,990 each) over the next 16 quarters.

Example 2. The facts are the same as in Example 1, except that the applicable interest rate used by the plan when the loan is refinanced is significantly lower due to a reduction in market rates of interest and, under the terms of the refinanced loan, the amount of the first 16 installments on the refinanced loan is equal to $2,848 and the amount of the next four installments on the refinanced loan is equal to $406. The $2,848 amount is the sum of $2,442 to repay the first loan by December 31, 2015 (the term of the first loan), plus $406 (which is the amount to repay, in level quarterly installments over five years beginning on January 1, 2012, the $6,678 excess of the refinanced loan over the January 1, 2012, balance of the first loan).

The transaction does not result in a deemed distribution because the terms of the new loan would satisfy the plan loan requirements (including the substantially level amortization requirements) determined as if the new loan consisted of two loans, one of which is in the amount of the first loan ($33,322) and is amortized in substantially level payments over a period ending December 31, 2015 (the last day of the term of the first loan) and the other of which is in the additional amount ($6,678) borrowed under the new loan. The transaction would also not result in a deemed distribution if the terms of the new loan provided for repayments to be made in level quarterly installments (of $2,931 each) over the next 16 quarters.

For the effective date of the final regulations relating to refinanced and multiple plan loans, see Q 14:16.

Q 14:15   Does the participant acquire basis if the loan is repaid after a deemed distribution?

Yes, if the participant repays the loan after a deemed distribution (see Q 14:9) of the loan, then the participant's investment in the contract (basis; see Q 13:3) under the plan increases by the amount of the cash repayments that the participant makes on the loan after the deemed distribution. However, loan repayments are not treated as after-tax contributions for other purposes (see Qs 6:34, 27:77). [Treas. Reg. § 1.72(p)-1, Q&A-21]

Example. Ben receives a $20,000 loan on January 1, 2011, to be repaid in 20 quarterly installments of $1,245 each. On December 31, 2011, the outstanding loan balance ($19,179) is deemed distributed as a result of a failure to make quarterly installment payments that were due on September 30, 2011, and December 31, 2011. On June 30, 2012, Ben repays $5,147 (which is the sum of the three installment payments that were due on September 30, 2011, December 31, 2011, and March 31, 2012 with interest thereon to June 30, 2012, plus the installment payment that was due on June 30, 2012). Thereafter, Ben resumes making the installment payments of $1,245 from September 30, 2012 through December 31, 2015. The loan repayments made after December 31, 2011, through December 31, 2015, total $22,577. Because

Ben repaid $22,577 after the deemed distribution that occurred on December 31, 2011, he has basis equal to $22,577 as of December 31, 2015.

For the effective date of the final regulations relating to participant loans, see Q 14:16.

Q 14:16   What effective date applies to participant loans?

The rules regarding participant loans are generally applicable to assignments, pledges, and loans made after August 13, 1982 (the statutory effective date). The final regulations discussed in Qs 14:1 through 14:3, 14:5 through 14:13, and 14:15 apply to assignments, pledges, and loans made on or after January 1, 2002 (the regulatory effective date). [Treas. Reg. § 1.72(p)-1, Q&A-22(a), Q&A-22(b)] The regulations that were finalized in Qs 14:13 and 14:14 apply to assignments, pledges, and loans made on or after January 1, 2004. [Treas. Reg. § 1.72(p)-1, Q&A-22(d)]

A plan is permitted to apply the final regulations discussed in Qs 14:13 and 14:15 to a loan made before the regulatory effective date and after the statutory effective date if there had not been any deemed distribution (see Q 14:1) before the transition date. If there had been a deemed distribution before the transition date, the final regulations could be applied to the loan beginning on any January 1, but only if the plan reported, in Box 1 of Form 1099-R, a gross distribution of an amount at least equal to the initial default amount. The initial default amount is the amount that would be reported as a gross distribution under Q 14:9, and the transition date is the January 1 on which a plan begins applying the final regulations discussed in Qs 14:13 and 14:15 to a loan. If a plan applies the final regulations to such a loan, then the plan, in its reporting and withholding on or after the transition date, must not attribute basis (see Qs 13:3, 14:9) to the participant based upon the initial default amount. [Treas. Reg. § 1.72(p)-1, Q&A-22(c)(1), Q&A-22(c)(2)]

The plan must treat the excess (the loan transition amount) as a loan amount that remains outstanding and must include the excess in the participant's income at the time of the actual distribution if the following events occur:

1. The plan attributed basis to the participant based on the deemed distribution of the loan;

2. The plan subsequently made an actual distribution to the participant before the transition date; and

3. Immediately before the transition date, the initial default amount (or if less, the amount of the basis so attributed) exceeds the participant's basis.

[Treas. Reg. § 1.72(p)-1, Q&A-22(c)(2)(iv)]

Example 1. In 1998, when Joann's account balance under a plan was $50,000, she received a loan from the plan. Joann made the required repayments until 1999, when there was a deemed distribution of $20,000 as a result of a failure to repay the loan. For 1999, as a result of the deemed distribution, the plan reported, in Box 1 of Form 1099-R, a gross distribution of $20,000 (the initial default amount) and, in Box 2 of Form 1099-R, a taxable amount of $20,000. The plan then recorded an increase in Joann's basis for the same amount ($20,000). Thereafter, the plan disregarded the interest that accrued on the loan after the 1999 deemed distribution (see Q 14:13). Thus, as of December 31, 2001, the total taxable amount reported by the plan as a result of the deemed distribution was $20,000 and the plan's records showed that Joann's basis was the same amount ($20,000).

As of January 1, 2002, the plan decided to apply the final regulations to the loan. Accordingly, it reduced Joann's basis by the initial default amount of $20,000 so that her remaining tax basis in the plan was zero. Thereafter, the amount of the outstanding loan was not treated as part of the account balance. Joann attained age 59½ in the year 2003 and received a distribution of the full account balance under the plan consisting of $60,000 in cash and the loan receivable. At that time, the plan's records reflected an offset of the loan amount against the loan receivable in Joann's account and a distribution of $60,000 in cash. For the year 2003, the plan had to report a gross distribution of $60,000 in Box 1 of Form 1099-R and a taxable amount of $60,000 in Box 2 of Form 1099-R.

Example 2. The facts are the same as in Example 1, except that in 1999, immediately prior to the deemed distribution, Joann's account balance under the plan totaled $50,000 and her basis was $10,000. For 1999, the plan reported, in Box 1 of Form 1099-R, a gross distribution of $20,000 (the initial default amount) and reported, in Box 2 of Form 1099-R, a taxable amount of $16,000 (the $20,000 deemed distribution − $4,000 of basis [$10,000 × ($20,000/$50,000)] allocated to the deemed distribution). The plan then recorded an increase in basis equal to the $20,000 deemed distribution, so that Joann's remaining tax basis as of December 31, 1999, totaled $26,000 ($10,000 − $4,000 + $20,000). Thereafter, the plan disregarded the interest that accrued on the loan after the 1999 deemed distribution. Thus, as of December 31, 2001, the total taxable amount reported by the plan as a result of the deemed distribution was $16,000, and the plan's records showed that Joann's basis was $26,000.

As of January 1, 2002, the plan decided to apply the final regulations to the loan. Accordingly, it reduced Joann's basis by the initial default amount of $20,000, so that her remaining tax basis in the plan was $6,000. Thereafter, the amount of the outstanding loan was not treated as part of the account balance. Joann attained age 59½ in the year 2003 and received a distribution of the full account balance under the plan consisting of $60,000 in cash and the loan receivable. At that time the plan's records reflected an offset of the loan amount against the loan receivable in Joann's account and a distribution of $60,000 in cash. For the year 2003, the plan had to report a gross distribution of $60,000 in Box 1 of Form 1099-R and a taxable amount of $54,000 ($60,000 − $6,000) in Box 2 of Form 1099-R.

Example 3. In 1993, when Samantha's account balance in a plan was $100,000, she received a loan of $50,000 from the plan. Samantha made the required loan repayments until 1995, when there was a deemed distribution of $28,919 as a result of a failure to repay the loan. For 1995, as a result of the deemed distribution, the plan reported, in Box 1 of Form 1099-R, a gross distribution of $28,919 (the initial default amount) and, in Box 2 of Form 1099-R, a taxable amount of $28,919. For 1995, the plan also recorded an increase in Samantha's basis for the same amount ($28,919). Each year thereafter through 2001, the plan reported a gross distribution equal to the interest accruing that year on the loan balance, reported a taxable amount equal to the interest accruing that year on the loan balance reduced by Samantha's basis allocated to the gross distribution, and recorded a net increase in her tax basis equal to the taxable amount. As of December 31, 2001, the taxable amount reported by the plan as a result of the loan totalled $44,329, and the plan's records show that Samantha's basis totalled the same amount ($44,329).

As of January 1, 2002, the plan decided to apply the final regulations. Accordingly, it reduced Samantha's tax basis by the initial default amount of $28,919, so that her remaining basis in the plan was $15,410 ($44,329 − $28,919). Thereafter, the amount of the outstanding loan was not treated as part of the account balance. Samantha attained age 59½ in the year 2003 and received a distribution of the full account balance under the plan consisting of $180,000 in cash and the loan receivable equal to the $28,919 outstanding loan amount in 1995 plus interest accrued thereafter to the payment date in 2003. At the time, the plan's records reflected an offset of the loan amount against the loan receivable in Samantha's account and a distribution of $180,000 in cash. For the year 2003, the plan had to report a gross distribution of $180,000 in Box 1 of Form 1099-R and a taxable amount of $164,590 in Box 2 of Form 1099-R ($180,000 reduced by the remaining tax basis of $15,410).

Example 4. The facts are the same as in Example 1, except that in 2000, after the deemed distribution, Joann received a $10,000 hardship distribution (see Q 27:14). At the time of the hardship distribution, Joann's account balance under the plan totalled $50,000. For 2000, the plan reported, in Box 1 of Form 1099-R, a gross distribution of $10,000 and, in Box 2 of Form 1099-R, a taxable amount of $6,000 (the $10,000 actual distribution − $4,000 of basis [$10,000 × ($20,000/$50,000)] allocated to this actual distribution). The plan then recorded a decrease in basis equal to $4,000, so that Joann's remaining basis as of December 31, 2000, totalled $16,000 ($20,000 − $4,000). After 1999, the plan disregarded the interest that accrued on the loan after the 1999 deemed distribution. Thus, as of December 31, 2001, the total taxable amount reported by the plan as a result of the deemed distribution plus the 2000 actual distribution was $26,000, and the plan's records showed that Joann's basis was $16,000.

As of January 1, 2002, the plan decided to apply the final regulations to the loan. Accordingly, it reduced Joann's basis by the initial default amount of $20,000, so that her remaining basis in the plan was reduced from $16,000 to zero. However, because the $20,000 total default amount exceeded $16,000, the plan recorded a loan transition amount of $4,000 ($20,000 − $16,000). Thereafter, the amount of the outstanding loan, other than the $4,000 loan transition amount, was not treated as part of the account balance. Joann attained age 59 in the year 2003 and received a distribution of the full account balance under the plan consisting of $60,000 in cash and the loan receivable. At that time, the plan's records reflected an offset of the loan amount against the loan receivable in Joann's account and a distribution of $60,000 in cash. The plan had to report in Box 1 of Form 1099-R a gross distribution of $64,000 and in Box 2 of Form 1099-R a taxable amount for Joann for the year 2003 equal to $64,000 (the sum of the $60,000 paid in the year 2003 plus $4,000 as the loan transition amount).

Q 14:17   Is interest paid on a participant loan deductible?

The deductibility of interest on a loan from a qualified retirement plan (see Q 14:2) is first determined under the general rules governing the deductibility of interest. Notwithstanding the general rules, interest on a loan to a participant is never deductible if the loan is made to a key employee (see Q 26:23), whether or not the plan is top-heavy, or if the loan is secured by elective contributions made under a 401(k) plan (see Qs 27:1, 27:16). [I.R.C. §§ 72(p)(3), 163; Priv. Ltr. Rul. 8933018]

IRS has ruled that a participant could deduct interest he paid on a bona fide mortgage loan (see Q 14:9) obtained from a qualified retirement plan, even though the amount of the mortgage loan over $50,000 (see Q 14:4) was deemed to be a taxable distribution to the participant. [Field Serv. Adv. 200047022]

See Q 1:17 for additional information relating to interest charged on plan loans.

Q 14:18   Is spousal consent needed for a participant loan?

Yes, if the qualified retirement plan is subject to the automatic survivor benefit requirements (see Q 10:1) and if the participant's accrued benefit (see Q 9:2) is used as security for the loan (see Q 10:11). Consent is required even if the accrued benefit is not the primary security for the loan. Spousal consent is not required, however, if the total accrued benefit subject to the security is $5,000 or less (see Q 10:61). Spousal consent must be obtained within 180 days of the date that the loan is so secured, and in the same manner as the consent to the waiver of the qualified joint and survivor annuity (see Q 10:8) or qualified preretirement survivor annuity (see Q 10:9) is obtained (see Q 10:21). For purposes of spousal consent, any renegotiation, extension, renewal, or other revision of a loan is treated as a new loan. [I.R.C. § 417(a)(4); Treas. Reg. § 1.401(a)-20, Q&A-24; Prop. Treas. Reg. § 1.401(a)-20, Q&A-24]

Q 14:19   How is a participant loan treated for rollover purposes?

The only type of distribution related to a plan loan that cannot be an eligible rollover distribution is a deemed distribution (see Qs 14:1, 15:9). [Treas. Reg. § 1.72(p)-1, Q&A-12] In contrast, when a participant terminates employment and the participant's accrued benefit (see Q 9:2) is offset by the amount of an unpaid plan loan balance, the plan loan offset amount (see Q 14:10) can be an eligible rollover distribution (see Q 14:20). Thus, an amount equal to the plan loan offset amount can be rolled over by the participant (or spousal distributee) to an eligible retirement plan within the 60-day period (see Q 34:34) unless the plan loan offset amount fails to be an eligible rollover distribution for another reason.

An offset amount to repay a plan loan can be an eligible rollover distribution whether or not the offset occurs after the participant's employment has terminated. Similarly, a plan loan offset amount can be an eligible rollover distribution even if the offset occurs because the loan is accelerated or is treated as if it were in default (e.g., where the plan treats a loan as in default upon termination of employment or within a specified period thereafter). [Treas. Reg. § 1.402(c)-2, Q&A-9(a), Q&A-9(b); Priv. Ltr. Rul. 200617037]

The transfer of an eligible rollover distribution, including a note evidencing a participant's plan loan, from one qualified retirement plan to another does not cause the transferred amounts to be treated as a deemed distribution. [Priv. Ltr. Ruls. 9729042, 9617046]

Q 14:20   Must a direct rollover option be provided for a plan loan offset amount that is an eligible rollover distribution?

A plan will *not* fail to satisfy the direct rollover requirement merely because the plan does not permit a participant to elect a direct rollover (see Q 34:20) of a plan loan offset amount (see Q 14:10) that is an eligible rollover distribution. Nevertheless, the amount by which a participant's accrued benefit (see Q 9:2) is offset to repay a plan loan can be an eligible rollover distribution (see Q 14:19). Thus, an amount equal to the plan loan offset amount can be rolled over by the participant to an eligible retirement plan (see Q 34:16) within 60 days (see Q 34:34) unless the plan loan offset amount fails to be an eligible rollover distribution for another reason. [I.R.C. § 402(c); Treas. Reg. §§ 1.401(a)(31)-1, Q&A-16, 1.402(c)-2, Q&A-9; Priv. Ltr. Rul. 200617037]

> **Example 1.** In 2011, Dale has an account balance of $10,000 in Stu'N Dale Corporation's profit sharing plan, of which $3,000 is represented by a plan loan secured by her account balance. The plan does not provide any direct rollover option with respect to plan loans. Upon termination of employment in 2011, Dale, who is under age 70½, elects a distribution of her entire account balance, and her outstanding loan is offset against the account balance on distribution. Dale elects a direct rollover of $7,000. When Dale's account balance was offset by the amount of the $3,000 unpaid loan balance, she received a plan loan offset amount (equivalent to $3,000) that is an eligible rollover distribution. Dale may roll over $3,000 to an eligible retirement plan within 60 days.

> **Example 2.** The facts are the same as in Example 1, except that the plan provides that, upon termination of employment, Dale's account balance is

automatically offset by the amount of the unpaid loan balance. Dale terminates employment but does not request a distribution from the plan. The $3,000 offset amount attributable to the plan loan in this example is treated in the same manner as the $3,000 offset amount in Example 1.

Example 3. The facts are the same as in Example 2, except that, instead of providing for an automatic offset upon termination of employment, the plan requires full repayment of the loan by Dale within 30 days of termination. Dale terminates employment, does not elect a distribution from the plan, and also fails to repay the plan loan within 30 days. The plan declares the plan loan in default and executes on the loan by offsetting Dale's account balance by $3,000. The $3,000 offset amount in this example is treated in the same manner as the $3,000 offset amount in Examples 1 and 2. The result in this example is the same even though the plan treats the loan as in default before offsetting Dale's accrued benefit by the amount of the unpaid loan.

Example 4. Stuart, who is age 60, has an account balance in the Lori-Dana Corp. 401(k) plan. In 2008, Stuart made a plan loan that is secured by elective contributions, and, in 2011, Stuart stops repayment. In 2011, Stuart is taxed on a deemed distribution equal to the amount of the unpaid loan balance. The deemed distribution is *not* an eligible rollover distribution. Because Stuart has not separated from service or experienced any other event that permits the distribution of his elective contributions that secure the loan, the plan is prohibited from executing on the loan. Accordingly, Stuart's account balance is not offset by the amount of the unpaid loan balance at the time he stops repayment on the loan. Thus, there is no distribution of an offset amount that is an eligible rollover distribution in 2011. However, Stuart has basis (see Qs 13:3, 14:15) in his account balance to the extent of the deemed distribution. In 2012, Stuart separates from service and is eligible, and elects, to receive a total distribution of his account balance. As part of the distribution to Stuart, his account balance is offset by the amount of the unpaid loan balance. Although an offset amount can generally be part of an eligible rollover distribution, the portion of the distribution to Stuart that equals the amount of the prior deemed distribution will not be eligible for rollover because it is not includible in his gross income and also because the offset amount cannot be rolled over by means of a direct rollover.

Q 14:21 Are there any other requirements applicable to participant loans?

Yes. Another set of requirements must be met to prevent a loan to a participant from being subject to an excise tax. An excise tax is imposed on certain prohibited transactions (e.g., loans) between a plan and a disqualified person (see chapter 24 for details). However, an exemption is provided for any loan by a qualified retirement plan (see Q 14:2) to a participant who is a disqualified person (see Q 24:4) if the following requirements are met:

1. The loan must be available to all participants on a reasonably equivalent basis;

2. Loans must not be made available to highly compensated employees (see Q 3:2) in amounts greater than the amounts made available to other employees;

3. The loan must be made in accordance with specific provisions in the plan;

4. The loan must bear a reasonable rate of interest (see Q 1:17); and

5. The loan must be adequately secured.

[I.R.C. §§ 4975(c), 4975(d); ERISA § 408(b)(1); Rev. Rul. 89-14, 1989-1 C.B. 111]

DOL has advised that plan fiduciaries may reasonably interpret loan prohibitions implemented by the Sarbanes-Oxley Act of 2002 (see Q 1:24) to deny plan loans to officers and directors without violating their fiduciary duties or the requirement that loans be available to all participants on a reasonably equivalent basis. [DOL Field Assistance Bull. 2003-1]

One of the requirements is that the loan must be adequately secured. A loan will be considered to be adequately secured if the security posted for such loan is something in addition to and supporting a promise to pay, which is so pledged to the plan that it may be sold, foreclosed upon, or otherwise disposed of upon default of repayment of the loan, and the value and liquidity of the security is such that it may reasonably be anticipated that loss of principal or interest will not result from the loan. The adequacy of the security will be determined in light of the type and amount of security that would be required in the case of an otherwise identical transaction in a normal commercial setting between unrelated parties on arm's-length terms. A participant's vested accrued benefit (see Qs 9:1, 9:2) under a plan may be used as security for a participant loan to the extent of the plan's ability to satisfy the participant's outstanding obligation in the event of default. [DOL Reg. § 2550.408b-1(f)(1)] According to IRS, the loan may be secured by the participant's entire vested accrued benefit; but, according to the DOL, no more than one-half of the vested accrued benefit may be used to secure the loan. [I.R.C. § 401(a)(13)(A); Treas. Reg. § 1.401(a)-13(d)(2); DOL Reg. § 2550.408b-1(f)(2); DOL Op. Ltr. 89-30A]

> **Example.** Stephanie has a vested accrued benefit of $18,000 and borrows $10,000. Although the $10,000 loan satisfies the amount limitations (see Q 14:4) and is secured by Stephanie's vested accrued benefit, DOL requires that Stephanie post additional security of $1,000 because the $10,000 loan exceeds one-half of her vested accrued benefit of $9,000 ($18,000/2).

A loan may be both a deemed distribution (see Qs 14:1, 14:8) and a prohibited transaction so that the borrowing participant may be subject to both income tax and excise tax. [Geib, 80 T.C.M. 931 (2000); Medina, 112 T.C. 51 (1999)] A deemed distribution is not a correction of a prohibited transaction (see Q 24:6). [Treas. Reg. § 1.72(p)-1, Q&A-16]

Before sending a notice of deficiency with respect to the excise tax, IRS is required to notify DOL and provide DOL with a reasonable opportunity to obtain a correction of the prohibited transaction or to comment on the imposition of the excise tax. [I.R.C. § 4975(h)] An IRS notification to DOL informing it of a series of prohibited transactions was sufficient, even though IRS failed to identify all disqualified persons involved in the prohibited transactions. IRS concluded that each disqualified person need not be specifically named for the notice to be adequate. [Field Serv. Adv. 200113016]

Chapter 15

Life Insurance and Death Benefits

Although the primary purpose of a qualified retirement plan is to pay retirement benefits, the plan may also provide life insurance coverage for participants. This chapter examines the limits on life insurance coverage and the tax consequences of including insurance in a qualified retirement plan. A discussion of how death benefit payments by qualified retirement plans are taxed is also included.

Q 15:1 Must a qualified retirement plan provide a death benefit to participants?

Generally, a qualified retirement plan is not required to provide a death benefit with respect to employer contributions if the employee dies while a participant in the plan. However, in the case of married participants, a qualified retirement plan is required to provide a death benefit to the participant's surviving spouse unless an election and consent to waive such benefits have been made. [I.R.C. §§ 401(a)(11), 411(a)(3), 417(a)] One court ruled that a plan's prospective elimination of a death benefit for its participants did not violate the anti-cutback rule (see Q 9:25), because the death benefit was not an accrued benefit (see Q 9:2) or retirement-type subsidy (see Q 9:33) protected from elimination by the anti-cutback rule. [Kerber v. Qwest Pension Plan, 2009 WL 2096221 (10th Cir. 2009)]

For details on qualified preretirement survivor annuities (QPSAs) and qualified joint and survivor annuities (QJSAs), see chapter 10.

Q 15:2 May a qualified retirement plan provide life insurance coverage for participants?

Yes, but the primary purpose of a company's qualified retirement plan must be to pay retirement benefits to participants. Any life insurance coverage provided under the qualified retirement plan must be incidental to the provision of retirement benefits (see Q 15:4).

In November 1997, two IRS representatives questioned the acceptability of the acquisition by a qualified retirement plan of second-to-die insurance (e.g., a policy usually covering both the participant and the participant's spouse). This position was premised on two basic rules applicable to qualified retirement plans. The first is the exclusive benefit rule that requires qualified retirement plans to be maintained for the exclusive benefit of employees (see Q 4:1).

Under the IRS reasoning, maintaining life insurance on someone other than an employee violates this requirement. The second problem is the definitely determinable requirement that is applicable to pension plans (see Q 2:20; this requirement applies to all pension plans). The IRS representatives opined that maintaining life insurance on an individual other than a participant would be a violation of the definitely determinable requirement. [Rev. Rul. 69-523, 1969-2 C.B. 90]

The IRS representatives advised that the above prohibition also applies to profit sharing plans (see Q 2:6). Although the definitely determinable requirement does not apply to profit sharing plans, the exclusive benefit rule does. The reliance on Revenue Ruling 69-523 appears to be misplaced because a prior IRS revenue ruling and IRS regulations permit a profit sharing plan to provide incidental amounts of life, accident, and health insurance for a participant *or* his family with funds allocated to the participant's account. [Rev. Rul. 61-164, 1961-2 C.B. 99; Treas. Reg. § 1.401-1(b)(1)(ii)]

Whether defined benefit plans that include life insurance products may still use the traditional type of split-funded cost method will be discussed in future proposed regulations, according to IRS representatives. The representatives stated, however, that it is difficult to use this funding method because PPA (see Q 1:33) requires that the plan liabilities be valued using specific market rates of interest, while the cash value portion of the assets grows at insurance company valuation rates. Split-funding also uses a level funding method, spreading the cost over time, while PPA requires use of the unit credit method that is essentially a year-by-year type of funding. Thus, the typical model of a split-funded defined benefit plan with life insurance may disappear. It may be possible, however, to use the envelope funding method. With split-funding, a portion of the lump-sum benefit payable to a participant at retirement will be provided by the cash surrender value of the policy on the participant's life. In addition to the annual policy premium, an annual contribution to the plan (i.e., side fund) is made to fund the portion of the lump-sum benefit not provided by the policy. Under the envelope method, the annual cost is divided into two components—the death benefit cost and the retirement cost. The death benefit cost is calculated using plan actuarial assumptions in conformance with PPA, and is essentially the one-year term cost of the death benefit under the plan. The retirement cost is an annual contribution to the plan to fund the entire lump-sum benefit, again using PPA methods and assumptions. Because the actuarial cost under the envelope method is the sum of the two parts, the insurance premium is considered to be a part of the annual cost and not an addition to it. For example, if the one-year actuarial death benefit term cost is $20,000 and the PPA determined retirement cost is $50,000, the total required contribution is $70,000; however, if the insurance premium is $15,000, then $55,000 is contributed to the side fund.

See Q 15:13 for a discussion of the life insurance subtrust technique, and also see Q 15:21 for a further discussion of second-to-die insurance.

Q 15:3 Is a company allowed a deduction for life insurance purchased under a qualified retirement plan?

The portion of employer contributions to its qualified retirement plan that is used to purchase life insurance on behalf of plan participants is deductible. If the employer pays the life insurance premiums directly to the insurance company and reports the premium payments as plan contributions, the payments are deductible as plan contributions because the invoice for the premiums is to the plan, not to the employer, and it is a liability of the plan that is being satisfied by the employer's contribution.

However, if life insurance is provided under a qualified retirement plan for a self-employed individual (see Q 6:60), the cost of current life insurance protection (see Qs 15:6–15:8) is neither deductible nor considered as a contribution for purposes of determining the maximum amount of the contribution that may be made on behalf of an owner-employee (see Q 5:32). [I.R.C. § 404(e); Treas. Reg. § 1.404(e)-1A(g)]

See Q 15:13 for a discussion of the life insurance subtrust technique.

Q 15:4 What limits apply to the amount of life insurance that can be purchased for participants under a qualified retirement plan?

The basic restriction is that the amount of life insurance coverage must be incidental to the plan's retirement benefits. [Treas. Reg. § 1.401-1(b)(1)]

For a defined contribution plan (see Q 2:2), life insurance coverage is considered incidental if less than 50 percent of the company's contributions to the plan on behalf of the participant is used to purchase whole life insurance or no more than 25 percent is used to purchase term life insurance. [Rev. Rul. 54-51, 1954-1 C.B. 147; Rev. Rul. 57-213, 1957-1 C.B. 157; Rev. Rul. 60-83, 1960-1 C.B. 157; Rev. Rul. 66-143, 1966-1 C.B. 79; Rev. Rul. 76-353, 1976-2 C.B. 112; Priv. Ltr. Rul. 8725088] IRS has concluded that the limitation regarding term life insurance also applies to universal life insurance and that the entire premium is subject to the incidental test. [Field Serv. Adv. 1999633]

Although there is no limit if the life insurance is purchased with company contributions accumulated in a profit sharing plan for two years or longer (see Q 1:48), IRS has never officially addressed if doing so would cause the excess premium payment to be includible in the insured participant's income. The author understands that IRS withdrew a proposed letter to that effect; however, in November 2000, an IRS representative opined that the excess premium payment should be treated as a taxable distribution to the insured participant.

For a defined benefit plan (see Q 2:3), life insurance coverage is generally considered incidental if the amount of the insurance does not exceed 100 times the participant's projected monthly benefit. For example, if a participant can expect a $1,000 monthly benefit, life insurance coverage of up to $100,000 can be provided for the participant under the defined benefit plan. However, life insurance coverage may exceed the 100 times limit and still be considered incidental. [Rev. Rul. 60-83, 1960-1 C.B. 157; Rev. Rul. 61-121, 1961-2 C.B. 65; Rev. Rul. 68-31, 1968-1 C.B. 151; Rev. Rul. 68-453, 1968-2 C.B. 163; Rev. Rul. 74-307, 1974-2 C.B. 126] See Q 15:2 for a recent development concerning split-funded defined benefit plans.

The incidental limitations do not apply to life insurance purchased with voluntary employee contributions (see Q 1:50). [Rev. Rul. 69-408, 1969-2 C.B. 58]

Q 15:5 Does the purchase of life insurance affect retirement benefits?

If part of the company's contributions to its defined contribution plan (see Q 2:2) goes toward the purchase of life insurance coverage, there may be less available for participants at retirement. This will be so if the return on the investment in life insurance is less than the return on the trust fund investments. Although retirement benefits may be reduced, death benefits will be substantially increased.

Using company contributions to pay for life insurance under a defined benefit plan (see Q 2:3) does not affect the amount of a participant's retirement benefit. However, because participants are promised a fixed level of benefits at retirement, the company may have to increase its contributions to cover any shortfall in funding for those benefits resulting from the use of company contributions to pay insurance premiums.

Q 15:6 What are the tax consequences to participants when their employer's qualified retirement plan provides life insurance protection?

The tax law allows participants to postpone payment of income taxes on retirement benefits payable to them from a qualified retirement plan. Participants pay no tax until they receive those benefits. They do, however, incur some tax cost when their employer's qualified retirement plan provides life insurance protection. Because participants receive a present benefit—current life insurance protection—they must include the value of that benefit in their gross incomes for the year in which employer contributions or trust earnings are used to pay life insurance premiums.

A participant must pay tax on the term cost of insurance protection paid for with employer contributions or trust earnings if, upon death, the proceeds of the life insurance policy on the participant's life are payable to either (1) the participant's estate or beneficiary or (2) the trustee of the plan if the trustee is required by the plan's provisions to pay such proceeds to the participant's estate or beneficiary. [I.R.C. § 72(m)(3)(B); Treas. Reg. § 1.72-16(b)]

The amount included in a participant's gross income, which is determined under special IRS tables that contain the current life insurance protection costs (see Q 15:7), is often well below the premium paid by the plan for the insurance.

[IRS Notice 2002-8, 2002-1 C.B. 398 (revoking IRS Notice 2001-10, 2001-1 C.B. 459, which rendered obsolete Rev. Rul. 55-747, 1955-2 C.B. 228); Rev. Rul. 66-110, 1966-1 C.B. 12; Rev. Rul. 67-154, 1967-1 C.B. 11]

If a self-employed individual (see Q 6:60) is covered by a life insurance policy under a qualified retirement plan, the individual will not be taxed because the cost of the current life insurance protection is not deductible by the employer (see Q 15:3). [I.R.C. §§ 72(m)(3)(B), 404(e); Treas. Reg. § 1.404(e)-1A(g)]

Q 15:7   What is the cost of current life insurance protection?

IRS rulings set forth the method of calculating the amount of a participant's current taxable income as a result of receiving life insurance protection under a company's qualified retirement plan (see Q 15:6). [IRS Notice 2002-8, 2002-1 C.B. 398 (revoking IRS Notice 2001-10, 2001-1 C.B. 459, which rendered obsolete Rev. Rul. 55-747, 1955-2 C.B. 228); Rev. Rul. 66-110, 1966-1 C.B. 12; Rev. Rul. 67-154, 1967-1 C.B. 11]

The participant's current taxable amount may be determined by applying the one-year premium term rate (the Table 2001 rates) at the participant's age to the difference between the face amount of the policy and its cash surrender value at the end of the year.

The Table 2001 rates are set forth below:

**Interim Table of One-Year Term Premiums
for $1,000 of Life Insurance Protection**

Attained Age	Section 79 Extended and Interpolated Annual Rates	Attained Age	Section 79 Extended and Interpolated Annual Rates
0	$ 0.70	13	$ 0.28
1	0.41	14	0.33
2	0.27	15	0.38
3	0.19	16	0.52
4	0.13	17	0.57
5	0.13	18	0.59
6	0.14	19	0.61
7	0.15	20	0.62
8	0.16	21	0.62
9	0.16	22	0.64
10	0.16	23	0.66
11	0.19	24	0.68
12	0.24	25	0.71

Interim Table of One-Year Term Premiums
for $1,000 of Life Insurance Protection *(cont'd)*

Attained Age	Section 79 Extended and Interpolated Annual Rates	Attained Age	Section 79 Extended and Interpolated Annual Rates
26	$ 0.73	57	$ 5.20
27	0.76	58	5.66
28	0.80	59	6.06
29	0.83	60	6.51
30	0.87	61	7.11
31	0.90	62	7.96
32	0.93	63	9.08
33	0.96	64	10.41
34	0.98	65	11.90
35	0.99	66	13.51
36	1.01	67	15.20
37	1.04	68	16.92
38	1.06	69	18.70
39	1.07	70	20.62
40	1.10	71	22.72
41	1.13	72	25.07
42	1.20	73	27.57
43	1.29	74	30.18
44	1.40	75	33.05
45	1.53	76	36.33
46	1.67	77	40.17
47	1.83	78	44.33
48	1.98	79	49.23
49	2.13	80	54.56
50	2.30	81	60.51
51	2.52	82	66.74
52	2.81	83	73.07
53	3.20	84	80.35
54	3.65	85	88.76
55	4.15	86	99.16
56	4.68	87	110.40

**Interim Table of One-Year Term Premiums
for $1,000 of Life Insurance Protection** *(cont'd)*

Attained Age	Section 79 Extended and Interpolated Annual Rates	Attained Age	Section 79 Extended and Interpolated Annual Rates
88	$ 121.85	94	$ 206.70
89	133.40	95	228.35
90	144.30	96	250.01
91	155.80	97	265.09
92	168.75	98	270.11
93	186.44	99	281.05

Example. Keren, age 35, is a participant in her company's qualified retirement plan. The plan provides Keren with a life insurance policy in the face amount of $40,000. At year-end, the policy had a cash surrender value of $2,000. Keren must include $37.62 in her current taxable income ([[($40,000 + $2,000) × $.99] − 1,000).

Q 15:8   Must the Table 2001 rates be used to determine the cost of pure life insurance included in a participant's gross income?

No. If the insurance company's rates for individual one-year term policies available to all standard risks on an initial issue insurance basis are lower, the lower rates may be utilized. [Rev. Rul. 66-110, 1966-1 C.B. 12; Rev. Rul. 67-154, 1967-1 C.B. 11; Priv. Ltr. Rul. 9023044]

Participants may continue to determine the value of current life insurance protection by using the insurer's lower published premium rates that are available to all standard risks for initial issue one-year term insurance, subject to the following additional limitations. Before the effective date of future guidance, for periods after December 31, 2003, IRS will not consider an insurer's published premium rates to be available to all standard risks who apply for term insurance unless (1) the insurer generally makes the availability of such rates known to persons who apply for term insurance coverage from the insurer, and (2) the insurer regularly sells term insurance coverage through the insurer's normal distribution channels. [IRS Notice 2002-8, 2002-1 C.B. 398 (revoking IRS Notice 2001-10, 2001-1 C.B. 459)]

The rate tables published by the parent corporation of an insurance company that issued the policy could not be used because the parent corporation and the issuing company were not the same insurer and the parent corporation's rate tables were not available to all standard risks and were developed for five-year term insurance. [Priv. Ltr. Rul. 9452004] IRS has also ruled that an insurance company's rates could not be used because they were not the insurer's current published one-year initial issue individual term rates available to all standard risks. [Priv. Ltr. Rul. 199918060]

Q 15:9   Are loans from insurance policies purchased under qualified retirement plans taxable?

If a participant receives a loan from an insurance policy purchased under a qualified retirement plan (as well as any assignment or pledge of the policy), it is treated as a loan made from the plan.

Generally, such loans are not taxable. However, if the policy loan exceeds the Code limitations on loans from qualified retirement plans, the loan is treated as a taxable distribution to the participant. [I.R.C. §§ 72(p)(2), 72(p)(5)] See chapter 14 for details.

Q 15:10   Who receives the proceeds from life insurance purchased under a qualified retirement plan when a participant dies before retirement?

Generally, if a participant dies while working for the company, the proceeds from life insurance purchased under a qualified retirement plan will be paid to designated beneficiaries. [Kuhn v. Metropolitan Life Ins. Co., No. 5:98-cv-82 (W.D. Mich. 1999)] One court concluded that a designation of beneficiary form that contained numerous errors sufficiently showed a deceased plan participant's intent to change the beneficiary of his life insurance policy because he evidenced his intent to change beneficiaries and he undertook positive actions to effectuate the change. [Metropolitan Life Ins. Co. v. Johnson, 297 F.3d 558 (7th Cir. 2002); *but see* Metropolitan Life Ins. Co. v. Parker, 436 F.3d 1109 (9th Cir. 2006)] If the participant fails to designate a beneficiary or if the sole designated beneficiary predeceases the participant, the life insurance proceeds generally will be paid to the participant's estate in accordance with the provisions of the policy. When a widow named her daughter as beneficiary of a life insurance policy under her employer's profit sharing plan and subsequently remarried, the court ruled that the surviving spouse, and not the daughter, was entitled to the insurance proceeds. [Howard v. Branham & Baker Coal Co., 968 F.2d 1214 (6th Cir. 1992); *see also* Metropolitan Life Ins. Co. v. Clark, 2005 WL 3419998 (6th Cir. 2005)] An employee participated in a qualified retirement plan, the plan purchased a policy on his life, and he designated his wife as beneficiary. When the employee terminated employment with the company, he elected, with his wife's consent, to take a lump-sum payment of his benefits from the plan, which included the cash surrender value of the policy. The plan did not surrender the policy and never changed the beneficiary. After the former employee died, his wife, the plan, and the company all claimed that they were entitled to the policy proceeds. A settlement dividing the proceeds between the wife and the company was upheld, and the court concluded that the plan was not entitled to any portion of the proceeds. [I.R.M. Defined Benefit Pension v. U.S. Life Ins. Co., No. 95-2029 (4th Cir. 1996)] (See Qs 10:1 through 10:36 for a discussion of the automatic survivor annuity requirements and their effect on the participant's right to designate a beneficiary.)

Where a life insurance plan expressly allowed changes of beneficiary to be made with the insurance company on forms other than those supplied by the plan, and further provided that changes predating the insured's death could be filed posthumously, one court held that a deceased employee's will that specifically disposed of the insurance proceeds was a valid change of beneficiary and therefore excluded his ex-wife, even though he never filed a change of the original designation of his ex-wife as beneficiary. [Liberty Life Assurance Co. of Boston v. Kennedy, 2004 WL 205843 (11th Cir. 2004)] A decedent did not remove his ex-wife as the designated beneficiary of a life insurance policy after their divorce, even though the divorce decree designated the decedent's minor children as beneficiaries until they reached the age of majority. The ex-wife contended that she remained the designated beneficiary under the policy. The second wife countered that the divorce decree constituted a qualified domestic relations order (QDRO; see Q 36:1), and the court held that the decree was a QDRO since it named alternate payees (see Q 36:5) of the insurance proceeds. The court also concluded that the estate of the decedent was the appropriate beneficiary since the minor children replaced the ex-wife, the minor children's beneficiary status lapsed upon their majority, and thus the estate was the proper beneficiary under the terms of the policy in the absence of a designated beneficiary. [Seaman v. Johnson, 2004 U.S. App. LEXIS 4400 (6th Cir. 2004); see also Moore v. Estate of Moore, 2005 Mich. App. LEXIS 1055 (Mich. App., 2d Cir. 2005); The Guardian Life Ins. Co. of America v. Finch v. Galaway, 2004 U.S. App. LEXIS 26800 (5th Cir. 2004)]

If there is a death benefit under the plan (other than life insurance) and there is no designated beneficiary, the provisions of the plan will determine who will receive the death benefit. [Retirement Comm. of the Rouge Steel Tax Efficient Sav. Plan for Hourly Employees v. Cortese, No. 00-CV-71233 (E.D. Mich. 2000); Jensen v. Estate of McGowan, 697 P.2d 1380 (_____ 1985)] One court ruled that the death benefit could be paid to the persons designated by a deceased participant on an unsigned beneficiary designation form. [O'Shea v. First Manhattan Co. Thrift Plan & Trust, No. 94-9004 (2d Cir. 1995)] However, in another case, the court held otherwise because the participant, who was unaware of the missing signature, had not substantially complied with the beneficiary designation process. The court determined that the plan administrator (see Q 20:1) did not have the authority to waive the signature requirement. [Bank Am. Pension Plan v. McMath, No. C 97-3242 (N.D. Cal. 2000); Bank Am. Pension Plan v. McMath, 206 F.3d 821 (9th Cir. 2000)] In yet another case, where the participant executed an improper beneficiary designation form naming his son as beneficiary, the court held that the death benefit should be paid according to the terms of the plan (to the son and daughter) even though a plan representative had provided the wrong form. [Schmidt v. Sheet Metal Workers, 128 F.3d 541 (7th Cir. 1997)] A plan participant designated his stepdaughter as beneficiary by name and did not describe the relationship. The plan provided that any designation of a nonspouse beneficiary would be given effect if it included a description of the relationship between the participant and the beneficiary. The plan committee decided that the relationship designation was merely a formality to help locate a beneficiary, as opposed to a material omission, and determined that the participant's beneficiary designation was valid. The court concluded that the committee's determination on the validity of the participant's designation of his stepdaughter as beneficiary was reasonable, and should be upheld, based on the following five factors: (1) whether a plan administrator's interpretation of plan terms is reasonable; (2) whether any of the plan's terms are rendered inconsistent or meaningless by the plan administrator's interpretation; (3) whether the plan administrator's interpretation of plan terms would conflict with ERISA; (4) whether the terms at issue have been interpreted consistently; and (5) whether the plan administrator's interpretation is contrary to the plan's clear language. [Alliant Techsystem, Inc. 401(k) Plan v. Marks v. Irwin Bank & Trust, as Guardian of the Estate of Marier, No. 05-3614 (8th Cir. 2006)]

In a case in which a deceased participant had not removed the former spouse as the designated beneficiary, the court ruled that ERISA preempted a state statute that purported to nullify the former spouse's right to receive the death benefit, and the beneficiary designation remained effective. [Iron Workers Mid-S. Pensions Fund v. Stoll, No. 91-0513 (E.D. La. 1991)] Another court ruled that ERISA did not preempt a state statute that revoked the spouse's status as a beneficiary of nonprobate assets upon dissolution of the marriage. The court reasoned that the state statute had no effect on plan administration and did not frustrate the purposes of ERISA. [Egelhoff v. Egelhoff, 139 Wash. 2d 557 (1999)] However, the United States Supreme Court reversed and ruled that ERISA preempted the state statute because the statute had an impermissible connection to an ERISA plan. [Egelhoff v. Egelhoff, 532 U.S. 141 (2001)] In another case, on October 1, 1986, the interest of a participant in a company pension plan became vested (see Q 9:1), as did the interest of his wife as his designated beneficiary. In 1988, the plan was terminated; and, in order to satisfy its obligations to the participants, the plan purchased annuity contracts from an insurance company. The annuity contracts contained a provision permitting the annuitant to change the beneficiary designation. The decedent and his wife divorced in 1994 and entered into a settlement agreement whereby each waived any right to an interest in any pension plans, retirement plans, profit sharing plans, and so forth. At the time of the decedent's death in 2005, he had remarried but never changed the annuity beneficiary designation. His surviving spouse, as the executor of his estate, commenced an action against the former wife and the insurance company, claiming that the former wife had waived her interest in the annuity and that all payments should be made to the estate. The former wife contended that her rights in the plan vested on the date of the decedent's retirement, at which time she was still his wife and designated beneficiary, and that her interest was therefore non-assignable under ERISA (see Qs 4:27, 36:7). The estate contended that the annuity was a private contract governed by state law and that, under state law, the former wife had waived her interest in the annuity. The district court ruled in favor of the former wife, but the appellate court noted that ERISA permits the termination of a plan where the employer obligates itself to purchase annuities to provide the benefit the employee would have otherwise enjoyed under the plan. The court then held that the purchase of the annuities terminated the plan and that termination severed the applicability of ERISA. The dispute was thus to be determined pursuant to state law, and the case was remanded to the district court for adjudication of the estate's claims pursuant to state law. [Hallingby v. Hallingby, 574 F.3d 51 (2d Cir. 2009)]

An employee purchased annuity contracts and designated his first wife as beneficiary. The divorce decree made no reference to the contracts, and state law at the time of the divorce held that a former spouse's rights as an insurance beneficiary were not terminated by a divorce unless the divorce decree expressly provided otherwise. Between the dates of the employee's second marriage and his death, state law was changed to create a presumption directly opposite to that which previously existed. Under the new law, a divorce revoked any disposition of property made by a divorced individual to a former spouse unless the divorce decree expressly provided otherwise. Both wives claimed entitlement to the proceeds of the annuity contracts, and the court upheld the new law and ruled in favor of the second wife. [Stillman v. TIAA-CREF, No. 02-4020 (10th Cir. 2003)]

The United States Supreme Court has resolved a split of authority among the federal courts by unanimously concluding that (1) the waiver by a former spouse of a plan interest in a divorce decree that did not constitute a QDRO does not violate the anti-alienation rule (see Qs 4:27, 36:7) and (2) plan administrators are not required to honor waivers expressed in external documents that do not comply with plan terms and procedures governing beneficiary designations. As a consequence of the decision, a former spouse who attempted to waive her rights in a participant's plan account remained entitled to the benefits because the participant had not designated a new beneficiary prior to his death. [Kennedy v. Plan Administrator for DuPont Savings and Investment Plan, 129 S. Ct. 865 (2009)]

One court determined that the fact that a deceased participant designated his former wife as beneficiary of the death benefit under a qualified retirement plan did not change the designation of his mother as beneficiary for life insurance under an employee benefits plan because each plan provided different benefits payable upon the death of the participant with independent procedures for designating beneficiaries. [Steamship Trade Ass'n Int'l Longshoremen's Ass'n v. Bowman, No. 00-1907 (4th Cir. 2001)] Where a participant changed beneficiaries of his qualified retirement plan from his wife to others without spousal consent, the court determined that the participant's wife was entitled to his plan benefits. [Edelman v. Smith Barney, Inc., No. 98-Civ-691 (S.D.N.Y. 1999)] For more details, see Q 10:21.

Courts have concluded that a nonparticipant spouse who predeceased the participant spouse could not bequeath her community property interest in his pension plan to a third party. [Boggs v. Boggs, 520 U.S. 833 (1997); Albamis v. Rogers, 937 F.2d 1450 (9th Cir. 1991)]

Where an agent under a power of attorney improperly used the power to change the beneficiary of a qualified retirement plan death benefit, the court overturned the new beneficiary designation and reinstated the original beneficiary designation. [Taylor v. Kemper Fin. Servs. Co., 1999 U.S. Dist. LEXIS 14989 (N.D. Ill. 1999)] Another court ruled that a new beneficiary designation could be overturned and the original beneficiary designation reinstated if the change was made because of undue influence on the participant by the beneficiary. [Tinsley v. General Motors Corp., 227 F.3d 700 (6th Cir. 2000)]

A plan participant was married; and, when the couple separated, a formal judgment of separation was entered by a state court but no divorce decree was ever obtained. Some years later, after an interim second marriage, the participant married another woman and remained married to her until his death. Both the first and third wives applied for surviving spouse benefits under the plan. The court concluded that state law applied in determining who was the surviving spouse because the plan itself did not include a definition. The law of the participant's domicile at death was deemed controlling, and state law recognized the concept of putative marriage. A putative marriage is one that was entered into in good faith by at least one of the parties but is invalid by reason of an existing impediment on the part of one or both of the parties. Where such a marriage exists, the putative spouse has the same right to property acquired during the relationship as if she were the lawful spouse, and the court ruled in favor of the third wife. [Central States, Southeast & Southwest Areas Pension Fund v. Gray, No. 02 C 8381 (N.D. Ill. 2003)]

A plan participant removed his daughter as beneficiary of his retirement plan benefits and replaced her with another individual whom he described as attorney and executor. The court concluded that the new beneficiary was to receive the benefits in his personal capacity and not in his capacity as executor of the deceased participant's estate. [Duggins v. Fluor Daniel, Inc., 217 F.3d 317 (5th Cir. 2000)] One court ruled that, under the language of an employer's retirement plan, an executor of a deceased beneficiary's estate could not make a valid disclaimer of the deceased beneficiary's interest in a deceased participant's benefits under the plan. According to the court, the term "beneficiary" under the plan did not encompass a personal representative, executor, or administrator who disclaims on behalf of the beneficiary. Thus, the proceeds of the deceased's interest in the plan had to pass according to the plan. [Nickel v. Estate of Estes, 122 F.3d 294 (5th Cir. 1997)]

Where a husband and wife died simultaneously in an accident, one court determined that the husband's plan benefits should be paid to the wife's estate. The wife was designated as the primary beneficiary, and the plan document provided that the contingent beneficiary would receive the plan benefits only if the primary beneficiary died *before* the participant. Because they died simultaneously and it could not be proved who died first, the plan benefits became payable to the wife and not the contingent beneficiary. [Tucker v. Shreveport Transit Mgmt. Inc., 2000 WL 1224721 (5th Cir. 2000)]

The surviving spouse of a plan participant, who was receiving plan benefits, disappeared and was declared presumed dead 15 years later. After being apprised of her disappearance, the plan ceased benefit payments. The court ruled that the surviving spouse's estate was not entitled to any benefit payments after notification of her disappearance. [Estate of Cornwell v. AFL-CIO, 328 F.3d 672 (D.C. Cir. 2003)]

A plan participant designated his wife as primary beneficiary and his son as secondary beneficiary of any death benefit payable under the plan. The participant's wife was convicted in the death of her husband, which, under state law, precluded her from receiving the plan death benefit. The distribution of the death benefit to the son was includible in his gross income. [D.N. v. United States, 2009 WL 4781902 (D. Ore. 2009)]

Q 15:11   How are proceeds from life insurance purchased under a qualified retirement plan taxed for income tax purposes?

The amount of the proceeds that is equal to the cash surrender value of the policy is included in the beneficiary's gross income. Any proceeds in excess of the cash surrender value of the insurance policy are not subject to federal income tax. However, the beneficiary's taxable amount is reduced by the current life insurance protection costs that were included in the deceased participant's gross income during such participant's lifetime (see Qs 13:3, 15:6, 15:7; the current life insurance protection costs are treated as a tax-free return of the participant's investment). [Treas. Reg. § 1.72-16(b)] If the proceeds are also subject to estate tax (see Q 15:12), the beneficiary will be entitled to an income tax deduction for the estate tax attributable to the proceeds. [I.R.C. § 691(c); Field Serv. Adv. 200011023; *see also* Priv. Ltr. Rul. 200444021]

If the participant's surviving spouse receives the proceeds, payment of income tax may be postponed by rolling over the taxable amount of the proceeds to an IRA or to a qualified retirement plan in which the surviving spouse participates. In that case, the surviving spouse will not incur income tax liability until withdrawals are made from the IRA or from the plan. For details on rollovers, see chapter 34.

If all of the benefits payable under the qualified retirement plan—including the life insurance proceeds—are distributed within one taxable year, the recipient may be able to elect forward averaging income tax treatment for the entire distribution. See chapter 13 for more details.

Q 15:12   Are proceeds from life insurance purchased under a qualified retirement plan included in the participant's estate for tax purposes?

Yes. Life insurance proceeds (and other death benefits) paid under a qualified retirement plan are included in the participant's gross estate. [I.R.C. § 2039] See Q 15:13 for a discussion of the life insurance subtrust technique.

Q 15:13   Does a retirement plan fail to qualify because it contains an irrevocable subtrust feature relating to insurance policies on the life of a participant?

The use of the subtrust technique entails creating an irrevocable life insurance subtrust within a qualified retirement plan (i.e., within the plan's master trust). The insured participant is usually the owner or majority owner of the entity (plan sponsor) establishing the retirement plan. The participant surrenders all rights to change the beneficiary of the policy by making an irrevocable beneficiary designation of the special trustee of the subtrust, and the plan is amended to deny the participant the right to have the policy distributed at retirement. Ownership of the policy is then transferred to the special trustee, and the participant then has no control over the policy. The purpose of the subtrust is to purchase an insurance policy on the participant's life, using deductible plan contributions, and having the insurance proceeds be excludable from the participant's estate for estate tax purposes. [I.R.C. §§ 2037, 2039, 2042] Although many practitioners believed that using the subtrust technique would disqualify the plan, many others did not. In a yet-to-be-published technical advice memorandum (TAM), IRS attacks the subtrust technique on plan qualification grounds.

Facts

The plan, a defined benefit plan (see Q 2:3), was established in 1972; and the plan sponsor resolved to terminate the plan as of December 31, 1996, at which time the sole owner of the plan sponsor was the sole plan participant ("A"). A's daughter had also been a participant, but she had received her benefit some years prior to the proposed termination date.

A was approximately age 51 when the plan was established; normal retirement age (see Q 10:55) under the plan is age 55; and A was approximately age 76 as of the proposed termination date.

Under the plan, the accrued benefit (see Q 9:2) of a participant who remains active beyond the normal retirement age will be increased according to a formula set forth in the plan document. The plan also provides that a participant may elect to commence benefits in any one of three optional forms. One such form is a segregation of the actuarial equivalent of the accrued benefit into a separate account within the plan's trust. The funds in the separate account are invested at the direction of the plan's trustees and are credited or charged with investment gains and losses. Upon subsequent retirement or death, the value of the separate account will be distributed, either as a lump-sum payment or in installments. The plan provides that, in the absence of a participant's written designation to the contrary, the designated beneficiary will be the participant's surviving spouse.

When A was approximately age 74, he elected to have his accrued benefit segregated into a separate account, which was then credited with all the funds then held within the plan.

In 1995, the plan was amended. One amendment increased the level of death benefits payable with respect to participants who died prior to the commencement of benefits. The other amendment added a subtrust feature to the plan. Prior to the 1995 amendments, the only death benefit provided under the plan was the payment of the accrued benefit to the beneficiary of a participant who died prior to commencement of benefits (subject to the survivor annuity requirements; see Q 10:9). The 1995 amendments provided for the purchase of insurance on the life of A, in a face amount not to exceed 100 times the projected monthly normal retirement benefit or such amounts as would satisfy the $66^2/_3\%/33^1/_3\%$ rule based on the theoretical individual level premium reserve (see Q 15:4). IRS commented that it was unclear whether the trustee was actually required to obtain coverage equal to the greater of the two amounts. Thus, it was uncertain whether the amount of insurance coverage under the plan was definitely determinable. If benefits are not definitely determinable, the plan would not be qualified (see Q 15:2).

The 1995 amendments also provided that all policies purchased on the life of A were nontransferable, other than to A himself, and that the benefit payable on A's death before commencement of benefits would be equal to the sum of:

1. The QJSA;
2. The proceeds of insurance policies maintained on A's life; and
3. The actuarial equivalent of the accrued benefit, reduced by the sum of (a) the actuarial equivalent of the QJSA and (b) the cash value of the insurance policies.

Both before and after the 1995 amendments, the only provision made by the plan regarding death benefits of participants who had already commenced receiving their retirement benefits were those incorporated into the particular benefit option chosen by the participant (e.g., the survivor benefit under a QJSA; see Q 10:8).

Regarding the subtrust feature, the plan, as amended, provided that, notwithstanding any of its other provisions, all insurance policies purchased on A's life would be owned by named special trustees; and, in the event of A's death, the special trustees would administer the policy proceeds in accordance with a specified irrevocable trust agreement. Under other specified circumstances, the special trustees could sell the policies to A at a cost equal to their then cash values or, if greater, their interpolated terminal reserves (see Q 15:21).

The amended plan stated that the trustees could not distribute the policies on A's life to him as partial or full payment of his benefits and could not convert the policies into annuities providing benefits to him. The amended plan further stated that the cash values of the policies could not be used to provide benefits to A during his lifetime. The amended plan precluded further amendments or modifications in any way to the new provisions addressing the insurance policies on A's life.

In September 1995, the plan purchased an insurance policy on A's life. In December 1996, A created the specified irrevocable life insurance trust for the benefit of his wife and descendants. The plan provided that any insurance proceeds collected by the special trustees would thereafter be administered in accordance with the terms of the insurance trust. The trust granted the wife a right to the greater of 5 percent of the insurance proceeds or $5,000, plus any investment earnings on the insurance proceeds. The special trustees could, at their discretion, pay out more to A's wife, if they deemed higher amounts to be appropriate. The trustees would distribute the trust funds, at the death of the later to die of A and his wife, to A's children and grandchildren.

In 1996, A's separate account, other than the insurance policy, was transferred to an IRA.

Applicable Law

A plan will be qualified only if under the trust instrument it is impossible, at any time prior to the satisfaction of all liabilities with respect to employees and their beneficiaries, for any part of the corpus or income to be used for, or diverted to, purposes other than the exclusive benefit of the employees or their beneficiaries (see Q 4:1). [I.R.C. § 401(a)(2)]

A qualified plan is prohibited from discriminating in favor of highly compensated employees (HCEs; see Qs 3:2, 4:10–4:21). [I.R.C. § 401(a)(4)]

Under any defined benefit plan, the accrued benefit payable to a participant who has not died prior to the annuity starting date (see Q 10:3) must be paid in the form of a QJSA. There are certain exceptions to this requirement. In particular, a participant may elect to waive the QJSA; however, such election is valid only if the participant's spouse consents to such election (see Qs 10:20, 10:21). [I.R.C. §§ 401(a), 417(a)]

A qualified plan is prohibited from providing for the alienation or assignment of benefits provided under the plan. Alienation or assignment includes any arrangement (direct or indirect, revocable or irrevocable) whereby a party acquires from a participant a right or interest enforceable against the plan in any part of a plan benefit payment that is, or may become, payable to the participant (see Q 4:27). [I.R.C. § 401(a)(13)]

There are rules regarding the transfer of assets or liabilities from one plan to another (see Q 9:55). [I.R.C. § 414(*l*)]

A trust forming part of a retirement plan will constitute a qualified trust only if it is part of a retirement plan established by an employer for the exclusive benefit of the employees or their beneficiaries. [Treas. Reg. § 1.401-1(a)(3)] The term "beneficiaries" includes the estate of the employee, dependents of the employee, persons who are the natural objects of the employee's bounty, and any persons designated by the employee to share in the benefits of the plan after the death of the employee. [Treas. Reg. § 1.401-1(b)(4)]

A retirement plan is a plan established and maintained by an employer primarily to provide systematically for the payment of definitely determinable benefits to the employees over a period of years, usually for life, after retirement. A retirement plan may provide for the payment of a benefit due to disability and may also provide for the payment of incidental death benefits through insurance or otherwise. However, a plan is not a retirement plan if it provides for the payment of benefits not customarily included in a retirement plan. [Treas. Reg. § 1.401-1(b)(1)(i)]

The nondiscrimination requirements must be satisfied by both the form and operation of the plan. All benefits, rights, and features provided under the plan must be made available in the plan in a nondiscriminatory manner; and certain rules are used in testing whether all benefits, rights, and features under a plan are being provided in a nondiscriminatory manner. All benefits, rights, and features provided under a plan must satisfy both a current availability test and an effective availability test. [Treas. Reg. §§ 1.401(a)(4)-1(a), 1.401(a)(4)-1(b)(3), 1.401(a)(4)-4] See Q 4:20 for details.

Rules, in question-and-answer format, are provided for the survivor annuity requirements (see Q 10:1). Separate accounts under defined benefit plans are subject to the survivor annuity requirements. Even if the plan's assets are invested in one trust, more than one plan will exist if a portion of the assets is not available to pay some of the benefits. [Treas. Reg. §§ 1.401(a)-20, Q&A-15, 1.414(*l*)-1(b)(i)]

A retirement plan will fail to be qualified if it contains a provision permitting a participant to irrevocably elect, prior to retirement, to have all or part of his or her nonforfeitable interest in the plan, which would otherwise become payable to the participant during his or her lifetime, paid only to the participant's designated beneficiary after the participant's death. [Rev. Rul. 56-656, 1956-2 C.B. 280] The stated rationale for this holding was the belief that payments to persons other than the participant should be merely incidental to the plan's purpose of distributing benefits to the participant.

Analysis

The general issue raised by the IRS Area Office is whether the subtrust feature causes the plan to fail qualification. The IRS Area Office proposes that the subtrust feature causes such a failure because:

1. It violates the exclusive benefit requirement;
2. It violates the survivor annuity requirements; and
3. It creates a prohibited assignment or alienation.

Before proceeding with its analysis, IRS noted that there was a question as to whether the very purchase of the insurance policy covering A's life caused the plan to become disqualified in September 1995. On the one hand, the plan permits the trustees to make investments in insurance policies; but, on the other hand, the plan (as amended by the 1995 Amendments) states that, if insurance is purchased on behalf of a participant, the new provisions govern the amount of death benefit payable upon the death of the participant. The latter plan provision addresses death benefits only in the context of participants who die prior to the commencement of their benefit. At the time the insurance policy covering A's life was purchased, his benefit had already been segregated into a separate account; and, under the terms of the plan, this segregation was a commencement of his benefit.

Thus, IRS saw a question as to whether A was eligible to receive insurance coverage afforded by the policy that was purchased in September 1995. If A was not so eligible, then the plan operated in violation of its terms and failed of qualification as of September 1995. Because the IRS Area Office has not asked the IRS National Office to opine on this question and in view of the various other issues to be discussed below, IRS proceeded under the assumption that the purchase of the insurance policy in September 1995 was not a disqualifying event.

Regarding the question of compliance with survivor annuity requirements, IRS noted that the terms of the irrevocable life insurance trust did not require that all its assets be distributed to A's spouse (and, indeed, the special trustees could limit distributions to the spouse even if against her wishes). Thus, the use of funds in the segregated account to purchase the insurance policy (the proceeds of which must be distributed in accordance with the terms of the trust) would have required spousal consent. If the plan failed to secure such consent, then it would be a violation of the survivor annuity requirements.

IRS noted that the parties who would benefit from the insurance proceeds are the spouse and heirs of A. Because these persons are the natural objects of A's bounty, IRS was not inclined to consider this a prohibited assignment or alienation. However, IRS did recognize that the terms of the subtrust prohibited the cash value of the insurance policy from being used to provide any benefits to A during his lifetime.

Aside from the issues raised by the IRS Area Office, the subtrust feature causes the plan to fail qualification for two additional reasons: (i) failing to satisfy the nondiscrimination requirements and (ii) failing to satisfy the incidental death benefit requirement.

The subtrust feature applies only to A, who is an HCE. The restriction of the subtrust feature to A, to the exclusion of any other participant who might be covered under the plan, causes the plan to make the feature effectively available on a basis that substantially favors a particular HCE. As such, the plan fails to satisfy the nondiscrimination requirements and, as a result, fails qualification even in the absence of any other issue discussed in the TAM.

The subtrust feature causes the plan to violate the incidental benefit requirement because the plan prevents the cash value of the insurance policy from being used to provide benefits to A during his lifetime. Such a provision is not a benefit within the intendment of a qualified retirement plan. Thus, the plan violates the requirement that death benefits be incidental and, as a result of this violation, fails qualification even in the absence of any other issue discussed in the TAM.

One of the 1995 Amendments provided that no amendment could be made to the plan that had the effect of causing assets or income of the plan to be used for purposes other than for the exclusive benefit of participants and beneficiaries. The exclusive benefit requirement has never been interpreted to mean that the provision of retirement benefits is the only permissible purpose of a retirement plan. In addition to retirement benefits, a plan is permitted to provide death benefits (through insurance or otherwise). Thus, although IRS found that the subtrust feature caused the plan to violate various qualification requirements, the exclusive benefit requirement is not one of the violated requirements.

A plan is a single plan only if all of its assets are available to pay all of the benefits under the plan. More than one plan will exist if a portion of plan assets is not available to pay some of the benefits. Thus, in the instant case, the purchase of an insurance policy on A's life, along with the plan provision that prevents the cash value of that policy from being used to provide benefits to him during his lifetime, caused the plan to cease being a single plan. Consequently, the subtrust cannot be viewed as being a part of the plan. Furthermore, because the cash value of the insurance policy cannot be used to benefit A during his lifetime, the only benefit provided to him under the subtrust is life insurance protection. Thus, the subtrust cannot be a qualified plan. Accordingly, IRS takes the view that the purchase of the insurance policy using funds in A's separate account constituted a taxable distribution of those funds, which distribution took place in September 1995.

Conclusion

A plan will fail qualification if it contains an irrevocable subtrust feature as described in the TAM. IRS concluded that the plan does contain such a feature; and, accordingly, IRS concluded that the plan has failed qualification.

In addition, IRS concluded that the plan's subtrust feature causes the plan to fail to satisfy the requirement that death benefits be incidental to the plan's primary purpose of providing retirement benefits. The plan also fails of qualification because it discriminates in favor of HCEs. IRS also concluded that the exclusive benefit rule was not violated. Finally, IRS concluded that, given the provisions of the plan regarding the purchase of insurance policies on A's life, the use of funds in his separate account for this purpose constituted a distribution that is taxable to him.

Although the TAM considered a subtrust contained in a defined benefit plan, the author believes that many of the conclusions reached by IRS are equally applicable to subtrusts contained in defined contribution plans (see Q 2:2).

Q 15:14 Can a participant recover the cost of current life insurance protection tax free when qualified retirement plan benefits are distributed?

Yes. When an insurance policy purchased under a qualified retirement plan is distributed to a participant who had reported the cost of current life insurance protection as income (see Q 15:6), the total current life insurance protection costs that were included in gross income can be recovered tax free from the benefits received under the plan (see Q 13:3). However, these costs can be recovered only if the original insurance policy is distributed to the employee. If the life insurance is surrendered and the cash value and investment fund are used to purchase an annuity, the current life insurance protection costs are not part of the participant's cost for the annuity because the benefits will not be provided under the same contract. In addition, if the policy is surrendered by the plan's trustee and the cash surrender value is distributed to the participant, the participant's current life insurance protection costs are not recoverable. However, if the participant elects an annuity settlement option under the original policy, the current life insurance protection costs are recoverable. [I.R.C. § 72; Treas. Reg. § 1.72-16(b); Rev. Rul. 67-336, 1967-2 C.B. 66]

The amount distributed by a qualified retirement plan to a participant is taxable in the year of distribution (see Q 13:1). If property is distributed to the participant, the amount includible in the participant's gross income is the fair market value of the property. A life insurance policy constitutes property, and the participant must include in gross income the cash value of the policy at the time of distribution. The reserve accumulation in a life insurance policy constitutes the source of and approximates the amount of such cash value.

A participant who receives an insurance policy as a distribution from a qualified retirement plan uses the stated cash surrender value of the policy as its fair market value for purposes of determining the amount includible in income. However, this practice is not appropriate where the total policy reserves, including life insurance reserves (if any), together with any reserves for advance premiums, dividend accumulations, etc., represent a much more accurate approximation of the fair market value of the policy than does the policy's stated cash surrender value.

Example. Harvey is a participant in the Fran Electric Supply Corp. defined benefit plan. On January 1, 2004, $400,000 of plan assets were used to purchase an insurance policy on Harvey's life, and the policy was distributed to Harvey on January 1, 2006, two years after the date of purchase. The policy provides a stated cash surrender value for each of the first five policy years, as set forth in the table below. The total end-of-year reserves held by the insurance company for the policy also are set forth in the table.

Year	Surrender Value	Reserves
1	$106,000	$406,949
2	112,360	426,597
3	119,012	447,052
4	126,248	468,178
5	489,908	489,908

As the total reserves for the policy at the end of year two, $426,597, substantially exceed the policy's cash surrender value, $112,360, the reserves represent a much more accurate approximation of the fair market value of the policy when distributed than does the policy's cash surrender value. Accordingly, the amount includible in Harvey's gross income by reason of the distribution of the policy at the end of year two is the $426,597 reserve, not the $112,360 stated cash surrender value at that date.

In the case of a distribution in excess of Harvey's accrued benefit (see Q 9:2) resulting from valuing the policy at $112,360 rather than $426,597, the distribution would not be treated as a distribution to Harvey from a qualified retirement plan and, depending upon the facts and circumstances of the case, could be treated as a reversion to the employer (see Q 25:52). Such a distribution could also disqualify the plan because a number of qualification issues are raised.

[I.R.C. §§ 72, 402(a), 807(d); Treas. Reg. §§ 1.72-16(c)(2)(ii), 1.402(a)-1(a)(1)(iii), 1.402(a)-1(a)(2); IRS Notice 89-25, 1989-1 C.B. 662, Q&A-10; Ann. 95-99, 1995-48 I.R.B. 10]

IRS has issued guidance addressing abuses in the use of insurance-funded defined benefit plans. For details, see Qs 15:15–15:17.

Q 15:15   What is the value of a life insurance policy?

Generally, any amount actually distributed by a qualified retirement plan is taxable to the distributee in the taxable year of the distributee in which distributed. [I.R.C. §§ 72, 402(a)] The current regulations provide, in general, that a distribution of property by a plan is taken into account by the distributee at its fair market value and that, upon the distribution of an annuity or life insurance contract, the entire cash value of the contract must be included in the distributee's income. Prior to August 29, 2005, the regulations did not define "fair market value" or "entire cash value," and questions arose regarding the interaction between these two provisions and whether entire cash value included a reduction for surrender charges.

PTCE 92-6 (see Q 15:21) permits a qualified retirement plan to sell individual life insurance contracts and annuities to various individuals and entities for the cash surrender value of the contracts, provided certain conditions are met. The preamble to the predecessor of PTCE 92-6 notes that, for federal income tax purposes, the value of an insurance policy is not the same as, and may exceed, its cash surrender value, and that a purchase of an insurance policy at its cash surrender value may therefore be a purchase of property for less than its fair market value. The regulations did not address the consequences of a sale of property by a plan to a plan participant or beneficiary for less than the fair market value of that property. In this regard, the preamble states that the federal income tax consequences of such a bargain purchase must be determined in accordance with generally applicable federal income tax rules but that any income realized by a participant or relative of such participant upon such a purchase under the conditions of the PTCE will not be deemed a distribution from the plan to such participant for qualified retirement plan purposes.

IRS has finalized proposed amendments to the existing regulations to clarify that the requirement that a distribution of property must be included in the distributee's income at fair market value is controlling in those situations where the existing regulations provide for the inclusion of the entire cash value. Thus, the final regulations provide that, in those cases where a qualified retirement plan distributes a life insurance contract, retirement income contract, endowment contract, or other contract providing insurance protection, the fair market value of such a contract (i.e., the value of all rights under the contract, including any supplemental agreements thereto and whether or not guaranteed) is generally included in the distributee's income and not merely the entire cash value of the contract. [Treas. Reg. §§ 1.402(a)-1(a)(1)(iii), 1.402(a)-1(a)(2)] The final regulations also provide that if a plan transfers property to a participant or beneficiary for consideration that is less than the fair market value of the property, the transfer will be treated as a distribution by the plan to the participant or beneficiary to the extent the fair market value of the distributed property exceeds the amount received in exchange. Thus, in contrast to the statement to the contrary in the preamble to the PTCE, any bargain element in the sale would be treated as a distribution under Section 402(a). It is also intended that any bargain element would be treated as a distribution for other purposes of the Code, including the limitations on in-service distributions from certain plans (see Q 10:58) and the limitations of Section 415 (see Q 6:11). In a case that arose before the finalization of the proposed amendments, the court concluded that the bargain element of the sale of a life insurance policy to the insured plan participant represented taxable income and that the value of the policy was its entire cash value without reduction for surrender charges. [Matthies, 134 T.C. No. 6 (2010)]

As noted above, for these purposes, fair market value was not defined. In a prior ruling, IRS ruled that, in situations similar to those in which an employer purchases and pays the premiums on an insurance policy on the life of one of its employees and subsequently sells such policy (on which further premiums must be paid), the value of such policy for computing taxable gain in the year of purchase should be determined under the method of valuation prescribed in the gift tax regulations. [Treas. Reg. § 25.2512-6] Under this method, the value of such a policy is not its cash surrender value but the interpolated terminal reserve at the date of sale plus the proportionate part of any premium paid by the employer prior to the date of the sale which is applicable to a period subsequent to the date of the sale. The gift tax regulations also provide that if because of the unusual nature of the contract such approximation is not reasonably close to the full value, this method may not be used. Thus, this method may not be used to determine the fair market value of an insurance policy where the reserve does not reflect the value of all of the relevant features of the policy.

In IRS Notice 89-25, IRS addressed the question of what amount is includible in income where a participant receives a distribution from a qualified retirement plan that includes a life insurance policy with a value substantially higher than the cash surrender value stated in the policy (see Q 15:14). The Notice noted the practice of using cash surrender value as fair market value for these purposes and concluded that this practice is not appropriate where the total policy reserves, including life insurance reserves (if any), together with any reserves for advance premiums, dividends accumulations, etc., represent a much more accurate approximation of the policy's fair market value. Since the Notice was issued, life insurance contracts have been marketed that are structured in a manner that results in a temporary period during which neither a contract's reserves nor its cash surrender value represent the fair market value of the contract. For example, some life insurance contracts may provide for large surrender charges and other charges that are not expected to be paid because they are expected to be eliminated or reversed in the future (under the contract or under another contract for which the first contract is exchanged), but this future elimination or reversal is not always reflected in the calculation of the contract's reserve. If such a contract is distributed prior to the elimination or reversal of those charges, both the cash surrender value and the reserve under the contract could significantly understate the fair market value of the contract. Thus, in some cases, it would not be appropriate to use either the net surrender value (i.e., the contract's cash value after reduction for any surrender charges) or, because of the unusual nature of the contract, the contract's reserves to determine the fair market value of the contract. Accordingly, the Notice should not be interpreted to provide that a contract's reserves (including life insurance reserves, if any, together with any reserves for advance premiums, dividend accumulations, etc.) are always an accurate representation of the contract's fair market value.

For example, it would not be appropriate to use a contract's reserve or the net surrender value of the contract as fair market value at the time of distribution if under that contract those amounts are significantly less than the aggregate of: (1) the premiums paid from the date of issue through the date of distribution, plus (2) any amounts credited (or otherwise made available) to the policyholder with respect to those premiums (including interest, dividends, and similar income items), or, in the case of variable contracts, all adjustments made with respect to the premiums paid during that period that reflect investment return and the current market value of segregated asset accounts, minus (3) reasonable mortality charges and reasonable charges (other than mortality charges) actually charged from the date of issue to the date of distribution and expected to be paid. The following example provides an illustration of a contract where it would not be appropriate to use a contract's reserve or its net surrender value as its fair market value.

> **Example.** Casey participates in a qualified retirement plan. In Year 1, the plan acquires a life insurance contract on Casey's life that is not a variable contract and has a face amount of $1,400,000. In that year and for the next four years, the plan pays premiums of $100,000 per year on the contract. The contract provides for a surrender charge that is fixed for the first five years of the contract and decreases ratably to zero at the end of ten years. The contract also imposes reasonable mortality and other charges. The contract provides a stated cash surrender value for each of the first ten years (the first five years are guaranteed), as set forth in the table below. The reserves under the contract, including life insurance reserves and reserves for advance premiums, dividend accumulations, etc., at the end of the fifth year are $150,000.

Year	Premium	Net Surrender Value	Cash Value Determined Without Reduction for Surrender Charges
1	$100,000		
2	100,000		
3	100,000		
4	100,000		
5	100,000	$100,000	$450,000
6		195,000	475,000
7		290,000	500,000
8		385,000	525,000
9		480,000	550,000
10		575,000	575,000

At the end of Year 5, Casey retired and received a distribution of the insurance contact that was purchased on his life. The proposed regulations clarify that the contract is included in Casey's income at its fair market value rather than the $100,000 net surrender value. Furthermore, Casey could not treat the $150,000 reserve as of the end of the fifth year as the fair market value, because this amount is less than the amount a willing buyer would pay a willing seller for such a contract, with neither party being under a compulsion to buy and sell and both having reasonable knowledge of the relevant facts.

IRS recognized that taxpayers could have difficulty determining the fair market value of a life insurance contact after the clarification that IRS Notice 89-25 should not be interpreted to provide that a contract's reserves (including life insurance reserves, if any, together with any reserves for advance premiums, dividend accumulations, etc.) are always an accurate representation of the contract's fair market value. In connection with this guidance, the IRS issued a revenue procedure that provided interim rules under which the cash value (without reduction for surrender charges) of a life insurance contract distributed from a qualified retirement plan could be treated as the fair market value of that contract. After receiving many comments concerning the safe harbors set forth in that revenue procedure, IRS determined that adjustments to the safe harbors were appropriate, issued a new revenue procedure, and superseded the prior revenue procedure. [Rev. Proc. 2005-25, 2005-1 C.B. 962]

Safe Harbor Formulas for Fair Market Value. The revenue procedure provides two safe harbor formulas that, if used to determine the value of an insurance contract, retirement income contract, endowment contract, or other contract providing life insurance protection that is distributed or otherwise transferred from a qualified retirement plan, will meet the definition of fair market value.

Safe Harbor for Non-Variable Contracts. The fair market value of an insurance contract, retirement income contract, endowment contract, or other contract providing life insurance protection may be measured as the greater of:

A. The sum of the interpolated terminal reserve and any unearned premiums plus a pro rata portion of a reasonable estimate of dividends expected to be paid for that policy year based on company experience, and

B. The product of the PERC amount (the amount described below based on premiums, earnings, and reasonable charges) and the applicable average surrender factor also described below.

The PERC amount is the aggregate of:

1. The premiums paid from the date of issue through the valuation date without reduction for dividends that offset those premiums, plus

2. Dividends applied to purchase paid-up insurance prior to the valuation date, plus

3. Any amount of credit (or otherwise made available) to the policyholder with respect to premiums, including interest and similar income items (whether credited or made available under the contract or to some other account), but not including dividends used to offset premiums and dividends used to purchase paid-up insurance, minus

4. Explicit or implicit reasonable mortality charges and reasonable charges (other than mortality charges), but only if those charges are actually charged on or before the valuation date and those charges are not expected to be refunded, rebated, or otherwise reversed at a later date, minus

5. Any distributions (including distributions of dividends and dividends held on account), withdrawals, or partial surrenders taken prior to the valuation date.

Safe Harbor for Variable Contracts. If the insurance contract, retirement income contract, endowment contract, or other contract providing insurance protection being valued is a variable contract, the fair market value may be measured as the greater of:

A. The sum of the interpolated terminal reserve and any unearned premiums plus a pro rata portion of a reasonable estimate of dividends expected to be paid for that policy year based on company experience, and

B. The product of the variable PERC amount (the amount described below based on premiums, earnings, and reasonable charges) and the applicable average surrender factor.

The variable PERC amount is the aggregate of:

1. The premiums paid from the date of issue through the valuation date without reduction for dividends that offset those premiums, plus

2. Dividends applied to increase the value of the contract (including dividends used to purchase paid-up insurance) prior to the valuation date, plus or minus

3. All adjustments (whether credited or made available under the contract or some other account) that reflect the investment return and the market value of segregated asset accounts, minus

4. Explicit or implicit reasonable mortality charges, but only if those charges are actually charged on or before the valuation date and those charges are not expected to be refunded, rebated, or otherwise reversed at a later date, minus

5. Any distributions (including distributions of dividends and dividends held on account), withdrawals, or partial surrenders taken prior to the valuation date.

Average Surrender Factor. In the case of a distribution or sale from a qualified retirement plan, if the contract provides for explicit surrender charges, the average surrender factor is the unweighted average of the applicable surrender factors over the ten years beginning with the policy year of the distribution or sale. For this purpose, the applicable surrender factor for a policy year is equal to the greater of (1) 0.70 or (2) a fraction, the numerator of which is the projected amount of cash that would be available if the policy were surrendered on the first day of the policy year (or, in the case of the policy year of the distribution or sale, the amount of cash that was actually available on the first day of that policy year) and the denominator of which is the projected (or actual) PERC amount as of that same date. The applicable surrender factor for a year in which there is no surrender charge is 1.00. A surrender charge is permitted to be taken into account only if it is contractually specified at issuance and expressed in the form of nonincreasing percentages or amounts.

Application of Safe Harbor Formulas. The safe harbors must be interpreted in a reasonable manner, consistent with the purpose of identifying the fair market value of a contract. Thus, for example, if income is calculated with respect to premiums paid under the contract, that amount must be included in item 3 of the formulas, even if the income can be realized only through an exchange right that gives rise to a springing cash value under another policy. Similarly, if a mortality charge or other amount charged under a contract can be expected to be directly or indirectly returned to the contract holder (whether through the contract, a supplemental agreement, or under a verbal understanding and regardless of whether there is a guarantee), the charge is not permitted to be subtracted under item 4 in the formulas. In addition, a surrender charge cannot be taken into account in determining an average surrender factor if it may be waived or otherwise avoided or was created for purposes of the transfer or distribution. Furthermore, at no time are these rules to be interpreted in a manner that allows the use of these formulas to understate the fair market value of the life insurance contracts and associated distributions or transfers. For example, if the insurance contract has not been in force for some time, the value of the contract is best established through the sale of the particular insurance contract by the insurance company (i.e., as the premiums paid for that contract).

Date as of Which Fair Market Value Is Determined. In the case of a distribution or sale of a contract from a qualified retirement plan, the date as of which the fair market value will be determined is the date of that distribution or sale.

Treatment of Dividends Held on Deposit. Dividends held on deposit with respect to an insurance contract are not included in the fair market value of the contract. However, such dividends are taxable income to the employee at the time the rights to those dividends are transferred to that individual. For example, if a qualified retirement plan distributes a contract to an employee along with the rights to dividends held on deposit with respect to that contract, the employee must take into income both the fair market value of the contract and the value of the dividends held on deposit. This is the case regardless of whether the dividends on deposit are paid directly to the employee at the time the contract is distributed or merely made available for payment at a later time.

Treatment of Loans. If a participant receives a loan from a life insurance contract held by a qualified retirement plan and the contract is subsequently distributed to the participant in satisfaction of the participant's benefit under the plan, the reduction in the value of the distribution in order to repay the participant's loan from the plan constitutes a plan loan offset amount, which is treated as a distribution from the plan (see Q 14:10).

Effective Date. The revenue procedure applies to distributions, sales, and other transfers made on or after February 13, 2004. However, for periods before May 1, 2005, taxpayers may rely on the safe harbors of the revenue procedure; and, for periods on or after February 13, 2004, and before May 1, 2005, taxpayers may also rely on the safe harbors in the prior revenue procedure.

Q 15:16   Must life insurance policies acquired by a plan satisfy the nondiscrimination requirements?

A plan that is funded, in whole or in part, with life insurance contracts does not satisfy the requirements prohibiting discrimination (see Qs 4:10–4:21) in favor of HCEs (see Q 3:2) where (1) the plan permits HCEs, prior to distribution of retirement benefits, to purchase those life insurance contracts prior to distribution, and (2) any rights under the plan for non-highly compensated employees (NHCEs; see Q 3:12) to purchase life insurance contracts from the plan prior to distribution of retirement benefits are not of inherently equal or greater value than the purchase rights of HCEs.

A plan satisfies the nondiscrimination requirements only if all benefits, rights, and features provided under the plan are made available under the plan in a nondiscriminatory manner (see Q 4:20). Benefits, rights, and features (i.e., optional forms of benefit, ancillary benefits, and other rights or features) are made available under the plan in a nondiscriminatory manner only if each benefit, right, or feature satisfies the current and effective availability requirements. In general, a benefit, right, or feature satisfies the current availability requirements for a plan year if the group of employees to whom the benefit, right, or feature is currently available during the plan year satisfies the minimum coverage requirements (without regard to the average benefit percentage test; see Q 5:15).

Another right or feature is any right or feature applicable to employees under the plan (other than a benefit formula, an optional form of benefit, or an ancillary benefit) that can be expected to have meaningful value. A distinct other right or feature exists if a right or feature is not available on substantially the same terms as another right or feature. The right to a particular form of investment, including, for example, a particular class or type of employer securities (taking into account, in determining whether different forms of investment exist, any differences in conversion, dividend, voting, liquidation preference, or other rights conferred under the security) is a distinct other right or feature. Similarly, differences in insurance contracts (e.g., differences in cash value growth terms or different exchange features) that may be purchased from a plan can create distinct other rights or features even if the terms under which the contracts are purchased from the plan are the same.

An optional form of benefit, ancillary benefit, or other right or feature is permitted to be aggregated with another optional form of benefit, ancillary benefit, or other right or feature if one of the two is, in all cases, of inherently equal or greater value than the other, and the optional form of benefit, ancillary benefit, or other right or feature that is of inherently equal or greater value separately satisfies the current and effective availability requirements. For this purpose, one benefit, right, or feature is of inherently equal or greater value than another benefit, right, or feature only if, at any time and under any conditions, it is impossible for any employee to receive a smaller amount of a less valuable right under the first benefit, right, or feature than under the second benefit, right, or feature.

Example. The PhiLinda Rollin' Dolen Corporation maintains Plan A, a qualified retirement plan that provides an incidental death benefit (see Q 15:4) for each participant and holds a life insurance contract on the life of each participant to fund that incidental death benefit. Before distributions to a participant under Plan A commence, each participant is offered the opportunity to purchase from Plan A the life insurance contract under which the participant is insured for its cash surrender value.

The PhiLinda Rollin' Dolen Corporation has NHCEs that are not excludable employees, and the features of the life insurance contracts covering the lives of HCEs are different from the features of the life insurance contracts covering the lives of NHCEs. In addition, because of these differences in the features of the contracts, the rights that the NHCEs have to purchase the life insurance contracts under which they are insured are not of inherently equal or greater value than the rights that HCEs have to purchase the life insurance contracts under which they are insured.

To the extent the purchase from Plan A of a life insurance contract by an HCE is a distribution alternative with respect to benefits, such a purchase right is an optional form of benefit under Plan A. Even in situations in which this purchase right is not an optional form of benefit, this purchase right is another right or feature. The purchase rights for the HCEs are distinct optional forms of benefit or other rights or features from the purchase rights for NHCEs because of differences in the life insurance contracts (analogous to a conversion right applicable to a security). This purchase right for HCEs does not satisfy the current availability requirement because the right to purchase the contracts of a type available to the HCEs is not available to any NHCEs and therefore is not available to a group that satisfies the minimum coverage requirement. Moreover, under the facts presented, this purchase right of HCEs cannot satisfy the nondiscrimination requirements through aggregation with any other optional form of benefit, ancillary benefit, or other right or feature (such as the purchase right for NHCEs) because no other optional form of benefit, ancillary benefit, or other right or feature under the plan that would enable the aggregated benefits to be available to a group that satisfies the minimum coverage requirement is of inherently equal or greater value. Thus, Plan A fails to satisfy the nondiscrimination requirements.

[Rev. Rul. 2004-21, 2004-1 C.B. 544]

See Q 15:13 for a discussion of the life insurance subtrust technique.

Q 15:17   How are 412(i) plans affected by IRS life insurance rulings?

A 412(i) plan, a defined benefit plan funded entirely with insurance products, has many advantages (see Qs 2:25, 8:11). PPA (see Q 1:33) deleted Section 412(i) and replaced it with Section 412(e)(3). For purposes of *The Pension Answer Book*, a fully insured plan will still be referred to as a 412(i) plan.

A defined benefit plan (see Q 2:3) cannot be a 412(i) plan if the plan holds life insurance contracts and annuity contracts for the benefit of a participant that provides for benefits at normal retirement age (see Q 10:55) in excess of the participant's benefits at normal retirement age under the terms of the plan.

Employer contributions under a defined benefit plan that are used to purchase life insurance coverage for a participant in excess of the participant's death benefit provided under the plan are not fully deductible when contributed, but are carried over to be treated as contributions in future years and deductible in future years when other contributions to the plan that are taken into account for the taxable year are less than the maximum amount deductible for the year (see Q 12:20).

Example 1. Arnie Inwood Corporation maintains Plan A, a defined benefit plan that is funded solely by life insurance contracts and annuities with level annual premiums for each participant commencing with the date the individual becomes a participant in the plan (or, in the case of an increase in benefits, commencing at the time the increase becomes effective) and ending with the individual's attainment of normal retirement age. Plan A is intended to be a 412(i) plan. The amounts that will be accumulated under the insurance contracts and annuity contracts for the benefit of a participant at normal retirement age, assuming premiums are paid and determined by applying annuity purchase rates guaranteed under the contracts, will provide for benefits in excess of the participant's benefits at normal retirement age under the terms of the plan.

Plan A is not a 412(i) plan because the participant's benefit under Plan A payable at normal retirement age is not equal to the amount provided at normal retirement age with respect to the contracts held on behalf of the participant; and, thus, Plan A fails to satisfy the equal benefit requirements. Accordingly, Plan A is subject to the minimum funding requirements, with charges and credits to the funding standard account determined using the reasonable funding method selected for the plan under generally applicable rules and using reasonable actuarial assumptions. Such reasonable funding method and such reasonable actuarial assumptions are also used to determine the deductible amount of contributions. In addition, the exception from the accrual rules that applies to § 412(i) plans does not apply to Plan A.

Example 2. Jill Atlantic Bridge Corporation maintains Plan B. With respect to Jill, Plan B provides a death benefit that meets the definition of an incidental death benefit. The assets of Plan B include life insurance contracts on Jill's life with a face amount in excess of her death benefit under Plan B. Premiums with respect to Jill include an annual premium for the waiver of the entire premium payment if she becomes disabled. Upon the death of a covered employee, the portion of the proceeds of the life insurance contract that exceeds the life benefit payable to Jill's beneficiary under the plan is applied to the payment of premiums under the plan with respect to other participants.

The fact that the life insurance contracts on Jill's life provide for death benefits in excess of the death benefits under the plan would not cause Plan B to fail to satisfy the requirements to be a 412(i) plan, if Plan B otherwise met those requirements. Similarly, the fact that the life insurance contracts on Jill's life provide for death benefits that would fail to satisfy the incidental benefit rule if payable to Jill's beneficiary under the plan does not cause Plan B to fail to satisfy the incidental death benefit rule because those excess death benefits under the life insurance contracts are not payable to her beneficiary. However, a portion of the corporation's contributions is attributable to the purchase of life insurance coverage that is in excess of the incidental death benefit payable under Plan B. The portion of the contributions that is attributable to such excess life insurance coverage does not constitute normal cost and is not deductible as part of normal cost for the taxable year in which contributed. Rather, that portion of the corporation's contributions is used to provide a source of funds to pay future premiums (i.e., premiums on other participants) that will come due after the participant's death. Accordingly, the nondeductible portion of the contributions under Plan B that is paid for life insurance protection for Jill is carried over to be treated as contributions in later years and deductible when the employer contributions are less than the maximum deductible limit (e.g., in years in which excess death benefits under Plan B are used to satisfy the corporation's obligation to pay future premiums on other participants). Similarly, the corporation's contributions to pay premiums for the disability waiver for Jill do not constitute normal cost and are not deductible as part of normal costs for the taxable year in which contributed. Rather, that portion of the contributions is used to provide a source of funds to pay future premiums that will come due after she becomes disabled. Accordingly, the nondeductible portion of the corporation's contributions that is paid for the disability waiver for Jill is carried over to be treated as contributions in later years and deductible when the employer contributions are less than the maximum deductible limit (e.g., if and when she becomes disabled).

Transactions that are the same as, or substantially similar to, the transaction described in Example 2 are identified as listed transactions effective February 13, 2004, provided that the employer has deducted amounts used to pay premiums on a life insurance contract for a participant with a death benefit under the contract that exceeds the participant's death benefit under the plan by more than $100,000.

[Rev. Rul. 2004-20, 2004-1 C.B. 546; Bhatia v. Dischino, 2010 WL 1236406 (N.D. Tex. 2010)]

IRS has detailed a method by which defined benefit plans in the 412(i) audit program may resolve abusive tax avoidance transactions by recalculating contributions from the inception of the plan as if the minimum funding rules applied. [Employee Plan News, Vol. 7 (Spring 2007)]

For an excellent discussion of fully insured plans, see Landsberg, "Section 412(i) Fully Insured Defined Benefit Plans and the Perils of Unintended Consequences," *Journal of Pension Planning & Compliance*, Vol. 30, No. 3.

Q 15:18   Is the cost of current life insurance protection recovered tax free by a deceased participant's beneficiary?

Yes. Current life insurance protection costs can be recovered tax free by the beneficiary of the life insurance proceeds in the event of the participant's death(see Q 15:11). [Treas. Reg. § 1.72-16(c); Rev. Rul. 63-76, 1963-1 C.B. 23]

Q 15:19   What advantage does a participant gain when the company's qualified retirement plan provides life insurance protection?

By purchasing life insurance protection through the company's qualified retirement plan, the participant is able to shift a personal expense (not tax-deductible) to the plan without adverse tax consequences (see Q 15:3).

The income tax advantage of buying life insurance through the company's qualified retirement plan is even greater for a participant who could otherwise buy insurance only by paying a very high premium because of ill health. Instead of making large out-of-pocket premium payments, the participant merely includes the cost of current life insurance protection (see Q 15:6) in gross income.

Q 15:20   May a qualified retirement plan purchase a life insurance policy from a plan participant or from the employer?

Generally, a prohibited transaction (see Q 24:1) occurs if there is a sale of property between a qualified retirement plan and a party in interest (see Q 24:3). Thus, a purchase by a qualified retirement plan of a life insurance policy from a plan participant or from the participant's employer would constitute a prohibited transaction. However, the Department of Labor (DOL) is authorized to grant a class exemption (see Q 24:26) under which a party in interest or disqualified person (see Q 24:4) who meets the requirements of the class exemption will automatically be entitled to relief from the prohibited transaction rules.

DOL has granted a class exemption so that the prohibited transaction rules do not apply to the sale of a life insurance policy to a qualified retirement plan from a plan participant on whose life the policy was issued, or from an employer, any of whose employees are covered by the plan, if:

1. The plan pays no more than the lesser of
   a. The cash surrender value of the policy;
   b. If the plan is a defined benefit plan (see Q 2:3), the value of the participant's accrued benefit (see Q 9:2) at the time of the sale (determined under any reasonable actuarial method); or
   c. If the plan is a defined contribution plan (see Q 2:2), the value of the participant's account balance (see Q 9:2);
2. The sale does not involve any policy that is subject to a loan that the plan assumes; and
3. The sale does not contravene any provision of the plan.

The exemption is also available for plan participants who are owner-employees (see Q 5:32) or shareholder-employees (i.e., a more-than-5-percent shareholder) of an S corporation (see Q 14:21).
[PTCE 92-5 (57 Fed. Reg. 5019)]

It is the view of DOL that, where the cash surrender value of a policy is zero, the requirements of PTCE 92-5 are met where there is a transfer of the policy by the participant to the plan for no consideration. DOL also noted that because the policy has no cash surrender value at the time of the transaction, compliance with PTCE 92-5 requires that the plan not pay any consideration. Similarly, the transfer of a term policy by the participant to the plan for no consideration meets the requirements of PTCE 92-5, and the plan may not pay any consideration for the term policy. [DOL Op. Ltr. 2002-12A]

Q 15:21   May a qualified retirement plan sell a life insurance policy to a plan participant or to the employer?

Generally, a prohibited transaction (see Q 24:1) occurs if there is a sale of property between a qualified retirement plan and a party in interest (see Q 24:3). Thus, a sale by a qualified retirement plan of a life insurance policy to a plan participant or to the participant's employer would constitute a prohibited transaction. However, DOL is authorized to grant a class exemption (see Q 24:26) under which a party in interest or disqualified person (see Q 24:4) who meets the requirements of the class exemption will automatically be entitled to relief from the prohibited transaction rules.

DOL has granted a class exemption so that the prohibited transaction rules do not apply to the sale of a life insurance policy by a qualified retirement plan to (1) the insured participant under the plan; (2) a relative or member of the family of the participant [ERISA § 3(15); I.R.C. § 4975(e)(6)]; (3) an employer, any of whose employees are covered by the plan; or (4) another qualified retirement plan, if:

1. The participant is the insured under the policy;
2. The relative is the beneficiary under the policy;
3. The policy would, but for the sale, be surrendered by the plan;
4. With respect to a sale of the policy to the employer, a relative, or another plan, the insured participant is first informed of the proposed sale and is given the opportunity to purchase the policy from the plan but delivers to the plan a written election not to purchase the policy and a written consent to the sale by the plan; and
5. The amount received by the plan as consideration for the sale is at least equal to the amount necessary to put the plan in the same cash position as it would have been in had it retained the policy, surrendered it, and made a distribution to the participant of the participant's vested (see Q 9:1) interest under the plan. See Q 15:15 concerning the value of a life insurance policy.

The exemption is also available for plan participants who are owner-employees (see Q 5:32) or shareholder-employees (i.e., a more-than-5-percent shareholder) of an S corporation (see Q 28:2). [PTCE 92-6 (57 Fed. Reg. 5189)]

A sale of a policy by a plan to a partnership composed of the insured participant and the participant's children does not come within the exemption because the partnership is not a relative even though all of the other partners are relatives of the participant. A sale, however, directly to the children could come within the exemption.

DOL has expanded the exemption to include the following three situations:

1. The sale may be to multiple relatives of the insured participant who are the sole beneficiaries under the policy.
2. The term "policy" includes second-to-die insurance covering the participant and the participant's spouse.
3. The sale may be for a partial interest in the policy. [DOL Op. Ltr. 98-07A; *see also* DOL Op. Ltr. 2006-03A]

With regard to the second situation, DOL stated that it assumed that applicable law and the plan permitted the acquisition and ownership by the plan of a policy covering the joint lives of a participant and spouse. This caveat is important because of IRS statements relating to the acquisition by a plan of second-to-die insurance (see Q 15:2).

DOL has also expanded the exemption to include a sale of a policy by a plan to a personal or private trust established by or for the benefit of the insured plan participant or by or for the benefit of one or more relatives of the insured plan participant. The amendment of the exemption is retroactively effective to February 12, 1992. [67 Fed. Reg. 56,313; 67 Fed. Reg. 31,835]

Q 15:22 How are death benefit payments under a qualified retirement plan taxed?

Death benefits payable under a qualified retirement plan are generally included in the deceased participant's gross estate. For the exceptions, see Q 15:23. [I.R.C. § 2039; Priv. Ltr. Rul. 200105058] If the death benefits are payable to a charitable organization, an estate tax charitable deduction is allowable; and, if the death benefits are payable to a charitable remainder trust, a partial estate tax charitable deduction is allowable. [I.R.C. § 2055; Priv. Ltr. Ruls. 200230018, 9818009]

The participant's beneficiary is subject to income tax on death benefit payments. The income tax treatment depends on how the beneficiary receives the death benefit payments. Forward averaging treatment may be available for a lump-sum distribution (see Q 13:12). If an annuity is purchased, ordinary income tax rates apply to amounts received under the annuity contract (see Q 13:4). A transfer of funds from a qualified retirement plan to the temporary administrator of a deceased participant's estate is a distribution includible in the estate's gross income in the year of receipt. [Machat, 75 T.C.M. 2194 (1998); Priv. Ltr. Rul. 9320006] If the death benefits are subject to both estate tax and income tax, the beneficiary will be entitled to an income tax deduction for the estate tax attributable to the death benefits. [I.R.C. § 691(c); Priv. Ltr. Rul. 200316008; Field Serv. Adv. 200011023] Where the participant's estate is the beneficiary, the estate is not allowed an estate tax deduction for the income tax paid by the estate with respect to the death benefit distribution. [Priv. Ltr. Rul. 200444021] Similarly, the value of the deceased participant's qualified retirement plan death benefits is not discounted to reflect the potential income tax liability that will be incurred by the beneficiary upon receipt. [Estate of Smith v. United States, No. 04-20194 (5th Cir. 2004)]

However, death benefits paid upon an individual's death to a charitable organization or to a charitable remainder trust are not subject to income tax because the charitable beneficiary is exempt from tax (see Q 13:3). [I.R.C. §§ 501(a), 664(c); Priv. Ltr. Ruls. 200234019, 200230018, 200221011, 9818009] Where a decedent designated his estate as beneficiary of his plan benefits, the decedent's will named a charity as the residual beneficiary of his estate, and the estate assigned the plan benefits to the charity, the estate was not required to include the plan benefits in its gross income. [Priv. Ltr. Rul. 200845029, 200526010, 200520004; *see also* Priv. Ltr. Rul. 201027031; *but see* CCA 200644020]

For rules on the taxation of life insurance proceeds, see Qs 15:11 and 15:18; and, for a discussion of the life insurance subtrust technique, see Q 15:13.

Q 15:23   Are any death benefit payments received from a qualified retirement plan excluded from estate tax?

Yes. The repeal of the $100,000 estate tax exclusion by the Tax Reform Act of 1984 (TRA '84) does not apply to a participant who was receiving benefit payments (i.e., was in pay status) under the plan prior to 1985 and who, prior to July 18, 1984, irrevocably elected the form of the benefit that the beneficiary would receive.

Furthermore, the total estate tax exclusion previously available if the participant had died before 1983 continues to apply if the participant was receiving benefit payments (i.e., was in pay status) under the plan prior to 1983 and had already irrevocably elected the form of benefit that the beneficiary would receive.

The estate tax exclusion remains available if the participant terminated employment before 1985 (in the case of the $100,000 exclusion) or 1983 (in the case of the total exclusion), irrevocably elected the form of benefit to be paid in the future, and was not in pay status as of the applicable date. [I.R.C. § 2039; TEFRA § 245(c) (as amended by TRA '84 § 525); Temp. Treas. Reg. § 20.2039-1T, Q&A-1; Priv. Ltr. Rul. 8630028] This exclusion applies only to qualified retirement plans and *not* to IRAs. [Sherrill v. United States, No. 2:04-CV-509 (N.D. In. 2006); Rev. Rul. 92-22, 1992-1 C.B. 313; Priv. Ltr. Rul. 9828003, 9221030, 9144046; S. Rep., 1986-3 C.B. 1019]

A participant was in pay status on the applicable date with respect to an interest in the plan if the participant irrevocably elected the form of benefit and received at least one payment under such form of benefit. [Temp. Treas. Reg. § 20.2039-1T, Q&A-2]

As of the applicable date, an election of the form of benefit is irrevocable if, as of such date, a written election had been made specifying the form of distribution (e.g., lump sum, annuity) and the period over which the distribution would be made (e.g., life annuity, term certain). An election is considered revocable if the form or period of the distribution could be determined or altered after the applicable date, but it will not be considered revocable just because the beneficiaries were not designated as of such date or could be changed thereafter. [Temp. Treas. Reg. § 20.2039-1T, Q&A-3]

Q 15:24   Is a deceased participant's estate entitled to a marital deduction for death benefit payments received by the surviving spouse from a qualified retirement plan?

A marital deduction is allowed for any property included in the deceased participant's estate that passes from the decedent to the surviving spouse. [I.R.C. § 2056]

Death benefit payments from a qualified retirement plan to a deceased participant's surviving spouse will qualify for the marital deduction and will be deducted from the deceased participant's gross estate for estate tax purposes. This deduction will also be available if the surviving spouse receives the death benefit payments in the form of a QPSA (see Q 10:9) and the deceased participant's executor does not elect to forgo the deduction. [I.R.C. §§ 2039, 2056(b)(7)(C); Treas. Reg. § 301.9100-8; Priv. Ltr. Ruls. 199904023, 9245033, 9232036, 9204017, 9008003; *see also* Rev. Rul. 2006-26, 2006-1 C.B. 939; Priv. Ltr. Ruls. 2006-26, 2006-1 C.B. 939 200241012, 199931033, 9830004, 9738010, 9729015, 9704029; *but see* Priv. Ltr. Rul. 9220007]

See Q 30:47 for a discussion of the marital deduction QTIP election and illustrative examples.

Chapter 16

10 Percent Tax on Early Distributions

Distributions from qualified retirement plans and IRAs are generally includible in the individual's gross income. In addition, if an individual receives a distribution prior to attainment of age 59½, the individual's income tax may be increased by an amount equal to 10 percent of the portion includible in gross income. However, a number of exceptions apply to the imposition of this additional tax. This chapter examines the 10 percent additional tax on early distributions and discusses the exceptions that may apply.

Q 16:1 What is the 10 percent additional tax on early distributions?

If an individual receives a distribution from a qualified plan (see Q 16:2), the individual's tax for the taxable year in which the distribution is received is increased by an amount equal to 10 percent of the portion of the distribution includible in gross income, unless an exception applies (see Q 16:3). [I.R.C. § 72(t)(1); Holmes, T.C.M. 2010–42; Prough, T.C.M. 2010–20; Haigh, 97 T.C.M. 1794 (2009); Hughes, 96 T.C.M. 314 (2008); Jennings, No. 4939-06S (Tax Ct. 2008); Atkin, 95 T.C.M. 1364 (2008); Huynh, 95 T.C.M. 1111 (2008); Sharma, T.C. Summ. Op. 2008-98; Leon and Tilley, T.C. Summ. Op. 2008-86; Thompson, 94 T.C.M. 430 (2007); Jackson, 93 T.C.M. 1211 (2007); Belmont, 93 T.C.M. 1034 (2007); Lewis, 93 T.C.M. 934 (2007); Bhattacharyya, 93 T.C.M. 711 (2007); Kaldi, T.C. Summ. Op. 2007-45; Jordan, 91 T.C.M. 1129 (2006); Seidel, 89 T.C.M. 972 (2005); Jensen, 86 T.C.M. 293 (2003); Bougas III, 86 T.C.M. 9 (2003); Armstrong v. United States, A4-02-042 (D.N.D. 2003); Coleman-Stephens, T.C. Summ. Op. 2003-91; Cabirac, 120 T.C. 163 (2003); Williams, 85 T.C.M. 1113 (2003); Machen v United States, 00-478T (Fed. Cl. 2001); Czepiel v. Comm'r, 00-1257 (1st Cir. 2000); Jones, 80 T.C.M. 76 (2000); Bunney, 114 T.C. 259 (2000); Robertson, 79 T.C.M. 1725 (2000); Deal, 78 T.C.M. 638 (1999); Scott v Comm'r, No. 98-2780 (5th Cir. 1999); Roman v. Comm'r, No. 98-2780 (11th Cir. 1999); Schmalzer, 76 T.C.M. 803 (1998); Keenan, 76 T.C.M. 748 (1998); Bach, 75 T.C.M. 1722 (1998); Roundy v. Comm'r, 122 F.3d 835 (9th Cir. 1997); Reese, 74 T.C.M. 232 (1997); Chiu, 73 T.C.M. 2679 (1997); Burton, 73 T.C.M. 1729 (1997); Robinson, 72 T.C.M. 1320 (1996); Siano v. United States, Civ. 95-1618

(W.D. Pa. 1996); Malesa, 72 T.C.M. 495 (1996); Coffield, 72 T.C.M. 338 (1996); Hobson, 71 T.C.M. 3172 (1996); Montgomery, 71 T.C.M. 3154 (1996); Ross, 70 T.C.M. 1596 (1995); Grow, 70 T.C.M. 1576 (1995); Orgera, 70 T.C.M. 1488 (1995); Copley, 70 T.C.M. 1040 (1995); Wittstadt, Jr., 70 T.C.M. 994 (1995); Huff, 68 T.C.M. 674 (1994)] The constructive receipt doctrine applies. A distribution from an IRA in the form of a check was includible in income in the year of receipt even though the IRA owner did not deposit or cash the check until several years later. A cash basis taxpayer is considered to constructively receive income as of the date a check is received unless there are substantial limitations placed on the use of the check. [Millard, 90 T.C.M. 136 (2005)] IRA assets invested in collectibles are treated as distributions for income tax purposes (see Q 30:1) and may also be subject to the 10 percent additional tax. [Minteer v. Comm'r, 05-74551 (9th Cir. 2006)]

The tax, an additional income tax, is imposed upon the recipient of the distribution and applies only to the portion of the distribution includible in the recipient's gross income. Thus, the portion of a distribution that represents a return of basis is subject to neither income tax (see Q 13:3) nor the additional income tax, and this may also apply to net unrealized appreciation on employer securities distributed from a qualified retirement plan (see Qs 13:18, 28:71). [IRS Notice 87-16, Q&A-D9, 1987-1 C.B. 446; Villaroel v. Comm'r, 202 F.3d 271 (6th Cir. 2000); *see also* Seidel, 89 T.C.M. 972 (2005) In addition, if a distribution from a qualified plan is exempt from income tax by virtue of a tax treaty, the additional tax will not be imposed. [Priv. Ltr. Rul. 9253049]

> **Example.** Ben receives a $40,000 distribution from the BML Corp. profit sharing plan of which $5,000 represents a recovery of basis. Because no exception applies, an additional tax of $3,500 [($40,000–$5,000) × 10%] is imposed upon Ben.

An individual had to include in income the total amount of a distribution he received, despite the fact that an IRS employee who had provided assistance to him with the preparation of his return erroneously reported only 10 percent of the distribution as income. Because no exception applied, the 10 percent additional tax was also imposed on the entire distribution. [Bradley, T.C. Summ. Op. 2006-11] Another individual was liable for the 10 percent additional tax on an early distribution made to his former wife prior to their divorce. The husband did not qualify for relief as an innocent spouse because he had knowledge of the distribution and filed a joint income tax return with his then wife. [Packer, No. 8413-03S (Tax Ct. 2006)]

The additional tax applies to an individual who made an irrevocable election to defer receipt of a distribution prior to both the effective date and the date of enactment of the additional tax, and then received a distribution thereafter. [O'Connor, 67 T.C.M. 2708 (1994); Bullard, 65 T.C.M. 1844 (1993); Shimota v. United States, 21 Cl. Ct. 510 (1990), *aff'd*, 943 F.2d 1312 (Fed. Cir. 1991); Panos, 64 T.C.M. 542 (1992)]

The state of California imposes a $2\frac{1}{2}$ percent additional tax on early distributions, and IRS has concluded that such additional tax is deductible for federal income tax purposes. [Office of Chief Counsel IRS Memo. 20072201F]

Throughout this chapter, the 10 percent additional tax on early distributions is referred to as the penalty tax.

See Q 1:28 for a discussion of the Katrina Emergency Tax Relief Act of 2005 and other developments for their effect on the taxation of distributions, including the penalty tax and other issues.

Q 16:2 What is a qualified plan for purposes of the penalty tax?

For purposes of the penalty tax, the term "qualified plan" means:

1. A qualified retirement plan (i.e., a defined contribution plan or a defined benefit plan; see Qs 1:5, 2:2, 2:3);
2. A 403(b) plan (see Q 35:1);
3. An IRA, including traditional IRAs, Roth IRAs, SEP IRAs, and SIMPLE IRAs (see Qs 30:1, 31:1, 32:1, 33:2).

[I.R.C. §§ 72(t)(1), 4974(c)]

For purposes of this chapter, a 403(b) plan is treated as a qualified retirement plan.

After former participants started an action against the employer claiming that some of the excess qualified retirement plan assets should have been allocated to them, the employer placed some of the assets in an escrow account. Distributions from the escrow account to the former participants following settlement of the suit were not distributions from a qualified retirement plan, so the penalty tax was not imposed. [Priv. Ltr. Rul. 9006055] One court ruled that a payment of pension benefits resulting from an arbitration award that was paid through a state retirement system constituted a distribution from a qualified plan and was subject to the penalty tax. [Kute v. United States, 191 F.3d 371 (3d Cir. 1999); *see also* O'Connor, 67 T.C.M. 2708 (1994)]

Q 16:3 Are there exceptions to the penalty tax?

The penalty tax is imposed upon the recipient of a distribution from a qualified plan (see Q 16:2), unless the distribution is:

1. Made on or after the date the employee attained age 59½ (see Q 16:4);
2. Made to a beneficiary (or to the estate of the employee) after the death of the employee (see Q 16:5);
3. Attributable to the employee's disability (see Q 16:6);
4. Part of a series of substantially equal periodic payments (not less frequently than annually) made for the life (or life expectancy) of the employee, or the joint lives (or joint life expectancy) of such employee and the employee's beneficiary (see Qs 16:7–16:9);
5. Made to an employee after separation from service after attainment of age 55 (see Q 16:10);
6. Made on account of an IRS levy (see Q 16:11);

7. An amount not in excess of the total medical expenses deductible for the year under Section 213 by the employee (see Q 16:12);

8. A payment to an alternate payee pursuant to a QDRO (see Q 16:13);

9. Made to an unemployed individual for health insurance premiums (see Q 16:14);

10. Made for qualified higher education expenses (see Q 16:15);

11. A qualified first-time homebuyer distribution (see Q 16:16);

12. A corrective distribution (see Q 16:17); or

13. A dividend paid with respect to certain stock held by an ESOP (see Q 16:18).

[I.R.C. §§ 72(t)(2)(A)-(F)]

For purposes of these exceptions, the term "employee" includes a participant in a qualified retirement plan (see Q 1:5) and, in the case of an IRA, the individual for whose benefit the IRA was established. [I.R.C. § 72(t)(5)]

Certain of the exceptions apply to distributions from both qualified retirement plans and IRAs; however, some apply only to distributions from qualified retirement plans and not from IRAs, while others apply only to distributions from IRAs and not from qualified retirement plans.

Neither financial hardship nor personal difficulties is an exception to the penalty tax. To avoid the penalty tax, the distribution must come within one of the enumerated exceptions. [Carder, 7422-07S (Tax Ct. 2008); Cole, 91 T.C.M. 888 (2006); Reese, No. 5598-05S (Tax Ct. 2006); Reimann, No. 10877-03S (Tax Ct. 2005); Vulic, 87 T.C.M. 1036 (2004); Gallagher, 81 T.C.M. 1149 (2001); Robertson, 79 T.C.M. 1725 (2000); Deal, 78 T.C.M. 638 (1999); Arnold, 111 T.C. 250 (1998); Peaslee, 77 T.C.M. 1195 (1999); Pulliam, 72 T.C.M. 307 (1996)] The penalty tax was imposed even though the individual had received erroneous advice from IRS employees in preparing her income tax return. [Deal, 78 T.C.M. 638 (1999); see also Bradley, T.C. Summ. Op. 2006-11] The penalty tax was also imposed where a plan participant was precluded from making repayments on his plan loan because he had filed a voluntary petition in bankruptcy. [White, No. 1815-04S (Tax Ct. 2005)]

Under PPA (see Q 1:33), the penalty tax does not apply to a qualified reservist distribution. A qualified reservist distribution is a distribution:

1. From an IRA or attributable to elective deferrals under 401(k) plan (see Q 27:1) or a 403(b) plan (see Q 35:1);

2. Made to an individual who (by reason of being a member of a military reserve unit) was ordered or called to active duty for a period in excess of 179 days or for an indefinite period; and

3. That is made during the period beginning on the date of such order or call to duty and ending at the close of the active duty period.

An individual who receives a qualified reservist distribution may, at any time during the two-year period beginning on the date after the end of the active duty period, make one or more contributions to an IRA of such individual in an aggregate amount not to exceed the amount of such distribution. The dollar limitations otherwise applicable to contributions to IRAs do not apply to any such contribution, and no deduction is allowed for any such contribution.

This provision applies to individuals ordered or called to active duty after September 11, 2001, and before December 31, 2007. The two-year period for making recontributions of qualified reservist distributions does not end before August 17, 2008. The December 31, 2007 expiration date has been repealed, and this provision is now permanent.

[I.R.C. § 72(t)(2)(G) (as amended by HEART Act § 107(a)); HEART Act § 107(b)]

Because the above provision added by PPA is retroactive, an eligible reservist who already paid the penalty tax can claim a refund by using Form 1040X to amend the return for the year in which the retirement distribution was received. An eligible reservist should write "active duty reservist," at the top of Form 1040X. In Form 1040X, Part II Explanation of Changes, the reservist should write the date called to active duty, the amount of the retirement distribution, and the amount of early withdrawal penalty paid. [IR 2006-152 (Sept. 28, 2006)]

The penalty tax does not apply to permissible withdrawals from eligible automatic contribution arrangements (EACAs; see Qs 27:5, 27:7).

See Qs 30:29 and 31:21 for a discussion of penalty-free economic-stimulus payment withdrawals from IRAs and Roth IRAs.

Q 16:4   What does age 59½ mean?

If a distribution from a qualified plan (see Q 16:2) is made on or after the date on which the employee attains age 59½ (see Q 16:3), the penalty tax is not imposed. [I.R.C. § 72(t)(2)(A)(i)] This exception applies to distributions from both qualified retirement plans and IRAs.

Although there is no provision defining age 59½, it is believed that it means the actual date on which the employee attains age 59½. For example, if an individual's date of birth is June 30, 1951, the individual's 59th birthday is June 30, 2010 and age 59½ is attained on December 30, 2010; however, if the individual's 59th birthday is July 1, 2010, age 59½ is attained on January 1, 2011.

Example. Steve's date of birth is May 3, 1952, and he receives a first distribution from his IRA on October 7, 2011 and a second distribution from his IRA on December 9, 2011. Assuming no other exception applies, the first distribution occurs before attainment of age 59½ (that is, before November 3, 2011) and the penalty tax will be imposed, but the second distribution will be penalty tax free.

A married couple who were both under age 59½ and who used their IRAs to make a down payment on a personal residence were subject to the penalty tax because no other exception applied. [Harris, 67 T.C.M. 1983 (1994)] A husband and a wife each had an IRA; and the husband had attained age 59½, but the wife had not. By mistake, the wife withdrew $20,000 from her IRA instead of the husband withdrawing from his IRA. The penalty tax was assessed against the wife. [Owens, T.C. Summ. Op. 2004-29]

Q 16:5   How does the exception for death work?

The penalty tax does not apply if an early distribution is made because of the death of the employee (see Q 16:3). [I.R.C. § 72(t)(2)(A)(ii); Priv. Ltr. Ruls. 9842058, 9608042, 9418034] This exception applies to distributions from both qualified retirement plans and IRAs and also applies whether the distribution is to a beneficiary designated by the employee or to the employee's estate.

> **Example.** Zane, age 52, dies, and his profit sharing plan account is paid to his 20-year-old daughter, Zora. Even though neither Zane nor Zora attained age 59½, the penalty tax is not imposed on the distribution.

A surviving spouse who is the beneficiary of a deceased spouse's IRA may choose either to retain the IRA in the name of the deceased spouse or to elect to treat the deceased spouse's IRA as that of the surviving spouse (see Qs 30:49, 30:50). This choice may result in the imposition of the penalty tax upon subsequent IRA distributions to the surviving spouse. [Gee, 127 T.C. No. 1 (2006); Priv. Ltr. Rul. 200110033; *see also* Sears, T.C.M. 2010–146 and Priv. Ltr. Rul. 200450057]

> **Example 1.** Zane, age 52, designates his 45-year-old wife, Zeena, as beneficiary of his IRA. After Zane's death, Zeena retains the IRA in Zane's name and commences distributions from his IRA. The penalty tax will not be imposed because the distribution is made to the beneficiary after the employee's death.

> **Example 2.** The facts are the same as in Example 1, except that Zeena elects to treat the IRA as her own. The penalty tax will be imposed because the exception for death does not apply in this situation; however, another exception may possibly apply (see Q 16:7).

An individual participated in two qualified retirement plans and also had a SEP (see Q 32:1). The individual designated his wife as the sole beneficiary of all three plans. After the individual's death, the two plans established separate beneficiary accounts for the wife. IRS ruled that the wife could establish a new IRA in the name of the deceased husband, naming herself as beneficiary, and then have the benefits of all three plans transferred directly to the new IRA. Thereafter, IRA distributions to the wife prior to her attaining age 59½ will not be subject to the penalty tax because the exception for death applies. [Priv. Ltr. Rul. 200650023]

Q 16:6   When is an individual disabled?

The penalty tax does not apply if an early distribution is made because of the employee's disability (see Q 16:3). [I.R.C. § 72(t)(2)(A)(iii); Dart, T.C. Summ. Op. 2008-158; Rideaux, T.C. Summ. Op. 2006-74; Meyer, 85 T.C.M. 760 (2003); Coleman-Stephens, T.C. Summ. Op. 2003-91; Fohrmeister, 73 T.C.M. 2483

(1997); Dwyer, 106 T.C. 337 (1996); Kovacevic, 64 T.C.M. 1076 (1992); Kane, 63 T.C.M. 2753 (1992); Priv. Ltr. Ruls. 201011036, 200126037, 9810033, 9745033, 9621043, 9418034] This exception applies to distributions from both qualified retirement plans and IRAs.

To come within the exception for disability:

1. The individual must be unable to engage in any substantial gainful activity due to a medically determinable physical or mental impairment;

2. The disability must be expected to result in death or to be of a long-continued and indefinite duration; and

3. The individual must furnish proof of the disability in the form and manner required by IRS.

[I.R.C. § 72(m)(7)]

In determining whether an individual's impairment renders the individual unable to engage in any substantial gainful activity, primary consideration is given to the nature and severity of the impairment. Consideration is also given to other factors such as the individual's education, training, and work experience. The substantial gainful activity is the activity, or a comparable activity, in which the individual customarily engaged prior to the arising of the disability or prior to retirement if the individual was retired at the time the disability arose. [Treas. Reg. § 1.72-17A(f)(1); Lukovsky, T.C.M. 2010–117; Dollander, 98 T.C.M. ___ (2009); Machlay, T.C. Summ. Op. 2009-21; Kopty, 94 T.C.M. 480 (2007); Warrington, T.C. Summ. Op. 2007-122; Dykes, T.C. Summ. Op. 2007-101; Kaldi, T.C. Summ. Op. 2007-45; Johnson, T.C. Summ. Op. 2006-62; Haas, No. 7524-04S (Tax Ct. 2005); Thomas, No. 10824-03S (Tax Ct. 2005); Robertson, 88 T.C.M. 294 (2004)]

Whether or not the impairment in a particular case constitutes a disability will be determined with reference to all the facts in the case. The following are examples of impairments that would ordinarily be considered as preventing substantial gainful activity:

1. Loss of use of two limbs;

2. Certain progressive diseases that have resulted in the physical loss or atrophy of a limb, such as diabetes, multiple sclerosis, or Buerger's disease;

3. Diseases of the heart, lungs, or blood vessels that have resulted in major loss of heart or lung reserve as evidenced by X-ray, electrocardiogram, or other objective findings, so that, despite medical treatment, breathlessness, pain, or fatigue is produced on slight exertion, such as walking several blocks, using public transportation, or doing small chores;

4. Cancer that is inoperable or progressive;

5. Damage to the brain or a brain abnormality that has resulted in severe loss of judgment, intellect, orientation, or memory;

6. Mental diseases (e.g., psychosis or severe psychoneurosis) requiring continued institutionalization or constant supervision of the individual;

7. Loss or diminution of vision to the extent that the affected individual has a central visual acuity of no better than 20/200 in the better eye after best correction, or has a limitation in the fields of vision such that the widest diameter of the visual fields subtends an angle no greater than 20 degrees;

8. Permanent and total loss of speech; and

9. Total deafness uncorrectable by a hearing aid.

The existence of one or more of the impairments described above (or of an impairment of greater severity) will not, however, in and of itself always permit a finding that an individual is disabled. Any impairment, whether of lesser or greater severity, must be evaluated in terms of whether it does in fact prevent the individual from engaging in the individual's customary or any comparable substantial gainful activity. [Treas. Reg. § 1.72-17A(f)(2)]

An impairment must be expected either to continue for a long and indefinite period or to result in death. Ordinarily, a terminal illness because of disease or injury would result in disability. The term "indefinite" is used in the sense that it cannot reasonably be anticipated that the impairment will, in the foreseeable future, be so diminished as no longer to prevent substantial gainful activity. For example, an individual who suffers a bone fracture that prevents the individual from working for an extended period of time will not be considered disabled, if recovery can be expected in the foreseeable future; however, if the fracture persistently fails to knit, the individual would ordinarily be considered disabled. [Treas. Reg. § 1.72-17A(f)(3); Williams, T.C. Summ. Op. 2004-57]

An impairment that is remediable does not constitute a disability. An individual will not be deemed disabled if, with reasonable effort and safety, the impairment can be diminished to the extent that the individual will not be prevented by the impairment from engaging in the customary or any comparable substantial gainful activity. [Treas. Reg. § 1.72-17A(f)(4)]

An individual's depression caused by his wife's untimely death from cancer at age 53 and the September 11, 2001 attacks (the individual worked near the World Trade Center and lost a number of friends and neighbors, including persons who had attended his wife's funeral) was ruled not to qualify as a disability. [Kowsh, 96 T.C.M. 123 (2008)] One court ruled that an individual suffering from AIDS was subject to the penalty tax because, during the year of the distribution from his IRA, he was able to engage in substantial gainful activity. [West, T.C. Summ. Op. 2002-30] However, another individual who suffered from AIDS, had a nervous breakdown, and took a leave of absence from work was ruled unable to engage in substantial gainful activity and was not subject to the penalty tax. [Meyer, 85 T.C.M. 760 (2003)] Distributions from a wife's IRA to pay household expenses after her husband became disabled did not come within the exception for disability and, therefore, were subject to the penalty tax. [Boulden, 70 T.C.M. 216 (1995)] Similarly, a husband did not qualify for the exception to the penalty tax because his spouse was disabled. The exception for a disability only applies to a plan participant, and the wife was not a vested participant of the plan by virtue of state community property laws. [Barkley, 88 T.C.M. 634 (2004)]

Q 16:7   What are substantially equal periodic payments if the series of payments commenced before 2003?

One of the exceptions to the penalty tax is for a distribution from a qualified plan that is part of a series of substantially equal periodic payments (not less frequently than annually) made over the life (or life expectancy) of the employee (see Q 16:3) or the joint lives (or joint life expectancy) of the employee and the employee's designated beneficiary. [I.R.C. § 72(t)(2)(A)(iv)] This exception applies to distributions from both a qualified retirement plan and an IRA; however, if the distribution is made from a qualified retirement plan, this exception applies *only* if the series of payments commences after the employee separates from service (see Q 13:10). [I.R.C. § 72(t)(3)(B)]

According to IRS, a series of payments that commenced before 2003 will be considered to be substantially equal periodic payments if they are made according to one of the methods set forth below:

1. Payments will be treated as satisfying this requirement if the annual payment is determined using a method that would be acceptable for purposes of calculating required minimum distributions (the RMD method). See chapter 11 for details.

2. Payments will also be treated as substantially equal periodic payments if the amount to be distributed annually is determined by amortizing the employee's account balance over a number of years equal to the employee's life expectancy (or the joint life and last survivor expectancy of the employee and the employee's beneficiary) at an interest rate that does not exceed a reasonable interest rate on the date that payments commence (the fixed amortization method).

Example 1. V & S Corporation established a profit sharing plan many years ago. Vicente, age 50, had an account balance in the plan of $1,000,000 and terminated employment in 1996. In 1997, if Vicente commenced receiving $86,790 a year from the plan, the annual payments were considered substantially equal periodic payments and were not subject to the penalty tax. This was because Vicente had a life expectancy of 33.1 years and amortizing $1,000,000 over 33.1 years at an interest rate of 8 percent resulted in an annual payment of $86,790.

3. As a third permissible method, payments will be treated as substantially equal periodic payments if the amount to be distributed annually is determined by dividing the employee's account balance by an annuity factor (the present value of an annuity of $1 per year beginning at the employee's age attained in the first distribution year and continuing for the life of the employee), with such annuity factor derived using a reasonable mortality table and an interest rate that does not exceed a reasonable interest rate on the date that payments commence (the fixed annuitization method).

Example 2. S & V Corporation established a money purchase pension plan many years ago. Sabine, age 50, had an account balance in the plan of $900,000 and terminated employment in 1992. If the annuity factor for a $1 per year annuity for Sabine is 11.109 (assuming an interest rate of 8 percent and using the UP-1984 mortality table), Sabine would receive an annual distribution of $81,015 ($900,000 ÷ 11.109). As substantially equal periodic payments, no penalty tax would apply.

[IRS Notice 89-25 Q&A-12, 1989-1 C.B. 662; Priv. Ltr. Ruls. 200309028, 200214029, 200203072, 200131011, 200118057, 200115039, 200113022, 200105066, 200103078]

Under the above examples, the annual payment remains constant (at least until Vicente and Sabine attain age 59½; see Q 16:9). However, IRS has approved a method whereby the annual payments may increase from year to year, as illustrated in the example below. [Priv. Ltr. Rul. 9047043]

> **Example 3.** In Example 2, assume that the first year of distribution was 1993, when the dollar limitation for the annual benefit under a defined benefit plan was $115,641 (see Q 6:11). In 2001, the dollar limitation increased to $140,000. In 2001, Sabine could receive an annual distribution of $98,080 ($81,015 × $140,000 ÷ $115,641).

With regard to the fixed annuitization method, IRS has allowed an individual to use both an interest factor that may change from year to year and an annuity factor based upon attained age each year. [Priv. Ltr. Ruls. 200051052, 200031058] IRS has also ruled that IRA distributions constituted a series of substantially equal periodic payments even though the annual distribution amount would be increased by a consumer price index or other percentage adjustment in each subsequent year. [Priv. Ltr. Ruls. 200033048, 200031059, 9536031] However, a percentage adjustment was not permitted after the employee had received level annual payments for several years. [Priv. Ltr. Rul. 199943050] Where an individual contended that distributions from his IRA were based upon the fixed amortization method, but the court found that the individual received distributions in differing amounts over several years, received distributions from different IRAs, and failed to establish his account balance in the IRAs, the penalty tax was imposed. [Kulzer, T.C. Summ. Op. 2008-28; *see also* Carlson, T.C. Summ. Op. 2008-22] IRS representatives have opined that any mortality table used for Section 401(a)(4) purposes or used for current estate tax purposes would be considered reasonable and that any interest rate up to 120 percent of the federal midterm rate at the time of the calculation would be considered reasonable.

An individual with more than one IRA can take periodic payments from one IRA without taking periodic payments from the others. Also, the account balances of the other IRAs need not be considered in calculating the amount of the periodic payment from the distributing IRA. However, the individual can consider the account balances of all IRAs, calculate the amount of the periodic payments from each IRA, and then take the periodic payments from only one IRA. [IRS Notice 88-38, 1988-1 C.B. 524; Priv. Ltr. Ruls. 200309028, 200119060, 9816028, 9747045, 9505022, 9243054, 9050030] To calculate substantially equal periodic payments from a single IRA, the entire IRA account balance, not a portion thereof, must be used. [Priv. Ltr. Rul. 9705033]

See Q 16:8 regarding a series of payments that commences after 2002, and see Q 16:9 regarding modifications of the periodic payments.

Q 16:8   What are substantially equal periodic payments if the series of payments commences after 2002?

If a series of payments commences on or after January 1, 2003, the payments will be considered to be substantially equal periodic payments if they are made in accordance with one of the following three calculations:

1. *The required minimum distribution (RMD) method.* The annual payment for each year is determined by dividing the account balance for that year by the number from the chosen life expectancy table for that year. Under this method, the account balance, the number from the chosen life expectancy table, and the resulting annual payments are redetermined for each year. If this method is chosen, there will not be deemed to be a modification in the series of substantially equal periodic payments, even if the amount of payments changes from year to year, provided there is not a change to another method of determining the payments (see Q 16:9).

2. *The fixed amortization method.* The annual payment for each year is determined by amortizing in level amounts the account balance over a specified number of years determined using the chosen life expectancy table and the chosen interest rate. Under this method, the account balance, the number from the chosen life expectancy table, and the resulting annual payment are determined once for the first distribution year, and the annual payment is the same amount in each succeeding year.

3. *The fixed annuitization method.* The annual payment for each year is determined by dividing the account balance by an annuity factor that is the present value of an annuity of $1 per year beginning at the individual's age and continuing for the life of the individual (or the joint lives of the individual and beneficiary). The annuity factor is derived using the mortality table in Appendix B of Revenue Ruling 2002-62 and using the chosen interest rate. Under this method, the account balance, the annuity factor, the chosen interest rate, and the resulting annual payment are determined once for the first distribution year, and the annual payment is the same amount in each succeeding year.

[Rev. Rul. 2002-62, § 2.01, 2002-2 C.B. 710; Priv. Ltr. Ruls. 200544023, 200532062]

Where an individual failed to establish that the distributions from his individual retirement annuities (see Q 30:3) satisfied any one of the three calculations to be considered substantially equal periodic payments, the penalty tax was imposed. [Prough, T.C.M. 2010–20]

The life expectancy tables that can be used to determine distribution periods are:

1. The uniform lifetime table set forth at the end of this Q 16:8;
2. The single life expectancy table (see Q 11:24); or
3. The joint and last survivor table (see Q 11:24).

The number that is used for a distribution year is the number shown from the table for the employee's (or IRA owner's) age on such individual's birthday in that year. If the joint and survivor table is being used, the age of the beneficiary on the beneficiary's birthday in that year is also used. In the case of the RMD method, the same life expectancy table that is used for the first distribution year must be used in each following year. Thus, if the individual uses the single life expectancy table for the RMD method in the first distribution year, the same table must be used in subsequent distribution years.

[Rev. Rul. 2002-62, § 2.02(a), 2002-2 C.B. 710]

If the joint life and last survivor table is used, the survivor must be the actual beneficiary of the employee with respect to the account for the year of the distribution. If there is more than one beneficiary, the identity and age of the beneficiary used for purposes of each of the permissible methods are determined under the rules for determining the designated beneficiary for purposes of the RMD rules (see Qs 11:14, 11:15). The beneficiary is determined for a year as of January 1 of the year, without regard to changes in the beneficiary in that year or beneficiary determinations in prior years. For example, if an individual starts distributions from an IRA in 2006 at age 50 and a 25-year-old and 55-year-old are beneficiaries on January 1, the 55-year-old is the designated beneficiary, and the number for the individual from the joint and last survivor table (age 50 and age 55) would be 38.3, even though later in 2006 the 55-year-old is eliminated as a beneficiary. However, if that beneficiary is eliminated or dies in 2006, under the RMD method, that individual would not be taken into account in future years. If, in any year there is no beneficiary, the single life expectancy table is used for that year. [Rev. Rul. 2002-62, § 2.02(b), 2002-2 C.B. 710]

The interest rate that may be used is any interest rate that is not more than 120 percent of the federal midterm rate for either of the two months immediately preceding the month in which the distribution begins. [Rev. Rul. 2002-62, § 2.02(c), 2002-2 C.B. 710] If the interest rate used exceeds the guidelines, the distributions will not be substantially equal periodic payments and the penalty tax will be imposed unless another exception applies. [Farley, Jr., T.C. Summ. Op. 2003-43; Priv. Ltr. Rul. 200437038] The individual is permitted to use a lesser interest rate and, by doing so, can tailor the amount of the substantially equal periodic payments.

The account balance that is used to determine payments must be determined in a reasonable manner based on the facts and circumstances. For example, for an IRA with daily valuations that made its first distribution on July 15, 2006, it would be reasonable to determine the yearly account balance when using the RMD method based on the value of the IRA from December 31, 2005, to July 15, 2006. For subsequent years, under the method, it would be reasonable to use the value either on the December 31 of the prior year or on a date within a reasonable period before that year's distribution. [Rev. Rul. 2002-62, § 2.02(d), 2002-2 C.B. 710]

Under all three permissible methods, substantially equal periodic payments are calculated with respect to an account balance as of the first valuation date selected. Thus, a modification to the series of payments will occur if, after such date, there is (1) any addition to the account balance other than gains or losses, (2) any nontaxable transfer of a portion of the account balance to another retirement plan, or (3) a rollover by the individual of the amount received resulting in such amount not being taxable (see Q 16:9). [Rev. Rul. 2002-62, § 2.02(e), 2002-2 C.B. 710] However, IRS ruled that adjustments in the payment stream could be made without a modification having occurred. In the first two cases approved by IRS, the IRA owner proposed to determine the annual payments from the IRA using the fixed amortization method; but, rather than making a fixed annual payment, the owner proposed to recalculate the amount of the annual payment each year. For subsequent years, the owner would recalculate the annual distribution for each succeeding year by using the IRA account balance as of December 31 of the prior year, determining life expectancy as of the owner's age in each subsequent year using the single life table (see Q 11:24), and using 120 percent of the federal mid-term rate as of December 31 of the prior year. [Priv. Ltr. Ruls. 200432021, 200432024; see also Priv. Ltr. Ruls. 200551033, 200551032] In the third case approved by IRS, the IRA owner proposed to determine the annual payments from the IRA using the fixed annuitization method; but, rather than making a fixed annual payment, the owner proposed to recalculate the amount of the annual payment each year. For subsequent years, the annual distribution amount would be determined by dividing the IRA account balance as of December 31 of the prior year by an annuity factor that is equal to the cost of an annual $1 per year life annuity, with such annuity factor (based on the owner's age in that distribution year) calculated using 120 percent of the federal mid-term rate as of December 31 of the prior year and the Appendix B mortality table. [Priv. Ltr. Rul. 200432023; see also Priv. Ltr. Rul. 200943044] An individual commenced receiving a series of withdrawals from his IRA and, at about the same time, requested an IRS ruling that the methodology constituted a series of substantially equal periodic payments. After IRS disapproval of the methodology, the individual redetermined the annual distribution, which IRS approved and which resulted in a smaller annual distribution. The individual was permitted to redeposit the excess withdrawal to his IRA (see Q 34:36). [Priv. Ltr. Rul. 200442033]

Under a qualified retirement plan, upon the occurrence of a distributable event, a participant could elect to receive a portion of the plan account in a single-sum payment with the balance of the account to be distributed in the form of an annuity. Whether or not the participant rolled over the single-sum payment to an IRA (see Q 34:1), IRS ruled that the portion distributed as an annuity would be treated as a series of substantially equal periodic payments. [Priv. Ltr. Rul. 200550039]

The rules set forth above are effective for any series of payments commencing on or after January 1, 2003, and were permitted to be used for distributions that commenced in 2002. If a series of payments commenced in a year prior to 2003 that satisfied the prior rules (see Q 16:7), the method of calculating the payments in the series is permitted to be changed at any time to the RMD method, including use of a different life expectancy table. [Rev. Rul. 2002-62, § 3, 2002-2 C.B. 710]

Individual's Age	Life Expectancy	Individual's Age	Life Expectancy
10	86.2	41	55.4
11	85.2	42	54.4
12	84.2	43	53.4
13	83.2	44	52.4
14	82.2	45	51.5
15	81.2	46	50.5
16	80.2	47	49.5
17	79.2	48	48.5
18	78.2	49	47.5
19	77.3	50	46.5
20	76.3	51	45.5
21	75.3	52	44.6
22	74.3	53	43.6
23	73.3	54	42.6
24	72.3	55	41.6
25	71.3	56	40.7
26	70.3	57	39.7
27	69.3	58	38.7
28	68.3	59	37.8
29	67.3	60	36.8
30	66.3	61	35.8
31	65.3	62	34.9
32	64.3	63	33.9
33	63.3	64	33.0
34	62.3	65	32.0
35	61.4	66	31.1
36	60.4	67	30.2
37	59.4	68	29.2
38	58.4	69	28.3
39	57.4	70	27.4
40	56.4	71	26.5

Individual's Age	Life Expectancy	Individual's Age	Life Expectancy
72	25.6	94	9.1
73	24.7	95	8.6
74	23.8	96	8.1
75	22.9	97	7.6
76	22.0	98	7.1
77	21.2	99	6.7
78	20.3	100	6.3
79	19.5	101	5.9
80	18.7	102	5.5
81	17.9	103	5.2
82	17.1	104	4.9
83	16.3	105	4.5
84	15.5	106	4.2
85	14.8	107	3.9
86	14.1	108	3.7
87	13.4	109	3.4
88	12.7	110	3.1
89	12.0	111	2.9
90	11.4	112	2.6
91	10.8	113	2.4
92	10.2	114	2.1
93	9.6	115 and older	1.9

[Rev. Rul. 2002-62, app. A, 2002-2 C.B. 710]

See Q 16:9 regarding modifications of the periodic payments.

Q 16:9   What happens if the substantially equal periodic payments are modified?

There is a special recapture provision. If the amount of the periodic payments (see Qs 16:7, 16:8) is modified (other than by reason of death or disability; see Qs 16:5, 16:6) before the *later* of (1) the end of the five-year period beginning with the date of the first payment or (2) the employee's attainment of age 59½ (see Q 16:4), the penalty tax that would have been imposed on all payments, plus interest, is imposed in the year in which the modification occurs. [I.R.C. § 72(t)(4); Arnold, 111 T.C. 250 (1998); Priv. Ltr. Ruls. 200033048, 9821056, 9818055]

Example 1. Harriet commences receiving substantially equal annual payments from her qualified retirement plan after retirement at age 50. Harriet ceases receiving payments at age 58 after eight annual payments. The recapture tax will apply because, even though Harriet has received more than five annual payments, she is not age 59½. Harriet must pay the recapture tax in the year in which she reaches age 58. The recapture amount will be 10 percent of the total of the eight annual payments. Interest will also be imposed.

Example 2. Harriet commenced receiving substantially equal annual payments from her IRA at age 58. Harriet ceases receiving payments at age 61 after three annual payments. The recapture tax will apply because, even though Harriet has attained age 59½, she ceased receiving payments before the end of the five-year period. Harriet must pay the recapture tax in the year in which she reaches age 61. The recapture amount will be 10 percent of the total of the annual payments received by Harriet before she attained age 59½. Interest will also be imposed.

Under the three permissible methods, substantially equal periodic payments are calculated with respect to an account balance as of the first valuation date (see Q 16:8). Thus, a modification to the series of payments will occur if, after such date, there is (1) any addition to the account balance other than gains or losses, (2) any nontaxable transfer of a portion of the account balance to another retirement plan, or (3) a rollover by the individual of the amount received resulting in such amount not being taxable. [Rev. Rul. 2002-62, § 2.02(e), 2002-2 C.B. 710; Priv. Ltr. Ruls. 200925044, 200720023] An individual had received annual distributions (in equal quarterly payments) from his IRA in substantially equal periodic payments. After receiving the final quarterly payment but before the end of the five-year period, the individual rolled over a qualified retirement plan distribution to his IRA. IRS ruled that the rollover was a modification. [Priv. Ltr. Rul. 200634033] IRS ruled that an individual was not subject to the penalty tax where the financial advisor erroneously rolled over an amount from one of the individual's IRAs into another IRA from which the individual was taking substantially equal periodic payments. [Priv. Ltr. Rul. 200616046; *see also* Priv. Ltr. Ruls. 200929021, 200631025, and 200628029]

Where an IRA owner desired to increase the periodic payments because the return on the IRA investments was greater than anticipated, IRS concluded that the increase would be an impermissible modification and the penalty tax would be imposed retroactively. [Priv. Ltr. Ruls. 199943050, 9821056] In a similar situation, IRS ruled that, although the increased payments constituted an impermissible modification, the increased payments satisfied the exception for substantially equal periodic payments. Hence, the recapture tax was imposed upon the initial stream of payments, but the penalty tax was not imposed upon the new increased stream of payments. [Priv. Ltr. Ruls. 200033048, 199909059] During one year in which an IRA owner was receiving periodic payments, she took an additional distribution that satisfied the exception for qualified higher education expenses (see Q 16:15). The court concluded that a distribution satisfying this statutory exception did not constitute a modification of the series of substantially equal periodic payments. [Benz, 132 T.C. No. 15 (2009)]

Where an IRA owner desired to cease receiving periodic payments and roll over the IRA to a qualified retirement plan (see Q 34:38), IRS similarly ruled that cessation would be a modification resulting in the retroactive imposition of the penalty tax. [Priv. Ltr. Rul. 9818055] A change in the monthly distribution date is ministerial and not a modification of the periodic payment method; therefore, the penalty tax will not be imposed on either the current or prior distributions. [Priv. Ltr. Rul. 9514026] An individual's correction of a mathematical error of less than .2 percent to his 2003 annual distribution payment from his IRAs was not a modification, ruled IRS. [Priv. Ltr. Rul. 200601044]

IRS has ruled that, where a portion of the husband's IRA was transferred to an IRA of the former spouse pursuant to a divorce decree (see Q 30:51) and the substantially equal periodic payments to the husband were reduced but the aggregate annual amount of the distributions to the husband and former spouse did not change substantially, a modification of the periodic payment method did not occur. [Priv. Ltr. Rul. 9739044] In a similar situation, IRS ruled that a former spouse did not have to continue receiving a proportionate amount of the periodic payments after a portion of the husband's IRA was transferred to her IRA, but IRS did not rule as to whether the former husband could proportionately reduce his periodic payments or had to continue them in the same amount. [Priv. Ltr. Rul. 200027060] However, IRS subsequently ruled that the periodic payments could be proportionately reduced. [Priv. Ltr. Ruls. 201030038, 200214034, 200202076, 200202075, 200202074, 200052039, 200050046] IRS has ruled similarly concerning the reduction in annual distributions from a qualified retirement plan after the participant became divorced. [Priv. Ltr. Rul. 200225040]

IRS has promulgated new life expectancy tables for purposes of calculating required minimum distributions (see Qs 11:1, 11:24). IRS has advised that these new tables also may be used to determine an employee's (or IRA owner's) life expectancy, or the joint life expectancy of an employee (or IRA owner) and designated beneficiary, for purposes of calculating the amount of substantially equal periodic payments. One method (see Q 16:7) allows use of the methodology underlying the minimum distribution calculations for separate accounts in which the account balance in the prior year is divided by life expectancy or joint life expectancy. Under this method, the payments are not equal but are treated as substantially equal if the life expectancy is determined in a consistent manner. A series of substantially equal periodic payments determined under this methodology will not be considered to have been modified merely because the new tables are used in the future to determine the annual periodic payments rather than the prior tables. If a series of payments commenced in a year prior to 2003 that satisfied the prior rules (see Q 16:7), the method of calculating the payments in the series is permitted to be changed at any time to the RMD method (see Q 16:8), including use of a different life expectancy table. [Rev. Rul. 2002-62, § 3, 2002-2 C.B. 710]

If, as a result of following an acceptable method of determining substantially equal periodic payments, an individual's assets in an individual account plan (see Q 2:2) or an IRA are exhausted, the individual will not be subject to the penalty tax as a result of not receiving substantially equal periodic payments, and the resulting cessation of payments will not be treated as a modification of the series of payments. [Rev. Rul. 2002-62, § 2.03(a), 2002-2 C.B. 710]

An individual who begins distributions in a year using either the fixed amortization method or the fixed annuitization method (see Qs 16:7, 16:8) may in any subsequent year switch to the RMD method to determine the payment for the year of the switch and all subsequent years, and the change in method will not be treated as a modification. Once the change is made, the RMD method must be followed in all subsequent years. Any subsequent change will be a modification. [Rev. Rul. 2002-62, § 2.03(b), 2002-2 C.B. 710] RMDs from defined contribution plans (see Q 2:2) and IRAs are suspended for calendar year 2009 (see Q 11:1). The suspension does not apply to payments that are part of a series of substantially equal periodic payments under the RMD method. Therefore, if these payments are skipped for 2009 (other than for death or disability) before age 59½, or before five years from the date of the first payment have elapsed, all the payments made under the series will be subject to the recapture tax. [IRS Notice 2009-82, Q&A-9, 2009-41 I.R.B.]

An individual was receiving substantially equal periodic payments from his IRA, but the IRA custodian failed to make the entire required distribution during the taxable year. After discovery of the error, the custodian made a make-up distribution in the next taxable year. IRS ruled that the underpayment was not a modification. [Priv. Ltr. Rul. 200503036; *see also* Priv. Ltr. Ruls. 200930053, 200840054, and 200835033]

Q 16:10   How does the age 55 requirement work?

If an employee receives a distribution from a qualified retirement plan after separation from service and separation occurs during or after the calendar year in which the employee attains age 55, the penalty tax will not apply. Thus, it appears that a 54-year-old employee will not be subject to the penalty tax on a distribution made after separation from service as long as the employee attains age 55 during the calendar year in which separation occurs. [I.R.C. § 72(t)(2)(A)(v); IRS Notice 87-13 Q&A-20, 1987-1 C.B. 432; Williams, T.C. Summ. Op. 2008-53; Olintz, No. 763-05S (Tax Ct. 2006); Priv. Ltr. Ruls. 200215032, 200038050, 199919039, 9429026, 9224056; *but see* Priv. Ltr. Rul. 9135060 (the employee retired at age 50), *replaced by* Priv. Ltr. Rul. 9241063 (based on different facts)]

Example. Monroe participated in a profit sharing plan until 2008 when he retired at age 55. In 2010, at age 57, Monroe received a single-sum distribution of his plan benefits. Since Monroe separated from service during or after the calendar year in which he attained age 55, his receipt of benefits will not be subject to the penalty tax.

This exception does *not* apply to a distribution from an IRA. [I.R.C. § 72(t)(3)(A)]

Q 16:11   How is a distribution made on account of an IRS levy treated?

One court ruled that the penalty tax applies to voluntary distributions and not to involuntary withdrawals. Hence, the court did not apply the penalty tax when IRS levied against an individual's qualified retirement plan account (see Q 4:29). [Larotonda, 89 T.C. 287 (1987)] In another case, the court did not apply the penalty tax when an involuntary IRA withdrawal resulted from a decree of forfeiture to the government over which the IRA owner had no control. [Murillo, 75 T.C.M. 1564 (1998)] The penalty tax will not apply to a distribution made on account of an IRS levy on an individual's qualified retirement plan benefits or IRA. [I.R.C. § 72(t)(2)(A)(vii)]

> **Example.** On January 25, 2011, IRS levies John's entire IRA of $22,000. Even though John has not attained age 59½, the distribution due to the IRS levy will not be subject to the penalty tax; however, John must include the $22,000 in his gross income for 2011.

IRS announced that it will not assess the penalty tax on levies in the case of a decree of forfeiture. [Chief Couns. Notice N(36) 00002; Action on Decision, 1999-1 C.B. 332] IRS has also ruled that a court may garnish a participant's benefit from a qualified retirement plan to satisfy a fine or restitution order imposed in a federal criminal action and that a distribution made pursuant to an order of garnishment will not be subject to the penalty tax. [Priv. Ltr. Rul. 200426027] IRS also announced that, after serving a notice of levy on a state retirement fund, IRS cannot exercise the taxpayer's right to suspend membership in the fund in order to obtain an immediate distribution of the taxpayer's assets in the fund where the taxpayer has not yet attained retirement age. [Chief Couns. Advice 200819001]

This exception does not apply if there is no levy on the qualified retirement plan benefits or IRA. Thus, the exception does not apply if IRS has not levied upon the individual and the individual withdraws funds to pay taxes in order to avoid a levy or the individual withdraws funds to obtain the release of a levy on other interests. [Kallmyer, T.C. Summ. Op. 2002-52; *see also* Amesbury, T.C.M. 2010–_____]

Q 16:12   How does the exception for medical expenses work?

The penalty tax will not apply to early distributions from a qualified retirement plan or an IRA that are used to pay medical expenses in excess of 7½ percent of adjusted gross income (AGI). This exception applies whether or not the individual itemizes deductions for the taxable year. [I.R.C. § 72(t)(2)(B); Mitchell, 91 T.C.M. 1172 (2006); Berry, 87 T.C.M. 812 (2004)]

> **Example 1.** Jennifer, age 25, incurred medical expenses of $3,000 in 2010 and withdrew $3,000 from her IRA that year. Jennifer's AGI (including the $3,000 IRA withdrawal) for 2010 was $22,000. For 2010, Jennifer could deduct $1,350 of her medical expenses [$3,000 − (7.5% × $22,000)]. Whether or not Jennifer itemizes deductions on her 2010 return, $1,350 of her IRA withdrawal is exempt from the penalty tax.

The medical expense payments and the plan or IRA distributions must occur in the same tax year. [Evers, T.C. Summ. Op. 2008-140; Kimball, T.C. Summ. Op. 2004-2]

Example 2. Jennifer incurred medical expenses of $3,000 in 2009, withdraws $3,000 from her IRA in 2010, and incurs no medical expenses in 2010. The entire $3,000 IRA withdrawal is subject to the penalty tax because the payment of the expenses and the receipt of the withdrawal occurred in different tax years.

Q 16:13 How are alternate payees treated?

The penalty tax on early distributions from qualified retirement plans (see Q 36:33) does not apply to any distribution to an alternate payee (see Q 36:5) pursuant to a QDRO (see Q 36:1). [I.R.C. § 72(t)(2)(C); Seidel, 89 T.C.M. 972 (2005); Priv. Ltr. Ruls. 9051041, 9013007, 8935041] Because of this exception, the penalty tax will not be imposed on the participant if the alternate payee is a nonspouse or non-former spouse (e.g., a child) (see Q 36:30) and will not be imposed on a spouse or former spouse alternate payee (see Q 36:31).

A spouse or former spouse alternate payee may be eligible to roll over the distribution (see Q 36:32). However, if, for example, the alternate payee rolls over the distribution to an IRA and commences distributions before age 59½ (see Q 16:4), the penalty tax will be imposed, unless an exception applies (see Q 36:33).

Although the QDRO rules do not apply to IRAs, the transfer of an individual's interest in an IRA to the individual's spouse or former spouse under a divorce or separation agreement is not considered a taxable transfer made by such individual; and, therefore, the penalty tax will not be imposed because the tax applies only to amounts includible in income (see Qs 16:1, 30:51, 36:8). [I.R.C. §§ 72(t)(3)(A), 408(d)(6); Priv. Ltr. Ruls. 200214029, 200202076, 200202075, 200202074, 9739044, 9016077] However, if the spouse or former spouse commences distributions before 59½, the penalty tax will be imposed, unless an exception applies. [Cohen, 88 T.C.M. 330 (2004)] The penalty tax was imposed when an amount was transferred from an individual's IRA to his former spouse in a garnishment proceeding for arrearages in child support payments. [Vorwald, 73 T.C.M. 1697 (1997)] The penalty tax was also imposed where, pursuant to a divorce decree, the individual withdrew funds from a plan and/or his IRA and then paid the funds to his former wife. [Simpson, I, 86 T.C.M. 470 (2003); Bougas III, 86 T.C.M. 9 (2003); Czepiel v. Comm'r, 00-1257 (1st Cir. 2000); Baas, 83 T.C.M. 1744 (2002); Jones, 80 T.C.M. 76 (2000); Bunney, 114 T.C. 259 (2000)]

Q 16:14 How does the exception for health insurance premiums work?

The penalty tax does not apply to distributions to an individual from an IRA for the payment of health insurance premiums with respect to the individual and the individual's spouse and dependents after the individual has separated from service. For this exception to apply, the individual must have received unemployment compensation for 12 consecutive weeks under federal or state law, and the distributions must be made during a taxable year in which the unemployment compensation is paid or during the next year. This exception does not apply to distributions made after an individual's reemployment if the individual has been employed for at least 60 days after the initial separation from service. A self-employed individual (see Q 6:60) is treated as meeting the requirements for unemployment compensation except for the fact that the individual had been self-employed. [I.R.C. § 72(t)(2)(D); Priv Ltr. Rul. 200920052] In addition, for this exception to apply, the health insurance premium must be paid by the individual in the taxable year of the distribution. [Davis, T.C. Summ. Op. 2009-61] This exception does *not* apply to distributions from qualified retirement plans.

Q 16:15   What are qualified higher education expenses?

Penalty-free withdrawals from IRAs, *not* from qualified retirement plans, can be made for qualified higher education expenses. [I.R.C. §§ 72(t)(2)(E), 72(t)(7)] During one year in which an IRA owner was receiving substantially equal periodic payments (see Q 16:8), she took an additional distribution that satisfied the exception for qualified higher education expenses. The court concluded that a distribution satisfying this statutory exception did not constitute a modification of the series of substantially equal periodic payments (see Q 16:9). [Benz, 132 T.C. No. 15 (2009)] Where an individual withdrew funds from a qualified retirement plan, used the distribution to pay for qualified higher education expenses, and no other exception applied, the penalty tax was imposed. [Domanico, No. 18992-04S (Tax Ct. 2006); Barbee, No. 9408-04S (Tax Ct. 2006); Jones, No. 6936-04S (Tax Ct. 2005); Uscinski, 89 T.C.M. 1337 (2005); McGovern, T.C. Summ. Op. 2003-137] Had the individual rolled over the plan distribution to an IRA (see Q 16:22) and then withdrawn the funds from the IRA to pay such expenses, the IRA withdrawal would have satisfied the exception and the penalty tax would not have been imposed. For the exception to be available, the qualified higher education expenses must be incurred by the individual in the taxable year of the distribution. [Duronio, 93 T.C.M. 1112 (2007); Lodder-Beckert, 90 T.C.M. 4 (2005); Ambata, No. 19592-04S (Tax Ct. 2005)

Qualified higher education expenses mean expenses for tuition, fees, books, supplies, and equipment required for the enrollment or attendance of the individual (including the individual's spouse or child or grandchild of the individual or the individual's spouse) at an eligible education institution. If the individual is at least a half-time student at an eligible educational institution, qualified higher education expenses will also include room and board (generally the school's posted room and board charge for students living on-campus, or $2,500 per year for students living off-campus and not at home). [I.R.C. §§ 529(e)(3), 530(b)(2)(A), 530(b)(2)(B); IRS Notice 98-49, Q&A C-2, 1998-2 C.B. 365; IRS Notice 97-60, § 3, Q&A-15, 1997-2 C.B. 310] Where a computer was not required for a student's enrollment or attendance at a university, the cost of the computer was not a qualified higher education expense. [Gorski, T.C. Summ. Op. 2005-112]

For room and board to be a qualified higher education expense, a student will be considered to be enrolled at least half-time if the student is enrolled for at least half the full-time academic workload for the course of study the student is pursuing as determined under the standards of the institution where the student is enrolled. The institution's standard for a full-time workload must equal or exceed the standards established by the Department of Education under the Higher Education Act of 1965. A student will not be treated as an eligible student if convicted of a federal or state felony charge for the possession or distribution of a controlled substance. [I.R.C. §§ 25A(b)(3), 529(e)(3)(B)(i); IRS Notice 97-60, § 1, Q&A-3, 1997-2 C.B. 310]

The individual's qualified higher education expenses are reduced by:

1. Any payments paid for, or on behalf of, the individual under a scholarship or fellowship grant excludable from gross income under Section 117;

2. Certain other tax-free educational benefits (such as employer-provided educational assistance excludable from gross income under Section 127);

3. Expenses paid with income from United States savings bonds excludable under Section 135; or

4. Any other payment, other than a gift, bequest, devise, or inheritance excludable under Section 102(a), that is for the individual's education expenses or attributable to the individual's enrollment at an eligible educational institution, and that is excludable from gross income. [I.R.C. §§ 25A(g)(2), 530(b)(2)(A)]

An eligible educational institution is any college, university, vocational school, or other postsecondary educational institution that is described in Section 481 of the Higher Education Act of 1965 and, therefore, is eligible to participate in the student aid programs administered by the Department of Education. This category includes virtually all accredited public, nonprofit, and proprietary postsecondary educational institutions. [I.R.C. § 530(b)(3); IRS Notice 97-60, § 3, Q&A-16, 1997-2 C.B. 310] High schools are not eligible educational institutions. [Nolan, 94 T.C.M. 378 (2007)]

Q 16:16   What is a qualified first-time homebuyer distribution?

Penalty-free withdrawals from IRAs, *not* from qualified retirement plans, can be made if the distribution is a qualified first-time homebuyer distribution. [I.R.C. § 72(t)(2)(F); Fulcher, T.C. Summ. Op. 2003-157] Where an individual withdrew funds from a qualified retirement plan, used the distribution to pay a portion of the cost of a new home, and no other exception applied, the penalty tax was imposed. [Jones, No. 6936-04S (Tax Ct. 2005); Joseph, T.C. Summ. Op. 2003-153] Had the individual rolled over the plan distribution to an IRA (see Q 16:22) and then withdrawn the funds from the IRA to pay such portion, the IRA withdrawal would have satisfied the exception and the penalty tax would not have been imposed.

First-time homebuyers are individuals (and spouses) who did not own an interest in a principal residence during the two years prior to the purchase of a home and who were not in an extended period for filing with respect to the gain from the sale of a principal residence. Penalty-free withdrawals can be made for the acquisition, construction, or reconstruction costs of a principal residence for a first-time homebuyer who is the individual or the individual's spouse, child, or grandchild, or ancestor of the individual or the individual's spouse. The distribution has to be used within 120 days to pay the costs of acquiring, constructing, or reconstructing a residence. If there is a delay in acquisition, construction, or reconstruction, the distribution can be redeposited in an IRA within 120 days without imposition of income or penalty taxes. [Priv. Ltr. Rul. 200423033] The aggregate amount of payments or distributions received by an individual that may be treated as qualified first-time homebuyer distributions for any taxable year may not exceed $10,000 reduced by the aggregate amounts treated as qualified first-time homebuyer distributions with respect to the individual for all prior taxable years. In other words, there is a $10,000 lifetime limit. [I.R.C. § 72(t)(8)] Individuals who used a distribution to pay off a mortgage on their residence acquired seven years earlier did not qualify as first-time homebuyers. [Sharma, T.C. Summ. Op. 2008-98; *see also* Davis, T.C. Summ. Op. 2009-61]

An individual cannot have two principal residences at the same time. [Suarez, No. 19455-03S (Tax Ct. 2005)] For the exception to apply to a married couple, each spouse must qualify as a first-time homebuyer. [Olup, T.C. Summ. Op. 2005-183]

Q 16:17   How are corrective distributions treated?

Corrective distributions of excess aggregate contributions, excess deferrals, or excess aggregate contributions from qualified retirement plans are not subject to the penalty tax (see Qs 27:28, 27:31, 27:64, 27:85).

Corrective distributions from IRAs are also not subject to the penalty tax (see Q 30:9).

Q 16:18   How are dividends paid to ESOP participants treated?

Dividends paid in cash directly to ESOP (see Q 28:1) participants by the employer and dividends paid to the ESOP and then distributed in cash to participants are treated as paid separately from any other payments from the ESOP. Thus, a deductible dividend is treated as a plan distribution and as paid under a separate contract providing only for payment of deductible dividends. A deductible dividend is a taxable distribution even though an employee has basis (see Q 13:3), but the distribution is not subject to the penalty tax (see Q 28:12). [I.R.C. §§ 72(e)(5)(D), 72(t)(2)(A)(vi), 402; Temp. Treas. Reg. § 1.404(k)-1T, Q&A-3]

Q 16:19   What is an involuntary cash-out?

A qualified retirement plan may provide for an involuntary distribution if the present value of an employee's benefit is $5,000 or less (see Qs 10:42, 10:61). Thus, a plan may require a single-sum distribution to terminating employees whose benefits have a present value of $5,000 or any lower amount. [I.R.C. §§ 411(a)(11), 417(e); Treas. Reg. §§ 1.401(a)(4)-4(b)(2)(ii)(C), 1.401(a)-4, Q&A-4, 1.411(d)-4, Q&A-2(b)(2)(v)]

If an involuntary distribution occurs before the employee is age 59½ and no exception applies (see Q 16:3), the penalty tax will be imposed, unless the distribution is rolled over (see Q 16:22). [IRS Notice 87-13, Q&A-20, 1987-1 C.B. 432]

Q 16:20   How is the cost of life insurance protection treated?

If a qualified retirement plan provides life insurance protection for a participating employee, the participant must include in gross income the term cost of the insurance protection paid for with employer contributions or trust earnings if, upon death, the proceeds of the life insurance policy on the participant's life are payable to either (1) the participant's estate or beneficiary or (2) the trustee of the plan if the trustee is required by the plan's provisions to pay such proceeds to the participant's estate or beneficiary (see Q 15:6). [I.R.C. § 72(m)(3)(B); Treas. Reg. § 1.72-16(b)]

The amount includible in the participant's gross income is not treated as a distribution for purposes of the penalty tax. [IRS Notice 89-25, Q&A-11, 1989-1 C.B. 662]

Q 16:21   How are loans treated?

Loans from qualified retirement plans are subject to a number of limitations and requirements. An amount received by a participant (or beneficiary) as a loan from a qualified retirement plan is treated as having been received as a distribution from the plan (a deemed distribution), unless the loan satisfies the applicable limitations and requirements. A deemed distribution may be includible in gross income; and, in addition, a taxable plan loan may also be subject to the penalty tax, unless an exception applies. [I.R.C. §§ 72(p)(1), 72(p)(5); Treas. Reg. § 1.72(p)-1, Q&A-1, Q&A-11; Billups, T.C. Summ. Op. 2009-86; Marquez, T.C. Summ. Op. 2009-80; Duncan, 90 T.C.M. 35 (2005); Plotkin, 81 T.C.M. 1395 (2001); Medina, 112 T.C. 51 (1999); Patrick, 75 T.C.M. 1629 (1998); Chapman, 73 T.C.M. 2405 (1997); Estate of Gray, 70 T.C.M. 556 (1995); Earnshaw, 69 T.C.M. 2353 (1995)]

For details on plan loans, see chapter 14.

Q 16:22   What is the effect of a rollover?

The penalty tax can be avoided if an early distribution qualifies for rollover treatment and it is rolled over into an eligible retirement plan. See chapter 34 for more information on rollovers.

Where an individual received a distribution from a qualified retirement plan because the insurance company holding plan assets was liquidated or because the financial institution holding plan assets failed, the penalty tax was imposed. In both cases, the courts held that there is no differentiation between voluntary and involuntary distributions and that the individual could have avoided the penalty by doing a timely rollover. [Swihart, 76 T.C.M. 855 (1998); Aronson, 98 T.C. 283 (1992); *see also* Atkin, 95 T.C.M. 1364 (2008)] IRS has also advised that the penalty tax may be imposed on individuals who withdrew funds from their IRAs to make new investments, believed that the new investments qualified for rollover treatment, but subsequently discovered that their funds had been embezzled. [Field Serv. Adv. 199933038]

Q 16:23   Do any special rules apply to IRAs?

IRA assets invested in collectibles are treated as distributions for tax purposes (that is, taxed as current income; and, if the individual has not attained age 59½ (see Q 16:4), the penalty tax also is imposed (see Q 30:2)). [I.R.C. § 408(m); Rev. Rul. 92-73, 1992-2 C.B. 224; Priv. Ltr. Rul. 8940067]

A retirement account is not treated as an IRA if an individual engages in a prohibited transaction (see Q 24:1) with respect to the retirement account. The account is treated as having distributed all its assets to the individual on the first day of the taxable year in which the prohibited transaction occurs. If an individual uses the IRA or any portion thereof as security for a loan, the portion used is treated as a distribution to the individual (see Q 30:45). [I.R.C. §§ 408(e)(2), 408(e)(4); Priv. Ltr. Rul. 9725029]

If an individual borrows any money from or against an individual retirement annuity, the annuity contract ceases to be a qualified individual retirement annuity as of the first day of the year. Because of the borrowing, the individual must include in gross income for the year the fair market value of the annuity as of the first day of such year (see Q 30:3). [I.R.C. § 408(e)(3); Griswold, 85 T.C. 869 (1985)]

In addition to including the deemed distributions in gross income, the individual will be subject to the penalty tax if the individual has not attained age 59½ on the date of the deemed distribution.

Example 1. Stuart attained age 59½ on April 30, 2011 and engaged in a prohibited transaction with his IRA on May 14, 2011. Stuart is subject to the penalty tax because he was not age 59½ on January 1, 2011, the date of the deemed distribution.

Example 2. The facts are the same as in Example 1, except that Stuart uses his IRA as security for a loan on May 14, 2011. Stuart is not subject to the penalty tax because he was age 59½ on May 14, 2011, the date of the deemed distribution.

Q 16:24 Does a special rule apply to SIMPLE IRAs?

A special rule applies to a payment or distribution received from a SIMPLE IRA (see Q 33:3) during the two-year period beginning on the date on which the individual first participated in any SIMPLE IRA plan maintained by the individual's employer (the two-year period). Under this special rule, if the penalty tax applies to a distribution within the two-year period, the penalty tax is increased from 10 percent to 25 percent. If one of the exceptions to the application of the penalty tax applies (see Q 16:3), the exception will also apply to distributions within the two-year period and the 25 percent penalty tax will not apply. [I.R.C. § 72(t)(6); IRS Notice 98-4, Q&A I-2, 1998-1 C.B. 269]

The two-year period begins on the first day on which contributions made by the individual's employer are deposited in the individual's SIMPLE IRA. [IRS Notice 98-4, Q&A I-5, 1998-1 C.B. 269]

Q 16:25 Do different rules apply to Roth IRAs?

A qualified distribution from a Roth IRA is not includible in gross income (see Q 31:27) and, therefore, cannot be subject to the penalty tax (see Q 16:1). However, to the extent that a distribution from a Roth IRA is includible in the individual's gross income, the distribution may also be subject to the penalty tax. Since a Roth IRA is treated in most cases in the same manner as an IRA, the exceptions that apply to the imposition of the penalty tax on IRA distributions will also apply to Roth IRA distributions (see Q 16:3). [I.R.C. §§ 72(t), 408A(a); Treas. Reg. § 1.408A-6, Q&A-5(a)]

The amount includible in gross income because of a rollover or conversion of an IRA to a Roth IRA is not subject to the penalty tax even if the penalty tax would otherwise apply. [I.R.C. § 408A(d)(3)(A)(ii)] However, an individual is prevented from receiving a premature distribution while retaining the benefit of the nonpayment of the penalty tax. If converted amounts are withdrawn within the five-year period beginning with the year of the rollover or conversion, then, to the extent attributable to amounts that were includible in income due to the rollover or conversion, the amount withdrawn will be subject to the penalty tax unless an exception applies. [I.R.C. § 408A(d)(3)(F)] See Q 31:49 for details.

Q 16:26 How is the penalty tax reported?

The penalty tax is reported on Form 5329, Additional Taxes on Qualified Plans (Including IRAs) and Other Tax-Favored Accounts, which is attached to the individual's income tax return for the year of the distribution. Although the payor is not liable to withhold any amount on account of the penalty tax, the individual may have estimated tax liability with respect to the penalty tax. [IRS Notice 87-13, Q&A-20, 1987-1 C.B. 432]

IRS has concluded that math error procedures cannot be used to assess the penalty tax. This means that a notice of deficiency must be issued. [Service Center Advice 200250019]

Q 16:27   Is the penalty tax dischargeable in bankruptcy?

The additional tax on early distributions is treated as a penalty, not a tax, for bankruptcy law purposes. Thus, IRS does not have priority status over other creditors. [*In re* Cassidy, Jr., Nos. 91-1180, 91-1244 (10th Cir. 1992); see also Q 8:22] However, one court concluded that the penalty was a nondischargeable penalty so that post-bankruptcy discharge collection efforts by IRS did not violate the bankruptcy discharge injunction. [*In re* Mounier, No. 93-02297 (Bankr. S.D. Cal. 1998)]

Chapter 17

Saver's Credit

An eligible individual is allowed a nonrefundable tax credit for the taxable year in an amount equal to the applicable percentage of the individual's qualified retirement savings contributions for the year up to $2,000. This chapter describes the saver's credit and includes a sample notice that employers can give to employees explaining the credit.

Q 17:1 What is the saver's credit?

The saver's credit is a nonrefundable income tax credit (see Q 17:8) for certain taxpayers with adjusted gross income (AGI) that does not exceed $50,000 (indexed for inflation; see Q 17:6). The credit is equal to a specified percentage of certain (1) employee contributions made to an employer-sponsored retirement plan and (2) individual or spousal contributions to an IRA (see Q 30:1), including a Roth IRA (see Q 31:1). [I.R.C. § 25B; Ann. 2001-106, Q&A-1, 2001-2 C.B. 416]

AGI is modified by disregarding the foreign earned income exclusion and foreign housing exclusion or deduction under Section 911, the exclusion of income from American Samoa, Guam, or the Northern Mariana Islands under Section 931, and the exclusion of income from Puerto Rico under Section 933, and is referred to in this chapter as modified AGI. [I.R.C. § 25B(e)]

The amount of an individual's saver's credit in a taxable year cannot exceed the amount of tax that the individual would otherwise pay (not counting any refundable credits or the adoption credit) in the taxable year. If the individual's tax liability is reduced to zero because of other nonrefundable credits, then the individual will not be entitled to the saver's credit. [I.R.C. § 25B(g); Ann. 2001-106, Q&A-13, 2001-2 C.B. 416] The amount of the individual's saver's credit will not change the amount of the individual's refundable tax credits. A refundable tax credit, (e.g., the earned income credit or the refundable amount of the child tax credit) is an amount that the individual would receive as a refund even if the individual did not otherwise owe any taxes.

Initially, the saver's credit was available only for taxable years beginning in 2002 through the taxable year beginning in 2006. [I.R.C. § 25B(h); Ann.

2001-106, Q&A-1, 2001-2 C.B. 416] However, PPA (see Q 1:33) has made the saver's credit permanent. [PPA § 812 deleting I.R.C. § 25B(h)]

In a July 12, 2007, letter to the Acting IRS Commissioner, two members of the Senate Finance Committee requested that IRS improve targeted advertising to ensure that eligible taxpayers are made aware that they can use the saver's credit, permit taxpayers to claim the credit on Form 1040EZ, and refer to the saver's credit consistently in all IRS forms and publications. IRS did so and reminded low- and moderate-income workers that they can take steps to save for retirement and qualify for the saver's credit in 2007 and future years. [IRS News Rel. IR-2007-187 (Nov. 9, 2007); *see also* IRS News Rel. IR-2008-134 (Dec. 1, 2008)]

Q 17:2   Who is eligible for the saver's credit?

An eligible individual is an individual who has attained age 18 by the end of the taxable year and who is not a full-time student or claimed as a dependent on another taxpayer's federal income tax return for the year. [I.R.C. § 25B(c); Ann. 2001-106, Q&A-2, 2001-2 C.B. 416]

For this purpose, students include individuals who, during some part of each of five months during the year, are (1) enrolled at a school that has a regular teaching staff, course of study, and regularly enrolled body of students in attendance or (2) taking an on-farm training course given by such a school or a state, county, or local government. A student is a full-time student if the individual is enrolled for the number of hours or courses the school considers to be full time. [I.R.C. §§ 25B(c)(2)(B), 152(f)(2); Ann. 2001-106, Q&A-2, 2001-2 C.B. 416]

Q 17:3   What is the maximum annual contribution eligible for the saver's credit?

The maximum is $2,000 per year. [I.R.C. § 25B(a); Ann. 2001-106, Q&A-3, 2001-2 C.B. 416] The maximum amount is not indexed for inflation.

See Q 17:9 for the treatment of married individuals.

Q 17:4   Can the annual contribution amount eligible for the saver's credit be reduced?

Yes. The eligible individual's (see Q 17:2) qualified retirement savings contributions (see Q 17:5) for the taxable year are reduced by the sum of distributions received by the individual during the testing period from qualified retirement plans, 403(b) plans (see Q 35:1), IRAs (see Q 30:1), Roth IRAs (see Q 31:1), and Section 457 plans. [I.R.C. § 25B(d)(2)(A); Ann. 2001-106, Q&A-4, 2001-2 C.B. 416] The testing period, with respect to a taxable year, is the period that includes:

1. The taxable year;
2. The two preceding taxable years; and

3. The period after the taxable year to the due date (including extensions) for filing the individual's federal income return for the taxable year.

[I.R.C. § 25B(d)(2)(A); Ann. 2001-106, Q&A-4, 2001-2 C.B. 416]

Distributions received by the individual's spouse are treated as received by the individual if the individual and spouse filed a joint return for *both* (1) the taxable year for which the credit is claimed and (2) the taxable year during which the spouse received the distribution. [I.R.C. § 25B(d)(2)(D); Ann. 2001-106, Q&A-4, 2001-2 C.B. 416]

In the case of a distribution from a Roth IRA, this reduction applies to any such distribution, whether or not taxable, that is not rolled over. An amount does not count as a distribution for purposes of the reduction if the distribution is a return of a contribution to an IRA (including a Roth IRA) made for the taxable year and (1) the distribution is made before the due date (including extensions) of the individual's tax return for that year, (2) no deduction is taken with respect to the contribution, and (3) the distribution includes any income attributable to the contribution (see Q 30:9). [Ann. 2001-106, Q&A-4, 2001-2 C.B. 416]

Example 1. Richard contributes $3,000 to a 401(k) plan during 2010; but Richard took a $500 IRA withdrawal during 2010 and had taken a $900 IRA withdrawal during 2009, and neither of these withdrawals was rolled over. The amount of Richard's 2010 plan contribution eligible for the credit is $1,600 ($3,000 − $500 − $900), instead of the $2,000 that would have been eligible for the credit if no withdrawals had been taken.

Example 2. The facts are the same as in Example 1, except that Richard took a $500 nontaxable Roth IRA withdrawal during 2010 and had taken a $900 nontaxable plan distribution of voluntary contributions during 2009. The amount of Richard's 2010 plan contribution eligible for the credit is still $1,600.

Because of the testing period, a distribution can affect four taxable years.

Example 3. Richard took a distribution from an IRA on April 7, 2008, that was not rolled over. The distribution reduces Richard's qualified retirement savings contributions for (1) 2007, because the testing period includes the period after the taxable year (2007) to the due date (including extensions) for filing Richard's federal income tax return for 2007; (2) 2008, because that is the taxable year of the distribution; (3) 2009, because 2008 is within the two preceding taxable years; and (4) 2010, because 2008 is also within the two preceding taxable years.

The following distributions will *not* reduce the eligible individual's qualified retirement savings contributions:

1. Plan loans that are treated as distributions (see Qs 14:9, 14:10);
2. Certain corrective distributions (see Qs 27:28, 27:31, 27:64, 27:85, 30:9);
3. Dividends paid with respect to certain stock held by an ESOP (see Q 28:12); and
4. Rollovers from an IRA to a Roth IRA (see Q 31:44). [I.R.C. § 25B(d)(2)(C)]

Q 17:5   What are qualified retirement savings contributions?

Qualified retirement savings contributions for the taxable year are the sum of the eligible individual's (see Q 17:2):

1. Elective contributions to a 401(k) plan (see Q 27:1), SEP (see Q 32:9), SIMPLE plan (see Q 33:1), 403(b) plan (see Q 35:1), and Section 457 plan;
2. Voluntary employee contributions (see Q 27:77);
3. IRA contributions (see Q 30:1);
4. Roth IRA contributions (see Q 31:1).

[I.R.C. § 25B(d)(1); Ann. 2001-106, Q&A-5, 2001-2 C.B. 416]

For purposes of the saver's credit, an employee contribution will be voluntary as long as it is not required as a condition of employment. [Ann. 2001-106, Q&A-5, 2001-2 C.B. 416]

An amount contributed to an individual's IRA is not a contribution eligible for the saver's credit if (1) the amount is distributed to the individual before the due date (including extensions) of the individual's tax return for the year for which the contribution was made, (2) no deduction is taken with respect to the contribution, and (3) the distribution includes any income attributable to the contribution (see Q 30:9). [Ann. 2001-106, Q&A-5, 2001-2 C.B. 416]

A qualified retirement savings contribution can also represent an investment in the contract (i.e., basis; see Qs 13:3, 30:24). [I.R.C. § 25B(f)]

Q 17:6   What is the saver's credit rate?

The saver's credit rate is based on the eligible individual's (see Q 17:2) modified AGI (see Q 17:1) for the taxable year for which the credit is claimed. Under PPA (see Q 1:33), the income limits applicable to the saver's credit are indexed beginning in 2007. Indexed amounts are rounded to the nearest multiple of $500. Under the indexed income limits, the income limits for single taxpayers are one-half that for married taxpayers filing a joint return and for heads of household are three-fourths that for married taxpayers filing a joint return. [I.R.C. § 25B(b)] For 2010, the indexed amounts are as follows:

Modified AGI

Joint Return		*Head of Household*		*All Other Cases*		
Over	*Not Over*	*Over*	*Not Over*	*Over*	*Not Over*	*Applicable Percentage*
$ 0	$33,500	$ 0	$25,125	$ 0	$16,750	50%
33,500	36,000	25,125	27,000	16,750	18,000	20
36,000	55,500	27,000	41,625	18,000	27,750	10
55,500		41,625		27,750		0

[I.R.C. § 25B(b); Rev. Proc. 2009-50, 2009-2 C.B. 617; Ann. 2001-106, Q&A-6, 2001-2 C.B. 416]

Example 1. In 2010, Ben, age 26, is not married, is not a full-time student, and is not claimed as a dependent on another taxpayer's federal income tax return for that year. For 2010, Ben's modified AGI is $16,000; he contributes $2,000 to a 401(k) plan in which he participates; and he files his return on April 15, 2011. From January 1, 2008, through April 15, 2011, Ben does not receive any plan or IRA distributions. For 2010, Ben is allowed a $1,000 tax credit ($2,000 × 50%).

Example 2. The facts are the same as in Example 1, except that Ben's modified AGI is $17,000. His tax credit is $400 ($2,000 × 20%).

Example 3. The facts are the same as in Example 1, except that Ben withdrew $2,000 from his Roth IRA on January 15, 2008. Ben is allowed no tax credit [($2,000 − $2,000) × 50%] because of the distribution to him during the testing period (see Q 17:4). The result would be the same if Ben's Roth IRA withdrawal occurred on April 15, 2011.

Q 17:7   Does the saver's credit affect an eligible individual's entitlement to any deduction or exclusion that would otherwise apply to the contributions?

No. Eligible individuals (see Q 17:2) entitled to deduct IRA contributions or to exclude plan contributions from gross income will be able to deduct or exclude those amounts and also claim the saver's credit. [Ann. 2001-106, Q&A-7, 2001-2 C.B. 416]

Since a deductible IRA contribution or the exclusion of a plan contribution will reduce the individual's modified AGI (see Q 17:1), the individual may then qualify for the saver's credit, or possibly a higher credit rate, as a result.

Example 1. Stanley, a single individual, has compensation of $18,700 and no other income. If Stanley makes a $2,000 deductible IRA contribution, his modified AGI will decrease to $16,700 and qualify Stanley for a 50 percent saver's credit. If Stanley contributed only $1,000, his credit rate would be 20 percent; and, if Stanley contributed only $200, his credit rate would be 10 percent.

Example 2. The Miller's Tale Corporation maintains a 401(k) plan that matches 50 percent of a participant's contribution to a maximum of 3 percent of compensation. Vera, a single individual, earns $16,700 in 2010, has no other income, and elects to contribute $1,000 to the plan. Vera will benefit in three ways:

1. With a marginal income tax rate of 15 percent, the contribution reduces Vera's income tax by $150.
2. Vera gets a saver's credit of $500 (50% × $1,000).
3. The employer match is $501 (3% × $16,700).

Q 17:8   What taxes can the saver's credit offset?

The saver's credit may be used against both an individual's income tax liability and alternative minimum tax liability, but the credit cannot create a tax refund (see Q 17:1). [I.R.C. §§ 25B(a), 25B(g); Ann. 2001-106, Q&A-8, Q&A-13, 2001-2 C.B. 416]

Q 17:9   How are married taxpayers treated?

Qualified retirement savings contributions (see Q 17:5) by or for either or both spouses, up to $2,000 per year for each spouse, can give rise to the saver's credit. Since the saver's credit is allowed to an eligible taxpayer (see Q 17:2), a married couple filing a joint return can utilize the saver's credits allowable to both spouses (see Q 17:6). [I.R.C. § 25B(a); Ann. 2001-106, Q&A-9, 2001-2 C.B. 416]

> **Example 1.** In 2010, Steve and Sallie are married. Both are eligible individuals, have modified AGI (see Q 17:1) of $30,000, and both contribute $2,000 to 401(k) plans. Steve and Sallie timely file their 2010 joint federal income tax return, and neither receives a plan or IRA distribution during the testing period (see Q 17:4). For 2010, Steve and Sallie are allowed a $2,000 saver's credit [($2,000 + $2,000) × 50%].

> **Example 2.** The facts are the same as in Example 1, except that Steve contributes $2,000 to his IRA and $2,000 to a spousal IRA (see Q 30:25) on behalf of Sallie. For 2010, Steve and Sallie are allowed a $2,000 saver's credit.

Q 17:10   Are salary reduction and voluntary employee contributions that are eligible for the saver's credit taken into account in the ADP and ACP tests?

Yes. Salary reduction contributions to a 401(k) plan (see Q 27:1), whether or not those contributions give rise to the saver's credit, are taken into account in the nondiscrimination test for salary reduction contributions (the ADP test; see Q 27:18) for plans subject to that test. Also, voluntary employee contributions to a qualified retirement plan, whether or not those contributions give rise to the saver's credit, are taken into account in the nondiscrimination test for voluntary employee contributions (the ACP test; see Q 27:77) for plans subject to that test. [Ann. 2001-106, Q&A-10, 2001-2 C.B. 416]

Q 17:11   Can an individual claim the saver's credit for an amount contributed to a plan pursuant to automatic enrollment?

Yes. Any amount that is treated as an elective contribution on behalf of an eligible individual (see Q 17:2) to an employer plan (see Q 17:5) can give rise to the saver's credit (see Qs 27:5, 35:11). [I.R.C. § 25B(d)(1); Ann. 2001-106, Q&A-11, 2001-2 C.B. 416]

Q 17:12   Can an individual take a projected saver's credit into account in figuring the allowable number of withholding allowances on Form W-4?

Yes. For information on converting credits into withholding allowances, see IRS Publication 919, "How Do I Adjust My Withholding?" [Ann. 2001-106, Q&A-12, 2001-2 C.B. 416]

Q 17:13   Is there a sample notice that employers can use to help explain the saver's credit to employees?

Yes. Employers are encouraged to tell their employees about the credit. Employers can inform employees in any way they choose, including use of the notice set out below.

Notice to Employees Regarding Saver's Credit

This notice explains how you may be able to pay less tax by contributing to [insert name of employer's plan] (the Plan) or to an individual retirement arrangement (IRA).

Beginning in 2002, if you make contributions to the Plan or to an IRA, you may be eligible for a tax credit, called the "saver's credit." This credit could reduce the federal income tax you pay dollar-for-dollar. The amount of the credit you can get is based on the contributions you make and your credit rate. The credit rate can be as low as 10 percent or as high as 50 percent, depending on your adjusted gross income—the lower your income, the higher the credit rate. The credit rate also depends on your filing status. See the tables at the end of this notice to determine your credit rate.

The maximum contribution taken into account for the credit for an individual is $2,000. If you are married filing jointly, the maximum contribution taken into account for the credit is $2,000 each for you and your spouse.

The credit is available to you if you:

- Are 18 or older
- Are not a full-time student
- Are not claimed as a dependent on someone else's return, and
- Have adjusted gross income (shown on your tax return for the year of the credit) that does not exceed:
  — $50,000 if you are married filing jointly
  — $37,500 if you are a head of household with a qualifying person, or
  — $25,000 if you are single or married filing separately (see Q 17:6)

Example 1. Sharon and Fred are married and file their federal income tax return jointly. For 2002, their adjusted gross income would have been $34,000 if they had not made any retirement contributions. During 2002, Sharon elected to have $2,000 contributed to her employer's 401(k) plan. Fred made a deductible contribution of $2,000 to an IRA for 2002. As a result of these contributions, their 2002 adjusted gross income is $30,000. If their federal income tax would have been $3,000 (after applying any other credits to which they are entitled) without having made any retirement contributions, then their federal income tax as a result of making the $4,000 retirement contributions will be only $400 after application of the saver's credit and other tax benefits for the retirement contributions. Thus, by saving $4,000 for their retirement, Sharon and Fred have also reduced their taxes by $2,600.

The annual contribution eligible for the credit may have to be reduced by any taxable distributions from a retirement plan or IRA that you or your spouse receive during the year you claim the credit, during the two preceding years, or during the period after the end of the year for which you claim the credit and before the due date for filing your return for that year. A distribution from a Roth IRA that is not rolled over is taken into account for this reduction, even if the distribution is not taxable. After these reductions, the maximum annual contribution eligible for the credit per person is $2,000.

Example 2. Harriet's adjusted gross income for 2002 is low enough for her to be eligible for the credit that year, and she defers $3,000 of her pay to her employer's 401(k) plan during 2002. During 2001, Harriet took a $400 hardship withdrawal from her employer's plan; and, during 2002, she takes an $800 IRA withdrawal. Harriet's 2002 saver's credit will be based on contributions of $1,800 ($3,000 − $400 − $800).

The amount of your saver's credit will not change the amount of your refundable tax credits. A refundable tax credit, such as the earned income credit or the refundable amount of your child tax credit, is an amount that you would receive as a refund even if you did not otherwise owe any taxes.

The amount of your saver's credit in any year cannot exceed the amount of tax that you would otherwise pay (not counting any refundable credits or the adoption credit) in any year. If your tax liability is reduced to zero because of other nonrefundable credits, such as the Hope Scholarship Credit, then you will not be entitled to the saver's credit.

Credit Rates (see Q 17:6 for the 2010 individual AGI amounts)

If your income tax filing status is "married filing joint," and your adjusted gross income is:	Your saver's credit rate is:
$0 − $30,000	50% of contribution
$30,001 − $32,500	20% of contribution
$32,501 − $50,000	10% of contribution
Over $50,000	credit not available

*If your income tax filing status is
"head of household" and your
adjusted gross income is:*   *Your saver's credit rate is:*

$0 – $22,500   50% of contribution
$22,501 – $24,375   20% of contribution
$24,376 – $37,500   10% of contribution
Over $37,500   credit not available

*If your income tax filing status is
"single" "married filing separate," or
"qualifying widow(er)," and
your adjusted gross income is:*   *Your saver's credit rate is:*

$0 – $15,000   50% of contribution
$15,001 – $16,250   20% of contribution
$16,251 – $25,000   10% of contribution
Over $25,000   credit not available

[Ann. 2001-106, Q&A-13, 2001-2 C.B. 416]

Chapter 18

Determination Letters

Before a company commits itself to making substantial contributions to a retirement plan, it must be certain that the plan qualifies for favorable tax treatment. This chapter discusses the procedure for submitting the retirement plan to IRS for an advance ruling on the plan's tax status.

Q 18:1   What is an IRS determination letter?

Although it is not required, an employer has the option of seeking an advance determination as to the qualified status of its retirement plan by IRS, rather than waiting for IRS to review the plan in connection with an audit. This written advance determination is called a determination letter. A favorable determination letter indicates that, in the opinion of IRS, the terms of the plan conform to the requirements of the Code. For more details, see chapter 4. [Rev. Proc. 2010-6, 2010-1 I.R.B. 193; IRS Pub. 794]

A determination letter may also be requested when the retirement plan is amended or terminated.

Q 18:2   Is a fee charged for a request for a determination letter?

Yes. IRS charges a user fee for each request for a determination letter (as well as for letter rulings, opinion letters, and other similar rulings or determinations). [I.R.C. § 7528(c)] Each request must be accompanied by payment of the user fee (check or money order, payable to the United States Treasury) attached to IRS Form 8717, User Fee for Employee Plan Determination, Opinion, and Advisory Letter Request. IRS will exercise discretion in deciding whether to immediately return any determination letter request not accompanied by full payment. In those cases where the submission is not immediately returned, a reasonable amount of time will be given in order to submit the proper fee. The fee is refundable only in certain situations (e.g., if IRS refuses to rule on an issue properly requested, or issues an erroneous ruling, or if the ruling issued is not responsive).

The amount of the user fee depends on the type of request, whether a multiple employer plan (see Qs 8:7, 18:16) is involved, whether a master and prototype plan (M&P plan; see Q 2:27) or a volume submitter plan (see Q 2:28) is involved, and whether the request covers the average benefit test (see Q 5:17) or any general test (see Qs 4:13, 4:18). Some examples are listed below:

Determination Request without General or Average Benefit Test	User Fee
Individually designed plans (Form 5300)	$1,000
Adopters of M&P plans and volume submitter plans (Form 5307)	$ 300
Terminations (Form 5310)	$1,000

Determination Request with General or Average Benefit Test	
Individually designed plans (Form 5300)	$1,800
Adopters of M&P plans and volume submitter plans (Form 5307)	$1,000
Terminations (Form 5310)	$1,800

[Rev. Proc. 2010-8, 2010-1 I.R.B. 234; Form 8717]

An eligible employer is not required to pay a user fee for any determination letter request with respect to the qualified status of a retirement plan that the employer maintains if the request is made before the later of (1) the last day of the fifth plan year that the plan is in existence or (2) the end of any remedial amendment period beginning within the first five years of the plan. An application for a defined contribution plan (see Q 2:2) from an eligible employer for a plan that was first effective on or after January 2, 1997 will automatically meet this requirement, and an application for a defined benefit plan (see Q 2:3) from an eligible employer for a plan that was first effective on or after January 3, 1996 will automatically meet this requirement. An eligible employer is an employer that had no more than 100 employees who received at least $5,000 in compensation from the employer for the preceding year and has at least one non-highly compensated employee (see Q 3:12) who is participating in the plan. The determination of eligible employer status is made as of the date of the determination letter request. [I.R.C. §§ 408(p)(2)(C)(i)(I), 7528(b)(2); Instructions to Form 8717]

The sponsor of a prototype or similar plan that the sponsor intends to market to participating employers is required to pay a user fee for a request for a notification letter, opinion letter, or similar ruling. An eligible employer that adopts a prototype plan, however, is not required to pay a user fee for a determination letter request with respect to the employer's plan.

[IRS Notice 2003-49, 2003-2 C.B. 294, *amplifying* IRS Notice 2002-1, 2002-1 C.B. 283]

IRS has advised that the user fees for most employer plans determination letters will increase on February 1, 2011. [*Employee Plans News*, Special Ed., July 2010]

Q 18:3 Must an employer apply for a determination letter?

No. However, the advantage of obtaining a favorable determination letter is that the employer is afforded some assurance that its retirement plan is qualified and will remain so if it qualifies in operation (see Q 18:4), if it is not amended (other than as may be required by IRS), and if there is no change in law. Receipt of a favorable determination letter allows the employer to make contributions to the retirement plan with the knowledge that its deductions for those contributions will most likely be allowed should IRS audit its tax returns.

See Q 4:7 for a discussion of timely filed determination letter requests and an employer's ability to recover its contributions to a disqualified retirement plan.

IRS has implemented a staggered remedial amendment period system (see Q 18:6) for individually designed plans (see Q 2:26). The system was implemented initially to stagger the expiration of individually designed plans' remedial amendment periods for EGTRRA 2001 (see Q 1:21). [Rev. Proc. 2007-44, 2007-2 C.B. 54, *superseding and modifying* Rev. Proc. 2005-66, 2005-2 C.B. 509, *modifying* Ann. 2004-32, 2004-1 C.B. 860; QAB 2006-4 (Aug. 29, 2006); QAB 2006-2 (Jan. 23, 2006, revised July 5, 2006)] With respect to M&P plans (see Q 2:27) and volume submitter plans (see Q 2:28), IRS established regular six-year amendment/approval cycles for all pre-approved plans, beginning with the submission of these plans for EGTRRA 2001 opinion and advisory letters. [Rev. Proc. 2007-44, 2007-2 C.B. 54, *superseding and modifying* Rev. Proc. 2005-66, 2005-2 C.B. 509, *modifying* Rev. Proc. 2005-16, 2005-1 C.B. 674 and Ann. 2004-32, 2004-1 C.B. 860]

See Q 18:7 for details.

Q 18:4 What does the term "qualifies in operation" mean?

Generally, a retirement plan qualifies in operation if it is maintained according to the terms on which the favorable determination letter was issued. However, conditions may develop in operation that may jeopardize the qualification of the retirement plan. Examples of common operational features that arise after issuance of a favorable determination letter and that may adversely affect the favorable determination include the following:

- Failure to meet nondiscrimination requirements (see Q 4:10)
- Failure to meet coverage requirements (see Q 5:15)
- Contributions or benefits in excess of the limitations under Section 415 (see chapter 6)

- Not providing top-heavy minimums (see chapter 26)
- Failure of a 401(k) plan (see Q 27:1) to meet special nondiscrimination tests (see Qs 27:18, 27:77)

[IRS Pub. 794]

Q 18:5   What are the limitations of a favorable determination letter?

A determination letter applies only to qualification requirements regarding the form of the retirement plan. For example, a determination letter does not consider whether actuarial assumptions are reasonable for funding purposes (see Qs 2:20, 8:12) or whether a specific contribution is deductible. The determination as to whether a retirement plan qualifies is made from the information in the written plan document and the supporting information submitted by the employer. Therefore, the determination letter may not be relied upon if:

1. There has been a misstatement or omission of material facts;
2. The facts subsequently developed are materially different from the facts on which the determination was made; or
3. There is a change in applicable law.

[Rev. Proc. 2010-6, § 21, 2010-1 I.R.B. 193; IRS Pub. 794]

IRS revoked a previously issued favorable determination letter on a prospective, rather than a retroactive, basis because IRS had all of the necessary information when it made its favorable determination, and the employer had relied in good faith on the determination letter. [Priv. Ltr. Rul. 9508003; I.R.C. § 7805(b)] Similarly, where a determination letter was subsequently revoked by IRS, the revocation was applied prospectively. With respect to the original request, there was no misstatement or omission of material facts, the facts at the time of the transaction were not materially different from the facts on which the determination was based, and there had been no change in applicable law. [Priv. Ltr. Rul. 9519001]

Also, the determination letter applies only to the employer and its participants on whose behalf the determination letter was issued. A determination letter may include one or more caveats that affect the scope of reliance represented by the letter (see Q 18:23).

A plan sponsor has a certain amount of flexibility in determining the scope of the determination letter to be issued for its plan since the sponsor is given the option to elect whether the determination letter should consider certain requirements. Specifically, a plan sponsor may choose whether a plan will be reviewed for compliance with the nondiscrimination in amount requirement (see Q 4:11) and whether a plan will be reviewed for compliance with the minimum coverage requirement (see Q 5:15). A plan sponsor may also request IRS to determine whether specific benefits, rights, or features under the plan satisfy the current availability requirement (see Q 4:20); but in no event will any plan be reviewed to determine whether any benefit, right, or feature under the plan satisfies the effective availability requirement (see Q 4:20). [Rev. Proc. 2010-6, § 5, 2010-1 I.R.B. 193]

Plan sponsors can elect to have a plan reviewed for compliance with the form requirements only or with both the form requirements and the coverage and nondiscrimination requirements (see Qs 4:10, 5:15, 5:23) that the plan sponsor elects to have considered. For example, a plan sponsor need not provide demographic data for the ratio percentage test (see Q 5:16) but may choose to do so to have this considered in the determination letter.

IRS will generally not include in the determination letter separate caveats for the coverage and nondiscrimination requirements. A letter may be relied on with regard to specific determination requests made with the application, provided the relevant information and demonstrations are retained by the applicant. Failure to retain copies of demonstrations or other information submitted with the application may limit the scope of reliance on issues for which the demonstrations were provided.

[Rev. Proc. 2010-6, § 5, 2010-1 I.R.B. 193; Ann. 2001-77, 2001-2 C.B. 83; IRS Pub. 794]

IRS has a new Favorable Determination Letter 4577 for adopters of pre-approved defined contribution plan documents. Unlike other determination letters, such as Letter 2002, Letter 4577 will *not* include the adoption dates of plan documents and amendments. IRS expects that this change will accelerate the processing of certain Form 5307 applications. Plan sponsors may rely on Letter 4577 for all plan amendments listed on line 3 of Form 5307 (see Q 18:13) that conform the plan to the applicable Cumulative List (see Q 18:11). As with all favorable determination letters, the applicant must retain Form 5307 and all documents submitted with the application to maintain reliance. [*Employee Plans News*, Summer 2010]

Q 18:6 When should a retirement plan be submitted for IRS approval?

A retirement plan should be submitted for IRS approval as early as possible. Amendments needed to qualify a retirement plan can be made retroactively until the company's federal income tax return for the year is due (including extensions) or at a later time if allowed by IRS. This period of time during which an amendment regarding a disqualifying provision may be made retroactively is referred to as the remedial amendment period. A disqualifying provision includes a provision of a new plan, the absence of a provision from a new plan, or an amendment to an existing plan that causes the plan to fail to satisfy the qualification requirements (see Q 4:1) as of the date the plan or amendment is first made effective. [I.R.C. § 401(b); Treas. Reg. § 1.401(b)-1(b)(i)] IRS generally extends the remedial amendment period with respect to new laws (e.g., EGTRRA 2001).

If the retirement plan is submitted to IRS within the remedial amendment period, IRS will extend the time limit for amending the plan. If the retirement plan is submitted after the remedial amendment period, IRS may not allow the company to amend its plan retroactively, particularly if the changes that need to be made are significant. [I.R.C. § 401(b); Treas. Reg. § 1.401(b)-1] See Q 18:7 regarding the EGTRRA 2001 remedial amendment period and Q 18:11 of *The 2007 Pension Answer Book* regarding the GUST remedial amendment period.

Q 18:7   When should an individually designed plan be amended and submitted for EGTRRA 2001?

IRS has implemented a system of staggered remedial amendment periods for individually designed plans (see Q 2:26). This system had been implemented initially to stagger the expiration of individually designed plans' remedial amendment periods for EGTRRA 2001 (see Q 18:6).

The system establishes regular five-year cycles for plan amendments and determination letter renewals for individually designed plans. The cycles, which are based on employer identification numbers (EINs), ensure that employers will not have to submit determination letter applications more frequently than every five years.

On February 1, 2006, IRS began accepting applications for determination letters for individually designed plans that took into account the requirements of EGTRRA 2001 as well as other changes in qualification requirements and guidance reflected in the applicable Cumulative List (see Q 18:11). According to the following chart, an individually designed plan's EGTRRA 2001 remedial amendment period is also extended to the end of the five-year cycle in which the remedial amendment period would otherwise end.

If the EIN of the employer ends in	The plan's cycle is	The last day of the EGTRRA remedial amendment period is	The next five-year remedial amendment cycle ends on
1 or 6	Cycle A	January 31, 2007	January 31, 2012
2 or 7	Cycle B	January 31, 2008	January 31, 2013
3 or 8	Cycle C	January 31, 2009	January 31, 2014
4 or 9	Cycle D	January 31, 2010	January 31, 2015
5 or 0	Cycle E	January 31, 2011	January 31, 2016

Example. Linda Corp. adopts a new plan on January 1, 2009, and its EIN ends in 0. Since the plan's cycle is Cycle E, the initial remedial amendment period is extended to January 31, 2011, so that any required retroactive remedial amendments, including EGTRRA 2001 amendments, must be adopted by January 31, 2011. The subsequent five-year cycle ends on January 31, 2016.

Exceptions to the general rule for determining a plan's five-year remedial amendment cycle include the following:

1. For a plan that is a multiemployer plan (see Q 29:2), the plan's five-year remedial amendment cycle is Cycle D.

2. For a plan that is a multiple employer plan (see Q 8:9), the plan's five-year remedial amendment cycle is Cycle B.

3. For a plan that is a governmental plan under Section 414(d), the plan's five-year remedial amendment cycle is Cycle C. However, IRS implemented a one-time modification to permit sponsors of governmental plans to submit for determination letters during Cycle C or Cycle E. Additionally, because the option is only a one-time modification, the filing cycle for the governmental plan will continue to be Cycle C. Accordingly, the determination letter for a governmental plan filed during Cycle E will expire at the end of the next Cycle C (i.e., January 31, 2014). [Rev. Proc. 2009-36, 2009-35 I.R.B. 304; *Employee Plans News*, Special Ed., Nov. 5, 2008]

4. For a plan maintained by multiple members of a controlled group (see Q 5:31) or an affiliated service group (see Q 5:35), the plan's five-year remedial amendment cycle is determined with reference to the last digit of the EIN that is or will be used to report the plan on Form 5500 (see Q 21:2).

5. If more than one plan is maintained by members of a controlled group or an affiliated service group, the employers may elect that the five-year remedial amendment cycle for all plans maintained by any members of the group (other than multiemployer plans or multiple employer plans) will be Cycle A. The election must be made jointly by all members of the controlled or affiliated service group.

6. If more than one plan is maintained by a controlled group that is a parent-subsidiary controlled group organization, an election may be made that the remedial amendment cycle be determined by reference to the last digit of the parent's EIN. This election is to be made by the parent, in the case of a parent-subsidiary controlled group.

In the case of a merger or acquisition, a change in plan sponsorship, or a plan spin-off, a plan's five-year remedial amendment cycle is determined as follows:

1. If plans with different five-year remedial amendment cycles are merged, the five-year remedial amendment cycle of the merged plan is thereafter determined with respect to the employer that maintains the merged plan.

2. If one employer acquires another employer and maintains its plan, the five-year remedial amendment cycle of the plan is thereafter determined with respect to the employer that is maintaining the plan.

3. If there is a change in the EIN, controlled group status, affiliated service group status, etc., of the employer that maintains a plan, the five-year remedial amendment cycle of the plan is thereafter determined with respect to the employer that maintains the plan.

4. If a portion of a plan is spun off, the five-year remedial amendment cycle of the spun-off plan is determined with respect to the employer that maintains the spun-off plan.

5. If a self-employed person with no employees submits a determination letter application based upon the last digit of the individual's social security number (SSN) instead of the EIN for the first determination letter

submitted, the determination letter application will be processed based upon the SSN with the other on-cycle determination letter applications. However, subsequent five-year remedial amendment cycles will be determined based upon the last digit of the employer's EIN.

6. If a plan changes its status by becoming or ceasing to be a multiemployer plan or a multiple employer plan, the five-year remedial amendment cycle of the plan is thereafter determined on the basis of the changed status of the plan.

As a result of one of the cycle-changing events described above, a plan's five-year remedial amendment cycle may change. In such case, a cover letter or attachment to the determination letter application with respect to the plan should note the cycle change and explain why there was a change in the plan's cycle. All relevant information directly related to the cycle-changing event should be submitted with the determination letter application. For example, if the cycle-changing event was a plan merger or spin-off, the determination letter application should include the corporate resolutions or actions that relate to the merger or spin-off.

[Rev. Proc. 2007-44, 2007-2 C.B. 54, *superseding and modifying* Rev. Proc. 2005-66, 2005-2 C.B. 509]

Q 18:8   Can an individually designed plan submit off-cycle?

In general, plan sponsors of individually designed plans (see Q 2:26) that wish to preserve reliance on a plan's favorable determination letter must apply for a new determination letter for each remedial amendment cycle (see Q 18:7) during the last 12 months of the plan's remedial amendment cycle—that is, between February 1 and January 31 of the last year of the cycle. This is referred to as "on-cycle" filing. Determination letters issued for individually designed plans will include a statement that the letter may not be relied on after the end of the plan's first five-year remedial amendment cycle that ends more than 12 months after the application was received and will include the specific expiration date. Thus, determination letters issued for applications filed more than 12 months before the end of a five-year remedial amendment cycle may not be relied on after that cycle. In appropriate circumstances, IRS may extend the expiration dates of determination letters for a particular cycle year or years.

If an application for a determination letter is submitted before or after the last 12-month period of a plan's remedial amendment cycle (that is, the 12-month period beginning on February 1 and ending on January 31 of the last year of the cycle), the application is filed off-cycle. The off-cycle filing will be reviewed using the same Cumulative List that would be used for an application that was filed on-cycle on the same date as the off-cycle filing date. This means that the determination letter issued for the plan may not take into account any or all of the changes in qualification requirements for which the plan must be amended within the plan's current remedial amendment cycle. Further, the determination letter may not be relied on after the end of the plan's first five-year remedial amendment cycle that ends more than 12 months after the application is received. Consequently, the plan may need to be further amended within the cycle and another determination letter application will need to be filed within the last 12 months of the cycle if the plan sponsor wishes to preserve reliance on a determination letter.

Example. Dymond Corp. Pension Plan is in Cycle E because Dymond Corp.'s EIN ends in "0". Accordingly, the initial five-year remedial amendment cycle for the plan ends January 31, 2011, and the subsequent five-year remedial amendment cycle ends January 31, 2016. Dymond Corp. submitted a determination letter application on March 1, 2009. The 2008 Cumulative List was used to review the determination letter submission. Since the initial five-year remedial amendment cycle will expire on January 31, 2011, a new determination letter application must be submitted during the last 12 months of the remedial amendment cycle (between February 1, 2010 to January 31, 2011) to continue to have reliance on a determination letter after that date.

Generally, an off-cycle application will not be reviewed until all on-cycle plans have been reviewed and processed. However, the following types of applications will be given the same priority as on-cycle applications:

- A terminating plan
- A new individually designed plan whose next regular on-cycle submission period ends at least two years after the end of the off-cycle submission period during which the plan sponsor submits its application
- An off-cycle application submitted in accordance with published guidance issued by IRS specifying that a determination letter must be submitted in connection with a particular event

In addition, a sponsor of a plan may request that an off-cycle application be given the same priority review as an on-cycle application due to urgent business need. IRS will consider such requests based on the facts and circumstances. However, it is expected that such an application will be given the same priority as an on-cycle application only in limited cases where exceptional circumstances exist.

Although a new plan may file off-cycle and receive priority review as described above, a new plan is not required to be submitted for a determination letter off-cycle because the initial remedial amendment period for a new plan is extended to the end of the applicable remedial amendment cycle in which the remedial amendment period would otherwise end.

[Rev. Proc. 2007-44, §§ 13,14, 2007-2 C.B. 54, *superseding and modifying* Rev. Proc. 2005-66, 2005-2 C.B. 509]

Q 18:9 When should a pre-approved plan be amended and submitted for EGTRRA 2001?

IRS implemented six-year amendment/approval cycles for all pre-approved plans—that is, M&P plans (see Q 2:27) and volume submitter plans (see Q 2:28)—beginning with the submission of these plans for EGTRRA 2001 opinion and advisory letters. With respect to pre-approved plans, a sponsor is any person that (1) has an established place of business in the United States where it is accessible during every business day and (2) represents to IRS that it has at least 30 employer-clients, each of whom is reasonably expected to timely adopt the sponsor's basic plan document. An M&P mass submitter is any person that (1) has an established place of business in the United States where it is accessible during every business day and (2) submits opinion letter applications on behalf of at least 30 unaffiliated sponsors, each of whom is sponsoring, on a word-for-word identical basis, the same basic plan document. A national sponsor is a sponsor that has either (1) 30 or more adopting employers in each of 30 or more states or (2) 3,000 or more adopting employers.

Sponsors and practitioners maintaining pre-approved plans generally have until January 31 of the calendar year following the opening of the six-year remedial amendment cycle to submit applications for opinion and advisory letters. However, sponsors and practitioners maintaining mass submitter plans and national sponsors generally have until October 31 of the calendar year in which the six-year remedial amendment cycle opens to submit opinion and advisory applications. A later deadline of January 31, 2006, applied for the initial EGTRRA application for sponsors and practitioners who maintained mass submitter plans and national sponsors who submitted applications for defined contribution M&P and volume submitter plans and a later deadline of January 31, 2008 applied for the initial EGTRRA application for sponsors and practitioners who maintain mass submitter plans and national sponsors who submitted applications for defined benefit M&P and volume submitter plans.

Defined contribution plans (see Q 2:2) and defined benefit plans (see Q 2:3) have different six-year amendment/approval cycles. In general, sponsors of M&P plans and practitioners maintaining volume submitter plans must apply for new opinion or advisory letters for the plans every six years according to the following chart:

Defined contribution plans

Initial EGTRRA application due:	*Next application due:*
Non-Mass Submitter Sponsors:	
February 17, 2005	February 1, 2011
through January 31, 2006	through January 31, 2012
Mass Submitters and National Sponsors:	
February 17, 2005	February 1, 2011
through January 31, 2006	through October 31, 2011

Defined benefit plans

Initial EGTRRA application due:	*Next application due:*
Non-Mass Submitter Sponsors:	
February 1, 2007	February 1, 2013
through January 31, 2008	through January 31, 2014

Defined benefit plans
Initial EGTRRA application due: *Next application due:*

Mass Submitters and National
Sponsors:
   February 1, 2007   February 1, 2013
   through January 31, 2008   through October 31, 2013

Sponsors will have until January 31 of the year that marks the end of the plan's first year of the six-year remedial amendment cycle to timely submit these specimen plans for opinion and advisory letters. Adopting employers will generally have two years in which to timely adopt the pre-approved plans.

IRS began accepting applications for opinion letters and advisory letters on February 17, 2005, for defined contribution pre-approved plans that took into account the requirements of EGTRRA 2001 as well as other changes in qualification requirements and guidance reflected in the 2004 Cumulative List (see Q 18:11). The submission period for these pre-approved plans ended on January 31, 2006. IRS began accepting applications for opinion and advisory letters for pre-approved defined benefit plans on February 1, 2007. [IRS Notice 2007-3, 2007-1 C.B. 255]

IRS expects that it will complete review of the pre-approved plans within approximately two years from the date the applications are submitted. For example, it was expected that review of the defined contribution pre-approved plans would be completed by early 2008. When IRS completes its review process, it will designate a uniform deadline for all adopting employers to timely adopt the pre-approved plans. The deadline will provide approximately a two-year window for adoption of amendments. IRS issued the opinion and advisory letters for EGTRRA 2001 pre-approved defined contribution plans on March 31, 2008, or, in some cases, as soon as possible thereafter. Employers using the pre-approved plan documents to restate their plans for EGTRRA 2001 were required to adopt the EGTRRA 2001–approved plan document by April 30, 2010. IRS began accepting applications for individual determination letters submitted by adopters of these pre-approved plans on May 1, 2008. The procedures for filing such applications are clarified and revised as follows:

1. An application for a determination letter that was filed on Form 5307 (see Q 18:13) generally did not need to include the plan's EGTRRA 2001 good-faith amendments that were adopted prior to the adoption of the EGTRRA 2001–restated plan or any interim plan amendments, regardless of when adopted, unless the plan was a volume submitter plan that did not authorize the practitioner to amend the plan on behalf of the adopting employer. IRS, however, may have requested evidence of adoption of good-faith and interim amendments during the course of its review of a particular plan. Applications filed on Form 5307 for volume submitter plans that did not authorize the practitioner to amend the plan on behalf of the adopting employer must have included the plan's EGTRRA 2001 good-faith amendments and any interim amendments that were adopted for qualification changes on the 2004 Cumulative List.

2. An application for a determination letter on a pre-approved plan that was required to file Form 5300 (see Q 18:13) only because the plan was a multiple employer (see Q 8:9) volume submitter plan or because the employer was requesting a determination regarding partial termination (see Q 25:5), affiliated service group status, (see Qs 5:35, 5:36) or leased employees (see Q 5:58) was reviewed on the basis of the Cumulative List that was used to review the underlying pre-approved plan (that is, the 2004 Cumulative List) as if the application had been filed on Form 5307. IRS's review of the application did not consider changes in the qualification requirements subsequent to the 2004 Cumulative List. Except in the case of volume submitter plans that did not authorize the practitioner to amend the plan on behalf of the adopting employer, an application described in this paragraph did not need to include the plan's EGTRRA 2001 good-faith amendments that were adopted prior to the adoption of the EGTRRA 2001–restated plan or any interim plan amendments, regardless of when adopted. IRS, however, may have requested evidence of adoption of good-faith and interim amendments during the course of its review of a particular plan. An application for a volume submitter plan that was described in this paragraph but which did not authorize the practitioner to amend on behalf of the adopting employer must have included the plan's EGTRRA 2001 good-faith amendments and any interim amendments that were adopted for qualification changes on the 2004 Cumulative List.

3. An application for a determination letter on any other pre-approved plan that was required to file Form 5300 was reviewed on the basis of the Cumulative List in effect on the date the application was filed. The application must have included a copy of the plan's timely signed and dated good-faith EGTRRA 2001 amendments, interim amendments, and other plan amendments for all the changes in qualification requirements on the Cumulative List that was in effect when the application was filed. Applications described in this paragraph included (1) applications for determination letters on M&P plans that had been amended by the adopting employer in a manner other than to choose among options permitted under the plan, and (2) applications for determination letters on volume submitter plans that had been modified by the adopting employer in a manner that was too extensive or complex or otherwise determined by IRS to be incompatible with the purposes of the volume submitter program.

IRS extended the deadline for restating pre-approved defined contribution plans and, if applicable, submitting determination letter applications to July 30, 2010 for sponsors of those plans affected by a federally declared disaster. [Notice 2010-48, 2010-27 I.R.B. 9]

[Rev. Proc. 2009-6, § 9, 2009-1 I.R.B. 189; Ann. 2008-23, 2008-1 C.B. 731]

IRS issued the opinion and advisory letters for EGTRRA 2001 pre-approved defined benefit plans on March 31, 2010 or, in some cases, as soon as possible thereafter. Employers using a preapproved plan document to restate a defined benefit plan for EGTRRA and the 2006 Cumulative List will be required to adopt the EGTRRA-approved plan document by April 30, 2012. IRS commenced accepting applications for individual determination letters submitted by adopters of the preapproved plans on May 1, 2010. [Ann. 2010-20, 2010-15 I.R.B. 551]

An employer's plan is treated as a pre-approved plan and is therefore eligible for a six-year amendment/approval cycle if:

1. The employer is either a prior adopter, a new adopter, an intended adopter, or the adopter of a replacement plan, and

2. The sponsor or practitioner maintaining an existing or interim pre-approved plan timely submits an opinion or advisory letter application for the plan:

   a. By the application deadline of October 31 or January 31, whichever is applicable, in the first year of the six-year remedial amendment cycle for pre-approved plans, and

   b. Receives a favorable current opinion or advisory letter from IRS before the employer adopts the plan.

[Rev. Proc. 2007-44, 2007-2 C.B. 54, *superseding and modifying* Rev. Proc. 2005-66, 2005-2 C.B. 509, *modifying* Rev. Proc. 2005-16, 2005-1 C.B. 674]

Example. Neal, Inc. maintains a volume submitter defined contribution plan. The sponsor timely submitted the EGTRRA 2001 volume submitter specimen plan on or before January 31, 2006, and received an opinion letter dated March 31, 2008. Neal, Inc. had until April 30, 2010 to adopt the EGTRRA 2001 approved version of the volume submitter plan.

Applications for opinion or advisory letters submitted by sponsors and practitioners are generally processed in the order received. If a sponsor or practitioner of an M&P or volume submitter plan with a valid opinion or advisory letter from the immediately preceding six-year cycle (or, for the initial six-year cycle, a valid opinion or advisory letter for GUST) submits an application for an opinion or advisory letter after the scheduled due date, then the review of the plan will be delayed and may not be completed by the time the review of timely submitted pre-approved plans is completed for other sponsors and practitioners (approximately two years). As a result, an employer adopting such a plan may have less than two years to adopt the late submitted pre-approved plan, that is, less time than an employer adopting a pre-approved plan that had been submitted by the deadline. [Rev. Proc. 2007-49, 2007-2 C.B. 141]

IRS has relaxed the restrictions on off-cycle applications for new pre-approved plans if certain requirements are met. Sponsors or practitioners will not be precluded from submitting an off-cycle application for an opinion or advisory letter because they previously submitted an on-cycle application. To get this relief, the new application for a plan must be word-for-word identical to a mass submitter plan that has received a favorable EGTRRA opinion or advisory letter, or for which an application for such a letter is pending. Further, the new application must be filed according to the procedures governing mass submitter plans. [Rev. Proc. 2008-56, 2008-2 C.B. 826]

In the event of changes in qualification requirements resulting from future guidance, or other regulatory or statutory changes that were not taken into account in issuing the opinion letter, an approved M&P plan must be amended by the sponsor and, if necessary, the employer to retain its approved status if any provisions therein fail to meet the requirements of law, regulations, or other guidelines affecting qualification. Failure to so amend could result in the loss of a plan's qualified status. However, this does not change the applicable period during the six-year cycle when sponsors must request opinion letters, which will still occur only once every six years. Sponsors are required to make reasonable and diligent efforts to ensure that each employer who, to the best of the sponsor's knowledge, continues to maintain the plan as an M&P plan amends its plan when necessary. [Rev. Proc. 2005-16, § 8, 2005-1 C.B. 674] In one case, because the employer apparently did not adopt the amendments required to conform to the provisions of EGTRRA and to the minimum distribution requirements of the Code, it was held that the IRS agent should proceed to examine the plan and issue an adverse determination letter holding that the plan be disqualified if that was the result of the examination. [Priv. Ltr. Rul. 200913053]

Q 18:10 Were good-faith EGTRRA 2001 plan amendments required?

Generally, in order to be within the EGTRRA 2001 remedial amendment period, a plan was required to adopt a good-faith EGTRRA 2001 plan amendment. A plan is required to have a good-faith EGTRRA 2001 plan amendment in effect for a year if:

1. The plan is required to implement a provision of EGTRRA 2001 for the year or the plan sponsor chooses to implement an optional provision of EGTRRA 2001 for the year, and

2. The plan language, prior to the amendment, is not consistent either with the provision of EGTRRA 2001 or with the operation of the plan in a manner consistent with EGTRRA 2001, as applicable.

Good-faith EGTRRA 2001 amendments had to be adopted no later than the later of (1) the end of the plan year in which the amendments were required to be, or were optionally, put into effect or (2) the end of the GUST remedial amendment period. In limited situations, an amendment may have been required to be adopted earlier to avoid a decrease or elimination of Section 411(d)(6) protected benefits (see Q 10:45).

[IRS Notice 2001-42, 2001-2 C.B. 70]

The remedial amendment period with respect to all disqualifying provisions of a new plan (i.e., plans that have been put into effect after December 31, 2001), and all disqualifying provisions arising from a plan amendment adopted after December 31, 2001, had been extended to the EGTRRA 2001 remedial amendment period. The time by which good-faith EGTRRA 2001 amendments had to be adopted was not extended.

[Rev. Proc. 2004-25, 2004-1 C.B. 791]

Example. Poncho Pension Plan was put into effect during 2002, and the EGTRRA 2001 good-faith amendments were adopted at that time. The remedial amendment period for all disqualifying provisions of the plan, whether or not related to EGTRRA 2001, will be extended to the EGTRRA 2001 remedial amendment period.

IRS provided guidance relating to the effective dates for certain amendments required by EGTRRA 2001 and provided sample plan amendments that could have been adopted or used in drafting good-faith amendments for individually designed and pre-approved plans. [IRS Notice 2001-57, 2001-2 C.B. 279; IRS Notice 2001-56, 2001-2 C.B. 277]

Q 18:11   What is the Cumulative List?

The Cumulative List is the annual list of changes required by IRS to be reflected in the following year's opinion, advisory, or determination letter submissions. No reliance can be provided for changes in a plan that are not included in the applicable Cumulative List. The Cumulative List is updated and published annually to identify statutory, regulatory, and guidance changes that will be considered by IRS in its review of both pre-approved and individually designed plans (see Qs 2:26–2:28) whose remedial amendment cycles (see Qs 18:7–18:9) are scheduled to end on January 31 of the second calendar year following publication of the list.

For example, sponsors or practitioners maintaining non–mass submitter defined contribution pre-approved plans had until January 31, 2006, to submit opinion and advisory letter applications that were reviewed by IRS based upon the 2004 Cumulative List; and sponsors or practitioners maintaining non-mass submitter defined benefit pre-approved plans had until January 31, 2008 to submit opinion and advisory letter applications that were reviewed by IRS based upon the 2006 Cumulative List. [IRS Notice 2007-3, 2007-1 C.B. 255; IRS Notice 2004–84, 2004-2 C.B. 1030] Similarly, Cycle A individually designed plans that were submitted for determination letters between February 1, 2006 and January 31, 2007 were reviewed by IRS on the basis of the Cumulative List issued in the latter part of 2005; Cycle B individually designed plans that were submitted for determination letters between February 1, 2007 and January 31, 2008 were reviewed by IRS on the basis of the 2006 Cumulative List; Cycle C individually designed plans that were submitted for determination letters between February 1, 2008 and January 31, 2009 were reviewed by IRS on the basis of the 2007 Cumulative List; Cycle D individually designed plans that were submitted for determination letters between February 1, 2009 and January 31, 2010 were reviewed by IRS on the basis of the 2008 Cumulative List; and Cycle E individually designed plans that are being submitted for determination letters between February 1, 2010 and January 31, 2011 will be reviewed by IRS on the basis of the 2009 Cumulative List. [IRS Notice 2009-98, 2009-52 I.R.B. 974; IRS Notice 2008-108, 2008-2 C.B. 1275; IRS Notice 2007-94, 2007-2 C.B. 1179; IRS Notice 2007-3, 2007-1 C.B. 255; IRS Notice 2005-101, 2005-2 C.B. 1219]

In general, IRS will not consider in its review of any opinion, advisory or determination letter application any:

1. Guidance issued after the October 1 preceding the date the applicable Cumulative List is issued;

2. Statutes enacted after the October 1 preceding the date the applicable Cumulative List is issued;

3. Qualification requirements that become effective in a calendar year after the calendar year in which the submission period begins with respect to the applicable Cumulative List; or

4. Statutes that are first effective in the year in which the submission period begins with respect to the applicable Cumulative List for which there is no guidance identified on the applicable Cumulative List.

[Rev. Proc. 2007-44, 2007-2 C.B. 54, *superseding and modifying* Rev. Proc. 2005-66, 2005-2 C.B. 509; Rev. Proc. 2005-16, 2005-1 C.B. 674]

Q 18:12 What is the general procedure for requesting a determination letter?

Requests for determination letters should be addressed to EP Determinations at the following address:

Internal Revenue Service
P.O. Box 12192
Covington, KY 41012-0192

Applications shipped by Express Mail or a delivery service should be sent to:

Internal Revenue Service
201 West Rivercenter Blvd.
Attn: Extracting Stop 312
Covington, KY 41011

The filing of the application, when accompanied by all required information and documents, will generally serve to provide IRS with the information required to make the requested determination. However, in making the determination, IRS may require the submission of additional information. Information submitted to IRS in connection with an application for a determination letter may be subject to public inspection.

Documents that should accompany the request include the following:

- Copy of the plan and trust
- Executed power of attorney (if the application is made on behalf of the employer)
- Appropriate IRS application form (e.g., Form 5300, Form 5307, or Form 5310)
- Form 8717 and applicable user fee (see Q 18:2)
- Copy of latest favorable determination letter, if any

- Schedule Q (Form 5300), Elective Determination Requests (this schedule is optional)

[Rev. Proc. 2010-6, § 6, 2010-1 I.R.B. 193]

IRS has advised that determination letter application forms are in the process of being revised. [Retirement News for Employers, Vol. 4, Summer 2007] Form 5307, Application for Determination for Adopters of Master or Prototype or Volume Submitter Plans, was revised March 2008.

Before the actual application may be filed with IRS, notice of the filing must first be given to all interested parties (see Q 18:19).

See Qs 18:13 through 18:18 regarding procedures for requesting determination letters.

Q 18:13   What is the procedure for requesting a determination letter for initial qualification or amendment of a plan?

A determination letter request for initial qualification, amendment, restatement, or partial termination of a plan must follow additional procedures in addition to those required in Q 18:12. The following forms must be filed with a determination letter request:

- Form 5300, Application for Determination for Employee Benefit Plan, must be filed for individually designed defined contribution plans (see Q 2:2), defined benefit plans (see Q 2:3), and collectively bargained plans

- Form 5307, Application for Determination for Adopters of Master or Prototype or Volume Submitter Plans, must be filed for an M&P plan and a volume submitter plan

- Form 5309, Application for Determination of Employee Stock Ownership Plan, must be filed together with Form 5300, if the application relates to an employee stock ownership plan (ESOP; see chapter 28)

In general, individually designed plans must be restated when they are submitted for determination letter applications. For this purpose, submission of a working copy of the plan in a restated format will suffice.

In addition to the plan and trust instrument and all plan amendments made to the date of the application, the applicant must send IRS any amendments that are adopted and/or proposed after the date of the determination letter application and before IRS issues the determination letter. The applicant must submit a cover letter that references the date that the pending application was submitted, the identity of the employer and the plan, and any other helpful identifying information. The amendments must be attached to the letter. This additional information must be sent to:

Internal Revenue Service
TE/GE Correspondence Unit
P.O. Box 2508, Room 4024
Cincinnati, OH 45201

In general, a determination letter may not be relied upon for any period preceding the beginning of the remedial amendment cycle for which the letter is issued. Thus, for example, if an application for a determination letter includes a plan amendment that was effective before the beginning of the plan's current remedial amendment cycle, the determination letter may not be relied upon with respect to the effect of the amendment for the period preceding the beginning of the cycle.

With respect to an M&P plan, the determination letter request must include the following additional information:

- An adoption agreement showing which elections the employer is making with respect to the elective provisions contained in the plan
- A copy of the plan's most recent opinion letter
- In the case of a determination letter request for an M&P plan that uses a separate trust or custodial account, a copy of the employer's trust or custodial account document

An employer that amends any provision of an M&P plan or its adoption agreement (other than to choose among the options offered by the sponsoring organization or sponsor), or an employer that chooses to discontinue participation in such a plan as amended by its sponsoring organization or sponsor and does not substitute another approved plan is considered to have adopted an individually designed plan. The requirements relating to the issuance of determination letters for an individually designed plan will then apply to such plan. In addition, an application submitted by an employer with respect to an M&P plan will be treated as an application for an individually designed plan if it is executed prior to the time the M&P plan is approved.

With respect to a volume submitter plan, the determination letter request must include the following additional information:

- A copy of the advisory letter for the practitioner's volume submitter specimen plan
- A written representation made by the volume submitter practitioner which states that the plan and trust instrument are word-for-word identical to the approved specimen plan and, if they are not, an explanation as to how the plan and trust instrument differ from the approved specimen plan, describing the location, nature, and effect of each deviation from the language of the approved specimen plan

Deviations from the language of the approved specimen plan will be evaluated based on the extent and complexities of the changes. If the changes are determined not to be compatible with the volume submitter program, IRS may require the adopter to file Form 5300 and pay the higher user fee (see Q 18:2). In addition, an employer will not be treated as having adopted a volume submitter plan if the employer has signed or otherwise adopted the plan prior to the date of the volume submitter specimen plan's advisory letter. In this case, the determination letter application for the employer's plan may not be filed on Form 5307 and will not be eligible for a reduced user fee.

[Rev. Proc. 2010-6, §§ 7, 9, 2010-1 I.R.B. 193; Ann. 2001-77, 2001-2 C.B. 83]

Q 18:14 Are there procedures for approval of M&P and volume submitter plans?

IRS has issued a revenue procedure that includes procedures for issuing opinion and advisory letters with respect to M&P plans (see Q 2:27) and volume submitter plans (see Q 2:28). While IRS will continue to maintain the two programs separately, narrowing the differences between the M&P and volume submitter programs makes it appropriate to set forth the rules for both programs in a single revenue procedure.

Generally, M&P plans will continue to consist of a basic plan document and adoption agreement that may not be amended by adopting employers, except by choosing among permitted options under the adoption agreement, without the loss of M&P status. Likewise, volume submitter plans will continue to be allowed in either an adoption agreement or individually designed format to be amended by adopting employers without the loss of volume submitter status, provided the extent and complexity of the amendments are not inconsistent with the purpose of the volume submitter program.

The revenue procedure contains the following additional procedures:

1. Adopting employers of nonstandardized defined contribution M&P plans may adopt an allocation formula that is designed to be cross-tested for nondiscrimination (see Q 4:22).
2. Volume submitter plans may, but are not required to, include a provision that allows a volume submitter practitioner to amend the plan on behalf of adopting employers for changes in law.

Commencing February 17, 2005, and ending January 31, 2006, IRS accepted applications for opinion and advisory letters for defined contribution pre-approved plans that took into account the requirements of EGTRRA 2001, as well as other changes in qualification requirements and guidance reflected in the 2004 Cumulative List (see Q 18:11); and, commencing February 1, 2007 and ending January 31, 2008, IRS accepted applications for opinion and advisory letters for defined benefit pre-approved plans that took into account the requirements of EGTRRA 2001, as well as other changes in qualification requirements and guidance reflected in the 2006 Cumulative List.

[Rev. Proc. 2005-16, 2005-1 C.B. 674 *modified by* Ann. 2005-36, 2005-1C.B. 1095 *and* Ann. 2005-37, 2005-1 C.B. 1096; IRS Notice 2007-3, 2007-1 C.B. 255; IRS Notice 2004-84, 2004-2 C.B. 1030]

Q 18:15   What are the reliance procedures for M&P and volume submitter plans?

Adopting employers of nonstandardized M&P and volume submitter plans can rely on a favorable opinion or advisory letter issued to the M&P or volume submitter sponsor if the employer adopts a plan that is identical to an approved M&P or volume submitter plan and chooses only options permitted under the terms of the approved plan. These employers can forgo filing Form 5307 (see Q 18:13) and rely on a favorable opinion or advisory letter issued to the M&P or volume submitter sponsor with respect to the qualification requirements, with the following limitations:

1. Except as provided below, adopting employers of nonstandardized M&P plans and volume submitter plans cannot rely on a favorable opinion or advisory letter with respect to:

   a. The nondiscrimination requirements (see Q 4:10), the minimum coverage requirement (see Q 5:15), the minimum participation requirement (see Q 5:23), the definition of compensation (see Q 6:64), or the permitted disparity rules (see chapter 7); or

   b. If the employer maintains or has ever maintained another plan covering some of the same participants, the contribution and benefit limitations (see Qs 6:11, 6:34) or the top-heavy rules (see chapter 26).

2. Adopting employers of nonstandardized M&P plans and volume submitter plans can rely on the opinion or advisory letter with respect to the minimum coverage requirement and minimum participation requirement if 100 percent of all nonexcludable employees benefit under the plan.

3. Adopting employers of nonstandardized M&P plans that elect a safe harbor allocation or benefit formula and a safe harbor compensation definition can rely on an opinion letter with respect to the nondiscrimination requirements, the 401(k) rules (see chapter 27), and the employer matching and employee contribution requirements (see Q 27:86).

4. Adopting employers of nonstandardized safe harbor M&P plans that require adopting employers to elect a safe harbor allocation or benefit formula are entitled to the same reliance as adopting employers of nonstandardized plans except that they have automatic reliance with respect to the nondiscriminatory amounts requirement if they elect a safe harbor definition of compensation.

5. Adopting employers of standardized M&P plans that maintain or have ever maintained another plan can rely on a favorable opinion letter except with respect to the contribution and benefit limitations and the top-heavy rules.

6. Adopting employers of standardized M&P defined benefit plans can rely on an opinion letter with respect to the minimum participation requirement if the plan satisfies the requirement with respect to its prior benefit structure or is deemed to satisfy the requirement under regulations.

7. Adopting employers of standardized M&P plans cannot rely on an opinion letter with respect to:

a. Whether the timing of any amendment (or series of amendments) satisfies the nondiscrimination requirements (see Q 4:21); or

b. Whether the plan satisfies the effective availability requirement with respect to any benefit, right, or feature (see Q 4:20).

[Rev. Proc. 2010-6, § 8, 2010-1 I.R.B. 193; Rev. Proc. 2005-16, § 19, 2005-1 C.B. 674]

Q 18:16   What are the special application procedures for multiple employer plans?

A determination letter applicant for a multiple employer plan (see Q 8:9) can request either (1) a letter for the plan according to item 1 below or (2) a letter for the plan and a letter for each employer maintaining the plan if a separate Form 5300 is filed with respect to that employer according to item 2 below. Accordingly, the following rules apply:

1. An applicant requesting a letter for the plan should submit one Form 5300 for the plan that is filed on behalf of the controlling member. The optional minimum coverage questions and Schedule Q (see Q 18:12) should be omitted and the design-based safe harbor (see Qs 4:12, 4:14) questions may be included or omitted. In this case, the user fee (see Q 18:2) for a single employer plan applies. An employer maintaining a multiple employer plan can rely on a favorable determination letter issued for the plan except with respect to the nondiscrimination requirements (see Q 4:10), the minimum participation requirement (see Q 5:23), the minimum coverage requirement (see Q 5:15), the permitted disparity rules (see chapter 7), the definition of compensation (see Q 6:64), and, if the employer maintains or has ever maintained another plan, the top-heavy rules (see chapter 26) and the contribution and benefit limitations (see Qs 6:11, 6:34).

2. An applicant requesting a letter for the plan and an employer must submit the filing required in item 1 above and a separate Form 5300 (completed through line 8) for each employer requesting a separate letter. Each employer may elect to respond to the Form 5300 questions regarding minimum coverage and design-based safe harbors and to file Schedule Q to request a determination on the average benefit test (see Q 5:17), the general test (see Qs 4:13, 4:18), or any other nondiscrimination requirement addressed by Schedule Q. In this case, the user fee is determined under the user fee schedules for multiple employer plans and treating the entire application as a general test or average benefit test application if any employer requests a determination on either of these tests.

[Rev. Proc. 2010-6, § 10, 2010-1 I.R.B. 193]

Q 18:17   Is there a special procedure regarding minor amendments?

Because there is no longer a special procedure for minor amendments, where a determination letter for a plan amendment is requested, individually designed plans must be restated, M&P plans must submit an amended adoption agreement, and volume submitter plans must either submit an amended adoption agreement or a restated plan (see Qs 18:12, 18:13) within the applicable submission cycle (see Qs 18:7-18:9).

Prior to July 9, 2007, Form 6406, Short Form Application for Determination for Minor Amendment of Employee Benefit Plan, may have been filed to request a determination letter on a minor plan amendment. See Q 18:17 of *The 2008 Pension Answer Book* for details.

[Rev. Proc. 2010-6, §§ 7, 9, 11, 2010-1 I.R.B. 193]

Q 18:18   What is the procedure for requesting a determination letter for a plan termination?

Form 5310, Application for Determination for Terminating Plan, should be used when the employer intends to terminate a retirement plan, other than a multiemployer plan covered by the PBGC (see Qs 25:11, 29:2). Form 5300 should be filed in the case of the termination of a multiemployer plan covered by the PBGC. Form 6088, Distributable Benefits From Employee Pension Benefit Plans, is required to be included with the filing of the termination of a defined benefit plan (see Q 2:3) or an *underfunded defined contribution plan* (see Q 2:2). With respect to a collectively bargained underfunded defined contribution plan, Form 6088 is required only if the plan benefits employees who are not collectively bargained employees or more than 2 percent of the participants are professional employees. A separate Form 6088 is required for each employer participating in a multiple employer plan (see Q 8:9). Generally, IRS will not issue a determination letter with respect to the termination unless the retirement plan has been amended to comply with the applicable provisions of law that are in effect at the time of termination (see Q 25:62). [Rev. Proc. 2010-6, § 12, 2010-1 I.R.B. 193; Instructions to Form 6088]

For details with regard to requesting a determination letter for an affiliated service group, see Q 5:36.

Q 18:19   What are the requirements regarding notice to employees?

All interested parties must be given notice that an application for a determination letter will be made. Generally, this means that all current employees eligible to participate in the retirement plan must be notified. A notice must be provided not less than ten days and not more than 24 days before the application is filed. This time period applies to all methods of providing the notice to interested parties such as electronic medium, posting, in person, or mail. [I.R.C. § 7476(b); Treas. Reg. §§ 1.7476-1, 1.7476-2, 601.201(o)(3)(xv); Rev. Proc. 2010-6, § 18, 2010-1 I.R.B. 193] An employer that mailed notice of an impending determination letter request to the last known address of each interested party fulfilled the notice requirement. [Halliburton Co., 64 T.C.M. 713 (1992)]

In addition to receiving notice, interested parties have the following rights:

1. To submit written comments with respect to the qualification of such plans to IRS;

2. To request DOL to submit a comment to IRS on behalf of the interested parties; and

3. To submit written comments to IRS on matters with respect to which DOL was requested to comment but declined.

[Rev. Proc. 2010-6, § 17, 2010-1 I.R.B. 193]

The notice must contain the following information:

1. Brief description of the class of interested parties to whom the notice is addressed;

2. Name of plan, plan identification number, and name of plan administrator;

3. Name and identification number of the applicant;

4. That an application for a determination letter will be sent to IRS, the address of the IRS office, and the purpose of the application (e.g., initial qualification);

5. Description of class of employees eligible to participate;

6. Statement of whether IRS has ever issued a determination letter as to the qualified status of the plan;

7. Description of the procedures for interested parties to submit comments to IRS or to request DOL to do so;

8. The specific dates by which a comment to IRS or DOL must be received;

9. The number of interested parties needed in order for DOL to comment; and

10. The procedure whereby certain additional information may be obtained by the interested parties. This additional information consists of:

    a. An updated copy of the plan and related trust agreement;

    b. A copy of the application;

    c. Other documents, whether sent to or from IRS in connection with this application; and

    d. Any other information that affects the rights of the interested parties.

An employer that fails to give proper notice to interested parties is barred from appealing IRS's refusal to issue a determination letter to the Tax Court. [I.R.C. § 7476(b); Treas. Reg. §§ 601.201(o)(3)(xviii)-601.201(o)(3)(xx); Rev. Proc. 2010-6, § 18, 2010-1 I.R.B. 193]

In one case, two retired employees who were receiving benefits from a pension plan and who erroneously received a notice regarding an IRS application with respect to a plan amendment lacked standing to challenge the plan's tax-qualified status because only current employees qualify as interested parties. According to the court, the mere fact that the former employees erroneously received a notice to interested parties did not confer standing on them. [Flynn v. Comm'r, No. 00-1457 (D.C. Cir. 2001)]

In order to continue to advance the goal of permitting plan sponsors to use electronic media in administering their retirement plans, under final regulations issued by IRS, notice may be provided to interested parties by any method that reasonably ensures that all interested parties will receive the notice. The method used must be reasonably calculated to provide timely and adequate notice to all interested parties.

If notice to interested parties is delivered using an electronic medium, it must be a medium reasonably accessible to the distributee. Furthermore, (1) the electronic medium must be reasonably designed to provide the notice in a manner no less understandable to the distributee than a written paper document, and (2) at the time the notice is provided the distributee must be advised that the distributee may request and receive a written paper notice at no charge.

> **Example 1.** Denise Corp. is amending its profit sharing plan and applying for a determination letter. For present employees, Denise Corp. provides the notice by posting the notice at those locations within the principal places of employment of the interested parties that are customarily used for employer notices to employees with regard to labor-management relations matters. Denise Corp. satisfies the notice to interested parties requirement.

> **Example 2.** Captain Allen, Inc. is amending its pension plan and applying for a determination letter. Employees located at worksites 1 through 4 have access to computers at their workplace; however, employees located at worksite 5 do not have access to computers. For present employees with access to computers (worksites 1 through 4), Captain Allen, Inc. provides the notice by posting the notice on its web site. (Captain Allen, Inc. customarily posts employer notices to employees at worksites 1 through 4 with regard to labor-management relations matters on its web site.) For present employees without access to computers (worksite 5), Captain Allen, Inc. provides the notice by posting the notice at worksite 5 in a location that is customarily used for employer notices to employees with regard to labor-management relations matters. Captain Allen, Inc. also sends the notice by e-mail to each collective-bargaining representative of interested parties who are present employees covered by a collective bargaining agreement, using the e-mail address previously provided by such collective-bargaining representative. Captain Allen, Inc. satisfies the notice to interested parties requirement.

[Treas. Reg. § 1.7476-2]

IRS has issued proposed regulations (see Q 20:5) setting forth rules that clarify existing procedures regarding the use of electronic media to provide notices to plan participants and includes notice to interested parties.

Q 18:20   What happens to an application for a determination letter after it is sent to IRS?

After IRS receives an application for a determination letter concerning the qualification of a plan, an acknowledgment, Notice 3336 that includes a document locator number is sent to the applicant.

After data entry for the application is completed at the Processing Center in Covington, Kentucky, the application is sent to the Cincinnati office for review by one of the Employee Plans Specialists. Applications are processed in the order they are received.

Some applications are approved based on the information submitted. If this is the case, the applicant will receive a favorable determination letter without further contact from IRS. If additional information is required or if other changes or plan amendments are needed, an Employee Plans Specialist will contact the applicant by fax, phone, or mail. The specialist may be from the Cincinnati office or from another IRS office. Typically a determination letter will be issued after the additional information and/or amendments are submitted. If IRS determines that the plan is not qualified, IRS will discuss its findings with the applicant. Furthermore, if an agreement cannot be reached, IRS will provide the applicant with a complete explanation of the applicant's appeal rights (see Q 18:22).

Q 18:21   How long does it take to obtain a determination letter?

Generally, a determination letter is issued within 180 days after the application is filed. Notice 3336 (see Q 18:20) generally provides an estimate of the time period required to process the application (typically, 145 days).

IRS has a maximum of 270 days to rule after it receives an application for a determination. If IRS fails to act within this period, the employer can ask the Tax Court for a favorable ruling (technically, a declaratory judgment) notwithstanding IRS's inaction (see Q 18:22).

On the other hand, IRS must wait at least 60 days after it receives the application before it can issue a determination letter. This gives IRS a chance to review any comments made by interested parties (see Q 18:19).

An applicant for a determination letter has the right to have a conference with the EP Determinations manager (see Q 18:12) concerning the status of the application if the application has been pending for at least 270 days. The status conference may be by phone or in person, as mutually agreed upon. During the conference, any issues relevant to the processing of the application may be addressed, but the conference will not involve substantive discussion of technical issues. No tape, stenographic, or other verbatim recording of a status conference may be made by any party. Subsequent status conferences may also be requested if at least 90 days have passed since the last preceding status conference. A request for a status conference with the EP Determinations manager should be made in writing and sent to the specialist assigned to review the application.

[I.R.C. § 7476; Rev. Proc. 2010-6, §§ 6, 19, 2010-1 I.R.B. 193]

Q 18:22   What alternatives are available to an applicant if IRS proposes to issue an adverse determination letter?

Generally, IRS is inclined to issue a favorable determination letter to an applicant even if this means accepting amendments in proposed form as a basis for closing a case. There are circumstances, however, in which the applicant cannot satisfy IRS (by amendment or otherwise) that a favorable determination letter should be issued. Three courses of action are then available to the applicant. The applicant can:

1. Request IRS to seek technical advice from EP Technical;
2. Withdraw the application; or
3. Appeal the proposed adverse determination letter.

Requests for technical advice are made only when the issue involved satisfies certain criteria established by IRS. Chances of going this route are remote.

Withdrawal of an application at best restores the status quo. The applicant's request for a determination letter may be withdrawn by a written request at any time prior to the issuance of a final adverse determination letter. However, IRS may consider the information submitted in connection with the withdrawn request in a subsequent examination. Generally, the user fee will not be refunded if the application is withdrawn.

Appeal is the usual course of action. An appeal may be taken to the Appeals Office, and if the EP Determinations manager's (see Q 18:12) position is sustained, the applicant must petition the Tax Court for a declaratory judgment that its retirement plan is qualified on or before the 91st day after the date of issuance of the final adverse determination. [Hamlin Dev. Co., 65 T.C.M. 2071 (1993)] Failure to exhaust all IRS administrative remedies bars an applicant from proceeding in the Tax Court. [Joseph P. Clawson, M.D., Inc., P.S., Profit & Pension Trusts, 65 T.C.M. 2452 (1993)] However, an employer whose plan qualification request is unduly delayed by IRS is deemed to have exhausted administrative remedies. [I.R.C. § 7476; Rev. Proc. 2010-6, §§ 6, 20, 2010-1 I.R.B. 193; Tipton & Kalmbach, Inc., 43 T.C.M. 1345 (1982)]

Q 18:23   Once a favorable determination letter is issued, may IRS subsequently revoke such qualification?

Courts have generally held that in order for IRS to revoke a prior favorable determination letter, a material change of fact must have occurred since the time of the initial IRS review of the employer's retirement plan (see Q 18:5). However, the failure to amend a retirement plan on a timely basis after initial IRS approval may cause the plan to lose its qualified status (see Q 4:8). [Boggs v. Comm'r, 784 F.2d 1166 (4th Cir. 1986); Lansons, Inc., 622 F.2d 774 (5th Cir. 1980); Mills, Mitchell & Turner, 65 T.C.M. 2127 (1993); Hamlin Dev. Co., 65 T.C.M. 2071 (1993); Kollipara Rajsheker, M.D., Inc., 64 T.C.M. 1153 (1992); Attardo, 62 T.C.M. 313 (1991); Stark Truss Co., 62 T.C.M. 169 (1991); Basch Eng'g, Inc., 59 T.C.M. 482 (1990); Halligan, 51 T.C.M. 1203 (1986)]

In one case, a favorable determination letter was conditioned on limiting the deduction for contributions to the retirement plan and requiring the participant to include a corresponding amount in his income; the participant, however, refused to include the amount in his income. The court found that the plan was not qualified because the participant did not comply with the conditions of the determination letter. [TCS Mfg., Inc. Employees Pension Trust, 60 T.C.M. 1312 (1990)]

See chapter 19 regarding IRS correction programs.

Chapter 19

IRS and DOL Correction Programs

IRS has implemented a comprehensive system of correction programs that is intended to resolve disqualifying plan defects without the sanction of plan disqualification. DOL has established a program that is designed to encourage the voluntary and timely correction of fiduciary breaches while avoiding civil actions and penalties. This chapter discusses the programs available to plan sponsors and fiduciaries regarding plan violations and breaches.

Q 19:1   Will a retirement plan with disqualifying defects be disqualified?

In order to be qualified, a retirement plan must meet certain requirements (see Q 4:1). A plan that does not meet these requirements both in form and operation has a disqualifying defect and may be disqualified. If a plan is disqualified, it will lose certain tax benefits (see Q 1:6). The lost benefits include the following:

1. Deductions may not be allowed for certain contributions. [I.R.C. § 404(a)]

2. Plan earnings may become taxable. [I.R.C. § 501(a)]

3. Employer contributions may be includible in a participant's gross income (see Q 4:26). [I.R.C. § 402(b)(1)]

4. The vested accrued benefit of a highly compensated employee (HCE; see Q 3:2) may be includible in gross income (see Q 4:26). [I.R.C. § 402(b)(4)(A)]

5. Tax-free rollovers may not be allowed (see Q 34:39). [I.R.C. § 402(c)]

However, IRS provides a comprehensive system of correction programs in order for plan sponsors to correct qualification failures so that a plan with a disqualifying defect remains qualified. The system—Employee Plans Compliance Resolution System (EPCRS; see Q 19:2)—is continually being revised and updated in order to meet the needs of retirement plan sponsors and enforce compliance. Furthermore, EPCRS may be used by an employer that offers a plan that is intended to be a 403(b) plan (see Q 35:1) but that has failed to satisfy the requirements because of certain types of failures. EPCRS permits an employer to correct these failures and thereby provide its employees with retirement benefits on a tax-favored basis. In addition, EPCRS may be used to correct failures with respect to SEPs (see Q 32:1) and SIMPLE IRAs (see Q 33:2). PPA (see Q 1:33) clarifies that IRS has full authority to establish and implement EPCRS and directs IRS to improve and continue to update EPCRS. [PPA § 1101] [Rev. Proc. 2008-50, 2008-2 C.B. 464]

Q 19:2 What is the Employee Plans Compliance Resolution System (EPCRS)?

EPCRS is the IRS system that coordinates compliance programs for the correction of plan qualification failures (see Q 19:5); with respect to 403(b) plans (see Q 35:1), 403(b) failures (see Q 19:6); and, with respect to SEPs (see Q 32:1) and SIMPLE IRAs (see Q 33:2), not satisfying the requirements of Sections 408(k) and 408(p), respectively.

EPCRS is based on the following general principles:

1. Plan sponsors should be encouraged to establish administrative practices and procedures that ensure that plans are properly operated.
2. Plan sponsors should maintain plan documents satisfying the qualification requirements.
3. Plan sponsors should make voluntary and timely correction of any plan failures, whether involving discrimination in favor of HCEs (see Q 3:2), plan operations, the terms of the plan document, or adoption of a plan by an ineligible employer (see Qs 19:5, 19:6).
4. Voluntary compliance is promoted by providing for IRS-approved limited fees for voluntary corrections, thereby reducing the uncertainty regarding potential liability.
5. Fees and sanctions should be graduated in a series of steps so that there is always an incentive to correct promptly.
6. Sanctions for qualification failures identified on audit should be reasonable in light of the nature, extent, and severity of the violation.
7. Administration of EPCRS should be consistent and uniform.
8. Taxpayers should be able to rely on the availability of EPCRS in taking corrective actions to maintain the qualified status of their plans.

[Rev. Proc. 2008-50, § 1.02, 2008-2 C.B. 464]

Q 19:3 What are the basic elements of EPCRS?

EPCRS includes the following basic elements:

1. *Self-Correction Program (SCP; see Q 19:17).* A plan sponsor that has established compliance practices and procedures may, at any time, without paying any fee or sanction, correct insignificant operational failures (see Q 19:18) under a qualified plan or a 403(b) plan (see Q 35:1), or a SEP (see Q 32:1) or SIMPLE IRA (see Q 33:2), provided the SEP or SIMPLE IRA is established and maintained pursuant to a document

approved by IRS. In addition, in the case of a qualified plan that is the subject of a favorable determination letter (see Q 19:7) or in the case of a 403(b) plan the plan sponsor generally may correct even significant operational failures without payment of any fee or sanction.

2. *Voluntary Correction Program with Service Approval (VCP; see Q 19:20)*. A plan sponsor, at any time before audit, may pay a limited fee and receive IRS approval for correction of a qualified plan, 403(b) plan, SEP, or SIMPLE IRA. Under VCP, there are special procedures for Anonymous Submissions (see Q 19:23) and Group Submissions (see Q 19:24).

3. *Correction on Audit (Audit CAP; see Q 19:28)*. If a failure (other than a failure corrected through SCP or VCP) is identified on audit, the plan sponsor may correct the failure and pay a sanction. The sanction imposed will bear a reasonable relationship to the nature, extent, and severity of the failure, taking into account the extent to which correction occurred before audit.

[Rev. Proc. 2008-50, § 1.03, 2008-2 C.B. 464]

Q 19:4   What are the basic eligibility requirements for EPCRS?

SCP (see Q 19:17) is available only for operational failures (see Qs 19:5, 19:6). Qualified plans and 403(b) plans (see Q 35:1) are eligible for SCP with respect both insignificant and significant operational failures (see Qs 19:18, 19:19). SEPs (see Q 32:1) and SIMPLE IRAs (see Q 33:2) are eligible for SCP with respect to insignificant operational failures only.

Qualified plans, 403(b) plans, SEPs, and SIMPLE IRAs are eligible for VCP (see Q 19:20). VCP provides general procedures for correction of all qualification failures (see Q 19:5): operational failure, plan document failure, demographic failure, and employer eligibility failure.

Audit CAP (see Q 19:28) is available for qualified plans, 403(b) plans, SEPs, and SIMPLE IRAs in order to correct all failures found on examination that have not been corrected in accordance with SCP or VCP.

IRS may extend EPCRS to other arrangements (e.g., Section 457 plans).

Additional specific rules regarding eligibility for EPCRS are as follows:

1. *Effect of examination*. If the plan or plan sponsor is under examination (see Q 19:8), VCP is not available. However, while the plan or plan sponsor is under examination, insignificant operational failures (see Q 19:18) can be corrected under SCP; and, if correction has been substantially completed before the plan or plan sponsor is under examination, significant operational failures (see Q 19:19) can be corrected under SCP.

2. *Favorable letter requirement*. The provisions of SCP relating to significant operational failures are available for a qualified plan only if the plan has received a favorable letter (see Q 19:7). The provisions of SCP relating to insignificant operational failures are available for a SEP only if the plan

document consists of either (a) a Form 5305-SEP or 5305A-SEP (see Q 32:14) adopted by an employer or (b) a current favorable opinion letter for a plan sponsor that has adopted a prototype SEP. The provisions of SCP relating to insignificant operational failures are available for a SIMPLE IRA only if the plan document consists of either (a) a Form 5305-SIMPLE or 5304-SIMPLE (see Q 33:18) adopted by an employer or (b) a current favorable opinion letter for a plan sponsor that has adopted a prototype SIMPLE IRA.

3. *Established practices and procedures.* In order to be eligible for SCP, formal or informal practices and procedures reasonably designed to promote and facilitate overall compliance with the requirements for plan qualification must have been established. A plan document alone does not constitute evidence of established procedures. In order to use SCP, these established procedures must have been in place and routinely followed, and an operational failure must have occurred through an oversight or mistake in applying them, because of an inadequacy in the procedures, or because the failure relates to transferred assets (see Q 19:9) and did not occur after the end of the first plan year that begins after the corporate merger, acquisition, or other similar transaction.

4. *Correction by plan amendment.*

   a. A plan sponsor may use VCP and Audit CAP for a qualified plan to correct plan document, demographic, and operational failures by a plan amendment, including correcting an operational failure by plan amendment to conform the terms of the plan to the plan's prior operations, provided that the amendment complies with the requirements for plan qualification.

   b. Generally, SCP is not available to correct an operational failure by plan amendment. However, in limited circumstances, SCP may be used to correct a compensation limitation failure, a hardship distribution failure, and a failure regarding the inclusion of an ineligible employee (see Q 19:32).

5. *Submission for a determination letter.*

   a. Under VCP and Audit CAP, a determination letter (see Q 18:1) will be issued to correct a nonamender failure, or to correct a failure in either a VCP filing submitted for a terminating plan or a terminating plan under examination. In addition, a determination letter may be issued to correct a failure in a plan that is either submitted under VCP or being examined during the last 12 months of the plan's remedial amendment cycle (see Qs 18:6–18:9). IRS reserves the right to require the submission of a determination letter application with respect to any amendment proposed or adopted to correct any qualification failure under VCP or Audit CAP.

   b. In the case of any correction of an operational failure through plan amendment under SCP, as permitted under 4 above, a plan sponsor must submit a determination letter application. The determination letter application must be submitted before the end of the plan's applicable remedial amendment period, and the amendment under SCP must be identified as such in the cover letter.

6. *Availability of correction of employer eligibility failure.* SCP is not available to correct an employer eligibility failure.

7. *Availability of correction of a terminated plan.* Correction of qualification failures in a terminated plan may be made under VCP and Audit CAP, whether or not the trust is still in existence.

8. *Availability of correction of an orphan plan.* An orphan plan (see Q 19:10) that is terminating may be corrected under VCP and Audit CAP, provided that the party acting on behalf of the plan is an eligible party (see Q 19:10).

9. *Availability of correction of Section 457 plans.* Submissions relating to Section 457 plans will be accepted by IRS on a provisional basis outside of EPCRS through standards that are similar to EPCRS.

10. *Egregious failures.* SCP is not available to correct operational failures that are egregious. For example, if an employer has consistently and improperly covered only HCEs (see Q 3:2) or if a contribution to a defined contribution plan (see Q 2:2) for an HCE is several times greater than the annual addition limit (see Q 6:12), the failure would be considered egregious. VCP is available to correct egregious failures; however, these failures are subject to increased fees (see Q 19:27). Audit CAP is also available to correct egregious failures.

11. *Diversion or misuse of plan assets.* SCP, VCP, and Audit CAP are not available to correct failures relating to the diversion or misuse of plan assets.

12. *Abusive tax avoidance transactions.* With respect to SCP, in the event that the plan or the plan sponsor has been a party to an abusive tax avoidance transaction, SCP is not available. With respect to VCP, if IRS determines that the plan or plan sponsor was, or may have been, a party to an abusive tax avoidance transaction, then the matter will be referred to the IRS Employee Plans Tax Shelter Coordinator. With respect to Audit CAP, regarding an abusive tax avoidance transaction, the matter may be referred to the IRS Employee Plans Tax Shelter Coordinator.

[Rev. Proc. 2008-50, § 4, 2008-2 C.B. 464]

Q 19:5   What is a qualification failure?

A qualification failure is any failure that adversely affects the qualification of a plan. The four types of qualification failures—plan document failure, operational failure, demographic failure, and employer eligibility failure—are defined as:

1. *Plan document failure.* A plan document failure means a plan provision (or the absence of a plan provision) that, on its face, violates the requirements of Section 401(a) or 403(a). Thus, for example, the failure of a plan to be amended to reflect a new qualification requirement within the plan's applicable remedial amendment period (see Qs 18:6-18:9) is a plan

document failure. In addition, if a plan has not been timely or properly amended during an applicable remedial amendment period for adopting good faith or interim amendments with respect to disqualifying provisions, the plan is considered to have a plan document failure. A plan document failure includes any qualification failure that is a violation of the requirements of Section 401(a) or 403(a) and that is not an operational failure, demographic failure, or employer eligibility failure.

2. *Operational failure.* An operational failure means a qualification failure (other than an employer eligibility failure) that arises solely from the failure to follow plan provisions. For example, a failure to follow the terms of a plan providing for the satisfaction of the requirements of Section 401(k) (see chapter 27) is considered to be an operational failure. A plan does not have an operational failure to the extent the plan is permitted to be amended retroactively to reflect the plan's operations (see Q 18:6). In the situation where a plan sponsor timely adopted a good faith or interim amendment that is not a disqualifying provision and the plan was not operated in accordance with the terms of such interim amendment, the plan is considered to have an operational failure.

3. *Demographic failure.* A demographic failure means a failure to satisfy the nondiscrimination requirements (see Q 4:10), the minimum participation requirement (see Q 5:23), or the minimum coverage requirement (see Q 5:15) and that is not an operational failure or an employer eligibility failure. The correction of a demographic failure generally requires a corrective amendment to the plan that adds benefits or increases existing benefits.

4. *Employer eligibility failure.* An employer eligibility failure means the adoption of a plan intended to include a cash-or-deferred arrangement (CODA; see Q 27:2) and satisfy the requirements of Section 401(a) or 403(b) by an employer that fails to meet the employer eligibility requirements to establish a 401(k) plan. An employer eligibility failure is not a plan document, operational, or demographic failure.

[Rev. Proc. 2008-50, § 5.01(2), 2008-2 C.B. 464]

Q 19:6   What is a 403(b) failure?

With respect to a 403(b) plan (see Q 35:1), a 403(b) failure is any operational, demographic, or employer eligibility failure defined as follows:

1. *Operational failure.* With respect to a 403(b) plan, any of the following failures:

   a. To satisfy the requirements relating to the availability of salary reduction contributions (see Qs 35:14–35:16);

   b. To satisfy the nondiscrimination testing for matching and employee contributions (see Q 35:18);

   c. To satisfy the compensation limit requirement (see Q 35:18);

   d. To satisfy the prohibitions on distributions (see Q 35:34);

    e. To satisfy the incidental death benefit rules (see Q 35:36);

    f. To pay RMDs (see Q 35:36);

    g. To give employees the right to elect a direct rollover (see Q 35:38);

    h. To satisfy the limit on elective deferrals (see Q 35:25);

    i. Involving contributions or allocations of excess amounts; or

    j. To satisfy any other applicable requirements that (i) results in the loss of 403(b) status for the plan or the loss of 403(b) status for the custodial accounts or annuity contracts under the plan and (ii) is not a demographic failure, an eligibility failure, or a failure related to the purchase of annuity contracts, or contributions to custodial accounts, on behalf of individuals who are not employees of the employer.

2. *Demographic failure.* With respect to a 403(b) plan, a failure to satisfy the nondiscrimination, minimum participation, or minimum coverage requirements (see Qs 35:14–35:17).

3. *Employer eligibility failure.* With respect to a 403(b) plan, any of the following:

    a. A plan of an ineligible employer;

    b. A failure to satisfy the nontransferability requirement (see Q 35:13);

    c. A failure to initially establish or maintain a custodial account (see Q 35:6); or

    d. A failure to purchase (initially or subsequently) either an annuity contract from an insurance company (unless grandfathered) or a custodial account from a regulated investment company utilizing a bank or an approved non-bank trustee/custodian (see Q 35:6).

[Rev. Proc. 2008-50, § 5.02(2), 2008-2 C.B. 464]

Q 19:7   What is a favorable letter?

Favorable letter means a current favorable determination letter (see Q 18:1) for an individually designed plan (including a volume submitter plan that is not identical to an approved volume submitter plan (see Q 2:28)), a current favorable opinion letter for a plan sponsor that has adopted a master or prototype plan (see Q 2:27), or a current favorable advisory letter and certification that the plan sponsor has adopted a plan that is identical to an approved volume submitter plan. A plan has a current favorable determination letter, opinion letter, or advisory letter if:

1. The plan has a favorable determination letter, opinion letter, or advisory letter that considers the law changes incorporated in the plan sponsor's most recently expired remedial amendment cycle (see Q 18:6).

2. For plans with respect to whom the initial remedial amendment cycle has not expired, the favorable determination letter, opinion letter, or advisory letter that considers GUST.

3. The plan is initially adopted or effective after December 31, 2001, and the plan sponsor timely submits an application for a determination letter or adopts an approved master or prototype plan or volume submitter plan within the plan's remedial amendment period.

4. The plan is terminated prior to the expiration of the plan's applicable remedial amendment cycle and the plan was amended to reflect the provisions of any legislation that was in effect when the plan was terminated.

[Rev. Proc. 2008-50, § 5.01(4), 2008-2 C.B. 464]

Q 19:8   What is "under examination"?

"Under examination" means (1) a plan that is under an Employee Plans examination (i.e., an examination of a Form 5500 series (see Q 21:1) or other Employee Plans examination), (2) a plan sponsor that is under an Exempt Organizations examination (i.e., an examination of a Form 990 series or other Exempt Organizations examination), or (3) a plan that is under investigation by the Criminal Investigation Division of IRS.

A plan that is under an Employee Plans examination includes any plan for which the plan sponsor has received verbal or written notification from Employee Plans of an impending Employee Plans examination, or of an impending referral for an Employee Plans examination, and also includes any plan that has been under an Employee Plans examination and is now in appeal or in litigation for issues raised in an Employee Plans examination.

A plan is considered to be under examination if it is aggregated for purposes of satisfying the nondiscrimination requirements (see Q 4:10), the minimum participation requirement (see Q 5:23), or the minimum coverage requirement (see Q 5:15) with a plan that is under examination. In addition, a plan is considered to be under examination with respect to a failure of a qualification requirement if the plan is aggregated with another plan for purposes of satisfying that qualification requirement and that other plan is under examination. Examples of such qualification requirements include the top-heavy requirement (see chapter 25), the annual addition limitation (see Q 6:34), and the elective contribution limitation (see Q 27:51).

An Employee Plans examination also includes the case where a plan sponsor has applied for a determination letter with respect to plan amendment or plan termination (see Q 25:63) and is notified by an IRS agent that there is a possible qualification failure (e.g., a partial termination; see Q 25:5).

[Rev. Proc. 2008-50, § 5.07, 2008-2 C.B. 464]

Q 19:9   What are transferred assets?

Transferred assets are plan assets that were received, in connection with a corporate merger, acquisition, or other similar employer transaction, by the plan in a transfer (including a merger or consolidation of plan assets) from a plan sponsored by an employer that was not a member of the same controlled group (see Q 5:31) as the plan sponsor. If a transfer of plan assets related to the same employer transaction is accomplished through several transfers, then the date of the transfer is the date of the first transfer. [Rev. Proc. 2008-50, § 5.01(7), 2008-2 C.B. 464]

Q 19:10 What is an orphan plan?

With respect to VCP (see Q 19:20) and Audit CAP (see Q 19:28), an orphan plan means any qualified plan with respect to which an eligible party has determined that the plan sponsor (1) no longer exists, (2) cannot be located, or (3) is unable to maintain the plan. An orphan plan does not include any plan terminated pursuant to DOL regulations governing the termination of abandoned individual account plans (see Q 25:64).

Eligible party means:

1. A court-appointed representative with authority to terminate the plan and dispose of the plan's assets;
2. In the case of an orphan plan under investigation by DOL, a person or entity that has accepted responsibility for terminating the plan and distributing the plan's assets; or
3. In the case of a qualified plan to which Title I of ERISA has never applied (see Q 20:39), a surviving spouse who is the sole beneficiary of a plan that provided benefits to a participant who was (a) the sole owner of the business that sponsored the plan and (b) the only participant in the plan.

[Rev. Proc. 2008-50, § 5.03, 2008-2 C.B. 464]

Q 19:11 What are the correction principles and rules of general applicability under EPCRS?

Generally, a failure (see Qs 19:5, 19:6) is not corrected unless full correction is made with respect to all participants and beneficiaries and for all taxable years (whether or not the statute of limitations has run). Even if correction is made for a closed taxable year, the tax liability associated with that year will not be redetermined because of the correction. Correction is determined taking into account the terms of the plan at the time of the failure. Correction should be accomplished taking into account the following principles:

1. *Restoration of benefits.* The correction method should restore the plan to the position it would have been in had the failure not occurred, including restoration of current and former participants and beneficiaries to the benefits and rights they would have had.
2. *Reasonable and appropriate correction.* The correction should be reasonable and appropriate for the failure. Depending on the nature of the failure, there may be more than one reasonable and appropriate correction for the failure. For qualified plans, any permitted correction method (see Qs 19:31, 19:32) is deemed to be a reasonable and appropriate

method of correcting the related qualification failure. Any permitted correction method applicable to a 403(b) plan (see Q 35:1), SEP, or SIMPLE IRA is deemed to be a reasonable and appropriate method of correcting the related failure (see Qs 19:6, 19:16). Whether any other particular correction method is reasonable and appropriate is determined taking into account the applicable facts and circumstances and the following principles:

    a. The correction method should, to the extent possible, resemble one already provided for.

    b. The correction method for failures relating to nondiscrimination should provide benefits for nonhighly compensated employees (NHCEs; see Q 3:12).

    c. The correction method should keep assets in the plan, except to the extent that there are already rules providing for correction by distribution to participants or return of assets to the employer.

    d. The correction method should not violate another applicable specific requirement. If an additional failure is created as a result of the use of a correction method, then that failure also must be corrected.

3. *Consistency requirement.* Generally, where more than one correction method is available, the correction method should be applied consistently in correcting all operational failures of that type for that plan year. Similarly, earnings adjustment methods should be applied consistently with respect to corrective contributions or allocations for a plan year.

4. *Principles regarding corrective allocations and corrective distributions.*

    a. Corrective allocations under a defined contribution plan (see Q 2:2) should be based upon the terms of the plan and other applicable information at the time of the qualification failure and should be adjusted for earnings and forfeitures that would have been allocated to the participant's account if the failure had not occurred. The corrective allocation need not be adjusted for losses.

    b. A corrective allocation to a participant's account because of a failure to make a required allocation in a prior limitation year (see Q 6:58) will not be considered an annual addition (see Q 6:34) with respect to the participant for the limitation year in which the correction is made, but will be considered an annual addition for the limitation year to which the corrective allocation relates. However, the normal rules regarding deductions apply (see chapter 12).

    c. Corrective allocations should come only from employer contributions (including forfeitures if the plan permits their use to reduce employer contributions).

    d. In the case of a defined benefit plan (see Q 2:3), a corrective distribution for an individual should be increased to take into account the delayed payment, consistent with the plan's actuarial adjustments.

5. *Special exceptions to full correction.* In general, a failure must be fully corrected. Although the mere fact that correction is inconvenient or

burdensome is not enough to relieve a plan sponsor of the need to make full correction, full correction may not be required in certain situations because it is unreasonable or not feasible. Even in these situations, the correction method adopted must be one that does not have significant adverse effects on participants and beneficiaries or the plan and that does not discriminate significantly in favor of HCEs (see Q 3:2). The following exceptions specify those situations in which full correction is not required:

    a. *Reasonable estimates.* If it is not possible to make a precise calculation or the probable difference between the approximate and the precise restoration of a participant's benefits is insignificant and the administrative cost of determining precise restoration would significantly exceed the probable difference, reasonable estimates may be used in calculating appropriate correction.

    b. *Delivery of very small benefits.* If the total corrective distribution due a participant or beneficiary is $75 or less, the plan sponsor is not required to make the corrective distribution if the reasonable direct costs of processing and delivering the distribution to the participant or beneficiary would exceed the amount of the distribution.

    c. *Recovery of small overpayments.* Generally, for a submission under VCP (see Q 19:20), if the total amount of an overpayment (see Q 19:13) made to a participant or beneficiary is $100 or less, the plan sponsor is not required to seek the return of the overpayment.

    d. *Locating lost participants.* Reasonable actions must be taken to find all current and former participants and beneficiaries to whom additional benefits are due, but who have not been located after a mailing to the last known address (see Q 25:43).

    e. *Small excess amounts.* Generally, under VCP or Audit CAP, if the total amount of an excess amount (see Q 19:13) with respect to the benefit of a participant or beneficiary is $100 or less, the plan sponsor is not required to distribute or forfeit such excess amount.

    f. *Orphan plans.* IRS retains the discretion to determine under VCP and Audit CAP whether full correction will be required in a terminating orphan plan (see Q 19:10).

  6. *Correction principle for loan failures.* In the case of a loan failure that is corrected (see Q 19:15), the participant is generally responsible for paying the corrective payment. However, with respect to the failure regarding a defaulted loan, the employer should pay a portion of the correction payment on behalf of the participant equal to the interest that accumulates as a result of such failure.

  7. *Correction for exclusions of employees for elective contributions or after-tax employee contributions.* If a qualified plan has an operational failure (see Q 19:5) that consists of excluding an employee who should have been eligible to make an elective contribution (see Qs 27:3, 27:16) under a CODA (see Q 27:2) or an after-tax employee contribution (see Q 27:74), the employer should contribute to the plan on behalf of the excluded

employee an amount that makes up for the value of the lost opportunity to the employee to have a portion of the employee's compensation contributed to the plan accumulated with earnings tax free in the future.

8. *Reporting.* Any distributions from the plan should be properly reported.

Generally, none of the correction programs is available to correct failures that can be corrected under the Code and related regulations. For example, as a general rule, a plan document failure that is a disqualifying provision for which the remedial amendment period has not expired can be corrected by operation of the Code through a retroactive remedial amendment.

[Rev. Proc. 2008-50, §§ 6.01, 6.02, 6.08, 2008-2 C.B. 464]

Q 19:12   How is an employer eligibility failure corrected?

The permitted correction of an employer eligibility failure (see Q 19:6) is the cessation of all contributions (including salary reduction and after-tax contributions) beginning no later than the date the application under VCP is filed. Pursuant to VCP correction, the assets in such a plan are to remain in the trust, annuity contract, or custodial account and are to be distributed no earlier than the occurrence of one of the applicable distribution events.

Cessation of contributions is not required if continuation of contributions would not be an employer eligibility failure. For example, a tax-exempt employer may maintain a 401(k) plan after 1996 (see Q 27:1).

[Rev. Proc. 2008-50, § 6.03, 2008-2 C.B. 464]

Q 19:13   What is an excess amount?

With respect to a qualified plan, "excess amount" means a qualification failure (see Q 9:5) due to a contribution, allocation, or similar credit that is made on behalf of a participant or beneficiary to a plan in excess of the maximum amount permitted to be contributed, allocated, or credited on behalf of the participant or beneficiary under the terms of the plan or that exceeds a limitation on contributions or allocations. Excess amounts include: (1) an elective deferral or after-tax employee contribution that is in excess of the maximum contribution under the plan; (2) an elective deferral or after-tax employee contribution made in excess of the annual addition (see Q 6:34); (3) an elective deferral in excess of the dollar limitation (see Q 27:51); (4) an excess contribution or excess aggregate contribution under Sections 401(k) or 401(m); (5) an elective deferral or after-tax employee contribution that is made with respect to compensation in excess of the compensation limitation (see Q 6:45); and (6) any other employer contribution that exceeds certain limitations under the Code. Excess amounts are limited to contributions, allocations, or annual additions under a defined contribution plan, after-tax employee contributions to a defined benefit plan, and contributions or allocations that are to be made to a separate account (with actual earnings) under a defined benefit plan. [Rev. Proc. 2008-50, § 5.01(3)(a), 2008-2 C.B. 464]

With respect to a 403(b) plan (see Q 35:1), "excess amount" means any amount returned to ensure that the plan satisfies the requirements of Sections 401(a)(30) (see Q 35:25), 415 (see Q 35:29), or 403(b)(2) (for plan years prior to January 1, 2002). In addition, excess amount includes (for all plan years) any distributions required to ensure that the plan complies with the applicable requirements of Section 403(b) (see Q 35:11). [Rev. Proc. 2008-50, § 5.02(3), 2008-2 C.B. 464]

"Excess allocation" means an excess amount for which the Code or regulations do not provide any corrective mechanism. [Rev. Proc. 2008-50, § 5.01(3)(b), 2008-2 C.B. 464]

"Overpayment" means a qualification failure due to a payment being made to a participant or beneficiary that exceeds the amount payable to the participant or beneficiary under the terms of the plan or that exceeds a limitation provided in the Code or regulations. Overpayments include both payments from a defined benefit plan and payments from a defined contribution plan. [Rev. Proc. 2008-50, § 5.01(3)(c), 2008-2 C.B. 464]

Q 19:14   How are excess amounts treated?

A distribution of an excess amount (see Q 19:13) is not eligible for the favorable tax treatment accorded to distributions from qualified plans (such as eligibility for rollover; see Q 34:1). To the extent that a current or prior distribution was a distribution of an excess amount, distribution of that excess amount is not an eligible rollover distribution (see Q 34:9). Thus, for example, if such a distribution was contributed to an IRA (see Q 30:1), the contribution is not a valid rollover contribution (see Q 34:8) for purposes of determining the amount of excess contributions to the individual's IRA. A distribution of excess amounts is generally treated in the same manner as corrective disbursements of elective deferrals (see Q 27:63). The distribution must be reported on Forms 1099-R for the year of distribution with respect to each participant or beneficiary receiving such a distribution. In addition, the employer must notify the recipients that the excess amount was distributed and was not eligible for rollover.

[Rev. Proc. 2008-50, § 6.06, 2008-2 C.B. 464]

Q 19:15   Are there special rules relating to the correction of plan loan failures?

Unless correction is made in accordance with 1, 2, or 3 below, a deemed distribution (see Q 14:8) in connection with a failure relating to a loan to a participant made from a qualified plan or a 403(b) plan (see Q 35:1) must be reported on Form 1099-R with respect to the affected participant and any applicable income tax withholding amount that was required to be paid in connection with the failure must be paid by the employer. As part of VCP (see Q 19:20), the deemed distribution may be reported on Form 1099-R with respect to the affected participant for the year of correction (instead of the year of the failure).

A deemed distribution corrected under 1, 2, or 3, as follows, is not required to be reported on Form 1099-R, and repayments made do not result in the affected participant having additional basis (see Q 13:3) in the plan for purposes of determining the tax treatment of subsequent distributions from the plan to the affected participant:

1. *Loans in excess of the dollar limitation* (see Q 14:4). A failure to comply with plan provisions requiring that loans comply with the dollar limitation may be corrected by a corrective repayment to the plan based on the excess of the loan amount over the maximum loan amount. After the corrective payment is made, the applicant may reform the loan to amortize the remaining principal balance as of the date of repayment over the remaining period of the original loan. This is permissible as long as the recalculated payments over the remaining period would not cause the loan to violate the maximum duration permitted (see Qs 14:5, 14:6). The maximum duration is determined from the date the original loan was made. In addition, the amortization payments determined for the remaining period must comply with the level amortization requirements.

2. *Loan terms that do not satisfy the maximum term or level amortization requirements* (see Qs 14:5, 14:6). For a failure of loan repayment terms to provide for a repayment schedule that complies with the maximum repayment terms or the level amortization rules, the failure may be corrected by a reamortization of the loan balance in accordance with the requirements over the remaining period measured from the original date of the loan.

3. *Defaulted loans.* A failure to repay the loan in accordance with the loan terms may be corrected by (a) a lump-sum repayment equal to the additional repayments that the affected participant would have made to the plan if there had been no failure to repay the plan, plus interest accrued on the missed repayments, (b) reamortizing the outstanding balance of the loan, including accrued interest, over the remaining payment schedule of the original term of the loan, or (c) any combination of (a) or (b).

[Rev. Proc. 2008-50, § 6.07, 2008-2 C.B. 464]

Q 19:16 Are there special rules regarding corrections of SEPs and SIMPLE IRAs?

Generally, the correction for a SEP (see Q 32:1) or a SIMPLE IRA (see Q 33:2) is expected to be similar to the correction required for a qualified plan with a similar qualification failure (i.e., plan document failure, operational failure, demographic failure, and employer eligibility failure). In any case in which correction is not feasible for a SEP or SIMPLE IRA or in any other case determined by IRS at its discretion, IRS may provide for a different correction and a special fee (see Q 19:27).

If the failure involves a violation of the deferral percentage test (see Q 32:12) applicable to a salary reduction SEP (see Q 32:9), there are several methods to correct the failure. This failure may be corrected in one of the following ways:

1. The plan sponsor may make contributions that are 100 percent vested to all eligible NHCEs (see Q 3:12) necessary to raise the deferral percentage needed to pass the test. This amount may be calculated as either the same percentage of compensation or the same flat dollar amount.

2. The plan sponsor may effect distribution of excess contributions, adjusted for earnings through the date of correction, to HCEs (see Q 3:2) to correct the failure. The plan sponsor must also contribute to the SEP an amount equal to the total amount distributed. This amount must be allocated to (a) current employees who were NHCEs in the year of the failure, (b) current NHCEs who were NHCEs in the year of the failure, or (c) employees (both current and former) who were NHCEs in the year of the failure.

The plan sponsor should correct undercontributions to a SEP or a SIMPLE IRA by contributing make-up amounts that are fully vested, adjusted for earnings credited from the date of the failure to the date of correction.

An "excess amount" under a SEP or SIMPLE IRA is an amount contributed on behalf of an employee that is in excess of an employee's benefit under the plan or an elective deferral in excess of the limitations of elective deferrals (see Q 32:10) or the deferral percentage test.

If an excess amount is attributable to elective deferrals, the plan sponsor may effect distribution of the excess amount, adjusted for earnings through the date of correction, to the affected participant. The amount distributed to the affected participant is includible in gross income in the year of distribution. The distribution is reported on Form 1099-R for the year of distribution with respect to each participant receiving the distribution. In addition, the plan sponsor must inform affected participants that the distribution of an excess amount is not eligible for favorable tax treatment accorded to distributions from a SEP or a SIMPLE IRA (and, specifically, is not eligible for a rollover (see Q 34:1)). If the excess amount is attributable to employer contributions, the plan sponsor may effect distribution of the employer excess amount, adjusted for earnings through the date of correction, to the plan sponsor. The amount distributed to the plan sponsor is not includible in the gross income of the affected participant, and the plan sponsor is not entitled to a deduction for such employer excess amount. The distribution is reported on Form 1099-R issued to the participant indicating the taxable amount as zero.

If an excess amount is retained in the SEP or SIMPLE IRA, a special fee (see Q 19:27), in addition to the VCP submission fee, will apply. The plan sponsor is not entitled to a deduction for an excess amount retained in the SEP or SIMPLE IRA. In the case of an excess amount retained in a SEP that is attributable to a failure regarding contribution limits (see Q 32:6), the excess amount, adjusted for earnings through the date of correction, must reduce the affected participants' applicable contribution limit for the year following the year of correction (or for the year of correction if the plan sponsor so chooses), and subsequent years, until the excess is eliminated.

If the total excess amount in a SEP or SIMPLE IRA, whether attributable to elective deferrals or employer contributions, is $100 or less, the plan sponsor is not required to distribute the excess amount and the special fee will not apply.

[Rev. Proc. 2008-50, § 6.10, 2008-2 C.B. 464]

Q 19:17 What is the Self-Correction Program (SCP)?

SCP allows a plan sponsor that has established compliance practices and procedures (1) at any time without paying any fee or sanction to correct insignificant operational failures (see Q 19:18) under a qualified plan, a 403(b) plan, a SEP, or a SIMPLE IRA, provided the SEP or SIMPLE IRA is established and maintained on a document approved by IRS and (2) in the case of a qualified plan that is the subject of a favorable determination letter or a 403(b) plan, to correct significant operational failures (see Q 19:19) within a required period without payment of any fee or sanction.

[Rev. Proc. 2008-50, §§ 1.03, 7, 8, 9, 2008-2 C.B. 464]

Q 19:18 What are the requirements for self-correction of insignificant operational failures?

Under SCP (see Q 19:17), a plan sponsor of a qualified plan, a 403(b) plan (see Q 35:1), a SEP (see Q 32:1), or a SIMPLE IRA (see Q 33:2) may correct an operational failure (see Qs 19:5, 19:6) at any time if, given all the facts and circumstances, the operational failure is insignificant. This self-correction procedure is available even if the plan or plan sponsor is under examination (see Q 19:8). The factors to be considered in determining whether or not an operational failure is insignificant include, but are not limited to, the following:

1. Whether other failures occurred during the period being examined (for this purpose a failure is not considered to have occurred more than once merely because more than one participant is affected by the failure);

2. The percentage of plan assets and contributions involved in the failure;

3. The number of years the failure occurred;

4. The number of participants affected relative to the total number of participants in the plan;

5. The number of participants affected as a result of the failure relative to the number of participants that could have been affected by the failure;

6. Whether correction was made within a reasonable time after discovery; and

7. The reason for the failure (e.g., data errors).

No single factor is determinative. In addition, factors 2, 4, and 5, above should not be interpreted to exclude small businesses. In the case of a plan with more than one operational failure in a single year, or operational failures that occur in more than one year, the operational failures are eligible for correction only if all of the operational failures are insignificant in the aggregate. Significant operational failures (see Q 19:19) that have been corrected and operational failures corrected under VCP (see Q 19:20) are not taken into account for purposes of determining if operational failures are insignificant in the aggregate.

Example 1. Eric Corp. established a money purchase pension plan in 1992 that provides for an employer contribution equal to 10 percent of compensation. During its examination of the plan for the 2007 plan year, IRS discovered that the employee responsible for entering data into the employer's computer made minor arithmetical errors in transcribing the compensation data with respect to six out of the plan's 40 participants, resulting in excess allocations to those six participants' accounts. Under these facts, the number of participants affected by the failure relative to the number of participants that could have been affected is insignificant, and the failure is due to minor data errors. Thus, the failure occurring in 2007 would be eligible for correction.

Example 2. In 1991, Marsha Inc. established a profit sharing plan. In 2007, the allocations for 50 of the 250 participants were subject to the annual addition limitation (see Q 6:34). In 2010, during its examination of the plan for the 2007 plan year, IRS discovered that the annual additions allocated to the accounts of three participants exceeded the maximum limitation. Marsha Inc. contributed $3,500,000 to the plan, and the amount of the excess totaled $4,550. Under these facts, because (1) the number of participants affected by the failure relative to the total number of participants who could have been affected by the failure and (2) the monetary amount of the failure relative to the total employer contribution to the plan for 2007 are insignificant, the failure is eligible for correction.

Example 3. The facts are the same as in Example 2, except that the failure occurred during 2007, and 2009. In addition, the three participants affected by the failure were not identical each year. The fact that the failures occurred during more than one year did not cause the failures to be significant; accordingly, the failures are still eligible for correction.

Example 4. The facts are the same as in Example 2, except that the annual additions of 18 of the 50 participants whose benefits were limited exceeded the maximum limitations during 2007 and the amount of the excesses ranged from $1,000 to $9,000, and totaled $150,000. Under these facts, taking into account (1) the number of participants affected by the failure relative to the total number of participants who could have been affected by the failure for 2007 and (2) the monetary amount of the failure relative to the total employer contribution, the failure is significant. Accordingly, the failure that occurred in 2007 is ineligible for correction as an insignificant failure.

Example 5. Public School maintains for its 200 employees a salary reduction 403(b) plan (see Q 35:11). The business manager has primary responsibility for administering the plan, in addition to other administrative functions within Public School. During the 2007 plan year, a former employee should have received an additional required minimum distribution of $278, another participant received an impermissible hardship withdrawal of $2,500, and another participant made elective deferrals of which $1,000 was in excess of the limit. Under these facts, even though multiple failures occurred in a single plan year, the failures will be eligible for correction under SCP because, in the aggregate, the failures are insignificant.

[Rev. Proc. 2008-50, § 8, 2008-2 C.B. 464]

Example 6. Gary, Inc. established a profit sharing plan in 1985. During its examination of the plan for the 1998 plan year, IRS discovered that, when providing data to the plan's third party administrator, the company reported years of participation as years of service, resulting in 12 out of 80 participants not being vested in accordance with the plan's vesting schedule. None of the affected participants had terminated employment; therefore, correction was made by revising (on paper) the vested percentages of the affected participants. IRS determined that the operational failures were insignificant because no other qualification failures were discovered, only 15 percent of the total participants were affected, corrective distributions were not necessary, and the operational failures were caused by miscommunications.

[Western Region IRS/Practitioner Benefits Conference, Case Studies (Sept. 18, 1998)]

Q 19:19   What are the requirements for self-correction of significant operational failures?

Under SCP (see Q 19:17), a plan sponsor of a qualified plan or a 403(b) plan (see Q 35:1) may correct an operational failure (see Qs 19:5, 19:6), even if significant, if the correction is either completed or substantially completed by the last day of the correction period.

The last day of the correction period for an operational failure is the last day of the second plan year following the plan year for which the failure occurred. However, in the case of a failure to satisfy the ADP test (see Q 27:18) or the ACP test (see Q 27:77), the correction period does not end until the last day of the second plan year following the plan year that includes the last day of the additional period for correction (see Qs 27:34, 27:82). The correction period for an operational failure that occurs for any plan year ends on the first date the plan or plan sponsor is under examination (see Q 19:8) for that plan year.

In the case of an operational failure that relates only to transferred assets (see Q 19:9), or to a plan assumed in connection with a corporate merger, acquisition, or other similar employer transaction, the correction period does not end until the last day of the first plan year that begins after the corporate merger, acquisition, or other similar employer transaction between the plan sponsor and the sponsor of the transferor plan.

Correction of an operational failure is substantially completed by the last day of the correction period only if:

1. a. During the correction period, the plan sponsor is reasonably prompt in identifying the operational failure, formulating a correction method, and initiating correction in a manner that demonstrates a commitment to completing correction of the operational failure as expeditiously as practicable, and

   b. Within 120 days after the last day of the correction period, the plan sponsor completes correction of the operational failure, or

2. a. During the correction period, correction is completed with respect to 65 percent of all participants affected by the operational failure, and

   b. Thereafter, the plan sponsor completes correction of the operational failure with respect to the remaining affected participants in a diligent manner.

In order to complete correction by plan amendment (see Q 19:4), the appropriate determination letter application must be submitted before the end of the plan's applicable remedial amendment period (see Q 18:6).

Example 1. In 2004, Hildy Corp. established a profit sharing plan with a 401(k) feature and received a favorable determination letter. During 2009, the plan administrator discovers that, despite established practices and procedures, several employees eligible to participate in the plan for 2008 were excluded. The administrator also finds that, for 2008, additional employees made excess elective deferrals and top-heavy minimum contributions were not made. During the 2009 plan year, the plan sponsor makes corrective contributions on behalf of the excluded employees, distributes the excess deferrals to the affected participants, and makes a top-heavy minimum contribution on behalf of all participants entitled to that contribution. Each corrective contribution and distribution is credited with earnings at a rate appropriate for the plan from the date the corrective contribution or distribution should have been made to the date of correction. The operational failures for the 2008 plan year are properly corrected within the correction period.

Example 2. In 1993, Sophie Corp. established Sophie Plan, a profit sharing plan, and received a favorable determination letter. In April 2009, Sophie Corp. purchased all of the stock of Hannah Corp., a wholly owned subsidiary of Emma Corp. Employees of Hannah Corp. participated in Emma Plan, a profit sharing plan sponsored by Emma Corp. The plan assets attributable to the account balances of the employees of Hannah Corp. who had participated in Emma Plan were transferred to Sophie Plan. As part of this agreement, Emma Corp. represented that its plan is tax qualified. Effective July 1, 2009, Sophie Plan accepted the transfer of plan assets from Emma Plan. After the transfer, it was determined that all the participants in one division of Hannah Corp. had been incorrectly excluded from allocation of the profit sharing contributions for the 2004 and 2005 plan years. During 2010, Sophie Corp. made corrective contributions on behalf of the affected participants. The corrective contributions were credited with earnings at a rate appropriate for the plan from the date the corrective contributions should have been made to the date of correction. Under these facts, Sophie Corp. has, within the correction period, corrected the operational failures for the 2004 and 2005 plan years with respect to the assets transferred to its plan.

[Rev. Proc. 2008-50, § 9, 2008-2 C.B. 464]

Example 3. Jane Corporation established a profit sharing plan in 1988 and received a favorable determination letter in 1996. In 1998, due to the relocation of its main office, a partial termination occurred, but the affected participants did not become fully vested. During 1999, a third party administrator discovered the operational failure that was corrected by fully vesting all affected participants. During an audit, IRS determined that the plan had established practices and procedures, the operational failures were corrected within the two-year correction period, and the correction method was reasonable and appropriate; therefore, the plan was eligible for SCP. [Western Region IRS/Practitioner Benefits Conference, Case Studies (Sept. 18, 1998)]

Q 19:20   What is the Voluntary Correction Program with Service Approval (VCP)?

VCP enables a sponsor, at any time prior to audit, to voluntarily disclose to IRS qualification failures (see Qs 19:5, 19:6) it has discovered in its plan, pay a limited fee, and receive approval for correction.

[Rev. Proc. 2008-50, §§ 1.03, 10, 2008-2 C.B. 464]

Q 19:21   What are the general requirements of VCP?

The requirements under VCP (see Q 19:20) will be met with respect to failures submitted if the plan sponsor pays the compliance fee (see Q 19:27) and implements the corrective actions in accordance with the compliance statement (see Q 19:22).

Only the failures raised by the plan sponsor or failures identified by IRS in processing the VCP application will be addressed and covered. Consideration under VCP does not preclude or impede a subsequent examination of the plan sponsor or the plan by IRS with respect to the taxable year or years involved with respect to matters that are outside the compliance statement. However, a plan sponsor's statements describing failures are made only for purposes of VCP and will not be regarded by IRS as an admission of a failure for purposes of any subsequent examination. Except in unusual circumstances, a plan that has been properly submitted under VCP will not be examined while the submission is pending. This practice regarding concurrent examination does not extend to other plans of the plan sponsor. Thus, any plan of the plan sponsor that is not pending under VCP could be subject to examination.

In any case in which a determination letter is submitted (see Q 19:4), the plan sponsor must submit a copy of the amendment, the appropriate application form (i.e., Form 5300 series), and the appropriate user fee (see Q 18:2) concurrently and to the same address as the VCP submission.

A submission of a plan under the determination letter program does not constitute a submission under VCP. If the plan sponsor discovers a qualification failure (see Q 19:5), the qualification failure may not be corrected as part of the determination letter process. The plan sponsor may use SCP (see Q 19:17) and VCP instead, as applicable. If, in connection with a determination letter application, IRS discovers a qualification failure, IRS may issue a closing agreement with respect to the failure identified or, if appropriate, refer the case to Employee Plans examinations. In either case, the fee relating to VCP will not apply (see Q 19:27); generally, the fee structure relating to Audit CAP will apply (see Q 19:29). However, if, in connection with a determination letter application, IRS discovers that the plan has not been amended timely for tax legislation changes, a special fee structure will apply (see Q 19:29).

Upon receipt of a submission under VCP, IRS will review whether the eligibility requirements and the submission requirements are satisfied. If IRS determines that a VCP submission is seriously deficient, IRS reserves the right to return the submission, including any compliance fee, without contacting the plan sponsor.

Once IRS determines that a request for consideration under VCP is acceptable, IRS will consult with the plan sponsor to discuss the proposed corrections and the plan's administrative procedures.

If additional information is required, IRS will generally contact the plan sponsor and explain what is needed to complete the submission. The plan sponsor will have 21 days from the date of this contact to provide the requested information.

If additional, unrelated failures are discovered by the plan sponsor after the initial VCP submission, the sponsor may request that such failures be added to the submission. IRS retains the discretion to reject the inclusion of such failures if the request is not timely (e.g., if the plan sponsor makes its request when processing of the VCP submission is substantially complete). If IRS discovers an unrelated failure while the VCP request is pending, the failure generally will be added to the failures under consideration in the submission. However, IRS retains the discretion to determine that a failure is outside the scope of the voluntary request for consideration because it is not voluntarily brought forward by the plan sponsor.

If IRS initially determines that it cannot issue a compliance statement because the parties cannot agree upon correction or a change in administrative procedures, the plan sponsor will be offered a conference. If resolution cannot be reached, the matter will be closed, the compliance fee will not be returned, and the case may be referred for examination.

If agreement is reached, IRS will send to the plan sponsor a compliance statement specifying the corrective action required. If the original submission is subsequently materially modified, then, unless the plan sponsor has submitted a penalty of perjury statement with respect to such subsequent modifications, the plan sponsor will be required to sign the compliance statement.

[Rev. Proc. 2008-50, § 10, 2008-2 C.B. 464]

Q 19:22   What is a compliance statement?

The compliance statement issued for a VCP submission addresses the failures identified, the terms of correction, including any revision of administrative procedures, and the time period within which proposed corrections must be implemented, including any changes in administrative procedures. The compliance statement also provides that IRS will not treat the plan as failing to satisfy the applicable requirements of the Code on account of the failures if the conditions of the compliance statement are satisfied.

The compliance statement is conditioned on (1) there being no misstatement or omission of material facts in connection with the submission and (2) the implementation of the specific corrections and satisfaction of any other conditions in the compliance statement.

The compliance statement is binding upon both IRS and the plan sponsor or eligible organization (see Q 19:24) with respect to the specific tax matters identified therein for the periods specified, but does not preclude or impede an examination of the plan by IRS relating to matters outside the compliance statement, even with respect to the same taxable year or years to which the compliance statement relates.

The plan sponsor must implement the specific corrections and administrative changes set forth in the compliance statement within 150 days of the date of the compliance statement. Any request for an extension of this time period must be made in advance and in writing and must be approved IRS.

Once the compliance statement has been issued (based on the information provided), the plan sponsor cannot request a modification of the compliance terms except by a new request for a compliance statement. However, if the requested modification is minor and is postmarked within the correction period provided for in the compliance statement, the compliance fee for the modification will be the lesser of one-half the original compliance fee or $1,500.

Once the compliance statement has been issued, IRS may require verification that the corrections have been made and that any plan administrative procedures required by the statement have been implemented. If IRS determines that the plan sponsor did not implement the corrections and procedures within the stated time period, the plan may be referred for examination consideration.

[Rev. Proc. 2008-50, § 10, 2008-2 C.B. 464]

Q 19:23   What special rules relate to the Anonymous Submission procedure?

The Anonymous Submission procedure permits submission of qualified plans, 403(b) plans (see Q 36:1), SEPs (see Q 32:1), and SIMPLE IRAs (see Q 33:2) under VCP (see Q 19:20) without initially identifying the applicable plan(s), the plan sponsor(s), or the eligible organization (see Q 19:24). The general requirements relating to VCP (see Qs 19:21, 19:25, 19:26) apply to these submissions. However, information identifying the plan or the plan sponsor may be redacted, and the power of attorney and penalty of perjury statement need not be included with the initial submission; but, for purposes of processing the submission, the state of the plan sponsor must be identified. In addition, if a determination letter application will be submitted as part of the submission, the application should not be submitted until the time all identifying information is provided to IRS. Once IRS and the plan representative reach agreement with respect to the submission, IRS will contact the plan representative in writing indicating the terms of the agreement. The plan sponsor will have 21 days to identify the plan and plan sponsor. If the plan sponsor does not submit the identifying material within 21 days of the letter of agreement, the matter will be closed and the compliance fee will not be returned.

Until the plan and plan sponsor are identified to IRS, a submission under the Anonymous Submission procedure does not preclude or impede an examination of the plan sponsor or its plan(s). Thus, a plan submitted under the Anonymous Submission procedure that comes under examination prior to the date the plan and plan sponsor identifying materials are received by IRS will no longer be eligible for VCP.

[Rev. Proc. 2008-50, § 10.10, 2008-2 C.B. 464]

Q 19:24   What special rules relate to Group Submissions?

An eligible organization may submit a VCP request (see Q 19:20) for a qualified plan, a 403(b) plan (see Q 35:1), a SEP (see Q 32:1), or a SIMPLE IRA (see Q 33:2) under a Group Submission for operational failures (see Q 19:5), plan document failures (see Q 19:5), and employer eligibility failures (see Q 19:5).

For purposes of a Group Submission, the term "eligible organization" means either:

1. A sponsor of a master or prototype plan;
2. A volume submitter practitioner;
3. An insurance company or other entity that has issued annuity contracts or provides services with respect to assets for 403(b) plans; or
4. An entity that provides its clients with administrative services with respect to qualified plans, 403(b) plans, SEPs, or SIMPLE IRAs.

An eligible organization is not eligible to make a Group Submission unless the submission includes a failure resulting from a systemic error involving the eligible organization that affects at least 20 plans. If, at any time before IRS issues the compliance statement, the number of plans that have the same failure falls below 20, the eligible organization must notify IRS that it is no longer eligible to make a Group Submission (and the compliance fee will be retained).

A Group Submission is subject to the same procedures as any VCP submission (see Qs 19:21, 19:25, 19:26), except that the eligible organization is responsible for performing the procedural obligations imposed on the plan sponsor.

The eligible organization must provide notice to all plan sponsors of the plans included in the Group Submission. The notice must be provided at least 90 days before the eligible organization provides IRS with certain required information. The purpose of the notice is to provide each plan sponsor with information relating to the Group Submission request. The notice should explain the reason for the Group Submission and inform the plan sponsor that the plan sponsor's plan will be included in the Group Submission unless the plan sponsor responds within the 90-day period to exclude the plan sponsor's plan from the Group Submission.

When an eligible organization receives an unsigned compliance statement on the proposed correction and agrees to the terms of the compliance statement, the eligible organization must return to IRS within 120 days not only the signed compliance statement and any additional compliance fee (see Q 19:27), but also a list containing:

1. The employers' tax identification numbers for the plan sponsors of the plans to whom the compliance statement may be applicable;

2. The plans by name, plan number, type of plan, number of plan partici-pants, and trust's tax identification numbers;

3. A certification that each plan sponsor received notice of the Group Submission; and

4. A certification that each plan sponsor timely filed the Form 5500 return for each plan.

Only those plans for which correction is actually made within 240 days of the date of the signed compliance statement (or within such longer period as may be agreed to by IRS at the request of the eligible organization) will be covered by that statement.

If a plan sponsor of a plan that is eligible to be included in the Group Submission is notified of an impending employee plans examination after the eligible organization filed the Group Submission application, the plan sponsor's plan will be included in the Group Submission. However, with respect to such plan, the Group Submission will not preclude or impede an examination of the plan with respect to any failures not identified in the Group Submission application at the time the plan comes under examination.

[Rev. Proc. 2008-50, § 10.11, 2008-2 C.B. 464]

Q 19:25   What are the general application procedures for VCP?

In general, a request under VCP (see Q 19:20) consists of a letter from the plan sponsor (that may be a letter from the plan sponsor's representative) or eligible organization (see Q 19:24) to IRS that contains a description of the failures, a description of the proposed methods of correction, and other proce-dural items, and includes supporting information and documentation.

The letter must contain the following:

1. A statement identifying the type of plan submitted (e.g., qualified plan, 403(b) plan (see Q 35:1), SEP (see Q 32:1), or SIMPLE IRA (see Q 33:2)) and, if applicable, whether the submission is a Group Submission (see Q 19:24), an Anonymous Submission (see Q 19:23), or a nonamender submission, a multiemployer (see Q 29:2) or multiple employer plan (see Q 8:9) submission, or an orphan plan (see Q 19:10) submission. In addition, if the submission involves a qualified plan, the statement should also identify the type of qualified plan being submitted (e.g., defined benefit (see Q 2:3), money purchase pension (see Q 2:4), profit sharing (see Q 2:6), stock bonus (see Q 2:13), 401(k) (see Q 2:12), or ESOP (see Q 2:14)).

2. A complete description of the failures and the years in which the failures occurred, including closed years (that is, years for which the statutory period has expired).

3. Identifying information for the applicant including name and employer identification number.

4. Plan data including information relating to the number of participants and amount of plan assets.

5. An explanation of how and why the failures arose.

6. A detailed description of the method for correcting the failures that the plan sponsor has implemented or proposes to implement. Each step of the correction method must be described in narrative form. The description must include the specific information needed to support the suggested correction method. This information includes, for example, the number of employees affected and the expected cost of correction (both of which may be approximated if the exact number cannot be determined at the time of the request), the years involved, and calculations or assumptions the plan sponsor used to determine the amounts needed for correction.

7. A description of the methodology that will be used to calculate earnings or actuarial adjustments on any corrective contributions or distributions (indicating the computation periods and the basis for determining earnings or actuarial adjustments).

8. Specific calculations for each affected employee or a representative sample of affected employees. The sample calculations must be sufficient to demonstrate each aspect of the correction method proposed.

9. The method that will be used to locate and notify former employees and beneficiaries or an affirmative statement that no former employees or beneficiaries were affected by the failures or will be affected by the correction.

10. A description of the measures that have been or will be implemented to ensure that the same failures will not recur.

11. If relief from excise tax or income tax is sought, a specific request with an explanation supporting such request.

12. A specific request for relief from reporting a corrected participant loan as a deemed distribution or to report the loan as a deemed distribution in the year of correction instead of the year in which the deemed distribution occurred.

13. A statement that, to the best of the plan sponsor's knowledge, neither the plan nor the plan sponsor is under examination.

14. A statement that neither the plan nor the plan sponsor has been a party to an abusive tax avoidance transaction, or a brief identification of any abusive tax avoidance transaction to which the plan or the plan sponsor has been a party.

15. If a submission includes a failure that refers to transferred assets (see Q 19:9) and occurred prior to the transfer, a description of the transaction (including the dates of the employer change and the plan transfer).

16. A statement, if applicable, that the plan is currently being considered in a determination letter application that is not related to the VCP application.

17. In case of a submission of a 403(b) plan statement that the plan sponsor has contacted all other entities involved with the plan and has been assured of cooperation in implementing the applicable correction to the extent necessary. For example, if the plan's failure is the failure to satisfy the limit on elective deferrals (see Q 35:26), the plan sponsor must, prior to making the VCP application, contact the insurance company or custodian with control over the plan's assets to assure cooperation in effecting a distribution of the excess deferrals and the earnings thereon. An application under VCP must also contain a statement as to the type of employer (e.g., a tax-exempt organization) submitting the VCP application.

18. A Group Submission must be signed by the eligible organization or an authorized representative and accompanied by a copy of the relevant portions of the plan document(s).

19. If the plan is an orphan plan (see Q 19:10), whether relief from the compliance fee is being requested and supporting rationale for such relief.

A streamlined submission procedure should be used if all of the qualification failures the plan sponsor proposes to correct through VCP are described below and the plan sponsor proposes to correct such failures using a correction method provided in Appendix F of Revenue Procedure 2008-50. A streamlined application consists of the Appendix F, the appropriate schedule(s) for the failure(s) and all other documents required as indicated on the applicable schedule. IRS reserves the right to request additional information in connection with its processing of the streamlined application. The failure to provide the information required in the format provided in Appendix F may result in a delay in the processing of the submission.

The failures eligible for the streamlined application procedure and the applicable Appendix F schedules are described as follows:

1. *Schedule 1:* The plan sponsor failed to timely adopt (a) interim amendments or (b) amendments required to reflect the changed operation of the

plan on account of the plan sponsor's decision to implement optional law changes.

2. *Schedule 2:* The plan sponsor failed to timely adopt amendments to comply with required legislative or regulatory changes.

3. *Schedule 3:* The plan is a SEP or a SARSEP and experienced one or more of the failures included on Appendix F.

4. *Schedule 4:* The plan is a SIMPLE IRA and experienced one or more of the failures included on Appendix F.

5. *Schedule 5:* The plan sponsor failed to properly administer loans and the failure solely relates to employees who are neither key employees nor self-employed individuals.

6. *Schedule 6:* The plan sponsor failed to satisfy the criteria for an employer to sponsor either a 403(b) plan or a 401(k) plan.

7. *Schedule 7:* The plan failed to distribute elective deferrals made in excess of the limit.

8. *Schedule 8:* The plan failed to make required minimum distributions.

9. *Schedule 9:* The plan experienced one or more of the following failures:

   a. Failure to limit compensation;

   b. Hardship distribution failure;

   c. Loans permitted in operation but not permitted by plan document; or

   d. Early inclusion of otherwise eligible employee(s).

[Rev. Proc. 2008-50, §§ 11.01, 11.02, 11.03, app. F, 2008-2 C.B. 464]

Q 19:26   What documents are required for a VCP submission?

A VCP (see Q 19:20) submission must be accompanied by the following documents:

1. *Plan document.* A copy of the entire plan document or the relevant portions of the plan document. For example, in a case involving improper exclusion of eligible employees from a profit sharing plan with a cash or deferred arrangement, relevant portions of the plan document include the eligibility, allocation, and cash or deferred arrangement provisions of the basic plan document (and the adoption agreement, if applicable), along with applicable definitions in the plan. If the plan is a 403(b) plan and a plan document is not available, a written description of the plan, and sample salary reduction agreements if relevant, should be submitted. In the case of a SEP and a SIMPLE IRA, the entire plan document should be submitted.

2. *Determination letter application.* In any case in which correction of a qualification failure is made by plan amendment, other than the adoption of a model amendment or a prototype or volume submitter plan for which the plan sponsor has reliance, the plan sponsor must submit a copy of the

plan document in restated form, the appropriate application form (i.e., Form 5300, 5307 or 5310), and the appropriate user fee.

3. *Date fee due.* Generally, the VCP fee (see Q 19:27) and, if applicable, the determination letter user fee, must be included with the submission. All fees must be submitted by check made payable to the U.S. Treasury.

4. *Additional fee due for SEPs, SIMPLE IRAs, and Group Submissions.* In the case of a SEP, a SIMPLE IRA, or a Group Submission, the initial fee described must be included in the submission and any additional fee is due at the time the compliance statement is signed by the plan sponsor and returned to the IRS, or when agreement has been reached between IRS and the plan sponsor regarding correction of the failure(s).

5. *Signed submission.* The submission must be signed by the plan sponsor or the sponsor's authorized representative.

6. *Power of attorney requirements.* To sign the submission or to appear before IRS in connection with the submission, the plan sponsor's representative must comply with certain requirements.

7. *Penalty of perjury statement.* A penalty of perjury statement must accompany a request, and it must be signed by the plan sponsor, not the plan sponsor's representative.

8. *Checklist.* IRS will be able to respond more quickly to a VCP request if the request is carefully prepared and complete. A checklist prepared by IRS is designed to assist plan sponsors and their representatives in preparing a submission that contains the required information and documents. The checklist must be completed, signed, and dated by the plan sponsor or the plan sponsor's representative and should be placed on top of the submission.

9. *Designation.* The letter to IRS should indicate in the upper right hand corner the type of plan submitted under VCP (i.e., qualified plan, 403(b) plan, SEP, or SIMPLE IRA). In addition, if the submission is a Group Submission, an Anonymous Submission, a nonamender submission, a multiemployer (see Q 29:2) or multiple employer plan (see Q 8:9) submission, or an orphan plan (see Q 19:10) submission, the letter should so indicate.

10. *Acknowledgement letter.* IRS will acknowledge receipt of a VCP submission if the plan sponsor or the plan sponsor's representative completes an acknowledgement form provided by IRS and includes it in the submission.

11. *VCP mailing address.* All VCP submissions and accompanying determination applications, if applicable, should be mailed to:

> Internal Revenue Service
> Attention: SE:T:EP:RA:VC
> P.O. Box 27063
> McPherson Station
> Washington, D.C. 20038-7063

12. *Maintenance of copies of submissions.* Plan sponsors and their representatives should maintain copies of all correspondence submitted to IRS with respect to their VCP requests.

13. *Assembling the submission.* IRS will be able to process a submission more quickly if the submission package contains all of the required items and is assembled in a preferred order.

[Rev. Proc. 2008-50, §§ 11.04-11.15, app. C, app. D, app. E, 2008-2 C.B. 464]

Q 19:27   What are the compliance fees for VCP?

In general, the compliance fees for submissions under VCP (see Qs 19:20, 19:25, 19:26) are determined in accordance with a graduated range of fees based on the number of participants in the plan. All fees must be submitted by check made payable to the U.S. Treasury and, generally, must be included with the initial submission.

The compliance fee for a submission under VCP for qualified plans and 403(b) plans (see Q 35:1), including Anonymous Submissions (see Q 19:23), is determined in accordance with the following chart.

Number of Participants	Fee
20 or fewer	$ 750
21 to 50	1,000
51 to 100	2,500
101 to 500	5,000
501 to 1,000	8,000
1,001 to 5,000	15,000
5,001 to 10,000	20,000
Over 10,000	25,000

If (1) the VCP submission involves the failure to satisfy the minimum distribution requirements (see chapter 11) for 50 or fewer participants, (2) such failure is the only failure of the submission, and (3) the failure would result in the imposition of the excise tax (see Q 11:67), the compliance fee is $500.

If (1) the VCP submission involves the failure of participant loans to comply with the requirements of the Code, (2) the failure does not affect more than 25 percent of the plan sponsor's participants in any of the year(s) in which the failure occurred, and (3) the failure is the only failure of the submission, the compliance fee is reduced by 50 percent.

IRS has the discretion to waive the VCP fee in the case of a terminating orphan plan (see Q 19:10). In such case, the submission must include a request for a waiver of the VCP fee.

The compliance fee for plans that have not been amended for tax legislation changes within the plan's remedial amendment period is determined in accordance with the above chart. However, the applicable fee is reduced by 50 percent for nonamenders that submit under VCP within a one-year period following the expiration of the plan's remedial amendment period for complying with tax law changes. For example, the fee for a plan that was not amended for GUST with 700 participants submitted within the one-year period following the expiration of the plan's remedial amendment period for GUST changes would be $4,000.

Notwithstanding the above, the compliance fee for a submission that contains only a failure to amend the plan timely with respect to interim amendments or amendments required to implement optional law changes is $375.

The compliance fee for a Group Submission (see Q 19:24) is based on the number of plans affected by the failure as described in the compliance statement. The initial fee for the first 20 plans is $10,000. An additional fee is due equal to the product of the number of plans in excess of 20 multiplied by $250, up to a maximum of $50,000. If more than one master or prototype plan (see Q 2:27) is submitted as a Group Submission (see Q 19:24), each master or prototype plan is considered a separate Group Submission for purposes of the compliance fee.

The compliance fee for a SEP (see Q 32:1) or a SIMPLE IRA (see Q 33:2), including an Anonymous Submission, is $250. IRS reserves the right to impose a fee schedule pursuant to the above chart in appropriate cases. In any case in which a SEP or SIMPLE IRA correction is not similar to a correction for a similar qualification failure, IRS may impose an additional fee. If the failure involves an excess amount to a SEP or a SIMPLE IRA and the plan sponsor retains the excess amount in the SEP or SIMPLE IRA, a fee equal to at least 10 percent of the excess amount, excluding earnings, will be imposed. This is in addition to the SEP or SIMPLE IRA compliance fee set forth above.

In cases involving failures that are egregious, the compliance fee for qualified plans, 403(b) plans, SEPs, and SIMPLE IRAs is the greater of the general fee or an amount equal to a negotiated percentage (not to exceed 40 percent) of the maximum payment amount (MPA; see Q 19:30).

Compliance fees are determined based on the total number of plan participants. For new plans and ongoing plans, the number of plan participants is determined from the most recently filed Form 5500 series (see Q 21:1). In the case of a terminated plan, the Form 5500 used must be the one filed for the plan year prior to the plan year for which the final Form 5500 was filed. If the submission involves a plan with transferred assets and no new incidents of the failure occurred after the end of the second plan year that begins after the corporate merger, acquisition, or other similar employer transaction, the plan sponsor may calculate the number of plan participants based on the Form 5500 information that would have been filed by the plan sponsor for the plan year that includes the employer transaction if the transferred assets were maintained as a separate plan.

[Rev. Proc. 2008-50, § 12, 2008-2 C.B. 464]

Q 19:28   What are the requirements of Audit CAP?

If IRS identifies a qualification failure (see Q 19:5) or a 403(b) failure (see Q 19:6) (other than a failure that has been corrected in accordance with SCP (see Q 19:17) or VCP (see Q 19:20)) upon an examination of a qualified plan, 403(b) plan (see Q 35:1), SEP (see Q 32:1), or SIMPLE IRA (see Q 33:2), Audit CAP is available if the plan sponsor corrects the failure, pays a sanction (see Q 19:29), satisfies any additional requirements, and enters into a closing agreement with IRS. Payment of the sanction generally is required at the time the closing agreement is signed. All sanction amounts should be submitted by certified or cashier's check made payable to U.S. Treasury.

Depending on the nature of the failure, IRS will discuss the appropriateness of the plan's existing administrative procedures with the plan sponsor. If existing administrative procedures are inadequate for operating the plan in conformance with the applicable requirements of the Code, the closing agreement may be conditioned upon the implementation of stated procedures. In addition, for qualified plans, the plan sponsor may be required to obtain a favorable letter (see Q 18:1) before the closing agreement is signed.

If IRS and the plan sponsor cannot reach an agreement with respect to the correction of the failure(s) or the amount of the sanction, the plan will be disqualified or, in the case of a 403(b) plan, SEP, or SIMPLE IRA, EPCRS will not be available. A closing agreement constitutes an agreement between IRS and the plan sponsor that is binding with respect to the tax matters identified therein for the periods specified.

[Rev. Proc. 2008-50, § 13, 2008-2 C.B. 464]

Q 19:29   What is the sanction under Audit CAP?

The sanction under Audit CAP (see Q 19:28) is a negotiated percentage of the MPA (see Q 19:30). Sanctions will not be excessive and will bear a reasonable relationship to the nature, extent, and severity of the failures, based on the following factors:

1. The steps taken by the plan sponsor to ensure that the plan had no failures (see Qs 19:5, 19:6);
2. The steps taken to identify failures that may have occurred;
3. The extent to which correction has progressed before the examination was initiated;
4. The number and type of employees affected by the failures;
5. The number of NHCEs (see Q 3:12) who would be adversely affected if the plan were not treated as qualified or as satisfying the 403(b) plan, SEP, or SIMPLE IRA requirements;
6. Whether the failure is a failure to satisfy the nondiscrimination requirements (see Q 4:10), the minimum participation requirement (see Q 5:23), or the minimum coverage requirement (see Q 5:15);
7. Whether the failure is solely an employer eligibility failure;

8. The period over which the failure occurred; and

9. The reason for the failure (e.g., data errors).

Factors relating only to qualified plans also include:

1. Whether the plan is the subject of a favorable letter (see Q 19:7), and

2. Whether the failure(s) was discovered during the determination letter process.

In the case of any participant loan that did not comply with the requirements of the Code, the MPA will include the tax IRS could collect as a result of the loan not being excluded from gross income.

If one of the failures discovered during an employee plan examination includes the failure to timely amend the plan for relevant legislation, it is expected that the sanction will be greater than the applicable fee. An additional factor taken into account with respect to a participant loan that did not comply with the requirements of the Code is the extent to which the failure is a result solely of action (or inaction) of the employer or its agents (or to the extent to which the failure is a result of the employee's or beneficiary's actions or inaction).

If the examination involves a plan with transferred assets and IRS determines that no new incidents of the failures that relate to the transferred assets occur after the end of the second plan year that begins after the corporate merger, acquisition, or other similar employer transaction occurred, the sanction under Audit CAP will not exceed the sanction that would apply if the transferred assets were maintained as a separate plan.

[Rev. Proc. 2008-50, § 14, 2008-2 C.B. 464]

> **Example 1.** Jackie-Lynn Corp. established a profit sharing plan in 1988 that was timely amended and received a favorable determination letter in 1996. The newly hired third party administrator discovered that the compensation of four NHCEs in 1996 and 1997 was incorrectly calculated, resulting in the annual addition exceeding the limitation. While preparing a request to IRS under EPCRS, Jackie-Lynn Corp. received notice of an audit for the 1996 plan year. The operational failures were corrected by placing the excess annual additions in a suspense account, and the closing agreement's sanction equaled $12,960 (20 percent of the plan's $64,800 MPA). [Western Region IRS/Practitioners Benefits Conference, Case Studies (Sept. 18, 1998)]

> **Example 2.** The Steve S Corporation established a 401(k) plan in 1982 that was timely amended and received favorable determination letters in 1987 and 1996. As of the end of the 1995 plan year, the plan benefited four HCEs (see Q 3:3) and 48 NHCEs. The accountant assumed that the third party administrator (TPA) would conduct the ADP test (see Q 27:18), while the TPA assumed that the accountant would do so. During an examination, IRS discovered that the plan failed the ADP test for 1995 and 1996. At the request of IRS, Steve S Corporation corrected the failure by contributing qualified nonelective contributions, and the closing agreement's sanction equaled

$20,875 (25 percent of the plan's $83,500 MPA). [Western Region IRS/Practitioners Benefits Conference, Case Studies (Sept. 18, 1998)]

The compliance fee for nonamenders not voluntarily identified by the plan sponsor, but instead discovered by IRS in connection with the determination letter application process, is determined in accordance with the following chart:

Number of Participants	EGTRRA, Subsequent Legislation	GUST, § 401(a) (9) Regs	UC '92, OBRA '93	TRA '86	TEFRA, DEFRA, REA	ERISA
20 or less	$ 2,500	$ 3,000	$ 3,500	$ 4,000	$ 4,500	$ 5,000
21–50	5,000	6,000	7,000	8,000	9,000	10,000
51–100	7,500	9,000	10,500	12,000	13,500	15,000
101–500	12,500	15,000	17,500	20,000	22,500	25,000
501–1,000	17,500	21,000	24,500	28,000	31,500	35,000
1,001–5,000	25,000	30,000	35,000	40,000	45,000	50,000
5,001–10,000	32,500	39,000	45,500	52,000	58,500	65,000
Over 10,000	40,000	48,000	56,000	64,000	72,000	80,000

This fee schedule applies if the only failure in the submission is the nonamender failure.

[Rev. Proc. 2008-50, § 14.04, 2008-2 C.B. 464]

Q 19:30   What is the Maximum Payment Amount (MPA)?

The MPA for qualified plans means a monetary amount that is approximately equal to the tax IRS could collect upon plan disqualification and is the sum for the open taxable years of the:

1. Tax on the trust;

2. Additional income tax resulting from the loss of employer deduction for plan contributions (and any interest or penalties applicable to the plan sponsor's tax return);

3. Additional income tax resulting from income inclusion for participants in the plan, including the tax on plan distributions that have been rolled over to other qualified trusts or eligible retirement plans (and any interest or penalties applicable to the participants' returns); and

4. Any other tax that results from a qualification failure that would apply but for the correction under EPCRS.

[Rev. Proc. 2008-50, § 5.01(5), 2008-2 C.B. 464]

The MPA for 403(b) plans (see Q 35:1) means a monetary amount that is approximately equal to the tax IRS could collect as a result of the 403(b) failure and is the sum for the open taxable years of the:

1. Additional income tax resulting from income inclusion for employees or other participants, including the tax on distributions that have been rolled over to other qualified trusts or eligible retirement plans and any interest or penalties applicable to the participants' returns; and

2. Any other tax that results from a 403(b) failure that would apply but for the correction under EPCRS.

[Rev. Proc. 2008-50, § 5.02(4), 2008-2 C.B. 464]

Q 19:31   Does IRS have listed failures and permitted correction methods?

IRS sets forth operational failures (see Q 19:5) and correction methods relating to qualified plans. In each case, the method described corrects the operational failure. Corrective allocations and distributions should reflect earnings and actuarial adjustments. The correction methods are acceptable under SCP (see Q 19:17) and VCP (see Q 19:20). Additional correction methods and earnings adjustment methods (see Q 19:32) set forth by IRS are also acceptable under SCP and VCP. To the extent a failure listed below could occur under a 403(b) plan (see Q 35:1), SEP (see Q 32:1), or SIMPLE IRA (see Q 33:2), the correction method listed for such failure may be used to correct the failure. The listed failures and their permitted correction methods include:

1. *Failure to provide top-heavy minimums (see Qs 26:35, 26:41).* In a defined contribution plan (see Q 2:2), the permitted correction method is to contribute and allocate the required top-heavy minimums in the manner provided for in the plan on behalf of non-key employees (see Q 26:27) (and any other employee required to receive top-heavy allocations under the plan). In a defined benefit plan (see Q 2:3), the minimum required benefit must be accrued in the manner provided in the plan.

2. *Failure to satisfy the ADP test or the ACP test (see Qs 27:18, 27:77).* The permitted correction method is to make qualified nonelective contributions (see Q 27:17) on behalf of the NHCEs (see Q 3:12) to the extent necessary to raise the actual deferral percentage (ADP; see Q 27:19) or actual contribution percentage (ACP; see Q 27:78) of the NHCEs to the percentage needed to pass the test or tests. The contributions must be made on behalf of all eligible NHCEs and must be the same percentage of compensation. See Q 19:32 for an additional correction method.

3. *Failure to distribute excess deferrals (see Q 27:50).* The permitted correction method is to distribute the excess deferral to the employee and to report the amount as taxable in the year of deferral and the year distributed. A distribution to an HCE (see Q 3:3) is included in the ADP test (see Q 27:11); a distribution to a NHCE (see Q 3:12) is not included in the ADP test.

4. *Failure to include an eligible employee as a participant in the plan (see chapter 5).*

a. With respect to plans with employer-provided contributions or benefits (which are not 401(k) plans (see Q 27:1)), the permitted correction method is to make a contribution to the plan on behalf of employees excluded from a defined contribution plan or to provide benefit accruals for employees excluded from a defined benefit plan.

b. With respect to plans subject to Sections 401(k) or 401(m) (see Q 27:73), the corrective contribution for an improperly excluded employee is the following:

   (i) If the employee was not provided the opportunity to elect and make elective deferrals (see Qs 27:3, 27:16) to a 401(k) plan that does not satisfy the safe harbor contribution requirements (see Q 27:42), the employer must make a qualified nonelective contribution (QNEC; see Q 27:17) to the plan on behalf of the employee that compensates the employee for the missed deferral opportunity. The missed deferral opportunity is equal to 50 percent of the employee's missed deferral, and the missed deferral is determined by multiplying the actual deferred percentage (ADP; see Q 27:18) for the employee's group in the plan (either highly compensated or nonhighly compensated) for the year of exclusion by the employee's compensation for that year.

   (ii) If the employee should have been eligible for, but did not receive an allocation of, employer matching contributions under a non-safe harbor plan because the employee was not given the opportunity to make elective deferrals, the employer should make a QNEC on behalf of the affected employee. The QNEC will be equal to the matching contribution the employee would have received had the employee made a deferral equal to the missed deferral determined in (i) above.

   (iii) If the employee was not provided the opportunity to elect and make elective deferrals to a safe harbor 401(k) plan that uses a rate of matching contributions to satisfy the safe harbor requirements (see Q 27:43), then the missed deferral is deemed equal to the greater of 3 percent of compensation or the maximum deferral percentage for which the employer provides a matching contribution rate that is at least as favorable as 100 percent of the elective deferral made by the employee. This estimate of the missed deferral replaces the estimate based on the ADP test in a traditional 401(k) plan. The required QNEC on behalf of the excluded employee is equal to (A) the missed deferral opportunity, which is an amount equal to 50 percent of the missed deferral, plus (B) the matching contribution that would apply based on the missed deferral. If an employee was not provided the opportunity to elect and make elective deferrals to a safe harbor 401(k) plan that uses nonelective contributions to satisfy the safe harbor requirements, then the missed deferral is deemed equal to 3 percent of compensation. The required QNEC on behalf of the excluded employee is equal to (A) 50 percent of the missed deferral, plus (B) the nonelective contribution required to be made on behalf of the employee. The QNEC required to compensate the employee for the missed deferral opportunity and the corresponding matching or nonelective contribution is adjusted for earnings until the corrective QNEC is made on behalf of the affected employee.

(iv) If the employee should have been eligible to elect and make after-tax employee contributions (see Q 27:74), the employer must make a QNEC to the plan on behalf of the employee that is equal to the missed opportunity for making after-tax employee contributions. The missed opportunity for making after-tax employee contributions is equal to 40 percent of the employee's missed after-tax contributions, and the employee's missed after-tax contributions are equal to the actual contribution percentage (ACP; see Q 27:77) for the employee's group (either highly compensated or nonhighly compensated) times the employee's compensation, but with the resulting amount not to exceed applicable plan limits.

(v) If the employee was improperly excluded from an allocation of employer matching contributions because the employee was not given the opportunity to make after-tax employee contributions, the employer should make a QNEC on behalf of the affected employee. The QNEC is equal to the matching contribution the employee would have received had the employee made an after-tax employee contribution equal to the missed after-tax employee contribution determined under (iv) above.

c. With respect to plans allowing Roth contributions, for employees who were improperly excluded from plans, the permitted correction is the same as described under b. above. Thus, for example, the corrective employer contribution required to replace the missed deferral opportunity is made in accordance with the method described in b.(ii) above if the plan is not a safe harbor plan or b.(iii) above in the case of a safe harbor plan. However, none of the corrective contributions made by the employer may be treated as designated Roth contributions (and may not be included in an employee's gross income) and thus may not be contributed or allocated to a designated Roth account. The corrective contribution must be allocated to an account established for receiving a QNEC or any other employer contribution in which the employee is fully vested and subject to the withdrawal restrictions that apply to elective deferrals.

d. With respect to plans permitting catch-up contributions:

(i) If an eligible employee was not provided the opportunity to elect and make catch-up contributions to a 401(k) plan, the employer must make a QNEC to the plan on behalf of the employee that replaces the "missed deferral opportunity" attributable to the failure to permit an eligible employee to make a catch-up contribution. The missed deferral opportunity for catch-up contributions is equal to 50 percent of the employee's missed deferral attributable to catch-up contributions. For this purpose, the missed deferral attributable to catch-up contributions is one half of the applicable catch-up contribution limit for the year in which the employee was improperly excluded.

(ii) If an employee was precluded from making catch-up contributions, the plan sponsor should ascertain whether the affected employee would have been entitled to an additional matching contribution on account of the missed deferral. If the employee would have been entitled to an additional matching contribution, then the employer must make a QNEC for the matching contribution on behalf of the affected employee. The QNEC is equal to the additional matching contribution the employee would have received had the employee made a deferral equal to the missed deferral.

e. With respect to a failure to implement an employee election:

(i) For eligible employees who filed elections to make elective deferrals under the plan which the plan sponsor failed to implement on a timely basis, the plan sponsor must make a QNEC to the plan on behalf of the employee to replace the "missed deferral opportunity." The missed deferral opportunity is equal to 50 percent of the employee's "missed deferral." The missed deferral is determined by multiplying the employee's elected deferral percentage by the employee's compensation. If the employee elected a dollar amount for an elective deferral, the missed deferral would be the specified dollar amount.

(ii) For eligible employees who filed elections to make after-tax employee contributions under the plan which the plan sponsor failed to implement on a timely basis, the plan sponsor must make a QNEC to the plan on behalf of the employee to replace the employee's missed opportunity for after-tax employee contributions. The missed opportunity for making after-tax employee contributions is equal to 40 percent of the employee's "missed after-tax contributions." The missed after-tax employee contribution is determined by multiplying the employee's elected after-tax employee contribution percentage by the employee's compensation.

(iii) In the event of failure described in e.(i) or (ii), if the employee would have been entitled to an additional matching contribution had either the missed deferral or after-tax employee contribution been made, then the employer must make a QNEC for the matching contribution on behalf of the affected employee. The QNEC is equal to the matching contribution the employee would have received had the employee made a deferral equal to the missed deferral.

The methods for correcting these failures do not apply until after the correction of other qualification failures. Thus, for example, if, in addition to the failure of excluding an eligible employee, the plan also failed the ADP or ACP test, the correction methods described above cannot be used until after correction of the ADP or ACP test failures. See Q 19:32 for an additional correction method.

f. IRS has provided additional guidance with respect to correcting the failure of not implementing the automatic enrollment feature in a 401(k) plan (see Q 27:5). The correction method depends on whether the failure to implement automatic enrollment arose from the erroneous exclusion of an eligible employee or the failure to execute the employee's election.

Example 1. Jody Corp. 401(k) Plan provides that, unless the participant elects otherwise, compensation will be reduced by 3 percent and contributed to the plan. For 2008, the ADP for NHCEs was 4 percent. Mark, an NHCE, became eligible to participate in Jody Corp. 401(k) Plan on January 1, 2008. Due to an oversight, Jody Corp. did not give Mark the plan's enrollment materials that included a description of the plan and the procedures to elect to contribute an amount other than the automatic enrollment deferral percentage. Mark did not make a specific election, and the plan did not implement its automatic enrollment provision. As a result, Mark did not make any elective contribution to the plan in 2008. Mark earned $30,000 in compensation in 2008. Since Mark was erroneously excluded from the plan, his missed deferral is determined using the applicable ADP for 2008 and equals $1,200 (4% × $30,000). The corrective contribution required to be contributed to the plan and allocated to Mark's account is $600 (50% × $1,200).

Example 2. The facts are the same as Example 1, except that after receiving the plan's enrollment materials, Mark did not submit an election form. By not making an affirmative election, Mark has expressed his desire to contribute at the plan's automatic enrollment deferral percentage of 3 percent, but the plan did not implement the automatic enrollment provision. In this case, Mark's missed deferral is $900 (3% × $30,000), and the corrective contribution is $450 (50% × $900).

[Retirement News for Employers, Volume 6/Summer 2009]

5. *Failure to timely pay required minimum distributions (RMDs; see chapter 11).* In a defined contribution plan, the permitted correction method is to distribute the RMDs. The amount to be distributed for each year in which the failure occurred should be determined by dividing the adjusted account balance on the applicable valuation date by the applicable divisor. In a defined benefit plan, the permitted correction method is to distribute the RMDs, plus an interest payment representing the loss of use of such amount.

6. *Failure to obtain participant and/or spousal consent for certain distributions (see chapter 10).* The permitted correction method is to give the affected employees a choice between providing informed consent for the

distribution actually made or receiving a qualified joint and survivor annuity (QJSA; see Q 10:8). If participant and/or spousal consent cannot be obtained, the participant must receive a QJSA based on the monthly amount that would have been provided under the plan at the retirement date. This annuity may be actuarially reduced to take into account distributions already received by the participant. However, the portion of the QJSA payable to the spouse upon the death of the participant may not be actuarially reduced to take into account prior distributions to the participant. An alternative permitted correction method is to give each affected participant a choice between (a) providing informed consent for the distribution actually made, (b) receiving a qualified joint and survivor annuity (QJSA; see Q 10:8), or (c) receiving a single-sum payment equal to the actuarial present value of that survivor annuity benefit.

7. *Failure to limit annual additions (see Q 6:34).* For limitation years beginning before January 1, 2009, the permitted correction method is to place the excess annual additions into an unallocated suspense account to be used as an employer contribution in the succeeding years. The permitted correction for failure to limit annual additions that are elective deferrals is to distribute the elective deferrals. For limitation years beginning on or after January 1, 2009, the failure to limit annual additions is corrected in accordance with the correction of excess allocations (see Q 19:13). In general, an excess allocation is corrected in accordance with the reduction of account balance correction method. Under this method, the account balance of an employee who received an excess allocation is reduced by the excess allocation (adjusted for earnings). If the excess allocation would have been allocated to other employees in the year of the failure had the failure not occurred, then that amount (adjusted for earnings) is reallocated to those employees in accordance with the plan's allocation formula. If the improperly allocated amount would not have been allocated to other employees absent the failure, that amount (adjusted for earnings) is placed in a separate account that is not allocated on behalf of any participant or beneficiary (an unallocated account) established for the purpose of holding excess allocations, adjusted for earnings, to be used to reduce employer contributions (other than elective deferrals) in the current year or succeeding year(s). While such amounts remain in the unallocated account, the employer is not permitted to make contributions to the plan other than elective deferrals. Excess allocations that are attributable to elective deferrals or after-tax employee contributions, (along with earnings attributable thereto) must be distributed to the participant. If an excess allocation consists of annual additions attributable to both employer contributions and elective deferrals or after-tax employee contributions, then the correction of the excess allocation is completed by first distributing the unmatched employee's after-tax contributions (adjusted for earnings) and then the unmatched employee's elective deferrals (adjusted for earnings). If any excess remains, and is attributable to either elective deferrals or after-tax employee contributions that are matched, the excess is apportioned first to after-tax employee contributions with the associated matching employer contributions and

then to elective deferrals with the associated matching employer contributions. Any matching contribution or nonelective employer contribution (adjusted for earnings) which constitutes an excess allocation is then forfeited and placed in an unallocated account established for the purpose of holding excess allocations to be used to reduce employer contributions in the current year and succeeding year(s). Such unallocated account is adjusted for earnings. While such amounts remain in the unallocated account, the employer is not permitted to make contributions (other than elective deferrals) to the plan. See Q 19:32 for an additional correction method.

[Rev. Proc. 2008-50, § 6.06, 2008-2 C.B. 464]

8. *Failure regarding orphan plans (see Q 19:10).* If (1) a plan has one or more failures that result from either the employer having ceased to exist, the employer no longer maintaining the plan, or similar reasons and (2) the plan is an orphan plan, the permitted correction is to terminate the plan and distribute plan assets to participants and beneficiaries. This correction must satisfy the following conditions: (1) The correction must comply with conditions, standards, and procedures under DOL regulations relating to abandoned plans (see Q 25:64), (2) The qualified termination administrator must have reasonably determined whether, and to what extent, the survivor annuity requirements apply to any benefit payable under the plan and takes reasonable steps to comply with those requirements (if applicable), (3) Each participant and beneficiary must have been provided a nonforfeitable right to his or her accrued benefits as of the date of deemed termination, and (4) Participants and beneficiaries must receive notification of their rights (see Q 20:20). In addition, IRS reserves the right to pursue appropriate remedies against any party who is responsible for the plan, such as the plan sponsor, plan administrator, or owner of the business, even in its capacity as a participant or beneficiary under the plan. In any case in which a 403(b) failure results from the employer having ceased involvement with respect to specific assets (including an insurance annuity contract) held under a defined contribution plan on behalf of a participant who is a former employee or on behalf of a beneficiary, a permitted correction is to distribute those plan assets to the participant or beneficiary.

[Rev. Proc. 2008-50, app. A, 2008-2 C.B. 464]

Q 19:32　What additional correction methods may be used to correct an operational failure?

In addition to the permitted correction methods listed by IRS (see Q 19:31), plan sponsors may use other correction methods to correct operational failures (see Q 19:5) to comply with the qualified plan rules. If an operational failure is corrected in the specific manner described in an applicable correction method, IRS will treat the correction as acceptable under SCP (see Q 19:17) and VCP (see Q 19:20). To the extent a failure included below could occur under a 403(b) plan (see Q 35:1), SEP (see Q 32:1), or SIMPLE IRA (see Q 33:2), the correction method listed for such failure may be used to correct the failure. The correction methods include the following:

1. *Failure to satisfy the ADP test or the ACP test (see Qs 27:13, 27:86).* In addition to the listed permitted correction method (see Q 19:31), the failure may be corrected by using the one-to-one correction method. Under the one-to-one correction method, an excess contribution amount is determined and assigned to HCEs (see Q 3:3). That excess contribution amount (adjusted for earnings) is either distributed to HCEs or forfeited from the HCEs' accounts. That same dollar amount (i.e., the excess contribution amount, adjusted for earnings) is contributed to the plan and allocated to NHCEs (see Q 3:12).

   Example 1. Cody Corp. maintains a profit sharing plan with a CODA. In 2009, it was discovered that for 2007 the ADP test was not met. Cody Corp. uses the one-to-one correction method to correct the failure to satisfy the ADP test for 2007. Accordingly, the excess contributions (with earnings), in the amount of $7,649, are distributed to the HCEs. In addition, a corrective contribution, in the amount of $7,649, the sum of the amounts distributed to the HCEs, is made to the plan. The corrective contribution is allocated to the account balances of eligible NHCEs for 2007 pro rata, based on their compensation for 2007.

2. *Failure to include an eligible employee or a participant in the plan (see chapter 5).* In addition to the listed permitted correction method (see Q 19:31) regarding the failure to include an eligible employee from nonelective contributions in a profit sharing plan (see Q 2:6), the failure may be corrected by using the reallocation correction method. Under the reallocation correction method, the account balance of the excluded employee is increased by an amount that is equal to the allocation the employee would have received, the account balances of other participants are reduced accordingly, and the increases and reductions are reconciled, as necessary.

   Example 2. Molly, Inc. maintains a profit sharing plan, and for 2008 five employees who met the eligibility requirements were inadvertently excluded from participating in the plan. The contribution resulted in an allocation on behalf of each of the eligible employees, other than the excluded employees, equal to 10 percent of compensation. If the five excluded employees had shared in the original allocation, the allocation made on behalf of each employee would have equaled 9 percent of compensation. Molly, Inc. uses the reallocation correction method to correct the failure to include the five eligible employees. Thus, the account balances are adjusted to reflect what would have resulted from the correct allocation of the employer contribution for the 2008 plan year among all eligible employees, including the five excluded employees. The inclusion of the excluded employees in the allocation of that contribution would have resulted in each eligible employee, including each excluded employee, receiving an allocation equal to 9 percent of compensation. Accordingly, the account balance of each excluded employee is increased by 9 percent of the employee's 2008 compensation, adjusted for earnings, and the account balance of each of the eligible employees other than the excluded employees is reduced by 1 percent of the employee's 2008 compensation, adjusted for earnings.

3. *Failure to apply the proper vesting percentage (see chapter 9).* A failure in a defined contribution plan to apply the proper vesting percentage to a participant's account balance that results in a forfeiture of too large a portion of the participant's account balance may be corrected using the contribution correction method or the reallocation method.

   Example 3. Cary Corp. maintains a profit sharing plan providing that forfeitures of account balances are reallocated among the account balances of other participants on the basis of compensation. During the 2008 plan year, Andrea terminated employment and received a single-sum distribution of the vested portion of her account balance. However, an incorrect determination of Andrea's vested percentage was made, resulting in Andrea's receiving a distribution of less than the amount to which she was entitled under the plan. The remaining portion of Andrea's account balance was forfeited and reallocated. Cary Corp. uses the contribution correction method to correct the improper forfeiture by making a contribution on behalf of Andrea equal to the incorrectly forfeited amount (adjusted for earnings) and increasing Andrea's account balance accordingly. No reduction is made from the account balances of participants who received an allocation of the improper forfeiture.

   Example 4. The facts are the same as in Example 3, except that Cary Corp. uses the reallocation correction method to correct the improper forfeiture. Andrea's account balance is increased by the amount that was improperly forfeited (adjusted for earnings), and the account balance of each participant who shared in the allocation of the improper forfeiture is reduced by the amount of the improper forfeiture that was allocated to that participant's account (adjusted for earnings).

4. *Failures relating to exceeding defined benefit plan or defined contribution plan limits.* If payments from a defined benefit plan exceed the retirement benefit limits (see Q 6:11), the excess can be corrected by returning the overpayment or reducing future payments. If annual additions under a defined contribution plan exceed the limits (see Q 6:34), then, in addition to the listed correction method (see Q 19:31), the previously paid excess can be repaid to the plan or, in the case of certain terminated employees who have received a distribution of elective deferrals, nonvested contributions can be forfeited.

5. *Failure to limit compensation (see Q 6:45).* If contributions to a defined contribution plan have been allocated based on compensation in excess of the annual limit, (a) the account balance of the participant who received the allocation may be reduced by the improperly allocated amount, and the excess allocation may be used to reduce future employer contributions, or (b) additional plan contributions may be made for other participants under VCP and SCP.

Example 5. Phyllis, Inc. maintains an 8-percent-of-compensation money purchase pension plan. For the 2008 plan year, Mark, a participant in the plan, had compensation of $250,000 and he received a contribution of $20,000 (8% × $250,000) rather than a contribution of $18,400 (8% × $230,000), resulting in an improper allocation of $1,600 ($20,000 − $18,400). The failure is corrected using the reduction of account balance method by reducing Mark's account balance by $1,600 (adjusted for earnings) and crediting that amount to an unallocated account to be used to reduce future employer contributions.

Example 6. The facts are the same as in Example 5, except that Phyllis, Inc. corrects the failure under VCP using the contribution correction method by (1) amending the plan to increase the contribution percentage for all participants for the 2008 plan year and (2) contributing an additional amount (adjusted for earnings) for those participants for that plan year. The plan is amended to increase the contribution percentage by .7 percentage points ($1,600 ÷ $230,000), from 8 percent to 8.7 percent. In addition, each participant for the 2008 plan year receives an additional contribution of .7 percent multiplied by that participant's compensation for 2008.

6. *Failure of making hardship distributions (see Q 27:14) and loans from a plan that does not provide for such provisions.* If hardship distributions that were not permitted under plan terms have been made, then, a corrective plan amendment may be made under VCP and SCP if the plan as amended satisfies the qualification requirements and would have satisfied the qualification requirements had the amendment been adopted when hardship distributions were first made available. In addition, if loans have been made to participants from a plan that does not provide for plan loans, then a corrective plan amendment may be made under VCP and SCP if the plan as amended satisfies the qualification requirements and would have satisfied the qualification requirements had the amendment been adopted when plan loans were first made available.

Example 7. MPS Corporation maintains a 401(k) plan and although plan provisions in 2007 did not provide for hardship distributions, beginning in 2007 hardship distributions were made currently and effectively available to all employees. Hardship distributions were made to a number of participants during 2007 and 2008, creating an operational failure. The failure was discovered in 2009. MPS Corporation corrects the failure under VCP by adopting a plan amendment effective January 1, 2007, to provide a hardship distribution option that is available to all employees.

7. *Early inclusion of otherwise eligible employee failure.* The operational failure of including an otherwise eligible employee in the plan who either (a) has not completed the plan's minimum age or service requirements, or (b) has completed the plan's minimum age or service requirements but became a participant in the plan on a date earlier than the applicable plan entry date, may be corrected under VCP and SCP by using the plan amendment correction method. This method allows the plan to be amended retroactively to change the eligibility or entry date provisions to

provide for the inclusion of the ineligible employee to reflect the plan's actual operations. Furthermore:

a. The amendment must satisfy the qualification requirements at the time it is adopted;

b. The amendment would have satisfied the qualification requirements had the amendment been adopted at the earlier time when it is effective; and

c. The employees affected by the amendment are predominantly NHCEs (see Q 3:12).

Example 8. Jilly TS Inc. maintains a 401(k) plan applicable to all of its employees who have at least six months of service. The plan provides that Jilly TS Inc. will make matching contributions based upon an employee's salary reduction contributions. In 2009, it is discovered that all four employees who were hired in 2008 were permitted to make salary reduction contributions to the plan effective with the first weekly paycheck after they were employed. Three of the four employees are NHCEs. Jilly TS Inc. matched these employees' salary reduction contributions in accordance with the plan's matching contribution formula. Jilly TS Inc. corrects the failure under SCP by adopting a plan amendment, effective for employees hired on or after January 1, 2008, to provide that there is no service eligibility requirement under the plan and submitting the amendment to IRS for a determination letter.

[Rev. Proc. 2008-50, app. B, §§ 1, 2, 2008-2 C.B. 464]

Q 19:33 How is a corrective contribution or allocation adjusted for earnings?

In general, whenever the appropriate correction method for an operational failure (see Q 19:5) in a defined contribution plan (see Q 2:2) includes a corrective contribution or allocation that increases one or more employees' account balances, the contribution or allocation must be adjusted for earnings and forfeitures. IRS has provided earnings adjustment methods that may be used to adjust a corrective contribution or allocation for earnings in a defined contribution plan. A corrective contribution or allocation that increases an employee's account balance is adjusted to reflect an earnings amount that is based on the earnings rate (or rates) for the period of the failure. In the case of an exclusion of an eligible employee from a plan contribution, the beginning of the period of the failure is the date on which contributions were made for other employees for the year of the failure. For administrative convenience, for purposes of calculating the earnings rate for corrective contributions for a plan year during which an employee was improperly excluded from making periodic elective deferrals or employee after-tax contributions or from receiving periodic matching contributions, the employer may treat the date on which the contributions would have been made as the midpoint of the plan year for which the failure occurred.

The earnings rate generally is based on the investment results that would have applied to the corrective contribution or allocation if the failure had not occurred. If a plan permits employees to direct the investment of account balances into more than one investment fund, the earnings rate is based on the rate applicable to the employee's investment choices for the period of the failure. For administrative convenience, if most of the employees for whom the corrective contribution or allocation is made are NHCEs (see Q 3:12), the rate of return of the fund with the highest earnings rate under the plan for the period of the failure may be used to determine the earnings rate for all corrective contributions or allocations. If the employee had not made any applicable investment choices, the earnings rate may be based on the earnings rate under the plan as a whole (i.e., the average of the rates earned by all of the funds in the valuation periods during the period of the failure weighted by the portion of the plan assets invested in the various funds during the period of the failure).

For administrative convenience, the earnings rate applicable to the corrective contribution or allocation for a valuation period with respect to any investment fund may be assumed to be the actual earnings rate for the plan's investments in that fund during that valuation period. For example, the earnings rate may be determined without regard to any special investment provisions that vary according to the size of the fund. Further, the earnings rate applicable to the corrective contribution or allocation for a portion of a valuation period may be a pro rata portion of the earnings rate for the entire valuation period, unless the application of this rule would result in either a significant understatement or overstatement of the actual earnings during that portion of the valuation period. The earnings amount generally may be allocated in accordance with any of the following methods:

- Plan allocation method
- Specific employee allocation method
- Bifurcated allocation method, or
- Current period allocation method

Example. Paul Inc. maintains a profit sharing plan that provides only for nonelective contributions. The plan has a single investment fund. Under the plan, assets are valued annually (the last day of the plan year) and earnings for the year are allocated in proportion to account balances as of the last day of the prior year. Plan contributions for 1998 were made on March 31, 1999. On April 20, 2001, Paul Inc. determines that an operational failure occurred for 1998 because an employee, JoAnne, was improperly excluded from the plan. Paul Inc. decides to correct the failure by using the IRS-listed correction method for the exclusion of an eligible employee from nonelective contributions in a profit sharing plan (see Q 19:31). Under this method, Paul Inc. determines that this failure is corrected by making a contribution on behalf of JoAnne of $5,000 (adjusted for earnings). The earnings rate under the plan for 1999 was 20 percent and for 2000 was 10 percent. On May 15, 2001, when Paul Inc. determines that a contribution to correct the failure will be made on

June 1, 2001, a reasonable estimate of the earnings rate under the plan from January 1, 2001 to June 1, 2001 is 12 percent.

The $5,000 corrective contribution on behalf of JoAnne is adjusted to reflect an earnings amount based on the earnings rates for the period of the failure (March 31, 1999, through June 1, 2001) and the earnings amount is allocated using the plan allocation method. Paul Inc. determines that a pro rata simplifying assumption may be used to determine the earnings rate for the period from March 31, 1999, to December 31, 1999, because that rate does not significantly understate or overstate the actual earnings for that period. Accordingly, Paul Inc. determines that the earnings rate for that period is 15 percent (9/12 of the plan's 20 percent earnings rate for the year). The total corrective amount adjusted for earnings equals $7,084 [$5,000 + $750 ($5,000 × 15%) + $575 (($5,000 + $750) × 10%) + $759 (($5,000 + $750 + $575) × 12%)].

[Rev. Proc. 2008-50, app. B, § 3, 2008-2 C.B. 464]

Q 19:34 Can excise taxes be resolved under EPCRS?

In general, EPCRS is not available for events for which the Code provides tax consequences other than plan disqualification (such as the imposition of an excise tax or additional income tax). For example, funding deficiencies (see Q 8:22), prohibited transactions (see Q 24:1), and failures to file Form 5500 (see Q 21:10) cannot be corrected under EPCRS.

As part of VCP (see Q 19:20) and Audit CAP (see Q 19:28), if the failure involves the failure to satisfy the minimum distribution requirements (see chapter 11), in appropriate cases IRS will waive the excise tax (see Qs 11:67–11:71) applicable to plan participants. The waiver will be included in the compliance statement (see Q 19:22), or in the closing agreement (see Q 19:28) in the case of Audit CAP. The plan sponsor, as part of the submission, must request the waiver, and, in cases where the participant subject to the excise tax is an owner-employee (see Q 5:32) or a 10 percent owner of a corporation, the plan sponsor must also provide an explanation supporting the request.

As part of VCP, if the failure involves a correction that requires the plan sponsor to make a plan contribution that is not deductible, in appropriate cases IRS will not pursue the excise tax on such nondeductible contributions (see Q 12:9). The plan sponsor, as part of the submission, must request the relief and provide an explanation supporting the request.

As part of VCP, if a failure results in excess contributions (see Q 27:25) under a plan, IRS will not pursue the excise tax (see Q 27:34) in appropriate cases. For example, where correction is made for any case in which the ADP test (see Q 27:18) was timely performed but, due to reliance on inaccurate data, an insufficient amount of excess elective contributions was distributed to highly compensated employees (HCEs; see Q 3:2), the excise tax will be waived. The plan sponsor, as part of the submission, must provide a detailed description of the failure and the reason for it not having been corrected.

As part of VCP, in appropriate cases, IRS will not pursue the excise tax relating to excess contributions made to an IRA under any of the following circumstances:

1. As part of the proposed correction for overpayments, the participant or beneficiary ("recipient") removes the overpayment (plus earnings) from the recipient's IRA and returns that amount to the plan;

2. As part of the proposed correction for excess amounts, the recipient removes the excess amount (plus earnings) from the recipient's IRA and reports that amount (reduced by any applicable after-tax employee contribution) as a taxable distribution for the year in which the excess amount (plus earnings) is removed from the recipient's IRA; or

3. In the case of an overpayment that was not made pursuant to a distributable event, the plan sponsor, as part of the submission, must request relief from the excise tax under Code Section 4973 and provide an explanation supporting the request.

As part of VCP, in the appropriate cases, IRS will not pursue the 10 percent additional income tax under Code Section 72(t) (or will pursue only a portion thereof) if, as part of the proposed correction for overpayments that were not made pursuant to a distributable event, the participant or beneficiary ("recipient") removes the amount improperly distributed and rolled over (plus earnings) from the recipient's IRA and returns that amount to the plan. The plan sponsor, as part of the submission, must request the relief and provide an explanation supporting the request.

[Rev. Proc. 2008-50, § 6.09, 2008-2 C.B. 464]

Q 19:35 Can plan officials correct fiduciary breaches and avoid DOL penalties?

Yes. A plan fiduciary (see Q 23:1), plan sponsor, party in interest (see Q 24:3), or other person in a position to correct a breach may avoid assessment of civil penalties under ERISA Section 502(l) (see Q 23:51) for possible breaches of fiduciary duties by correcting such breaches and reporting them to DOL's Employee Benefits Security Administration (EBSA) pursuant to EBSA's Voluntary Fiduciary Correction Program (VFC Program; see Q 19:36). The VFC Program is designed to benefit workers by encouraging the voluntary and timely correction of possible fiduciary breaches of ERISA. [DOL Notice, 71 Fed. Reg. 20,261 (Apr. 19, 2006)]

Q 19:36 What is the Voluntary Fiduciary Correction Program (VFC Program)?

The VFC Program is designed to encourage the voluntary and timely correction of possible fiduciary breaches by allowing the avoidance of potential ERISA civil actions initiated by DOL and the assessment of civil penalties under ERISA Section 502(l) (see Q 23:51). The VFC Program was adopted by EBSA on a permanent basis in March 2002 and has recently been revised by the addition of certain changes that simplify and expand the original VFC Program.

Under the VFC Program, plan officials may voluntarily apply for relief from EBSA enforcement actions when they fully and accurately correct violations by:

1. Identifying all violations and determining whether they fall within the transactions covered by the VFC Program;

2. Following the process for correcting specific violations;

3. Calculating and restoring losses and profits with interest and distributing supplemental benefits to participants; and

4. Filing an application with the appropriate EBSA regional office, and including with the filing documentation showing evidence of corrected financial transactions.

[DOL Notice, 71 Fed. Reg. 20,261 (Apr. 19, 2006), revising DOL Notice, 70 Fed. Reg. 17,515 (Apr. 6, 2005)]

Q 19:37   What is the effect of the VFC Program?

EBSA generally will issue to the applicant a no action letter with respect to a breach (see Q 19:38) identified in the application if the eligibility requirements (see Q 19:39) are satisfied and a plan official (see Q 19:38) corrects the breach in accordance with the other requirements and procedures of the VFC Program (see Qs 19:40–19:43). Pursuant to the no action letter it issues, EBSA will not initiate a civil investigation under Title I of ERISA regarding the applicant's responsibility for any transaction described in the no action letter or assess a civil penalty under either ERISA Section 501(i) or 501(l) (see Q 23:51) on the correction amount (see Q 19:41) paid to the plan or its participants.

The following limitations apply on the effect of the VFC Program:

1. Any no action letter issued is limited to the breach and applicants identified therein. The method of calculating the correction amount is only intended to correct the specific breach described in the application.

2. A no action letter does not imply DOL approval of matters not included therein, including steps that the fiduciaries take to prevent recurrence of the breach described in the application and to ensure the plan's future compliance with Title I of ERISA.

3. Any no action letter is conditioned on the truthfulness, completeness, and accuracy of the statements made in the application and any material misrepresentations or omissions will void the no action letter.

4. If an application fails to satisfy the terms of the VFC Program, EBSA reserves the right to investigate and take any other action with respect to the transaction and/or plan that is the subject of the application, including refusing to issue a no action letter.

5. Compliance with the terms of the VFC Program will not preclude:

   a. EBSA or any other governmental agency from conducting a criminal investigation of the transaction identified in the application;

   b. EBSA's assistance to such other agency; or

   c. EBSA making the appropriate referrals of criminal violations.

6. Compliance with the terms of the VFC Program will not preclude EBSA from taking any of the following actions:

   a. Seeking removal from positions of responsibility with respect to a plan or other non-monetary injunctive relief against any person responsible for the transaction at issue;

   b. Referring information regarding the transaction to IRS; or

   c. Imposing civil penalties based on the failure or refusal to file a timely, complete, and accurate annual return/report (Form 5500; see Q 21:2). Amended annual returns/reports may be required if possible breaches of ERISA have been identified, or if action is taken to correct possible breaches in accordance with the VFC Program.

7. The issuance of a no action letter does not affect the ability of any other government agency, or any other person, to enforce any rights or carry out any authority they may have, with respect to matters described in the no action letter.

   Example 1. A plan fiduciary causes the plan to purchase real estate from the plan sponsor under circumstances to which no prohibited-transaction exemption (see Q 24:20) applies. In connection with this transaction, the purchase causes the plan assets to be no longer diversified, a violation of ERISA (see Q 23:81). If the application reflects full compliance with the requirements of the VFC Program, the no action letter would apply to the violation of the prohibited transaction rules, but would not apply to the violation of the diversification requirement. [ERISA §§ 404(a)(1)(C), 406(a)(1)(A)]

The correction criteria under the VFC Program represent EBSA's enforcement policy and are provided for informational purposes, but are not intended to confer enforceable rights on any person who purports to correct a violation. Applicants are advised that the term "correction" as used in the VFC Program is not necessarily the same as "correction" pursuant to the prohibited transaction rules (see Q 24:6). Correction may not be achieved under the VFC Program by engaging in a new prohibited transaction. However, IRS has indicated that the tax treatment of a breach and correction under the VFC Program (including the income and employment tax consequences to participants, beneficiaries, and plan sponsors) is determined under the Code and that, except in those instances where the fiduciary breach or its correction involve a tax abuse, a correction under the VFC Program for a breach that constitutes a prohibited transaction generally will constitute correction for purposes of Section 4975 and a correction under the VFC Program for a breach that also constitutes an operational failure (see Q 19:5) generally will constitute correction for purposes of EPCRS (see Q 19:2).

EBSA reserves the right to conduct an investigation and take any other enforcement action relating to the transaction identified in a VFC Program application in certain circumstances, such as prejudice to DOL that may be caused by the expiration of the statute of limitations period, material misrepresentations, or significant harm to the plan or its participants that is not cured by the correction provided under the VFC Program. EBSA may also conduct a civil investigation and take any other enforcement action relating to matters not covered by the VFC Program application or relating to other plans sponsored by the same plan sponsor, while a VFC Program application involving the plan or the plan sponsor is pending.

EBSA will maintain the confidentiality of any documents submitted under the VFC Program, to the extent permitted by law. However, EBSA has an obligation to make referrals to IRS and to refer to other agencies evidence of criminality and other information for law enforcement purposes.

[DOL Notice, 71 Fed. Reg. 20,261 § 2 (Apr. 19, 2006)]

Q 19:38   What important terms apply for the VFC Program?

For purposes of the VFC Program, the following definitions are applicable:

1. *Breach.* Any transaction which is or may be a breach of the fiduciary responsibilities contained in Part 4 of Title I of ERISA.

2. *Plan official.* A plan fiduciary (see Q 23:1), plan sponsor, party in interest (see Q 24:3) with respect to a plan, or other person who is in a position to correct a breach.

3. *Under investigation.* A plan or potential applicant shall be considered to be under investigation if:

   a. EBSA is conducting an investigation of the plan;

   b. EBSA is conducting an investigation of the potential applicant or plan sponsor in connection with an act or transaction directly related to the plan;

   c. Any governmental agency is conducting a criminal investigation of the plan or of the potential applicant or plan sponsor in connection with an act or transaction directly related to the plan;

   d. IRS is conducting an employee plans examination of the plan; or

   e. PBGC, any state attorney general, or any state insurance commissioner is conducting an investigation or examination of the plan or of the applicant or plan sponsor in connection with an act or transaction directly related to the plan, unless the applicant notifies EBSA, in writing, of such an investigation or examination at the time of the application;and the plan, a plan official, or any authorized plan representative has received a written or oral notice of an investigation or examination described in a through e above.

[DOL Notice, 71 Fed. Reg. 20,261 § 3 (Apr. 19, 2006)]

Q 19:39   What are the eligibility conditions for the VFC Program?

Eligibility for the VFC Program is conditioned on the following:

1. Neither the plan nor the applicant is under investigation (see Q 19:38);
2. The application contains no evidence of potential criminal violations; and
3. EBSA has not conducted an investigation that resulted in written notice to a plan fiduciary (see Q 23:1) that the transaction, for which the potential applicant could otherwise have sought relief under the VFC Program, has been referred to IRS.

[DOL Notice, 71 Fed. Reg. 20,261 § 4 (Apr. 19, 2006)]

Q 19:40   What are the conditions of valuation for the VFC Program?

Many corrections require that the current or fair market value of an asset be determined as of a particular date, usually either the date the plan originally acquired the asset or the date of the correction, or both. In order to be acceptable as part of a VFC Program correction, the valuation must meet the following conditions:

1. If there is a generally recognized market for the property (e.g., the New York Stock Exchange), the fair market value of the asset is the average value of the asset on such market on the applicable date, unless the plan document specifies another objectively determined value (e.g., the closing price).
2. If there is no generally recognized market for the asset, the fair market value of that asset must be determined in accordance with generally accepted appraisal standards by a qualified, independent appraiser and reflected in a written appraisal report signed by the appraiser.
3. An appraiser is qualified if the appraiser has met the education, experience, and licensing requirements that are generally recognized for appraisal of the type of asset being appraised.
4. An appraiser is independent if the appraiser is not one of the following, does not own or control any of the following, and is not owned or controlled by, or affiliated with, any of the following:
   a. The prior owner of the asset, if the asset was purchased by the plan;
   b. The purchaser of the asset, if the asset was, or is now being sold, by the plan;
   c. Any other owner of the asset, if the plan is not the sole owner;
   d. A fiduciary of the plan (see Q 23:1);
   e. A party in interest (see Q 24:3) with respect to the plan (except to the extent the appraiser becomes a party in interest when retained to perform this appraisal for the plan); or
   f. The VFC Program applicant.

[DOL Notice, 71 Fed. Reg. 20,261 § 5 (Apr. 19, 2006)]

Q 19:41   What is the correction amount under the VFC Program?

For purposes of the VFC Program, the correction amount is the amount that must be paid to the plan as a result of the breach in order to make the plan whole. In most instances, the correction amount will be a combination of the principal amount involved in the transaction, the lost earnings amount, and any interest on lost earnings. However, in circumstances where the restoration of profits amount exceeds the lost earnings amount and any interest on lost earnings, the correction amount will be a combination of the principal amount and the restoration of profits amount.

With respect to the correction amount, the following items are applicable:

1. *Principal amount.* The amount that would have been available to the plan for investment or distribution on the date of the breach had the breach not occurred. Generally, the principal amount is the base amount on which lost earnings and, if applicable, restoration of profits is calculated. The principal amount also includes, where appropriate, any transaction costs associated with entering into the transaction that constitutes the breach.

2. *Loss date.* The date that the plan lost the use of the principal amount.

3. *Recovery date.* The date that the principal amount is restored to the plan.

4. *Lost earnings.* The amount that would have been earned by the plan on the principal amount but for the breach. Lost earnings will be calculated according to the following:

   a. *Initial calculation.* Lost earnings will be calculated by: (i) determining the applicable corporate underpayment rate(s) established under Section 6621(a)(2) for each quarter (or portion thereof) for the period beginning with the loss date and ending with the recovery date; (ii) determining, by reference to Revenue Procedure 95-17, the applicable factor(s) for such quarterly underpayment rate(s) for each quarter (or portion thereof) of the period beginning with the loss date and ending with the recovery date; and (iii) multiplying the principal amount by the first applicable factor to determine the amount of earnings for the first quarter (or portion thereof). If the loss date and recovery date are within the same quarter, the initial calculation is complete. If the recovery date is not in the same quarter as the loss date, the applicable factor for each subsequent quarter (or portion thereof) must be applied to the sum of the principal amount and all earnings as of the end of the immediately preceding quarter (or portion thereof), until lost earnings have been calculated for the entire period, ending with the recovery date.

   b. *Payment of lost earnings after recovery date.* If lost earnings are not paid to the plan on the recovery date along with the principal amount, payment of lost earnings will include interest on the amount of lost earnings. Such interest will be calculated in the same manner as lost earnings described in a. above for the period beginning on the recovery date and ending on the date the lost earnings are paid to the plan.

c. *Special rule for transactions causing large losses.* If the amount of lost earnings and any interest added to such lost earnings exceed $100,000, the amount of lost earnings and interest, if any, to be paid to the plan will be determined in accordance with a. and b. above, substituting the applicable underpayment rates under Section 6621(c)(1) for the rates under Section 6621(a)(2).

d. *Method of calculation.* For purposes of calculating lost earnings and interest, if any, a plan official may either (i) use the online calculator or (ii) perform a manual calculation. The application will include sufficient information to verify the correctness of the amounts to be paid to the plan.

5. *Restoration of profits.* If the principal amount was used for a specific purpose such that a profit on the use of the principal amount is determinable, the plan official must calculate the restoration of profits amount and compare it to the lost earnings amount to determine the correction amount. Restoration of profits is a combination of two amounts: (i) the amount of profit made on the use of the principal amount by the fiduciary or party in interest who engaged in the breach and (ii) if the profit is returned to the plan on a date later than the date on which the profit was realized, the amount of interest earned on such profit from the date the profit was realized to the date on which the profit is paid to the plan. If the restoration of profits amount exceeds lost earnings and interest, if any, the restoration of profits amount must be paid to the plan instead of lost earnings.

a. *Calculation of interest.* Interest shall be calculated by: (i) determining the applicable corporate underpayment rate(s) established under Section 6621(a)(2) for each quarter (or portion thereof) for the period beginning with the date the profit was realized and ending with the date on which the profit is paid to the plan; (ii) determining, by reference to Revenue Procedure 95-17, the applicable factor(s) for such quarterly underpayment rate(s) for each quarter (or portion thereof) of the period beginning with the date the profit was realized and ending with the date on which the profit is paid to the plan; and (iii) multiplying the first applicable factor by the profit on the principal amount, to determine the amount of interest for the first quarter (or portion thereof). If the date the profit was realized and the date the profit is paid to the plan are within the same quarter, the initial calculation is complete. If the date the profit was realized is not in the same quarter as the date the profit was paid to the plan, the applicable factor for each subsequent quarter (or portion thereof) must be applied to the sum of the profit on the principal amount and all interest as of the end of the immediately preceding quarter (or portion thereof), until interest has been calculated for the entire period, ending with the date the profit is paid to the plan.

b. *Special rule for transactions resulting in large restorations.* If the amount of restoration of profits exceeds $100,000, the amount of any interest on the restoration of profits to be paid to the plan will be determined in accordance with a. above, substituting the applicable underpayment rates under Section 6621(c)(1) for the rates under Section 6621(a)(2).

    c. *Method of calculation.* For purposes of calculating the interest amount for restoration of profits, a plan official may either (i) use the online calculator or (ii) perform a manual calculation. The application will include sufficient information to verify the correctness of the amounts to be paid to the plan.

  6. *Online calculator.* An internet-based compliance assistance tool provided on EBSA's Web site that permits applicants to calculate the amount of lost earnings, any interest on lost earnings, and the interest amount for restoration of profits, if applicable, for certain transactions. The online calculator will be updated as necessary.

The fiduciary, plan sponsor, or other plan official, not the plan, must pay the costs of correction. The costs of correction include, where appropriate, such expenses as closing costs, prepayment penalties, or sale or purchase costs associated with correcting the transaction.

Plans will have to make supplemental distributions to former employees, beneficiaries receiving benefits, or alternate payees (see Q 36:5) if the original distributions were too low because of the breach. The applicant must demonstrate proof of payment to participants and beneficiaries whose current location is known to the plan and/or applicant. For individuals whose location is unknown, applicants must demonstrate that they have segregated adequate funds to pay the missing individuals and that the applicant has commenced the process of locating the missing individuals. The costs of such efforts are part of the costs of correction.

Where correction under the VFC Program requires distributions in amounts less than $20 to former employees and the applicant demonstrates that the cost of making the distribution exceeds the amount of the payment to which such individual is entitled, the applicant need not make distributions to such individuals. However, the applicant must pay to the plan as a whole the total of such *de minimis* amounts not distributed to such individuals.

[DOL Notice, 71 Fed. Reg. 20,261 § 5 (Apr. 19, 2006)]

The principles of the above correction calculations are illustrated by the following example:

Example. Jason Inc.'s pay periods end every other Friday; and, each pay period, participant contributions total $10,000, which reasonably can be segregated from Jason Inc.'s general assets by ten business days following the end of each pay period. Jason Inc. should have remitted participant contributions for the pay period ending March 2, 2001 to the Jason Inc. 401(k) Plan by March 16, 2001, the loss date, but actually remitted them on April 13, 2001, the recovery date. In early 2004, a plan official discovers that participant contributions for this pay period were not remitted on a timely basis. To comply with the VFC Program, the plan official determined that all lost earnings would be repaid on January 30, 2004. Based on the above facts: the principal amount is $10,000, the loss date is March 16, 2001, the recovery date is April 13, 2001, and the number of days late is 28 (recovery date less loss date).

Step 1. The plan official must calculate lost earnings, based on the principal amount, that should have been paid on the recovery date. The first period of time is from March 16, 2001, to March 31, 2001 (15 days). The Code underpayment rate is 9 percent, and, using Revenue Procedure 95-17, the factor for 15 days at 9 percent is 0.003705021, so that $10,000 × 0.003705021 = $37.05. The plan is due $10,037.50 as of March 31, 2001. The second period of time is April 1, 2001 through April 13, 2001 (13 days). The Code underpayment rate is 8 percent, and, using Revenue Procedure 95-17, the factor for 13 days at 8 percent is 0.002853065, so that $10,037.50 × 0.002853065 = $28.64. Therefore, lost earnings of $65.69 ($37.05 + $28.64) must be paid to the plan.

Step 2. If lost earnings are paid to the plan after the recovery date, the plan official must calculate the amount of interest on the lost earnings (determined in Step 1) that must also be paid to the plan. This calculation is shown by the chart on page 19-51. The Interest column is the previous time period's Amount Due multiplied by the Factor, and the Amount Due is the previous Amount Due plus Interest. The calculation in the first row is based on the $65.69 lost earnings. The plan is also owed $11.64. This is the amount of interest on $65.69 (lost earnings on the principal amount) accrued between April 13, 2001, the recovery date, when the principal amount $10,000 was paid to the plan, and January 30, 2004, the date chosen to repay lost earnings. Therefore, the plan official must pay $77.33 to the plan on January 30, 2004, as lost earnings ($65.69) plus interest on lost earnings ($11.64) for the pay period ending March 2, 2001, in addition to the principal amount ($10,000) that was paid on April 13, 2001. This total corresponds with the final Total Due in the chart.

1st Day	To	Days	Underpayment Rate	Rev. Proc. Table	Factor	Interest	Amount Due
4/14/01	6/30/01	78	8%	21	.017240956	1.132558	66.82256
7/1/01	9/30/01	92	7%	19	.017798686	1.189354	68.01191
10/1/01	12/31/01	92	7%	19	.017798686	1.210523	69.22243
1/1/02	3/31/02	90	6%	17	.014903267	1.031640	70.25408
4/1/02	6/30/02	91	6%	17	.015070101	1.058736	71.31281
7/1/02	9/30/02	92	6%	17	.015236961	1.086591	72.39940
10/1/02	12/31/02	92	6%	17	.015236961	1.103147	73.50255
1/1/03	3/31/03	90	5%	15	.012404225	0.911742	74.41429
4/1/03	6/30/03	91	5%	15	.012542910	0.933372	75.34766
7/1/03	9/30/03	92	5%	15	.012681615	0.955530	76.30319
10/1/03	12/31/03	92	4%	13	.010132630	0.773152	77.07634
1/1/04	1/30/04	30	4%	61	.003283890	0.253110	77.32945
					Total Interest:	$11.64	

[DOL Notice, 71 Fed. Reg. 20,261 § 5, app. D (Apr. 19, 2006)]

Q 19:42   What are the application procedures for the VFC Program?

In order to be valid, each application must meet the following requirements:

1. *Preparer.* The application must be prepared by a plan official (see Q 19:38) or the plan official's authorized representative.

2. *Contact person.* Each application must include the name, address, and telephone number of a contact person.

3. *Detailed narrative.* The applicant must provide a detailed narrative describing the breach (see Q 19:38) and the corrective action. The narrative must include:

    a. A list of all persons materially involved in the breach and its correction;

    b. The employer identification number and address of the plan sponsor and administrator (see Q 20:1);

    c. The date the plan's most recent Form 5500 (see Q 21:2) was filed;

    d. An explanation of the breach, including the date it occurred;

    e. An explanation of how the breach was corrected, by whom, and when; and

    f. (i) If the applicant performs a manual calculation, specific calculations demonstrating how principal amount (see Q 19:41) and lost earnings (see Q 19:41) or, if applicable, restoration of profits (see Q 19:41) were computed;

    (ii) If the applicant uses the online calculator, the data elements required to be input into the online calculator; and

    (iii) An explanation of why payment of lost earnings or restoration of profits was chosen to correct the breach.

4. *Supporting documentation.* The applicant must also include:

    a. Copies of the relevant portions of the plan document and any other pertinent documents;

    b. Documentation that supports the narrative description of the transaction and correction;

    c. Documentation establishing the lost earnings amount;

    d. Documentation establishing the amount of restoration of profits, if applicable;

    e. All documents relating to the eligible breaches and acceptable correction methods under the VFC Program (see Q 19:43); and

    f. Proof of payment of principal amount and lost earnings or restoration of profits.

5. *Penalty of perjury statement.* Each application must also include a penalty of perjury statement. The statement must be signed and dated by a plan fiduciary with knowledge of the transaction that is the subject of the application and the authorized representative of the applicant, if any. In addition, each plan official applying under the VFC Program must execute the penalty of perjury statement.

6. *Checklist.* The checklist provided by DOL must be completed, signed, and submitted with the application.

7. *Where to apply.* The application should be mailed to the appropriate regional EBSA office.

[DOL Notice, 71 Fed. Reg. 20,261 § 6, apps. B,C,E (Apr. 19, 2006)]

Q 19:43   What are the eligible transactions and acceptable corrections under the VFC Program?

EBSA has identified certain breaches (see Q 19:38) and methods of correction that are suitable for the VFC Program. Any plan official (see Q 19:38) may correct a breach listed in accordance with the applicable correction method and the rules for acceptable corrections (see Q 19:41). The following correction methods are strictly construed and are the only acceptable correction methods under the VFC Program for the transactions described. EBSA will not accept applications concerning correction of breaches other than the following:

1. Delinquent participant contributions and participant loan repayments to retirement plans (see Q 19:44);

2. Loans (see Q 19:45):

    a. Loan at fair market interest rate to a party in interest (see Q 24:3);

    b. Loan at below-market interest rate to a party in interest;

    c. Loan at below-market interest rate to a person who is not a party in interest;

    d. Loan at below-market interest rate solely due to a delay in perfecting the plan's security interest;

3. Participant loans (see Q 19:46):

    a. Loans failing to comply with plan provisions for amount, duration, or level amortization;

    b. Default loans;

4. Purchases, sales, and exchanges (see Q 19:47):

    a. Purchase of an asset (including real property) by a plan from a party in interest;

    b. Sale of an asset (including real property) by a plan to a party in interest;

    c. Sale and leaseback of real property to employer;

    d. Purchase of an asset (including real property) by a plan from a person who is not a party in interest at a price more than fair market value;

    e. Sale of an asset (including real property) by a plan to a person that is not a party in interest at a price less than fair market value;

5. Holding of an illiquid asset previously purchased by a plan;

6. Payment of benefits without properly valuing plan assets (see Q 19:48);

7. Plan expenses (see Q 19:49):

    a. Duplicative, excessive, or unnecessary compensation paid by a plan;

b. Expenses improperly paid by a plan; and

c. Payment of dual compensation to a plan fiduciary.

[DOL Notice, 71 Fed. Reg. 20,261 § 7 (Apr. 19, 2006)]

Q 19:44   How are delinquent participant contributions and participant loan repayments corrected under the VFC Program?

The following rules apply to the correction of delinquent participant contributions to retirement plans.

1. *Description of transaction.* An employer receives directly from participants, or withholds from employees' paychecks, certain amounts for either contribution to a retirement plan or repayment of participants' plan loans. Instead of forwarding the contributions for investment in accordance with the provisions of the plan and within the required time frames (see Q 23:32), the employer retains the contributions for a longer period of time. Similarly, in the case of participant loan repayments, instead of applying such repayments to outstanding loan balances within the required time frame and in accordance with the provisions of the plan, the employer retains such repayments for a longer period of time.

2. *Correction of transaction.*

   a. *Unpaid contributions or participant loan repayments.* The plan should be paid the principal amount (see Q 19:41) plus the greater of (i) lost earnings (see Q 19:41) on the principal amount or (ii) restoration of profits (see Q 19:41) resulting from the employer's use of the principal amount. The loss date (see Q 19:41) for each contribution is the earliest date on which the contributions reasonably could have been segregated from the employer's general assets. In no event will the loss date be later than the applicable maximum time period.

   b. *Late contributions or participant loan repayments.* If the participant contributions or loan repayments were remitted to the plan outside of the time period, the only correction required is to pay to the plan the greater of (i) lost earnings or (ii) restoration of profits resulting from the employer's use of the principal amount. Any penalties, late fees, or other charges will be paid by the employer and not from participant loan repayments.

3. *Documentation.* In addition to the required documentation (see Q 19:42), the following additional documents should also be submitted:

   a. A statement from a plan official identifying the earliest date on which the participant contributions and/or repayments reasonably could have been segregated from the employer's general assets and supporting documentation.

   b. If restored participant contributions and/or repayments (exclusive of lost earnings): (i) total $50,000 or less or (ii) exceed $50,000 and were remitted to the plan within 180 days from the date such amounts were received by the employer, or the date such amounts otherwise would have been payable to the participants in cash, additional information includes:

A. A narrative describing the applicant's contribution and/or repayment remittance practices before and after the period of unpaid or late contributions and/or repayments and

B. Summary documents demonstrating the amount of unpaid or late contributions and/or repayments; and

C. If restored participant contributions and/or repayments (exclusive of lost earnings) exceed $50,000 and were remitted more than 180 days after the date such amounts were received by the employer, or the date such amounts otherwise would have been payable to the participants in cash, additional information includes:

   (i) A narrative describing the applicant's contribution and/or repayment remittance practices before and after the period of unpaid or late contributions and/or repayments;

   (ii) For participant contributions and/or repayments received from participants, a copy of the accounting records that identify the date and amount of each contribution received; and

   (iii) For participant contributions and/or repayments withheld from employees' paychecks, a copy of the payroll documents showing the date and amount of each withholding.

[DOL Notice, 71 Fed. Reg. 20,261 § 7.1 (Apr. 19, 2006)]

A prohibited-transaction class exemption (PTCE; see Q 19:50) provides relief from the penalty taxes (see Q 24:5) on the prohibited transaction (see Q 24:1) applicable to the above breach (see Q 19:38).

Q 19:45 How are certain loans corrected under the VFC Program?

The following rules apply to the correction of certain loans.

1. Loan at fair market interest rate to a party in interest (see Q 24:3) with respect to the plan:

   a. *Description of transaction.* A plan made a loan to a party in interest at an interest rate no less than that for loans with similar terms to a borrower of similar creditworthiness.

   b. *Correction of transaction.* The loan should be repaid in full, including any prepayment penalties. An independent commercial lender must also confirm in writing that the loan was made at a fair market interest rate for a loan with similar terms to a borrower of similar creditworthiness.

   c. *Documentation.* In addition to the required documentation (see Q 19:42), a narrative describing the process used to determine the fair market interest rate should also be submitted.

A PTCE (see Q 19:50) provides relief from the penalty taxes (see Q 24:5) on the prohibited transaction (see Q 24:1) applicable to the above breach (see Q 19:38).

2. Loan at below-market interest rate to a party in interest with respect to the plan:

   a. *Description of transaction.* A plan made a loan to a party in interest with respect to the plan at an interest rate which, at the time the loan was made, was less than the fair market interest rate for loans with similar terms to a borrower of similar creditworthiness.

   b. *Correction of transaction.* The loan should be repaid in full, including any prepayment penalties. The principal amount, plus the greater of (i) the lost earnings or (ii) the restoration of profits, should be paid to the plan. For purposes of this transaction, the principal amount is equal to the excess of the interest payments that would have been received if the loan had been made at the fair market interest rate (from the beginning of the loan until the recovery date) over interest payments actually received under the loan terms during such period. For purposes of the VFC Program, the fair market interest rate must be determined by an independent commercial lender.

   c. *Documentation.* In addition to the required documentation, additional documents including a copy of the independent commercial lender's fair market interest rate determination and a copy of the independent fiduciary's written approval of the fair market interest rate determination should also be submitted.

   Example 1. The Howard Corp. Pension Plan made to Gayle, a party in interest, a $150,000 mortgage loan, secured by a first deed, at a fixed interest rate of 4 percent per annum to be fully amortized over 30 years. The fair market interest rate for comparable loans, at the time this loan was made, was 7 percent per annum. Gayle or the plan official must repay the loan in full plus any applicable prepayment penalties. Gayle or the plan official also must pay the difference between what the plan would have received through the recovery date had the loan been made at 7 percent and what, in fact, the plan did receive from the commencement of the loan to the recovery date, plus lost earnings on that amount.

3. Loan at below-market interest rate to a person who is not a party in interest with respect to the plan:

   a. *Description of transaction.* A plan made a loan to a person who is not a party in interest with respect to the plan at an interest rate which, at the time the loan was made, was less than the fair market interest rate for loans with similar terms to a borrower of similar creditworthiness.

   b. *Correction of transaction.*

      (i) The principal amount, plus lost earnings through the recovery date should be paid to the plan.

(ii) Each loan payment has a principal amount equal to the excess of (A) interest payments that would have been received until the recovery date if the loan had been made at the fair market interest rate over (B) the interest actually received under the loan terms.

(iii) From the inception of the loan to the recovery date, the amount to be paid to the plan is the lost earnings on the series of principal amounts.

(iv) From the recovery date to the maturity date of the loan, the amount to be paid to the plan is the present value of the remaining principal amounts. Instead of calculating the present value, it is acceptable for administrative convenience to pay the sum of the remaining principal amounts.

c. *Documentation.* In addition to the required documentation, additional documents including a narrative describing the process used to determine the fair market interest rate at the time the loan was made and a copy of the independent commercial lender's fair market interest rate determination should also be submitted.

Example 2. The Laurie Ltd. Pension Plan made to Joel a $150,000 mortgage loan, secured by a first deed, at a fixed interest rate of 4 percent per annum to be fully amortized over 30 years. The fair market interest rate for comparable loans, at the time this loan was made, was 7 percent per annum. Joel or the plan official must pay the excess of what the plan would have received through the recovery date had the loan been made at 7 percent over what, in fact, the plan did receive from the commencement of the loan to the recovery date, plus lost earnings on that amount. The plan official must pay on the recovery date the difference in the value of the remaining payments on the loan between the 7 percent and the 4 percent for the duration of the time the plan is owed repayments on the loan.

4. Loan at below-market interest rate solely due to a delay in perfecting the plan's security interest:

a. *Description of transaction.* For purposes of the VFC Program, if a plan made a purportedly secured loan to a person who is not a party in interest with respect to the plan, but there was a delay in recording or otherwise perfecting the plan's interest in the loan collateral, the loan will be treated as an unsecured loan until the plan's security interest was perfected.

b. *Correction of transaction.*

(i) The principal amount, plus lost earnings, through the date the loan became fully secured should be paid to the plan.

(ii) The principal amount is equal to the excess of the loan payment that would have been received if the loan had been made at the fair market rate for an unsecured loan over the loan payment actually received under the loan terms during the period.

    (iii) In addition, if the delay in perfecting the loan's security caused a permanent change in the risk characteristics of the loan, the fair market interest rate for the remaining term of the loan must be determined by an independent commercial lender. In that case, the correction amount includes an additional payment to the plan. The amount to be paid to the plan is the present value of the remaining principal amounts from the date the loan is fully secured to the maturity date of the loan. Instead of calculating the present value, it is acceptable for administrative convenience to pay the sum of the remaining principal amounts.

  c. *Documentation.* In addition to the required documentation, additional documents including a narrative describing the process used to determine the fair market interest rate for the period that the loan was unsecured and a copy of the independent commercial lender's fair market interest rate determination should also be submitted.

[DOL Notice, 71 Fed. Reg. 20,261 § 7.2 (Apr. 19, 2006)]

Q 19:46 How are certain participant loans corrected under the VFC Program?

The following rules apply to the correction of certain participant loans.

1. Loans failing to comply with plan provisions for amount, duration, or level amortization (see Qs 14:4–14:6):

  a. *Description of transaction.* A plan extended a loan to a plan participant, and the loan terms did not comply with applicable plan provisions, which incorporated the requirements of the Code concerning:

    (i) The amount of the loan;

    (ii) The duration of the loan; or

    (iii) The level amortization of the loan repayment.

  b. *Correction of transaction.* Plan officials must make a voluntary correction of the loan with IRS approval under VCP (see Q 19:20).

  c. *Documentation.* The applicant is not required to submit any of the supporting documentation (see Q 19:42), except that the applicant must provide (i) proof of payment and (ii) a copy of the IRS compliance statement (see Q 19:22).

2. Default loans:

  a. *Description of transaction.* A plan extended a loan to a plan participant, and at origination the loan complied with applicable plan provisions that incorporated the requirements of the Code. During the loan repayment period, the plan official responsible for loan administration failed to properly withhold a number of loan repayments from the participant's wages and included the amount of such repayments in the participant's wages based on administrative or systems processing errors. The failure to withhold is a breach (see Q 19:38).

b. *Correction of transaction.* Plan officials must make a voluntary correction of the loan with IRS approval under VCP.

c. *Documentation.* The applicant is not required to submit any of the supporting documentation, except that the applicant must provide (i) proof of payment and (ii) a copy of the IRS compliance statement.

[DOL Notice, 71 Fed. Reg. 20,261 § 7.3 (Apr. 19, 2006)]

Q 19:47   How are certain purchases, sales, and exchanges corrected under the VFC Program?

The following rules apply to the correction of certain purchases, sales, and exchanges.

1. Purchase of an asset (including real property) by a plan from a party in interest (see Q 24:3):

    a. *Description of transaction.* A plan purchased an asset with cash from a party in interest with respect to the plan.

    b. *Correction of transaction.* The transaction must be corrected by the sale of the asset back to the party in interest who originally sold the asset to the plan or to a person who is not a party in interest. The plan must receive the higher of (i) the fair market value of the asset at the time of resale, without a reduction for the costs of sale, plus restoration to the plan of the party in interest's investment return from the proceeds of the sale, to the extent they exceed the plan's net profits from owning the property or (ii) the principal amount, plus the greater of (A) lost earnings on the principal amount or (B) the restoration of profits, if any. For this transaction, the principal amount is the plan's original purchase price. As an alternative, the plan may retain the asset and receive (i) the greater of (A) lost earnings or (B) the restoration of profits, if any, on the principal amount and (ii) the amount by which the principal amount exceeded the fair market value of the asset at the time of the original purchase, plus the greater of (A) lost earnings or (B) restoration of profits, if any, on such excess, provided an independent fiduciary determines that the plan will realize a greater benefit from this correction than it would from the resale of the asset described above.

    c. *Documentation.* In addition to the required documentation (see Q 19:42), the following documents should also be submitted:

        (i) Documentation of the plan's purchase of the real property, including the date of the purchase, the plan's purchase price, and the identity of the seller;

        (ii) A narrative describing the relationship between the original seller of the asset and the plan;

        (iii) The qualified, independent appraiser's report addressing the fair market value of the asset purchased by the plan, both at the time of the original purchase and at the recovery date; and

(iv) If applicable, a report of the independent fiduciary's determination that the plan will realize a greater benefit by receiving the alternative correction amount and retaining the asset.

Example 1. Paulette Retirement Plan purchased from Paulette Inc., the plan sponsor, a parcel of real property and uses the property as an office. The plan official obtains from a qualified, independent appraiser an appraisal of the property reflecting the fair market value of the property at the time of purchase at $100,000, although the plan paid $120,000 for the property and $5,000 in transaction costs. As of the recovery date, the property is valued at $110,000. To correct the transaction, Paulette Inc. repurchases the property for $120,000 with no reduction for the costs of sale and reimburses the plan for $5,000, the initial costs of sale. Paulette Inc. also must pay the plan the greater of the plan's lost earnings or the sponsor's investment return on these amounts. The determination of an independent fiduciary is not required because the applicant is correcting the transaction by selling the asset back to the party in interest.

Example 2. On February 1, 2006, Barry Corp. Pension Plan purchased from a party in interest a parcel of commercial real estate for $120,000, the fair market value, and incurred $5,000 in costs of sale. Barry Corp. Pension Plan initially uses the property as an office. At the same time that it is discovered that the original purchase was a prohibited transaction, the plan enters into a lucrative lease with an unrelated party for use of the property to begin January 1 of the following year. As of the recovery date, the property is valued at $150,000. Lost earnings are calculated through September 30, 2009, the anticipated recovery date, as $26,098.23 on the principal amount of $125,000 (purchase price plus transaction costs). The increase in the fair market value, $30,000, is greater than lost earnings or restoration of profits. Because the property is rapidly appreciating in value and because the plan official expects to realize significant rental income from the property, the plan official would like to correct by retaining the property rather than selling the asset back to the party in interest. The plan official must obtain a determination by an independent fiduciary that the plan will realize a greater benefit by retaining the asset than by selling the asset back to the party in interest. Because the original purchase price was the same as the fair market value and the increase in the fair market value is greater than any earnings or investment return on the original purchase price, the only cash payment to the Barry Corp. Pension Plan involved in this correction is the $5,000 in costs of sale, plus lost earnings.

A PTCE (see Q 19:50) provides relief from the penalty taxes (see Q 24:5) on the prohibited transaction (see Q 24:1) applicable to the above breach (see Q 19:38) when the purchase of an asset is at fair market value.

2. Sale of an asset (including real property) by a plan to a party in interest:

   a. *Description of transaction.* A plan sold an asset for cash to a party in interest with respect to the plan.

b. *Correction of transaction.* The plan may repurchase the asset from the party in interest at the lower of the price for which it sold the property or the fair market value of the property as of the recovery date plus restoration to the plan of the party in interest's net profits from owning the property, to the extent they exceed the plan's investment return from the proceeds of the sale. As an alternative, the plan may receive the principal amount plus the greater of (i) lost earnings or (ii) the restoration of profits, if any, provided an independent fiduciary determines that the plan will realize a greater benefit from this correction than it would from the repurchase of the asset.

c. *Documentation.* In addition to the required documentation, additional documents such as the appraiser's report, description of sale, and independent fiduciary's determination, if applicable, must also be submitted.

Example 3. My Son Jay, Inc. Pension Plan sold a parcel of unimproved real property to the plan sponsor who did not make any profit on the use of the property. As part of the correction, the plan official obtains an appraisal of the property reflecting the fair market value of the property as of the date of sale from a qualified, independent appraiser. The appraiser values the property at $130,000, although the plan sold the property to My Son Jay, Inc. for $120,000. The plan did not incur any transaction costs during the original sale. As of the recovery date, the appraiser values the property at $140,000. The plan corrects the transaction by repurchasing the property at the original sale price of $120,000, with the party in interest assuming the costs of the reversal of the sale transaction. The determination of an independent fiduciary is not required because the applicant is correcting the transaction by repurchasing the property from the party in interest.

Example 4. Assume the same facts as in Example 3, except that the appraiser values the property as of the recovery date at $100,000, and the plan fiduciaries believe that the property will continue to decrease in value based on environmental studies conducted in adjacent areas. Based on the determination of an independent fiduciary that the plan will realize a greater benefit by receiving the principal amount plus the greater of lost earnings or restoration of profits, the transaction is corrected by a cash settlement, rather than by repurchasing the asset.

A PTCE provides relief from the penalty taxes on the prohibited transaction applicable to the above breach when the sale of an asset is at fair market value.

3. Sale and leaseback of real property to employer:

a. *Description of transaction.* The plan sponsor sold a parcel of real property to the plan, which then was leased back to the sponsor, in a transaction that is not otherwise exempt.

b. *Correction of transaction.* The transaction must be corrected by the sale of the parcel of real property back to the plan sponsor or to a person who is not a party in interest with respect to the plan. The plan must receive the higher of (i) the fair market value of the asset at the time of resale, without a reduction for the costs of sale or (ii) the principal amount, plus the greater of (A) lost earnings on the principal amount or (B) the restoration or profits, if any. If the plan has not been receiving rent at fair market value, as determined by a qualified, independent appraiser, the sale price of the real property should not be based on the historic below-market rent that was paid to the plan.

c. *Documentation.* In addition to the required documentation, additional documents including the appraiser's report, a copy of the lease, and documentation of the plan's purchase and sale of the real property should also be submitted.

Example 5. Doris Inc. Retirement Plan purchased at fair market value (FMV) from Doris Inc., the plan sponsor, an office building that served as its primary business site. Simultaneously, Doris Inc. leased the building from the plan at below market rental rate. The plan official obtains from a qualified independent appraiser (see Q 24:21) an appraisal of the property reflecting the FMV of the property and rent. To correct the transaction, Doris Inc. purchases the property from the plan at the higher of the appraised value at the time of the resale or the original sales price and also pays the lost earnings. Because the rent paid to the plan was below the market rate, Doris Inc. must also make up the difference between the rent paid under the terms of the lease and the amount that should have been paid, plus lost earnings on this amount.

A PTCE provides relief from the penalty taxes on the prohibited transaction applicable to the above breach when the sale and leaseback are at fair market value.

4. Purchase of an asset (including real property) by a plan from a person who is not a party in interest with respect to the plan at a price more than fair market value:

a. *Description of transaction.* A plan acquired an asset from a person who is not a party in interest with respect to the plan, without determining the asset's fair market value. As a result, the plan paid more than it should have for the asset.

b. *Correction of transaction.* The principal amount is the difference between the actual purchase price and the asset's fair market value at the time of purchase. The plan must receive the principal amount plus the lost earnings.

c. *Documentation.* In addition to the required documentation, additional documents including the appraiser's report and description of purchase should also be submitted.

Example 6. Lisa L. Pension Plan bought unimproved land without obtaining a qualified, independent appraisal. Upon discovering that the purchase price was $10,000 more than the appraised fair market value, the plan official pays Lisa L. Pension Plan the principal amount of $10,000 plus lost earnings.

5. Sale of an asset (including real property) by a plan to a person who is not a party in interest with respect to the plan at a price less than fair market value:

   a. *Description of transaction.* A plan sold an asset to a person who is not a party in interest with respect to the plan, without determining the asset's fair market value. As a result, the plan received less than it should have from the sale.

   b. *Correction of transaction.* The principal amount is the amount by which the fair market value of the asset as of the recovery date exceeds the price at which the plan sold the property. The plan must receive the principal amount plus lost earnings.

   c. *Documentation.* In addition to the required documentation, additional documents including the appraiser's report and description of original sale should also be submitted.

   Example 7. Sue Corporation Profit Sharing Plan sold unimproved land without taking steps to ensure that the plan received fair market value. Upon discovering that the sale price was $10,000 less than the fair market value, the plan official pays the plan the principal amount of $10,000 plus lost earnings.

6. Holding of an illiquid asset previously purchased by a plan:

   a. *Description of transaction.* A plan is holding an asset previously purchased from (i) a party in interest for which relief was available under a statutory or administrative prohibited transaction exemption, (ii) a party in interest at no greater than the fair market value, (iii) a person who was not a party in interest in an acquisition in which a plan fiduciary fails to appropriately discharge his or her fiduciary duties, or (iv) a person who was not a party in interest in an acquisition in which a plan fiduciary appropriately discharged his or her fiduciary duties. Currently, a plan fiduciary determines that such asset is an illiquid asset because:

      (i) The asset failed to appreciate, failed to provide a reasonable rate of return, or caused a loss to the plan;

      (ii) The sale of the asset is in the best interest of the plan; and

      (iii) Following reasonable efforts to sell the asset to a person who is not a party in interest, the asset cannot immediately be sold for its original purchase price or its current fair market value, if greater. Examples of assets that may meet this definition include, but are not limited to, restricted and thinly traded stock, limited partnership interests, real estate, and collectibles.

   b. *Correction of transaction.* The transaction may be corrected by the sale of the asset to a party in interest, provided the plan receives the higher of:

      (i) The fair market value of the asset at the time of the resale, without a reduction for the cost of sale, or

(ii) The principal amount plus lost earnings. This correction provides relief for both the original purchase of the asset, if required, and the sale of the illiquid asset by the plan to a party in interest; relief from the prohibited transaction excise tax also is provided if the plan official satisfies the applicable conditions of the prohibited transaction class exemption relating to the VFC Program (see Q 19:50). For this transaction, the principal amount is the plan's original purchase price.

c. *Documentation.* In addition to the required documentation, the following documents should also be submitted:

(i) Documentation regarding the plan's original purchase of the asset;

(ii) The qualified independent appraiser's report addressing the fair market value of the asset purchased;

(iii) A narrative describing the plan's efforts to sell the asset to persons who are not parties in interest;

(iv) A statement from a plan official attesting that the asset failed to appreciate, the sale of the asset is in the best interest of the plan, the asset is an illiquid asset, and the plan made reasonable efforts to sell the asset to persons who are not parties in interest; and

(v) In the case of an illiquid asset that is real estate, a statement from a plan official attesting that no party in interest owns real estate that is contiguous to the plan's parcel of real estate.

Example 8. Allyson Inc. Pension Plan purchases undeveloped real property from a party in interest for $60,000 in June 2004. In April 2009, plan officials determine that the property is an illiquid asset. A qualified independent appraiser appraises the property at a current fair market value of $20,000. Allyson Inc., the plan sponsor, pays the plan the principal amount of $60,000 plus lost earnings, and plan officials transfer the property from the plan to the plan sponsor. The plan officials also comply with the applicable terms of the related exemption.

Example 9. Boca Mike, Inc. Retirement Plan purchases a limited partnership interest for $60,000 in July 2004 from an unrelated party after plan fiduciaries properly fulfill their fiduciary duties with respect to the purchase. In April 2009, plan officials determine that the interest is an illiquid asset because the interest has failed to generate a reasonable rate of return. A qualified independent appraiser appraises the interest at a current fair market value of $80,000. Boca Mike, Inc., the plan sponsor, pays the plan the fair market value of $80,000 without a reduction for the costs of the sale, which is greater than the principal amount plus lost earnings, and plan officials transfer the interest from the plan to the plan sponsor. The plan officials also comply with the applicable terms of the related exemption.

A PTCE provides relief from the penalty taxes on the prohibited transaction applicable to the above breach.

[DOL Notice, 71 Fed. Reg. 20,261 § 7.4 (Apr. 19, 2006)]

Q 19:48   How are certain improperly valued benefit payments corrected under the VFC Program?

The following rules apply to the correction of certain benefit payments without properly valuing plan assets on which payment is based.

1. *Description of transaction.* A defined contribution plan (see Q 2:2) pays benefits based on the value of the plan's assets. If one or more of the plan's assets are not valued at current value, the benefit payments are not correct. If the plan's assets are overvalued, the current benefit payments will be too high; and, if the plan's assets are undervalued, the current benefit payments will be too low.

2. *Correction of transaction.* Establish the correct value of the improperly valued asset for each plan year, starting with the first plan year in which the asset was improperly valued. Restore to the plan for distribution to the affected plan participants, or restore directly to the plan participants, the amount by which all affected participants were underpaid distributions to which they were entitled under the terms of the plan, plus lost earnings (see Q 19:41). The participant account balances must be adjusted accordingly, and amended annual returns/reports (Forms 5500; see Q 21:2) must be filed for the last three plan years or all plan years, if less.

3. *Documentation.* In addition to the required documentation, the following additional documents should also be submitted:

   a. A copy of the independent appraiser's report;

   b. A written statement confirming the date that the amended annual returns/reports were filed;

   c. Proof of payment to the plan and copies of the adjusted participant account balances if losses are restored; and

   d. Proof of payment if supplemental distributions are made.

   Example 1. On December 31, 2006, Rugman Irving Profit Sharing Plan purchased a 20-acre parcel of real property for $500,000, which represented a portion of the plan's assets. The plan has carried the property on its books at cost, rather than at fair market value (FMV). Emily, a participant, left the company on January 1, 2008, and received a distribution, which included her portion of the value of the property. Emily's account balance represented 2 percent of the plan's assets. A qualified independent appraiser has determined the FMV of the property as of December 31, 2007, was $400,000. Therefore, Emily was overpaid by $2,000 (($500,000 − $400,000) × 2%). The plan officials corrected the transaction by paying to the plan the $2,000 principal amount plus lost earnings. The plan administrator also filed amended Forms 5500 for the applicable plan years to reflect the proper values and will include the correct asset valuation in the 2009 Form 5500 when that form is filed.

   Example 2. Assume the same facts as in Example 1, except that the property had appreciated in value to $600,000 as of December 31, 2007. Emily would have been underpaid by $2,000. The correction consists of locating Emily and distributing to her the $2,000 principal amount plus lost earnings, as well as filing the amended Forms 5500.

[DOL Notice, 71 Fed. Reg. 20,261 § 7.5 (Apr. 19, 2006)]

Q 19:49   How are certain improper plan expenses corrected under the VFC Program?

The following rules apply to the correction of certain improper plan expenses.

1. Duplicative, excessive, or unnecessary compensation paid by a plan:

   a. *Description of transaction.* A plan used plan assets to pay compensation, including commissions or fees, to a service provider (such as an attorney, accountant, recordkeeper, actuary, financial advisor, or insurance agent), and the compensation was:

      (i) Excessive in amount for the services provided to the plan;

      (ii) Duplicative, in that a plan paid two or more providers for the same service; or

      (iii) Unnecessary for the operation of the plan, in that the services were not helpful and appropriate in carrying out the purposes for which the plan is maintained.

   b. *Correction of transaction.*

      (i) Restore to the plan the principal amount plus the greater of (A) lost earnings or (B) restoration of profits resulting from the use of the principal amount.

      (ii) For the transaction described in (a)(i) above, the principal amount is the difference between (A) the amount actually paid by the plan to the service provider and (B) the reasonable market value of such services.

      (iii) For the transactions described in (a)(ii) above, the principal amount is the difference between (A) the total amount of compensation paid to the service providers and (B) the least amount of compensation paid to one of the service providers for the duplicative services.

      (iv) For the transactions described in (a)(iii) above, the principal amount is the amount of compensation paid by the plan to the service provider for the unnecessary services.

   c. *Documentation.* In addition to the required documentation (see Q 19:42), additional documents including a written estimate of the market value of services and the cost of services should also be submitted.

      Example 1. Abby Inc. Pension Plan hired Debra, an investment advisor, who advised the plan's trustees about how to invest the plan's entire portfolio. In accordance with the plan document, the trustees instructed Debra to limit the plan's investments to equities and bonds. In exchange for her services, the Plan paid Debra 3 percent of the value of the portfolio's assets. If the trustees had inquired they would have learned that comparable investment advisors charged 1 percent of the value of the assets for the type of portfolio that the plan maintained. To correct the transaction, Abby Inc. Pension Plan must be paid the principal amount of 2 percent of the value of the plan's assets plus lost earnings.

Example 2. Annie Corp. Pension Plan paid John, a travel agent, to arrange a fishing trip for the plan's investment advisor as a way of rewarding the advisor because the plan's investment return for the year exceeded the plan's investment goals by 10 percent. An internal auditor discovered the charge on the plan's record books. To correct the transaction, Annie Corp. Pension Plan must be paid the principal amount, which is the total amount paid to John, plus the higher of lost earnings or restoration of profits.

2. Expenses improperly paid by a plan:

   a. *Description of transaction.* A plan used plan assets to pay expenses, including commissions or fees, that should have been paid by the plan sponsor to a service provider (such as an attorney, accountant, recordkeeper, actuary, financial advisor, or insurance agent) for:

      (i) Services provided in connection with the administration and maintenance of the plan (plan expenses) in circumstances where a plan provision requires that such plan expenses be paid by the plan sponsor, or

      (ii) Services provided in connection with the establishment, design, or termination of the plan (settlor expenses) that relate to the activities of the plan sponsor in its capacity as settlor.

   b. *Correction of transaction.*

      (i) Restore to the plan the principal amount, plus the greater of (A) lost earnings or (B) restoration of profits resulting from the use of the principal amount.

      (ii) The principal amount is the entire amount improperly paid by the plan to the service provider for expenses that should have been paid by the plan sponsor.

   c. *Documentation.* In addition to the required documentation, additional documents including copies of the plan's accounting records regarding the expenses paid by the plan to the service provider should also be submitted.

Example 3. Pointer John Inc., the plan sponsor of Pointer John Inc. Pension Plan, is considering amending its defined contribution plan to add a 5 percent matching contribution. The company hired an actuary to estimate the cost of providing this matching contribution over the next ten years. In exchange for these services, the plan paid the actuary $10,000. Several months after the actuary's bill has been paid, a plan official realizes that one of the company's employees erroneously paid the bill from the defined contribution plan's assets. The bill should have been paid by the company because the bill related to settlor expenses. To correct the transaction, the plan must be paid the principal amount ($10,000), plus lost earnings or restoration of profits.

A PTCE (see Q 19:50) provides relief from the penalty taxes (see Q 24:5) on the prohibited transaction (see Q 24:1) applicable to the above breach (see Q 19:38) relating to payment of settlor expenses.

3. Payment of dual compensation to a plan fiduciary:

    a. *Description of transaction.* A plan pays a fiduciary for services rendered to the plan when the fiduciary already receives full-time pay from an employer or an association of employers, whose employees are participants in the plan, or from an employee organization whose members are participants in the plan. The plan's payments to the plan fiduciary are not mere reimbursements of expenses properly and actually incurred by the fiduciary.

    b. *Correction of transaction.*

       (i) Restore to the plan the principal amount plus the greater of (A) lost earnings or (B) restoration of profits resulting from the fiduciary's use of the principal amount for the same period.

      (ii) The principal amount is the amount of compensation paid to the fiduciary by the plan.

    c. *Documentation.* In addition to the required documentation, additional documents including copies of the plan's accounting records regarding the compensation should also be submitted.

[DOL Notice, 71 Fed. Reg. 20,261 § 7.6 (Apr. 19, 2006)]

Q 19:50   Is there a prohibited-transaction class exemption (PTCE) in conjunction with the VFC Program?

A PTCE (see Q 24:26) provides relief from the penalties imposed (see Q 24:5) with respect to certain eligible transactions identified in the VFC Program. The PTCE does not provide relief for a transaction identified in the VFC Program that is not specifically described in the PTCE. The eligible transactions described in the PTCE that are provided relief are:

1. The failure to transmit participant contributions to a retirement plan within the required time frames (see Q 19:44) and/or the failure to transmit participant loan repayments to a retirement plan within a reasonable time after withholding or receipt by the employer;

2. A loan at fair market interest rate to a party in interest (see Q 24:3) with respect to a plan (see Q 19:45);

3. The purchase or sale of an asset (including real property) between a plan and a party in interest at fair market value (see Q 19:47);

4. The sale of real property to a plan by the employer and leaseback of the property to the employer, at fair market value and fair market rental value, respectively (see Q 19:47);

5. The purchase of an asset (including real property) by a plan where the asset has later been determined to be illiquid; and

6. Use of plan assets to pay expenses, including commissions or fees, to a service provider for services provided in connection with the establishment, design, or termination of the plan (settlor expenses).

In order to be eligible for the PTCE, the following conditions must be met:

1. With respect to a transaction in item 1 above, the contributions or payments must have been transmitted to the retirement plan not more than 180 days from the date the amounts were received by the employer;

2. With respect to the transactions in items 2, 3, 4, and 5 above, the plan assets involved in the transaction did not in the aggregate exceed 10 percent of the fair market value of all the assets of the plan;

3. The fair market value of any plan asset involved in a transaction described in item 3, 4, or 5 above was determined in accordance with the VFC Program (see Q 19:40);

4. The terms of a transaction described in item 2, 3, 4, 5, or 6 above were at least as favorable to the plan as the terms generally available in arm's-length transactions between unrelated parties;

5. With respect to any transaction described above, the transaction was not part of an agreement, arrangement, or understanding designed to benefit a party in interest;

6. With respect to any transaction described above, the applicant has not taken advantage of the relief provided by the VFC Program during the three-year period prior to submission of the current application;

7. With respect to a transaction involving a sale of an illiquid asset, the plan paid no brokerage fees or commissions in connection with the sale of the asset; and

8. With respect to any transaction described in 6 above, the amount of plan assets involved in the transaction or series of related transactions did not, in the aggregate, exceed the lesser of $10,000 or 5 percent of the fair market value of all of the assets of the plan at the time of the transaction.

Certain limited exceptions from condition 6 above apply to broker-dealers, service providers, non-fiduciaries, and individuals acting without knowledge.

The PTCE also requires that the applicant meet the requirements of the VFC Program (see Qs 19:40–19:43) and receives a no action letter (see Q 19:37) with respect to such transaction.

Furthermore, notice under the PTCE must be given to interested persons within 60 days following the date of submission of an application under the VFC Program. The notice must include an objective description of the transaction and the steps taken to correct it, and it must be written in a manner reasonably calculated to be understood by the average plan participant or beneficiary.

The notice requirement will not apply where: (1) the applicant has met all of the other VFC Program requirements; (2) the amount of the excise tax that otherwise would be imposed would be less than or equal to $100; (3) the amount of the excise tax that otherwise would be imposed was paid to the plan and allocated to the participants and beneficiaries in the same manner as provided under the plan with respect to plan earnings; and (4) the applicant provides a copy of a completed IRS Form 5330 (see Q 21:18) or written documentation containing the information required by IRS Form 5330 and proof of payment with the submission of the application for the sole purpose of determining whether the excise tax due is less than or equal to $100.

[PTCE 2002-51, 71 Fed. Reg. 20,135 (amended Apr. 19, 2006)]

Chapter 20

Operating the Plan

By clearly placing the responsibility for administering a qualified retirement plan with the plan administrator, ERISA gave that role considerable significance. This chapter explains who the plan administrator is, what the plan administrator's responsibilities are, and which records must be maintained.

Q 20:1 Who is the plan administrator?

Generally, the plan administrator is a person specifically designated by the qualified retirement plan as the administrator (1) by name, (2) by reference to the person or group holding a named position, (3) by reference to a procedure for designating an administrator, or (4) by reference to the person or group charged with the specific responsibilities of plan administrator. If no person or group is designated, the employer is the administrator (in the case of a qualified retirement plan maintained by a single employer). The employer's board of directors (in the case of a corporation) may authorize a person or group to fulfill the responsibilities of administrator. In any case, if a plan administrator cannot be determined, the plan administrator is the person or persons actually responsible for control, disposition, or management of the property received by the qualified retirement plan. [ERISA § 3(16)(A); I.R.C. § 414(g); Treas. Reg. § 1.414(g)-1]

The employer was held liable as plan administrator where the named administrator was inactive or was not solely responsible for plan administration, and where the employer retained some control over benefit decisions. [Rosen v. TRW, Inc., 979 F.2d 191 (11th Cir. 1992); Law v. Ernst & Young, 956 F.2d 364 (1st Cir. 1992)] In another case, the court held that despite contrary language in the plan booklet, the employer was a plan administrator because it exercised control over plan administration. [Hamilton v. Allen-Bradley Co., No. 99-11766 (11th Cir. 2001)] A company that acquired all of the shares of stock of another company became the successor plan administrator of the acquired company's profit sharing plan. [DOL/PWBA v. Syncom Techs., Office of Admin. Law Judges, No. 1998-RIS-28 (June 23, 2000)] However, where a retirement plan specifically designated an administrator, the employer, who was not the named administrator, could not be held liable for failure to provide requested information. [Jones v. Allied Signal Inc., 16 F.3d 141 (7th Cir. 1994); McKinsey v. Sentry Ins., No. 92-3194 (10th Cir. 1993)]

For more details and examples, see Qs 20:9 and 22:13.

Q 20:2   Can officers or owners of the company function as the plan administrator?

Yes. In small companies, a company officer or owner usually is designated as plan administrator (see Q 20:1). In large companies, three or more people (a committee) may be designated collectively as plan administrator.

Q 20:3   What are the basic responsibilities of the plan administrator?

The plan administrator (see Q 20:1) is responsible for managing the day-to-day affairs of the qualified retirement plan. Specifically, these responsibilities include the following:

1. Hiring attorneys, accountants, consultants, and, for certain qualified retirement plans, actuaries;
2. Determining eligibility for plan participation, vesting, and accrual of benefits;
3. Advising participants or beneficiaries of their rights and settlement options;
4. Ruling on claims for benefits;
5. Directing distribution of benefits;
6. Preparing reports for IRS, DOL, and PBGC (see chapter 21);
7. Preparing reports for participants and responding to information requests by participants (see Q 22:13); and
8. Keeping service records, benefit records, vesting records, and participant information.

IRS, DOL, and PBGC released guidance regarding the use of electronic technologies (e.g., telephonic response systems, computers, e-mail) for plan administration. These technologies may be used to satisfy various requirements for notice, election, consent, recordkeeping, and participant disclosure (see Q 20:4).

Generally, the decision of a plan administrator with discretionary authority to interpret a plan document may not be changed unless the interpretation is arbitrary or capricious. [Saffle v. Sierra Pac. Power Co. Bargaining Unit Long Term Disability Income Plan, 1996 U.S. App. LEXIS 13329 (9th Cir. 1996); Gallo v. Amoco Corp., No. 96-1518 (7th Cir. 1996)]

Q 20:4   May electronic media be used for plan administration?

A plan administrator (see Q 20:1) may use electronic media for transactions involving plan participants and beneficiaries. The use of electronic technologies will not affect the qualified status of a plan unless a specific provision of the Code sets forth rules regarding the media through which the transaction may be conducted. As a result of developments in electronic technologies, a variety of electronic media (e.g., e-mail, the Internet, intranet systems, and automated telephone systems) are now available for many plan transactions. IRS has provided guidance that electronic media may be used in the following transactions:

- Participant enrollment in a plan
- Designation of contribution rate
- Designation of beneficiaries (other than those requiring spousal consent; see Q 10:21)
- Direct rollover election (see Q 34:17)
- Investment allocation elections (see Q 23:15)
- Inquiries about account and general plan information

The above list is not exhaustive as to the types of transactions conducted through electronic media.

[IRS Notice 99-1, 1999-1 C.B. 269]

IRS has issued specific guidance for electronic technologies with respect to the direct rollover notice (see Q 20:20), participants' consent for distribution and the tax withholding notice (see Q 20:10).

IRS has issued regulations (see Q 20:5) setting forth rules that clarify and expand existing procedures regarding the use of electronic media to provide notices to plan participants and beneficiaries and to transmit elections or consents relating to retirement plans.

The regulations coordinate the existing notice and election rules under the Code and regulations relating to certain employee benefit arrangements with the requirements of the Electronic Signatures in Global and National Commerce Act (E-SIGN Act; see Q 20:7) and set forth the exclusive rules relating to the use of electronic media to satisfy any requirement under the Code that a communication to or from a participant, with respect to the participant's rights under the employee benefit arrangement, be in writing or in written form. The standards set forth in the regulations also function as a safe harbor when an electronic medium is used for any communication that is not required to be in writing.

The regulations apply to any notice, election, or similar communication provided to or made by a participant or beneficiary under a qualified retirement plan, 403(b) plan (see Q 35:1), SEP (see Q 32:1), SIMPLE plan (see Q 33:1), or Section 457 Plan.

The regulations do not apply to any notice, election, consent, or disclosure required under the provisions of Title I or IV of ERISA over which DOL or PBGC has interpretative and regulatory authority. For example, see Q 20:23 regarding the summary plan description (SPD) and Q 20:24 regarding the summary annual report (SAR) for which DOL has regulatory authority.

DOL has issued guidance for electronic technologies with respect to the furnishing of documents to participants (see Q 20:23) and the maintenance and storage of plan records (see Q 20:7).

PBGC has issued guidance with respect to methods of issuing certain notices, including electronic notices (see Q 20:23) and the rules for maintaining records by electronic means (see Q 20:7).

Q 20:5 Has IRS issued regulations regarding the use of electronic media?

Regulations issued by IRS provide rules relating to the use of electronic media to provide applicable notices to plan participants and beneficiaries and to transmit participant elections or consents relating to retirement plans. These new rules must be satisfied in order to use electronic media to provide an applicable notice or to transmit a participant election if the notice or election is required by IRS to be in writing or in written form.

An applicable notice that is provided using electronic media is treated as being provided in writing if the requirements contained in paragraph 1 below are satisfied and either the consent requirements contained in paragraph 2 below are satisfied or the requirements for exemption from the consent requirements contained in paragraph 3 below are satisfied. A participant election that is transmitted using electronic media is treated as being provided in writing if the requirements contained in paragraphs 1 and 4 below are satisfied.

1. The requirements related to the design of an electronic system are:
   a. The electronic system must take into account the content of a notice and must be reasonably designed to provide the information in the notice to a recipient in a manner that is no less understandable to the recipient than a written paper document.
   b. The electronic system must be designed to alert the recipient, at the time an applicable notice is provided, to the significance of the information in the notice and provide any instructions needed to access the notice, in a manner that is readily understandable.
2. The consent requirements are satisfied if the following conditions are met:
   a. *Consent.* The recipient must affirmatively consent to the delivery of the applicable notice using electronic media. This consent must be either:
      (i) Made electronically in a manner that reasonably demonstrates that the recipient can access the applicable notice in the electronic form that will be used to provide the notice, or
      (ii) Made using a written paper document, but only if the recipient confirms the consent electronically in a manner that reasonably demonstrates that the recipient can access the applicable notice in the electronic form that will be used to provide the notice.
   b. *Withdrawal of consent.* The consent requirement in a. above is not satisfied if the recipient withdraws consent before the applicable notice is delivered.

c. *Required disclosure statement.* The recipient, prior to consenting, must be provided with a clear and conspicuous statement containing the following disclosures:

(i) *Right to receive paper document.* The statement informs the recipient of any right to have the applicable notice be provided using a written paper document or other nonelectronic form; and the statement informs the recipient how, after having provided consent to receive the applicable notice electronically, the recipient may, upon request, obtain a paper copy of the applicable notice and whether any fee will be charged for such copy.

(ii) *Right to withdraw consent.* The statement informs the recipient of the right to withdraw consent to receive electronic delivery of an applicable notice on a prospective basis at any time and explains the procedures for withdrawing that consent and any conditions, consequences, or fees in the event of the withdrawal.

(iii) *Scope of the consent.* The statement informs the recipient whether the consent to receive electronic delivery of an applicable notice applies only to the particular transaction that gave rise to the applicable notice or to other identified transactions that may be provided or made available during the course of the parties' relationship.

(iv) *Description of the contact procedures.* The statement describes the procedures to update information needed to contact the recipient electronically.

(v) *Hardware or software requirements.* The statement describes the hardware and software requirements needed to access and retain the applicable notice.

d. *Post-consent change in hardware or software requirements.* If, after a recipient provides consent to receive electronic delivery, there is a change in the hardware or software requirements needed to access or retain the applicable notice and such change creates a material risk that the recipient will not be able to access or retain the applicable notice in electronic format:

(i) The recipient must receive a statement of the revised hardware or software requirements for access to and retention of the applicable notice, and the right to withdraw consent to receive electronic delivery without the imposition of any fees for the withdrawal and without the imposition of any condition or consequence that was not previously disclosed.

(ii) The recipient must reaffirm consent to receive electronic delivery.

e. *Prohibition on oral communications.* For purposes of these consent rules, neither an oral communication nor a recording of an oral communication is an electronic record.

3. *Exemption from consumer consent requirements.* The consent requirements contained in paragraph 2 above are not required if the following conditions are satisfied:

    a. *Effective ability to access.* The electronic medium used to provide an applicable notice must be a medium that the recipient has the effective ability to access, and

    b. *Free paper copy of applicable notice.* At the time the applicable notice is provided, the recipient must be advised that request may be made to receive the applicable notice in writing on paper at no charge; and, upon request, that applicable notice must be provided to the recipient at no charge.

4. *Special rules for participant elections.* The rules are satisfied if the following conditions are met:

    a. *Effective ability to access.* The electronic medium under a system used to make a participant election must be a medium that the individual who is eligible to make the election is effectively able to access.

    b. *Authentication.* The electronic system used in delivering a participant election is reasonably designed to preclude any person other than the appropriate individual from making the election.

    c. *Opportunity to review.* The electronic system provides the individual making the participant election with a reasonable opportunity to review, confirm, modify, or rescind the terms of the election before the election becomes effective.

    d. *Confirmation of action.* The person making the participant election, within a reasonable time, receives a confirmation of the effect of the election under the terms of the plan through either a written paper document or an electronic medium.

    e. *Participant elections, including spousal consents, that are required to be witnessed by a plan representative or a notary public.* In the case of a participant election that is required to be witnessed by a plan representative or a notary public (e.g., a spousal consent under Section 417; see Q 10:21), an electronic notarization acknowledging a signature (in accordance with Section 101(g) of E-SIGN and state law applicable to notary publics) will not be denied legal effect so long as the signature of the individual is witnessed in the physical presence of the plan representative or notary public.

[Treas. Reg. § 1.401(a)-21]

Example 1. Perrin, Inc. Profit Sharing Plan, a qualified retirement plan, permits participants to request benefit distributions from the plan on its Internet site. Under the plan's system for such transactions, a participant must enter the participant's account number and personal identification number (PIN), and this information must match the information in the plan's records in order for the transaction to proceed. If a participant requests a distribution from the plan's website, then, at the time of the request for distribution, a disclosure statement appears on the computer screen that explains that the participant can consent to receive the Section 402(f) Notice (see Q 20:20) electronically. In the disclosure statement, the plan provides information relating to the consent, including how to receive a paper copy of the notice, how to withdraw the consent, the hardware and software requirements, and the procedures for accessing the Section 402(f) Notice, which is in a file format from a specific spreadsheet program. After reviewing the disclosure statement, the participant consents to receive the Section 402(f) Notice via e-mail by selecting the consent button at the end of the disclosure statement. As a part of the consent procedure, the participant must demonstrate that the participant can access the spreadsheet program by answering a question from the spreadsheet program, which is in an attachment to an e-mail. Once the participant correctly answers the question, the Section 402(f) Notice is then delivered to the participant via e-mail. The delivery of the Section 402(f) Notice satisfies the consent requirements.

Example 2. Hildy Corp. has a qualified retirement plan that permits participants to request benefit distributions from the plan by e-mail. Under the plan's system for such transactions, a participant must enter the participant's account number and PIN and this information must match the information in the plan's records in order for the transaction to proceed. If a participant requests a distribution by e-mail, the plan administrator (see Q 20:1) provides the participant with a Section 411(a)(11) Notice (see Q 10:61) in an attachment to an e-mail. Hildy Corp.'s plan sends the e-mail with a request for a computer-generated notification that the message was received and opened. The e-mail instructs the participant to read the attachment for important information regarding the request for a distribution. In addition, the e-mail also provides that the participant may request the Section 411(a)(11) Notice on a written paper document and that, if the participant requests the notice on a written paper document, it will be provided at no charge. Hildy Corp.'s plan receives notification indicating that the e-mail was received and opened by the participant. The participant is effectively able to access the e-mail system used to make a participant election and consents to the distribution by e-mail. Within a reasonable period of time after the participant's consent to the distribution by e-mail, the plan administrator, by e-mail, sends confirmation of the terms (including the form) of the distribution to the participant and advises the participant that the participant may request the confirmation on a written paper document that will be provided at no charge. The delivery of the Section 411(a)(11) Notice and the transmission of the participant's consent to a distribution satisfy the requirements for exemption from consent and participant elections.

Example 3. Stan Inc. Retirement Plan, a qualified retirement plan, permits participants to request distributions by e-mail on the employer's e-mail system. Under this system, a participant must enter the participant's account number and PIN. This information must match that in the plan's records in order for the transaction to proceed. If a participant requests a distribution by e-mail, the plan administrator provides the participant with a Section 411(a)(11) Notice by e-mail. The e-mail also provides that the participant may request the Section 411(a)(11) Notice on a written paper document and that, if the participant requests the notice on a written paper document, it will be provided at no charge. Sue, a participant, requests a distribution and receives the Section 411(a)(11) Notice from the plan administrator by reply e-mail.

However, before Sue elects a distribution, she terminates employment. Following termination of employment, Sue no longer has access to the employer's e-mail system. The plan does not satisfy the participant election requirements because Sue is not effectively able to access the electronic medium used to make the participant election. The plan must provide Sue with the opportunity to transmit the participant election through another system that she is effectively able to access, such as the automated telephone systems.

Q 20:6   Which records should a plan administrator maintain?

The plan administrator (see Q 20:1) is required to maintain records relating to the operation of the qualified retirement plan that will provide in sufficient detail the necessary information from which required reports (to IRS, DOL, and PBGC) may be verified, explained, or clarified. These records must be kept available for at least six years after the filing date of the reports. [ERISA § 107] One court concluded that plan trustees do have the fiduciary duty to keep records that are sufficient to verify the information that the trustees provided on the plan's annual report (see Q 21:1), even though they have no obligation to furnish participants or beneficiaries with financial records containing an itemization of expenditures incurred in managing a plan. [Shaver v. Operating Eng'rs Local 428 Pension Trust Fund, 332 F.3d 1198 (9th Cir. 2003)]

The plan administrator must also maintain records to determine the benefits due or that may become due in order to be able to report that information to any plan participant who:

1. Requests the information (but not more than once in any 12-month period);
2. Terminates service with the company; or
3. Has a one-year break in service (but not more than once with respect to consecutive one-year breaks in service; see Q 5:10).

[ERISA § 209]

Thus, a plan administrator should maintain the following records:

Service. Precise records must be kept of time worked by all employees so that determinations of eligibility, vesting, or benefit accrual may be substantiated. These records have to be maintained for many years, even though a participant may have terminated employment and distributions may have been made.

Benefits. Detailed records should be maintained to project benefits for highly paid participants to ensure that their benefits do not exceed the limitations provided by law. These records should also be maintained if a qualified retirement plan provides for deferred payment of benefits. For example, a participant who terminates employment at a young age might not receive benefits until a later age.

Vesting. The vesting alternatives under ERISA and the Code require calculations under specific formulas. In some cases, participants may be under different vesting schedules, requiring meticulous administrative records. For example, if a vesting schedule is changed by amendment, certain participants may elect to remain under the old vesting schedule (see Q 9:7). See also Qs 26:30 through 26:34 regarding vesting under top-heavy plans, which may require dual record-keeping for vesting purposes.

Deductible employee contributions. Although no longer permitted, separate accounting for past contributions, if any, is still required (see Q 6:40).

Plan administrators are also required to retain all plan records necessary to support or validate PBGC premium payments. The records, which include actuarial calculations, must be kept for six years after the filing due date and must be submitted to PBGC no later than 45 days after written request for such records. [PBGC Reg. § 4007.10]

See Q 20:7 regarding the use of electronic media for plan records.

Q 20:7   May electronic media be used for the maintenance and retention of plan records?

Electronic media may be used for purposes of complying with the records maintenance and retention requirement of ERISA (see Q 20:6). Electronic media may be used if:

1. The electronic recordkeeping system has reasonable controls to ensure the integrity, accuracy, authenticity, and reliability of the records kept in electronic form;

2. The electronic records are maintained in reasonable order and in a safe and accessible place, and in such manner as they may be readily inspected or examined (e.g., the recordkeeping system should be capable of indexing, retaining, preserving, retrieving, and reproducing the electronic records);

3. The electronic records are readily convertible into legible and readable paper copy as may be needed to satisfy ERISA's reporting and disclosure requirements;

4. The electronic recordkeeping system is not subject, in whole or in part, to any agreement or restriction that would, directly or indirectly, compromise or limit a person's ability to comply with any of ERISA's reporting and disclosure requirements; and

5. Adequate records management practices are established and implemented (e.g., following procedures for labeling of electronically maintained or retained records, providing a secure storage environment, creating backup electronic copies and selecting an off-site storage location, observing a quality assurance program evidenced by regular evaluations of the electronic recordkeeping system including periodic checks of electronically maintained or retained records, and retaining paper copies of records that cannot be clearly, accurately, or completely transferred to an electronic recordkeeping system).

All electronic records must exhibit a high degree of legibility and readability when displayed on a video display terminal and when reproduced in paper form. Original paper records may be disposed of any time after they are transferred to an electronic recordkeeping system that complies with the requirements. However, such original records may not be discarded if the electronic record would not constitute a duplicate or substitute record under the terms of the plan and applicable federal or state law.

[DOL Reg. § 2520.107-1]

The Electronic Signatures in Global and National Commerce Act (E-SIGN Act) provides federal standards for using electronic signatures and electronic records. In general, the Act provides a means for expanded use of electronic signatures and records by benefit plans, to the extent the affected participants have access to electronic communications. [Pub. L. No. 106-229 (June 30, 2000)] The DOL final regulation is consistent with the goals of E-SIGN Act and is designed to facilitate voluntary use of electronic records while ensuring continued accuracy, integrity, and accessibility of employee benefit plan information and records required to be kept by law. [Preamble to DOL Reg. § 2520.107-1]

PBGC has issued regulations regarding the use of electronic media to satisfy the record and retention requirements. These regulations are substantially the same as the DOL regulations discussed above. [PBGC Reg. §§ 4000.51–4000.54]

Q 20:8 May the plan administrator rely on information gathered by those performing ministerial functions?

Yes, provided the plan administrator (see Q 20:1) has exercised prudence in selecting and retaining these people. The plan administrator should consider whether those gathering information are competent, honest, and responsible. [DOL Reg. § 2509.75-8, FR-11]

Q 20:9 What penalty is imposed for failure to comply with recordkeeping requirements and requests for information?

If a plan administrator (see Q 20:1) does not maintain records necessary to make required benefit status reports to participants (see Q 20:6), DOL may impose a penalty of $10 ($11 after adjustment for inflation) for each affected participant unless there is reasonable cause for the failure. [ERISA § 209(b); DOL Reg. § 2575.209b-1] Furthermore, a plan administrator who fails to comply with a request for information that is required to be furnished to a participant may be liable for penalties of up to $100 ($110 after adjustment for inflation) a day from the date of failure to comply (see Q 20:23). [ERISA § 502(c)(1)(B); DOL Reg. § 2575.502c-1]

In one case, where the plan administrator failed to timely respond to a request by a participant's surviving spouse for certain documents, including the plan document, to determine his status as a plan beneficiary, the court assessed a penalty of $35,050 ($50 × 701 days). The fact that the plan merged with another plan and its records were in disarray was determined to be an insufficient reason for the delay. [Lowe v. McGraw-Hill Cos., 2004 WL 502201 (7th Cir. 2004)] In another case, the imposition of penalties was not an abuse of discretion where the court stated that the requirement to supply plan documents upon request to plan participants applied to current and former employees who were, or could become, eligible to receive a benefit. This group included former employees with a colorable claim that they would prevail in a suit for benefits. Factors such as the bad faith or intentional conduct of the plan administrator, the length of the delay, the number of requests made, the documents withheld, and the prejudice to the participant could be considered to determine whether to impose a penalty. [Gorini v. AMP Inc., Nos. 02-3431, 02-3900 (3d Cir. 2004)] The court in another case, assessed a penalty of $100 per day per document, but only for one participant, for failure to supply requested information to over 70 participants; the penalty was divided among all such participants. The district court's basis for its ruling that there had been no showing of prejudice or bad faith was not an abuse of discretion. [Bartling v. Fruehauf Corp, 29 F.3d 1062 (6th Cir. 1994)] In another case, the court held that a plan administrator who failed to provide plan documents in a timely manner to a participant could be assessed penalties even though the participant was not prejudiced by the delay and the delay was not due to the plan administrator's bad faith if the cause of the failure was not beyond the control of the plan administrator. [Glocker v. W.R. Grace & Co., 1995 U.S. App. LEXIS 33874 (4th Cir. 1995)]

However, in another case, although the court agreed that the participant was entitled to receive a detailed breakdown of his monthly benefit, it did not penalize the plan administrator for failing to provide such information because the court had no reliable evidence that the administrator knew it was obligated to provide this data. [Maiuro v. Federal Express Corp., No. 92-4518 (D.N.J. 1994)] In yet another case, a court's failure to assess a penalty against a government agency for failing to comply with a request for a plan document was not considered an abuse of power because an award of monetary damages is a matter within the court's discretion. [Hennessy v. Federal Deposit Ins. Corp., 58 F.3d 908 (3d Cir. 1995)]

For more details, see Q 22:13.

Q 20:10   Is withholding required on the distribution of benefits from a retirement plan?

An eligible rollover distribution (see Q 34:8) is subject to automatic 20 percent withholding unless the distribution is transferred by a direct rollover (see Q 34:17) to an eligible retirement plan (see Q 34:16) that permits the acceptance of rollover distributions. [I.R.C. §§ 401(a)(31), 3405(c); Treas. Reg. §§ 1.401(a)(31)-1, Q&A-1(b)(1), 1.402(c)-2, Q&A-1(b)(3), 31.3405(c)-1, Q&A-1(a), Q&A-8]

Distributions other than eligible rollover distributions are subject to elective withholding provisions and are not subject to the mandatory 20 percent withholding. Form W-4P, Withholding Certificate for Pension or Annuity Payments, is used to inform payors whether income tax is to be withheld and on what basis. The elective withholding rules apply to both periodic payments (e.g., annuities) and nonperiodic payments (e.g., lump-sum distributions) that are not eligible rollover distributions. The payor of a distribution is required to give notice to a payee of the payee's right not to have tax withheld. Special rules apply to notice given through electronic media (see Qs 20:4, 20:5). The option to elect out of withholding is not available if the payment is delivered outside the United States or its possessions, unless the payee certifies to the payor that the payee is not (1) a U.S. citizen or resident alien or (2) a tax-avoiding expatriate under Section 877. [I.R.C. §§ 3405(a), 3405(b), 3405(e); Treas. Reg. §§ 31.3405(c)-1, Q&A-1(a), 35.3405-1, Q&As d-35, d-36; IRS Notice 87-7, 1987-1 C.B. 420]

However, IRS has ruled that plan administrators (see Q 20:1) are not required to withhold tax on installment distributions to nonresident aliens to the extent that the distributions are in substantially equal payments if the nonresident alien performed services for the employer outside the United States and at least 90 percent of the plan's participants are citizens of the United States. [I.R.C. §§ 871(f), 1441(c)(7); Priv. Ltr. Rul. 9537028]

Because required minimum distributions (RMDs; see Q 11:1) are generally not eligible rollover distributions, they are not subject to the mandatory 20 percent withholding rules. Accordingly, because RMDs for 2009 were not required to be paid from defined contribution plans (see Q 11:1), any 2009 RMDs paid from a defined contribution plan on or before December 31, 2009 were subject to the optional withholding rules. However, the 2009 RMDs paid between January 1, 2010 and April 1, 2010 were subject to the mandatory 20 percent withholding rules if they otherwise qualified as eligible rollover distributions. [*Employee Plans News*, Vol. 9/Winter 2010]

The withholding requirements for distributions from qualified retirement plans to nonresident aliens follow the rules under Section 1441 that generally require withholding at a 30 percent flat rate, rather than Section 3405 that allows for graduated withholding rates and governs withholding from pension distributions to U.S. citizens. [Treas. Reg. §§ 1.1441-0–1.1441-4; Preamble to Treas. Reg. §§ 1.1441-0–1.1441-4; IRS Notice 99-25, 1999-1 C.B. 1070] IRS has issued guidance with respect to withholding in connection with payments from a defined benefit plan to nonresident aliens. The IRS guidance provides detailed rules for determining the U.S. source portion of a pension distribution from a defined benefit plan in cases where the retiree has performed services both in the United States and abroad during his or her employment. [Rev. Proc. 2004-37, 2004-1 C.B. 1099]

In addition to withholding, plan administrators are also subject to record-keeping and reporting responsibilities (see Q 21:19).

Q 20:11   Does 20 percent automatic withholding apply if a participant elects to receive only a portion of the distribution?

If a participant elects to have a portion of the distribution paid to an eligible retirement plan (see Q 34:16) in a direct rollover (see Q 34:17) and to receive the remainder of the distribution, the 20 percent withholding requirement (see Q 20:10) applies only to the portion of the distribution that the participant receives. There is no 20 percent withholding for the portion of the distribution that is paid to an eligible retirement plan in a direct rollover. [Treas. Reg. § 31.3405(c)-1, Q&A-6]

Q 20:12 May a participant elect to have more than 20 percent withheld from an eligible rollover distribution?

Yes. A participant and a plan administrator (see Q 20:1) may enter into an agreement to withhold more than 20 percent of the eligible rollover distribution (see Qs 20:6, 34:8). [I.R.C. § 3402(p); Treas. Reg. § 31.3405(c)-1, Q&A-3]

Q 20:13 Is there any liability for failure to withhold income taxes?

Yes. Generally, the plan administrator (see Q 20:1) or payor will be liable for the tax that should have been withheld as well as any penalties if a taxable distribution is made from a retirement plan and the recipient of the distribution does not elect out of the withholding or if automatic withholding applies (see Q 20:10). [I.R.C. §§ 3405(d), 6672(a); Temp. Treas. Reg. § 35.3405-1T, Q&A G-2, Q&A G-20] With respect to an eligible rollover distribution, if the plan administrator reasonably relies on information provided by the participant, the plan administrator will not be liable for any taxes that should have been withheld solely because the distribution is paid to a plan that is not an eligible retirement plan (see Q 34:16). Although the plan administrator is not required to verify independently the accuracy of information provided by the distributee, the plan administrator's reliance on the information furnished must be reasonable. [Treas. Reg. § 31.3405(c)-1, Q&A-7]

Q 20:14 Which types of retirement plans are subject to the withholding rules on distributions?

All qualified and nonqualified retirement plans—including individual retirement accounts (IRAs; see Q 30:1) of any type—are subject to the general withholding rules. Only an eligible rollover distribution (see Q 34:8) is subject to automatic 20 percent withholding (see Q 20:10). [I.R.C. § 3405]

Q 20:15 If property other than cash is distributed, how is withholding accomplished?

The plan administrator (see Q 20:1) or payor must withhold on distributions of property even if this requires selling all or part of the property. However, the participant may remit to the administrator sufficient cash to satisfy the withholding obligation. [Treas. Reg. § 31.3405(c)-1, Q&A-9; Temp. Treas. Reg. § 35.3405-1T, Q&A F-2, Q&A F-3]

Q 20:16   Is there an exception from withholding for distributions of employer securities?

Yes. The maximum amount withheld on any distribution (including any eligible rollover distribution; see Q 34:8) may not exceed the sum of the cash and the fair market value of other property (excluding employer securities and plan loan offset amounts; see Q 14:11) received in the distribution. Thus, although employer securities must be included in the aggregate amount that is subject to 20 percent withholding, the total amount required to be withheld from an eligible rollover distribution is limited to the sum of cash and the fair market value of property received by the participant, excluding any amount of the distribution that is an employer security. If the distribution consists solely of employer securities or of employer securities and cash (not in excess of $200) in lieu of fractional shares, no amount is required to be withheld. [I.R.C. §§ 402(e)(4)(E), 3405(e)(8); Treas. Reg. § 31.3405(c)-1, Q&A-11]

Q 20:17   If the amount of an eligible rollover distribution is less than $200, must tax be withheld?

No. If the amount of the eligible rollover distribution (see Q 34:8) is less than $200, the plan administrator (see Q 20:1) need not withhold tax. However, all eligible rollover distributions received within one taxable year of the distributee under the same plan must be aggregated for purposes of determining whether the $200 floor is reached. If the plan administrator (or payor) does not know at the time of the first distribution (that is less than $200) whether there will be additional eligible rollover distributions during the year for which aggregation is required, the plan administrator need not withhold from the first distribution. If distributions are made within one taxable year under more than one plan of an employer, the plan administrator (or payor) may, but need not, aggregate distributions for purposes of determining whether the $200 floor is reached. However, once the $200 floor is reached, the sum of all payments during the year must be used to determine the amount required to be withheld. [Treas. Reg. § 31.3405(c)-1, Q&A-14]

Q 20:18   How are participant loans treated for the withholding rules?

For details, see Q 14:11.

Q 20:19   When did the automatic withholding rules become effective?

The automatic withholding rules are applicable to eligible rollover distributions (see Q 34:8) made after December 31, 1992, even if the event giving rise to the distribution occurred before January 1, 1993, or even if the eligible rollover distribution is part of a series of payments that began before January 1, 1993. [Treas. Reg. §§ 1.401(a)(31)-1, Q&A-1(c), 1.402(c)-2, Q&A-1(c), 31.3405(c)-1, Q&A-1(c)]

Example. Richie terminated employment with The Greatest Helaine Corporation in 1992 but does not receive his pension plan benefits until 2011. Even though Richie's employment was terminated in 1992 (before the rules became effective), the distribution of his benefits in 2011 is subject to the automatic withholding rules.

Q 20:20 Must a recipient receive an explanation of the tax effects of a distribution from a qualified retirement plan?

The plan administrator (see Q 20:1) is required, within a reasonable time before making an eligible rollover distribution (see Q 34:8) to provide the distributee with a written explanation of the direct rollover provisions and other special tax rules. This explanation is known as the Section 402(f) Notice. The posting of a Section 402(f) Notice does not satisfy this requirement. The notice must be provided, individually, to each distributee (see Q 34:29).

A participant's consent to a distribution is not valid unless the participant receives a notice of the participant's rights under the plan no more than 180 days and no less than 30 days prior to the annuity starting date (see Q 10:3). For years that began before 2007, the 180-day period was 90 days. [ERISA § 205(c)(7)(A); IRS Notice 2007-7, § VIII, 2007-1 C.B. 395]. However, a participant may waive the 30-day requirement and, therefore, need not wait 30 days after receipt of the Section 402(f) Notice for a direct rollover (see Q 34:17) to be made if:

1. The participant is given the opportunity to consider the decision of whether or not to elect a direct rollover for at least 30 days after the notice is provided; and

2. The plan administrator provides information to the participant clearly indicating that the participant has a right to this period for making the decision.

IRS has provided a model amendment that plan sponsors may adopt in order to allow participants to waive the 30-day notice requirement. The waiver does not apply to the qualified joint and survivor annuity (QJSA) notice (see Q 10:29). Therefore, waivers are only available to profit sharing, stock bonus, and 401(k) plans that are exempt from the automatic survivor benefit requirements (see Q 10:6). However, see Q 10:20 regarding the waiver of the 30-day minimum waiting period with respect to the QJSA notice.

[I.R.C. § 402(f); Treas. Reg. §§ 1.401(a)(31)-1, Q&A-1(b)(2), 1.402(f)-1, Q&A-1 through Q&A-4; Rev. Proc. 93-47, 1993-2 C.B. 578; IRS Notice 93-26, 1993-1 C.B. 308]

See Q 10:20 regarding the timing of the maximum QJSA explanation period and Q 10:57 regarding the timing of the notice with respect to the right to defer the receipt of benefits.

There is a penalty of $10 for each recipient who is not given timely notice unless there is reasonable cause for the failure. [I.R.C. § 6652(i)]

In one case, the court held that the administrator had a duty to provide tax information to the participant, but that the administrator did not have a duty to ensure that the participant actually read the material and was not required to give advice regarding every possible investment option and tax consequence. [Bouteiller v. Vulcan Iron Works, Inc, 834 F. Supp. 207 (E.D. Mich. 1993)] Courts have held that a participant could not recover money damages for failure of the plan administrator to give notice of the rollover option upon distribution of the participant's benefits, even though the participant, because he failed to roll over the distribution, was taxed on the distribution. [Fraser v. Lintas: Campbell-Ewald, 56 F.3d 722 (6th Cir. 1995); Novak v. Andersen Corp, 962 F.2d 757 (8th Cir. 1992)]

Plan administrators can satisfy the notice requirement by providing each recipient of an eligible rollover distribution with a copy of one of the model IRS notices. IRS provides two safe harbor notices that simplify the presentation and description of the participant's options upon receiving an eligible rollover distribution. One notice is intended for distributions of non-Roth amounts, and the other is intended solely for distributions of Roth amounts. If a distribution includes both Roth and non-Roth amounts, both notices must be provided. The model notices reflect all provisions of current law, including EGTRRA (see Q 1:21), PPA (see Q 1:33), TIPRA (see Q 1:31), HEART (see Q 1:35), and WRERA (see Q 1:36).

Although the safe harbor notices may be distributed on a word-for-word basis, employers may customize the notice by deleting sections that do not apply to their plans. Alternatively, employers or service providers can develop their own Section 402(f) notices if they choose to do so, as long as the legal requirements are met. It is expected that IRS will publish a Spanish translation of the safe harbor notices. The required notification regarding the automatic rollover provisions (see Qs 34:18, 34:19) is also incorporated in the safe harbor notices.

The complete model notices are lengthy, and the following is the introduction and general information portion of the notice for non-Roth amounts:

YOUR ROLLOVER OPTIONS

You are receiving this notice because all or a portion of a payment you are receiving from the [INSERT NAME OF PLAN] (the "Plan") is eligible to be rolled over to an IRA or an employer plan. This notice is intended to help you decide whether to do such a rollover.

This notice describes the rollover rules that apply to payments from the Plan that are not from a designated Roth account (a type of account with special tax rules in some employer plans). If you also receive a payment from a designated Roth account in the Plan, you will be provided a different notice for that payment, and the Plan administrator or the payor will tell you the amount that is being paid from each account.

Rules that apply to most payments from a plan are described in the "General Information About Rollovers" section. Special rules that only apply in certain circumstances are described in the "Special Rules and Options" section.

GENERAL INFORMATION ABOUT ROLLOVERS

How can a rollover affect my taxes?

You will be taxed on a payment from the Plan if you do not roll it over. If you are under age 59½ and do not do a rollover, you will also have to pay a 10% additional income tax on early distributions (unless an exception applies). However, if you do a rollover, you will not have to pay tax until you receive payments later and the 10% additional income tax will not apply if those payments are made after you are age 59½ (or if an exception applies).

Where may I roll over the payment?

You may roll over the payment to either an IRA (an individual retirement account or individual retirement annuity) or an employer plan (a tax-qualified plan, Section 403(b) plan, or governmental Section 457(b) plan) that will accept the rollover. The rules of the IRA or employer plan that holds the rollover will determine your investment options, fees, and rights to payment from the IRA or employer plan (for example, no spousal consent rules apply to IRAs and IRAs may not provide loans). Further, the amount rolled over will become subject to the tax rules that apply to the IRA or employer plan.

How do I do a rollover?

There are two ways to do a rollover. You can do either a direct rollover or a 60 day rollover.

If you do a direct rollover, the Plan will make the payment directly to your IRA or an employer plan. You should contact the IRA sponsor or the administrator of the employer plan for information on how to do a direct rollover.

If you do not do a direct rollover, you may still do a rollover by making a deposit into an IRA or eligible employer plan that will accept it. You will have 60 days after you receive the payment to make the deposit. If you do not do a direct rollover, the Plan is required to withhold 20% of the payment for federal income taxes (up to the amount of cash and property received other than employer stock). This means that, in order to roll over the entire payment in a 60 day rollover, you must use other funds to make up for the 20% withheld. If you do not roll over the entire amount of the payment, the portion not rolled over will be taxed and will be subject to the 10% additional income tax on early distributions if you are under age 59½ (unless an exception applies).

How much may I roll over?

If you wish to do a rollover, you may roll over all or part of the amount eligible for rollover. Any payment from the Plan is eligible for rollover, except:

- Certain payments spread over a period of at least 10 years or over your life or life expectancy (or the lives or joint life expectancy of you and your beneficiary)
- Required minimum distributions after age 70$\frac{1}{2}$ (or after death)
- Hardship distributions
- ESOP dividends
- Corrective distributions of contributions that exceed tax law limitations
- Loans treated as deemed distributions (for example, loans in default due to missed payments before your employment ends)
- Cost of life insurance paid by the Plan
- Contributions made under special automatic enrollment rules that are withdrawn pursuant to your request within 90 days of enrollment
- Amounts treated as distributed because of a prohibited allocation of S corporation stock under an ESOP (also, there will generally be adverse tax consequences if you roll over a distribution of S corporation stock to an IRA).

The Plan administrator or the payor can tell you what portion of a payment is eligible for rollover.

If I don't do a rollover, will I have to pay the 10% additional income tax on early distributions?

If you are under age 59$\frac{1}{2}$, you will have to pay the 10% additional income tax on early distributions for any payment from the Plan (including amounts withheld for income tax) that you do not roll over, unless one of the exceptions listed below applies. This tax is in addition to the regular income tax on the payment not rolled over.

The 10% additional income tax does not apply to the following payments from the Plan:

- Payments made after you separate from service if you will be at least age 55 in the year of the separation
- Payments that start after you separate from service if paid at least annually in equal or close to equal amounts over your life or life expectancy (or the lives or joint life expectancy of you and your beneficiary)
- Payments from a governmental defined benefit pension plan made after you separate from service if you are a public safety employee and you are at least age 50 in the year of the separation
- Payments made due to disability
- Payments after your death
- Payments of ESOP dividends
- Corrective distributions of contributions that exceed tax law limitations

- Cost of life insurance paid by the Plan
- Contributions made under special automatic enrollment rules that are withdrawn pursuant to your request within 90 days of enrollment
- Payments made directly to the government to satisfy a federal tax levy
- Payments made under a qualified domestic relations order (QDRO)
- Payments up to the amount of your deductible medical expenses
- Certain payments made while you are on active duty if you were a member of a reserve component called to duty after September 11, 2001 for more than 179 days
- Payments of certain automatic enrollment contributions requested to be withdrawn within 90 days of the first contribution.

If I do a rollover to an IRA, will the 10% additional income tax apply to early distributions from the IRA?

If you receive a payment from an IRA when you are under age 59½, you will have to pay the 10% additional income tax on early distributions from the IRA, unless an exception applies. In general, the exceptions to the 10% additional income tax for early distributions from an IRA are the same as the exceptions listed above for early distributions from a plan. However, there are a few differences for payments from an IRA, including:

- There is no exception for payments after separation from service that are made after age 55.
- The exception for qualified domestic relations orders (QDROs) does not apply (although a special rule applies under which, as part of a divorce or separation agreement, a tax-free transfer may be made directly to an IRA of a spouse or former spouse).
- The exception for payments made at least annually in equal or close to equal amounts over a specified period applies without regard to whether you have had a separation from service.
- There are additional exceptions for (1) payments for qualified higher education expenses, (2) payments up to $10,000 used in a qualified first time home purchase, and (3) payments after you have received unemployment compensation for 12 consecutive weeks (or would have been eligible to receive unemployment compensation but for self employed status).

Will I owe State income taxes?

This notice does not describe any State or local income tax rules (including withholding rules).

[Notice 2009-68, 2009-39 I.R.B. 423]

IRS has issued regulations (see Q 20:5) setting forth rules that clarify existing procedures regarding the use of electronic media to provide notices to plan participants and includes the Section 402(f) Notice.

If a benefit is immediately distributable, a participant must be informed of the right, if any, to defer receipt of the distribution and of the consequences of failing to defer. [IRS Notice 2007-7, § VIII, 2007-1 C.B. 395; Prop. Treas. Reg. § 1.411-(a)11] The safe harbor notices do not include this information, and it is recommended that service providers customize the Section 402(f) safe harbor notice by adding this information to that notice. See Q 10:61 for details.

See chapter 34 for details on rollovers.

Q 20:21   Must a separate Section 402(f) Notice be given for each distribution in a series of periodic payments?

No. The plan administrator (see Q 20:1) can satisfy the Section 402(f) Notice requirement (see Q 20:20) with respect to each payment in the series by providing the notice to the distributee prior to the first payment, and then providing the notice at least once annually for as long as the payments continue. [Treas. Reg. § 1.402(f)-1, Q&A-3]

Q 20:22   Must notice be given for a blackout period?

One of the provisions of the Sarbanes-Oxley Act of 2002 (see Q 1:24) requires plan administrators (see Q 20:1) to provide at least 30 days advance notice of blackout periods to participants and beneficiaries under individual account plans (see Q 2:2).

"Blackout period" means any period for which any ability of participants or beneficiaries under the plan, which is otherwise available under the terms of such plan, to direct or diversify assets credited to their accounts, to obtain loans from the plan, or to obtain distributions from the plan is temporarily suspended, limited, or restricted if such suspension, limitation, or restriction is for any period of more than three consecutive business days. A blackout period does not include a suspension, limitation, or restriction which:

1. Occurs by reason of the application of the securities laws of the Securities and Exchange Act of 1934;
2. Is a regularly scheduled suspension, limitation, or restriction under the plan (or change thereto), provided that such suspension, limitation, or restriction (or change) has been disclosed to affected plan participants and beneficiaries;
3. Occurs by reason of a QDRO (see Q 36:1); or
4. Occurs by reason of an act or a failure to act on the part of an individual participant or by reason of an action or claim by a party unrelated to the plan involving the account of an individual participant.

The notice must be written in a manner calculated to be understood by the average plan participant and must include:

1. The reason for the blackout period;
2. A description of the rights otherwise available to participants and beneficiaries under the plan that will be temporarily suspended, limited, or restricted by the blackout period (e.g., the right to direct or diversify assets

in individual accounts, to obtain loans from the plan, to obtain distributions from the plan), including identification of any investments subject to the blackout period;

3. The length of the blackout period by reference to:

   a. The expected beginning and ending dates of the blackout period, or

   b. The calendar week during which the blackout period is expected to begin and end;

4. In the case of investments affected, a statement that the participants or beneficiaries should evaluate the appropriateness of their current investment decisions in light of their inability to direct or diversify assets in their accounts during the blackout period;

5. In any case in which the notice is not furnished at least 30 days in advance of the last date on which affected participants and beneficiaries could exercise affected rights immediately before the commencement of the blackout period:

   a. statement that federal law generally requires that notice be furnished to affected participants and beneficiaries at least 30 days in advance of the last date on which participants and beneficiaries could exercise the affected rights immediately before the commencement of a blackout, and

   b. An explanation of the reasons why at least 30 days advance notice could not be furnished; and

6. The name, address, and telephone number of the plan administrator or other contact responsible for answering questions about the blackout period.

The notice must be furnished to all affected participants and beneficiaries at least 30 days, but not more than 60 days, in advance of the last date on which such participants and beneficiaries could exercise the affected rights immediately before the commencement of any blackout period. The requirement to give at least 30 days advance notice will not apply in any case in which:

1. A deferral of the blackout period in order to comply with the 30-day requirement would result in a plan violation under ERISA Section 404(a)(1)(A) or (B);

2. The inability to provide the advance notice of a blackout period is due to events that were unforeseeable or circumstances beyond the reasonable control of the plan administrator; or

3. The blackout period applies only to one or more participants or beneficiaries solely in connection with their becoming, or ceasing to be, participants or beneficiaries of the plan as a result of a merger, acquisition, divestiture, or similar transaction involving the plan or plan sponsor.

In any case in which notice cannot be timely given, the administrator must furnish the notice to all affected participants and beneficiaries as soon as reasonably possible under the circumstances, unless such notice in advance of the termination of the blackout period is impracticable.

The regulations also provide a model notice that may be used to assist plan administrators in discharging their notice obligation.

[ERISA § 101(i); DOL Reg. § 2520.101-3]

A plan administrator who fails to comply with the blackout notice rules may be liable for penalties of up to $100 a day. [ERISA § 502(c)(7); DOL Reg. § 2560.502c-7]

A blackout notice is not required for one-participant plans (including plans that cover the spouse of the owner) and plans that cover only partners (or only partners and their spouses). [ERISA § 101(i)]

Q 20:23 What documents can a participant obtain?

A participant is entitled to obtain, without charge and without request, a summary plan description (SPD; see Q 22:1), a summary of material modifications (see Q 22:8) to the plan, and a summary annual report (SAR; see Q 20:24). Upon request, other documents must be furnished to a participant by the plan administrator (see Q 20:1). [ERISA § 104(b)(4)] One court held that participants were entitled to receive copies of a plan's actuarial reports because they were necessary for the operation of a pension plan and these were other instruments under which the plan was established or operated. [Bartling v. Fruehauf Corp, 29 F.3d 1062 (6th Cir. 1994)] Another court held that a list of plan participants was not an instrument under which the plan was operated; and, therefore, the plan administrator was not required to provide the list to a committee representing retired participants because participants only have a right to obtain documents that provide information regarding plan benefits. [Hughes Salaried Retirees Action Comm. v. Administrator of the Hughes Non-Bargaining Ret. Plan, 72 F.3d 686 (9th Cir. 1995)] One court concluded that plan trustees have no obligation to furnish participants or beneficiaries with financial records containing an itemization of expenditures incurred in managing a plan; however, the trustees do have the fiduciary duty to keep records that are sufficient to verify the information that the trustees provided on the plan's annual report (see Q 21:1). [Shaver v. Operating Eng'rs Local 428 Pension Trust Fund, 332 F.3d 1198 (9th Cir. 2003)] Since former employees are not participants, former employees are not entitled to plan documents unless they have an expectation of returning to covered employment or have a colorable claim for benefits. [Szoke v. Deloitte & Touche L.L.P., 1995 U.S. Dist. LEXIS 2517 (S.D.N.Y. 1995)] In another case, a plan administrator was not liable for penalties for failure to timely respond to a participant's information request because the request had not been sufficiently specific to notify the administrator of the nature of the information sought. [Kollman v. Hewitt Assocs., LLC, No. 05-5018, No. 05-5207, No. 06-1558 (3d Cir. 2007)]

The plan administrator of a single-employer plan is required to provide to plan participants and beneficiaries written notice of limitations on benefits and benefit accruals within 30 days after the plan has become subject to certain funding based restrictions (see Q 8:6) and may be liable for penalties of up to $1,000 a day for each violation. [ERISA §§ 101(j), 502(c)(4)]

In addition, for plan years beginning after December 31, 2007, each administrator of a multiemployer plan (see Q 29:2) is required to furnish upon request (1) a copy of any periodic actuarial report received by the plan for any plan year, (2) a copy of any quarterly, semi-annual, or annual financial report prepared for the plan by any plan investment manager, advisor, or other fiduciary, and (3) a copy of an application filed with IRS requesting an extension of the amortization periods (see Q 8:30). DOL may assess a civil penalty of not more than $1,000 a day for each violation. [ERISA §§ 101(k), 502(c)(4); DOL Reg. § 2520.101-6]

For more details and other examples, see Q 22:13.

The plan administrator may furnish the required documents through electronic media if:

1. Appropriate and necessary measures are taken to ensure that the system for furnishing documents:
   a. Results in actual receipt by participants of transmitted information and documents (e.g., return-receipt electronic mail feature is used or periodic reviews or surveys to confirm receipt of transmitted information are conducted), and
   b. Protects the confidentiality of personal information relating to the individual's accounts and benefits (e.g., incorporating in the system measures designed to preclude unauthorized receipt of or access to such information by individuals other than the individual for whom the information is intended);
2. Electronically delivered documents are prepared and furnished in a manner consistent with the applicable style, format, and content requirements;
3. Each participant, beneficiary, or other individual is provided notice, through electronic means or in writing, apprising the individual of the document to be furnished electronically, the significance of the document (e.g., the document describes changes in plan benefits), and the individual's right to request and receive a paper version of each such document; and
4. Upon request, the participant, beneficiary, or other individual is provided a paper version of the electronically furnished document.

Furthermore, the furnishing of documents through electronic media may only be made to the following individuals:

1. A participant who:
   a. Has the ability to effectively access documents furnished in electronic form at any location where the participant is reasonably expected to perform duties as an employee, and
   b. With respect to whom access to the employer's or plan sponsor's electronic information system is an integral part of those duties; or
2. A participant, beneficiary, or any other person entitled to documents under Title I of ERISA (e.g., alternate payee (see Q 36:5)) who:

a. Has affirmatively consented, in electronic or non-electronic form, to receive documents through electronic media and has not withdrawn such consent;

b. In the case of documents to be furnished through the Internet or other electronic communication network, has affirmatively consented or confirmed consent electronically, in a manner that reasonably demonstrates the individual's ability to access information in the electronic form that will be used to provide the information that is the subject of the consent, and has provided an address for the receipt of electronically furnished documents;

c. Prior to consenting, is provided, in electronic or non-electronic form, a clear and conspicuous statement indicating:

    (i) The types of documents to which the consent would apply;

    (ii) That consent can be withdrawn at any time without charge;

    (iii) The procedures for withdrawing consent and for updating the participant's, beneficiary's, or other individual's address for receipt of electronically furnished documents or other information;

    (iv) The right to request and obtain a paper version of an electronically furnished document, including whether the paper version will be provided free of charge; and

    (v) Any hardware and software requirements for accessing and retaining the documents; and

d. Following consent, if a change in hardware or software requirements needed to access or retain electronic documents creates a material risk that the individual will be unable to access or retain electronically furnished documents:

    (i) Is provided with a statement of the revised hardware or software requirements for access to and retention of electronically furnished documents;

    (ii) Is given the right to withdraw consent without charge and without the imposition of any condition or consequence that was not disclosed at the time of the initial consent; and

    (iii) Again consents to the receipt of documents through electronic media.

[DOL Reg. § 2520.104b-1(c)]

The E-SIGN Act (see Q 20:7) provides federal standards for using electronic signatures and electronic records. The DOL final regulation takes into account provisions of E-SIGN Act relating to consumer disclosure and consent with regard to electronic communications. [Preamble to DOL Reg. § 2520.104b-1(c)]

PBGC has issued regulations regarding methods for providing an issuance by electronic media. These regulations are substantially the same as the DOL regulations discussed above. [PBGC Reg. §§ 4000.11–4000.15]

Effective for plan years beginning after December 31, 2006, a plan administrator of a defined contribution plan (other than a one-participant plan) must furnish a benefit statement:

1. At least once each calendar quarter to each participant or beneficiary who has the right to direct the investment of assets in his or her account under the plan;

2. At least once each calendar year to a participant or beneficiary who has his or her own account under the plan but does not have the right to direct the investment of the assets of the account; and

3. Upon written request to a plan beneficiary not described in (1) or (2) above.

The benefit statement must indicate the total benefits accrued and the nonforfeitable benefits, if any, that have accrued or the earliest date on which benefits will become nonforfeitable. The statement must also include an explanation of any permitted disparity or any floor-offset arrangement that may be applied in determining any accrued benefits. A benefit statement for a defined contribution plan must include the value of each investment to which assets in a participant's account have been allocated.

For a benefit statement covering a defined contribution plan that must be provided at least once each calendar quarter to participants who have the right to direct the investment of their account assets, the statement must include an explanation of any limitations or restrictions on any right of the participant or beneficiary to direct the investment. The notice must include an explanation regarding the importance of a well-balanced and diversified investment portfolio and a statement of the risk that holding more than 20 percent of a portfolio in the securities of one entity may not be adequately diversified.

Until DOL issues regulations, the new requirements will be treated as being met, if the plan administrator has acted in good faith. DOL has issued the following guidance regarding good-faith compliance:

1. *Statements using multiple documents.* Multiple documents may be used to comply with the requirement to provide a benefit statement. Thus, for example, a plan administrator may be the source for vesting information, while the plan's brokerage firm may be the source for investment-related information.

2. *Manner of furnishing statements.* Benefit statements may be provided in written, electronic, or other appropriate forms.

3. *Dates for furnishing statements.* A benefit statement provided no later than 45 days following the appropriate period (quarter or year) will be considered good-faith compliance.

4. *Provision for plan loans will not require quarterly statements.* An individual account plan that is not otherwise required to provide quarterly statements will not be required to do so merely because the plan permits participants to take plan loans.

5. *Explanations of limits on directing investments.* A benefit statement for an individual account plan that permits participants to direct their investments must include an explanation of any limitations or restrictions on a participant's or beneficiary's right under the plan to direct an investment. Pending further guidance, a benefit statement need only explain limitations and restrictions under the plan and does *not* need to address limitations and restrictions imposed by investment funds, other investment vehicles, or state and federal securities laws.

6. *Explanation of importance of diversification.* A benefit statement for an individual account plan that permits participants to direct their investments must include an explanation of the importance of diversifying investments and the risk of holding too much of one security. Pending the development of a model statement for this explanation, the following language will be considered good-faith compliance:

> To help achieve long-term retirement security, you should give careful consideration to the benefits of a well-balanced and diversified investment portfolio. Spreading your assets among different types of investments can help you achieve a favorable rate of return, while minimizing your overall risk of losing money. This is because market or other economic conditions that cause one category of assets, or one particular security, to perform very well often cause another asset category, or another particular security, to perform poorly. If you invest more than 20% of your retirement savings in any one company or industry, your savings may not be properly diversified. Although diversification is not a guarantee against loss, it is an effective strategy to help you manage investment risk.

> In deciding how to invest your retirement savings, you should take into account all of your assets, including any retirement savings outside of the plan. No single approach is right for everyone because, among other factors, individuals have different financial goals, different time horizons for meeting their goals, and different tolerances for risk.

> It is also important to periodically review your investment portfolio, your investment objectives, and the investment options under the plan to help ensure that your retirement savings will meet your retirement goals.

7. *Providing participants with notice of diversification rights.* Plans must provide notice of the diversification rights under ERISA Section 101(m).

8. *Directing participants to DOL website.* A benefit statement for an individual account plan that permits participants to direct their investments must include a notice directing participants to the DOL website for sources of information on individual investing and diversification. The plan administrator should direct participants to http://www.dol.gov/ebsa/investing.html. [FAB 2006-03 (Dec. 20, 2006)]

Because many individual account plans that do not permit participants and beneficiaries to direct the investment of assets in their individual accounts may not be able to comply within the 45-day period in 3 above, DOL has provided additional guidance. Plan administrators of those individual account plans will be treated as acting in good faith compliance if statements are furnished to participants and beneficiaries on or before the date on which the Form 5500 is filed by the plan (but not later than the date, including extensions, the form is required to be filed) for the plan year to which the statement relates. [FAB 2007-03 (Oct. 12, 2007)]

A plan administrator of a defined benefit plan (other than a one-participant plan) must furnish a benefit statement:

1. At least once every three years to each participant with a nonforfeitable accrued benefit and who is employed by the employer maintaining the plan at the time the statement is to be furnished, and

2. To a participant or beneficiary of the plan upon written request.

The information furnished under 1. above may be based on reasonable estimates. The annual statement requirements will be treated as met if at least once a year the plan administrator provides to participants notice of availability of the benefit statement and the ways in which the participant may obtain the statement.

DOL was required to develop one or more model benefit statements by August 18, 2007. These statements are to be written in a manner calculated to be understood by the average plan participant and that are to be used by plan administrators in complying with the requirement to provide benefit statements to participants and beneficiaries. As of yet, the model benefit statements have not been developed. [ERISA § 105(a)]

Q 20:24 What is a summary annual report?

The summary annual report (SAR) is a summary of the information contained in the annual report (see Q 21:1). The plan administrator (see Q 20:1) must furnish an SAR to each participant and each beneficiary receiving benefits within nine months after the close of the plan year. If IRS has granted an extension for filing the annual report, the deadline to furnish the SAR is extended until two months after the extended due date of the annual report.

Example. A calendar year profit sharing plan is granted an extension to file its Form 5500 for plan year ended December 31, 2009, until October 15, 2010 (i.e., 2½ months after the July 31, 2010, due date). The summary annual report must be furnished no later than December 15, 2010.

[ERISA §§ 103(b)(3), 104(b)(3); DOL Reg. § 2520.104b-10]

For plan years beginning after 2007, defined benefit plans are no longer required to provide SARs. [ERISA § 104(b)(3)]

Q 20:25 How should a plan administrator handle oral inquiries from participants?

Numerous questions by participants can be expected. The plan administrator can insist that inquiries be in writing unless the effect of that request is to make it difficult for participants to inquire about the plan (e.g., if the participants are not fluent in English). One court ruled that the obligation to issue a foreign language version of a plan's SPD does not extend to the denial of benefit claims made by participants (see Q 22:14). [Diaz v. United Agric. Employee Welfare Benefit Plan & Trust, 50 F.3d 1478 (9th Cir. 1995)]

The danger, of course, in responding orally to complex questions about the plan is that since there is no record of what was said, a participant may claim at a later date that the information provided by the plan administrator was misleading. Thus, the plan administrator should limit the number of individuals authorized by the plan to answer questions concerning the plan or its benefits. Such a policy should be strictly adhered to and conveyed to participants. Those authorized to answer questions should maintain a log for recording inquiries. They should also respond in writing to inquiries that they believe may affect an individual's benefits in order to have a record of what was said.

Q 20:26 May the plan administrator or trustee choose the form of distribution that will be made to a participant?

No. See Qs 10:45 through 10:52 regarding discretion with respect to distributions from a qualified retirement plan.

Q 20:27 Can innocent errors in the operation of a qualified retirement plan result in disqualification of the plan?

Yes. One qualified retirement plan, for example, was disqualified (i.e., lost its tax-favored status) after IRS determined that the plan was discriminatory because contributions had been allocated solely for the benefit of a shareholder-employee when, in fact, five additional employees were eligible for coverage. It did not matter that this situation resulted from an honest mistake. Furthermore, the company's offer to cure the discrimination retroactively was rejected. Although the Code authorizes retroactive corrections for defects in the retirement plan itself (see Q 18:6), there is no statutory authority for a retroactive correction of a mistake in the operation of the retirement plan. However, IRS has implemented a system of correction programs to resolve disqualifying plan defects without seeking plan disqualification (see chapter 19). [I.R.C. § 401(b); Myron v. United States, 550 F.2d 1145 (9th Cir. 1977); *see also* Buzzetta Constr. Corp., 92 T.C. 641 (1989)]

Q 20:28 Can a qualified retirement plan be amended?

Yes, but ERISA requires that a plan provide a procedure for amending the plan and for identifying the persons who have authority to amend the plan.

[ERISA § 402(b)(3)] The U.S. Supreme Court held that a plan provision stating that the company reserves the right to modify or amend the plan was a sufficient amendment procedure so that the employer could amend its plan. [Curtiss-Wright Corp. v. Schoonejongen, 514 U.S. 73 (1995)]

A purported plan amendment, which would have rendered a participant's spouse ineligible to receive benefits as a surviving spouse, was held to be ineffective because plan trustees apparently did not follow the plan's detailed amendment procedures. [Overby v. National Assn. of Letter Carriers, 595 F.3d 1290 (D.C. Cir. 2010)]

Q 20:29   What is the actuary's role in administering a qualified retirement plan?

The actuary's primary function is to determine the amount needed by an employer's defined benefit plan (see Q 2:3) to pay promised retirement benefits to participants. Assumptions and methods used by the actuary are basic to the application of the minimum funding standards (see Q 8:1). The actuary is called upon to certify the amount of tax-deductible dollars the employer must contribute to its defined benefit plan.

If a defined benefit plan is not funded solely through insurance, the services of an enrolled actuary—that is, an actuary licensed to practice before the government agencies responsible for administering ERISA—are required. Some enrolled actuaries may work for insurance companies, and others may be employed by accounting firms or firms specializing in actuarial services. [ERISA §§ 3041, 3042, 3043; I.R.C. § 7701(a)(35)]

Q 20:30   What is the trustee's role in administering a qualified retirement plan?

The trustee holds title to plan assets and is responsible for managing them unless this responsibility has been delegated to an investment manager. For details on the trustee's investment responsibilities, see chapter 23.

Q 20:31   What is the accountant's role in administering a qualified retirement plan?

The accountant's role may entail preparing statements of plan assets, auditing the plan's books and records, and preparing reports to government agencies. Plans with 100 or more participants (large plan filers; see Q 21:2), and certain plans with less than 100 participants (small plan filers; see Q 21:2) that do not meet the small plan audit waiver requirements (see Q 21:16), require special reports by an independent qualified public accountant (see Q 21:16).

Q 20:32   Is there a bonding requirement?

Generally, every fiduciary (anyone who has some discretionary authority or control over the plan or its assets; see chapter 23), and anyone who handles funds or other property of the plan, must be bonded. The bonding requirements are intended to protect employee benefit plans from risk of loss due to fraud or dishonesty on the part of persons who handle plan funds or other property (see Q 20:36). The bond is sometimes referred to as an ERISA fidelity bond.

The bond must cover at least 10 percent of the amount handled by the bonded individual; it may not be for less than $1,000 and need not be for more than $500,000. Effective for plan years beginning after December 31, 2007, the maximum bond amount increased to $1 million in the case of a plan that holds employer securities. [ERISA §§ 3(21), 412]

EBSA has provided guidance on the ERISA fidelity bond requirements. [FAB 2008-04 (Nov. 25, 2008)]

Q 20:33 · What losses must an ERISA fidelity bond cover?

An ERISA fidelity bond must protect the plan against loss by reason of acts of fraud or dishonesty on the part of persons required to be bonded, whether the person acts directly or through connivance with others. [ERISA § 412; DOL Reg. § 2580.412-1] The term "fraud or dishonesty" for this purpose encompasses risks of loss that might arise through dishonest or fraudulent acts in handling plan funds or other property. This includes, but is not limited to, larceny, theft, embezzlement, forgery, misappropriation, wrongful abstraction, wrongful conversion, willful misapplication, and other similar acts where losses result. The bond must provide recovery for losses occasioned by such acts even though no personal gain accrues to the person committing the act. Deductibles or other similar features that transfer risk to the plan are prohibited. [DOL Reg. § 2580.412-1; FAB 2008-04, Q-1 (Nov. 25, 2008)]

A fidelity bond is different than fiduciary liability insurance, which generally insures the plan against losses caused by breaches of fiduciary responsibilities and is not required under ERISA. Whether a plan purchases fiduciary liability insurance is subject, generally, to ERISA's fiduciary standards (see chapter 23). [FAB 2008-04, Q-2 (Nov. 25, 2008)]

Q 20:34 Who must be bonded?

Every person who handles funds or other property (see Q 20:36) of an employee benefit plan is required to be bonded unless covered under one of the exemptions (see Q 20:37). Those required to be bonded include the plan administrator (see Q 20:1) and those officers and employees of the plan or plan sponsor who handle plan funds by virtue of their duties relating to the receipt, safe-keeping, and disbursement of funds. They may also include other persons, such as service providers, whose duties and functions involve access to plan funds or decision-making authority that can give rise to a risk of loss through fraud or dishonesty. Where a plan administrator, service provider, or other plan official is an entity, such as a corporation or association, the bonding requirements apply to the natural persons who perform handling functions on behalf of the entity. [DOL Reg. §§ 2580.412-1, 2580.412-3, 2580.412-6; FAB 2008-4, Q-5 (Nov. 25, 2008)]

Q 20:35   What are funds or other property for purposes of the bonding requirement?

The term "funds or other property" is intended to encompass all property that is or may be used as a source for the payment of benefits to plan participants. It includes property in the nature of quick assets (e.g., cash, checks, negotiable instruments) and property that is readily convertible into cash for distribution as benefits.

Although the term does not include permanent assets used in plan operation (land, buildings, furniture, and fixtures), land and buildings that are investments of a qualified retirement plan will be covered by the term "other property." [DOL Reg. § 2580.412-4; FAB 2008-4, Q-17 (Nov. 25, 2008)]

Q 20:36   What is handling of funds?

A person handles funds or other property of a qualified retirement plan whenever that person's duties or activities are such that there is risk that the funds or other property could be lost if that person, acting alone or with others, engaged in dishonest or fraudulent conduct. Under this definition, handling is generally considered to include situations in which there is:

1. Physical contact with cash, checks, or property;
2. The power to secure physical possession of the cash, checks, or similar property;
3. The authority to cause a transfer of property such as mortgages or securities to oneself or another; or
4. Disbursement of funds or other property including the power to sign or endorse checks.

[DOL Reg. § 2580.412-6; FAB 2008-4, Q-18 (Nov. 25, 2008)]

Q 20:37   Are any fiduciaries exempt from the bonding requirements?

Yes. A bond generally is not required from:

1. A bank that is subject to federal regulation and is federally insured;
2. A savings and loan association subject to federal regulation if it is the plan administrator; and
3. An insurance company that provides or underwrites, in accordance with state law, plan benefits for any plan other than one established or maintained for the insurance company's employees.

[ERISA § 412(a); DOL Reg. §§ 2580.412-23 through 2580.412-32; FAB 2008-4, Q-15 (Nov. 25, 2008)]

A subsidiary of a bank holding company met the conditions for exemption from the bonding requirements since it (a) was a corporation under the laws of the U.S. or of any state, (b) was authorized under those laws to exercise trust powers or to conduct an insurance business, (c) was subject to supervision or examination by federal or state authority, and (d) met certain capital requirements. [EBSA Op. Ltr. 2004-07A]

An entity that is registered as a broker or dealer is exempt from the bonding requirement under ERISA if that entity is subject to the fidelity bond requirements of a self-regulatory organization. [ERISA § 412(a)]

Q 20:38   May a party in interest provide a bond in satisfaction of the bonding requirements?

Generally, a bond may not be procured from a party in interest (see Q 24:3) or from any entity in which the qualified retirement plan or a party in interest, directly or indirectly, has any significant control or financial interest. However, a bond can be procured from a party in interest where the financial interest or control is not incompatible with an unbiased exercise of judgment. Thus, a bond may be obtained from a party in interest providing multiple services to plans. For example, if an insurance company providing life insurance for a plan is affiliated with a surety company, a bond may be obtained from the surety company. [ERISA § 412(c); DOL Reg. §§ 2580.412-33 through 2580.412-36]

Q 20:39   Is bonding required for a plan with only one participant?

In the case of a qualified retirement plan covering only the owner (i.e., the shareholder or sole proprietor), or the owner and the owner's spouse, the qualified retirement plan is not subject to the bonding requirements. However, if the plan's only participant is not the owner, this exception does not apply. Furthermore, if a partnership's qualified retirement plan covers only partners (or partners and their spouses), the qualified retirement plan is not subject to the bonding requirements (see Q 23:13). [DOL Reg. § 2510.3-3]

Q 20:40   Are SEPs and SIMPLE IRAs subject to the bonding requirements?

There is no specific exemption for a SEP (see Q 32:1) or SIMPLE IRA (see Q 33:2). Such plans are generally structured in such a way, however, that, if any person does handle funds or other property (see Q 20:36) of such plans, that person will fall under one of the financial institution exemptions (see Q 20:37). [FAB 2008-04, Q-16 (Nov. 25, 2008)]

Q 20:41   Can a bond insure more than one plan?

Yes. More than one plan may be named as an insured under the same bond. Any such bond must, however, allow for a recovery by each plan in an amount at least equal to that which would have been required for each plan under separate bonds. Thus, if a person covered under a bond has handling functions (see Q 20:36) in more than one plan insured under that bond, the amount of the bond must be sufficient to cover such person for at least 10 percent of the total amount that person handles in all the plans insured under the bond, up to the maximum required amount for each plan (see Q 20:32). [DOL Reg. § 2580.412-16(c); FAB 2008-04, Q-23 (Nov. 25, 2008)]

> **Example.** Y is covered under a bond that insures two separate plans, Plan A and Plan B. Both plans hold employer securities. Y handles $12,000,000 in funds for Plan A and $400,000 for Plan B. Accordingly, Plan A must be able to recover under the bond up to a maximum of $1,000,000 for losses caused by Y, and Plan B must be able to recover under the bond up to a maximum of $40,000 for losses caused by Y.

If the bond insures more than one plan, a claim by one plan may not reduce the amount of coverage available to other plans insured on the bond. Further, in order to meet the requirement that each plan insured on a multi-plan bond be protected, the bonding arrangement must ensure that payment of a loss sustained by one plan will not reduce the amount of required coverage available to other plans insured under the bond. [DOL Reg. § 2580.412-16(d); FAB 2008-04, Q-24 (Nov. 25, 2008)]

Q 20:42 Can bonds use an omnibus clause to name plans as insureds?

Yes. An omnibus clause is sometimes used as an alternative way to identify multiple plans as insureds on one bond, rather than specifically naming on the bond each individual plan in a group of plans. By way of example, an omnibus clause might name as insured "all employee benefit plans sponsored by ABC Company." ERISA does not prohibit using an omnibus clause to name plans insured on a bond, as long as the omnibus clause clearly identifies the insured plans in a way that would enable the insured plans' representatives to make a claim under the bond. [FAB 2008-04, Q-32 (Nov. 25, 2008)]

Q 20:43 If the funds handled increase during the plan year, must the bond be increased?

No. With respect to each covered person, the bond amount must be fixed annually. The bond must be fixed or estimated at the beginning of the plan's reporting year as soon after the date when such year begins as the necessary information from the preceding reporting year can practicably be ascertained. The amount of the bond must be based on the highest amount of funds handled (see Q 20:36) by the person in the preceding plan year. [DOL Reg. §§ 2580.412-11, 2580.412-14, 2580.412-19; FAB 2008-04, Q-41 (Nov. 25, 2008)]

Chapter 21

Reporting to Government Agencies

Once a qualified retirement plan has been put into operation, the plan administrator has the responsibility of filing certain information returns, reports, and statements with the agencies that administer the federal pension laws: IRS, DOL, and PBGC. This chapter sets forth guidelines for the plan administrator to follow in meeting these reporting requirements.

Q 21:1 What are the annual reporting requirements?

Each employer (subject to a limited exception) (see Q 21:2) that maintains a qualified retirement plan is required to file an annual report. The annual report is commonly referred to as the Form 5500 series return/report.

The appropriate Form 5500 series return/report (Form 5500, 5500-SF, or 5500-EZ) must be filed for each qualified retirement plan (see Q 21:2) for each plan year in which the plan has assets. Therefore, the year of complete distribution of all plan assets is the last year for which a Form 5500 must be filed (see Q 21:8). [I.R.C. §§ 6058, 6059]

Q 21:2 Which Form 5500 series return/report is required for a particular qualified retirement plan?

Qualified retirement plans must file either Form 5500, Annual Return/Report of Employee Benefit Plan, Form 5500-SF, Short Form Annual Return/Report of Small Employee Benefit Plan, or Form 5500-EZ, Annual Return of One-Participant (Owners and Their Spouses) Retirement Plan.

Effective January 2010, with respect to filings for 2009, Form 5500 and Form 5500-SF are required to be filed with DOL under the ERISA Filing Acceptance System 2 (EFAST2), an all-electronic system (see Q 21:3).

Form 5500 consists of (1) the main Form 5500, which includes identifying information; (2) one or more of nine schedules that focus on particular subject matter for filing requirements; and (3) supplemental documents or materials that may also be required to be attached. Generally, a Form 5500 filed for a retirement plan that covers fewer than 100 participants as of the beginning of the plan year should be completed following the requirements for a "small plan," and a Form 5500 filed for a plan that covers 100 or more participants as of the beginning of the plan year should be completed following the requirements for a "large plan."

In lieu of completing and filing Form 5500, Form 5500-SF may be used by certain small plans. Plans that meet the following eligibility conditions may voluntarily choose to file Form 5500-SF:

1. The plan must have had fewer than 100 participants at the beginning of the plan year;

2. The plan must meet the conditions for being exempt from the requirement to be audited annually by an independent qualified public accountant, but not by virtue of enhanced bonding (see Q 21:16);

3. At all times during the plan year, the plan must be 100 percent invested in certain secure investments that have a readily determinable fair market value;

4. The plan must not hold any employer securities (see Q 23:86) at any time during the plan year; and

5. The plan must not be a multiemployer plan (see Q 29:2).

[2009 Instructions for Form 5500-SF]

A one-participant plan that is required to file an annual return for 2009 must file a paper Form 5500-EZ or, if eligible, electronically file Form 5500-SF. A one-participant plan may not file Form 5500. A one-participant plan is defined as a qualified retirement plan that covers only:

1. The owner of a business or both the owner and spouse; and the business, whether or not incorporated, is wholly owned by the owner, or both the owner and spouse; or

2. Partners (or the partners and their spouses) in a business partnership.

For plan years beginning after December 31, 2006, for purposes of determining a one-participant plan, the term "partner" has been modified to include an individual who owns more than 2 percent (2%) of an S corporation (see Q 28:2).

Prior to 2009, Form 5500-EZ could not be used if the plan sponsor was a member of an affiliated service group (see Q 5:35), controlled group of corporations (see Q 5:31), or group of businesses under common control (see Q 5:29) or if it leased employees (see Q 5:59). In addition, if the plan satisfied the coverage requirements (see Q 5:15) only when combined with another plan, Form 5500-EZ could not be used. New characteristic codes have been added to identify these features on Form 5500-EZ.

Employers with one or more one-participant plans that have total assets of $250,000 or less at the end of the plan year need not file Form 5500-EZ. For plan years beginning prior to January 1, 2007, the asset amount was $100,000.

Example. A plan meets all the requirements for filing Form 5500-EZ and its total assets (either alone or in combination with one or more one-participant plans maintained by the employer) exceed $250,000 at the end of the 2009 plan year. Form 5500-EZ must be filed for each of the employer's one-participant plans, including those with less than $250,000 in assets for the 2009 plan year.

Filers of Form 5500-EZ are not required to file any schedules or attachments (see Qs 21:6, 21:7); however, such filers are required to collect and retain a completed Schedule MB (see Q 21:7) for multiemployer defined benefit plans and certain money purchase plans, if applicable, and a completed and signed Schedule SB (see Q 21:7) for single-employer defined benefit plans, if applicable. The requirement to both perform an annual valuation and maintain the minimum funding standard account for all plans subject to the minimum funding requirements (see Q 8:1) continues.

Foreign plans are not eligible to file Form 5500 regardless of whether the plan was previously required to file an annual return on Form 5500. Every foreign plan that is required to file an annual return for 2009 must instead file a paper Form 5500-EZ. A foreign plan is a retirement plan that is maintained outside the United States primarily for nonresident aliens and is required to file an annual return if the employer who maintains the plan is (1) a domestic employer, or (2) a foreign employer with income derived from sources within the United States if contributions to the plan are deducted on its U.S. income tax return.

[2009 Instructions for Form 5500-EZ]

Q 21:3   How is the Form 5500 series return/report filed?

Forms 5500 and 5500-SF and accompanying schedules are required to be filed electronically for plan years beginning on or after January 1, 2009. Beginning January 2010, an all-electronic system called EFAST2 will receive those electronic annual returns/reports.

Form 5500-EZ cannot be submitted electronically and must be submitted on paper with IRS. However, a one-participant plan (see Q 21:2) that is eligible to file Form 5500-EZ may elect to file Form 5500-SF electronically with EFAST2 rather than filing Form 5500-EZ on paper with IRS. Although uncommon, it is possible to have a one-participant plan that covers 100 or more participants. For example, a large law firm could sponsor a plan covering only partners and their spouses and qualify as a one-participant plan. A one-participant plan that covers 100 or more participants is not eligible to file Form 5500-SF and must file Form 5500-EZ on paper with IRS.

Filers may electronically file the annual return/report using (1) EFAST2-approved third-party software or (2) IFILE. IFILE is the Form 5500 and Form 5500-SF annual return/report preparation and submission application that is on DOL's website www.efast.dol.gov and is offered as an alternative to EFAST2-approved third-party software.

Effective January 1, 2010, prior year delinquent and amended filings of the Form 5500 returns/reports must be submitted electronically through EFAST2 and may not be submitted on paper through the initial EFAST system. A limited exception was available for delinquent and amended filings where the filer had the option to submit the forms through EFAST on paper until October 15, 2010. After October 15, 2010, even 2008 plan year filings must be submitted electronically through EFAST2.

A delinquent or amended Form 5500 return/report submitted electronically through EFAST2 for plan years prior to 2009 must use the current filing year Form 5500, schedules, and instructions except as provided below. The current filing year forms take the place of the Form 5500 that would have been filed in the prior year. The electronic filing on the current filing year Form 5500 must indicate in the appropriate space at the beginning of the Form 5500 the plan year for which the annual return/report is being filed. However, filers using EFAST2 must use the actual (original) schedules (see Qs 21:6, 21:7) associated with the plan year for which the annual return/report relates with respect to the following schedules:

- Schedule B, SB, or MB (Actuarial Information)
- Schedule E (ESOP Annual Information)
- Schedule P (Annual Return of Fiduciary of Employee Benefit Trust)
- Schedule R (Retirement Plan Information)
- Schedule T (Qualified Pension Plan Coverage Information)

For example, with respect to a delinquent 2007 Form 5500 return/report for a defined benefit plan, the 2007 Schedules B and R and all required attachments for these schedules must be included and attached as pdf images to the current filing year Form 5500. The filer has the option of using either the current filing year or the original Schedule C. Because Schedule E does not apply to a defined benefit plan, and Schedule P and Schedule T were not applicable to 2007 plan year filings, all other required schedules and attachments should be completed using the current year filing forms and instructions. The entire filing should then be filed electronically in accordance with EFAST2 electronic filing requirements.

Schedule SSA should not be attached to any EFAST2 filing; the most current year Form 8955-SSA should be submitted to the IRS (see Q 21:6).

[EBSA FAQs, EFAST2 All-Electronic System, www.efast.dol.gov]

Prior to January 1, 2010 and the 2009 filings, Form 5500 was filed with DOL and processed under EFAST, the initial computerized system designed for processing the 5500 series forms and predecessor to EFAST2. Form 5500 could have been filed in one of the following formats:

1. Hand print or
2. Machine print

The machine print format required completion by computer software from EFAST-approved vendors; and the hand print format permitted completion by typewriter, by hand, or by computer software from EFAST-approved vendors. The hand print form was published with a pre-printed bar code at the bottom of each page, and all the required attachments were filed by mail. Hand print forms could not be filed electronically. The machine print form and all the required attachments could be filed in the following ways:

1. By modem, using an approved EFAST transmitter;

2. By mailing magnetic tape, floppy diskettes, or CD-ROMs containing the Form 5500 data; or

3. By mailing a paper version of the machine print form.

Q 21:4   Are there special filing rules for large plans and small plans?

Yes. Qualified retirement plans with 100 or more participants (large plans; see Q 21:2) are required to file Form 5500 and certain special schedules, and plans with fewer than 100 participants (small plans; see Q 21:2) need not file these schedules. If the number of participants is between 80 and 120 and a Form 5500 was filed for the prior plan year, the employer may elect to complete the current Form 5500 in the same category (large plan or small plan) as was filed for the prior Form 5500. For example, if a Form 5500 annual return/report was filed for the 2008 plan year as a small plan, including Schedule I if applicable, and the number of participants in 2009 is 120 or less, the employer may elect to complete the 2009 Form 5500 and schedules in accordance with the instructions for a small plan, including for eligible filers, filing Form 5500-SF instead of Form 5500. This rule appears to create an anomaly if the number of plan participants increases from below 100 in year 1 to between 100 and 120 in year 2 and subsequent years. For example, a qualified retirement plan with 95 participants in year 1 files as a small plan filer; and, in year 2, if the plan has 105 participants, it may again file as a small plan filer. Each year thereafter, if the plan has between 100 and 120 participants, the plan may file as a small plan filer for each such year. [DOL Reg. § 2520.103-1(d); 2009 Instructions for Form 5500]

Q 21:5   What special schedules must accompany the Form 5500 series return/report?

The Form 5500 return/report consists of the main Form 5500, which includes identifying information and, depending upon the type of filer, one or more of nine schedules, including three for pensions (see Q 21:6) and six for general reporting (see Q 21:7). All schedules must identify the name of the plan, the sponsor's employer identification number, and the plan number.

If a small plan files Form 5500-SF (see Q 21:2), the only schedules that are required to be filed are Schedule SB (Form 5500) (see Q 21:6) or Schedule MB (Form 5500) (see Q 21:6), if applicable. [2009 Instructions for Form 5500-SF]

Q 21:6   What pension schedules must accompany Form 5500?

Certain pension schedules must be attached to Form 5500 (see Q 21:4).

Schedule SB (Form 5500), Single-Employer Defined Benefit Plan Actuarial Information, is used for single-employer or multiple-employer defined benefit plans, and Schedule MB (Form 5500), Multiemployer Defined Benefit Plan and Certain Money Purchase Plan Actuarial Information, is used for multiemployer defined benefit plans or certain money purchase pension plans where a waiver of the minimum funding standard (see Q 8:1) is currently being amortized. [I.R.C. § 6059; 2009 Instructions for Form 5500] Commencing with the 2008 plan year filings, Schedule SB (Form 5500) and Schedule MB (Form 5500) replaced Schedule B (Form 5500). An IRS representative has opined that Schedule B must be filed for the plan year in which a defined benefit plan terminates but need not be filed for the plan year after the year in which the plan terminates (see Qs 8:33, 25:63). [IRS Spec. Rul. (July 27, 1993)]

Schedule R (Form 5500), Retirement Plan Information, must be attached to Form 5500 from a defined benefit plan, a plan subject to the minimum funding standards, or any plan from which a distribution was made during the year. The purpose of this schedule is to report certain information on plan distributions, funding, and the adoption of amendments increasing the value of benefits in a defined benefit plan. Multiemployer defined benefit plans are required to provide additional information, and all defined benefit plans (single-employer, multiple-employer, and multiemployer) with 1,000 or more participants are required to provide financial asset breakdown information. For the 2009 plan year, additional information required by WRERA (see Q 1:36) is filed as attachments to Schedule R. Also, effective 2009, certain ESOP information formerly reported on Schedule E is now reported on Schedule R. [2009 Instructions for Schedule R (Form 5500)]

Schedule E (Form 5500), ESOP Annual Information, has been eliminated for plan years beginning on or after January 1, 2009. Previously, Schedule E was completed by an employer or plan administrator (see Q 20:1) of a qualified retirement plan that included employee stock ownership plan (ESOP) benefits (see Q 28:1). If applicable, the completed Schedule E was attached to Form 5500. Effective 2009, certain ESOP information formerly reported on Schedule E is now reported on Schedule R.

Schedule SSA (Form 5500), Annual Registration Statement Identifying Separated Participants With Deferred Vested Benefits, has been eliminated for plan years beginning on or after January 1, 2009. Previously, Schedule SSA was used to inform IRS of plan participants who separated from service but were not paid retirement benefits. In general, a separated plan participant with deferred vested benefits was required to be reported no later than on the Schedule SSA filed for the plan year following the plan year in which the separation occurred. [I.R.C. § 6057; 2008 Instructions for Schedule SSA (Form 5500)] As part of the transition to EFAST2 (see Q 21:3), the prior Schedule SSA is being replaced with Form 8955-SSA that will be filed directly with IRS. The 2009 filing of Form 8955-SSA may be delayed until the time the 2010 Form 5500 filing is due. At that time, preparers should expect that both the 2009 and 2010 Form 8955-SSA will be due. The data to be collected will be nearly identical to that required on Schedule SSA.

Q 21:7   What financial reporting schedules must accompany Form 5500?

Certain financial reporting schedules must be attached to Form 5500 (see Q 21:4).

Schedule A (Form 5500), Insurance Information, must be attached to Form 5500 if any benefits are provided by an insurance company, insurance service, or other similar organization. This includes investment contracts with insurance companies, such as guaranteed investment contracts and pooled separate accounts. [ERISA § 103(e); 2009 Instructions for Schedule A (Form 5500)]

Schedule C (Form 5500), Service Provider Information, must be attached to Form 5500 by large plans (see Q 20:2) to report:

1. Service providers receiving, directly or indirectly, $5,000 or more in compensation for services rendered to the plan during a plan year, and

2. Information relating to the termination of an accountant or enrolled actuary.

Schedule D (Form 5500), DFE/Participating Plan Information, is used for filing information on relationships between plans and master trust investment accounts, common/collective trusts, insurance company pooled separate accounts, and group insurance arrangements, collectively known as Direct Filing Entities (DFEs).

Schedule G (Form 5500), Financial Transaction Schedules, must be attached to Form 5500 by large plans (see Q 21:2) to report loans or fixed income obligations in default or deemed uncollectible, leases in default or classified as uncollectible, and nonexempt prohibited transactions.

Schedule H (Form 5500), Financial Information, must be attached to Form 5500 by large plans. This schedule includes financial statements and questions involving investments, financial transactions, handling of plan assets, and the accountant's opinion.

Schedule I (Form 5500), Financial Information-Small Plan, must be attached to Form 5500 by small plans (see Q 21:2). This schedule includes simplified financial statements and questions involving investments, financial transactions, and handling of plan assets.

Schedule P (Form 5500), Annual Return of Fiduciary of Employee Benefit Trust, has been eliminated for plan years beginning on or after January 1, 2006. Previously, the Schedule P was completed by a fiduciary (trustee or custodian) and filed as an attachment to Form 5500 (and, prior to 2005, Form 5500-EZ). It was strongly recommended that Schedule P be filed because it started the running of the statute of limitations under Section 6501(a) for the trust (see Q 21:14). IRS has confirmed that filing Form 5500 and 5500-EZ *without* Schedule P will nonetheless start the running of the statute of limitations on the plan filing. [Ann. 2007-63, 2007-2 C.B. 236; 2006 Instructions to Form 5500]

Q 21:8   When is a Form 5500 series return/report due?

The appropriate Form 5500 series return/report is due by the last day of the seventh month following the close of the plan year (July 31 for calendar-year plans), unless the due date is extended (see Q 21:9). Note that the due date relates to the plan year and not to the employer's taxable year. [ERISA § 104]

> **Example.** Allaire Corporation files its federal income tax return on a calendar-year basis. Allaire Corporation maintains a qualified retirement plan with a plan year end of January 31. For the plan year ending January 31, 2011, the Form 5500 series return/report is due August 31, 2011.

For a short plan year, the Form 5500 series return/report is due by the last day of the seventh month after the short plan year ends. A short plan year ends on the date of a change in a plan's accounting period or upon the complete distribution of assets with respect to a plan termination (see chapter 25). Generally, if a current Form 5500 series return/report was not available before the due date for the short plan year return, the latest form available could have been used. [2008 Instructions for Form 5500; DOL Troubleshooter's Guide to Filing Form 5500 (May 2001)] Short 2009 plan year filers whose due date to submit their 2009 filing was before January 1, 2010 were given an automatic extension to electronically file their complete Form 5500 within 90 days after the 2009 filing system was available on the DOL website. This special extension was granted to encourage such short 2009 plan year filers to file their 2009 Form 5500 annual return/report electronically under EFAST2. Short 2009 plan year filers whose due date to submit their 2009 filing was before January 1, 2010, and who chose not to take advantage of the special extension, were required to use plan year 2008 forms and submit their 2009 filing to EFAST on or before the due date for their short plan year filing. Short 2010 plan year filers may *not* use the 2009 forms for filing; they must use the 2010 forms, schedules, and instructions. [2008 and 2009 Instructions for Form 5500]

Q 21:9   May the due date for filing a Form 5500 series return/report be extended?

Yes. An automatic extension of the due date for filing is available to an employer if all of the following conditions are met:

1. The plan year coincides with the employer's taxable year;
2. The employer has been granted an extension of time to file its federal income tax return to a date later than the due date for its Form 5500 series return/report; and
3. A copy of the income tax extension is attached to the Form 5500 series return/report.

[2009 Instructions for Form 5500]

> **Example 1.** Winston Corporation files its federal income tax return on a calendar-year basis and maintains a qualified retirement plan with a calendar-plan year. Winston Corporation receives an extension to file its

federal income tax return to September 15, 2011. The due date for filing the Form 5500 series return/report is automatically extended to September 15, 2011.

Example 2. The facts are the same as in Example 1, except that Winston Corporation maintains a qualified retirement plan with a plan year end of January 31. The due date for filing the Form 5500 series return/report is not automatically extended because the plan year does not coincide with the tax year.

Furthermore, an extension of up to two and one-half months will be automatically approved for filing the Form 5500 series return/report by filing Form 5558, Application for Extension of Time To File Certain Employee Plan Returns with IRS—not DOL—on or before the regular due date. A signature is not required if the request is for an extension to file the Form 5500 series return/report. Effective for the 2009 plan year filings, filers will not be required (or allowed) to attach to the electronic filing copies of either the Form 5558 or the acknowledgment letter that plan sponsors were receiving. Prior to the 2009 plan year filings, a photocopy of Form 5558, or the acknowledgment letter approving such request, was required to be attached to the Form 5500 series return/report. [Ann. 99-37, 1999-1 C.B. 907; Instructions to Form 5558]

Example 3. The facts are the same as in Example 2, except that Winston Corporation files Form 5558 no later than August 31, 2011. The due date for filing the Form 5500 series return/report is extended to November 15, 2011.

Q 21:10   What penalties may be imposed for late filing of the Form 5500 series return/report?

One or more of the following five penalties may be imposed or assessed for late or incomplete filings after the date they are due unless there was reasonable cause for the improper filing:

1. DOL may assess a civil penalty against a plan administrator (see Q 20:1) of up to $1,000 a day ($1,100 after adjustment for inflation) for the late filing of a Form 5500 series return/report. [DOL Reg § 2575.502c-2] In addition, a Form 5500 series return/report rejected by DOL because it lacks material information will be treated as if it had not been filed. In other words, the plan administrator can be assessed a penalty for an incomplete as well as an untimely but complete filing.

2. A penalty of $25 a day (up to a maximum of $15,000) is imposed for each day a Form 5500 series return/report is overdue.

3. A plan administrator who fails to include all required separated participants in a timely filed annual registration statement (Schedule SSA (prior to 2009); see Q 21:6) is subject to a penalty of $1 a day for each separated participant (the maximum penalty is $5,000).

4. A penalty of $1,000 is imposed if an actuarial report (Schedule MB or Schedule SB; see Q 21:6) is not filed for a defined benefit plan.

5. A penalty of $1 a day (up to a maximum of $1,000) is imposed if a notification of change of status of a plan is not filed on time.

[ERISA §§ 104(a)(4), 502(c)(2); I.R.C. §§ 6652(d)(1), 6652(d)(2), 6652(e), 6692]

Penalties assessed against a plan administrator were within DOL's discretion where subsequent to DOL's initial rejection of Form 5500, the plan administrator mistakenly sent a corrected form to IRS, not DOL. DOL waived 90 percent of the penalty, but assessed the remaining 10 percent because the plan administrator failed to show reasonable cause. [DOL, PWBA v. Rhode Island Bricklayers & Allied Craftsmen Pension Fund, DOL/ALJ (Boston, Mass.), No. 94-RIS-64 (May 30, 1995)] Also, DOL's assessment of a penalty for failure to file a correct annual report (Form 5500) despite numerous opportunities to correct errors in the form was upheld by an administrative law judge. [DOL, PWBA v. Northwestern Inst. of Psychiatry, DOL/ALJ (Camden, N.J.), No. 93-RIS-23 (Dec. 21, 1993)] In another case, IRS could not collect penalties from a plan sponsor for failure to file returns where the plan sponsor established that it had mailed them, and IRS was unable to rebut the presumption that it had received the returns. [*In re* Boedecker, 1993 Bankr. LEXIS 1873 (Bankr. D. Mont. 1993)]

DOL has opined that a penalty for the late filing of Form 5500 does not constitute a reasonable expense of administering a plan; and, therefore, the penalty is a liability of the plan administrator and not a liability of the plan. [DOL Info. Ltr. (Feb. 23, 1996)]

See Q 21:11 regarding the DFVC Program.

Q 21:11   What is the Delinquent Filer Voluntary Compliance Program?

DOL established the Delinquent Filer Voluntary Compliance (DFVC) Program to encourage, through the assessment of reduced civil penalties (see Q 21:10), delinquent plan administrators (see Q 20:1) to comply with the annual reporting requirements (see Q 21:1). The DFVC Program is not available to plan administrators who have been notified of a failure to file the annual report at issue. IRS late-filer penalty letters will not disqualify a plan from participating in the DFVC Program; however, a DOL Notice of Intent to Assess a Penalty will always disqualify a plan.

In order to comply with the DFVC Program, the plan administrator must file a complete Form 5500 return/report (see Q 21:2), including all required schedules and attachments, for each plan year for which the plan administrator is seeking relief. This filing must be filed electronically pursuant to EFAST2 (see Q 21:3). Form 5500, Part I, box D should be checked. When preparing reports for years prior to 2008, the filer must use the current year Form 5500 (the 2009 form at this time) and the related schedules (see Q 21:3). Each form or schedule must identify the applicable prior plan year to which the filing applies in the Plan Year Beginning and Plan Year Ending fields at the top of each form. The insertion of a plan year other than a current year serves as notification to EFAST2 processing that most edit checks are to be turned off and ensures EFAST2 will accept the filing. Some schedules that have been eliminated or modified and were required for an earlier reporting year are required to be filed in their original format. These schedules must be converted to a pdf file and attached as "Other Attachment."

Furthermore, the plan administrator should submit to DOL a paper copy of the Form 5500 return/report, without schedules and attachments and include payment of the applicable penalty amount. This separate submission should be sent by mail to:

> DFVC Program-DOL
> P.O. Box 70933
> Charlotte, NC 28272-0933

The applicable penalty amount is determined as follows:

1. With respect to a small plan filer (see Q 21:2), the applicable penalty amount is $10 per day for each day the annual return/report is filed after the date on which the annual report was due (without regard to any extensions), not to exceed the greater of $750 per annual return/report or, in the case of a DFVC Program submission relating to more than one delinquent annual filing for the plan, $1,500 per plan.

2. With respect to a large plan filer (see Q 21:2), the applicable penalty amount is $10 per day for each day the annual return/report is filed after the date on which the annual report was due (without regard to any extensions), not to exceed the greater of $2,000 per annual return/report or, in the case of a DFVC Program submission relating to more than one delinquent annual filing for the plan, $4,000 per plan.

The penalty should be paid by the plan administrator and may not be paid from the assets of the plan.

[DOL Notice, 67 Fed. Reg. 15,051 (Mar. 28, 2002); 2009 Instructions for Form 5500; EBSA FAQs, The Delinquent Filer Voluntary Compliance Program, www. efast.dol.gov]

IRS will not impose penalties (see Q 21:10) on a late filer who satisfies the requirements of the DFVC Program. The late filer does not need to file a separate application for relief with IRS, as IRS will coordinate with DOL which late filers are eligible for relief.

Form 5500-EZ (see Q 21:2) filers are not eligible for relief because such plans are not subject to Title 1 of ERISA, and they are ineligible to participate in the DFVC Program.

[IRS Notice 2002-23, 2002-1 C.B. 742]

Q 21:12   Are there any criminal penalties for violations of the reporting requirements?

Yes. Willful violations of the reporting and disclosure requirements of ERISA can result in penalties up to a maximum of $100,000 in the case of an individual ($500,000 for any other entity), 10-year imprisonment, or both. [ERISA § 501]

In addition, it is a criminal offense to knowingly make a false statement or conceal or fail to disclose any fact needed to prepare reports required by Title I of ERISA. The maximum penalties are a $10,000 fine, five-year imprisonment, or both. [18 U.S.C. § 1027] This provision has been applied to the following:

1. A service provider who provided the plan with false information regarding his profits, which the plan needed to complete its Form 5500. [United States v. Martorano, 767 F.2d 63 (3d Cir. 1985)]

2. A participant who submitted false information to his plan. [United States v. Bartkus, 816 F.2d 255 (6th Cir. 1987)]

Q 21:13   Does a plan administrator's reliance on a third party to timely file the Form 5500 series return/report constitute reasonable cause for late filing?

No. One court has upheld the imposition by IRS of a $5,000 penalty against an employer for the late filing of the Form 5500 series return/report, even though the employer relied on a bank to file the return on time, because the responsibility for timely filing remains with the employer or plan administrator (see Q 20:1). [I.R.C. § 6058(a); Alton Ob-Gyn, Ltd. v. United States, 789 F.2d 515 (7th Cir. 1986)]

Q 21:14   Does the statute of limitations apply to the Form 5500 series return/report?

IRS has confirmed that for plan years beginning after December 31, 2006, filing the Form 5500 series return/report *without* Schedule P (Form 5500) (see Q 21:7) will start the running of the statute of limitations on the plan filing.

For plan years beginning prior to January 1, 2007, the filing of Schedule P with the Form 5500 return/report (2005, for the Form 5500-EZ) started the running of the statute of limitations for any tax-exempt trust that was part of a qualified retirement plan. [I.R.C. §§ 6033(a), 6501(a)]

One court has held that the filing of the Form 5500 series return/report for 1980 without Schedule P attached started the running of the statute of limitations because the form disclosed the plan's trustees and was signed by a trustee under penalty of perjury. However, the 1979 Form 5500 series return/report did not start the running of the statute of limitations because it did not disclose the plan's trustees. [Martin Fireproofing Profit Sharing Plan & Trust, 92 T.C. 1173 (1989)]

Q 21:15   Does the filing of the Form 5500 series return/report start the statute of limitations running with regard to a prohibited transaction?

Yes, it does, if it discloses the transaction. Although Form 5330 is the appropriate form to report a prohibited transaction for the purpose of computing any excise taxes that may be owed (see Qs 21:18, 24:5), IRS conceded in one case that the filing of a Form 5500 series return/report that adequately discloses the facts of the transaction is sufficient to start the three-year statute of limitations running for prohibited transactions. [Rutland, 89 T.C. 1137 (1987)] In one case, the trustee of a pension plan paid excise taxes on a prohibited transaction and filed Form 5330 some years after Form 5500 had been filed. Subsequently, the trustee filed for a refund when it discovered that the transaction was not prohibited. IRS denied the refund because the claim was made more than three years after Form 5500 had been filed even though the claim was made within three years of the Form 5330 filing. The court concluded that the filing of Form 5500, and not the filing of Form 5330, started the three-year statute of limitations applicable to refund claims. [Imperial Plan, Inc. v. United States, 95 F.3d 25 (9th Cir. 1996)]

However, the six-year statute of limitations may be applicable if the Form 5500 series return/report does not disclose a prohibited transaction. [Thoburn, 95 T.C. 132 (1990)]

Q 21:16   Must a plan engage an independent accountant when it files its Form 5500 series return/report?

If a plan is a large plan filer (see Q 21:2), a certified public accountant or licensed public accountant (or an individual certified by DOL) must, in most cases, conduct an audit of the plan's books and records and issue an opinion, which must be included in the annual report, covering:

1. The financial statements and schedules covered by the annual report;
2. The accounting principles and practices reflected in the report;
3. The consistency of the application of those principles and practices; and
4. Any changes in accounting principles having a material effect on the financial statements.

[ERISA §§ 103(a)(3), 109(b); DOL Reg. § 2520.103-1(b)(5); 2009 Instructions for Schedule H (Form 5500)]

If a plan is a small plan filer (see Q 21:2), an accountant's audit and opinion are also required; however, in order for a small plan to be eligible to waive the annual audit requirements:

1. At least 95 percent of the plan's assets must be qualifying plan assets, or
2. Any person handling plan assets that are not qualifying plan assets must be bonded, and
3. The summary annual report (SAR; see Q 20:24) must contain additional information.

Qualifying plan assets are:

1. Qualifying employer securities (see Q 23:86);
2. Loans to plan participants (see Q 14:1);
3. Any assets held by:
   a. A bank or similar financial institution,
   b. An insurance company qualified to do business under the laws of a state,
   c. An organization registered as a broker-dealer under the Securities and Exchange Act of 1934, or
   d. Any other organization authorized to act as a trustee for IRAs (see Q 30:2);
4. Shares issued by an investment company registered under the Investment Company Act of 1940;
5. Investment and annuity contracts issued by any insurance company qualified to do business under the laws of a state; and
6. For individual account plans (see Q 2:2), any assets over which the participant or beneficiary exercises control and for which the participant or beneficiary receives, at least annually, a statement from a regulated financial institution (referred to in 3 and 5 above) describing the assets held or issued by the financial institution and their amount.

[DOL Reg. § 2520.104-46(b)(1)(ii)]

Small plans filers for which at least 95 percent of the assets, as of the last day of the preceding plan year, constitute qualifying plan assets will not be subject to bond requirements in order to qualify for the waiver. However, handlers of non-qualifying assets in plans where less than 95 percent of the assets are qualifying plan assets must be bonded, but not for an amount that is less than the value of the non-qualifying plan assets. If a bond is acquired pursuant to ERISA Section 412 (i.e., a fidelity bond is required in an amount no less than 10 percent of the funds handled; see Q 20:32), the bond requirement with respect to the small plan audit waiver may be satisfied.

Example 1. Liz Ltd. Retirement Plan, a calendar year plan, has total assets of $600,000 as of the end of the plan year. A fidelity bond covering $60,000 (10% × $600,000) has been acquired. The assets include investments in various bank, insurance company, and mutual fund products of $520,000; investments in qualifying employer securities of $40,000; participant loans totaling $20,000; and a $20,000 investment in a real estate limited partnership. Because the only asset of the plan that does not constitute a qualifying plan asset is the $20,000 real estate investment and the investment represents less than 5 percent of the plan's total assets, no bond would be required as a condition for the small plan audit waiver.

Example 2. Jimmy Co. Pension Plan, a calendar year plan, has total assets of $600,000 as of the end of the plan year, of which $558,000 constitutes qualifying plan assets and $42,000 constitutes non-qualifying plan assets. A fidelity bond covering $60,000 (10% × $600,000) has been acquired. Under these circumstances, no additional bond would be required as a condition for the small plan audit waiver because the fidelity bond covering $60,000 is greater than $42,000 (i.e., 7% of the assets in the plan do not constitute qualifying plan assets).

Example 3. Sunshine Co. Pension Plan, a calendar year plan, has total assets of $600,000 as of the end of the plan year, of which $510,000 constitutes qualifying plan assets and $90,000 constitutes nonqualifying plan assets. A fidelity bond covering $60,000 (10% × $600,000) has been acquired. Because 15 percent of the assets in the plan (i.e., $90,000) do not constitute qualifying plan assets, the plan, as a condition to electing the small plan audit waiver for the next plan year, must ensure that a fidelity bond be acquired in an amount equal to at least $90,000 (15% × $600,000). Since the plan already has a fidelity bond covering $60,000, increasing the coverage to $90,000, would be sufficient to meet the audit waiver requirement.

[DOL Reg. § 2520.104-46(b)(1)(iii); EBSA FAQs (Mar. 3, 2004)]

The SAR must include, in addition to any other required information:

1. The name of each regulated financial institution holding qualifying plan assets, and the amount of such assets reported by the institution as of the end of the plan year;

2. The name of the surety company issuing the bond if the plan has more than 5 percent of its assets in non-qualifying plan assets;

3. A notice indicating that participants and beneficiaries may, upon request and without charge, examine, or receive copies of, evidence of the required bond and statements received from the regulated financial institutions describing the qualifying plan assets; and

4. A notice stating that participants and beneficiaries should contact DOL if they are unable to examine or obtain copies of the regulated financial institution statements or evidence of the required bond, if applicable.

[DOL Reg. § 2520.104-46(b)(1)(i)(B); 2008 Instructions for Schedule I (Form 5500)]

DOL has stated that both large plan and small plan filers must use current value to determine realized and unrealized gains and losses, not the historical cost method. [DOL Notice (Jan. 26, 1990); DOL News Rel. 91-2 (1991)]

A 403(b) plan that is subject to Title I of ERISA (see Q 35:51) is not required to include an accountant's opinion with its Form 5500. [DOL Info. Ltr. (Nov. 15, 1996)]

Q 21:17   Where are the Form 5500 series return/reports filed?

The 2009 Form 5500 and Form 5500-SF, with any required schedules, statements, and attachments, should be electronically filed with DOL using the

EFAST2 processing system (see Q 21:3). Form 5500-EZ should be filed on paper and sent by mail or private delivery service to the following address:

Department of the Treasury
Internal Revenue Service
Ogden, UT 84201-0020

[2009 Instructions for Form 5500, 2009 Instructions for Form 5500-SF, 2009 Instructions for Form 5500-EZ]

Q 21:18 Which special returns must be filed with IRS?

Although the Form 5500 series return/report (other than Form 5500-EZ) is filed with DOL, certain special returns must be filed with IRS.

Form 5310, Application for Determination for Terminating Plan, is filed with IRS as part of an application for a determination letter (see chapter 18) concerning the termination of a qualified retirement plan. Although there is no legal requirement to file for a determination letter regarding a plan's termination, it is strongly suggested that Form 5310 be filed with IRS (see Q 25:63).

Form 5310-A, Notice of Plan Merger or Consolidation, Spinoff, or Transfer of Plan Assets or Liabilities; Notice of Qualified Separate Lines of Business, is filed to notify IRS of a consolidation, merger, spinoff, or transfer of plan assets and liabilities. Form 5310-A must be filed at least 30 days before the event. See Q 9:55 for details and Q 9:56 for filing exceptions. Form 5310-A is also filed to notify IRS that the employer treats itself as operating qualified separate lines of business (see Qs 5:47, 5:49).

Another special return filed with IRS is Form 5330, Return of Excise Taxes Related to Employee Benefit Plans. Form 5330 is used to report and pay the tax on the following:

- Prohibited transactions (see Q 21:16, chapter 24)
- Failure to meet minimum funding standards (see Q 8:1)
- Failure to pay liquidity shortfall (see Q 8:32)
- Certain ESOP dispositions (see chapter 28)
- Nondeductible contributions to qualified retirement plans (see chapter 12)
- Excess contributions to 401(k) plans (see Qs 27:25, 27:34)
- Certain prohibited allocations of qualified securities by an ESOP (see chapter 28)
- Reversions of qualified retirement plan assets to employers (see Q 25:52)
- Failure to provide notice of significant reduction in future accruals (see Q 9:50)
- Multiemployer plans in endangered or critical status (see Q 8:8)

[I.R.C. §§ 4971, 4972, 4975, 4978, 4979, 4979A, 4980, 4980F; Instructions to IRS Form 5330]

Form 5330 is generally due on or before the last day of the seventh month after the end of the taxable year of the employer or other person required to file Form 5330. An extension of up to six months may be requested by filing Form 5558 (see Q 21:9). However, Form 5558 does not extend the time to pay taxes. To report reversions, Form 5330 must be filed by the last day of the month following the month in which the reversion occurred. To report the failure to provide notice of significant reduction in future accruals, Form 5330 must be filed by the last day of the month following the month in which the failure occurred. To report excess contributions to 401(k) plans, Form 5330 must be filed by the last day of the 15th month after the close of the plan year to which the excess contributions relate.

Another special return filed with IRS, Form 5329, Additional Taxes on Qualified Plans (Including IRAs) and Other Tax-Favored Accounts, is used to report any excise tax or additional tax owed in connection with a qualified retirement plan or IRA. Form 5329 is used to report and pay the tax on the following:

- Excess contributions to a traditional IRA (see Q 30:9), Roth IRA (see Q 31:8), Coverdell ESA, and Archer MSA
- Certain taxable distributions from education accounts
- Early distributions (see Qs 16:1, 30:41, 31:32)
- Excess accumulations (failure to make a required minimum distribution; see Qs 11:67–11:71, 30:43)

Form 5329 should generally be attached to and filed by the same due date (including extensions) as the taxpayer's Form 1040, U.S. Individual Income Tax Return. If a taxpayer is subject *only* to the tax on early distributions (and distribution code 1 is correctly shown in Box 7 of Form 1099-R; see Q 21:19), Form 5329 need not be filed and the tax should be reported on Form 1040.

[I.R.C. §§ 72(t), 4973, 4974; 2009 Instructions for Form 5329]

Q 21:19 Which form is used to report qualified retirement plan distributions?

Form 1099-R, Distributions From Pensions, Annuities, Retirement or Profit-Sharing Plans, IRAs, Insurance Contracts, etc., is used to report distributions from qualified retirement plans, including periodic payments, nonperiodic payments that are not total distributions, and total distributions. Those receiving qualified retirement plan payments must receive Form 1099-R by January 31 of the year after the payment. [Rev. Proc. 92-86, 1992-2 C.B. 495; 2010 Instructions for Form 1099-R]

A plan sponsor or plan administrator (see Q 20:1) may furnish the required Form 1099-R electronically to recipients if the consent, format, posting, and notification requirements are satisfied. [IRS Notice 2004-10, 2004-1 C.B. 433]

Form 1099-R information is summarized on Form 1096, Annual Summary and Transmittal of U.S. Information Returns, which must be filed with IRS by the last day in February. After December 31, 2008, the only acceptable method of filing electronically will be through the Filing Information Returns Electronically (FIRE) System. [2010 Instructions for Form 1096; IRS Pub. 1220]

The failure to timely file a required report can result in a $25 per day penalty up to a maximum of $15,000. [I.R.C. § 6652(e)]

Generally, the filing of Form 1099-R with respect to each payee satisfies information reporting requirements with respect to income tax withholding. For failing to report withholding taxes or to keep necessary records, IRS may impose a penalty of $50 for each affected individual, up to a maximum of $50,000 in a calendar year. [I.R.C. §§ 6047(d), 6704; Temp. Treas. Reg. § 35.3405-1T, Q&A E-9]

Form 945, Annual Return of Withheld Federal Income Tax, is used to report nonpayroll items, including pension withholding. Semiweekly depositors are required to complete and file Form 945-A, Annual Record of Federal Tax Liability, with Form 945. Form 945 must be filed only for a calendar year in which withholding is required. [Treas. Reg. § 31.6011(a)-4(b); Ann. 94-13, 1994-5 I.R.B 50; 2009 Instructions for Forms 945, 945-A]

Q 21:20   Are there additional DOL reporting requirements?

Summary plan descriptions (SPDs; see Q 22:1) and summary description of material modifications (SMMs; see Q 22:8) as well as other documents relating to plans must be provided to DOL upon request. The penalty for failure to comply with such a request is up to $100 per day ($110 after adjustment for inflation), up to a maximum of $1,000 per request ($1,100 after adjustment for inflation). No penalty will be imposed if the failure is due to matters reasonably beyond the control of the plan administrator (see Q 20:1). [ERISA §§ 101, 104, 502(c)(6)]

Some of these reports must also be distributed to participants. See chapter 22 for more details.

Q 21:21   Which types of plans are exempt from the reporting requirements of DOL?

There is a general exemption for individual retirement accounts (IRAs; see chapter 30), governmental plans, church plans, and excess benefit plans (unfunded plans providing benefits above the limits on contributions and benefits for tax purposes). [ERISA § 4(b)]

There is also an exemption for "plans without employees"—that is, plans in which the only participants are either an individual and the individual's spouse, if that individual is the only owner of the business (whether incorporated or not), or the partners in a partnership and the partners' spouses. In the case of any other family relationship, the exemption does not apply. For example, if the only plan participants are brothers, or father and son, the reporting requirements apply unless they are partners. This exemption does not apply to the requirement to file a Form 5500 series return/report (see Q 21:2). [DOL Reg. § 2510.3-3]

Generally, 403(b) plans (see Q 35:1) established pursuant to salary reduction arrangements will not be subject to Title I of ERISA and, therefore, not be required to file Form 5500. See Q 35:51 for details.

Q 21:22   What are the payment and filing requirements of PBGC?

ERISA requires payment of premiums to PBGC (see Q 25:10). There are two kinds of annual premiums: (1) the flat-rate premium (see Q 21:30), which applies to all plans, and (2) the variable-rate premium (see Q 21:30), which applies only to single-employer plans.

Every covered plan under ERISA Section 4021 (see Q 25:11) must make a premium filing each year. The due dates for these filings vary based on plan size (see Q 21:24).

Electronic filing is mandatory for all plans. My Plan Administration Account (My PAA) is a secure Web-based application that enables pension plan professionals to electronically submit premium filings to PBGC in accordance with PBGC's regulations. Electronic filings may be prepared using My PAA's data entry screens or with compatible private-sector software. PBGC may grant exemptions from the electronic filing requirement for good cause in appropriate circumstances.

[2010 Premium Payment Instructions PBGC]

Q 21:23   Who must file with PBGC?

The plan administrator (see Q 20:1) of each pension plan covered under ERISA Section 4021 (see Q 25:11) is required annually to file the prescribed premium information and pay the premium due in accordance with PBGC's (see Q 25:10) premium regulations and instructions. If a plan is covered, a premium filing must be made even if no premium is owed.

Premium filings must be made and premiums must be paid through and including the plan year in which any of the following occurs:

1. Plan assets are distributed in satisfaction of all benefit liabilities pursuant to the plan's termination.
2. A trustee is appointed for the plan. [ERISA § 4042]
3. The plan ceases to exist by transferring all of its assets and liabilities to one or more other plans in a merger or consolidation.
4. The plan ceases to be a covered plan.

[ERISA § 4021]

Example 1. A calendar-year plan terminates in a standard termination with a termination date of September 30, 2009. On April 7, 2010, assets are distributed in satisfaction of all benefit liabilities. The plan administrator must file and make the premium payments for the 2009 and 2010 plan years.

Example 2. A plan with a plan year beginning July 1 and ending June 30 terminates in a distress termination with a termination date of April 28, 2010. On July 7, 2010, a trustee is appointed to administer the plan under ERISA Section 4042. Premium filings and payments must be made for both the 2009 and 2010 plan years because a trustee was not appointed until after the beginning of the 2010 plan year.

[2010 Premium Payment Instructions PBGC]

A pension plan was not required to pay premiums to PBGC for the plan year following the plan year in which the plan filed for a standard termination (see Q 25:13) and distributed plan benefits and all surplus assets under the first six categories of ERISA Section 4044(a) (see Q 25:38), except for assets attributable to employee contributions and subject to a lawsuit. [PBGC Op. Ltr. No. 93-11]

Q 21:24   When are PBGC premium filings due?

A filing includes both the submission of required data and the payment of any required premium. In general, if a filing is not made by the due date, late payment charges will apply. Late payment charges include both interest charges and penalty charges (see Q 21:32).

The date by which a filing must be made varies depending on the number of participants for whom premiums were owed in the prior plan year. Generally, the filing due dates vary based on the plan size. For this purpose, plan size is based on the number of participants for whom flat-rate premiums (see Q 21:30) were payable for the plan year preceding the premium payment year. Plan size is determined as follows:

1. *Small plans (prior year participant count is less than 100):* Both the flat-rate premium and the variable-rate premium (see Q 21:30) are due by the last day of the 16th full calendar month following the end of the plan year preceding the premium payment year. For example, April 30, 2011 is the due date for 2010 calendar-year plans.

2. *Mid-size plans (prior year participant count is 100 or more but less than 500):*
   a. The due date for the flat-rate premium is the 15th day of the tenth full calendar month in the plan year. For example, October 15, 2010 is the due date for 2010 calendar-year plans.
   b. The due date for the variable-rate premium is the 15th day of the tenth full calendar month in the plan year. However, if the premium funding target (see Q 21:29) is not yet known, an estimated variable-rate premium may be paid and an amended filing made at a later date to reconcile the final variable-rate premium with the estimate. Note that this reconciliation date is the same date all premiums are due for small

plans. For example, April 30, 2011 is the due date for 2010 calendar-year plans.

3. *Large plans (prior year participant count is 500 or more):*

    a. The due date for the flat-rate premium is the last day of the second full calendar month in the plan year. For example, the due date is the last day of February for calendar-year plans. However, if the final flat-rate premium is not known by that time, an estimate may be paid and a reconciliation filing made at a later date to reconcile the final flat-rate premium with the estimate. Note that for plans that pay a variable-rate premium, this reconciliation date is the same date the variable-rate premium is due.

    b. The due date for the variable-rate premium is the same as for mid-size plans.

Example. A preexisting calendar-year plan had 525 participants on December 31, 2008 and 490 participants on December 31, 2009. Because the participant count was 500 or more as of the participant count date for the 2009 premium payment year (i.e., December 31, 2008), the plan is considered a large plan for the 2010 premium payment year and the 2010 flat-rate premium is due on March 1, 2010. For 2010, the flat-rate premium due is based on 490 participants (the participant count on December 31, 2009). The fact that premiums are due for fewer than 500 participants for 2010 does not negate the fact that the early flat-rate premium due date applies for 2010.

However, for the 2011 premium payment year, the plan will be considered a mid-size plan because the participant count for 2010 was more than 100 and less than 500 participants. Therefore, for 2011, the flat-rate premium is not due until October 17, 2011.

If a premium filing due date falls on a Saturday, Sunday, or federal holiday, the due date is extended automatically to the next business day. Additionally, PBGC may grant disaster relief by waiving late filing and payment penalties for certain plans that are unable to meet the filing deadline as a result of a major disaster (e.g., a hurricane).

Because plan size for due date purposes is based on the participant count for the prior plan year, a new plan or a newly covered plan is not considered a small, mid-size, or large plan for this purpose regardless of how many participants are in the plan. Thus, the above rules do not apply to new or newly covered plans (see Q 21:25). There are also special due date rules for preexisting plans that are changing plan years (see Q 21:26).

[PBGC Reg. § 4007.11; 2010 Premium Payment Instructions PBGC]

Q 21:25 Are there special rules for new and newly covered plans?

New plans and newly covered plans are not classified as small, mid-size, or large plans, because those classifications are based on the number of partici-pants for whom premiums were payable for the plan year preceding the premium payment year. Therefore, special due date rules apply to these first-time filers. For new plans and newly covered plans, both the flat-rate premium and the variable-rate premium are due on the later of:

1. The last day of the 16th full calendar month that began on or after the first day of the premium payment year in the case of a newly covered plan, or on or after the effective date in the case of a new plan, or

2. 90 days after the plan adoption date.

Example 1. A new calendar-year plan was adopted and effective on January 1, 2010 and had 650 participants on that date. Although there are more than 500 participants, the plan is not considered a large plan for 2010, because plan size is based on the number of participants for whom 2009 premiums were required to be paid. Because the plan is a new plan, the 2010 flat-rate premium is not due on March 1, 2010 (the flat-rate premium due date applicable for preexisting large plans). Instead, the plan would be required to pay its flat-rate and variable-rate premiums by May 2, 2011. As a new plan, its 2010 participant count date is January 1, 2010 (the first day of the plan year), and so the 2010 flat-rate premium is based on a participant count of 650 as of January 1, 2010.

In 2011, this plan will be considered a large plan because the participant count for the 2010 premium payment year was above 500. As a large plan, the 2011 flat-rate premium will be due on February 28, 2011. Note that this is before the date that the 2010 premium payments are due (May 2, 2011). The 2011 variable-rate premium will be due on October 17, 2011.

Example 2. A new plan is adopted on December 1, 2010 and has a July 1 through June 30 plan year. The plan became effective on December 1, 2010. The filing due date for the plan's first year (December 1, 2010 through June 30, 2011) is April 2, 2012, regardless of the participant count on the participant count date (December 1, 2010).

Example 3. A professional service employer maintains a plan with a calendar plan year. If this plan has never had more than 25 active participants since September 2, 1974, it is not a covered plan under ERISA Section 4021. On October 18, 2010, the plan, which always had 25 or fewer active participants, has 26 active participants. It is now a covered plan and will continue to be a covered plan regardless of how many active participants the plan has in the future. Note that the premium payment year begins on January 1, 2010, even though the plan did not become covered until after that date. The due date for the plan's first premium filing is May 2, 2011 (the last day of the 16th full calendar month that began on or after the first day of the premium payment year).

[PBGC Reg. § 4007.11; 2010 Premium Payment Instructions PBGC]

Q 21:26   How does a change in the plan year affect the due dates for filing PBGC forms?

For a plan that changes its plan year, the filing due dates for the short year are unaffected by the change in plan year. For the first plan year under the new cycle, the due date is whichever is later:

1. Thirty days following the date on which a plan amendment changing the plan year was adopted, or

2. The date the filing would otherwise be due.

Example 1. By plan amendment adopted on December 1, 2010, a small plan changes from a plan year beginning January 1 to a plan year beginning June 1. This results in a short plan year beginning January 1, 2010 and ending May 31, 2010. Both the flat-rate and variable-rate premiums for the short plan year are due May 2, 2011. For the new plan year beginning June 1, 2010, the due date for the flat-rate and variable-rate premium is the date the filing would otherwise be due (September 30, 2011), because that is later than 30 days after the date the plan amendment changing the plan year was adopted (December 31, 2010).

Example 2. By plan amendment adopted on January 7, 2011 and made retroactively effective to April 1, 2010, a mid-size plan changes from a plan year beginning March 1 to a plan year beginning April 1. For the March 1, 2010 through March 31, 2010 short plan year, both the flat-rate and variable-rate premiums are due December 15, 2010. For the new plan year beginning April 1, 2010, the due date for the flat-rate premium and variable-rate premium is 30 days after the adoption of the plan amendment changing the plan year (February 7, 2011), because that is later than the date the premium would otherwise be due (January 17, 2011).

Example 3. By plan amendment adopted on July 8, 2010 and made retroactively effective to May 1, 2010, a large plan changes from a plan year beginning February 1 to a plan year beginning May 1. The plan has always had 500 or more participants. For the February 1, 2010 through April 30, 2010 short plan year, the flat-rate premium is due March 31, 2010, and the variable-rate premium is due November 15, 2010. For the new plan year beginning May 1, 2010, the due date for the flat-rate premium is 30 days after the adoption of the plan amendment changing the plan year (August 8, 2010), because that is later than the date the flat-rate premium would otherwise be due (June 30, 2010). The variable-rate premium for the first plan year in the new cycle is due on the date the variable-rate premium would otherwise be due (February 15, 2011), because that is later than 30 days after the adoption of the plan amendment (August 8, 2010).

[PBGC Reg. § 4007.11; 2010 Premium Payment Instructions PBGC]

Q 21:27   How are filings with PBGC completed?

In order to report certain required data and submit any required premium payment to PBGC (see Q 25:10), a complete premium filing must be prepared. The two types of filings are:

1. Estimated flat-rate premium filings for large plans required to pay the flat-rate premium early in the year, and

2. Comprehensive premium filings for all other purposes.

A comprehensive premium filing is used to report:

1. The flat-rate premium and related data for all plans;

2. The variable-rate premium and related data for single-employer plans; and

3. Additional data, such as identifying information and miscellaneous plan-related or filing-related data, for all plans. For large plans, the comprehensive premium filing also serves to reconcile an estimated flat-rate premium paid earlier in the year.

The PBGC Comprehensive Premium Filing is the form used to make the comprehensive premium filing. PBGC Form 1-ES, Estimated Premium Payment is used for the estimated flat-rate premium filings for large plans.

Although e-filing of premium information through My PAA (see Q 21:22) is mandatory, premium payments may be made either within My PAA or outside of My PAA. If payment is made within My PAA, payment may be made by electronic funds transfer using automated clearing house (ACH), by electronic check, or by credit card. If payment is made outside of My PAA, payment may be made by electronic funds transfer or paper check.

[2010 Premium Payment Instructions PBGC]

Q 21:28   How are participants counted for premium filing purposes?

Plan participants must be counted because flat-rate premiums are based on the number of participants. In addition, the number of participants for the prior plan year affects when a filing for the current plan year is due.

The date on which participants are counted for premium purposes is called the "participant count date." The participant count date is the last day of the plan year preceding the premium payment year, except as follows:

1. If the plan is a new plan, the participant count date is the first day of the premium payment year,

2. If the plan is a newly covered plan, the participant count date is the first day of the premium payment year, or

3. If the plan is the transferee plan in a merger or the transferor plan in a spinoff to a new plan, and the transaction meets the conditions described below, the participant count date is the first day of the premium payment year. A plan merger or spinoff is covered by this rule if:

a. A merger is effective on the first day of the transferee (the continuing) plan's plan year, or a spinoff is effective on the first day of the transferor plan's plan year, and

b. The merger or spinoff is not *de minimis,* as defined in the regulations.

Example 1. An ongoing plan changes its plan year from a calendar year to a plan year that begins June 1, effective June 1, 2010. The participant count date for the January 1, 2010 through May 31, 2010 plan year is December 31, 2009, and for the June 1, 2010 through May 31, 2011 plan year is May 31, 2010.

Example 2. A new calendar-year plan is adopted February 18, 2010, retroactively effective as of January 1, 2010. The participant count date is January 1, 2010.

Example 3. A new calendar-year plan is adopted January 1, 2010, effective April 1, 2010. The participant count date is April 1, 2010.

For premium purposes, "participant" means an individual (whether active, inactive, retired, or deceased) with respect to whom the plan has benefit liabilities. Beneficiaries and alternate payees (see Q 36:5) are not counted as participants. However, a deceased participant will continue to be counted as a participant if there are one or more beneficiaries or alternate payees who are receiving or have a right to receive benefits earned by the participant.

An individual is not counted as a participant after all benefit liabilities with respect to the individual are distributed through the purchase of irrevocable commitments from an insurer or otherwise. In addition, a non-vested individual is not counted as a participant after:

1. A deemed "zero-dollar cashout";

2. A one-year break in service (see Q 5:10) under plan rules; or

3. Death.

[PBGC Reg. §§ 4006.2, 4006.5(d), 4006.5(e), 4006.6; 2010 Premium Payment Instructions PBGC]

Q 21:29 How are unfunded vested benefits determined?

The term "unfunded vested benefits" is used to describe the underfunding measure on which the variable-rate premium is based. For variable-rate premium purposes, unfunded vested benefits means the excess, if any, of:

1. The premium funding target, over

2. The fair market value of plan assets.

Both the premium funding target and the fair market value of assets are measured on the funding valuation date for the premium payment year. For premium purposes, this date is called the UVB valuation date to distinguish it from the participant count date. The premium funding target is the liability measure underlying the UVB calculation. It is determined the same way the funding target is determined (see Q 8:2), except that only vested benefits are included and a special premium discount rate structure is used.

[2010 Premium Payment Instructions PBGC]

Q 21:30 What must plan sponsors pay as an insurance premium to PBGC?

For plan years beginning after December 31, 2005, with respect to single-employer plans, the flat-rate portion of the premium is $30 per participant; and, with respect to multiemployer plans (see Q 29:2), the flat-rate portion of the premium is $8 per participant. [ERISA §§ 4006(a)(3)(A)(i), 4006(a)(3)(A)(iii)]

For plan years beginning on or after January 1, 2007, the flat-rate portion of the premium will be automatically adjusted each year to reflect increases in the national average wage index that is currently used for Social Security indexing. The rate will be rounded to the nearest multiple of $1. [ERISA §§ 4006(a)(3)(F), 4006(a)(3)(G)] For plan years beginning in 2010, with respect to single-employer plans, the flat-rate portion of the premium increased to $35, and, with respect to multiemployer plans, the flat-rate portion remained at $9. For single-employer plans that began in 2009, the flat-rate portion was $34; for such plans that began in 2008, the flat-rate portion was $33; and, for such plans that began in 2007, the flat-rate portion was $31. For multiemployer plans that began in 2009, the flat-rate portion remained at $9; for such plans that began in 2008, the flat-rate portion was $9; and, for such plans that began in 2007, the flat-rate portion remained at $8. [PBGC Notice Dec. 1, 2009]

In addition, each plan year, with respect to single-employer plans, a variable-rate component of the premium is determined based on a plan's unfunded vested benefits and is equal to $9 for every $1,000 of unfunded vested benefits, divided by the number of participants for whom premiums are being paid as of the close of the preceding plan year. [ERISA § 4006(a)(3)(E); PBGC Reg. §§ 4006.3, 4006.5]

> **Example 1.** For the plan year beginning September 1, 2010 and ending August 31, 2011, a defined benefit plan with 100 participants has unfunded vested benefits of $1,000,000. For purposes of computing the variable-rate premium, the amount based on the unfunded vested benefits is $9,000 [($1,000,000 ÷ $1,000) × $9]. The variable rate for the plan is $90 per participant ($9,000 ÷ 100). The total premium due for this year is $125 per participant. This consists of the $35 flat rate and the $90 variable-rate portion.

Effective for plan years beginning after December 31, 2006, for plans of small employers, those with 25 or fewer employees, the PBGC variable rate premium for each participant will not exceed $5 multiplied by the number of participants in the plan as of the close of the preceding plan year. This is not simply a $5 cap per participant, but the cap grows geometrically with plan size. [ERISA § 4006(a)(3)(H); PBGC Reg. § 4006.3]

Example 2. A defined benefit plan had 20 participants as of December 31, 2009. For 2010, the variable-rate premium for all 20 participants cannot exceed $2,000 (($5 × 20) × 20).

For plan years beginning after December 31, 2007, the variable rate premium will be based on the plan's unfunded vested benefits valued using a three segmented yield curve of investment-grade corporate bonds. Furthermore, the rule providing that no variable rate premium is required if contributions for the prior year were at least equal to the full funding limit will no longer apply. [PBGC Notice, 72 Fed. Reg. 6012 (Feb. 8, 2007); ERISA § 4006(a)(3)]

For plan years beginning after December 31, 2005, with respect to a single-employer plan that terminates in a distress or involuntary manner (see Qs 25:15, 25:22), a premium of $1,250 per participant, per year, for three years is imposed. Generally, the three-year period during which the premium applies starts with the first month following the month in which the termination date occurs. However, with respect to terminations during a bankruptcy reorganization proceeding, the three-year period does not start until after the bankruptcy proceeding has been concluded. Furthermore, plans that terminate during a bankruptcy reorganization proceeding where the bankruptcy filing was made before October 18, 2005 are exempt. [ERISA §§ 4006(a)(7), 4041(c)(2)(B), 4042; PBGC Reg. § 4006.7]

Q 21:31   May premiums be prorated for a short plan year?

Premium payors are allowed to pay a prorated premium for the following short plan years:

- A short first year of a new or newly covered plan;
- A short year created by a change in plan year;
- A short year created by distribution of plan assets pursuant to plan termination; or
- A short year created by the appointment of a trustee for a single-employer plan under ERISA Section 4042 (see Q 25:22).

The proration is based on the number of full and partial months in the short plan year.

[2010 Premium Payment Instructions PBGC]

Q 21:32   What happens if the premium payment is late?

Late payment charges, including both interest and penalty charges, are assessed if PBGC receives a premium payment after the due date. The interest charge is based on the number of days the payment is late, and accrues at the rate imposed under Section 6601(a) (the rate for late payment of taxes). The late payment penalty rate is (1) 1 percent per month on any amount of unpaid premium that is paid on or before the date PBGC issues a written notice to any person liable for the plan's premium that there may be a premium delinquency, or (2) 5 percent per month on any amount of unpaid premium that is paid after that date. PBGC regulations provide that the late payment penalty will be no more than 100 percent of the unpaid premiums and no less than the lesser of $25 or the amount of unpaid premium. [PBGC Reg. §§ 4007.7, 4007.8; PBGC Statement of Policy, 61 Fed. Reg. 63,874 (Dec. 2, 1996); 2010 Premium Payment Instructions PBGC]

Q 21:33   Can the late penalty charges be waived?

Generally, if the plan administrator (see Q 20:1) can show substantial hardship or otherwise demonstrate good cause, PBGC may waive the penalty (but not interest) charge (see Q 21:32). In addition to waiving premium penalties on the basis of reasonable cause, PBGC may waive the penalty for provisions of law, for legal errors, during pendency of PBGC procedures, and for other appropriate circumstances. [PBGC Reg. §§ 4007.8(b), 4007.8(c), Part 4007, apps 21–25; 2010 Premium Payment Instructions PBGC]

The late penalty (see Q 21:32) is automatically waived in the following situations:

1. With respect to large plans (see Q 21:24), no penalty will be charged until the date the flat-rate reconciliation filing is due (see Q 21:24) if the premium that was paid by the flat-rate premium due date equals at least the lesser of:

   a. 90 percent of the full flat-rate premium, or

   b. An amount equal to the participant count for the year before the premium payment year multiplied by the applicable flat-rate premium for the premium payment year.

2. With respect to large plans, no penalty will be charged until the date the reconciliation is due if a flat-rate premium payment was not made by the premium due date because either:

   a. Fewer than 500 participants were erroneously reported for the plan year preceding the premium payment year, or

   b. The due date for paying the flat-rate premium for the plan year preceding the premium payment year is later than the due date for paying the flat-rate premium for the premium payment year.

3. With respect to large and mid-size plans (see Q 21:24), no penalty will be charged until the date the reconciliation is due or (if earlier) the date the reconciliation filing is made if, by the plan's variable-rate premium due date (see Q 21:24):

   a. The plan administrator reports:

      i. The fair market value of the plan's assets for the premium payment year; and

      ii. An estimate of the premium funding target (see Q 21:29) that is certified by an enrolled actuary to be a reasonable estimate that:

(A) Takes into account the most current data available to the enrolled actuary;

(B) Has been determined in accordance with generally accepted actuarial principles and practices; and

(C) Uses the calculation methodology (alternative or standard) in effect for the plan year; and

b. The plan administrator pays at least the amount of variable-rate premium determined from the value of assets and estimated premium funding target so reported.

[PBGC Reg. §§ 4007.8(f) through 4007.8(j); 2010 Comprehensive Premium Payment Instructions PBGC]

Q 21:34   Must PBGC be notified when certain significant events affecting a single-employer defined benefit plan occur?

Yes. The plan administrator (see Q 20:1) or contributing sponsor may be required to notify PBGC of a reportable event. ERISA Section 4043 and PBGC regulations include a list of reportable events. With respect to certain reportable events, the plan administrator and each contributing sponsor are required to notify PBGC within 30 days after that person knows or has reason to know that a reportable event has occurred, unless a waiver or extension applies. Examples of these events include:

• Plan disqualification (notice is waived)

• Decrease in benefits (notice is waived)

• Active participation reduction (notice is waived for certain small plans and funding exceptions)

• Termination or partial termination (notice is waived)

• Inability to pay benefits when due (notice is waived for plans with more than 100 participants)

• Failure to meet minimum funding standards (see Q 8:1) (notice is waived if payment is made within 30 days or PBGC Form 200 is filed (see Q 21:35), and for certain small employers failing to make quarterly contributions (see Q 8:32))

• Bankruptcy (notice is waived for foreign entity)

• Liquidation (notice is waived for certain funding exceptions, foreign entities, and 10 percent *de minimis* exception)

• Change in sponsor or controlled group (see Q 5:31) (notice is waived for certain funding exceptions, foreign entities, and 10 percent *de minimis* exception)

• Transfer of benefit liabilities (notice is waived for complete plan transfer, 3 percent *de minimis* exception, and funding exception)

• Application for minimum funding waiver (see Q 8:25)

[PBGC Reg. §§ 4043.1–4043.35; PBGC Tech. Update 08-2]

If a required quarterly contribution for the 2010 plan year is not timely made and the failure to make the contribution is not motivated by financial inability, the reporting requirement:

1. Is waived if the plan had fewer than 25 participants for the prior plan year, and

2. If the plan had at least 25 but fewer than 100 participants for the prior year, will be considered satisfied if a simplified notice is filed with PBGC by the time the first missed-quarterly reportable event report for the 2010 plan year would otherwise be due.

[PBGC Tech. Update 09-4]

In certain circumstances, each contributing sponsor (but *not* the plan administrator) must notify PBGC at least 30 days *before* the occurrence of a reportable event. This advance notice applies only to privately held companies that are members of a controlled group that maintain plans with aggregate unfunded vested benefits of more than $50 million and an aggregate funded vested benefit percentage of less than 90 percent. Examples of these events include:

- Change in sponsor or controlled group (notice is waived for small plan and 5 percent *de minimis* exception)
- Liquidation (notice is waived for 5 percent *de minimis* exception)
- Bankruptcy (notice is extended until ten days after event has occurred)
- Application for minimum funding waiver (notice is extended until ten days after event has occurred)

[PBGC Reg. §§ 4043.61–4043.68]

PBGC may assess a penalty of up to $1,000 per day ($1,100 after adjustment for inflation) for failure to provide the required notice. [PBGC Reg. § 4043.3(e)]

PBGC Form 10, Post-Event Notice of Reportable Events, may be used to notify PBGC that a reportable event has occurred, and PBGC Form 10-Advance, Advance Notice of Reportable Events, may be used to notify PBGC in advance that a reportable event will occur.

[Instructions to PBGC Form 10 and PBGC Form 10-Advance]

PBGC has issued proposed regulations that would make significant changes to its regulations on reportable events and conform the regulations with the funding rules arising from PPA (see Q 1:33). The proposed regulations would eliminate most of the automatic waivers and extensions in the existing reportable events regulations. PBGC believes that the current rules are depriving it of early warnings that would enable it to mitigate distress situations. Furthermore, PBGC believes that the increased reporting burden stemming from the elimination of most of the automatic waivers and extensions is justified by PBGC's need for timely information that may contribute to plan continuation or the minimizing of funding shortfalls.

[Preamble to PBGC Prop. Reg. §§ 4043.1–4043.81]

Q 21:35   Are there any other notification requirements to PBGC?

Yes. PBGC must be notified by filing Form 200, Notice of Failure to Make Required Contributions, within ten days of the due date for a required plan contribution (see Q 8:16) if the aggregate unpaid balance, including interest, exceeds $1 million. [ERISA § 302(f)(4)]

Also, for plan years beginning after 2007, each contributing sponsor for a single-employer plan, and each member of the contributing sponsor's controlled group, must file annual actuarial and financial information with PBGC if (1) the funding target attainment percentage (FTAP; see Q 8:6) at the end of the preceding plan year is less than 80 percent, (2) the conditions for imposing a lien for missed plan contributions exceeding $1 million have been met, or (3) any portion of minimum funding waivers exceeding $1 million remains unpaid (see Qs 8:22, 8:23). Effective for plan years beginning after December 31, 2007, PBGC is waiving reporting for a controlled group if the aggregate plan underfunding does not exceed $15 million (disregarding those plans with no underfunding). However, the waiver does not apply if the reporting is required for any reason other than having an FTAP below 80 percent. For plan years beginning prior to 2008, there was a threshold requirement of $50 million aggregate unfunded vested benefits. [ERISA § 4010; PBGC Reg. §§ 4010.1–4010.14]

PBGC has issued final regulations that require the financial and actuarial information that underfunded plans are required to submit to be filed electronically in a standardized format. [PBGC Reg. § 4010.3; PBGC News Rel. No. 06-20 (Jan. 27, 2006)]

Q 21:36   How are forms filed with PBGC?

PBGC has issued regulations that consolidate the methods that may be used to send a filing to PBGC or provide an issuance to a third party. The regulations provide rules with respect to:

1. Methods of filings with PBGC including electronic filings;
2. Methods of issuing certain notices including electronic notices;
3. The determination of the date on which (a) a filing is treated as made or (b) an issuance is provided;
4. The computation of time periods; and
5. The rules for maintaining records by electronic means.

The regulations allow the filing of any submission, other than premiums (see Q 21:24), by hand, mail, or commercial delivery service, and refer the filer to PBGC's web site, http://www.pbgc.gov for current information on electronic filing that includes permitted methods, fax numbers, and e-mail addresses. [PBGC Reg. §§ 4000.1–4000.4]

See Q 20:23 regarding PBGC rules with respect to providing an issuance by electronic media. [PBGC Reg. §§ 4000.11–4000.15]

In general, PBGC will treat the submission as filed or the issuance as provided on the date it is sent if certain requirements are met. The requirements depend upon the method used to send the submission or issuance as follows:

- If the U.S. Postal Service is used, the filing date is the date the submission is mailed if it is properly addressed and first class mail (or equivalent) is used.

- If a commercial delivery service is used, the filing date is the date the submission is deposited with the delivery service if it is reasonable to expect the submission to arrive at the proper address on the second business day.

- If hand delivery is used, the filing date is the date of receipt of the hand delivered submission at the proper address.

- If a computer disk is sent, the filing date is determined as if a paper version of the submission was sent and the electronic disk complies with any technical requirements and a contact person is identified in writing.

- If electronic delivery is used, the filing date is the date the submission is electronically transmitted to the proper address and the electronic submission complies with any technical requirements and a contact person is included in the e-mail.

[PBGC Reg. §§ 4000.21–4000.31]

According to the regulations, when computing a time period, whether forwards or backwards, the day after (or before) the act, event, or default that begins the period is day one, the next day is day two, and so on. [PBGC Reg. §§ 4000.41–4000.43]

See Q 20:7 regarding PBGC rules with respect to the use of electronic media to satisfy the record maintenance and retention requirements. [PBGC Reg. §§ 4000.51–4000.54]

Chapter 22

Summary Plan Descriptions

One of the major obligations of a plan administrator is the preparation of a summary of the plan for distribution to participants and
beneficiaries. This chapter examines summary plan descriptions
(SPDs)—what they are, the information they must contain, and
how to avoid their legal pitfalls.

Q 22:1   What is a summary plan description?

An SPD is a booklet that describes the plan's provisions and the participants'
benefits, rights, and obligations in simple language. The SPD is the primary
source of supplying information regarding the plan document, and plan administrators (see Q 20:1) must provide the SPD to each plan participant and each
beneficiary receiving benefits under the plan (see Q 22:2). [ERISA §§ 101(a),
102(a)(1), 104(b)]

An SPD must contain certain information (see Q 22:4), and many courts have
ruled that it is a legally binding document (see Q 22:5).

Q 22:2   When must an SPD be furnished to a participant?

An SPD must be furnished to each participant and beneficiary no later than
(1) 90 days after becoming a participant or first receiving benefits, as the case
may be, or (2) within 120 days after the plan first becomes subject to the reporting and disclosure requirements of ERISA. [ERISA §§ 3(7), 3(8), 104(b)] Electronic media may be used to fulfill this requirement. [DOL Reg. §§ 2520.104b-1,
2520.107]

In the case of a new plan that provides that it is effective only upon IRS
approval, the 120-day period does not begin until the day after such condition is
satisfied (i.e., the day after IRS issues a favorable determination letter; see
Q 18:1). [DOL Reg. § 2520.104b-2(a)(3)] Conversely, if the plan is adopted
retroactively, the 120-day period begins to run at the time of adoption.

Penalties have been assessed against a plan administrator (see Qs 20:1,
22:13) for failure to provide plan participants and beneficiaries with an SPD.

[ERISA § 502(c); Leyda v. AlliedSignal, Inc., 2003 WL 55876 (2d Cir. 2003); Keogan v. Towers, Perrin, Forster & Crosby, Inc., 2003 U.S. Dist. LEXIS 7999 (D. Minn. 2003); Sunderlin v. First Reliance Standard Life Ins. Co., 2002 U.S. Dist. LEXIS 22646 (W.D.N.Y. 2002); Jackson v. E.J. Brach Corp., No. 94 C 6350 (N.D. Ill. 1996); Sacks v. Gross, Sklar & Metzger, P.C., No. 88-5009 (E.D. Pa. 1992)] One court ruled that a participant who never received an SPD could sue the plan administrator for damages regardless of whether or not his request for the SPD was in writing because the plan administrator was obligated to furnish the SPD within 90 days of enrollment. [Crotty v. Cook, 121 F.3d 541 (9th Cir. 1997)] However, another court ruled that a former plan participant who requested a copy of the SPD had to do so in writing. [ERISA § 104(b)(4); Amat v. Seafarers Int'l Union, 2002 WL 511540 (E.D. La. 2002)] Sending an SPD to a participant via first-class mail is acceptable. If a dispute arises as to whether or not an SPD was provided by mail to a participant, the plan administrator must prove that the SPD was mailed; the plan administrator is not required to prove that the SPD was received. Evidence that an SPD was always sent by first-class mail to a participant's last known address was satisfactory proof. [Campbell v. Emery Air Freight Corp, No. 93-6568 (E.D. Pa. 1995)]

In another case, the court determined that the failure of an employer to provide an SPD did not negate the knowing waiver of ERISA claims by an employee who was aware of his potential eligibility for benefits at the time he signed the release. [Finz v. Schlesinger, 957 F.2d 78 (2d Cir. 1992)] Failure to distribute the SPD was not a breach of fiduciary duty where it was undisputed that other materials were sent to an eligible employee that informed him of his obligation to enroll in the plan to receive benefits, concluded one court. [Brenner v. Johns Hopkins Univ., 2004 U.S. App. LEXIS 2339 (4th Cir. 2004)]

A plan administrator can refuse to provide an SPD to a deceased participant's son who was not a beneficiary. [Keys v. Eastman Kodak Co., 739 F. Supp. 135 (W.D.N.Y. 1990)]

Q 22:3 Must the SPD be filed with the Department of Labor?

The requirement that the SPD be filed with DOL has been eliminated. However, the SPD must be provided to DOL upon request, and the penalty for failure to comply with DOL's request is up to $110 per day but not in excess of $1,100 per request. No penalty will be imposed if the failure is due to matters reasonably beyond the control of the plan administrator (see Q 20:1). [ERISA §§ 101, 102, 104, 502(c)(6); DOL Reg. § 2575.502c-6]

DOL has issued regulations in connection with the elimination of required filings. Additional regulations clarify the liability for penalties that may be assessed. If more than one person is responsible as a plan administrator, all such individuals will be jointly and severally responsible for penalties due to a failure to provide requested documents to DOL. Any fine assessed will be the personal liability of the administrator, not the plan. Therefore, fines paid from plan assets would not constitute reasonable expenses under ERISA Section 403 or 404. Prior to any penalty being assessed, DOL must provide notice of its intent to penalize, the amount of the penalty, the period to which the penalty applies, and the reasons for the penalty. Administrators may initiate an adjudicatory proceeding but must first comply with all procedures relating to administrative reviews. [DOL Reg. §§ 2520.102-104b, 2560.502c-2(a), 2560.502c-6, 2570.110-121]

In addition to the SPD (including any summary description of material modifications (SMM; see Q 22:8) or changes in the information required to be included in the SPD), DOL may request any other document with respect to which a participant or beneficiary has requested, in writing, a copy from the plan administrator and which the plan administrator has failed or refused to furnish to the participant or beneficiary. [DOL Reg. § 2520.104a-8(a)(1)] Multiple requests for the same or similar document or documents are considered separate requests for the purpose of assessing penalties. [DOL Reg. § 2520.104a-8(a)(2)]

For the purposes of these rules, a participant or beneficiary includes a person who is:

1. A participant or beneficiary within the meaning of ERISA;
2. An alternate payee under a qualified domestic relations order (see Qs 36:1, 36:5) or prospective alternate payee (spouses, former spouses, children, or other dependents); or
3. A representative of any of the foregoing.

[ERISA §§ 3(7), 3(8); DOL Reg. § 2520.104a-8(b)]

A document will be deemed to be furnished to DOL on the date the document is received by it at the address specified in the request; or, if a document is delivered by certified mail, the date on which the document is mailed to DOL at the address specified in the request. [DOL Reg. § 2520.104a-8(d)]

Q 22:4   What information must an SPD contain?

An SPD must contain the following information:

1. Name of the plan.
2. Name and address of the employer whose employees are covered by the plan.
3. Employer identification number (EIN) assigned by IRS to the employer.
4. Plan number.
5. Type of plan (e.g., defined benefit plan, money purchase pension plan, profit sharing plan). Due to the fact that participant and beneficiary rights and obligations may be substantially affected by whether a defined contribution plan (see Q 2:2) is intended to comply with ERISA Section 404(c) (see Qs 23:14, 23:15), references to ERISA Section 404(c) must be included. While existing regulations require participants and beneficiaries to be provided with an explanation that the plan is intended to constitute an ERISA Section 404(c) plan, DOL wanted to emphasize administrators' notification duties by including the reference to ERISA Section 404(c).

Also added to the types of plans are 401(k) plans (see Q 27:1) and cash balance plans (see Q 2:23). [DOL Reg. §§ 2520.102-3(d), 2550.404c-1(b)(2)(i)(B)(1)(i); Prop. DOL Reg. § 2550.404(c)-1(b)(2)(i)(B)(1)]

6. Type of administration of the plan (e.g., employer self-administration, contract administration, insurer administration).

7. Name, business address, and business telephone number of the plan administrator.

8. Name of the person designated as agent for the service of legal process and the address at which the agent may be served (and a statement that a plan trustee or administrator may also be served).

9. Name, title, and business address of each trustee.

10. Plan's requirements regarding eligibility for participation and benefits, including the plan's normal retirement age. The SPD is required to include either a description of the plan's procedures covering qualified domestic relations order (QDRO; see Q 36:1) determinations or a statement indicating that participants and beneficiaries can obtain a free copy of such procedures (see Q 36:21) from the plan administrator. If an SPD contains the QDRO description, it should include sufficient information to allow prospective alternate payees (see Q 36:5) to exercise their rights. DOL believes that participants and beneficiaries should be aware that QDRO determination procedures exist and that the SPD is the most appropriate vehicle for communicating information about them. [DOL Reg. § 2520.103-3(j)(1)]

11. Statement describing any joint and survivor benefits.

12. Description of the benefits and vesting provisions of the plan, including contingent top-heavy provisions, and circumstances that may result in disqualification, ineligibility, or denial, loss, forfeiture, or suspension of benefits.

13. Statement as to whether the plan is maintained pursuant to one or more collective bargaining agreements and, if so, a statement that copies of such agreements are available to participants and beneficiaries.

14. Statement as to whether the plan is covered by termination insurance from PBGC and, if so, a description of the guaranty provisions. The SPD of a defined benefit plan (see Q 2:3) is required to disclose that benefits are insured by PBGC, summarize the termination insurance rules, and indicate where additional PBGC information can be obtained. An SPD meets these requirements if it includes a model statement set forth in the regulations. [DOL Reg. § 2520.102-3(m)(3)]

15. Plan's fiscal year end.

16. Source of contributions to the plan (employer and/or employee contributions) and the method used to calculate the amount of the contributions (a defined benefit plan need only state that the contribution is actuarially determined).

17. Identity of any funding medium (e.g., insurance company, trust fund) used for the accumulation of assets to provide benefits.

18. Plan's provisions governing termination of the plan, including the rights and benefits of participants and the disposition of assets. DOL has added to, and clarified, the regulations by requiring plan administrators to include in the SPD a summary of plan provisions governing (a) the authority of the plan sponsor or others to terminate the plan or eliminate plan benefits, and the circumstances under which plan benefits may be amended or terminated; (b) the benefits, rights, and obligations of participants and beneficiaries on plan termination (including the termination's effect on the accrual and vesting of benefits) and on the amendment or elimination of benefits; and (c) the allocation and disposition of plan assets upon plan termination. DOL has further noted that any description of exceptions, limitations, reductions, or other restrictions, which includes plan amendment and termination provisions, must not be minimized, rendered obscure, or otherwise made to appear unimportant. [DOL Reg. § 2520.102-3(1)]

19. Plan's procedures regarding claims for benefits and the remedies available for disputing denied claims.

20. Statement of ERISA rights available to plan participants. DOL has amended the model statement that may be used to furnish participants and beneficiaries with the statement of ERISA rights. The amendment includes clarifications to the language discussing types of documents participants and beneficiaries have the right to examine and receive upon request, and an updated description of the penalty for an administrator's failure to provide requested documents as up to $110 a day (changed from up to $100 a day) and that this amount has been increased to take inflation into account. DOL has also added a sentence indicating that issues involving the qualified status of domestic relations orders (see Qs 36:1, 36:2) may be pursued in federal court. [DOL Reg. § 2520.102-3(t)(2)]

[DOL Reg. § 2520.102-3]

One court has ruled that a plan description that did not include all of the items enumerated above was still an SPD. [International Union of Operating Eng'rs-Employers Constr. Indus. Pension, Welfare & Training Funds v. Karr, No. 91-38546 (9th Cir. 1993)] A multiemployer plan (see Q 29:2) had a policy of requiring a claimant to prove entitlement to additional benefits if the claimant believed an employer underreported the claimant's earnings, but the policy was not set forth in the SPD. The court held that the SPD did not comply with ERISA and DOL regulations (see item 12 above). [Wilkins v. Mason Tenders' District Council Pension Fund, 445 F.3d 572 (2d Cir. 2006)] Another court concluded that the conversion of an employer's defined benefit plan to a cash balance plan (see Q 2:23) violated the Section 204(h) Notice requirements (see Q 9:36). The court also ruled that the information presented in the SPD and SMM (see Q 22:8) regarding the conversion had material omissions that prevented plan participants from determining the full effect of the conversion on their retirement benefits. [Amara v. CIGNA Corp., 348 Fed. Appx. 627 (2d Cir. 2009)] ERISA does not require an SPD to describe or illustrate every method by which a plan benefit may be limited under different early retirement options offered under the plan. [McCarthy v. Dun & Bradstreet Corp., 482 F.3d 184 (2d Cir. 2007)]

Bear in mind that technical jargon is out—the idea is simplicity and the goal is clarity. The SPD should be understood by the average plan participant. Clarifying examples and illustrations are recommended. The SPD must not mislead or misinform, and important terms should be defined (see Q 22:5). Benefits should not be exaggerated, and restrictions and limitations should be described and not be minimized. In other words, the SPD must not be slanted in a way that emphasizes the benefits provided by the plan or plays down any plan terms that might cause a participant to lose benefits or fail to qualify for them. [ERISA § 102(b); DOL Reg. §§ 2520.102-2, 2520.102-3; DOL ERISA Tech. Rel. 84-1; DOL Op. Ltr. 85-05A; Haymond v. Eighth Dist. Elec. Benefit Fund, No. 01-4119 (10th Cir. 2002); Williams v. Midwest Operating Eng'rs Welfare Fund, 1997 U.S. App. LEXIS 26986 (7th Cir. 1997); *but see* Sprague v. General Motors Corp., 133 F.3d 388 (6th Cir. 1998)]

One court ruled that a statement in an SPD informing participants of their right to file a claim to recover benefits in state or federal court was merely a statutorily required disclosure rather than a freely negotiated forum selection clause. [Cruthis v. Metropolitan Life Ins. Co., No. 03-2648 (7th Cir. 2004)]

Q 22:5 Is an SPD a legally binding document?

Because an SPD is the primary source of information concerning the terms of the plan (see Q 22:1), the trend is to permit employees to rely on the SPD when it conflicts with the terms of the plan document. Plan administrators (see Q 20:1) must make sure that they do not make any false or misleading representations in an SPD because the plan may be bound by a statement in the SPD that is inconsistent with the plan, even if the inconsistency is inadvertent (see Q 22:6). [Haus v. Bechtel Jacobs Co., LLC, 2007 U.S. App. LEXIS 14706 (6th Cir. 2007); Bouboulis v. Transport Workers Union of America, 442 F.3d 55 (2d Cir. 2006); Burstein v. Retirement Account Plan for Employees of Allegheny Health Educ. & Research Fund, 2003 WL 21509028 (3d Cir. 2003); Abbruscato v. Empire Blue Cross & Blue Shield, 274 F.3d 90 (2d Cir. 2001); Devlin v. Empire Blue Cross & Blue Shield, 247 F.3d 76 (2d Cir. 2001); Rhorer v. Raytheon Eng'rs & Construc-tors, Inc., 181 F.3d 634 (5th Cir. 1999); Barker v. Ceridian Corp., No. 99-1434 (8th Cir. 1999); Buce v. National Serv. Indus., Inc., 1999 WL 1049347 (N.D. Ga. 1999); Fallo v. Piccadilly Cafeterias, Inc., 1998 U.S. App. LEXIS 10719 (5th Cir. 1998); Dodson v. Woodmen of the World Life Ins. Soc'y, 1997 U.S. App. LEXIS 5141 (8th Cir. 1997); Williams v. Midwest Operating Eng'rs Welfare Fund, 1997 U.S. App. LEXIS 26986 (7th Cir. 1997); Curcio v. John Hancock Mut. Life. Ins. Co., 33 F.3d 226 (3d Cir. 1994); Nelson v. EG&G Energy Measurements Group, Inc., 1994 U.S. App. LEXIS 27853 (9th Cir. 1994); Aiken v. Policy Mgmt. Sys. Corp., 1993 U.S. App. LEXIS 34398 (4th Cir. 1993); Brumm v. Bert Bell NFL Ret. Plan, No. 92-3346 (8th Cir. 1993); Pierce v. Security Trust Life Ins. Co., 1992 U.S. App. LEXIS 15562 (4th Cir. 1992); Hansen v. Continental Ins. Co., 940 F.2d 971 (5th Cir. 1991); Heidgerd v. Olin Corp., No. 89-7869 (2d Cir. 1990); Edwards v. State Farm Mut. Auto. Ins. Co., 851 F.2d 134 (6th Cir. 1988); McKnight v.

Southern Life & Health Ins. Co., 758 F.2d 1566 (11th Cir. 1985); Hoover v. Exxon Mobil Corp., 2004 U.S. Dist. LEXIS 5484 (E.D. Pa. 2004); Mauser v. Raytheon Co. Pension Plan for Salaried Employees, No. 97-10215 (D. Mass. 1998); Allport v. Griffis, 1997 U.S. Dist. LEXIS (N.D. Ill. 1997); Gregory v. Texasgulf, Inc., No. B-84-88 (D. Conn. 1990); *but see* Sprague v. General Motors Corp., 133 F.3d 388 (6th Cir. 1998)]

Courts have held that, where an SPD conflicts with formal plan documents, the provisions of the SPD prevail as a matter of law. [Frommert v. Conkright, 433 F.3d 254 (2d Cir. 2006); Marolt v. Alliant Techsystems, Inc., No. 97-2817 (8th Cir. 1998); *see also* Wilkins v. Mason Tenders' District Council Pension Fund, 445 F.3d 572 (2d Cir. 2006)] However, another court ruled that, even though there may have been a conflict between the plan and the SPD, the plan administrator's interpretation was neither arbitrary nor capricious because the plan language could be interpreted in more than one way. [White v. Employee Ret. Plan of Amoco Corp & Participating Cos., No. 96 CV 4298 (N.D. Ill. 2000); *see also* Kelly v. Retirement Pension Plan for Certain Home Office Employees of Provident Mut., 2003 WL 2207-0527 (3d Cir. 2003)] Where a plan document is silent as to the grant of decision-making discretion to the plan administrator, but includes the right of amendment as well as a provision stating that the document will prevail over a conflict with the SPD, a provision in the SPD purporting to grant this discretion to the administrator, but also acknowledging the primacy of the plan document, is ineffective to create the necessary discretion to warrant review of the administrator's benefit decisions under the deferential arbitrary and capricious standard, concluded one court. [Jobe v. Medical Life In. Co., 598 F.3d 478 (8th Cir. 2010)] Where there was a conflict between the plan document and the SPD, courts have concluded that the provision more favorable to the employee controls and that the burden of uncertainty created by careless or inaccurate drafting of the SPD must be placed on those who do the drafting. [Gravelle v. Bank One Corp., 2009 WL 1649193 (6th Cir. 2009); Skinner v. Northrop Grumman Retirement Plan B, 2009 WL 1416725 (9th Cir. 2009); Banuelos v. Construction Laborers' Trust Funds For Southern California, No. 02-57096 (9th Cir. 2004); Bergt v. Retirement Plan for Pilots Employed by Mark Air, Inc., 293 F.3d 1139 (9th Cir. 2002)] However, courts have ruled that an asserted ambiguity in the SPD did not prevail over clear language in the plan. [Walter v. Monsanto Co. Pension Plan, 2009 WL 1651378 (S.D. Ill. 2009); Zirnhelt v. Michigan Consol. Gas Co., 526 F.3d 282 (6th Cir. 2008)] The spouse of a deceased plan participant was not entitled to benefits under an ambiguous SPD, where the plan administrator reasonably exercised discretionary authority to construe the plan terms and deny benefits. [Weiss v. Northern California Retail Clerks Unions and Food Employers Joint Pension Plan, 2007 WL 579776 (9th Cir. 2007)] One court concluded that, despite the difference in language between the plan and the SPD, the rules for eligibility for early retirement benefits were actually the same. [Jessup v. Alcoa, Inc., 2007 WL 957523 (8th Cir. 2007)]

However, some courts have ruled that a participant must show reliance on a faulty SPD in order to recover denied benefits. [Skinner v. Northrop Grumman Retirement Plan B, 2010 WL 679061 (__. D. Cal. 2010); Bocchino v. Trustees of

District Council Ironworkers Funds of Northern New Jersey, 2009 WL 2038645 (3d Cir. 2009); Greeley v. Fairview Health Services, 2007 U.S. App. LEXIS 3797 (8th Cir. 2007); Fenton v. John Hancock Mut. Life Ins. Co., Nos. 02-1960, 03-1277, 03-1278 (1st Cir. 2005); Mauser v. Raytheon Co. Pension Plan for Salaried Employees, 2001 WL 68364 (1st Cir. 2001); Andersen v. Chrysler Corp, 1996 U.S. App. LEXIS 28496 (7th Cir. 1996); Maxa v. John Alden Life Ins. Co., No. 91-2203MN (8th Cir. 1992); Bachelder v. Communications Satellite Corp., 837 F.2d 519 (1st Cir. 1988); Govoni v. Bricklayers, Masons, & Plasterers Pension Fund, 732 F.2d 250 (1st Cir. 1984); Thompson v. Federal Express Corp., 1992 U.S. Dist. LEXIS 19334 (M.D. Ga. 1992); Freund v. Gerson, 610 F. Supp. 69 (S.D. Fla. 1985)] One court ruled that a participant must show *either* reliance upon or prejudice flowing from a faulty SPD, but not both. [Aiken v. Policy Mgmt. Sys. Corp., 1993 U.S. App. LEXIS 34398 (4th Cir. 1993)] However, in another case, the same court previously ruled that a participant could not have relied on the SPD to his detriment, even though the SPD and the plan language conflicted with respect to the amount of his distribution. [Fuller v. FMC Corp., 1993 U.S. App. LEXIS 19448 (4th Cir. 1993)] Another court concluded that a participant need not demonstrate reliance on a deficient SPD, rather only likely prejudice need be demonstrated. [Burke v. Kodak Ret. Income Plan, 336 F.3d 103 (2d Cir. 2003); *see also* Goldinger v. DatexOhmeda Cash Balance Plan, 2010 WL 1270191 (__.D. Wash. 2010) and Tocker v. Philip Morris Cos., Inc., 2006 U.S. App. LEXIS 29141 (2d Cir. 2006)] The same court also concluded that its prejudice standard established for ERISA claims based on deficient SPDs is also applicable to claims based on the complete absence of an SPD. [Weinreb v. Hospital for Joint Diseases Orthopaedic Institute, 2005 U.S. App. LEXIS 5701 (2d Cir. 2005); *see also* Watson v. Consolidated Edison Co. of N.Y., Inc., 2010 WL 1564654 (2d Cir. 2010)]

An SPD gave adequate notice that a participant may receive only benefits guaranteed by PBGC (see Q 25:16) upon the termination of an underfunded defined benefit plan; therefore, the participant was not improperly denied benefits under the plan when reduced benefits were received. [Arnold v. Arrow Transp. Co., No. 89-35280 (9th Cir. 1991)] However, where a rehired participant was advised that his plan benefits were reduced by other benefits previously distributed to him, another court ruled that a statement in the SPD that a participant's benefits *may* also be reduced was wholly inadequate to provide meaningful notice of the potential loss of benefits. [Layaou v. Xerox Corp., No. 95-cv-6388L (W.D.N.Y. 2004); Layaou v. Xerox Corp., 238 F.3d 205 (2d Cir. 2001)]

Where an SPD did not expressly set forth whether severance payments were included in the definition of compensation for plan purposes, the plan administrator was permitted to look to extrinsic evidence to determine that such payments were not included. [Krawczyk v. Harnischfeger Corp., 1994 U.S. App. LEXIS 32973 (7th Cir. 1994)] Where a plan defined compensation as excluding bonuses, overtime, and commissions, but the SPD used the term "compensation" without further definition, the court concluded that the plan's definition was controlling because there was no direct conflict. [Anderson v. Mrs Grissom's Salads, Inc., 2000 U.S. App. LEXIS 14511 (6th Cir. 2000)] Another court concluded that if an SPD is accurate and comprehensive enough to satisfy the

ERISA requirements (see Q 22:4), the fact that the SPD is silent on a particular issue does not prevent a plan administrator from relying on the more detailed terms of the plan. [Mers v. Marriott Int'l Group Accidental Death & Dismemberment Plan, 1998 U.S. App. LEXIS 9399 (7th Cir. 1998); *see also* Bolone v. TRW Sterling Plant Pension Plan, 2005 WL 1027569 (6th Cir. 2005); Straus v. Prudential Employee Sav. Plan, No. CV 02-3067 (E.D.N.Y. 2003)]

One court ruled that an employer is not bound by an erroneous statement in a separate booklet distributed to employees with the SPD, because the SPD was consistent with the plan. However, the court implied that an employer might be bound by an erroneous statement in the SPD. [Alday v. Container Corp. of Am., 906 F.2d 660 (11th Cir. 1990)] Other courts have held that a booklet describing plan benefits did not contain sufficient information to rise to the status of an SPD (see Q 22:4). Therefore, even though the booklet was in conflict with the actual plan document, the employee could not rely upon the booklet. [Palmisano, II v. Allina Health Sys., Inc., No. 98-3619 (8th Cir. 1999); Hicks v. Fleming Cos., 961 F.2d 537 (5th Cir. 1992); Pisciotta v. Teledyne Indus., Inc., 91 F.3d 1326 (9th Cir. 1996)] Another court concluded that documents prepared by an employer summarizing the level of benefits that would be paid by a defined benefit plan (see Q 2:3) did not bind the plan because the documents relied upon by the participants were written by the employer, not by the plan, and were not SPDs. Both the plan and the SPD contained provisions limiting the annual retirement benefit. [Helfrich v. Carle Clinic Ass'n, P.C., 328 F.3d 915 (7th Cir. 2003)]

A court concluded that an employer breached its fiduciary duty when the SPD and plan benefits counselor provided incomplete and misleading information about the plan's lump-sum distribution option (see Q 23:19). [Estate of Becker v. Eastman Kodak Co., 1997 U.S. App. LEXIS 17937 (2d Cir. 1997)]

Q 22:6 What is the purpose of a disclaimer clause?

Disclaimer language (see below) is a possible, though unreliable, means of insulating plan assets and the plan administrator (see Q 20:1) from liability should the SPD prove to be misleading, incomplete, or contradictory to the provisions of the plan. Participants and their beneficiaries are placed on notice that the plan itself is the controlling document and that they should not rely solely upon the representations in the SPD. [Kolentus v. Avco Corp., 798 F.2d 949 (7th Cir. 1986)]

The following is a sample disclaimer clause:

> Please read this summary carefully. This summary is written in simple, nontechnical language, and it is intended to help you to understand how this plan will benefit you and your loved ones. The plan and trust documents are also available for you to read. Although these documents are written in technical language, they may be helpful to you.
>
> If it appears to you that any of the provisions of the plan or trust documents is not in agreement with the statements made in this summary, please bring this to the attention of the plan administrator. Keep in mind that, if there is any conflict between this summary and the

provisions of the plan or trust documents, the terms of the plan or trust will govern. You should rely solely on the provisions of the plan and trust documents.

However, it has been held that employees can rely on an SPD despite a disclaimer where the SPD favors the employees [Pierce v. Security Trust Life Ins. Co., 1992 U.S. App. LEXIS 15562 (4th Cir. 1992)] and that an employer cannot disavow a disclaimer when the SPD favors the employer but the plan favors the employees. [Glocker v. W.R. Grace & Co., No. 91-2262 (4th Cir. 1992)]

Q 22:7   Will a disclaimer in an SPD be recognized in a lawsuit?

At present, there are no governmental prohibitions against the use of a disclaimer in an SPD. Nothing is risked, therefore, by including the disclaimer (see Q 22:6).

The courts have held that a participant or beneficiary cannot use an SPD to sue for relief under ERISA unless the lawsuit also asserts a claim arising under the plan itself. However, the courts have left the door open for a participant to sue on other than ERISA grounds on the basis of inaccurate or misleading statements in the SPD. In any event, it is reasonable to expect that a claim based on willful or negligent misrepresentations in an SPD would be upheld even when a disclaimer is included in the SPD. [O'Brien v. Sperry Univac, 458 F. Supp. 1179 (D.D.C. 1978); McKnight v. Southern Life & Health Ins. Co., 758 F.2d 1566 (11th Cir. 1985); *see also* Feifer v. Prudential Ins. Co. of Am., 2002 WL 31239308 (2d Cir. 2002)]

Q 22:8   What happens if the plan is changed?

Any change in the provisions of the plan or in the administration of the plan that constitutes a material modification (see Q 22:9) must be disclosed to participants and beneficiaries in the form of a summary description of material modifications (SMM) to the plan. The SMM must be distributed within 210 days after the close of the plan year in which the material modification is adopted. [DOL Reg. § 2520.104b-3] Electronic media may be used to fulfill this requirement. [DOL Reg. §§ 2520.104b-1, 2520.107]

One court concluded that a booklet that described the material modifications to an ERISA plan's life insurance coverage constituted a legitimate modification of the plan and that an inaccurate personalized worksheet distributed with the booklet was not enforceable. [Crosby v. Rohm & Haas Co., 2007 U.S. App. LEXIS 6084 (6th Cir. 2007)]

The requirement that the SMM be filed with DOL has been eliminated. However, the SMM must be provided to DOL upon request, and the penalty for failure to comply with DOL's request is up to $110 per day but not in excess of $1,100 per request. No penalty will be imposed if the failure is due to matters reasonably beyond the control of the plan administrator (see Q 20:1). [ERISA §§ 101, 102, 104; DOL Reg. § 2575.502c-6] See Q 22:3 for further details.

Q 22:9   What constitutes a reportable material modification?

Basically, a material modification exists when there is a change or modification to any of the information required to be included in the SPD (see Q 22:4). [DOL Reg. § 2520.104b-3]

For example, the elimination of a special retirement benefit that allowed participants not eligible for normal retirement benefits to qualify for reduced retirement benefits was held to be a material modification of a plan. [Baker v. Lukens Steel Co., 793 F.2d 509 (3d Cir. 1986)] One court concluded that the conversion of an employer's defined benefit plan to a cash balance plan (see Q 2:23) violated the Section 204(h) Notice requirements (see Q 9:36). The court also ruled that the information presented in the SPD and SMM (see Q 22:8) regarding the conversion had material omissions that prevented plan participants from determining the full effect of the conversion on their retirement benefits. [Amara v. CIGNA Corp., 348 Fed. Appx. 627 (2d Cir. 2009)]

Q 22:10   How often is an updated SPD due?

Generally, every five years the plan administrator (see Q 20:1) is required to furnish to each participant and each beneficiary receiving benefits under the plan an updated SPD that incorporates all plan amendments made within that five-year period. The updated SPD must be furnished no later than 210 days after the end of the fifth plan year after the previous SPD. This requirement for an updated SPD must be met even if SMMs have been issued (see Q 22:8). However, even if there have been no amendments to the plan, another copy of the original SPD must be distributed every ten years. [ERISA § 104(b); DOL Reg. § 2520.104b-2] The updated SPD is not required to be filed with DOL (see Q 22:3).

Q 22:11   How is the five-year period for an updated SPD measured?

Each time an SPD is distributed, the five-year period begins anew. If the plan distributes an updated SPD less than five years after the previous one was distributed, a new five-year period begins at that time. [DOL Reg. § 2520. 104b-2(b)]

Example. The plan administrator of the Ess-Cee-Jay Corporation profit sharing plan distributed the first SPD on March 1, 2005. On January 3, 2006, the vesting provisions of the calendar-year plan were amended and an SMM (see Q 22:8) was timely distributed on July 29, 2007 (210 days after the end of the plan year of the amendment). An updated SPD will be due on July 29, 2011 (210 days after December 31, 2010, the end of the plan year of the fifth anniversary of the original SPD). If a new SPD (instead of the SMM) had been distributed on July 29, 2007, the next SPD would be due July 29, 2013.

Q 22:12   What happens if the plan is terminated?

If the plan terminates before the date by which an original or an updated SPD is required, the SPD requirement is waived if, and only if, all distributions to participants and beneficiaries have been completed.

Q 22:13   What documents other than an SPD can a participant obtain?

Other than an SPD, a participant is entitled to obtain, without charge and without request, an SMM (see Q 22:8) to the plan and a summary annual report (see Q 20:24). Because detailed information about a defined benefit plan must be provided to participants in an annual funding notice, effective for plan years beginning after December 31, 2007, the requirement to provide a summary annual report to participants will not apply to defined benefit plans. [ERISA § 104(b)(3) (as amended by PPA § 503(c)(1)); PPA § 503(f)]

Upon request, other documents must be furnished to a participant by the plan administrator (see Q 20:1). These include:

1. A statement of the participant's total accrued benefits;
2. The plan instrument;
3. The latest annual report (Form 5500 series return);
4. The trust agreement; and
5. The collective bargaining agreement or any other document under which the plan is established.

The request must be in writing. [ERISA § 104(b)(4); Christensen v. The Qwest Pension Plan, 462 F.3d 913 (8th Cir. 2006); Amat v. Seafarers Int'l Union, 2002 WL 511540 (E.D. La. 2002)] Electronic media may be used to comply with the request. [DOL Reg. §§ 2520.104b-1, 2520.107] A reasonable charge (not to exceed $.25 per page) may be imposed for copies of these items (other than the annual benefit statement). [ERISA § 105(a); DOL Reg. § 2520.104b-30] The plan administrator's failure to provide these documents within 30 days after the participant's request may subject the plan administrator to penalties, attorneys' fees, and costs (see Qs 22:4, 23:61). [ERISA §§ 502(c)(1), 502(g)(1); Cromer-Tyler v. Teitel, 2008 WL 4335938 (11th Cir. 2008); Zirnhelt v. Michigan Consol. Gas Co., 526 F.3d 282 (6th Cir. 2008); Lowe v. McGraw-Hill Cos., 2004 WL 502201 (7th Cir. 2004); Gorini v. AMP Inc., Nos. 02-3431, 02-3900 (3d Cir. 2004); McGrath v. Lockheed Martin Corp., 2002 WL 31269646 (6th Cir. 2002); Cherry v. Toussaint, 2002 WL 31479004 (2d Cir. 2002); McConnell, Jr. v. William F. Costigan & Co., P.C., 2002 U.S. Dist. LEXIS 15826 (S.D.N.Y. 2002); Lampkins v. Golden, No. 95-2001 (6th Cir. 1996); Boone v. Leavenworth Anesthesia, Inc., No. 92-3349 (10th Cir. 1994); Lee v. Benefit Plans Administrator of ARMCO, Inc., No. H-90-3642 (S.D. Tex. 1992)] An appellate court concluded that it was an abuse of discretion for the district court not to have awarded the participant penalties for the plan's failure to furnish requested information. [Leister v. Dovetail, Inc., 2008 WL 4659364 (7th Cir. 2008)] One court ruled that penalties could be assessed against a plan administrator for distributing a misleading SPD. [Anderson v. Mrs. Grissom's Salads, Inc., 2000

U.S. App. LEXIS 14511 (6th Cir. 2000)] Another court determined that, upon the written request of a participant's attorney, a plan administrator (see Q 20:1) is required to disclose pension benefit information, even if the request is not accompanied by a written authorization from the participant. [Minadeo v. ICI Paints, 398 F.3d 751 (6th Cir. 2005); *see also* Daniels v. Thomas & Betts Corp., 263 F.3d 66 (3d Cir. 2001); *but see* Bartling v. Fruehauf Corp., 29 F.3d 1062 (6th Cir. 1994)] In addition, the failure may result in a participant's complaint to the local DOL field office, with the possibility of an ensuing investigation of the plan. [Thomas v. Jeep-Eagle Corp., 746 F. Supp. 863 (E.D. Wis. 1990)]

One court concluded that the imposition of penalties on a plan for failure to provide requested information was inappropriate where the individual's request was general in nature as to the existence of any retirement plan coverage she might have had and not for specific information. [Davenport v. Harry N. Abrams, Inc., 249 F.3d 130 (2d Cir. 2001)] Another court found that the request was not sufficiently specific to notify the administrator of the documents sought. [Kollman v. Hewitt Assocs., LLC, 2007 U.S. App. LEXIS 11272 (3d Cir. 2007)] Although a request for information need not be served upon or mailed personally to the plan administrator for the administrator to be assessed a civil penalty, one court held that to impose personal liability for delays in responding to information requests, the request must actually be received by the administrator. [Romero v. Smith Kline Beecham, 2002 U.S. App. LEXIS 22576 (3d Cir. 2002)] In another case, no penalty was imposed on the employer for a ten-month delay in providing plan information, because the employee did not show that any damage resulted from the delay or that bad faith or intentional delay existed on the part of the employer. [Plotkin v. Bearings Ltd., 1992 U.S. Dist. LEXIS 7787 (E.D.N.Y. 1992)] However, in another case, the court held that a showing of injury or prejudice was not required and a substantial penalty was assessed against the employer. [Moothart v. Bell, 21 F.3d 1499 (10th Cir. 1994)] Another court concluded that criminal conduct by a plan participant did not excuse the plan administrator's refusal to produce documents. However, because the participant had not shown injury or damage, only a nominal penalty was awarded. [Blazejewski v. Wm. E. Gipson, D.D.S., P.C., 1999 U.S. Dist. LEXIS 18028 (N.D. Ill. 1999)] Where an employee received inaccurate written benefit statements and oral communications, the employer was not bound by the inaccurate representations, because the terms of the plan controlled. [Miller v. Coastal Corp., 978 F.2d 622 (10th Cir. 1992)]

Participants in an employee stock ownership plan (ESOP; see Q 28:1) were not entitled to copies of the ESOP's determination letter (see Q 18:1) or to appraisal or evaluation reports of company stock because the papers were not formal or legal documents under which the plan was set up or managed. [Faircloth v. Lundy Packing Co., 91 F.3d 648 (4th Cir. 1996)] Similarly, another court concluded that a defined benefit plan (see Q 2:3) was not required to disclose actuarial valuation reports to a participant because such documents are not instruments under which the plan is established or operated. [Board of Trustees of the CWA/ITU Negotiated Pension Fund v. Weinstein, 107 F.3d 139 (2d Cir. 1997)]

For an individual to receive a penalty award for a plan's failure to provide requested plan documents and other relevant information, the individual must actually be either a participant or beneficiary at the time the litigation is commenced. Thus, the penalty would not be assessed if it is shown that the individual had no colorable claim to benefits under the plan at the time of commencement. [Morrison v. Marsh & McLennan Cos., Inc., 439 F.3d 295 (6th Cir. 2006)] An employee was dismissed and received her plan benefits; ten years later, she requested plan documents and commenced an action. The court ruled that the employee was not entitled to the documents, because she had no expectation of returning to employment with the employer and had no colorable claim for benefits. In addition, the court concluded that the state law six-year statute of limitations had expired. [Szoke v. Deloitte & Touche L.L.P., 1995 U.S. Dist. LEXIS 2517 (S.D.N.Y. 1995)] Another court applied the state's two-year statute of limitations on breach of fiduciary duty actions, rather than the four-year statute applicable to fraud actions, in a claim relating to a plan administrator's failure to supply a beneficiary with requested plan information. [Hatteburg v. Red Adair Co., 2003 WL 22510848 (5th Cir. 2003)] In another case, an employee with a nonfrivolous but ultimately unsuccessful claim for benefits was deemed to be a participant entitled to receive requested plan information and entitled to a penalty award for the company's failure to do so. [Sedlack v. Braswell Serv. Group, Inc., Nos. 96-2650, 96-2651 (4th Cir. 1998)] A worker who failed to demonstrate that he was an employee, as opposed to an independent contractor, was not entitled to plan documents he requested. [Mulzet v. R.L. Reppert Inc., 2002 WL 31761696 (3d Cir. 2002)]

One court ruled that an employer's issuance of benefit statements to an employee showing accruals of retirement benefits prevented the employer from relying on another plan provision to deny the employee retirement benefits. [Spink v. Lockheed Corp, 125 F.3d 1257 (9th Cir. 1997)]

For other examples, see Q 20:23.

DOL was directed to develop one or more model benefit statements that could be used by plan administrators in complying with the benefit statement requirements. The use of the model statement is optional. It is intended that the model statement include items such as the amount of vested accrued benefits as of the statement date that are payable at normal retirement age under the plan, the amount of accrued benefits that are forfeitable but that may become vested under the terms of the plan, information on how to contact the Social Security Administration to obtain a participant's personal earnings and benefit estimate statement, and other information that may be important to understanding benefits earned under the plan. DOL was also given the authority to promulgate any interim final rules as determined appropriate to carry out the benefit statement requirements. [PPA § 508(b)] DOL has issued guidance implementing the periodic pension benefit statement requirements enacted by PPA. [DOL Field Assistance Bull. 2006-3]

After the issuance of Field Assistance Bulletin 2006-03, it came to the attention of DOL that many individual account plans that do not permit participants and beneficiaries to direct the investment of assets in their individual accounts may not be able to comply within the 45-day period set forth in the Bulletin. It was represented that many of these plans are profit sharing plans (see Q 2:6) and the sponsors of those plans do not determine or make profit sharing contributions until after the sponsor's business tax return is completed. Similarly, non-participant directed individual account plans sponsored by partnerships cannot make contribution determinations until completion of the partnership tax return. It also was represented that many such plans are dependent on securing third-party valuations for those assets that do not have a readily ascertainable value. Compliance with the 45-day good-faith period, therefore, would appear to be impossible or very expensive for many of these plans unless the benefit statements were based on data from the end of the prior plan year. It was further represented that much of the required information is compiled in connection with the preparation of the plan's Form 5500 Annual Return/Report (see Q 21:2); and, accordingly, the time frame for furnishing benefit statements should correspond to the required filing of the plan's Form 5500. DOL concluded that plan administrators of individual account plans that do not provide for participant direction of investments will be treated as acting in good-faith compliance when statements are furnished to participants and beneficiaries on or before the date on which Form 5500 is filed by the plan (but in no event later than the date, including extensions, on which Form 5500 is required to be filed by the plan) for the plan year to which the statement relates. Field Assistance Bulletin 2006-03 is superseded as it relates to the dates for furnishing pension benefit statements to participants and beneficiaries of individual account plans that do not permit participants and beneficiaries to direct the investment of assets in their individual accounts. [ERISA § 105(a)(1)(A)(ii); DOL Field Assistance Bull. 2007-03]

See Q 20:23 for details.

Q 22:14 Is there any special requirement if many plan participants cannot read English?

Yes. If a sufficient number of plan participants (generally, 25 percent for plans with less than 100 participants, 10 percent for plans with 100 or more participants) are literate only in the same non-English language, then the plan administrator (see Qs 20:1, 22:1) must give these participants an SPD with a notice written in their own language. This notice must inform such participants of the availability of assistance sufficient to enable them to become informed as to their rights under the plan. [DOL Reg. § 2520.102-2(c)] One court has ruled that the foreign language notice rules do not extend to the denial of benefit claims made by participants (see Q 10:66). [Diaz v. United Agric. Employee Welfare Benefit Plan & Trust, 1995 U.S. App. LEXIS 6112 (9th Cir. 1995)]

Chapter 23

Fiduciary Responsibilities

Plan administrators, trustees, and fiduciaries must take special care to fulfill their responsibilities; investing plan assets carelessly can mean financial ruin. This chapter examines the meaning of fiduciary responsibility under ERISA, when a fiduciary can be held personally liable for losses sustained by the plan, how liability can be avoided, and guidelines for investing plan assets.

Q 23:1 Who is a fiduciary under ERISA?

A fiduciary under ERISA is any person who:

1. Exercises any discretionary authority or control over the plan's management;

2. Exercises any authority or control over the management or disposition of the plan's assets;

3. Renders investment advice for a fee or other compensation with respect to plan funds or property; or

4. Has any discretionary authority or responsibility in the plan's administration.

[ERISA § 3(21)(A)]

The test for determining fiduciary status is a functional one; if a person or entity has or may exercise any of the functions described in ERISA Section 3(21)(A), the person or entity will be deemed to be a fiduciary. [Finkel v. Romanowicz, 2009 WL 2432723 (2d Cir. 2009); Best v. Cyrus, 310 F.3d 932 (6th Cir. 2002); Michael Hamilton, Indep. Fiduciary, SCIW Health & Welfare Trust Fund v. Carell, 2001 WL 276977 (6th Cir. 2001); Board of Trustees of Bricklayers & Allied Craftsmen Local 6 of N.J. Welfare Fund v. Wettlin Assocs., Inc., No. 00-1382 (3d Cir. 2001); IT Corp. v. General Am. Life Ins. Co., 107 F.3d 1415 (9th Cir. 1997); Blatt v. Marshall & Lassman, 812 F.2d 810 (2d Cir. 1987); Eaves v. Penn, 587 F.2d 453 (10th Cir. 1978); Meyer v. Berkshire Life Ins. Co., 2003 U.S. Dist. LEXIS 6107 (D. Md. 2003); Crowley v. Corning, Inc., No. 02-CV-6172 (W.D.N.Y. 2002); Keach v. U.S. Trust Co., N.A., 2002 U.S. Dist. LEXIS 22281 (C.D. Ill. 2002); Reich v. Hosking, 1996 U.S. Dist. LEXIS 5975 (E.D. Mich. 1996); Daniels v. National Employee Benefit Servs., Inc., 1994 U.S. Dist. LEXIS 9485

(N.D. Ohio 1994)] One court concluded that a plan participant could not sue the plan's administrative and investment committees for breaching their fiduciary duties under ERISA by selling stock holdings for a large loss because the committees do not qualify as "persons" that can be sued for breach of fiduciary duty under ERISA. [Tatum v. R.J. Reynolds Tobacco Co., 2007 U.S. Dist. LEXIS 39801 (M.D. N.C. 2007] A mutual fund provider was not a functional fiduciary where the trust agreement gave the plan sponsor, and not the mutual fund provider, control over which investment options would be available to plan participants. [Hecker v. Deere & Co., 556 F. 3d 575 (7th Cir. 2009); *see also* Zang v. Paychex, Inc., No. 08-CV-60461 (W.D.N.Y. 2010)]

Fiduciary status may involve a question of fact; a provision of an oral agreement that a broker was not to be considered an ERISA fiduciary was not dispositive of the issue. [Schiffli Embroidery Workers Pension Fund v. Ryan, Beck & Co., No. 91-5433 (D.N.J. 1994)] A provision in a written agreement that an insurance company retained to administer a plan was not a named fiduciary did not prevent the insurance company from being deemed a fiduciary based upon its activities and, in any event, was not binding upon a plaintiff participant who was not a party to the agreement. [IT Corp. v. General Am. Life, 107 F.3d 1415 (9th Cir. 1997)] If a third-party administrator exceeds the bounds of its agreement requiring only ministerial actions to assume discretionary authority, it will be considered a fiduciary. [Harold Ives Trucking Co. v. Spradley & Coker, Inc., 1999 U.S. App. LEXIS 9529 (8th Cir. 1999)] One court rejected former trustees' argument that amending a multiemployer plan (see Q 29:2) to increase benefits for retirees despite the plan's fiscal deterioration was not an act within their fiduciary capacity. A trustee is not acting as a fiduciary when amending a single-employer plan (see Q 29:2); however, the court ruled, that principal does not apply to trustees of a multiemployer plan. [Burke v. Bodewes, No. 00-CV-65C (W.D.N.Y. 2003)]

An officer and shareholder who decided which creditors to pay and elected not to remit funds due to a plan was deemed an ERISA fiduciary. [LoPresti v. Terwilliger, 126 F.3d 34 (2d Cir. 1997)] An employer which had appointed a plan administrator was not a de facto co-administrator of its plan; accordingly, it could not be liable for benefits due thereunder. [Crocco v. Xerox Corp, 137 F.3d 105 (2d Cir. 1998)] A company's officers and directors who had no discretion or control over the management or assets of the company's plan did not become fiduciaries merely because they hired a third-party administrator to service the plan and assigned plan management duties to the company's human resources department. [Briscoe v. Fine, 444 F.3d 478 (6th Cir. 2006)]

Courts may differ as to whether certain actions constitute fiduciary duties. Calculating pension benefits was considered a fiduciary duty in one case [Pineiro v. PBGC, 2003 U.S. Dist. LEXIS 15034 (S.D.N.Y. 2003)], but not in another. [Jos F Cunningham Pension Plan v. Mathiew, No. 97-2230 (4th Cir. 1998)]

An independent distribution consultant appointed by the Security and Exchange Commission (SEC) to develop and implement a plan to distribute mutual fund settlement proceeds correcting trade irregularities, but with no control over plan assets, is not a fiduciary. Moreover, proceeds from certain settlements between the SEC and various mutual fund companies would not be considered plan assets (see Q 23:32) until distributed from the settlement fund and received by the appropriate plan fiduciaries. [DOL Field Assistance Bull. 2006-01]

DOL announced plans to issue proposed regulations to expand the current regulatory definition of "fiduciary" to include more persons, such as pension consultants, as fiduciaries. As a result of the proposed regulatory change, these persons would become subject to ERISA's fiduciary responsibility rules. [DOL Fact Sheet, Jan. 2010]

DOL provided guidance concerning the duties of fiduciaries with respect to alleged abuses involving mutual funds. [DOL News Rel. (Feb. 17, 2004)] DOL has also launched a nationwide campaign, "Getting It Right—Know Your Fiduciary Responsibilities," to educate employers and service providers about their fiduciary responsibilities under ERISA. The campaign focuses on the legal obligations of plan sponsors and other fiduciaries, including:

1. Understanding the terms of their plans.
2. Selecting and monitoring service providers.
3. Making timely contributions to funds.
4. Avoiding prohibited transactions.
5. Making timely disclosures to plan participants and the government.

[DOL News Rel. (May 19, 2004)]

Q 23:2 Can a person be a fiduciary for a limited purpose and not be considered a fiduciary with respect to other activities?

Yes. A person may be a fiduciary for a limited purpose and also perform other, nonfiduciary roles with regard to the same plan. [John Hancock Mut. Life Ins. Co. v. Harris Trust & Sav. Bank, 510 U.S. 86 (1993)] In this case, the U.S. Supreme Court ruled that certain pension plan assets held in the general accounts of insurance companies constituted plan assets. They were therefore subject to the fiduciary responsibility rules of ERISA, including the rules prohibiting certain transactions involving the assets of an employee benefit plan. ERISA Section 401 was amended to relieve insurers holding plan assets in a general account from any liability for acts prior to its enactment and, for a defined period, for future acts that otherwise might constitute a claim under ERISA. [ERISA § 401(c)] Accordingly, trustees' claims for fiduciary breach against an insurer with respect to alleged mismanagement of funds in its general account were barred by the amendment, while claims of mismanagement with respect to funds held in separate accounts remained viable. [Adkins v. John Hancock Mut. Life Ins. Co., No. 96-741-Civ-J-20 (M.D. Fla. 1997)] See Q 23:90 for a discussion of DOL regulations clarifying the status of plan assets held in insurance company general accounts.

Under a contract between the employer, which was also the plan trustee, and an insurance company, a defined benefit plan (see Q 2:3) was established whereby the insurance company, as plan administrator (see Q 20:1), allocated investment income to the plan. According to the contract, the trustee was able to withdraw free funds, which were excess investment funds. The insurance company initially allowed the trustee to roll over the free funds at book value, so that the plan would not experience the losses that would have resulted if the funds were withdrawn in accordance with the contract. Subsequently, the insurance company refused the trustee's request to do so. The court noted that the transfer of the free funds was outside the terms of the contract and stated that the insurance company's fiduciary duty did not include an obligation to release the free funds to the trustee in a manner different from that specified in the contract, even though doing so would benefit the plan. The court held that the insurance company's discretionary authority did not extend to any concession that it could conceivably make to the trustee and further held that, even though the insurance company was required to exercise its managerial discretion with respect to the free funds in accordance with ERISA's fiduciary duty provisions, it only had a fiduciary duty to the plan to the extent that it exercised discretion over its various plan duties and responsibilities. [Harris Trust & Sav. Bank v. John Hancock Mut. Life Ins. Co., 2002 WL 1902607 (2d Cir. 2002)]

Q 23:3   Are all actions by fiduciaries that affect a plan within the definition of fiduciary duties?

No. Courts have held that various actions by plan fiduciaries that affect a plan, such as plan formation, amendment, or termination, are employer or settlor functions not falling within the purview of ERISA Section 3(21)(A) and, accordingly, not subject to fiduciary duties to participants. [Beck v. PACE Int'l Union, 2007 WL 1661301 (S. Ct. 2007); Hughes Aircraft Co. v. Jacobson, 525 U.S. 432 (1999); Schultz v. Windstream Communications, Inc., 2010 WL 1266858 (8th Cir. 2010); Gromala v. Royal & Sunalliance, 2004 WL 259226 (6th Cir. 2004); Hartline v. Sheet Metal Workers' Nat'l Pension Fund, No. 01-7078 (D.C. Cir. 2002); Reynolds v. Edison Int'l, 2000 U.S. App. LEXIS 24895 (9th Cir. 2000); Sengpiel v. B.F. Goodrich Co., 156 F.3d 660 (6th Cir. 1998); Brillinger v. General Elec. Co., 130 F.3d 61 (2d Cir. 1997); American Flint Glass Workers Union v. Beaumont Glass Co, 62 F.3d 574 (3d Cir. 1995); Sutton v. Weirton Steel, Div. of Nat'l Steel Corp., 724 F.2d 406 (4th Cir. 1983); Dall v. Chinet Co., No. 97-48-P-C (D. Me. 1998); *see also* DOL Field Assistance Bull. 2002-2] DOL has advised that an employer that eliminated retiree life insurance benefits under its welfare plan and instituted similar benefits for the same retirees under its pension plan would be engaging in settlor activities and not be subject to the fiduciary standards, notwithstanding any potential economic benefits to the employer. [DOL Adv. Op. 2003-04A]

An amendment to a plan that benefited an employer by increasing the reversion of surplus assets (see Q 23:81) was not considered a breach of fiduciary duty; the amendment related to the design of plan benefits and not to the administration of the plan. Accordingly, it was not subject to ERISA's fiduciary duty standards. [Engelhart v. Consolidated Rail Corp., No. 92-7056 (E.D. Pa. 1993)] The adoption of an amended multiemployer plan (see Q 29:2) by the plan trustees that conflicted with a supplemental agreement between a union and an employer association was not a breach of fiduciary duty because the supplemental agreement was not a document governing the plan and the trustees were not acting as fiduciaries. [Gard v. Blankenburg, 2002 WL 261817 (6th Cir. 2002)] Similarly, the spin-off by a corporation of a division with a transfer of plan assets to fund a new plan for the former employees of the division was considered a settlor, as opposed to a fiduciary, function. [Flanigan v. General Elec. Co., 242 F.3d 78 (2d Cir. 2001)] Amendments to multiemployer plans, however, may be subject to ERISA's fiduciary duties if inherently unfair, not rationally related to the plan's overall purposes, and enacted to further interests apart from the pension fund. [Walling v. Brady, 125 F.3d 114 (3d Cir. 1997)] A multiemployer plan board of trustees' action to amend the plan definition of "final average earnings" and apply it to plan retirees constituted a breach of fiduciary duty because such an act impaired the vested right of retirees to receive benefits under the plan. [Walker v. Board of Trustees, Reg'l Transp. Dist. & Amalgamated Transit Union Div. 1001 Pension Fund, No. 02-1173 (10th Cir. 2003)] To some extent, the determination of fiduciary status may depend on how and who makes the decision. Thus, a decision by an employer not to grant severance pay to certain employees was not considered a fiduciary action when made by individual managers as opposed to a separate committee of the employer. [Noorily v. Thomas & Betts Corp, 188 F.3d 153 (3d Cir. 1999)]

Trustees of a multiemployer plan did not have a fiduciary duty to advise an employee that his employer had violated the collective bargaining agreement in not making required contributions, even though such failure caused the employee to lose service credit and, accordingly, receive lower benefits. [Bagsby v. Central States, Southeast & Southwest Areas Pension Funds, No. 97-6209 (6th Cir. 1998)] Another court concluded that an employer did not breach its fiduciary duty by funding its contributions to a profit sharing plan (see Q 2:6) by reducing its employees' share of net profits because the amounts were not owed to the employees as compensation and, hence, were employer, not employee, contributions. [Beatty v. North Cent. Cos., Nos. 01-1908, 01-2010 (8th Cir. 2002)]. A financially distressed employer did not breach its fiduciary duty when it amended its pension plan to reduce its contributions from 25 percent of each participant's compensation to zero and failed to resume funding of the plan despite stating its intention to do so. [Kaldi v. Sioux Valley Physician Partners, Inc., 2007 WL 925245 (8th Cir. 2007)]

In a suit alleging breach of ERISA fiduciary duties by an employee who claimed he was discharged wrongfully to deprive him of option rights, the court held that the employer was not acting as a plan administrator when terminating the employee so there was no breach of fiduciary duty. The court considered the nature of the employer's action and not the intent behind such action in determining the capacity in which the employer acted. [Long v. Excel Telecomms. Corp., 1999 U.S. Dist. LEXIS 17663 (N.D. Tex. 1999)]

Q 23:4   Is it a breach of fiduciary duty to misrepresent future benefits?

The U.S. Supreme Court concluded that nothing in ERISA requires a plan sponsor to disclose information about its future intentions regarding employee benefit plans; however, if an employer makes disclosure about plans, it has a fiduciary duty not to make misrepresentations. [Varity Corp. v. Howe, 516 U.S. 489 (1996)]

Although a decision to amend or terminate a plan may be a business decision that is not regulated by ERISA, misrepresentations regarding future benefits do fall within ERISA and, if material and relied upon, are actionable. Accordingly, in responding to inquiries, disclosure must be made of specific changes that are seriously being considered for purposes of implementation at an appropriate corporate level having authority to adopt such proposed changes. [Winkel v. Kennecott Holdings Corp., 2001 WL 23163 (10th Cir. 2001); Bradney v. E.I. DuPont de Nemours & Co. Pension & Ret. Plan, 229 F.3d 1150 (6th Cir. 2000); Bins v. Exxon Co., U.S.A., 220 F.3d 1042 (9th Cir. 2000); McAuley v. International Bus. Machs. Corp., 165 F.3d 1038 (6th Cir. 1999); Rabley v. Eastman Kodak Co., 1999 U.S. App. LEXIS 23372 (2d Cir. 1999); Wayne v. Pacific Bell, 189 F.3d 982 (9th Cir. 1999); Vartanian v. Monsanto Co., 1997 U.S. App. LEXIS 35324 (1st Cir. 1997); Fischer v. Philadelphia Elec. Co., 96 F.3d 1533 (3d Cir. 1996); Berlin v. Michigan Bell Telephone Co., 858 F.2d 1154 (6th Cir. 1988); Hudson v. General Dynamics Corp., No. 3:96cv1317 (D. Conn. 2001); *but see* Bettis v. Thompson, No. H-93-2976 (S.D. Tex. 1996)] Misrepresentations occasioned by clerical error, however, are not actionable. [Easa v. Florists' Transworld Delivery Ass'n, No.97-CV-73006 (E.D. Mich. 1998)]

One court ruled that an employer did not breach its fiduciary duty by failing to disclose the possibility of an early retirement plan to an employee who was considering retirement because, at the time the employee inquired about an early retirement plan, the employer had not given serious consideration to implementing such a plan. [Chichelo v. Hoffman La-Roche Inc., No. 01-2055 (3d Cir. 2002); *see also* Rashid v. First Energy Corp. Pension Plan, 2006 U.S. App. LEXIS 14121 (3d Cir. 2006); Peterson v. AT&T, 2005 WL 751925 (3d Cir. 2005); Adams v. Sun Co., 2002 WL 31255490 (3d Cir. 2002); Reimering v. Retirement Pension Plan of the Cal. State Auto. Ass'n, No. 01-15505 (9th Cir. 2002)] The same court also determined that a former employee could not sustain a suit for breach of fiduciary duty against his former employer and the plan committee for failing to inform him of a plan amendment that was under serious consideration because the amendment only became effective after his employment was terminated. [Nydes v. Equitable Res. Inc., No. 01-2396 (3d Cir. 2002)] The same court also concluded that the serious consideration test applies to multiemployer plans (see Q 29:2) as well as single-employer plans. [Mushalla v. Teamsters Local No. 863 Pension Fund, 2002 WL 1835429 (3d Cir. 2002)] Another court concluded that a voluntary severance package offered by the employer six weeks after a plan participant took early retirement was a separate plan, not an amendment to an existing retirement plan, even though the participant had asked his supervisor and members of the employer's human resources department if the employer intended to offer such a package. Consequently, the employer was a fiduciary only with regard to the existing plan and not to the severance package. [Beach v. Commonwealth Edison Co., No. 03-3907 (7th Cir. 2004)] However, one court determined that an employer did not have an affirmative duty to communicate the status of its internal deliberations regarding a possible change to its early retirement plan even if it was seriously considering a change. In rejecting a bright-line serious consideration test adopted by several other courts, the court adopted an approach that takes into account whether employees would consider the information material in making benefit-related decisions. [Martinez v. Schlumberger, Ltd., 338 F.3d 407 (5th Cir. 2003); *see also* Ballone v. Eastman Kodak Co., 109 F.3d 117 (2d Cir. 1997)] Another court determined that employees who had retired before an involuntary termination benefit program was under serious consideration were nonetheless entitled to the benefits since they had been actively misled by the employer regarding the program's future availability. [Mathews v. Chevron Corp, 362 F.3d 1172 (9th Cir. 2004); *see also* Wayne v. Pacific Bell, 238 F.3d 1048 (9th Cir. 2001)] An employer breached its fiduciary duties when it deliberately kept critical information regarding the status of early retirement programs from the employees, including human resources personnel who counseled other employees about retirement, ruled one court. [Broga v. Northeast Utils., 315 F. Supp. 2d 212 (D. Conn. 2004)] An employer did not breach its fiduciary duties because there was no causal connection between its alleged misrepresentations and the employees' entitlement to receive certain benefits. [Ferrer v. Chevron Corp., 2007 WL 1087257 (5th Cir. 2007)]

In what may become an important decision, one court concluded that former plan participants could not claim a breach of fiduciary duty solely on the basis of alleged oral misrepresentations that purported to alter plan terms, because oral promises cannot vary the terms of an ERISA plan. [Ladouceur v. Credit Lyonnais, 584 F.3d 510 (2d Cir. 2009)]

Q 23:5   Is a fiduciary required to respond fully and accurately to all inquiries by or on behalf of a participant?

Yes. Misleading communications, misrepresentations, or omissions to participants may constitute a breach of fiduciary duty. [Griggs v. E.I. DuPont de Nemours & Co., 385 F.3d 440 (4th Cir. 2004); James v. Pirelli Armstrong Tire Corp., 2002 U.S. App. LEXIS 1907 (6th Cir. 2002); Bourjolly v. Koenig, No. 99-2179 (8th Cir. 2000); Estate of Becker v. Eastman Kodak Co., 1997 U.S. App. LEXIS 17937 (2d Cir. 1997); Jordan v. Federal Express Corp., 116 F.3d 1005 (3d Cir. 1997); Kurz v. Philadelphia Elec. Co., 96 F.3d 1544 (3d Cir. 1996); Drennan v. General Motors Corp., 977 F.2d 246 (6th Cir. 1992); Adams v. The Brink's Co., No. 02-00044 (W.D. Va. 2005); Gore v. Crozer Chester Med. Ctr., No. 96-8192(E.D. Pa. 1997)] It is not necessary to find that the plan administrator (see Q 20:1) had knowingly deceived the participant. To the contrary, a breach of fiduciary duty claim is viable for misleading communications made either negligently or intentionally. [McGrath v. Lockheed Martin Corp., 2002 WL 31269646 (6th Cir. 2002); Krohn v. Huron Mem'l Hosp., 173 F.3d 542 (6th Cir. 1999)] A fiduciary may also have a duty to notify a participant of an interpretation of an ambiguous material plan provision if the participant might misinterpret the provision to the participant's detriment. [Harte v. Bethlehem Steel Corp., 214 F.3d 446 (3d Cir. 2000) However, one court ruled that a breach of fiduciary duty did not occur where the employer had provided a participant with incorrect benefits projections for a number of years before she retired. [Hart v. Equitable Life Assurance Soc'y, 2003 WL 22148771 (2d Cir. 2003); *see also* Christensen v. The Qwest Pension Plan, 462 F.3d 913 (8th Cir. 2006); *but see* Schaffer v. Westinghouse Savannah River Co., 2005 U.S. App. LEXIS 4164 (4th Cir. 2005); DOL Reg. § 2509.75-8, FR-11]

In certain circumstances, misleading communications or misrepresentations may constitute fraud under state law on the theory that they do not relate to an ERISA plan and, accordingly, are not preempted by ERISA (see Q 23:56). [Spink v. Lockheed, 125 F.3d 1257 (9th Cir. 1997)] A statement of present intent that is later changed does not constitute a breach of fiduciary duty. [Frahm v. Equitable Life Assurance Soc'y of the United States, 137 F.3d 955 (7th Cir. 1998); Sprague v. General Motors Corp., 133 F.3d 388 (6th Cir. 1998)]

Q 23:6   Will courts enforce promises to plan participants to prevent injustice when there is reliance, even though the promise is not in accordance with the terms of a plan?

At times, courts will enforce promises of this nature based upon the theory of ERISA promissory estoppel. The elements of this claim vary among the circuit courts. The tenth circuit does not recognize it. [Miller v. Coastal Corp, 978 F.2d 622 (10th Cir. 1992)] The first and eighth circuits have expressed doubts as to whether they would recognize estoppel. [City of Hope Nat'l Med. Ctr. v. Healthplus, Inc., 156 F.3d 223 (1st Cir. 1998); Jensen v. Sipco, Inc., 38 F.3d 945 (8th Cir. 1994)] The fourth circuit appears to recognize equitable or promissory estoppel. [Schaffer v. Westinghouse Savannah River Co., 2005 U.S. App. LEXIS 4164 (4th Cir. 2005)] The fourth circuit, however, would not permit benefits to be granted in accordance with erroneous projections, even under a theory of equitable estoppel; to do so, said the court, would effectively allow informal communications to change the terms of a formal plan. [Clark v. BASF Corp. Salaried Employees' Pension Plan, No. 04-2024 (4th Cir. 2005)] In other circuits that recognize promissory estoppel, a common element is extraordinary circumstances. The second circuit also requires that there is a promise, which is relied on, causing injury, and there would be injustice if the promise were not enforced. [Ladouceur v. Credit Lyonnaise, 2005 U.S. App LEXIS 27967 (2d Cir. 2005); Arnold v. Lucks, 392 F.3d 512 (2d Cir. 2004); Aramony v. United Way Replacement Benefit Plan, 191 F.3d 140 (2d Cir. 1999); Devlin v. Transportation Communications Int'l Union, 173 F.3d 94 (2d Cir. 1999)] However, the second circuit more recently ruled that former plan participants could not claim a breach of fiduciary duty solely on the basis of alleged oral misrepresentations that purported to alter plan terms, because oral promises cannot vary the terms of an ERISA plan. [Ladouceur v. Credit Lyonnais, 584 F.3d 510 (2d Cir. 2009); *see also* Watson v. Consolidated Edison Co. of N.Y., Inc., 2010 WL 1564654 (2d Cir. 2010)] The fifth circuit may find promissory estoppel in extraordinary circumstances where there is reasonable and detrimental reliance upon a material misrepresentation. [Weir v. Federal Asset Disposition Ass'n, 123 F.3d 281 (5th Cir. 1997)] However, in a later case, it appears that the fifth circuit would require only a demonstration of reasonable reliance. [Melo v. Sara Lee Corp., 2005 U.S. App. LEXIS 25218 (5th Cir. 2005)] The sixth circuit ruled that a beneficiary could invoke equitable estoppel in situations involving unambiguous plan provisions where a plaintiff could demonstrate traditional estoppel elements. One required element, according to the court, includes the fact that the defendant engaged in intended deception or such gross negligence that it amounted to constructive fraud. Also required, the court indicated, are: (1) a written representation; (2) plan provisions that, though unambiguous, do not allow for individual calculation of benefits; and (3) extraordinary circumstances in which the balance of equities strongly favors the application of estoppel. In this instance, the sixth circuit believed, all of these elements could be fulfilled by facts alleged by the beneficiary. [Bloemker v. Laborers' Local 265 Pension Fund, No. 09-3536 (6th Cir. 2010)] The seventh circuit appears to limit estoppel to welfare (not pension) plans and requires that the promise be in writing and that there is some element of willfulness. It does not permit estoppel class certification (see Q 23:41). [Gallegos v. Mt. Sinai Med. Ctr., 210 F.3d 803 (7th Cir. 2000); Trustmark Life Ins. Co. v. University of Chicago Hosps., 207 F.3d 876 (7th Cir. 2000); Shields v. Local 705, Int'l Bhd. of Teamsters, 188 F.3d 895 (7th Cir. 1999); Frahm v. Equitable Life Assurance Soc'y, 137 F.3d 955 (7th Cir. 1998); Retired Chicago Police Ass'n v. City of Chicago, 7 F.3d 584 (7th Cir. 1993)] In the third circuit, extraordinary circumstances are equivalent to fraud or similar inequitable conduct. [Kurz v. Philadelphia Elec. Co., 96 F.3d 1544 (3d Cir. 1996)] The third circuit has also stated that an equitable estoppel requires three elements: (1) a material misrepresentation; (2) reasonable and detrimental reliance; and (3) extraordinary circumstances. [Pell v. E.I. DuPont de Nemours & Co., Inc., 539 F.3d 292 (3d Cir. 2008)] In the sixth, ninth, and eleventh circuits, estoppel can be invoked with respect to ambiguous plan provisions, not unambiguous plan provisions. [Sprague v. General Motors Corp., 133 F.3d 388 (6th Cir. 1998); Greany v. Western Farm Bureau Life Ins. Co., 973 F.2d 812 (9th Cir. 1992); Kane v. Aetna Life Ins., 893 F.2d 1283 (11th Cir. 1990)] The eleventh circuit recognizes equitable estoppel as a very narrow doctrine that is appropriate only where (1) the relevant plan provisions at issue are ambiguous and (2) the plan provider or administrator has made representations to the participant that constitute an informal interpretation of the ambiguity. [Waschak v. The Acuity Brands, Inc. Senior Management Benefit Plan, 2010 WL 2543137 (11th Cir. 2010)] The eleventh circuit has held that an employer which allegedly misled employees into accepting positions with a successor company did not breach its fiduciary duty and that the employees' reliance on the employer's alleged misrepresentation was not detrimental. [Hammond v. Reynolds Metals Co., 2007 WL 675652 (11th Cir. 2007)] The ninth circuit has also ruled that, although plaintiffs are usually entitled to recover under the theory of equitable estoppel, participants in ERISA plans cannot recover benefits under equitable estoppel if the plan is a trust fund and the recovery of benefits would contradict the plan's written terms. [Kessler v. ADT Sec. Sys., Inc., No. 01-15594 (9th Cir. 2002)]

Q 23:7 Does a person who performs ministerial duties within guidelines furnished by others acquire fiduciary status?

No. Those performing purely ministerial functions within guidelines established by others are not plan fiduciaries. DOL regulations list the following job categories as ministerial:

1. Application of rules to determine eligibility for participation or benefits;

2. Calculation of service and compensation for benefit purposes;

3. Preparing communications to employees;

4. Maintaining participants' service and employment records;

5. Preparing reports required by government agencies;

6. Calculating benefits;

7. Explaining the plan to new participants and advising participants of their rights and options under the plan;

8. Collecting contributions and applying them as specified in the plan;

9. Preparing reports covering participants' benefits;

10. Processing claims; and

11. Making recommendations to others for decisions with respect to plan administration.

[DOL Reg. § 2509.75-8, D-2; Stahly v. Salomon Smith Barney, Inc., 2009 WL 725056 (9th Cir. 2009); Arizona State Carpenters Pension Trust Fund v. Citibank (Ariz.), 1997 U.S. App. LEXIS 23587 (9th Cir. 1997); Flacche v. Sun Life Assurance Co. of Can., No. 91-3462 (6th Cir. 1992); Flanagan Lieberman Hoffman & Swaim v. Transamerica Life Ins. & Annuity Co., 2002 U.S. Dist. LEXIS 21327 (S.D. Ohio 2002); Demaio v. Cigna Corp., No. 89-0724 (E.D. Pa. 1993); Reichling v. Continental Bank, 813 F. Supp. 197 (E.D.N.Y. 1993)]

Trustees were not fiduciaries to the extent they lacked discretion over the investment of plan assets, so they did not violate their fiduciary duties by investing all plan assets in group annuity contracts because the plan itself required such investment and the trustees had no discretion. [Arakelian v. National W. Life Ins. Co., No. 84-1953 (D.D.C. 1990)] However, a directed trustee can be a fiduciary, but a different standard is applied to investments made by the trustee at the direction of another (see Q 23:19). [ERISA § 403(a); DOL Field Assistance Bull. 2004-03; In re WorldCom, Inc. ERISA Litigation, 2005 WL 221263 (S.D.N.Y. 2005)] Because a human resources manager was not a fiduciary, a court concluded that a participant was not entitled to rely on the manager's misstatements regarding the participant's right to continue plan coverage. [Estate of Weeks v. Advance Stores Co., 2004 U.S. App. LEXIS 10637 (4th Cir. 2004)] In another case, a human resources representative who provided inaccurate pension estimates was not a plan fiduciary, and the employer did not breach a fiduciary duty owing to the inaccurate estimates. [Livick v. The Gillette Co., 524 F.3d 24 (1st Cir. 2008)] Also, plan sponsor managers were not acting in a fiduciary capacity when they made erroneous statements to plan participants regarding benefits and, therefore, were not liable for a fiduciary breach. [Adams v. The Brink's Co., No. 06-1744 (4th Cir. 2008)]

A broker or dealer registered under the Securities Exchange Act of 1934 is not deemed to be a fiduciary solely because the broker-dealer executes securities transactions on behalf of the plan in the ordinary course of its business, provided:

1. The broker-dealer is not affiliated with a plan fiduciary, and
2. The plan fiduciary specifies:
    a. The security to be purchased or sold;
    b. The price range within which the security may be purchased or sold;
    c. The time span (not exceeding five days) during which the security may be purchased or sold; and
    d. The minimum or maximum quantity of the security that may be purchased or sold within such price range.

[DOL Reg. § 2510.3-21(d)(1)]

Q 23:8   What is rendering investment advice for the purpose of determining fiduciary status?

A person is rendering investment advice to a plan only if such person (1) makes recommendations as to valuing, buying, holding, or selling securities or other property and (2) has, directly or indirectly, (a) discretionary authority or control over buying or selling securities or other property for the plan, whether or not pursuant to an agreement, arrangement, or understanding, or (b) regularly renders advice to the plan pursuant to a mutual agreement, arrangement, or understanding that such advice will serve as a primary basis for plan investment decisions and that such advice will be based on the particular needs of the plan regarding such matters as investment policies or strategy, overall portfolio composition, or diversification of plan investments. [DOL Reg. § 2510.3-21(c)(1); DOL Op. Ltr. 95-17A; Ellis v. Rycenga Homes, Inc., 2007 WL 1032367 (W.D. Mich. 2007); Dudley Supermarket, Inc. v. Transamerica Life Ins. & Annuity Co., 302 F.3d 1 (1st Cir. 2002)] A financial services firm that attended trust meetings and prepared quarterly financial reports for the plan was not a plan fiduciary. The firm's actions were considered ministerial tasks that did not give rise to fiduciary liability and, thus, did not constitute the rendering of investment advice for a fee. [Stahly v. Salomon Smith Barney, Inc., 2009 WL 725056 (9th Cir. 2009)]

DOL has opined that:

1. A person directing a plan's investments constitutes the exercise of authority and control over the management of plan assets, so the person would be a plan fiduciary, even if such person were chosen by a participant and had no other connection to the plan.
2. The conclusion is the same if the plan is a self-directed account plan (see Q 23:14). A person selected by a participant in this type of plan to manage the participant's investments would be liable for imprudent investment decisions because these decisions would not have been due to the participant's exercise of control.
3. Merely advising a participant to roll over to an IRA a distribution that is permitted under the plan to take advantage of investment options that are not available under the plan, even when combined with a recommendation on how to invest that distribution, does not constitute investment advice.

4. A recommendation by an advisor, who is not otherwise a plan fiduciary, that a participant take a permissible distribution from a plan and roll it over to an IRA so that the advisor will earn management or investment fees related to the IRA is not investment advice or an exercise of authority or control over plan assets that would make the person a fiduciary. [DOL Op. Ltr. 2005-23A]

A broker's practice of recommending investments will not make that broker a fiduciary in the absence of any agreement, arrangement, or understanding referred to in item (2)(b) above. [Thomas, Head & Greisen Employees Trust v. Buster, 24 F.3d 1114 (9th Cir. 1994); Farm King Supply, Inc. Integrated Profit Sharing Plan & Trust v. Edward D. Jones & Co., 884 F.2d 288 (7th Cir. 1989)] However, a broker may be considered a fiduciary if the broker engages in unauthorized buying and selling of plan assets. [Olson v. E.F. Hutton & Co., No. 91-1416 (8th Cir. 1992)]

Although a broker may be a fiduciary because it rendered advice for a fee, the broker's fiduciary duty is limited to those fiduciary duties it performed; thus, the broker had no duty to inform a fund client regarding the reasons a dishonest employee's employment was terminated. [Glaziers & Glassworkers Union Local 252 Annuity Fund v. Newbridge Sec., Inc, 93 F.3d 1171 (3d Cir. 1996)] An investment advisor was also not prohibited from enforcing a restrictive covenant signed by an asset manager employed by it because this was considered an internal business matter not subject to the rule requiring a fiduciary to act exclusively in the best interests of the plans it managed. [Frank Russell Co. v. Wellington Mgmt. Co., 1998 WL 481230 (3d Cir. 1998)]

The person rendering investment advice can be a fiduciary even though compensated on a commission basis since commissions constitute a fee or other compensation (see Q 23:1). [Reich v. McManus, 1995 U.S. Dist. LEXIS 5661 (N.D. Ill. 1995)]

DOL announced plans to issue proposed regulations to expand the current regulatory definition of "fiduciary" to include more persons, such as pension consultants, as fiduciaries. [DOL Fact Sheet, Jan. 2010]

Q 23:9   What is a named fiduciary?

Every plan is required to have at least one named fiduciary (i.e., one or more persons designated in the plan by name or title as responsible for operating the plan). The purpose of the requirement is to enable employees and other interested parties to ascertain the person responsible for plan operations. A plan covering employees of a corporation can designate the corporation as the named fiduciary. However, DOL regulations suggest that "a plan instrument which designates a corporation as 'named fiduciary' should provide for designation by the corporation of specified individuals or other persons to carry out specified fiduciary responsibilities under the plan . . . ." [ERISA § 402(a)(1); DOL Reg. § 2509.75-5, FR-1, FR-3] There is a conflict among the circuit courts as to whether officer-shareholders of the named fiduciary may be deemed fiduciaries. [*Compare* Kayes v. Pacific Lumber Co., 51 F.3d 1449 (9th Cir. 1995) (finding fiduciary status), *with* Confer v. Custom Eng'g Co., 952 F.2d 34 (3d Cir. 1991) (rejecting fiduciary status)]

Q 23:10 Are attorneys, accountants, actuaries, insurance agents, insurers, custodians, consultants, and others who provide services to a plan considered plan fiduciaries?

No. They are not considered plan fiduciaries solely because they render such services. Many cases hold that attorneys, accountants, actuaries, service providers, and consultants do not possess or exert the necessary discretionary authority or control regarding management of the plan to cause them to be fiduciaries under ERISA. [Zang v. Paychex, Inc., No. 08-CV-60461 (W.D.N.Y. 2010) (mutual fund provider); Bhatia v. Dischino, 2010 WL 1236406 (N.D. Tex. 2010) (actuary); Pender v. Bank of America Corp., 2010 WL 1434297 (D. N.C. 2010) (accountants); DOL v. Payea, 2009 WL 2046135 (__. D. Mich. 2009) (depository bank); Hecker v. Deere & Co., 556 F.3d 575 (7th Cir. 2009) (mutual fund provider); *In re* Mushroom Transportation Co., Inc., No. 02-3754 (3d Cir. 2004) (bank and law firm); Gerosa v. Savasta & Co., 329 F.3d 317 (2d Cir. 2003) (actuary); Hamilton v. Carell, 2001 WL 276977 (6th Cir. 2001) (consultant); CSA 401(k) Plan v. Pension Prof'ls, Inc., 1999 U.S. App. LEXIS 30404 (9th Cir. 1999) (third-party administrator); Custer v. Sweeney, 1996 U.S. App. LEXIS 17852 (4th Cir. 1996) (attorney); Chapman v. Klemick, 3 F.3d 1508 (11th Cir. 1993) (attorney); Kaniewski v. Equitable Life Assurance Soc'y, No. 92-3604 (6th Cir. 1993) (insurance company); Schloegel v. Boswell, 994 F.2d 266 (5th Cir. 1993) (insurance agent); Useden v. Acker, No. 90-5445 (11th Cir. 1991) (attorneys and bank); Mertens v. Hewitt Assocs., 948 F.2d 607 (9th Cir. 1991), *aff'd,* 508 U.S. 248 (1993) (actuaries); Consolidated Beef Indus., Inc. v. New York Life Ins. Co., Nos. 90-5131, 90-5164 (8th Cir. 1991) (insurance company and agent); Pappas v. Buck Consultants, Inc., 923 F.2d 531 (7th Cir. 1991) (actuaries); Anoka Orthopaedic Assocs., P.A. v. Lechner, 910 F.2d 514 (8th Cir. 1990) (attorneys and consultants); Painters of Phila. Dist. Council No. 21 Welfare Fund v. Price Waterhouse, 879 F.2d 1146 (3d Cir. 1989) (accountants); Flanagan Lieberman Hoffman & Swaim v. Transamerica Life Ins. & Annuity Co, 2002 U.S. Dist. LEXIS 21327 (S.D. Ohio 2002) (administrative service provider); A Ronald Sirna, Jr., P.C. Profit Sharing Plan v. Prudential Sec., Inc., No. 95 Civ. 8422 (S.D.N.Y. 1997) (administrative service provider); Pension Plan of Pub. Serv. Co. of N.H. v. KPMG Peat Marwick, 1993 U.S. Dist. LEXIS 2254 (D.N.H. 1993) (accountants)]

However, they will be regarded as fiduciaries if they exercise discretionary authority or control over the management or administration of the plan or some authority or control over plan assets even if such activities are unauthorized. [DOL Reg. § 2509.75-5, D-1; John Hancock Mut. Life Ins. Co. v. Harris Trust & Sav. Bank, 510 U.S. 86 (1993); Rud v. Liberty Life Assur. Co. of Boston, 438 F.3d 772 (7th Cir. 2006); Chao v. Day, 436 F.3d 234 (D.C. Cir. 2006); David P. Coldesina Employee Profit Sharing Plan and Trust v. Estate of Simper, 407 F.3d 1126 (10th Cir. 2005); Srein v. Frankford Trust Co., No. 01-4516 (3d Cir. 2003); Dudley Supermarket, Inc. v. Transamerica Life Ins. & Annuity Co., 302 F.3d 1 (1st Cir. 2002); Barron v. UNUM Life Ins. Co. of Am., No. 01-1065 (4th Cir.

2001); Midwest Cmty. Health Serv. v. American United Life Ins. Co., No. 00-2360 (7th Cir. 2001); Patelco Credit Union v. Sahri, 2001 WL 964972 (9th Cir. 2001); Arizona State Carpenters Pension Trust Fund v. Citibank (Ariz.), 1997 U.S. App. LEXIS 23587 (9th Cir. 1997); Reich v. Lancaster, 55 F.3d 1034 (5th Cir. 1995); Sheldon Co. Profit-Sharing Plan & Trust v. Smith, 1995 U.S. App. LEXIS 20708 (6th Cir. 1995); Olson v. E.F. Hutton & Co., No. 91-1416 MN (8th Cir. 1992); Meyer v. Berkshire Life Ins. Co., 2003 U.S. Dist. LEXIS 6107 (D. Md. 2003); Bouton v. Thompson, 764 F. Supp. 20 (D. Conn. 1991); Brock v. Self, 632 F. Supp. 1509 (W.D. La. 1986); DOL Op. Ltr. 2005-23A]

One court concluded that an attorney who had represented a plan and one of the plan's trustees was not liable as a plan fiduciary for a letter provided to a successor trustee that erroneously confirmed the legality of a prohibited transaction (see Q 24:1). [Mellon Bank v. Levy, 2003 U.S. App. LEXIS 16118 (3d Cir. 2003)] A plan's trustees sued an insurance company in state court claiming, among other matters, breach of fiduciary duty based upon the actions of an agent of the insurance company. The company had the case removed to federal court and, in doing so, waived a defense that it was not a fiduciary. The court rejected the company's later argument that it had not conceded its fiduciary status. [Meyer v. Berkshire Life Ins. Co., 372 F.3d 261 (4th Cir. 2004)]

An insurance company that held plan assets in its general account was not considered a fiduciary; however, if the assets were held in a separate account for that particular plan, the insurance company may be deemed a fiduciary. [Tool v. National Employee Benefit Servs., Inc., No. C96-0296 (N.D. Cal. 1996)] See Q 23:90 for a discussion of DOL regulations clarifying the status of plan assets held in insurance company general accounts, and see Q 23:2 for a discussion of ERISA Section 401(c).

DOL has opined that the inclusion of certain limitation of liability and indemnification provisions in contracts between plans and plan service providers would not be per se imprudent or per se unreasonable. However, liability limit and indemnification provisions that purport to apply to fraud or willful misconduct by the plan service provider would be void as against public policy, so that it would be imprudent and unreasonable for a plan fiduciary to agree to those terms. [DOL Op. Ltr. 2002-08A; ERISA §§ 404(a)(1)(B), 408(b)(2)]

The Securities and Exchange Commission (SEC) has advised that some pension plan consultants may not be fully disclosing potential conflicts of interest that could affect the objectivity of advice they are giving to clients. To encourage the disclosure and review of information regarding potential conflicts of interest, the SEC has developed, in conjunction with DOL, a set of questions designed to assist plan fiduciaries in the evaluation of the objectivity of a pension consultant's recommendations, as follows:

1. Are you registered with the SEC or a state securities regulator as an investment advisor? If so, have you provided me with all the disclosures required under those laws (including Part II of Form ADV)?

2. Do you or a related company have relationships with money managers that you recommend, consider for recommendation, or otherwise mention to the plan for our consideration? If so, describe those relationships.

3. Do you or a related company receive any payments from money managers you recommend, consider for recommendation, or otherwise mention to the plan for our consideration? If so, what is the extent of these payments in relation to your other income (revenue)?

4. Do you have any policies or procedures to address conflicts of interest or to prevent these payments or relationships from being considered when you provide advice to your clients?

5. If you allow plans to pay your consulting fees using the plan's brokerage commissions, do you monitor the amount of commissions paid and alert plans when consulting fees have been paid in full? If not, how can a plan make sure it does not overpay its consulting fees?

6. If you allow plans to pay your consulting fees using the plan's brokerage commissions, what steps do you take to ensure that the plan receives the best execution for its securities trades?

7. Do you have any arrangements with broker-dealers under which you or a related company will benefit if money managers place trades for their clients with such broker-dealers?

8. If you are hired, will you acknowledge in writing that you have a fiduciary obligation as an investment advisor to the plan while providing the consulting services we are seeking?

9. Do you consider yourself a fiduciary under ERISA with respect to the recommendations you provide the plan?

10. What percentage of your plan clients utilize money managers, investment funds, brokerage services, or other service providers from whom you receive fees?

[SEC News Release 2005-81 (June 1, 2005); SEC News Release 2005-75 (May 16, 2005)]

See Q 23:12 for a discussion of proposed regulations designed to provide plan fiduciaries with sufficient information to evaluate the reasonableness of compensation and fees directly and indirectly paid to certain service providers (including affiliates), and to assess the potential for conflicts of interest that may affect the performance of a service provider. Also, DOL announced plans to issue proposed regulations to expand the current regulatory definition of "fiduciary" to include more persons, such as pension consultants, as fiduciaries. As a result of the proposed regulatory change, these persons would become subject to ERISA's fiduciary responsibility rules. [DOL Fact Sheet, Jan. 2010]

Q 23:11   If service providers are not considered fiduciaries, are they nonetheless responsible for the services they provide?

Yes. Although not fiduciaries, they may be liable to the plan or plan sponsors based upon traditional theories of negligence, malpractice, or fraud. [Penny/ Ohlmann/Nieman, Inc. v. Miami Valley Pension Corp., 399 F.3d 692 (6th Cir. 2005); Milkis Enterprises, Inc. v. Retirement Plan Consultants, 2005 WL 913087 (E.D. Pa. 2005); Leblanc v. Cahill, 153 F.3d 134 (4th Cir. 1998); Steiner Corp. v.

Johnson & Higgins of Cal., No. 96-4044 (10th Cir. 1998); Padeh v. Zagoria, 1995 U.S. Dist. LEXIS 14255 (S.D. Fla. 1995); Clayton v. Peat Marwick, No. 94-2005 (C.D. Cal. 1994); Berlin City Ford, Inc. v. Roberts Planning Group, 864 F. Supp. 292 (D.N.H. 1994); Horton v. Cigna Individual Fin. Servs. Co., 1993 U.S. Dist. LEXIS 8639 (N.D. Ill. 1993); Hanovi Corp. v. San Francisco Pension Corp, 1993 U.S. Dist. LEXIS 18314 (N.D. Cal. 1993); Mazur v. Gaudet, 826 F. Supp. 188 (E.D. La. 1992)]

One court concluded that plan trustees were able to sustain an action against the plan's actuary even though the actuary was not a plan fiduciary because ERISA does not preempt "run-of-the-mill" state law professional negligence claims against nonfiduciaries. [Gerosa v. Savasta & Co., 329 F.3d 317 (2d Cir. 2003)] According to one court, ERISA did not preempt state law misrepresentation and negligence claims brought against a nonfiduciary life insurance company and a provider of a fully insured plan (see Q 23:57). [Hausmann v. Union Bank of California, N.A., 2009 WL 1325810 (D.C. Cal. 2009); see also Patel v. Pacific Life Ins. Co., 2009 WL 1456526 (__.D. Tex. 2009)]

DOL has opined that the inclusion of certain limitation of liability and indemnification provisions in contracts between plans and plan service providers would not be per se imprudent or per se unreasonable. However, liability limit and indemnification provisions that purport to apply to fraud or willful misconduct by the plan service provider would be void as against public policy, so that it would be imprudent and unreasonable for a plan fiduciary to agree to those terms. [DOL Op. Ltr. 2002-08A; ERISA §§ 404(a)(1)(B), 408(b)(2)]

See Q 23:12 for a discussion of proposed regulations designed to provide plan fiduciaries with sufficient information to evaluate the reasonableness of compensation and fees directly and indirectly paid to certain service providers (including affiliates), and to assess the potential for conflicts of interest that may affect the performance of a service provider.

Q 23:12   Has DOL issued regulations concerning service providers?

DOL has issued proposed regulations that are designed to provide plan fiduciaries (see Q 23:1) with sufficient information to evaluate the reasonableness of compensation and fees directly and indirectly paid to certain service providers (including affiliates), and to assess the potential for conflicts of interest that may affect the performance of a service provider. [ERISA § 408(b)(2); DOL Prop. Reg. § 2550.408b-2(c)]

No contract or arrangement to provide services to an employee benefit plan, or any extension or renewal of such contract or arrangement, by:

1. A service provider that provides or may provide any services to the plan pursuant to the contract or arrangement as a fiduciary either within the meaning of ERISA or under the Investment Advisers Act of 1940;

2. A service provider that provides or may provide any one or more of the following services to the plan pursuant to the contract or arrangement: banking, consulting, custodial, insurance, investment advisory (plan or

participants), investment management, record keeping, securities or other investment brokerage, or third party administration; or

3. A service provider that receives or may receive indirect compensation or fees in connection with providing any one or more of the following services to the plan pursuant to the contract or arrangement: accounting, actuarial, appraisal, auditing, legal, or valuation;

is reasonable unless the requirements discussed in this Q 23:12 are satisfied. [DOL Prop. Reg. § 2550.408b-2(c)(l)(i)]

The terms of the contract or arrangement must be in writing. [DOL Prop. Reg. § 2550.408b-2(c)(1)(ii)

The terms of the contract or arrangement (including any extension or renewal of such contract or arrangement) must require the service provider to disclose in writing, to the best of the service provider's knowledge, the information set forth below in items 1 through 6 and must include a representation by the service provider that, before the contract or arrangement was entered into (or extended or renewed), all such information was provided to the fiduciary (i.e., the responsible plan fiduciary) with authority to cause the employee benefit plan to enter into (or extend or renew) the contract or arrangement:

1. All services to be provided to the plan pursuant to the contract or arrangement and, with respect to each such service, the compensation or fees to be received by the service provider, and the manner of receipt of such compensation or fees. For these purposes:

    a. Compensation or fees include money or any other thing of monetary value (for example, gifts, awards, and trips) received, or to be received, directly from the plan or plan sponsor or indirectly (i.e., from any source other than the plan, the plan sponsor, or the service provider) by the service provider or its affiliate in connection with the services to be provided pursuant to the contract or arrangement or because of the service provider's or affiliate's position with the plan. An affiliate of a service provider is any person directly or indirectly (through one or more intermediaries) controlling, controlled by, or under common control with the service provider, or any officer, director, agent, or employee of, or partner with, the service provider.

    b. Compensation or fees may be expressed in terms of a monetary amount, formula, percentage of the plan's assets, or per capita charge for each participant or beneficiary of the plan. The manner in which compensation or fees is expressed must contain sufficient information to enable the responsible plan fiduciary to evaluate the reasonableness of such compensation or fees.

    c. If a service provider offers a bundle of services to the plan that is priced as a package, rather than on a service-by-service basis, then only the service provider offering the bundle of services must provide the required disclosures. The service provider must disclose all services and the aggregate compensation or fees to be received, directly or indirectly, by the service provider, any affiliate or subcontractor of such service provider, or any other party in connection with the bundle of services. The service provider will not be required to disclose the allocation of such compensation or fees among its affiliates, subcontractors, or other parties, except to the extent such party receives or may receive compensation or fees that are a separate charge directly against the plan's investment reflected in the net value of the investment or that are set on a transaction basis, such as finder's fees, brokerage commissions, and soft dollars (research or other products or services other than execution in connection with securities transactions).

   d. A description of the manner of receipt of compensation or fees must state whether the service provider will bill the plan, deduct fees directly from plan accounts, or reflect a charge against the plan investment and must describe how any prepaid fees will be calculated and refunded when a contract or arrangement terminates;

2. Whether the service provider (or an affiliate) will provide any services to the plan as a fiduciary either within the meaning of ERISA or under the Investment Advisers Act of 1940;

3. Whether the service provider (or an affiliate) expects to participate in, or otherwise acquire a financial or other interest in, any transaction to be entered into by the plan in connection with the contract or arrangement and, if so, a description of the transaction and the service provider's participation or interest therein;

4. Whether the service provider (or an affiliate) has any material financial, referral, or other relationship or arrangement with a money manager, broker, or client of the service provider, other service provider to the plan, or any other entity that creates or may create a conflict of interest for the service provider in performing services pursuant to the contract or arrangement and, if so, a description of such relationship or arrangement;

5. Whether the service provider (or any affiliate) will be able to affect its own compensation or fees, from whatever source, without the prior approval of an independent plan fiduciary, in connection with the provision of services pursuant to the contract or arrangement (for example, as a result of incentive, performance-based, float, or other contingent compensation) and, if so, a description of the nature of such compensation; and

6. Whether the service provider (or an affiliate) has any policies or procedures that address actual or potential conflicts of interest or that are designed to prevent either the compensation or fees or the relationships or arrangements from adversely affecting the provision of services to the plan pursuant to the contract or arrangement and, if so, an explanation of these policies or procedures and how they address such conflicts of interest or prevent an adverse effect on the provision of services. [DOL Prop. Reg. § 2550.408(b)-2(c)(l)(iii)]

The terms of the contract or arrangement must require that the service provider disclose to the responsible plan fiduciary any material change to the information required to be disclosed no later than 30 days from the date on which the service provider acquires knowledge of the material change. [DOL Prop. Reg. § 2550.408b-2(c)(l)(iv)]

The terms of the contract or arrangement must require that the service provider disclose all information related to the contract or arrangement and any compensation or fees received thereunder that is required by the responsible plan fiduciary or plan administrator (see Q 20:1) in order to comply with the reporting and disclosure requirements of Title I of ERISA and the regulations, forms, and schedules issued thereunder. [DOL Prop. Reg. § 2550.408b-2(c)(i)(v)]

The service provider must comply with its disclosure obligations under the contract or arrangement as described above. [DOL Prop. Reg. § 2550.408(b)-2(c)(1)(vi)] See Q 24:26 for a proposed PTCE that would relieve a plan fiduciary of liability for a prohibited transaction that results from the failure by the service provider to comply with the disclosure regulations.

No contract or arrangement is reasonable if it does not permit termination by the plan without penalty to the plan on reasonably short notice under the circumstances to prevent the plan from becoming locked into an arrangement that has become disadvantageous. A long-term lease that may be terminated prior to its expiration (without penalty to the plan) on reasonably short notice under the circumstances is not generally an unreasonable arrangement merely because of its long term. A provision in a contract or other arrangement that reasonably compensates the service provider or lessor for loss upon early termination of the contract, arrangement, or lease is not a penalty. For example, a minimal fee in a service contract that is charged to allow recoupment of reasonable start-up costs is not a penalty. Similarly, a provision in a lease for a termination fee that covers reasonably foreseeable expenses related to the vacancy and reletting of the office space upon early termination of the lease is not a penalty. Such a provision does not reasonably compensate for loss if it provides for payment in excess of actual loss or if it fails to require mitigation of damages. [DOL Prop. Reg. § 2550.408b-2(c)(2)]

DOL issued final regulations that will become effective on July 16, 2011. [DOL Reg. §§ 2550.408b-2(c)(1), 2550.408b-2(c)(3)]

Q 23:13 Do the fiduciary responsibility rules of ERISA apply to a Keogh plan?

Yes, if the plan covers common-law employees as well as self-employed individuals (see Q 6:60), the fiduciary responsibility provisions of ERISA are applicable. However, the fiduciary responsibility provisions of ERISA do not apply to plans that cover only self-employed individuals. A plan covering only the owner-employee (see Q 5:32) and the owner-employee's spouse is not a plan providing retirement income to employees. Plans in which only sole proprietors or partners participate are not considered employee benefit plans, and sole proprietors, partners, and their spouses are not considered employees for ERISA's fiduciary responsibility rules. [ERISA § 3(3); DOL Reg. §§ 2510.3-3(b), 2510.3-3(c); Robertson v. Alexander Grant & Co., 798 F.2d 868 (5th Cir. 1986); Schwartz v. Gordon, 761 F.2d 864 (2d Cir. 1985); Olsavsky v. Casey, 1992 U.S. Dist. LEXIS 18495 (D. Conn. 1992)]

Q 23:14   What is a self-directed account plan?

A self-directed account plan is an individual account plan described in ERISA Section 3(34) that permits a participant to make an independent choice from a broad range of investment alternatives regarding the manner in which any portion of the assets in the participant's individual account is invested. [ERISA § 404(c); DOL Reg. §§ 2550.404c-1(a)(1), 2550.404c-1(b)(1)]

According to DOL, a self-directed account plan must:

1. Include at least three investment options with materially different risk and return characteristics;

2. Provide enough information to allow the participant to make informed investment decisions for every investment alternative offered;

3. Enable diversification of investments; and

4. Allow participants independent control to change investments at least quarterly, and more frequently if volatile investments are offered.

[DOL Reg. §§ 2550.404c-1(a)(1), 2550.404c-1(c)(2)]

The participant or beneficiary must be provided or have the opportunity to obtain sufficient information to make informed investment decisions with regard to investment alternatives available under the plan, and incidents of ownership appurtenant to such investments. A participant or beneficiary will be considered to have sufficient information if the participant or beneficiary is provided by an identified plan fiduciary (or a person or persons designated by the plan fiduciary to act on its behalf):

1. An explanation that the plan is intended to constitute an ERISA Section 404(c) plan and that the fiduciaries of the plan may be relieved of liability for any losses that are the direct and necessary result of investment instructions given by such participant or beneficiary;

2. Identification of any designated investment managers;

3. The information required to be disclosed as discussed further on in this Q 23:14; and

4. In the case of plans that offer an investment alternative that is designed to permit a participant or beneficiary to directly or indirectly acquire or sell any employer security (employer security alternative), a description of the procedures established to provide for the confidentiality of information relating to the purchase, holding, and sale of employer securities, and the exercise of voting, tender, and similar rights, by participants and beneficiaries, and the name, address, and phone number of the plan fiduciary responsible for monitoring compliance with the procedures.

[DOL Prop. Reg. § 2550.404c-1(b)(2)(i)(B)]

A participant must be provided, either directly or on request, with the following information (based on the latest information available to the plan):

1. A description of the annual operating expenses of each investment alternative, and the aggregate amount of these expenses expressed as a percentage of average net assets;

2. Copies of any prospectuses, financial statements, and reports available to the plan;

3. A list of the assets in the portfolio of each alternative, and, for any asset that is a fixed-rate investment contract, the name of the issuer, the term, and the rate of return; and

4. Information on the value of shares of the alternatives available under the plan, as well as the past and current investment performance determined (net of expenses) on a reasonable and consistent basis.

[DOL Reg. § 2550.404c-1(b)(2)(i)(B)(2); Tussey v. ABB, Inc., No. 06-04305-CV (W.D. Mo. 2008)]

A plan offers a broad range of investment alternatives only if the available investment alternatives are sufficient to provide the participant with a reasonable opportunity (1) to affect materially the potential return on amounts in the account and the degree of risk to which these amounts are subject and (2) to permit the participant to choose from at least three investment alternatives, each of which is diversified and has materially different risk and return characteristics so that the participant may achieve a portfolio with aggregate risk and return characteristics within the range normally appropriate for the participant and with appropriate diversification. [DOL Reg. § 2550.404c-1(b)(3)(i)]

DOL has opined that the delivery of a mutual fund profile designed to comply with Securities Act Section 10(b) to participants and beneficiaries immediately before or immediately after their investment in the mutual fund satisfied DOL requirements if the most recent prospectus in the plan's possession is a profile. The profile satisfies the requirements because it provides a clear summary of key information about a mutual fund that is useful to such participants and/or beneficiaries; however, delivery of a Section 10(a) prospectus is required if the most recent prospectus is a Section 10(a) prospectus or if the participant specifically requests a Section 10(a) prospectus. [DOL Op. Ltr. 2003-11A] The delivery of a mutual fund's summary prospectus will satisfy the obligation to deliver a prospectus to participants and beneficiaries. [DOL Field Assistance Bull. 2009-03]

Participants must also be advised that, if DOL requirements are satisfied, the plan's fiduciaries may be protected against liability for investment losses incurred as a result of the investment instructions given by participants to the fiduciaries. This does not serve to relieve a fiduciary from its duty to prudently select and monitor any designated investment manager or designated investment alternative offered under the plan. [DOL Reg. § 2550.404c-1(d)(2); DOL Prop. Reg. § 2550.404c-1(d)(2)(iv); Lingis v. Motorola, Inc., 2009 WL 1708097 (N.D. Ill. 2009)] The plan's fiduciaries remain liable, however, for choosing and monitoring the investment options available to participants in a prudent manner. [ERISA § 404(a)(1)(B); In re Unisys Sav. Plan Litig., 173 F.3d 145 (3d Cir. 1999)] One court held that the trustees of an individual account plan remained liable for investment losses because the trustee failed to abide by required plan procedures when the plan converted to a self-directed account plan. [Allison v. Bank One-Denver, 289 F.3d 1223 (10th Cir. 2002)] The trustee of a plan that gave participants discretion to direct the investments in their accounts, but that did not meet the requirements to be a self-directed account plan, was still shielded from a breach of fiduciary duty claim by an implied exception to the rule that trustees have exclusive authority over the management of plan assets. [ERISA § 403(a); DOL Reg. § 2550.404c-1(a)(2); Jenkins v. Yager, 444 F.3d 916 (7th Cir. 2006)] One court, however, ruled that an employer could not rely on the self-directed account plan rules as an affirmative defense to allegations regarding the selection of an employer stock fund among designated investment options. [*In re* Tyco International Ltd., Multidistrict Litigation, 2009 WL 921147 (D. N.H. 2009); *but see* Rogers v. Baxter International, Inc., No. 04-C-6476 (N.D. Ill. 2010)]

DOL has provided guidance concerning educational materials that may be circulated to participants by employers without such employers being considered investment advisors. [DOL Reg. § 2509.96-1]

DOL has issued interim final rules implementing the provisions of the Sarbanes-Oxley Act of 2002 (see Q 1:24) that require administrators (see Q 20:1) of individual account plans to provide participants and beneficiaries with a 30-day advance notice of any blackout period (see Q 20:22) during which their rights to direct or diversify investments of their accounts or to obtain a loan or receive a distribution under the plan would be temporarily suspended, limited, or restricted for more than three consecutive business days. The interim final rules, which became effective January 26, 2003 and apply to blackout periods commencing on or after that date, generally follow the provisions of ERISA as added by the Act. In addition, however, the rules require the notice to:

1. Disclose the expected ending date of the blackout period;

2. Contain a statement advising participants and beneficiaries to review their investment in light of their inability to direct or diversify account assets during the blackout period; and

3. Provide an explanation of why a notice may not have been furnished within the specified time period.

Furthermore, the rules place a 60-day ceiling on the time within which the advance notice must be provided. DOL has also provided a Model Notice to assist plan administrators in complying with the applicable requirements.

[ERISA § 101(i); DOL Reg. §§ 2520.101-3, 2570.130-141]

Effective for plan years beginning after December 31, 2006, a participant is treated as exercising control with respect to assets in an individual account plan if such amounts are invested in a default arrangement in accordance with DOL regulations until the participant makes an affirmative election regarding investments. Such regulations must provide guidance on the appropriateness of certain investments for designation as default investments under the arrangement, including guidance regarding appropriate mixes of default investments and asset classes that DOL considers consistent with long-term capital appreciation or long-term capital preservation (or both), and the designation of other default investments. DOL was directed to issue regulations concerning the default arrangement.

In order for this treatment to apply, notice of the participant's rights and obligations under the arrangement must be provided. Under the notice requirement, within a reasonable period before the plan year, the plan administrator must give each participant notice of the rights and obligations under the arrangement that is sufficiently accurate and comprehensive to apprise the participant of such rights and obligations and is written in a manner calculated to be understood by the average participant. The notice must include an explanation of the participant's rights under the arrangement to specifically elect to exercise control over the assets in the participant's account. In addition, the participant must have a reasonable period of time after receipt of the notice and before the assets are first invested to make such an election. The notice must also explain how contributions made under the arrangement will be invested in the absence of any investment election by the employee.

[ERISA § 404(c)(5)]

DOL issued regulations implementing the fiduciary relief, under which participants or beneficiaries in an individual account plan will be treated as exercising control over the assets in their accounts with respect to the amount of contributions and earnings that, in the absence of an investment election by the participant, are invested by the plan in accordance with the regulations. If participants or beneficiaries are treated as exercising control over the assets in their accounts, no person who is otherwise a fiduciary will be liable for any loss, or by reason of any breach, that results from such participant's or beneficiary's exercise of control. Except for the requirement that the plan offer a broad range of investment alternatives, a plan need not meet the requirements for an ERISA Section 404(c) plan in order for a plan fiduciary to obtain the relief under the regulations. [DOL Reg. § 2550.404c-5(a)(1)] The standards set forth apply solely for purposes of determining whether a fiduciary meets the requirements of the regulations. Such standards are not intended to be the exclusive means by which fiduciaries must satisfy their responsibilities under ERISA with respect to the investment of assets in the individual account of a participant or beneficiary. [DOL Reg. § 2550.404c-5(a)(2)]

Except as provided below, a fiduciary of an individual account plan that permits participants or beneficiaries to direct the investment of assets in their accounts and that meets the conditions described below will not be liable for any loss, or by reason of any breach, that is the direct and necessary result of (1) investing all or part of a participant's or beneficiary's account in a qualified default investment alternative (QDIA), or (2) investment decisions made by an investment manager or an investment company in connection with the management of a QDIA. Nothing in the regulations will:

1. Relieve a fiduciary from the duties to prudently select and monitor any QDIA under the plan or from any liability that results from a failure to satisfy these duties, including liability for any resulting losses;

2. Relieve an investment manager from its fiduciary duties or from any liability that results from a failure to satisfy these duties, including liability for any resulting losses; or

3. Provide relief from the prohibited-transaction provisions (see Q 24:1), or from any liability that results from a violation of those provisions, including liability for any resulting losses. [DOL Reg. § 2550.404c-5(b)]

With respect to the investment of assets in the individual account of a participant or beneficiary, a fiduciary will qualify for the above fiduciary relief if:

1. Assets are invested in a QDIA;

2. The participant or beneficiary on whose behalf the investment is made had the opportunity to direct the investment of the assets in the account but did not direct the investment of the assets;

3. The participant or beneficiary on whose behalf an investment in a QDIA may be made is furnished a notice at least 30 days in advance of the date of plan eligibility, or at least 30 days in advance of the date of any first investment in a QDIA on behalf of a participant or beneficiary, or on or before the date of plan eligibility provided the participant has the opportunity to make a permissible withdrawal (see Q 27:5); and within a reasonable period of time of at least 30 days in advance of each subsequent plan year;

4. A fiduciary provides to a participant or beneficiary certain material relating to a participant's or beneficiary's investment in a QDIA;

5. Any participant or beneficiary on whose behalf assets are invested in a QDIA may transfer, in whole or in part, such assets to any other investment alternative available under the plan with a frequency consistent with that afforded to a participant or beneficiary who elected to invest in the QDIA, but not less frequently than once within any three-month period. Except as provided in this item 5, any such transfer, or any permissible withdrawal, by a participant or beneficiary of assets invested in a QDIA, in whole or in part, resulting from a participant's or beneficiary's election to make such a transfer or withdrawal during the 90-day period beginning on the date of the participant's first elective contribution, or other first investment in a QDIA on behalf of a participant or beneficiary, will not be subject to any restrictions, fees, or expenses (including surrender charges, liquidation or exchange fees, redemption fees, and similar expenses charged in connection with the liquidation of, or transfer from, the investment). The preceding sentence does not apply to fees and expenses that are charged on an ongoing basis for the operation of the investment itself (such as investment management fees, distribution and/or service fees, 12b-1 fees, or legal, accounting, transfer agent, and similar administrative expenses) and that are not imposed, or do not vary, based on a participant's or beneficiary's decision to withdraw, sell, or transfer assets out of the QDIA. Following the end of the 90-day period, any transfer or permissible withdrawal will not be subject to any restrictions, fees, or expenses not otherwise applicable to a participant or beneficiary who elected to invest in that QDIA; and

6. The plan offers a broad range of investment alternatives. [DOL Reg. §§ 2550.404c-1(b)(2)(i)(B)(1)(viii), 2550.404c-1(b)(2)(i)(B)(1)(ix), 2550.404c-1(b)(3), 2550.404c-5(c); DOL Prop. Reg. § 2550.404c-1(b)(2)(i)(B)]

The notice must be written in a manner calculated to be understood by the average plan participant and contain the following:

1. A description of the circumstances under which assets in the individual account of a participant or beneficiary may be invested on behalf of the participant and beneficiary in a QDIA; and, if applicable, an explanation of the circumstances under which elective contributions (see Qs 27:5, 27:16) will be made on behalf of a participant, the percentage of such contributions, and the right of the participant to elect not have such contributions made on the participant's behalf (or to elect to have such contributions made at a different percentage);

2. An explanation of the right of participants and beneficiaries to direct the investment of assets in their individual accounts;

3. A description of the QDIA, including a description of the investment objectives, risk, and return characteristics (if applicable), and fees and expenses attendant to the investment alternative;

4. A description of the right of the participants and beneficiaries on whose behalf assets are invested in a QDIA to direct the investment of those assets to any other investment alternative under the plan, including a description of any applicable restrictions, fees, or expenses in connection with such transfer; and

5. An explanation of where the participants and beneficiaries can obtain investment information concerning the other investment alternatives available under the plan. [DOL Reg. § 2550.404c-5(d)]

A QDIA means an investment alternative available to participants and beneficiaries that:

1. Does not hold or permit the acquisition of employer securities (see Q 23:86), except:

   a. Employer securities held or acquired by an investment company registered under the Investment Company Act of 1940 or a similar pooled investment vehicle regulated and subject to periodic examination by a State or Federal agency and with respect to which investment in such securities is made in accordance with the stated investment objectives of the investment vehicle and independent of the plan sponsor or an affiliate thereof, or

   b. With respect to a QDIA described in item 4c below, employer securities acquired as a matching contribution (see Q 27:75) from the employer/plan sponsor, or employer securities acquired prior to management by the investment management service to the extent the investment management service has discretionary authority over the disposition of such employer securities;

2. Satisfies the requirements regarding the ability of a participant or beneficiary to transfer, in whole or in part, the investment from the QDIA to any other investment alternative available under the plan;

3. Is managed by an investment manager, as defined in ERISA Section 3(38), a trustee of the plan, or the plan sponsor, or a committee comprised

primarily of employees of the plan sponsor, which is a named fiduciary (see Q 23:9); an investment company registered under the Investment Company Act of 1940; or an investment product or fund; and

4. Constitutes one of the following:

   a. An investment fund product or model portfolio that applies generally accepted investment theories, is diversified so as to minimize the risk of large losses and that is designed to provide varying degrees of long-term appreciation and capital preservation through a mix of equity and fixed income exposures based on the participant's age, target retirement date (such as normal retirement age under the plan), or life expectancy. Such products and portfolios change their asset allocations and associated risk levels over time with the objective of becoming more conservative (i.e., decreasing risk of losses) with increasing age. For these purposes, asset allocation decisions for such products and portfolios are not required to take into account risk tolerances, investments, or other preferences of an individual participant. An example of such a fund or portfolio may be a life-cycle or targeted-retirement-date fund or account.

   b. An investment fund product or model portfolio that applies generally accepted investment theories, is diversified so as to minimize the risk of large losses and that is designed to provide long-term appreciation and capital preservation through a mix of equity and fixed income exposures consistent with a target level of risk appropriate for participants of the plan as a whole. For these purposes, asset allocation decisions for such products and portfolios are not required to take into account the age, risk tolerances, investments, or other preferences of an individual participant. An example of such a fund or portfolio may be a balanced fund.

   c. An investment management service with respect to which a fiduciary, applying generally accepted investment theories, allocates the assets of a participant's individual account to achieve varying degrees of long-term appreciation and capital preservation through a mix of equity and fixed income exposures, offered through investment alternatives available under the plan, based on the participant's age, target retirement date (such as normal retirement age under the plan), or life expectancy. Such portfolios are diversified so as to minimize the risk of large losses and change their asset allocations and associated risk levels for an individual account over time with the objective of becoming more conservative (i.e., decreasing risk of losses) with increasing age. For these purposes, asset allocation decisions are not required to take into account risk tolerances, investments, or other preferences of an individual participant. An example of such a service may be a managed account.

   d. An investment product or fund designed to preserve principal and provide a reasonable rate of return, whether or not such return is guaranteed, consistent with liquidity. Such investment product must (1) seek to maintain, over the term of the investment, the dollar value that is equal to the amount invested in the product, and (2) be offered by a State or federally regulated financial institution. Such an investment product will constitute a QDIA for not more than 120 days after the date of the participant's first elective contribution.

e. An investment product or fund designed to preserve principal; provide a rate of return generally consistent with that earned on intermediate investment grade bonds; and provide liquidity for withdrawals by participants and beneficiaries, including transfers to other investment alternatives. Such investment product or fund must meet the following requirements: (1) there are no fees or surrender charges imposed in connection with withdrawals initiated by a participant or beneficiary, and (2) principal and rates of return are guaranteed by a State or federally regulated financial institution. An investment product or fund described in this paragraph (e) constituted a QDIA solely for purposes of assets invested in such product or fund before December 24, 2007.

f. An investment fund product or model portfolio that otherwise meets these requirements will not fail to constitute a product or portfolio for purposes of paragraphs (a) and (b) solely because the product or portfolio is offered through variable annuity or similar contracts or through common or collective trust funds or pooled investment funds and without regard to whether such contracts or funds provide annuity purchase rights, investment guarantees, death benefit guarantees, or other features ancillary to the investment fund product or model portfolio. [DOL Reg. § 2550.404c-5(e)]

Title I of ERISA supersedes any State law that would restrict the inclusion in any plan of an automatic contribution arrangement. An automatic contribution arrangement is an arrangement (or the provisions of a plan) under which:

1. A participant may elect to have the plan sponsor make payments as contributions under the plan on the individual's behalf or receive such payments directly in cash;

2. A participant is treated as having elected to have the plan sponsor make such contributions in an amount equal to a uniform percentage of compensation provided under the plan until the participant specifically elects not to have such contributions made (or specifically elects to have such contributions made) at a different percentage; and

3. Contributions are invested in accordance with the regulations. [ERISA § 514(e)(1); DOL Reg. § 2550.404c-5(f)(1)]

A State law that would directly or indirectly prohibit or restrict the inclusion in any pension plan of an automatic contribution arrangement is superseded as to any pension plan, regardless of whether such plan includes an automatic contribution arrangement. [DOL Reg. § 2550.404c-5(f)(2)] The administrator of an automatic contribution arrangement will be considered to have satisfied the notice requirements if notices are furnished in accordance with the regulations. [DOL Reg. § 2550.404c-5(f)(3)] Nothing precludes a pension plan from including an automatic contribution arrangement that does not meet the conditions of the regulations. [DOL Reg. § 2550.404(c)-5(f)(4)]

Subsequent to the issuance of the final regulations, DOL released a field assistance bulletin providing further guidance concerning the QDIA regulations. [DOL Field Assistance Bull. 2008-03]

A plan sponsor that chooses to create and manage a QDIA itself may be relieved of liability for decisions to invest all or part of a participant's or beneficiary's account in a QDIA only if the plan sponsor is a named fiduciary. The plan sponsor would not be relieved of liability for the management of the QDIA or the prudent selection and monitoring of the QDIA. [DOL Field Assistance Bull. 2008-03, Q-1]

Relief is available under the QDIA regulations for assets invested in a default investment prior to the effective date of the regulations if all conditions of the QDIA regulations are satisfied with respect to such assets. The relief available under the QDIA regulations is not limited to assets that are invested in a QDIA on or after the effective date of the regulations. If the notice and other requirements for relief under the QDIA regulations are satisfied, the fiduciary will, except to the extent otherwise limited by the regulations, be relieved of liability with respect to all assets invested in the QDIA, without regard to whether the assets were contributed prior to the effective date of the regulations. The fiduciary will have the benefit of the relief under the QDIA regulations for fiduciary decisions made on or after the date that all requirements of the QDIA regulations have been satisfied. However, relief is not available for fiduciary decisions made prior to the effective date of the QDIA regulations, such as decisions by a fiduciary to invest assets in a default investment. [DOL Field Assistance Bull. 2008-03, Q-2]

A fiduciary could obtain the relief referred to in the preceding paragraph with respect to assets invested in a QDIA on behalf of participants and beneficiaries who elect to invest in a default investment prior to the effective date of the regulations. The relief available under the QDIA regulations would extend to all assets invested in a QDIA on behalf of participants and beneficiaries who, on or after the effective date of the regulations, fail to give investment direction after being provided the required notice without regard to whether the participant or beneficiary made an earlier affirmative election to invest in the default investment. The result may be significant where plan records cannot establish that an investment was the direct and necessary result of a participant's or beneficiary's exercise of control for purposes of the self-directed account rules. For example, assume that, prior to the effective date of the QDIA regulations, plan sponsor PS used Default A as the default investment for its plan, an investment that would not qualify as a QDIA under the regulations. Following publication of the QDIA regulations, PS decides to change to Default B, an investment that would qualify as a QDIA under the regulations, but PS is unable to distinguish between those participants and beneficiaries who directed that their assets be invested in Default A and those participants and beneficiaries who were defaulted into Default A. If PS distributes a new investment election form to all participants and beneficiaries invested in Default A, relief under the QDIA regulations would be available to PS with respect to assets that are moved into Default B and held in the plan accounts of participants and beneficiaries who failed to respond to the investment election form if all of the requirements of the regulations are otherwise satisfied with respect to such participants and beneficiaries. Alternatively, if Default A is an investment that would qualify as a QDIA under the regulations and PS complies with the notice and other requirements necessary to establish Default A as a QDIA, PS would be relieved of liability in accordance with the QDIA regulations with respect to all assets invested in Default A, without regard to whether the assets were the result of a default investment. [DOL Field Assistance Bull. 2008-03, Q-3]

One of the conditions for fiduciary relief under the QDIA regulations is that the participant or beneficiary on whose behalf an investment in a QDIA is made must have had the opportunity to direct the investment of assets in the plan account, but did not direct such investment. Although fiduciary relief may vary based on the particular facts and circumstances, if participants and beneficiaries are not provided the opportunity to direct the investment of plan assets that result from non-elective contributions such as QNECs (see Q 27:17), or the proceeds from litigation or other settlements, at least one of the conditions for fiduciary relief will not have been satisfied, and relief would not be available under the QDIA regulations. To the extent a participant or beneficiary is, in fact, given the opportunity to direct the investment of such contributions, or after such amounts are allocated to a participant's or beneficiary's plan account and the participant or beneficiary is subsequently provided the opportunity to direct the investment of those assets, the relief may be available. [DOL Field Assistance Bull. 2008-03, Q-4]

The fiduciary relief is available to a 403(b) plan (see Q 35:1) if the program is a pension plan covered by Title I of ERISA (see Q 35:51). [DOL Field Assistance Bull. 2008-3, Q-5]

The notice must include a description of the QDIA, including a description of the fees and expenses attendant to the investment alternative. In the absence of further guidance, DOL believes that participants and beneficiaries generally should be provided information concerning: (1) the amount and description of any shareholder-type fees such as sales loads, sales charges, deferred sales charges, redemption fees, surrender charges, exchange fees, account fees, purchase fees, and mortality and expense fees, and (2) for investments with respect to which performance may vary over the term of the investment, the total annual operating expenses of the investment expressed as a percentage (e.g., expense ratio). In this regard, DOL noted that it is currently developing a proposed regulation that would establish disclosure requirements, including requirements applicable to the disclosure of plan and investment fee and expense information, for participant directed individual account plans. DOL anticipates that furnishing the information required under that regulation would satisfy the required investment-related fee and expense disclosures. With regard to the form of disclosure of the fee and expense information, DOL noted that there is nothing in the QDIA regulations that would preclude the use of separate, but simultaneously furnished, documents to satisfy the notice requirements. Accordingly, in the absence of additional guidance, the furnishing of a prospectus or profile prospectus of an investment alternative subject to the Securities

Act of 1933, along with the other required information, could be used to satisfy the required disclosure. [DOL Field Assistance Bull. 2008-03, Q-6]

It is DOL's view that plans that wish to use electronic means by which to satisfy their notice requirements may rely on either guidance issued by DOL (see Q 20:23) or guidance issued by IRS (see Q 20:5) relating to use of electronic media. Accordingly, in the absence of further guidance, DOL's views extend only to the QDIA regulations' notice requirement. However, DOL currently is working on a separate regulatory initiative concerning the broader application of disclosure by electronic means. [DOL Field Assistance Bull. 2008-03, Q-7]

Plan sponsors do not have to combine the QDIA notice with a notice required by a qualified automatic contribution arrangement (QACA) or an eligible automatic contribution arrangement (EACA). Although DOL did coordinate with IRS to ensure that plan sponsors could comply with the notice requirements of the Code (applicable to QACAs and EACAs) and ERISA (applicable to self-directed accounts) with a single, stand alone document, plan sponsors are not required to combine these notices. Some plan sponsors offering a QACA will not seek the fiduciary relief provided by ERISA Section 404(c)(5). Alternatively, a plan sponsor could select a QDIA and avail itself of the fiduciary relief provided by ERISA Section 404(c)(5) under circumstances other than automatic enrollment or under an automatic enrollment provision that is not intended to qualify as a QACA or EACA. Plan sponsors are free to satisfy these notice requirements independently if they choose to do so. For plan sponsors that wish to combine these notices, DOL coordinated with IRS to provide a sample notice available on the internet that may be used to help a plan sponsor satisfy these notice content requirements. [DOL Field Assistance Bull. 2008-03, Q-8] See Qs 27:5–27:7 for a detailed discussion of QACAs and EACAs.

The timing requirements for the IRS and DOL notices are not consistent. Under the DOL's QDIA regulations, an initial notice generally must be provided at least 30 days in advance of a participant's date of plan eligibility or any first investment in a QDIA, or on or before the date of plan eligibility (if the participant has the opportunity to make a permissible withdrawal under the EACA). An annual notice also must be provided at least 30 days in advance of each subsequent plan year. Under IRS proposed regulations on QACAs and EACAs, IRS articulated the timing requirements for the required notices. Specifically, a notice must be provided within a reasonable period of time before the beginning of each plan year or a reasonable period of time before an employee first becomes eligible under the plan. A notice is deemed to satisfy these timing requirements if the notice is provided at least 30 days (and not more than 90 days) before the beginning of each plan year or, if an employee did not receive the annually required notice because it was provided before the date of eligibility for the plan, at least by the employee's eligibility date (and not more than 90 days before the employee's eligibility date). Although the timing provisions for these notices are not identical, plan sponsors can easily satisfy both requirements for a plan year. A plan sponsor can satisfy the annual notice requirements under the QDIA regulations and the IRS's proposed regulations if a notice is provided at least 30, and not more than 90, days before the beginning of each plan year. For example, the sponsor of a calendar-year plan may choose to distribute a notice on November 1 of each year. A notice distributed on September 1 would not necessarily comply with IRS rules, because September 1 is more than 90 days before the first day of the subsequent plan year. Further, a plan that includes an EACA and permits an employee to withdraw default contributions during the 90-day period following the date of the employee's first elective contribution can satisfy DOL's initial notice requirement, as well as IRS's special rule for employees who do not receive the annually required notice on or before, but no more than 90 days before, an employee's date of plan eligibility. For example, if a new employee is immediately eligible for participation on the first day of employment, June 1, the distribution of a notice to that employee on June 1 would satisfy both regulations. [DOL Field Assistance Bull. 2008-03, Q-9]

While the QDIA regulations generally provide for disclosure through a separate notice, DOL has indicated that it anticipates that the QDIA notice requirements and the QACA and EACA notice requirements can be satisfied in a single disclosure document. It is DOL's view that the information required to be disclosed in a safe harbor notice (see Q 27:46) is sufficiently related to the information required to be disclosed in the QDIA notice that combining the notices would improve, rather than complicate, the disclosure of plan information to participants and beneficiaries. [DOL Field Assistance Bull. 2008-03, Q-10]

Generally, for a 90-day period following the first investment in a QDIA on behalf of a participant or beneficiary, any transfer or withdrawal of assets from the QDIA by a participant or beneficiary cannot be subject to any restrictions, fees, or expenses (including surrender charges, liquidation or exchange fees, redemption fees, and similar expenses charged in connection with the liquidation of, or transfer from, the investment). DOL included this requirement to ensure that participants and beneficiaries would not be restricted from or penalized for moving assets out of the QDIA during the period of time that they would be most likely to opt out of the plan or redirect their plan investments. To the extent that any such fees or expenses otherwise assessed to the account of a participant or beneficiary or the plan generally, the assessment of the fees or expenses would not serve to inhibit a participant's or beneficiary's decision to opt out of the investment alternative and the policy objective would be satisfied. [DOL Field Assistance Bull. 2008-03, Q-11] For purposes of this requirement, the 90-day condition on restrictions, fees, or expenses does not apply to participants or beneficiaries who have existing assets invested in the plan as of the effective date of the QDIA regulations. For example, if a plan, prior to the effective date of the QDIA regulations, used a balanced fund as its default investment, and the balanced fund qualifies as a QDIA under the QDIA regulations, the plan sponsor may wish to continue to use this fund as its default investment and obtain relief under the regulations. With respect to existing assets, the plan sponsor is not subject to the restriction for the 90-day period following the effective date of the regulations (or the date the balanced fund becomes a QDIA). Of course, assets invested in the QDIA cannot be subject to any restrictions, fees, or expenses that are not otherwise applicable to participants and beneficiaries who elected to invest in the QDIA. However, if a new participant is enrolled in the plan on or after the effective date of the QDIA regulations, the restriction will apply with respect to the first elective contribution or other investment that is made into the balanced fund QDIA on behalf of that participant. [DOL Field Assistance Bull. 2008-03, Q-12]

Any transfer or permissible withdrawal from a QDIA resulting from a participant's or beneficiary's election to make such a transfer or withdrawal during the 90-day period beginning on the date of the participant's first elective contribution, or other first investment in QDIA, must not be subject to any restrictions, fees, or expenses, other than certain ongoing administrative and investment fees. DOL explained that this provision was intended to prevent the imposition of any restriction, fee, or expense on a transfer or permissible withdrawal of assets, whether assessed by the plan, the plan sponsor, or as part of an underlying investment product or portfolio. DOL also provided a few examples of restrictions that might inhibit a participant's or beneficiary's decision to withdraw, sell, or transfer assets out of a QDIA during this 90-day period. One of the cited examples was a "round-trip" restriction on the ability of the participant or beneficiary to reinvest within a defined period of time. DOL concluded that the reference to round-trip restrictions was too broad and should not have been included as an example of an impermissible restriction. Round-trip restrictions, unlike fees and expenses assessed directly upon liquidation of, or transfer from, an investment, generally affect only a participant's ability to reinvest in the QDIA for a limited period of time. This is not a restriction prohibited by the final regulations. However, to the extent that a round-trip restriction would affect a participant's or beneficiary's ability to liquidate or transfer from a QDIA or restrict a participant's or beneficiary's ability to invest in any other investment alternative available under the plan, it would be impermissible for purposes of the final regulations. [DOL Field Assistance Bull. 2008-03, Q-13; preamble to final regulations before technical correction; preamble to final regulations with technical correction]

Each of the QDIA categories described in the QDIA regulations requires that the investment fund product, model portfolio, or investment management service be diversified so as to minimize the risk of large losses and be designed to provide varying degrees of long-term appreciation and capital preservation through a mix of equity and fixed income exposures. DOL did not intend to include funds, products, or services with no fixed income exposure. Although an investment option with no fixed income component may be appropriate for certain individuals actively directing their own investments, DOL determined that a QDIA should have some fixed income exposure. Similarly, a fund, product, or service with no equity exposure cannot qualify as a QDIA under the QDIA regulations. The regulations do not establish minimum fixed income or equity exposures necessary to satisfy the requirement for a mix within a QDIA. DOL continues to believe that such a determination is best left to the discretion of the entities described in the QDIA regulations in assessing the appropriateness of a particular QDIA; and, therefore, DOL does not plan to provide further guidance on the issue. [DOL Field Assistance Bull. 2008-03, Q-14]

The QDIA regulations require that defaulted participants be provided material in accordance with the regulations governing self-directed account plans. The QDIA regulations are not intended to require that all of the referenced information be furnished automatically, without regard to whether some of the information for such plans is required to be provided only upon request of a participant or beneficiary. Defaulted participants should be furnished neither less nor more material than would be provided to participants who direct their own investments in a self-directed account plan. The disclosure rules, therefore, are intended to operate in the same manner as under the regulations applicable to such plans. That is, for purposes of the QDIA regulations, defaulted participants are required to be automatically furnished, in the case of registered investment companies, the most recent prospectus or profile prospectus and furnished any material relating to voting, tender, or similar rights provided to the plan. In addition, plans are required to furnish either automatically or upon request certain information concerning the plan's investment alternatives, such as annual operating expenses and the value of shares or units in the investment alternatives. [DOL Field Assistance Bull. 2008-03, Q-15]

A plan sponsor can use two different QDIAs, for example, one for its automatic contribution arrangement and another for rollover contributions. Nothing in the QDIA regulations limits the ability of a plan sponsor to use more than one QDIA. [DOL Field Assistance Bull. 2008-03, Q-16]

In the case of an individual account plan sponsored by a single employer, a committee that is established by a plan sponsor and comprised primarily of employees of the plan sponsor and that, pursuant to the documents and instruments governing the plan, is a named fiduciary of the plan can be treated as managing a QDIA. [DOL Field Assistance Bull. 2008-03, Q-17]

The 120-day capital preservation QDIA permits investment in a capital preservation product for a 120-day period following a participant's first elective contribution to an EACA. This QDIA is intended to provide administrative flexibility to plans that satisfy the EACA requirements and allow employees to make permissible withdrawals. Accordingly, a plan fiduciary that uses the 120-day capital preservation QDIA for the investment of assets other than assets contributed pursuant to an EACA will not obtain fiduciary relief under the regulations. For example, use of the 120-day capital preservation QDIA for a rollover from an IRA or other plan would not relieve a plan sponsor of liability under the QDIA regulations (unless the rollover was made during the 120-day period following a participant's first EACA contribution). [DOL Field Assistance Bull. 2008-03, Q-18] A plan sponsor is not required to use any of the QDIAs described in the regulations for its plan, including the 120-day capital preservation QDIA. The 120-day capital preservation QDIA was included in the regulations to afford plan sponsors the flexibility of using a capital preservation investment alternative for the investment of contributions during the period of time when employees are most likely to opt out of plan participation. [DOL Field Assistance Bull. 2008-03, Q-19] A plan sponsor cannot manage the 120-day capital preservation QDIA because the investment fund or product must be offered by a State or federally regulated financial institution. [DOL Field Assistance Bull. 2008-03, Q-20]

A plan sponsor is not required to distribute a notice 30 days before the effective date of the QDIA regulations to obtain relief for prior contributions to a stable value fund or product, but the relief provided by the QDIA regulations generally will not take effect until 30 days after the required initial notice is furnished to participants and beneficiaries. For example, if a plan sponsor distributed the initial notice on January 1, 2008 to participants and beneficiaries who were defaulted into a stable value fund prior to the effective date of the regulations, and assuming all other requirements of the regulations had been satisfied, the fiduciary relief provided by the regulations would have been available to the plan sponsor on January 31, 2008 (i.e., 30 days later). Of course, regardless of the date on which fiduciary relief is available to the plan sponsor, the relief will extend only to assets that were invested in the stable value product or fund on or before the effective date of the final regulations. [DOL Field Assistance Bull. 2008-03, Q-21] The QDIA regulations provide grandfather-type relief for assets invested in certain stable value products or funds prior to the effective date of the regulations. Following publication of the QDIA regulations, DOL determined that the description of stable value products and funds may limit the availability of the grandfather-type relief, contrary to the intention of DOL. Accordingly, to ensure broad application of this relief to stable value products and funds, DOL amended the QDIA regulations to provide that relief is available with respect to an investment product or fund designed to preserve principal; provide a rate of return generally consistent with that earned on intermediate investment grade bonds; and provide liquidity for withdrawals by participants and beneficiaries, including transfers to other investment alternatives. Two additional conditions apply: (1) no fees or surrender charges can be imposed in connection with withdrawals from the product or fund initiated by a participant or beneficiary, and (2) the product or fund must invest primarily in investment products that are backed by State or federally regulated financial institutions. For example, the product or fund may be issued directly by a State or federally regulated financial institution. Alternatively, the principal and accrued interest on the product or fund may be backed by contracts issued by such institutions. [DOL Field Assistance Bull. 2008-03, Q-22]

Effective for plan years beginning after December 31, 2007, other changes are made with regard to self-directed account plans as discussed below.

The special rule providing relief from fiduciary liability in the case of a self-directed account plan does not apply in connection with a blackout period in which the participant's or beneficiary's ability to direct the investment of account assets is suspended by a plan sponsor or fiduciary. However, if a plan sponsor or fiduciary meets the requirements of ERISA in connection with authorizing and implementing a blackout period, any person who is otherwise a fiduciary is not liable under ERISA for any loss occurring during the blackout period. By August 17, 2007, DOL is directed to issue interim final regulations providing guidance, including safe harbors, on how plan sponsors or other affected fiduciaries can satisfy their fiduciary responsibilities during any black-out period. [ERISA §§ 404(c)(1), 404(c)(1)(A)(ii), 404(c)(1)(B)-(C)]

In addition, the special rule is amended with respect to a case in which a qualified change in investment options offered under the plan occurs. In such a case, for purposes of the special rule, a participant or beneficiary who has exercised control over the investment of account assets before a change in investment options is not treated as not exercising control over such assets in connection with the change if certain requirements are met.

For this purpose, a qualified change in investment options is a change in the investment options offered to a participant or beneficiary under the terms of the plan, under which:

1. The participant's account is reallocated among one or more new investment options offered instead of one or more investment options that were offered immediately before the effective date of the change, and
2. The characteristics of the new investment options, including characteristics relating to risk and rate of return, are, immediately after the change, reasonably similar to the characteristics of the investment options offered immediately before the change.

The following requirements must be met in order for the rule to apply:

1. At least 30 but not more than 60 days before the effective date of the change in investment options, the plan administrator furnishes written notice of the change to participants and beneficiaries, including information comparing the existing and new investment options and an explanation that, in the absence of affirmative investment instructions from the participant or beneficiary to the contrary, the account of the participant or beneficiary will be invested in new options with characteristics reasonably similar to the characteristics of the existing investment options;
2. The participant or beneficiary has not provided to the plan administrator, in advance of the effective date of the change, affirmative investment instructions contrary to the proposed reinvestment of the participant's or beneficiary's account; and
3. The investment of the participant's or beneficiary's account as in effect immediately before the effective date of the change was the product of the exercise by such participant or beneficiary of control over the assets of the account.

[ERISA § 404(c)(4)]

DOL has also issued proposed regulations that would require employers and plan administrators, in satisfaction of their fiduciary duties, to provide participants and beneficiaries in participant-directed plans with plan and investment-related information, including details of fees and expenses assessed to their individual accounts. The proposed regulations, which, when finalized, would apply to plan years beginning on or after January 1, 2009, would specifically require the disclosure of investment-related fee and expense information (e.g., sales loads, deferred sales charges, redemption fees, service charges, exchange fees, account fees, purchase fees, and the expense ratio for the total operating expenses of the investment) to be made in a chart or similar format that would allow for a comparison of the plan's investment options. The investment of plan assets is a fiduciary act governed by the fiduciary standards of ERISA. Fiduciaries must discharge their duties with respect to the plan prudently and solely in the interest of participants and beneficiaries. Where the documents and instruments governing an individual account plan provide for the allocation of investment responsibilities to participants or beneficiaries, fiduciaries must take steps to ensure that such participants and beneficiaries, on a regular and periodic basis, are made aware of their rights and responsibilities with respect to the investment of assets held in, or contributed to, their accounts and are provided sufficient information regarding the plan, including fees and expenses, and regarding designated investment alternatives, including fees and expenses attendant thereto, to make informed decisions with regard to the management of their individual accounts. [DOL Prop. Reg. § 2550.404a-5(a)]

For plan years beginning on or after January 1, 2009, the fiduciary (or fiduciaries) of an individual account plan must comply with the disclosure requirements set forth below with respect to each participant or beneficiary that, pursuant to the terms of the plan, has the right to direct the investment of assets held in, or contributed to, such person's individual account. Compliance will satisfy the duty to make the required regular and periodic disclosures. [DOL Prop. Reg. § 2550.404a-5(b)]

A fiduciary (or a person or persons designated by the fiduciary to act on its behalf) must provide to each participant or beneficiary the following plan-related information, based on the latest information available to the plan:

1. On or before the date of plan eligibility and at least annually thereafter (i.e., at least once in any 12-month period, without regard to whether the plan operates on a calendar or fiscal year basis): (a) an explanation of the circumstances under which participants and beneficiaries may give investment instructions; (b) an explanation of any specified limitations on such instructions under the terms of the plan, including any restrictions on transfer to or from a designated investment alternative; (c) a description of or reference to plan provisions relating to the exercise of voting, tender, and similar rights appurtenant to an investment in a designated investment alternative as well as any restrictions on such rights; (d) an identification of any designated investment alternatives offered under the plan; and (e) an identification of any designated investment managers. Not later than 30 days after the date of adoption of any material change to this information, each participant and beneficiary must be furnished a description of such change.

2. On or before the date of plan eligibility and at least annually thereafter, an explanation of any fees and expenses for plan administrative services (e.g., legal, accounting, recordkeeping) that, to the extent not otherwise included in investment-related fees and expenses, may be charged to the plan and the basis on which such charges will be allocated (e.g., pro rata, per capita) to, or affect the balance of, each individual account, and, at

least quarterly (i.e., at least once in any three-month period, without regard to whether the plan operates on a calendar- or fiscal-year basis), (a) a statement that includes the dollar amount actually charged during the preceding quarter to the participant's or beneficiary's account for administrative services and (b) a description of the services provided to the participant or beneficiary for such amount (e.g., recordkeeping).

3. On or before the date of plan eligibility and at least annually thereafter, an explanation of any fees and expenses that may be charged against the individual account of a participant or beneficiary for services provided on an individual, rather than plan, basis (e.g., fees attendant to processing plan loans (see Q 14:1) or qualified domestic relations orders (QDROs; see Q 36:1), fees for investment advice or similar services charged on an individual basis), and, at least quarterly, (a) a statement that includes the dollar amount actually charged during the preceding quarter to the participant's or beneficiary's account for individual services and (b) a description of the services provided to the participant or beneficiary for such amount (e.g., fees attendant to processing plan loans).

[DOL Prop. Reg. §§ 2550.404(a)-5(c), 2550.404(a)-5(h)(4), 2550.404(a)-5(h)(5)]

In addition to the above, a fiduciary (or a person or persons designated by the fiduciary to act on its behalf), based on the latest information available to the plan, must provide identifying information, performance data, benchmarks, and fee and expense information on or before the date of plan eligibility. [DOL Prop. Reg. § 2550.404(a)-5(d)]

A designated investment alternative is any investment alternative designated by the plan into which participants and beneficiaries may direct the investment of assets held in, or contributed to, their individual accounts. This term does not include "brokerage windows," "self-directed brokerage accounts," or similar plan arrangements that enable participants and beneficiaries to select investments beyond those designated by the plan. [DOL Prop. Reg. § 2550.404(a)-5(h)(1)] A fiduciary must provide to each participant or beneficiary, on or before the date of plan eligibility and at least annually thereafter, with respect to each designated investment alternative offered under the plan, (1) the name of the designated investment alternative; (2) an internet website address that is sufficiently specific to lead participants and beneficiaries to supplemental information regarding the designated investment alternative, including the name of the investment's issuer or provider, the investment's principal strategies and attendant risks, the assets comprising the investment's portfolio, the investment's portfolio turnover, the investment's performance, and related fees and expenses; (3) the type or category of the investment (e.g., money market fund, balanced (stocks and bonds) fund, large-cap fund); and (4) the type of management utilized by the investment (e.g., actively managed, passively managed). [DOL Prop. Reg. § 2550.404(a)-5(d)(1)(i)]

Average annual total return is the average annual profit or loss realized by a designated investment alternative at the end of a specified period, calculated in the same manner as average annual total return is calculated under Item 21 of Securities and Exchange Commission Form N-1A with respect to an open-end management investment company registered under the Investment Company Act of 1940. [DOL Prop. Reg. § 2550.404(a)-5(h)(2)] For designated investment alternatives with respect to which the return is not fixed, a fiduciary must provide the average annual total return (percentage) of the investment for the following periods, if available: one-year, five-year, and ten-year, measured as of the end of the applicable calendar year; as well as a statement indicating that an investment's past performance is not necessarily an indication of how the investment will perform in the future. In the case of designated investment alternatives with respect to which the return is fixed for the term of the investment, a fiduciary must provide both the fixed rate of return and the term of the investment. [DOL Prop. Reg. § 2550.404(a)-5(d)(1)(ii)] For designated investment alternatives with respect to which the return is not fixed, a fiduciary must provide the name and returns of an appropriate broad-based securities market index over the one-year, five-year, and ten-year periods comparable to the performance data periods provided above, and which is not administered by an affiliate of the investment provider, its investment advisor, or a principal underwriter, unless the index is widely recognized and used. [DOL Prop. Reg. § 2550.404a-5(d)(1)(iii)]

Total annual operating expenses are the annual operating expenses of the designated investment alternative (e.g., investment management fees, distribution, service, and administrative expenses) that reduce the rate of return to participants and beneficiaries, expressed as a percentage, calculated in the same manner as total annual operating expenses are calculated under Instruction 3 to Item 3 of Securities and Exchange Commission Form N-1A with respect to an open-end management investment company registered under the Investment Company Act of 1940. [DOL Prop. Reg. § 2550.404(a)-5(h)(3)]

For designated investment alternatives with respect to which the return is not fixed, a fiduciary must provide (1) the amount and a description of each shareholder-type fee (i.e., fees charged directly against a participant's or beneficiary's investment), such as sales loads, sales charges, deferred sales charges, redemption fees, surrender charges, exchange fees, account fees, purchase fees, and mortality and expense fees; (2) the total annual operating expenses of the investment expressed as a percentage (e.g., expense ratio); and (3) a statement indicating that fees and expenses are only one of several factors that participants and beneficiaries should consider when making investment decisions. In the case of designated investment alternatives with respect to which the return is fixed for the term of the investment, a fiduciary must provide the amount and a description of any shareholder-type fees that may be applicable to a purchase, transfer, or withdrawal of the investment in whole or in part. [DOL Prop. Reg. § 2550.404a-5(d)(1)(iv)]

The above requirements to provide information to a participant on or before the date of plan eligibility may be satisfied by furnishing to the participant the most recent annual disclosure furnished to participants and beneficiaries and any material changes to the information furnished to participants and beneficiaries. [DOL Prop. Reg. § 2550.404a-5(d)(1)(v)]

A fiduciary must furnish the information described above in a chart or similar format that is designed to facilitate a comparison of such information for each designated investment alternative available under the plan, as well as (1) a statement indicating the name, address, and telephone number of the fiduciary (or a person or persons designated by the fiduciary to act on its behalf) to contact for the provision of the information required to be provided upon request, as described below, and (2) a statement that more current investment-related information (e.g., fee and expense and performance information) may be available at the listed internet website addresses. Nothing, however, precludes a fiduciary from including additional information that the fiduciary determines appropriate for such comparisons, provided such information is not inaccurate or misleading. [DOL Prop. Reg. § 2550.404a-5(d)(2)] DOL has provided a model comparative chart in the Appendix to the proposed regulations. A fiduciary must provide to each investment participant or beneficiary, subsequent to an investment in a designated investment alternative, any materials provided to the plan relating to the exercise of voting, tender, and similar rights appurtenant to the investment, to the extent that such rights are passed through to such participant or beneficiary under the terms of the plan, and also provide to each participant or beneficiary, either at the times specified above, or upon request, the following information relating to designated investment alternatives:

1. Copies of prospectuses (or any short-form or summary prospectus, the form of which has been approved by the Securities and Exchange Commission) for the disclosure of information to investors by entities registered under either the Securities Act of 1933 or the Investment Company Act of 1940, or similar documents relating to designated investment alternative that are provided by entities that are not registered under either of these Acts;

2. Copies of any financial statements or reports, such as statements of additional information and shareholder reports, and of any other similar materials relating to the plan's designated investment alternatives, to the extent such materials are provided to the plan;

3. A statement of the value of a share or unit of each designated investment alternative as well as the date of the valuation; and

4. A list of the assets comprising the portfolio of each designated investment alternative that constitute plan assets (see Q 23:23) and the value of each such asset (or the proportion of the investment which it comprises).

[DOL Prop. Reg. §§ 2550.404a-5(d)(3), 2550.404a-5(d)(4)]

Certain of the information required to be disclosed may be provided as part of the plan's summary plan description (SPD; see Q 22:1) or as part of a pension benefit statement (see Q 22:13), if such SPD or pension benefit statement is furnished at a frequency that comports with the timing requirements discussed above. Certain other information required to be disclosed may be included as part of a pension benefit statement. A fiduciary that uses and accurately completes the model format set forth in the Appendix will be deemed to have satisfied the comparative format requirements. Except with respect to the dollar amounts required to be included, fees and expenses may be expressed in terms of a monetary amount, formula, percentage of assets, or per capita charge. The information required to be prepared by the fiduciary for disclosure must be written in a manner calculated to be understood by the average plan participant. [DOL Prop. Reg. § 2550.404a-5(e)]

Nothing in the proposed regulations is intended to relieve a fiduciary of its duty to prudently select and monitor providers of services to the plan or designated investment alternatives offered under the plan. [DOL Prop. Reg. § 2550.404a-5(f)] The required disclosures must be furnished in a manner consistent with DOL requirements, including use of electronic media. [DOL Reg. § 2520.104b-1; DOL Prop. Reg. § 2550.404a-5(g)] Plan fiduciaries breached their duty of prudence because they failed to adequately investigate alternatives to the retail share classes of the mutual fund or to request an easily obtainable waiver of minimum investment requirements applicable to the institutional class of shares, causing plan participants to incur a significant amount of unnecessary fees. [Tibble v. Edison International, No. CV 07 5359SW (C.D. Cal. 2010)]

See Qs 24:10–24:13 for a detailed discussion of the prohibited-transaction exemption for investment advice.

Q 23:15   Is a participant or beneficiary who self-directs an individual account considered a fiduciary?

No. If the plan permits self-directed accounts (see Q 23:14), participants will not be considered fiduciaries solely because they exercise control over assets in their individual accounts. The consequences are twofold. First, other plan fiduciaries generally would have no co-fiduciary liability on account of participants' investment decisions. Second, because the participants are not fiduciaries, no prohibited transaction under ERISA would result if their exercise of control over the assets in their accounts caused the trust to engage in transactions with parties in interest (see Q 24:3). [ERISA § 404(c); DOL Reg. §§ 2550.404c-1(a), 2550.404c-1(d)]

Q 23:16   Are any individuals prohibited from serving as fiduciaries?

Yes. A person who has been convicted of any of a wide range of crimes, including robbery, bribery, extortion, and fraud, cannot serve as a plan fiduciary for a period of 13 years after the conviction or after the end of imprisonment, whichever is later. A person who knowingly violates the rule is subject to a maximum fine of $10,000, five years' imprisonment, or both. [ERISA § 411]

One court has gone further and permanently barred former plan fiduciaries from acting as fiduciaries or providing services to plans in the future. [Beck v. Levering, No. 91-6174 (2d Cir. 1991)]

Q 23:17   Can a trustee be appointed for life or be subject to removal only for just cause?

No. DOL has ruled that the appointment of a trustee for life, or the ability to remove a trustee only upon misfeasance or incapacity to perform the duties of the position, is inconsistent with ERISA's fiduciary responsibility provisions. [DOL Op. Ltr. 85-41A; Levy v. Local Union No. 810, 20 F.3d 516 (2d Cir. 1994); Partenza v. Brown, No. 98 Civ. 4265 (S.D.N.Y. 1998); Mobile, Ala.-Pensacola, Fla. Bldg. & Constr. Trades Council v. Daugherty, 684 F. Supp. 270 (S.D. Ala. 1989)]

Trustees did not breach their fiduciary duty by approving a trust amendment that transferred the power to appoint and remove trustees from a single joint council of local unions to three joint councils. The amendment only affected the distribution of power among the various unions and did not entrench current trustees. [International Bhd. of Teamsters v. New York State Teamsters Council Health & Hosp. Fund, 1990 U.S. App. LEXIS 8409 (2d Cir. 1990)]

Q 23:18   Are fiduciaries subject to removal?

Yes. Fiduciaries may be removed for failing to fulfill their obligations and duties. [ERISA §§ 409, 502(a)(2); Chao v. Malkani, 452 F.3d 290 (4th Cir. 2006); Chao v. Merino, 452 F.3d 174 (2d Cir. 2006); Felber v. Estate of Regan, 1997 U.S. App. LEXIS 16069 (8th Cir. 1997); Marshall v. Snyder, 572 F.2d 894 (2d Cir. 1978); Harris Trust & Sav. Bank v. John Hancock Mut. Life Ins. Co., No. 83 Civ. 5401 (S.D.N.Y. 2000); Oscar A. Samos, M.D., Inc. v. Dean Witter Reynolds, Inc., No. 91-0209 (D.R.I. 1991)]

A court did not abuse its discretion when it refused to remove plan fiduciaries because the plan fiduciaries had not violated their fiduciary duties. [Landgraff v. Columbia/HCA Healthcare Corp., 2002 WL 203208 (6th Cir. 2002)]

Q 23:19   What is a fiduciary's basic duty?

The basic duty of a fiduciary is to act solely in the interest of the plan's participants and beneficiaries and for the exclusive purpose of providing benefits for participants and their beneficiaries. [Waller v. Blue Cross of Cal., 1994 U.S. App. LEXIS 16490 (9th Cir. 1994)] One court concluded that plan trustees have no obligation to furnish participants or beneficiaries with financial records containing an itemization of expenditures incurred in managing a plan; however, the trustees do have the fiduciary duty to keep records that are sufficient to verify the information that the trustees provided on the plan's annual report. [Shaver v. Operating Eng'rs Local 428 Pension Trust Fund, 332 F.3d 1198 (9th Cir. 2003)]

DOL has provided guidance concerning employee benefit plan investments in economically targeted investments (i.e., investments selected for the economic benefits they create apart from their investment return to the employee benefit plan). ERISA's plain text establishes a clear rule that, in the course of discharging their duties, fiduciaries may never subordinate the economic interests of the plan to unrelated objectives and may not select investments on the basis of any factor outside the economic interests of the plan except in very limited circumstances enumerated below.

With regard to investing plan assets, DOL has interpreted the prudence requirements as they apply to the investment duties of fiduciaries of employee benefit plans. The prudence requirements are satisfied if (1) the fiduciary making an investment or engaging in an investment course of action has given appropriate consideration to those facts and circumstances that, given the scope of the fiduciary's investment duties, the fiduciary knows or should know are relevant and (2) the fiduciary acts accordingly. This includes giving appropriate consideration to the role that the investment or investment course of action plays (in terms of such factors as diversification, liquidity, and risk/return characteristics) with respect to that portion of the plan's investment portfolio within the scope of the fiduciary's responsibility.

Other facts and circumstances relevant to an investment or investment course of action would, in the view of DOL, include consideration of the expected return on alternative investments with similar risks available to the plan. It follows that, because every investment necessarily causes a plan to forgo other investment opportunities, an investment will not be prudent if it would be expected to provide a plan with a lower rate of return than available alternative investments with commensurate degrees of risk or is riskier than alternative available investments with commensurate rates of return.

ERISA's plain text does not permit fiduciaries to make investment decisions on the basis of any factor other than the economic interests of the plan. Situations may arise, however, in which two or more investment alternatives are of equal economic value to a plan. DOL has recognized in past guidance that, under these limited circumstances, fiduciaries can choose between the investment alternatives on the basis of a factor other than the economic interests of the plan. DOL has interpreted the statute to permit this selection because (1) ERISA requires fiduciaries to invest plan assets and to make choices between investment alternatives, (2) ERISA does not itself specifically provide a basis for making the investment choice in this circumstance, and (3) the economic interests of the plan are fully protected by the fact that the available investment alternatives are, from the plan's perspective, economically indistinguishable.

Given the significance of ERISA's requirement that fiduciaries act solely in the interest of participants and beneficiaries, DOL believes that, before selecting an economically targeted investment, fiduciaries must have first concluded that the alternative options are truly equal, taking into account a quantitative and qualitative analysis of the economic impact on the plan. ERISA's fiduciary standards do not permit fiduciaries to select investments based on factors outside the economic interests of the plan until they have concluded, based on economic factors, that alternative investments are equal. A less rigid rule would allow fiduciaries to act on the basis of factors outside the economic interests of the plan in situations where reliance on those factors might compromise or subordinate the interests of plan participants and their beneficiaries. DOL rejects a construction of ERISA that would render its tight limits on the use of plan assets illusory and that would permit plan fiduciaries to expend trust assets to promote myriad public policy preferences.

A plan fiduciary's analysis is required to comply with, but is not necessarily limited to, the prudence requirements. In evaluating the plan portfolio, as well as portions of the portfolio, the fiduciary is required to examine the level of diversification, degree of liquidity, and the potential risk/return in comparison with available alternative investments. The same type of analysis must also be applied when choosing between investment alternatives. Potential investments should be compared to other investments that would fill a similar role in the portfolio with regard to diversification, liquidity, and risk/return. In light of the rigorous requirements established by ERISA, DOL believes that fiduciaries who rely on factors outside the economic interests of the plan in making investment choices and subsequently find their decision challenged will rarely be able to demonstrate compliance with ERISA absent a written record demonstrating that a contemporaneous economic analysis showed that the investment alternatives were of equal value.

Example 1. A plan owns an interest in a limited partnership that is considering investing in a company that competes with the plan sponsor. The fiduciaries may not replace the limited partnership investment with another investment based on this fact unless they prudently determine that a replacement investment is economically equal or superior to the limited partnership investment and would not adversely affect the plan's investment portfolio, taking into account factors including diversification, liquidity, risk, and expected return. The competition of the limited partnership with the plan sponsor is a factor outside the economic interests of the plan and, thus, cannot be considered unless an alternative investment is equal or superior to the limited partnership.

Example 2. A multiemployer plan (see Q 29:2) covering employees in a metropolitan area's construction industry wants to invest in a large loan for a construction project located in the same area because it will create local jobs. The plan has taken steps to ensure that the loan poses no prohibited transaction issues (see Q 24:1). The loan carries a return fully commensurate with the risk of nonpayment. Moreover, the loan's expected return is equal to or greater than construction loans of similar quality that are available to the plan. However, the plan has already made several other loans for construction projects in the same metropolitan area, and this loan could create a risk of large losses to the plan's portfolio due to lack of diversification. The fiduciaries may not choose this investment on the basis of the local job creation factor because, due to lack of diversification, the investment is not of equal economic value to the plan.

Example 3. A plan is considering an investment in a bond to finance affordable housing for people in the local community. The bond provides a return at least as favorable to the plan as other bonds with the same risk rating. However, the bond's size and lengthy duration raises a potential risk regarding the plan's ability to meet its predicted liquidity needs. Other available bonds under consideration by the plan do not pose this same risk. The return on the bond, although equal to or greater than the alternatives, would not be sufficient to offset the additional risk for the plan created by the role that this bond would play in the plan's portfolio. The plan's fiduciaries may not make this investment based on factors outside the economic interests of the plan because it is not of equal or greater economic value to other investment alternatives.

Example 4. A plan sponsor adopts an investment policy that favors plan investment in companies meeting certain environmental criteria (so-called green companies). In carrying out the policy, the plan's fiduciaries may not simply consider investments only in green companies. They must consider all investments that meet the plan's prudent financial criteria. The fiduciaries may apply the investment policy to eliminate a company from consideration only if they appropriately determine that other available investments provide equal or better returns at the same or lower risks and would play the same role in the plan's portfolio.

Example 5. A collective investment fund, which holds assets of several plans, is designed to invest in commercial real estate constructed or renovated with union labor. Fiduciaries of plans that invest in the fund must determine that the fund's overall risk and return characteristics are as favorable, or more favorable, to the plans as other available investment alternatives that would play a similar role in their plans' portfolios. The fund's managers may select investments constructed or improved with union labor after an economic analysis indicates that these investment options are equal or superior to their alternatives. The managers will best be able to justify their investment choice by recording their analysis in writing. However, if real estate investments that satisfy both ERISA's fiduciary requirements and the union labor criterion are unavailable, the fund managers may have to select investments without regard to the union labor criterion.

[DOL Reg. §§ 2509.08-1, 2550.404a-1; DOL Int. Bull. 2008-1]

DOL has also provided guidance with regard to the obligations of plan fiduciaries concerning shareholder rights. The interpretive bulletin sets forth DOL's interpretation of ERISA Sections 402, 403, and 404 as they apply to voting of proxies on securities held in employee benefit plan investment portfolios and the maintenance of and compliance with statements of investment policy, including proxy voting policy. In addition, the interpretive bulletin provides guidance on the appropriateness under ERISA of active monitoring of corporate management by plan fiduciaries.

The fiduciary act of managing plan assets that are shares of corporate stock includes the management of voting rights appurtenant to those shares of stock. As a result, responsibility for voting or deciding not to vote proxies lies exclusively with the plan trustee except to the extent that either (1) the trustee is subject to the direction of a named fiduciary (see Q 23:9) or (2) the power to manage, acquire, or dispose of the relevant assets has been delegated by a named fiduciary to one or more investment managers. Where the authority to manage plan assets has been delegated to an investment manager, no person other than the investment manager has authority to make voting decisions for proxies appurtenant to such plan assets except to the extent that the named fiduciary has reserved to itself (or to another named fiduciary so authorized by the plan document) the right to direct a plan trustee regarding the voting of proxies. In this regard, a named fiduciary, in delegating investment management authority to an investment manager, could reserve to itself the right to direct a trustee with respect to the voting of all proxies or reserve to itself the right to direct a trustee as to the voting of only those proxies relating to specified assets or issues.

If the plan document or investment management agreement provides that the investment manager is not required to vote proxies, but does not expressly preclude the investment manager from voting proxies, the investment manager would have exclusive responsibility for proxy voting decisions. Moreover, an investment manager would not be relieved of its own fiduciary responsibilities by following directions of some other person regarding the voting of proxies, or by delegating such responsibility to another person. If, however, the plan document or the investment management contract expressly precludes the investment manager from voting proxies, the responsibility for voting proxies would lie exclusively with the trustee. The trustee, however, may be subject to the directions of a named fiduciary if the plan so provides.

The exercise of fiduciary duties requires that, in voting proxies, regardless of whether the vote is made pursuant to a statement of investment policy, the responsible fiduciary must consider only those factors that relate to the economic value of the plan's investment and must not subordinate the interests of the participants and beneficiaries in their retirement income to unrelated objectives. Votes must be cast only in accordance with a plan's economic interests. If the responsible fiduciary reasonably determines that the cost of voting (including the cost of research, if necessary, to determine how to vote) is likely to exceed the expected economic benefits of voting, or if the exercise of voting results in the imposition of unwarranted trading or other restrictions, the fiduciary has an obligation to refrain from voting. In making this determination, objectives, considerations, and economic effects unrelated to the plan's economic interests cannot be considered. The fiduciary's duties also require that the named fiduciary appointing an investment manager periodically monitor the activities of the investment manager with respect to the management of plan assets, including decisions made and actions taken by the investment manager with regard to proxy voting decisions. The named fiduciary must carry out this responsibility solely in the participants' and beneficiaries' interest in the economic value of the plan assets and without regard to the fiduciary's relationship to the plan sponsor.

It is DOL's view that compliance with the duty to monitor necessitates proper documentation of the activities that are subject to monitoring. Thus, the investment manager or other responsible fiduciary would be required to maintain accurate records as to proxy voting decisions, including, where appropriate, cost-benefit analyses. Moreover, if the named fiduciary is to be able to carry out its responsibilities in determining whether the investment manager is fulfilling its fiduciary obligations in investing plan assets in a manner that justifies the continuation of the management appointment, the proxy voting records must enable the named fiduciary to review not only the investment manager's voting procedure with respect to plan-owned stock, but also to review the actions taken in individual proxy voting situations.

The fiduciary obligations of prudence and loyalty to plan participants and beneficiaries require the responsible fiduciary to vote proxies on issues that may affect the economic value of the plan's investment. However, fiduciaries also need to take into account costs when deciding whether and how to exercise their shareholder rights, including the voting of shares. Such costs include, but are not limited to, expenditures related to developing proxy resolutions, proxy voting services, and the analysis of the likely net effect of a particular issue on the economic value of the plan's investment. Fiduciaries must take all of these factors into account in determining whether the exercise of such rights (e.g., the voting of a proxy), independently or in conjunction with other shareholders, is expected to have an effect on the economic value of the plan's investment that will outweigh the cost of exercising such rights. With respect to proxies appurtenant to shares of foreign corporations, a fiduciary, in deciding whether to purchase shares of a foreign corporation, should consider whether any additional difficulty and expense in voting such shares is reflected in their market price.

The maintenance by a plan of a statement of investment policy designed to further the purposes of the plan and its funding policy is consistent with the fiduciary obligations set forth in ERISA. Because the fiduciary act of managing plan assets that are shares of corporate stock includes the voting, where appropriate, of proxies appurtenant to those shares of stock, a statement of proxy voting policy would be an important part of any comprehensive statement of investment policy. A statement of investment policy is a written statement that provides the fiduciaries who are responsible for plan investments with guidelines or general instructions concerning various types or categories of investment management decisions that may include proxy voting decisions. A statement of investment policy is distinguished from directions as to the purchase or sale of a specific investment at a specific time or as to voting specific plan proxies.

In plans where investment management responsibility is delegated to one or more investment managers appointed by the named fiduciary, inherent in the authority to appoint an investment manager, the named fiduciary responsible for appointment of investment managers has the authority to condition the appointment on acceptance of a statement of investment policy. Thus, such a named fiduciary may expressly require, as a condition of the investment management agreement, that an investment manager comply with the terms of a statement of investment policy that sets forth guidelines concerning investments and investment courses of action that the investment manager is authorized or is not authorized to make. Such investment policy may include a policy or guidelines on the voting of proxies on shares of stock for which the investment manager is responsible. Such guidelines must be consistent with the fiduciary obligations and the interpretive bulletin and may not subordinate the economic interests of the plan participants to unrelated objectives. In the absence of such an express requirement to comply with an investment policy, the authority to manage the plan assets placed under the control of the investment manager would lie exclusively with the investment manager. Although a trustee may be subject to the direction of a named fiduciary, an investment manager who has authority to make investment decisions, including proxy voting decisions, would never be relieved of its fiduciary responsibility if it followed the direction as to specific investment decisions from the named fiduciary or any other person.

Statements of investment policy issued by a named fiduciary authorized to appoint investment managers would be part of the documents and instruments governing the plan. An investment manager to whom such investment policy applies would be required to comply with such policy, insofar as the policy directives or guidelines are consistent with Titles I and IV of ERISA. Therefore, if, for example, compliance with the guidelines in a given instance would be imprudent, then the investment manager's failure to follow the guidelines would not violate the requirement to follow the documents and instruments governing the plan. Moreover, the investment manager would not be shielded from liability for imprudent actions taken in compliance with a statement of investment policy.

The plan document or trust agreement may expressly provide a statement of investment policy to guide the trustee or may authorize a named fiduciary to issue a statement of investment policy applicable to a trustee. Where a plan trustee is subject to an investment policy, the trustee's duty to comply with such investment policy would also be analyzed under ERISA. Thus, the trustee would be required to comply with the statement of investment policy unless, for example, it would be imprudent to do so in a given instance.

Maintenance of a statement of investment policy by a named fiduciary does not relieve the named fiduciary of its obligations with respect to the appointment and monitoring of an investment manager or trustee. In this regard, the named fiduciary appointing an investment manager must periodically monitor the investment manager's activities with respect to management of the plan assets. Moreover, compliance would require maintenance of proper documentation of the activities of the investment manager and of the named fiduciary of the plan in monitoring the activities of the investment manager. In addition, in DOL's view, a named fiduciary's determination of the terms of a statement of investment policy is an exercise of fiduciary responsibility, and, as such, statements may need to take into account factors such as the plan's funding policy and its liquidity needs as well as issues of prudence, diversification, and other fiduciary requirements of ERISA.

An investment manager of a pooled investment vehicle that holds assets of more than one employee benefit plan may be subject to a proxy voting policy of one plan that conflicts with the proxy voting policy of another plan. If the investment manager determines that compliance with one of the conflicting voting policies would violate the standard of care (for example, by being imprudent or not solely in the economic interest of plan participants), the investment manager would be required to ignore the policy and vote in accordance with ERISA's obligations. If, however, the investment manager reasonably concludes that application of each plan's voting policy is consistent with ERISA's obligations, such as where the policies reflect different but reasonable judgments or where the plans have different economic interests, ERISA would generally require the manager, to the extent permitted by applicable law, to vote the proxies in proportion to each plan's interest in the pooled investment vehicle. An investment manager may also require participating investors to accept the investment manager's own investment policy statement, including any statement of proxy voting policy, before they are allowed to invest, which may help to avoid such potential conflicts. As with investment policies originating from named fiduciaries, a policy initiated by an investment manager and adopted by the participating plans would be regarded as an instrument governing the participating plans, and the investment manager's compliance with such a policy would be governed by ERISA.

An investment policy that contemplates activities intended to monitor or influence the management of corporations in which the plan owns stock is consistent with a fiduciary's obligations under ERISA where the responsible fiduciary concludes that there is a reasonable expectation that such monitoring or communication with management, by the plan alone or together with other shareholders, will enhance the economic value of the plan's investment in the corporation, after taking into account the costs involved. Such a reasonable expectation may exist in various circumstances, for example, where plan investments in corporate stock are held as long-term investments or where a plan may not be able to easily dispose of such an investment. Active monitoring and communication activities would generally concern such issues as the independence and expertise of candidates for the corporation's board of directors and assuring that the board has sufficient information to carry out its responsibility to monitor management. Other issues may include such matters as consideration of the appropriateness of executive compensation, the corporation's policy regarding mergers and acquisitions, the extent of debt financing and capitalization, the nature of long-term business plans, the corporation's investment in training to develop its work force, other workplace practices, and financial and non-financial measures of corporate performance that are reasonably likely to affect the economic value of the plan. Active monitoring and communication may be carried out through a variety of methods, including by means of correspondence and meetings with corporate management as well as by exercising the legal rights of a shareholder. In creating an investment policy, a fiduciary must consider only factors that relate to the economic interest of participants and their beneficiaries in plan assets and must not use an investment policy to promote myriad public policy preferences.

Plan fiduciaries risk violating the exclusive purpose rule where they exercise their fiduciary authority in an attempt to further legislative, regulatory, or public policy issues through the proxy process. In such cases, DOL would expect fiduciaries to be able to demonstrate in enforcement actions their compliance with the exclusive purpose and prudence requirements. The mere fact that plans are shareholders in the corporations in which they invest does not itself provide a rationale for a fiduciary to spend plan assets to pursue, support, or oppose such proxy proposals. Because of the heightened potential for abuse in such cases, the fiduciaries must be prepared to articulate a clear basis for concluding that the proxy vote, the investment policy, or the activity intended to monitor or influence the management of the corporation is more likely than not to enhance the economic value of the plan's investment before expending plan assets.

The use of plan assets by plan fiduciaries to further policy or political issues through proxy resolutions that have no connection to enhancing the economic value of the plan's investment in a corporation would, in DOL's view, violate the prudence and exclusive purpose requirements. For example, the likelihood that the adoption of a proxy resolution or proposal requiring corporate directors and officers to disclose their personal political contributions would enhance the economic value of a plan's investment in the corporation appears sufficiently remote that the expenditure of plan assets to further such a resolution or proposal clearly raises compliance issues.

[DOL Reg. § 2509.08-2; DOL Int. Bull. 2008-2]

The existence of a conflict of interest may be weighed as a factor in determining whether an abuse of discretion occurred, but this fact alone will not eliminate the usual deference granted to the plan administrator (see Q 20:1). In order for a participant to challenge the administrator's decision, the participant must show, by material and probative evidence beyond the mere fact of an apparent conflict of interest, that the administrator's self-interest caused it to breach its fiduciary obligations to the participant; and, even if the participant succeeds in making such a showing, the plan can still rebut the presumption that the conflict affected its decision to deny benefits. [Alford v. DCH Found. Group Long-Term Disability Plan, Nos. 01-56090, 01-56178 (9th Cir. 2002); *see also* Donachy v. Motion Control Industries, 2009 WL 1553650 (3d Cir. 2009)] A fiduciary must also act prudently, diversify the investment of the plan's assets, and act in a manner consistent with the plan's documents. [California Ironworkers Field Pension Trust v. Loomis Sayles & Co., 259 F.3d 1036 (9th Cir. 2001); Laborers Nat'l Pension Fund v. ANB Mgmt. & Trust Co., 173 F.3d 313 (5th Cir. 1999); *see also In re* Syncor ERISA Litigation, 516 F.3d 1095 (9th Cir. 2008)].

A trustee did not breach its fiduciary duty when it invested all plan funds in employer stock because the plan itself required such investment upon the direction of the plan administrator and the trustee had no discretion; and an employer did not breach its fiduciary duty when former employee stock ownership plan (ESOP; see Q 28:1) participants who elected cash distributions, rather than employer stock, were not advised by the employer that it had commenced preliminary discussions to sell the company at a price substantially in excess of the current market price. [ERISA §§ 403(a), 404(a); Ershick v. United Mo. Bank of Kan. City, N.A., 948 F.2d 660 (10th Cir. 1991); Sweeney v. Kroger Co., 773 F. Supp. 1266 (E.D. Mo. 1991); *see also* Kirschbaum v. Reliant Energy, Inc., 526 F.3d 243 (5th Cir. 2008)] Where 401(k) plan (see Q 27:1) assets were substantially invested in employer stock, one court concluded that plan fiduciaries did not have an obligation to make a special disclosure to plan participants about personal sales of employer stock. [Nelson v. Hodowal, 512 F.3d 347 (7th Cir. 2008)] The court also concluded that plan fiduciaries had no duty to diversify investments of the ESOP because of the fraudulent overstatement of circulation figures, and the corresponding fraudulent increase in advertising rates, where there was no red flag to alert the fiduciaries about the fraudulent activity. The fiduciaries were not in a position to be aware of the fraud, and there was no evidence that the fraud actually affected the company's stock price. [Pugh v. Tribune Co., 2008 WL 867739 (7th Cir. 2008)]

DOL has clarified the responsibilities of a directed trustee under ERISA. The named fiduciary, not the directed trustee, is primarily responsible for ensuring the prudence of investment plan decisions; and a directed trustee is required to question the directing fiduciary's instructions regarding transactions involving publicly traded securities only in rare circumstances. DOL also specifically addressed the responsibilities of a directed trustee in determining whether a direction is proper, that is, consistent with the plan's terms and not contrary to ERISA. [DOL Field Assistance Bull. 2004-03; *In re* WorldCom, Inc. ERISA Litigation, 2005 WL 221263 (S.D.N.Y. 2005)]

A trustee breached its fiduciary duties when it distributed plan assets to the plan administrator at the administrator's direction because the plan provided that distributions could be made *only* to the participant or beneficiaries. [Buse v. Vanguard Group of Inv. Cos., 1996 U.S. Dist. LEXIS 9152 (E.D. Pa. 1996)] The manager of multiemployer plans breached his fiduciary duty by unilaterally giving himself and his son periodic salary raises without first obtaining approval of the plans' trustees. [LaScala v. Scrufari, 2007 WL 603106 (6th Cir. 2007)] One court concluded that a trustee breached his fiduciary duties because the trustee had a responsibility to ensure that plan contributions and loan repayments were made to the plan, even though he was not specifically directed to do so under the plan document. [Best v. Cyrus, 310 F.3d 932 (6th Cir. 2002)] An investment management company did not commit a breach of fiduciary duty by liquidating poorly performing bonds in a plan even though the liquidation caused a significant loss to the plan. [Ulico Casualty Co. v. Clover Capital Mgmt., Inc., 2004 U.S. Dist. LEXIS 18643 (N.D.N.Y. 2004)]

A trustee who distributed the assets of a terminated plan in such manner as to benefit himself breached his fiduciary duty to the other plan participants and beneficiaries. [Solis v. Current Development Corp., 557 F.3d 772 (7th Cir. 2009)] A trustee's transfer of excess plan assets to the employer before participants received all their benefits violated the trustee's fiduciary duty to the participants (see Q 23:83). [PBGC v. Fletcher, No. MO-89-CA-179 (W.D. Tex. 1990)] Trustees breached their fiduciary duty to a participant's widow by failing to distribute plan benefits to her as soon as the amount payable was determined as required by the plan, and a company breached its fiduciary duty when it unreasonably delayed implementing a plan participant's request to transfer his plan account from a common stock fund to a fixed-income investment fund. [Carich v. James River Corp., No. 90-35567 (9th Cir. 1992); Sherwood Group, Inc. v. Meselsohn, No. 88 Civ. 3650 (S.D.N.Y. 1990); *see also* Piazza v. Corning Inc., 2005 U.S. Dist. LEXIS 30113 (W.D.N.Y. 2005)] Not surprisingly, one court ruled that the fiduciary of a deceased participant's retirement plans breached its duty by distributing the participant's death benefits to the participant's husband while he was under indictment for her murder because the fact that the husband was under indictment provided the fiduciary with reasonable notice that he could become ineligible for benefits. [Atwater v. Nortel Networks, Inc., No. 1:04CV00503 (M.D. N.C. 2005)]

Plan participants brought suit alleging that the defendants breached their fiduciary duties by failing to diversify plan assets, to remove plan fiduciaries or monitor plan fiduciaries, and to disclose material information affecting the plans. The defendants argued that securities laws prohibit them from disclosing negative financial news to plan participants before disclosing the same to the general public because doing so would constitute illegal insider trading. The court held that plan fiduciaries cannot use the securities laws to shield themselves from potential liability for alleged breaches of fiduciary duties. [*In re* Xcel Energy, Inc., Securities, Derivative & ERISA Litigation, No. 02-2677 (D. Minn. 2004)] In another case, the court concluded that, where the same person was a fiduciary of both plans subject to ERISA and plans not subject to ERISA, fiduciary duty under ERISA did not require favoring ERISA plans over non-ERISA plans. [Securities and Exchange Comm. v. Capital Consultants, LLC, No. 03-35406 (9th Cir. 2005)]

In selecting a service provider for an ERISA-covered plan, fiduciaries must consider the quality of the services provided, not merely the cost thereof, with the fiduciaries' decision made with the interests of beneficiaries being primary, taking all steps necessary to prevent conflicting interests from affecting the decision [DOL Info. Ltr. (Feb. 19, 1998); Wsol, Sr. v. Fiduciary Mgmt. Assocs., Inc., Nos. 00-2703, 01-1685 (7th Cir. 2001); Bussian v. R.J.R. Nabisco, Inc., 2000 WL 1145395 (5th Cir. 2000)]

DOL opined that the purchase by an ESOP of the plan sponsor's stock from personal trusts is not a prohibited transaction (see Q 24:1), even if the plan sponsor serves as trustee of both the ESOP and the personal trusts. DOL stated that the stock acquisitions were exempt from the prohibited transaction provisions, as long as the transactions were for adequate consideration and no commission was charged for them. DOL cautioned, however, that the exemption of the stock purchases from the prohibited transaction provisions was not determinative of whether the fiduciary obligations under ERISA had been met. [DOL Op. Ltr. 2002-04A]

One court concluded that a claim for breach of fiduciary duty is not subject to the same administrative exhaustion requirement as a claim for benefits (see Q 10:66). [Galvan v. SBC Pension Benefit Plan, No. 04-51214 (5th Cir. 2006)]

DOL has issued a booklet entitled "Protect Your Pension" to help participants understand basic rules governing plan contributions and investments. [DOL News Rel. 96-415]

Q 23:20   What is the applicable standard of care for a fiduciary?

A fiduciary is subject to the prudent person standard of care; that is, the fiduciary must act "with the care, skill, prudence, and diligence under the circumstances then prevailing that a prudent person acting in a like capacity and familiar with such matters would use in the conduct of an enterprise of a like character and with like aims." [ERISA § 404(a)(1)(B); Edgar v. Avaya, Inc., 2007 WL 2781847 (3d Cir. 2007); DiFelice v. US Airways, Inc., 497 F.3d 410 (4th Cir. 2007); California Ironworkers Field Pension Trust v. Loomis Sayles & Co., 259 F.3d 1036 (9th Cir. 2001); Kowalewski v. Detweiler, 770 F. Supp. 290 (D. Md. 1991)] The prudence requirement is an objective standard focusing on a fiduciary's conduct in arriving at an investment decision and not on the results of that decision. [Johnson v. Radian Group, Inc., 2009 WL 2137241 (E.D. Pa. 2009)] A good-faith reliance upon expert advice later found erroneous has been held not to be a breach of the standard. [Riley v. Murdock, No. 95-2414 (4th Cir. 1996); Morgan v. Independent Drivers Ass'n Pension Plan, 975 F.2d 1467 (10th Cir. 1992); *but see* Reich v. Autrey, No. 94-515-CIV-J-20 (M.D. Fla. 1997)]

One court ruled that a claim by plan participants and beneficiaries that the employer breached its fiduciary duties by failing to adequately investigate and monitor an investment of plan assets in a hedge fund should be dismissed, because the plan was a defined benefit plan (see Q 2:3) with a substantial surplus. [Harley v. Minn Mining & Mfg. Co., 284 F.3d 901 (8th Cir. 2002)]

ERISA does not, however, prohibit dual loyalties. Accordingly, a bank serving as trustee did not breach its fiduciary duty to the plan by refusing to continue to extend credit to an unrelated corporation in which the plan had invested plan assets. [Friend v. Sanwa Bank Cal., 1994 U.S. App. LEXIS 24805 (9th Cir. 1994)] An investment manager may also render services to an ERISA plan and others, recommending different investments in the same field so long as such differing investments do not harm the plan. [Salovaara v. Eckert, No. 94 C 3430 (S.D.N.Y. 1998)]

Q 23:21 How does the prudent person standard apply to trustees or investment managers?

A trustee or other fiduciary responsible for investing the plan's assets must, in order to satisfy the prudent person standard, consider the following factors:

1. The composition of the portfolio with regard to diversification;

2. The liquidity and current return of the portfolio relative to the anticipated cash flow requirements of the plan; and

3. The projected return of the portfolio relative to the funding objectives of the plan.

In addition, the trustee or other fiduciary must determine that the particular investment or investment strategy is reasonably designed to further the purposes of the plan, taking into consideration the risk of loss and the opportunity for gain (or other return) associated with the investment or the investment strategy. [Edgar v. Avaya, Inc., 2007 WL 2781847 (3d Cir. 2007); DiFelice v. US Airways, Inc., 497 F.3d 410 (4th Cir. 2007); California Ironworkers Field Pension Trust v. Loomis Sayles & Co., 259 F.3d 1036 (9th Cir. 2001); Laborers Nat'l Pension Fund v. Northern Trust Quantitative Advisors, Inc., 173 F.3d 313 (5th Cir. 1999); Gilbert v. EMG Advisors, Inc., 1999 WL 160382 (9th Cir. 1999); DOL Reg. § 2550.404a-1] DOL has advised that a fiduciary of a defined benefit plan (see Q 2:3) may consider the liability obligations of the plan and the risks associated with those liability obligations in determining a prudent investment strategy for the plan. [DOL Op. Ltr. 2006-08A]

The standard for prudent investment conduct focuses on the process undertaken at the time the challenged investment is made. Procedural prudence is the primary inquiry, not the success or failure of the investment. The test is whether, at the time the fiduciary engaged in the investment transaction, the fiduciary employed appropriate methods to investigate the merits of the investment and to structure the investment. [Donovan v. Mazzola, 716 F.2d 1226 (9th Cir. 1983); *see also* Bunch v. W.R. Grace & Co., 2009 WL 211054 (1st Cir. 2009); Kanawi v. Bechtel Corp., 590 F. Supp. 2d 1213 (N.D. Cal. 2008); Roth v. Sawyer-Cleator Lumber Co., 16 F.3d 915 (8th Cir. 1994); Fink v. National Sav. & Trust Co., 772 F.2d 951 (D.C. Cir. 1985); Katsoros v. Cody, 744 F.2d 270 (2d Cir. 1984)] An investment management company did not commit a breach of fiduciary duty by liquidating poorly performing bonds in a plan even though the liquidation caused a significant loss to the plan. [Ulico Casualty Co. v. Clover Capital Mgmt., Inc., 2004 U.S. Dist. LEXIS 18643 (N.D.N.Y. 2004)] DOL has promulgated fiduciary responsibility rules relating to investments in derivatives. [DOL Info. Ltr. (May 21, 1996)]

One court concluded that amendments to a 401(k) plan (see Q 27:1) that removed a category of stock from investment options under the plan was a settlor activity (see Q 23:3) but did not relieve plan fiduciaries of their discretion to determine the prudence of retaining existing investments in that category of stock. [Tatum v. R.J. Reynolds Tobacco Co., 392 F.3d 636 (4th Cir. 2004)] Subsequently, a lower court ruled that a plan participant could not sue the plan's administrative and investment committees for breaching their fiduciary duties under ERISA by selling stock holdings for a large loss because the committees do not qualify as "persons" that can be sued for breach of fiduciary duty under ERISA. [Tatum v. R.J. Reynolds Tobacco Co., 2007 U.S. Dist. LEXIS 39801 (M.D. N.C. 2007]

DOL posted guidance on its website on the duties of plan fiduciaries who believe they may have had exposure to losses on investments with entities related to Bernard L. Madoff Investment Securities LLC. The guidance also provided steps that could be taken to assess and protect the interests of plans, participants, and beneficiaries. [DOL News Rel. and Statement (Feb. 2009)]

Q 23:22   Would a transaction involving the plan that benefits the employer result in a breach of fiduciary duty?

Not necessarily. A transaction that incidentally benefits the employer will not violate the rule that a fiduciary act solely in the interest of the plan's participants and beneficiaries as long as the fiduciary correctly concludes, on the basis of a careful, thorough, and impartial inquiry, that the transaction is in the interests of participants and beneficiaries. [Andrade v. Parsons Corp., No. 90-56202 (9th Cir. 1992); Phillips v. Amoco Oil Co., 799 F.2d 1464 (11th Cir. 1986); Donovan v. Bierwirth, 680 F.2d 263 (2d Cir. 1982)]

However, management trustees of an ESOP (see Q 28:1) breached their fiduciary duty by not voting the ESOP shares at a shareholder meeting. If their conflicting loyalties to the company and the participants prevented them from properly representing the participants, they should have sought advice from a competent, independent advisor (see Q 28:52). [Newton v. Van Otterloo, No.

S89-610 (N.D. Ill. 1991)] Even where a breach of fiduciary duty occurs, plaintiffs must establish that they were damaged by the breach. [Howard v. Shay, No. CV 91-146 (C.D. Cal. 1998)]

Q 23:23   What are plan assets?

Under PPA (see Q 1:33), the term "plan assets" will be defined under regulations to be issued by DOL. However, under the regulations, the assets of any entity (see Q 23:25) are not to be treated as plan assets if, immediately after the most recent acquisition of any equity interest (see Q 23:27) in the entity, less than 25 percent of the total value of each class of equity interest in the entity (disregarding certain interests) is held by benefit plan investors (see Q 23:30). For this purpose, an entity is considered to hold plan assets only to the extent of the percentage of the equity interest held by benefit plan investors, which means an employee benefit plan subject to the fiduciary rules of ERISA, any plan to which the prohibited-transaction rules (see Q 24:1) of the Code applies, and any entity whose underlying assets include plan assets by reason of a plan's investment in such entity. [ERISA § 3(42)]

A plan's investment in a registered investment company, such as a mutual fund, does not by itself cause the fund's investment adviser or principal underwriter to be deemed to be a fiduciary (see Q 23:1) or a party in interest (see Q 24:3), except insofar as such investment company or its investment adviser or principal underwriter acts in connection with an employee benefit plan covering employees of the investment company, the investment adviser, or its principal underwriter. In addition, where a plan invests in a security issued by a registered investment company, the assets of the plan are deemed to include the security but are not, solely by reason of such investment, deemed to include any assets of such investment company. [ERISA §§ 3(21)(B), 401(b)(1)] A target-date or lifecycle mutual fund, which automatically rebalances to a more conservative asset allocation as the participant approaches the target retirement date, may consist of shares of affiliated mutual funds. In DOL's view, a mutual fund's investment in the shares of affiliated mutual funds would not, by itself, affect the application of the exclusion of mutual funds from the plan asset rules under ERISA. Accordingly, the fact that a target-date or lifecycle mutual fund's assets consist of shares of affiliated mutual funds does not, on that basis alone, make the assets of the target-date or lifecycle mutual fund plan assets of investing employee benefit plans or make the investment advisers to such mutual funds fiduciaries to the investing plans. [DOL Op. Ltr. 2009-04A]

Two company officers, not named as plan fiduciaries (see Q 23:9), were nonetheless acting in a fiduciary capacity and were criminally liable for diverting plan assets in the form of employer contributions owed to the company's plans. The court ruled that employer contributions to ERISA plans became assets of the plans when they became due and payable and that unpaid employer contributions are assets held in trust for the benefit of the plan and not for the employer's benefit. [ERISA § 403; United States v. Jackson, Jr., 524 F.3d 532 (4th Cir. 2008); United States v. Carey, 524 F.3d 532 (4th Cir. 2008); *but see In re* M & S Grading, Inc., 2008 WL 4133863 (8th Cir. 2008)] Another court, however, concluded that employer contributions do not become plan assets until the contributions are actually made to the plan unless the plan documents otherwise provide. [*In re* Halpin, 2009 WL 1272632 (2d Cir. 2009)] See Q 29:6 for additional information.

Q 23:24   Must the assets of the plan be segregated?

Yes. The plan's assets (see Q 23:23) must be segregated from the employer's property and held in trust. [ERISA § 403(a); Herman v. Goldstein, 2000 WL 1269746 (2d Cir. 2000)]

Q 23:25   What are plan assets when a plan invests in another entity?

Generally, the plan's assets (see Q 23:23) will include its investment in an entity but not any of the underlying assets of such entity. However, if the plan's equity interest in an entity is neither a publicly offered security nor a security issued by an investment company registered under the Investment Company Act of 1940, the plan's assets will include both the equity interest and an undivided interest in each of the underlying assets (the look-through rule; see Q 23:26). In that event, any person who has any authority or control over the management of the underlying assets or provides investment advice for a fee with respect to such assets is a fiduciary of the investing plan (see Q 23:1). [DOL Reg. § 2510.3-101(a); DOL Op. Ltr. 2002-01A; DOL Info. Ltr. (Jan. 6, 2004)]

Q 23:26   Are there any exceptions to the look-through rule?

Yes. The look-through rule (see Q 23:25) will not apply if:

1. The equity interest (see Q 23:27) is in an operating company (see Q 23:28), or
2. The amount of equity participation in the entity by benefit plan investors is not significant (see Qs 23:29, 23:30).

[DOL Reg. § 2510.3-101(a)(2); DOL Op. Ltr. 2002-01A]

Q 23:27   What is an equity interest and a publicly offered security?

An equity interest is any interest in an entity other than an instrument that is treated as debt under applicable local law and that does not have substantial equity features. Examples of equity interests include an interest in profits of a partnership, an undivided interest in property, and a beneficial interest in a trust.

A publicly offered security is a security that is freely transferable, is part of a widely held class of securities, and is covered under certain federal securities registration rules.

Example 1. A plan acquires debentures issued by the Gigolo Corporation pursuant to a private offering. All of Gigolo's shareholders are benefit plan investors. Gigolo is engaged primarily in investing and reinvesting in precious metals on behalf of its shareholders, so it is not an operating company. By their terms, the plan's debentures are convertible into common stock of Gigolo at the plan's option. At the time the plan acquired the debentures, the conversion feature was incidental to Gigolo's obligation to pay interest and principal. The plan's assets do not include an interest in the underlying assets of Gigolo because the plan has not acquired an equity interest in Gigolo.

Example 2. Assume the same facts as in Example 1, except the plan exercises its option to convert the debentures into common stock, thereby acquiring an equity interest in Gigolo. Assuming that the common stock is not a publicly traded security and that there has been no change in the composition of the other equity investors in Gigolo, the plan's assets would then include an undivided interest in the underlying assets of Gigolo. As a result, employees of Gigolo with authority or control over the assets of Gigolo would be fiduciaries of the plan.

[DOL Reg. §§ 2510.3-101(b), 2510.3-101(j)(1)]

The Securities and Exchange Commission (SEC) has approved a rule allowing any member of the National Association of Securities Dealers (NASD) who is designated by a named fiduciary (see Q 23:9) as an investment manager of equity securities to vote proxies in accordance with fiduciary responsibilities. [SEC Order Approving Proposed Rule Change by Nat'l Ass'n of Securities Dealers, 60 Fed. Reg. 25,749]

Q 23:28 What is an operating company?

An operating company is generally an entity that is engaged primarily, directly or through subsidiaries, in the production or sale of a product or service other than investment of capital. Also, a venture capital operating company or a real estate operating company will be treated as an operating company. [DOL Reg. § 2510.3-101(c); DOL Op. Ltr. 2002-01A]

An entity is a venture capital operating company if at least 50 percent of its assets (other than short-term investments made pending long-term commitments) are invested in an operating company (other than a venture capital operating company) as to which the investing entity has and exercises the right to participate substantially in or influence the management of the operating company. [DOL Reg. § 2510.3-101(d)]

An entity is a real estate operating company if at least half of its assets are invested in managed or developed real estate and the investing entity has the right to participate substantially and directly in the management or development activities. In addition, the investing entity, in the ordinary course of its business, must actually engage in real estate management or development activities. [DOL Reg. § 2510.3-101(e)]

Q 23:29   What level of participation of benefit plan investors is considered significant?

Equity participation in an entity is significant on any date if, immediately after the most recent acquisition or redemption of any equity interest (see Q 23:27), 25 percent or more of the value of any class of equity interest in the entity is held by benefit plan investors (see Qs 23:23, 23:30). [DOL Reg. § 2510.3-101(f)(1); DOL Op. Ltr. 2005-19A; DOL Op. Ltr. 89-05A]

Q 23:30   What is a benefit plan investor?

A benefit plan investor includes:

1. An employee benefit plan as defined by ERISA;
2. An individual retirement account (see Q 30:2) or individual retirement annuity (see Q 30:3); or
3. Any entity whose underlying assets include plan assets as a result of a plan's investment in that entity (see Q 23:25).

[ERISA § 3(42) (as added by PPA § 611(f)); PPA § 611(h)(1); DOL Reg. § 2510.3-101(f)(2)]

Q 23:31   Are there any investments by a plan that may never satisfy the exceptions to the look-through rule?

Yes. If a plan acquires or holds an interest in any entity (other than a licensed insurance company) established or maintained to provide any pension or welfare benefit to participants or beneficiaries of the investing plan, none of the exceptions may apply (see Qs 23:24, 23:26). As a result, the assets of the plan will include its investment and an undivided interest in the underlying assets of that entity.

> **Example.** A qualified retirement plan acquires a beneficial interest in a trust that is not an insurance company licensed to do business in a state. Under this arrangement, the trust will provide the plan benefits that are promised to the participants and beneficiaries under the terms of the plan. The plan's assets include its beneficial interest in the trust and an undivided interest in each of the trust's underlying assets. Thus, persons with authority or control over trust assets would be fiduciaries of the qualified retirement plan.

[DOL Reg. §§ 2510.3-101(h)(2), 2510.3-101(j)(12)]

Q 23:32   When are participant contributions considered plan assets?

Participant contributions, whether by direct payment by the participants or by withholding by the employer from participants' wages, must become assets of plans such as 401(k) plans (see Q 27:1) no later than the 15th business day of the month following the month in which the withholding actually occurred. Nonetheless, participant contributions to a plan will be considered plan assets as of the earliest date on which the contributions can reasonably be segregated from the general assets of the employer. [DOL Reg. § 2510.3-102; Bannistor v. Ullman, 287 F.3d 394 (5th Cir. 2002); *see also* Paul v. C.T. Enterprises, Inc., 394 F.3d 213 (4th Cir. 2005) and United States v. Whiting, 471 F.3d 792 (7th Cir. 2006)] DOL has advised that these rules also apply to multiemployer defined contribution plans (see Q 29:2). [DOL Field Assistance Bull. 2003-04A]

DOL has issued final regulations, applicable primarily to defined contribution plans (see Q 2:2) with fewer than 100 participants, that would provide a safe harbor period for employers to remit contributions from participants into retirement plans. The assets of the plan include amounts that a participant or beneficiary pays to an employer, or amounts that a participant has withheld from wages by an employer, for contribution or repayment of a participant loan (see chapter 14) to the plan, as of the earliest date on which such contributions or repayments can reasonably be segregated from the employer's general assets. In the case of a plan with fewer than 100 participants at the beginning of the plan year, any amount deposited with the plan not later than the seventh business day following the day on which such amount is received by the employer (in the case of amounts that a participant or beneficiary pays to an employer) or the seventh business day following the day on which such amount would otherwise have been payable to the participant in cash (in the case of amounts withheld by an employer from a participant's wages) will be deemed to be contributed or repaid to the plan on the earliest date on which such contributions or participant loan repayments can reasonably be segregated from the employer's general assets. The safe harbor is an optional alternative method of compliance and does not establish the exclusive means by which participant contribution or participant loan repayment amounts will be considered to be contributed or repaid to a plan by the earliest date on which such contributions or repayments can reasonably be segregated from the employer's general assets. [DOL Reg. §§ 2510.3-102(a), 2510.3-102(e)]

Except for the safe harbor, in no event will the date for reasonable segregation from the employer's general assets occur later than the 15th business day of the month following the month in which the participant contribution or participant loan repayment amounts are received by the employer (in the case of amounts that a participant or beneficiary pays to an employer) or the 15th business day of the month following the month in which such amounts would otherwise have been payable to the participant in cash (in the case of amounts withheld by an employer from a participant's wages). [DOL Reg. § 2510.3-102(b)(1)] In limited circumstances, an employer may elect an extension of ten business days. This does not apply to the safe harbor. An employer may not elect an extension more than twice in any plan year unless the employer pays to the plan an amount representing interest on the participant contributions that were subject to all the extensions within such plan year. [DOL Reg. §§ 2510.3-102(d), 2510.3-102(e)]

Example 1. Marilan Corporation sponsors a 401(k) plan, and there are 30 participants in the plan. Marilan Corporation has one payroll period for its employees and uses an outside payroll processing service to pay employee wages and process deductions. Marilan Corporation has established a system under which the payroll processing service provides payroll deduction information to it within one business day after the issuance of paychecks. Marilan Corporation checks this information for accuracy within five business days and then forwards the withheld employee contributions to the plan. The amount of the total withheld employee contributions is deposited with the plan on the seventh business day following the date on which the employees are paid. Under the safe harbor, when the participant contributions are deposited with the plan on the seventh business day following a pay date, the participant contributions are deemed to be contributed to the plan on the earliest date on which such contributions can reasonably be segregated from Marilan Corporation's general assets.

Example 2. Harv-San Tailor Corporation is a large national corporation that sponsors a 401(k) plan with 600 participants. Harv-San Tailor Corporation has several payroll centers and uses an outside payroll processing service to pay employee wages and process deductions. Each payroll center has a different pay period. Each center maintains separate accounts on its books for purposes of accounting for that center's payroll deductions and provides the outside payroll processor the data necessary to prepare employee paychecks and process deductions. The payroll processing service issues the employees' paychecks and deducts all payroll taxes and elective employee deductions. The payroll processing service forwards the employee payroll deduction data to the corporation on the date of issuance of paychecks. Harv-San Tailor Corporation checks this data for accuracy and transmits this data, along with the employee 401(k) deferral funds, to the plan's investment firm within three business days. The plan's investment firm deposits the employee 401(k) deferral funds into the plan on the day they are received from the corporation. The assets of the 401(k) plan would include the participant contributions no later than three business days after the issuance of paychecks.

Salary reduction contributions under a SIMPLE IRA plan (see Q 33:1) must become plan assets on the earliest date the contributions can be reasonably segregated from the employer's general assets, but no later than the 30th day following the month in which the participant contribution amounts would otherwise have been payable to the participant. [DOL Reg. § 2510.3-102(b)(2)]

IRS has issued guidance explaining how an employer must compute the amount involved for purposes of paying the 15 percent excise tax imposed on a prohibited transaction (see Q 24:5) for being late in transmitting a participant's elective deferrals to a 401(k) plan. The ruling shows by way of an example that the amount involved is based on interest on those elective deferrals. Further, it indicates that the interest is cumulative and the amount keeps running until the employer properly separates the funds from its general assets and pays it into the plan. [Rev. Rul. 2006-38, 2006-2 C.B. 80]

The president of an employer was liable to a multiemployer plan for unpaid contributions after the employer stopped making contributions and filed for bankruptcy because such unpaid contributions were deemed plan assets over which the president exercised discretionary authority and committed a breach of fiduciary duty to the plan by paying corporate expenses instead of making the required plan contributions (see Q 29:6). [PMTA-ILA Containerization Fund v. Rose, 1995 U.S. Dist. LEXIS 10877 (E.D. Pa. 1995)] An employer and its officer who breached their fiduciary duties by delaying the deposit of employee contributions to a plan were liable for the interest that would have been earned on the delayed contributions. [Wilson v. United Int'l Investigative Servs. 401(k) Sav. Plan, 2002 U.S. Dist. LEXIS 22259 (E.D. Pa. 2002)] DOL has clarified the responsibility of named fiduciaries (see Q 23:9) and trustees for the collection of delinquent employer and employee contributions. The guidance is intended to brief field investigators on the responsibilities of plan fiduciaries and trustees to monitor and collect delinquent employer and employee contributions owed to plans covered by ERISA. [DOL Field Assistance Bull. 2008-01]

DOL has opined that participant loan repayments (see chapter 14) are sufficiently similar to plan contributions, so that such repayments (whether made to the employer for purposes of being forwarded to the plan or withheld from employee wages by the employer for forwarding to the plan) become plan assets as of the earliest date on which the repayments can reasonably be segregated from the employer's general assets. [DOL Op. Ltr. 2002-02A] The safe-harbor proposed regulation discussed in this Q 23:32 applies to participant loan repayments.

DOL has also opined that plan fiduciaries may not use plan assets to further public policy debates and political activities through proxy resolutions that have no connection to enhancing the value of the plan's investment in a corporation. [DOL Op. Ltr. 2007-07A]

Q 23:33   What expenses relating to the plan may be paid out of plan assets?

Generally, plan assets are held exclusively to provide benefits to participants or beneficiaries and to defray reasonable expenses of administering the plan (see Q 23:19). Plan assets may therefore be used to pay plan expenses that are reasonably related to plan administration and authorized by the plan, such as actuarial services required under ERISA. [ERISA § 103(a)(4)(A); Shaver v. Operating Eng'rs Local 428 Pension Trust Fund, 332 F.3d 1198 (9th Cir. 2003)] Selecting the service provider is an exercise of discretionary authority subject to ERISA's fiduciary standards. Accordingly, a responsible plan fiduciary should engage in an objective process designed to elicit information necessary to assess the qualifications of the proposed service provider, the quality of the work product, and the reasonableness of the fees charged with respect to the services provided. [DOL Info. Ltr. (Dec. 1, 1997)]

Services provided in connection with establishing the plan, terminating the plan, and other plan design functions would not properly be paid out of the plan; reasonable expenses incurred in connection with implementing those decisions would generally be payable by the plan. Services with respect to obtaining an IRS determination letter (see Q 18:1), to amend the plan to comply with changes in the law, for routine nondiscrimination testing, to comply with ERISA disclosure requirements, and to communicate plan information to participants normally can be paid from the plan. Payment of Pension Benefit Guaranty Corporation (PBGC) premiums is proper if the plan is silent or explicitly states that the plan may pay the premiums. However, the payment would be improper if the document indicates that the plan sponsor will pay them. [ERISA §§ 403(c)(1), 404(a)(1); DOL Info. Ltr. (Mar. 2, 1987); DOL Op. Ltr. 2001-01A] Questions concerning expenses that may properly be paid from a plan may be directed to:

Office of Regulations and Interpretations
Employee Benefits Security
Administration Room N-5669
200 Constitution Ave.
Washington, DC 20210
Attention: Settlor Expense Guidance

See Q 23:34 for additional information.

Q 23:34　How can expenses paid out of plan assets be allocated?

DOL has issued guidance addressing the allocation of plan expenses among participants in a defined contribution plan (see Q 2:2). [DOL Field Assistance Bull. 2003-3]

The guidance states that plan sponsors and fiduciaries have significant flexibility in establishing rules for allocating expenses among participants in defined contribution plans, including whether plan expenses are allocated on a pro rata or per capita basis when charged to the plan as a whole, or whether expenses will be charged to individual participants. For whether a particular expense is properly charged to the plan in the first instance, see Q 23:33.

ERISA does not specifically address how plan expenses may be allocated among participants and beneficiaries. According to DOL, a plan sponsor has considerable discretion in determining how expenses will be allocated in the plan document, and a method of allocating expenses set forth in the plan document becomes part of defining the benefit entitlements under the plan and must be followed by a plan fiduciary unless inconsistent with other ERISA requirements. If the plan document does not set forth a method of allocating expenses, the fiduciary must select an allocation method that is consistent with general fiduciary duties, including the duty to act solely in the interest of plan participants and beneficiaries (see Q 23:19). An allocation method does not fail to be solely in the interest of participants merely because it disfavors one class of participants versus another, provided that a rational basis exists for the method selected.

The guidance sets forth that a pro rata allocation of expenses based on account balances would be permissible in most cases. However, a per capita method would also be reasonable for allocating fixed administrative expenses, such as recordkeeping, legal, auditing, and annual report expenses. Expenses for investment advisory services could be allocated on either a pro rata or per capita basis without regard to actual utilization by particular participants, or else could be charged directly to the accounts of the participants who utilize the service. It would presumably not be prudent for a fiduciary to charge an expense tied directly to account balances, such as investment fees, on a per capita basis. Plan expenses for the following defined contribution plan activities may be charged to the accounts of the specific participant or beneficiary:

1. Processing hardship withdrawals;
2. Calculating benefits under different distribution options;
3. Making distributions; and
4. Processing QDROs (see Q 36:22).

Different allocation methods may apply to different participant groups, and a plan may charge vested separated participant accounts with a pro rata or per capita share of plan expenses without regard to whether the accounts of active participants are similarly charged. IRS has ruled that a defined contribution plan may charge a pro rata share of the plan's reasonable administrative expenses to the accounts of former employees, even though the employer pays the expenses allocable to the accounts of current employees. [Rev. Rul. 2004-10, 2004-1 C.B. 484]

DOL notes that the summary plan description (SPD; see Q 22:1) must describe any provision resulting in the imposition of a fee or charge on a participant or beneficiary that is a condition to the receipt of benefits under the plan, as well as any circumstances that may result in the offset or reduction of benefits.

It should be noted that the guidance issued by DOL applies specifically to defined contribution plans, and not to defined benefit plans (see Q 2:3).

Q 23:35 What are the consequences if plan assets are used improperly?

An improper payment of plan assets for expenses other than reasonable plan administration expenses would be a breach of fiduciary duty and would subject the fiduciary to personal liability for the breach (see Q 23:36). In addition, the payment may be a prohibited transaction if the payment is made to, on behalf of, or for the benefit of a party in interest (see Qs 24:8, 24:20) and does not qualify for a statutory or administrative exemption under ERISA or the Code (see Qs 24:19–24:21). Finally, the payment may be considered a violation of the exclusive benefit provision of the Code and result in plan disqualification (see Q 4:1).

A defined benefit plan (see Q 2:3) sponsored by both an employer and a union had assets in excess of that required for funding the plan's future liabilities. In a new collective bargaining agreement, in exchange for an increase in the plan benefits, the employer was permitted discretion to determine the amount and timing of its future contributions. Using that discretion, the employer discontinued plan contributions; however, as to contributions from the union, the employer opined that permitting the union to discontinue payments to the plan would contravene labor law. The employer then requested that the union make payments to the employer, instead of the plan, in the amount the employer had to declare in its financial statements as attributable to its costs of pension benefits. The issue was how to characterize the payments from the union to the employer. The court concluded that the payments from the union to the employer made to reimburse costs of providing pension benefits were not plan contributions and, therefore, were not plan assets or subject to ERISA's fiduciary duty rules. [Bottle Beer Drivers, Warehousemen & Helpers Teamsters Local 843 v. Anheuser Busch, Inc., 2004 WL 938462 (3d Cir. 2004)]

Q 23:36   Can a fiduciary be held liable for a breach of duty?

Yes. ERISA permits a civil action to be brought by a participant, beneficiary, or other fiduciary against a fiduciary for a breach of duty. The fiduciary is personally liable for any losses to the plan resulting from the breach of duty, and any profits obtained by the fiduciary through the use of plan assets must be turned over to the plan. [ERISA §§ 409(a), 502(a)(2)] The fiduciary is not liable to the plan participant, only to the plan itself. [LaRue v. DeWolff, Boberg & Assocs., Inc., 450 F.3d 570 (4th Cir. 2006); Murchison v. Murchison, 2006 WL 994508 (D.C. Cir. 2006)] Another court ruled otherwise, holding that plan participants could pursue their claims seeking compensation for their individual plan losses resulting from an alleged breach of fiduciary duty. [Tullis v. UMB Bank, 2008 WL 215535 (6th Cir. 2008)] The United States Supreme Court resolved this conflict and unanimously ruled that ERISA allows participants to bring suit to recover losses from fiduciary breaches that impair the value of the plan assets held in their individual accounts, even if the financial solvency of the entire plan is not threatened by the alleged fiduciary breach. [LaRue v. DeWolff, Boberg & Assocs., Inc., 552 U.S. 248 (2008); *see also* Rogers v. Baxter International, Inc., 2008 WL 867741 (7th Cir. 2008) and Young v. Principal Financial Group, Inc., 2008 WL 1776590 (S.D. Ia. 2008); *but see* Cook v. Campbell, 2008 WL 2039501 (M.D. Ala. 2008)] The proposition by a participant in a cash balance plan (see Q 2:23) that the Supreme Court decision should be extended beyond individual account plans was rejected. [Fisher v. The Penn Traffic Co., 2009 WL 910388 (2d Cir. 2009)] The Supreme Court declined to review the *Fisher* decision. [Fisher v. The Penn Traffic Co., *cert. den.*, 130 S. Ct. 494 (2009)] The court may require other appropriate relief, including removal of the fiduciary (see Q 23:18). There is a question whether fiduciaries are liable to third parties if their breach may be considered in the best interests of plan beneficiaries. [General Am. Life Ins. Co. v. Castonguay, 984 F.2d 1518 (9th Cir. 1993)]

Two corporate officers who were trustees (i.e., fiduciaries) of the corporation's ESOP (see Q 28:1) withdrew over $2,000,000 in ESOP contributions immediately after they were made to meet the corporation's expenses. Promissory notes that provided that the funds would be replaced with corporate stock of equal value were issued to the ESOP by the corporation. After the corporation transferred most of its operating assets to another company, it transferred stock to the ESOP. The number of shares transferred was based on the value of the stock when the funds were initially withdrawn and did not account for the asset transfer. DOL claimed that the stock was virtually worthless after the asset transfer and brought suit for the amount withdrawn plus interest. The court ruled in favor of DOL and also held that the trustees had the burden of proving the amount of the loss to the ESOP. [Secretary of the United States DOL v. Gilley, 2002 WL 856995 (6th Cir. 2002); *see also* Chao v. USA Mining Inc., No. 1:04-CV-138 (E.D. Tenn. 2007)]

One court concluded that a breach of fiduciary duty claim under ERISA could not be supported where misrepresentations made by the employer and relied on by an employee related to a non-ERISA plan. [Bell v. Pfizer, Inc., 2010 WL 3385949 (2d Cir. 2010)]

Q 23:37 Can a claim for breach of fiduciary duty be time barred?

Yes. ERISA contains what is known as a statute of limitations requiring that claims alleging a breach of fiduciary duty be commenced within a certain period of time or be barred. ERISA generally provides that, unless there is fraud or concealment, no action may be commenced with respect to a fiduciary's breach of any responsibility, duty, or obligation or with respect to a violation after the earlier of:

1. Six years after (a) the date of the last action that constituted a part of the breach or violation, or (b) in the case of an omission, the latest date on which the fiduciary could have cured the breach or violation, or

2. Three years after the earliest date on which the plaintiff had actual knowledge of the breach or violation; except that in the case of fraud or concealment, such action may be commenced not later than six years after the date of discovery of such breach or violation.

[ERISA § 413; Browning v. Tiger's Eye Benefits Consulting, 313 Fed. Appx. 656 (4th Cir. 2009); Ranke v. Sanofi-Synthelabo, Inc., 2006 U.S. App. LEXIS 2015 (3d Cir. 2006); Tinley v. Gannett Co., 2003 WL 68076 (3d Cir. 2003); Million v. Trustees of the Cent. States, Southeast & Southwest Areas Pension Fund, 2002 WL 31412401 (6th Cir. 2002); Richard B. Roush, Inc. Profit Sharing Plan v. New England Mut. Life Ins. Co., 311 F.3d 581 (3d Cir. 2002); C.B. Richard Ellis Investors, L.L.C. v. Sonnenblick, No. 01-55918 (9th Cir. 2002); Woods v. Halliburton Co., 2002 WL 31379873 (10th Cir. 2002); Minnkota Ag Prods., Inc. v. Norwest Bank N.D., Nat'l Ass'n, No. 01-2524 (8th Cir. 2002); *In re* Unisys Corp. Retiree Med. Benefit ERISA Litig., 242 F.3d 497 (3d Cir. 2001); Montrose Med. Group Participants Sav. Plan v. Bulger, No. 00-3430 (3d Cir. 2001); Corral v. Southern Cal. Gas Co., 2000 U.S. App. LEXIS 925 (9th Cir. 2000); Babock v. Hartmax Corp., 1999 WL 538091 (5th Cir. 1999); Spangler v. Altec Int'l Ltd. P'ship, 199 U.S. App. LEXIS 2114 (7th Cir. 1999); Spragg v. Pacific Telesis Corp., 1999 WL 51489 (9th Cir. 1999); Brown v. American Life Holdings, Inc., 190 F.3d 856 (8th Cir. 1999); Jefferson v. R.R. Donnelly & Sons Co., No. 00 C 8609 (N.D. Ill. 2001); Jeffries v. Pension Trust Fund of the Pension, Hospitalization & Benefit Plan of the Elec. Indus., No. 99 Civ. 4174 (S.D.N.Y. 2001); Adelman v.

Neurology Consultants, No. 99-113 (E.D. Pa. 2000); Wilson Land Corp. v. Smith Barney, Inc., 1999 U.S. Dist. LEXIS 12879 (W.D.N.C. 1999); Mayes v. Local 106, Int'l Union of Operating Eng'rs, No. 93-CV-716 (N.D.N.Y. 1999)]

Courts are divided as to what constitutes actual knowledge. Some courts have held that actual knowledge of a breach or violation requires that the individual have actual knowledge of all material facts necessary to understand that some claim exists, which facts could include necessary opinions of experts, knowledge of a transaction's harmful consequences, or even actual harm. [Reich v. Lancaster, 68 F.3d 951 (5th Cir. 1995); Gluck v. Unisys Corp, 960 F.2d 1168 (3d Cir. 1992); International Union v. Murata Erie N. Am., 980 F.2d 889 (3d Cir. 1992)] However, other courts have held that actual knowledge requires only knowledge of all the relevant facts of the conduct or transaction constituting the violation and not that the facts establish a valid ERISA claim. Under this standard, it is not necessary that an individual have knowledge of every last detail of a transaction or knowledge of its illegality. It is knowledge of the transaction that triggers the running of the statute of limitations, not knowledge of the law. [Bishop v. Lucent Technologies, Inc., No. 07-3435 (6th Cir. 2008); Wright v. Heyne, 349 F.3d 321 (6th Cir. 2003); Rush v. Martin Peterson Co., 83 F.3d 894 (7th Cir. 1996); Brock v. Nellis, 809 F.2d 753 (11th Cir. 1987); Blanton v. Anzalone, 760 F.2d 989 (9th Cir. 1985)] One court adopted a hybrid view whereby actual knowledge occurs when an individual has knowledge of all material facts necessary to understand that a fiduciary has breached its duty or otherwise violated ERISA. While the individual need not have knowledge of the relevant law, knowledge of all facts necessary to constitute a claim is necessary. [Caputo v. Pfizer, Inc, 267 F.3d 181 (2d Cir. 2001)] Possession of an SPD (see Q 22:1) by former plan participants was not actual knowledge that triggered the three-year statute of limitations without evidence that the participants had read and understood the plan terms or SPD. [Harris v. Finch, Pruyn & Co., Inc., 2008 WL 2064972 (N.D.N.Y. 2008)]

A clear repudiation of benefits in response to an informal inquiry that is known or should be known by the participant may start the statute of limitations. [Carey v. International Bhd. of Elec. Workers Local 363 Pension Plan, 1999 U.S. App. LEXIS 32699 (2d Cir. 1999)]; *see also* Chuck v. Hewlett Packard Co., 2006 U.S. App. LEXIS 18579 (9th Cir. 2006)]

In addition to a claim being barred by the statute of limitations, a claim can be barred by the judicial doctrine of res judicata (i.e., a case already adjudicated). Where a plan and its participants attempted to sue the plan's former fiduciary in a court for breach of fiduciary duty, the claim was barred by res judicata because it had not been brought in the employer's earlier bankruptcy proceeding. [Browning v. Levy, 2002 WL 377025 (6th Cir. 2002)]

One court ruled that ERISA does not contain a statute of limitations for bringing suit on benefit claims (see Qs 10:65, 10:66). Therefore, an ERISA benefit plan cannot start the statute of limitations running on a participant's cause of action for benefits before the participant can even file suit under the plan's terms. [White v. Sun Life Assur. Co. of Canada, 2007 WL 1218209 (4th Cir. 2007)]

Q 23:38   May a participant or beneficiary sue a fiduciary for a personal wrong with respect to an ERISA plan?

Yes. ERISA permits plan participants to sue for equitable relief on their own behalf when harmed by a fiduciary's breach of duty. [ERISA § 502(a); Varity Corp. v. Howe, 516 U.S. 489 (1996)] Monetary damages and legal relief are not available. [Fisher v. The Penn Traffic Co., 2009 WL 910388 (2d Cir. 2009); Kendall v. Employees Retirement Plan of Avon Products, 561 F.3d 112 (2d Cir. 2009); Paulsen v. CNF Inc., 559 F.3d 1061 (9th Cir. 2009)] ERISA also provides the basis for an action against a nonfiduciary who participates in a prohibited transaction (see Q 24:1). [ERISA § 406; Leblanc v. Cahill, 153 F.3d 134 (4th Cir. 1998); Quint v. Freda, 1999 U.S. Dist. LEXIS 1384 (S.D.N.Y. 1999)] One court ruled that plan participants cannot bring an action for breach of fiduciary duty under ERISA Section 502(a)(2) unless the relief sought would benefit the plan as a whole. [Milofsky v. American Airlines Inc., 404 F.3d 338 (5th Cir. 2005)] However, on rehearing, the decision was reversed. [Milofsky v. American Airlines, Inc., No. 03-11087 (5th Cir. 2006)] In a similar case, another court determined that two plan participants could proceed with their breach of fiduciary duty action even though the alleged breaches of fiduciary duty that caused the plan to sustain losses only affected a portion of the plan's participants. [*In re* Schering-Plough Corp. ERISA Litigation, 420 F.3d 231 (3d Cir. 2005)] An individual plan participant could not maintain an ERISA Section 502(a)(2) breach of fiduciary duty claim against plan trustees in a representative capacity, ruled one court, without taking some procedural steps to protect the interests of other plan participants. [Coan v. Kaufman, 457 F.3d 250 (2d Cir. 2006)] Another court concluded that a plan participant was not entitled to recover additional benefits because he brought suit under ERISA Section 502(a)(3), under which the recovery of monetary benefits is not available, and should have brought suit under ERISA Section 502(a)(1)(B). [Crosby v. Bowater Inc. Retirement Plan for Salaried Employees of Great Northern Paper Inc., 382 F.3d 587 (6th Cir. 2004) *see also* Young v. Principal Financial Group, Inc., 2008 WL 1776590 (S.D. Ia. 2008)]. An accounting firm was not subject to equitable remedies under ERISA Section 502(a)(3). The firm successfully argued that services it rendered in designing, utilizing, and administering a client's 401(k) plan (see Q 27:1) and cash balance plan (see Q 2:23) did not make the firm liable as a nonfiduciary for knowingly participating in alleged breaches by the plans' fiduciaries. [Pender v. Bank of America Corp., 2010 WL 1434297 (D. N.C. 2010)] Because the relief sought by the participant was under ERISA Section 502, the court concluded that the state's ten-year statute of limitations for breach of a written contract was applicable. [Leister v. Dovetail, Inc., 2008 WL 4659364 (7th Cir. 2008)]

An injunction, sought by former employees as equitable relief under ERISA Section 502(a)(3) to prevent a plan's reduction of their monthly benefits, was actually a claim for monetary damages and thus not available as equitable relief, determined another court. [Ramsey v. Formica Corp., 398 F.3d 421 (6th Cir. 2005)] An appeals court affirmed the dismissal of a denial of benefits case, ruling that relabeling the relief sought to restitution or surcharge does not change the nature of the remedy from monetary to equitable and that monetary damages are not available under ERISA. [Estate of Siade v. Group Health Plan, Inc., 2006 U.S. App. LEXIS 1144 (8th Cir. 2006)]

The assignee of a participant's claim under a valid assignment may also pursue a claim for breach of fiduciary duty. [Texas Life, Accident, Health & Hosp. Serv. Ins. Guar. Ass'n v. Gaylord Entm't Co., 105 F.3d 210 (5th Cir. 1997); I.V. Servs. of Am., Inc. v. Inn Dev. & Mgmt., Inc., 1998 U.S. Dist. LEXIS 7776 (D. Mass. 1998); *but see* State of Connecticut v. Health Net, Inc., 2004 WL 2009481 (11th Cir. 2004)] However, an assignee of an assignee of a participant's claim lacks standing to sue on behalf of the participant. [Simon v. Value Behavioral Health, 208 F.3d 1073 (9th Cir. 2001)]

A person designated by a participant as a beneficiary as well as a participant pursuant to the terms of a plan has standing to sue under ERISA. [ERISA § 502(a); Mein v. Carus Corp, No. 00-2618 (7th Cir. 2001); O'Connell v. Kenney, No. 3:03CV0845 (D. Conn. 2003); Neuma, Inc. v. E.I. DuPont de Nemours & Co., 1998 U.S. Dist. LEXIS 9761 (N.D. Ill. 1998)] A person whose claim to be a beneficiary was denied in an earlier lawsuit has no standing to bring a later action for benefits. [Dunn v. Harris Corp., 2009 WL 2868888 (11th Cir. 2009)] A participant's estate also may sue to the same extent as the deceased participant. [Sanders v. International Soc'y for Performance Improvement, No. 97-CV-740 (D.C. 1999)] One court has ruled that an independent contractor who becomes covered under the terms of an employer's plan, while not a participant under the plan's terms, is nevertheless a beneficiary protected by ERISA. [Hollis v. Provident Life & Accident Ins. Co., 259 F.3d 410 (5th Cir. 2001)] Another court ruled that, in determining whether an individual has standing to claim ERISA's protection as a plan beneficiary, it is not necessary that the individual establish that the claim is meritorious; rather, the claim must be one that has a colorable chance of succeeding in a suit for benefits, even where the claimant has a mistaken, but reasonable, belief that the claim is meritorious. [Daniels v. Thomas & Betts Corp., 263 F.3d 66 (3d Cir. 2001)]

A participant did not have standing to bring an action against the company president for taking a distribution from the plan because the distribution was from the president's own plan account. [Cunningham v. Adams, 2004 U.S. App. LEXIS 16448 (10th Cir. 2004)]

Q 23:39 May a former participant sue a fiduciary for a personal wrong with respect to an ERISA plan?

A participant who has received all benefits due from a plan has standing to sue, even though such individual is no longer a participant or beneficiary. [Harris v. Amgen, Inc., 2009 WL 2020785 (9th Cir. 2009); Vaughn v. Bay Environmental Mgmt., Inc., 2008 WL 4276603 (9th Cir. 2008); Lanfear v. Home Depot, Inc., 2008 WL 2916390 (11th Cir. 2008); Evans v. Akers, 534 F.3d 65 (1st Cir. 2008); *In re* Mutual Funds Investment Litigation, 529 F.3d 207 (4th Cir. 2008); Bridges v. American Elec. Power Co., Inc., 498 F.3d 442 (6th Cir. 2007); Harzewski v. Guidant Corp., 489 F.3d 799 (7th Cir. 2007); Graden v. Conexant Systems, Inc., 496 F.3d 291 (3d Cir. 2007); *but see* Ericson v. Greenberg & Co.,

P.C., 2004 WL 2931048 (3d Cir. 2004), Gurecki v. Northeast Med. Assocs., P.C., No. 98-7289 (3d Cir. 1999), Crawford v. Lamantia, 34 F.3d 28 (1st Cir. 1994), Kuntz v. Reese, 785 F.2d 1410 (9th Cir. 1986), LaLonde v. Textron, Inc., 2006 U.S. Dist. LEXIS 8483 (D.R.I. 2006), and Nahigian v. Leonard, 2002 U.S. Dist. LEXIS 22815 (D. Mass. 2002)] Former employees with a colorable claim for benefits, however, are considered participants with standing to sue under ERISA. [Firestone Tire & Rubber Co. v. Bruch, 489 U.S. 101 (1989); Chastain v. AT&T, 07-6288 (10th Cir. 2009); Piazza v. EBSCO Indus., Inc., 2001 WL 1523333 (11th Cir. 2001); Waters Corp. v. Millipore Corp., 1998 U.S. App. LEXIS 6761 (1st Cir. 1998); Borowski v. International Bus. Machs. Corp., 165 F.3d 13 (2d Cir. 1998); Christensen v. Chesebrough-Pond's, Inc., 862 F. Supp. 22 (D. Conn. 1994)] Also, former employees who took early retirement based upon representations of their employer that were not truthful have standing to sue under ERISA with respect to such misrepresentations. [Mullins v. Pfizer, 899 F. Supp. 69 (D. Conn. 1995); Ogden v. Michigan Bell Tel. Co., 657 F. Supp. 328 (E.D. Mich. 1986)] See Q 23:4 for a discussion of representations concerning future benefits.

A distribution of a vested benefit to a participant after initiation of a lawsuit does not divest the participant of standing to maintain the action. [Bridges v. American Elec. Power Co., Inc., 498 F.3d 442 (6th Cir. 2007); Crotty v. Cook, 121 F.3d 541 (9th Cir. 1997); Schultz v. PLM Int'l Inc., 127 F.3d 1139 (9th Cir. 1997)] However, for purposes of ERISA Section 510, which prohibits terminating an employee for exercising a right under a plan, participant status and standing are determined at the time of the alleged ERISA breach. [McBride v. PLM Int'l, Inc., 1999 U.S. App. LEXIS 11366 (9th Cir. 1999)] A plan participant retained standing to bring a claim of breach of fiduciary duty under ERISA even after the plan was terminated and administration was taken over by PBGC (see Q 25:10), concluded another court. [Wilmington Shipping Co. v. New England Life Ins. Co., 2007 WL 2216008 (4th Cir. 2007)] An employee who never became a plan participant, but who claimed having suffered losses because of fiduciary breaches, lacked standing to sue. [Caltagirone v. NY Community Bancorp, Inc., 2007 WL 4467655 (2d Cir. 2007)] However, one court held that a plan participant had standing to sue even though he sought redress for alleged breaches committed before he commenced participation in the plan. [Braden v. Wal-Mart Stores, Inc., 2009 WL 4062105 (8th Cir. 2009)]

Under the Pension Annuitants Protection Act (PPA '94; see Q 1:18), a former participant who receives an annuity upon termination of a plan, however, has standing to sue if the purchase of the annuity violated fiduciary standards. DOL has stated that fiduciaries must justify their actions in purchasing anything other than the safest annuity available (see Q 23:19), and this applies to both defined benefit plans (see Q 2:3) and defined contribution plans (see Q 2:2). [DOL Interpretive Bull. 95-1; DOL Op. Ltr. 2002-14A] PPA (see Q 1:33) directed DOL to issue final regulations clarifying that the selection of an annuity contract as an optional form of distribution from a defined contribution plan is not subject to the safest available annuity requirement under DOL Interpretive Bull. 95-1 and is subject to all otherwise applicable fiduciary standards. The regulations are intended to clarify that the plan sponsor or other applicable plan fiduciary is required to act in accordance with the prudence standards of ERISA (see Q 23:20).

It is not intended that there be a single safest available annuity contract since the plan fiduciary must select the most prudent option specific to its plan and its participants and beneficiaries. Furthermore, it is not intended that the regulations restate all of the facts contained in DOL Interpretive Bull. 95-1. [PPA § 625]

DOL has released final regulations to comply with the PPA annuity provider selection provisions. Previously, both defined benefit and defined contribution plans were required to meet the safest available annuity standard in selecting an annuity provider to distribute benefits. The final regulations require only defined benefit plans offering an annuity option to meet the higher safest available annuity standard. [DOL Reg. § 2509.95-1]

When an individual account plan purchases an annuity from an insurer as a distribution of benefits to a participant or beneficiary, the plan's liability for the payment of those benefits is transferred to the annuity provider. The selection of an annuity provider in connection with a benefit distribution, or a benefit distribution option made available to participants and beneficiaries under the plan, is governed by the fiduciary standards. Fiduciaries must discharge their duties with respect to the plan solely in the interest of the participants and beneficiaries, and the fiduciary must act for the exclusive purpose of providing benefits to the participants and beneficiaries and defraying reasonable plan administration expenses. In addition, a fiduciary is required to act with the care, skill, prudence, and diligence under the prevailing circumstances that a prudent person acting in a like capacity and familiar with such matters would use. [ERISA § 404(a)(1)(B)]

Effective December 8, 2008, the final regulations establish a safe harbor for satisfying the fiduciary duties in selecting an annuity provider and contract for benefit distributions from an individual account plan, and set forth an optional means for satisfying these fiduciary responsibilities. The regulations do not establish minimum requirements or the exclusive means for satisfying these responsibilities. [DOL Reg. § 2550.404a-4(a)]

As a safe harbor, the selection of an annuity provider for benefit distributions from an individual account plan satisfies the prudent person standard of care requirements if the fiduciary:

1. Engages in an objective, thorough, and analytical search for the purpose of identifying and selecting providers from which to purchase annuities;

2. Appropriately considers information sufficient to assess the ability of the annuity provider to make all future payments under the annuity contract;

3. Appropriately considers the cost (including fees and commissions) of the annuity contract in relation to the benefits and administrative services to be provided under such contract;

4. Appropriately concludes that, at the time of the selection, the annuity provider is financially able to make all future payments under the annuity contract and the cost of the annuity contract is reasonable in relation to the benefits and services to be provided under the contract; and

5. If necessary, consults with an appropriate expert or experts for purposes of compliance with the foregoing requirements.[DOL Reg. § 2550.404a-4(b)]

For purposes of the foregoing requirements, the time of selection may be either (1) the time when the annuity provider and contract are selected for distribution of benefits to a specific participant or beneficiary or (2) the time when the annuity provider is selected to provide annuity contracts at future dates to participants or beneficiaries, provided that the selecting fiduciary periodically reviews the continuing appropriateness of the conclusion described in 4. above, taking into account the factors described in 2., 3., and 5. above. A fiduciary is not required to review the appropriateness of this conclusion with respect to any annuity contract purchased for any specific participant or beneficiary. [DOL Reg. § 2550.404a-4(c)]

Q 23:40   May participants asserting they were not timely paid in full claim a breach of fiduciary duty?

Courts are divided as to whether participants who have been paid in full but complain that such payments were not timely so that they were deprived of the value of the use of their benefits may seek judicial relief under ERISA. [*Compare* Clair v. Harris Trust & Sav. Bank, 190 F.3d 495 (7th Cir. 1999), Holmes v. Pension Plan of Bethlehem Steel Corp., 213 F.3d 124 (3d Cir. 2000), *and* Fotta v. Trustees of the United Mine Workers of Am., Health & Ret. Fund, 165 F.3d 209 (3d Cir. 1998) (upholding such right), *with* Walsh v. Eastman Kodak Co., 53 F. Supp. 2d 569 (W.D.N.Y. 1999), *and* Dunnigan v. Metropolitan Life Ins. Co., 2000 WL 264322 (S.D.N.Y. 2000) (denying such right); *but see* Rego v. Westvaco Corp., 2003 WL 264702 (4th Cir. 2003); Strom v. Goldman, Sachs & Co., 202 F.3d 138 (2d Cir. 1999)]

Q 23:41   May a class action be brought for an alleged ERISA violation?

Yes, in an appropriate case. Class actions by one or more representatives of a class are permitted under Rule 23 of the Federal Rules of Civil Procedure upon meeting the requirements of the rule, including (1) the class is so numerous that joinder of all members is impracticable, (2) there are questions of law or fact common to the class, (3) the claims of the representative party are typical of the class, and (4) the representative party will fairly and adequately protect the interests of the class. Also, separate actions would create a risk of inconsistent or varying results or be binding upon others similarly situated as a practical matter, or the party opposing the class has acted or refused to act on grounds generally applicable to the class, or common questions of law or fact predominate over any questions affecting only individual members so that a class action is superior to other available methods to adjudicate the controversy. The unnamed class members in a class action suit need not exhaust their administrative remedies (see Q 10:66) as a condition to being allowed to be members of the class. [*In re* Household Int'l Tax Reduction Plan, 441 F.3d 500 (7th Cir. 2006)] One court concluded that a release of claims signed by a named representative of a class action alleging breach of fiduciary duty cast doubt on the representative's ability to meet the typicality (item 3) and adequacy (item 4) requirements necessary for class certification. [*In re* Schering Plough ERISA Litig., No. 08-4814 (3d Cir. 2009)]

Typical class actions include allegations that plan fiduciaries acted imprudently in making or maintaining investments of plan assets [Donovan v. Estate of Fitzsimmons, 778 F.2d 298 (7th Cir. 1985)]; breach of plan terms [United Steelworkers of Am. v. IVACO, No. 1:01-CV-0426 (N.D. Ga. 2002)]; improper reductions in plan benefits [Garpar v. Linvatec Corp, 167 F.R.D. 51 (N.D. Ill. 1996)]; fiduciary duty to inform or avoid misinforming [Bunnion v. Consolidated Rail Corp., 1998 WL 372644 (E.D. Pa. 1998), Walsh v. Northrop Grumman Corp., 162 F.R.D. 440 (E.D.N.Y. 1995)]; claims involving interpretation of benefit provisions [Vizcaino v. Microsoft Corp., 120 F.3d 1006 (9th Cir. 1997)]; breach of fiduciary obligations in connection with the sale of plan stock below fair market value [Piazza v. EBSCO Indus., Inc., 2001 WL 1523333 (11th Cir. 2001); Sommers Drug Stores Co. Employee Profit Sharing Trust v. Corrigan Enters., Inc., 883 F.2d 345 (5th Cir. 1989)]; and claims of a class of nonvested pension participants to benefits [Morales v. Pan Am. Life Ins. Co., 914 F.2d 83 (5th Cir. 1990)]. A representative of a subclass of participants where less than all participants were damaged may sue on behalf of that subclass. [Kuper v. Lovenko, 66 F.3d 1447 (6th Cir. 1995); *see also* Milofsky v. American Airlines, Inc., No. 03-11087 (5th Cir. 2006)]

One court approved the settlement of a class action between an employer and plan participants concerning breaches of fiduciary duty with respect to the investment of plan funds in the employer's stock. The settlement included a structural change to the plan permitting greater diversification of plan investments but did not include a monetary payment to the plan or to the plan participants. [IKON Office Solutions, Inc. Sec. Litig. v. IKON, 2002 WL 1837960 (E.D. Pa. 2002)]

The United States Supreme Court has held that non-named class members who object to a proposed class settlement in a timely manner at a fairness hearing may bring an appeal without first having intervened in the action. [Devlin v. Scardelletti, 2002 WL 1270617 (U.S. 2002)]

Q 23:42   May participants sue a sponsor derivatively for delinquent contributions?

No. A plan's trustees have discretion to decide whether to sue to enforce a plan's rights; accordingly, participants have standing to sue the trustees but do not have standing to sue derivatively on behalf of the plan for delinquent contributions. [Moore v. American Fed'n of Television & Radio Artists, 216 F.3d 1236 (11th Cir. 2000)]

Q 23:43   May a plan or employer sue to redress an ERISA violation?

Courts are divided as to whether a plan, as opposed to the plan fiduciaries, may sue under ERISA. One court has permitted a plan to sue under ERISA for unpaid contributions, whereas another court dismissed a suit by a plan for breach of fiduciary duty and restitution of profits unjustly retained, concluding that the plan did not have standing to assert an ERISA violation. [Chicago Graphics Arts Health & Welfare Fund v. Jefferson Smurfit Corp., 1995 U.S. Dist. LEXIS 14228 (N.D. Ill. 1995); Pedre Co. v. Robins, 1995 U.S. Dist. LEXIS 14253 (S.D.N.Y. 1995)]

An employer acting as a fiduciary did not have standing to sue an insurance company also acting as a fiduciary when the insurance company denied a participant's claim for benefits. [Coyle & Delany Co. v. Blue Cross & Blue Shield of Va., Inc., 1996 U.S. App. LEXIS 32913 (4th Cir. 1996)]

Q 23:44   Can fiduciaries of a transferee plan sue fiduciaries of a transferor plan?

Yes. One court has held that fiduciaries of a transferee plan have standing to sue the fiduciaries of a transferor plan in connection with a breach of fiduciary duties. [Modern Woodcrafts, Inc. v. Hawley, 354 F. Supp. 1000 (D. Conn. 1982)] Another court agreed and also extended the right to sue to the purchaser of the business that sponsored the transferee plan. [Pilkington P.L.C. v. Perelman, 72 F.3d 1396 (9th Cir. 1995)] A federal common law action for restitution was also permitted where funds were mistakenly transferred from one plan to another. [State St. Bank & Trust Co. v. Denman Tire Corp., No. 00-1650 (1st Cir. 2001)]

Q 23:45   Is a jury trial available in an action against a fiduciary?

Courts have generally determined that a jury trial is not available in an action alleging breach of fiduciary duty, especially when the relief sought is equitable in nature. [Thomas v. Oregon Fruit Prod. Co., 228 F.3d 991 (9th Cir. 2000); Powers v. Montana Res. Inc., 2000 U.S. App. LEXIS 29772 (9th Cir. 2000); Adams v. Cyprus Amax Mineral Co., 149 F.3d 1156 (10th Cir. 1998); Pane v. RCA Corp., 36 F.3d 1508 (5th Cir. 1995); Houghton v. SIPCO, 38 F.3d 953 (8th Cir. 1994); Spinelli v. Gaughan, 12 F.3d 853 (9th Cir. 1993); Blake v. Union Mut. Stock Life Ins. Co. of Am., 906 F.2d 1525 (11th Cir. 1990); Chilton v. Savannah Foods & Indus., Inc., 814 F.2d 620 (11th Cir. 1986); Mein v. Pool Co. Disability Plan, 1998 U.S. Dist. LEXIS 170 (D. Colo. 1998); Richards v. General Motors Corp., 1994 U.S. Dist. LEXIS 4045 (E.D. Mich. 1994); Henley v. Lokey Oldsmobile-Countryside, Inc., 1993 U.S. Dist. LEXIS 3742 (M.D. Fla. 1993); Landry v. Air Line Pilots Ass'n, Int'l, AFL-CIO, No. 86-3196 (E.D. La. 1991); *but see* Sheet Metal Workers Local 19 v. Keystone Heating & Air Conditioning, 934 F.2d 35 (3d Cir. 1991); Algie v. RCA Global Communication, Inc., 891 F. Supp. 875 (S.D.N.Y. 1994); McDonald v. Artcraft Elec. Supply Co., 774 F. Supp. 29 (D.D.C. 1991)]

The defendants were entitled to a jury trial, concluded one court, because the claim for breach of fiduciary duty was in the nature of the legal claim for compensatory damages and not an equitable claim for restitution. The court noted that, despite the purported merger of law and equity in federal rules, the distinction remained. Applying a two-step test, the court ruled that, although breach of fiduciary duty claims were historically equitable, the trustee's claim was in the nature of a legal remedy because the defendants never possessed the funds in question and were not unjustly enriched. Since the remedy sought was legal in nature, the defendants were entitled to a jury trial. [Pereira v. Farace, Nos. 03-5053, 03-5055 (2d Cir. 2005); *see also* Great-West Life & Annuity Ins. Co. v. Knudson, 534 US 204 (2002) and Chao v. Meixner, 2007 WL 4225069 (N.D. Ga. 2007)] A jury trial was permitted in an action seeking compensatory and punitive damages against a plan administrator for failing to remit expenses allegedly covered by a plan. [*Ex parte* Met Life Ins. Co., No. 1941855 (Ala. 1996)] A jury trial was also permitted in a case alleging that an employer failed to notify an employee of a new early retirement program since the relief sought was not equitable in nature. [Mullins v. Pfizer, 899 F. Supp. 69 (D. Conn. 1995); *see also* Ellis v. Rycenga Homes, Inc., 2007 WL 1032367 (W.D. Mich. 2007)]

A jury trial may be available when an ERISA claim is combined with either a common-law or statutory claim where the plaintiff is entitled to a jury trial under the United States Constitution. [Stewart v. KHD Deutz of Am. Corp., 1996 U.S. App. LEXIS 3243 (8th Cir. 1996)]

Q 23:46 Can an ERISA claim be subject to arbitration?

Yes. ERISA does not require that ERISA claims be decided only by the courts; accordingly, arbitration clauses will be enforced as a matter of federal common law even if the dispute concerns an ERISA dispute, construction of contract language, or defenses such as alleged waiver, delay, or estoppel. [VanVels v. Betten, Sr., 2007 U.S. Dist. LEXIS 7003 (W.D. Mich. 2007); Williams v. Imhoff, 203 F.3d 758 (10th Cir. 2000); Wood v. Prudential Ins. Co. of Am., 207 F.3d 674 (3d Cir. 2000); Kramer v. Smith Barney, 1996 U.S. App. LEXIS 8861 (5th Cir. 1996); Pritzker v. Merrill Lynch Pierce Fenner & Smith, Inc., 7 F.3d 1110 (3d Cir. 1993); Bird v. Shearson Lehman/Am. Express, Inc., 926 F.2d 116 (2d Cir. 1991); Board of Trustees of the Ironworkers Local 498 Supplemental Pension Fund v. Linder, 2002 U.S. Dist. LEXIS 17403 (N.D. Ill. 2002); Bevere v. Oppenheimer & Co., 1994 U.S. Dist. LEXIS 17703 (D.N.J. 1994); Witkowski v. Welch, No. 90-0924 (E.D. Pa. 1993); Fabian Fin. Servs. v. Kurt H. Volk Inc. Profit Sharing Plan, 768 F. Supp. 728 (C.D. Cal. 1991); *but see* International Ass'n of Machinists, Dist. 10 v. Waukesha Engine Div., 17 F.3d 1994 (7th Cir. 1994); Johnson v. Francis Xavier Cabrini Hosp. of Seattle, 910 F.2d 594 (9th Cir. 1990)] In certain circumstances, arbitration may be ordered with respect to a claim against a party to an arbitration agreement while the court stays the action with regard to other defendants who are not parties to the arbitration agreement. [Schorr v. G.B. Res., 1992 WL 183392 (S.D.N.Y. 1992)]

A plan participant who sued the plan's investment advisor for breach of fiduciary duty was not bound by an arbitration clause contained in an investment management agreement that governed the relationship between the plan's trustees and the investment advisor, where the participant neither signed the agreement nor sought to enforce its terms. [Comer v. Micor, Inc., 2006 WL 231643 (9th Cir. 2006)]

Q 23:47   Can a fiduciary be liable for a breach of fiduciary duty that occurred prior to the fiduciary's appointment?

No. A fiduciary cannot be held liable for a breach of fiduciary duty that was committed prior to the fiduciary becoming a fiduciary. Although the fiduciary may not be liable for the original breach, if the fiduciary knows about the breach, the fiduciary should take steps to remedy the situation. Failure to do so may constitute a subsequent independent breach of fiduciary duty by the successor fiduciary.

Example. Sallie has no existing relationship with the plan. She negotiates an agreement to provide investment advice to the plan that will render her a fiduciary. She will not be liable for any investment decisions made prior to her becoming a fiduciary that are held to have been imprudent and, consequently, a fiduciary breach.

[ERISA § 409(b); Barker v. American Mobil Power Corp., 1995 U.S. App. LEXIS 31979 (9th Cir. 1995); Baeten v. Van Ess, 446 F. Supp. 868 (E.D. Wis. 1977); DOL Op. Ltr. 76-95]

Q 23:48   Can a fiduciary be liable for failing to act?

Yes. A breach of fiduciary duty can occur by reason of omission as well as commission. A plan administrator breached his fiduciary duty by not investing plan assets, liquidating assets only to pay benefits, not making an effort to collect obligations owed to the plan, and holding an unspecified sum of plan funds in cash at his home. [Newport v. Elms, 1992 U.S. Dist. LEXIS 9130 (E.D. La. 1992)] Investing plan assets in a money market fund was not a fiduciary breach where the fiduciary did not have sufficient information to invest the assets for individual accounts and the participants suffered no damages. [King v. National Human Res. Comm., Inc., No. 99-1313 (7th Cir. 2000)]

A fiduciary may also be liable for not investigating his suspicions that a plan was not being operated properly by other fiduciaries. [Barker v. American Mobil Power Corp., 1995 U.S. App. LEXIS 31979 (9th Cir. 1995)] Plaintiffs, however, have the burden of establishing that a loss resulted from the fiduciary's failure to act. [Silverman v. Mutual Benefit Life Ins. Co., 138 F.3d 98 (2d Cir. 1998)]

Q 23:49 Can a qualified retirement plan set off a fiduciary's liability to a plan for breach of fiduciary duty against the fiduciary's benefits from the plan?

Yes. A qualified retirement plan can set off a fiduciary's liability to a plan for breach of fiduciary duty against the fiduciary's benefits from the plan, notwithstanding ERISA's anti-alienation provision (see Qs 4:26, 4:27). [Coar v. Kazimir, 990 F.2d 1413 (3d Cir. 1993); United States v. Gaudet, No. 91-3647 (5th Cir. 1992); Friedlander v. Doherty, 851 F. Supp. 515 (N.D.N.Y. 1994)]

A participant's benefit in a qualified retirement plan may be reduced to satisfy liabilities of the participant to the plan due to (1) the participant's being convicted of committing a crime involving the plan, (2) a civil judgment (or consent order or decree) entered by a court in an action brought in connection with a violation of the fiduciary rules, or (3) a settlement agreement between DOL or PBGC (see Q 23:51) and the participant in connection with a violation of the fiduciary rules. The court order establishing such liability must require that the participant's benefit in the plan be applied to satisfy the liability. If the participant is married at the time the benefit is offset to satisfy the liability, spousal consent (see Q 10:21) to such offset is required unless the spouse is also required to pay an amount to the plan in the judgment, order, decree, or settlement or the judgment, order, decree, or settlement provides a joint and 50 percent survivor annuity for the spouse (see Q 10:8). [ERISA §§ 206(d)(4), 206(d)(5); I.R.C. §§ 401(a)(13)(C), 401(a)(13)(D)]

Q 23:50 Can retirement benefits be waived to settle a potential suit?

Yes. ERISA's anti-alienation provision (see Qs 4:26, 4:27) does not prohibit a knowing and voluntary waiver of benefits by a former trustee in connection with a settlement agreement concerning a potential claim against the trustee. [Rhoades v. Casey, 1999 WL 1037798 (5th Cir. 1999)]

Q 23:51 Does DOL impose a penalty for breaches of fiduciary duty?

Yes. DOL imposes a penalty of 20 percent of the amount payable for breaches of fiduciary duties (or knowing participation therein), pursuant to a court order or settlement agreement with DOL. DOL may waive or reduce the penalty if the fiduciary or other person (1) acted responsibly and in good faith or (2) will not otherwise be able to restore all plan losses without severe financial hardship. [ERISA § 502(*l*); Rodrigues v. Herman, 121 F.3d 1352 (9th Cir. 1997); Huffer v. Herman, 2001 WL 345455 (S.D. Ohio 2001); Citywide Bank of Denver v. Herman, 1997 U.S. Dist. LEXIS 15067 (D. Colo. 1997)] A settlement by a fiduciary with DOL does not prohibit a beneficiary from later suing for the same wrong, nor does a resolution of a claim by a beneficiary against a fiduciary bar DOL from proceeding against the fiduciary on the same facts. [Herman v. South Carolina Nat'l Bank, 140 F.3d 1413 (11th Cir. 1998); Jackson v. Truck Drivers' Union Local 42 Health & Welfare Fund, 933 F. Supp. 1124 (D. Mass. 1996)]

An excise tax is imposed on entity managers who knowingly approve prohibited tax shelter transactions. If any entity manager of a tax-exempt entity approves the entity as (or otherwise causes the entity to be) a party to a prohibited tax shelter transaction at any time during the taxable year, and the entity manager knows, or has reason to know, that the transaction is a prohibited tax shelter transaction, the entity manager must pay an excise tax for the taxable year. The amount of the tax imposed on an entity manager who approves the entity as a party to a prohibited tax shelter transaction is $20,000 for each approval (or other act causing participation). The term "tax-exempt entity" includes a qualified retirement plan.

In general, a person who decides that the assets of the plan are to be invested in a prohibited tax shelter transaction is the entity manager. Except for a self-directed account plan (see Q 23:14), a participant or beneficiary generally is not an entity manager. For example, a participant or beneficiary is not an entity manager merely by reason of choosing among pre-selected investment options. Depending on the circumstances, the person who is responsible for determining the pre-selected investment options may be an entity manager.

The excise tax is effective for taxable years ending after May 17, 2006 (with respect to transactions occurring before, on, and after May 17, 2006), except that no excise tax applied to income or proceeds that were properly allocable to any period on or before the date which was 90 days after May 17, 2006.

[I.R.C. § 4965]

IRS issued a notice to ensure that qualified retirement plans and other tax-exempt entities and other affected parties are aware of the new excise taxes and disclosure rules that target certain potentially abusive tax shelter transactions to which a tax-exempt entity is a party. [IRS Notice 2006-65, 2006-2 C.B. 102] In addition, IRS issued final regulations that became effective on July 6, 2010. See Q 1:31 for details.

Q 23:52   Can plan officials correct fiduciary breaches and avoid DOL penalties?

Yes. A plan fiduciary, plan sponsor, party in interest (see Q 24:3), or other person in a position to correct a breach may avoid assessment of civil penalties under ERISA Section 502(1) for possible breaches of fiduciary duties by correcting such breaches and reporting them to DOL's Employee Benefits Security Administration (EBSA) pursuant to EBSA's Voluntary Fiduciary Correction Program (VFC Program). DOL has expanded and simplified its original VFC Program; and, for a detailed discussion of the VFC Program, see Qs 19:36 through 19:50.

Q 23:53   Can a nonfiduciary be held liable for a breach of fiduciary duty?

Yes. Claims for restitution, as opposed to monetary damages, against nonfiduciary parties in interest (see Q 24:3) are permitted under ERISA. [Harris Trust & Sav. Bank v. Salomon Smith Barney, Inc., 530 U.S. 238 (2000); Landwehr v. Du-Pree, 72 F.3d 726 (9th Cir. 1995); DeLaurentis v. Job-Shop Technical Servs., Inc., 1996 U.S. Dist. LEXIS 593 (E.D.N.Y. 1996); Carpenters Local Union No. 64 Pension Fund v. Silverman, 1995 U.S. Dist. LEXIS 8663 (S.D.N.Y. 1995)] ERISA does not authorize suits by plan participants for money damages against nonfiduciaries who knowingly participate in a fiduciary's breach of fiduciary duty. [Mertens v. Hewitt Assocs., 508 U.S. 248 (1993); Buckley Dement, Inc. v. Travelers Plan Adm'rs of Ill., Inc., 39 F.3d 784 (7th Cir. 1994); Slice v. Sons of Norway, No. 93-2301 (8th Cir. 1994); Reich v. Rowe, 20 F.3d 25 (1st Cir. 1994); Colleton Reg'l Hosp. v. M.R.S. Med. Review Sys., Inc., 866 F. Supp. 896 (D.S.C. 1994); Blevins Screw Prods., Inc. v. Prudential Bache Sec., Inc., 835 F. Supp. 984 (E.D. Mich. 1993)]

The DOL 20 percent penalty tax (see Q 23:51) may be imposed against nonfiduciaries. Nonfiduciaries may be liable for participating in a prohibited transaction (see Q 24:3). [Herman v. South Carolina Nat'l Bank, 140 F.3d 1413 (11th Cir. 1998); Reich v. Compton, 1995 U.S. App. LEXIS 13619 (3d Cir. 1995)]

Q 23:54   Can individuals controlling a fiduciary be jointly and severally liable for a fiduciary's breach of duty?

Yes, on the theory that the controlling individual is responsible for the fiduciary's actions. [Lowen v. Tower Asset Mgmt., Inc., 829 F.2d 1209 (2d Cir. 1987); *but see* Confer v. Custom Eng'g Co., 952 F.2d 34 (3d Cir. 1991)] A nonfiduciary insurance company was not liable for breach of fiduciary duty by its soliciting agent, admittedly a fiduciary, where the agent acted outside the scope of his employment without the knowledge or participation of the insurance company. [Kral, Inc. v. Southwestern Life Ins. Co., 1993 U.S. App. LEXIS 20656 (5th Cir. 1993)]

Q 23:55   Can fiduciaries be liable for the actions of their agents who are not fiduciaries?

Yes. [Taylor v. Peoples Natural Gas Co., 49 F.3d 982 (3d Cir. 1995)] Such liability may be determined under a federal common law of agency rule of imputing the knowledge of an agent to its principal. [Steinberg v. Mikkelsen, 1995 U.S. Dist. LEXIS 15588 (E.D. Wis. 1995)]

Q 23:56   Can a nonfiduciary be liable on a rationale outside of ERISA?

Yes. A depository and custodial agent or plan administrator who was not an ERISA fiduciary may be liable for breach of common law fiduciary obligations, breach of an implied covenant of good faith and fair dealing, negligence, and common law fraud under traditional theories not preempted by ERISA (see Qs 23:10, 23:57). [Arizona State Carpenters Pension Trust Fund v. Citibank (Ariz.), 1997 U.S. App. LEXIS 23587 (9th Cir. 1997); Mornstein v. National Ins. Servs., Inc., 93 F.3d 715 (11th Cir. 1996); Skilstaf, Inc. v. Adminitron, 6 F. Supp. 2d 1210 (M.D. Ala. 1999); Zandi-Dulabi v. Pacific Ret. Plans Inc., 1993 U.S. Dist. LEXIS 8700 (N.D. Cal. 1993); *but see* Garren v. John Hancock Mut. Life Ins. Co., 1997 U.S.App. LEXIS 13598 (11th Cir. 1997)] See Q 23:11 concerning the obligations of nonfiduciary service providers.

One court concluded that plan trustees were able to sustain an action against the plan's actuary even though the actuary was not a plan fiduciary because ERISA does not preempt "run-of-the-mill" state law professional negligence claims against nonfiduciaries. [Gerosa v. Savasta & Co., 329 F.3d 317 (2d Cir. 2003); *see also* Penny/Ohlmann/Nieman, Inc. v. Miami Valley Pension Corp., 399 F.3d 692 (6th Cir. 2005); Milkis Enterprises, Inc. v. Retirement Plan Consultants, 2005 WL 913087 (E.D. Pa. 2005)] Another court concluded that ERISA did not preempt state law misrepresentation and negligence claims brought against a nonfiduciary life insurance company and a provider of a fully insured plan (see Q 23:57). [Hausmann v. Union Bank of California, N.A., 2009 WL 1325810 (D.C. Cal. 2009); *see also* Patel v. Pacific Life Ins. Co., 2009 WL 1456526 (__.D. Tex. 2009)]

Q 23:57   Can an ERISA claim be barred by state law?

No. ERISA contains a preemption section providing that, with certain exceptions, ERISA supersedes ". . . any and all State laws insofar as they may now or hereafter relate to any employee benefit plan . . ." regulated thereunder. [ERISA § 514; Dudley Supermarket, Inc. v. Transamerica Life Ins. & Annuity Co., 302 F.3d 1 (1st Cir. 2002); Hollis v. Provident Life & Accident Ins. Co., 259 F.3d 410 (5th Cir. 2001); Central States, Southeast & Southwest Areas Pension Fund v. Howell, 227 F.3d 672 (6th Cir. 2000); Michelin Tire Corp v. Trustees of the Warehouse Employees Union Local 169 & Employers Joint Pension Plan, No. 96-1354 (3d Cir. 1999); Commonwealth Edison Co. v. Vega, 174 F.3d 870 (7th Cir. 1999)]

ERISA accordingly generally supersedes state statutory and case law concerning trusts, tort, and contract law, although general principles of such law often form the basis of a federal common law under ERISA. [Tucker v. Shreveport Transit Mgmt. Inc. Sportran 401(k) Plan Inc., No. 99-30219 (5th Cir. 2000); Best Int'l U.S.A. v. Tucker & Clark, No. 3:99-CV-1556 (N.D. Tex. 2000)] ERISA preempted a state law that revoked an ex-spouse's status as a beneficiary on the dissolution of the marriage because the state statute had an impermissible connection with the plan by binding administrators to a particular choice of rules for determining beneficiary status. [Egelhoff v. Egelhoff, 532 U.S. 141 (2001)] ERISA also may preempt state law discrimination claims. [Wood v. Prudential Ins. Co. of Am., 207 F.3d 674 (3d Cir. 2000)] The purpose of preemption is to encourage employers to adopt plans by standardizing regulatory requirements applicable to plan administration. [Grahm v. Balcor Co., 146 F.3d 1052 (9th Cir. 1998)]

State law claims by plan participants against plan attorneys for excessive compensation were preempted by ERISA since such attorneys were parties in interest (see Q 24:3) although not fiduciaries so that such claims would constitute prohibited transactions (see Q 24:1). [Rutledge v. Seyfarth, Shaw, Fairweather & Geraldson, 2000 WL 16550 (9th Cir. 2000)]

State laws regulating insurance, banking, securities, and generally applicable criminal law are exceptions to ERISA preemption. [ERISA §§ 514(b)(2), 514(b)(4); UNUM Life Ins. Co. of Am. v. Ward, 526 U.S. 358 (1999); *but see* Smith v. Provident Bank, 170 F.3d 609 (6th Cir. 1999)] ERISA also did not preempt state law claims for fraud and breach of contract arising from a legal settlement between an employer and an employee as opposed to the employer's administration of the plan. [Brokaski v. Delco Sys. Operations, 2000 WL 222616 (9th Cir. 2000)] Another ruled that ERISA did not preempt a state breach of fiduciary claim against a majority shareholder brought by an ESOP (see Q 28:1), which was a minority shareholder. [Hoeppner v. Jens Howard Elec. Co., 2002 Ohio App. LEXIS 5982 (10th Dist. 2002)] State law claims for fraud, misrepresentation, breach of contract, or negligence may not have a sufficient connection to a plan or its administration to be preempted. [Patel v. Pacific Life Ins. Co., 2009 WL 1456526 (__.D. Tex. 2009); Hausmann v. Union Bank of California, N.A., 2009 WL 1325810 (D.C. Cal. 2009); Thrailkill v. Amsted Indus., No. 99-4244-CV-C-5 (W.D. Mich. 2000); ANB Bankcorp, Inc. v. Equitable Life Assurance Soc'y of the United States, No. 99-CV-469-K (N.D. Okla. 2000); Swanson v. Liquid Sugars, Inc., No. 99-4903 (N.D. Cal. 2000); Analytical Surveys, Inc. v. Intercare Health Plans, Inc., No. IP 99-1422 (S.D. Ind. 2000); *see also* E.I. DuPont de Nemours & Co. v. Sawyer, No. 06-20865 (5th Cir. 2008)]

Q 23:58   May a fiduciary be held liable for breaches committed by a co-fiduciary?

Yes, if the fiduciary:

1. Knowingly participates in or tries to conceal a co-fiduciary's breach;
2. Enables a co-fiduciary to commit a breach by failing to meet the fiduciary's specific responsibilities; or
3. Knowing of a co-fiduciary's breach, fails to make a reasonable effort to remedy it. [ERISA § 405(a)]

Example. Ben and Jason are co-trustees. The trust specifies that they cannot invest in commodity futures. If Ben suggests to Jason that he invest part of the plan assets in commodity futures and Jason does so, both Ben and Jason may be held personally liable for any losses sustained by the plan. Similarly, if Jason invests in commodity futures and tells Ben about it, Ben could be held personally liable for any losses if he conceals the investment or fails to make a reasonable effort to correct it.

The co-fiduciary may be liable for failing to perform the co-fiduciary's fiduciary duties, even if the co-fiduciary is not aware of the other fiduciary's breach. [Russo v. Unger, 1991 WL 254570 (S.D.N.Y. 1991)] Fiduciaries may also be liable where, by not following the procedures set forth in the plan, they enable a co-fiduciary to embezzle plan assets. [Silverman v. Mutual Benefit Life Ins. Co., 138 F.3d 98 (2d Cir. 1998); Mazur v. Gaudet, 826 F. Supp. 188 (E.D. La. 1992)]

Q 23:59   What should a fiduciary do if a co-fiduciary commits a breach of duty?

The fiduciary must try to remedy the breach. For example, if an improper investment was made, the fiduciary might consider disposing of the asset. Alternatively, the fiduciary might notify the company of the breach, institute a lawsuit against the co-fiduciary, or bring the matter before DOL. The fiduciary's resignation as a protest against the breach, without making reasonable efforts to prevent it, will not relieve the fiduciary of liability. [ERISA § 405(a)(3); DOL Reg. § 2509.75-5] A fiduciary may not be liable for the theft of assets by a co-fiduciary if there is no evidence that the assets could be recovered. [Silverman v. Mutual Benefit Life Ins. Co., 138 F.3d 98 (2d Cir. 1998)] A fiduciary may also remain liable after an effective resignation if the fiduciary fails to make adequate provision for the continued prudent management of plan assets. [Ream v. Frey, 1997 U.S. App. LEXIS 2649 (3d Cir. 1997)]

Q 23:60   Can a breaching fiduciary obtain contribution or indemnity from other breaching co-fiduciaries?

There is a split among the courts as to whether there is a right of contribution or indemnity among fiduciaries in plans governed by ERISA so that a passive trustee can seek indemnification from an active trustee. Some cases hold that no such right exists. [Call v. Sumitomo Bank of Cal., 881 F.2d 626 (9th Cir. 1989); Kim v. Fujikawa, 871 F.2d 1427 (9th Cir. 1989); Meoli v. American Med. Servs. of San Diego, No. 97 CV 1222 (S.D. Cal. 1999); Roberts v. Taussig, 39 F. Supp. 2d 1010 (N.D. Ohio 1999); Physicians Healthchoice, Inc. v. Trustees of the Auto. Employee Benefit Trust, 764 F. Supp. 1360 (__.D. Mich. 1991)]

Other cases, however, hold that a fiduciary's right to seek contribution and indemnity is a fundamental principle of the law governing trusts and that those remedies should be incorporated into a federal common law of ERISA. [Smith v. Local 819 IBT Pension Plan, 2002 WL 1020724 (2d Cir. 2002); Chemung Canal Trust Co. v. Sovran Bank/Md., 939 F.2d 12 (2d Cir. 1991); Free v. Briody, 732 F.2d 1331 (7th Cir. 1984); Green v. Wm. Mason & Co., No. 96-1730 (D.N.J. 1997); Youngberg v. Bekins Co., No. S-95-896LKK (E.D. Cal. 1996); Duncan v. Santaniello, 1995 U.S. Dist. LEXIS 14381 (D. Mass. 1995); Cohen v. Baker, 1994 U.S. Dist. LEXIS 1595 (E.D. Pa. 1994); Maher v. Strachan Shipping Co., 817 F. Supp. 43 (E.D. La. 1993), rev'd on other grounds, 1995 U.S. App. LEXIS 32042 (5th Cir. 1995)] Such federal common law would include a system of proportional fault among fiduciaries. [In re Masters, Mates & Pilots Pension Plan & IRAP Litig., 957 F.2d 1020 (2d Cir. 1993)]

A right of contribution under ERISA may also have been endorsed by implication in a decision of the United States Supreme Court that resolved a conflict among the circuits by holding that defendants in an action under Section 10(b) of the Securities Exchange Act of 1934 have a right to contribution as a matter of federal law. [Musick, Peeler & Garrett v. Employers Ins. of Wausau, No. 92-34 (U.S. 1993)]

Q 23:61 Does ERISA authorize punitive or extra-contractual damages to a beneficiary for breach of fiduciary duty?

No. The United States Supreme Court has held that punitive damages are not available to a beneficiary in an action against the plan fiduciary for an alleged breach of fiduciary duty where the alleged breach was the untimely processing of the beneficiary's claim for benefits. Remedies available to the beneficiary in such instances would include only recovery of the benefits owed, clarification of the beneficiary's right to present or future benefits, or removal of the breaching fiduciary. [Massachusetts Mut. Life Ins. Co. v. Russell, 473 U.S. 134 (1985)] Extra-contractual compensatory damages are also not available in a suit against a fiduciary under ERISA. [Helfrich v. PNC Bank, Ky., Inc., No. 00-5148 (6th Cir. 2001); Glencoe v. Teachers Ins. & Annuity Ass'n of Am., No. 99-2417 (4th Cir. 2000); Rogers v. Hartford Life & Accident Ins. Co., 1999 WL 68260 (5th Cir. 1999); Nero v. Industrial Molding Corp., 1999 WL 68258 (5th Cir. 1999); Shih v. Commercial Ass'n for Sec. & Health, 809 F. Supp. 80 (D. Colo. 1992)]

However, the Supreme Court expressly left open certain issues—for instance, whether a plan, as opposed to a participant or beneficiary, could recover punitive damages and whether a participant or beneficiary could recover such damages when the injurious conduct was not a breach of fiduciary duty but a violation of other sections of ERISA or of the terms of the plan. Most courts since the *Russell* decision have concluded that punitive or extra-contractual damages under such circumstances are similarly unavailable under ERISA. [Millsap v. McDonnell Douglas Corp., No. 03-5124 (10th Cir. 2004); Farr v. US W. Communications, Inc., 151 F.3d 908 (9th Cir. 1998); Fraser v. Lintas: Campbell-Ewald, 56 F.3d 722 (6th Cir. 1995); Medina v. Anthem Life Ins. Co., 1993 U.S. App. LEXIS 1317 (5th Cir. 1993); Lafoy v. HMO Colo., 988 F.2d 97 (10th Cir. 1993); Novak v. Andersen Corp., 962 F.2d 757 (8th Cir. 1992); Harsch v. Eisenberg, 956 F.2d 651 (7th Cir. 1992); McRae v. Seafarers' Welfare Plan, 920 F.2d 819 (11th Cir. 1991); Reinking v. Philadelphia Am. Life Ins. Co., 910 F.2d 1210 (4th Cir. 1990); Drinkwater v. Met Life Ins. Co., 846 F.2d 821 (1st Cir. 1988); Bone v. Association Mgmt. Servs., Inc., 632 F. Supp. 493 (S.D. Miss. 1986); *but see Ex parte* Met Life Ins. Co., No. 1941855 (Ala. 1996); D'Amore v. Stangle & Denigris Inc., 1995 U.S. Dist. LEXIS 18313 (D. Conn. 1995); California Digital Defined Benefit Pension Plan v. Union Bank, 705 F. Supp. 489 (C.D. Cal. 1989)]

One court concluded that a fiduciary could recover punitive damages from another fiduciary who was guilty of malicious conduct. [Ampere Auto. Corp. v. Employee Benefit Plans, Inc., No. 92 C 2580 (N.D. Ill. 1993)] Another court upheld an arbitrator's award of punitive damages in favor of a plan against its investment manager, although acknowledging that the arbitrator may have misinterpreted applicable law. [Shearson Lehman Bros. v. Neurosurgical Assocs. of Ind., 1995 U.S. Dist. LEXIS 12161 (S.D. Ind. 1995)]

Q 23:62 Does ERISA authorize the recovery of attorneys' fees, costs, and interest?

Yes. A court may, in its discretion, award reasonable attorneys' fees and costs to a prevailing party in an action by a participant, beneficiary, or fiduciary. [ERISA § 502(g)(1)] However, the United States Supreme Court has ruled that, in an ERISA action, there is no requirement that a litigant be the prevailing party in order to be awarded attorneys' fees and costs. The court concluded that the claimant was entitled to an award where she had achieved some degree of success on the merits of her case. [Hardt v. Reliance Standard Life Ins. Co., 130 S. Ct. 2149 (2010)]

Courts have examined the following five factors in deciding whether to award fees and costs, not all of which must be present to justify an award:

- Opponent's culpability or bad faith
- Opponent's ability to pay
- Deterrent effect on others in similar circumstances
- Whether action benefited all plan participants or the plan as a whole
- Relative merits of parties' positions

[Reilly v. Charles M. Brewer Ltd. Money Purchase Pension Plan, No. 08-16750 (9th Cir. 2009); Bauer Mechanical, Inc. v. Joint Arbitration Bd. of Plumbing, 562 F.3d 784 (7th Cir. 2009); Cromer-Tyler v. Teitel, 2008 WL 4335938 (11th Cir. 2008); Starr v. Metro Systems, Inc., 461 F.3d 1036 (8th Cir. 2006); Moon v. UNUM Provident Corp., 461 F.3d 639 (6th Cir. 2006); Pease v. Hartford Life and Accident Ins. Co., 449 F.3d 435 (2d Cir. 2006); Stark v. PPM America, 354 F.3d 666 (7th Cir. 2004); Lowe v. McGraw-Hill Cos., Inc., 361 F.3d 335 (7th Cir. 2004); Seitzman v. Sun Life Assurance Co. of Can., Inc., 311 F.3d 477 (2d Cir. 2002); Mizzell v. Provident Life & Accident Ins. Co., 2002 WL 461715 (9th Cir. 2002); Johannssen v. District No. 1—Pac. Coast Dist., MEBA Pension Plan, 292 F.3d 159 (4th Cir. 2002); Fritcher v. Health Care Serv. Corp., 301 F.3d 811 (7th Cir. 2002); Hess v. Hartford Life & Accident Ins. Co., 274 F.3d 456 (7th Cir. 2001); White v. Sundstrand Corp., 256 F.3d 580 (7th Cir. 2001); Riley v. Administrator of the Supersaver 401k Capital Accumulation Plan for Employees of Participating AMR Corp. Subsidiaries, 209 F.3d 780 (5th Cir. 2000); Schwartz v. Gregori, 1998 WL 801361 (6th Cir. 1998); Denzler v. Questech, Inc., No. 94-2109 (4th Cir. 1996); Eddy v. Colonial Life Ins. Co. of Am., 59 F.3d 201 (D.C. Cir. 1995); McPherson v. Employees' Pension Plan of Am. Re-Insurance Co., 1994 U.S. App. LEXIS 22777 (3d Cir. 1994); Commercial Elec., Inc. v. IBEW Local 1168, No. 92-15268 (9th Cir. 1993); Meredith v. Navistar Int'l Transp. Co., 935 F.2d 124 (7th Cir. 1991); Eaves v. Penn, 587 F.2d 453 (10th Cir. 1978); Depenbrock v. Cigna Corp., No. 01-6161 (E.D. Pa. 2004); Surgical Consultants, P.C. v. Division 1181 ATU, 1999 U.S. Dist. LEXIS 14611 (E.D.N.Y. 1999); Hylaszek v. Aetna Life Ins. Co., 1999 U.S. Dist. LEXIS 16165 (N.D. Ill. 1999); Cunningham v. Gibson Elec. Co., 1999 U.S. Dist. LEXIS 12408 (N.D. Ill. 1999); Maryland Elec. Indus. Health Fund v. Triangle Sign & Serv. Div. of Lok-Tite Indus., Inc., 1993 U.S. Dist. LEXIS 2606 (D. Md. 1993); St. Laurent v. New Haven Terminal, Inc., 1993 U.S. Dist. LEXIS 17331 (D. Conn. 1993); Lanning v.

Maxwell, 1992 U.S. Dist. LEXIS 14089 (D. Kan. 1992); Ursic v. Bethlehem Mines, 719 F.2d 670 (3d Cir. 1983)]

The seventh circuit stands alone in applying not only the five-factor test but also a test based on whether the party against whom fees is sought had substantial justification for its position. [Herman v. Central States, Southeast and Southwest Areas Pension Fund, 423 F.3d 684 (7th Cir. 2005)] One court concluded that the first and fifth factors so strongly militated against a fee award that it did not consider the other three factors. [DiGiacomo v. Teamsters Pension Trust Fund of Phila. and Vicinity, 2005 WL 3048719 (3d Cir. 2005)] On the other hand, an appeals court held that the lower court had abused its discretion in awarding fees to a prevailing fiduciary where the lower court addressed only three factors and omitted any analysis of the third and fourth factors. [Mid Atlantic Medical Services, LLC v. Sereboff, 407 F.3d 212 (4th Cir. 2005)] Similarly, where a court considered only two of the five factors, a higher court remanded the matter to the lower court for reconsideration, with instructions to consider all five factors. [Toy v. Plumbers & Pipefitters Local Union No. 74 Pension Plan, 2009 WL 692398 (3d Cir. 2009)]

An attorney's fee award of $45,000 was upheld, even though the plan benefits recovered by the claimant as a result of the litigation were approximately $650. The plan sponsor's argument that the disproportionate size of the award was punitive and invalid was rejected, and the court ruled that fees need not be proportional to the amount recovered to be reasonable. [Tomasko v. Ira H. Weinstock, P.C. No. 08-4673 (3d Cir. 2009)] Similarly, in an action by three multiemployer plans (see Q 29:2) to recover approximately $2,000 of delinquent contributions, an attorney's fee award of approximately $51,000 was approved. [Anderson v. AB Painting and Sandblasting Inc., 578 F.3d 542 (7th Cir. 2009)]

One court concluded that an insurer's initial offer to settle a benefit claim, which was rejected by the claimant, did not bar the claimant from requesting attorney fees after the insurer litigated the full claim in court. [Kamlet v. Hartford Life and Accident Ins. Co., 2006 U.S. App. LEXIS 10976 (11th Cir. 2006)]

In one case, a prevailing defendant's claim for fees was rejected because it was not sought on a timely basis. [Bender v. Freed, 2006 WL 240562 (7th Cir. 2006)] In another case, where the plaintiff was awarded fees, the plan, on appeal, contended that the lower court had failed to apply the five-factor test. The plan lost its appeal because the court determined that the plan waived the argument by failing to mention the test in its one-sentence objection to plaintiff's fee application. [Gorman v. Carpenters' & Millwrights' Health Benefit Trust Fund, 410 F.3d 1194 (10th Cir. 2005)]

The trial court may also award simple or compound prejudgment interest. [Skrevedt v. E.I. DuPont de Nemours & Co., 2006 U.S. Dist. LEXIS 89411 (D. Del. 2006); Skrevedt v. E.I. DuPont de Nemours & Co., Nos. 02-3620, 02-4283 (3d Cir. 2004); Parke v. First Reliance Standard Life Ins. Co., 368 F.3d 999 (8th Cir. 2004); Mary Helen Coal Corp. v. Hudson, No. 99-2181 (4th Cir. 2000); Fotta v. Trustees of the United Mine Workers of Am., 165 F.3d 209 (3d Cir. 1998); Russo v. Unger, 845 F. Supp. 124 (S.D.N.Y. 1994)] It may not, however, grant an award based on the plan's actual rate of return. [Holmes v. Pension Plan of Bethlehem Steel Corp., 213 F.3d 124 (3d Cir. 2000)] Also, it should not look to state laws concerning prejudgment interest and attorneys' fees. [Ford v. Uniroyal Pension Plan, 154 F.3d 613 (6th Cir. 1998); see Q 23:57] Where a participant brought a successful breach of fiduciary duty claim against a plan's trustee, a court concluded that the participant was not entitled to prejudgment interest on the plan's losses because the breaches did not result in the trustee's unjust enrichment. [White v. Martin, 2003 U.S. Dist. LEXIS 15785 (D. Minn. 2003)]

In a successful suit by a fiduciary to recover delinquent contributions, a court awarded attorneys' fees that it considered mandatory, not discretionary, under ERISA Section 502(g)(2), as opposed to ERISA Section 502(g)(1) governing fees to a party prevailing in a suit alleging breach of a fiduciary duty. [Northwest Adm'rs v. Albertson's, 1996 U.S. App. LEXIS 33640 (9th Cir. 1996)] ERISA Section 502(g)(1) provides for recovery of attorney's fees and costs incurred in an action brought under ERISA. However, because the retirees were seeking reimbursement of expenses incurred while recovering benefits in a bankruptcy court under the bankruptcy code, and *not* under ERISA, their attempt to recover under ERISA Section 502(g)(1) was without merit, ruled one court. [Michaels v. Breedlove, 2004 WL 2806519 (3d Cir. 2004)]

A plan prevailed in a suit brought by a participant for increased benefits and was awarded a judgment for attorney's fees; however, the plan was not permitted to satisfy the judgment from the participant's plan benefits because of the anti-alienation rule (see Q 9:25). [Martorana v. The Bd. of Trustees of Steamfitters Local Union 420 Health, Welfare and Pension Fund, 404 F.3d 797 (3d Cir. 2005)] In another case, a plan trustee that filed an interpleader action to determine the beneficiary of a deceased participant's benefits, but became involved in years of litigation with several defendants, was not entitled to attorney fees because it acted in bad faith throughout the case. [First Trust Corp. v. Bryant, 410 F.3d 842 (6th Cir. 2005)]

ERISA permits benefit plans to indemnify fiduciaries and third-party administrators for attorneys' fees in cases in which the parties settle before the fiduciaries' liability is judicially determined, concluded one court. [Martinez v. Barasch, 2006 U.S. App. LEXIS 6914 (S.D.N.Y. 2006)]

Q 23:63   What method is used to calculate reasonable attorneys' fees?

The "lodestar/multiplier" method has been used to determine reasonable attorneys' fees. The lodestar is a reasonable hourly rate multiplied by the number of hours reasonably spent on the case. The multiplier is then applied to increase or decrease the lodestar amount on the basis of other relevant factors, including whether the attorneys had a sure source of compensation for their services, but not whether the attorneys had a contingent fee arrangement. [Hensley v. Eckerhart, 461 U.S. 424 (1983); Van Gerwen v. Guarantee Mut. Life Co., 214 F.3d 1041 (9th Cir. 2000); Brytus v. Spang & Co., 203 F.3d 238 (3d Cir. 2000); McElwaine v. US W., Inc., 176 F.3d 1167 (9th Cir. 1999); Florin v. Nationsbank of Ga., 1994 U.S. App. LEXIS 24337 (7th Cir. 1994); D'Emanuele v.

Montgomery Ward & Co., 904 F.2d 1379 (9th Cir. 1990); Adams v. Bowater, Inc., 2004 U.S. Dist. LEXIS 9247 (D. Me. 2004)]

One court awarded fees based on a decreasing percentage scale depending on the recovery obtained. [Cooper v. The IBM Personal Pension Plan, 2005 U.S. Dist. LEXIS 17071 (S.D. Ill. 2005)]

Q 23:64   Can attorneys' fees be denied to a prevailing party?

Yes. Attorneys' fees may be denied after trial even if the complaining party is successful. [Janeiro v. Urological Surgery Professional Assn., 457 F.3d 130 (1st Cir. 2006); Leyda v. AlliedSignal, Inc., 2003 WL 55876 (2d Cir. 2003); Gard v. Blakenburg, 2002 WL 261817 (6th Cir. 2002); Central States, Southeast & Southwest Areas Pension Fund v. Hunt Truck Lines, Inc., 272 F.3d 1000 (7th Cir. 2001); Sheldon Co. Profit-Sharing Plan & Trust v. Smith, 1995 U.S. App. LEXIS 20708 (6th Cir. 1995); Administrative Committee of the Wal-Mart Stores, Inc. Plan v. Varco, 2004 U.S. Dist. LEXIS 12174 (N.D. Ill. 2004)]

Q 23:65   Can attorneys' fees be awarded although not all requested relief is granted?

Yes. Attorneys' fees may be awarded although not all relief requested is granted or when substantive issues are settled out of court. [Freeman v. Continental Ins. Co., No. 92-8316 (11th Cir. 1993); Spain v. Aetna Life Ins. Co., 1993 U.S. App. LEXIS 33975 (9th Cir. 1993); Caruthers v. Procter & Gamble, 1998 U.S. Dist. LEXIS 1250 (D. Kan. 1998); Alba v. Upjohn Co, 1997 U.S. Dist. LEXIS 3448 (D. Mass. 1997)] Attorneys' fees were awarded to a defendant where the plaintiff withdrew his ERISA claim before trial. [McNaboc v. NVF Co., 2002 U.S. Dist. LEXIS 21287 (D. Del. 2002)]

Also, attorneys' fees can be awarded in suits seeking injunctive relief and not monetary damages. [Cefali v. Buffalo Brass Co., No. 87-102L (W.D.N.Y. 1990)]

Q 23:66   Can attorneys' fees be awarded in proportion to the success of a prevailing party?

Yes. Attorneys' fees may also be awarded in proportion to the success of the prevailing party so that if a plaintiff sued to redress two wrongs and received relief on only one, a court could award half of the plaintiff's fees. [Christian v. DuPont-Waynesboro Health Care Plan, 1998 U.S. Dist. LEXIS 9343 (W.D. Va. 1998)]

Q 23:67   Can attorneys' fees be awarded to a defendant when the court determines that it lacked jurisdiction or that ERISA did not apply?

No. Attorneys' fees may not be awarded to a defendant prevailing on an argument that the court lacked jurisdiction to hear the dispute because the court would then also have no jurisdiction to award such fees. [In re Knight, 207 F.3d

1115 (9th Cir. 2000); Cliburn v. Police Jury Ass'n, 165 F.3d 315 (5th Cir. 1999)] By the same reasoning, a court concluded that a party who succeeded in defeating a claim that ERISA applied to a transaction was not entitled to attorneys' fees under ERISA for defending the claim. [Frosco v. Pyramid Cos. III, 2001 U.S. App. LEXIS 815 (2d Cir. 2000)]

Q 23:68   Can attorneys' fees be awarded for administrative proceedings?

Courts are divided as to whether attorneys' fees are recoverable for administrative proceedings. [*Compare* Kahane v. UNUM Life Ins. Co. of America, 2009 WL 805817 (11th Cir. 2009), Hahnemann University Hospital v. All Shore, Inc., 514 F.3d 300 (3d Cir. 2008), Parke v. First Reliance Standard Life Ins. Co., 368 F.3d 999 (8th Cir. 2004), Peterson v. Continental Cas. Co., 282 F.3d 112 (2d Cir. 2002), Anderson v. Procter & Gamble Co., 220 F.3d 449 (6th Cir. 2000), Thomke v. Connecticut Gen. Life Ins. Co., 1994 U.S. App. LEXIS 2972 (9th Cir. 1994), Cann v. Carpenters' Pension Trust Fund, 989 F.2d 313 (9th Cir. 1993), Harsch v. Eisenberg, 956 F.2d 651 (7th Cir. 1992), LaSelle v. Public Serv. Co. of Colo., 988 F. Supp. 1348 (D. Colo. 1997), *and* Mintenkenbaugh v. Central States Southeast & Southwest Areas Health & Welfare Fund, 1996 U.S. Dist. LEXIS 22553 (W.D. Ky. 1996) (refusing to award attorneys' fees), *with* Hamilton v. Bank of N.Y., 1995 U.S. Dist. LEXIS 10464 (D. Del. 1995), *and* Chicago Graphic Arts Health & Welfare Fund v. Jefferson Smurfit Corp., 1995 U.S. Dist. LEXIS 18203 (N.D. Ill. 1995) (awarding attorneys' fees)]

Q 23:69   Is there a presumption for awarding attorneys' fees to a prevailing plaintiff or against awarding fees to a prevailing defendant?

Courts are divided as to whether there is a presumption for awarding attorneys' fees to a prevailing plaintiff or against awarding fees to a prevailing defendant. [Grosz-Salomon v. Paul Revere Life Ins. Co., 238 F.3d 1154 (9th Cir. 2001); Martin v. Arkansas Blue Cross & Blue Shield, No. 00-3420 (8th Cir. 2001) (presumption for the award of fees to a prevailing plaintiff); Kayes v. Pacific Lumber, Inc., 51 F.3d 1449 (9th Cir. 1995); Welsh v. Burlington N., Inc., 54 F.3d 1331 (8th Cir. 1995); New York State Teamsters Council Health & Hosp. Fund v. Estate of De Perno, Nos. 93-7870, 93-7896 (2d Cir. 1994) (once a fiduciary breach has been established, the burden may shift to the defendant fiduciary to show why costs, including attorneys' fees, should not be awarded); Florence Nightingale Nursing Serv. v. Blue Cross/Blue Shield, 41 F.3d 1476 (11th Cir. 1995); Todd v. AIG Life Ins. Co., 47 F.3d 1448 (5th Cir. 1995); Ellison v. Shenango, Inc. Pension Bd., 956 F.2d 1268 (3d Cir. 1992); Armistead v. Vernitron Corp., 944 F.2d 1287 (6th Cir. 1991); Cottrill v. Sparrow, Johnson & Ursillo, Inc., 1996 U.S. App. LEXIS 29939 (1st Cir. 1996) (declines to establish a presumption for the award of fees to a prevailing plaintiff); Shockley v. Alyeska Pipeline Serv. Co, 130 F.3d 403 (9th Cir. 1998) (rejects proposition that the courts disfavor awards of attorneys' fees to ERISA defendants, stating that ERISA's attorneys' fees provision is neutral and does not favor one side or the other in ERISA fee cases); *but see* Salovaara v. Eckert, 222 F.3d 19 (2d Cir. 2000); Flanagan v. Inland Empire Elec. Workers Pension Plan, 3 F.3d 1246 (9th Cir. 1993); Zimmer v. Reliance Standard Life Ins. Co., 1999 WL 76896 (S.D.N.Y. 1999); Anita Founds., Inc v. ILGWU Nat'l Ret. Fund, 902 F.2d 185 (2d Cir. 1990); and Nachwalter v. Christie, 805 F.2d 956 (11th Cir. 1986), for the proposition that the standards for awarding fees to a prevailing defendant are more difficult than those for awarding fees to a prevailing plaintiff)]

One court held that the proper rule for determining an award of attorneys' fees is that there is no presumption that a successful plaintiff should receive an award in the absence of exceptional circumstances. However, the court said, this does not mean that there is a presumption against fees, and the defendant usually bears the burden of attorneys' fees for the prevailing plaintiff. [Tomasko v. Ira H. Weinstock, P.C., 255 Fed Appx. 676 (3d Cir. 2007); *see also* Tomasko v. Ira H. Weinstock, P.C., No. 08-4673 (3d Cir. 2009)]

In one instance, a court awarded attorneys' fees and costs under the Equal Access to Justice Act, 28 U.S.C. § 2412, to a plan administrator (see Q 20:1) who successfully defended a suit by DOL alleging that the administrator breached certain fiduciary duties. [Herman v. Schwent, 1999 WL 333416 (8th Cir. 1999)] Another court awarded a partial fee to a prevailing defendant because of the plaintiff's near frivolous claims and because the plaintiff unnecessarily prolonged the litigation. [Moore v. Lafayette Life Ins. Co., 458 F.3d 416 (6th Cir. 2006)]

Q 23:70   Can attorneys' fees be awarded to losing plaintiffs?

No. No court has awarded attorneys' fees to a plaintiff who has not been at least partially successful, although several opinions in dicta have stated that attorneys' fees could in rare instances be awarded to losing plaintiffs where the suit benefited a class of participants and most of the factors of the five-part test (see Q 23:62) favored an award. [Andrews v. Blue Cross/Blue Shield of Nebraska, 165 Fed. Appx. 650 (10th Cir. 2006); McElwaine v. US W., Inc., 176 F.3d 1167 (9th Cir. 1999); Groves v. Modified Ret. Plan for Hourly Paid Employees of Johns Manville Corp. & Subsidiaries, 803 F.2d 109 (3d Cir. 1986); Huss v. Green Springs Health Servs., Inc., 1999 U.S. Dist. LEXIS 10014 (E.D. Pa. 1999); Chicago Area International Brotherhood of Teamsters Health & Welfare Trust Fund v. Dietz & Kolodenko Co., 1996 U.S. Dist. LEXIS 421 (N.D. Ill. 1996); Bishop v. Osborn Transp., Inc., 687 F. Supp. 1526 (N.D. Ala. 1988); Petro v. Flinkote Co., 633 F. Supp. 10 (N.D. Ohio 1986)] A plan may also provide for awarding attorneys' fees to nonprevailing parties in any nonfrivolous dispute. [Krumme v. West Point Stevens, Inc., 2000 WL 1920451 (2d Cir. 2000)]

Where an appeals court reversed a district court's award of benefits, it also automatically reversed a fee award to the no-longer-prevailing plaintiff, holding that it is always an abuse of discretion to award attorney's fees to a losing party. [Webb v. Careten Ins. Co., 188 Fed. Appx. 391 (6th Cir. 2006); *see also* Antolik v. Saks Inc., 463 F.3d 796 (8th Cir. 2006)]

One court ordered a prevailing plaintiff's attorney to pay the losing defendant's legal fees because the attorney continued to prosecute the case after the plaintiff had received all the relief he was entitled to under ERISA. [Moreno v. St. Francis & Health Ctr., 2002 WL 171980 (N.D. Ill. 2002)] Another court awarded attorneys' fees not to the prevailing plaintiff but to the losing defendant because the plan had subjected its beneficiaries to burdensome litigation. [Carpenters Health and Welfare Trust for Southern California v. Vonderharr, 384 F.3d 667 (9th Cir. 2004)]

Q 23:71 Can attorneys' fees be awarded if the prevailing party is represented by in-house staff counsel?

Yes. A prevailing party may be awarded what it would have paid to independent attorneys if the party was represented by its in-house staff counsel. [Central States, Southeast and Southwest Areas Pension Fund v. Central Cartage Co., 1996 U.S. App. LEXIS 756 (7th Cir. 1996)]

Q 23:72 Can attorneys' fees be awarded to a prevailing consultant or association?

No. An award of attorneys' fees to a defendant, who was a consultant to a plan, in an action brought by the plan was improper since the plan was not a participant, beneficiary, or fiduciary as required under ERISA Section 502(g). [Corder v. Howard Johnson & Co., 53 F.3d 225 (9th Cir. 1994)] Also, an award of attorneys' fees to an association successfully challenging a state law as preempted by ERISA was denied for the same reason. [Self-Insurance Inst. of Am., Inc. v. Korioth, 53 F.3d 694 (5th Cir. 1995)]

Q 23:73 Are communications between an attorney and a plan administrator subject to the attorney-client privilege?

If the attorney gives advice with respect to settlor functions (see Q 23:3), the privilege will apply. If the advice, however, concerns fiduciary questions or questions with respect to plan administration, the privilege may not apply on the theory that the attorney represents the beneficiaries of the trust, not the trustee. [United States v. Mett, 178 F.3d 1058 (9th Cir. 1999); United States v. Doe, 162 F.3d 554 (9th Cir. 1998); In re Long Island Lighting Co., 129 F.3d 268 (2d Cir. 1997); Fischel v. Equitable Life Assurance, No. C96-4202 (N.D. Cal. 2000); Hudson v. General Dynamics, 1999 U.S. Dist. LEXIS 18950 (D. Conn. 1999); Wsol v. Fiduciary Mgmt. Assocs., Inc., 1999 U.S. Dist. LEXIS 19002 (N.D. Ill. 1999)]

Q 23:74 Can the plan contain a provision relieving a fiduciary of personal liability?

No. [IT Corp. v. General Am. Life, 107 F.3d 1415 (9th Cir. 1997); Martin v. Nations Bank of Ga., N.A., 1993 U.S. Dist. LEXIS 6322 (N.D. Ga. 1993)] The plan may, however, buy insurance to cover liability or losses due to acts or omissions of fiduciaries if the insurance company is given a right to sue the breaching fiduciary. [ERISA § 410] If misrepresentations are made in the insurance application by one fiduciary, the policy may be voided as against all fiduciaries, some of whom may be without coverage through no fault of their own; otherwise, the insurance company would suffer hardship by providing coverage for a risk it never meant to insure. A fiduciary may buy insurance to cover the fiduciary's own liability. [Mazur v. Gaudet, 826 F. Supp. 188 (E.D. La. 1992)] The fiduciary may also be indemnified from a nonplan source, such as the plan sponsor. [DOL Reg. § 2509.75-4]

Q 23:75   Can a plan contain a provision permitting indemnification of a fiduciary?

Yes. A plan may provide for indemnification of expenses of a fiduciary who successfully defends against a claim of breach of fiduciary duty. [Packer Eng'g, Inc. v. Kratville, No. 91-2976 (7th Cir. 1992)] ERISA permits benefit plans to indemnify fiduciaries and third-party administrators for attorneys' fees in cases in which the parties settle before the fiduciaries' liability is judicially determined, concluded one court. [Martinez v. Barasch, 2006 U.S. App. LEXIS 6914 (S.D.N.Y. 2006)]

Q 23:76   Is a release executed by a plan beneficiary freeing plan fiduciaries from past liability under ERISA valid?

Yes. A release that is part of a settlement of a bona fide dispute over past fiduciary breaches is valid as is a release where there was an uncertainty as to legal rights and a clear expression of an intent to be bound that would have been sufficient under applicable state law. [Stadler v. McCullouch, No. 95-1380 (3d Cir. 1996)]

A release will not, however, be valid where entitlement is clear and without doubt or relating to the performance of future fiduciary duties. [Blessing v. Struthers-Dunn, Inc., 1985 WL 3569 (E.D. Pa. 1985)] A general release also will not bar an ERISA claim unless that was the intent and purpose of the parties to the transaction. [Auslander v. Helfand, 1997 U.S. Dist. LEXIS 20597 (D. Md. 1997)]

According to one court, an insurer breached its fiduciary duty by relying on a general release from future claims signed by a participant involving a plan sponsored by her first employer to deny her benefits under another plan sponsored by a later employer because the release was not a written term of the plan under which she was seeking benefits. [Barron v. UNUM Life Ins. Co. of Am., No. 01-1065 (4th Cir. 2001)]

Q 23:77   Can fiduciary responsibility be delegated?

Yes. For example, the trust instrument can provide that one trustee has responsibility for one-half of the plan assets and a second trustee has responsibility for the other half of the plan assets. Neither trustee would be liable for the acts of the other except under the co-fiduciary liability rule of ERISA Section 405(a) (see Q 23:58). [ERISA § 405(b)]

If the plan expressly so provides, the named fiduciaries can allocate among themselves or delegate to others their fiduciary duties, other than the management or control of the plan's assets. The management or control of the plan's assets can be delegated only to an investment manager. [ERISA §§ 405(c)(1), 402(c)(3)]

An effective allocation or delegation will generally relieve the named fiduciary from liability for the acts of the person to whom such duties are allocated or delegated. The named fiduciary, however, is not relieved of liability under the co-fiduciary rules of ERISA Section 405(a). [ERISA § 405(c)(2)] Such rules specifically exclude investment managers. [ERISA § 405(d)] Accordingly, a trustee bank was not liable as a co-fiduciary for breaches by an investment manager. [Beddall v. State St. Bank & Trust Co., 137 F.3d 12 (1st Cir. 1998)]

Q 23:78   What is the liability of an investment manager for its decisions regarding investment of plan assets?

An investment manager is a bank, insurance company, or investment advisor registered with the SEC or state in which it maintains its principal office that acknowledges in writing that it is a fiduciary with respect to the plan (see Q 23:1). Therefore, any failure to comply with fiduciary standards may result in a breach of fiduciary duty, and the investment manager will be liable for any losses to the plan resulting from the breach. In addition, the investment manager may be required to disgorge any profits derived from the breach. [California Ironworkers Field Pension Trust v. Loomis Sayles & Co., 259 F.3d 1036 (9th Cir. 2001)]

An investment manager who bought and sold on behalf of a plan was found to have engaged in churning the plan's portfolio when the manager directed approximately 94 transactions over 17 months, resulting in a loss of $47,000, while the broker received commissions of $9,700 in one three-month period. The investment manager was held liable for the losses to the plan and was ordered to return the commissions to the plan. [Dasler v. E.F. Hutton & Co., 694 F. Supp. 624 (D. Minn. 1988)]

A bank trustee whose duties were limited to following the directions of another fiduciary was not liable for losses to the plan. [DiFelice v. U.S. Airways, Inc., 497 F.3d 410 (4th Cir. 2007); Maniace v. Commerce Bank of Kan. City, 40 F.3d 264 (8th Cir. 1994); In re Coca-Cola Enterprises Inc., ERISA Litig., 2007 WL 1810211 (D. Ga. 2007); but see Moench v. Robertson, 62 F.3d 553 (3d Cir. 1995); Kuper v. Iovenko, 66 F.3d 1447 (6th Cir. 1995); FirsTier Bank, N.A. v. Zeller, 16 F.3d 907 (8th Cir. 1994)] A trustee of an ESOP may have breached its fiduciary duties in not notifying participants that it would mirror participants' votes when the trustee voted unallocated shares. Because of the lack of notice, the trustee had a fiduciary duty to act independently in determining how to vote the unallocated shares. [Herman v. NationsBank of Ga., N.A., 135 F.3d 1409 (11th Cir. 1998)] For further details, see Q 28:1.

Q 23:79   Are there any limits on the investments a qualified retirement plan can make?

There are no specific dollar or percentage limits placed on the amount a qualified retirement plan can invest in any particular type of asset (other than qualifying employer securities or qualifying employer real property; see Q 23:81). Nor are there any limits on the types of investments that can be made. Investments in such tangible assets as real estate, gold, art, or diamonds are permitted, even though these investments may not generate current income for the plan and generally lack liquidity. However, see the discussion regarding a fiduciary's standard of care at Qs 23:19 and 23:20.

Limits on investments in qualifying employer securities or qualifying employer real property are discussed at Q 23:82. The consequences of investments by self-directed accounts in collectibles are discussed at Q 23:87.

Q 23:80   May a qualified retirement plan borrow to make investments?

Yes. There is no prohibition against any particular method by which a qualified retirement plan invests its assets. However, securities purchased on margin are considered acquisition indebtedness, subject to the tax on unrelated business taxable income (UBTI)—both dividends and gains—resulting from such acquisition indebtedness. [I.R.C. §§ 511, 514; Ocean Cove Corp. Ret. Plan & Trust v. United States, 657 F. Supp. 776 (S.D. Fla. 1987); Elliot Knitwear Profit Sharing Plan v. Comm'r, 614 F.2d 347 (3d Cir. 1980), *aff'g* 71 T.C. 765 (1979)] Gains realized from the short sale of publicly traded securities through a broker are not income derived from acquisition indebtedness and, hence, do not constitute UBTI. [Rev. Rul. 95-8, 1995-1 C.B. 293; Priv. Ltr. Ruls. 9703027, 9637053] Trading in commodity futures contracts does not constitute debt-financed property and also does not constitute UBTI. [Priv. Ltr. Ruls. 8338138, 8110164, 8107114, 8104998, 8044023]

When a plan borrows money to acquire or improve real estate, the debt generally is not considered acquisition indebtedness, so the income or gain from the real estate is not treated as UBTI. [I.R.C. § 514(c)(9)]

Q 23:81   What is the diversification requirement?

A trustee (or any other fiduciary responsible for investing plan assets) is required to discharge the trustee's duties "by diversifying the investments of the plan so as to minimize the risk of large losses, unless under the circumstances it is clearly not prudent to do so." [ERISA § 404(a)(1)(C)]

The degree of investment concentration that would violate the diversification rule cannot be stated as a fixed percentage but depends on the facts and circumstances of each case, including the following factors:

- The purposes of the plan
- The amount of plan assets
- Financial and industrial conditions

- The type of investment made
- Diversification along geographic lines
- Diversification along industry lines
- The date the investment matures

For example, if the trustee is investing in real estate mortgages, the trustee should not invest a disproportionate amount in mortgages within a particular area or on a particular type of property even if that investment would result in social gains to a particular community. [H.R. Conf. Rep. No. 1280, 93d Cong., 2d Sess., *reprinted in* 1974 U.S.C.C.A.N. 5038, 5084, 5085] DOL settled three suits alleging that trustees violated their fiduciary duties by purchasing Z-Bonds and other investments from the same broker-dealer when the trustees agreed to repay $3 million to the plans plus $600,000 in ERISA Section 502(1) penalties (see Q 24:5). [DOL News Rel. (Sept. 16, 1999]

One court held that trustees violated the diversification rule when over 65 percent of the plan's assets were invested in commercial first mortgages secured by property located in one area. The lack of diversification caused too much risk that the value of the assets would decline if there were a severe economic downturn in the area where the property securing the mortgages was located. As a result, the investments in the aggregate were held to be imprudent. [Brock v. Citizens Bank of Clovis, 841 F.2d 344 (10th Cir. 1988)] However, other courts have held that investing over 70 percent and 63 percent of a plan's assets in real estate did not necessarily mean that the investments were imprudent. [Reich v. King, 1994 U.S. Dist. LEXIS 16763 (D. Md. 1994); Metzler v. Graham, 1997 U.S. App. LEXIS 10752 (5th Cir. 1997)]

Another court held that an investment company that invested over 70 percent of a plan's assets in long-term government bonds did not properly diversify plan assets because the investment company failed to determine the plan's particular cash flow needs and was forced to sell some bonds at a loss to meet the plan's need for cash. [GIW Indus., Inc. v. Trevor, Stewart, Burton & Jacobsen, Inc., 845 F.2d 729 (11th Cir. 1990)] However, other courts have found that no violation occurred with an investment of almost 90 percent of a plan's assets in one profitable investment or that the failure to diversify was not an imprudent act. [Etter v. J. Pease Constr. Co., Inc., 963 F.2d 1005 (7th Cir. 1992); Lanka v. O'Higgins, No. 88-CV-922 (N.D.N.Y. 1992)]

The diversification requirement may be met by investing plan assets in a bank's pooled investment fund (see Q 23:88), a mutual fund (see Q 23:89), or insurance or annuity contracts if the bank, mutual fund, or insurance company diversifies its investments. One court explained that a violation of the diversification requirement occurs where the plan investments as a whole are not sufficiently diversified. A violation does not occur if the specific investment fund is not diversified, as long as the plan offers a range of diversified investment options. [Young v. General Motors Investment Mgmt. Corp., 325 Fed. Appx. 31 (2d Cir. 2009)]

The diversification requirement generally does not apply to an investment in employer securities by an ESOP, depending on the exact language of the ESOP.

Where it does not apply, there may still be a presumption that an ESOP fiduciary did not violate ERISA by investing plan assets in employer securities. [*In re* Radioshack ERISA Litig., 2008 WL 1808329 (__. D. Tex. 2008); Moench v. Robertson, 62 F.3d 553 (3d Cir. 1995); Ershick v. United Mo. Bank of Kan. City, N.A., 948 F.2d 660 (10th Cir. 1991)] However, an ESOP must offer certain participants the right to elect to diversify the stock acquired after 1986 and allocated to their accounts (see Qs 28:53–28:63). For further details, see Q 28:1.

Q 23:82   Must a plan make only blue chip investments?

No. DOL says, "[A]lthough securities issued by a small or new company may be a riskier investment than securities issued by a blue chip company, the investment in the former company may be entirely proper under . . . [the] prudence rule." [Preamble to DOL Reg. § 2550.404a-1]

The degree of risk that the trustee takes in making investments depends in part on the type of plan the employer maintains. In a defined contribution plan (see Q 2:2), benefits received by a plan participant are based on the employer's contributions, increased or decreased by the return on plan investments. Thus, it may be appropriate to consider some speculative investments in a defined contribution plan.

In a defined benefit plan (see Q 2:3), a rate of return on investments above that assumed by the actuary reduces required contributions, and a rate of return below the assumed rate increases required contributions. Thus, investments will normally be of a nature that will return at least as much as the actuary has assumed. It is likely, therefore, that speculative investments in a defined benefit plan will have less appeal than in a defined contribution plan. DOL has advised that a fiduciary of a defined benefit plan may consider the liability obligations of the plan and the risks associated with those liability obligations in determining a prudent investment strategy for the plan. [DOL Op. Ltr. 2006-08A]

Q 23:83   How can a trustee or other plan fiduciary be protected from lawsuits for failure to meet the prudent person rule?

In acting prudently, trustees or other fiduciaries should also act defensively, building a record to defend their actions. For example, fiduciaries should:

- Keep detailed records of the actions taken and the factors that went into the decisions;
- Make sure these records describe in detail the relevant circumstances prevailing at the time—that is, outline the conditions under which the action was taken; and
- Make sure all reasonable steps have been taken to acquire the information needed to make informed decisions.

Q 23:84   May a qualified retirement plan invest in employer securities or employer real property?

A plan subject to ERISA generally may not acquire or hold qualifying employer securities (see Q 23:86) or qualifying employer real property (see Q 23:85) if the total fair market value of such assets exceeds 10 percent of the fair market value of the plan's assets at the time of acquisition. The 10 percent limitation does not apply to an eligible individual account plan that specifically authorizes such investments. An eligible individual account plan is defined as:

- A profit sharing, stock bonus, thrift, or savings plan
- An ESOP, or
- A money purchase pension plan in existence on the date of ERISA's enactment that invested primarily in qualifying employer securities at that time

[ERISA § 407; DOL Op. Ltr. 2003-10A]

Individual account plans that are part of a floor offset arrangement—an arrangement under which the plan's benefits are taken into account in determining a participant's benefits under a defined benefit plan—established after December 17, 1987, do not fall within this exception. [ERISA § 407(d)(3)(C); DOL Op. Ltr. 2004-04A] In addition, the two plans that constitute the floor offset arrangement will be treated as a single plan for purposes of the 10 percent limit.

Example. Ben Corporation and Jason Corporation each have floor offset arrangements with assets of $200,000 divided equally between their defined benefit and profit sharing plans. Ben Corporation established its floor offset arrangement in 1985; Jason Corporation's was established in 1988. Up to $10,000 of the assets of Ben Corporation's defined benefit plan and up to $100,000 (which is 100 percent of the assets) of Ben Corporation's profit sharing plan can be invested in qualifying employer securities—for a total of $110,000. In contrast, the amount of Jason Corporation's qualifying employer securities held by the floor offset arrangement may not exceed $20,000 (10 percent of its assets in the aggregate). [ERISA § 407(d)(9)]

With respect to elective contributions (and earnings thereon) made to a 401(k) plan (see Q 27:1) for plan years beginning after 1998, generally, employers will not be permitted to force employees to invest more than 10 percent of that amount in employer securities and employer real property unless the assets were acquired before January 1, 1999, were acquired on or after January 1, 1999, under a written agreement binding on that date and at all times thereafter, or the plan is an ESOP. [ERISA § 407(b)(2)] See Qs 28:53 and 28:64 for a discussion of new diversification requirements concerning employer securities.

Q 23:85   What is qualifying employer real property?

Employer real property is real property leased to an employer of employees covered by the plan or an affiliate of the employer. Such real property is qualifying only if it is dispersed geographically, suitable for more than one use, and held without violation of the other ERISA fiduciary rules (except the diversification and prohibited transaction rules, which do not apply). [ERISA §§ 406(d)(2), 406(d)(4)]

Q 23:86   What are qualifying employer securities?

Employer securities are stock, marketable obligations, or certain publicly traded partnership interests issued by an employer of employees covered by the plan or an affiliate of the employer. Stock or partnership interests acquired by a plan other than an eligible individual account plan after December 17, 1987, will be qualifying employer securities only if (1) not more than 25 percent of the aggregate amount of stock of the same class issued and outstanding at the time of acquisition is held by the plan and (2) at least 50 percent of such aggregate amount is held by persons independent of the issuer. For stock acquired on or before December 17, 1989, plans had until December 31, 1992, to comply with the new rules. [ERISA §§ 407(d)(5), 407(f); DOL Op. Ltr. 2003-14A; DOL Op. Ltr. 97-25A]

Q 23:87   What does earmarking investments mean?

Earmarking in a defined contribution plan (see Q 2:2) allows each participant, on a nondiscriminatory basis, an opportunity to invest funds contributed to the plan on the participant's behalf as the participant sees fit in any investment vehicle that the trustees are willing to administer. Traditional retirement plan investments—blue chip stocks, bonds, and real estate—can be passed over in favor of more speculative investments such as new stock issues, diamonds, gold, art, and antiques. However, amounts invested in collectibles under an earmarked plan will be treated as distributions for tax purposes. Collectibles are defined as works of art, rugs, antiques, precious metals, stamps, coins, and any other tangible property specified as a collectible by IRS. [I.R.C. § 408(m)]

There is no place for earmarking of employer contributions in a defined benefit plan (see Q 2:3) since there are no individual accounts and investment gains or losses affect the amount the employer must contribute to the plan rather than the level of benefits payable to participants. However, earmarking of voluntary or rollover contributions by participants may be appropriate. Earmarking in a self-directed account plan (see Q 23:14) has the added advantage of possibly relieving the plan's trustees of liability for poor investment decisions made by the participant.

Q 23:88   What are pooled investment funds?

Pooled investment funds are commingled funds maintained by a bank on behalf of many qualified retirement plans. When a bank is appointed as trustee and the qualified retirement plan's assets are invested by the bank, the company retains only a limited choice in directing the investment of the plan's assets.

Generally, the bank has a dual fund arrangement—a fixed-income fund and a common stock fund—that permits the company to direct the proportion of its contributions invested in each fund. The pooling of funds makes it possible to offer small plans the economies and security of a large plan. This investment vehicle may be particularly attractive to small and medium-sized plans, such as plans in which the annual contribution is below $100,000. To participate in a pooled investment fund, the company maintaining the plan must adopt the bank's collective trust as part of its own trust and authorize investments in the bank's trust.

A trustee must, of course, be prudent in selecting and retaining the bank that directs the plan's investments.

Q 23:89   Can plan assets be invested in a mutual fund?

Yes. Mutual funds are a common investment vehicle, especially for small plans desiring professional investment management but not wishing to retain a bank's trusteeship or for plans that are too small to participate in a bank's pooled investment fund (see Q 23:23). A trustee must, of course, be prudent in selecting and retaining the mutual fund in which plan assets are invested, taking into account the wide variety of funds available with different investment goals.

Q 23:90   Can assets in an insurance company's general accounts be considered assets of an ERISA plan?

Yes. DOL issued proposed regulations clarifying the status of plan assets (see Q 23:23) held in insurance company general accounts that were designed to be administratively feasible and to protect the interests and rights of the plan and its participants and beneficiaries. DOL issued final regulations in January 2000 providing a safe harbor for insurers that issued nonguaranteed policies to plans on or before December 31, 1998, so that the insurers' general accounts are not treated as plan assets.

Under the final regulations, when a plan acquires a policy (other than a guaranteed benefit policy) issued by an insurer on or before December 31, 1998 (i.e., a transition policy), that is supported by assets of the insurer's general account, the plan's assets include the policy but not any of the underlying assets of the insurer's general account, provided the insurer satisfies the requirements of the safe harbor, in which event no person will be liable under the reporting and disclosure requirements of ERISA or its fiduciary responsibility provisions or prohibited transaction rules (see Q 24:1) for conduct occurring before the effective dates of the regulations on the basis of a claim that the insurer's assets (other than plan assets held in a separate account) are plan assets. [DOL Info. Ltr. (Jan. 6, 2004)]

To meet the safe harbor, an insurer must:

1. Disclose to plan fiduciaries specified information. First, the insurer must describe the method by which expenses and income are allocated to a contract before entering into it as well as additional information explaining the extent to which alternative contract arrangements supported by

assets of insurers' separate accounts are available, and other information concerning such separate accounts;

2. Allow plans to terminate or discontinue a policy on 90 days' notice to the insurer, and to elect, without penalty, either: (a) a lump-sum payment, or (b) annual installment payments over a ten-year period, with interest; and

3. Give plans written notice of insurer-initiated amendments 60 days before the amendments take effect. [DOL Reg. § 2550.401c]

The final regulations contain a cure provision allowing insurers that have made reasonable, good-faith efforts to comply with the regulations to take advantage of the safe harbor, notwithstanding an initial failure to comply with one or more of the requirements of the regulations. For the cure to apply, the insurer must:

1. Have established written procedures reasonably designed to ensure compliance and to detect instances of noncompliance;

2. Comply with the regulations within 60 days from the earlier of the insurer's detection of a problem or the receipt of written notice of noncompliance from the plan;

3. Credit interest on any amounts due the plan on termination or discontinuance of the policy, if not paid within 90 days of receipt of notice from the plan; and

4. Make the plan whole for any losses resulting from noncompliance. [DOL Reg. § 2550.401c]

Chapter 24

Prohibited Transactions

Both ERISA and the Code prohibit certain classes of transactions between a retirement plan and parties in interest to the plan, regardless of the fairness of the particular transaction involved or the benefit to the plan. In addition, fiduciaries are prohibited from engaging in certain conduct that would affect their duty of loyalty to the plan. This chapter examines the nature of prohibited transactions, the penalties that apply when a prohibited transaction occurs, and the statutory, administrative, and class exemptions to the prohibited-transaction rules.

Q 24:1   What is a prohibited transaction?

A prohibited transaction occurs under ERISA if a plan fiduciary (see Q 23:1) causes the retirement plan (see Q 24:4) to engage in a transaction that the fiduciary knows or should know constitutes a *direct* or *indirect*:

1. Sale, exchange, or lease of any property between the plan and a party in interest (see Q 24:3);

2. Loan or other extension of credit between the plan and a party in interest; [Priv. Ltr. Rul. 9238003]

3. Furnishing of goods, services, or facilities between the plan and a party in interest;

4. Transfer of plan assets to a party in interest or the use of plan assets by or for the benefit of a party in interest; or

5. Acquisition of employer securities or employer real property in excess of the limits set by law (see Q 23:84). [ERISA § 406(a)(1)]

There are three key concepts in the area of prohibited transactions. First, a prohibited transaction may be either direct or indirect. Second, a prohibited transaction involves both a plan and a party in interest. Third, a prohibited transaction occurs between a plan and a party in interest in either direction. For example, a prohibited transaction might consist of a transfer of assets from a party in interest to a plan or a transfer of assets from a plan to a party in interest. [Priv. Ltr. Rul. 9713002] A fiduciary must act prudently in determining whether a party-in-interest relationship exists prior to entering a transaction, and actual knowledge of illegality is not required. [Marshall v. Kelly, 465 F. Supp. 341 (W.D. Okla. 1978); *see also* Donovan v. Schmoutey, 592 F. Supp. 1361 (D. Nev. 1984); Freund v. Marshall & Ilsley Bank, 485 F. Supp. 629 (W.D. Wis. 1979)]

In addition, ERISA prohibits a fiduciary from:

1. Dealing with plan assets (see Q 23:23) in the fiduciary's own interest or for the fiduciary's own account;

2. Acting in any transaction involving the plan on behalf of a party whose interests are adverse to the interests of the plan or its participants or beneficiaries; or

3. Receiving any consideration for the fiduciary's own personal account from any person dealing with the plan in connection with any transaction involving plan assets. [ERISA § 406(b)]

DOL has opined that the use of plan assets to promote union organizing or to advance union goals in collective bargaining negotiations is prohibited. [DOL Op. Ltr. 2008-05A] DOL has determined that tuition reimbursement payments made by a union-sponsored trust to provide reimbursement to affiliated local unions for the expenses incurred by members in completing a welding program would not constitute a prohibited transaction if the reimbursement was pursuant to a clear agreement and the trust was not charged any interest or required to make other payments. [ERISA §§ 406(b)(1), 408(b)(2); DOL Op. Ltr. 2007-04A]

There is an exemption from the prohibited-transaction rules for certain transactions between a plan and a common or collective trust fund or a pooled investment fund that is maintained by a party in interest to the plan. [ERISA § 408(b)(8); I.R.C. § 4975(d)(8); DOL Op. Ltr. 2005-09A] DOL has ruled that a company which served as a fiduciary and administrator (see Q 20:1) for its own qualified retirement plan could receive fees from certain mutual funds that were selected by the company as investment options for plan participants as reimbursement for direct expenses incurred in providing the administrative services without violating ERISA. Although ERISA prohibits a fiduciary from receiving a fee or other consideration for its personal account from a party dealing with the plan in connection with a transaction involving the plan assets, a fiduciary may receive reimbursement of direct expenses without violating ERISA as long as the fiduciary does not receive compensation or other consideration. The term "reimbursement" is not defined, but DOL interpreted the term to include the fees from the mutual funds to the extent that the plan and the company expressly agreed to use the fees to reduce or eliminate the plan's liability for the company's direct expenses incurred in providing services to the plan. Therefore, the company would not violate ERISA by receiving fees from the mutual funds as long as the company credited all payments against its direct expenses incurred from providing services for the plan, for which the plan would otherwise be liable. [ERISA § 406(b)(3); DOL Reg. § 2550.408b-2(e)(3); DOL Op. Ltr. 97-19A; *see also* DOL Op. Ltr. 99-03A]

DOL has opined that a company that sponsored a qualified retirement plan would engage in a prohibited transaction if it provided and charged fees for trustee services that exceeded direct expenses incurred in providing those services and that the trustee services provided by the company could not be exempted as ancillary services. [ERISA § 408(b)(6); DOL Op. Ltr. 2001-10A] A trust company's receipt of 12b-1 fees (i.e., fees a mutual fund pays from fund assets to cover the costs of marketing and selling fund shares and the costs of providing shareholder services) and subtransfer fees from mutual funds with investment advisors that are the trust company's affiliates, for services in connection with employee benefit plan investments in the mutual funds, is not a prohibited transaction where the decision to invest in those funds is made by an employee benefit plan fiduciary or participant who is independent of both the trust company and its affiliates. [ERISA §§ 406(b)(1), 406(b)(3); DOL Op. Ltr. 2003-09A] The investment in a mutual fund by a defined contribution plan (see Q 2:2) may be a prohibited transaction where one of the members of the board which serves as the plan's trustee is the president and chief executive officer of the investment advisor that administers the mutual fund. The same board member is involved in the mutual fund's day-to-day operations; and, therefore, the board member's interest in the mutual fund could affect his best judgment as a plan fiduciary with regard to decisions involving the investment of the plan's assets. However, a prohibited transaction could be avoided if the board member removes himself from all decisions regarding the investment of the plan's assets in the mutual fund. [DOL Op. Ltr. 2005-04A]

DOL has granted prohibited transaction exemptions (see Q 24:20) to allow an investment company to receive fees for advising defined contribution plan participants how to allocate their plan accounts among the company's mutual funds and to allow the asset management affiliates of five financial services firms to purchase securities from underwriting or selling syndicates on behalf of the firms' plans, where the affiliates participate as managers or syndicate members and where the affiliates also serve as the plan fiduciaries. [PTEs 97-60, 2000-25 through 2000-29] Also, DOL has opined that a company's model asset allocation portfolio that would offer individual investment advice and asset allocation services in the company's funds for participants would not be a *per se* violation of the prohibited-transaction rules as a consequence of any receipt of increased investment advisory fees because of such investments since the investment recommendations would not be the result of the company's exercise of authority, control, or responsibility. [DOL Op. Ltr. 2001-09A]

DOL has also opined that an entity which acts as a registered investment advisor, a registered commodity trading advisor, and a registered commodity pool operator with respect to qualified retirement plans does not engage in prohibited transactions as a fiduciary by charging performance-based fees for services. The investment advisor is subject to the general fiduciary rules and must not use any of the authority, control, or responsibility that makes it a fiduciary to cause a plan to pay additional fees for its services or pay additional fees to a party in which the fiduciary has an interest that may affect its judgment as a fiduciary. [DOL Op. Ltr. 99-16A] If services rendered to a plan by a broker-dealer/registered representative are limited to executing trades at the direction of plan participants, the representative would not be providing investment advice or investment advisory services to the plan and its participants.

[DOL Op. Ltr. 2005-11A] According to DOL, the purchase by an employee stock ownership plan (ESOP; see Q 28:1) of the plan sponsor's stock from personal trusts is not a prohibited transaction even if the plan sponsor serves as trustee of both the ESOP and the personal trusts, as long as the transactions are for adequate consideration and no commission is charged. [DOL Op. Ltr. 2002-04A]

Transactions executed through an alternative trading system whereby fiduciaries negotiate for the purchase of securities on behalf of plans are not prohibited transactions, even if they take place between the plan and a party in interest, so long as the parties' identities are *not* disclosed to each other, according to DOL. DOL pointed to the Conference Committee Report accompanying ERISA Section 406, which states that "an ordinary 'blind' purchase or sale of securities" is not a prohibited transaction even if one of the parties involved turns out to be a party in interest. DOL cautioned that, although the sheer size of the system's subscribers and its number of trades, as well as its procedures and software, would normally assure anonymity, the system allowed for the parties to identify themselves if they chose, in which case the transactions would be prohibited. [DOL Op. Ltr. 2004-05A] See Q 24:21 for a discussion of the new statutory prohibited-transaction exemption for electronic communication network.

In one case, a party in interest sold publicly traded securities of an unrelated corporation for cash and a noninterest bearing, demand promissory note to a qualified retirement plan established by the professional corporation through which the individual conducted his practice. The individual conceded that the sale of the stock constituted a prohibited transaction but contended that the excise tax (see Q 24:5) should not apply because the transaction would qualify as a prudent investment if judged under the highest fiduciary standards. The court upheld the imposition of the excise tax and affirmed the principle that the prohibited-transaction restrictions were *per se* prohibitions with specifically defined exemptions and that no good-faith exception exists. [Leib, 88 T.C. 1474 (1987)] In another case, the individuals who were parties in interest also argued that they should not be subject to the excise tax because they acted in good faith and on the advice of their attorneys and investment counselors in engaging in the prohibited transactions and further argued that the plan was not harmed and in fact was better off as a result of the transactions. The court rejected these arguments as irrelevant and noted that the language and the legislative history of the statutory provisions at issue indicated a congressional intention to create a blanket prohibition against certain transactions whether the transaction was entered into prudently or in good faith, or whether the plan benefited as a result. In essence, "good intentions and a pure heart are no defense." [Rutland, 89 T.C. 1137 (1987); *see also* Donovan v. Cunningham, 716 F.2d 1455 (5th Cir. 1983); M&R Inv. Co. v. Fitzsimmons, 685 F.2d 283 (9th Cir. 1982); Cutair v. Marshall, 590 F.2d 523 (3d Cir. 1979)] An attorney who wrote an opinion letter to a lending bank regarding the effectiveness of a mortgage on property that was sold by a plan trustee to the plan was not liable as a plan fiduciary or a party in interest, even though the sale was later deemed to be a prohibited transaction. [Mellon Bank, N.A. v. Levy, 2003 U.S. App. LEXIS 16118 (3d Cir. 2003)] A violation of the exclusive benefit rule (see Q 4:1) does not automatically constitute a prohibited transaction, which the court said is a term of art for certain specified transactions. [Borrelli v. Internal Revenue Service, 2005 WL 3150533 (2d Cir. 2005)]

In a case of potentially far-reaching consequences, the United States Supreme Court held that a prohibited transaction did *not* occur when an employer conditioned eligibility for plan benefits under a special early retirement program on the employee's execution of a broad waiver covering potential Age Discrimination in Employment Act (ADEA) and other employment-related claims against the employer. [Lockheed Corp. v. Spink, 517 U.S. 882 (1996)]

Receipt of commissions by a fiduciary's wholly owned subsidiary on loans from a plan to unrelated borrowers is a prohibited transaction. [Murphy v. Dawson, No. 88-2992 (4th Cir. 1989)] A plan's payment of legal fees to the attorneys defending a trustee in a criminal prosecution is a prohibited transaction between the plan and the trustee. [O'Malley v. Comm'r, 972 F.2d 150 (7th Cir. 1992), *aff'g* 96 T.C. 644 (1991)] An attorney hired by a union to provide legal services to its pension plan, who was paid pension benefits he was not entitled to under the terms of the plan, was liable for restitution of benefits he received because, as a service provider to the plan, he was a party in interest. Thus, his use of plan funds was a prohibited transaction, concluded the court. [Dietz v. Cahill, No. 94-CV-6633L (W.D.N.Y. 1996)] Loans from a law firm's qualified retirement plan to clients of the law firm pending settlement of their lawsuits are prohibited transactions because the loans benefit the law firm's business. [Priv. Ltr. Ruls. 9238001, 9118001] Similarly, a loan from a plan to a partnership in which a trustee had a 39 percent interest was a prohibited transaction between the plan and the trustee because of the loan's benefit to the partnership in which the trustee had a significant interest. [Priv. Ltr. Rul. 9119002] An investment by a qualified retirement plan in a participating mortgage loan made to a limited partnership in which the plan investment advisor held a 7.5 percent interest was a prohibited transaction because the ownership interest created a conflict of interest resulting in the advisor's having divided loyalties. [Priv. Ltr. Rul. 9208001] DOL opined that transactions between plans and a limited partnership designed to be a collective investment vehicle, including initial and subsequent contributions to and distributions from the partnership, would not be prohibited transactions. However, DOL cautioned that the appropriate plan fiduciaries would still be required to act solely in the interests of the plan participants and beneficiaries in exercising their duties. [DOL Op. Ltr. 2003-15A] Where insurance policies were sold to a qualified retirement plan at a time when the owner of the insurance agency was a plan fiduciary, a prohibited transaction occurred. [Clasby, 77 T.C.M. 1546 (1999)] A plan's hiring of contractors employed by a plan fiduciary to construct an addition to the plan's facility would be a prohibited transaction. [DOL Op. Ltr. 99-09A]

A prohibited transaction did not occur, determined one court, where a participant utilized his qualified retirement plan assets to repay the employer in restitution for theft because the participant was not compelled or forced to allow garnishment of his benefits or to liquidate his benefits. [Greve v. J.H. Patterson

Co., No. 96 C 50424 (N.D. Ill. 1999)] Another court concluded that a prohibited transaction did not occur where members of a local union used settlement proceeds of a lawsuit to reimburse the national union for advanced litigation costs even though the national union was a party in interest. [Jordan v. Michigan Conf. of Teamsters Welfare Fund, 2000 WL 301034 (6th Cir. 2000)]

The mere retention of an investment management company—a party in interest because it was half-owned by a corporation that also wholly owned a company sponsoring the qualified retirement plan—to manage the plan's assets did not result in a prohibited transaction because the sponsoring company, not the plan, paid the investment management fees. [DOL Op. Ltr. 91-14A] A bank trustee that purchased the stock of its parent corporation at the direction of an unaffiliated named fiduciary did not engage in a prohibited transaction. [DOL Op. Ltr. 92-23A] However, a bank trustee's receiving income from the float on benefit checks it issues to plan participants is a prohibited transaction. [DOL Op. Ltr. 93-24A] DOL has advised that if a bank trustee has openly negotiated with an independent plan fiduciary to retain float attributable to outstanding benefit checks as part of its overall compensation, then the bank trustee's use of the float would not be self-dealing because the bank trustee would not be exercising its fiduciary authority or control for its own benefit. Thus, to avoid problems, bank trustees should, as part of their fee negotiations, provide full and fair disclosure regarding the use of float on outstanding benefit checks. DOL has formulated guidance for the disclosure of specific information regarding compensation earned in the form of float and concerning the selection and monitoring process to be engaged in by the responsible fiduciary. [DOL Field Assistance Bull. 2002-3] DOL opined that the provision of administrative services to a pension fund and a welfare fund by a newly formed corporation that was owned by the funds would not constitute prohibited transactions because such services would be treated as intra-plan transactions with respect to each of the funds. [DOL Reg. § 2510.3-101(h)(3); DOL Op. Ltr. 2005-03A]

DOL has opined that overdraft protection services provided by a bank to plans, for which the bank is a party in interest, are not prohibited transactions between plan fiduciaries and parties in interest, provided the services furnished and the compensation paid are both reasonable. However, such overdraft protection services are still subject to general standards of fiduciary conduct. [DOL Op. Ltr. 2003-02A] Bank fees paid by qualified retirement plans for certain services provided to mutual funds, and not for investment advisory services, are not prohibited transactions, DOL opined. [DOL Op. Ltr. 93-12A; PTE 77-4] The payment of fees to a plan trustee by plans investing in mutual funds, and the waiver of investment advisory fees by the mutual funds' investment advisor, meet the requirements of a prohibited-transaction exemption. [DOL Op. Ltr. 93-13A; PTE 77-4] To satisfy the requirements of PTE 77-4, a prospectus must be furnished to an independent plan fiduciary. If a prospectus is not available, this requirement will be met if all the information required under the form used to register an open-end investment company and certain additional information are provided to the fiduciary. [DOL Op. Ltr. 94-34A] DOL has described the circumstances under which the payment of certain administrative fees by mutual fund companies to defined contribution plan service providers will not violate the prohibited-transaction rules [DOL Op. Ltr. 97-15A], and DOL has also described when a plan service provider will be considered a fiduciary. [DOL Op. Ltr. 97-16A]

An individual, who was the sole participant and the plan administrator of a qualified retirement plan, did not engage in a prohibited transaction when he requested the plan's trustee to loan plan assets to a corporation in which he held an 18 percent interest, one court has ruled. The participant did not use his fiduciary authority, control, or responsibility to make the loan to the other corporation. The plan's trustee had sole discretion to make investment decisions and independently approved the loan. As a result, the participant did not deal with the income or assets of the plan in his own interest or for his own account. [Greenlee, 72 T.C.M. 394 (1996); *but see* Flahertys Arden Bowl, Inc. v. Comm'r, 271 F.3d 763 (8th Cir. 2001), where the court ruled that the participant was a fiduciary under the Code even though he was not a fiduciary under ERISA; see Qs 24:3, 24:4] The sole owner of a corporation, which maintained a qualified retirement plan, was both the sole trustee and plan administrator (see Q 20:1). The plan made a series of loans to three corporations in which the owner held a minority interest. Even though the owner may not have derived a direct monetary benefit from the loans, the court concluded that the loans constituted prohibited transactions because plan assets were used for his benefit and that "he sat on both sides of the table." [Rollins, 88 T.C.M. 447 (2004)]

An employer and an individual who was the employer's president, controlling shareholder, and a plan trustee were found jointly and severally liable for the excise tax on a series of prohibited transactions. Plan assets were taken without loan agreements and used to repay employer debts; a trust checking account was used as an expense account to pay the individual's wife, relatives, and other persons; and loans by the plan to third parties were repaid to the employer. These transactions violated both the proscription on self-dealing by a plan fiduciary and the prohibition on any direct or indirect transfer to, or use by or for the benefit of, a disqualified person (see Q 24:4) of the income or assets of a plan. [Priv. Ltr. Rul. 9424001; *see also* Pension Benefit Guar. Corp. v. Hoyte, 20 Employee Benefits Cas. (BNA) 2684 (S.D.N.Y. 1997)] A prohibited transaction occurs when a party in interest repays plan loans by transferring property to the plan because the repayment constitutes a sale or exchange of property between the plan and the party in interest. [Morrissey, 76 T.C.M. 1006 (1998); Priv. Ltr. Ruls. 9713002, 9701001]

Where plan participants borrowed substantial assets from a qualified retirement plan and the loans were treated as taxable distributions, courts have ruled that the loans also constituted prohibited transactions and excise taxes were assessed (see chapter 14, Q 24:8). [Geib, 80 T.C.M. 931 (2000); Medina, 112 T.C. 51 (1999); Field Serv. Adv. 200047022]

One court ruled that DOL may sue parties in interest who were not fiduciaries, but who were involved in a prohibited transaction. [Herman v. South Carolina Nat'l Bank, 135 F.3d 1409 (11th Cir. 1998)] Another court ruled that a cause of action may exist against a person who participates in a prohibited transaction even though the person is neither a fiduciary nor a party in interest (see Q 24:3). [ERISA § 502(a)(3); Leblanc v. Cahill, 2001 WL 119998 (4th Cir. 2001)] A court allowed a class action to proceed against PBGC (see Q 25:10) based on PBGC's alleged participation in a prohibited transaction. The court held that PBGC could be held liable for participating in a prohibited transaction as a nonfiduciary. [Coleman v. PBGC, 2000 WL 527010 (D.D.C. 2000)]

For a discussion of statutory, administrative, and class exemptions, see Qs 24:8, 24:20, and 24:26.

Q 24:2 Can one event give rise to more than one prohibited transaction?

One case involved the sale of property by disqualified persons (see Q 24:4) to a qualified retirement plan. The disqualified persons included the corporation that maintained the plan, officers, directors, and employees of the corporation, and participants of the plan. In 1976, disqualified persons sold property owned by them to the plan for $430,000. The plan paid cash, assumed an outstanding mortgage on the property, and issued a promissory note to the parties as consideration for the purchase. In 1977, the plan leased the property to the corporation for use as its corporate headquarters. The plan failed to report the transactions as prohibited transactions (see Q 21:15). In 1978, the parties filed an application for exemption from the prohibited-transaction restrictions with DOL (see Qs 24:20, 24:24). After the application was denied, two of the parties purchased the property from the plan for $430,000 in June 1980 and paid an additional $20,000 as further consideration for the purchase in December 1982.

The court determined that the parties engaged in three separate prohibited transactions: (1) the sale of the property to the plan; (2) the issuance of the promissory note to the parties by the plan; and (3) the lease of the property by the plan to the corporation.

The parties argued that they should not be subjected to double taxation in having both the sale of the property to the plan and the plan's issuance of the promissory note treated as separate prohibited transactions. Alternatively, the parties argued that the amount involved (see Q 24:5) in the sale transaction should be reduced by the amount of the promissory note. The court held that each of the enumerated prohibited transactions was designed to guard against particular instances of overreaching by a person able to exert influence over the affairs of a plan. Further, the court found no indication in ERISA or in the legislative history that the prohibited-transaction restrictions were intended to be mutually exclusive. [Rutland, 89 T.C. 1137 (1987); *see also* Priv. Ltr. Ruls. 9713002, 9701001]

Q 24:3 Who is a party in interest?

Under ERISA, the following are parties in interest with respect to a plan:

1. Any fiduciary (see Q 23:1), counsel, or employee of the plan;
2. A person providing services to the plan;

3. An employer any of whose employees are covered by the plan, and any direct or indirect owner of 50 percent or more of such employer;

4. A relative (i.e., spouse, ancestor, lineal descendant, or spouse of a lineal descendant) of any of the persons described in (1), (2), or (3) above;

5. An employee organization, any of whose members are covered by the plan;

6. A corporation, partnership, estate, or trust of which at least 50 percent is owned by any person or organization described in (1), (2), (3), (4), or (5) above;

7. Officers, directors, 10-percent-or-more shareholders, and employees of any person or organization described in (2), (3), (5), or (6) above; and

8. A 10-percent-or-more partner of or joint venturer with any person or organization described in (2), (3), (5), or (6) above.

[ERISA §§ 3(14), 3(15)]

A fiduciary must act prudently in determining whether a party-in-interest relationship exists prior to entering a transaction, and actual knowledge of illegality is not required. [Marshall v. Kelly, 465 F. Supp. 341 (W.D. Okla. 1978); *see also* Donovan v. Schmoutey, 592 F. Supp. 1361 (D. Nev. 1984); Freund v. Marshall & Ilsley Bank, 485 F. Supp. 629 (W.D. Wis. 1979)]

In one case, a court rejected DOL's contention that a corporation was the alter ego (see Q 29:7) of a labor union that was a party in interest to a pension plan and found that the plan's loan and sale of a mortgage note to the corporation was not a prohibited transaction; however, the court also ruled that DOL could bring a civil action against a nonfiduciary who participated in a prohibited transaction (see Qs 23:53, 24:1). [Reich v. Compton, 57 F.3d 270 (3d Cir. 1995)] Another court ruled that a nonfiduciary who unknowingly violated the prohibited-transaction rules by receiving money that his employer had wrongfully taken from the company's plan could be held liable for the violation as a party in interest and could also be ordered to make restitution to the plan. [Landwehr v. Du-Pree, 72 F.3d 726 (9th Cir. 1995)] The United States Supreme Court has unanimously concluded that a plan does have a private right of recovery against a nonfiduciary party in interest to recover losses resulting from a prohibited transaction because ERISA permits the imposition of civil liabilities on nonfiduciary parties in interest for their participation in prohibited transactions. [ERISA §§ 406, 502(a); Harris Trust & Sav. Bank v. Salomon Smith Barney, Inc., 530 U.S. 238 (2000)]

DOL has opined that an international union that owned less than 10 percent of the stock of a holding company whose wholly owned subsidiary administered welfare and pension plans that were managed by employers and local unions affiliated with the international union was not a party in interest solely because of the stock ownership. [PWBA Gen. Info. Ltr. (June 3, 1993)]

In another case, a plan that covered employees of Corporation A loaned funds to Corporation B that was formed by children of the majority owners of A. The plan received guarantees from two of the children; but, within a year of the loan transaction and with most of the loan unpaid, the plan released the guarantors from their guarantees. The court concluded that the guarantors were parties in interest since they were related to the majority owners of A and that the release of the guarantors was a direct or indirect transfer of plan assets to, or for the benefit of, a party in interest and, hence, a prohibited transaction. The release of the guarantees benefited the guarantors at the expense of the plan in that the plan no longer had the same security to enable it to collect on the outstanding amount of its loan and the guarantees were assets of the plan. [Reich v. Polera Bldg. Corp., 1996 U.S. Dist. LEXIS 1365 (S.D.N.Y. 1996)]

Q 24:4 How do the prohibited-transaction provisions under the Code differ from the prohibited-transaction provisions under ERISA?

The prohibited-transaction provisions under the Code are in many respects the same as those under ERISA. However, the Code uses the term "disqualified person" rather than "party in interest" (see Q 24:3) and does not require knowledge on the part of a fiduciary that the transaction or conduct is prohibited. The definitions of the term "party in interest" under ERISA and "disqualified person" under the Code are nearly identical, but the term "party in interest" is slightly more inclusive (i.e., the ERISA, but not the Code, definition includes counsel to and employees of the plan, and all employees—not only highly compensated employees—of the employer). [I.R.C. § 4975(e)(2)] A disqualified person is:

1. A fiduciary;
2. A person providing services to the plan;
3. An employer any of whose employees are covered by the plan;
4. An employee organization any of whose members are covered by the plan;
5. An owner, direct or indirect, of 50 percent or more of the employer or employee organization, whether a partnership, corporation, trust, or unincorporated enterprise;
6. A member of the family (i.e., spouse, ancestor, lineal descendant, or spouse of a lineal descendant) of any individual described in (1), (2), (3), or (5) above;
7. A corporation, partnership, or trust or estate of which (or in which) 50 percent or more is owned directly or indirectly by persons described in (1), (2), (3), (4), or (5) above;
8. An officer, director (or an individual having powers or responsibilities similar to those of officers or directors), a 10-percent-or-more shareholder, or a highly compensated employee (earning 10 percent or more of the yearly wages of an employer) of a person described in (3), (4), (5), or (7) above; or
9. A 10-percent-or-more partner or joint venturer of a person described in (3), (4), (5), or (7) above.

Plans that cover only a sole shareholder and/or the shareholder's spouse and plans that cover only partners are not subject to ERISA and, therefore, are not subject to ERISA's prohibited-transaction provisions. However, such plans are subject to the prohibited-transaction provisions of the Code. [DOL Reg. §§ 2510.3-3(b), 2510.3-3(c)] In addition, the prohibited-transaction provisions under the Code apply to IRAs and Roth IRAs, while ERISA's prohibited-transaction provisions do not. [I.R.C. §§ 4975(c), 4975(e)(1)] If a plan permits self-directed accounts (see Q 23:14), participants will not be considered fiduciaries under ERISA solely because they exercise control over assets in their individual accounts (see Q 23:15). However, such a participant is a fiduciary under the Code. Where a participant directed his plan account to make loans to a corporation of which the participant owned 57 percent of the stock, the corporation was a disqualified person and was subject to the prohibited-transaction penalty provisions of the Code. [Flahertys Arden Bowl, Inc. v. Comm'r, 271 F.3d 763 (8th Cir. 2001); *see also* Pension Benefit Guar. Corp. v. Hoyte, 20 Employee Benefits Cas. (BNA) 2684 (S.D.N.Y. 1997)]

A partnership that received a loan from its defined contribution plans (see Q 2:2) was a disqualified person because the general partners, who were fiduciaries of the plans, owned, directly or indirectly, 50 percent or more of the partnership. The general partners, husband and wife, each owned a one-third interest in the partnership. Under the attribution rules, each spouse was deemed to own two-thirds; thus, each spouse owned 50 percent or more of the partnership (see Q 24:3). [Davis v. United States, No. 93-2047 (4th Cir. 1995)]

Once a disqualified person enters into a prohibited transaction, the person remains liable for any excise taxes (see Q 24:5) until correction of the prohibited transaction is completed (see Q 24:6). A person's status at the time of the prohibited transaction determines whether the person has a relationship to the plan or the employer or related parties that fits within one of the definitions of disqualified person. One court reasoned that it would not serve the purpose of ERISA to allow an otherwise disqualified person to avoid liability by merely changing his legal status after he had engaged in the prohibited transaction. Thus, an individual who had terminated his employment and stockholdings in the employer before the prohibited transaction occurred should not be treated as a disqualified person; whereas an individual who divested himself of stockholdings by the date of the prohibited transaction, but did not terminate employment until after the prohibited transaction occurred, was a disqualified person. [Rutland, 89 T.C. 1137 (1987)]

Q 24:5 What penalties may be imposed on a party in interest or disqualified person for engaging in a prohibited transaction?

Under the Code, a penalty tax equal to 15 percent of the amount involved in the transaction is imposed on the disqualified person (see Q 24:4) (other than a fiduciary acting solely in that capacity) for each year or part thereof that the transaction remains uncorrected (first-tier excise tax). The amount involved is determined by considering the transaction to be separate and continuing prohibited transactions on the day it occurred and on the first day of each subsequent taxable year. Thus, the 15 percent penalty tax carries over from year to year *and* a new 15 percent penalty tax is imposed each year. Because it is *both* a continuing transaction and a new transaction each year, the penalty tax pyramids. An additional tax (second-tier excise tax) equal to 100 percent of the amount involved is imposed if the prohibited transaction is not timely corrected (see Q 24:6). [I.R.C. §§ 4975(a), 4975(b); Treas. Reg. §§ 53.4941(c)-1(b)(2)(ii), 53.4941(e)-1(e)(1); Rev. Rul. 2002-43, 2002-2 C.B. 85; Geib, 80 T.C.M. 931 (2000); Rollins, 88 T.C.M. 447 (2004); Morrissey, 76 T.C.M. 1006 (1998); Davis v. United States, 93-2047 (4th Cir. 1995); Lambos, 88 T.C. 1440 (1987)] Moreover, parties who engage in a prohibited transaction can be liable, in addition to the penalty tax, for another penalty for failure to file Form 5330 (see Q 21:18). [Geib, 80 T.C.M. 931 (2000); Janpol, 102 T.C. 499 (1994); Janpol, 101 T.C. 518 (1993)]

Before sending a notice of deficiency with respect to the excise tax, IRS is required to notify DOL and provide DOL with a reasonable opportunity to obtain a correction of the prohibited transaction or to comment on the imposition of the excise tax. [I.R.C. § 4975(h)] An IRS notification to DOL informing it of a series of prohibited transactions was sufficient even though IRS failed to identify all disqualified persons involved in the prohibited transactions. IRS concluded that each disqualified person need not be specifically named for the notice to be adequate. [Field Serv. Adv. 200118016]

The 15 percent penalty tax was increased by TRA '97 from 10 percent for prohibited transactions occurring after *August 5, 1997*, after the 10 percent penalty tax had been increased by SBA '96 from 5 percent for prohibited transactions occurring after *August 20, 1996*. Because the amount involved is determined by considering the transaction to be separate and continuing prohibited transactions on the day it occurred and on the first day of each subsequent taxable year, if the prohibited transaction first occurred prior to August 5, 1997, and continued into the next taxable year, the penalty tax will be 15 percent of the amount involved for such subsequent taxable year. [Rev. Rul. 2002-43, 2002-2 C.B. 85]

The amount involved in a prohibited transaction generally means the greater of the amount of money and the fair market value of the other property given, or the amount of money and the fair market value of the other property received. Fair market value must be determined as of the date on which the prohibited transaction occurs. If the use of money or other property is involved, the amount involved is the greater of the amount paid for the use or the fair market value of the use for the period for which the money or other property is used. In addition, as previously stated, transactions involving the use of money or other property are treated as giving rise to a prohibited transaction occurring on the date of the actual transaction plus a new prohibited transaction on the first day of each succeeding taxable year or portion of a succeeding taxable year that is within the taxable period. The taxable period is the period of time beginning with the date of the prohibited transaction and ending with the earliest of (1) the date correction is completed; (2) the date of mailing of a notice of deficiency; or

(3) the date on which the tax is assessed. [Treas. Reg. §§ 53.4941(c)-1(b)(2)(ii), 53.4941(e)-1(e)(1); Rev. Rul. 2002-43, 2002-2 C.B. 85]

Example 1. During September 2002, a qualified retirement plan purchased property from a disqualified person for $10,000. The fair market value of the property was $5,000. The amount involved in the transaction is $10,000 (the greater of the amount received by the disqualified person or the fair market value of the property). The initial excise tax is $1,500 (15% × $10,000).

Example 2. A disqualified person borrowed money from a plan in a prohibited transaction. The fair market value of the use of the money and the actual interest on the loan is $1,000 per month. The loan was made on July 1, 1995, and repaid on December 31, 1996 (date of correction). The disqualified person's taxable year is the calendar year. On July 31, 1997, the disqualified person filed a delinquent Form 5330 for the 1995 plan year and a timely Form 5330 for the 1996 plan year (see Q 21:18). No notice of deficiency with respect to the tax had been mailed to the disqualified person, and no assessment of the tax had been made before the time the disqualified person filed Forms 5330.

When a loan is a prohibited transaction, the loan is treated as giving rise to a prohibited transaction on the date the transaction occurs, and an additional prohibited transaction occurs on the first day of each succeeding taxable year within the taxable period. Each prohibited transaction has its own separate taxable period that begins on the date the prohibited transaction occurred or is deemed to occur and ends on the date of the correction. The taxable period that begins on the date the loan occurs runs from July 1, 1995 (date of loan), through December 31, 1996 (date of correction). Therefore, in this example, there were two prohibited transactions: the first occurred on July 1, 1995, and the second occurred on January 1, 1996. A 5 percent tax is imposed on the amount involved for each taxable year or part thereof in the taxable period of each prohibited transaction.

The amount involved to be reported on Form 5330 filed for 1995 is $6,000 (6 months × $1,000 of interest). The amount of tax due is $300 (5% × $6,000). Any interest and penalties imposed for the delinquent filing of Form 5330 for 1995 will be billed separately to the disqualified person.

The taxable period for the second prohibited transaction ran from January 1, 1996 through December 31, 1996 (date of correction). Because there were two prohibited transactions with taxable periods running during 1996, the penalty tax is due for the 1996 taxable year for both prohibited transactions. The penalty tax to be reported on Form 5330 filed for 1996 includes both the prohibited transaction of July 1, 1995, with an amount involved of $6,000, resulting in a tax due of $300 (5% × $6,000) and the second prohibited transaction of January 1, 1996, with an amount involved of $12,000 (12 months × $1,000 of interest), resulting in a tax due of $600 (5% × $12,000). The total penalty tax for 1996 is $900 ($300 + $600).

If the loan was not repaid until December 31, 1997, the penalty tax to be reported on Form 5330 filed for 1997 includes the prohibited transaction of

July 1, 1995, with an amount involved of $6,000, resulting in a tax due of $300 (5% × $6,000); the second prohibited transaction of January 1, 1996, with an amount involved of $12,000 (12 months × $1,000 of interest), resulting in a tax due of $600 (5% × $12,000); and a third prohibited transaction of January 1, 1997, with an amount involved of $12,000 (12 months × $1,000 of interest), resulting in a tax due of $1,200 (10% × $12,000). The total penalty tax for 1997 would be $2,100 ($300 + $600 + $1,200).

If the loan was not repaid until December 31, 1998, the penalty tax to be reported on Form 5330 filed for 1998 includes the prohibited transaction of July 1, 1995, with an amount involved of $6,000, resulting in a tax due of $300 (5% × $6,000); the second prohibited transaction of January 1, 1996, with an amount involved of $12,000 (12 months × $1,000 of interest), resulting in a tax due of $600 (5% × $12,000); the third prohibited transaction of January 1, 1997, with an amount involved of $12,000 (12 months × $1,000 of interest), resulting in a tax due of $1,200 (10% × $12,000); and a fourth prohibited transaction of January 1, 1998, with an amount involved of $12,000 (12 months × $1,000 of interest), resulting in a tax due of $1,800 (15% × $12,000). The total penalty tax for 1998 would be $3,900 ($300 + $600 + $1,200 + $1,800).

IRS has determined what the amount involved is if an employer does not timely pay elective deferrals (see Q 27:16) to a qualified retirement plan. Under the ruling, the employer sponsors a 401(k) plan (see Q 27:1). The employees are paid on a payment date following the close of each payroll period. Pursuant to the terms of the plan, during a specific payroll period, a portion of the pay of each employee was withheld in accordance with a cash-or-deferred election (see Q 27:3) made by the employee. The aggregate amount withheld for all employees for that payroll period totaled $100,000. Although the employer could reasonably segregate this amount from its general assets and transmit it to the plan on December 8, 2004, the employer failed to do so and did not correct the failure until December 30, 2005. The applicable interest rate for underpayments was five percent on both December 8, 2004, and January 1, 2005.

IRS ruled that the failure to transmit the contribution until December 30, 2005, constitutes a prohibited transaction for 2004 and a prohibited transaction for 2005. Accordingly, (1) the amount involved for the 2004 prohibited transaction is interest on $100,000 from December 8, 2004, to December 31, 2004, and (2) the amount involved for the 2005 prohibited transaction is interest on the new balance owed to the plan after increasing the principal as a result of there not being a correction of the 2004 prohibited transaction and is calculated from January 1, 2005, to December 30, 2005. The taxable period for the 2004 prohibited transaction begins on December 8, 2004 and ends on December 30, 2005 (the date of the correction), and the taxable period for the 2005 prohibited transaction begins on January 1, 2005, and ends on December 30, 2005 (the date of the correction).

For purposes of calculating the excise tax on a timely filed Form 5330 for a failure to transmit participant contributions or amounts that would have otherwise been payable to the participant in cash, the applicable interest rate for underpayments on the date of the prohibited transaction is an appropriate rate used to calculate the amount involved. The following illustrates the application of this rate to the facts above (and taking into account only the first-tier excise tax):

Calculation of the Amount Involved

No.	Date	Principal	Interest Rate	Time	Amount Involved
1.	12/8/2004	$100,000	5%	.0628415 (28/366)	$314
2.	1/1/2005	$100,314	5%	.9972602 (364/365)	$5,002

Calculation of First-Tier Excise Tax

Act No.	Date of Prohibited Transaction	Taxable Period	2004 Taxable Year	2005 Taxable Year
1.	12/8/2004	12/8/04 to 12/30/04	$314	$314
2.	1/1/2005	1/1/05 to 12/30/05	-0-	$5,002
			$314	$5,316
			× 15%	× 15%
			$ 47	$ 797

Accordingly, the first-tier excise tax totals $844 ($47 + $797).

[Rev. Rul. 2006-38, 2006-2 C.B. 80; I.R.C. § 6621(A)(2)]

IRS has authority to abate the penalty tax. [I.R.C. § 4962]

If a taxpayer files Form 5330, pays the prohibited transaction penalty tax, and later determines that it overpaid the penalty tax, a claim for refund may be made. To be timely, a refund claim must be filed within three years from the time the return was filed or two years from the time the tax was paid, whichever period expires later. One court concluded that, for purposes of the prohibited-transaction excise tax, the relevant return is the plan's annual return (Form 5500; see Q 21:1), not Form 5330. [Imperial Plan, Inc. v. United States, 95 F.3d 25 (9th Cir. 1996); I.R.C. §§ 6501(*l*)(1), 6511(f)]

Example. For its 2004 plan year, B. Karsh Travel Corp. filed Form 5500 on July 31, 2005. After being advised that the corporation had engaged in a prohibited transaction during the 2004 plan year, the corporation filed a delinquent Form 5330 and paid the penalty tax on December 16, 2005. On December 1, 2008, B. Karsh Travel Corp. filed a claim for refund alleging that it overpaid the penalty tax. Although the claim for refund was filed within the three-year period following its filing of Form 5330, the claim was too late because it was more than three years after Form 5500 was filed (i.e., July 31, 2008) and more than two years after the penalty tax was paid (i.e., December 16, 2007).

Under ERISA, any fiduciary (see Q 23:1) who engages in a prohibited transaction is personally liable for any losses to the plan and must restore to the plan any profit made by the fiduciary through the use of the plan's assets. A plan trustee was ordered to disgorge profits he earned from the resale of property he purchased with funds improperly borrowed from the plan because he had used plan assets to obtain financing for his purchase on more favorable terms than were otherwise available, thereby improving his financial circumstances and increasing his profits. [Felber v. Estate of Regan, 1997 U.S. App. LEXIS 16069 (8th Cir. 1997)] Also, the civil penalty imposed by DOL for certain breaches of fiduciary duty applies to prohibited transactions (see Q 23:36), but the penalty is reduced by any penalty tax imposed under Section 4975. [ERISA §§ 409(a), 502(*l*)] Where a former participant alleged that his employer breached its fiduciary duty by engaging in a prohibited transaction, the court dismissed his claim on the grounds that the relief sought must benefit the plan as a whole and not just an individual participant. [ERISA § 502(a)(2); Owen v. Soundview Fin. Group, Inc., No. 99-7994 (2d Cir. 2000)] One court has ruled that the Double Jeopardy Clause of the United States Constitution does not bar the imposition of the civil penalty against a plan trustee who was convicted of embezzling funds from qualified retirement plans. [DOL v. Rutledge, No. 92-7011 (11th Cir. 1993)]

A DOL consent judgment regarding prohibited transactions entered into by a trustee of a qualified retirement plan was not binding upon IRS because the definition of a prohibited transaction under the Code differs from the ERISA definition and because the consent judgment specifically indicated it was made without admitting or denying DOL's allegations, concluded one court. Therefore, the prohibited transaction penalties assessed against the trustee by IRS were upheld. [Baizer v. Comm'r, 204 F.3d 1231 (9th Cir. 2000)]

Q 24:6   How is a prohibited transaction corrected?

A prohibited transaction is corrected by undoing the transaction to the extent possible, but in any event placing the plan in a financial position no worse than the position it would have been in had the party in interest (see Q 24:3) acted under the highest fiduciary standards. [I.R.C. § 4975(f)(5)]

If a prohibited transaction is not corrected during the taxable period, an additional tax equal to 100 percent of the amount involved may be imposed (second-tier excise tax). The term "taxable period" means, with respect to a prohibited transaction, the period beginning with the date on which the prohibited transaction occurs and ending on the earliest of:

1. The date of mailing a notice of deficiency with respect to the first-tier excise tax (see Q 24:5) under Section 6212;

2. The date on which the first-tier excise tax is assessed; or

3. The date on which correction of the prohibited transaction is completed. [I.R.C. §§ 4975(b), 4975(f)(2)]

If a prohibited transaction is corrected during the taxable period, then the 100 percent tax imposed with respect to the prohibited transaction (including interest, additions to the tax, and additional amounts) will not be assessed, and if assessed will be abated, and if collected will be credited or refunded as an overpayment. The goal, if possible, is correction of the prohibited transaction, rather than the collection of the 100 percent tax. [I.R.C. § 4961; IRS Litig. Guideline Mem. (TL-83)]

A subsidiary that sold customer loans to its parent corporation's profit sharing plan was not entitled to an exemption from the initial tax (first-tier excise tax) on prohibited transactions (see Q 24:5) because no class exemption (see Q 24:26) was available since the plan trustee was also the sole shareholder and president of the parent corporation and president of the subsidiary. The plan could not cure the prohibited transaction by retroactively appointing an unrelated co-trustee (see Q 24:24). However, the subsidiary was not assessed the second-tier excise tax because the plan timely sold the loans. [Westoak Realty & Inv. Co. v. Comm'r, 999 F.2d 308 (8th Cir. 1993), aff'g 63 T.C.M. 2502 (1992)]

Where the sole shareholder of a corporation made loans from its qualified retirement plans and repaid the loans and accrued interest by transferring his interest in two parcels of real estate to the plans, the shareholder was liable for the first-tier excise tax because the transfer was a prohibited sale or exchange (see Q 24:1) and also for the second-tier excise tax because the prohibited transaction was never corrected. In this case, the assessed first-tier and second-tier excise taxes exceeded $1,500,000. [Morrissey, 76 T.C.M. 1006 (1998)] An individual's partial repayment of prohibited loans was insufficient to correct the entire transaction. [Geib, 80 T.C.M. 931 (2000)]

A sole shareholder's transfer of assets from the employer's two retirement plans to the employer's checking account constituted a prohibited transaction. Furthermore, the sole shareholder's payments to former participants from the employer's assets and from his own funds did not correct the prohibited transaction because the plans were not restored to the same financial position they would have been in had the prohibited transaction not occurred. The employer and the shareholder were found jointly and severally liable for both the first-tier and second-tier excise taxes. [Priv. Ltr. Rul. 9316001]

One court ruled that a prohibited transaction corrected itself because it was an extremely successful investment, thereby enabling the disqualified persons (see Q 24:4) to avoid additional assessments of both the first-tier excise tax and the second-tier excise tax. [Zabolotny v. Comm'r, 7 F.3d 774 (8th Cir. 1993)] IRS disagrees that the prohibited transaction was self-correcting and announced that although it will follow the decision in cases arising within the Eighth Circuit, it will not adhere to the decision on a nationwide basis. [Non-acq, 1994-1 C.B. 1; Action on Decision 1994-004 (May 31, 1994)]

On occasion, a prohibited transaction is required to correct a prohibited transaction. For example, a sale of assets to a plan by the plan sponsor is a prohibited transaction; and if to undo the transaction the plan sponsor wishes to purchase those assets from the plan, that, too, is a prohibited transaction. Therefore, to undo the transaction, an exemption must be obtained (see Q 24:20). DOL has issued a class exemption (see Q 24:26) that covers transactions specifically authorized by DOL under a settlement agreement and thus permits the proposed corrective action to be taken without an individual exemption. To be exempt, the following conditions must be met:

1. The transaction (i.e., corrective action) must have been authorized by DOL pursuant to a settlement agreement and must follow a DOL investigation.

2. The transaction must be described in writing by the terms of the settlement agreement.

3. The parties in interest must give advance written notice of the transaction to all affected participants and beneficiaries at least 30 days before the settlement agreement.

4. The notice and method of distribution must be approved in advance by the DOL office that negotiated the settlement.

5. The notice must include a description of the transaction, the approximate date on which the transaction will occur, the address of the DOL office that negotiated the settlement agreement, and a statement informing participants and beneficiaries of their right to forward comments to the DOL office.

[PTCE 94-71 (59 Fed. Reg. 51,216)]

A prohibited transaction can be corrected by an in-kind distribution of property to a participant in connection with the termination of a plan (see Q 25:1) when the participant who receives the property is not the party in interest who sold it to the plan. This correction is possible because rescission is not required if the property is transferred to a third party in an arm's-length transaction. [Treas. Reg. § 53.4941(e)-1(c)(3)(ii)]

PPA (see Q 1:33) provides a prohibited-transaction exemption (see Q 24:8) for a transaction in connection with the acquisition, holding, or disposition of any security or commodity if the transaction is corrected within a certain period, generally within 14 days of the date the disqualified person (or other person knowingly participating in the transaction) discovers, or reasonably should have discovered, the transaction was a prohibited transaction. For this purpose, correct means, with respect to a transaction, (1) to undo the transaction to the extent possible and in any case to make good to the plan or affected account any losses resulting from the transaction, and (2) to restore to the plan or affected account any profits made through the use of assets of the plan. If the exemption applies, no excise tax will be assessed against the transaction, any tax assessed will be abated, and any tax collected will be credited or refunded as a tax overpayment.

The exemption does not apply to any transaction between a plan and a plan sponsor or its affiliates that involves the acquisition or sale of an employer security (see Q 23:86) or the acquisition, sale, or lease of employer real property (see Q 23:85). In addition, in the case of a disqualified person (or other person knowingly participating in the transaction), the exemption does not apply if, at the time of the transaction, the person knew (or reasonably should have known) that the transaction would constitute a prohibited transaction.

This provision applies to any transaction that the fiduciary or disqualified person discovers, or reasonably should have discovered, after August 17, 2006, constitutes a prohibited transaction.

[ERISA § 408(b)(20); I.R.C. §§ 4975(d)(23), 4975(f)(11) (as amended by WRERA 2008 § 106(c))]

Q 24:7 May a plan purchase insurance to cover any losses to the plan resulting from a prohibited transaction?

Yes, a plan may carry insurance to protect itself from loss due to the conduct of a fiduciary (see Q 23:1). However, a plan cannot contain a provision relieving a fiduciary from liability for actions taken with respect to a prohibited transaction. [ERISA § 410]

Q 24:8 Are there any statutory exceptions to the prohibited-transaction provisions?

There are numerous statutory exceptions to the prohibited-transaction provisions. Some of the most common are the following:

1. Loans made by a plan to a party in interest (see Q 24:3) who is a plan participant or beneficiary if such loans (1) are available to all participants and beneficiaries on a reasonably equivalent basis, (2) are not made available to highly compensated employees (see Q 3:2) in an amount greater than the amount made available to other employees, (3) are made in accordance with specific provisions regarding such loans set forth in the plan, (4) bear a reasonable rate of interest, and (5) are adequately secured. For more details on plan loans, see chapter 14.

2. Services rendered by a party in interest to a plan that are necessary for the establishment or operation of the plan if no more than reasonable compensation is paid. DOL has found no violation when a fiduciary received investment management fees from a plan. [DOL Op. Ltrs. 93-06A, 92-08A]

3. A loan to an employee stock ownership plan (ESOP), provided the loan is primarily for the benefit of plan participants and beneficiaries and the interest rate is not in excess of a reasonable interest rate (see Q 28:7).

4. Ancillary services provided by a federal or state supervised bank or similar financial institution that is a fiduciary (see Q 23:1) to the plan, provided (1) the bank or similar financial institution has adopted adequate internal safeguards to ensure that provision of the ancillary service is consistent with sound banking and financial practice and (2) no more than reasonable compensation is paid for such services.

5. The acquisition or sale by a plan of qualifying employer securities (see Q 23:86) or the acquisition, sale, or lease by a plan of qualifying employer

real property (see Q 23:85) if (1) the acquisition, sale, or lease is for adequate consideration; (2) no commission is charged; and (3) the restrictions and limitations of ERISA Section 407 are satisfied. [Cosgrove v. Circle K Corp., 1997 U.S. App. LEXIS 3853 (9th Cir. 1997)]

[ERISA §§ 3(18)(B), 408(b), 408(e); I.R.C. §§ 3409(l)(2), 4975(d); DOL Op. Ltr. 90-04A]

In one case, disqualified persons (see Q 24:4) sold their interest in land, including mineral rights, to an ESOP (see Q 28:1). Because the mineral rights were not leased to the employer and, with respect to the land leased, such properties were not dispersed geographically, the land did not constitute qualifying employer real property and the exemption did not apply. [Zabolotny, 97 T.C. 385 (1991); *but see* Zabolotny v. Comm'r, 7 F.3d 774 (8th Cir. 1993), *non-acq,* 1994-1 C.B. 1; A.O.D. 1994-004 (May 31, 1994)] In another case, a real estate transaction between a disqualified person and a profit sharing plan did not satisfy the requirements for an exemption because the property was never leased to the corporation sponsoring the plan or to an affiliate and was not composed of a substantial number of land parcels dispersed geographically. [Pearland Inv. Co., 62 T.C.M. 1221 (1991); *see also* Rutland, 89 T.C. 1137 (1987); Lambos, 88 T.C. 1440 (1987)] DOL has ruled that the ERISA definition, and not the Code definition, of "employer securities" controls for purposes of determining prohibited-transaction exemptions. [DOL Op. Ltr. 96-08A]

IRS ruled that the contribution of stock options granted by the employer to its 401(k) plan (see Q 27:1) would be deductible by the employer to the extent of the fair market value of the options granted. [Priv. Ltr. Rul. 9712033] However, IRS announced that it would reexamine its ruling. [Ann. 97-45, 1997-17 I.R.B. 20] No reference was made in the ruling concerning potential prohibited-transaction issues. The employer made an application to DOL for an exemption from the prohibited-transaction rules (see Q 24:20). [Exemption Application No. D-10269 (61 Fed. Reg. 68,794)] However, DOL representatives have opined that a 401(k) plan cannot hold a right to allow any of its participants to purchase employer securities at a fixed price for an entire year. Although the right is an option and the option is an employer security, it is not a qualifying employer security and holding it in the plan constitutes a prohibited transaction. After almost six years, IRS revoked its ruling and advised that it is still considering these issues. [Priv. Ltr. Rul. 200401021]

DOL has opined that loans from plans that are made available to participants of different bargaining units only after their collective bargaining agreements are renegotiated will be treated as being available to participants on a reasonably equivalent basis, as long as all bargaining units approve the loan feature within a reasonable period of time. Therefore, the loans will be exempt from ERISA's prohibited-transaction provisions. [DOL Op. Ltr. 95-19A] DOL has also opined that a plan's agreement to settle a lawsuit against a service provider, arising out of the underlying service arrangement, could qualify for ERISA's exemption from the prohibited-transaction rules for plans that reasonably contract with parties in interest for services necessary for the operation of the plan, provided that certain conditions are satisfied. [DOL Op. Ltr. 95-26A]

The statutory exceptions to the prohibited-transaction rules do not fail to apply merely because a transaction involves the sale of employer securities to an ESOP maintained by an S corporation by a shareholder-employee, a family member of the shareholder-employee, or a corporation controlled by the shareholder-employee (see Q 28:2). Thus, the statutory exemptions for such a transaction (including the exemption for a loan to the ESOP to acquire employer securities in connection with such a sale or a guarantee of such a loan) apply. [I.R.C. § 4975(f)(6)]

One court concluded that loans from a qualified retirement plan to a fiduciary were prohibited transactions and rejected the fiduciary's claim that the loans benefited the plan participants. [Zacky, 87 T.C.M. 1378 (2004)]

A plan may suspend an employee's obligation to pay a plan loan during the period of the employee's military service without engaging in a prohibited transaction (see Q 1:16).

In addition to the new prohibited-transaction exemption discussed in Q 24:6, see Q 24:9 for new statutory exceptions to the prohibited-transaction provisions.

Q 24:9 Did PPA add new statutory prohibited-transaction exemptions?

With one exception (see Q 24:10), effective for transactions occurring after August 17, 2006, PPA (see Q 1:33) adds a number of a new statutory exceptions to the prohibited-transaction provisions. [PPA §§ 601(a)(3), 601(b)(4), 611(h)(1)] A number of the new exceptions codify previously issued prohibited-transaction class exemptions (see Q 24:26). The new statutory exemptions are for:

1. Investment advice (see Q 24:10).
2. Block trading (see Q 24:14).
3. Electronic communication network (see Q 24:15).
4. Service providers (see Q 24:16).
5. Foreign exchange transactions (see Q 24:17).
6. Cross-trading (see Q 24:18).

Q 24:10 What is the prohibited-transaction exemption for investment advice?

PPA (see Q 1:33) adds a new category of prohibited-transaction exemption (see Q 24:8) in connection with the provision of investment advice through an eligible investment advice arrangement to participants and beneficiaries of a defined contribution plan (see Q 2:2) who direct the investment of their accounts under the plan and to beneficiaries of IRAs (see Q 30:1). If the requirements are met, the following are exempt from prohibited-transaction treatment: (1) the provision of investment advice; (2) an investment transaction (i.e., a sale, acquisition, or holding of a security or other property) pursuant to the advice; and (3) the direct or indirect receipt of fees or other compensation in connection with the provision of the advice or an investment transaction pursuant to the advice. These prohibited-transaction exemptions do not in any manner alter existing individual or class exemptions provided by statute or administrative action.

DOL is also directed, in consultation with IRS, to determine, based on certain information to be solicited by DOL, whether there is any computer model investment advice program that meets the requirements of the provision and may be used by IRAs. The determination is to be made by December 31, 2007. If DOL determines there is such a program, the exemptions described above apply in connection with the use of the program with respect to IRA beneficiaries. If DOL determines that there is not such a program, it is directed to grant a class exemption from prohibited-transaction treatment (as discussed below) for the provision of investment advice, investment transactions pursuant to such advice, and related fees to beneficiaries of such arrangements.

These exemptions apply in connection with the provision of investment advice by a fiduciary adviser under an eligible investment advice arrangement. An eligible investment advice arrangement is an arrangement (1) meeting certain requirements (discussed below) and (2) which either provides that any fees (including any commission or compensation) received by the fiduciary adviser for investment advice or with respect to an investment transaction with respect to plan assets do not vary depending on the basis of any investment option selected, or uses a computer model under an investment advice program as described below in connection with the provision of investment advice to a participant or beneficiary. In the case of an eligible investment advice arrangement with respect to a defined contribution plan (see Q 2:2), the arrangement must be expressly authorized by a plan fiduciary other than (1) the person offering the investment advice program, (2) any person providing investment options under the plan, or (3) any affiliate of (1) or (2).

If an eligible investment advice arrangement provides investment advice pursuant to a computer model, the model must (1) apply generally accepted investment theories that take into account the historic returns of different asset classes over defined periods of time, (2) use relevant information about the participant or beneficiary, (3) use prescribed objective criteria to provide asset allocation portfolios comprised of investment options under the plan, (4) operate in a manner that is not biased in favor of any investment options offered by the fiduciary adviser or related person, and (5) take into account all the investment options under the plan in specifying how a participant's or beneficiary's account should be invested without inappropriate weighting of any investment option. An eligible investment expert must certify, before the model is used and in accordance with rules prescribed by DOL, that the model meets these requirements. The certification must be renewed if there are material changes to the model as determined under regulations. For this purpose, an eligible investment expert is a person who meets requirements prescribed by DOL and who does not bear any material affiliation or contractual relationship with any investment adviser or related person.

In addition, if a computer model is used, the only investment advice that may be provided under the arrangement is the advice generated by the computer model, and any investment transaction pursuant to the advice must occur solely at the direction of the participant or beneficiary. This requirement does not preclude the participant or beneficiary from requesting other investment advice, but only if the request has not been solicited by any person connected with carrying out the investment advice arrangement.

In the case of an eligible investment advice arrangement with respect to a defined contribution plan, an annual audit of the arrangement for compliance with applicable requirements must be conducted by an independent auditor (i.e., unrelated to the person offering the investment advice arrangement or any person providing investment options under the plan) who has appropriate technical training or experience and proficiency and who so represents in writing. The auditor must issue a report of the audit results to the fiduciary that authorized use of the arrangement. In the case of an eligible investment advice arrangement with respect to IRAs, an audit is required at such times and in such manner as prescribed by DOL.

Before the initial provision of investment advice, the fiduciary adviser must provide written notice (which may be in electronic form) containing various information to the recipient of the advice, including information relating: (1) the role of any related party in the development of the investment advice program or the selection of investment options under the plan; (2) past performance and rates of return for each investment option offered under the plan; (3) any fees or other compensation to be received by the fiduciary adviser or affiliate; (4) any material affiliation or contractual relationship of the fiduciary adviser or affiliates in the security or other property involved in the investment transaction; (5) the manner and under what circumstances any participant or beneficiary information will be used or disclosed; (6) the types of services provided by the fiduciary adviser in connection with the provision of investment advice; (7) the adviser's status as a fiduciary of the plan in connection with the provision of the advice; and (8) the ability of the recipient of the advice separately to arrange for the provision of advice by another adviser that could have no material affiliation with and receive no fees or other compensation in connection with the security or other property. This information must be maintained in accurate form and must be provided to the recipient of the investment advice, without charge, on an annual basis, on request, or in the case of any material change.

Any notification must be written in a clear and conspicuous manner, calculated to be understood by the average plan participant, and sufficiently accurate and comprehensive so as to reasonably apprise participants and beneficiaries of the required information. DOL is directed to issue a model form for the disclosure of fees and other compensation as required by the provision. The fiduciary adviser must maintain for at least six years any records necessary for determining whether the requirements for the prohibited-transaction exemption were met. A prohibited transaction will not be considered to have occurred solely because records were lost or destroyed before the end of six years due to circumstances beyond the adviser's control.

In order for the exemption to apply, the following additional requirements must be satisfied: (1) the fiduciary adviser must provide disclosures applicable under securities laws; (2) an investment transaction must occur solely at the direction of the recipient of the advice; (3) compensation received by the fiduciary adviser or affiliates in connection with an investment transaction must be reasonable; and (4) the terms of the investment transaction must be at least as favorable to the plan as an arm's-length transaction would be.

For purposes of the provision, fiduciary adviser is a person who is a fiduciary of the plan by reason of the provision of investment advice to a participant or beneficiary and who is also: (1) registered as an investment adviser under the Investment Advisers Act of 1940 or under State laws; (2) a bank, a similar financial institution supervised by the United States or a State, or a savings association (as defined under the Federal Deposit Insurance Act), but only if the advice is provided through a trust department that is subject to a periodic examination and review by Federal or State banking authorities; (3) an insurance company qualified to do business under State law; (4) registered as a broker or dealer under the Securities Exchange Act of 1934; (5) an affiliate of any of the preceding; or (6) an employee, agent, or registered representative of any of the preceding who satisfies the requirements of applicable insurance, banking, and securities laws relating to the provision of advice. A person who develops the computer model or markets the investment advice program or computer model is treated as a person who is a plan fiduciary by reason of the provision of investment advice and is treated as a fiduciary adviser, except that DOL may prescribe rules under which only one fiduciary adviser may elect treatment as a plan fiduciary. Affiliate is an affiliated person as defined under Section 2(a)(3) of the Investment Company Act of 1940, and registered representative is a person described in Section 3(a)(18) of the Securities Exchange Act of 1934 or a person described in Section 202(a)(17) of the Investment Advisers Act of 1940.

Subject to certain requirements, an employer or other person who is a plan fiduciary, other than a fiduciary adviser, is not treated as failing to meet the fiduciary requirements of ERISA solely by reason of the provision of investment advice as permitted under this provision or of contracting for or otherwise arranging for the provision of the advice. This rule applies if (1) the advice is provided under an arrangement between the employer or plan fiduciary and the fiduciary adviser for the provision of investment advice by the fiduciary adviser as permitted under this provision; (2) the terms of the arrangement require compliance by the fiduciary adviser with the requirements of this provision; and (3) the terms of the arrangement include a written acknowledgement by the fiduciary adviser that the fiduciary adviser is a plan fiduciary with respect to the advice.

This provision does not exempt the employer or a plan fiduciary from fiduciary responsibility under ERISA for the prudent selection and periodic review of a fiduciary adviser with whom the employer or plan fiduciary has arranged for the provision of investment advice. The employer or plan fiduciary does not have the duty to monitor the specific investment advice given by a fiduciary adviser. Nothing in the fiduciary responsibility provisions of ERISA will be construed to preclude the use of plan assets (see Q 23:23) to pay for reasonable expenses in providing investment advice.

Under this provision, DOL must determine, in consultation with IRS, whether there is any computer model investment advice program that can be used by IRAs and that meets the above requirements. The determination is to be made on the basis of information to be solicited by DOL as described below. Under this provision, a computer model investment advice program must (1) use relevant information about the beneficiary, (2) take into account the full range of investments, including equities and bonds, in determining the options for the investment portfolio of the beneficiary, and (3) allow the account beneficiary, in directing the investment of assets, sufficient flexibility in obtaining advice to evaluate and select options.

As soon as practicable after August 17, 2006, DOL, in consultation with IRS, must solicit information as to the feasibility of the application of computer model investment advice programs for IRAs, including from (1) at least the top 50 trustees of IRAs, determined on the basis of assets held by such trustees, and (2) other persons offering such programs based on nonproprietary products. The information solicited by DOL from such trustees and other persons is to include information on their computer modeling capabilities with respect to the current year and the preceding year, including their capabilities for investment accounts they maintain. If a person from whom DOL solicits information does not provide such information within 60 days after the solicitation, the person is not entitled to use any class exemption granted by DOL as required under this provision (as discussed below) unless such failure is due to reasonable cause and not willful neglect.

The exemptions provided with respect to an eligible investment advice arrangement involving a computer model do not apply to IRAs. If DOL determines that there is a computer model investment advice program that can be used by IRAs, the exemptions with respect to an eligible investment advice arrangement involving a computer model can apply to IRAs.

If, as a result of the study of this issue, DOL determines that there is not such a program, it must grant a class exemption from prohibited-transaction treatment for (1) the provision of investment advice by a fiduciary adviser to beneficiaries of IRAs; (2) investment transactions pursuant to the advice; and (3) the direct or indirect receipt of fees or other compensation in connection with the provision of the advice or an investment transaction pursuant to the advice. Application of the exemptions are to be subject to conditions as are set forth in the class exemption and as are (1) in the interests of the IRA and its beneficiary and protective of the rights of the beneficiary, and (2) necessary to ensure the requirements of the applicable exemptions and the investment advice provided utilizes prescribed objective criteria to provide asset allocation portfolios comprised of securities or other property available as investments under the IRA. Such conditions could require that the fiduciary adviser providing the advice (1) adopt written policies and procedures that ensure the advice provided is not biased in favor of investments offered by the fiduciary adviser or a related person, and (2) appoint an individual responsible for annually reviewing the advice provided to determine that the advice is provided in accordance with the policies and procedures in (1).

If DOL later determines that there is any computer model investment advice program that can be used by IRAs, the class exemption ceases to apply after the later of (1) the date two years after DOL's later determination or (2) the date three years after the date the exemption first took effect.

Any person may request DOL to make a determination with respect to any computer model investment advice program as to whether it can be used by IRAs, and DOL must make such determination within 90 days of the request. If DOL determines that the program cannot be so used, within 10 days of the determination, it must notify the House Committees on Ways and Means and Education and the Workforce and the Senate Committees on Finance and Health, Education, Labor, and Pensions thereof and the reasons for the determination.

The above provisions are effective with respect to investment advice provided after December 31, 2006.

[ERISA §§ 408(b)(14), 408(g); I.R.C. §§ 4975(d)(17) (as amended by WRERA 2008 § 106(a)(2)(A)), 4975(f)(8) (as amended by WRERA 2008 § 106(a)(2)(B))]

DOL issued guidance concerning the new prohibited-transaction exemption for investment advice by asking and answering the following three questions.

1. Did enactment of the new investment advice provisions invalidate or otherwise affect prior guidance issued by DOL concerning investment advice?

No. It is the view of DOL that enactment of the new exemption allows the provision of investment advice to plan participants under circumstances that would, in the absence of an exemption, have constituted a prohibited transaction prior to the enactment of PPA. Except for providing that persons who develop or market computer models or who market investment advice programs using such models are fiduciaries, and requiring advisers to expressly acknowledge their fiduciary status, the new exemption does not alter ERISA's framework for determining fiduciary status or recast otherwise permissible forms of investment advice as prohibited. For this reason, it is the view of DOL that the new provisions do not invalidate or otherwise affect prior DOL guidance relating to investment advice and that such guidance continues to represent DOL's views.

Guidance of particular note in this regard includes: Interpretive Bulletin 96-1, in which DOL identified categories of investment-related information and materials that do not constitute investment advice; Advisory Opinion Nos. 97-15A (see Q 24:1) and 2005-10A (see Q 30:46), in which DOL explained that a fiduciary investment adviser could provide investment advice with respect to investment funds that pay it or an affiliate additional fees without engaging in a prohibited transaction if those fees are offset against fees that the plan otherwise is obligated to pay to the fiduciary; and Advisory Opinion 2001-09A (see Q 24:1) in which DOL concluded that the provision of fiduciary investment advice, under circumstances where the advice provided by the fiduciary with respect to investment funds that pay additional fees to the fiduciary is the result of the application of methodologies developed, maintained, and overseen by a party independent of the fiduciary, would not result in prohibited transactions.

2. To what extent are the standards for selecting and monitoring a fiduciary adviser different from the standards applicable to plan fiduciaries who offer an investment advice program with respect to which relief under the statutory exemption for investment advice is not required?

It is the view of DOL that, with the exception of certain requirements regarding compliance with the conditions of the statutory exemption, the same fiduciary duties and responsibilities apply to the selection and monitoring of an investment adviser for participants and beneficiaries in a participant-directed individual account plan, regardless of whether the program of investment advice services is one to which the statutory exemption applies.

A plan fiduciary will not be treated as failing to meet the requirements of ERISA solely by reason of the provision of investment advice or solely by reason of contracting or arranging for the provision of investment advice pursuant to an eligible investment advice arrangement but subject to the provision that addresses a fiduciary's duty to select and review the investment advice provider prudently. This principle is consistent with DOL's guidance provided in Interpretive Bulletin 96-1 regarding the provision of investment advice generally. Accordingly, it is DOL's view that a plan sponsor or other fiduciary will not fail to meet the requirements of ERISA solely by reason of offering a program of investment advice services to participants or beneficiaries that is not an eligible investment advice arrangement.

Plan fiduciaries have a duty to prudently select and periodically monitor the advisory program; however, fiduciaries have no duty to monitor the specific investment advice given by the fiduciary adviser to any particular recipient of advice. It is the view of DOL that these principles are consistent with those set forth in DOL regulations (see Q 23:14) and, therefore, are equally applicable to plan fiduciaries who select a program of investment advice services with respect to which relief under the investment advice statutory exemption is not required.

Thus, it is DOL's view that a plan sponsor or other fiduciary that prudently selects and monitors an investment advice provider will not be liable for the advice furnished by such provider to the plan's participants and beneficiaries, whether or not that advice is provided pursuant to the statutory exemption. DOL notes, however, that a fiduciary may have co-fiduciary liability if, for example, it knowingly participates in a breach committed by another fiduciary (see Q 23:58).

Although the Interpretive Bulletin does not address the monitoring of specific investment advice provided to a particular plan participant or beneficiary, DOL believes that fiduciaries selecting advisory programs are subject to the same fiduciary duty to prudently select and monitor investment advisers regardless of whether the advice arrangement was established under the exemption. Accordingly, it is the view of DOL that, like fiduciaries offering programs of investment advice services with respect to which exemptive relief is not required have no duty to monitor the specific investment advice given by the investment advice provider to any particular recipient of the advice.

With regard to the prudent selection of service providers generally, DOL has indicated that a fiduciary should engage in an objective process that is designed to elicit information necessary to assess the provider's qualifications, quality of services offered, and reasonableness of fees charged for the service. The process also must avoid self-dealing, conflicts of interest, or other improper influence. In applying these standards to the selection of investment advisers for plan participants, DOL anticipates that the process utilized by the responsible fiduciary will take into account the experience and qualifications of the investment adviser, including the adviser's registration in accordance with applicable federal and/or state securities law, the willingness of the adviser to assume fiduciary status and responsibility under ERISA with respect to the advice provided to participants, and the extent to which advice to be furnished to participants and beneficiaries will be based upon generally accepted investment theories.

In monitoring investment advisers, DOL anticipates that fiduciaries will periodically review, among other things, the extent to which there have been any changes in the information that served as the basis for the initial selection of the investment adviser, including whether the adviser continues to meet applicable federal and state securities law requirements, and whether the advice being furnished to participants and beneficiaries was based upon generally accepted investment theories. Fiduciaries also should take into account whether the investment advice provider is complying with the contractual provisions of the engagement; utilization of the investment advice services by the participants in relation to the cost of the services to the plan; and participant comments and complaints about the quality of the furnished advice. With regard to comments and complaints, DOL notes that, to the extent that a complaint or complaints raise questions concerning the quality of advice being provided to participants, a fiduciary may have to review the specific advice at issue with the investment adviser.

Plan assets can be used to pay reasonable expenses in providing investment advice to participants and beneficiaries. Again, this provision is consistent with the long-held view of DOL, provided that the service provider rendering investment advice is selected and monitored prudently. Consistent with this guidance, fiduciaries selecting programs of investment advice services with respect to which exemptive relief is not required may use plan assets to pay reasonable expenses in providing investment advice (and/or investment education) to plan participants and beneficiaries.

3. For purposes of an eligible investment advice arrangement, is an affiliate of a fiduciary adviser subject to the level fee requirement?

The investment advice exemption applies only to investment advice provided by a fiduciary adviser under an eligible investment advice arrangement. Included within the meaning of eligible investment advice arrangement is an arrangement that, among other things, provides that any fee (including any commission or other compensation) received by the fiduciary adviser for investment advice or with respect to the sale, holding, or acquisition of any security or other property for purposes of investment of plan assets do not vary depending on the basis of any investment option selected.

A fiduciary adviser is a person who is a fiduciary of the plan by reason of providing investment advice and who is a registered investment adviser, a bank or similar financial institution, an insurance company, or a registered broker-dealer; an affiliate of such registered investment adviser, bank, insurance company, or broker-dealer; or an employee, agent, or registered representative of any such entity.

Only the fees or other compensation of the fiduciary adviser may not vary. In this regard, DOL notes that, in contrast to other provisions of the investment advice exemption and the eligible investment advice arrangement, the fee provision references only the fiduciary adviser, not the fiduciary adviser or an affiliate. Inasmuch as a person can be fiduciary adviser only if that person is a fiduciary of the plan by virtue of providing investment advice, an affiliate of a registered investment adviser, a bank or similar financial institution, an insurance company, or a registered broker-dealer will be subject to the varying fee limitation only if that affiliate is providing investment advice to plan participants and beneficiaries.

Also consistent with past DOL guidance, if the fees and compensation received by an affiliate of a fiduciary that provides investment advice do not vary or are offset against those received by the fiduciary for the provision of investment advice, no prohibited transaction would result solely by reason of providing investment advice and thus there would be no need for a prohibited-transaction exemption. It is DOL's view, therefore, that Congress did not intend for the requirement that fees not vary depending on the basis of any investment options selected to extend to affiliates of the fiduciary adviser, unless, of course, the affiliate is also a provider of investment advice to a plan.

DOL further notes that, although fiduciary advisers are generally limited to certain types of entities, employees, agents, or registered representatives of those entities are also permitted to qualify as fiduciary advisers if they satisfy the requirements of applicable insurance, banking, and securities laws relating to the provision of the advice. As with affiliates, such an individual must not only be an employee, agent, or registered representative of one of those entities, but also must provide investment advice in such person's capacity as employee, agent, or registered representative. It is the view of DOL that where an individual acts as an employee, agent, or registered representative on behalf of an entity engaged to provide investment advice to a plan, that individual, as well as the entity, must be treated as the fiduciary adviser. In such instances, therefore, both the individual and the entity would be treated as fiduciary advisers and subject to the fee provision. DOL interprets the requirement that fees received by a fiduciary adviser not vary on the basis of any investment option selected as meaning that the fees or other compensation (including salary, bonuses, awards, promotions, or any other thing of value) received, directly or indirectly, from an employer, affiliate, or other party, by a fiduciary adviser (or used for the adviser's benefit) may not be based, in whole or part, on the investment options selected by participants or beneficiaries.

In general, a party seeking to avail itself of a statutory or administrative exemption from the prohibited-transaction provisions bears the burden of establishing compliance with the conditions of the exemption. With regard to the exemptive relief accorded an eligible investment advice arrangement, it is the expectation of DOL that parties offering investment advisory services will maintain, and be able to demonstrate compliance with, policies and procedures designed to ensure that fees and compensation paid to fiduciary advisers, at both the entity and individual level, do not vary on the basis of any investment option selected. Moreover, it is anticipated that compliance with such policies and procedures will be reviewed as part of the required annual audit and addressed in the required report.

[DOL Field Assistance Bull. 2007-1; ERISA §§ 3(21)(A)(ii), 408(b)(14), 408(g)(2)(A)(i), 408(g)(3), 408(g)(5), 408(g)(10), 408(g)(11)(A); DOL Reg. § 2509.96-1(e)]

DOL issued, but then withdrew, final regulations providing guidance on a prohibited-transaction exemption for investment advice provided under self-directed individual account plans (see Q 23:14) and IRAs (see Q 24:11). DOL issued proposed regulations to replace the withdrawn final regulations and advised that the proposed regulations are nearly identical to the withdrawn final regulations.

For a discussion of the proposed regulations and the definition of pertinent terms, see Q 24:11.

Q 24:11   Has DOL issued regulations concerning the prohibited-transaction exemption for investment advice?

Yes, and the final regulations that were issued in 2009 applied to transactions occurring on or after November 18, 2009. [74 Fed. Reg. 23,951] DOL first extended the effective date to May 17, 2010 and then, three days later, withdrew the final regulations. [74 Fed. Reg. 59,092, 74 Fed. Reg. 60,156] According to DOL, it decided to withdraw the regulations based on public comments that raised sufficient doubts as to whether the conditions of the final regulations and the class exemption associated with the regulations could adequately protect the interests of plan participants and beneficiaries. DOL then issued proposed regulations that will become effective 60 days after the final regulations are published and will apply to transactions occurring on or after the 60th day. [DOL Prop. Reg. § 2550.408g-1(f)]

The proposed regulations provide relief from the prohibited-transaction provisions for certain transactions in connection with the provision of investment advice to participants and beneficiaries. The regulations implement the statutory exemption (see Q 24:10), and the requirements and conditions set forth in the proposed regulations apply solely for purposes of the statutory exemption. Accordingly, no inferences should be drawn with respect to requirements applicable to the provision of investment advice not addressed by the proposed regulations. [DOL Prop. Reg. § 2550.408g-1(a)(1)]

Nothing contained in ERISA, the Code, or the proposed regulations imposes an obligation on a plan fiduciary (see Q 23:1) or any other party to offer, provide, or otherwise make available any investment advice to a participant or beneficiary, or invalidates or otherwise affects prior regulations, exemptions, or interpretive or other guidance issued by DOL pertaining to the provision of investment advice and the circumstances under which such advice may or may not constitute a prohibited transaction. [DOL Prop. Reg. §§ 2550.408g-1(a)(2), 2550.408g-1(a)(3)]

ERISA and the Code provide an exemption for transactions in connection with the provision of investment advice to a participant or a beneficiary if the investment advice is provided by a fiduciary adviser under an eligible investment advice arrangement. An eligible investment advice arrangement is an arrangement that meets the requirements relating to the use of either fee-leveling or computer models, or both. [DOL Prop. Reg. §§ 2550.408g-1(b)(1), 2550.408g-1(b)(2)]

An arrangement that uses fee-leveling is an eligible investment advice arrangement if:

1. Any investment advice is based on generally accepted investment theories that take into account the historic risks and returns of different asset classes over defined periods of time, although nothing precludes any investment advice from being based on generally accepted investment theories that take into account additional considerations;

2. Any investment advice takes into account investment management and other fees and expenses attendant to the recommended investments;

3. Any investment advice takes into account, to the extent furnished by a plan, participant, or beneficiary, information relating to age, time horizons (e.g., life expectancy, retirement age), risk tolerance, current investments in designated investment options, other assets or sources of income, and investment preferences of the participant or beneficiary. A fiduciary adviser must request such information, but nothing requires that any investment advice take into account information requested, but not furnished, by a participant or beneficiary or precludes requesting and taking into account additional information that a plan or a participant or beneficiary may provide;

4. No fiduciary adviser (including any employee, agent, or registered representative) that provides investment advice receives from any party (including an affiliate of the fiduciary adviser), directly or indirectly, any fee or other compensation (including commissions, salary, bonuses, awards, promotions, or other things of value) that is based in whole or in part on a participant's or beneficiary's selection of an investment option; and

5. The requirements relating to the arrangement being authorized by a plan fiduciary, an annual audit, disclosure, and certain other conditions hereinafter discussed are satisfied.

[DOL Prop. Reg. § 2550.408g-1(b)(3)]

An arrangement that uses computer models is an eligible investment advice arrangement if the only investment advice provided under the arrangement is advice that is generated by a computer model described below under an investment advice program and with respect to which the requirements relating to the arrangement being authorized by a fiduciary, an annual audit, disclosure, and certain other conditions hereinafter discussed are satisfied. [DOL Prop. Reg. § 2550.408g-1(b)(4)]

A computer model must be designed and operated to:

1. Apply generally accepted investment theories that take into account the historic risks and returns of different asset classes over defined periods of time, although nothing precludes a computer model from applying generally accepted investment theories that take into account additional considerations;

2. Take into account investment management and other fees and expenses attendant to the recommended investments;

3. Request from a participant or beneficiary and, to the extent furnished, utilize information relating to age, time horizons (e.g., life expectancy, retirement age), risk tolerance, current investments in designated investment options, other assets or sources of income, and investment preferences, provided, however, that nothing precludes a computer model from requesting and taking into account additional information that a plan or a participant or beneficiary may provide;

4. Utilize appropriate objective criteria to provide asset allocation portfolios composed of investment options available under the plan;

5. Avoid investment recommendations that inappropriately favor investment options offered by the fiduciary adviser or a person with a material affiliation or material contractual relationship with the fiduciary adviser over other investment options, if any, available under the plan, or inappropriately favor investment options that may generate greater income for the fiduciary adviser or a person with a material affiliation or material contractual relationship with the fiduciary adviser; and

6. Except as provided in the next sentence, take into account all designated investment options available under the plan without giving inappropriate weight to any investment option. A computer model will not be treated as failing to meet these requirements merely because it does not make recommendations relating to the acquisition, holding, or sale of an investment option that constitutes an investment primarily in qualifying employer securities (see Q 23:86); constitutes an investment fund, product, or service that allocates the invested assets of a participant or

beneficiary to achieve varying degrees of long-term appreciation and capital preservation through equity and fixed income exposures, based on a defined time horizon (such as retirement age or life expectancy) or level of risk of the participant or beneficiary, provided that, contemporaneous with the provision of investment advice generated by the computer model, the participant or beneficiary is also furnished a general description of such funds, products, or services and how they operate; or constitutes an annuity option with respect to which a participant or beneficiary may allocate assets toward the purchase of a stream of retirement income payments guaranteed by an insurance company, provided that, contemporaneous with the provision of investment advice generated by the computer model, the participant or beneficiary is also furnished a general description of such options and how they operate. [DOL Prop. Reg. § 2550.408g-1(b)(4)(i)]

Prior to utilization of the computer model, the fiduciary adviser must obtain a written certification from an eligible investment expert that the computer model meets the above requirements. If, following certification, a computer model is modified in a manner that may affect its ability to meet the above requirements, the fiduciary adviser must, prior to utilization of the modified model, obtain a new certification from an eligible investment expert that the computer model, as modified, meets the above requirements. An eligible investment expert is a person that, through employees or otherwise, has the appropriate technical training or experience and proficiency to analyze, determine, and certify whether a computer model meets the above requirements, except that an eligible investment expert does not include any person that has any material affiliation or material contractual relationship with the fiduciary adviser, with a person with a material affiliation or material contractual relationship with the fiduciary adviser, or with any employee, agent, or registered representative of the foregoing. [DOL Prop. Reg. §§ 2550.408g-1(b)(4)(ii), 2550.408g-1(b)(4)(iii)]

A certification by an eligible investment expert must:

1. Be in writing;
2. Contain:
   a. An identification of the methodology or methodologies applied in determining whether the computer model meets the above requirements;
   b. An explanation of how the applied methodology or methodologies demonstrated that the computer model met the above requirements;
   c. A description of any limitations that were imposed by any person on the eligible investment expert's selection or application of methodologies for determining whether the computer model meets the above requirements;
   d. A representation that the methodology or methodologies were applied by a person or persons with the educational background, technical

training, or experience necessary to analyze and determine whether the computer model meets the above requirements; and

   e. A statement certifying that the eligible investment expert has determined that the computer model meets the above requirements; and

3. Be signed by the eligible investment expert.

[DOL Prop. Reg. § 2550.408g-1(b)(4)(iv)]

The selection of an eligible investment expert is a fiduciary act governed by ERISA. [ERISA § 404(a)(1); DOL Prop. Reg. § 2550.408g-1(b)(4)(v)]

Except as provided, the arrangement pursuant to which investment advice is provided to participants and beneficiaries must be expressly authorized by a plan fiduciary (or, in the case of an IRA, the IRA beneficiary) other than the person offering the arrangement, any person providing designated investment options under the plan, or any affiliate of either. However, in the case of an IRA, an IRA beneficiary will not be treated as an affiliate of a person solely by reason of being an employee of such person. In the case of an arrangement pursuant to which investment advice is provided to participants and beneficiaries of a plan sponsored by the person offering the arrangement or a plan sponsored by an affiliate of such person, the authorization may be provided by the plan sponsor of such plan, provided that the person or affiliate offers the same arrangement to participants and beneficiaries of unaffiliated plans in the ordinary course of its business. For purposes of the authorization, a plan sponsor will not be treated as a person providing a designated investment option under the plan merely because one of the designated investment options of the plan is an option that permits investment in securities of the plan sponsor or an affiliate. [DOL Prop. Reg. § 2550.408g-1(b)(5)]

The fiduciary adviser must, at least annually, engage an independent auditor, who has appropriate technical training or experience and proficiency, and so represents in writing to the fiduciary adviser, to conduct an audit of the investment advice arrangements for compliance with the requirements of the regulations and, within 60 days following completion of the audit, issue a written report to the fiduciary adviser and, except with respect to an arrangement with an IRA, to each fiduciary who authorized the use of the investment advice arrangement, setting forth the specific findings of the auditor regarding compliance of the arrangement with the requirements of the regulations. [DOL Prop. Reg. § 2550.408g-1(b)(6)(i)]

With respect to an arrangement with an IRA, the fiduciary adviser, within 30 days following receipt of the report from the auditor, must furnish a copy of the report to the IRA beneficiary or make such report available on its website, provided that such beneficiaries are provided information, with the information required to be disclosed, concerning the purpose of the report, and how and where to locate the report applicable to their account; and, in the event that the report of the auditor identifies noncompliance with the requirements of the regulations, within 30 days following receipt of the report from the auditor, must send a copy of the report to DOL at the following address:

Investment Advice Exemption Notification
U.S. Department of Labor
Employee Benefits Security Administration
Room N-1513
200 Constitution Ave., NW.
Washington, DC 20210

[DOL Prop. Reg. § 2550.408g-1(b)(6)(ii)]

An auditor is considered independent if it does not have a material affiliation or material contractual relationship with the person offering the investment advice arrangement to the plan or with any designated investment options under the plan. The auditor must review sufficient relevant information to formulate an opinion as to whether the investment advice arrangements, and the advice provided pursuant thereto, offered by the fiduciary adviser during the audit period were in compliance with the regulations. Nothing precludes an auditor from using information obtained by sampling, as reasonably determined appropriate by the auditor, investment advice arrangements, and the advice pursuant thereto, during the audit period. The selection of an auditor is a fiduciary act governed by ERISA. [ERISA § 404(a)(1); DOL Prop. Reg. § 2550.408g-1(b)(6)(iii)-(v)]

The fiduciary adviser must provide, without charge, to a participant or a beneficiary before the initial provision of investment advice with regard to any security or other property offered as an investment option, a written notification of:

1. The role of any party that has a material affiliation or material contractual relationship with the fiduciary adviser in the development of the investment advice program and in the selection of investment options available under the plan;

2. The past performance and historical rates of return of the designated investment options available under the plan, to the extent that such information is not otherwise provided;

3. All fees or other compensation that the fiduciary adviser or any affiliate thereof is to receive (including compensation provided by any third party) in connection with the provision of the advice; the sale, acquisition, or holding of any security or other property pursuant to such advice; or any rollover or other distribution of plan assets or the investment of distributed assets in any security or other property pursuant to such advice;

4. Any material affiliation or material contractual relationship of the fiduciary adviser or affiliates thereof in the security or other property;

5. The manner, and under what circumstances, any participant or beneficiary information provided under the arrangement will be used or disclosed;

6. The types of services provided by the fiduciary adviser in connection with the provision of investment advice by the fiduciary adviser, including, with respect to a computer model arrangement, any limitations on the ability of a computer model to take into account an investment primarily in qualifying employer securities;

7. The adviser acting as a fiduciary of the plan in connection with the provision of the advice; and

8. The right of a recipient of the advice to separately arrange for the provision of advice by another adviser that could have no material affiliation with and receive no fees or other compensation in connection with the security or other property.

[DOL Prop. Reg. § 2550.408g-1(b)(7)(i)]

The required notification must be written in a clear and conspicuous manner and in a manner calculated to be understood by the average plan participant and must be sufficiently accurate and comprehensive to reasonably apprise such participants and beneficiaries of the information required to be provided in the notification. The appendix to the proposed regulations (see Q 24:12) contains a model disclosure form that may be used to provide notification of the information described above. Use of the model form is not mandatory. However, use of an appropriately completed model disclosure form will be deemed to satisfy these requirements with respect to such information. The notification may be provided in written or electronic form (see Q 20:23). [DOL Prop. Reg. §§ 2550. 408g-1(b)(7)(ii), 2550.408g-1(b)(7)(iii)]

With respect to the information required to be disclosed, the fiduciary adviser must, at all times during the provision of advisory services to the participant or beneficiary pursuant to the arrangement, (1) maintain accurate, up-to-date information in a form that is consistent with the preceding paragraph; (2) provide, without charge, accurate, up-to-date information to the recipient of the advice no less frequently than annually; (3) provide, without charge, accurate information to the recipient of the advice upon request of the recipient; and (4) provide, without charge, to the recipient of the advice any material change to the information at a time reasonably contemporaneous with the change in information. [DOL Prop. Reg. § 2550.408g-1(b)(7)(iv)]

The other conditions that an eligible investment advice arrangement must satisfy are:

1. The fiduciary adviser provides appropriate disclosure, in connection with the sale, acquisition, or holding of the security or other property, in accordance with all applicable securities laws;

2. Any sale, acquisition, or holding of a security or other property occurs solely at the direction of the recipient of the advice;

3. The compensation received by the fiduciary adviser and affiliates thereof in connection with the sale, acquisition, or holding of the security or other property is reasonable; and

4. The terms of the sale, acquisition, or holding of the security or other property are at least as favorable to the plan as an arm's-length transaction would be.

[DOL Prop. Reg. § 2250.408g-1(b)(8)]

The proposed regulations define a number of pertinent terms with respect to eligible investment advice arrangements. [DOL Prop. Reg. § 2550.408g-1(c)]

"Designated investment option" means any investment option designated by the plan into which participants and beneficiaries may direct the investment of assets held in, or contributed to, their individual accounts. The term does not include brokerage windows, self-directed brokerage accounts, or similar plan arrangements that enable participants and beneficiaries to select investments beyond those designated by the plan. [DOL Prop. Reg. § 2550.408g-1(c)(1)]

"Fiduciary adviser" means, with respect to a plan, a person who is a fiduciary of the plan by reason of the provision of investment advice by the person to the participant or beneficiary of the plan and who is:

1. Registered as an investment adviser under the Investment Advisers Act of 1940 or under the laws of the state in which the fiduciary maintains its principal office and place of business;
2. A bank or similar financial institution or a savings association, but only if the advice is provided through a trust department of the bank or similar financial institution or savings association which is subject to periodic examination and review by federal or state banking authorities;
3. An insurance company qualified to do business under the laws of a state;
4. A person registered as a broker or dealer under the Securities Exchange Act of 1934;
5. An affiliate of a person described in any of 1. through 4.; or
6. An employee, agent, or registered representative of a person described in 1. through 5. who satisfies the requirements of applicable insurance, banking, and securities laws relating to the provision of advice.

[ERISA §§ 3(21)(A)(ii), 408(b)(4); DOL Prop. Reg. § 2550.408g-1(c)(2)(i)]

Generally, a fiduciary adviser includes any person who develops the computer model or markets the computer model or investment advice program. [DOL Prop. Reg. § 2550.408g-1(c)(2)(ii)]

A "registered representative" of another entity means a person described in Section 3(a)(18) of the Securities Exchange Act of 1934 (substituting the entity for the broker or dealer referred to in such section) or a person described in Section 202(a)(17) of the Investment Advisers Act of 1940 (substituting the entity for the investment adviser referred to in such section). [DOL Prop. Reg. § 2250.408g-1(c)(3)]

"IRA" means an individual retirement account (see Q 30:2), an individual retirement annuity (see Q 30:3), an Archer MSA, a health savings account, a Coverdell education savings account, or a trust, plan, account, or annuity that, at any time, has been determined by IRS to be any of the foregoing. [I.R.C. §§ 220(d), 223(d), 530; DOL Prop. Reg. § 2550.408g-1(c)(4)]

An "affiliate" of another person means:

1. Any person directly or indirectly owning, controlling, or holding with power to vote, 5 percent or more of the outstanding voting securities of such other person;

2. Any person 5 percent or more of whose outstanding voting securities are directly or indirectly owned, controlled, or held with power to vote, by such other person;

3. Any person directly or indirectly controlling, controlled by, or under common control with, such other person; and

4. Any officer, director, partner, co-partner, or employee of such other person.

[DOL Prop. Reg. § 2550.408g-1(c)(5)]

A person with a "material affiliation" with another person means any affiliate of the other person; any person directly or indirectly owning, controlling, or holding, 5 percent or more of the interests of such other person; and any person 5 percent or more of whose interests are directly or indirectly owned, controlled, or held, by such other person. "Interest" means with respect to an entity the combined voting power of all classes of stock entitled to vote or the total value of the shares of all classes of stock of the entity if the entity is a corporation; the capital interest or the profits interest of the entity if the entity is a partnership; or the beneficial interest of the entity if the entity is a trust or unincorporated enterprise. [DOL Prop. Reg. § 2550.408g-1(c)(6)]

Persons have a "material contractual relationship" if payments made by one person to the other person pursuant to contracts or agreements between the persons exceed 10 percent of the gross revenue, on an annual basis, of such other person. [DOL Prop. Reg. § 2550.408g-1(c)(7)]

"Control" means the power to exercise a controlling influence over the management or policies of a person other than an individual. [DOL Prop. Reg. § 2550.408g-1(c)(8)]

The fiduciary adviser must maintain, for a period of not less than six years after the provision of investment advice, any records necessary for determining whether the applicable requirements have been met. A prohibited transaction will not be considered to have occurred solely because the records are lost or destroyed prior to the end of the six-year period due to circumstances beyond the control of the fiduciary adviser. [DOL Prop. Reg. § 2550.408g-1(d)]

The relief from the prohibited transaction provisions of ERISA and the sanctions imposed by the Code do not apply to any transaction in connection with the provision of investment advice to an individual participant or beneficiary with respect to which the applicable conditions of the regulations have not been satisfied. In the case of a pattern or practice of noncompliance with any of the applicable conditions, the relief will not apply to any transaction in connection with the provision of investment advice provided by the fiduciary adviser during the period over which the pattern or practice extended. [DOL Prop. Reg. § 2550.408g-1(e)]

As previously discussed, a person who develops a computer model or who markets a computer model or investment advice program used in an eligible investment advice arrangement is treated as a fiduciary of a plan by reason of the provision of investment advice to the plan participant or beneficiary, and also is treated as a fiduciary adviser. However, DOL may prescribe rules under which only one fiduciary adviser may elect to be treated as a fiduciary with respect to the plan. [DOL Prop. Reg. § 2550.408g-2(a)]

If an election is made, then the person identified in the election will be the sole fiduciary adviser treated as a fiduciary by reason of developing or marketing the computer model, or marketing the investment advice program, used in an eligible investment advice arrangement. The election must be in writing and must:

1. Identify the investment advice arrangement, and the person offering the arrangement, with respect to which the election will be effective;
2. Identify a person who:
   a. Is described as a fiduciary adviser;
   b. Develops the computer model, or markets the computer model or investment advice program, with respect to the arrangement; and
   c. Acknowledges that it elects to be treated as the only fiduciary, and fiduciary adviser, by reason of developing such computer model, or marketing such computer model or investment advice program;
3. Be signed by the person;
4. Be furnished to the fiduciary who authorized the arrangement; and
5. Be maintained as discussed above.

[DOL Prop. Reg. §§ 2550.408g-2(b)(1), 2550.408g-2(b)(2)]

Q 24:12   Has DOL provided a model disclosure form for use with eligible investment advice arrangements?

DOL issued, but then withdrew, final regulations that authorize fiduciary advisers to provide individualized investment advice under eligible investment advice arrangements. DOL then issued proposed regulations (see Q 24:11); and, as an appendix to the proposed regulations, DOL provided the following model disclosure form:

Fiduciary Adviser Disclosure

This document contains important information about [enter name of Fiduciary Adviser] and how it is compensated for the investment advice provided to you. You should carefully consider this information in your evaluation of that advice.

[enter name of Fiduciary Adviser] has been selected to provide investment advisory services for the [enter name of Plan]. [enter name of Fiduciary Adviser] will be providing these services as a fiduciary under the Employee Retirement Income Security Act (ERISA). [enter name of Fiduciary Adviser), therefore, must act prudently and with only your interest in mind when providing you recommendations on how to invest your retirement assets.

Compensation of the Fiduciary Adviser and Related Parties

[enter name of Fiduciary Adviser] (is/is not) compensated by the plan for the advice it provides. (if compensated by the plan, explain what and how compensation is charged (e.g., asset-based fee, flat fee, per advice)). (If applicable, [enter name of Fiduciary Adviser] is not compensated on the basis of the investment(s) selected by you.)

Affiliates of [enter name of Fiduciary Adviser] (if applicable enter, and other parties with whom [enter name of Fiduciary Adviser] is related or has a material financial relationship) also will be providing services for which they will be compensated. These services include: [enter description of services, e.g., investment management, transfer agent, custodial, and shareholder services for some/all the investment funds available under the plan.]

When [enter name of Fiduciary Adviser] recommends that you invest your assets in an investment fund of its own or one of its affiliates and you follow that advice, [enter name of Fiduciary Adviser] or that affiliate will receive compensation from the investment fund based on the amount you invest. The amounts that will be paid by you will vary depending on the particular fund in which you invest your assets and may range from __% to __%. Specific information concerning the fees and other charges of each investment fund is available from [enter source, such as: your plan administrator, investment fund provider (possibly with Internet Web site address)]. This information should be reviewed carefully before you make an investment decision.

(if applicable enter, [enter name of Fiduciary Adviser] or affiliates of [enter name of Fiduciary Adviser] also receive compensation from non-affiliated investment funds as a result of investments you make as a result of recommendations of [enter name of Fiduciary Adviser]. The amount of this compensation also may vary depending on the particular fund in which you invest. This compensation may range from __% to __%. Specific information concerning the fees and other charges of each investment fund is available from [enter source, such as: your plan administrator, investment fund provider (possibly with Internet Web site address)]. This information should be reviewed carefully before you make an investment decision.

(if applicable enter, In addition to the above, [enter name of Fiduciary Adviser] or affiliates of [enter name of Fiduciary Adviser] also receive other fees or compensation, such as commissions, in connection with the sale, acquisition or holding of investments selected by you as a result of recommendations of [enter name of Fiduciary Adviser]. These amounts are: [enter description of all other fees or compensation to be received in connection with sale, acquisition or holding of investments]. This information should be reviewed carefully before you make an investment decision.

(if applicable enter, When [enter name of Fiduciary Adviser] recommends that you take a rollover or other distribution of assets from the plan, or recommends how those assets should subsequently be invested, [enter name of Fiduciary Adviser] or affiliates of [enter name of Fiduciary Adviser] will receive additional fees or compensation. These amounts are: [enter description of all other fees or compensation to be received in connection with any rollover or other distribution of plan assets or the investment of distributed assets]. This information should be reviewed carefully before you make a decision to take a distribution.

Consider Impact of Compensation on Advice

The fees and other compensation that [enter name of Fiduciary Adviser] and its affiliates receive on account of assets in [enter name of Fiduciary Adviser] (enter if applicable, and non-[enter name of Fiduciary Adviser]) investment funds are a significant source of revenue for the [enter name of Fiduciary Adviser] and its affiliates. You should carefully consider the impact of any such fees and compensation in your evaluation of the investment advice that [enter name of Fiduciary Adviser] provides to you. In this regard, you may arrange for the provision of advice by another adviser that may have no material affiliation with or receive compensation in connection with the investment funds or products offered under the plan. This type of advice is/is not available through your plan.

Investment Returns

While understanding investment-related fees and expenses is important in making informed investment decisions, it is also important to consider additional information about your investment options, such as performance, investment strategies and risks. Specific information related to the past performance and historical rates of return of the investment options available under the plan (has/has not) been provided to you by [enter source, such as: your plan administrator, investment fund provider]. (If applicable enter. If not provided to you, the information is attached to this document).

For options with returns that vary over time, past performance does not guarantee how your investment in the option will perform in the future; your investment in these options could lose money.

Parties Participating in Development of Advice Program or Selection of Investment Options

Name, and describe role of, affiliates or other parties with whom the fiduciary adviser has a material affiliation or contractual relationship that participated in the development of the investment advice program (if this is an arrangement that uses computer models) or the selection of investment options available under the plan.

Use of Personal Information

Include a brief explanation of the following—

What personal information will be collected;

How the information will be used;

Parties with whom information will be shared;

How the information will be protected; and

When and how notice of the Fiduciary Adviser's privacy statement will be available to participants and beneficiaries.

Should you have any questions about [enter name of Fiduciary Adviser] or the information contained in this document, you may contact [enter name of contact person for fiduciary adviser, telephone number, address].

Q 24:13 Has DOL prescribed a class exemption in connection with the prohibited-transaction exemption for investment advice?

In 2004, DOL issued final regulations providing relief from the prohibited-transaction provisions for certain transactions in connection with the provision of investment advice to participants and beneficiaries (see Q 24:11). The regulations implemented the statutory exemption (see Q 24:10) and also prescribed a class exemption (see Q 24:26) for certain transactions not therein covered by the statutory exemption. Subsequently, the final regulations and the class exemption were withdrawn. In 2010, DOL issued proposed regulations concerning the provision of investment advice (see Q 24:11); however, the proposed regulations did not retain the class exemption.

Q 24:14 What is the prohibited-transaction exemption for block trading?

PPA (see Q 1:33) provides prohibited-transaction exemptions (see Q 24:8) for a purchase or sale of securities or other property (as determined by DOL) between a plan and a disqualified person (see Q 24:4), other than a fiduciary, involving a block trade if: (1) the transaction involves a block trade; (2) at the time of the transaction, the interest of the plan (together with the interests of any other plans maintained by the same plan sponsor) does not exceed 10 percent of the aggregate size of the block trade; (3) the terms of the transaction, including the price, are at least as favorable to the plan as an arm's-length transaction with an unrelated party; and (4) the compensation associated with the transaction must be no greater than the compensation associated with an arm's-length transaction with an unrelated party. For purposes of the provision, block trade is any trade of at least 10,000 shares or with a market value of at least $200,000 that will be allocated across two or more unrelated client accounts of a fiduciary. Examples of property other than securities that DOL may apply the exemption to include, but are not limited to, futures contracts and currency.

This exemption is effective for transactions occurring after August 17, 2006.

[ERISA § 408(b)(15); I.R.C. § 4975(d)(18)]

Q 24:15   What is the prohibited-transaction exemption for electronic communication network?

PPA (see Q 1:33) provides a prohibited-transaction exemption (see Q 24:8) for a transaction involving the purchase or sale of securities (or other property as determined under regulations) between a plan and a party in interest (see Q 24:3) if: (1) the transaction is executed through an electronic communication network, alternative trading system, or similar execution system or trading venue that is subject to regulation and oversight by (a) the applicable Federal regulating entity or (b) a foreign regulatory entity as DOL may determine under regulations; (2) either (a) neither the execution system nor the parties to the transaction take into account the identity of the parties in the execution of trades, or (b) the transaction is effected under rules designed to match purchases and sales at the best price available through the execution system in accordance with applicable rules of the SEC or other relevant governmental authority; (3) the price and compensation associated with the purchase and sale are not greater than an arm's-length transaction with an unrelated party; (4) if the disqualified person (see Q 24:4) has an ownership interest in the system or venue, the system or venue has been authorized by the plan sponsor or other independent fiduciary for this type of transaction; and (5) not less than 30 days before the first transaction of this type executed through any such system or venue, a plan fiduciary is provided written notice of the execution of the transaction through the system or venue.

Examples of other property for purposes of the exemption include, but are not limited to, futures contracts and currency.

This exemption is effective for transactions occurring after August 17, 2006.

[ERISA § 408(b)(16); I.R.C. § 4975(d)(19)]

Q 24:16   What is the prohibited-transaction exemption for service providers?

PPA (see Q 1:33) provides a prohibited-transaction exemption (see Q 24:8) for certain transactions (such as sales of property, loans, and transfers or use of plan assets) between a plan and a person that is a party in interest (see Q 24:3) solely by reason of providing services (or solely by reason of having certain relationships with a service provider), but only if, in connection with the transaction, the plan receives no less, or pays no more, than adequate consideration. For this purpose, adequate consideration means: (1) in the case of a security for which there is a generally recognized market, the price of the security prevailing on a national securities exchange registered under the Securities Exchange Act of 1934, taking into account factors such as the size of the transaction and marketability of the security, or, if the security is not traded on such a national securities exchange, a price not less favorable to the plan than the offering price for the security as established by the current bid and asked prices quoted by persons independent of the issuer and of any disqualified person, taking into account factors such as the size of the transaction and marketability of the security; and (2) in the case of an asset other than a security for which there is a generally recognized market, the fair market value of the asset as determined in good faith by a fiduciary or named fiduciaries in accordance with regulations. The exemption does not apply to a fiduciary (or an affiliate) who has or exercises any discretionary authority or control with respect to the investment of the assets involved in the transaction or provides investment advice with respect to the assets.

This exemption is effective for transactions occurring after August 17, 2006.

[ERISA § 408(b)(17); I.R.C. § 4975(d)(20)]

Q 24:17   What is the prohibited-transaction exemption for foreign exchange transactions?

PPA (see Q 1:33) provides a prohibited-transaction exemption (see Q 24:8) for foreign exchange transactions between a bank or broker-dealer (or an affiliate or either) and a plan in connection with the sale, purchase, or holding of securities or other investment assets (other than a foreign exchange transaction unrelated to any other investment in securities or other investment assets) if: (1) at the time the foreign exchange transaction is entered into, the terms of the transaction are not less favorable to the plan than the terms generally available in comparable arm's-length foreign exchange transactions between unrelated parties or the terms afforded by the bank or the broker-dealer (or any affiliate thereof) in comparable arm's-length foreign exchange transactions involving unrelated parties; (2) the exchange rate used for a particular foreign exchange transaction may not deviate by more than three percent from the interbank bid and asked rates at the time of the transaction for transactions of comparable size and maturity as displayed on an independent service that reports rates of exchange in the foreign currency market for such currency; and (3) the bank or broker-dealer (and any affiliate of either) does not have investment discretion or provide investment advice with respect to the transaction.

This exemption is effective for transactions occurring after August 17, 2006.

[ERISA § 408(b)(18) (as amended by WRERA 2008 § 106(b)(1)); I.R.C. § 4975(d)(21) (as amended by WRERA 2008 § 106(b)(2)(C))]

Q 24:18   What is the prohibited-transaction exemption for cross-trading?

PPA (see Q 1:33) provides prohibited-transaction exemptions (see Q 24:8) for a transaction involving the purchase and sale of a security between a plan and any other account managed by the same investment manager if certain requirements are met. These requirements are:

1. The transaction is a purchase or sale for no consideration other than cash payment against prompt delivery of a security for which market quotations are readily available;

2. The transaction is effected at the independent current market price of the security;

3. No brokerage commission fee (except for customary transfer fees, the fact of which is disclosed) or other remuneration is paid in connection with the transaction;

4. A fiduciary (other than the investment manager engaging in the cross trades or any affiliate) for each plan participating in the transaction authorizes in advance of any cross trades (in a document that is separate from any other written agreement of the parties) the investment manager to engage in cross trades at the investment manager's discretion, after the fiduciary has received disclosure regarding the conditions under which cross trades may take place (but only if the disclosure is separate from any other agreement or disclosure involving the asset management relationship), including the written policies and procedures of the investment manager;

5. Each plan participating in the transaction has assets of at least $100,000,000, except that, if the assets of a plan are invested in a master trust containing the assets of plans maintained by employers in the same controlled group (see Q 5:31), the master trust has assets of at least $100,000,000;

6. The investment manager provides to the plan fiduciary who has authorized cross trading a quarterly report detailing all cross trades executed by the investment manager in which the plan participated during such quarter, including the following information as applicable: the identity of each security bought or sold, the number of shares or units traded, the parties involved in the cross trade, and the trade price and the method used to establish the trade price;

7. The investment manager does not base its fee schedule on the plan's consent to cross trading and no other service (other than the investment opportunities and cost savings available through a cross trade) is conditioned on the plan's consent to cross trading;

8. The investment manager has adopted, and cross trades are effected in accordance with, written cross-trading policies and procedures that are fair and equitable to all accounts participating in the cross-trading program and that include a description of the manager's pricing policies and procedures, and the manager's policies and procedures for allocating cross trades in an objective manner among accounts participating in the cross-trading program; and

9. The investment manager has designated an individual responsible for periodically reviewing purchases and sales to ensure compliance with the written policies and procedures and, following such review, the individual must issue an annual written report no later than 90 days following the period to which it relates, signed under penalty of perjury, to the plan fiduciary who authorized the cross trading, describing the steps performed during the course of the review, the level of compliance, and any specific instances of noncompliance. The written report must also notify

the plan fiduciary of the plan's right to terminate participation in the investment manager's cross-trading program at any time.

No later than 180 days after August 17, 2006, DOL, after consultation with the SEC, was directed to issue regulations regarding the content of policies and procedures required to be adopted by an investment manager under the requirements for the exemption.

This exemption is effective for transactions occurring after August 17, 2006. [ERISA § 408(b)(19); I.R.C. § 4975(d)(22)]

DOL has issued final regulations concerning cross-trading that became effective on February 4, 2009. [DOL Reg. § 2550.408b-19]

For purposes of the final regulations, the following pertinent terms are defined:

1. "Account" includes any single customer or pooled fund or account.

2. "Compliance officer" means an individual designated by the investment manager who is responsible for periodically reviewing the cross-trades made for the plan to ensure compliance with the investment manager's written cross-trading policies and procedures and the requirements of ERISA Section 408(b)(19)(H).

3. "Plan fiduciary" means a person described in ERISA Section 3(21)(A) (see Q 23:1) with respect to a plan (other than the investment manager engaging in the cross-trades or an affiliate) who has the authority to authorize a plan's participation in an investment manager's cross-trading program.

4. "Investment manager" means a person described in ERISA Section 3(38).

5. "Plan" means any employee benefit plan as described in ERISA Section 3(3) to which Title I applies or any plan defined in Section 4975(e)(1).

6. "Cross-trade" means the purchase and sale of a security between a plan and any other account managed by the same investment manager.

[DOL Reg. § 2550.408b-19(c)]

There is exempted from the prohibited-transaction rules any cross-trade of securities if certain conditions are satisfied. Among other conditions, the exemption requires that the investment manager adopt, and effect cross-trades in accordance with, written cross-trading policies and procedures that are fair and equitable to all accounts participating in the cross-trading program and that include:

1. A description of the investment manager's pricing policies and procedures, and

2. The investment manager's policies and procedures for allocating cross-trades in an objective manner among accounts participating in the cross-trading program. [ERISA § 408(b)(19); DOL Reg. §§ 2550.408b-19(a)(1), 2550.408b-19(a)(2)]

A plan fiduciary for each plan participating in the cross-trades is required to receive in advance of any cross-trades disclosure regarding the conditions under which the cross-trades may take place, including the written policies and procedures. This disclosure must be in a document that is separate from any other agreement or disclosure involving the asset management relationship. The policies and procedures furnished to the authorizing fiduciary must conform with the requirements of the regulations. [ERISA §§ 408(b)(19)(D), 408(d)(19)(H); DOL Reg § 2550.408b-19(a)(3)]

The standards set forth in the final regulations apply solely for purposes of determining whether an investment manager's written policies and procedures satisfy the content requirements. Accordingly, such standards do not determine whether the investment manager satisfies the other requirements for relief under the exemption for cross-trades. [ERISA § 408(b)(19)(H); DOL Reg. § 2550.408b-19(a)(4)]

The final regulations specify the content of the written policies and procedures required to be adopted by an investment manager and disclosed to the plan fiduciary prior to authorizing cross-trading in order for transactions to qualify for relief under the exemption. [DOL Reg. § 2550.408b-19(b)(1)]

The content of the policies and procedures must be clear and concise and written in a manner calculated to be understood by the plan fiduciary authorizing cross-trading. Although no specific format is required for the investment manager's written policies and procedures, the information contained in the policies and procedures must be sufficiently detailed to facilitate a periodic review by the compliance officer of the cross-trades and a determination by such compliance officer that the cross-trades comply with the investment manager's written cross-trading policies and procedures. [DOL Reg. § 2550.408b-19(b)(2)]

An investment manager's policies and procedures must be fair and equitable to all accounts participating in its cross-trading program and reasonably designed to ensure compliance with the applicable requirements. Such policies and procedures must include:

1. A statement of policy that describes the criteria that will be applied by the investment manager in determining that execution of a securities transaction as a cross-trade will be beneficial to both parties to the transaction;

2. A description of how the investment manager will determine that cross-trades are effected at the independent current market price of the security, including the identity of sources used to establish such price;

3. A description of the procedures for ensuring compliance with the $100,000,000 minimum asset size requirement. A plan or master trust will satisfy the minimum asset size requirement as to a transaction if it satisfies the requirement upon its initial participation in the cross-trading program and on an annual basis thereafter;

4. A statement that any investment manager participating in a cross-trading program will have conflicting loyalties and responsibilities to the parties involved in any cross-trade transaction and a description of how the investment manager will mitigate such conflicts;

5. A requirement that the investment manager allocate cross-trades among accounts in an objective and equitable manner and a description of the allocation method(s) available to and used by the investment manager for assuring an objective allocation among accounts participating in the cross-trading program. If more than one allocation methodology may be used by the investment manager, a description of what circumstances will dictate the use of a particular methodology;

6. Identification of the compliance officer responsible for periodically reviewing the investment manager's compliance and a statement of the compliance officer's qualifications for this position;

7. A statement that the cross-trading statutory exemption requires satisfaction of several objective conditions in addition to the requirements that the investment manager adopt and effect cross-trades in accordance with written cross-trading policies and procedures; and

8. A statement that specifically describes the scope of the annual review conducted by the compliance officer. [DOL Reg. § 2550.408b-19(b)(3)(i)]

An investment manager may include such other policies and procedures not required by the final regulations as the investment manager may determine appropriate to comply with the requirements of the exemption. [DOL Reg. § 2550.408b-19(b)(3)(ii)]

Q 24:19 Can an employer's contribution of property to a qualified retirement plan be a prohibited transaction?

According to DOL and IRS, the contribution of property to a pension plan (e.g., defined benefit or money purchase pension plan; see Qs 2:3, 2:4) is a prohibited transaction because the contribution discharges the employer's legal obligation to contribute cash to the plan. On the other hand, if the plan is not a pension plan (e.g., profit sharing plan; see Q 2:6), the contribution of property is not a prohibited transaction because it is purely voluntary and does not relieve the employer of an obligation to make cash contributions to the plan. However, if the employer is obligated to contribute a percentage of net profit to a profit sharing plan, a contribution of property will be a prohibited transaction. No matter what type of plan is involved, a transfer of encumbered property will be treated as a sale or exchange (i.e., prohibited transaction). [DOL Interpretive Bull. 94-3; DOL Op. Ltrs. 90-05A, 81-69A; *see also* Priv. Ltr. Rul. 9145006]

The United States Supreme Court, agreeing with both DOL and IRS, ruled that the transfer of unencumbered property to a defined benefit plan is a prohibited transaction because it constitutes a sale or exchange within the meaning of the Code. [Comm'r v. Keystone Consol. Indus., Inc., 508 U.S. 152 (1993)] The assignment of an employer's accounts receivable to its pension plan to satisfy the employer's funding obligation is a prohibited transaction because it constitutes a sale or exchange of property between a plan and a disqualified person. [Baizer v. Comm'r, 204 F.3d 1231 (9th Cir. 2000)]

IRS representatives have opined that the contribution of property to a pension plan is a prohibited transaction even if the owner of the employer is the sole plan participant, that the plan trustee must sell the property to an unrelated third party to correct the transaction, and that the contribution of property, although a prohibited transaction, is still a contribution for purposes of the minimum funding requirements (see Q 8:1).

Where an employer contributed shares of its stock to an ESOP (see Q 28:1), IRS concluded that, for purposes of determining whether such contribution was a prohibited transaction, the ERISA definition, and not the Code definition, applied to determine if the shares were qualifying employer securities (see Q 23:86). [Chief Couns. Adv. 200109010; *see also* DOL Op. Ltr. 2003-14A]

Q 24:20   Can a party in interest obtain an exemption from the prohibited-transaction restrictions?

DOL may grant an exemption from the prohibited-transaction rules if the exemption is (1) administratively feasible, (2) in the interests of the plan and of its participants and beneficiaries, and (3) protective of the rights of the plan's participants and beneficiaries. [ERISA § 408(a); I.R.C. § 4975(c)(2)]

IRS has granted DOL primary authority to issue rulings and regulations on, and grant exemptions from, the prohibited-transaction restrictions. A specific statement explaining how the proposed exemption satisfies the requirements listed above and detailed information concerning the proposed transaction are required. [DOL Reg. §§ 2570.30–2570.52; *see also* 73 Fed. Reg. 18,301] DOL has issued proposed regulations that would update the procedures governing the filing and processing of applications for exemptions from the prohibited trans-action provisions. The proposed rules would consolidate existing policies, clarify the types of information and documentation required to submit a complete filing, expand the methods for transmitting filings to include electronic submissions, and require a summary statement designed to make complex exemptions more understandable to participants and other interested parties. [DOL Prop. Reg. §§ 2570.30–2570.52]

To comply with the provisions of a qualified domestic relations order (QDRO; see Q 36:1), a participant was permitted to make a loan to the plan because the plan contained insufficient liquid assets to effect a transfer to the IRA (see Q 30:1) of the alternate payee (see Q 36:5). [DOL Op. Ltr. 94-29A; PTCE 80-26 (45 Fed. Reg. 28,545)]

DOL has provided, in a booklet, examples of common transactions for which exemptions are requested and has set forth the factors that DOL ordinarily would consider and that should be addressed by the applicants. [Exemption Procedures Under Federal Pension Law (DOL 1995)]

Example 1. Esskay-H Corporation sponsors a qualified retirement plan. The plan owns a parcel of real property that it wishes to sell to Esskay-H Corporation. These are the factors that DOL ordinarily would consider and that should be addressed by the applicants:

1. The plan pays no commissions or other expenses in connection with the sale.

2. If there is no generally recognized market for the property, the fair market value of the property must be determined by a qualified independent appraiser (see Q 24:21) and reflected in a qualified appraisal report (see Q 24:22). If there is a generally recognized market for the property, the fair market value of the property is the value objectively determined by reference to the price on such market on the date of the transaction.

3. If the party in interest (see Q 24:3) engaging in the transaction (or a related entity) caused the plan to invest in the property, then the plan should receive no less than the greater of its cost of acquiring and holding the property (e.g., original purchase price, insurance, real estate taxes) or the current fair market value of the property at the time of the sale, provided, however, that a purchase price in excess of such fair market value may not be required if the applicant provides sufficient documentation that the plan's original investment was consistent with ERISA's fiduciary standards, or the sale is made from a one-participant plan, an IRA (see Q 30:1) not subject to Title I of ERISA, or an individual account or accounts in the plan and the affected participant voluntarily consents to the sale. In order to complete consideration of the application, DOL needs to know the background history of the property: from whom was it acquired (party in interest), date of acquisition, and price paid. Information must also be furnished concerning whether the property has been used by or leased to anyone, including parties in interest, since its acquisition by the plan. DOL also needs to know why the plan proposes to sell the property, and whether it has made any efforts to sell the property to an unrelated third party.

4. Where the sale of property eliminates an ongoing prohibited transaction (such as a prohibited lease to a party in interest), DOL will not grant an exemption unless the prohibited transaction is corrected (see Q 24:6) and the party in interest pays the appropriate excise taxes (see Q 24:5).

5. If the sale of the property will result in a contribution to the plan under the Code, the applicant must represent that such contribution will not result in any violation of the requirements for qualification or, if there would be a violation, that it will be remedied without any adverse consequences for the plan (see chapter 4).

Example 2. UU-Pee-H Corporation wishes to borrow $100,000 from its plan. These are the factors that DOL would ordinarily consider and that should be addressed by the applicants:

1. At the time the loan is made, the sum of the principal amount of the loan, plus the amount of all other plan loans and leases to the party in interest (or a related entity), does not exceed 25 percent of the aggregate fair market value of the assets of the plan (or self-directed account; see Qs 23:14, 23:87). The aggregate fair market value is determined as of the plan's most recent valuation date (no more than 12 months before the transaction). This 25 percent limitation is a continuing requirement that must be met throughout the term of the loan.

2. The exemption request must include a statement that the terms of the loan (e.g., interest rate, repayment schedule, duration of the loan) are not less favorable to the plan than those obtainable in an arm's-length transaction between unrelated parties. The exemption request must also set forth the basis for this determination. To assure comparability with arm's-length loans, a statement from a third party in the business of lending money under similar circumstances may be required.

3. The loan is secured by collateral having a fair market value at the time the loan is made that is at least 150 percent of the principal amount of the loan if the collateral is real property, and at least 200 percent of the principal amount of the loan if the collateral is personal property or accounts receivable.

4. The collateral securing the loan has been appraised by a qualified independent appraiser who has issued a qualified appraisal report. The property securing the loan is insured against casualty loss in an amount not less than the amount of the outstanding principal of the loan (plus accrued but unpaid interest), and the plan is a named beneficiary of the policy.

5. The plan's security interest must be perfected in the manner required by applicable state law. For example, if recording is required for perfection, the security agreement must be recorded with the appropriate government officials.

6. Unless the loan is from a self-directed account or an IRA, a qualified independent fiduciary (see Q 24:23) who has the experience necessary to effectively review and monitor loans of this type:

   a. Reviewed the terms of the loan and compared the terms with the terms for similar loans between unrelated parties;

   b. Examined the plan's overall investment portfolio, considered the plan's liquidity and diversification requirements, in light of the proposed transaction, and determined whether the proposed transaction complies with the plan's investment objectives and policies;

   c. Stated that such fiduciary believes that the proposed transaction is in the best interests of the plan and its participants and beneficiaries and explained in detail the reasons for such opinion; and

   d. Agreed to monitor the loan and the conditions of the exemption on behalf of the plan throughout the term of the loan, taking all appropriate actions to safeguard the interests of the plan and has stated that such fiduciary will be given the authority to so act.

Example 3. Ceekayell Corporation sponsors a plan for its employees. Ceekayell Corporation wishes to sell a parcel of land to the plan which then will be leased back to it. These are the factors that DOL ordinarily would consider and that should be addressed by the applicants:

1. At the time when the sale and leaseback transactions are effectuated, the sum of the fair market value of the property, plus the amount of all other plan loans and leases to such party in interest (or a related entity), does

not exceed 25 percent of the aggregate fair market value of the plan's assets. The aggregate fair market value is determined as of the plan's most recent valuation date (no more than 12 months before the transaction). This 25 percent limitation is a continuing requirement which must be met throughout the term of the lease.

2. Both the fair market value of the property acquired by the plan and the fair market rental value of the property to be leased to the party in interest have been appraised by a qualified independent appraiser and reflected in a qualified appraisal report.

3. The exemption request must include a representation that the terms of the lease (e.g., rent, duration, allocation of expenses) are not less favorable to the plan than those obtainable in an arm's-length transaction between unrelated parties. The exemption request must also set forth the basis for this determination (e.g., comparable to the terms of similar leases between unrelated parties).

4. A qualified independent fiduciary who has the experience necessary to effectively review and monitor transactions of this type reviewed the terms of the purchase by the plan and of the lease and compared them with the terms of similar transactions involving unrelated parties and must have satisfied the other requirements of paragraph 6 of Example 2.

5. The lease must provide for periodic adjustments (no less frequently than every year) to the rents payable thereunder, so that the rents will be no less than the fair market rental value of the leased premises at the time of the adjustment. Generally, the initial rent will be the floor rental during the term of the lease, even if the fair market rental value has decreased. The adjustment may be made by using the consumer price index, or by retaining a qualified independent appraiser satisfactory to the qualified independent fiduciary. The qualified independent fiduciary will determine which method is appropriate for making such adjustment; the method need not be the same for all periods.

Example 4. A-Essell Corporation wishes to raise capital by issuing, to all holders of its stock, rights that will entitle such shareholders to acquire additional shares. A-Essell Corporation's profit sharing plan currently owns shares of stock of the corporation and, thus, is entitled to acquire these rights. This prohibited transaction involves stock rights that are not considered qualifying employer securities (see Q 23:86). Although the plan is a holder of stock of the employer that is a qualifying employer security, when a business decision is made to issue stock rights to all shareholders of the employer, the plan's acquisition and holding of such rights would be prohibited in the absence of an administrative exemption. These are the factors that DOL would ordinarily consider and that should be addressed by the applicants:

1. The plan's acquisition of the stock rights results from a business decision on behalf of the plan's sponsor in its capacity as issuer of the securities, rather than in its capacity as plan fiduciary.

2. The plan is treated in the same manner as any other holder of the affected class of securities.

3. If the plan provides for self-directed investment of the assets in each participant's account, all decisions with respect to the plan's acquisition, holding, and control of the rights are made by the individual plan participants.

4. With respect to plans other than those providing for self-directed accounts, a qualified independent fiduciary who is qualified to review and monitor transactions of this type:

    a. Examined the plan's overall investment portfolio, considered the plan's liquidity and diversification requirements, and considered the plan's investment objectives and policies in light of the receipt of the stock rights; and

    b. Will exercise the authority for all decisions regarding the acquisition, holding, and control of the rights, including the decision as to whether the plan should exercise or sell the rights acquired through the offering.

5. If the employer securities to be received upon exercise of the stock rights would otherwise violate ERISA Section 407, the exemption will include additional relief for the receipt and holding of such securities provided that the securities are disposed of by the plan within an agreed-upon period of time from their receipt by the plan or another prohibited transaction exemption is obtained. There is a general prohibition on the acquisition of additional employer securities by a defined benefit plan (see Q 2:3) if the plan already holds qualifying employer securities up to the limit imposed under ERISA (see Q 23:84).

Example 5. Jayemkay Corporation sponsors a defined benefit plan and wishes to lease a parcel of land owned by the plan to use as a parking lot. These are the factors that DOL ordinarily would consider and that should be addressed by the applicants:

1. At the time the lease is entered into, the sum of the fair market value of the leased property, plus the amount of all other plan loans and leases to such party in interest (or a related entity), does not exceed 25 percent of the aggregate fair market value of the plan's assets, such aggregate fair market value to be determined as of the plan's most recent valuation date (but no more than 12 months before the transaction). This 25 percent limitation is a continuing requirement that must be met throughout the term of the lease.

2. The other factors set forth in Example 3 regarding the lease.

Q 24:21   Who is a qualified independent appraiser?

A qualified independent appraiser is any individual or entity that is qualified to serve in that capacity and that is independent of the party in interest (see Q 24:3) engaging in the transaction and its affiliates. The qualified independent appraiser must represent in writing its qualifications to serve in that capacity and must also detail any relationship it may have with the party in interest engaging in the transaction with the plan, or its affiliates, that could enable the party in interest or its affiliates to control or materially influence the actions of the appraiser, or vice versa.

If the property in question is real property, the appraiser should be an M.A.I., or a member of a similar sanctioning body. If the property is an asset other than real property, the appraiser must demonstrate that it has experience in valuing assets of that type.

If an individual is to serve as the qualified independent appraiser, less than 1 percent of the appraiser's annual income (generally measured on the basis of the prior year's income, but including amounts received for performing the appraisal) may be derived from the party in interest and its affiliates. If an entity is to serve as the qualified independent appraiser, less than 1 percent of the entity's annual income (generally measured on the basis of the prior year's income, but including amounts received for performing the appraisal) may come from business derived from the party in interest and its affiliates. [Exemption Procedures Under Federal Pension Law (DOL 1995)]

Q 24:22   What is a qualified appraisal report?

The appraisal must be in writing and set forth the methods used in determining the fair market value and the reasons used for the valuation in light of those methods. The appraisal should be no more than one year old; if an appraisal report older than one year is submitted, there must be a written update by the qualified independent appraiser (see Q 24:21) reaffirming the prior appraisal as of the date of the transaction. The document submitted by the qualified independent appraiser should describe the methodology used to determine the fair market value of the property and explain why such methodology best represented the fair market value of the property. The appraisal must take into account any special benefit that the party in interest (see Q 24:3) may derive from the property such as the fact that it owns an adjacent parcel of property or would gain voting control over a company. [Exemption Procedures Under Federal Pension Law (DOL 1995)]

Q 24:23   Who is a qualified independent fiduciary?

A qualified independent fiduciary is any individual or entity that is qualified (i.e., knowledgeable as to its duties and responsibilities as an ERISA fiduciary (see Qs 23:1, 23:20) and knowledgeable as to the subject transaction) to serve in that capacity and that is independent of the party in interest (see Q 24:3) engaging in the transaction and its affiliates. Thus, for example, the independent fiduciary cannot be an affiliate of the person engaging in the transaction under the exemption.

The qualified independent fiduciary must represent in writing its qualifications to serve in that capacity and must also detail any relationship it may have with the party in interest engaging in the transaction with the plan, or its affiliates, in order to determine whether such fiduciary may be subject to improper influence by a party to the transaction other than the plan, or whether such fiduciary has an interest that may conflict with the interests of the plan for which it acts. In addition, the qualified independent fiduciary must represent that it understands its ERISA duties and responsibilities in acting as a fiduciary with respect to the plan.

The general rule for individual exemption requests involving a financial institution serving as the qualified independent fiduciary is that less than 1 percent of the financial institution's deposits and less than 1 percent of its outstanding loans (both in dollar amounts) are attributable to the deposits and loans of the party in interest and its affiliates.

If an individual is to serve as the qualified independent fiduciary, less than 1 percent of the fiduciary's annual income (generally measured on the basis of the prior year's income) may be derived from the party in interest and its affiliates. Fixed, nondiscretionary retirement income would not be included for purposes of this test. If an entity is to serve as the qualified independent fiduciary, less than 1 percent of the entity's annual income (generally measured on the basis of the prior year's income) may come from business derived from the party in interest and its affiliates. While in certain cases DOL has permitted an independent fiduciary to receive as much as 5 percent of its annual income from the party in interest and its affiliates, these cases have involved unusual circumstances, and the general standard of independence remains a 1 percent test.

[Exemption Procedures Under Federal Pension Law (DOL 1995)]

Q 24:24   Can a prohibited-transaction exemption be granted retroactively?

Yes, but only under very limited circumstances. DOL generally will grant a retroactive exemption only if the applicant acted in good faith and the safeguards necessary for the grant of a prospective exemption were in place when the prohibited transaction occurred. DOL generally will not grant a retroactive exemption if the transaction resulted in a loss to the plan or was inconsistent with the general fiduciary responsibility provisions of ERISA Sections 403 and 404. [DOL Tech. Rel. 85-1]

Q 24:25   Can a prohibited-transaction exemption be used to benefit the owner of a closely held corporation?

Yes. Although the continued well-being of the plan is the prime consideration in qualifying for an exemption from the prohibited-transaction restrictions, the fact that the corporation or a shareholder also benefits from the transaction will not preclude the granting of an exemption. For example, it may be possible for the corporation to borrow from its cash-rich qualified retirement plan or to sell assets to the plan to improve the business's cash flow without incurring a penalty. As the following case histories illustrate, DOL is willing to approve an exemption even if the corporation or shareholder will reap a substantial benefit from the transaction with the qualified retirement plan.

Business financing. DOL granted an exemption to permit the acquisition, ownership, management, development, leasing, financing, or sale of real property (including the acquisition, ownership, or sale of any joint venture or partnership interest in such property), or the borrowing or lending of money in connection therewith, between a party in interest and the plans. [PTE 96-16]

Loan to company. DOL granted an exemption for a series of loans by a plan to a leasing company, a party in interest, and a guarantee of the loans by the employer, also a party in interest, provided, among other conditions, that (1) the total amount of the outstanding loans does not exceed 20 percent of the plan's assets at any time, (2) each loan agreement is signed on behalf of the plan by a qualified independent fiduciary (see Q 24:23), (3) all terms and conditions of the loans are at least as favorable to the plan as those the plan could obtain in an arm's-length transaction with an unrelated third party, and (4) the qualified independent fiduciary determines that each loan is prudent and in the best interests of the plan and protective of the plan and its participants and beneficiaries. [PTE 2004-14]

Exchange of assets. An exemption was granted by DOL to permit the exchange of an unimproved tract of land owned by the plan and allocated to the individually directed plan account of a party in interest for another unimproved tract of land owned jointly by the party in interest and her husband. [PTE 2004-17]

Selling an unwanted asset. Exemptions were permitted by DOL for the sale of improved real property by the plan to an individual who was a party in interest with respect to the plan. [PTEs 96-51, 96-13]

Sale by party in interest to plan. DOL granted an exemption to permit the sale of real property by a party in interest to the plan, provided, among other conditions, that (1) the fair market value of the property is established by a qualified independent appraiser (see Q 24:21), (2) the plan will not pay any commissions or other expenses with respect to the transaction, and (3) a qualified independent fiduciary determines that the transaction is in the best interest of the plan and its participants and beneficiaries. [PTE 2004-18]

Lease of facilities. An exemption was granted to permit the leasing of certain improved real property owned by the plan to the employer, the plan sponsor and a party in interest, provided (1) all terms and conditions of the lease are at least as favorable to the plan as those that the plan could obtain in an arm's-length transaction with an unrelated party, (2) the lease is a triple net lease under which the employer is obligated to pay for all costs of maintenance, repair, and taxes related to the property, (3) the interests of the plan for all purposes under the lease are represented by a qualified independent fiduciary, and (4) the rent paid by the employer is no less than the fair market rental value of the property. [PTE 2004-04]

Loan to plan. DOL granted an exemption to permit (1) the extension of credit to the plan (loan) by the employer, the plan sponsor, with respect to the plan's investments in annuity accounts and (2) the plan's potential repayment of the loan. [PTE 96-04]

With the publication of PTCE 96-62 (see Q 24:26), which provides for expedited processing of certain prohibited-transaction exemption requests that are not published, the number of published individual exemption requests has declined.

Q 24:26   What is a prohibited-transaction class exemption?

In addition to the statutory and administrative exemptions from the prohibited-transaction rules, DOL can grant a class exemption under which a party in interest or disqualified person (see Qs 24:3, 24:4) who meets the requirements of the class exemption will automatically be entitled to relief from the prohibited-transaction rules.

The following is a brief summary of some of the transactions for which prohibited-transaction class exemptions (PTCEs) have been issued. Many of these exemptions have detailed requirements that are not summarized here.

PTCE 2006-16. PTCE 2006-16 amends and replaces PTCEs 81-6 and 82-63. PTCE 81-6 exempts the lending of securities by employee benefit plans to certain banks and broker-dealers, and PTCE 82-63 exempts certain compensation arrangements for the provision of securities lending services by a plan fiduciary (see Q 23:1) to an employee benefit plan. The final amendment incorporates the exemptions into one renumbered exemption, and expands the relief that was provided in PTCEs 81-6 and 82-63 to include additional parties and additional forms of collateral subject to the specified conditions. The exemption affects participants and beneficiaries of employee benefit plans, persons who lend securities on behalf of such plans, and parties in interest who engage in securities lending transactions with such plans. The effective date of this amendment is January 2, 2007, and the revocation of PTCEs 81-6 and 82-63 is effective on January 2, 2007. [71 Fed. Reg. 63,786]

PTCE 2006-06. In conjunction with the issuance of three final regulations to facilitate the termination of individual account plans (see Q 2:2) and the distribution of benefits where the plans have been abandoned by their sponsoring employers, DOL has also issued PTCE 2006-06 that permits a qualified termination administrator of an abandoned individual account plan to select and pay fees to itself or to an affiliate for performing termination-related services to the plan. DOL has issued final regulations and a related amendment to PTCE 2006-06 to allow rollovers into inherited IRAs for missing nonspouse beneficiaries (see Qs 25:64, 34:33). [71 Fed. Reg 20,856; DOL Reg. §§ 2520.103-13, 2550.404(a)(3), 2578.1]

PTCE 2004-16. PTCE 2004-16 permits a plan fiduciary, which is also the employer maintaining the plan, to establish an IRA at a financial institution that is the employer or an affiliate, on behalf of its separated employees, in connection with a mandatory distribution. The exemption permits plan fiduciaries to select a proprietary product as the initial investment for an IRA, and also provides relief from what would otherwise be a prohibited transaction for the receipt of certain fees by IRA providers in connection with the establishment or maintenance of the IRA and the initial investment of a mandatory distribution. This PTCE was issued concurrently with final regulations providing a fiduciary responsibility safe harbor for automatic rollovers (see Q 34:17) and affects plan sponsors, plan fiduciaries, and IRA providers and accountholders. The class exemption became effective for mandatory distributions made on or after March 28, 2005. [69 Fed. Reg. 57,964]

PTCE 2004-07. PTCE 2004-07 permits the acquisition, holding, and sale of certain publicly traded shares of beneficial interest in a real estate investment trust (REIT) that is structured under state law as a business trust (trust REIT) by individual account plans sponsored by the trust REIT or its affiliates. The exemption is designed to provide relief for plans sponsored by a trust REIT that wish to invest in REIT-issued securities. Shares issued by a trust REIT are not stock. Trust REITs had not been allowed to offer employer securities as an investment option. An individual account plan maintained by a corporate REIT, however, could invest up to 100 percent of its assets in the stock issued by the REIT, if permitted under the provisions of the plan. The treatment of corporate REITs and trust REITs will now be equalized. [69 Fed. Reg. 23,220]

PTCE 2003-39. PTCE 2003-39 has been issued for the purpose of facilitating settlements of litigation between plans and parties in interest. The exemption, which is retroactively effective to January 1, 1975, allows: (a) the release by a plan of a claim against a party in interest in exchange for consideration given by the party in interest to the plan in settlement of the claim, and (b) the provision by a plan, under the terms of a settlement, of an extension of credit to a party in interest whereby the party in interest would repay, in installments, the settlement amounts owed to the plan. [68 Fed. Reg. 75,632] DOL has adopted an amendment that expands the categories of assets that may be accepted by plans in the settlement of litigation, subject to certain conditions. Among other things, the amendment permits the receipt of non-cash assets in settlement of a claim (including the promise of future employer contributions), but only in instances where the consideration can be objectively valued. The amendment also modifies PTCE 2003-39 to permit plans to acquire, hold, or sell employer securities such as warrants and stock rights that are received in settlement of litigation, including bankruptcy proceedings, and clarifies the duties of the independent fiduciary charged with settling litigation on behalf of a plan. [75 Fed. Reg. 33,830]

PTCE 2002-51. PTCE 2002-51 was issued in conjunction with DOL's Voluntary Fiduciary Correction (VFC) Program (see Qs 19:36–19:50), which is designed to encourage the voluntary and timely correction of possible fiduciary breaches by allowing the avoidance of potential ERISA civil actions initiated by DOL, as well as the assessment of civil penalties under ERISA. The PTCE provides limited relief from excise taxes for transactions involving: (a) failure to timely remit participant contributions to plans or to transmit participant loan repayments to a plan within a reasonable time after withholding or receipt by the employer, (b) loans made at a fair market interest rate by plans to parties in interest, (c) purchase or sales of assets (including real property) between plans and parties in interest at fair market value, and (d) sales of real property to plans by employers and leaseback of the property at fair market value and fair market rental value, respectively. [67 Fed. Reg. 70,623] DOL has expanded and simplified the VFC Program and, in connection therewith, has issued an amendment to the PTCE to cover transactions involving illiquid plan assets. [71 Fed. Reg. 20,135]

PTCE 2002-13. PTCE 2002-13 amends numerous previously issued PTCEs to define the term "employee benefit plan," as such term is used in those PTCEs, to include plans described in Section 4975(e)(1). Included in the term are qualified retirement plans, qualified annuity plans, and IRAs. The amendment affects individuals with beneficial interests in such plans, as well as the financial institutions that provide services and products to the plans. [67 Fed. Reg. 9483]

PTCE 2002-12. PTCE 2002-12 permits cross-trades of securities among index and model-driven funds managed by investment managers. Those affected by the exemption include participants and beneficiaries of employee benefit plans with assets invested in index or model-driven funds, large pension plans, and other large amounts involved in portfolio restructuring programs, as well as the funds and their investment managers. The exemption provides relief for (1) the purchase and sale of securities between an index or model-driven fund and another such fund, at least one of which holds plan assets (see Q 22:23) subject to ERISA, and (2) the purchase and sale of securities between such funds and certain large accounts pursuant to portfolio restructuring programs of large accounts. The exemption also applies to cross-trades between two or more large accounts if such cross-trades occur as part of a single cross-trading program involving both funds and large accounts pursuant to which securities are cross-traded solely as a result of the objective operation of the program. The exemption is effective as of April 15, 2002. [67 Fed. Reg. 6613] See Q 24:24 for a discussion of the new statutory prohibited-transaction exemption for cross trading.

PTCE 98-5. PTCE 98-5 permits certain foreign exchange transactions between employee benefit plans and certain banks and broker-dealers which are parties in interest, where the transactions are executed understanding instructions (i.e., a written authorization from a plan fiduciary, who is independent of the bank or broker-dealer, to make the transactions specified by the authorization under instructions provided in the authorization). [63 Fed. Reg. 63,503] See Q 24:23 for a discussion of the new statutory prohibited-transaction exemption for foreign exchange transactions.

PTCE 97-41. PTCE 97-41 allows (prospectively and retroactively to October 1, 1988) employee benefit plans to purchase shares of a registered investment company (fund), the investment advisor for which is a bank or plan advisor that also serves as a fiduciary of the plan, in exchange for plan assets transferred in-kind from a collective investment fund (CIF) maintained by the bank or plan advisor. The exemption allows the bank or plan advisor to convert an employee benefit plan's assets currently managed through a CIF into a fund by transferring the assets out of the CIF and into the fund without the bank or plan advisor being considered to have dealt with the plan assets in its own interest. [62 Fed. Reg. 42,830]

PTCE 97-11. PTCE 97-11 allows broker-dealers to provide free or low-cost brokerage services to IRA, SEP, SIMPLE IRA, and Keogh plan customers if certain conditions are met. ERISA provides that receipt of reduced or no-cost services by an individual under an arrangement in which plan assets are taken into account for purposes of pricing the services is a prohibited transaction. However, PTCE 93-33 discussed in this question allows banks to consider IRA or

Keogh plan account balances in determining eligibility to receive reduced or no-cost banking services. The exemption permits broker-dealers to provide similar incentives to IRA, SEP, SIMPLE IRA, and Keogh plan customers without engaging in a prohibited transaction. The following conditions would have to be satisfied:

1. The IRA, SEP, SIMPLE IRA, or Keogh plan must be established and maintained for the exclusive benefit of the participant, a spouse, or a beneficiary;

2. The services offered must be of the type the broker-dealer could offer that are consistent with federal and state laws;

3. The services must be provided in the ordinary course of business by brokers not only to customers who qualify for such services and who maintain IRAs, SEPs, SIMPLE IRAs, or Keogh plans with the broker-dealers but also to customers who are eligible for the services and who do not maintain IRA, SEPs, SIMPLE IRAs, or Keogh plans with the broker-dealer;

4. The account value or the fees incurred by the IRA, SEP, SIMPLE IRA, or Keogh plan must be the same as for any account eligible to receive reduced or no-cost services;

5. The total of all fees for the broker-dealer's services to the IRA, SEP, SIMPLE IRA, or Keogh plan cannot exceed reasonable compensation;

6. IRA, SEP, SIMPLE IRA, and Keogh plan customers must be eligible for the same services offered to other customers with the same account values or who generate the same amount of fees; and

7. Investment performance on IRA, SEP, SIMPLE IRA, and Keogh plan investments must be no less favorable than that of identical investments made by customers ineligible for the reduced or no-cost investment services. [62 Fed. Reg. 5855] PTCE 97-11 has been extended to apply to Roth IRAs (see Q 31:1) [DOL Op. Ltr. 98-03A; 64 Fed. Reg. 1042] and to apply to individual retirement annuities (see Q 30:3). [67 Fed. Reg. 76,425]

PTCE 96-62. PTCE 96-62 creates a class exemption from the prohibited-transaction rules for certain prospective transactions that are substantially similar to at least two other transactions for which exemptions have been granted within the last 60 months. Consideration of these requests for exemption will be made under expedited procedures and as class exemptions, rather than as an individual exemption, if certain conditions are met. Substantially similar means alike in all material aspects, as determined by DOL. However, there is no requirement of substantial similarity between the type of plan involved in the proposed transaction and the type of plans involved in the previously granted individual exemptions. In addition, there must be little, if any, risk of abuse or loss to the plan participants and beneficiaries as a result of the transaction. [61 Fed. Reg. 39,988] Because of the success of the expedited procedures, the number of requests for individual exemptions relating to routine transactions decreased. This created a problem because exemptions granted under PTCE 96-62 cannot be relied on by other parties wishing to receive similar exemptions because the PTCE 96-62 exemption was limited only to those transactions that were the subject of that specific exemption. DOL was concerned that parties seeking authorization for transactions under the expedited procedures would not be able to find two substantially similar non-expedited individual exemptions that were granted within the 60-month time period. To alleviate this problem, DOL has expanded PTCE 96-62 to permit a party to base its submission on substantially similar transactions described in either (1) two individual exemptions granted within the past 60 months, or (2) one individual exemption granted within the past 120 months and one transaction that received final authorization under the expedited procedures within the past 60 months. [67 Fed. Reg. 44,622]

PTCE 96-23. PTCE 96-23 allows in-house asset managers (INHAMs) to engage in a wide variety of party-in-interest transactions without violating ERISA Section 406(a)(1)(A) (see Qs 24:1, 24:3). INHAMs are exempted from transactions in which either affiliates of the employer or the parent corporation are involved, so long as they are service providers to the plan. Transactions between an INHAM and individuals who are not service providers would still be prohibited. Thus, for example, an INHAM would still be prohibited from doing an individual transaction with the president of the plan sponsor. The transaction cannot be designed to specifically favor a party in interest.

An INHAM is an organization that is:

1. Either (a) a direct or indirect wholly owned subsidiary of an employer or of a parent organization of the employer or (b) a membership nonprofit corporation, a majority of whose members are officers or directors of such an employer or parent corporation, and

2. A registered investment advisor that has under its management and control total assets attributable to plans maintained by affiliates of the INHAM in excess of $50 million.

The employer or parent corporation's plans must have at least $250 million in plan assets. The INHAM must have discretionary authority to negotiate the transactions, although the plan sponsor may retain the right to veto or approve transactions involving amounts of $5 million or more. [61 Fed. Reg. 15,975] DOL has proposed an amendment to expand the definition of INHAM to include a subsidiary that is 80 percent or more owned by the employer or parent company. Additionally, the plan assets under management requirement would be increased from $50 million to $85 million. The proposed amendment would ease the restrictions on parties-in-interest to engage in transactions with the plan if the parties are co-joint venturers. Under the amendment, a co-joint venturer may engage in a transaction with a plan only if the joint venture relationship is the entity's sole relationship to the employer or if the entity is both a joint venturer and a service provider or an entity with a relationship to a service provider. The party-in-interest dealing with the plan may not be the INHAM or a person related to the INHAM. An INHAM is related to a party-in-interest if the party owns a 5 percent or more interest in the INHAM or if the INHAM (or a person controlling, or controlled by, the INHAM) owns a 5 percent or more interest in the party-in-interest. DOL proposes to increase the 5 percent threshold to 10 percent. In addition, the proposed amendment would expand the relief relating to the leasing of office or commercial space owned by a plan managed by an INHAM to an employer with respect to the plan or an affiliate of the employer. Under the proposed amendment, the relief would be expanded to include additional situations involving existing leases with an employer or an affiliate beyond foreclosure situations, provided that the decision to acquire the office or commercial space subject to the lease is made by the INHAM. [75 Fed. Reg. 33,642]

PTCE 95-60. PTCE 95-60 allows (prospectively and retroactively to January 1, 1975) certain transactions engaged in by insurance company general accounts in which an employee benefit plan has an interest if certain specified conditions are met. An additional exemption is provided for plans to engage in transactions with persons who provide services to insurance company general accounts. The exemption also permits transactions relating to the origination and operation of certain asset pool investment trusts in which a general account has an interest as a result of the acquisition of certificates issued by the trust. The exemption affects participants and beneficiaries of employee benefit plans, insurance company general accounts, and other persons engaging in the described transactions. [60 Fed. Reg. 35,925]

PTCE 94-20. PTCE 94-20 permits an employee benefit plan and a broker-dealer or bank or any affiliate that is a party in interest to enter into a foreign currency exchange transaction if the transaction is directed by an independent fiduciary and meets certain arm's-length tests. [59 Fed. Reg. 8022] See Q 24:23 for a discussion of the new statutory prohibited-transaction exemption for foreign exchange transactions.

PTCE 93-33. PTCE 93-33 allows banks to offer services at reduced or no cost to persons who maintain IRAs, SEPs, and Keogh plans, provided that the services offered are the same as those offered by the bank in the ordinary course of business to customers who do not maintain such plans or IRAs (see Q 30:46). The exemption covers investments in securities for which market quotations are readily available, but excludes investments in securities offered by a bank exclusively to IRAs and Keogh plans. [59 Fed. Reg. 22,686, 58 Fed. Reg. 13,053] PTCE 93-33 has been extended to apply to Roth IRAs (see Q 31:1), Education IRAs (now called Coverdell Education Savings Accounts), and SIMPLE IRAs (see Q 33:2).[DOL Op. Ltr. 98-03A; PTCE 97-11 (62 Fed. Reg. 5855; 64 Fed. Reg. 1042)] DOL has opined that the contribution of a $100 cash credit by an insurer or bank to an individual's newly created health savings account (HSA) as a means of encouraging the individual to participate in an HSA is not a prohibited transaction. [DOL Op. Ltr. 2004-09A]

PTCE 93-1. PTCE 93-1 permits banks, credit unions, and other financial institutions to give cash or other premiums as an incentive to open, or make contributions to, an IRA or Keogh plan (see Q 30:46). [58 Fed. Reg. 3567]

PTCE 86-128. PTCE 86-128 allows broker-dealers who are plan fiduciaries to effect or execute securities transactions for a fee paid by the plan, if certain requirements are satisfied. The exemption also allows sponsors of pooled separate accounts and other pooled investment funds to use their affiliates to effect or execute securities transactions for such accounts if certain conditions are met. [51 Fed. Reg. 41,686; *see also* 73 Fed. Reg. 21,987] DOL has proposed an amendment to PTCE 86-128 that would allow employee benefit plan fiduciaries who are also discretionary plan trustees to effect or execute securities transactions on behalf of those plans. [67 Fed. Reg. 31,838]

PTCE 84-24. PTCE 84-24 provides relief for certain transactions relating to the purchase, with plan assets, of investment company securities or insurance or annuity contracts, and the payment of associated sales commissions to insurance agents or brokers, pension consultants, or investment company principal underwriters that are parties in interest with respect to such plan. [49 Fed. Reg. 13,209, *as corrected by* 49 Fed. Reg. 24,819] PTCE 84-24, amended PTCE 77-9 [42 Fed. Reg. 32,395, *as amended by* 44 Fed. Reg. 1479] Currently, relief is not available under PTCE 84-24 if an affiliate of the insurance agent or broker, pension consultant, insurance company, or investment company principal underwriter is a plan trustee that has investment discretion over any of the assets of the plan. DOL has, however, adopted an amendment that extends relief to transactions relating to the purchase by plans of investment company securities or insurance or annuity contracts, and the receipt of associated sales commissions by an insurance agent or broker, pension consultant, or investment company principal underwriter in situations where an affiliate of the insurance agent or broker, pension consultant, or investment company principal underwriter is a trustee with investment discretion over plan assets that are not involved in the transaction. [71 Fed. Reg. 5887]

PTCE 84-14. PTCE 84-14 permits parties in interest to engage in various transactions involving plan assets that would otherwise be prohibited transactions if, among other conditions, the plan assets are managed by persons defined in the exemption as qualified professional asset managers (QPAMs). QPAMs can be banks, savings and loans, insurance companies, and investment managers that are regulated by applicable state or federal law and meet certain financial standards. A major condition of the exemption is the requirement that the QPAM maintain independence from the entities in which the plan invests by retaining full authority over the terms of transactions and investment decisions. [49 Fed. Reg. 9494, *as amended by* 50 Fed. Reg. 41,430 and 70 Fed. Reg. 49,305; DOL Op. Ltr. 2003-07A] DOL has adopted an amendment to PTCE 84-14 to allow financial service entities to act as QPAMs for their own plans. [75 Fed. Reg. 38,837] DOL has opined that transactions between a broker-dealer and a separate 401(k) plan account (see Q 27:1) managed by a QPAM are covered by PTCE 84-14, despite the plan participants receiving investment advice from a subsidiary of the broker-dealer for a fee. Because neither the broker-dealer nor its subsidiary would have the authority to appoint or terminate the QPAM, the subsidiary's provision of investment advice to participants, for a fee, would not violate the PTCE. [DOL Op. Ltr. 2007-01A] PTCE 84-14 contains a 10-percent-of-assets exception. DOL has opined that where a pooled investment fund that holds plan assets invests in a second pooled investment fund that also holds plan assets, the second fund is not required to look through to (and thus count separately) the plan assets invested in the first fund. [DOL Op. Ltr. 2007-02A]

PTCE 80-26. PTCE 80-26 permits the lending of money or other extension of credit from a party in interest or disqualified person to an employee benefit plan, and the repayment of such loan or other extension of credit in accordance with its terms or other written modifications thereof, if:

1. No interest or other fee is charged to the plan, and no discount for payment in cash is relinquished by the plan, in connection with the loan or extension of credit;

2. The proceeds of the loan or extension of credit are used only:

   a. for the payment of ordinary operating expenses of the plan, including the payment of benefits in accordance with the terms of the plan and periodic premiums under an insurance or annuity contract, or

   b. for a purpose incidental to the ordinary operation of the plan;

3. The loan or extension of credit is unsecured;

4. The loan or extension of credit is not directly or indirectly made by an employee benefit plan; and

5. The loan or extension of credit is made pursuant to a written agreement if the duration of the loan or extension of credit is more than 60 days. [45 Fed. Reg. 28,545, as amended by 71 Fed. Reg. 17,917]

PTCE 79-13. PTCE 79-13 permits the acquisition and sale of shares of a closed-end mutual fund that is registered under the Investment Company Act of 1940 by an employee benefit plan covering only employees of the mutual fund, the investment advisor of the fund, or any affiliate thereof (whether or not the mutual fund, investment advisor, or affiliate is a fiduciary of the plan). [44 Fed. Reg. 25,533]

PTCE 77-4. PTCE 77-4 provides that certain restrictions do not apply to the purchase or sale by plan of registered shares issued by an open-end investment company where a plan fiduciary is also an investment advisor to the investment company, if specified conditions are satisfied, such as the plan must not pay a sales commission in connection with the purchase or sale. [42 Fed. Reg. 18,732] DOL has opined that the prohibition on sales commissions does not apply to brokerage commissions paid incident to transactions of shares of registered open-end investment companies to brokers unaffiliated with the fund, investment advisor, or any affiliates. However, DOL cautioned that, if a plan fiduciary who is also an investment advisor to a fund remits commissions to a broker-dealer who is an affiliate of the advisor or the fund, the commission payments would be separate prohibited transactions with no relief available under PTCE 77-4. [DOL Op. Ltr. 2002-05A]

PTCE 77-3. PTCE 77-3 permits the acquisition and sale of shares of an open-end mutual fund registered under the Investment Company Act of 1940 by an employee benefit plan covering only employees of the mutual fund, the investment advisor, or principal underwriter of the mutual fund, or any affiliate thereof (whether or not such mutual fund, investment advisor, principal underwriter, or affiliate is a fiduciary of the plan). [42 Fed. Reg. 18,734; DOL Op. Ltr. 2006-06A] A life insurance company's investment in its own mutual funds of its employees' qualified retirement plan assets was not a prohibited transaction because the conditions of PTCE 77-3 were satisfied. [Mehling v. N.Y. Life Ins. Co., No. 99-CV-5417 (E.D. Pa. 2001)]

PTCE 75-1. PTCE 75-1 permits certain transactions among employee benefit plans, broker-dealers, reporting dealers, and banks. Under this exemption, the prohibited-transaction provisions of ERISA will not apply to the purchase or sale of securities between a broker-dealer registered under the Securities and Exchange Act of 1934, an employee benefit plan during the existence of an underwriting or selling syndicate with respect to such securities, or a reporting dealer who is a market maker. The exemption also allows the extension of credit between a broker-dealer and a plan. [40 Fed. Reg. 50,845] Amendments have been adopted whereby a plan may engage in certain transactions with broker-dealers, reporting dealers, and banks that are plan fiduciaries as long as the institutions and their affiliates do not have investment authority over or provide investment advice with regard to the plan's assets involved in the transaction. [71 Fed. Reg. 5883]

DOL has opined that, under PTCE 91-38, a bank's wholly owned subsidiary, which is a trust company that is trustee for collective investment funds in which employee benefit plans invest, will be considered a bank for purposes of the class exemption covering bank collective investment funds. [DOL Op. Ltr. 2006-07A] DOL has also advised that a state-licensed branch of a non-U.S. bank would qualify as a bank or trust company for purposes of the prohibited transaction exemption authorized under ERISA Section 408(b)(8) (see Q 24:1) and as a bank for purposes of PTCE 91-38, as long as the state banking authority regulated such branches with the same level of oversight it would apply to state-chartered banks in the state. [DOL Op. Ltr. 2007-03A]

Concurrent with the issuance of final regulations that require contracts between plan fiduciaries and service providers to disclose specified information (see Q 23:12), DOL has incorporated in the final regulations a PTCE that relieves a plan fiduciary of liability for a prohibited transaction that results from the failure by a service provider to comply with the disclosure regulations. In order for the relief under the PTCE to apply, the plan fiduciary must have reasonably believed that the contract complied with the governing requirements and must not have had reason to know that the service provider would fail to comply with the disclosure requirements. The PTCE will become effective on July 16, 2011.

DOL has proposed an amendment to certain underwriter exemptions, which are a group of individual prohibited transaction exemptions that permit plans to hold securities representing interests in investment trusts, but which require that trustees of the investment trusts to be independent of the securities' underwriters. The amendment would allow investment trust trustees to be affiliates of the underwriters of the securities. [67 Fed. Reg. 36,028]

See Qs 15:20 and 15:21 for PTCEs regarding the purchase and sale of life insurance policies and Qs 30:45 and 31:33 regarding application of the prohibited-transaction rules to IRAs and Roth IRAs.

Chapter 25

Termination of the Plan

To qualify for tax-favored status, an employer's qualified retirement plan must be permanent. Nevertheless, an employer may amend the plan, terminate the plan, or stop contributing to the plan. This chapter examines how these actions may affect plan participants and the plan status, and discusses the rules regarding the termination of qualified retirement plans.

Q 25:1 Once a qualified retirement plan is established, may the employer terminate it?

Yes. Although the employer must have intended the plan to be permanent, it may be terminated if the plan permits it. In addition, in the case of a defined benefit plan (see Q 2:3) covered by Title IV of ERISA (see Qs 25:9, 25:11, 25:12), the applicable termination rules must be satisfied.

Defined contribution plans (see Q 2:2) and defined benefit plans not covered by Title IV of ERISA are not subject to these rules. However, the plan administrator (see Q 20:1) of a defined benefit plan or an individual account plan subject to the minimum funding requirements (see Qs 2:2, 8:1) must furnish a written notice concerning a plan amendment that provides for a significant reduction in the rate of future benefit accrual (see Q 9:37). This notice is called the Section 204(h) Notice (see Q 9:38). The plan administrator is required to provide in this notice, in a manner calculated to be understood by the average plan participant, sufficient information (as defined in regulations) to allow participants to understand the effect of the amendment. [I.R.C. § 4980F; ERISA § 204(h)] See Qs 9:37 through 9:53 for a more detailed discussion of the Section 204(h) Notice.

See Q 25:61 regarding the application of ERISA Section 204(h) to a terminated plan covered by Title IV of ERISA.

In one case, a plan covered by Title IV of ERISA was terminated by the adoption of a board resolution and not by a plan amendment (see Q 25:2). Since the employer complied with the requirements for a standard termination (see Q 25:13), the court ruled that the plan was not required to be amended to cease benefit accruals prior to its termination. [Aldridge v. Lily-Tulip, Inc. Salary Ret. Plan Benefits Comm., 1994 U.S. App. LEXIS 36300 (11th Cir. 1994)]

Q 25:2   May a qualified retirement plan be terminated by a formal declaration of the plan sponsor's board of directors?

Although the plan sponsor's board of directors should adopt a resolution authorizing the termination of a qualified retirement plan, certain substantive and/or notice requirements must also be met to implement a plan termination (see Qs 25:1, 25:13, 25:15, 25:60, 25:63).

The date that a plan subject to PBGC jurisdiction is deemed to terminate can be no earlier than the date determined under applicable PBGC provisions (see Q 25:28). Despite a resolution terminating a company's defined benefit plan (see Q 2:3), the plan was deemed not terminated because PBGC's notice and filing requirements were not followed. Therefore, since the ongoing plan did not meet the minimum participation requirement (see Q 5:23), the plan was disqualified. [Gant, 76 T.C.M. 994 (1998)] Where a plan sponsor never notified PBGC of its intention to terminate its defined benefit plan, PBGC properly established the date on which the sponsor ceased operations as the plan's involuntary termination date, not the date ten years earlier when the plan sponsor informed its employees that the plan was being terminated. [PBGC v. Mize Co., No. 92-1351 (4th Cir. 1993)]

In the case of any other qualified retirement plan, the date of termination is generally established by the terms of the plan and by the actions of the company officials (e.g., a meeting of the board of directors). Despite a resolution terminating a company's money purchase pension plan (see Q 2:4), the plan was deemed not terminated taking into account all the facts and circumstances such as the participants not being notified, the annual reports (see Q 21:2) stating the plan was not terminated, and the conversion of the plan into a profit sharing plan (see Q 2:6). Therefore, since the ongoing plan did not meet the minimum participation requirement, the plan was disqualified. [Gant, 76 T.C.M. 994 (1998)]

[ERISA § 4041(a)(1); Treas. Reg. § 1.411(d)-2; Phillips v. Bebber, Nos. 89-2184, 89-2189 (4th Cir. 1990); Rev. Rul. 89-87, 1989-2 C.B. 81; Rev. Rul. 79-237, 1979-2 C.B. 190]

An independent plan administrator (see Q 20:1) may terminate a pension plan despite the plan sponsor's desire to continue the plan. [Delgrosso v. Spang & Co., No. 82-2672 (W.D. Pa. 1991); ERISA § 4041(a)] Pension plan trustees who terminated a plan after a plan sponsor changed the plan's funding method acted in good faith and did not breach their fiduciary duties (see Qs 23:19, 23:20). [Morgan v. Independent Drivers Ass'n Pension Plan, 1992 U.S. App. LEXIS 22927 (10th Cir. 1992)] In another case, a bankruptcy trustee who assumed the position of the employer-debtor was ordered by the court to terminate the company's defined benefit plan. Upon reconsideration, the court ruled that only the plan administrator had authority to terminate the plan and, because the employer-debtor was not the plan administrator, the bankruptcy trustee did not have this authority. [*In re* Esco Mfg. Co., No. 93-1681 (5th Cir. 1995)]

In one case, a participant in a qualified retirement plan sued to have the plan disqualified and terminated because the rate of return on the plan's investments was unfavorable. The court ruled that there is no requirement that a retirement plan's investments grow at a specified rate or that its participants be satisfied with the rate of return. The court further explained that it does not have the power to terminate a plan; it can only review the qualified status of a plan. [Sonier, 78 T.C.M. 313 (1999)]

However, IRS has declared that a termination will not occur if plan assets are not distributed as soon as administratively feasible, even if the plan has been terminated in accordance with Title IV of ERISA (see Q 25:63).

Q 25:3 Which factors may cause a qualified retirement plan to be terminated?

A defined benefit plan covered by the Title IV program (see Qs 25:11, 25:12) will be considered to be terminated only if the conditions and procedures prescribed by PBGC are satisfied (see Qs 25:2, 25:13, 25:15).

Whether a defined contribution plan (see Q 2:2) is terminated is generally a question to be determined with regard to all the facts and circumstances in a particular case. For example, a plan may be terminated when, in connection with the winding up of the company's trade or business, the company begins to discharge its employees (see Q 25:5). However, a plan is not terminated merely because a company consolidates or replaces that plan with a comparable plan (see Q 25:6). [Treas. Reg. § 1.401-6(b)] Similarly, a plan is not terminated merely because the company sells or otherwise disposes of its trade or business if the acquiring company continues the plan as a separate and distinct plan of its own or consolidates or replaces that plan with a comparable plan.

Q 25:4 What is the effect of a plan termination on a participant's accrued benefit?

A qualified retirement plan must provide that (1) upon its full or partial termination or (2) in the case of a profit sharing plan upon complete discontinuance of contributions under the plan, "the rights of all affected employees to benefits accrued to the date of such termination, partial termination, or discontinuance, to the extent funded as of such date, or the amounts credited to the employees' accounts, are nonforfeitable" (see Q 9:13). [I.R.C. § 411(d)(3)]

The practical effect of a plan termination, therefore, is that each affected participant becomes 100 percent vested in the participant's accrued benefit (see Q 9:2) as of the date of termination if the plan has sufficient assets to cover the benefit. In one case, where there was a partial termination (see Q 25:5) of an employee stock ownership plan (ESOP; see Q 28:1), the court held that the terminated participants were not required to be vested in unallocated assets held in a suspense account because these assets were not accrued benefits. [Rummel v. Consolidated Freightways, Inc., 1992 U.S. Dist. LEXIS 15144 (N.D. Cal. 1992)]

If a profit sharing plan (see Q 2:6) is amended to add a cash-or-deferred arrangement (see Q 27:2) and a matching contribution (see Q 27:75) but discontinues its regular profit sharing contribution, IRS has opined that a discontinuance of contributions requiring full vesting has not occurred because this is a facts-and-circumstances determination. Ceasing one type of employer contribution while commencing another type of employer contribution is not a discontinuance of a plan requiring full vesting.

Generally, a participant who is partially vested need not become 100 percent vested upon termination of the plan if the participant separates from service and is paid the vested accrued benefit prior to the date of termination. However, a partially vested participant who terminates service, is not paid the vested accrued benefit, and does not incur a one-year break in service (see Q 5:10) prior to the date of termination must become 100 percent vested upon termination of the plan. Some IRS district offices have interpreted the above rule to require that all nonvested former participants with breaks in service of less than five years who have not been paid their vested accrued benefits be fully vested (see Q 9:17). [I.R.C. §§ 411(a)(6)(B), 411(a)(6)(C); Penn v. Howe-Baker Eng'rs, Inc., No. 89-2257 (5th Cir. 1990); Gen. Couns. Mem. 39,310 (Nov. 29, 1984)]

Despite the requirement that an employee must become fully vested upon plan termination, one court concluded that the partially vested benefit of a previously terminated participant who had yet to receive a distribution of his vested benefit can be forfeited upon plan termination if the employer is liquidated at the same time. [Borda v. Hardy, Lewis, Pollard & Page, P.C., 138 F.3d 1062 (6th Cir. 1998); see also Flanagan v. Inland Empire Elec. Worker's Pension Plan & Trust, 3 F.3d 1246 (9th Cir. 1993)] In another case, the court upheld a plan administrator's decision to deny full credit to employees who were laid off prior to a plan's termination. The court reasoned that "a person is unaffected by a plan's termination unless either he or she was employed by the plan-sponsoring employer at the time of the plan's termination or his or her discharge was directly linked to the plan's termination." [Bayer v. Holcroft/Loftus, Inc., 769 F. Supp. 225 (E.D. Mich. 1991)] However in another case, where an employee terminated employment and did not receive a distribution of benefits, and the company terminated the plan one month later, the court ruled that the company's determination that upon termination of employment employees immediately forfeited their account balances would violate ERISA and concluded that the employee became fully vested upon plan termination. [Kerkhof v. MCI Worldcom, Inc., No. 99-118-P-H (D. Me. 2000)]

An issue that has been resolved by IRS involves whether converting or merging a money purchase pension plan (see Q 2:4) into a profit sharing plan (see Q 2:6) requires full vesting of benefits. IRS has determined that the conversion or merger of a money purchase pension plan into a profit sharing plan does not result in a partial termination of the money purchase pension plan; and, therefore, the participants do not become 100 percent vested. However, a Section 204(h) Notice (see Qs 9:37–9:53) must be provided to affected individuals in a money purchase pension plan that is converted or merged into a profit sharing plan (see Q 25:60). [Rev. Rul. 2002-42, 2002-2 C.B. 76]

See Q 25:5 regarding partial terminations.

Q 25:5   What is a partial termination?

Generally, whether or not a partial termination of a qualified retirement plan has occurred will be determined on the basis of all the facts and circumstances. Under applicable regulations, a partial termination may be found to have occurred when a significant group of employees covered by the plan is excluded from coverage, as a result of either an amendment to the plan or their discharge by the employer. One court concluded that if various corporate transactions occurring in different years are sufficiently related, then participant terminations from the different years can be aggregated for purposes of determining whether a partial termination has occurred. Thus, a partially vested terminated participant could be entitled to full vesting by virtue of a partial termination resulting from employee terminations occurring in future years. [Matz v. Household Int'l Tax Reduction Inv. Plan, 2001 WL 1027275 (7th Cir. 2001); *see also* Matz v. Household Int'l Tax Reduction Inv. Plan, 2003 WL 22227138 (N.D. Ill. 2003)] The court also adopted a rebuttable presumption that a partial termination occurs where there is a 20 percent or greater reduction in the number of plan participants. In addition, the court ruled that if the reduction is below 10 percent, no partial termination occurs and that if the reduction is above 40 percent, partial termination is conclusively presumed. The case was remanded to the district court to consider the tax motives and determine other issues, such as whether a series of terminations should be treated as a single termination, whether terminated participants should include employees who left voluntarily, and whether participants should include those who were employed by reorganized entities. [Matz v. Household Int'l Tax Reduction Inv. Plan, 2004 U.S. App. LEXIS 23284 (7th Cir. 2004)] IRS ruled that if the turnover rate is at least 20 percent, there is a presumption that a partial termination has occurred. The turnover rate is determined by dividing the number of participating employees who had an employer-initiated severance from employment during the applicable period by the sum of all of the participating employees at the start of the applicable period and the employees who became participants during the applicable period. The applicable period depends on the circumstances: a plan year, in the case of a plan year that is less than 12 months, the plan year plus the immediately preceding plan year, or a longer period if there are a series of related severances from employment. [Rev. Rul. 2007-43, 2007-2 C.B. 45]

A partial termination may be held to have occurred when benefits or employer contributions are reduced or the eligibility or vesting requirements under the plan are made less liberal. However, according to IRS, a reduction in future benefit accruals or employer contributions, or a situation in which the eligibility or vesting requirements under the plan are made less liberal, does not necessarily constitute a partial termination. Instead, in order to bring about a partial termination in such a situation (1) a potential for reversion (see Q 25:49) must have been created or increased, (2) prohibited discrimination has occurred or the potential for discrimination has been increased (see Q 4:10), and/or (3) situations similar to those noted above are found. [IRS Doc. 6678 (4-81), Explanation for Worksheet, Form 6677, Plan Termination Standards] The merger or conversion of a money purchase pension plan (see Q 2:4) into a profit sharing (see Q 2:6) plan does not result in a partial termination of the money purchase pension plan. [Rev. Rul. 2002-42, 2002-2 C.B. 76] If a partial termination of a qualified retirement plan occurs, the provisions of the Code and regulations apply only to the part of the plan that is terminated. [Treas. Reg. §§ 1.401-6(b)(2), 1.411(d)-2(b)(3)]

IRS has ruled the freezing of accruals under a defined benefit plan (see Qs 2:3, 26:14), so that a partial termination of the plan occurs, does not constitute a plan termination for purposes of determining whether service with the employer after the plan was established may be disregarded toward vesting (see Q 9:11) if accruals resume under the plan. Therefore, all years of service with the employer following the establishment of the previously frozen plan must be taken into account for purposes of vesting. If, instead, the accruals are earned under a new plan maintained by the same employer and the new plan is merged with the frozen plan, then the same conclusion results, so that, after the merger, service after the frozen plan was established must be taken into account for purposes of vesting in any benefit accruals under the new plan. [Rev. Rul. 2003-65, 2003-1 C.B. 1035; Treas. Reg. § 1.411(a)-5(b)(3)(iii)]

> **Example 1.** After review of all the facts and circumstances, it was determined that a partial termination did not occur where the number of plan participants declined from 3,800 in 1989 to 3,000 in 1990, and then to 1,900 in 1991. Employee layoffs were caused by two separate events—an initial downturn in business in 1989–1990 due to a slow economy and a subsequent downturn in 1990–1991 due to the imposition of a federal luxury tax. The court also noted that the layoffs did not financially impair the plan and were not improperly motivated. [Administrative Comm. of Sea Ray Employees' Stock Ownership & Profit Sharing Plan v. Robinson, 1999 WL 11495 (6th Cir. 1999)]

> **Example 2.** An amendment to a defined benefit plan that eliminated an after-tax contributory feature resulting in the loss of contributory benefits for certain participants did not create a partial termination. Although between 29 percent and 39 percent of all plan participants suffered a decrease in future benefit accruals following the amendment, a determination of whether a defined benefit plan ceases or decreases future benefit accruals under the plan must be made by reference to the plan as a whole and not to a part of the plan. Since the impact of the amendment on the entire plan was to increase future benefit accruals in the aggregate for all plan participants, there was no reduction in future benefit accruals. The court found that there was no partial termination because there was no decrease in future benefit accruals as a result of the amendment and no increase in the potential for a reversion to the employer. [Gluck v. Unisys Corp., No. 90-1510 (E.D. Pa. 1995)]

> **Example 3.** A partial termination occurred where the employees of two subsidiaries became participants in a union plan, were no longer active participants in the company's plan, and the number of participants decreased to 958 from 1,564. [Priv. Ltr. Rul. 9523025]

> **Example 4.** A profit sharing plan was not partially terminated where layoffs due to a sharp decline in the company's business resulted in a 19.85 percent

reduction in the number of plan participants. The facts did not show employer abuse, bad faith, or misconduct (i.e., no reversion was created, the financial health of the plan was not adversely affected, and there was no discrimination in favor of highly compensated participants). Furthermore, the employer rehired a significant number of terminated employees in succeeding years. [Halliburton Co., 100 T.C. 216 (1993), *aff'd*, unpublished opinion (5th Cir. 1994); *see also* Baker, 68 T.C.M. 48 (1994) (same record as Halliburton)] However, a partial termination did occur where a company sold most of its operating assets and did not make continued employment available to 83 percent of its employees. [Collingnon v. Reporting Servs. Co., 1992 U.S. Dist. LEXIS 10070 (C.D. Ill. 1992)]

Example 5. Where between 40 and 70 percent of employees were laid off after completion of a project, and the union pension plan defined "partial termination" as a layoff of more than 20 percent of employees, the terminated employees became 100 percent vested. [Duncan v. Northern Alaska Carpenters Ret. Fund, No. 90-133-DA (D. Or. 1992)] Similarly, a partial termination occurred when a multiemployer plan experienced two reductions of over 50 percent in participation. [Thayer v. Alaska Teamster-Employer Pension Trust, No. A90-147 (D. Alaska 1992)]

Example 6. An employer discharged 132 of the 395 employees participating in its qualified retirement plan. Of the discharged employees, 65 were not fully vested. The court originally held that no partial termination occurred because the 65 nonvested discharged participants represented only 16.4 percent of all 395 participants. Upon reconsideration, the court held that all discharged plan participants must be taken into account, including vested participants. Thus, a partial termination occurred because 33.4 percent of all plan participants, a significant group, were discharged. [Weil v. Retirement Plan Admin. Comm. of the Terson Co., 913 F.2d 1045 (2d Cir. 1991); *see also* Matz v. Household Int'l Tax Reduction Inv. Plan, 2004 U.S. App. 2004 LEXIS 23284 (7th Cir. 2004) which also held that all plan participants should be counted in determining whether a partial termination has occurred]

Example 7. Two major oil companies (Gulf and Chevron) merged their operations in 1984 and merged their pension plans in 1986. The merger of operations resulted in a partial termination with respect to the significant number of Gulf plan participants (almost 10,000) who were discharged (prior to the merger of the plans) because of the merger of operations. A second partial termination occurred with respect to Gulf plan participants who were still employed by Chevron at the time of the merger of the plans. That merger resulted in a substantial reduction in future benefit accruals to those employees, thereby increasing the potential reversion to Chevron upon termination of the plan. [*In re* Gulf Pension Litig., No. 86-4365 (S.D. Tex. 1991)]

Example 8. A partial termination of a qualified retirement plan occurred when the employer's business was closed and 12 of the 15 participating employees were discharged upon refusing the opportunity to transfer to the employer's new business location. [Rev. Rul. 73-284, 1973-1 C.B. 139; *see also* Rev. Rul. 81-27, 1981-1 C.B. 228]

Example 9. In two successive years, an employer experienced reductions in its workforce of 34 percent and 51 percent, respectively, as a result of adverse economic conditions. The court ruled that, based on all the facts and circumstances, a partial termination occurred in each year. [Tipton & Kalmbach, Inc., 83 T.C. 154 (1984)]

Example 10. A corporation maintaining pension and profit sharing plans operated two divisions: one manufactured paint and the other produced other types of wall coverings. As a result of a split-off of one of the divisions to a new corporation, 16 employees (representing 14.7 percent of the participating employees) were transferred and were no longer eligible to participate in the original corporation's plans. In reviewing these facts, a court held that there was not a "significant percentage" of participants affected by the corporation's actions and that a partial termination of the plans did not occur. [Babb v. Olney Paint Co., 764 F.2d 240 (4th Cir. 1985); *see also* Kreis v. Charles O. Townley, M.D. & Assocs., P.C., 833 F.2d 74 (6th Cir. 1987)]

If a determination letter on the continued qualification of the plan after a possible partial termination is desired, Form 5300 (see Q 18:12) should be filed with IRS.

Q 25:6   Does the adoption of a new qualified retirement plan to replace another plan result in a termination of the original plan?

Not necessarily. A qualified retirement plan is not considered to be terminated if it is either replaced by or converted into a comparable plan. For this purpose, a comparable plan is defined as a qualified retirement plan covered by the same limitations on deductions as the original plan. Since stock bonus plans (see Q 2:13), ESOPs (see Q 28:1), and profit sharing plans (see Q 2:6) are generally covered by the same limitations on deductions, these plans are considered to be comparable (see Q 25:4). [Treas. Reg. §§ 1.381(c)(11)-1(d)(4), 1.401-6(b)(1)] IRS has determined that the merger or conversion of a money purchase pension plan into a profit sharing plan does not result in a partial termination of the money purchase pension plan; and, therefore, the participants do not become 100 percent vested. However, the assets that originated in the money purchase pension plan must retain their money purchase pension plan attributes (e.g., automatic survivor benefit requirements (see Q 10:1) and distribution restrictions and limitations (see Qs 1:4, 10:56)). [Rev. Rul. 2002-42, 2002-2 C.B. 76; Rev. Rul. 94-76, 1994-2 C.B. 46]

On the other hand, a defined benefit plan covered by Title IV is considered to be terminated if an amendment is adopted to convert the plan to a defined contribution plan, such as a profit sharing plan, an ESOP, or a stock bonus plan. However, the amendment will not take effect unless and until the requirements for a standard or distress termination under Title IV are satisfied (see Qs 25:13, 25:15). [ERISA § 4041(e)]

Furthermore, an employer's transfer of excess assets from its terminated defined benefit plan to its defined contribution plan constitutes a reversion resulting in taxable income and excise tax, followed by a contribution to the defined contribution plan (see Qs 25:49, 25:52). [Lee Eng'g Supply Co., 101 T.C. 189 (1993); IRS Notice 88-58, 1988-1 C.B. 546; Gen. Couns. Mem. 39,744 (July 14, 1988)] See Q 25:53 regarding qualified replacement plans.

Q 25:7 Can termination of a qualified retirement plan affect its tax-favored status for earlier years?

Yes. The termination of a plan, or the complete discontinuance of contributions to a profit sharing plan, can result in the retroactive disqualification of the plan, causing the disallowance of tax deductions for the employer. This will depend on whether the plan was intended as a permanent program for the exclusive benefit of employees or a temporary device to set aside funds for the benefit of highly compensated employees (HCEs; see Q 3:2) and whether the plan was discriminatory in operation.

Generally, IRS will not treat the termination as a device to benefit HCEs (see Q 4:21) if the termination is caused by a change in circumstances that would make it financially impractical to continue the plan. When termination of the plan occurs within a few years of its adoption, the reasons for termination will be examined closely. IRS will assume the plan was not temporary if the termination is for a "valid business reason" or on account of "business necessity."

Form 5310, Application for Determination for Terminating Plan, provides some insight into IRS's views as to what reasons for plan termination it considers valid, notwithstanding the presumed permanence of the plan. The listed reasons include:

- A change in ownership by merger
- The liquidation or dissolution of the employer
- A change in ownership by sale or transfer
- The existence of adverse business conditions
- The adoption of a new plan

If the plan termination is due to adverse business conditions, IRS requires an explanation of why such adverse conditions require the plan's termination.

When the termination occurs after ten years of active operation, IRS will usually not challenge the plan on these grounds even though a valid business reason for the termination is lacking. [Rev. Rul. 72-239, 1972-1 C.B. 107]

A qualified retirement plan will not satisfy Section 401(a)(4) if the plan's termination discriminates significantly in favor of HCEs (see Qs 3:2, 4:21). The determination of discrimination is based on all relevant facts and circumstances. [Treas. Reg. § 1.401(a)(4)-5(a)]

In one case, a plan trustee, who was also the sole stockholder of the company, was removed because he breached his fiduciary duty by purposely undervaluing the property held in a terminated plan so that he and his spouse would receive a windfall profit. [Solis v. Consulting Fiduciaries, Inc., 557 F.3d 772 (7th Cir. 2009)] See chapter 23 regarding fiduciary responsibilities.

Q 25:8   Is there a limit on the annual amount that a pension plan may pay to certain participants?

A defined benefit plan (and a money purchase pension plan with an accumulated funding deficiency; see Q 8:22) must provide that the annual payments to certain employees are restricted to an amount equal to a straight life annuity that is the actuarial equivalent of the accrued benefit and other benefits to which the employee is entitled under the plan (other than a Social Security supplement) plus the amount an employee would be entitled to receive under a Social Security supplement. The restrictions apply to distributions to all HCEs (see Q 3:2). However, in any given year, the plan may limit the preceding restricted group to those 25 HCEs whose compensation was the highest.

The above restrictions are not applicable if:

1. The distribution to a restricted HCE is less than 1 percent of plan assets after the payment of the benefit;

2. The value of the plan assets is at least 110 percent of the plan's current liabilities; or

3. The value of the benefit payable to the restricted HCE does not exceed $5,000. [I.R.C. § 411(a)(11)(A)]

Distributions in excess of the limit will be permitted if the participant enters into an escrow agreement, posts a bond, or provides a bank letter of credit.

[Treas. Reg. § 1.401(a)(4)-5(b); Rev. Rul. 92-76, 1992-2 C.B. 76]

With respect to a multiple employer plan (see Q 8:9) composed of tax-exempt employers, IRS ruled that (1) the determination of whether the value of the benefits payable to a restricted employee is less than 1 percent of all current liabilities may be made without disaggregating the plan into separate plans for each employer and (2) the meaning of the high-25 group for determining restricted employees means one of the 25 non-excludable HCEs with the greatest amount of compensation of each participating employer. [Priv. Ltr. Rul. 200449043]

For purposes of determining the 25 highest paid HCEs, IRS has ruled that all current and former employees of the controlled group (see Q 5:31) are taken into account, even though they are not members of the qualified separate line of business (see Q 5:47). [Priv. Ltr. Rul. 200248029]

In one case, the rules were satisfied where an agreement between an employee and trustee provided for repayment of the restricted amount if the plan terminated and repayment was necessary and, to secure repayment, single-sum distributions that equaled at least 125 percent of the restricted amount were rolled over to an IRA from the defined benefit plan and a defined contribution plan. [Priv. Ltr. Rul. 200606051] In another case, a defined benefit plan was not disqualified and the payment of a restricted amount to an HCE was allowed where an escrow agreement was entered into to secure repayment of 100 percent of the restricted amount and a letter of credit equal to 25 percent of the restricted amount was issued. [Priv. Ltr. Rul. 9631031] Similarly, distribution of the restricted amount was allowed where the participant agreed to establish a bank letter of credit or federal surety bond in an amount equal to at least 100 percent of the restricted amount. [Priv. Ltr. Rul. 9743051] A repayment agreement that was part of an IRA arrangement into which restricted distributions from a defined benefit plan were transferred satisfied the repayment (escrow) requirements where the participant agreed to repay the restricted amount if the plan terminated and repayment was necessary. [Priv. Ltr. Rul. 9514028] IRS representatives have opined that payments under a QDRO (see Q 36:1) relating to the benefits of a restricted employee are subject to the limitation on distributions.

Where a participant's election of a lump-sum distribution was a restricted benefit, the distribution arrangement was modified so that the benefit payments did not exceed the restrictions. IRS ruled that the final payment, which will be substantially larger than the other payments and will be made within ten years from the date of the first payment, will be an eligible rollover distribution (see Q 34:8). [Priv. Ltr. Rul. 201031042]

Prior to the issuance of regulations under Section 401(a)(4), a plan that substantially funded benefits for older, higher-paid employees at a more rapid pace than for younger, lower-paid employees (e.g., a defined benefit plan) was limited in the amount that it could pay out. [Treas. Reg. § 1.401-4(c)]

Similar to the current rules, the full benefit was allowed to be paid if there was adequate provision for repayment of any part of the distribution representing the restricted portion. A participant, part of the restricted group, who was to receive a large distribution, agreed to provide the plan trustee with a security agreement and letter of credit to fund his obligation to repay the plan if necessary. The agreement did not violate the restriction. [Rev. Rul. 81-135, 1981-1 C.B. 203; Priv. Ltr. Rul. 9210037] An escrow agreement imposed on an HCE's IRA as a result of a pre-1994 distribution could be released where the value of plan assets exceeded 110 percent of the plan's liabilities. [Priv. Ltr. Ruls. 9419040, 9417031]

See Q 8:6 for the rules regarding benefit restrictions for defined benefit plans that are underfunded or have liquidity problems.

Q 25:9   What is Title IV of ERISA?

Title IV of ERISA established the rules regarding the termination of many defined benefit plans (see Q 2:3). In addition, it established an insurance program to guarantee that participants and beneficiaries will receive certain pension benefits promised under an employer's defined benefit plan if the plan does not have sufficient assets to cover certain benefits in the event of the plan's termination. The program was designed to be self-financed, funded with premiums paid by sponsors of covered plans.

Q 25:10   What is the Pension Benefit Guaranty Corporation (PBGC)?

ERISA established PBGC as a wholly owned government corporation to administer the termination rules and to establish the mechanism for insuring benefits under Title IV. [ERISA § 4002]

Q 25:11   What pension plans are insured by PBGC?

To be entitled to coverage, the plan must be a defined benefit plan (see Q 2:3). In addition, the plan must:

1. Have been in effect for at least one year;
2. Be maintained by an employer engaged in commerce or in an industry or activity that affects commerce, or by a labor organization that represents employees who are engaged in commerce or in activities affecting commerce; and
3. Be a qualified pension plan, or have been operated in practice as a qualified pension plan for the five plan years prior to the termination.

[ERISA § 4021(a)]

In one case, the court ruled that an employer was not liable to the PBGC for its terminated pension plan's underfunding because the plan was not qualified and, thus, was not insured by PBGC. [PBGC v. Artra Group Inc., No. 90 C 5358 (N.D. Ill. 1991)]

PBGC has stated that with respect to defined benefit plans that terminated prior to September 26, 1980 and were not amended to comply with the minimum vesting schedules, benefits are guaranteed only to the extent that they were vested under the express terms of the plan. [Policy Submission of Bd. of Dirs. of PBGC (Jan. 14, 1993); *see also* Page v. PBGC, 968 F.2d 1310 (D.C. Cir. 1992)]

Q 25:12   Are any qualified defined benefit plans exempt from PBGC coverage?

Excluded from plan termination insurance coverage are defined benefit plans (see Q 2:3) that are established and maintained:

1. For government employees (or to which the Railroad Retirement Acts apply);
2. For church employees, unless the plan elects under Section 410(d) to be covered and has notified PBGC that it wishes to have this section of the law apply to it;
3. Outside the United States for nonresident aliens;
4. Exclusively for one or more substantial owners (i.e., the sole owner of the trade or business, a more-than-10-percent partner, or a more-than-10-percent shareholder); or
5. By professional service employers that at no time have had more than 25 active participants.

In addition to the aforementioned plans, all defined contribution plans (e.g., profit sharing, money purchase pension, ESOPs, stock bonus; see Q 2:2) as well as certain nonqualified plans are excluded from Title IV coverage. [ERISA § 4021(b)]

A defined benefit plan becomes exempt as exclusively for the benefit of the substantial owner when (1) all nonowner employees have retired and received their plan benefits and (2) the owner remains as the only plan participant. [PBGC Op. Ltr. No. 90-6]

Q 25:13   What is a standard termination?

A single-employer defined benefit plan may be voluntarily terminated under Title IV's standard termination procedures only if it is determined that when the final distributions are made, the assets of the plan will be sufficient to cover all benefit liabilities (see Q 25:14) as of the termination date. In addition:

1. The plan administrator (see Q 20:1) must provide a 60-day advance notice of termination to affected parties (see Qs 25:25, 25:29);

2. A notice containing specified information (completed by the plan administrator), together with an enrolled actuary's certification, must be filed with PBGC (see Q 25:30);

3. A notice containing required information must be provided to participants and beneficiaries regarding benefits to be paid (see Q 25:31); and

4. PBGC must not have issued a notice of noncompliance stating that it has reason to believe that the standard termination requirements have not been met or that the plan does not have sufficient assets for benefit liabilities (see Q 25:33).

[ERISA § 4041(b)]

Q 25:14   What are benefit liabilities?

Benefit liabilities under a single-employer defined benefit plan are defined as "the benefits of employees and their beneficiaries under the plan (within the meaning of § 401(a)(2) of the Internal Revenue Code of 1986)." [ERISA § 4001(a)(16)]

If a plan does not have sufficient assets for benefit liabilities, the plan sponsor may consider making a contribution to the plan. Also, a contributing sponsor, or a member of a controlled group (see Q 5:31) of a contributing sponsor, may make a commitment to contribute any additional sums necessary to make the plan sufficient. [PBGC Reg. § 4041.21(b)(1)] However, because of the rules relating to deductibility of contributions and funding requirements, the contribution may not be deductible. In this circumstance, some limited relief is offered whereby contributions made to a plan under a standard termination are deductible, but only to the extent that they are guaranteed by PBGC. [I.R.C. § 404(g)] See Q 12:18 for details.

Alternatively, in order to facilitate the termination of a plan in a standard termination, a majority owner (i.e., an individual who owns 50 percent or more of the company) may agree to forgo receipt of all or part of the majority owner's benefit. To be valid:

1. The agreement must be in writing;
2. If the plan requires the spouse to consent to a distribution in a form other than a qualified joint and survivor annuity (QJSA; see Q 10:8), the spouse, if any, must consent in writing;
3. The agreement and spousal consent must be made no earlier than the date the Notice of Intent to Terminate (NOIT; see Q 25:26) is issued and no later than the date of the last distribution; and
4. The agreement must not be inconsistent with a qualified domestic relations order (QDRO; see Q 36:1).

[PBGC Reg. § 4041.21(b)(2)]

Q 25:15   What is a distress termination?

If a defined benefit plan (see Q 2:3) cannot satisfy the conditions for a standard termination (see Q 25:13), it can be voluntarily terminated only if the conditions for a distress termination of a single-employer plan are satisfied. This type of termination may occur if the employer contributing to the plan and each member of its controlled group (see Q 5:31) meet at least one of the following conditions:

1. Liquidation in bankruptcy or insolvency proceeding.
2. Reorganization in bankruptcy or insolvency proceeding. In addition, the bankruptcy petition must be filed prior to the proposed date of plan termination, and the bankruptcy or other appropriate court must determine that, unless the plan is terminated, the employer and all the members of the controlled group will be unable to pay their debts under a reorganization plan and unable to continue without a reorganization.
3. Termination of the plan is required to enable payment of debts while staying in business or to avoid unreasonably burdensome pension costs caused by a decline of the employer's covered workforce.

One court ruled that an employer satisfied the financial requirements for a distress termination of a pension plan because, if the plan was not terminated, the employer would be unable to pay all of its debts pursuant to a plan of reorganization and would be unable to continue in business outside of a Chapter 11 reorganization. The termination was approved subject to a determination that there was no violation of a collective bargaining agreement (see Q 25:23). [*In re* U.S. Airways Group, Inc., No. 02-83984 (Bankr. E.D. Va. 2003)] On appeal, the bankruptcy court's order terminating the plan was affirmed because the court concluded that reversal at this late stage would undermine the reorganization plan and interests of third parties relying upon the plan. [*In re* U.S. Airways Group, Inc., No. 03-1825 (4th Cir. 2004)] In another case, a request for approval of a distress termination of a number of pension plans was granted where the employer demonstrated that, unless the plans were terminated, it could not pay all of its debts under a plan of reorganization and continue in business outside of bankruptcy. [*In re* Wire Rope Corp. of Am., Inc., 2002 WL 31890196 (Bankr. W.D. Mo. 2002)] When a debtor in a Chapter 11 reorganization sought to terminate multiple pension plans simultaneously under the reorganization test, the Third Circuit ruled that the test should be applied to all of the plans in the aggregate, and not to each plan separately. [*In re* Kaiser Aluminum Corp., No. 05-2695 (3d. Cir. 2006)]

A bankruptcy court held that an employer did not have to submit a reorganization plan and disclosure statement before the court could determine whether it was financially necessary for the employer to terminate its defined benefit plan under the distress termination procedures. [*In re* Sewell Mfg. Co., 1996 Bankr. LEXIS 468 (Bankr. N.D. Ga. 1996)]

If PBGC determines that the requirements of a distress termination have been met, additional information may be required of the plan administrator and the enrolled actuary in order to determine the sufficiency of plan assets. PBGC must then notify the plan administrator as soon as possible after reaching its determination. Where PBGC was unable to determine if a plan seeking a distress termination had sufficient assets to provide guaranteed benefits and no agreement was reached between the plan administrator (see Q 20:1) and PBGC, the court ruled that PBGC could institute the plan termination (see Q 25:22). [PBGC v. Cafeteria Operators, LP, 2004 U.S. Dist. LEXIS 15927 (N.D. Tx. 2004)]

[ERISA § 4041(c)]

In one case, it was held that participants in a spun-off defined benefit plan that was subsequently terminated in a distress termination lacked standing under ERISA to sue for breach of fiduciary duty, and the PBGC's decision not to pursue an enforcement action against the plan's fiduciaries was not subject to judicial review. However, the court held that ERISA did not preempt the participants' potential state law claim for professional negligence against the plan's actuary (see Q 23:57). [Paulsen v. CNF Inc., No. 07-15142 (9th Cir. 2009)]

For plan years beginning after December 31, 2005, with respect to a single-employer plan that terminates in a distress manner, a premium of $1,250 per participant, per year, for three years is imposed. Generally, the three-year period during which the premium applies starts with the first month following the month in which the termination date occurs. However, with respect to terminations during a bankruptcy reorganization proceeding, the three-year period does not start until after the bankruptcy proceeding has been concluded. Plans that terminate during a bankruptcy reorganization proceeding where the bankruptcy filing was made before October 18, 2005 are exempt. [ERISA §§ 4006(a)(7), 4041(c)(2)(B); PBGC Reg. § 4006.7] One court, in reversing the bankruptcy court, ruled that an employer that terminated a defined benefit plan while undergoing a bankruptcy reorganization could not avoid paying a termination premium to the PBGC by classifying the termination premium as an unsecured, pre-petition claim that was dischargeable. [PBGC v. Oneida, Ltd., 562 F.3d 154 (2d Cir. 2009)]

Effective August 17, 2006, in the case of a distress termination, information provided to PBGC must be furnished to an affected party within 15 days after receipt of a request from the affected party. [ERISA § 4041(c)(2)(D); PBGC Reg. § 4041.51]

Q 25:16   What benefits under a single-employer defined benefit plan are guaranteed by PBGC?

When a single-employer defined benefit plan terminates under the distress termination procedures, PBGC will guarantee the payment of "certain benefits." The characteristics of this type of benefit are that:

1. It is a pension benefit;
2. It is nonforfeitable (see Q 25:17) on the date of plan termination; and
3. A participant must be entitled to the benefit. The benefit will be guaranteed to the extent that it does not exceed the limitations set forth in ERISA and its regulations (see Qs 25:18–25:21). [ERISA §§ 4022(a), 4022(b); PBGC Reg. § 4022.3]

Under a special rule, a qualified preretirement survivor annuity (see Q 10:9) is not treated as forfeitable solely because the participant has not died as of the termination date. [ERISA § 4022(e)]

PBGC has extended its guarantees to benefits attributable to a period of service that begins before a plan's termination date and ends on the termination date during which the participant was serving in the uniformed services as defined in USERRA (see Q 1:16) and to which the participant is entitled under USERRA, even if the reemployment occurs after the plan's termination date. [PBGC Reg. § 4022.11]

A company that sold off divisions with underfunded pension liabilities was liable to PBGC for those liabilities after the sold divisions failed because a principal purpose of the sale was to evade termination liability (see Q 29:24). Although the court held that the reasonable chance of success of an entity that acquires a business with unfunded pension liabilities is not an independent part of the test for predecessor liability, evidence of the transferee's viability nonetheless can be considered in determining whether a transferor's primary purpose for entering a transaction was to evade termination liability. [PBGC v. White Consol. Indus., Inc., 2000 WL 769718 (3d Cir. 2000); ERISA § 4069]

Q 25:17   Does PBGC guarantee a benefit that becomes nonforfeitable solely as a result of the plan's termination?

No. Although the plan must provide for 100 percent vesting upon termination (see Q 25:4), a benefit that vests because of this rule is not a guaranteed benefit. [ERISA § 4022(a)]

Q 25:18   Are there any limitations on the amount of the benefit PBGC will guarantee?

Yes. PBGC's guarantee may be subject to one or more statutorily prescribed benefit limitations (see Qs 25:19–25:21). For example, the guarantee may not exceed the maximum monthly benefit limitation amount, which is expressed in terms of an annuity that is payable for the life of the participant commencing at age 65. The maximum guaranteed benefit is adjusted annually to reflect cost-of-living increases (see Q 25:19).

Furthermore, the guaranteed benefit may not exceed the actuarial equivalent of a monthly benefit in the form of a life annuity commencing at age 65. Accordingly, if a benefit is payable at an earlier age, the maximum guaranteed benefit is actuarially reduced to reflect the earlier commencement of the receipt of the benefit. This reduction does not apply to a disability benefit. [ERISA § 4022(b); PBGC Reg. § 4022.23]

If PBGC is trustee of a terminated underfunded single-employer defined benefit plan (see Q 2:3) and a benefit is in pay status, benefit payments continue (subject to limits; see Q 25:19) in the form in which they are being paid. PBGC distributes benefits not yet in pay status that are valued in excess of $5,000 in the automatic form of distribution payable under the plan and generally does not make single-sum distributions unless the value of the benefit does not exceed $5,000 (see Q 10:60).

PBGC provides the following additional annuity benefit distribution options to participants and beneficiaries whose benefits are not in pay status:

- Straight-life annuity
- Five-year, ten-year, and 15-year certain-and-continuous annuities
- Joint and 50 percent, 75 percent, and 100 percent survivor annuities
- Joint and 50 percent survivor annuity under which the participant's benefit increases to the unreduced level if the named beneficiary dies before the participant

[PBGC Reg. § 4022.8]

Q 25:19   What is the maximum guaranteed monthly benefit?

The maximum guaranteed monthly benefit for plans terminating in 2010 remains at $4,500.00. This amount applies even though a participant may not retire and receive the benefit until years after the termination of the plan. [ERISA § 4022(b)(3); PBGC News Rel. No. 10-02]

The maximum guaranteed benefit has been adjusted for inflation and was initially $750.00 in 1974. For the prior five years, the adjusted amounts were as follows:

Year	Adjusted Amount
2009	$4,500.00
2008	4,312.50
2007	4,125.00
2006	3,971.59
2005	3,801.14

Q 25:20 What is the effect on PBGC's guarantees of a plan amendment prior to the plan's termination?

If an amendment is adopted within five years of the termination and adds a new benefit or increases the value of a benefit for any participant who is not a majority owner, PBGC's guarantee will be subject to a phase-in rule. Such increases include any changes that advance a participant's entitlement (such as liberalization of the participation or vesting requirement), a reduction in the normal or early retirement ages, or a change in the form of benefit. Increases due to salary increases or additional years of service are not subject to this rule. Under this five-year phase-in rule, a benefit increase will be subject to the following formula: multiply the number of years a benefit increase has been in effect by the greater of 20 percent of the monthly increase or $20 per month (but not in excess of the actual increase). [ERISA § 4022(b)(7); PBGC Reg. §§ 4022.2, 4022.25] The PBGC guarantee for benefits for plant shutdowns and other unpredictable, contingent events is phased in over a five-year period at the rate of 20 percent of the guaranteed benefit per year. [ERISA § 4022(b)(8)]

With respect to a plan termination for which a Notice of Intent to Terminate (NOIT; see Q 25:25) is provided after December 31, 2005, the guaranteed benefit phase-in rules vary, depending upon how much of the business the participant owns. For substantial owners, the same 60-month phase-in rule that applies to non-owner participants applies. For majority owners, a stricter phase-in rule applies. Under this rule, the amount of benefits guaranteed is determined by multiplying (a) a fraction (not to exceed one), where the numerator is the number of years from (i) the later of the effective date of the amendment or the plan adoption date to (ii) the termination date, and the denominator is 10; by (b) the amount of benefits that would be guaranteed under the phase-in rules for participants who are not majority owners.

For majority owners the phase-in occurs over a 10-year period and depends on the number of years the plan has been in effect. In addition, the majority owner's guaranteed benefit is limited so that it cannot be more than the amount phased in over 60 months for other participants.

A substantial owner is an individual who during the 60-month period ending on the date the plan termination occurs, owns:

1. The entire interest in an unincorporated trade or business;

2. More than 10 percent of either the capital interest or the profits of a partnership; or

3. More than 10 percent in value of either the voting stock or all the stock of a corporation.

A majority owner is an individual who during the 60-month period ending on the date the plan termination occurs, owns:

1. The entire interest in an unincorporated trade or business;

2. 50 percent or more of either the capital interest or the profits of a partnership; or

3. 50 percent or more in value of either the voting stock or all the stock of a corporation.

A PBGC representative has stated that, if a substantial owner is also a majority owner, the individual will be treated as a majority owner for purposes of applying the above rules.

[ERISA § 4022(b)(5)]

With respect to a plan termination for which a NOIT was provided before January 1, 2006, any benefits provided under a plan to a participant who was a substantial owner, and thereafter any amendment benefiting a substantial owner, was subject to a 30-year phase-in rule. [ERISA § 4022(b)(5); PBGC Reg. § 4022.26] In one case, a substantial owner was precluded from receiving PBGC benefits after amendment and termination of the plan, because, under the original plan, the substantial owner would not have received any benefits. [Brown v. PBGC, 1993 U.S. Dist. LEXIS 6764 (D.D.C. 1993)]

A defined benefit plan subject to PBGC coverage (see Q 25:11) cannot be amended to increase plan liabilities while the employer is in bankruptcy. Exceptions to this prohibition allow any plan amendment that either:

1. Provides *de minimis* increases and is reasonable;

2. Would leave the plan with a funded current liability percentage of 100 percent or more;

3. Only repeals a retroactive plan amendment under Code Section 412(c)(8); or

4. Is required as a condition of qualification.

An amendment to a defined benefit plan of an employer in bankruptcy that provided for less than a 1 percent increase in current liability was determined to be a *de minimis* increase in the plan's liabilities. Even though the increase in the sum of the normal cost and net amortization charges was greater than 3 percent, the plan had a credit balance in an amount 60 times greater than the sum of the normal cost and net amortization charges. [Priv. Ltr. Rul. 200403097; *see also* Priv. Ltr. Rul. 200334038, where plan amendments were determined to be reasonable and to provide for *de minimis* increases in liabilities because the sum of the increased liability resulting from the amendments was less than 3 percent; *see also* Priv. Ltr. Rul. 200319010, where an amendment that permitted the payment of special cash payments to certain surviving spouses of deceased plan participants was not reasonable.]

[I.R.C. § 401(a)(33); ERISA §§ 204(i), 4022(f)]

If a plan terminates after an employer enters bankruptcy, the date of the bankruptcy filing is substituted for the termination date for purposes of determining the maximum PBGC benefit guarantee and for purposes of determining the asset allocation for retirees or those who could have retired three years prior to the termination date. [ERISA § 4022(g); Prop. PBGC Reg. § 4022]

Q 25:21   What is the effect of the plan's disqualification on the guaranteed benefit?

PBGC will not guarantee any benefits that accrue after IRS has disqualified a plan or an amendment. [ERISA § 4022(b)(6); PBGC Reg. § 4022.27]

Q 25:22   Can PBGC initiate the termination of a plan?

Yes. PBGC may institute termination proceedings in federal court if it finds that:

1. Minimum funding standards (see Q 8:1) have not been satisfied;
2. The plan will be unable to pay benefits when due;
3. A distribution of more than $10,000 was made to a substantial owner in any 24-month period for reasons other than death, and, after the distribution, there are unfunded vested liabilities; or
4. The possible long-run liability of the employer to PBGC is expected to increase unreasonably if the plan is not terminated.

[ERISA § 4042(a)]

Where PBGC began involuntary termination proceedings, the court upheld PBGC's chosen termination date, a significant date, because it is the date on which benefit accruals cease and a factor in determining the amount that PBGC may recover from the employer. On PBGC's earlier termination date, participants did not have a justifiable expectation of accrual of vested shutdown benefits; but, if the later union chosen termination date would have applied, PBGC would have faced an unreasonable increase of $95 million in liabilities. [PBGC v. Republic Technologies Int'l, LLC, 386 F.3d 659 (6th Cir. 2004)] In another case, a plan's termination date, as selected by PBGC as part of the plan's involuntary termination, was appropriate because reasonable notice to participants had been provided by PBGC. If a later date had been chosen, PBGC could have suffered long-term harm, because the sponsor would have owed an additional $88 million. [PBGC v. United Airlines, Inc., 2007 WL 57271 (4th Cir. 2007)] Similarly, where PBGC determined that its liability would increase unreasonably if a company's defined benefit plans were terminated after bankruptcy reorganization, PBGC was allowed to terminate the plans prior to reorganization. [PBGC v. Fel, 798 F. Supp. 239 (D.N.J. 1992)] In another case, the court upheld the decision of PBGC to terminate defined benefit plans where the record included reports that the plans were underfunded and there was no prospect that the plans would be properly funded in the future. [Pan Am. World Airways, Inc. Coop. Ret. Income Plan v. Pension Comm. of Pan Am. World Airways, Inc., Nos. 91 Civ. 5016 (MBM), 91 Civ. 5017 (MBM) (S.D.N.Y. 1991)] However, PBGC must institute termination proceedings whenever it determines that a single-employer defined benefit plan does not have enough assets to pay benefits that are currently due. [ERISA § 4042(a)] In one case, after PBGC announced its intention to terminate a plan, in an attempt to forestall or prevent the termination, PBGC entered into a settlement agreement where the plan would be terminated if a significant event occurred in the future. Once a significant event occurred some years later, PBGC was obliged to carry out the termination. [Allied Pilots Ass'n v. PBGC, 334 F.3d 93 (D.C. Cir. 2003)] Where PBGC was unable to determine if a plan seeking a distress termination (see Q 25:15) had sufficient assets to provide guaranteed benefits and no agreement was reached between the plan administrator (see Q 20:1) and PBGC, the court ruled that PBGC could institute the plan termination. [PBGC v. Cafeteria Operators, LP, 2004 U.S. Dist. LEXIS 15927 (N.D. Tx. 2004)]

PBGC was subject to fiduciary duties (see chapter 23), concluded one court, when it served as a trustee of an involuntarily terminated pension plan and, therefore, had a fiduciary duty to issue benefit determination statements to participants in a timely manner (see Qs 25:30, 25:31). [Pineiro v. PBGC, 1997 U.S. Dist. LEXIS 18810 (S.D.N.Y. 1997)] Furthermore, participants of the terminated plan could sue PBGC for breach of fiduciary duty in the calculation of guaranteed benefits. [Pineiro v. PBGC, 1999 WL 19513 (S.D.N.Y. 1999)]

PBGC may also cease the termination of a plan and restore the plan to its status prior to termination if circumstances change. In a much publicized case, the United States Supreme Court allowed PBGC to restore terminated defined benefit plans. LTV Corporation (LTV) filed for bankruptcy. At that time, LTV maintained three underfunded defined benefit plans all covered by PBGC. PBGC instituted proceedings to involuntarily terminate the plans. Subsequently, LTV established new plans that provided benefits lost by the termination. In effect, the new "follow-on" plans provided benefits equal to the difference between the promised benefits under the terminated plans and PBGC guaranteed benefits. PBGC objected and determined to restore the plans. The Supreme Court upheld PBGC's authority to return responsibility for funding the terminated plans to the plan sponsor. [PBGC v. LTV Corp., 496 U.S. 633 (1990)] The PBGC restoration order was held enforceable because PBGC was not required to consider whether restoration would lead to the retermination of the plans or whether the bankruptcy court would approve contributions to the restored plans. [PBGC v. LTV Corp., No. 87 Civ. 7261 (S.D.N.Y. 1990)] Employers may be discouraged from using "follow-on" plans to shift the burden of paying benefits from the plan sponsor to PBGC. [ERISA § 4047]

Since the minimum funding standards (see Q 8:1) do not apply between the dates of termination and restoration and the plan will be underfunded, or become more underfunded, during this period, PBGC will issue a restoration payment schedule that provides for the amortization of the restored plan's unfunded liabilities over a period of up to 30 years after the PBGC restoration order. The restoration payment schedule is used to determine the minimum funding standards for the unfunded prerestoration plan liabilities. Restored plans must reimburse PBGC for any guaranteed benefit payments (see Q 25:16) made by PBGC while the plan was terminated, and PBGC insurance premiums (see Q 21:23) must be paid on behalf of restored plans. [Treas. Reg. § 1.412(c)(1)-3; PBGC Reg. §§ 4047.1–4047.5]

With respect to a single-employer plan that terminates in an involuntary manner, a premium of $1,250 per participant, per year, for three years is imposed. Generally, the three-year period during which the premium applies starts with the first month following the month in which the termination date occurs. However, with respect to terminations during a bankruptcy reorganization proceeding, the three-year period does not start until after the bankruptcy proceeding has been concluded. Plans that terminate during a bankruptcy reorganization proceeding where the bankruptcy filing was made before October 18, 2005 are exempt. [ERISA §§ 4006(a)(7), 4042; PBGC Reg. § 4006.7]

Furthermore, in the case of an involuntary termination, information provided to PBGC must be furnished to an affected party within 15 days after receipt of a request from the affected party. [ERISA § 4042(c)(3); PBGC Reg. § 4042.4]

Q 25:23   Can a plan covered by Title IV be terminated if the termination would violate an existing collective bargaining agreement?

The authority of PBGC to terminate a plan under these circumstances will depend on whether the termination is initiated by the plan administrator (see Q 20:1) or PBGC. If the plan administrator attempts to terminate the plan under the standard or distress termination provisions (see Qs 25:13, 25:15), PBGC may not proceed with the termination. However, PBGC's authority to institute involuntary termination proceedings for such a plan is not limited by the fact that the termination would violate the collective bargaining agreement (CBA). [ERISA § 4041(a)(3); PBGC Op. Ltr. No. 87-4]

One court concluded that an agreement between PBGC and the plan sponsor that called for PBGC to consider whether or not it should take over and terminate a retirement plan was in accordance with ERISA; and, as the court explained, although a corporation's plan termination may not override a CBA, ERISA allows PBGC to terminate a plan regardless of the terms of a CBA. [*In re* UAL Corp., 428 F.3d 677 (7th Cir. 2005)]

Q 25:24   Is there any restriction on the form of a benefit paid by a terminating defined benefit plan?

Yes. The general rule is that a benefit be paid in annuity form, unless the participant elects an optional form of benefit under the terms of the plan. [ERISA § 4041(b)(3)(A)(i); PBGC Reg. § 4041.28] However, an exception exists for small amounts of benefits. PBGC and any other plan administrator (see Q 20:1) of a terminating plan may choose to pay a benefit in a single payment without the consent of the participant if the present value of the benefit is $5,000 or less. [PBGC Reg. §§ 4022.7, 4041.28; PBGC Op. Ltr. No. 90-5] A direct rollover (see Q 34:17) is the default option for an involuntary distribution that exceeds $1,000 and does not exceed $5,000 (see Qs 34:18, 34:19).

See Qs 25:36 and 25:42 through 25:46 regarding missing participants.

Q 25:25 Who must be notified of the company's intention to terminate a defined benefit plan covered by Title IV—and when must this notice be given?

The plan administrator (see Q 20:1) must provide to all affected parties (see Q 25:29) written notice of the company's intention to terminate a defined benefit plan covered by Title IV (Notice of Intent to Terminate-NOIT) at least 60 days and no more than 90 days before the proposed date of termination. [ERISA § 4041(a)(2); PBGC Reg. § 4041.23]

Q 25:26 What information must be included in the NOIT?

According to regulations issued by PBGC, the plan administrator (see Q 20:1) must issue the NOIT (see Q 25:25) to each affected party (see Q 25:29) individually. Each notice must be either hand delivered or delivered by first-class mail or courier service to the affected party's last known address. The notice may be issued by electronic means reasonably calculated to ensure actual receipt by the affected party.

The NOIT must include the following information:

1. *Identifying information.* The name and plan number of the plan; the address and employer identification number of each contributing sponsor; and the name, address, and telephone number of the person who may be contacted by an affected party with questions concerning the plan's termination.

2. *Intent to terminate plan.* A statement that the plan administrator intends to terminate the plan in a standard termination as of a specified proposed termination date and will notify the affected party if the proposed termination date is changed to a later date or if the termination does not occur.

3. *Sufficiency requirement.* A statement that, in order to terminate in a standard termination, plan assets must be sufficient to provide all plan benefits under the plan.

4. *Cessation of accrual.* A statement (as applicable) that:

   a. Benefit accruals will cease as of the termination date but will continue if the plan does not terminate;

   b. A plan amendment has been adopted under which benefit accruals will cease, in accordance with ERISA Section 204(h) (see Qs 9:36, 25:60), as of the proposed termination date or a specified date before the proposed termination date, whether or not the plan is terminated; or

   c. Benefit accruals ceased, in accordance with ERISA Section 204(h), as of a specified date before the NOIT was issued.

5. *Annuity information.* If required, the annuity information contained in Q 25:32.

6. *Benefit information.* A statement that each affected party entitled to plan benefits will receive a written notification regarding the party's plan benefits.

7. *Summary plan description.* A statement as to how an affected party entitled to receive the latest updated SPD (see Q 22:1) can obtain it.

8. *Continuation of monthly benefits.* For persons who are, as of the proposed termination date, in pay status, a statement (as applicable):

   a. That their monthly (or other periodic) benefit amounts will not be affected by the plan's termination, or

   b. Explaining how their monthly (or other periodic) benefit amounts will be affected under plan provisions.

9. *Extinguishment of guarantee.* A statement that after plan assets have been distributed in full satisfaction of all plan benefits with respect to a participant or a beneficiary of a deceased participant, either by the purchase of irrevocable commitments (annuity contracts) or by an alternative form of distribution provided for under the plan, the PBGC no longer guarantees that participant's or beneficiary's plan benefits.

[PBGC Reg. § 4041.23]

PBGC has developed a model NOIT that plan administrators may use. Also, participants in terminated plans must be informed about state guarantees that apply to the annuity providers (see Q 25:32). [PBGC Reg. § 4041.27; PBGC Standard Termination Filing Instructions Booklet]

Q 25:27 What is the relevance of the date of plan termination?

The termination date is critical for determining the rights of the participants and beneficiaries to the benefits under the plan that are guaranteed by PBGC, the employer's liability to PBGC for any underfunding, and PBGC's exposure for guaranteed benefits. [ERISA § 4048; Audio Fidelity Corp. v. PBGC, 624 F.2d 513 (4th Cir. 1980)]

Q 25:28 What factors are considered by PBGC in establishing a defined benefit plan's termination date?

The date of termination will depend on whether the termination is filed by the plan administrator (see Q 20:1) under the standard or distress termination procedures (see Qs 25:13, 25:16) or whether PBGC has initiated the termination (see Q 25:22). However, in a termination other than one initiated by PBGC, the date must be prospective and at least 60 days after the NOIT is issued to affected parties (see Qs 25:2, 25:25, 25:29). [ERISA § 4041(a)(2); Phillips v. Bebber, Nos. 89-2184, 89-2189 (4th Cir. 1990)]

Q 25:29　Who is an affected party?

An affected party, for purposes of a termination subject to PBGC's jurisdiction, is:

- A participant
- A beneficiary of a deceased participant
- A beneficiary who is an alternate payee under a QDRO (see chapter 36)
- Any employee organization that represents plan participants or that represented plan participants within five years prior to the issuance of the NOIT (see Q 25:25)
- PBGC (in the case of a distress termination; see Q 25:15), or
- Any person designated in writing to receive notice on behalf of an affected party

[ERISA §§ 4001(a)(21), 4041(a)(2), 4041(c)(1)(A); PBGC Reg. § 4001.2]

Q 25:30　Are there any other notice requirements if the company intends to terminate a defined benefit plan in a standard termination?

Yes. Notice must be provided to PBGC by filing PBGC Form 500, Standard Termination Notice Single-Employer Plan Termination. PBGC Schedule EA-S, Standard Termination Certification of Sufficiency, attached to Form 500, must be used by the enrolled actuary to certify that the plan is projected to have sufficient assets to provide all benefit liabilities. [ERISA § 4041(b)(2)(A)]

Form 500 should be filed no later than 180 days after the proposed termination date. [PBGC Reg. § 4041.25]

In addition, no later than the date on which the notice is filed with PBGC, the plan administrator (see Q 20:1) must provide each participant and beneficiary with a Notice of Plan Benefits (see Q 25:31). [ERISA § 4041(b)(2)(B)]

Q 25:31　What information must be included in the Notice of Plan Benefits?

The plan administrator (see Q 20:1) must issue a notice to each affected party (other than an employee organization; see Q 25:29) that (1) specifies the amount of the individual's benefits as of the proposed termination date and the form of benefit on the basis of which the amount was determined and (2) includes the following information used in determining the individual's benefits:

- Length of service
- Age of the participant or beneficiary
- Wages

- Assumptions (including the interest rate)
- Such other information as PBGC may require

[ERISA § 4041(b)(2)(B); PBGC Reg. § 4041.24]

Q 25:32　Are there any special rules regarding the purchase of annuity contracts?

Yes. PBGC requires plan administrators (see Q 20:1) to inform participants of the identity of the insurer or insurers from whom irrevocable commitments (i.e., annuity contracts) may be purchased prior to the distribution of plan assets. This information must be included in the NOIT (see Q 25:25). If the identity of the insurer is not known, the information must be provided to participants no later than 45 days prior to the date of distribution.

Participants in terminated plans must also be informed about state guarantees that apply to their benefits in the event that the annuity providers encounter financial difficulty. The plan administrator must include a statement informing the affected party:

1. That once the plan distributes a benefit in the form of an annuity purchased from an insurance company, the insurance company takes over the responsibility for paying that benefit;
2. That all states have established guaranty associations to protect policy holders in the event of an insurance company's financial failure;
3. That a guaranty association is responsible for all, part, or none of the annuity if the insurance company cannot pay;
4. That each guaranty association has dollar limits on the extent of its guaranty coverage, along with a general description of the applicable dollar coverage limits;
5. That in most cases the policy holder is covered by the guaranty association for the state where the policy holder lives at the time the insurance company fails to pay; and
6. How to obtain the addresses and telephone numbers of guaranty association offices from the PBGC.

With respect to the state guarantees, PBGC has developed a model notice that plan administrators may use.

[PBGC Reg. § 4041.27; PBGC Standard Termination Filing Instructions Booklet]

See Q 25:37 regarding the selection of an annuity.

Q 25:33　After the notice is filed with PBGC, does PBGC have to act within designated time limits?

Yes. Within 60 days after the plan administrator (see Q 20:1) notifies PBGC (see Q 25:30), PBGC must issue to the plan administrator a notice of noncompliance if it determines (1) based on the notice provided by filing Form 500 (see Q 25:30), or based on information provided by affected parties (see Q 25:29) or otherwise obtained by PBGC, that there is reason to believe that the plan assets are not sufficient for benefit liabilities (see Q 25:14) or (2) that any of the notice requirements (see Qs 25:25, 25:30, 25:31) have not been met. PBGC is not required to issue a notice of noncompliance for failure to satisfy the procedural requirements in (2) above and may elect not to if it determines that issuance of the notice would be inconsistent with the interests of participants and beneficiaries. [ERISA § 4041(b)(2)(C); PBGC Reg. §§ 4041.26, 4041.31]

Q 25:34 May the 60-day period for PBGC to issue a notice of noncompliance be extended?

Yes. PBGC and the plan administrator (see Q 20:1) may extend the 60-day period (see Q 25:33) for the noncompliance notice by jointly signing a written agreement before expiration of the initial 60-day period. Additional extensions are also permitted. [ERISA § 4041(b)(2)(C); PBGC Reg. § 4041.26]

Q 25:35 Assuming that PBGC does not issue a notice of noncompliance, when should final distribution of assets occur?

The plan administrator (see Q 20:1) must complete the distribution of assets, pursuant to a standard termination, no later than 180 days after expiration of the 60-day (or extended) period (see Qs 25:34, 25:34), assuming that plan assets are sufficient to meet benefit liabilities (see Q 25:14), determined as of the termination date, when the final distribution occurs. [ERISA § 4041(b)(2)(D); PBGC Reg. § 4041.28(a)]

The distribution deadline will automatically be extended until the 120th day after the plan's receipt of a favorable IRS determination letter (see Q 18:1) if on or before the date that the plan administrator files PBGC Form 500 (see Q 25:30), the plan administrator submitted to IRS a request for a determination letter with respect to the plan's termination.

[PBGC Reg. § 4041.28(a)(1)(ii)]

PBGC may in its discretion extend certain deadlines. PBGC will grant such an extension where it finds compelling reasons why it is not administratively feasible for the plan administrator (or other persons acting on behalf of the plan administrator) to take the action until the later date and the delay is brief. The PBGC shall consider:

1. The length of the delay and
2. Whether ordinary business care and prudence in attempting to meet the deadline is exercised.

Any request for an extension that is filed later than the 15th day before the applicable deadline shall include a justification for not filing the request earlier.

PBGC will not:

- Extend the 60-day time limit for issuing the NOIT (see Q 25:25)
- Waive the requirement that the Notice of Plan Benefits (see Q 25:30) be issued by the time the plan administrator files PBGC Form 500 with PBGC
- Extend the deadline for filing the post-distribution certification (see Q 25:41)

[PBGC Reg. § 4041.30]

Q 25:36   What is the method for the final distribution of assets?

The plan administrator (see Q 20:1) must distribute the plan's assets, pursuant to a standard termination (see Q 25:13), in accordance with the required allocation of assets (see Q 25:38). In distributing the assets, the plan administrator must:

1. Purchase irrevocable commitments from an insurer to provide for all benefit liabilities (and any other benefits to which assets are required to be allocated) (see Q 25:37), or

2. Otherwise fully provide the benefit liabilities (and any other benefits to which assets are required to be allocated) in accordance with the plan's provisions and any applicable PBGC regulations, including the transfer of assets to PBGC on behalf of a missing participant.

[ERISA §§ 4041(b)(3), 4050] See Qs 25:42 through 25:46 regarding missing participants.

The Supreme Court ruled that an employer who received a $5 million reversion from its overfunded terminated defined benefit plan was under no fiduciary obligation to consider a merger of its plan with an existing multiemployer plan as an alternative to the purchase of annuities to meet its obligations in a standard termination because merger is not a permissible method of plan termination. [Beck v PACE Int'l Union, 2007 WL 1661301 (S. Ct. 2007)]

In one case, the court agreed with PBGC that the annuity starting date for valuing a terminated plan's lump-sum distribution payments is the distribution date, not the termination date, even though a plan amendment provided that the annuity starting date was the termination date. Accordingly, use of the lower interest rate resulted in additional benefits due the participants. [PBGC v. Wilson N. Jones Mem'l Hosp., 374 F.3d 362 (5th Cir. 2004)]

PBGC has issued guidance that lump-sum valuations for single-employer plans terminating prior to January 1, 2008 in a standard termination should use interest rate and mortality assumptions effective prior to January 1, 2008 (the PPA effective date) even when the final distribution occurs after December 31, 2007. [PBGC Tech. Update 07-3] PBGC has issued additional guidance regarding lump-sum valuations for single-employer plans terminating on or after January 1, 2008. For a plan that terminates in 2008 through 2011, the applicable interest rate is determined based on the applicable phase-in percentage (see Q 10:62) in effect for the plan year in which the lump sum is paid (not for the plan year in which the plan terminates). Accordingly, if a plan's termination date occurs during the phase-in period, the specific interest rates used to calculate the minimum value of a lump-sum payment (determined in accordance with the stability period (see Q 10:62) and lookback month (see Q 10:62) in effect on the termination date) reflect the weighting of the 30-year Treasury yields and the new PPA rates under Section 417(e)(3)(D) on the distribution date. Annual updates to the applicable mortality table are part of the base mortality table prescribed by IRS under Section 430(h)(3), which is projected to improve using specified factors. Because the annual updates are part of the base mortality table, they are included in the law in effect on the termination date. Accordingly, for a plan with a termination date on or after the first day of the first plan year beginning in 2008, a lump sum would be determined based on the applicable mortality table as specified by IRS on the plan's termination date, taking into account projected mortality improvements under the table through the plan year containing the distribution date.

> **Example.** A calendar-year plan is amended in 2008 to reflect PPA minimum lump-sum assumptions, terminates on July 1, 2009, and has a one-year stability period and a two-month lookback. A lump sum paid in 2010 is calculated based on the phase-in percentage for the plan year beginning in 2010 and the November 2009 rates. Accordingly, a lump sum paid in 2010 would be determined using a blended rate based on a 60 percent weighting of the November 2009 segment rates and a 40 percent weighting of the November 2009 30-year Treasury rate. [PBGC Tech. Update 08-4]

In order to have a valid termination, the benefits of all participants must be distributed. Before a reversion of excess assets occurs (see Q 25:49), all plan liabilities must first be satisfied. [I.R.C. § 401(a)(2); ERISA § 4044(d)]

Participants in a defined benefit plan for which a standard termination notice was filed with PBGC were not entitled to a pro rata share of the plan's surplus assets where the plan was never terminated under ERISA because the employer had never completed all of the required steps to terminate a defined benefit plan and still paid benefits to some participants. [Jensen v. Moore Wallace North America, Inc., No. 66-4388 (6th Cir. 2007)]

Q 25:37   Is PBGC or the employer liable to participants if an insurer fails to make payments under annuity contracts?

When irrevocable commitments (i.e., annuity contracts) have been purchased to pay all benefit liabilities, the plan termination process is completed and the PBGC guarantee obligation ends. [PBGC Op. Ltr. No. 91-1] Similarly, employers are not liable to participants if an insurer fails to meet its obligations under the annuity contracts. The purchase of annuity contracts that irrevocably provide for the payment of all benefit liabilities satisfies the employer's obligation with respect to the termination. [PBGC Op. Ltr. No. 91-4] Employees who participated in a defined benefit plan, for whom group annuities were purchased from an insurance company upon the plan's termination in 1986, were entitled to over $1 million resulting from the sale of stock received as part of the insurance company's demutualization, because the court determined that the employees and not the plan sponsor were the owners of the annuity contracts. [Bank of New York v. Janowick, 470 F.3d 264 (6th Cir. 2006)]

However, fiduciaries must select the insurer that issues the annuity contracts in a way that satisfies their fiduciary duty to plan participants (see Q 23:19). Fiduciaries of defined benefit plans may be liable for purchasing annuities without adequately evaluating the insurer's financial condition. [DOL News Rel. 91-281] Plan fiduciaries have a duty to select the safest annuity provider available unless it is in the interests of participants and beneficiaries to do otherwise. For example, when the safest available annuity is only marginally safer but disproportionately more expensive than competing annuities, the participants are likely to bear a significant portion of the increased cost. [PWBA Interpretive Bull. 95-1] DOL has limited the application of Interpretive Bulletin 95-1 to the selection of annuity providers for defined benefit plans only and has issued guidance that establishes a safe harbor for selecting annuity providers for individual account plans. [DOL Reg. §§ 2509.95-1, 2550.404a-4] In one case, the court held that an employer may have breached its fiduciary duty by not acting prudently when it selected a company to provide annuities for a terminated pension plan. [Waller v. Blue Cross of Cal., 1994 U.S. App. LEXIS 16490 (9th Cir. 1994)] In another case, a company agreed to pay $4.07 million to DOL as part of a settlement involving the improper selection of a group annuity provider to fund pension benefits. The money will be distributed to the participants and beneficiaries of the terminated pension plan. [DOL News Rel. 95-143]

A qualified retirement plan participant, beneficiary, or fiduciary can bring an action for appropriate relief if the purchase of an insurance or annuity contract in connection with the termination of a person's status as a plan participant would violate fiduciary standards. [ERISA § 502(a)(9)]

See Q 25:32 regarding notice requirements with respect to insurers providing annuity benefits for terminating plans.

Q 25:38   How are plan assets allocated when a defined benefit plan is terminated?

There are six categories into which plan assets must be divided upon termination of a single-employer defined benefit plan. The assets are assigned to these categories, starting with the first category, until the value of the assets has been exhausted. On termination of a defined benefit plan, the assets are allocated in the following order:

1. Employee voluntary contributions;

2. Employee mandatory contributions;

3. Annuity payments in pay status at least three years before the termination of the plan (including annuity payments that would have been in pay status for at least three years if the employee had retired then) based on the provisions of the plan in effect during the five years before termination of the plan under which the benefit would be the least;

4. All other guaranteed insured benefits, determined without regard to the aggregate limit on benefits guaranteed with respect to a participant under all multiemployer and single-employer plans;

5. All other vested benefits; and

6. All other benefits under the plan (see Q 25:39).

[ERISA § 4044(a)]

Q 25:39   What does the phrase "all other benefits under the plan" cover?

According to PBGC and IRS, the statutory language in ERISA Section 4044(a)(6) encompasses only those benefits that participants have accrued as of the date of termination (or in the case of benefit subsidies protected by REA, benefits to which participants may become entitled in the future). [PBGC Op. Ltr. No. 87-11; Gen. Couns. Mem. 39,665]

The United States Supreme Court has agreed with the PBGC and IRS positions and held that the "all other accrued benefits" category under ERISA Section 4044(a)(6) covers participants' accrued forfeitable benefits, but not unaccrued benefits. [Mead Corp. v. Tilley, 490 U.S. 714 (1989); *see also* May v. Houston Post Pension Plan, No. 89-2249 (5th Cir. 1990); Blessitt v. Retirement Plan for Employees of Dixie Engine Co., 848 F.2d 1164 (11th Cir. 1988)] After remand by the Supreme Court, the Fourth Circuit ruled that the unaccrued subsidized early retirement benefits of participants who satisfied the service requirement but not the age requirement to be eligible for the subsidized benefits at the time of plan termination constituted contingent liabilities that the plan required to be satisfied before excess assets could be returned to the employer (see Q 25:49). [Tilley v. Mead Corp, No. 86-3858 (4th Cir. 1991)]

One court held that unaccrued early retirement subsidies did not automatically vest upon plan termination where the participants did not meet the age and service eligibility requirements for early retirement subsidies. [Berard v. Royal Elec., Inc., 795 F. Supp. 519 (D.R.I. 1992)]

Another court held that a plan sponsor was not required to place additional funds in the pension plan upon the plan's termination in 1986 in order to satisfy the participants' contingent, forfeitable right to subsidized early retirement benefits. However, the court noted that, for terminations initiated after October 16, 1987, the law changed, and a plan sponsor would be prevented from limiting its liability upon its own failure to fund. [Aldridge v. Lily-Tulip, Inc. Salary Ret. Plan Benefits Comm., No. 90-8686 (11th Cir. 1992)]

Q 25:40   Can a distribution of plan assets be reallocated?

Yes. The traditional rules provide that if the asset allocation discriminates in favor of HCEs (see Q 3:2), the allocation (see Q 25:38) may be changed to the extent necessary to avoid the prohibited discrimination (see Q 25:8).

A qualified retirement plan will be considered discriminatory if a plan amendment or series of plan amendments discriminates significantly in favor of HCEs. For this purpose, a plan amendment includes the termination of a plan and any change in the benefits, rights, or features under a plan (see Qs 4:20, 4:21). [Treas. Reg. § 1.401(a)(4)-5(a)(1)]

However, the law also provides that a defined benefit plan cannot terminate in a standard termination (see Q 25:13) unless it has sufficient assets to cover all benefit liabilities of the plan, which would obviate any such reallocation. [ERISA § 4041(b)(1)(D)]

One court upheld a reallocation of excess plan assets solely to 13 management employee-participants upon a plan termination that occurred after 102 plan participants terminated employment and received annuity contracts in satisfaction of their entire plan benefits. Those 102 former employees were not entitled to share in the reallocation because they were not plan participants when the plan was terminated. [Teagardener v. Republic-Franklin, Inc., No. 89-3865 (6th Cir. 1990)] In another case, former employees, who were participants in a defined contribution plan (see Q 2:2) that matched employee contributions with company stock from an unallocated account under the plan, were not entitled to receive a share of the surplus in that account after all of the company stock was sold. Furthermore, although a partial termination (see Q 25:5) may have occurred, the court concluded that the surplus assets in the unallocated account were new benefits and, therefore, not protected as accrued benefits. [Bennett v. Conrail Matched Sav. Plan Admin. Comm., 1999 WL 86842 (3d Cir. 1999)]

Q 25:41 Must PBGC be notified once final distribution of assets is completed?

Yes. Within 30 days after the last distribution date of plan benefits (through priority category 6; see Q 25:38) for any affected party, the plan administrator (see Q 20:1) must file with PBGC a notice certifying that the assets have been distributed in accordance with the required order of allocation of assets and that all benefits have been distributed in accordance with either method of distribution described in Q 25:36. PBGC Form 501, Post-Distribution Certification for Standard Termination, has been designed for this purpose. The due date for Form 501 is unaffected by the timing of any distribution of residual assets, whether to the employer (see Q 25:49) or to participants and beneficiaries (see Q 25:40). Form 501 also requires information regarding the insurers, if any, from whom annuity contracts have been purchased and the forms and amounts of distributions. [ERISA § 4041(b)(3)(B); PBGC Reg. § 4041.29]

See Q 25:45 regarding missing participants.

PBGC may assess a penalty, not to exceed $1,000 a day ($1,100 after adjustment for inflation), for failure to provide any required notice or other material information. [ERISA § 4071] However, according to PBGC, the penalty for failure to file Form 501 should not exceed $25 per day for the first 90 days of delinquency, and $50 per day thereafter. For plans with fewer than 100 participants, the penalty will be proportionately reduced with a minimum penalty of $5 per day. In general, the total penalty should not exceed $100 multiplied by the number of participants. PBGC may reduce or eliminate the penalty where reasonable cause is shown. [PBGC Statement of Policy, 60 Fed. Reg. 36,837 (July 18, 1995); PBGC Standard Termination Filing Instructions Booklet]

Although the statutory deadline to file Form 501 is 30 days after the last distribution date (see Q 25:35), PBGC will assess a penalty for the late filing of Form 501 only if it is filed more than 90 days after the distribution deadline. [PBGC Reg. § 4041.29]

Q 25:42   May benefits due missing participants be paid to PBGC?

Yes. Administrators (see Q 20:1) of plans that terminate under the standard termination procedures (see Q 25:13) may provide benefits for a participant or beneficiary who cannot be located either through the purchase of an annuity from an insurer or by paying funds on behalf of the missing individual to PBGC (see Q 25:44). If funds are paid to PBGC, PBGC will search for the participant or beneficiary and pay benefits to those who are located. [ERISA § 4050]

PBGC's missing participant program has been extended to defined contribution plans and other plans that are not subject to PBGC. Also, PBGC must issue regulations for terminated multiemployer plans similar to the missing participant regulations that apply to single-employer defined benefit plans. These provisions are effective for distributions made after final regulations implementing them are prescribed. At this time, regulations have not been prescribed. [ERISA § 4050]

Q 25:43   Is a diligent search required before paying a missing participant's benefit to PBGC?

Yes. A diligent search must be made for each missing participant before the designated benefit is paid to PBGC. A search is diligent only if the search:

1. Begins not more than six months before the NOIT (see Q 25:25) is issued;
2. Includes inquiry of any plan participants and beneficiaries of the missing participant; and
3. Includes use of a commercial locator service to search for the missing participant.

[PBGC Reg. § 4050.4]

If a participant cannot be located, a request can be sent to IRS or the Social Security Administration. IRS has issued instructions and information on the use of its letter-forwarding program. Written requests should explain the need for letter forwarding, list the Social Security number of the individual being sought, and include the letter to be forwarded. There is no charge for requests involving less than 50 potential recipients. [Rev. Proc. 94-22, 1994-1 C.B. 608]

Q 25:44   What is the method of distribution for missing participants?

The plan administrator (see Q 20:1) must purchase an irrevocable commitment from an insurer or pay PBGC a designated benefit, and provide PBGC with certain information and certifications. The amount of the designated benefit is determined under special rules and will depend on whether the benefit required under the plan is a mandatory lump sum, *de minimis* lump sum, no lump sum, or elective lump sum. [ERISA § 4050(a); PBGC Reg. § 4050.5]

An additional $300 must be added to each designated benefit greater than $5,000 as an adjustment for expenses. [PBGC Reg. § 4050.2]

Q 25:45   What procedures apply with respect to missing participants?

The plan administrator (see Q 20:1) of a plan with one or more missing participants must file Schedule MP (Missing Participant Information) with PBGC Form 501 (see Q 25:41) and pay PBGC the value of benefits payable to any missing participant for whom the plan administrator did not purchase an irrevocable commitment. The Schedule MP includes the information PBGC needs to identify and locate missing participants to whom it will pay benefits, to compute and pay those benefits, and to direct individuals for whom the plan purchased annuities to the appropriate insurance company.

Attachment A (Annuity Purchase Information) must be filed with Schedule MP if the plan purchased an irrevocable commitment for one or more missing participants and Attachment B (Individual Information) must be filed with Schedule MP for each missing participant for whom amounts are paid to PBGC. Payment of these amounts must be sent to PBGC with a payment voucher.

Generally, the filing due date for the Schedule MP (including attachments) and payment of designated benefits is the same as that for PBGC Form 501 (see Q 25:41).

Q 25:46   If PBGC locates a missing participant, how is distribution made?

If a missing participant is located, PBGC will pay a single sum if this amount is $5,000 or less and no participant or spousal consent is required. If the single-sum benefit is greater than $5,000, PBGC will pay the benefit, subject to actuarial assumptions set by PBGC at the time of the transfer, in the same forms and at the same times as a guaranteed benefit, including a single sum, if the plan had provided for payment in this form. [PBGC Reg. §§ 4050.7(b), 4050.8-4050.12]

Q 25:47   Does PBGC perform post-termination audits for compliance with the Title IV requirements?

Yes. PBGC selectively conducts post-termination compliance audits. The data request may include copies of the following:

- The plan and trust documents
- Applicable labor contracts
- Applicable insurance contracts to fund the plan
- Actuarial reports and enrolled actuary's worksheets
- The plan's financial statement as of the termination date
- Benefit data for each participant
- Election and spousal consent forms

The plan administrator (see Q 20:1) or sponsor should maintain records relating to the plan's termination for six years after Form 501 (see Q 25:41) is filed with PBGC. [PBGC Reg. § 4041.5]

Q 25:48 Does an employer incur any liability to PBGC for the payment of benefits to plan participants of an underfunded terminated plan?

Yes. When PBGC incurs liabilities for benefits in the case of a distress termination (see Q 25:15) or a termination instituted by the PBGC (see Q 25:22), it can obtain reimbursement from the contributing employer or a member of its controlled group (see Q 5:31). If more than one employer jointly sponsors a plan, the liability to PBGC is separately applicable to each such entity.

Any trade or business, whether or not incorporated, can be a member of the contributing employer's controlled group if a prescribed control or ownership test is satisfied. In that case, it will be jointly and severally liable to reimburse PBGC. [ERISA §§ 4001(b), 4062(b)] Although a company did not control the operation of its subsidiary's business at the time of the subsidiary's plan termination, it did own at least 80 percent of the subsidiary's stock and therefore was liable to PBGC for the plan's unfunded benefit liabilities. [PBGC v. East Dayton Tool & Die Co., No. 93-3185 (6th Cir. 1994)]

The liability of a contributing employer or member of its controlled group generally is the total amount of the unfunded benefit liabilities to all participants and beneficiaries as of the termination date, plus interest at a reasonable rate calculated from the termination date. [ERISA § 4062(b)]

If the liability to PBGC is not paid, a lien in favor of PBGC arises in an amount equal to the lesser of (1) the unfunded benefit liabilities or (2) 30 percent of the collective net worth of the contributing employers of a plan and members of the controlled group (but treating as zero any negative net worth). [ERISA §§ 4062(d)(1), 4068(a)]

Q 25:49 May excess assets remaining after the standard termination of a defined benefit plan be returned to the employer after payment of all plan benefit liabilities?

Yes, provided that the distribution does not contravene any other provision of law, the excess was the result of an "erroneous actuarial computation," and the plan specifically permits the distribution of excess assets in this situation (see Qs 25:36, 25:50–25:52). [ERISA § 4044(d); Treas. Reg. § 1.401-2; Shepley v. New Coleman Holdings, Inc., 1999 WL 186182 (2d Cir. 1999); Int'l Union of Elec. Workers v. Murata Erie N. Am., Inc., No. 94-3267 (3d Cir. 1994)]

In one case, the employer received $3.5 million of excess funds as a result of actuarial error. The section of the plan containing a general prohibition against reversion of funds had to be read in conjunction with another section that contained a specific exception allowing for a reversion after the satisfaction of all liabilities. [Parrett v. American Ship Bldg. Co., 990 F.2d 854 (6th Cir. 1993)] In another case, an employer recovered $275 million to use in expanding and improving its ongoing business [Walsh v. Great Atl. & Pac. Tea Co., 4 Employee Benefits Cas. (BNA) 2577 (3d Cir. 1983)]; and, in another, the court held that a reversion of $600,000 of excess assets to the receiver of the insolvent employer did not violate ERISA's exclusive benefit rule (see Q 4:1). [Outzen v. FDIC, No. 90-8077 (10th Cir. 1991)]

In another case, the court held that a 1959 plan provision that "in no event and under no circumstances" could plan assets be returned to the employer precluded any subsequent amendment to the plan to allow such a reversion upon termination of the plan [Bryant v. International Fruit Prods., Inc., 793 F.2d 118 (6th Cir. 1986)]; and another court held that plan participants were entitled to excess assets upon plan termination because an amendment providing for a reversion of excess assets to the employer was not properly executed according to plan procedures. [Albedyll v. Wisconsin Porcelain Co. Revised Ret. Plan, 947 F.2d 246 (7th Cir. 1991)] Similarly, the employer was not entitled to the excess assets upon plan termination where the plan did not specifically provide for a reversion even though the reversion provision had existed in an earlier version of the plan and was provided for in the trust agreement. [Rinard v. Eastern Co., 978 F.2d 265 (6th Cir. 1992)] However, in another case, an employer was entitled to surplus plan assets despite the plan's ambiguous language that surplus assets would be "referred" to the employer instead of "reverted" to the employer. [Dame v. First Nat'l Bank of Omaha, 217 F.3d 1018 (8th Cir. 2000)]

In yet another case, a board resolution required that all assets be distributed to participants, although the plan permitted reversions. The court determined that this resolution informally amended the plan to require that excess assets be distributed to plan participants. [Horn v. Berdon, Inc. Defined Benefit Pension Plan, No. 89-55391 (9th Cir. 1991)] However, in another case, former employees were not entitled to a pro rata share of excess assets recouped by their former employer when the employer terminated its retirement plan because the employees, who were laid off before they reached the plan's early retirement age, were not entitled to retirement benefits. [Fuller v. FMC Corp., 1993 U.S. App. LEXIS 19448 (4th Cir. 1993)]

A participant's waiver assigning his pension plan benefits to the employer constituted a prohibited assignment or alienation (see Q 4:27) and resulted in his receipt of a taxable distribution (see Q 13:1). The court ruled that the waived benefits did not represent excess assets reverting to the employer. [Gallade, 106 T.C. 355 (1996)]

Further, if an overfunded plan with mandatory employee contributions is terminated, certain assets attributable to such contributions must be distributed to participants and beneficiaries. [ERISA § 4044(d)(3)(B)]

Q 25:50 May a defined benefit plan that did not originally provide for distribution of excess assets to the employer be amended to authorize such a distribution?

Yes. However, for defined benefit plans covered by PBGC (see Qs 25:11, 25:12), any amendment providing for a reversion, or increasing the amount that may revert to the employer, is not effective before the fifth calendar year following the date of the adoption of such an amendment. A special rule provides that a distribution to the employer will not be treated as failing to satisfy this rule if the plan has been in effect for fewer than five years.

For plans that, as of December 17, 1987, had no provision relating to the distribution of plan assets to the employer, the new rule applies to such amendments that were adopted more than one year after the effective date of the new law. For plans that, as of December 17, 1987, provided for the distribution of plan assets to the employer, the new law applies to any amendment made after December 17, 1987. [ERISA § 4044(d)(2)]

In one case, participants in one plan that was merged into a plan of another employer were not entitled to any portion of the surplus assets of the merged plan at the time of the merger because the merged plan reserved the employer's right to amend the plan to allow for the reversion of surplus assets on plan termination. The fact that the merger resulted in a partial termination (see Q 25:5) of the merged plan did not prevent amendment of the surviving plan to allow for the reversion of the surplus assets at the time of the merger. However, two other plans that were simultaneously merged into the surviving plan did provide an irrevocable provision for the reallocation of excess assets to plan participants upon plan termination. Thus, the surviving plan could not be amended to allow reversion of the surplus assets of those plans at the time of the merger. Although the surplus assets were not required to be distributed until complete termination, the court considered the two merged plans as terminated as of the day prior to the merger and ordered the distribution of the surplus assets to the participants. [Borst v. Chevron Corp., U.S. App. LEXIS 29473 (5th Cir. 1994); *In re* Gulf Pension Litig., No. 86-4365 (S.D. Tex. 1991)]

Q 25:51 May an employer terminate a defined benefit plan to recover any excess assets and adopt a new defined benefit plan covering the same employees?

Yes, if the plan specifically permits the recovery of excess assets and:

1. All employees covered by the original plan are given notice of the termination and adoption;
2. All accrued benefits are vested as of the termination date and annuities are purchased to cover those benefits;

3. The plan's funding method is changed to take into consideration the termination and adoption, and IRS approves the change in funding method;

4. No other termination and adoption will be made in the next 15 years; and

5. The new plan is intended to be permanent.

[PBGC News Rel. 84-23, on the Joint Implementation Guidelines for Termination of Defined Benefit Plans]

Legislation has sought to deter employers from terminating plans in order to recover excess assets (see Q 25:52).

IRS ruled that the potential right to the excess amount from an overfunded defined benefit plan was properly treated as an asset of a target corporation at the time of its acquisition by the acquiring corporation. Furthermore, the tax benefit rule required that the overfunded amount, to the extent of deductible contributions, be included in the target corporation's income to the extent it received the tax benefit. [Priv. Ltr. Rul. 9650002]

Q 25:52   Is the employer liable for any taxes on the reversion?

Yes. The amount of the reversion is taxable to the employer as ordinary income. Furthermore, a nondeductible excise tax equal to 50 percent of the amount of the reversion is imposed upon the employer; however, the excise tax is reduced from 50 percent to 20 percent if the employer either establishes a qualified replacement plan (see Q 25:53) or amends the defined benefit plan to provide pro rata benefit increases (see Q 25:54). The 20 percent excise tax applies to an employer who, as of the date of plan termination, is in bankruptcy under Chapter 7 or in similar proceedings under state law. In one case, an employer that had ceased doing business was subject to the 20 percent excise tax on the reversion of assets from its defined benefit plan since the reversion occurred after the employer entered into voluntary judicially supervised liquidation proceedings under state law that were similar to bankruptcy liquidation proceedings. [Priv. Ltr. Rul. 9851053] In another case, a bankrupt corporation was subject to the 50 percent excise tax on the reversion of assets from its defined benefit plan because the exception that allowed the 20 percent excise tax on reversions resulting from an employer's Chapter 7 bankruptcy did not apply since the corporation had ceased doing business while it was in Chapter 11 bankruptcy. [Priv. Ltr. Rul. 9847034] For an exception to the excise tax, see Q 25:55. [I.R.C. §§ 4980(a), 4980(d)]

The excise tax applies to direct and indirect reversions. An indirect reversion includes the use of plan assets for the benefit of the employer on plan termination and, therefore, would include the use of plan assets to satisfy an obligation of the employer. [I.R.C. § 4980(c)(2)(A); Priv. Ltr. Rul. 9136017] In one case, IRS ruled that an employer's proposed use of surplus assets in its defined benefit plan to provide matching contributions for its 401(k) plan would be a reversion and result in taxable income to the employer. Furthermore, the employer would be liable for the excise tax on reversions. [Priv. Ltr. Rul. 9723033]

A reversion received by a tax-exempt organization from its terminated defined benefit plan is generally not subject to the excise tax on reversions [I.R.C. § 4980(c)(1)(A); Priv. Ltr. Ruls. 200122035, 9320050, 9120029] The reversion to a tax-exempt organization, a member of a controlled group (see Q 5:31) that included both tax-exempt and for-profit entities, was not includible as unrelated business taxable income (see Q 1:6) and was not subject to the excise tax on reversions because the plan covered only employees of the tax-exempt entities and no tax deduction was ever taken for contributions. [Priv. Ltr. Rul. 200222035] However, in another case, because two of the three corporations maintaining a plan were nonexempt, IRS ruled that the total reversion was subject to the excise tax. Since the surplus was attributable to contributions made by a tax-exempt corporation and its for-profit affiliates, the plan was not maintained, at all times, by an employer exempt from tax. [Priv. Ltr. Rul. 9837036] Since a tax exempt employer never received a tax benefit from contributions made to its plan, the employer did not realize unrelated business taxable income from the recovery of surplus assets upon the plan's termination. However, the employer was subject to the excise tax on reversions because it had previously been subject to the tax on unrelated business taxable income, and therefore had not at all times been exempt from tax. [Priv. Ltr. Rul. 200334043] In another case, the excise tax did not apply because the employer was a foreign corporation not subject to corporate income taxes. [Priv. Ltr. Rul. 200152049] An exception to the excise tax also exists for certain reversions transferred to an ESOP (see chapter 27). [I.R.C. § 4980(c)(3); Priv. Ltr. Rul. 9138065]

A reversion does not include any distribution to the employer allowable under Section 401(a)(2) in the case of a plan other than a multiemployer plan by reason of mistake of fact or, in the case of any plan, by reason of the failure of the plan to initially qualify or the failure of the contributions to be deductible. [I.R.C. § 4980(c)(2)(B)] In one case, the overfunded amount in a terminated defined benefit plan that was established as a spin-off of a prior plan was returned to the company. IRS determined that the return of this amount did not constitute an employer reversion, because the amount was the result of erroneous actuarial computations and not deductible because it exceeded the amount required to make the plan sufficient for benefit liabilities. [Priv. Ltr. Rul. 200851045]

IRS has ruled that the transfer of liabilities attributable to the employees of a contributing employer from a multiemployer defined benefit plan (see Q 29:2) that was expected to become insolvent to an overfunded defined benefit plan of the contributing employer did not cause the employer to recognize income or create a reversion. [Priv. Ltr. Rul. 199935076] Similarly, an employer's transfer of liabilities from an underfunded defined benefit plan to an overfunded defined benefit plan did not constitute a reversion of plan assets to the employer [Priv. Ltr. Rul. 9318035], and the merger of three overfunded defined benefit plans sponsored by a parent company's subsidiaries into the parent company's underfunded defined benefit plan did not constitute a reversion of plan assets. [Priv. Ltr. Rul. 9224032] Furthermore, an employer's transfer of a portion of the assets and liabilities of its defined benefit plan to a new defined benefit plan for certain former employees was not a termination of the original defined benefit plan, and the transfer of plan assets was not considered a reversion of plan assets. [Priv. Ltr. Rul. 9046046] A dissolved corporation did not have a deficiency resulting from its failure to report reversion income from its terminated defined benefit plan because it was entitled to an offsetting deduction for reasonable compensation paid to its sole shareholder-employee who reported the income as a reversion rather than compensation on his tax return. [Souris, 72 T.C.M. 830 (1996)]

The return of an excess advance payment to a defined benefit plan did not constitute an employer reversion because the excess advance was at all times held separately from the plan and was never contributed to the plan. [Priv. Ltr. Rul. 200727024]

Courts have ruled that the excise tax imposed on a reversion is not considered a penalty for bankruptcy purposes and, therefore, has priority status over the claims of unsecured creditors. [*In re* Juvenile Shoe Corp. of Am., No. 95-2289 (8th Cir. 1996); *In re* C-T of Va., Inc., No. 91-2397 (4th Cir. 1992); Priv. Ltr. Rul. 200005001] However, see Q 8:21 regarding the excise tax relating to the minimum funding standards.

Form 5330 (see Q 21:18) is used to report the reversion and pay the excise tax. If the 20 percent rate is used, the employer must explain why it qualifies for the lower rate. IRS has ruled that an employer is required to file a separate Form 5330 for each reversion and cannot amend a Form 5330 filed with respect to a reversion received in one year to report a reversion in a subsequent year. [Field Serv. Adv. 200226001]

Q 25:53   What is a qualified replacement plan?

The 50 percent excise tax on reversions is reduced to 20 percent if the employer, in connection with the termination of its defined benefit plan, establishes or maintains a qualified replacement plan (see Q 25:52). [I.R.C. § 4980(d)(2)]

Qualified replacement plans must satisfy the following requirements:

1. At least 95 percent of the active participants in the terminated plan who remain as employees of the employer after the termination must be active participants in the replacement plan.

2. The replacement plan must receive a transfer from the terminated plan of an amount equal to at least 25 percent of the maximum amount of the reversion (less the present value of any benefit increases due to plan amendments within the 60-day period prior to plan termination). The amount that is transferred to the replacement plan is not includible in the employer's income and is not subject to the excise tax on reversions; and, concomitantly, the employer is not permitted a tax deduction for the transfer.

3. If the replacement plan is a defined contribution plan, the amount transferred to it must be allocated to the accounts of participants in the

plan year in which the transfer occurs or be credited to a suspense account and allocated from the account to the participant accounts no less rapidly than ratably over seven plan years beginning with the year of the transfer. If the limitation on annual additions to defined contribution plans (see Q 6:34) prevents any amount in the suspense account from being allocated to a participant by the end of the seven-year period, that amount will be allocated to the accounts of other participants. If any amount credited to the suspense account is not allocated as of the termination date of a replacement plan, it must be allocated to the accounts of participants as of such date. Any amount that cannot be so allocated will be treated as an employer reversion subject to the excise tax. [Priv. Ltr. Rul. 9224033]

Example 1. Lauren, Inc. maintains a defined benefit plan that has excess assets of $200,000. As part of the termination of this plan, it establishes a qualified replacement plan funded with $50,000. Lauren's excise tax on the reversion is $30,000 (20% × $150,000), and Lauren also reports $150,000 of income. Assuming that Lauren is taxed at 34 percent on its income, it will owe $51,000 in income tax on the reversion and end up with $69,000 [$200,000 − ($50,000 + $30,000 + $51,000)] after paying both taxes and funding the replacement plan.

IRS has determined that an amount greater than 25 percent of the excess assets may be transferred to a qualified replacement plan. According to IRS, the transfer of more than 25 percent of the amount of excess assets to a qualified replacement plan does not result in an employer reversion; and, therefore, the amount transferred is not includible in the gross income of the employer and is not treated as an employer reversion for purposes of the excise tax. [Rev. Rul. 2003-85, 2003-2 C.B. 291]

Example 2. The facts are the same as in Example 1, except that the qualified replacement plan is funded with $200,000, the full amount of the excess assets. The additional transfer of $150,000 is neither subject to excise tax nor reportable as taxable income.

Prior to the issuance of Revenue Ruling 2003-85, it appeared that more than 25 percent of the excess assets could not be transferred to a qualified replacement plan. Consequently, the following discussion with respect to the 25-percent rule may apply only to those cases that arose before the issuance of the Revenue Ruling.

An existing plan constituted a qualified replacement plan where at least 95 percent of the active participants in the terminated defined benefit plan who remained employees of the company after the termination were active participants in the existing plan and the requirements of (2) and (3) above were met. [Priv. Ltr. Ruls. 200344025, 9627030] Because certain employees elected out of the predecessor defined benefit plan and were not accruing benefits on the plan's termination date, they were not considered active participants as of the termination date and, therefore, were not considered in determining whether the plan satisfied the 95 percent requirement in (1) above. [Priv. Ltr. Rul. 9252035] Amounts transferred to a qualified replacement plan can be used as matching contributions (see Qs 27:80, 27:81) if the requirements of (3) above are satisfied. [Priv. Ltr. Rul. 9302027; *see also* Priv. Ltr. Ruls. 200109052; 200031055] Similarly, as part of a sale of a company, the 20 percent excise tax applied to the reversion of the seller's overfunded defined benefit plan where 25 percent of the excess was transferred to the buyer's 401(k) plan. The transferred amount was to be used as the employer match for future elective deferrals by the former participants in the defined benefit plan. [Priv. Ltr. Rul. 200107038] IRS ruled that a 401(k) plan (see Q 27:1) would be a qualified replacement plan where it received 25 percent of the reversion amount of a terminated defined benefit plan to be used to make matching contributions based on a percentage of each participant's pre-tax contribution and at least 95 percent of the active participants in the terminated defined benefit plan who remained as employees were active participants in the 401(k) plan. [Priv. Ltr. Rul. 200208037] A company that transferred 25 percent of its terminated plan's surplus assets to a newly established 401(k) plan was subject to the 20 percent tax where the transferred amounts were to be allocated as employer discretionary profit sharing contributions and/or employer matching contributions. [Priv. Ltr. Rul. 9834036; *see also* Priv. Ltr. Rul. 200045031] IRS ruled that a defined contribution plan was a qualified replacement plan and that the amounts transferred from the terminated defined benefit plan could be allocated as employer nonelective contributions, but could not be allocated as matching contributions because these amounts were contributed before the cash-or-deferred elections were made, before the employees' performance of service with respect to which the elective deferrals were made, and before the employee deferrals were made. In addition, if the amounts transferred to the suspense account in the defined contribution plan cannot be allocated due to the Section 415 limitations, the remaining suspense account may be transferred to the company and treated as a reversion subject to the 20 percent excise tax at the end of the seven-plan-year period, provided the amount remaining in the suspense account totals an amount that is less than 75 percent of the amount initially transferred to the defined contribution plan. [Priv. Ltr. Ruls. 200836035, 200836034) Where a company spun off from its plan a separate retiree plan, terminated the retiree plan, and transferred 25 percent of the surplus assets to a replacement plan, the 20 percent excise tax rate applied to the reversion. [Priv. Ltr. Rul. 9645029]

An amendment to a defined benefit plan that increased the value of benefits, was adopted more than 60 days prior to the date of its termination, and was made effective on the date of termination, was not considered part of the 25 percent reversion amount; and, therefore, the value of such increases was not subject to the excise tax as it met the requirement of (2) above. [Priv. Ltr. Rul. 200051045]

Where 100 percent of the surplus of a terminated defined benefit plan was transferred to a qualified replacement plan and allocated to participants, IRS ruled that the 20 percent excise tax should be imposed on 75 percent of the surplus and that the surplus transferred was not a taxable distribution to participants. [Priv. Ltr. Ruls. 9839031, 9839030, 9823051; *but see* Priv. Ltr. Ruls. 200227041, 200227040, where IRS modified Priv. Ltr. Rul. 9839030 and ruled that assets transferred in excess of 25 percent of the reversion amount would be included in the gross income of the company and are considered as contributions to the qualified replacement plan, subject to the deduction rules of Section 404 of the Code (see chapter 12)] In another case, IRS ruled that 25 percent *and only 25 percent* of the surplus transferred from a terminated defined benefit plan to a profit sharing plan is not includible in income. Any amount greater than 25 percent of the surplus is a reversion and includible in the company's gross income, and the company is subject to the excise tax with respect to the transfer or reversion of the remaining 75 percent of the surplus. If more than 25 percent of the surplus is transferred to the profit sharing plan, its tax qualified status becomes an issue and such amount is regarded as a contribution subject to the deduction limits of the Code; therefore, to the extent that any part of the transferred amount in excess of 25 percent exceeds the deductible limits, the company is subject to an excise tax (see Q 12:9). [Priv. Ltr. Rul. 200212035]

In order to qualify, the asset transfer must be a "direct transfer from the terminated plan to the replacement plan . . . before any employer reversion." [I.R.C. § 4980(d)(2)(B)(i)] In one case, the employer deposited funds from the terminated plan into its own account and subsequently transferred those funds into a replacement profit sharing plan. The court ruled that the new plan did not satisfy the requirements of a qualified replacement plan because the transfer was an "indirect transfer." [Southern Aluminum Castings Co. v. United States, 788 F. Supp. 1200 (S.D. Ala. 1991)]

Two or more qualified plans may be treated as one plan for purposes of determining whether a plan is a qualified replacement plan. [I.R.C. § 4980 (d)(5)(D)(i)] In one case, where a portion of 25 percent of the residual assets of a terminated defined benefit plan was transferred to a 401(k) plan and the remaining portion was transferred to a new defined benefit plan, IRS ruled that both plans together constituted a qualified replacement plan and the 20 percent tax rate applied to the reversion. [Priv. Ltr. Rul. 9803027]

Q 25:54   What is a pro rata benefit increase?

If, in connection with the termination of its defined benefit plan, the employer amends the plan, effective as of the date of termination, to provide pro rata benefit increases in the accrued benefits (see Q 9:2) of qualified participants equal to at least 20 percent of the amount of the reversion, the 50 percent excise tax on the reversion will be reduced to 20 percent (see Q 25:52). [I.R.C. § 4980(d)(3); Priv. Ltr. Rul. 9236043]

The pro rata increase must benefit all qualified participants. Qualified participants include active participants, participants in pay status, certain beneficiaries, and individuals who have a nonforfeitable right to an accrued benefit under the terminated plan as of the termination date and whose service terminated during the period beginning three years before the termination date. The 20 percent excise tax, rather than the 50 percent tax, was imposed on an employer reversion at plan termination because the employer provided for pro rata benefit increases to qualified participants equal to 20 percent of the surplus assets remaining after satisfaction of plan obligations. [Priv. Ltr. Rul. 9335047]

In one case, no excise tax was imposed where all of the excess assets were used to increase plan benefits and pay plan expenses, and there was, in fact, no reversion to the employer. [Priv. Ltr. Rul. 200317049]

Q 25:55   Are transfers to a retiree health account subject to the excise tax on reversions?

If a defined benefit plan (see Q 2:3) is overfunded and the plan termination would expose the employer to the excise tax on reversions (see Q 25:52), the amount of the excess assets can be reduced by a qualified transfer of assets to a postretirement health benefits account that is part of the plan. The amount transferred is not considered a reversion subject to either income or excise taxes. One qualified transfer can be made during each tax year, but no later than December 31, 2013, of the amount reasonably estimated to be required to pay qualified current retiree health liabilities for the year. The amount of a qualified transfer, however, cannot exceed the amount of excess plan assets as of the last valuation date before the transfer. All accrued benefits (see Q 9:2) of all plan participants must become fully vested (see Q 25:4) as if the plan terminated at the time of a qualified transfer. [I.R.C. §§ 401(h), 420; Priv. Ltr. Rul. 9419037; ERISA Tech. Rel. No. 91-1]

In order to make the transfers to health benefits accounts, the employer must meet a minimum cost requirement that requires employer provided retiree health expenditures be maintained for covered retirees, their spouses, and dependents at a minimum dollar level for a five-year cost maintenance period. The minimum cost requirements are not met if the employer significantly reduces retiree health coverage during the cost maintenance period. [Treas. Reg. § 1.420-1]

Statutory benefits paid under Federal Black Lung Law and Illinois Black Lung Law in connection with sickness, hospitalization, and medical expenses were determined to be applicable health benefits for purposes of a retiree health benefit account. [Priv. Ltr. Rul. 200112063]

IRS has issued procedures for requesting determination letters regarding the effect on the qualified plan status of a transfer of excess pension assets to a retiree health benefit account. [Rev. Proc. 92-24, 1992-1 C.B. 739]

Pension plans may transfer excess pension assets to retiree medical accounts to fund future retiree health benefit and collectively bargained retiree health benefit plans. [IRC § 420(f)]

Q 25:56   If an employer wants to withdraw from a plan maintained by two or more unrelated employers, would the withdrawal be considered a plan termination?

No. The general rule is that such a withdrawal would not constitute a plan termination. However, the withdrawal of one or more employers may result in a partial termination of the plan (see Q 25:5). [Treas. Reg. § 1.411(d)-2(b)]

Q 25:57   What is a complete discontinuance of contributions under a profit sharing plan?

Instead of directly defining a complete discontinuance, IRS describes what it is and what it is not.

First, IRS regulations distinguish a complete discontinuance from a suspension of contributions under a plan that is "merely a temporary cessation of contributions by the employer." The regulations provide that "a complete discontinuance of contributions may occur although some amounts are contributed by the employer under the plan if such amounts are not substantial enough to reflect the intent on the part of the employer to continue to maintain the plan. The determination of whether a complete discontinuance of contributions under the plan has occurred will be made with regard to all the facts and circumstances in the particular case, and without regard to the amount of any contributions made under the plan by employees." [Treas. Reg. § 1.411(d)-2(d)]

Second, the regulations state that, in any case in which a suspension of a profit sharing plan is considered a discontinuance, the discontinuance becomes effective no later than the last day of the taxable year that follows the last taxable year for which a substantial contribution was made under the profit sharing plan. [Treas. Reg. § 1.411(d)-2(d)(2)]

> **Example.** Brian Corporation maintains a calendar-year profit sharing plan. The last "substantial" contribution made by the corporation was on July 2, 2010. If a discontinuance of contributions is deemed to occur, it will become effective no later than December 31, 2011.

Employees who become eligible to enter a plan subsequent to its discontinuance receive no benefits, nor do any additional benefits accrue to any of the participants unless employer contributions are resumed. IRS, therefore, takes the position that discontinuance of contributions is equivalent to a plan termination.

What if an employer has no profits? IRS says that the failure of an employer to make contributions to its profit sharing plan for five consecutive years due solely to the absence of current or accumulated earnings and profits is not a discontinuance of contributions if the plan requires the employer to resume contributions as soon as it has profits. [Rev. Rul. 80-146, 1980-1 C.B. 90] Since current or accumulated profits are no longer required for the employer to make tax-deductible contributions to a profit sharing plan, such failure to make contributions may ripen into a discontinuance. [I.R.C. § 401(a)(27)]

Q 25:58   Must a profit sharing plan provide for full vesting of benefits upon a complete discontinuance of contributions?

Yes. A Tax Court decision upheld IRS's position that a profit sharing plan did not qualify merely because it did not provide for full vesting of participants' accrued benefits on complete discontinuance of contributions. Even though IRS conceded that there never was a discontinuance of contributions, and that no employee's rights to benefits were ever adversely affected, the absence of such a provision from a plan was, according to the court, a sufficient defect in the instrument to disqualify the plan, resulting in the disallowance of the employer deduction. [Tionesta Sand & Gravel, Inc., 73 T.C. 758 (1980), *aff'd,* unpublished opinion (3d Cir. Feb. 27, 1981)]

Q 25:59   Can a plan amendment result in the termination of the plan?

Yes. If benefits or employer contributions to the plan are reduced, or vesting or eligibility requirements are made less liberal, the plan is considered to be curtailed. Full vesting of a portion of the benefits may be required if IRS decides that the curtailment is a partial termination of the plan (see Q 25:5).

If an employer seeks to amend a defined benefit plan covered by Title IV to convert it to a defined contribution plan, the termination rules of Title IV must be satisfied first before the former plan is treated as terminated (see Q 25:6). [ERISA § 4041(e)]

Q 25:60   Can a plan be amended to reduce or stop benefit accruals?

Yes, but if the amendment provides for a significant reduction in the rate of future benefit accrual, a Section 204(h) Notice (see Q 9:38) must be provided. In general, the Section 204(h) Notice must be provided at least 45 days before the effective date of a plan amendment that significantly reduces future accruals. In the case of a small plan, the Section 204(h) Notice must be provided at least 15 days before the effective date of the applicable amendment. For this purpose, a small plan is a plan that the plan administrator (see Q 20:1) reasonably expects to have fewer than 100 participants (see Q 9:44). This rule applies to amendments to defined benefit plans and to defined contribution plans subject to the funding standards of ERISA Section 302, namely, money purchase pension plans and target benefit plans. [ERISA § 204(h)]

The plan administrator is required to provide in this notice, in a manner calculated to be understood by the average plan participant, sufficient information (as defined in regulations) to allow participants to understand the effect of the amendment. [I.R.C. § 4980F; ERISA § 204(h)] In one case, prior to the change in law, the court ruled that a company's notice violated ERISA Section 204(h) when the notice came before the plan amendment was adopted and after the amendment's effective date—exactly the opposite of what ERISA required at that time. [Production & Maint. Employees' Local 504 v. Roadmaster Corp., Nos. 89-1464, 90-2698 (7th Cir. 1992)] See Qs 9:37 through 9:53 for a more detailed discussion of the Section 204(h) Notice.

Q 25:61   How do Section 4980F and ERISA Section 204(h) apply to terminated plans covered by Title IV of ERISA?

An amendment providing for the cessation of benefit accruals on a specified future date and for the termination of a plan is subject to Section 4980F and ERISA Section 204(h) (see Qs 9:37–9:53). [Treas. Reg. § 54.4980F-1(b), Q&A-17]

See Q 9:52 for details.

Q 25:62   Must terminating plans be amended for changes in the law?

Yes. A plan that terminates after the effective date of a change in law, but prior to the date that amendments are otherwise required (see Q 4:8), must still be amended to comply with the applicable provisions of law that are in effect at the time of plan termination. Because such a terminated plan would no longer be in existence by the required amendment date and therefore could not be amended on that date, the plan must be amended in connection with the plan termination. [Rev. Proc. 2009-6, § 12.06, 2009-1 I.R.B. 189]

Q 25:63   Must IRS be notified when a plan terminates?

Just as there is no legal requirement to file a request for a favorable determination letter (see Q 18:1) with IRS with regard to a new or amended plan, there is no requirement regarding a plan's termination. However, a plan administrator (see Q 20:1) must notify IRS on the Form 5500 series return/report (see Q 21:1) for the year in which the plan terminates. In addition, a Form 5500 series return/report must be filed every year (even after a plan terminates) until all assets are distributed from the trust. An IRS representative has opined that Schedule B (see Qs 8:33, 21:6) must be filed for the plan year in which a defined benefit plan (see Q 2:3) terminates but need not be filed for the plan year after the year in which the plan terminates. [Spec. Rul. (July 27, 1998)]

It is strongly suggested that plan administrators file Form 5310 (see Q 21:18) with IRS requesting a favorable determination letter with regard to a plan's termination. Form 6088, Distributable Benefits From Employee Pension Benefit Plans, must be attached to Form 5310 with respect to the termination of a defined benefit plan or an *underfunded defined contribution plan* (see Q 18:18). [Rev. Proc. 2009-6, § 12, 2009-1 I.R.B. 189; Instructions to Form 6088] IRS has developed guidelines when examining plans for compliance with qualification requirements (see Q 4:1) where a plan was terminated and a determination letter request was not submitted to IRS. [Ann. 94-101, 1994-35 I.R.B. 53]

IRS has issued a revenue ruling explaining that a termination of a qualified retirement plan is not complete until the final distribution of plan assets. However, if the "terminated" retirement plan fails to distribute its assets as soon as administratively feasible following the established plan termination date, IRS will not treat the plan as being terminated. [Rev. Rul. 89-87, 1989-2 C.B. 81]

The ruling provides that whether a distribution is made as soon as administratively feasible will be determined under all the facts and circumstances of the given case; but, generally, a distribution that is not completed within one year following the date of plan termination specified by the employer will be presumed not to have been completed as soon as administratively feasible. If a plan's assets are not distributed as soon as administratively feasible, the plan is considered to be an ongoing plan and must meet the requirements of Section 401(a) in order to maintain its qualified status. For example, such a plan remains subject to the minimum funding requirements under Section 412 (see Q 8:1) and the information reporting requirements of Sections 6057 and 6058 (and, in the case of a defined benefit plan, the actuarial reporting requirements of Section 6059). It is not clear under the ruling whether a pending determination letter request on the plan's termination or a delay caused by the termination procedures of Title IV of ERISA (applicable to certain defined benefit plans) will excuse a distribution delay of more than one year. However, one IRS key district has advised that, if the determination letter request is submitted timely, distributions completed within six months after the issuance of the determination letter will be treated as having been made as soon as administratively feasible. [EP/EO Baltimore Key District Newsl. (Apr. 1991)]

Q 25:64 Are there special rules applicable to the termination of abandoned plans?

DOL has issued regulations to facilitate the termination of individual account plans (see Q 2:2) and the distribution of benefits where the plans have been abandoned by their sponsors. The regulations, which were issued in conjunction with a prohibited-transaction class exemption (PTCE; see Q 24:26), were developed to help prevent participants and beneficiaries of abandoned plans from losing favorable tax treatment otherwise accorded distributions from qualified retirement plans. Under the regulations, any determination that a plan is abandoned, and any related termination activities, may only be performed by a qualified termination administrator (QTA). A person or entity may only be a QTA for a plan if it is eligible to serve as a trustee or issuer of an individual retirement plan (see Qs 30:1, 30:2) and if it holds the plan's assets.

A plan generally would be considered to be abandoned if no contributions to, or distributions from, the plan have been made for at least 12 consecutive months, or other facts indicate the plan's abandonment, and, after reasonable efforts to locate the plan sponsor, the QTA determines that the sponsor no longer exists, cannot be located, or is unable to maintain the plan.

A QTA must make reasonable efforts to locate or communicate with the plan sponsor by sending a Notice of Intent to Terminate Plan. If the QTA does not receive acknowledgment of delivery, it will be deemed to have made a reasonable effort to locate or communicate with the plan sponsor if the QTA contacts plan service providers to obtain a current address and attempts further deliveries to that current address, again by a method that requires acknowledgment of delivery.

The Notice of Intent to Terminate Plan must include:

1. The name and address of the QTA;
2. The name of the plan;
3. The account number or other identifying information relating to the plan;
4. A statement that the plan may be terminated and benefits distributed if the plan sponsor fails to contact the QTA within 30 days;
5. Contact information for the person, office, or department that the plan sponsor must contact about the plan;
6. A statement that, if the plan is terminated, notice of the termination will be provided to DOL's Employee Benefits Security Administration (EBSA);
7. A statement regarding the plan sponsor's potential liability as a fiduciary (see Q 23:1) or plan administrator (see Q 20:1); and
8. A statement that the plan sponsor may contact DOL for more information about the termination process.

If a QTA determines that the plan has been abandoned, the termination date generally is the 90th day following the date of the letter from EBSA acknowledging receipt of the notice of plan abandonment. Notice is provided to EBSA by filing a Notification of Plan Abandonment and Intent to Serve as Qualified Termination Administrator that must include the following information:

1. Information about the QTA, including contact information, a statement that the QTA qualifies as such, and information about whether the QTA or its affiliate is or has been under investigation by IRS, DOL, or the Securities and Exchange Commission within the past 24 months;
2. Information about the plan, its sponsor, and the estimated number of plan participants;
3. The QTA's findings on the plan's abandonment;
4. Plan asset information, including the estimated value, the period that the assets have been held by the QTA (if less than 12 months), and the identification of any assets with no readily ascertainable value;
5. Service provider information, including contact information and a list of the services provided; and
6. A statement that the notice is true, complete, and provided under penalty of perjury.

The QTA must take all steps necessary or appropriate to wind down the plan, including:

1. Locating and updating the plan's records;
2. Calculating the benefits payable to the plan participants and beneficiaries;
3. Reporting delinquent contributions to DOL;
4. Hiring service providers to assist in winding down the plan;

5. Paying reasonable plan expenses;

6. Providing a Notice of Plan Termination notifying the participants of the termination, the estimated values of their account balances, the benefit distribution options available under the plan, the identity of the QTA, and the results of a failure to make a benefit distribution election (along with information about the IRA provider and fees in the case of an involuntary rollover to an IRA; see Qs 34:18, 34:19);

7. Distributing the plan benefits;

8. Filing a Special Terminal Report for Abandoned Plans; and

9. Filing a Final Notice to EBSA within two months after the QTA completes the other listed requirements.

The PTCE provides relief from the fiduciary restrictions regarding transactions by a plan and a party in interest (see Q 24:3), and on self dealing and participation in transactions where the fiduciary's interests are adverse to those of the plan.

The regulations provide a safe harbor when making distributions on behalf of participants and beneficiaries who fail to make an election. The regulations provide that (1) in the case of a distribution to a participant or surviving spouse the distribution be rolled over to an IRA and (2) in the case of a distribution to a nonspouse beneficiary the distribution be rolled over to an inherited IRA (see Q 34:33).

[DOL Reg. §§ 2520.103-13, 2550.404a-3, 2578.1; PTCE 2006-06, 71 Fed. Reg. 20,856 (as amended Oct. 7, 2008, 73 Fed. Reg. 58,629)]

Chapter 26

Top-Heavy Plans

A qualified retirement plan that primarily benefits key employees—a top-heavy plan—can qualify for tax-favored status only if, in addition to the regular qualification requirements, it meets several special requirements. This chapter examines what top-heavy plans are and the special requirements these plans must satisfy.

Q 26:1 What is a top-heavy defined benefit plan?

A defined benefit plan (see Q 2:3) is top-heavy if, as of the determination date (see Q 26:20), the present value of the accrued benefits of all key employees (see Qs 26:2, 26:23) exceeds 60 percent of the present value of the accrued benefits of all employees. [I.R.C. § 416(g)(1)(A)(i); Treas. Reg. § 1.416-1, Q T-1(c)]

Q 26:2 How are accrued benefits calculated for purposes of determining whether a qualified retirement plan is top-heavy?

Solely for determining whether the present value of cumulative accrued benefits for key employees (see Q 26:23) exceeds 60 percent of the present value of cumulative accrued benefits for all employees, the accrued benefit of an employee (other than a key employee) is determined by the method that is used for benefit accrual purposes under all qualified retirement plans maintained by the employer or, if there is no such single method used under all the plans, as if the benefit accrues no more rapidly than the slowest permitted rate under the fractional accrual rule. [I.R.C. § 416(g)(4)(F)]

Q 26:3 What is a top-heavy defined contribution plan?

A defined contribution plan (see Q 2:2) is top-heavy if, as of the determination date (see Q 26:20), the total of the accounts of all key employees (see Q 26:23) exceeds 60 percent of the total of the accounts of all employees. [I.R.C. § 416(g)(1)(A)(ii); Treas. Reg. § 1.416-1, Q T-1(c), Q M-16]

Q 26:4 Which qualified retirement plans are subject to the top-heavy rules?

Generally, all defined benefit plans (see Q 2:3) and defined contribution plans (see Q 2:2) are subject to the top-heavy rules. A simplified employee pension (SEP) is also subject to the top-heavy rules (see Qs 26:6, 32:1). [Treas. Reg. § 1.416-1, Q G-1] SIMPLE plans (see Q 33:1), however, are *not* subject to the top-heavy rules. [I.R.C. §§ 401(k)(11)(D)(ii), 416(g)(4)(G)]

A 401(k) plan (see Q 27:1) that satisfies the safe harbor 401(k) rules (see Q 27:40) and satisfies the ACP test safe harbor for matching employer contributions (see Q 27:89) will be exempt from the top-heavy rules. [I.R.C. § 416(g)(4)(H)] This exemption applies if the 401(k) plan consists *solely* of a CODA and matching contributions. Where a plan allows for 401(k) contributions, matching contributions, and discretionary profit sharing contributions, but where no profit sharing contribution is made such that the only current contributions are elective deferrals and the safe harbor match, then the plan is not top-heavy and no top-heavy minimum would be required. A plan that is amended to reduce or suspend safe harbor contributions during the year will be subject to the top-heavy rules (see Q 27:94).

> **Example 1.** Carmine Corporation maintains a profit sharing plan containing a CODA that provides for safe harbor matching contributions. The plan also provides for an employer discretionary nonelective contribution. The plan is a calendar-year plan and covers all employees who have one year of service and are age 21 or over. Other than elective contributions and the matching contributions, no other contributions are made to the plan for 2010, and there are no forfeitures. The plan meets the requirements for the exemption, and is, therefore, not subject to the top-heavy rules for 2010 because no other contributions are made to the plan other than elective contributions and the safe harbor match.

> **Example 2.** The facts are the same as in Example 1, except that Carmine Corporation makes a discretionary nonelective contribution for 2010. In this case, the plan does not meet the requirements for the exemption and, therefore, is subject to the top-heavy rules for 2010.

> **Example 3.** The facts are the same as in Example 1, except that forfeitures are allocated to participants' accounts for 2010 in the same manner as nonelective contributions. In this case, the plan does not meet the requirements for the exemption and, therefore, is subject to the top-heavy rules for 2010.

> **Example 4.** The facts are the same as in Example 1, except that employees are permitted to make elective contributions immediately upon commencement of employment, but NHCEs are not eligible for matching contributions until they have completed one year of service. Since this will result in a greater rate of matching contributions for highly compensated employees (HCEs; see Q 3:2) than for non-highly compensated employees (NHCEs; see Q 3:12), the matching contributions do not satisfy the safe harbor requirements. In this case, the plan does not meet the requirements for the exemption and, therefore, is subject to the top-heavy rules for 2010.

However, certain plans that provide for early participation may satisfy the safe harbor requirements with respect to the portion of the plan that covers employees who have completed the minimum age and service requirements (see Q 5:2), while satisfying the ADP test (see Q 27:18) for the eligible employees who have not completed the minimum age and service requirements. Unless a plan meets the requirements to be exempt from the top-heavy rules, no portion of the plan will satisfy the exemption. [Rev. Rul. 2004-13, 2004-1 C.B. 485; IRS Notice 2000-3, Q&A-10, 2000-1 C.B. 413]

The top-heavy rules do not apply to a plan that consists solely of (1) a qualified automatic contribution arrangement (QACA; see Qs 27:5, 27:6) and (2) matching contributions satisfying the limitations applicable to SIMPLE 401(k) plans (see Q 33:31). [IRC §§ 401(m)(12), 416(g)(4)(H)]

Q 26:5   Is a multiple employer plan subject to the top-heavy rules?

Yes. A multiple employer plan is subject to the top-heavy rules. A multiple employer plan is a qualified retirement plan to which more than one employer contributes and that is not the subject of a collective bargaining agreement.

If five employers contribute to a multiple employer plan and the accrued benefits of the key employees (see Q 26:23) of one employer exceed 60 percent of the accrued benefits of all employees of that employer, the plan is top-heavy with respect to that employer. If the retirement plan fails to satisfy the top-heavy rules for the employees of that employer, all five employers will be maintaining a retirement plan that is not qualified. [I.R.C. § 413(c); Treas. Reg. § 1.416-1, Q G-2, Q T-2]

Q 26:6   What is a top-heavy simplified employee pension?

A SEP (see Q 32:1) is top-heavy if, as of the determination date (see Q 26:20), the total of the accounts of all key employees (see Q 26:23) exceeds 60 percent of the total of the accounts of all employees. However, at the employer's election, top-heavy status may be determined by taking into account only the total employer contributions to the SEP, rather than account balances. [I.R.C. §§ 408(k)(1), 416(i)(6)]

Q 26:7   Which factors must be considered in determining whether a qualified retirement plan is top-heavy?

To determine whether a qualified retirement plan is top-heavy, it is necessary to consider:

1. Which employers must be treated as a single employer (see Q 26:12);
2. What the determination date is for the plan year (see Q 26:20);
3. Which employees are or formerly were key employees (see Q 26:23);
4. Which former employees have not performed any services for the employer during the one-year period ending on the determination date;

5. Which plans of such employers are required or permitted to be aggregated in determining top-heavy status (see Qs 26:8, 26:9); and

6. The present value of the accrued benefits (under a defined benefit plan) or the account balances (under a defined contribution plan) of key employees, former key employees, and non-key employees (see Qs 26:1, 26:3).

[I.R.C. § 416(g)(4)(E); Treas. Reg. § 1.416-1, Q T-1(a)]

Q 26:8   What is a required aggregation group?

A required aggregation group consists of each retirement plan of the employer in which a key employee (see Q 26:23) is a participant in the plan year containing the determination date (see Q 26:20) and any other retirement plan of the employer that enables a retirement plan covering a key employee to satisfy the coverage and nondiscriminatory benefit requirements (see Qs 4:10, 5:15). [I.R.C. § 416(g)(2)(A); Treas. Reg. § 1.416-1, Q T-6]

Example 1. Elaine Corporation maintains a defined benefit plan covering key employees and other salaried, non-key employees and also maintains a second defined benefit plan covering hourly, non-key employees. The first defined benefit plan by itself does not satisfy the coverage or nondiscriminatory benefit requirements, but does so when the two plans are considered together. The two defined benefit plans constitute a required aggregation group.

Example 2. Jamie, a sole proprietor, terminated her qualified retirement plan in 2010. In 2011, Jamie incorporates and establishes a corporate qualified retirement plan. In determining whether the corporate plan is top-heavy, Jamie's terminated retirement plan and the corporate retirement plan are part of a required aggregation group.

See Q 26:47 for a discussion of a special rule affecting aggregation groups.

Q 26:9   What is a permissive aggregation group?

A permissive aggregation group consists of each retirement plan of the employer that is required to be aggregated (see Q 26:8) and any other retirement plan of the employer that is not part of the required aggregation group but that satisfies the coverage and nondiscriminatory benefit requirements (see Qs 4:10, 5:15) when considered together with the required aggregation group. [I.R.C. § 416(g)(2)(A)(ii); Treas. Reg. § 1.416-1, Q T-7]

Example. The facts are the same as those in Example 1 in Q 26:8, except that the first defined benefit plan by itself satisfies the coverage and nondiscriminatory benefit requirements, but the second defined benefit plan needs to be aggregated with the first plan to meet these requirements. Since the second plan covers no key employees and does not enable the first plan to meet the requirements, the second plan is not part of a required aggregation group with the first plan, but both plans form a permissive aggregation group.

Q 26:10   Must collectively bargained retirement plans be aggregated with other retirement plans of the employer?

Collectively bargained retirement plans (see Q 29:2) that include a key employee (see Q 26:23) must be included in the required aggregation group for the employer (see Q 26:8). Collectively bargained retirement plans that do not include a key employee may be included in a permissive aggregation group (see Q 26:9). However, the special qualification requirements applicable to top-heavy plans (see Q 26:22) generally do not apply to collectively bargained retirement plans, whether or not they include a key employee. [I.R.C. §§ 416(i)(4), 7701(a)(46); Treas. Reg. § 1.416-1, Q T-3, Q T-7, Q T-8]

Q 26:11   What is a top-heavy group?

If a required aggregation group (see Q 26:8) is a top-heavy group, each retirement plan that is required to be included in the aggregation group is treated as a top-heavy plan. If, however, the group is not top-heavy, no retirement plan in the required aggregation group is treated as a top-heavy plan.

If a permissive aggregation group (see Q 26:9) is top-heavy, only those retirement plans that are part of the required aggregation group are subject to the special qualification requirements (see Q 26:22) placed on top-heavy plans. Retirement plans that are not part of the required aggregation group are not subject to these added requirements. If a permissive aggregation group is not top-heavy, on the other hand, the top-heavy requirements do not apply to any retirement plan in the group.

An aggregation group is a top-heavy group if, as of the determination date (see Q 26:20), the sum of (1) the present value of the accumulated accrued benefits for key employees (see Q 26:23) under all defined benefit plans included in the group and (2) the account balances of key employees under all defined contribution plans included in the group exceeds 60 percent of the same amount determined for all employees under all retirement plans included in the group. [I.R.C. § 416(g)(2)(B); Treas. Reg. § 1.416-1, Q T-9, Q T-10, Q T-11]

Example 1. Nat Corporation maintains a defined benefit plan covering key employees and other salaried, non-key employees and also maintains a second defined benefit plan covering hourly, non-key employees that enables the first plan to satisfy the coverage and nondiscriminatory benefit requirements. Since this is a required aggregation group, if the present value of the total accrued benefits for all key employees exceeds 60 percent of the present value of the total accrued benefits for all employees under both plans, both plans are considered top-heavy plans and minimum top-heavy benefits must be provided for all non-key employees. If, however, each plan satisfied the coverage and nondiscriminatory benefit requirements separately, the two plans would not constitute an aggregation group and only the first plan would be a top-heavy plan.

Example 2. The facts are the same as in Example 1, except that the second plan does not satisfy the coverage and nondiscriminatory benefit requirements on its own and consequently needs to be aggregated with the first plan to do so. In this case, because a permissive aggregation group exists, only those plans that are part of a required aggregation group must provide top-heavy minimum benefits. Therefore, only the first plan, not the second plan, is required to provide the top-heavy minimum benefits.

See Q 26:47 for a discussion of a special rule affecting aggregation groups.

Q 26:12 How are separate retirement plans of related employers treated for purposes of the top-heavy rules?

The aggregation group rules (see Qs 26:8, 26:9) and the top-heavy group rules (see Q 26:11) apply to all retirement plans of related employers if the related employers are treated as a single employer for retirement plan purposes. [I.R.C. §§ 414(b), 414(c), 414(m); Treas. Reg. § 1.416-1, Q T-1(b)]

See Q 26:47 for a discussion of a special rule affecting aggregation groups.

Q 26:13 How is a terminated retirement plan treated for purposes of the top-heavy rules?

A terminated retirement plan must be aggregated with the employer's other retirement plans if it (1) was maintained within the one-year period ending on the determination date (see Q 26:20) for the plan year in question and (2) would be part of a required aggregation group (see Q 26:8) for that plan year had it not been terminated. (A terminated retirement plan is a retirement plan that has formally terminated, has ceased crediting service for benefit accruals and vesting, and has been or is distributing plan assets to the participants.)

No additional vesting, benefit accruals, or contributions must be provided for participants in a terminated retirement plan. [I.R.C. § 416(g)(3); Treas. Reg. § 1.416-1, Q T-4]

Q 26:14 How is a frozen retirement plan treated for purposes of the top-heavy rules?

A frozen retirement plan must provide minimum benefits or contributions (see Qs 26:35, 26:41) and provide top-heavy vesting (see Q 26:30). (A frozen retirement plan is a retirement plan that has ceased crediting service for benefit accruals, but has not distributed all assets to the participants.) [Treas. Reg. § 1.416-1, Q T-5]

With respect to frozen defined benefit plans, service during a plan year in which the plan benefits no key employee (see Q 5:20) will be excluded from the determination of the minimum annual benefit. [I.R.C. § 416(c)(1)(C)(iii)]

Q 26:15   What happens if an employee ceases to be a key employee?

If an employee ceases to be a key employee (see Q 26:23) and continues to work for the employer, that employee is treated as a non-key employee and the employee's accrued benefit under the defined benefit plan and account balance under the defined contribution plan are disregarded for purposes of determining whether the retirement plan is top-heavy for each plan year following the last plan year for which the employee was a key employee. [I.R.C. § 416(g)(4)(B); Treas. Reg. § 1.416-1, Q T-1(d), Q T-12]

Q 26:16   How are plan distributions to employees treated for purposes of determining whether the qualified retirement plan is top-heavy?

The present value of the accrued benefit of an employee in a defined benefit plan, or the account balance of an employee in a defined contribution plan, includes any amount distributed with respect to the employee under the plan within the one-year period ending on the determination date (see Q 26:20). However, if the distribution is made for a reason other than severance from employment, death, or disability, a five-year period will apply instead of the one-year period. This rule applies whether or not the employee is a key employee (see Q 26:23) and applies to distributions made to a beneficiary of an employee (see Q 26:29). [I.R.C. § 416(g)(3); Treas. Reg. § 1.416-1, Q T-30]

If the employee does not render any services to the employer at any time during the one-year period ending on the determination date (see Q 26:20), the present value of the employee's accrued benefit or account balance is not taken into account for purposes of top-heavy plan testing. [I.R.C. § 416(g)(4)(E); Treas. Reg. § 1.416-1, Q T-1(d)]

Q 26:17   Are death benefits treated as distributions for purposes of determining whether a qualified retirement plan is top-heavy?

Death benefits (see Q 26:16) up to the present value of the deceased participant's accrued benefit immediately prior to death are treated as distributions for top-heavy testing purposes, but any death benefits in excess of this amount are not taken into account. For example, the distribution from a defined contribution plan, including the cash value of life insurance policies, of a participant's account balance due to the participant's death is treated as a distribution for top-heavy testing purposes. [Treas. Reg. § 1.416-1, Q T-31]

Q 26:18   How are rollovers and transfers treated for purposes of determining whether a retirement plan is top-heavy?

The rules for handling rollovers and plan-to-plan transfers depend on whether the rollovers and transfers are unrelated (both initiated by the employee and made from a qualified retirement plan maintained by one employer to a qualified retirement plan maintained by another employer) or related (either not initiated by the employee or made to a qualified retirement plan maintained by the same or a related employer).

In the case of unrelated rollovers or transfers, (1) the qualified retirement plan making the distribution always counts the distribution (see Q 26:16) and (2) the qualified retirement plan accepting the rollover or transfer does not consider it if it was accepted after 1983, but considers it if it was accepted prior to 1984.

In the case of related rollovers or transfers, the qualified retirement plan making the rollover or transfer does not count it as a distribution, but the qualified retirement plan accepting the rollover or transfer counts it. The rules for related rollovers do not depend on whether the rollover or transfer was accepted prior to 1984. [I.R.C. § 416(g)(4)(A); Treas. Reg. § 1.416-1, Q T-32]

IRS representatives have opined that if a participant makes a direct rollover (see Q 34:17) of a distribution from a terminated retirement plan to another plan of the same employer, the amount rolled over will be counted in the recipient plan's top-heavy determination because it is a related rollover. However, IRS representatives have also opined that if a participant rolls over a distribution from a terminated retirement plan to an IRA and later rolls over the IRA assets into another plan of the same employer (see Q 34:38), the amount rolled over will *not* be counted in the recipient plan's top-heavy determination because it is an unrelated rollover.

Q 26:19   How are employee contributions treated for purposes of determining whether a qualified retirement plan is top-heavy?

For purposes of determining the present value of accumulated accrued benefits under a defined benefit plan and the sum of the account balances under a defined contribution plan, benefits derived from both employer contributions and employee contributions (whether mandatory or voluntary) are taken into account. However, accumulated deductible employee contributions (see Q 6:40) under a qualified retirement plan are disregarded. [Treas. Reg. § 1.416-1, Q T-28]

Q 26:20   When is the determination date?

The date on which a qualified retirement plan is determined to be top-heavy is called the determination date. The determination date for a new retirement plan is the last day of the first plan year; for an existing plan, it is the last day of the preceding plan year. [I.R.C. § 416(g)(4)(C); Treas. Reg. § 1.416-1, Q T-22]

Example. Charles Corporation established a calendar-year defined contribution plan on January 1, 2011. On December 31, 2011 (the last day of the first plan year), the accounts of the key employees exceed 60 percent of all employees' accounts under the plan. For 2011, the plan is top-heavy. The plan will also be top-heavy for the 2012 plan year because the determination date for the 2012 plan year is the last day of the 2011 plan year.

According to IRS representatives, if an employer maintains a retirement plan that is top-heavy and later establishes a new retirement plan, the new plan is not considered a new plan for purposes of the first year determination date rule. Therefore, top-heavy minimum benefits or contributions (see Qs 26:35, 26:41) must be provided in both plans.

Q 26:21 If the employer has more than one qualified retirement plan, when is the top-heavy determination made?

When two or more retirement plans are aggregated (see Qs 26:8, 26:9), the present value of the accrued benefits or account balances is determined separately for each plan as of each plan's determination date (see Q 26:20). The retirement plans are then aggregated by adding the results of each plan as of the determination dates that fall within the same calendar year. The combined results indicate whether or not the retirement plans are top-heavy. [Treas. Reg. § 1.416-1, Q T-23]

Example. David Corporation maintains two qualified retirement plans, Plan A and Plan B, each covering a key employee. Plan A's plan year commences July 1 and ends June 30. Plan B's plan year is the calendar year. For Plan A's plan year commencing July 1, 2010, the determination date is June 30, 2010. For Plan B's 2011 plan year, the determination date is December 31, 2010. These plans must be aggregated.

On the respective determination dates of each plan, separate calculations of the present value of the accrued benefits of all employees are made. The determination dates, June 30, 2010, and December 31, 2010, fall within the same calendar year. Accordingly, the present values of accrued benefits or account balances with respect to each of these determination dates are combined for purposes of determining whether the plans are top-heavy. If, after combining the two, the total results show that the plans are top-heavy, Plan A will be top-heavy for the plan year commencing July 1, 2010, and Plan B will be top-heavy for the 2011 calendar plan year.

Q 26:22 Are there special qualification requirements that apply to top-heavy plans?

Yes. In addition to the qualification requirements that apply to all retirement plans, a top-heavy plan must satisfy the following requirements:

1. Minimum vesting (see Q 26:30); and
2. Minimum benefits or contributions (see Qs 26:35, 26:41).

[I.R.C. § 416(a); Treas. Reg. § 1.416-1, Q T-35, Q T-36, Q T-37]

Q 26:23 Who is a key employee?

A key employee is an employee who, at any time during the plan year, is:

1. An officer (see Q 26:24) having annual compensation greater than $130,000 (subject to cost-of-living adjustments);

2. A 5 percent owner (see Q 26:26); or

3. A 1 percent owner whose annual compensation exceeds $150,000 (see Q 26:26).

The $130,000 annual compensation amount is adjusted for increases in cost of living only if the adjustment is $5,000 or greater and then is made in multiples of $5,000 (i.e., rounded down to the next-lowest multiple of $5,000). For example, an increase in the cost of living of $4,999 will result in no adjustment, and an increase of $9,999 will create an upward adjustment of $5,000. For plan years that begin in 2010, the $130,000 amount remained at $160,000. [I.R.C. § 416(i)(1)(A); IRS Notice 2009-94, 2009-2 C.B. 848]

For the five plan years that began prior to 2010, the amount was:

Plan Year Beginning in	Amount
2009	$160,000
2008	150,000
2007	145,000
2006	140,000
2005	135,000

Q 26:24 Who is an officer of the employer for top-heavy plan purposes?

The determination as to whether an employee is an officer is made on the basis of all the facts and circumstances—including, for example, the source of the employee's authority, the term for which the employee was elected or appointed, and the nature and extent of the employee's duties. As generally accepted in connection with corporations, the term "officer" means an administrative executive who is in regular and continued service. It implies continuity of service and excludes those employed for a special and single transaction, or those with only nominal administrative duties. So, for example, all the employees of a bank who have the title of vice-president or assistant vice-president are not automatically considered officers. An employee who does not have the title of an officer but has the authority of an officer is an officer for purposes of the key employee test. [Rev. Rul. 80-314, 1980-2 C.B. 152; Treas. Reg. § 1.416-1, Q T-13]

The number of employees that can be considered officers is equal to 10 percent of all employees, or three, whichever is greater. In no case, however, can the total number of officers exceed 50. Thus, if the employer has fewer than 30 employees, no more than three can be considered officers. [I.R.C. § 416(i)(1)(A); Treas. Reg. § 1.416-1, Q T-14]

For purposes of determining the number of officers taken into account, the following employees are excluded:

1. Employees who have not completed six months of service by the end of the year;

2. Employees who normally work less than 17½ hours per week during the year;

3. Employees who normally work six months or less during any year;

4. Employees who are not age 21 by the end of the year;

5. Certain nonresident aliens; and

6. Union employees if they constitute 90 percent of the employer's workforce and the retirement plan covers only non-union employees.

[I.R.C. §§ 414(q)(5), 416(i)(1)(A); Temp. Treas. Reg. § 1.414(q)-1T, Q&A-9(b)]

Q 26:25   Do any organizations other than corporations have officers?

Sole proprietorships, partnerships, unincorporated associations, trusts, and labor organizations may have officers. [Treas. Reg. § 1.416-1, Q T-15]

Q 26:26   Who is a 5 percent owner or a 1 percent owner for top-heavy plan purposes?

A 5 percent owner is a person who owns, directly or indirectly, *more than* 5 percent of the shares of stock of the corporation. A 1 percent owner is a person who owns, directly or indirectly, *more than* 1 percent of the shares of stock of the corporation. A 1 percent owner is a key employee (see Q 26:23) only if such owner's annual compensation from the employer is more than $150,000. [I.R.C. § 416(i)(1)(A)(iv)]

If the employer is not a corporation, the ownership test is applied to the person's capital or profits interest in the employer. In determining ownership percentages, each employer, whether related or unrelated (see Q 5:31), is treated as a separate entity. But for purposes of determining whether an employee has compensation of more than $150,000, compensation from each related entity is aggregated. The definition of compensation is Section 415 compensation (see Qs 6:41, 26:43. [I.R.C. §§ 416(i)(1)(B), 416(i)(1)(C); Treas. Reg. § 1.416-1, Q T-16, Q T-17, Q T-18, Q T-20, Q T-21]

For purposes of determining ownership, an individual is considered as owning the shares of stock owned by his or her spouse, children, grandchildren, and parents. In addition, shares of stock owned by a corporation, partnership, estate, or trust can be attributed to the individual, and vice versa. If the employer is not a corporation, similar principles apply. [I.R.C. §§ 318(a), 416(i)(1)(B)(iii); Treas. Reg. §§ 1.318-1–1.318-4, 1.416-1, Q T-18]

Q 26:27   Who is a non-key employee?

Any employee who is not a key employee (see Q 26:23) is a non-key employee. [I.R.C. § 416(i)(2)]

Q 26:28   Who is a former key employee?

A former key employee is an individual who, when employed by the employer, was once a key employee (see Q 26:23).

Example. Melanie, who was a 5 percent owner of Whitney Corp. in 2010, sold all of her interest in the corporation before the end of the year and retired. Even though Melanie is no longer an employee or owner, she will be treated as a former key employee in 2011 and thereafter.

Former key employees are non-key employees and are excluded entirely from the calculation in determining top-heaviness. [Treas. Reg. § 1.416-1, Q T-1(d), Q T-12]

Q 26:29   How is a beneficiary treated under the top-heavy plan rules?

For purposes of the top-heavy plan rules, the terms "key employee," "former key employee," and "non-key employee" include their beneficiaries. [I.R.C. § 416(i)(5); Treas. Reg. § 1.416-1, Q T-12]

Q 26:30   What is the minimum vesting requirement for a top-heavy plan?

A top-heavy plan must contain either a three-year vesting provision or a six-year graded vesting provision. [I.R.C. § 416(b)(1); Treas. Reg. § 1.416-1, Q V-1]

Under three-year vesting, an employee who completes at least three years of service (see Q 26:31) must be 100 percent vested. Under six-year graded vesting, an employee must become vested as determined by the following table:

Completed Years of Service	Vested Percentage
2	20
3	40
4	60
5	80
6 or more	100

Because of recent changes in the vesting requirements, the top-heavy minimum vesting rules are not as significant as they once were. Specifically, for plan years beginning after December 31, 2006, the minimum top-heavy vesting provisions are applicable to all employer contributions to defined contribution plans (see Qs 2:2, 9:4). An applicable defined benefit plan (see Q 2:23) must provide that each employee who has completed at least three years of service has a nonforfeitable right to 100 percent of the employee's accrued benefit derived from employer contributions. In the case of a plan in existence on June 29, 2005, the vesting requirements for an applicable defined benefit plan generally applies to years beginning after December 31, 2007 (see Q 9:4).

Accordingly, it appears that the top-heavy vesting rules are applicable only to defined benefit plans (see Q 2:3) other than applicable defined benefit plans. [I.R.C. §§ 411(a)(2), 411(a)(13)]

Q 26:31 Which years of service must be taken into account for minimum vesting purposes?

The rules for determining an employee's years of service for vesting under non-top-heavy plans (see chapter 9) also apply for the minimum vesting requirements under top-heavy plans. Thus, years of service completed before 1984 (the year the top-heavy rules went into effect) and years of service completed after 1983 (including years when the plan is not top-heavy) are counted for minimum vesting purposes. [I.R.C. § 416(b)(2); Treas. Reg. § 1. 416-1, Q V-2]

Q 26:32 Which benefits must be subject to the minimum top-heavy vesting requirement?

All benefits must be subject to the minimum top-heavy vesting requirement. These benefits include benefits accrued before a retirement plan becomes top-heavy. However, when a retirement plan becomes top-heavy, the accrued benefit of an employee who does not have an hour of service after the plan becomes top-heavy is not required to be subject to the minimum vesting requirement. [Treas. Reg. § 1.416-1, Q V-3]

Q 26:33 When a top-heavy plan ceases to be top-heavy, may the vesting schedule be changed?

Yes. When a top-heavy plan ceases to be top-heavy, the vesting schedule may be changed to one that would otherwise be permitted. However, in changing the vesting schedule, any portion of the benefit that was nonforfeitable before the plan ceased to be top-heavy must remain nonforfeitable, and any employee with three or more years of service must be given the option of remaining under the prior (i.e., top-heavy) vesting schedule (see Q 9:7). [I.R.C. § 411(a)(10); Treas. Reg. § 1.416-1, Q V-7]

Q 26:34 Which top-heavy vesting schedule is more favorable to the employer?

It depends on how long the employees usually stay with the employer.

Example. Rena Corporation adopted a profit sharing plan on January 1, 2010, and contributes 10 percent of each participant's compensation per year. Bob completes a year of service on January 1, 2011, and enters the plan. Bob earns $10,000 a year. Set forth below is a calculation of Bob's benefits under the six-year graded and three-year cliff vesting schedules (see Q 26:30):

Plan Year	6-Year Contribution/ Account Balance	6-Year Vesting Percentage/ Vested Benefits	3-Year Contribution/ Account Balance	3-Year Vesting Percentage/ Vested Benefits
1	0 / 0		0 / 0	
2	$1,000 / $1,000	20% / $200	$1,000 / $1,000	0% / $0
3	$1,000 / $2,000	40% / $800	$1,000 / $2,000	100% / $2,000
4	$1,000 / $3,000	60% / $1,800	$1,000 / $3,000	100% / $3,000
5	$1,000 / $4,000	80% / $3,200	$1,000 / $4,000	100% / $4,000
6	$1,000 / $5,000	100% / $5,000	$1,000 / $5,000	100% / $5,000

In plan year 2, less vested benefits are provided under the three-year cliff vesting schedule; in plan years 3, 4, and 5, less vested benefits are provided under the six-year graded vesting schedule. Thus, if employees customarily leave before completing three years of service, three-year cliff vesting is more favorable to the employer; if they leave after completing three years of service, the six-year graded schedule is more favorable to the employer. After six years of service, both schedules provide equal benefits.

As an alternative, Rena Corporation could require employees to complete two years of service to become eligible, but then employees must be 100 percent vested immediately (see Q 9:13). With a two-year service requirement and 100 percent immediate vesting, Bob's benefits would be as follows:

Plan Year	Contribution/ Account Balance	Vesting Percentage/ Vested Benefits
1	0 / 0	
2	0 / 0	
3	$1,000 / $1,000	100% / $1,000

Plan Year	Contribution/ Account Balance	Vesting Percentage/ Vested Benefits
4	$1,000 $2,000	100% $2,000
5	$1,000 $3,000	100% $3,000
6	$1,000 $4,000	100% $4,000

In plan year 2, the least vested benefits occur under three-year cliff or with the two-year service requirement; in plan years 3 and 4, the least vested benefits occur under six-year graded; in plan years 5 and 6, and in all subsequent plan years, the least vested benefits occur with the two-year service requirement. Therefore, if employees customarily leave after completing five or more years of service, the two-year service requirement will be most favorable to the employer maintaining a top-heavy plan.

Q 26:35 What is the minimum benefit requirement for a top-heavy defined benefit plan?

Under a top-heavy defined benefit plan, the accrued benefit when expressed as an annual retirement benefit (see Q 26:36) of a non-key employee (see Q 26:27) must not be less than the employee's average compensation (see Q 26:38) multiplied by the lesser of:

1. 2 percent times the number of years of service (see Q 26:39) or

2. 20 percent.

Benefits attributable to employer contributions are considered, but benefits attributable to employee contributions must be ignored.

[I.R.C. §§ 416(c)(1)(A), 416(c)(1)(B); Treas. Reg. § 1.416-1, Q M-1, Q M-2, Q M-5, Q M-6]

Q 26:36 What does annual retirement benefit mean for the minimum benefit requirement?

Annual retirement benefit means a benefit attributable to employer contributions payable annually in the form of a single life annuity (with no ancillary benefits) beginning at the retirement plan's normal retirement age (see Q 10:55). [I.R.C. § 416(c)(1)(E); Treas. Reg. § 1.416-1, Q M-2(d)]

If benefits under the defined benefit plan are payable in a form other than a straight life annuity (under a straight life annuity, payments terminate upon the death of the annuitant), the minimum benefit is adjusted downward to a benefit that is equivalent to a straight life annuity. For example, if the annuity payments under the defined benefit plan are guaranteed for a period of ten years (that is, if the participant dies within the ten-year period, payments will be made to the participant's beneficiary for the rest of the period), the minimum annual retirement benefit (see Q 26:35) is reduced by 10 percent. [Treas. Reg. § 1.416-1, Q M-3]

Q 26:37 What is the minimum benefit required if the employee receives benefits other than at normal retirement age?

If the benefit commences at a date other than at normal retirement age (see Q 10:55), the employee must receive an amount that is at least the actuarial equivalent of the minimum single life annuity benefit (see Qs 26:35, 26:36) commencing at normal retirement age. The employee may receive a lower benefit if the benefit commences before normal retirement age and must receive a higher benefit if the benefit commences after normal retirement age. [Treas. Reg. § 1.416-1, Q M-3]

Q 26:38 What does the term "participant's average compensation" mean for the minimum benefit requirement?

A participant's average compensation means the participant's total compensation (see Q 6:41) averaged over a period of no more than five consecutive years (the testing period) during which the participant had the greatest aggregate compensation from the employer. [I.R.C. §§ 415(c)(3), 416(c)(1)(D)(i); Treas. Reg. § 1.416-1, Q M-2(c), Q T-21]

A year need not be taken into account during the testing period if it ends in a plan year beginning before 1984 or begins after the close of the last plan year in which the plan was a top-heavy plan. [I.R.C. § 416(c)(1)(D)(iii); Treas. Reg. § 1.416-1, Q M-2(c)]

Q 26:39 Which years of service are taken into account in determining the minimum annual benefit under a top-heavy defined benefit plan?

A year of service generally means a year during which the employee completes 1,000 hours of service. The rules for determining years of service parallel those for calculating vesting (see Qs 9:4, 9:10–9:12). However, the following years of service are not taken into account for determining the minimum annual retirement benefit:

1. A year of service within which ends a plan year for which the defined benefit plan is not top-heavy; and
2. A year of service completed in a plan year beginning before 1984.

With respect to frozen defined benefit plans, service during a plan year in which the plan benefits no key employee (see Q 5:20) will be excluded from the determination of the minimum annual benefit.

[I.R.C. § 416(c)(1)(C); Treas. Reg. § 1.416-1, Q M-2(b)]

The minimum annual benefit under a top-heavy defined benefit plan (see Q 26:35) is the lesser of (1) 2 percent of the employee's compensation multiplied by the employee's years of service or (2) 20 percent of the employee's compensation. This determination of the employee's total years of service is important only if the total is less than ten, because if years of service equal or exceed ten, the 20 percent minimum can be used.

In one circumstance, IRS representatives opined that the top-heavy minimum accrued benefit commenced to accrue when the employee became a participant. According to the facts, a non-key employee was hired January 1, 1985, and became eligible to participate in the company's defined benefit plan on January 1, 1988. For purposes of the top-heavy rules, IRS representatives stated that the minimum accrued benefit starts to accrue when an employee becomes a participant, so that in the circumstances of the above case, the accrued benefit as of January 1, 1988 was zero.

Q 26:40 Which employees must receive a minimum benefit in a top-heavy defined benefit plan?

Each non-key employee (see Q 26:27) who is a participant and who has at least 1,000 hours of service during the year must receive a minimum benefit in a top-heavy defined benefit plan for that period. A non-key employee may not fail to receive a minimum benefit merely because the employee was not employed on a specified date (e.g., the last day of the plan year). Similarly, a non-key employee who is excluded from participation (or who accrues no benefit) because either (1) the employee's compensation is below a stated amount or (2) the employee fails to make mandatory employee contributions must nevertheless accrue a minimum benefit. [Treas. Reg. § 1.416-1, Q M-1, Q M-4]

Q 26:41 What is the minimum contribution requirement for a top-heavy defined contribution plan?

Under a top-heavy defined contribution plan, the employer's contribution for each non-key employee (see Q 26:27) must not be less than 3 percent of compensation (see Q 26:43). However, if the highest contribution percentage rate for a key employee (see Q 26:23) is less than 3 percent of compensation, the 3 percent minimum contribution rate is reduced to the rate that applies to the key employee. [I.R.C. §§ 416(c)(2)(A), 416(c)(2)(B); Treas. Reg. § 1.416-1, Q M-1, Q M-7, Q M-8, Q M-9]

> **Example.** Aviva Corporation established a calendar-year defined contribution plan (see Q 2:2) on January 1, 2010. The plan is top-heavy and contains a contribution formula of 2 percent of compensation below the taxable wage base (see Q 7:7) and 4 percent of compensation in excess of the taxable wage base. Andrea, the highest-paid key employee, earns $130,000, and the contribution on her behalf is $3,064 [(2% × $106,800) + (4% × $23,200 ($130,000 − $106,800))]. Because her contribution rate is 2.36 percent

($3,064 ÷ $130,000), Aviva Corporation has to contribute only 2.36 percent of compensation for each non-key employee.

Contributions to a 401(k) plan (see Q 27:1) deemed not top-heavy under the safe harbor exception (see Q 26:4), but that belongs to a top-heavy aggregation group (see Q 26:11), may be taken into account in determining whether any other plan in the group meets the minimum contribution requirements. [I.R.C. § 416(g)(4)(H)]

> **Example.** Sharon Corp., Marin Corp., and Taryn Corp. are members of an aggregation group. Sharon Corp.'s 401(k) plan is deemed to have satisfied the top-heavy rules because it satisfied the safe harbor 401(k) rules and the ACP test safe harbor for matching employer contributions. The defined contribution plans of Marin Corp. and Taryn Corp. do not satisfy the safe harbor requirements. The group's highest employer contribution rate for a key employee is 3.3 percent. When combined, the total of Marin Corp. and Taryn Corp. non-key employee compensation is $180,000 and the employer contributions for non-key employees equal $4,950, which results in a 2.75 percent contribution rate. Therefore, if Sharon Corp. is excluded, the aggregation group would be required to make an additional employer contribution for non-key employees. However, Sharon Corp.'s non-key employee compensation of $100,000 and its employer contributions for non-key employees of $4,100 may be added to the group's compensation and employer contributions. Thus, the group's total non-key employee compensation is $280,000 ($180,000 + $100,000) and its total employer contributions for non-key employees is $9,050 ($4,950 + $4,100), resulting in a contribution rate of 3.23 percent ($9,050 ÷ $280,000). As this exceeds the 3 percent requirement, the group does not need to make an additional contribution to the plan.

Catch-up contributions (see Q 27:52) with respect to the *current* plan year are not taken into account for top-heavy purposes. Thus, if the only contributions made for a plan year for key employees are catch-up contributions, the applicable percentage is 0 percent, and no top-heavy minimum contribution is required for the year. However, catch-up contributions for *prior* years are taken into account for top-heavy purposes. Therefore, catch-up contributions for *prior* years are included in the account balances that are used in determining whether the plan is top-heavy. [Treas. Reg. § 1.414(v)-1(d)(3)(i)]

Q 26:42   Do forfeitures affect the minimum contribution requirement?

Under the minimum contribution rules (see Q 26:41), reallocated forfeitures are considered as employer contributions. For example, if no amount is contributed by the employer under a profit sharing plan for any key employee but forfeitures are allocated to key employees, contributions may be required under the minimum contribution rules for non-key employees. [Treas. Reg. § 1.416-1, Q M-7]

Q 26:43   What does participant's compensation mean for purposes of the minimum contribution requirement?

The term "participant's compensation" means the participant's total compensation from the employer during the year (see Q 6:41)—even though compensation, as defined in the plan, may exclude certain forms of compensation (e.g., bonuses). [I.R.C. §§ 415(c)(3), 416(c)(2)(A); Treas. Reg. § 1.416-1, Q M-7, Q T-21]

Q 26:44   Which employees must receive the top-heavy defined contribution plan minimum contribution?

Those non-key employees (see Q 26:27) who are participants and have not separated from service at the end of the plan year, whether or not they have completed 1,000 hours of service, must receive the top-heavy defined contribution plan minimum contribution. A non-key employee who is excluded from participation (or who accrues no benefit) because (1) the employee declines to make mandatory contributions to the plan or (2) the employee declines to make elective contributions under a 401(k) plan (see Qs 26:46, 27:16) is considered an employee covered by the plan for purposes of the minimum contribution requirement. [Treas. Reg. § 1.416-1, Q M-10]

Q 26:45   Can Social Security benefits or contributions be used to satisfy the minimum benefit and contribution requirements?

No. A top-heavy plan cannot take benefits or contributions under Social Security into account to satisfy the minimum benefit requirement (see Q 26:35) or the minimum contribution requirement (see Q 26:41). Thus, the required minimum benefit or contribution for a non-key employee may not be eliminated or reduced by providing for permitted disparity (see Q 7:1) in the plan. [I.R.C. § 416(e); Treas. Reg. § 1.416-1, Q M-11]

Q 26:46   Can elective contributions under a 401(k) plan be used to satisfy the top-heavy minimum contribution rules?

No. Elective contributions to a 401(k) plan (see Q 27:16) on behalf of non-key employees may not be treated as employer contributions for the purpose of satisfying the top-heavy minimum contribution requirement. However, in determining the percentage at which contributions are made for the key employee with the highest percentage, elective contributions on behalf of key employees are taken into account (see Qs 26:41, 26:44, 26:47). [Treas. Reg. § 1.416-1, Q M-20]

Q 26:47   Can qualified nonelective contributions and matching contributions under a 401(k) plan be used to satisfy the top-heavy minimum contribution rules?

Qualified nonelective contributions to a 401(k) plan (see Q 27:17) may be taken into account for the purpose of satisfying the minimum top-heavy contribution requirement. Also, matching contributions to a 401(k) plan may be taken into account for the purpose of satisfying the minimum top-heavy contribution requirement (see Qs 26:41, 26:44, 26:46). [I.R.C. § 416(c)(2)(A); Treas. Reg. § 1.416-1, Q M-18, Q M-19]

The safe harbor nonelective contributions made to a safe harbor 401(k) plan (see Q 27:42) may be taken into account for the purpose of satisfying the minimum top-heavy contribution requirement, but the safe harbor matching contributions (see Q 27:43) may not be taken into account for this purpose. [IRS Notice 98-52, 1998-2 C.B. 634] A 401(k) plan that satisfies the safe harbor 401(k) rules (see Q 27:40) and satisfies the ACP test safe harbor for matching employer contributions (see Q 27:89) will be exempt from the top-heavy rules (see Q 26:4). [I.R.C. § 416(g)(4)(H)] Furthermore, if a plan that meets the safe harbor 401(k) rules is a member of a top-heavy aggregation group, matching contributions under the plan may be taken into account in determining whether any other plan in the group meets the minimum contribution requirement (see Q 26:41).

Q 26:48   Must an employer that has both a top-heavy defined benefit plan and a top-heavy defined contribution plan provide both a minimum benefit and a minimum contribution for non-key employees?

No. If a non-key employee (see Q 26:27) participates in both a top-heavy defined benefit plan and a top-heavy defined contribution plan maintained by an employer, the employer is not required to provide the non-key employee with both the minimum benefit and the minimum contribution.

There are four safe harbor rules a top-heavy plan may use in determining which minimum an employee must receive. Because the defined benefit minimums are generally more valuable, if each employee covered under both a top-heavy defined benefit plan and a top-heavy defined contribution plan receives the defined benefit minimum, receipt of that minimum will satisfy the standards. A safe harbor defined contribution minimum is provided by IRS. If the contributions and forfeitures under the defined contribution plan equal 5 percent of compensation in each year the plan is top-heavy, that minimum will also satisfy the standards.

The other two safe harbor rules are:

1. Using a floor offset under which the defined benefit minimum is provided in the defined benefit plan and is offset by the benefits provided under the defined contribution plan (see Q 2:22); and

2. Proving by use of a comparability analysis that the plans provide aggregate benefits at least equal to the defined benefit minimum.

[I.R.C. § 416(f); Treas. Reg. § 1.416-1, Q M-12, Q M-13, Q M-15; Rev. Rul. 76-259, 1976-2 C.B. 111]

Example. Alicia, a non-key employee, participates in a top-heavy money purchase pension plan that provides an annual contribution rate of 5 percent of compensation and a top-heavy defined benefit plan that provides a retirement benefit equal to 8 percent of compensation. The employer is not required to provide an additional retirement benefit for Alicia under the defined benefit plan.

Q 26:49   What is the limitation on compensation that may be taken into account under a top-heavy plan?

Only the first $200,000 (adjusted for cost-of-living increases) of an employee's compensation (see Qs 6:45, 6:46) may be taken into account, regardless of whether the plan is top-heavy. The annual compensation limit remained at $245,000 for plan years that begin in 2010. An adjustment to the annual compensation limit will be made only if it is $5,000 or greater and then is made in multiples of $5,000 (i.e., rounded down to the next lowest multiple of $5,000). For example, an increase in the cost-of-living of $4,999 will result in no adjustment, and an increase of $9,999 will create an upward adjustment of $5,000. [I.R.C. § 401(a)(17); IRS Notice 2009-94, 2009-2 C.B. 848]

For the five years prior to 2010, the compensation limits were as follows:

Year	Compensation Limit
2009	$245,000
2008	230,000
2007	225,000
2006	220,000
2005	210,000

Q 26:50   Must every qualified retirement plan incorporate the top-heavy plan requirements?

The additional rules for top-heavy plans are tax-qualification requirements. A top-heavy plan will be a qualified retirement plan, and a trust forming part of a top-heavy plan will be a qualified trust, only if the additional requirements are met. Other than governmental plans and collectively bargained plans that are not top-heavy, any retirement plan qualifies for tax-favored status only if the plan includes provisions that will automatically take effect if the plan becomes a top-heavy plan and also has provisions that will meet the additional qualification requirements for top-heavy plans. [I.R.C. § 401(a)(10)(B); Treas. Reg. § 1.416-1, Q G-1,Q T-38]

Chapter 27

401(k) Plans

Qualified plans containing cash-or-deferred arrangements, commonly known as 401(k) plans, are the most popular and widely offered employee benefit plans. This chapter describes how a 401(k) plan operates and the special qualification requirements that must be satisfied, including the special qualification requirements applicable to qualified retirement plans that provide for employer matching contributions and/or employee voluntary contributions. This chapter also discusses the 401(k) final regulations promulgated by IRS and designated Roth contributions and accounts.

Q 27:1 What is a 401(k) plan?

A 401(k) plan is a qualified profit sharing or stock bonus plan (see Qs 2:6, 2:13) that contains a cash-or-deferred arrangement (CODA; see Q 27:2). A pre-ERISA money purchase pension plan and a rural cooperative plan may also contain a CODA. [I.R.C. §§ 401(k)(1), 401(k)(6), 401(k)(7); Treas. Reg. §§ 1.401(k)-1(a)(1), 1.401(k)-6, 1.410(b)-9]

Under a CODA, an eligible employee may make a cash-or-deferred election (see Q 27:3) to have the employer make a contribution to the plan on the employee's behalf or pay an equivalent amount to the employee in cash. The amount contributed to the plan under the CODA on behalf of the employee is called an elective contribution (see Q 27:16). Subject to certain limitations (see Qs 27:18, 27:51), elective contributions are excluded from the employee's gross income for the year in which they are made and are not subject to taxation until distributed. United States resident aliens who were not green card holders were allowed to make contributions to a pension scheme in a foreign country while they were employed in the United States. The pension plan in the foreign country generally corresponded with a similar scheme in the United States for purposes of the treaty between the United States and the contracting country. The contributions that the participants made were deductible from their income for United States income tax to the extent the amounts did not exceed the elective contribution limits. So long as the taxpayers were United States residents and not United States citizens or lawful permanent residents, they could claim the benefits of the treaty and exclude benefit accruals under the foreign plan's scheme prior to receiving any distributions from the plan. [Priv. Ltr. Ruls. 200602046, 200602045]

A 401(k) plan may be a stand-alone plan (permitting elective contributions only) or may also permit other types of employer contributions and/or after-tax employee contributions. However, a 401(k) plan is the only method available under which employees may defer compensation on an elective, pretax basis to a qualified retirement plan. Technically, a 401(k) plan means a plan consisting solely of elective contributions under a CODA (i.e., a stand-alone plan); however, references in *The Pension Answer Book* to a 401(k) plan include a plan containing a CODA that also permits other types of contributions.

For years beginning before 1997, state and local governments and tax-exempt organizations were prohibited from maintaining 401(k) plans, unless the plan was established prior to May 6, 1986, in the case of a plan sponsored by a state or local government, or prior to July 2, 1986, in the case of a plan sponsored by a tax-exempt organization. This prohibition did not apply to a rural cooperative plan. For years beginning after 1996, 401(k) plans are available to tax-exempt organizations, but remain unavailable to state and local governments other than a rural cooperative plan. [I.R.C. § 401(k)(4)(B); Treas. Reg. § 1.401(k)-1(e)(4); Priv. Ltr. Ruls. 200028042, 9842064, 9638039, 9625053, 9612029, 9550030] IRS ruled that a state bar association could establish a 401(k) plan because it was not considered an instrumentality of a state or local government. [Priv. Ltr. Rul. 9749014; *see also* Priv. Ltr. Rul. 200313017] IRS also ruled that an agency of the federal government, which contracted with individuals for personnel services abroad, could establish a 401(k) plan because the agency was not considered a government employer. [Priv. Ltr. Rul. 200116050; *see also* Priv. Ltr. Rul. 200347019]

DOL has published a booklet entitled "A Look at 401(k) Plan Fees." According-ing to DOL, more and more employees are investing in their futures through 401(k) plans. Employees who participate in 401(k) plans assume responsibility for their retirement income by contributing part of their salary and, in many instances, by directing their own investments (see Q 23:14). Each 401(k) plan participant will need to consider the investment objectives, the risk and return characteristics, and the performance over time of each investment option offered by the plan in order to make sound investment decisions. Fees and expenses are one of the factors that will affect the investment returns and will impact the participant's retirement income. The information contained in this booklet answers some common questions about the fees and expenses that may be paid by a 401(k) plan. It highlights the most common fees and encourages each 401(k) plan participant to:

1. Make informed investment decisions;
2. Consider fees as one of several factors in decision making;
3. Compare all services received with the total cost; and
4. Realize that cheaper is not necessarily better.

DOL and IRS have also jointly published a booklet entitled "401(k) Plans for Small Businesses." IRS has posted on its website "401(k) Plan Potential Mistakes," a document that provides tips on how to identify, correct, and avoid 11 common errors associated with 401(k) plans. The document lists in table format the potential mistakes, and a summary of how to identify, correct, and avoid each mistake.

On December 29, 2004, IRS issued comprehensive final regulations setting forth the requirements (including the nondiscrimination requirements) for CODAs under Section 401(k) and for matching contributions and employee contributions under Section 401(m). The final regulations apply for plan years beginning on or after January 1, 2006. However, plan sponsors were permitted to apply the final regulations to any plan year that ended after December 29, 2004, provided the plan applied all the rules of the final regulations, to the extent applicable, for that plan year and all subsequent plan years. IRS cautioned, however, that a decision to apply the regulations in the middle of a plan year could be successfully implemented only if the plan was operated in accordance with the regulations for that year. [Treas. Reg. § 1.401(k)-1(g); Preamble to final regulations]

IRS also issued final regulations concerning automatic contribution arrangements and permissible withdrawals from such arrangements (see Qs 27:5–27:7).

For a discussion of designated Roth contributions and accounts, see Qs 27:96–27:110.

Effective for plan years beginning on or after January 1, 2010, employers with 500 or fewer employees may establish a combined defined benefit/401(k) plan. [I.R.C. § 414(x); ERISA § 210(e)] See Q 27:67 for details.

IRS will be sending compliance questionnaires to approximately 1,200 401(k) plan sponsors. Data gathered from the results of this compliance check will help IRS with guidance, compliance, and determining where to focus outreach efforts regarding 401(k) plans. The compliance check can be completed on-line, at IRS's website (http://www.irs.gov), after receiving the paper work notice to complete the questionnaire. [*Retirement News for Employers*, Spring 2010]

Q 27:2   What is a cash-or-deferred arrangement (CODA)?

A plan, other than a profit sharing (see Q 2:6), stock bonus (see Q 2:13), pre-ERISA money purchase pension, or rural cooperative plan, does not satisfy the qualification requirements (see Q 4:1) if the plan includes a CODA; but a profit sharing, stock bonus, pre-ERISA money purchase, or rural cooperative plan does not fail to satisfy the qualification requirements merely because the plan includes a CODA. A CODA is part of a plan if any contributions to the plan, or accruals or other benefits under the plan, are made or provided pursuant to the CODA. [I.R.C. §§ 401(k)(1), 401(k)(6), 401(k)(7); Treas. Reg. §§ 1.401(k)-1(a)(1), 1.401(k)-6]

A CODA is an arrangement under which an eligible employee may make a cash-or-deferred election (see Q 27:3) with respect to contributions to, or

accruals or other benefits under, a plan that is intended to satisfy the qualification requirements. [Treas. Reg. § 1.401(k)-1(a)(2)(i)] However, a CODA does
not include an arrangement under which amounts contributed under a plan at
an employee's election are designated or treated at the time of contribution as
after-tax employee contributions (e.g., by treating the contributions as taxable
income subject to applicable withholding requirements), but a designated Roth
contribution (see Q 27:96) is not treated as an after-tax contribution for this
purpose. A contribution can be an after-tax employee contribution even if the
employee's election to make after-tax employee contributions is made before
the amounts subject to the election are currently available (see Q 27:3) to the
employee. [Treas. Reg. § 1.401(k)-1(a)(2)(ii)] A CODA does not include an
arrangement under an employee stock ownership plan (ESOP; see Q 28:1) under
which dividends are either distributed or invested pursuant to an election made
by participants or their beneficiaries (see Q 28:14). [Treas. Reg. § 1.401(k)-
1(a)(2)(iii)]

The extent to which elective contributions (see Q 27:16) constitute plan
assets is determined in accordance with regulations and rulings issued by DOL
(see Q 23:32). [Treas. Reg. § 1.401(k)-1(a)(2)(iv)]

Q 27:3 What is a cash-or-deferred election?

A cash-or-deferred election is any direct or indirect election (or modification
of an earlier election) by an employee to have the employer either:

1. Provide an amount to the employee in the form of cash (or some other
   taxable benefit) that is not currently available, or
2. Contribute an amount to a trust, or provide an accrual or other benefit,
   under a plan deferring the receipt of compensation.

[I.R.C. § 401(k)(2)(A); Treas. Reg. §§ 1.401(k)-1(a)(3)(i), 1.401(k)-6]

For purposes of determining whether an election is a cash-or-deferred
election, it is irrelevant whether the default that applies in the absence of an
affirmative election is described in item 1 or 2 above. [Treas. Reg. § 1.401(k)-
1(a)(3)(ii)] See Q 27:5 for a discussion of automatic enrollment.

A cash-or-deferred election can be made only with respect to an amount that
is not currently available to the employee on the date of the election. Further, a
cash-or-deferred election can be made only with respect to amounts that would
(but for the cash-or-deferred election) become currently available after the later
of the date on which the employer adopts the CODA (see Q 27:2) or the date on
which the arrangement first becomes effective. A contribution is made pursuant
to a cash-or-deferred election only if the contribution is made after the election
is made. [Treas. Reg. §§ 1.401(k)-1(a)(3)(iii)(A), 1.401(k)-1(a)(3)(iii)(B)]

Contributions are made pursuant to a cash-or-deferred election only if the
contributions are made after the employee's performance of service with respect
to which the contributions are made (or when the cash or other taxable benefit
would be currently available, if earlier). The timing of contributions will not be

treated as failing to satisfy this requirement merely because contributions for a pay period are occasionally made before the services with respect to that pay period are performed, provided the contributions are made early in order to accommodate bona fide administrative considerations (e.g., the temporary absence of the bookkeeper with responsibility to transmit contributions to the plan) and are not paid early with a principal purpose of accelerating deductions. [Treas. Reg. § 1.401(k)-1(a)(3)(iii)(C)]

Cash or another taxable benefit is currently available to the employee if it has been paid to the employee or if the employee is able currently to receive the cash or other taxable benefit at the employee's discretion. An amount is not currently available to an employee if there is a significant limitation or restriction on the employee's right to receive the amount currently. Similarly, an amount is not currently available as of a date if the employee may under no circumstances receive the amount before a particular time in the future. The determination of whether an amount is currently available to an employee does not depend on whether it has been constructively received by the employee for income tax purposes. [Treas. Reg. § 1.401(k)-1(a)(3)(iv)] If an employee has received compensation from the employer, the employee's return of the compensation to the employer followed by the employer's contribution of the returned compensation to the employer's plan does not constitute a cash-or-deferred election. IRS representatives have opined that, if an employee receives tip income directly from the employer's customers, the employee cannot give the tip monies to the employer and have the tip income deferred and contributed to the employer's 401(k) plan; once received by the employee, it is too late to defer the tip income. With respect to severance pay and accumulated vacation pay, IRS representatives have opined that an elective contribution can be made only by an active employee. Consequently, if such payments are available prior to termination of employment, a participant can make a cash-or-deferred election if the plan so permits; but, if the participant has terminated employment and such payments are thereafter made, the election cannot be made.

IRS ruled that an employer's contribution of an employee's unused vacation pay to its 401(k) plan was not made under a cash-or-deferred election but constituted a nonelective contribution by the employer (see Q 27:17). As a nonelective contribution, IRS concluded that the contributed unused vacation pay was not subject to payroll taxes (see Q 27:71). The employer's vacation policy was "use it or lose it"; if an employee did not use all accrued vacation by year-end, it was forfeited. Had unused vacation not been forfeited and had the employee had the option to receive compensatory pay, the contribution would have been an elective contribution (see Q 27:16) subject to payroll taxes. [Priv. Ltr. Ruls. 200311043, 199940043, 9635002] IRS similarly ruled that, under a program whereby an employee could exchange up to five days of unused sick leave for the employer's contribution to a 401(k) plan, the contribution constituted a nonelective employer contribution and not a contribution made pursuant to a salary reduction agreement. [Priv. Ltr. Rul. 200247050] IRS also ruled that defined benefit plan (see Q 2:3) participants' choice to make an election to cease future participation in the plan and to become eligible to receive employer contributions in a second plan was not a cash-or-deferred election because there was no reduction in their compensation. [Priv. Ltr. Rul. 200213029] However, IRS did conclude that contributions by an employer of excess funds from its disability plan to its 401(k) plan were pursuant to a cash-or-deferred election because the employees had the option of receiving the excess funds in cash. [Priv. Ltr. Rul. 200149036] An employer proposed to amend its 401(k) plan to allow participants to redirect their contributions to a vacation and holiday fund into the plan as elective contributions. The proposed amendment would make amounts directed into the vacation fund unavailable until six months after they were contributed to the fund. Because a plan is qualified only if the arrangement provides that the amount each eligible employee may defer as an elective contribution is available to the employee in cash and the amounts to be deferred would not be available in cash to the employee, IRS ruled that the proposed amendment would violate the cash availability requirement and that the plan would, therefore, lose its qualified status. [Treas. Reg. § 1.401(k)-1(e)(2)(i); Priv. Ltr. Rul. 200350019]

See Q 27:4 for the latest developments concerning contributions to a plan of the dollar equivalent of a participant's unpaid time off.

A cash-or-deferred election does not include a one-time irrevocable election made no later than the employee's first becoming eligible under the plan or certain other plans or arrangements of the employer (whether or not such other plan or arrangement has terminated) to have contributions equal to a specified amount or percentage of the employee's compensation (including no amount of compensation) made by the employer on the employee's behalf to the plan and a specified amount or percentage of the employee's compensation (including no amount of compensation) divided among all other plans or arrangements of the employer (including plans or arrangements not yet established) for the duration of the employee's employment with the employer, or in the case of a defined benefit plan (see Q 2:3) to receive accruals or other benefits (including no benefits) under such plans. Thus, for example, employer contributions made pursuant to a one-time irrevocable election described in this paragraph are not treated as having been made pursuant to a cash-or-deferred election and are not includible in an employee's gross income. In the case of an irrevocable election made on or before December 23, 1994:

1. The election does not fail to be treated as a one-time irrevocable election merely because an employee was previously eligible under another plan of the employer (whether or not such other plan has terminated), and

2. In the case of a plan in which partners may participate, the election does not fail to be treated as a one-time irrevocable election merely because the election was made after commencement of employment or after the employee's first becoming eligible under any plan of the employer, provided that the election was made before the first day of the first plan year beginning after December 31, 1988, or, if later, March 31, 1989. [I.R.C. § 219(g)(5)(A); Treas. Reg. §§ 1.401(k)-1(a)(3)(v), 1.402(a)-(1)(d)]

An amount generally is includible in an employee's gross income for the taxable year in which the employee actually or constructively receives the amount; and, generally, an employee is treated as having received an amount that is contributed to a qualified retirement plan pursuant to the employee's cash-or-deferred election, even if the election to defer is made before the year in which the amount is earned or before the amount is currently available. However, contributions made by an employer on behalf of an employee to a qualified CODA (see Q 27:9) are not treated as distributed or made available to the employee or as contributions made to the plan by the employee merely because the arrangement includes provisions under which the employee has an election as to whether the contribution will be made to the plan or received by the employee in cash. [I.R.C. § 402(e)(3); Treas. Reg. §§ 1.401(k)-1(a)(3)(vi), 1.402(a)-1(d)]

Example 1. An employer maintains a profit sharing plan under which each eligible employee has an election to defer an annual bonus payable on January 30 each year. The bonus equals 10 percent of compensation during the previous calendar year. Deferred amounts are not treated as after-tax employee contributions. The bonus is currently available on January 30. An election made prior to January 30 to defer all or part of the bonus is a cash-or-deferred election, and the bonus deferral arrangement is a CODA.

Example 2. An employer maintains a profit sharing plan that provides for discretionary profit sharing contributions and under which each eligible employee may elect to reduce compensation by up to 10 percent and to have the employer contribute such amount to the plan. The employer pays each employee every two weeks for services during the immediately preceding two weeks. The employee's election to defer compensation for a payroll period must be made prior to the date the amount would otherwise be paid. The employer contributes to the plan the amount of compensation that each employee elected to defer, at the time it would otherwise be paid to the employee, and does not treat the contribution as an after-tax employee contribution. The election is a cash-or-deferred election, and the contributions are elective contributions.

Example 3. The facts are the same as in Example 2, except that the employer makes a $10,000 contribution on January 31 of the plan year that is in addition to the contributions that satisfy the employer's obligation to make contributions with respect to cash-or-deferred elections for prior payroll periods. Employee A makes an election on February 15 to defer $2,000 from compensation that is not currently available, and the employer reduces the employee's compensation to reflect the election. None of the additional $10,000 contributed January 31 is a contribution made pursuant to Employee A's cash-or-deferred election, because the contribution was made before the election was made. Accordingly, the employer must make an additional contribution of $2,000 in order to satisfy its obligation to contribute an amount to the plan pursuant to Employee A's election. The $10,000 contribution may be allocated under the plan terms providing for discretionary profit sharing contributions.

Example 4. The facts are the same as in Example 3, except that Employee A had an outstanding election to defer $500 from each payroll period's compensation. The $10,000 additional payment that is contributed early is not made early in order to accommodate bona fide administrative considerations. None of the additional $10,000 contributed January 31 is a contribution made pursuant to Employee A's cash-or-deferred election for future payroll periods, because the contribution was made before the earlier of Employee A's performance of services to which the contribution is attributable or when the compensation would be currently available. Furthermore, the exception for early contributions does not apply. Accordingly, the employer must make an additional contribution of $500 per payroll period in order to satisfy its obligation to contribute an amount to the plan pursuant to Employee A's election. The $10,000 contribution may be allocated under the plan terms providing for discretionary profit sharing contributions.

Example 5. Employer B establishes a money purchase pension plan (see Q 2:4) in 1986. This is the first qualified retirement plan established by Employer B. All salaried employees are eligible to participate under the plan. Hourly-paid employees are not eligible to participate under the plan. In 2000, Employer B establishes a profit sharing plan under which all employees (both salaried and hourly) are eligible. Employer B permits all employees on the effective date of the profit sharing plan to make a one-time irrevocable election to have Employer B contribute 5 percent of compensation on their behalf to the plan and make no other contribution to any other plan of Employer B (including plans not yet established) for the duration of the employee's employment with Employer B, and have their salaries reduced by 5 percent. The election provided under the profit sharing plan is not a one-time irrevocable election with respect to the salaried employees of Employer B who, before becoming eligible to participate under the profit sharing plan, became eligible to participate under the money purchase pension plan. The election under the profit sharing plan is a one-time irrevocable election with respect to the hourly employees because they were not previously eligible to participate under another plan of the employer.

IRS approved an arrangement under which a highly compensated employee (HCE; see Q 3:3) may defer compensation under a nonqualified plan (see Qs 1:11–1:13) and retain the amounts in that plan until the employer performs the actual deferral percentage (ADP) test (see Q 27:18) and the actual contribution percentage (ACP) test (see Q 27:77) to determine the maximum amount of elective contributions that can be made for that plan year under the employer's qualified 401(k) plan. Once the employer determines the maximum amount of elective contributions that can be made for the plan year, an appropriate amount of funds will be transferred to the qualified 401(k) plan from the nonqualified plan so that the maximum amount allowable can be deferred. IRS also ruled that the elective contributions are determined for the year made, not the year in which they are transferred. [Priv. Ltr. Ruls. 200116046, 200012083, 199924067, 9807027, 9752018, 9701057, 9530038]

USERRA (see Q 1:16) provides that any qualified retirement plan contribution that is contingent upon the making of contributions or deferrals by the employee is due the reemployed person only if the employee makes up the missed contributions or deferrals. A makeup of employee contributions or deferrals may be contributed by the employee over a period of time equal to three times the period of absence due to military service, but not to exceed five years.

IRS explained how to correct an employer's failure to execute an employee's election to defer amounts to a 401(k) plan. The problem can be rectified by making a qualified nonelective contribution (QNEC; see Q 27:17) to the plan on behalf of the employee, and the error can be fixed through the Employee Plans Compliance Resolution System (EPCRS; see Q 19:2). The remedy requires the employer to make a corrective contribution of 50 percent of the missed deferral (adjusted for earnings) on behalf of the affected employee. The employee is fully vested (see Q 9:1) in those contributions, and the contributions are subject to the same withdrawal restrictions (see Q 27:14) that apply to elective deferrals. Before correcting for the exclusion, however, the plan must evaluate whether, in the event that the employee had made the missed deferral, it would still pass the applicable ADP test. The ADP test should be corrected according to the plan's terms before implementing any corrective contribution on behalf of the employee. In addition, the missed deferral amount should be reduced, if necessary, to ensure that the employee's elective deferrals (the sum of deferrals actually made and the missed deferrals, for which a corrective contribution may be required) comply with all other applicable plan and legal limits.

In the following examples, the employees are nonhighly compensated employees (NHCEs; see Q 3:12).

Example 1. Sandy's elective deferral election at the start of 2007 was never processed by the employer's payroll system. As a result, Sandy received taxable compensation amounts that should have been contributed to the plan during the first six months of the year. The facts in this example include: (1) the plan's ADP for NHCEs of 5 percent; (2) Sandy's election form agreeing to a deferral of 10 percent of pay; and (3) her compensation of $20,000 for the six months that no deferrals were made. Assuming that the plan passes the ADP test and that no changes must be made to the missed deferral amounts on account of plan or legal limits, the amount of the corrective contribution the employer must make on Sandy's behalf is $1,000 [50% of her missed deferral amount (10% × $20,000)].

Example 2. Harvey elected to defer 5 percent of his compensation in 2007. The plan includes bonuses in the definition of compensation that is used for an employee making elective contributions. Harvey was able to make deferrals on his base compensation, but the payroll system overlooked his bonus. The facts here entail: (1) an ADP of 3 percent; (2) Harvey's base compensation of $19,000; and (3) his bonus of $2,000. Assuming that the plan passes the ADP test and that no changes must be made to the missed deferral amounts on account of plan or legal limits, the corrective contribution required on behalf of Harvey is $50 [50% of $100 (5% × $2,000)].

The correction applies only to missed deferrals. The corrective contribution also must be adjusted for earnings from the date that the elective deferrals should have been made through the date of the corrective contribution. IRS recommended that employers (1) establish systems to ensure that employees are provided the opportunity to make deferrals/after-tax contributions to the plan according to the plan's terms and (2) work to ensure that third party plan administrators have sufficient understanding of the plan's terms to operate the plan accordingly. [*Retirement News for Employers*, Fall 2007]

Q 27:4 Can the dollar equivalent of unused paid time off be contributed to a qualified retirement plan?

Two revenue rulings issued by IRS address issues relating to the contribution to a plan of the dollar equivalent of unused paid time off. The issues raised in the first ruling are discussed below.

ISSUES

1. Do the amendments described below to an existing profit sharing plan requiring or permitting certain annual contributions of the dollar equivalent of unused paid time off cause the plan to fail to meet the qualification requirements (see Q 4:1) and the requirements, if applicable, relating to 401(k) plans?

2. When is a participant required to recognize gross income with respect to the contributions to the profit sharing plan and payments to the participant as described below?

FACTS

For purposes of each situation below, it is assumed that the employer is a C corporation; that each participant is an individual who accounts for gross income under the cash receipts and disbursements method of accounting and has a calendar year taxable year; that all employees of the employer are eligible to participate in the paid time off plan (PTO plan) on substantially the same terms and conditions; that, prior to its amendment, the PTO plan qualifies as a bona fide sick and vacation leave plan; that all payments for paid time off (whether paid for used or unused time off) are made from the general assets of the employer; and that the employer has two-week pay periods. For this purpose, a paid time off plan refers to a sick and vacation leave plan under which a participant may take paid leave without regard to whether the leave is due to illness or incapacity.

Situation 1: Company Z maintains the Company Z PTO Plan (Z PTO Plan), under which all participants are granted up to 240 hours of paid time off each January 1 (prorated for new hires commencing employment during the calendar year), with the number of hours depending solely on the participant's number of years of service. For this purpose, salaried employees are treated as working eight hours per work day. Under the Z PTO Plan, no unused paid time off hours remaining as of the close of business on December 31 may be carried over to the following year.

Company Z also maintains the Company Z Profit Sharing Plan (Z Profit Sharing Plan). The Z Profit Sharing Plan includes a CODA (see Q 27:2) thatprovides for elective contributions (see Q 27:14) and that does not provide for catch-up contributions (see Q 27:50). The Z Profit Sharing Plan has a calendar year plan year and limitation year (see Q 6:58).

In December 2008, Company Z amended the Z Profit Sharing Plan and the Z PTO Plan, effective January 1, 2009, to provide that (1) the dollar equivalent of any unused paid time off as of the close of business on December 31 is forfeited under the Z PTO Plan and the dollar equivalent of the amount forfeited is contributed to the Z Profit Sharing Plan and allocated to the participant's account as of December 31, to the extent the contribution (in combination with prior annual additions) does not exceed the applicable limitations (see Q 6:34), and (2) the dollar equivalent of any remaining paid time off is paid to the employee by February 28 of the following year. Under the Z Profit Sharing Plan, the amounts attributable to paid time off are in addition to other contributions under the plan and are treated as nonelective contributions (see Q 27:15). For these purposes, the dollar equivalent of the unused paid time off is determined as the number of hours of unused paid time off multiplied by the participant's hourly rate of compensation as of December 31 of that year (determined for salaried employees by treating the employee as working eight hours per work day).

A is an employee of Company Z who participates in the Z PTO Plan and the Z Profit Sharing Plan. As of the close of business on December 31, 2009, A has 20 hours of unused paid time off and earns $25 per hour; and, therefore, the dollar equivalent of A's unused paid time off is $500. Because of the application of the annual addition limitations, Company Z may contribute only $400 of unused paid time off to the Z Profit Sharing Plan for allocation to A's account in the 2009 limitation year (in combination with prior annual additions).

Company Z contributes $400 to the Z Profit Sharing Plan on behalf of A on February 28, 2010, and allocates this amount to A's account under the Z Profit Sharing Plan as of December 31, 2009. Company Z pays A the remaining $100 in cash on February 28, 2010.

Situation 2: Company Y maintains the Company Y PTO Plan (Y PTO Plan), under which participants ratably accrue up to 240 hours of paid time off each calendar year on a pay-period basis beginning on January 1 and at the end of the year may carry over to the following year an amount of unused paid time off not to exceed a specified number of hours (the carryover limit). For this purpose, salaried employees are treated as working eight hours per work day. The dollar equivalent of any unused paid time off for a year in excess of the carryover limit is paid to the participant by February 28 of the following year.

Company Y also maintains the Company Y Section 401(k) Plan (Y 401(k) Plan). The Y 401(k) Plan includes a CODA that provides for elective contributions and that does not provide for catch-up contributions. The Y 401(k) Plan has a calendar year plan year and limitation year.

In December 2008, Company Y amended the Y 401(k) Plan and the Y PTO Plan, effective January 1, 2009, to provide that a participant may elect to reduce all or part of the dollar equivalent of any unused paid time off that may not be carried over to the following year and have that amount contributed by Company Y to the Y 401(k) Plan and allocated to the participant's account as of the beginning of the third pay period of the following year, to the extent that the contribution (in combination with prior annual additions) does not exceed the applicable limitations and to the extent that the contributions (in combination with prior elective deferrals) do not exceed the applicable limitation (see Q 27:49). Under the terms of the Y 401(k) Plan, contributions of the dollar equivalent of paid time off are in addition to other contributions under the Y 401(k) Plan and are treated as elective contributions (for example, the same distribution restrictions apply; see Q 27:14). The dollar equivalent of any unused paid time off that is not contributed to the Y 401(k) Plan under the terms of the amended Y PTO Plan is paid to the participant by February 28 of the following year. For these purposes, the dollar equivalent of the unused paid time off is determined as the number of hours of unused paid time off multiplied by the participant's hourly rate of compensation as of December 31 of the initial year (determined for salaried employees by treating the employee as working eight hours per work day).

B is an employee of Company Y who participates in the Y PTO Plan and the Y 401(k) Plan. As of the close of business on December 31, 2009, B has 15 hours of unused paid time off in excess of the carryover limit and earns $30 per hour, so the dollar equivalent of B's unused paid time off in excess of the carryover limit is $450.

Pursuant to a valid and timely election, B elects to have 60 percent of the dollar equivalent of the unused paid time off in excess of the carryover limit, or $270, contributed to the Y 401(k) Plan, the contribution of which would not cause the plan to exceed the elective deferral or annual addition limitations for the applicable year. On February 1, 2010, Company Y contributes $270 to the Y 401(k) Plan and allocates $270 to B's account under the plan as of February 1, 2010. Under the terms of the Y 401(k) Plan, this amount is treated as a contribution for the 2010 plan year. Company Y pays B the remaining $180 on February 1, 2010.

ANALYSIS

Situation 1: The amendment of the Z Profit Sharing Plan to require certain contributions of the dollar equivalent of unused paid time off to the Z Profit Sharing Plan does not cause the Z Profit Sharing Plan to fail to meet the qualification requirements, provided that the contributions made pursuant to the arrangement satisfy the nondiscrimination requirements (see Q 4:9), in combination with other contributions and forfeitures allocated for the year. Because A is not provided a right to elect a payment of the dollar equivalent of the unused paid time off in lieu of a plan contribution, Company Z's contribution of $400 to the Z Profit Sharing Plan is not an elective contribution that is made pursuant to a cash-or-deferred election (see Q 27:3). Rather,

Company Z's contribution to the Z Profit Sharing Plan is a nonelective employer contribution.

The amount contributed and allocated for each participant will vary based on the amount of the participant's unused paid time off. Thus, contributions for unused paid time off are likely to preclude a plan from satisfying a design-based safe harbor (see Q 4:11). Therefore, testing based on the contributions made for individual participants generally will be required.

The contributions made pursuant to the arrangement must also not exceed the annual addition limitations (in combination with prior annual additions). Because the contribution of $400 on behalf of A was allocated to A's account as of December 31, 2009, and made February 28, 2010 (before the end of the 30-day period following the deadline for Company Z to file its income tax return), it is subject to the annual addition limitations applicable for the 2009 limitation year (see Q 6:35) and is taken into account for nondiscrimination purposes for the 2009 plan year. Under the facts presented, the contribution of $400 does not cause the plan to exceed the annual addition limitations for 2009.

If the nondiscrimination requirements are met, the amount contributed will be includible in A's gross income only when distributed to A. Like any other distribution from the Z Profit Sharing Plan, the distribution of amounts attributable to the dollar equivalent of the unused paid time off is subject to an additional 10 percent tax on early distributions (see Q 16:1) unless the distribution satisfies one of the exceptions (see Q 16:3), such as being made on or after the date on which the participant attains age 59½ or after the participant separates from service after attainment of age 55.

Under the Z PTO Plan as amended, the dollar equivalent of unused paid time off is not paid, set apart, or otherwise made available so that A may draw on it either (1) during the 2009 calendar year or (2) upon conversion in 2009 to a contribution to a qualified retirement plan or cash payment in 2010. Therefore, under the doctrine of constructive receipt, such amount is not includible in A's gross income in 2009. In addition, the amendment to the Z PTO Plan and the operation of the plan in accordance with the terms of the amendment do not cause the Z PTO Plan to fail to qualify as a bona fide sick and vacation leave plan. The $100 payment is includible in A's gross income in 2010, the taxable year in which it is paid to A.

Situation 2: The amendment of the Y 401(k) Plan to permit certain contributions of the dollar equivalent of unused paid time off to the Y 401(k) Plan does not cause the Y 401(k) Plan to fail to meet the requirements applicable to 401(k) plans, provided that the contributions (taking into account other contributions, prior deferrals, and prior annual additions, as applicable) satisfy the nondiscrimination requirements applicable to 401(k) plans and the applicable limitations on elective deferrals and the annual addition.

Because B is provided a right to elect either a payment of cash or a plan contribution for the dollar equivalent of unused paid time off that may not be carried over to the subsequent year, Company Y's contribution of $270 to the Y

401(k) Plan and allocation to B's account under the plan is an elective contribution. Because the contribution is made on February 1, 2010 and is not treated as allocated for 2009, it is taken into consideration for the nondiscrimination requirements applicable to 401(k) plans and the limitations on elective deferrals and the annual addition for 2010.

Under the facts presented, the allocation of $270 would not cause the Y 401(k) Plan to exceed the annual addition limitations for the 2010 limitation year. Although the dollar equivalent of the unused paid time off was made available to B in 2010, the $270 is not treated as made available to B if the amount was contributed to the plan as part of a CODA. If the requirements applicable to 401(k) plans and elective deferrals are met, the contribution will have been made pursuant to a CODA and will be includible in B's gross income only when distributed to B. Like any other distribution from the Y 401(k) Plan, the distribution of amounts attributable to the dollar equivalent of the unused paid time off is subject to an additional 10 percent penalty tax unless the distribution satisfies one of the exceptions.

Under the Y PTO Plan, as amended, the dollar equivalent of unused paid time off is not paid, set apart, or otherwise made available so that B may draw on it either (1) during the 2009 calendar year or (2) upon conversion in 2009 to a contribution to a qualified retirement plan or cash payment in 2010. Therefore, under the doctrine of constructive receipt, such amount is not includible in B's gross income in 2009. In addition, the amendment to the Y PTO Plan and the operation of the plan in accordance with the terms of the amendment do not cause the Y PTO Plan to fail to qualify as a bona fide sick and vacation leave plan. The $180 payment is includible in B's gross income in 2010, the taxable year in which it is paid to B.

HOLDING

1. Under the facts presented, the amendments requiring or permitting certain contributions of the dollar equivalent of unused paid time off to a profit sharing plan do not cause the plan to fail to meet the qualification requirements, provided that the contributions satisfy the applicable requirements relating to nondiscrimination and annual additions and, where applicable, relating to 401(k) plans and elective deferrals.

2. Under the facts presented, assuming the applicable qualification requirements are satisfied, a participant does not include in gross income contributions of the dollar equivalent of unused paid time off to the profit sharing plan until distributions are made to the participant from the plan and does not include in gross income an amount paid for the dollar equivalent of unused paid time off that is not contributed to the profit sharing plan until the taxable year in which the amount is paid to the participant.

[Rev. Rul. 2009-31, 2009-2 C.B. 395]

The same issues are raised in the second ruling, but in the context of contributions made at a participant's termination of employment.

ISSUES

1. Do the amendments described below to an existing profit sharing plan requiring or permitting certain contributions to the plan of the dollar equivalent of unused paid time off at a participant's termination of employment cause the plan to fail to meet the qualification requirements and the requirements, if applicable, relating to 401(k) plans?

2. When is a participant required to recognize gross income with respect to the contributions to the profit sharing plan and payments to the participant as described below?

FACTS

For purposes of each situation below, it is assumed that the employer is a C corporation; that each participant is an individual who accounts for gross income under the cash receipts and disbursements method of accounting and has a calendar year taxable year; that all employees of the employer are eligible to participate in the paid time off plan (the PTO plan) on substantially the same terms and conditions; that, prior to its amendment, the PTO plan qualifies as a bona fide sick and vacation leave plan; that payments under the PTO plan for unused paid time off constitute payment for unused accrued bona fide sick, vacation, or other leave; that all payments for paid time off (whether paid for used or unused time off) are made from the general assets of the employer; and that the employer has two-week pay periods. For this purpose, a paid time off plan refers to a sick and vacation pay or leave plan under which a participant may take paid leave without regard to whether the leave is due to illness or incapacity.

Situation 1: Company X maintains the Company X PTO Plan (X PTO Plan), under which all participants are granted up to 240 hours of paid time off each January 1 (prorated for new hires commencing employment during the calendar year), with the number of hours depending solely on the participant's number of years of service. For this purpose, salaried employees are treated as working eight hours per work day. Under the X PTO Plan, a participant at the end of the year may carry over to the following year an amount of unused paid time off not to exceed a specified number of hours (the carryover limit), and any hours of unused paid time off in excess of the carryover limit are forfeited. If a participant terminates employment, the dollar equivalent of any hours of unused paid time off remaining at the termination of employment are paid to the terminated participant within 60 days after the termination of employment, with the dollar equivalent determined as the number of hours of unused paid time off multiplied by the terminated participant's hourly rate of compensation for the pay period during which the participant terminates employment (determined for salaried employees by treating the employee as working eight hours per work day).

Company X also maintains the Company X Profit Sharing Plan (X Profit Sharing Plan). The X Profit Sharing Plan includes a CODA that provides for elective contributions and that does not provide for catch-up contributions. The

X Profit Sharing Plan has a calendar year plan year and limitation year. The X Profit Sharing Plan provides that amounts for unused paid time off paid by the later of two-and-one-half months after termination of employment with Company X or the end of the limitation year that includes the date of the severance from employment are treated as compensation under the plan for purposes of the annual addition limitation, to the extent permissible. The X Profit Sharing Plan provides that Section 415 compensation (see Q 6:41) is determined using only amounts actually paid during the limitation year.

In December 2008, Company X amended the X Profit Sharing Plan and the X PTO Plan, effective January 1, 2009, to provide that the dollar equivalent of any unused paid time off at the time of a participant's termination of employment is forfeited under the X PTO Plan and is contributed to the X Profit Sharing Plan and allocated to the participant's account as of the first day of the second pay period beginning immediately after the participant's termination of employment, to the extent the contribution (in combination with prior annual additions) does not exceed the applicable limitations. Under the X Profit Sharing Plan, contributions of the dollar equivalent of paid time off are in addition to other contributions under the plan and are treated as nonelective contributions. Under the terms of the X PTO Plan, the dollar equivalent of any unused paid time off that is not contributed to the X Profit Sharing Plan is paid to the terminated participant within 60 days after the termination of employment. For these purposes, the dollar equivalent of the unused paid time off is determined as the number of hours of unused paid time off multiplied by the terminated participant's hourly rate of compensation for the pay period during which the participant terminates employment (determined for salaried employees by treating the employee as working eight hours per work day).

C is an employee of Company X who participates in the X PTO Plan and the X Profit Sharing Plan. C's employment terminates on October 1, 2009. As of the close of business on October 1, 2009, C has 12 hours of unused paid time off, and earns $25 per hour, and so has unused paid time off with a dollar equivalent of $300. The 12 hours does not exceed the sum of the hours in the remaining work days for 2009 plus the carryover limit.

A contribution of $300 to the X Profit Sharing Plan on behalf of C, in combination with prior annual additions, would not cause C's total contributions and annual additions to exceed the limitations for the 2009 limitation year. Company X contributes $300 to the X Profit Sharing Plan on October 19, 2009, and allocates this amount to C's account under the X Profit Sharing Plan, effective as of October 19, 2009.

Situation 2: The facts are the same as in Situation 1, except that C's employment terminates on December 28, 2009, and any payment for unused paid time off on account of termination will be paid to C in 2010 and will be the only payment of compensation that C will receive from Company X in 2010. C has 12 hours of unused paid time off and earns $25 per hour and, therefore, has unused paid time off with a dollar equivalent of $300. The 12 hours of unusedpaid time off does not exceed the sum of the hours in the remaining work days for 2009 plus the carryover limit. The $300 does not exceed the annual addition applicable dollar limit for 2010. Company X contributes $150 to the X Profit Sharing Plan on January 18, 2010, and allocates the amount to C's account under the X Profit Sharing Plan as of January 18, 2010. This contribution is not treated as a contribution to the X Profit Sharing Plan for 2009. Company X pays the remaining $150 to C on January 18, 2010.

Situation 3: Company W maintains the Company W PTO Plan (W PTO Plan), under which participants ratably accrue up to 240 hours of paid time off each calendar year on a pay-period basis beginning on January 1. For this purpose, salaried employees are treated as working eight hours per work day. Under the W PTO Plan, a specified number of unused paid time off hours remaining as of the close of business on December 31 may be carried over to the following year, and any hours of unused paid time off in excess of the carryover limit are forfeited. If a participant terminates employment, the dollar equivalent of any hours of unused paid time off remaining at the termination of employment are paid to the terminated participant within 60 days after the termination of employment, with the dollar equivalent determined as the number of hours of unused paid time off multiplied by the terminated participant's hourly rate of compensation for the pay period during which the participant terminates employment (determined for salaried employees by treating the employee as working eight hours per work day).

Company W also maintains the Company W Section 401(k) Plan (W 401(k) Plan). The W 401(k) Plan includes a CODA that does not provide for catch-up contributions. The W 401(k) Plan has a calendar year plan year and limitation year. The W 401(k) Plan provides that amounts contributed to the plan are taken into account for the year in which falls the date the amounts are allocated to the participant's account under the plan. The W 401(k) Plan also provides that amounts for unused paid time off paid by the later of two-and-one-half months after termination of employment with Company W or the end of the limitation year that includes the date of the severance from employment are treated as Section 415 compensation, to the extent permissible. The W 401(k) Plan provides that compensation is determined by including only amounts actually paid during the limitation year.

In December 2008, Company W amended the W 401(k) Plan and the W PTO Plan, effective January 1, 2009, to provide that a participant may elect to reduce all or part of the dollar equivalent of any unused paid time off at the time of a participant's termination of employment and have that amount contributed by Company W and allocated to the participant's account under the W 401(k) Plan as of the first day of the second pay period beginning immediately after the participant's termination of employment, to the extent that the contribution (in combination with prior annual additions) does not exceed the applicable annual addition limitations and to the extent the contributions (in combination with prior elective deferrals) do not exceed the applicable elective deferral limitation. Under the terms of the W 401(k) Plan, contributions of the dollar equivalent ofpaid time off are in addition to other contributions and treated as elective contributions. Under the terms of the W PTO Plan, the dollar equivalent of any unused paid time off that is not contributed to the W 401(k) Plan is paid to the employee on the first day of the second pay period beginning immediately after the participant's termination of employment. For these purposes, the dollar equivalent of the unused paid time off is determined as the number of hours of unused paid time off multiplied by the terminated participant's hourly rate of compensation for the pay period during which the participant terminates employment (determined for salaried employees by treating the employee as working eight hours per work day).

D is an employee of Company W who participates in the W PTO Plan and the W 401(k) Plan. D terminates employment on October 1, 2009. As of the close of business on October 1, 2009, D has 15 hours of unused paid time off, and earns $20 per hour, and so has unused paid time off with a dollar equivalent of $300. The 15 hours does not exceed the sum of the hours in the remaining work days for 2009 plus the carryover limit.

D has a valid and timely election in effect to have 70 percent of the dollar equivalent of the unused paid time off contributed to the W 401(k) Plan. The contribution of $210 (70% x $300) would not exceed the applicable limitations for elective deferrals and the annual addition. Company W contributes $210 to the W 401(k) Plan on October 19, 2009, and allocates that amount to D's account under the W 401(k) Plan as of October 19, 2009. Company W pays the remaining $90 to D on October 19, 2009.

Situation 4: The facts are the same as in Situation 3, except that D's employment terminates on December 28, 2009, and any payment for unused paid time off on account of termination will be paid to D in 2010 and will be the only payment of compensation that D will receive from Company W in 2010. As of the close of business on December 28, 2009, D has 15 hours of unused paid time off, and earns $20 per hour, and so has unused paid time off with a dollar equivalent of $300. The 15 hours does not exceed the sum of the hours in the remaining work days for 2009 plus the carryover limit.

D has a valid and timely election in effect to have 70 percent of the dollar equivalent of the unused paid time off contributed to the W 401(k) Plan. The contribution of $210 (70% x $300) would not exceed the applicable limitations for elective deferrals and the annual addition. Company W contributes $210 to the W 401(k) Plan on January 18, 2010 and allocates that amount to D's account under the W 401(k) Plan as of January 18, 2010. Company W pays the remaining $90 to D on January 18, 2010.

ANALYSIS

Situation 1: The amendment to the X Profit Sharing Plan to require certain contributions of the dollar equivalent of unused paid time off to the X Profit Sharing Plan does not cause the X Profit Sharing Plan to fail to meet the qualification requirements, provided that the contributions satisfy thenondiscrimination requirements (in combination with other contributions and forfeitures allocated for the year). Because C is not provided a right to elect a payment of cash for unused paid time off in lieu of a plan contribution, Company X's contribution of $300 to the X Profit Sharing Plan is not an elective contribution that is made pursuant to a cash-or-deferred election. Rather, Company X's contribution to the X Profit Sharing Plan is a nonelective employer contribution.

The amount contributed and allocated for each participant will vary based on the amount of the participant's unused paid time off. Thus, the contributions for unused paid time off are likely to preclude a plan from satisfying a design-based safe harbor. Therefore, testing based on the contributions made for individual participants generally will be required.

The contributions made pursuant to the arrangement must also not exceed the annual addition limitations (in combination with prior annual additions). Because the contribution of $300 was allocated to C's account as of October 19, 2009, and made on that date (before the end of the 30-day period following the deadline for Company X to file its income tax return), the contribution is subject to the annual addition limitations applicable for the 2009 limitation year and is taken into account for nondiscrimination purposes for the 2009 plan year. Under the facts presented, the contribution of $300 (in combination with prior annual additions) does not exceed the annual addition limitations for 2009.

If the nondiscrimination requirements are met, the amount contributed will be included in C's gross income only when the amount is distributed to C. Like any other distribution from the X Profit Sharing Plan, the distribution of amounts attributable to the dollar equivalent of unused paid time off is subject to an additional 10 percent penalty tax unless the distribution satisfies one of the exceptions.

The amendment to the X PTO Plan and the operation of the plan in accordance with the terms of the amendment do not cause the X PTO Plan to fail to qualify as a bona fide sick and vacation leave plan.

Situation 2: The amendment to the X Profit Sharing Plan to require certain contributions of the dollar equivalent of unused paid time off to the X Profit Sharing Plan does not cause the X Profit Sharing Plan to fail to meet the qualification requirements, provided that the contributions made pursuant to the amendment satisfy the nondiscrimination requirements (in combination with other contributions and forfeitures allocated for the year). Because C is not provided a right to elect a payment of cash for unused paid time off in lieu of a contribution to the X Profit Sharing Plan, Company X's contribution of $150 to the X Profit Sharing Plan is not an elective contribution that is made pursuant to a cash-or-deferred election. Rather, Company X's contribution to the X Profit Sharing Plan is a nonelective employer contribution.

The contributions made pursuant to the arrangement must also not exceed the annual addition limitations (in combination with prior annual additions). Because the contribution is allocated to C's account on January 18, 2010, and made on that date (before the end of the 30-day period following the deadline for Company X to file its income tax return), the contribution is subject to the annual addition limitations applicable for the 2010 limitation year and is taken into account for nondiscrimination purposes for the 2010 plan year. Under the facts, none of the $300 exceeds the applicable annual addition dollar limit for

2010, so the $150 contribution also would not exceed the applicable annual addition dollar limit. However, the $150 contribution must also not exceed 100 percent of compensation for the 2010 limitation year. Because the $150 contribution is a nonelective contribution, it is not taken into account as Section 415 compensation. However, because the paid time off could have been carried over and used in 2010 had C remained employed, the payment of the remaining $150 to C on January 18 can be included as Section 415 compensation for 2010. Accordingly, the allocation of $150 to C's account will provide an allocation of 100 percent of compensation and will not exceed the annual addition limitations for the 2010 limitation year.

If the nondiscrimination requirements are met, the amount contributed will be included in C's gross income only when the amount is distributed to C. Like any other distribution from the X Profit Sharing Plan, the distribution of amounts attributable to the dollar equivalent of unused paid time off is subject to an additional 10 percent penalty tax unless the distribution satisfies one of the exceptions.

Under the facts of Situation 2, C terminates employment in 2009, but the contribution to the X Profit Sharing Plan and the cash payment to C occur in 2010. Under the X PTO Plan as amended, the dollar equivalent of unused paid time off is not paid, set apart, or otherwise made available so that C may draw on it either (1) during the 2009 calendar year or (2) upon conversion in 2009 to a contribution to a qualified retirement plan or cash payment in 2010. Therefore, such amount is not includible in C's gross income in 2009 under the doctrine of constructive receipt. In addition, the amendment to the X PTO Plan and the operation of the plan in accordance with the terms of the amendment do not cause the X PTO Plan to fail to qualify as a bona fide sick and vacation leave plan. The $150 payment is includible in C's gross income in 2010, the taxable year in which it is paid to C.

Situation 3: The amendment to the W 401(k) Plan to permit certain contributions of the dollar equivalent of unused paid time off to the W 401(k) Plan does not cause the W 401(k) Plan to fail to meet the qualification requirements or the requirements relating to 401(k) plans, provided that the contributions (taking into account other contributions, prior deferrals, and prior annual additions, as applicable) satisfy the 401(k) plan nondiscrimination requirements and the applicable limitations relating to elective deferrals and annual additions.

Because D is provided a right to elect either a payment of cash or a plan contribution for the dollar equivalent of unused paid time off that may not be carried over to the following year, Company W's contribution of $210 to the W 401(k) Plan is an elective contribution. Because the contribution is allocated to D's account as of October 19, 2009, and is made on that date (before the end of the 30-day period following the deadline for Company W to file its income tax return), the contribution is subject to the limitations applicable for the 2009 limitation year. The contribution is also subject to the limitations on elective deferrals applied for 2009 and the actual deferral percentage (ADP) nondiscrimination testing (see Q 27:18) for the 2009 plan year.

Under the facts presented, the allocation of $210 to D's account (in combination with prior annual additions) does not cause the plan to exceed the annual addition limitations. Although the dollar equivalent of the unused paid time off was made available to D in 2009, the $210 is not treated as made available to D because the amount was contributed to the plan as part of a CODA. Accordingly, if the nondiscrimination requirements relating to 401(k) plans and the limitations on elective deferrals are met, the amount contributed will be included in D's gross income only when the amount is distributed to D. Like any other distributions from the W 401(k) Plan, the distribution of amounts attributable to the dollar equivalent of unused paid time off is subject to the additional 10 percent penalty tax if the distribution does not meet one of the exceptions.

In addition, the amendment to the W PTO Plan and the operation of the plan in accordance with the terms of the amendment do not cause the W PTO Plan to fail to qualify as a bona fide sick and vacation leave plan. The $90 payment is includible in D's gross income in 2009, the taxable year in which it is paid to D.

Situation 4: The amendment to the W 401(k) Plan to permit certain contributions of the dollar equivalent of unused paid time off to the W 401(k) Plan does not cause the W 401(k) Plan to fail to meet the qualification requirements or the requirements applicable to 401(k) plans, provided that the contributions (taking into account other contributions, prior deferrals, and prior annual additions, as applicable) satisfy the nondiscrimination requirements relating to 401(k) plans, and the applicable limitations on elective deferrals and annual additions.

Because D is provided a right to elect either a payment of cash or a plan contribution for the dollar equivalent of unused paid time off that may not be carried over to the following year, Company W's contribution of $210 to the W 401(k) Plan is an elective contribution. Because the contribution is made on January 18, 2010, and is allocated as of that date (before the end of the 30-day period following the deadline for Company W to file its income tax return), the contribution is subject to the annual addition limitations applicable for the 2010 limitation year. The contribution is also subject to the limitations on elective deferrals applied for 2010 and the ADP nondiscrimination testing for the 2010 plan year.

As an elective contribution, the $210 may be treated as Section 415 compensation, so that D's total 2010 compensation for annual addition purposes is $300 (the $210 elective contribution plus the $90 payment). Under the facts presented, the allocation of $210 to D's account (in combination with prior annual additions) will not cause the plan to exceed the annual addition limitations. Although the dollar equivalent of the unused paid time off was made available to D in 2010, the $210 will not be treated as made available to D because the amount was contributed to the plan as part of a CODA. Accordingly, if the nondiscrimination requirements and the limitations are met, the amount contributed will be included in D's gross income only when the amount is distributed to D. Like any other distributions from the W 401(k) Plan, the distribution of amounts attributable to the dollar equivalent of unused paid time off is subject to the additional 10 percent penalty tax if the distribution does not meet one of the exceptions.

Under the facts of Situation 4, D terminates employment in 2009, but the contribution to the W Profit Sharing Plan and the cash payment to D occur in 2010. Under the W PTO Plan as amended, the dollar equivalent of unused paid time off is not paid, set apart, or otherwise made available so that D may draw on it either (1) during the 2009 calendar year or (2) upon conversion in 2009 to a contribution to a qualified retirement plan or cash payment in 2010. Therefore, such amount is not includible in D's gross income in 2009 under the doctrine of constructive receipt. In addition, the amendment to the W PTO Plan and the operation of the plan in accordance with the terms of the amendment do not cause the W PTO Plan to fail to qualify as a bona fide sick and vacation leave plan. The $90 payment is includible in D's gross income in 2010, the taxable year in which it is paid to D.

HOLDING

1. Under the facts presented, the amendments requiring or permitting certain contributions of the dollar equivalent of unused paid time off to a profit sharing plan do not cause the plan to fail to meet the qualification requirements, provided that the contributions satisfy the applicable requirements relating to nondiscrimination and, where applicable, relating to 401(k) plans and elective deferrals.

2. Under the facts presented, assuming the applicable qualification requirements are satisfied, a participant does not include in gross income contributions of the dollar equivalent of unused paid time off to the profit sharing plan until distributions are made to the participant from the plan and does not include in gross income an amount paid for the dollar equivalent of unused paid time off that is not contributed to the profit sharing plan until the taxable year in which the amount is paid to the participant.

[Rev. Rul. 2009-32, 2009-2 C.B. 398]

Q 27:5   What is an automatic contribution arrangement?

Initially, an automatic contribution arrangement was referred to as a negative election 401(k) plan. Under a negative election 401(k) plan, an employee is deemed to have elected to have the employer contribute a percentage of the employee's compensation to the plan under a cash-or-deferred election (see Q 27:3) unless the employee specifically elects in writing not to defer compensation. In other words, the employee does not make an affirmative election to contribute. IRS ruled that this type of plan was permissible. [Rev. Rul. 2000-8, 2000-1 C.B. 617]. For purposes of determining whether an election is a cash-or-deferred election, it is irrelevant whether the default that applies in the absence of an affirmative election is that the employee receives an amount in cash or some other taxable benefit or that the employer contributes an amount to a plan or provides an accrual or other benefit under a plan deferring the receipt of compensation. [Treas. Reg. § 1.401(k)-1(a)(3)(ii)]

The first negative election 401(k) plan approved by IRS contained, among others, the following provisions:

1. The employer maintains a calendar-year profit sharing plan that contains a CODA (see Q 27:2) and also provides for matching contributions (see Q 27:75). Under the plan an employee, including a newly hired employee, may elect to have the employer make contributions on the employee's behalf to the plan in lieu of receiving that amount as cash compensation that would otherwise be payable to the employee. The employee may designate the amount of these compensation reduction contributions as a percentage of the employee's compensation, subject to certain limitations set forth in the plan.

2. Under the plan, if a newly hired employee does not affirmatively elect to receive cash or have a specified amount contributed to the plan, the employee's compensation is automatically reduced by 3 percent and this amount is contributed to the plan. An election not to make compensation reduction contributions or to contribute a different percentage of compensation can be made at any time. The election is effective for the first pay period and subsequent pay periods (until superseded by a subsequent election) if filed when the employee is hired or if filed within a reasonable period thereafter ending before the compensation for the first pay period is currently available. Thus, if an employee files an election to receive cash in lieu of compensation reduction contributions and the election is filed when the employee is hired or within a reasonable period thereafter ending before the compensation is currently available, then no compensation reduction contributions for the first pay period or subsequent pay periods are made on the employee's behalf to the plan until the employee makes a subsequent affirmative election to reduce compensation. Elections filed at a later date are effective for payroll periods beginning in the month next following the date the election is filed.

3. At the time an employee is hired, the employee receives a notice that explains the automatic compensation reduction election and the employee's right to elect to have no such compensation reduction contributions made to the plan or to alter the amount of those contributions, including the procedure for exercising that right and the timing for implementation of any such election. The employee is subsequently notified annually of the employee's compensation reduction percentage and the right to change the percentage.

4. The plan also provides that, for each employee who has at least one year of service, the employer will make matching contributions on account of the employee's compensation reduction contributions up to a specified percentage of the employee's compensation. The plan does not permit voluntary employee contributions (see Q 27:74). According to IRS, if the plan permitted employee contributions, then the amount contributed to the plan would have to be designated or treated, at the time of the

contribution, as pretax compensation reduction contributions or after-tax employee contributions.

IRS also concluded that a negative election 401(k) plan could apply the same provisions as discussed above to both current and newly hired employees. IRS expanded the provisions of the plan to include the following:

1. The plan is amended, effective the next January 1, to apply the same rule to both current and newly hired employees. Thus, under the plan as amended, if an employee hired before January 1 who has not elected compensation reduction contributions of at least 3 percent of compensation does not affirmatively elect during a specified reasonable period ending on the January 1 effective date to receive cash or have a specified amount contributed to the plan, the employee's compensation is automatically reduced by 3 percent and this amount is contributed to the plan beginning with the first pay period that begins after the January 1 effective date.

2. Under the terms of the plan as amended, if a current employee files an election to receive cash in lieu of compensation reduction contributions and the election is filed during the reasonable period ending on the January 1 effective date, then no compensation reduction contributions for the first pay period beginning on or after the January 1 effective date or for subsequent pay periods are made on the employee's behalf to the plan until the employee makes a subsequent affirmative election to reduce compensation. In the case of a current employee who has a compensation reduction contribution election in effect for less than 3 percent, who does not make a new compensation reduction contribution election during the reasonable period ending on the January 1 effective date, and whose compensation is therefore automatically reduced by 3 percent beginning on that January 1, if that employee thereafter makes an affirmative election to reduce compensation by another amount (or no amount), then that affirmative election will continue in effect until the employee makes a subsequent affirmative election for a different amount.

3. At the beginning of the reasonable period ending on the January 1 effective date, each current employee receives a notice that explains the new automatic compensation reduction election and the employee's right to elect to have no such compensation reduction contributions made to the plan or to alter the amount of those contributions, including the procedure for exercising that right and the timing for implementation of any such election. Thereafter, each employee receives the annual notice described above in paragraph 3 relating to the first negative election 401(k) plan.

Negative election provisions may be included in both custom-designed plans (see Q 2:26) and prototype plans (see Q 2:27). [Ann. 2000-60, 2000-2 C.B. 149] IRS subsequently advised that the employer could use any percentage of pay as the automatic contribution percentage (i.e., more than 3 percent), that the contribution percentage could escalate over time, and that automatic enrollment could apply to future raises or bonuses, as long as the applicable notice requirements are met. [IRS Gen. Info. Ltr. (Mar. 17, 2004); Preamble to final regulations]

DOL advised IRS that, under Title I of ERISA, fiduciaries of a plan must ensure that the plan is administered prudently and solely in the interest of plan participants and beneficiaries. While ERISA Section 404(c) may serve to relieve certain fiduciaries from liability where participants or beneficiaries exercise control over the assets in their individual accounts, DOL took the position that participants or beneficiaries will not be considered to have exercised control if they are merely apprised of investments that will be made on their behalf in the absence of instructions to the contrary (see Q 23:14). Effective for plan years beginning after December 31, 2006, a participant in an individual account plan, including a 401(k) plan, will be deemed to have exercised actual control over assets in the participant's plan account if the plan's fiduciaries make default investments for the participant in accordance with guidance provided by DOL. See Q 23:14 for a discussion of regulations issued by DOL.

As discussed below, for plan years beginning after December 31, 2007, Section 401(k)(13) authorizes a 401(k) plan to contain an automatic enrollment arrangement.

Under PPA (see Q 1:33), a 401(k) plan that contains an automatic contribution arrangement that satisfies certain requirements (a qualified automatic contribution arrangement; QACA) is treated as meeting the ADP test (see Q 27:18) with respect to elective deferrals (see Q 27:16) and the ACP test (see Q 27:77) with respect to matching contributions (see Q 27:75). [I.R.C. §§ 401(k)(13)(A), 401(m)(12)]

A QACA must meet certain requirements with respect to (1) automatic deferral; (2) matching or nonelective contributions (see Q 27:17); and (3) notice to employees. [I.R.C. § 401(k)(13)(B)]

A QACA must provide that, unless an employee elects otherwise, the employee is treated as making an election to make elective deferrals equal to a stated percentage of compensation not in excess of 10 percent *and* at least equal to (1) three percent of compensation for the first year the deemed election applies to the participant; (2) four percent during the second year; (3) five percent during the third year; and (4) six percent during the fourth year and thereafter. The stated percentage must be applied uniformly to all eligible employees. Eligible employees are all employees eligible to participate in the arrangement, other than employees eligible to participate in the arrangement immediately before the date on which the arrangement became a QACA arrangement with an election in effect (either to participate at a certain percentage or not to participate). [I.R.C. § 401(k)(13)(C)] See Q 27:8 for a discussion of escalation features.

An automatic contribution arrangement satisfies the contribution requirement if the employer either (1) satisfies a matching contribution requirement or (2) makes a nonelective contribution to a defined contribution plan (see Q 2:2) of at least three percent of an employee's compensation on behalf of each NHCE (see Q 3:12) who is eligible to participate in the automatic contribution arrangement.

A plan generally satisfies the matching contribution requirement if, under the arrangement, (1) the employer makes a matching contribution on behalf of each NHCE that is equal to 100 percent of the employee's elective deferrals as do not exceed one percent of compensation and 50 percent of the employee's elective deferrals as exceed one percent but do not exceed six percent of compensation, and (2) the rate of match with respect to any elective deferrals for HCEs is not greater than the rate of match for NHCEs. [I.R.C. §§ 401(k)(13)(D)(i) (as amended by WRERA 2008 § 109(b)(1)), 401(k)(13)(D)(iv)]

A plan including an automatic contribution arrangement that provides for matching contributions is deemed to satisfy the ACP test if, in addition to meeting the safe harbor contribution requirements applicable to the QACA, (1) matching contributions are not provided with respect to elective deferrals in excess of six percent of compensation; (2) the rate of matching contribution does not increase as the rate of an employee's elective deferrals increases; and (3) the rate of matching contribution with respect to any rate of elective deferral of an HCE (see Q 3:3) is no greater than the rate of matching contribution with respect to the same rate of deferral of an NHCE. [I.R.C. § 401(k)(13)(D)(ii)]

Any matching or other employer contributions taken into account in determining whether the requirements for a QACA are satisfied must vest at least as rapidly as under two-year cliff vesting. That is, employees with at least two years of service must be 100 percent vested with respect to such contributions. Furthermore, any such matching or other employer contributions are subject to the withdrawal rules applicable to elective contributions (see Q 27:14). [I.R.C. § 401(k)(13)(D)(iii)] Permitted disparity may not be taken into account for purposes of satisfying the QACA requirements. [I.R.C. § 401(k)(13)(D)(iv)]

Under a notice requirement, each employee eligible to participate in the arrangement must receive notice of the arrangement that is sufficiently accurate and comprehensive to apprise the employee of such rights and obligations and is written in a manner calculated to be understood by the average employee to whom the arrangement applies. The notice must explain (1) the employee's right under the arrangement to elect not to have elective contributions made on the employee's behalf or to elect to have contributions made in a different amount, and (2) how contributions made under the automatic enrollment arrangement will be invested in the absence of any investment election by the employee. The employee must be given a reasonable period of time after receipt of the notice and before the first election contribution will be made to make an election with respect to contributions and investments. [I.R.C. § 401(k)(13)(E)] If the notice requirement is not satisfied, an ERISA penalty of $1,100 per day applies. [ERISA § 502(c)(4)]

A defined contribution plan is treated as meeting the requirements with respect to matching contributions if the plan is a QACA and meets the limitation on matching contributions applicable to a SIMPLE 401(k) plan (see Q 33:31). [I.R.C. § 401(m)(12)] The top-heavy rules (see Q 26:4) do not apply to a plan that consists solely of (1) a QACA and (2) matching contributions satisfying the limitations applicable to SIMPLE 401(k) plans. [I.R.C. § 416(g)(4)(H)] The rules for automatic contribution arrangements apply with respect to matching contributions under a 403(b) plan (see Q 35:1). [I.R.C. § 403(b)(12)]

DOL and IRS have jointly issued a publication, *Automatic Enrollment 401(k) Plans for Small Businesses*, to help small employers understand automatic enrollment for 401(k) plans offered to their employees. [DOL News Rel. No. 09-53-NAT (Jan. 15, 2009)] For a discussion of final regulations issued by IRS, see Q 27:6.

IRS provided guidance to enable employers maintaining 401(k) plans featuring automatic contribution arrangements to correct the erroneous exclusion of eligible employees and the failure to execute an employee's election (or nonelection) under the arrangement. The prescribed corrective mechanisms, as illustrated by IRS, require the employer to make a corrective contribution of 50 percent of the missed deferral (adjusted for earnings) for the affected employee. However, the calculation of the amount of the missed deferral varies in accordance with the circumstances of the automatic contribution arrangement.

In the event a plan erroneously excludes an employee from participating in the arrangement, a corrective contribution may be made.

Example 1. ABC sponsors a 401(k) plan pursuant to which an employee, absent a contrary election, will be enrolled in the plan with an automatic deferral equal to 3 percent of compensation. Norman, an NHCE, became eligible to participate in the plan on January 1, 2008. However, due to an oversight, he was not provided with enrollment materials that described the plan and detailed the procedures by which an employee could elect to contribute an amount other than the prescribed automatic deferral percentage. As a result, Norman was not automatically enrolled in the plan and did not make any elective contributions to the plan in 2008. In determining the corrective contribution, the employee's missed deferral is based on the average ADP (see Q 27:19) for other employees in the employee's category (i.e., NHCEs). The ADP for the plan's NHCEs was 4 percent. Pursuant to this formula, Norman's missed deferral is $1,200 [4% ADP for NHCEs x $30,000 (Norman's compensation for 2008)]. The required corrective contribution would be $600 (50% x the $1,200 missed deferral). In addition, the corrective contribution will be adjusted for earnings from the date the elective deferral should have been made through the date of the corrective contribution.

An alternative correction mechanism applies where a plan sponsor provides an employee with enrollment materials, but fails to implement the employee's election or nonelection.

Example 2. Rosee became eligible to participate in ABC's plan on January 1, 2008. The plan sponsor furnished Rosee with the plan's enrollment materials in November 2007. At that time, Rosee did not make a specific election; and by not making an affirmative election to participate in the plan, Rosee expressed the desire to contribute at the plan's automatic enrollment deferral percentage of 3 percent of compensation. However, the plan failed to execute this election. Consequently, Rosee did not make any elective contributions to the plan in 2008. In determining the amount of the corrective contribution, Rosee's missed deferral is based on her elected deferral percentage. Pursuant to this formula, Rosee's missed deferral is $900 [3% (her elected deferral percentage) x $30,000 (her compensation for 2008)]. The required corrective contribution would, thus, be $450 (50% x $900 missed deferral). In addition, the corrective contribution will be adjusted for earnings from the date the elective deferral should have been made through the date of the corrective contribution.

IRS recommended that employers periodically review the records of eligible employees who are not making elective deferrals to the plan. Plan records for such employees should contain affirmative election requests that the elective deferral be reduced from the automatic contribution arrangement default percentage to zero. Absent such an affirmative election, it is likely that the plan's automatic contribution arrangement provisions were not properly implemented.

[*Retirement News for Employers*, Summer 2009]

If a QACA allows an employee to elect to make permissible withdrawals of erroneous contributions, the amount withdrawn is included in the employee's gross income in the year of the distribution. The 10 percent penalty tax (see Q 16:1) is not imposed with respect to the distribution, and the arrangement is not treated as violating any restriction on distributions by allowing the withdrawal (see Q 27:14). With respect to distributions to an employee as a result of this election, employer matching contributions are forfeited or subject to other treatment that IRS may prescribe. [I.R.C. § 414(w)(1)] A permissible withdrawal is any withdrawal from an eligible automatic contribution arrangement (EACA) that is made pursuant to an employee election and consists of elective contributions and earnings attributable to those contributions. [I.R.C. § 414(w)(2)(A)]. The election must be made within 90 days of the first elective contribution with respect to the employee under the arrangement. [I.R.C. § 414(w)(2)(B)] The amount of any distributions under this election must be equal to the amount of elective contributions made with respect to the first payroll period to which the EACA applies to the employee and any succeeding payroll period beginning before the effective date of the election (and earnings attributable to those contributions). [I.R.C. § 414(w)(2)(C)]

An EACA for purposes of the special rules for withdrawals is an arrangement:

1. Under which a participant may elect to have the employer make payments as contributions under the plan or to the participant directly in cash;
2. Under which the participant is treated as having elected to have the employer make contributions in an amount equal to a uniform percentage of compensation provided under the plan until the participant elects not to have the contributions made or changes the percentage at which the contributions are made; and
3. That satisfies certain notice requirements described below. [I.R.C. § 414(w)(3) (as amended by WRERA 2008 § 109(b)(4))]

Within a reasonable period before each plan year, the plan administrator (see Q 20:1) must give to each employee who is a participant in an automatic contribution arrangement for such plan year a notice of the employee's rights and obligations under the arrangement. The notice must be sufficiently accurate and comprehensive to inform employees of their rights and obligations and must be written in a manner that is understandable by the average employee to whom the arrangement applies. The notice must include an explanation of the employee's right to elect not to have elective contributions made on the employee's behalf or to elect to change the contribution percentage. The employee must be given a reasonable amount of time to make the election before the first elective contribution is made. Finally, the notice must explain how the contributions will be invested in the absence of any investment election by the employee. [I.R.C. § 414(w)(4)] IRS has posted a sample "Automatic Enrollment Notice" on its website that may be used by sponsors of QACAs that authorize EACA withdrawals to satisfy the applicable notice requirements. The notice may also be used to comply with certain ERISA notice requirements and the default investment regulations (see Q 23:14) that must be satisfied in order for a fiduciary to secure relief from liability stemming from default investments and to ensure ERISA preemption of state restrictions on automatic contribution arrangements discussed further on in this Q 27:5. See Q 29:3 for a discussion of DOL regulations concerning the imposition of the penalty for failure to provide the notice.

For purposes of the special rules for withdrawals, "applicable employer plan" means:

1. Qualified retirement plans;
2. 403(b) plans under which amounts are contributed by an individual's employer;
3. Governmental Section 457 plans;
4. Simplified employee pensions (SEPs) that provide for a salary reduction arrangement (see Q 32:9); and
5. SIMPLE IRA plans (see Q 33:2).

[I.R.C. § 414(w)(5) (as amended by WRERA 2008 § 109(b)(5))]

A withdrawal is not taken into account for purposes of applying the participation and discrimination standards for CODAs or for purposes of applying the limitation on elective deferrals (see Q 27:51). [I.R.C. § 414(w)(6) (as amended by WRERA 2008 § 109(b)(6))] Erroneous automatic contributions are added as a permitted forfeiture with respect to the treatment of forfeited matching contributions for purposes of the minimum vesting standards and for purposes of exempting CODAs from disqualification due to the distribution of excess contributions (see Q 27:33). For a discussion of final regulations issued by IRS, see Q 27:7.

IRS gave guidance facilitating automatic enrollment by providing two sample plan amendments that can be adopted or used in drafting plan amendments to add certain automatic contribution features to 401(k) plans. The first sample amendment can be used to add a basic automatic contribution arrangement with, if elected by an adopting employer, an escalation feature. The second sample amendment can be used to add an EACA with, if elected by an adopting employer, an escalation feature. [IRS Notice 2009-65, 2009-2 C.B. 413] For a discussion of an IRS ruling concerning escalation features, see Q 27:8.

Q 27:6   Has IRS issued final regulations concerning QACAs?

IRS issued final regulations on February 24, 2009.

A CODA (see Q 27:2) is a QACA (see Q 27:5) if it is an automatic contribution arrangement where the default election under that arrangement is a contribution equal to the qualified percentage described below multiplied by the eligible employee's compensation from which elective contributions (see Q 27:16) are permitted to be made under the CODA. For plan years beginning on or after January 1, 2010, the compensation used for this purpose must be safe harbor compensation (see Q 27:41). [Treas. Reg. § 1.401(k)-3(j)(1)(i)]

An automatic contribution arrangement is a CODA that provides, in the absence of an eligible employee's affirmative election, that a default election applies under which the employee is treated as having made an election to have a specified contribution made on the employee's behalf under the plan. The default election begins to apply with respect to an eligible employee no earlier than a reasonable period of time after receipt of the notice describing the automatic contribution arrangement. The default election ceases to apply with respect to an eligible employee for periods of time with respect to which the employee has an affirmative election that is currently in effect to have elective contributions made in a different amount on the employee's behalf (in a specified amount or percentage of compensation), or not have elective contributions made on the employee's behalf. [Treas. Reg. § 1.401(k)-3(j)(1)(ii)]

An automatic contribution arrangement will not fail to be a QACA merely because the default election is not applied to an employee who was an eligible employee under the CODA (or a predecessor arrangement) immediately prior to the effective date of the QACA and on that effective date had an affirmative election in effect (that remains in effect) to have elective contributions made on the employee's behalf (in a specified amount or percentage of compensation), or not have any elective contributions made on the employee's behalf. [Treas. Reg. § 1.401(k)-(j)(1)(iii)]

A percentage is a qualified percentage only if it: (1) is uniform for all employees (except to the extent provided below); (2) does not exceed 10 percent; and (3) satisfies the minimum percentage requirements. [Treas. Reg. § 1.401(k)-3(j)(2)(i)]

The minimum percentage requirement is satisfied only if the percentage that applies for the initial period is at least 3 percent. For this purpose, the initial period begins when the employee first has contributions made pursuant to a default election under an arrangement that is intended to be a QACA for a plan year and ends on the last day of the following plan year. The minimum percentage requirement is satisfied only if the percentage that applies for the plan year immediately following the last day of the initial period is at least

4 percent; if the percentage that applies for the next plan year is at least 5 percent; and if the percentage that applies for all plan years thereafter is at least 6 percent. [Treas. Reg. § 1.401(k)-3(j)(2)(ii)] See Q 27:8 for a discussion of escalation features.

A plan does not fail to satisfy the uniform percentage requirement merely because:

1. The percentage varies based upon the number of years (or portions of years) since the beginning of the initial period for an eligible employee;
2. The rate of elective contributions under a cash-or-deferred election (see Q 27:3) that is in effect for an employee immediately prior to the effective date of the default percentage under the QACA is not reduced;
3. The rate of elective contributions is limited so as not to exceed the limits applicable to compensation (see Qs 27:21, 27:41), the dollar limitation on elective contributions (see Q 27:51), determined with or without catch-up contributions (see Q 27:52), and the annual addition limitation (see Qs 6:34, 27:51, 27:52); or
4. The default election is not applied during the period an employee is not permitted to make elective contributions because, on account of a hardship distribution (see Q 27:14), the employee's ability to make elective contributions has been suspended for six months (see Q 27:44).

[Treas. Reg. §§ 1.401(k)-1(d)(3)(iv)(E)(2), 1.401(k)-3(c)(6)(v)(B), 1.401(k)-3(j)(2)(iii)]

The minimum percentages are based on the date the initial period begins, regardless of whether the employee is eligible to make elective contributions under the plan after that date. Thus, for example, if an employee is ineligible to make contributions under the plan for six months because the employee had a hardship withdrawal and the six-month period includes a date as of which the default minimum percentage is increased, then the default percentage must reflect that increase when the employee is permitted to resume contributions. However, for purposes of determining the date the initial period begins, a plan is permitted to treat an employee who for an entire plan year did not have contributions made pursuant to a default election under the QACA as if the employee had not had such contributions made for any prior plan year as well. [Treas. Reg. § 1.401(k)-3(j)(2)(iv)]

A CODA satisfies the contribution requirements only if it satisfies the safe harbor contribution requirements (see Q 27:40), as modified by the rules discussed below. In addition, a CODA satisfies the notice requirement (see Q 27:5) only if the notice satisfies the additional requirements discussed below. [Treas. Reg. § 1.401(k)-3(k)(1)]

In applying the safe harbor matching contribution requirement (see Q 27:43) in the case of a CODA, the basic matching formula is modified so that each eligible NHCE (see Q 3:12) must receive the sum of: (1) 100 percent of the employee's elective contributions that do not exceed one percent of the employee's safe harbor compensation and (2) 50 percent of the employee's elective contributions that exceed one percent of the employee's safe harbor compensation but that do not exceed six percent of the employee's safe harbor compensation. [Treas. Reg. § 1.401(k)-3(k)(2)]

A QACA will not fail to satisfy the safe harbor contribution requirements, as applicable, merely because the safe harbor contributions are not QNECs or QMACs (see Q 27:17) provided that (1) the contributions are subject to the withdrawal restrictions that apply to QNECs and QMACs (see Q 27:14) and (2) any employee who has completed two years of service has a nonforfeitable right to the account balance attributable to the safe harbor contributions (see Q 27:5). [Treas. Reg. § 1.401(k)-3(k)(3)]

Each employee eligible to participate in the arrangement must receive a notice that explains:

1. The level of elective contributions that will be made on the employee's behalf if the employee does not make an affirmative election;
2. The employee's right under the arrangement to elect not to have elective contributions made on the employee's behalf (or to elect to have such contributions made in a different amount or percentage of compensation); and
3. How contributions under the arrangement will be invested (including, in the case of an arrangement under which the employee may elect among two or more investment options, how contributions will be invested in the absence of an investment election by the employee).

[Treas. Reg. §§ 1.401(k)-3(k)(4)(i), 1.401(k)-3(k)(4)(ii)]

In addition, the notice must be provided sufficiently early so that the employee has a reasonable period of time after receipt of the notice to make the elections. However, the requirement that an employee have a reasonable period of time after receipt of the notice to make an alternative election does not permit a plan to make the default election effective any later than the earlier of (1) the pay date for the second payroll period that begins after the date the notice is provided and (2) the first pay date that occurs at least 30 days after the notice is provided. [Treas. Reg. §§ 1.401(k)-3(k)(4)(i), 1.401(k)-3(k)(4)(iii)]

See Qs 27:49 and 27:94 for a discussion of proposed regulations issued by IRS.

Q 27:7　Has IRS issued final regulations concerning permissible withdrawals from EACAs?

PPA (see Q 1:33) added Section 414(w), which provides rules under which certain employees are permitted to elect to make a withdrawal of default elective contributions from an EACA (see Q 27:5). The final regulations set forth the rules applicable to permissible withdrawals. [Treas. Reg. § 1.414(w)-1(a)] Section 414(w) applies to plan years beginning on or after January 1, 2008. However, the final regulations apply to plan years beginning on or after January 1, 2010. For plan years that begin in 2008, a plan must operate in accordance with a good-faith interpretation of Section 414(w). For this purpose, a plan that operates in accordance with the final regulations will be treated as operating in accordance with a good-faith interpretation. [Treas. Reg. § 1.414(w)-1(f)]

For purposes of the final regulations, a number of terms are defined:

1. An applicable employer plan is a:
   a. Qualified retirement plan;
   b. Section 403(b) plan (see Q 35:1);
   c. Governmental Section 457 plan;
   d. Simplified employee pension (SEP) providing for a salary reduction arrangement (see Q 32:9); or
   e. SIMPLE IRA plan (see Q 33:2).

2. An automatic contribution arrangement is an arrangement that provides for a cash-or-deferred election (see Q 27:3) and specifies that, in the absence of a covered employee's affirmative election, a default election applies under which the employee is treated as having elected to have default elective contributions made on the employee's behalf under the plan. The default election begins to apply with respect to an eligible employee no earlier than a reasonable period of time after receipt of the notice describing the automatic arrangement. This default election ceases to apply with respect to an eligible employee for periods of time with respect to which the employee has an affirmative election that is currently in effect to not have any default elective contributions made on the employee's behalf, or have contributions made in a different amount or percentage of compensation (see Q 27:5).

3. Covered employee is an employee who is covered under the automatic contribution arrangement, determined under the terms of the plan. A plan must provide whether an employee who makes an affirmative election remains a covered employee. If a plan provides that an employee who makes an affirmative election remains a covered employee, then the employee must continue to receive a notice (see Q 27:5) and the plan may be eligible for the excise tax relief with respect to excess amounts distributed within six months after the end of the plan year (see Qs 27:34, 27:87). Such an employee will also have the default election reapply if the plan provides that the employee's prior affirmative election no longer remains in effect and the employee does not make a new affirmative election.

4. Default elective contributions are the contributions that are made at a specified level or amount under an automatic contribution arrangement in the absence of a covered employee's affirmative election that are elective contributions (see Q 27:16) or contributions made to a governmental Section 457 plan that would be elective contributions if they were made under a qualified retirement plan.

[Treas. Reg. § 1.414(w)-1(e)]

An EACA is an automatic contribution arrangement under an applicable employer plan that is intended to be an EACA for the plan year and that satisfies the uniformity requirement and the notice requirement discussed below. An EACA need not cover all employees who are eligible to elect to have contributions made on their behalf under the applicable employer plan. [Treas. Reg. § 1.414(w)-1(b)(1)]

An EACA must provide that the default elective contribution is a uniform percentage of compensation. An arrangement does not violate the uniformity requirement merely because the percentage varies in a manner that is permitted under the rules applicable to EACAs (see Q 27:5), except that the rules are applied without regard to whether the arrangement is intended to be a QACA. [Treas. Reg. §§ 1.414(w)-1(b)(2)(i), 1.414(w)-1(b)(2)(ii)]

All automatic contribution arrangements that are intended to be EACAs within a plan (or within the disaggregated plan) are aggregated (see Q 27:12). Thus, for example, if a single plan covering employees in two separate divisions has two different automatic contribution arrangements that are intended to be EACAs, the two automatic contribution arrangements can constitute EACAs only if the default elective contributions under the arrangements are the same percentage of compensation. However, if the different automatic contribution arrangements cover employees in portions of the plan that are mandatorily disaggregated, then there is no requirement to aggregate those automatic contribution arrangements under the uniformity requirements. [Treas. Reg. § 1.414(w)-1(b)(2)(iii)]

There is also a notice requirement that is satisfied for a plan year if each covered employee is given notice of the employee's rights and obligations under the arrangement. The notice must be sufficiently accurate and comprehensive to apprise the employee of such rights and obligations and be written in a manner calculated to be understood by the average employee to whom the arrangement applies. The notice must be in writing; however, see Q 20:4 for rules permitting the use of electronic media to provide applicable notices. [Treas. Reg. § 1.414(w)-1(b)(3)(i)]

The notice must include the provisions required in the notice for QACAs (see Q 27:6) to the extent those provisions apply to the arrangement. A notice is not considered sufficiently accurate and comprehensive unless the notice accurately describes:

1. The level of the default elective contributions that will be made on the employee's behalf if the employee does not make an affirmative election;

2. The employee's rights to elect not to have default elective contributions made to the plan on the employee's behalf or to have a different percentage of compensation or different amount of contribution made to the plan on the employee's behalf;

3. How contributions made under the arrangement will be invested in the absence of any investment election by the employee; and

4. The employee's rights to make a permissible withdrawal, if applicable, and the procedures to elect such a withdrawal.

[Treas. Reg. § 1.414(w)-1(b)(3)(ii)]

The timing requirement is satisfied if the notice is provided within a reasonable period before the beginning of each plan year or, in the plan year the employee is first eligible to make a cash-or-deferred election (or first becomes covered under the automatic contribution arrangement as a result of a change in employment status), within a reasonable period before the employee becomes a covered employee. In addition, a notice satisfies the timing requirements only if it is provided sufficiently early so that the employee has a reasonable period of time after receipt of the notice in order to make the election. The timing requirement is satisfied if, within a period of at least 30 days (and no more than 90 days) before the beginning of each plan year, the notice is given to each employee covered under the automatic contribution arrangement for the plan year. In the case of an employee who does not receive the notice within the period described in the previous sentence because the employee becomes eligible to make a cash-or-deferred election (or becomes covered under the automatic contribution arrangement as a result of a change in employment status) after the 90th day before the beginning of the plan year, the timing requirement is deemed to be satisfied if the notice is provided no more than 90 days before the employee becomes eligible to make a cash-or-deferred election (or becomes covered under the automatic contribution arrangement as a result of a change in employment status), and no later than the date that affords the employee a reasonable period of time after receipt of the notice to make the election. If it is not practicable for the notice to be provided on or before the date specified in the plan on which an employee becomes eligible to make a cash-or-deferred election, the notice will nonetheless be treated as provided timely if it is provided as soon as practicable after that date and the employee is permitted to elect to defer from all types of compensation that may be deferred under the plan earned beginning on that date. [Treas. Reg. § 1.414(w)-(b)(3)(iii)]

If the plan so provides, any employee who has default elective contributions made under the EACA may elect to make a withdrawal of such contributions (and earnings attributable thereto) in accordance with certain requirements. An applicable employer plan that includes an EACA will not fail to satisfy the prohibition on in-service withdrawals (see Q 27:14) merely because it permits withdrawals that satisfy the timing and amount requirements discussed below. [Treas. Reg. § 1.414(w)-1(c)(1)]

A covered employee's election to withdraw default elective contributions must be made no later than 90 days after the date of the first default elective contribution under the EACA and must be effective no later than the latest effective date of the election. A plan is permitted to set an earlier deadline for making this election; but, if a plan provides that a covered employee may withdraw default elective contributions, then the election period for the covered employee must be at least 30 days. The date of the first default elective contribution is the date that the compensation that is subject to the cash-or-deferred election would otherwise have been included in gross income. The effective date of an election cannot be after the earlier of (1) the pay date for the second payroll period that begins after the date the election is made and (2) the first pay date that occurs at least 30 days after the election is made.

For purposes of determining the date of the first default elective contribution under the EACA, a plan is permitted to treat an employee who for an entire plan year did not have default elective contributions made under the EACA as if the employee has not had such contributions for any prior plan year as well. The determination of whether an election is made no later than 90 days after the date of the first default elective contribution under the EACA must take into account any other EACA that is required to be aggregated with the EACA. [Treas. Reg. § 1.414(w)-1(c)(2)]

A distribution satisfies the amount and timing of distributions requirements if the distribution is equal to the amount of default elective contributions made under the EACA through the effective date of the election (adjusted for allocable gains and losses to the date of distribution). If default elective contributions are separately accounted for in the participant's account, the amount of the distribution will be the total amount in that account. However, if default elective contributions are not separately accounted for under the plan, the amount of the allocable gains and losses will be determined under rules similar to those provided for the distribution of excess contributions (see Q 27:26). The distribution amount may be reduced by any generally applicable fees. However, the plan may not charge a higher fee for a distribution of permissible withdrawals than would apply to any other distributions of cash. The distribution must be made in accordance with the plan's ordinary timing procedures for processing distributions and making distributions. [Treas. Reg. § 1.414(w)-1(c)(3)]

The amount of the withdrawal is includible in the eligible employee's gross income for the taxable year in which the distribution is made. However, any portion of the distribution consisting of designated Roth contributions (see Q 27:96) is not included in an employee's gross income a second time. The portion of the withdrawal that is treated as an investment in the contract (see Q 13:3) is determined without regard to any plan contributions other than those distributed as a withdrawal of default elective contributions. The withdrawal is not subject to the 10 percent tax on early withdrawals (see Q 16:1). The amount of the withdrawal is reported on Form 1099-R, "Distributions From Pensions, Annuities, Retirement or Profit-Sharing Plans, IRAs, Insurance Contracts, etc.," as described in the applicable instructions. The amount of the withdrawal is not taken into account in determining the limitation on elective deferrals (see Q 27:51). [Treas. Reg. § 1.414(w)-1(d)(1)]

In the case of any such withdrawal, employer matching contributions with respect to the amount withdrawn that have been allocated to the participant's account (adjusted for allocable gains and losses) must be forfeited. A plan is permitted to provide that employer matching contributions will not be made with respect to any such withdrawal if the withdrawal has been made prior to the date as of which the match would otherwise be allocated. [Treas. Reg. § 1.414(w)-1(d)(2)]

A withdrawal may be made without regard to any notice or consent otherwise required (see Qs 10:20, 10:61). [Treas. Reg. § 1.414(w)-1(d)(3)]

The corrective distribution rules are not limited to arrangements meeting the requirements of a qualified enrollment feature.

Any State law that would directly or indirectly prohibit or restrict the inclusion in a plan of an automatic contribution arrangement is preempted. The State preemption rules are not limited to arrangements that meet the requirements of a qualified enrollment feature. [ERISA § 514(e)]

Although QACAs became effective for plan years beginning after December 31, 2007, the preemption of conflicting State regulations became effective on August 17, 2006. [PPA § 902(g)]

See Qs 27:49 and 27:94 for a discussion of proposed regulations issued by IRS, and see Q 27:8 for a discussion of escalation features.

Q 27:8 Can an automatic contribution arrangement include an escalation feature?

A revenue ruling issued by IRS addresses how an automatic contribution arrangement (see Q 27:5) can work where the 401(k) plan has an escalation feature. In a plan with an escalation feature, the amount of an employee's compensation contributed to the plan is increased periodically according to the terms of the plan without any affirmative election being made by the employee. The issues raised in the ruling are described below.

ISSUES

1. Will default contributions to a profit sharing plan fail to be considered elective contributions (see Q 27:16) merely because they are made pursuant to an automatic contribution arrangement under which an eligible employee's default contribution percentage automatically increases in plan years after the first plan year of the eligible employee's participation in the automatic contribution arrangement based in part on increases in the eligible employee's plan compensation?

2. Will default contributions under an automatic contribution arrangement fail to satisfy the qualified percentage requirement (including uniformity and minimum percentage requirements) relating to a QACA (see Qs 27:5, 27:6; providing an automatic enrollment nondiscrimination safe harbor) or the uniformity requirement relating to an EACA (see Qs 27:5, 27:7; permitting 90-day withdrawals) merely because default contributions are made pursuant to an arrangement under which the default contribution percentage for all eligible employees increases on a date other than the first day of a plan year?

FACTS

Situation 1: Employer X maintains Plan A, a profit sharing plan intended to satisfy the requirements of Sections 401(a), 401(k), and 401(m), and maintained on a calendar-year basis. Plan A is not intended to satisfy the requirements to be a QACA or an EACA.

Under Plan A, any eligible employee of Employer X may affirmatively elect to receive compensation entirely in cash or to have Employer X make specified contributions on the eligible employee's behalf to Plan A in lieu of receiving those amounts as cash compensation. Subject to certain limitations set forth in Plan A, the eligible employee may designate the amount of these elective contributions as a percentage of the eligible employee's plan compensation, defined under Plan A as base pay (excluding overtime, bonuses, and other special compensation).

Under Plan A, if any eligible employee of Employer X does not affirmatively elect to receive cash or to have a specified amount contributed to Plan A, default contributions are automatically contributed to Plan A (with a corresponding reduction in the eligible employee's cash compensation) beginning with the first pay period of the first plan year of the eligible employee's participation in the automatic contribution arrangement. For that first plan year, the default contribution percentage is 4 percent of plan compensation. Any eligible employee may elect at any time not to make elective contributions (including not to make default contributions) or to have Employer X contribute to Plan A a different percentage of plan compensation.

Employer X usually provides annual increases in base pay for its employees effective for pay periods beginning on or after the employment anniversary date for each employee. Under Plan A, for plan years after the first plan year of the eligible employee's participation in the automatic contribution arrangement, the default contribution percentage is automatically increased beginning with the first pay period that begins on or after the eligible employee's employment anniversary date. The increase in the default contribution percentage is equal to the greater of (1) one percentage point, or (2) a number of percentage points calculated as 30 percent of the percentage increase in the eligible employee's base pay for such first pay period over the eligible employee's base pay for the immediately preceding pay period (rounded to the nearest whole percentage). However, under Plan A, the default contribution percentage may never exceed 11 percent. For example, the default contribution percentage for an employee with default contributions beginning in 2009 would increase by one percentage point each plan year for pay periods beginning on or after the employee's employment anniversary date (to 5 percent in 2010, 6 percent in 2011, etc., up to 11 percent in 2016 and later plan years), even if base pay were not to increase. If the employee's base pay were to increase by at least 5 percent during one or more plan years before 2016, the default contribution percentage would increase to 11 percent even earlier.

Eligible employees are provided notices satisfying the timing and content requirements (see Q 27:15) that explain the default contribution percentage, automatic increases in the default contribution percentage in plan years after the first plan year, and the eligible employees' right to elect to have no elective contributions (including no default contributions) made to Plan A or to alter the amount of those contributions.

Plan A provides that elective contributions are immediately nonforfeitable (see Q 27:13) and, if the eligible employee has not attained age 59½, cannot be distributed prior to the eligible employee's death or severance from employment, except in the case of hardship (see Q 27:14). Plan A also provides that, for each eligible employee, Employer X will make matching contributions (see Q 27:75) to Plan A on account of the eligible employee's elective contributions up to a specified percentage of the eligible employee's plan compensation.

Plan A provides that default contributions and related matching contributions will, absent a contrary election, be invested in a qualified default investment alternative (QDIA; see Q 23:14).

Situation 2: Employer Y maintains Plan B, a profit sharing plan intended to satisfy the requirements of Sections 401(a), 401(k), and 401(m), and maintained on a calendar-year basis. Plan B is also intended to satisfy the requirements to be a QACA or an EACA.

Under Plan B, any eligible employee of Employer Y may affirmatively elect to receive compensation entirely in cash or to have Employer Y make specified contributions on the eligible employee's behalf to Plan B in lieu of receiving those amounts as cash compensation. Subject to certain limitations set forth in Plan B, the eligible employee may designate the amount of these elective contributions as a percentage of the eligible employee's plan compensation, as defined under Plan B.

Under Plan B, if any eligible employee of Employer Y does not affirmatively elect to receive cash or to have a specified amount contributed to Plan B, default contributions are automatically contributed to Plan B (with a corresponding reduction in the eligible employee's cash compensation) beginning with the first pay period of the first plan year of the eligible employee's participation in the automatic contribution arrangement. For that first plan year, the default contribution percentage is 3 percent of plan compensation. Any eligible employee may elect at any time not to make elective contributions (including not to make default contributions) or to have Employer Y contribute to Plan B a different percentage of plan compensation.

Employer Y usually provides annual increases in compensation for its employees effective for pay periods beginning on or after April 1 each year. Under Plan B, for plan years after the first plan year of the eligible employee's participation in the automatic contribution arrangement, the default contribution percentage is automatically increased beginning with the first pay period that begins on or after April 1. The increase in the default contribution percentage is equal to one percentage point. However, under Plan B, the default contribution percentage may never exceed 10 percent.

Eligible employees are provided notices satisfying the timing and content requirements (see Qs 27:6, 27:7) that explain the default contribution percentage, automatic increases to the default contribution percentage in plan years after the first plan year, and the eligible employees' right to elect to have no elective contributions (including no default contributions) made to Plan B or to alter the amount of those contributions.

Plan B provides that elective contributions are immediately nonforfeitable and, if the eligible employee has not attained age 59½, cannot be distributed prior to the eligible employee's death or severance from employment, except in the case of hardship or in the case of a distribution that satisfies the permissible withdrawal rules (see Q 27:7). Plan B also provides that, for each eligible employee, Employer Y will make specified matching contributions to Plan B on account of the eligible employee's elective contributions up to a specified percentage of the eligible employee's plan compensation under a matching formula that satisfies the matching contribution rules (see Qs 27:5, 27:6).

Plan B provides that default contributions and related matching contributions will, absent a contrary election, be invested in a QDIA.

ANALYSIS

Situation 1: The default contributions made for an eligible employee in Situation 1 are elective contributions made pursuant to a cash-or-deferred election (see Q 27:3) and satisfy the requirement that the amount that each eligible employee may defer as an elective contribution be available to the eligible employee in cash (or some other taxable benefit). The election is a cash-or-deferred election, and the contributions are elective contributions even though the contributions are made pursuant to a default election in the absence of an affirmative election.

Because a default contribution percentage can be increased or otherwise changed over time pursuant to a plan-specified schedule, the default contributions in Situation 1 do not cease to be elective contributions merely because default contribution percentages increase over time and such increases are, in part, determined by reference to the amount of, and are scheduled to take effect at or by reference to the time of, future increases in base pay.

The structure of increases in the default contribution percentage for years after the first plan year of an eligible employee's participation in the automatic contribution arrangement results in default contribution percentages for eligible employees that are not uniform percentages of plan compensation for all eligible employees, and the percentages do not vary based solely on the number of years (or portions of years) since the beginning of the initial period (see Q 27:6). However, because the automatic contribution arrangement in Situation 1 is not intended to be an EACA or a QACA, this nonuniformity is permissible.

Situation 2: The default contributions described in Situation 2 are elective contributions made pursuant to cash-or-deferred elections and satisfy the requirement that the amount that each eligible employee may defer as an elective contribution be available to the eligible employee in cash (or some other taxable benefit). The election is a cash-or-deferred election, and the contributions are elective contributions even though the contributions are made pursuant to a default election in the absence of an affirmative election.

The default contributions described in Situation 2 do not cause the arrangement to fail to satisfy the requirements for a QACA and an EACA. In particular, the provisions in Plan B under which, for plan years after the first plan year of an eligible employee's participation in the automatic contribution arrangement, the default contribution percentage is automatically increased beginning with the first pay period that begins on or after April 1, do not cause Plan B to fail the uniformity requirement (see Qs 27:6, 27:7). The increases are eligible for an exception to the uniformity requirement because they apply in the same manner to all eligible employees for whom the same number of years or portions of years have elapsed since default contributions were first made for them under the automatic contribution arrangement.

Also, the default contribution percentages for each plan year after the first plan year satisfy the minimum default contribution percentage requirements (see Qs 27:5, 27:6) for periods beginning both before and on or after April 1 of such a plan year. This is because the minimum default contribution percentage of 4 percent is not required to apply until after the end of the plan year following the first plan year of an eligible employee's participation in the automatic contribution arrangement, whereas, under Plan B, the increased default contribution percentage of 4 percent applies earlier, beginning with the first pay period that begins on or after April 1 of the plan year following the first plan year. Similarly, the minimum default contribution percentages of 5 percent and 6 percent are satisfied under Plan B earlier than required. Alternatively, if under Plan B increased default contribution percentages had not begun to apply until April 1 of the second plan year following the first plan year, the minimum default contribution percentage requirements could have been satisfied by using an initial default contribution percentage of 4 percent (rather than 3 percent).

HOLDINGS

1. Default contributions to a profit sharing plan will not fail to be considered elective contributions merely because they are made pursuant to an automatic contribution arrangement under which an eligible employee's default contribution percentage automatically increases in plan years after the first plan year of the eligible employee's participation in the automatic contribution arrangement based in part on increases in the eligible employee's plan compensation.

2. Default contributions under an automatic contribution arrangement will not fail to satisfy the qualified percentage requirement (including uniformity and minimum percentage requirements) relating to a QACA or the uniformity requirement relating to an EACA merely because default contributions are made pursuant to an arrangement under which the default contribution percentage for all eligible employees increases on a date other than the first day of a plan year.

[Rev. Rul. 2009-30, 2009-2 C.B. 391]

Q 27:9   What is a qualified CODA?

A qualified CODA is a CODA (see Q 27:2) that satisfies the coverage and nondiscrimination requirements (see Q 27:12), the nonforfeitability requirement (see Q 27:13), the distribution limitation (see Q 27:14), and certain additional requirements (see Q 27:15). [Treas. Reg. § 1.401(k)-1(a)(4)(i)]

Except for the recharacterization of excess contributions (see Q 27:30), elective contributions (see Q 27:16) under a qualified CODA (including designated Roth contributions (see Q 27:96)) are treated as employer contributions. [Treas. Reg. §§ 1.401(k)-1(a)(4)(ii), 1.401(k)-2(b)(3)] Except if the ADP test (see Q 27:18) is not satisfied or excess contributions are recharacterized, elective contributions under a qualified CODA are neither includible in an employee's gross income at the time the cash would have been includible in the employee's gross income (but for the cash-or-deferred election) nor at the time the elective contributions are contributed to the plan. [Treas. Reg. §§ 1.401(k)-1(a)(4)(iii), 1.402(a)-1(d)(2)(i)]

Elective contributions (including elective contributions that are designated Roth contributions) under a qualified CODA satisfy the nondiscrimination requirements with respect to amounts (see Q 4:12) if and only if the amount of elective contributions satisfies the ADP test or the ADP test safe harbor (see Q 27:40). [Treas. Reg. §§ 1.401(a)(4)-1(b)(2)(ii)(B), 1.401(k)-1(a)(4)(iv)(A)]

A plan that includes a qualified CODA must also satisfy the nondiscrimination requirements with respect to benefits, rights, and features (see Q 4:20). For example, the right to make each level of elective contributions under a CODA and the right to make designated Roth contributions are rights or features subject to the nondiscrimination requirements. Thus, for example, if all employees are eligible to make a stated level of elective contributions under a CODA, but that level of contributions can be made only from compensation in excess of a stated amount, such as the Social Security taxable wage base (see Q 7:7), the arrangement will generally favor HCEs (see Q 3:3) with respect to the availability of elective contributions and thus will generally not satisfy the nondiscrimination requirements. [Treas. Reg. §§ 1.401(a)(4)-4(e)(3)(i), 1.401(a)(4)-4(e)(3)(iii)(D), 1.401(k)-1(a)(4)(iv)(B)]

A qualified CODA is treated as a separate plan that must satisfy the minimum coverage requirement (see Q 5:15). The determination of whether a CODA satisfies the minimum coverage requirement must be made without regard to the modifications to the disaggregation rules (see Q 27:12). [Treas. Reg. §§ 1.401(a)(4)-11(g)(3)(vii)(A), 1.401(k)-1(a)(4)(iv)(C)]

Q 27:10   What is a nonqualified CODA?

A nonqualified CODA is a CODA (see Q 27:2) that fails to satisfy one or more of the coverage and nondiscrimination requirements (see Q 27:12), the nonforfeitability requirement (see Q 27:13), the distribution limitation (see Q 27:14), and certain additional requirements (see Q 27:15). [Treas. Reg. § 1.401(k)-1(a)(4)(i)]

Except as specifically provided otherwise, elective contributions (see Q 27:16) under a nonqualified CODA are treated as nonelective employer contributions. [Treas. Reg. § 1.401(k)-1(a)(5)(ii)] Elective contributions under a nonqualified CODA are includible in an employee's gross income at the time the cash or other taxable amount that the employee would have received, but for the cash-or-deferred election (see Q 27:3), would have been includible in the employee's gross income. [Treas. Reg. §§ 1.401(k)-1(a)(5)(iii), 1.402 (a)-1(d)(1)]

A profit sharing, stock bonus, pre-ERISA money purchase pension, or rural cooperative plan (see Q 27:1) does not fail to satisfy the qualification requirements (see Q 4:1) merely because the plan includes a nonqualified CODA. In determining whether the plan satisfies the qualification requirements, the nondiscrimination tests applicable to 401(k) plans and 401(m) plans (see Q 27:73) may not be used. [Treas. Reg. §§ 1.401(a)(4)-1(b)(2)(ii)(B), 1.401(k)-1(a)(5)(iv)(A), 1.410(b)-9]

The amount of employer contributions under a nonqualified CODA is treated as satisfying the qualification requirements if the arrangement is part of a collectively bargained plan that automatically satisfies the minimum coverage requirement (see Q 5:15). [Treas. Reg. §§ 1.401(a)(4)-1(c)(5), 1.401(k)-1(a)(5)(iv)(B), 1.410(b)-2(b)(7)] Additionally, the nondiscrimination and minimum coverage requirements do not apply to a governmental plan maintained by a state or local government or political subdivision thereof (or agency or instrumentality thereof). [I.R.C. §§ 401(a)(5), 410(c)(1)(A), 414(d); Treas. Reg. § 1.401(k)-1(a)(5)(iv)(B)]

Example. For the 2011 plan year, BJC Corporation maintains a collectively bargained plan that includes a CODA. Employer contributions under the CODA do not satisfy the ADP test. The arrangement is a nonqualified CODA. The employer contributions under the CODA are considered to be nondiscriminatory, and the elective contributions are generally treated as employer contributions. However, the elective contributions are includible in each employee's gross income.

Q 27:11   What rules apply to CODAs of self-employed individuals?

Generally, a partnership or sole proprietorship is permitted to maintain a CODA (see Q 27:2), and individual partners or owners are permitted to make cash-or-deferred elections (see Q 27:3) with respect to compensation attributable to services rendered to the entity, under the same rules that apply to other CODAs. For example, any contributions made on behalf of an individual partner or owner pursuant to a CODA of a partnership or sole proprietorship are elective contributions (see Q 27:16) unless they are designated or treated as after-tax employee contributions (see Q 27:74). In the case of a partnership, a CODA includes any arrangement that directly or indirectly permits individual partners to vary the amount of contributions made on their behalf. The elective contributions under such an arrangement are includible in income and are not deductible unless the arrangement is a qualified CODA (see Q 27:9). Also, even if the arrangement is a qualified CODA, the elective contributions are includible in gross income and are not deductible to the extent they exceed the applicable limit (see Q 27:51). [Treas. Reg. §§ 1.401(a)-30, 1.401(k)-1(a)(6)(i), 1.402(a)-(1)(d)]

Matching contributions (see Q 27:75) made on behalf of a self-employed individual (see Q 6:62) are not treated as elective contributions made pursuant to a cash-or-deferred election, without regard to whether such matching contributions indirectly permit individual partners to vary the amount of contributions made on their behalf. [Treas. Reg. § 1.401(k)-1(a)(6)(ii)]

A partner's compensation is deemed currently available (see Q 27:3) on the last day of the partnership taxable year, and a sole proprietor's compensation is deemed currently available on the last day of the individual's taxable year. Accordingly, a self-employed individual may not make a cash-or-deferred election with respect to compensation for a partnership or sole proprietorship taxable year after the last day of that year. See Q 27:22 for the rules regarding when these contributions are treated as allocated. [Treas. Reg. § 1.401(k)-1(a)(6)(iii)]

The earned income (see Q 6:61) of a self-employed individual for a taxable year constitutes payment for services during that year. Thus, for example, if a partnership provides for cash advance payments during the taxable year to be made to a partner based on the value of the partner's services prior to the date of payment (and which do not exceed a reasonable estimate of the partner's earned income for the taxable year), a contribution of a portion of these payments to a profit sharing plan in accordance with an election to defer the portion of the advance payments does not fail to be made pursuant to a cash-or-deferred election merely because the contribution is made before the amount of the partner's earned income is finally determined and reported. However, see Q 27:22 for rules on when earned income is treated as received. [Treas. Reg. § 1.401(k)-1(a)(6)(iv)]

A partnership, like any other employer, may allow each of its employees (including partners who are treated as employees) to make a one-time irrevocable election (see Q 27:3) to have a specified amount or percentage of compensation (including no amount) contributed by the employer throughout the employee's employment or, in the case of a defined benefit plan (see Q 2:3), to receive accruals or other benefits (including no benefits) under the plan. This permits partners to elect different rates of employer contributions; however, since this arrangement is not treated as a CODA, these employer contributions must satisfy the nondiscrimination requirements (see Qs 4:10–4:26) without relying on the ADP test (see Q 27:18). If a partnership suffers a loss (i.e., has negative earned income) for its taxable year, IRS representatives have opined that all of the elective contributions on behalf of partners must be refunded because no deferrals are permissible. As a result of that refund, the partners are not treated as benefiting under the plan for purposes of the minimum coverage requirement (see Q 5:15). The partners also are disregarded for purposes of applying the general nondiscrimination tests and are excluded for purposes of applying the ADP test; the partners are not treated as receiving zero allocations.

Q 27:12   What are the coverage and nondiscrimination requirements?

A CODA (see Q 27:2) satisfies the coverage and nondiscrimination requirements for a plan year only if:

1. The group of eligible employees under the CODA satisfies the minimum coverage requirement (see Q 5:15), including the average benefit percentage test (see Q 5:17), if applicable, and

2. The CODA satisfies the ADP test (see Q 27:18), the ADP test safe harbor provisions (see Q 27:40), the ADP safe harbor provisions relating to automatic contribution arrangements (see Qs 27:5, 27:6), or the SIMPLE 401(k) plan provisions (see Q 33:31).

[Treas. Reg. § 1.401(k)-1(b)(1)]

A governmental plan maintained by a state or local government or political subdivision thereof (or agency or instrumentality thereof) is treated as meeting these requirements. [Treas. Reg. § 1.401(k)-1(b)(2)]

The final regulations are designed to provide simple, practical rules that accommodate legitimate plan changes. At the same time, the rules are intended to be applied by employers in a manner that does not make use of changes in plan testing procedures or other plan provisions to inflate inappropriately the ADP (see Q 27:19) for non-highly compensated employees (NHCEs; see Q 3:12), which is used as a benchmark for testing the ADP for HCEs (see Q 3:3) or to otherwise manipulate the nondiscrimination testing requirements. Further, the minimum coverage and nondiscrimination requirements are part of the overall requirement that benefits or contributions not discriminate in favor of HCEs. Therefore, a plan will not be treated as satisfying these requirements if there are repeated changes to plan testing procedures or plan provisions that have the effect of distorting the ADP so as to increase significantly the permitted ADP for HCEs, or otherwise manipulate the nondiscrimination rules, if a principal purpose of the changes was to achieve such a result. [Treas. Reg. § 1.401(k)-1(b)(3)]

The final regulations contain the exclusive rules for aggregating and disaggregating plans and CODAs for purposes of satisfying all of the requirements applicable to 401(k) plans. [Treas. Reg. § 1.401(k)-1(b)(4)(i)]

Except as otherwise specifically provided below, all CODAs included in a plan are treated as a single CODA, and a plan must apply a single ADP test or satisfy the ADP safe harbor provisions with respect to all such arrangements within the plan. Thus, for example, if two groups of employees are eligible for separate CODAs under the same plan, all contributions under both CODAs must be treated as made under a single CODA subject to a single test, even if they have significantly different features, such as different limits on elective contributions. [Treas. Reg. § 1.401(k)-1(b)(4)(ii)]

For these purposes, the term "plan" means a plan after application of the mandatory disaggregation rules and the permissive aggregation rules, as modified below. Thus, for example, two plans that are treated as a single plan pursuant to the permissive aggregation rules are treated as a single plan for purposes of Section 401(k) and Section 401(m). A single testing method must apply with respect to all CODAs under a plan. Thus, in applying the permissive aggregation rules, an employer may not aggregate plans that apply inconsistent testing methods. For example, a plan that applies the current year testing method may not be aggregated with another plan that applies the prior year testing method (see Qs 27:19, 27:35). Similarly, an employer may not aggregate a plan using the ADP safe harbor provisions and another plan that is using the ADP test. [Treas. Reg. §§ 1.401(k)-1(b)(4)(iii), 1.410(b)-7(a), 1.410(b)-7(b), 1.410(b)-7(c), 1.410(b)-7(d)]

If a CODA is included in a plan that is mandatorily disaggregated, the CODA must be disaggregated in a consistent manner. For example, in the case of an employer that is treated as operating qualified separate lines of business (see Q 5:47), if the eligible employees under a CODA are in more than one qualified separate line of business, only those employees within each qualified separate line of business may be taken into account in determining whether each disaggregated portion of the plan complies with the 401(k) plan requirements, unless the employer is applying the special rule for employer-wide plans with respect to the plan. Similarly, if a CODA under which employees are permitted to participate before they have completed the minimum age and service requirements (see Q 27:18) applies the separate testing rule for determining whether the plan complies with the minimum coverage requirement, then the arrangement must be treated as two separate arrangements, one comprising all eligible employees who have met the age and service requirements and one comprising all eligible employees who have not met the age and service requirements, unless the plan is disregarding all NHCEs who have not met the minimum age and service requirements. Restructuring may not be used to demonstrate compliance with the 401(k) plan requirements. [I.R.C. § 410(b); Treas. Reg. §§ 1.401(a)(4)-9(c)(3)(ii), 1.401(k)-1(b)(4)(iv), 1.410(b)-7(b), 1.414(a)-1(c)(2)(ii)]

The mandatory disaggregation rules relating to 401(k) plans and 401(m) plans (see Q 27:73) and employee stock ownership plans (ESOP; see Q 28:1) and non-ESOP portions of a plan do not apply. Accordingly, an ESOP and a non-ESOP, which are different plans, are permitted to be aggregated for these purposes. [Treas. Reg. §§ 1.401(k)-1(b)(4)(v)(A), 1.410(b)-7(b), 1.410(b)-7(c)(1), 1.410(b)-7(c)(2)]

Notwithstanding the general rule that a plan that benefits employees who are included in a unit of employees covered by a collective bargaining agreement (see Q 29:6) and employees who are not included in the collective bargaining unit is treated as comprising separate plans, an employer can treat two or more separate collective bargaining units as a single collective bargaining unit for purposes of the 401(k) plan requirements, provided that the combinations of units is determined on a basis that is reasonable and reasonably consistent from year to year. Thus, for example, if a plan benefits employees in three categories (e.g., employees included in collective bargaining unit A, employees included in collective bargaining unit B, and employees not included in any collective bargaining unit), the plan can be treated as comprising three separate plans, each of which benefits only one category of employees. However, if collective bargaining units A and B are treated as a single collective bargaining unit, the plan will be treated as comprising only two separate plans, one benefiting all employees who are included in a collective bargaining unit and another benefiting all other employees. Similarly, if a plan benefits only employees who are included in collective bargaining unit A and employees who are included in collective bargaining unit B, the plan can be treated as comprising two separate plans. However, if collective bargaining units A and B are treated as a single collective bargaining unit, the plan will be treated as a single plan. An employee is treated as included in a unit of employees covered by a collective bargaining agreement if and only if the employee is a collectively bargained employee. [I.R.C. § 410(b); Treas. Reg. §§ 1.401(k)-1(b)(4)(v)(B), 1.410(b)-6(d)(2), 1.410(b)-7(c)]

The portion of the plan that is maintained pursuant to a collective bargaining agreement is treated as a single plan maintained by a single employer that employs all the employees benefiting under the same benefit computation formula and covered pursuant to that collective bargaining agreement. The rules discussed in the preceding paragraph (including the permissive aggregation of collective bargaining units) apply to the resulting deemed single plan in the same manner as they would to a single employer plan, except that the plan administrator (see Q 20:1) is substituted for the employer where appropriate and that appropriate fiduciary obligations are taken into account. The noncollectively bargained portion of the plan is treated as maintained by one or more employers, depending on whether the noncollectively bargaining unit employees who benefit under the plan are employed by one or more employers. [Treas. Reg. § 1.401(k)-1(b)(4)(v)(C)]

Example 1. Jorge's Chicago Club, Ltd. maintains a profit sharing plan that includes a CODA in which all of its employees are eligible to participate. For purposes of applying the minimum coverage requirement, Jorge's Chicago Club, Ltd. is treated as operating qualified separate lines of business. However, Jorge's Chicago Club, Ltd. applies the special rule for employer-wide plans to the portion of its profit sharing plan that consists of elective contributions (see Q 27:16) under the CODA (and to no other plans or portions of plans). Under these facts, the 401(k) plan requirements must be applied on an employer-wide rather than a qualified separate line of business basis.

Example 2. Susan's Thirty-Two, Inc. maintains a profit sharing plan that includes a CODA in which all of its employees are eligible to participate. For purposes of applying the minimum coverage requirement, the plan treats the CODA as two separate plans, one for the employees who have completed the minimum age and service eligibility conditions and the other for employees who have not completed the conditions. The plan provides that it will satisfy the ADP test safe harbor provisions with respect to the employees who have met the minimum age and service conditions and that it will meet the ADP test with respect to the employees who have not met the minimum age and service conditions. Under these facts, the CODA must be disaggregated on a consistent basis with the disaggregation of the plan. Thus, ADP testing must be applied by comparing the ADP for eligible HCEs who have not completed the minimum age and service conditions with the ADP for eligible NHCEs for the applicable year who have not completed the minimum age and service conditions.

Example 3. Daniella Sports Star Co., Inc. maintains a stock bonus plan including an ESOP. The plan also includes a CODA for participants in the ESOP and non-ESOP portions of the plan. The ESOP and non-ESOP portions of the stock bonus plan are a single CODA for 401(k) plan purposes. However, the ESOP and non-ESOP portions of the plan are still treated as separate plans for purposes of satisfying the minimum coverage requirement.

Q 27:13   What is the nonforfeitability requirement?

The amount attributable to an employee's elective contributions (see Q 27:16) must be immediately nonforfeitable (i.e., 100 percent vested; see Q 9:1), must be disregarded for purposes of applying vesting requirements to other contributions or benefits (see Qs 9:4, 26:30), and must remain nonforfeitable even if the employee makes no additional elective contributions under a CODA (see Q 27:2). An amount is immediately nonforfeitable if it is immediately nonforfeitable within the meaning of Section 411 and would be nonforfeitable under the plan regardless of the age and service of the employee or whether the employee is employed on a specific date. An amount that is subject to forfeitures or suspensions does not satisfy the nonforfeitability requirement. [Treas. Reg. § 1.401(k)-1(c)]

Example. Jason and Casey are covered by Ben Corp.'s profit sharing plan, which includes a CODA. All employees participating in the plan have a nonforfeitable right to a percentage of their account balance (see Q 9:2) derived from all contributions (including elective contributions) as shown in the following table:

Completed Years of Service	Nonforfeitable Percentage
Less than 1	0
2	20
3	40
4	60
5	80
6 or more	100

The CODA does not satisfy the nonforfeitability requirement, because elective contributions are not immediately nonforfeitable. Thus, the CODA is a nonqualified CODA (see Q 27:10).

Q 27:14   When may distributions be made from a 401(k) plan?

Contrary to the usual rule for a profit sharing or stock bonus plan (see Qs 2:6, 2:13), a qualified 401(k) plan may not permit a distribution from the plan of amounts attributable to elective contributions (see Q 27:16) merely because of the completion of a stated period of participation or the lapse of a fixed number of years (see Q 1:48). [I.R.C. § 401(k)(2)(B)(ii)]

Amounts attributable to elective contributions may not be distributed before one of the following events, and any distributions so permitted must also satisfy the additional requirements discussed below (to the extent applicable):

1. The employee's death, disability, or severance from employment;
2. In the case of a profit sharing or stock bonus plan, the employee's attainment of age 59½ or the employee's hardship; or
3. The termination of the plan.

[Treas. Reg. § 1.401(k)-1(d)(1)]

An employee has a severance from employment when the employee ceases to be an employee of the employer maintaining the plan. An employee does not have a severance from employment if, in connection with a change of employment, the employee's new employer maintains such plan with respect to the employee. For example, a new employer maintains a plan with respect to an employee by continuing or assuming sponsorship of the plan or by accepting a transfer of plan assets and liabilities (see Q 9:55) with respect to the employee. [Treas. Reg. § 1.401(k)-1(d)(2)]

A distribution is treated as made after an employee's hardship if and only if it is made on account of the hardship. For purposes of this rule, a distribution is made on account of hardship only if the distribution both is made on account of an immediate and heavy financial need of the employee and is necessary to satisfy the financial need. The determination of the existence of an immediate and heavy financial need and of the amount necessary to meet the need must be made in accordance with nondiscriminatory and objective standards set forth in the plan. [Treas. Reg. § 1.401(k)-1(d)(3)(i)]

A distribution on account of hardship must be limited to the maximum distributable amount. The maximum distributable amount is equal to the employee's total elective contributions as of the date of distribution, reduced by the amount of previous distributions of elective contributions. Thus, the maximum distributable amount does not include earnings, qualified nonelective contributions (QNECs; see Q 27:17), or qualified matching contributions (QMACs; see Q 27:17), unless grandfathered. If the plan so provides, the maximum distributable amount may be increased for amounts credited to the employee's account as of a date specified in the plan that is no later than December 31, 1988, or, if later, the end of the last plan year ending before July 1, 1989. Thus, the maximum amount available to a participant for a hardship withdrawal consists of the amount of all such contributions and earnings thereon as of the applicable date, plus elective contributions made thereafter. [I.R.C. § 401(k)(2)(B)(i)(IV); Treas. Reg. § 1.401(k)-1(d)(3)(ii)]

Whether an employee has an immediate and heavy financial need is determined based on all the relevant facts and circumstances. Generally, for example, the need to pay the funeral expenses of a family member would constitute an immediate and heavy financial need. A distribution made to an employee for the purchase of a boat or television would generally not constitute a distribution made on account of an immediate and heavy financial need. A financial need may be immediate and heavy even if it was reasonably foreseeable or voluntarily incurred by the employee. A distribution is deemed to be on account of an immediate and heavy financial need of the employee if the distribution is for:

1. Expenses for (or necessary to obtain) medical care that would be deductible (determined without regard to whether the expenses exceed 7½ percent of adjusted gross income) and which includes expenses for the care of a spouse or dependent;

2. Costs directly related to the purchase of a principal residence for the employee (excluding mortgage payments);

3. Payment of tuition, related educational fees, and room and board expenses, for up to the next 12 months of postsecondary education for the employee or the employee's spouse, children, or dependents;

4. Payments necessary to prevent the eviction of the employee from the employee's principal residence or foreclosure on the mortgage on that residence;

5. Payments for burial or funeral expenses for the employee's deceased parent, spouse, children, or dependents; or

6. Expenses for the repair of damage to the employee's principal residence that would qualify for the casualty deduction (determined without regard to whether the loss exceeds 10 percent of adjusted gross income). [Treas. Reg. § 1.401(k)-1(d)(3)(iii)]

A 401(k) plan that permits hardship distributions of elective contributions to a participant only for expenses described in items 1 through 6 above may, beginning August 17, 2006, permit distributions for expenses described in items 1, 3, or 5 (relating to medical, tuition, and funeral expenses, respectively) for a primary beneficiary under the plan. For this purpose, a primary beneficiary under the plan is an individual who is named as a beneficiary under the plan and has an unconditional right to all or a portion of the participant's account balance under the plan upon the death of the participant. A plan that adopts these expanded hardship provisions must still satisfy all the other requirements applicable to hardship distributions, such as the requirement that the distribution be necessary to satisfy the financial need. These rules also apply to 403(b) plans (see Q 35:35). [IRS Notice 2007-7, § III, Q&A-5(a), 2007-1 C.B. 395]

Example. Ellen participates in a 401(k) plan and designates her brother Steve, who is not her dependent, as a beneficiary of her plan account. The plan permits hardship distributions of elective contributions to a participant only for expenses described in items 1 through 6 above. The plan may be amended to permit Ellen to take a hardship distribution from the plan to pay for Steve's medical expenses to the same extent she could take a distribution to pay medical expenses of one of her dependents.

IRS learned that some employers had concerns about adding provisions during a plan year to their safe harbor plans (see Q 27:40) in order to take advantage of changes to the rules for hardship withdrawals, where the pre-year safe harbor notice (see Q 27:46) did not include information about the added provision. IRS announced that a plan will not fail to satisfy the requirements to be a safe harbor plan merely because of mid-year changes to implement changes concerning hardship withdrawals. [Ann. 2007-59, 2007-1 C.B. 1448]

A distribution is treated as necessary to satisfy an immediate and heavy financial need of an employee only to the extent the amount of the distribution is not in excess of the amount required to satisfy the financial need. For this purpose, the amount required to satisfy the financial need may include any amounts necessary to pay any federal, state, or local income taxes or penalties reasonably anticipated to result from the distribution. [Treas. Reg. § 1.401(k)-1(d)(3)(iv)(A)]

A distribution is not treated as necessary to satisfy an immediate and heavy financial need of an employee to the extent the need may be relieved from other resources that are reasonably available to the employee. This determination generally will be made on the basis of all the relevant facts and circumstances. The employee's resources are deemed to include those assets of the employee's spouse and minor children that are reasonably available to the employee. Thus, for example, a vacation home owned by the employee and the employee's spouse, whether as community property, joint tenants, tenants by the entirety, or tenants in common, generally will be deemed a resource of the employee. However, property held for the employee's child under an irrevocable trust or under the Uniform Gifts to Minors Act (or comparable state law) is not treated as a resource of the employee. [Treas. Reg. § 1.401(k)-1(d)(3)(iv)(B)]

An immediate and heavy financial need generally may be treated as not capable of being relieved from other resources that are reasonably available to the employee if the employer relies upon the employee's representation (made in writing or such other form as may be prescribed by IRS), unless the employer has actual knowledge to the contrary, that the need cannot reasonably be relieved:

1. Through reimbursement or compensation by insurance or otherwise;
2. By liquidation of the employee's assets;
3. By cessation of elective contributions or employee contributions (see Q 27:74) under the plan;
4. By other currently available distributions (including distribution of ESOP dividends; see Q 28:14) and nontaxable (at the time of the loan) loans under plans maintained by the employer or by any other employer; or
5. By borrowing from commercial sources on reasonable commercial terms in an amount sufficient to satisfy the need.

[Treas. Reg. § 1.401(k)-1(d)(3)(iv)(C)]

A need cannot reasonably be relieved by one of the actions described above if the effect would be to increase the amount of the need. For example, the need for funds to purchase a principal residence cannot reasonably be relieved by a plan loan if the loan would disqualify the employee from obtaining other necessary financing. [Treas. Reg. § 1.401(k)-1(d)(3)(iv)(D)]

A distribution is deemed necessary to satisfy an immediate and heavy financial need of an employee if each of the following requirements is satisfied:

1. The employee has obtained all other currently available distributions (including distribution of ESOP dividends, but not hardship distributions) and nontaxable (at the time of the loan) loans under the plan and all other plans maintained by the employer, and

2. The employee is prohibited, under the terms of the plan or an otherwise legally enforceable agreement, from making elective contributions and employee contributions to the plan and all other plans maintained by the employer for at least six months after receipt of the hardship distribution. [Treas. Reg. § 1.401(k)-1(d)(3)(iv)(E)]

The phrase "plans maintained by the employer" means all qualified and nonqualified plans of deferred compensation maintained by the employer, including a CODA (see Q 27:2) that is part of a cafeteria plan within the meaning of Section 125. However, it does not include the mandatory employee contribution portion of a defined benefit plan (see Q 2:3) or a health or welfare benefit plan (including one that is part of a cafeteria plan). In addition, the phrase also includes a stock option, stock purchase, or similar plan maintained by the employer. [Treas. Reg. § 1.401(k)-1(d)(3)(iv)(F)]

IRS may prescribe additional guidance of general applicability expanding the list of deemed immediate and heavy financial needs and prescribing additional methods for distributions to be deemed necessary to satisfy an immediate and heavy financial need. [Treas. Reg. § 1.401(k)-1(d)(3)(v)]

IRS has addressed how the plan sponsor should verify that the required conditions for a hardship distribution have been met, and what plan sponsors should do when it is discovered that such a distribution has been made without the conditions having been met. In order to find such a mistake, IRS recommends that plan sponsors review: (1) the plan document to determine when distributions may occur; (2) each plan distribution and its related documentation showing the reason for the distribution; and (3) whether distributions designated as hardship distributions were made in accordance with the terms of the plan. The company should take reasonable steps to ensure that a participant who receives a hardship distribution without meeting the plan's conditions for such a distribution returns the erroneously distributed amounts to the plan. The participant should also be advised that to the extent any amounts are not returned, they are not eligible for tax-favored treatment, such as rollovers to IRAs or other retirement plans. IRS recommends that a formal approval process should be installed to ensure that hardship distributions comply with the terms of the plan, including documenting the reason for the hardship and certification of the unavailability of other sources of money. Company officials with the authority to authorize distributions should be made aware of the formal process and the dangers of approving distributions based upon verbal or informal requests. IRS also recommends the use of the Employee Plans Compliance Resolution System (EPCRS; see Q 19:2) to correct the mistake. If the plan is not the subject of an IRS examination, the plan should be able to correct the mistake using either the Self-Correction Program (SCP; Q 19:17) or the Voluntary Correction Program (VCP; see Q 19:20). If the plan is under IRS examination, mistakes are generally corrected by a closing agreement under the Audit Closing Agreement Program (Audit CAP; see Q 19:28). However, if the mistake is an isolated instance, the mistake may still be eligible for correction under SCP. [*Retirement News for Employers*, Spring 2008] IRS has also advised employers and employees concerning the tax consequences of hardship distributions. [*Retirement News for Employers*, Summer 2009]

A distribution may not be made upon termination of the plan if the employer establishes or maintains an alternative defined contribution plan (see Q 2:2). The determination of the identity of the employer is applied as of the date of plan termination, and a plan is an alternative defined contribution plan only if it is a defined contribution plan that exists at any time during the period beginning on the date of plan termination and ending 12 months after distribution of all assets from the terminated plan. However, if, at all times during the 24-month period beginning 12 months before the date of plan termination, fewer than 2 percent of the employees who were eligible under the defined contribution plan that includes the CODA as of the date of plan termination are eligible under the other defined contribution plan, the other plan is not an alternative defined contribution plan. In addition, a defined contribution plan is not treated as an alternative defined contribution plan if it is an ESOP (see Q 28:1), a SEP (see Q 32:1), a SIMPLE IRA plan (see Q 33:2), a 403(b) plan (see Q 35:1), or a Section 457 plan. [Treas. Reg. §§ 1.401(k)-1(d)(4)(i), 1.401(k)-6, 1.410(b)-9] A distribution upon plan termination must be a lump-sum distribution (see Q 13:5). [I.R.C. § 402(e)(4)(D); Treas. Reg. § 1.401(k)-1(d)(4)(ii)]

Amounts attributable to elective contributions may not be distributed on account of any event not described above, such as completion of a stated period of plan participation or the lapse of a fixed number of years. For example, if excess deferrals (and income) for an employee's taxable year are not distributed within the time prescribed (see Q 27:63), the amounts may be distributed only on account of an event described above. The cost of life insurance (see Q 15:6) is not treated as a distribution. The making of a loan is not treated as a distribution, even if the loan is secured by the employee's accrued benefit attributable to elective contributions or is includible in the employee's income; however, the reduction, by reason of default on a loan, of an employee's accrued benefit derived from elective contributions is treated as a distribution (see Q 14:10). A plan does not fail to satisfy these requirements merely by reason of a dividend distribution from an ESOP. These limitations generally continue to apply to amounts attributable to elective contributions (including QNECs and QMACs taken into account for the ADP test) that are transferred to another qualified retirement plan of the same or another employer. Thus, the transferee plan will generally fail to satisfy the qualification requirements and these special requirements applicable to 401(k) plans if transferred amounts may be distributed before the specified times. In addition, a CODA fails to satisfy these limitations if it transfers amounts to a plan that does not provide that the transferred amounts may not be distributed before the specified times. The transferor plan does not fail to comply with the preceding sentence if it reasonably concludes that the transferee plan provides that the transferred amounts may not be distributed before the specified times. What constitutes a basis for a reasonable conclusion is determined under standards comparable to those under the rules related to acceptance of rollover distributions (see Q 34:27). The limitations cease to apply after the transfer, however, if the amounts could have been distributed at the time of the transfer (other than on account of hardship) and the transfer is an elective transfer (see Q 9:32). The limitations also do not apply to amounts that have been paid in a direct rollover (see Q 34:17) to the plan after being distributed by another plan. [Treas. Reg. § 1.401(k)-1(d)(5)]

> **Example 1.** Jennifer, Inc. maintains a profit sharing plan that includes a CODA. Elective contributions under the arrangement may be withdrawn for any reason after two years following the end of the plan year in which the contributions were made. Because the plan permits distributions of elective contributions before the occurrence of one of the permissible events, the CODA is a nonqualified CODA (see Q 27:10) and the elective contributions are currently includible in income.

> **Example 2.** SKH Inc. maintains Plan W, a profit sharing plan that includes a CODA. Plan W provides for distributions upon a participant's severance from employment, death, or disability. All employees of SKH Inc. and its wholly owned subsidiary, WPH Inc., are eligible to participate in Plan W. SKH Inc. agrees to sell all issued and outstanding shares of WPH Inc. to an unrelated entity, SWK Inc. effective on December 31, 2007. Following the transaction, WPH Inc. will be a wholly owned subsidiary of SWK Inc. Additionally, individuals who are employed by WPH Inc. on the effective date of the sale continue to be employed by WPH Inc. following the sale. Following the transaction, all employees of WPH Inc. will cease to participate in Plan W and will become eligible to participate in the CODA maintained by SWK Inc., Plan X. No assets will be transferred from Plan W to Plan X, except in the case of a direct rollover. WPH Inc. ceases to be a member of SKH Inc. controlled group (see Q 5:31) as a result of the sale. Therefore, employees of WPH Inc. who participated in Plan W will have a severance from employment and are eligible to receive a distribution from Plan W.

> **Example 3.** CKL Corp. maintains a profit sharing plan that includes a CODA. The plan, the only plan maintained by CKL Corp., does not provide for loans. However, the plan provides that elective contributions may be distributed to an eligible employee on account of hardship using the deemed immediate and heavy financial need provisions and provisions regarding distributions necessary to satisfy financial need. Caroline is an eligible employee in the plan with an account balance of $50,000 attributable to elective contributions made by her. The total amount of elective contributions made by Caroline,

who has not previously received a distribution from the plan, is $20,000. Caroline requests a $15,000 hardship distribution of her elective contributions to pay six months of college tuition and room and board expenses for her dependent. At the time of the distribution request, the sole asset of Caroline that is reasonably available to her is a savings account with an available balance of $10,000. A distribution is made on account of hardship only if the distribution both is made on account of an immediate and heavy financial need of the employee and is necessary to satisfy the financial need. A distribution for payment of up to the next 12 months of post-secondary education and room and board expenses for Caroline's dependent is deemed to be on account of an immediate and heavy financial need of Caroline. A distribution is treated as necessary to satisfy Caroline's immediate and heavy financial need to the extent the need may not be relieved from other resources reasonably available to her. Caroline's $10,000 savings account is a resource that is reasonably available to the employee and must be taken into account in determining the amount necessary to satisfy her immediate and heavy financial need. Thus, Caroline may receive a distribution of only $5,000 of her elective contributions on account of this hardship, plus an amount necessary to pay any federal, state, or local income taxes or penalties reasonably anticipated to result from the distribution.

Example 4. The facts are the same as in Example 3. Adam, another employee of CKL Corp., has an account balance of $25,000, attributable to his elective contributions. The total amount of elective contributions made by Adam, who has not previously received a distribution from the plan, is $15,000. Adam requests a $10,000 distribution of his elective contributions to pay six months of college tuition and room and board expenses for his child. Adam makes a written representation (with respect to which CKL Corp. has no actual knowledge to the contrary) that the need cannot reasonably be relieved:

1. Through reimbursement or compensation by insurance or otherwise;
2. By liquidation of the employee's assets;
3. By cessation of elective contributions or employee contributions under the plan;
4. By other distributions or nontaxable (at the time of the loan) loans from plans maintained by the employer or by any other employer; or
5. By borrowing from commercial sources on reasonable commercial terms in an amount sufficient to satisfy the need.

A distribution for payment of up to the next 12 months of post-secondary education and room and board expenses for Adam's child is deemed to be on account of Adam's immediate and heavy financial need. In addition, because CKL Corp. can rely on Adam's written representation, the distribution is considered necessary to satisfy his immediate and heavy financial need. Therefore, Adam may receive a $10,000 distribution of his elective contributions on account of hardship, plus an amount necessary to pay any federal, state, or local income taxes or penalties reasonably anticipated to result from the distribution.

Example 5. The facts are the same as in Example 3, except the plan provides for hardship distributions using the safe harbor rule. Accordingly, the plan provides for a six-month suspension of an eligible employee's elective contributions and employee contributions to the plan after the receipt of a hardship distribution by such eligible employee. A distribution for payment of up to the next 12 months of post-secondary education and room and board expenses for Caroline's dependent is deemed to be on account of Caroline's immediate and heavy financial need. In addition, because Caroline is not eligible for any other distribution or loan from the plan and the plan suspends her elective contributions and employee contributions following receipt of the hardship distribution, the distribution will be deemed necessary to satisfy Caroline's immediate and heavy financial need (and Caroline is not required to first liquidate her savings account). Therefore, Caroline may receive a $15,000 distribution of her elective contributions on account of hardship, plus an amount necessary to pay any federal, state, or local income taxes or penalties reasonably anticipated to result from the distribution.

Example 6. JMK Corp. maintains a pre-ERISA money purchase pension plan that includes a CODA and that is not a rural cooperative plan. Elective contributions under the arrangement may be distributed to an employee on account of hardship. Hardship is a permissible distribution event only in a profit sharing, stock bonus, or rural cooperative plan. Since elective contributions under the arrangement may be distributed before a permissible distribution event occurs, the CODA does not satisfy the distribution limitation and is not a qualified CODA (see Q 27:9). Moreover, the plan is not a qualified retirement plan because a money purchase pension plan may not provide for payment of benefits upon hardship. [Treas. Reg. § 1.401-1(b) (1)(i)]

See Q 1:28 for a discussion of the Katrina Emergency Tax Relief Act of 2005 and other developments for their effect on distributions, loans, and other issues.

Under PPA (see Q 1:33), a 401(k) plan will not violate the distribution restrictions by reason of making a qualified reservist distribution (see Q 16:3).

A company proposed to allow participants to pay for long-term care insurance from the company's 401(k) plan. IRS concluded that such payments would result in taxable distributions to the participants. The use of accounts for the purpose of paying long-term care insurance premiums was considered a distribution from the plan, and participants would be taxed on the distributions. In addition, the plan would fail to comply with the distribution restrictions if it made distributions for insurance premiums to the participants. [Priv. Ltr. Rul. 200806013]

Under SBJA 2010 (see Q 1:38), eligible retirement plan distributions from 401(k) plans made after September 27, 2010 may be rolled over to a designated Roth account (see Q 27:96) within the plan. Any amount required to be included in gross income for the 2010 taxable year is included in income in equal amounts for the 2011 and 2012 taxable years unless the taxpayer elects otherwise (see Q 31:49).

Q 27:15   What additional requirements are there for qualified CODAs?

In addition to the coverage and nondiscrimination requirements (see Q 27:12), the nonforfeitability requirement (see Q 27:13), and the distribution limitation (see Q 27:14), a CODA (see Q 27:2) must be part of a profit sharing, stock bonus, pre-ERISA money purchase, or rural cooperative plan (see Q 27:1) that otherwise satisfies the qualification requirements (see Q 4:1) taking into account the CODA. A plan that includes a CODA may provide for other contributions, including employer contributions (other than elective contributions; see Q 27:16), employee contributions (see Q 27:74), or both. However, except as may be expressly permitted, elective contributions and matching contributions (see Q 27:75) taken into account for the ADP test (see Qs 27:18, 27:23) may not be taken into account for purposes of determining whether any other contributions under any plan (including the plan to which the contributions are made) satisfy the qualification requirements. [Treas. Reg. § 1.401-1(e)(1)]

A CODA must provide that the amount that each eligible employee may defer as an elective contribution is available to the employee in cash. Thus, for example, if an eligible employee is provided the option to receive a taxable benefit (other than cash) or to have the employer contribute on the employee's behalf to a profit sharing plan an amount equal to the value of the taxable benefit, the arrangement is not a qualified CODA. Similarly, if an employee has the option to receive a specified amount in cash or to have the employer contribute an amount in excess of the specified cash amount to a profit sharing plan on the employee's behalf, any contribution made by the employer on the employee's behalf in excess of the specified cash amount is not treated as made pursuant to a qualified CODA, but would be treated as a matching contribution. This cash availability requirement applies even if the CODA is part of a cafeteria plan within the meaning of Section 125. [Treas. Reg. § 1.401(k)-1(e)(2)(i)] A CODA must provide an employee with an effective opportunity to make (or change) a cash-or-deferred election (see Q 27:3) at least once during each plan year. Whether an employee has an effective opportunity is determined based on all the relevant facts and circumstances, including the adequacy of notice of the availability of the election, the period of time during which an election may be made, and any other conditions on elections. [Treas. Reg. § 1.401(k)-1(e)(2)(ii)]

The portion of an employee's benefit subject to the nonforfeitability requirement and the distribution limitation must be determined by an acceptable separate accounting between that portion and any other benefits. Separate accounting is not acceptable unless contributions and withdrawals are attributed to the separate accounts and gains, losses, and other credits or charges are separately allocated on a reasonable and consistent basis. The separate accounting requirement applies at the time the elective contribution is contributed to the plan and continues to apply until the contribution is distributed under the plan. These requirements are treated as satisfied if all amounts held under a plan that includes a qualified CODA (and, if applicable, under another plan to which QNECs and QMACs are made; see Q 27:17) are subject to the nonforfeitability requirement and the distribution limitation. [Treas. Reg. § 1.401(k)-1(e)(3)]

A CODA cannot require an employee to complete more than one year of service (see Q 5:8) to be eligible to make a cash-or-deferred election (see Q 27:3). [Treas. Reg. § 1.401(k)-1(e)(5)]

To be a qualified CODA, no other benefit may be conditioned (directly or indirectly) upon the employee's electing to make or not to make elective contributions under the arrangement. The preceding sentence does not apply to:

1. Any matching contribution made by reason of such an election;
2. Any benefit, right, or feature (such as a plan loan) that requires, or results in, an amount to be withheld from an employee's pay (e.g., to pay for the benefit or to repay the loan), to the extent the CODA restricts elective contributions to amounts available after such withholding from the employee's pay (after deduction of all applicable income and employment taxes);
3. Any reduction in the employer's top-heavy contributions (see Q 26:47) because of matching contributions that resulted from the elective contributions; or
4. Any benefit that is provided at the employee's election under a cafeteria plan in lieu of an elective contribution under a qualified CODA. [Treas. Reg. § 1.401(k)-1(e)(6)(i)]

Other benefits include, but are not limited to, benefits under a defined benefit plan (see Q 2:3); nonelective contributions under a defined contribution plan; the availability, cost, or amount of health benefits; vacations or vacation pay; life insurance; dental plans; legal services plans; loans (including plan loans); financial planning services; subsidized retirement benefits; stock options; property subject to Section 83; and dependent care assistance. Also, increases in salary, bonuses, or other cash remuneration (other than the amount that would be contributed under the cash-or-deferred election) are other benefits. The ability to make after-tax employee contributions is a benefit, but that benefit is not contingent upon an employee's electing to make or not make elective contributions under the arrangement merely because the amount of elective contributions reduces dollar-for-dollar the amount of after-tax employee contributions that may be made. Additionally, benefits under any other plan or arrangement (whether or not qualified) are not contingent upon an employee's electing to make or not to make elective contributions under a CODA merely because the elective contributions are or are not taken into account as compensation under the other plan or arrangement for purposes of determining benefits. [Treas. Reg. § 1.401(k)-1(e)(6)(ii)]

Any benefit under an excess benefit plan that is dependent on the employee's electing to make or not to make elective contributions is not treated as contingent, and deferred compensation under a nonqualified plan of deferred compensation that is dependent on an employee's having made the maximum elective deferrals or the maximum elective contributions permitted under the terms of the plan also is not treated as contingent. [ERISA § 3(36); Treas. Reg. § 1.401(k)-1(e)(6)(iii)] Except as otherwise provided in the preceding sentence, participation in a nonqualified deferred compensation plan is treated as contingent to the extent that an employee may receive additional deferred compensation under the nonqualified plan to the extent the employee makes or does not make elective contributions. [Treas. Reg. § 1.401(k)-1(e)(6)(iv)] A loan or distribution of elective contributions is not a benefit conditioned on an employee's electing to make or not make elective contributions under the arrangement merely because the amount of the loan or distribution is based on the amount of the employee's account balance. [Treas. Reg. § 1.401(k)-1(e)(6)(v)]

> **Example 1.** Jason Corp. maintains a CODA for all of its employees. Jason Corp. also maintains a nonqualified deferred compensation plan for two highly paid executives, Ben and Casey. Under the terms of the nonqualified deferred compensation plan, Ben and Casey are eligible to participate only if they do not make elective contributions under the CODA. Participation in the nonqualified plan is a contingent benefit because Ben's and Casey's participation is conditioned on their electing not to make elective contributions under the CODA.

> **Example 2.** Jason Corp. maintains a CODA for all its employees. Jason Corp. also maintains a nonqualified deferred compensation plan for two highly paid executives, Ben and Casey. Under the terms of the arrangements, Ben and Casey may defer a maximum of 10 percent of their compensation and may allocate their deferral between the CODA and the nonqualified deferred compensation plan in any way they choose (subject to the overall 10 percent maximum). Because the maximum deferral available under the nonqualified deferred compensation plan depends on the elective deferrals made under the CODA, the right to participate in the nonqualified plan is a contingent benefit.

The plan must provide for satisfaction of either the ADP test (see Q 27:18) or the ADP test safe harbor (see Q 27:40); and, if with respect to that alternative there are optional choices, which of the optional choices will apply. For example, a plan that uses the ADP test must specify whether it is using the current year testing method or prior year testing method (see Qs 27:18, 27:35–27:39). Additionally, a plan that uses the prior year testing method must specify whether the ADP for eligible NHCEs (see Q 3:12) for the first plan year is (1) 3 percent or (2) the actual ADP for the eligible NHCEs for the first plan year (see Q 27:37). Similarly, a plan that uses the safe harbor method must specify whether the safe harbor contribution will be the nonelective safe harbor contribution or the matching safe harbor contribution and is not permitted to provide that ADP testing will be used if the requirements for the safe harbor are not satisfied. In addition, a plan that uses the safe harbor method relating to automatic contribution arrangements (see Qs 27:5, 27:6) must specify the default percentages that apply for the plan year and whether the safe harbor contribution will be the nonelective safe harbor contribution or the matching safe harbor contribution, and is not permitted to provide that ADP testing will be used if the requirements for the safe harbor are not satisfied. A plan may incorporate by reference the provisions of the ADP test if that is the nondiscrimination test being applied. IRS may, in guidance of general applicability, specify the options that will apply under the plan if the nondiscrimination test is incorporated by reference. [Treas. Reg. § 1.401(k)-1(e)(7)]

With respect to compensation that is paid (or would be paid but for a cash-or-deferred election) in plan years beginning on or after July 1, 2007, a CODA satisfies the additional requirements for qualified CODAs only if cash-or-deferred elections can only be made with respect to amounts that are compensation (see Q 6:41). Thus, for example, the arrangement is not a qualified CODA if an eligible employee who is not in qualified military service (see Q 27:51) and who is not permanently and totally disabled can make a cash-or-deferred election with respect to an amount paid after severance from employment, unless the amount is paid by the later of 2 months after severance from employment or the end of the year that includes the date of severance from employment (see Q 6:8). [I.R.C. §§ 22(e)(3), 414(u), 415(c)(3); Treas. Reg. §§ 1.401(k)-1(e)(8), 1.415(c)-2]

Q 27:16   What are elective contributions?

Elective contributions are those contributions made to a plan by the employer on an employee's behalf pursuant to the employee's cash-or-deferred election (see Q 27:3) pursuant to a CODA (see Q 27:2), whether or not the arrangement is a qualified CODA (see Qs 27:9, 27:10). [Treas. Reg. § 1.401(k)-6] Elective contributions are sometimes referred to as elective deferrals.

Elective contributions cannot be used to satisfy the top-heavy minimum contribution requirement (see Q 26:46). However, a 401(k) plan that satisfies the safe harbor rules (see Q 27:40) and satisfies the ACP safe harbor for matching employer contributions (see Q 27:89) will be exempt from the top-heavy rules. [I.R.C. § 416(g)(4)(H)] This exemption applies if the 401(k) plan consists *solely* of a CODA and matching contributions.

> **Example 1.** A 401(k) plan provides for safe harbor matching contributions. The plan also permits the employer to make a nonelective contribution (see Q 27:17) for any plan year at the employer's discretion. The nonelective contribution is subject to five-year vesting (see Q 9:4) and is allocated to participants' accounts in the same ratio that each participant's compensation bears to the compensation of all participants. The plan is a calendar-year plan and covers all employees of the employer (including HCEs; see Q 3:3) who have one year of service and are age 21 or older. Other than elective contributions and the matching contributions, no other contributions are made to the plan for 2010, and there are no forfeitures. The plan is not subject to the top-heavy rules for 2010 because no nonelective contribution is made; and, therefore, five-year vesting is permissible (see Q 26:30).

> **Example 2.** The facts are the same as in Example 1, except the employer makes a discretionary nonelective contribution to the plan for 2010. Because of the discretionary nonelective contribution, the plan is subject to the top-heavy rules for 2010 and five-year vesting is not permissible.

> **Example 3.** The facts are the same as in Example 1, except forfeitures occur in 2010 due to the severance from employment of a participant who was not fully vested in amounts attributable to discretionary nonelective contributions made in a prior year. Pursuant to the terms of the plan, forfeitures are

allocated to participants' accounts for 2010 in the same manner as nonelective contributions. Because the allocation of forfeitures to participants' accounts does not satisfy the requirements for safe harbor nonelective contributions, the plan is subject to the top-heavy rules for 2010, and five-year vesting is not permissible.

Example 4. The facts are the same as in Example 1, except employees are permitted to make elective contributions immediately upon commencement of employment, but NHCEs (see Q 3:12) are not eligible for matching contributions until they have completed one year of service with the employer. Since newly hired NHCEs who make elective contributions will not be eligible to receive any matching contributions until they have completed one year of service, this will result in a greater rate of matching contributions for HCEs than for NHCEs; and, thus, the matching contributions do not satisfy the safe harbor requirements. Further, since all eligible NHCEs under the plan do not receive safe harbor nonelective contributions or safe harbor matching contributions, the matching contributions made under the plan do not satisfy the safe harbor requirements. Consequently, the plan is subject to the top-heavy rules for 2010 and five-year vesting is not permissible. However, certain plans that provide for early participation may satisfy the safe harbor requirements with respect to the portion of the plan that covers employees who have completed the minimum age and service requirements (see Q 5:2), while satisfying the ADP test (see Q 27:18) for the eligible employees who have not completed the minimum age and service requirements. Unless a plan meets the requirements to be exempt from the top-heavy rules, no portion of the plan will satisfy the exemption.

[Rev. Rul. 2004-13, 2004-1 C.B. 485; IRS Notice 2000-3, Q&A-10, 2000-1 C.B. 413]

With respect to elective contributions (and earnings thereon) made for plan years beginning after 1998, generally, employers will not be permitted to force employees to invest more than 10 percent of that amount in employer securities and employer real property unless the assets were acquired before January 1, 1999, were acquired on or after January 1, 1999, under a written agreement binding on that date and at all times thereafter, or the plan is an ESOP (see Qs 23:84, 28:1). [ERISA § 407(b)(2); EGTRRA 2001 § 655]

An employee is permitted to designate all or a portion of the elective contribution as being includible in the employee's gross income as an after-tax contribution (see Qs 27:96–27:110).

See Q 23:32 for a discussion of when participant contributions are considered plan assets and Qs 27:49 and 27:94 for a discussion of proposed regulations issued by IRS.

Q 27:17 What are qualified nonelective contributions (QNECs) and qualified matching contributions (QM~~A~~ ?

A nonelective contribution is an employer contribution made to the plan (other than a matching contribution) that the employee could not have elected to receive in cash or in other benefits instead of being contributed to the plan. [Treas. Reg. § 1.401(k)-6]

A matching contribution is any:

1. Employer contribution (including a contribution made at the employer's discretion) to a defined contribution plan (see Q 2:2), on account of an employee contribution (see Q 27:74), to a plan maintained by the employer;

2. Employer contribution (including a contribution made at the employer's discretion) to a defined contribution plan on account of an elective deferral (see Q 27:16); and

3. Forfeiture allocated on the basis of employee contributions, matching contributions, or elective deferrals.

[Treas. Reg. §§ 1.401(k)-6, 1.401(m)-1(a)(2)]

To be qualified, nonelective contributions (QNECs) and matching contributions (QMACs) must satisfy the nonforfeitability (see Q 27:13) and distribution (see Q 27:14) requirements as though they were elective contributions when contributed to the plan, without regard to whether the contributions are actually taken into account under the ADP test (see Q 27:18) or the ACP test (see Q 27:77). A matching contribution does not fail to qualify as a QMAC solely because it is forfeitable as a result of being a matching contribution with respect to an excess deferral (see Q 27:63), excess contribution (see Q 27:25), or excess aggregate contribution (see Q 27:82), or it is forfeitable because the employee has made a permissible withdrawal under an EACA (see Qs 27:5, 27:7). [Treas. Reg. § 1.401(k)-6]

Q 27:18 What is the actual deferral percentage (ADP) test?

A qualified 401(k) plan must meet a special ADP test that is designed to limit the extent to which elective contributions (see Q 27:16) made on behalf of HCEs (see Q 3:3) may exceed the elective contributions made on behalf of NHCEs (see Q 3:12). [I.R.C. § 401(k)(3)(A)]

A CODA (see Q 27:2) satisfies the ADP test for a plan year only if:

1. The ADP (see Q 27:19) for the eligible HCEs for the plan year is not more than the ADP for the eligible NHCEs for the applicable year (see Q 27:19) multiplied by 1.25, or

2. The excess of the ADP for the eligible HCEs for the plan year over the ADP for the eligible NHCEs for the applicable year is not more than two percentage points, and the ADP for the eligible HCEs for the plan year is not more than the ADP for the eligible NHCEs for the applicable year multiplied by 2.0.

[Treas. Reg. § 1.401(k)-2(a)(1)(i)]

If, for the applicable year for determining the ADP of the NHCEs for a plan year, there are no eligible NHCEs (i.e., all of the eligible employees under the CODA for the applicable year are HCEs), the arrangement is deemed to satisfy the ADP test for the plan year. [I.R.C. § 401(k)(3)(A); Treas. Reg. § 1.401(k)-2(a)(1)(ii)]

A 401(k) plan may elect to disregard NHCEs eligible to participate in the plan before they complete one year of service and attain age 21. To make this election, the plan must satisfy the minimum coverage requirement (see Q 5:15), taking into account only those employees who do not meet the plan's minimum age and service requirements. Instead of applying two separate tests, a plan can adopt a single ADP test that compares the ADP for HCEs who are eligible to participate (including those who have not satisfied the plan's minimum age and service requirements) and the ADP for NHCEs who are eligible to participate and who have met the plan's minimum age and service requirements. [I.R.C. § 401(k)(3)(F); Treas. Reg. § 1.401(k)-2(a)(1)(iii)]

IRS has ruled that employees who have not satisfied a plan's eligibility requirements for participation (see Qs 1:44, 5:2), but who are permitted to make rollover contributions (see Q 34:1), need not be taken into account for purposes of the ADP test. [Rev. Rul. 96-48, 1996-2 C.B. 31] Employees of a tax-exempt charitable organization (see Q 35:3) who are eligible to make salary reduction contributions under a 403(b) plan (see Q 35:1) may be treated as excludable employees for purposes of testing a 401(k) plan if (1) no employee of *any* tax-exempt charitable organization is eligible to participate in the 401(k) plan and (2) at least 95 percent of the employees who are not employees of *any* such organization are eligible to participate in the 401(k) plan. [Treas. Reg. § 1.410(b)-6(g); EGTRRA 2001 § 664] In addition to 401(k) plans, the regulations apply to 401(m) plans (see Qs 27:73, 27:77).

An alternative method, the ADP test safe harbor, may be used to satisfy the ADP test. If the plan satisfies the requirements of the safe harbor rule, the ADP test will automatically be satisfied. Thus, the employer may choose either to satisfy the ADP test or to use the safe harbor rule. For details of the ADP test safe harbor, see Qs 27:40 through 27:50.

For the treatment of catch-up contributions on the ADP test, see Q 27:56.

Q 27:19 How is the ADP calculated for purposes of the test?

The ADP for a group of eligible employees (either eligible HCEs or eligible NHCEs; see Qs 3:3, 3:12) for a plan year or applicable year is the average of the ADRs (see Q 27:20) of the eligible employees in that group for that year. The ADP for a group of eligible employees is calculated to the nearest hundredth of a percentage point. [I.R.C. § 401(k)(3)(B); Treas. Reg. § 1.401(k)-2(a)(2)(i)]

Example 1. Lenny of Lido Corp., with six eligible employees, adopts a 401(k) plan for calendar year 2011. Each employee may elect to receive up to 15 percent of compensation (or the maximum dollar amount, adjusted for inflation, if less) in cash or to have part or all of this amount contributed to the plan as an elective contribution. The employees make the following elections for the first plan year:

HCEs	Compensation	Elective Contribution	Percentage of Compensation
A	$120,000	$12,000	10.0
B	100,000	7,500	7.5
			17.5

NHCEs	Compensation	Elective Contribution	Percentage of Compensation
C	$40,000	$2,000	5.0
D	35,000	0	0.0
E	30,000	1,050	3.5
F	30,000	1,050	3.5
			12.0

The ADP for the HCEs is 8.75 percent (17.5% ÷ 2); the ADP for the NHCEs is 3 percent (12% ÷ 4). The plan fails the ADP test (see Q 27:18) because the ADP of the HCEs is more than the ADP of the NHCEs multiplied by 1.25 and the ADP of the HCEs exceeds the ADP of the NHCEs by more than two percentage points.

See Q 27:25 for a discussion of excess contributions.

The ADP test is applied using the prior year testing method or the current year testing method. Under the prior year testing method, the applicable year for determining the ADP for the eligible NHCEs is the plan year immediately preceding the plan year for which the ADP test is being performed. Under the prior year testing method, the ADP for the eligible NHCEs is determined using the ADRs for the eligible employees who were NHCEs in that preceding plan year, regardless of whether those NHCEs are eligible employees or NHCEs in the plan year for which the ADP test is being calculated. Under the current year testing method, the applicable year for determining the ADP for the eligible NHCEs is the same plan year as the plan year for which the ADP test is being performed. Under either method, the ADP for eligible HCEs is the average of the ADRs of the eligible HCEs for the plan year for which the ADP test is being performed. [Treas. Reg. § 1.401(k)-2(a)(2)(ii)] See Qs 27:35–27:39 for additional rules for the prior year testing method.

Example 2. Ellen of New City Corporation's 401(k) plan has a 10 percent ADP for HCEs and an 8 percent ADP for NHCEs for the 2010 plan year (the first plan year). The plan met the ADP test because 10 percent did not exceed 8 percent multiplied by 1.25.

Example 3. Ellen of New City Corporation's 401(k) plan has a 10 percent ADP for HCEs and a 6 percent ADP for NHCEs for the 2011 plan year (the second plan year). The plan would not meet the ADP test because (1) 10 percent exceeds 6 percent multiplied by 1.25 and (2) the ADP of HCEs exceeds the ADP of NHCEs by more than two percentage points. However, because the ADP of the NHCEs for the *2010 plan year* (the *prior year*), 8 percent, is used, the plan will meet the ADP test because 10 percent does not exceed 8 percent multiplied by 1.25.

Q 27:20 How is the actual deferral ratio (ADR) of an employee calculated for purposes of the ADP test?

The ADR of an eligible employee for a plan year or applicable year (see Q 27:19) is the sum of the employee's elective contributions taken into account with respect to such employee for the year (see Q 27:22) and the QNECs and QMACs taken into account with respect to such employee for the year (see Q 27:23), divided by the employee's compensation taken into account for the year (see Q 27:21). The ADR is calculated to the nearest hundredth of a percentage point. If no elective contributions, QNECs, or QMACs are taken into account for the ADP test (see Q 27:18) with respect to an eligible employee for the year, the ADR of the employee is zero. For example, if Gerri's compensation is $50,000 and she made elective contributions of $3,000, her ADR is 6 percent ($3,000 ÷ $50,000). [I.R.C. § 401(k)(3)(B); Treas. Reg. § 1.401(k)-2(a)(3)(i)]

The ADR of an HCE (see Q 3:3) who is an eligible employee in more than one CODA (see Q 27:2) of the same employer is calculated by treating all contributions with respect to such HCE under any such arrangement as being made under the CODA being tested. Thus, the ADR for such an HCE is calculated by accumulating all contributions under any CODA that would be taken into account under the ADP test for the plan year, if the CODA under which the contribution was made applied the ADP test and had the same plan year. For example, in the case of a plan with a 12-month plan year, the ADR for the plan year of that plan for an HCE who participates in multiple CODAs of the same employer is the sum of all contributions during such 12-month period that would be taken into account with respect to the HCE under all such arrangements in which the HCE is an eligible employee, divided by the HCE's compensation for that 12-month period (determined using the compensation definition for the plan being tested), without regard to the plan year of the other plans and whether those plans are satisfying the ADP test or the ADP test safe harbor (see Q 27:40). [I.R.C. § 401(k)(3)(A); Treas. Reg. § 1.401(k)-2(a)(3)(ii)]

Example 1. Stephanie, an HCE with compensation of $120,000, is eligible to make elective contributions under Plan S and Plan T, two profit sharing plans maintained by SKH Corp. with calendar-year plan years, each of which includes a CODA. During the current plan year, Stephanie makes elective contributions of $6,000 to Plan S and $4,000 to Plan T. Under each plan, the ADR for Stephanie is determined by dividing her total elective contributions under both arrangements by her compensation taken into account under the plan for the year. Therefore, Stephanie's ADR under each plan is 8.33% ($10,000 ÷ $120,000).

Example 2. The facts are the same as in Example 1, except that Plan T defines compensation (for deferral and testing purposes) to exclude all bonuses paid to an employee. Plan S defines compensation (for deferral and testing purposes) to include bonuses paid to an employee. During the current year, Stephanie's compensation included a $10,000 bonus. Therefore,

Stephanie's compensation under Plan T is $110,000 and her compensation under Plan S is $120,000. Stephanie's ADR under Plan T is 9.09% ($10,000 ÷ $110,000); and, under Plan S, her ADR is 8.33% ($10,000 ÷ $120,000).

Example 3. WPH Corp. sponsors two profit sharing plans, Plan U and Plan V, each of which includes a CODA. Plan U's plan year begins on July 1 and ends on June 30. Plan V has a calendar-year plan year. Compensation under both plans is limited to the participant's compensation during the period of participation. Bill is an HCE who participates in both plans. Bill's monthly compensation and elective contributions to each plan for the 2010 and 2011 calendar years are as follows:

Calendar Year	Monthly Compensation	Monthly Elective Contribution to Plan U	Monthly Elective Contribution to Plan V
2010	$ 10,000	$ 500	$ 400
2011	$ 11,500	$ 700	$ 550

Under Plan U, Bill's ADR for the plan year ended June 30, 2011, is equal to his total elective contributions under Plan U and Plan V for the plan year ending June 30, 2011, divided by his compensation for that period. Therefore, Bill's ADR under Plan U for the plan year ending June 30, 2011, is [($900 × 6) + ($1,250 × 6)] ÷ [($10,000 × 6) + ($11,500 × 6)], or 10 percent. Under Plan V, Bill's ADR for the plan year ended December 31, 2010, is equal to total elective contributions under Plan U and V for the plan year ending December 31, 2010, divided by his compensation for that period. Therefore, Bill's ADR under Plan V for the plan year ending December 31, 2010, is ($10,800 ÷ $120,000), or 9 percent.

Example 4. The facts are the same as Example 3, except that Bill first becomes eligible to participate in Plan U on January 1, 2011. Under Plan U, Bill's ADR for the plan year ended June 30, 2011, is equal to his total elective contributions under Plan U and V for the plan year ending June 30, 2011, divided by his compensation for that period. Therefore, Bill's ADR under Plan U for the plan year ending June 30, 2011, is [($400 × 6) + ($1,250 × 6)] ÷ [($10,000 × 6) + ($11,500 × 6)], or 7.67 percent.

Q 27:21   What does compensation mean for purposes of the ADP test?

For purposes of determining the availability of making elective contributions (see Q 27:16) by an employee, the term "compensation" must satisfy a general nondiscriminatory definition—that is, the definition cannot discriminate in favor of HCEs (see Q 3:3). An employer may elect to include or exclude elective contributions in the definition of compensation (see Qs 6:64–6:68). [I.R.C. §§ 401(k)(9), 414(s); Treas. Reg. §§ 1.401(k)-6, 1.414(s)-1]

The period used to determine an employee's compensation for a plan year must be either the plan year or the calendar year ending within the plan year. Whichever period is selected must be applied uniformly to determine the compensation of every eligible employee under the plan for that plan year. A plan may, however, limit the period taken into account under either method to that portion ,of the plan year or calendar year in which the employee was an eligible employee, provided that this limit is applied uniformly to all eligible employees under the plan for that plan year. In the case of an HCE who participates in more than one CODA of the same employer (see Q 27:20), period of participation includes periods under another plan for which elective contributions are aggregated. [Treas. Reg. § 1.401(k)-6] Where a participant terminates employment at the end of the calendar year and is paid for unused vacation time in the following calendar year, IRS representatives opined that, since the participant does not perform services in the following calendar year, the payment is not considered compensation for that year.

The amount of compensation used for purposes of the ADP test (see Q 27:18) cannot exceed $200,000 (adjusted for inflation). An adjustment will be made only if it is $5,000 or greater and then will be made in multiples of $5,000 (i.e., rounded down to the next lowest multiple of $5,000). For example, an increase in the cost-of-living of $4,999 will result in no adjustment, and an increase of $9,999 will create an upward adjustment of $5,000. The adjustment applies to plan years beginning in the calendar year in which the adjustment is effective. For plan years that begin in 2011, the compensation limit remained at $245,000. [I.R.C. § 401(a)(17); IRS Notice 2009-94, 2009-2 C.B. 848]

Example. Lillian Limited adopted a 401(k) plan on January 1, 2010. In 2010, A, B, and C were HCEs, and D, E, and F were NHCEs.

Compensation and Deferrals

Employee	Compensation	Deferral	ADR	Average
A	$245,000	$13,475	5.50%	
B	180,000	9,000	5.00	7.97%
C	70,000	9,380	13.40	
D	40,000	4,800	12.00	
E	35,000	2,100	6.00	6.00%
F	20,000	0	0.00	

The ADP test is satisfied in 2010 (see Q 27:18).

Assume that Lillian earns $25,000 a month during 2010, makes elective contributions from January 1 to June 30, suspends making deferrals from July through September, and resumes deferrals from October through December. Lillian is considered an eligible employee for the entire year because an eligible employee is one who would be eligible to make elective contributions but for a suspension due to, among other reasons, an election not to participate. Even though Lillian earned $300,000 for the year, the $245,000 compensation limit is used to determine her ADR (see Q 27:20). Even if Lillian suspended her elective contributions for the remainder of the year after earning $120,000, the divisor would still be $245,000. If Lillian chose not to make any elective contributions for 2010, her ADR would be zero ($0 ÷ $245,000). [Treas. Reg. § 1.401(k)-6]

Q 27:22 What elective contributions are counted for purposes of the ADP test?

An elective contribution (see Q 27:16) is taken into account in determining the ADR (see Q 27:20) for an eligible employee for a plan year or applicable year (see Q 27:19) for purposes of the ADP test (see Q 27:18) only if each of the following requirements is satisfied:

1. The elective contribution is allocated to the eligible employee's account under the plan as of a date within that year. For purposes of this rule, an elective contribution is considered allocated as of a date within a year only if (a) the allocation is not contingent on the employee's participation in the plan or performance of services on any date subsequent to that date and (b) the elective contribution is actually paid to the plan no later than the end of the 12-month period immediately following the year to which the contribution relates.

2. The elective contribution relates to compensation that either (a) would have been received by the employee in the year but for the employee's election to defer or (b) is attributable to services performed by the employee in the year and, but for the employee's election to defer, would have been received by the employee within 2½ months after the close of the year, but only if the plan provides for elective contributions that relate to compensation that would have been received after the close of a year to be allocated to such prior year rather than the year in which the compensation would have been received. [Treas. Reg. § 1.401(k)-2(a)(4)(i)]

Failure by the employer to pay over elective contributions to the plan in a timely manner may subject the employer to prohibited-transaction excise taxes (see Q 23:32, 24:1). IRS has determined what the amount involved is for purposes of calculating the excise tax if an employer does not timely pay elective contributions to the plan (see Q 24:5).

A partner's distributive share of partnership income is treated as received on the last day of the partnership taxable year, and a sole proprietor's compensation is treated as received on the last day of the individual's taxable year. Thus, an elective contribution made on behalf of a partner or sole proprietor is treated as allocated to the partner's or individual's account for the plan year that includes the last day of the partnership's or individual's taxable year, provided the above requirements are met (see Q 27:11). [Treas. Reg. § 1.401(k)-2(a)(4)(ii)]

Elective contributions of an HCE (see Q 3:3) must include any excess deferrals, even if those excess deferrals are distributed (see Qs 27:63–27:65). [Treas. Reg. § 1.401(k)-2(a)(4)(iii)]

The following elective contributions are not taken into account for purposes of the ADP test:

1. Elective contributions that do not satisfy the above requirements are not taken into account in determining the ADR of an eligible employee for the plan year or applicable year with respect to which the contributions were made or for any other plan year. Instead, the amount of the elective contributions must satisfy the nondiscrimination requirements

(see Q 4:10) without regard to the ADP test for the plan year for which they are allocated under the plan as if they were nonelective contributions and were the only nonelective contributions for that year.

2. Elective contributions of an NHCE do not include any excess deferrals to the extent the excess deferrals exceed the applicable limit (see Q 27:51); however, to the extent that the excess deferrals are not so prohibited, they are included in elective contributions even if distributed.

3. Elective contributions that are treated as catch-up contributions (see Qs 27:52–27:61) are not taken into account for the plan year for which the contributions were made or for any other plan year.

4. Except to the extent necessary to demonstrate satisfaction of the ACP test (see Q 27:77), elective contributions taken into account for the ACP test are not taken into account.

5. Additional elective contributions made pursuant to USERRA (see Q 1:16) by reason of an eligible employee's qualified military service are not taken into account for the plan year for which the contributions are made or for any other plan year.

6. Default elective contributions made under an EACA that are distributed as a permissible withdrawal (see Qs 27:5, 27:7) for plan years beginning on or after January 1, 2008, for the plan year for which the contributions are made, or for any other plan year.

[Treas. Reg. § 1.401(k)-2(a)(5)]

Q 27:23   Can QNECs and QMACs be taken into account for purposes of the ADP test?

QNECs and QMACs (see Q 27:17) may be taken into account in determining the ADR (see Q 27:20) for an eligible employee for purposes of the ADP test (see Q 27:18) for a plan year or applicable year (see Q 27:19) but only to the extent the contributions satisfy the requirements discussed in this Q 27:23. [Treas. Reg. § 1.401(k)-2(a)(6)]

The QNEC or QMAC must be allocated to the employee's account as of a date within that year (see Q 27:22). Consequently, under the prior year testing method (see Qs 27:19, 27:35–27:39), in order to be taken into account in calculating the ADP for the eligible NHCEs (see Q 3:12) for the applicable year, a QNEC or QMAC must be contributed no later than the end of the 12-month period immediately following the applicable year even though the applicable year is different than the plan year being tested. [Treas. Reg. § 1.401(k)-2(a)(6)(i)]

The amount of nonelective contributions, including those QNECs taken into account for the ADP test and those QNECs taken into account for the ACP test (see Q 27:77), must satisfy the nondiscrimination requirements (see Q 4:10). The amount of nonelective contributions, excluding those QNECs taken into account for the ADP test and those QNECs taken into account for the ACP test, must satisfy the nondiscrimination requirements. [Treas. Reg. § 1.401(k)-2(a)(6)(ii)] A 401(k) plan uses matching contributions to satisfy the top-heavy requirement (see Qs 26:41, 26:47); all NHCEs receive a 3 percent matching contribution, and one non-key HCE (see Qs 3:3, 26:27) receives a 3 percent nonelective contribution to satisfy the top-heavy requirements. IRS representatives have opined that such a plan will fail the coverage test for nonelective contributions.

The plan that contains the CODA (see Q 27:2) and the plan or plans to which the QNECs or QMACs are made must be plans that would be permitted to be aggregated. If the plan year of the plan that contains the CODA is changed to satisfy the requirement that aggregated plans have the same plan year, QNECs and QMACs may be taken into account in the resulting short plan year only if such QNECs and QMACs could have been taken into account under an ADP test for a plan with the same short plan year. [Treas. Reg. § 1.401(k)-2(a)(6)(iii)]

QNECs cannot be taken into account for a plan year for an NHCE to the extent such contributions exceed the product of that NHCE's compensation and the greater of 5 percent or two times the plan's representative contribution rate. Any QNEC taken into account under an ACP test (including the determination of the representative contribution rate) is not permitted to be taken into account for purposes of the ADP test (including the determination of the representative contribution rate). The plan's representative contribution rate is the lowest applicable contribution rate of any eligible NHCE among a group of eligible NHCEs that consists of half of all eligible NHCEs for the plan year (or, if greater, the lowest applicable contribution rate of any eligible NHCE in the group of all eligible NHCEs for the plan year and who is employed by the employer on the last day of the plan year). The applicable contribution rate for an eligible NHCE is the sum of the QMACs taken into account under the ADP test for the eligible NHCE for the plan year and the QNECs made for the eligible NHCE for the plan year, divided by the eligible NHCE's compensation for the same period. However, QNECs that are made in connection with an employer's obligation to pay prevailing wages under the Davis-Bacon Act, Public Law 71-798, Service Contract Act of 1965, Public Law 89-286, or similar legislation can be taken into account for a plan year for an NHCE to the extent such contributions do not exceed 10 percent of that NHCE's compensation. [Treas. Reg. § 1.401(k)-2(a)(6)(iv)]

QMACs may be used for the ADP test only to the extent that such QMACs are matching contributions that are not precluded from being taken into account under the ACP test for the plan year (see Q 27:80). [Treas. Reg. § 1.401(k)-2(a)(6)(v)]

QNECs and QMACs cannot be taken into account for the ADP test to the extent such contributions are taken into account for purposes of satisfying any other ADP test, any ACP test, the ADP test safe harbor (see Q 27:40), the ACP test safe harbor (see Q 27:89), or the requirements of SIMPLE 401(k) plans (see Q 33:25). Thus, for example, matching contributions that are made for the safe harbor matching contribution requirement cannot be taken into account under the ADP test. Similarly, if a plan switches from the current year testing method to the prior year testing method, QNECs that are taken into account under the current year testing method for a year may not be taken into account under the prior year testing method for the next year.

Example 1. Plan U is a calendar year profit sharing plan that contains a CODA and uses the current year testing method and provides that elective contributions are included in compensation. The following amounts are contributed under Plan U for the 2010 plan year: QNECs equal to 2 percent of each employee's compensation; contributions equal to 6 percent of each employee's compensation that are not immediately vested under the terms of the plan; and 3 percent of each employee's compensation that the employee may elect to receive as cash or to defer under the plan. Both types of nonelective contributions are made for the HCEs (employees M and N) and the NHCEs (employees O through S) for the plan year and are contributed after the end of the plan year but before the end of the following plan year. In addition, neither type of nonelective contributions is used for any other ADP or ACP test.

For the 2010 plan year, the compensation, elective contributions, and ADRs (see Q 27:20) of employees M through S are shown in the following table:

Employee	Compensation	Elective Contributions	ADR
M	$ 100,000	$ 3,000	3%
N	100,000	2,000	2
O	60,000	1,800	3
P	40,000	0	0
Q	30,000	0	0
R	5,000	0	0
S	20,000	0	0

The elective contributions alone do not satisfy the ADP test because the ADP for the HCEs, consisting of employees M and N, is 2.5 percent and the ADP for the NHCEs is 0.6 percent.

The 2 percent QNECs satisfy the timing requirement because the QNECs are paid within 12 months after the plan year for which allocated. All nonelective contributions also satisfy the nondiscrimination requirements because all employees receive an 8 percent nonelective contribution and the nonelective contributions, excluding the QNECs, is 6 percent for all employees. In addition, the QNECs are not disproportionate because no QNEC for an NHCE exceeds the product of the plan's applicable contribution rate (2 percent) and that NHCE's compensation. The 2 percent QNECs may be taken into account in applying the ADP test: however, the 6 percent nonelective contributions may not be taken into account because they are not QNECs. If the 2 percent QNECs are taken into account, the ADP for the HCEs is 4.5 percent and the ADP for the NHCEs is 2.6 percent. Because 4.5 percent is not more than two percentage points greater than 2.6 percent, and not more than two times 2.6, the CODA satisfies the ADP test.

Example 2. The facts are the same as in Example 1, except the plan uses the prior year testing method. In addition, the NHCE ADP for the 2009 plan year (the prior plan year) is 0.8 percent, and no QNECs are contributed for the 2009 plan year during 2009 or 2010.

In 2011, it is determined that the elective contributions alone do not satisfy the ADP test for 2010 because the 2010 ADP for the eligible HCEs, consisting of employees M and N, is 2.5 percent and the 2009 ADP for the eligible NHCEs is 0.8 percent. An additional QNEC of 2 percent of compensation is made for each eligible NHCE in 2011 and allocated for 2009.

The 2 percent QNECs that are made in 2011 and allocated for the 2009 plan year do not satisfy the timing requirement for the applicable year for the 2009 plan year because they were not contributed before the last day of the 2010 plan year. Accordingly, the 2 percent QNECs may not be taken into account in applying the ADP test for the 2010 plan year. The CODA fails to be a qualified CODA unless the ADP failure is corrected (see Qs 27:25–27:34).

Example 3. The facts are the same as in Example 1, except that the ADP for the HCEs is 4.6 percent and there is no 6 percent nonelective contribution under the plan. The employer would like to take into account the 2 percent QNEC in determining the ADP for the NHCEs but not in determining the ADP for the HCEs.

The elective contributions alone fail the ADP test because the HCE ADP for the plan year (4.6 percent) exceeds 0.75 percent (0.6% × 1.25) and 1.2 percent (0.6% × 2).

The 2 percent QNECs may not be taken into account in determining the ADP of the NHCEs because they fail to satisfy the nondiscrimination requirements. This is because the amount of nonelective contributions, excluding those QNECs that would be taken into account under the ADP test, would be 2 percent of compensation for the HCEs and 0 percent for the NHCEs. Therefore, the CODA fails to be a qualified CODA unless the ADP failure is corrected.

Example 4. The facts are the same as in Example 3, except that Employee R receives a QNEC in an amount of $500 and no QNECs are made on behalf of the other employees.

If the QNEC could be taken into account, the ADP for the NHCEs would be 2.6 percent and the plan would satisfy the ADP test. The QNEC is disproportionate and cannot be taken into account to the extent it exceeds the greater of 5 percent and two times the plan's representative contribution rate (0 percent), multiplied by Employee R's compensation. The plan's representative contribution rate is 0 percent because it is the lowest applicable contribution rate among a group of NHCEs that is at least half of all NHCEs, or all the NHCEs who are employed on the last day of the plan year. Therefore, the QNEC may be taken into account under the ADP test only to the extent it does not exceed 5 percent times Employee R's compensation (or $250), and the CODA fails to satisfy the ADP test and must be corrected.

Example 5. The facts are the same as in Example 3, except that the plan changes from the current year testing method to the prior year testing method for the following plan year (2011 plan year). The ADP for the HCEs for the 2011 plan year is 3.5 percent.

The 2 percent QNECs may not be taken into account in determining the ADP for the NHCEs for the applicable year (2010 plan year) in satisfying the ADP test for the 2011 plan year because they were taken into account in satisfying the ADP test for the 2010 plan year. Accordingly, the NHCE ADP for the applicable year is 0.6 percent. The elective contributions for the plan year fail the ADP test because the HCE ADP for the plan year (3.5 percent) exceeds the ADP limit of 1.2 percent [the greater of 0.75% (0.6% × 1.25) and 1.2% (0.6% × 2)], determined using the applicable year ADP for the NHCEs. Therefore, the CODA fails to be a qualified CODA unless the ADP failure is corrected.

Example 6. JMK Corp. maintains Plan X, a profit sharing plan that contains a CODA and that uses the current year testing method. Plan X provides for employee contributions, elective contributions, and matching contributions. Matching contributions on behalf of NHCEs are QMACs and are contributed during the 2010 plan year. Matching contributions on behalf of HCEs are not QMACs, because they fail to satisfy the nonforfeitability requirement. The elective contributions and matching contributions with respect to HCEs for the 2010 plan year are shown in the following table:

	Elective Contributions	Total Matching Contributions	Matching Contributions that are not QMACs	QMACs
HCEs	15%	5%	5%	0%

The elective contributions and matching contributions with respect to the NHCEs for the 2010 plan year are shown in the following table:

	Elective Contributions	Total Matching Contributions	Matching Contributions that are not QMACs	QMACs
NHCEs	11%	4%	0%	4%

The plan fails to satisfy the ADP test because the ADP for HCEs (15 percent) is more than 1.25 percent of the ADP for NHCEs (11 percent) and more than two percentage points greater than 11 percent. However, the plan provides that QMACs may be used to meet the ADP test provided that they are not used for any other ADP or ACP test. QMACs equal to 1 percent of compensation are taken into account for each NHCE in applying the ADP test. After this adjustment, the applicable ADP and ACP (taking into account the disproportionate matching contribution rule) for the plan year are as follows:

	ADP	*ACP*
HCEs	15%	5%
NHCEs	12	3

The elective contributions and QMACs taken into account for purposes of the ADP test satisfy the test because the ADP for HCEs (15 percent) is not more than the ADP for NHCEs multiplied by 1.25 (12% × 1.25 = 15%).

Q 27:24   Is there a simple rule to follow in determining whether the ADP test is satisfied?

Yes. If the ADP (see Qs 27:18, 27:19) for the NHCEs (see Q 3:12) is less than 2 percent, the ADP for the HCEs (see Q 3:3) can be up to two times higher. If the ADP for the NHCEs is between 2 percent and 8 percent, the ADP for the HCEs can be two percentage points higher. If the ADP for the NHCEs is more than 8 percent, the ADP for the HCEs can be up to 1.25 times higher.

For example, a 4 percent ADP for the NHCEs means that an ADP of 6 percent (4% + two percentage points) for the HCEs is not discriminatory. Likewise, an ADP of 10 percent for the NHCEs permits an ADP of 12.5 percent (10% × 1.25) for the highly compensated group. [I.R.C. § 401(k)(3)]

Q 27:25   What is an excess contribution under the ADP test?

An excess contribution for a plan year is the excess of the elective contributions (including QNECs and QMACs that are treated as elective contributions; see Qs 27:17, 27:23) made on behalf of HCEs (see Q 3:3) for the plan year over the maximum amount of such contributions permitted under the ADP test (see Q 27:18) for such plan year. [I.R.C. § 401(k)(8)(B); Treas. Reg. § 1.401(k)-6]

Excess contributions can be corrected. A CODA (see Q 27:2) does not fail to satisfy the ADP test if the employer, in accordance with the terms of the plan that includes the CODA, uses any of the following correction methods:

1. The employer makes QNECs or QMACs that are taken into account for the ADP test and, in combination with other amounts taken into account, allow the CODA to satisfy the test.
2. Excess contributions are distributed.
3. Excess contributions are recharacterized.

[Treas. Reg. § 1.401(k)-2(b)(1)(i)]

A plan may provide for the use of any of the correction methods described above, may limit elective contributions in a manner designed to prevent excess contributions from being made, or may use a combination of these methods to avoid or correct excess contributions. A plan may permit an HCE to elect whether any excess contributions will be recharacterized or distributed. If the plan uses a combination of correction methods, any QNEC or QMAC must be taken into account before application of the distribution or recharacterization correction methods. [Treas. Reg. § 1.401(k)-2(b)(1)(ii)]

A failure to satisfy the ADP test may not be corrected using any other method. Thus, excess contributions for a plan year may not remain unallocated or be allocated to a suspense account for allocation to one or more employees in any future year. In addition, excess contributions may not be corrected using retroactive correction rules. [Treas. Reg. §§ 1.401(a)(4)-11(g)(3)(vii), 1.401(a)(4)-11(g)(5), 1.401(k)-2(b)(1)(iii)]

For a discussion of correction methods and the consequences of making excess contributions, see Qs 27:26 through 27:34; and, for a discussion of rules that apply for plan years beginning after December 31, 2007, see Q 27:5.

Q 27:26   How is an excess contribution corrected by distribution?

Correction through a distribution generally involves a four-step process. First, the plan must determine the total amount of excess contributions that must be distributed under the plan. Second, the plan must apportion the total amount of excess contributions among HCEs (see Q 3:3). Third, the plan must determine the income allocable to excess contributions. Finally, the plan must distribute the apportioned excess contributions and allocable income (see Q 27:27). See Q 27:28 for rules relating to the tax treatment of these distributions and Q 27:29 for other rules relating to these distributions. [I.R.C. §§ 401(k)(8)(A)(i), 401(k)(8)(C); Treas. Reg. § 1.401(k)-2(b)(2)(i); IRS Notice 2008-30, Q&As 19-21, 2008-1 C.B. 638]

The following procedures must be used to determine the total amount of the excess contributions to be distributed:

1. The amount of excess contributions attributable to a given HCE for a plan year is the amount (if any) by which the HCE's contributions taken into account for the ADP test (see Qs 27:18, 27:22, 27:23) must be reduced for the HCE's ADR (see Q 27:20) to equal the highest permitted ADR under the plan. To calculate the highest permitted ADR under a plan, the ADR of the HCE with the highest ADR is reduced by the amount required to cause that HCE's ADR to equal the ADR of the HCE with the next highest ADR. If a lesser reduction would enable the arrangement to satisfy the requirements of paragraph 3 below, only this lesser reduction is used in determining the highest permitted ADR.

2. The process described in paragraph 1 above must be repeated until the arrangement would satisfy the requirements of paragraph 3 below. The sum of all reductions for all HCEs determined under paragraph 1 above is the total amount of excess contributions for the plan year.

3. A CODA (see Q 27:2) satisfies the ADP test if the arrangement would satisfy the requirements of the ADP test if the ADR for each HCE were determined after the reductions described in paragraph 1 above.

[Treas. Reg. § 1.401(k)-2(b)(2)(ii)]

The following procedures must be used in apportioning the total amount of excess contributions determined above among the HCEs:

1. The contributions of the HCE with the highest dollar amount of contributions taken into account for the ADP test are reduced by the amount required to cause that HCE's contributions to equal the dollar amount of the contributions taken into account for the HCE with the next highest dollar amount of contributions taken into account. If a lesser apportionment to the HCE would enable the plan to apportion the total amount of excess contributions, only the lesser apportionment would apply.

2. The amount of contributions taken into account with respect to an HCE who is an eligible employee in more than one plan of an employer is determined by taking into account all contributions otherwise taken into account with respect to such HCE under any plan of the employer during the plan year of the plan being tested as being made under the plan being tested (see Q 27:20). However, the amount of excess contributions apportioned for a plan year with respect to any HCE must not exceed the amount of contributions actually contributed to the plan for the HCE for the plan year.

3. The procedure in paragraph 1 above must be repeated until the total amount of excess contributions has been apportioned.

[Treas. Reg. § 1.401(k)-2(b)(2)(iii)]

For plan years beginning on or after January 1, 2008, the income allocable to excess contributions is equal to the allocable gain or loss through the end of the plan year. [Treas. Reg. §§ 1.401(k)-2(b)(2)(iv)(A), 1.401(k)-2(b)(2)(iv)(D)]

A plan may use any reasonable method for computing the income allocable to excess contributions, provided that the method does not violate the nondiscrimination requirements (see Q 4:10), is used consistently for all participants and for all corrective distributions under the plan for the plan year, and is used by the plan for allocating income to participant's accounts. A plan will not fail to use a reasonable method for computing the income allocable to excess contributions merely because the income allocable to excess contributions is determined on a date that is no more than seven days before the distribution. [Treas. Reg. § 1.401(k)-2(b)(2)(iv)(B)]

A plan may allocate income to excess contributions for the plan year by multiplying the income for the plan year allocable to the elective contributions and other amounts taken into account (including contributions made for the plan year) by a fraction, the numerator of which is the excess contributions for the employee for the plan year and the denominator of which is the sum of the (1) account balance attributable to elective contributions and other contributions taken into account as of the beginning of the plan year and (2) any additional amount of such contributions made for the plan year. [Treas. Reg. § 1.401(k)-2(b)(2)(iv)(C)]

IRS has indicated that it would approve an arrangement whereby an excess contribution could be transferred to a nonqualified plan (see Qs 1:11–1:13), provided that both the cash-or-deferred election (see Q 27:3) and the election to transfer the excess contribution to the nonqualified plan are made before the beginning of the plan year (i.e., before the participant earns the contributed funds).

The following examples illustrate the application of the distribution correction method. For purposes of these examples, none of the plans provides for catch-up contributions (see Q 27:52).

Example 1. Plan P, a calendar year profit sharing plan that includes a CODA, provides for distribution of excess contributions to HCEs to the extent necessary to satisfy the ADP test. For the 2010 plan year, Jamie, an HCE, has elective contributions of $12,000 and $200,000 in compensation, for an ADR of 6 percent, and James, a second HCE, has elective contributions of $8,960 and compensation of $128,000, for an ADR of 7 percent. The ADP for the NHCEs is 3 percent for the 2010 plan year. Under the ADP test, the ADP of the two HCEs under the plan may not exceed 5 percent (i.e., two percentage points more than the ADP of the NHCEs under the plan). The ADP for the two HCEs under the plan is 6.5 percent. Therefore, there must be a correction of excess contributions for the 2010 plan year.

The total amount of excess contributions for the HCEs is determined as follows: the elective contributions of James (the HCE with the highest ADR) are reduced by $1,280 in order to reduce his ADR to 6 percent ($7,680 ÷ $128,000), which is the ADR of Jamie.

Because the ADP of the HCEs determined after the $1,280 reduction to James still exceeds 5 percent, further reductions in elective contributions are necessary in order to reduce the ADP of the HCEs to 5 percent. The elective contributions of Jamie and James are each reduced by 1 percent of compensation ($2,000 and $1,280 respectively). Because the ADP of the HCEs determined after the reductions equals 5 percent, the plan would satisfy the ADP test.

The total amount of excess contributions [$4,560 ($1,280 + $2,000 + $1,280)] is apportioned among the HCEs first to the HCE with the highest amount of elective contributions. Therefore, Jamie is apportioned $3,040 (the amount required to cause his elective contributions to equal the next highest dollar amount of elective contributions). Because the total amount of excess contributions has not been apportioned, further apportionment is necessary. The balance ($1,520) of the total amount of excess contributions is apportioned equally between Jamie and James ($760 to each).

Therefore, the CODA will satisfy the ADP test if, by the end of the 12-month period following the end of the 2010 plan year, Jamie receives a corrective distribution of excess contributions equal to $3,800 ($3,040 + $760) and allocable income and James receives a corrective distribution of $760 and allocable income.

Example 2. The facts are the same as in Example 1, except Jamie's ADR is based on $3,000 of elective contributions to this plan and $9,000 of elective contributions to another plan of the employer.

The total amount of excess contributions [$4,560 ($1,280 + $2,000 + $1,280)] is apportioned among the HCEs first to the HCE with the highest amount of elective contributions. The amount of elective contributions for Jamie is $12,000. Therefore, Jamie is apportioned $3,040 (the amount required to cause his elective contributions to equal the next highest dollar amount of elective contributions). However, no more than the amount actually contributed to the plan may be apportioned to an HCE. Accordingly, no more than $3,000 may be apportioned to Jamie. Therefore, the remaining $1,560 must be apportioned to James.

The CODA will satisfy the ADP test if, by the end of the 12-month period following the end of the 2010 plan year, Jamie receives a corrective distribution of excess contributions equal to $3,000 (total amount of elective contributions actually contributed to the plan for Jamie) and allocable income and James receives a corrective distribution of $1,560 and allocable income.

If an HCE has made an excess contribution and a part thereof is attributable to a designated Roth contribution, see Q 27:96 for a modification to the correction methods.

Q 27:27   When must distribution of an excess contribution be made?

Within 12 months after the close of the plan year in which the excess contribution arose, the plan must distribute to each HCE (see Q 3:3) the excess contributions apportioned to such HCE and the allocable income (see Q 27:26). Except as otherwise provided in this Q 27:27 and Q 27:33, a distribution of excess contributions must be in addition to any other distributions made during the year and must be designated as a corrective distribution by the employer. In the event of a complete termination of the plan during the plan year in which an excess contribution arose, the corrective distribution must be made as soon as administratively feasible after the date of termination of the plan, but in no event later than 12 months after the date of termination. If the entire account balance of an HCE is distributed prior to when the plan makes a distribution of excess contributions, the distribution is deemed to have been a corrective distribution of excess contributions (and allocable income) to the extent that a corrective distribution would otherwise have been required. [Treas. Reg. § 1.401(k)-2(b)(2)(v)]

Q 27:28   What is the tax treatment of corrective distributions of excess contributions?

For plan years beginning on or after January 1, 2008, a corrective distribution of excess contributions and allocable income (see Q 27:26) is includible in the employee's gross income for the employee's taxable year in which distributed. [Treas. Reg. § 1.401(k)-2(b)(2)(vi)(A)] See Q 27:34 for additional rules relating to the employer excise tax on amounts distributed more than two-and-one-half months (six months in the case of certain plans that include an EACA; see Qs 27:5, 27:6) after the end of the plan year.

Regardless of when the corrective distribution is made, it is not subject to the 10 percent tax on early distributions (see Qs 16:1, 16:17). [I.R.C. § 401(k)(8)(D); Treas. Reg. § 1.401(k)-2(b)(2)(vi)(A)] Corrective distributions cannot be rolled over to an eligible retirement plan (see Q 34:8).

Corrective distributions of excess contributions and attributable income from designated Roth accounts are not qualified distributions (see Q 27:105).

Q 27:29 What other rules apply to corrective distributions of excess contributions?

A corrective distribution of excess contributions (and allocable income; see Q 27:26) may be made under the terms of the plan without regard to any notice or consent to the employee or the employee's spouse (see Qs 10:21, 10:61). Excess contributions are treated as employer contributions for purposes of the deduction rules (see Q 12:1) and the annual addition limitation (see Q 6:34) even if distributed from the plan. A distribution of excess contributions (and allocable income) is not treated as a distribution for purposes of determining whether the plan satisfies the minimum distribution requirements (see Q 11:27). Any distribution of less than the entire amount of excess contributions (and allocable income) with respect to any HCE is treated as a pro rata distribution of excess contributions and allocable income. [Treas. Reg. § 1.401(k)-2(b)(2)(vii)]

Q 27:30 How is an excess contribution corrected by recharacterization?

Excess contributions are recharacterized only if the excess contributions that would have to be distributed if the plan was correcting through distribution of excess contributions (see Q 27:26) are recharacterized as described in Q 27:31, and all of the conditions set forth in Q 27:32 are satisfied. [I.R.C. § 401(k)(8)(A)(ii); Treas. Reg. § 1.401(k)-2(b)(3)(i)]

Q 27:31 What is the tax treatment of a recharacterized excess contribution?

Recharacterized excess contributions are includible in the employee's gross income as if such amounts were distributed (see Q 27:28). The recharacterized excess contributions are treated as employee contributions for purposes of Section 72, the nondiscrimination requirements (see Q 4:10), the ACP test (see Q 27:77), the distribution limitation (see Q 27:14), and the ADP test (see Q 27:18). This requirement is not treated as satisfied unless the payor or plan administrator (see Q 20:1) timely reports the recharacterized excess contributions as employee contributions to IRS and the employee. [Treas. Reg. § 1.401(k)-2(b)(3)(ii)]

Q 27:32 What other rules apply to recharacterized excess contributions?

Excess contributions may not be recharacterized after 2½ months after the close of the plan year to which the recharacterization relates. Recharacterization is deemed to have occurred on the date on which the last of those HCEs (see Q 3:3) with excess contributions to be recharacterized is notified (see Q 27:31). [Treas. Reg. § 1.401(k)-2(b)(3)(iii)(A)]

The amount of recharacterized excess contributions, in combination with the employee contributions actually made by the HCE, may not exceed the maximum amount of employee contributions (determined without regard to the ACP test; see Q 27:77) permitted under the provisions of the plan as in effect on the first day of the plan year. [Treas. Reg. § 1.401(k)-2(b)(3)(iii)(B)]

Recharacterized excess contributions continue to be treated as employer contributions for all purposes of the Code, except as set forth in Q 27:31. Thus, for example, recharacterized excess contributions remain subject to the nonforfeitability requirement (see Q 27:13); must be deducted under Section 404; and are treated as employer contributions for the annual addition limitation (see Q 6:34). [Treas. Reg. § 1.401(k)-2(b)(3)(iii)(C)]

Q 27:33 What rules apply to all excess contribution corrections?

The amount of excess contributions (and allocable income) to be distributed (see Q 27:26) or the amount of excess contributions recharacterized (see Q 27:30) with respect to an employee for a plan year is reduced by any amounts previously distributed to the employee from the plan to correct excess deferrals for the employee's taxable year ending with or within the plan year (see Q 27:63). The amount required to be distributed to correct an excess deferral to an employee for a taxable year is reduced by any excess contributions (and allocable income) previously distributed or excess contributions recharacterized with respect to the employee for the plan year beginning with or within the taxable year. The amount of excess contributions includible in the gross income of the employee, and the amount of excess contributions reported by the payor or plan administrator (see Q 20:1) as includible in the gross income of the employee, does not include the amount of the reduction. [I.R.C. § 402(g)(2); Treas. Reg. §§ 1.401(k)-2(b)(4)(i), 1.402(g)-1(e)(6)]

A matching contribution (see Q 27:75) is taken into account for purposes of the nondiscrimination requirements (see Q 4:10) even if the match is with respect to an elective contribution that is distributed or recharacterized. This requires that, after correction of excess contributions, each level of matching contributions be currently and effectively available to a group of employees. Thus, a plan that provides the same rate of matching contributions to all employees will not meet the nondiscrimination requirements if elective contributions are distributed to HCEs (see Q 3:3) to the extent needed to meet the ADP test (see Q 27:18), while matching contributions attributable to those elective contributions remain allocated to the HCEs' accounts. A plan may forfeit matching contributions attributable to excess contributions, excess aggregate contributions (see Q 27:82), or excess deferrals to avoid a violation of the nondiscrimination requirements. A QMAC (see Q 27:23) is not treated as forfeitable (see Q 27:13) merely because under the plan it is forfeited to avoid a violation or because it is a permissible withdrawal under an EACA (see Qs 27:5,

27:7). [I.R.C. §§ 401(k)(8)(E) (as amended by WRERA 2008 § 109(b)(2)), 411(a)(3)(G) (as amended by WRERA 2008 § 109(b)(2); Treas. Reg. §§ 1.401(a)(4)-4(e)(3)(iii)(G), 1.401(k)-2(b)(4)(ii), 1.401(k)-2(b)(4)(iii), 1.411(a)-4(b)(7)]

If excess contributions are distributed or recharacterized, the CODA (see Q 27:2) is treated as meeting the ADP test regardless of whether the ADP (see Q 27:19) for the HCEs, if recalculated after the distributions or recharacterizations, would satisfy the test. [Treas. Reg. § 1.401(k)-2(b)(4)(iv)]

Example. For the 2010 plan year, Steve, an HCE, has elective contributions of $8,500 and $85,000 in compensation, for an ADR (see Q 27:20) of 10 percent, and Sallie, an HCE, has elective contributions of $9,600 and compensation of $160,000, for an ADR of 6 percent. As a result, the ADP for the two HCEs under the plan is 8 percent [(10% + 6%) ÷ 2]. The ADP for the NHCEs is 3 percent. Under the ADP test, the ADP of the two HCEs under the plan may not exceed 5 percent (i.e., two percentage points more than the ADP of the NHCEs under the plan).

The total excess contributions for the HCEs is determined as follows:

Step 1. The elective contributions of Steve (the HCE with the highest ADR) are reduced by $3,400 in order to reduce his ADR to 6 percent ($5,100 ÷ $85,000), which is the ADR of Sallie. Because the ADP of the HCEs still exceeds 5 percent, the ADP test is not satisfied and further reductions in elective contributions are necessary. The elective contributions of Steve and Sallie are each reduced by 1 percent of compensation ($850 and $1,600, respectively). Because the ADP of the two HCEs now equals 5 percent, the ADP test is satisfied, and no further reductions in elective contributions are necessary.

Step 2. The total excess contributions for the HCEs that must be distributed equal $5,850, the total reductions in elective contributions under Step 1 ($3,400 + $850 + $1,600).

The $5,850 in total excess contributions for the 2010 plan year is then distributed as follows:

Step 3. The plan distributes $1,100 in elective contributions to Sallie (the HCE with the highest dollar amount of elective contributions) in order to reduce the dollar amount of her elective contributions to $8,500, which is the dollar amount of the elective contributions of Steve.

Step 4. Because the total amount distributed ($1,100) is less than the total excess contributions ($5,850), Step 3 must be repeated. As the dollar amounts of remaining elective contributions for both Steve and Sallie are equal, the remaining $4,750 of excess contributions is then distributed equally to Steve and Sallie in the amount of $2,375 each.

Under this example, Steve must receive a total distribution of $2,375 of excess contributions, and Sallie must receive a total distribution of $3,475 of excess contributions. This is true even though the ADR of Steve exceeded the ADR of Sallie. The plan is now treated as satisfying the nondiscrimination test even though the ADP would fail to satisfy the test if recalculated after distributions [7.21% ($6,125 ÷ $85,000) + 3.83% ($6,125 ÷ $160,000) = 11.04% ÷ 2 = 5.52%].

A CODA does not fail to meet the ADP test merely because excess contributions that are catch-up contributions (see Q 27:52) and exceed the ADP limit are not corrected. [Treas. Reg. § 1.401(k)-2(b)(4)(v)]

Q 27:34 What happens if excess contributions are not timely corrected?

If a plan does not correct excess contributions (see Q 27:25) within two-and-one-half months after the close of the plan year for which the excess contributions are made, the employer will be liable for a 10 percent excise tax on the amount of the excess contributions. QNECs and QMACs properly taken into account (see Q 27:23, 27:25) for a plan year may enable a plan to avoid having excess contributions, even if the contributions are made after the close of the two-and-one-half-month period. [I.R.C. § 4979(f); Treas. Reg. §§ 1.401(k)-2(b)(5)(i), 54.4979-1]

If excess contributions are not corrected within 12 months after the close of the plan year for which they were made, the CODA will fail to satisfy the ADP test (see Q 27:18) for the plan year for which the excess contributions are made and all subsequent plan years during which the excess contributions remain in the plan. [I.R.C. § 401(k)(8); Treas. Reg. § 1.401(k)-2(b)(5)(ii)]

In the case of excess contributions under a plan that includes an EACA (see Qs 27:5, 27:6), six months is substituted for two-and-one-half months. The additional time applies to a distribution of excess contributions for a plan year beginning on or after January 1, 2010 only where all the eligible NHCEs (see Q 3:12) and eligible HCEs (see Q 3:3) are covered employees under the EACA for the entire plan year (or for the portion of the plan year that the eligible NHCEs and eligible HCEs are eligible employees). No tax is imposed on any excess contribution to the extent the contribution (together with any income allocable thereto) is corrected before the close of the first two and one-half months of the following plan year (six months in the case of a plan that includes an EACA). The extension to six months applies to a distribution of excess contributions for a plan year beginning on or after January 1, 2010, only where all the eligible NHCEs and eligible HCEs are covered employees under an EACA. In the case of an EACA, QMACs and QNECs properly taken into account may enable a plan to avoid excess contributions, even if made after the close of the six-month period. [Treas. Reg. §§ 1.401(k)-2(b)(5)(iii), 54.4979-1(c)]

Q 27:35 Are there additional rules that apply to the prior year testing method for the ADP test?

The current year testing method is the testing method under which the applicable year is the current plan year, and the prior year testing method is the testing method under which the applicable year is the prior plan year. [Treas. Reg. § 1.401(k)-6]

For the prior year testing method, additional rules apply to:

1. Change in the testing method (see Q 27:36).
2. Calculation of the ADP under the prior year testing method for the first plan year (see Q 27:37).
3. Plans using different testing methods for the ADP and ACP tests (see Q 27:38).
4. Plan coverage changes (see Q 27:39).

[Treas. Reg. § 1.401(k)-2(c)]

Q 27:36   Can the testing method be changed?

A plan is permitted to change from the prior year testing method to the current year testing method (see Q 27:35) for any plan year. A plan is permitted to change from the current year testing method to the prior year testing method only in situations described below. A plan that uses the safe harbor method (see Q 27:40) is treated as using the current year testing method for that plan year. [Treas. Reg. § 1.401(k)-2(c)(1)(i)]

The situations in which a plan can change to the prior year testing method are as follows:

1. The plan is not the result of the aggregation of two or more plans, and the current year testing method was used under the plan for each of the five plan years preceding the plan year of the change (or, if lesser, the number of plan years the plan has been in existence, including years in which the plan was a portion of another plan).
2. The plan is the result of the aggregation of two or more plans and, for each of the plans that are being aggregated (the aggregating plans), the current year testing method was used for each of the five plan years preceding the plan year of the change (or, if lesser, the number of plan years since that aggregating plan has been in existence, including years in which the aggregating plan was a portion of another plan).
3. A disposition or acquisition occurs; and, (a) as a result of the transaction, the employer maintains both a plan using the prior year testing method and a plan using the current year testing method, and (b) the change from the current year testing method to the prior year testing method occurs within the transition period.

[I.R.C. § 410(b)(6)(C); Treas. Reg. §§ 1.401(k)-2(c)(1)(ii), 1.410 (b)-2(f)]

Notification to or filing with IRS of a change from the current year to the prior year testing method is not required in order for the change to be valid. However, the plan must reflect such a change. [Treas. Reg. § 1.401(k)-1(e)(7)]

Example. The facts are the same as in Examples 2 and 3 of Q 27:19; and, for the 2012 plan year (the third plan year), Ellen of New City Corporation's 401(k) plan has a 10 percent ADP for HCEs and an 8 percent ADP for NHCEs. The plan does not meet the ADP test because (1) 10 percent exceeds 6 percent (the ADP for NHCEs for 2011, the *prior plan year*) multiplied by 1.25 and (2) the ADP of HCEs exceeds the *prior plan year's* ADP of NHCEs by more than two percentage points. However, Ellen of New City Corporation may elect to base the 2012 ADP test on the ADP for NHCEs for the current plan year, 2012. If this election is made, the plan will meet the ADP test because 10 percent does not exceed 8 percent multiplied by 1.25.

Q 27:37 How is the ADP calculated under the prior year testing method for the first plan year?

If, for the first plan year of any plan (other than a successor plan), the plan uses the prior year testing method (see Q 27:35), the plan is permitted to use either (1) that first plan year as the applicable year for determining the ADP (see Q 27:19) for eligible NHCEs (see Q 3:12) or (2) 3 percent as the ADP for eligible NHCEs, for applying the ADP test (see Q 27:18) for that first plan year. A plan (other than a successor plan) that uses the prior year testing method but has elected for its first plan year to use that year as the applicable year is not treated as changing its testing method in the second plan year and is not subject to the limitations on double counting on QNECs (see Q 27:23) for the second plan year. [Treas. Reg. § 1.401(k)-2(c)(2)(i)]

The first plan year of any plan is the first year in which the plan provides for elective contributions (see Q 27:16). Thus, the first plan year rule does not apply to a plan for a plan year if for such plan year the plan is aggregated with any other plan that provided for elective contributions in the prior year. [Treas. Reg. § 1.401(k)-2(c)(2)(ii)]

A plan is a successor plan if 50 percent or more of the eligible employees for the first plan year were eligible employees under a qualified CODA (see Q 27:9) maintained by the employer in the prior year. If a plan that is a successor plan uses the prior year testing method for its first plan year, the ADP for the group of NHCEs for the applicable year must be determined in accordance with Q 27:39. [Treas. Reg. § 1.401(k)-2(c)(2)(iii)]

Q 27:38 May a plan use different testing methods for the ADP and ACP tests?

Except as otherwise provided below, a plan may use the current year testing method or prior year testing method (see Q 27:35) for the ADP test (see Q 27:18) for a plan year without regard to whether the current year testing method or prior year testing method is used for the ACP test (see Q 27:77) for that year. For example, a plan may use the prior year testing method for the ADP test and the current year testing method for its ACP test for the plan year. However, plans that use different testing methods cannot use:

1. The recharacterization method (see Q 27:30) to correct excess contributions for a plan year;

2. The rules to take elective contributions into account under the ACP test rather than the ADP test (see Q 27:81); or

3. The rules to take QMACs into account under the ADP test rather than the ACP test (see Q 27:23).

[Treas. Reg. § 1.401(k)-2(c)(3)]

Q 27:39 What happens if there are plan coverage changes?

A plan that uses the prior year testing method (see Q 27:35) and experiences a plan coverage change during a plan year satisfies the ADP test (see Q 27:18) for that year only if the plan provides that the ADP (see Q 27:19) for the NHCEs (see Q 3:12) for the plan year is the weighted average of the ADPs for the prior year subgroups. If a plan coverage change occurs and 90 percent or more of the total number of the NHCEs from all prior year subgroups are from a single prior year subgroup, then, in lieu of using the weighted averages, the plan may provide that the ADP for the group of eligible NHCEs for the prior year under the plan is the ADP of the NHCEs for the prior year of the plan under which that single prior year subgroup was eligible.

The following definitions apply:

1. "Plan coverage change" means a change in the group or groups of eligible employees under a plan on account of (a) the establishment or amendment of a plan, (b) a plan merger or spinoff, (c) a change in the way plans are combined or separated (e.g., permissively aggregating plans not previously aggregated or ceasing to permissively aggregate plans), (d) a reclassification of a substantial group of employees that has the same effect as amending the plan (e.g., a transfer of a substantial group of employees from one division to another division), or (e) a combination of any of the foregoing.

2. "Prior year subgroup" means all NHCEs for the prior plan year who, in the prior year, were eligible employees under a specific plan maintained by the employer that included a qualified CODA (see Q 27:9) and who would have been eligible employees in the prior year under the plan being tested if the plan coverage change had first been effective as of the first day of the prior plan year instead of first being effective during the plan year. The determination of whether an NHCE is a member of a prior year subgroup is made without regard to whether the NHCE terminated employment during the prior year.

3. "Weighted average of the ADPs for the prior year subgroups" means the sum, for all prior year subgroups, of the adjusted ADPs for the plan year.

4. "Adjusted ADP" means the ADP for the prior plan year of the specific plan under which the members of the prior year subgroup were eligible employees on the first day of the prior plan year, multiplied by a fraction, the numerator of which is the number of NHCEs in the prior year subgroup and denominator of which is the total number of NHCEs in all prior year subgroups.

Example 1. Regent Advisory Services, Inc. maintains two calendar year plans, Plan O and Plan P, each of which includes a CODA. The plans were not permissively aggregated for the 2010 plan year. Both plans use the prior year testing method. Plan O had 300 eligible employees who were NHCEs for the 2010 plan year, and their ADP for that year was 6 percent. Sixty of the eligible employees who were NHCEs for the 2010 plan year under Plan O terminated their employment during that year. Plan P had 100 eligible employees who were NHCEs for 2010, and the ADP for those NHCEs for that plan was 4 percent. Plan O and Plan P are permissively aggregated for the 2011 plan year (see Q 27:12).

The permissive aggregation of Plan O and Plan P for the 2011 plan year is a plan coverage change that results in treating the plans as one plan (Plan OP). Therefore, the prior year ADP for the NHCEs under Plan OP for the 2011 plan year is the weighted average of the ADPs for the prior year subgroups: the Plan O prior year subgroup and the Plan P prior year subgroup.

The Plan O prior year subgroup consists of the 300 employees who, in the 2010 plan year, were eligible NHCEs under Plan O and who would have been eligible under Plan OP for the 2010 plan year if Plan O and Plan P had been permissively aggregated for that plan year. The Plan P prior year subgroup consists of the 100 employees who, in the 2010 plan year, were eligible NHCEs under Plan P and would have been eligible under Plan OP for the 2010 plan year if Plan O and Plan P had been permissively aggregated for that plan year.

The weighted average of the ADPs for the prior year subgroups is the sum of the adjusted ADP for the Plan O prior year subgroup and the adjusted ADP for the Plan P prior year subgroup. The adjusted ADP for the Plan O prior year subgroup is 4.5 percent, calculated as follows: 6 percent (the ADP for the NHCEs under Plan O for the 2010 plan year) × 300/400 (the number of NHCEs in the Plan O prior year subgroup divided by the total number of NHCEs in all prior year subgroups). The adjusted ADP for the Plan P prior year subgroup is 1 percent, calculated as follows: 4 percent (the ADP for the NHCEs under Plan P for the 2010 plan year) × 100/400 (the number of NHCEs in the Plan P prior year subgroup divided by the total number of NHCEs in all prior year subgroups). Thus, the prior year ADP for NHCEs under Plan OP for the 2011 plan year is 5.5 percent (the sum of adjusted ADPs for the prior year subgroups, 4.5% + 1.0%).

The determination of whether an NHCE is a member of a prior year subgroup is made without regard to whether that NHCE terminated employment during the prior year. Thus, the prior ADP for the NHCEs under Plan OP for the 2011 plan year is unaffected by the termination of the 60 NHCEs covered by Plan O during the 2010 plan year.

Example 2. The facts are the same as Example 1, except that the 60 employees who terminated employment during the 2010 plan are instead spun-off to another plan.

The permissive aggregation of Plan O and Plan P for the 2011 plan year is a plan coverage change that results in treating the plans as one plan (Plan OP), and the spin-off of the 60 employees is a plan coverage change. Therefore, the prior year ADP for the NHCEs under Plan OP for the 2011 plan year is the weighted average of the ADPs for the prior year subgroups: the Plan O prior year subgroup and the Plan P prior year subgroup.

For purposes of determining the prior year subgroups, the employees who would have been eligible employees in the prior year under the plan being tested are determined as if both plan coverage changes had first been effective as of the first day of the prior plan year. The Plan O prior year subgroup consists of the 240 employees who, in the 2010 plan year, were eligible NHCEs under Plan O and would have been eligible under Plan OP for the 2010 plan year if the spin-off had occurred at the beginning of the 2010 plan year and Plan O and Plan P had been permissively aggregated for that plan year. The Plan P prior year subgroup consists of the 100 employees who, in the 2010 plan year, were eligible NHCEs under Plan P and would have been eligible under Plan OP for the 2010 plan year if Plan O and Plan P had been permissively aggregated for that plan year.

The weighted average of the ADPs for the prior year subgroups is the sum of the adjusted ADP with respect to the prior year subgroup consisting of eligible NHCEs from Plan O and the adjusted ADP with respect to the prior year subgroup consisting of eligible NHCEs from Plan P. The adjusted ADP for the prior year subgroup consisting of eligible NHCEs under Plan O is 4.23 percent, calculated as follows: 6 percent (the ADP for the NHCEs under Plan O for the 2010 plan year) × 240/340 (the number of NHCEs in that prior year subgroup divided by the total number of NHCEs in all prior year subgroups). The adjusted ADP for the prior year subgroup consisting of the eligible NHCEs from Plan P is 1.18 percent, calculated as follows: 4 percent (the ADP for the NHCEs under Plan P for the 2010 plan year) × 100/340 (the number of NHCEs in that prior year subgroup divided by the total number of NHCEs in all prior year subgroups. Thus, the prior year ADP for NHCEs under Plan OP for the 2011 plan year is 5.41 percent (the sum of adjusted ADPs for the prior year subgroups, 4.23% + 1.18%).

Example 3. The facts are the same as in Example 1, except that instead of Plan O and Plan P being permissively aggregated for the 2011 plan year, 200 of the employees eligible under Plan O were spun off from Plan O and merged into Plan P.

The spin-off from Plan O and merger to Plan P for the 2011 plan year are plan coverage changes for Plan P. Therefore, the prior year ADP for the NHCEs under Plan P for the 2011 plan year is the weighted average of the ADPs for the prior year subgroups under Plan P. There are two subgroups under Plan P for the 2011 plan year. The Plan O prior year subgroup consists of the 200 employees who, in the 2010 plan year, were eligible NHCEs under Plan O and who would have been eligible under Plan P for the 2010 plan year if the spin-off and merger had occurred on the first day of the 2010 plan year. The Plan P prior year subgroup consists of the 100 employees who, in the 2010 plan year, were eligible NHCEs under Plan P for the 2010 plan year.

The weighted average of the ADPs for the prior year subgroups is the sum of the adjusted ADP for the Plan O prior year subgroup and the adjusted ADP for the Plan P prior year subgroup. The adjusted ADP for the Plan O prior year subgroup is 4 percent, calculated as follows: 6 percent (the ADP for the NHCEs under Plan O for the 2010 plan year) × 200/300 (the number of NHCEs in the Plan O prior year subgroup divided by the total number of NHCEs in all prior year subgroups). The adjusted ADP for the Plan P prior year subgroup is 1.33 percent, calculated as follows: 4 percent (the ADP for the NHCEs under Plan P for the 2010 plan year) × 100/300 (the number of NHCEs in the Plan P prior year subgroup divided by the total number of NHCEs in all prior year subgroups). Thus, the prior year ADP for NHCEs under Plan P for the 2011 plan year is 5.33 percent (the sum of adjusted ADPs for the two prior year subgroups, 4.0% + 1.33%).

The spin-off from Plan O for the 2011 plan year is a plan coverage change for Plan O. Therefore, the prior year ADP for the NHCEs under Plan O for the 2011 plan year is the weighted average of the ADPs for the prior year subgroups under Plan O. In this case, there is only one prior year subgroup under Plan O, the employees who were NHCEs of Employer B for the 2010 plan year and who were eligible for the 2010 plan year under Plan O. Because there is only one prior year subgroup under Plan O, the weighted average of the ADPs for the prior year subgroup under Plan O is equal to the NHCE ADP for the prior year (2010 plan year) under Plan O, or 6 percent.

Example 4. Esteban Ltd. maintains a calendar year plan, Plan Q, which includes a CODA that uses the prior year testing method. Plan Q covers employees of Division A and Division B. In 2010, Plan Q had 500 eligible employees who were NHCEs, and the ADP for those NHCEs for 2010 was 2 percent. Effective January 1, 2011, Esteban Ltd. amends the eligibility provisions under Plan Q to exclude employees of Division B, effective January 1, 2011. In addition, effective on that same date, Esteban Ltd. establishes a new calendar year plan, Plan R, which includes a CODA that uses the prior year testing method. The only eligible employees under Plan R are the 100 employees of Division B who were eligible employees under Plan Q.

Plan R is a successor plan because all of the employees were eligible employees under Plan Q in the prior year. Therefore, Plan R cannot use the first plan year rule.

The amendment to the eligibility provisions of Plan Q and the establishment of Plan R are plan coverage changes for Plan Q and Plan R. Accordingly, each plan must determine the NHCE ADP for the 2011 plan year under the rules for plan coverage changes.

The prior year ADP for NHCEs under Plan Q is the weighted average of the ADPs for the prior year subgroups. Plan Q has only one prior year subgroup because the only NHCEs who would have been eligible employees under Plan Q for the 2010 plan year if the amendment to the Plan Q eligibility provisions had occurred as of the first day of that plan year were eligible employees under Plan Q. Therefore, for purposes of the 2011 plan year under

Plan Q, the ADP for NHCEs for the prior year is the weighted average of the ADPs for the prior year subgroups, or 2 percent, the same as if the plan amendment had not occurred.

Similarly, Plan R has only one prior year subgroup because the only NHCEs who would have been eligible employees under Plan R for the 2010 plan year if the plan were established as of the first day of that plan year were eligible employees under Plan Q. Therefore, for purposes of the 2011 testing year under Plan R, the ADP for NHCEs for the prior year is the weighted average of the ADPs for the prior year subgroups, or 2 percent, the same as that of Plan Q.

Example 5. The facts are the same as in Example 4, except that the provisions of Plan R extend eligibility to 50 hourly employees who previously were not eligible employees under any qualified CODA maintained by Esteban Ltd. Plan R is a successor plan because 100 of Plan R's 150 eligible employees were eligible employees under another qualified CODA maintained by Esteban Ltd. in the prior year. Therefore, Plan R cannot use the first plan year rule. The establishment of Plan R is a plan coverage change that affects Plan R. Because the 50 hourly employees were not eligible employees under any qualified CODA of Esteban Ltd. for the prior plan year, they do not comprise a prior year subgroup. Accordingly, Plan R still has only one prior year subgroup. Therefore, for purposes of the 2011 testing year under Plan R, the ADP for NHCEs for the prior year is the weighted average of the ADPs for the prior year subgroups, or 2 percent, the same as that of Plan Q.

[Treas. Reg. § 1.401(k)-2(c)(4)]

Q 27:40   Does a safe harbor rule apply for purposes of satisfying the ADP test?

Yes. A CODA (see Q 27:2) satisfies the ADP safe harbor provision for a plan year if the arrangement satisfies the safe harbor nonelective contribution requirement (see Q 27:42) or the safe harbor matching contribution requirement (see Q 27:43) for the plan year, the notice requirement (see Q 27:46), the plan year requirement (see Q 27:47), and additional rules (see Qs 27:48–27:50), as applicable. The contribution requirement cannot be satisfied by taking permitted disparity (see Q 7:1) into account. [I.R.C. § 401(k)(12); Treas. Reg. § 1.401(k)-3(a)]

See Qs 27:5, 27:6 for a discussion of the safe harbor provisions for EACAs and Qs 27:49 and 27:94 for a discussion of proposed regulations issued by IRS.

Q 27:41   What is safe harbor compensation?

Safe harbor compensation means compensation as defined in Q 27:21, provided, however, that the rule that generally permits a definition of compensation to exclude all compensation in excess of a specified dollar amount does not apply in determining the safe harbor compensation of NHCEs (see Q 3:12). Thus, for example, the plan may limit the period used to determine safe harbor compensation to the eligible employee's period of participation. [I.R.C. § 401(k)(12)(C); Treas. Reg. §§ 1.401(k)-3(b)(2), 1.401(k)-6]

Q 27:42　What is the safe harbor nonelective contribution requirement for the ADP test?

The safe harbor nonelective contribution requirement is satisfied if, under the terms of the plan, the employer is required to make a QNEC (see Q 27:17) on behalf of each eligible NHCE (see Q 3:12) equal to at least 3 percent of the employee's safe harbor compensation (see Q 27:41). [Treas. Reg. § 1.401(k)-3(b)(1)]

Q 27:43　What is the safe harbor matching contribution requirement for the ADP test?

The safe harbor matching contribution requirement is satisfied if, under the terms of the plan, QMACs (see Q 27:17) are made on behalf of each eligible NHCE (see Q 3:12) in an amount determined under the basic matching formula or under an enhanced matching formula. [I.R.C. § 401(k)(12)(B)(i); Treas. Reg. § 1.401(k)-3(c)(1)]

Under the basic matching formula, each eligible NHCE receives QMACs in an amount equal to the sum of:

1. 100 percent of the amount of the employee's elective contributions (see Q 27:16) that do not exceed 3 percent of the employee's safe harbor compensation (see Q 27:41), and

2. 50 percent of the amount of the employee's elective contributions that exceed 3 percent of the employee's safe harbor compensation but that do not exceed 5 percent of the employee's safe harbor compensation.

[Treas. Reg. § 1.401(k)-3(c)(2)]

Under an enhanced matching formula, each eligible NHCE receives a matching contribution under a formula that, at any rate of elective contributions by the employee, provides an aggregate amount of QMACs at least equal to the aggregate amount of QMACs that would have been provided under the basic matching formula. In addition, under an enhanced matching formula, the ratio of matching contributions on behalf of an employee under the plan for a plan year to the employee's elective contributions may not increase as the amount of an employee's elective contributions increases. [Treas. Reg. § 1.401(k)-3(c)(3)]

The safe harbor matching contribution requirement is not satisfied if the ratio of matching contributions made on account of an HCE's (see Q 3:3) elective contributions under the CODA (see Q 27:2) for a plan year to those elective contributions is greater than the ratio of matching contributions to elective contributions that would apply with respect to any eligible NHCE with elective contributions at the same percentage of safe harbor compensation. [Treas. Reg. § 1.401(k)-3(c)(4)]

The safe harbor matching contribution requirement will not fail to be satisfied merely because safe harbor matching contributions are made on both elective contributions and employee contributions (see Q 27:74) if safe harbor matching contributions are made with respect to the sum of elective contributions and employee contributions on the same terms as safe harbor matching contributions are made with respect to elective contributions. Alternatively, the safe harbor matching contribution requirement will not fail to be satisfied merely because safe harbor matching contributions are made on both elective contributions and employee contributions if safe harbor matching contributions on elective contributions are not affected by the amount of employee contributions. The safe harbor matching contribution requirement will not fail to be satisfied merely because the plan provides that safe harbor matching contributions will be made separately with respect to each payroll period (or with respect to all payroll periods ending with or within each month or quarter of a plan year) taken into account under the plan for the plan year, provided that safe harbor matching contributions with respect to any elective contributions made during a plan year quarter are contributed to the plan by the last day of the immediately following plan year quarter. [Treas. Reg. § 1.401(k)-3(c)(5)]

Q 27:44   What restrictions are permissible on elective contributions by NHCEs?

The safe harbor matching contribution requirement (see Q 27:43) is not satisfied if elective contributions (see Q 27:16) by NHCEs (see Q 3:12) are restricted, unless the restrictions are permitted as discussed below.

A plan may limit the frequency and duration of periods in which eligible employees may make or change cash-or-deferred elections (see Q 27:3) under a plan. However, an employee must have a reasonable opportunity, including a reasonable period after receipt of the notice (see Q 27:45), to make or change a cash-or-deferred election for the plan year. For this purpose, a 30-day period is deemed to be a reasonable period to make or change a cash-or-deferred election.

A plan is permitted to limit the amount of elective contributions that may be made by an eligible employee under a plan, provided that each NHCE who is an eligible employee is permitted (unless the employee is restricted due to Code limitations) to make elective contributions in an amount that is at least sufficient to receive the maximum amount of matching contributions available under the plan for the plan year, and the employee is permitted to elect any lesser amount of elective contributions. However, a plan may require eligible employees to make cash-or-deferred elections in whole percentages of compensation or whole dollar amounts.

A plan may limit the types of compensation that may be deferred by an eligible employee under a plan, provided that each eligible NHCE is permitted to make elective contributions under a definition of compensation that would be a reasonable definition of compensation (see Q 6:67). Thus, the definition of compensation from which elective contributions may be made is not required to satisfy the nondiscrimination requirement (see Q 6:68).

A plan may limit the amount of elective contributions made by an eligible employee under a plan because of the limitations on the amount of elective deferrals (see Q 27:51) or on the amount of the annual addition (see Q 6:34), or because, on account of a hardship distribution, an employee's ability to make elective contributions has been suspended for six months (see Q 27:14).

[Treas. Reg. § 1.401(k)-3(c)(6)]

Q 27:45 Has IRS provided examples for the ADP test safe harbor matching contribution requirement?

Yes, and the following examples illustrate the safe harbor matching contribution requirement (see Qs 27:41, 27:43, 27:44).

Example 1. Beginning January 1, 2011, SBK Corp. maintains Plan L covering employees in Divisions D and E, each of which includes HCEs (see Q 3:3) and NHCEs (see Q 3:12). Plan L contains a CODA (see Q 27:2) and provides QMACs (see Q 27:17) equal to 100 percent of each eligible employee's elective contributions (see Q 27:16) up to 3 percent of compensation and 50 percent of the next 2 percent of compensation. For purposes of the matching contribution formula, safe harbor compensation is defined as all compensation within the meaning of Section 415(c) (3) (see Qs 6:41, 27:41). Also, each employee is permitted to make elective contributions from all safe harbor compensation and may change a cash-or-deferred election at any time. Plan L limits the amount of an employee's elective contributions for purposes of the limits on elective deferrals (see Q 27:51) and the annual addition (see Q 6:34) and, in the case of a hardship distribution, suspends an employee's ability to make elective contributions for six months (see Q 27:14). All contributions under Plan L are nonforfeitable (see Q 27:13) and are subject to withdrawal restrictions (see Q 27:14). Plan L provides for no other contributions, and SBK Corp. maintains no other plans. Plan L is maintained on a calendar year basis, and all contributions for a plan year are made within 12 months after the end of the plan year. Based on these facts, matching contributions under Plan L are safe harbor matching contributions because they are QMACs equal to the basic matching formula. Accordingly, Plan L satisfies the safe harbor matching contribution requirement.

Example 2. The facts are the same as in Example 1, except that instead of providing a basic matching contribution, Plan L provides a QMAC equal to 100 percent of each eligible employee's elective contributions up to 4 percent of safe harbor compensation. Plan L's formula is an enhanced matching formula because each eligible NHCE receives safe harbor matching contributions at a rate that, at any rate of elective contributions, provides an aggregate amount of QMACs at least equal to the aggregate amount of QMACs that would have been received under the basic safe harbor matching formula, and the rate of matching contributions does not increase as the rate of an employee's elective contributions increases. Accordingly, Plan L satisfies the safe harbor matching contribution requirement.

Example 3. The facts are the same as in Example 2, except that instead of permitting each employee to make elective contributions from all compensation within the meaning of Section 415(c)(3), each employee's elective contributions under Plan L are limited to 15 percent of the employee's compensation. The definition of compensation under Plan L is a reasonable definition of compensation. Plan L will not fail to satisfy the safe harbor matching contribution requirement merely because Plan L limits the amount of elective contributions and the types of compensation that may be deferred by eligible employees, provided that each eligible NHCE may make elective contributions equal to at least 4 percent of the employee's safe harbor compensation.

Example 4. The facts are the same as in Example 1, except that Plan L provides that only employees employed on the last day of the plan year will receive a safe harbor matching contribution. Even if the plan that provides for employee contributions and matching contributions satisfies the minimum coverage requirement (see Q 5:15) taking into account this last day requirement, Plan L will not satisfy the safe harbor matching contribution requirement because safe harbor matching contributions are not made on behalf of all eligible NHCEs who make elective contributions. The result would be the same if, instead of providing safe harbor matching contributions, Plan L provides for a 3 percent safe harbor nonelective contribution (see Q 27:42) that is restricted to eligible employees under the CODA who are employed on the last day of the plan year.

Example 5. The facts are the same as in Example 1, except that instead of providing QMACs under the basic matching formula to employees in both Divisions D and E, employees in Division E are provided QMACs under the basic matching formula, while safe harbor matching contributions continue to be provided to employees in Division D under the enhanced matching formula described in Example 2. Even if Plan L satisfies the nondiscrimination requirements with respect to each rate of matching contributions available to employees under the plan, the plan will fail to satisfy the safe harbor matching contribution requirement because the rate of matching contributions with respect to HCEs in Division D at a rate of elective contributions between 3 percent and 5 percent would be greater than that with respect to NHCEs in Division E at the same rate of elective contributions. For example, an HCE in Division D who would have a 4 percent rate of elective contributions would have a rate of matching contributions of 100 percent, while an NHCE in Division E who would have the same rate of elective contributions would have a lower rate of matching contributions.

Q 27:46   What is the notice requirement for the ADP test safe harbor rules?

Each eligible employee must be given notice of the employee's rights and obligations under the plan, and the notice must satisfy the content requirement and the timing requirement discussed below. The notice must be in writing or in such other form as may be approved by IRS. See Qs 20:4 and 20:5 for a discussion of the use of electronic media to provide notices to plan participants. [Treas. Reg. § 1.401(k)-3(d)(1)]

The content requirement is satisfied if the notice is sufficiently accurate and comprehensive to inform the employee of the employee's rights and obligations under the plan and written in a manner calculated to be understood by the average employee eligible to participate in the plan. [Treas. Reg. § 1.401(k)-3(d)(2)(i)] A notice is not considered sufficiently accurate and comprehensive unless the notice accurately describes:

1. The safe harbor nonelective contribution or safe harbor matching contribution formula used under the plan (including a description of the levels of safe harbor matching contributions, if any, available under the plan (see Qs 27:42, 27:43));

2. Any other contributions under the plan or matching contributions to another plan on account of elective contributions (see Q 27:16) or employee contributions (see Q 27:74) under the plan (including the potential for discretionary matching contributions) and the conditions under which such contributions are made;

3. The plan to which safe harbor contributions will be made (if different from the plan containing the CODA; see Q 27:2);

4. The type and amount of compensation that may be deferred under the plan (see Q 27:41);

5. How to make cash-or-deferred elections (see Q 27:3), including any administrative requirements that apply to such elections;

6. The periods available under the plan for making cash-or-deferred elections (see Q 27:44);

7. Vesting and withdrawal provisions applicable to contributions under the plan (see Qs 27:13, 27:14); and

8. Information that makes it easy to obtain additional information about the plan (including an additional copy of the summary plan description (SPD; see Q 22:1)) such as telephone numbers, addresses and, if applicable, electronic addresses of individuals or offices from whom employees can obtain such plan information.

[Treas. Reg. § 1.401(k)-3(d)(2)(iii)]

A plan will not fail to satisfy the content requirements merely because, in the case of information relating to any other contributions under the plan, the plan to which safe harbor contributions will be made, or the type and amount of compensation that may be deferred under the plan, the notice cross-references the relevant portions of an SPD that provides the same information and that has been provided (or is concurrently provided) to employees. [Treas. Reg. § 1.401(k)-3(d)(2)(ii)]

The timing requirement is satisfied if the notice is provided within a reasonable period before the beginning of the plan year (or, in the year an employee becomes eligible, within a reasonable period before the employee becomes eligible). The determination of whether a notice satisfies this timing requirement is based on all of the relevant facts and circumstances. The timing requirement is deemed to be satisfied if at least 30 days (and no more than 90 days) before the beginning of each plan year, the notice is given to each eligible employee for the plan year. In the case of an employee who does not receive the notice within the period described in the previous sentence because the employee becomes eligible after the 90th day before the beginning of the plan year, the timing requirement is deemed to be satisfied if the notice is provided no more than 90 days before the employee becomes eligible (and no later than the date the employee becomes eligible). Thus, for example, the preceding sentence would apply in the case of any employee eligible for the first plan year under a newly established plan that provides for elective contributions or in the case of the first plan year in which an employee becomes eligible under an existing plan that provides for elective contributions. [Treas. Reg. § 1.401(k)-3(d)(3)]

IRS representatives have opined that an exact percentage must be shown in the notice if the plan is using the safe harbor matching contribution formula to meet the minimum required contribution requirement. However, if the plan is meeting the requirement by making a nonelective contribution, the percentage may be expressed as "at least 3 percent," thereby giving the employer the ability to contribute greater than 3 percent if it so desires.

IRS representatives also opined in a case where a safe harbor notice is provided to participants 30 days before the plan year begins that the plan "might" contribute a 3 percent safe harbor nonelective contribution in the coming plan year. During the plan year, the plan sponsor decides to qualify under the safe harbor rules by making a 3 percent nonelective contribution, and a supplemental notice is sent to all participants that such a contribution would indeed be made that year. As to what plan amendment must be made, IRS representatives opined that, for the first year a plan will be using the safe harbor, the plan must be amended before the end of the year in which the safe harbor would apply. Because a "maybe" notice is being used, the plan must specify the use of ADP current year testing (see Qs 27:18, 27:35) as of the beginning of the plan year until the employer decides to make the required contribution to use the safe harbor. Once that decision has been made, the plan must be amended to provide that the plan is using the safe harbor. Only one amendment needs to be made electing safe harbor status if it is intended that the plan will follow the safe harbor contribution requirements in future years. However, if the plan sponsor intends to use the "maybe" notice in the subsequent year, the amendment either must specify that it is effective only for the year in which it is adopted, or the amendment must specify that the safe harbor rules are being followed for the current year and that the testing method is being changed back to the ADP current year method as of the first day of the following year. If the plan sponsor fails to amend the plan after the safe harbor notice has been given to participants, the ADP test will have to be done because the plan did not specify otherwise.

See Qs 27:5, 27:6 for the notice requirement in the case of an EACA.

Q 27:47   What is the plan year requirement for the ADP test safe harbor rules?

Except as provided in this Q 27:47 or in Q 27:48, a plan will fail to satisfy the safe harbor requirements and the safe harbor requirements relating to automatic contribution arrangements (see Qs 27:5, 27:6) unless plan provisions that satisfy the safe harbor rules are adopted before the first day of the plan year and remain in effect for an entire 12-month plan year. In addition, except as provided in Q 27:49, a plan that includes provisions that satisfy the safe harbor rules will not satisfy the coverage and nondiscrimination requirements (see Q 27:12) if it is amended to change such provisions for that plan year. Moreover, if, as described in Q 27:50, safe harbor matching or nonelective contributions (see Q 27:40) will be made to another plan for a plan year, provisions under that other plan specifying that the safe harbor contributions will be made and providing that the contributions will be QNECs or QMACs (see Q 27:23) must also be adopted before the first day of that plan year. [Treas. Reg. § 1.401(k)-3(e)(1)]

A newly established plan (other than a successor plan; see Q 27:37) will not be treated as violating the plan year requirement merely because the plan year is less than 12 months, provided that the plan year is at least three months long (or, in the case of a newly established employer that establishes the plan as soon as administratively feasible after the employer comes into existence, a shorter period). Similarly, a CODA (see Q 27:2) will not fail to satisfy the plan year requirement if it is added to an existing profit sharing, stock bonus, or pre-ERISA money purchase pension plan (see Q 27:1) for the first time during that year provided that (1) the plan is not a successor plan and (2) the CODA is made effective no later than three months prior to the end of the plan year. [Treas. Reg. § 1.401(k)-3(e)(2)]

A plan that has a short plan year as a result of changing its plan year will not fail to satisfy the plan year requirement merely because the plan year has less than 12 months, provided that (1) the plan satisfied the plan year requirement for the immediately preceding plan year, and (2) the plan satisfies such requirement for the immediately following plan year (or for the immediately following 12 months if the immediately following plan year is less than 12 months). [Treas. Reg. § 1.401(k)-3(e)(3)]

A plan that terminates during a plan year will not fail to satisfy the plan year requirement merely because the final plan year is less than 12 months, provided that the plan satisfies the requirement through the date of termination and either:

1. The plan would satisfy the requirements in Q 27:49, treating the termination of the plan as a reduction or suspension of safe harbor matching contributions, other than the requirement that employees have a reasonable opportunity to change their cash-or-deferred elections (see Q 27:3) and, if applicable, employee contribution elections, or

2. The plan termination is in connection with a disposition or acquisition or the employer incurs a substantial business hardship (see Q 8:24). [Treas. Reg. § 1.401(k)-3(e)(4); Prop. Treas. Reg. § 1.401(k)-3(e)(4)(ii)]

See Q 27:46 for a discussion of opinions expressed by IRS representatives.

Q 27:48   What rules apply to plan amendments adopting the ADP test safe harbor nonelective contributions?

Notwithstanding, the plan year requirement (see Q 27:47), a plan that provides for the use of the current year testing method (see Q 27:35) may be amended after the first day of the plan year and no later than 30 days before the last day of the plan year to adopt the safe harbor nonelective contribution method (see Q 27:42), effective as of the first day of the plan year but only if the plan provides contingent and follow-up notices. Such a plan amendment for a plan year may provide for the use of the safe harbor nonelective contribution method, and a plan sponsor is not limited in the number of years for which it is permitted to adopt an amendment providing for the safe harbor nonelective contribution method. [Treas. Reg. § 1.401(k)-3(f)(1)]

A plan satisfies the requirement to provide the contingent notice if it provides a notice that would satisfy the notice requirement (see Q 27:46), except that, in lieu of setting forth the safe harbor contributions used under the plan, the notice specifies that the plan may be amended during the plan year to include the safe harbor nonelective contribution and that, if the plan is amended, a follow-up notice will be provided. [Treas. Reg. § 1.401(k)-3(f)(2)]

A plan satisfies the requirement to provide a follow-up notice if no later than 30 days before the last day of the plan year, each eligible employee is given a notice that states that the safe harbor nonelective contributions will be made for the plan year. The notice must be in writing or in such other form as may be prescribed by IRS and is permitted to be combined with a contingent notice provided for the next plan year. [Treas. Reg. § 1.401(k)-3(f)(3)]

See Q 27:46 for a discussion of opinions expressed by IRS representatives.

Q 27:49   Is it permissible to reduce or suspend an ADP test safe harbor matching or nonelective contribution?

A plan that provides for safe harbor matching contributions (see Q 27:43) will not fail to satisfy the ADP test (see Q 27:18) for a plan year merely because the plan is amended during a plan year to reduce or suspend safe harbor matching contributions on future elective contributions and, if applicable, employee contributions provided that:

1. All eligible employees are provided a supplemental notice;
2. The reduction or suspension of safe harbor matching contributions is effective no earlier than the later of 30 days after eligible employees are provided the supplemental notice and the date the amendment is adopted;
3. Eligible employees are given a reasonable opportunity (including a reasonable period after receipt of the supplemental notice) prior to the reduction or suspension of safe harbor matching contributions to change

their cash-or-deferred elections (see Q 27:3) and, if applicable, their employee contribution elections;

4. The plan is amended to provide that the ADP test will be satisfied for the entire plan year in which the reduction or suspension occurs using the current year testing method (see Q 27:35); and

5. The plan satisfies all other CODA requirements with respect to amounts deferred through the effective date of the amendment.

[Treas. Reg. § 1.401(k)-3(g)(1)]

The supplemental notice is satisfied if each eligible employee is given a notice in writing or such other form as prescribed by IRS that explains (1) the consequences of the amendment that reduces or suspends matching contributions on future elective contributions and, if applicable, employee contributions, (2) the procedures for changing their cash-or-deferred elections and, if applicable, their employee contribution elections, and (3) the effective date of the amendment. [Treas. Reg. § 1.401(k)-3(g)(2)]

Under proposed regulations issued by IRS, it is permissible to reduce or suspend an ADP test safe harbor nonelective contribution. A plan that provides for safe harbor nonelective contributions (see Q 27:42) will not fail to satisfy the ADP test for the plan year merely because the plan is amended during the plan year to reduce or suspend safe harbor nonelective contributions, provided that:

1. The employer incurs a substantial business hardship (see Q 8:24);

2. The amendment is adopted after May 18, 2009;

3. All eligible employees are provided the supplemental notice;

4. The reduction or suspension of safe harbor nonelective contributions is effective no earlier than the later of 30 days after eligible employees are provided the supplemental notice and the date the amendment is adopted;

5. Eligible employees are given a reasonable opportunity (including a reasonable period after receipt of the supplemental notice) prior to the reduction or suspension of nonelective contributions to change their cash-or-deferred elections and, if applicable, their employee contribution elections;

6. The plan is amended to provide that the ADP test will be satisfied for the entire plan year in which the reduction or suspension occurs using the current year testing method; and

7. The plan satisfies all other CODA requirements with respect to safe harbor compensation paid through the effective date of the amendment.

[Prop. Treas. Reg. §§ 1.401(k)-3(e)(4)(ii), 1.401(k)-3(g)(1)]

With regard to the supplemental notice, the first requirement is changed to an explanation of the consequences of the amendment that reduces or suspends future safe harbor contributions. [Prop. Treas. Reg. § 1.401(k)-3(g)(2)]

See Q 27:46 for a discussion of opinions expressed by IRS representatives.

Q 27:50   What other rules apply to the ADP test safe harbor requirements?

A contribution is taken into account for the safe harbor requirements for a plan year if and only if the contribution would be taken into account for such plan year for the ADP test (see Q 27:18) or the ACP test (see Q 27:77). Thus, for example, a safe harbor matching contribution (see Q 27:43) must be made within 12 months of the end of the plan year. Similarly, an elective contribution (see Q 27:16) that would be taken into account for a plan year (see Q 27:22) must be taken into account for such plan year for the safe harbor requirements, even if the compensation would have been received after the close of the plan year. [Treas. Reg. § 1.401(k)-3(h)(1)]

A safe harbor nonelective contribution (see Q 27:42) used to satisfy the nonelective contribution requirement may also be taken into account for purposes of determining whether a plan satisfies the nondiscrimination requirements (see Q 4:10). Thus, these contributions are not subject to the limitations on QNECs (see Q 27:23) but are subject to the rules generally applicable to nonelective contributions for purposes of the nondiscrimination requirements. However, to the extent they are needed to satisfy the safe harbor contribution requirement or the safe harbor contribution requirement relating to automatic contribution arrangements (see Qs 27:5, 27:6), safe harbor nonelective contributions may not be taken into account under any plan for permitted disparity purposes (see Q 7:1). [I.R.C. §§ 401(k)(12)(E)(ii), 401(k)(13)(D)(iv); Treas. Reg. § 1.401(k)-3(h)(2)]

The alternative nondiscrimination rule for certain plans that provide for early participation (see Q 27:18) do not apply for the safe harbor requirements or the safe harbor requirements relating to automatic contribution arrangements. Thus, a plan is not treated as satisfying the safe harbor requirements with respect to the eligible employees who have not completed the minimum age and service requirements unless the plan satisfies the safe harbor requirements with respect to such eligible employees. However, a plan is permitted to treat the plan as two separate plans and apply the safe harbor requirements to one plan and apply the ADP test to the other plan. See Example 2 in Q 27:12. [Treas. Reg. § 1.401(k)-3(h)(3)]

Safe harbor matching or nonelective contributions may be made to the plan that contains the CODA or to another qualified defined contribution plan (see Q 2:2). If safe harbor contributions are made to another defined contribution plan, the safe harbor plan must specify the plan to which the safe harbor contributions are made, and the contribution requirements (see Qs 27:42, 27:43) must be satisfied in the other defined contribution plan in the same manner as if the contributions were made to the plan that contains the CODA. Consequently, the plan to which the contributions are made must have the same plan year as the plan containing the CODA, and each employee eligible under the plan containing the CODA must be eligible under the same conditions under the other defined contribution plan. The plan to which the safe harbor contributions are made need not be a plan that can be aggregated with the plan that contains the CODA. [Treas. Reg. § 1.401(k)-3(h)(4)]

Safe harbor matching or nonelective contributions cannot be used to satisfy the safe harbor requirements with respect to more than one plan. [Treas. Reg. § 1.401(k)-3(h)(5)]

Q 27:51   Is there a dollar limitation on the amount of elective contributions?

An employee's elective contributions (see Q 27:16) under all plans in which the employee participates (even if not maintained by the same employer) during the taxable year (including simplified employee pensions (SEPs) that offer salary reduction arrangements (see Q 32:9), 403(b) plans that offer salary reduction arrangements (see Q 35:1), designated Roth contributions (see Q 27:96), and SIMPLE plans (see Q 33:1)) are limited to an applicable dollar amount, and the amount of the elective contributions in excess of the applicable dollar amount (excess deferrals) is included in such individual's gross income for the year, except to the extent the excess deferrals are composed of designated Roth contributions and thus are already includible in gross income. A designated Roth contribution is treated as an excess deferral only to the extent that the total amount of designated Roth contributions for an individual exceeds the applicable limit for the taxable year or the designated Roth contributions are identified as excess deferrals and the individual receives a distribution of the excess deferrals and allocable income (see Qs 27:62, 27:64). [I.R.C. § 402(g)(1); Treas. Reg. §§ 1.402(g)-1(a), 1.402(g)-(1)(b), 1.402(g)-1(d)(1); IRS Notice 2005-75, 2005-2 C.B. 929]

The 2006 $15,000 limit on elective contributions is adjusted for inflation; however, an adjustment will be made only if it is $500 or greater and then will be made in multiples of $500 (i.e., rounded down to the next lowest multiple of $500). For example, an increase in the cost-of-living of $499 will result in no adjustment, and an increase of $999 will create an upward adjustment of $500. [I.R.C. § 402(g)(4); Treas. Reg. § 1.402(g)-1(d)(1)] For 2010, the limit on elective contributions remained at $16,500. [IRS Notice 2009-94, 2009-2 C.B. 848] For the prior five years, the applicable dollar amount was:

For taxable years beginning in calendar year	The applicable dollar amount
2009	$16,500
2008	15,500
2007	15,500
2006	15,000
2005	14,000

Since a CODA (see Q 27:2) is part of a defined contribution plan, the amount of a participant's elective contributions is also subject to the limitation on annual additions (see Q 6:34). For annual addition limitation purposes, compensation includes elective contributions. [I.R.C. § 415(c)(3)(D)] For the treatment of catch-up contributions to a 401(k) plan, see Q 27:52.

A 401(k) plan is not qualified unless the plan provides that the elective contributions on behalf of an employee under the plan and all other plans of the employer may not exceed the applicable limit for the employee's taxable year beginning in the calendar year. The plan may incorporate the applicable limit by reference. [I.R.C. § 401(a)(30); Treas. Reg. § 1.401(a)-30(a)]

Make-up contributions by an employer or employee to a 401(k) plan on behalf of reemployed veterans that are required by USERRA (see Q 1:16) are not subject to the generally applicable plan contribution limits or limits on deductible contributions with respect to the year in which the contributions are made. Moreover, the make-up contributions will not be considered in applying the limits to any other contributions made during the year. However, the make-up contributions (including elective contributions) may not exceed the aggregate amount of contributions that would have been permitted under the applicable limits for the year for which the contributions are made if the individual had continued to be employed by the employer during the period of military service. Because the limits are subject to cost-of-living adjustments, the amount of a make-up contribution may vary. For example, a reemployed veteran may make an elective contribution under a 401(k) plan of $15,500 for the 2007 plan year. However, the make-up contribution would be limited to $14,000 if the contribution related to the 2005 plan year.

Q 27:52   What are salary reduction catch-up contributions?

An individual who participates in a 401(k) plan, who will attain age 50 by the end of the plan year and for whom no other elective contributions (see Q 27:16) may otherwise be made for the plan year because of the application of any limitation contained in the Code (e.g., the annual limit on elective contributions) or of the plan, will be able to make additional elective contributions (i.e., catch-up contributions) to the plan for that plan year.

The maximum catch-up contribution that an eligible individual may make for the taxable year is the *lesser* of:

1. The applicable dollar amount, or
2. The individual's compensation for the year reduced by all of the individual's other elective contributions for the year to 401(k) plans, salary reduction SEPs (see Q 32:9), SIMPLE plans (see Q 33:1), 403(b) plans (see Q 35:1), and Section 457 plans.

The 2006 $5,000 limitation is adjusted for inflation in $500 increments in the same manner as the adjustment to the elective contribution dollar limitation (see Q 27:51). For 2010, the limit on catch-up contributions remained at $5,500. [IRS Notice 2009-94, 2009-2 C.B. 848] For the prior five years, the applicable dollar amount was:

For taxable years beginning in calendar year	The applicable dollar amount
2009	$ 5,500
2008	5,000
2007	5,000
2006	5,000
2005	4,000

Example 1. In 2010, Ann is an HCE (see Q 3:3), who is over age 50 and participates in a 401(k) plan sponsored by her employer, Williamson of Williamsburg, Inc. The maximum annual elective contribution limit is $16,500 for 2010 and, after application of the ADP test (see Q 27:18), the maximum elective contribution Ann may make for 2010 is $9,000. Ann may make an additional catch-up contribution of $5,500 for 2010.

Example 1A. The facts are the same as in Example 1, except that the maximum annual elective contribution limit increases to $17,000 and the maximum additional catch-up contribution limit increases to $6,000 in 2011. Ann may make an additional catch-up contribution of $6,000 in 2011.

Example 2. Sallie, who is over age 50, participates in a 401(k) plan and, for 2010, has compensation of $60,000. For 2010, the maximum elective contribution limit is $16,500; but, under the terms of the plan, the maximum permitted elective contribution is 10 percent of compensation or, in Sallie's case, $6,000. Sallie can contribute up to $11,500 for 2010 ($6,000 under the terms of the plan and an additional catch-up contribution of $5,500).

Example 2A. The facts are the same as in Example 2, except that the maximum annual elective contribution limit increases to $17,000 and the maximum additional catch-up contribution limit increases to $6,000 in 2011. Sallie may make an additional catch-up contribution of $6,000 in 2011.

Catch-up contributions are not subject to any other contribution limits and are not taken into account in applying other contribution limits; and, therefore, they are not considered, for example, for the elective contribution limitation, the deduction for plan contributions (see Q 12:15), or the annual addition limitation (see Q 6:34). In addition, catch-up contributions are not subject to the nondiscrimination rules (see Q 4:10), including, among others, the ADP test and the ACP test (see Q 27:77). However, a plan fails to meet the nondiscrimination requirements with respect to benefits, rights, and features (see Q 4:20) unless the plan allows all eligible individuals participating in the plan to make the same election with respect to catch-up contributions. For purposes of this rule, all plans of related employers are treated as a single plan.

[I.R.C. § 414(v); Treas. Reg. §§ 1.414(v)-1(c)(2)(i), 1.414(v)-1(c)(2)(iii); IRS Notice 2005-75, 2005-2 C.B. 929]

IRS published final regulations concerning catch-up contributions. For details, see Qs 27:53 through 27:61.

Q 27:53 What important terms apply to catch-up contributions?

An applicable employer plan will not be treated as failing to meet any requirement of the Code solely because the plan permits a catch-up eligible participant to make catch-up contributions. With respect to an applicable employer plan, catch-up contributions are elective deferrals (see Q 27:16) made by a catch-up eligible participant that exceed any of the applicable limits (see Q 27:54) and that are treated under the applicable employer plan as catch-up contributions, but only to the extent they do not exceed the catch-up contribution limit (see Qs 27:55, 27:58). To the extent provided in Q 27:56, catch-up contributions are disregarded for purposes of various statutory limits. In addition, unless otherwise provided in Q 27:57, all catch-up eligible participants of the employer must be provided the opportunity to make catch-up contributions in order for an applicable employer plan to comply with the universal availability requirement. [I.R.C. §§ 402(g)(3), 414(v); Treas. Reg. §§ 1.402(g)-2, 1.414(v)-1(a)(1)]

Except as specifically provided to the contrary, elective deferrals treated as catch-up contributions remain subject to statutory and regulatory rules otherwise applicable to elective deferrals. For example, catch-up contributions under an applicable employer plan that is a 401(k) plan are subject to the nonforfeitability and distribution restrictions (see Qs 27:13, 27:14). In addition, the plan is permitted to provide a single election for catch-up eligible participants, with the determination of whether elective deferrals are catch-up contributions being made under the terms of the plan. [Treas. Reg. § 1.414(v)-1(a)(2)]

The term "applicable employer plan" means a 401(k) plan and also includes salary reduction SEPs (see Q 32:9), SIMPLE plans (see Q 33:1), 403(b) plans (see Q 35:1), and a Section 457 plan. [Treas. Reg. § 1.414(v)-1(g)(1)]

The term "elective deferral" includes a contribution to a Section 457 plan. [I.R.C. § 402(g)(3); Treas. Reg. § 1.414(v)-1(g)(2)]

An employee is a catch-up eligible participant for a taxable year if:

1. The employee is eligible to make elective deferrals under an applicable employer plan, and

2. The employee's 50th or higher birthday would occur before the end of the employee's taxable year.

[Treas. Reg. § 1.414(v)-1(g)(3)]

A participant who is projected to attain age 50 before the end of the taxable year is deemed to be age 50 as of the first day of such year. Thus, a participant who will attain age 50 on or before the last day of such year can be a catch-up eligible participant as of the beginning of that year, rather than at the participant's 50th birthday; and this is true even if the participant dies or terminates employment during that year before attaining age 50. [I.R.C. § 414(v)(5)(A); Treas. Reg. § 1.414(v)-1(g)(3)(ii)]

For illustrative examples, see Q 27:61.

Q 27:54 When do elective deferrals exceed an applicable limit for catch-up contribution purposes?

An applicable limit for purposes of determining catch-up contributions for a catch-up eligible participant (see Q 27:53) is any of the following:

1. *Statutory limit.* A statutory limit is a limit on elective deferrals (see Q 27:53) or annual additions (see Q 6:34) permitted to be made (without regard to catch-up contributions) with respect to an employee for a year. [I.R.C. §§ 401(a)(30), 402(h), 403(b), 408, 415(c), or 457(b)(2)]

2. *Employer-provided limit.* An employer-provided limit is any limit on the elective deferrals an employee is permitted to make (without regard to catch-up contributions) that is contained in the terms of the plan, but that is not required under the Code. Thus, for example, if, in accordance with the terms of the plan, HCEs (see Q 3:3) are limited to a deferral percentage of 10 percent of compensation, this limit is an employer-provided limit that is an applicable limit with respect to the HCEs.

3. *Actual deferral percentage (ADP) limit.* In the case of a 401(k) plan that would fail the ADP test (see Q 27:18) if it did not make a correction (see Qs 27:25–27:34), the ADP limit is the highest amount of elective deferrals that can be retained in the plan by an HCE. In the case of a salary reduction SEP (see Q 32:9) that would fail the average deferral percentage test if it did not make a correction (see Q 32:14), the ADP limit is the highest amount of elective deferrals that can be made by any HCE.

[Treas. Reg. § 1.414(v)-1(b)(1)]

IRS representatives have opined that a participant's cessation of elective contributions because of a hardship withdrawal (see Q 27:14) is a statutory limit.

Except as provided below, the amount of elective deferrals in excess of an applicable limit is determined as of the end of the plan year by comparing the total elective deferrals for the plan year with the applicable limit for the plan year. In addition, except as provided below, in the case of a plan that provides for separate employer-provided limits on elective deferrals for separate portions of plan compensation within the plan year, the applicable limit for the plan year is the sum of the dollar amounts of the limits for the separate portions. For example, if a plan sets a deferral percentage limit for each payroll period, the applicable limit for the plan year is the sum of the dollar amounts of the limits for the payroll periods. If the plan limits elective deferrals for separate portions of the plan year, then, solely for purposes of determining the amount that is in excess of an employer-provided limit, the plan may provide, as an alternative method, that the applicable limit for the plan year is the product of the employee's plan year compensation and the time-weighted average of the deferral percentage limits, rather than determining the employer-provided limit as the sum of the limits for the separate portions of the year. Thus, for example, if, in accordance with the terms of the plan, HCEs are limited to 8 percent of compensation during the first half of the plan year and 10 percent of compensation for the second half of the plan year, the plan is permitted to provide that the applicable limit for an HCE is 9 percent of the employee's plan year compensation. A plan using the alternative method is permitted to provide that the applicable limit for the plan year is determined as the product of the catch-up eligible participant's compensation used for purposes of the ADP test and the time-weighted average of the deferral percentage limits. This alternative calculation is available regardless of whether the deferral percentage limits change during the plan year. [Treas. Reg. § 1.414(v)-1(b)(2)(i)]

In the case of an applicable limit that is applied on the basis of a year other than the plan year (e.g., the calendar-year limit on elective deferrals), the determination of whether elective deferrals are in excess of the applicable limit is made on the basis of such other year. [Treas. Reg. § 1.414(v)-1(b)(2)(ii)]

For illustrative examples, see Q 27:61.

Q 27:55   What is the catch-up contribution limit?

Elective deferrals (see Q 27:16) with respect to a catch-up eligible participant (see Q 27:53) in excess of an applicable limit (see Q 27:54) are treated as catch-up contributions as of a date within a taxable year only to the extent that such elective deferrals do not exceed the catch-up contribution limit, reduced by elective deferrals previously treated as catch-up contributions for the taxable year. The catch-up contribution limit for a taxable year is generally the applicable dollar catch-up limit for such taxable year (see Q 27:52). However, an elective deferral is not treated as a catch-up contribution to the extent that the elective deferral, when added to all other elective deferrals for the taxable year under any applicable employer plan (see Q 27:53) of the employer, exceeds the participant's compensation for the taxable year. [Treas. Reg. §§ 1.414(v)-1(c)(1), 1.414(v)-1(c)(2)(i), 1.414(v)-1(c)(2)(iii)] See Q 27:60 for additional details.

For purposes of determining the maximum amount of permitted catch-up contributions for a catch-up eligible participant, the determination of whether an elective deferral is a catch-up contribution is made as of the last day of the plan year or, for annual addition limitation purposes (see Q 6:34), as of the last day of the limitation year (see Q 6:58), except that, with respect to elective deferrals in excess of an applicable limit that is tested on the basis of the taxable year or calendar year (e.g., the dollar limit on elective deferrals (see Q 27:51)), the determination of whether such elective deferrals are treated as catch-up contributions is made at the time they are deferred. [Treas. Reg. § 1.414(v)-1(c)(3)]

For illustrative examples, see Q 27:61.

Q 27:56   How are catch-up contributions treated?

Catch-up contributions are not taken into account in applying the elective deferral dollar limit (see Q 27:51), the salary reduction SEP dollar limit (see Q 32:10), the SIMPLE plan elective deferral dollar limit (see Qs 33:10, 33:30), the 403(b) plan elective deferral limit (see Q 35:34), or the annual addition limitation (see Q 6:34) to other contributions or benefits under an applicable employer plan (see Q 27:53) or any other plan of the employer. [I.R.C. § 414(v)(3)(A)(i); Treas. Reg. § 1.414(v)-1(d)(1)]

Elective deferrals that are treated as catch-up contributions with respect to a 401(k) plan because they exceed a statutory or employer-provided limit are subtracted from the catch-up contribution eligible participant's (see Q 27:53) elective deferrals for the plan year for purposes of determining the ADR (see Q 27:20) of a catch-up eligible participant. [Treas. Reg. § 1.414(v)-1(d)(2)(i)]

For purposes of the correction of excess contributions (see Q 27:25), elective deferrals under the plan treated as catch-up contributions for the plan year and not taken into account in the ADP test under the preceding paragraph are subtracted from the catch-up eligible participant's elective deferrals under the plan for the plan year. [Treas. Reg. § 1.414(v)-1(d)(2)(ii)]

A 401(k) plan that satisfies the ADP test through correction must retain any elective deferrals that are treated as catch-up contributions (see Q 27:55) because they exceed the ADP limit (see Q 27:54). In addition, a 401(k) plan is not treated as failing to satisfy the correction rules (see Qs 27:25–27:34) merely because elective deferrals described in the preceding sentence are not distributed or recharacterized as employee contributions. Notwithstanding the fact that elective deferrals are not distributed, such elective deferrals are still considered to be excess contributions; and, accordingly, matching contributions with respect to such elective deferrals are permitted to be forfeited (see Q 27:83). [I.R.C. § 411(a)(3)(G) (as amended by WRERA 2008 § 109(b)(2)); Treas. Reg. § 1.414(v)-1(d)(2)(iii)]

Example 1. Jean (age 45) and David (age 54) are HCEs (see Q 3:3) who, for 2010, defer $16,500 and $15,500, respectively, to Case Corp.'s 401(k) plan. The plan fails the ADP test for 2010 and is required to make a total corrective distribution of $1,000, plus earnings. The plan may not recharacterize the corrective distribution as a catch-up contribution for David. Jean must receive the corrective distribution as the HCE with the highest dollar amount of deferrals. However, because Jean is not eligible to make catch-up contributions, the corrective distribution may not be recharacterized as a catch-up contribution; but, if Jean had been age 50, the amount could be recharacterized as a catch-up contribution.

Example 2. A 401(k) plan's HCEs, John (age 52) and Martha (age 54), defer $21,500 and $16,500 to the plan, respectively, for 2010. John's excess deferral ($5,000) is treated as a catch-up contribution and excluded from the ADP test. However, the plan still fails the ADP test and is required to make a corrective distribution of $1,500, plus earnings. Because Martha and John are treated as deferring the same dollar amount, each, generally, would receive a corrective distribution of $750. However, because Martha has not exceeded the catch-up limit, the plan may recharacterize the $750 corrective distribution to her as a catch-up contribution. By contrast, John must receive the entire $750 corrective distribution.

Catch-up contributions with respect to the current plan year are not taken into account for top-heavy purposes (see Q 26:3). However, catch-up contributions for prior years are taken into account for top-heavy purposes. Therefore, catch-up contributions for prior years are included in the account balances that are used in determining whether the plan is top-heavy. [Treas. Reg. § 1.414(v)-1(d)(3)(i)]

Catch-up contributions with respect to the current plan year are not taken into account for minimum coverage purposes (see Q 5:15). Thus, catch-up contributions are not taken into account in determining the average benefit percentage (see Q 5:19) for the year if benefit percentages are determined based on current year contributions. However, catch-up contributions for prior years are taken into account for minimum coverage purposes. Therefore, catch-up contributions for prior years are included in the account balances that are used in determining the average benefit percentage if allocations for prior years are taken into account. [Treas. Reg. § 1.414(v)-1(d)(3)(ii)]

An applicable employer plan (see Q 27:53) does not violate the nondiscrimination requirements (see Qs 4:10–4:17) merely because the group of employees for whom catch-up contributions are currently available (i.e., the catch-up eligible participants; see Q 27:55) is not a group of employees that would satisfy the minimum coverage requirement. In addition, a catch-up eligible participant is not treated as having a right to a different rate of allocation of matching contributions merely because an otherwise nondiscriminatory schedule of matching rates is applied to elective deferrals that include catch-up contributions. [Treas. Reg. § 1.414(v)-1(d)(4)]

For additional examples, see Q 27:61.

Q 27:57 What is the universal availability requirement for catch-up contribution purposes?

An applicable employer plan (see Q 27:53) that offers catch-up contributions and that is otherwise subject to the nondiscrimination requirements (see Qs 4:10–4:17) will not satisfy these requirements unless all catch-up eligible participants (see Q 27:53) who participate under any applicable employer plan maintained by the employer are provided with the effective opportunity to make the same dollar amount of catch-up contributions. A plan fails to provide an effective opportunity to make catch-up contributions if it has an applicable limit (e.g., an employer-provided limit; see Q 27:54) that applies to a catch-up eligible participant and does not permit the participant to make elective deferrals in excess of that limit. An applicable employer plan does not fail to satisfy the universal availability requirement solely because an employer-provided limit does not apply to all employees or different limits apply to different groups of employees. However, a plan may not provide lower employer-provided limits for catch-up eligible participants. [Treas. Reg. § 1.414(v)-1(e)(1)(i)]

An applicable employer plan does not fail to satisfy the universal availability requirement merely because the plan allows participants to defer an amount equal to a specific percentage of compensation for each payroll period and for each payroll period permits each catch-up eligible participant to defer a pro rata share of the applicable dollar catch-up limit in addition to that amount. Also, an applicable employer plan does not fail to satisfy the universal availability requirement merely because it restricts the elective deferrals of an employee (including a catch-up eligible participant) to amounts available after other withholding from the employee's pay (e.g., after deduction of all applicable income and employment taxes). For this purpose, an employer limit of 75 percent of compensation or higher will be treated as limiting employees to amounts available after other withholdings. [Treas. Reg. § 1.414(v)-1(e)(1)(ii)]

An applicable employer plan does not fail to satisfy the universal availability requirement merely because union employees are not provided the opportunity to make catch-up contributions. [Treas. Reg. § 1.414(v)-1(e)(2)]

If an applicable employer plan satisfies the universal availability requirement before an acquisition or disposition and would fail to satisfy the universal availability requirement merely because of such event, then the applicable employer plan will continue to be treated as satisfying this requirement through the end of the transition period. [I.R.C. § 410(b)(6)(C)(ii); Treas. Reg. §§ 1.410(b)-2(f), 1.414(v)-1(e)(4)]

Prior to the promulgation of the final regulations, IRS issued additional guidance on the universal availability requirement. Consequently, a plan would not have been treated as failing to satisfy the nondiscrimination requirements for 2002 solely because different plans maintained by the same employer adopted catch-up contributions beginning on different dates during 2002, provided that all such plans began offering catch-up contributions no later than October 1, 2002. In addition, until the issuance of further guidance, an applicable employer plan that permits catch-up contributions will not fail to satisfy the nondiscrimination or universal availability requirements solely because another applicable employer plan maintained by the employer that is qualified under Puerto Rico law does not provide for catch-up contributions. [IRS Notice 2002-4, 2002-1 C.B. 298]

An IRS representative has opined that the separate line of business exception (see Q 5:44) cannot be used to satisfy the universal availability requirement for catch-up contribution purposes.

Q 27:58 If an employer sponsors multiple plans, how are catch-up contributions treated?

All applicable employer plans (see Q 27:53), other than Section 457 eligible governmental plans, maintained by the same employer are treated as one plan, and all Section 457 eligible governmental plans maintained by the same employer are treated as one plan. Thus, the total amount of catch-up contributions under all applicable employer plans of an employer (other than Section 457 eligible governmental plans) is limited to the applicable dollar catch-up limit (see Q 27:52) for the taxable year, and the total amount of catch-up contributions for all Section 457 eligible governmental plans of an employer is limited to the applicable dollar catch-up limit for the taxable year. [I.R.C. § 414(v)(2)(D); Treas. Reg. § 1.414(v)-1(f)(1)]

An applicable employer plan is permitted to allow a catch-up eligible participant (see Q 27:53) to defer amounts in excess of an employer-provided limit (see Q 27:54) under that plan without regard to whether elective deferrals (see Q 27:16) made by the participant have been treated as catch-up contributions for the taxable year under another applicable employer plan aggregated with such plan. However, to the extent elective deferrals under another plan maintained by the employer have already been treated as catch-up contributions during the taxable year, the elective deferrals under the plan may be treated as catch-up contributions only up to the amount remaining under the catch-up limit for the year. Any other elective deferrals that exceed the employer-provided limit may not be treated as catch-up contributions and must satisfy the otherwise applicable nondiscrimination rules. For example, the right to make contributions in excess of the employer-provided limit is another right or feature that must satisfy the nondiscrimination requirements (see Q 4:20) to the extent that the contributions are not catch-up contributions. Also, contributions in excess of the employer-provided limit are taken into account under the ADP test (see Q 27:18) to the extent they are not catch-up contributions. [Treas. Reg. § 1.414(v)-1(f)(2)]

If a catch-up eligible participant makes additional elective deferrals in excess of an applicable limit under more than one applicable employer plan that is aggregated, the applicable employer plan under which elective deferrals in excess of an applicable limit are treated as catch-up contributions is permitted to be determined in any manner that is not inconsistent with the manner in which such amounts were actually deferred under the plan. [Treas. Reg. § 1.414(v)-1(f)(3)]

Q 27:59   Are catch-up contributions excludable from gross income?

Elective deferrals that exceed the dollar limit (see Q 27:51) are excludable from gross income to the extent the amount of the elective deferrals do not exceed the catch-up contribution limit (see Q 27:52) for the taxable year. [I.R.C. § 402(g)(1)(C); Treas. Reg. § 1.402(g)-2]

For illustrative examples, see Q 27:61.

Q 27:60   How are catch-up contributions reported?

Employers are required to report participants' elective deferrals (see Q 27:16) on Form W-2 in box 12 using Codes D through H and S. For employees' catch-up contributions (see Q 27:52), employers must report the elective deferral catch-up contributions in the totals reported for Codes D through H and S.

The reporting of catch-up contributions is addressed in the Instructions for Forms 1099-R and 5498.

[Ann. 2001-93, 2001-2 C.B. 416]

Q 27:61   Has IRS provided examples regarding catch-up contributions?

Yes. The following examples illustrate the application of the final regulations (see Qs 27:53–27:59). For purposes of the examples, except as specifically provided, the plan year is the calendar year. In addition, it is assumed that the participant's elective deferrals under all plans of the employer do not exceed the participant's compensation, that the taxable year of the participant is the calendar year, and that any correction is made through distribution of excess contributions (see Q 27:26). [Treas. Reg. § 1.414(v)-1(h)]

Example 1. Steve is eligible to make elective deferrals under a 401(k) plan. The plan does not limit elective deferrals except as necessary to comply with the elective deferral dollar limit and the annual addition limitation (see Q 6:34). In 2010, Steve is 55 years old. The plan also provides that a catch-up eligible participant (see Q 27:53) is permitted to defer amounts in excess of the elective deferral dollar limit up to the applicable dollar catch-up limit for the year. Steve defers $19,500 during 2010.

Steve's elective deferrals in excess of the limit ($3,000) do not exceed the applicable dollar catch-up limit for 2010 ($5,500). The $3,000 is a catch-up contribution, and it is not taken into account in determining Steve's ADR (see Qs 27:20, 27:56).

Example 2. Madeleine and Mac, who are HCEs (see Q 3:3) each earning $120,000, are eligible to make elective deferrals under a 401(k) plan. The plan limits elective deferrals as in Example 1 and also provides that no HCE may make an elective deferral at a rate that exceeds 10 percent of compensation. However, the plan also provides that a catch-up eligible participant is permitted to defer amounts in excess of 10 percent during the plan year up to the applicable dollar catch-up limit for the year. In 2010, Madeleine and Mac are both 55 years old and both elect to defer 10 percent of compensation plus a pro rata portion of the $5,500 applicable dollar catch-up limit for 2010. Madeleine continues this election in effect for the entire year, for a total elective contribution for the year of $17,500. However, in July 2010, after deferring $8,750, Mac discontinues making elective deferrals.

Once Madeleine's elective deferrals for the year exceed the elective deferral dollar limit ($16,500), subsequent elective deferrals are treated as catch-up contributions as they are deferred, provided that such elective deferrals do not exceed the catch-up contribution limit for the taxable year. Since the $1,000 in elective deferrals made after Madeleine reaches the $16,500 limit for the calendar year does not exceed the applicable dollar catch-up limit for 2010, the entire $1,000 is treated as a catch-up contribution.

As of the last day of the plan year, Madeleine has exceeded the employer-provided limit (see Q 27:54) of 10 percent [$12,000 (10% × $120,000)] by an additional $4,500. Because the additional $4,500 in elective deferrals does not exceed the $5,500 applicable dollar catch-up limit for 2010, reduced by the $1,000 in elective deferrals previously treated as catch-up contributions, the entire $4,500 of elective deferrals is treated as a catch-up contribution.

In determining Madeleine's ADR, $5,500 of catch-up contributions are subtracted from her elective deferrals for the plan year (see Q 27:56). Accordingly, Madeleine's ADR is 10 percent ($12,000 ÷ $120,000). In addition, for purposes of applying the excess contribution rules, Madeleine is treated as having elective deferrals of $12,000.

Mac's elective deferrals for the year do not exceed an applicable limit for the plan year. Accordingly, Mac's $8,750 of elective deferrals must be taken into account in determining his ADR.

Example 3. The facts are the same as in Example 2, except that the plan is amended to change the maximum permitted deferral percentage for HCEs to 7 percent, effective for deferrals after April 1, 2010. Madeleine, who has earned $40,000 in the first three months of the year and has been deferring at a rate of 10 percent of compensation plus a pro rata portion of the $5,500 applicable dollar catch-up limit for 2010, reduces the 10-percent-of-pay deferral rate to 7 percent for the remaining nine months of the year (while continuing to defer a pro rata portion of the $5,500 applicable dollar catch-up limit for 2010). During those nine months, Madeleine earns $80,000. Thus, her total elective deferrals for the year are $15,100 ($4,000 for the first three months of the year plus $5,600 for the last nine months of the year plus an additional $5,500 throughout the year).

The employer-provided limit for Madeleine for the plan year is $9,600 ($4,000 for the first three months of the year + $5,600 for the last nine months of the year). Accordingly, Madeleine's elective deferrals for the year that are in excess of the employer-provided limit are $5,500 (the excess of $15,100 − $9,600), which does not exceed the applicable dollar catch-up limit of $5,500.

Alternatively, the plan may provide that the employer-provided limit is determined as the time-weighted average of the different deferral percentage limits over the course of the year (see Q 27:54). In this case, the time-weighted average limit is 7.75 percent for all participants, and the applicable limit for Madeleine is 7.75 percent of $120,000, or $9,300. Accordingly, Madeleine's elective deferrals for the year that are in excess of the employer-provided limit are $5,800 (the excess of $15,100 − $9,300). Because the amount of Madeleine's elective deferrals in excess of the employer-provided limit ($5,800) exceeds the applicable dollar catch-up limit for the taxable year, only $5,500 of her elective deferrals may be treated as catch-up contributions. In determining Madeleine's ADR, the $5,500 of catch-up contributions are subtracted from her elective deferrals for the plan year. Accordingly, Madeleine's ADR is 8 percent ($9,600 ÷ $120,000). In addition, for purposes of applying the excess contribution rules Madeleine is treated as having elective deferrals of $9,600.

Example 4. The facts are the same as in Example 1. In addition to Steve, Elizabeth is an HCE who is eligible to make elective deferrals under the plan. During 2010, Elizabeth, who is 51 years old, elects to defer $15,000.

The ADP test (see Q 27:18) is run for the plan (after excluding the $3,000 in catch-up contributions from Steve's elective deferrals), but the plan needs to take corrective action in order to pass the ADP test. After applying the excess contribution rules to allocate the total excess contributions, the maximum deferrals that may be retained by any HCE is $13,500. The ADP limit under the plan of $13,500 is an applicable limit (see Q 27:54). Accordingly, $1,500 of Elizabeth's elective deferrals exceed the applicable limit. Similarly, $3,000 of Steve's elective deferrals (other than the $3,000 of elective deferrals treated as catch-up contributions because they exceed the elective deferral dollar limit) exceed the applicable limit.

The $1,500 of Elizabeth's elective deferrals that exceed the applicable limit are less than the applicable dollar catch-up limit and are treated as catch-up contributions. The plan must retain Elizabeth's $1,500 in elective deferrals, and the plan is not treated as failing to satisfy the excess contribution rules merely because the elective deferrals are not distributed to Elizabeth.

The $3,000 of Steve's elective deferrals that exceed the applicable limit are greater than the portion of the applicable dollar catch-up limit ($2,500) that remains after treating the $3,000 of elective deferrals in excess of the elective deferral dollar limit as catch-up contributions. Accordingly, $2,500 of Steve's elective deferrals are treated as catch-up contributions. The plan must retain Steve's $2,500 in elective deferrals, and the plan is not treated as failing to satisfy the excess contribution rules merely because the elective deferrals are not distributed to him. However, $500 of Steve's elective deferrals cannot be treated as catch-up contributions and must be distributed to him in order to satisfy the excess contribution rules.

Example 5. Dylan is an HCE who is a catch-up eligible employee under a 401(k) plan, with a plan year ending October 31, 2010. The plan does not limit elective deferrals except as in Example 1. The plan permits all catch-up eligible participants to defer an additional amount equal to the applicable dollar catch-up limit for the year ($5,500) in excess of the elective deferral dollar limit. Dylan did not exceed the limit in 2009 and did not exceed the ADP limit for the plan year ending October 31, 2009. Dylan made $3,200 of deferrals in the period November 1, 2009 through December 31, 2009 and an additional $17,000 of deferrals in the first ten months of 2010, for a total of $20,200 in elective deferrals for the plan year.

Once Dylan's elective deferrals for the calendar year 2010 exceed $16,500, subsequent elective deferrals are treated as catch-up contributions at the time they are deferred, provided that such elective deferrals do not exceed the applicable dollar catch-up limit for the taxable year. Since the $500 in elective deferrals made after Dylan reaches the $16,500 limit for the calendar year does not exceed the applicable dollar catch-up limit for 2010, the entire $500 is a catch-up contribution. The entire $500 is subtracted from Dylan's $20,200 in elective deferrals for the plan year ending October 31, 2010 in determining his ADR for that plan year.

The ADP test is run (after excluding the $500 in excess elective deferrals), but the plan needs to take corrective action in order to pass the ADP test. After applying the excess contribution rules to allocate the total excess contributions, the maximum deferrals that may be retained by any HCE for the plan year ending October 31, 2010 (the ADP limit) is $15,800.

Elective deferrals that exceed the elective deferral dollar limit are also subtracted from Dylan's elective deferrals for purposes of applying the rules. Accordingly, for purposes of correcting the failed ADP test, Dylan is treated as having contributed $19,700 of elective deferrals. The amount of elective deferrals that would have to be distributed to Dylan is $3,900 ($19,700 − $15,800), which is less than the excess of the applicable dollar catch-up limit ($5,500) over the elective deferrals previously treated as catch-up contributions for the taxable year ($500). The plan must retain Dylan's $3,900 in elective deferrals and is not treated as failing to satisfy the excess contribution rules merely because the elective deferrals are not distributed to Dylan.

Even though Dylan's elective deferrals for calendar year 2010 have exceeded the elective deferral dollar limit, he can continue to make elective deferrals during the last two months of the calendar year, since his catch-up contributions for the taxable year are not taken into account in applying the elective deferral dollar limit for 2010. Thus, Dylan can make an additional contribution of $3,900 [$16,500 − ($17,000 − $4,400)] without exceeding the elective deferral dollar limit for the calendar year and without regard to any additional catch-up contributions. Dylan may also make additional catch-up contributions of $1,100 (the $5,500 applicable dollar catch-up limit for 2010, reduced by the $4,400 ($500 + $3,900) of elective deferrals previously treated as catch-up contributions during the taxable year). The $1,100 of catch-up contributions will not be taken into account in the ADP test for the plan year ending October 31, 2011.

Example 6. The facts are the same as in Example 5, except that Dylan exceeded the elective deferral dollar limit for 2009 by $1,300 prior to October 31, 2009, and made $600 of elective deferrals in the period November 1, 2009 through December 31, 2009 (which were catch-up contributions for 2009). Thus, Dylan made $17,600 of elective deferrals for the plan year ending October 31, 2010.

Once Dylan's elective deferrals for the calendar year 2010 exceed $16,500, subsequent elective deferrals are treated as catch-up contributions as they are deferred, provided that such elective deferrals do not exceed the applicable dollar catch-up limit for the taxable year. Since the $500 in elective deferrals made after Dylan reaches the $16,500 limit for calendar year 2010 does not exceed the applicable dollar catch-up limit for 2010, the entire $500 is a catch-up contribution. The entire $500 is subtracted from Dylan's elective deferrals in determining his ADR for the plan year ending October 31, 2010. In addition, the $600 of catch-up contributions from the period November 1, 2009, to December 31, 2009, is subtracted from his elective deferrals in determining his ADR. Thus, the total elective deferrals taken into account in determining Dylan's ADR for the plan year ending October 31, 2010 is $16,500 ($17,600 in elective deferrals for the current plan year – $1,100 in catch-up contributions).

The ADP test is run (after excluding the $1,100 in elective deferrals in excess of the elective deferral dollar limit), but the plan needs to take corrective action in order to pass the ADP test. After allocating the total excess contributions, the maximum deferrals that may be retained by any HCE (the ADP limit) is $15,800.

Elective deferrals that exceed the elective deferral dollar limit are also subtracted from Dylan's elective deferrals for purposes of applying the excess contribution rules. Accordingly, for purposes of correcting the failed ADP test, Dylan is treated as having contributed $16,500 of elective deferrals. The amount of elective deferrals that would have to be distributed to Dylan is $700 ($16,500 – $15,800), which is less than the excess of the applicable dollar catch-up limit ($5,500) over the elective deferrals previously treated as catch-up contributions under the plan for the taxable year ($500). The plan must retain Dylan's $700 in elective deferrals and is not treated as failing to satisfy the excess contribution rules merely because the elective deferrals are not distributed to Dylan.

Even though Dylan's elective deferrals for calendar year 2010 have exceeded the elective deferral dollar limit, he can continue to make elective deferrals during the last two months of the calendar year, since his catch-up contributions for the taxable year are not taken into account in applying the elective deferral dollar limit for 2010. Thus, Dylan can make an additional contribution of $700 [$16,500 – ($17,000 – $1,200)] without exceeding the elective deferral dollar limit for the calendar year and without regard to any additional catch-up contributions. Dylan may also make additional catch-up contributions of $4,300 (the $5,500 applicable dollar catch-up limit for 2010, reduced by $1,200 ($500 + $700) in elective deferrals previously treated as catch-up contributions during taxable year 2010). The $4,300 of catch-up contributions will not be taken into account in the ADP test for the plan year ending October 31, 2011.

Example 7. Mac, who is 58 years old, is an HCE who earns $100,000. Mac participates in a 401(k) plan, Plan S, for the first six months of the year and then transfers to another 401(k) plan, Plan E, sponsored by the same employer, for the second six months of the year. Plan S limits HCE's elective deferrals to 6 percent of compensation for the period of participation, but permits catch-up eligible participants to defer amounts in excess of 6 percent during the plan year, up to the applicable dollar catch-up limit for the year. Plan E limits elective deferrals to 8 percent of compensation for the period of participation, but permits catch-up eligible participants to defer amounts in excess of 8 percent during the plan year, up to the applicable dollar catch-up limit for the year. Mac, who earned $50,000 in the first six months of the year, defers $6,000 under Plan S. Mac also deferred $7,000 under Plan E.

As of the last day of the plan year, Mac has $3,000 in elective deferrals under Plan S that exceed the employer-provided limit of $3,000. Under Plan E, Mac has $3,000 in elective deferrals that exceed the employer-provided limit of $4,000. The total amount of elective deferrals in excess of employer-provided limits, $6,000, exceeds the applicable dollar catch-up limit by $500. Accordingly, $500 of the elective deferrals in excess of the employer-provided limits are not catch-up contributions and are treated as regular elective deferrals (and are taken into account in the ADP test). The determination of which elective deferrals in excess of an applicable limit are treated as catch-up contributions is permitted to be made in any manner that is not inconsistent with the manner in which such amounts were actually deferred under Plan S and Plan E.

Example 8. KC Corporation sponsors a 401(k) plan that provides for matching contributions equal to 50 percent of elective deferrals that do not exceed 10 percent of compensation. Elective deferrals for HCEs are limited, on a payroll-by-payroll basis, to 10 percent of compensation. KC Corporation pays employees on a monthly basis. The plan also provides that elective contributions are limited to the elective deferral dollar limits and other applicable statutory limits and provides for catch-up contributions. Under the plan, for purposes of calculating the amount to be treated as catch-up contributions (and to be excluded from the ADP test), amounts in excess of the 10 percent limit for HCEs are determined at the end of the plan year based on compensation used for purposes of ADP testing (testing compensation), a definition of compensation that is different from the definition used under the plan for purposes of calculating elective deferrals and matching contributions during the plan year (deferral compensation).

Casey, an HCE, is a catch-up eligible participant with deferral compensation of $10,000 per monthly payroll period. Casey defers 10 percent per payroll period for the first ten months of the year and is allocated a matching contribution each payroll period of $500. Casey also defers an additional $4,000 during the first ten months of the year. Casey then reduces deferrals during the last two months of the year to 5 percent of compensation and is allocated a matching contribution of $250 for each of the last two months of the plan year. For the plan year, Casey has $15,000 in elective deferrals and $5,500 in matching contributions.

Casey's testing compensation is $118,000. At the end of the plan year, based on 10 percent of testing compensation, or $11,800, the plan determines that Casey has $3,200 in deferrals that exceed the 10 percent employer-provided limit. The plan excludes $3,200 from ADP testing and calculates Casey's ADR as $11,800 divided by $118,000, or 10 percent. Although Casey has not been allocated a matching contribution equal to 50 percent of $11,800, because the plan provides that matching contributions are calculated based on elective deferrals during the payroll period as a percentage of deferral compensation, the plan is not required to allocate an additional $400 of matching contributions to Casey.

Q 27:62 To what time period does the dollar limitation on elective contributions apply?

The limitation on elective contributions (see Q 27:51) applies on the basis of the participant's tax year. In most cases, this is the calendar year. The limitation applies without regard to:

1. The plan year of the plan under which the elective contributions are made;
2. When the participant elects to make the contributions; or
3. When the elective contributions are made to the plan.

[I.R.C. §§ 401(a)(30), 402(g)(1); Treas. Reg. §§ 1.401(a)-30(a), 1.402(g)-1(a)]

Q 27:63 How are excess deferrals corrected?

If an excess deferral is included in a participant's gross income for any taxable year, then, not later than March 1 following the close of the taxable year, the participant may allocate the amount of the excess deferral among the plans under which it arose (assuming more than one plan) and may notify each such plan of the portion allocated to it. If any designated Roth contributions (see Q 27:96) were made to a plan, the notification must also identify the extent, if any, to which the excess deferrals are composed of designated Roth contributions. Regulations issued by IRS extend the March 1 date to April 15. A plan may provide that the participant is deemed to have notified the plan of excess deferrals (including the portion of excess deferrals that is composed of designated Roth contributions) to the extent the participant has excess deferrals for the taxable year calculated by taking into account only elective deferrals under the plan and other plans of the same employer and the plan may provide the extent to which such excess deferrals are composed of designated Roth contributions. A plan may instead provide that the employer may notify the plan on behalf of the individual under these circumstances. [I.R.C. § 402(g)(2)(A)(i); Treas. Reg. § 1.402(g)-1(e)(2)(i)]

Not later than April 15 following the close of the taxable year in which the excess deferral arose, the plan may distribute to the participant the amount allocated to it by the participant plus any income allocable to that amount through the end of the taxable year. This distribution may be made notwithstanding any other provision of law. [I.R.C. § 402(g)(2)(A)(ii); Treas. Reg. § 1.402(g)-1(e)(2)(ii)] IRS representatives have opined that the April 15 date is not extended if it falls on a weekend or holiday.

A corrective distribution of an excess deferral may also be made during the same year in which the excess deferral arose. Such a distribution may be made only if the following conditions are satisfied:

1. The participant designates the distribution as an excess deferral;
2. The corrective distribution is made after the date on which the plan received the excess deferral; and
3. The plan designates the distribution as a distribution of an excess deferral. [Treas. Reg. § 1.402(g)-1(e)(3)(i)]

With respect to the first condition, if any designated Roth contributions were made to a plan, the notification must identify the extent, if any, to which the excess deferrals are composed of designated Roth contributions. A plan may provide that a participant is deemed to have notified the plan of excess deferrals (including the portion of excess deferrals that is composed of designated Roth contributions) for the taxable year calculated by taking into account only elective deferrals under the plan and other plans of the same employer, and the plan may provide the extent to which such excess deferrals are composed of designated Roth contributions. A plan may instead provide that the employer may make the designation on behalf of the participant under these circumstances. [Treas. Reg. § 1.402(g)-1(e)(3)(i)]

Corrective distributions must be provided for under the terms of the plan. A plan may require that the notification and designations referred to above must be in writing, and may also require that the participant certify or otherwise establish that the specified amount is an excess deferral. [Treas. Reg. § 1.402(g)-1(e)(4)]

Q 27:64   What are the tax consequences of making excess deferrals?

Excess deferrals for a taxable year are included in the employee's gross income for the taxable year in which they were made. However, the income allocable to excess deferrals is included in the employee's gross income for the taxable year in which it is distributed. [I.R.C. §§ 402(g)(1), 402(g)(2)(C)(ii); Treas. Reg. §§ 1.402(g)-1(a), 1.402(g)-1(e)(8)(i)]

Example. In 2010, Jennifer, age 26, defers $17,000 under a 401(k) plan. Earnings attributable to the excess deferral [$500 ($17,000 − $16,500)] are $25. If Jennifer withdraws $525 ($500 + $25) by April 15, 2011, $500 is taxable in 2010 and $25 in 2011.

The 10 percent penalty tax on early distributions (see Qs 16:1, 16:17) does not apply to a corrective distribution of an excess deferral, nor is it subject to the spousal consent requirements (see Q 10:21). [Treas. Reg. §§ 1.402(g)-1(e)(7), 1.402(g)-1(e)(8)(i)]

If excess deferrals are not timely distributed, the amount of the excess deferrals is included in the employee's gross income for the taxable year in which the excess deferrals arose and will again be included in the employee's gross income in the year when they are actually distributed. Accordingly, failure to make a corrective distribution of excess deferrals within the specified period causes double taxation on such deferrals. [Treas. Reg. § 1.402(g)-1(e)(8)(iii)] These rules generally apply to distributions of excess deferrals that are designated Roth contributions (see Q 27:96) and the attributable income. Thus, if a designated Roth account (see Q 27:96) includes any excess deferrals, any distribution of amounts attributable to those excess deferrals is includible in gross income (without adjustment for any return of investment; see Q 13:3). In addition, such distributions cannot be qualified distributions (see Qs 27:98, 27:105) and are not eligible rollover distributions (see Q 34:8). For this purpose, if a designated Roth account includes any excess deferrals, any distributions from the account are treated as attributable to those excess deferrals until the total amount distributed from the designated Roth account equals the total of such deferrals and attributable income. [Prop. Treas. Reg. § 1.402(g)-1(e)(8)(iv)]

A plan may use any reasonable method for computing the income allocable to excess deferrals, provided that the method is nondiscriminatory, is used consistently for all participants and for all corrective distributions under the plan for the plan year, and is used by the plan for allocating income to participants' accounts. IRS has provided a safe harbor procedure for calculating the income. Under this method, the income for the plan year allocated to the excess deferral is determined by multiplying the income allocable to all deferrals in the taxable year by the employee's excess deferral for the taxable year and then dividing the result by the sum of (1) the employee's total account balance attributable to deferrals at the start of the year and (2) the employee's new deferrals during the taxable year. [Treas. Reg. § 1.402(g)-1(e)(5)]

Q 27:65   Are excess deferrals distributed after year end to an employee nevertheless counted for purposes of the ADP test?

Whether or not excess deferrals are timely distributed to an employee after the end of the employee's taxable year, any excess deferrals of HCEs (see Q 3:3) are still counted for purposes of the ADP test (see Q 27:18); excess deferrals of NHCEs (see Q 3:12) are not taken into account. [I.R.C. § 402(g)(2)(B); Treas. Reg. § 1.402(g)-1(e)(1)(ii)]

Q 27:66   Is there a tax credit for elective contributions?

An eligible individual will be allowed a nonrefundable tax credit for the taxable year in an amount equal to the applicable percentage of the individual's qualified retirement savings contributions for the year up to $2,000.

See chapter 17 for details.

Q 27:67   What is a combined 401(k) plan?

A combined 401(k) plan is a plan that permits both elective contributions (those contributions that are made pursuant to a CODA; see Qs 27:2, 27:16) and other types of employer contributions. By establishing a combined plan, the employer can failsafe the 401(k) plan so that it will always satisfy the ADP test (see Q 27:18). [Treas. Reg. § 1.401(k)-2(a)(6)]

Example. W & M Regel Corporation adopts a profit sharing plan with a CODA in 2011. Each employee may elect to receive up to 6 percent of compensation in cash or to have that amount contributed to the plan as an elective contribution. In 2011, all HCEs (see Q 3:3) elect to have 6 percent of their compensation contributed to the plan, and all other employees elect to receive cash. W & M Regel Corporation also makes a nonelective contribution to the plan equal to

4 percent of each NHCE's (see Q 3:12) compensation. The nonelective contribution is qualified because it is subject to the same nonforfeitability and distribution provisions as the elective contributions (see Q 27:17).

Effective for plan years beginning on or after January 1, 2010, certain employers may establish a combined defined benefit/401(k) plan. [I.R.C. § 414(x) (as amended by WRERA 2008 § 109(c)(1)); ERISA § 210(e) (as amended by WRERA 2008 § 109(c)(2))]

PPA (see Q 1:33) provides rules for an eligible combined plan. An eligible combined plan is a plan:

1. That is maintained by an employer that is a small employer at the time the plan is established;
2. That consists of a defined benefit plan (see Q 2:3) and an applicable defined contribution plan (see Q 2:2);
3. The assets of which are held in a single trust forming part of the plan and are clearly identified and allocated to the defined benefit plan and the applicable defined contribution plan to the extent necessary for the separate application of the Code and ERISA; and
4. That meets certain benefit, contribution, vesting, and nondiscrimination requirements as discussed below.

For this purpose, an applicable defined contribution plan is a defined contribution plan that includes a qualified CODA. A small employer is an employer that employed an average of at least two, but not more than 500, employees on business days during the preceding calendar year and at least two employees on the first day of the plan year.

Except as specified in PPA, the provisions of the Code and ERISA are applied to any defined benefit plan and any applicable defined contribution plan that are part of an eligible combined plan in the same manner as if each were not part of the eligible combined plan. Thus, for example, the limits on contributions and benefits apply separately to contributions under an applicable defined contribution plan (see Q 6:34) that is part of an eligible combined plan and to benefits under the defined benefit plan (see Q 6:11) that is part of the eligible combined plan. In addition, the spousal protection rules apply to the defined benefit plan, but not to the applicable defined contribution plan except to the extent provided under present law (see Q 10:6). Moreover, although the assets of an eligible combined plan are held in a single trust, the funding rules apply to a defined benefit plan that is part of an eligible combined plan on the basis of the assets identified and allocated to the defined benefit plan (see Q 8:1), and the limits on investing defined benefit plan assets in employer securities or real property apply to such assets (see Q 23:84). Similarly, separate participant accounts are required to be maintained under the applicable defined contribution plan that is part of the eligible combined plan, and earnings (or losses) on participants' account are based on the earnings (or losses) with respect to the assets of the applicable defined contribution plan (see Q 2:2).

A defined benefit plan that is part of an eligible combined plan is required to provide each participant with a benefit of not less than the applicable percentage of the participant's final average pay. The applicable percentage is the lesser of (1) 1 percent multiplied by the participant's years of service or (2) 20 percent. For this purpose, final average pay is determined using the consecutive-year period (not exceeding five years) during which the participant has the greatest aggregate compensation. If the defined benefit plan is an applicable defined benefit plan (i.e., cash balance plan; see Q 2:23), the plan is treated as meeting this benefit requirement if each participant receives a pay credit for each plan year of not less than the percentage of compensation determined in accordance with the following table:

Participant's Age as of Beginning of Plan Year	Percentage
30 or less	2%
Over 30, but less than 40	4%
Over 40, but less than 50	6%
50 or over	8%

A defined benefit plan that is part of an eligible combined plan must provide the required benefit to each participant, regardless of whether the participant makes elective deferrals to the applicable defined contribution plan that is part of the eligible combined plan. Any benefits provided under the defined benefit plan (including any benefits provided in addition to required benefits) must be fully vested after three years of service (see Q 9:1).

Certain automatic enrollment and matching contribution requirements must be met with respect to an applicable defined contribution plan that is part of an eligible combined plan. First, the qualified CODA must constitute an automatic contribution arrangement, under which each employee eligible to participate is treated as having elected to make deferrals of 4 percent of compensation unless the employee elects otherwise (i.e., elects not to make deferrals or to make deferrals at a different rate). Participants must be given notice of their right to elect otherwise and must be given a reasonable period of time after receiving notice in which to make an election. In addition, participants must be given notice of their rights and obligations within a reasonable period before each year (see Q 27:5).

Under the applicable defined contribution plan, the employer must be required to make matching contributions on behalf of each employee eligible to participate in the arrangement in an amount equal to 50 percent of the employee's elective deferrals up to 4 percent of compensation, and the rate of matching contribution with respect to any elective deferrals for HCEs (see Q 3:3) must not be greater than the rate of match for NHCEs. Matching contributions in addition to the required matching contributions may also be made. The employer may also make nonelective contributions under the applicable defined contribution plan, but any nonelective contributions are not taken into account in determining whether the matching contribution requirement is met. Any matching contributions under the applicable defined contribution plan (including any in excess of required matching contributions) must be fully vested when made. Any nonelective contributions made under the applicable defined contribution plan must be fully vested after three years of service.

An applicable defined contribution plan satisfies the ADP test on a safe-harbor basis (see Q 27:40). Matching contributions under an applicable defined contribution plan must satisfy the ACP test or may satisfy the matching contribution safe harbor (see Q 27:76), as modified to reflect the matching contribution requirements applicable under PPA.

Nonelective contributions under an applicable defined contribution plan and benefits under a defined benefit plan that are part of an eligible combined plan are generally subject to the nondiscrimination rules (see Q 4:10). However, neither a defined benefit plan nor an applicable defined contribution plan that is part of an eligible combined plan may be combined with another plan in determining whether the nondiscrimination requirements are met. The permitted disparity rules (see Q 7:1) do not apply in determining whether an applicable defined contribution plan or a defined benefit plan that is part of an eligible combined plan satisfies (1) the contribution or benefit requirements or (2) the nondiscrimination requirements.

An applicable defined contribution plan and a defined benefit plan that are part of an eligible combined plan are treated as meeting the top-heavy requirements (see Chapter 26).

All contributions, benefits, and other rights and features (see Q 4:20) that are provided under a defined benefit plan or an applicable defined contribution plan that is part of an eligible combined plan must be provided uniformly to all participants. This requirement applies regardless of whether nonuniform contributions, benefits, or other rights or features could be provided without violating the nondiscrimination rules. However, it is intended that a plan will not violate the uniformity requirement merely because benefits accrued for periods before a defined benefit or defined contribution plan became part of an eligible combined plan are protected (as required under the anti-cutback rules; see Q 9:25).

An eligible combined plan is treated as a single plan for purposes of annual reporting. Thus, only a single Form 5500 is required (see Q 21:1). All of the information required under present law with respect to a defined benefit plan or a defined contribution plan must be provided on the Form 5500 for the eligible combined plan. In addition, only a single summary annual report must be provided to participants (see Q 20:24).

The provisions of PPA relating to default investment options and the preemption of state laws with respect to automatic enrollment arrangements are applicable to eligible combined plans (see Q 27:5). It is intended that, when an eligible combined plan terminates, the PBGC guarantee applies only to benefits under the defined benefit portion of the plan (see Q 25:16). In the case of a termination of the defined benefit plan and the applicable defined contribution plan forming part of an eligible combined plan, the plan administrator (see Q 20:1) must terminate each plan separately.

Q 27:68   Can a CODA be part of a thrift or savings plan?

Yes. A thrift or savings plan (see Q 2:11) is a plan in which employee or elective contributions and employer contributions are made on a matching basis. The matching contributions by the employer encourage greater participation by the NHCEs (see Q 3:12) and may be important in satisfying the ADP test (see Q 27:18).

For example, if the employer makes a $.50 matching contribution for every $1.00 of elective contributions made by the employee, the employee receives an immediate 50 percent return on the investment and has a greater incentive to participate in the plan.

The ADP test can be automatically satisfied by making matching contributions (see Q 27:43).

Q 27:69   How does a CODA affect the employer's tax-deductible contributions?

Because a CODA (see Q 27:2) must be part of a profit sharing or stock bonus plan (see Q 27:1), the limitation on an employer's tax-deductible contributions to such type of plan applies—25 percent of total compensation paid to all participants (see Qs 12:8, 12:15). [I.R.C. § 404(a)(3)(A)]

If any employee of the employer is covered by both a defined contribution plan and a defined benefit plan, a special tax-deduction limitation applies (see Q 12:21). [I.R.C. § 404(a)(7)]

The deduction for contributions to a 401(k) plan that are attributable to services rendered by participants after the end of the employer's taxable year will not be allowed because compensation must be earned before it can be deferred and contributed to the plan. [Rev. Rul. 2002-73, 2002-2 C.B. 805; Rev. Rul. 2002-46, 2002-2 C.B. 117; Rev. Rul. 90-105, 1990-2 C.B. 69; IRS Notice 2002-48, 2002-2 C.B. 130; IRS Coordinated Issue Paper UIL No. 9300.23-00 (Sept. 24, 2004); IRS Coordinated Issue Paper UIL No. 404.11-00 (Oct. 23, 1996); IRS Appeals Settlement Guidelines UIL No. 9300.01-1 (Oct. 1. 2004); Field Serv. Adv. 200107012; Chief Couns. Adv. 200038004]

Example 1. JMK Corp. maintains a 401(k) plan, which provides for matching contributions (see Q 27:75). JMK Corp.'s taxable year is the fiscal year ending June 30. The plan has a calendar plan year and was amended to provide for JMK Corp.'s board of directors to set a minimum contribution for a plan year to be allocated first toward elective deferrals (see Q 27:16) and matching contributions, with any excess to be allocated to participants as of the end of the plan year in proportion to compensation earned during the plan year. Pursuant to this plan amendment, JMK Corp.'s board adopted a resolution on June 15, 2010, setting a minimum contribution of $80,000 for the 2010 calendar plan year. By December 31, 2010 (the last day of the plan year), JMK Corp. had contributed $80,000 to the plan. These amounts consisted of (1) $38,000 for elective deferrals and matching contributions attributable to compensation earned by the plan participants before the end of JMK Corp.'s taxable year ending June 30, 2010 (pre-year end service contributions) and (2) $42,000 for elective deferrals and matching contributions attributable to compensation earned by plan participants after the end of JMK Corp.'s taxable year ending June 30, 2010 (post-year end service contributions). JMK Corp. made each contribution attributable to compensation earned during each pay period contemporaneously with the issuance of wage payments for the pay period.

JMK Corp. receives an extension of time to March 15, 2011 to file the income tax return for its taxable year ending June 30, 2010 (2010 taxable year). On the income tax return for its 2010 taxable year, which was timely filed on March 1, 2011, JMK Corp. claimed a deduction for the entire $80,000 for elective deferrals and matching contributions made to the plan during the plan's 2010 calendar plan year, relating to both pre-year end service contributions and post-year end service contributions. The total amount contributed and claimed by JMK Corp. as a deduction did not exceed 25 percent of the total compensation otherwise paid or accrued during JMK Corp.'s 2010 taxable year to participants under the plan.

The plan amendment and the board resolution setting a minimum contribution for the plan year established a liability, prior to the end of JMK Corp.'s taxable year, to make that contribution. However, JMK Corp.'s post-year end service contributions still are attributable to compensation earned by plan participants after the end of the taxable year. Neither the plan amendment nor the board resolution bears on when that compensation is earned. Thus, for example, the post-year end service contributions in these circumstances are still on account of that subsequent taxable year rather than on account of JMK Corp.'s 2010 taxable year, and so cannot be deemed paid at the end of JMK Corp.'s 2010 taxable year. Therefore, JMK Corp.'s post-year end service contributions are not deductible for its 2010 taxable year. This applies regardless of whether the employer's liability to make a minimum contribution is fixed before the close of the taxable year.

Example 2. The facts are the same as in Example 1, but there are two variations, neither of which involves contributions after the end of the taxable year. One variation involves an actual payment to the plan before the end of the taxable year in anticipation of deferrals and matching contributions to occur after the end of the taxable year (but before the end of the overlapping plan year). The other variation involves such a prepayment, combined with a guaranteed minimum contribution. Because these variations involve actual payments before the end of the taxable year, the payments are deductible for JMK Corp.'s 2010 taxable year.

IRS has issued final and temporary regulations that may require individuals, trusts, partnerships and their partners, C corporations, and S corporations and their shareholders to file a statement with their income tax or information returns reporting certain tax avoidance transactions involving contributions to

401(k) plans attributable to compensation earned after the close of the taxable year. IRS has included in tax avoidance transactions those transactions in which taxpayers claim deductions for contributions to a 401(k) plan or matching contributions to a defined contribution plan where the contributions are attributable to compensation earned by plan participants after the end of the taxable year. In general, a separate statement will be required for each reportable transaction for each taxable year in which an individual's or an entity's federal income tax liability is affected by its participation in such a transaction. [Treas. Reg. §§ 1.6011-4, 54.6011-4; Rev. Proc. 2003-25, 2003-1 C.B. 601; IRS Notice 2001-51, 2001-2 C.B. 190] IRS has concluded that the two variations described in Example 2 are not reportable transactions. [IRS Notice 2002-48, 2002-2 C.B. 130]

A number of changes affecting the employer's tax deductible contributions to a 401(k) plan have been made. See Q 27:52 for the treatment of catch-up contributions. However, the employer's tax deductible contribution can be maximized by adopting a combined 401(k) plan (see Q 27:67). [I.R.C. § 404(n)]

Example 3. In 2011, Marcy, age 50, is the sole employee of Pioneer Plans Corporation, and the corporation adopts a profit sharing plan with a CODA. In 2011, Marcy has a salary of $116,000 after making an elective contribution of $16,500 and a catch-up contribution of $5,500. Marcy's compensation for the year is $138,000 ($116,000 + $16,500 + $5,500; see Q 6:12), and the corporation makes a contribution to the plan of $32,500 for Marcy's benefit. Since the catch-up contribution is not considered for the annual addition limitation (see Q 27:70), Marcy's annual addition is $49,000 ($32,500 + $16,500) and does not exceed the limitation of the lesser of $49,000 or 100 percent of compensation. In addition, the entire $54,500 ($32,500 + $16,500 + $5,500) contributed to the plan in 2011 is deductible because elective and catch-up contributions are not considered employer contributions and are not subject to the employer deduction limitation relating to the 25-percent-of-compensation limitation for profit sharing plan contributions.

Example 4. The facts are the same as in Example 3, except that the annual addition limitation increases to $51,000 for the 2011 limitation year (see Q 6:12), but the elective and catch-up contribution limitations do not increase for 2011. The corporation can now make a contribution of $34,500 to the plan for Marcy's benefit. Marcy's annual addition is $51,000 ($34,500 + $16,500), and the entire $56,500 ($34,500 + $16,500 + $5,500) is deductible. If the limitation on elective contributions increases to $17,000 in 2011 and Marcy makes an elective contribution of that amount, the corporation's contribution for Marcy's benefit will be limited to $34,000 because her annual addition cannot exceed $51,000 ($34,000 + $17,000).

Example 5. The facts are the same as in Example 3, except that Marcy and her husband, Van, also age 50, are the only employees of Pioneer Plans Corporation, and Van earns the same salary and makes the same elective and catch-up contributions. The entire $113,000 ($56,500 + $56,500) contributed to the plan in 2011 is deductible.

Example 6. The facts are the same as in Example 5, except that Marcy's daughter, Cloie, is also an employee of Pioneer Plans Corporation. Cloie has compensation of $10,000 (before her elective contribution), makes an elective contribution of $7,850, and is allocated a plan contribution of $2,150. Her annual addition is $10,000 ($2,150 + $7,850) and does not exceed the limitation of the lesser of $49,000 or 100 percent of compensation. The entire $123,000 ($56,500 + $56,500 + $10,000) contributed to the plan in 2011 is deductible.

Q 27:70   How does a CODA affect the annual addition limitation?

Because a CODA must be part of a profit sharing or stock bonus plan (see Q 27:1), the limitation on annual additions to defined contribution plans applies (see Qs 6:34, 27:51). In computing the annual addition, elective contributions (see Q 27:16) made under a qualified CODA are considered employer contributions. [I.R.C. § 415(c); Treas. Reg. § 1.401(k)-1(a)(4)(ii); Rev. Proc. 92-93, 1992-2 C.B. 505]

IRS has explained how a plan can correct the mistake of failing to limit contributions for a participant. According to IRS, if contributions for a participant include both employer and employee elective contributions, correction for contributions that exceed the employee's annual addition limitation should be made in the following manner:

Step 1: Distribute unmatched elective contributions (adjusted for earnings) to the affected participant. If any excess remains, proceed to Step 2.

Step 2: Distribute elective contributions (adjusted for earnings) that are matched, and forfeit related matching contributions (adjusted for earnings). If any excess remains, proceed to Step 3.

Step 3: Forfeit other profit sharing contributions.

The employer should report the corrective distribution made to the participant on Form 1099-R. The participant should include the distribution as income but is not subject to the 10 percent tax on early distributions (see Q 16:17). The participant may not roll over the corrective distribution to another qualified retirement plan or to an IRA (see Q 34:8).

The plan sponsor should transfer the forfeited employer contributions (profit sharing or matching) to an unallocated account. These amounts are used to reduce employer contributions in the current year and, if applicable, later years.

[*Retirement News for Employers*, Winter 2009]

A number of changes have been made to the annual addition limitation. See Qs 27:52 and 27:69 for the treatment of catch-up contributions; see Qs 6:34 and 6:36 for a discussion of changes affecting the annual addition limitation; and see Qs 12:8, 12:9, 12:15, and 12:21 for a discussion of changes to the deduction limits.

Q 27:71   Are elective contributions subject to payroll taxes?

Yes. Elective contributions (see Q 27:16) made under a CODA (see Q 27:2) are included in the Social Security taxable wage base (see Q 7:7) for both employer and employee withholding purposes. Elective contributions are also subject to the Federal Unemployment Tax Act (FUTA). [Social Security Act Amendments of 1983 § 324(d)]

Elective contributions are also included for purposes of measuring the annual increases in Social Security average wages, which will affect the calculation of both the taxable earnings base and benefit computations. [Social Security Act § 209]

Q 27:72   Does a 401(k) plan require registration with the Securities and Exchange Commission?

The Securities and Exchange Commission (SEC) has expressed its opinion that CODAs (see Q 27:2) do not require registration of plan interests or employer stock purchased by the plan, but that a salary reduction plan under which an employee accepts a reduction in salary to obtain a contribution of a like amount by the employer to a qualified profit sharing plan (see Q 2:6) may create plan interests that are securities. [SEC Rel. No. 33-6281; Diasonics, Inc., SEC, Div. of Corp. Fin. (Dec. 23, 1982)]

In a case in which the employer adopted a wage reduction program that consisted of eligibility to participate in an ESOP (see Q 28:1) and profit sharing plan in return for a reduction in wages, the court held that, in order to be considered an investment contract subject to protection under the Securities Acts of 1933 and 1934, there must be (1) an investment of money (2) in a common enterprise (3) with profits derived from the efforts of other persons. Since the wage reduction program constituted an investment of money, the ESOP is a common enterprise, and profits (i.e., dividends and appreciation in value) would result primarily from efforts of management and employees, each employee's interest in the ESOP was an investment contract. [Uselton v. Commercial Lovelace Motor Freight, Inc., Nos. 88-1253, 88-1750 (10th Cir. 1991); see also International Bhd. of Teamsters v. Daniel, 439 U.S. 551 (1979); SEC v. W.J. Howey Co., 328 U.S. 293 (1946)]

In another case, the court ruled that the Securities Acts applied to employee claims involving an ESOP because (1) the plan, as an ESOP, lacked the primary indicia of a pension plan (i.e., payment of benefits only upon retirement), (2) participation was voluntary, (3) the ESOP was contributory because participants gave up a percentage of income, and (4) participants acquired common stock, a security specifically enumerated in the Securities Act of 1933. [Hood v. Smith's Transfer Corp., 762 F. Supp. 1274 (W.D. Ky. 1991)]

For a discussion of these issues, see BW Berglund and J Henshaw, Securities Law Issues Relating to Employee Benefit Plans, 27 *J. Pension Plan. & Compliance* No. 2, at p. 54 (Summer 2001).

Q 27:73   What is a 401(m) plan?

A 401(m) plan is a defined contribution plan (see Q 2:2) to which employee contributions (see Q 27:74) and/or matching contributions (see Q 27:75) are made for a plan year. [I.R.C. § 401(m)] A 401(m) plan must satisfy the nondiscrimination requirements (see Q 27:76).

On December 29, 2004, IRS issued comprehensive final regulations setting forth the requirements (including the nondiscrimination requirements) for CODAs (see Q 27:2) under Section 401(k) and for employee contributions and matching contributions under Section 401(m). The final regulations apply for plan years beginning on or after January 1, 2006. However, plan sponsors were permitted to apply the final regulations to any plan year that ended after December 29, 2004, provided the plan applied all the rules of the final regulations, to the extent applicable, for that plan year and all subsequent plan years. IRS cautioned, however, that a decision to apply the regulations in the middle of a plan year could only be successfully implemented if the plan was operated in accordance with the regulations for that year. [Treas. Reg. § 1.401(m)-l(d); Preamble to final regulations]

Q 27:74   What are employee contributions?

Employee contributions are contributions to a plan that are designated or treated at the time of contribution as after-tax employee contributions (e.g., by treating the contributions as taxable income subject to applicable withholding requirements) and are allocated to an individual account for each eligible employee to which attributable earnings and losses are allocated. Employee contributions include:

1. Employee contributions to the defined contribution portion of a defined benefit plan (see Q 2:3) to the extent they are allocated to a separate account for each individual participant;

2. Employee contributions applied to the purchase of whole life insurance protection or survivor benefit protection under a defined contribution plan (see Q 15:2);

3. Amounts attributable to excess contributions that are recharacterized as employee contributions (see Q 27:31); and

4. Employee contributions to a 403(b) plan (see Q 35:1). [Treas. Reg. § 1.401(m)-1(a)(3)(i)]

Employee contributions do not include designated Roth contributions (see Q 27:96), repayment of loans (see Q 14:1), rollover contributions (see Q 34:1), repayment of distributions (see Q 9:22), or employee contributions that are transferred to the plan from another plan. [Treas. Reg. § 1.401(m)-1(a)(3)(ii)]

Employee contributions to a qualified cost-of-living arrangement are treated as employee contributions to a defined contribution plan (see Q 2:2), without regard to the requirement that the employee contributions be allocated to an individual account to which attributable earnings and losses are allocated. [I.R.C. § 415(k)(2)(B); Treas. Reg. § 1.401(m)-1(a)(3)(iii)]

Employee contributions are sometimes referred to as voluntary contributions. See Q 23:32 for a discussion of when employee contributions are considered plan assets.

Q 27:75   What are matching contributions?

Matching contributions are any:

1. Employer contribution (including a contribution made at the employer's discretion) to a defined contribution plan (see Q 2:2) on account of an employee contribution (see Q 27:74) to a plan maintained by the employer;

2. Employer contribution (including a contribution made at the employer's discretion) to a defined contribution plan on account of an elective deferral (see Q 27:21); and

3. Forfeiture allocated on the basis of employee contributions, matching contributions, or elective deferrals (see Q 9:19).

[I.R.C. §§ 401(m)(4)(A), 401(m)(4)(B); Treas. Reg. § 1.401(m)-1(a)(2)(i)]

Whether an employer contribution is made on account of an employee contribution or an elective deferral is determined on the basis of all the relevant facts and circumstances, including the relationship between the employer contribution and employee actions outside the plan. An employer contribution made to a defined contribution plan on account of contributions made by an employee under an employer-sponsored savings arrangement that are not held in a plan that is intended to be a qualified retirement plan or other arrangement is not a matching contribution. [Treas. Reg. §§ 1.401(m)-1(a)(2)(ii), 1.402(g)-1(b)]

Employer contributions are not matching contributions made on account of elective deferrals if they are contributed before the cash-or-deferred election (see Q 27:3) is made or before the employees' performance of services with respect to which the elective deferrals are made (or when the cash that is subject to the cash-or-deferred elections would be currently available, if earlier). In addition, an employer contribution is not a matching contribution made on account of an employee contribution if it is contributed before the employee contribution. This does not apply to a forfeiture that is allocated as a matching contribution. In addition, an allocation of shares from an ESOP loan suspense account (see Q 28:7) will not fail to be treated as a matching contribution solely because the employer contribution that resulted in the release and allocation of those shares from the suspense account is made before the employees' performance of services with respect to which the elective deferrals are made (or when the cash that is subject to the cash-or-deferred elections would be currently available, if earlier) provided that the contribution is for a required payment that is due under the loan terms, and the contribution is not made early with a principal purpose of accelerating deductions. The timing of contributions will not be treated as failing to satisfy these requirements merely because contributions are occasionally made before the employees' performance of services with respect to which the elective deferrals are made (or when the cash that is subject to the cash-or-deferred elections would be currently available, if earlier) in order to accommodate bona fide administrative considerations and are not paid early with a principal purpose of accelerating deductions. [Treas. Reg. § 1.401(m)-1(a)(2)(iii)]

Q 27:76   What nondiscrimination requirements apply to 401(m) plans?

A defined contribution plan (see Q 2:2) does not satisfy the qualification requirements (see Q 4:1) for a plan year unless the amount of employee contributions (see Q 27:74) and matching contributions (see Q 27:75) to the plan for the plan year satisfies the nondiscrimination requirements (see Q 4:10). The amount of employee contributions and matching contributions under a plan satisfies the nondiscrimination requirements with respect to amounts if and only if the amount of employee contributions and matching contributions satisfies the nondiscrimination test and the additional requirements discussed below. A plan that provides for employee contributions or matching contributions must satisfy the nondiscrimination requirements relating to benefits, rights, and features (see Q 4:20) in addition to the nondiscrimination requirement regarding amounts (see Q 4:12). For example, the right to make each level of employee contributions and the right to each level of matching contributions under the plan are benefits, rights, or features subject to the nondiscrimination requirements. [Treas. Reg. § 1.401(m)-1(a)(1)]

The matching contributions and employee contributions under a plan satisfy the nondiscrimination in amount requirement for a plan year only if the plan satisfies:

1. The ACP test (see Q 27:77);
2. The ACP safe harbor provisions (see Q 27:89);
3. The ACP safe harbor provisions relating to automatic contribution arrangements (see Q 27:89); or
4. The SIMPLE 401(k) plan provisions (see Q 33:31).

[I.R.C. § 401(m); Treas. Reg. § 1.401(m)-1(b)(1)]

This requirement is treated as satisfied with respect to employee contributions and matching contributions under a collectively bargained plan (or the portion of a plan) that automatically satisfies the minimum coverage requirement (see Q 5:15). Additionally, the coverage and nondiscrimination requirements do not apply to a governmental plan maintained by a state or local government or political subdivision thereof (or agency or instrumentality thereof). [Treas. Reg. §§ 1.401(a)(4)-1(c)(5), 1.401(m)-1(b)(2), 1.410(b)-2(b)(7)]

The anti-abuse provision and the rules for aggregating and disaggregating plans that apply to 401(k) plans (see Q 27:12) also apply to 401(m) plans. An employer may not aggregate a plan that is using the ACP safe harbor provisions or the ACP safe harbor provisions relating to automatic contribution arrangements and another plan that is using the ACP test. [Treas. Reg. §§ 1.401(m)-1(b)(3), 1.401(m)-1(b)(4)]

The group of employees who are eligible to make employee contributions or eligible to receive matching contributions must satisfy the coverage requirements as if those employees were covered under a separate plan. The determination of whether the separate plan satisfies the coverage requirements must be made without regard to the modifications to the disaggregation rules. In addition, except as expressly permitted, employee contributions, matching contributions, and elective contributions taken into account for the ACP test may not be taken into account for purposes of determining whether any other contributions under any plan (including the plan to which the employee contributions or matching contributions are made) satisfy the qualification requirements. [Treas. Reg. § 1.401(m)-1(c)(1)]

The plan must provide for satisfaction of either the ACP test or the ACP test safe harbor and, if with respect to that alternative there are optional choices, which of the optional choices will apply. For example, a plan that uses the ACP test must specify whether it is using the current year testing method or prior year testing method (see Qs 27:19, 27:35–27:39). Additionally, a plan that uses the prior year testing method must specify whether the ACP for eligible NHCEs for the first plan year is 3 percent or the ACP for the eligible NHCEs for the first plan year (see Q 27:37). Similarly, a plan that uses the safe harbor method or the safe harbor method relating to automatic contribution arrangements must specify the default percentages that apply for the plan year and whether the safe harbor contribution will be the nonelective safe harbor contribution or the matching safe harbor contribution and is not permitted to provide that ACP testing will be used if the requirements for the safe harbor are not satisfied. A plan may incorporate by reference the provisions of the ACP test if that is the nondiscrimination test being applied. IRS may, in guidance of general applicability, specify the options that will apply under the plan if the nondiscrimination test is incorporated by reference. [Treas. Reg. § 1.401(m)-1(c)(2)]

See Q 27:5 for a discussion of new rules that apply for plan years beginning after December 31, 2007.

Q 27:77   What is the actual contribution percentage (ACP) test?

A plan satisfies the ACP test for a plan year only if:

1. The ACP for the eligible HCEs (see Q 3:3) for the plan year is not more than the ACP for the eligible NHCEs (see Q 3:12) for the applicable year (see Q 27:19) multiplied by 1.25, or

2. The excess of the ACP for the eligible HCEs for the plan year over the ACP for the eligible NHCEs for the applicable year is not more than two percentage points, and the ACP for the eligible HCEs for the plan year is not more than the ACP for the eligible NHCEs for the applicable year multiplied by 2.0.

[I.R.C. § 401(m)(2); Treas. Reg. § 1.401(m)-2(a)(1)(i)]

Similar to the 401(k) plan (see Q 27:18) if, for the applicable year there are no eligible NHCEs (i.e., all of the eligible employees under the plan for the applicable year are HCEs), the plan is deemed to satisfy the ACP test for the plan year. [Treas. Reg. § 1.401(m)-2(a)(1)(ii)] The special rule that applies for early participation in a 401(k) plan (see Q 27:18) also applies to a 401(m) plan with ACP being substituted for ADP. [I.R.C. § 401(m)(5)(C); Treas. Reg. § 1.401(m)-2(a)(1)(iii)]

USERRA (see Q 1:16) provides that any qualified retirement plan benefit or contribution that is contingent upon the making of contributions or deferrals by the employee is due the reemployed person only if the employee makes up the missed contributions or deferrals. A makeup of employee contributions or deferrals may be contributed by the employee over a period of time equal to three times the period of absence due to military service, but not to exceed five years. For example, if a participant in a 401(k) plan that provides employer matching contributions is called to 12 months of active military duty, the employee would have 36 months after returning to employment to make up the missed deferrals. As the deferrals are made up, the corresponding employer matching contributions would be credited to the participant's account under the plan.

IRS has ruled that employees who have not satisfied a plan's eligibility requirements for participation (see Qs 1:44, 5:2), but who are permitted to make rollover contributions (see Q 34:1), need not be taken into account for purposes of the ACP test. [Rev. Rul. 96-48, 1996-2 C.B. 31] Employees of a tax-exempt charitable organization (see Q 35:3) who are eligible to make salary reduction contributions under a 403(b) plan (see Q 35:1) may be treated as excludable employees for purposes of testing a 401(k) plan or a plan providing for matching contributions under the same general arrangement as the 401(k) plan of the employer (i.e., 401(m) plan) if (1) no employee of *any* tax-exempt charitable organization is eligible to participate in the 401(k) or 401(m) plan and (2) at least 95 percent of the employees who are not employees of *any* such organization are eligible to participate in the 401(k) or 401(m) plan. [Treas. Reg. § 1.410(b)-6(g); EGTRRA 2001 § 664] In addition to 401(m) plans, the regulations apply to 401(k) plans (see Q 27:18).

An alternative method, the ACP test safe harbor, may be used to satisfy the ACP test. If the plan satisfies the requirements of the safe harbor rule, the ACP test will automatically be satisfied. Thus, the employer may choose either to satisfy the ACP test or to use the safe harbor rule. For details of the ACP test safe harbor, see Qs 27:89 through 27:95.

Q 27:78 How is the ACP calculated for purposes for the test?

The ACP for a group of eligible employees (either eligible HCEs or eligible NHCEs; see Qs 3:3, 3:12) for a plan year or applicable year is the average of the actual contribution ratios (ACRs; see Q 27:79) of eligible employees in the group for that year. The ACP for a group of eligible employees is calculated to the nearest hundredth of a percentage point. [I.R.C. § 401(m)(3); Treas. Reg. § 1.401 (m)-2(a)(1)(i)]

The ACP test (see Q 27:77) is applied using the prior year testing method or the current year testing method. Under the prior year testing method, the applicable year for determining the ACP for the eligible NHCEs is the plan year immediately preceding the plan year for which the ACP test is being calculated. Under the prior year testing method, the ACP for the eligible NHCEs is determined using the ACRs for the eligible employees who were NHCEs in that preceding plan year, regardless of whether those NHCEs are eligible employees or NHCEs in the plan year for which the ACP test is being performed. Under the current year testing method, the applicable year for determining the ACP for eligible NHCEs is the same plan year as the plan year for which the ACP test is being calculated. Under either method, the ACP for the eligible HCEs is determined using the ACRs of eligible employees who are HCEs for the plan year for which the ACP test is being performed. [Treas. Reg. § 1.401(m)-2(a)(2)(ii)] See Q 27:88 for additional rules for the prior year testing method.

Q 27:79   How is the actual contribution ratio (ACR) of an employee calculated for purposes of the ACP test?

The ACR of an eligible employee for the plan year or applicable year (see Q 27:78) is the sum of the employee contributions (see Q 27:74) and matching contributions (see Q 27:75) taken into account with respect to such employee (see Q 27:80) and the QNECs and elective contributions taken into account (see Q 27:81) for the year, divided by the employee's compensation (see Q 27:21) taken into account for the year. The ACR is calculated to the nearest hundredth of a percentage point. If no employee contributions, matching contributions, elective contributions, or QNECs are taken into account with respect to an eligible employee for the year, the ACR of the employee is zero. [I.R.C. § 401(m)(3); Treas. Reg. § 1.401(m)-2(a)(3)(i)]

The ACR of an HCE (see Q 3:3) who is an eligible employee in more than one plan of an employer to which employee contributions or matching contributions are made is calculated in the same manner as the ADR of an HCE who is an eligible employee in more than one CODA of the same employer (see Q 27:20). [I.R.C. § 401(m)(2)(B); Treas. Reg. § 1.401(m)-2(a)(3)(ii)]

> **Example.** Terry, an HCE with compensation of $120,000, is eligible to make employee contributions under Plan S and Plan T, two calendar-year profit sharing plans of KSS Corp. Plan S and Plan T use the same definition of compensation. Plan S provides a match equal to 50 percent of each employee's contributions and Plan T has no match. During the current plan year, Terry elects to contribute $4,000 in employee contributions to Plan T and $4,000 in employee contributions to Plan S. There are no other contributions made on behalf of Terry. Each plan must calculate Terry's ACR by dividing the total employee contributions by her and matching contributions under both plans by $120,000. Therefore, Terry's ACR under each plan is 8.33 percent [($4,000 + $4,000 + $2,000) ÷ $120,000].

See Q 27:20 for additional examples of the application of the parallel rule for multiple CODAs.

Q 27:80   What employee and matching contributions are counted for purposes of the ACP test?

An employee contribution (see Q 27:74) is taken into account in determining the ACR (see Q 27:79) for an eligible employee for the plan year or applicable year (see Q 27:78) in which the contribution is made. For purposes of the preceding sentence, an amount withheld from an employee's pay (or a payment by the employee to an agent of the plan) is treated as contributed at the time of such withholding (or payment) if the funds paid are transmitted to the trust within a reasonable period after the withholding (or payment). Excess contributions that are recharacterized (see Qs 27:30–27:32) are taken into account as employee contributions for the plan year that includes the time at which the excess contribution is includible in the gross income of the employee (see Q 27:31). A matching contribution (see Q 27:75) is taken into account in determining the ACR for an eligible employee for a plan year or applicable year only if each of the following requirements is satisfied:

1. The matching contribution is allocated to the employee's account under the terms of the plan as of a date within that year;

2. The matching contribution is made on account of (or the matching contribution is allocated on the basis of) the employee's elective deferrals (see Q 27:16) or employee contributions for that year; and

3. The matching contribution is actually paid to the plan no later than the end of the 12-month period immediately following the year that contains that date.

[Treas. Reg. § 1.401(m)-2(a)(4)]

Matching contributions that do not satisfy the above requirements may not be taken into account in the ACP test (see Q 27:77) for the plan year with respect to which the contributions were made, or for any other plan year. Instead, the amount of the matching contributions must satisfy the nondiscrimination requirements (see Q 4:10) without regard to the ACP test for the plan year for which they are allocated under the plan as if they were nonelective contributions and were the only nonelective contributions for that year. [Treas. Reg. § 1.401(m)-2(a)(5)(i)]

A matching contribution with respect to an elective deferral for an NHCE (see Q 3:12) is not taken into account under the ACP test to the extent it exceeds the greatest of:

1. 5 percent of compensation;

2. The employee's elective deferrals for a year; and

3. The product of two times the plan's representative matching rate and the employee's elective deferrals for a year.

[Treas. Reg. § 1.401(m)-2(a)(5)(ii)(A)]

The plan's representative matching rate is the lowest matching rate for any eligible NHCE among a group of NHCEs that consists of half of all eligible NHCEs in the plan for the plan year who make elective deferrals for the plan year (or, if greater, the lowest matching rate for all eligible NHCEs in the plan who are employed by the employer on the last day of the plan year and who make elective deferrals for the plan year). [Treas. Reg. § 1.401(m)-2(a)(5)(ii)(B)] The matching rate for an employee generally is the matching contributions made for such employee divided by the employee's elective deferrals for the year. If the matching rate is not the same for all levels of elective deferrals for an employee, the employee's matching rate is determined assuming that an employee's elective deferrals are equal to 6 percent of compensation. [Treas. Reg. § 1.401(m)-2(a)(5)(ii)(C)]

If a plan provides a match with respect to the sum of the employee's employee contributions and elective deferrals, that sum is substituted for the amount of the employee's elective deferrals above and employees who make either employee contributions or elective deferrals are taken into account for calculation of the representative matching rate. Similarly, if a plan provides a match with respect to the employee's employee contributions, but not elective deferrals, the employee's employee contributions are substituted for the amount of the employee's elective deferrals and employees who make employee contributions are taken into account for calculation of the representative matching rate. [Treas. Reg. § 1.401(m)-2(a)(5)(ii)(D)]

QMACs that are taken into account for the ADP test (see Q 27:23) are not taken into account in determining an eligible employee's ACR. [Treas. Reg. § 1.401(m)-2(a)(5)(iii)]

A plan that satisfies the ACP safe harbor requirements (see Qs 27:89–27:95) or the ACP safe harbor requirements relating to automatic contribution arrangements for a plan year but nonetheless must satisfy the ACP test because it provides for employee contributions for such plan year is permitted to apply the ACP test disregarding all matching contributions with respect to all eligible employees. In addition, a plan that satisfies the ADP safe harbor requirements (see Qs 27:40–27:50) for a plan year using QMACs but does not satisfy the ACP safe harbor requirements or the ACP safe harbor requirements relating to automatic contribution arrangements for such plan year is permitted to apply the ACP test by excluding matching contributions with respect to all eligible employees that do not exceed 4 percent ($3\frac{1}{2}$ percent in the case of a plan that satisfies the ADP safe harbor relating to automatic contribution arrangements; see Qs 27:5, 27:6) of each employee's compensation. If a plan so disregards matching contributions, the disregard must apply with respect to all eligible employees. [Treas. Reg. § 1.401(m)-2(a)(5)(iv)]

A matching contribution that is forfeited because the contribution to which it relates is treated as an excess contribution (see Q 27:25), excess deferral (see Q 27:63), excess aggregate contribution (see Q 27:82), or default elective contribution that is distributed as a permissible withdrawal under an EACA (see Qs 27:5, 27:7) is not taken into account. [Treas. Reg. § 1.401(m)-2(a)(5)(v)]

Additional employee contributions and matching contributions made by reason of an eligible employee's qualified military service under USERRA (see

Q 1:16) are not taken into account for the plan year for which the contributions are made, or for any other plan year. [Treas. Reg. § 1.401(m)-2(a)(5)(vi)]

Q 27:81 Can QNECs and elective contributions be taken into account for purposes of the ACP test?

QNECs (see Q 27:17) and elective contributions (see Q 27:16) may be taken into account in determining the ACR (see Q 27:79) for an eligible employee for a plan year or applicable year (see Q 27:78), but only to the extent the contributions satisfy the requirements discussed in this Q 27:81. [Treas. Reg. § 1.401(m)-2(a)(6)]

The QNECs must be allocated to the employee's account as of a date within that year (see Q 27:22), and the elective contribution must satisfy the compensation requirement (see Q 27:22). Consequently, under the prior year testing method (see Q 27:35), in order to be taken into account in calculating the ACP (see Q 27:77) for the group of eligible NHCEs (see Q 3:12) for the applicable year, a QNEC must be contributed no later than the end of the 12-month period following the applicable year even though the applicable year is different than the plan year being tested. [Treas. Reg. § 1.401(m)-2(a)(6)(i)]

Elective contributions may be taken into account for the ACP test (see Q 27:77) only if the CODA (see Q 27:2) under which the elective contributions are made is required to satisfy the ADP test (see Q 27:18) and then, only to the extent that the CODA would satisfy that test, including such elective contributions in the ADP for the plan year or applicable year. Thus, for example, elective deferrals made pursuant to a salary reduction agreement under a 403(b) plan (see Q 35:1) are not permitted to be taken into account in an ACP test. Similarly, elective contributions under a CODA that is using the ADP test safe harbor (see Q 27:40) cannot be taken into account in an ACP test. In addition, for plan years ending on or after November 8, 2007, elective contributions that are not permitted to be taken into account for the ADP test for the plan year (see Q 27:22) are not permitted to be taken into account for the ACP test. [Treas. Reg. § 1.401(m)-2(a)(6)(ii)]

The amount of nonelective contributions, including those QNECs taken into account for the ACP test and those QNECs taken into account for the ADP test (see Q 27:23), and the amount of nonelective contributions, excluding those QNECs taken into account for the ACP test and those QNECs taken into account for the ADP test, satisfies the nondiscrimination requirements (see Q 4:10). [Treas. Reg. § 1.401(m)-2(a)(6)(iii)]

The plan that provides for employee or matching contributions and the plan or plans to which the QNECs or elective contributions are made must be plans that would be permitted to be aggregated. If the plan year of the plan that provides for employee or matching contributions is changed to satisfy the requirement that aggregated plans have the same plan year, QNECs and elective contributions may be taken into account in the resulting short plan year only if such QNECs and elective contributions could have been taken into account under an ADP test for a plan with that same short plan year (see Q 27:23). [Treas. Reg. § 1.401(m)-2(a)(6)(iv)]

QNECs cannot be taken into account for an applicable year for an NHCE to the extent such contributions exceed the product of that NHCE's compensation and the greater of 5 percent and two times the plan's representative contribution rate. Any QNEC taken into account in an ADP test (including the determination of the representative contribution rate) is not permitted to be taken into account for purposes of the ACP test (including the determination of the representative contribution rate). The plan's representative contribution rate is the lowest applicable contribution rate of any eligible NHCE among a group of eligible NHCEs that consists of half of all eligible NHCEs for the plan year (or, if greater, the lowest applicable contribution rate of any eligible NHCE in the group of all eligible NHCEs for the applicable year and who is employed by the employer on the last day of the applicable year). The applicable contribution rate for an eligible NHCE is the sum of the matching contributions taken into account under the ACP test for the employee for the plan year and the QNECs made for that employee for the plan year, divided by that employee's compensation for the same period. However, QNECs that are made in connection with an employer's obligation to pay prevailing wages under the Davis-Bacon Act, Public Law 71-798, Service Contract Act of 1965, Public Law 89-286, or similar legislation can be taken into account for a plan year for an NHCE to the extent such contributions do not exceed 10 percent of that NHCE's compensation. [Treas. Reg. § 1.401(m)-2(a)(6)(v)]

QNECs cannot be taken into account to the extent such contributions are taken into account for purposes of satisfying any other ACP test, any ADP test, the ADP test safe harbor (see Q 27:40), the ACP test safe harbor (see Q 27:89), or the requirements of SIMPLE 401(k) plans (see Q 33:25). Thus, for example, QNECs that are made for the ADP safe harbor nonelective contribution requirement (see Q 27:42) cannot be taken into account under the ACP test. Similarly, if a plan switches from the current year testing method to the prior year testing method (see Q 27:36), QNECs that are taken into account under the current year testing method for a plan year may not be taken into account under the prior year testing method for the next plan year. [Treas. Reg. § 1.401(m)-2(a)(6)(vi)]

Example 1. Lisa Ltd. maintains Plan U, a profit sharing plan under which $.50 matching contributions are made for each dollar of employee contributions. Plan U uses the current year testing method. The chart below shows the average employee contributions (as a percentage of compensation) and matching contributions (as a percentage of compensation) for Plan U's HCEs and NHCEs for the 2011 plan year:

	Matching Contributions	Elective Contributions	ACP
HCEs	4%	2%	6%
NHCEs	3%	1.5%	4.5%

The matching rate for all NHCEs is 50 percent; and, thus, the matching contributions are not disproportionate. Accordingly, they are taken into account in determining the ACR of eligible employees. Because the ACP for the HCEs (6.0%) exceeds 5.63 percent (4.5% × 1.25), Plan U does not satisfy the ACP test. However, because the ACP for the HCEs does not exceed the ACP for the NHCEs by more than 2 percentage points and the ACP for the HCEs does not exceed the ACP for the NHCEs multiplied by 2.0 (4.5% × 2.0 = 9%), the plan satisfies the ACP test.

Example 2. Employees A through F are eligible employees in Plan V, a profit sharing plan of Marsha Management Corp. that includes a CODA and permits employee contributions. Under Plan V, a $.50 matching contribution is made for each dollar of elective contributions and employee contributions. Plan V uses the current year testing method and does not provide for elective contributions to be taken into account in determining an eligible employee's ACR. For the 2011 plan year, Employees A and B are HCEs and the remaining employees are NHCEs. The compensation, elective contributions, employee contributions, and matching contributions for the 2011 plan year are shown in the following table:

Employee	Compensation	Elective Contributions	Employee Contributions	Matching Contributions
A	$190,000	$15,000	$ 3,500	$9,250
B	100,000	5,000	10,000	7,500
C	85,000	12,000	0	6,000
D	70,000	9,500	0	4,750
E	40,000	10,000	0	5,000
F	10,000	0	0	0

The matching rate for all NHCEs is 50 percent; and, thus, the matching contributions are not disproportionate. Accordingly, they are taken into account in determining the ACR of eligible employees, as shown in the following table:

Employee	Compensation	Elective Contributions	Employee Contributions	ACR
A	$190,000	$ 3,500	$9,250	6.71%
B	100,000	10,000	7,500	17.50
C	85,000	0	6,000	7.06
D	70,000	0	4,750	6.79
E	40,000	0	5,000	12.50
F	10,000	0	0	0.00

The ACP for the HCEs is 12.11 percent [(6.71% + 17.50%) ÷ 2]. The ACP for the NHCEs is 6.59 percent [(7.06% + 6.79% + 12.50% + 0.00%) ÷ 4]. Plan V fails to satisfy the ACP test because the ACP of HCEs is more than 125 percent of the ACP of the NHCEs ($6.59\% \times 1.25 = 8.24\%$). In addition, Plan V fails to satisfy the ACP test because the ACP for the HCEs exceeds the ACP of the other employees by more than two percentage points ($6.59\% + 2\% = 8.59\%$). Therefore, the plan fails to satisfy the ACP test unless the ACP failure is corrected.

Example 3. The facts are the same as Example 2, except that the plan provides that the NHCEs' elective contributions may be used to meet the ACP test to the extent needed. The $10,000 of elective contributions for Employee E may be taken into account in determining the ACP rather than the ADP to the extent that the plan satisfies the ADP test excluding from the ADP this $10,000. In this case, if the $10,000 were excluded from the ADP for the NHCEs, the ADP for the HCEs is 6.45 percent $[(7.89\% + 5.00\%) \div 2]$ and the ADP for the NHCEs would be 6.92 percent $[(14.12\% + 13.57\% + 0\% + 0\%) \div 4]$, and the plan would satisfy the ADP test excluding from the ADP the elective contributions for NHCEs that are taken into account for the ACP test. After taking into account the $10,000 of elective contributions for Employee E in the ACP test, the ACP for the NHCEs is 12.84% $[(7.06\% + 6.79\% + 37.50 \% + 0\%) \div 4]$. Therefore the plan satisfies the ACP test because the ACP for the HCEs (12.11%) is less than 1.25 times the ACP for the NHCEs.

Example 4. The facts are the same as Example 2, except that Plan V provides for a higher than 50 percent match rate on the elective contributions and employee contributions for all NHCEs. The match rate is defined as the rate, rounded up to the next whole percent, necessary to allow the plan to satisfy the ACP test, but not in excess of 100 percent. In this case, an increase in the match rate from 50 percent to 74 percent will be sufficient to allow the plan to satisfy the ACP test. Thus, for the 2010 plan year, the compensation, elective contributions, employee contributions, and matching contributions at a 74 percent match rate of the eligible NHCEs (employees C through F) are shown in the following table:

Employee	Compensation	Elective Contributions	Matching Contributions	Employee Contributions
C	$85,000	$12,000	$0	$8,880
D	70,000	9,500	0	7,030
E	40,000	10,000	0	7,400
F	10,000	0	0	0

The matching rate for all NHCEs is 74 percent; and, thus, the matching contributions are not disproportionate. Therefore, the matching contributions may be taken into account in determining the ACP for the NHCEs. The ACP for the NHCEs is 9.75 percent $[(10.45\% + 10.04\% + 18.50\% + 0.00\%) \div 4]$. Because the ACP for the HCEs (12.11%) is less than 1.25 times the ACP for the NHCEs, the plan satisfies the ACP test.

Example 5. The facts are the same as Example 4, except that Employee E's elective contributions are $2,000 (rather than $10,000) and the $2,000 of elective contributions for Employee E are taken into account in determining the ACP rather than the ADP. In addition, Plan V provides that the higher match rate is not limited to 100 percent and applies only for a specified group of NHCEs. The only member of that group is Employee E. Under the plan provision, the higher match rate is a 400 percent match. Thus, for the 2011 plan year, the compensation, elective contributions, employee contributions, and matching contributions of the eligible NHCEs (employees C through F) are shown in the following table:

Employee	Compensation	Elective Contributions	Employee Contributions	Matching Contributions
C	$ 85,000	$ 12,000	$ 0	$ 6,000
D	70,000	9,500	0	4,750
E	40,000	2,000	0	8,000
F	10,000	0	0	0

If the entire matching contribution made on behalf of Employee E were taken into account under the ACP test, Plan V would satisfy the test, because the ACP for the NHCEs would be 9.71 percent [(7.06% + 6.79% + 25.00% + 0.00%) ÷ 4]. Because the ACP for the HCEs (12.11%) is less than 1.25 times what the ACP for the NHCEs would be, the plan would satisfy the ACP test. However, matching contributions for an eligible NHCE that exceed the greatest of (1) 5 percent of compensation, (2) the employee's elective deferrals, (3) and two times the product of the plan's representative matching rate and the employee's elective deferrals, cannot be taken into account in applying the ACP test. The plan's representative matching rate is the lowest matching rate for any eligible employee in a group of NHCEs that is at least half of all eligible employees who are NHCEs in the plan for the plan year who make elective contributions for the plan year. For Plan V, the group of NHCEs who make such contributions consists of Employees C, D, and E. The matching rates for these three employees are 50 percent, 50 percent, and 400 percent, respectively. The lowest matching rate for a group of NHCEs that is at least half of all the NHCEs who make elective contributions (or two NHCEs) is 50 percent. Because 400 percent is more than twice the plan's representative matching rate and the matching contributions exceed 5 percent of compensation, the full amount of matching contributions is not taken into account. Only $2,000 of the matching contributions made on behalf of Employee E (matching contributions that do not exceed the greatest of 5 percent of compensation, the employee's elective deferrals, or the product of 100 percent (two times the representative matching rate) and the employee's elective deferrals) may be taken into account under the ACP test. Accordingly, the ACP for the NHCEs is 5.96 percent [(7.06% + 6.79% + 10.00% + 0.00%) ÷ 4], and the plan fails to satisfy the ACP test unless the ACP failure is corrected.

Example 6. The facts are the same as Example 2, except that Plan V provides a QNEC equal to 13 percent of pay for Employee F that will be taken into account under the ACP test to the extent permissible.

A QNEC cannot be taken into account in determining an NHCE's ACR to the extent it exceeds the greater of 5 percent and the product of the employee's compensation and the plan's representative contribution rate. The plan's representative contribution rate is two times the lowest applicable contribution rate for any eligible employee in a group of NHCEs that is at least half of all eligible employees who are NHCEs in the plan for the plan year. For Plan V, the applicable contribution rates for Employees C, D, E, and F are 7.06 percent, 6.79 percent, 12.5 percent, and 13 percent, respectively. The lowest applicable contribution rate for a group of NHCEs that is at least half of all the NHCEs is 12.50 percent (the lowest applicable contribution rate for the group of NHCEs that consists of Employees E and F).

The plan's representative contribution rate is two times 12.50 percent or 25.00 percent. Accordingly, the QNECs for Employee F can be taken into account under the ACP test only to the extent they do not exceed 25.00 percent of compensation. In this case, all of the QNECs for Employee F may be taken into account under the ACP test. After taking into account the QNECs for Employee F, the ACP for the NHCEs is 9.84 percent [(7.06% + 6.79% + 12.50% + 13.00%) ÷ 4]. Because the ACP for the HCEs (12.11%) is less than 1.25 times the ACP for the NHCEs, the plan satisfies the ACP test.

Q 27:82   What is an excess aggregate contribution under the ACP test?

An excess aggregate contribution for a plan year is the excess of the aggregate amount of employee contributions (see Q 27:74) and matching contributions (see Q 27:75) made on behalf of HCEs (see Q 3:3) for the plan year over the maximum amount of such contributions that are permitted under the ACP test (see Q 27:77). Any QNECs (see Q 27:17) and elective contributions (see Q 27:16) treated as matching contributions for purposes of the ACP test (see Q 27:81) are treated as matching contributions under this definition. However, QMACs that are treated as elective contributions for purposes of meeting the ADP test (see Q 27:23) are not treated as matching contributions under this definition. [I.R.C. § 401(m)(6)(B); Treas. Reg. § 1.401(m)-5]

Excess aggregate contributions can be corrected. A plan that provides for employee contributions or matching contributions does not fail to satisfy the ACP test if the employer, in accordance with the terms of the plan, uses either of the following correction methods:

1. The employer makes additional contributions that are taken into account for the ACP test that, in combination with the other contributions taken into account, allow the plan to satisfy the test.

2. Excess aggregate contributions are distributed or forfeited.

[I.R.C. § 401(m)(6); Treas. Reg. § 1.401(m)-2(b)(i)]

A plan may provide for the use of either of the correction methods described above, may limit employee contributions or matching contributions in a manner that prevents excess aggregate contributions from being made, or may use a combination of these methods, to avoid or correct excess aggregate contributions. If a plan uses a combination of correction methods, any contributions made by the employer must be taken into account before any distribution or forfeiture is made. [Treas. Reg. § 1.401(m)-2(b)(ii)]

A failure to satisfy the ACP test may not be corrected using any other method. Thus, excess aggregate contributions for a plan year may not be corrected by forfeiting vested matching contributions, distributing nonvested matching contributions, recharacterizing matching contributions, or not making matching contributions required under the terms of the plan. Similarly, excess aggregate contributions for a plan year may not remain unallocated or be allocated to a suspense account for allocation to one or more employees in any future year. In addition, excess aggregate contributions may not be corrected using the retroactive correction rules. [Treas. Reg. §§ 1.401(a)(4)-11(g)(3)(vii), 1.401(a)(4)-11(g)(5), 1.401(m)-2(b)(iii)]

For a discussion of the distribution or forfeiture correction method and the consequences of making an excess aggregate contribution, see Qs 27:83 through 27:87; and, for a discussion of rules that apply for plan years beginning after December 31, 2007, see Q 27:5.

Q 27:83   How is an excess aggregate contribution corrected by distribution or forfeiture?

Correction through a distribution generally involves the same four-step process that applies to the excess contribution distribution method for the ADP test (see Q 27:26). However, in lieu of distribution, the apportioned matching contribution may be forfeited, if forfeitable (see Q 27:84). For plan years beginning on or after January 1, 2008, the income allocable to excess aggregate contributions is equal to the allocable gain through the end of the plan year. [I.R.C. § 401(m)(6)(C); Treas. Reg. § 1.401(m)-2(b)(i)–(iv); IRS Notice 2008-30, Q&As 19-21, 2008-1 C.B. 638]

See Q 27:85 for rules relating to the tax treatment of corrective distributions and Q 27:86 for other rules relating to corrective distributions.

The following examples illustrate the application of the distribution correction method. See also Q 27:26 for additional examples of the parallel correction rules applicable to CODAs. For purposes of these examples, none of the plans provides for catch-up contributions (see Q 27:52).

Example 1. Irish Gary, Inc. maintains a plan that provides for employee contributions (see Q 27:74) and fully vested matching contributions (see Q 27:75). The plan provides that failures of the ACP test (see Q 27:77) are corrected by distribution. In 2011, the ACP for the eligible NHCEs (see Q 3:12) is 6 percent. Thus, the ACP for the eligible HCEs (see Q 3:3) may not exceed 8 percent. The three HCEs who participate have the following compensation, contributions, and ACRs (see Q 27:79):

Employee	Compensation	Employee Contributions and Matching Contributions	ACR	Average
A	$200,000	$14,000	7%	
B	150,000	13,500	9	9.33%
C	100,000	12,000	12	

The total amount of excess aggregate contributions for the HCEs is determined as follows: the matching and employee contributions of Employee C (the HCE with the highest ACR) is reduced by 3 percent of compensation (or $3,000) in order to reduce the ACR of that HCE to 9 percent, which is the ACR of Employee B.

Because the ACP of the HCEs determined after the $3,000 reduction still exceeds 8 percent, further reductions in matching contributions and employee contributions are necessary in order to reduce the ACP of the HCEs to 8 percent. The employee contributions and matching contributions for Employees B and C are reduced by an additional .5 percent of compensation or $1,250 ($750 and $500, respectively). Because the ACP of the HCEs determined after the reductions now equals 8 percent, the plan would satisfy the ACP test.

The total amount of excess aggregate contributions ($4,250) is apportioned among the HCEs first to the HCE with the highest amount of matching contributions and employee contributions. Therefore, Employee A is apportioned $500 (the amount required to cause A's matching contributions and employee contributions to equal the next highest dollar amount of matching contributions and employee contributions). Because the total amount of excess aggregate contributions has not been apportioned, further apportionment is necessary. The balance ($3,750) of the total amount of excess aggregate contributions is apportioned equally between Employees A and B ($1,500 to each, the amount required to cause their contributions to equal the next highest dollar amount of matching contributions and employee contributions). Because the total amount of excess aggregate contributions has not been apportioned, further apportionment is necessary. The balance ($750) of the total amount of excess aggregate contributions is apportioned equally among Employees A, B, and C ($250 to each, the amount required to allocate the total amount of excess aggregate contributions for the plan).

Therefore, the plan will satisfy the ACP test if, by the end of the 12-month period following the end of the 2011 plan year (see Q 27:84), Employee A receives a corrective distribution of excess aggregate contributions equal to $2,250 ($500 + $1,500 + $250) and allocable income, Employee B receives a corrective distribution of $250 and allocable income, and Employee C receives a corrective distribution of $1,750 ($1,500 + $250) and allocable income.

Example 2. Jennifer is the sole HCE who is eligible to participate in a CODA (see Q 27:2) maintained by Kate Corp. The plan that includes the arrangement, Plan X, permits employee contributions and provides a fully vested matching contribution equal to 50 percent of elective contributions. Plan X is a calendar-year plan and corrects excess contributions by recharacterization (see Q 27:30) and provides that failures of the ACP test are corrected by distribution. For the 2011 plan year, Jennifer's compensation is $200,000, and her elective contributions are $15,000. The ADPs and ACPs for Jennifer and the other eligible employees under Plan X are shown in the following table:

	ADR	ACR
Jennifer	7.5%	3.75%
NHCEs	4%	2%

In February 2012, Kate Corp. determines that Jennifer's ADR must be reduced to 6 percent, or $12,000, which requires a recharacterization of $3,000 as an employee contribution. This increases Jennifer's ACR to 5.25 percent ($7,500 in matching contributions plus $3,000 recharacterized as employee contributions, divided by $200,000 in compensation). Since Jennifer's ACR must be limited to 4 percent for Plan X to satisfy the ACP test, Plan X must distribute 1.25 percent, or $2,500, of Jennifer's employee contributions and matching contributions together with allocable income. If $2,500 in matching contributions and allocable income is distributed, this will correct the excess aggregate contributions and will not result in a discriminatory rate of matching contributions.

Example 3. The facts are the same as in Example 2, except that Jennifer also had elective contributions under Plan Y, maintained by Hepner, Inc., an employer unrelated to Kate Corp. In January 2012, Jennifer requests and receives a distribution of $1,200 in excess contributions from Plan X. Pursuant to the terms of Plan X, Jennifer forfeits the $600 match on the excess contributions to correct a discriminatory rate of match. The $3,000 that would otherwise have been recharacterized for Plan X to satisfy the ADP test is reduced by the $1,200 already distributed as an excess contribution, leaving $1,800 to be recharacterized. Jennifer's ACR is now 4.35 percent ($7,500 in matching contributions plus $1,800 in recharacterized contributions less $600 forfeited matching contributions attributable to the excess contributions, divided by $200,000 in compensation). The matching and employee contributions for Jennifer must be reduced by .35 percent of compensation in order to reduce the ACP of the HCEs to 4 percent. The plan must provide for forfeiture of additional matching contributions to prevent a discriminatory rate of matching contributions.

Example 4. The facts are the same as in Example 3, except that Jennifer does not request a distribution of excess contributions until March 2012. Hepner, Inc., has already recharacterized $3,000 as employee contributions. The amount of excess contributions is reduced by the amount of excess contributions that are recharacterized. Because the amount recharacterized is greater than the excess contributions, Plan X is neither required nor permitted to make a distribution of excess contributions, and the recharacterization has corrected the excess contributions.

Example 5. For the 2011 plan year, Ben defers $10,000 under Plan M and $6,000 under Plan N. Plans M and N, which have calendar plan years are maintained by unrelated employers. Plan M provides a fully vested, 100 percent matching contribution, does not take elective contributions into account under Section 401(m) or take matching contributions into account under Section 401(k), and provides that excess contributions and excess aggregate contributions are corrected by distribution. Under Plan M, Ben is allocated excess contributions of $600 and excess aggregate contributions of $1,600. Ben timely requests and receives a distribution of the $1,000 excess contribution from Plan M and, pursuant to the terms of Plan M, forfeits the corresponding $1,000 matching contribution. No distribution is required or permitted to correct the excess contributions because $1,000 has been distributed by Plan M as excess contributions. The distribution required to correct the excess aggregate contributions (after forfeiting the matching contribution) is $600 ($1,600 in excess aggregate contributions minus $1,000 in forfeited matching contributions). If Ben had corrected the excess contributions of $1,000 by withdrawing $1,000 from Plan N, Plan M would have had to correct the $600 excess contributions in Plan M by distributing $600. Since Ben then would have forfeited $600 (instead of $1,000) in matching contributions, he would have had $1,000 ($1,600 in excess aggregate contributions minus $600 in forfeited matching contributions) remaining of excess aggregate contributions in Plan M. These would have been corrected by distributing an additional $1,000 from Plan M.

Example 6. Jason is the sole HCE in a profit sharing plan under which the employer matches 100 percent of employee contributions up to 2 percent of compensation and 50 percent of employee contributions up to the next 4 percent of compensation. For the 2011 plan year, Jason has compensation of $100,000 and makes a 7 percent employee contribution of $7,000. Jason receives a 4 percent matching contribution or $4,000. Thus, Jason's ACR is 11 percent. The ACR for the NHCEs is 5 percent, and the employer determines that Jason's ACR must be reduced to 7 percent to satisfy the ACP test. In this case, the plan satisfies the ACP test if it distributes the unmatched employee contributions of $1,000 plus $2,000 of matched employee contributions with their related matches of $1,000. This would leave Jason with 4 percent employee contributions and 3 percent matching contributions for an ACR of 7 percent. Alternatively, the plan could distribute all matching contributions and satisfy the ACP test. However, the plan could not distribute $4,000 of Jason's employee contributions without forfeiting the related matching contributions because this would result in a discriminatory rate of matching contributions.

Example 7. Casey is an HCE in Daniel, Inc.'s profit sharing plan, which matches 100 percent of employee contributions up to 5 percent of compensation. The matching contribution is vested at the rate of 20 percent per year. In 2011, Casey makes $5,000 in employee contributions and receives $5,000 of matching contributions. Casey is 60 percent vested in the matching contributions at the end of the 2011 plan year. In February 2012, Daniel, Inc. determines that Casey has excess aggregate contributions of $1,000. The plan provides that only matching contributions will be distributed as excess aggregate contributions.

Daniel, Inc. has two options available in distributing Casey's excess aggregate contributions. The first option is to distribute $600 of vested matching contributions and forfeit $400 of nonvested matching contributions. These amounts are in proportion to Casey's vested and nonvested interests in all matching contributions. The second option is to distribute $1,000 of vested matching contributions leaving the nonvested matching contributions in the plan. If the second option is chosen, the plan must also provide a separate vesting schedule for vesting these nonvested matching contributions. This is necessary because the nonvested matching contributions must vest as rapidly as they would have had no distribution been made. Thus, 50 percent must vest in each of the next two years.

The plan will not satisfy the nondiscriminatory availability requirement if only nonvested matching contributions are forfeited because the effect is that matching contributions for HCEs vest more rapidly than those for NHCEs.

Example 8. Levy Ltd. maintains a calendar year profit sharing plan that includes a CODA. Elective contributions are matched at the rate of 100 percent. After-tax employee contributions are permitted under the plan only for NHCEs and are matched at the same rate. No employees make excess deferrals. Caroline, an HCE, makes an $8,000 elective contribution and receives an $8,000 matching contribution. Levy Ltd. performs the ADP and ACP tests. To correct failures of the ADP and ACP tests, the plan distributes to Caroline $1,000 of excess contributions and $500 of excess aggregate contributions. After the distributions, Caroline's contributions for the year are $7,000 of elective contributions and $7,500 of matching contributions. As a result, Caroline has received a higher effective rate of matching contributions than NHCEs ($7,000 of elective contributions matched by $7,500 is an effective matching rate of 107 percent). If this amount remains in Caroline's account without correction, it will cause the plan to fail to satisfy the nondiscrimination requirements, because only an HCE receives the higher matching contribution rate. The remaining $500 matching contribution may be forfeited (but not distributed), if the plan so provides. The plan could instead correct the discriminatory rate of matching contributions by making additional allocations to the accounts of NHCEs.

Q 27:84   When must distribution or forfeiture of an excess aggregate contribution be made?

Within 12 months after the close of the plan year in which the excess aggregate contribution (see Q 27:83) arose, the plan must distribute to each HCE (see Q 3:3) the contributions apportioned to such HCE and the allocable income (see Q 27:83) to the extent it is vested (see Q 9:1) or forfeit such amount, if forfeitable. Except as otherwise provided in this Q 27:84, a distribution of excess aggregate contributions must be in addition to any other distributions made during the year and must be designated as a corrective distribution by the employer. In the event of a complete termination of the plan during the plan year in which an excess aggregate contribution arose, the corrective distribution must be made as soon as administratively feasible after the date of termination of the plan, but in no event later than 12 months after the date of termination. If the entire account balance of an HCE is distributed prior to when the plan makes a distribution of excess aggregate contributions, the distribution is deemed to have been a corrective distribution of excess aggregate contributions (and allocable income) to the extent that a corrective distribution would otherwise have been required. [Treas. Reg. § 1.401(m)-2(b)(2)(v)]

Q 27:85   What is the tax treatment of corrective distributions of excess aggregate contributions?

For plan years beginning on or after January 1, 2008, a corrective distribution of excess aggregate contributions (and allocable income; see Q 27:83) is includible in the employee's gross income in the employee's taxable year in which distributed. The portion of the distribution that is treated as an investment in the contract (see Q 13:3) and is therefore not subject to tax is determined without regard to any plan contributions other than those distributed as excess aggregate contributions. [Treas. Reg. § 1.401(m)-2(b)(2)(vi)(A)]

Regardless of when the corrective distribution is made, it is not subject to the 10 percent tax on early distributions (see Qs 16:1, 16:17). Corrective distributions cannot be rolled over to an eligible retirement plan (see Q 34:8). [I.R.C. § 401(m)(7)(A); Treas. Reg. § 1.401(m)-2(b)(2)(vi)(A)] See Q 27:87 for additional rules relating to the employer excise tax on amounts distributed more than two-and-one-half months (six months in the case of an EACA; see Qs 27:5, 27:6) after the end of the plan year.

Corrective distributions of excess aggregate contributions and attributable income from designated Roth accounts are not qualified distributions (see Q 27:105).

Q 27:86   What other rules apply to corrective distributions of excess aggregate contributions?

A corrective distribution of excess aggregate contributions (and allocable income) may be made under the terms of the plan without regard to any notice or consent to the employee or the employee's spouse (see Qs 10:21, 10:61). A distribution of excess aggregate contributions (and allocable income) is not treated as a distribution for purposes of determining whether the plan satisfies the minimum distribution requirements (see Q 11:27). Any distribution of less than the entire amount of excess aggregate contributions (and allocable income) with respect to any HCE (see Q 3:3) is treated as a pro rata distribution of excess aggregate contributions and allocable income.

Excess aggregate contributions (other than amounts attributable to employee contributions; see Q 27:74), including forfeited matching contributions (see Q 27:75), are treated as employer contributions for purposes of the deduction rules (see Q 12:1) and the annual addition limitation (see Q 6:34) even if distributed from the plan. Forfeited matching contributions that are reallocated to the accounts of other participants for the plan year in which the forfeiture occurs are treated as annual additions for the participants to whose accounts they are reallocated and for the participants from whose accounts they are forfeited.

A matching contribution may not be distributed merely because the contribution to which it relates is treated as an excess contribution (see Q 27:25), excess deferral (see Q 27:63), or excess aggregate contribution. A matching contribution is taken into account under the nondiscrimination rules (see Q 4:10) even if the match is distributed, unless the distributed contribution is an excess aggregate contribution. This requires that, after correction of excess aggregate contributions, each level of matching contributions be currently and effectively available to a group of employees that satisfies the nondiscrimination requirements (see Q 4:20). Thus, a plan that provides the same rate of matching contributions to all employees will not meet the nondiscrimination requirements if employee contributions are distributed to HCEs to the extent needed to meet the ACP test (see Q 27:77), while matching contributions attributable to employee contributions remain allocated to the HCEs' accounts. This is because the level of matching contributions will be higher for a group of employees that consists entirely of HCEs. A plan may forfeit matching contributions attributable to excess contributions, excess aggregate contributions, and excess deferrals to avoid a violation of the nondiscrimination requirements. A plan is permitted to provide for which contributions will be distributed to satisfy the ACP test so as to avoid discriminatory matching rates that would otherwise violate the nondiscrimination requirements. For example, the plan may provide that unmatched employee contributions will be distributed before matched employee contributions. If the distributions and forfeitures are made, the employee contributions and matching contributions are treated as meeting the ACP test regardless of whether the ACP for the HCEs, if recalculated after the distributions and forfeitures, would satisfy the test.

[Treas. Reg. § 1.401(m)-2(b)(3)]

Q 27:87   What happens if excess aggregate contributions are not timely corrected?

If a plan does not correct excess aggregate contributions (see Q 27:32) within two-and-one-half months after the close of the plan year for which the excess aggregate contributions are made, the employer will be liable for a 10 percent excise tax on the amount of the excess aggregate contributions. In the case of excess aggregate contributions under a plan that includes an EACA (see Qs 27:5, 27:6), six months is substituted for two and one-half months. The additional time applies to a contribution of excess aggregate contributions for a plan year beginning on or after January 1, 2010, only where all the eligible NHCEs (see Q 3:12) and eligible HCEs (see Q 3:3) are covered employees under the EACA for the entire plan year (or for the portion of the plan year that the eligible NHCEs and eligible HCEs are eligible employees). No tax is imposed on any excess aggregate contribution to the extent the contribution (together with any income allocable thereto) is corrected before the close of the first two-and-one-half months of the following plan year (six months in the case of a plan that includes an EACA). The extension to six months applies to a distribution of excess aggregate contributions for a plan year beginning on or after January 1, 2010, only where all the eligible NHCEs and eligible HCEs are covered employees under an EACA for the entire plan year (or the portion of the plan year that the eligible NHCEs and eligible HCEs are eligible employees under the plan). QNECs or elective contributions taken into account (see Q 27:81) may permit a plan to avoid excess aggregate contributions, even if made after the close of the two-and-one-half month, or six-month, period for distributing excess aggregate contributions without the excise tax. [I.R.C. § 4979(f); Treas. Reg. §§ 1.401(m)-2(b)(4)(i), 1.401(m)-2(b)(4)(iii), 54.4979-1] IRS representatives have opined that, if the last day of the two-and-one-half-month period falls on a weekend or holiday, the period is extended to the next business day.

If excess aggregate contributions are not corrected within 12 months after the close of the plan year for which they were made, the plan will fail to satisfy the nondiscrimination requirements (see Q 4:10) for the plan year for which the excess aggregate contributions are made and all subsequent plan years during which the excess aggregate contributions remain in the plan. [I.R.C. § 401(m)(6)(A); Treas. Reg. § 1.401(m)-2(b)(4)(ii)]

Q 27:88 Are there additional rules that apply to the prior year testing method for the ACP test?

The current year testing method is the testing method under which the applicable year is the current plan year, and the prior year testing method is the testing method under which the applicable year is the prior plan year. [Treas. Reg. § 1.401(m)-5] The additional rules that apply to the ADP test also generally apply to the ACP test (see Qs 27:35–27:39). [Treas. Reg. § 1.401(m)-2(c)]

Example. Stephanie Corporation maintains two plans, Plan N and Plan P, each of which provides for employee contributions or matching contributions. The plans were not permissively aggregated (see Q 27:12) for the 2010 testing year. Both plans use the prior year testing method. Plan N had 300 eligible employees who were NHCEs for 2010, and their ACP for that year was 6 percent. Plan P had 100 eligible employees who were NHCEs for 2010, and the ACP for those NHCEs for that plan was 4 percent. Plan N and Plan P are permissively aggregated for the 2011 plan year.

The permissive aggregation of Plan N and Plan P for the 2011 testing year is a plan coverage change that results in treating the plans as one plan (Plan NP). Therefore, the prior year ACP for the NHCEs under Plan NP for the 2011 testing year is the weighted average of the ACPs for the prior year subgroups.

The first step in determining the weighted average of the ACPs for the prior year subgroups is to identify the prior year subgroups. With respect to the 2011 testing year, an employee is a member of a prior year subgroup if the employee was an NHCE of Stephanie Corporation for the 2010 plan year, was an eligible employee for the 2010 plan year under any 401(k) plan maintained by Stephanie Corporation, and would have been an eligible employee in the 2010 plan year under Plan NP if Plan N and Plan P had been permissively aggregated for that plan year. The NHCEs who were eligible employees under separate plans for the 2010 plan year comprise separate prior year subgroups. Thus, there are two prior year subgroups under Plan NP for the 2011 testing year: the 300 NHCEs who were eligible employees under Plan N for the 2010 plan year and the 100 NHCEs who were eligible employees under Plan P for the 2010 plan year.

The weighted average of the ACPs for the prior year subgroups is the sum of the adjusted ACP with respect to the prior year subgroup that consists of the NHCEs who were eligible employees under Plan N, and the adjusted ACP with respect to the prior year subgroup that consists of the NHCEs who were eligible employees under Plan P. The adjusted ACP for the prior year subgroup that consists of the NHCEs who were eligible employees under Plan N is 4.5 percent, calculated as follows: 6 percent (the ACP for the NHCEs under Plan N for the prior year) × 300/400 (the number of NHCEs in that prior year subgroup divided by the total number of NHCEs in all prior year subgroups), which equals 4.5 percent. The adjusted ACP for the prior year subgroup that consists of the NHCEs who were eligible employees under Plan P is 1 percent, calculated as follows: 4 percent (the ACP for the NHCEs under Plan P for the prior year) × 100/400 (the number of NHCEs in that prior year subgroup divided by the total number of NHCEs in all prior year subgroups), which equals 1 percent. Thus, the prior year ACP for NHCEs under Plan NP for the 2011 testing year is 5.5 percent (the sum of adjusted ACPs for the prior year subgroups, 4.5% + 1.0%).

For examples of parallel rules applicable to the ADP test, see Q 27:39.

Q 27:89   Does a safe harbor rule apply for purposes of satisfying the ACP test?

Yes. A 401(m) plan (see Q 27:73) satisfies the ACP safe harbor provision for a plan year if the arrangement satisfies the safe harbor nonelective contribution requirement (see Q 27:42) or the safe harbor matching contribution requirement (see Q 27:43) for the plan year, the limitation on matching contributions (see Q 27:90), the notice requirement (see Q 27:91), the plan year requirement (see Q 27:92), and additional rules (see Qs 27:93–27:95), as applicable. For plan years beginning on or after January 1, 2008, a safe harbor rule also applies to an automatic contribution arrangement (see Qs 27:5, 27:6). In both cases, the safe harbor contribution requirement must be satisfied without taking into account permitted disparity (see Q 7:1). [I.R.C. § 401(m)(11); Treas. Reg. § 1.401(m)-3(a)]

Q 27:90   Is there a limitation on matching contributions?

A plan that provides for matching contributions must limit such contributions as follows:

1. The ratio of matching contributions on behalf of an employee under the plan for a plan year to the employee's elective contributions (see Q 27:16) and employee contributions (see Q 27:74) must not increase as the amount of an employee's elective contributions and employee contributions increases.

2. Matching contributions must not be made with respect to elective contributions or employee contributions that exceed 6 percent of the employee's safe harbor compensation (see Q 27:41), and matching contributions that are discretionary must not exceed 4 percent of the employee's safe harbor compensation.

3. The ratio of matching contributions on behalf of an HCE (see Q 3:3) to that HCE's elective contributions or employee contributions (or the sum of elective contributions and employee contributions) for that plan year must be no greater than the ratio of matching contributions to elective contributions or employee contributions (or the sum of elective contributions and employee contributions) that would apply with respect to any NHCE (see Q 3:12) for whom the elective contributions or employee contributions (or the sum of elective contributions and employee contributions) are the same percentage of safe harbor compensation.

[I.R.C. § 401(m)(11)(B); Treas. Reg. §§ 1.401(m)-3(d)(2), 401(m)-3(d)(3), 1.401(m)-3(d)(4)]

An employee is taken into account for purposes of item 3 if the employee is an eligible employee under the CODA (see Q 27:2) with respect to which the safe harbor contributions (see Qs 27:42, 27:43) are being made for a plan year. A plan will not fail to satisfy item 3 merely because the plan provides that matching contributions will be made separately with respect to each payroll period (or with respect to all payroll periods ending with or within each month or quarter of a plan year) taken into account under the plan for the plan year, provided that matching contributions with respect to any elective contributions or employee contributions made during a plan year quarter are contributed to the plan by the last day of the immediately following plan year quarter. [Treas. Reg. § 1.401(m)-3(d)(4)]

The rules for determining the ACR of an HCE eligible under more than one plan (see Qs 27:20, 27:79) apply for purposes of determining the rate of matching contributions. However, a plan will not fail to satisfy the safe harbor matching contribution requirements merely because an HCE participates during the plan year in more than one plan that provides for matching contributions, provided that (1) the HCE is not simultaneously an eligible employee under two plans that provide for matching contributions maintained by an employer for a plan year, and (2) the period used to determine compensation for purposes of determining matching contributions under each such plan is limited to periods when the HCE participated in the plan. [Treas. Reg. § 1.401(m)-3(d)(5)]

A plan does not satisfy the safe harbor requirements if elective contributions or employee contributions by NHCEs are restricted. A plan may limit:

1. The frequency and duration of periods in which eligible employees may make or change contribution elections under a plan. However, an employee must have a reasonable opportunity (including a reasonable period after receipt of the notice; see Q 27:91) to make or change a contribution election for the plan year. A 30-day period is deemed to be a reasonable period to make or change a contribution election.

2. The amount of contributions that may be made by an eligible employee under a plan, provided that each NHCE who is an eligible employee is permitted (unless the employee is restricted under item 5) to make contributions in an amount that is at least sufficient to receive the maximum amount of matching contributions available under the plan for the plan year, and the employee is permitted to elect any lesser amount of contributions. However, a plan may require eligible employees to make contribution elections in whole percentages of compensation or whole dollar amounts.

3. The types of compensation that may be deferred or contributed by an eligible employee under a plan, provided that each eligible NHCE is permitted to make contributions under a definition of compensation that would be a reasonable definition of compensation (see Q 6:67). Thus, the definition of compensation from which contributions may be made is not required to satisfy the nondiscrimination requirement (see Q 6:68).

4. The amount of contributions made by an eligible employee under a plan because of the limitations on the amount of elective deferrals (see Q 27:51) or the annual addition (see Q 6:34), or because, on account of a hardship distribution, an employee's ability to make contributions has been suspended for six months (see Q 27:14).

[Treas. Reg. § 1.401(m)-3(d)(6)]

Q 27:91   Is there a notice requirement for the ACP test safe harbor?

The notice requirement that applies for purposes of the ADP test safe harbor (see Q 27:46) also applies for purposes of the ACP test safe harbor (see Q 27:89). [I.R.C. § 401(m)(11)(A)(ii); Treas. Reg. § 1.401(m)-3(e)]

Q 27:92   Is there a plan year requirement for the ACP test safe harbor?

The plan year requirement that applies for purposes of the ADP test safe harbor (see Q 27:47) also applies for purposes of the ACP test safe harbor (see

Q 27:89) and the ACP test safe harbor relating to an automatic contribution arrangement (see Qs 27:5, 27:6). [Treas. Reg. § 1.401(m)-3(f); Prop. Treas. Reg. § 1.401(m)-3(f)(4)(ii)]

Q 27:93 What rules apply to plan amendments adopting safe harbor nonelective contributions for purposes of the ACP test?

Notwithstanding, the plan year requirement (see Q 27:47), a plan that provides for the use of the current year testing method (see Q 27:35) may be amended after the first day of the plan year and no later than 30 days before the last day of the plan year to adopt the safe harbor nonelective contribution method (see Q 27:42), effective as of the first day of the plan year but only if the plan provides contingent and follow-up notices. [Treas. Reg. § 1.401(m)-3(g)] See Q 27:48 for further details.

Q 27:94 Is it permissible to reduce or suspend an ACP test safe harbor matching or nonelective contribution?

A plan that provides for safe harbor matching contributions (see Q 27:43) will not fail to satisfy the ACP test (see Q 27:77) for a plan year merely because the plan is amended during a plan year to reduce or suspend safe harbor matching contributions on future elective contributions and, if applicable, employee contributions, provided that:

1. All eligible employees are provided the supplemental notice;

2. The reduction or suspension of safe harbor matching contributions is effective no earlier than the later of 30 days after eligible employees are provided the supplemental notice and the date the amendment is adopted;

3. Eligible employees are given a reasonable opportunity (including a reasonable period after receipt of the supplemental notice) prior to the reduction or suspension of safe harbor matching contributions to change their cash-or-deferred elections (see Q 27:3) and, if applicable, their employee contribution elections;

4. The plan is amended to provide that the ACP test will be satisfied for the entire plan year in which the reduction or suspension occurs using the current year testing method (see Q 27:35); and

5. The plan satisfies all other ACP test requirements with respect to amounts deferred through the effective date of the amendment.

[Treas. Reg. § 1.401(m)-3(h)(1)]

The supplemental notice of suspension requirement is satisfied if each eligible employee is given a notice in writing or such other form as prescribed by IRS that explains (1) the consequences of the amendment that reduces or suspends matching contributions on future elective contributions and, if applicable, employee contributions, (2) the procedures for changing their cash-or-deferred election and, if applicable, their employee contribution elections, and (3) the effective date of the amendment. [Treas. Reg. §§ 1.401(k)-3(g)(2), 1.401(m)-3(h)(2)]

Under proposed regulations issued by IRS, it is permissible to reduce or suspend an ACP test safe harbor nonelective contribution. A plan that provides for safe harbor nonelective contributions (see Q 27:40) will not fail to satisfy the ACP test for the plan year merely because the plan is amended during the plan year to reduce or suspend safe harbor nonelective contributions, provided that:

1. The employer incurs a substantial business hardship (see Q 8:24);
2. The amendment is adopted after May 18, 2009;
3. All eligible employees are provided the supplemental notice;
4. The reduction or suspension of safe harbor nonelective contributions is effective no earlier than the later of 30 days after eligible employees are provided the supplemental notice and the date the amendment is adopted;
5. Eligible employees are given a reasonable opportunity (including a reasonable period after receipt of the supplemental notice) prior to the reduction or suspension of nonelective contributions to change their cash-or-deferred elections and, if applicable, their employee contribution elections;
6. The plan is amended to provide that the ACP test will be satisfied for the entire plan year in which the reduction or suspension occurs using the current year testing method; and
7. The plan satisfies all other ACP test requirements with respect to safe harbor compensation paid through the effective date of the amendment.

[Prop. Treas. Reg. §§ 1.401(m)-3(f)(4)(ii), 1.401(m)-3(h)(1)]

With regard to the supplemental notice, the first requirement is changed to an explanation of the consequences of the amendment that reduces or suspends future safe harbor contributions. [Prop. Treas. Reg. §§ 1.401(k)-3(g)(2), 1.401(m)-3(h)(2)]

Q 27:95   What other rules apply to the ACP test safe harbor requirements?

A contribution is taken into account for a plan year if and only if the contribution would be taken into account for such plan year (see Q 27:50). [Treas. Reg. § 1.401(k)-3(j)(1)]

A safe harbor nonelective contribution (see Q 27:42) used to satisfy the nonelective contribution requirement may also be taken into account for purposes of determining whether a plan satisfies the nondiscrimination requirements (see Q 27:50). [Treas. Reg. § 1.401(m)-3(j)(2)]

The alternative nondiscrimination rule for certain plans that provides for early participation (see Q 27:18) does not apply for the safe harbor requirements for 401(m) plans (see Q 27:73) or for automatic contribution arrangements (see Qs 27:5, 27:6). Thus, a plan is not treated as satisfying the safe harbor requirements with respect to the eligible employees who have not completed the minimum age and service requirements unless the plan satisfies the safe harborrequirements with respect to such eligible employees. [Treas. Reg. § 1.401(m)-3(j)(3)]

Safe harbor matching or nonelective contributions may be made to another qualified defined contribution plan (see Q 2:2). Consequently, each NHCE under the plan providing for matching contributions must be eligible under the same conditions under the other defined contribution plan, and the plan to which the contributions are made must have the same plan year as the plan providing for matching contributions (see Q 27:50). [Treas. Reg. § 1.401(m)-3(j)(4)]

Safe harbor matching or nonelective contributions cannot be used to satisfy the safe harbor requirements with respect to more than one plan. [Treas. Reg. § 1.401(m)-3(j)(5)]

If the plan provides for employee contributions, in addition to satisfying the safe harbor requirements, it must also satisfy the ACP test. See Q 27:80 for special rules under which the ACP test is permitted to be performed disregarding some or all matching when the safe harbor is satisfied with respect to the matching contributions. [Treas. Reg. § 1.401(m)-3(j)(6)]

Q 27:96   What are designated Roth contributions?

Effective for taxable years beginning on or after January 1, 2006, a plan may permit an employee who makes elective contributions (see Q 27:16) under a qualified CODA (see Q 27:9) to designate some or all of those contributions as designated Roth contributions. Although designated Roth contributions are elective contributions under a qualified CODA, unlike pre-tax elective contributions, they are currently includible in gross income. However, a qualified distribution of designated Roth contributions is excludable from gross income (see Q 27:98). [I.R.C. § 402A; Treas. Reg. § 1.401(k)-1(f)]

The IRS final regulations provide special rules relating to designated Roth contributions under a 401(k) plan and a definition of designated Roth contributions. Under the regulations, a designated Roth contribution is defined as an elective contribution under a qualified CODA that, to the extent permitted under the plan, is:

1. Designated irrevocably by the employee at the time of the cash-or-deferred election (see Q 27:3) as a designated Roth contribution that is being made in lieu of all or a portion of the pre-tax elective contributions the employee is otherwise eligible to make under the plan;

2. Treated by the employer as includible in the employee's income at the time the employee would have received the contribution amounts in cash if the employee had not made the cash-or-deferred election (e.g., by treating the contributions as wages subject to applicable withholding requirements); and

3. Maintained by the plan in a separate account. [I.R.C. § 402A(c)(1); Treas. Reg. §§ 1.401(k)-1(f)(1), 1.401(k)-6, 1.401(m)-5]

Designated Roth contributions are made in lieu of all or a portion of elective contributions that the employee is otherwise eligible to make under the CODA. If a CODA offered only designated Roth contributions, an employee participating in the arrangement would not be electing to make such contributions in lieu of elective contributions the employee was otherwise eligible to make under the plan. Thus, the final regulations clarify that, in order to provide for designated Roth contributions, a qualified CODA must also offer pre-tax elective contributions. [Preamble to final regulations]

The regulations provide that, under a separate accounting requirement, contributions and withdrawals of designated Roth contributions must be credited and debited to a designated Roth account maintained for the employee, and the plan must maintain a record of the employee's investment in the contract (i.e., designated Roth contributions that have not been distributed) with respect to the employee's designated Roth account. In addition, gains, losses, and other credits or charges must be separately allocated on a reasonable and consistent basis to the designated Roth account and other accounts under the plan (see Q 27:107). However, forfeitures may not be allocated to the designated Roth account, and no contributions other than designated Roth contributions and certain rollover contributions are permitted to be allocated to a designated Roth account. For example, matching contributions (see Q 27:75) are not permitted to be allocated to a designated Roth account. The separate accounting requirement applies at the time the designated Roth contribution is contributed to the plan and must continue to apply until the designated Roth contribution account is completely distributed. [I.R.C. §§ 402A(b)(2), 402A(c)(3); Treas. Reg. §§ 1.401(k)-1(f)(2), 1.401(k)-6; Preamble to final regulations]

A designated Roth contribution must satisfy the requirements applicable to elective contributions made under a qualified CODA. Thus, designated Roth contributions are subject to the nonforfeitability and distribution restrictions (see Qs 27:13, 27:14) applicable to elective contributions, are taken into account under the ADP test (see Q 27:18) in the same manner as pre-tax elective contributions, and are treated as employer contributions for many purposes. Similarly, designated Roth accounts are subject to the minimum distribution rules in the same manner as pre-tax elective contributions (see Qs 11:4, 11:9, 11:23), and designated Roth contributions may be treated as catch-up contributions (see Q 27:52) and serve as the basis for participant loans (see Q 14:1). [Treas. Reg. § 1.401(k)-1(f)(3)(i); Preamble to final regulations]

The rules regarding frequency of elections apply in the same manner to both pre-tax elective contributions and designated Roth contributions; thus, an employee must have an effective opportunity to make (or change) an election to make designated Roth contributions at least once during each plan year (see Q 27:15). [Treas. Reg. § 1.401(k)-1(f)(4)(i)] In the case of a plan that provides for both pre-tax elective contributions and designated Roth contributions and in which, under the automatic enrollment provision (see Q 27:5), the default in the absence of an affirmative election is to make a contribution under the CODA, the plan terms must provide the extent to which the default contributions are pre-tax elective contributions and the extent to which the default contributions are designated Roth contributions. If the default contributions under the plan are designated Roth contributions, then an employee who has not made an affirmative election is deemed to have irrevocably designated the contributions as designated Roth contributions. [I.R.C. § 402A(c)(1)(B); Treas. Reg. § 1.401(k)-1(f)(4)(ii)]

There are correction methods that a plan may use if it fails to satisfy the ADP test for a year (see Q 27:25). The final regulations amend the rules relating to these correction methods to permit an HCE (see Q 3:3) with elective contributions for a year that includes both pre-tax elective contributions and designated Roth contributions to elect whether excess contributions should be attributed to pre-tax elective contributions or designated Roth contributions. There is no requirement that the plan provide this option, and a plan may provide for one of the correction methods without permitting an HCE to make such an election. [Treas. Reg. § 1.401(k)-2(b)(1)(ii); Preamble to final regulations]

The final regulations provide that a distribution of excess contributions is not includible in income to the extent it represents a distribution of designated Roth contributions. However, the income allocable to a corrective distribution of excess contributions that are designated Roth contributions is includible in gross income in the same manner as income allocable to a corrective distribution of excess contributions that are pre-tax elective contributions (see Qs 27:26, 27:105). The regulations also provide a similar rule under the correction methods that a plan may use if it fails to satisfy the ACP test (see Qs 27:82, 27:83, 27:105). [Treas. Reg. §§ 1.401(k)-2(b)(vi)(B), 1.401(k)-2(b)(vi)(C), 1.401(m)-2(b)(2)(vi)(B), 1.401(m)-2(b)(2)(vi)(C)]

A direct rollover (see Q 34:17) from a designated Roth account under a qualified CODA may only be made to another designated Roth account under a qualified retirement plan or 403(b) plan (see Q 35:1) or to a Roth IRA (see Q 31:1), and only to the extent the direct rollover is permitted. The lifetime minimum distribution rules will be avoided by rolling over a designated Roth account to a Roth IRA (see Q 31:26). In addition, a plan is permitted to treat the balance of the participant's designated Roth account and the participant's other accounts under the plan as accounts held under two separate plans for purposes of applying the special rule under which a plan will satisfy the direct rollover requirement even though the plan administrator (see Q 20:1) does not permit any distributee to elect a direct rollover with respect to eligible rollover distributions (see Q 34:8) during a year that are reasonably expected to total less than $200 (see Q 34:25). Thus, if a participant's balance in the designated Roth account is less than $200, the plan is not required to offer a direct rollover election with respect to that account or to apply the automatic rollover provisions with respect to that account. [I.R.C. §§ 401(a)(31), 402(c), 402A(c)(3), 402A(e)(1); Treas. Reg. § 1.401(k)-1(f)(3)(ii)] See Qs 27:100, 27:101 for more details.

There are other aspects of designated Roth contributions that must be reflected in plan terms and are not addressed in the final regulations. For example, while a plan is permitted to allow an employee to elect the character of a distribution (i.e., whether the distribution will be made from the designated Roth contribution account or other accounts), the extent to which a plan so permits must be set forth in the terms of the plan. [Preamble to final regulations]

Although designated Roth contributions under a qualified CODA bear some similarity to contributions to a Roth IRA (e.g., contributions to either type of account are after-tax contributions, and qualified distributions from either type of account are excludable from gross income), there are many differences between these types of arrangements. For example, an individual is ineligible to make Roth IRA contributions if the individual's modified adjusted gross income exceeds certain limits (see Q 31:16), but no comparable income limits are imposed on an individual's eligibility to make designated Roth contributions under a CODA. In addition, a traditional IRA may be converted to a Roth IRA (see Q 31:44), but a pre-tax elective contribution account under a qualified CODA cannot be converted to a designated Roth account. Also, specific ordering rules apply to distributions from Roth IRAs (see Q 31:29). However, specific ordering rules for distributions from designated Roth accounts do not apply, so the rules applicable to distributions from qualified retirement plans apply to determine the character of distributions from such accounts (see Qs 13:1, 13:3). [Preamble to final regulations] However, under SBJA 2010 (see Q 1:38), eligible retirement plan distributions from 401(k) plans made after September 27, 2010 may be rolled over to a designated Roth account within the plan. Any amount required to be included in gross income for the 2010 taxable year is included in income in equal amounts for the 2011 and 2012 taxable years unless the taxpayer elects otherwise (see Q 31:49).

The final regulations apply to plan years beginning on or after January 1, 2006. [Treas. Reg. § 1.401(k)-1(f)(5)]

See Q 27:97 for the sample plan amendment released by IRS for designated Roth contributions in 401(k) plans, and see Qs 27:98–27:110 for a discussion of final regulations published by IRS concerning the taxation of distributions from designated Roth accounts under a 401(k) plan. See also Q 31:43 for a discussion of the coordination between designated Roth accounts and Roth IRAs.

Q 27:97 Has IRS provided a sample plan amendment for designated Roth contributions?

IRS has provided a sample plan amendment regarding designated Roth contributions (see Q 27:96) that individual plan sponsors and sponsors of pre-approved plans (see Qs 2:26-2:28) can adopt or use in drafting individual-ized plan amendments. Because the amendment is a sample plan amendment, sponsors are not required to adopt the amendment verbatim. In fact, it may be necessary for plan sponsors to modify the sample amendment to conform to their plan's terms. In addition, some plan sponsors may need to revise the sample amendment to conform the amendment to the administration of the plan. An issue not addressed in the sample amendment is the extent to which an employee can elect that a distribution (other than a corrective distribution of excess distributions) will be made from either the designated Roth account or any other account of the employee under the plan. A plan sponsor is permitted to (and may find it necessary to conform the amendment to the plan's operation) revise the amendment (including the default provisions of the amendment) to address this issue.

Plan sponsors who want to provide for designated Roth contributions in their 401(k) plans must adopt a discretionary amendment. The deadline to adopt a discretionary amendment is the end of the plan year in which the amendment is effective. The timely adoption of the amendment must be evidenced by a written document that is signed and dated by the employer (including an adopting employer of a pre-approved plan).

IRS will not treat the adoption of the sample plan amendment or an individualized plan amendment that reflects the qualification requirements of the regulations relating to designated Roth contributions as affecting the pre-approved status of a master and prototype (M&P) or volume submitter plan. That is, such amendment to an M&P plan that is adopted by an employer will not cause the plan to fail to be an M&P plan. Similarly, such amendment to a volume submitter plan that is adopted by an employer will not cause the plan to fail to be a volume submitter plan. In either case, the amendment will not result in the loss of reliance on a favorable opinion, advisory, or determination letter (see Q 18:1). In the case where the amendment causes the plan to fail to satisfy the qualification requirements (see Q 4:1), the plan will not be disqualified if a remedial amendment that corrects the failure is adopted before the end of the remedial amendment period.

The format of the sample plan amendment generally follows the design of pre-approved plans, including all M&P plans, that employ a basic plan document and an adoption agreement. Thus, the sample plan amendment includes language designed for inclusion in a basic plan document and language designed for inclusion in an adoption agreement to allow the employer to indicate whether, or when, the corresponding basic plan document provision will be effective in the employer's plan and to select among options related to the application of the basic plan document provision. Sponsors of plans that do not use an adoption agreement should modify the format of the amendment to incorporate the appropriate adoption agreement options in the terms of the amendment. In such case, the notes in the adoption agreement portion of the sample amendment should not be included in the amendment that will be signed and dated by the employer. Designated Roth contributions are referred to as Roth elective deferrals and designated Roth accounts are referred to as Roth elective deferral accounts in the sample amendment, which is set forth below.

Article _____.

ROTH ELECTIVE DEFERRALS

Section 1. General Application

1.1 This article will apply to contributions beginning with the effective date specified in the adoption agreement but in no event before the first day of the first taxable year beginning on or after January 1, 2006.

1.2 As of the effective date under section 1.1, the plan will accept Roth elective deferrals made on behalf of participants. A participant's Roth elective deferrals will be allocated to a separate account maintained for such deferrals as described in section 2.

1.3 Unless specifically stated otherwise, Roth elective deferrals will be treated as elective deferrals for all purposes under the plan.

Section 2. Separate Accounting

2.1 Contributions and withdrawals of Roth elective deferrals will be credited and debited to the Roth elective deferral account maintained for each participant.

2.2 The plan will maintain a record of the amount of Roth elective deferrals in each participant's account.

2.3 Gains, losses, and other credits or charges must be separately allocated on a reasonable and consistent basis to each participant's Roth elective deferral account and the participant's other accounts under the plan.

2.4 No contributions other than Roth elective deferrals and properly attributable earnings will be credited to each participant's Roth elective deferral account.

Section 3. Direct Rollovers

3.1 Notwithstanding section _____, a direct rollover of a distribution from a Roth elective deferral account under the plan will only be made to another Roth elective deferral account under an applicable retirement plan described in § 402A(e)(1) or to a Roth IRA described in § 408A, and only to the extent the rollover is permitted under the rules of § 402(c).

3.2 Notwithstanding section _____, unless otherwise provided by the employer in the adoption agreement, the plan will accept a rollover contribution to a Roth elective deferral account only if it is a direct rollover from another Roth elective deferral account under an applicable retirement plan described in § 402A(e)(1) and only to the extent the rollover is permitted under the rules of § 402(c).

3.3 The plan will not provide for a direct rollover (including an automatic rollover) for distributions from a participant's Roth elective deferral account if the amount of the distributions that are eligible rollover distributions is reasonably expected to total less than $200 during a year. In addition, any distribution from a participant's Roth elective deferral account is not taken into account in determining whether distributions from a participant's other accounts are reasonably expected to total less than $200 during a year. However, eligible rollover distributions from a participant's Roth elective deferral account are taken into account in determining whether the total amount of the participant's account balances under the plan exceeds $1,000 for purposes of mandatory distributions from the plan.

3.4 The provisions of the plan that allow a participant to elect a direct rollover of only a portion of an eligible rollover distribution but only if the amount rolled over is at least $500 is applied by treating any amount distributed from the participant's Roth elective deferral account as a separate distribution from any amount distributed from the participant's other accounts in the plan, even if the amounts are distributed at the same time.

Section 4. Correction of Excess Contributions

4.1 In the case of a distribution of excess contributions, a highly compensated employee may designate the extent to which the excess amount is composed of pre-tax elective deferrals and Roth elective deferrals but only to the extent such types of deferrals were made for the year.

4.2 If the highly compensated employee does not designate which type of elective deferrals are to be distributed, the plan will distribute pre-tax elective deferrals first.

Section 5. Definition

5.1 Roth Elective Deferrals. A Roth elective deferral is an elective deferral that is:

(a) Designated irrevocably by the participant at the time of the cash or deferred election as a Roth elective deferral that is being made in lieu of all or a portion of the pre-tax elective deferrals the participant is otherwise eligible to make under the plan; and

(b) Treated by the employer as includible in the participant's income at the time the participant would have received that amount in cash if the participant had not made a cash or deferred election.

(Adoption Agreement Provisions)

Article _____, Roth Elective Deferrals: (Check and complete, if applicable)

_____ shall apply to contributions after January 1, 2006.

_____ shall apply to contributions after _____ (Enter a date later than January 1, 2006)

(Note: If neither option is chosen, the amendment will not be effective even if the amendment is signed and dated.)

Section _____, Direct Rollovers: (Check, if applicable)

The plan:

_____will not

accept a direct rollover from another Roth elective deferral account under an applicable retirement plan as described in § 402A(e)(1).

(Note: The default position is that the plan will accept a direct rollover of Roth elective deferrals from another Roth elective deferral account. The default position will apply unless this option is checked.)

Employer's signature and date

[Notice 2006-44, 2006-1 C.B. 889; Notice 2005-95, 2005-2 C.B. 1172; Rev. Proc. 2005-66, 2005-2 C.B. 509]

Q 27:98   How is a distribution from a designated Roth account taxed?

The taxation of a distribution from a designated Roth account (see Q 27:96) depends on whether or not the distribution is a qualified distribution. A qualified distribution from a designated Roth account is not includible in the distributee's gross income. Except as otherwise provided below, a qualified distribution is a distribution that is made after the five-taxable-year period of participation (see Q 27:99) has been completed and that is:

1. Made on or after the date on which the employee attains age 59½;
2. Made to a beneficiary (or to the employee's estate) on or after the death of the employee; and
3. Attributable to the employee's being disabled (see Q 16:6). [Treas. Reg. § 1.402A-1, Q&A-1, Q&A-2(a), Q&A-2(b)]

A distribution from a designated Roth account is not a qualified distribution to the extent it consists of a distribution of excess deferrals and attributable income (see Qs 27:63, 27:64). See Q 27:105 for other amounts that are not treated as qualified distributions, including excess contributions (see Q 27:34) and excess aggregate contributions (see Q 27:82), and income on any of these excess amounts. [Treas. Reg. § 1.402A-1, Q&A-2(c)]

Except as provided in Q 27:105, a distribution from a designated Roth account that is not a qualified distribution is taxable to the distributee (see Qs 13:1, 13:3). For this purpose, a designated Roth account is treated as a separate contract. Thus, except as otherwise provided for a rollover (see Q 27:100), if a distribution is made before the annuity starting date (see, Q 10:3), the portion of any distribution that is includible in gross income as an amount allocable to income on the contract and the portion not includible in gross income as an amount allocable to investment in the contract (also known as basis) is determined treating the designated Roth account as a separate contract. Similarly, in the case of any amount received as an annuity, if a distribution is made on or after the annuity starting date, the portion of any annuity payment that is includible in gross income as an amount allocable to income on the contract and the portion not includible in gross income as an amount allocable to investment in the contract is determined treating the designated Roth account as a separate contract. For these purposes, designated Roth contributions (see Q 27:96) are contributions that are includible in gross income. [I.R.C. §§ 72(b), 72(d), 72(e)(8), 72(f)(1), 72(f)(2); Treas. Reg. § 1.402A-1, Q&A-3]

A prohibited allocation under an S corporation ESOP is a deemed distribution that is not an eligible rollover distribution (see Qs 28:3, 34:8). With respect to a designated Roth account, such a deemed distribution does not constitute a qualified distribution.

See Q 31:43 for a discussion of the coordination between designated Roth accounts and Roth IRAs.

Q 27:99   What is the five-taxable-year period of participation for a qualified distribution from a designated Roth account?

The five-taxable-year period of participation for a plan is the period of five consecutive taxable years that begins with the first day of the first taxable year in which the employee makes a designated Roth contribution to any designated Roth account (see Q 27:96) established for the employee under the same plan and ends when five consecutive taxable years have been completed. For this purpose, the first taxable year in which an employee makes a designated Roth contribution is the year in which the amount is includible in the employee's gross income. Notwithstanding the preceding, however, a contribution that is returned as an excess deferral (see Q 27:63) or excess contribution (see Q 27:26) does not begin the five-taxable-year period of participation. Similarly, a contribution returned as a permissible withdrawal under a qualified automatic enrollment arrangement (see Q 27:5) does not begin the five-taxable-year period of participation. Because of the requirement of the five-taxable-year period, no qualified distribution can occur before the taxable year beginning in 2011. [I.R.C. § 402A(d)(2); Treas. Reg. § 1.402A-1, Q&A-4(a)]

Generally, an employee's five-taxable-year period of participation is determined separately for each plan in which the employee participates. Thus, if an employee has elective deferrals made to designated Roth accounts under two or more plans, the employee may have two or more different five-taxable-year periods of participation, depending on when the employee first had contributions made to a designated Roth account under each plan. However, if a direct rollover contribution (see Q 34:17) of a distribution from a designated Roth account under another plan is made by the employee to the plan, the five-taxable-year period of participation begins on the first day of the employee's taxable year in which the employee first had designated Roth contributions made to such other designated Roth account, if earlier than the first taxable year in which a designated Roth contribution is made to the plan. See Q 27:100 for additional rules on determining the start of the five-taxable-year period of participation in the case of an indirect rollover. [I.R.C. § 402A(c)(3); Treas. Reg. § 1.402A-1, Q&A-4(b)]

The beginning of the five-taxable-year period of participation is not redetermined for any portion of an employee's designated Roth account. This is true even if the entire designated Roth account is distributed during the five-taxable-year period of participation, and the employee subsequently makes additional designated Roth contributions under the plan. [Treas. Reg. § 1.402A-1, Q&A-4(c)]

The rule in the preceding paragraph applies if the employee dies or the account is divided pursuant to a qualified domestic relations order (QDRO; see Q 36:1); and, thus, a portion of the account is not payable to the employee and is payable to the employee's beneficiary or an alternate payee (see Q 36:5). In the case of distribution to an alternate payee or beneficiary, generally, the age, death, or disability of the employee is used to determine whether the distribution to an alternate payee or beneficiary is qualified. However, if an alternate payee or a spousal beneficiary rolls the distribution into a designated

Roth account in a plan maintained by such individual's own employer, such individual's age, disability, or death is used to determine whether a distribution from the recipient plan is qualified. In addition, if the rollover is a direct rollover (see Q 34:17) contribution to the alternate payee's or spousal beneficiary's own designated Roth account, the five-taxable-year period of participation under the recipient plan begins on the earlier of the date the employee's five-taxable-year period of participation began under the distributing plan or the date the five-taxable-year period of participation applicable to the alternate payee's or spousal beneficiary's designated Roth account began under the recipient plan. [Treas. Reg. § 1.402A-1, Q&A-4(d)]

If a designated Roth contribution is made by a reemployed veteran for a year of qualified military service (see Q 27:51) that is before the year in which the contribution is actually made, the contribution is treated as having been made in the year of qualified military service to which the contribution relates, as designated by the reemployed veteran. Reemployed veterans may identify the year of qualified military service for which a contribution is made for other purposes, such as for entitlement to a match, and the treatment for the five-taxable-year period of participation rule follows that identification. In the absence of such designation, for purposes of determining the first year of the five years of participation, the contribution is treated as relating to the first year of qualified military service for which the reemployed veteran could have made designated Roth contributions under the plan or, if later, the first taxable year in which designated Roth contributions could be made under the plan. [Treas. Reg. § 1.402A-1, Q&A-4(e)]

See Q 31:43 for a discussion of the coordination between designated Roth accounts and Roth IRAs.

Q 27:100   How do the taxation rules apply to a distribution from a designated Roth account that is rolled over?

An eligible rollover distribution (see Q 34:8) from a designated Roth account (see Q 27:96) is permitted to be rolled over into another designated Roth account or a Roth IRA (see Q 31:1), and the amount rolled over is not currently includible in gross income. To the extent that a portion of a distribution from a designated Roth account is not includible in income (determined without regard to the rollover), if that portion of the distribution will be rolled over into a designated Roth account, the rollover must be accomplished through a direct rollover (see Qs 34:8, 34:17) of the entire distribution (that is, a 60-day rollover (see Q 34:34) to another designated Roth account is not available for this portion of the distribution). For this purpose, any amount paid in a direct rollover is treated as a separate distribution from any amount paid directly to the employee. If a distribution from a designated Roth account is instead made to the employee, the employee would still be able to roll over the entire amount (or any portion thereof) into a Roth IRA within the 60-day period. [I.R.C. 402A(c)(3); Treas. Reg. § 1.402A-1, Q&A-5(a)] IRS has issued two safe harbor explanations that may be provided to recipients of eligible rollover distributions, the second of which applies to a distribution from a designated Roth account (see Qs 20:20, 34:29). [IRS Notice 2009-68, 2009-2 C.B. 423]

In the case of an eligible rollover distribution from a designated Roth account that is not a qualified distribution (see Q 27:98), if the entire amount of the distribution is not rolled over, the part that is rolled over is deemed to consist first of the portion of the distribution that is attributable to income. [I.R.C. § 72(e)(8); Treas. Reg. § 1.402A-1, Q&A-5(b)]

If an employee receives a distribution from a designated Roth account, the portion of the distribution that would be includible in gross income is permitted to be rolled over into a designated Roth account under another plan. In such a case, additional reporting by the recipient plan is required (see Q 27:110). In addition, the employee's period of participation under the distributing plan is not carried over to the recipient plan for purposes of satisfying the five-taxable-year period of participation requirement under the recipient plan (see Q 27:99). Generally, the taxable year in which the recipient plan accepts such rollover contribution is the taxable year that begins the participant's new five-taxable-year period of participation. However, if the participant is rolling over to a plan in which the participant already has a pre-existing designated Roth account with a longer period of participation, the starting date of the recipient account is used to measure the participant's five-taxable-year period of participation. [Treas. Reg. § 1.402A-1, Q&A-5(c)]

> **Example.** Sallie receives a $14,000 eligible rollover distribution that is not a qualified distribution from her designated Roth account, consisting of $11,000 of investment in the contract and $3,000 of income. Within 60 days of receipt, Sallie rolls over $7,000 of the distribution into a Roth IRA. The $7,000 is deemed to consist of $3,000 of income and $4,000 of investment in the contract. Because the only portion of the distribution that could be includible in gross income (the income) is rolled over, none of the distribution is includible in Sallie's gross income.

These rollover rules apply for taxable years beginning on or after January 1, 2006. [Treas. Reg. § 1.402A-1, Q&A-5(e)]

IRS learned that some employers had concerns about adding provisions during a plan year to their safe harbor plans (see Q 27:40) in order to take advantage of changes to the rules concerning a qualified Roth contribution program, where the pre-year safe harbor notice (see Q 27:46) did not include information about the added provision. IRS announced that a plan will not fail to satisfy the requirements to be a safe harbor plan merely because of mid-year changes to implement a qualified Roth contribution program. [Ann. 2007-59, 2007-1 C.B. 1448] IRS also announced that sponsors of prototype Roth IRAs must amend their documents in order to allow the rollover of amounts from designated Roth accounts. [Ann. 2007-55, 2007-1 C.B. 1384]

See Q 31:43 for a discussion of the coordination between designated Roth accounts and Roth IRAs.

Q 27:101   In the case of a rollover contribution to a designated Roth account, how is the amount that is treated as investment in the contract determined?

If a distribution from a designated Roth account (see Q 27:96) is rolled over to another designated Roth account in a direct rollover (see Q 34:17), the amount of the rollover contribution allocated to investment in the contract in the recipient-designated Roth account is the amount that would not have been includible in gross income if the distribution had not been rolled over. Thus, if an amount that is a qualified distribution (see Q 27:98) is rolled over, the entire amount of the rollover contribution is allocated to investment in the contract. [Treas. Reg. § 1.402A-1, Q&A-6(a)]

If the entire account balance of a designated Roth account is rolled over to another designated Roth account in a direct rollover and, at the time of the distribution, the investment in the contract exceeds the balance in the designated Roth account, the investment in the contract in the distributing plan is included in the investment in the contract of the recipient plan. [Treas. Reg. § 1.402A-1, Q&A-6(b)]

Under SBJA 2010 (see Q 1:38), eligible retirement plan distributions from 401(k) plans made after September 27, 2010 may be rolled over to a designated Roth account within the plan. Any amount required to be included in gross income for the 2010 taxable year is included in income in equal amounts for the 2011 and 2012 taxable years unless the taxpayer elects otherwise (see Q 31:49).

See Q 31:43 for a discussion of the coordination between designated Roth accounts and Roth IRAs.

Q 27:102   After a qualified distribution from a designated Roth account has been made, how is the remaining investment in the contract of the account determined?

The portion of any qualified distribution that is treated as a recovery of investment in the contract is determined in the same manner as if the distribution were not a qualified distribution (see Q 27:98). Thus, the remaining investment in the contract in a designated Roth account (see Q 27:96) after a qualified distribution is determined in the same manner after a qualified distribution as it would be determined if the distribution were not a qualified distribution. [Treas. Reg. § 1.402A-1, Q&A-7]

Example 1. Fernando receives a $12,000 distribution, which is a qualified distribution that is attributable to his being disabled (see Q 16:6), from his designated Roth account. Immediately prior to the distribution, the account consisted of $21,850 of investment in the contract (i.e., designated Roth contributions) and $1,150 of income. For purposes of determining recovery of investment in the contract, the distribution is deemed to consist of $11,400 of investment in the contract [$12,000 × $21,850 ÷ ($1,150 + $21,850)] and $600 of income [$12,000 × $1,150 ÷ ($1,150 + $21,850)]. Immediately after the distribution, Fernando's designated Roth account consists of $10,450 of investment in the contract and $550 of income. This determination of the remaining investment in the contract will be needed if Fernando subsequently is no longer disabled and takes a nonqualified distribution from the designated Roth account.

There is no relationship between the accounting for designated Roth contributions as investment in the contract and their treatment as elective deferrals available for a hardship distribution (see Q 27:14). A plan that makes a hardship distribution from elective deferrals that includes designated Roth contributions must separately determine the amount of elective deferrals available for hardship and the amount of investment in the contract attributable to designated Roth contributions. Thus, the entire amount of a hardship distribution is treated as reducing the otherwise maximum distributable amount for purposes of applying the rule that generally limits hardship distributions to the principal amount of elective deferrals made less the amount of elective deferrals previously distributed from the plan, even if a portion of the distribution is treated as income. [Treas. Reg. § 1.402A-1, Q&A-8(a)]

Example 2. Assume the same facts as in Example 1, except that, instead of being disabled, Fernando is receiving a hardship distribution. In addition, Fernando has made elective deferrals that are not designated Roth contributions totaling $20,000 and has received no previous distributions of elective deferrals from the plan. The adjustment to the investment in the contract is the same as in Example 1; but, for purposes of determining the amount of elective deferrals available for future hardship distribution, the entire amount of the distribution is subtracted from the maximum distributable amount. Thus, Fernando has only $29,850 ($41,850 − $12,000) available for hardship distribution from his designated Roth account.

See Q 31:43 for a discussion of the coordination between designated Roth accounts and Roth IRAs.

Q 27:103   Can an employee have more than one separate contract for designated Roth contributions under a qualified retirement plan?

Except as otherwise provided in the next paragraph, for purposes of determining income, there is only one separate contract for an employee with respect to the designated Roth contributions (see Q 27:96) under a plan. Thus, if a plan maintains one separate account for designated Roth contributions made under the plan and another separate account for rollover contributions received from a designated Roth account (see Q 27:96) under another plan (so that the rollover account is not required to be subject to the distribution restrictions otherwise applicable to the account consisting of designated Roth contributions made under the plan), both separate accounts are considered to be one contract for purposes of applying the income determination rules to the distributions from either account. [I.R.C. § 72; Treas. Reg. § 1.402A-1, Q&A-9(a)]

If a separate account with respect to an employee's accrued benefit (see Q 9:1) consisting of designated Roth contributions is established and maintained for an alternate payee (see Q 36:5) pursuant to a QDRO (see Q 36:1) and another designated Roth account is maintained for the employee, each account is treated as a separate contract. The alternate payee's designated Roth account is also a separate contract with respect to any other account maintained for that alternate payee. Similarly, if separate accounts are established and maintained for different beneficiaries after the death of an employee, the separate account for each beneficiary is treated as a separate contract and is also a separate contract with respect to any other account maintained for that beneficiary under the plan that is not a designated Roth account. When the separate account is established for an alternate payee or for a beneficiary (after an employee's death), each separate account must receive a proportionate amount attributable to investment in the contract. [Treas. Reg. § 1.402A-1, Q&A-9(b)]

Q 27:104   What is the tax treatment of employer securities distributed from a designated Roth account?

If a distribution of employer securities from a designated Roth account is not a qualified distribution (see Q 27:98), the net unrealized appreciation rules apply (see Qs 13:18, 28:71). Thus, in the case of a lump-sum distribution that includes employer securities, unless the taxpayer elects otherwise, net unrealized appreciation attributable to the employer securities is not includible in gross income; and such net unrealized appreciation is not included in the basis of the distributed securities and is capital gain to the extent such appreciation is realized in a subsequent taxable transaction. In the case of a qualified distribution of employer securities from a designated Roth account, the distributee's basis in the distributed securities for purposes of subsequent disposition is their fair market value at the time of distribution. [Treas. Reg. § 1.402A-1, Q&A-10]

Q 27:105   Are there certain distributions from a designated Roth account that cannot be qualified distributions?

Each of the following cannot be a qualified distribution (see Q 27:98):

1. Elective contributions (see Q 27:16) and employee contributions (see Q 27:74) that are returned to the employee, together with the income allocable thereto, in order to comply with the Section 415 limitations (see Q 27:70);

2. Corrective distributions of excess contributions (see Q 27:26) and excess deferrals (see Q 27:63) and corrective distributions of excess aggregate contributions (see Q 27:83), together with the income allocable to these corrective distributions;

3. Loans in default that are deemed distributions (see Chapter 14);

4. Dividends paid by employer stock ownership plan (ESOP) employer securities (see Q 28:12);

5. The costs of current life insurance protection (see Q 15:7);

6. Prohibited allocations that are treated as deemed distributions (see Q 28:3); and

7. Distributions that are permissible withdrawals from an EACA (see Qs 27:5, 27:7).

Loans that are treated as deemed distributions or dividends paid on employer securities are not qualified distributions even if the deemed distributions occur or the dividends are paid after the employee attains age 59½ and the five-taxable-year period of participation has been satisfied (see Q 27:99). However, if a dividend is reinvested, the amount of such a dividend is not precluded from being a qualified distribution if later distributed. Further, an amount is not precluded from being a qualified distribution merely because it is an amount not eligible for rollover. Thus, a hardship distribution (see Q 27:14) is not precluded from being a qualified distribution. [I.R.C. § 402(c)(4); Treas. Reg. § 1.402(c)-2, Q&A-4; Treas. Reg. § 1.402A-1, Q&A-11]

Q 27:106   How do the plan loan rules apply to a designated Roth account?

If any amount from a designated Roth account (see Q 27:96) is included in a loan to an employee, notwithstanding the general rule that the designated Roth account is treated as a separate contract, the plan aggregation rules (see Q 14:4) apply for purposes of determining the maximum amount the employee is permitted to borrow from the plan and such amount is based on the total of the designated Roth contribution amounts and the other amounts under the plan. To the extent a loan is from a designated Roth account, the repayment requirement (see Q 14:6) must be satisfied separately with respect to that portion of the loan and with respect to the portion of the loan from other accounts under the plan. [Treas. Reg. § 1.402A-1, Q&A-12]

Q 27:107   How can the separate accounting requirement for a designated Roth account be violated?

Any transaction or accounting methodology involving an employee's designated Roth account (see Q 27:96) and any other accounts under the plan or plans of an employer that has the effect of directly or indirectly transferring value from another account into the designated Roth account violates the separate accounting requirement (see Q 27:96). However, any transaction that merely exchanges investments between accounts at fair market value will not violate the separate accounting requirement. [Treas. Reg. § 1.402A-1, Q&A-13(a)]

In the case of an annuity contract that contains both a designated Roth account and any other accounts, IRS may prescribe additional guidance of general applicability to provide additional rules for allocation of income, expenses, gains, and losses among the accounts under the contract. [Treas. Reg. § 1.402A-1, Q&A-13(b)] The separate accounting requirement applies to designated Roth accounts for taxable years beginning on or after January 1, 2006. [Treas. Reg. § 1.402A-1, Q&A-13(c)]

Q 27:108   How is an annuity contract that is distributed from a designated Roth account treated?

A qualified plan distributed annuity contract (see Q 34:14) that is distributed from a designated Roth account is not treated as a distribution; instead, the amounts paid under the annuity contract are treated as distributions. Thus, the period after the annuity contract is distributed and before a payment from the annuity contract is made is included in determining whether the five-year period of participation is satisfied (see Q 27:99). Further, for purposes of determining if a distribution is a qualified distribution (see Q 27:98), the determination of whether a distribution is made on or after the date the employee attains age 59½, made to a beneficiary or the estate of the employee on or after the employee's death, or attributable to the employee's being disabled is made based on the facts at the time the distribution is made from the annuity contract. Thus, for example, if an employee first makes a designated Roth contribution to a designated Roth account in 2006 at age 56, receives a distributed annuity contract in 2007 purchased only with assets from the designated Roth account, and then receives a distribution from the contract in 2011 at age 60, the distribution is a qualified distribution. [Treas. Reg. § 1.402A-1, Q&A-14]

Q 27:109 What is the effective date of the designated Roth account distribution rules?

Except as otherwise provided in Qs 27:100 and 27:107, the final regulations apply for taxable years beginning on or after January 1, 2007. [Treas. Reg. § 1.402A-1, Q&A-15]

See Q 31:43 for a discussion of the coordination between designated Roth accounts and Roth IRAs.

Q 27:110 What are the reporting and recordkeeping requirements with respect to designated Roth accounts?

The plan administrator (see Q 20:1) or other responsible party with respect to a plan with a designated Roth account (see Q 27:96) is responsible for keeping track of the five-taxable-year period of participation (see Q 27:99) for each employee and the amount of investment in the contract (unrecovered designated Roth contributions) on behalf of such employee. For purposes of the preceding sentence, in the absence of actual knowledge to the contrary, the plan administrator or other responsible party is permitted to assume that the employee's taxable year is the calendar year. In the case of a direct rollover (see Q 34:18) from another designated Roth account, the plan administrator or other responsible party of the recipient plan can rely on reasonable representations made by the plan administrator or responsible party with respect to the plan with the other designated Roth account. [Treas. Reg. § 1.402A-2, Q&A-1]

If an amount is distributed from a designated Roth account, the plan administrator or other responsible party must provide a statement as described below in the following situations:

1. In the case of a direct rollover of a distribution from a designated Roth account under a plan to a designated Roth account under another plan, the plan administrator or other responsible party must provide to the plan

administrator or responsible party of the recipient plan either a statement indicating the first year of the five-taxable-year period and the portion of the distribution that is attributable to investment in the contract or a statement that the distribution is a qualified distribution (see Q 27:98).

2. If the distribution is not a direct rollover to a designated Roth account under another plan, the plan administrator or responsible party must provide to the employee, upon request, the same information described in paragraph 1, except the statement need not indicate the first year of the five-taxable-year period. [I.R.C. § 6047(f); Treas. Reg. § 1.402A-2, Q&A-2(a)]

The statement must be provided within a reasonable period following the direct rollover or distributee request, but in no event later than 30 days following the direct rollover or distributee request. [Treas. Reg. § 1.402A-2, Q&A-2(b)]

To the extent required in IRS forms and instructions to such forms, if a qualified retirement plan accepts a rollover contribution (other than a direct rollover contribution) of the portion of the distribution from a designated Roth account that would have been includible in gross income, the plan administrator or other responsible party for the recipient plan must notify IRS of its acceptance of the rollover contribution no later than the due date for filing Form 1099-R, Distributions From Pensions, Annuities, Retirement or Profit-Sharing Plans, IRAs, Insurance Contracts, etc. The forms and instructions will specify the address to which the notification is required to be sent and will require inclusion of the employee's name and social security number, the amount rolled over, the year in which the rollover contribution was made, and such other information as IRS may require in order to determine that the amount rolled over is a valid rollover contribution. [Treas. Reg. § 1.402A-2, Q&A-3]

The reporting and recordkeeping requirements are applicable for taxable years beginning on or after January 1, 2007. [Treas. Reg. § 1.402A-2, Q&A-4]

For a discussion of regulations regarding coordination between designated Roth accounts and Roth IRAs, see Q 31:43.

Q 27:111 Are 401(k) plan benefits exempt from the participants' creditors?

In 1992, the United States Supreme Court held that a participant's interest in a qualified retirement plan is exempt from the claims of creditors in a bankruptcy proceeding, thereby resolving the conflict among the courts of appeals. [Patterson v. Shumate, 504 U.S. 753 (1992)]

On April 20, 2005, President Bush signed into law the Bankruptcy Abuse Prevention and Consumer Protection Act of 2005, which contains provisions that protect the qualified retirement plan assets of bankruptcy filers. See Q 1:27 for a discussion of the salient provisions of this Act. [*In re* Skvorecz, 2007 WL 1378348 (Bankr. D. Col. 2007)] One court concluded that a debtor's repayment of a 401(k) plan loan did not constitute a payment of secured debts or a necessary expense that could be deducted from the debtor's monthly income for purposes of applying the means test under Chapter 7 of the Bankruptcy Code. The court acknowledged that debtors in Chapter 13 proceedings are expressly authorized to deduct 401(k) loan repayments in the calculation of disposable income. However, the court cautioned, bankruptcy law does not provide a comparable right for Chapter 7 debtors. [Egjebjerg v. Anderson, 574 F.3d 1045 (9th Cir. 2009)] In Chapter 13 proceedings, a bankruptcy court approved plans in which it was proposed that debtors would repay 401(k) plan loans through their employers' payroll deductions and, after the loans were repaid, then continue the payroll deductions in order to make contributions to the 401(k) plans. The court concluded that, under the Bankruptcy Code, neither a debtor's bankruptcy estate nor disposable income under Chapter 13 includes the debtor's contributions, or loan repayments, to specified retirement plans. [*In re* Seafort, 2009 WL 1767627 (Bankr. D. Ken. 2009)] However, this decision was reversed by the appellate court. The debtors had not been making elective contributions (see Q 27:16) on the date of the bankruptcy filing, and the court concluded that bankruptcy protection is not provided under Chapter 13 for elective contributions that begin after the bankruptcy filing. Because property of the estate and exclusions from the bankruptcy estate must both be determined on the date of the bankruptcy filing, only elective contributions that are being made at the time of the bankruptcy filing are excluded from the bankruptcy estate. [Seafort v. Burden, 2010 WL 3564709 (6th Cir. 2010)] In addition, because loan repayments to the 401(k) plan would cease during the proposed Chapter 13 bankruptcy plan, another court determined that the bankruptcy plan had to be based upon a calculation of the debtor's projected disposable income over the period of the bankruptcy plan, and not just on the debtor's actual disposable income at the time of the submission of the bankruptcy plan. [McCarty v. Lasowski, 575 F.3d 815 (8th Cir. 2009); *see also* Hamilton v. Lanning, 130 S. Ct. 2464 (2010) and Nowlin v. Peake, 576 F.3d 258 (5th Cir. 2009)] The following discussion may apply only to those cases that arose before the October 17, 2005, effective date of the Act.

One court ruled that a participant's 401(k) plan benefits were excluded from his bankruptcy estate despite the participant's right under the plan to obtain distribution of his benefits because the 401(k) plan contained an anti-alienation provision. [Manufacturers Bank & Trust Co., Forest City, La. v. Holst, No. C 96-3038 (N.D. La. 1996)] Another court concluded that amounts contributed by a debtor to a 401(k) plan within the year preceding the bankruptcy filing could not be excluded, under state law, from the bankruptcy estate. [*In re* Bellwoar, No. 03-15455 (E.D. Pa. 2003)]

IRS could levy upon a participant's 401(k) plan account if the participant had an immediate right to elect normal retirement benefits, even though he elected to defer retirement. However, the plan administrator (see Q 20:1) could not be forced to distribute the assets under the levy until the participant obtained an immediate right to receive the benefits. Since the participant deferred his retirement, the benefits were not yet payable to him. [Chief Counsel Advice 200032004] IRS also ruled, however, that a federal court seeking to collect a fine in an individual's criminal case would not violate the anti-alienation rule (see Q 4:28) by garnishing his 401(k) plan account balance. [Priv. Ltr. Rul. 200342007]

One court ruled that IRS possessed valid tax liens against a debtor's 401(k) plan benefits. [*In re* Piper, 02-12096 (Bankr. D. Mass. 2003)] The 401(k) plan account of a participant was not exempt from an IRS levy for collection of unpaid federal taxes, despite the discharge of the participant's tax liabilities in bankruptcy, where the levy had attached prior to the filing of the bankruptcy petition, determined another court. [Iannone, 122 T.C. 287 (2004)] However, another court concluded that IRS could not levy against a participant's 401(k) plan benefits because they were exempt under ERISA. [ERISA § 206(d); *In re* Wingfield, 2002 U.S. Dist. LEXIS 15885 (E.D. Va. 2002)]

See Qs 4:27 through 4:30 for more details.

Chapter 28

Employee Stock Ownership Plans

An employee stock ownership plan (ESOP) is a special breed of qualified retirement plan. In addition to providing retirement benefits for employees, an ESOP can be used as a market for company stock, as a method of increasing the company's cash flow, as an estate planning tool for the owner of a closely held corporation, and as a means of financing the company's growth. This chapter examines the requirements for establishing and maintaining an ESOP and explains how an ESOP works.

Q 28:1 What is an employee stock ownership plan?

An ESOP is essentially a defined contribution plan (see Q 2:2) whose funds must be invested primarily in employer securities (see Q 28:8). There is no specific percentage requirement, and "primarily" is a flexible term that takes into account facts and circumstances such as the investment performance of the employer securities. Generally, the funds may come from any or all of the following sources: (1) company contributions of cash or employer securities (see Q 28:27), (2) an exempt loan to the ESOP (see Q 28:7), or (3) a defined contribution plan converted to an ESOP (see Q 28:31). The "primarily" requirement does not apply to a stock bonus (see Q 28:6) component of an ESOP. [Thompson, Jr. v. Avondale Indus, Inc, 2003 U.S. Dist. LEXIS 2318 (ED La 2003)] The amount of tax-deductible contributions to an ESOP is generally determined in the same manner as for other defined contribution plans (see Qs 12:1–12:17), although there is a special rule increasing the deductible amount of employer contributions used to repay exempt loans to the ESOP (see Q 28:19). [I.R.C. §§ 404(a)(3), 404(a)(9), 409, 4975(e)(7); Treas. Reg. §§ 54.4975-11(a)(2), 54.4975-11(b); DOL Op. Ltr. 83-006A]

ESOP assets will be considered invested in employer securities in a variety of circumstances. If an ESOP receives cash or other assets for employer securities as part of a reorganization, the assets will satisfy the requirement if they are invested in employer securities within 90 days (or an extended period if granted by IRS) of the acquisition of cash or other assets. Cash received by an ESOP as the result of an exempt loan, earnings, dividends, or other cash contributions will satisfy the requirement if invested in employer securities within 60 days of the contribution. Cash or cash equivalents allocated to a participant's account will be deemed to be invested in employer securities if the value of those benefits does not exceed 2 percent of the value of the allocated securities. Also, amounts transferred to an ESOP following a reversion from a terminated defined benefit plan will meet the investment requirement if the amounts are invested in employer securities within 90 days of the transfer, and such amounts will not be subject to the excise tax on employer reversions (see Q 25:52). The 90-day period may be extended by IRS. [I.R.C. § 4980(c)(3); IRS Notice 88-56, 1988-1 C.B. 540, 18; Priv. Ltr. Ruls. 200507016, 200127054, 9803025, 9452045, 9448045, 9419030, 9402021] IRS has ruled that an ESOP did not fail to satisfy the requirement that an ESOP be designed to invest in qualifying employer securities after it transferred assets and stock in connection with a merger. [Priv. Ltr. Rul. 200018058]

An ESOP that holds in a suspense account the stock of a subsidiary company spun off from the parent company sponsoring the ESOP, which stock was purchased with a reversion amount from a terminated defined benefit plan, can sell the stock of the subsidiary and use the proceeds to buy stock of the sponsoring parent company. The ESOP cannot, however, use the proceeds to buy any assets other than the sponsoring parent's stock, because such a transaction would be a violation of the ESOP exception to the tax on employer reversions. [Priv. Ltr. Rul. 9411038] Participants in an ESOP are permitted to make elective contributions under the plan's cash-or-deferred arrangement (see Qs 27:2, 27:16) prior to the allocation of all stock held in a suspense account purchased with reversion amounts from a terminated defined benefit plan, provided the elective contributions are not made until after required allocations are made from the suspense account for the plan year and the combined amounts do not exceed the annual addition limitation (see Q 28:26). In addition, stock held in the suspense account could be used for matching contributions, subject to the annual addition limitation. [I.R.C. § 4980(c)(3)(C); Priv. Ltr. Rul. 9350025]

The funds are held in trust for the benefit of employees and their beneficiaries and are used to buy employer securities from shareholders or from the company itself. When a participant retires or leaves, the participant receives the vested interest in the ESOP in the form of cash or employer securities. However, an ESOP may preclude a participant from obtaining a distribution of employer securities if the company's corporate charter or bylaws restrict the ownership of substantially all employer securities to employees or the ESOP. [I.R.C. § 409(h)(2)]

Participants can exercise a put option and put the employer securities back to the company for their fair market value if the securities are not readily tradable on an established market (see Q 28:70). To keep the employer securities from falling into the hands of competitors, either the ESOP or the company may be given the right of first refusal if the participant attempts to sell the securities. However, a participant generally can demand a distribution of benefits in the form of employer securities and cannot be required to sell the securities back to the company. [I.R.C. §§ 409(h)(1), 409(h)(7); Treas. Reg. § 54.4975-7(b)(9)] However, a different rule applies to an ESOP established by an S corporation (see Q 28:2). IRS has ruled that where a recapitalization involved an exchange of one class of stock for a new class of stock and the new class of stock did not qualify as employer securities, the ESOP participants were not required to have the right to demand distribution of plan benefits in the form of the new stock. [Priv. Ltr. Rul. 200010060]

IRS has ruled that neither the transfer of damages from a settlement fund to an ESOP nor the proposed manner of allocation of the fund adversely affected the qualified status of the plan (see Q 1:5), the allocation did not result in taxable income to the ESOP participants, distributions of the settlement fund were not subject to the consent requirements (see Q 10:61), and distributions by the plan were eligible rollover distributions (see Q 34:8). [Priv. Ltr. Rul. 200604039]

The basic purpose of an ESOP is the investment of plan assets in employer securities. [Priv. Ltr. Rul. 9724001] Courts have ruled that an ESOP trustee did not breach its fiduciary duty (see Q 23:19) to plan participants by investing plan assets in employer securities, even though the employer was in serious financial decline, because the trustee had no discretion and was required to act upon the direction of the company's ESOP committee. [Summers v. State Street Bank & Trust Co., 453 F.3d 404 (7th Cir. 2006); Maniace v. Commerce Bank of Kan. City, 40 F.3d 264 (8th Cir. 1994); Ershick v. United Mo. Bank of Kan. City, N.A., 948 F.2d 660 (10th Cir. 1991); see also Kirschbaum v. Reliant Energy, Inc., 526 F.3d 243 (5th Cir. 2008) and In re Radioshack ERISA Litig., 2008 WL 1808329 (__. D. Tex. 2008)] In another case, the court ruled that a participant's claim of breach of fiduciary duty against the plan administrator (see Q 20:1) for losses incurred after the employer's bankruptcy was not dismissed because, despite the plan requirement that funds be invested in the employer securities, the plan administrator still had a fiduciary obligation to prudently invest or diversify plan assets. [Rankin v. Rots, 278 F. Supp. 2d 853 (E.D. Mich. 2003); see also In re Syncor ERISA Litig., 516 F.3d 1095 (9th Cir. 2008), In re WorldCom, Inc. ERISA Litig., 2005 WL 221263 (S.D.N.Y. 2005), and In re WorldCom, Inc. ERISA Litig., 263 F. Supp. 2d 725 (S.D.N.Y. 2003); DOL Field Assistance Bull. 2004-03] Where 401(k) plan (see Q 27:1) assets were substantially invested in employer securities, the court concluded that plan fiduciaries did not have an obligation to make a special disclosure to plan participants about personal sales of employer securities. [Nelson v. Hodowal, 512 F.3d 347 (7th Cir. 2008)]

One court decided that the trustees of an ESOP violated their fiduciary duties when they established a competing business, knowing that the new business would decrease the value of the ESOP's assets. [Neyer, Tiseo & Hindo, Ltd. v. Russell, 1993 U.S. Dist. LEXIS 12011 (E.D. Pa. 1993)] Another court ruled that fiduciaries of an ESOP did not breach their fiduciary duty when they failed to diversify the ESOP's assets during an 18-month period in which the value of employer securities declined by 80 percent. The court stated that an ESOP fiduciary is presumed to have acted prudently in investing in employer securities but that this presumption can be overcome by a showing that the fiduciary abused its discretion. [Kuper v. Iovenko, 66 F.3d 1447 (6th Cir. 1995); see also Johnson v. Radian Group, Inc., 2009 WL 2137241 (E.D. Pa. 2009), In re Computer Sciences Corp. ERISA Litig., 2009 WL 2156696 (9th Cir. 2009), Lingis v. Motorola, Inc., 2009 WL 1708097 (N.D. Ill. 2009), Brieger v. Tellabs, Inc., 2009 WL 1565203 (__. D. Ill. 2009), Shirk v. Fifth Third Bancorp, No. 05-cv-049 (__.D. Ohio 2009),

Edgar v. Avaya, Inc., 2007 WL 2781847 (3d Cir. 2007), DiFelice v. US Airways, Inc., 497 F.3d 410 (4th Cir. 2007), Moench v. Robertson, 62 F.3d 553 (3d Cir. 1995), and Herman v. Mercantile Bank, 143 F.3d 419 (8th Cir. 1998)] One court stated that ERISA waives the duty to diversify ESOP assets. [Steinman v. Hicks, 352 F.3d 1101 (7th Cir. 2003); *see also* In re Coca-Cola Enterprises Inc., ERISA Litig., 2007 WL 1810211 (D. Ga. 2007), Wright v. Oregon Metallurgical Corp., 360 F.3d 1090 (9th Cir. 2004) and *In re* McKesson HBOC, Inc. ERISA Litig., No. C-00-20030 (N.D. Cal. 2005)] Another court concluded that plan fiduciaries had no duty to diversify investments of the ESOP because of the fraudulent overstatement of circulation figures, and the corresponding fraudulent increase in advertising rates, where there was no red flag to alert the fiduciaries about the fraudulent activity. The fiduciaries were not in a position to be aware of the fraud, and there was no evidence that the fraud actually affected the company's stock price. [Pugh v. Tribune Co., 2008 WL 867739 (7th Cir. 2008); *see also* Rogers v. Baxter International, Inc., 2008 WL 867741 (7th Cir. 2008)] Plan fiduciaries did not breach their duties under ERISA by continuing to offer an employer stock fund as a plan investment option despite a significant drop in the value of the stock. The ERISA Section 404(c)–compliant (see Q 23:14) 401(k) plan provided sufficient cautions of the risks involved in investing in employer stock to enable the plan participants to exercise control over their accounts and, thereby, shield plan fiduciaries from liability for losses resulting from the participants' investment decisions. [Rogers v. Baxter International, Inc., No. 04-C-6476 (N.D. Ill. 2010)]

An ESOP of a subsidiary corporation held unallocated shares of the parent corporation. After the merger of the subsidiary's ESOP into the parent's ESOP, the unallocated shares would be allocated to all plan participants and not only to the participants employed by the subsidiary. The court ruled that the subsidiary's ESOP suffered no loss; and, thus, the participants in the subsidiary's ESOP could not sustain a claim for breach of fiduciary duty. [Fox v. Herzog Heine Geduld, Inc., No. 06-1333 (3d Cir. 2007)] A trustee of an ESOP may have breached its fiduciary duty when it failed to notify the participants that the trustee would vote the ESOP's stock not yet allocated to participant accounts in the same percentages as directed by the participants with regard to the stock already allocated to participant accounts; because of the lack of notice, the trustee had a fiduciary duty to act independently in determining how to vote the unallocated stock (see Qs 28:30, 28:52). [Herman v. Nations Bank of Ga., N.A., 126 F.3d 1354 (11th Cir. 1997)] In the same case, the court later held that the participants were not fiduciaries with respect to the voting of unallocated shares because of the lack of notice. [Herman v. Nations Bank of Ga., N.A., 135 F.3d 1409 (11th Cir. 1998)]

One court ruled that a bank trustee violated its fiduciary duty when the ESOP purchased employer stock for more than fair market value even though the trustee had relied on an outside valuation report and informal DOL opinion. [Reich v. Valley Nat'l Bank of Ariz., 837 F. Supp. 1259 (S.D.N.Y. 1993)] Another court concluded that fiduciaries of an ESOP breached their fiduciary duties by purchasing shares of stock on behalf of the ESOP without adequate investigation and by overpaying for the shares even though the fiduciaries had retained an analyst to perform a valuation. [Chao v. Hall Holding Co., 285 F.3d 415 (6th Cir. 2002)] Concerning the sale of employer securities, another court ruled that fiduciaries breached their fiduciary duties when they approved a sale of employer securities by the ESOP to a related party at a price based solely on an independent appraisal report and did not meaningfully discuss, review, or question the report. The court refused to adopt a per se rule insulating fiduciaries from liability by relying on an independent appraiser's report, particularly where there was the potential for self-dealing. [Howard v. Shay, 100 F.3d 1484 (9th Cir. 1996); *see also* Howard v. Shay, No. CV 91-146 (C.D. Cal. 1998); Reich v. Hall Holding Co., 990 F. Supp. 955 (N.D. Ohio 1998); Donovan v. Cunningham, 716 F.2d 1455 (5th Cir. 1983)] However, another court concluded that a trust company exercised sufficient due diligence in advising an ESOP concerning a repurchase of employer stock from a company's officers and directors, even though the business climate subsequently changed, resulting in the company's bankruptcy. [Keach v. U.S. Trust Co., 419 F.3d 626 (7th Cir. 2005)] The relevant inquiry, said one court, is whether the fiduciary acted with the prudence required of a fiduciary under the prevailing circumstances at the time of the transaction (see Q 23:20). [Henry v. Champlain Enterprises, Inc., 445 F.3d 610 (2d Cir. 2006)]

A trustee of an ESOP did not violate its fiduciary duties to ESOP participants when it repaid loans with the cash proceeds from the sale of corporate stock in a suspense account even though it was not technically required to do so, concluded one court. [Benefits Comm. of Saint-Gobain Corp. v. Key Trust Co. of Ohio, N.A., Trustee of the Furon Co. ESOP, 313 F.3d 919 (6th Cir. 2002)] Where an ESOP owns all of the shares of the employer and a group of executives is responsible for managing the employer and the ESOP, excessive compensation paid to the group could be a breach of fiduciary duty. [Eckelkamp v. Beste, 2002 WL 31890079 (8th Cir. 2002); *see also* Johnson v. Couturier, 572 F.3d 1067 (9th Cir. 2009)]

A terminated ESOP participant received all shares of employer stock credited to his ESOP account and promptly sold the shares. Seven months later the employer was sold, and the buyer purchased the ESOP shares for a significantly greater price per share. The court held that the employer did not commit a fiduciary breach by failing to inform the participant that a sale of the employer was being considered. [Olson v. Chem-Trend, Inc, 1995 U.S. Dist. LEXIS 11016 (E.D. Mich. 1995)] Another court concluded that an employer's former employees were not entitled to a distribution of cash surplus from an ESOP where the surplus resulted from a successful tender offer for the employer's stock. [Bennett v. Conrail Matched Sav. Plan Admin. Comm., 1999 WL 86842 (3d Cir. 1999)]

DOL opined that the purchase by an ESOP of the plan sponsor's stock from personal trusts is not a prohibited transaction (see Q 23:1), even if the plan sponsor serves as trustee of both the ESOP and the personal trusts. DOL stated that the stock acquisitions were exempt from the prohibited transactions provisions, as long as the transactions were for adequate consideration and no commission was charged for them. DOL cautioned, however, that the exemption of the stock purchases from the prohibited transaction provisions was not determinative of whether the fiduciary obligations under ERISA had been met. [DOL Op. Ltr. 2002-04A]

Two corporate officers who were trustees of the corporation's ESOP withdrew over $2,000,000 in ESOP contributions immediately after they were made to meet the corporation's expenses. Promissory notes that provided that the funds would be replaced with corporate stock of equal value were issued to the ESOP by the corporation. After the corporation transferred most of its operating assets to another company, it transferred stock to the ESOP. The number of shares transferred was based on the value of the stock when the funds were initially withdrawn and did not account for the asset transfer. DOL claimed that the stock was virtually worthless after the asset transfer and brought suit for the amount withdrawn plus interest. The court ruled in favor of DOL and also held that the trustees had the burden of proof regarding the value of the stock. [Secretary of the United States DOL v. Gilley, 2002 WL 856995 (6th Cir. 2002)]

One court concluded that an underestimation of the number of retiring employees entitled to single-sum distributions from an ESOP that caused serious cash flow problems for the company and decimated the value of the ESOP's shares did not constitute a breach of fiduciary duty. [Armstrong v. Amsted Indus., Inc., 2004 U.S. Dist. LEXIS 14776 (N.D. Ill. 2004)] A claim of mismanagement against company officers brought by ESOP plan participants was not preempted by ERISA merely because the alleged mismanagement adversely affected the value of the ESOP holding company stock, concluded one court, so that the action could be brought in state court. [Husvar v. Rapoport, No. 01-4254 (6th Cir. 2003); *see also* Ervast v. Flexible Prods. Co, 2003 WL 22203472 (11th Cir. 2003)]

In 2002, DOL's Regional Enforcement Project in San Francisco found the following problems with ESOPs:

1. Improper valuation of employee securities;
2. Failure to properly allocate stock to individual participant accounts;
3. Failure to pass through voting rights to plan participants;
4. Outright fraud and embezzlement; and
5. ESOP loans that are not primarily for the benefit of plan participants.

See Q 28:2 for rules applicable to S corporations that establish ESOPs.

Q 28:2   Can an ESOP be a shareholder of an S corporation?

An S corporation is a small business corporation for which an election is in effect for the taxable year, and a small business corporation is a domestic corporation which is not an ineligible corporation and which does *not:*

- Have more than 100 shareholders
- Have as a shareholder a person (other than an estate, certain trusts, a qualified retirement plan, or a Section 501(c)(3) organization (see Q 35:3)) who is not an individual

- Have a nonresident alien as a shareholder
- Have more than one class of stock (see Q 28:8)

A qualified retirement plan, including an ESOP, can be a shareholder of an S corporation. [I.R.C. § 1361] With regard to the 100-shareholder limit for S corporations, the ESOP, not the participants, is treated as the shareholder. Thus, if the ESOP owns all of the employer securities (see Q 28:8), there is only one S corporation shareholder. In addition, where the ESOP of an S corporation permitted each participant to elect once each year to withdraw the S corporation cash distributions allocated to the participant's account, IRS ruled that the election did not create an impermissible second class of stock. [Priv. Ltr. Rul. 199906044] A floor price agreement guaranteeing a minimum price at which stock would be repurchased after having been distributed to participants in an ESOP was disregarded in determining whether the outstanding shares conferred identical rights. [Treas. Reg. § 1.1361-1(*l*)(2)(iii)(B); Priv. Ltr. Rul. 200914019] IRS has ruled that a corporation's status as an S corporation will not be affected merely because its ESOP makes distributions of the corporation's stock and one or more ESOP participants elect to make a direct rollover (see Q 34:17) of the stock to an IRA, provided that:

1. The terms of the ESOP require that the S corporation repurchase its stock immediately upon the ESOP's distribution of the stock to an IRA;

2. The S corporation actually repurchases the S corporation stock contemporaneously with, and effective on the same day as, the distribution, or the ESOP is permitted to assume the rights and obligations of the S corporation to repurchase the stock immediately upon the distribution to an IRA and the ESOP actually repurchases the stock contemporaneously with, and effective on the same day as, the distribution; and

3. No income (including tax-exempt income), loss, deduction, or credit attributable to the distributed S corporation stock is allocated to the participant's IRA. [Rev. Proc. 2004-14, 2004-1 C.B. 489; Priv. Ltr. Rul. 200633013]

ESOPs established or maintained by S corporations need not give participants the right to demand their distributions in the form of employer securities if they have the right to receive such distributions in cash. This is true even if the corporation's corporate charter or bylaws do not restrict ownership to employees or the ESOP (see Q 28:1). Alternatively, the ESOP can distribute stock but require that the recipient resell the stock immediately to the employer. In either case, the recipient must receive at least fair market value for the stock. This alleviates the problem of the 100-shareholder rule and also prevents the recipient from rolling over the stock to an IRA since an IRA cannot be an S corporation shareholder. [I.R.C. § 409(h)(2); Priv. Ltr. Rul. 200744021]

If an ESOP owns S corporation employer securities, the ESOP's proportionate share of the S corporation income is not considered in computing the ESOP's unrelated business taxable income (see Qs 1:6, 30:11). [I.R.C. § 512(e)(3); Priv. Ltr. Rul. 200029055] IRS also ruled that any gain realized from the disposition of

S corporation employer securities will be exempt from the unrelated business income tax. [Priv. Ltr. Rul. 200029055]

A plan's different distribution media (i.e., cash or in-kind) constitute different optional forms of benefit (see Qs 10:37, 10:45). Consequently, an amendment that eliminates a particular distribution medium under a plan eliminates an optional form of benefit and may be treated as reducing accrued benefits in violation of the anti-cutback rule (see Qs 9:25, 9:31) to the extent that the amendment applies to benefits accrued as of the later of the adoption date or the effective date of the amendment. However, an ESOP does not violate the anti-cutback rule merely because it modifies distribution options in a nondiscriminatory manner. [I.R.C. § 411(d)(6)(C)] The ESOP exception has been expanded to S corporations. An ESOP will not violate the anti-cutback rule merely because the S corporation employer maintaining the plan eliminates, or retains the discretion to eliminate, optional forms of benefit by substituting cash distributions for distributions in the form of employer securities. [Treas. Reg. § 1.411(d)-4, Q&A-2(d)(2)(ii), Q&A-11]

A statutory exemption from the prohibited-transaction rules has been created for ESOPs established or maintained by S corporations (see Q 28:67).

A shareholder of an S corporation who sells employer securities to an ESOP *cannot* elect to defer recognition of all or part of the gain by purchasing qualified replacement property (see Qs 28:34–28:48). It is unclear whether a shareholder of a C corporation (i.e., a corporation that is not an S corporation) can sell employer securities to an ESOP, elect nonrecognition treatment, and then have the C corporation elect to be treated as an S corporation. [I.R.C. § 1041(c)(1)(A)]

An S corporation *cannot* deduct dividends it pays on employer securities held by an ESOP (see Qs 28:10–28:12). [I.R.C. § 404(k)(1)] Since income taxes are generally not imposed on S corporations, the inability to deduct dividends should not be significant. Earnings (whether dividends or otherwise) paid by an S corporation to an ESOP with respect to stock allocated to participant accounts cannot be used to repay an exempt loan (see Q 28:7), unless the plan provides that employer securities with a fair market value of not less than the amount of the distribution are allocated to the employee's account for the year in which the distribution would have been so allocated. [I.R.C. § 4975(f)(7)] Also, such earnings paid on unallocated shares in the ESOP suspense account can be used to repay the exempt loan. If an ESOP owns S corporation stock, the S corporation may not deduct any accrued expenses for any ESOP participant, including plan contributions based on accrued compensation. A taxpayer, including an S corporation, may only deduct an expense in the same tax year that the payment is reported as income by a related party. A related party includes any person who directly or indirectly owns any of the S corporation's stock. Therefore, if an ESOP holds S corporation stock, the participants indirectly own stock in the S corporation. The participants do not include accrued compensation in their income until the year in which they receive it; and, therefore, the S corporation cannot deduct any compensation (including any bonus or vacation pay) accrued to the participants. The S corporation also cannot deduct any plan contributions for the participants that are based on accrued compensation. [I.R.C. §§ 267(a)(2), 267(e)(1)(B)(ii); *IRS Employee Plan News* (Aug. 2, 2010)]

IRS did not abuse its discretion by retroactively revoking an ESOP's favorable determination letter (see Qs 18:1, 18:4) after the ESOP was terminated where it was later found that the ESOP had never satisfied the minimum coverage requirements (see Q 5:15). [Yarish Consulting, Inc., T.C.M. 2010-74]

Areas of uncertainty include the following:

1. Whether the 10 percent early withdrawal tax (see Q 16:1) applies to S corporation distributions to an ESOP that are, in turn, distributed by the ESOP to participants. This penalty tax does not apply to dividends (see Qs 28:12, 28:19); however, S corporation distributions technically do not constitute dividends.

2. Whether the $5,000 cash-out limit participant consent rule (see Q 10:61) applies to S corporation distributions to an ESOP that are, in turn, distributed by the ESOP to participants. This limitation does not apply to dividends; but, again, S corporation distributions technically do not constitute dividends. [I.R.C. §§ 404(k)(1), 411(a)(11)(C)]

The expanded deduction rules relating to leveraged ESOPs do *not* apply to S corporations (see Q 28:9). [I.R.C. § 404(a)(9)(C)]

See Qs 28:3 and 28:5 for additional developments affecting ESOPs for S corporations.

Q 28:3   How does EGTRRA 2001 affect ESOPs of S corporations?

Under EGTRRA 2001 (see Q 1:21), certain allocations of employer securities in an S corporation are prohibited. If there is a nonallocation year with respect to an ESOP maintained by an S corporation: (1) the amount allocated in a prohibited allocation to an individual who is a disqualified person is treated as distributed to such individual (i.e., the value of the prohibited allocation is includible in the gross income of the individual receiving the prohibited allocation); (2) an excise tax is imposed on the S corporation equal to 50 percent of the amount involved in a prohibited allocation; and (3) an excise tax is imposed on the S corporation with respect to any synthetic equity owned by a disqualified person. [I.R.C. §§ 409(p), 4979A; Treas. Reg. § 1.409(p)-1; IRS Notice 2002-2, Q&A-15, 2002-1 C.B. 285]

IRS issued temporary regulations in 2003 that also served as the text of proposed regulations. The 2003 regulations provided guidance on identifying disqualified persons, on determining whether an ESOP has a nonallocation year, and on the definition of synthetic equity. In 2004, IRS issued a ruling (see Q 28:5) that addressed three factual situations involving an S corporation with qualified subchapter S subsidiaries (QSUBs). IRS issued later temporary regulations that again served as the text of proposed regulations. The later temporary regulations were effective generally for plan years that began on or after January 1, 2005. On December 19, 2006, IRS issued final regulations that adopt the provisions of the later temporary and proposed regulations with certain modifications. The final regulations apply for plan years beginning on or after January 1, 2006. For plan years beginning before January 1, 2006, the later temporary and proposed regulations apply. [Preamble to final regulations; Treas. Reg. § 1.409(p)-1(i)]

An ESOP holding employer securities (see Q 28:8) consisting of stock in an S corporation must provide that no portion of the assets of the plan attributable to (or allocable in lieu of) such employer securities may, during a nonallocation year, accrue under the ESOP, or be allocated directly or indirectly under any qualified retirement plan of the employer (including the ESOP), for the benefit of any disqualified person (a prohibited allocation). [Treas. Reg. § 1.409(p)-1(b)(1)]

There is a prohibited allocation if there is either an impermissible accrual or an impermissible allocation. The amount of the prohibited allocation is equal to the sum of the impermissible accrual plus the amount of the impermissible allocation (if any). [Treas. Reg. § 1.409(p)-1(b)(2)(i)] There is an impermissible accrual to the extent that employer securities consisting of stock in an S corporation owned by the ESOP and any assets attributable thereto are held under the ESOP for the benefit of a disqualified person during a nonallocation year. For this purpose, assets attributable to stock in an S corporation include any distributions made on S corporation stock held in a disqualified person's account in the ESOP (including earnings thereon), plus any proceeds from the sale of S corporation securities held for a disqualified person's account in the ESOP (including any earnings thereon). Thus, in the event of a nonallocation year, all S corporation shares and all other ESOP assets attributable to S corporation stock, including distributions, sales proceeds, and earnings on either the distribution or proceeds, held for the account of such disqualified person in the ESOP during that year are an impermissible accrual for the benefit of that person, whether attributable to contributions in the current year or in prior years. [Treas. Reg. § 1.409(p)-1(b)(2)(ii)].

An impermissible allocation occurs during a nonallocation year to the extent that a contribution or other annual addition (see Q 6:34) is made with respect to the account of a disqualified person, or the disqualified person otherwise accrues additional benefits, directly or indirectly under the ESOP or any other qualified retirement plan of the employer (including a release and allocation of assets from a suspense account), that, for the nonallocation year, would have been added to the account of the disqualified person under the ESOP and invested in employer securities consisting of stock in an S corporation owned by the ESOP but for a provision in the ESOP that precludes such addition to the account of a disqualified person, and investment in employer securities during a nonallocation year. [Treas. Reg. § 1.409(p)-1(b)(2)(iii)]

If a plan year is a nonallocation year, the amount of any prohibited allocation in the account of a disqualified person as of the first day of the plan year is treated as distributed from the ESOP (or other plan of the employer) to the disqualified person on the first day of the plan year. In the case of an impermissible accrual or impermissible allocation that is not in the account of a disqualified person as of the first day of the plan year, the amount of the prohibited allocation is treated as distributed on the date of the prohibited allocation. Thus, the fair market value of assets in the disqualified person's account that constitutes an impermissible accrual or allocation is included in gross income (to the extent in excess of any investment in the contract allocable to such amount; see Q 13:3) and is subject to the 10 percent tax on early distributions unless an exception applies (see Q 16:1). A deemed distribution is not an actual distribution from the ESOP. Thus, the amount of the prohibited allocation is not an eligible rollover distribution (see Q 34:8). However, with respect to any subsequent distribution from the ESOP, the amount that the disqualified person previously took into account as income as a result of the deemed distribution is treated as an investment in the contract. [Treas. Reg. § 1.409(p)-1(b)(2)(iv)(A)] If there is a prohibited allocation, then the plan fails to satisfy the ESOP requirements and ceases to be an ESOP. In such a case, the exemption from the excise tax on prohibited transactions for loans to leveraged ESOPs (see Q 28:7) would cease to apply to any loan (with the result that the employer would owe an excise tax with respect to the previously exempt loan). As a result of these failures, the plan would lose the prohibited transaction exemption for loans to an ESOP. Finally, a plan that does not operate in accordance with its terms to reflect the prohibited allocation provisions fails to satisfy the qualification requirements (see Q 4:1), which would cause the corporation's S election to terminate. [I.R.C. §§ 1362, 4975(e)(7), 4979A(a); Treas. Reg. § 1.409(p)-1(b)(2)(iv)(B)]

> **Example 1.** Caroline Corporation, an S corporation, establishes an ESOP in 2010, with a calendar plan year. The ESOP is a qualified retirement plan that includes terms providing that a prohibited allocation will not occur during a nonallocation year. On December 31, 2010, all of the 1,000 outstanding shares of stock of Caroline Corporation, with a fair market value of $30 per share, are contributed to the ESOP and allocated among accounts established within the plan for the benefit of Caroline Corporation's three employees, Ben, Jason, and Casey, based on their compensation for 2010. As a result, on December 31, 2010, Ben's account includes 800 of the shares ($24,000); Jason's account includes 140 of the shares ($4,200); and Casey's account includes the remaining 60 shares ($1,800). The plan year 2010 is a nonallocation year, Ben and Jason are disqualified persons on December 31, 2010, and a prohibited allocation occurs for them on December 31, 2010.

> On December 31, 2010, Ben and Jason each has a deemed distribution as a result of the prohibited allocation, resulting in income of $24,000 for Ben and $4,200 for Jason. Caroline Corporation owes an excise tax based on an amount involved of $28,200. The plan ceases to be an ESOP on the date of the prohibited allocation (December 31, 2010) and also fails to satisfy the qualification requirements on that date due to the failure to comply with the provisions requiring compliance with the prohibited allocation rules. As a result of having an ineligible shareholder, Caroline Corporation ceases to be an S corporation on December 31, 2010.

An ESOP may prevent a nonallocation year or a prohibited allocation during a nonallocation year by providing for assets (including S corporation securities) allocated to the account of a disqualified person (or a person reasonably expected to become a disqualified person absent a transfer) to be transferred into a separate portion of the plan that is not an ESOP or to another qualified retirement plan of the employer that is not an ESOP. Any such transfer must be effectuated by an affirmative action taken no later than the date of the transfer, and all subsequent actions (including benefit statements) generally must be consistent with the transfer having occurred on that date. In the event of such a transfer involving S corporation securities, the recipient plan is subject to tax on unrelated business taxable income (UBTI; see Q 1:6). [I.R.C. § 512; Treas. Reg. §§ 1.409(p)-1(b)(2)(v)(A), 54.4975-11(a)(5)] If a transfer is made from an ESOP to a separate portion of the plan or to another plan of the employer that is not an ESOP, then both the ESOP and the plan or portion that is not an ESOP do not fail to satisfy the nondiscrimination requirements relating to the availability of benefits, rights, or features (see Q 4:20) merely because of the transfer. Further, subsequent to the transfer, that plan will not fail to satisfy these requirements merely because of the benefits, rights, or features with respect to the transferred benefits if those benefits, rights, or features would satisfy these requirements if the mandatory disaggregation rule for ESOPs did not apply. [Treas. Reg. §§ 1.409(p)-1(b)(2)(v)(B); 1.410(b)-7(c)(2)] IRS has provided sample plan language that plan administrators of ESOPs holding S corporation stock may use to transfer assets from the accounts of disqualified persons to a separate portion of the plan or to another plan of the employer that is not an ESOP in order to prevent a nonallocation year. [*Employee Plans News Special Edition* (July 2008)]. In March 2009, IRS revised the sample plan language.

A nonallocation year means a plan year of an ESOP during which, at any time, the ESOP holds any employer securities that are shares of an S corporation and either:

1. Disqualified persons own at least 50 percent of the number of outstanding shares of stock in the S corporation (including deemed-owned ESOP shares), or
2. Disqualified persons own at least 50 percent of the sum of: (a) the outstanding shares of stock in the S corporation (including deemed-owned ESOP shares) and (b) the shares of synthetic equity in the S corporation owned by disqualified persons. [Treas. Reg. § 1.409(p)-1(c)(1)]

Rules of attribution apply to determine ownership of shares in the S corporation (including deemed-owned ESOP shares) and synthetic equity. However, for this purpose, the provision relating to options to acquire stock is disregarded and the members of an individual's family include members of the individual's family as discussed below. In addition, an individual is treated as owning deemed-owned ESOP shares of that individual notwithstanding the employee trust exception. [I.R.C. §§ 318(a), 318(a)(2)(B)(i); Treas. Reg. § 1.409(p)-1(c)(2)]

A person is treated as owning stock if the person has an exercisable right to acquire the stock, the stock is both issued and outstanding, and the stock is held by persons other than the ESOP, the S corporation, or a related entity. This rule applies only if treating persons as owning the shares results in a nonallocation year. This rule does not apply to a right to acquire stock of an S corporation held by a shareholder that is subject to federal income tax that would not be taken into account in determining if an S corporation has a second class of stock, provided that a principal purpose of the right is not the avoidance or evasion of the prohibited allocation rules. In addition, this rule does not apply for purposes of determining ownership of deemed-owned ESOP shares or whether an interest constitutes synthetic equity. [Treas. Reg. §§ 1.409(p)-1(c)(4); 1.1361-1(*l*)(2)(iii), 1.1361-1(*l*)(4)(iii)(C)] If any share is treated as owned by more than one person, then that share is counted as a single share and that share is treated as owned by disqualified persons if any of the owners is a disqualified person. [Treas. Reg. § 1.409(p)-1(c)(5)]

A disqualified person means any person for whom:

1. The number of such person's deemed-owned ESOP shares of the S corporation is at least 10 percent of the number of the deemed-owned ESOP shares of the S corporation;
2. The aggregate number of such person's deemed-owned ESOP shares and synthetic equity shares of the S corporation is at least 10 percent of the sum of: (a) the total number of deemed-owned ESOP shares and (b) the person's synthetic equity shares of the S corporation;
3. The aggregate number of the S corporation's deemed-owned ESOP shares of such person and of the members of such person's family is at least 20 percent of the number of deemed-owned ESOP shares of the S corporation; or
4. The aggregate number of the S corporation's deemed-owned ESOP shares and synthetic equity shares of such person and of the members of such person's family is at least 20 percent of the sum of: (a) the total number of deemed-owned ESOP shares and (b) the synthetic equity shares of the S corporation owned by such person and other persons of such person's family. [Treas. Reg. § 1.409(p)-1(d)(1)]

Each member of the family of any person who is a disqualified person under items 3 and 4 above and who owns any deemed-owned ESOP shares or synthetic equity shares is a disqualified person. A member of the family means, with respect to an individual:

1. The spouse of the individual;
2. An ancestor or lineal descendant of the individual or the individual's spouse;
3. A brother or sister of the individual or of the individual's spouse and any lineal descendant of the brother or sister; and
4. The spouse of any individual described in item 2 or 3 above. [Treas. Reg. §§ 1.409(p)-1(d)(2)(i), 1.409(p)-1(d)(2)(ii)]

A spouse of an individual who is legally separated from such individual under a decree of divorce or separate maintenance is not treated as such individual's spouse. [Treas. Reg. § 1.409(p)-1(d)(2)(iii)] IRS concluded that the plan year of an S corporation's ESOP was not a nonallocation year because none of the individuals who were participants in the plan were disqualified persons. No individual owned more than 10 percent of the total number of deemed-owned shares. [Priv. Ltr. Rul. 200804023]

Example 2. An S corporation has 800 outstanding shares of which 100 are owned by Steve and 700 are held in an ESOP during 2010, including 200 shares held in Steve's ESOP account, 65 shares held in the ESOP account of Stephanie, 65 shares held in the ESOP account of Bill, who is Stephanie's husband, and 14 shares held in the ESOP account of Jennifer, who is the daughter of Stephanie and Bill. There are no unallocated suspense account shares in the ESOP. The S corporation has no synthetic equity. Steve is a disqualified person during 2010 because his account in the ESOP holds at least 10 percent of the shares owned by the ESOP (200 is 28.6 percent of 700). Although, during 2010, none of Stephanie, Bill, or Jennifer is individually a disqualified person, because each of their accounts holds less than 10 percent of the shares owned by the ESOP, each of them is a disqualified person because Stephanie and members of her family own at least 20 percent of the deemed-owned ESOP shares (144 [65 + 65 + 14] ÷ 700 = 20.6%). As a result, disqualified persons own at least 50 percent of the outstanding shares of the S corporation during 2010 (Steve's 100 directly owned shares, Steve's 200 deemed-owned shares, Stephanie's 65 deemed-owned shares, Bill's 65 deemed-owned shares, and Jennifer's 14 deemed-owned shares are 55.5 percent of 800).

Example 3. An S corporation has shares that are owned by an ESOP and various individuals. Caroline and Adam are married and have a son Ben. Stephanie and Bill are married and have a daughter Jennifer. Ben and Jennifer are married. Stephanie has a brother Jamie. Their percentages of the deemed-owned ESOP shares of the S corporation are as follows: Adam has 6 percent, Ben has 7 percent, and Stephanie has 8 percent. None of Caroline, Bill, Jennifer, and Jamie has any deemed-owned ESOP shares, and the S corporation has no synthetic equity. However, Caroline and Jamie each owns directly a number of shares of the outstanding shares of the S corporation.

Ben is a disqualified person (because Ben's family consists of Caroline, Adam, himself, Stephanie, Bill, and Jennifer; and, in the aggregate, those persons own more than 20 percent of the deemed-owned ESOP shares), and Jennifer is also a disqualified person (because Jennifer's family consists of Caroline, Adam, Ben, Stephanie, Bill, and herself; and, in the aggregate those persons own more than 20 percent of the deemed-owned ESOP shares). Further, Adam and Stephanie are each a disqualified person because each is a member of a family that includes one or more disqualified persons and each has deemed-owned ESOP shares. However, Caroline, Bill, and Jamie are not disqualified persons. For example, Caroline does not own more than 10 percent of the deemed-owned ESOP shares; and Caroline's family, which consists of herself, Adam, Ben, and Jennifer, owns, in the aggregate, only 13 percent of the deemed-owned ESOP shares (Jennifer's parents are not members of Caroline's family because the family members of a person do not include the parents-in-law of the person's descendants). Further, for purposes of determining whether the ESOP has a nonallocation year, the shares directly owned by Caroline and Jamie would be taken into account as shares owned by disqualified persons under the attribution rules.

A person is treated as owning such person's deemed-owned ESOP shares. Deemed-owned ESOP shares owned by a person mean, with respect to any person:

1. Any shares of stock in the S corporation constituting employer securities that are allocated to such person's account under the ESOP, and

2. Such person's shares of the stock in the S corporation that is held by the ESOP but is not allocated to the account of any participant or beneficiary (with such person's share to be determined in the same proportion as the shares released and allocated from a suspense account under the ESOP for the most recently ended plan year for which there were shares released and allocated from a suspense account or, if there has been no such prior release and allocation from a suspense account, then determined in proportion to a reasonable estimate of the shares that would be released and allocated in the first year of loan repayment). [Treas. Reg. § 1.409(p)-1(e)]

Synthetic equity is treated as owned by a person in the same manner as stock is treated as owned by a person, directly or under the attribution rules. [Treas. Reg. § 1.409(p)-1(f)(1)]

Synthetic equity includes any stock option, warrant, restricted stock, deferred issuance stock right, stock appreciation right payable in stock, or similar interest or right that gives the holder the right to acquire or receive stock of the S corporation in the future. Rights to acquire stock in an S corporation with respect to stock that is, at all times during the period when such rights are effective, both issued and outstanding and held by a person other than the ESOP, the S corporation, or a related entity are not synthetic equity but only if that person is subject to federal income taxes. A right of first refusal to acquire stock held by an ESOP is not treated as a right to acquire stock of an S corporation if the right to acquire stock would not be taken into account in determining if an S corporation has a second class of stock and the price at which the stock is acquired under the right of first refusal is not less than the price determined under a fair valuation formula (see Q 28:70). The right of first refusal must also comply with certain other requirements. This provision does not apply if, based on the facts and circumstances, IRS finds that the right to acquire stock held by the ESOP constitutes an avoidance or an evasion of the prohibited allocation rules. [I.R.C. § 409(h); Treas. Reg. §§ 1.409(p)-1(f)(2)(i), 1.1361-1(*l*)(2)(iii)(A), 54.4975-7(b)(9), 54.4975-11(d)(5)] Synthetic equity also includes a right to a future payment (payable in cash or any other form other than stock of the S corporation) from an S corporation that is based on the value of the stock of the S corporation, such as appreciation in such value. Thus, for example, synthetic equity includes a stock appreciation right with respect to stock of an S corporation that is payable in cash or a phantom stock unit with respect to stock of an S corporation that is payable in cash. [Treas. Reg. § 1.409(p)-1(f)(2)(ii)]

Synthetic equity includes a right to acquire stock or other similar interest in a related entity to the extent of the S corporation's ownership, and also includes a right to acquire assets of an S corporation or a related entity other than either rights to acquire goods, services, or property at fair market value in the ordinary course of business or fringe benefits excluded from gross income. [I.R.C. § 132; Treas. Reg. § 1.409(p)-1(f)(2)(iii)] Synthetic equity also includes any of the following with respect to an S corporation or a related entity: any remuneration to which Section 404(a)(5) applies; remuneration for which a deduction would be permitted under Section 404(a)(5) if separate accounts were maintained; any right to receive property to which Section 83 applies (including a payment to a trust described in Section 402(b) or to an annuity described in Section 403(c)) in a future year for the performance of services; any transfer of property (to which Section 83 applies) in connection with the performance of services to the extent that the property is not substantially vested by the end of the plan year in which transferred; and a split-dollar life insurance arrangement entered into in connection with the performance of services (other than one under which, at all times, the only economic benefit that will be provided under the arrangement is current life insurance protection). Synthetic equity also includes any other remuneration for services under a plan, method, or arrangement deferring the receipt of compensation to a date that is after the 15th day of the third calendar month following the end of the entity's taxable year in which the related services are rendered. However, synthetic equity does not include benefits under a plan that is an eligible retirement plan (see Q 34:16) and does not include any interest described to the extent that:

1. The interest is nonqualified deferred compensation (within the meaning of Section 3121(v)(2)) that was outstanding on December 17, 2004;

2. The interest is an amount that was taken into account prior to January 1, 2005, for purposes of taxation (or income attributable thereto); and

3. The interest was held before the first date on which the ESOP acquires any employer securities. [Treas. Reg. §§ 1.61-22(b), 1.61-22(d)(3), 1.83-3(e), 1.83-3(i), 1.409(p)-1(f)(2)(iv), 31.3121(v)(2)-1(d)]

Synthetic equity does not include shares that are deemed-owed ESOP shares (or any rights with respect to deemed-owned ESOP shares to the extent such rights are specifically permitted under the put option provisions; see Q 28:70). [Treas. Reg. § 1.409(p)-1(f)(2)(v)]

Related entity means any entity in which the S corporation holds an interest and which is a partnership, a trust, an eligible entity that is disregarded as an entity that is separate from its owner, or a QSub (see Q 28:5). [Treas. Reg. §§ 1.409(p)-1(f)(3), 301.7701-3]

In the case of synthetic equity that is determined by reference to shares of stock of the S corporation, the person who is entitled to the synthetic equity is treated as owning the number of shares of stock deliverable pursuant to such synthetic equity. In the case of synthetic equity that is determined by reference to shares of stock of the S corporation, but for which payment is made in cash or other property (besides stock of the S corporation), the number of shares of synthetic equity treated as owned is equal to the number of shares of stock having a fair market value equal to the cash or other property (disregarding lapse restrictions). Where such synthetic equity is a right to purchase or receive S corporation shares, the corresponding number of shares of synthetic equity is determined without regard to lapse restrictions or to any amount required to be paid in exchange for the shares. Thus, for example, if a corporation grants an employee of an S corporation an option to purchase 100 shares of the corporation's stock, exercisable in the future only after the satisfaction of certain performance conditions, the employee is the deemed owner of 100 synthetic equity shares of the corporation as of the date the option is granted. If the same employee were granted 100 shares of restricted S corporation stock (or restricted stock units), subject to forfeiture until the satisfaction of performance or service conditions, the employee would likewise be the deemed owner of 100 synthetic equity shares from the grant date. However, if the same employee were granted a stock appreciation right with regard to 100 shares of S corporation stock (whether payable in stock or in cash), the number of synthetic equity shares the employee is deemed to own equals the number of shares having a value equal to the appreciation at the time of measurement (determined without regard to lapse restrictions). [Treas. Reg. §§ 1.83-3(i), 1.409(p)-1(f)(4)(i)]

In the case of synthetic equity that is determined by reference to shares of stock (or similar interests) in a related entity, the person who is entitled to the synthetic equity is treated as owning shares of stock of the S corporation with the same aggregate value as the number of shares of stock (or similar interests) of the related entity (with such value determined without regard to any lapse restriction). [Treas. Reg. § 1.409(p)-1(f)(4)(ii)]

In the case of any synthetic equity to which neither of the preceding paragraphs apply, the person who is entitled to the synthetic equity is treated as owning on any date a number of shares of stock in the S corporation equal to the present value (on that date) of the synthetic equity (with such value determined without regard to any lapse restriction) divided by the fair market value of a share of the S corporation's stock as of that date. A year is a nonallocation year if certain thresholds are met at any time during that year. However, for purposes of this paragraph, an ESOP may provide that the number of shares of S corporation stock treated as owned by a person who is entitled to synthetic equity to which this paragraph applies is determined annually (or more frequently), as of the first day of the ESOP's plan year or as of any other reasonable determination date or dates during the plan year. If the ESOP so provides, the number of shares of synthetic equity to which this paragraph applies that are treated as owned by that person for any period from a given determination date through the date immediately preceding the next following determination date is the number of shares treated as owned on the given determination date. [Treas. Reg. §§ 1. 409(p)-1(f)(4)(iii)(A), 1.409-1(f)(4)(iii)(B)]

In addition, if the terms of the ESOP so provide, then the number of shares of synthetic equity with respect to grants of synthetic equity to which this paragraph applies may be fixed for a specified period from a determination date identified under the ESOP through the day before a determination date that is not later than the third anniversary of the identified determination date. Thus, the ESOP must provide for the number of shares of synthetic equity to which this paragraph applies to be redetermined not less frequently than every three years, based on the S corporation share value on a determination date that is not later than the third anniversary of the identified determination date and the aggregate present value of the synthetic equity to which this paragraph applies (including all grants made during the three-year period) on that determination date. However, additional accruals, allocations, or grants (to which this paragraph applies) that are made during such three-year period are taken into account on each determination date during that period, based on the number of synthetic equity shares resulting from the additional accrual, allocation, or grant (determined as of the determination date on or next following the date of the accrual, allocation, or grant). If, as permitted under this paragraph, an ESOP provides for the number of shares of synthetic equity to be fixed for a specific period from a determination date to a subsequent determination date, then that subsequent determination date can be changed to a new determination date, subject to the following conditions:

1. The change in the subsequent determination date must be effectuated through a plan amendment adopted before the new determination date;

2. The new determination date must be earlier than the prior determination date (that is, the new determination date must be earlier than the determination date applicable in the absence of the plan amendment);

3. The conditions discussed in the third sentence of this paragraph must be satisfied measured from the new determination date; and

4. Except to the extent permitted by IRS, the change must be adopted in connection with either a change in the plan year of the ESOP or a merger, consolidation, or transfer of plan assets of the ESOP under Section 414(*l*) (and the new determination date must be consistent with the plan year change or Section 414(*l*) event). [Treas. Reg. § 1.409(p)-1(f)(4)(iii)(c)]

The number of synthetic shares otherwise determined is decreased ratably to the extent that shares of the S corporation are owned by a person who is not an ESOP and who is subject to federal income taxes. For example, if an S corporation has 200 outstanding shares, of which individual A owns 50 shares and the ESOP owns the other 150 shares, and individual B would be treated as owning 100 synthetic equity shares of the S corporation but for this paragraph, then, under the rule of this paragraph, the number of synthetic shares treated as owned by B is decreased from 100 to 75 (because the ESOP only owns 75 percent of the outstanding stock of the S corporation, rather than 100 percent). [Treas. Reg. § 1.409(p)-1(f)(4)(iv)]

If a synthetic equity right includes (directly or indirectly) a right to purchase or receive shares of S corporation stock that have per-share voting rights greater than the per-share voting rights of one or more shares of S corporation stock held by the ESOP, then the number of shares of deemed-owned synthetic equity attributable to such right is not less than the number of shares that would have the same voting rights if the shares had the same per-share voting rights as shares held by the ESOP with the least voting rights. For example, if shares of S corporation stock held by the ESOP have one voting right per share, then an individual who holds an option to purchase one share with 100 voting rights is treated as owning 100 shares of synthetic equity. [Treas. Reg. § 1.409(p)-1(f)(4)(v)]

Whether the principal purpose of the ownership structure of an S corporation involving synthetic equity constitutes an avoidance or evasion of the prohibited allocation rules is determined by taking into account all of the surrounding facts and circumstances, including all features of the ownership of the S corporation's outstanding stock and related obligations (including synthetic equity), any shareholders who are taxable entities, and the cash distributions made to shareholders, to determine whether, to the extent of the ESOP's stock ownership, the ESOP receives the economic benefits of ownership in the S corporation that occur during the period that stock of the S corporation is owned by the ESOP. Among the factors indicating that the ESOP receives these economic benefits include shareholder voting rights, the right to receive distributions made to shareholders, and the right to benefit from the profits earned by the S corporation, including the extent to which actual distributions of profits are made from the S corporation to the ESOP and the extent to which the ESOP's ownership interest in undistributed profits and future profits is subject to dilution as a result of synthetic equity. For example, the ESOP's ownership interest is not subject to dilution if the total amount of synthetic equity is a relatively small portion of the total number of shares and deemed-owned shares of the S corporation. [Treas. Reg. § 1.409(p)-1(g)(2)]

Taking into account the standard in the preceding paragraph, the principal purpose of the ownership structure of an S corporation constitutes an avoidance or evasion in any case in which:

1. The profits of the S corporation generated by the business activities of a specific individual or individuals are not provided to the ESOP, but are instead substantially accumulated and held for the benefit of that individual or individuals on a tax-deferred basis within an entity related to the S corporation, such as a partnership, trust, or corporation (such as in a subsidiary that is a disregarded entity), or any other method that has the same effect of segregating profits for the benefit of such individual or individuals (such as nonqualified deferred compensation);

2. The individual or individuals for whom profits are segregated have rights to acquire 50 percent or more of those profits directly or indirectly (for example, by purchase of the subsidiary); and

3. A nonallocation year would occur if the prohibited allocation rules were separately applied with respect to either the separate entity or whatever method has the effect of segregating profits for the individual or individuals, treating such entity as a separate S corporation owned by an ESOP (or, in the case of any other method of segregation of profits, by treating those profits as the only assets of a separate S corporation owned by an ESOP). [Treas. Reg. § 1.409(p)-1(g)(3)]

Any ownership structure described above results in a nonallocation year; and, in addition, under such ownership structure, each individual is treated as a disqualified person and that person's interest in the separate entity is treated as synthetic equity. IRS may provide that a nonallocation year occurs in any case in which the principal purpose of the ownership structure of an S corporation constitutes an avoidance or evasion of the prohibited allocation rules. For any year that is a nonallocation year, IRS may treat any person as a disqualified person. [I.R.C. § 409(p)(7)(B); Treas. Reg. § 1.409(p)-1(c)(3)]

For examples illustrating the prohibited allocation rules, see Q 28:4; and, for additional information on S corporation ESOPs, see Q 28:5.

Q 28:4   Has IRS provided examples regarding the S corporation ESOP prohibited allocation rules?

Yes. The following examples illustrate the application of the final regulations issued by IRS concerning the prohibited allocation rules (see Q 28:3).

Example 1. This example relates to the determination of disqualified persons and nonallocation year if there is no synthetic equity. CDL Corporation is a calendar-year S corporation that maintains an ESOP. CDL has a single class of common stock, of which there are a total of 1,200 shares outstanding, and has no synthetic equity. In 2010, individual A, who is not an employee of CDL (and is not related to any employee of the corporation), owns 100 shares directly, individual B, who is an employee of the corporation, owns 100 shares directly, and the remaining 1,000 shares are owned by the ESOP. The ESOP's 1,000 shares are allocated to the accounts of individuals who are employees of CDL (none of whom are related) as set forth in columns 1 and 2 in the following table:

1	2	3	4
	Deemed-Owned ESOP Shares	Percentage Deemed-Owned	Disqualified
Shareholders	(total of 1,000)	ESOP Shares	Person
B	330	33%	Yes
C	145	14.5%	Yes
D	75	7.5%	No
E	30	3%	No
F	20	2%	No
Other participants	400 (none exceeds 10 shares)	1% or less	No

As shown in column 4, individuals B and C are disqualified persons for 2010 because each owns at least 10 percent of CDL's deemed-owned ESOP shares. However, the synthetic equity shares owned by any person do not affect the calculation for any other person's ownership of shares. 2010 is not a nonallocation year because disqualified persons do not own at least 50 percent of CDL's outstanding shares (the 100 shares owned directly by B, B's 330 deemed-owned ESOP shares, plus C's 145 deemed-owned ESOP shares equal only 47.9 percent of the 1,200 outstanding shares of CDL).

Example 2. This example relates to the determination of disqualified persons and nonallocation year if there is synthetic equity. The facts are the same as in Example 1, except that, as shown in column 4, individuals E and F have options to acquire 110 and 130 shares, respectively, of CDL common stock from CDL:

1	2	3	4	5	6
Shareholders	Deemed-Owned ESOP Shares (total of 1,000)	Percentage Deemed-Owned ESOP Shares	Options (240)	Shareholder Percentage of Deemed-Owned ESOP plus Synthetic Equity Shares	Disqualifed Person
B	330	33%			Yes (col. 3)
C	145	14.5%			Yes (col. 3)
D	75	7.5%			No
E	30	3%	110	11.1% ([30 + 91.7] divided by 1,091.7)	Yes (col. 5)
F	20	2%	130	11.6% ([20 + 108.3] divided by 1,108.3)	Yes (col. 5)
Other participants	400 (none exceeds 10 shares)	1% or less			No

Individual E's synthetic equity shares are counted in determining whether E is a disqualified person for 2010, and individual F's synthetic equity shares are counted in determining whether F is a disqualified person for 2010. Therefore, E's option to acquire 110 shares of the S corporation converts into 91.7 shares of synthetic equity (110 times the ratio of the 1,000 deemed-owned ESOP shares to the sum of the 1,000 deemed-owned ESOP shares plus the 200 shares held outside the ESOP by A and B). Similarly, F's option to acquire 130 shares of the S corporation converts into 108.3 shares of synthetic equity (130 times the ratio of the 1,000 deemed-owned ESOP shares to the sum of the 1,000 deemed-owned ESOP shares plus the 200 shares held outside the ESOP by A and B). However, the synthetic equity shares owned by any person do not affect the calculation for any other person's ownership of shares. Accordingly, as shown in column 6, individuals B, C, E, and F are disqualified persons for 2010.

The 100 shares owned directly by B, B's 330 deemed-owned ESOP shares, C's 145 deemed-owned ESOP shares, E's 30 deemed-owned ESOP shares, E's 91.7 synthetic equity shares, F's 20 deemed-owned ESOP shares, plus F's 108.3 synthetic equity shares total 825 and equal 58.9 percent of 1,400, which is the sum of CDL's 1,200 outstanding shares and the 200 shares of synthetic equity shares of CDL held by disqualified persons. Thus, 2010 is a nonallocation year for CDL's ESOP because disqualified persons own at least 50 percent of the total shares of outstanding stock of CDL and the total synthetic equity shares of CDL held by disqualified persons. In addition, independent of the preceding conclusion, 2010 would be a nonallocation year because disqualified persons own at least 50 percent of CDL's outstanding shares because the 100 shares owned directly by B, B's 330 deemed-owned ESOP shares, C's 145 deemed-owned ESOP shares, E's 30 deemed-owned ESOP shares, plus F's 20 deemed-owned ESOP shares equal 52.1 percent of CDL's 1,200 outstanding shares.

Example 3. This example relates to the determination of the number of shares of synthetic equity. JKH Corporation is a calendar-year S corporation that maintains an ESOP. JKH has a single class of common stock of which there are a total of 1,000 shares outstanding, all of which are owned by the ESOP. JKH has no synthetic equity, except for four grants of nonqualified deferred compensation that are made to an individual during the period from 2006 through 2012, as set forth in column 2 in the following table, and the ESOP uses the special rules to determine the number of shares of synthetic equity owned by that individual with a determination date of January 1 and the triennial rule redetermining value, as shown in columns 4 and 5:

1	2	3	4	5
Determination Date	Present Value of Nonqualified Deferred Compensation on Determination Date	Share Value on Determination Date	New Shares of Synthetic Equity on Determination Date	Aggregate Number of Synthetic Equity Shares on Determination Date
January 1, 2006	A grant is made on January 1, 2006, with a present value of $1,000. An additional grant of nonqualified deferred compensation with a present value of $775 is made on March 1, 2006.	$10 per share	100	100

1	2	3	4	5
Determination Date	Present Value of Nonqualified Deferred Compensation on Determination Date	Share Value on Determination Date	New Shares of Synthetic Equity on Determination Date	Aggregate Number of Synthetic Equity Shares on Determination Date
January 1, 2007	An additional grant is made on December 31, 2006, with a present value of $800 on January 1, 2007. The March 1, 2006, grant has a present value on January 1, 2007, of $800.	$8 per share	200	300
January 1, 2008	No new grants made.	$12 per share		300
January 1, 2009	An additional grant is made on December 31, 2008, with a present value of $3,000 on January 1, 2009. The grants made during 2006 through 2008 have an aggregate present value on January 1, 2009, of $3,750.	$15 per share	200	450

1	2	3	4	5
Determination Date	Present Value of Nonqualified Deferred Compensation on Determination Date	Share Value on Determination Date	New Shares of Synthetic Equity on Determination Date	Aggregate Number of Synthetic Equity Shares on Determination Date
January 1, 2010	No new grants are made.	$11 per share		450
January 1, 2011	No new grants are made.	$22 per share		450
January 1, 2012	No new grants are made. The grants made during 2006 through 2009 have an aggregate present value on January 1, 2012, of $7,600.	$20 per share		380

The grant made on January 1, 2006, is treated as 100 shares until the determination date in 2009. The grant made on March 1, 2006, is not taken into account until the 2007 determination date, and its present value on that date, along with the then present value of the grant made on December 31, 2006, is treated as a number of shares that are based on the $8-per-share value on the 2007 determination date, with the resulting number of shares continuing to apply until the determination date in 2009. On the January 1, 2009, determination date, the grant made on the preceding day is taken into account at its present value of $3,000 on January 1, 2009, and the $15-per-share value on that date with the resulting number of shares (200) continuing to apply until the next determination date. In addition, on the January 1, 2009, determination date, the number of shares determined under other grants made between January 1, 2006, and December 31, 2008, must be revalued. Accordingly, the aggregate value of all nonqualified deferred compensation granted during that period is determined to be $3,750 on January 1, 2009, and the corresponding number of shares of synthetic equity based on the $15-per-share value is determined to be 250 shares on the 2009 determination date, with the resulting aggregate number of shares (450) continuing to apply until the determination date in 2012. On the January 1, 2012, determination date, the aggregate value of all nonqualified deferred compensation is determined to be $7,600, and the corresponding number of shares of synthetic equity based on the $20-per-share value on the 2012 determination date is determined to be 380 shares (with the resulting number of shares continuing to apply until the determination date in 2015, assuming no further grants are made).

See Q 28:5 for more information regarding ESOPs of S corporations.

Q 28:5   What has IRS done to stop abusive transactions involving S corporation ESOPs?

In addition to the regulations issued by IRS concerning prohibited allocations in S corporation ESOPs (see Qs 28:3, 28:4), IRS issued a ruling, effective for plan years ending after October 20, 2003, to shut down abusive transactions involving S corporation ESOPs, and such abusive transactions are listed transactions for tax-shelter disclosure purposes. [Rev. Rul. 2004-4, 2004-1 C.B. 414]

In the ruling, IRS describes three situations and asks (1) are the individuals disqualified persons, (2) does the related ESOP have a nonallocation year, and (3) are any disqualified persons treated as owning synthetic equity (see Q 28:3)?

Situation 1: Before 2003, Individuals A and B own, either directly or indirectly, in whole or in part, a domestic professional services corporation. In addition, before 2003, individuals C, D, and E each owns, either directly or indirectly, in whole or in part, his or her own domestic professional services corporation. A, B, C, D, and E (Taxpayers) are employees of their respective domestic professional services corporations (Service Recipient Corporations).

In 2003, a new corporation (S Corp.) is formed, and elects to be treated as an S corporation. S Corp. forms a subsidiary corporation for each Taxpayer (QSubs A through E) and files a qualified subchapter S subsidiary (QSub) election for each subsidiary. S Corp. contributes cash in exchange for 100 percent of the issued and outstanding stock of each QSub. Each Taxpayer is designated as an officer and investment manager for Taxpayer's respective QSub. In addition, each QSub grants its respective Taxpayer a nonqualified stock option to acquire substantially all or a majority of the shares of the QSub.

At the same time that S Corp. is formed, it establishes an ESOP, which holds 100 percent of the stock of S Corp. All the employees of S Corp. and the QSubs participate in the ESOP, with the exception of Taxpayers A through E.

Taxpayers A through E and their support staff terminate their existing employee relationship with their respective Service Recipient Corporations and become employees of the respective QSub. The customers of Taxpayers A through E stop doing business with the Service Recipient Corporations and begin doing business with the respective QSub of Taxpayers A through E.

Taxpayers A through E receive salary payments from their respective QSub in an amount substantially less than the income to S Corp. generated by the business activities of that Taxpayer after deduction for expenses. S Corp. treats the subsidiaries as valid QSubs and treats the income generated by each QSub each year, and earnings thereon, as earned by S Corp. The payments to the Taxpayers for current salary are deducted by S Corp. as an ordinary and necessary business expense. However, since S Corp. is wholly owned by the ESOP, S Corp.'s net earnings are not taxed currently.

Amounts of income to S Corp. generated by the business activities of each Taxpayer (net of expenses) but not paid to Taxpayers within two and one-half months after the end of the year accumulate in each Taxpayer's respective QSub, for example, in a brokerage account in each subsidiary, over which the respective Taxpayer has investment control as the investment manager of the subsidiary. A through E can access the amounts accumulated in their respective QSub by exercising their option to purchase shares in the QSub. If each Taxpayer's option to purchase shares of QSub stock were synthetic equity of S Corp., then each Taxpayer would own at least 10 percent of the sum of the outstanding shares of S Corp. plus the synthetic equity shares of S Corp.

Situation 2: The facts are the same as in Situation 1, except that instead of five individuals, there are 11 individuals (Taxpayers A through K) each of whom is an employee of a Service Recipient Corporation owned either directly or indirectly, in whole or in part, by the Taxpayer. As in Situation 1, amounts of income to S Corp. generated by the business activities of each Taxpayer (net of expenses) but not paid to the Taxpayer accumulate in each Taxpayer's respective QSub, and each Taxpayer has the right to acquire stock in that Taxpayer's QSub under the same terms as described in Situation 1. If each Taxpayer's option to purchase shares of QSub stock were synthetic equity of S Corp., then each Taxpayer would own less than 10 percent of the sum of the outstanding shares of S Corp. plus the synthetic equity shares of S Corp.

Situation 3: Before 2003, Corporation M is an S corporation with 200 employees, wholly owned by an ESOP that was established after March 14, 2001, in which substantially all of its employees participate. Before 2003, Individual A (Taxpayer) operated a professional services corporation as a separate business. In 2003, Corporation M forms a QSub for A by contributing cash in exchange for 100 percent of the issued and outstanding stock of the QSub. As in Situation 1, A and A's support staff terminate their existing employment relationship with A's Service Recipient Corporation and become employees of the QSub; A's customers become customers of the QSub; amounts of income to S Corp. generated by the business activities of A (net of expenses) but not paid to A accumulate in A's QSub; and A has the right to acquire stock in the QSub under the same terms as described in Situation 1. A does not participate in the Corporation M ESOP. If A's option to purchase shares of the QSub were synthetic equity of S Corp., then A would own less than 10 percent of the total of the outstanding shares of S Corp. plus the synthetic equity shares of S Corp.

In each situation described above, the ownership structure of the S corporation is designed to allow one or more Taxpayers, each operating a business for a Taxpayer's own benefit, to take advantage of the tax-exempt status of the S corporation that results from the ownership of its outstanding stock by the ESOP. The ownership structure thereby avoids current taxation of the profits of each Taxpayer's separate business, while each Taxpayer retains the right to at least 50 percent of the business through the right to acquire shares in the QSub. Because the profits of each business are being segregated and accumulated in each Taxpayer's QSub, the ESOP is owner of the business only in form, not in substance, to the extent that the Taxpayer has a right to the profits by exercising the Taxpayer's option to acquire the shares of the QSub. Thus, the ESOP is not providing benefits to rank-and-file employees that reflect its ownership share in the S corporation.

In Situation 1, each Taxpayer is using options on QSub stock to retain ownership of his or her separate business, with the profits of that business being segregated from the profits of the businesses of the other QSubs. In this way, the structure is designed to divert the profits of each business away from the ESOP. If each QSub were an S corporation directly owned by an ESOP, each Taxpayer's right to acquire shares of that corporation would be synthetic equity. Accordingly, the structure described in Situation 1 is similar to other forms of synthetic equity, such as the right to acquire stock in a related entity that is the only significant asset of an S corporation (owned by an ESOP). Further, the economic effect is similar to nonqualified deferred compensation for services rendered to the QSub which is declared to be synthetic equity.

Consequently, the options granted to each Taxpayer in Situation 1 to acquire shares in the QSub for that Taxpayer's business should be treated as synthetic equity in S Corp. Accordingly, IRS has determined that the options are synthetic equity. Because these options are synthetic equity in Situation 1, each Taxpayer is a 10 percent owner of the number of deemed-owned shares of S Corp. Taxpayers A through E are thus disqualified persons; and, because disqualified persons A through E own an aggregate of at least 50 percent of the shares, 2003 is an nonallocation year for the ESOP.

A group of individuals with the same right to acquire the accumulated profits of their businesses as described in Situation 1 should not avoid the application of the prohibited allocation rules merely because each individual's right to acquire the accumulated profits of that individual's business does not have a value equal to at least 10 percent of the value of S Corp. because more than ten separate businesses are combined (as described in Situation 2). In fact, Congress anticipated the combining of more than ten businesses as a means of avoiding the application of these rules and gave this ownership structure as an example of the type of situation where exercise of the authority granted to IRS would be appropriate.

Further, an individual with the same right to acquire the accumulated profits of that individual's business, similar to the rights described in Situation 1, should not avoid the application of the prohibited allocation rules merely because the business is combined, as in Situation 3, with the business of an S corporation owned by an ESOP that otherwise fulfills Congressional intent by providing broad-based coverage and benefits to rank-and-file employees. The rank-and-file employees in Situation 3 are not sharing in the profits of the

Taxpayer's separate business through the ESOP's ownership share to the extent that the profits of that business are being accumulated for the benefit of that Taxpayer. With respect to that Taxpayer's separate business, the ownership structure of the S corporation is designed to avoid or evade the application of these rules.

In all three situations, the accumulation of profits for the benefit of a specific individual is comparable to the operation of an S corporation owned by an ESOP. Moreover, as in Situation 1, if any one of these businesses were the only business activity of S Corp., the option held by the Taxpayers would be synthetic equity that would result in a nonallocation year and each Taxpayer being a disqualified person if those shares of synthetic equity were at least 50 percent of the shares of stock of S Corp. plus the total synthetic equity shares.

Accordingly, IRS has determined that a nonallocation year occurs and the individual is a disqualified person in any case in which (i) shares of an S corporation are employer securities held by an ESOP, (ii) the profits of the S corporation generated by the business activities of a specific individual are accumulated and held for the benefit of that individual in a QSub or similar entity (such as a limited liability company), (iii) these profits are not paid to the individual as compensation within two and one-half months after the end of the year in which earned, and (iv) the individual has rights to acquire shares of stock (or similar interests) of the QSub or similar entity representing 50 percent or more of the fair market value of the stock of such QSub or similar entity. In addition, IRS has determined that such individual's right to acquire shares of stock (or similar interests) of the QSub or similar entity is synthetic equity. For purposes of this paragraph, the rights of the individual are determined after taking into account the attribution rules.

As a result, in Situations 2 and 3, the Taxpayer's right to acquire the shares of the QSub is synthetic equity, each individual Taxpayer (A through K in Situation 2, and A in Situation 3) is a disqualified person, and a nonallocation year occurs. The respective Taxpayers in Situations 2 and 3 are disqualified persons regardless of whether, at any time, a particular Taxpayer owns synthetic equity shares of S Corp. equal to at least 10 percent of the sum of the outstanding shares of S Corp. plus the synthetic equity shares of S Corp.

The same conclusions would apply with respect to Situations 1, 2, and 3 even if the support staff of the Taxpayers were to continue to be employed by their respective Service Recipient Corporations, the Service Recipient Corporations were to continue to provide substantially the same services for their customers, any of the Taxpayers or their support staff were to be employees of S Corp. (instead of employees of a QSub), or any of the Taxpayers were to participate in the ESOP.

IRS intends to reflect the guidance in this ruling in regulations, effective for plan years ending after October 20, 2003. It is expected that the regulations will apply to similar transactions that have the effect of reserving profits from an individual's business activities to provide similar tax benefits to the individual, either with the use of a QSub or through the use of another method.

In appropriate cases, IRS may challenge other tax benefits claimed by any individual involved in this type of business structure. For example, in the appropriate case, IRS may take the position for income tax purposes that, even though the Taxpayer purported to transfer the business (including the employment of the support staff) to the QSub, the Taxpayer never relinquished ownership of the business and, therefore, should still be taxed on the profits. IRS might also take the position that the subsidiary is not a QSub. Alternatively, if the support staff of the Taxpayers were to continue to be employed by their respective Service Recipient Corporations and the Service Recipient Corporations were to continue to provide substantially the same services for their customers, IRS might assert that the Taxpayers continue to be employed by their respective Service Recipient Corporation, with the related tax consequences.

In conclusion:

1. With respect to Situation 1, (a) A through E are disqualified persons with respect to the ESOP, (b) the ESOP has a nonallocation year, and (c) the options to acquire stock in QSubs A through E are synthetic equity to which the excise tax applies (see Q 28:3)

2. With respect to Situation 2, (a) A through K are disqualified persons with respect to the ESOP, (b) the ESOP has a nonallocation year, and (c) A through K are each treated as owning synthetic equity in the form of each individual's option to acquire shares of the corresponding QSub.

3. With respect to Situation 3, (a) A is a disqualified person with respect to the ESOP, (b) the ESOP has a nonallocation year, and (c) A is treated as owning synthetic equity in the form of A's option to acquire shares of the corresponding QSub.

The ruling applies for plan years ending after October 20, 2003, but is not effective before March 15, 2004 if (1) all interests in a QSub held by individuals who would be disqualified persons under the ruling were distributed to those individuals as compensation on or before March 15, 2004 and (2) no such individual had been a participant in the ESOP at any time after October 20, 2003 and before March 15, 2004. In addition, for purposes of the excise tax, an individual's interest in a QSub that constituted synthetic equity under the ruling was disregarded to the extent such interest was distributed to the individual as compensation on or before March 15, 2004.

Arrangements that are the same as, or substantially similar to, the described transactions are listed transactions with respect to the S corporation and each individual who is a disqualified person under the ruling. [Treas. Reg. §§ 1.6011-4(b)(2), 301.6111-2(b)(2), 301.6112-1(b)(2)]

Independent of their classification as listed transactions, such transactions may already be subject to the disclosure requirements, the tax shelter registration requirements, or the list maintenance requirements. [I.R.C. §§ 6011, 6111, 6112] Persons required to register these tax shelters who have failed to do so may be subject to penalty, and persons required to maintain lists of investors who have failed to do so (or who fail to provide such lists when requested by IRS) may be subject to penalty. [I.R.C. §§ 6707(a), 6708(a)] In addition, IRS may impose penalties on parties involved in transactions or substantially similar transactions, including the accuracy-related penalty. [I.R.C. § 6662]

IRS has also issued guidance reflecting its attempt to challenge abusive tax avoidance transactions involving S corporations and tax-exempt entities. The targeted transactions are structured to improperly shift taxation away from taxable S corporation shareholders to an exempt party, such as a qualified retirement plan, in order to defer or avoid taxes. [IRS Notice 2004-30, 2004-1 C.B. 828]

IRS issued letters to approximately 1,700 businesses and retirement plan sponsors alerting them to new income and excise taxes applicable to S corporation ESOPs and warning of the consequences of participating in abusive schemes involving ESOPs and S corporations. The letters were mailed to S corporation ESOPs reporting ten or fewer participants. In addition, the IRS letters called attention to other abuses connected with S corporation ESOPs. The IRS determined that many existing arrangements designed to take advantage of the benefits of S corporation ESOP rules would not only involve taxation under the prohibited allocation rules but would also violate qualification requirements, such as the coverage rules (see Q 5:15). When an ESOP is not qualified under such circumstances, the subchapter S corporation may be taxable as a C corporation, and any highly compensated ESOP participant may be taxed on the value of such participant's account balance. [IR-2004-155 (Dec. 22, 2004)]

Q 28:6   How is an ESOP different from a stock bonus plan?

A stock bonus plan (see Q 2:13) permits, but does not require, current investments in employer securities (see Q 28:12). [Thompson, Jr. v. Avondale Indus., Inc., 2003 U.S. Dist. LEXIS 2318 (E.D. La. 2003)] An ESOP must invest primarily (see Q 28:1) in employer securities. [Priv. Ltr. Rul. 9724001] Further, an ESOP, but not a stock bonus plan, may borrow from the employer or use the employer's credit to acquire employer securities. [ERISA § 407(d)(6); I.R.C. § 4975(d)(3); Priv. Ltr. Rul. 200634061]

Q 28:7   What is an exempt loan?

Generally, the lending of money by the employer to a qualified retirement plan is a prohibited transaction (see Q 24:1). However, an employer's loan or guarantee of a loan to an ESOP will not be a prohibited transaction if the loan satisfies the requirements for being an exempt loan. The exempt loan requirements include the following:

1. The loan must be primarily for the benefit of participants and beneficiaries of the ESOP;

2. The proceeds of the loan must be used to acquire qualifying employer securities (see Q 28:8) or to repay an exempt loan or a prior exempt loan;

3. The interest rate of the loan must be reasonable;

4. The loan must be without recourse against the ESOP and without collateral other than qualifying employer securities acquired (or refinanced) with the proceeds of the exempt loan; and

5. The loan must provide for the release from encumbrance of employer securities used as collateral as the loan is repaid.

[I.R.C. § 4975(d)(3); Treas. Reg. §§ 54.4975-7(b), 54.4975-11(c); Priv. Ltr. Ruls. 200634061, 200223066, 9431055, 9417033, 9417032]

One court concluded that a bank which accepted employer securities as collateral for a loan to an ESOP was not entitled to funds in a malpractice settlement fund belonging to the ESOP because the funds did not represent proceeds of the pledged securities. The bank argued that it was entitled to the proceeds of the settlement fund because the fund represented collateral on the bank's loan to the ESOP. The court conceded that a security interest attaches to assets that replace damaged or destroyed collateral, but determined that the employer securities, which were the bank's collateral, were worthless from the time the bank acquired the securities. The fund, therefore, did not represent the diminished value of the securities, but a disposition of the malpractice liability of the ESOP's advisors. [McDannold v. Star Bank, N.A., 261 F.3d 478 (6th Cir. 2001)]

The refinancing of an exempt loan will not create a prohibited transaction if the refinancing is carried out primarily for the benefit of the ESOP participants and beneficiaries and satisfies the other requirements set forth above. [Priv. Ltr. Ruls. 9704030, 9704021, 9652024, 9610028, 9530015] DOL has stated that the obligations of a fiduciary under ERISA apply to the refinancing of an exempt loan and has set forth guidelines on how to comply with these fiduciary obligations. [ERISA §§ 404(a), 408(b)(3); DOL Reg. § 2550.408b-3; DOL Field Assistance Bull. 2002-1 (Sept. 26, 2002)] IRS has also ruled that extending the maturity date and repayment period of an ESOP loan did not cause the loan to lose its exempt status. [Priv. Ltr. Ruls. 9649050, 9645023] IRS concluded that a loan continued to be an exempt loan after the ESOP acquired common stock of its new parent corporation after a merger. [Priv. Ltr. Rul. 9608040] A subsidiary's exempt loan incurred to acquire its parent company's ESOP stock did not create a prohibited transaction when, once the subsidiary was sold, the parent redeemed the subsidiary's unallocated ESOP stock held in the plan suspense account as security for the ESOP loan repayment and used the proceeds received from the redemption to repay the loan. IRS also ruled that the redemption proceeds were a permissible source for the loan repayment. [Priv. Ltr. Ruls. 9701058, 9701048, 9621034]

DOL has opined that a loan to an ESOP is an exempt loan even if ESOP assets other than those pledged as collateral are used to repay the loan. However, if the employer securities purchased with the proceeds of the loan were not pledged as collateral, repayment of the loan could violate ERISA's general fiduciary responsibility rules. [DOL Op. Ltr. 93-35A; ERISA § 408(b)(3); DOL Reg. § 2550.408b-3(e)]

The sale of employer securities held in a suspense account (i.e., employer securities not yet allocated to participants) under the ESOP in order to repay an exempt loan with any excess funds being allocated to the participants just prior to the termination of the ESOP satisfied the requirement that the transaction be for the primary benefit of participants and beneficiaries. [Priv. Ltr. Ruls. 9837032, 9648054, 9640027, 9624002, 9437035] IRS has also ruled that an ESOP that was being terminated could sell employer securities held in the suspense account to the employer, use the proceeds to repay the exempt loan, and allocate the remaining employer securities to the participants with the allocations not being treated as annual additions (see Q 6:34). [Priv. Ltr. Ruls. 200733029, 200716027, 200536031, 200536028, 200321020, 200243055, 200213033, 200210065; Treas. Reg. § 1.415-6(b)(2)(i)] Where the ESOP was terminated for financial and business reasons, IRS ruled that the repayment of an exempt loan in connection with distributions from the plan did not cause the loan to violate the exemption requirements. [Priv. Ltr. Ruls. 200733029, 200408032] The proceeds from the sale of shares held by an ESOP, which resulted from the sale of the employer in a merger transaction, could be used to repay the plan's exempt loan without causing the loan to lose its exemption from the prohibited transaction rules. [Priv. Ltr. Rul. 200514026]

The amendment of an ESOP and the write-down of loans to the ESOP because of the decline in value of the employer securities did not cause the remaining ESOP loan to fail to qualify as an exempt loan. [Priv. Ltr. Ruls. 9506030, 9437039, 9237037] However, IRS has ruled that the accelerated release of employer securities held in a suspense account under the ESOP can cause the loan to fail to satisfy the requirements of an exempt loan. [Priv. Ltr. Rul. 9447057; Treas. Reg. § 54.4975-7(b)(8)(i)] On the other hand, IRS concluded that the accelerated payment of an exempt loan did not cause the loan to fail to satisfy the exemption requirements because the payment was primarily for the benefit of the ESOP participants, since it was made in connection with the merger of the ESOP into another qualified retirement plan. [Priv. Ltr. Rul. 200006054]

IRS has ruled that salary reduction contributions to a 401(k) plan (see Q 27:1) are *employer contributions* and may be used to repay an exempt loan [Priv. Ltr. Rul. 9503002], but DOL has suggested that these contributions are *employee contributions* and, as such, may cause a prohibited transaction to occur.

With respect to an ESOP maintained by an S corporation (see Q 28:2), rules similar to those applicable to C corporations now apply to S corporations so that an ESOP does not jeopardize its status as an ESOP or the loan's status as exempt merely because it uses distributions from the S corporation stock purchased with the loan proceeds to amortize the loan. This rule does not apply to distributions paid on stock that has been allocated to an employee's account, unless the plan provides that employer securities with a fair market value of not less than the amount of the dividend is allocated to the employee's account for the year in which the dividend would have been so allocated. [I.R.C. § 4975 (f)(7)]

Q 28:8   What are employer securities?

Employer securities include common stock issued by the employer that is readily tradable on an established securities market. If the employer has no readily tradable common stock, employer securities include employer-issued common stock that has a combination of voting power and dividend rights at least the equal of the class of common stock with the greatest voting power and the class of common stock with the greatest dividend rights. Noncallable preferred stock that is convertible into common stock that meets the requirements of employer securities also qualifies if the conversion price is reasonable. Nonvoting common stock of an employer is treated as employer securities if the employer has a class of nonvoting common stock outstanding and the specific shares that the plan acquires have been issued and outstanding for at least 24 months. [I.R.C. §§ 409(*l*), 4975(e)(8); Priv. Ltr. Rul. 200744021]

IRS has ruled that common stock of a corporation held by its subsidiary's ESOP that is traded over-the-counter on the National Association of Securities Dealers Automated Quotation (NASDAQ) Small Cap Market qualifies as employer securities readily tradable on an established securities market. [Priv. Ltr. Rul. 9529043; *see also* Priv. Ltr. Rul. 9514021] However, stock listed on the Over The Counter Bulletin Board (OTCBB) or the National Association of Securities Dealers (NASD) pink sheet is not readily tradable. [Priv. Ltr. Ruls. 200052014, 9036039, 8910067] IRS has also ruled that stock of a foreign corporation traded on the New York Stock Exchange was readily tradable employer securities. [Priv. Ltr. Rul. 200237026]

Employer securities also include stock issued by a member of a controlled group of corporations (see Q 5:31) that includes the employer if the stock meets the same requirements as qualifying employer-issued stock. If a U.S. corporation is a wholly owned subsidiary of a foreign corporation whose stock is not tradable on an established U.S. securities market, the U.S. subsidiary is deemed to have no readily tradable common stock and employer securities may include both stock of the foreign parent and stock of the U.S. subsidiary. [I.R.C. § 409(*l*); Priv. Ltr. Ruls. 9219038, 9135059, 8610082; *see also* Priv. Ltr. Rul. 200935046] Common stock of a parent corporation does not constitute employer securities with respect to the employees of a partnership partially owned by the parent's subsidiary because a partnership cannot be a member of a controlled group of corporations. Consequently, the employees of the partnership could not participate in the ESOP maintained by the parent corporation. [Gen. Couns. Mem. 39,880; Priv. Ltr. Rul. 9236042] However, IRS ruled otherwise where the two partners of the partnership were the parent corporation that maintained the ESOP and one of its wholly owned subsidiary corporations or were wholly owned subsidiary corporations of the parent corporation and the partnership elected to be classified as an association taxable as a corporation. [Treas. Reg. § 301.7701-3; Priv. Ltr. Ruls. 200008040, 199916055, *see also* Priv. Ltr. Rul. 200125090] IRS has also ruled that a limited liability company (LLC) wholly owned by a parent corporation and five LLCs owned by the first LLC were members of the parent corporation's controlled group for purposes of participating in the parent corporation's ESOP, even though five of the six LLCs had not elected to be classified as an association taxable as a corporation. [Priv. Ltr. Rul. 199949046; *see also* Priv. Ltr. Ruls. 200116051, 200111053]

An S corporation may not have more than one class of stock outstanding, although it may have voting common stock and nonvoting common stock as long as all other rights and preferences are identical (see Q 28:2).

Where an employer contributed shares of its stock to an ESOP, IRS concluded that, for purposes of determining whether such contribution was a prohibited transaction, the ERISA definition, and not the Code definition, applied to determine if the shares were qualifying employer securities (see Q 23:85). [Chief Couns. Adv. 200109010]

Q 28:9   What is the limitation on tax-deductible contributions to an ESOP?

Generally, the limitation on the deduction for employer contributions to an ESOP is 25 percent of covered compensation. [I.R.C. § 404(a)(3)] In addition to an employer being able to deduct up to 25 percent of covered compensation for contributions to a leveraged ESOP (an ESOP that borrows to acquire employer securities (see Q 28:7)) used to repay loan principal, the employer can also deduct an unlimited amount for contributions used to pay interest on the loan. [I.R.C. § 404(a)(9); Priv. Ltr. Ruls. 200732028, 200436015, 9548036]

Example. Ben-Jen Corporation contributes 30 percent of participants' compensation to its ESOP to repay principal and interest on the ESOP loan; 25 percent is used to repay loan principal; and 5 percent is used for interest payments. The entire 30 percent contribution is deductible.

See Q 28:2 for rules applicable to an ESOP maintained by an S corporation, and see chapter 12 for rules applicable to the deduction limitations.

Q 28:10   Are dividends paid on employer securities held by an ESOP ever deductible by the employer?

Yes. The employer may be allowed to deduct dividends it pays on employer securities (see Q 28:8) held by an ESOP that it maintains or held by an ESOP maintained by another member of a controlled group (see Qs 5:31, 28:8) that includes the employer. [Priv. Ltr. Ruls. 200350017, 200049041, 200006053, 200005039]

To be deductible, the dividend must be:

1. Paid in cash to the ESOP participants or their beneficiaries;
2. Paid to the ESOP and distributed to the participants or beneficiaries not later than 90 days after the close of the plan year in which paid; or
3. Used to make payments on an exempt loan. (For employer securities acquired by the ESOP after August 4, 1989, the deduction for dividends used for loan repayment is applicable only if the dividends are on

employer securities acquired with the proceeds of the loan being repaid.) [Priv. Ltr. Ruls. 200828036, 200828035, 199948029, 9701058]

The deduction is allowed for the taxable year of the employer during which the dividend is paid, distributed, or used to repay an exempt loan. [I.R.C. §§ 404(k), 409(*l*)(4); Priv. Ltr. Ruls. 200350017, 200033047, 200018056, 199938040, 199923047, 199921056, 199910057] Only the corporation paying the dividend is entitled to the deduction with respect to applicable employer securities (see Q 28:22) held by an ESOP. Thus, no deduction is permitted to a corporation maintaining the ESOP if that corporation does not pay the dividend. [Prop. Treas. Reg. § 1.404(k)-2, Q&A-1, Q&A-2]

> **Example.** S is a United States corporation that is wholly owned by P, an entity organized under the laws of a foreign country that is classified as a corporation for federal income tax purposes. P is not engaged in a United States trade or business and has a single class of common stock that is listed on a stock exchange in a foreign country. In addition, these shares are listed on the New York Stock Exchange, in the form of American Depositary Shares, and are actively traded through American Depositary Receipts (ADRs). S maintains an ESOP for its employees. The ESOP holds ADRs of P and receives a dividend with respect to those employer securities, and the dividends received by the ESOP constitute applicable dividends.
>
> P, as the payor of the dividend, is entitled to a deduction with respect to the dividends, although, as a foreign corporation, P does not obtain a United States tax benefit from the deduction. No corporation other than the corporation paying the dividend is entitled to the deduction; thus, because S did not pay the dividends, S is not entitled to a deduction. The answer would be the same if P is a United States C corporation.

If dividends on employer securities allocated to a participant are used to repay an exempt loan, the ESOP must provide that employer securities with a fair market value equal to the dividends be allocated to such participant in lieu of the dividends. [I.R.C. § 404(k)(2)(B); Priv. Ltr. Rul. 9132024] When convertible preferred stock was sold by shareholders to an ESOP, IRS ruled that dividends paid by the employer and used to make loans to the ESOP to purchase the stock were deductible dividends. [Priv. Ltr. Rul. 9836022]

An employer's cash distribution to an ESOP in redemption of a portion of the ESOP's stock may be considered a dividend and deductible by the employer. [I.R.C. §§ 301, 302, 316; Priv. Ltr. Rul. 9211006] An employer which redeemed stock from its ESOP in an amount equal in value to a participant's vested account balance upon a termination of employment was allowed to claim a paid dividend deduction. The court concluded that the stock was owned by the ESOP rather than by the participants, the redemption was essentially equivalent to a dividend, and the redemption did not result in a meaningful reduction of the ESOP's proportionate interest in the employer. [Boise Cascade Corp. v. United States, 329 F.3d 751 (9th Cir. 2003)]. To the contrary, IRS has ruled that amounts paid by an employer to redeem stock from its ESOP pursuant to a participant's election are payments in exchange for stock and not deductible dividends (see Q 28:23). [Rev. Rul. 2001-6, 2001-1 C.B. 491; Priv. Ltr. Rul. 9612001; *see also* Nestlé Purina Petcare Co. v. Comm'r, 09-1381 (8th Cir. 2010); Conopco, Inc. v. United States, 07-3564 (3d Cir. 2009), General Mills, Inc. v. United States, 08-1638 (8th Cir. 2009), and Chrysler Corp. v. Comm'r, No. 03-1214 (6th Cir. 2006)] Additional arguments advanced by IRS to support its position that redemption payments are not deductible dividends are:

1. The payments in redemption of stock are not dividends and, therefore, cannot be deducted as applicable dividends (see Qs 28:14, 28:15);

2. Even if the payments are dividends, they are nondeductible stock reacquisition expenses; and

3. Treating such payments as deductible dividends is inappropriate because such treatment would vitiate important protections for ESOP participants and would duplicate an earlier deduction by the corporation for the same economic expense (e.g., a deduction for a prior contribution of stock that is being redeemed). [I.R.C. §§ 162(k), 404(a), 404(k); IRS Chief Counsel Notice CC-2004-038 (Oct. 1, 2004)]

It is important to note that IRS has authority to disallow the deduction if the dividends constitute an evasion of taxation or are unreasonably excessive in amount (see Q 28:23). [I.R.C. § 404(k)(5)(A); Steel Balls, Inc. v. Comm'r, 95-3431 (8th Cir. 1996); Priv. Ltr. Rul. 9304003]

Example. Lev-Hep Corporation repays an exempt loan with dividends on employer securities acquired with the exempt loan proceeds. Because the dividend rate is 70 percent, an extraordinary dividend far in excess of the dividend Lev-Hep Corporation can be reasonably expected to pay on a recurring basis, the dividends are not deductible.

Under final regulations issued by IRS, payments to reacquire stock held by an ESOP, including reacquisition payments that are used to make benefit distributions to participants or beneficiaries, are not deductible because those payments do not constitute applicable dividends and the treatment of those payments as applicable dividends would constitute, in substance, an avoidance or evasion of taxation. The final regulations apply with respect to payments to reacquire stock that are made on or after August 30, 2006. [Treas. Reg. § 1.404(k)-3, Q&A-1, Q&A-2] With respect to amounts paid or received on or after August 30, 2006, no deduction that would otherwise be allowable is allowed for any amount paid or incurred by a corporation in connection with the reacquisition of its stock or the stock of any related person. Amounts paid or incurred in connection with the reacquisition of stock include amounts paid by a corporation to reacquire its stock from an ESOP. This prohibition, however, does not apply to any:

1. Deduction allowable for interest;

2. Deduction for amounts that are properly allocable to indebtedness and amortized over the term of such indebtedness;

3. Deduction for dividends paid (within the meaning of Section 561); or

4. Amount paid or incurred in connection with the redemption of any stock in a regulated investment company that issues only stock which is

redeemable upon the demand of the shareholder. [I.R.C. §§ 163, 404(k)
(2)(A), 465(b)(3)(C); Treas. Reg. § 1.162(k)-1]

Although dividends paid on employer securities held by an ESOP may be
deductible by the employer from gross income, they are not deductible for
alternative minimum tax purposes. [Schuler Indus., Inc. v. United States, 109
F.3d 753 (Fed Cir. 1997); Snap-Drape, Inc. v. Comm'r, 98 F.3d 194 (5th Cir.
1996); Illinois Cereal Mills, Inc. v. United States, 93-2223 (C.D. Ill. 1994); Treas.
Reg. § 1.56(g)-1(d)(3)(iii)(E)] In addition, the deductibility of dividends may be
subject to the uniform capitalization rules (see Q 12:22). [Field Serv. Adv.
200137016]

See Q 28:2 for rules applicable to an ESOP maintained by an S corporation.

In addition to the deductions permitted for dividends paid with respect to
employer securities that are held by an ESOP, an employer is entitled to deduct
dividends that, at the election of plan participants or their beneficiaries, are (1)
payable in cash directly to plan participants or beneficiaries, (2) paid to the plan
and subsequently distributed to the participants or beneficiaries in cash no later
than 90 days after the close of the plan year in which the dividends are paid to
the plan, or (3) paid to the plan and reinvested in qualifying employer securities.
Dividends reinvested in qualifying employer securities must be 100 percent
vested (see Q 28:21). IRS is authorized to disallow the deduction for any ESOP
dividend if it determines that the dividend constitutes, in substance, the
avoidance or evasion of taxation (see Q 28:23). [I.R.C. §§ 404(k)(2)(A),
404(k)(4)(B), 404(k)(5)(A), 404(k)(7); Priv. Ltr. Rul. 200350017]

IRS has issued guidance on the deduction for reinvested dividends. See Qs
28:13 through 28:25 for details.

Q 28:11   Are dividends paid to participants deductible even if participants can elect whether or not to receive them in a current cash payment?

Yes. Dividends actually paid in cash to plan participants are deductible
despite a plan provision that permits participants to elect to receive or not to
receive payment of dividends. [I.R.C. § 404(k)(2)(A)(iii); IRS Notice 2002-2,
2002-1 C.B. 285, Q&A-1(a); Priv. Ltr. Rul. 9618009; *see also* Priv. Ltr. Ruls.
200350017, 200018056, 199938040]

See Q 28:2 for rules applicable to an ESOP maintained by an S corporation
and 28:13 through 28:25 for new rules relating to dividends reinvested in
employer securities.

Q 28:12   How are dividends paid to ESOP participants taxed?

Dividends paid in cash directly to ESOP participants by the employer and
dividends paid to the ESOP and then distributed in cash to participants are
treated as paid separately from any other payments from the ESOP. Thus, a
deductible dividend is treated as a plan distribution and as paid under a separate

contract providing only for payment of deductible dividends. A deductible dividend is a taxable distribution even though an employee has basis (see Q 13:3), but the distribution is not subject to the 10 percent tax on early distributions (see Qs 16:1, 16:18, 28:19). [I.R.C. §§ 72(e)(5)(D), 72(t)(2)(A)(vi), 402; Temp. Treas. Reg. § 1.404(k)-1T, Q&A-3]; IRS has ruled that dividends paid in cash to ESOP participants are not wages subject to the FICA tax. [Priv. Ltr. Rul. 200033047; I.R.C. §§ 3101, 3111]

A distribution of a participant's entire account balance from an ESOP is eligible for treatment as a lump-sum distribution (see Qs 13:5, 13:18, 28:71) even if the participant received dividend distributions with respect to employer securities held by the ESOP in earlier years. [Priv. Ltr. Ruls. 199947041, 9045048, 9024083]

For distributions made before 2009, employers must report deductible dividends on Form 1099-DIV; but, if the dividend is paid in the same year that a total distribution is made to the participant, the entire amount should be reported on Form 1099-R. Participants must report the dividend distribution on their tax returns as a plan distribution and not as investment income. IRS is directed to establish procedures for information returns and reports with respect to deductible dividend payments. [I.R.C. § 6047(e); Ann. 85-168, 1985-48 I.R.B. 40; Ann. 85-180, 1985-1 C.B. 24] However, distributions from a plan that are made in 2009 or later years and that are deductible dividends must be reported on a Form 1099-R that does not report any other distributions in accordance with the instructions to the form. Accordingly, if there are other distributions from the plan in such years that are not deductible dividends, they must be reported on a separate Form 1099-R. It is anticipated that the instructions will require a special code in box 7 of the form to indicate the special tax treatment and rollover restrictions applicable to deductible dividends. Payments of deductible dividends made directly from the corporation to the plan participants or their beneficiaries are reported on Form 1099-DIV in accordance with the instructions to that form. [Ann. 2008-56, 2008-2 C.B. 1192]

Q 28:13   What is the effective date of the deduction for reinvested dividends?

A deduction for applicable dividends (see Q 28:15) paid on applicable employer securities (see Q 28:22) of a C corporation held by an ESOP is permitted. Effective for taxable years of the corporation beginning on or after January 1, 2002, the definition of applicable dividend has been amended to allow a deduction for dividends paid on applicable employer securities held by the ESOP and with respect to which participants or beneficiaries are provided an election to have the dividend paid in cash, paid to the ESOP and distributed in cash not later than 90 days after the close of the plan year in which paid, or paid to the ESOP and reinvested in qualifying employer securities (see Q 28:8). The deduction is available both with respect to dividends that the participant or beneficiary elects to reinvest and with respect to dividends that the participant or beneficiary elects to receive in cash. [I.R.C. § 404(k)(2)(A); IRS Notice 2002-2, sec. II, 2002-1 C.B. 285; Priv. Ltr. Rul. 200350017]

In order for dividends with respect to which an election is provided to be applicable dividends for a taxable year beginning on or after January 1, 2002, the election provided must comply with certain requirements (see Qs 28:14, 28:15). [IRS Notice 2002-2, Q&A-1(a), 2002-1 C.B. 285]

A dividend subject to an election by ESOP participants is an applicable dividend if the election provided with respect to the dividend complies with certain requirements, and if, based on the timing rules (see Q 28:16), the deduction for the dividend is allowed for a taxable year beginning on or after January 1, 2002. [IRS Notice 2002-2, Q&A-1(b), 2002-1 C.B. 285]

Q 28:14   What dividend elections can be offered to ESOP participants?

The election provided to ESOP participants with respect to dividends paid on applicable employer securities (see Q 28:22) must be offered in accordance with the terms of the plan and offer participants an election between:

1. Either (a) the payment of dividends in cash to participants or (b) the payment to the ESOP and distribution in cash to participants not later than 90 days after the close of the plan year in which the dividends are paid by the corporation, and

2. The payment of dividends to the ESOP and reinvestment in employer securities.

An ESOP can also offer participants a choice among the options described in 1 and the option described in 2. [I.R.C. § 404(k)(2)(A)(iii); IRS Notice 2002-2, Q&A-2, 2002-1 C.B. 285; Priv. Ltr. Rul. 200350017]

Q 28:15   What are the requirements for participant elections?

In order for dividends subject to an election to be applicable dividends, the election must be provided in a manner that satisfies the following requirements:

1. A participant must be given a reasonable opportunity before a dividend is paid or distributed in which to make the election.

2. A participant must have a reasonable opportunity to change a dividend election at least annually.

3. If there is a change in the plan terms governing the manner in which the dividends are paid or distributed to participants, a participant must be given a reasonable opportunity to make an election under the new plan terms prior to the date on which the first dividend subject to the new plan terms is paid or distributed.

An ESOP does not fail to comply with these requirements solely because it provides that, if a participant fails to make an affirmative dividend election, one of the options offered to participants is treated as a default election. [I.R.C. § 404(k)(2)(A)(iii); IRS Notice 2002-2, Q&A-3, 2002-1 C.B. 285]

Q 28:16   When are dividends with respect to which an election is provided deductible?

Dividends reinvested in employer securities (see Q 28:8) pursuant to an election (see Q 28:15) are deductible in the *later* of the taxable year of the corporation in which (1) the dividends are reinvested in employer securities at the participant's election or (2) the participant's election become irrevocable. An election is not considered made until the date the election becomes irrevocable. Therefore, dividends are not considered to be reinvested at the participant's election prior to the time when the participant's election becomes irrevocable (see the example in Q 28:17). Dividends paid to participants or paid to the ESOP and distributed to participants within 90 days after the end of the plan year are deductible in the taxable year of the corporation in which the dividend is paid or distributed to the participant. [I.R.C. § 404(k)(2)(A)(iii); IRS Notice 2002-2, Q&A-4, 2002-1 C.B. 285; Priv. Ltr. Rul. 200350017]

See Q 28:10 for a discussion of regulations relating to which corporation may take the deduction and the accompanying example.

Q 28:17   Where dividends on employer securities are paid to participants, can earnings on these dividends also be deducted?

A deduction for dividends paid on applicable employer securities (see Q 28:22) is allowed where the dividends are paid to participants by the ESOP not later than 90 days after the close of the plan year in which the dividends are paid by the corporation. [I.R.C. § 404(k)(2)(A)(ii)]

Earnings on dividends held in the plan do not constitute dividends and, accordingly, are not deductible. Investment losses attributable to the dividends, or the reduction of the dividend amount paid to the ESOP by the corporation through tax withholding (e.g., by a foreign country with respect to dividends paid by a foreign corporation) or other means, reduce the amount of dividend that is available for reinvestment or distribution to participants and therefore reduce the amount that is deductible. [IRS Notice 2002-2, Q&A-5(a), 2002-1 C.B. 285]

For example, assume that dividends of $2 per share are paid to an ESOP and invested in employer securities prior to the time when participants elect either to have the dividends reinvested in employer securities or to receive a distribution of the dividends within 90 days after the end of the plan year. During the period between when the dividends are paid by the corporation to the ESOP and when participant elections become irrevocable, the fund suffers investment losses of 50 percent, so that the amount of the dividend remaining is $1 per share. The deduction available with respect to participants who elect reinvestment is determined based on $1 of dividends per share. During the period between when participant elections become irrevocable and dividends are distributed to participants who elect a distribution, the fund suffers further losses, so that the amount of the dividend remaining is $.75. The ESOP pays the remaining dividends ($.75 per share) and is allowed a deduction with respect to participants who elect a distribution based on a dividend of $.75 per share, regardless of whether nondividend amounts are paid to participants by the ESOP.

A plan is not treated as violating certain requirements of the Code merely by reason of any payments of an applicable dividend (see Q 28:15). The distribution of amounts not attributable to dividends from a participant's account does not constitute a payment or distribution of an applicable dividend and, accordingly, could be treated as violating these requirements. [I.R.C. §§ 404(k)(2)(A), 404(k)(5)(B); IRS Notice 2002-2, Q&A-5(a), 2002-1 C.B. 285]

> **Example.** Carmine Corporation is a calendar year C corporation that maintains an ESOP that accumulates dividends during the year for distribution within 90 days after the end of the plan year. In 2010, the ESOP is amended to provide participants with an election with respect to dividends paid by Carmine Corporation in 2010. A participant's election to have a dividend distributed or reinvested in employer securities becomes irrevocable when the dividend is paid to the ESOP. The ESOP provides that dividends are invested in employer securities as soon as possible after the dividend is paid to the ESOP for those participants who elect to have dividends reinvested in employer securities. All 2010 dividends that participants elect to reinvest are actually reinvested in employer securities during 2010. The ESOP also provides that the dividends to be distributed based on participant elections are invested in a short-term investment fund. This fund does not incur losses prior to the distribution of the dividends. Distributions are made to participants during the first 90 days of 2011.
>
> Carmine Corporation is entitled to a deduction for 2010 for the amount of the dividends reinvested in employer securities in 2010. Carmine Corporation is also entitled to a deduction for 2011 for the amount of dividends distributed to participants in 2011. Because Carmine Corporation did not incur any losses with respect to the dividends that were accumulated for distribution, Carmine Corporation's deduction is equal to the dividends paid by it.

Q 28:18   How are dividends that are paid or reinvested treated?

The payment or reinvestment of dividends subject to an election (see Q 28:14) does not constitute an employer contribution, employee contribution, or forfeiture for annual addition limitation purposes (see Q 6:34); and, consequently, these dividends are not annual additions. In addition, these dividends are not elective deferrals, elective contributions, or employee contributions (see Q 27:77). [I.R.C. §§ 401(k), 401(m), 402(g), 404(k)(2)(A)(iii), 415(c); IRS Notice 2002-2, Q&A-6, 2002-1 C.B. 285]

Q 28:19   If, pursuant to an election, dividends are paid to the plan and reinvested in qualifying employer securities, how are those dividends treated under the ESOP?

Dividends that are reinvested in qualifying employer securities (see Q 28:8) at the participant's election (see Qs 28:14, 28:15) lose their identity as dividends and are treated as earnings in the same manner as dividends with respect to which a participant is not provided an election. Therefore, for example, dividends reinvested at a participant's election are no longer eligible for the exception to the 10 percent tax on early distributions (see Q 16:18). Similarly, such amounts are no longer treated as dividends for other purposes.

In contrast, dividends paid in cash to a participant pursuant to an election are taxable (see Q 28:12) and are not subject to the consent requirements (see Q 10:21) or the restrictions on distributions from 401(k) plans (see Q 27:14). In addition, dividends paid to participants are not eligible rollover distributions (see Q 34:9), even if the dividends are distributed at the same time as amounts that do constitute an eligible rollover distribution. Therefore, if, prior to the date a participant receives a distribution, such participant has made an irrevocable election offered by the ESOP to have dividends distributed (see Qs 28:14–28:16), any dividends subject to that election are distributed as dividends and are not eligible rollover distributions. The corporation is allowed a deduction with respect to such dividends for the year in which the distribution is paid to the participant.

[I.R.C. § 404(k)(2)(A)(iii); IRS Notice 2002-2, Q&A-7, 2002-1 C.B. 285]

Q 28:20   How do ESOP dividends affect hardship distributions?

A distribution is made on account of hardship from a 401(k) plan (see Q 27:1) only if the distribution is made on account of an immediate and heavy financial need of the employee and is necessary to satisfy the financial need. A distribution is deemed necessary to satisfy an immediate and heavy financial need of an employee if the employee has obtained all distributions currently available under all plans maintained by the employer (see Q 27:14). For purposes of satisfying these hardship distribution requirements, a participant in an ESOP that offers a dividend reinvestment election (see Qs 28:14, 28:15) must elect to receive dividends to the extent currently available to the participant under the ESOP. [IRS Notice 2002-2, Q&A-8, 2002-1 C.B. 285]

Q 28:21   What are the vesting requirements for dividends with respect to which a corporation is allowed a deduction?

Participants must be fully vested (see Q 9:1) in dividends with respect to which a corporation claims a deduction. Since a corporation is permitted to offer participants an election between receipt of a dividend in cash or reinvestment in employer securities (see Q 28:8) under the ESOP and is allowed a deduction without regard to the participant's election (see Qs 28:14, 28:15), an ESOP must provide that a participant is fully vested in any dividend with respect to which the participant is offered an election. An ESOP can comply with this requirement by providing that participants are fully vested in dividends with respect to which an election is offered, without regard to whether the participant is vested in the employer securities with respect to which the dividend is paid. Alternatively, an ESOP can comply with this requirement by offering an election only to vested participants. [I.R.C. §§ 404(k)(2)(B)(iii), 404(k)(7); Treas. Reg. § 1.401(a)(4)-4(b)(2)(ii)(2)(B); IRS Notice 2002-2, Q&A-9, 2002-1 C.B. 285]

Q 28:22   In order for an applicable dividend to be deductible, when must the plan be an ESOP?

The applicable dividends (see Qs 28:13, 28:14) must be paid with respect to applicable employer securities. Applicable employer securities are employer securities (see Q 28:8) held on the record date for a dividend by an ESOP maintained by the corporation paying such dividend or any other corporation which is a member of the controlled group of corporations that includes such corporation (see Q 5:31). In order to satisfy this requirement, the ESOP must be designated as an ESOP no later than the record date for such dividend and must comply with other requirements as of a date no later than the record date. The retroactive designation of a plan as an ESOP does not satisfy the requirement that a plan be designated as an ESOP no later than the record date. [I.R.C. §§ 404(k)(1), 404(k)(3), 409(*l*)(4), 4975(e); IRS Notice 2002-2, Q&A-10, 2002-1 C.B. 285]

Q 28:23   When does the payment of a dividend constitute an avoidance or evasion of taxation?

IRS may disallow a deduction for any dividend if it determines that the dividend constitutes, in substance, an avoidance or evasion of taxation. This includes the authority to disallow a deduction for unreasonable dividends. With respect to reinvested dividends (see Q 28:14), a dividend paid on common stock that is primarily and regularly traded on an established securities market is presumed to be a reasonable dividend. In the case of a corporation with no outstanding common stock (determined on a controlled group basis; see Q 5:31) that is primarily and regularly traded on an established securities market, a determination regarding whether the dividend is reasonable is made by comparing the dividend rate on the stock held by the ESOP with the dividend rate for common stock of comparable corporations whose stock is primarily and regularly traded on an established securities market. Whether a closely held corporation is comparable to a corporation whose stock is primarily and regularly traded on an established securities market is determined by comparing relevant corporate characteristics such as industry, size of the corporation, earnings, debt-equity structure, and dividend history.

It is the position of IRS that payments in redemption of stock held by an ESOP that are used to make distributions to terminating ESOP participants constitute an evasion of taxation and are not applicable dividends. Moreover, any deduction for such payments in redemption of stock is barred (see Q 28:10). The final regulations (see Q 28:10) issued by IRS apply to amounts paid or received on or after August 30, 2006, and with respect to payments to reacquire stock that are made on or after August 30, 2006. [I.R.C. §§ 162(k), 404(k)(2)(A)(iii), 404(k)(5)(A); Treas. Reg. §§ 1.162(k)-1, 1.404(k)-3, Q&A-1, Q&A-2, 54.49757-(b)(1)(iv); Rev. Rul. 2001-6, 2001-1 C.B. 491; IRS Chief Counsel Notice CC-2004-038 (Oct. 1, 2004)]

Q 28:24 Can an ESOP offer a dividend election to a participant who has terminated employment?

A participant who terminates employment but does *not* receive a distribution of benefits continues to be a participant in the ESOP. An ESOP may provide that the same election (see Q 28:14) is offered to all participants, including both active participants and participants who are no longer active participants in the ESOP, and the corporation is allowed a deduction with respect to all dividends subject to the election. [I.R.C. § 404(k)(2)(A)(iii); Treas. Reg. §§ 1.401(a)(4)-5(d), 1.410(b)-2(c)(1); IRS Notice 2002-2, Q&A-12, 2002-1 C.B. 285]

Q 28:25 When does an ESOP have to be amended for the changes made by EGTRRA 2001?

IRS has implemented a system that staggers remedial amendment periods for individually designed plans (see Q 2:26). This new system establishes regular five-year cycles for plan amendments and determination letter renewals for individually designed plans. An ESOP is subject to these five-year cycles, which are based on employer identification numbers (EINs). On February 1, 2006, IRS began accepting applications for determination letters for individually designed plans that took into account the requirements of EGTRRA 2001 as well as other changes and qualification requirements. [Rev. Proc. 2005-66, 2005-2 C.B. 509] See Q 18:7 for details.

For purposes of determining whether a plan provision is a disqualifying provision, a plan sponsor will not fail to have adopted a timely good faith amendment solely because the amendment does not specifically address the IRS guidance. For example, an amendment does not fail to be a timely good faith amendment solely because it does not address vesting of dividends with respect to which an election is provided (see Q 28:21). However, the plan must operate in accordance with the IRS guidance, effective as of January 1, 2002.

[I.R.C. §§ 401(b), 4975(e); Rev. Proc. 2004-25, 2004-1 C.B. 791; IRS Notice 2002-2, Q&A-13, 2002-1 C.B. 285; IRS Notice 2001-42, 2001-2 C.B. 70]

Q 28:26 What is the limit on the amount that may be added to an ESOP participant's account each year?

The amount that can be added to a participant's account (the annual addition) is limited to the lesser of $40,000 (adjusted for inflation) or 100 percent of the participant's compensation (see Qs 6:12, 6:34). [I.R.C. §§ 415(c)(1), 415(c)(2); Treas. Reg. § 1.415(c)-1(f)(2)(i)]

If no more than one-third of the employer's contributions for the year are allocated to HCEs (see Q 3:3), contributions applied to pay interest on a loan, as well as forfeitures of ESOP stock acquired through a loan, are disregarded for purposes of computing the annual addition. [I.R.C. § 415(c)(6); Treas. Reg. § 1.415(c)-1(f)(3); Priv. Ltr. Rul. 200014043] If forfeitures are not disregarded, the annual addition amount is based upon the fair market value of the forfeitures on the date of allocation. [Priv. Ltr. Rul. 9638046] For purposes of calculating the annual addition, an ESOP may provide for the release of employee securities (see Q 28:8) from the suspense account (see Q 28:7) based upon their fair market value rather than their original purchase price. [Treas. Reg. § 1.415(c)-1(f)(2)(ii)]

Dividends on employer securities (see Q 28:8) held by an ESOP may not be considered part of the annual addition (see Q 28:18) so that contributions to an ESOP might be effectively increased; however, in one case, the dividends were so excessive in amount that the court agreed with IRS that the dividends were part of the annual addition and disqualified the ESOP (see Qs 1:5, 1:6). [I.R.C. § 404(k); Steel Balls, Inc. v. Comm'r, 95-3431 (8th Cir. 1996)] Only compensation paid in the course of employment with the employer maintaining the ESOP is considered; commissions, bonuses, and management fees paid to an employee as an independent contractor are not included as compensation. Thus, where plan contributions allocated to the account of a participant exceeded the annual addition limitation, the ESOP lost its qualified status. [Van Roekel Farms, Inc. v. Comm'r, 2001 U.S. App. LEXIS 14201 (8th Cir. 2001); Howard E. Clendenen, Inc. v. Comm'r, 207 F.3d 1071(8th Cir. 2000); Roblene, Inc, 77 T.C.M. 1998 (1999)]

IRS has ruled that, where an employer used loan proceeds to distribute excess capital to its ESOP and a portion of the distribution attributable to allocated stock was paid to participant accounts, the distribution was not an annual addition because it was not an employer or employee contribution or a forfeiture. [Priv. Ltr. Rul. 9801030; *see also* Priv. Ltr. Ruls. 200213033, 200210065, 200147056, 200034039]

IRS has also ruled that the receipt of foreign earned income by participants in a corporation's ESOP while the participants were employed by the corporation's subsidiary did not adversely affect the qualified status of the plan. [Priv. Ltr. Rul. 200205050]

Q 28:27 Can a company obtain a tax deduction for stock contributions to its ESOP?

Yes. One of the basic advantages of using an ESOP is the ability to use either cash or employer securities (see Q 28:8) for the company's contributions. A company strapped for cash can make its contributions in authorized but unissued securities and still get a tax deduction for the full amount of the contribution. Thus, for example, a company with an annual payroll of $500,000 that contributes $125,000 (25 percent of $500,000) to its ESOP in the form of employer securities is allowed a tax deduction of $125,000. The contribution in the form of employer securities not only keeps cash in the company but also provides a cash flow from the tax savings realized by the deduction.

The amount of the contribution is the fair market value of the employer securities even though there is no cost to the company (see Q 12:5). [J.P. Emco v. United States, 90-617T (Fed. Cl. 1996)]

Note, however, that a contribution of employer securities to a money purchase pension ESOP could be a prohibited transaction (see Q 24:19).

Q 28:28   Can an ESOP provide for permitted disparity?

A qualified retirement plan designated as an ESOP after November 1, 1977, may not provide for permitted disparity (i.e., integration with Social Security; see chapter 7). An ESOP providing for permitted disparity before that date can continue to do so, but the plan cannot be amended to increase the integration level or the integration percentage. [Treas. Reg. § 54.4975-11(a)(7)(ii)]

Q 28:29   How can a company use an ESOP to help finance the acquisition of another company?

A purchasing company that needs cash to acquire another company (the target) may obtain the necessary cash by arranging a bank loan to its ESOP. The ESOP gets the borrowed cash to the purchasing company by buying employer securities (see Q 28:8) of the purchasing company. The purchasing company then buys the target's assets or stock with the cash. The bank loan is paid off through tax-deductible cash contributions by the purchasing company to the ESOP.

Another approach is to have the ESOP itself buy the stock of the target with the borrowed funds, and then exchange the target stock for newly issued stock of its own company. This approach is riskier, however, because the exchange of stock may be considered a prohibited transaction under ERISA (see Q 24:1). Before proceeding in this way, a DOL exemption request should be considered (see Q 24:20).

A third approach is for the company itself to borrow the cash and buy the target directly, using the cash flow created by a tax deduction for the stock contributions to the ESOP to help finance the purchase. This approach has the advantages of avoiding prohibited-transaction problems and producing less dilution of the purchasing company's stock.

An ESOP of a company that was acquired by another company was treated as a qualified retirement plan and an ESOP because it was not a mere conduit for the acquiring company's ESOP. The acquisition required the acquired company to establish an ESOP with the intention to merge its ESOP into the acquiring company's previously established ESOP, and the merging of the two ESOPs resulted in an entity consisting of the assets and liabilities of both plans. IRS ruled that the acquired company's ESOP did not violate the exclusive benefit rule (see Q 4:1) even though the acquired company's ESOP was created primarily to allow shareholders to claim favorable tax treatment (see Q 28:34) and even though the ESOP was never intended to be a permanent program. [Priv. Ltr. Rul. 9705004]

Q 28:30   Are ESOPs used by publicly traded companies to defend against unwanted takeovers?

Yes. By establishing an ESOP that purchases stock on the open market, management hopes to place a block of stock in the presumably friendly hands of its employees. However, to the extent that publicly traded stock (i.e., a registration-type class of securities) is allocated to participants, each participant must be given the opportunity to direct the ESOP as to the voting of the allocated shares. With respect to unallocated stock, the trustees and other fiduciaries must take special care to be sure they are acting solely in the interest of ESOP participants and beneficiaries (see Qs 28:1, 28:51). [I.R.C. § 409(e)]

Shareholders of the target company and the potential acquiring company may challenge the voting of the ESOP's stock. In one case, an ESOP that acquired 14 percent of the stock of a publicly traded company in response to a takeover threat was upheld as fundamentally fair to the shareholders of the public company. The ESOP required that unallocated stock be voted in the same proportion as allocated stock. [Shamrock Holdings v. Polaroid, 559 A.2d 257 (Del. Ch. 1989); *but see* Herman v. Nations Bank of Ga., N.A., 126 F.3d 1354 (11th Cir. 1997)]

However, the trustees of NCR's leveraged ESOP, established in the midst of AT&T's takeover threat, were enjoined from voting the ESOP's convertible preferred NCR stock in a special shareholders' meeting at which AT&T was expected to try to replace NCR's board of directors. Even though the ESOP required the trustees to vote unallocated stock in the same proportion as allocated stock, NCR's directors approved the establishment of the ESOP without adequate information about its fairness to NCR shareholders. The ESOP's purpose was to entrench management and prevent AT&T's takeover. [NCR Corp. v. AT&T, 761 F. Supp. 475 (S.D. Ohio 1991); Menowitz v. NCR Corp., No. C-3-91-12 (S.D. Ohio 1991)]

Q 28:31   Can a profit sharing plan be converted to an ESOP?

Yes. If the company currently has a profit sharing plan and wants to replace it with an ESOP, the company has three alternatives. It can:

1. Continue the profit sharing plan and make future contributions to both the profit sharing plan and the ESOP.

2. Terminate the profit sharing plan. This results in the immediate 100 percent vesting of all the accounts of plan participants (see Q 25:4). The assets under the profit sharing plan can be either distributed currently or maintained in the plan for distribution as employees retire or separate from service.

3. Adopt the ESOP as a continuation of the profit sharing plan. Replacement of the profit sharing plan will not be considered a termination of the plan for vesting purposes. Employer securities must be purchased with plan assets because an ESOP must invest primarily in employer securities (see Qs 28:1, 28:8).

Plan fiduciaries must beware that the conversion of a profit sharing plan into an ESOP may, depending on the purpose and financial consequences of the conversion, be a violation of the prudent person rule (see Q 23:20). In other words, if the business goes sour after the conversion, it is likely that participants will bring a claim against the fiduciaries for making an imprudent investment. The courts have been sympathetic to such claims. [Eaves v. Penn, 587 F.2d 453 (10th Cir. 1978); Bradshaw v. Jenkins, No. C83-771R (W.D. Wash. 1984); Baker & Goss v. Smith, 2 Employee Benefits Cas. 1380 (__Pa. 1981); *but see* McDannold v. Star Bank, N.A., 261 F.3d 478 (6th Cir. 2001); Andrade v. Parsons Corp., No. CV 85-3344-RJK (C.D. Cal. 1990)]

In a reverse situation, an ESOP was converted to a profit sharing plan after the employer participated in a corporate merger and the ESOP sold the employer securities. At the time, the ESOP established an escrow account to cover possible liabilities of the employer; and, a few years later, the escrow was released and allocated that year to the profit sharing plan participants as income. The plan administrator (see Q 20:1) denied the claim of a former participant, who had terminated employment before the release of the escrow, that he was entitled to share in the escrow funds, and the court upheld the plan administrator. [Becker v. Midwest Stamping & Mfg. Co. Profit Sharing Plan & Trust Admin. Comm., 2000 U.S. App. LEXIS 15805 (6th Cir. 2000)]

Q 28:32 How can an ESOP be used as an estate planning tool for the owner of a closely held corporation?

The bulk of an owner's estate frequently consists of the value of the stock in the owner's corporation. If the value of that stock is not established before the owner's death, an arbitrary figure—one based on a compromise between an IRS valuation expert and the estate's expert—may be used to determine the amount of estate taxes due. The establishment of an ESOP before the owner's death may ease this burden on the estate because the fair market value of the stock acquired by the ESOP would be determined by an independent appraiser (see Q 28:72) beforehand, reducing the chances of a dispute with IRS. [I.R.C. § 401(a)(28)]

The ESOP can also provide cash to pay the estate taxes and administration expenses of a deceased majority shareholder. The tax law provides various solutions to the liquidity problems of an estate that consists mostly of the stock of a closely held corporation. If the estate fails to qualify for this special treatment, it may be able to raise the cash through the sale of stock to the ESOP.

For example, assume that the estate of a deceased shareholder fails to meet the requirements that permit it to pay the estate tax in installments over a period of up to 15 years. The estate tax is then due within nine months of the shareholder's death. By selling the deceased shareholder's stock to the ESOP, the estate can raise the cash it needs. However, one court has indicated that a premium price paid by the ESOP to purchase a majority of a corporation's stock from the estates of two shareholders may be unreasonable corporate waste. [RCM Sec. Fund v. Stanton, No. 90-7047 (2d Cir. 1991)]

The ESOP can also rescue an estate of a deceased shareholder that cannot avail itself of the benefits of a Section 303 redemption. This provision of the Code permits the redemption of a portion of a deceased shareholder's stock for the express purpose of paying estate taxes and administration expenses. If an estate fails to qualify, the proceeds of a redemption of the deceased shareholder's stock are likely to be subject to income tax as a dividend. This result can be avoided by having the ESOP buy the stock from the estate. The sale to the ESOP does not have the danger of being treated as a dividend.

Generally, a sale to the corporation or to the ESOP will result in no gain at all because the estate's basis for the stock it sells will equal the fair market value of the stock on the deceased shareholder's date of death, and the purchase price paid by the corporation or the ESOP will likely be this amount (see Q 13:18). [I.R.C. §§ 302, 303, 1014, 6166]

Q 28:33 How can an ESOP be used to provide a market for the stock of controlling shareholders in a closely held corporation?

An ESOP is a mechanism that enables controlling shareholders to sell all or a portion of their shares to the employees, who would be the logical buyers if they could obtain the financing.

The transaction clearly benefits the shareholders by allowing them to cash out their interests in the corporation. It also benefits the corporation because the shares may be purchased with pretax dollars (i.e., annual cash contributions to the ESOP), resulting in a substantial reduction in the cash required to finance the transaction.

Another advantage of this type of transaction is that it provides for the continuity of management by enabling new employees to acquire stock as older employees and shareholders retire without diluting the equity of the remaining shareholders. That is, the ESOP, by purchasing outstanding shares from existing shareholders, avoids the diluting effect that would be involved if the ESOP purchased newly issued shares from the corporation.

There may, however, be some dilution of earnings to the extent that the ESOP creates expenses that the corporation would not otherwise have. Even this may not be the case if the corporation previously had a profit sharing plan and the ESOP is installed simply as a replacement for the profit sharing plan (see Q 28:31).

An existing buy-sell agreement between two controlling shareholders, a father and son, giving each the option to buy the other's shares at a below-market price, may pose a problem. IRS ruled that the father's sale of some of his shares to an ESOP at market value (after the son's waiver of his rights under the agreement) would be a taxable gift by the son to his father to the extent the ESOP's purchase price exceeds the option price under the buy-sell agreement. [Priv. Ltr. Rul. 9117035]

Q 28:34 May gain on the sale of securities to an ESOP be deferred?

Yes. A shareholder who sells qualified securities (see Q 28:36) to an ESOP may elect to defer recognition of all or part of the gain, which would otherwise be recognized as long-term capital gain, by purchasing qualified replacement property (see Q 28:37) within the replacement period (see Q 28:38). If the shareholder makes an election (see Q 28:40), gain is immediately taxable only to the extent that the amount realized on the sale exceeds the cost of the replacement property. If the sale to the ESOP is an installment sale, any taxable gain (that is, the gain relating to the portion of the proceeds not invested in qualified replacement property within the replacement period) must be reported on the installment basis, unless the seller elects otherwise. [I.R.C. §§ 453, 1042; Temp. Treas. Reg. § 1.1042-1T, Q&A-1; Priv. Ltr. Ruls. 9705004, 9631002, 9102021, 9102017]

This advantage is not available to a shareholder of an S corporation who sells employer securities to an ESOP (see Q 28:2). Where a corporation terminated its S corporation election, thereby becoming a C corporation, and shortly thereafter a shareholder sold a portion of his shares to an ESOP, IRS ruled that the shares were qualified securities and that the shareholder was eligible to defer recognition of the gain on the shares sold to the ESOP. [Priv. Ltr. Rul. 200003014]

IRS ruled that, if the shareholder dies before purchasing qualified replacement property, the deceased shareholder's estate may acquire the replacement property to preserve the deferral of the gain. [Priv. Ltr. Rul. 9644024]

Note. If the selling shareholders' interests in the ESOP are in excess of 20 percent of the total account balances for all employees, IRS may consider the sale to the ESOP to be a distribution under Section 301 and not a sale. [Rev. Proc. 87-22, 1987-1 C.B. 718]

Q 28:35 Are all taxpayers eligible to elect deferral of gain upon the sale of securities to an ESOP?

All taxpayers (including grantor trusts) other than S corporation shareholders and C corporations (see Qs 28:2, 28:34) can make the election (see Q 28:41). [I.R.C. § 1042(c)(7); Priv. Ltr. Ruls. 200003014, 199934006, 9705004, 9631002, 9442015, 9141046]

However, only the taxpayer who sells the qualified securities (see Q 28:36) is eligible to make the election. A trust with eight individual beneficiaries sold its stock to an ESOP, elected to defer recognition of the gain, and purchased qualified replacement property (see Q 28:37) with a portion of the proceeds. Soon thereafter, the trust was divided into eight equal separate trusts, one for each beneficiary. The separate trusts are not eligible to defer gain by acquiring replacement property with the remaining proceeds because the original trust and the resulting eight separate trusts are not the same taxpayer. [Priv. Ltr. Rul. 9143013]

Where a partnership sold the qualified securities, the election was a partnership decision; therefore, no individual partner was eligible to elect deferral of gain. [Priv. Ltr. Ruls. 9846005, 9508001]

IRS ruled that, if the taxpayer dies before purchasing qualified replacement property, the deceased taxpayer's estate may acquire the replacement property to preserve the deferral of the gain. [Priv. Ltr. Rul. 9644024]

Q 28:36 What are qualified securities?

Qualified securities are employer securities (see Q 28:8) that (1) are issued by a domestic C corporation (see Q 28:2) that for one year before and immediately after the sale has no readily tradable stock outstanding, (2) have not been received by the seller as a distribution from a qualified retirement plan or pursuant to an option or other right to acquire stock granted by the employer, and (3) as of the time of the sale, have been held by the seller for more than three years. Shares of common stock are not qualified securities if the employer's stock had been traded over the counter on NASDAQ within one year of the sale to the ESOP (see Q 28:8). [I.R.C. §§ 1042(b)(4), 1042(c)(1); Temp. Treas. Reg. § 1.1042-1T, Q&A-1(b); Priv. Ltr. Ruls. 9830028, 9215026, 9036039] However, stock listed on the Over The Counter Bulletin Board (OTCBB) or the NASD pink sheet is not readily tradable. [Priv. Ltr. Ruls. 200052014, 9036039, 8910067]

Where a corporation terminated its S corporation election (see Q 28:2), thereby becoming a C corporation, and shortly thereafter a shareholder sold a portion of his shares to an ESOP, IRS ruled that the shares were qualified securities and that the shareholder's holding period for purposes of the three-year holding requirement would include the time during which the corporation was an S corporation. [Priv. Ltr. Rul. 200003014] Where an individual transferred stock to a partnership which, in turn, sold the stock to an ESOP, the period of time the individual owned the stock was added to the period of time the partnership owned the stock for purposes of the three-year requirement. [Priv. Ltr. Ruls. 200243001, 9846005] Shareholders' holding period of qualifying securities in a domestic C corporation included the shareholders' holding period of their membership interests in a predecessor limited liability company that had been previously merged into the C corporation. [Priv. Ltr. Rul. 200827018]

Q 28:37 What is qualified replacement property?

Qualified replacement property is any security issued by a domestic operating corporation that did not have passive investment income (e.g., rents, royalties, dividends, or interest) that exceeded 25 percent of its gross receipts in its taxable year preceding the purchase. The domestic operating corporation may be an S corporation (see Q 28:2). [Priv. Ltr. Ruls. 9801055, 9801054,

9801053] Securities of the corporation that issued the employer securities (see Q 28:8), and of any corporation that is a member of a controlled group of corporations with such corporation (see Q 5:31), cannot be qualified replacement property. An operating corporation is a corporation that uses more than 50 percent of its assets in the active conduct of a trade or business. Banks and insurance companies are considered operating corporations. [I.R.C. §§ 409(*l*), 1042(c)(4); Priv. Ltr. Rul. 9432009] Shares of stock of a newly formed domestic corporation constituted qualified replacement property, ruled IRS. As a newly formed corporation, it did not have passive investment income in excess of 25 percent of its gross receipts for the taxable year preceding the taxable year in which the shares were sold. Moreover, at the time the shares were sold or before the close of the replacement period, more than 50 percent of the assets were used in the active conduct of a trade or business. [Priv. Ltr. Rul. 9720026; *see also* Priv. Ltr. Ruls. 9801055, 9801054, 9801053] B Corporation, a domestic corporation that was incorporated by the shareholders of A Corporation as a building management company to purchase, own, lease, and manage commercial real estate qualified as an operating corporation; shares of stock received by the individuals, the shareholders that formed B Corporation, upon reinvestment of the proceeds received from the sale of A Corporation's stock to an ESOP, constituted qualified replacement property; and the sale of A Corporation stock and subsequent purchase of B Corporation stock by the individuals qualified for nonrecognition, ruled IRS. [Priv. Ltr. Rul. 200337003]

A sale of employer securities to an ESOP in exchange for a promissory note, followed by a transfer of the note to an unrelated corporation in exchange for shares of its stock, qualifies for deferral treatment (see Q 28:34) because the stock of the unrelated corporation constitutes qualified replacement property. [Priv. Ltr. Rul. 9321067]

Q 28:38   What is the replacement period?

The replacement period is the period beginning three months before the date of sale to the ESOP and ending 12 months after the sale. The qualified replacement property (see Q 28:37) must be purchased during this period. [I.R.C. § 1042(c)(3); Temp. Treas. Reg. § 1.1042-1T, Q&A-3(c)]

IRS ruled that, if the shareholder dies before purchasing qualified replacement property, the deceased shareholder's estate may acquire the replacement property to preserve the deferral of the gain. [Priv. Ltr. Rul. 9644024]

Q 28:39   What other conditions apply before the deferral of gain is permitted?

After the sale, the ESOP must own at least 30 percent of either (1) each class of outstanding stock of the corporation or (2) the total value of all outstanding stock of the corporation. Also, the selling shareholder must have held the stock for at least three years. Where an individual transferred stock to a partnership which, in turn, sold the stock to an ESOP, the period of time the individual owned the stock was added to the period of time the partnership owned the stock for purposes of the three-year requirement. [I.R.C. §§ 1042(b)(2), 1042(b)(4), 1223(2); Priv. Ltr. Ruls. 200243001, 9846005] Where a corporation terminated its S corporation election (see Q 28:2), thereby becoming a C corporation, and shortly thereafter a shareholder sold a portion of his shares to an ESOP, IRS ruled that the shareholder's holding period for purposes of the three-year holding requirement would include the time during which the corporation was an S corporation. [Priv. Ltr. Rul. 200003014]

As part of the election (see Q 28:40), the selling shareholder must file with IRS a verified written statement of the corporation sponsoring the ESOP consenting to the application of the excise taxes on early dispositions and prohibited allocations of the qualified securities (see Qs 28:45–28:47). [I.R.C. § 1042(b)(3); Temp. Treas. Reg. § 1.1042-1T, Q&A-2(a)] IRS ruled that because of the failure to file a verified written statement of consent, the deferral of gain was not permitted. [Priv. Ltr. Rul. 9733001; *see also* Priv. Ltr. Rul. 200519030]

IRS has ruled that the 30 percent requirement was satisfied when the employer merged its two plans, one of which held about 25 percent of the employer's outstanding shares and the other about 11 percent. [Priv. Ltr. Rul. 9639071]

Q 28:40   How does the selling shareholder elect not to recognize gain?

The election not to recognize the gain realized upon the sale of qualified securities (see Q 28:36) is made in a statement of election attached to the selling shareholder's income tax return filed on or before the due date (including extensions) for the taxable year in which the sale occurs. The election is irrevocable. If the selling shareholder does not make a timely election, the shareholder may not subsequently make an election on an amended return or otherwise. No discretionary extension of time to file the election can be granted by IRS because the deadline for filing an election to defer gain on sales of qualified securities is prescribed by statute. [I.R.C. § 1042(c)(6); Temp. Treas. Reg. § 1.1042-1T, Q&A-3; Estate of Clause, 122 T.C. 115 (2004); Priv. Ltr. Ruls. 200519030, 9733001, 9438016, 8932048; *but see* Priv. Ltr. Rul. 200906009] If the selling shareholder dies before purchasing qualified replacement property, the deceased shareholder's estate may acquire the replacement property and make the election on the deceased's final income tax return. [Priv. Ltr. Rul. 9644024]

The statement of election must provide that the selling shareholder elects to treat the sale of securities as a sale of qualified securities and must contain the following information:

- Description of the qualified securities sold, including the type and number of shares
- Date of the sale of the qualified securities
- Adjusted basis of the qualified securities
- Amount realized upon the sale of the qualified securities
- Identity of the ESOP to which the qualified securities were sold

- Names and taxpayer identification numbers of the others involved, if the sale was part of a single interrelated transaction including other sales of qualified securities, and the number of shares sold by the other sellers

[Temp. Treas. Reg. § 1.1042-1T, Q&A-3]

If the selling shareholder has purchased qualified replacement property (see Q 28:37) at the time of the election, a statement of purchase must be attached to the statement of election. The statement of purchase must describe the qualified replacement property, give the date of the purchase and the cost of the property, declare such property to be the qualified replacement property, and be notarized within 30 days after the purchase of the qualified replacement property. [Temp. Treas. Reg. § 1.1042-1T, Q&A-3] Where the statement of purchase was not executed within the 30-day period but qualified replacement property had been acquired, IRS ruled that the selling shareholder had substantially complied with the statutory requirements. [Priv. Ltr. Ruls. 200339010, 200246027, 9852004, 9821022, 9735046]

If the selling shareholder has not purchased qualified replacement property at the time of the filing of the statement of election, the notarized statement of purchase described above must be attached to the shareholder's income tax return filed for the following taxable year. The statement of purchase must be filed with the IRS district where the election was originally filed if the return is not filed with such district. [I.R.C. § 1042(a)(1); Temp. Treas. Reg. § 1.1042-1T, Q&A-3]

IRS has ruled that notarization after the 30-day period did not invalidate the election and that an election that substantially complied with the rules was valid even though the notarized statement did not declare that the property purchased with the sales proceeds was intended to be qualified replacement property. [Priv. Ltr. Ruls. 200423018, 200324013, 200019002, 199944025, 199944009, 199934006]

In order to facilitate compliance concerning identification of qualified replacement property through notarization of the statements of purchase, IRS has proposed an amendment to provide that the notarization requirements for the statement of purchase are satisfied if the selling shareholder's statement of purchase is notarized not later than the time the selling shareholder files the income tax return for the taxable year in which the sale of qualified securities occurred in any case in which any qualified replacement property was purchased by such time and during the qualified replacement period. If qualified replacement property was purchased after the filing date and during the qualified replacement period, the statement of purchase must be notarized not later than the time the selling shareholder's income tax return is filed for the taxable year following the year for which the election was made. [Temp. Treas. Reg. § 1.1042-1T, Q&A-3(b)]

Q 28:41   What is the basis of qualified replacement property?

If the selling shareholder makes an election not to recognize the gain (see Q 28:40), the basis of the qualified replacement property (see Q 28:37) purchased during the replacement period (see Q 28:38) is reduced by an amount equal to the amount of gain that was not recognized. If more than one item of qualified replacement property is purchased, the basis of each item is reduced by an amount determined by multiplying the total gain not recognized by a fraction whose numerator is the cost of such item of property and whose denominator is the total cost of all such items of property. [I.R.C. § 1042(d); Temp. Treas. Reg. § 1.1042-1T, Q&A-4; Priv. Ltr. Ruls. 9102021, 9102017]

If the selling shareholder dies, the basis of the qualified replacement property becomes the property's fair market value at the date of the selling shareholder's death. [Priv. Ltr. Ruls. 9339005, 9109024] However, if the selling shareholder dies before purchasing qualified replacement property, the deceased shareholder's estate may acquire the replacement property to preserve the deferral of the gain; but IRS ruled that there is no step-up in basis so that the basis of the qualified replacement property will reflect the unrecognized gain on the sale to the ESOP. [Priv. Ltr. Rul. 9644024]

> **Example.** Esau sold 1,000 shares of XYZ Corp. stock to XYZ Corp.'s ESOP on May 1, 2009 for $1,000,000. Esau's basis was $100,000. Esau died on December 4, 2009 without having purchased qualified replacement property; and, on April 2, 2010, the administrator of Esau's estate acquired $1,000,000 of qualified replacement property. The gain of $900,000 ($1,000,000 − $100,000) is deferred. On September 4, 2010, the administrator sells the replacement property for $1,050,000. The estate recognizes a gain of $950,000 ($1,050,000 − $100,000).

Q 28:42   What happens if the taxpayer who elects nonrecognition treatment later disposes of the qualified replacement property?

If the taxpayer disposes of any qualified replacement property (see Q 28:37), gain must be recognized unless exempted (see Q 28:43) to the extent not previously recognized in connection with the acquisition of the qualified replacement property, notwithstanding any other provision of the law that might defer recognition (see Q 28:41). A special recapture rule applies if the taxpayer controls the corporation that issued the qualified replacement property and the corporation disposes of a substantial portion of its assets other than in the ordinary course of its trade or business. [I.R.C. § 1042(e)]

A taxpayer's transfer of qualified replacement property to a revocable trust created by the taxpayer is not a disposition, and the division of a trust that acquired qualified replacement property into eight separate trusts is not a disposition (see Q 28:35). Furthermore, the distribution of qualified replacement property by a trust to its beneficiary is not a disposition. [Priv. Ltr. Ruls. 9533038, 9411003, 9327080, 9226027, 9143013, 9141046] In addition, a transfer to an irrevocable trust created by the taxpayer that is a grantor trust for income tax purposes is not a disposition. [I.R.C. § 671; Priv. Ltr. Rul. 200239035] Similarly, a transfer to a grantor retained annuity trust that is structured as a grantor trust for income tax purposes is not a disposition. [Priv. Ltr. Ruls. 200709012, 200709011]

IRS has also ruled that the transfer of an interest in a partnership which owned the qualified replacement property was not a disposition and that the conversion of a business trust into a limited partnership or the conversion of a partnership into a limited liability company did not result in the disposition of qualified replacement property. [Priv. Ltr. Ruls. 200243001, 9846005, 9814020] However, a shareholder, who sold qualified securities to an ESOP, reinvested the proceeds in qualified replacement property, elected to defer recognition of gain from the sale, and contributed the qualified replacement property to a partnership in exchange for a partnership interest, recognized gain on the contribution to the extent that gain on the sale was deferred. Although the contribution of property to a partnership is usually a nonrecognition event, the shareholder's contribution was a disposition of the qualified replacement property; thus, gain was recognized. [Rev. Rul. 2000-18, 2000-1 C.B. 847; I.R.C. § 721]

Contributions of qualified replacement property to a charitable remainder trust constitute a disposition of such property but do not result in a recapture of the deferred gain because of the nature of the trust. [Priv. Ltr. Ruls. 9732023, 9728048, 9715040, 9547023, 9547022] The same result occurs if the contribution is made directly to a charitable organization. [Priv. Ltr. Ruls. 9533038, 9515002]

Q 28:43 Do all dispositions of qualified replacement property result in the recapture of gain?

No. The following dispositions are exempted from the recapture provisions:

- Dispositions upon death
- Dispositions by gift
- Subsequent sales of the qualified replacement property to an ESOP pursuant to Section 1042
- Transfers in a corporate reorganization, provided no corporation involved in the reorganization is controlled by the taxpayer holding the qualified replacement property

[I.R.C. § 1042(e)(3); Priv. Ltr. Ruls. 9846005, 9533038, 9515002, 9339005]

Where a partnership owned the qualified replacement property, a gift of a partnership interest was ruled not to be a disposition of the qualified replacement property. [Priv. Ltr. Rul. 200243001] An individual's transfer of qualified replacement property to his spouse pursuant to a marital separation agreement incident to their divorce was treated as a gift and exempted from the recapture provisions. [I.R.C. § 1041(b)(1); Priv. Ltr. Rul. 201024005]

Q 28:44   What is the statute of limitations when a selling shareholder elects nonrecognition of the gain on the sale of qualified securities?

If any gain is realized, but not recognized, by the selling shareholder on the sale of any qualified securities (see Q 28:36), the statute of limitations with respect to such nonrecognized gain will not expire until three years from the date of IRS receipt of:

1. A notarized statement of purchase that includes the cost of the qualified replacement property (see Q 28:40);

2. A written statement of the selling shareholder's intent not to purchase qualified replacement property (see Q 28:37) within the replacement period (see Q 28:38); or

3. A written statement of the selling shareholder's failure to purchase qualified replacement property within the replacement period.

If the selling shareholder files a statement of intent not to purchase or failure to purchase qualified replacement property, the statement must be accompanied, if appropriate, by an amended return for the taxable year in which the gain from the sale of the qualified securities was realized. The amended return must report any gain from the sale of qualified securities that is required to be recognized in the taxable year in which the gain was realized due to a failure to meet the nonrecognition requirements. [I.R.C. § 1042(f); Temp. Treas. Reg. § 1.1042-1T, Q&A-5]

Q 28:45   What happens if the ESOP disposes of qualified securities within three years of their acquisition?

An excise tax is imposed on the amount realized on the disposition (see Q 28:46) of qualified securities (see Q 28:36) if:

1. The ESOP acquires any qualified securities in a sale for which nonrecognition treatment was elected (see Q 28:40);

2. The ESOP disposes of any of such qualified securities during the three-year period after the date on which any qualified securities were acquired; and

3. Either (a) the total number of shares of employer securities (see Q 28:8) held by the ESOP after such disposition is less than the total number of shares of employer securities held immediately after the sale for which nonrecognition treatment was elected or (b) the value of the employer securities held by the ESOP immediately after such disposition is less than 30 percent of the total value of all employer securities outstanding at that time.

[I.R.C. § 4978(a); Temp. Treas. Reg. § 54.4978-1T, Q&A-1]

Q 28:46   What is the amount of the excise tax on the disposition of qualified securities?

The tax is 10 percent of the amount realized on the disposition that is allocable to qualified securities acquired within the three-year period following their acquisition. [I.R.C. § 4978(b); Temp. Treas. Reg. § 54.4978-1T, Q&A-2]

A disposition is any sale, exchange, or distribution. However, the excise tax will not apply to any disposition of qualified securities that is made by reason of:

- Death of the employee
- Retirement of the employee after the employee has attained age 59
- Disability of the employee (see Q 16:6)
- Separation from service by the employee for any period that results in a one-year break in service (see Q 5:10; Priv. Ltr. Rul. 200135044)

In addition, dispositions necessary to comply with the diversification requirements (see Q 28:53) and exchanges pursuant to corporate reorganizations will not trigger the excise tax. [I.R.C. § 4978(d); Temp. Treas. Reg. § 54.4978-1T, Q&A-3]

The excise tax is imposed on the corporation or corporations that made the verified written statement of consent to the application of such excise tax on the disposition of employer securities (see Qs 28:39, 28:40). [I.R.C. § 4978(c); Temp. Treas. Reg. § 54.4978-1T, Q&A-4]

Q 28:47   Are there any restrictions on the allocation of qualified securities acquired by the ESOP in a transaction in which the seller elected nonrecognition of gain?

Yes. None of the employer securities (see Q 28:8) acquired by the ESOP in a nonrecognition transaction may be directly or indirectly allocated to or accrue to the benefit of the selling shareholder or a member of the shareholder's family during the nonallocation period (see Q 28:48), or to an owner of more than 25 percent (subject to attribution rules) of any class of employer stock at any time. The family-member restriction does not apply if the family member is a lineal descendant of the shareholder and the total amount allocated to all such lineal descendants does not exceed more than 5 percent of the employer securities held by the plan that are attributable to the sale to the plan by a person related to such descendants. In addition, a person will not be treated as a 25 percent shareholder if such person was not a 25 percent shareholder at any time during the one-year period ending on the date of sale of the employer securities to the plan or on the date the employer securities are allocated to participants. [I.R.C. §§ 318(a), 409(n)(1), 409(n)(3); Priv. Ltr. Rul. 9707015]

Example. Steve, the owner of 40 percent of the outstanding shares of stock of Ess & Jay Ltd., sold all of his shares to the company's ESOP and elected nonrecognition treatment. Steve's shares were attributed to his son, Jamie, an ESOP participant. Because Jamie was treated as an owner of more than 25 percent of Ess & Jay Ltd.'s shares immediately before the sale, Jamie is prohibited from receiving an allocation of any of the shares purchased by the ESOP from his father.

For purposes of determining whether the prohibition against an accrual of qualified securities (see Q 28:36) is satisfied, the allocation of any contributions or other assets that are not attributable to qualified securities sold to the ESOP must be made without regard to the allocation of the qualified securities. In effect, this allocation restriction operates to prohibit any direct or indirect accrual of benefits under all qualified retirement plans of an employer. [I.R.C. § 409(n)(1); Temp. Treas. Reg. § 1.1042-1T, Q&A-2(c); Priv. Ltr. Rul. 9041071]

Example. Stephanie, Caroline, and James own 50, 25, and 25 shares, respectively, of the 100 outstanding shares of common stock of Ess & Ess Corporation. The corporation establishes an ESOP that obtains a loan, and the loan proceeds are used to purchase the 100 shares of qualified securities from Stephanie, Caroline, and James, all of whom elect nonrecognition treatment with respect to the gain realized on their sale of such securities. No part of the assets of the ESOP attributable to the 100 shares of qualified securities may accrue under the ESOP for the benefit of Caroline or James during the nonallocation period or to Stephanie at any time. These restrictions also generally apply to any person who is a member of any of their families. Furthermore, no other assets of the ESOP may accrue to the benefit of such individuals in lieu of the receipt of assets attributable to such qualified securities.

The prohibited allocation is treated as a distribution to the person receiving such allocation. Also, there is an excise tax imposed on the employer equal to 50 percent of the amount involved in a prohibited allocation of qualified securities acquired by an ESOP after October 23, 1986. [I.R.C. §§ 409(n)(2), 4979A]

IRS representatives have opined that where the corporation which issued the qualified securities was acquired by another corporation in a stock-for-stock transaction, the nonallocation rules continue to apply to the new stock.

If the nonallocation rules affect an essential employee, the employer may consider adopting a nonqualified plan (see Qs 1:11–1:13), such as an incentive stock option plan, a nonqualified stock option plan, a restricted stock plan, a phantom stock plan, a stock appreciation rights plan, or a nonqualified stock bonus plan.

Q 28:48   What is the nonallocation period?

The nonallocation period, for purposes of the nonrecognition provisions regarding sales of stock to an ESOP (see Qs 28:34–28:47), is the period beginning on the date of sale and ending on the later of (1) the date that is ten years after the date of sale or (2) the date of the plan allocation attributable to the final payment of acquisition indebtedness incurred in connection with the sale. [I.R.C. § 409(n)(3)(C)]

Q 28:49   How can an ESOP be used to facilitate a buyout of shareholders in a closely held corporation?

An ESOP can be used to purchase all or a portion of the stock of minority shareholders, inactive shareholders, and outside shareholders. In these instances, the primary advantage is that the corporation purchases the shares with pretax dollars. From the minority shareholder's point of view, it is generally irrelevant whether the shares are purchased by the corporation or by the ESOP, since the shareholder would generally be entitled to the same tax treatment in either case. However, the sale of the stock to the ESOP is more likely to be treated as a sale (and not a distribution of property) than a sale of stock to the corporation. [Priv. Ltr. Rul. 8931040]

The purchase of stock from existing shareholders can be financed in a number of ways, depending on the size of the payroll, the assets of the ESOP, and the needs and objectives of the selling shareholder. If the selling shareholder needs immediate liquidity, the ESOP may use any cash on hand and borrow funds either from the corporation or from an outside lender to purchase the shareholder's stock for cash.

If the selling shareholder does not need immediate liquidity, the shareholder may prefer to receive interest by selling the stock to the ESOP on an installment-sale basis in return for an interest-bearing note. An installment sale has the advantages of spreading out the tax over a number of years and fixing the price of the shares at the time of the sale.

Finally, the shareholder may simply sell a portion of the shares each year on a serial-sale basis. This is the approach usually taken when the shareholder is not yet ready to sell a block of stock at one time.

Note. In order to meet qualification requirements and avoid a prohibited transaction (see Q 24:1), an independent appraiser (see Q 28:72) must determine the purchase price in each transaction on the basis of the stock's fair market value at the time of sale (see Q 28:1). [I.R.C. §§ 401(a)(28)(C), 4975(d)(13); ERISA § 408(e)] One court ruled that a sale of stock by the majority shareholder to an ESOP was a prohibited transaction because the shareholder did not prove that the purchase price was equal to fair market value or that the price was determined in good faith after a prudent investigation. [Eyler v. Comm'r, 88 F.3d 445 (7th Cir. 1996)]

Q 28:50   How can an ESOP be used to finance a business?

Under conventional financing, a corporation that needs to raise $1 million for working capital or expansion purposes borrows the funds from a bank or other lender and repays the loan with after-tax dollars. Although the interest component of each debt payment is a deductible expense to the corporation, the principal repayment is not deductible and is, therefore, considered an after-tax payment.

By use of an ESOP, it is possible to arrange the financing so that both the interest and principal repayments are tax deductible. This is accomplished either by having the ESOP rather than the corporation borrow the $1 million or by having the corporation reloan the proceeds to the ESOP. The ESOP uses the loan proceeds to purchase $1 million worth of newly issued stock from the corporation. The corporation has the $1 million needed for working capital or expansion purposes, and the ESOP owns $1 million worth of the corporation's stock. Thereafter, the corporation may make an annual tax-deductible contribution to the plan consisting of (1) an amount of up to 25 percent of covered payroll for the purpose of repaying the loan principal plus (2) an unlimited amount used to pay interest on the loan (see Q 28:9). [I.R.C. § 404(a)(9)]

In the case of a typical private corporation, the lender may demand both a pledge agreement, pledging the shares of stock as collateral for the loan, and a guarantee agreement from the corporation. Under the guarantee agreement, the corporation agrees to make annual contributions to the ESOP sufficient to amortize the loan and, in the event that the corporation fails to make such contributions, to pay the loan directly.

Q 28:51 May an ESOP enter into an agreement obligating itself to purchase stock when a shareholder dies?

No. An ESOP may, however, be given an option to buy stock when the shareholder dies. [Treas. Reg. § 54.4975-11(a)(7)(i)]

Q 28:52 Must plan participants be given voting rights with respect to their stock?

If the employer securities (see Q 28:8) are registered with the Securities and Exchange Commission (SEC), participants must be given full voting rights with respect to stock allocated to their accounts. DOL has opined that fiduciaries of a collectively bargained ESOP must pass through decisions concerning tender offers or proxy voting to the plan's participants and vote as directed, unless doing so would violate ERISA. According to DOL, even if the plan provides the trustees with the discretion to vote shares and circumstances justify not voting as directed, trustees cannot disregard the participants' directions unless obeying the directions would violate ERISA. [DOL Priv. Ltr. Rul. (Sept. 28, 1995)]

An ESOP maintained by an employer that does not have registration-type securities (e.g., a closely held corporation) is required to pass through voting rights to participants with stock allocated to their accounts only with respect to any corporate merger or consolidation, recapitalization, reclassification, liquidation, dissolution, sale of substantially all assets of a trade or business, or other similar transaction prescribed by regulations. The plan may authorize the trustees of an ESOP maintained by such an employer to vote such allocated stock on a one vote per participant basis. [I.R.C. § 409(e)] IRS ruled that an ESOP is *not* required to pass through voting rights to participants with stock allocated to their accounts *unless* state corporation law requires one of the enumerated corporate matters to be submitted to a shareholder vote. [Priv. Ltr. Rul. 9705004]

These voting requirements do not apply to stock held by the ESOP in a suspense account (i.e., stock not yet allocated to participants). The trustees have discretion in voting unallocated stock and allocated stock not subject to the pass-through rule, but they must vote such stock in accordance with their fiduciary duty to plan participants and beneficiaries (see Qs 23:19, 28:1). [Central Trust Co., N.A. v. American Advents Corp., 771 F. Supp. 871 (S.D. Ohio 1991)]

The pass-through voting requirements are not violated when trustees vote the shares of stock that are allocated to participants' accounts and for which no voting directions are timely received. The participants were entitled to direct the votes but failed to timely communicate their directions to the trustees. [Rev. Rul. 95-57, 1995-2 C.B. 62]

Q 28:53 What is diversification of investments in an ESOP?

A qualified participant in an ESOP must be permitted to direct the ESOP as to the investment of up to 25 percent of the participant's account during the 90-day period following each plan year in the qualified election period. With the final diversification election during the qualified election period, the participant may elect to diversify up to 50 percent of the participant's account. [I.R.C. § 401(a)(28)(B)] For discussion of these diversification rules, see Qs 28:54-28:63. However, these diversification rules do not apply to an applicable defined contribution plan. [I.R.C. § 401(a)(28)(b)(v)]

Generally effective for plan years beginning after December 31, 2006, new diversification requirements apply to applicable defined contribution plans. See Q 28:64 for a discussion of transitional guidance issued by IRS concerning the new diversification requirements and the required notice and for a discussion of a final regulation issued by DOL; see Q 28:65 for a discussion of final regulations issued by IRS; and see Q 28:66 for more information on the required notice.

Q 28:54 Who is a qualified participant?

A qualified participant is any employee who has completed at least ten years of participation in the ESOP and has attained age 55. [I.R.C. § 401(a)(28)(B)(iii); Hess v. Reg-Ellen Machine Tool Corp., Nos. 04-3408, 04-3415 (7th Cir. 2005); *see also* Hess v. Reg-Ellen Machine Tool Corp. ESOP, No. 06-2797 (7th Cir. 2007)]

When an ESOP is terminated and a successor ESOP adopted, a participant's years of participation in both ESOPs can be aggregated for purposes of the ten-year requirement. [Priv. Ltr. Rul. 9213006]

See Qs 28:53 and 28:64 for a discussion of new diversification requirements that apply to certain ESOPs.

Q 28:55   What is the qualified election period?

The qualified election period is the six-plan-year period beginning with the plan year after the first plan year in which the employee is a qualified participant (see Q 28:54). [I.R.C. § 401(a)(28)(B)(iv)]

Example. Joe of Rockville Centre Ltd. maintains an ESOP with a calendar-year plan year. Mitzi completed ten years of participation in the ESOP in 2009 when she was age 56. Thus, Mitzi became a qualified participant in the plan year beginning January 1, 2010. Mitzi will be eligible to make diversification elections during the election periods in 2011, 2012, 2013, 2014, 2015, and 2016.

See Qs 28:53 and 28:64 for a discussion of new diversification requirements that apply to certain ESOPs.

Q 28:56   What must an ESOP do to satisfy the diversification requirements?

A qualified participant (see Q 28:54) must be given the opportunity to make a diversification election within 90 days after the close of each plan year within the qualified election period (see Q 28:54) with respect to a cumulative amount of at least 25 percent of the participant's account (50 percent for the last election period). The ESOP can satisfy this requirement by offering any of the following:

1. To distribute all or part of the amount subject to the diversification election;

2. At least three other distinct investment options; or

3. To transfer the portion of the account balance subject to the diversification election to another qualified defined contribution plan (see Q 2:2) of the employer that offers at least three investment options.

The ESOP must complete diversification in accordance with a diversification election within 90 days after the end of the period during which the election could be made for the plan year. [I.R.C. § 401(a)(28)(B)(ii); IRS Notice 88-56, Q-13, 1988-1 C.B. 540]

If this requirement is satisfied by the distribution of all or part of the amount subject to the diversification election, the distribution will be an eligible rollover distribution subject to the 20 percent income tax withholding rules (see Q 20:10).

See Qs 28:53 and 28:64 for a discussion of new diversification requirements that apply to certain ESOPs.

Q 28:57   What is the effect of the diversification or distribution of a participant's employer securities?

Amounts diversified pursuant to a diversification election are generally treated as amounts not held by an ESOP and are no longer subject to the statutory provisions governing amounts held by an ESOP. Thus, for example, a qualified participant (see Q 28:54) cannot demand that the distribution of diversified amounts be made in the form of employer securities (see Q 28:8). [IRS Notice 88-56, Q-16, 1988-1 C.B. 540]

Amounts distributed in satisfaction of the diversification requirements that consist of employer securities are subject to a participant's put option (see Q 28:70). Distributions in satisfaction of the diversification requirements do not violate the restrictions regarding distributions before a participant's termination of employment or certain other events. [IRS Notice 88-56, Q-14, 1988-1 C.B. 540; I.R.C. § 409(h)]

See Qs 28:53 and 28:64 for a discussion of new diversification requirements that apply to certain ESOPs.

Q 28:58 Are all employer securities held by an ESOP subject to diversification?

No. Only employer securities (see Q 28:8) acquired by or contributed to an ESOP after December 31, 1986, are subject to the diversification requirements. Therefore, employer securities allocated to participant accounts after December 31, 1986, will not be subject to diversification if they were acquired or contributed before that date. [IRS Notice 88-56, Q-1, 1988-1 C.B. 540]

Also, if an ESOP received cash contributions prior to January 1, 1987, and subsequently—but within certain time limits—used the contributions to acquire employer securities, those securities will be deemed to have been acquired before January 1, 1987, and will not be subject to the diversification rules. [IRS Notice 88-56, Q-3, 1988-1 C.B. 540]

An ESOP acquired employer securities prior to January 1, 1987, received cash for the securities after a tender offer, and then used the proceeds of the tender offer to acquire stock of the new parent corporation. IRS ruled that the new parent corporation's stock was deemed to have been acquired prior to January 1, 1987, and, therefore, was not subject to the diversification requirements. [Priv. Ltr. Ruls. 200234070, 9608040] However, employer securities that will be transferred from a profit sharing plan to an ESOP pursuant to the employer's restructuring will not be treated as having been acquired prior to January 1, 1987, and, therefore, will be subject to the diversification requirements. [Priv. Ltr. Rul. 200317031]

See Qs 28:53 and 28:64 for a discussion of new diversification requirements that apply to certain ESOPs.

Q 28:59 Are dividends paid to an ESOP subject to the diversification rules?

Yes. Dividends paid after December 31, 1986, in the form of employer securities (see Q 28:8), or in cash or other property used to acquire employer securities (see Q 28:10), are subject to the diversification rules. This is true even though the dividends are paid with respect to employer securities acquired by the ESOP before January 1, 1987. [IRS Notice 88-56, Q-1, 1988-1 C.B. 540]

However, the diversification rules will not apply to securities acquired with cash dividends paid before January 1, 1987, if the acquisition occurred within 60 days of the date of payment of the dividend. [IRS Notice 88-56, Q-1, Q-3, 1988-1 C.B. 540]

See Qs 28:53 and 28:64 for a discussion of new diversification requirements that apply to certain ESOPs.

Q 28:60   How is the determination made as to which employer securities are subject to diversification?

An ESOP may separately account for employer securities (see Q 28:8) contributed or acquired after December 31, 1986, and those contributed before January 1, 1987. If the ESOP does not maintain separate accounts for securities based on the date of acquisition, any securities allocated after 1986 will be presumed to consist, first, of securities acquired or contributed after 1986 and, second, of securities acquired or contributed before 1987. [IRS Notice 88-56, Q-4, 1988-1 C.B. 540]

An ESOP may, under certain circumstances, use an alternative formula to determine the portion of a qualified participant's (see Q 28:54) account attributable to employer securities acquired or contributed after December 31, 1986. Under this formula, the number of securities in a qualified participant's account deemed acquired or contributed after December 31, 1986, is determined by multiplying the number of shares allocated to a qualified participant's account by a fraction representing, as of the plan valuation date closest to the date on which the individual becomes a qualified participant, the portion of the total shares that were acquired by or contributed to the ESOP after December 31, 1986. This formula is available only if the IRS model plan amendments to conform to the TRA '86 changes were adopted by the ESOP sponsor on or before January 1, 1989. [IRS Notice 88-56, Q-5, 1988-1 C.B. 540; IRS Notice 87-2, 1987-1 C.B. 396]

> **Example.** Floyd Corporation adopted the model plan amendments with respect to its ESOP. On January 1, 2009—the plan's valuation date—the ESOP held 100,000 shares of Floyd Corporation's stock. Of those 100,000 shares, 75,000 were acquired by the ESOP after December 31, 1986. Michelle, a participant in the ESOP with 40 shares allocated to her account, became a qualified participant on January 8, 2010. The number of shares allocated to Michelle's account that are subject to the diversification requirements is 30 $(75,000 \div 100,000 \times 40)$. If Michelle does not elect to diversify within 90 days after the close of the 2010 plan year, and eight more shares are allocated to her account on January 1, 2011, the number of shares in her account subject to diversification increases to 36 $[(75,000 \div 100,000) \times (40 + 8)]$. [IRS Notice 88-56, Q-9, 1988-1 C.B. 540]

See Qs 28:53 and 28:64 for a discussion of new diversification requirements that apply to certain ESOPs.

Q 28:61   May any qualified participants in ESOPs that hold employer securities acquired after December 31, 1986, be excluded from making the diversification election?

Yes. If an ESOP holds and allocates to a qualified participant's (see Q 28:54) account a *de minimis* amount of employer securities (see Q 28:12) acquired after December 31, 1986 (see Qs 28:59, 28:60), it will not be required to offer diversification to that participant. A fair market value of $500 or less will be considered to be a *de minimis* amount for this purpose, although an ESOP may elect to use a lower threshold. If the *de minimis* level is exceeded later in the qualified election period (see Q 28:55), then all employer securities allocated to the qualified participant that were acquired or contributed after December 31, 1986, are subject to diversification. [IRS Notice 88-56, Q-7, Q-8, 1988-1 C.B. 540]

See Qs 28:53 and 28:64 for a discussion of new diversification requirements that apply to certain ESOPs.

Q 28:62   May employer securities acquired before 1987 be diversified?

Yes. The shares diversified need not be those actually acquired after 1986 (see Qs 28:58, 28:60). The number of shares that must be available for diversification is nevertheless determined by the number of shares acquired or contributed after December 31, 1986. The diversified shares, however, must be employer securities (see Q 28:8) that, immediately prior to diversification, were subject to the put option and right to demand requirements of Section 409(h) (see Qs 28:1, 28:70). [IRS Notice 88-56, Q-10, 1988-1 C.B. 540]

See Qs 28:53 and 28:64 for a discussion of new diversification requirements that apply to certain ESOPs.

Q 28:63   May an ESOP permit a qualified participant to elect diversification of amounts in excess of that required by statute?

Yes, an ESOP may permit diversification of amounts in excess of the minimum requirements (see Q 28:55). However, such amounts are not treated as available for diversification or as diversified in accordance with Section 401(a)(28)(B). Amounts in excess of the minimum diversification requirements remain subject to the participant's right under Section 409(h) to demand distribution in the form of employer securities (see Q 28:8). [IRS Notice 88-56, Q-11, 1988-1 C.B. 540]

See Qs 28:53 and 28:64 for a discussion of new diversification requirements that apply to certain ESOPs.

Q 28:64   Has IRS issued transitional guidance on the new diversification requirements?

In order to be a qualified retirement plan, certain defined contribution plans (see Q 2:2) must satisfy diversification requirements, and IRS issued transitional guidance. [IRS Notice 2006-107, 2006-2 C.B. 1114] IRS extended the transitional guidance until regulations to be issued become effective (see Q 28:65). [IRS Notice 2008-7, 2008-1 C.B. 276]

Part III of the notice provides transitional guidance and applies pending the issuance of further guidance.

A.   *Scope of Application.*

Diversification requirements are imposed for defined contribution plans that hold publicly traded employer securities. Employer securities are securities issued by an employer of employees covered by the plan or by an affiliate of such employer. [I.R.C. § 401(a)(35)(G)(iv); ERISA § 407(d)(1)] Publicly traded employer securities are employer securities that are readily tradable on an established securities market. For this purpose, if a plan holds employer securities that are not publicly traded, then, except as may be provided in regulations issued by IRS, those employer securities are nevertheless treated as publicly traded employer securities if an employer corporation, or any member of the controlled group of corporations (see Q 5:31) that includes an employer corporation, has issued a class of stock that is a publicly traded employer security. For this purpose, an employer corporation is any corporation that is an employer maintaining the plan, and a controlled group of corporations has the meaning given under Section 1563(a), except that 50 percent is substituted for 80 percent wherever it occurs in Section 1563. [I.R.C. § 401(a)(35)(G)(v)]

However, under the notice, a plan (and an investment option described in C below) is not treated as holding employer securities to which the diversification requirements apply with respect to any securities held by either an investment company registered under the Investment Company Act of 1940 or a similar pooled investment vehicle that is regulated and subject to periodic examination by a state or federal agency and with respect to which investment in the securities is made both in accordance with the stated investment objectives of the investment vehicle and independent of the employer and any affiliate thereof, but only if the holdings of the investment company or similar investment vehicle are diversified so as to minimize the risk of large losses.

In addition, the diversification requirements do not apply to an ESOP if: (1) there are no contributions held in the plan (or earnings thereunder) that are elective deferrals, employee after-tax contributions, or matching contributions that are subject to testing (see Qs 27:18, 27:76) and (2) the plan is a separate plan from any other plan maintained by the employer. Thus, an ESOP is subject to the diversification requirements if either the ESOP holds any contributions to which testing applies (or earnings thereon) or the ESOP is a portion of a plan that holds any amounts that are not part of the ESOP. [I.R.C. § 414(*l*); Treas. Reg. § 1.414(*l*)-1]

B. *Applicable Individuals Who Have Diversification Rights.*

Applicable individuals are provided with diversification rights with respect to publicly traded employer securities held in the plan. The diversification rights apply with respect to elective deferrals and employee contributions (and earnings thereon) and are required to be available to (1) any participant, (2) any alternate payee (see Q 36:5) who has an account under the plan, and (3) any beneficiary of a deceased participant. For this purpose, employee contributions include both employee after-tax contributions and rollover contributions held under the plan. The diversification rights apply with respect to other employer contributions (and earnings thereon) and are required to be available to each applicable individual who is either (1) a participant who has completed at least three years of service, (2) an alternate payee who has an account under the plan with respect to a participant who has completed at least three years of service, or (3) a beneficiary of a deceased participant. For purposes of the notice, persons who are entitled to receive diversification rights are applicable individuals. [I.R.C. §§ 401(a)(35)(B), 401(a)(35)(C)]

For purposes of the diversification requirements relating to employer contributions and the transitional rule described in E below, the date on which a participant completes three years of service (see Q 9:10) occurs immediately after the end of the third vesting computation period provided for under the plan that constitutes the completion of a third year of service. However, for a plan that uses the elapsed time method (see Q 5:9) of crediting service for vesting purposes (or a plan that provides for immediate vesting without using a vesting computation period or the elapsed time method of determining vesting), the date on which a participant completes three years of service is the third anniversary of the participant's date of hire. [I.R.C. §§ 401(a)(35)(C), 411(a)(5)]

C. *Basic Divestiture Rules.*

An applicable individual is required to be permitted to elect to direct the plan to divest any publicly traded employer securities held in such individual's account under the plan and to reinvest an equivalent amount in other investment options offered under the plan with respect to the portion of the account that is subject to the diversification requirements to the extent applicable. This diversification right applies only when publicly traded employer securities are held under the plan and allocated to the participant's or beneficiary's account.

The investment options offered must include not less than three investment options, other than employer securities, to which the applicable individual may direct the proceeds of the divestment of employer securities, and each investment option must be diversified and have materially different risk and return characteristics. For this purpose, investment options that satisfy the requirements of the DOL regulations (see Q 23:14) are treated as being diversified and having materially different risk and return characteristics. [I.R.C. § 401(a)(35)(D)(i)]

D. *Restrictions or Conditions on Divestiture Rights.*

1. *Conditions or Restrictions.* A plan is not treated as failing to meet the diversification requirements merely because the plan limits the time for divestment and reinvestment to periodic, reasonable opportunities occurring no less frequently than quarterly. A plan is prohibited from imposing restrictions or conditions with respect to the investment of employer securities that are not imposed on the investment of other assets of the plan. For purposes of this prohibition, except as described below, a restriction or condition with respect to employer securities includes: (i) a restriction on an applicable individual's rights to divest an investment in employer securities that is not imposed on an investment that is not in employer securities and (ii) a benefit that is conditioned on investment in employer securities. Thus, the following are examples of prohibited restrictions or conditions:

a. A plan allows applicable individuals the right to divest employer securities on a periodic basis (such as quarterly), but permits divestiture of another investment on a more frequent basis (such as daily). However, see paragraph 4 below for a transitional rule.

b. A plan under which a participant who divests the account of employer securities receives less favorable treatment (such as a lower rate of matching contributions) than a participant whose account remains invested in employer securities.

Similarly, the following are examples of restrictions or conditions that are not prohibited, provided that the limitations apply without regard to a prior exercise of rights to divest employer securities:

a. A provision that limits the extent to which an individual's account balance can be invested in employer securities. Thus, a provision that does not allow more than 10 percent of an individual's account balance to be invested in employer securities is permitted.

b. A provision under which an employer securities investment fund is closed; that is, other amounts invested under the plan cannot be transferred into an investment in a class of employer securities (and no contributions are permitted to be invested in that class of employer securities).

However, a provision under which, if a participant divests the account balance with respect to investment in a class of employer securities, the participant is not permitted for a period of time thereafter to reinvest in that class of employer securities is a restriction that is prohibited, because this limitation takes into account a prior exercise of rights to divest employer securities. [I.R.C. §§ 401(a)(35)(D)(ii)(I), 401(a)(35)(D)(ii)(II)]

2. *Permitted Restrictions.* A restriction imposed by reason of the application of securities laws or a restriction that is reasonably designed to ensure compliance with such laws is not an impermissible restriction or condition. Thus, for example, for purposes of ensuring compliance with Rule 10b-5 of the Securities and Exchange Commission, a plan may limit divestiture rights for participants

who are subject to Section 16(b) of the Securities Exchange Act of 1934 to a period (such as three to 12 days) following publication of the employer's quarterly earnings statements. In addition, an impermissible restriction or condition does not include the imposition of fees or other investment options under the plan merely because fees are not imposed with respect to investments in employer securities. Further, a plan may restrict the application of otherwise applicable diversification rights under the plan for up to 90 days following an initial public offering of the employer's stock.

3. *Transition Rule Through March 30, 2007 for Continuation of Existing Restrictions or Conditions.* For the period from January 1, 2007 through March 30, 2007, a plan does not impose a restriction or condition merely because the plan restricts diversification rights with respect to employer securities pursuant to a plan provision that was in effect on December 18, 2006. However, any such restriction that continues to be imposed on or after March 31, 2007 violates the impermissible restriction or condition rule.

4. *Transition Rule for 2007 for Grandfathered Investments.* For the period prior to January 1, 2008, a plan does not impose a prohibited restriction or condition merely because the plan, as in effect on December 18, 2006, (i) does not impose an otherwise applicable restriction on a stable value fund or (ii) allows applicable individuals the right to divest employer securities on a periodic basis, but permits divestiture of another investment on a more frequent basis, provided that the other investment is not a generally available investment (e.g., the other investment is available only to a fixed class of participants). However, any such restriction that continues to be imposed after December 31, 2007 violates the impermissible restrictions or condition rule.

E. *Transition Rule under § 401(a)(35)(H).*

A special transition rule is provided under which, for employer securities acquired in a plan year beginning before January 1, 2007, the diversification rights with respect to employer contributions apply only to the applicable percentage of the number of shares of those securities. The applicable percentage is 33 percent for the first plan year to which diversification applies, 66 percent for the second plan year, and 100 percent for all subsequent plan years. If a plan holds more than one class of securities, the transition rule applies separately with respect to each class. This transition rule does not apply to a participant who, before the first plan year beginning after December 31, 2005, had attained age 55 and completed at least three years of service.

F. *Notice under ERISA Section 101(m).*

In addition to amending the Code and ERISA to provide applicable individuals with the divestiture rights discussed in the notice, PPA (see Q 1:33) also added ERISA Section 101(m), which requires plans to notify applicable individuals of these rights. Specifically, plan administrators (see Q 20:1) must provide a notice to applicable individuals not later than 30 days before the first date on which the individuals are eligible to exercise their rights. The notice must set forth the diversification rights and describe the importance of diversifying the investment of retirement account assets. ERISA Section 101(m) became effective for plan years beginning after December 31, 2006.

Although some plans were required to comply with the diversification requirements as early as January 1, 2007, DOL advised IRS that Section 101(m) does not require plans to furnish notices before January 1, 2007. Pursuant to this interpretation, plans with plan years beginning on or after January 1, 2007, but before February 1, 2007, were not required to furnish the model notice included herein (or a notice otherwise meeting the requirements of Section 101(m)) earlier than January 1, 2007. DOL, however, encouraged plans to furnish notice on the earliest possible date.

G. *Model Notice.*

PPA directs IRS to prescribe a model notice for purposes of ERISA Section 101(m). The model notice below was issued pursuant to that directive.

The model notice may have to be adapted to reflect particular plan provisions. For example, changes would generally be necessary if either the plan has more than one class of employer securities, the plan provides the same diversification rights for participants without regard to whether they have three years of service, some of the plan's investment options are closed, the plan receives participant elections electronically, or the transition rule is being applied.

Notice of Your Rights Concerning Employer Securities

This notice informs you of an important change in Federal law that provides specific rights concerning investments in employer securities (company stock). Because you may now or in the future have investments in company stock under the [*insert name of plan*], you should take the time to read this notice carefully.

Your Rights Concerning Employer Securities

For plan years beginning after December 31, 2006, the Plan must allow you to elect to move any portion of your account that is invested in company stock from that investment into other investment alternatives under the Plan. This right extends to all of the company stock held under the Plan, except that it does not apply to your account balance attributable to [*identify any accounts to which the rights apply only after three years of service*] until you have three years of service. [*Insert description of any advance notice requirement before a diversification election becomes effective.*] You may contact the person identified below for specific information regarding this new right, including how to make this election. In deciding whether to exercise this right, you will want to give careful consideration to the information below that describes the importance of diversification. All of the investment options under the Plan are available to you if you decide to diversify out of company stock.

The Importance of Diversifying Your Retirement Savings

To help achieve long-term retirement security, you should give careful consideration to the benefits of a well-balanced and diversified investment portfolio. Spreading your assets among different types of investments can help you achieve a favorable rate of return, while minimizing your overall risk of losing money. This is because market or other economic conditions that cause one category of assets, or one particular security, to perform very well often cause another asset category, or another particular security, to perform poorly. If you invest more than 20% of your retirement savings in any one company or industry, your savings may not be property diversified. Although diversification is not a guarantee against loss, it is an effective strategy to help you manage investment risk.

In deciding how to invest your retirement savings, you should take into account all of your assets, including any retirement savings outside of the Plan. No single approach is right for everyone because, among other factors, individuals have different financial goals, different time horizons for meeting their goals, and different tolerances for risk. Therefore, you should carefully consider the rights described in this notice and how these rights affect the amount of money that you invest in company stock through the Plan.

It is also important to periodically review your investment portfolio, your investment objectives, and the investment options under the Plan to help ensure that your retirement savings will meet your retirement goals.

For More Information

If you have any questions about your rights under this new law, including how to make this election, contact [*enter name and contact information*].

Effective October 9, 2007, DOL amended its regulations to reflect the addition of the notice requirements relating to the diversification rights. The conforming amendments do not change the existing penalty assessment procedures or the related procedures for contesting penalty assessments. Rather, the changes merely extend DOL's existing procedures for assessing civil penalties for violations relating to blackout notices (see Q 20:23) to include violations of the notice requirements relating to diversification rights. These conforming changes primarily add references to ERISA Section 101(m) next to existing references to ERISA Section 101(i) throughout the regulation. [ERISA §§ 101(m), 204(j), 502(c)(7); DOL Reg. § 2560.502c-7]

IRS issued proposed regulations relating to the diversification requirements. Until the regulations go into effect, IRS Notice 2006-107 will continue to apply. For this purpose, the transitional relief provided for the period prior to January 1, 2008 will continue to apply after 2007 until the regulations go into effect. In addition, plans are also permitted to apply the proposed regulations for plan years before the regulations go into effect. [Prop. Treas. Reg. § 1.401(a)(35)-1; preamble to proposed regulations]

Plan amendments adopting the diversification requirements do not have to be made until the last day of the first plan year that begins on or after January 1, 2010. [IRS Notice 2009-97, 2009-2 C.B. ___]

See Q 28:65 for a discussion of the final regulations issued by IRS.

Q 28:65   When are the final regulations concerning the new diversification requirements effective?

Although the statutory effective date of the new diversification requirements became effective for plan years beginning after December 31, 2006, the regulatory effective/applicability date of the final regulations is effective and applicable for plan years beginning on or after January 1, 2011. [Treas. Reg. §§ 1.401(a)(35)-1(g)(1)(i), 1.401(a)(35)-1(g)(2)] Plan amendments adopting the diversification requirements do not have to be made until the last day of the first plan year that begins on or after January 1, 2010. [IRS Notice 2009-97, 2009-2 C.B. ___]

With respect to the final regulations, the following definitions are important:

1. *Applicable defined contribution plan:* Except as otherwise provided, an applicable defined contribution plan (see Q 2:2) means any defined contribution plan that holds employer securities (see Q 28:8) which are publicly traded. An ESOP is not an applicable defined contribution plan if the plan is a separate plan with respect to any other defined benefit plan (see Q 2:3) or defined contribution plan maintained by the same employer or employers and holds no contributions (or earnings thereunder) that are (or were ever) subject to Section 401(k) (see Q 27:1) or 401(m) (see Q 27:73). Thus, an ESOP is an applicable defined contribution plan if the ESOP is a portion of a larger plan (whether or not that larger plan includes contributions that are subject to Section 401(k) or 401(m)). A plan is not considered to hold amounts ever subject to Section 401(k) or 401(m) merely because the plan holds amounts attributable to rollover amounts in a separate account that were previously subject to Section 401(k) or 401(m). A one-participant plan is not an applicable defined contribution plan. A defined contribution plan holding employer securities that are not publicly traded is treated as an applicable defined contribution plan if any employer maintaining the plan or any member of a controlled group of corporations that includes such employer has issued a class of stock that is publicly traded. A controlled group of corporations has the meaning given such term by Section 1563(a), except that "50 percent" is substituted for "80 percent" each place it appears (see Q 5:31). This rule does not apply to a plan if (1) no employer maintaining the plan (or a parent corporation with respect to such employer) has issued stock that is publicly traded, and (2) no employer maintaining the plan (or parent corporation with respect to such employer) has issued any special class of stock that grants to the holder or issuer particular rights, or bears particular risks for the holder or issuer, with respect to any employer maintaining the plan (or any member of a controlled group of corporations that includes such employer) that has issued any stock that is publicly traded. [I.R.C. §§ 401(a)(35) (E)(iv), 414(l); Treas. Reg. § 1.401(a)(35)-1(f)(2)]

2. *Employer security:* Employer security has the meaning given such term by ERISA Section 407(d)(1). Subject to rules discussed below, a plan (and an investment option) is not treated as holding employer securities to the extent the employer securities are held indirectly as part of a broader fund that is (1) a regulated investment company described in Section 851(a); (2) a common or collective trust fund or pooled investment fund maintained by a bank or trust

company supervised by a State or a federal agency; (3) a pooled investment fund of an insurance company that is qualified to do business in a State; (4) an investment fund managed by an investment manager within the meaning of ERISA Section 3(38) for a multiemployer plan (see Q 29:2); or (5) any other investment fund designated by IRS in revenue rulings, notices, or other guidance. This exception applies only if the investment in the employer securities is held in a fund under which (1) there are stated investment objectives of the fund and (2) the investment is independent of the employer (or employers) and any affiliate thereof. An investment in employer securities in a fund is not considered to be independent of the employer (or employers) and any affiliate thereof if the aggregate value of the employer securities held in the fund is in excess of ten percent of the total value of all of the fund's investments for the plan year. The determination of whether the value of employer securities exceeds ten percent of the total value of the fund's investments for the plan year is made as of the end of the preceding plan year. The determination can be based on the information in the latest disclosure of the fund's portfolio holdings that was filed with the SEC in that preceding plan year. [Treas. Reg. § 1.401(a)(35)-1(f)(3)]

3. *Parent corporation:* A parent corporation is any corporation (other than the employer corporation) in an unbroken chain of corporations ending with the employer corporation if each of the corporations other than the employer corporation owns stock possessing 50 percent or more of the total combined voting power of all classes of stock in one of the other corporations in such chain. [I.R.C. § 424(e); Treas. Reg. § 1.401(a)(35)-1(f)(4)]

4. *Publicly traded:* A security is publicly traded if it is readily tradable on an established securities market. Except as provided by revenue rulings, notices, or other guidance, a security is readily tradable on an established securities market if (1) the security is traded on a national securities exchange that is registered under Section 6 of the Securities Exchange Act of 1934 or (2) the security is traded on a foreign national securities exchange that is officially recognized, sanctioned, or supervised by a governmental authority and the security is deemed by the SEC as having a ready market under SEC Rule 15c3-1. [Treas. Reg. § 1.401(a)(35)-1(f)(5)]

A trust that is part of an applicable defined contribution plan is not qualified unless the plan (1) satisfies the diversification election requirements for elective deferrals (see Q 27:16) and employee contributions (see Q 27:74); (2) satisfies the diversification election requirements for employer nonelective contributions (see Q 27:17); (3) satisfies the investment option requirement; and (4) does not apply any restrictions or conditions on investments in employer securities that violate the requirements relating thereto discussed below. [I.R.C. § 401(a)(35); Treas. Reg. § 1.401(a)(35)-1(a)]

With respect to any individual described in this paragraph, if any portion of the individual's account under an applicable defined contribution plan attributable to elective deferrals, employee contributions, or rollover contributions (see Q 34:1) is invested in employer securities, then the plan satisfies the diversification requirements if the individual may elect to divest those employer securities and reinvest an equivalent amount in other investment options. The plan may limit the time for divestment and reinvestment to periodic, reasonable opportunities occurring no less frequently than quarterly. An individual is described in this paragraph if the individual is (1) a participant; (2) an alternate payee (see Q 36:5) who has an account under the plan; or (3) a beneficiary of a deceased participant. [Treas. Reg. § 1.401(a)(35)-1(b)]

With respect to any individual described in this paragraph, if a portion of the individual's account under an applicable defined contribution plan attributable to employer nonelective contributions is invested in employer securities, then the plan satisfies the requirements of this paragraph if the individual may elect to divest those employer securities and reinvest an equivalent amount in other investment options. The plan may limit the time for divestment and reinvestment to periodic, reasonable opportunities occurring no less frequently than quarterly. An individual is described in this paragraph if the individual is (1) a participant who has completed at least three years of service; (2) an alternate payee who has an account under the plan with respect to a participant who has completed at least three years of service; or (3) a beneficiary of a deceased participant. For purposes of this paragraph, a participant completes three years of service on the last day of the vesting computation period provided for under the plan that constitutes the completion of the third year of service (see Q 9:10). However, for a plan that uses the elapsed time method of crediting service for vesting purposes (or a plan that provides for immediate vesting without using a vesting computation period or the elapsed time method of determining vesting), a participant completes three years of service on the day immediately preceding the third anniversary of the participant's date of hire. [I.R.C. § 411(a)(5); Treas. Reg. § 1.401(a)(35)-1(c)]

In the case of the portion of an account to which the preceding paragraph applies and that consists of employer securities acquired in a plan year beginning before January 1, 2007, the requirements apply only to the applicable percentage of such securities. The applicable percentage is determined as follows:

Plan year	Applicable percentage
1st	33
2nd	66
3rd and following	100

[I.R.C. § 401(a)(35)(H); Treas. Reg. §§ 1.401(a)(35)-1(g)(3)(i), 1.401(a)(35)-1(g)(3)(ii)(A)] The application of this transition rule is illustrated by the following example. Suppose that the account of a participant with at least three years of service held 120 shares of employer common stock contributed as matching contributions before the diversification requirements became effective. In the first year for which diversification applies, 33 percent (i.e., 40 shares) of that stock is subject to the diversification requirements. In the second year for which diversification applies, a total of 66 percent of 120 shares of stock (i.e., 79 shares, or an additional 39 shares) is subject to the diversification requirements. In the third year for which diversification applies, 100 percent of the stock, or all 120 shares, is subject to the diversification requirements. In addition, in each year, employer stock in the account attributable to elective deferrals and employee after-tax contributions is fully subject to the diversification requirements, as is any new stock contributed to the account.

A special effective date applies with respect to employer matching and nonelective contributions (and earnings thereon) that are invested in employer securities that, as of September 17, 2003, (1) consist of preferred stock and (2) are held within an ESOP, under the terms of which the value of the preferred stock is subject to a guaranteed minimum. Under the special rule, the diversification requirements apply to such preferred stock for plan years beginning after the earlier of (1) December 31, 2007 or (2) the first date as of which the actual value of the preferred stock equals or exceeds the guaranteed minimum. When the new diversification requirements become effective for the plan under the special rule, the applicable percentage of employer securities held on the effective date that is subject to diversification is determined without regard to the special rule. [Treas. Reg. § 1.401(a)(35)-1(g)(3)(ii)(B)]

This transition rule does not apply to an individual who is a participant who attained age 55 and had completed at least three years of service before the first day of the first plan year beginning after December 31, 2005. The transition rule applies separately with respect to each class of securities. [Treas. Reg. §§ 1.401(a)(35)-1(g)(3)(iii), 1.401(a)(35)-1(g)(3)(iv)]

An applicable defined contribution plan must offer no less than three investment options, other than employer securities, to which an individual who has the right to divest may direct the proceeds from the divestment of employer securities. Each of the three investment options must be diversified and have materially different risk and return characteristics. For this purpose, investment options that constitute a broad range of investment alternatives within the meaning of DOL regulations (see Q 23:14) are treated as being diversified and having materially different risk and return characteristics. [Treas. Reg. § 1.401(a)(35)-1(d); DOL Reg. § 2550.404c-1(b)(3)]

Except as provided below, an applicable defined contribution plan violates the requirements concerning restrictions or conditions on investments in employer securities if the plan imposes restrictions or conditions that are not imposed on the investment of other assets of the plan. A restriction or condition with respect to employer securities means (1) a restriction on an individual's right to divest an investment in employer securities that is not imposed on an investment that is not employer securities or (2) a benefit that is conditioned on investment in employer securities. A plan violates these requirements if it imposes a restriction or condition described in the preceding or following sentence either directly or indirectly. A plan imposes an indirect restriction on an individual's right to divest an investment in employer securities if, for example, the plan provides that a participant who divests the account balance with respect to the investment in employer securities is not permitted for a period of time thereafter to reinvest in employer securities. A plan does not impose an indirect restriction or condition merely because there are tax conse-quences that result from an individual's divestment of an investment in employer securities. Thus, the loss of the special treatment for net unrealized appreciation with respect to employer securities (see Qs 13:18, 28:71) is disregarded. Similarly, a plan does not impose an impermissible restriction or condition merely because it provides that an individual may not reinvest divested amounts in the same employer securities account but is permitted to invest such divested amounts in another employer securities account where the only relevant difference between the separate accounts is the cost (or other basis) of the trust in the shares held in each account. [I.R.C. § 402(e)(4); Treas. Reg. §§ 1.401(a)(35)-1(e)(1), 1.402(a)-1(b)]

An applicable defined contribution plan does not violate the requirements concerning restrictions or conditions merely because it imposes a restriction or a condition discussed in this paragraph. A plan is permitted to impose a restriction or condition on the divestiture of employer securities that is either required in order to ensure compliance with applicable securities laws or is reasonably designed to ensure compliance with applicable securities laws. For example, it is permissible for a plan to limit divestiture rights for participants who are subject to Section 16(b) of the Securities Exchange Act of 1934 to a reasonable period (such as three to 12 days) following publication of the employer's quarterly earnings statements because it is reasonably designed to ensure compliance with Rule 10b-5 of the SEC. An applicable defined contribu-tion plan is permitted to restrict the application of the diversification require-ments for up to 90 days after the plan becomes an applicable defined contribution plan (for example, a plan becoming an applicable defined contri-bution plan because the employer securities held under the plan become publicly traded). In the case where an investment fund no longer meets the requirement that the investment must be independent of the employer (includ-ing the situation where the fund no longer meets the percentage limitation rule), the plan does not fail to satisfy the diversification requirements merely because it does not offer those rights with respect to that investment fund for up to 90 days after the investment fund ceases to meet those requirements. [Treas. Reg. § 1.401(a)(35)-1(e)(2)]

An applicable defined contribution plan does not violate the requirements concerning restrictions or conditions merely because it imposes an indirect restriction or condition discussed in this paragraph. A plan is permitted to limit the extent to which an individual's account balance can be invested in employer securities, provided the limitation applies without regard to a prior exercise of rights to divest employer securities. For example, a plan does not impose an impermissible restriction merely because the plan prohibits a participant from investing additional amounts in employer securities if more than ten percent of that participant's account balance is invested in employer securities. A plan is permitted to impose reasonable restrictions on the timing and number of investment elections that an individual can make to invest in employer securi-ties, provided that the restrictions are designed to limit short-term trading in the employer securities. For example, a plan could provide that a participant may not elect to invest in employer securities if the employee has elected to divest employer securities within a short period of time, such as seven days, prior to the election to invest in employer securities. The plan has not provided an indirect benefit that is conditioned on investment in employer securities merely because the plan imposes fees on other investment options that are not imposed on the investment in employer securities. In addition, the plan has not provided a restriction on the right to divest an investment in employer securities merely because the plan imposes a reasonable fee for the divestment of employer securities. A plan is permitted to allow transfers to be made into or out of a stable value or similar fund more frequently than a fund invested in employer securities. Thus, a plan that includes a broad range of investment alternatives, including a stable value or similar fund, does not impose an impermissible restriction merely because it permits transfers into or out of that fund more frequently than other funds under the plan, provided that the plan would otherwise satisfy the requirements concerning restrictions or conditions (taking into account any restrictions or conditions imposed with respect to the other investment options under the plan). For these purposes, a stable value fund or similar fund means an investment product or fund designed to preserve or guarantee principal and provide a reasonable rate of return, while providing liquidity for benefit distributions or transfers to other investment alternatives. A plan is permitted to provide for transfer out of a qualified default investment alternative (QDIA; see Q 23:14) more frequently than a fund invested in employer securities. A plan is permitted to prohibit any further investment in employer securities. Thus, a plan is not treated as imposing an indirect restriction merely because it provides that an employee who divests an investment in employer securities is not permitted to reinvest in employer securities, but only if the plan does not permit additional contributions or other investments to be invested in employer securities. For this purpose, a plan does not provide for further investment in employer securities merely because dividends paid on employer securities under the plan are reinvested in employer securities (see Q 28:14). An employer stock fund does not fail to be a frozen fund merely because of the allocation of employer securities that are released as matching contributions from the plan's suspense account that holds employer securities acquired with an exempt loan (see Q 28:7). This applies only to employer securities that were acquired in a plan year beginning before January 1, 2007 with the proceeds of an exempt loan that is not refinanced after the end of the last plan year beginning before January 1, 2007. [Treas. Reg. § 1.401(a)(35)-1(e)(3); DOL Reg. §§ 2550.404c-5(e)(4)(iv)(A), 2550.404c-5(e)(4)(v)(A)]

IRS may provide for additional permitted restrictions or conditions or permitted indirect restrictions or conditions in revenue rulings, notices, or other guidance. [Treas. Reg. § 1.401(a)(35)-1(e)(4)]

Q 28:66   What is the notice requirement for the new diversification requirements?

An applicable individual (see Q 28:65) must be notified of the right to divest the account under an applicable defined contribution plan (see Q 28:65) of employer securities. Not later than 30 days before the first date on which an applicable individual is eligible to exercise such right with respect to any type of contribution, the plan administrator (see Q 20:1) must provide the individual with a notice setting forth such right and describing the importance of diversifying the investment of plan account assets. Under the diversification provision, an applicable individual's right to divest the account of employer securities attributable to elective deferrals (see Q 27:16) and employee after-tax contributions (see Q 27:74) and the right to divest the account of employer securities attributable to other contributions (i.e., nonelective employer contributions and employer matching contributions; see Qs 27:17, 27:75) may become exercisable at different times. Thus, to the extent the applicable individual is first eligible to exercise such rights at different times, separate notices are required.

The notice must be written in a manner calculated to be understood by the average plan participant and may be delivered in written, electronic, or other appropriate form to the extent such form is reasonably accessible to the applicable individual. IRS has regulatory authority over the required notice and was directed to prescribe a model notice to be used for this purpose.

In the case of a failure to provide a required notice of diversification rights, DOL may assess a civil penalty against the plan administrator of up to $100 a day from the date of the failure. For this purpose, each violation with respect to any single applicable individual is treated as a separate violation.

The provision of the notice generally applies to plan years beginning after December 31, 2006. Under a transition rule, if notice would otherwise be required to be provided before 90 days after August 17, 2006, notice was not required until 90 days after such date.

[ERISA §§ 101(m), 502(c)(7)]

For further discussion of the notice requirement and the model notice issued by IRS, see Q 28:64.

Q 28:67 Is a loan from a shareholder to an ESOP a prohibited transaction?

Not necessarily. Although ERISA generally prohibits loans (or loan guarantees) between a qualified retirement plan and a disqualified person (a 10-percent-or-more shareholder, for example), a loan (or a loan guarantee) by a disqualified person to an ESOP is not a prohibited transaction (see Q 24:1) if the loan qualifies as an exempt loan (see Q 28:7). [ERISA § 408(b)(3); I.R.C. § 4975(d)(3)]

The statutory exceptions to the prohibited-transaction rules do not fail to apply merely because a transaction involves the sale of employer securities (see Q 28:8) to an ESOP maintained by an S corporation (see Q 28:2) by a shareholder-employee (see Q 14:21), a family member of the shareholder-employee, or a corporation controlled by the shareholder-employee. Thus, the statutory exemptions for such a transaction (including the exemption for a loan to the ESOP to acquire employer securities in connection with such a sale or a guarantee of such a loan) apply. [I.R.C. § 4975(f)(6)]

Q 28:68 Must distributions under an ESOP commence by specified dates?

Yes. As a qualification requirement, with regard to distributions attributable to stock acquired after December 31, 1986, an ESOP must provide that, if a participant elects (and, if applicable, the participant's spouse consents), the distribution of the participant's account balance will begin not later than one year after the end of the plan year:

1. In which the individual terminates employment by reason of reaching retirement age, disability (see Q 16:6), or death; or

2. That is the fifth plan year following the plan year in which the individual otherwise terminates employment (unless the individual is reemployed by the employer before such time).

For purposes of this rule, the individual's account balance is deemed not to include any employer securities (see Q 28:8) acquired with the proceeds of an exempt loan (see Q 28:7) until the end of the plan year in which such loan is repaid in full. In addition to these requirements, the ESOP must comply with the minimum distribution requirements (see chapter 11). [I.R.C. §§ 401(a)(9), 409(o)(1)(A), 409(o)(1)(B)]

Q 28:69 Must distributions under an ESOP be made at certain intervals?

With regard to distributions attributable to stock acquired after December 31, 1986, an ESOP must provide that (unless the participant elects otherwise) the distribution of the participant's account balance will be in substantially equal periodic payments (not less frequently than annually) over a period not longer than five years. If the participant's account balance exceeds $500,000, the distribution period may be extended one year for each $100,000 (or part thereof) by which the account balance exceeds $500,000. However, the distribution period cannot exceed ten years. [I.R.C. § 409(o)(1)(C)]

Both of the dollar amounts are adjusted for inflation. However, an adjustment will be made only if it is $5,000 or greater and then will be made in multiples of $5,000 (i.e., rounded down to the next lowest multiple of $5,000). For example, an increase in the cost-of-living of $4,999 will result in no adjustment, and an increase of $9,999 will create an upward adjustment of $5,000. For 2010, the respective amounts are $985,000 and $195,000. [IRS Notice 2009-94, 2009-2 C.B. 848; I.R.C. §§ 409(o)(2), 415(d)]

Q 28:70 When can participants exercise their put option?

Participants can exercise a put option and put the employer securities back to the company for their fair market value if the securities are not readily tradable on an established market (see Q 28:8). The put option must last for a period of at least 60 days following the date of distribution of employer securities. If the option is not exercised, the participant must be given the opportunity to sell the stock to the employer during an additional 60-day period in the following plan year. [I.R.C. § 409(h)(4)]

If a put option is exercised with respect to stock distributed in a total distribution, the employer must pay for the stock in substantially equal periodic payments (not less frequently than annually) over a period beginning no later than 30 days after the exercise of the put option and ending no later than five years thereafter. Reasonable interest and adequate security must be provided for unpaid amounts. For this purpose, a total distribution is a distribution of the balance of the recipient's account within one calendar year. [I.R.C. § 409(h)(5); Treas. Reg. § 54.4975-7(b)(12)(iv); Merrimac Paper Co., Inc. v. Harrison, 420 F.3d 53 (1st Cir. 2005)] The employer's unsecured promissory notes are not adequate security. [Cofer v. Audichron Co., 7 Employee Benefits Cas. (BNA) 2104 (N.D. Ga. 1986); Treas. Reg. § 1.503(b)-1(b)(1); Rev. Rul. 80-269, 1980-2 C.B. 191; Ann. 95-33, 1995-19 I.R.B. 14; Priv. Ltr. Rul. 9438002]

If the stock is distributed in installments, the employer must pay for the stock no later than 30 days after the put option is exercised. [I.R.C. § 409(h)(6)]

One court ruled that ESOP participants whose put options were not honored by the sponsoring company could not sue the ESOP trustees under ERISA because the put options were binding on the company and not the ESOP. [Flynn v. Ballinger, No. C94-0190 (N.D. Cal. 1994)] An employer established a plan that consisted of both an ESOP portion and a 401(k) plan (see Q 27:1) portion. Participants who received employer securities were given a put option. The plan was amended and eliminated the put option from the 401(k) portion. The court concluded that the put option was an optional form of benefit and that its elimination violated the anti-cutback rule (see Q 9:25). [Goodin v. Innovative Technical Solutions, Inc., 2007 U.S. Dist. LEXIS 31320 (D. Hawaii 2007)]

A company maintained an ESOP that contained a put option provision. When exercised, the option required the company to repurchase its stock from the retirees. Two employees retired and exercised their put options. The ESOP purchased the stock, instead of the company, in exchange for a promissory note payable over a period of years that was secured by the stock sold. Shortly thereafter, the company went bankrupt, rendering the stock worthless. The court held that the ESOP trustees may be liable for breach of fiduciary duty because the decline in value of the stock due to the company's bankruptcy constituted a loss to the plan that was brought about by the trustees' decisions. [Roth v. Sawyer-Cleaton Lumber Co., 1995 U.S. App. LEXIS 19919 (8th Cir. 1995)]

Q 28:71   How are distributions from an ESOP taxed?

Distributions from an ESOP are generally taxed like any other distribution from a qualified retirement plan (see chapter 13). If appreciated employer securities (see Q 28:8) are included in a lump-sum distribution, the recipient may defer tax on the net unrealized appreciation until the securities are sold (see

Q 13:18). [Priv. Ltr. Ruls. 200935046, 200927040, 200537041, 200509032, 200507016; IRS Pub. 575; *see also* Priv. Ltr. Rul. 200615007] It is imperative that the distribution of the employer securities be part of a lump-sum distribution. [Priv. Ltr. Rul. 200434022; *see also* Priv. Ltr. Rul. 200433020] This special rule applies even where the participant receives a distribution of employer securities from an ESOP and immediately exercises the put option to sell the securities to the employer (see Q 28:70). Therefore, even if a participant immediately exchanges the securities for cash, the participant is entitled to exclude the net unrealized appreciation from ordinary income and treat the appreciation as capital gain realized upon the sale of the securities. [Priv. Ltr. Rul. 200841042] This advantage may not be available to ESOP participants if the ESOP is maintained by an S corporation because such an ESOP need not give participants the right to demand their distributions in the form of employer securities (see Q 28:2).

If the appreciated employer securities are rolled over to an IRA, a subsequent distribution of the securities or the sales proceeds thereof from the IRA would be taxed as ordinary income and the benefits of the net unrealized appreciation will have been lost. [Priv. Ltr. Rul. 200442032] An IRA is not prohibited from holding a promissory note. Where an individual received the balance of his ESOP benefits in the form of a promissory note providing for four equal annual installment payments, the promissory note was eligible to be rolled over into an IRA. [Priv. Ltr. Rul. 200846024]

An employee who received a plan distribution on or within three months after the one-year anniversary of his second termination of employment with a wholly owned subsidiary was entitled to net unrealized appreciation treatment with respect to the distribution of the parent company's securities from his participant's ESOP account. Net unrealized appreciation treatment was available to the employee despite the fact that he received a distribution of his participant's deferral and matching accounts after his first separation from service with the subsidiary. However, a second employee who received a distribution of his participant's ESOP account within one tax year was not entitled to net unrealized appreciation treatment. The employee had already received a distribution of his participant's deferral, matching, and profit sharing accounts and would not receive a distribution of his ESOP account until a later date due to the delayed distribution provisions under the plan. A distribution to a third employee from her participant's ESOP account was not entitled to net unrealized appreciation treatment. This employee had received a distribution from her ESOP account in a prior tax year because her plan loan, which was due and payable upon termination of employment, was not repaid and, thus, was defaulted and offset by a portion of her ESOP account (see Q 14:10). [Priv. Ltr. Rul. 200634059]

Even if an employee receives appreciated employer securities and defers income tax on the net unrealized appreciation, the basis of the securities may be subject to the 10 percent penalty tax on early withdrawals unless an exception applies (see Q 16:1). [Villarroel v. Comm'r, 202 F.3d 271 (6th Cir. 2000)]

IRS has ruled that an ESOP is required to adjust its basis in S corporation stock (see Q 28:2) for the ESOP's pro rata share of the corporation's items and that, upon distribution of S corporation stock by an ESOP to a participant, the stock's net unrealized appreciation is determined using the ESOP's adjusted basis in the stock. [Rev. Rul. 2003-27, 2003-1 C.B. 597] The basis of each shareholder's stock in an S corporation is increased for any period by the sum of the following items determined with respect to that shareholder for such period: (1) certain items of income, (2) any nonseparately computed income, and (3) the excess of the deductions for depletion over the basis of the property subject to depletion. The basis of each shareholder's stock in an S corporation is decreased for any period (but not below zero) by the sum of the following items determined with respect to that shareholder for such period: (1) distributions by the corporation that were not includible in the income of the shareholder, (2) certain items of loss and deduction, (3) any nonseparately computed loss,(4) any expense of the corporation not deductible in computing its taxable income and not properly chargeable to capital account, and (5) the amount of the shareholder's deduction for depletion for any oil and gas property held by the S corporation to the extent such deduction does not exceed the proportionate share of the adjusted basis of such property allocated to such shareholder. [I.R.C. § 1367(a)]

Example. JKH Corporation, a calendar-year S corporation, maintains an ESOP. The ESOP holds 100 shares of JKH stock that it purchased on January 1, 2010, for $10,000 with employer contributions. The ESOP's pro rata share of JKH's income for the corporation's 2010 taxable year is $1,000 (composed entirely of nonseparately computed income of $10 per share) that the ESOP properly reports on Form 5500 (see Q 21:1). The ESOP makes no distributions to its shareholders during 2010.

Jennifer is an employee of JKH and a participant in the ESOP. The plan holds five shares of JKH stock for the benefit of Jennifer from January 1 to December 31, 2010. On December 31, 2010, the plan distributes the five shares of JKH stock to Jennifer, subject to her right to require JKH to repurchase the shares under a fair valuation formula (see Q 28:70). On that date, the fair market value of the five shares is $580.

The ESOP's pro rata share of JKH's nonseparately computed income for its 2010 taxable year increases the basis of each share of JKH stock held by the plan by $10. Therefore, the basis of each of the five shares of stock held by the plan for the benefit of Jennifer is increased by $10 from $100 to $110. The amount of net unrealized appreciation in the JKH stock is $30, the excess of the market value of the stock at the time of distribution ($580) over the plan's adjusted basis in the stock ($550). Unless Jennifer rolls the distributed stock over into an eligible retirement plan (see Q 34:16), she will have $550 of income as a result of the distribution.

The amount of taxable income that may be offset by some loss carryovers and recognized built-in losses when a loss corporation experiences a change in ownership is limited. IRS has issued final regulations addressing whether a distribution of shares in a loss corporation by a qualified retirement plan results in a change in ownership and triggers special limitations. Under the regulations, when a qualified retirement plan distributes shares in a loss corporation, the plan participant is treated as having received the shares at the same time and in the same manner as the plan for purposes of testing for a change in ownership. In addition, the distribution itself gives rise to a testing date. The final regulations are effective for distributions from qualified retirement plans after June 23, 2006. [I.R.C. § 382; Treas. Reg. § 1.382-10]

Q 28:72 Which factors are used to value employer securities that are not readily tradable?

Employer securities that are not readily tradable (see Q 28:8) must be valued by an independent appraiser. [I.R.C. § 401(a)(28)(C)]

The valuation of employer securities must be reasonable, written, made in good faith, and based on all relevant factors used to determine fair market value. Relevant factors include:

- Nature of the business and history of the enterprise
- Economic outlook in general and condition of specific industry
- Book value of the securities and financial condition of the business
- Earning capacity of the company
- Dividend-paying capacity of the company
- Existence of goodwill
- Market price of similar stocks
- Marketability of securities, including an assessment of the company's ability to meet its put obligations
- Existence of a control premium, which means a block of security that provides actual control of the company (control must be actual control that is not dissipated within a short period of time)

[Prop. DOL Reg. § 2510.3-18]

One court has ruled that fiduciaries breached their fiduciary duties when they approved a sale of employer securities by the ESOP to a related party at a price based solely on an independent appraisal report and did not meaningfully discuss, review, or question the report. The court refused to adopt a per se rule insulating fiduciaries from liability by relying on an independent appraiser's report, particularly where there was the potential for self-dealing (see Q 28:1). [Howard v. Shay, 100 F.3d 1484 (9th Cir. 1996); see also Howard v. Shay, No. CV 91-146 (C.D. Cal. 1998); Reich v. Hall Holding Co., 990 F. Supp. 955 (N.D. Ohio 1998); Donovan v. Cunningham, 716 F.2d 1455 (5th Cir. 1983)] Other courts have ruled that a bank trustee violated its fiduciary duty when the ESOP purchased employer stock for more than fair market value even though the trustee had relied on an outside valuation report and informal DOL opinion, and that fiduciaries of an ESOP breached their fiduciary duties by purchasing shares of stock on behalf of the ESOP without adequate investigation and by overpaying for the shares even though the fiduciary had retained an analyst to perform a valuation. [Reich v. Valley Nat'l Bank of Ariz., 837 F. Supp. 1259 (S.D.N.Y. 1993); Chao v. Hall Holding Co., 285 F.3d 415 (6th Cir. 2002)] The relevant inquiry, said one court, is whether the fiduciary acted with the prudence required of a fiduciary under the prevailing circumstances at the time of the transaction (see Q 23:20). [Henry v. Champlain Enterprises, Inc., 445 F.3d 610 (2d Cir. 2006)] Another court concluded that the bank trustee had to consider the effect of the employer's acquisition of another company and concomitant assumption of large debt. [Armstrong v. LaSalle Bank Nat'l Ass'n, 446 F.3d 728 (7th Cir. 2006)]

Participants in an ESOP were not entitled to copies of the plan's determination letter (see Q 18:1) or to appraisal or evaluation reports of company stock because the papers were not formal or legal documents under which the plan was set up or managed. [Faircloth v. Lundy Packing Co., 91 F.3d 648 (4th Cir. 1996)]

Q 28:73   Can employees' interests in an ESOP be investment contracts under the Securities Acts of 1933 and 1934?

Yes, says one court. The company solicited new employees to participate in its wage reduction program, which constituted eligibility to participate in the company's ESOP and profit sharing plan in return for a reduction in wages. The court held that, in order to be considered an investment contract subject to protection under the Securities Acts of 1933 and 1934, there must be (1) an investment of money (2) in a common enterprise (3) with profit derived from the efforts of other persons. Since the wage reduction program constituted an investment of money, the ESOP is a common enterprise, and profits (i.e., dividends and appreciation in value) would result primarily from efforts of management and employees, each employee's interest in the ESOP was an investment contract. [Uselton v. Commercial Lovelace Motor Freight, Inc., Nos. 88-1253, 88-1750 (10th Cir. 1991); *see also* International Bhd. of Teamsters v. Daniel, 439 U.S. 551 (1979); SEC v. W.J. Howey Co., 328 U.S. 293 (1946)]

Another court has ruled that the Securities Acts applied to employee claims involving an ESOP because (1) the plan, as an ESOP, lacked the primary indicia of a pension plan (i.e., payment of benefits only upon retirement), (2) participation was voluntary, (3) the ESOP was contributory because participants gave up a percentage of income, and (4) participants acquired common stock, a security specifically enumerated in the Securities Act of 1933. [Hood v. Smith's Transfer Corp., 762 F. Supp. 1274 (W.D. Ky. 1991)]

For a discussion of these issues, see B.W. Berglund & J. Henshaw, *Securities Law Issues Relating to Employee Benefit Plans,* 27 J. Pension Plan. & Compliance No. 2, at p. 54 (Summer 2001).

Q 28:74 Is a participant's interest in an ESOP exempt from bankruptcy?

In 1992, the United States Supreme Court held that a participant's interest in a qualified retirement plan is exempt from the claims of creditors in a bankruptcy proceeding, thereby resolving the conflict among the courts of appeals. [Patterson v. Shumate, 504 U.S. 753 (1992)]

See Qs 4:28 through 4:30 for more details and Q 1:27 for a discussion of The Bankruptcy Abuse Prevention and Consumer Protection Act of 2005.

Chapter 29

Multiemployer Plans

Many companies maintain qualified retirement plans established under collective bargaining agreements. Frequently, more than one employer is required to contribute to the plan. How these multiemployer plans work, their basic advantages, and the system for guaranteeing benefits are examined in this chapter.

Q 29:1 What kind of retirement plan is used to provide retirement benefits for union workers?

Retirement plans are subject to collective bargaining. Often a retirement plan negotiated by a union is set up on an industrywide (sometimes regional) basis. An employer, out of necessity or voluntarily, will negotiate to join this industrywide retirement plan. In other cases, the employer may find it possible or desirable to have a separate (individual) retirement plan for its own employees as a result of negotiations with the union.

If the employer decides to go with an individual retirement plan, the plan is virtually identical to those plans adopted in nonunion situations. The only differences are that the retirement plan covers union workers and that the benefits result from the collective bargaining process. All of the requirements for qualification as a tax-favored retirement plan that apply to retirement plans that do not cover union employees apply to the individual collectively bargained retirement plan.

If, on the other hand, the employer decides to provide benefits under an industrywide or areawide retirement plan, commonly referred to as a multiemployer plan (see Q 29:2), an entirely different set of rules applies (in addition to some of the basic requirements). [I.R.C. §§ 413(a), 413(b); *see also* ERISA §§ 4201–4225] For example, hours of service that are credited to a participant for purposes of eligibility, vesting, and accrual of benefits are determined under different rules. [I.R.C. § 413(b)] The minimum funding requirements applicable to qualified retirement plans are modified, and the time to adopt certain retroactive plan amendments is extended. [I.R.C. §§ 412(b)(7), 412(d)(2)] IRS has issued guidance in the form of questions and answers concerning the election that can be made for certain multiemployer plans to defer charges for net experience losses. [I.R.C. § 412(b)(7)(F); Notice 2005-40, 2005-1 C.B. 1088]

Also, the provisions governing plan termination differ greatly from the rules for single-employer plans. [*Compare* ERISA §§ 4041, 4041A] However, other requirements for qualification that apply to retirement plans that do not cover union employees also apply to multiemployer plans; and, if a multiemployer plan does not meet the qualification requirements, the plan will not qualify for tax-exempt status as a labor organization. [I.R.C. § 501(c)(5); Treas. Reg. § 1.501(c)(5)-1(b); Tupper v. United States, 1998 U.S. App. LEXIS 535 (1st Cir. 1998); Stichting Pensioenfonds Voor de Gezonheid v. United States, 129 F.3d 195 (D.C. Cir. 1997); *but see* Morganbesser v. United States, 984 F.2d 560 (2d Cir. 1993)]

IRS noted that the use of a nonqualified plan (see Qs 1:11–1:13) designed to provide benefits in excess of the defined benefit plan limitations on benefits (see Q 6:11) paid by a multiemployer defined benefit plan did not affect the qualified (see Qs 1:5, 1:6) status of the multiemployer plan. [Priv. Ltr. Ruls. 200115027, 200018061, 200004042]

Under PPA (see Q 1:33), the funding rules for multiemployer plans are separated from the single-employer plan funding rules. The same general framework remains, but changes have been made for plan years beginning after December 31, 2007 that:

1. Reduce the amortization periods for certain supplemental costs to 15 years;
2. Change the amortization extension and funding waiver interest rate to the plan rate;
3. Tighten the reasonableness requirement for actuarial assumptions;
4. Eliminate the alternative minimum funding standard;
5. Make available an automatic five-year amortization extension with an additional five-year extension; and
6. Provide for deemed approval of changes in the use of the shortfall funding method. [I.R.C. § 431; ERISA § 304]

IRS issued a revenue procedure permitting multiemployer plan sponsors to request an extension of the amortization period for unfunded liability for up to ten years if certain conditions are met. A plan sponsor may request an automatic extension not in excess of five years and an alternative extension not in excess of ten years in the same application. IRS will automatically grant the portion of an application requesting an extension of five years or less. The grant of the portion of an application that includes a request for an extension of over five but not exceeding ten years is discretionary on the part of IRS.

The request for an extension of an amortization period must be submitted to IRS in the form of a letter ruling, along with appropriate authorization, certification by the plan's actuary, and a user fee (see Q 18:2). Notice must be provided to each employee organization representing employees covered by the plan, to each contributing employer, and to each participant, beneficiary, and alternate payee (see Q 36:5) of the plan within 14 days prior to the date of submission of the request. Appendix A of the revenue procedure contains a

Model Notice that will allow sponsors to comply with the notice requirement. All extension requests must be submitted by the last day of the first plan year for which the extension is intended to take effect. IRS will consider applications received after this date only upon a showing of good cause. The plan actuary must provide IRS with annual certification of a plan's funding status not later than the 90th day of each plan year, even if an application for an extension has been made. The actuary's certification may not take into account any extension application before the application receives a favorable ruling. [Rev. Proc. 2008-2, 2008-2 C.B. 1211]

Furthermore, under PPA, multiemployer plans that are so underfunded as to be in endangered or critical status are required to adopt funding improvement and rehabilitation plans and take certain actions to improve their funding status over a multiyear period. Excise taxes and civil penalties may apply if a plan does not adopt or comply with a required funding improvement or rehabilitation plan. [I.R.C. §§ 412(b)(3), 432, 4971(g); ERISA §§ 302(b)(3), 305, 502(a)(3), 502(c)(8)] IRS provided guidance for the sponsors of significantly underfunded multiemployer defined benefit plans, regarding elections (Section 204 election), which were provided in WRERA 2008 (see Q 1:36), of (1) a temporary freeze to their status as endangered or critical (or neither) and/or (2) an extension of the funding improvement period or rehabilitation period that applies to such plans. IRS has described the effect of the Section 204 elections and provided procedures for making the elections and providing the notices required regarding the elections. [IRS Notice 2009-31, 2009-1 C.B. 856] IRS extended the election date. The earliest deadline was extended to June 30, 2009. IRS also enabled plan sponsors, not yet able to reach agreement as to whether to make a Section 204 election, to make a timely election and automatically revoke the election later, if necessary. [IRS Notice 2009-42, 2009-1 C.B. 1011]

IRS set forth additional circumstances in which it will automatically approve a request to revoke a Section 204 election and has amplified IRS Notices 2009-31 and 2009-42. A request for revocation of a Section 204 election will be approved automatically by IRS, regardless of whether the election was the subject of arbitration, if the following requirements are met:

1. The request for revocation of the election must be submitted to IRS by the due date for the adoption of a funding improvement plan, rehabilitation plan, or update, whichever is applicable for the election year after taking the revocation into account. In the case of a plan where the decision to make a Section 204 election is the subject of an arbitration process, the deadline for submitting the request for revocation is the later of the due date under the preceding sentence or 30 days following the resolution of the arbitration.

2. Notice under Section 432(b)(3)(D) of the plan's actual certified status for the election year must be provided no later than 30 days after the request for revocation is submitted. The notice is also required to include a statement that the election was revoked and to explain the consequences of the revocation.

3. The plan sponsor must have complied with the requirements of Section 432(d)(1)(A) and (B) or Section 432(f)(4), as applicable, during the plan's funding plan adoption period or rehabilitation plan adoption period, determined as though a Section 204 election had never been made. This requirement does not apply to a plan where revocation results from the resolution of arbitration.

A request for revocation that is eligible for automatic approval must be signed by an authorized trustee who is a current member of the board of trustees that is the plan sponsor, and a copy of the plan's Section 204 election must be attached. The request for revocation must be mailed to IRS at the following address (which is also the address to which a Section 204 election is sent):

Internal Revenue Service
EPCU
Group 7602
SE:TEGE:EP
Room 1700 – 17th Floor
230 S. Dearborn Street
Chicago, IL 60604

The request for revocation may not be submitted electronically.

IRS may approve requests for revocations in circumstances other than those set forth above. Such requests are not eligible for automatic approval under this procedure, but must instead be made in accordance with Revenue Procedure 2009-4.

[Rev. Proc. 2009-43, 2009-2 C.B. 460]

In addition, DOL has issued proposed regulations that would establish procedures for assessing civil penalties against sponsors of multiemployer plans in endangered or critical status that fail to adopt a funding improvement or rehabilitation plan. [DOL Prop. Reg. § 2560.502c-8]

The plan sponsor will be liable for civil penalties assessed for:

1. Each violation by such sponsor of the requirement to adopt by the deadline a funding improvement plan or rehabilitation plan with respect to a multiemployer plan that is in endangered or critical status, or

2. In the case of a plan in endangered status that is not in seriously endangered status, a failure by the plan to meet the applicable benchmarks by the end of the funding improvement period with respect to the plan.

Violations or failures mean a failure or refusal, in whole or in part, to adopt a funding improvement or rehabilitation plan or to meet the applicable benchmarks at the prescribed relevant times and in the prescribed manners.

[DOL Prop. Reg. § 2560.502c-8(a)]

The amount assessed for each separate violation will be determined by DOL, taking into consideration the degree or willfulness of the failure or refusal to comply with the specific requirements referred to above. However, the amount assessed for each violation will not exceed $1,100 a day (or such other maximum amount as may be established by regulation), computed from the date of the plan sponsor's failure or refusal to comply with the specific requirements. [DOL Prop. Reg. § 2560.502c-8(b)] Prior to the assessment of any penalty, DOL will provide to the plan sponsor of the plan a written notice indicating DOL's intent to assess a penalty, the amount of such penalty, the period to which the penalty applies, and the reason(s) for the penalty. [DOL Prop. Reg. § 2560.502c-8(c)] DOL may determine that all or part of the penalty amount in the notice of intent to assess a penalty will not be assessed on a showing that the plan sponsor complied with the requirements, or on a showing by the plan sponsor of mitigating circumstances regarding the degree or willfulness of the noncompliance. [DOL Prop. Reg. § 2560.502c-8(d)]

Upon issuance by DOL of a notice of intent to assess a penalty, the plan sponsor will have 30 days from the date of service of the notice to file a statement of reasonable cause explaining why the penalty, as calculated, should be reduced, or not be assessed, for the reasons set forth above. Such statement must be made in writing and set forth all the facts alleged as reasonable cause for the reduction or nonassessment of the penalty. The statement must contain a declaration by the plan sponsor that the statement is made under the penalties of perjury. [DOL Prop. Reg. § 2560.502c-8(e)] Failure to file a statement of reasonable cause within the 30-day period will be deemed to constitute a waiver of the right to appear and contest the facts alleged in the notice of intent, and such failure will be deemed an admission of the facts alleged in the notice for purposes of any proceeding involving the assessment of a civil penalty. Such notice will then become a final order of DOL 45 days from the date of service of the notice. [DOL Reg. § 2570.131(g); DOL Prop. Reg. § 2560.502c-8(f)]

DOL, following a review of all of the facts in a statement of reasonable cause alleged in support of nonassessment or a complete or partial waiver of the penalty, will notify the plan sponsor, in writing, of its determination on the statement of reasonable cause and its determination of whether to waive the penalty, in whole or in part, and/or assess a penalty. If it is the determination of DOL to assess a penalty, the notice will indicate the amount of the penalty assessment, not to exceed the amount described above. Except as provided below, a notice issued indicating DOL's determination to assess a penalty will become a final order 45 days from the date of service of the notice. [DOL Reg. §§ 2570.131(g), 2570.131(m); DOL Prop. Reg. § 2560.502c-8(g)]

A notice will not become a final order if, within 30 days from the date of the service of the notice, the plan sponsor or a representative thereof files a request for a hearing and files an answer to the notice. The answer opposing the proposed sanction must be in writing and supported by reference to specific circumstances or facts surrounding the notice of determination. [DOL Reg. §§ 2570.130 through 2570.141; DOL Prop. Reg. § 2560.502c-8(h)] Service of a notice must be made (1) by delivering a copy to the plan sponsor or representative thereof; (2) by leaving a copy at the principal office, place of business, or residence of the plan sponsor or representative thereof; or (3) by mailing a copy to the last known address of the plan sponsor or representative thereof. If service is accomplished by certified mail, service is complete upon mailing. If service is by regular mail, service is complete upon receipt by the addressee. When service of a notice from DOL is by certified mail, five days will be added to the time allowed by these rules for the filing of a statement or a request for hearing and answer, as applicable. [DOL Prop. Reg. § 2560.502c-8(i)]

If more than one person is responsible as plan sponsor for the violations, all such persons will be jointly and severally liable for such violations. Any person or persons against whom a civil penalty has been assessed pursuant to a final order will be personally liable for the payment of such penalty. [DOL Prop. Reg. § 2560.502c-8(j)]

Q 29:2 What is a multiemployer plan?

Generally, a multiemployer plan is a plan established under a collective bargaining agreement (CBA) that is maintained by two or more unrelated employers. From a technical or legal standpoint, however, the multiemployer plan is defined as a plan:

1. To which more than one employer is required to contribute;
2. That is maintained under a CBA between an employee organization and more than one employer; and
3. That meets any additional requirements that may be issued by the Department of Labor (DOL). [ERISA § 3(37); I.R.C. § 414(f); Priv. Ltr. Rul. 200306038]

The multiemployer plan should be distinguished from the single-employer plan. Although the multiemployer plan is established through negotiations between employers, an association of employers, or a trade association and the union representing the plan participants, the single-employer plan is established or maintained by only one employer, either unilaterally or through a CBA. Generally, the sponsoring single employer has the ultimate responsibility for the administration of the plan. In contrast, responsibility for a multiemployer plan lies with a board of trustees composed of both union and employer representatives. [ERISA § 3(37)(A); Labor-Management Relations Act § 302(c)(5)] However, DOL has opined that a plan created from the merger of two single-employer defined benefit plans (see Q 2:3) was not a multiemployer plan. The plan was maintained pursuant to CBAs between two employers and two or more unions; but DOL determined that the plan was not a multiemployer plan because: (1) it was not maintained by a substantial number of unaffiliated contributing employers; (2) employee relationships with any particular employer maintaining the plan did not tend to be short term; (3) benefits under the plan were more closely related to service with a single employer than to years of service; and (4) the administrative cost of maintaining the separate rate single-employer plans was not significantly greater than that of maintaining the merged plan. [DOL Op. Ltr. 2002-07A] A multiemployer plan may be able to expel a member employer from the plan. [Borntrager v. Central States, Southeast and Southwest Areas Pension Fund, No. 04-1720 (8th Cir. 2005)]

IRS has discovered some plans incorrectly identifying themselves as multi-employer plans. IRS explained that this mistake results from a misunderstanding of the term "multiemployer." Some employers that have more than one employer in their plan sponsorship, such as controlled groups (see Q 5:31) or affiliated service groups (see Q 5:35), mistakenly believe that they are multiemployer plans. IRS also reported that some plans are failing to identify themselves as multiemployer plans when indeed they are. Plans also need to identify that employees are subject to a CBA. [*IRS Employee Plan News*, Summer 2006] Certain plans that irrevocably elected multiemployer status after enactment of the Multiemployer Pension Plan Amendments Act of 1980 were permitted to revoke that election, and certain plans sponsored by tax-exempt employers were permitted to irrevocably elect multiemployer status. Plans had to make the revocation or election by August 17, 2007. [I.R.C. § 414(f)(6); ERISA § 3(37)(G); PBGC Notice, July 23, 2007 (72 Fed. Reg. 40,176)] Any election is effective starting with any plan year beginning on or after January 1, 1999 and ending before January 1, 2008, as designated by the plan in the election. [I.R.C. § 414(f)(6)(B)]. The plan administrator (see Q 20:1) making an election must provide notice of the pending election no later than 30 days before the election is made to each plan participant and beneficiary, each labor organization representing such participants or beneficiaries, and each employer that has an obligation to contribute to the plan, describing the principal differences between the guarantee programs under Title IV (see Qs 25:16–25:19, 29:11–29:14) and the benefit restrictions under Title I (see Qs 8:6, 29:1) for single-employer and multiemployer plans, along with such other information the plan administrator chooses to include. DOL has published a Model Notice of Pending Election of Multiemployer Plan Status. [71 Fed. Reg. 69,594]

DOL has opined that business owners who provide services to their businesses may be participants in a multiemployer plan. [ERISA § 3(37); DOL Op. Ltr. 2006-04A; DOL Op. Ltr. 99-04A; *see also* Arnold v. Lucks, 392 F.3d 512 (2d Cir. 2004)]

The refusal to comply with the request of a participating employer in a multiemployer plan that the plan's trustees transfer the plan's liability to pay benefits for the employer's employees and an amount of funds equal to the employer's contributions to a new single-employer plan has been upheld because a multiemployer plan is not *required* to permit an asset transfer to another plan. [ERISA § 4234; Ganton Techs., Inc. v. National Indus. Group Pension Plan, 1996 U.S. App. LEXIS 1758 (2d Cir. 1996); Caterino v. Barry, 8 F.3d 878 (1st Cir. 1993); Vornado, Inc. v. Trustees of the Retail Store Employees' Union Local 1262, 829 F.2d 416 (3d Cir. 1987)] The amendment of a multiemployer plan to permit the acceptance of contributions to be accounted for on a notional basis did not affect the tax-exempt status of the plan, ruled IRS. The special contributions had an effect on the potential withdrawal liability (see Q 29:16) of employers; however, all of the assets arising from the special contributions were available to pay the benefits of all employees covered by the plan. In addition, the employers' special contributions did not fail to be fully deductible since the contributed amount was included in the funding method used by the plan. [Priv. Ltr. Rul. 200508028]

PPA (see Q 1:33) provides that, in the case of a multiemployer plan, it is unlawful for the plan sponsor or any other person to discriminate against any contributing employer for exercising rights under ERISA or for giving information or testifying in any inquiry or proceeding related to ERISA before Congress. [ERISA § 510]

Effective for plan years beginning after 2007, upon written request, each multiemployer plan administrator must furnish specified financial information for the plan to any plan participant or beneficiary, employee representative, or any contributing employer. The information that must be made available includes a copy of any:

1. Periodic actuarial report (including any sensitivity testing) received by the plan for any plan year that has been in the plan's possession for at least 30 days;

2. Quarterly, semiannual, or annual financial report prepared for the plan by any plan investment manager, advisor, or other fiduciary that has been in the plan's possession for at least 30 days; and

3. Application requesting an extension of amortization periods, as well as any determination made upon this application by IRS. [ERISA § 101(k)(1)]

Any actuarial or financial report required to be provided is subject to confidentiality limits. These required reports may not (1) include any individually identifiable information regarding any plan participant, beneficiary, employee, fiduciary, or contributing employer, or (2) reveal any proprietary information about the plan, any contributing employer, or entity providing services to the plan. [ERISA § 101(k)(2)(C)]

Multiemployer financial plan information must be provided to the participant, beneficiary, or contributing employer requesting it within 30 days after the request. [ERISA § 101(k)(2)(A)] The actuarial or other financial reports may be provided in a written, electronic, or other appropriate form to the extent that the form is reasonably accessible to persons and to employers requesting a copy of the form. [ERISA § 101(k)(2)(B)] Anyone entitled to a copy of any actuarial or financial report is not entitled to receive more than one copy of any report during any 12-month period. The person required to provide the report may impose a reasonable charge to cover the cost of copying, mailing, and other expenses involved in furnishing copies of the reports. DOL is authorized to impose a limit on what constitutes a reasonable charge. [ERISA § 101(k)(3)]

DOL may impose a penalty of up to $1,000 per day for each violation of the requirement to provide, upon request, actuarial or other financial information to any plan participant or beneficiary, employee representative, or contributing employer. [ERISA § 502(c)(c)], See Q 29:3 for a discussion of DOL final regulations.

DOL has issued proposed regulations on the obligation of multiemployer plan administrators to disclose certain actuarial and financial information to participants and others. [DOL Prop. Reg. §§ 2520.101-6, 2520.104b-30]

DOL has opined that the use of plan assets to promote union organizing or to advance union goals in collective bargaining negotiations is prohibited (see Q 24:1). [DOL Op. Ltr. 2008-05A]

Q 29:3   Can DOL impose monetary penalties for the failure or refusal to furnish certain information or notices?

A plan administrator (see Q 20:1) may be liable for penalties assessed by DOL for the failure or refusal to furnish actuarial, financial, or funding information (see Q 29:2) or a notice of potential withdrawal liability (see Q 29:16). A failure or refusal to furnish these items means a failure or refusal to furnish, in whole or in part, these items at the relevant times and manners prescribed by ERISA. [ERISA §§ 101(k), 101(*l*), 502(c)(4), 514(e)(3); DOL Reg. § 2560.502c-4(a)]

The amount assessed for each separate violation will be determined by DOL, taking into consideration the degree or willfulness of the failure or refusal to furnish these items. However, the amount assessed for each violation will not exceed $1,000 a day (or such other maximum amount as may be established by regulation pursuant to the Federal Civil Penalties Inflation Adjustment Act of 1990, as amended), computed from the date of the plan administrator's failure or refusal to furnish these items. For purposes of calculating the amount to be assessed, a failure or refusal to furnish the item, with respect to any person entitled to receive such item, will be treated as a separate violation. [DOL Reg. § 2560.502c-4(b)]

Prior to the assessment of any penalty, DOL must provide the plan administrator with a written notice indicating intent to assess a penalty, the amount of such penalty, the number of individuals on which the penalty is based, the period to which the penalty applies, and the reason(s) for the penalty. [DOL Reg. § 2560.502c-4(c)] DOL may determine that all or part of the penalty amount in the notice of intent to assess a penalty should not be assessed on a showing that the plan administrator complied with the applicable requirements, or on a showing by such person of mitigating circumstances regarding the degree or willfulness of the noncompliance. [DOL Reg. § 2560.502c-4(d)]

Upon issuance by DOL of a notice of intent to assess a penalty, the plan administrator will have 30 days from the date of service of the notice to file a statement of reasonable cause explaining why the penalty, as calculated, should be reduced, or not be assessed, for the reasons set forth in the preceding paragraph. Such statement must be made in writing and set forth all the facts alleged as reasonable cause for the reduction or non-assessment of the penalty. The statement must contain a declaration by the plan administrator that the statement is made under penalties of perjury. [DOL Reg. § 2560.502c-4(e)] Failure to file a statement of reasonable cause within the 30-day period will be deemed to constitute a waiver of the right to appear and contest the facts alleged in the notice of intent, and such failure will be deemed an admission of the facts alleged in the notice for purposes of any proceeding involving the assessment of a penalty. Such notice will then become a final order of DOL 45 days from the date of service of the notice. [DOL Reg. §§ 2560.502c-4(f), 2570.131(g)]

DOL, following a review of all of the facts in a statement of reasonable cause alleged in support of non-assessment or a complete or partial waiver of the penalty, will notify the plan administrator, in writing, of its determination on the statement of reasonable cause and of its determination of whether to waive the penalty in whole or in part and/or assess a penalty. If it is the determination of DOL to assess a penalty, the notice will indicate the amount of the penalty assessment, not to exceed the amount described above. This notice is considered a pleading. Except as provided in the next paragraph, the notice indicating DOL's determination to assess a penalty will become a final order 45 days from the date of service of the notice. [DOL Reg. §§ 2560.502c-4(g), 2570.131(m)]

A notice issued pursuant to the preceding paragraph will not become a final order if, within 30 days from the date of the service of the notice, the plan administrator or a representative thereof files a request for a hearing and files an answer to the notice. The answer opposing the proposed sanction must be in writing and supported by reference to specific circumstances or facts surrounding the notice of determination issued. [DOL Reg. §§ 2560.502c-4(h), 2570. 130–2570.141]

Service of a notice must be made by (1) delivering a copy to the plan administrator or representative thereof; (2) leaving a copy at the principal office, place of business, or residence of the plan administrator or representative thereof; or (3) mailing a copy to the last known address of the plan administrator or representative thereof. If service is accomplished by certified mail, service is complete upon mailing. If service is by regular mail, service is complete upon receipt by the addressee. When service of a notice is by certified mail, five days will be added to the time allowed by these rules for the filing of a statement or a request for hearing and answer as applicable. A statement of reasonable cause will be considered filed upon (1) mailing, if accomplished using United States Postal Service certified mail or express mail; (2) receipt by the delivery service, if accomplished using a designated private delivery service; (3) transmittal, if transmitted in a manner specified in the notice of intent to assess a penalty as a method of transmittal to be accorded such special treatment; or (4) in the case of any other method of filing, upon receipt by DOL at the address provided in the notice of intent to assess a penalty. [DOL Reg. § 2560.502c-4(i)]

If more than one person is responsible as plan administrator for the failure to furnish the required items, as applicable, all such persons will be jointly and severally liable for such failure. For purposes of the notice of potential withdrawal liability, administrator includes the plan sponsor. Any person or persons against whom a penalty has been assessed will be personally liable for the payment of such liability. [DOL Reg. § 2560.502c-4(j)]

The regulations became effective on March 3, 2008.

Q 29:4   Is a retirement plan maintained by two or more affiliated companies considered a multiemployer plan?

No. In considering whether more than one employer is required to contribute to the plan, employers that are under common control (see Qs 5:29, 5:31) are considered as only one employer. Thus, a plan that requires contributions from two or more companies that are controlled by the same interests is not a multiemployer plan because only one employer is required to contribute to the plan; multiemployer plans require more than one unrelated employer (see Q 29:2). [ERISA § 3(37)(B)]

Q 29:5 What are the basic advantages of a multiemployer plan?

The multiemployer plan has been developed to meet the needs of industries (e.g., construction, transportation, mining) that usually use craftsmen and draw their employees from a limited pool of workers within a specific geographical area. A multiemployer plan can benefit a particular industry because it:

1. Permits mobile employees to take their pension benefits with them when they move from one participating employer to another within the same industry;
2. Stabilizes pension costs among participating employers, reducing competitive wrangling for select employees;
3. Makes possible economies of scale because of the pooling of pension resources, either increasing benefits or reducing employer costs; and
4. Reduces administrative costs through use of experienced and knowledgeable administrators and trustees.

An employee who worked full time for two unrelated employers, both of which contributed to the same multiemployer plan, was entitled only to one pension benefit and not to a double benefit. [Pochoday v. Building Serv. 32B-J Pension Fund, No. 00-9097 (2d Cir. 2001)] Where a union member, whose employer had not contributed to the union's pension plan on his behalf for a portion of his career, presented detailed evidence that he had been engaged in covered employment during this period, the plan's denial of retirement benefits for this period was arbitrary and capricious, ruled one court [Glascoe v. Central States, Southeast & Southwest Areas Pension Fund, 2002 WL 486391 (6th Cir. 2002)] One court concluded that the method used by a multiemployer plan to calculate pension benefits for participants who had service with multiple employers was a reasonable interpretation of plan provisions and had to be upheld. [Otto v. Western Pennsylvania Teamsters and Employers Pension Fund, No. 04-2307 (3d Cir. 2005)] Another court ruled that an employee was not entitled to pension benefits for services performed for his employer for the period during which the employer had not been a signatory to a collective bargaining agreement (CBA), even though, during that same period, the employer was part of a controlled group of corporations (see Q 5:31) that included signatories to the CBA. [Yates v. UMWA 1974 Pension Plan, No. 05-2224 (4th Cir. 2006)]

DOL has opined that the use of plan assets to promote union organizing or to advance union goals in collective bargaining negotiations is prohibited (see Q 24:1). [DOL Op. Ltr. 2008-05A]

Q 29:6   Must an employer contribute to a multiemployer plan?

Every employer who is obligated to make contributions to a multiemployer plan under the terms of the plan or under the terms of a collective bargaining agreement (CBA) must make contributions in accordance with the terms and conditions of the plan or the agreement. [ERISA § 515] Effective for years beginning after December 31, 2007, the deduction limit for contributions to a multiemployer defined benefit plan (see Q 2:3) is increased. [I.R.C. § 404(a)(1)(D)] For plan years beginning after December 31, 2007, employers must make contributions to or under the multiemployer plan for any plan year which, in the aggregate, are sufficient to ensure that the plan does not have an accumulated funding deficiency as of the end of the plan year. If an employer is a member of a controlled group (see Q 5:31) or an affiliated service group (see Q 5:35), each member of the group is jointly and severally liable for the contribution. [I.R.C. §§ 412(b), 412(d)(3); ERISA §§ 302(b), 302(d)(3)]

One court concluded that plan participants do not have standing to sue derivatively on behalf of a plan against employers for unpaid fund contributions even though the participants alleged that the plan trustees breached their fiduciary duties by refusing to sue the employers. [Moore v. American Fed'n of Television & Radio Artists, 216 F.3d 1236 (11th Cir. 2000)] However, another court determined that a union had standing on behalf of its members to sue three sureties for delinquent contributions. The court applied a three-pronged test in determining that the union had standing to bring the action: (1) the union members had standing to sue in their own right for unpaid wages and benefits; (2) the protection of members' rights is germane to the union's purposes; and (3) neither the claim asserted nor the relief requested required the participation of the union's individual members. [Ironworkers Dist Council of the Pac. Northwest v. George Sollit Corp., No. CO1-1668C (D. Wash. 2002)]

In a lawsuit brought by a plan participant, another court ruled that the plan and its trustees did not breach their fiduciary duties when they entered into an agreement with a contributing employer that relieved the employer of its plan contribution obligations for a five-month period. [Sprague v. Central States, Southeast & Southwest Areas Pension Fund, 2001 WL 1243414 (7th Cir. 2001)] DOL has opined that trustees of a multiemployer plan that have established delinquent contribution procedures pursuant to the authority of their trust agreement, which could only be amended by the trustees, are not required to adopt delinquent contribution procedures specified in a CBA that conflicted with the trust provisions. DOL did not address whether a trust agreement could mandate that delinquent contribution procedures be subject to collective bargaining or empower an employer association or union to amend the terms of the trust agreement; but DOL did note, however, that whether the employers who signed the CBA are bound by the delinquent contribution procedures in the trust agreement is dependent on the facts of each case. [DOL Op. Ltr. 2002-06A]

In an action by a multiemployer plan to enforce ERISA Section 515, if a judgment in favor of the plan is awarded, the court shall award to the plan:

1. The unpaid contributions;

2. Interest on the unpaid contributions;

3. An amount equal to the greater of (a) interest on the unpaid contributions or (b) liquidated damages provided for under the plan in an amount not in excess of 20 percent (or such higher percentage as may be permitted under federal or state law) of the amount determined by the court under paragraph 1;

4. Reasonable attorneys' fees and costs of the action, to be paid by the employer; and

5. Such other legal or equitable relief as the court deems appropriate.

[ERISA § 502(g)(2); Anderson v. AB Painting & Sandblasting, Inc., 578 F.3d 542 (7th Cir. 2009); Iron Workers' Local No. 25 Pension Fund v. MCS Gen. Contractors, 2000 U.S. App. LEXIS 22688 (6th Cir. 2000)]

An employer cannot escape liability for interest, liquidated damages or double interest, attorneys' fees, and costs by paying delinquent contributions before the entry of a judgment, as long as plan contributions were unpaid at the time the suit was filed. [UAW Local 259 Social Security Dept. v. Metro Auto Center, 2007 WL 2472237 (3d Cir. 2007); Iron Workers Dist. Council of W. N.Y. & Vicinity Welfare & Pension Funds v. Hudson Steel Fabricators & Erectors, Inc., 1995 U.S. App. LEXIS 30924 (2d Cir. 1995)] Such awards are mandatory, not discretionary, and also apply to postsuit, prejudgment, voluntary payments of amounts that were delinquent when the suit was filed. [Northwest Adm'rs v. Albertson's, 1996 U.S. App. LEXIS 33640 (9th Cir. 1996)] One court held that an employer was required under a CBA to pay liquidated damages for delinquent contributions to a multiemployer plan because the damages caused by the delinquent contributions were difficult or impossible to assess and the amount of damages required by the liquidated damages clause under the CBA was a reasonable prediction of the harm suffered by the plan. [Trustees of Bricklayers Pension Trust Fund, Metropolitan Area v. Rosati, Inc., No. 00-1245 (6th Cir. 2001)] The routine audit fees of a multiemployer plan may not be part of a judgment award to the plan; however, the plan could recover attorneys' fees at the market rate rather than at the rate they were actually charged, concluded one court. [Board of Trustees v. JPR Inc., 1998 U.S. App. LEXIS 3165 (D.C. Cir. 1998)] A multiemployer plan received an award for delinquent contributions, union dues, prejudgment interest, and liquidated damages. The plan also requested an award of audit costs. The court concluded that the plan failed to provide information necessary to support an award of reasonable audit costs and did not carry its burden of demonstrating that the audit costs should be recovered. [Trustees of Chicago Plastering Inst. Pension Trust v. Cork Plastering, Inc., 2007 WL 3449493 (N.D. Ill. 2007)] One court determined that an employer was liable for additional contributions to multiemployer plans based on an audit of a ten-year period for which the employer had retained only four years of payroll records. The fact that the audit lacked the exactness that would have been possible if the employer had kept records for the entire audit period did not warrant a rejection of the auditor's finding. [Trustees of Chicago Plastering Institute Pension Fund v. R.G. Construction Services, Inc., 2009 WL 1733036 (___.D. Ill. 2009)] An employer that stopped making payments to a multiemployer plan had to pay past due interim withdrawal liability payments, future payments, interest for past due amounts, attorneys' fees, and liquidated damages to the plan, even though there was disagreement as to whether the employer was merely engaged in labor disputes at the time the payments stopped or had completely withdrawn from the plan. [Central States, Southeast & Southwest Areas Pension Fund v. Bomar Nat'l, Inc., No. 00-2472 (7th Cir. 2001)] Attorneys' fees can include billings of law clerks, paralegals, and other non-attorneys and costs can include charges for electronic legal research, postage, photocopies, courier services, facsimile charges, long distance phone charges, and court reporter services, provided that separate billing for these services and expenses is the prevailing practice in the local community. [Trustees of the Construction Industry and Laborers Health and Welfare Trust v. Redland Ins. Co., 2006 U.S. App. LEXIS 22230 (9th Cir. 2006)] However, an award of attorneys' fees to the prevailing defendant in a suit for plan contributions brought by the trustees of a multiemployer plan was upheld because the trustees' suit was not substantially justified. [Sullivan v. William Randolph, Inc., 504 F.3d 665(7th Cir. 2007)]

An employer was held liable for the payment of delinquent contributions to a multiemployer plan because its defenses were precluded by ERISA Section 515. The court stated that only three defenses to a delinquency action have been recognized by the circuit courts that have considered the issue:(1) the multiemployer plan contributions are illegal; (2) the CBA is void from its inception (e.g., fraud in the execution); and (3) the employees have voted to decertify the union as their bargaining representative. [Louisiana Bricklayers & Trowel Trades Pension Fund & Welfare Fund v. Alfred Miller Gen. Masonry Contracting Co, No. 97-30594 (5th Cir. 1998)] However, courts have ruled that, even if a CBA is declared void from its inception by the National Labor Relations Board, it is not void from inception for purposes of ERISA. Consequently, contributions to the multiemployer plan required by the CBA must be made from the date of the agreement until the date the CBA is declared void. [Mackillop v. Lowe's Market, Inc., 1995 U.S. App. LEXIS 16769 (9th Cir. 1995); *see also* Alaska Trowel Trades Funds v. Lopshire, 1996 U.S. App. LEXIS 33535 (9th Cir. 1996)] One court concluded that, although a union representative made some fraudulent statements about the nature of a CBA signed by a company representative, there was no fraud in the execution of the CBA because the document was clearly labeled a CBA; thus, the company was liable for delinquent plan contributions. [Laborers' Pension Fund v. A&C Envtl., Inc., 2002 WL 1895541 (7th Cir. 2002)] One court, however, concluded that an employer's claim that it had properly terminated its obligations to a multiemployer plan pursuant to a termination clause in the CBA was a permissible defense against the plan's action for delinquent contributions, since evaluating the merits of the defense involved a straightforward inquiry. [Plumbers & Pipefitters Local Union No. 572 Health & Welfare Fund v. A&H Mechanical Contractors, Inc., 2004 WL 1208873 (6th Cir. 2004)] Another court permitted a defense of abandonment. An employer executed a CBA that obligated it to contribute to a multiemployer plan, which agreement contained specific termination provisions requiring the employer to give the union written notice if it intended to terminate the CBA. The employer provided the required termination notice to the union, which the union acknowledged; but the union later sent two letters stating that the employer's notice was untimely and threatened arbitration proceedings. The employer ceased making contributions to the plan, and no further demands for fund contributions were made. Ten years later, the fund commenced a law suit seeking back payment of the contributions. The court ruled in favor of the employer on the grounds that the union had abandoned its challenge to the termination because no action to obtain contributions was taken for over ten years, despite initial threats of arbitration, and that the employer was, therefore, entitled to assume that the CBA had been terminated and that no further contributions were required. [Laborers Health & Welfare Trust Fund for N. Cal. v. Leslie G. Delbon Co., Nos. 98-16407, 98-16488 (9th Cir. 2000)] On somewhat similar but otherwise different facts, other courts have come to different conclusions. [Teamster & Employers Welfare Trust of Ill. v. Gorman Bros. Ready Mix, No. 01-2029 (7th Cir. 2002); Trustees of the Mich. Laborers' Health Care Fund v. Gibbons, 209 F.3d 587 (6th Cir. 2000); Northwestern Ohio Adm'rs v. SEA Builders Corp, No. 3:99cv07406 (N.D. Ohio 2000)]

Special assessments made by trustees of a multiemployer plan against family-controlled construction companies, in which the owner or the owner's spouse was treated as an employee, that required the companies to contribute for hours in excess of those actually worked were held to be invalid. [La Barbera v. J.D. Collyer Equip. Corp., 337 F.3d 132 (2d Cir. 2003)]

One court determined that an employer was not required to make contributions after the CBA expired because the participation agreement signed contemporaneously with the CBA did not require contributions after the expiration of the CBA. [Central States, Southeast & Southwest Areas Pension Fund v. General Materials, Inc., No. 07-1392/1473 (6th Cir. 2008); *see also* Dugan v. R.J. Corman R.R., 2003 U.S. App. LEXIS 19521 (7th Cir. 2003)] In another case, however, even though the CBA had expired, an employer was held liable for delinquent contributions because its conduct demonstrated an intent to be bound by the expired agreement. [Laborers' Pension Fund & Laborers' Welfare Fund v. Blackmore Sewer Constr., Inc., Nos. 00-1112, 00-1975 (7th Cir. 2002); Michigan Bricklayers & Allied Craftsmen Health Care Fund v. Northwestern Constr., Inc., 1997 U.S. App. LEXIS 15440 (6th Cir. 1997)] Similarly, another court concluded that an employer could be liable for delinquent contributions where the CBA expired, the employer did not sign two later agreements, but continued to submit monthly remittance reports. [Brown v. C. Volante Corp, 1999 WL 807724 (2d Cir. 1999)] An employer was held liable for plan contributions under a CBA for the entire period covered by the CBA, even before signing a formal letter of consent, because the employer's course of conduct, making payments in accordance with the CBA, demonstrated the employer's assent to the CBA. [Line Construction Benefit Fund v. Allied Electrical Contractors, Inc., 591 F.3d 576 (7th Cir. 2010)] Courts have determined that an employer, which did not make contributions to a multiemployer plan because of an additional agreement with the union that was not disclosed to the plan, was liable for contributions to the plan and associated damages since the plan was entitled to rely on the disclosed agreement requiring contributions. [Northwest Adm'rs, Inc. v. Sacramento

Stucco, No. C 96-2998 (N.D. Cal. 2000); Central States, Southeast & Southwest Areas Pension Fund v. Transport, Inc., 1999 WL 446838 (7th Cir. 1999)] An employer was required to make contributions to a multiemployer plan based on the terms of the plan, not on the unwritten terms of a CBA. [New York State Teamsters Conference Pension & Retirement Fund v. United Parcel Service, Inc., 2004 U.S. App. LEXIS 18289 (2d Cir. 2004)] Another employer which made contributions to a multiemployer plan pursuant to an unwritten CBA was bound to the CBA and was required to cooperate with an audit to determine ERISA compliance. [Bricklayers Local 21 of Illinois Apprenticeship and Training Program v. Banner Restoration, Inc., 2004 U.S. App. LEXIS 20783 (7th Cir. 2004)] Another court ruled that an employer could be liable for multiemployer plan contributions under a CBA even though the agreement was signed by the association of which the employer was a member and not by the employer itself because an employer can delegate authority to the association to sign the CBA. [National Leadburners Benefit Funds v. O.G. Kelley & Co., 1997 U.S. App. LEXIS 32273 (6th Cir. 1997)] One court concluded that the CBA signed by an employer's predecessor bound the employer as an assignee even though the employer had not signed the CBA and that nonmembers could be liable for plan contributions. [Building Serv. 32B-J Pension Fund v. Vanderveer Estates Holding, LLC, No. 00 Civ. 0364 (S.D.N.Y. 2000)] However, where an employer argued that it joined an association only to receive current industry information and never received a copy of the association's bylaws or the CBA, the employer was not liable for plan contributions, ruled the court, because mere membership in the association was insufficient to form a basis to infer that the employer agreed to be bound by the CBA. [Alston v. Kay E. Parking Corp., No. 95 Civ. 0962 (S.D.N.Y. 1997)] Another court determined that a multiemployer plan was not entitled to summary judgment against an employer for unpaid contributions pursuant to CBAs between the employer's multiemployer organization and a union because the organizational membership application the employer signed did not expressly provide that the employer was designating the organization as representative with regard to any CBAs. [Moriarty v. Pepper, Nos. 01-1034, 01-1080 (7th Cir. 2001)]

One court ruled that, where a union's CBA with a contractor was ambiguous concerning the employees it covered and the geographic area to which it applied and the union had overlapping jurisdiction with a number of other unions that had CBAs with the same contractor, it could not be assumed that all multiemployer plan contributions not paid by the contractor were owed to members of one union. [Carpenters Fringe Benefit Funds of Ill. v. McKenzie Eng'g, 217 F.3d 578 (8th Cir. 2000)] Another court concluded that an employer obligated to make contributions to a multiemployer plan for eligible employees was not similarly obligated, under the terms of the governing CBAs, to make contributions for leased employees. [Central Pennsylvania Teamsters Pension Fund v. Power Packaging, Inc., No. 04-2867 (3d Cir. 2005)]

Where an employer is consistently delinquent in making its contributions to a multiemployer plan, the plan may be able to obtain a court order requiring that future contributions be made on a timely basis even without a showing of irreparable harm. [Trustees for Michigan Carpenters Council Pension Fund v. WWA, Inc., No. 99-1144 (6th Cir. 2000)]

One court concluded that an employer's contributions to a multiemployer plan within the 90-day period before it filed for bankruptcy protection was not an avoidable preference because the payments were made for contemporaneous new value (i.e., the employees' services); thus, the plan was not required to return the contributions to the bankruptcy trustee. [Jones Truck Lines, Inc. v. Central States, Southeast and Southwest Areas Pension, Health & Welfare Funds, 130 F.3d 323 (8th Cir. 1997)] Monthly multiemployer plan contributions arising during the 180-day period preceding the bankruptcy filing date were entitled to priority unsecured status, ruled one court. [*In re* Cornell and Co., No. 96-31650 (Bankr. E.D. Pa. 1998)] An assignee/trustee which received a general assignment for the benefit of creditors from an employer in bankruptcy was not liable for the employer's unpaid contributions, concluded one court, because (1) the assignee was not obligated, under the law governing assignments, to perform the employer's duties under the CBA; (2) the assignment instrument did not obligate the assignee to such duties; (3) the assignee had no ownership relationship with the employer; and (4) it was not necessary for the purposes of ERISA to construe the term "employer" to include an assignee for the benefit of creditors. [Mason Tenders Dist. Council Welfare Fund v. Logic Constr. Corp., No. 97 Civ. 5212 (S.D.N.Y. 1998)] Other courts have ruled that a bankrupt employer's debt to multiemployer plans is dischargeable, holding that a fiduciary relationship under ERISA does not necessarily create a fiduciary relationship under the Federal Bankruptcy Code. [Bd. of Trustees of Ohio Carpenters Pension Fund v. Bucci, 2007 WL 1891736 (6th Cir. 2007); Hunter v. Philpott, 373 F.3d 1186 (8th Cir. 2004); *but see In re* Hemmeter, 242 F.3d 1186 (9th Cir. 2001)] One court determined that a multiemployer plan's judgment lien for unpaid contributions against an employer did not take priority over a previously perfected security interest. [Chicago Dist. Council of Carpenters Pension Fund v. Tessio Constr. Co., No. 02-C-4987 (N.D. Ill. 2003)] In an employer's bankruptcy proceeding, unpaid plan contributions were held to be assets of the employer and, thus, subject to the priority interests of the employer's creditors because the contributions were employer, not employee, contributions as they had not been deducted from the employee's pay. [*In re* M & S Grading, Inc., 2008 WL 4133863 (8th Cir. 2008)] Another court concluded that employer contributions do not become plan assets until the contributions are actually made to the plan unless the plan documents otherwise provide. [*In re* Halpin, 2009 WL 1272632 (2d Cir. 2009)]

Two related companies were not liable for a third company's unpaid pension contributions because they were not parties to the CBA creating the obligation to contribute to the pension plan and had not withheld or disguised their corporate identities in order to defraud the pension plan. [Central States, Southeast & Southwest Areas Pension Fund v. Central Transp., Inc., No.95-2055 (7th Cir. 1996); *see also* Hawaii Carpenters Trust Funds v. Birtcher/BCI, 1997 U.S. App. LEXIS 6340 (9th Cir. 1997)] One court concluded that an employer which employed several employees for whom contributions were made to a multiemployer plan by an unrelated entity, a signatory of the CBA, was not obligated for contributions for all of its employees because the employer was not a signatory of the agreement. [Trustees of Bay Area Painters & Tapers Pension Fund v. H.L. Heggstead, Inc., No. C 96-02694 (N.D. Cal. 1998)] A corporation that was required by the CBA to make contributions on behalf of owner-drivers could not do so legally because they were independent contractors and not employees. The court ruled that making contributions on behalf of independent contractors would be a violation of the Labor Management Relations Act (LMRA). [Mazzei v. Rock-N-Around Trucking, Inc., No. 00-1473 (7th Cir. 2001)]

An employer that did not contribute to a multiemployer plan on behalf of its casual drivers was found liable to the plan for interest and contributions. The employer classified each new full-time driver it hired as a casual driver (a classification not eligible for fringe benefits) for periods of up to four years. Because the employees assigned casual driver status by the employer did not meet the ordinary definition of casual employee (i.e., short term, temporary, or sporadic), the court held that the employer had an obligation to contribute to the plan on their behalf. [Brown-Graves Co. v. Central States, Southeast & Southwest Areas Pension Fund, 206 F.3d 680 (6th Cir. 2000); see also Dugan v. R.J. Corman R.R., 2003 U.S. App. LEXIS 19521 (7th Cir. 2003); Central States, Southeast & Southwest Areas Pension Fund v. Groesbeck Lumber & Supply, Inc., No. 99 C 1947 (N.D. Ill. 2000)] One court concluded that the ERISA definition of "employee," and not the definition used in the LMRA, had to be used to interpret a CBA even though the trust agreements were established prior to ERISA. [ERISA § 3(6); Moriarty v. Svec, 233 F.3d 955 (7th Cir. 2000)] Another court determined that, although certain pre-apprentice employees were not covered under the multiemployer plan, the employer's responsibility to contribute on their behalf was established under the CBA. [Iron Workers' Local No. 25 Pension Fund v. MCS Gen. Contractors, 2000 U.S. App. LEXIS 22688 (6th Cir. 2000)] A master CBA prevailed over a local CBA so that an employer was required to contribute to a multiemployer plan for part-time employees. [Central States, Southeast & Southwest Areas Pension Fund v. Kroger Co, 226 F.3d 903 (7th Cir. 2000)] An employer was required to contribute on behalf of non-union workers to a multiemployer plan because the workers did the general type of work described in the CBA. The CBA did not define "journeymen and apprentices"; but, because the workers came within the dictionary definition and they performed the work described in the CBA, the workers were covered by the CBA. [Plumber, Steamfitter & Shipfitter Indus. Pension Plan & Trust v. Siemens Bldg. Techs. Inc., 228 F.3d 964 (9th Cir. 2000)] An Ohio employer was not obligated to make contributions to a Michigan bricklayers union fund when the Ohio employer did work in Michigan with carpenters union employees from Ohio, ruled one court, because the use of the term "traveling contractor" in the CBA of the Ohio bricklayers union was ambiguous. [Trustees of the BCA Local 32 Ins. Fund v. Ohio Ceiling & Partition Co., 2002 WL 31245970 (6th Cir. 2002)] However, another court upheld a multiemployer plan's claim against a contractor for plan contributions based on construction projects performed in another state with a subcontractor's nonunion employees in violation of a CBA. [Flynn v. Dick Corp., 2007 WL 817389 (D.C. Cir. 2007)] One court concluded that an employer was obligated to make plan contributions for all employees covered under a CBA, despite a handwritten clause on related documents that limited contributions to only union employees, because under ERISA the plan administrator (see Q 20:1) was entitled to disregard the employer's intent and to enforce the typewritten plan terms. [Northwestern Ohio Adm'rs, Inc. v. Walcher & Fox, Inc., Nos. 00-3536, 00-3538 (6th Cir. 2001)]

See Qs 29:7 and 29:8 for further details.

Q 29:7   What is an alter ego corporation?

An "alter ego" corporation can be held liable for the delinquent contributions of a company obligated to make contributions to a multiemployer plan. [Flynn v. R.C. Tile, 353 F.3d 953 (D.C. Cir. 2004); Flynn v. Greg Anthony Constr. Co., 2003 U.S. App. LEXIS 23024 (6th Cir. 2003); Massachusetts Carpenters Cent. Collection Agency v. Belmont Concrete Corp., 1998 U.S. App. LEXIS 5988 (1st Cir. 1998); IBEW Local Union No. 100 Pension Trust Fund v. Dale Elec. Inc., No. 96-16054 (9th Cir. 1998); Boilermaker-Blacksmith Nat'l Pension Fund v. Gendron, No. 98-2317 (D. Kan. 2000); United Food & Commercial Workers Union v. Fleming Foods E., Inc., No. 95-2587 (D.N.J. 2000); Bourgal v. Robco Contracting Enters., Ltd., No. CV 93-2664 (E.D.N.Y. 1997); Chicago Dist. Council of Carpenters Pension Fund v. PMQT, Inc., No. 94 C 6785 (N.D. Ill. 1996); *see also* Burke v. Hamilton Installers, 2008 WL 2275909 (2d Cir. 2008)]

One court held that one corporation was not the alter ego of another because the two companies did not have identical control and management and transactions between the two companies were negotiated at arm's length. [Greater Kan. City Laborers Pension Fund v. Superior Gen. Contractors, Inc., 104 F.3d 1050 (8th Cir. 1997); *see also* Trustees of the Resilient Floor Decorators Insurance Fund v. A&M Installations, Inc., 2005 U.S. App. LEXIS 93 (6th Cir. 2005); Minnesota Laborers Health & Welfare Fund v. Scanlan, 2004 WL 235203 (8th Cir. 2004); Massachusetts Carpenters Cent. Collection Agency v. AA Bldg. Erectors, Inc., 343 F.3d 18 (1st Cir. 2003); United Food & Commercial Workers & Participating Food Indus. Tri-state Health & Welfare Fund v. Cinnaminson Supermarket, Inc., No. 98-5452 (3d Cir. 1999)] However, another court concluded that a successor company was liable for a predecessor's delinquent contributions. The successor company shared the same management and warehouse facilities as the predecessor company and leased all of the predecessor's machinery and equipment, thus establishing sufficient continuity of operations to create successor liability. [Chicago Dist. Council of Carpenters Pension Fund v. Artistry Woodworking, Inc., No. 92 C 2069 (N.D. Ill. 1997)] An employer and principal owner of a funeral home and livery service, inherited from his father, was held liable for delinquent contributions for the livery service employees because continuity of business operations existed before and after the father's death and the livery service was the alter ego of the funeral home. In addition, the court concluded that ERISA preempted the state's law of successor liability under which a successor entity does not assume the liability of its predecessor. [Moriarty v. Svec, 1998 WL 865438 (7th Cir. 1998)] A company that was not a signatory to a CBA (see Q 29:6) was not liable for contributions to multiemployer plans, even if the company was deemed to be a joint employer with a company that was a signatory. [Trustees of the Screen Actors Guild-Producers Pension and Health Plans v. NYCA, Inc., 2009 WL 2032464 (9th Cir. 2009)]

An employer declared bankruptcy and owed contributions to a multiem-ployer plan administered in Virginia. The plan commenced an action against the employer in a Virginia court and also served process on a board member and a related company, both Indiana residents, alleging that both of them were alter egos of the bankrupt employer and, thus, also responsible for the delinquent contributions. The court concluded that the Virginia court had jurisdiction over both of them, even when neither had any ties to Virginia, and that they were required, once served, to dispute their alter ego status in Virginia. [ERISA § 502(e)(2); Board of Trustees, Sheet Metal Workers' Nat'l Pension Fund v. Elite Erectors, Inc., 212 F.3d 1031 (7th Cir. 2000); *but see* Central States, Southeast & Southwest Areas Pension Fund v. Reimer Express World Corp, 230 F.3d 934 (7th Cir. 2000)]

A multiemployer plan successfully brought an action against an employer for delinquent contributions; and, when the plan was unable to collect the judg-ment, it sued a second employer as the alter ego successor of the first employer. The court concluded that where an alter ego claim is being asserted and the proof of liability depends on facts and theories that differ significantly from the facts and theories used to obtain the initial judgment, an independent basis for federal jurisdiction must be provided for the alter ego action. Thus, the court determined that the plan could not enforce the judgment which was based on ERISA and the LMRA against the second employer in federal court without providing an independent basis for federal jurisdiction (i.e., basis other than ERISA or the LMRA). [Ellis v. All Steel Construction Inc., 389 F.3d 1031 (10th Cir. 2004); *see also* Sandlin v. Corporate Interiors Inc., 972 F.2d 1212 (10th Cir. 1992); Peacock v. Thomas, 516 U.S. 349 (1996); *but see* Board of Trustees, Sheet Metal Workers' Nat'l Pension Fund v. Elite Erectors, Inc., 212 F.3d 1031 (7th Cir. 2000)]

Q 29:8 Can corporate officers be liable for unpaid employer contributions?

One court held that the president of an employer that was obligated to contribute to a multiemployer plan was personally liable for unpaid plan contributions even though he was not provided with copies of the collective bargaining or trust agreements before signing a counterpart agreement. [Employee Painters' Trust v. J & B Finishes, 1996 U.S. App. LEXIS 3416 (9th Cir. 1996)] After its corporate charter was revoked, the corporation continued to conduct business and an officer signed CBAs on behalf of the corporation. The court concluded that the officers of the corporation who carried on new business were personally liable for unpaid plan contributions. [Shaw v. Jenkins, 2001 WL 327730 (S.D. Ohio 2001)] Another court held that an employer's president committed a fiduciary breach by failing to make plan contributions and was personally liable to the plan for the unpaid contributions. The court concluded that the unpaid contributions became plan assets when they became due and owing to the plan. Because the president exercised discretionary authority over these amounts, he was a fiduciary (see Q 23:1) and, therefore, committed a breach when he used the amounts to pay corporate expenses rather than plan contributions. Thus, he was liable to the plan for the losses caused by his breach (see Q 23:32). [ERISA § 409(a); PMTA-ILA Containerization Fund v. Rose, 1995 U.S. Dist. LEXIS 10877 (E.D. Pa. 1995)] However, another court ruled otherwise and held that classifying contributions as plan assets does not necessarily transfer fiduciary status onto corporate officers, and personal liability for delinquent plan contributions could not be imposed upon an unknowing restaurant owner. [Hotel Employees and Restaurant Employees Int'l Union Welfare Fund v. Billy's 1870, 2004 U.S. Dist. LEXIS 15685 (N.D. Ill. 2004)] Yet another court concluded that unpaid contributions did not become plan assets when they became due and owing to the plan; hence, the employer's former officers were not liable for the unpaid contributions. [Manley v. Fischer, No. 96-Civ-0561 (S.D.N.Y. 1998); see also ITPE v. Hall, 334 F.3d 1011 (11th Cir. 2003)] One court held that, even if the unpaid contributions were plan assets, the corporate officers were not fiduciaries because they did not exercise authority or control over the management or disposition of plan assets. [In re Luna, 406 F.3d 1192 (10th Cir. 2005)] However, another court concluded that, even though unpaid contributions were not plan assets, the sole director and shareholder of the employer was personally liable because all circumstances warranted piercing the corporate veil. [Trustees of the Nat'l Elevator Indus. Pension, Health Benefit & Educ. Funds v. Lutyk, 332 F.3d 188 (3d Cir. 2003)] Another court declined to impose personal liability on a corporate officer because, in New York, an agent who signs an agreement on behalf of a disclosed principal is not individually bound to the terms of the agreement unless there is clear and explicit evidence of the agent's intention to substitute or add the officer's personal liability for, or to, that of the principal. [Mason Tenders Dist. Council Welfare Fund v. Thomsen Constr. Co., No. 01-9225 (2d Cir. 2002); Cement & Concrete Workers Dist. Council Welfare Fund, Pension Fund, Legal Servs. Fund & Sec. Fund v. Lollo, 35 F.3d 29 (2d Cir. 1994); see also Operating Eng'rs Local No. 49 Health & Welfare Fund v. Listul Erection Corp., 2002 U.S. Dist. LEXIS 17508 (D. Minn. 2002); Mason Tenders Dist. Council Welfare Fund v. Massucci, No. 95 Civ. 9139 (S.D.N.Y. 1997); Cement & Concrete Workers Dist. Council Welfare Fund, Pension Fund, Legal Servs. Fund & Sec. Fund v. Lollo, Nos. 97-7013, 97-7023 (2d Cir. 1998)] However, one court ruled, without qualification, that there is no personal liability for delinquent contributions under ERISA. [Schuck, Jr. v. DAK Elec. Contracting Corp., No. CV 95-2454 (E.D.N.Y. 1998)] A corporate officer who occasionally signed company checks for contributions to multiemployer plans was not personally liable for unpaid contributions because he did not exercise discretionary control over plan assets. [Teamsters Health & Welfare Funds of Phila. & Vicinity v. World Transp., Inc., No. 00-5562 (E.D. Pa. 2003)] The owners of an insolvent corporation were held not to be personally liable for unpaid plan contributions because the plan did not provide satisfactory evidence that the owners had used the corporation to fraudulently avoid paying the plan contributions. [Carpenters District Council of Kansas City Pension Fund v. JNL Construction Co., Inc., 596 F.3d 491 (8th Cir. 2010)]

A state statute making the ten largest shareholders of a closely held corporation personally liable for unpaid pension plan contributions was preempted by ERISA, concluded one court. [Romney v. Lin, 1996 U.S. App. LEXIS 22017 (2d Cir. 1996), *reh'g denied*, 1997 U.S. App. LEXIS 1044 (2d Cir. 1997)] The same court upheld the dismissal of a multiemployer plan's suit against a general contractor to recover unpaid contributions due from a bankrupt subcontractor because the state statute allowing a lien against money owed to the general contractor was preempted by ERISA. [Plumbing Indus. Bd., Plumbing Local Union No. 1 v. E.W. Howell Co., 1997 U.S. App. LEXIS 24047 (2d Cir. 1997)] Another court determined that a general contractor, which had not signed the CBA, was not liable for unpaid plan contributions of its subcontractors, which had signed the CBA, despite state statutes to the contrary, because ERISA preempted the state statutes. [IBEW, Local Union No. 46 v. Trig Elec. Constr. Co., No. 68504-5 (Wash. 2000)]

Q 29:9 May a multiemployer plan return mistaken employer contributions?

IRS has issued final regulations that provide rules and procedures by which multiemployer plans may return mistaken employer contributions to employers. Generally, plans are required to prohibit the diversion of corpus or income for purposes other than for the exclusive benefit of employees or their beneficiaries (see Q 4:1). The final regulations provide a narrow exception to this general rule, under which plans will not violate this prohibition if a contribution is returned within six months after the date on which a plan administrator (see Q 20:1) determines that the contribution was the result of a mistake of fact or law. The employer must, however, establish a right to the refund of the mistakenly contributed amount by filing a claim with the plan administrator within six months after the date on which the plan administrator determines that the mistake occurred. The employer must also demonstrate that an excessive contribution has been made due to a mistake of fact or law. [I.R.C. § 401(a)(2); Treas. Reg. § 1.401(a)(2)-1]

One court ruled that employers have a right under ERISA to sue for the return of mistakenly made contributions. [ERISA § 502(e); Trustees of Operating Eng'r Pension Trust v. Tab Contractors, Inc. v. International Union of Operating Eng'r Local 12, 2002 WL 31188791 (D. Nev. 2002)] Another court concluded that an employer could not use alleged overpayments to a multiemployer pension fund to offset its liability for unpaid contributions, interest, and liquidated damages because, even though the employer had not signed a new CBA, it made increased contributions without protest under the new CBA and the increase in contributions could not be characterized as overpayments. [Operating Eng'r Local 139 Health Benefits Fund v. Gustafson Constr. Corp., 2001 WL 818856 (7th Cir. 2001)] According to another court, an employer does not have standing under ERISA to make a counterclaim against a multiemployer plan for repayment of contributions that were mistakenly paid to the plan, even though ERISA permits the return of contributions that were made in error, because employers are not specifically listed as a party authorized to sue under ERISA. [ERISA §§ 402(c)(2)(A), 502; Amalgamated Cotton Garment & Allied Indus. Ret. Fund v. Youngworld Stores Group, Inc., No. 99 CIV 3852 (S.D.N.Y. 2001)] Another court declared that an employer which mistakenly made plan contributions on behalf of an employee may be entitled to a refund upon a balancing of the equities, including whether the plan made payments to the employee, whether the refund would have an adverse financial impact on the plan, and whether other beneficiaries of the plan would be negatively affected. [Laborers' Health & Welfare Fund for S. Cal. v. W.A. Rasic Constr. Corp., Nos. 96-56168, 96-56250 (9th Cir. 1998); *see also* Ennen v. Sheet Metal Workers Nat'l Pension Fund, No. TH 98-119-C-T/H (S.D. Ind. 2000)]

Q 29:10   How are hours of service credited to an employee under a multiemployer plan?

For purposes of participation and vesting, a multiemployer plan is treated as if all participating employers constitute a single employer. Thus, with certain exceptions, all covered service with an employer participating in the plan as well as all contiguous noncovered service with that same employer are taken into account. For purposes of the accrual of benefits, only covered service is counted. [DOL Reg. § 2530.210; I.R.C. §§ 413(a), 413(b); Gauer v. Connors, 953 F.2d 97 (4th Cir. 1991); Rev. Rul. 85-130, 1985-2 C.B. 137]

The determination of covered service is functional. Full-time employees performed covered service even though their employers claimed they were casual employees under the collective bargaining agreement. [Central States, Southeast & Southwest Areas Pension Fund v. Independent Fruit & Produce Co., No. 89-1927 (8th Cir. 1990); *see also* Brown-Graves Co. v. Central States, Southeast & Southwest Areas Pension Fund, 206 F.3d 680 (6th Cir. 2000)]

See Q 9:5 for a discussion of the application of the minimum vesting standards to multiemployer plans.

Q 29:11   Are benefits under a multiemployer plan guaranteed?

Yes. Pension Benefit Guaranty Corporation (PBGC) has the authority to insure the benefits of a defined benefit multiemployer plan. Although a multiemployer plan usually combines the features of a defined benefit plan (see Q 2:3) and a defined contribution plan (see Q 2:2) (i.e., both benefits and contributions are fixed), the courts have said that a multiemployer plan is a defined benefit plan. Therefore, the benefits under a multiemployer plan are guaranteed by PBGC. [Connolly v. PBGC, 581 F.2d 729 (9th Cir. 1978); PBGC v. Defoe Shipbuilding Co., 639 F.2d 311 (6th Cir. 1981)]

Note, however, that the benefits under a multiemployer plan are guaranteed only if the plan becomes insolvent (see Q 29:12). [ERISA § 4022A(a)(2)]

Q 29:12   When is a multiemployer plan insolvent?

A multiemployer plan is considered insolvent when its available resources are insufficient to pay benefits when due for the plan year or when the plan is determined by the plan sponsor to be insolvent while the plan is in reorganization. The plan's available resources include cash, marketable securities, earnings, payments due from withdrawn employers, and employer contributions, minus reasonable administration expenses and amounts owed to PBGC for financial assistance. [I.R.C. § 418E; ERISA § 4245]

A sponsor of a multiemployer plan in reorganization must perform a test at the end of the first plan year in reorganization, and every three years thereafter as long as the plan is in reorganization, to determine whether the plan will become insolvent during any of the next five plan years. If the sponsor determines that insolvency is possible in any of the next five plan years, the solvency determination must be made annually, instead of every three years, until the plan potentially will not be insolvent for at least the next five plan years. This provision is effective for determinations made in plan years beginning after December 31, 2007. [I.R.C. § 418E(d)(1); ERISA § 4245(d)(1)]

PBGC (see Q 29:11) divided a multiemployer plan into two separate plans in an effort to extend the solvency of the plan. [PBGC News Rel. (May 26, 2010)]

Q 29:13   What level of benefits is guaranteed?

The level of guaranteed benefits is generally lower than the guarantees provided under single-employer defined benefit plans. However, benefits accrued through July 29, 1980 that are payable to retirees or beneficiaries as of that date or to vested participants who were within three years of normal retirement age (see Q 10:55) as of that date are guaranteed in accordance with the higher ERISA single-employer rules. [ERISA §§ 4022A(a), 4022A(c), 4022A(h)]

PBGC (see Q 29:11) previously guaranteed 100 percent of the first $5 of monthly benefits per year of service. The next $15 of monthly benefits or, if less, the accrual rate over $5 per month per year of service was guaranteed at 75 percent for strong plans and 65 percent for weaker plans.

PBGC's maximum guarantee limit has been increased. Under the new guarantee limit, the guarantee increased to 100 percent of the first $11 of the monthly benefit accrual rate and 75 percent of the next $33 for each year of service. For example, for a worker with 30 years of service and a benefit accrual rate of $23 per month, the maximum guarantee is $600 per month ($7,200 per year), an increase from the old guarantee of $487.50 per month ($5,850 per year), determined as follows:

$$[(100\% \times \$11) + (75\% \times \$12)] \times 30 \text{ years} =$$
$$\$600 \text{ per month} \times 12 \text{ months} = \$7,200 \text{ per year}$$

Similarly, for a worker with 20 years of service and a benefit accrual rate of $25 per month, the maximum guarantee is $430 per month ($5,160 per year), an increase from the old guarantee of $325 per month ($3,900 per year), determined as follows:

$$[(100\% \times \$11) + (75\% \times \$14)] \times 20 \text{ years} =$$
$$\$430 \text{ per month} \times 12 \text{ months} = \$5{,}160 \text{ per year}$$

The increased guarantee limit applies to any multiemployer plan that did not receive PBGC financial assistance within the one-year period that ended on December 21, 2000. The old guarantee limit remains in place for participants in multiemployer plans that received financial assistance during that year.

[ERISA § 4022A(c); PBGC Tech. Update 00-7 (Dec. 26, 2000)]

Q 29:14   What benefits are not guaranteed by PBGC?

PBGC will not guarantee benefits that have been in effect under the multi-employer plan for less than 60 months. Also, benefit improvements that have not been in effect for at least 60 months are not guaranteed.

This differs from coverage provided for single-employer plans, which phase in benefit guarantees of 20 percent a year, with a minimum phase-in of $20 each month, during the five-year period following the implementation of a benefit improvement (see Q 25:21). [ERISA §§ 4022(b), 4022A(b)]

Q 29:15   How did the Pension Funding Equity Act of 2004 affect multiemployer defined benefit plans?

The administrator (see Q 20:1) of a defined benefit plan (see Q 2:3) which is a multiemployer plan is required for each plan year to furnish a plan funding notice to each plan participant and beneficiary, to each labor organization representing such participants or beneficiaries, to each employer that has an obligation to contribute under the plan, and to PBGC. [ERISA § 101(f)] Any administrator who fails to meet this requirement with respect to a participant or beneficiary may, in a court's discretion, be personally liable to such participant or beneficiary in the amount of up to $100 a day from the date of such failure or refusal, and the court may in its discretion order such other relief as it deems proper. [ERISA § 502(c)(1)]

DOL has proposed regulations, including a model notice, to implement this requirement. [DOL Prop. Reg. § 2520.101-4]

In general, the proposed regulations require the administrator of a multiem-ployer defined benefit plan to furnish annually a notice of the plan's funded status to the plan's participants and beneficiaries and other specified interested parties. [DOL Prop. Reg. § 2520.101-4(a)(1)] There is a limited exception to the requirement to furnish the annual funding notice. Under the exception, the plan administrator of a plan receiving financial assistance from PBGC is not required to furnish the annual funding notice to the parties otherwise entitled to such notice. [DOL Prop. Reg. § 2520.101-4(a)(2)]

The notice must include:

1. The name of the plan;
2. The address and phone number of the plan administrator and the plan's principal administrative officer (if different from the plan administrator);
3. The plan sponsor's employer identification number;
4. The plan number;
5. A statement as to whether the plan's funded current liability percentage for the plan year to which the notice relates is at least 100 percent (and, if not, the actual percentage);
6. A statement of the market value of the plan's assets (and valuation date), the amount of benefit payments, and the ratio of the assets to the payments for the plan year to which the notice relates;
7. A summary of the rules governing insolvent multiemployer plans (see Q 29:12), including the limitations on benefit payments and any potential benefit reductions and suspensions (and the potential effects of such limitations, reductions, and suspensions on the plan);
8. A general description of the benefits under the plan that are eligible to be guaranteed by PBGC, along with an explanation of the limitations on the guarantee and the circumstances under which such limitations apply (see Q 29:13); and
9. Any additional information that the plan administrator elects to include, provided that such information is necessary or helpful to understanding the mandatory information in the notice. [DOL Prop. Reg. § 2520.101-4(b)]

Notices must be written in a manner calculated to be understood by the average plan participant (see Q 22:4). [DOL Reg. § 2520.102-2; DOL Prop. Reg. § 2520.101-4(c)] Notices (except for notices to PBGC) must be furnished in a manner consistent with the requirements of DOL Reg. § 2520.104b-1 (see Q 22:2). [DOL Prop. Reg. § 2520.101-4(e)]

Notices must be furnished within nine months after the close of the plan year, unless IRS has granted an extension of time to file the annual report (see Q 21:1), in which case the notice must be furnished within two months after the close of the extension period. [DOL Prop. Reg. § 2520.101-4(d)]

Persons entitled to notice include:

1. Each participant covered under the plan on the last day of the plan year to which the notice relates;
2. Each beneficiary receiving benefits under the plan on the last day of the plan year to which the notice relates;
3. Each labor organization representing participants under the plan on the last day of the plan year to which the notice relates.
4. Each employer that, as of the last day of the plan year to which the notice relates, is a party to the CBA(s) pursuant to which the plan is maintained or which otherwise may be subject to withdrawal liability (see Q 29:16); and
5. PBGC. [DOL Prop. Reg. § 2520.101-4(f)]

Set forth below is the model notice published by DOL:

Annual Funding Notice for [Insert name of pension plan]

Introduction

This notice, which federal law requires all multiemployer plans to send annually, includes important information about the funding level of [insert name, number, and EIN of plan] (Plan). This notice also includes information about rules governing insolvent plans and benefit payments guaranteed by the Pension Benefit Guaranty Corporation (PBGC), a federal agency. This notice is for the plan year beginning [insert beginning date] and ending [insert ending date] (Plan Year).

Plan's Funding Level

The Plan's "funding current liability percentage" for the Plan year was [insert percentage—see instructions below]. In general, the higher the percentage, the better funded the plan. The funded current liability percentage, however, is not indicative of how well a plan will be funded in the future or if it terminates.

(Instructions: For purposes of computing the "funded current liability percentage," insert ratio of actuarial value of assets to current liability, expressed as a percentage. If the percentage is equal to or greater than 100 percent, you may insert "at least 100 percent.")

Plan's Financial Information

The market value of the Plan's assets as of [insert valuation date] was [insert amount]. The total amount of benefit payments for the Plan Year was [enter amount]. The ratio of assets to benefit payments is [enter amount calculated by dividing the value of plan assets by the total benefit payments]. This ratio suggests that the Plan's assets could provide for approximately [enter amount calculated above] years of benefit payments in annual amounts equal to what was paid out in the Plan Year. However, the ratio does not take into account future changes in total benefit payments or plan assets.

Rules Governing Insolvent Plans

The law has special rules governing insolvent multiemployer pension plans. A plan is insolvent for a plan year if its available financial resources are not sufficient to pay benefits when due for the plan year.

An insolvent plan must reduce benefit payments to the highest level that can be paid from the plan's available financial resources. If such resources are not enough to pay benefits at a level specified by law (see Benefit Payments Guaranteed by the PBGC, below), the plan must apply to the PBGC for financial assistance. The PBGC, by law, will loan the plan the amount necessary to pay benefits at the guaranteed level. Reduced benefits may be restored if the plan's financial condition improves.

A plan that becomes insolvent must provide prompt notification of the insolvency to participants and beneficiaries, contributing employers, labor unions representing participants, and PBGC. In addition, participants and beneficiaries also must receive information regarding whether, and how, their benefits will be reduced or affected as a result of the insolvency, including loss of a lump sum option. This information will be provided for each year the plan is insolvent.

Benefit Payments Guaranteed by the PBGC

The PBGC guarantees only vested benefits. Specifically, it guarantees a monthly benefit payment equal to 100 percent of the first $11 of the Plan's monthly benefit accrual rate, plus 75 percent of the next $33 of the accrual rate, times each year of credited service. The maximum guaranteed payment for a vested retiree, therefore, is $35.75 per month times each year of credited service.

Example 1: If a participant with 10 years of credited service has an accrued monthly benefit of $500, the accrual rate for purposes of determining the PBGC guarantee would be determined by dividing the monthly benefit by the participant's years of service ($500/10), which equals $50. The guaranteed mount for a $50 monthly accrual rate is equal to the sum of $11 plus $24.75 (.75 × $33), or $35.75. Thus, the participant's guaranteed monthly benefit is $357.50 ($35.75 × 10).

Example 2: If the participant in Example 1 has an accrued monthly benefit of $200, the accrual rate for purposes of determining the guarantee would be $20 (or $200/10). The guaranteed amount for a $20 monthly accrual rate is equal to the sum of $11 plus $6.75 (.75 × $9), or $17.75. Thus, the participant's guaranteed monthly benefit would be $177.50 ($17.75 × 10).

In calculating a person's monthly payment, the PBGC will disregard any benefit increases that were made under the plan within 60 months before insolvency. Similarly, the PBGC does not guarantee pre-retirement death benefits to a spouse or beneficiary (e.g., a qualified pre-retirement survivor annuity), benefits above the normal retirement benefit, disability benefits not in pay status, or non-pension benefits, such as health insurance, life insurance, death benefits, vacation pay, or severance pay.

Where To Get More Information

For more information about this notice, you may contact [enter name of plan administrator and, if applicable, principal administrative officer], at [enter phone number and address]. For more information about the PBGC and multiemployer benefit guarantees, go to PBGC's Web site, http://www.pbgc.gov, or call PBGC toll-free at 1-800-400-7242 (TTY/TDD users may call the Federal relay service toll free at 1-800-877-8339 and ask to be connected to 1-800-400-7242).

[DOL Prop. Reg. § 2520.101-4(g)]

IRS has issued guidance in the form of questions and answers concerning the election that can be made for certain multiemployer plans to defer charges for net experience losses. [I.R.C. § 412(b)(7)(F); Notice 2005-40, 2005-1 C.B. 1088]

PPA (see Q 1:33) changes the information that must be provided in the notice and accelerates the time when the notice must be provided.

In addition to the information required under present law, the annual funding notice must include the following additional information, as of the end of the plan year in which the notice relates:

1. A statement of the number of participants who are retired or separated from service and receiving benefits, retired or separated participants who are entitled to future benefits, and active participants;

2. A statement setting forth the funding policy of the plan and the asset allocation of investments under the plan (expressed as percentages of total assets);

3. An explanation containing specific information of any plan amendment, scheduled benefit increase or reduction, or other known event taking effect in the current plan year and having a material effect on plan liabilities or assets for the year (as defined in regulations); and

4. A statement that a person may obtain a copy of the plan's annual report upon request, through the Internet website, or through an Intranet website maintained by the applicable plan sponsor.

Furthermore, the notice must provide:

1. A statement as to whether the plan's funded percentage (as defined under the minimum funding rules for multiemployer plans) for the plan year to which the notice relates and the two preceding plan years, is at least 100 percent (and, if not, the actual percentages);

2. A statement of the value of the plan's assets and liabilities for the plan year to which the notice relates and the two preceding plan years;

3. Whether the plan was in endangered or critical status (see Q 29:1) and, if so, a summary of the plan's funding improvement or rehabilitation plan and a statement describing how a person can obtain a copy of the plan's funding improvement or rehabilitation plan and the actuarial or financial data that demonstrate any action taken by the plan toward fiscal improvement; and

4. A statement that the plan administrator will provide, on written request, a copy of the plan's annual report to any labor organization representing participants and beneficiaries and any employer that has an obligation to contribute to the plan.

The annual funding notice must be provided within 120 days after the end of the plan year to which it relates. DOL is required to publish a model notice not later than August 17, 2007. In addition, DOL is given the authority to promulgate any interim final rules as appropriate to carry out the requirement that a model notice be published.

These provisions are effective for plan years beginning after December 31, 2007. Under a transition rule, any requirement to report a plan's funding target attainment percentage or funded percentage for a plan year beginning before January 1, 2008, is met if (1) in the case of a plan year beginning in 2006, the plan's funded current liability percentage is reported, and (2) in the case of a plan year beginning in 2007, the funding target attainment percentage or funded percentage as determined using such methods of estimation as IRS may provide is reported.

[ERISA § 101(f)]

Q 29:16   What is the financial liability of an employer that withdraws from a multiemployer plan?

An employer that withdraws from a multiemployer plan is liable for its proportionate share of unfunded vested benefits (UVBs), determined as of the date of withdrawal. The liability is imposed upon withdrawal without reference to the plan's termination. However, one court concluded that multiple instances of withdrawal liability can occur and that a multiemployer plan can recalculate an employer's withdrawal liability every year. [ERISA §§ 4205, 4211(c)(2); Central States, Southeast & Southwest Areas Pension Fund v. Safeway, Inc., 2000 WL 1481134 (7th Cir. 2000)] One court concluded that an agreement by a union to indemnify a contributing employer for its withdrawal liability to a multiemployer plan was enforceable. [Pittsburgh Mack Sales & Service, Inc. v. International Union of Operating Engineers, Local No. 66, 580 F.3d 185 (3d Cir. 2009)]

The employer's withdrawal liability is based on the plan's total unfunded liability for vested benefits, not the lesser guaranteed benefits that apply to single-employer terminations. The method used to determine the employer's share can vary from plan to plan (see Q 29:28).

The result is that an employer that withdraws from an underfunded multi-employer plan may have to continue to contribute to the plan at approximately the same dollar level after withdrawal as before withdrawal until the liability is fully paid. In some cases, the withdrawing employer can make payments over a 20-year period (see Q 29:39).

PBGC (see Q 29:11) has approved the adoption by a multiemployer plan of a special withdrawal liability rule. [ERISA § 4203(f); DOL Reg. §§ 4203.1, 4203. 4(a); PBGC Notice, Aug. 6, 2003 (68 Fed. Reg. 46,068)]

Effective for plan years beginning after 2007, upon written request, a multiemployer plan sponsor or administrator must provide to any employer who has an obligation to contribute to the plan a notice of:

1. The estimated amount of what the employer's withdrawal liability would be if the employer withdrew on the last day of the plan year preceding the date of the request, and

2. An explanation of how this estimated withdrawal liability amount was determined, including (a) the actuarial assumptions and methods used to determine the value of plan liabilities and assets; (b) the data regarding employer contributions, UVBs, and annual changes in the plan's UVBs, and (c) the application of any relevant limits on the estimated withdrawal liability. [ERISA § 101(l)(1)]

In connection with the participant, the term "employer contribution" means a contribution made by an employer as an employer of the participant. [ERISA § 101(l)(1)]

Any required notice of potential withdrawal liability must be provided to the requesting employer within 180 days after the request is made and in a form and manner to be prescribed in DOL regulations. Subject to DOL regulations, a period longer than 180 days may be allowed for plans that determine withdrawal liability under ERISA §§ 4211(c)(4) and (5) (see Q 29:28). [ERISA § 101(*l*)(2)(A)] The notice of potential withdrawal liability may be provided in a written, electronic, or other appropriate form to the extent that the form is reasonably accessible to persons and to employers requesting a copy of the form. [ERISA § 101(*l*)(2)(B)] Anyone entitled to the notice of potential withdrawal liability is not entitled to receive more than one copy of any notice during any 12-month period. The person required to provide the notice may impose a reasonable charge to cover the cost of copying, mailing, and other expenses involved in furnishing copies of the notice. DOL is authorized to impose a limit on what constitutes a reasonable charge. [ERISA § 101(*l*)(3)] DOL may impose a penalty of up to $1,000 per day for each violation of the requirement to provide, upon request, the notice of potential withdrawal liability. [ERISA § 502(c)(4)]

See Q 9:5 for a discussion of the application of the minimum vesting standards to multiemployer plans, and see Q 29:3 for a discussion of DOL proposed regulations concerning the imposition of the penalty for failure to provide the notice.

Q 29:17   Can withdrawal liability be assessed against any employer that withdraws from a multiemployer plan?

Withdrawal liability applies only to withdrawals that occur on or after September 26, 1980. The United States Supreme Court has ruled that the withdrawal liability provisions of ERISA are constitutional. [Connolly v. PBGC, 475 U.S. 211 (1986); *see also* Central States, Southeast & Southwest Areas Pension Fund v. Midwest Motor Express, Inc., 1999 WL 371671 (7th Cir. 1999)]

When an employer temporarily ceased contributions to a multiemployer plan prior to September 26, 1980, but a complete withdrawal (see Q 29:19) did not occur until thereafter, the employer was assessed withdrawal liability, and the United States Supreme Court ruled that the assessment did not violate the employer's right to due process of law and did not constitute an unconstitutional taking of property without just compensation. [Concrete Pipe & Prods. of Cal., Inc. v. Construction Laborers Pension Trust for S. Cal., 508 U.S. 602 (1993)] However, an employer who, prior to September 26, 1980, entered into a binding agreement to withdraw and ceased business operations before the end of 1980 was not assessed withdrawal liability. [Crown Cork & Seal Co. v. Central States, Southeast & Southwest Areas Pension Fund, 982 F.2d 857 (3d Cir. 1992)]

For withdrawal liability purposes, one court concluded that an employer is an entity that is either contractually obligated to contribute to a multiemployer plan or obligated under applicable labor-management relations law. [ERISA § 4212(a); Central States, Southeast & Southwest Areas Pension Fund v. International Comfort Products, LLC, 2009 WL 3400630 (6th Cir. 2009); *see also* Laborers Health and Welfare Trust Fund for N. California v. Advanced Lightweight Concrete Co., Inc., 484 U.S. 539 (1988)]

A law firm that advised a client to pay its legal bills and other liabilities before satisfying a court order to reimburse a multiemployer plan for delinquent withdrawal liability payments was held to be in civil contempt of court. [Chicago Truck Drivers, Helpers & Warehouse Workers Union Pension Fund v. Brotherhood Leasing v. Gula v. Dysart, Taylor, Lay, Cotter & McMonigle, P.C., No. 02-3622 (8th Cir. 2005)]

Q 29:18   What steps are involved in determining multiemployer plan withdrawal liability?

The withdrawal liability process consists of five phases:

1. Determining whether the employer has withdrawn (see Q 29:19);
2. Computing the withdrawn employer's share of the plan's UVBs (see Q 29:28);
3. Determining whether any reductions apply to the withdrawal liability (see Q 29:30);
4. Notifying the employer of the amount of the withdrawal liability (see Q 29:40); and
5. Collecting the liability (see Q 29:44).

[ERISA §§ 4201, 4202]

Q 29:19   When is a participating employer considered to have withdrawn from a multiemployer plan?

An employer is considered to have withdrawn, and therefore is subject to withdrawal liability, when it (1) permanently ceases to have an obligation to contribute to the multiemployer plan or (2) permanently ceases all covered operations under the plan.

Special rules apply for determining whether there is a complete or partial withdrawal (see Q 29:21) of employers in the following industries:

- Building and construction
- Trucking
- Household goods moving
- Public warehousing
- Retail food
- Certain segments of the entertainment industry

[ERISA § 4203; PBGC Reg. § 4203.1; PBGC Notice (70 Fed. Reg. 71,562)]

The key issue is whether the employer's obligation to contribute has ceased. [Central States, Southeast & Southwest Areas Pension Fund v. Hunt Truck Lines, Inc., 204 F.3d 236 (7th Cir. 2000); Connors v. Barrick Gold Exploration, Inc., 962 F.2d 1076 (D.C. Cir. 1992)] An employer was deemed to have withdrawn from a multiemployer plan on the day after the CBA expired, because that was the first day that the employer no longer had an obligation to contribute. [Technical

Metallurgical Services, Inc. v. Plumbers and Pipefitters Nat'l. Pension Fund, No. 06-40321 (5th Cir. 2007)] If the employer is no longer obligated to make contributions to the multiemployer plan, it cannot escape withdrawal by either continuing to make payments or getting another company to agree to make contributions on its behalf. [Connors v. B & W Coal Co., 646 F. Supp. 164 (D.D.C. 1986)] However, the result may be different if another company signs an agreement undertaking the obligation on behalf of the original employer. [ILGWU Nat'l Ret. Fund v. Distinctive Coat Co., 6 Employee Benefits Cas. (BNA) 2631 (S.D.N.Y. 1985)] An employer withdrawing from a multiemployer plan incurred withdrawal liability in spite of a termination agreement that effectively relieved it of liability in exchange for severance payments and salary enhancements where the employer's principal purpose was to avoid paying its share of existing UVBs (see Q 29:28). [ERISA § 4212(c); Supervalu v. Board of Trustees of the Southwestern Penn. & Md. Area Teamsters and Employers Pension Fund, 2007 WL 2429345 (3d Cir. 2007); *see also* Teamsters Joint Council No. 83 of The Virginia Pension Fund v. Weidner Realty Assocs., 2010 WL 1734975 (4th Cir. 2010)]

In an arbitration, it was held that although the passage of some time may be necessary for a determination of whether a cessation of covered operations is permanent, once it is determined to be permanent, the date of withdrawal will relate back to the date when contributions ceased. [E.H. Hatfield Enters., Inc. v. UMW 1950 & 1974 Pension Plans, 9 Employee Benefits Cas. (BNA) 1980 (1988) (Jaffe, Arb.)] In another case, a general contractor was not required to continue making contributions after it subcontracted the covered employees' work to a non-union employer. [Board of Trustees of the Chicago Plastering Inst. Pension Trust Fund v. William A. Duguid Co., No. 87 C 10768 (N.D. Ill. 1991)]

An employer's withdrawal liability was not a claim that could be discharged in bankruptcy where the multiemployer plan had no enforceable right to payment at the time of confirmation of bankruptcy because the employer had not actually withdrawn from the plan before the confirmation proceeding had occurred. If an employer wants its withdrawal liability discharged in bankruptcy, the court said it must completely withdraw from the plan before confirmation. An employer cannot remain a participating employer and simultaneously have its withdrawal liability forgiven if it later decides to withdraw. Because withdrawal liability is based on an employer's share of UVBs at withdrawal, there can be no pre-withdrawal breach of ERISA giving rise to a right to payment by a plan. Thus, a claim cannot exist before actual withdrawal. [CPT Holdings, Inc. v. Industrial & Allied Employees Union Pension Plan, Local 73, 1998 WL 842239 (6th Cir. 1998)]

Q 29:20 Can an employer be held liable for withdrawal liability as a result of circumstances such as decertification of the union or a plant closing?

Yes. The issue is whether the employer's obligation to contribute to the multiemployer plan has ceased or whether all covered operations under the plan have ceased. If the answer is yes to either, then the circumstances that led to the cessation of the obligation to contribute or to the cessation of all covered operations are irrelevant. For example, an employer may be subject to withdrawal liability if the employer's employees vote to decertify the union representing them; however, if the employer continues to be obligated to contribute to the plan, decertification does not constitute withdrawal until the obligation ceases. Similarly, withdrawal liability may be triggered by a plant closing or merger of a facility. [ERISA §§ 4203, 4205, 4212; Central States, Southeast & Southwest Areas Pension Fund v. Schilli Corp., 2005 WL 2008224 (7th Cir. 2005)]

Q 29:21   Does a participating employer have any liability if there is a partial withdrawal from the multiemployer plan?

Yes. Withdrawal liability applies when a participating employer partially withdraws from the multiemployer plan. Generally, a partial withdrawal occurs when:

1. There is at least a 70 percent decline in the employer's contribution base units (e.g., hours worked) [PBGC Op. Ltr. 93-2];

2. The employer ceases to have an obligation to contribute to the plan under at least one, but not all, of its CBAs and continues the same type of work in the geographical area covered by the agreement; or

3. The employer ceases to have an obligation to contribute to the plan for work performed at one or more, but fewer than all, of its facilities (see Q 29:22) covered under the agreement.

A 70 percent decline in contribution base units occurs if, during the plan year and each of the preceding two plan years (the three-year testing period), the number of contribution base units for which the employer was required to make plan contributions did not exceed 30 percent of the number of contribution base units for the high base year. The high base year is determined by averaging the employer's contribution base units for the two plan years for which such units were the highest within the five plan years preceding the three-year testing period.

[ERISA §§ 4205, 4208; Penske Logistics, LLC v. Freight Drivers and Helpers Local 557 Pension Fund, 2010 WL 1583074 (3d Cir. 2010); Central States, Southeast & Southwest Areas Pension Fund v. Safeway, Inc., 2000 WL 1481134 (7th Cir. 2000); Chicago Truck Drivers, Helpers & Warehouse Workers Union (Indep.) Pension Fund v. Leaseway Transp. Corp., 1996 U.S. App. LEXIS 1858 (7th Cir. 1996)]

Partial withdrawal liability was assessed where a company closed two shipping terminals and transferred the work from union employees to nonunion employees at another location. [Nestle Holdings, Inc. v. Central States, Southeast & Southwest Areas Pension Fund, 342 F.3d 801 (7th Cir. 2003)]

See Q 29:42 for a discussion of a new procedure applicable to disputes involving withdrawal liability.

Q 29:22   What is a facility for purposes of a partial withdrawal?

The term "facility" has been determined by PBGC to be a discrete economic unit of an employer. For example, the term will ordinarily apply to a single retail store rather than to a group of stores in a metropolitan area. [PBGC Op. Ltr. Nos. 86-2, 82-33, 82-22; May Stern & Co. v. Western Pa. Teamsters & Employers Pension Fund, 8 Employee Benefits Cas. (BNA) 2202 (1987) (Nagle, Arb.)]

Q 29:23   Is withdrawal liability affected if employers are under common control?

Employers under common control (see Qs 5:29, 5:31) are considered as only one employer. Withdrawal liability can be assessed against all members of the commonly controlled group, even if only one member of the commonly controlled group is required to contribute to the multiemployer plan. [ERISA § 4001(b); DOL Op. Ltr. 82-13; McDougall and Central States, Southeast & Southwest Areas Pension Fund v. Pioneer Ranch Limited Partnership and Whiting, 2007 U.S. App. LEXIS 16585 (7th Cir. 2007); Minnesota Laborers Health & Welfare Fund v. Scanlan, 2004 WL 235203 (8th Cir. 2004); ILGWU Nat'l Ret. Fund v. Meredith Grey, Inc., 2003 U.S. App. LEXIS 26271 (2d Cir. 2003); NYSA-ILA Pension Trust Fund v. Montague Assocs., Inc., No. 94 Civ. 3604 (S.D.N.Y. 1996); Central States, Southeast & Southwest Areas Pension Fund v. Slotky, 956 F.2d 1369 (7th Cir. 1992); Central States, Southeast & Southwest Areas Pension Fund v. Newbury Transp. Corp, 1992 U.S. Dist. LEXIS 1757 (N.D. Ill. 1992); Central States, Southeast & Southwest Areas Pension Fund v. Chatham Props., 929 F.2d 260 (6th Cir. 1991); IUE AFL-CIO Pension Fund v. Barker & Williamson, Inc., 788 F.2d 118 (3d Cir. 1986); O'Connor v. DeBolt Transfer, Inc., 737 F. Supp. 1430 (W.D. Pa. 1990); Board of Trustees of the W. Conference of Teamsters Pension Trust Fund v. Salt Creek Terminals, Inc., No. C85-2270R (W.D. Wash. 1986); Connors v. Calvert Dev. Co., 622 F. Supp. 877 (D.D.C. 1985)] One court ruled that, in determining whether a partnership and a withdrawing employer are jointly liable for withdrawal liability, the lack of an economic nexus between them is irrelevant; the proper inquiry is whether they are under common control. [Connor v. Incoal, Inc., 1993 U.S. App. LEXIS 13168 (D.C. Cir. 1993)] A general partner of a partnership that was a member of a controlled group was held personally responsible for a company's withdrawal liability because, under partnership law, partners were personally liable for obligations of the partnership. [Teamsters Pension Trust Fund of Phila. & Vicinity v. Domenic Cristinzio, Inc., No. 96-6596 (E.D. Pa. 1998)] However, one court ruled that while Federal Rule of Civil Procedure 4(k)(a) allows for worldwide service of process, a multiemployer plan could not pursue a withdrawal liability assessment against the Canadian parents of a domestic U.S. corporation where the parent corporations lacked minimum contacts with the forum state. [Central States, Southeast & Southwest Areas Pension Fund v. Reimer Express World Corp., 230 F.3d 934 (7th Cir. 2000)] An entity that failed to arbitrate (see Q 29:42) the issue of whether it was a member of a controlled group waived its ability to contest that issue. [Trucking Employees of N.J. Welfare Fund, Inc. v. Bellezza Co., 2003 WL 262505 (3d Cir. 2003)]

The merger of subsidiary corporations into the parent, followed by the parent's selective contribution of assets and assignment of liabilities to newly created subsidiaries, did not shield the parent from withdrawal liability, because the reorganization did not meet the safe harbor requirements (see Q 29:24). [Centra, Inc. v. Central States, Southeast & Southwest Areas Pension Fund, 2009 WL 253574 (7th Cir. 2009] An acquiring corporation was liable for the withdrawal liability payments of the acquired corporation even after the acquired corporation was discharged in bankruptcy because of the acquiring corporation's control both before and after the bankruptcy reorganization. [Teamsters Joint Council No. 83 v. Centra, Inc., No. 90-1815 (4th Cir. 1991)] However, a public entity that hired a private company to manage a marine terminal was not considered the employer of the private company's employees. [Seaway Port Auth. of Duluth v. Duluth-Superior ILA Marine Ass'n Restated Pension Plan, 920 F.2d 503 (8th Cir. 1990)]

The employer of leased employees for withdrawal liability purposes is not necessarily the same as under the Code (see Qs 5:58–5:63). In one case, a company leased truck drivers to another company and made interim withdrawal liability payments (see Q 29:44) after the lease ended. Although both companies may be considered employers, the issue of each company's withdrawal liability to the plan is subject to arbitration (see Q 29:43). [Global Leasing, Inc. v. Henkel Corp., 744 F. Supp. 595 (D.N.J. 1990); see also New York State Teamsters Conf. Pension and Retirement Fund v. Express Services, Inc., 426 F.3d 640 (2d Cir. 2005)] In other cases, a company that leased truck drivers from another company was held not to be an employer for withdrawal liability purposes since it had no contractual liability to contribute to the plan. [Transpersonnel, Inc. v. Roadway Express, Inc., No. 04-2321 (7th Cir. 2005); Rheem Mfg. Co v. Central States, Southeast & Southwest Areas Pension Fund, No. 95-1073 (8th Cir. 1995); see also Central Pennsylvania Teamsters Pension Fund v. Power Packaging, Inc., No. 04-2867 (3d Cir. 2005)] In determining whether a corporation was the employer, one court applied a contributing obligor test. Under this test, only a party that is obligated to contribute to a plan is an employer. The court noted that the corporation was not contractually bound to contribute to the plan and, therefore, was not subject to withdrawal liability. [Tampa Bay Int'l Terminals, Inc. v. Tampa Maritime Ass'n-Int'l Longshoremen's Ass'n Pension Plan & Trust, No. 95-2776 (11th Cir. 1996)] A company which had a call option on all of the shares of stock of another company which was delinquent in its partial withdrawal liability payments (see Q 29:21) was held not to be responsible for the withdrawal liability. The call option did not make the companies members of a commonly controlled group. [Central States, Southeast & Southwest Areas Pension Fund v. Quickie Transp. Co., 2000 WL 468241 (7th Cir. 2001)]

Where the shareholders of a bankrupt company also operated a real estate business that leased property to the company and the leasing of property was considered a trade or business, the shareholders were liable for the withdrawal liability of the company as members of a commonly controlled group. [Central States, Southeast & Southwest Areas Pension Fund v. Ditello, 974 F.2d 887 (7th Cir. 1992)] In other cases, sole proprietors were found personally liable for the withdrawal liability of their failed companies because their real estate investments constituted a business and the individuals had common control over both the failed company and the sole proprietorship. [Central States, Southeast & Southwest Areas Pension Fund v. Personnel, Inc., 974 F.2d 789 (7th Cir. 1992); Central States, Southeast & Southwest Areas Pension Fund v. Koder, 970 F.2d 1067 (7th Cir. 1992); Central States, Southeast & Southwest Areas Pension Fund v. Landvatter, 1993 U.S. Dist. LEXIS (N.D. Ill. 1993); see also Central States, Southeast & Southwest Areas Pension Fund v. Nieman, 2002 WL 485311 (7th Cir. 2002)] However, a shareholder of a bankrupt corporation was not liable for its withdrawal liability even though he owned and leased real property. In the first case, the rental of two apartments above the garage of the shareholder's residence did not constitute a trade or business. [Central States, Southeast & Southwest Areas Pension Fund v. White, 2001 WL 818782 (7th Cir. 2001)] In the second case, because the real property was subject to triple net leases, the court ruled that it was a passive investment and did not constitute a trade or business. [Central States, Southeast & Southwest Areas Pension Fund v. Fulkerson, 238 F.3d 891 (7th Cir. 2001)] In another case involving real property, a multiemployer plan failed to show that a real estate partnership was a member of a controlled group responsible for the withdrawal liability of a bankrupt slaughterhouse. [Teamsters Joint Council No. 83 of The Virginia Pension Fund v. Weidner Realty Assocs., 2010 WL 1734975 (4th Cir. 2010)] In another case, a court determined that a lender that loaned money to the owner of two companies in exchange for stock in one of the companies was not liable for the withdrawal liability of the owner's other company because the lender was not under common control with the other company. [Central States, Southeast & Southwest Areas Pension Fund v. Wolk, No. 98 C 1484 (N.D. Ill. 2001)] A majority owner of a business, which had ceased making contributions to a multiemployer plan, obtained a capital interest in another company. The court ruled that, for withdrawal liability common control purposes, acquisition of a partnership interest is not necessary to establish common control if the majority owner owned a requisite percentage of a capital interest in the other company. [Central States, Southeast & Southwest Areas Pension Fund v. Creative Dev. Co, 2000 WL 1639459 (5th Cir. 2000)]

One court ruled that an individual's estate planning trust was jointly and severally liable for the withdrawal liability of a company owned by the individual who established the trust. The trust had leased property to the company and another entity under the individual's control and was thus a trade or business under common control. [Vaughn v. Sexton, 975 F.2d 498 (8th Cir. 1992)]

One court concluded that an action for withdrawal liability payments filed by a multiemployer plan could proceed against the alter egos (see Q 29:7) of a bankrupt corporation. [Board of Trustees of Teamsters Local 863 Pension Fund v. Foodtown, Inc., 2002 WL 1575075 (3d Cir. 2002); see also Burke v. Hamilton Installers, 2008 WL 2275909 (2d Cir. 2008)] Another court concluded that alter-ego and veil-piercing (see Q 29:8) claims are available to trustees of a multiemployer plan seeking to hold a bankrupt company's corporate affiliates and individual owners liable for withdrawal payments. [Brown v. Astro Holdings, Inc., 2005 U.S. Dist. LEXIS 18406 (E.D. Pa. 2005)]

Q 29:24   Does a withdrawal occur if there is a change in business structure?

No, provided the change in corporate structure does not cause an interruption in the employer's contributions or obligations under the multiemployer plan. [ERISA § 4218]

Changes in corporate structure include the following:

- Reorganization involving a mere change in identity, form, or place of organization
- Liquidation into a parent corporation
- Merger, consolidation, or division
- Change to an unincorporated form of business enterprise

[ERISA § 4069(b)]

The incorporation of a sole proprietorship or partnership does not constitute a withdrawal if the successor corporation continues to have an obligation to contribute and does so. [PBGC Op. Ltr. 83-18] One court ruled that a successor corporation was automatically liable for a predecessor sole proprietorship's delinquent contributions to a multiemployer plan because the successor corporation had the same ownership, management, and type of business as the predecessor sole proprietorship and was therefore the alter ego of the predecessor sole proprietorship (see Q 29:10). [Downey v. General Interiors, Inc., Nos. 92-16711, 92-16797 (9th Cir. 1994); see also U.A. Local 343 of the United Ass'n of Journeymen & Apprentices of the Plumbing & Pipefitting Indus. of the United States & Can., AFL-CIO v. Nor-Cal Plumbing, Inc., No. 92-15749 (9th Cir. 1994)]

Similarly, changes in the composition of an employer-partnership (e.g., sale of partnership interests to new partners) do not result in a withdrawal if the partnership continues to have an obligation to contribute and continues to honor that obligation. [Park S. Hotel Corp. v. New York Hotel Trades Council, 851 F.2d 578 (2d Cir. 1988); Connors v. B&W Coal Co., 646 F. Supp. 164 (D.D.C. 1986); but see E.H. Hatfield Enters., Inc. v. UMW 1950 & 1974 Pension Plans, 9 Employee Benefits Cas. 1980 (1988) (Jaffe, Arb.)] Assignees of a partnership interest were not subject to withdrawal liability because they were assignees and not partners. [Connors v. Middle Fork Corp., No. 89-0698 (GHR) (D.D.C. 1992)]

A sale of one subsidiary in a corporate group did not result in a complete withdrawal of that corporate group from a multiemployer plan because another subsidiary in the group continued to contribute to the plan, and withdrawal liability was not imposed. [Central States, Southeast & Southwest Areas Pension Fund v. Sherwin-Williams Co., 1995 U.S. App. LEXIS 35273 (7th Cir. 1995)] Similarly, withdrawal liability was not imposed when two of three subsidiaries of a parent corporation ceased operations because the parent continued to contribute to the fund on behalf of the third subsidiary. However, the parent's withdrawal liability was triggered when it sold the third subsidiary to an unrelated purchaser even though the purchaser continued to make contributions to the plan. The court held that the corporate restructuring exception applies only when the withdrawal does not result *solely* because of a change in corporate restructuring. The alleged corporate restructuring was the sale of the third subsidiary. Refusing to view the sale of the third subsidiary in isolation, the court found that the parent's withdrawal did not result *solely* because of the sale of the third subsidiary. Instead, withdrawal was the net effect of a series of transactions (the second subsidiary ceasing operations four years after the first subsidiary, and the third subsidiary being sold ten months afterwards) that altogether resulted in the severance of the parent's common ownership of all three corporations. [Penn Cent. Corp v. Western Conference of Teamsters Pension Trust Fund, 1996 U.S. App. LEXIS 1143 (9th Cir. 1996)]

Where two U.S. shipping companies that contributed to a multiemployer plan withdrew from certain shipping operations and entered into a joint venture establishing a new company to handle those operations, the court held that the joint venture creation of a new company, where the two companies continued to exist in the same corporate form, did not qualify under the corporate restructuring exception. [Bowers v. Andrew Weir Shipping, Ltd., 1994 U.S. App. LEXIS 15524 (2d Cir. 1994)]

Q 29:25 Does a withdrawal occur if there is a suspension of contributions during a labor dispute?

No withdrawal occurs as a result of the temporary suspension of contributions during a labor dispute. However, a withdrawal may occur if the cessation of contributions is permanent even though the cessation occurred during a labor dispute. [ERISA § 4218; PBGC Op. Ltrs. 82-2, 82-21; Combs v. Adkins Coal Co., 597 F. Supp. 122 (D.D.C. 1984)] An employer that stopped making payments to a multiemployer plan had to pay past due interim withdrawal liability payments and future payments to the plan, even though there was disagreement as to whether the employer was merely engaged in labor disputes at the time the payments stopped or had completely withdrawn from the plan. [Central States, Southeast & Southwest Areas Pension Fund v. Bomar Nat'l, Inc., No. 00-2472 (7th Cir. 2001)]

Q 29:26 Who determines when a withdrawal from a multiemployer plan occurs?

The plan sponsor determines whether and when an employer has withdrawn from the multiemployer plan. [ERISA §§ 3(16)(B), 4202]

Q 29:27 Is a sale of employer assets considered a withdrawal from a multiemployer plan?

If the assets sold by the employer represent all of its covered operations, there may be a complete withdrawal. However, if only part of the employer's operation is sold, a partial withdrawal (see Q 29:21) may result. The withdrawal liability of the selling employer is limited to a maximum amount. [ERISA § 4225]

Withdrawal liability is assessed without regard to any transaction entered into by an employer if a principal purpose of the transaction is to avoid or evade withdrawal liability. Consequently, a parent company's sale of a subsidiary subjected the parent to withdrawal liability because a principal purpose of the sale was to avoid or evade withdrawal liability even though there were business reasons for disposing of the subsidiary. [Sherwin-Williams Co. v. New York State Teamsters Conference Pension & Ret. Fund, No. 97-3480 (6th Cir. 1998)]

The selling employer is relieved of primary withdrawal liability only if the following conditions are satisfied:

1. The purchasing company is an unrelated party that assumes substantially the same contribution obligation;
2. The purchasing company posts a bond for the following five plan years; and
3. The contract of sale provides that the selling employer is secondarily liable if the purchasing company completely or partially withdraws during the following five plan years and fails to pay its withdrawal liability. [Central States, Southeast & Southwest Areas Pension Fund v. Nitehawk Express, Inc., 2000 WL 1092663 (7th Cir. 2000); Central States, Southeast & Southwest Areas Pension Fund v. Hunt Truck Lines, Inc., 204 F.3d 236 (7th Cir. 2000); PBGC Op. Ltr. 92-1]

If the above conditions are not satisfied, the purchasing company is not responsible for any of the seller's withdrawal liability. However, a purchasing company was held liable for the seller's withdrawal liability under an indemnification agreement entered into between the parties. [Lear Siegler Diversified Holdings Corp. v. Regal-Beloit Corp., No. 97C4018 (N.D. Ill. 1999)] PBGC is authorized to grant individual or class exemptions or variances from the requirement that the purchasing company post a bond if it determines that the request for exemption or variance would more effectively or equitably carry out the purposes of Title IV of ERISA and would not significantly increase the risk of financial loss to the plan. [ERISA § 4204(c); PBGC Reg. § 4204.22(b); PBGC Notice of Exemption, 58 Fed. Reg. 60,707 (Nov. 17, 1993); PBGC Notice of Exemption, 57 Fed. Reg. 7408 (Mar. 2, 1992)] Also, if the purchaser withdraws after the sale, the determination of the purchaser's withdrawal liability takes into account the seller's required contribution for the year of the sale and the four preceding years. [ERISA § 4204]

If the selling employer distributes all or substantially all of its assets or liquidates before the expiration of the five-year period, it must post a bond or establish an escrow account. [ERISA § 4204(a)(3)] When a selling employer converted its assets to cash before the expiration of the five-year period, it did not incur withdrawal liability even though it failed to post the required bond because the purchasing company had not failed to make contributions during the period. The plan's sole remedy was to enforce the bond requirement. [Central States, Southeast & Southwest Areas Pension Fund v. Bell Transit Co., No. 93-2519 (7th Cir. 1994)]

In one case, the purchasing company continued to contribute on behalf of the selling company's employees pursuant to its own CBA that was essentially identical to that of the selling employer. The court held that no withdrawal had occurred. [Dorns Transp., Inc. v. Teamsters Pension Trust Fund of Phila. & Vicinity, 787 F.2d 897 (3d Cir. 1986)] In another case, the court ruled that when the purchasing company assumed substantially the same contribution obligation as the seller and subsequent events caused a reduction in workforce and contributions, withdrawal liability could not be assessed against the selling employer because the sale of assets did not cause the reduction in contributions and the reduction was neither abusive nor significantly harmful to the plan. [IAM Nat'l Pension Fund Benefit Plan A v. Dravo Corp., 7 Empl. Ben. Cas. 1892 (D.D.C. 1986)]

A parent company sold one of its subsidiaries to an unrelated entity, relieving the parent of primary withdrawal liability. Subsequently, the parent closed facilities owned by two other subsidiaries. In calculating the parent's withdrawal liability, the contribution history of the previously sold subsidiary could not be considered. [Borden, Inc. v. Bakery & Confectionery Union & Indus. Int'l Pension, 974 F.2d 528 (4th Cir. 1992)] However, where a parent corporation sold all of its shares of stock in a subsidiary and not the assets of the subsidiary, the court concluded that since the primary purpose of the sale was avoidance of withdrawal liability, the parent remained liable for the subsidiary's withdrawal liability. [Santa Fe Pac. Corp. v. Central States, Southeast & Southwest Areas Pension Fund, Nos. 93-2736, 93-2899 (7th Cir. 1994)]

Also, at least one court has held that a company that purchased a selling company's assets for cash may still be liable for the selling company's delinquent contributions in some circumstances. [Upholsterer's Int'l Union Pension Fund v. Artistic Furniture of Pontiac, 920 F.2d 1323 (7th Cir. 1990)] Moreover, where a pension fund agreement provided that participants' service with a withdrawing employer would include service with a predecessor employer, the withdrawing employer was required to pay the withdrawal liability of the predecessor employer from whom it had purchased assets. [Artistic Carton Co v. Paper Indus. Union-Mgmt. Pension Fund, 971 F.2d 1346 (7th Cir. 1992)]

Q 29:28 How is a withdrawing employer's share of the multiemployer plan's UVBs computed?

The withdrawing employer's share of the multiemployer plan's UVBs (see Q 29:16) may be computed under a statutory method or a PBGC-approved alternative method. The four statutory methods are:

1. The presumptive method;
2. The modified presumptive method;
3. The rolling-five method; and
4. The direct attribution method.

The presumptive method is generally used to determine withdrawal liability unless the plan is amended to permit the use of an alternative method. [ERISA § 4211; PBGC Reg. § 4211.1]

The plan may adopt a statutory alternative method, but such an alternative may not be applied to an employer without its consent if it withdrew before the adoption of the alternative method. An assessment of withdrawal liability was found to be erroneous and unenforceable where the fund used a calculation method adopted after the employer had withdrawn. [ERISA § 4214(a); Jos. Schlitz Brewing Co. v. Milwaukee Brewery Workers' Pension Plan, 1993 U.S. App. LEXIS 20658 (7th Cir. 1993); Sigmund Cohn Corp v. District No. 15 Machinists Pension Fund, No. CV 91-2691 (RJD) (E.D.N.Y. 1992)] In calculating the employers' withdrawal liability using the direct attribution method, a plan attributed all of the service credits of two employees to the withdrawing employers as their last employer, although those employees earned some of the plan service credits while employed elsewhere. The plan adopted the direct attribution method for assessing withdrawal liability and rules providing that in the absence of reliable records, participants' service would be attributed to the employer using a last employer assumption. The court concluded that a plan may use the last employer assumption to allocate withdrawal liability using the direct attribution method, either as a simplifying actuarial assumption that is reasonable under the particular circumstances or as a permissible plan rule that an employer may agree to be bound by under general contracting principles. [Isb Liquidating Co. v. District No. 15 Machinists' Pension Fund, 127 F. Supp. 2d 192 (E.D.N.Y. 2001)]

PBGC has issued a final regulation modifying the presumptive and modified presumptive methods of allocating UVBs, and plans may adopt these modifications without prior PBGC approval. [PBGC Reg. § 4211.11(a)] In addition, final PBGC regulations contain rules for determining the allocation of UVBs for an employer that withdraws from a multiemployer plan after the plan has merged with another multiemployer plan and rules concerning the partial withdrawal of an employer from a multiemployer plan and its subsequent reentry into the plan. [PBGC Reg. §§ 4211.1–4211.37]

One court ruled that death, disability, and early retirement benefits provided in a defined benefit multiemployer plan are nonforfeitable under ERISA and are therefore properly included in calculations used to determine an employer's withdrawal liability. [United Foods, Inc. v. Western Conference of Teamsters Pension Trust Fund, Nos. 93-15765 et al. (9th Cir. 1994)] Another court ruled that, for purposes of assessing withdrawal liability, benefits credited to participants for service with the employer before the employer began contributing to the plan were nonforfeitable, even though the past service credits were subject to cancellation by the trustees if the employer withdrew from the plan. [Almacs, Inc. v. New England Teamsters & Trucking Indus. Pension Fund, 1993 U.S. Dist. LEXIS 10977 (D.R.I. 1993)] Multiple instances of withdrawal liability can occur, and a multiemployer plan can recalculate an employer's withdrawal liability every year, ruled one court. [ERISA §§ 4205, 4211(c)(2); Central States, Southeast & Southwest Areas Pension Fund v. Safeway, Inc., 2000 WL 1481134 (7th Cir. 2000)]

PBGC issued final regulations implementing provisions of PPA (see Q 1:33) to change the allocation of UVBs to withdrawing employers from a multiemployer plan and make adjustments in determining an employer's withdrawal liability when a multiemployer plan is in critical status (see Q 29:1). PBGC also provided guidance on simplified methods for applying the statutory requirements that multiemployer plans in critical status disregard certain benefit reductions in determining the plan's UVBs for purposes of determining an employer's withdrawal liability. [PBGC Tech. Update 10-3]

A plan using the presumptive withdrawal liability method, including a construction industry plan, may be amended to substitute a plan year that is designated in a plan amendment and for which the plan has no UVBs, for the plan year ending before September 26, 1980. This provision is referred to as the statutory fresh start option. For plan years ending before the designated plan year and for the designated plan year, the plan will be relieved of the burden of calculating changes in UVBs separately for each plan year and allocating those changes to the employers that contributed to the plan in the year of the change. As the plan must have no UVBs for the designated plan year, employers withdrawing from the plan after the modification is effective will have no liability for UVBs arising in plan years ending before the designated plan year. The regulations reflect this new statutory modification to the presumptive method.

In addition, the regulations permit plans to substitute a new plan year for the plan year ending before September 26, 1980, *without regard* to the amount of a plan's UVBs at the end of the newly designated plan year. This amendment is referred to as a regulatory fresh start option. This change will allow plans using the presumptive method to aggregate the multiple liability pools attributable to prior plan years and the designated plan year. It will thus allow such plans to allocate the plan's UVBs as of the end of the designated plan year among the employers that have an obligation to contribute under the plan for the first plan year ending on or after such date. The plan will allocate UVBs based on the employer's share of the plan's contributions for the five-year period ending with the designated plan year. Thereafter, such plans would apply the regular rules under the presumptive method to segregate changes in the plan's UVBs by plan year and to allocate individual plan year liabilities among the employers obligated to contribute under the plan in that plan year.

PBGC believes this modification to the presumptive method will ease the administrative burdens of plans that have difficulty obtaining the actuarial and contributions data necessary to compute each employer's allocable share of annual changes in UVBs occurring in plan years as far back as 1980. However, this modification does not apply to a construction plan, because PBGC's authority is limited to adjustments in the denominators of the allocation fractions for such plans.

PBGC will also permit plans using the modified presumptive method to designate a plan year that would substitute for the last plan year ending before

September 26, 1980, thus providing another regulatory fresh start option. This amendment provides for the allocation of substantially all of a plan's UVBs among employers that have an obligation to contribute under the plan, while enabling plans to split a single liability pool for plan years ending after September 25, 1980, into two liability pools: one based on the plan's UVBs as of the end of the newly designated plan year, allocated among employers who have an obligation to contribute under the plan for the plan year immediately following the designated plan year, and a second based on the UVBs as of the end of the plan year prior to the withdrawal (offset in the manner described above for the modified presumptive method). For a period of time, this modification would reduce new employers' liability for UVBs of the plan before the employer's participation, which could assist plans in attracting new employers and preserving the plan's contribution base. The modification would not require PBGC approval for adoption.

For each of these modifications, the regulations clarify that a plan's UVBs, determined with respect to plan years ending after the plan year designated in the plan amendment, are reduced by the value of the outstanding claims for withdrawal liability that can reasonably be expected to be collected from employers who withdrew from the plan in or before the designated plan year.

PPA establishes additional funding rules for multiemployer plans in endangered or critical status (see Q 29:1). The sponsor of a plan in critical status (i.e., a plan that is less than 65 percent funded and/or meets any of the other defined tests) is required to adopt a rehabilitation plan that will enable the plan to cease to be in critical status within a specified period of time or to forestall possible insolvency. As deemed appropriate by the plan sponsor, based upon the outcome of collective bargaining over benefit and contribution schedules, the rehabilitation plan may include reductions to adjustable benefits. However, any benefit reductions must be disregarded in determining a plan's UVBs for purposes of an employer's withdrawal liability. Also, a plan is limited in its payment of lump sums and similar benefits after a notice of the plan's critical status is sent, but any such benefit limits must be disregarded in determining a plan's UVBs for purposes of determining an employer's withdrawal liability.

Adjustable benefits include benefits, rights, and features under the plan, such as post-retirement death benefits, 60-month guarantees, disability benefits not yet in pay status; certain early retirement benefits, retirement-type subsidies, and benefit payment options; and benefit increases that would not be eligible for a guarantee on the first day of the initial critical year because the increases were adopted (or, if later, took effect) less than 60 months before such date. An amendment reducing adjustable benefits may not affect the benefits of any participant or beneficiary whose benefit commencement date is before the date on which the plan provides notice that the plan is or will be in critical status for a plan year; the level of a participant's accrued benefit at normal retirement age also is protected.

A plan actuary must use actuarial assumptions that, in the aggregate, are reasonable and, in combination, offer the actuary's best estimate of anticipated experience in determining the UVBs of a plan for purposes of determining an employer's withdrawal liability (absent regulations setting forth such methods and assumptions). For purposes of determining withdrawal liability, UVBs mean the amount by which the value of nonforfeitable benefits under the plan exceeds the value of plan assets.

The regulations amend the definition of "nonforfeitable benefits" and the definition of "UVBs" to include adjustable benefits that have been reduced by a plan sponsor, to the extent such benefits would otherwise be nonforfeitable benefits (see Q 9:1).

Each employer otherwise obligated to make contributions for the initial plan year and any subsequent plan year that a plan is in critical status must pay a surcharge to the plan for such plan year, until the effective date of a CBA (see Q 29:6)(or other agreement pursuant to which the employer contributes) that includes terms consistent with the rehabilitation plan adopted by the plan sponsor. However, any employer surcharges must be disregarded in determining an employer's withdrawal liability, except for purposes of determining the UVBs attributable to an employer (the direct attribution method) or a comparable approved method.

The presumptive, modified presumptive, and rolling-five methods of allocating UVBs allocate the liability pools among participating employers based on the employers' contribution obligations for the five-year period ending with the date the liability pool arose or the plan year immediately preceding the plan year of the employer's withdrawal (depending on the method or liability pool). The numerator of the allocation fraction is the total amount required to be contributed by the withdrawing employer for the five-year period, and the denominator of the allocation fraction is the total amount contributed by all employers under the plan for the five-year period. The regulations exclude amounts attributable to the employer surcharge from the contributions that are otherwise includible in the numerator and the denominator of the allocation fraction under the presumptive, modified presumptive, and rolling-five methods. A simplified method for the application of this principle is provided below in the form of an illustration of the exclusion of employer surcharge amounts from the allocation fraction.

Example. Plan X is a multiemployer plan that has vested benefit liabilities of $200 million and assets of $130 million as of the end of its 2015 plan year. During the 2015 plan year, there were three contributing employers. Two of three employers were in the plan for the entire five-year period ending with the 2015 plan year. One employer was in the plan during the 2014 and 2015 plan years only. Each employer had a $4 million contribution obligation each year under a CBA. In addition, for the 2011, 2012, and 2013 plan years, employers were liable for the automatic employer surcharge at a rate of 5 percent of required contributions in 2011 and 10 percent of required contributions in 2012 and 2013. The following table shows the contributions and surcharges owed for the five-year period.

	Employer A ($ in millions)		Employer B ($ in millions)		Employer C ($ in millions)	
Year	Contribution	Surcharge	Contribution	Surcharge	Contribution	Surcharge
2011	$ 4	$0.2	$ 4	$0.2		
2012	4	0.4	4	0.4		
2013	4	0.4	4	0.4		
2014	4	.0	4	.0	$4	$0
2015	4	.0	4	.0	4	0
Five-year total	$20	$1.0	$20	$1.0	$8	$0

Employers A, B, and C contributed $48 million during the five-year period, excluding surcharges, and $50 million including surcharges. Under the rolling-five method, the UVBs allocable to an employer are equal to the plan's UVBs as of the end of the last plan year preceding the withdrawal, multiplied by a fraction equal to the amount the employer was required to contribute to the plan for the last five plan years preceding the withdrawal over the total amount contributed by all employers for those five plan years (other adjustments are also required).

Employer A's share of the plan's UVBs in the event it withdraws in 2016 is $29.17 million, determined by multiplying $70 million (the plan's UVBs at the end of 2015) by the ratio of $20 million to $48 million. Employer B's allocable UVBs are identical to Employer A's, and the amount allocable to Employer C is $11.66 million ($70 million multiplied by the ratio of $8 million to $48 million). The $2.0 million attributable to the automatic employer surcharge is excluded from contributions in the allocation fraction.

The changes relating to modifications to the statutory methods for determining an employer's share of UVBs are applicable to employer withdrawals from a plan that occur on or after January 29, 2009. The change relating to the presumptive method made by PPA is applicable to employer withdrawals occurring on or after January 1, 2007. The changes relating to the effect of PPA benefit adjustments and employer surcharges for purposes of determining an employer's withdrawal liability are applicable to employer withdrawals from a plan occurring in plan years beginning on or after January 1, 2008.

[PBGC Prop. Reg. §§ 4211.2, 4211.4, 4211.12(c), 4211.12(d), 4219.2; preamble to proposed regulations]

Q 29:29   Can withdrawal liability be imposed if the multiemployer plan has no UVBs?

Yes. Even if a multiemployer plan as a whole has no UVBs (see Q 29:16), each of the statutory methods of calculating withdrawal liability except the rolling-five method (see Q 29:28) may result in liability for a withdrawing employer. Under the statutory methods, the withdrawing employer is deemed responsible for the vested benefits of its employees. Accordingly, withdrawal liability may be imposed even if plan assets would be sufficient to fund this liability. [RXDC, Inc. v. Oil, Chem. & Atomic Workers Union-Indus. Pension Fund, No. 781, F. Supp. 1516 (D. Colo. 1992); Wise v. Ruffin, 914 F.2d 570 (4th Cir. 1990); Ben Hur Constr. Co. v. Goodwin, 784 F.2d 876 (8th Cir. 1986); PBGC Withdrawal of Notice of Interpretation, 56 Fed. Reg. 12,288 (Mar. 22, 1991); *but see* Berkshire Hathaway, Inc. v. Textile Workers Pension Fund, 874 F.2d 53 (1st Cir. 1989)]

Q 29:30 May multiemployer plan withdrawal liability be waived or reduced?

There are numerous circumstances under which multiemployer plan withdrawal liability can be either waived or reduced. These waivers are designed to protect small employers and employers in certain industries.

For example, an employer's liability is waived in full if its share is less than the lesser of $50,000 or .75 percent of the total unfunded liability of the plan. If the employer's share is between $50,000 and $150,000, it is reduced but not eliminated. The plan may increase the $50,000 and $150,000 limits to $100,000 and $250,000, respectively. [ERISA § 4209]

Also, waivers of withdrawal liabilities are provided in the construction industry on a mandatory basis when the employer leaves the area. A similar waiver is provided in certain cases for plans covering the entertainment industry. In both cases, there is no withdrawal liability unless the employer either continues to perform the same work in the same jurisdiction or resumes the same work in the same jurisdiction within five years and does not renew its obligation to contribute to the plan. PBGC may exclude certain employers in the entertainment industry from the waiver provision if PBGC determines that it is necessary to protect the plan's participants. [ERISA §§ 4203(b), 4203(c)]

Plans in industries other than construction or entertainment may be amended to provide for special withdrawal liability rules if PBGC finds that the rules apply to an industry in which the characteristics that make the use of the special rules appropriate are clearly shown and that the rules would not pose a significant risk to PBGC. [PBGC Notice, 74 Fed. Reg. 9114 (March 2, 2009); PBGC Notice of Approval, 56 Fed. Reg. 49,804 (Oct. 1, 1991)]

Employers that withdraw from a plan that receives substantially all its contributions from employers in the trucking, public warehousing, or household goods moving industries may post a five-year bond instead of making withdrawal liability payments. If the withdrawal of an employer that posted a bond substantially damages the plan, PBGC may require that the bond be paid to the plan. A bond could not be posted by an employer that withdrew from a plan that received approximately 62 percent of its contributions from employers primarily involved in the trucking business; the plan did not receive substantially all its contributions from truckers. [ERISA § 4203(d); Continental Can Co. v. Chicago Truck Drivers, Helpers & Warehouse Workers Union Pension Fund, 916 F.2d 1154 (7th Cir. 1990)]

One court concluded that an agreement by a union to indemnify a contributing employer for its withdrawal liability to a multiemployer plan was enforceable. [Pittsburgh Mack Sales & Service, Inc. v. International Union of Operating Engineers, Local No. 66, 580 F.3d 185 (3d Cir. 2009)]

Q 29:31   What happens if an employer reenters a plan after a prior withdrawal?

PBGC has issued regulations providing for the reduction or abatement of withdrawal liability under certain circumstances. A reentering employer that seeks an abatement of its complete withdrawal liability must formally apply for the waiver by the date of the first scheduled withdrawal liability payment falling due after the employer resumes covered operations or, if later, at least 15 days from the date the employer resumes covered operations under the multiemployer plan. The application must:

1. Identify the withdrawn employer and the date it withdrew;
2. Identify the reentered employer and all trades and businesses under common control with the employer as of both the date of withdrawal and the date of resumption of covered operations;
3. Set forth the list of operations for which the employer is obligated to contribute to the plan; and
4. Include the date the employer resumes covered operations.

[ERISA § 4207(a); PBGC Reg. § 4207.3]

PBGC has issued regulations that allow multiemployer plans to adopt alternative rules for reduction or waiver of complete withdrawal liability. A plan sponsor is required to submit a written request for PBGC approval of a plan amendment adopting the alternative rules. The request must contain the following information:

1. The name and address of the plan and the telephone number of the plan sponsor or its duly authorized representative;
2. The sponsor's nine-digit employer identification number (EIN) and the three-digit plan identification number (PIN);
3. A copy of the executed amendment, including the date on which the amendment was adopted, its proposed effective date, and the full text of the alternative rules;
4. A copy of the plan's most recent actuarial valuation report;
5. A certification that notice of the adoption of the amendment and of the request for PBGC approval has been given to all employers with an obligation to contribute to the plan and to all employee organizations representing employees covered by the plan; and
6. In addition, the plan may submit any other information that it believes is pertinent to its request.

PBGC may require the plan sponsor to submit additional information in order to review the request. PBGC will approve a plan amendment if it determines that the alternative rules contained therein are consistent with the purposes of ERISA. However, PBGC will not approve an abatement rule if its implementation would be adverse to the interest of plan participants and beneficiaries or the rule would increase PBGC's risk of loss with respect to the plan.

[ERISA § 4207(b); PBGC Reg. § 4207.10]

Q 29:32   What withdrawal liability payments must the employer make while the abatement determination is made?

The reentering employer may post a bond or establish an escrow account equal to 70 percent of the required withdrawal liability payments, in which case, pending the abatement determination, no withdrawal liability payments need be made. [PBGC Reg. § 4207.4]

Q 29:33   What is required for abatement of an employer's withdrawal liability upon reentry to the multiemployer plan?

An employer that completely withdraws from a multiemployer plan and subsequently reenters the plan will have its liability abated if it resumes covered operations under the plan and assumes a postentry level of contribution base units (see Q 29:21) that exceeds 30 percent of the employer's prewithdrawal amount. [PBGC Reg. § 4207.5]

Q 29:34   What are the effects of an abatement?

If the plan sponsor determines that the reentering employer is eligible for abatement:

1. The employer has no obligation to make future withdrawal liability payments to the multiemployer plan with respect to its complete withdrawal;
2. The employer's liability for a subsequent withdrawal will be calculated under modified rules;
3. The bond will be canceled or amounts held in the escrow account (see Q 29:32) will be returned to the employer; and
4. Any withdrawal liability payments made by the employer will be refunded by the plan.

[PBGC Reg. § 4207.3(c)]

Q 29:35   What are the effects of a nonabatement?

If the plan sponsor determines that the employer is not eligible for abatement:

1. The sponsor notifies the employer of its determination;

2. Within 30 days of the sponsor's notice, the bond posted or the escrow account established by the employer (see Q 29:32) must be paid to the multiemployer plan;

3. Within 30 days of the sponsor's notice, the employer must make the balance of the withdrawal liability payment not covered by the bond or escrow account;

4. The employer must resume its withdrawal liability payments under the plan schedule; and

5. The employer will be treated as a new employer for purposes of any future application rules.

[PBGC Reg. § 4207.3(d)]

Q 29:36   How can a reentering employer elect nonabatement?

A reentering employer can elect nonabatement by not filing the application for a waiver of its withdrawal liability (see Q 29:31) upon its reentry to the multiemployer plan. [PBGC Reg. § 4207.3]

Q 29:37   Does the value of the employer affect the amount of its withdrawal liability?

Yes. If all, or substantially all, of the employer's assets are sold in an arm's-length transaction to an unrelated party and the purchasing company does not assume the withdrawal liability (see Q 29:27), the employer's withdrawal liability is limited to the greater of (1) the UVBs (see Qs 29:16, 29:28) attributable to its employees or (2) a percentage of the employer's liquidation or dissolution value, as determined under the following table:

Liquidation or Dissolution Value of Employer After Sale	Percentage
Not more than $2,000,000	30% of the amount
More than $2,000,000, but not more than $4,000,000	$600,000, plus 35% of the amount in excess of $2,000,000
More than $4,000,000, but not more than $6,000,000	$1,300,000, plus 40% of the amount in excess of $4,000,000
More than $6,000,000, but not more than $7,000,000	$2,100,000, plus 45% of the amount in excess of $6,000,000
More than $7,000,000, but not more than $8,000,000	$2,550,000, plus 50% of the amount in excess of $7,000,000
More than $8,000,000, but not more than $9,000,000	$3,050,000, plus 60% of the amount in excess of $8,000,000
More than $9,000,000, but not more than $10,000,000	$3,650,000, plus 70% of the amount in excess of $9,000,000
More than $10,000,000	$4,350,000, plus 80% of the amount in excess of $10,000,000

However, the withdrawal liability is not included in determining the liquidation or dissolution value of the employer. [ERISA § 4225; PBGC Op.Ltr. 93-3]

For sales occurring on or after January 1, 2007, the above table is changed as follows:

Liquidation or Dissolution Value of Employer After Sale	*Percentage*
Not more than $5,000,000	30% of the amount
More than $5,000,000, but not more than $10,000,000	$1,500,000, plus 35% of the amount in excess of $5,000,000
More than $10,000,000, but not more than $15,000,000	$3,250,000, plus 40% of the amount in excess of $10,000,000
More than $15,000,000, but not more than $17,500,000	$5,250,000, plus 45% of the amount in excess of $15,000,000
More than $17,500,000, but not more than $20,000,000	$6,375,000, plus 50% of the amount in excess of $17,500,000
More than $20,000,000, but not more than $22,500,000	$7,625,000, plus 60% of the amount in excess of $20,000,000
More than $22,500,000, but not more than $25,000,000	$9,125,000, plus 70% of the amount in excess of $22,500,000
More than $25,000,000	$10,875,000, plus 80% of the amount in excess of $25,000,000

[ERISA § 4225(a)(2)]

Q 29:38   Does an insolvent employer have withdrawal liability?

Yes, but that liability may be limited. An insolvent employer in liquidation or dissolution is liable for the first 50 percent of its normal withdrawal liability, and the remainder of its liability is limited to the employer's value, as of the commencement of liquidation or dissolution, reduced by the first 50 percent. [ERISA § 4225(b); PBGC Op. Ltr. 93-3]

An employer is insolvent if its liabilities, including withdrawal liability, exceed its assets as of the commencement of liquidation or dissolution. However, the employer's liquidation or dissolution value is determined without regard to withdrawal liability. [ERISA § 4225(d); Trustees of Amalgamated Ins. Fund v. Geltman Indus., Inc., 784 F.2d 926 (9th Cir. 1986)] An employer in Chapter 11 reorganization, however, is not said to be in liquidation or dissolution and so may not have its withdrawal liability cut in half. [Granada Wines, Inc. v. New England Teamsters & Trucking Indus. Pension Fund, 748 F.2d 42 (1st Cir. 1984)] However, see Q 29:19 for a discussion of whether or not an employer's withdrawal liability is dischargeable in bankruptcy.

Q 29:39   What is the 20-year cap on a withdrawing employer's liability?

The withdrawing employer's liability is paid over the number of years required to amortize the liability in level annual installments. The annual liability payments are basically equal to the annual payments of the employer's plan contributions before withdrawal. If the annual payments will not amortize the withdrawal liability in 20 years, the withdrawal liability is reduced to the amount that can be paid off in the 20-year period. [ERISA § 4219(c)]

The United States Supreme Court has ruled that the word "amortize" assumes interest charges and that interest begins to accrue on the first day of the plan year following withdrawal. [ERISA §§ 4219(c)(1)(A)(i), 4219(c)(4); Milwaukee Brewery Workers' Pension Plan v. Jos. Schlitz Brewing Co., No. 93-768 (U.S. 1995)]

Q 29:40   When is the employer notified of its liability for withdrawal from a multiemployer plan?

The plan sponsor must notify the employer of the amount of its liability "as soon as practicable" after the employer's withdrawal. At the same time, the plan sponsor will demand payment in accordance with a schedule of payments. In one case, a notice given to an employer two years after the withdrawal liability arose was considered timely. In another case, timely notice was given 12 years after withdrawal because the withdrawing employer never notified the plan sponsor and, for some reason, continued to make contributions to the plan. [ERISA § 4219(b); Brentwood Fin. Corp. v. Western Conference of Teamsters Pension Fund, 902 F.2d 1456 (9th Cir. 1990); Giroux Bros. Transp., Inc. v. New England Teamsters & Trucking Indus. Pension Fund, No. 95-1032 (1st Cir.1996)] In another case, notice given five and one-half years after the withdrawal liability arose was not considered timely. [Teamsters Pension Trust Fund of Phila. & Vicinity v. Custom Cartage Co., 1991 U.S. Dist. LEXIS 11566 (E.D. Pa. 1991)] However, a notice given before the actual date of withdrawal is not timely and does not give rise to withdrawal liability. The court concluded that the plan could later give a new, timely notice in order to obtain interim payments (see Q 29:44). [Central States, Southeast & Southwest Areas Pension Fund v. Hunt Truck Lines, Inc., 204 F.3d 236 (7th Cir. 2000)]

Notice of, and demand for, withdrawal liability made to one member of a commonly controlled group is sufficient to constitute notice and demand to all members of the group. Thus, courts have held an entity within a commonly controlled group liable for the withdrawal liability of another group member even though only the withdrawing employer received actual notice of the withdrawal liability. The rationale for this is that all trades or businesses under common control are treated as a single employer and, thus, notice to one is notice to all (see Q 29:23). [Chicago Truck Drivers v. El Paso Co., 525 F.3d 591 (7th Cir. 2008); IAM Nat'l Fund v. Slyman Indus., Inc., 901 F.2d 127 (D.C. Cir. 1990); Teamsters Pension Trust Fund-Bd. of the W. Conference v. Allyn Transp. Co., 832 F.2d 502 (9th Cir. 1987); IUE AFL-CIO Pension Fund v. Barker & Williamson, Inc., 788 F.2d 118 (3d Cir. 1986); Board of Trustees of Trucking

Employees of North Jersey Welfare Fund, Inc. v. Gotham Fuel Corp., 860 F. Supp. 1044 (D.N.J. 1993); Board of Trustees of Trucking Employees of North Jersey Welfare Fund, Inc. v. Able Truck Rental Corp., 822 F. Supp. 1091 (D.N.J. 1993); Central States, Southeast & Southwest Areas Pension Fund v. Landvatter, 1993 U.S. Dist. LEXIS 13 (N.D. Ill. 1993); Central States, Southeast & Southwest Areas Pension Fund v. Bay, 684 F. Supp. 483 (E.D. Mich. 1988); Board of Trustees of the W. Conference of Teamsters Pension Trust Fund v. Salt Creek Terminals, Inc., No. C85-2270R (W.D. Wash. 1986); Connors v. Calvert Dev. Co., 622 F. Supp. 877 (D.D.C. 1985)]

The date when one employer in a commonly controlled group receives notice of withdrawal liability is used to determine the timeliness of any group member's request to arbitrate disputes concerning the withdrawal liability (see Q 29:42). [McDonald v. Centra, No. S 89-1734 (D. Md. 1990); Teamster Pension Trust Fund of Phila. v. Laidlaw Indus., Inc., 745 F. Supp. 1016 (D. Del. 1990)] However, one court permitted a husband and wife who jointly owned an unincorporated farm to arbitrate the amount of withdrawal liability assessed against the husband's manufacturing company. The plan sponsor's notice of withdrawal liability demanded payment only from the husband's corporation and other commonly controlled corporations. [ILGWU Nat'l Ret. Fund v. Minotola Indus., Inc., 88 Civ. 9131 (S.D.N.Y. 1991)]

ERISA Section 4301 imposes a three-or six-year statute of limitations on civil actions with respect to multiemployer plans, including issues of withdrawal liability. Because the statute of limitations begins to run when notice and demand for payment of withdrawal liability is not met by the withdrawing employer, an action brought more than six years thereafter is not timely. [Board of Trustees of Trucking Employees of North Jersey Welfare Fund Inc.–Pension Fund v. Kero Leasing Corp., 2004 U.S. App. LEXIS 14258 (3d Cir. 2004); Central States, Southeast & Southwest Areas Pension Fund v. Navco, 1993 U.S. App. LEXIS 20367 (7th Cir. 1993); Joyce v. Clyde Sandoz Masonry, 871 F.2d 1119 (Fed. Cir. 1989); Central States, Southeast & Southwest Areas Pension Fund v. Mississippi Warehouse Corp., 1994 U.S. Dist. LEXIS 5888 (N.D. Ill. 1994); Central States, Southeast & Southwest Areas Pension Fund v. Van Vorst Indus., Inc., 1992 U.S. Dist. LEXIS 1867 (N.D. Ill. 1992)] However, one court held that the six-year statute of limitations began to run when an employer in the construction industry withdrew from the plan (i.e., the date on which the employer resumed covered work within five years from the date on which it ceased making plan contributions; see Q 29:30). [Board of Trustees of the Constr. Laborers Pension Trust for S. Cal. v. Thibodo, 1994 U.S. App. LEXIS 24499 (9th Cir. 1994)] Other courts have held that the six-year statute of limitations commences with each withdrawal liability payment due date; that is, each scheduled payment is a separate obligation that has its own statute of limitations period. [Board of Trustees of the Dist. No. 15 Machinists' Pension Trust v. Kahle Eng'g Corp., 1994 U.S. App. LEXIS 36945 (3d Cir. 1994); Carriers Container Council v. Mobile S.S. Ass'n, 948 F.2d 1219 (11th Cir. 1991)] A plan's action to collect withdrawal liability from an employer that stopped making payments in 1982 was not barred by the statute of limitations. The statute did not start running until the plan demanded payment in 1987. [ILGWU Nat'l Ret. Fund v. Smart Modes of Cal., Inc., 735 F. Supp. 103 (S.D.N.Y. 1990)]

The United States Supreme Court has now resolved this issue and concluded that ERISA's six-year statute of limitations on a multiemployer plan's action to collect unpaid withdrawal liability from an employer that withdrew from the plan does not commence to run until the employer fails to make payment on the schedule set by the plan. The Court determined that, since the act of withdrawing from a plan does not violate ERISA, withdrawal cannot trigger the statute of limitations and that the statute of limitations is not triggered until two events take place: (1) the plan must calculate the employer's withdrawal liability, set a payment schedule, and demand payment from the employer, and (2) the employer must default on an installment due and payable under the schedule. Of even greater significance, the Court also ruled that each missed installment payment creates a separate cause of action with its own six-year limitations period. However, if the trustees elect to accelerate the liabilities by demanding payment in full following an employer's default, the six-year period commences when the liability is accelerated. [Bay Area Laundry & Dry Cleaning Pension Trust Fund v. Ferbar Corp. of Cal., Inc., 522 U.S. 192 (1997)] Despite this United States Supreme Court decision, one court ruled that the statute of limitations commenced to run on the date the employer ceased operations; and, since the plan filed suit more than six years thereafter, the statute had expired. In this case, the employer filed for bankruptcy, the plan filed a proof of claim in bankruptcy, a few weeks later the employer ceased operations, two weeks thereafter the plan sent the employer a notice and demand for payment of withdrawal liability to be paid in 14 equal installments, the employer never made any withdrawal liability payments, and the plan brought suit more than six years later. [Central States, Southeast & Southwest Areas Pension Fund v. Basic Am. Indus., Inc., 252 F.3d 911 (7th Cir. 2001)]

Q 29:41 Is the initial determination of a withdrawing employer's liability presumptively correct?

When an employer withdraws from a multiemployer plan, the plan sponsor determines the amount of the withdrawing employer's liability (see Qs 29:16, 29:18). The initial determination is presumed to be correct. To overcome this presumption, the employer must demonstrate, by a preponderance of evidence, that the actuarial assumptions and methods used by the plan's actuary are unreasonable or that a significant error has been made in applying the assumptions or methods. In one case, a plan's actuarial calculations were not unreasonable in the aggregate even though the interest rate assumption may have been unreasonably low. [ERISA § 4221(a)(3); Combs v. Classic Coal Corp, 931 F.2d 96 (D.C. Cir. 1991)]

A number of employers have raised unsuccessful constitutional challenges to the presumption of correctness accorded plan sponsors' determinations of withdrawal liability. [Keith Fulton & Sons, Inc. v. New England Teamsters & Trucking Indus. Pension Fund, 762 F.2d 1137 (1st Cir. 1985); Board of Trustees of the W. Conference of Teamsters Pension Trust Fund v. Thompson Bldg.

Materials, Inc., 749 F.2d 1396 (9th Cir. 1984); Washington Star Co. v. International Typographical Union Negotiated Pension Plan, 729 F.2d 1502 (D.C. Cir. 1984); Textile Workers Pension Fund v. Standard Dye & Finishing Co., 725 F.2d 843 (2d Cir. 1984); Republic Indus., Inc. v. Teamsters Joint Council No. 83 of Va. Pension Fund, 718 F.2d 628 (4th Cir. 1983); Centennial State Carpenters Pension Trust Fund v. Woodworkers of Denver, Inc., 615 F. Supp. 1063 (D. Colo. 1985)]

However, two courts have held that the presumption of correctness of the determination of the amount of the withdrawing employer's liability by plan sponsors who owe a fiduciary duty to the plan and who are therefore biased in favor of the plan is unconstitutional. [United Retail & Wholesale Employees Teamsters Union Local No. 115 Pension Plan v. Yahn & McDonnell, Inc., 787 F.2d 128 (3d Cir. 1986), *aff'd per curiam sub nom.* PBGC v. Yahn & McDonnell, Inc., 481 U.S. 735 (1987); Robbins v. Pepsi-Cola Metro. Bottling Co., 636 F. Supp. 641 (N.D. Ill. 1986)] In affirming the Third Circuit's decision that the presumption in favor of the correctness of a plan sponsor's initial determination regarding withdrawal liability is unconstitutional, the Supreme Court split four to four. Thus, the decision is binding only with respect to the parties in the case. As a result, the conflict among the circuits continues.

See Q 29:42 for a discussion of a new procedure applicable to disputes involving withdrawal liability.

Q 29:42 May an employer contest the determination of its liability for withdrawing from a multiemployer plan?

Yes. When the employer receives notice of its withdrawal liability (see Q 29:40) from the plan sponsor, it may, within 90 days of its receipt of such notice, ask the plan sponsor to review any specific matter relating to its determination, point out any inaccuracy in its determination, or provide additional information to the trustees bearing on their determination. The plan sponsor must also comply with an employer's request for an explanation of its calculation of the employer's withdrawal liability even if the employer has not yet requested arbitration. [ERISA §§ 4219(b)(2), 4221(e); John J. Nissen Baking Co. v. New England Teamsters & Trucking Indus. Pension Fund, 737 F. Supp. 679 (D. Me. 1990)]

One court concluded that an employer, *following* its withdrawal from a plan, did not have a right to the same detailed information regarding the calculation of withdrawal liability to which it would have been entitled *before* its withdrawal from the plan. After the employer withdrew from the plan, the plan sponsor notified the employer of the amount and payment schedule for its withdrawal liability. In response, the employer made a written request to the plan sponsor seeking additional detailed information in order to evaluate the withdrawal liability computations it had been given. The employer commenced an action after the plan sponsor merely provided plan documents and a contribution history but did not provide additional requested information for the basis of its withdrawal liability calculations. The court ruled that the employer was not entitled to additional information beyond that which it had already received from the plan sponsor. ERISA Section 4221(e) requires a plan sponsor to furnish information necessary for an employer to compute its own withdrawal liability in order to determine whether to withdraw from the plan. However, under post-withdrawal circumstances, the procedures set forth in ERISA Section 4219(b) apply. Under the latter section, once the employer withdrew from the plan, the plan sponsor was only required to notify the employer of its withdrawal liability and demand payment in accordance with a payment schedule, as the plan sponsor had done. [Reliable Liquors v. Truck Drivers & Helpers Local Union No. 355 Pension Fund, No. 02-3854 (D. Md. 2003)]

The plan sponsor has 120 days to respond to an employer's request that it reconsider its earlier determination of withdrawal liability. If it takes no action, then the employer must request arbitration within 60 days after the expiration of the 120-day period or it may be estopped from disputing the amounts owed in a later court action to collect the withdrawal liability (see Q 29:43). The plan sponsor, however, is required to undertake a "reasonable review" of the employer's contentions and notify the employer of its decision, setting forth the basis for its decision and the reasons behind any change in its liability determination. The employer must request arbitration within 60 days of its receipt of this second notice even though 120 days may not have elapsed since the employer requested a review of its withdrawal liability. [ERISA § 4221(a)(1)]

The plan sponsor, too, may request arbitration within 60 days of either (1) notification to the employer of its decision after review of the employer's dispute of the liability determination or (2) the expiration of 120 days after the employer requests review of the plan sponsor's initial determination. Alternatively, both the plan sponsor and the employer may jointly request arbitration within 180 days of the initial demand for payment of withdrawal liability. [ERISA §§ 4219(b), 4221(a); PBGC Reg. § 4221.3]

The time limits set forth above are strictly enforced. In one case, an employer erroneously mailed its timely arbitration request to the plan sponsor, not to the arbitration association as required under the plan. The court refused to order arbitration, even though the arbitration request was hand delivered to the arbitration association immediately upon discovery of the error two days after the deadline. [Central States, Southeast & Southwest Areas Pension Fund v. T.W. Servs., No. 89 C 7415 (N.D. Ill. 1989)]

The standard of review for *factual findings* made by an arbitrator requires that there be a presumption, rebuttable only by a clear preponderance of the evidence, that the findings of fact made by the arbiter are correct. [ERISA § 4221(c)] However, one court has ruled that a review of an arbitrator's *legal* conclusions as to plan withdrawal liability should be de novo (that is, reviewed anew) and is not entitled to the presumption of correctness. [Trustees of the Cent. Pension Fund of the Int'l Union of Operating Eng'rs & Participating Employers v. Wolf Crane Serv., Inc., 374 F.3d 1035 (11th Cir. 2004)]

Where companies against which withdrawal liability claims were asserted disputed whether they were employers, one court ruled that the employer-status question was subject to the determination of the court and was not a question to be submitted to an arbitrator. [New York State Teamsters Conf. Pension and Retirement Fund v. Express Services, Inc., 426 F.3d 640 (2d Cir. 2005)]

Under PPA (see Q 1:33), if (1) a plan sponsor determines that a complete or partial withdrawal of an employer has occurred or an employer is liable for withdrawal liability payments with respect to the complete or partial withdrawal from the plan and (2) such determination is based in whole or in part on a finding by the plan sponsor that a principal purpose of any transaction that occurred after December 31, 1998, and at least five years (two years in the case of a small employer) before the date of complete or partial withdrawal was to evade or avoid withdrawal liability, the person against which the withdrawal liability is assessed may elect to use a special rule relating to required payments. Under the special rule, if the electing person contests the plan sponsor's determination with respect to withdrawal liability payments through an arbitration proceeding, through a claim brought in a court of competent jurisdiction, or as otherwise permitted by law, the electing person is not obligated to make the withdrawal liability payments until a final decision in the arbitration proceeding, or in court, upholds the plan sponsor's determination. The special rule applies only if the electing person (1) provides notice to the plan sponsor of its election to apply the special rule within 90 days after the plan sponsor notifies the electing person of its liability, and (2) if a final decision on the arbitration proceeding, or in court, of the withdrawal liability dispute has not been rendered within 12 months from the date of such notice, the electing person provides to the plan, effective as of the first day following the 12-month period, a bond issued by a corporate surety, or an amount held on escrow by a bank or similar financial institution satisfactory to the plan, in an amount equal to the sum of the withdrawal liability payments that would otherwise be due for the 12-month period beginning with the first anniversary of such notice. The bond or escrow must remain in effect until there is a final decision in the arbitration proceeding, or in court, of the withdrawal liability dispute. At such time, the bond or escrow must be paid to the plan if the final decision upholds the plan sponsor's determination. If the withdrawal liability dispute is not concluded by 12 months after the electing person posts the bond or escrow, the electing person must, at the start of each succeeding 12-month period, provide an additional bond or amount held in escrow equal to the sum of the withdrawal liability payments that would otherwise be payable to the plan during that period.

A small employer is an employer which, for the calendar year in which the transaction occurred, and for each of the three preceding years on average (1) employs no more than 500 employees and (2) is required to make contributions to the plan on behalf of not more than 250 employees.

This procedure is effective for any person that receives a notification of withdrawal liability and demand for payment on or after August 17, 2006, with respect to a transaction that occurred after December 31, 1998.

[ERISA § 4221(b); PBGC Prop. Reg. § 4219.1]

Q 29:43   Does the employer run any risk if it does not demand arbitration of the plan sponsor's claim for withdrawal liability?

Yes. An employer that fails to initiate arbitration within the statutory periods (see Q 29:42) risks being barred from disputing the plan's determination of withdrawal liability in a subsequent court action by the plan sponsor to recover that liability. [United National Retirement Fund v. Veranda Marketing Co., 2009 WL 2025163 (___.D.N.Y. 2009); Board of Trustees, Sheet Metal Workers' Nat'l. Pension Fund v. BES Services, Inc., 469 F.3d 369 (4th Cir. 2006); ILGWU Nat'l Ret. Fund v. Meredith Grey, Inc., 2003 U.S. App. LEXIS 26271 (2d Cir. 2003); Trucking Employees of N. Jersey Welfare Fund, Inc. v. Bellezza Co., 2003 WL 262505 (3d Cir. 2003); Rao v. Prest Metals, 2001 WL 720454 (___.D.N.Y. 2001); Teamsters Pension Trust Fund of Phila. & Vicinity v. Domenic Cristinzio, Inc., No. 96-6596 (E.D. Pa. 1998); Philadelphia Marine Trade Ass'n-ILA Pension Fund v. Rose, No. 95-1767 (3d Cir. 1996); Einhorn v. Jos. Paolino & Sons, Inc., No. 95-5824 (E.D. Pa. 1996); Chicago Truck Drivers, Helpers & Warehouse Workers Union (Indep.) Pension Fund v. R. Sumner Trucking Co., 1992 U.S. Dist. LEXIS 1877 (N.D. Ill. 1992); Trustees of the Colo. Pipe Indus. Pension Trust v. Howard Elec. & Mechanical, Inc., 909 F.2d 1379 (10th Cir. 1990); New York State Teamsters Conference Pension & Ret. Fund v. McNicholas Transp. Co., 848 F.2d 20 (2d Cir. 1988); ILGWU Nat'l Ret. Fund v. Levy Bros. Frocks, Inc., 846 F.2d 879 (2d Cir. 1988); Robbins v. Admiral Merchs. Motor Freight,Inc., 846 F.2d 1054 (7th Cir. 1988); Teamsters Pension Trust Fund-Bd. of Trustees v. Allyn Transp. Co., 832 F.2d 502 (9th Cir. 1987); IAM Nat'l Pension Fund v. Clinton Engines Corp., 825 F.2d 415 (D.C. Cir. 1987)]

Additionally, courts will generally dismiss an employer's action to challenge a determination of withdrawal liability when arbitration has been bypassed. [Central States, Southeast & Southwest Areas Pension Fund v. Carstensen Freight Lines, Inc., No. 99-2256 (7th Cir. 2000); Central States, Southeast & Southwest Areas Pension Fund v. Progressive Drivers Servs. Inc., No. 95 C 4084 (N.D. Ill. 1996); McDonald v. Centra, Inc., No. 90-2483 (4th Cir. 1991); Caleb v. Smith & Son of Ohio, Inc., 946 F.2d 1059 (S.D.N.Y. 1991); Mason & Dixon Tank Lines, Inc. v. Central States, Southeast & Southwest Areas Pension Fund, 852 F.2d 156 (6th Cir. 1988); Flying Tiger Line v. Teamsters Pension Trust Fund, 830 F.2d 1241 (3d Cir. 1987); Central States, Southeast & Southwest Areas Pension Fund v. Conaway, 1991 U.S. Dist. LEXIS 5096 (N.D. Ill. 1991)] However, an employer has been permitted to proceed in court in the absence of arbitration when only statutory or constitutional issues, not factual issues, were raised. [IAM Nat'l Pension Fund Benefit Plan C v. Stockton Tri Indus., 727 F.2d 1204 (D.C. Cir. 1984); Central States, Southeast & Southwest Areas Pension Fund v. Skyland Leasing Co., 691 F. Supp. 6 (W.D. Mich. 1987)] Where companies against which withdrawal liability claims were asserted disputed whether they were employers, one court ruled that the employer-status question was subject to the determination of the court and was not a question to be submitted to an arbitrator. [New York State Teamsters Conf. Pension and Retirement Fund v. Express Services, Inc., 426 F.3d 640 (2d Cir. 2005)] There is no right to a jury trial in a suit contesting the enforcement of withdrawal liability because the arbitrator is the fact finder. [Connors v. Ryan's Coal Co., 923 F.2d 1461 (11th Cir. 1991)]

Even if the employer attempts to initiate arbitration but does not do so properly—that is, in accordance with the rules of the plan—it may be held to have waived its right to contest the claim. For example, merely expressing a desire for arbitration and requesting information on how to proceed is not the equivalent of initiation of arbitration within the meaning of the plan's rules. [Robbins v. Braver Lumber & Supply Co., No. 85 C 08332 (N.D. Ill. 1987)]

One court ruled that, even though the employer successfully challenged the plan's claim against it for withdrawal liability, the employer was not entitled to attorneys' fees because the plan's position was substantially justified. [Central States, Southeast & Southwest Areas Pension Fund v. Paramount Liquor Co., 203 F.3d 442 (7th Cir. 2000); *but see* Continental Can Co v. Chicago Truck Drivers, Helpers & Warehouse Workers Union Pension Fund, 921 F.2d 126 (7th Cir. 1990), which held that a party successfully defending an arbitrator's award was presumptively entitled to attorneys' fees]

See Q 29:42 for a discussion of a new procedure applicable to disputes involving withdrawal liability.

Q 29:44   When are withdrawal liability payments due?

The plan sponsor sets the schedule of payments. The first payment is due no later than 60 days after demand (see Q 29:40), and subsequent payments are usually made quarterly.

Even if the employer contests the determination of liability either with the plan sponsor or through arbitration, the employer is not relieved of its obligation to begin payment of the withdrawal liability. [ERISA §§ 4219(c)(2), 4219(c)(3), 4221(d); Central States, Southeast & Southwest Areas Pension Fund v. O'Neill Bros. Transfer & Storage Co., 2010 WL 3421164 (7th Cir. 2010); Central States, Southeast & Southwest Areas Pension Fund v. Bomar Nat'l, Inc., No. 00-2472 (7th Cir. 2001); Bridge v. Wright Indus., Inc., No. 96 CV 8113 (N.D. Ill. 1998); Central States, Southeast & Southwest Areas Pension Fund v. National Cement Prods. Co., No. 97C4031 (N.D. Ill. 1998); Galgay v. Beaverbrook Coal Co., 1997 U.S. App. LEXIS 1463 (3d Cir. 1997); Central States, Southeast & Southwest Areas Pension Fund v. Ten D, Inc., 1992 U.S. Dist. LEXIS 5524 (N.D. Ill. 1992); DeBreceni v. Merchants Terminal Corp., 889 F.2d 1 (1st Cir. 1989)] Further, courts have ordered an employer that refused to make withdrawal liability payments pending arbitration to pay the plan's attorneys' fees and costs. [Trustees of the Plumbers & Pipefitters Nat'l Pension Fund v. Mar-Len, Inc., 30 F.3d 621 (5th Cir. 1994); Retirement Fund of the Fur Mfg. Indus. v. Getto & Getto, Inc., 714 F. Supp. 651 (S.D.N.Y. 1989)] In addition, one court ordered an employer that was not subject to withdrawal liability to pay liquidated damages for its failure to make interim payments while challenging the withdrawal liability assessment, and another court issued a contempt order against the employer and its president. [Central States, Southeast & Southwest Areas Pension Fund v. Lady Baltimore Foods, Inc., 960 F.2d 1339 (7th Cir. 1992); Central States, Southeast & Southwest Areas Pension Fund v. Wintz Props., 1998 WL 568768 (7th Cir. 1998)]

In limited situations, an employer may be relieved from making withdrawal liability payments pending arbitration upon a showing of the employer's likelihood of success in arbitration and irreparable harm to be suffered due to payment. [Robbins v. McNicholas Transp. Co, 819 F.2d 682 (7th Cir. 1987)] The employer must provide evidence of irreparable harm after first demonstrating that the pension fund lacks a "colorable claim" for the assessment of withdrawal liability. [Trustees of the Plumbers & Pipefitters Nat'l Pension Fund v. Mar-Len, Inc., 30 F.3d 621 (5th Cir. 1994); Trustees of the Chicago Truck Drivers, Helpers & Warehouse Workers Union (Indep.) Pension Fund v. Rentar Indus., Inc., 951 F.2d 152 (7th Cir. 1991); NYSA-ILA Pension Trust Fund v. Lykes Bros., No. 96 Civ. 5616 (S.D.N.Y. 1997)] However, in cases where an arbitration proceeding initiated by the employer was still pending, the court ruled that it was premature for the plan to request payment of the total amount of the employer's withdrawal liability. [Chicago Truck Drivers, Helpers & Warehouse Workers Union (Indep.) Pension Fund v. Century Motor Freight, Inc., 125 F.3d 526 (7th Cir. 1997); New York State Teamsters Conference Pension & Ret. Fund v. CDC Haulage Corp, 1996 U.S. Dist. LEXIS 2706 (N.D.N.Y. 1996); PBGC Reg. § 4219.31(c)(iii)]

The bankruptcy or insolvency of the parent member of a controlled group does not relieve the subsidiary controlled group members of their obligation to make withdrawal liability payments (see Q 29:23) even if the liquidation or dissolution of the insolvent parent may reduce the amount of the withdrawal liability (see Q 29:38). [Central States, Southeast & Southwest Areas Pension Fund v. Chatham Props., 929 F.2d 260 (6th Cir. 1991)]

A default will not occur, however, until 60 days after a demand for payment is made (see Q 29:46).

See Q 29:42 for a discussion of a new procedure applicable to disputes involving withdrawal liability.

Q 29:45　May a multiemployer plan return mistaken withdrawal liability payments?

IRS has issued final regulations that provide rules and procedures by which multiemployer plans may return mistaken withdrawal liability payments to employers. Generally, plans are required to prohibit the diversion of corpus or income for purposes other than for the exclusive benefit of employees or their beneficiaries (see Q 4:1). The final regulations provide a narrow exception to the general rule under which plans will not violate this prohibition if a payment is returned within six months after the date on which a plan administrator determines that the payment was the result of a mistake of fact or law. The employer must, however, establish a right to the refund of the mistakenly paid amount by filing a claim with the plan administrator within six months after the date on which the plan administrator determines that the mistake occurred. The employer must also demonstrate that an excessive overpayment has been made due to a mistake of fact or law. [I.R.C. § 401(a)(2); Treas. Reg. § 1.401(a)(2)-1]

If, after review, the plan sponsor or arbitrator determines that the employer has overpaid, the employer is entitled to a lump-sum refund with interest. [PBGC

Reg. § 4219.32(c); Huber v. Casablanca Indus., Inc., 916 F.2d 85 (3d Cir. 1990)] A multiemployer plan that mistakenly overcharged withdrawing employers for withdrawal liability can refund the overcharged amounts to the employers as long as the refunds are made within six months of the discovery of the error. [ERISA § 403(c)(2)(A)(ii); DOL Op. Ltr. 95-24A]

Q 29:46   What happens if a withdrawal liability payment is missed?

If a payment is not made by the due date, interest is charged from that date until the payment is actually made. [ERISA § 4219(c)(3); Carriers Container Council, Inc. v. Mobile S.S. Ass'n, Inc., 896 F.2d 1330 (11th Cir. 1990)] A default generally occurs 60 days after the employer gets written notice from the plan sponsor of failure to make a payment when due. If the payment is not made within the 60 days, the entire amount of the withdrawal liability plus interest becomes due immediately. [ERISA § 4219(c)(5); PBGC Reg. §§ 4219.31, 4219.32; Huber v. Casablanca Indus., Inc., 916 F.2d 85 (3d Cir. 1990); Local 807 Labor-Mgmt. Pension Fund v. ABC Fast Freight Forwarding Corp., No. 82 C 3356 (E.D.N.Y. 1984)] One court ruled that a company that paid its interim withdrawal liability payments in full only after the plan commenced an action to recover the delinquent payments is subject to ERISA's statutory penalties for late payment. [Bridge v. Transpersonnel, Inc., 2004 U.S. Dist. LEXIS 18242 (N.D. Ill. 2004)]

An employer must make withdrawal liability payments even if the National Labor Relations Board has exclusive jurisdiction to determine whether the employer must continue to make plan contributions after the expiration of the collective bargaining agreement. [Trustees of the Colo. Pipe Indus. Pension Trust v. Howard Elec. & Mech., Inc., 909 F.2d 1379 (10th Cir. 1990)]

Q 29:47   Are owners of the employer personally liable for withdrawal liability?

Generally, shareholders of corporations are not personally liable for amounts the employer cannot pay. [ILGWU Nat'l Ret. Fund v. Pantagis, No. 97 Civ. 4604 (S.D.N.Y. 1998); Operating Eng'r Pension Trust v. Reed, 726 F.2d 513 (9th Cir. 1984); *but see* Laborers Clean-Up Contract Admin. Trust Fund v. Uriarte Clean-Up Serv., Inc., 736 F.2d 516 (9th Cir. 1984)] Controlling or dominant shareholders are not considered employers for withdrawal liability purposes. [Scarbrough v. Perez, 870 F.2d 1079 (6th Cir. 1989); DeBreceni v. Graf Bros. Leasing, Inc., 828 F.2d 877 (1st Cir. 1987); Connors v. P&M Coal Co., 801 F.2d 1373 (D.C. Cir. 1986)] A state law under which the ten largest shareholders of a closely held corporation can be held liable for unpaid plan contributions was held to be preempted by ERISA. [Romney v. Lin, 1996 U.S. App. LEXIS 22017 (2d Cir. 1996), *reh'g denied,* 1997 U.S. App. LEXIS 1044 (2d Cir. 1997); *but see* Sasso v. Vachris, 66 N.Y.2d 28 (1985)] However, shareholders were held personally liable when they did not observe corporate formalities and removed assets from the corporation. [Plumbers' Pension Fund, Local 130, UA v. A-Best Plumbing & Sewer, Inc., 1992 U.S. Dist. LEXIS 3110 (N.D. Ill. 1992); *see also* Schaffer, Jr. v. Charles Benjamin, Inc., No. 92-1312 (3d Cir. 1992)]

However, a shareholder of a dissolved corporation may be personally liable to the extent of corporate assets distributed to the shareholder upon dissolution. [Retirement Fund of the Fur Mfg. Indus. v. Robert Goldberg Furs, Inc., 88 Civ. 6033 (JES) (S.D.N.Y. 1991); Central States, Southeast & Southwest Areas Pension Fund v. Minneapolis Van & Warehouse Co., 764 F. Supp. 1289 (N.D. Ill. 1991); Retirement Fund of the Fur Mfg. Indus. v. Strassberg & Tama, Inc., 88 Civ. 6034 (MBM) (S.D.N.Y. 1989)]

A corporate officer is not personally liable for withdrawal liability payments solely by virtue of the individual's capacity as an officer of the withdrawing employer. [Cement & Concrete Workers Dist. Council Welfare Fund, Pension Fund, Legal Servs. Fund & Sec. Fund v. Lollo, 35 F.3d 29 (2d Cir. 1994); Blankenship v. Omni Catering, Inc., No. 92-55871 (9th Cir. 1994); Seymour v. Hull & Moreland Eng'g, Inc., 605 F.2d 1105 (9th Cir. 1979); Connors v. BMC Coal Co., 634 F. Supp. 74 (D.D.C. 1986); Connors v. Darryll Waggle Constr., Inc., 631 F. Supp. 1188 (D.D.C. 1986)]

Partners or sole proprietors are personally liable, but assets that would be exempt under bankruptcy law are also exempt from satisfaction of the withdrawal liability obligation. Furthermore, a husband and wife who jointly operated a farm were personally liable for the unpaid withdrawal liability of a corporation controlled by the husband because the farm and corporation were under common control (see Q 29:23). [ERISA § 4225(c); Connors v. Ryan's Coal Co., 923 F.2d 1461 (11th Cir. 1991); Board of Trustees of the W. Conference of Teamsters Pension Trust Fund v. H.F. Johnson, Inc., 830 F.2d 1009 (9th Cir. 1987)] Despite the fact that ERISA does not expressly create withdrawal liability for partners, a general partner of a partnership that was a member of a controlled group was held personally responsible for a company's withdrawal liability because, under partnership law, partners are personally liable for obligations of the partnership, ruled one court. [Teamsters Pension Trust Fund of Phila. & Vicinity v. Domenic Cristinzio, Inc., No. 96-6596 (E.D. Pa. 1998)] However, the spouse of an unincorporated business owner is not personally liable for the business owner's withdrawal liability unless it can be shown that she intended to form a partnership with her husband with respect to the business. [Chicago Truck Drivers, Helpers & Warehouse Union (Indep.) Pension Fund v. Steinberg, 32 F.3d 269 (7th Cir. 1994); Central States, Southeast & Southwest Areas Pension Fund v. Johnson, 991 F.2d 387 (7th Cir. 1993); Chicago Truck Drivers, Helpers & Warehouse Workers Union (Indep.) Pension Fund v. Slotky, 9 F.3d 1251 (7th Cir. 1993)]

Q 29:48 Are withdrawal liability claims entitled to priority in bankruptcy proceedings?

It has been held that withdrawal liability is considered a general unsecured claim and is not entitled to priority in bankruptcy proceedings because it is not an administrative expense claim. [Trustees of the Amalgamated Ins. Fund v. McFarlin's, Inc., 789 F.2d 98 (2d Cir. 1986)] However, the discharge in bankruptcy of a corporation that owed contributions and withdrawal liability to a multiemployer plan did not preclude the plan from later seeking recovery from a new corporation that had acquired the assets of the old corporation. [Chicago Truck Drivers, Helpers & Warehouse Workers Union (Indep.) Pension Fund v. Tasemkin, Inc., 59 F.3d 48 (7th Cir. 1995)]

An employer's withdrawal liability was not a claim that could be discharged in bankruptcy where the multiemployer plan had no enforceable right to payment at the time of confirmation of bankruptcy because the employer had not actually withdrawn from the plan before the confirmation proceeding had occurred. If an employer wants its withdrawal liability discharged in bankruptcy, the court said it must completely withdraw from the plan before confirmation. An employer cannot remain a participating employer and simultaneously have its withdrawal liability forgiven if it later decides to withdraw. Because withdrawal liability is based on an employer's share of UVBs (see Q 29:16) at withdrawal, there can be no pre-withdrawal breach of ERISA giving rise to a right to payment by a plan. Thus, a claim cannot exist before actual withdrawal. [CPT Holdings, Inc. v. Industrial & Allied Employees Union Pension Plan, Local 73, 1998 WL 842239 (6th Cir. 1998)]

Q 29:49   May multiemployer plans be merged?

Yes; but a merger, or a transfer of assets and liabilities, between multiemployer plans must satisfy four requirements unless otherwise provided by PBGC:

1. PBGC must receive 120 days' advance notice of the transaction;
2. Accrued benefits must not be reduced;
3. There must be no reasonable likelihood that benefits will be suspended as a result of plan insolvency; and
4. An actuarial valuation of each affected plan must have been performed.

[ERISA §§ 4231(a), 4231(b)]

PBGC's regulation on mergers and transfers between multiemployer plans prescribes procedures for requesting a determination that a merger or transfer satisfies applicable requirements, allows PBGC to waive the 120-day notice requirement, and sets higher-level and lower-level requirements for safe harbor plan solvency tests and for valuation standards. Whether the higher-level or lower-level requirements applied depended on whether a significant transfer was involved.

Transactions involving plans that have been terminated by mass withdrawal (see Q 29:50) are rare. PBGC concluded that the current regulation did not make clear whether, and if so how, the merger and transfer rules apply to these cases. Since such plans have no contributing employers, and transactions involving them present more risk than most others, PBGC determined that it was important to specify how the merger and transfer rules apply to them. The amended regulations clarify that transactions involving such plans are subject to the merger and transfer rules and (except for *de minimis* transactions) are governed by the higher-level valuation standard and safe harbor solvency test. Terminated plans, like other plans, could satisfy the plan solvency requirement without recourse to the safe harbor test by demonstrating that benefits are not likely to be suspended.

The amended regulations also extend to *de minimis* terminated plan transactions the requirement that actuarial valuation reports be submitted to PBGC.

Both plans involved in a significant transfer were subject to the higher-level valuation standard and safe harbor solvency test, even if only one of the plans was significantly affected. The standard for determining whether a plan is significantly affected is generally the same as the standard for determining whether a transfer was a significant transfer under the prior regulations. A transferor plan is significantly affected if the assets transferred equal or exceed 15 percent of its pretransfer assets. A transferee plan is significantly affected if the unfunded accrued benefits transferred equal or exceed 15 percent of its pretransfer assets. The amended regulations no longer automatically apply the higher-level valuation standard and safe harbor solvency test to both plans involved in a significant transfer if only one of the plans is significantly affected. Instead, the higher-level standard and test are just applied to the significantly affected plan. In addition, as discussed above, the higher-level standard and test are applied to any plan that is involved in a non-*de minimis* terminated plan transaction.

The prior regulations required that a compliance determination request for a significant transfer include copies of all actuarial valuations performed within the five years preceding the proposed effective date of the transfer. Since this could not be done where the last plan year preceding the proposed effective date was in progress when the compliance determination request was filed, the amended regulations call for the valuations performed within the five years preceding the compliance determination request.

The amended regulations also modify the higher-level valuation standard slightly so that the actuarial assumptions and methods used in the premerger valuation are those expected to be used for the surviving plan after the merger.

Under the prior regulations, the requirement for 120 days' notice could be waived only if PBGC was satisfied that failure to complete the transaction in a shorter time would harm participants or beneficiaries. PBGC typically completes its reviews in 60 to 90 days, and there is usually no reason to wait the full 120 days. The amended regulations permit a merger or transfer to be consummated if (1) the plan sponsor demonstrates that failure to complete the merger or transfer in less than 120 days would cause harm to participants and beneficiaries, (2) PBGC determines that the transaction complies with the merger and transfer rules, or (3) PBGC completes its review of the transaction.

[PBGC Reg. §§ 4231.1–4231.10]

Q 29:50   What is a mass withdrawal from a multiemployer plan?

A mass withdrawal is one form of multiemployer plan termination (see Q 29:51). A mass withdrawal occurs if:

1. Every employer withdraws from the plan or
2. The obligation of all employers to contribute to the plan ceases.

[ERISA § 4041A(a)(2)]

If a mass withdrawal occurs, all withdrawing employers lose the benefit of the waiver or reduction of small liabilities (see Q 29:30) and the 20-year cap (see Q 29:39), and the plan's UVBs (see Q 29:16) are fully allocated among all of the withdrawing employers. For this purpose, the withdrawal of substantially all employers by agreement or arrangement is considered a mass withdrawal. [ERISA §§ 4209, 4219(c); PBGC Reg. §§ 4219.1, 4219.2, 4219.11–4219.19]

To ensure that all UVBs are fully allocated among all liable employers, a determination is required of the plan's UVBs as of end of the plan year in which the plan terminates, based on the value of the plan's nonforfeitable benefits as of that date less the value of plan assets (benefits and assets valued in accordance with assumptions specified by PBGC), less the outstanding balance of any initial withdrawal liability (assessments without regard to the occurrence of a mass withdrawal) and any redetermination liability (assessments for *de minimis* and 20-year cap reduction amounts) that can reasonably be expected to be collected. [PBGC Reg. § 4219.15(b)] Each liable employer's share of this reallocation liability is equal to the amount of the reallocation liability multiplied by a fraction (1) the numerator of which is the sum of the employer's initial withdrawal liability and any redetermination liability and (2) the denominator of which is the sum of all initial withdrawal liabilities and all the redetermination liabilities of all liable employers. [PBGC Reg. § 4219.15(c)(1)]

PBGC believes the current allocation fraction for reallocation liability must be modified to address those situations in which employers, which would otherwise be liable for reallocation liability, have little or no initial withdrawal liability or redetermination liability and, therefore, have a zero (or understated) reallocation liability. Such situations may arise, for example, where an employer withdraws from the plan before the mass withdrawal valuation date, but has no withdrawal liability under the modified presumptive and rolling-five methods because either (1) the plan has no UVBs as of the end of the plan year preceding the plan year in which the employer withdrew or (2) the plan did not require the employer to make contributions for the five-year period preceding the plan year of withdrawal. In these cases, if the employer's withdrawal is later determined to be part of a mass withdrawal for which reallocation liability applies, the employer would not be liable for any portion of the reallocation liability.

A plan's status may change from funded to underfunded between the end of the plan year before the employer withdraws and the mass withdrawal valuation date as a result of differences in the actuarial assumptions used by the plan's actuary in determining UVBs, or due to investment losses that reduce the value of the plan's assets, among other reasons. Likewise, an employer may not have paid contributions for purposes of the allocation fraction used to determine the employer's initial withdrawal liability if the plan provided for a contribution holiday under which employers were not required to make contributions. PBGC believes the absence of initial withdrawal liability should not generally exempt an otherwise liable employer from reallocation liability. Shifting reallocation liability away from some employers increases the allocable share of other employers in a mass withdrawal, increases the risk of a loss of benefits to participants, and increases the financial risk to PBGC. To ensure that reallocation liability is allocated broadly among all liable employers, PBGC replaces the current allocation fraction based on initial withdrawal liability with a new allocation fraction for determining an employer's allocable share of reallocation liability. The new fraction allocates the plan's UVBs based on the average of the employer's contribution base units relative to the combined averages of the plan's total contribution base units for the three plan years preceding each employer's withdrawal from the plan. The numerator consists of the withdrawing employer's average contribution base units during the three plan years preceding the withdrawal (that is, the three plan years divided by three). The denominator is the sum of the averages of all withdrawing employers' contribution base units for the three plan years preceding each employer's withdrawal. A contribution base unit is a unit with respect to which an employer has an obligation to contribute under a multiemployer plan (e.g., an hour worked). [PBGC Reg. §§ 4219.15(c)(1), 4219.15(c)(3)]

The changes in the fraction for allocating reallocation liability are applicable to plan terminations by mass withdrawals (or by withdrawals of substantially all employers pursuant to an agreement or arrangement to withdraw) that occur on or after January 29, 2009. The changes relating to plan terminations by mass withdrawals (or withdrawals of substantially all employers pursuant to an agreement or arrangement to withdraw) occurring for plan years beginning on or after January 1, 2008. [Preamble to final regulations]

PBGC has given guidance as to the administration of multiemployer plans that have terminated by mass withdrawal. Generally, the plan sponsor must periodically determine whether the value of nonforfeitable benefits exceeds the value of plan assets. If so, the plan sponsor must reduce benefits other than accrued benefits guaranteed by PBGC (see Q 29:13), suspend certain benefit payments, or seek financial assistance in the form of a PBGC loan (see Q 29:51) to the extent necessary to ensure the plan's sufficiency. Under these circumstances, the reduction of accrued benefits does not cause plan disqualification (see Q 9:26). [ERISA § 4281; I.R.C. § 411(a)(3)(F); PBGC Reg. §§ 4281.1–4281.47] Effective July 12, 2006, PBGC has amended its regulation on morality assumptions used for valuations in multiemployer plans following mass withdrawals to conform the regulation to the amendments made to the morality tables under the regulations for withdrawals from single-employer plans. [PBGC Reg. § 4281.14]

Generally, the plan sponsor of a plan that terminates by mass withdrawal can only pay benefits that were nonforfeitable at plan termination without first obtaining PBGC approval. Thus, PBGC approval is not needed to pay a qualified preretirement survivor annuity (QPSA; see Q 10:9) to the surviving spouse of a participant who died before the plan termination date. Further, the plan sponsor does not need PBGC approval to pay the QPSA for a participant who died after the plan termination date unless the plan sponsor has determined that plan assets are not sufficient to pay all nonforfeitable plan benefits. [ERISA § 4041A(c); PBGC Op. Ltr. 91-2]

Q 29:51   What is the liability of an employer upon termination of a multiemployer defined benefit plan?

For multiemployer plans, plan termination does not mean dissolution of the plan and does not result in PBGC involvement as the provider of benefits. Instead, termination means mass withdrawal (see Q 29:50), the amendment of the plan to freeze vested benefits and to give no credit for further service, or the conversion of the plan into a defined contribution plan. Employers must continue to contribute to the frozen plan in order to fund the plan's unfunded liabilities. The plan administrator (see Q 20:1) must notify PBGC after the effective date of termination and follow PBGC reporting requirements and rules regarding administration of terminated multiemployer plans. [ERISA § 4041A; PBGC Reg. §§ 4041.21, 4041A.1–4041A.44]

PBGC funds are available only if a plan becomes insolvent (see Q 29:12). These PBGC funds are only loans and must be repaid. [ERISA §§ 4022A(a), 4261]

If, upon termination of a multiemployer plan, there are excess assets, such excess cannot revert to the employers. [ERISA § 403(c)(1); DOL Op. Ltr. 94-39A] One court concluded that the reversion of surplus employer contributions from a multiemployer plan to one of the contributing employers would also violate ERISA's exclusive benefit rule (see Q 4:1). [Resolution Trust Corp. v. Financial Insts. Ret. Fund, No. 95-5016 (10th Cir. 1995)] However, a multiemployer plan that suffered the withdrawal of all but one employer 16 months prior to the plan's termination constituted a single-employer plan and, therefore, could distribute excess assets to the last employer. Although the exception to the exclusive benefit rule for reversion of assets is limited to single-employer plans, the plan was eligible for the exception because it had been converted to a single-employer plan more than a year prior to termination. The distribution of excess assets was limited, however, to funds attributable to the last employer's contributions and could be distributed only to the last employer or its successor. [Hawkeye Nat'l Life Ins. Co. v. AVIS Indep. Corp., 1997 U.S. App. LEXIS 19198 (8th Cir. 1997)]

Q 29:52   May a multiemployer plan exclude some newly adopting employers from withdrawal liability?

Yes. A multiemployer plan may adopt a rule under which an employer may withdraw from the plan without liability within six years after joining the plan or, if less, the number of years required for vesting under the plan. This free-look rule is applicable to the employer only if it (1) contributes less than 2 percent of all employer contributions to the plan each year and (2) has not previously used this rule with respect to the plan.

In addition, for the free-look rule to be enforceable, the plan must (1) be amended to permit the rule, (2) have an eight-to-one assets-to-benefits payable ratio in the year before the employer joins the plan, and (3) provide that an employee's service before the employer joined the plan will not be counted in determining benefits. Prior to 2007, plans primarily covering employees in the building and construction industry were not permitted to adopt the free-look rule. [ERISA § 4210]

One court held that the free-look rule did not apply to an employer after it was acquired by another employer because both employers were then under common control and the acquiring employer was ineligible to use the free-look rule (see Q 29:23). [Central States, Southeast & Southwest Areas Pension Fund v. Hoosier Dairy, Inc., No. 90 C 3795 (N.D. Ill. 1991)]

Chapter 30

Individual Retirement Plans

Anyone who receives compensation may set aside a sum of money each year for retirement in a tax-deferred account known as an individual retirement plan (IRA). EGTRRA 2001 increased the IRA contribution limits and provided a credit for IRA contributions made by eligible individuals. However, not all IRA contributions are deductible. This chapter examines how IRAs and designated nondeductible IRAs work.

Q 30:1   What is an individual retirement plan?

An individual retirement plan is a personal retirement plan. This type of plan allows employees, self-employed individuals (see Q 6:60), and certain other individuals, whether or not they participate in qualified retirement plans (including Keogh plans, simplified employee pensions (SEPs), SIMPLE plans, 403(b) plans, and governmental plans), to establish IRAs and make annual contributions to them. For active plan participants, however, these contributions might not be deductible (see Q 30:14). [I.R.C. §§ 219, 408]

There are two types of individual retirement plans: (1) individual retirement accounts (see Q 30:2) and (2) individual retirement annuities (see Q 30:3). Both types are commonly referred to as IRAs. Required minimum distributions (RMDs) from IRAs are suspended for calendar year 2009 (see Q 30:42). IRS has advised that, pending issuance of further guidance, IRAs do not have to be amended to reflect the suspension. [IRS Notice 2009-82, Q&A-1, 2009-41 I.R.B.]

A working spouse may set up an IRA for the nonworking spouse (see Q 30:25). In addition, certain divorced or separated persons may make deductible contributions to IRAs even though they receive no wages or salary (see Q 30:5).

Deductible contributions to an IRA are tax deductible whether or not the individual itemizes deductions [I.R.C. § 62(a)(7)]; and, generally, earnings on all amounts contributed to any IRA accumulate on a tax-deferred basis (see Qs 30:11, 30:12). [I.R.C. § 408(e)]

For a discussion of deemed IRAs, see Q 30:36; and, for a discussion of Roth IRAs, see chapter 31.

Q 30:2   What are the basic characteristics of an individual retirement account?

An IRA is a trust or custodial account established in the United States for the exclusive benefit of an individual and the individual's beneficiaries. The trust instrument (or custodial agreement) must provide that:

1. Except in the case of rollover contributions (see chapter 34), all contributions must be in cash (see Q 30:10) and annual contributions to the IRA may not exceed the dollar amount in effect for the taxable year (see Q 30:5);

2. The trustee must be either a bank or a person who demonstrates an ability to properly administer the trust;

3. No portion of the trust's assets may be invested in life insurance contracts;

4. The individual's interest must be nonforfeitable;

5. The trust assets must not be commingled with other property, except in a common trust or investment fund (see Q 30:11); and

6. Certain distribution requirements apply (see Qs 30:42, 30:43, 30:50).

[I.R.C. §§ 408(a), 408(h); Nichola, 63 T.C.M. 2150 (1992)]

An IRA must be a trust created or organized in the United States and must be maintained at all times as a domestic trust in the United States. [Treas. Reg. § 1.408-2(b)] Trusts that are parts of qualified retirement plans and IRAs may pool their assets in a group trust without affecting the exempt status of the separate trusts. [Rev. Rul. 81-100, 1981-1 C.B. 326] A trust will be treated as a domestic trust if:

1. A court within the United States is able to exercise primary supervision over the administration of the trust (court test), and

2. One or more United States persons have the authority to control all substantial decisions of the trust (control test).

In applying the control test, all individuals with power over substantial decisions, whether acting as a fiduciary (see Q 23:1) or not, are considered. However, a special rule for certain trusts provides that these trusts are deemed to satisfy the control test if control of substantial trust decisions is made only by United States fiduciaries. IRS has added to the categories of trusts that may use the special control test group trusts consisting of qualified retirement plan trusts and IRA trusts that meet the requirements of Rev. Rul. 81-100. [I.R.C. § 7701(a)(30)(E); Treas. Reg. § 301.7701-7(d)(1)(iv)]

Because the trust or custodial account must be established in the United States, amounts withdrawn by an individual from his IRA and then transferred by him to an account or trust with a foreign bank were includible in the individual's income. [I.R.C. § 408(a); Keenan, 76 T.C.M. 748 (1998); Chiu, 73 T.C.M. 2679 (1997); *see also* Bichindaritz, 90 T.C.M. 639 (2005)]

One of the requirements set forth above relates to the qualification of an IRA trustee. The trustee (or custodian) must be a bank, thrift institution, insurance company, brokerage firm, or other person who demonstrates to IRS that such person will administer the account in a manner consistent with the requirements of the law. An accountant was held not to be qualified to serve as an IRA trustee. [I.R.C. §§ 408(a)(2), 408(h), 408(n), 581; Treas. Reg. § 1.408-2(b)(2); Ann. 2002-12, 2002-1 C.B. 553; Schoof, 110 T.C. 1 (1998)] IRS has updated its list of entities that have been approved to serve as nonbank trustees or custodians. [Ann. 2007-47, 2007-1 C.B. 1260]

No portion of IRA assets may be invested in life insurance contracts. [I.R.C. § 408(a)(3)] IRS ruled that a loan from an IRA to a tax-exempt religious organization was neither a prohibited investment in insurance nor a prohibited transaction (see Q 30:45). The IRA owner proposed to make a loan to the organization, and the promissory note from the organization to the IRA would include a security agreement. The promissory note would be secured by a collateral assignment of an insurance policy on the IRA owner's life. The organization was not a disqualified person with respect to the IRA, and the IRA owner had no control, ownership, or financial interest in the organization; therefore, the transaction was not prohibited, and the IRA did not cease to be an IRA. In addition, the organization would be the purchaser and owner of the insurance policy, and the IRA would be neither an owner nor a beneficiary of the policy. Thus, the transaction did not constitute a prohibited investment in a life insurance contract. [Priv. Ltr. Rul. 200741016]

An IRA, generally, cannot be a shareholder of an S corporation (see Q 28:2), and IRA assets should not be invested in collectibles (works of art, rugs, antiques, metals, gems, stamps, coins, alcoholic beverages, or other items of tangible personal property specified by IRS). There is a limited exception whereby an IRA may hold shares of an S corporation that is a bank, but only if such shares were held by the IRA on October 22, 2004. [Taproot Administrative Services, Inc., 133 T.C. No. 9 (2009); Rev. Rul. 92-73, 1992-2 C.B. 224; I.R.C. §§ 1361(c)(2)(A)(vi), 1361(c)(2)(B)(vi); Treas. Reg. § 1.1361-1(h)(1)(vii)] Amounts invested in collectibles are treated as distributions for tax purposes (that is, taxed as current income; if the individual is under age 59½, a 10 percent penalty tax for a premature withdrawal also applies (see Q 30:41)). [Minteer v. Comm'r, 05-74551 (9th Cir. 2006)] However, gold, silver, or platinum coins issued by the U.S. government or any type of coin issued under the laws of any state, and certain gold, silver, platinum, or palladium bullion will not be considered collectibles. An interest in a portion of a gold coin portfolio is not considered a collectible. [I.R.C. §§ 408(m)(3), 1361; Rev. Rul. 92-73, 1992-2 C.B. 224; Priv. Ltr. Rul. 8940067] The exception for coins and bullion applies only if the coins and bullion are in possession of the IRA trustee. IRS has ruled that IRA investments in coins and bullion that are in the physical possession of an entity other than the IRA trustee are collectibles and will be treated as IRA distributions. [Priv. Ltr. Rul. 200217059] IRS has also ruled that an IRA trustee was permitted to purchase shares of an investment trust formed to hold gold bullion without that purchase being treated as a taxable distribution from the IRA or as the acquisition of a collectible. The investment trust, formed to allow investment in publicly traded, exchange-listed securities in the gold market, planned to make shares available to IRAs. Provided the IRA trustee did not distribute trust shares or bullion to the IRA owners, no taxable distribution will have occurred. [Priv. Ltr. Ruls. 200732027, 200732026, 200446032]

Even though an individual's interest in an IRA must be nonforfeitable, the nonforfeitable status of the IRA did not provide the IRA owner with a preference over other depositors in the distribution of an insolvent bank's assets where the individual had lost his IRA assets as a result of the bank's failure. [I.R.C. § 408(a)(4); Goldblatt v. FDIC, No. 95-56426 (9th Cir. 1997)]

An account that is identified as an IRA and meets the statutory requirements is treated as an IRA, even if the owner later claims it is not an IRA because the owner made an untimely rollover contribution that is an excess contribution (see Q 30:9). [Michel, 58 T.C.M. 1019 (1989)]

Q 30:3   What are the basic characteristics of an individual retirement annuity?

An individual retirement annuity is an annuity contract or endowment contract issued by an insurance company. However, an endowment contract issued after November 6, 1978, cannot qualify. The contract must be nontransferable and nonforfeitable. Premiums may not be fixed, nor may they exceed the dollar amount in effect for the taxable year (see Q 30:5). Distributions must satisfy the minimum distribution requirements and must be made by specified dates in order to avoid penalties for insufficient distributions (see Qs 30:42, 30:43, 30:48). [I.R.C. § 408(b); Treas. Reg. § 1.408-3(e)(1)(ix)]

With respect to a contract that would otherwise qualify as an individual retirement annuity, but for the fact that contract premiums are invested at the direction of the individual in publicly available securities, IRS will treat the contract as an individual retirement annuity and will not treat the individual as owning the assets associated with the contract, provided that no additional federal tax liability would have been incurred if the consideration for the contract had instead been held as part of an IRA (see Q 30:2). However, the general account of an insurance company will be treated as a common investment or trust fund (see Q 30:11). [Rev. Proc. 99-44, 1999-2 C.B. 598; Rev. Rul. 82-55, 1982-1 C.B. 12; Rev. Rul. 82-54, 1982-1 C.B. 11; Rev. Rul. 81-225, 1981-2 C.B. 12; Rev. Rul. 80-274, 1980-2 C.B. 27; Rev. Rul. 77-85, 1977-1 C.B. 12]

Participation in a group annuity may be used instead of an individual annuity contract. Only part of the premium for an endowment contract builds an annuity; the rest buys current life insurance protection. The part of the premium that pays for current life insurance protection is not tax deductible. [I.R.C. §§ 219(d)(3), 408(a)(3), 408(b); Priv. Ltr. Rul. 8439026]

If an individual borrows any money from or against an individual retirement annuity, the annuity contract ceases to be a qualified individual retirement annuity as of the first day of the year. Because of the borrowing, the individual must include in gross income for the year the fair market value of the annuity as of the first day of such year. [I.R.C. § 408(e)(3); Griswold, 85 T.C. 869 (1985)]

Despite the requirement that the entire interest of the owner of an individual retirement annuity must be nonforfeitable, in a novel case, one court concluded that this requirement did not protect a convicted racketeer's annuity contract from forfeiture to the government in a criminal proceeding. [I.R.C. § 408(b)(4); United States v. Infelise, 159 F.3d 300 (7th Cir. 1998)]

Q 30:4   Who is eligible to set up an IRA?

Any individual who has not attained age 70½ by the end of the taxable year and who receives compensation may establish an IRA (see Q 30:5). [I.R.C. § 219(d)(1); Treas. Reg. § 1.219-1(b)(2)(ii)] An individual attains age 70½ as of the date six months after the individual's 70th birthday. For example, an individual whose date of birth is June 30, 1940 attains age 70½ on December 30, 2010, and an individual whose date of birth is August 31, 1940, attains age 70½ on February 28, 2011.

> **Example.** Gary was born on June 30, 1940, and his 70th birthday was June 30, 2010. Gary becomes 70½ on December 30, 2010, and cannot make an IRA contribution for 2010. Lynn was born on July 1, 1940, and she becomes age 70½ on January 1, 2011. Lynn can make an IRA contribution for 2010.

An IRA may also be established as a vehicle for deferring taxes on eligible rollover distributions from qualified retirement plans, 403(b) plans (see Q 35:1), and governmental Section 457 plans, including distributions received after attainment of age 70½ and distributions to surviving spouses of plan participants. For details, see chapter 34.

For taxable years beginning on or after January 1, 2004, members of the armed forces may treat combat pay as compensation for purposes of the IRA contribution and deduction rules. [I.R.C. §§ 112, 219(f)(7)]

Q 30:5   How much may be contributed to an IRA?

An individual may contribute to an IRA 100 percent of compensation up to a maximum dollar amount. [I.R.C. §§ 219(b)(1), 408(a)(1), 408(b)(2)(B)] The contribution limit can be doubled if a spousal IRA is also established (see Q 30:25). [I.R.C. § 219(c)] However, there is no dollar limit with respect to a rollover contribution (see Q 34:2). IRS has ruled that wrap fees paid by IRA owners from non-IRA funds to their IRA trustees were not IRA contributions. The fees were charged as part of different investment programs offered to IRA owners by an investment advisory company for its services. [Priv. Ltr. Rul. 200507021] An IRA owner suffered a significant loss in her IRA because of her financial advisor's breach of fiduciary duty, and an arbitration panel awarded her compensatory damages. IRS allowed the IRA owner to contribute the amount of the compensatory damages to her IRA as a restorative payment. [Priv. Ltr. Rul. 200724040; *see also* Priv. Ltr. Ruls. 200852034, 200850054, and 200738025]

IRS has provided a safe harbor definition of compensation for the purpose of determining eligibility to make an IRA contribution. Under the safe harbor, compensation is the amount properly shown on Form W-2, Box 1 (wages, tips, and other compensation) less the amount properly shown in Box 11 (nonqualified plans). [I.R.C. § 219(f)(1); Rev. Proc. 91-18, 1991-1 C.B. 522]

Compensation includes taxable alimony and separate maintenance payments. A divorced or separated spouse who receives taxable alimony, but no other compensation, is able to make contributions to an IRA. Unemployment compensation benefits, IRA distributions, and capital gains are not compensation for purposes of calculating IRA contributions. Where an individual's only income consisted of interest, dividends, and pension distributions, he had no compensation to support the deduction of his IRA contribution. Deferred compensation and amounts received as a pension or annuity are not treated as compensation and cannot be used as a basis for contributions to an IRA even if the safe harbor definition of compensation is used. A separation pay allowance received by an employee is considered deferred compensation for this purpose. Also, a fee paid by a husband to his wife for services rendered in connection with their jointly held investments is not compensation to her, nor is a payment by a husband to his wife where, in fact, the wife did not render any services to the husband's business. [I.R.C. § 219(f)(1); Treas. Reg. § 1.219-1(c); Bell, No. 3524-05S (Tax Ct. 2006); Clarke, 77 T.C.M. 2188 (1999); Russell, 71 T.C.M. 3184 (1996); King, 71 T.C.M. 3033 (1996); Shelley, 68 T.C.M. 584 (1994); Bingo, 61 T.C.M. 2782 (1991); Priv. Ltr. Ruls. 8535001, 8519051]

In a novel ruling, a farmer transferred hogs to his wife, who was a bona fide employee, as compensation for her services to his farming business. IRS ruled that the hogs constituted compensation and could be used as a basis for contributions to an IRA. [Priv. Ltr. Rul. 9202003]

A contribution made to an IRA for the year in which an individual attains age $70^1/_2$ (see Q 30:4), or any year thereafter, is a nondeductible excess contribution (see Q 30:9) that cannot be treated as a designated nondeductible IRA contribution (see Q 30:20). [I.R.C. §§ 219(d)(1), 408(o)]

An estate cannot make an IRA contribution on behalf of the decedent or to the spousal IRA of the decedent's spouse for the year in which the decedent died. [Priv. Ltr. Rul. 8439066]

The maximum dollar amount applicable to IRA contributions is as follows:

For taxable years beginning in	The maximum amount is
2008 and thereafter	$5,000
2005 through 2007	4,000
2002 through 2004	3,000

[I.R.C. §§ 219(b)(1)(A), 219(b)(5)(A), 408(a)(1), 408(b)(2)(B)]

For a discussion of catch-up contributions, see Q 30:6; for a discussion of indexing for inflation, see Q 30:7; and, for a discussion of a tax credit for IRA contributions, see Q 30:8.

For taxable years beginning on or after January 1, 2004, members of the armed forces may treat combat pay as compensation for purposes of the IRA contribution and deduction rules. [I.R.C. §§ 112, 219(f)(7)] Differential wage payments are also included in compensation for purposes of the annual limitations on contributions to IRAs (see Q 1:35).

Effective for taxable years beginning after 2006 and before 2010, an applicable individual could have elected to make additional IRA contributions of up to $3,000 per year for 2007-2009. An applicable individual must have been a participant in a 401(k) plan (see Q 27:1) under which the employer matched at least 50 percent of the employee's contributions to the plan with stock of the employer. In addition, in a taxable year preceding the taxable year of an additional contribution (1) the employer (or any controlling corporation of the employer) must have been a debtor in a bankruptcy case, and (2) the employer or any other person must have been subject to an indictment or conviction resulting from business transactions related to the bankruptcy. The individual must also have been a participant in the 401(k) plan on the date six months before the bankruptcy case was filed. An applicable individual who elected to make these additional IRA contributions was not permitted to make IRA catch-up contributions that apply to individuals age 50 and older. [I.R.C. § 219(b)(5)(C)]

A widow rolled over her deceased husband's plan benefits into an IRA, but her financial adviser misappropriated the funds. Following a lawsuit, funds were paid to the widow, who then placed the funds into her IRA. IRS treated the funds paid to the IRA as a restorative payment, not as a contribution. [Priv. Ltr. Rul. 200714030; Rev. Rul. 2002-45, 2002-2 C.B. 116] For additional information, see Q 12:2.

Q 30:6   What are catch-up IRA contributions?

An individual who has attained age 50 by the close of the taxable year may make the following additional catch-up IRA contributions:

For taxable years beginning in	The catch-up amount is
2006 and thereafter	$1,000
2002 through 2005	500

[I.R.C. § 219(b)(5)(B)]

The following table shows the maximum dollar contribution limits, including the catch-up amount for an individual age 50 or over:

For taxable years beginning in	The maximum amount is
2008 and thereafter	$6,000
2006 and 2007	5,000
2005	4,500
2002 through 2004	3,500

Example. During 2008, Terry attained age 52. Terry was unmarried, did not participate in a qualified retirement plan, and earned $55,000 in 2008. Terry could have contributed up to $6,000 to her IRA.

Individuals who made permissible additional IRA contributions in 2007, 2008, or 2009 were not eligible to make catch-up IRA contributions in the same year (see Q 30:5).

See Q 30:7 for a discussion of indexing for inflation.

Q 30:7 Is the IRA contribution limit indexed for inflation?

The maximum contribution limit to deductible IRAs (see Q 30:5) and the maximum contribution limit to designated nondeductible IRAs (see Q 30:20) is subject to cost-of-living increases for taxable years beginning on or after January 1, 2009. [I.R.C. § 219(b)(5)(C)]

For taxable years beginning after 2008, the $5,000 maximum IRA contribution amount (see Q 30:5) will be subject to cost-of-living adjustments; however, an adjustment will be made only if it is $500 or greater and then will be made in multiples of $500 (i.e., rounded down to the next lowest multiple of $500). For example, an increase in the cost-of-living of $499 will result in no adjustment, and an increase of $999 will create an upward adjustment of $500. Therefore, the cost-of-living must increase by 10 percent before the first adjustment to the $5,000 limit will occur (10% × $5,000 = $500). For the taxable year beginning in 2010, the $5,000 amount is unchanged.

The catch-up IRA contribution amount (see Q 30:6) is *not* subject to cost-of-living adjustments.

Q 30:8 Is there a tax credit for IRA contributions?

An eligible individual will be allowed a nonrefundable tax credit for the taxable year in an amount equal to the applicable percentage of the individual's qualified retirement savings contributions for the year up to $2,000.

See chapter 17 for details.

Q 30:9 Is a penalty imposed on an excess contribution to an IRA?

If an individual contributes more to an IRA than the amount allowable (see Q 30:5), the excess contribution is subject to a 6 percent excise tax. Further, the penalty will be charged each year the excess contribution remains in the IRA. [I.R.C. §§ 4973(a), 4973(b); Bach, 75 T.C.M. 1722 (1998); Rodoni, 105 T.C. 29 (1995); Wittstadt, Jr., 70 T.C.M. 994 (1995); Conway v. United States, Civ. MJG-93-1707 (D. Md. 1995); Dorsey, 69 T.C.M. 2041 (1995); Shelley, 68 T.C.M. 584 (1994); Martin, 67 T.C.M. 2960 (1994); Priv. Ltr. Ruls. 200904029, 200128061]

The individual can avoid the penalty by withdrawing the excess contribution, along with the net income allocable to the excess, before the due date (including extensions) of the individual's federal income tax return for the year of the excess contribution. The net income on the excess contribution is treated as gross income for the taxable year in which the excess contribution was made. [I.R.C. §§ 408(d)(4), 4973(b)] Where excess contributions were not withdrawn timely because of errors made by the IRA custodian, excise taxes were not imposed. [Childs, 71 T.C.M. 3163 (1996); Thompson, 71 T.C.M. 3160 (1996)]

If the individual does not withdraw the excess contribution before such filing deadline, the 6 percent excise tax must be paid for the year of the excess contribution. To avoid the 6 percent excise tax for the following year, the remaining excess contribution can be eliminated by either withdrawing such amount from the IRA or making a contribution for such year equal to the maximum allowable amount (see Q 30:5) reduced by the remaining excess contribution. [I.R.C. § 4973(b)]

The excess contribution rules apply to Roth IRAs (see Q 31:8). For purposes of determining the amount of the excess contribution, a contribution to a regular IRA will be aggregated with the contribution to the Roth IRA. [I.R.C. §§ 4973(a), 4973(b), 4973(f)]

Example 1. For 2010, Jennifer Kate, age 21, contributes $5,500 to an IRA. An excess contribution of $500 has been made ($5,500–$5,000).

Example 2. For 2010, Jennifer Kate, age 21, contributes $4,500 to her deductible IRA and $1,000 to her Roth IRA. An excess contribution of $500 has been made ($4,500 + $1,000 − $5,000). Jennifer Kate can avoid the penalty by withdrawing $500, along with the net income allocable to the excess, from either IRA or a portion from one IRA and the balance from the other IRA by the due date (including extensions) of her 2010 federal income tax return.

In order to assist individuals who wish to change the nature of an IRA contribution, contributions to an IRA (and earnings thereon) may be transferred in a trustee-to-trustee transfer from any IRA to another IRA by the due date for the individual's return for the year of the contribution (including extensions). Any such transferred contributions will be treated as if contributed to the transferee IRA (and not to the transferor IRA). Trustee-to-trustee transfers include transfers between IRA trustees as well as IRA custodians, apply to transfers from and to IRA accounts and annuities, and apply to transfers between IRA accounts and annuities with the same trustee or custodian. A transfer is permitted only if no deduction is allowed with respect to the contribution to the transferor IRA. [I.R.C. §§ 408A(d)(6), 408A(d)(7)]

Example 3. For 2010, Jennifer Kate is eligible to contribute $5,000 to her deductible IRA, but only $3,250 to her Roth IRA (see Q 31:16). Mistakenly, Jennifer Kate contributes $5,000 to her Roth IRA. Before the due date (including extensions) for filing her 2010 federal income tax return, Jennifer Kate can do a trustee-to-trustee transfer of $1,750 (plus the earnings thereon) from her Roth IRA to her deductible IRA instead of withdrawing the excess contribution and earnings.

As previously discussed, an IRA contribution will not be included in the IRA owner's gross income when distributed as a returned contribution if (1) it is received by the IRA owner on or before the day prescribed by law, including extensions, for filing the IRA owner's federal income tax return for the year of the contribution, (2) no deduction is allowed with respect to the contribution, and (3) the distribution is accompanied by the amount of net income attributable to the contribution. [I.R.C. § 408(d)(4)]

The method for calculating net income generally bases the calculation of the amount of net income attributable to a contribution on the actual earnings and losses of the IRA during the time the IRA held the contribution. For purposes of returned contributions, the net income attributable to a contribution made to an IRA is determined by allocating to the contribution a pro rata portion of the earnings on the IRA assets during the period the IRA held the contribution. This attributable net income is calculated by using the following formula:

$$\text{Net income} = \text{Contribution} \times \frac{\text{Adjusted Closing Balance} - \text{Adjusted Opening Balance}}{\text{Adjusted Opening Balance}}$$

The following terms are pertinent:

1. Adjusted opening balance is the fair market value of the IRA at the beginning of the computation period plus the amount of any contributions or transfers (including the contribution that is distributed as a returned contribution and recharacterizations of contributions (see Q 31:9)) made to the IRA during the computation period.

2. Adjusted closing balance is the fair market value of the IRA at the end of the computation period plus the amount of any distributions or transfers (including recharacterizations of contributions) made from the IRA during the computation period.

3. Computation period is the period beginning immediately prior to the time that the contribution being returned was made to the IRA and ending immediately prior to the removal of the contribution. If more than one contribution was made as a regular contribution and is being returned from the IRA, the computation period begins immediately prior to the time the first contribution being returned was contributed.

4. Regular contribution is an IRA contribution made by the IRA owner that is neither a trustee-to-trustee transfer from another IRA nor a rollover from another IRA or retirement plan.

When an IRA asset is not normally valued on a daily basis, the fair market value of the asset at the beginning of the computation period is deemed to be the most recent, regularly determined, fair market value of the asset, determined as of a date that coincides with or precedes the first day of the computation period. In addition, solely for these purposes, recharacterized contributions are taken into account for the period they are actually held in a particular IRA. Under this method, net income may be a negative number.

In the case of an IRA that has received more than one regular contribution for a particular taxable year, the last regular contribution made to the IRA for a particular taxable year is deemed to be the contribution that is distributed as a returned contribution up to the amount of the contribution identified by the IRA owner as the amount distributed as a returned contribution. In the case of an individual who has multiple IRAs, the net income calculation is performed only on the IRA containing the contribution being returned and that IRA is the IRA that must distribute the contribution.

If an IRA is established with a contribution and no other contributions or distributions are made to or from that IRA, then the subsequent distribution of the entire IRA will satisfy the requirement that the return of a contribution be accompanied by the amount of net income attributable to the contribution.

The following examples illustrate the net income calculation:

Example 4. On May 1, 2010, when Bobbi's IRA is worth $4,800, she makes a $1,600 regular contribution to her IRA. Bobbi requests that $400 of the May 1, 2010, contribution be returned to her; and, on February 1, 2011, when the IRA is worth $7,600, the IRA custodian distributes to Bobbi the $400 plus attributable net income. During this time, no other contributions have been made to the IRA and no distributions have been made.

The adjusted opening balance is $6,400 ($4,800 + $1,600), and the adjusted closing balance is $7,600. Thus, the net income attributable to the $400 May 1, 2010, contribution is $75 [$400 × ($7,600 − $6,400) ÷ $6,400]. Therefore, the total to be distributed on February 1, 2011, is $475 ($400 + $75).

Example 5. Beginning in January 2010, Peter contributes $400 on the 15th of each month by payroll deduction (see Q 30:34) to an IRA for 2010, resulting in an excess regular contribution of $800 for the year. Peter requests that the $800 excess regular contribution be returned to him; and, on March 1, 2011, when the IRA is worth $16,000, the IRA custodian distributes to Peter the $800 plus attributable net income. The excess regular contributions to be returned are deemed to be the last two made in 2010: (1) the $400 December 15 contribution and (2) the $400 November 15 contribution. On November 15, the IRA was worth $11,000 immediately prior to the contribution. No distributions or transfers have been made from the IRA and no contributions or transfers, other than the monthly contributions (including $400 made in January and February 2011), have been made.

As of the beginning of the computation period (November 15), the adjusted opening balance is $12,600 [$11,000 + $400 + $400 + $400 + $400], and the adjusted closing balance is $16,000. Thus, the net income attributable to the excess regular contributions is $216 [$800 × ($16,000 − $12,600) ÷ $12,600]. Therefore, the total to be distributed as returned contributions on March 1, 2011 to correct the excess regular contribution is $1,016 [$800 + $216].

[Treas. Reg. §§ 1.408-4(c), 1.408-11]

An audit conducted by the Treasury Inspector General for Tax Administration (TIGTA) disclosed that noncompliance with IRA excess contribution rules continues to grow, resulting in significant revenue loss to the federal government. [Audit Rept. No. 201040043, TIGTA News Rel., May 2010]

For a discussion of the method for recharacterized contributions, see Q 31:9.

Q 30:10   May contributions other than cash be made to an IRA?

Except in the case of a rollover contribution, all contributions to an IRA must be in cash. [I.R.C. § 408(a)(1)]

Q 30:11   Can an IRA be subject to income tax?

An IRA is subject to the tax imposed on unrelated business taxable income (UBTI).

If a trade or business regularly carried on by a partnership of which a tax-exempt organization (e.g., IRA) is a member is an unrelated trade or business as to the organization, it must include its share of the partnership's income from the unrelated trade or business and its share of the directly connected deductions in computing its UBTI. An IRA purchased a limited partnership interest in a nonpublicly traded partnership; and, in the case of an IRA, unrelated trade or business means any trade or business regularly carried on by the IRA or a partnership of which it is a member. Although the IRA custodian does not participate in the management of the partnership and the IRA's liability is limited to the amount of the investment, IRS concluded that the business income passed through to the IRA as a limited partner was UBTI.

The partnership in which the IRA invested also owned and operated a distributed warehouse. It financed the construction of the warehouse and leased part of its floor space to an unrelated third-party tenant from which it received rental income. Although rents from real property are generally excluded from UBTI, there is included in UBTI as an item of gross income with respect to debt-financed property an amount based upon the average acquisition indebtedness on the property. If property, regardless of how acquired, is acquired subject to a mortgage or other similar lien, the amount of the indebtedness secured by the mortgage or lien is considered an indebtedness of the organization incurred in acquiring the property even though the organization did not assume or agree to pay the indebtedness. IRS therefore concluded that income derived by the partnership from the rental of the warehouse and received by the IRA is generated by debt-financed property and is UBTI.

Because there is a specific deduction of $1,000 in computing UBTI, except for purposes of computing net operating loss, the IRA was required to pay income tax on the UBTI to the extent that UBTI exceeded $1,000.

[I.R.C. §§ 408(e)(1), 511, 512, 513, 514; Priv. Ltr. Rul. 9703026]

IRS has also ruled that a qualified retirement plan that invests funds in a common trust fund has UBTI from the trust fund to the same extent as it would have had it made the same investment directly. A common trust fund is a fund maintained by a bank or trust company for the collective investment of funds contributed to the fund by the bank in its capacity, for example, as a trustee. A common trust fund is not subject to taxation, but its income is included in the gross income of the participants (e.g., a qualified retirement plan) in the fund. Therefore, if a common trust fund operated an active business, income from that business would be UBTI when passed through to the qualified retirement plan. [Rev. Rul. 98-41, 1998-2 C.B. 256; Rev. Rul. 67-301, 1967-2 C.B. 146; I.R.C. § 584; Treas. Reg. § 1.584-2(c)(3)] This ruling should be equally applicable to an IRA. [Priv. Ltr. Rul. 200148074]

Q 30:12 Does the wash-sale rule apply to an IRA?

The issue presented is whether or not a loss on a sale of stock or securities will be disallowed if an individual sells stock or securities for a loss and causes the individual's IRA or Roth IRA (see Q 31:1) to purchase substantially identical stock or securities within 30 days before or after the sale.

Example. Steve owns 100 shares of Essjaykay Company stock with a basis of $1,000. On December 20, 2010, Steve sells the 100 shares for $600 for a loss of $400. On December 21, 2010, Steve causes his IRA or Roth IRA to purchase 100 shares of Essjaykay Company stock for $605. The sale and purchase of stock are executed with different, unrelated market participants, and Steve is not a dealer in stock or securities.

In the case of any loss claimed to have been sustained from any sale or other disposition of shares of stock or securities where it appears that, within a period beginning 30 days before the date of such sale or disposition and ending 30 days after such date, the taxpayer has acquired (by purchase or by an exchange on which the entire amount of gain or loss is recognized by law), or has entered into a contract or option so to acquire, substantially identical stock or securities, then no deduction will be allowed unless the taxpayer is a dealer in stock or securities and the loss is sustained in a transaction made in the ordinary course of such business. [I.R.C. § 1091(a)] If the loss on the sale of the stock or securities is disallowed, then the basis is the basis of the stock or securities sold, increased or decreased, as the case may be, by the difference, if any, between the price at which the stock or securities were acquired and the price at which the substantially identical stock or securities were sold. [I.R.C. § 1091(d)]

IRS concluded that, even though an IRA or a Roth IRA is a tax-exempt trust, Steve has nevertheless been deemed to have accrued 100 shares of Essjaykay Company stock on December 21, 2010, by virtue of the purchase of the shares by his IRA or Roth IRA. Therefore, Steve's loss on the sale of his Essjaykay Company stock is disallowed, and the basis in his IRA or Roth IRA is not increased. [Rev. Rul. 2008-5, 2008-1 C.B. 271]

Q 30:13   Can active participants in qualified retirement plans also make deductible IRA contributions?

Not necessarily. If an individual is an active participant in a qualified retirement plan (see Qs 30:14, 30:15) for any part of a plan year ending with or within the individual's taxable year, IRA contributions cannot be deducted if the individual's modified adjusted gross income (AGI) exceeds certain specified amounts (see Qs 30:14, 30:17). For married couples, the active participation of one spouse does not cause the other spouse to be treated as an active participant (see Qs 30:15–30:17). [I.R.C. § 219(g)] These rules apply even if the individual is unaware that the individual is an active participant in the employer's qualified retirement plan. [Baumann, 70 T.C.M. 61 (1995)]

Q 30:14   What is active participation?

Generally, active participation refers to participation in a qualified retirement plan, SEP (see chapter 32), SIMPLE plan (see chapter 33), 403(b) plan (see Q 35:1), or governmental plan (see Q 30:15). [I.R.C. § 219(g)(5); Rosetti, 85 T.C.M. 1472 (2003); Wade, 81 T.C.M. 1613 (2001); Bradkamp, T.C. Summ. Op. 2001-5; Tolley, Jr., 73 T.C.M. 2877 (1997); Fuhrman, 73 T.C.M. 1792 (1997); Freese, 71 T.C.M. 3004 (1996); Porter v. Comm'r, 856 F.2d 1205 (8th Cir. 1988)] A schoolteacher who participated in a qualified state retirement plan was an active participant. [Neumeister v. Comm'r, 00-1517 (6th Cir. 2001)] An individual's status as an active participant must be reported on Form W-2.

Q 30:15   Who is an active participant?

An active participant in a defined benefit plan (see Q 2:3) is an individual who participates or meets the eligibility requirements for participation at any time during the plan year ending with or within the individual's taxable year. Thus, an individual is an active participant if the individual is eligible but declines to participate or fails to complete the minimum period of service or to make an employee contribution necessary to accrue a benefit. However, an individual who elects pursuant to the plan not to participate will be considered to be ineligible for participation for the period to which the election applies; but, in the case of a defined benefit plan, such an election is effective no earlier than the first plan year commencing after the date of the election. An individual is not an active participant if the employer has frozen benefit accruals (unless pre-freeze benefit accruals increase as compensation increases). An individual who accrues no additional benefits in a plan year ending with or within the individual's taxable year by reason of attaining a specified age is not an active participant by reason of participation in the plan. [Treas. Reg. § 1.219-2(b); Prop. Treas. Reg. § 1.219-2(f)(1); Rosetti, 85 T.C.M. 1472 (2003); Wartes, 65 T.C.M. 2058 (1993); Ann. 91-11, 1991-4 I.R.B. 80; IRS Notice 88-131, 1988-2 C.B. 546; IRS Notice 87-16, 1987-1 C.B. 446; Priv. Ltr. Rul. 8948008] An employee who made mandatory contributions to a public employees' plan was an active participant even though he never accrued service credits. [Starnes, No. 13869-07S (Tax Ct. 2008)] An individual was eligible to participate in her employer's cash balance plan (see Q 2:23) but, during 15 years of employment, never accrued a benefit because she never worked 1,000 hours or more during any plan year. The individual was held to be an active participant. [Colombell, No. 23979-04S (Tax Ct. 2006)]

An individual is an active participant in a money purchase pension or target benefit plan (see Qs 2:4, 2:5) if an employer contribution or forfeiture is required to be allocated to the individual's account for the plan year ending with or within the individual's taxable year. Thus, an individual who separates from service before the beginning of a calendar year may still be an active participant for such calendar year if, under the terms of the plan, the individual is eligible to receive an allocation for the plan year ending in such calendar year. [Treas. Reg. § 1.219-2(c)]

An individual is treated as an active participant under a profit sharing or stock bonus plan (see Qs 2:6, 2:13) if any employer contribution is added or any forfeiture is allocated to the individual's account during the individual's taxable year. A contribution is added to the individual's account on the later of the date the contribution is made or allocated. [Treas. Reg. § 1.219-2(d); Tolley, Jr., 73 T.C.M. 2877 (1997)]

An individual is not an active participant in a defined contribution plan (see Q 2:2) if only earnings (rather than contributions or forfeitures) are allocated to the individual's account.

An individual is treated as an active participant for any taxable year in which the individual makes a voluntary or mandatory employee contribution or an elective contribution under a 401(k) plan (see Q 27:1). However, an individual is not an active participant merely because the individual is eligible but chooses not to make such elective contribution. [Treas. Reg. § 1.219-2(e); Prop. Treas. Reg. § 1.219-2(f)(1); Naemi, T.C. Summ. Op. 2001-158]

The determination of whether an individual is an active participant is made without regard as to whether the individual's rights are nonforfeitable. [I.R.C. § 219(g); Castillo, No. 4698-02S (Tax Ct. 2003); Naemi, T.C. Summ. Op. 2001-158; Wade, 81 T.C.M. 1613 (2001); Bradkamp, T.C. Summ. Op. 2001-5; Nicolai, 73 T.C.M. 2157 (1997); Freese, 71 T.C.M. 3004 (1996); Morales-Caban, 66 T.C.M. 995 (1993); Wartes, 65 T.C.M. 2058 (1993)]

An individual was treated as an active participant in her employer's qualified retirement plan even though she was unaware of her eligibility to participate, and actual inclusion, in the plan. [Baumann, 70 T.C.M. 61 (1995)] An individual who was employed by a local school district, but who participated in a qualified state retirement plan, was treated as an active participant. [Neumeister v. Comm'r, 00-1517 (6th Cir. 2001)]

For married couples filing jointly, the active participation of one spouse does not cause the other spouse to be treated as an active participant (see Qs 30:16, 30:17). In addition, in the case of a married couple filing separate tax returns who do not live together at any time during the taxable year, the active participant status of one spouse does not affect the status of the other spouse; each spouse is treated as a single individual. [I.R.C. § 219(g)(4); Tolley, Jr., 73

T.C.M. 2877 (1997); Baumann, 70 T.C.M. 61 (1995); Bermingham, 67 T.C.M. 2200 (1994); Wartes, 65 T.C.M. 2058 (1993); Felber, 64 T.C.M. 261 (1992)]

Q 30:16   What level of income affects an active participant's deduction limitation?

Modified adjusted gross income (AGI) over the applicable dollar amount results in a limit on the IRA deduction for active participants (see Q 30:17). Effective for taxable years beginning after December 31, 2006, the applicable dollar amounts for a taxpayer filing a joint return and for any unmarried taxpayer (but not for married individuals filing separate returns) are subject to cost-of-living adjustments. Any increase is rounded to the nearest multiple of $1,000. [I.R.C. § 219(g)(8)] For 2010, the applicable dollar amount for a taxpayer filing a joint return remained at $89,000, but, for any unmarried taxpayer, increased to $56,000. [Rev. Proc. 2009-50, 2009-2 C.B. 617] For the five years prior to 2010, the applicable dollar amounts were:

1. For a taxpayer filing a joint return:

For taxable years beginning in	The applicable dollar amount is
2009	$89,000
2008	85,000
2007	83,000
2006	75,000
2005	70,000

2. For any unmarried taxpayer;

For taxable years beginning in	The applicable dollar amount is
2009	$55,000
2008	53,000
2007	52,000
2006	50,000
2005	50,000

3. Zero for married individuals filing separate returns. [Rosetti, 85 T.C.M. 1427 (2003)]

[I.R.C. § 219(g)(3)(B)]

However, married individuals filing separately who live apart during the entire year are treated as not married for this purpose so that the applicable dollar amount for each individual is the dollar amount applicable to an unmarried taxpayer. [I.R.C. §§ 219(g)(3)(B), 219(g)(4); IRS Notice 87-16, 1987-1 C.B. 446]

For purposes of the IRA deduction limit, AGI is modified and calculated without taking into account any deductible IRA contributions made for the taxable year or certain exclusions for foreign earned income, United States savings bond redemptions, amounts paid to the individual or expenses incurred by the individual's employer for qualified adoption expenses, and deductions for interest on education loans and qualified tuition and related expenses, but taking into account any taxable Social Security benefits (see Q 30:19) and passive loss limitations applicable to the individual. For example, the AGI-based phaseout of the exemption from the disallowance for passive losses is applied taking into account the amount of the conversion that is includible in AGI, and then the amount of the conversion is subtracted from AGI in determining whether an individual is eligible to make an IRA contribution. [I.R.C. § 219(g)(3)(A)] For married couples, AGI is the combined AGI of both spouses, even though the Code refers to the AGI of the taxpayer in the singular form. [I.R.C. §§ 219(g)(2)(A)(i), 219(g)(3)(b)(i); Flank, No. 11503-05S (Tax Ct. 2006); Ho, 89 T.C.M. 1410 (2005)]

For 2011, it is anticipated that the applicable dollar amount for a taxpayer filing a joint return will increase to $90,000, but, for any unmarried taxpayer, will remain at $56,000.

Q 30:17 If an individual is an active participant in a qualified retirement plan, what are the applicable IRA deduction limits?

The amount that may be deducted is the contribution limitation (see Q 30:5) reduced by an amount that bears the same ratio to the contribution limitation as the amount by which the taxpayer's modified AGI exceeds the applicable dollar amount (see Q 30:16) bears to $20,000 in the case of a taxpayer filing a joint return and $10,000 in the case of any unmarried taxpayer. Thus, for 2010, a married couple, both of whom are active participants, who have AGI of at least $109,000 cannot make a deductible IRA contribution. For married couples, AGI is the combined AGI of both spouses, even though the Code refers to the AGI of the taxpayer in the singular form. [I.R.C. §§ 219(g)(2)(A)(i), 219(g)(2)(A)(ii), 219(g)(3)(B)(i); Flank, No. 11503-05S (Tax Ct. 2006); Ho, 89 T.C.M. 1410 (2005)] Prior to 2007, the phaseout amount for married individuals filing a joint return was $10,000. [I.R.C. § 219(g)(2)(A)(ii)]

Example 1. Bob and Judy are married, are active participants in their employer's qualified retirement plan, and file a joint return for 2010. Their AGI for 2010 is $104,000, and each earns over $5,000. Both Bob and Judy may make a deductible IRA contribution of up to $1,250, computed as follows:

AGI	$104,000
Less: Applicable dollar amount	89,000
Difference	$ 15,000

Reduction in $5,000 limitation ($5,000 × ($15,000 ÷ $20,000))	$3,750
Maximum deductible IRA contribution ($5,000 − $3,750)	$1,250

Example 1A. For 2011, assume the same facts as in Example 1, except that the applicable dollar amount increases to $91,000. Both Bob and Judy may make a deductible IRA contribution of up to $1,750, computed as follows:

AGI	$104,000
Less: Applicable dollar amount	91,000
Difference	$ 13,000
Reduction in $5,000 limitation ($5,000 × ($13,000 ÷ $20,000))	$ 3,250
Maximum deductible IRA contribution ($5,000 − $3,250)	$ 1,750

[I.R.C. § 219(g)(2)(A); IRS Notice 87-16, 1987-1 C.B. 446]

The reduction in the maximum dollar limitation is rounded to the next lowest $10 in the case of a reduction that is not a multiple of $10. [I.R.C. § 219(g)(2)(C)] For individuals whose modified AGI is not above the level that would totally eliminate a deductible IRA contribution, there is a $200 minimum IRA deduction allowable. [I.R.C. § 219(g)(2)(B)]

Example 2. In 2010, Norman, an unmarried individual who is an active participant in his employer's qualified retirement plan, has AGI of $65,900. He may make a deductible IRA contribution of $200, computed as follows:

AGI	$ 65,900
Less: Applicable dollar amount	56,000
Difference	$ 9,900
Reduction in $5,000 limitation ($5,000 × ($9,900 ÷ $10,000))	$ 4,950
Maximum deductible IRA contribution (greater of $200 or $5,000 − $4,950)	$ 200

Example 2A. For 2011, assume the same facts as in Example 2, except that the applicable dollar amount increases to $57,000. Norman may make a deductible IRA contribution of $550, computed as follows:

AGI	$65,900
Less: Applicable dollar amount	57,000
Difference	$ 8,900
Reduction in $5,000 limitation ($5,000 × ($8,900 ÷ $10,000))	$ 4,450
Maximum deductible IRA contribution (greater of $200 or $5,000 − $4,450)	$ 550

An individual is not considered an active participant in a qualified retirement plan merely because the individual's spouse is an active participant; however, the maximum deductible IRA contribution for an individual who is not an active participant, but whose spouse is, is phased out for taxpayers with modified AGI between $150,000 and $160,000. [I.R.C. § 219(g)(7)] The applicable dollar amount of $150,000 is also subject to cost-of-living adjustments and increased to $167,000 in 2010. [I.R.C. § 219(g)(8); Rev. Proc. 2009-50, 2009-2 C.B. 617] For 2011, it is anticipated that the applicable dollar amount will increase to $169,000.

Example 3. In 2010, Rita is an active participant in a qualified retirement plan, and her husband, Sonny, is not. The combined AGI of Rita and Sonny for the year is $200,000. Neither Rita nor Sonny is entitled to make deductible contributions to an IRA for 2010.

Example 3A. Assume the same facts as in Example 3, except that the combined AGI of Rita and Sonny is $125,000. Sonny, the nonparticipant spouse, can make a $5,000 deductible contribution to an IRA. However, no deductible contribution can be made for Rita.

Q 30:18   Does the receipt of Social Security benefits affect deductible IRA contributions?

If an individual is an active participant in a qualified retirement plan (see Qs 30:14, 30:15), the deduction for IRA contributions is subject to a phaseout if modified AGI exceeds certain specified amounts (see Qs 30:16, 30:17). An individual's AGI includes the taxable portion of Social Security benefits. [I.R.C. §§ 219(g)(3)(A)(i), 219(g)(3)(B)]

The determination of the taxable portion of Social Security benefits depends in part upon the individual's modified AGI. In determining modified AGI, the individual may subtract deductible IRA contributions. Therefore, a deductible IRA contribution may cause a reduction in the taxable portion of Social Security benefits, and the individual must compute taxable Social Security benefits twice. The first computation is for the purpose of determining the tentative amount of Social Security benefits that must be included in gross income if the individual did not make any IRA contribution. This first computation determines the amount of hypothetical AGI for purposes of the IRA phaseout provision. The second computation actually determines the amount of taxable Social Security benefits by taking into account the deductible IRA contribution that was determined under the first computation. [I.R.C. § 86(b)(2); Ann. 88-38, 1988-10 I.R.B. 60; Conf. Rep. No. 99-841, 1986-3 (vol. 4) C.B. 377; IRS Pub. 590]

Unlike an income-tax-free rollover from one IRA to another (see Qs 34:1, 34:3), a rollover or conversion of an IRA to a Roth IRA is taxable to the same extent as if the amount distributed from the IRA were not rolled over at all (see Qs 31:44, 31:50). [I.R.C. § 408A(d)(3)(A)(i); Treas. Reg. § 1.408A-4, Q&A-7(a)] An individual's income from converting his IRA to a Roth IRA was included as an item of income for purposes of determining the taxability of his Social Security benefits. [Helm, T.C. Summ. Op. 2002-138]

**Q 30:19   May an individual who is ineligible to make a fully
deductible IRA contribution make a nondeductible IRA
contribution?**

Yes. An individual who is ineligible to make a deductible IRA contribution to
the full extent of the contribution limitation (see Q 30:5) may make a designated
nondeductible IRA contribution (see Q 30:20). [I.R.C. § 408(o)]

For details on Roth IRAs, see chapter 31.

Q 30:20   What is a designated nondeductible IRA contribution?

A designated nondeductible IRA contribution is a nondeductible IRA contribution to the extent of the excess of (1) the lesser of the dollar amount in effect
for the taxable year (or an increased amount when a spousal IRA is also
involved; see Q 30:25) or 100 percent of compensation over (2) the IRA
deduction limit with respect to the individual (but see Q 30:21). [I.R.C. § 408(o)]

**Q 30:21   May an individual who is eligible to make a deductible
IRA contribution elect to treat such a contribution as
nondeductible?**

Yes. An individual is permitted to make such an election and might do so if,
for example, the individual had compensation for the taxable year but had no
taxable income for the taxable year after taking into account other deductions.
[I.R.C. § 408(o)(2)(B)(ii)]

An individual who is eligible to make a deductible IRA contribution or a
designated nondeductible IRA contribution (see Q 30:20) is permitted to make
a nondeductible contribution to a Roth IRA, but only to the extent that a
deductible IRA contribution and/or a designated nondeductible contribution is
not made for that year (see Q 31:4).

**Q 30:22   Is an individual required to report a designated
nondeductible contribution on the tax return?**

Yes. An individual who makes a designated nondeductible contribution (see
Q 30:20) to an IRA (or who receives any amount from an IRA) must include the
following information on the income tax return for the applicable taxable year:

1. The amount of designated nondeductible contributions for the year;

2. The amount of distributions from IRAs for the year;

3. The excess (if any) of (a) the aggregate amount of designated nondeductible contributions for all preceding taxable years over (b) the aggregate
   amount of distributions from IRAs that were excludable from gross
   income for such taxable years;

4. The aggregate balance of all IRAs of the individual as of the end of the
   taxable year; and

5. Such other information as IRS may prescribe.

[I.R.C. § 408(o)(4); Ann. 99-18, 1999-1 C.B. 853]

If the required information is not provided on the individual's tax return for a taxable year, all IRA contributions are considered to have been deductible and, therefore, are taxable upon withdrawal from the IRA. However, an individual may change a designation of a contribution from deductible to nondeductible (or vice versa) by filing an amended return before the expiration of the statute of limitations on assessment of tax for such year. [IRS Notice 87-16, 1987-1 C.B. 446]

There is a $50 penalty for failure to report the required information, and a $100 penalty for overstating the amount of designated nondeductible contributions—unless the taxpayer can demonstrate that the error was due to reasonable cause. [I.R.C. §§ 408(o)(4), 6693(b)]

Q 30:23 What is the tax treatment of IRA withdrawals by an individual who has made both deductible and nondeductible contributions?

The amount includible in an individual's income is determined by subtracting from the amount of the IRA withdrawal an amount that bears the same ratio to the amount withdrawn as the individual's aggregate nondeductible IRA contributions bear to the aggregate balance of all IRAs of the individual (including rollover IRAs, SEPs, and SIMPLE IRAs). [I.R.C. §§ 408(d)(1), 408(d)(2); Schmalzer, 76 T.C.M. 803 (1998); Priv. Ltr. Rul. 200904029]

The formula for determining the nontaxable portion of an IRA distribution is:

$$\frac{\text{Total nondeductible contributions}}{\substack{\text{Aggregate IRA year-end account balances +}\\ \text{amount of IRA distributions}}} \times \substack{\text{IRA}\\ \text{distributions}} = \substack{\text{Nontaxable portion of}\\ \text{distribution}}$$

[IRS Notice 87-16, 1987-1 C.B. 446]

Example. Assume that Anne has made aggregate deductible IRA contributions into two IRAs for 2008 and 2009 of $1,800 and aggregate nondeductible IRA contributions of $2,200 during those two years. In January 2010, Anne withdrew $1,000 from one IRA. At the end of 2010, the account balance of both IRAs was $4,500. Of the $1,000 withdrawn during 2010, $400 is treated as a partial return of nondeductible contributions, calculated as follows:

$$\frac{\text{Total nondeductible contributions (\$2,200)}}{\substack{\text{Aggregate IRA year-end account balances (\$4,500) +}\\ \text{amount of IRA distributions during year (\$1,000)}}} = \frac{\$2,200}{\$5,500} \times \$1,000 = \$400$$

The balance of the withdrawn amount ($1,000 − $400 = $600) is includible in income on Anne's 2010 tax return.

Since a Roth IRA (see Qs 31:1, 31:28) is a discrete account, the above rules will not apply to distributions from a Roth IRA, and a Roth IRA will not be considered in determining the aggregate balance of all of the individual's IRAs.

If a distribution from an IRA is rolled over to an eligible retirement plan (see Q 34:16) that is not an IRA, the distribution will be attributed first to amounts other than designated nondeductible contributions. [I.R.C. § 408(d)(3)(H)] Thus, if an individual receives a distribution from an IRA, a portion thereof is not rolled over, and/or a portion of the distribution represents designated nondeductible contributions, the pro rata allocation of the portion not rolled over will apply only to that distribution (without considering any other IRA of the individual) in order to determine the taxable portion of the distribution not rolled over.

> **Example.** Anne has two IRAs; IRA A of $50,000, all of which is attributable to deductible contributions, and IRA G of $75,000, of which $10,000 represents designated nondeductible contributions. In 2010, Anne receives a distribution of $65,000 from IRA G and rolls over $25,000 to a qualified retirement plan. To determine what portion of the $40,000 distribution that was not rolled over is taxable, IRA A is not taken into account. After deducting the $25,000 rollover from IRA G, the remaining $50,000 ($75,000 − $25,000) consists of $10,000 of basis and $40,000 of possible income. Therefore, of the $40,000 not rolled over, $32,000 is a taxable distribution [($40,000 ÷ $50,000) × $40,000].

An individual rolled over a distribution from a 401(k) plan (see Q 27:1) to an IRA and erroneously characterized the rollover as a designated nondeductible contribution. The individual received a distribution of his entire IRA some years later and claimed that most of the distribution was nontaxable. The court thought otherwise and concluded that the entire distribution was taxable. [Sternberg v. IRS, 04-1325 (2d Cir. 2005)] An individual who received an IRA distribution was taxed on the full amount because his claim that a portion of the distribution was not taxable could not be supported. [Hoang, 91 T.C.M. 899 (2006)]

Q 30:24   What is the tax treatment of IRA withdrawals by an individual who has made only nondeductible contributions?

The amount includible in an individual's income is determined in the same manner as set forth in Q 30:23. [I.R.C. §§ 408(d)(1), 408(d)(2); IRS Notice 87-16, 1987-1 C.B. 446]

> **Example 1.** Assume that Eric has made aggregate nondeductible IRA contributions to his IRA of $4,400 and has never made a deductible IRA contribution. In January 2010, Eric withdraws $2,000 from his IRA; and, at the end of 2010, the IRA account balance was $9,000. Of the $2,000 withdrawn during 2010, $800 is treated as a partial return of nondeductible contributions, calculated as follows:

$$\frac{\text{Total nondeductible contributions (\$4,400)}}{\begin{array}{c}\text{Aggregate IRA year-end account balances (\$9,000)} + \\ \text{amount of IRA distributions during year (\$2,000)}\end{array}} = \frac{\$4,400}{\$11,000} \times \$2,000 = \$800$$

The balance of the withdrawn amount ($2,000 – $800 = $1,200) is includible in income on Eric's 2009 tax return.

Nondeductible IRA contributions, but not deductible IRA contributions, represent basis (see Q 13:3) and that is why a portion of the distribution is nontaxable. Because of this rule, the individual can have a loss on the IRA, but the individual can only take the loss for income tax purposes when *all* of the amounts in *all* of the individual's IRAs have been distributed.

Example 2. Assume that Mihal has made aggregate nondeductible IRA contributions to her IRA of $2,000 and has never made a deductible IRA contribution. The $2,000 represents Mihal's basis. On December 31, 2009, when the IRA balance was $2,400, Mihal withdrew $600. Of the $600 withdrawal, $500 is nontaxable and Mihal's basis is reduced to $1,500 ($2,000 – $500). In 2010, Mihal's IRA investment decreases in value from $1,800 to $1,300, and Mihal withdraws the entire remaining IRA balance. Since the amount distributed ($1,300) is less than Mihal's remaining basis ($1,500), Mihal can take the $200 loss on her 2010 federal income tax return as a miscellaneous itemized deduction. As a miscellaneous itemized deduction, it is subject to the 2 percent of adjusted gross income limit and could subject Mihal to the alternative minimum tax (AMT).

Even if an individual has made deductible IRA contributions, a loss may be recognized if all IRAs have been distributed and the amounts distributed are less than the individual's unrecovered basis.

[IRS Notice 89-25, 1989-1 C.B. 662, Q&A-7]

An individual rolled over a distribution from a 401(k) plan (see Q 27:1) to an IRA and erroneously characterized the rollover as a designated nondeductible contribution. The individual received a distribution of his entire IRA some years later and claimed that most of the distribution was nontaxable. The court thought otherwise and concluded that the entire distribution was taxable. [Sternberg v. IRS, 04-1325 (2d Cir. 2005)]

Q 30:25   What is a spousal IRA?

If only one spouse is working, the working spouse may make an additional contribution to an IRA (a spousal IRA) on behalf of the nonworking spouse (provided a joint income tax return is filed). A spousal IRA is available even if both spouses work if the spouse for whom the spousal IRA is set up consents to being treated as having no compensation, for IRA purposes, for the taxable year.

The total amount of allowable annual contributions to the working spouse's IRA and to the spousal IRA is double the dollar amount in effect for the taxable year (or 100 percent of the working spouse's earnings if less). The contributions to both IRAs need not be split equally between the spouses. However, the maximum IRA contribution on behalf of either spouse is the dollar amount in effect for the taxable year. [I.R.C. § 219(c)]

Example 1. Caroline is married to Adam, and they file a joint return. Their modified AGI for 2010 is $70,000, all of which is earned by Caroline. Caroline and Adam may each make a deductible IRA contribution of up to $5,000.

See Q 30:16 for rules relating to the active participation issue.

Example 2. Bill, an active participant in his employer's qualified retirement plan, is married to Stephanie, and they file a joint return. Their modified AGI for 2010 is $94,000, all of which is earned by Bill. Bill may make a deductible IRA contribution of up to $3,750, computed as follows:

AGI	$94,000
Less: Applicable dollar amount	89,000
Difference	$ 5,000
Reduction in $5,000 limitation ($5,000 × ($5,000 ÷ $20,000))	$ 1,250
Maximum deductible IRA contribution ($5,000 − $1,250)	$ 3,750

However, a $5,000 deductible spousal IRA contribution can be made on behalf of Stephanie because their combined modified AGI does not exceed $166,000 in 2010 (see Q 30:17).

[I.R.C. §§ 219(c)(1), 219(g)(2)(A), 219(g)(7); IRS Notice 87-16, 1987-1 C.B. 446]

If the working spouse has reached age 70½, then as long as the working spouse continues to receive compensation, the working spouse can make deductible contributions to the nonworking spouse's IRA. The nonworking spouse must, however, be less than age 70½, and the maximum contribution on behalf of the nonworking spouse is the dollar amount in effect for the taxable year. [I.R.C. § 219(d)(1)]

If the working spouse dies, a contribution may be made to a spousal IRA by the surviving spouse if a joint income tax return is filed for the year for which the contribution was made. [Priv. Ltr. Rul. 8527083]

The maximum permitted IRA contributions is generally limited by the individual's earned income. Previously it was possible for the nonworking (or lesser earning) spouse and the working spouse to make IRA contributions in excess of the couple's combined earned income. The following example illustrates what was permissible.

Example. Suppose Howard and Barbara retired in the middle of January 1999. In that year, Howard earned $1,000, and Barbara earned $500. Both were active participants in a qualified retirement plan (see Q 29:19). Their modified AGI was $60,000, and they made no Roth IRA contributions. Before application of the income phase-out rules (see Q 29:21), the maximum deductible IRA contribution that Howard could make was $1,000. After application of the income phase-out rules, Howard's maximum contribution was $200, and he contributed that amount to an IRA. Howard could then make a nondeductible contribution of $800 ($1,000 – $200).

Barbara's maximum permitted deductible contribution before the income phase-out was $1,300 (the sum of their combined earned income ($1,500), less Howard's deductible IRA contribution ($200)). Under the income phase-out, Barbara's deductible contribution was limited to $200, and she could then make a nondeductible contribution of $1,100 ($1,300 – $200).

Thus, the total permitted contributions for Howard and Barbara were $2,300 ($1,000 for Howard plus $1,300 for Barbara). The combined contribution was not limited to $1,500, their combined earned income.

Now, the contributions for the spouse with the lesser income cannot exceed the combined earned income of both spouses reduced by the contributions made by the spouse with the greater income. In the above example, Barbara's nondeductible IRA contribution is now limited to $300 [($1,000 + $500) – ($1,000 + $200)]. [I.R.C. § 219(c)(1)(B)(ii)]

Q 30:26 When must IRA contributions be made?

A deductible or nondeductible contribution to an IRA must be made by the due date, not including extensions, for filing the return. [I.R.C. § 219(f)(3)]

Example. Betty wants to make a contribution to her IRA for 2010. Betty can do so any time in 2010, or she can wait until her 2010 tax return is due, April 15, 2011. Even if Betty obtains an extension to file her return to October 17, 2011, her IRA contribution is due by April 15, 2011.

An IRA contribution is timely if it is received by the IRA sponsor in an envelope bearing a post office cancellation date no later than the due date of the individual's federal income tax return, not including extensions. [Priv. Ltr. Ruls. 8628047, 8611090, 8551065, 8536085] Previously, taxpayers could only use the United States Postal Service, but IRS is now authorized to name private delivery services meeting specific criteria that taxpayers may use in lieu of the Postal Service. [I.R.C. § 7502; IRS Notice 2004-83, 2004-2 C.B. 1030; Estate of Cranor, 81 T.C.M. 1111 (2001); Diller v. Comm'r, No. 97-7171 (3d Cir. 1997); *see also* IRS Notice 2002-17, 2002-1 C.B. 567]

An individual claimed a deduction for an IRA contribution he, in fact, never made and was, of course, denied the deduction. [Edmonds, 76 T.C.M. 710 (1998)]

IRS has added the deadline for IRA contributions to the list of tax-related deadlines that may be postponed by reason of a Presidentially declared disaster. IRS is allowed to disregard a period of up to one year in determining whether IRA contributions were made within the time prescribed. [I.R.C. § 7508A(b); Treas. Reg. § 301.7508A-1; IRS Notice 2002-27, 2002-1 C.B. 489; IRS Notice 2001-68, 2001-2 C.B. 504; IRS Notice 2001-61, 2001-2 C.B. 305]

For taxable years beginning on or after January 1, 2004, members of the armed forces may treat combat pay as compensation for purposes of the IRA contribution and deduction rules. [I.R.C. §§ 112, 219(f)(7)] For the time to make additional catch-up contributions, see Q 30:5.

Q 30:27 Can an IRA deduction be claimed before the contribution is actually made?

Yes, as long as the contribution is made by the due date, not including extensions, for filing the return. [Rev. Rul. 84-18, 1984-1 C.B. 88]

Example. Danielle files her 2010 return on February 4, 2011, and claims a deduction of $5,000 for an IRA contribution that she has not made. If she makes the contribution by the due date of the return, April 15, 2011, the deduction is allowed.

Q 30:28 May an individual borrow money to fund an IRA?

Yes. The deductibility of the interest paid on the loan is determined under the general rules applicable to interest payments. The interest payments are not subject to the rule prohibiting interest deductions on loans incurred to purchase or carry tax-exempt assets because the income earned on the IRA is tax deferred, not tax exempt (see Q 30:11). [I.R.C. § 163; Priv. Ltr. Rul. 8527082]

Q 30:29 May an individual make a contribution to an IRA with a credit card?

Yes, according to IRS. An individual established an IRA at a bank and funded the IRA with a cash advance drawn on his bank credit card. The bank executed the transaction pursuant to written instructions of the individual. IRS ruled that if, by April 15, a cash advance was drawn on the individual's credit card, credited to the IRA, and designated as a contribution for the previous year, the individual could deduct the contribution for the previous year, provided the bank honored its obligation to make payment on the credit card cash advance. [Priv. Ltr. Rul. 8622051]

Q 30:30 Can an individual's income tax refund be directly deposited into an IRA?

IRS was directed to develop forms under which all or a portion of an individual's income tax refund may be deposited in an IRA of the individual (or the spouse of the individual in the case of a joint return). This does not modify the rules relating to IRAs, including the rules relating to timing and deductibility of contributions. [PPA § 830] IRS developed Form 8888, Direct Deposit of Refund to More Than One Account. However, if the individual wants the refund deposited to only one account, Form 8888 should not be used. Instead, the individual can request a direct deposit of the refund on the tax return being filed (e.g., Form 1040). [Instructions to Form 8888]

IRS announced that economic-stimulus payments directly deposited into IRAs could be withdrawn tax-free and penalty-free. This relief was designed to help taxpayers who may have been unaware that, by choosing direct deposit for their entire regular tax refund, they were also choosing to have their stimulus payment directly deposited as well. If a taxpayer elected a split refund (Form 8888), however, the stimulus payment was paid by a paper check. This relief was available for amounts withdrawn from IRAs that were less than or equal to a taxpayer's directly deposited stimulus payment. To qualify for this relief, funds had to be taken out by April 15, 2009, in most cases. Without this relief, taxes, penalties, and other special rules would apply to amounts removed from these accounts. Regular refunds were not eligible for this relief. In general, the deadline for these withdrawals was the due date or extended due date for filing a 2008 return. This meant April 15, 2009 for most taxpayers, or October 15, 2009 for those who obtained tax-filing extensions. [IRS News Rel. IR-2008-68 (Apr. 30, 2008); Ann. 2008-44, 2008-2 C.B. 982]

Q 30:31   Does the payment of a fee to the trustee of an IRA reduce the amount otherwise allowable as a contribution to the IRA?

No. The payment of a fee to the trustee for the establishment and maintenance of an IRA, or for various other administrative services performed, is not considered a contribution to an IRA for purposes of the annual contribution limit (see Q 30:5) or the excess contribution penalty (see Q 30:9). Moreover, the trustee fees may be deductible as expenses incurred for the production of income. [I.R.C. § 212; Rev. Rul. 84-146, 1984-2 C.B. 61; Priv. Ltr. Ruls. 8432109, 8329049]

IRS has ruled that wrap fees paid by IRA owners from non-IRA funds to their IRA trustees were not IRA contributions. The fees were charged as part of different investment programs offered to IRA owners by an investment advisory company for its services. [Priv. Ltr. Rul. 200507021] However, the payment of brokerage commissions incurred for the purchase or sale of IRA assets is considered a contribution to the IRA subject to the annual contribution limit. [Rev. Rul. 86-142, 1986-2 C.B. 60; Priv. Ltr. Rul. 8711095] This rule also applies to commissions paid to insurance agents attributable to the purchase of individual retirement annuities. [Priv. Ltr. Rul. 8747072]

Q 30:32   What is an employer-sponsored IRA?

An employer may establish IRAs for its employees (and for the nonworking spouses of these employees). The contributions are deductible by the employer and includible as compensation income by the employee, subject to Social Security and unemployment taxes. Whether the employee can deduct the contribution is determined under the rules generally applicable to IRA contributions (see Qs 30:13–30:17). The assets of the employer-sponsored IRAs may be held in a common trust fund (see Q 30:11). [I.R.C. §§ 219(f)(5), 408(c)]

If the employer contributes less than the maximum allowed (100 percent of compensation up to the dollar amount in effect for the taxable year; increased to double the dollar amount in effect for the taxable year in the case of a spousal IRA), the employee can contribute the difference (see Qs 30:5–30:8, 30:25).

Example. Jamie's employer contributes $4,500 to an IRA on his behalf for 2010. Because Jamie earns more than $5,000 a year, the maximum allowable contribution is $5,000. Jamie, who is not married, can contribute an additional $500 to the IRA.

There is no requirement that an employer-sponsored IRA cover a certain number or group of employees. In fact, the employer may discriminate in favor of highly compensated employees (HCEs; see Q 3:3). [I.R.C. § 408(c); Cline v. Industrial Maint. Eng'g & Contracting Co., 2000 WL 282584 (9th Cir. 2000)]

An IRA is not considered employer sponsored merely because the employer acts as trustee or custodian of its employees' IRAs. However, the employer is a disqualified person (see Qs 24:3, 24:4) with respect to the IRA, so the employer must be careful to avoid engaging in a prohibited transaction (see Q 24:1) that would disqualify the IRA (see Q 30:45). For example, the purchase of stock of the employer's parent company by the employer as IRA custodian may be considered a prohibited transaction. [DOL Adv. Op. 90-20A]

Q 30:33 Can employer-sponsored IRAs help an employer that has a qualified retirement plan satisfy coverage requirements?

No. An employer maintaining a qualified retirement plan cannot satisfy the coverage requirements that must be met by taking into consideration the fact that employees not covered under the plan are covered by an employer-sponsored IRA.

For details on coverage requirements, see chapter 5.

Q 30:34 What is a payroll-deduction IRA?

An employer may choose to play a limited role in promoting retirement savings (IRAs) for its employees by establishing a payroll-deduction program in conjunction with a financial institution (e.g., a bank, insurance company, mutual fund, or brokerage firm). Each employee is allowed to set up an IRA with the sponsoring institution, and the amount the employee wishes to contribute to the IRA each pay period is deducted from the employee's paycheck by the employer. An employer may permit its employees to contribute to IRAs by direct deposit through payroll deduction. [Ann. 99-2, 1999-1 C.B. 305]

Q 30:35 Does a payroll-deduction IRA expose the employer to ERISA liabilities and compliance requirements?

A payroll-deduction IRA is not considered a pension plan subject to ERISA as long as the employer does not endorse the program. The employer will not be considered to have endorsed the program and will be free of ERISA responsibilities if all of the following conditions are met:

1. Materials distributed to the employees, either by the employer or by the IRA sponsor, clearly say that:

   a. The program is completely voluntary;

   b. The employer is not endorsing the sponsor or its investment program;

   c. There are other IRA investments available to employees outside the payroll-deduction program;

   d. An IRA may not be appropriate for everyone; and

   e. The tax consequences are the same whether or not payroll deductions are used to make the IRA contributions.

2. The employer is not the IRA sponsor or an affiliate of the sponsor.

3. No significant investments will be made in securities of the employer.

4. If the payroll-deduction IRA is the result of a collective bargaining agreement, no investments designed to provide more jobs, loans, or similar direct benefits to union members are permitted.

[DOL Reg. §§ 2509.99-1, 2510.3-2(d); DOL Interpretive Bull. 99-1]

In addition, the employer must promptly transfer the funds it deducts from its employees' paychecks to the IRA sponsor or it risks the imposition of some ERISA responsibilities. [DOL Op. Ltr. 81-80A]

Q 30:36   What is a deemed IRA?

A qualified retirement plan or a 403(b) plan (see Q 35:1) may permit employees to make voluntary employee contributions (see Qs 27:74, 35:19) to a separate account or annuity that (1) is established under the plan and (2) meets the requirements applicable to either IRAs or Roth IRAs. In such event, the separate account or annuity will be deemed an IRA or a Roth IRA, as applicable, for all purposes of the Code. For example, the reporting requirements applicable to IRAs apply. The deemed IRA, and contributions thereto, are not subject to the qualification rules pertaining to the plan. In addition, the deemed IRA, and contributions thereto, are not taken into account in applying such rules to any other contributions under the plan. The deemed IRA, and contributions thereto, are subject to the exclusive benefit and fiduciary rules of ERISA to the extent otherwise applicable to the plan but are not subject to the ERISA reporting and disclosure, participation, vesting, funding, and enforcement requirements applicable to the plan. [I.R.C. § 408(q); ERISA § 4(c)] However, ERISA Section 4(c) has been amended, so that a deemed IRA, and contributions to it, are subject to the ERISA administration and enforcement rules, and ERISA is intended to apply to a deemed IRA in a manner similar to a SEP (see Q 30:38).

Similar to an employer-sponsored IRA (see Q 30:32), it appears that an employer has wide discretion in determining who is eligible to make deemed IRA contributions because there are no coverage or nondiscrimination requirements.

Among the advantages of a deemed IRA are the ability to:

1. Permit additional employee contributions to plans, including both regular deemed IRA contributions and, presumably, rollover contributions from an employee's existing IRA into the deemed IRA (see Q 34:3), and

2. Retain plan assets in the plan by allowing distributions from the plan to be rolled over into the plan's traditional deemed IRA and using the deemed IRA as the default IRA for automatic cash-outs (see Q 34:17).

DOL has advised that the establishment of deemed IRAs as part of a governmental plan would not subject the plan to any provisions of Title I of ERISA if the plan, taking into account the deemed IRAs, continues to meet the definition of a governmental plan. [DOL Op. Ltr. 2003-01A]

Plan sponsors that want to provide for deemed IRAs must have such provisions in their plan documents and must have deemed IRAs in effect for employees no later than the date deemed IRA contributions are accepted from such employees. However, plan sponsors that wanted to provide for deemed IRAs for plan years beginning before January 1, 2004 (but after December 31, 2002) were not required to have such provisions in their plan documents before the end of such plan years. Plan sponsors must have adopted a good-faith EGTRRA 2001 plan amendment. [IRS Notice 2001-57, 2001-2 C.B. 279]. To satisfy the requirements for the EGTRRA 2001 remedial amendment period, the provisions must reflect a reasonable, good-faith interpretation of the statute. [IRS Notice 2001-42, 2001-2 C.B. 70] The sample plan amendment set forth below is a reasonable, good-faith interpretation of EGTRRA 2001. In addition to the sample plan amendment, a plan that intends to comply with the deemed IRA provisions must also contain language that satisfies Section 408 or 408A, relating to traditional and Roth IRAs, respectively. IRS has provided sample language (a Listing of Required Modifications or LRMs) that satisfies Sections 408 and 408A on IRS's Web Site at www.irs.gov/ep. A plan will satisfy the reasonable, good-faith interpretation of the EGTRRA 2001 requirement with respect to IRA language if the language addresses every applicable point in the IRA LRMs.

The following sample plan amendment may be adopted *only* by plans trusteed by a person eligible to act as a trustee of an IRA (see Q 30:2) and plans that designate an insurance company to issue annuity contracts (see Q 30:3). Additional language that satisfies Section 408 or 408A must also be added to the plan.

SECTION _____. DEEMED IRAs

1. Applicability and effective date. This section shall apply if elected by the employer in the adoption agreement and shall be effective for plan years beginning after the date specified in the adoption agreement.

2. Deemed IRAs. Each participant may make voluntary employee contributions to the participant's—[insert "traditional" or "Roth"] IRA under the plan. The plan shall establish a separate—[insert "account" or "annuity"] for the designated IRA contributions of each participant and

any earnings properly allocable to the contributions, and maintain separate recordkeeping with respect to each such IRA.

3. Reporting duties. The—[insert "trustee" or "issuer"] shall be subject to the reporting requirements of section 408(i) of the Internal Revenue Code with respect to all IRAs that are established and maintained under the plan.

4. Voluntary employee contributions. For purposes of this section, a voluntary employee contribution means any contribution (other than a mandatory contribution within the meaning of section 411(c)(2) of the Code) that is made by the participant and which the participant has designated, at or prior to the time of making the contribution, as a contribution to which this section applies.

5. IRAs established pursuant to this section shall be held in—[insert "a trust" or "an annuity"] separate from the trust established under the plan to hold contributions other than deemed IRA contributions and shall satisfy the applicable requirements of sections 408 and 408A of the Code, which requirements are set forth in section—[insert the section of the plan that contains the IRA requirements].

(Adoption agreement provisions)

Section _____ of the plan, Deemed IRAs: (check one)

_____ shall be effective for plan years beginning after December 31, (enter a year later than 2001).

_____shall not apply.

[Rev. Proc. 2003-13, 2003-1 C.B. 317]

Trusts that are parts of deemed IRAs may pool their assets in a group fund without affecting the exempt status of the separate trusts (see Q 30:2). [Rev. Rul. 2004-67, 2004-2 C.B. 28; Rev. Rul. 81-100, 1981-1 C.B. 326]

IRS has issued regulations that provide guidance to employers wanting to adopt deemed IRAs or deemed Roth IRAs (see Q 30:37).

Q 30:37   Has IRS issued regulations regarding deemed IRAs?

In addition to the sample plan amendment published by IRS (see Q 30:36), IRS has issued regulations. [Treas. Reg. § 1.408(q)-1] The regulations apply to deemed IRAs established on or after August 1, 2003. [Treas. Reg. § 1.408(q)-1(h)(4)]

A qualified employer plan is a qualified retirement plan, a 403(b) plan (see Q 35:1), or a governmental Section 457 plan. [Treas. Reg. § 1.408(q)-1(h)(1)] A voluntary employee contribution is any contribution (other than a mandatory contribution; see Q 6:37) that is made by an individual as an employee under a qualified employer plan that allows employees to elect to make contributions to deemed IRAs and with respect to which the individual has designated the contribution as a contribution to a deemed IRA. [Treas. Reg. § 1.408(q)-1(h)(2)]

A qualified employer plan may permit employees to make voluntary employee contributions to a separate account or annuity established under the plan. If the requirements applicable to deemed IRAs are met, such account or annuity is treated in the same manner as an IRA or Roth IRA (see Q 31:1), and contributions to such an account or annuity are treated as contributions to an IRA or Roth IRA and not to the qualified employer plan. The account or annuity is referred to as a deemed IRA. [Treas. Reg. § 1.408(q)-1(a)]

If the account or annuity meets the requirements applicable to traditional IRAs, the account or annuity is deemed to be a traditional IRA; and, if the account or annuity meets the requirements applicable to Roth IRAs, the account or annuity is deemed to be a Roth IRA. Simplified employee pensions (SEPs; see Q 32:1) and SIMPLE IRAs (see Q 33:2) may not be used as deemed IRAs. [Treas. Reg. § 1.408(q)-1(b)]

Except as provided below, the qualified employer plan and the deemed IRA are treated as separate entities under the Code and are subject to the separate rules applicable to qualified employer plans and IRAs, respectively. Issues regarding eligibility, participation, disclosure, nondiscrimination, contributions, distributions, investments, and plan administration are generally to be resolved under the separate rules (if any) applicable to each entity under the Code. [Treas. Reg. § 1.408(q)-1(c)]

The following exceptions to the treatment of a deemed IRA and the qualified employer plan as separate entities apply:

1. The plan document of the qualified employer plan must contain the deemed IRA provisions, and a deemed IRA must be in effect at the time the deemed IRA contributions are accepted. Notwithstanding the preceding sentence, employers that provided deemed IRAs for plan years beginning before January 1, 2004 (but after December 31, 2002), are not required to have such provisions in their plan documents before the end of such plan years.

2. The requirements regarding commingling of assets (see Q 30:2) do not apply to deemed IRAs. Accordingly, the assets of a deemed IRA may be commingled for investment purposes with those of the qualified employer plan. However, the restrictions on the commingling of plan and IRA assets with other assets apply to the assets of the qualified employer plan and the deemed IRA. [Treas. Reg. § 1.408(q)-1(d)]

Rules applicable to distributions from qualified employer plans under the Code do not apply to distributions from deemed IRAs. Instead, the rules applicable to distributions from IRAs apply to distributions from deemed IRAs. Also, any restrictions that a trustee, custodian, or insurance company is permitted to impose on distributions from traditional and Roth IRAs may be imposed on distributions from deemed IRAs (for example, early withdrawal penalties on annuities). The required minimum distribution (RMD) rules (see chapter 11) must be met separately with respect to the qualified employer plan and the deemed IRA. The determination of whether a qualified employer plan satisfies the RMD rules is made without regard to whether a participant satisfies the RMD requirements with respect to the deemed IRA that is established under such plan. [Treas. Reg. § 1.408(q)-1(e)]

The trustee or custodian of an IRA must be a bank; or, if the trustee is not a bank, the trustee must have received approval from IRS to serve as a nonbank trustee or nonbank custodian (see Q 30:2). IRS has issued final regulations that provide that a governmental unit may qualify as a nonbank trustee of a deemed IRA that is part of its qualified retirement plan. [Treas. Reg. § 1.408-2(e)(8)]

Deemed IRAs that are individual retirement accounts (see Q 30:2) may be held in separate individual trusts, a single trust separate from a trust maintained by the qualified employer plan, or in a single trust that includes the qualified employer plan. A deemed IRA trust must be created or organized in the United States for the exclusive benefit of the participants. If deemed IRAs are held in a single trust that includes the qualified employer plan, the trustee must maintain a separate account for each deemed IRA. In addition, the written governing instrument creating the trust must satisfy the requirements applicable to IRAs. If deemed IRAs are held in a single trust that includes the qualified employer plan, the prohibition against investment in life insurance contracts is treated as satisfied if no part of the separate accounts of any of the deemed IRAs is invested in such contracts, regardless of whether the separate account for the qualified employer plan invests in such contracts. The rules requiring each Roth IRA to be clearly designated as a Roth IRA will not fail to be satisfied solely because Roth deemed IRAs and traditional deemed IRAs are held in a single trust, provided that the trustee maintains separate accounts for the Roth deemed IRAs and traditional deemed IRAs of each participant, and each of those accounts is clearly designated as such. [Treas. Reg. § 1.408(q)-1(f)(2)]

Deemed IRAs that are individual retirement annuities (see Q 30:3) may be held under a single annuity contract or under separate annuity contracts. However, the contract must be separate from any annuity contract or annuity contracts of the qualified employer plan. In addition, the contract must satisfy the requirements applicable to individual retirement annuities, and there must be separate accounting for the interest of each participant in those cases where the individual retirement annuities are held under a single annuity contract. [Treas. Reg. § 408(q)-1(f)(3)]

The deductibility of voluntary employee contributions to a traditional deemed IRA is determined in the same manner as if they were made to any other traditional IRA. Thus, for example, taxpayers with compensation that exceeds certain limits may not be able to make contributions to deemed IRAs, or the deductibility of such contributions may be limited (see Qs 30:5, 30:6, 30:13–30:18). However, the rules regarding the taxable year in which amounts paid by an employer to an individual retirement plan are includible in the employee's income are not applicable to deemed IRAs (see Q 30:32). [Treas. Reg. § 1.408(q)-1(f)(4)]

The same rules apply to rollovers and transfers to and from deemed IRAs as apply to rollovers and transfers to and from other IRAs. Thus, for example, the plan may provide that an employee may request and receive a distribution of the deemed IRA account balance and may roll it over to an eligible retirement plan, regardless of whether that employee may receive a distribution of any other plan benefits (see chapter 34). [Treas. Reg. § 1.408(q)-1(f)(5)]

The availability of a deemed IRA is not a benefit, right, or feature of the qualified employer plan (see Q 4:19); and, therefore, the employer is not required to offer deemed IRAs to all employees. [Treas. Reg. § 1.408(q)-1(f)(6)]

Neither the assets held in the deemed IRA portion of the qualified employer plan, nor any benefits attributable thereto, are taken into account for purposes of determining the benefits of employees and their beneficiaries under the plan or determining the plan's assets or liabilities. [Treas. Reg. § 1.408(q)-1(f)(7)]

If the qualified employer plan fails to satisfy the qualification requirements applicable to it, either in form or operation, any deemed IRA that is an IRA and that is included as part of the trust of that qualified employer plan does not satisfy the deemed IRA requirements. Accordingly, any account maintained under such a plan as a deemed IRA ceases to be a deemed IRA at the time of the disqualifying event. In addition, the deemed IRA also ceases to satisfy the requirements relating to IRAs and Roth IRAs. Also, if any one of the deemed IRAs fails to satisfy the IRA or Roth IRA requirements and the assets of that deemed IRA are included as part of the trust of the qualified employer plan, the deemed IRA requirements are not satisfied and the plan will fail to satisfy the plan's qualification requirements. [Treas. Reg. § 1.408(q)-1(g)(1)]

If the qualified employer plan fails to satisfy its qualification requirements, either in form or operation, but the assets of a deemed IRA are held in a separate trust (or where a deemed IRA is an individual retirement annuity), then the deemed IRA does not automatically fail to satisfy the applicable requirements relating to IRAs and Roth IRAs. Instead, its status as an IRA will be determined by considering whether the account or the annuity satisfies the IRA or Roth IRA requirements (including, in the case of IRAs, the prohibition against the commingling of assets). Also, if a deemed IRA fails to satisfy the requirements of a qualified IRA and the assets of the deemed IRA are held in a separate trust (or where the deemed IRA is an individual retirement annuity), the qualified employer plan will not fail the qualification requirements applicable to it solely because of the failure of the deemed IRA. [Treas. Reg. § 1.408(q)-1(g)(2)]

Q 30:38   How does a simplified employee pension (SEP) differ from an employer-sponsored IRA?

A SEP allows a company to contribute the lesser of $40,000 (subject to cost-of-living adjustments) or 100 percent of an eligible employee's compensation (see Q 6:45) to an IRA established by the employee. The employer-sponsored IRA limit is the lesser of the dollar amount in effect for the taxable year (double the dollar amount in effect for the taxable year with a spousal IRA) or 100 percent of compensation (see Qs 30:5–30:8, 30:25). SEPs must comply with coverage and nondiscrimination requirements, while an employer-sponsored IRA may discriminate in favor of HCEs (see Qs 3:3, 30:32).

For details on how a SEP and SIMPLE IRA work, see chapter 32 and chapter 33.

Q 30:39 Are there restrictions on IRA distributions?

No. Unlike qualified retirement plans, an individual may withdraw all or any part of an IRA at any time. Also, spousal consent to a withdrawal is not necessary, and there are no limitations as to the form of distribution (see chapter 10).

However, minimum annual distributions must start by April 1 of the year after the year in which the individual reaches age 70½ (see Q 30:42), and a penalty tax is imposed for insufficient distributions (see Q 30:43). [I.R.C. §§ 408(a)(6), 408(b)(3); *see also* I.R.C. § 401(a)(9)]

Also, additional taxes may apply to distributions before an individual reaches age 59½ (see Q 30:41).

Q 30:40 How are distributions from an IRA taxed?

Generally, a recipient of a payment or distribution from an IRA must include the amount received in gross income for the year of receipt. [I.R.C. § 408(d)(1); Cohen, 88 T.C.M. 330 (2004); Hendricks, 82 T.C.M. 893 (2001); Pena, 81 T.C.M. 1534 (2001); Gallagher, 81 T.C.M. 1149 (2001); Copley, 70 T.C.M. 1040 (1995)] One court concluded that an IRA beneficiary received shares of stock from her deceased brother's IRA in the year of transfer, not the year the new stock certificate was issued. As the sole beneficiary of her brother's IRA, which consisted mainly of shares of stock, she requested that the brokerage company transfer the funds in the IRA to her personal account by means of a journal entry. The brokerage company complied, but a new stock certificate was not issued until the following year. Although the beneficiary argued that she had not received the shares of stock until the new certificate was issued, the court held that the shares were received and constituted income to her in the year she exercised control, the year she requested the transfer. [Olson, 88 TCM 185 (2004)]

IRS ruled that amounts paid from a husband's IRA to a trust for the benefit of his former wife pursuant to a court order were taxable to the husband as IRA owner. [Chief Couns. Adv. 200923027] Where an individual mistakenly closed his IRA and received a distribution of the entire balance, the distribution was includible in the individual's income in the year of distribution. [Metcalf v. Comm'r, 02-72889 (9th Cir. 2003)] Amounts withdrawn by an individual from his IRA and then transferred by him to an account or trust with a foreign bank were includible in the individual's income (see Q 30:2). [Keenan, 76 T.C.M. 748 (1998); Chiu, 73 T.C.M. 2679 (1997)] The constructive receipt doctrine applies. A distribution from an IRA in the form of a check was includible in income in the year of receipt even though the IRA owner did not deposit or cash the check until several years later. A cash basis taxpayer is considered to constructively receive income as of the date a check is received unless there are substantial limitations placed on the use of the check. [Millard, 90 T.C.M. 136 (2005)] A prison inmate was taxable on distributions received from his late father's IRAs. His novel argument that he was exempt from taxation because he was prohibited from voting for president of the United States by virtue of his status as a prison inmate was without merit and rejected by the court. [Cutler 94 T.C.M. 498 (2007)]

The naming of a trust as the beneficiary of an individual's IRA does not constitute a distribution from the IRA even though the individual is the creator, trustee, and sole beneficiary of the trust because no amount was actually distributed from the IRA to either the individual or the trust. Amounts embezzled from an IRA by an officer of the IRA trustee and then restored to the IRA by the trustee are not taxable distributions. [Gen. Couns. Mem. 39,858; Priv. Ltr. Ruls. 9253054, 9234016] An individual was a beneficiary of his deceased father's IRA. The individual, who received Medicaid payments due to a disability, sought to avoid income that would negatively affect his eligibility for Medicaid. A trust was created by a court, based on a petition by the individual's guardian. The guardian was trustee, and the individual was the sole beneficiary and owner of the trust. The trust was intended to qualify as a special needs trust, the assets of which would not be considered with respect to the individual's Medicaid eligibility. IRS ruled that the trust was a grantor trust for income tax purposes; and, therefore, the transfer of the individual's beneficial interest in the share of the IRA to the trust was not a sale or disposition of that share for income tax purposes. [Priv. Ltr. Rul. 200620025; *see also* Priv. Ltr. Rul. 200826008]

IRA distributions are taxed as ordinary income. IRA distributions are not eligible for capital gains treatment or the forward averaging method that may apply to lump-sum distributions from qualified retirement plans (see Q 13:14). [I.R.C. § 408(d)(1); Costanza, 50 T.C.M. 280 (1985)] However, IRA distributions made upon an individual's death to a charitable organization or to a charitable remainder trust are not subject to income tax because the charitable beneficiary is exempt from tax (see Q 13:3). [I.R.C. §§ 501(a), 664(c); Priv. Ltr. Ruls. 200234019, 199901023, 9818009, 9723038, 9341008, 9237020] Where a decedent designated his estate as beneficiary of his plan benefits, the decedent's will named a charity as the residual beneficiary of his estate, and the estate assigned the plan benefits to the charity, the estate was not required to include the plan benefits in its gross income. [Priv. Ltr. Ruls. 200845029, 200520004] This is also applicable to IRA benefits. [Priv. Ltr. Ruls. 200850004, 200826028, 200617020; *see also* Doby, No. 17756-03S (Tax Ct. 2006)]

If the IRA is paid out all in one year, the individual pays income tax on the entire amount in one year. If distributions are received as an annuity or over a period of years, tax payments are spread over several years. If the individual has made only deductible IRA contributions, the entire amount of each IRA distribution is fully taxable. If, however, the individual has made nondeductible contributions to any IRA, a portion of all IRA distributions, even distributions made from an IRA to which only deductible contributions have been made, will be considered a tax-free return of the individual's nondeductible contributions (see Qs 30:23, 30:24). For purposes of determining what portion of an IRA distribution is taxable, the following special rules apply:

1. All IRAs, SEPs (see Q 32:1), and SIMPLE IRAs (see Q 33:2) maintained by the individual are aggregated;

2. All distributions during the year are treated as one distribution;

3. The aggregate account balance is determined as of the end of the year and includes distributions made during the year; and

4. The individual's overall nondeductible contributions are determined as of the end of the year.

[I.R.C. § 408(d)(2)]

A distribution from a rollover IRA (see Q 34:2) established by a surviving spouse with a distribution from the deceased spouse's 403(b) plan (see Q 35:1) is fully taxable. The surviving spouse does not receive a basis (see Q 13:3) equal to the fair market value of the amount rolled over. [Priv. Ltr. Rul. 9031046] However, when an individual rolled over the entire distribution to an IRA and was informed the following year by the trustee of the qualified retirement plan that the individual's benefits had been erroneously overvalued, IRS ruled that the amount distributed to the individual to repay the employer would not be includible in the individual's income (see Q 34:41). [Priv. Ltr. Rul. 9118020]

If a distribution from an IRA is premature, the amount distributed is taxed as ordinary income and a penalty tax may be imposed (see Q 30:41). [I.R.C. § 72(t)] A distribution from an IRA is not taxable if there is a valid rollover of the distribution to another IRA, or to the same IRA (see Qs 34:3, 34:4). An individual received a distribution from a qualified retirement plan and rolled over the distribution to an IRA. Even though the rollover was not timely (see Q 34:35), the individual reported the rollover as timely and nontaxable on her income tax return for that year. When a distribution from the IRA was made some years later, the individual claimed that the IRA distribution was nontaxable because the plan distribution should have been taxable originally (the statute of limitations had expired). The court determined that a duty of consistency barred the claim that the IRA distribution was not taxable. [Estate of Ashman v. Comm'r, 2000 WL 1593403 (9th Cir. 2000)] An individual rolled over a distribution from a 401(k) plan (see Q 27:1) to an IRA and erroneously characterized the rollover as a designated nondeductible contribution. The individual received a distribution of his entire IRA some years later and claimed that most of the distribution was nontaxable. The court thought otherwise and concluded that the entire distribution was taxable. [Sternberg v. IRS, 04-1325 (2d Cir. 2005] An individual who received an IRA distribution was taxed on the full amount because his claim that a portion of the distribution was not taxable could not be supported. [Hoang, 91 T.C.M. 899 (2006)] Another individual who received an IRA distribution was taxed on the full amount because he provided no evidence that a rollover was made. [Bhattacharyya, 93 T.C.M. 711 (2007)]

A sale of assets held in an individual's IRA is not a distribution to the individual when the sale proceeds are retained by the IRA custodian. [Priv. Ltr. Rul. 9331055] A taxable distribution was not made to an IRA owner who received a check from the IRA custodian to purchase shares of a closely held corporation, which shares were issued to the IRA. Most important, the check was payable to the corporation and not to the IRA owner, so that the IRA owner was acting as agent for the IRA custodian. [Ancira, 119 T.C. 135 (2002)] The division of a decedent's IRA into four separate IRAs, one for each beneficiary, is not a distribution to the beneficiaries. [Priv. Ltr. Rul. 200008044; *see also* Rev. Rul. 78-406, 78-2 C.B. 157 and Priv. Ltr. Rul. 200945011] Similarly, the assignment of IRAs in satisfaction of beneficiaries' percentage shares of an estate did not cause either the estate or any beneficiary to have taxable income. [Priv. Ltr. Rul. 200234019] The payment of a fee directly from the IRA to a company for services in connection with transferring IRA assets between mutual funds is not a taxable distribution to the IRA owner. [Priv. Ltr. Rul. 8747072]

A disclaimer of IRA benefits by the beneficiary of a deceased IRA owner that satisfies the requirements of state law and the Code (see Q 11:17) is not an assignment of income, does not violate the nonforfeitability requirement (see Q 30:2) or the nontransferability requirement (see Q 30:3), and will be taxable to the actual recipient and not to the disclaiming beneficiary. [Gen. Couns. Mem. 39,858; I.R.C. §§ 408(a)(4), 408(b)(1), 2518(b)] A married couple's agreement to divide the husband's IRA, a community property asset, into separate equal shares that could be disposed of separately by each spouse did not constitute a distribution or transfer of amounts from the IRA for income tax purposes so that no amount was includible in either individual's gross income because the reclassification of community property into separate property did not constitute an actual distribution or payment from the IRA. [I.R.C. § 408(g); Priv. Ltr. Rul. 9439020] However, if the wife then transferred her separate share of her husband's IRA to an IRA in her own name, the wife would receive a taxable distribution. [Priv. Ltr. Rul. 199937055]

A levy by IRS (see Q 30:52) on an individual's IRA to satisfy the individual's tax liabilities is a constructive receipt of income and, therefore, a taxable distribution to the individual. [I.R.C. §§ 72(e)(2), 408(d)(1); Schroeder, 78 T.C.M. 566 (1999); Murillo, 75 T.C.M. 1564 (1998), *acq.*, Action on Decision, 1999-1 C.B. 332; Pilipski, 66 T.C.M. 984 (1993)] The transfer of a debtor's IRA to the debtor's bankruptcy estate is not a taxable distribution; but, when the bankruptcy estate received a distribution from the IRA, the estate, not the debtor, was taxable. [I.R.C. §§ 408(d)(1), 1398(f)(1); Treas. Reg. § 1.408-4(a); *In re* Vogt, 2000 WL 222134 (Bankr. E.D. Va. 2000)] A withdrawal from an IRA that was applied toward the purchase of a residence constituted a taxable distribution to the individual. [Clarke, 68 T.C.M. 398 (1994)]

A wife was not entitled to innocent spouse relief where she had actual knowledge of IRA withdrawals made by her husband and not reported as income on their joint income tax return. [Stringham, No. 22346-03S (Tax Ct. 2006)] An individual was liable for the accuracy-related penalty of 20 percent of the underpayment of the tax due on her IRA distributions because her understatement of the tax was substantial and without reasonable cause. The court found that it was not reasonable for the individual to rely on the statements of friends rather than consulting a professional. Therefore, the court concluded, the individual did not act with reasonable cause and in good faith with respect to any portion of the underpayment of tax and was liable for the accuracy-related penalty. [Snyder, No. 13874-04S (Tax Ct. 2006)]

Eligible taxpayers are allowed to make one-time transfers from an IRA or a Roth IRA (see Q 31:1) to a health savings account (HSA). These distributions are generally excluded from gross income and are not subject to the early distribution penalty tax. The amount contributed to the HSA through a qualified HSA funding distribution is not allowed as a deduction and counts against the taxpayer's maximum annual HSA contribution for the tax year of the distribution. Additionally, testing period rules apply.

See Q 1:28 for a discussion of the Katrina Emergency Tax Relief Act of 2005 and other developments for their effect on the taxation of distributions and other issues.

Q 30:41   Is a penalty imposed on a premature distribution from an IRA?

A distribution from an IRA before the individual for whose benefit the IRA was established reaches age 59½ is subject to a 10 percent penalty tax (i.e., the tax is increased by an amount equal to 10 percent of the amount includible in gross income).

For a complete discussion of the 10 percent penalty tax on early withdrawals and the exceptions that may apply, see chapter 16.

Q 30:42   What is the minimum distribution requirement?

Once distributions from an IRA are required to begin (see Q 30:39), the owner must withdraw a certain amount during each year or be subject to a penalty for insufficient distributions (see Q 30:43). IRS representatives have opined that an IRA owner may roll over funds from an IRA to a qualified retirement plan and delay required minimum distributions (RMDs) until retirement if the IRA owner is a non-5 percent owner of the plan sponsor (see Q 11:5).

IRS issued final regulations detailing the methods for satisfying the minimum distribution requirement. The final regulations indicate that distributions from an IRA are subject to requirements similar to those governing minimum distributions from qualified retirement plans. RMDs for the 2009 distribution calendar year were suspended. For a complete discussion of the minimum distribution requirement, see chapter 11 and, specifically with regard to IRAs, Qs 11:56 through 11:66.

See Q 30:50 for the minimum distribution requirements after the death of the IRA owner.

Q 30:43   What is the penalty imposed for insufficient distributions from an IRA?

An annual nondeductible 50 percent excise tax is imposed on the difference between the minimum required distribution from an IRA (see Q 30:42) and the amount distributed. [I.R.C. § 4974] IRS can waive the excise tax if the shortfall resulted from a reasonable error and the individual is taking steps to correct the situation. [I.R.C. § 4974(d)] IRS representatives have opined that an IRA owner may roll over funds from an IRA to a qualified retirement plan and delay RMDs until retirement if the IRA owner is a non-5 percent owner of the plan sponsor (see Q 11:5). RMDs for the 2009 distribution calendar year have been suspended.

For a complete discussion of minimum required distributions, see chapter 11 and, specifically with regard to the excise tax, Qs 11:67 through 11:71.

Q 30:44   Can an individual make a charitable contribution directly from an IRA?

PPA (see Q 1:33) provides an exclusion from gross income for otherwise taxable IRA distributions from a traditional or a Roth IRA (see Q 31:1) in the case of qualified charitable distributions. This exclusion does not apply to simplified employee pensions (see Q 32:1) or SIMPLE IRAs (see Q 33:2). The exclusion cannot exceed $100,000 per taxpayer per taxable year, and, initially, applied only for taxable years 2006 and 2007. A provision of The Emergency Economic Stabilization Act of 2008 extended this exclusion to taxable years 2008 and 2009. At this time, this exclusion has not been extended to 2010 or a later year. Special rules apply to determining the amount of an IRA distribution that is otherwise taxable. The rules regarding taxation of IRA distributions (see Q 30:40) and the deduction of charitable contributions continue to apply to distributions from an IRA that are not qualified charitable distributions. Qualified charitable distributions are taken into account for purposes of the minimum distribution rules applicable to traditional IRAs (see Q 30:42) to the same extent the distribution would have been taken into account under such rules had the distribution not been directly distributed as a qualified charitable distribution. RMDs for the 2009 distribution calendar year were suspended (see Q 30:42). An IRA does not fail to qualify as an IRA merely because qualified charitable distributions have been made from the IRA.

A qualified charitable distribution is any distribution from an IRA directly by the IRA custodian or trustee to an organization described in Section 170(b)(1)(A) (other than an organization described in Section 509(a)(3) or a donor advised fund (as defined in Section 4966(d)(2)). Distributions are eligible for the exclusion *only* if made on or after the date the IRA owner attains age 70½.

The exclusion applies only if a charitable contribution deduction for the entire distribution otherwise would be allowable, determined without regard to the generally applicable percentage limitations. Thus, for example, if the deductible amount is reduced because of a benefit received in exchange, or if a deduction is not allowable because the donor did not obtain sufficient substantiation, the exclusion is not available with respect to any part of the IRA distribution.

If the IRA owner has any IRA that includes nondeductible contributions (see Q 30:23), a special rule applies in determining the portion of a distribution that is includible in gross income (but for this provision) and thus is eligible for qualified charitable distribution treatment. Under the special rule, the distribution is treated as consisting of income first, up to the aggregate amount that would be includible in gross income (but for this provision) if the aggregate balance of all IRAs having the same owner were distributed during the same year. In determining the amount of subsequent IRA distributions includible in income, proper adjustments will be made to reflect the amount treated as a qualified charitable distribution under the special rule.

Distributions that are excluded from gross income by reason of this provision are not taken into account in determining the deduction for charitable contributions under Section 170.

The following examples illustrate the determination of the portion of an IRA distribution that is a qualified charitable distribution. In each example, it is assumed that the requirements for qualified charitable distribution treatment are otherwise met (e.g., the applicable age requirement and the requirement that contributions are otherwise deductible) and that no IRA distributions occur during the year.

Example 1. Steve has a traditional IRA with a balance of $100,000, consisting solely of deductible contributions and earnings, and he has no other IRA. The entire IRA balance is distributed in a distribution to a qualified charitable organization. Absent this provision, the entire distribution of $100,000 would be includible in Steve's income. Accordingly, under this provision, the entire distribution of $100,000 is a qualified charitable distribution. As a result, no amount is included in Steve's income and the distribution is not taken into account in determining the amount of his charitable deduction for the year.

Example 2. Sallie has a traditional IRA with a balance of $100,000, consisting of $20,0000 of nondeductible contributions and $80,000 of deductible contributions and earnings, and she has no other IRA. In a distribution to a qualified charitable organization, $80,000 is distributed from the IRA. Absent this provision, a portion of the distribution from the IRA would be treated as a nontaxable return of nondeductible contributions. The nontaxable portion of the distribution would be $16,000, determined by multiplying the amount of the distribution ($80,000) by the ratio of the nondeductible contributions to the account balance ($20,000 ÷ $100,000). Accordingly, $64,000 of the distribution ($80,000 minus $16,000) would be includible in income.

However, under this provision, the distribution is treated as consisting of income first, up to the total amount that would be includible in gross income (but for this provision) if all amounts were distributed from all IRAs otherwise taken into account in determining the amount of IRA distributions. The total amount that would be includible in income if all amounts were distributed from the IRA is $80,000. Accordingly, under this provision, the entire $80,000 distributed to the charitable organization is treated as includible in income (before application of this provision) and is a qualified charitable distribution. As a result, no amount is included in Sallie's income and the distribution is not taken into account in determining the amount of her charitable deduction for the year. In addition, for purposes of determining the tax treatment of other distributions from the IRA, $20,000 of the amount remaining in the IRA is treated as Sallie's nondeductible contributions (i.e., not subject to tax upon distribution).

[I.R.C. § 408(d)(8); IRS News Rel. IR-2006-192 (Dec. 14, 2006)]

IRS issued guidance concerning the use of IRAs to make charitable contributions. [IRS Notice 2007-7, § IX, 2007-1 C.B. 395]

The income exclusion for qualified charitable distributions only applies to the extent that the aggregate amount of qualified charitable distributions made during 2006 and/or 2007 with respect to an IRA owner does not exceed $100,000. Thus, if an IRA owner maintains multiple IRAs in a taxable year, and qualified charitable distributions are made from more than one of these IRAs, the maximum total amount that may be excluded for that year by the IRA owner is $100,000. For married individuals filing a joint return, the limit is $100,000 per individual IRA owner. [IRS Notice 2007-7, § IX, Q&A-34, 2007-1 C.B. 395] The income exclusion also applies for taxable years 2008 and 2009.

Qualified charitable distributions may be made to an organization described in Section 170(b)(1)(A), other than supporting organizations or donor-advised funds. [IRS Notice 2007-7, § IX, Q&A-35, 2007-1 C.B. 395]

Generally, the exclusion for qualified charitable distributions is available for distributions from any type of IRA (including a Roth IRA and a deemed IRA (see Q 30:36)) that is neither an ongoing SEP IRA nor an ongoing SIMPLE IRA. For this purpose, a SEP IRA or a SIMPLE IRA is treated as ongoing if it is maintained under an employer arrangement under which an employer contribution is made for the plan year ending with or within the IRA owner's taxable year in which the charitable contributions would be made. [IRS Notice 2007-7, § IX, Q&A-36, 2007-1 C.B. 395]

The exclusion from gross income for qualified charitable distributions is available for distributions from an IRA maintained for the benefit of a beneficiary (i.e., inherited IRA (see Q 30:48)) after the death of the IRA owner *if* the beneficiary has attained age 70½ before the distribution is made. [IRS Notice 2007-7, § IX, Q&A-37, 2007-1 C.B. 395]

The charitable contribution provision is applicable to distributions made at any time in 2006. Thus, a distribution made in 2006 that satisfies all of the requirements is a qualified charitable distribution even if it was made before August 17, 2006. [IRS Notice 2007-7, § IX, Q&A-38, 2007-1 C.B. 395]

For purposes of determining the amount of charitable contributions that may be deducted, qualified charitable distributions that are excluded from income are not taken into account. However, qualified charitable distributions must still satisfy the requirements to be deductible charitable contributions under Section 170 (other than the percentage limits), including the substantiation requirements. [IRS Notice 2007-7, § IX, Q&A-39, 2007-1 C.B. 395]

A qualified charitable distribution is not subject to withholding because an IRA owner that requests such distribution is deemed to have elected out of withholding. For purposes of determining whether a distribution requested by an IRA owner satisfies all of the requirements, the IRA trustee, custodian, or issuer may rely upon reasonable representations made by the IRA owner. [IRS Notice 2007-7, § IX, Q&A-40, 2007-1 C.B. 395]

If a check from an IRA is made payable to an eligible charitable organization and delivered by the IRA owner to the charitable organization, the payment to the charitable organization will be considered a direct payment by the IRA trustee to the charitable organization. [IRS Notice 2007-7, § IX, Q&A-41, 2007-1 C.B. 395]

The amount distributed in a qualified charitable distribution is an amount distributed from the IRA for purposes of the required minimum distribution rules. [IRS Notice 2007-7, § IX, Q&A-42, 2007-1 C.B. 395]

If an amount intended to be a qualified charitable distribution is paid to a charitable organization but fails to satisfy all of the requirements, the amount paid is treated as (1) a distribution from the IRA to the IRA owner that is includible in gross income and (2) a contribution from the IRA owner to the charitable organization that is subject to the charitable deduction rules (including the percentage limits). [IRS Notice 2007-7, § IX, Q&A-43, 2007-1 C.B.395]

DOL, which has interpretive jurisdiction with respect to prohibited transactions (see Q 30:45), has advised IRS that a distribution made by an IRA trustee directly to an eligible charitable organization will be treated as a receipt by the IRA owner and, thus, would not constitute a prohibited transaction. This would be true even if the individual for whose benefit the IRA is maintained had an outstanding pledge to the receiving charitable organization. [IRS Notice 2007-7, § IX, Q&A-44, 2007-1 C.B. 395]

Q 30:45   What happens if an individual engages in a prohibited transaction with regard to the IRA?

A retirement account is not treated as an IRA if an individual engages in a prohibited transaction (see Q 24:1) with respect to the retirement account. The account is treated as having distributed all its assets to the individual on the first day of the taxable year in which the prohibited transaction occurs. [I.R.C. § 408(e)(2); Priv. Ltr. Rul. 9725029] Thus, the individual will include the deemed distribution in income (see Q 30:40) and possibly be subject to the 10 percent penalty tax (see Q 30:41). One court ruled that an individual's loan from his IRA was a prohibited transaction that disqualified the IRA, even though he repaid the loan two months later. [*In re* Hughes, 293 B.R. 528 (Bankr. M.D. Fla. 2003)] Because an individual engaged in a prohibited transaction with his IRA, the IRA was not exempt from claims of creditors (see Q 30:52). In addition, two other IRAs of the individual lost their exempt status because, after the prohibited transaction occurred, funds from the first IRA were rolled over to the other two IRAs (see Q 34:42). [*In re* Willis, __ (Bankr. __.D. Fla. 2009)] IRS ruled that a transaction engaged in by an IRA was subject to a conflict of interest and could constitute a prohibited transaction. [Priv. Ltr. Rul. 200945040]

If an individual uses the IRA or any portion thereof as security for a loan, the portion used is treated as a distribution to the individual. [I.R.C. § 408(e)(4)] If an individual borrows from an IRA, the IRA is treated as having distributed all its assets to the individual (see Qs 30:3, 34:4). However, IRS representatives have opined that an individual may roll over funds from an IRA to a qualified retirement plan (see Q 34:7) and then make a loan from the plan. See chapter 14 for details.

An individual is a disqualified person (see Q 24:4) with respect to the individual's IRA, so the individual's guarantee of a loan to the IRA is a prohibited transaction. [I.R.C. §§ 4975(c)(1), 4975(e)(2); DOL Op. Ltr. 90-23A] DOL advised that the grant by an IRA owner to a brokerage firm of a security interest in his non-IRA accounts in order to cover indebtedness of, or arising from, his IRA would be a prohibited transaction, because it was akin to a guarantee by the IRA owner. [DOL Op. Ltr. 2009-03A] However, a loan from an IRA to a tax-exempt church was not a prohibited transaction. The church was not a disqualified person with respect to the IRA, and the IRA owner had no control, ownership, or financial interest in the church (see Q 30:2). [Priv. Ltr. Rul. 200741016] DOL also opined that a proposed sale and leaseback of a building and land to an IRA by members of the IRA holder's family would be a prohibited transaction. [DOL Op. Ltr. 93-33A] Similarly, according to DOL, the purchase by an IRA of notes of a corporation whose majority owners are members of the IRA owner's family would be a prohibited transaction, where the IRA owner has investment discretion over the IRA (i.e., a self-directed IRA). [DOL Op. Ltr. 2006-09A] According to DOL, a lease transaction between a limited liability company owned in part by an IRA and an S corporation (see Q 28:2) owned in part by one of the IRA owners constitutes a prohibited transaction. [DOL Op. Ltr. 2006-01A] The use of an IRA to purchase a personal residence is a prohibited transaction resulting in a taxable distribution to the IRA holder. [Harris, 67 T.C.M. 1983 (1994)]

According to DOL, allowing an IRA owner to instruct the IRA custodian to purchase an interest in a partnership would not be a prohibited transaction because the transaction would be between the IRA and the partnership, and the partnership would not be a disqualified person. The IRA owner, who was the general partner of an investment club formed by various family members, owned a 6.5 percent interest in the club/partnership, and he desired to have his IRA purchase an interest in the partnership. The investment club's assets were managed by an outside brokerage firm, and the IRA owner received no compensation. Due to his status in the partnership and his control over the investment of his assets, the IRA owner was a disqualified person; however, since he owned only a 6.5 percent interest in the partnership, the partnership itself was not a disqualified person. Therefore, transactions between the IRA and the partnership would not be prohibited. [DOL Op. Ltr. 2000-10A]

An individual established an IRA, and the IRA acquired shares of stock of a corporation formed by the individual and of which he was a director. The payment of dividends by the corporation to the IRA did not constitute a prohibited transaction. [Swanson, 106 T.C. 76 (1996)]

IRS has ruled that the addition of certain policy credits to IRAs pursuant to a conversion of an insurance mutual holding company into a stock company did not appear to constitute a prohibited transaction, but further advised that DOL had the authority to address this issue. [Priv. Ltr. Rul. 200128061] IRS has also ruled that a postnuptial agreement that provided for the division of an individual's IRA between the spouses in the event of their divorce was not a prohibited transaction (see Q 30:51). [Priv. Ltr. Rul. 200215061]

DOL has granted a class exemption permitting purchases and sales by IRAs of American Eagle bullion coins from or to authorized purchasers even if the authorized purchasers are disqualified persons (see Qs 24:3, 24:4). [PTCE 91-55 (56 Fed. Reg. 49,209)] There is a limited exception to the prohibited-transaction rules whereby an IRA may sell shares of bank stock to the IRA owner, but only if such shares were held by the IRA on October 22, 2004. [I.R.C. § 4975(d)(16)]

An excise tax is imposed on entity managers who knowingly approve prohibited tax-shelter transactions. If any entity manager of a tax-exempt entity approves the entity as (or otherwise causes the entity to be) a party to a prohibited tax-shelter transaction at any time during the taxable year, and the entity manager knows, or has reason to know, that the transaction is a prohibited tax-shelter transaction, the entity manager must pay an excise tax for the taxable year. The amount of the tax imposed on an entity manager who approves the entity as a party to a prohibited tax-shelter transaction is $20,000 for each approval (or other act causing participation). The term "tax-exempt entity" includes both an IRA and a Roth IRA (see Q 31:1). In general, a person who decides that the assets of the IRA are to be invested in a prohibited tax-shelter transaction is the entity manager. The excise tax is effective for taxable years ending after May 17, 2006 (with respect to transactions occurring before, on, and after May 17, 2006), except that no excise tax applies to income or proceeds that are properly allocable to any period on or before the date which is 90 days after May 17, 2006. [I.R.C. § 4965 (as added by TIPRA § 516(a)); TIPRA § 516(d)(1)] IRS issued a notice to ensure that IRAs and other tax-exempt entities and other affected parties are aware of the new excise taxes and disclosure rules that target certain potentially abusive tax shelter transactions to which a tax-exempt entity is a party. [IRS Notice 2006-65, 2006-2 C.B. 102] In addition, IRS issued final regulations that became effective on July 6, 2010. See Q 1:31 for details.

Q 30:46   Will the receipt of reduced or no-cost services by a customer who directs the IRA to invest in a bank's financial products constitute a prohibited transaction?

Banks are permitted to provide IRA holders or their family members with institutional services either at reduced costs or at no cost, such as free checking. The services offered must be the same as those offered by the bank in the ordinary course of its business to customers who do not maintain IRAs at the bank. Therefore, a prohibited transaction (see Q 24:1) will not occur when an

IRA holder, who is a fiduciary with respect to the IRA, uses IRA assets to obtain services from the bank. [I.R.C. § 4975(c)(1); PTCE 93-33 (59 Fed. Reg. 22,686, 58 Fed. Reg. 31,053)] Broker-dealers are permitted to do the same. [PTCE 97-11 (64 Fed. Reg. 11,042)]

Banks and other financial institutions can offer cash or other premiums as incentives for opening IRAs or for making additional IRA contributions. The value of the premium on deposits up to $5,000 is limited to $10 and on deposits in excess of $5,000 is limited to $20. Free group-term life insurance can be offered to IRA holders annually if the face amount of the insurance does not exceed the lesser of $5,000 or the value of the account. [PTCE 93-1 (58 Fed. Reg. 3567)]

A bank requested a prohibited-transaction exemption regarding its providing investment advice to IRA holders and its later receipt of advisory and non-advisory fees from third party investment companies to which the IRA assets are directed. DOL first determined that the bank did not require an exemption, and then opined that the bank's receipt of the third-party fees would meet the exemption requirements if the bank reduced the management fees charged to the IRAs by the amount of the third-party fees and if receiving the third-party fees did not cause the bank's compensation to exceed the amount of the management fees agreed to with the IRA holders. [I.R.C. § 4975(d)(2); DOL Op. Ltr. 2005-10A]

See Q 24:26 for additional information.

Investment advisors for IRAs would not be eligible to use the computer model exceptions, only the fee arrangement exception for an eligible investment advice arrangement. See Q 24:9 for details.

Q 30:47 Are amounts remaining in an IRA at death subject to federal estate taxes?

The entire amount in the IRA is included in the decedent's gross estate. [I.R.C. § 2039]; Sherrill v. United States, No. 2:04-CV-509 (N.D. In. 2006) IRS has ruled that the value of a decedent's IRA would not be discounted for federal estate tax purposes to take into account the potential income tax payable by the beneficiaries upon receiving distributions from the IRA. [Priv. Ltr. Rul. 200247001; see also Estate of Kahn, 125 T.C. 227 (2005) and Estate of Smith v. United States, No. 04-20194 (5th Cir. 2004)]

An IRA may constitute qualified terminable interest property (QTIP) for which an estate tax marital deduction may be elected. IRS has allowed a QTIP election where the surviving spouse can compel that all IRA income be paid to a trust that, in turn, pays out all such income received from the IRA, plus all trust income, to the surviving spouse annually during lifetime. IRS also allowed a QTIP election for an IRA that pays the greater of all IRA income or the required minimum distribution (RMD; see chapter 11) to a QTIP trust that then pays an amount equal to the IRA income and all trust income to the surviving spouse. [I.R.C. § 2056(b)(7); Rev. Rul. 2000-2, 2000-1 C.B. 305; Priv. Ltr. Ruls.

199931033, 9830004, 9738010, 9729015, 9704029, 9551015] Where a decedent designated a qualified domestic trust (QDOT) for the benefit of his noncitizen spouse as the beneficiary of his IRA, IRS permitted a QTIP election to be made. [Priv. Ltr. Ruls. 200241012, 9544038] Where a decedent designated his noncitizen spouse as beneficiary of his IRA, the spouse created a QDOT for her own benefit, and the spouse then designated the QDOT as beneficiary of the IRA, IRS ruled that the IRA qualified for the estate tax marital deduction. [Priv. Ltr. Ruls. 199904023, 9623063; *see also* Priv. Ltr. Rul. 9746049]

To qualify for QTIP or QDOT treatment, all IRA income must be paid or available to the surviving spouse. IRS has revised the definition of "income" applicable to trusts to take into account certain state statutory changes to the concepts of income and principal. Amounts allocated between income and principal pursuant to applicable state law would be respected if state law provides for a reasonable apportionment of the trust's total return for the year between the income and remainder beneficiaries, taking into account ordinary income, capital gains, and, in some circumstances, unrealized appreciation. The regulations are intended to permit trustees to implement a total return investment strategy and to follow applicable state laws designed to treat the income and remainder beneficiaries impartially. However, the regulations still retain the existing rule that trust provisions that depart fundamentally from traditional concepts of income and principal will generally be disregarded. With respect to the estate tax marital deduction, the regulations provide that a spouse's interest would satisfy the income standard if the spouse is entitled to income as defined under a state statute that provides for a reasonable apportionment of the trust's total return between the income and remainder beneficiaries and that meets the requirements of the regulations. In addition, a conforming amendment is made providing rules regarding distributions of income from a QDOT. [Treas. Reg. §§ 1.643(b)-1, 20.2056(b)-5, 20.2056A-5(c)(2)]

In a revenue ruling, IRS asked: If a marital trust described in Situations 1, 2, or 3 below is the named beneficiary of a decedent's IRA (or defined contribution plan; see Q 2:2), under what circumstances is the surviving spouse considered to have a qualifying income interest for life in the IRA (or plan) and in the trust for both the IRA and the trust to qualify for QTIP treatment? The facts presented in the ruling are similar to those in Example 1 of Q 11:25.

Situation 1—Authorized Adjustments Between Income and Principal. The trust is governed by the laws of State X. State X has adopted a version of the Uniform Principal and Income Act (UPIA), including a provision similar to Section 104(a) of the UPIA providing that, in certain circumstances, the trustee is authorized to make adjustments between income and principal to fulfill the trustee's duty of impartiality between the income and remainder beneficiaries. More specifically, State X has adopted a provision providing that adjustments between income and principal may be made, as under Section 104(a) of the UPIA, where trust assets are invested under State X's prudent investor standard, the amount to be distributed to a beneficiary is described by reference to the trust's income, and the trust cannot be administered impartially after applying State X's statutory rules regarding the allocation of receipts and disbursements to income and principal. In addition, State X's statute incorporates a provision similar to Section 409(c) of the UPIA providing that, when a payment is made from an IRA to a trust: (1) if no part of the payment is characterized as interest, a dividend, or an equivalent payment, and all or part of the payment is required to be distributed currently to the beneficiary, the trustee must allocate 10 percent of the required payment to income and the balance to principal; and (2) if no part of the payment made is required to be distributed from the trust or if the payment received by the trust is the entire amount to which the trustee is contractually entitled, the trustee must allocate the entire payment to principal. State X's statute further provides that, similar to Section 409(d) of the UPIA, if in order to obtain an estate tax marital deduction for a trust a trustee must allocate more of a payment to income, the trustee is required to allocate to income the additional amount necessary to obtain the marital deduction.

For each calendar year, the trustee determines the total return of the assets held directly in the trust, exclusive of the IRA, and then determines the respective portion of the total return that is to be allocated to principal and to income under State X's version of Section 104(a) of the UPIA in a manner that fulfills the trustee's duty of impartiality between the income and remainder beneficiaries. The amount allocated to income is distributed to the surviving spouse as income beneficiary of the trust, in accordance with the terms of the trust instrument. Similarly, for each calendar year, the trustee determines the total return of the assets held in the IRA and then determines the respective portion of the total return that would be allocated to principal and to income under State X's version of Section 104(a) of the UPIA in a manner that fulfills a fiduciary's duty of impartiality. This allocation is made without regard to, and independent of, the trustee's determination with respect to trust income and principal. If the surviving spouse exercises the withdrawal power, the trustee withdraws from the IRA the amount allocated to income (or the RMD, if greater), and distributes to her the amount allocated to income of the IRA.

Situation 2—Unitrust Income Determination. The trust is governed by the laws of State Y. Under State Y law, if the trust instrument specifically provides or the interested parties consent, the income of the trust means a unitrust amount of 4 percent of the fair market value of the trust assets valued annually. In accordance with procedures prescribed by the State Y statute, all interested parties authorize the trustee to administer the trust and to determine withdrawals from the IRA in accordance with this provision. The trustee determines an amount equal to 4 percent of the fair market value of the IRA assets and an amount equal to 4 percent of the fair market value of the trust's assets, exclusive of the IRA, as of the appropriate valuation date. In accordance with the terms of the trust, the trustee distributes the amount equal to 4 percent of the trust assets, exclusive of the IRA, to the surviving spouse, annually. In addition, if the surviving spouse exercises the withdrawal power, the trustee withdraws from the IRA the greater of the RMD amount or the amount equal to 4 percent of the value of the IRA assets, and distributes to the surviving spouse at least the amount equal to 4 percent of the value of the IRA assets.

Situation 3—"Traditional" Definition of Income. The trust is governed by the laws of State Z. State Z has not enacted the UPIA and, therefore, does not have provisions comparable to Sections 104(a) and 409(c) and (d) of the UPIA. Thus, in determining the amount of IRA income the surviving spouse can compel the trustee to withdraw from the IRA, the trustee applies the law of State Z regarding the allocation of receipts and disbursements to income and principal, with no power to allocate between income and principal. As in Situations 1 and 2, the income of the trust is determined without regard to the IRA, and the income of the IRA is separately determined based on the assets of the IRA.

In Situation 1, under Section 104(a) of the UPIA as enacted by State X, the trustee of the trust allocates the total return of the assets held directly in the trust (i.e., assets other than those held in the IRA) between income and principal in a manner that fulfills the trustee's duty of impartiality between the income and remainder beneficiaries. The trustee makes a similar allocation with respect to the IRA. The allocation of the total return of the IRA and the total return of the trust in this manner constitutes a reasonable apportionment of the total return of the IRA and the trust between the income and remainder beneficiaries. Under the terms of the trust, the income of the IRA so determined is subject to the surviving spouse's withdrawal power, and the income of the trust, so determined, is payable to her annually. Accordingly, the IRA and the trust meet the all-income requirement; and, therefore, the surviving spouse has a qualifying income interest for life in both the IRA and the trust because she has the power to unilaterally access all of the IRA income, and the income of the trust is payable to her annually.

Depending upon the terms of the trust, the impact of State X's version of Sections 409(c) and (d) of the UPIA may have to be considered. State X's version of Section 409(c) of the UPIA provides in effect that an RMD from the IRA will be allocated 10 percent to income and 90 percent to principal. This 10 percent allocation to income, standing alone, does not satisfy the requirements, because the amount of the RMD is not based on the total return of the IRA (and therefore the amount allocated to income does not reflect a reasonable apportionment of the total return between the income and remainder beneficiaries). The 10 percent allocation to income also does not represent the income of the IRA under applicable state law without regard to a power to adjust between principal and income. State X's version of Section 409(d) of the UPIA, requiring an additional allocation to income if necessary to qualify for the marital deduction, may not qualify the arrangement for QTIP treatment because savings clauses may be ineffective to reform an instrument for federal transfer tax purposes. Based on the facts in Situation 1, if the surviving spouse exercises the withdrawal power, the trustee is obligated under the trust's terms to withdraw the greater of all of the income of the IRA or the annual RMD and to distribute at least the income of the IRA to the surviving spouse. Thus, in this case, State X's version of Section 409(c) or (d) of UPIA would only operate to determine the portion of the RMD amount that is allocated to trust income, and (because trust income is determined without regard to the IRA or distributions from the IRA) would not affect the determination of the amount distributable to the surviving spouse. Accordingly, in Situation 1, the all-income requirement is satisfied. However, if the terms of a trust do not require the distribution to the surviving spouse of at least the income of the IRA in the event that she exercises the right to direct the withdrawal from the IRA, then this requirement may not be satisfied unless the trust's terms provide that State X's version of Section 409(c) of the UPIA is not to apply.

In Situation 2, the trustee determines the income of the trust (excluding the IRA) and the income of the IRA under a statutory unitrust regime pursuant to which "income" is defined as a unitrust amount of 4 percent of the fair market value of the assets determined annually. The determination of what constitutes trust income and the income of the IRA in this manner satisfies the requirements. The trust distributes the income, determined in this manner, to the surviving spouse annually, and she has the power to compel the trustee annually to withdraw and distribute to her the income of the IRA, determined in this manner. Accordingly, in Situation 2, because the surviving spouse has the power to unilaterally access all income of the IRA, and the income of the trust is payable to her annually, the IRA and the trust meet the all-income requirement. The result would be the same if State Y had enacted both the statutory unitrust regime and a version of Section 104(a) of the UPIA and the income of the trust is determined under Section 104(a) of the UPIA as enacted by State Y, and the income of the IRA is determined under the statutory unitrust regime (or vice versa). Under these circumstances, trust income and IRA income are each determined under state statutory provisions applicable to the trust that satisfy the requirements; and, therefore, the surviving spouse has a qualifying income interest for life in both the IRA and the trust.

In Situation 3, the surviving spouse has the power to compel the trustee to withdraw the income of the IRA as determined under the law (whether common or statutory) of a jurisdiction that has not enacted Section 104(a) of UPIA. Under the terms of the trust, if the surviving spouse exercises this power, the trustee must withdraw the greater of the RMD amount or the income of the IRA, and at least the income of the IRA must be distributed to her. Accordingly, in Situation 3, the IRA and the trust meet the all-income requirement; and, therefore, the surviving spouse has a qualifying income interest for life in both the IRA and the trust, because she receives the income of the trust (excluding the IRA) at least annually and she has the power to unilaterally access all of the IRA income. The result would be the same if State Z had enacted Section 104(a) of the UPIA, but the trustee decided to make no adjustments pursuant to that provision.

In Situations 1, 2, and 3, the income of the IRA and the income of the trust (excluding the IRA) are determined separately and without taking into account that the IRA distribution is made to the trust. In order to avoid any duplication in determining the total income to be paid to the surviving spouse, the portion of the IRA distribution to the trust that is allocated to trust income is disregarded in determining the amount of trust income that must be distributed to the surviving spouse.

The result in Situations 1, 2, and 3 would be the same if the terms of the trust directed the trustee annually to withdraw all of the income from the IRA and to distribute to the surviving spouse at least the income of the IRA (instead of granting the surviving spouse the power, exercisable annually, to compel the trustee to do so). Furthermore, if, instead of the trust being the named beneficiary of the decedent's interest in the IRA, the trust is the named beneficiary of a decedent's interest in a defined contribution plan, the same principles would apply regarding whether the surviving spouse is considered to have a qualifying income interest for life in the plan.

Therefore, if a marital trust is the named beneficiary of a decedent's IRA (or a defined contribution plan), the surviving spouse, under the circumstances described in Situations 1, 2, and 3 will be considered to have a qualifying income interest for life in the IRA (or plan) and in the trust for purposes of an election to treat both the IRA (or plan) and the trust as QTIP. If the marital deduction is sought, the QTIP election must be made for both the IRA and the trust.

IRS advised that the principles illustrated in Situations 1 and 2 will not be applied adversely to taxpayers for taxable years beginning prior to May 30, 2006, in which the trust was administered pursuant to a state statute granting the trustee a power to adjust between income and principal or authorized a unitrust payment in satisfaction of the income interest of the surviving spouse. [Rev. Rul. 2006-26, 2006-1 C.B. 939; Rev. Rul. 75-440, 1975-2 C.B. 372; Rev. Rul. 65-144, 1965-1 C.B. 422]

IRA distributions made upon an individual's death to a charitable organization are not subject to estate tax because the distributions qualify for the charitable estate tax deduction. [I.R.C. § 2055; Priv. Ltr. Rul. 9723038; *see also* Priv. Ltr. Rul. 200652028] If the IRA distributions are made to a charitable remainder trust, a portion of the distribution (i.e., the value of the charitable remainder interest) will qualify for the charitable estate tax deduction. [Priv. Ltr. Rul. 199901023]

If the IRA benefits are subject to both estate tax and income tax, the beneficiary will be entitled to an income tax deduction for the estate tax attributable to the IRA benefits. [I.R.C. § 691(c); Rev. Rul. 92-47, 1992-1 C.B. 198; Rev. Rul. 69-297, 1969-1 C.B. 131; ILM 200644020; Priv. Ltr. Ruls. 200633009, 200316008, 200247001; Field Serv. Adv. 200011023] Where the IRA owner's estate is the beneficiary, the estate is not allowed an estate tax deduction for the income tax paid by the estate with respect to the IRA distributions. [Priv. Ltr. Rul. 200444021]

Where three individuals were designated as beneficiaries of a decedent's IRA; and, pursuant to a court-approved settlement, the three individuals transferred the inherited IRAs (see Q 30:48) to an inherited IRA of a fourth individual, IRS ruled that the transfers were not taxable gifts. [Priv. Ltr. Rul. 200707158]

Where a participant in a 401(k) plan (see Q 27:1) rolled over a distribution of his plan benefits to an IRA (see Q 34:8), upon his death, the IRA beneficiaries, and not his wife, were entitled to the IRA. The automatic survivor rules (see Q 10:6) do not apply to IRAs. [Charles Schwab & Co. v. Dibickero, 2010 WL 200276 (9th Cir. 2010)]

Q 30:48   What is an inherited IRA?

An IRA becomes an inherited IRA after the death of the IRA owner unless the sole beneficiary is the IRA owner's surviving spouse (see Q 30:49). The nonspouse beneficiary cannot make a tax-deductible contribution to an inherited IRA, and distributions from an inherited IRA do not qualify for rollover treatment. If a trust is named as beneficiary of an IRA, the IRA will be an inherited IRA even if the surviving spouse is the sole trust beneficiary; and, since an inherited IRA cannot be rolled over, distributions from the IRA will be taxable to the beneficiary. However, IRS has ruled in a number of cases that, if the surviving spouse is the sole trust beneficiary, the surviving spouse can do a rollover (see Q 34:6). When an IRA owner designated a trust for the benefit of his surviving spouse as the beneficiary of his IRA, a partial rollover was allowed. The surviving spouse was empowered to withdraw $50,000 each year from the trust and to elect the form of distribution from the IRA to the trust, provided that no less than the RMD amount was distributed to the trust each year. IRS ruled that the surviving spouse could roll over to her own IRA each year the portion of the $50,000 annual withdrawal that exceeded that year's RMD (see Q 34:6). (See Q 30:42 for the applicable minimum distribution requirements.) [I.R.C. §§ 219(d)(4), 408(d)(3)(C); Jankelovits, 96 T.C.M. 460 (2008); Priv. Ltr. Ruls. 9649045, 9416037, 9322005, 9321032; Rev. Rul. 92-47, 1992-1 C.B. 198]

The beneficiary of an inherited IRA can have the IRA funds transferred directly to a new IRA (see Q 34:6) *if* the new IRA is maintained in the name of the decedent. This type of transfer is not a rollover and does not result in a taxable distribution to the beneficiary. [Rev. Rul. 78-406, 78-2 C.B. 157; Priv. Ltr. Ruls. 9810033, 9802046, 9751041, 9737030; *but see* Priv. Ltr. Rul. 200228023] An IRA owner died after commencing to receive RMDs. The IRA owner designated his wife as the sole beneficiary (see Q 11:14) and did not name any contingent beneficiary. The IRA owner's wife died seven days later without (1) disclaiming the IRA (see Q 11:17); (2) taking any distributions from the IRA; (3) electing to treat the IRA as her own (see Q 11:60); or (4) naming any beneficiary. As a result, the right to receive the IRA passed by the deceased wife's will to their two children. The deceased wife's personal representatives proposed to subdivide the IRA into two sub-IRAs, with each sub-IRA being titled "IRA owner (deceased) for the benefit of a specific beneficiary under the will of the wife (deceased)" and to accomplish the subdivision by trustee-to-trustee transfers. IRS ruled that neither the Code nor the RMD regulations precluded the posthumous division of an IRA into more than one IRA, and that the division did not constitute a transfer for purposes of the income in respect of a decedent rules (see Q 30:47), a taxable distribution (see Q 30:40), or a rollover (see Q 34:6). [Priv. Ltr. Rul. 200945011; IRC §§ 408(d)(1), 408(d)(3), 691(a)(2); Rev. Rul. 92-47, 1992-1 C.B. 198]

The beneficiary of an inherited IRA cannot convert the IRA to an inherited Roth IRA (see Q 31:44). [IRC §§ 408(d)(3)(C), 408A(e)(1)(B)(i)] One court ruled that an inherited IRA is not exempt from claims of creditors in a bankruptcy proceeding (see Q 30:52). [*In re* Chilton, No. 08-43414 (Bankr. E.D. Tex. 2010)] However, other courts ruled otherwise and held that a debtor's inherited IRA was exempted from the bankruptcy estate. [*In re* Nessa, 2010 WL 128313 (8th Cir. 2010); *In re* Tabor, 1:09bk-05277 (Bankr. M.D. Pa. 2010)]

The beneficiary of an inherited IRA was able to make charitable cc
directly from the IRA during 2009 (see Q 30:44).

Q 30:49   Do special rules apply if the beneficiary is the IRA own
surviving spouse?

Yes. For details, see Q 11:60.

A surviving spouse who is the beneficiary of a deceased spouse's IRA may
roll the IRA distribution into the surviving spouse's own IRA. [Priv. Ltr. Ruls.
9831032, 9711032, 9534027, 9433031] Such rollover was allowed when the deceased spouse named his estate as beneficiary of his IRA, and his surviving spouse was the sole beneficiary of the estate (see Q 34:6). [I.R.C.
§ 402(c)(9)]

An IRA owner died, his surviving spouse rolled over the IRA distribution to her
own IRA, and the surviving spouse designated beneficiaries to receive her IRA
after her death. After the surviving spouse died, the court ruled that her
beneficiaries were entitled to the IRA proceeds and not the contingent
beneficiaries named by the husband (that is, those who would have received the
original IRA had the wife predeceased the husband). [Bank One, Milwaukee,
N.A. v. Fueger, 1996 Misc. App. LEXIS 358 95-1771 (Wis. Ct. App. 1st Dist. 1996)]

Q 30:50   What minimum distribution requirements apply after the
IRA owner's death?

Generally, the minimum distribution rules applicable to qualified retirement
plans apply to distributions from IRAs. [I.R.C. §§ 408(a)(6), 408(b)(3)] RMDs
for the 2009 distribution calendar year were suspended. For a complete discussion of the minimum distribution rules, see chapter 11 and, specifically with
regard to IRAs, Qs 11:56 through 11:66.

Q 30:51   May an IRA be transferred incident to divorce?

Yes. A transfer of an individual's interest in an IRA to the individual's spouse
or former spouse under a divorce decree or a written instrument incident to the
divorce is not a taxable distribution or transfer (see Q 36:5). After the transfer,
the transferred interest is treated as the IRA of the transferee spouse or former
spouse. [I.R.C. § 408(d)(6); Cohen, 88 T.C.M. 330 (2004); Priv. Ltr. Ruls.
201030038, 200211049, 200050046, 200027060, 9739044, 9006066] IRS has also
ruled that a postnuptial agreement that provided for the division of an individual's IRA between the spouses in the event of their divorce was not a prohibited
transaction (see Q 30:45). [Priv. Ltr. Rul. 200215061]

When an individual and his spouse entered into a private separation agreement providing for a division of the individual's IRA, the transfer to the spouse
was taxable to the individual because the agreement was not incident to a decree
of divorce or legal separation. [Priv. Ltr. Ruls. 9422060, 9344027] The same
result would arise if the transfer to the spouse occurs prior to the execution of a

marital settlement agreement or the entry of a divorce decree. [Field Serv. Adv. 199935055] Furthermore, if funds are withdrawn from an IRA and paid over to the former spouse by the IRA owner to satisfy a divorce decree, the withdrawal will be taxable to the IRA owner. [Jones, 80 T.C.M. 76 (2000); Bunney, 114 T.C. 259 (2000); Czepiel, 78 T.C.M. 378 (1999), aff'd, 00-1257 (1st Cir. 2000); Harris, 62 T.C.M. 406 (1991)] Similarly, an amount transferred from an individual's IRA to his former spouse in a garnishment proceeding for arrearages in child support payments is taxable to the IRA owner. [Vorwald, 73 T.C.M. 1697 (1997)] IRS also ruled that amounts paid from a husband's IRA to a trust for the benefit of his former wife pursuant to a court order were taxable to the husband as IRA owner. [Chief Couns. Adv. 200923027]

If an individual, incident to a divorce, is required to transfer some or all of the assets in an IRA to a spouse or former spouse, there are two methods commonly used to make the transfer:

1. *Changing the Name on the IRA.* If all the assets in an IRA are to be transferred, the individual can make the transfer by changing the name on the IRA from the individual's name to the name of the spouse or former spouse.

2. *Direct Transfer.* The individual directs the trustee (or custodian) of the IRA to transfer the affected assets directly to the trustee of a new or existing IRA set up in the name of the spouse or former spouse; or, if the spouse or former spouse is allowed to keep his or her portion of the IRA assets in the individual's existing IRA, the individual can direct the trustee to transfer the assets permitted to be kept by the individual directly to a new or existing IRA set up in the individual's name. The name on the IRA containing the spouse's or former spouse's portion of the assets would then be changed to show the spouse's ownership.

[IRS Pub. 590]

When a decedent had designated his wife as the beneficiary of his IRA and failed to change the beneficiary after their divorce, the court ruled that the ex-spouse released her interest in the IRA when she executed a divorce settlement agreement stating that any IRAs were the sole and exclusive property of the depositor. [Kruse v. Todd, Nos. S89A0554, S89A0555 (Ga. 1990)] However, another court ruled otherwise. [Walden v. Walden, No. 2950772 (Ala. Civ. App. 1996)] Other courts have also ruled otherwise because the settlement agreement contained only a general waiver provision and did not express a specific intention to surrender any rights as the beneficiary of the IRA or because the marital dissolution decree did not expressly address the ex-spouse's status as beneficiary of the IRA. [East v. Paine Webber, Inc., No. 506 (Md. Ct. Spec. App. 2000); Maccabees Mut. Life Ins. Co v. Morton, No. 90-8618 (11th Cir. 1991); Schultz v. Schultz, No. 17/97-1391 (La. 1999)]

One court determined that a husband's bankruptcy filing did not protect his IRA from his wife's claims during their divorce proceeding, even though the divorce court did not divide the marital property until after the bankruptcy petition had been filed, because the wife had an equitable interest in the IRA that arose before the bankruptcy petition was filed. [Davis v. Cox, 2004 WL 110848 (1st Cir. 2004)]

Q 30:52   Can an IRA be reached by judgment creditors?

The United States Supreme Court has ruled that, under Section 522(d)(10)(E) of the Bankruptcy Code, IRAs are exempt from claims of creditors. [Rousey v. Jacoway, 544 U.S. 1561 (2005); *but see In re* Benson, 2007 WL 915202 (Bankr. Ct. Pa. 2007)]. On April 20, 2005, President Bush signed into law the Bankruptcy Abuse Prevention and Consumer Protection Act of 2005, which contains provisions that will protect the retirement assets of bankruptcy filers. See Q 1:27 for a discussion of the salient provisions of this Act.

Although an IRA may be exempt from claims of creditors, one court ruled that a debtor's inherited IRA (see Q 30:48) is not an exempt asset of the debtor's bankruptcy estate. [*In re* Chilton, No. 08-43414 (Bankr. E.D. Tex. 2010)] However, other courts ruled otherwise and held that a debtor's inherited IRA was exempted from the bankruptcy estate. [*In re* Nessa, 2010 WL 128313 (8th Cir. 2010); *In re* Tabor, 1:09bk-05277 (Bankr. M.D. Pa. 2010)] Another court ruled that, because an individual engaged in a prohibited transaction with his IRA (see Q 30:45), the IRA was not exempt from claims of creditors. In additic two other IRAs of the individual lost their exempt s   ᵃft prohibited transaction occurred, funds from the first IR other two IRAs (see Q 34:42). [*In re* Willis, __ (Bankr.

Since the Act did not become effective until Octobe do not apply to bankruptcy cases that commenced Consequently, the following discussion may apply only before the October 17, 2005, effective date of the $1 million limit may be increased if the interests of justi at this time whether the Act is exclusive or whether continue to be protected by case law.

Prior to the Supreme Court decision and the ena federal courts held that IRAs could be exempted fr estate under Section 522(d)(10)(E) of the Bankruptc WL 2079956 (3d Cir. 2008); *In re* Bramlette, 2005 W 2005); Rousey v. Jacoway, 2003 WL 22382955 (8th 259 B.R. 467 (1st Cir. 2001); *In re* Brucher, 243 F.3 McKown, 203 F.3d 1188 (9th Cir. 2000); *In re* Carmic   J F.3d 375 (5th Ci.. 1996)] Generally, it depended on state law because ERISA does not apply to IRAs. [*In re* Greenfield, 2003 WL 396689 (Bankr. S.D. Cal. 2003); *In re* Bissell, 2000 WL 1733281 (Bankr. E.D. Va. 2000); *In re* Nelson, No. WW-94-1446 (9th Cir. 1995); *In re* Zott, 225 B.R. 160 (Bankr. E.D. Mich. 1998); Johnston v. Mayer, No. 97-1366 (Bankr. E.D. Va. 1998)] Some courts have ruled that an IRA can be reached by all judgment creditors because the money deposited in the IRA is contributed voluntarily, set aside for the depositor's own benefit, and subject to the depositor's control, and the IRA is revocable at will. Additionally, some courts will consider the special needs of the depositor. [*In re* Bashara, 293 B.R.

216 (Bankr. D. Neb. 2003); *In re* Dale, 2002 WL 1869013 (6th Cir. 2002); *In re* Brucher, 243 F.3d 242 (6th Cir. 2001); *In re* Savage, 2000 WL 665739 (Bankr. D. Ark. 2000); *In re* Carmichael, 100 F.3d 375 (5th Cir. 1996); *In re* Brewer, No. 92-25198-BM (Bankr. W.D. Pa. 1993); *In re* Huebner, 986 F.2d 1222 (8th Cir. 1993); Velis v. Kardanis, 949 F.2d 78 (3d Cir. 1991); *In re* Swenson, No. 90A-04222 (Bankr. D. Utah 1991); *In re* Damast, No. 90-1815 (Bankr. D.N.H. 1991); *In re* Ree, No. 89-00723-W (N.D. Okla. 1990); *In re* Lownsberry, No. 89-B-07144-J (D. Colo. 1989); Schoneman v. Schoneman, No. 62-852 (Kan. Ct. App. 1989); *In re* Gillett, 46 B.R. 642 (S.D. Fla. 1985); *In re* Montavon, 52 B.R. 99 (D. Minn. 1985)]

Conversely, other courts have ruled that an IRA (or a portion thereof) is exempt property under state law. [*In re* Davis, 2004 WL 1873999 (3d Cir. 2004); *In re* Howard, 2004 WL 1780996 (Bankr. Ga. 2004); *In re* Tomlin, 315 B.R. 439 (Bankr. Mich. 2004); Rawlinson v. Kendall, 209 B.R. 501 (9th Cir. 1997); *In re* Yuhas, 1997 U.S. App. LEXIS 931 (3d Cir. 1997); *In re* Meehan, 102 F.3d 1209 (11th Cir. 1997); *In re* Barshak, No. 96-1423 (3d Cir. 1997); *In re* Seltzer, 1996 U.S. App. LEXIS 33336 (9th Cir. 1996); *In re* Hyde, 200 B.R. 694 (N.D. Ala. 1996); *In re* Solomon, 1995 U.S. App. LEXIS 29795 (4th Cir. 1995); *In re* Nelson, No. WW-94-1446 (9th Cir. 1995); *In re* Bates, 1994 Bankr. LEXIS 1977 (Bankr. D. Me. 1994); *In re* Walker, No. 90-5171 (10th Cir. 1992); *In re* Templeton, Jr., No. 92 B04870 (Bankr. N.D. Ill. 1992); *In re* Kulp, No. 90-1190 (10th Cir. 1991); Reliance Ins. Co. v. Ziegler, Nos. 90-1628, 90-1799, 90-2068 (7th Cir. 1991); *In re* Volpe, No. 90-8496 (5th Cir. 1991); *In re* Suarez, No. 90-18947 BKC-AJC (Bankr. S.D. Fla. 1991); *In re* Shumaker, 124 B.R. 820 (Bankr. D. Mont. 1991); *In re* Barlage, 121 B.R. 352 (D. Minn. 1990); *In re* Galvin, No. 89-21638-7 (D. Kan. 1990); *In re* Herrscher, No. B-88-07650-PHX-RGM (D. Ariz. 1990); *In re* Ewell, No. 89-1736-8P7 (Bankr. M.D. Fla. 1989); *In re* Maitin, No. 3-88-02890 (Bankr. E.D. Tenn. 1989); *In re* Laxson, 102 B.R. 85 (N.D. Tex. 1989)] One court ruled that a state statute provided only limited bankruptcy exemption for a debtor's IRA, even though a higher court had previously determined that the same state statute exempted a debtor's entire IRA from bankruptcy. [*In re* Mooney, 2000 WL 575951 (Bankr. C.D. Cal. 2000); *In re* McKown, 203 F.3d 1188 (9th Cir. 2000)] One court ruled that an individual's loan from his IRA was a prohibited transaction that disqualified the IRA (see Q 30:45), even though he repaid the loan two months later. The loan repayment did not reinstate or requalify his IRA; and, consequently, the individual was not entitled to a bankruptcy exemption for the former IRA after he filed for bankruptcy. [*In re* Hughes, 293 B.R. 528 (Bankr. M.D. Fla. 2003)]

One court concluded that a SEP (see Q 32:1) of a trustee of a qualified retirement plan against whom judgment was rendered for breach of fiduciary duty was subject to garnishment because IRAs such as SEPs are excepted from ERISA's anti-alienation provision. A participant in the plan obtained a judgment against the plan's trustee for breach of fiduciary duty. The court ordered the trustee's SEP garnished to satisfy the judgment, and the trustee appealed on the grounds that the SEP was exempt from garnishment under ERISA's anti-alienation provision and under state law that protected IRAs from garnishment. The court ruled that ERISA's anti-alienation provision contains a qualification that excepts IRAs such as SEPs and also held that, even if the SEP were exempted from garnishment under state law, the state law related to or had a connection with ERISA plans, in that it exempted all IRAs from garnishment where ERISA specifically would allow garnishment. Therefore, the state exemption statute was preempted by ERISA, and the SEP was subject to garnishment. [Lampkins v. Golden, 2002 U.S. App. LEXIS 900 (6th Cir. 2002)] This case can be distinguished because it did not involve a claim in bankruptcy, and this legal distinction was relevant in another case that held that a state law provision exempting IRAs from a debtor's bankruptcy estate was not preempted by ERISA. [*In re* Mitchell, 2002 WL 31444051 (Bankr. N.D. Ohio 2002)]

If a debtor's IRA is distributed to the bankruptcy estate, the estate, not the debtor, receives a taxable distribution. [*In re* Vogt, 2000 WL 222134 (Bankr. E.D. Va. 2000)] Courts have ruled that an IRA received by a debtor from a former spouse pursuant to a divorce agreement was exempt property under state law. [*In re* Brackett, 259 B.R. 768 (M.D. Fla. 2001); Chapman v. Wells, 557 N.W.2d (N.D. 1996)] However, another court ruled that a debtor in bankruptcy was not entitled to exempt, under a state exemption statute, his interest in his ex-wife's IRA because the statute only protected IRA funds derived from a debtor's employment and, because the source of the IRA funds was his ex-wife's employment, his interest in her IRA was not exempt from bankruptcy. [Anderson v. Seaver, 269 B.R. 27 (8th Cir. 2001)]

One court has held that an IRA, upon the depositor's death, passed directly to the named beneficiary and did not become part of the deceased depositor's estate subject to the claims of creditors. [Estate of Davis, 6 Employee Benefits Cas. (BNA) 2491 (Cal. Ct. App. 1985)] Shortly before a debtor filed a voluntary bankruptcy proceeding, he rolled over an IRA, which was not entirely exempt from attachment by creditors under state law, to a qualified retirement plan, which was entirely exempt (see Q 4:28). The court determined that the rollover was not a fraudulent conveyance *per se* and further ruled that the plan assets were exempt from attachment by creditors. [*In re* Stern, 2003 U.S. App. LEXIS 1828 (9th Cir. 2003); *see also In re* Ferch, 333 B.R. 718 (Bankr. W.D. Tx. 2005)]

Although state law may exempt an IRA from judgment creditors [*e.g.,* Conn. Gen. Stat. § 52-321a; Fla. Stat. Ann. § 222.21; 735 Ill. Comp. Stat. 5/12-1006; Md. Code Ann., Cts. & Jud. Proc. § 11-504(h); Mass. Gen. Laws, ch 235, § 34A; Mich. Comp. Laws § 600.6023; N.J. Stat. Ann. § 25:2-1(b); N.Y. C.P.L.R. § 5205(c)(2); Ohio Rev. Code Ann. § 2329.66(A)(10); 42 Pa. Cons. Stat. § 8124; Tex. Prop. Code Ann. § 42.0021; Wash. Rev. Code § 6.15.020; *In re* Dubroff, 119 F.3d 75 (2d Cir. 1997)], an exemption provided by state law is ineffective against the execution and creation of statutory liens of the United States for federal taxes. [*In re* Piper, 02-12096 (Bankr. D. Mass. 2003); *In re* Jacobs, 147 B.R. 106 (Bankr. W.D. Pa. 1992); Leuschner v. First W. Bank & Trust Co., 261 F.2d 705 (9th Cir. 1958); Knox v. Great W. Life Assurance Co., 212 F.2d 784 (8th Cir. 1954)] Consequently, IRS can levy on an individual's IRA to satisfy the individual's liability for taxes and can also assert a tax lien against an individual's IRA (see Q 30:40). [I.R.C. § 6321; Treas. Reg. § 1.401(a)-13(b)(2); Sillavan v. United States, 2002 U.S. Dist. LEXIS 2127 (N.D. Ala. 2002); Schroeder, 78

T.C.M. 566 (1999); *In re* Saunders, 1999 Bankr LEXIS 947 (Bankr. S.D. Fla. 1999); *In re* Deppisch, 97-35005 (S.D. Ohio 1998); *In re* Aylward, 208 B.R. 565 (Bankr. M.D. Fla. 1997); *In re* Deming, 92-17755F (Bankr. E.D. Pa. 1994); *In re* Schreiber, 1994 Bankr. LEXIS 49 (N.D. Ill. 1994); Pilipski, 66 T.C.M. 984 (1993); *see also* United States v. Grico, 99-202-01 (E.D. Pa. 2003); *but see* Leissner, T.C.M. 2003-191] IRS also concluded that only the IRA custodian must be served with a notice of levy on an IRA. [Chief Couns. Advice 201036016] One court ruled that an IRA custodian was not liable to the IRA owner when it liquidated mutual fund shares held in the IRA and delivered the cash to IRS in response to an IRS levy. [Kane v. Capital Guardian Trust Co., No. 97-3030 (10th Cir. 1998)] Another court concluded that a convicted racketeer's individual retirement annuity (see Q 30:3) was not immune from seizure by the government in a criminal proceeding. [United States v. Infelise, 159 F.3d 300 (7th Cir. 1998); *see also* United States v. Vondette, 352 F.3d 772 (2d Cir. 2003); United States v. Norton, 2002 U.S. Dist. LEXIS 17052 (W.D. Va. 2002)] Where a plan participant transferred his benefits to an IRA without spousal consent (see Q 10:21), the court stated that IRS could levy against the entire IRA even though the participant's wife had not consented to the transfer. [Kopec v. Kopec, 1999 WL 96144 (E.D.N.Y. 1999)] Another court ruled that an IRA owner could be required to withdraw funds from his IRA to satisfy an order of restitution. [United States v. Kalani, No. S3 98 CR 1238-06 (S.D.N.Y. 2003); *see also* United States v. Weiss, 2003 WL 22138504 (2d Cir. 2003)]

IRS concluded that a federal tax lien did not attach to the proceeds of a decedent's IRA because no assessment or lien arose prior to death, the IRA passed directly to the beneficiary of the IRA and not to the decedent's estate, and all of the decedent's rights in the IRA became extinguished at his death. [Priv. Ltr. Rul. 199937002]

See Q 34:42 for a discussion of rollover IRAs.

Q 30:53   What are the IRA reporting requirements?

The reporting requirements by IRA trustees apply to contributions to and distributions from IRAs, even if the IRA is revoked. Thus, Form 5498, IRA Contribution Information, must be filed to report a contribution to an IRA even if the IRA is later revoked. An exception is made for amounts transferred from one IRA to another IRA. In this case, the transferor IRA trustee will generally have reported an IRA contribution on Form 5498 when the IRA was established (and when additional contributions were made). Therefore, the transferee IRA trustee should not file a Form 5498 upon the establishment of the transferred IRA.

In addition, Form 1099-R, Distribution From Pensions, Annuities, Retirement or Profit-Sharing Plans, IRAs, Insurance Contracts, etc., must be filed for all distributions, even those made on account of revocation. Distributions should be reported as taxable in the year distributed. [Ann. 2000-86, 2000-2 C.B. 456]

Form 5498 is used both to report any contributions made to an IRA and to report the fair market value of any IRA balance as of December 31 of the tax year. In addition, the IRA trustee is required to report the fair market value of the

IRA as of December 31 to the IRA owner by the following January 31. Generally, if the fair market value of the IRA is zero on December 31, no reporting of the fair market value is required. However, the IRA trustee still may be required to file a Form 5498 to report any contribution made for the year.

If both an IRA contribution and revocation of the IRA occur in the same calendar year, the contribution must be reported. The fair market value on December 31 need not be reported because the account balance is zero on that day. However, if the IRA is revoked in the year after it is established, both the contribution and the fair market value must be reported. [Rev. Proc. 91-70, 1991-2 C.B. 899; I.R.C. §§ 408(i), 6047(d)]

IRA trustees must identify to IRS on Form 5498 each IRA for which a minimum distribution is required to be made to an IRA owner. The IRA trustee does not need to report the amount of the RMD to the IRS; however, the IRA trustee must provide additional information regarding the IRA to the IRA owner required to receive an RMD. The IRA trustee either must report the amount of the RMD for the IRA to the IRA owner or must advise the IRA owner that a minimum distribution with respect to the IRA is required for the year, offer to calculate the amount of the RMD for the IRA owner upon request, and then, if requested, calculate the amount and provide it to the IRA owner. Reporting is only required with respect to IRA owners, and no reporting is required with respect to beneficiaries at this time. [Treas. Reg. § 1.408-8, Q&A-10; IRS Notice 2002-27, 2002-1 C.B. 814] IRS has announced that IRA trustees can satisfy the minimum distribution reporting requirements with regard to IRA owners by using one or both of the two alternatives and has clarified that an IRA trustee may use both alternatives, so that one may be used for some IRA owners and the other alternative for other IRA owners. [IRS Notice 2003-3, 2003-1 C.B. 258]

IRA trustees may furnish the required Form 1099-R and Form 5498 electronically to recipients if the trustee satisfies the consent, format, posting, and notification requirements. [IRS Notice 2004-10, 2004-1 C.B. 433]

IRS issued guidance to financial institutions on the reporting rules applicable to the suspension of RMDs for 2009 (see Q 30:42). IRS advised issuers of the 2008 Form 5498 not to put a check in box 11 indicating whether the taxpayer must take an RMD. However, if a financial institution issued a Form 5498 with box 11 checked, IRS did not consider the form incorrectly issued as long as the IRA owner was notified by the financial institution no later than March 31, 2009 that no RMD was required for 2009. In addition, the RMD information required under IRS Notice 2002-27 did not have to be sent to IRA owners for 2009. [IRS Notice 2009-9, 2009-51 C.B. 419]

Chapter 31

Roth IRAs

Although contributions to a Roth IRA are not deductible, distributions may be income tax free. Contributions to a Roth IRA may be made after an individual attains age 70½, and the minimum distribution rules do not apply during the individual's lifetime. An individual may also be eligible to roll over all or part of an IRA to a Roth IRA or convert an IRA into a Roth IRA. In addition, EGTRRA 2001 increased the Roth IRA contribution limits and provided a credit for Roth IRA contributions made by eligible individuals. Explained in this chapter are all of the rules and requirements applicable to Roth IRAs.

Q 31:1   What is a Roth IRA?

A Roth IRA is an individual retirement plan that is designated at the time of establishment as a Roth IRA. Except as otherwise provided in this chapter, a Roth IRA is treated in the same manner as an IRA. [I.R.C. §§ 408A(a), 408A(b); Treas. Reg. § 1.408A-1, Q&A-1] The term "traditional IRA" means an IRA or a SEP IRA (see Q 32:1), but does not include a SIMPLE IRA (see Q 33:2) or a Roth IRA. [Treas. Reg. § 1.408A-8, Q&A-1] In this chapter, the term "regular IRA" means deductible and designated nondeductible IRAs. Where a Roth IRA should be treated in the same manner as an IRA, cross-references are made to questions in chapter 30.

There are several significant differences between traditional IRAs and Roth IRAs under the Code. For example, eligibility to contribute to a Roth IRA is subject to special modified adjusted gross income (AGI) limits (see Q 31:16); contributions to a Roth IRA are never deductible (see Q 31:14); qualified distributions from a Roth IRA are not includible in gross income (see Q 31:27); the required minimum distribution (RMD) rules do not apply to a Roth IRA during the lifetime of the owner (see Q 31:36); and contributions to a Roth IRA can be made after the owner has attained age 70½ (see Q 31:3). [Treas. Reg. § 1.408A-1, Q&A-2]

A Roth IRA is a trust (or custodial account) established in the United States (see Q 30:2) for the exclusive benefit of an individual or the individual's beneficiaries. The trust instrument must provide that:

1. Except in the case of rollover contributions (see Q 31:39), all contributions must be in cash (see Q 31:12) and annual contributions to the Roth IRA may not exceed the dollar amount in effect for the taxable year (see Q 31:4);

2. The trustee must be either a bank or a person who demonstrates an ability to properly administer the trust (see Q 30:2);

3. No portion of the trust's assets may be invested in life insurance contracts (see Q 30:2);

4. The individual's interest must be nonforfeitable;

5. The trust assets must not be commingled with other property, except in a common trust or investment fund (see Q 30:11); and

6. Certain distribution requirements apply (see Q 31:37).

[I.R.C. §§ 408(a), 408A(a)]

The document establishing the Roth IRA must clearly designate the IRA as a Roth IRA, and this designation generally cannot be changed at a later date. Thus, an IRA that is designated as a Roth IRA generally cannot later be treated as a traditional IRA (see Q 31:47). [Treas. Reg. § 1.408A-2, Q&A-2]

Generally, earnings on all amounts contributed to a Roth IRA accumulate on a tax-free basis (see Q 31:13). [I.R.C. §§ 408(e)(1), 408A(a)] Because a Roth IRA is generally treated in the same manner as an IRA, certain investments should not be made with Roth IRA assets (see Q 30:2). A Roth IRA cannot be a shareholder of an S corporation (see Q 28:2). [Taproot Administrative Services, Inc., 133 T.C. No. 9 (2009); Rev. Rul. 92-73, 1992-2 C.B. 224; Treas. Reg. § 1.1361-1(h)(1)(vii)]

IRS has issued two model forms for use by financial institutions to offer Roth IRAs to their customers: Form 5305-R, Roth Individual Retirement Trust Account, and Form 5305-RA, Roth Individual Retirement Custodial Account. [IRS Notice 98-49, Q&A-1, 1998-2 C.B. 365] Contributions to a Roth IRA must be maintained as a separate trust or custodial account from contributions to an IRA (see Q 30:2) or to a designated nondeductible IRA (see Q 30:20). Separate accounting within a single trust or custodial account is not permitted. [Ann. 97-122, 1997-50 I.R.B. 63]

Trusts that are parts of Roth IRAs may pool their assets in a group trust without affecting the exempt status of the separate trusts (see Q 30:2). [Rev. Rul. 2004-67, 2004-2 C.B. 28; Rev. Rul. 81-100, 1981-1 C.B. 326]

A SEP IRA or a SIMPLE IRA may not be designated as a Roth IRA (see Q 31:46). [I.R.C. § 408A(f)]

Q 31:2 Can a Roth IRA be in the form of an individual retirement annuity?

Yes. An individual retirement annuity (see Q 30:3) is an annuity contract issued by an insurance company. The contract must be nontransferable and nonforfeitable, premiums may not be fixed or exceed the dollar amount in effect for the taxable year (see Q 31:4), and distributions must satisfy certain distribution requirements. [I.R.C. §§ 408(b), 408A(b); Treas. Reg. § 1.408-3(b)] For further details, see Q 30:3.

Contributions to a Roth individual retirement annuity must be maintained as a separate annuity contract from an individual retirement annuity, and separate accounting within a single annuity contract is not permitted. [Ann. 97-122, 1997-50 I.R.B. 63]

IRS has issued a Roth IRA form, Form 5305-RB, Roth Individual Retirement Annuity Endorsement, that is a model annuity endorsement agreement. A Roth individual retirement annuity is established after the annuity contract, which includes Form 5305-RB, is executed by the individual and the insurance company. [IRS Notice 98-49, Q&A-1, 1998-2 C.B. 365; Ann. 98-58, 1998-2 C.B. 58]

Q 31:3   Who is eligible to set up a Roth IRA?

Only an individual can establish a Roth IRA. Unlike an IRA (see Q 30:4), contributions to a Roth IRA may be made even *after* the individual for whom the account is maintained has attained age 70½. [I.R.C. § 408A(c)(4); Treas. Reg. § 1.408A-2, Q&A-1] A parent or guardian of a minor child may establish a Roth IRA on behalf of the minor child, and a Roth IRA may be established on behalf of an individual who lacks the legal capacity to do so. [Preamble to final regulations]

An employer or an association of employees can establish a trust to hold contributions of employees or members made under a Roth IRA. Each employee's or member's account in the trust is treated as a separate Roth IRA that is subject to the generally applicable Roth IRA rules. The employer or association of employees may do certain acts otherwise required by an individual, for example, establishing and designating a trust as a Roth IRA. [I.R.C. § 408(c); Treas. Reg. § 1.408A-2, Q&A-3]

If the surviving spouse of a Roth IRA owner treats a Roth IRA as the surviving spouse's own (see Q 31:41) as of a date, the Roth IRA is treated from that date forward as though it were established for the benefit of the surviving spouse and not the original Roth IRA owner. Thus, for example, the surviving spouse is treated as the Roth IRA owner for purposes of applying the minimum distribution requirements (see Qs 31:26, 31:37). Similarly, the surviving spouse is treated as the Roth IRA owner rather than a beneficiary for purposes of determining the amount of any distribution from the Roth IRA that is includible in gross income (see Q 31:27) and whether the distribution is subject to the 10 percent penalty tax on early distributions (see Q 31:32). [Treas. Reg. § 1.408A-2, Q&A-4]

In addition to accepting annual contributions, a Roth IRA may be used to hold amounts rolled over, transferred, or considered transferred from a non-Roth IRA (see Q 31:39). [I.R.C. § 408A(d)(3)(as amended by WRERA 2008 § 108(d)(2)); Treas. Reg. § 1.408A-3, Q&A-1; Instructions to Forms 5305-R and 5305-RA]

See Q 31:16 for a discussion of restrictions on who can make Roth IRA contributions and Q 31:44 for a discussion of restrictions on who can roll over or convert an IRA into a Roth IRA.

For a discussion of deemed Roth IRAs, see Q 31:24.

Q 31:4   How much may be contributed to a Roth IRA?

An individual may contribute to a Roth IRA 100 percent of compensation up to a maximum dollar amount, provided that the individual's modified AGI (see Q 31:16) does not exceed a threshold amount. The contribution limit can be doubled if a spousal Roth IRA (see Q 31:18) is also established. However, there is no dollar limit with respect to a rollover contribution (see Q 31:39). [I.R.C. §§ 408A(c)(2), 408A(c)(6)(B); Treas. Reg. § 1.408A-3, Q&A-3] In this chapter, "AGI" means modified adjusted gross income.

The contribution limits on Roth IRAs and regular IRAs are coordinated so that the maximum total annual contributions that can be made by an individual to all of these IRAs is the dollar amount in effect for the taxable year or, if less, the amount of the individual's compensation. If an individual makes contributions to both a regular IRA and a Roth IRA, the maximum limit for the Roth IRA is the lesser of (1) the dollar amount in effect for the taxable year or, if less, the compensation amount, reduced by the regular IRA contribution, and (2) the maximum allowable Roth IRA contribution amount if AGI exceeds the threshold amount. Employer contributions, including elective deferrals, made under a SEP (see Q 32:1) or SIMPLE IRA plan (see Q 33:2) on behalf of the individual (including a self-employed individual; see Q 6:60) do *not* reduce the amount of the individual's maximum Roth IRA contribution. [I.R.C. §§ 408(A)(c)(2), 408A(f); Treas. Reg. § 1.408A-3, Q&A-3]

> **Example.** Stephanie is eligible to contribute $5,000 in 2010 to both a deductible IRA and a Roth IRA. If Stephanie contributes $5,000 to her deductible IRA, she cannot make a contribution to a Roth IRA; if Stephanie contributes less than $5,000 to her deductible IRA, she can contribute the difference to a Roth IRA; and, if Stephanie forgoes making any contribution to her deductible IRA, she can contribute $5,000 to a Roth IRA.

In most cases, it appears that, on an after-income tax basis, it will be wiser to forgo making a deductible IRA contribution and to make a Roth IRA contribution (see Q 31:27).

A Roth IRA is generally treated in the same manner as an IRA, and IRS has provided a safe harbor definition of compensation for the purpose of determining eligibility to make an IRA contribution. [I.R.C. §§ 219(f)(1), 408A(a); Treas. Reg. § 1.408A-3, Q&A-4; Rev. Proc. 91-18, 1991-1 C.B. 522] Differential wage payments are also included in compensation for purposes of the annual limitations on contributions to Roth IRAs. For a discussion of the safe harbor definition and what does or does not constitute compensation, see Q 30:5.

An estate cannot make an IRA contribution on behalf of the decedent or to the spousal IRA of the decedent's spouse for the year in which the decedent died. [Priv. Ltr. Rul. 8439066]

IRS provided guidance aimed at shutting down abuses involving indirect contributions to Roth IRAs. IRS provides that these abuses satisfy the listkeeping and registration requirements for tax shelter arrangements that are listed transactions (see Q 28:5). The guidance addresses situations in which value is shifted into an individual's Roth IRA through transactions involving entities owned by the individual. The guidance applies to any arrangement that has the effect of transferring value to the Roth IRA corporation comparable to a contribution to the Roth IRA. [IRS Notice 2004-8, 2004-1 C.B. 333; Chief Couns. Adv. 200917030; *but see* Chief Couns. Adv. 200929005] However, IRS concluded that the penalty for failing to make the required disclosure of a Roth IRA listed transaction should not be treated as a joint and several liability of the husband and wife who filed a joint return. Consequently, if only one spouse engaged in a listed transaction, it would be reasonable to assess the penalty only against the participating spouse. [I.R.C. § 6707A; Chief Couns. Adv. 200938022]

See Q 31:8 for a discussion of excess contributions and Q 31:16 for a discussion of restrictions on who can make Roth IRA contributions.

The maximum dollar amount applicable to Roth IRA contributions is as follows:

For taxable years beginning in	The maximum amount is
2008 and thereafter	$5,000
2005 through 2007	4,000
2002 through 2004	3,000

[I.R.C. §§ 219(b)(1)(A)]

For a discussion of catch-up contributions, see Q 31:5; for a discussion of indexing for inflation, see Q 31:6; and, for a discussion of a tax credit for Roth IRA contributions, see Q 31:7.

Although not specifically set forth, it appears that the special rules discussed in the last two paragraphs of Q 30:5 apply to Roth IRAs.

Q 31:5 What are catch-up Roth IRA contributions?

An individual who has attained age 50 by the close of the taxable year may make the following additional catch-up Roth IRA contributions:

For taxable years beginning in	The maximum catch-up amount is
2006 and thereafter	$1,000
2002 through 2005	500

[I.R.C. § 219(b)(5)(B)]

The following table shows the maximum dollar contribution limits, including the catch-up amount for an individual age 50 or over:

For taxable years beginning in	The maximum amount is
2008 and thereafter	$6,000
2006 and 2007	5,000
2005	4,500
2002 through 2004	3,500

Example 1. During 2008, Ben attained age 52. Ben was unmarried and earned $55,000 in 2008. Ben could have contributed up to $6,000 to his Roth IRA.

If the special rule discussed in the last paragraph of Q 30:5 applied to Roth IRAs, then individuals who made permissible additional contributions in 2007, 2008, or 2009 were not eligible to make catch-up contributions in the same year.

See Q 31:6 for a discussion of indexing for inflation.

Q 31:6   Is the Roth IRA contribution limit indexed for inflation?

The maximum contribution limit to deductible IRAs and the maximum contribution limit to Roth IRAs are subject to cost-of-living increases for taxable years beginning on or after January 1, 2009. [I.R.C. § 219(b)(5)(C)]

For taxable years beginning after 2008, the $5,000 maximum Roth IRA contribution amount (see Q 31:4) will be subject to cost-of-living adjustments; however, an adjustment will be made only if it is $500 or greater and then will be made in multiples of $500 (i.e., rounded down to the next lowest multiple of $500). For example, an increase in the cost-of-living of $499 will result in no adjustment, and an increase of $999 will create an upward adjustment of $500. Therefore, the cost-of-living must increase by 10 percent before the first adjustment to the $5,000 limit will occur (10% × $5,000 = $500). For the taxable year beginning in 2010, the $5,000 amount is unchanged.

The catch-up IRA contribution amount (see Q 31:5) is *not* subject to cost-of-living adjustments.

Q 31:7   Is there a tax credit for Roth IRA contributions?

An eligible individual will be allowed a nonrefundable tax credit for the taxable year in an amount equal to the applicable percentage of the individual's qualified retirement savings contributions for the year up to $2,000.

See chapter 17 for details.

Q 31:8   Is a penalty imposed on an excess contribution to a Roth IRA?

If an individual contributes more to a Roth IRA than the amount allowable, the excess contribution is subject to a 6 percent excise tax. Further, the penalty will be charged each year the excess contribution remains in the Roth IRA. [I.R.C. §§ 4973(a), 4973(f); Treas. Reg. § 1.408A-3, Q&A-7; Spec. Couns. Adv. 200148051]

The individual can avoid the penalty by withdrawing the excess contribution, along with the net income allocable to the excess, before the due date (including extensions) of the individual's federal income tax return for the year of the excess contribution. The net income on the excess contribution is treated as gross income for the taxable year in which the excess contribution was made. [I.R.C. §§ 408(d)(4), 4973(f); Treas. Reg. § 1.408A-3, Q&A-7]

If the individual does not withdraw the excess contribution before such filing deadline, the 6 percent excise tax must be paid for the year of the excess contribution. To avoid the 6 percent excise tax for the following year, the remaining excess contribution can be eliminated by either withdrawing such amount or making a contribution for such year equal to the maximum allowable amount reduced by the remaining excess contribution. [I.R.C. § 4973(f)]

Although the excess contribution penalties apply separately to an individual's Roth IRAs and regular IRAs, for purposes of determining the amount of the excess contribution, a contribution to a regular IRA is aggregated with the contribution to the Roth IRA. Aggregate excess contributions that are not distributed from a Roth IRA on or before the federal income tax return due date (with extensions) for the year of the contributions are reduced and treated as a deemed Roth IRA contribution for each subsequent taxable year to the extent that the Roth IRA owner does not actually make regular IRA and Roth IRA contributions for such years. [I.R.C. §§ 4973(a), 4973(b), 4973(f); Treas. Reg. § 1.408A-3, Q&A-7]

> **Example 1.** For 2010, Caroline, age 40, contributes $5,500 to a Roth IRA. An excess contribution of $500 has been made ($5,500 − $5,000).

> **Example 2.** For 2010, Caroline, age 40, contributes $4,500 to a deductible IRA and $1,000 to a Roth IRA. An excess contribution of $500 has been made ($4,500 + $1,000 − $5,000). Caroline can avoid the penalty by withdrawing $500, along with the net income allocable to the excess, from either IRA or a portion from one IRA and the balance from the other IRA by the due date (including extensions) of her 2010 federal income tax return. If Caroline does not make the withdrawal, the $500 excess contribution would be an excess contribution to her Roth IRA because an individual's contributions are applied first to a regular IRA, then to a Roth IRA.

For a discussion of how to calculate the net income allocable to an excess contribution, see Q 30:9; and for a discussion of recharacterized contributions, see Q 31:9.

Q 31:9   What are recharacterized contributions?

An IRA owner can recharacterize certain contributions (i.e., treat a contribution made to one type of IRA as made to a different type of IRA) for a taxable year. If an individual makes a contribution to an IRA (the first IRA) for a taxable year and then transfers the contribution (or a portion of the contribution) in a trustee-to-trustee transfer from the trustee of the first IRA to the trustee of another IRA (the second IRA), the individual can elect to treat the contribution as having been made to the second IRA, instead of to the first IRA. A transfer between the first IRA and the second IRA will not fail to be a trustee-to-trustee transfer merely because both IRAs are maintained by the same trustee. Redesignating the first IRA as the second IRA will be treated as a transfer of the entire account balance from the first IRA to the second IRA.

This recharacterization election can be made only if the trustee-to-trustee transfer from the first IRA to the second IRA is made on or before the due date (including extensions) for filing the individual's federal income tax return for the taxable year for which the contribution was made to the first IRA. In many cases, IRS has granted an extension of time for an individual to elect to recharacterize a Roth IRA as a traditional IRA. [Priv. Ltr. Ruls. 201026041, 201022026, 201016095, 201004037, 200950059, 200948065, 200938040, 200928044, 200924062, 200921036, 200919064, 200909073, 200906059, 200840055, 200839039, 200826040; *but see* Spec. Couns. Adv. 200148051] In another ruling, IRS granted an extension for recharacterization and also granted the individual an extension of time to take required minimum distributions (RMDs) from the recharacterized IRA (see Q 31:26). [Priv. Ltr. Rul. 200213030] IRS has granted these extensions where the conversion of the traditional IRA to a Roth IRA was invalid, primarily because the IRA owner's AGI exceeded $100,000 (see Q 31:44). However, IRS has the authority to grant an extension of time for a recharacterization even though the conversion was valid if:

1. The individual acted reasonably and in good faith, and
2. Granting relief will not prejudice the interests of the government.

[Treas. Reg. §§ 301.9100-1, 301.9100-3]

A conversion that is accomplished through a rollover of a distribution from a traditional IRA in a taxable year that, 60 days after the distribution (see Q 34:35), is contributed to a Roth IRA in the next taxable year is treated as a contribution for the earlier taxable year. IRS has added the deadline for a recharacterization to the list of tax-related deadlines that may be postponed by reason of a Presidentially declared disaster. IRS is allowed to disregard a period of up to one year in determining whether a recharacterization was made within the time prescribed.

[I.R.C. §§ 408A(d)(6), 408A(d)(7), 7508A(b); Treas. Reg. §§ 1.408A-5, Q&A-1, 301.7508A-1; IRS Notice 2002-27, 2002-1 C.B. 489; IRS Notice 2001-68, 2001-2 C.B. 504; IRS Notice 2001-61, 2001-2 C.B. 305; Ann. 99-104, 1999-2 C.B. 555; Ann. 99-57, 1999-1 C.B. 1256]

The net income attributable to the amount of a contribution that is being recharacterized must be transferred to the second IRA along with the contribution. If the amount of the contribution being recharacterized was contributed to a separate IRA and no distributions or additional contributions have been made from or to that IRA at any time, then the contribution is recharacterized by the trustee of the first IRA transferring the entire account balance of the first IRA to the trustee of the second IRA. In this case, the net income (or loss) attributable to the contribution being recharacterized is the difference between the amount of the original contribution and the amount transferred. [Treas. Reg. §§ 1.408-4(c)(2)(ii), 1.408A-5, Q&A-2]

The contribution that is being recharacterized as a contribution to the second IRA is treated as having been originally contributed to the second IRA on the same date and (in the case of a regular contribution) for the same taxable year that the contribution was made to the first IRA. Thus, for example, no deduction would be allowed for a contribution to the first IRA, and any net income transferred with the recharacterized contribution is treated as earned in the second IRA, and not the first IRA. [Treas. Reg. § 1.408A-5, Q&A-3]

If an amount is contributed to the first IRA in a tax-free transfer, the amount cannot be recharacterized as a contribution to the second IRA. However, if an amount is initially contributed to an IRA for a taxable year, then is moved (with net income attributable to the contribution) in a tax-free transfer to another IRA (the first IRA), the tax-free transfer can be disregarded, so that the initial contribution that is transferred from the first IRA to the second IRA is treated as a recharacterization of that initial contribution. Thus, if a contribution to an IRA for a year is followed by one or more tax-free transfers between IRAs prior to the recharacterization, then the contribution is treated as if it remained in the initial IRA. Consequently, an individual may elect to recharacterize an initial contribution made to the initial IRA that was involved in a series of tax-free transfers by making a trustee-to-trustee transfer from the last IRA in the series to the second IRA. In this case, the contribution to the second IRA is treated as made on the same date (and for the same taxable year) as the date the contribution being recharacterized was made to the initial IRA. [Treas. Reg. § 1.408A-5, Q&A-4, Q&A-7]

If an amount is erroneously rolled over or transferred from a traditional IRA to a SIMPLE IRA (see Q 33:2), the contribution can subsequently be recharacterized as a contribution to another traditional IRA; but employer contributions (including elective deferrals) under a SIMPLE IRA plan or a SEP (see Q 32:1) cannot be recharacterized as contributions to another IRA. However, an amount converted from a SEP IRA or SIMPLE IRA to a Roth IRA may be recharacterized as a contribution to a SEP IRA or SIMPLE IRA, including the original SEP IRA or SIMPLE IRA. [Treas. Reg. § 1.408A-5, Q&A-4, Q&A-5]

Recharacterizing a contribution is never treated as a rollover for purposes of the one-rollover-per-year limitation (see Qs 31:40, 34:5) even if the contribution would have been treated as a rollover contribution by the second IRA if it had been made directly to the second IRA, rather than as a result of recharacterization of a contribution to the first IRA. [Treas. Reg. § 1.408A-5, Q&A-8]

Example 1. In 2009, Jamie convered the entire amount in his regular IRA to a Roth IRA. Jamie thereafter determines that he was ineligible to have made a conversion in that year (see Q 31:44). Accordingly, prior to the due date (plus extensions) for filing his federal income tax return for 2009, Jamie decided to recharacterize the conversion contribution. Jamie instructed the trustee of the Roth IRA (first IRA) to transfer in a trustee-to-trustee transfer the amount of the contribution, plus net income, to the trustee of a new regular IRA (second IRA). Jamie notified the trustee of the first IRA and the trustee of the second IRA that he was recharacterizing his IRA contribution (see Q 31:11). On his federal income tax return for 2009, Jamie treated the original amount of the conversion as having been contributed to the second IRA and not the Roth IRA. As a result, the contribution was treated as having been made to the second IRA and not to the Roth IRA. The result would be the same if the conversion amount had been transferred in a tax-free transfer to another Roth IRA prior to the recharacterization.

Example 2. In 2010, Bill makes a $5,000 contribution for 2010 to his regular IRA (first IRA). Prior to the due date (plus extensions) for filing his federal income tax return for 2010, Bill decides that he would prefer to contribute to a Roth IRA instead. Bill instructs the trustee of the first IRA to transfer in a trustee-to-trustee transfer the amount of the contribution, plus attributable net income, to the trustee of a Roth IRA (second IRA). Bill notifies the trustee of the first IRA and the trustee of the second IRA that he is recharacterizing his $5,000 contribution for 2009 (see Q 31:11). On his federal income tax return for 2010, Bill treats the $5,000 as having been contributed to the Roth IRA for 2010 and not to the regular IRA. As a result, the contribution is treated as having been made to the Roth IRA for 2010 and not to the regular IRA. The result would be the same if the conversion amount had been transferred in a tax-free transfer to another regular IRA prior to the recharacterization.

Example 3. The facts are the same as in Example 2, except that the $5,000 contribution is initially made to a Roth IRA and the recharacterizing transfer is made to a regular IRA. On Bill's federal income tax return for 2010, he treats the $5,000 as having been contributed to the regular IRA for 2010 and not the Roth IRA. As a result, the contribution is treated as having been made to the regular IRA for 2010 and not to the Roth IRA. The result would be the same if the contribution had been transferred in a tax-free transfer to another Roth IRA prior to the recharacterization, except that the only Roth IRA trustee the individual must notify is the one actually making the recharacterization transfer.

Example 4. In 2010, Adam receives a distribution from regular IRA 1 and contributes the entire amount to regular IRA 2 in a rollover contribution (see Q 34:3). In this case, Adam cannot elect to recharacterize the contribution by transferring the contribution amount, plus net income, to a Roth IRA, because an amount contributed to an IRA in a tax-free transfer cannot be recharacterized. However, Adam may be eligible to convert (other than by recharacterization) the amount in regular IRA 2 to a Roth IRA (see Q 31:44).

Example 5. Stephanie makes a $5,000 contribution to a regular IRA on January 1, 2011, for 2010. On April 15, 2011, when the $5,000 has increased to $5,500, Stephanie recharacterizes the contribution by transferring the $5,500 to a Roth IRA. In this case, Stephanie's contribution to the Roth IRA for 2010 is $5,000. The $500 of earnings is not treated as a contribution to the Roth IRA. The results would be the same if the $5,000 had decreased to $4,500 prior to the recharacterization.

Example 6. In December 2010, Caroline receives a distribution from her traditional IRA of $300,000 and, in January 2011, she contributes the $300,000 to a Roth IRA as a conversion contribution. In April 2011, when the $300,000 has increased to $350,000, Caroline recharacterizes the conversion contribution by transferring the $350,000 to a traditional IRA. In this case, Caroline's conversion contribution for 2010 is $0, because the $300,000 conversion contribution and the earnings of $50,000 are disregarded. The results would be the same if the $300,000 had decreased to $250,000 prior to the recharacterization. Further, since the conversion is disregarded, the $300,000 is not includible in gross income in 2010.

As previously discussed, a contribution made to one type of IRA may be recharacterized as having been made to another type of IRA if (1) the recharacterization transfer occurs on or before the date prescribed by law for filing the IRA owner's federal income tax return for the year for which the contribution was made, (2) no deduction is allowed with respect to the contribution to the transferor IRA, and (3) the transfer is accompanied by any net income allocable to the contribution. If a contribution being recharacterized is in an IRA that at any time contained other contributions, the net income attributable to the contribution being recharacterized is calculated under the old method (see Q 30:9), except that net income can be a negative amount. If an IRA is established with a contribution and no other contributions or distributions are made, then the subsequent recharacterization transfer of the entire IRA will satisfy the requirement that the transfer be accompanied by any net income allocable to the contribution. [I.R.C. § 408A(d)(6); Treas. Reg. § 1.408A-5, Q&A-2]

The method for calculating net income generally bases the calculation of the amount of net income attributable to a contribution on the actual earnings and losses of the IRA during the time the IRA held the contribution. For purposes of recharacterizations, the net income attributable to IRA contributions is determined by allocating to the contribution a pro rata portion of the earnings on the IRA assets during the period the IRA held the contribution. This attributable net income is calculated by using the following formula:

$$\text{Net income} = \text{Contribution} \times \frac{(\text{Adjusted Closing Balance} - \text{Adjusted Opening Balance})}{\text{Adjusted Opening Balance}}$$

The following terms are pertinent:

1. Adjusted opening balance is the fair market value of the IRA at the beginning of the computation period plus the amount of any contributions

or transfers (including the contribution that is being recharacterized and any other recharacterizations) made to the IRA during the computation period.

2. Adjusted closing balance is the fair market value of the IRA at the end of the computation period plus the amount of any distributions or transfers (including contributions returned (see Q 30:9) and recharacterizations of contributions) made from the IRA during the computation period.

3. Computation period is the period beginning immediately prior to the time the particular contribution being recharacterized is made to the IRA and ending immediately prior to the recharacterizing transfer of the contribution. If a series of regular contributions was made to the IRA and consecutive contributions in that series are being recharacterized, the computation period begins immediately prior to the time the first of the regular contributions being recharacterized was made.

When an IRA asset is not normally valued on a daily basis, the fair market value of the asset at the beginning of the computation period is deemed to be the most recent, regularly determined, fair market value of the asset, determined as of a date that coincides with or precedes the first day of the computation period. In addition, solely for purposes of determining net income, recharacterized contributions are taken into account for the period they are actually held in a particular IRA.

In the case of an individual with multiple IRAs, the net income calculation is performed only on the IRA containing the particular contribution to be recharacterized and that IRA is the IRA from which the recharacterizing transfer must be made. In the case of multiple contributions made to an IRA for a particular year that are eligible for recharacterization, the IRA owner can choose (by date and by dollar amount, not by specific assets acquired with those dollars) which contribution, or portion thereof, will be recharacterized.

If an IRA is established with a contribution and no other contributions or distributions are made, then the subsequent recharacterization transfer of the entire IRA will satisfy the requirement that the transfer be accompanied by any net income allocable to the contribution.

The following examples illustrate the new method net income calculation:

Example 7. On March 1, 2009, when Susan's Roth IRA was worth $80,000, she made a $160,000 conversion contribution to the Roth IRA. Subsequently, Susan discovered that she was ineligible to make a Roth conversion contribution in 2009 (see Q 31:44), and so she requested that the $160,000 be recharacterized to a traditional IRA. Pursuant to this request, on March 1, 2010, when the IRA was worth $225,000, the Roth IRA custodian transferred to a traditional IRA the $160,000 plus allocable net income. No other contributions had been made to the Roth IRA, and no distributions had been made.

The adjusted opening balance was $240,000 ($80,000 + $160,000), and the adjusted closing balance was $225,000. Thus, the net income allocable to the

$160,000 was minus $10,000 [$160,000 × ($225,000 – $240,000) ÷ $240,000]. Therefore, in order to recharacterize the March 1, 2009, $160,000 conversion contribution on March 1, 2010, the Roth IRA custodian had to transfer from Susan's Roth IRA to her traditional IRA $150,000 [$160,000 – $10,000].

Example 8. On April 1, 2011, when Jeff's traditional IRA is worth $100,000, he converts the entire amount, consisting of 100 shares of stock in Wiener Corp. and 100 shares of stock in Krevat Corp., by transferring the shares to a Roth IRA. At the time of the conversion, the 100 shares of stock in Wiener Corp. are worth $50,000 and the 100 shares of stock in Krevat Corp. are also worth $50,000. Jeff decides that he would like to recharacterize the Wiener Corp. shares back to a traditional IRA. However, Jeff may choose only by dollar amount the contribution or portion thereof that will be recharacterized. On the date of transfer, November 1, 2011, the 100 shares of stock in Wiener Corp. are worth $40,000, and the 100 shares of stock in Krevat Corp. are worth $70,000. No other contributions have been made to the Roth IRA, and no distributions have been made.

If Jeff requests that $50,000 (which was the value of the Wiener Corp. shares at the time of conversion) be recharacterized, the net income allocable to the $50,000 is $5,000 [$50,000 × ($110,000 – $100,000) ÷ $100,000]. Therefore, in order to recharacterize $50,000 of the April 1, 2011, conversion contribution on November 1, 2011, the Roth IRA custodian must transfer from Jeff's Roth IRA to a traditional IRA assets with a value of $55,000 ($50,000 + $5,000).

If, on the other hand, Jeff requests that $40,000 (which was the value of the Wiener Corp. shares on November 1) be recharacterized, the net income allocable to the $40,000 is $4,000 [$40,000 × ($110,000 – $100,000) ÷ $100,000]. Therefore, in order to recharacterize $40,000 of the April 1, 2011, conversion contribution on November 1, 2011, the Roth IRA custodian must transfer from Jeff's Roth IRA to a traditional IRA assets with a value of $44,000 ($40,000 + $4,000).

Regardless of the amount of the contribution recharacterized, the determination of that amount (or of the net income allocable thereto) is not affected by whether the recharacterization is accomplished by the transfer of shares of Wiener Corp. or of shares of Krevat Corp.

[Treas. Reg. § 1.408A-5, Q&A-2(c)]

See Q 31:10 for a strategy to change the result in Example 8.

Q 31:10 Can an individual choose which Roth IRA assets to recharacterize?

In many cases, an individual chooses to recharacterize a Roth IRA conversion (see Q 31:9) because the converted traditional IRA assets have decreased in value. The conversion of an IRA into a Roth IRA is a taxable event, and the IRA owner includes the converted amount in gross income (see Q 31:49). Consequently, if the converted IRA assets decrease in value, the individual is subjected to a greater income tax than necessary. By recharacterizing the Roth IRA conversion back to a traditional IRA and then reconverting the traditional IRA again to a Roth IRA, the individual's income tax burden will be reduced.

> **Example.** When Ben's IRA is worth $100,000, he converts it to a Roth IRA, and Ben will include $100,000 in gross income. Six months later, Ben's Roth IRA is worth only $70,000. Ben recharacterizes the conversion back to a traditional IRA and does not include the $100,000 in gross income. If, when Ben is again eligible to convert his IRA to a Roth IRA (see Q 31:48), his IRA is still worth $70,000, Ben will include only $70,000 in gross income, so Ben's income tax will be reduced.

If, in the Example, some of Ben's Roth IRA investments decreased in value and others increased in value, Ben could not recharacterize only the depreciated investments and avoid taking into account the appreciation in the other investments. [IRS Notice 2000-39, 2000-2 C.B. 132] This is illustrated in Example 8 of Q 31:9. If, in Example 8, Jeff had established two Roth IRAs and rolled over or transferred the 100 shares of stock in Wiener Corp. to one Roth IRA and the 100 shares of stock of Krevat Corp. to the second Roth IRA, Jeff could recharacterize the first Roth IRA and effectively transfer only $40,000, instead of $44,000, back to a traditional IRA.

Q 31:11   How does an individual make the election to recharacterize a contribution?

An individual makes the recharacterization election by notifying, on or before the date of the transfer, both the trustee of the first IRA and the trustee of the second IRA that the individual has elected to treat the contribution as having been made to the second IRA, instead of the first IRA. The notification of the election must include the following information:

1. The type and amount of the contribution to the first IRA that will be recharacterized;

2. The date on which the contribution was made to the first IRA and the year for which it was made;

3. A direction to the trustee of the first IRA to transfer, in a trustee-to-trustee transfer, the amount of the contribution and net income allocable to the contribution to the trustee of the second IRA; and

4. The names of the trustee of the first IRA and the trustee of the second IRA and any additional information needed to make the transfer.

The election and the trustee-to-trustee transfer must occur on or before the due date (including extensions) for filing the individual's federal income tax return for the taxable year for which the recharacterized contribution was made to the first IRA, and the election cannot be revoked after the transfer. An individual who makes this election must report the recharacterization and must treat the contribution as having been made to the second IRA, instead of the first IRA, on the individual's federal income tax return for the taxable year.

The election to recharacterize a contribution may be made on behalf of a deceased IRA owner by the decedent's executor, administrator, or other person responsible for filing the final federal income tax return of the decedent. [Treas. Reg. § 1.408A-5, Q&A-6]

IRS has issued final regulations that add the deadline for a recharacterization to the list of tax-related deadlines that may be postponed by reason of a Presidentially declared disaster. The regulations allow IRS to disregard a period of up to one year in determining whether a recharacterization was made within the time prescribed. [I.R.C. § 7508A(b); Treas. Reg. § 301.7508A-1; IRS Notice 2002-27, 2002-1 C.B. 489; IRS Notice 2001-68, 2001-2 C.B. 504; IRS Notice 2001-61, 2001-2 C.B. 305]

Q 31:12   May contributions other than cash be made to a Roth IRA?

Except in the case of a rollover contribution (see Q 31:39), all contributions to a Roth IRA must be in cash. [I.R.C. §§ 408(a)(1), 408A(a)]

Q 31:13   Can a Roth IRA be subject to income tax?

Since a Roth IRA is treated in most cases in the same manner as an IRA, a Roth IRA, although generally not subject to income tax, can be subject to the tax imposed on unrelated business taxable income. [I.R.C. §§ 408A(a), 408(e)(1)] See Qs 30:11 and 30:12 for details.

Q 31:14   Is a Roth IRA contribution deductible?

No. No deduction is allowed for a contribution to a Roth IRA. [I.R.C. § 408A(c)(1); Treas. Reg. § 1.408A-1, Q&A-2; Ann. 97-122, 1997-50 I.R.B. 63]

Q 31:15   Can an active participant in a qualified retirement plan make a Roth IRA contribution?

An individual who is an active participant in a qualified retirement plan may deduct annual IRA contributions if the individual's AGI does not exceed certain limits (see Qs 30:13–30:17).

Active participant-status does not affect an individual's eligibility to contribute to a Roth IRA. If an individual cannot make a deductible contribution to an IRA, the individual may still be eligible to make a contribution to a Roth IRA. [I.R.C. § 408A(c)(2)]

Example 1. Jamie, who is unmarried and an active participant in his employer's qualified retirement plan, has AGI of $66,000 for 2010. Although Jamie cannot make a deductible IRA contribution for 2010, he can contribute $5,000 to a Roth IRA for 2010.

Example 2. The facts are the same as in Example 1, except that Jamie's AGI is $55,000. Jamie may contribute $2,500 to a deductible IRA and another $2,500 to a Roth IRA, or he may forgo making a deductible IRA contribution, in whole or in part, and contribute the forgone amount to the Roth IRA.

Q 31:16   Are there restrictions on who can contribute to a Roth IRA?

The maximum annual contribution that may be made to a Roth IRA is the *lesser* of the dollar amount in effect for the taxable year or the individual's compensation for the year (see Q 31:4). The maximum annual contribution that can be made to a Roth IRA phases out for:

1. A single individual with AGI between $95,000 (applicable dollar amount) and $110,000;

2. A married individual filing a joint return with AGI between $150,000 (applicable dollar amount) and $160,000; and

3. A married individual filing a separate return with AGI between zero (applicable dollar amount) and $10,000.

[I.R.C. §§ 408A(c)(2), 408A(c)(3)(A), 408A(c)(3)(B)(ii); Treas. Reg. § 1.408A-3, Q&A-3]

However, married individuals filing separately who live apart during the entire year are treated as not married for this purpose so that the applicable dollar amount for each such married individual is the dollar amount applicable to an unmarried individual. [I.R.C. §§ 219(g)(4), 408A(c)(3)(C); Treas. Reg. § 1.408A-3, Q&A-3]

Beginning in 2007, the applicable dollar amounts for single individuals and married individuals filing a joint return are subject to cost-of-living adjustments. Any increase is rounded to the nearest multiple of $1,000. [I.R.C. § 408A(c)(3)(C)] For 2010, the applicable dollar amount for a single individual is $105,000 and $167,000 for a married individual filing a joint return. [Rev. Proc. 2009-50, 2009-2 C.B. 617] For 2011, it is anticipated that the applicable dollar amount for a single individual will increase to $107,000 and, for a married individual filing a joint return, will increase to $169,000.

For purposes of the Roth IRA contribution limit, AGI is modified and calculated without taking into account certain exclusions for foreign earned income, United States savings bond redemptions, amounts paid to the individual or expenses incurred by the individual's employer for qualified adoption expenses, and deductions for interest on education loans and qualified tuition and related expenses, but taking into account any taxable Social Security benefits (see Q 31:17) and passive loss limitations applicable to the individual. In addition, AGI is calculated without taking into account (1) amounts includible in income as a result of a conversion of an IRA into a Roth IRA (see Q 31:42) or (2) deductible IRA contributions made for the taxable year. For example, the AGI-based phaseout of the exemption from the disallowance for passive losses is applied taking into account the amount of the conversion that is includible in AGI, and then the amount of the conversion is subtracted from AGI in determining whether an individual is eligible to make a Roth IRA contribution. [I.R.C. §§ 219(g)(3)(A), 408A(c)(3)(B)(i); Treas. Reg. § 1.408A-3, Q&A-5, Q&A-6]

Example 1. Jamie, a single taxpayer, has AGI of $114,000 for 2010. Jamie may make a contribution of up to $2,000 to a Roth IRA, computed as follows:

AGI	$114,000
Less: Applicable dollar amount	105,000
Difference	$ 9,000
Reduction in $5,000 limitation ($5,000 × ($9,000 ÷ $15,000))	$ 3,000
Maximum Roth IRA contribution ($5,000 − $3,000)	$ 2,000

Example 1A. For 2011, assume the same facts as in Example 1, except that the applicable dollar amount increases to $107,000. Jamie may make a contribution of up to $2,667 to a Roth IRA, computed as follows:

AGI	$114,000
Less: Applicable dollar amount	107,000
Difference	$ 7,000
Reduction in $5,000 limitation ($5,000 × ($7,000 ÷ $15,000))	$ 2,333
Maximum Roth IRA contribution ($5,000 − $2,333)	$ 2,667

Example 2. Caroline and Adam are married, file a joint return for 2010, and have AGI of $175,000. Caroline and Adam may each contribute up to $1,000 to a Roth IRA, computed as follows:

AGI	$175,000
Less: Applicable dollar amount	167,000
Difference	$ 8,000
Reduction in $5,000 limitation ($5,000 × ($8,000 ÷ $10,000))	$ 4,000
Maximum Roth IRA contribution ($5,000 − $4,000)	$ 1,000

Example 2A. For 2011, assume the same facts as in Example 2, except that the applicable dollar amount increases to $170,000. Caroline and Adam may each contribute up to $2,500 to a Roth IRA, computed as follows:

AGI	$175,000
Less: Applicable dollar amount	170,000
Difference	$ 5,000
Reduction in $5,000 limitation ($5,000 × ($5,000 ÷ $10,000))	$ 2,500
Maximum Roth IRA contribution ($5,000 − $2,500)	$ 2,500

Example 2B. Assume the same facts as in Examples 2 and 2A, except that Caroline and Adam file separate returns for 2010 and 2011, and each has AGI of more than $10,000. Since both Caroline and Adam have AGI of more than the $10,000 threshold amount, neither of them may contribute to a Roth IRA for either 2010 or 2011.

Example 3. In 2010, Ben, who is not married, has AGI of $112,500. For 2010, Ben contributes $2,800 to a deductible IRA and $2,200 to a Roth IRA. Because Ben's $2,200 Roth IRA contribution does not exceed the phased-out maximum Roth IRA contribution of $2,500 and because Ben's total IRA contributions do not exceed $5,000, Ben's Roth IRA contribution does not exceed the maximum permissible contribution.

The reduction in the maximum dollar limitation is rounded to the next lowest $10 in the case of a reduction that is not a multiple of $10. [I.R.C. §§ 219(g)(2)(C), 408A(c)(3)(A); Treas. Reg. § 1.408A-3, Q&A-3] For individuals whose AGI is not above the level that would totally eliminate a Roth IRA contribution, there is a $200 minimum Roth IRA contribution allowable. [I.R.C. §§ 219(g)(2)(B), 408A(c)(3)(A); Treas. Reg. § 1.408A-3, Q&A-3]

Example 4. In 2010, Norman, an unmarried individual, has AGI of $119,500. He may make a Roth IRA contribution of $200, computed as follows:

AGI	$119,500
Less: Applicable dollar amount	105,000
Difference	$ 14,500
Reduction in $5,000 limitation ($5,000 × ($14,500 ÷ $15,000))	$ 4,833
Maximum Roth IRA contribution (greater of $200 or $5,000 − $4,833)	$ 200

Example 4A. For 2011, assume the same facts as in Example 4, except that the applicable dollar amount increases to $107,000. Norman may make a Roth IRA contribution of $833, computed as follows:

AGI	$119,500
Less: Applicable dollar amount	107,000
Difference	$ 12,500
Reduction in $5,000 limitation ($5,000 × ($12,500 ÷ $15,000))	$ 4,167
Maximum Roth IRA contribution (greater of $200 or $5,000 − $4,167)	$ 833

An individual who is ineligible to make a deductible IRA contribution or a Roth IRA contribution to the full extent of the contribution limitation (see

Qs 30:5, 31:15) may make a designated nondeductible IRA contribution (see Q 30:20). [I.R.C. § 408(o)]

Example 5. Bill, who is married and an active participant in his employer's qualified retirement plan, has with his wife Stephanie AGI of $177,000 for 2010. Because Bill cannot make either a deductible IRA contribution or a Roth IRA contribution, he may make a designated nondeductible IRA contribution of up to $5,000.

Example 6. The facts are the same as in Example 5, except that their AGI is $172,000. Although Bill cannot make a deductible IRA contribution, he can contribute $2,500 to a Roth IRA and $2,500 to a designated nondeductible IRA.

Contributions to a SEP (see Q 32:1) or SIMPLE IRA (see Q 33:2) do not affect an individual's eligibility to contribute to a Roth IRA. [I.R.C. § 408A(f); Treas. Reg. § 1.408A-3, Q&A-3].

An individual who receives a military death gratuity or payment under the Servicemembers' Group Life Insurance (SGLI) program may contribute an amount up to the sum of the gratuity and SGLI payments received to a Roth IRA, notwithstanding the annual contribution limit and the income phase-out of the contribution limit that otherwise apply to contributions to Roth IRAs. The contribution will be considered a qualified rollover contribution (see Q 31:39) if the contribution is made before the end of the one-year period beginning on the date on which the amount is received. This provision generally applies with respect to death from injuries occurring on or after June 17, 2008. See Q 1:35 for details.

Q 31:17   Does the receipt of Social Security benefits affect Roth IRA contributions?

A Roth IRA contribution is subject to a phaseout if AGI exceeds certain specified amounts (see Q 31:16). Since an individual's AGI includes the taxable portion of Social Security benefits, the receipt of such benefits may affect an individual's eligibility to make a Roth IRA contribution. However, because a Roth IRA contribution is not deductible, an interrelated computation is not required as may occur when calculating a deductible IRA contribution (see Q 30:18). [I.R.C. §§ 219(g)(3)(A)(i), 408A(c)(3)]

Although amounts includible in income as a result of a conversion of an IRA into a Roth IRA are not taken into account in the calculation of an individual's AGI for purposes of the Roth IRA contribution limit (see Q 31:16), such income is included as an item of income for purposes of determining the taxability of the individual's Social Security benefits. [Helm, T.C. Summ. Op. 2002-138]

Q 31:18   What is a spousal Roth IRA?

If only one spouse is working, the working spouse may make an additional contribution to a Roth IRA (a spousal Roth IRA) on behalf of the nonworking spouse (provided a joint income tax return is filed). A spousal Roth IRA is available even if both spouses work if the spouse for whom the spousal Roth IRA is set up consents to being treated as having no compensation, for both Roth IRA and regular IRA purposes, for the taxable year. The total amount of allowable annual contributions to the working spouse's Roth IRA and to the spousal Roth IRA is double the dollar amount in effect for the taxable year (or 100 percent of the working spouse's earnings if less). However, if the married couple's AGI exceeds $167,000 (see Q 31:16), the maximum Roth IRA contribution amount commences to be phased out. [I.R.C. §§ 219(c), 408A(a), 408A(c)(2); Treas. Reg. § 1.408A-3, Q&A-4]

> **Example 1.** Caroline is married to Adam, and they file a joint return. Their AGI for 2010 is $70,000, all of which is earned by Caroline. Caroline may make a contribution of up to $5,000 to her Roth IRA and another $5,000 contribution to a spousal Roth IRA on behalf of Adam.

> **Example 2.** Stephanie, an active participant in her employer's qualified retirement plan, is married to Bill, and they file a joint return. Their AGI for 2010 is $109,000, all of which is earned by Stephanie. Stephanie may not make a deductible IRA contribution (see Q 31:15); however, Stephanie can contribute $5,000 to her Roth IRA, and a $5,000 spousal Roth IRA contribution can be made on behalf of Bill because their combined AGI does not exceed $167,000.

Q 31:19 When must Roth IRA contributions be made?

A contribution to a Roth IRA must be made by the due date, *not* including extensions, for filing the individual's federal income tax return. [I.R.C. §§ 219(f)(3), 408A(c)(7); Treas. Reg. § 1.408A-3, Q&A-2]

> **Example.** Betty wants to make a contribution to her Roth IRA for 2010. Betty can do so any time in 2010, or she can wait until her 2010 tax return is due, April 15, 2011. Even if Betty obtains an extension to file her return to October 17, 2011, her Roth IRA contribution is due by April 15, 2011.

IRS has added the deadline for IRA contributions to the list of tax-related deadlines that may be postponed by reason of a Presidentially declared disaster. IRS is allowed to disregard a period of up to 90 days in determining whether IRA contributions were made within the time prescribed. [I.R.C. § 7508A(b); Treas. Reg. § 301.7508A-1] It appears that the postponement does not apply to Roth IRA contributions because a Roth IRA is not considered a qualified retirement plan. [I.R.C. § 4974(c); *but see* IRS Notice 2002-27, 2002-1 C.B. 489; IRS Notice 2001-68, 2001-2 C.B. 504; IRS Notice 2001-61, 2001-2 C.B. 305]

For additional details, see Q 30:26.

Q 31:20 May an individual make a contribution to a Roth IRA with a credit card?

Because a Roth IRA is in most cases treated in the same manner as an IRA, the answer should be "yes." [I.R.C. § 408A(a)] For details, see Q 30:29.

Q 31:21 Can an individual's income tax refund be directly deposited into a Roth IRA?

IRS was directed to develop forms under which all or a portion of an individual's income tax refund may be deposited in a Roth IRA of the individual (or the spouse of the individual in the case of a joint return). This does not modify the rules relating to Roth IRAs, including the rules relating to timing of contributions. [PPA § 830] IRS developed Form 8888, Direct Deposit of Refund to More Than One Account. However, if the individual wants the refund deposited to only one account, Form 8888 should not be used. Instead, the individual can request a direct deposit of the refund on the tax return being filed (e.g., Form 1040). [Instructions to Form 8888]

IRS announced that economic-stimulus payments directly deposited into Roth IRAs could be withdrawn tax-free and penalty-free. This relief was designed to help taxpayers who may have been unaware that, by choosing direct deposit for their entire regular tax refund, they were also choosing to have their stimulus payment directly deposited as well. If a taxpayer elected a split refund (Form 8888), however, the stimulus payment was paid by a paper check. This relief was available for amounts withdrawn from Roth IRAs that were less than or equal to a taxpayer's directly deposited stimulus payment. To qualify for this relief, funds had to be taken out by April 15, 2009, in most cases. Without this relief, taxes, penalties, and other special rules would apply to amounts removed from these accounts. Regular refunds were not eligible for this relief. In general, the deadline for these withdrawals was the due date or extended due date for filing a 2008 return. This meant April 15, 2009, for most taxpayers, or October 15, 2009, for those who obtained tax-filing extensions. [IRS News Rel. IR-2008-68 (Apr. 30, 2008); Ann. 2008-44, 2008-2 C.B. 982]

Q 31:22 Does the payment of a fee to the trustee of a Roth IRA reduce the amount otherwise allowable as a contribution to the Roth IRA?

Because a Roth IRA is in most cases treated in the same manner as an IRA, the answer should be "no." [I.R.C. § 408A(a)] For details, see Q 30:31.

Q 31:23 What is a payroll-deduction Roth IRA?

An employer may choose to play a limited role in promoting retirement savings for its employees by establishing a payroll-deduction program in conjunction with a financial institution (e.g., a bank, insurance company, mutual fund, or brokerage firm). Each employee is allowed to set up a Roth IRA with the sponsoring institution, and the amount the employee wishes to contribute to the Roth IRA each pay period is deducted from the employee's paycheck by the employer. An employer may permit its employees to contribute to Roth IRAs by direct deposit through payroll deduction (see Qs 30:34, 30:35). [Ann. 99-2, 1999-1 C.B. 305]

Q 31:24   What is a deemed Roth IRA?

For plan years beginning on or after January 1, 2003, a qualified retirement plan or 403(b) plan (see Q 35:1) may permit employees to make voluntary employee contributions (see Qs 27:74, 35:19) to a separate account or annuity that (1) is established under the plan and (2) meets the requirements applicable to either IRAs or Roth IRAs. In such event, the separate account or annuity will be deemed an IRA or a Roth IRA, as applicable, for all purposes of the Code. For example, the reporting requirements applicable to Roth IRAs apply (see Q 31:51). The deemed Roth IRA, and contributions thereto, are not subject to the qualification rules pertaining to the plan. In addition, the deemed Roth IRA, and contributions thereto, are not taken into account in applying such rules to any other contributions under the plan. The deemed Roth IRA, and contributions thereto, are subject to the exclusive benefit and fiduciary rules of ERISA to the extent otherwise applicable to the plan but are not subject to the ERISA reporting and disclosure, participation, vesting, funding, and enforcement requirements applicable to the plan. [I.R.C. § 408(q); ERISA § 4(c)] However, ERISA Section 4(c) has been amended, so that a deemed Roth IRA, and contributions to it, will be subject to the ERISA administration and enforcement rules, and ERISA is intended to apply to a deemed Roth IRA in a manner similar to a SEP (see Q 32:1).

Similar to an employer-sponsored IRA (see Q 30:32), it appears that an employer has wide discretion in determining who is eligible to make deemed Roth IRA contributions because there are no coverage or nondiscrimination requirements. In addition, an employee could presumably roll over an existing Roth IRA into the deemed Roth IRA.

Trusts that are parts of deemed IRAs may pool their assets in a group trust without affecting the exempt status of the separate trusts (see Q 30:2). [Rev. Rul. 2004-67, 2004-2 C.B. 28; Rev. Rul. 81-100, 1981-1 C.B. 326]

For additional information regarding deemed Roth IRAs and deemed IRAs, see Q 30:36; and, for a discussion of regulations issued by IRS, see Q 30:37.

Q 31:25   Are there restrictions on Roth IRA distributions?

No. Unlike qualified retirement plans, an individual may withdraw all or any part of a Roth IRA at any time. Also, spousal consent (see Q 10:21) to a withdrawal is not necessary, and there are no limitations as to the form of distribution. However, distributions from a Roth IRA may be subject to income and penalty taxes (see Qs 31:27, 31:32).

Q 31:26   Does the minimum distribution requirement apply to a Roth IRA during the owner's lifetime?

Unlike an IRA, the minimum distribution requirement does not apply during the lifetime of the Roth IRA owner. [I.R.C. § 408A(c)(5); Treas. Reg. §§ 1. 408A-1, Q&A-2, 1.408A-6, Q&A-14]

Because the lifetime minimum distribution requirement does not apply:

1. The Roth IRA owner need not commence distributions by April 1 of the calendar year following the calendar year in which the owner attains age 70½ (see Q 11:58).

2. The Roth IRA owner can delay indefinitely when distributions will commence.

3. The Roth IRA owner can arbitrarily determine each year how much, if any, the owner wishes to withdraw.

4. The penalty for insufficient distributions can never be imposed upon the Roth IRA owner (see Q 31:38).

A recharacterization of a Roth IRA back to a traditional IRA may trigger an RMD from the traditional IRA (see Q 31:9). [Priv. Ltr. Rul. 200213030] RMDs for the 2009 distribution calendar year were suspended (see Q 30:42).

For a complete discussion of the minimum distribution requirement, see chapter 11 and, specifically with regard to IRAs, Qs 11:56 through 11:66.

Q 31:27   Are distributions from a Roth IRA taxable?

Qualified distributions from a Roth IRA are not includible in gross income. [I.R.C. § 408A(d)(1); Treas. Reg. § 1.408A-6, Q&A-1]

A qualified distribution is a distribution from a Roth IRA that satisfies a five-year holding period requirement (see Q 31:28) and that is:

1. Made on or after the date on which the individual attains age 59½;

2. Made to a beneficiary (or to the individual's estate) on or after the death of the individual;

3. Attributable to the individual's being disabled (see Q 16:6); or

4. A qualified special purpose distribution.

[I.R.C. § 408A(d)(2)(A); Treas. Reg. § 1.408A-6, Q&A-1]

Example 1. Bill established a Roth IRA in 2006 when he was age 37 and makes a contribution each year until he reaches age 60. At age 60, Bill's Roth IRA is worth $200,000, consisting of $48,000 in contributions and $152,000 in accumulated earnings. Bill may withdraw all or any part of his Roth IRA income tax free because the five-year holding period requirement has been satisfied and Bill is over age 59½.

If the distribution from the Roth IRA is not a qualified distribution, then, subject to an ordering rule (see Q 31:29), only the portion of the distribution allocable to earnings on the contributions will be included in the individual's income. [Treas. Reg. § 1.408A-6, Q&A-4; Widemon, 88 T.C.M. 13 (2004)]

Example 2. Assume in Example 1 that, in 2010, Bill withdrew all of his Roth IRA consisting of $8,000 in contributions and $1,500 in earnings. The entire earnings of $1,500 will be includible in Bill's gross income in 2010.

A qualified special purpose distribution means a qualified first-time home-buyer distribution (see Q 16:16). [I.R.C. § 408A(d)(5); Treas. Reg. § 1.408A-6, Q&A-1; IRS Notice 98-49, Q&A C-2, 1998-2 C.B. 365]

> **Example 3.** Assume the same facts as in Example 2, except that the distribution is a qualified first-time homebuyer distribution. The entire earnings of $1,500 is still includible in Bill's income because the five-year holding period requirement has not been satisfied. If the withdrawal occurs in 2011, the requirement will be satisfied and, hence, income tax free.

An amount distributed from a Roth IRA will not be included in gross income to the extent it is rolled over to another Roth IRA on a tax-free basis (see Q 31:40). Corrective distributions that are returned to the Roth IRA owner are not includible in gross income, because any amount distributed as a corrective distribution is treated as if it had never been contributed. However, any net income required to be distributed together with the contributions is includible in gross income for the taxable year in which the contributions were made (see Q 31:8). A distribution that is not a qualified distribution, and is neither contributed to another Roth IRA in a qualified rollover contribution nor constitutes a corrective distribution, is includible in the Roth IRA owner's gross income to the extent that the amount of the distribution, when added to the amount of all prior distributions from the owner's Roth IRAs (whether or not they were qualified distributions) and reduced by the amount of those prior distributions previously includible in gross income, exceeds the Roth IRA owner's contributions to all of the owner's Roth IRAs. [Treas. Reg. § 1.408A-6, Q&A-1, Q&A-2; Widemon, 88 T.C.M. 13 (2004); *Retirement News for Employers*, Winter 2010]

To the extent that Roth IRA distributions are includible in gross income, elective withholding rules may apply. [I.R.C. § 3405; Treas. Reg. § 1.408A-6, Q&A-12] IRA distributions are includible in an individual's income for federal tax withholding purposes (see Qs 20:10, 20:14, 30:40). However, an exception from withholding is provided for distributions for which it is reasonable to believe an exclusion from gross income applies. This exception from withholding has been extended to distributions from Roth IRAs. [I.R.C. § 3405(e)(1)(B)]

See Q 31:30 for a discussion of having a tax-deductible loss on a distribution from a Roth IRA, and Q 31:32 for a discussion of the penalty tax that may be imposed on distributions from a Roth IRA.

See Q 30:44 for a discussion of qualified charitable distributions.

Q 31:28 What is the five-year holding period requirement?

A payment or distribution from a Roth IRA is not a qualified distribution (see Q 31:27) if the payment or distribution is made within the five-taxable-year period beginning with the first taxable year for which the individual made a contribution to a Roth IRA (or the individual's spouse made a contribution to a spousal Roth IRA; see Q 31:18) established for the individual. [I.R.C. § 408A(d)(2)(B); Treas. Reg. § 1.408A-6, Q&A-1, Q&A-2]

All Roth IRAs, whether or not maintained in separate accounts, are treated as a single Roth IRA. [I.R.C. §§ 408A(d)(2), 408A(d)(4); Treas. Reg. § 1.408A-6, Q&A-1] The five-taxable-year period begins on the first day of the taxable year for which the individual is *deemed to make a contribution* to the individual's initial Roth IRA and ends on the last day of the fifth consecutive taxable year beginning with the first taxable year. [Treas. Reg. § 1.408A-6, Q&A-2]

As is the case with IRAs generally, contributions to a Roth IRA may be made for a year by the due date for the individual's federal income tax return for the year (determined without regard to extensions) (see Q 31:19). In the case of a contribution to a Roth IRA made after the end of the taxable year, the five-taxable-year period begins with the taxable year to which the contribution relates, rather than the year in which the contribution is actually made. [I.R.C. § 408A(d)(2)(B)]

Thus, each Roth IRA owner has only one five-taxable-year period for all the Roth IRAs of which the individual is the owner. The amount of any contribution distributed as a corrective distribution (see Q 31:9) is treated as if it had never been contributed. [Treas. Reg. § 1.408A-6, Q&A-2; *Retirement News for Employers*, Winter 2010]

Example 1. Sallie made a $100 contribution to her Roth IRA for 2005 on April 15, 2006. Sallie then made annual contributions to her Roth IRA for each year 2006 through 2009. On January 1, 2010, the five-year holding period requirement was satisfied with respect to her entire Roth IRA.

Example 2. The facts are the same as in Example 1, except that, for each year 2006–2009, Sallie established four new Roth IRAs for a total of five separate Roth IRAs. On January 1, 2010, the five-year holding period requirement was met with respect to all five Roth IRAs. This is so because the period for each of Sallie's Roth IRAs commenced with the first taxable year for which a contribution was made to her initial Roth IRA.

An individual may be eligible to roll over an IRA to a Roth IRA or to convert an IRA into a Roth IRA (see Q 31:44). A subsequent rollover or conversion does not start a new five-year holding period. [I.R.C. § 408A(d)(2)(B); Treas. Reg. § 1.408A-6, Q&A-2]

Example 3. On April 26, 2006, Terry established a Roth IRA and contributed $2,000. On January 17, 2007, Terry rolled over a distribution from her IRA to her Roth IRA. The five-year holding period requirement will be met on January 1, 2011.

Example 4. The facts are the same as in Example 3, except that Terry made a second IRA rollover contribution to a new Roth IRA on March 11, 2009. Since both Roth IRAs are treated as a single Roth IRA, the five-year holding period requirement will be met for both of Terry's Roth IRAs on January 1, 2011.

Because only a single five-year holding period applies to all of an individual's Roth IRAs, it is not necessary for the individual to maintain separate Roth IRAs for contributions and conversions. However, to simplify the identification of funds distributed from Roth IRAs, individuals are encouraged to maintain conversion contributions for each taxable year in a separate Roth IRA (see Q 31:49). [Instructions to Forms 5305-R and 5305-RA]

The beginning of the five-taxable-year period is not redetermined when the Roth IRA owner dies. Thus, in determining the five-taxable-year period, the period the Roth IRA is held in the name of a beneficiary, or in the name of a surviving spouse who treats the decedent's Roth IRA as the surviving spouse's own, includes the period it was held by the decedent. The five-taxable-year period for a Roth IRA held by an individual as a beneficiary of a deceased Roth IRA owner is determined independently of the five-taxable-year period for the beneficiary's own Roth IRA. However, if a surviving spouse treats the Roth IRA as the surviving spouse's own, the five-taxable-year period with respect to any of the surviving spouse's Roth IRAs (including the one that the surviving spouse treats as his or her own) ends at the earlier of the end of either the five-taxable-year period for the decedent or the five-taxable-year period applicable to the surviving spouse's own Roth IRAs. [Treas. Reg. § 1.408A-6, Q&A-7]

Q 31:29   What are the ordering rules?

An ordering rule applies for purposes of determining what portion of a nonqualified distribution (i.e., a distribution from a Roth IRA that is not a qualified distribution; see Q 31:27) is includible in income. Under the ordering rule, distributions from a Roth IRA are treated as made from contributions first, and all of an individual's Roth IRAs are treated as a single Roth IRA. Thus, no portion of a distribution from a Roth IRA is treated as attributable to earnings (and therefore possibly includible in gross income) until the total of all distributions from all the individual's Roth IRAs exceeds the amount of contributions. [I.R.C. §§ 408A(d)(1), 408A(d)(4); Treas. Reg. § 1.408A-6, Q&A-8; Widemon, 88 T.C.M. 13 (2004)]

> **Example 1.** Lee establishes a Roth IRA in 2005 at age 41 and contributes $2,000 each year from 2005 through 2014. On February 1, 2015, Lee's Roth IRA contains $30,000, consisting of contributions of $20,000 and earnings of $10,000, and he withdraws $20,000. Although the five-year holding period requirement (see Q 31:28) has been satisfied, the withdrawal is not a qualified distribution (see Q 31:27). However, no part of the withdrawal is includible in Lee's gross income because his Roth IRA contributions ($20,000) are deemed recovered first under the ordering rule.

> **Example 2.** The facts are the same as in Example 1, except that Lee withdraws $18,000 on December 31, 2014 and an additional $3,000 on February 1, 2015. The $18,000 withdrawal in 2014 is nontaxable. However, of the $3,000 withdrawal in 2015, $2,000 is treated as attributable to contributions and $1,000 is treated as attributable to earnings. Thus, in 2015, Lee must include $1,000 in gross income.

> **Example 3.** The facts are the same as in Example 1, except that Lee maintained five separate Roth IRAs, withdrew an aggregate of $20,000 from four Roth IRAs, and left intact his fifth Roth IRA containing $10,000. The $20,000 is still nontaxable because all of Lee's Roth IRAs are treated as a

single Roth IRA for this purpose so that the entire $20,000 is attributable to contributions.

Roth IRAs and non-Roth IRAs are treated separately for determining the taxability of distributions. [I.R.C. § 408A(d)(4)]

If an individual has (1) a Roth IRA that contains both IRA conversion contributions (see Q 31:44) and other contributions, (2) more than one Roth IRA some of which contain IRA conversion contributions and others of which contain other contributions, or (3) one or more Roth IRAs that contain only IRA conversion contributions, then the ordering rule has within it a second ordering rule. For this rule also, all of an individual's Roth IRAs are treated as a single Roth IRA. Under the second ordering rule, distributions from an individual's Roth IRA are treated as made from contributions to the Roth IRA (or from all of the individual's Roth IRAs if more than one) in the following order:

1. From regular Roth IRA contributions (i.e., contributions not attributable to conversion contributions).

2. From conversion contributions from IRAs (starting with the amounts first converted) with withdrawals of converted amounts being treated as coming first from converted amounts that were includible in income.

3. From earnings.

Therefore, earnings will be treated as withdrawn after the withdrawal of regular Roth IRA contributions and conversion contributions from IRAs. [I.R.C. § 408A(d)(4); Treas. Reg. § 1.408A-6, Q&A-8; *Retirement News for Employers*, Winter 2010]

For purposes of determining the source of distributions, the following rules apply:

1. All distributions from all of an individual's Roth IRAs made during a taxable year are aggregated.

2. All regular contributions made for the same taxable year to all the individual's Roth IRAs are aggregated and added to the undistributed total regular contributions for prior taxable years. Regular contributions for a year include contributions made in the following taxable year that are identified as made for the taxable year (see Q 30:27). For example, a regular contribution made in 2010 for 2009 is aggregated with the contributions made in 2009 for 2009.

3. All conversion contributions received during the same taxable year by all the individual's Roth IRAs are aggregated.

4. A distribution from an individual's Roth IRA that is rolled over to another Roth IRA of the individual is disregarded for purposes of determining the amount of both contributions and distributions.

5. Any excess contribution distribution (including net income) is disregarded in determining the amount of contributions, earnings, and distributions.

If an individual recharacterizes a contribution made to a regular IRA (first IRA) by transferring the contribution to a Roth IRA (second IRA), then the contribution to the Roth IRA is taken into account for the same taxable year for which it would have been taken into account if the contribution had originally been made to the Roth IRA and had never been contributed to the regular IRA. Thus, the contribution to the Roth IRA is treated as contributed to the Roth IRA on the same date and for the same taxable year that the contribution was made to the regular IRA.

If an individual recharacterizes a regular or conversion contribution made to a Roth IRA (first IRA) by transferring the contribution to a regular IRA (second IRA), the contribution to the Roth IRA and the recharacterizing transfer are disregarded in determining the amount of both contributions and distributions for the taxable year with respect to which the original contribution was made to the Roth IRA.

The effect of income or loss occurring after the contribution to the first IRA is disregarded in determining the amounts described in the preceding paragraphs. Thus, for these purposes, the amount of the contribution is determined based on the original contribution.

[Treas. Reg. § 1.408A-6, Q&A-9]

> **Example 1.** In 1998, Norman converted $80,000 in his traditional IRA to a Roth IRA. Norman had a basis of $20,000 in the conversion amount and so had to include the remaining $60,000 in gross income. Norman also made a regular contribution of $2,000 in 1998. If a distribution of $2,000 was made to Norman anytime in 1998, it was treated as made entirely from the regular contributions, so there were no income tax consequences as a result of the distribution.

> **Example 2.** The facts are the same as in Example 1, except that Norman also made a $2,000 regular contribution in each year 1999 through 2002 and he did not take a distribution in 1998. A distribution of $85,000 was made to Norman in 2002. The distribution was treated as made from the $10,000 of regular contributions (the total regular contributions made in the years 1998–2002), $60,000 of conversion contributions that were includible in gross income, and $15,000 of conversion contributions that were not includible in gross income. As a result, no amount of the distribution was includible in gross income; however, because the distribution was allocable to a conversion made within the previous five years, the $60,000 was subject to the 10 percent penalty tax as if it were includible in gross income for 2002, unless an exception applied.

> **Example 3.** The facts are the same as in Example 4, except no distribution occurred in 2002. In 2003, the entire balance in the account, $170,000 ($90,000 of contributions and $80,000 of earnings), was distributed to Norman. The distribution was treated as made from $10,000 of regular contributions, $60,000 of conversion contributions that were includible in gross income, $20,000 of conversion contributions that were not includible in gross income, and $80,000 of earnings. As a result, for 2003, Norman had to

include in gross income the $80,000 allocable to earnings, unless the distribution was a qualified distribution; and, if it was not a qualified distribution, the $80,000 would be subject to the 10 percent penalty tax, unless an exception applied.

Example 4. Shirley converted $20,000 to a Roth IRA in 1998 and $15,000 (in which amount Shirley had a basis of $2,000) to another Roth IRA in 1999. No other contributions were made. In 2003, a $30,000 distribution that was not a qualified distribution was made to Shirley. The distribution was treated as made from $20,000 of the 1998 conversion contribution and $10,000 of the 1999 conversion contribution that was includible in gross income. As a result, for 2003, no amount was includible in gross income; however, because $10,000 was allocable to a conversion contribution made within the previous five taxable years, that amount was subject to the 10 percent penalty tax as if the amount were includible in gross income for 2003, unless an exception applied. The result would be the same whichever of Shirley's Roth IRAs made the distribution.

Example 5. The facts are the same as in Example 4, except that the distribution was a qualified distribution. The result is the same as in Example 4, except that no amount would be subject to the 10 percent penalty tax because it was a qualified distribution.

See Q 31:9 for a discussion of IRA and Roth IRA recharacterizations and additional examples.

Q 31:30 Can an individual have a tax-deductible loss on a Roth IRA distribution?

Roth IRA contributions represent basis (see Q 13:3) and that is why all or a portion of the distribution is nontaxable (see Q 31:27). Because of this rule, the individual can have a loss on a Roth IRA, but the individual can only take the loss for income tax purposes when *all* of the amounts in *all* of the individual's Roth IRAs have been distributed.

Example. Assume that Jason has made aggregate contributions to his Roth IRA of $2,000. The $2,000 represents Jason's basis. On December 31, 2009, when the Roth IRA balance was $2,400, Jason withdrew $500. All of the $500 withdrawal is nontaxable, and Jason's basis is reduced to $1,500 ($2000 − $500). In 2010, Jason's Roth investment decreases in value from $1,900 to $1,300, and Jason withdraws the entire remaining Roth IRA balance. Since the amount distributed ($1,300) is less than Jason's remaining basis ($1,500), Jason can take the $200 loss on his 2010 federal income tax return as a miscellaneous itemized deduction. As a miscellaneous itemized deduction, it is subject to the 2 percent of adjusted gross income limit and could subject Jason to the alternative minimum tax (AMT).

Q 31:31   Can an individual make a gift of a Roth IRA?

Yes; but a Roth IRA owner's transfer of the Roth IRA to another individual by gift constitutes an assignment of the owner's rights under the Roth IRA. At the time of the gift, the assets of the Roth IRA are deemed distributed to the owner and, accordingly, are treated as no longer held in a Roth IRA. Thus, the deemed distribution may be includible in the Roth IRA owner's gross income (see Qs 31:27–31:29). [Treas. Reg. § 1.408A-6, Q&A-19]

Q 31:32   Can a penalty be imposed on a distribution from a Roth IRA?

A qualified distribution from a Roth IRA is not includible in gross income (see Q 31:27) and is not subject to the 10 percent penalty tax on early distributions. However, to the extent that a distribution is includible in the individual's gross income, the distribution may also be subject to the 10 percent penalty tax on early distributions (i.e., the tax is increased by an amount equal to 10 percent of the amount includible in gross income). Because a Roth IRA is treated in most cases in the same manner as an IRA, the exceptions that apply to the imposition of the 10 percent penalty tax on IRA distributions will also apply to Roth IRA distributions (see chapter 16 for details). [I.R.C. §§ 72(t), 408A(a); Treas. Reg. § 1.408A-6, Q&A-5(a)]

Example 1. Steve establishes a Roth IRA when he is age 58 and contributes the maximum amount each year. At age 61, Steve withdraws all of the funds from his Roth IRA. The portion of the withdrawal attributable to earnings will be includible in Steve's gross income that year because the five-year holding period requirement has not been satisfied (i.e., it is not a qualified distribution; see Q 31:28). However, the 10 percent penalty tax will not be incurred because Steve has attained age 59½.

Example 2. Lisa establishes a Roth IRA when she is age 40 and contributes the maximum amount each year. Three years later, Lisa withdraws all of the funds from her Roth IRA consisting of $9,000 in contributions and $1,000 in earnings. The entire earnings of $1,000 will be includible in Lisa's gross income that year and will be subject to the 10 percent penalty tax unless an exception applies.

Example 3. The facts are the same as in Example 2, except that the distribution constitutes a qualified first-time homebuyer distribution. The entire earnings of $1,000 is still includible in Lisa's gross income, but the 10 percent penalty tax does not apply because the distribution is a qualified special purpose distribution (see Q 31:27).

If a qualified rollover contribution (see Q 31:39) is made from an IRA to a Roth IRA, the 10 percent penalty tax does not apply; however, distributions from the rollover Roth IRA may be subject to the penalty tax (see Q 31:49). [I.R.C. §§ 408A(d)(3)(A)(ii), 408A(e)]

Q 31:33 What happens if an individual engages in a prohibited transaction with regard to a Roth IRA?

Because a Roth IRA is an individual retirement plan and a Roth IRA is treated in most cases in the same manner as an individual retirement plan, the same rules should apply. [I.R.C. §§ 408A(a), 408A(b); Treas. Reg. § 1.408A-1, Q&A-1(b)]

A retirement account is not treated as an IRA if an individual engages in a prohibited transaction (see Q 24:1) with respect to the retirement account. The account is treated as having distributed all its assets to the individual on the first day of the taxable year in which the prohibited transaction occurs. [I.R.C. § 408(e)(2); Priv. Ltr. Rul. 9725029]

If an individual uses an IRA or any portion thereof as security for a loan, the portion used is treated as a distribution to the individual. [I.R.C. § 408(e)(4)]

For further details, see Q 30:45.

Q 31:34 Will the receipt of reduced or no-cost services by a customer who directs the Roth IRA to invest in a bank's financial products constitute a prohibited transaction?

Because a Roth IRA is an individual retirement plan and a Roth IRA is treated in most cases in the same manner as an individual retirement plan, the same rules should apply. [I.R.C. §§ 408A(a), 408A(b)] For further details, see Q 30:46.

Q 31:35 May a Roth IRA be transferred incident to divorce?

Because a Roth IRA is an individual retirement plan and a Roth IRA is treated in most cases in the same manner as an individual retirement plan, the same rules should apply. [I.R.C. §§ 408A(a), 408A(b)] For further details, see Q 30:51.

Q 31:36 Are amounts remaining in a Roth IRA at death subject to federal estate taxes?

The entire amount in a Roth IRA is included in the decedent's gross estate for federal estate tax purposes. [I.R.C. § 2039] However, distributions from a Roth IRA after the owner's death may be income tax free (see Qs 31:27, 31:37). [Treas. Reg. § 1.408A-6, Q&A-14(c)]

Because a Roth IRA is treated in most cases in the same manner as an IRA, the federal estate tax rules applicable to IRAs should also apply to Roth IRAs. [I.R.C. §§ 408A(a), 408A(b)] For details, see Q 30:47.

Q 31:37 What minimum distribution requirements apply after a Roth IRA owner's death?

Although the minimum distribution requirements do not apply during the lifetime of a Roth IRA owner (see Q 31:26), the post-death minimum distribution requirements *do* apply. Because the lifetime minimum distribution requirements do not apply, the Roth IRA owner can never die *after* the required beginning date (RBD)—death always occurs *before* the RBD (see Q 11:58). [I.R.C. §§ 401(a)(9)(B), 408A(c)(5); Treas. Reg. § 1.408A-6, Q&A-14]

If the Roth IRA owner dies before the entire balance in the Roth IRA has been distributed and the surviving spouse is not the sole beneficiary, the entire remaining Roth IRA balance must at the owner's election (or if the owner has not elected, at the election of the beneficiary or beneficiaries) be distributed as follows:

1. By December 31 of the year containing the fifth anniversary of the Roth IRA owner's death, or

2. Over the life expectancy of the designated beneficiary (see Qs 11:14–11:19), starting no later than December 31 of the year following the year of the owner's death.

These rules are essentially the same as those that apply to non-Roth IRA distributions to a nonspouse beneficiary where the owner dies before the RBD. An individual required to receive minimum distributions from a traditional IRA or SIMPLE IRA (see Q 33:2) cannot choose to take the amount of the minimum distributions from a Roth IRA. Similarly, an individual required to receive minimum distributions from a Roth IRA cannot choose to take the amount of the minimum distributions from a traditional IRA or SIMPLE IRA. In addition, an individual required to receive minimum distributions as a beneficiary under a Roth IRA can only satisfy the minimum distributions for one Roth IRA by distributing from another Roth IRA if the Roth IRAs were inherited from the same decedent. [Treas. Reg. § 1.408A-6, Q&A-15]

If the Roth IRA owner dies before the entire balance in the Roth IRA has been distributed and the surviving spouse is the sole beneficiary, the surviving spouse is then treated as the Roth IRA owner (see Q 31:41). Because the lifetime minimum distribution requirements will not apply to the surviving spouse, the surviving spouse can delay indefinitely when distributions will commence. [Forms 5305-R, 5305-RA; IRS Notice 98-49, 1998-2 C.B. 365] If the surviving spouse of a Roth IRA owner treats a Roth IRA as the surviving spouse's own as of a date, from that date forward, the Roth IRA is treated as though it were established for the benefit of the surviving spouse and not the original Roth IRA owner. Thus, for example, in addition to the surviving spouse being treated as the Roth IRA owner for purposes of applying the minimum distribution requirements, the surviving spouse is treated as the Roth IRA owner rather than a beneficiary for purposes of determining the amount of any distribution from the Roth IRA that is includible in gross income and whether the distribution is subject to the 10 percent penalty tax on early distributions (see Q 31:32). [Treas. Reg. §§ 1.408A-2, Q&A-4, 1.408A-6, Q&A-3]

RMDs for the 2009 distribution calendar year were suspended. For a complete discussion of the minimum distribution rules, see chapter 11 and, specifically with regard to IRAs, Qs 11:56 through 11:66.

A distribution from a Roth IRA is a qualified distribution (see Q 31:27) if it is made to a beneficiary (or to the estate of the Roth IRA owner) on account of the owner's death and the five-year holding period requirement (see Q 31:28) is satisfied. Therefore, distributions from a Roth IRA after the death of the owner may be income tax free to the recipient. [I.R.C. §§ 408A(d)(1), 408A(d)(2)(A)(ii), 408A(d)(2)(B); Treas. Reg. 1.408A-6, Q&A-14(c)]

> **Example 1.** Archie establishes a Roth IRA in 2007 and contributes $2,000 for each year of 2007, 2008, 2009, and 2010. Archie dies in October 2011, and the entire Roth IRA consisting of $6,000 in contributions and $1,500 in earnings is paid to his son Leach in December of that year. The $1,500 earnings portion of the Roth IRA will be includible in Leach's gross income because the five-year holding period requirement has not been satisfied.

> **Example 2.** The facts are the same as in Example 1, except that the distribution is delayed until January 2012. Because the five-year holding period requirement has now been satisfied, the distribution to Leach is income tax free.

> **Example 3.** The facts are the same as in Example 1, except that Leach withdraws $6,000 in December 2011 and the balance of the Roth IRA in January 2012. The first distribution is income tax free under the ordering rule (see Q 31:29), and the second distribution is income tax free as a qualified distribution.

Q 31:38 May a penalty be imposed for insufficient distributions from a Roth IRA?

An annual nondeductible 50 percent excise tax is imposed on the difference between the minimum required distribution from a Roth IRA and the amount distributed. [I.R.C. § 4974]

Because the minimum distribution requirements do not apply during the Roth IRA owner's lifetime (see Q 31:26), this penalty for insufficient distributions can never be imposed while the Roth IRA owner is alive. However, because the minimum distribution requirements do apply after the owner's death (see Q 31:37), failure to satisfy those requirements could result in the imposition of this excise tax.

For a complete discussion of the minimum distribution rules, see chapter 11 and, specifically with regard to the excise tax, Qs 11:67 through 11:71.

Q 31:39 What is a qualified rollover contribution?

No rollover contribution may be made to a Roth IRA unless it is a qualified rollover contribution. A qualified rollover contribution is a rollover contribution to a Roth IRA from another Roth IRA or from an IRA, provided that certain requirements are satisfied. [I.R.C. §§ 408A(c)(6), 408A(e); Treas. Reg. § 1. 408A-3, Q&A-1; Instructions to Forms 5305-R and 5305-RA]

For distributions made after December 31, 2007, a Roth IRA can accept rollovers from eligible retirement plans in addition to another Roth IRA or an IRA. For further details on qualified rollover contributions, see Qs 31:40 through 31:49 and, specifically, Q 31:43 for a discussion of the coordination between designated Roth accounts and Roth IRAs. See Q 31:16 for a special qualified rollover contribution provision.

Q 31:40   May a Roth IRA be rolled over to another Roth IRA?

Yes. A rollover contribution to a Roth IRA from another Roth IRA is a qualified rollover contribution (see Q 31:39). [I.R.C. §§ 408A(c)(6), 408A(e); Instructions to Forms 5305-R and 5305-RA] All or part of the investments held in a particular Roth IRA may be withdrawn and transferred (rolled over) to another Roth IRA without tax or penalty. This gives the Roth IRA owner flexibility by enabling the owner to shift investments. For example, the owner may shift from one annuity Roth IRA to another or, seeking higher interest or dividends, from one trusteed Roth IRA to another.

To make the switch, certain requirements must be met. To be a qualified rollover contribution:

1. The amount distributed to the individual from the Roth IRA must be transferred to the other Roth IRA not later than 60 days after receipt. [Duralia, 67 T.C.M. 3084 (1994)]

2. If property, other than cash, is received from the Roth IRA, that same property must be transferred to the other Roth IRA. [I.R.C. § 408(d)(3)(A)]

An individual withdrew funds from an IRA, invested the funds in securities, and rolled over the securities to a new IRA. Because the same property was not contributed to the new IRA, it did not qualify as a rollover contribution. [Lemishow, 110 T.C. 110 (1998)]

If a rollover from a particular Roth IRA has been made during the preceding 12-month period, a second rollover from that Roth IRA is not permitted. [I.R.C. §§ 408(d)(3)(B), 408A(e); Treas. Reg. § 1.402(c)-2, Q&A-16; Martin, 63 T.C.M. 3122 (1992); Priv. Ltr. Rul. 8502044]

Example 1. On January 5, 2011, Adam receives a first distribution from Roth IRA X and, on January 19, 2011, deposits the distribution in Roth IRA Y. Because Adam did not receive any distributions from Roth IRA X during the preceding 12-month period, the rollover from Roth IRA X to Roth IRA Y is permitted.

Example 2. On November 21, 2011, Adam receives a second distribution from Roth IRA X and, on January 4, 2012, deposits this distribution in Roth IRA Y. Even though the distribution is rolled over within the 60-day period, this rollover is *not* permitted because Adam received the first rollover distribution from Roth IRA X within the preceding 12-month period. [Priv. Ltr. Rul. 9308050]

However, more than one transfer between Roth IRAs may be made during a 12-month period if the individual has the funds in a Roth IRA transferred from the Roth IRA *directly* to another Roth IRA. Because this type of transfer is not considered a rollover, the 12-month waiting period does not apply. To avoid any adverse consequences that might result to Adam in Example 2, Adam could have had the funds in Roth IRA X transferred directly to Roth IRA Y. [Priv. Ltr. Ruls. 9826042, 9438019, 9416037, 9106044, 9034068; IRS Pub. 590; *see also* Martin, 63 T.C.M. 3122 (1992); Martin, 67 T.C.M. 2960 (1994); Priv. Ltr. Ruls.200027064, 199948039, 9308050] If the individual has more than one Roth IRA, a separate 12-month waiting period applies for each Roth IRA. [Prop. Treas. Reg. § 1.408-4(b)(4)(ii)] A rollover from an IRA to a Roth IRA (see Q 31:44) is not treated as a rollover contribution for purposes of the 12-month waiting period rule. [I.R.C. § 408A(e); Treas. Reg. § 1.402(c)-2, Q&A-16]

The 60-day rollover period commences with the date of receipt; and, if the rollover is not made within that period, the distribution is deemed received in the calendar year of receipt, not the calendar year in which the 60-day period expires. [Robinson, 72 T.C.M. 1320 (1996)] The 60-day rollover period is measured in calendar days. If the 60th day falls on a Saturday, Sunday, or holiday, the rollover period is not extended to the next business day. [Priv. Ltr. Rul. 200606055]

> **Example 3.** Bill receives a distribution from his Roth IRA on December 1, 2010 and does not roll over the distribution to another Roth IRA. The distribution is deemed received by Bill in 2010, and not in 2011 when the 60-day rollover period expires.

WRERA 2008 (see Q 1:36) clarified that a qualified rollover contribution to a Roth IRA from another Roth IRA or a designated Roth account was not subject to the gross income inclusion, adjusted gross income limit, and filing status requirements that applied to rollovers from non-Roth eligible retirement plans (see Q 31:44). [I.R.C. § 408A(c)(3)(B) (as amended by WRERA 2008 § 108(d)(1))] For a discussion of the coordination between designated Roth accounts and Roth IRAs, see Q 31:43; and, for further details concerning the 60-day rollover period, see Q 34:36.

Q 31:41   May a beneficiary of a Roth IRA roll over the proceeds at the death of the Roth IRA owner?

If the beneficiary is *not* the surviving spouse of the Roth IRA owner, the minimum distribution requirements apply so that the Roth IRA proceeds must be distributed, or commence to be distributed, to the beneficiary by a specified date (see Qs 31:37, 31:38). [I.R.C. §§ 401(a)(9)(B), 408A(c)(5); Forms 5305-R, 5305-RA] Consequently, a Roth IRA acquired by a beneficiary upon the death of a nonspouse is an inherited Roth IRA and does not qualify for rollover treatment (see Q 30:48). [Priv. Ltr. Rul. 200013041] Furthermore, the nonspouse beneficiary cannot make contributions to an inherited Roth IRA. [I.R.C. § 408(d)(3)(C); Priv. Ltr. Ruls. 9630034, 9504045, 9305025, 9250040, 9014071, 8623054] Although the beneficiary of an inherited Roth IRA cannot make a rollover to a Roth IRA in the beneficiary's name, the beneficiary of an inherited Roth IRA can have the Roth IRA funds transferred directly to a new Roth IRA (see Q 31:40) *if* the new Roth IRA is maintained in the name of the decedent. This type of transfer is not a rollover and does not result in a distribution to the beneficiary. [Priv. Ltr. Ruls. 9810033, 9802046, 9751041, 9737030] Where a nonspouse beneficiary received a distribution from an inherited IRA and contributed the distribution to a new IRA in the decedent's name, IRS ruled that the distribution was includible in the nonspouse beneficiary's gross income because a trustee-to-trustee transfer did not occur. [Priv. Ltr. Rul. 200228023]

If the Roth IRA owner dies before the entire balance in the Roth IRA has been distributed and the surviving spouse is the *sole* beneficiary, the surviving spouse is then treated as the Roth IRA owner. [Forms 5305-R, 5305-RA] Alternatively, a surviving spouse who is the beneficiary of a deceased spouse's Roth IRA (or who is not the sole beneficiary) may roll over the distribution into the surviving spouse's own Roth IRA. [I.R.C. § 408(d)(3)(C); Priv. Ltr. Ruls. 9831032, 9711032, 9534027, 9433031] IRS has ruled that a surviving spouse who received a distribution from her deceased husband's IRA could redeposit (roll over) all or any portion of the distribution into the deceased husband's IRA. [I.R.C. § 408(d)(3)(D); Priv. Ltr. Rul. 200010054]

IRS has ruled that a surviving spouse may roll over funds received from the deceased spouse's IRA even though the surviving spouse was not specifically named as beneficiary. For details, see Qs 34:6 and 34:33. See Q 31:42 for new rollover rules and also Q 31:43 for a discussion of the coordination between designated Roth accounts and Roth IRAs.

Q 31:42   May a qualified retirement plan distribution be rolled over to a Roth IRA?

For taxable years beginning after December 31, 2007, qualified retirement plan and 403(b) plan (see Q 35:1) benefits may be directly rolled over to a Roth IRA. [I.R.C. §§ 408A(d)(3) (as amended by WRERA 2008 § 108(d)), 408A(e)] The rules that apply to a rollover or conversion of an IRA into a Roth IRA (see Q 31:44) also apply to a rollover from a qualified retirement plan or 403(b) plan to a Roth·IRA.

A distribution from a qualified retirement plan may only be rolled over to an eligible retirement plan; and, for taxable years beginning before January 1, 2008, an eligible retirement plan did not include a Roth IRA (see Q 34:16). [I.R.C. § 402(c)(8)(B); Priv. Ltr. Rul. 200220029] Furthermore, a rollover contribution to a Roth IRA from a qualified retirement plan was not a qualified rollover contribution (see Q 31:39). [I.R.C. § 408A(e); Treas. Reg. § 1.408A-4, Q&A-5] A rollover contribution to a Roth IRA from a 403(b) contract was also precluded. [I.R.C. § 403(b)(8); Treas. Reg. § 1.408A-4, Q&A-5]

As noted, for distributions made on or before December 31, 2007, a Roth IRA could only accept a rollover contribution of amounts distributed from another Roth IRA, from a non-Roth IRA (i.e., traditional IRA or SIMPLE IRA; see Q 33:2), or from a designated Roth account (see Q 27:96). These rollover contributions to

Roth IRAs are qualified rollover contributions (see Q 31:39). A qualified rollover contribution from a non-Roth IRA to a Roth IRA is a conversion (see Q 31:44). An individual who rolls over an amount from a non-Roth IRA to a Roth IRA must include in gross income any portion of the conversion amount that would be includible in gross income if the amount were distributed without being rolled over. For distributions before 2010, a conversion contribution was permitted only if the IRA owner's adjusted gross income (AGI) did not exceed certain limits (see Q 31:44). [IRS Notice 2008-30, 2008-1 C.B. 638]

For distributions made after December 31, 2007, distributions from a qualified retirement plan may be rolled over to a Roth IRA. The rollover can be made through a direct rollover (see Q 34:17) from the plan to the Roth IRA or an amount can be distributed from the plan and contributed (rolled over) to the Roth IRA within 60 days (see Qs 34:34-34:36). In either case, the amount rolled over must be an eligible rollover distribution (see Q 34:8) and there is included in gross income any amount that would be includible if the distribution were not rolled over (see Q 31:44). In addition, for taxable years beginning before January 1, 2010, an individual could not make a qualified rollover contribution from an eligible retirement plan other than a Roth IRA if, for the year the eligible rollover distribution was made, the individual had AGI exceeding $100,000 or was married and filed a separate return. [IRS Notice 2008-30, Q&A-1, 2008-1 C.B. 638] A qualified rollover contribution now includes distributions from 403(b) contracts and governmental Section 457 plans. [IRS Notice 2008-30, Q&A-2, 2008-1 C.B. 638]

The 10 percent penalty tax on early distributions (see Q 16:1) does not apply to rollovers from an eligible retirement plan other than a Roth IRA. However, as with conversions, if a taxable amount rolled into a Roth IRA from an eligible retirement plan other than a Roth IRA is distributed within five years, the penalty tax applies to such distribution as if it were includible in gross income (see Q 31:49). [IRS Notice 2008-30, Q&A-3, 2008-1 C.B. 638]

A plan is required to follow a distributee's election to have an eligible rollover distribution paid in a direct rollover to an eligible retirement plan specified by the distributee. [IRS Notice 2008-30, Q&A-4, 2008-1 C.B. 638] The plan administrator (see Q 20:1) was not responsible for assuring that the distributee was eligible to make a rollover to a Roth IRA. However, a distributee that was ineligible to make a rollover to a Roth IRA could have recharacterized the contribution (see Qs 31:9, 31:47). [IRS Notice 2008-30, Q&A-5, 2008-1 C.B. 638]

An eligible rollover distribution paid to an employee or the employee's spouse is subject to 20 percent mandatory withholding (see Qs 20:10, 34:33). An eligible rollover distribution that a distributee elects to have paid directly to an eligible retirement plan (including a Roth IRA) is not subject to mandatory withholding, even if the distribution is includible in gross income. Also, a distribution that is directly rolled over to a Roth IRA by a nonspouse beneficiary (see Q 34:33) is not subject to mandatory withholding. However, a distributee and a plan administrator or payor are permitted to enter into a voluntary withholding agreement with respect to an eligible rollover distribution that is directly rolled over from an eligible retirement plan to a Roth IRA (see Q 20:10). [IRS Notice 2008-30, Q&A-6, 2008-1 C.B. 638]

In the case of a distribution from an eligible retirement plan other than a Roth IRA, the AGI and filing status of the beneficiary were used to determine eligibility to make a qualified rollover contribution to a Roth IRA. A plan may, but was not required to, permit rollovers by nonspouse beneficiaries, and a rollover by a nonspouse beneficiary must be made by a direct trustee-to-trustee transfer. Effective for plan years beginning after December 31, 2009, this provision is mandatory and a plan is required to offer a direct rollover of a distribution to a nonspouse beneficiary (see Q 34:33). A nonspouse beneficiary who was ineligible to make a qualified rollover contribution to a Roth IRA could have recharacterized the contribution. A surviving spouse who makes a rollover to a Roth IRA may elect either to treat the Roth IRA as the surviving spouse's own or to establish the Roth IRA in the name of the decedent, with the surviving spouse as the beneficiary (see Q 31:41). A nonspouse beneficiary cannot elect to treat the Roth IRA as the beneficiary's own. In the case of a rollover where the beneficiary does not treat the Roth IRA as the beneficiary's own, minimum distributions from the Roth IRA are required (see Q 31:37). [IRS Notice 2008-30, Q&A-7, 2008-1 C.B. 638; *Retirement News for Employers*, Fall 2009]

IRS has explained how a former plan participant who initially requested the plan administrator to roll over the participant's plan account to an IRA may change that instruction and have the rollover instead made to a Roth IRA. IRS said that the course of action depends on whether or not the rollover to the IRA has been completed. If the rollover has not been completed, the participant should communicate with the plan administrator and change the rollover designation from an IRA to a Roth IRA. The plan administrator will complete Form 1099-R (Distributions From Pension, Annuities, Retirement or Profit-Sharing Plans, IRAs, Insurance Contracts, etc.) so that it properly reflects the rollover to the Roth IRA. However, if the participant elected to receive the distribution and make the rollover, the participant can simply roll the distribution over to a Roth IRA within 60 days of receipt. IRS noted, however, that the participant would have to replace the 20 percent mandatory withholding to accomplish a rollover of the entire plan account. If the plan administrator has completed the initial rollover request or the participant has completed the rollover, the participant may then roll over or convert the IRA into a Roth IRA. [*Retirement News for Employers,* Spring 2009]

IRS has clarified the consequences of making a rollover from an eligible retirement plan to a Roth IRA. [IRS Notice 2009-75, 2009-2 C.B. 436]

If an eligible rollover distribution from an eligible retirement plan is rolled over to a Roth IRA and the distribution is not made from a designated Roth account, then the amount that would be includible in gross income were it not part of a qualified rollover contribution is included in the distributee's gross income for the year of the distribution. For this purpose, the amount included in gross income is equal to the amount rolled over, reduced by the amount of any after-tax contributions (see Qs 6:38, 6:39) that are included in the amount rolled over, in the same manner as if the distribution had been rolled over to a non-Roth IRA that was the participant's only non-Roth IRA and that non-Roth IRA had then been immediately converted to a Roth IRA. Thus, the special rules relating to net unrealized appreciation (see Q 13:18) and certain optional methods for calculating tax available to participants born on or before January 1, 1936 (see Q 13:19) are not applicable. [IRS Notice 2009-75, 2009-2 C.B. 436, Q&A-1(a)]

Except for a distribution from a designated Roth account, an eligible rollover distribution made before January 1, 2010 from an eligible retirement plan may not be rolled over to a Roth IRA unless, for the year of the distribution, the distributee's AGI does not exceed $100,000 and, in the case of a married distributee, the distributee files a joint federal income tax return with the distributee's spouse. The $100,000 limit and the requirement that a married distributee file a joint return do not apply to distributions made on or after January 1, 2010. If an eligible rollover distribution made before 2010 is ineligible to be rolled over to a Roth IRA either because the distributee's AGI exceeds $100,000 or because a married distribute does not file a joint return, the distribution can be rolled over into a non-Roth IRA and then the non-Roth IRA can be converted, on or after January 1, 2010, into a Roth IRA. [IRS Notice 2009-75, 2009-2 C.B. 436, Q&A-2(a)]

See Q 31:43 for a discussion of the coordination between designated Roth accounts and Roth IRAs and the consequences of making a rollover from a designated Roth account to a Roth IRA.

Q 31:43   What is the coordination between designated Roth accounts and Roth IRAs?

An eligible rollover distribution (see Q 34:8) from a designated Roth account (see Q 27:96) may be rolled over to a Roth IRA. [Treas. Reg. § 1.408A-10, Q&A-1] Also, an individual may establish a Roth IRA and roll over an eligible rollover distribution from a designated Roth account to that Roth IRA even if such individual is not eligible to make regular contributions or was not eligible to make conversion contributions, because of the AGI limits (see Qs 31:16, 31:44). [Treas. Reg. § 1.408A-10, Q&A-2] IRS has announced that sponsors of prototype Roth IRAs must amend their documents in order to allow the rollover of amounts from designated Roth accounts. [Ann. 2007-55, 2007-2 C.B. 1384]

Distributions from Roth IRAs are deemed to consist first of regular contributions, then of conversion contributions, and finally of earnings (see Q 31:29). The amount of a rollover contribution that is treated as a regular contribution is the portion of the distribution that is treated as investment in the contract (see Q 27:101), and the remainder of the rollover contribution is treated as earnings. Thus, the entire amount of any qualified distribution (see Q 27:98) from a designated Roth account that is rolled over into a Roth IRA is treated as a regular contribution to the Roth IRA. Accordingly, a subsequent distribution from the Roth IRA in the amount of that rollover contribution is not includible in gross income (see Q 31:29). [Treas. Reg. § 1.408A-10, Q&A-3(a)] If the entire account balance of a designated Roth account is distributed to an employee and only a portion of the distribution is rolled over to a Roth IRA within the 60-day period (see Q 34:35) and, at the time of the distribution, the investment in the contract exceeds the balance in the designated Roth account, the portion of the investment in the contract that exceeds the amount used to determine the taxable amount of the distribution is treated as a regular contribution. [Treas. Reg. § 1.408A-10, Q&A-3(b)]

The five-taxable-year period for determining a qualified distribution from a Roth IRA begins with the earlier of the taxable year for which the individual is deemed to make a contribution to the individual's initial Roth IRA (see Q 31:28) or the taxable year in which a rollover contribution from a designated Roth account is made to a Roth IRA. The five-taxable-year period for this purpose and the five-taxable-year period of participation for a qualified distribution from a designated Roth account (see Q 27:99) are determined independently. [Treas. Reg. § 1.408A-10, Q&A-4]

Example 1. Sallie began making designated Roth contributions under her employer's 401(k) plan in 2009. Sallie, who is over 59½, takes a distribution from her designated Roth account in 2011, prior to the end of the five-taxable-year period of participation used to determine qualified distributions from a designated Roth account. The distribution is an eligible rollover distribution, and Sallie rolls it over to her Roth IRA, which was established in 2006 (i.e., established for more than five years). Any subsequent distribution from the Roth IRA of the amount rolled in, plus earnings thereon, would not be includible in gross income because it would be a qualified distribution.

Example 2. The facts are the same as in Example 1, except that the Roth IRA is Sallie's first Roth IRA and is established with the rollover in 2011, which is the only contribution made to the Roth IRA. If a distribution is made from the Roth IRA prior to the end of the five-taxable-year period used to determine qualified distributions from a Roth IRA (which begins in 2011, the year of the rollover which established the Roth IRA), the distribution would not be a qualified distribution, and any amount of the distribution that exceeded the portion of the rollover contribution that consisted of investment in the contract is includible in Sallie's gross income.

Example 3. The facts are the same as in Example 2, except that the distribution from the designated Roth account and the rollover to the Roth IRA occur in 2014 (after the end of the five-taxable-year period of participation used to determine qualified distributions from a designated Roth account). If a distribution is made from the Roth IRA prior to the expiration of the five-taxable-year period used to determine qualified distributions from a Roth IRA, the distribution would not be a qualified distribution, and any amount of the distribution that exceeded the amount rolled in is includible in Sallie's gross income.

Amounts distributed from a Roth IRA may be rolled over or transferred only to another Roth IRA and are not permitted to be rolled over to a designated Roth account. The same rule applies even if all the amounts in the Roth IRA are attributable to a rollover distribution from a designated Roth account in a plan. [Treas. Reg. § 1.408A-10, Q&A-5]

These regulations apply for taxable years beginning on or after January 1, 2006. [Treas. Reg. § 1.408A-10, Q&A-6]

IRS has clarified the consequences of making a rollover from a designated Roth account to a Roth IRA. If an eligible rollover distribution made from a designated Roth account in an eligible retirement plan is rolled over to a Roth IRA, the amount rolled over is not includible in the distributee's gross income, whether or not the distribution is a qualified distribution (see Q 31:27) from the designated Roth account. [IRS Notice 2009-75, 2009-2 C.B. 436, Q&A-1(b)] There are no restrictions based on the limitations and joint filing requirements that apply to a rollover of an eligible rollover distribution made from a designated Roth account under an eligible retirement plan to a Roth IRA. [IRS Notice 2009-75, 2009-2 C.B. 436, Q&A-2(b)]

Under SBJA 2010 (see Q 1:36B), eligible retirement plan distributions from 401(k) and 403(b) plans (see Qs 27:1, 35:1) made after September 27, 2010 may be rolled over to a designated Roth account within the plan. Any amount required to be included in gross income for the 2010 taxable year is included in income in equal amounts for the 2011 and 2012 taxable years unless the taxpayer elects otherwise (see Q 31:49).

Q 31:44 May an individual roll over or convert an IRA into a Roth IRA?

Effective for taxable years beginning after December 31, 2009, the $100,000 income limit discussed in this Q 31:44 is eliminated. Thus, taxpayers, including married taxpayers filing separate returns, are permitted to make such conversions without regard to their AGI. [TIPRA § 512(c)] By eliminating the AGI limitation on conversions of IRAs into Roth IRAs, most individuals will be able to circumvent the AGI limitation for making contributions to Roth IRAs (see Q 31:16). This is because an individual who is ineligible to make a Roth IRA contribution may be eligible to make a deductible IRA contribution, and an individual who is ineligible to make either a Roth IRA contribution or a deductible IRA contribution may be eligible to make a nondeductible IRA contribution (see Qs 30:5, 30:6, 30:17, 30:20). In 2010 and thereafter, the individual can then immediately convert the IRA or designated nondeductible IRA into a Roth IRA without any AGI limitation. See Q 31:49 for available income tax elections.

For taxable years beginning before January 1, 2010, an individual could have made a qualified rollover contribution (see Q 31:39) to a Roth IRA from an IRA unless for the taxable year of the distribution to which the contribution related:

1. The individual's AGI (see Q 31:16) exceeded $100,000, or
2. The individual was married and filed a separate return (i.e., the individual and spouse did not file a joint federal income tax return).

[I.R.C. § 408A(c)(3)(B)(prior to repeal by TIPRA § 512(c)); Treas. Reg. § 1. 408A-4, Q&A-1(a), Q&A-2; Forms 5305-R, 5305-RA]

The only exception to this joint filing requirement was for an individual who lived apart from the spouse for the entire taxable year. In that case, such individual could be treated as not married, file a separate return, and be subject to the $100,000 limit on the individual's separate AGI. In all other cases, a married individual filing a separate return was not permitted to convert an amount to a Roth IRA, regardless of the individual's AGI. [I.R.C. §§ 219(g)(4), 408A(c) (3)(C); Treas. Reg. § 1.408A-4, Q&A-2(b)]

Although amounts includible in income as a result of a conversion of an IRA into a Roth IRA was not taken into account in the calculation of an individual's AGI (see Q 31:16), such income was included as an item of income for purposes of determining the taxability of the individual's Social Security benefits and could have caused the individual's AGI to exceed the threshold amount. [Helm, T.C. Summ. Op. 2002-138] An individual's AGI did not include RMDs (see chapter 11) from IRAs *solely* for purposes of determining eligibility to roll over or convert an IRA into a Roth IRA. The RMD, however, was not, and still will not be, eligible for such a rollover or conversion and will be includible in the individual's gross income. [I.R.C. § 408A(c)(3)(C)(i)(prior to repeal by TIPRA § 512(c)); Treas. Reg. §§ 1.408A-3, Q&A-6, 1.408A-4, Q&A-6; Joint Committee on Taxation's General Explanation of Tax Legislation Enacted in 1998, Tit. VII, D] Although the IRS regulation was silent regarding RMDs from qualified retirement plans, IRS indicated that an individual's AGI also did not include RMDs from such plans. [IRS Pub. 590] However, RMDs for 2009 were suspended (see Q 11:1). Thus, distributions during 2009 that would have been RMDs were not excluded from an individual's AGI. This paragraph is applicable only to taxable years beginning before January 1, 2010.

In order to be eligible for a conversion, an amount must be eligible to be rolled over, and a rollover of an RMD is prohibited. If a minimum distribution is required for a year with respect to an IRA, the first dollars distributed during that year are treated as consisting of the RMD until an amount equal to the RMD for that year has been distributed. Any amount converted is treated as a distribution from a traditional IRA and a rollover contribution to a Roth IRA, not as a trustee-to-trustee transfer. Thus, in a year for which a minimum distribution is required (including the calendar year in which the individual attains age 70½), an individual may not convert the assets of an IRA (or any portion of those assets) to a Roth IRA to the extent that the RMD for the traditional IRA for the year has not been distributed. If an RMD is contributed to a Roth IRA, it is treated as having been distributed and then contributed as a regular contribution to a Roth IRA. The amount of the RMD is not a conversion contribution. [Treas. Reg. § 1.408A-4, Q&A-6]

As with rollovers generally, including a rollover from one Roth IRA to another, a rollover from an IRA to a Roth IRA must satisfy the 60-day rule (see Q 31:40). However, with regard only to rollovers from an IRA to a Roth IRA, the 12-month rule does *not* apply so that multiple rollovers within a 12-month period may be made from an IRA to a Roth IRA. [I.R.C. § 408A(e); Treas. Reg. § 1.408A-4, Q&A-1]

Example. On October 8, 2010, James received a distribution from his IRA and, on October 25, 2010, deposited the distribution in his Roth IRA. On January 3, 2011, James receives a second distribution from his IRA and, on

February 7, 2011, deposits this distribution in his Roth IRA. Because both rollovers satisfy the 60-day rule and rollovers from IRAs to Roth IRAs are disregarded for the 12-month rule, both rollovers are qualified rollover contributions.

Instead of receiving a distribution from an IRA and rolling it over into a Roth IRA, an individual may effect a conversion of an IRA into a Roth IRA. [I.R.C. § 408A(d)(3)(C); Treas. Reg. § 1.408A-4, Q&A-1(b)] A conversion is treated in the same manner as a rollover. If an individual wishes to roll over the entire balance in an IRA to a Roth IRA, the individual can simply sign Form 5305-R or Form 5305-RA and direct the IRA trustee or custodian to change the IRA to a Roth IRA. If the individual wishes to roll over less than the entire balance, the individual can do a trustee-to-trustee transfer without taking an actual distribution. A conversion or trustee-to-trustee transfer is the preferred method because the 60-day rule will automatically be satisfied. Where a participant in a qualified retirement plan received an eligible rollover distribution but died within 60 days of receiving the distribution without having completed a rollover into an IRA, the executor of his estate was able to complete the rollover as the participant's fiduciary. [Gunther v. United States, 537 F. Supp. 126 (W.D. Mich. 1982)] Even assuming this would apply to a rollover from an IRA to a Roth IRA, this problem would be avoided by effecting a conversion of an IRA into a Roth IRA or by doing a trustee-to-trustee transfer. However, IRS ruled otherwise and did not permit the decedent's executor to complete the rollover. [Priv. Ltr. Rul. 200415011] In another ruling, IRS permitted the decedent's wife, who had been the sole beneficiary of the decedent's IRA, to complete the rollover by contributing the distribution to an IRA established in the decedent's name. [Priv. Ltr. Rul. 200444029] See Q 34:34 for further details.

Effectively, an amount can be converted by any of three methods:

1. An amount distributed from an IRA is contributed (rolled over) to a Roth IRA within the 60-day period;
2. An amount in an IRA is transferred in a trustee-to-trustee transfer from the trustee of the IRA to the trustee of the Roth IRA; or
3. An amount in an IRA is transferred to a Roth IRA maintained by the same trustee.

Any converted amount is treated as a distribution from the IRA and a qualified rollover contribution to the Roth IRA, even if the conversion is accomplished by means of a trustee-to-trustee transfer or a transfer between IRAs of the same trustee. A transaction that is treated as a failed conversion (see Q 31:47) is not a conversion. [Treas. Reg. § 1.408A-4, Q&A-1(c), Q&A-1(d); *see also* Priv. Ltr. Rul. 200437037] However, the beneficiary of an inherited IRA (see Q 30:48) cannot convert the IRA to an inherited Roth IRA. [I.R.C. §§ 408(d)(3)(C), 408A(e)(1)(B)(i)]

Q 31:45 May an IRA rollover or conversion be made if the individual is receiving substantially equal periodic payments?

Yes. Not only is the conversion amount itself not subject to the 10 percent early distribution tax (see Q 31:32), but the conversion amount is also not treated as a distribution for purposes of determining whether a modification has occurred (see Qs 16:7, 16:9). Distributions from the Roth IRA that are part of the original series of substantially equal periodic payments will be nonqualified distributions from the Roth IRA until they meet the requirements for being a qualified distribution (see Q 31:27).

The additional 10 percent tax will not apply to the extent that these nonqualified distributions are part of a series of substantially equal periodic payments. However, if the original series of substantially equal periodic payments does not continue to be distributed in substantially equal periodic payments from the Roth IRA after the conversion, the series of payments will have been modified and, if this modification occurs within five years of the first payment or prior to the individual becoming disabled (see Q 16:6) or attaining age 59½ (see Q 16:4), the individual will be subject to the recapture tax (see Q 16:9).

[Treas. Reg. § 1.408A-4, Q&A-12]

Q 31:46   May an individual roll over or convert a SEP or SIMPLE IRA into a Roth IRA?

A qualified rollover contribution (see Q 31:39) includes a rollover contribution to a Roth IRA from an IRA. [I.R.C. §§ 408A(c)(6), 408A(d)(3)(as amended by WRERA 2008 § 108(d)(2)), 408A(e); Treas. Reg. § 1.408A-4, Q&A-1] Both a SEP (see Q 32:1) and a SIMPLE IRA (see Q 33:2) are IRAs. However, a SEP or SIMPLE IRA may not be designated as a Roth IRA. [I.R.C. § 408A(f)]

An amount in an individual's SEP IRA can be converted to a Roth IRA on the same terms as an amount in any other traditional IRA (see Q 31:44). An amount in an individual's SIMPLE IRA can be converted to a Roth IRA on the same terms as a conversion from a traditional IRA, except that an amount distributed from a SIMPLE IRA during a two-year period that begins on the date that the individual first participated in any SIMPLE IRA plan maintained by the individual's employer cannot be converted to a Roth IRA (see Qs 33:17, 33:18). A distribution of an amount from an individual's SIMPLE IRA during this two-year period is not eligible to be rolled over into an IRA that is not a SIMPLE IRA and thus cannot be a qualified rollover contribution. This two-year period applies separately to the contributions of each of an individual's employers maintaining a SIMPLE IRA plan. Once an amount in a SEP IRA or SIMPLE IRA has been converted to a Roth IRA, it is treated as a contribution to a Roth IRA for all purposes. Future contributions under the SEP or under the SIMPLE IRA plan may not be made to the Roth IRA. [Treas. Reg. § 1.408A-4, Q&A-4]

Q 31:47   May an individual reverse a rollover or conversion of an IRA into a Roth IRA?

In order to assist individuals who erroneously convert IRAs into Roth IRAs, contributions to a Roth IRA (and earnings thereon) may be transferred in a trustee-to-trustee transfer from the Roth IRA to a non-Roth IRA by the due date for the individual's federal income tax return for the year of the contribution (including extensions). Any such transferred contributions will be treated as if contributed to the transferee IRA (and not to the transferor IRA). Trustee-to-trustee transfers include transfers between IRA trustees as well as IRA custodians, apply to transfers from and to IRA accounts and annuities, and apply to transfers between IRA accounts and annuities with the same trustee or custodian. [I.R.C. §§ 408A(d)(6), 408A(d)(7); Treas. Reg. §§ 1.408A-4, Q&A-3, 1.408A-5, Q&A-1 through Q&A-9; Ann. 99-104, 1999-2 C.B. 555; Ann. 99-57, 1999-1 C.B. 1256; IRS Notice 98-49, § B, Q&A-1, 1998-2 C.B. 365]

> **Example 1.** In 2009, Michael believed that his AGI would not exceed $100,000 and converted his IRA into a Roth IRA. When Michael's 2009 federal income tax return was prepared, his AGI (excluding the converted amount) was actually $102,000. Michael had until April 15, 2010, to reverse the conversion by transferring his Roth IRA, including the earnings on the converted amount, to an IRA. If Michael received an extension to file his return, he had until October 15, 2010.

> **Example 2.** In 2009, Richard believed that his AGI would not exceed $100,000 (excluding the converted amount) and converted his IRA into a Roth IRA. Richard received an extension to file his 2009 federal income tax return and filed the return on September 23, 2010 disclosing AGI of $98,000 (excluding the converted amount). In 2012, a partnership in which Richard was a partner is audited for calendar year 2009; and, as a result of the audit, Richard's AGI for 2009 increases to $101,000 (excluding the converted amount). Because Richard's AGI for 2009 exceeded $100,000, he was not permitted to convert his IRA to a Roth IRA; and, because October 15, 2010 has passed, he cannot correct the conversion. Consequently, Richard's 2009 conversion is an excess contribution to a Roth IRA and subject to the 6 percent excess contribution penalty tax for 2009, 2010, 2011, and, possibly, 2012 unless a timely withdrawal is made (see Q 31:8). In addition, net income on the converted amount is treated as gross income for the taxable year in which the excess contribution was made.

The term "failed conversion" means a transaction in which an individual contributes to a Roth IRA an amount transferred or distributed from a traditional IRA or SIMPLE IRA (including a transfer by redesignation) in a transaction that does not constitute a conversion (see Q 31:44). [Treas. Reg. § 1.408A-8, Q&A-1(b)(4); *see also* Priv. Ltr. Rul. 200437037]

If a failed conversion amount is recharacterized as a contribution to a traditional IRA, the failed conversion amount will be treated as having been contributed to the traditional IRA and not to the Roth IRA. If the contribution is not properly recharacterized, the contribution will be treated as a regular contribution to the Roth IRA and, thus, an excess contribution subject to the excess contribution penalty tax to the extent that it exceeds the individual's regular contribution limit. This is the result regardless of which conversion method was utilized (i.e., rollover, trustee-to-trustee transfer, or redesignation). [Treas. Reg. § 1.408A-4, Q&A-3]

See Q 31:9 for a discussion of recharacterized contributions, IRS extensions of time to recharacterize, and the examples therein illustrating the recharacterization rules.

Q 31:48   Can multiple recharacterizations be made?

An IRA owner who converts an amount from a traditional IRA to a Roth IRA during any taxable year and then transfers that amount back to a traditional IRA by means of a recharacterization (see Qs 31:9, 31:47) may not reconvert that amount from the traditional IRA to a Roth IRA before the beginning of the taxable year following the taxable year in which the amount was converted to a Roth IRA or, if later, the end of the 30-day period beginning on the day on which the IRA owner transfers the amount from the Roth IRA back to a traditional IRA by means of a recharacterization (regardless of whether the recharacterization occurs during the taxable year in which the amount was converted to a Roth IRA or the following taxable year). Thus, any attempted reconversion of an amount prior to the time permitted is a failed conversion (see Q 31:47) of that amount. [Treas. Reg. § 1.408A-5, Q&A-9(a)(1)] For this purpose, a failed conversion of an amount resulting from a failure to satisfy the AGI or joint filing requirement (see Q 31:44) is treated as a conversion in determining whether an IRA owner has previously converted that amount. [Treas. Reg. § 1.408A-5, Q&A-9(a)(2)]

> **Example.** Casey converted his IRA into a Roth IRA in 2010 and recharacterized this 2010 conversion on October 8, 2011. Casey must wait until November 8, 2011 (31 days) to reconvert back to a Roth IRA. Casey does not have to wait until 2012 to reconvert because the original conversion was done in 2010 and 2011 is the year after the conversion, so the 30-day period is the longer time period.

Q 31:49   What are the tax consequences of an IRA rollover or conversion into a Roth IRA?

Unlike an income tax-free rollover from one IRA to another (see Qs 34:1, 34:3), a rollover or conversion of an IRA to a Roth IRA (see Q 31:44) is taxable to the same extent as if the amount distributed from the IRA was not rolled over at all. [I.R.C. § 408A(d)(3)(A)(i); Treas. Reg. § 1.408A-4, Q&A-7(a)]

> **Example 1.** In 2011, Brian converts his IRA (his only IRA) to a Roth IRA. The entire amount of Brian's IRA will be includible in his gross income that year.

> **Example 2.** In 2011, Claire converts her designated nondeductible IRA (see Q 30:20; her only IRA) to a Roth IRA. Because Claire's contributions to her IRA were not deductible, only the portion of her IRA attributable to earnings will be includible in her gross income that year.

> **Example 3.** In 2011, Ben converts his designated nondeductible IRA to a Roth IRA, but Ben also has a deductible IRA that he does not convert. The amount taxable that year to Ben is determined by subtracting from the amount of the conversion an amount that bears the same ratio to the amount

of the conversion as Ben's aggregate nondeductible IRA contributions bear to the aggregate balance of both of Ben's IRAs (see Q 30:23).

The amount includible in gross income because of the rollover or conversion of an IRA to a Roth IRA is not subject to the 10 percent penalty tax on early distributions even if the penalty tax would otherwise apply (see Q 16:1). [I.R.C. § 408A(d)(3)(A)(ii); Treas. Reg. § 1.408A-4, Q&A-7(b)]

> **Example 4.** In Example 1, assume that Brian has not attained age 59½ and no other exception to the penalty tax is applicable. Even though the entire amount in Brian's IRA will be taxable, no portion of the conversion will be subject to the 10 percent penalty tax.

Conversion amounts includible in gross income may be subject to the elective withholding rules. [Treas. Reg. § 1.408A-6, Q&A-13] Since conversion amounts are includible in gross income, the individual could become liable for estimated tax underpayment penalties. IRS has advised that it is not authorized to abate such penalties. [Special Couns. Adv. 200105062]

Although the amount includible in gross income because of a rollover or conversion of an IRA to a Roth IRA is not subject to the 10 percent penalty tax, an individual is prevented from receiving a premature distribution (i.e., within five years) while retaining the benefit of the nonpayment of the 10 percent early withdrawal penalty tax. If converted amounts are withdrawn within the five-year period beginning with the year of the rollover or conversion, then, to the extent attributable to amounts that were includible in income due to the rollover or conversion, the amount withdrawn will be subject to the 10 percent penalty unless an exception applies. [I.R.C. § 408A(d)(3)(F); Treas. Reg. § 1.408A-6, Q&A-5(a), Q&A-5(b); Kitt v. United States, 2002 WL 27527 (Fed. Cir. 2002); *IRS Employee Plans News*, Winter 2010; *Retirement News for Employers*, Winter 2010]

This five-year period for purposes of determining whether the penalty tax applies to a distribution allocable to a conversion contribution is separately determined for each conversion contribution, and need not be the same as the five-year holding period used for purposes of determining whether a distribution is a qualified distribution (see Qs 31:27, 31:28). For example, if a taxpayer who received a distribution from a traditional IRA on December 31, 2009, made a conversion contribution by contributing the distributed amount to a Roth IRA on February 25, 2010, in a qualifying rollover contribution and made a regular contribution for 2009 on the same date, the five-year period for purposes of penalty tax began on January 1, 2010, while the five-year holding period for purposes of qualified distributions began on January 1, 2009. [Treas. Reg. § 1.408A-6, Q&A-5(c); *IRS Employee Plans News*, Winter 2010; *Retirement News for Employers*, Winter 2010]

> **Example.** On April 3, 2006, Sallie converted her $80,000 traditional IRA to her first Roth IRA. The five-year holding period used for purposes of determining whether a distribution is a qualified distribution began on January 1, 2006. On March 6, 2010, Sallie made a $5,000 contribution to her second Roth IRA. On December 1, 2010, when Sallie was age 60, she withdrew

$7,000 from her first Roth IRA, which withdrawal was not a qualified distribution. Because of the ordering rules (see Q 31:29), the $7,000 withdrawal is not includible in Sallie's gross income, since $5,000 is deemed to be from the contribution to her second Roth IRA and $2,000 is deemed to be from the conversion contribution to her first Roth IRA. Had Sallie been age 59 on December 1, 2010, then, even though no portion of the withdrawal would be includible in her gross income, the $2,000 attributable to the conversion contribution would be subject to the 10 percent penalty tax on early distributions, unless another exception applies (see Q 16:3), because the withdrawal was made within five years from January 1, 2006, the commencement of the five-year holding period for her first Roth IRA.

If the owner of a Roth IRA dies prior to the end of the five-year period relating to qualified distributions (see Q 31:28) or prior to the end of the five-year period relating to conversions, the different types of contributions in the Roth IRA are allocated, if there are multiple beneficiaries, to each beneficiary on a pro rata basis. Thus, for example, if a Roth IRA owner died in 2008 when the Roth IRA contained a regular contribution of $2,000, a conversion contribution of $6,000, and earnings of $1,000, and the owner left the Roth IRA equally to four children, each child receives one-quarter of each type of contribution. Pursuant to the ordering rules, an immediate distribution of $2,000 to one of the children will be deemed to consist of $500 of regular contributions, $1,500 of conversion contributions, and no amount of earnings. [Treas. Reg. § 1.408A-6, Q&A-11]

IRS has issued final regulations clarifying the amount of income that must be reflected when a traditional IRA annuity is converted to a Roth IRA. The final regulations are applicable to any conversion in which an annuity contract is distributed or treated as distributed from a traditional IRA on or after August 19, 2005. However, for annuity contracts distributed or treated as distributed from a traditional IRA on or before December 31, 2008, taxpayers may instead apply the valuation methods in the previously issued temporary regulations and Revenue Procedure 2006-13. [Treas. Reg. § 1.408A-4, Q&A-14(c)]

Where part or all of a traditional IRA that is an individual retirement annuity (see Q 30:3) is converted to a Roth IRA, for purposes of determining the amount includible in gross income as a distribution, the amount that is treated as distributed is the fair market value of the annuity contract on the date the annuity contract is converted. Similarly, where a traditional IRA that is an individual retirement account (see Q 30:2) holds an annuity contract as an account asset and the traditional IRA is converted to a Roth IRA, for purposes of determining the amount includible in gross income as a distribution, the amount that is treated as distributed with respect to the annuity contract is the fair market value of the annuity contract on the date that the annuity contract is distributed or treated as distributed from the traditional IRA. These rules also apply to conversions from SIMPLE IRAs (see Q 33:2). [Treas. Reg. § 1.408A-4, Q&A-14(a)(1)] The preceding does not apply to a conversion of a traditional IRA to the extent the conversion is accomplished by the complete surrender of an annuity contract for its cash value and the reinvestment of the cash proceeds in a Roth IRA, but only if the surrender extinguishes all benefits and other characteristics of the contract. In such a case, the cash from the surrendered contract is the amount reinvested in the Roth IRA. [Treas. Reg. 1.408A-4, Q&A-14(a)(2)]

If, with respect to an annuity, there is a comparable contract issued by the company which sold the annuity, the fair market value of the annuity may be established by the price of the comparable contract. If the conversion occurs soon after the annuity was sold, the comparable contract may be the annuity itself and, thus, the fair market value of the annuity may be established through the sale of the particular contract by the company (that is, the actual premiums paid for such contract). If, with respect to an annuity, there is no comparable contract available in order to make the comparison, the fair market value may be established through an approximation that is based on the interpolated terminal reserve at the date of the conversion, plus the proportionate part of the gross premium last paid before the date of the conversion that covers the period extending beyond that date. This is referred to as the gift tax method. [Treas. Reg. § 1.408A-4, Q&A-14(b)(2)]

As an alternative to the gift tax method, the accumulation method may be used for an annuity contract that has not been annuitized. The fair market value of such an annuity contract is permitted to be determined using the methodology provided in Q 11:36, with the following modifications:

1. All front-end loads and other non-recurring charges assessed in the 12 months immediately preceding the conversion must be added to the account value;

2. Future distributions are not to be assumed in the determination of the actuarial present value of additional benefits; and

3. The exclusions set forth in the second paragraph of Q 11:36 are not to be taken into account. [Treas. Reg. § 1.408A-4, Q&A-14(b)(3)]

If, because of the unusual nature of the contract, the value determined under one of the above methods does not reflect the full value of the contract, that method may not be used. Additional guidance regarding the fair market value of an individual retirement annuity, including formulas to be used for determining fair market value, may be issued by IRS in revenue rulings, notices, or other guidance. [Treas. Reg. § 1.408A-4, Q&A-14(b)(1)]

The income limit for rolling over or converting an IRA into a Roth IRA will be eliminated for taxable years beginning after December 31, 2009 (see Q 31:44). If a conversion to a Roth IRA occurs after 2010, the taxable portion of the conversion amount will be includible in gross income for the year of the conversion (see Examples 1, 2, and 3 of this Q 31:49). However, if the conversion occurs in 2010, then, unless the individual elects otherwise, none of the income from the conversion will be included in gross income in 2010; but, one-half of the income resulting from the conversion will be includible in gross income in 2011 and the other one-half in 2012.

Example 5. Steve's IRA has a $20,000 balance, consisting of deductible contributions and earnings. Steve does not have a Roth IRA. In February

2010, Steve converts his IRA to a Roth IRA; and, as a result of the conversion, $20,000 is includible in gross income. Unless Steve elects otherwise (i.e., unless he elects to include the entire conversion in income for 2010), $10,000 of the income resulting from the conversion will be included in income in 2011 and $10,000 in 2012.

Unless IRS provides a form and/or a procedure for making the election, presumably, an individual would elect not to have the two-tax-year-spread period apply by simply including in gross income on the individual's 2010 tax return the entire amount of the taxable portion of the conversion.

An individual is prevented from receiving a premature distribution from a Roth IRA that received amounts from a converted IRA while retaining the benefit of the two-tax-year-spread period. Thus, for premature distributions of converted amounts, there is an acceleration of income inclusion, and the 10 percent early withdrawal penalty tax may apply. Under the income inclusion rule, the amount that will be included in an individual's gross income for any taxable year beginning in 2010, or the first taxable year in the two-tax-year-spread period (i.e., 2011), will be:

1. The aggregate distributions from the individual's Roth IRAs for the taxable year that are allocable to the portion of the qualified rollover contribution (including conversions) required to be included in gross income, plus

2. The lesser of:
   a. One-half of the amount includible in income as a result of the conversion, and
   b. The aggregate amount that must be included in gross income as a result of the conversion for all taxable years in the two-year period (without regard to the amount of the premature distribution of rolled over amounts), reduced by amounts included in gross income for all preceding taxable years.

Example 6. Sallie has an IRA with a value of $20,000, consisting of deductible contributions and earnings, and she has no Roth IRA. Sallie converts her IRA to a Roth IRA in January 2010. As a result of the conversion, $20,000 is includible in gross income. Unless Sallie elects otherwise, $10,000 of the income resulting from the conversion normally would be included in income in 2011, and $10,000 in 2012. Assume, however, that, in May 2010, Sallie takes a $4,000 distribution from the Roth IRA that is not a qualified distribution. Under the ordering rules, all of the $4,000 distribution is attributable to amounts includible in income as a result of the conversion. Under the income inclusion rule, the $4,000 is included in income in 2010 ($4,000 taxable conversion distribution + $0 previously included in income). In 2011, the amount included in income is $10,000: $0 distribution + the lesser of (a) $10,000 (one-half of the amount resulting from the conversion income) or (b) $16,000 (i.e., $20,000 taxable conversion income – $4,000 previously included in income). In 2012, the amount included in income is $6,000: $0 distribution + the lesser of (a) $10,000 one-half of the income resulting from the conversion or (b) $20,000 – ($4,000 included in income in 2010 + $10,000 included in income in 2011).

If an individual who converted an IRA into a Roth IRA in 2010 dies before 2012 (when all of the conversion income will have been included in income under the two-year rule), the remaining conversion income is included in income for the taxable year of death. However, if the individual's surviving spouse acquires the individual's entire interest in any Roth IRA into which the IRA was converted in 2010, the spouse may elect to continue the two-year spread by including in income the remaining amounts of the conversion income over the remainder of the two-year period. The amounts would be includible in the spouse's gross income in the taxable years ending with (or within) the taxable years of the deceased individual in which the amounts would have been includible. This election cannot be made or changed after the due date for filing the tax return for the spouse's taxable year that includes the date of death.

[I.R.C. §§ 408A(d)(3)(A)(iii); 408A(d)(3)(E)(i)]

It appears that, after 2012, a large Roth IRA conversion could trigger the imposition of the new health care taxes on a taxpayer's investment income and wages.

Q 31:50   Can a Roth IRA be reached by judgment creditors?

It may have depended on state law because ERISA does not apply to Roth IRAs. Some state statutes may exempt an IRA from judgment creditors by making a specific reference to Section 408. Since a Roth IRA is created under Section 408A, not Section 408, such a state statute would not encompass a Roth IRA. However, see Q 30:52 for new developments.

Q 31:51   What are the Roth IRA reporting requirements?

Generally, the reporting requirements applicable to IRAs (see Q 30:53) other than Roth IRAs also apply to Roth IRAs, except that the trustee of a Roth IRA must include on Forms 1099-R and 5498 additional information as described in the instructions thereto. Any conversion of amounts from an IRA other than a Roth IRA to a Roth IRA is treated as a distribution for which a Form 1099-R must be filed by the trustee maintaining the non-Roth IRA. In addition, the owner of such IRAs must report the conversion by completing Form 8606. In the case of a recharacterization (see Q 31:9), IRA owners must report such transactions in the manner prescribed in the instructions to the applicable federal tax forms.

A trustee maintaining a Roth IRA is permitted to rely on reasonable representations of a Roth IRA contributor or distributee for purposes of fulfilling reporting obligations.

[Treas. Reg. § 1.408A-7, Q&A-1, Q&A-2; Ann. 99-106, 1999-2 C.B. 561; IRS Notice 98-49, 1998-2 C.B. 365; Ann. 99-18, 1999-1 C.B. 853; Ann. 99-5, 1999-1 C.B. 325; Ann. 98-113, 1998-2 C.B. 793]

IRS has provided a method for reporting IRA recharacterizations and reconversions by IRA trustees after December 31, 2000. The reporting method retains the existing requirement that recharacterized amounts be identified separately from other types of distributions and contributions to IRAs; but the method specifies that each recharacterization or reconversion occurring after December 31, 2000, whether or not the same trustee is involved, must be reported as provided for on Forms 5498 and 1099-R and the accompanying instructions. The forms and their instructions were changed to include the following rules:

1. Recharacterizations that occur after the year for which the contributions being recharacterized were made and recharacterizations that occur in the same year as the year for which the contributions being recharacterized were made must be reported on separate Forms 1099-R.

2. All prior year recharacterizations from the same originating IRA must be reported together on a single Form 1099-R using Code R in Box 7, and all same-year recharacterizations from the same originating IRA must be reported on a single Form 1099-R using the new code in Box 7.

3. Recharacterizations are reported in a new box on Form 5498 titled "Recharacterized contributions," and the checkbox titled "Rechar." has been eliminated.

4. All recharacterized contributions received by an IRA in the same year may be totaled and reported on one Form 5498 or each recharacterized contribution can be reported on a separate Form 5498.

5. Reconversions are reported on Forms 1099-R and 5498 in the same manner as other conversions.

[IRS Notice 2000-30, 2000-1 C.B. 1266]

Because of the reporting requirements discussed above, the following changes were made to the distribution codes:

1. Code N is added for reporting a *Recharacterized IRA contribution made for 2001*.

2. Code R is changed to report a *Recharacterized IRA contribution made for 2000*.

Only two distribution codes can be entered in Box 7 on Form 1099-R. Therefore, payers were able only to report a distribution as the result of an excess contribution to a Roth IRA by using Code J with Code 8 or P. Payers could not use Code 1, 2, 3, or 4 if Codes J and 8 or P applied. To alleviate this reporting problem, the following changes have been made to the distribution codes:

1. Code J is changed to report an *Early distribution from a Roth IRA, no known exception*.

2. Code T is added to report a *Roth IRA distribution, exception applies*.

Therefore, payers can use only the following codes for a Roth IRA distribution:

1. Code J for an early distribution from a Roth IRA, no known exception. (Do not use Code 1 with Code J. However, Code 5, 8, or P, if applicable, must be used.)

2. Code T for a distribution from a Roth IRA, exception applies. (Do not use Code 2, 3, 4, or 7 with Code T. However, Code 5, 8, or P, if applicable, must be used.)

[Ann. 2000-86, 2000-2 C.B. 456]

For 2003 and subsequent years, IRA trustees may furnish the required Form 1099-R and Form 5498 electronically to recipients if the trustee satisfies the consent, format, posting, and notification requirements. [IRS Notice 2004-10, 2004-1 C.B. 433]

See Q 30:53 for additional details.

Chapter 32

Simplified Employee Pensions

Complex and burdensome rules may cause the owner of a small business to think twice before adopting a qualified retirement plan. But then both the company and the owner forgo significant tax benefits. The simplified employee pension offers a practical alternative with respect to the institution of a retirement program. Requirements for establishing and maintaining a SEP are explained in this chapter.

Q 32:1 What is a simplified employee pension (SEP)?

A SEP is an individual retirement account or individual retirement annuity (IRA) established for an employee to which the employer makes discretionary, direct tax-deductible contributions. [I.R.C. § 408(k); Prop. Treas. Reg. § 1.408-7(c)(1)]

For a discussion on IRAs, see chapter 30.

Q 32:2 Who is eligible to participate in a SEP?

Each employee age 21 or over who earns at least $450 during the year (adjusted for cost-of-living increases) and has performed services for the employer in at least three of the immediately preceding five calendar years must participate in the SEP. Employees covered by a collective bargaining agreement in which retirement benefits were the subject of good-faith bargaining and employees who are nonresident aliens may be excluded from participation. All employees, including part-time employees, not excluded under one of the above statutory exclusions must participate in the SEP. [I.R.C. § 408(k)(2); Prop. Treas. Reg. § 1.408-7(d)] A deduction was disallowed where an S corporation had only two employees, a husband and wife, and a contribution to the SEP was made only for the husband. Because no SEP contribution was made for the other employee, the wife, the participation requirements were not met. [Brown, No. 4460-07S (Tax Ct. 2008)]

The $450 compensation requirement is adjusted for cost-of-living increases. However, an adjustment will be made only if it is $50 or greater, and then will be made in multiples of $50 (i.e., rounded down to the next lowest multiple of

$50). For example, a $49 cost-of-living increase will result in no adjustment, and an increase of $99 will create an upward adjustment of $50. [I.R.C. §§ 408(k)(2)(C), 408(k)(8)] For 2010, the $450 amount remained at $550. [IRS Notice 2009-94, 2009-2 C.B. 848]

For the five years prior to 2010, the compensation amounts were as follows:

Year	Compensation Limit
2009	$550
2008	500
2007	500
2006	450
2005	450

Example. JTS Corporation, a calendar-year corporation, maintains a SEP. Mindy commenced employment on October 1, 2007. Mindy worked 250 hours in 2007 and 900 hours each year in 2008, 2009, and 2010. If Mindy is at least age 21 and earns $550 or more, she must participate in the SEP in 2010.

An employer may not require that an employee be employed as of a particular date in order for a contribution to be made on the employee's behalf. [Prop. Treas. Reg. § 1.408-7(d)(3)] Accordingly, a SEP cannot have a last-day-of-the-year employment requirement. If the employee is otherwise eligible, the employee must share in any SEP contribution. For example, eligible employees who die or terminate employment before the contribution is made must receive an allocation. [IRS FAQs regarding SEPs]

If contributions are made for a particular year, contributions must be made on behalf of eligible employees over age 70½, even though the employees may already have started to receive required minimum distributions from the SEP and may not make contributions to their own IRAs (see chapter 11, Q 30:4). [I.R.C. § 219(b)(2)]

For purposes of participation in a SEP, the rules regarding controlled businesses, affiliated service groups, and leased employees are applicable (see Qs 5:29, 5:35, 5:58). [I.R.C. §§ 414(b), 414(c), 414(m)(4), 414(n)(3); Priv. Ltr. Rul. 9026056]

Q 32:3 Does the prohibition against discrimination in favor of highly compensated employees apply to a SEP?

Yes. A SEP may not discriminate in favor of highly compensated employees (HCEs; see Q 3:3). Contributions must bear a uniform relationship to the compensation of each employee. The annual compensation limit is $200,000, adjusted for cost-of-living increases (see Qs 6:45, 6:46). [I.R.C. §§ 401(a)(17), 408(k)(3), 408(k)(8)]

The annual compensation limit is adjusted for increases in cost of living only if the adjustment is $5,000 or greater and then is made in multiples of $5,000 (i.e., rounded down to the next lowest multiple of $5,000). For example, an increase in the cost of living of $4,999 will result in no adjustment, and an increase of $9,999 will create an upward adjustment of $5,000 (see Q 6:46). [I.R.C. § 401(a)(17)] For plan years that begin in 2010, the $200,000 compensation limit remained at $245,000. [IRS Notice 2009-94, 2009-2 C.B. 848] For the five plan years that began prior to 2010, the compensation limits were as follows:

Year	Compensation Limit
2009	$245,000
2008	230,000
2007	225,000
2006	220,000
2005	210,000

Example. In 2010, Jill Corporation has three employees: the business owner earning $300,000 and two other employees earning $20,000 each. Since all three employees meet the eligibility requirements and the SEP may take into account only the first $245,000 of compensation paid to an employee, only $285,000 ($245,000 plus $40,000) would be counted for purposes of determining the amount of the contribution to the SEP. Assuming Jill Corporation wants to contribute the maximum amount allowed on behalf of the owner (see Q 32:6), it should use a 20 percent formula for its contribution. The contribution on behalf of the owner would be $49,000 (20% × $245,000), and the contribution for the other two employees would be $4,000 each (20% × $20,000).

If the SEP is top-heavy, the employer contributions on behalf of each eligible non-key employee must generally be at least 3 percent of compensation. [I.R.C. §§ 408(k)(1)(B), 416(c)(2), 416(e)] For details on top-heavy plans, see chapter 26.

One court ruled that an employer may have discriminated against an employee by requiring that the employee choose between a standard salary and a lower salary plus a contribution to the employer's SEP. [Garratt v. Walker, 164 F.3d 1249 (10th Cir. 1998)]

Q 32:4 May a SEP provide for permitted disparity?

Yes. The permitted disparity (or integration) rules applicable to defined contribution plans also apply to employer contributions to SEPs. These rules permit a limited disparity between the contribution percentages applicable to compensation below and above the integration level (see Q 7:6). Generally, the integration level is the taxable wage base (TWB; see Q 7:7), or some percentage of the TWB, in effect as of the beginning of the plan year. [I.R.C. §§ 401(*l*)(2), 408(k)(3)(D)]

A SEP will not be considered discriminatory if the excess contribution percentage (ECP; see Q 7:4) does not exceed the base contribution percentage (BCP; see Q 7:5) by more than the lesser of (1) the BCP or (2) the greater of 5.7 percentage points or the percentage equal to the rate of tax attributable to the old age insurance portion of the Old Age, Survivors' and Disability Insurance (OASDI) as of the beginning of the plan year (see Qs 7:3–7:8). [I.R.C. § 401(*l*)(2)]

> **Example.** Sharon Corporation establishes a SEP for the 2010 calendar year. The SEP provides that each participant will receive an allocation of 5 percent of compensation up to the taxable wage base ($106,800 in 2010) and 10.7 percent of compensation in excess of the taxable wage base. The SEP does not meet the permitted disparity requirements, because the ECP, 10.7 percent, exceeds the BCP, 5 percent, by more than the lesser of 5 percentage points or 5.7 percentage points. However, if the ECP was reduced to 10 percent, the plan would meet the permitted disparity requirements.

For details on permitted disparity, see chapter 7.

Q 32:5   Are contributions made to a SEP on an employee's behalf forfeitable?

No. Employer contributions under a SEP must fully vest when made and are nonforfeitable. Employers may not condition any contribution to a SEP on the employee's retaining any portion of the contribution in the account and may not prohibit withdrawals from a SEP. The employee may take a distribution from the SEP at any time and at the employee's discretion, but the distribution must then be included in income (see Q 32:19). [I.R.C. § 408(k)(4)]

Q 32:6   How much may be contributed to an employee's IRA through a SEP?

An employer's total contribution to its SEP may vary annually at the employer's discretion. [Prop. Treas. Reg. § 1.408-7(c)(1)] The employer's annual contribution to a SEP on behalf of each employee is limited to the lesser of (1) 25 percent of the employee's compensation (not including the SEP contribution) or (2) $40,000. The $40,000 amount is subject to cost-of-living adjustments; however, an adjustment will be made only if it is $1,000 or greater and then will be made in multiples of $1,000 (see Q 6:12). For 2010, the $40,000 limitation amount remained at $49,000. For the purpose of the 25 percent limitation, compensation is defined as compensation under Section 414(s) (see Q 6:66) includible in the employee's gross income. If the employer's contribution exceeds the above limitation, the excess contribution is includible in the employee's income and regarded as having been contributed by the employee to the IRA under the SEP. [I.R.C. §§ 402(h)(2), 415(c)(1)(A), 415(d)(1)(C), 415(d)(4)(B); IRS Notice 2009-94, 2009-2 C.B. 848] For the five limitation years ended prior to 2010, the adjusted dollar limitation was:

Limitation Year Ending in	Adjusted Limit
2009	$49,000
2008	46,000
2007	45,000
2006	44,000
2005	42,000

A 6 percent excise tax is imposed on an excess contribution to an IRA, and this tax is applicable to SEPs (see Q 30:9). [I.R.C. § 4973]

The employee may contribute an additional amount to a personal IRA (see Q 30:5), even though the employee is a participant in a SEP. However, for the purpose of determining the deductibility of the IRA contribution, the employee will be considered an active participant because of the employee's participation in the SEP (see Q 30:15). [I.R.C. §§ 219(g)(5)(A)(v), 408(j); IRS Notice 87-16, 1987-1 C.B. 446]

Q 32:7   How much can an employer deduct for contributions to a SEP?

Subject to the $40,000 annual addition limitation for each employee (see Q 32:6), the employer may deduct no more than 25 percent of the total compensation (see Q 12:15) paid to all participating employees during the calendar year ending with or within the employer's taxable year (or during the taxable year in the case of a SEP maintained on the basis of the employer's taxable year). [I.R.C. §§ 404(h)(1)(C), 415 (c)(1)(A)]

An excess contribution is deductible in succeeding taxable years in order of time, subject to the percentage limitation. If the employer maintains both a SEP and a defined contribution plan (see Q 2:2), the deduction limitation for the defined contribution plan contribution is reduced by the amount of the allowable deduction for the SEP contribution with respect to the participants in such plan. [I.R.C. § 404(h)(2)]

Q 32:8   When are contributions to a SEP deductible?

Contributions to a SEP are deductible:

1. In the case of a SEP maintained on a calendar-year basis, for the taxable year within which the calendar year ends; or

2. In the case of a SEP maintained on the basis of the taxable year of the employer (that is not a calendar year), for such taxable year.

[I.R.C. § 404(h)(1)(A)]

The contribution must be made no later than the due date of the employer's return for the taxable year (including extensions). [I.R.C. § 404(h)(1)(B)]

Q 32:9 May an employer maintain a salary reduction SEP?

For years beginning after 1996, an employer may not establish a salary reduction SEP. However, an employer may continue to make contributions to a salary reduction SEP that was established in a year beginning before 1997, and employees hired in a year beginning after 1996 may participate in the salary reduction SEP. [I.R.C. § 408(k)(6)] Effectively, salary reduction SEPs have been replaced by SIMPLE plans. For details, see chapter 33.

For years beginning before 1997, an employer that had fewer than 26 employees who were eligible to participate at any time during the preceding calendar year could have established and maintained a SEP whereby each employee was permitted to elect to have contributions made to the SEP or to receive the contributions in cash under procedures similar to a 401(k) plan. At least 50 percent of the eligible employees of the employer must have elected to defer part of their compensation to the SEP. [I.R.C. § 408(k)(6)] These requirements continue to be applicable to a salary reduction SEP that was established before 1997 and that is currently maintained after 1996.

> **Example.** In 1996, SOS Corp. established a salary reduction SEP and in 2009 had 28 eligible employees. Elective deferrals may not be made to the SEP in 2010 because SOS Corp. had more than 25 eligible employees in 2009. If SOS Corp. has less than 26 eligible employees in 2010, elective deferrals may be made to the SEP in 2011, provided that at least 50 percent of the employees make elective deferrals in 2011.

A tax credit is provided with respect to elective contributions to a SEP. An eligible individual will be allowed a nonrefundable tax credit for the taxable year in an amount equal to the applicable percentage of the individual's qualified retirement savings contributions for the year up to $2,000. [I.R.C. § 25B] For a discussion of the tax credit, see chapter 17.

A salary reduction SEP that contains an eligible automatic contribution arrangement (EACA; see Q 27:5) is permitted to allow employees, within 90 days after the date of the first default elective contribution, to elect to receive a distribution based on the default elective contributions and avoid the additional income tax on early withdrawals (see Q 16:1). [I.R.C. § 414(w)(5) as amended by WRERA 2008 § 109(b)(5)]

Q 32:10 What are the limits on elective deferrals to a SEP?

Elective deferrals under a SEP (see Q 32:9) are treated like elective deferrals under a 401(k) plan and are subject to an applicable dollar limitation. The 2006 $15,000 limitation on elective deferrals is adjusted for inflation in $500 increments, and the base period for calculating the inflation adjustment is the calendar quarter beginning July 1, 2005. [I.R.C. §§ 401(a)(30), 402(g)(1), 402(g)(4), 408(k)(6)(A)(iv)] For 2010, the limitation remained at $16,500. [IRS Notice 2009-94, 2009-2 C.B. 848] For the prior five years, the applicable dollar amount was:

For taxable years beginning in calendar year	The applicable dollar amount
2009	$16,500
2008	15,500
2007	15,500
2006	15,000
2005	14,000

Q 32:11   What are salary reduction catch-up contributions?

An individual who is age 50 may be permitted to make an additional elective deferral (i.e., catch-up contribution) to a SEP up to the applicable dollar amount. The 2006 $5,000 amount is adjusted for cost-of-living increases in $500 increments. [I.R.C. § 414(v)] For 2010, the limit on catch-up contributions remained at $5,500. [IRS Notice 2009-94, 2009-2 C.B. 848] For the prior five years, the applicable dollar amount was:

For taxable years beginning in calendar year	The applicable dollar amount
2009	$5,500
2008	5,000
2007	5,000
2006	5,000
2005	4,000

For further details on the catch-up contributions, see Qs 27:52 through 27:61.

Q 32:12   Is there a special nondiscrimination test for salary reduction SEPs?

Yes. Under a salary reduction SEP (see Q 32:9), the deferral percentage for each HCE (see Q 3:3) cannot exceed 125 percent of the average deferral percentage for all eligible non-highly compensated employees (NHCEs; see Q 3:12). The deferral percentage for an employee for a year is the ratio of (1) the amount of elective employer contributions actually paid over to the SEP on behalf of the employee for the year to (2) the employee's compensation for the year. [I.R.C. §§ 408(k)(6)(A)(iii), 408(k)(6)(D)]

The above calculation is different from the calculation applicable to a 401(k) plan (see Qs 27:18, 27:19). Under a 401(k) plan, after the actual deferral percentage (ADP) is calculated separately for each employee, the average of the ADP for all HCEs cannot exceed 125 percent of the average of the ADP for all NHCEs. Also, an alternative test is available under a 401(k) plan. If the average

ADP for HCEs does not exceed the average ADP for NHCEs multiplied by 2, and the average ADP for HCEs does not exceed the average ADP for the NHCEs by more than two percentage points, then the ADP test will be satisfied even if the first test is not satisfied.

Example. Prior to 1997, L&S Corporation established a salary reduction SEP. In 2010, the deferral percentage for each HCE equals 5.5 percent. The average deferral percentage for the NHCEs equals 4 percent. The special nondiscrimination test is not satisfied because 5.5 percent is greater than 5 percent (125% × 4%). If the salary reduction SEP were a 401(k) plan, the requirement would be met because 5.5 percent does not exceed 4 percent by more than two percentage points and 5.5 percent is less than 4 percent multiplied by 2.

Furthermore, with respect to a 401(k) plan, but not a salary reduction SEP, satisfaction of the ADP test has been simplified (see Qs 27:18, 27:40). For example, the ADP of the HCEs for the current plan year may be tested against the ADP of the NHCEs for the preceding plan year or a safe harbor contribution may be made.

Example. Prior to 1997, Jo Anne Corp. established a salary reduction SEP. For 2010, the deferral percentage for each HCE equals 10 percent, and the average deferral percentage for the NHCEs equals 6 percent. For 2009, the average deferral percentage for the NHCEs equaled 8 percent. The special nondiscrimination test is not satisfied in 2010 because 10 percent is greater than 7.5 percent (125% × 6%). If the salary reduction SEP were a 401(k) plan, the requirement would be met because 10 percent does not exceed 8 percent multiplied by 125 percent.

Q 32:13 How is a SEP established?

Generally, any employer may establish a SEP. SEPs are available to both C and S corporations, partnerships, and sole proprietorships. In one case, an individual taxpayer's work relationship with the State Department was that of an independent contractor, and, as such, was entitled to deduct her contribution to a SEP. Although some of the evidence indicated an employee status, the totality of the facts pointed toward an independent contractor status. [Levine, 89 T.C.M. 1063 (2005)] In another case, the court determined that a SEP was not established by an individual or by an employer on his behalf where the contribution was not made by an employer on his behalf, but was made by the individual who was not self-employed and, therefore, not eligible to establish a SEP. [Ramsey, 71 T.C.M. 2816 (1996)] IRS announced a settlement initiative for United States citizens and permanent residents who are common-law employees of foreign embassies and consular offices in the United States and who erroneously established SEPs. As common-law employees, they were not self-employed and, therefore, not eligible to establish SEPs. [Ann. 2006-95, 2006-2 C.B. 1105]

In order to establish a SEP, the employer must execute a written instrument within the time prescribed for making deductible contributions (see Q 32:8).

This instrument must include the name of the employer, the participation requirements, the allocation formula, and the signature of a responsible official. [I.R.C. § 408(k)(5); Prop. Treas. Reg. § 1.408-7(b)]

The SEP may be set up in one of three ways:

1. By a model SEP (see Q 32:14), that is, executing Form 5305-SEP or, prior to 1997, Form 5305A-SEP in the case of a salary reduction SEP (see Q 32:9);

2. By a master or prototype plan for which a favorable opinion letter has been issued; or

3. By an individually designed plan.

In order to retain certain tax benefits, the SEP document must be timely updated to comply with law changes. Specifically, IRS required sponsors of SEPs to update their plan documents to reflect EGTRRA by the end of 2002, or shortly thereafter in some cases. [Rev. Proc. 2002-10, 2002-1 C.B. 401; *Retirement News for Employers*, Volume 5/Winter 2009]

See Q 32:25 regarding correction of failures with respect to SEPs.

Q 32:14   When may an employer use a model SEP?

IRS has designed a model SEP agreement to be used by employers wishing to implement SEPs with relatively little paperwork. This is done by completing Form 5305-SEP or, prior to 1997, 5305A-SEP for salary reduction SEPs. The form is not filed with IRS, but is retained by the employer and distributed to all participating employees. This fulfills the employer's reporting and disclosure obligations relating to the adoption of the agreement and also satisfies the notification requirements. However, a model SEP may not be used:

1. By an employer currently maintaining another qualified retirement plan;

2. By members of an affiliated service group, a controlled group of corporations, or trades or businesses under common control, unless all eligible employees of all members participate in the SEP (see Qs 5:29, 5:35);

3. By an employer that uses the services of leased employees (see Q 5:58);

4. If any eligible employee has not established an IRA (see Q 32:1); or

5. If the contribution formula considers permitted disparity (see chapter 7).

To adopt a model SEP, the plan must be maintained on a calendar-year basis.

[Instructions to Forms 5305-SEP and 5305A-SEP]

Use of a nonmodel SEP requires the employer to distribute certain other summaries regarding the SEP. Once an employee becomes eligible to participate in the SEP, the employer must furnish certain specific information to the employee, including an explanation of participation requirements, the formula allocating employer contributions, the name of the person designated to supply any additional SEP information, and an explanation of the terms of the IRA accepting the SEP contribution. [Prop. Treas. Reg. § 1.408-6; DOL Reg. § 2520. 104-49]

IRS has ruled that where a company terminated its defined benefit plan, the company's individually designed SEP satisfied the requirements under the Code (including the special limitation regarding participation in both a defined benefit plan and a defined contribution plan) and qualified as a SEP. [Priv. Ltr. Ruls. 9709008, 9706009, 9652029]

Q 32:15   Can a dissolved partnership's SEP be continued by its successor sole proprietors?

No. A SEP adopted by a partnership is not considered a plan covering its employees after the partnership is dissolved, even though the former partners continue to operate the same business as sole proprietors. A sole proprietor must adopt a new SEP in order to continue making deductible contributions for the employees. [Priv. Ltr. Rul. 8450051]

Q 32:16   What are the annual reporting requirements of a SEP?

Once a SEP is established, there is limited annual reporting to both IRS and participants. There is no requirement that the employer file the Form 5500 series (see Q 21:1) for the SEP. The trustee or issuer of the IRA is required to furnish annual information regarding contributions to the SEP and the fair market value of assets in the SEP. For this purpose, Form 5498 must be filed with IRS by May 31. [Prop. Treas. Reg. § 1.408-5; Instructions to IRS Form 5498]

The information on Form 5498 must also be supplied to the participants. The employer maintaining the SEP must notify each participant of the SEP contribution made on the employee's behalf on Form W-2 by the later of January 31 following the contribution year or 30 days after the contribution. [I.R.C. § 408(l); Prop. Treas. Reg. § 1.408-9; Instructions to IRS Form 5498]

Q 32:17   Are SEP contributions taxable to the employee?

No. Both employer contributions and employee elective deferrals under the SEP (see Q 32:9) are excludable from the employee's gross income. [I.R.C. § 402(h)]

Notwithstanding the exclusion from gross income, SEP contributions made under a salary reduction agreement are subject to the Federal Insurance Contributions Act (FICA) and the Federal Unemployment Tax Act (FUTA) taxes, but SEP contributions under a non-salary reduction arrangement are not subject to such taxes. [I.R.C. §§ 3121(a)(5)(C), 3306(b)(5)(C)]

Q 32:18   How are SEP assets managed?

The assets of a SEP are managed by a financial institution and not by individual trustees, although the employee may be permitted to direct the investment of the employee's account. The SEP must be established with a bank, thrift institution, insurance company, brokerage firm, or other entity that is eligible to be an IRA custodian. Each individual who participates in the SEP may set up or use a personal IRA for investment purposes. If the participant does not have an IRA, the employer must establish one for the participant.

Similar to an individual's personal IRA, the participant may make trustee-to-trustee transfers and change the investment manager of the SEP. Since IRA rules govern the types of investments in a SEP, SEP assets cannot be lent to participants or invested in life insurance contracts, collectibles, or any other assets in which IRAs may not invest (see Qs 30:2, 30:45). [I.R.C. §§ 408(a)(3), 408(e)(4), 408(m)]

Q 32:19   How are distributions from a SEP taxed?

Generally, the same rules that apply to IRA distributions apply to distributions from a SEP. Distributions from a SEP are includible in ordinary income in the year received; and, as with an IRA, favorable tax elections (e.g., special averaging) are not available for distributions from a SEP.

If a withdrawal from a SEP is premature (that is, a distribution is made before the individual reaches age 59½, becomes disabled, or dies), the amount withdrawn, in addition to ordinary income tax, is subject to a 10 percent penalty tax. Similar to distributions from an IRA, an exception to the 10 percent penalty tax exists if the individual receives a distribution from the SEP in substantially equal periodic payments. [I.R.C. §§ 72(t)(1), 72(t)(2)(A)(iv)] See chapter 16 for details and other exceptions.

Distributions from a SEP must begin no later than April 1 of the calendar year following the year in which the participant reaches age 70½. If the required minimum distribution (RMD; see chapter 11) is not made, a penalty tax is imposed equal to 50 percent of the amount by which such RMD exceeds the actual amount distributed during the taxable year (see Q 30:42). [I.R.C. §§ 401(a)(9), 4974(a)]

RMDs from SEPs for calendar year 2009 were suspended (see Q 11:56). [IRC § 401(a)(9)(H) (as added by WRERA 2008 § 201(a); WRERA 2008 § 201(c)(1))]

If the employee has at any time made nondeductible IRA contributions, the amount includible in income upon a distribution from a SEP is determined in accordance with an allocation formula (see Q 30:23). [I.R.C. §§ 402(h)(3), 408(d)]

The assets of a decedent's SEP are included in the decedent's gross estate. [I.R.C. § 2039]

The provision under PPA that allowed individuals age 70½ or older to distribute up to $100,000 of their IRA balance to charitable organizations in 2006 and in 2007 without recognizing income and without taking a charitable deduction did not apply to distributions from an ongoing SEP IRA (see Q 30:44). For this purpose, a SEP IRA was treated as ongoing if it was maintained under an employer arrangement under which an employer contribution was made for the plan year ending with or within the IRA owner's taxable year in which the charitable contributions would have been made. The Emergency Economic Stabilization Act of 2008 extended this PPA provision to 2008 and 2009. [I.R.C. § 408(d)(8); IRS Notice 2007-7, § IX, Q&A-36, 2007-1 C.B. 395] At this time, this provision has not been extended to 2010 or a later year.

Q 32:20   How may assets be moved from a SEP without penalty?

An employee may wish to move funds from an IRA under the SEP to another IRA for higher interest rates, different investment alternatives, or more favorable withdrawal and transfer terms. Similar to IRAs, there are two ways to move assets from the SEP without penalty. One method is through a rollover, whereby the employee withdraws all or part of the amount from the SEP account and rolls over that amount to another IRA, or even the same IRA, within 60 days. Assets withdrawn, but not timely rolled over, will be included in the employee's income and may be subject to penalty taxes. Also, such rollovers may not be made more frequently than once every 12 months; otherwise, the subsequent rollover will be included in the employee's income and may be subject to penalty taxes. [I.R.C. § 408(d)(3)]

The second, and more advisable, way to move funds from an IRA under a SEP to another IRA is through a trustee-to-trustee transfer of funds. Under this method, the employee directs the trustee of the IRA to transfer the IRA funds directly to the trustee of a second IRA. There are no restrictions on the number of trustee-to-trustee transfers that may be made to or from a SEP.

For more details, see chapter 34.

Q 32:21   May a distribution from a qualified retirement plan be rolled over into a SEP?

Yes. If, within 60 days after receipt, a participant rolls over an eligible rollover distribution from a qualified retirement plan to an IRA funded as a SEP, the rollover amount will not be includible in income. [I.R.C. § 402(c); Priv. Ltr. Rul. 8630068] Furthermore, an eligible rollover distribution from an IRA may be rolled over into a qualified retirement plan, 403(b) plan (see Q 35:1), or Section 457 plan. [I.R.C. § 408(d)(3)]

For details on rollovers, see chapter 34.

Q 32:22   What advantages does a SEP offer to the business owner?

The greatest advantage a SEP offers over qualified retirement plans is the minimal amount of paperwork and bookkeeping necessary to start and maintain the plan. Costs for consultants (lawyers, accountants, or actuaries) are sharply reduced, possibly even eliminated. Another advantage of a SEP is the flexibility it affords with respect to contributions. The employer can contribute any amount it wishes, up to a maximum set by law (see Q 32:6), or it can choose not to make any contribution at all. Although this is generally true for profit sharing plans also, it is not true for pension plans. In addition, the employer's fiduciary duty (see chapter 23) is reduced because participants in a SEP choose their own investments when they establish IRAs. Furthermore, a SEP may be established after the end of the employer's taxable year (see Qs 32:8, 32:13).

Q 32:23 What are the drawbacks to the adoption of a SEP?

Eligibility rules for a SEP tend to be less restrictive than the rules for qualified retirement plans, and this can increase the employer's costs. Many of the employees who need not be covered under a qualified retirement plan must be covered under a SEP. For example, a SEP must include part-time and seasonal workers, regardless of how few hours they worked during the year (assuming they satisfy the compensation requirement and have worked for the employer in at least three of the previous five years; see Q 32:2).

Another drawback to a SEP is that employees must be fully vested at all times (see Q 32:5). A qualified retirement plan does not operate this way; vesting can be gradually phased in to favor longer-term employees (see chapter 9).

Also, although SEPs are subject to fewer reporting requirements, employers may not be aware of many of the rules applicable to SEPs. For example, the employer must determine which employees are eligible, which are HCEs (see Q 3:3), and which are key employees (see Q 26:23). In addition, ADP and top-heavy tests may need to be performed. (See Qs 32:2, 32:3, 32:12.) IRS has issued proposed examination guidelines that provide employee plan examiners with technical background and guidance regarding issues that should be considered during the examination of a SEP. [Ann. 97-42, 1997-17 I.R.B. 19]

Q 32:24 Can a SEP be reached by judgment creditors?

The United States Supreme Court has ruled that, under Section 522(d)(10)(E) of the Bankruptcy Code, IRAs are exempt from claims of creditors. [Rousey v. Jacoway, 544 U.S. 1561 (2005)]

The Bankruptcy Abuse Prevention and Consumer Protection Act of 2005 (see Q 1:27) contains provisions that protect the retirement assets of bankruptcy filers. The legislation protects all retirement plan assets from creditors during bankruptcy proceedings by exempting those assets from the debtor's bankruptcy estate. An individual's bankruptcy estate would not include retirement funds to the extent that those funds are in a qualified retirement plan, SEP, SIMPLE plan (see Q 33:1), 403(b) plan (see Q 35:1), IRA (see Q 30:1), Roth IRA (see Q 31:1), or Section 457 plan. The Act does not condition the exemption for IRA assets to those necessary for the support of the debtor and dependents. However, the amount of IRA assets that is protected during bankruptcy proceedings is limited to $1 million (adjusted for inflation); but amounts attributable to rollovers (see Q 34:1) from qualified retirement plans and 403(b) plans (not SEPs or SIMPLE plans) do not count toward the $1 million limit. The

$1 million limit may be increased if the interests of justice so require. The limit applies to traditional and Roth IRAs but not to SEPs or SIMPLE plans. [Act § 224]

Because the Act did not become effective until October 17, 2005, its provisions do not apply to bankruptcy cases that commenced before the effective date. Consequently, see Q 30:52 for a discussion of those cases that arose before the October 17, 2005 effective date of the Act.

Q 32:25 What IRS correction programs apply to a SEP?

The Employee Plans Compliance Resolution System (EPCRS; see Q 19:2) may be used to correct failures with respect to SEPs. A SEP that is maintained under a plan document approved by IRS is eligible for SCP (see Q 19:17) with respect to insignificant failures (see Q 19:18) and is eligible for VCP (see Q 19:20) under the special procedure VCSEP. A SEP is also eligible for Audit CAP (see Q 19:28).

Audits of SEPs revealed that some sponsors had not timely updated their plans to comply with EGTRRA. EPCRS may be used to correct these failures. [*Retirement News for Employers*, Vol. 5/ Winter 2009]

For details on IRS correction programs, see chapter 19.

Chapter 33

Savings Incentive Match Plan for Employees

Small employers may be reluctant to establish qualified retirement plans because of the complexity of the rules relating to such plans and the cost of complying with such rules. In order to encourage small employers to adopt retirement plans, the savings incentive match plan for employees (SIMPLE plan) was created. This chapter explains the requirements for establishing and maintaining a SIMPLE plan.

Q 33:1 What is the savings incentive match plan for employees (SIMPLE plan)?

The SIMPLE plan is a simplified retirement plan for small businesses that allows employees to make elective contributions and requires employers to make matching or nonelective contributions. The SIMPLE plan may be structured either as a SIMPLE IRA plan (see Q 33:2) or as a SIMPLE 401(k) plan (see Q 33:25). SIMPLE plans are generally not subject to the nondiscrimination rules applicable to qualified retirement plans, including the top-heavy rules (see chapters 4 and 26). [I.R.C. §§ 401(k)(11), 408(p), 416(g)(4)(G); Treas. Reg. § 1.401(k)-4; IRS Notice 98-4, Q&A I-6, 1998-1 C.B. 269]

Q 33:2 What is a SIMPLE IRA plan?

A SIMPLE IRA plan is a written arrangement that provides a simplified tax-favored retirement plan for small employers. If an employer establishes a SIMPLE IRA plan, each employee may choose whether to have the employer make payments as contributions under the SIMPLE IRA plan or to receive these payments directly in cash. An employer that chooses to establish a SIMPLE IRA plan must make either matching contributions or nonelective contributions (see Q 33:12). All contributions under a SIMPLE IRA plan are made to SIMPLE IRAs. [I.R.C. § 408(p); IRS Notice 98-4, Q&A A-1, 1998-1 C.B. 269]

Contributions under a SIMPLE IRA plan may only be made to a SIMPLE IRA and not to any other type of IRA. A SIMPLE IRA is an individual retirement account (see Q 30:2) or an individual retirement annuity (see Q 30:3) to which the only contributions that may be made are contributions under a SIMPLE IRA plan and rollovers or transfers from another SIMPLE IRA. [IRS Notice 98-4, Q&A A-2, 1998-1 C.B. 269]

Q 33:3   Must a SIMPLE IRA plan be maintained on a calendar-year basis?

Yes. A SIMPLE IRA plan may *only* be maintained on a calendar-year basis. Thus, for example, employer eligibility to establish a SIMPLE IRA plan (see Q 33:4) and SIMPLE IRA plan contributions (see Qs 33:10, 33:12) are determined on a calendar-year basis. [I.R.C. § 408(p)(6)(C); IRS Notice 98-4, Q&A A-3, 1998-1 C.B. 269]

Q 33:4   Who may adopt a SIMPLE IRA plan?

Employers who employed 100 or fewer employees who earned $5,000 or more in compensation (see Q 33:7) for the preceding calendar year (the 100-employee limitation) may adopt a SIMPLE IRA plan. For purposes of the 100-employee limitation, all employees employed at any time during the calendar year are taken into account, regardless of whether they are eligible to participate in the SIMPLE IRA plan (see Q 33:6). Thus, employees who are excludable (union employees, air pilots, and nonresident aliens; see Q 5:5) or who have not met the plan's minimum eligibility requirements must be taken into account. Employees also include self-employed individuals (see Q 6:60) who received earned income (see Q 6:61) from the employer during the year. [I.R.C. § 408(p)(2)(C)(i)(I); IRS Notice 98-4, Q&A B-1, 1998-1 C.B. 269]

> **Example.** In 2010, Alexandra, Ltd. employed 140 employees, 110 of whom were union employees and for whom retirement benefits were the subject of good-faith bargaining. Although Alexandra, Ltd. may exclude all union employees from participation in a SIMPLE IRA plan and therefore only 30 employees could be eligible to participate, Alexandra, Ltd. may not establish a SIMPLE IRA plan in 2011 because the company employed more than 100 employees during 2010.

An employer that previously maintained a SIMPLE IRA plan is treated as satisfying the 100-employee limitation for the two calendar years (the two-year grace period) immediately following the calendar year for which it last satisfied the 100-employee limitation. However, if the failure to satisfy the 100-employee limitation is due to an acquisition, disposition, or similar transaction involving the employer, then the SIMPLE IRA plan may be maintained during a transition period that begins on the date of the transaction and ends on the last day of the second calendar year following the calendar year in which the transaction occurs. [I.R.C. §§ 408(p)(2)(C)(i)(II), 408(p)(10), 410(b)(6)(C)(i); IRS Notice 98-4, Q&A B-2, 1998-1 C.B. 269]

> **Example.** Steven Corp. employs 60 employees and maintains a SIMPLE IRA plan. Andrew Inc. employs 80 employees and sponsors a qualified defined benefit plan. Following the purchase of Andrew Inc. on June 1, 2010, Steven

Corp. may continue to maintain the SIMPLE IRA plan during the period from June 1, 2010, to December 31, 2012. The coverage under the SIMPLE IRA plan may not be significantly changed, and only individuals who would have been employees of Steven Corp. had the transaction not occurred may be eligible to participate.

A SIMPLE IRA plan generally may not be established if the employer maintains another qualified plan under which *any* of its employees receives an allocation of contributions (in the case of a defined contribution plan; see Q 2:2) or has an increase in an accrued benefit (in the case of a defined benefit plan; see Q 2:3) for any plan year beginning or ending in that calendar year (the only plan requirement). For this purpose, a qualified plan includes a:

1. Qualified retirement plan;
2. Qualified annuity plan (I.R.C. § 403(a));
3. 403(b) plan (see Q 35:1);
4. Simplified employee pension (SEP; see Q 32:1); and
5. SIMPLE IRA plan.

[I.R.C. § 408(p)(2)(D); IRS Notice 98-4, Q&A B-3, 1998-1 C.B. 269]

However, an employer can make contributions under a SIMPLE IRA plan for a calendar year even though it maintains another qualified plan if the other qualified plan maintained by the employer covers only union employees (as long as retirement benefits were the subject of good-faith bargaining), and the SIMPLE IRA plan excludes these employees.

If the failure to satisfy the exclusive plan requirement is due to an acquisition, disposition, or similar transaction involving the employer, the SIMPLE IRA plan may be maintained during a transition period that begins on the date of the transaction and ends on the last day of the second calendar year following the calendar year in which the transaction occurs. [I.R.C. §§ 408(p)(2)(D)(i), 408(p)(10); IRS Notice 98-4, Q&A B-3, 1998-1 C.B. 269]

Tax-exempt employers and governmental entities are permitted to maintain SIMPLE IRA plans. [IRS Notice 98-4, Q&A B-4, 1998-1 C.B. 269]

Q 33:5 Do the employer-aggregation and leased-employee rules apply to SIMPLE IRA plans?

For purposes of applying the SIMPLE IRA plan rules, certain related employers (trades or businesses under common control) are treated as a single employer. These related employers include controlled groups of corporations (see Q 5:31), partnerships or sole proprietorships under common control (see Q 5:33), and affiliated service groups (see Q 5:35). In addition, leased employees (see Q 5:58) are treated as employed by the employer. [IRS Notice 98-4, Q&A B-5, 1998-1 C.B. 269]

Example. Benjamin owns Adam Company, a computer rental agency, which has 80 employees who received $5,000 or more in compensation in

2010. Benjamin also owns Caroline Company, which repairs computers and has 60 employees who received $5,000 or more in compensation in 2010. Benjamin is the sole proprietor of both businesses. Since both Adam Company and Caroline Company are sole proprietorships under common control, all of the employees of both entities are treated as employees of a single employer. Thus, for purposes of the SIMPLE IRA plan rules, all 140 employees are treated as employed by Benjamin. Therefore, neither Adam Company nor Caroline Company is eligible to establish a SIMPLE IRA plan for 2011.

Q 33:6   Who is eligible to participate in a SIMPLE IRA plan?

Each employee who received at least $5,000 in compensation (see Q 33:7) from the employer during any two preceding calendar years (whether or not consecutive) and who is reasonably expected to receive at least $5,000 in compensation during the calendar year must be eligible to participate in the SIMPLE IRA plan for the calendar year. An employer may elect to exclude from participation union employees (as long as retirement benefits were the subject of good-faith bargaining), air pilots, and nonresident aliens (see Q 5:5). If the failure to satisfy the participation rules is due to an acquisition, disposition, or similar transaction involving the employer, then the SIMPLE IRA plan may be maintained during a transition period that begins on the date of the transaction and ends on the last day of the second calendar year following the calendar year in which the transaction occurs. The rules regarding controlled businesses, affiliated service groups, and leased employees are applicable (see Q 33:5). Thus, for example, if two related employers must be aggregated, all employees of either employer who satisfy the eligibility criteria must be allowed to participate in the SIMPLE IRA plan. [I.R.C. §§ 408(p)(4), 408(p)(10); IRS Notice 98-4, Q&A C-1, 1998-1 C.B. 269]

An employer may impose less-restrictive eligibility requirements by eliminating or reducing the prior-year compensation requirement, the current-year compensation requirement, or both. The employer, however, cannot impose any other conditions for participation in a SIMPLE IRA plan. [IRS Notice 98-4, Q&A C-2, 1998-1 C.B. 269]

> **Example 1.** Arlene Inc. may maintain a SIMPLE IRA plan for employees who received $3,000 or more in compensation for any preceding calendar year.

> **Example 2.** Ron Corporation may not maintain a SIMPLE IRA plan only for employees who have attained age 21 regardless of their compensation.

An employee may participate in a SIMPLE IRA plan even if the employee also participates in a plan of an unrelated employer for the same year. However, the employee's salary reduction contributions (see Qs 27:16, 32:9, 33:9, 33:10, 35:11) are subject to an aggregate limit on elective deferrals (see Q 27:51). [IRS Notice 98-4, Q&A C-3, 1998-1 C.B. 269]

Q 33:7   What does compensation mean for a SIMPLE IRA plan?

In the case of an individual who is not a self-employed individual (see Q 6:50), compensation means the amount described in Section 6051(a)(3) (wages, tips, and other compensation from the employer subject to income tax withholding under Section 3401(a)) and amounts described in Section 6051(a)(8), *including* elective contributions (see Q 33:9) made under a SIMPLE IRA plan. For purposes of applying the 100-employee limitation (see Q 33:4) and determining whether an employee is eligible to participate in a SIMPLE IRA plan (i.e., whether the employee had $5,000 in compensation for any two preceding years; see Q 33:6), an employee's compensation also includes the employee's elective deferrals under a 401(k) plan (see Q 27:1), a salary reduction SEP (see Q 32:9), and a 403(b) plan (see Q 35:1). [IRS Notice 98-4, Q&A C-4, 1998-1 C.B. 269]

In the case of a self-employed individual, compensation means net earnings from self-employment determined under Section 1402(a), *prior to* subtracting any contributions made under the SIMPLE IRA plan on behalf of the individual (see Q 6:61). [IRS Notice 98-4, Q&A C-5, 1998-1 C.B. 269]

Q 33:8   What contributions may be made to an employee's SIMPLE IRA?

Contributions to an employee's SIMPLE IRA are limited to employee elective contributions (see Q 33:9) and required employer matching contributions or nonelective contributions (see Q 33:12). These are the only contributions that may be made under a SIMPLE IRA plan, except for certain rollover contributions (see Q 33:17). [I.R.C. §§ 408(p)(2)(A)(i), 408(p)(2)(A)(iii); IRS Notice 98-4, Q&A D-1, 1998-1 C.B. 269]

All contributions made to an employee's SIMPLE IRA must be nonforfeitable. Thus, all contributions made by the employer vest immediately (see Q 9:1). [I.R.C. § 408(p)(3); IRS Notice 98-4, Q&A F-1, 1998-1 C.B. 269]

Q 33:9   What is an employee elective contribution under a SIMPLE IRA plan?

An employee elective or salary reduction contribution is a contribution made pursuant to an employee's election (see Q 33:13) to have an amount contributed to the employee's SIMPLE IRA, rather than have the amount paid directly to the employee in cash. An employee must be permitted to elect to have salary reduction contributions made at the level specified by the employee, expressed as a percentage of compensation for the year. Additionally, an employer may permit an employee to express the level of salary reduction contributions as a specific dollar amount. An employer may not place any restrictions on the amount of an employee's salary reduction contributions (e.g., by limiting the contribution percentage), except to the extent needed to comply with the annual limit on the amount of salary reduction contributions (see Q 33:10). [I.R.C. § 408(p)(2)(A)(ii); IRS Notice 98-4, Q&A D-2, 1998-1 C.B. 269]

A SIMPLE IRA plan that contains an eligible automatic contribution arrangement (EACA; see Q 27:5) is permitted to allow employees, within 90 days after the date of the first default elective contribution, to elect to receive a distribution based on the default elective contributions and avoid the additional income tax on early withdrawals (see Q 16:1). [I.R.C. § 414(w)(5) as amended by WRERA 2008 § 109(b)(5)]

IRS has issued guidance designed to facilitate automatic enrollment in a SIMPLE IRA plan and has provided a sample plan amendment that a prototype sponsor of a SIMPLE IRA plan, using a designated financial institution (see Q 33:19), can use in drafting an amendment to add an automatic enrollment arrangement (see Q 27:5). [IRS Notice 2009-66, 2009-39 I.R.B. 418; IRS Notice 2009-67, 2009-39 I.R.B. 420]

An employer matching contribution (see Q 33:12) made on behalf of a self-employed individual (see Q 6:60) is not treated as an employee elective contribution. [I.R.C. § 408(p)(8)]

Q 33:10 What is the annual limit on employee elective contributions to a SIMPLE IRA?

An employee may make annual elective contributions to a SIMPLE IRA up to the applicable dollar amount.

The 2005 $10,000 limitation is adjusted for inflation in $500 increments, and the base period for calculating the inflation adjustment is the calendar quarter beginning July 1, 2004. [I.R.C. §§ 408(p)(2)(A)(ii), 408(p)(2)(E)] For 2010, the limitation remained at $11,500. [IRS Notice 2009-94, 2009-2 C.B. 848] For the prior five years, the applicable dollar amount was:

For years beginning in calendar year	The applicable dollar amount
2009	$11,500
2008	10,500
2007	10,500
2006	10,000
2005	10,000

An employer matching contribution (see Q 33:12) made on behalf of a self-employed individual (see Q 6:60) is not treated as an employee elective contribution. [I.R.C. § 408(p)(8)]

Q 33:11 What are salary reduction catch-up contributions?

An individual who participates in a SIMPLE IRA (see Q 33:2) or a SIMPLE 401(k) plan (see Q 33:25), who has attained age 50 by the end of the calendar year, and for whom no other elective contributions may otherwise be made for the calendar year because of the application of any limitation contained in the

Code or of the plan, will be able to make additional elective contributions (i.e., catch-up contributions) to the plan for that calendar year.

The maximum catch-up contribution that an eligible individual may make for the calendar year is the *lesser* of:

1. The applicable dollar amount, or
2. The individual's compensation for the year reduced by all of the individual's other elective contributions for the year to 401(k) plans (see Q 27:1), salary reduction SEPs (see Q 32:9), SIMPLE plans, 403(b) plans (see Q 35:1), and Section 457 plans.

The 2006 $2,500 limitation is adjusted for inflation in $500 increments and the base period for calculating the inflation adjustment is the calendar quarter beginning July 1, 2005. [I.R.C § 414(v)(2)(B)(ii)] For 2010, the limit on catch-up contributions remained at $2,500. [IRS Notice 2009-94, 2009-2 C.B. 848] For the prior five years, the applicable dollar amount was:

For years beginning in calendar year	The applicable dollar amount
2009	$2,500
2008	2,500
2007	2,500
2006	2,500
2005	2,000

For further details, see Qs 27:52 through 27:61.

Q 33:12   What must an employer contribute under a SIMPLE IRA plan?

An employer must make either a matching contribution or a nonelective contribution.

Under a SIMPLE IRA plan, an employer is generally required to match the employee's elective contribution (see Q 33:9) on a dollar-for-dollar basis up to a limit of 3 percent of the employee's compensation (see Q 33:7) for the entire calendar year. [I.R.C. §§ 408(p)(2)(A)(iii), 408(p)(2)(C)(ii)(I); IRS Notice 98-4, Q&A D-4, 1998-1 C.B. 269]

The 3 percent limit on matching contributions is permitted to be reduced for a calendar year at the election of the employer, but only if:

1. The limit is not reduced below 1 percent;
2. The limit is not reduced for more than two years out of the five-year period that ends with (and includes) the year for which the election is effective; and

3. Employees are notified of the reduced limit within a reasonable period of time before the 60-day election period during which employees can enter into salary reduction agreements (see Q 33:13).

In determining whether the limit was reduced below 3 percent for a year, any year before the first year in which an employer (or a predecessor employer) maintains a SIMPLE IRA plan will be treated as a year for which the limit was 3 percent. If an employer chooses to make nonelective contributions for a year, that year also will be treated as a year for which the limit was 3 percent. [I.R.C. §§ 408(p)(2)(C)(ii)(II), 408(p)(2)(C)(ii)(III); IRS Notice 98-4, Q&A D-5, 1998-1 C.B. 269]

For purposes of the 3 percent employer match, the annual compensation limit (see Q 6:45) does *not* apply.

Example 1. Peter Corp. establishes a SIMPLE IRA plan in 2010, and Ilene, a participant, earns compensation of $383,334. If Ilene elects to defer $11,500, Peter Corp. must match an additional $11,500 (3% × $383,334), so that a total of $23,000 will be contributed to Ilene's SIMPLE IRA.

As an alternative to making matching contributions, an employer may elect to make a nonelective contribution of 2 percent of compensation for each eligible employee. The employer's nonelective contributions must be made for each eligible employee regardless of whether the employee elects to make salary reduction contributions for the calendar year. The employer may, but is not required to, limit nonelective contributions to eligible employees who have at least $5,000 (or some lower amount selected by the employer) of compensation for the year. [I.R.C. § 408(p)(2)(B)(i); IRS Notice 98-4, Q&A D-6, 1998-1 C.B. 269]

An employer may substitute the 2 percent nonelective contribution for the matching contribution for a year, but only if:

1. Eligible employees are notified that a 2 percent nonelective contribution will be made instead of a matching contribution, and

2. This notice is provided within a reasonable period of time before the 60-day election period during which employees can enter into salary reduction agreements (see Q 33:13). [I.R.C. § 408(p)(2)(B)(i); IRS Notice 98-4, Q&A D-6, 1998-1 C.B. 269]

For purposes of the 2 percent nonelective contribution, the annual compensation limitation (i.e., $245,000 in 2010) *does* apply. [IRS Notice 98-4, Q&A D-6, 1998-1 C.B. 269; IRS Notice 2009-94, 2009-2 C.B. 848]

Example 2. The facts are the same as in Example 1, except that Peter Corp. has properly elected to make a nonelective contribution of 2 percent of compensation. In this case, the total contribution made to Ilene's SIMPLE IRA will equal $16,400 [$11,500 + $4,900 (2% × $245,000)].

Q 33:13   When must an employee be given the right to enter into a salary reduction agreement?

During the 60-day period immediately preceding January 1 of a calendar year (i.e., November 2 to December 31 of the preceding calendar year), an eligible employee must be given the right to enter into a salary reduction agreement for the calendar year or to modify a prior agreement (including reducing the amount subject to this agreement to $0). However, for the year in which the employee becomes eligible to make salary reduction contributions, the period during which the employee may enter into a salary reduction agreement or modify a prior agreement is a 60-day period that includes either the date the employee becomes eligible or the day before that date.

> **Example.** Stan Corp. establishes a SIMPLE IRA plan effective as of July 1, 2011, and Sue, an eligible employee, becomes eligible to make salary reduction contributions on that date. The 60-day period must begin no later than July 1, 2011, and cannot end before June 30, 2011.

During these 60-day periods, employees have the right to modify their salary reduction agreements without restrictions. In addition, for the year in which an employee becomes eligible to make salary reduction contributions, the employee must be able to commence these contributions as soon as the employee becomes eligible, regardless of whether the 60-day period has ended.

Nothing precludes a SIMPLE IRA plan from providing additional or longer periods for permitting employees to enter into salary reduction agreements or to modify prior agreements. For example, a SIMPLE IRA plan can provide a 90-day election period instead of the 60-day period. In addition, a SIMPLE IRA plan can provide quarterly election periods during the 30 days before each calendar quarter.

An employee must be given the right to terminate the salary reduction agreement for a calendar year at any time during the year. However, the plan may provide that an employee who terminates a salary reduction agreement at any time other than the periods described above will not be eligible to resume participation until the beginning of the next calendar year.

[I.R.C. § 408(p)(5); IRS Notice 98-4, Q&A E-1 through Q&A E-3, 1998-1 C.B. 269]

Q 33:14   What are the tax consequences of SIMPLE IRA plan contributions?

An employer may generally deduct contributions (including employee elective contributions; see Q 33:9) made under a SIMPLE IRA plan for the employer's taxable year with or within which the calendar year for which the contributions were made ends. [I.R.C. § 404(m)(2)(A); IRS Notice 98-4, Q&A I-7, 1998-1 C.B. 269]

> **Example.** BML Corporation's taxable year ends on June 30. Contributions that it makes under its SIMPLE IRA plan for calendar year 2010 (including

contributions made in 2010 before June 30, 2010) will be deductible in the taxable year ending June 30, 2011.

An employer may deduct the contributions for its taxable year only if the contributions are made by the date the employer's tax return is due (including extensions). An employer must contribute an employee's elective contributions to the employee's SIMPLE IRA no later than 30 days after the last day of the month for which the contributions are made and must make matching contributions by the date that its tax return for the tax year is due (including extensions) (see Q 33:20). [I.R.C. §§ 404(m), 408(p)(5)(A); IRS Notice 98-4, Q&A I-7, 1998-1 C.B. 269]

Because a SIMPLE IRA plan is not subject to the 25-percent-of-compensation deduction limitation (see Q 12:8), the employer may deduct *all* of the elective, matching, and nonelective contributions made under the SIMPLE IRA plan. [I.R.C. §§ 404(a)(3), 404(m)(1); IRS Notice 98-4, Q&A I-7, 1998-1 C.B. 269]

Contributions to a SIMPLE IRA are excludable from the employee's income and are not subject to federal income tax withholding. The employee's elective contributions are subject to tax under the Federal Insurance Contributions Act (FICA) and the Federal Unemployment Tax Act (FUTA). Matching and nonelective contributions to a SIMPLE IRA are not subject to FICA or FUTA. [IRS Notice 98-4, Q&A I-1, 1998-1 C.B. 269]

Q 33:15   When are distributions made from a SIMPLE IRA?

Amounts held in a SIMPLE IRA may be withdrawn at any time. An employer may not require an employee to retain any portion of the contributions in the employee's SIMPLE IRA or otherwise impose any withdrawal restrictions. [IRS Notice 98-4, Q&A F-2, 1998-1 C.B. 269]

Generally, the required minimum distribution (RMD) rules applicable to IRAs and qualified retirement plans apply to distributions from SIMPLE IRAs. See Qs 30:42, 30:50, and chapter 11 for details.

RMDs from SIMPLE IRAs for calendar year 2009 were suspended (see Q 11:56). [IRC § 401(a)(9)(H) (as added by WRERA 2008 § 201(a); WRERA 2008 § 201(c)(1))]

Q 33:16   What are the tax consequences of SIMPLE IRA distributions?

Generally, distributions from a SIMPLE IRA are taxed like distributions from a regular IRA; that is, the distributions are includible in the individual's income when withdrawn from the SIMPLE IRA and taxed as ordinary income (see Q 30:40). [I.R.C. § 402(k); IRS Notice 98-4, Q&A I-2, 1998-1 C.B. 269]

In addition to being subject to income tax, certain IRA distributions may be subject to a 10 percent penalty tax; that is, the tax is increased by an amount equal to 10 percent of the amount includible in gross income. A number of exceptions, however, apply to the imposition of this 10 percent penalty tax (see Q 30:41).

A special rule applies to a payment or distribution received from a SIMPLE IRA during the two-year period beginning on the date on which the individual first participated in any SIMPLE IRA plan maintained by the individual's employer (the two-year period). Under this special rule, if the penalty tax on early distributions applies to a distribution within the two-year period, the penalty tax is increased from 10 percent to 25 percent. If one of the exceptions to the application of the penalty tax applies (e.g., for amounts paid after age 59½, after death, or as part of a series of substantially equal periodic payments), the exception will also apply to distributions within the two-year period and the 25 percent penalty tax will *not* apply. [I.R.C. § 72(t)(6); IRS Notice 98-4, Q&A I-2, 1998-1 C.B. 269]

The two-year period begins on the first day on which contributions made by the individual's employer are deposited in the individual's SIMPLE IRA. [IRS Notice 98-4, Q&A I-5, 1998-1 C.B. 269]

The provision under PPA that allowed individuals age 70½ or older to distribute up to $100,000 of their IRA balance to charitable organizations in 2006 and in 2007 without recognizing income and without taking a charitable deduction did not apply to distributions from an ongoing SIMPLE IRA (see Q 30:44). For this purpose, a SIMPLE IRA was treated as ongoing if it was maintained under an employer arrangement under which an employer contribution was made for the plan year ending with or within the IRA owner's taxable year in which the charitable contributions would have been made. The Emergency Economic Stabilization Act of 2008 extended this PPA provision to 2008 and 2009. [I.R.C. § 408(d)(8); IRS Notice 2007-7, § IX, Q&A-36, 2007-1 C.B. 395] At this time, this provision has not been extended to 2010 or a later year.

Q 33:17   Are there any special rollover rules that apply to a distribution from a SIMPLE IRA?

A tax-free rollover may be made from one SIMPLE IRA to another; and a rollover may also be made from a SIMPLE IRA to a regular IRA (see Q 30:1), a qualified retirement plan, a 403(b) plan (see Q 35:1), or a Section 457 plan provided that the individual has participated in the SIMPLE IRA plan for the two-year period (see Q 33:16). Thus, a distribution from a SIMPLE IRA during the two-year period qualifies as a rollover contribution (and is not includible in gross income) *only* if the distribution is paid into another SIMPLE IRA and satisfies the other requirements for treatment as a rollover contribution (see Q 34:3). [I.R.C. §§ 408(d)(3)(A), 408(d)(3)(G); IRS Notice 98-4, Q&A I-3, 1998-1 C.B. 269]

> **Example.** In 2010, S&S Ltd. establishes a SIMPLE IRA plan covering two employees, Sallie and Stephen, both age 39. Both employees separate from service in 2011. Sallie rolls over the funds in her SIMPLE IRA to a regular IRA, and Stephen rolls over the funds in his to a SIMPLE IRA maintained by his new employer. In both cases, rollovers are made within the two-year period. Sallie's rollover is invalid because it was not made to a SIMPLE IRA. Thus, the rollover amount is a taxable distribution, and Sallie is also liable for the

25 percent penalty tax. Because Stephen's rollover is valid, there are no tax consequences.

During the two-year period, amounts in a SIMPLE IRA can be transferred to another SIMPLE IRA in a tax-free trustee-to-trustee transfer. If, during the two-year period, an amount is paid from a SIMPLE IRA directly to the trustee of a regular IRA, the payment is neither a tax-free trustee-to-trustee transfer nor a rollover contribution; the payment is considered a distribution from the SIMPLE IRA (and may be includible in income and subject to the penalty tax) and a contribution to the regular IRA that does not qualify as a rollover contribution. After the expiration of the two-year period, amounts in a SIMPLE IRA can be transferred in a tax-free trustee-to-trustee transfer to a regular IRA, a qualified retirement plan, a 403(b) plan, or a Section 457 plan. [IRS Notice 98-4, Q&A I-4, 1998-1 C.B. 269]

If the employee is no longer participating in the SIMPLE IRA plan (e.g., the employee has terminated employment) and the two-year period has expired, the employee may treat the SIMPLE IRA as a regular IRA. [I.R.C. § 408(d)(3)(G)]

Q 33:18   How is a SIMPLE IRA plan established?

An employer may establish a SIMPLE IRA plan effective on any date between January 1 and October 1 of the year, provided that the employer (or any predecessor employer) did not previously maintain a SIMPLE IRA plan. This requirement does not apply to a new employer that comes into existence after October 1 of the year the SIMPLE IRA plan is established if the employer establishes the SIMPLE IRA plan as soon as administratively feasible after the employer comes into existence. If an employer (or any predecessor employer) previously maintained a SIMPLE IRA plan, the employer may establish a new SIMPLE IRA plan effective only on January 1 of the year. A SIMPLE IRA plan may only be maintained on a calendar-year basis (see Q 33:3), and a SIMPLE IRA must be established for an employee prior to the first date by which a contribution is required to be deposited into the employee's SIMPLE IRA. [IRS Notice 98-4, Q&A K-1, Q&A K-2, 1998-1 C.B. 269]

IRS has issued two model forms that employers may use to establish a SIMPLE IRA plan. Form 5305-SIMPLE is a form that may be used by an employer establishing a SIMPLE IRA plan with a financial institution that is a designated financial institution (see Q 33:19). Form 5304-SIMPLE may be used by an employer establishing a SIMPLE IRA plan under which each eligible employee is permitted to select the financial institution for the investment of the employee's SIMPLE IRA assets. [IRS Notice 98-4, Q&A K-3, Q&A K-4, 1998-1 C.B. 269; Instructions to IRS Form 5304-SIMPLE and IRS Form 5305-SIMPLE]

Based on findings that many employers had failed to update their SIMPLE IRA plans for EGTRRA 2001 (see Q 1:21), IRS offered an extended time to update these plans. Employers that previously failed to amend their SIMPLE IRA plans for EGTRRA 2001 had until December 31, 2006 to either adopt the latest version of the IRS model SIMPLE IRA plan (revised August 2005) or adopt another SIMPLE IRA plan document that had been updated for EGTRRA 2001. According to IRS guidance, if a taxpayer used an IRS model SIMPLE IRA plan document with a revision date of March 2002 or August 2005, no further action was required as the plan was up-to-date. If the taxpayer used a SIMPLE IRA prototype plan, IRS advised the taxpayer to check with the document provider or the financial institution holding the SIMPLE IRA to confirm that the document included EGTRRA 2001 provisions. [Employee Plans News, Special Edition (March 10, 2006)]

See Q 33:39 regarding correction of failures with respect to SIMPLE IRAs.

An employer can terminate its SIMPLE IRA plan prospectively beginning with the next calendar year. An employer that chooses to terminate its SIMPLE IRA plan must notify the financial institution that handles the plan that it will not be making contributions for the next calendar year and that it wants to terminate the contract or agreement with the institution. The employer must also notify its employees within a reasonable time before the 60-day election period that it is discontinuing the SIMPLE IRA plan. It is not required to notify IRS that the SIMPLE IRA plan has been terminated. [*Employee Plans News*, Vol. 9/ Summer 2009]

Q 33:19   Who holds the SIMPLE IRA funds?

Generally, an employer must permit an employee to select the financial institution for the SIMPLE IRA to which the employer will make all contributions on behalf of the employee. However, instead of making SIMPLE IRA plan contributions to the financial institution selected by each employee, an employer may require that all contributions on behalf of all eligible employees under the SIMPLE IRA plan be made to SIMPLE IRAs at a particular financial institution if the following requirements are met:

1. The employer and the financial institution agree that the financial institution will be a designated financial institution (DFI) for the SIMPLE IRA plan;

2. The financial institution agrees that, if a participant so requests, the participant's SIMPLE IRA balance will be transferred without cost or penalty to another SIMPLE IRA or, after the two-year period (see Q 33:16) to a regular IRA at a financial institution selected by the participant; and

3. Each participant is given written notification describing the procedure to transfer the participant's SIMPLE IRA balance without cost or penalty as described in 2 above.

Only certain financial institutions, such as banks, savings and loan associations, insured credit unions, insurance companies, or IRS-approved nonbank trustees, may serve as DFIs.

[I.R.C. § 408(p)(7); IRS Notice 98-4, Q&A E-4, Q&A J-1, 1998-1 C.B. 269; Instructions to IRS Form 5305-SIMPLE]

A participant must be given a reasonable period of time each year in which to transfer the SIMPLE IRA balance without cost or penalty. A participant will be deemed to have been given a reasonable period of time if, for each calendar year, the participant has until the end of the 60-day period (see Q 33:13) to request a transfer of the balance attributable to SIMPLE IRA plan contributions for the calendar year following that 60-day period (or, for the year in which an employee becomes eligible to make salary reduction contributions, for the balance of that year) and subsequent calendar years. If the time or manner in which a participant may transfer the SIMPLE IRA balance without cost or penalty is limited, any such limitation must be disclosed as part of the written notification discussed above. [IRS Notice 98-4, Q&A J-2, 1998-1 C.B. 269]

> **Example 1.** Teri Corp. first establishes a SIMPLE IRA plan effective January 1, 2011, and intends to make all contributions to a DFI. For the 2011 calendar year, Teri Corp. provides the 60-day election period beginning November 2, 2010, and notifies each participant that a transfer of future SIMPLE IRA contributions may be made without cost or penalty if the participant contacts the DFI prior to January 1, 2011. For the 2011 calendar year, the notice requirement will be met.

> **Example 2.** The facts are the same as in Example 1, except that Jeff, a participant, does not request a transfer of his SIMPLE IRA balance by December 31, 2010, but requests a transfer of his current balance to another SIMPLE IRA on July 1, 2011. Jeff's current balance is not required to be transferred without cost or penalty because Jeff did not request the transfer prior to January 1, 2011. However, during the 60-day period preceding the 2012 calendar year, Jeff may request a transfer, without cost or penalty, of his balance attributable to contributions made for the 2012 calendar year and, if he so elects, for all future calendar years (but not his balance attributable to contributions for the 2011 calendar year).

> **Example 3.** The facts are the same as in Example 1, except that Jeff becomes an eligible employee on June 1, 2011, and the 60-day period begins on that date. For the 2011 calendar year, Jeff will be deemed to have been given a reasonable amount of time to request a transfer, without cost or penalty, of his balance attributable to contributions for the remainder of the 2011 calendar year if the DFI allows such a request to be made prior to July 31, 2011.

If the participant requests a transfer of the SIMPLE IRA balance within a reasonable time limit imposed by the plan (if the plan imposes a limit), the participant's balance must be transferred on a reasonably frequent basis. A transfer on a monthly basis will satisfy this requirement. [IRS Notice 98-4, Q&A J-3, 1998-1 C.B. 269]

To satisfy the without-cost-or-penalty requirement, a participant's balance must be transferred in a trustee-to-trustee transfer (see Q 33:17) directly to a SIMPLE IRA or, after the two-year period (see Q 33:16), to a regular IRA, a qualified retirement plan, a 403(b) plan, or a Section 457 plan (see Q 33:17), at the financial institution specified by the participant. A transfer is deemed to be made without cost or penalty if no liquidation, transaction, redemption, or termination fee, or any commission, load (whether front-end or back-end), or surrender charge, or similar fee or charge is imposed with respect to the balance being transferred. A transfer will not fail to be made without cost or penalty merely because contributions that a participant has elected to have transferred without cost or penalty are required to be invested in one specified investment option until transferred, even though a variety of investment options are available with respect to contributions that participants have not elected to transfer. [IRS Notice 98-4, Q&A J-4, 1998-1 C.B. 269]

The without-cost-or-penalty requirement is not violated merely because a DFI charges an *employer* an amount that takes into account the financial institution's responsibility to transfer balances upon participants' requests or otherwise charges an employer for transfers requested by participants, provided that the charge is *not* passed through to the participants who request transfers. [IRS Notice 98-4, Q&A J-5, 1998-1 C.B. 269]

Q 33:20   What are the employer notification requirements?

Employers maintaining SIMPLE IRA plans are not required to file annual reports. However, an employer must notify each employee, immediately before the employee's 60-day election period, of the employee's opportunity to enter into a salary reduction agreement or to modify a prior agreement (see Q 33:13). If applicable, this notification must disclose an employee's ability to select the financial institution that will serve as the trustee of the employee's SIMPLE IRA (see Q 33:19). The notification must also include the summary description (see Q 33:22). [I.R.C. §§ 408(l)(2)(A), 408(l)(2)(C); IRS Notice 98-4, Q&A G-1, 1998-1 C.B. 269]

An employer is deemed to provide the notification regarding a reduced matching contribution or a nonelective contribution (see Q 33:12) in lieu of a matching contribution within a reasonable period of time before the 60-day election period if, immediately before the 60-day election period, this notification is included with the notification of the employee's opportunity to enter into a salary reduction agreement. [IRS Notice 98-4, Q&A G-2, 1998-1 C.B. 269]

If the employer fails to provide one or more of the required notices, the employer will be liable for a penalty of $50 per day until the notices are provided. If the employer shows that the failure was due to reasonable cause, the penalty will not be imposed. [I.R.C. § 6693(c); IRS Notice 98-4, Q&A G-3, 1998-1 C.B. 269]

Q 33:21   When must the employer make contributions under a SIMPLE IRA plan?

The employer must make salary reduction contributions (see Q 33:9) to the financial institution (see Q 33:19) maintaining the SIMPLE IRA no later than the close of the 30-day period following the last day of the month in which amounts would otherwise have been payable to the employee in cash. Contributions under a SIMPLE IRA plan become plan assets as of the earliest date on which such contributions can reasonably be segregated from the employer's assets, but in no event later than the 30th day following the month in which such amounts would otherwise have been payable to the employee in cash. [I.R.C. § 408(p)(5)(A)(i); DOL Reg § 2510.3-102(b); IRS Notice 98-4, Q&A G-5, 1998-1 C.B. 269]

Matching and nonelective employer contributions (see Q 33:12) must be made to the financial institution maintaining the SIMPLE IRA no later than the due date for filing the employer's income tax return, including extensions, for the taxable year that includes the last day of the calendar year for which the contributions are made. [I.R.C. § 408(p)(5)(A)(ii); IRS Notice 98-4, Q&A G-6, 1998-1 C.B. 269]

If an eligible employee who is entitled to a contribution under a SIMPLE IRA plan is unwilling or unable to establish a SIMPLE IRA with any financial institution prior to the date on which the contribution is required to be made to the SIMPLE IRA of the employee, the employer may execute the necessary documents to establish a SIMPLE IRA on the employee's behalf with a financial institution selected by the employer. [IRS Notice 94-8, Q&A G-4, 1998-1 C.B.269]

Q 33:22   What is a summary description?

Each year, the trustee of a SIMPLE IRA must provide the employer maintaining the SIMPLE IRA plan with a summary description containing the following information:

1. The name and address of the employer and the trustee;
2. The requirements for eligibility for participation;
3. The benefits provided under the plan;
4. The time and method of making elections; and
5. The procedures for, and effect of, withdrawals (including rollovers) from the SIMPLE IRA.

This requirement also applies to the issuer of an annuity (see Q 33:2) established under a SIMPLE IRA plan.

[I.R.C. § 408(l)(2)(B); ERISA § 101(h)(2); IRS Notice 98-4, Q&A H-1, 1998-1 C.B. 269]

Q 33:23   What are the trustee administrative requirements?

The trustee must provide the summary description (see Q 33:22) to the employer early enough to allow the employer to meet its notification obligation (see Q 33:20). However, a trustee is not required to provide the summary description prior to agreeing to be the trustee of a SIMPLE IRA for the SIMPLE IRA plan. The trustee of a transfer SIMPLE IRA is not required to provide the summary description. A SIMPLE IRA is a transfer SIMPLE IRA if it is not a SIMPLE IRA to which the employer has made contributions under the SIMPLE IRA plan. [IRS Notice 98-4, Q&A H-1, 1998-1 C.B. 269]

The trustee must also provide an account statement to each individual for whom the SIMPLE IRA is maintained within 31 days after each calendar year.

The statement must reflect the account balance at the end of the year and the account activity during the year. [I.R.C. § 408(i); IRS Notice 98-4, Q&A H-2, 1998-1 C.B. 269]

The trustee must also file a report each calendar year with IRS. [I.R.C. § 408(i); IRS Notice 98-4, Q&A H-3, 1998-1 C.B. 269]

Trustees who fail to provide the summary description, the account statement, or the annual report are subject to a penalty of $50 for each day such failure continues. The penalty may be waived if the failure was due to reasonable cause. [I.R.C. §§ 6693(a), 6693(c); IRS Notice 98-4, Q&A H-1, Q&A H-2, Q&A H-3, 1998-1 C.B. 269]

All of these requirements also apply to the issuer of an annuity (see Q 33:2) established under a SIMPLE IRA plan.

Q 33:24 How are SIMPLE IRA distributions reported?

The payor of a designated distribution from an IRA must report the distribution on Form 1099-R, Distributions From Pensions, Annuities, Retirement or Profit-Sharing Plans, IRAs, Insurance Contracts, etc. A penalty may be imposed for failure to report a designated distribution from an IRA (including a SIMPLE IRA). [I.R.C. §§ 6047, 6721–6724; Treas. Reg. § 35.3405-1; IRS Notice 98-4, Q&A H-4, 1998-1 C.B. 269]

In addition, a SIMPLE IRA trustee is required to report on Form 1099-R whether a distribution to a participant occurred during the two-year period (see Q 33:16). A trustee is permitted to prepare this report on the basis of its own records with respect to the SIMPLE IRA account. A trustee may, but is not required to, take into account other adequately substantiated information regarding the date on which an individual first participated in any SIMPLE IRA plan maintained by the individual's employer. [IRS Notice 98-4, Q&A H-5, 1998-1 C.B. 269]

Q 33:25 What is a SIMPLE 401(k) plan?

A SIMPLE 401(k) plan is a 401(k) plan (see Q 27:1) maintained by an eligible employer (see Q 33:27) that satisfies the:

1. Contribution requirements (see Q 33:29),
2. Exclusive plan requirement (see Q 33:27), and
3. Vesting requirements (see Q 33:29).

[I.R.C. § 401(k)(11)(A); Treas. Reg. § 1.401(k)-4]

Except as otherwise provided, any term used in Section 401(k)(11) that is also used in Section 408(p) relating to SIMPLE IRA plans has the same meaning for the purposes of SIMPLE 401(k) plans. [I.R.C. § 401(k)(11)(D)(i)]

Q 33:26   Must a SIMPLE 401(k) plan be maintained on a calendar-year basis?

Yes. A SIMPLE 401(k) plan may *only* be maintained on a calendar-year basis. According to IRS guidance, the plan year of a SIMPLE 401(k) plan must be the whole calendar year. Thus, in general, a SIMPLE 401(k) plan can be established only on January 1 and terminated only on December 31. However, in the case of an employer that did not previously maintain a SIMPLE 401(k) plan, the establishment date can be as late as October 1 (or later in the case of an employer that comes into existence after October 1 and establishes the SIMPLE 401(k) plan as soon as administratively feasible). An employer maintaining a 401(k) plan (see Q 27:1) on a fiscal-year basis must convert the plan to a calendar year if it wishes to adopt the SIMPLE 401(k) plan provisions. [Treas. Reg. § 1.401(k)-4(g); Rev. Proc. 97-9, 1997-1 C.B. 624]

Q 33:27   Who may adopt a SIMPLE 401(k) plan?

Employers who employed 100 or fewer employees who earned $5,000 or more in compensation for the preceding calendar year may adopt a SIMPLE 401(k) plan. Rules regarding this 100-employee limitation, the two-year grace period, employer aggregation, and leased employees that are applicable to SIMPLE IRA plans (see Qs 33:4, 33:5) also apply to SIMPLE 401(k) plans. [Treas. Reg. § 1.401(k)-4(b); Rev. Proc. 97-9, 1997-1 C.B. 624]

Compensation for purposes of a SIMPLE 401(k) plan means the sum of wages, tips, and other compensation from the employer subject to federal income tax withholding (as described in Section 6051(a)(3)) and the employee's elective contributions made under any other plan, and if applicable, elective deferrals under a SIMPLE IRA plan (see Q 33:2), a salary reduction SEP (see Q 32:9), or a 403(b) plan (see Q 35:1), and compensation deferred under a Section 457 plan, required to be reported by the employer on Form W-2 (as described in Section 6051(a)(8)). In the case of a self-employed individual, compensation means net earnings from self-employment determined under Section 1402(a) prior to subtracting any contributions made under the SIMPLE 401(k) plan on behalf of the individual. [Treas. Reg. § 1.401(k)-4(e)(5)]

A SIMPLE 401(k) plan may not be established if the employer maintains another qualified plan (see Q 33:4) under which an employee who is eligible to participate in the SIMPLE 401(k) plan receives an allocation of contributions (in the case of a defined contribution plan; see Q 2:2) or has an increase in an accrued benefit (in the case of a defined benefit plan; see Q 2:3) for any plan year beginning or ending in that calendar year. For this purpose, a qualified plan includes a SIMPLE IRA plan. [I.R.C. § 401(k)(11)(C); Treas. Reg. § 1.401(k)-4(c)(1); Rev. Proc. 97-9, 1997-1 C.B. 624]

> **Example 1.** Mindy Corporation has 80 employees; 70 are employed in Division A and 10 in Division B. Mindy Corporation maintains a qualified retirement plan for Division A employees. In 2011, Mindy Corporation establishes a SIMPLE 401(k) plan for those employees in Division B. Mindy Corporation may establish a SIMPLE 401(k) plan for Division B employees

because those employees are not covered under another plan, provided that the plan satisfies all other requirements for qualification (see Q 33:32).

Example 2. The facts are the same as in Example 1, except that Mindy Corporation wishes to establish a SIMPLE IRA plan for the Division B employees. Mindy Corporation may not do so because it maintains another qualified plan.

Example 3. Perrin Inc. maintains a profit sharing plan with a June 30 year end, and for the plan year ending June 30, 2011, contributions are made. Perrin Inc. need not wait until calendar year 2012 to adopt a SIMPLE 401(k) plan; the company may adopt a SIMPLE 401(k) plan as of July 1, 2011 (see Q 33:26).

A special rule applies so that a SIMPLE 401(k) plan will not be treated as failing the above requirements if a participant in a SIMPLE 401(k) plan receives an allocation of forfeitures under another plan of the employer. [Treas. Reg. § 1.401(k)-4(c)(2)]

Similar to a SIMPLE IRA plan (see Q 33:4), a tax-exempt employer may establish a SIMPLE 401(k) plan; but, unlike a SIMPLE IRA plan, the general prohibition against governmental entities maintaining a 401(k) plan also applies to a SIMPLE 401(k) plan. [I.R.C. § 401(k)(4)(B)]

Q 33:28   Who is eligible to participate in a SIMPLE 401(k) plan?

A SIMPLE 401(k) plan may not condition participation on the completion of more than one year of service; however, like other qualified retirement plans, a SIMPLE 401(k) plan may impose a minimum age requirement or other conditions for participation (see Qs 5:2, 5:5). [I.R.C. §§ 401(k)(2)(D), 401(k)(11); Rev. Proc. 97-9, 1997-1 C.B. 624]

An employee may participate in a SIMPLE 401(k) plan even if the employee also participates in a plan of an unrelated employer for the same year. However, the employee's salary reduction contributions (see Qs 27:16, 33:30) are subject to an aggregate limit on elective deferrals (see Q 27:51).

Q 33:29   What contributions may be made to a SIMPLE 401(k) plan?

Contributions to a SIMPLE 401(k) plan are limited to employee elective contributions (see Q 33:30) and required employer matching contributions or nonelective contributions (see Q 33:31). These are the only contributions (other than certain rollover contributions; see Q 34:1) that may be made to a SIMPLE 401(k) plan. [I.R.C. § 401(k)(11)(B)(i); Treas. Reg. § 1.401(k)-4(e); Rev. Proc. 97-9, 1997-1 C.B. 624]

All contributions made to an employee's account under a SIMPLE 401(k) plan must be nonforfeitable. Thus, all contributions made by an employer vest immediately (see Q 9:1). [I.R.C. §§ 401(k)(11)(A)(iii), 408(p)(3); Treas. Reg. § 1.401(k)-4(f); Rev. Proc. 97-9, 1997-1 C.B. 624]

Q 33:30   What is an employee elective contribution to a SIMPLE 401(k) plan?

An employee elective, or salary reduction, contribution is a contribution made pursuant to an employee's cash-or-deferred election to have an amount contributed to the SIMPLE 401(k) plan, rather than have the amount paid directly to the employee in cash. An employee must be permitted to elect to have salary reduction contributions made at the level specified by the employee, expressed as a percentage of compensation for the year. [I.R.C. § 401(k) (11)(B)(i)(I); Rev. Proc. 97-9, 1997-1 C.B. 624]

The time periods regarding salary reduction agreements that are applicable to SIMPLE IRA plans (see Q 33:13) also apply to cash-or-deferred elections under SIMPLE 401(k) plans. For the plan year in which an employee first becomes eligible under a SIMPLE 401(k) plan, the employee must be permitted to make a cash-or-deferred election under the plan during a 60-day period that includes either the day the employee becomes eligible or the day before. For each subsequent plan year, each eligible employee must be permitted to make or modify his cash-or-deferred election during the 60-day period immediately preceding such plan year. The employer must notify each eligible employee within a reasonable time period prior to each 60-day election period, or on the day the election period starts, that the employee can make a cash-or-deferred election, or modify a prior election, if applicable, during that period. This is, however, in addition to any other election periods provided under the plan. An employee must be given the right to terminate the cash-or-deferred election for a calendar year at any time during the year. However, the plan may provide that an employee who terminates a cash-or-deferred election at any time other than the periods described above will not be eligible to resume participation until the beginning of the next calendar year. [I.R.C. § 401(k)(11)(B)(iii); Treas. Reg. §§ 1.401(k)-4(d)(2), 1.401(k)-4(d)(3); Rev. Proc. 97-9, 1997-1 C.B. 624]

The 2005 $10,000 limitation is adjusted for inflation in $500 increments and the base period for calculating the inflation adjustment will be the calendar quarter beginning July 1, 2004. For 2010, the limitation remained at $11,500. [IRS Notice 2009-94, 2009-2 C.B. 848] For the prior five years, the applicable dollar amount was:

For years beginning in calendar year	The applicable dollar amount
2009	$11,500
2008	10,500
2007	10,500
2006	10,000
2005	10,000

[I.R.C. §§ 401(k)(11)(B)(i)(I), 408(p)(2)(A)(ii), 408(p)(2)(E); Treas. Reg. § 1. 401(k)-4(e)(2); Rev. Proc. 97-9, 1997-1 C.B. 624; IRS Notice 2000-66, 2000-2 C.B. 600]

An employer matching contribution (see Q 33:31) made on behalf of a self-employed individual (see Q 6:60) is not treated as an employee elective contribution. [I.R.C. § 402(g)(8)]

The annual addition limitations applicable to a defined contribution plan apply to a SIMPLE 401(k) plan (see Q 6:34).

Q 33:31   What must an employer contribute to a SIMPLE 401(k) plan?

An employer must make either a matching contribution or a nonelective contribution.

Under a SIMPLE 401(k) plan, an employer is generally required to match the employee's elective contribution (see Q 33:30) on a dollar-for-dollar basis up to a limit of 3 percent of the employee's compensation (see Q 33:27) for the entire calendar year. [I.R.C. § 401(k)(11)(B)(i)(II); Treas. Reg. § 1.401(k)-4(e)(3); Rev. Proc. 97-9, 1997-1 C.B. 624]

Under a SIMPLE 401(k) plan, the employer does not have the option available under a SIMPLE IRA plan of reducing the matching contribution to less than 3 percent of each employee's compensation (see Q 33:12).

As an alternative to making matching contributions, an employer may elect to make a nonelective contribution of 2 percent of compensation for each eligible employee. The employer's nonelective contributions must be made for each eligible employee regardless of whether the employee makes a cash-or-deferred election for the calendar year. The employer may, but is not required to, limit nonelective contributions to eligible employees who have at least $5,000 (or some lower amount selected by the employer) of compensation for the year. [I.R.C. § 401(k)(11)(B)(ii); Treas. Reg. § 1.401(k)-4(e)(4); Rev. Proc. 97-9, 1997-1 C.B. 624]

The employer notice that is required to be given to eligible employees (see Q 33:30) must state whether the employer will make the 3 percent matching contribution or the 2 percent nonelective contribution. [I.R.C. § 401(k)(11)(B)(ii); Treas. Reg. § 1.401(k)-4(d)(3); Rev. Proc. 97-9, 1997-1 C.B. 624]

Under a SIMPLE 401(k) plan, for purposes of both the 3 percent matching contribution and the 2 percent nonelective contribution, the annual compensation limit (i.e., $245,000 in 2010) applies (see Q 6:45).

[I.R.C. § 401(a)(17); Rev. Proc. 97-9, 1997-1 C.B. 624]

Example 1. Marn Corporation adopted a SIMPLE 401(k) plan in 2010, and Steve earned compensation of $383,334. Steve elected to defer $11,500, but Marn Corporation could only make a matching contribution of $7,350 (3% × $245,000).

Example 2. The facts are the same as in Example 1, except that Marn Corporation adopted a SIMPLE IRA plan. In this case, Marn Corporation's matching contribution would have been $11,500 (3% × $383,334).

Q 33:32 What qualification requirements apply to SIMPLE 401(k) plans?

All qualification requirements applicable to qualified retirement plans (see Q 4:1) and certain requirements applicable to 401(k) plans (see Q 27:14) apply to SIMPLE 401(k) plans. However, SIMPLE 401(k) plans are *not* subject to:

1. The ADP test (see Q 27:18),
2. The ACP test (see Q 27:77), or
3. The top-heavy rules (see chapter 26).

[I.R.C. § 401(k)(11)(D)(ii); Treas. Reg. § 1.401(k)-4; Rev. Proc. 97-9, 1997-1 C.B. 624]

Q 33:33 What are the tax consequences of SIMPLE 401(k) plan contributions?

The rules regarding the employer's deduction for contributions to a 401(k) plan (see chapter 27) are generally applicable to a SIMPLE 401(k) plan. However, a SIMPLE 401(k) plan is not subject to the 25-percent-of-compensation deduction limitation. [I.R.C. § 404(a)(3)(A)]

With regard to the employee, the rules parallel those that apply to SIMPLE IRA plans (see Q 33:14).

The employer must make the employee elective contributions to the plan in accordance with DOL rules (see Q 23:32).

Q 33:34 What are the tax consequences of SIMPLE 401(k) plan distributions?

Since a SIMPLE 401(k) plan is a qualified retirement plan, the taxation of SIMPLE 401(k) plan distributions is the same.

See chapters 13 and 27 for details.

Q 33:35 How is a SIMPLE 401(k) plan established?

In general, a SIMPLE 401(k) plan must meet all the requirements of a qualified retirement plan (see Q 33:32). IRS had provided a model amendment that employers could have used to adopt a plan that contained the SIMPLE 401(k) provisions. Employers who adopted the model amendment did not have to file an application with IRS or pay a user fee. [Rev. Proc. 97-9, 1997-1 C.B. 624]

The above guidance appears to be obsolete due to the new rules regarding required amendments for EGTRRA 2001 (see Qs 18:7–18:11).

Q 33:36   What are the reporting requirements of a SIMPLE 401(k) plan?

Because the SIMPLE 401(k) plan is a qualified retirement plan, the same reporting and disclosure requirements are applicable.

See chapters 21 and 22 for details.

Q 33:37   Is there a tax credit for elective contributions to a SIMPLE plan?

An eligible individual will be allowed a nonrefundable tax credit for the taxable year in an amount equal to the applicable percentage of the individual's qualified retirement savings contributions for the year up to $2,000. [I.R.C. § 25B]

See chapter 17 for details on the tax credit.

Q 33:38   Is there an exception to the excise tax for nondeductible contributions to a SIMPLE plan?

Contributions to a SIMPLE IRA or a SIMPLE 401(k) plan that are not deductible when contributed solely because the contributions were not made in connection with a trade or business of the employer will not be taken into account for purposes of the 10 percent excise tax on nondeductible contributions to a qualified plan (see Q 12:9). For example, employers of household or domestic workers may make contributions to these plans without imposition of the excise tax. The excise tax exception does not apply to contributions made on behalf of the employer or a member of the employer's family. [I.R.C. § 4972(c)(6)]

Q 33:39   What correction programs apply to a SIMPLE plan?

The Employee Plans Compliance Resolution System (EPCRS; see Q 19:2) may be used to correct failures with respect to SIMPLE plans. Since a SIMPLE 401(k) is a qualified retirement plan, the same correction rules are applicable. In addition, EPCRS may be used to correct failures with respect to SIMPLE IRAs. A SIMPLE IRA that is maintained under a plan document approved by IRS is eligible for SCP (see Q 19:17) with respect to insignificant failures (see Q 19:18) and is eligible for VCP (see Q 19:20). A SIMPLE IRA is also eligible for Audit CAP (see Q 19:28).

Audits of SIMPLE IRAs reveal that some sponsors have not timely updated their plans to comply with EGTRRA. EPCRS may be used to correct these failures. [*Retirement News for Employers*, Vol. 5/ Winter 2009]

For details on IRS correction programs, see chapter 19.

Chapter 34

Rollovers

It is possible to postpone payment of taxes on certain distributions from a qualified retirement plan by transferring (rolling over) all or part of the distribution to an eligible retirement plan. In addition, money contributed to one IRA can be withdrawn and transferred to another IRA without tax or penalty. EGTRRA 2001 increased the opportunity to make rollovers. This chapter examines how rollovers work and describes the tax advantages and drawbacks involved.

Q 34:1   What is a rollover?

A rollover is a tax-free transfer of cash or other property from a qualified retirement plan to an individual and then from the individual to another qualified retirement plan. There are two types of rollovers to an IRA. First, amounts may be transferred from one IRA to another. Second, amounts may be transferred from a qualified retirement plan to an IRA. A rollover from one qualified retirement plan to another is also possible, as is a rollover to a qualified retirement plan from an IRA. [I.R.C. §§ 402(c), 408(d)(3); Priv. Ltr. Ruls. 9729042, 9315031]

A number of changes have been made to increase the opportunity to make rollovers. Among the changes are the following:

1. Rollovers can be made from a governmental Section 457 plan to an eligible retirement plan (see Q 34:16); rollovers can be made to a governmental Section 457 plan from an eligible retirement plan; and a governmental Section 457 plan is an eligible retirement plan. A non-governmental 457 plan is not an eligible retirement plan.

2. Rollovers can be made from a 403(b) contract (see Q 35:1) to an eligible retirement plan; rollovers can be made to a 403(b) contract from an eligible retirement plan; and a 403(b) contract is an eligible retirement plan.

3. Spousal rollovers (see Q 34:33) can be made to an IRA or another eligible retirement plan in which the spouse participates.

4. Death benefits payable to a nonspouse beneficiary of a deceased plan participant can be transferred directly to an IRA (see Q 34:33).

5. All or any portion of an IRA, except any portion representing a designated nondeductible IRA contribution (see Q 30:20), can be rolled over to an eligible retirement plan.

6. Amounts attributable to employee after-tax contributions (see Qs 6:37, 6:38) can be directly rolled over to a qualified retirement plan, 403(b) plan, or an IRA (see Q 34:8).

7. IRS is permitted to waive the 60-day requirement (see Qs 34:35, 34:36) in limited circumstances.

[I.R.C. §§ 401(a)(31), 402(c)(2)(A); Priv. Ltr. Rul. 200925049]

Required minimum distributions (RMDs) from defined contribution plans (see Q 2:2) and IRAs were suspended for calendar year 2009 (see Q 34:8). Payments to a plan participant in 2009 were not treated as ineligible for rollover on account of the suspension if the payments equaled the 2009 RMDs or were one or more payments in a series of substantially equal periodic distributions (that include the 2009 RMDs) made at least annually and expected to last for the life (or life expectancy) of the participant, the joint lives (or joint life expectancy) of the participant and the participant's designated beneficiary, or for a period of at least ten years (see Q 34:9). Accordingly, such payments could have been rolled over, provided all other applicable rules were satisfied. To assist plan participants who had received distributions in 2009 but were unsure of which amounts could be rolled over, IRS extended the 60-day rollover period (see Qs 34:35, 34:36) for any 2009 RMD and for any additional payments that were part of a series described in the preceding sentence to November 30, 2009. In the case of IRA owners who had received distributions of 2009 RMDs in 2009, IRS also extended the 60-day rollover period for any such distribution to November 30, 2009. However, because of the one rollover per year rule (see Q 34:3), which was unchanged by WRERA 2008 (see Q 1:36), no more than one distribution from an IRA in 2009 was eligible for this rollover relief. [IRS Notice 2009-82, 2009-41 I.R.B.]

An individual cannot roll over a distribution from a qualified retirement plan to an IRA of the individual's spouse (see Q 34:16). [Rodoni, 105 T.C. 29 (1995)] An individual who received a distribution from a qualified retirement plan and used the distribution to improve his residence and pay off a portion of his mortgage was taxable on the entire distribution. His argument that applying the distribution in this manner was akin to rolling over the distribution into his own private retirement plan was without merit. [Luke, 66 T.C.M. 615 (1993); *see also* Coffield, 72 T.C.M. 338 (1996); Grow, 70 T.C.M. 1576 (1995)] Amounts withdrawn by an individual from his IRA and then transferred by him to an account with a foreign bank were not treated as a rollover contribution and were, therefore, includible in the individual's income (see Q 30:2). [Chiu, 73 T.C.M. 2679 (1997)] Similarly, a United States citizen cannot roll over his account in a Canadian registered retirement savings plan to an IRA. [Priv. Ltr. Rul. 9833020; Rev. Rul. 89-95, 1989-2 C.B. 131; Rev. Proc. 89-45, 1989-2 C.B. 596] An individual cannot roll over distributions from an annuity contract funded solely by the individual's after-tax contributions. [Sadberry, 04-61160 (5th Cir. 2005)]

An IRA is not prohibited from holding a promissory note. Where an individual received the balance of his plan benefits in the form of a promissory note providing for four equal annual installment payments, the promissory note was eligible to be rolled over into an IRA. [Priv. Ltr. Rul. 200846024] The distribution of the entire amount credited to an individual under an annuity contract that had been distributed to the individual from a previously terminated qualified retirement plan was eligible to be rolled over into an IRA. [Priv. Ltr. Rul. 9338041; IRS Notice 93-26, 1993-1 C.B. 308] Settlement proceeds received by an individual from an insurance company that were intended to replace a portion of the individual's annuity amounts lost due to the alleged misconduct of insurance company employees and that were contributed to the individual's IRA constituted a valid rollover. [Priv. Ltr. Rul. 200452054; *see also* Priv. Ltr. Rul. 200534026] Additional distributions made from a trust created after an audit by Pension Benefit Guaranty Corporation (PBGC; see Q 25:10) established that participants had not received their entire benefits qualified for the same treatment as prior distributions and, therefore, could be rolled over to an eligible retirement plan. [Priv. Ltr. Rul. 200444045] Where an individual erroneously characterized a rollover as a nondeductible IRA contribution, he could not later claim that the withdrawal from the IRA of an amount equal to the rollover was not taxable. [Sternberg v. IRS, 04-1325 (2d Cir. 2005)]

Unemployment compensation will not be reduced for any retirement benefits that are not includible in income of the individual by reason of a rollover. This provision became effective for weeks beginning on or after August 17, 2006. [I.R.C. § 3304(a)(15) (as amended by WRERA 2008 § 111(b))]

IRS has issued guidelines to address potentially abusive retirement plan arrangements referred to as Rollovers as Business Start-ups (ROBS) that are designed to allow individuals to convert their existing retirement accounts into seed money for funding new businesses without first paying taxes on the distributions. See Q 4:2 for details.

Throughout this chapter, references to an IRA mean, except as otherwise noted, a deductible IRA (see Q 30:1). For a discussion of rollovers from an IRA to a Roth IRA (see Q 31:1) and from one Roth IRA to another Roth IRA, see Qs 31:40 and 31:44.

Q 34:2 What are IRA rollover accounts?

An IRA rollover account is an individual retirement plan to which certain distributions from an eligible retirement plan (see Q 34:16) have been transferred. The transfer is on a tax-free basis, and there is no dollar limit on the amount that may be transferred into an IRA rollover account. [I.R.C. §§ 402(c)(2), 408(d)(3)] A distribution from an eligible retirement plan may be rolled over to any type of individual retirement plan except an endowment contract (see Q 30:3). [I.R.C. §§ 402(c)(8)(B)(i), 402(c)(8)(B)(ii)] Because an accountant was not qualified to act as a trustee of an IRA (see Q 30:2), rollover contributions from other IRAs into the trust were taxable to the IRA owners. [Schoof, 110 T.C. 1 (1998)]

A distribution made before 2002 that included nondeductible employee contributions to a qualified retirement plan could not be rolled over to an IRA. Instead, they were returned to the employee tax free. [Coffield, 72 T.C.M. 338 (1996)] Where an individual relied on erroneous information given him on Form 1099-R (it did not disclose the amount of his nondeductible employee contributions) and rolled over the entire distribution to an IRA, IRS ruled that the individual could increase the dollar limit of the rollover by the amount of his nondeductible contributions and that such amount would not be included in income in the taxable year in which distributed to him. [I.R.C. § 408(d)(5); Priv. Ltr. Rul. 200337014] Any distribution made before 2002 that represented a participant's investment in the contract or basis (see Q 13:3) could not be rolled over and were received tax free. See Q 34:38 for details of a conduit IRA.

The following distributions made after 2001 can be rolled over to an IRA in addition to those previously allowed:

1. A distribution from a governmental Section 457 plan.
2. Amounts included in a distribution from a qualified retirement plan of employee after-tax contributions (see Qs 6:37, 6:38) or that represent basis, provided that a direct rollover is utilized (see Q 34:17).

[I.R.C. §§ 402(c)(2), 457(e)(16)]

Q 34:3   How does a rollover from one IRA to another work?

All or part of the money contributed to a particular IRA may be withdrawn and transferred (rolled over) to another IRA without tax or penalty. This gives the IRA participant flexibility by enabling the participant to shift investments. For example, the participant may shift from one annuity IRA to another or, seeking higher interest or dividends, from one trusteed IRA to another. [Priv. Ltr. Rul. 9820010]

To make the switch, certain requirements must be met. To qualify for a tax-free rollover:

1. The amount distributed to the individual from the old account must be transferred to the new account not later than 60 days after receipt (see Qs 34:35, 34:36). [Duralia, 67 T.C.M. 3084 (1994)]
2. If property, other than cash, is received from the old account, that same property must be transferred to the new account.

An individual withdrew funds from an IRA, invested the funds in securities, and rolled over the securities to a new IRA. Because the same property was not contributed to the new IRA, it did not qualify as a rollover contribution, and the entire amount of the withdrawal was taxable to the individual. [Lemishow, 110 T.C. 110 (1998); *see also* Priv. Ltr. Rul. 200647028] Where an individual received a distribution from an IRA and produced no documentary evidence of the date the distribution was received or deposited into another IRA, the distribution was taxable to the individual. [Edmonds, 76 T.C.M. 710 (1998); *see also* Kirshenbaum, T.C. Summ. Op. 2002-152]

If a tax-free rollover of a particular IRA has been made during the preceding 12-month period, a second (tax-free) rollover from that IRA is not permitted (see Q 34:5). [I.R.C. § 408(d)(3); Treas. Reg. § 1.402(c)-2, Q&A-16; Martin, 63 T.C.M. 3122 (1992); Priv. Ltr. Ruls. 200452047, 8502044]

Example 1. On January 5, 2011, Paul receives a first distribution from IRA X and, on January 19, 2011, deposits the distribution in IRA Y. Because Paul did not receive any distributions from IRA X during the preceding 12-month period, the rollover from IRA X to IRA Y is permitted.

Example 2. On November 21, 2011, Paul receives a second distribution from IRA X and, on January 4, 2012, deposits this distribution in IRA Y. Even though the distribution is rolled over within the 60-day period, this rollover is *not* permitted because Paul received the first rollover distribution from IRA X within the preceding 12-month period. [Priv. Ltr. Rul. 9308050]

To avoid the adverse consequences resulting to Paul in Example 2, Paul could have had the funds in IRA X transferred directly to IRA Y (see Q 34:5). Although IRS can waive the 60-day rollover requirement (see Q 34:36), it cannot waive the rule prohibiting an individual from making a rollover within one year of a previous rollover. [Priv. Ltr. Rul. 200850057]

Involuntary distributions made by the Resolution Trust Corporation from an IRA held in an insolvent financial institution may be rolled over to another IRA even if the amount had been rolled over to the IRA within the preceding 12-month period. [IRS Spec. Rul. (Feb. 5, 1991)]

See Q 34:7 for a discussion of rollovers from an IRA to a qualified retirement plan.

Q 34:4   May an individual borrow from an IRA?

No, but IRS has ruled that the requirements for a valid rollover are met when an individual receives a distribution from an IRA and the distribution is redeposited in the same IRA within 60 days (see Qs 34:35, 34:36). Such a transaction will constitute a tax-free rollover and not be subject to the excess contribution limits (see Q 30:7). [I.R.C. §§ 408(e), 4975(d); Priv. Ltr. Ruls. 9010007, 8826009]

Example. Susan has a $10,000 certificate of deposit (CD) maturing in 45 days. Susan has a $4,000 tuition payment due now and does not want to cash in the CD early. Susan withdraws $4,000 from her IRA and makes the tuition payment. When the CD matures, Susan immediately repays the $4,000 to her IRA. The withdrawal and redeposit are tax free.

Q 34:5   May more than one tax-free transfer between IRAs be made during a 12-month period?

Yes, but only if the individual has the funds in an IRA transferred from the IRA *directly* to another IRA (a trustee-to-trustee transfer). Because this type of transfer is not considered a rollover, the 12-month waiting period (see Q 34:3) does not apply. [Priv. Ltr. Ruls. 9826042, 9438019, 9416037, 9106044, 9034068; IRS Pub. 590; *see also* Martin, 63 T.C.M. 3122 (1992); Martin, 67 T.C.M. 2960 (1994); Priv. Ltr. Ruls. 200027064, 199948039, 9308050]

Further, if the individual has more than one IRA, a separate 12-month waiting period applies for each IRA. [Prop. Treas. Reg. § 1.408-4(b)(4)(ii)]

A rollover from an eligible retirement plan (other than an IRA; see Q 34:16) to an IRA (see Q 34:34) is not treated as a rollover contribution for purposes of the 12-month waiting period rule. [Treas. Reg. § 1.402(c)-2, Q&A-16]

Q 34:6 May a beneficiary of an IRA roll over the proceeds at the death of the owner of the IRA?

Yes, but only if the beneficiary is the *surviving spouse* of the IRA's owner (see Q 30:46). [I.R.C. § 408(d)(3)(C)(ii)(II); Priv. Ltr. Ruls. 9826055, 9820010, 9747045, 9426049, 9011035] This is true even if the surviving spouse has passed the required beginning date (RBD; see Q 11:5). [Priv. Ltr. Ruls. 199948039, 199930052, 9848042] IRS has ruled that a surviving spouse who received a distribution from her deceased husband's IRA could redeposit (roll over) all or any portion of the distribution into the deceased husband's IRA. [I.R.C. § 408(d)(3)(D); Priv. Ltr. Rul. 200010054]

IRS has ruled that a surviving spouse may roll over funds received from the deceased spouse's IRA if the funds were paid to the surviving spouse under the laws of intestacy (i.e., the decedent died without a will), as a beneficiary of the decedent's estate, as the result of a disclaimer (see Q 11:17), as a beneficiary of a trust created by the decedent, or by the exercise of a right of election, rather than as the individual designated as the beneficiary of the IRA. Generally, a rollover by the surviving spouse is permitted where there is no discretion on the part of someone other than the surviving spouse (e.g., the surviving spouse is the sole beneficiary of the estate or the surviving spouse may withdraw the funds from the trust). [Priv. Ltr. Ruls. 200950058 (trust), 200950053 (trust), 200943046 (trust), 200940031 (trust), 200938042 (disclaimer), 200935045 (trust), 200934046 (disclaimer, estate, and trust), 200928043 (trust), 200915063 (trust), 200905040 (trust), 200807025 (estate), 200720024 (estate), 200703035 (estate), 200650022 (estate), 200644031 (estate), 200634065 (estate), 200615032 (estate and trust), 200611037 (estate), 200532060 (disclaimer), 200438045 (right of election), 200433026 (estate and trust), 200324059 (intestacy), 200304038 (intestacy), 200150036 (right of election), 200129036 (intestacy), 200052040 (right of election)] Where the surviving spouse was a beneficiary of a trust to which the IRA was paid but did not have control over the trust, a rollover could not be done. [Priv. Ltr. Rul. 200618030]

An IRA owner designated a trust for the benefit of his surviving spouse as the beneficiary of his IRA. The surviving spouse was empowered to withdraw $50,000 each year from the trust and to elect the form of distribution from the IRA to the trust, provided that no less than the required minimum distribution (RMD) amount was distributed to the trust each year. IRS ruled that the surviving spouse could roll over to her own IRA each year the portion of the

$50,000 annual withdrawal that exceeded that year's RMD (see Q 34:11). [Priv. Ltr. Rul. 9649045; *see also* Priv. Ltr. Rul. 200944059]

An IRA acquired by a beneficiary upon the death of a nonspouse is an inherited IRA and does not qualify for rollover treatment, and an inherited IRA cannot be converted to a Roth IRA (see Qs 30:48, 31:44). [I.R.C. §§ 408(d)(3)(C), 408A(e)(1)(B)(i); Jankelovits, 96 T.C.M. 460 (2008); Priv. Ltr. Ruls. 200750019, 200513032, 200452047, 200452041, 9630034, 9504045, 9305025] Although the beneficiary of an inherited IRA cannot roll over the inherited IRA to an IRA in the beneficiary's name, IRS has ruled that the beneficiary of five inherited IRAs could consolidate them into a single IRA as long as the consolidated IRA was maintained in the deceased IRA owner's name. [Priv. Ltr. Ruls. 9802046, 9737030] A nonspouse beneficiary can do a trustee-to-trustee transfer as long as the new IRA is maintained in the name of the deceased IRA owner. [Rev. Rul. 78-406, 78-2 C.B. 157; *see also* Priv. Ltr. Rul. 200945011] Where a nonspouse beneficiary received a distribution from an inherited IRA and contributed the distribution to a new IRA in the decedent's name, IRS ruled that the distribution was includible in the nonspouse beneficiary's gross income because a trustee-to-trustee transfer did not occur. [Priv. Ltr. Rul. 200228023]

Where a surviving spouse was the beneficiary of her deceased husband's IRAs but had not yet received distributions before her death, the legal representative of the surviving spouse's estate was not permitted to do a rollover because that right was personal to the surviving spouse and could not be exercised by the legal representative. [Priv. Ltr. Rul. 200126038] An individual participated in two qualified retirement plans and also had a SEP (see Q 32:1). The individual designated his wife as the sole beneficiary of all three plans. After the individual's death, the two plans established separate beneficiary accounts for the wife. IRS ruled that the wife could establish a new IRA in the name of the deceased husband, naming herself as beneficiary and then have the benefits of all three plans transferred directly to the new IRA. [Priv. Ltr. Rul. 200650023]

See Q 11:60 concerning the special election that may be made by a surviving spouse.

Q 34:7   How does a rollover from an IRA to a qualified retirement plan work?

Certain distributions made from an IRA can be rolled over to a qualified retirement plan, a 403(b) contract (see Q 35:1), or a governmental Section 457 plan, whether or not the distributing IRA is a conduit IRA (see Q 34:38).

RMDs and distributions from inherited IRAs cannot be rolled over (see Q 34:6) to an eligible retirement plan (see Q 34:16). The nontaxable portion of an IRA distribution cannot be rolled over to an eligible retirement plan (other than another IRA) so that the maximum amount that can be rolled over from an IRA into a non-IRA eligible retirement plan is the taxable portion of the IRA distribution (without regard to the rollover). Thus, a designated nondeductible IRA contribution cannot be rolled over to a non-IRA eligible retirement plan (see Qs 29:22, 29:25). In addition, if employee after-tax contributions have been rolled over from a qualified retirement plan to an IRA (see Q 34:2), such amounts cannot be rolled back to a non-IRA eligible retirement plan, even if the IRA is a conduit IRA.

The rules for a rollover from one IRA to another (see Q 34:3) also apply to a rollover from an IRA to the non-IRA eligible retirement plan.

With regard to a rollover from an IRA to a non-IRA eligible retirement plan, the rollover distribution is treated as first coming from amounts in all of the individual's combined IRAs other than after-tax contributions. This maximizes the total amount of the IRA distribution eligible for rollover.

[I.R.C. § 408(d)(3); Priv. Ltr. Rul. 200925049]

> **Example 1.** In 2011, Stephanie has two IRAs, IRA A and IRA B. Stephanie made deductible contributions to IRA A, which has an account balance of $25,000; and she made $10,000 of designated nondeductible contributions to IRA B, which has an account balance of $35,000. Stephanie is eligible to roll over to her new employer's qualified retirement plan the sum of $50,000 because the amount remaining after the rollover will not be less than her basis of $10,000 [($25,000 + $35,000) − $50,000]. Stephanie could roll over her entire IRA B and $15,000 from IRA A, her entire IRA A and $25,000 from IRA B, or any other combination as long as the rollover does not exceed $50,000.

> **Example 2.** The facts are the same as in Example 1, except that Stephanie has a third IRA, IRA C, which has an account balance of $40,000, of which $35,000 is after-tax employee contributions rolled over by Stephanie from her prior employer's qualified retirement plan. Stephanie is now eligible to roll over an additional $5,000 ($40,000 − $35,000) to her new employer's plan.

Q 34:8 What types of distributions from a qualified retirement plan may be rolled over?

Only an eligible rollover distribution may be rolled over. [I.R.C. § 402(c); Treas. Reg. §§ 1.401(a)(31)-1, Q&A-1(c), 1.402(c)-2, Q&A-1(c); IRS Notice 2009-82, Q&A-7, 2009-41 I.R.B.] See Q 34:1 for a discussion of transition relief issued by IRS. An eligible rollover distribution is any distribution to an employee of all or any portion of the employee's qualified retirement plan benefit *except*:

1. An RMD (see Q 34:11);

2. A distribution that is one of a series of substantially equal periodic payments (at least annually) made (a) over the life or life expectancy of the employee or over the joint lives or joint life expectancy of the employee and the employee's beneficiary or (b) over a specified period of *ten or more years* (see Q 34:9);

3. A distribution made upon hardship of the employee (see Qs 1:46, 27:14);

4. The portion of any distribution that is not includible in gross income (determined without regard to the exclusion for net unrealized appreciation) (see Qs 13:3, 13:18) unless done by a direct rollover to an IRA or to a defined contribution plan (see Qs 2:2, 34:17) [Machen v. United States, 00-478T (Fed. Cl. 2001); Priv. Ltr. Ruls. 200337014, 9722040];

5. Elective contributions (see Q 27:16) and employee contributions (see Q 27:74) that are returned to the employee (together with the income allocable thereto) in order to comply with the Section 415 limitations (see Q 27:70);

6. Corrective distributions of excess contributions (see Q 27:26) and excess deferrals (see Q 27:63) and corrective distributions of excess aggregate contributions (see Q 27:83), together with the income allocable to these corrective distributions;

7. Loans in default that are deemed distributions (see chapter 14);

8. Dividends paid on employee stock ownership plan (ESOP) employer securities (see Q 28:12);

9. Distributions of premiums for accident or health insurance (see Q 1:49);

10. The costs of current life insurance protection (see Q 15:7);

11. Prohibited allocations in S corporation ESOPs that are treated as deemed distributions (see Q 28:3); and

12. A distribution that is a permissible withdrawal from an eligible automatic contribution arrangement (see Q 27:7).

[I.R.C. § 402(c)(4) (as amended by WRERA 2008 § 201(b)); Treas. Reg. §§ 1. 402(a)-1(e), 1.402(c)-2, Q&As-3, 4; Prop. Reg. § 1.402(c)-2, Q&A-4(h); Priv. Ltr. Ruls. 200411051, 200050049, 200038055, 200038051]

Effective for taxable years beginning after December 31, 2006, after-tax contributions may be rolled over from a qualified retirement plan to another qualified retirement plan (either a defined contribution or a defined benefit plan; see Q 2:3) or a 403(b) contract (see Q 35:1). However, the rollover must be a direct rollover, and the plan to which the rollover is made must separately account for after-tax contributions (and earnings thereon). [I.R.C. § 402(c)(2)(A)]

Where a participant in a 401(k) plan (see Q 27:1) rolled over a distribution of his plan benefits to an IRA, upon his death, the IRA beneficiaries, and not his wife, were entitled to the IRA. The automatic survivor rules do not apply to IRAs (see Q 10:6). [Charles Schwab & Co. v. Dibickero, 2010 WL 200276 (9th Cir. 2010)]

RMDs from IRAs and defined contribution plans (see Q 2:2) were suspended for calendar year 2009 (see Q 11:1). If all or a portion of a distribution during 2009 was an eligible rollover distribution because it was no longer an RMD, the distribution was not treated as an eligible rollover distribution for purposes of the direct rollover requirement (see Q 34:17) and the notice and written explanation of the direct rollover requirement (see Q 34:29), as well as the mandatory 20 percent income tax withholding for an eligible rollover distribution (see Q 20:10), to the extent the distribution would have been an RMD for 2009 absent this provision. Thus, for example, if a qualified retirement plan distributed an amount to an individual during 2009 that was an eligible rollover distribution but would have been an RMD for 2009, the plan was permitted, but not required, to offer the employee a direct rollover of that amount and to provide the employee with a written explanation of the requirement. If the employee received the distribution, the distribution was not subject to mandatory 20 percent income tax withholding and the employee would have rolled over the distribution by contributing it to an eligible retirement plan (see Q 34:16) within 60 days of receipt of the distribution (see Qs 11:41, 34:3). This was effective for calendar years beginning after December 31, 2008. However, the provision did not apply to any RMD for 2008 that was permitted to be made in 2009 by reason of an individual's RBD being April 1, 2009. [I.R.C. § 402(c)(4) (as amended by WRERA 2008 § 201(b); WRERA 2008 § 201(c)(1)] IRS clarified the circumstances under which a defined contribution plan had to withhold income tax from a 2009 RMD paid between January 1, 2010 and April 1, 2010. Although RMDs from defined contribution plans were suspended for calendar year 2009, IRS noted that some plans continued to pay RMDs. If a 2009 RMD was distributed between January 1, 2010 and April 1, 2010 (for example, to a participant who turned 70½ in 2009, but delayed taking the 2009 RMD until April 1, 2010), the mandatory 20 percent income tax withholding applied to that distribution unless the RMD was not an eligible rollover distribution for some other reason. If the amount distributed between January 1, 2010 and April 1, 2010 was the first distribution from the plan in 2010, the distribution was first applied to the 2010 RMD. The amount of the distribution up to the 2010 RMD was not an eligible rollover distribution and not subject to mandatory withholding; however, if the distribution was greater than the 2010 RMD, the excess was an eligible rollover distribution subject to mandatory withholding. [*IRS Employee Plan News*, Winter 2010; *Retirement News for Employers*, Winter 2010]

A plan offset amount (see Q 14:10) is an eligible rollover distribution. [Priv. Ltr. Rul. 200617037] However, a hardship distribution from a qualified retirement plan is not an eligible rollover distribution. IRS has issued the following guidance concerning hardship distributions:

1. *Pre-'89 401(k) plan amounts.* In many instances plan records do not make it possible to distinguish pre-'89 401(k) plan amounts from other amounts credited to an employee's account under the plan as of 1989 (see Q 27:14). The guidance provides that to the extent plan records are not available to segregate pre-'89 401(k) plan amounts from other 1989 amounts, all amounts in a participant's account as of the 1989 date will be treated as elective contributions. As such, they are ineligible for rollover when distributed as a hardship distribution.

2. *Satisfaction of another statutory event.* A hardship distribution will be treated as ineligible for rollover even though another statutory event has occurred (e.g., separation from service or attainment of age 59½) that

would have otherwise entitled the participant to receive a plan distribution without regard to the hardship.

3. *Allocation of basis.* A portion of a hardship distribution from a qualified retirement plan that is not includible in gross income may be allocated to the portion ineligible for rollover or to the portion eligible for rollover (or between the two portions) using any reasonable method. A qualified retirement plan must generally be consistent in the treatment of all distributions when applying this rule.

[IRS Notice 2000-32, 2000-2 C.B. 1]

An eligible rollover distribution is subject to automatic 20 percent withholding unless the distribution is transferred by a direct rollover (see Qs 20:10, 34:33) to an eligible retirement plan that permits the acceptance of rollover distributions. [Moon v. United States, No. 95-702T (Fed. Cl. 1997)] To be a qualified retirement plan, the plan *must* provide that if the distributee of an eligible rollover distribution elects to have the distribution paid directly to an eligible retirement plan, and specifies the eligible retirement plan to which the distribution will be paid, then the distribution will be paid to that eligible retirement plan in a direct rollover. Thus, the plan *must* give the distributee the option of having the distribution paid in a direct rollover to an eligible retirement plan specified by the distributee. [I.R.C. §§ 401(a)(31), 3405(c); Treas. Reg. §§ 1.401(a)(31)-1, Q&A-1(a), 1.402(c)-2, Q&A-1(a)] As previously discussed, these requirements are suspended for calendar year 2009. IRS has ruled that a court may garnish a participant's or beneficiary's benefit in a qualified retirement plan to satisfy a fine or restitution order imposed in a federal criminal action and that a single-sum payment made pursuant to a garnishment order constitutes an eligible rollover distribution and is subject to automatic 20 percent withholding. However, periodic payments made pursuant to such an order are not eligible rollover distributions and are not subject to automatic withholding. [Priv. Ltr. Rul. 200426027]

Where a participant's election of a lumpsum distribution was a restricted benefit (see Q 25:8), the distribution arrangement was modified so that the benefit payments did not exceed the restrictions. IRS ruled that the final payment, which will be substantially larger than the other payments and will be made within ten years from the date of the first payment, will be an eligible rollover distribution. [Priv. Ltr. Rul. 201031042] An individual participated in a qualified retirement plan that was terminated, and the individual received the distribution of his entire benefits in the form of an annuity contract. Subsequently, the individual received a distribution of the entire amount credited under the annuity contract and rolled the distribution over to an IRA. IRS ruled that the distribution from the annuity contract was an eligible rollover distribution. [Priv. Ltr. Rul. 9338041; IRS Notice 93-26, 1993-1 C.B. 308] IRS ruled that distributions from a settlement fund resulting from a class action lawsuit against qualified retirement plans were eligible rollover distributions. The settlement fund was treated as an extension of the plans that contributed to it, and all the amounts held in the fund came directly from the plans. [Priv. Ltr. Ruls. 200127055, 199905037; *see also* Priv. Ltr. Ruls. 200745022, 200452054; *but see* Priv. Ltr. Ruls. 200213032, 9241008] However, a United States citizen could not roll over his account in a Canadian registered retirement savings plan because the distribution was not an eligible rollover distribution. [Priv. Ltr. Rul. 9833020; Rev. Rul. 89-95, 1989-2 C.B. 131; Rev. Proc. 89-45, 1989-2 C.B. 596]

A surviving spouse was permitted to roll over a qualified retirement plan's single-sum distribution of previously unpaid monthly benefits, plus interest, that she was entitled to receive as her husband's surviving spouse (see Q 34:33). [Priv. Ltr. Rul. 9718037]

If a qualified retirement plan holds illiquid, nonmarketable assets, IRS has ruled that a distribution of both liquid assets and an interest in the illiquid assets can constitute an eligible rollover distribution. An independent, nonqualified trust is established, and the illiquid assets are transferred to the nonqualified trust. Each participant, in addition to receiving a distribution of liquid assets, receives a transferable certificate representing the participant's interest in the nonqualified trust. This total distribution may also qualify for favorable income tax treatment (see Q 13:7). [Priv. Ltr. Ruls. 9726032, 9507032, 9421041, 9418028, 9417041; *see also* Priv. Ltr. Rul. 200420036]

A provision within the income tax treaty between the United States and the United Kingdom may not be used by U.S. residents to make a tax-deferred rollover from a U.K. pension scheme to a U.S. retirement plan where the distribution would not qualify as an eligible rollover distribution. [CCA Memorandum AM 2008-009]

Q 34:9 What is a series of substantially equal periodic payments?

One of the exceptions to the 10 percent penalty tax (see Q 16:1) is for a distribution that is part of a series of substantially equal periodic payments. To determine whether a series of payments is a series of substantially equal periodic payments, and therefore not an eligible rollover distribution, generally the same principles are followed (see Q 16:7). Whether the series is one of substantially equal periodic payments over a specified period of *ten or more years* is generally determined at the time payments begin without regard to contingencies or modifications that have not yet occurred. For example, a joint and survivor annuity with a 50 percent survivor annuity to the participant's spouse will be treated as a series of substantially equal payments at the time payments commence, as will a joint and survivor annuity that provides for increased payments to the participant if the participant's spouse dies before the participant. [I.R.C. §§ 72(t)(2)(A)(iv), 402(c)(4)(A); Treas. Reg. § 1.402(c)-2, Q&A-5(a); Priv. Ltr. Rul. 200127027]

For purposes of determining whether a distribution is one of a series of payments that are substantially equal, Social Security supplements are disregarded. Similarly, a series of payments that is not substantially equal but that generally produces a series of substantially equal payments when expected Social Security payments are taken into account is treated as substantially equal for purposes of determining whether a distribution is an eligible rollover distribution.

Example. Judy will receive a life annuity from the PJK Corp. pension plan of $500 per month, plus a Social Security supplement consisting of payments of $200 per month until Judy reaches the age at which Social Security benefits begin. The $200 supplemental payments are disregarded so that each monthly payment of $700 made before the Social Security age and each monthly payment of $500 made after the Social Security age will be treated as one of a series of substantially equal periodic payments for life. Therefore, each monthly payment to Judy will not be an eligible rollover distribution. [Treas. Reg. § 1.402(c)-2, Q&A-5(b); Priv. Ltr. Rul. 9601054]

If the amount (or, if applicable, the method of calculating the amount) of the payments changes so that subsequent payments are not substantially equal to prior payments, a new determination must be made as to whether the remaining payments are a series of substantially equal periodic payments over a period. This determination is made without taking into account payments made or the years of payment that elapsed prior to the change. However, a new determination is not made merely because, upon the death of the employee, the spouse of the employee becomes the distributee. Thus, once distributions commence over a period that is at least as long as either the employee's life or ten years (e.g., as provided by a life annuity with a five-year- or ten-year-certain guarantee), then substantially equal payments to the survivor are not eligible rollover distributions (see Q 34:15) even though the payment period remaining after the death of the employee is or may be less than ten years. For example, substantially equal periodic payments made under a life annuity with a five-year term certain would not be an eligible rollover distribution even when paid after the death of the employee with only three years remaining under the term certain. [Treas. Reg. § 1.402(c)-2, Q&A-5(c)]

The following rules apply to determining whether a series of payments from a defined contribution plan (see Q 2:2) constitute substantially equal periodic payments for a period of at least ten years:

1. *Declining balance of years.* A series of payments from an account balance under a defined contribution plan will be considered substantially equal payments over a period, if, for each year, the amount of the distribution is calculated by dividing the account balance by the number of years remaining in the period. For example, a series of payments will be considered substantially equal payments over ten years if the series is determined as follows: in year 1, the annual payment is the account balance divided by 10; in year 2, the annual payment is the remaining account balance divided by 9; and so on until year 10 when the entire remaining balance is distributed.

2. *Reasonable actuarial assumptions.* If an employee's account balance under a defined contribution plan will be distributed in annual installments of a specified amount until the account balance is exhausted, then, for purposes of determining if the period of distribution is at least ten years, the period of years over which the installments will be distributed must be determined using reasonable actuarial assumptions. For example, if an employee has an account balance of $100,000, elects distributions of $12,000 per year until the account balance is exhausted, and

the future rate of return is assumed to be 8 percent per year, the account balance will be exhausted in approximately 14 years. Similarly, if the same employee elects a fixed annual distribution amount and the fixed annual amount is less than or equal to $10,000, it is reasonable to assume that a future rate of return will be greater than zero percent and, thus, the account will not be exhausted in less than ten years. [Treas. Reg. § 1.402(c)-2, Q&A-5(d)]

Where an individual elected to receive monthly payments from a qualified retirement plan over six years, each monthly payment was an eligible rollover distribution. [Priv. Ltr. Rul. 9429026]

RMDs from IRAs and defined contribution plans were suspended for calendar year 2009 (see Q 11:1). See Q 16:9 for a discussion applicable to the 10 percent penalty tax and Q 34:1 for a discussion of transition relief that was issued by IRS.

Q 34:10 If a payment is independent of a series of substantially equal periodic payments that are not eligible rollover distributions, can that payment be an eligible rollover distribution?

Yes. A payment is treated as independent of the payments in a series if the payment is substantially larger or smaller than the other payments in the series (see Q 34:9). An independent payment is an eligible rollover distribution if it is not otherwise excepted from the definition of eligible rollover distributions. This is the case regardless of whether the payment is made before, with, or after payments in the series. [Treas. Reg. § 1.402(c)-2, Q&A-6(a); Priv. Ltr. Rul. 9718037]

Example 1. Bob elects a single payment of half of his account balance under The Gordons of Greenwich, Inc. profit sharing plan, with the remainder of his account balance to be paid over his life expectancy. The single payment is treated as independent of the payments in the series and is an eligible rollover distribution unless otherwise excepted.

Example 2. If a participant's surviving spouse receives a survivor life annuity of $1,000 per month plus a single payment of $5,000, the single payment is treated as independent of the annuity payments and is an eligible rollover distribution unless otherwise excepted.

A plan participant was receiving substantially equal periodic payments from a qualified retirement plan. After his death, his wife elected not to continue the payments and to receive a single-sum payment of the present value of the remaining payments. IRS ruled that since the single-sum payment was substantially larger than the other payments in the series, the single-sum payment was an eligible rollover distribution except for the portion of the payment that was an RMD (see Q 34:11). [Priv. Ltr. Rul. 199940041]

If, due solely to reasonable administrative error or delay in payment, there is an adjustment after the annuity starting date (see Q 10:3) to the amount of any payment in a series of payments that otherwise would constitute a series of substantially equal payments, the adjusted payment or payments will be treated as part of the series of substantially equal periodic payments and will not be treated as independent of the payments in the series. For example, if, due solely to reasonable administrative delay, the first payment of a life annuity is delayed by two months and reflects an additional two months' worth of benefits, that payment will be treated as a substantially equal payment in the series rather than as an independent payment. The result will not change merely because the amount of the adjustment is paid in a separate supplemental payment. [Treas. Reg. § 1.402(c)-2, Q&A-6(b)(1)]

A supplemental payment from a defined benefit plan (see Q 2:3) to annuitants (e.g., retirees or beneficiaries) will be treated as part of a series of substantially equal payments, rather than as an independent payment, provided that the following conditions are met:

1. The supplement is a benefit increase for annuitants;
2. The amount of the supplement is determined in a consistent manner for all similarly situated annuitants;
3. The supplement is paid to annuitants who are otherwise receiving payments that would constitute substantially equal periodic payments; and
4. The aggregate supplement is less than or equal to the greater of 10 percent of the annual rate of payment for the annuity or $750 (or any higher amount prescribed by IRS). [Treas. Reg. § 1.402(c)-2, Q&A-6(b)(2); Priv. Ltr. Rul. 199914046]

If a payment in a series of payments from an account balance under a defined contribution plan (see Q 2:2) represents the remaining balance to the credit and is substantially less than the other payments in the series, the final payment must nevertheless be treated as a payment in the series of substantially equal payments and may not be treated as an independent payment if the other payments in the series are substantially equal and the payments are for a period of at least ten years. Thus, such final payment will not be an eligible rollover distribution. [Treas. Reg. § 1.402(c)-2, Q&A-6(b)(3)]

Q 34:11 When is a distribution from a plan a required minimum distribution (RMD)?

An RMD is not an eligible rollover distribution. If a minimum distribution is required for a calendar year, all amounts distributed during that calendar year are treated as RMDs as long as the total RMD for that calendar year has not been made. [Treas. Reg. § 1.402(c)-2, Q&A-7(a)]

Example. Linda is required to receive a minimum distribution from The Gordons of Greenwich, Inc. profit sharing plan in 2010 of $21,000. During 2010, Linda receives four quarterly distributions of $7,500 each. The first two distributions and $6,000 of the third distribution are RMDs. However, the remaining $1,500 of the third distribution and all of the fourth distribution are not RMDs because these are the amounts by which the total of the distributions exceeds the RMD.

If the total amount that is required to be distributed for a calendar year in order to satisfy the minimum distribution requirements is not distributed in that calendar year, the amount that was required but not distributed is added to the amount required to be distributed for the next calendar year in determining the portion of any distribution in the next calendar year that is a required distribution.

Example. Bob should have received, but did not receive, a minimum distribution in 2010 of $8,000. For 2011, Bob should receive a minimum distribution of $6,000. Bob's RMD for 2011 is $14,000.

Any amount paid before January 1 of the year in which the employee attains age 70½ will not be treated as an RMD and, thus, is an eligible rollover distribution if it otherwise qualifies. Conversely, any amount paid on or after January 1 of the year in which the employee attains age 70½ will be treated as an RMD and, hence, not an eligible rollover distribution. [Treas. Reg. § 1.402(c)-2, Q&A-7(b)]

Example. Shirley attains age 70½ on December 30, 2010, and has an RBD (see Q 11:5) of April 1, 2011. Shirley's RMD to be made on or before April 1, 2011, is $20,000, and she is paid that amount on June 21, 2010. Even though Shirley is only age 69 on June 21, 2010, the distribution is an RMD and, thus, is not an eligible rollover distribution.

Annuity payments from a defined benefit plan (see Q 2:3) may be RMDs even if annuity payments are made before the employee's RBD (see Qs 11:6, 11:35).

If the RMD has not yet been made to an employee, a distribution is then made to the employee that exceeds the RMD, and a portion of that distribution is excludable from gross income (see Q 13:3), the following rule applies for purposes of determining the amount of the distribution that is an eligible rollover distribution. The portion of the distribution that is excludable from gross income is first allocated toward satisfaction of the RMD and then the remaining portion of the RMD, if any, is satisfied from the portion of the distribution that is includible in gross income. [Treas. Reg. § 1.402(c)-2, Q&A-8; Priv. Ltr. Rul. 9840041]

Example. Norman is required to receive a minimum distribution of $4,000, and he receives a $4,800 distribution, of which $1,000 is excludable from income as a return of basis. First, the $1,000 return of basis is allocated toward satisfying the RMD. Then, the remaining $3,000 of the RMD is satisfied from the $3,800 of the distribution that is includible in gross income, so that the remaining balance of the distribution, $800, is an eligible rollover distribution if it otherwise qualifies.

Since the portion of a distribution that is excludable from gross income can now be directly rolled over (see Q 34:17) to an IRA or to a defined contribution plan (see Q 34:1), it is unclear whether the above example will remain applicable.

IRS has ruled that, if a participant dies before the RBD and the five-year rule (see Q 11:10) applies, a distribution to the surviving spouse beneficiary prior to the expiration of the fourth calendar year following the calendar year in which death occurred is not an RMD and, hence, is an eligible rollover distribution. [Priv. Ltr. Rul. 9850016; Treas. Reg. § 54.4974-2, Q&A-3(c)]

Example. Zeke, a participant in a profit sharing plan, died on December 15, 2010, and named his wife, Zelda, as beneficiary. If Zelda receives the death benefit on or before December 31, 2014, she may roll over the distribution to her IRA. If Zelda does not receive the distribution until calendar year 2015, the distribution is an RMD, and she may not do the rollover; it is not an eligible rollover distribution.

A participant in a qualified retirement plan sponsored by a company of which the participant was a 5 percent owner rolled over his account balance to another plan in which he participated. The second plan was sponsored by a company in which the participant was a non-5 percent owner. IRS ruled that the participant could delay RMDs from the second plan until retirement (see Q 11:5, example 5). [Priv. Ltr. Ruls. 200453026, 200453015]

RMDs from IRAs and defined contribution plans were suspended for calendar year 2009 (see Q 34:8). See Q 34:1 for a discussion of transition relief that was issued by IRS.

For a detailed discussion of the minimum distribution requirements, see chapter 11.

Q 34:12 May an employee roll over more than the plan administrator determines to be an eligible rollover distribution?

A plan administrator (see Q 20:1) may make certain assumptions in determining the amount of a distribution that is an eligible rollover distribution. The plan administrator may assume that, for the purpose of determining the RMD amount, there is no designated beneficiary (see Q 11:14). [Treas. Reg. § 1.401(a)(31)-1, Q&A-18] Even though the plan administrator calculates the portion of a distribution that is an RMD (and thus not an eligible rollover distribution) by assuming that there is no designated beneficiary, the portion of the distribution that is actually an RMD is determined by taking into account the designated beneficiary, if any. If, by taking into account the designated beneficiary, a greater portion of the distribution is an eligible rollover distribution, the employee may roll over the additional amount. [Treas. Reg. § 1.402(c)-2, Q&A-15]

Under the final regulations issued by IRS, this should be applicable only if the spouse of the employee is the sole designated beneficiary and the spouse is more than ten years younger than the employee (see Q 11:22).

Q 34:13 How are participant loans treated for rollover purposes?

For a discussion of how a participant loan is treated, see Q 14:19; for a discussion of whether a direct rollover (see Q 34:17) option must be provided for an offset amount that is an eligible rollover distribution, see Q 14:20.

Q 34:14   How is a qualified retirement plan distributed annuity contract treated?

A qualified retirement plan distributed annuity contract is an annuity contract purchased for a participant, and distributed to the participant, by a qualified retirement plan. [Treas. Reg. § 1.402(c)-2, Q&A-10(a)]

Amounts paid under a qualified retirement plan distributed annuity contract are eligible rollover distributions if they otherwise qualify. For example, if the employee surrenders the contract for a single-sum payment of its cash surrender value, the payment would be an eligible rollover distribution to the extent it is includible in gross income and not an RMD. This rule applies even if the annuity contract is distributed in connection with a plan termination. If any amount to be distributed under a qualified retirement plan distributed annuity contract is an eligible rollover distribution, the annuity contract must satisfy the direct rollover requirements in the same manner as a qualified retirement plan. In the case of a qualified retirement plan distributed annuity contract, the payor under the contract is treated as the plan administrator (see Q 20:1). [Treas. Reg. §§ 1.401(a)(31)-1, Q&A-17, 1.402(c)-2, Q&A-10(b); Priv. Ltr. Rul. 9338041; IRS Notice 93-26, 1993-1 C.B. 308]

An individual cannot roll over distributions from an annuity contract funded solely by the individual's after-tax contributions. [Sadberry, 04-61160 (5th Cir. 2005)]

Q 34:15   Can a person other than an employee receive an eligible rollover distribution?

If a distribution attributable to an employee is paid to the employee's *surviving spouse,* the rollover rules apply to the distribution in the same manner as if the spouse were the employee. The same rules apply if a distribution is paid to a spouse or former spouse as an alternate payee (see Q 36:5) under a qualified domestic relations order (QDRO; see Q 36:1). Therefore, a distribution to the surviving spouse of an employee (or to a spouse or former spouse as an alternate payee under a QDRO) can be an eligible rollover distribution. The surviving spouse is permitted to roll over an eligible rollover distribution in the same manner as if the spouse were the employee. In other words, the surviving spouse may roll over the distribution to a qualified retirement plan, 403(b) plan (see Q 35:1), or a governmental Section 457 plan in which the surviving spouse participates, or to an IRA. [I.R.C. § 402(c)(9); Treas. Reg. § 1.402(c)-2, Q&A-12(a); Priv. Ltr. Ruls. 200510039, 99940041, 9726032]

Distributions from a qualified retirement plan made prior to January 1, 2007 to a distributee other than the employee or the employee's surviving spouse (or spouse or former spouse as an alternate payee under a QDRO) could not be rolled over and, therefore, did not constitute eligible rollover distributions.

[Treas. Reg. § 1.402(c)-2, Q&A-12(b)] For distributions made after December 31, 2006, the benefits of a beneficiary other than a surviving spouse can be transferred *directly* to an IRA (see Q 34:33).

Q 34:16   What is an eligible retirement plan?

For *regular rollover purposes* (see Q 34:1), an eligible retirement plan means an IRA, a qualified retirement plan, a 403(b) plan (see Q 35:1), and a governmental Section 457 plan. [I.R.C. § 402(c)(8)(B); Treas. Reg. § 1.402(c)-2, Q&A-2]

For *direct rollover purposes* (see Q 34:17), an eligible retirement plan means an IRA, a defined contribution plan (see Q 2:2) but not a defined benefit plan (see Q 2:3), a 403(b) plan, and a governmental Section 457 plan. [I.R.C. §§ 401(a) (31)(D), 402(c)(8)(B)] However, IRS has advised that a qualified retirement plan *must* permit direct rollovers to defined contribution plans and *may* permit (but is not required to permit) direct rollovers to defined benefit plans. [Treas. Reg. § 1.401(a)(31)-1, Q&A-2] This rule also applies to the portion of a distribution from a qualified retirement plan that is excludable from gross income (see Q 34:1).

Eligible rollover distributions from qualified retirement plans, 403(b) plans, and governmental Section 457 plans generally may be rolled over to any of such plans; and, similarly, distributions from IRAs generally may be rolled over to any of such plans (see Q 34:7). A non-governmental 457 plan is not an eligible retirement plan.

An individual cannot roll over a distribution from a qualified retirement plan to an IRA of the individual's spouse because the spouse's IRA is not an eligible retirement plan. [Rodoni, 105 T.C. 29 (1995); Priv. Ltr. Rul. 9315031]

Q 34:17   What is a direct rollover?

A direct rollover is an eligible rollover distribution that is paid directly to an eligible retirement plan (see Q 34:16) for the benefit of the distributee (i.e., the distribution is made in the form of a direct trustee-to-trustee transfer from a qualified retirement plan to the eligible retirement plan). [I.R.C. § 401(a)(31); Treas. Reg. § 1.401(a)(31)-1, Q&A-3; Priv. Ltr. Ruls. 9617043, 9428042, 9331055]

A direct rollover may be accomplished by any reasonable means of direct payment to an eligible retirement plan. Reasonable means include a wire transfer or the mailing of a check to the eligible retirement plan. If the payment is made by wire transfer, the wire transfer must be directed only to the trustee of the eligible retirement plan. If payment is made by check, the check must be negotiable only by the trustee of the eligible retirement plan (see Q 34:20). In the case of an eligible retirement plan that does not have a trustee (e.g., an individual retirement annuity), the custodian of the plan or issuer of the contract under the plan, as appropriate, should be substituted for the trustee. [Treas. Reg. § 1.401(a)(31)-1, Q&A-3]

IRS has ruled that a plan amendment that changes the default method of payment to a direct rollover for involuntary distributions (see Q 10:61) when a distributee fails to affirmatively elect to make a direct rollover or to elect a cash payment does not adversely affect the qualification of the plan. In this case, a defined contribution plan (see Q 2:2) provides that, if a terminated employee's vested account balance (see Q 9:1) is $5,000 or less and the employee does not elect a direct rollover, the vested account balance will be paid in a single-sum cash payment to the employee. The plan is amended to provide that in the absence of an affirmative election on the part of the employee, the default form of payment of any involuntary cash-out from the plan that is between $1,000 and $5,000 will be a direct rollover to an IRA. The plan administrator (see Q 20:1) will establish an IRA (see Q 30:1) with a trustee unrelated to the employer on behalf of an employee who fails to elect the direct rollover or cash payment and will make initial investment decisions for the IRA. [Rev. Rul. 2000-36, 2000-2 C.B. 140]

EGTRRA 2001 (see Q 1:21) codified the conclusion reached by IRS in Revenue Ruling 2000-36. See Q 34:18 for a discussion of final regulations issued by DOL and Q 34:19 for a discussion of guidance issued by IRS concerning the automatic rollover rules.

For a discussion of the effect of the RMD rules on direct rollovers, see Q 11:41.

Q 34:18   Has DOL provided a safe harbor for automatic rollovers of mandatory distributions?

DOL has issued final regulations that apply to any rollover of a mandatory distribution made on or after March 28, 2005. [DOL Reg. § 2550.404a-2(e)] The regulations provide a safe harbor under which a fiduciary of a plan will be deemed to have satisfied such person's fiduciary duties in connection with an automatic rollover of a mandatory distribution. [DOL Reg. § 2550.404a-2(a)]

A fiduciary that meets the safe harbor is deemed to have satisfied such person's duties with respect to both the selection of an IRA provider and the investment of funds in connection with the rollover of mandatory distributions to an IRA. [DOL Reg. § 2550.404a-2(b)]

With respect to an automatic rollover of a mandatory distribution, a fiduciary will qualify for the safe harbor if:

1. The present value of the nonforfeitable accrued benefit (see Q 9:2) does not exceed $5,000;

2. The mandatory distribution is to an IRA;

3. In connection with the distribution of rolled-over funds to an IRA, the fiduciary enters into a written agreement with an IRA provider that provides:

   a. The rolled-over funds will be invested in an investment product designed to preserve principal and provide a reasonable rate of return, whether or not such return is guaranteed, consistent with liquidity;

   b. The investment product selected for the rolled-over funds will seek to maintain, over the term of the investment, the dollar value that is equal to the amount invested in the product by the IRA;

   c. The investment product selected for the rolled-over funds will be offered by a state or federally regulated financial institution, which is a bank or savings association, the deposits of which are insured by the Federal Deposit Insurance Corporation; a credit union, the member accounts of which are insured within the meaning of the Federal Credit Union Act; an insurance company, the products of which are protected by state guaranty associations; or an investment company registered under the Investment Company Act of 1940;

   d. All fees and expenses attendant to an IRA, including investments of such plan (e.g., establishment charges, maintenance fees, investment expenses, termination costs, and surrender charges), will not exceed the fees and expenses charged by the IRA provider for comparable IRAs established for reasons other than the receipt of a mandatory rollover distribution; and

   e. The participant on whose behalf the fiduciary makes an automatic rollover will have the right to enforce the terms of the contractual agreement establishing the IRA, with regard to the participant's rolled-over funds, against the IRA provider.

  4. Participants have been furnished a summary plan description (SPD; see Q 22:1), or a summary of material modifications (SMM; see Q 22:8), that describes the plan's automatic rollover provisions, including an explanation that the mandatory distribution will be invested in an investment product designed to preserve principal and provide a reasonable rate of return and liquidity, a statement indicating how fees and expenses attendant to the IRA will be allocated (i.e., the extent to which expenses will be borne by the account holder alone or shared with the distributing plan or plan sponsor), and the name, address, and phone number of a plan contact (to the extent not otherwise provided in the SPD or SMM) for further information concerning the plan's automatic rollover provisions, the IRA provider, and the fees and expenses attendant to the IRA; and

  5. Both the fiduciary's selection of an IRA and the investment of funds would not result in a prohibited transaction, unless such actions are exempted from the prohibited transaction provisions by a prohibited transaction class exemption (see Q 24:26). [DOL Reg. § 2550.404a-2(c); PTCE 2004-16]

A fiduciary will qualify for the protection afforded by the safe harbor with respect to a mandatory distribution of $1,000 or less, provided there is no affirmative distribution election by the participant and the fiduciary makes a rollover distribution of such amount into an IRA on behalf of such participant in accordance with the conditions described above. [DOL Reg. § 2550.404a-2(d)]

See Q 34:19 for a discussion of IRS guidance on automatic rollovers.

Q 34:19 Has IRS provided guidance concerning automatic rollovers of mandatory distributions?

After DOL promulgated final regulations concerning automatic rollovers of mandatory distributions (see Q 34:18), IRS provided guidance on this subject. The automatic rollover requirements apply to mandatory distributions made on or after March 28, 2005. [Notice 2005-5, 2005-1 C.B. 337; *see also Retirement News for Employers* (Winter 2007)]

The automatic rollover requirements apply to any mandatory distribution that is more than $1,000 and is an eligible rollover distribution (see Q 34:8) that is subject to the direct rollover requirements (see Q 34:17). Thus, in order for a plan that provides for such mandatory distributions to be qualified, it must satisfy the automatic rollover provisions. An eligible rollover distribution in the form of a plan loan offset amount is not subject to the automatic rollover provisions (see Q 14:20).

A mandatory distribution is a distribution that is made without the participant's consent and that is made to a participant before the participant attains the later of age 62 or normal retirement age (see Q 10:55). A distribution to a surviving spouse or alternate payee (see Q 36:5) is not a mandatory distribution for purposes of the automatic rollover requirements. Although mandatory distributions of accrued benefits (see Q 9:2) attributable to employer contributions with a present value exceeding $5,000 are generally prohibited, the automatic rollover provisions apply without regard to the amount of the distribution as long as the amount exceeds $1,000.

In order to satisfy the automatic rollover requirement, a plan must provide that, when making a mandatory distribution that exceeds $1,000 and that is an eligible rollover distribution, if, after receiving the Section 402(f) notice (see Q 20:20), a participant fails to elect to receive a mandatory distribution directly or have it paid in a direct rollover to an eligible retirement plan, the distribution will be paid in a direct rollover to an IRA.

A plan will not be treated as failing to operate in accordance with its terms (including the automatic rollover provisions) with respect to mandatory distributions merely because it does not process mandatory distributions for which the participant does not affirmatively elect direct rollover or direct payment due to a lack of sufficient administrative procedures for automatic rollovers, including establishing IRAs to accept automatic rollovers, provided the mandatory distributions are made on or before December 31, 2005.

If a participant receiving a mandatory distribution fails to elect to have such distribution paid to an eligible retirement plan in a direct rollover or to receive the distribution directly, the plan administrator (see Q 20:1) may execute the necessary documents to establish an IRA on the participant's behalf with a financial institution selected by the plan administrator. For this purpose, the plan administrator may use the participant's most recent mailing address in the records of the employer and plan administrator. The trustee or issuer of the IRA must provide a disclosure statement to the participant and provide a revocation period. The trustee or issuer of the IRA will not be treated as failing to satisfy the disclosure requirements merely because the disclosure statement is returned by the United States Postal Service as undeliverable after it was mailed to the participant using the address for the participant provided by the plan administrator as the participant's most recent mailing address in the records of the employer and plan administrator.

A mandatory distribution may be paid to a participant's IRA that is part of an employer-sponsored IRA (see Q 30:32) or to a participant's deemed IRA (see Q 30:36). A plan sponsor may amend or change a plan to eliminate a provision that requires the plan to make a mandatory single-sum distribution to participants without violating the anti-cutback rule (see Q 9:25). No spousal consent (see Q 10:21) is required before the annuity starting date (see Q 10:3) if the present value of the nonforfeitable benefit is not more than the $5,000 cash-out limit (see Q 10:61).

The automatic rollover rules apply to the entire amount of a mandatory distribution. Thus, for example, the portion of the distribution attributable to a rollover contribution is subject to the automatic rollover requirements even if that amount is excludable from the determination of whether the present value of the nonforfeitable accrued benefit exceeds $5,000 (see Q 10:61).

The plan administrator is required to notify the participant in writing (either separately or as part of the Section 402(f) notice) that, absent an affirmative election by the participant, the distribution will be paid to an IRA. The notice must identify the trustee or issuer of the IRA. A plan administrator will not be treated as failing to satisfy this notice requirement merely because the notice is sent using electronic media (see Q 20:5). Further, for an eligible rollover distribution paid as an automatic direct rollover, a plan administrator will not be treated as failing to satisfy this notice requirement with respect to an eligible rollover distribution merely because the notice is returned as undeliverable by the United States Postal Service after having been mailed to the participant using the participant's most recent mailing address in the records of the employer and plan administrator.

Plans that provide for mandatory distributions and that do not already include the automatic rollover provisions must adopt a good-faith plan amendment reflecting the automatic rollover requirements by the end of the first plan year ending on or after March 28, 2005. IRS has published a sample plan amendment that individual plan sponsors and sponsors (or volume submitter practitioners) of pre-approved plans can adopt or use in drafting individualized plan amendments. This sample plan amendment, or a plan amendment that is materially similar to this sample, will be a good-faith plan amendment. The adoption of this sample amendment by a sponsor (or volume submitter practitioner) of a pre-approved plan will not cause such a plan to be treated as an individually designed plan. If a plan is amended by a timely good-faith amendment reflecting the automatic rollover requirements, a plan amendment to a disqualifying provision related to the automatic rollover requirements can be made within the plan's remedial amendment period to the extent necessary to satisfy the automatic rollover requirements. [Rev. Proc. 2004-25, 2004-1 C.B. 791] To the extent necessary, such a remedial amendment may be made retroactively, effective as of March 28, 2005, or, if later, the date on which the plan becomes subject to the automatic rollover requirements.

The following is the sample amendment:

> In the event of a mandatory distribution greater than $1,000 in accordance with the provisions of section _____, if the participant does not elect to have such distribution paid directly to an eligible retirement plan specified by the participant in a direct rollover or to receive the distribution directly in accordance with section(s) _____, then the plan administrator will pay the distribution in a direct rollover to an individual retirement plan designated by the plan administrator.

Q 34:20   Is providing a distributee with a check for delivery to an eligible retirement plan a reasonable means of accomplishing a direct rollover?

Giving the distributee a check and instructing the distributee to deliver the check to the eligible retirement plan (see Q 34:16) is a reasonable means of direct payment (see Q 34:17), *provided that the check is made payable as follows*: [Name of the trustee] as trustee of [name of eligible retirement plan]. For example, if the name of the eligible retirement plan is "Individual Retirement Account of Jack N. Jill" and the name of the trustee is "ABC Bank," the payee line of the check should read "ABC Bank as trustee of Individual Retirement Account of Jack N. Jill."

Unless the name of the distributee is included in the name of the eligible retirement plan, the check also must indicate that it is for the benefit of the distributee. If the eligible retirement plan is not an IRA, the payee line of the check need not identify the trustee by name and may read "Trustee of the XYZ Corporation Savings Plan FBO Jane Plane." [Treas. Reg. § 1.401(a)(31)-1, Q&A-4]

If the plan does not make out the check to the trustee, a distribution, not a rollover, has occurred. [Ann. 95-99, 1995-48 I.R.B. 10] If that occurs, the distribution must be transferred into one or more eligible retirement plans within 60 days after receipt (see Q 34:34). However, the 60-day rollover period does not apply to a direct rollover if the plan makes out the check to the trustee. IRS ruled that, where the distributee gave the check to the trustee more than 60 days after receipt, the delay did not convert the rollover into a taxable distribution. [Priv. Ltr. Rul. 201005057]

Q 34:21   Is an eligible rollover distribution that is paid to an eligible retirement plan in a direct rollover includible in gross income?

No. An eligible rollover distribution that is paid to an eligible retirement plan (see Q 34:16) in a direct rollover (see Q 34:17) is not currently includible in the distributee's gross income. However, when any portion of the eligible rollover distribution is subsequently distributed from the eligible retirement plan, that portion will be includible in gross income, unless a part thereof represents basis (see Q 13:3). [I.R.C. § 402(c)(1); Treas. Reg. § 1.401(a)(31)-1, Q&A-5; Priv. Ltr. Rul. 9428042]

Q 34:22   What procedures may a plan administrator prescribe for electing a direct rollover?

The plan administrator (see Q 20:1) may prescribe any reasonable procedure for a distributee to elect a direct rollover (see Q 34:17). The procedure may include any reasonable requirement for information or documentation from the distributee. For example, it would be reasonable for the plan administrator to require the distributee to provide a statement from the plan designated by the distributee that it is, or is intended to be, an IRA or a qualified retirement plan and that it will accept the direct rollover for the benefit of the distributee. In the case of a designated recipient qualified retirement plan, it also would be reasonable for the plan administrator to require a statement that the plan is not excepted from the definition of an eligible retirement plan (i.e., is not a defined benefit plan; see Q 34:16). It would not be reasonable, however, for the plan administrator to require information or documentation or to establish procedures that effectively eliminate or substantially impair the distributee's ability to elect a direct rollover. For example, it would not be reasonable for the plan administrator to require the distributee to obtain an opinion from the distributee's attorney that the eligible retirement plan receiving the rollover is a qualified retirement plan or IRA. As another example, the plan administrator cannot require the trustee of an eligible retirement plan receiving a direct rollover to agree to return, upon demand, any portion of the distribution that the plan administrator subsequently claims was paid incorrectly. Likewise, the plan administrator cannot require a letter from the recipient plan indemnifying the distributing plan for any liability arising from the distribution. [Treas. Reg. § 1.401(a)(31)-1, Q&A-6; IRS Spec. Rul. (June 3, 1993)]

The plan administrator may establish a default procedure whereby a distributee who fails to make an affirmative election is treated as having either made or not made a direct rollover election. However, the plan administrator may not make a distribution under any default procedure unless the distributee has received an explanation of the default procedures and an explanation of the direct rollover option on a timely basis (see Q 34:29). [Treas. Reg. § 1.401(a)(31)-1, Q&A-7]

The plan administrator may establish a deadline after which the distributee may not revoke an election to make or not to make a direct rollover, but the plan administrator is not permitted to prescribe any deadline or time period that is more restrictive for the distributee than that which otherwise applies under the plan to a revocation of the form of distribution elected by the distributee. [Treas. Reg. § 1.401(a)(31)-1, Q&A-8]

Q 34:23 Can a distributee elect a partial direct rollover?

Yes. The plan administrator (see Q 20:1) must permit a distributee to elect to have a portion of an eligible rollover distribution paid to an eligible retirement plan (see Q 34:16) in a direct rollover (see Q 34:17) and to have the remainder paid to the distributee. The plan administrator is permitted to require that, if the distributee elects to have only a portion of an eligible rollover distribution paid to an eligible retirement plan in a direct rollover, that portion be equal to at least $500. If the entire amount of the eligible rollover distribution is $500 or less, the plan administrator need not allow the distributee to divide the distribution. [Treas. Reg. § 1.401(a)(31)-1, Q&A-9]

Q 34:24 Can a direct rollover be paid to two or more eligible retirement plans?

The plan administrator (see Q 20:1) is not required (but is permitted) to allow the distributee to divide an eligible rollover distribution into separate distributions to be paid to two or more eligible retirement plans (see Q 34:16) in direct rollovers (see Q 34:17). The plan administrator may require that the distributee select a single eligible retirement plan to which the eligible rollover distribution (or portion thereof) will be distributed in a direct rollover. [Treas. Reg. § 1.401(a)(31)-1, Q&A-10]

Q 34:25 Can there be a dollar limitation on a direct rollover?

Yes. A qualified retirement plan will satisfy the direct rollover requirement (see Q 34:17) even though the plan does not permit a distributee to elect a direct rollover with respect to eligible rollover distributions during a year that are reasonably expected to total less than $200 or any lower minimum amount specified by the plan administrator (see Q 20:1). [Treas. Reg. § 1.401(a)(31)-1, Q&A-11]

Q 34:26 How many elections are required for a series of periodic payments?

Each distribution in a series of substantially equal periodic payments may be an eligible rollover distribution (see Q 34:9).

Example. Joe participates in The Golfing Grace Corporation's profit sharing plan. Joe retires and elects to receive payment of his account balance in 60 substantially equal monthly payments. Each of the 60 monthly payments is an eligible rollover distribution, and Joe may make a direct rollover election.

A qualified retirement plan is permitted to treat a distributee's election to make or not to make a direct rollover with respect to one payment in a series of periodic payments as applying to all subsequent payments in the series, provided that:

1. The employee is permitted at any time to change, with respect to subsequent payments, a previous election to make or not to make a direct rollover, and

2. The written explanation (see Q 34:29) explains that the election to make or not to make a direct rollover will apply to all future payments unless the employee subsequently changes the election. [Treas. Reg. § 1.401(a)(31)-1, Q&A-12]

Q 34:27   Must a plan accept a direct rollover?

No. Although qualified retirement plans are required to provide distributees with the option to make a direct rollover (see Q 34:17) of their eligible rollover distributions to an eligible retirement plan (see Q 34:16), there is no requirement that an eligible retirement plan accept rollovers. Thus, an eligible retirement plan can refuse to accept rollovers. Alternatively, a plan can limit the circumstances under which it will accept rollovers. For example, a plan can limit the types of plans from which it will accept a rollover or limit the types of assets it will accept in a rollover (such as only cash or its equivalent). [Treas. Reg. § 1.401(a)(31)-1, Q&A-13]

If a plan accepts an invalid rollover contribution, the contribution will be treated, for purposes of applying the qualification requirements of the Code (see Q 4:1) to the receiving plan, as if it were a valid rollover contribution if the following two conditions are satisfied. First, when accepting the amount from the employee as a rollover contribution, the plan administrator (see Q 20:1) of the receiving plan reasonably concludes that the contribution is a valid rollover contribution. While evidence that the distributing plan is the subject of a determination letter (see Q 18:1) indicating that the distributing plan is qualified would be useful to the receiving plan administrator in reasonably concluding that the contribution is a valid rollover contribution, it is not necessary for the distributing plan to have such a determination letter in order for the receiving plan administrator to reach that conclusion. Second, if the plan administrator of the receiving plan later determines that the contribution was an invalid rollover contribution, the amount of the invalid rollover contribution, plus any earnings attributable thereto, is distributed to the employee within a reasonable time after such determination. [Treas. Reg. § 1.401(a)(31)-1, Q&A-14(a)]

An invalid rollover contribution is an amount that is accepted by a plan as a rollover or as a rollover contribution from a conduit IRA (see Q 34:38) but that is not an eligible rollover distribution from a qualified retirement plan or from a conduit IRA or that does not satisfy the other requirements for treatment as a rollover or a rollover contribution. [Treas. Reg. § 1.401(a)(31)-1, Q&A-14(b)(1)] A valid rollover contribution is a contribution that is accepted by a plan as a rollover or as a rollover contribution from a qualified retirement plan or from a conduit IRA and that satisfies the requirements for treatment as a rollover or a rollover contribution. [Treas. Reg. § 1.401(a)(31)-1, Q&A-14(b)(2)] See Q 34:1 for a discussion of the changes to the rollover rules.

Example 1. Meyers Casino Corp. maintains a profit sharing plan that permits any of its employees to make a rollover contribution to the plan. J.C. is an employee of Meyers Casino Corp., will not have attained age 70½ by the end of the year, and has a vested account balance in the Marty Park Ltd. pension plan (a plan maintained by J.C.'s prior employer). J.C. elects a single-sum distribution from the pension plan and elects that it be paid to the profit sharing plan in a direct rollover. J.C. provides the profit sharing plan administrator with a letter from the pension plan administrator stating that the Marty Park Ltd. pension plan has received a favorable determination letter from IRS. Based upon the letter, absent facts to the contrary, the profit sharing plan administrator may reasonably conclude that the Marty Park Ltd. pension plan is qualified and that the amount paid as a direct rollover is an eligible rollover distribution.

Example 2. The facts are the same as Example 1, except that, instead of the letter from the pension plan administrator relating to the favorable determination letter, J.C. provides the profit sharing plan administrator with a letter from the pension plan administrator representing that the Marty Park Ltd. pension plan satisfies the requirements of Section 401(a) (or representing that the plan is intended to satisfy the requirements of Section 401(a) and that the administrator of the Marty Park Ltd. pension plan is not aware of any plan provision or operation that would result in the disqualification of the Marty Park Ltd. pension plan). Based upon the letter, absent facts to the contrary, the profit sharing plan administrator may reasonably conclude that the Marty Park Ltd. pension plan is qualified and that the amount paid as a direct rollover is an eligible rollover distribution.

Example 3. Assume the same facts as in Example 1, except that J.C. elects to receive the distribution from the Marty Park Ltd. pension plan and wishes to make a rollover contribution rather than a direct rollover. When making the rollover contribution, J.C. certifies that, to the best of her knowledge, she is entitled to the distribution as an employee and not as a beneficiary, the distribution from the pension plan to be contributed to the Meyers Casino Corp. profit sharing plan is not one of a series of periodic payments, the distribution from the pension plan was received by her not more than 60 days before the date of the rollover contribution, and the entire amount of the rollover contribution would be includible in gross income if it were not being rolled over. As support for these certifications, J.C. provides the profit sharing plan administrator with two statements. The first is the letter described in Example 1, and the second is the distribution statement that accompanied the distribution check. The distribution statement indicates that the distribution is being made by the pension plan to J.C., indicates the gross amount of the distribution, and indicates that 20 percent was withheld for income tax. J.C. contributes to the profit sharing plan an amount not greater than the gross amount of the distribution, and the contribution is made within 60 days of the date of the distribution statement. Based on the certifications and documentation provided by J.C., absent facts to the contrary, the profit sharing plan administrator may reasonably conclude that the pension plan is qualified and that the distribution otherwise satisfies the requirements for treatment as a rollover contribution.

Example 4. The facts are the same as in Example 3, except that, rather than contributing the distribution from the pension plan to the profit sharing plan, J.C. contributes the distribution to an IRA. After the contribution of the distribution to the IRA, but before the year in which J.C. attains age $70\frac{1}{2}$, she requests a distribution from the IRA and decides to contribute it to the profit sharing plan as a rollover contribution. To make the rollover contribution, J.C. endorses the check received from the IRA as payable to the Meyers Casino Corp. profit sharing plan. In addition to providing the certifications described in Example 3 with respect to the distribution from the pension plan, J.C. certifies that, to the best of her knowledge, the contribution to the IRA was made not more than 60 days after the date she received the distribution from the pension plan, no amount other than the distribution from the pension plan has been contributed to the IRA, and the distribution from the IRA was received not more than 60 days earlier than the rollover contribution to the profit sharing plan. As support for these certifications, in addition to the two statements described in Example 3, J.C. provides copies of statements from the IRA. The statements indicate that the account is identified as an IRA, the account was established within 60 days of the date of the letter from the pension plan informing J.C. that an amount had been distributed, and the opening balance in the IRA does not exceed the amount of the distribution from the pension plan. There is no indication in the statements that any additional contributions have been made to the IRA since the account was opened. The date on the check from the IRA is less than 60 days before the date that J.C. makes the contribution to the profit sharing plan. Based on the certifications and documentation provided by J.C., absent facts to the contrary, the profit sharing plan administrator may reasonably conclude that the pension plan was qualified and that the contribution by J.C. satisfies the requirements for treatment as a rollover contribution.

Q 34:28   Is a direct rollover a distribution and rollover or a transfer of assets and liabilities?

A direct rollover (see Q 34:17) is a distribution and rollover of the eligible rollover distribution and not a transfer of assets and liabilities. If the spousal consent requirements (see Q 10:21) apply to the distribution, the requirements must be satisfied before the eligible rollover distribution may be distributed in a direct rollover. Similarly, the direct rollover is not a transfer of assets and liabilities that must satisfy the merger or consolidation requirements (see Q 9:53). Finally, a direct rollover is not a transfer of benefits for purposes of applying the optional forms of benefits requirement (see Q 10:45). Therefore, the eligible retirement plan (see Q 34:16) is not required to provide, with respect to amounts paid to it in a direct rollover, the same optional forms of benefits that were provided under the qualified retirement plan that made the direct rollover. [Treas. Reg. § 1.401(a)(31)-1, Q&A-15]

Q 34:29 Must distributees receive a written explanation of the rollover rules?

The plan administrator (see Q 20:1) is required, within a reasonable period of time (see Qs 20:20, 20:21) before making an eligible rollover distribution to provide the distributee with a written explanation known as a Section 402(f) Notice. The Section 402(f) Notice must be designed to be easily understood and must explain the following:

1. The rules under which the distributee may have the distribution paid in a direct rollover (see Q 34:17) to an eligible retirement plan (see Q 34:16);

2. The rules that require the withholding of tax on the distribution if it is not paid in a direct rollover (see Qs 20:10–20:18);

3. The rules under which the distributee will not be subject to tax if the distribution is contributed in a rollover to an eligible retirement plan within 60 days of receipt of the distribution (see Q 34:34);

4. If applicable, certain special rules regarding the taxation of the distribution (see chapter 13);

5. Information regarding when a later distribution from an eligible retirement plan receiving an eligible rollover distribution may be subject to restrictions and tax consequences that are different from those that would have been required under a plan that made the first distribution; and

6. If the plan administrator has established a default procedure whereby a distributee who fails to make an affirmative election is treated as having either made or not made a direct rollover election (see Q 34:22).

[I.R.C. § 402(f); Treas. Reg. §§ 1.401(a)(31)-1, Q&As-1(b)(2), 7, 1.402(c)-2, Q&A-1(b)(2), 1.402(f)-2, Q&As-1-4; Notice 93-26, 1993-1 C.B. 308]

IRS issued a model Section 402(f) Notice (see Q 20:20). [IRS Notice 2002-3, 2002-1 C.B. 289] IRS also issued a model Section 402(f) Notice in Spanish. [Ann. 2002-46, 2002-1 C.B. 834] An IRS representative advised that an updated model Section 402(f) Notice is among the items of pending guidance expected from IRS. IRS issued two safe harbor explanations that may be provided to recipients of eligible rollover distributions. [IRS Notice 2009-68, 2009-2 C.B. 423; *Retirement News for Employers*, Fall 2009]

One court has ruled that the failure of the plan administrator to give the Section 402(f) Notice to the recipient of a distribution did not entitle the recipient to money damages. [Fraser v. Lintas: Campbell-Ewald, 56 F.3d 722 (6th Cir. 1995)] A former participant who rolled over a plan distribution into an IRA and then withdrew a portion of the rollover could not hold the plan administrator responsible for not informing him that a subsequent distribution from the rollover IRA would be taxable. [Bouteiller v. Vulcan Iron Works, Inc., 834 F. Supp. 207 (E.D. Mich. 1993)]

IRS representatives have opined that the plan administrator cannot avoid having to distribute the Section 402(f) Notice by attaching it to the summary plan description (SPD; see Q 22:1) and placing a statement in the SPD that participants must read the notice at least 30 days prior to receiving a distribution.

RMDs from defined contribution plans (see Q 2:2) were suspended for calendar year 2009 (see Q 34:8).

For a discussion of the effect of the minimum distribution requirements on the Section 402(f) Notice and for a discussion of a change to the contents of the Section 402(f) Notice, see Q 20:20.

Q 34:30   How is a direct rollover reported to IRS?

IRS has advised that a direct rollover to an IRA should be reported on Form 1099-R (see Q 21:20) using code G in Box 7, and that a direct rollover to a qualified retirement plan should be reported using code H in Box 7. [Ann. 2000-86, 2000-2 C.B. 456; Ann. 95-99, 1995-48 I.R.B. 10; Ann. 94-40, 1994-12 I.R.B. 7; Rev. Proc. 93-31, 1993-2 C.B. 355; Ann. 93-20, 1993-6 I.R.B. 65]

If an individual receives from a qualified retirement plan both an RMD and a direct rollover within the same taxable year, two Forms 1099-R must be filed—one for the RMD and one for the direct rollover. [Ann. 94-46, 1994-13 I.R.B. 22]

Q 34:31   Is a rollover available for a distribution from a terminated retirement plan?

A participant who has not separated from service but who receives a distribution from a qualified retirement plan because of the plan's termination can roll over all or part of the distribution to postpone the payment of tax if it is an eligible rollover distribution. The distribution can be an eligible rollover distribution even if the participant continues to participate in another qualified retirement plan of the same employer (see Q 34:11). [I.R.C. § 402(c); Priv. Ltr. Ruls. 9729042, 9615042, 9507032, 9418028, 9338041; Notice 93-26, 1993-1 C.B. 308]

Q 34:32   May a person who is over age 70½ roll over a qualified retirement plan distribution?

An individual over age 70½ may roll over a distribution from a qualified retirement plan except to the extent that such distribution is an RMD (see Qs 34:6, 34:11). [I.R.C. §§ 401(a)(9), 402(c)(4)(B); Rev. Rul. 82-153, 1982-2 C.B. 86; Priv. Ltr. Rul. 9143078]

Q 34:33   Is a rollover of qualified retirement plan benefits available to a beneficiary of a deceased employee?

Yes. The spouse of an employee who receives an eligible rollover distribution (see Qs 34:11, 34:15) from a qualified retirement plan on account of the employee's death is permitted to roll over all or part of the distribution to an IRA or to another eligible retirement plan (see Q 34:16) in which the spouse participates. For distributions made prior to January 1, 2007, this applied only to a surviving spouse and not to a nonspouse beneficiary. [I.R.C. § 402(c)(9); Priv. Ltr. Ruls. 200826039, 199940041, 199928040, 9806012, 9729040, 9713018] If the employee dies before the RBD (see Q 11:5) and if the surviving spouse is the employee's sole beneficiary, a special spousal deferral rule applies (see Q 11:11). IRS has ruled that a surviving spouse, who received a distribution before the extended RBD, could do a rollover because the distribution was not an RMD (see Q 34:11) and thus was an eligible rollover distribution. [Priv. Ltr. Rul. 200222033].

IRS has also ruled that, if the deceased spouse's qualified retirement plan benefits are paid to a trust and the trust distributes the benefits to the surviving spouse, the surviving spouse may roll over the distribution. [Priv. Ltr. Ruls. 200621020, 200603036, 200509034, 200424007, 200208031, 200025062, 199943054, 199941050; *but see* Priv. Ltr. Ruls. 9437042, 9145041] Similarly, IRS has ruled that, if the deceased spouse's 403(b) plan (see Q 35:1) benefits are paid to a trust and the trust distributes the benefits to the surviving spouse, the surviving spouse may roll over the distribution to an IRA. [Priv. Ltr. Ruls. 200249008, 9749017]

If the deceased spouse's qualified retirement plan benefits are paid to the decedent's estate and the surviving spouse is the sole beneficiary of the decedent's residuary estate, IRS has ruled that the surviving spouse may roll over the distribution to an IRA [Priv. Ltr. Ruls. 200510032, 200344024, 200317040, 200305030, 200212036, 9850021, 9850016; *but see* Priv. Ltr. Rul. 9750063]; but the surviving spouse cannot roll over any part of the distribution that represents an RMD (see Q 34:11). [Priv. Ltr. Ruls. 199940041, 9638040, 9211059] IRS has also ruled that qualified retirement plan death benefits paid to the surviving spouse in satisfaction of her elective share rights under state law could be rolled over to an IRA. [Priv. Ltr. Rul. 9524020]

The surviving spouse was permitted to roll over the benefit to an IRA when the deceased spouse named a trust as the beneficiary of the death benefit payable from a qualified retirement plan, the trust beneficiaries disclaimed the benefit, and, as a result of the disclaimer, the benefit was paid to the surviving spouse (see Q 11:17). [Priv. Ltr. Ruls. 9450041, 9247026; *see also* Priv. Ltr. Ruls. 9835005, 9752072]

Generally, a rollover by the surviving spouse is permitted where there is no discretion on the part of someone other than the surviving spouse (e.g., the surviving spouse is the sole beneficiary of the estate or the surviving spouse may withdraw the funds from the trust).

The spouse may establish an IRA rollover account even if the spouse would not be eligible to establish a regular IRA. IRS has ruled that the surviving spouse could roll over the deceased spouse's plan benefits to an IRA of the deceased spouse. By rolling over the benefits to the deceased spouse's IRA, the surviving spouse, who had not yet attained age $59\frac{1}{2}$, could commence distributions from that IRA without imposition of the 10 percent penalty tax (see Q 16:5). [Priv. Ltr. Ruls. 9745033, 9608042, 9418034] IRS has also ruled that, even though the deceased spouse did not have an IRA, the surviving spouse could establish a new IRA in the name of the deceased spouse with the surviving spouse as the beneficiary and then do a rollover of the death benefit from a qualified retirement plan to the new IRA. Here, too, IRA distributions could be made to the surviving spouse without imposition of the 10 percent penalty tax. [Priv. Ltr. Ruls. 200650023, 200450057]

Because the distribution to a surviving spouse is an eligible rollover distribution, the distribution will be subject to automatic 20 percent withholding unless transferred by a direct rollover to an eligible retirement plan (see Qs 34:17, 34:34). [Priv. Ltr. Ruls. 9850021, 9402023, 9351041] However, in one case, the plan issued a check representing the deceased employee's entire benefit directly to the surviving spouse, *including* an amount equal to the entire amount withheld, and the surviving spouse was permitted to roll over the entire distribution to an IRA in her name. [Priv. Ltr. Rul. 200510039]

For distributions made after December 31, 2006, the benefits of a beneficiary other than a surviving spouse can be transferred *directly* to an IRA. The IRA is treated as an inherited IRA (see Q 30:48) of the nonspouse beneficiary. Thus, for example, distributions from the inherited IRA are subject to the distribution rules applicable to beneficiaries. This provision applies to amounts payable to a beneficiary under a qualified retirement plan, 403(b) plan, or a governmental Section 457 plan. Furthermore, except as otherwise provided by IRS, a trust that is maintained for the benefit of one or more designated beneficiaries must be treated as a designated beneficiary for purposes of the rollover available to nonspouse beneficiaries. In other words, the trustee of the trust can establish a rollover IRA for the benefit of a beneficiary of the trust (see Qs 11:14, 11:18). [I.R.C. § 402(c)(11) (as amended by WRERA 2008 §§ 108(f)(1), 108(f)(2)(B)); WRERA 2008 § 108(f)(2)(C); Priv. Ltr. Rul. 200717023]

IRS issued guidance concerning the nonspousal rollover rules. If a direct trustee-to-trustee transfer of any portion of a distribution from an eligible retirement plan is made to an IRA that is established for the purpose of receiving the distribution on behalf of a designated beneficiary (see Q 11:14) who is a nonspouse beneficiary, the transfer is treated as a direct rollover (see Q 34:17) of an eligible rollover distribution. The IRA of the nonspouse beneficiary is treated as an inherited IRA, and the new rules apply to distributions made after December 31, 2006. [IRS Notice 2007-7, § V, 2007-1 C.B. 395; *Retirement News for Employers*, Fall 2009]

A qualified retirement plan can offer a direct rollover of a distribution to a nonspouse beneficiary who is a designated beneficiary, provided that the distributed amount satisfies all of the requirements to be an eligible rollover distribution other than the requirement that the distribution be made to the participant or the participant's spouse. The direct rollover must be made to an IRA established on behalf of the designated beneficiary that will be treated as an inherited IRA. If a nonspouse beneficiary elects a direct rollover, the amount directly rolled over is not includible in gross income in the year of the distribution (see Q 34:1). [IRS Notice 2007-7, § V, Q&A-11, 2007-1 C.B. 395] In addition to qualified retirement plans, this applies to 403(b) plans and governmental Section 457 plans. [IRS Notice 2007-7, § V, Q&A-12, 2007-1 C.B. 395] Effective for plan years beginning after December 31, 2009, this provision is mandatory and a plan is required to offer a direct rollover of a distribution to a nonspouse beneficiary. [I.R.C. § 402(c)(11) (as amended by WRERA 2008 §§ 108(f)(1), 108(f)(2)(B)); WRERA 2008 § 108(f)(2)(C)]

The IRA must be established in a manner that identifies it as an IRA with respect to a deceased individual and also identifies the deceased individual and the beneficiary; for example, "Tom Smith as beneficiary of John Smith." [IRS Notice 2007-7, § V, Q&A-13, 2007-1 C.B. 395]

For plan years beginning before January 1, 2010, a plan is not required to offer a direct rollover of a distribution to a nonspouse beneficiary. If a plan does offer direct rollovers to nonspouse beneficiaries of some, but not all, participants, such rollovers must be offered on a nondiscriminatory basis, because the opportunity to make a direct rollover is a benefit, right, or feature (see Q 4:20). In the case of distributions from a terminated defined contribution plan, the plan will be considered to offer direct rollovers to nonspouse beneficiaries with respect to such distributions without regard to plan terms (see Qs 24:26, 25:64). [IRS Notice 2007-7, § V, Q&A-14, 2007-1 C.B. 395; *IRS Employee Plan News* (Feb. 13, 2007)] A direct rollover of a distribution by a nonspouse beneficiary is a rollover of an eligible rollover distribution only for those purposes. Accordingly, the distribution is not subject to the direct rollover requirements of Section 401(a)(31), the notice requirements (see Q 20:20), or the mandatory withholding requirements (see Q 34:34). If an amount distributed from a plan is *received* by a nonspouse beneficiary, the distribution is not eligible for rollover. [IRS Notice 2007-7, § V, Q&A-15, 2007-1 C.B. 395]

A plan may make a direct rollover to an IRA on behalf of a trust where the trust is the named beneficiary of a decedent, provided the beneficiaries of the trust meet the requirements to be designated beneficiaries (see Q 11:18). The IRA must be established in accordance with the above rules, with the trust identified as the beneficiary. In such a case, the beneficiaries of the trust are treated as having been designated as beneficiaries of the decedent for purposes of determining the distribution period if the trust meets certain requirements (see Qs 11:18, 11:19). [IRS Notice 2007-7, § V, Q&A-16, 2007-1 C.B. 395]

If the employee dies before the RBD, the RMDs for purposes of determining the amount eligible for rollover with respect to the nonspouse beneficiary are determined under either the five-year rule or the life expectancy rule (see Qs 11:9-11:12). Under either rule, no amount is an RMD for the year in which the employee dies. [IRS Notice 2007-7, § V, Q&A-17(a), 2007-1 C.B. 395]

Under the five-year rule, no amount is required to be distributed until the fifth calendar year following the year of the employee's death. In that year, the entire amount to which the beneficiary is entitled under the plan must be distributed. Thus, if the five-year rule applies with respect to a nonspouse beneficiary who is a designated beneficiary, for the first four years after the year the employee dies, no amount payable to the beneficiary is ineligible for direct rollover as an RMD. Accordingly, the beneficiary is permitted to directly roll over the beneficiary's entire benefit until the end of the fourth year (but, as described below, the five-year rule must also apply to the IRA to which the rollover contribution is made). On or after January 1 of the fifth year following the year in which the employee died, no amount payable to the beneficiary is eligible for rollover. [IRS Notice 2007-7, § V, Q&A-17(b), 2007-1 C.B. 395]

If the life expectancy rule applies, in the year following the year of death and each subsequent year, there is an RMD. See Q 11:23 to determine the applicable distribution period for the nonspouse beneficiary. The amount not eligible for rollover includes all undistributed RMDs for the year in which the direct rollover occurs and any prior year (even if the excise tax has been paid with respect to the failure in the prior years; see Qs 11:67-11:71). [IRS Notice 2007-7, § V, Q&A-17(c)(1), 2007-1 C.B. 395] If the five-year rule applies (see Q 11:12), the nonspouse designated beneficiary may determine the RMD under the plan using the life expectancy rule in the case of a distribution made prior to the end of the year following the year of death. However, in order to use this rule, the RMDs under the IRA to which the direct rollover is made must be determined under the life expectancy rule using the same designated beneficiary. [IRS Notice 2007-7, § V, Q&A-17(c)(2), 2007-1 C.B. 395] RMDs from IRAs and defined contribution plans (see Q 2:2) were suspended for calendar year 2009 (see Q 11:1). In a plan that permitted direct rollovers by nonspouse designated beneficiaries, the suspension extended the time for making the direct rollover if the participant died in 2008. The special rule provided that, if the five-year rule applied to a benefit under a plan, the nonspouse designated beneficiary could determine the RMD using the life expectancy rule in the case of a distribution made prior to the end of the year following the year of death. This special rule was modified so that, if the employee's death occurred in 2008, the nonspouse designated beneficiary had until the end of 2010 to make the direct rollover and use the life expectancy rule. [IRS Notice 2009-82, Q&A-3, 2009-41 I.R.B.]

If an employee dies on or after the RBD, for the year of the employee's death the RMD not eligible for rollover is the same as the amount that would have applied if the employee were still alive and elected the direct rollover (see Q 34:11). For the year after the year of the employee's death and subsequent years, see Q 11:24 to determine the applicable distribution period to use in calculating the RMD. As in the case of death before the employee's RBD, the amount not eligible for rollover includes all undistributed RMDs for the year in which the direct rollover occurs and any prior year, including years before the employee's death. [IRS Notice 2007-7, § V, Q&A-18, 2007-1 C.B. 395]

An IRA established to receive a direct rollover on behalf of a nonspouse designated beneficiary is treated as an inherited IRA, and the RMD requirements apply to the inherited IRA. The rules for determining the RMDs under the plan with respect to the nonspouse beneficiary also apply under the IRA. Thus, if the employee dies before the RBD and the five-year rule applied to the nonspouse designated beneficiary under the plan making the direct rollover, the five-year rule applies for purposes of determining RMDs under the IRA. If the life expectancy rule applied to the nonspouse designated beneficiary under the plan, the RMD under the IRA must be determined using the same applicable distribution period as would have been used under the plan if the direct rollover had not occurred. Similarly, if the employee dies on or after the RBD date, the RMD under the IRA for any year after the year of death must be determined using the same applicable distribution period as would have been used under the plan if the direct rollover had not occurred. [IRS Notice 2007-7, § V, Q&A-19, 2007-1 C.B. 395]

Confusion arose concerning the interaction of the special rule in Q&A-17 and the general rule enunciated in Q&A-19. IRS advised that the general rule of Q&A-19 is not intended to override the special rule in Q&A-17. [*IRS Employee Plan News* (Feb. 13, 2007)]

> **Example.** Plan participant A dies in 2010, prior to his RBD. The plan provides that, if a participant dies prior to the RBD and the participant designates a nonspouse as beneficiary, the five-year rule applies. A designated his child B as his only beneficiary. In 2010, B can roll over A's entire account balance into an inherited IRA and, in 2011, commence receiving RMDs under the life expectancy rule. If B delays the rollover to 2011, B must receive the 2011 RMD and, in 2012, commence receiving RMDs under the life expectancy rule. If B delays the rollover to 2012, 2013, or 2014, the five-year rule will apply and the entire IRA must be distributed on or before December 31, 2015. B cannot make a rollover on or after January 1, 2015 (see Q 11:12).

See Qs 34:6 and 34:15 for more details, and see Qs 24:26 and 25:64 regarding distributions from terminated plans to missing nonspouse beneficiaries.

Q 34:34 How does a rollover from a qualified retirement plan to an eligible retirement plan work?

The payout must be transferred into one or more eligible retirement plans (see Q 34:16) within 60 days after receipt (see Qs 34:35, 34:36). [Mostafa, 91 T.C.M. 1187 (2006); Priv. Ltr. Ruls. 200925049, 200219042] It is not necessary, however, to transfer the entire amount into an eligible retirement plan; but the portion not rolled over is taxed as ordinary income in the year received. No special tax treatment is available with respect to the portion of the distribution that is currently taxed (see Q 13:14). [I.R.C. § 402(c)(3); Reese, 74 T.C.M. 232 (1997); Orgera, 70 T.C.M. 1488 (1995); Barrett, 64 T.C.M. 1080 (1992); Tassinari, 48 T.C.M. 915 (1984); Priv. Ltr. Rul. 9243054]

However, unless the distribution is transferred by a direct rollover (see Q 34:17) to an eligible retirement plan, the distribution is subject to automatic 20 percent withholding (see Q 20:10). [Treas. Reg. § 1.402(c)-2, Q&A-11; Priv. Ltr. Rul. 9726032; Moon v. United States, No. 95-702T (Fed. Cl. 1997)]

Example. Fran is entitled to a distribution of $20,000 from her employer's profit sharing plan and is undecided about rolling over the distribution to her IRA. Since the distribution to Fran is an eligible rollover distribution, the plan will withhold $4,000 and distribute to Fran only $16,000; however, Fran is deemed to have received a distribution of $20,000. If Fran then decides to roll over the distribution, she must transfer an additional $4,000 to her IRA from her other funds within the 60-day period; otherwise, the withheld amount ($4,000) will be includible in her gross income. [Priv. Ltr. Rul. 200716029]

Where an employee received an eligible rollover distribution but died within 60 days of receiving the distribution without having completed a rollover into an IRA, the executor of his estate was able to complete the rollover as the employee's fiduciary. [Gunther v. United States, 537 F. Supp. 126 (W.D. Mich. 1982)] However, IRS has ruled that a decedent's executor could not complete a rollover of a distribution received by the decedent prior to his death. [Priv. Ltr. Rul. 200415011] IRS did not allow a decedent's executor to do a rollover of a distribution received by the decedent prior to her death because it was shown that the decedent had not intended to do a rollover. [Priv. Ltr. Rul. 200415011] IRS has also ruled that a transfer of assets from a decedent's qualified retirement plans to an IRA established prior to his death did not qualify as a direct rollover because, although the decedent took steps prior to his death to effectuate the intended transfer, the actual transfer did not occur during his lifetime. [Priv. Ltr. Rul. 200204038]

In other cases, however, IRS took a more liberal view. An IRA owner who suffered from memory loss withdrew funds from her IRA shortly before her death, and her executor was permitted to redeposit the funds in the decedent's IRA. [Priv. Ltr. Rul. 200516021; *see also* Priv. Ltr. Rul. 200924056] A retired plan participant requested a single-sum distribution from the plan and then died before receiving the check, which was made payable to an IRA in the decedent's name. Even though the IRA had not been established prior to death, IRS allowed the executor to establish the IRA in the decedent's name and do the rollover. [Priv. Ltr. Rul. 200453022] In another ruling, IRS permitted the decedent's wife, who had been the sole beneficiary of the decedent's IRA, to complete the rollover by contributing the distribution to an IRA established in the decedent's name. [Priv. Ltr. Rul. 200444029] IRS also allowed a surviving husband to complete the rollover by either redepositing the distribution into the deceased wife's old IRA or establishing a new IRA in her name. [Priv. Ltr. Rul 200520038] A wife wished to complete her husband's intended rollover; however, there was some confusion when her husband died prior to the receipt of two checks. IRS permitted the wife to roll over her late husband's IRA to an IRA established and maintained in her name. [Priv. Ltr. Rul. 200608029] All of these rulings were issued in connection with requests for waivers of the 60-day rollover period requirement (see Q 34:36). Where a plan participant established an IRA but died before the plan distribution was made, IRS permitted the IRA beneficiary (who also was the participant's beneficiary under the plan) to retitle the IRA to the name of the IRA owner, deceased, for the benefit of the beneficiary and then transfer the plan benefit to the retitled IRA (see Q 34:33). [Priv. Ltr. Ruls. 200717023, 200717022] A qualified retirement plan participant named her husband as beneficiary. IRS permitted the husband to establish an IRA in the name of his deceased wife with himself as the beneficiary and to have the plan benefits paid directly to the new IRA. IRS ruled that the new IRA was an inherited IRA (see Q 30:48) and that the husband did not elect to treat the new IRA as his own (see Qs 11:11, 11:60). [Priv. Ltr. Rul. 200936049]

A distribution from a qualified retirement plan may be rolled over into an IRA that has previously been established by a participant for purposes of the participant's annual contributions or into a new IRA established by the participant solely for purposes of making the rollover.

If the participant receives property other than money as part of the distribution from the plan and sells the property, the proceeds of sale may be rolled over to an IRA. The reverse, however, is not true. Where an individual received a distribution of money from a plan, invested the money in securities, and rolled over the securities to an IRA, the transfer to the IRA did not qualify as a rollover contribution; hence, the entire amount of the plan distribution was taxable to the individual. [I.R.C. § 402(c)(6); Lemishow, 110 T.C. 110 (1998)]

RMDs from IRAs and defined contribution plans (see Q 2:2) were suspended for calendar year 2009 (see Q 11:1). Distributions that included 2009 RMDs made from a plan could have been rolled over back into the same plan, provided the plan permitted such rollovers and the rollover satisfied all applicable requirements, taking into account the transition relief provided by IRS (see Q 34:1). [IRS Notice 2009-82, Q&A-6, 2009-41 I.R.B.]

Q 34:35   When does the 60-day rollover period begin?

IRS has held that if a distribution qualifying for rollover treatment is received by an individual in more than one payment, for purposes of the 60-day rollover period, that individual is deemed to have received all distributions on the day the last payment is received. [Priv. Ltr. Ruls. 9318044, 8434052] It was doubtful that this rule would remain effective because, in the example in Q 34:26, Joe should not be permitted to roll over all 60 payments within the 60-day period following the last payment. IRS has now stated that, if more than one distribution is received by an employee from a qualified retirement plan during a taxable year, the 60-day rule applies separately to each distribution. [Treas. Reg. § 1.402(c)-2, Q&A-11] Where an individual received the balance of his plan benefits in the form of a promissory note providing for four equal annual installment payments, the promissory note was eligible to be rolled over into an IRA. [Priv. Ltr. Rul. 200846024] Had the individual retained possession of the promissory note, none of the four installment payments would be eligible to be rolled over because the 60-day rollover period commenced with the date of receipt of the promissory note.

The distribution need not occur in any particular year. An individual who receives an eligible rollover distribution a number of years after termination of employment may still roll over the distribution. [Priv. Ltr. Ruls. 9604029, 9152041, 9049047]

The 60-day rollover period commences with the date of receipt; and, if the rollover is not made within that period, the distribution is taxable in the calendar year of receipt, not the calendar year in which the 60-day period expires. [I.R.C. § 402(c)(3); Treas. Reg. § 1.402(c)-2, Q-11; *In re* Williams, 269 B.R. 68 (Bankr. M.D. Fla. 2001); Robinson, 72 T.C.M. 1320 (1996); Priv. Ltr. Rul. 200745022]

> **Example.** Bruce receives an eligible rollover distribution from the Cutler Camp Counselor's pension plan on December 1, 2010 and does not roll over the distribution to an IRA or another qualified retirement plan. The distribution is includible in Bruce's income in 2010, and not in 2011 when the 60-day rollover period expires.

The 60-day rollover period is measured in calendar days. If the 60th day falls on a Saturday, Sunday, or holiday, the rollover period is *not* extended to the next business day. [Priv. Ltr. Ruls. 200951044, 200930052, 200606055] An individual who rolled over an IRA distribution after 64 days failed to comply with the 60-day rollover requirement. [Mostafa, 91 T.C.M. 1187 (2006); *see also* Atkin, 95 T.C.M. 1364 (2008)] The 60-day rollover period does not apply to a direct rollover if the plan makes out the check to the trustee (see Qs 34:17, 34:20). IRS ruled that, where the distributee gave the check to the trustee more than 60 days after receipt, the delay did not convert the rollover into a taxable distribution. [Priv. Ltr. Rul. 201005057]

An individual received a distribution from a qualified retirement plan and rolled over the distribution to an IRA. Even though the rollover was not timely, the individual reported the rollover as timely and nontaxable on her income tax return for that year. When a distribution from the IRA was made some years later, the individual claimed that the IRA distribution was nontaxable because the plan distribution should have been taxable originally (the statute of limitations had expired). The court determined that a duty of consistency barred the claim that the IRA distribution was not taxable. [Estate of Ashman v. Comm'r, 231 F.3d 541 (9th Cir. 2000)]

See Q 34:36 concerning extension of the 60-day requirement.

Q 34:36 Can the 60-day rollover period be extended?

IRS may waive the 60-day rollover period if the failure to waive such requirement would be against equity or good conscience, including cases of casualty, disaster, or other events beyond the reasonable control of the individual subject to such requirement. [I.R.C. §§ 402(c)(3)(B), 408(d)(3)(I)]

IRS has provided guidance clarifying the hardship conditions that will allow for a waiver of the 60-day time period during which an eligible rollover distribution must be rolled over to an eligible retirement plan (see Q 34:16). Except as provided below, an individual must apply for a hardship exception to the 60-day rollover requirement using the same procedure as that outlined for letter rulings, accompanied by a user fee of $90.

IRS will issue a ruling waiving the 60-day rollover requirement in cases where the failure to waive such requirement would be against equity or good conscience, including casualty, disaster, or other events beyond the reasonable control of the individual. In determining whether to grant a waiver, IRS will consider all relevant facts and circumstances, including:

1. Errors committed by a financial institution, other than as described below;

2. Inability to complete a rollover due to death, disability, hospitalization, incarceration, restrictions imposed by a foreign country, or postal error;

3. The use of the amount distributed (for example, in the case of payment by check, whether the check was cashed); and

4. The time elapsed since the distribution occurred.

No application to IRS is required if a financial institution receives funds on behalf of an individual prior to the expiration of the 60-day rollover period, the individual follows all procedures required by the financial institution for depositing the funds into an eligible retirement plan within the 60-day period (including giving instructions to deposit the funds into an eligible retirement plan), and, solely due to an error on the part of the financial institution, the funds are not deposited into an eligible retirement plan within the 60-day rollover period. Automatic approval is granted only if:

1. The funds are deposited into an eligible retirement plan within one year from the beginning of the 60-day rollover period, and

2. Had the financial institution deposited the funds as instructed, it would have been a valid rollover.

To be eligible for a waiver of the 60-day rollover period, either automatic or through application to IRS, the rules regarding the amount of money or other property that can be rolled over into an eligible retirement plan within the 60-day rollover period apply to deposits made pursuant to a waiver of the 60-day rollover period (see Qs 34:3, 34:34).

[Rev. Proc. 2004-8, 2004-1 C.B. 240; Rev. Proc. 2003-16, 2003-1 C.B. 305]

Waivers have been granted for a myriad of reasons. The most common reasons for granting waivers include financial institution error, miscommunication with financial institution, health, and medical condition; however, waivers have been granted for many other reasons. [Priv. Ltr. Ruls. 201039041 (60th day fell on a weekend and financial institution office was closed), 201036029 (prescription medication severely impaired ability to manage financial affairs), 201035038 (plan's failure to provide proper written notice of rollover rules and consequences), 201033041 (stress from loss of spouse), 201031039 (misleading advice), 201026042 (death of family member), 201026038 (medical and psychological problems), 201025085 (illness of taxpayer who missed rollover period by one day), 201024072 (taxpayer requested direct rollover, but processed as taxable distribution with income tax withholding), 201023073 (financial institution error), 201022025 (mental incapacity), 201022024 (victim of Ponzi scheme), 201021037 (financial company's failure to inform taxpayer of rollover option), 201015040 (distribution was unexpected and made without taxpayer's consent or knowledge), 201013073 (incorrect advice from financial institution), 201012055 (received duplicate distribution), 201010030 (financial advisor converted funds to his personal use), 201009017 (stress caused taxpayer to miss rollover deadline by three days by inadvertently using wrong date marked on her calendar), 201009016 (processing error resulted in unintended distribution), 201005059 (depressed following death of husband), 201001027 (financial advisor mistake), 200953033 (mental condition), 200952066 (60th day fell on bank holiday), 200951043 (caregiver to ill mother), 200951042 (financial institution error), 200949051 (mental and physical condition), 200948063 (sudden death of husband), 200946063 (financial institution error), 200938034 (financial institution refused to accept taxpayer's checks to roll over other IRAs), 200937040 (spouse died in medical facility after long illness), 200933038 (Alzheimer's disease), 200931063 (investment in a specific fund was not a qualified IRA investment), 200929022 (wife took distribution from her husband's retirement plan without his knowledge and consent), 200925046 (combination of medical condition and incorrect advice); 200921039 (financial representative made unauthorized distributions), 200920059 (distributions used by financial representative for unauthorized use), 200919066 (financial institution mistake), 200913070 (mentally incapacitated and unaware of tax consequences), 200912041 (divorcee did not receive written notice clarifying rollover rules), 200911046 (traveling to care for seriously ill mother), 200910068 (told age precluded rollover), 200909069 (medical condition impaired ability to accomplish a timely rollover), 200907046 (emergency eye surgery), 200906060 (surviving spouse did not realize that distributions received after decedent's death were from IRAs), 200905035 (plan administrator failed to provide proper written notice), 200903104 (rollover amounts were embezzled), 200851043 (murder of granddaughter), 200850056 (financial planner error), 200850055 (elderly taxpayer's mental state), 200847016 (memory loss from a medical condition), 200842048 (lack of information and advice from accountant and attorney), 200840053 (bank error), 200834021 (impaired ability to make sound financial decisions), 200833030 (suffered from dementia), 200828034 (financial institution advisor retained taxpayer's IRA distribution for personal use and left suicide note confessing to misappropriation), 200822028 (credit union employee error), 200814029 (irreversible neurological disease), 200752038 (plan sponsor failed to provide timely and accurate information concerning plan loan offset), 200746016 (erroneous advice), 200742027 (sudden hospitalization followed by death), 200740017 (Hurricane Katrina), 200737049 (error by company administering plan), 200729038 (first-time homebuyer's application to purchase residence was denied), 200725039 (IRA custodian erroneously made a second required minimum distribution), 200723033 (neurological disorder), 200722031 (plan distribution incorrectly made to estate and not to surviving spouse), 200719018 (admitted to hospital and then died), 200719017 (restorative payment), 200719015 (not advised of 60-day rollover requirement until three days after deadline), 200718037 (neurological disability), 200717027 (reliance on financial representative), 200716030 (family illness and death), 200715016 (plan administrator incorrectly made two distributions), 200714029 (unsophisticated in financial matters), 200709068 (misunderstanding caused in part by language barrier), 200708085 (did not realize that receipt of stock certificate was a distribution), 200706012 (deposited in wrong account), 200704034 (hurricane conditions), 200701027 (inability to access involuntarily distributed IRA funds relating to bankruptcy petition), 200701036 (mental and physical incapacities), 200651034 (taxpayer legally blind), 200650024 (taxpayer's new employer refused to accept his rolled over money from a former employer's plan), 200644030 (distress over death of spouse), 200642006 (failure to advise taxpayer of 60-day rollover requirement), 200642005 (recent divorcee attempted to roll over an amount withdrawn from an IRA in her married name to a new IRA in her maiden name), 200637035 (advised could not do a direct rollover), 200634055 (completed rollover on 61st day because bank was closed on 60th day), 200634064 (misunderstood instructions on financial institution's on-line site), 200628036 (misunderstanding regarding online transactions), 200628027 (confusing nature of custodian's web page), 200623076 (misappropriation of funds by investment firm during 60-day rollover period), 200621021 (told by financial institution employee she had 90 days), 200618026 (told had 120 days), 200615031 (distribution check sent to wrong address), 200614028 (daughter's hospitalization), 200613036 (inadvertently signed wrong form), 200613035 (mental health problems), 200611041 (unable to obtain clarification from financial institution as to eligibility for rollover), 200611039 (mailed check delayed by winter storm), 200611038 (improper guidance given by IRA custodian and attorney retained IRA distribution until rollover period had expired), 200609019 (spouse and financial representative both died), 200608034 (individual without authority liquidated taxpayer's IRA), 200608031 (individual inadvertently placed rollover in non-IRA account), 200608027 (grief due to daughter's death), 200608025 (providing care for infirm mother), 200606055 (60th day fell on weekend and believed had until next business day to complete rollover), 200606052 (told had 90 days for rollover), 200606050 (individual and husband both underwent surgery), 200605019 (misled by long-standing financial advisor), 200602053 (individual moved), 200602052 (miscommunication), 200602049 (unaware that deceased husband's annuity was an IRA), 200602047 (bouts of depression), 200549020 (deposited in wrong account), 200549019 (check sent to wrong address), 200547022 (mother-in-law became ill and died), 200546044 (hurricane damage), 200545055 (incorrect Form 1099-R issued by plan administrator), 200545053 (received incorrect address from financial advisor), 200544031 (age 94 and wore hearing aid), 200544030 (unfamiliar with financial matters and had cancer surgery), 200543064 (uncertainty as to fund ownership), 200540022 (unaware of 60-day rule), 200537040 (check not received in timely manner), 200537039 (erroneous tax information), 200535040 (financial firm erroneously assigned a valid IRA account number to a non-IRA account), 200532061 (delay in recovering funds after cancellation of IRA contracts), 200531031 (investment company never established new IRA), 200531030 (relative misappropriated funds and then died), 200527025 (use of wrong form), 200527024 (unintended closeout of IRA), 200524034 (inadvertently consolidated IRAs into non-IRA accounts), 200524033 (employee received a check from his employer after it declared bankruptcy, was unaware that the proceeds were from a qualified retirement plan, and deposited the check in a regular checking account, and employer had attached no documentation or explanation), 200524031 (hospitalized and not discharged until after 60-day period had expired), 200523031 (individual misaddressed the envelope with his check and forgot to sign the check), 200523030 (account manager failed to deposit some funds and deposited other funds into a non-IRA account), 200523029 (individual died two days before 60-day period expired), 200523027 (individual suffered from mental impairment due to brain tumors), 200522018 (individual did not calculate 60-day time period correctly), 200521036 (suffered from medical condition and was caregiver of daughter who also required medical attention), 200520038 (IRA owner died before completing rollover), 200516023 (preoccupied with care of seriously ill spouse), 200516022 (beneficiary spouse suffered from Alzheimer's disease), 200516021 (executrix of estate permitted to complete rollover in decedent's name where decedent suffered from memory loss), 200514027 (not fluent in English), 200512035 (nursing home resident duped by financial manager), 200512029 (bank could not accept rollover), 200512028 (not financially savvy), 200510033 (distribution of stock inadvertently placed in investment account), 200508030 (attending to terminally ill mother and mistakenly deposited distribution into regular savings account), 200508029 (unfamiliar with finances), 200508024 (spouse committed suicide), 200507017 (relied upon son, a registered representative), 200507015 (thought distribution was from a regular account, not an IRA), 200506028 (told could not roll over because over 59½), 200505026 (inexperienced in electronic transfers), 200503032 (distribution check sent to old address), 200502054 (bank would not accept self-directed IRA), 200502052 (individual was in war zone), 200502050 (trustee did not follow direct rollover request), 200445041 (English was tertiary language), 200445038 (received distribution in excess of RMD), 200442036 (rollover with a check drawn on a foreign account could not be completed within 60 days), 200440026 (distribution inadvertently rolled over to the non-IRA account because recipient filled out wrong application form), 200436023 (rollover could not be completed because plan had entered a blackout period), 200436012 (never received physical possession of distribution), 200435017 (believed rollover period was 90 days), 200433024 (distribution made pursuant to an invalid writ of execution), 200432031 (unauthorized withdrawal by child), 200432022 (serious illness and unaware of withdrawal), 200430037 (in process of moving to another state), 200430035 (erroneously advised that rollover period had expired), 200428034 (failure to receive check), 200428032 (bank refused to accept check), 200427027 (employer did not provide employee with either a written or oral explanation of rollover rules), 200426026 (struck in hit and run accident and unable to manage financial affairs), 200424009 (did not understand the rollover rules), 200423042 (unaware that distributions were from IRAs), 200423037 (not advised distribution was taxable), 200422054 (natural disaster), 200415012 (widow's mourning), 200410027 (not wearing hearing aids), 200409039 (check sent to incorrect zip code), 200406054 (severe weather conditions)]

Denials are less frequent; and, in most cases, the individual never contemplated doing a rollover and used the distribution for personal purposes. [Priv. Ltr. Ruls. 201035043 (chose only non-rollover option on election form), 201034025 (unable to support intention to do rollover), 201029021 (did not provide evidence of alleged financial institution error), 201015039 (taxpayer took a distribution and contributed it to what she believed was a self-directed IRA, but the legal and financial professionals with whom she consulted did not admit to any wrongdoing as to the advice taxpayer received), 201008048 (requested IRAs be closed and distributed to non-IRA account), 201003032 (taxpayer error, not financial institution error), 201003030 (simply forgot distribution was from IRA), 200952063 (failure to allow that memory problems or concerns for a skin condition prevented timely rollover), 200941037 (did not believe failure was due to propounded reasons), 200941032 (did not believe failure was due to confusing instructions on bank website), 200925048 (untimely rollover occurred because taxpayer was unsure of stock market conditions), 200919071 (thought had 90 days), 200914071 (did not follow advice of both English-and Spanish-speaking financial specialists), 200907049 (thought had 90 days for rollover but could have done it within 60 days), 200904031 (thought distributions from his IRAs would protect his savings), 200847022 (did not demonstrate inability to complete a timely rollover), 200840057 (insufficient documentation to indicate inability to do a timely rollover), 200835036 (used distribution to buy assets for new business), 200832026 (used distribution to buy trailer park lot), 200829030 (nothing prevented taxpayer from timely redepositing distribution), 200819020 (claim of financial institution error was incorrect), 200817059 (taxpayer had no intent to do rollover), 200809043 (taxpayer had prior experience dealing with IRA rollovers), 200804025 (unhappy with investment), 200751032 (not satisfied with investment earnings), 200738027 (taxpayer presented no evidence showing inability to properly handle financial affairs), 200736036 (failure to deposit funds in IRA deemed to be taxpayer's responsibility), 200730024 (unable to accomplish rollover due to change in work schedule and family vacation), 200727023 (included IRA with other funds to invest in jumbo CD), 200724039 (did not roll over plan loan offset), 200721023 (relied on friend's advice that distribution after age 59½ was tax-free), 200719016 (made loan to daughter), 200707160 (used funds as short-term loan), 200707157 (commingled funds in jointly held checking account), 200704042 (used distribution for future nursing home care), 200703045 (claim of grief not substantiated), 200643006 (ability to complete rollover timely was within taxpayer's control and never sought financial advice), 200637034 (withdrew IRA funds to cover tax liabilities and credit card debt), 200634062 (had no funds available for rollover on 60th day), 200628028 (used distribution as a short-term loan), 200624070 (taxpayer purposely deposited distribution into a non-IRA account), 200618028 (did not demonstrate intention or attempt to complete a timely rollover), 200617039 (it was inappropriate to permit retroactive correction of tax treatment choices deliberately made by taxpayer), 200613037 (taxpayer solely responsible for failure to make timely deposit), 200609023 (should have contacted a tax professional and had control of distribution at all times), 200601042 (individual did not open envelope containing check until after rollover period expired), 200549017 (took no steps to transfer distribution to an IRA for three years), 200546030 (transferred IRA to non-IRA account because of concern about losses), 200547024 (required to spend down IRA to qualify for Medicaid), 200546051 (withdrew IRA funds to purchase home), 200544027 (bought real estate), 200544025 (used to settle a personal obligation), 200540023 (used to pay for closing costs), 200526024 (contributed distribution to charities), 200518087 (withdrew IRA funds, put check into desk drawer, and forgot about it), 200518085 (withdrew IRA funds for home purchase and improvements and left unused portion in checking account), 200508027 (beneficiary spouse had signed a document consenting to the distribution, the 20-percent withholding, and the possibility that additional taxes could be due), 200452042 (used to pay her matrimonial attorney's fees), 200446030 (used to purchase real estate), 200436018 (used to pay home mortgage), 200433029 (disregarded professional advice and paid personal debts), 200433022 (used to pay personal debts), 200428031 (withdrawal made to avoid IRS levy), 200422058 (initially did not intend to do a rollover), 200422053 (distribution used to prevent foreclosure of home), 200421003 (deposited in separate personal account)]

Other requests were denied because the IRAs in question were inherited IRAs (see Q 34:6). An individual withdrew IRA funds to purchase his first home; and, 72 days later, he redeposited the funds into his IRA after his purchase offer was rejected. The individual's request for a waiver was denied because he had 120 days to redeposit his withdrawal in this situation (see Q 16:16). [Priv. Ltr. Rul. 200423033] A financial representative of the IRA trustee took distributions from IRAs and used the funds for his own benefit. IRS ruled that settlements received by the IRA owners could be recontributed; however, none of the IRA owners was allowed to contribute an amount that could be considered a reasonable amount of interest along with the distributed amount, because the 60-day requirement allows a rollover of the distributed amount but does not allow for the rollover of interest accrued during the distributed period. [Priv. Ltr. Ruls. 200922060, 200922059, 200922058, 200922057, 200922056]

IRS has added the deadline for rollover contributions to the list of tax-related deadlines that may be postponed by reason of a presidentially declared disaster. IRS is allowed to disregard a period of up to one year in determining whether rollover contributions were made within the time prescribed. [I.R.C. § 7508A(b); Treas. Reg. § 301.7508A-1; IRS Notice 2002-27, 2002-1 C.B. 489]

Q 34:37   When can a rollover to a qualified retirement plan be distributed?

If an eligible retirement plan (see Q 34:16) separately accounts for amounts attributable to rollover contributions to the plan, distributions of those amounts are not subject to the restrictions on permissible timing that apply to distributions of other amounts from the plan. Accordingly, the plan may permit the distribution of amounts attributable to rollover contributions at any time pursuant to an individual's request.

Thus, for example, if the receiving plan is a money purchase pension plan (see Q 2:4) and the plan separately accounts for amounts attributable to rollover contributions, a plan provision permitting the in-service distribution of those amounts will not cause the plan to fail to satisfy the prohibition against distributions before reaching normal retirement age (see Q 10:56).

However, a distribution of amounts attributable to a rollover contribution is subject to the survivor annuity requirements (see Q 10:1), the minimum distribution requirements (see Q 11:2), and the additional income tax on premature distributions (see Q 16:1), as applicable to the receiving plan. Thus, for example, if a distribution from an IRA is rolled over into a plan, any distribution from the plan of amounts attributable to the rollover would be subject to the exceptions from the penalty tax that apply to qualified retirement plans and not the exceptions that apply to IRAs (see Q 16:3).

The above does not apply to amounts received by a plan as a result of a merger, consolidation, or transfer of plan assets (see Q 9:55) or to plan-to-plan transfers otherwise permitted between 403(b) plans (see Q 35:1) and between governmental Section 457 plans.

[Rev. Rul. 2004-12, 2004-1 C.B. 478]

Q 34:38   Can amounts in a rollover IRA be transferred to a qualified retirement plan?

Prior to 2002, an IRA that contained only assets attributable to a rollover contribution from a qualified retirement plan could be rolled over to a second qualified retirement plan or to the original plan. This type of IRA is called a conduit IRA. Also, the recipient qualified retirement plan had to provide for the acceptance of rollovers (see Q 34:27). However, an RMD from a conduit IRA could not, and still cannot, be rolled over to either the original or any other qualified retirement plan (see Q 34:11). [I.R.C. §§ 402(c)(5), 408(d)(3)(A)(ii); Treas. Reg. § 1.408-4(b)(2); Priv. Ltr. Ruls. 9530037, 9518019, 9505023, 9108057]

Transferring money from one qualified retirement plan to another through a conduit IRA may provide a big tax advantage. The amount rolled over might remain eligible for special tax treatment (e.g., electing forward averaging tax treatment for a lump-sum distribution received from the second qualified retirement plan), although generally a trust-to-trust transfer provides more assurance of retaining eligibility for favorable tax treatment (see Q 13:5). [Priv. Ltr. Ruls. 9226076, 9151024, 9146045]

See Q 1:27 for a discussion of the Bankruptcy Abuse Prevention and Consumer Protection Act of 2005 and why rollover IRAs should be kept separate from regular IRAs, and also see Q 34:27 for a discussion of IRS regulations regarding rollovers from conduit IRAs.

Q 34:39   Can a distribution from a disqualified retirement plan be rolled over?

A distribution from a retirement plan that is retroactively disqualified is includible in income and is not eligible for a rollover to an IRA or to another eligible retirement plan (see Qs 34:16, 34:42). Rollover treatment is permitted for a distribution from a retirement plan that is qualified at the time of distribution, not at the time when contributions by the employer were made. [Treas. Reg. §§ 1.402(a)-1(a)(1)(ii), 1.402(a)-1(a)(1)(v), 1.402(b)-1(a), 1.402(b)-1(b); *In re*

Swift, 129 F.3d 792 (5th Cir. 1997); Weddel, 71 T.C.M. 1950 (1996); Fazi, 105 T.C. 436 (1995); Fazi, 102 T.C. 695 (1994); Cass v. Comm'r, 774 F.2d 740 (7th Cir. 1985); Baetens v. Comm'r, 777 F.2d 1160 (6th Cir. 1985); Woodson v. Comm'r, 651 F.2d 1094 (5th Cir. 1981); *but see* Greenwald v. Comm'r, 366 F.2d 538 (2d Cir. 1966)] See Q 34:27 for a discussion of IRS regulations regarding rollovers from a retirement plan that may not be qualified.

A payment made to an employee in settlement of the employee's claim for benefits from a qualified retirement plan was not eligible for rollover treatment because the settlement payment was made from the employer's general assets and not from a qualified retirement plan. [Priv. Ltr. Ruls. 200213032, 9241008; *but see* Priv. Ltr. Ruls. 200127055 and 199905037, where a settlement fund was treated as an extension of the qualified retirement plan]

Q 34:40 What are the tax advantages and disadvantages of rolling over a qualified retirement plan distribution to an IRA?

A rollover of a qualified retirement plan distribution to an IRA provides three distinct tax advantages:

1. Postponement of tax payments;
2. Possible reduction of tax liability on the eventual payout; and
3. Continued tax-free build-up of retirement savings.

The rollover defers tax on the qualified retirement plan payout and on the income earned in the IRA. Subsequently, tax liability on amounts in the IRA can be spread out by making withdrawals over a period of years.

Nevertheless, an IRA rollover has drawbacks. First, amounts in the IRA generally cannot be withdrawn without penalty before age 59½ (see chapter 16 for details). Second, IRA withdrawals are taxed as ordinary income with no special tax-reducing rules available (see Qs 13:14, 13:18). [I.R.C. §§ 72(t), 408(d); Costanza v. Comm'r, 50 T.C.M. 280 (1985)]

Whether the advantages of a rollover will outweigh the disadvantages depends on each individual situation; however, the rollover will be the better alternative in most situations.

Q 34:41 Can an IRA rollover be revoked?

Upon receipt of a lump-sum distribution from a qualified retirement plan, an individual may have the option of electing to roll over the distribution to another eligible retirement plan (see Q 34:16), having the tax on such distribution computed by using the forward averaging method (see Qs 13:14, 13:15), or having special rules apply to employer securities included in such distribution (see Q 13:18). Once the individual elects to roll over the distribution into an IRA, those funds become part of the IRA and are then subject to the rules governing IRAs. The amount timely rolled over to an IRA cannot be considered an excess contribution (see Q 30:9) and, therefore, cannot be withdrawn as such. [I.R.C. §§ 402(c)(5), 408(d)(5), 4973(b)] An individual cannot recharacterize a rollover contribution made to an IRA once the rollover has been made. Once an individual has chosen the form of a transaction for tax purposes, the individual cannot later disavow the form of the transaction merely because the tax consequences of the form chosen have become disadvantageous. [Barnes, Jr., 67 T.C.M. 2341; Barrett, 64 T.C.M. 1080 (1992); Hall, 61 T.C.M. 2236 (1991); Priv. Ltr. Ruls. 200442032, 8536098, 8536097]

For the IRA rollover to be tax free, the individual must irrevocably elect to treat the IRA contribution as a rollover contribution. Once any portion of the lump-sum distribution is irrevocably designated as a rollover contribution, the amount rolled over is not taxable and no part of the distribution is eligible for special income tax treatment. An irrevocable election is made by a written designation to the IRA sponsor (at the time of contribution) that it is a rollover contribution. In the case of a direct rollover (see Q 34:17), the individual is deemed to have irrevocably designated that the direct rollover is a rollover contribution. These same rules apply to a rollover by a surviving spouse (see Q 34:33). [Kopty, 94 T.C.M. 480 (2007); Treas. Reg. § 1.402(c)-2, Q&A-13; Priv. Ltr. Ruls. 200442032, 8815035]

However, when an individual rolled over the entire distribution to an IRA and was informed the following year by the trustee of the qualified retirement plan that the individual's benefits had been erroneously overvalued, IRS ruled that the amount distributed to the individual to repay the employer would not be includible in the individual's income. [Priv. Ltr. Rul. 9118020; *see also* Priv. Ltr. Rul. 200337014] In a later ruling, IRS concluded that the rollover of the erroneous excess amount should have been included in the individual's income at the time of the plan distribution, the excess rollover was an excess contribution subject to the 6 percent penalty tax, the distribution from the IRA to the individual of the excess contribution was not taxable to the individual, but the distribution of the earnings on the excess contribution was taxable to the individual in the year of distribution. [Priv. Ltr. Rul. 9633041]

Q 34:42   Can a rollover IRA be reached by judgment creditors?

See Q 1:27 for a discussion of the Bankruptcy Abuse Prevention and Consumer Protection Act of 2005 and its protection of rollover IRAs from claims of creditors. Although an IRA may be exempt from claims of creditors, one court ruled that a debtor's inherited IRA (see Q 30:48) is not an exempt asset of the debtor's bankruptcy estate. [*In re* Chilton, No. 08-43414 (Bankr. E.D. Tex. 2010)] However, another court ruled otherwise and held that a debtor's inherited IRA was exempted from her bankruptcy estate. [*In re* Nessa, 2010 WL 128313 (8th Cir. 2010)] Another court concluded that, because an individual engaged in a prohibited transaction with his IRA (see Q 30:45), the IRA was not exempt from claims of creditors (see Q 30:52). In addition, two other IRAs of the individual lost their exempt status because, after the prohibited transaction occurred, funds from the first IRA were rolled over to the other two IRAs. [*In re* Willis, ___(Bankr. ___.D. Fla. 2009)] The discussion below should apply only to matters arising before the Act's effective date of October 17, 2005.

Courts have ruled that a rollover IRA (see Qs 34:34, 34:38) is exempt from execution by judgment creditors under state law because ERISA does not apply to IRAs and the state elected to opt out of the federal scheme. [Youngblood v. FDIC, 29 F.3d 225 (5th Cir. 1994); *In re* Mann, No. 889-92426 (E.D.N.Y. 1992); N.Y.C.P.L.R. § 5205(c)] Other courts have concluded that a rollover IRA is not exempt from creditors. [*In re* Cesare, 1994 Bankr. LEXIS 1028 (Bankr. D. Conn. 1994)] Other courts have held that only a portion of the rollover IRA is exempt from creditors. [Phillips v. Bottoms, 2001 WL 33258528 (E.D. Va. 2001); *In re* Savage, 2000 WL 665739 (Bankr. D. Ark. 2000); *In re* Barshak, No. 96-1423 (3d Cir. 1997)] However, other courts have ruled that even though an IRA may not be exempt from bankruptcy (see Q 30:52), the portion of the IRA attributable to a rollover from a qualified retirement plan retains its exempt status. [*In re* Sheldon Modansky, No. 92 B 21976 (S.D.N.Y. 1993); *In re* Woods, 59 B.R. 221 (W.D. Wis. 1986)] One court ruled that an IRA was not exempt from claims of creditors because the rollover was from a retirement plan that was not qualified at the time of distribution (see Q 34:39). [*In re* Swift, 129 F.3d 792 (5th Cir. 1997)] However, another court concluded that the rollover IRA was exempt from the bankruptcy estate where the rollover was from a plan that had received a favorable determination letter from IRS (see Q 18:1). [*In re* Seferyn, 2008 WL 2059404 (Bankr. 10th Cir. 2008)]

One court ruled that an embezzler's pension plan benefits, initially protected by ERISA's anti-alienation provisions (see Q 4:28), maintained their exempt status after being rolled over into an IRA because state law exempted IRAs from creditors' claims absent a fraudulent conveyance. [Gilchinsky v. National Westminster Bank, Nos. A-0907-96TS, A-4544-96T2 (N.J. Super. Ct. App. Div. 1998); *but see* United States v. All Funds Distributed to, or on Behalf of, Weiss, 2003 WL 22138504 (2d Cir. 2003)] Another court concluded that, although qualified retirement plan benefits distributed to an alternate payee (see Q 36:5) pursuant to a QDRO (see Q 36:1) became part of the alternate payee's bankruptcy estate, because the QDRO required a rollover of the distribution to an IRA, state law would determine whether the rollover IRA was exempt from claims of creditors. [Johnston v. Mayer, C.M. No. 97-1366 (Bankr. E.D. Va. 1998)]

Chapter 35

403(b) Plans

One way for employees of certain organizations to accumulate funds for retirement is through a 403(b) plan. A 403(b) plan is a tax-favored deferred compensation arrangement that enables employees to exclude from income amounts contributed toward the purchase of annuity contracts. This chapter examines 403(b) plans—what they are, their tax advantages, and the myriad rules and requirements that apply to them. This chapter also discusses the many significant changes made by the final regulations issued by IRS in 2007.

Q 35:1 What is a 403(b) plan?

A 403(b) plan is a special type of deferred compensation arrangement that is available only to employees of certain organizations (see Q 35:2). The annuity contract is purchased by the employer on behalf of the employee, but a 403(b) plan must satisfy a number of requirements (see Q 35:13). [I.R.C. § 403(b)(1); Treas. Reg. § 1.403(b)-1] A 403(b) contract is a contract that satisfies those requirements, and a 403(b) plan is the plan of the employer under which the 403(b) contracts are maintained. [Treas. Reg. § 1.403(b)-2(b)(16)]

The employee can exclude from gross income, within certain specified limits, the amounts contributed toward the purchase of the annuity contract, and the employee does not have taxable income until payments under the contract are received (see Qs 35:23, 35:40). [Treas. Reg. § 1.403(b)-3(a)] However, this generally does not apply to designated Roth contributions (see Qs 35:11, 35:40, 35:49). In addition, earnings within the annuity contract accumulate tax free (see Q 35:6). A 403(b) plan has many of the same advantages as a qualified retirement plan. With the plethora of rules and requirements applicable to 403(b) plans, a violation of any one of them can cause the loss of the tax advantages.

If for any taxable year an employer contributes to more than one 403(b) contract for a participant or beneficiary, then all such contracts are treated as one contract for purposes of the requirements applicable to 403(b) plans and 403(b) contracts. [I.R.C. § 403(b)(5); Treas. Reg. §§ 1.403(b)-2(b)(16)(i), 1.403(b)-3(b)(1), 1.403(b)-7(f)]

Section 403(b) does not apply to any contributions or accruals under a defined benefit plan (see Q 2:3). [Treas. Reg. § 1.403(b)-10(f)]

On July 26, 2007, IRS issued final regulations. The final regulations are generally applicable for taxable years beginning after December 31, 2008. Thus, because individuals are almost uniformly on a calendar taxable year, the regulations generally began to apply on January 1, 2009. [Treas. Reg. § 1.403(b)-11(a)] In the case of a 403(b) plan maintained pursuant to one or more collective bargaining agreements (CBAs; see Q 29:2) that have been ratified and in effect on July 26, 2007, the final regulations do not apply before the earlier of (1) the date on which the last of the CBAs terminates (determined without regard to any extension thereof after July 26, 2007) or (2) July 26, 2010. [Treas. Reg. § 1.403(b)-11(b)]

If, on July 26, 2007, a plan excludes any of the following categories of employees, then the plan does not fail to satisfy the universal availability requirement (see Q 35:21) as a result of that exclusion before the first day of the first taxable year that begins after December 31, 2009:

1. Employees who make a one-time election to participate in a governmental plan that is not a 403(b) plan.

2. Professors who are providing services on a temporary basis to another educational organization (see Q 35:4) for up to one year and for whom 403(b) contract contributions are being made at a rate no greater than the rate each such professor would receive under the 403(b) plan of the original educational organization.

[Treas. Reg. § 1.403(b)-11(d)(i)]

If, on July 26, 2007, a plan excludes employees who are covered by a CBA from eligibility to make elective deferrals, the plan does not fail to satisfy the universal availability requirement as a result of that exclusion before the later of:

1. The first day of the first taxable year that begins after December 31, 2008, or

2. The earlier of (a) the date on which the related CBA terminates (determined without regard to any extension thereof after July 26, 2007) or (b) July 26, 2010.

[Treas. Reg. § 1.403(b)-11(d)(2)]

See Q 1:28 for a discussion of the Katrina Emergency Tax Relief Act of 2005 and other developments for their effect on distributions, loans, and other issues.

Q 35:2   What types of organizations can establish 403(b) plans?

Employees of only two types of organizations may participate in a 403(b) plan, and these organizations are referred to as eligible employers. An eligible employer is:

1. A State, but only with respect to an employee of the State performing services for a public school (see Q 35:4).

2. A Section 501(c)(3) organization with respect to any employee of the organization (see Q 35:3).

3. An employer of a minister, but only with respect to the minister (see Q 35:55).

4. A minister, but only with respect to a retirement income account established for the minister (see Q 35:55).

[I.R.C. §§ 170(b)(1)(A)(ii), 403(b)(1)(A); Treas. Reg. § 1.403(b)-2(a)(8)(i)]

An entity is not an eligible employer as a State if it treats itself as not being a State for any other purpose of the Code, and a subsidiary or other affiliate of an eligible employer is not an eligible employer if the subsidiary or other affiliate does not meet the definition of an eligible employer. [Treas. Reg. § 1.403(b)-2(a)(8)(ii)]

Employees of a limited liability company (LLC) will be treated as employed by a 501(c)(3) organization that owns the LLC's membership interest, and the employees will be eligible to participate in the organization's 403(b) plan, IRS has ruled. A 501(c)(3) organization that owns the membership interest of a single-member LLC wishes to extend participation in its 403(b) plan to the employees of the LLC. However, the single-member LLC is not a 501(c)(3) organization. Certain organizations that have a single owner can choose to be recognized as a separate entity from its owner or be disregarded as a separate entity for federal tax purposes. If the organization is disregarded, its activities are treated the same as a sole proprietorship or as a branch or division of its owner. The single-member LLC has not elected to be classified as a separate entity and, thus, is disregarded as a separate entity from its owner. Therefore, the employees of the single-member LLC will be treated as employees of the 501(c)(3) organization for 403(b) plan purposes. [Priv. Ltr. Rul. 200851044]

A 403(b) plan is limited to certain specific employers and employees (i.e., employees of a State public school, employees of a Section 501(c)(3) organization, and certain ministers), whereas a 401(k) plan is available to all employers, except a State or local government or any political subdivision, agency, or instrumentality thereof (see Q 27:1). An entity that is both a Section 501(c)(3) organization and an instrumentality of a State cannot have a 401(k) plan. However, an entity that is both an instrumentality of a State and a Section 501(c)(3) organization could cover any of its employees under a 403(b) plan, regardless of whether they are performing services for a public school. [I.R.C. §§ 401(k)(4)(B)(i), 401(k)(4)(B)(ii), 403(b)(1)(A)(i), 403(b)(1)(A)(ii)]

Q 35:3   What is a Section 501(c)(3) organization?

A Section 501(c)(3) organization is a nonprofit organization (a corporation, and any community chest, fund, or foundation) that meets the following conditions:

1. It is organized and operated exclusively for religious, charitable, scientific, testing for public safety, literary, or educational purposes; to foster national or international amateur sports competition (but only if no part

of its activities involves the provision of athletic facilities or equipment); or for the prevention of cruelty to children or animals;

2. No part of the net earnings of the organization may inure to the benefit of any private shareholder or individual;

3. No substantial part of the activities of the organization may consist of carrying on propaganda or otherwise attempting to influence legislation (except for certain lobbying activities by public charities); and

4. It does not participate in, or intervene in (including the publishing or distributing of statements), any political campaign on behalf of (or in opposition to) any candidate for public office.

[I.R.C. § 501(c)(3); Treas. Reg. §§ 1.403(b)-2(a)(18), 1.403(b)-10(g); Priv. Ltr. Rul. 200341023]

A cooperative hospital service organization established under Section 501(e) is treated as a Section 501(c)(3) organization and, therefore, may establish a 403(b) plan on behalf of its employees. [Rev. Rul. 72-309, 1972-2 C.B. 226]

State and municipal agencies and instrumentalities generally do not qualify as Section 501(c)(3) organizations; but, if an organization serves the exclusive purposes described above and is a separate entity from the government, then it may establish a 403(b) plan for its employees. [Rev. Rul. 60-384, 1960-2 C.B. 172; Rev. Rul. 67-290, 1967-2 C.B. 183]

An institution operated exclusively for educational purposes by a separate educational instrumentality may qualify both as a Section 501(c)(3) organization and as a public school (see Qs 35:2, 35:4). [Estate of Johnson, 56 T.C. 944 (1971); Priv. Ltr. Rul. 7817098]

The regulations include controlled group rules (see Q 5:31) for tax-exempt entities. Under these rules, the employer for a plan maintained by a Section 501(c)(3) organization (or any other tax-exempt organization under Section 501(a)) includes not only the organization whose employees participate in the plan, but also any other exempt organization that is under common control with such organization, based on 80 percent of the directors or trustees being either representatives of or directly or indirectly controlled by an exempt organization. The regulations include an anti-abuse rule and will also allow tax-exempt organizations to choose to be aggregated if they maintain a single plan covering one or more employees from each organization and the organizations regularly coordinate their day-to-day exempt activities. For a Section 501(c)(3) organization that makes contributions to a 403(b) plan, these rules will be generally relevant for purposes of the nondiscrimination requirements (see Qs 35:16–35:21), as well as the Section 415 contribution limitations (see Q 35:29), the special catch-up contributions (see Q 35:28), and the minimum distribution rules (see Q 35:37). The controlled group rules apply for taxable years beginning after December 31, 2008 (see Q 35:1). [Treas. Reg. § 1.414(c)-5; preamble to final regulations]

Example 1. Organization A is a Section 501(c)(3) organization and owns 80 percent or more of the total value of all classes of stock of corporation B, a for-profit organization. Organization A and corporation B are under common control.

Example 2. Organization M is a hospital, a Section 501(c)(3) organization, and organization N is a medical clinic, also a Section 501(c)(3) organization. N is located in a city, and M is located in a nearby suburb. There is a history of regular coordination of day-to-day activities between M and N, including periodic transfers of staff, coordination of staff training, common sources of income, and coordination of budget and operational goals. A single 403(b) plan covers professional and staff employees of both M and N. While a number of members of the board of directors of M are also on the board of directors of N, there is less than 80 percent overlap in board membership. Both organizations have approximately the same percentage of employees who are highly compensated (see Q 3:3) and have appropriate business reasons for being maintained in separate entities. M and N are not under common control, but may choose to treat themselves as under common control, assuming both of them act in a manner that is consistent with that choice for purposes of the nondiscrimination rules.

Example 3. Organizations O and P are each 501(c)(3) organizations. Each organization maintains a qualified retirement plan for its employees, but one of the plans would not satisfy the minimum coverage requirements (see Q 5:15) if the organizations were under common control. The two organizations are closely related; and, while the organizations have several trustees in common, the common trustees constitute fewer than 80 percent of the trustees of either organization. Organization O has the power to remove any of the trustees of P and to select the slate of replacement nominees. Under these facts, IRS treats the entities as under common control.

Q 35:4 What is a public school?

A public school is a State-sponsored educational organization that normally maintains a regular faculty and curriculum and normally has a regularly enrolled body of pupils or students in attendance at the place where educational activities are regularly carried on. [Treas. Reg. § 1.403(b)-2(a)(14)] A State is a State, a political subdivision of a State, or any agency or instrumentality of a State. For this purpose, the District of Columbia is treated as a State; in addition, for purposes of determining whether an individual is an employee performing services for a public school (see Q 35:5), an Indian tribal government is treated as a State. [Treas. Reg. § 1.403(b)-2(a)(20)] The term includes a federal public-supported school. [I.R.C. §§ 170(b)(1)(A)(ii), 403(b)(1)(A)(ii); Treas. Reg. § 1.170A-9(b)]

The term "educational organization" includes primary, secondary, preparatory, and high schools, colleges, and universities. If the organization engages in both educational and noneducational activities, it will qualify as an educational organization only if the noneducational activities are incidental to the primary educational purpose. [Treas. Reg. § 1.170A-9(b)(1)]

A State department of education may qualify as a part of a public school system if its services involve the operation or direction of the State's public school program. [Rev. Rul. 73-607, 1973-2 C.B. 145] A State agency created as part of a State educational department, which consists of accredited colleges and universities, community colleges, and junior colleges, is a public educational institution. [Priv. Ltr. Rul. 9438031] Employees of a school board insurance group were considered to have performed services for an educational institution; the insurance group was an agency or instrumentality of a State that permitted a local school board to pool resources with other school boards in order to take advantage of self-insurance options and other risk management programs. [Priv. Ltr. Rul. 199947040]

Teachers in private and parochial schools are employees of Section 501(c)(3) organizations (see Q 35:3).

IRS ruled that the trustee-to-trustee transfer of plan assets from one plan to another pursuant to a merger was not a distribution to the employees of the merged educational system. The amounts were not distributed or otherwise made available to the employees. [Priv. Ltr. Rul. 200601046]

To satisfy the requirements applicable to 403(b) contracts, the contract must be maintained pursuant to a plan (see Q 35:9). Concern was expressed that there may be a potential cost associated with satisfying the written plan requirement for those employers that do not have existing plan documents, such as public schools. To address this concern, IRS published guidance that includes model plan provisions that may be used by public school employers for this purpose. [Preamble to final regulations; Rev. Proc. 2007-71, 2007-2 C.B. 1184]

Q 35:5 Must there be an employer-employee relationship?

Whether an individual is associated with a Section 501(c)(3) organization (see Q 35:3) or a public school (see Q 35:4), the individual must be an *employee*, not an independent contractor, to be eligible to participate in a 403(b) plan. [I.R.C. § 403(b)(1)(A); Bruecher Foundation Services Inc., ___ (5th Cir. 2010); Feaster, T.C.M. 2010-157; Curry v. CTB McGraw-Hill, LLC, 2008 WL 4542863 (9th Cir. 2008); Ramirez, 94 T.C.M. 493 (2007); Jones, 94 T.C.M. 230 (2007); Peno Trucking, Inc., 93 T.C.M. 1027 (2007); Orion Contracting Trust, 92 T.C.M. 309 (2006); Levine, 89 T.C.M. 1063 (2005); Nu-Look Design, Inc. v. Comm'r, 03-2754 (3d Cir. 2004); Joseph M. Grey, Pub. Accountant, P.C. v. Comm'r, 02-4417 (3d Cir. 2004); Kolling v. American Power Conversion Corp., 2003 WL 22350886 (1st Cir. 2003); Kumpel, 86 T.C.M. 358 (2003); Ronald McLean E. Video, 85 T.C.M. 763 (2003); Mulzet v. R.L. Reppert Inc., 2002 WL 31761696 (3d Cir. 2002); Kiper v. Novartis Crop Protection, Inc., No. 00-528-B-M3 (M.D. La. 2002); Naughton, 84 T.C.M. 275 (2002); Priv. Ltr. Ruls. 200407014, 200341023] Thus, it is necessary to determine that an employer-employee relationship exists between the organization and the individual (see Q 5:1). [I.R.C. § 403(b)(1)(A); Treas. Reg. § 1.403(b)-1]

An employee is a common-law employee performing services for an employer and does not include a former employee or, as noted, an independent contractor. [Treas. Reg. § 1.403(b)-2(a)(9)]

Employees of a limited liability company (LLC) will be treated as employed by a 501(c)(3) organization that owns the LLC's membership interest, and the employees will be eligible to participate in the organization's 403(b) plan, IRS has ruled. A 501(c)(3) organization that owns the membership interest of a single-member LLC wishes to extend participation in its 403(b) plan to the employees of the LLC. However, the single-member LLC is not a 501(c)(3) organization. Certain organizations that have a single owner can choose to be recognized as a separate entity from its owner or be disregarded as a separate entity for federal tax purposes. If the organization is disregarded, its activities are treated the same as a sole proprietorship or as a branch or division of its owner. The single-member LLC has not elected to be classified as a separate entity and, thus, is disregarded as a separate entity from its owner. Therefore, the employees of the single-member LLC will be treated as employees of the 501(c)(3) organization for 403(b) plan purposes. [Priv. Ltr. Rul. 200851044]

An employee performing services for a public school means an employee performing services as an employee for a public school of a State (see Q 35:4). This definition is not applicable unless the employee's compensation for performing services for a public school is paid by the State. Further, a person occupying an elective or appointive public office is not an employee performing services for a public school unless such office is one to which an individual is elected or appointed only if the individual has received training, or is experienced, in the field of education. The term "public office" includes any elective or appointive office of a State. [Treas. Reg. § 1.403(b)-2(a)(10)]

IRS had provided guidelines for classifying individuals as either employees or independent contractors and listed 20 factors to be considered in establishing the existence of an employer-employee relationship. These guidelines did not specifically relate to 403(b) plans; however, they did provide guidance even though certain factors clearly may have been inapplicable to eligible employers (see Q 35:2). Control was the important element: if the organization controlled the relationship, the individual was an employee; if the individual controlled the relationship, the individual was an independent contractor. The 20 factors are described below:

1. *Instructions.* Is the individual subject to another person's instructions as to when, where, and how the work is to be performed? [Rev. Rul. 68-598, 1968-2 C.B. 464; Rev. Rul. 66-381, 1966-2 C.B. 449]

2. *Training.* Is the individual required to work with an experienced worker, to attend meetings, and to perform services in a particular manner? [Rev. Rul. 70-630, 1970-2 C.B. 229]

3. *Integration.* Are the individual's services integrated into business operations? [United States v. Silk, 331 U.S. 704 (1947)]

4. *Services rendered personally.* Must the services rendered by the individual be rendered personally? [Rev. Rul. 55-695, 1955-2 C.B. 410]

5. *Hiring, supervising, and paying assistants.* Does the individual have this responsibility? [Rev. Rul. 63-115, 1963-1 C.B. 178; Rev. Rul. 55-593, 1955-2 C.B. 610]

6. *Continuing relationship.* Are the individual's services of a temporary or permanent nature? [United States v. Silk, 331 U.S. 704 (1947)]

7. *Set hours of work.* Does the organization set the work hours of the individual? [Rev. Rul. 73-591, 1973-2 C.B. 337]

8. *Full time required.* Must the individual work substantially full time for the organization? [Rev. Rul. 56-694, 1956-2 C.B. 694]

9. *Doing work on employer's premises.* Who controls the place of work? [Rev. Rul. 56-694, 1956-2 C.B. 694]

10. *Order or sequence set.* Must the individual perform services in the order or sequence set by the organization? [Rev. Rul. 56-694, 1956-2 C.B. 694]

11. *Oral or written reports.* Is the individual required to submit regular reports? [Rev. Rul. 70-309, 1970-1 C.B. 199; Rev. Rul. 68-248, 1968-1 C.B. 431]

12. *Method of payment.* Is the individual paid by the hour or week, by the job, or by straight commission? [Rev. Rul. 74-389, 1974-2 C.B. 330]

13. *Expenses.* Are business and travel expenses paid by the individual or the organization? [Rev. Rul. 55-144, 1955-1 C.B. 483]

14. *Furnishing of tools and materials.* Who furnishes the tools, materials, and equipment? [Rev. Rul. 71-524, 1971-2 C.B. 346]

15. *Significant investment.* Who makes the investment in facilities used by the individual? [Rev. Rul. 71-524, 1971-2 C.B. 346]

16. *Realization of profit or loss.* Can the individual realize a profit or suffer a loss as a result of the work performed? [Rev. Rul. 70-309, 1970-1 C.B. 199]

17. *More than one organization.* Does the individual perform more than *de minimis* services for more than one unrelated organization at the same time? [Rev. Rul. 70-572, 1970-2 C.B. 221]

18. *General public.* Are the individual's services available to the general public on a regular and consistent basis? [Rev. Rul. 56-660, 1956-2 C.B. 693]

19. *Right to discharge.* Does the organization have the right to fire the individual? [Rev. Rul. 75-41, 1975-1 C.B. 323]

20. *Right to terminate.* Can the individual terminate the relationship without incurring liability? [Rev. Rul. 70-309, 1970-1 C.B. 199]

[Rev. Rul. 87-41, 1987-1 C.B. 296; Rev. Rul. 70-136, 1970-1 C.B. 12; Rev. Rul. 66-274, 1966-2 C.B. 446; Montesano v. Xerox Corp. Ret. Income Guarantee Plan, 256 F.3d 86 (2d Cir. 2001); Hensley v. Northwest Permanente P.C. Ret. Plan & Trust, 2001 WL 868044 (9th Cir. 2001); Administrative Comm. of the Time Warner, Inc. Benefit Plans v. Biscardi, No. 99 Civ. 12270 (S.D.N.Y. 2000); Day, 80 T.C.M. 834 (2000); Vizcaino v. Microsoft, C93-178D (W.D. Wash. 1998); Trombetta v. Cragin Fed. Bank for Sav. ESOP, 102 F.3d 1435 (7th Cir. 1996); Azad v. United States, 388 F.2d 74 (8th Cir. 1968); Haugen, 30 T.C.M. 1247 (1971); Ravel, 26 T.C.M. 885 (1967); Priv. Ltr. Ruls. 200234007, 9443002, 9429010, 9428012, 9149001; *see also* Revenue Act of 1978 § 530; SBA '96 § 1122; Ann. 96-13, 96-12 I.R.B. 33]

IRS replaced the 20-factor common-law test with a new procedure involving what it calls "categories of evidence." Under the new method, a business is to break down the factors pertaining to a given worker's status into three categories: behavioral control, financial control, and type of relationship. The behavior control category would include facts related to whether or not the business controls how the individual does the job (e.g., training and instructions given). The financial control category would comprise evidence related to the business aspects of the worker's job (e.g., the worker's investments and expenses). The type-of-relationship category would entail relational indicators (e.g., written contracts and length of association). [IRS Pub. 15-A (Employer's Supplemental Tax Guide)] IRS posted a revised document on its website providing answers to questions that may arise after it determines that an individual is an employee rather than an independent contractor. [Notice 989 (Rev. 7-2009) Commonly Asked Questions When IRS Determines Your Work Status is "Employee"]

An individual performs services for an educational organization if the individual is performing services as an employee directly or indirectly for such an institution. The principal, clerical employees, custodial employees, and teachers at a public elementary school are employees performing services *directly* for the educational institution. An employee who performs services involving the operation or direction of a state's or political subdivision's education program as carried on through educational institutions is an employee performing services *indirectly* for the institutions. An employee participating in an in-home teaching program is included because the program is merely an extension of the activities carried on by the educational institutions. [Priv. Ltr. Ruls. 9613013, 9613011, 9613005, 7801019, 7747057] Janitorial, custodial, and general clerical employees of a State department of education who are appointed by the commissioner of education are not persons occupying appointed public office, but are employees providing indirect services for an educational institution. Also, if an individual has a significant degree of executive or policymaking authority and the individual's position is based on educational training or experience, the individual will be considered to perform indirect services. [Rev. Rul. 73-607, 1973-2 C.B. 145]

IRS has ruled that employees of a State teachers' retirement system do not perform services directly or indirectly for an educational organization, and neither does a State employee who works in a department that is not part of an educational institution but supervises payroll and timekeeping for public schools. [Rev. Rul. 80-139, 1980-1 C.B. 88; Rev. Rul. 72-390, 1972-2 C.B. 227] However, employees of a school board insurance group do perform services for an educational organization. [Priv. Ltr. Rul. 199947040]

An individual can be both an employee of an organization and an independent contractor with regard to the same organization (see Q 6:62). [Reese, 63 T.C.M. 3129 (1992)]

IRS ruled that the trustee-to-trustee transfer of plan assets from one plan to another pursuant to a merger was not a distribution to the employees of the merged educational system. The amounts were not distributed or otherwise made available to the employees. The amounts transferred from the merged plan retained their employer and employee status for federal income tax purposes. The merged plan transferred appropriate records that had tracked the contributions between employer and employee, as well as pre-tax and post-tax contributions. The transferred amounts were not considered as part of the limitations on the benefits or contributions to the plan, since the amounts were not part of the annual benefit for purposes of determining the limitation. [Priv. Ltr. Rul. 200601046]

Q 35:6   What is an annuity contract?

For the 403(b) plan rules to apply, an annuity contract must be purchased for the employee; however, the term "annuity contract" was not defined. [I.R.C. § 403(b)(1)(A)] Except where a custodial account (see Q 35:7) is treated as an annuity contract, an annuity contract is a contract that is issued by an insurance company qualified to issue annuities in a State (see Q 35:4) and that includes payment in the form of an annuity, but does not include a contract that is a life insurance contract, an endowment contract, a health or accident insurance contract, or a property, casualty, or liability insurance contract. The regulations include a special transition rule relating to life insurance contracts issued before the effective date (see Q 35:8). [Treas. Reg. §§ 1.401(f)-1(d)(2), 1.401(f)-1(e), 1.401(f)-4(e), 1.403(b)-2(b)(2), 1.403(b)-8(c)(1), 1.403(b)-8(c)(2); preamble to final regulations] A limited exception is provided for certain State plans to be treated as qualifying as annuities. [Treas. Reg. § 1.403(b)-8(c)(3)] The term "annuity" also includes a face-amount certificate but does not include any contract or certificate that is transferable if a person other than a trustee is the owner of the contract or certificate. [I.R.C. § 401(g); Investment Company Act of 1940 § 2(a)(15)]

The annuity contract may be an individual contract for each employee or a group contract under which each employee has a separate account. The annuity contract may provide a fixed retirement benefit or a variable benefit that is based upon the performance of the underlying investments (i.e., a variable annuity contract). [Rev. Rul. 82-102, 1982-1 C.B. 62; Rev. Rul. 68-116, 1968-1 C.B. 177; Priv. Ltr. Ruls. 9636022, 9415016] With respect to a contract that would otherwise qualify as a 403(b) contract, but for the fact that contract premiums are invested at the direction of the individual in publicly available securities, IRS will treat the contract as a 403(b) contract and will not treat the individual as owning the assets associated with the contract, provided that no additional federal tax liability would have been incurred if the employer of the individual had instead paid an amount into a custodial account. [Rev. Proc. 99-44, 1999-2 C.B. 598; Rev. Rul. 82-55, 1982-1 C.B. 12; Rev. Rul. 82-54, 1982-1 C.B. 11; Rev. Rul. 81-225, 1981-2 C.B. 12; Rev. Rul. 80-274, 1980-2 C.B. 27; Rev. Rul. 77-85, 1977-1 C.B. 12]

A single group annuity contract may be used to fund benefits of both a qualified retirement plan and a 403(b) plan of an eligible employer (see Q 35:2), provided that the assets of both plans are separately accounted for and subaccounts are created for each employee to identify each plan's contributions. [Priv. Ltr. Rul. 9422053]

Contributions on behalf of employees to a credit union that maintains separate nonforfeitable special share accounts for each employee do not constitute the purchase of annuity contracts, and neither do contributions to a State teachers' retirement system or to a separately funded employee retirement reserve subject to State insurance department supervision. [Rev. Rul. 82-102, 1982-1 C.B. 62; Corbin v. United States, 760 F.2d 234 (8th Cir. 1985); Priv. Ltr. Rul. 9511040]

IRS has ruled that the addition of certain policy credits to 403(b) contracts pursuant to a conversion of a mutual holding insurance company into a stock company did not cause the 403(b) contracts to lose their qualification (see Q 35:13). The addition of the policy credits was not treated as a distribution; and, therefore, the following taxes were not applicable:

1. Income tax on distributions (see Q 35:40).
2. Penalty tax on early distributions (see Q 35:41).
3. Penalty tax on excess aggregate contributions (see Q 35:32).

IRS further ruled that the policy credits would constitute taxable income in the year of actual distribution and that the credits were investment earnings rather than an investment in the contract (see Q 35:40). [Priv. Ltr. Rul. 200128061]

Q 35:7   What is a custodial account?

A custodial account is treated as an annuity contract for purposes of the 403(b) plan rules. [I.R.C. § 403(b)(7); Treas. Reg. § 1.403(b)-8(d)(1)] A custodial account is defined as a plan, or a separate account under a plan, in which an amount attributable to 403(b) plan contributions (or amounts rolled over to a 403(b) contract) is held by a bank or other satisfactory party, if all amounts held in the account are invested in stock of a regulated investment company (i.e., mutual funds), the special restrictions on distributions with respect to a custodial account are satisfied (see Q 35:35), the assets held in the account cannot be used for, or diverted to, purposes other than for the exclusive benefit of plan participants or their beneficiaries (see Q 4:1), and the account is not part of a retirement income account (see Q 35:55). [I.R.C. §§ 401(f)(2), 403(b)(7), 408(n), 851(a); Treas. Reg. §§ 1.403(b)-8(d)(2), 1.408-2(b)(2); preamble to final regulations; Ann. 2004-72, 2004-2 C.B. 650; Priv. Ltr. Ruls. 200044044, 200014044, 986014, 9750057, 9716029, 9525067]

The requirement limiting investments to mutual funds is not satisfied if the account includes any assets other than stock of a regulated investment company. [Treas. Reg. § 1.403(b)-8(d)(3)] Trust assets held under a custodial account may be invested in a group trust with trust assets held under a qualified retirement plan or IRA. [Treas. Reg. § 1.403(b)-8(f) ; Priv. Ltr. Ruls. 200303041, 200242047, 9744022, 9540061; *see also* Rev. Rul. 81-100, 1981-1 C.B. 326]

Q 35:8   Can a 403(b) contract provide life insurance protection?

Neither a life insurance contract, an endowment contract, a health or accident insurance contract, nor a property, casualty, or liability insurance contract meets the definition of an annuity contract. However, if a contract issued by an insurance company qualified to issue annuities in a State (see Q 35:4) provides death benefits as part of the contract, then that coverage is permitted, assuming that those death benefits do not cause the contract to fail to satisfy any requirement applicable to 403(b) contracts, for example, assuming that those benefits satisfy the incidental benefit requirement (see Q 11:20). [Treas. Reg. §§ 1.401-1(b)(1)(i), 1.401(f)-1(c), 1.403(b)-8(c)(2)] This provision, however, does not apply to a life insurance contract issued before September 24, 2007. [Treas. Reg. § 1.403(b)-11(f)]

The life insurance protection must be incidental to the retirement annuity. To determine if the life insurance protection is incidental, the rules applicable to qualified retirement plans also apply to 403(b) contracts (see Q 15:4). [Treas. Reg. § 1.403(b)-1(c)(3) (prior to repeal); Priv. Ltr. Ruls. 9713022, 9626042, 9617042, 9601053] A separate insurance policy could have been purchased as part of a 403(b) plan, but the policy had to satisfy all of the requirements of a 403(b) contract (see Q 35:13). It was not required that both the annuity contract and the insurance policy be issued by the same insurance company. [Treas. Reg. §§ 1.403(b)-1(b)(4) (prior to repeal), 1.403(b)-1(c)(3) (prior to repeal); Priv. Ltr. Ruls. 9617042, 9336054, 9336053, 9327025, 9324044] If life insurance is provided as part of the 403(b) plan, the portion of the contribution providing current life insurance protection is includible in the employee's gross income (see Qs 15:6–15:8).

Q 35:9   Must a 403(b) contract be part of a plan or trust?

A contract does not satisfy the requirements applicable to 403(b) contracts unless it is maintained pursuant to a plan. For this purpose, a plan is a written defined contribution plan (see Q 2:2) that, in both form and operation, satisfies the requirements applicable to 403(b) plans. The plan must contain all the material terms and conditions for eligibility, benefits, applicable limitations, the contracts available under the plan, and the time and form under which benefit distributions would be made (see Q 35:13). A plan may contain certain optional features that are consistent with but not required for 403(b) plans, such as hardship withdrawal distributions (see Q 35:35), loans (see Q 35:38), plan-to-plan or annuity contract-to-annuity contract transfers (see Q 35:47), and acceptance of rollovers to the plan (see Q 35:42). However, if a plan contains any optional provisions, the optional provisions must meet, in both form and operation, the relevant requirements applicable to such provisions. [I.R.C. §§ 403(b)(1)(D), 403(b)(7)(B), 403(b)(12)(A); ERISA § 402(a)(1); Treas. Reg. §§ 1.403(b)-2(b)(13), 1.403(b)-2(b)(16)(ii), 1.403(b)-3(b)(3)(i); preamble to final regulations]

IRS has extended the January 1, 2009 deadline for sponsors of 403(b) plans to satisfy the written plan requirement. IRS will not treat a 403(b) plan as failing to satisfy the requirements of Section 403(b) and the final regulations during the 2009 calendar year, provided that:

1. On or before December 31, 2009, the sponsor of the plan has adopted a written 403(b) plan that is intended to satisfy the requirements of Section 403(b) (including the final regulations) effective as of January 1, 2009;

2. During 2009, the sponsor operates the plan in accordance with a reasonable interpretation of Section 403(b), taking into account the final regulations; and

3. Before the end of 2009, the sponsor makes its best efforts to retroactively correct any operational failure during the 2009 calendar year to conform to the terms of the written 403(b) plan, with such correction to be based on the general principles of correction set forth in EPCRS (see Q 19:6).

This relief applies solely with respect to the 2009 calendar year and may not be relied on with respect to the operation of the plan or correction of operational defects in any prior or subsequent year.

[IRS Notice 2009-3, 2009-1 C.B. 250]

The plan may allocate responsibility for performing administrative functions, including functions to comply with the requirements applicable to 403(b) plans and other tax requirements. Any such allocation must identify responsibility for compliance with the requirements of the Code that apply on the basis of the aggregated contracts issued to a participant under a plan, including loans and the conditions for obtaining a hardship withdrawal. A plan is permitted to assign such responsibilities to parties other than the eligible employer (see Q 35:2), but not to participants (other than employees of the employer a substantial portion of whose duties are administration of the plan), and may incorporate by reference other documents, including the insurance policy (see Q 35:8) or custodial account (see Q 35:7), which thereupon becomes part of the plan. [Treas. Reg. § 1.403(b)-3(b)(3)(ii); preamble to final regulations]

Because 403(b) plans are funded, in whole or in part, through individual annuity contracts, group annuity contracts, life insurance policies, and custodial accounts that must satisfy a number of requirements, a trust is not required. As an example, the employee will usually own and hold an individual annuity contract. However, a trust may be established for the purpose of making annuity contracts available to eligible employees. [Priv. Ltr. Rul. 9423031]

IRS has designed prototype plan (see Q 2:27) language and issued draft guidance on an opinion letter (see Q 18:1) program for 403(b) plans. IRS not only issued a draft revenue procedure to enable plan sponsors to obtain an opinion letter on their prototype plans but also released nearly 70 pages of sample plan language on its website. A prototype plan is a plan prepared by a funding organization or other person who expects at least 30 employers to adopt the plan, along with a required adoption agreement. The program for prototype plans will allow practitioners and financial organizations to obtain advance approval of the form of a prototype plan. Employers adopting the prototype plan will be able to rely on the IRS opinion that the form of the plan complies with the final regulations. After finalizing the draft revenue procedure, IRS will start accepting applications for opinions on prototype plans. The program will allow retroactive remedial plan amendments for years after 2009.

IRS will issue opinions on standardized plans that only provide for elective deferrals (see Q 35:11). IRS will also issue prototype opinions on nonstandardized plans, except for the application of the nondiscrimination rules to other types of contributions besides elective deferrals (such as matching contributions, nonelective employer contributions, and after-tax employee contributions; see Qs 35:10, 35:14, 35:18). IRS will not rule on a proposed plan with a vesting schedule (see Q 35:14) or a plan that applies only to churches and church-related organizations (see Q 35:55).

The prototype plan addresses essential requirements for plans with elective deferrals, such as eligibility and participation, contributions and limits, time and form of distributions, investments, plan termination and amendment, and adoption agreements. The sample plan also provides provisions for plans with additional employer or employee contributions besides salary deferral contributions.

At the same time, IRS is updating EPCRS to address 403(b) plans. Initially, plans will be able to correct problems in plan operations. After 2009, plans will be able to correct problems in both plan operations and plan documents. IRS will also develop a separate program for sponsors and employers to obtain an opinion on individually designed plans (see Q 2:26).

[Ann. 2009-34, 2009-1 C.B. 916]

Subsequent to the issuance of IRS Notice 2009-2 and Announcement 2009-34, IRS announced that it expects to publish a revenue procedure for obtaining an opinion letter that the form of a prototype or other pre-approved plan meets the requirements of Section 403(b) and the regulations thereunder. Thereafter, IRS intends to publish a revenue procedure for obtaining an individual determination letter for a 403(b) plan. The IRS announcement provides for a remedial amendment period and reliance for employers that, pursuant to the upcoming revenue procedures, either adopt a pre-approved plan with a favorable opinion letter or apply for an individual determination letter when available.

As one of the conditions for relief under IRS Notice 2009-3, a written 403(b) plan that is intended to satisfy the requirements of Section 403(b) and the regulations had to be adopted on or before December 31, 2009. If this condition was met and, pursuant to the upcoming revenue procedures, the employer sponsoring the plan either adopts a pre-approved plan that has received a favorable opinion letter from IRS or applies for an individual determination letter when available, the employer will have a remedial amendment period in which to amend the plan to correct any form defects retroactive to January 1, 2010. Further, such an employer will have reliance, beginning January 1, 2010, that the form of its written plan satisfies the requirements of Section 403(b) and the regulations, provided that, during the remedial amendment period, the pre-approved plan is adopted retroactive to January 1, 2010 or the plan is amended to correct any defects in the form of the plan retroactive to January 1, 2010.

An employer that first establishes a 403(b) plan after December 31, 2009 by adopting a written plan intended to satisfy the requirements of Section 403(b) and the regulations will also have reliance beginning on the effective date of the plan, provided the employer either adopts a pre-approved plan with a favorable opinion letter or applies for an individual determination letter and corrects any defects in the form of the plan retroactive to the plan's effective date.

The upcoming revenue procedures will include this remedial amendment provision and will address the time-frames for adopting a pre-approved plan or applying for a determination letter and other details regarding the remedial amendment period.

[Ann. 2009-89, 2009-2 C.B. ___]

Q 35:10 How are contributions made to a 403(b) contract?

A 403(b) contract must be purchased by the employer (see Q 35:2); therefore, in all cases, it is the employer that makes the contribution to the 403(b) contract. However, there are two main sources from which contributions are made:

1. Elective deferrals by the employee through salary reduction agreements (see Q 35:11).
2. Employer contributions that are made without regard to the employee's elective deferral or that match in some proportion the employee's elective deferral (see Qs 35:14, 35:18).

[I.R.C. §§ 403(b)(1)(A), 403(b)(1)(E); Treas. Reg. §§ 1.403(b)-2(b)(7), 1.403(b)-2(b)(17)(i); Priv. Ltr. Ruls. 9708021, 9643037]

In some cases, employees may be permitted to make voluntary, nondeductible contributions (see Qs 1:47, 27:73–27:95, 35:18).

Contributions to a 403(b) plan must be transferred to the insurance company issuing the annuity contract (or the entity holding assets of any custodial account that is treated as an annuity contract) within a period that is not longer than is reasonable for the proper administration of the plan. For purposes of this requirement, the plan may provide for elective deferrals for a participant under the plan to be transferred to the annuity contract within a specified period after the date the amounts would otherwise have been paid to the participant. For example, the plan could provide for elective deferrals under the plan to be contributed within 15 business days following the month in which these amounts would otherwise have been paid to the participant. [Treas. Reg. § 1.403(b)-8(b)] A participant is an employee for whom a 403(b) contract is currently being purchased, or an employee or former employee for whom a 403(b) contract has previously been purchased and who has not received a distribution of the employee's entire benefit under the contract. [Treas. Reg. § 1.403(b)-2(b)(12)]

Q 35:11 What is a salary reduction agreement?

The primary method for making contributions to a 403(b) contract is by the employee's taking a reduction in salary or forgoing an increase in salary. In either case, this is referred to as a salary reduction agreement. Amounts contributed by the employer to a 403(b) contract by reason of a salary reduction agreement are referred to as elective deferrals. [I.R.C. §§ 401(a)(30), 402(g)(3)(C), 403(b)(1)(E); Treas. Reg. § 1.403(b)-2(b)(7)] However, if a 403(b) plan requires an employee always to make contributions through a salary reduction agreement as a condition of employment, those contributions are not elective deferrals (see Q 35:26).

A salary reduction agreement must be legally binding, apply only to compensation earned by the employee after the agreement becomes effective, and be irrevocable with respect to compensation earned while the agreement is in effect. Multiple salary reduction agreements are permitted so that the frequency with which an employee can enter into a salary reduction agreement, the salary to which the agreement may apply, and the ability to revoke the agreement are determined under the rules applicable to cash-or-deferred elections under 401(k) plans (see Q 27:3). [SBA '96 § 1450(a)(1)] To the author's knowledge, there are no statutory or regulatory rules regarding frequency or the number of times an agreement may be revoked.

Example. Jamie is a teacher at Christie University. His monthly salary is $8,000; and, for 2010, he entered into a 4 percent salary reduction agreement. On July 1, 2010, he entered into a second salary reduction agreement for an additional 3 percent. The amounts contributed from the second 403(b) salary reduction agreement for the last six months of 2010 are not includible in his compensation because Jamie is permitted to enter into more than one salary reduction agreement during the year.

A contribution is not treated as made pursuant to a salary reduction agreement if it is made pursuant to a one-time irrevocable election by the employee at the time of initial eligibility to participate in the plan (see Q 27:3). [I.R.C. § 403(b)(12)(A)]

IRS has ruled that a negative election 401(k) plan is permissible. Under this type of plan, an employee is deemed to have elected to have the employer contribute a percentage of the employee's compensation to the plan under a cash-or-deferred election *unless* the employee specifically elects in writing *not* to defer compensation. [Rev. Rul. 2000-8, 2000-1 C.B. 617] With regard to 403(b) plans, IRS approved this concept. [Rev. Rul. 2000-35, 2000-2 C.B. 138] Negative election is now referred to as automatic contribution arrangement. For a discussion of automatic contribution arrangements and permissible withdrawals from such arrangements and the final regulations issued by IRS, see Qs 27:5–27:7.

An employee is permitted to designate all or a portion of the elective deferral as being includible in the employee's gross income as an after-tax contribution (see Q 35:49).

For 403(b) plans, effective as of November 16, 2004 (see Q 35:34), a salary reduction agreement is a plan or arrangement (whether evidenced by a written instrument or otherwise) whereby payment will be made by an employer, on behalf of an employee or the employee's beneficiary, under or to a 403(b) contract:

1. If the employee elects to reduce compensation pursuant to a cash-or-deferred election;

2. If the employee elects to reduce compensation pursuant to a one-time irrevocable election made at or before the time of initial eligibility to participate in such plan or arrangement (or pursuant to a similar arrangement involving a one-time irrevocable election); or

3. If the employee agrees as a condition of employment (whether such condition is set by statute, contract, or otherwise) to make a contribution that reduces compensation.

[Treas. Reg. § 31.3121(a)(5)-2]

Effective for taxable years beginning after December 31, 2008 (see Q 35:1), with respect to a 403(b) contract, an elective deferral means an employer contribution to purchase a 403(b) contract under a salary reduction agreement; but an elective deferral only includes a contribution that is made pursuant to a cash-or-deferred election. Thus, an elective deferral does not include a contribution that is made pursuant to an employee's one-time irrevocable election made on or before the employee's first becoming eligible to participate under the employer's plan or a contribution made as a condition of employment that reduces the employee's compensation. [I.R.C. § 403(b)(12)(A); Treas. Reg. §§ 1.402(g)(3)-1, 1.403(b)-2(b)(7), 1.403(b)-2(b)(17)(i)] An elective deferral includes a designated Roth contribution under a 403(b) contract (see Q 35:49). [Treas. Reg. §§ 1.403(b)-2(a)(17)(ii), 1.403(b)-3(c)(1), 1.403(b)-11(i)]

Q 35:12   Are amounts contributed to a 403(b) contract excluded from an employee's income?

Amounts contributed by an eligible employer (see Q 35:2) for the purchase of an annuity contract (see Q 35:6) for an employee are excluded from the gross income of the employee only if each of the requirements applicable to 403(b) contracts and 403(b) plans (see Q 35:13) is satisfied. In addition, amounts contributed by an eligible employer for the purchase of an annuity contract for an employee pursuant to a cash-or-deferred election (see Qs 27:3, 35:11) are not includible in an employee's gross income at the time the cash would have been includible in the employee's gross income (but for the cash-or-deferred election) if each of those requirements is satisfied. However, the preceding two sentences generally do not apply to designated Roth contributions (see Q 35:49). [I.R.C. § 403(b)(1); Treas. Reg. § 1.403(b)-3(a)]

Generally, the exclusion from gross income does not apply to contributions made for former employees. For this purpose, the contribution is not made for a former employee if the contribution is with respect to compensation that would otherwise be paid for a payroll period that begins before severance from employment (see Q 35:35). However, the exclusion from gross income does apply to contributions made for former employees with respect to certain compensation paid by the later of two months after severance from employment or the end of the limitation year that includes the date of severance from employment (see Q 6:43), and compensation paid to participants who are permanently and totally disabled or relating to qualified military service (see Qs 6:43, 6:44, 27:15). [Treas. Reg. § 1.403(b)-3(b)(4)]

The exclusion from gross income applies only to amounts held in an annuity contract, including a custodial account that is treated as an annuity contract (see Q 35:7) or a retirement income account that is treated as an annuity contract (see Q 35:55). [Treas. Reg. § 1.403(b)-8(a)]

Q 35:13   What requirements must a 403(b) contract satisfy?

In addition to the requirement that a 403(b) contract be purchased only by certain types of employers (see Q 35:2), a number of other requirements must be met:

1. The employee's rights under the 403(b) contract must be nonforfeitable (see Q 35:14). [I.R.C. § 403(b)(1)(C)]

2. The 403(b) contract must be nontransferable (see Q 35:15). [I.R.C. § 401(g)]

3. The 403(b) contract must provide for required minimum distributions (see Q 35:37). [I.R.C. § 403(b)(10)]

4. No distributions may be made from an *annuity contract* (as opposed to a custodial account) attributable to contributions made pursuant to a salary reduction agreement until the occurrence of certain specified events (see Q 35:35). [I.R.C. § 403(b)(11)]

5. No distributions may be made from a *custodial account* (as opposed to an annuity contract) before the occurrence of certain specified events (see Q 35:35). [I.R.C. § 403(b)(7)(A)(ii)]

6. The 403(b) contract must be purchased under a plan that satisfies minimum coverage and nondiscrimination requirements and that limits the amount of compensation that may be considered (see Qs 35:16–35:21). [I.R.C. §§ 403(b)(1)(D), 403(b)(12)]

7. Elective deferrals cannot exceed a specified amount (see Q 35:26). [I.R.C. § 403(b)(1)(E)]

8. The 403(b) contract must provide for direct rollovers (see Q 35:42). [I.R.C. § 403(b)(10)]

9. The 403(b) plan must provide that, in the case of an employee who dies while performing qualified military service, the survivors of the employee are entitled to any additional benefits provided under the plan had the employee resumed and then terminated employment on account of death (see Q 1:35). [I.R.C. § 401(a)(37) (as added by HEART Act § 104(a)); HEART Act § 104(d)(2)]

[I.R.C. § 403(b)(1)(B); Priv. Ltr. Ruls. 200345044, 200337013, 200319011, 200317031, 200304034, 200246037, 200245060, 200240052, 200231018]

Each 403(b) *contract,* not the 403(b) *plan,* must provide that elective deferrals made under the contract may not exceed the annual limit on elective deferrals. [I.R.C. § 403(b)(1)(E)] It is intended that the contract terms be given effect in order for this requirement to be satisfied. Thus, for example, if the contract issuer takes no steps to ensure that deferrals under the contract do not exceed the applicable limit, then the contract will not be treated as satisfying Section 403(b). This provision is intended to make clear that the exclusion of elective deferrals from gross income by employees who have not exceeded the annual limit on elective deferrals will not be affected to the extent other employees exceed the annual limit. However, if the occurrence of an uncorrected elective deferral made by an employee is attributable to reasonable error, the contract will not fail to satisfy Section 403(b), and only the portion of the elective deferral in excess of the annual limit will be includible in gross income.

IRS has updated its list of entities that have been approved to serve as nonbank custodians of custodial accounts. [Ann. 2007-47, 2007-1 C.B. 1260]

The regulations add to the requirements set forth above that the contract not be purchased under a qualified retirement plan or an eligible governmental Section 457 plan and that the annual additions to the contract not exceed the annual addition limitation (see Q 35:29). [Treas. Reg. §§ 1.403(b)-3(a)(1), 1.403(b)-3(a)(9)] All 403(b) contracts purchased for an individual by an employer are treated as purchased under a single contract. [I.R.C. § 403(b)(5); Treas. Reg. §§ 1.403(b)-2(a)(16)(i), 1.403(b)-3(b)(1)]

If a contract includes any amount that fails to satisfy all of the above requirements, then, except with respect to failure to satisfy the nonforfeitable requirements, excess contributions (see Q 35:31), and excess deferrals (see Q 35:26), the contract is not a 403(b) contract. Because all 403(b) contracts purchased for all individuals by an employer are treated as purchased under a single contract, then, except with respect to disaggregation of excess annual additions (see Q 35:31) or as otherwise provided in this paragraph, a failure to satisfy all of the requirements with respect to any contract issued to an individual by an employer adversely affects all contracts issued to that individual by that employer. [Treas. Reg. § 1.403(b)-3(d)(1)(i)]

A failure to operate in accordance with the terms of a plan adversely affects all of the contracts issued by the employer to the employee or employees with respect to whom the operational failure occurred. Such a failure does not adversely affect any other contract if the failure is neither a failure to satisfy the nondiscrimination requirements (a nondiscrimination failure) nor a failure of the employer to be an eligible employer (an employer eligibility failure). However, any failure that is not an operational failure adversely affects all contracts issued under the plan, including: (1) a failure to have contracts issued pursuant to a written defined contribution plan (see Q 35:9) which, in form, satisfies all of the requirements (a written plan failure); (2) a nondiscrimination failure; or (3) an employer eligibility failure. [Treas. Reg. § 1.403(b)-3(d)(1)(ii)]

If an annuity contract issued by an insurance company fails to be a 403(b) contract, the rules relating to nonqualified annuities apply, based on the value of the contract at the time of the failure. [I.R.C. § 403(c); Treas. Reg. § 1.403(b)-3(d)(1)(iii)]

Q 35:14   Must an employee's rights under a 403(b) contract be nonforfeitable?

Except for the failure to pay future premiums, the employee's rights under the 403(b) contract must be nonforfeitable at the time of the contributions for the purchase of the annuity contract. Nonforfeitable means being 100 percent vested (see Q 9:1). [I.R.C. § 403(b)(1)(C)] The nonforfeitability requirement is not violated if the 403(b) contract permits a return of contributions made as a result of a mistake of fact. [Gen. Couns. Mem. 38,992] IRS has ruled that employer nonmatching contributions to a 403(b) plan are not required to be 100 percent vested immediately and may be subject to a vesting schedule (see Q 9:4). [Priv. Ltr. Rul. 9529006]

Under the regulations, an employee's rights under a contract fail to be nonforfeitable unless the employee for whom the contract is purchased has at all times a fully vested and nonforfeitable right to all benefits provided under the contract. [Treas. Reg. § 1.403(b)-3(a)(2)]

If an annuity contract issued by an insurance company would qualify as a 403(b) contract but for the failure to satisfy the nonforfeitability requirement, then the contract is treated as a nonqualified annuity contract. [I.R.C. § 403(c); Treas. Reg. § 1.403(b)-3(d)(2)(i)]

On or after the date on which the participant's interest in a contract described in the preceding paragraph becomes nonforfeitable, the contract may be treated as a 403(b) contract if no election has been made under Section 83(b) with respect to the contract, the participant's interest in the contract has been subject to a substantial risk of forfeiture (as defined in Section 83) before becoming nonforfeitable, each contribution under the contract that is subject to a different vesting schedule is maintained in a separate account, and the contract has at all times satisfied the requirements applicable to 403(b) contracts other than the nonforfeitability requirement. Thus, for example, for the current year and each prior year, no contribution can have been made to the contract that would cause the contract to fail to be a 403(b) contract as a result of contributions exceeding the limitations on contributions (see Q 35:29) or to fail to satisfy the nondiscrimination rules (see Qs 35:16–35:21). [Treas. Reg. § 1.403(b)-3(d)(2)(ii)(A)]

If only a portion of a participant's interest in a contract becomes nonforfeitable in a year, then the portion that is nonforfeitable and the portion that fails to be nonforfeitable are each treated as separate contracts. In addition, if a contribution is made to an annuity contract in excess of the limitations on contributions and the excess is maintained in a separate account, then the portion of the contract that includes the excess contributions account and the remainder are each treated as separate contracts. Thus, if an annuity contract that includes an excess contributions account changes from forfeitable to nonforfeitable during a year, then the portion that is not attributable to the excess contributions account constitutes a 403(b) contract (assuming it otherwise satisfies the requirements to be a 403(b) contract) and is not included in gross income, and the portion that is attributable to the excess contributions account is included in gross income. [Treas. Reg. § 1.403(b)-3(d)(2)(ii)(B)]

Q 35:15   Must a 403(b) contract be nontransferable?

A 403(b) contract purchased after 1962 must be nontransferable. A 403(b) contract is transferable if the employee can transfer any portion of the employee's interest in the contract to any person other than the insurance company. Accordingly, a 403(b) contract is transferable if the employee can sell, assign, discount, or pledge as collateral for a loan or as security for the performance of an obligation or for any other purpose the employee's interest in the contract to any person other than the insurance company. A written agreement between the employee and the employer that the employee will not transfer the 403(b) contract is insufficient; the nontransferability provision must be part of the 403(b) contract itself. [I.R.C. § 401(g); Treas. Reg. §§ 1.401-9, 1.403(b)-3(a)(5); Rev. Rul. 74-458, 1974-2 C.B. 138]

The nontransferability requirement is not violated even though the employee can surrender the 403(b) contract to the insurance company, make a loan against the contract (see Q 35:38), designate a beneficiary, elect an optional method of settlement (e.g., a joint and survivor annuity), transfer amounts held under the 403(b) contract from one insurance company to another (see Q 35:47), or roll over a 403(b) contract distribution to another 403(b) contract, a qualified retirement plan, an IRA, or a governmental Section 457 plan (see Q 35:42). [In the Matter of Coppola, 2005 WL 17143365 (5th Cir. 2005)]

Q 35:16   Do the nondiscrimination requirements applicable to qualified retirement plans also apply to 403(b) plans?

Contributions to 403(b) plans may not discriminate in favor of highly compensated employees (HCEs; see Q 3:2); therefore, the same general nondiscrimination requirements that apply to qualified retirement plans will also be applicable to 403(b) plans. However, if the plan allows only elective deferrals (see Q 35:11), the general nondiscrimination requirements are replaced by a single nondiscrimination requirement (see Q 35:20). [I.R.C. §§ 403(b)(1)(D), 403(b)(12)(A)(i), 403(b)(12)(A)(ii); Treas. Reg. §§ 1.403(b)-3(a)(3), 1.403(b)-5; preamble to final regulations]

Contributions to an annuity contract do not satisfy the nondiscrimination requirements unless the contributions are made pursuant to a plan (see Q 35:9) and the terms of the plan satisfy the nondiscrimination requirements. [Treas. Reg. § 1.403(b)-5(c)] The regulations reflect only the nondiscrimination requirements of the Code and do not reflect ERISA requirements that may apply to 403(b) plans, such as vesting requirements (see Q 35:51). [Treas. Reg. § 1.403(b)-5(e)]

For a discussion of the nondiscrimination requirements, see Qs 4:10 through 4:23, and see Qs 5:29–5:31, 5:34, and 5:35 for a discussion of rules treating entities as a single employer for purposes of the nondiscrimination requirements. See also Q 35:17 relating to the limitation on compensation, Q 35:18 relating to matching and employee contributions, Q 35:19 relating to minimum coverage, and Q 35:21 relating to the universal availability requirement.

Q 35:17   Is there a limitation on the amount of compensation that may be taken into account under a 403(b) plan?

The same $200,000 compensation limitation (as adjusted for cost of living) that applies to qualified retirement plans also applies to 403(b) plans and 403(b) contracts. [I.R.C. §§ 401(a)(17), 403(b)(1)(D), 403(b)(12)(A)(i); Treas. Reg. §§ 1.401(a)(17)-1(a)(3), 1.403(b)-5(a)(1)(ii), 1.403(b)-5(a)(3)] For plan years that begin in 2010, the compensation cap remained at $245,000. [IRS Notice 2009-94, 2009-2 C.B. 848]

For further details, see Qs 6:45, 6:46, and 6:50.

Q 35:18   Can employer matching contributions and employee contributions be made to a 403(b) plan?

Yes, but the special nondiscrimination test applies as if the 403(b) plan were a qualified retirement plan. [I.R.C. §§ 403(b)(1)(D), 403(b)(12)(A)(i); Treas. Reg. § 1.403(b)-5(a)(1)(iii); Priv. Ltr. Rul. 9541038] For a discussion of this special test, see Qs 27:73 through 27:95.

A 403(b) plan is treated as satisfying the special test with respect to matching contributions if the plan satisfies the safe harbor contribution requirement, the notice requirement, and the matching contribution limitations. For purposes of applying these requirements, salary reduction contributions under a 403(b) plan are treated as elective contributions under a CODA (see Qs 27:1, 27:16). [IRS Notice 98-52, § VI, 1998-2 C.B. 634] For a discussion of the safe harbor rules, see Qs 27:89 through 27:95. For a discussion of proposed regulations issued by IRS regarding the permissibility of reducing or suspending an ADP test or an ACP test safe harbor nonelective contribution, see Qs 27:49 and 27:94.

Q 35:19   Are 403(b) plans subject to the minimum coverage requirement?

The minimum coverage requirement must be satisfied by the 403(b) plan unless the plan allows only elective deferrals (see Q 35:11). Thus, this requirement must be met if the 403(b) plan provides for contributions other than, or in addition to, elective deferrals (see Q 35:10). [I.R.C. §§ 403(b)(1)(D), 403(b)(12)(A)(i), 403(b)(12)(A)(ii); Treas. Reg. § 1.403(b)-5(a)(1)(iv)] For a discussion of the minimum coverage requirement, see Qs 5:15 through 5:22.

A 403(b) plan may require an employee to reach age 21 and to complete one year of service before becoming eligible to participate. If the employee's rights under the 403(b) contract are immediately nonforfeitable, as is usually the case (see Q 35:14), the service eligibility requirement may be increased to up to two years. If the 403(b) plan is adopted by a tax-exempt educational institution (see Q 35:2), the service eligibility requirement is no more than one year, and the employee's rights are immediately nonforfeitable, the age requirement may be increased to age 26. [I.R.C. §§ 410(a)(1), 170(b)(1)(A)(ii)] The 20-hour exclusion applicable to the special nondiscrimination requirement (see Q 35:20) cannot be used for determining employee eligibility, IRS representatives have opined.

Employees of a tax-exempt charitable organization (see Q 35:3) who are eligible to make salary reduction contributions under a 403(b) plan may be treated as excludable employees for purposes of testing a 401(k) plan (see Qs 27:1, 27:18) if (1) no employee of *any* tax-exempt charitable organization is eligible to participate in the 401(k) plan and (2) at least 95 percent of the employees who are not employees of *any* such organization are eligible to participate in the 401(k) plan. [Treas. Reg. § 1.410(b)-6(g)] In addition to 401(k) plans, the regulations apply to 401(m) plans (see Qs 27:73, 27:77).

Q 35:20   Is there a special nondiscrimination requirement if an employee may enter into a salary reduction agreement?

If any one employee may elect to have the employer make contributions to a 403(b) contract pursuant to a salary reduction agreement (see Q 35:11), then all employees of the employer must be permitted to elect to have the employer make salary reduction contributions of more than $200. This is the *only* nondiscrimination requirement that applies if the 403(b) plan allows just elective deferrals. Among the employees who may be excluded from this requirement are those who normally work less than 20 hours per week. [I.R.C. §§ 403(b)(1)(D), 401(b)(1)(E), 403(b)(12)(A)(ii); Treas. Reg. § 1.403(b)-5(a)(2)]

If a 403(b) plan provides for both elective deferrals and other contributions (i.e., employer contributions or employee contributions (see Q 35:10)), the nondiscrimination requirement discussed in this question applies to the elective deferrals, and the nondiscrimination requirements discussed in Qs 35:16 through 35:19 and 35:21 apply to the other contributions.

Q 35:21   What is the universal availability requirement?

In the case of an annuity contract (see Q 35:6) purchased by an eligible employer (see Q 35:2) other than a church (see Q 35:55), the contract must bepurchased under a plan (see Q 35:9) that satisfies the universal availability requirement. [I.R.C. § 403(b)(12)(A)(ii); Treas. Reg. §§ 1.403(b)-3(a)(3), 1.403(b)-3(b)(3), 1.403(b)-5(c), 1.403(b)-5(d)]

All employees of the eligible employer must be permitted to have elective deferrals contributed on their behalf if any employee of the eligible employer may elect to have the organization make elective deferrals. Further, the employee's right to make elective deferrals also includes the right to designate elective deferrals as designated Roth contributions (see Q 35:49). [Treas. Reg. § 1.403(b)-5(b)(1); preamble to final regulations] This is referred to as "universal availability."

An employee is not treated as being permitted to have elective deferrals contributed on the employee's behalf unless the employee is provided an effective opportunity that satisfies the universal availability requirement. Whether an employee has an effective opportunity is determined based on all the relevant facts and circumstances, including notice of the availability of the election, the period of time during which an election may be made, and any other conditions on elections. A 403(b) plan satisfies the effective opportunity requirement only if, at least once during each plan year, the plan provides an employee with an effective opportunity to make (or change) a cash-or-deferred election (see Q 27:3) between cash or a contribution to the plan. Further, an effective opportunity includes the right to have elective deferrals made on the employee's behalf up to the lesser of the applicable limits, including any permissible catch-up elective deferrals (see Qs 35:27, 35:28), or the applicable limits under the contract with the largest limitation, and applies to part-time employees as well as full-time employees. An effective opportunity is not considered to exist if there are certain other rights or benefits that are conditioned (directly or indirectly) upon a participant making or failing to made a cash-or-deferred election with respect to a contribution to a 403(b) contract. [Treas. Reg. §§ 1.401(k)-1(e)(6)(i), 1.403(b)-5(b)(2)]

In the case of a 403(b) plan that covers the employees of more than one Section 501(c)(3) organization (see Q 35:3), the universal availability requirement applies separately to each common-law entity (that is, applies separately to each Section 501(c)(3) organization). In the case of a 403(b) plan that covers the employees of more than one State (see Q 35:4) entity, this requirement applies separately to each entity that is not part of a common payroll. An employer may condition the employee's right to have elective deferrals made on the employee's behalf on the employee electing an elective deferral of more than $200 for a year. An employer that historically has treated one or more of its various geographically distinct units as separate for employee benefit purposes may treat each unit as a separate organization if the unit is operated independently on a day-to-day basis. Units are not geographically distinct if such units are located within the same Standard Metropolitan Statistical Area (SMSA). [Treas. Reg. § 1.403(b)-5(b)(3)]

A plan does not fail to satisfy the universal availability requirement merely because it excludes one or more of the types of employees listed below. If any employee listed in category 4 or 5 below has the right to have elective deferrals made on such employee's behalf, then no employee in that category may be excluded. [Treas. Reg. § 1.403(b)-(5)(b)(4)(i)]

The following types of employees may be excluded:

1. Employees eligible under another 403(b) plan, or under a Section 457(b) eligible governmental plan, of the employer that permits an amount to be contributed or deferred at the election of the employee, but only if the effective opportunity requirement is satisfied.

2. Employees eligible to make a cash-or-deferred election under a 401(k) plan of the employer, but only if the effective opportunity requirement is satisfied.

3. Non-resident aliens.

4. Certain student-employees.

5. Employees who normally work fewer than 20 hours per week. For this purpose, an employee normally works fewer than 20 hours per week if and only if (a) for the 12-month period beginning on the date the employee's employment commenced, the employer reasonably expects the employee to work fewer than 1,000 hours of service (see Q 5:9), and (b) for each plan year ending after the close of the 12-month period beginning on the date the employee's employment commenced (or, if the plan so provides, each subsequent 12-month period), the employee worked fewer than 1,000 hours of service in the preceding 12-month period. [Treas. Reg. §§ 1.403(b)-(5)(b)(4)(ii), 1.403(b)-5(b)(4)(iii)]

Contributions to an annuity contract do not satisfy the universal availability requirement unless the contributions are made pursuant to a plan (see Q 35:9) and the terms of the plan satisfy this requirement. [Treas. Reg. § 1.403(b)-5(c)] This requirement does not apply to a 403(b) contract purchased by a church (see Q 35:55). [Treas. Reg. § 1.403(b)-5(d)]

The universal availability requirement is in addition to other applicable legal requirements. Specifically, this requirement does not reflect the requirements of Title I of ERISA that may apply with respect to a 403(b) plan, such as the ERISA vesting requirements (see Q 35:51).

For a discussion of automatic contribution arrangements and permissible withdrawals from such arrangements and the final regulations issued by IRS, see Qs 27:5–27:7.

Q 35:22   Can a 403(b) plan take permitted disparity into account?

Yes. For a discussion of permitted disparity, see chapter 7.

Q 35:23   Is there a limit on the amount of contributions to a 403(b) contract that will be excludable from the employee's income?

The amount of contributions to a 403(b) contract that the employee may exclude from gross income for the taxable year (usually, the calendar year) is subject to two separate restrictions, both of which are applied on an annual basis:

1. The limit on elective deferrals (see Q 35:26). [I.R.C. §§ 401(a)(30), 402(g), 403(b)(1)(E)]

2. The overall limitation (see Q 35:29). [I.R.C. § 415(a)(2)(B)]

Generally, the employee can exclude from gross income for the taxable year employer contributions to a 403(b) contract equal to the *lesser of:*

1. The limit on elective deferrals for the *calendar year,* or

2. The overall limitation for the *limitation year* (see Q 6:58) ending with or within the employee's taxable year.

The limitation year is the calendar year, but the employee may elect to change the limitation year to another 12-month period. To do this, the employee must attach a statement to the employee's income tax return filed for the taxable year in which the change is made. However, if the employee is in control of an employer, the limitation year is the limitation year of that employer. [Treas. Reg. § 1.415(j)–1(e)]

An annuity contract will not be considered to be described in Section 403(b) if any of the following conditions exists:

1. The annual benefit under a defined benefit plan with respect to any participant for any limitation year exceeds the limitations (see Q 6:11).

2. The contributions and other additions credited under a defined contribution plan with respect to any participant for any limitation year exceed the limitations on contribution (see Q 6:34).

3. The annuity contract has been disqualified for any year (see Q 6:57).

[Treas. Reg. § 1.415(a)-1(b)(1)]

If the contributions and other additions under an annuity contract that otherwise satisfies the applicable requirements (see Q 35:13) exceed the limitations on contributions with respect to any participant for any limitation year (regardless of whether the annuity contract is a defined contribution plan or a defined benefit plan), then the portion of the contract that includes such excess annual addition fails to be a 403(b) annuity contract and the remaining portion of the contract is a 403(b) annuity contract. However, the status of the remaining portion of the contract as an annuity contract is not retained unless, for the year of the excess and each year thereafter, the issuer of the contract maintains separate accounts for each such portion. In addition, if the benefit under an annuity contract that is a defined benefit plan and that otherwise satisfies the applicable requirements exceeds the limitations on benefits with respect to any participant for any limitation year, then the contract fails to be a 403(b) annuity contract. [Treas. Reg. § 1.415(a)-1(b)(2)]

A 403(b) annuity contract includes custodial accounts (see Q 35:7) and retirement income accounts (see Q 35:55). [Treas. Reg. § 1.415(a)-1(b)(3)]

An employee is permitted to designate all or a portion of the elective deferral as being includible in the employee's gross income as an after-tax contribution (see Q 35:49).

Q 35:24 What does includible compensation mean?

Includible compensation means the amount of compensation received by the employee from an eligible employer (see Q 35:2) that is includible in gross income for the most recent period ending not later than the close of the employee's taxable year that may be counted as one year of service (see Q 35:25). An employee's includible compensation for the most recent one-year period of service excludes any amount received by an employee during such one-year period attributable to a taxable year that precedes the taxable year by more than five years. The amount of includible compensation is determined without regard to any community property laws. [I.R.C. § 403(b)(3); Treas. Reg. §§ 1.403(b)-2(b)(11), 1.415(c)-2(g)(1), 1.415(c)-2(g)(3); IRS Notice 2001-37, 2001-1 C.B. 1340]

In addition, the following items are *included:*

1. Certain foreign income even if not includible in gross income, and
2. Elective deferrals and similar pretax contributions of the employee, including qualified transportation fringe benefit plans.

The following items are *excluded* for the purposes of determining an employee's includible compensation:

1. Employer contributions to the 403(b) contract;
2. Employer contributions to a qualified retirement plan for the benefit of the employee;
3. Current life insurance protection costs (see Q 35:8); and
4. Compensation earned while the employer is not an eligible employer.

[I.R.C. § 403(b)(3); Treas. Reg. § 1.403(b)-2(b)(11); Rev. Rul. 79-221, 1979-2 C.B. 188; Rev. Rul. 68-304, 1968-1 C.B. 179]

In determining an employee's most recent one-year period of service, all service performed by the employee during the taxable year is first taken into account, but an employee's most recent one-year period of service may not be the same as the employer's most recent annual work period.

> **Example 1.** Bonnie, a contract bridge professor who reports her income on a calendar-year basis, is employed by Klein State University on a full-time basis during the university's 2008–2009 and 2009–2010 academic years (October through May). Bonnie's most recent one-year period of service consists of her service performed during January through May 2009 (which is part of the 2008–2009 academic year), and her service performed during October through December 2009 (which is part of the 2009–2010 academic year).

In the case of a part-time employee or a full-time employee who is employed for only part of a year, it is necessary to aggregate the most recent periods of service to determine the most recent one-year period of service. In such a case, service during the current taxable year is first taken into account, then service during the next preceding taxable year is taken into account, and so forth until service equals, in the aggregate, one year of service.

> **Example 2.** If Gary, an employee of The Klein Music Foundation, who reports his income on a calendar-year basis, is employed on a full-time basis during the months July through December 2008 (one-half year of service), July through December 2009 (one-half year of service), and October through December 2010 (one-quarter year of service), his most recent one-year period of service consists of his service during 2010 (one-quarter year of service), his service during 2009 (one-half year of service), and his service during the months October through December 2008 (one-quarter year of service).

IRS has ruled that former university employees who, pursuant to a corporate merger, were transferred to and became employees of a tax-exempt corporation did not separate from service for purposes of calculating benefits under the corporation's 403(b) plan. Years of service and amounts of includible compensation were determined as if the employees' prior employment had been with their new employer corporation. The former university employees performed substantially the same services in the same location. [Priv. Ltr. Rul. 9808039]

For purposes of the overall limitation (see Q 35:29), a former employee is deemed to have monthly includible compensation for the period through the end of the taxable year of the employee in which the employee ceases to be an employee and through the end of each of the next five taxable years. The amount of the monthly includible compensation is equal to one-twelfth of the former employee's includible compensation during the former employee's most recent year of service. Accordingly, nonelective employer contributions for a former employee must not exceed the annual addition limitation up to the lesser of the annual addition dollar amount or the former employee's annual includible compensation based on the former employee's average monthly compensation during the most recent year of service. [Treas. Reg. § 1.403(b)-4(d)(1)]

Example 3. Klein State University is a Section 501(c)(3) organization, operated on the basis of a June 30 fiscal year, that maintains a 403(b) plan for its employees. In 2008, Klein State amends the plan to provide for a temporary early retirement incentive under which the college will make a nonelective contribution for any participant who satisfies certain minimum age and service conditions and who retires before June 30, 2010. The contribution will equal 110 percent of the participant's rate of pay for one year and will be payable over a period ending no later than the end of the fifth fiscal year that begins after retirement. It is assumed that, under the facts and circumstances, the post-retirement contributions made for participants who satisfy the minimum age and service conditions and retire before June 30, 2010 do not discriminate in favor of former employees who are HCEs (see Q 3:2). Bonnie retires under the early retirement incentive on March 12, 2010, and Bonnie's annual includible compensation for the period from March 1, 2009 through February 28, 2010 (which is her most recent one year of service) is $30,000. The annual addition applicable dollar limit is assumed to be $49,000 for 2010 and $51,000 for 2011. Klein State contributes $30,000 for Bonnie for 2010 and $3,000 for her for 2011 (totaling $33,000, or 110 percent of $30,000). No other contributions are made to a 403(b) contract for Bonnie for those years. The contributions made for Bonnie do not exceed her includible compensation for 2010 or 2011.

Example 4. The Klein Music Foundation is a Section 501(c)(3) organization that maintains a 403(b) plan for its employees. The plan provides for the Foundation to make monthly nonelective contributions equal to 20 percent of the monthly includible compensation for each eligible employee. In addition, the plan provides for contributions to continue for five years following the retirement of any employee after age 64 and completion of at least 20 years of service (based on the employee's average annual rate of base salary in the preceding three calendar years ended before the date of retirement). It is assumed that, under the facts and circumstances, the post-retirement contributions made for participants who satisfy the minimum age and service conditions do not discriminate in favor of former employees who are HCEs. Gary retires on July 1, 2010 at age 64 after completion of 20 or more years of service. At that date, Gary's annual includible compensation for the most recently ended fiscal year of the Foundation is $72,000, and his average monthly rate of base salary for 2007 through 2009 is $5,000. The Foundation contributes $1,200 per month (20 percent of one-twelfth of $72,000) from January of 2010 through June of 2010 and contributes $1,000 (20 percent of $5,000) per month for Gary from July of 2010 through June of 2015. The annual addition applicable dollar limit is assumed to be at least $49,000 for 2010 through 2015. No other contributions are made to a 403(b) contract for Gary for those years. The contributions made for Gary do not exceed his includible compensation for any of the years from 2010 through 2014.

Example 5. Dane Public University maintains a 403(b) plan under which it contributes annually 10 percent of compensation for participants, including for the first five calendar years following the date on which the participant ceases to be an employee. The plan provides that, if a participant who is a former employee dies during the first five calendar years following the date on which the participant ceases to be an employee, a contribution is made that is equal to the lesser of (1) the excess of the individual's includible compensation for that year over the contributions previously made for the individual for that year or (2) the total contributions that would have been made on the individual's behalf thereafter if the individual had survived to the end of the five-year period.

Jane's annual includible compensation is $72,000 (so that her monthly includible compensation is $6,000). A $600 contribution is made for Jane for January of the first taxable year following retirement (10 percent of Jane's monthly includible compensation of $6,000). Jane dies during February of that year. The University makes a contribution for Jane for February equal to $11,400 (her monthly includible compensation for January and February, reduced by $600). The contribution does not exceed the amount of Jane's includible compensation for the taxable year for annual addition limitation purposes, but any additional contributions would exceed her includible compensation for such purposes.

Compensation may be treated as continuing for certain former employees who are disabled (see Q 6:41). [IRC § 415(e)(3)(C); Treas. Reg. §§ 1.403(b)-4(d)(3), 1.415(c)-2(g)(4)]

Q 35:25 How is a year of service determined?

A year of service means each full year during which an individual is a full-time employee of an eligible employer (see Q 35:2), plus fractional credit for each part of a year during which the individual is either a full-time employee of an eligible employer for a part of the year or a part-time employee of an eligible employer. In no case shall the number of years of service be less than one. [I.R.C. § 403(b)(4); Treas. Reg. § 1.403(b)-2(b)(21); Ravel, 26 T.C.M. 885 (1967)]

For purposes of determining a participant's includible compensation (see Q 35:24) and a participant's years of service for the catch-up rule (see Q 35:28) and for employer contributions for former employees (see Q 35:24), an employee must be credited with a full year of service for each year during which the individual is a full-time employee of the eligible employer, and a fraction of a year for each part of a year during which the individual is a full-time or part-time employee of the eligible employer. An individual's number of years of service equals the aggregate of the annual work periods during which the individual is employed by the eligible employer. [Treas. Reg. § 1.403(b)-4(e)(1)]

A year of service is based on the employer's annual work period, not the employee's taxable year. For example, in determining whether a university professor is employed full time, the annual work period is the school's academic year. However, in no case may an employee accumulate more than one year of service in a 12-month period. [Treas. Reg. § 1.403(b)-4(e)(2)] With respect to any 403(b) contract of an eligible employer, any period during which an individual is not an employee of that eligible employer is disregarded. [Treas. Reg. § 1.403(b)-4(e)(3)(i)]

Each annual work period during which an individual is employed full time by an eligible employer constitutes one year of service. In determining whether an individual is employed full time, the amount of work that the individual actually performs is compared with the amount of work that is normally required of individuals performing similar services from which substantially all of their annual compensation is derived. [Treas. Reg. § 1.403(b)-4(e)(4)]

An individual is treated as performing a fraction of a year of service for each annual work period during which the individual is a full-time employee for part of the annual work period and for each annual work period during which the individual is a part-time employee either for the entire annual work period or for a part of the annual work period. In determining the fraction that represents the fractional year of service for an individual employed full time for part of an annual work period, the numerator is the period of time (e.g., weeks or months) during which the individual is a full-time employee during that annual work period, and the denominator is the period of time that is the annual work period. In determining the fraction that represents the fractional year of service of an individual who is employed part time for the entire annual work period, the numerator is the amount of work performed by the individual, and the denominator is the amount of work normally required of individuals who perform similar services and who are employed full time for the entire annual work period. In determining the fraction representing the fractional year of service of an individual who is employed part time for part of an annual work period, the fractional year of service that would apply if the individual were a part-time employee for a full annual work period is multiplied by the fractional year of service that would apply if the individual were a full-time employee for the part of an annual work period. [Treas. Reg. § 1.403(b)-4(e)(5)]

In measuring the amount of work of an individual performing particular services, the work performed is determined based on the individual's hours of service (see Q 5:9), except that a plan may use a different measure of work if appropriate under the facts and circumstances. For example, a plan may provide for a university professor's work to be measured by the number of courses taught during an annual work period in any case in which that individual's work assignment is generally based on a specific number of courses to be taught. [Treas. Reg. § 1.403(b)-4(e)(6)]

In the case of a part-time employee or a full-time employee who is employed for only part of the year determined on the basis of the employer's annual work period, the employee's most recent periods of service are aggregated to determine the employee's most recent one-year period of service. In such a case, there is first taken into account the employee's service during the annual work period for which the last year of service's includible compensation is being determined; then there is taken into account the employee's service during the next preceding annual work period based on whole months; and so forth, until the employee's service equals, in the aggregate, one year of service. [Treas. Reg. § 1.403(b)-4(e)(7)]

If, at the close of a taxable year, an employee has, after application of all of the above rules, some portion of one year of service (but has accumulated less than one year of service), the employee is deemed to have one year of service. Other than for this purpose, fractional years of service are not rounded up. [Treas. Reg. § 1.403(b)-4(e)(8)]

Example 1. Adam is employed half time in 2009 and 2010 as a doctor by a hospital that is a Section 501(c)(3) organization. Adam earns $20,000 from the hospital in each of those years and retires on December 31, 2010. For purposes of determining Adam's includible compensation during his last year of service, Adam's most recent periods of service are aggregated to determine his most recent one-year period of service. In this case, since Adam worked half time in 2009 and 2010, the compensation he earned in those two years is aggregated to produce his includible compensation for his last full year in service. Thus, in this case, the $20,000 that Adam earned in 2009 and 2010 for his half-time work is aggregated, so that Adam has $40,000 of includible compensation for his most recent one year of service.

Example 2. Caroline is employed as a part-time professor by public Law School C during the first semester of its two-semester 2009–2010 academic year. While Caroline teaches one course generally for three hours a week during the first semester of the academic year, C's full-time faculty members generally teach for nine hours a week during the full academic year. For purposes of calculating how much of a year of service Caroline performs in the 2009–2010 academic year, the fraction is calculated as follows: because Caroline teaches one course at C for three hours per week for one semester and other faculty members at C teach nine hours per week for two semesters, Caroline is considered to have completed $3/18$ or $1/6$ of a year of service during the 2009–2010 academic year, determined as follows:

1. The fractional year of service if Caroline were a part-time employee for a full year is $3/9$ (number of hours worked divided by the usual number of hours of work required for that position).

2. The fractional year of service if Caroline were a full-time employee for half of a year is $1/2$ (one semester, divided by the usual two-semester annual work period).

3. These fractions are multiplied to obtain the fractional year of service: $3/9$ times $1/2$, or $3/18$, equals $1/6$ of a year of service.

An employee can earn a year of service only during a period in which the organization is an eligible employer. A teacher who changes employment from one school system to another in the same State cannot include years of service with the first school system for purposes of computing years of service for the second. [Rev. Rul. 69-629, 1969-2 C.B. 101]

Q 35:26   Is there a dollar limit on the amount of elective deferrals under a 403(b) contract?

Elective deferrals relate to amounts contributed to (1) a 403(b) contract under a salary reduction agreement (see Q 35:11), (2) a 401(k) plan pursuant to a cash-or-deferred arrangement (see Qs 27:1, 27:2), (3) a simplified employee pension (SEP) under a salary reduction agreement (see Q 32:9), and (4) a SIMPLE plan under a salary reduction agreement (see Qs 33:13, 33:30). [I.R.C. § 402(g)(3); Treas. Reg. §§ 1.402(g)-1(b), 1.403(b)-2(b)(7), 1.403(b)-2(b)(17)(i)] Elective deferrals also relate to any designated Roth contributions (see Q 35:49). [Treas. Reg. §§ 1.402(g)-1(b)(5), 1.403(b)-2(b)(17)(ii)]

An employee's elective deferrals under all plans in which the employee participates (even if not maintained by the same employer) during the taxable year are limited to an applicable dollar amount, and the amount of elective deferrals in excess of the applicable dollar amount (excess deferrals) is included in the employee's gross income, except to the extent the excess deferrals are composed of designated Roth contributions and, thus, are already includible in gross income. A designated Roth contribution is treated as an excess deferral only to the extent that the total amount of designated Roth contributions for an individual exceeds the applicable limit for the taxable year or the designated Roth contributions are identified as excess deferrals and the individual receives a distribution of the excess deferrals and allocable income (see Qs 27:63, 35:29). [I.R.C. § 402(g)(1); Treas. Reg. §§ 1.402(g)-1(a), 1.402(g)-1(d), 1.403(b)-4(c)(1); IRS Notice 2005-75, 2005-2 C.B. 929]

The 2006 $15,000 limit on elective deferrals is adjusted for inflation (see Q 27:51). For taxable years beginning in 2010, the applicable dollar amount remained at $16,500. [IRS Notice 2009-94, 2009-2 C.B. 848] For the prior five years, the applicable dollar amount was:

For taxable years beginning in calendar year	The applicable dollar amount
2009	$16,500
2008	15,500
2007	15,500
2006	15,000
2005	14,000

Because all of the employee's elective deferrals for the taxable year are aggregated, if the employee makes an elective deferral to a 403(b) contract of the applicable dollar amount for the taxable year, no amount may be contributed to a 401(k) plan, a SEP, or a SIMPLE plan under salary reduction agreements for that year. [I.R.C. §§ 401(a)(30); 402(g)(1), 402(g)(4), 403(b)(1)(E); Treas. Reg. §§ 1.402(g)-1(d)(2), 1.402(g)-1(d)(4); IRS Notice 87-13, 1987-1 C.B. 432] However, an employee can make an elective deferral to a 403(b) contract of the applicable dollar amount for the taxable year and can *also* make an elective deferral to a Section 457(b) plan of the applicable dollar amount for the same taxable year. [Priv. Ltr. Rul. 200934012] A 403(b) contract must require that all elective deferrals for an employee not exceed the limits, including elective deferrals for the employee under the contract and any other elective deferrals under the plan under which the contract is purchased and under all other plans, contracts, or arrangements of the employer. [Treas. Reg. § 1.403(b)-3(a)(4)]

Example 1. The Wagger State University, an eligible employer, offers its employees 403(b) contracts to which elective deferrals may be made. For the 2010 taxable year, two of Wagger's employees, Harold and Renee, contribute $3,500 and $8,500, respectively, to the 403(b) contract. Harold and Renee also participate in another employer's 401(k) plan for 2010. The maximum amounts that Harold and Renee may contribute under the 401(k) plan for their 2010 taxable year are $13,000 ($16,500 − $3,500) and $8,000 ($16,500 − $8,500), respectively.

Required contributions made by employees under a 403(b) plan are not subject to the limit on elective deferrals or treated as made pursuant to a salary reduction agreement if the required contributions are a condition of employment when made. [Priv. Ltr. Ruls. 199951048, 9610009, 9610008, 9610007] If an employee has the right or ability to terminate or modify an election, however, the contributions are elective deferrals even if the employee never exercises this right. [I.R.M. 7.7.1.13.5.1.1]

Example 2. Jason participates in a 403(b) plan; and, in order to receive employer contributions under the plan, Jason is required to elect to defer 3 percent of salary in the form of mandatory contributions. Jason has the option of revoking this election at any time, although Jason never terminates his election. The mandatory contributions are elective deferrals because Jason's election is revocable.

Example 3. Assume the same facts as in Example 2, except that the plan further provides that an election to terminate participation in the plan is irrevocable. Thus, an employee who terminates his election will be permanently excluded from participating in the plan. Even so, because the election to participate is revocable, the mandatory contributions are elective deferrals.

For a discussion of correcting excess deferrals and the tax consequences of making excess deferrals, see Qs 27:63 and 27:64.

See Q 35:30 for illustrative examples.

Q 35:27   What are elective deferral catch-up contributions?

An individual who participates in a 403(b) plan, who will attain age 50 by the end of the taxable year and for whom no other elective deferrals (see Q 35:26) may otherwise be made for the taxable year because of the application of any limitation contained in the Code (e.g., the annual limit on elective deferrals) or of the 403(b) plan will be able to make additional elective deferrals (i.e., catch-up contributions) for that taxable year.

The maximum catch-up contribution that an eligible individual may make for the taxable year is the *lesser* of:

1. The applicable dollar amount, or
2. The individual's compensation for the year reduced by all of the individual's other elective deferrals for the year to 403(b) contracts, 401(k) plans (see Q 27:1), salary reduction SEPs (see Q 32:9), SIMPLE plans (see Q 33:1), and Section 457 plans.

The 2006 $5,000 limitation is adjusted for inflation in $500 increments in the same manner as the adjustment to the elective deferral dollar limitation (see Q 27:51). For taxable years beginning in 2010, the applicable dollar amount remained at $5,500. [IRS Notice 2009-94, 2009-2 C.B. 848] For the prior five years, the applicable dollar amount was:

For taxable years beginning in calendar year	*The applicable dollar amount*
2009	$5,500
2008	5,000
2007	5,000
2006	5,000
2005	4,000

Catch-up contributions are not subject to any other contribution limits and are not taken into account in applying other contribution limits and, therefore, are not considered, for example, for the elective deferral limitation or the annual addition limitation (see Q 35:29). In addition, catch-up contributions are not subject to the nondiscrimination rules (see Qs 35:16, 35:20). However, a 403(b) plan fails to meet the nondiscrimination requirements with respect to benefits, rights, and features (see Q 4:20) unless the program allows all eligible individuals to make the same election with respect to catch-up contributions (see Q 35:21).

[I.R.C. § 414(v); Treas. Reg. §§ 1.403(b)-2(b)(4), 1.403(b)-4(c)(2)(i)]

IRS has promulgated regulations regarding catch-up contributions. For details, see Qs 27:53 through 27:61.

An eligible individual can both make an elective deferral catch-up contribution and utilize the special catch-up rule (see Q 35:28). [Treas. Reg. § 1.403(b)-4(c)(2)(ii)]

Q 35:28   Is there a special catch-up for certain organizations?

An employee who has completed 15 years of service (see Q 35:25), a qualified employee, with an educational organization, a hospital, a home health service agency, or a health and welfare service agency (a qualified organization) is eligible for a special catch-up rule, which increases the dollar limit. A health and welfare service agency is: (1) an organization whose primary activity is to provide services that constitute medical care (such as a hospice); (2) a Section 501(c)(3) organization (see Q 35:3) whose primary activity is the prevention of cruelty to individuals or animals; (3) an adoption agency; or (4) an agency that provides substantial personal services to the needy as part of its primary activity (such as a Section 501(c)(3) organization that provides meals to needy individuals, is a home health service agency, provides services to help individuals who have substance abuse problems, or provides help to the disabled). Under the catch-up rule, the dollar limit for the qualified employee's taxable year is increased by the *least* of the following amounts:

1. $3,000;
2. $15,000 reduced by amounts previously excluded from gross income in prior taxable years under this catch-up rule and by the aggregate amount of designated Roth contributions (see Q 35:49) for prior taxable years under this catch-up rule; or
3. $5,000 multiplied by the qualified employee's number of years of service (see Q 35:25) with the qualified organization, reduced by all prior elective deferrals under all plans of the qualified organization.

[I.R.C. § 402(g)(7); Treas. Reg. §§ 1.402(g)-1(d)(3), 1.403(b)-4(c)(3); preamble to final regulations; Priv. Ltr. Ruls. 200046040, 200025063]

Based upon the above limitation, under the catch-up rule, the dollar limit (see Q 35:26) for any taxable year cannot be increased by more than $3,000. Any catch-up contribution for an employee who is eligible for both an age 50 catch-up (see Q 35:27) and the special catch-up is treated first as a special catch-up to the extent a special catch-up is permitted, and then as an amount contributed as an age 50 catch-up (to the extent the age 50 catch-up amount exceeds the maximum special catch-up). [Treas. Reg. § 1.403(b)-4(c)(3)(iv)] An employee can make an elective deferral to a 403(b) contract of the applicable dollar amount for the taxable year and can *also* make an elective deferral to a Section 457(b) plan of the applicable dollar amount for the same taxable year. Furthermore, the employee can contribute the additional special catch-up amount to the 403(b) plan without reducing the contribution to the Section 457(b) plan. [Priv. Ltr. Rul. 200934012]

See Q 35:30 for illustrative examples.

Q 35:29 What is the overall limitation?

A 403(b) plan is treated as a defined contribution plan (see Q 2:2) for purposes of the limitations on contributions and, thus, is subject to the rules regarding the amount of annual additions (see Q 6:34) that may be made to a participant's account for a limitation year (see Qs 6:58, 35:23). In other words, the annual addition with respect to any limitation year may not exceed the *lesser* of $40,000, as adjusted for inflation (see Q 6:34), or 100 percent of compensation (see Q 35:24). [I.R.C. §§ 415(a)(2)(B), 415(c)(1), 415(c)(3)(E); Treas. Reg. §§ 1.415(c)-(1)(a)(1), 1.415(c)-1(a)(2)(iii); Priv. Ltr. Rul. 9529006] In the event that aggregating a 403(b) plan and a defined contribution plan causes the limitations on contributions applicable to a participant under the aggregated defined contribution plans to be exceeded for a particular limitation year, the excess of the contributions to the 403(b) plan plus the annual additions to the plan over such limitations is attributable to the 403(b) plan and therefore includible in the gross income of the participant for the taxable year with or within which that limitation year ends (see Q 6:57). [Treas. Reg. § 1.415(g)-1(b)(3)(iv)(C)]

For purposes of the annual addition limitation, the amount contributed toward the purchase of a 403(b) contract is treated as allocated to the employee's account as of the last day of the limitation year ending with or within the taxable year during which the contribution is made (see Q 6:36). [Treas. Reg. § 1.415(c)-1(b)(6)(i)] Excess elective deferrals distributed within the correction period (see Q 27:65) are not considered annual additions, but excess deferrals distributed after the correction period are counted. [Treas. Reg. §§ 1.402(g)-1(e)(1)(ii), 1.402(g)-1(e)(8)(iii)] These rules generally apply to distributions of excess deferrals that are designated Roth contributions (see Q 27:96) and the attributable income. Thus, if a designated Roth account (see Q 27:96) includes any excess deferrals, any distribution of amounts attributable to those excess deferrals is includible in gross income (without adjustment for any return of investment; see Q 13:3). In addition, such distributions cannot be qualified distributions (see Qs 27:98, 27:105) and are not eligible rollover distributions (see Q 34:8). For this purpose, if a designated Roth account includes any excess deferrals, any distributions from the account are treated as attributable to those excess deferrals until the total amount distributed from the designated Roth account equals the total of such deferrals and attributable income. [Treas. Reg. § 1.402(g)-1(e)(8)(iv)]

Certain individuals may make catch-up contributions (see Q 35:27), and a catch-up contribution will not be subject to, or be part of, the annual addition limitation. [I.R.C. § 414(v)(3)(A)]

One of the requirements that a 403(b) plan must satisfy is that the annual additions to the 403(b) contract may not exceed the applicable limitations treating contributions and other additions as annual additions (see Q 35:13). All 403(b) contracts purchased for an individual by an employer are treated as purchased under a single contract. The limitations do not apply to rollover contributions (see Q 35:45), but after-tax contributions are taken into account. [Treas. Reg. §§ 1.403(b)-3(a)(9), 1.403(b)-3(b), 1.403(b)-4(a), 1.403(b)-4(b)]

See Q 35:30 for illustrative examples.

In the case of a 403(b) plan, except as provided below, the participant on whose behalf the annuity contract is purchased is considered for purposes of the limitations on benefits and contributions to have exclusive control of the annuity contract. Accordingly, except as provided below, the participant, and not the participant's employer who purchased the 403(b) contract, is deemed to maintain the annuity contract, and such a 403(b) contract is not aggregated with a qualified retirement plan that is maintained by the participant's employer. [Treas. Reg. § 1.415(f)-1(f)(1)]

Where a participant on whose behalf a 403(b) contract is purchased is in control of any employer for a limitation year as discussed below (regardless of whether the employer controlled by the participant is the employer maintaining the 403(b) plan), the 403(b) contract for the benefit of the participant is treated as a defined contribution plan maintained by both the controlled employer and the participant for that limitation year. Accordingly, where a participant on whose behalf a 403(b) contract is purchased is in control of any employer for a limitation year, the 403(b) contract is aggregated with all other defined contribution plans maintained by that employer. In addition, in such a case, the 403(b) contract is aggregated with all other defined contribution plans maintained by the employee or any other employer that is controlled by the employee. Thus, for example, if a doctor is employed by a nonprofit hospital that provides him with a 403(b) contract, and the doctor also maintains a private practice as a shareholder owning more than 50 percent of a professional corporation, then any defined contribution plan of the professional corporation must be aggregated with the 403(b) plan for purposes of applying the limitations on contributions. For these purposes, it is immaterial whether the 403(b) contract is purchased as a result of a salary reduction agreement (see Q 35:11) between the employer and the participant. [Treas. Reg. § 1.415(f)-1(f)(2)(i)]

A participant is in control of an employer for a limitation year if, pursuant to the affiliated employer rules (see Q 6:7), a plan maintained by that employer would have to be aggregated with a plan maintained by an employer that is 100 percent owned by the participant. Thus, for example, if a participant owns 60 percent of the common stock of a corporation, the participant is considered to be in control of that employer for purposes of applying the preceding paragraph. [Treas. Reg. § 1.415(f)-1(f)(2)(ii)]

If a 403(b) plan is aggregated with a qualified retirement plan of a controlled employer, the plans must satisfy the limitations on contributions both separately and on an aggregate basis. In applying separately the limitations to the qualified retirement plan and to the 403(b) plan, compensation from the controlled employer may not be aggregated with compensation from the employer purchasing the 403(b) contract. [Treas. Reg. § 1.415(f)-1(f)(3)]

See Examples 6 and 7 of Q 6:56 for illustrations of these aggregation rules.

Q 35:30   Has IRS published examples illustrating the limitations on contributions to 403(b) contracts?

Yes, and the examples are as follows:

Example 1. *Facts illustrating application of the basic dollar limit.* Participant B, who is 45, is eligible to participate in a State university 403(b) plan in 2010. B is not a qualified employee (see Q 35:28). The plan permits elective deferrals, but no other employer contributions are made under the plan. The plan provides limitations on elective deferrals up to the maximum permitted (see Q 35:26) and the additional age 50 catch-up amount (see Q 35:27). For 2010, B will receive includible compensation (see Q 35:24) of $42,000 from the eligible employer. B desires to elect to have the maximum elective deferral possible contributed in 2010. For 2010, the basic dollar limit for elective deferrals is $16,500, and the additional dollar amount permitted under the age 50 catch-up is $5,500. B is not eligible for the age 50 catch-up in 2010 because B is 45 in 2010 or for the special catch-up because B is not a qualified employee. Accordingly, the maximum elective deferral that B may elect for 2010 is $16,500.

Example 2. *Facts illustrating application of the includible compensation limitation.* The facts are the same as in Example 1, except B's includible compensation is $14,000. Contributions may not exceed 100 percent of includible compensation. Accordingly, the maximum elective deferral that B may elect for 2010 is $14,000.

Example 3. *Facts illustrating application of the age 50 catch-up.* Participant C, who is 55, is eligible to participate in a State university 403(b) plan in 2010. The plan permits elective deferrals, but no other employer contributions are made under the plan. The plan provides limitations on elective deferrals up to the maximum permitted and the additional age 50 catch-up amount. For 2010, C will receive includible compensation of $48,000 from the eligible employer. C desires to elect to have the maximum elective deferral possible contributed in 2010. For 2010, the basic dollar limit for elective deferrals is $16,500, and the additional dollar amount permitted under the age 50 catch-up is $5,500. C does not have 15 years of service and thus is not a qualified employee. C is eligible for the age 50 catch-up in 2010 because C is 55 in 2010 but is not eligible for the special catch-up because C is not a qualified employee. Accordingly, the maximum elective deferral that C may elect for 2010 is $22,000 ($16,500 plus $5,500).

Example 4. *Facts illustrating application of both the age 50 and the special catch-up.* The facts are the same as in Example 3, except that C is a qualified employee for purposes of the special catch-up provisions. For 2010, the maximum additional elective deferral for which C qualifies under the special catch-up is $3,000. The maximum elective deferrals that C may elect for 2010 is $25,000. This is the sum of the basic limit on elective deferrals of $16,500, plus the $3,000 additional special catch-up amount for which C qualifies, plus the additional age 50 catch-up amount of $5,500.

Example 5. *Facts illustrating calculation of years of service with a predecessor organization for purposes of the special catch-up.* Participant A is an employee of hospital H and is eligible to participate in a 403(b) plan of H in 2010. A does not have 15 years of service with H, but A has previously made special catch-up deferrals to a 403(b) plan maintained by hospital P, which has since been acquired by H. The special catch-up amount for which A qualifies must be calculated taking into account A's prior years of service and elective deferrals with the predecessor hospital if and only if A did not have any severance from service in connection with the acquisition.

Example 6. *Facts illustrating application of the age 50 catch-up and the annual addition dollar limitation.* The facts are the same as in Example 4, except that the employer makes a nonelective contribution for each employee equal to 20 percent of C's compensation (which is $48,000). Thus, the employer makes a nonelective contribution for C for 2010 equal to $9,600. The plan provides that a participant is not permitted to make elective deferrals to the extent the elective deferrals would result in contributions in excess of the maximum and provides that contributions are reduced in the following order: the special catch-up elective deferrals are reduced first; the age 50 catch-up elective deferrals are reduced next; and then the basic elective deferrals are reduced. For 2010, the applicable dollar limit is $49,000. The maximum elective deferral that C may elect for 2010 is $25,000. This is the sum of the basic limit on elective deferrals of $16,500, plus the $3,000 additional special catch-up amount for which C qualifies, plus the additional age 50 catch-up amount of $5,500. The annual addition limit would not be exceeded because the sum of the $9,600 nonelective contribution and the $25,000 elective deferrals does not exceed the lesser of $54,000 (the sum of $49,000 plus the $5,000 additional age 50 catch-up amount) or $53,500 (the sum of C's includible compensation for 2010 ($48,000) plus the $5,500 additional age 50 catch-up amount).

Example 7. *Facts further illustrating application of the age 50 catch-up and the annual addition dollar limitation.* The facts are the same as in Example 6, except that C's includible compensation for 2010 is $60,000 and the plan provides for a nonelective contribution equal to 50 percent of includible compensation, so that the employer nonelective contribution for C for 2010 is $30,000 (50 percent of $60,000). The maximum elective deferral that C may elect for 2010 is $24,000. An elective deferral in excess of this amount would exceed the sum of the dollar limit plus the additional age 50 catch-up amount, because the sum of the employer's nonelective contribution of $30,000 plus an elective deferral in excess of $24,000 would exceed $54,000 (the sum of the $49,000 dollar limit plus the $5,000 additional age 50 catch-up amount). However, an elective deferral in excess of $22,000 would exceed the limitation on elective deferrals unless a special catch-up amount were permitted.

Example 8. *Facts further illustrating application of the age 50 catch-up and the annual addition dollar limitation.* The facts are the same as in Example 7, except that the plan provides for a nonelective contribution for C equal to $49,000 (the annual addition dollar limit). The maximum elective deferral that C may elect for 2010 is $5,500. An elective deferral in excess of this amount would exceed the sum of the dollar limit plus the additional age 50 catch-up amount ($5,500), because the sum of the employer's nonelective contribution of $49,000 plus an elective deferral in excess of $5,500 would exceed $54,500 (the sum of the $49,000 dollar limit plus the $5,500 additional age 50 catch-up amount).

Example 9. *Facts illustrating application of the age 50 catch-up and the annual addition includible compensation limitation.* The facts are the same as in Example 7, except that C's includible compensation for 2010 is $28,000, so that the employer nonelective contribution for C for 2010 is $14,000 (50 percent of $28,000). The maximum elective deferral that C may elect for 2010 is $19,500. An elective deferral in excess of this amount would exceed the sum of the compensation percentage limit plus the additional age 50 catch-up amount, because C's includible compensation is $28,000 and the sum of the employer's nonelective contribution of $14,000 plus an elective deferral in excess of $19,500 would exceed $33,500 (the sum of 100 percent of C's includible compensation plus the $5,500 additional age 50 catch-up amount).

Example 10. *Facts illustrating that elective deferrals cannot exceed compensation otherwise payable.* Employee D is age 60, has includible compensation of $16,000, and wishes to contribute elective deferrals of $20,000 for the year. No nonelective contributions are made for D. Because a contribution is an elective deferral only if it relates to an amount that would otherwise be included in the participant's compensation, the effective limitation on elective deferrals for a participant whose compensation is less than the dollar limit for elective deferrals is the participant's compensation. Thus, D cannot make elective deferrals in excess of D's actual compensation, which is $16,000, even though the dollar limit exceeds that amount.

Example 11. *Facts illustrating calculation of the special catch-up.* For 2010, employee E, who is age 50, is eligible to participate in a 403(b) plan of hospital H, which is a Section 501(c)(3) organization. H's plan permits elective deferrals and provides for an employer contribution of 10 percent of a participant's compensation. The plan provides limitations on elective deferrals up to the maximum permitted. For 2010, E's includible compensation is $50,000. E wishes to have the maximum elective deferral possible contributed in 2010. E has previously made $62,000 of elective deferrals under the plan, but has never made an election for a special catch-up elective deferral. For 2010, the basic dollar limit is $16,500, the additional dollar amount permitted under the age 50 catch-up is $5,500, E's employer will make a nonelective contribution of $5,000 (10 percent of $50,000 compensation), and E is a qualified employee of a qualified employer (see Q 35:28). The maximum elective deferral that E may elect for 2010 is $25,000. This is the sum of the basic limit of $16,500, plus the $3,000 maximum additional special catch-up amount for which E qualifies in 2010, plus the additional age 50 catch-up amount of $5,500. The limitation on the additional catch-up amount is not less than the first limitation of $3,000, because the second limitation is $15,000 ($15,000 minus zero) and the third limitation is $13,000 ($5,000 times 15, minus $62,000 of total deferrals in prior years). These conclusions would be unaffected if H were an eligible governmental employer that has a Section 457(b) eligible governmental plan and E were in the past to have made annual deferrals to that plan, because contributions to a Section 457(b) eligible governmental plan do not constitute elective deferrals; and these conclusions would also be the same if H had a 401(k) plan (see Q 27:1) and E were in the past to have made elective deferrals to that plan, assuming that those elective deferrals did not exceed $10,000 ($5,000 times 15, minus the sum of $62,000 plus $10,000, equals $3,000), so as to result in the third limitation being less than $3,000.

Example 12. *Facts illustrating calculation of the special catch-up in the next calendar year.* The facts are the same as in Example 11, except that, for 2011, E has includible compensation of $60,000. For 2011, E has previously made $87,000 of elective deferrals ($62,000 deferred before 2010, plus the $16,500 in basic elective deferrals in 2010, the $3,000 maximum additional special catch-up amount in 2010, plus the $5,500 age 50 catch-up amount in 2010). However, the $5,500 age 50 catch-up amount deferred in 2010 is disregarded for purposes of applying the limitation to determine the special catch-up amount. Thus, for 2011, only $81,500 of elective deferrals are taken into account in applying the third limitation. For 2011, the basic dollar limit for elective deferrals is assumed to be $17,000, the additional dollar amount permitted under the age 50 catch-up is assumed to be $5,500, and E's employer contributes $6,000 (10 percent of $60,000 compensation) as a non-elective contribution. The maximum elective deferral that E may elect for 2011 is $22,500. This is the sum of the basic limit on elective deferrals equal to $17,000, plus the additional age 50 catch-up amount of $5,500. E is not entitled to any additional special catch-up amount for 2011 due to the third limitation (16 times $5,000 equals $80,000, minus E's total prior elective deferrals of $81,500 equals zero for this purpose).

Q 35:31 What is an excess contribution?

An excess contribution is (1) the amount by which the contributions to a *custodial account* (see Q 35:7) for the employee's taxable year exceed the *lesser* of the amount excludable from gross income or the overall limitation (see Q 35:29) plus (2) any excess carried over from the preceding taxable year. Rollover contributions are not included (see Q 35:45). [I.R.C. §§ 4973(c)(1), 4973(c)(2); Prop. Treas. Reg. § 54.4973-1(d)]

If an excess contribution is made to a custodial account, the excess amount is subject to a 6 percent excise tax and the penalty will be charged each year the excess contribution remains in the custodial account. The excise tax is determined as of the close of the taxable year and cannot exceed 6 percent of the value of the custodial account. The excise tax is imposed on the employee, not on the employer. [I.R.C. § 4973(a); Prop. Treas. Reg. § 54.4973-1(e)]

An excess contribution can be corrected by either one or both of the following methods:

1. Making taxable distributions to the employee from the custodial account, or

2. Contributing in a subsequent taxable year less than the lower of the amount excludable from gross income or overall limitation applicable to the employee for that year.

[Treas. Reg. § 1.403(b)-7(c); IRS Pub. 571]

Form 5330, Return of Excise Taxes Related to Employee Benefit Plans, is used to report the excise tax and must be filed by the employer no later than the last day of the seventh month following the close of the taxable year.

This excise tax does *not* apply to contributions made to *annuity contracts;* it applies only with respect to *custodial accounts.*

If an excess annual addition (see Q 35:29) is made to a contract that otherwise satisfies the requirements applicable to 403(b) contracts (see Q 35:13), then the portion of the contract that includes such excess annual addition fails to be a 403(b) contract (and instead is a contract to which the nonqualified annuity rules apply) and the remaining portion of the contract is a 403(b) contract. This is not satisfied unless, for the year of the excess and each year thereafter, the issuer of the contract maintains separate accounts for each such portion. Thus, the entire contract fails to be a 403(b) contract if an excess annual addition is made and a separate account is not maintained with respect to the excess. [Treas. Reg. § 1.403(b)-3(b)(2)]

Any contribution made for a participant to a 403(b) contract for the taxable year that exceeds either the maximum annual contribution limit (see Q 35:29) or the maximum annual elective deferral limit (see Q 35:26) constitutes an excess contribution that is included in gross income for that taxable year. As noted, a contract to which a contribution is made that exceeds the maximum annual contribution limit is not a 403(b) contract unless the excess contribution is held in a separate account that constitutes a separate account for purposes of the nonqualified annuity rules. A contract does not fail to satisfy the requirements applicable to 403(b) contracts, the distribution rules (see Q 35:35), or the funding rules (see Q 35:12) solely by reason of a distribution of an excess contribution from the separate account. A 403(b) contract may provide that any excess deferral as a result of a failure to comply with the limitation for a taxable year with respect to any elective deferral made for a participant by the employer will be distributed to the participant, with allocable net income, no later than

April 15 of the following taxable year or as otherwise permitted (see Q 27:63). [Treas. Reg. §§ 1.403(b)-4(f), 1.403(b)-7(c)]

Example 1. Steve's employer makes a $51,000 contribution for 2010 to an individual annuity insurance policy for him that would otherwise be a 403(b) contract. The contribution does not include any elective deferrals, and the applicable annual addition limit is $49,000 for 2010. The $2,000 excess is put into a separate account under the policy. The employer includes $2,000 in Steve's gross income as wages for 2010 and, to the extent of the amount held in the separate account for the excess contribution, does not treat the amount as a 403(b) contract. The separate account for the excess contribution is a contract to which the nonqualified annuity rules apply, but the excess contribution does not cause the rest of the contract to fail to be a 403(b) contract.

Example 2. The facts are the same as in Example 1, except that the contribution is made to purchase mutual funds that are held in a custodial account, instead of an individual annuity insurance policy. The conclusion is the same as in Example 1, except that the purchase constitutes a transfer described in Section 83.

Example 3. The facts are the same as in Example 1, except that the amount held in the separate account for the excess contribution is subsequently distributed to Steve. The distribution is included in gross income to the extent provided under Section 72 relating to distributions from a nonqualified annuity contract.

Example 4. Sallie makes elective deferrals totaling $17,000 for 2010, when she is age 45, and the applicable limit on elective deferrals is $16,500. On April 14, 2011, the plan refunds the $500 excess along with applicable earnings of $65. The $565 payment constitutes a distribution of an excess deferral. The $500 excess deferral is included in Sallie's gross income for 2010. The additional $65 is included in her gross income for 2011; and, because the distribution is made by April 15, 2011, the $65 is not subject to the additional 10 percent penalty tax on early distributions (see Q 27:64).

Q 35:32 What are excess aggregate contributions?

Excess aggregate contributions are the excess of the aggregate amount of employee contributions and employer matching contributions (see Q 35:18) made on behalf of HCEs (see Q 3:3) for a plan year over the maximum amount of such contributions that are permitted under a special nondiscrimination test. [I.R.C. § 401(m)(6)(B)]

If excess aggregate contributions are made to any type of 403(b) contract, the excess amount is subject to a 10 percent excise tax. The excise tax is imposed on the employer, not on the HCEs. However, excess aggregate contributions can be corrected to avoid the 10 percent tax. [I.R.C. §§ 4979(a), 4979(f)]

Form 5330, Return of Excise Taxes Related to Employee Benefit Plans, is used to report the excise tax and must be filed by the employer no later than the last day of the 15th month following the close of the plan year to which the excess aggregate contributions relate.

For a discussion of the special nondiscrimination test and method of correction, see Qs 27:73 through 27:87.

Q 35:33   Is there a tax credit for elective deferrals?

An eligible individual is allowed a nonrefundable tax credit for the taxable year in an amount equal to the applicable percentage of the individual's qualified retirement savings contributions for the year up to $2,000.

See chapter 17 for details.

Q 35:34   Are elective deferrals subject to payroll taxes?

Yes. Elective deferrals, including designated Roth contributions (see Q 35:49), made under a salary reduction agreement (see Q 35:11) are included in the Social Security taxable wage base (see Q 7:7) for both employer and employee withholding purposes. Elective deferrals are also subject to the Federal Unemployment Tax Act (FUTA). [I.R.C. § 3121(v)(1)(A); Rev. Rul. 65-208, 1965-2 C.B. 383; Social Security Act Amendments of 1983 § 324(d); Chief Couns. Adv. 200333003; preamble to final regulations; Priv. Ltr. Rul. 200305006]

Regulations have been promulgated that define salary reduction agreements in a manner that expands the FICA tax treatment of contributions to 403(b) contracts. By expanding the definition of 403(b) salary reduction agreements beyond the definition of elective deferrals that applies for income tax purposes, the regulations effectively subject a wider variety of contributions to FICA tax. The regulations define a salary reduction agreement as including a plan or arrangement whereby a payment will be made if the employee elects to reduce compensation pursuant to a cash-or-deferred election (see Q 27:3). However, a salary reduction agreement now also includes a plan or arrangement under which a payment will be made if the employee elects to reduce compensation pursuant to a one-time irrevocable election made at or before the time of initial eligibility to participate in the plan or arrangement (see Q 35:11). In addition, the regulations provide that a salary reduction agreement will include a plan under which payments will be made if the employee agrees, as a condition of employment, to make a contribution that reduces the employee's compensation (see Q 35:11). [Treas. Reg. § 31.3121(a)(5)-2; University of Chicago v. United States, No. 07-3686 (7th Cir. 2008)]

Elective deferrals are also included for purposes of measuring the annual increases in Social Security average wages, which will affect the calculation of both the taxable earnings base and benefit computations. [Social Security Act § 209]

Q 35:35   Are there any prohibitions on distributions from 403(b) contracts?

Yes, but different rules apply depending upon whether the funding vehicle is an annuity contract or a custodial account (see Q 35:7).

If the funding vehicle is an annuity contract, distributions attributable to contributions made pursuant to a salary reduction agreement (see Q 35:11) may be paid only:

1. After the employee attains age 59½;
2. After severance from employment (see Q 27:14);
3. Upon the employee's death;
4. Because the employee becomes disabled (see Q 16:6); or
5. In the case of hardship (but excluding any earnings on such contributions).

[I.R.C. § 403(b)(11); Treas. Reg. §§ 1.403(b)-6(a), 1.403(b)-6(d)(1)(i); preamble to final regulations; Askew, No. 1486-04S (Tax Ct. 2005); Priv. Ltr. Rul. 200148077]

These restrictions do not apply to assets held under the annuity contract as of the end of the last year beginning before 1989. [Frank v. Aaronson, 120 F.3d 10 (2d Cir. 1997); TAMRA § 1011A(c)(11); Treas. Reg. § 1.403(b)-6(d)(1)(ii)] Furthermore, since these restrictions apply only to contributions made pursuant to a salary reduction agreement, there are no restrictions on distributions attributable to nonelective contributions (i.e., employer or employee contributions). In either case, distributions made prior to the employee's attainment of age 59½, even in the case of hardship, may be subject to the 10 percent penalty tax on early distributions (see chapter 16). However, under the regulations, an annuity contract is permitted to distribute retirement benefits (other than amounts attributable to elective deferrals) to the participant no earlier than upon the earliest of the participant's severance from employment or upon the prior occurrence of some event, such as after a fixed number of years, the attainment of a stated age, or disability. [Treas. Reg. § 1.403(b)-6(b)]

If the funding vehicle is a custodial account, distributions may not be paid or made available before the employee:

1. Dies;
2. Attains age 59½;
3. Severs from employment (see Q 27:14);
4. Becomes disabled (see Q 16:6); or
5. In case of contributions made pursuant to a salary reduction agreement, encounters financial hardship.

[I.R.C. § 403(b)(7)(A)(ii); Treas. Reg. §§ 1.403(b)-6(a), 1.403(b)-6(c), 1.403(b)-6(d)(1)(i); preamble to final regulations; Priv. Ltr. Rul. 200148077]

Other than elective deferrals, any amounts transferred out of a custodial account to an annuity contract or retirement income account, including earnings thereon, continue to be subject to these restrictions. [Treas. Reg. § 1.403(b)-6(c)] However, amounts attributable to elective deferrals are always subject to these restrictions. [Treas. Reg. § 1.403(b)-6(d)(1)(i)] The restriction on financial hardship distributions applies only to salary reduction contributions made in years beginning after 1988 and the earnings on all salary reduction contributions whenever made. Effectively, hardship distributions may be made only from the custodial account assets as of the end of the last year beginning before 1989, plus all subsequent salary reduction contributions. [TAMRA § 1011A(c)(1); Treas. Reg. § 1.403(b)-6(d)(1)(ii)] As with annuity contracts, hardship distributions may be subject to the 10 percent penalty tax on early distributions.

The regulations define hardship and apply the 401(k) plan rules (see Q 27:14). [Treas. Reg. § 1.403(b)-6(d)(2)] A hardship distribution from a 403(b) contract is not an eligible rollover distribution. Hence, a hardship distribution cannot be rolled over to an eligible retirement plan (see Q 34:17) and will not be subject to the 20 percent income tax withholding rules (see Q 35:42). [I.R.C. § 403(b)(8)(B)]

If an annuity contract or custodial account includes both elective deferrals and other contributions and the elective deferrals are not maintained in a separate account, then distributions may not be made earlier than the later of:

1. Any date permitted with respect to elective deferrals, and
2. Any date permitted with respect to contributions that are not elective deferrals.

[Treas. Reg. § 1.403(b)-6(d)(3)]

Severance from employment occurs on any date on which an employee ceases to be an employee of an eligible employer (see Q 35:2), even though the employee may continue to be employed either by another entity that is treated as the same employer where either that other entity is not an entity that can be an eligible employer (such as transferring from a Section 501(c)(3) organization to a for-profit subsidiary of the Section 501(c)(3) organization) or in a capacity that is not employment with an eligible employer (e.g., ceasing to be an employee performing services for a public school but continuing to work for the same State employer). Thus, severance from employment may occur if an employee transfers from one Section 501(c)(3) organization to another Section 501(c)(3) organization that is treated as the same employer or if an employee transfers from one public school to another public school of the same State employer. [Treas. Reg. §§ 1.403(b)-2(b)(19), 1.403(b)-6(h); preamble to final regulations]

The payment of fees from a 403(b) plan to an investment advisor who was responsible for managing the assets was neither a distribution nor a prohibited withdrawal. [Priv. Ltr. Rul. 9332040]

The restrictions on distributions from annuity contracts and custodial accounts do not apply to amounts held in a separate account for eligible rollover distributions (see Q 35:45) and do not prohibit distributions to an alternate payee pursuant to a qualified domestic relations order (QDRO) (see Q 35:48). [I.R.C. § 414(p)(10); Treas. Reg. §§ 1.403(b)-6(i), 1.403(b)-10(c); Blatt, 66 T.C.M. 1409 (1993); Priv. Ltr. Rul. 9619040]

For 403(b) plans that permit in-service distributions, the regulations do not apply to a contract issued by an insurance company before January 1, 2009. Any amendment to comply with the distribution requirements that is adopted before January 1, 2009, or such later date as may be permitted under guidance issued by IRS, does not violate ERISA Section 204(g) to the extent the amendment eliminates or reduces a right to receive benefit distributions during employment. [Treas. Reg. § 1.403(b)-11(e)]

Q 35:36   Are 403(b) contracts subject to the qualified joint and survivor annuity (QJSA) and qualified preretirement survivor annuity (QPSA) requirements?

Although the QJSA and QPSA requirements contained in the Code are not applicable to 403(b) contracts, parallel provisions contained in ERISA make these survivor annuity requirements applicable if the 403(b) plan is an employee pension benefit plan (see Q 35:51). Thus, if the 403(b) plan is exempt from Title I of ERISA, the QJSA and QPSA requirements do *not* apply. [ERISA §§ 3(2), 3(3), 205(a), 205(d) (as amended by PPA § 1004(b)(2)(A)-(C)), 205(e)]

If the 403(b) plan is not exempt from Title I, the survivor annuity requirements apply to a defined benefit plan (see Q 2:3), any individual account plan (see Q 2:2) subject to minimum funding requirements (see Q 8:1), and any participant under any other individual account plan unless:

1. The plan provides that, upon the participant's death, the participant's nonforfeitable benefit (reduced by any security interest held by the plan by reason of a loan outstanding to such participant) is payable in full to the participant's surviving spouse (unless the participant has elected with spousal consent that such benefit be paid instead to a designated beneficiary);

2. The participant does not elect the payment of benefits in the form of a life annuity; and

3. With respect to the participant, the plan is not a direct or indirect transferee plan.

[ERISA §§ 3(34), 3(35), 205(b)]

Because a 403(b) plan is not a defined benefit plan or an individual account plan subject to the minimum funding requirements, it appears that, if the 403(b) plan is not exempt from Title I, the QJSA requirement may apply only if the employee elects benefit payments in the form of a life annuity, and the QPSA requirement may apply only if the death benefit is not payable in full to the surviving spouse.

For a detailed discussion of the survivor annuity rules, see Qs 10:1 through 10:36.

Q 35:37   Do the minimum distribution requirements apply to 403(b) contracts?

Effective for benefits accruing after 1986, 403(b) contracts must satisfy the required minimum distribution (RMD) rules. These rules relate to both the time by which distributions from the 403(b) contract must begin and the amount that must be distributed from the 403(b) contract, and these rules are similar to those that apply to qualified retirement plans and IRAs. [I.R.C. § 403(b)(10); Treas. Reg. §§ 1.403(b)-3(a)(6), 1.403(b)-3(a)(8), 1.403(b)-6(e), 1.403(b)-6(g)]

No minimum distribution is required for calendar year 2009 from 403(b) contracts. For a complete discussion of the RMD rules, see chapter 11 and, specifically with regard to 403(b) contracts, Qs 11:52 through 11:55.

Q 35:38   Can an employee make a loan from a 403(b) contract?

Yes, but loans from 403(b) contracts are subject to the same limitations and requirements that apply to loans from qualified retirement plans. [I.R.C. § 72(p)(4)(A)(i)(III)] Interest paid by an employee on a loan from a 403(b) contract secured by amounts attributable to elective deferrals (see Q 35:26) is not deductible. [I.R.C. §§ 72(p)(3)(A), 72(p)(3)(B)(ii)]

The determination of whether the availability of a loan, the making of a loan, or a failure to repay a loan made from an issuer of a 403(b) contract to a participant or beneficiary is treated as a distribution (directly or indirectly), and the determination of whether the availability of the loan, the making of the loan, or a failure to repay the loan is in any other respect a violation of the requirements applicable to 403(b) contracts (see Q 35:13) depends on the facts and circumstances. Among the facts and circumstances are whether the loan has a fixed repayment schedule and bears a reasonable rate of interest, and whether there are repayment safeguards to which a prudent lender would adhere. Thus, for example, a loan must bear a reasonable rate of interest in order to be treated as not being a distribution. However, a plan loan offset is a distribution. [Treas. Reg. § 1.403(b)-6(f)]

The amount of any loan from a 403(b) contract to a participant or beneficiary (including any pledge or assignment treated as a loan) is treated as having been received as a distribution from the contract, except to the extent that the plan loan requirements have been satisfied. Thus, unless a loan satisfies such requirements, any amount loaned from a 403(b) contract to a participant or beneficiary (including any pledge or assignment treated as a loan) is includible in the gross income of the participant or beneficiary for the taxable year in which the loan is made. A deemed distribution is not an actual distribution for these purposes. [Treas. Reg. § 1.403(b)-7(d)]

When an employee who had previously made loans from a 403(b) contract terminated the contract without having repaid the loans, the outstanding loan balance was includible in income in the year of termination. Also, a taxable distribution occurs when an employee defaults on a loan under a 403(b) contract and the insurance company forecloses on the cash value of the annuity contract as used for security on the loan. [Dean, 65 T.C.M. 2757 (1993); IRS Spec. Rul. (Jan. 26, 1994)]

One court rejected a debtor's claim that the portion of his retirement account pledged to secure his alimony obligation was exempt property under the Bankruptcy Code. It held that, because the funds were validly pledged under State law, the assignment was a deemed distribution. This effectively removed those funds from the retirement account and made them non-exempt property that could be claimed by creditors in bankruptcy. The court held that the alimony payments were non-dischargeable and that the ex-wife's security interest in the plan was valid. [In the Matter of Coppola, 2005 WL 17143365 (5th Cir. 2005)]

For a discussion of the rules relating to loans, see chapter 14 and Q 35:39.

Q 35:39 Can a loan from a 403(b) contract be a prohibited transaction?

Although IRS and DOL share jurisdiction with regard to prohibited transactions, the Code restrictions and penalties imposed upon prohibited transactions do *not* apply to 403(b) plans or 403(b) contracts. Consequently, a loan to an employee from a 403(b) contract can never be a prohibited transaction for purposes of the Code (see Q 14:21). [I.R.C. § 4975(e)]

If the 403(b) plan is an employee pension benefit plan subject to ERISA (see Q 35:51), then the ERISA restrictions and penalties imposed upon prohibited transactions will apply to a loan to an employee from a 403(b) contract (see Qs 14:21, 24:1, 24:8). [ERISA §§ 406, 408(b)]

Q 35:40 How are distributions from a 403(b) contract taxed?

The amounts actually distributed from a 403(b) contract to a recipient employee or beneficiary are included in the recipient's income for the taxable year in which received. [I.R.C. §§ 72(m), 403(b)(1); Treas. Reg. § 1.403(b)-7(a); Askew, No. 1486-04S (Tax Ct. 2005); Priv. Ltr. Ruls. 9652020, 9617043, 9342056]

If the employee has an investment in the contract (also known as basis), a portion of the distribution from the 403(b) contract will be recovered tax free. [I.R.C. §§ 72(b), 72(c)]

An employee's investment in the contract (basis) includes:

1. The employee's voluntary contributions (see Qs 1:42, 35:18);
2. Current life insurance protection costs (see Q 35:8);
3. Employer contributions previously includible in the employee's income (see Q 35:29); and
4. Loans from the 403(b) contract to the employee that were treated as taxable distributions (see Q 35:38).

If amounts are received by the employee before the annuity starting date (see Q 10:3) and the employee has basis, a portion of the distribution bearing the same ratio as the basis bears to the employee's accrued benefit (see Q 9:2) as of the date of distribution is excludable from the employee's taxable income. If, on May 5, 1986, the 403(b) contract permitted the employee to withdraw voluntary contributions, pre-1987 basis will be recovered first and the pro rata recovery rule will apply only to the extent that amounts received exceed the employee's basis as of December 1, 1986. [I.R.C. § 72(e)]

If the employee has basis and receives annuity payments from the 403(b) contract, basis will be recovered under the annuity rules applicable to qualified retirement plans (see Q 13:4). If the employee receives the full value of the 403(b) contract in a lump-sum payment, the entire amount (less basis) will be taxable as ordinary income; the special averaging method that may be available for a lump-sum distribution from a qualified retirement plan (see Q 13:14) is *not* available for a lump-sum payment from a 403(b) contract. [I.R.C. §§ 402(d)(4)(A), 403(b)(1); Adamcewicz, 68 T.C.M. 276 (1994)] If dividends are paid to the employee under a 403(b) contract, the dividends constitute taxable income except to the extent excludable under the pro rata basis recovery rule. The payment of fees from a 403(b) contract to an investment advisor who is responsible for managing the assets is not a taxable distribution. [Priv. Ltr. Rul. 9332040]

A qualified retirement plan maintained by a State or local government employer may provide that a participant may make after-tax employee contributions in order to purchase permissive service credit, subject to certain limits. Permissive service credit is credit for a period of service recognized by the governmental plan only if the employee voluntarily contributes to the plan an amount (as determined by the plan) that does not exceed the amount necessary to fund the benefit attributable to the period of service and that is in addition to the regular employee contributions, if any, under the plan. In the case of any repayment of contributions and earnings to a governmental plan with respect to an amount previously refunded upon a forfeiture of service credit under the plan (or another plan maintained by a State or local government employer within the same State), any such repayment is not taken into account for purposes of the limits on contributions and benefits. Also, service credit obtained as a result of such a repayment is not considered permissive service credit for purposes of the limits. A participant may not use a rollover or direct transfer of benefits from a 403(b) contract to purchase permissive service credits or repay contributions and earnings with respect to a forfeiture of service credit. [I.R.C. § 415 (n)(3)(A)]

A participant in a State or local governmental plan will not be required to include in gross income a direct trustee-to-trustee transfer to a governmental defined benefit plan from a 403(b) contract if the transferred amount is used (1) to purchase permissive service credits under the plan or (2) to repay contributions and earnings with respect to an amount previously refunded under a forfeiture of service credit under the plan (or another plan maintained by a State or local government employer within the same state). [I.R.C. §§ 403(b)(13), 415(k)(3), 415(n)(3)(A); Treas. Reg. § 1.403(b)-10(b)(4)]

If an amount is distributed from a designated Roth account (see Qs 27:96, 35:49) under a 403(b) plan, the amount, if any, that is includible in gross income and the amount, if any, that may be rolled over to another 403(b) plan is determined under the rules applicable to a designated Roth account under a 401(k) plan (see Qs 27:98–27:110). Thus, the designated Roth account is treated as a separate contract, and the income-taxation rules must be applied separately to annuity payments with respect to a designated Roth account under a 403(b) plan and separately to annuity payments with respect to amounts attributable to any other contributions to the 403(b) plan. [Treas. Reg. §§ 1.403(b)-7(e), 1.403(b)-11(i)] For a discussion of the coordination of designated Roth accounts and Roth IRAs, see Q 31:43.

Q 35:41 May any additional taxes be imposed on the recipient of a distribution from a 403(b) contract?

The 10 percent penalty tax on early distributions (see chapter 16) and the 50 percent penalty tax for failure to make an RMD (see Qs 11:67–11:71) that may apply to distributions from qualified retirement plans and IRAs also apply to distributions from 403(b) contracts. [Treas. Reg. §§ 1.403(b)-6(e), 1.403(b)-7(a); Askew, No. 1486-04S (Tax Ct. 2005)]

Under PPA (see Q 1:33), the 10 percent penalty tax does not apply to qualified reservist distributions (see Q 16:3).

Q 35:42 Can distributions from a 403(b) contract be rolled over?

A 403(b) contract is required to provide that, if the distributee of an eligible rollover distribution (see Q 34:8) elects to have the distribution paid directly to an eligible retirement plan (see Q 34:16) and specifies the plan to which the distribution will be paid, then the distribution must be paid to that plan in a direct rollover (see Q 34:17). [I.R.C. § 403(b)(10); Treas. Reg. §§ 1.403(b)-3(a)(7), 1.403(b)-7(b)(2); Priv. Ltr. Rul. 9415016] The rules relating to the rollover of qualified retirement plan distributions also pertain to distributions from 403(b) plans and 403(b) contracts. A direct rollover is not includible in the gross income of a participant or beneficiary in the year rolled over. In addition, any payment made in the form of an eligible rollover distribution is not includible in gross income in the year paid to the extent the payment is contributed to an eligible retirement plan within 60 days after receipt, including the contribution to the eligible retirement plan of any property distributed. [I.R.C. §§ 403(b)(8), 403(b)(10); Treas. Reg. § 1.403(b)-7(b)(1); Tolliver, 62 T.C.M. 770 (1991); Priv. Ltr. Rul. 9744022]

To the extent that a portion of a distribution (including a distribution from a designated Roth account; see Qs 27:96, 35:49) would be excluded from gross income if it were not rolled over, if that portion of the distribution will be rolled over into an eligible retirement plan that is not an IRA, the rollover must be accomplished through a direct rollover of the entire distribution to a qualified retirement plan or 403(b) plan and that plan must agree to separately account for the amount not includible in income (so that a 60-day rollover to a qualified retirement plan or another 403(b) plan is not available for this portion of the distribution). Any direct rollover is a distribution that is subject to the distribution requirements (see Q 35:35). [Treas. Reg. §§ 1.403(b)-7(b)(1), 1.403(b)-7(b)(2)]

To ensure that the distributee of an eligible rollover distribution from a 403(b) contract has a meaningful right to elect a direct rollover, the distributee must be informed of the option. Thus, within a reasonable time before making the initial eligible rollover distribution, the payor must provide an explanation to the distributee of the right to elect a direct rollover and the income tax withholding consequences of not electing a direct rollover (see Q 34:29). [Treas. Reg. § 1.403(b)-7(b)(3)]

As in the case of an eligible rollover distribution from a qualified retirement plan, if a distributee of an eligible rollover distribution from a 403(b) contract does not elect to have the eligible rollover distribution paid to an eligible retirement plan in a direct rollover, the eligible rollover distribution is subject to 20 percent income tax withholding (see Q 20:10). [Treas. Reg. § 1.403(b)-7(b)(4)] The automatic rollover rules for certain mandatory distributions apply to 403(b) plans in the same manner as a qualified retirement plan (see Qs 34:17, 34:18). [Treas. Reg. § 1.403(b)-7(b)(5)]

A distribution from a 403(b) contract that is invested in a personal certificate of deposit is not a rollover. [Adamcewicz, 68 T.C.M. 276 (1994)] IRS representatives have opined that an individual who will receive benefits from a 403(b) contract in ten or more annual payments cannot roll over any of the payments to an eligible retirement plan (see Q 34:10). A direct rollover from a 403(b) contract to another 403(b) contract is a distribution and a rollover and not a transfer of funds between 403(b) contracts and, thus, does not affect the applicable law governing transfers of funds between 403(b) contracts. If a 403(b) contract is subject to restrictions regarding distributions, a rollover cannot be made while those restrictions apply because a direct rollover is a distribution that is subject to the distribution requirements. IRS representatives have opined that, if an employer terminates its 403(b) plan and replaces it with a 401(k) plan (see Q 27:1), a distributable event (see Q 35:35) has *not* occurred so that the employees cannot make rollovers to eligible retirement plans. However, a transfer of funds between 403(b) contracts may be permissible (see Q 35:47). [IRS Spec. Rul. (May 19, 1995); Frank v. Aaronson, 120 F.3d 10 (2d Cir. 1997)] See Q 34:37 for a discussion of when a rollover can be distributed.

A hardship distribution from a 403(b) contract (see Q 35:35) is not an eligible rollover distribution. Hence, a hardship distribution cannot be rolled over and will not be subject to the 20 percent income tax withholding rules. [I.R.C. § 403(b)(8)(B)] IRS issued the following guidance concerning hardship distributions:

1. *Pre-'89 403(b) plan amounts.* In many instances 403(b) plan records do not make it possible to distinguish pre-'89 403(b) plan elective deferral amounts from other amounts credited to an employee's 403(b) contract as of 1989 (see Q 35:35). The guidance provides that, to the extent plan records are not available to segregate pre-'89 403(b) plan elective deferral amounts from other 1989 amounts, all amounts in an employee's 403(b) contract as of the 1989 date will be treated as elective deferrals. As such, they are ineligible for rollover when distributed as a hardship distribution.

2. *Satisfaction of another statutory event.* A hardship distribution will be treated as ineligible for rollover even though another statutory event has occurred (e.g., separation from service or attainment of age 59) that would have otherwise entitled the employee to receive a distribution without regard to the hardship.

3. *Allocation of basis.* A portion of a hardship distribution from a 403(b) contract that is not includible in gross income may be allocated to the portion ineligible for rollover or to the portion eligible for rollover (or between the two portions) using any reasonable method. A 403(b) plan must generally be consistent in the treatment of all distributions when applying this rule. [IRS Notice 2000-32, 2000-2 C.B.1]

An alternate payee spouse or former spouse under a QDRO (see Qs 35:48, 36:1, 36:32) can roll over a distribution from a 403(b) contract to an eligible retirement plan. [I.R.C. § 402(e)(1); Blatt, 66 T.C.M. 1409 (1993)]

For taxable years beginning after December 31, 2007, 403(b) plan benefits may be directly rolled over to a Roth IRA (see Q 31:42). [I.R.C. §§ 408A(d)(3), 408A(c)]

See chapter 34 for a detailed discussion of rollovers.

Q 35:43 How are death benefit payments under a 403(b) contract taxed?

Death benefits payable under a 403(b) contract are generally included in the deceased employee's estate. For the exceptions, see Q 15:23. [I.R.C. § 2039] Death benefit payments from a 403(b) contract to a deceased employee's surviving spouse will qualify for the marital deduction and will be deducted from the decedent's gross estate for estate tax purposes (see Q 15:24). [I.R.C. § 2056]

For income tax purposes, the death benefit payable under a 403(b) contract will be taxed to the beneficiary in the same manner as the lifetime benefit would have been taxed to the employee (see Q 35:42). However, if the death benefit is also subject to estate tax, the beneficiary will be entitled to an income tax deduction for the estate tax attributable to the death benefit. [I.R.C. § 691(c); Treas. Reg. § 1.403(b)-2(b)(3); Field Serv. Adv. 200011023] For further details, see Q 15:22.

Q 35:44   Is a rollover of benefits under a 403(b) contract available to the beneficiary of a deceased employee?

Yes. The spouse of an employee who receives an eligible rollover distribution (see Q 34:8) from a 403(b) contract on account of the employee's death is permitted to roll over all or part of the distribution. The surviving spouse is permitted to roll over an eligible rollover distribution in the same manner as if the spouse were the employee. In other words, the surviving spouse may roll over the distribution to a 403(b) contract, qualified retirement plan, or a governmental Section 457 plan in which the surviving spouse participates, or to an IRA. [I.R.C. § 402(c)(9); Priv. Ltr. Ruls. 200444032, 200325008, 200317040, 200314029, 200107040, 200101039] The spouse may establish an IRA rollover account even if the spouse would not be eligible to establish a regular IRA. A 403(b) plan participant named her husband as beneficiary. IRS permitted the husband to establish an IRA in the name of his deceased wife with himself as the beneficiary and to have the 403(b) plan benefits paid directly to the new IRA. IRS ruled that the new IRA was an inherited IRA (see Q 30:48) and that the husband did not elect to treat the new IRA as his own (see Qs 11:11, 11:60). [Priv. Ltr. Rul. 200936049]

Under PPA (see Q 1:33), benefits of a beneficiary other than a surviving spouse may be transferred directly to an IRA. The IRA is treated as an inherited IRA of the nonspouse beneficiary. See Q 34:33 for more details.

Q 35:45   Can a 403(b) contract accept rollovers?

A 403(b) contract is an eligible retirement plan (see Q 34:16). A 403(b) contract may accept contributions that are eligible rollover distributions (see Q 34:8) made from another eligible retirement plan. Amounts contributed to a 403(b) contract as eligible rollover distributions are not taken into account for purposes of the contribution limitations and also are not subject to the distribution limitations if held in a separate account (see Q 35:35). [Treas. Reg. §§ 1.403(b)-4(a), 1.403(b)-6(i), 1.403(b)-10(d)(1)]

A 403(b) plan that receives an eligible rollover distribution that includes after-tax employee contributions (see Q 35:18) or designated Roth contributions (see Q 35:49) is required to obtain information regarding the employee's basis (see Q 35:40) in the amount rolled over. A 403(b) plan is permitted to receive an eligible rollover distribution that includes designated Roth contributions only if the plan permits employees to make elective deferrals that are designated Roth contributions. [Treas. Reg. §§ 1.403(b)-10(d)(2), 1.403(b)-11(i)]

Q 35:46   Can a 403(b) plan be terminated or frozen?

An employer may amend its 403(b) plan to eliminate future contributions for existing participants or to limit participation to existing participants and employees (to the extent consistent with the nondiscrimination requirements; see Qs 35:16–35:21). A 403(b) plan may contain provisions that permit plan termination and permit accumulated benefits to be distributed on termination.

However, in the case of a 403(b) contract that is subject to the distribution restrictions (see Q 35:35), termination of the plan and the distribution of accumulated benefits is permitted only if the employer (taking into account all entities that are treated as the employer under controlled group rules (see Q 35:3) on the date of the termination) does not make contributions to an alternative 403(b) contract that is not part of the plan during the period beginning on the date of plan termination and ending 12 months after distribution of all assets from the terminated plan. However, if at all times during the period beginning 12 months before the termination and ending 12 months after distribution of all assets from the terminated plan, fewer than 2 percent of the employees who were eligible under the 403(b) plan as of the date of plan termination are eligible under the alternative 403(b) contract, the alternative 403(b) contract is disregarded. To the extent a contract fails to satisfy the nonforfeitability requirement (see Q 35:14) at the date of plan termination, the contract is not, and cannot later become, a 403(b) contract. In order for a 403(b) plan to be considered terminated, all accumulated benefits under the plan must be distributed to all participants and beneficiaries as soon as administratively practicable after termination of the plan. A distribution includes delivery of a fully paid individual insurance annuity contract. The mere provision for, and making of, distributions to participants or beneficiaries upon plan termination does not cause a contract to cease to be a 403(b) contract. [Treas. Reg. §§ 1.403(b)-2(b)(1), 1.403(b)-10(a)(1)]

An employer that ceases to be an eligible employer (see Q 35:2) may no longer contribute to a 403(b) contract for any subsequent period, and the contract will fail to satisfy the exclusion from gross income rules (see Q 35:12) if any further contributions are made with respect to a period after the employer ceases to be an eligible employer. [Treas. Reg. § 1.403(b)-10(a)(2)]

Q 35:47   Can funds be transferred from one 403(b) contract to another?

If the conditions discussed below are met, a 403(b) contract held under a 403(b) plan is permitted to be exchanged for another 403(b) contract held under that 403(b) plan. Further, if the other conditions discussed below are met, a 403(b) plan is permitted to provide for the transfer of its assets, including any assets held in a custodial account (see Q 35:7) or retirement income account (see Q 35:55) that are treated as 403(b) contracts, to another 403(b) plan. Neither a qualified retirement plan nor a Section 457 eligible governmental plan may transfer assets to a 403(b) plan, and a 403(b) plan may not accept such a transfer. In addition, a 403(b) contract may not be exchanged for an annuity contract that is not a 403(b) contract. Neither a permitted plan-to-plan transfer nor a contract exchange is treated as a distribution for purposes of the distribution restrictions (see Q 35:35). Therefore, such a transfer or exchange may be made before severance from employment or another distribution event. Further, no amount is includible in gross income by reason of such a transfer or exchange. [Treas. Reg. § 1.403(b)-10(b)(1)(i); preamble to final regulations]

A 403(b) contract of a participant or beneficiary may be exchanged for another 403(b) contract of that participant or beneficiary under the same 403(b) plan if each of the following conditions are met:

1. The plan under which the contract is issued provides for the exchange.

2. The participant or beneficiary has an accumulated benefit immediately after the exchange that is at least equal to the accumulated benefit of that participant or beneficiary immediately before the exchange (taking into account the accumulated benefit of that participant or beneficiary under both 403(b) contracts immediately before the exchange).

3. The other contract is subject to distribution restrictions (see Q 35:35) with respect to the participant that are not less stringent than those imposed on the contract being exchanged, and the employer enters into an agreement with the issuer of the other contract under which the employer and the issuer will from time to time in the future provide each other with the following information:

    (a) Information necessary for the resulting contract, or any other contract to which contributions have been made by the employer, to satisfy the requirements applicable to 403(b) contracts (see Q 35:13), including information concerning the participant's employment and information that takes into account other 403(b) contracts or qualified retirement plans (such as whether a severance from employment has occurred for purposes of the distribution restrictions and whether the hardship withdrawal rules are satisfied).

    (b) Information necessary for the resulting contract, or any other contract to which contributions have been made by the employer, to satisfy other tax requirements (such as whether a plan loan satisfies the plan loan requirements (see Q 35:38) so that the loan is not a deemed distribution). [Treas. Reg. §§ 1.403(b)-2(b)(1), 1.403(b)-10(b)(2)(i); preamble to final regulations]

The condition in item 2 is satisfied if the exchange would satisfy Section 414(l)(1) if the exchange were a transfer of assets. [Treas. Reg. § 1.403(b)-10(b)(2)(ii)]

Subject to such conditions as IRS determines to be appropriate, it may issue rules of general applicability permitting an exchange of one 403(b) contract for another 403(b) contract for an exchange that does not satisfy item 3. Any such rules must require the resulting contract to set forth procedures that IRS determines are reasonably designed to ensure compliance with those requirements applicable to 403(b) contracts or other tax provisions that depend on either information concerning the participant's employment or information that takes into account other 403(b) contracts or other employer plans (such as whether a severance from employment has occurred for purposes of the distribution restrictions, whether the hardship withdrawal rules are satisfied, and whether a plan loan constitutes a deemed distribution). [Treas. Reg. § 1.403(b)-10(b)(2)(iii)]

This special rule for contracts received in an exchange does not apply to a contract received in an exchange that occurred on or before September 24, 2007 if the exchange (including the contract received in the exchange) satisfied such rules as IRS had prescribed in guidance of general applicability at the time of the exchange. [Treas. Reg. § 1.403(b)-11(g)]

A plan-to-plan transfer from a 403(b) plan to another 403(b) plan is permitted if each of the following conditions are met:

1. In the case of a transfer for a participant, the participant is an employee or former employee of the employer (or the business of the employer) for the receiving plan.

2. In the case of a transfer for a beneficiary of a deceased participant, the participant was an employee or former employee of the employer (or business of the employer) for the receiving plan.

3. The transferor plan provides for transfers.

4. The receiving plan provides for the receipt of transfers.

5. The participant or beneficiary whose assets are being transferred has an accumulated benefit immediately after the transfer at least equal to the accumulated benefit with respect to that participant or beneficiary immediately before the transfer.

6. The receiving plan provides that, to the extent any amount transferred is subject to any distribution restrictions, the receiving plan imposes restrictions on distributions to the participant or beneficiary whose assets are being transferred that are no less stringent than those imposed on the transferor plan.

7. If a plan-to-plan transfer does not constitute a complete transfer of the participant's or beneficiary's interest in the 403(b) plan, then the transferee plan treats the amount transferred as a continuation of a pro rata portion of the participant's or beneficiary's interest in the transferor 403(b) plan (e.g., a pro rata portion of the participant's or beneficiary's interest in any after-tax employee contributions).

[Treas. Reg. § 1.403(b)-10(b)(3)(i); preamble to final regulations]

The condition in item 4 is satisfied if the transfer would satisfy Section 414(*l*)(1). [Treas. Reg. § 1.403(b)-10(b)(3)(ii)]

A 403(b) plan may provide for the transfer of its assets to a qualified retirement plan to purchase permissive service credit under a defined benefit governmental plan or to make a repayment to a defined benefit governmental plan (see Q 35:40). [Treas. Reg. § 1.403(b)-10(b)(4); preamble to final regulations]

Additional plan-to-plan transfer rules may apply in the event that a plan-to-plan transfer is made to or from a 403(b) plan that is subject to Title I of ERISA (see Q 35:47). [ERISA § 208; Treas. Reg. §§ 1.403(b)-10(b)(1)(ii), 1.414(*l*)-1]

If cash is distributed from an annuity contract and the proceeds are reinvested in another annuity contract or in a custodial account, the distribution will not be a taxable transfer if:

1. The contract is issued by an insurance company that is subject to a rehabilitation, conservatorship, insolvency, or similar State proceeding at the time of the cash distribution;

2. The individual withdraws 100 percent of the cash distribution to which the individual is entitled under the annuity contract or, if less, the maximum amount permitted to be withdrawn under the terms of the State proceeding;

3. An exchange of the old annuity contract for the new annuity contract would qualify for tax-free treatment under Section 1035(a); and

4. The reinvestment is made within 60 days after receipt of the cash distribution and, if the cash distribution is restricted by the State proceeding to an amount less than the individual is entitled to, the individual assigns all rights to any future distributions to the issuer of the new annuity contract.

[Rev. Proc. 92-44, 1992-1 C.B. 875]

Additionally, an individual's exchange of an annuity contract issued by a life insurance company that has become subject to a rehabilitation, conservatorship, or Similar State proceeding for an annuity contract issued by another life insurance company will qualify as a tax-free exchange if the new contract is funded by a series of two or more payments from the old annuity contract. [Rev. Rul. 92-43, 1992-1 C.B. 288; Priv. Ltr. Rul. 9348051]

Q 35:48 Do the qualified domestic order (QDRO) rules apply to a 403(b) contract?

Any distribution from a 403(b) contract, including a distribution from a custodial account (see Q 35:7) or retirement income account (see Q 35:55), pursuant to a QDRO (see Q 36:1) is treated in the same manner as a distribution from a qualified retirement plan. Thus, for example, a 403(b) plan does not fail to satisfy the distribution restrictions (see Q 35:35) merely as a result of distribution made pursuant to a QDRO, so that such a distribution is permitted without regard to whether the employee from whose contract the distribution is made has had a severance from employment or another event permitting a distribution to be made. In the case of a plan that is subject to Title I of ERISA (see Q 35:51), the prohibition against assignment or alienation of plan benefits does not apply to an order that is determined to be a QDRO. [I.R.C. § 414(p)(9); ERISA §§ 206(d)(1), 206(d)(3); Treas. Reg. § 1.403(b)-10(c); preamble to final regulations]

Wherever used in this chapter 35, a beneficiary includes a person who is entitled to benefits in respect of a participant following the participant's death or an alternate payee (see Q 36:5) pursuant to a QDRO. [Treas. Reg. § 1.403(b)-2(b)(3)]

For a complete discussion of QDROs, see chapter 36.

Q 35:49   May a 403(b) plan include a qualified Roth contribution program?

A 403(b) plan is permitted to include a qualified Roth contribution program that enables an employee to elect to have all or a portion of the employee's elective deferrals (see Qs 35:11, 35:26) under the 403(b) plan treated as designated Roth contributions. Designated Roth contributions are elective deferrals that the employee designates (at such time and in such manner as IRS may prescribe) as not excludable from the employee's gross income. [I.R.C. § 402A; Treas. Reg. §§ 1.403(b)-2(b)(17)(ii), 1.403(b)-3(c)] For further details, see Q 27:96.

Under SBJA 2010 (see Q 1:38), eligible retirement plan distributions from 403(b) plans made after September 27, 2010 may be rolled over to a designated Roth account within the plan. Any amount required to be included in gross income for the 2010 taxable year is included in income in equal amounts for the 2011 and 2012 taxable years unless the taxpayer elects otherwise (see Q 31:49).

Q 35:50   May a 403(b) plan include deemed IRAs?

A 403(b) plan may permit employees to make voluntary employee contributions (see Q 35:18) to a separate account or annuity that (1) is established under the plan and (2) meets the requirements applicable to either IRAs or Roth IRAs. [Treas. Reg. § 1.403(b)-10(e)] See Qs 30:36 and 30:37 for details.

Q 35:51   Are 403(b) plans subject to the reporting and disclosure requirements of ERISA?

The answer to this question is dependent upon whether or not the 403(b) plan is subject to Title I of ERISA, and the 403(b) plan will be subject to Title I if it is an employee benefit pension plan. The term "employee benefit pension plan" means any plan, fund, or program established or maintained by an employer or by an employee organization, or by both, to the extent that such plan, fund, or program:

1. Provides retirement income to employees, or
2. Results in a deferral of income by employees for periods extending to the termination of covered employment or beyond.

[ERISA §§ 3(2), 3(3)]

A 403(b) plan established pursuant to salary reduction agreements (see Q 35:11) will *not* be "established or maintained by an employer" and, hence, *not* be subject to Title I, if the following requirements are satisfied:

1. Participation is completely voluntary for employees;
2. All rights under the 403(b) contract are enforceable solely by the employee, by a beneficiary of such employee, or by their authorized representative;
3. The sole involvement of the employer is limited to any of the following:
    (a) Permitting annuity contractors (e.g., insurance companies, mutual fund brokers) to publicize their products to employees;

(b) Requesting information concerning proposed funding media, products, or annuity contractors;

(c) Summarizing the information provided with respect to the proposed funding media or products made available, or the annuity contractors whose services are provided, in order to facilitate review and analysis by the employees;

(d) Collecting 403(b) contract contributions as required by salary reduction agreements, remitting the contributions to annuity contractors, and maintaining records of the contributions;

(e) Holding in the employer's name one or more group annuity contracts covering its employees;

(f) Limiting the funding media or products available to employees, or the annuity contractors who may approach employees, to a number and selection designed to afford employees a reasonable choice in light of all relevant circumstances; and

4. The employer receives no compensation other than reasonable compensation to cover expenses properly and actually incurred in the performance of the employer's duties pursuant to the salary reduction agreements.

[DOL Reg. § 2510.3-2(f); preamble to final regulations]

The safe harbor arrangement in the final regulations described above may make optional features, such as participant loans, available even if the 403(b) plan provider is responsible for any discretionary determinations. The employer may also refuse to include 403(b) contracts and accounts in its safe harbor arrangement with such optional features if that limitation is intended to reduce the employer's costs in offering the safe harbor arrangement or is designed to remove features that in operation could result in the employer being forced to take steps that would exceed the employer involvement permitted under the safe harbor. [DOL Field Assistance Bull. 2010-01, Q-14] An employer will exceed the safe harbor limitations on employer involvement if the employer hires a third-party administrator (TPA) to make discretionary decisions because the employer's selection of a TPA would be inconsistent with the safe harbor. DOL's Field Assistance Bulletin 2007-02, discussed further on in this Q 35:51, addressed the safe harbor conditions for tax-sheltered annuity arrangements to fall outside of Title I coverage and specifically noted that the documents governing the arrangement could identify parties other than the employer as responsible for administrative functions, including those related to tax compliance. As the Bulletin further noted, the documents should correctly describe the employer's limited role and allocate discretionary determinations to the annuity provider or other responsible third party selected by a person other than the employer. Moreover, an employer may limit the available providers it will make available in its safe harbor arrangement to those where the 403(b) contracts or accounts or other governing documents prepared by the provider state that the provider or another appropriate third party is responsible for discretionary decisions related to loans and hardship distributions. [DOL Field Assistance Bull. 2010-01, Q-15]

Generally, a safe harbor arrangement must offer participants a reasonable choice of both 403(b) plan providers and investment products. However, DOL recognizes that the cost of permitting employees to make contributions through payroll deductions may be significantly affected by the number of 403(b) plan contractors to which the employer must remit contributions. This may be particularly significant for small employers concerned about the administrative complexity of offering access to multiple 403(b) plan providers under a safe harbor 403(b) arrangement that normally requires a very limited financial commitment on the part of an employer in the form of affording payroll deductions. In DOL's view, an employer could, consistent with the safe harbor, limit the number of providers to which it will forward salary reduction contributions to one if employees are allowed to transfer or exchange, in accordance with IRS regulations, their interest to a 403(b) account of another provider. Also, there may be circumstances where an employer can demonstrate that increased administrative burdens and costs to the employer in offering a number of contractors under the arrangement would be sufficient to cause the employer to stop making its payroll system available to collect and remit payroll deduction contributions to any 403(b) plan contractor. In such cases, limiting available contractors to one offering a wide variety of investment products could be seen as affording employees a reasonable choice in light of all relevant circumstances as described above (e.g., a single insurance company's 403(b)-compliant arrangement with access to a broad range of affiliated investment products or a single 403(b)-compliant open architecture custodial account platform giving employees access to a broad range of unaffiliated mutual fund investment products). In any case where the employer limits the availability of providers in a 403(b) plan safe harbor arrangement, affording the employees a reasonable choice under the circumstances requires that limitations on or costs or assessments associated with an employee's ability to transfer or exchange contributions to another provider's contract or account be fully disclosed in advance of the employee's decision to participate in the program. [DOL Field Assistance Bull. 2010-01, Q-16]

An arrangement that otherwise meets the terms of the safe harbor will stay within the safe harbor if the written plan document (see Q 35:9) provides that salary deferrals will be discontinued to a provider that is not complying with the Code requirements (see Q 35:13). If the purpose of the provisions for discontinuing a provider from offering products to participants in the arrangement is necessary to maintain compliance with the Code, then including such provisions in the arrangement will not take it outside the safe harbor. [DOL Field Assistance Bull. 2010-01, Q-17] A safe harbor non–Title I arrangement may not authorize the employer to change 403(b) plan providers and unilaterally move employee funds from one provider to contracts or accounts of another provider. Although an employer can decide to limit the providers in a safe harbor arrangement to which it will forward employee salary reduction contributions, discretionary authority to exchange or move employee funds is inconsistent with the safe harbor requirements. [DOL Field Assistance Bull. 2010-01, Q-18]

DOL advised IRS that, although it does not appear that the regulations would mandate the establishment or maintenance of an employee pension benefit plan in order to satisfy its requirements, it leaves open the possibility that an employer may undertake responsibilities that would constitute establishing and maintaining an ERISA-covered plan. DOL further advised IRS that whether the manner in which any particular employer decides to satisfy particular responsibilities under the regulations will cause the employer to be considered to have established or to maintain a plan that is covered under Title I of ERISA must be analyzed on a case-by-case basis, applying the criteria set forth in the DOL regulations, including the employer's involvement as contemplated by the plan documents and in operation. [DOL Field Assistance Bull. 2007-02]

Consequently, unless the 403(b) plan comes within the above-mentioned exceptions, the program will be subject to the reporting and disclosure requirements of ERISA. If the 403(b) plan is subject to such requirements:

1. Form 5500 must be filed each year (see Qs 21:1–21:17),

2. A summary plan description (SPD) must be distributed to employees and beneficiaries (see Q 22:1),

3. A summary annual report must be distributed to employees and beneficiaries (see Q 22:13), and

4. An employee may request a statement of benefits (see Q 22:13).

Even if Form 5500 must be filed, DOL has advised that Schedule A (Insurance Information) need not be completed and attached to Form 5500. [DOL Info. Ltr. (Jan. 12, 1998)]

Where an employer ceased making contributions to a 403(b) plan on February 28, 1989 and only the employees continued to make contributions thereafter, DOL ruled that the program was an employee benefit pension plan subject to Title I. [DOL Op. Ltr. 94-30A] Church plans (see Q 35:55) are excluded from the requirements of Title I (see Q 21:21). [DOL Op. Ltrs. 2004-11A, 94-18A]

DOL provided transition relief for administrators of 403(b) plans that make good-faith efforts to comply with the 2009 plan year Form 5500 annual reporting and audit requirements with respect to annuity contracts and custodial accounts that were issued to current or former employees before January 1, 2009. [DOL Field Assistance Bull. 2009-02] DOL supplemented its Field Assistance Bulletin 2009-02 by issuing Field Assistance Bulletin 2010-01.

An annuity contract or custodial account need not be included in the Form 5500 or Form 5500-SF annual report if the employer provides information to the 403(b) plan provider concerning an employee's or former employee's employment status in connection with a contract or account that otherwise meets the conditions of Field Assistance Bulletin 2009-02 for being excluded from the plan's annual report. The annual reporting relief under the Bulletin will still be available even if the employer provides information to the 403(b) plan provider. Providing information, such as the contract owner's employment status, does not constitute involvement beyond that permitted under the Bulletin. On the other hand, where the employer must consent to, or make other discretionary decisions regarding, enforcement of the employee rights under the contract, the relief under the Bulletin is not available. Relief is also not available if, for example, the employer must certify in advance that an employee is eligible for a distribution that is permissible under the Code (see Q 35:35). Similarly, the Bulletin provides no relief if the employer has to approve a hardship distribution or a loan from the contract or account before the loan or distribution is made (see Q 35:38). [DOL Field Assistance Bull. 2010-01, Q-1] If an employer, through salary reduction, forwards an employee's loan repayments to a 403(b) contract provider, the employee's contract or account to which the loan repayments are being made must be included in the plan's annual report. Even if the loan repayments technically are not employee contributions, DOL would treat ongoing loan repayments forwarded by the employer like salary reduction employee contributions, giving the employer an ongoing role with the contract and provider beyond that envisioned in the Bulletin. On the other hand, the annual reporting relief in the Bulletin could apply to contracts or accounts that otherwise meet the conditions of the Bulletin for which employees make loan repayments in 2009 directly to the contract or custodial account providers. [DOL Field Assistance Bull. 2010-01, Q-2]

If the contract or account is known to the plan administrator and can be identified, it need not be included in the annual report if it meets the requirements of the Bulletin. The plan administrator (see Q 20:1) is not required to include in the plan's annual report a contract or account that meets the requirements of the Bulletin even if that contract or account is known to the administrator and can be identified. [DOL Field Assistance Bull. 2010-01, Q-3] If a plan administrator excludes some contracts or accounts from the plan's annual report because those contracts or accounts meet the requirements of the Bulletin, the administrator does not have to exclude all such contracts or accounts for reporting purposes. The plan administrator can decide to include contracts or accounts even if they meet such requirements. The plan administrator may decide that it is easier and less expensive for the plan to include such a contract or account in its Form 5500 or Form 5500-SF Annual Return/Report. [DOL Field Assistance Bull. 2010-10, Q-4]

The relief provided by the Bulletin applies to annual reports for both large and small 403(b) plans. The relief applies both for determining what annuity contracts or custodial accounts are treated as assets of the plan for purposes of the plan audit and for determining what plan assets must be identified on the plan's financial statements (including the Form 5500-SF or Schedules H or I of the Form 5500). The relief also applies for purposes of ascertaining the number of participants for reporting purposes, including the determination of whether or not the plan is a large plan required to submit as part of its Form 5500 the report of an independent qualified public accountant (IQPA). Employees whose only assets in the plan are contracts or accounts that meet the conditions of the Bulletin, and who are not otherwise eligible to make salary reduction contributions under the 403(b) plan, need not be counted as participants for these purposes. The Form 5500 and Form 5500-SF relief in the Bulletin does not address any other reporting or notice requirements under the Code or any other applicable federal or state law. [DOL Field Assistance Bull. 2010-01, Q-5]

403(b) annuity contracts and custodial accounts that meet the conditions in the Bulletin will not be treated as plan assets for purposes of ERISA's annual reporting and audit requirements. The Bulletin states that, with regard to those annuity contracts and custodial accounts that meet such conditions, the administrator of the plan is not required to treat either the annuity contracts or custodial accounts as part of the employer's Title I plan or as plan assets for purposes of ERISA's annual reporting requirements. Thus, the plan administrator may disregard such contracts or accounts for purposes of the reporting requirements. The Bulletin also provides that DOL will not reject a Form 5500 Annual Report on the basis of a qualified, adverse, or disclaimed opinion if the plan's IQPA engaged to audit the plan expressly states that the sole reason for such a qualified or adverse opinion or disclaimer of opinion was because such pre-2009 contracts were not covered by the audit or included in the plan's financial statements. [DOL Field Assistance Bull. 2010-01, Q-6]

Consistent with the obligation of employee benefit plan administrators to file complete and accurate annual reports, it is the obligation of the administrator to determine that the conditions of the Bulletin have been satisfied with respect to excluded contracts from such reports. Nonetheless, IQPAs engaged on behalf of participants to conduct employee benefit plan audits play an important role in bringing questions, issues, and irregularities discovered during the course of their audit engagement to the attention of the plan administrator. If an accountant, as part of the audit, discovers that contracts were incorrectly excluded under the Bulletin from the plan's financial statements, DOL expects that the accountant will alert the plan administrator. Also, plan administrators have an obligation to take reasonable steps to resolve questions concerning the exclusion of such contracts from their annual report. If a plan administrator and accountant do not agree with how to resolve issues relating to excluded contracts, DOL expects these issues to be noted in the audit report. [DOL Field Assistance Bull. 2010-01, Q-7] A plan excluded contracts and accounts meeting the conditions of the Bulletin from the Schedule of Assets Held for Investment (Form 5500, Schedule H, Line 4i) and Schedule of Reportable Transactions (Form 5500, Schedule H, Line 4j). Assuming all other required information is included, these schedules will be deemed to be presented in compliance with DOL's rules and regulations for reporting and disclosure. [DOL Field Assistance Bull. 2010-01, Q-8] Contracts and accounts that are excludable from reporting in the 2009 plan year financial statements may also be excluded from comparative financial statements included in the plan's 2009 annual report. [DOL Field Assistance Bull. 2010-01, Q-9]

The Bulletin does not provide plan administrators relief with respect to an annuity contract or custodial account exchanged in accordance with IRS requirements (see Q 35:47) for another contract or account with a new provider after January 1, 2009. Assume, for example, that an employee has a 403(b) annuity contract or custodial account that meets the conditions of the Bulletin and the employee decides to exchange that contract for a contract with a new provider after January 1, 2009. If the employer's authorization or approval of that exchange is required, even if just for tax compliance purposes, the new contract or account would not be eligible for annual reporting relief under the Bulletin. The new contract or account also would fail the requirement of having been issued before January 1, 2009. [DOL Field Assistance Bull. 2010-01, Q-10]

The annual reporting relief described in the Bulletin extends beyond the 2009 reporting year. DOL will not reject annual reports and accompanying audit reports required to be filed for years subsequent to 2009 solely because such reports exclude annuity contracts and custodial accounts meeting the conditions in the Bulletin. [DOL Field Assistance Bull. 2010-01, Q-11]

A plan administrator that determines it will not be able to comply fully with ERISA's annual reporting requirements for contracts that do not meet the conditions of the Bulletin must demonstrate a good-faith effort to comply. What constitutes a good-faith effort will depend on the facts and circumstances involved. Administrators of 403(b) plans that do not fully comply with the reporting requirements have the burden of demonstrating good faith and thus should document their efforts properly to account for and report on contracts and custodial accounts in their Form 5500 or Form 5500-SF Annual Returns/ Reports. Good faith would also generally require the plan administrator to implement internal controls to keep and maintain sufficient records on a going forward basis. In addition, ERISA requires a plan administrator to retain records necessary to verify or support information included in a Form 5500 annual report for six years from the date the annual report was filed, and also to maintain for as long as necessary records that are sufficient to determine the benefits due or which may become due under the plan (see Q 20:6). DOL has noted in other contexts relating to ERISA's record keeping requirements that whether lost or destroyed records can or should be reconstructed and whether the persons responsible for retention of the plan's records are or should be personally liable for the costs incurred in connection with the reconstruction of records or other consequences of their loss or destruction is necessarily dependent on the facts and circumstances of each case. [ERISA §§ 107, 209; DOL Field Assistance Bull. 2010-01, Q-12]

If an employer makes a final contribution to a contract or account in 2009 that is for 2008, the contract or account will be excludable from the plan's annual report under the Bulletin. This relief requires that the employer ceased having an obligation to make contributions (including salary reduction contributions), and actually ceased making contributions, to the contract or account before January 1, 2009. DOL has determined that final contributions to the contract or account attributable to 2008 that were not in fact deposited in the contract or account until 2009 will not be treated by DOL as constituting continuing contributions after January 1, 2009 that would make the contract or account ineligible for the relief provided by the Bulletin. [DOL Field Assistance Bull. 2010-01, Q-13]

DOL announced new outreach and compliance assistance efforts for 403(b) plans subject to Title I of ERISA. In addition to its issuance of Field Assistance Bulletin 2010-01, DOL also published a brochure entitled *Getting Ready for Changes in Filing Your Plan's Annual Return/Report Form 5500*. [DOL News Rel., Feb. 22, 2010]

Certain employee benefit pension plans are provided a limited exemption from, and alternative method of compliance with, certain annual reporting requirements. If the fully guaranteed benefits of a plan are provided exclusively through allocated insurance contracts or policies, the plan need not report certain financial information on the annual report, or engage an IQPA to examine the financial statements and schedules of the plan, including an IQPA's opinion concerning the plan's financial statements and schedules. [DOL Reg. § 2520.104-44(b)(2)] DOL opined that the traditional annuity offered by TIAA-CREF is not a fully allocated contract that qualifies for this exemption. [DOL Op. Ltr. 2010-01A]

Q 35:52 Do the fiduciary responsibility rules apply to 403(b) plans?

ERISA sets forth numerous rules relating to the duties, responsibilities, and liability of fiduciaries with respect to employee pension benefit plans (see Q 35:51). If a 403(b) plan is an employee pension benefit plan, the fiduciary responsibility rules of Title I of ERISA will apply. However, even if the 403(b) plan is covered by Title I, government plans are excluded from coverage, and this, by extension, excludes a 403(b) plan maintained by a public school (see Q 35:4) from the fiduciary responsibility rules. [ERISA § 3(32)]

A fiduciary of a 403(b) plan that is subject to Title I is prohibited from causing the 403(b) plan to engage in certain transactions with a party in interest (see Q 24:3) and from engaging in other conduct in the fiduciary's own interest with regard to the 403(b) plan. Violation of the proscription against engaging in prohibited transactions can result in substantial penalties being imposed on the offending fiduciary. [ERISA §§ 406, 502(i)]

A 403(b) plan may be a self-directed account plan—that is, a plan that permits an employee to make an independent choice, from a broad range of investment alternatives, regarding the manner in which the assets in the employee's 403(b) contract are invested (see Q 23:14). If the 403(b) plan permits a self-directed account, the employee will not be considered a fiduciary solely because the employee exercises control over assets in the 403(b) contract. The consequences of this are twofold. First, other fiduciaries generally would have no cofiduciary liability on account of the employee's investment decisions. Second, because the employee is not a fiduciary, no prohibited transaction under ERISA would result if the exercise of control over the assets caused the 403(b) contract to engage in transactions with parties in interest. [ERISA § 404(c); DOL Reg. §§ 2550.404c-1(a), 2550.404(c)-1(b)(1), 2550.404c-1(d)]

An excise tax is imposed on entity managers who knowingly approve prohibited tax-shelter transactions. If any entity manager of a tax-exempt entity approves the entity as (or otherwise causes the entity to be) a party to a prohibited tax-shelter transaction at any time during the taxable year, and the entity manager knows, or has reason to know, that the transaction is a prohibited tax-shelter transaction, the entity manager must pay an excise tax for the taxable year. The amount of the tax imposed on an entity manager who approves the entity as a party to a prohibited tax-shelter transaction is $20,000 for each approval (or other act causing participation). The term "tax-exempt entity" includes a 403(b) plan and a 403(b) contract. In general, a person who decides that the assets of the plan or contract are to be invested in a prohibited tax-shelter transaction is the entity manager. The excise tax is effective for taxable years ending after May 17, 2006 (with respect to transactions occurring before, on, and after May 17, 2006), except that no excise tax applies to income or proceeds that are properly allocable to any period on or before the date which is 90 days after May 17, 2006. [I.R.C. § 4965 (added by TIPRA § 516(a)); TIPRA § 516(d)(1)] IRS has issued a notice to ensure that 403(b) plans and other tax-exempt entities and other affected parties are aware of the new excise taxes and disclosure rules that target certain potentially abusive tax shelter transactions to which a tax-exempt entity is a party. [IRS Notice 2006-65, 2006-2 C.B. 102] In addition, IRS issued final regulations that became effective on July 6, 2010. See Q 1:31 for details.

See chapter 23 for a discussion of fiduciary responsibilities and chapter 24 for a discussion of prohibited transactions.

Q 35:53   Are 403(b) plan benefits exempt from claims of creditors?

In 1992, the United States Supreme Court held that a participant's interest in a qualified retirement plan is exempt from the claims of creditors in a bankruptcy proceeding, which, it was hoped, resolved the conflict among the courts of appeals. [Patterson v. Shumate, 504 U.S. 753 (1992)] On April 20, 2005, President Bush signed into law the Bankruptcy Abuse Prevention and Consumer Protection Act of 2005, which contains provisions that protect the 403(b) plan assets of bankruptcy filers. See Q 1:27 for a discussion of the salient provisions of this Act. Consequently, the following discussion may apply only to those cases that arose before the October 17, 2005 effective date of the Act.

ERISA and the Code require every qualified retirement plan to prohibit the assignment or alienation of benefits under the plan. [ERISA § 206(d)(1); I.R.C. § 401(a)(13)] Federal Bankruptcy Code Section 541(c)(2) excludes from the bankruptcy estate property of the debtor in a trust that is subject to a restriction on transfer enforceable under applicable nonbankruptcy law. The Supreme Court ruled that the anti-alienation provision contained in a qualified retirement plan constitutes a restriction on transfer enforceable under applicable nonbankruptcy law; and, accordingly, a debtor may exclude his interest in such a plan from the property of the bankruptcy estate. The Supreme Court referred to an "ERISA qualified" plan.

Not all 403(b) plans are subject to Title I of ERISA (see Q 35:51). Courts have held that 403(b) plan benefits were not subject to creditor claims; none of the courts relied upon the Supreme Court decision; and, in at least one case, the 403(b) plan was not subject to ERISA. [In re Grubbs, 325 B.R. 151 (Bankr. D. N.C. 2005); In re Gould, 04-11889 (Bankr. W.D. Pa. 2005); Will of King, N.Y.L.J., June 30, 2003 (Surr. Ct. Broome County); In re Gallet, N.Y.L.J., May 9, 2003 (Surr. Ct. N.Y. County); In re Barnes, 264 B.R. 415 (Bankr. D. Mich. 2001); In re Macintyre, 74 F.3d 186 (9th Cir. 1996); In re Johnson, 191 B.R. 75 (M.D. Pa. 1996)] One court concluded that 403(b) plan benefits were subject to creditor claims because the annuity contracts were not held in a trust (see Q 35:9). [Rhiel v. Adams, 2003 WL 22926926 (6th Cir. 2003)] However, another court rejected a debtor's claim that the portion of his retirement account pledged to secure his alimony obligation was exempt property under the Bankruptcy Code. It held that, because the funds were validly pledged under State law, the assignment was a deemed distribution (see Q 35:38). This effectively removed those funds from the retirement account and made them nonexempt property that could be claimed by creditors in bankruptcy. The court held that the alimony payments were non-dischargeable and that the ex-wife's security interest in the plan was valid. [In the Matter of Coppola, 2005 WL 17143365 (5th Cir. 2005)]

One court concluded that IRS had a secured claim against a debtor's 403(b) contracts to the extent of their value. The court ruled that restrictions on transfer contained in the annuity contracts (see Q 35:15) were inapplicable to federal tax liens (see Q 4:29) and, thus, were not enforceable under nonbankruptcy law and that the annuities constituted property of the bankruptcy estate with respect to IRS. For purposes of IRS's secured claim, the value of the annuities was to be fixed at the present value of the future stream of payments that the debtor would receive. [*In re* McIver, Jr., 262 B.R. 362 (Bankr. D. Md. 2001)] Another court held that IRS possessed valid tax liens against a debtor's 403(b) contracts. [*In re* Piper, 02-12096 (Bankr. D. Mass. 2003)]

Q 35:54   What IRS correction programs apply to 403(b) plans?

The Employee Plans Compliance Resolution System (EPCRS; see Q 19:2) is the IRS system that coordinates compliance programs for the correction of plan qualification failures (see Q 19:5) and, with respect to 403(b) plans, 403(b) failures (see Q 19:6). EPCRS may be used by 403(b) plans that are intended to satisfy the qualification requirements of the Code (see Qs 35:9, 35:13) but that have not satisfied these requirements because of certain types of failures. [Rev. Proc. 2006-27, 2006-1 C.B. 945]

For a detailed discussion of EPCRS and its applicability to 403(b) plans, see chapter 19.

Q 35:55   What special rules apply to 403(b) contracts purchased for church employees?

The term "church" means a church, a convention or association of churches, or an elementary or secondary school which is controlled, operated, or principally supported by a church or by a convention or association of churches. This term also includes a qualified church-controlled organization which is a church-controlled tax-exempt organization, *other than* an organization which offers goods, services, or facilities for sale, other than on an incidental basis, to the general public, other than goods, services, or facilities that are sold at a nominal charge that is substantially less than the cost of providing such goods, services, or facilities, and normally receives more than 25 percent of its support from either governmental sources or receipts from admissions, sales of merchandise, performance of services, or furnishing of facilities, in activities that are not unrelated trades or businesses, or both. [I.R.C. §§ 403(b)(12)(B), 3121(w)(3)(A), 3121(w)(3)(B); Treas. Reg. § 1.403(b)-2(b)(5)] A "church-related organization" means a church or a convention or association of churches, including an organization, whether a civil law corporation or otherwise, the principal purpose or function of which is the administration or funding of a plan or program for the provision of retirement benefits for the employees of a church or a convention or association of churches, if such organization is controlled by or associated with a church or a convention or association of churches. [I.R.C. § 414(e)(3)(A); Treas. Reg. § 1.403(b)-2(b)(6); Priv. Ltr. Ruls. 200816031, 200813044, 200747022, 200743036] Subject to any rules specifically applicable to ministers, an employee (see Q 35:5) also includes a minister when performing services in the exercise of the minister's ministry. [I.R.C. § 414(e)(5)(A); Treas. Reg. § 1.403(b)-2(b)(9)]

A retirement income account is a defined contribution program established or maintained by a church-related organization to provide 403(b) plan benefits for its employees or their beneficiaries. [I.R.C. § 403(b)(9)(B); Treas. Reg. § 1.403(b)-2(b)(15)] A retirement income account is treated as a 403(b) contract, and amounts paid by an employer to a retirement income account are treated as amounts contributed by the employer for a 403(b) contract for the employee on whose behalf the account is maintained. [I.R.C. §§ 403(b)(9)(A), 414(e), 414(i); Treas. Reg. § 1.403(b)-9(a)(1); Priv. Ltr. Ruls. 200708090, 200644032, 9819042, 9815060, 9625044, 9530031, 9451082] To be a retirement income account:

1. There must be sufficiently separate accounting for the retirement income account's interest in the underlying assets in order for it to be possible at all times to determine the retirement income account's interest in the underlying assets and to distinguish that interest from any interest that is not part of the retirement income account (see Q 2:2);

2. Investment performance must be based on gains and losses on those assets (see Q 2:2); and

3. The assets held in the account cannot be used for, or diverted to, purposes other than for the exclusive benefit of plan participants or their beneficiaries; and, for this purpose, assets are treated as diverted to the employer if there is a loan or other extension of credit from assets in the account of the employer (see Q 4:1).

[Treas. Reg. § 1.403(b)-9(a)(2)(i)]

Contributions to a 403(b) plan must be transferred to the entity holding assets of any retirement income account that is treated as an annuity contract within a period that is not longer than is reasonable for the proper administration of the plan (see Q 35:10). [Treas. Reg. §§ 1.403(b)-8(a), 1.403(b)-8(b)]

A retirement income account must be maintained pursuant to a program that is a plan (see Q 35:9), and the plan document must state (or otherwise evidence in a similarly clear manner) the intent to constitute a retirement income account. [Treas. Reg. § 1.403(b)-9(a)(2)(ii)] A trust that includes no assets other than assets of a retirement income account is treated as an organization that is exempt from taxation. [Treas. Reg. § 1.403(b)-9(a)(7)] Retirement income accounts, annuity contracts (see Q 35:6), and custodial accounts (see Q 35:7) can be used by church employees. [DOL Op. Ltrs. 2004-11A, 97-07A, 97-01A,

96-24A, 96-19A, 96-18A; Priv. Ltr. Ruls. 9849026, 9713021, 9704020, 9702035, 9643038] A retirement income account that is treated as an annuity contract is not a custodial account, even if it is invested solely in stock of a regulated investment company. [Treas. Reg. § 1.403 (b)-9(a)(4)] Retirement income account assets held in trust (including a custodial account that is treated as a trust) are subject to the same rules regarding combining of assets as custodial account assets (see Q 35:7). In addition, retirement income account assets are permitted to be commingled in a common fund with amounts devoted exclusively to church purposes (such as a fund from which unfunded pension payments are made to former employees of the church). However, unless otherwise permitted by IRS, no assets of the plan sponsor, other than retirement income account assets, may be combined with custodial account assets or any other assets permitted to be combined. [Treas. Reg. § 1.403(b)-8(f), 1.403(b)-9(a)(6)]

Generally, 403(b) contracts purchased by churches need not satisfy the minimum coverage and nondiscrimination requirements (see Qs 35:16–35:21). [I.R.C. §§ 403(b)(1)(D), 403(b)(12), 410(d)(1), 414(e), 3121(w)(3); Treas. Reg. § 1.403(b)-5(d); DOL Op. Ltr. 2000-02A; Priv. Ltr. Rul. 9725043] If a church plan makes an election to satisfy these requirements, the election is irrevocable. [I.R.C. § 410(d)(2)] The automatic rollover rules (see Q 34:17) apply to non-electing church plans. However, where the authority to amend the non-electing church plan is held by a church convention, these requirements will be treated as satisfied if the automatic rollover provisions are not applied to mandatory distributions from such plan that are made prior to the date that is 60 days after the close of the earliest church convention that occurs on or after January 1, 2006. [I.R.C. § 414(e)(3); IRS Notice 2005-15, Q&A-8, 2005-1 C.B. 337]

An election may be made by a church employee to increase the annual addition limitation (see Q 6:34). This election allows a contribution to a retirement income account in any year to be as much as $10,000 even if this amount is more than the 100-percent-of-compensation limit. Under this election, contributions in excess of the compensation limit may not exceed $40,000 for the lifetime of the employee. [I.R.C. § 415(c)(7)(A); Treas. Reg. §§ 1.403(b)-9(b), 1.415(c)-1(a)(3), 1.415(c)-1(d)]

Example 1. E is an employee of ABC Church earning $7,000 during each calendar year. E participates in a 403(b) plan maintained by ABC Church beginning in the year 2010. E's taxable year is the calendar year, and the limitation year for the plan coincides with the calendar year. ABC Church contributes $10,000 to be allocated to E's account under the plan for the year 2010.

This allocation is treated as not violating the limits because it does not exceed $10,000. Moreover, because an annual addition of $10,000 would otherwise exceed the limitation on contributions by $3,000, $3,000 is counted toward the aggregate limitation for year 2010. Accordingly, ABC Church may make such allocations for 13 years (for example, for years 2010 through 2022) without exceeding the aggregate limitation of $40,000. For the 14th year, ABC

Church could allocate only $8,000 to E's account (the sum of the $7,000 limitation and the remaining $1,000 of the $40,000 aggregate limitation).

Example 2. F is an employee of XYZ Church, and F's taxable year is the calendar year. F earns $2,000 during each calendar year for services F provides to XYZ Church, all of which are performed outside the United States during each calendar year. F participates in a 403(b) plan maintained by XYZ Church beginning in the year 2010. The limitation year for the plan coincides with the calendar year. XYZ Church contributes $10,000 to be allocated to F's account under the plan for the year 2010. F's adjusted gross income for each taxable year does not exceed $17,000.

This allocation is treated as not violating the limits because it does not exceed $10,000. Moreover, because an annual addition of $10,000 would otherwise exceed the limitation on contributions by $7,000 (the excess of $10,000 over the greater of the $2,000 compensation limitation or the $3,000 amount; see Q 35:26), XYZ Church may make such allocations for five years (for example, for years 2010 through 2014) without exceeding the aggregate limitation of $40,000. In year 2015, XYZ Church may contribute $8,000 to be allocated to F's account under the plan (the sum of the $3,000 limitation and the remaining $5,000 of the $40,000 aggregate limitation on annual additions in excess of the limits on contributions). For years after 2015, XYZ Church could allocate $3,000 per year to F's account.

A church employee with 15 years of service is eligible for the special catch-up election relating to the increased dollar amount of elective deferrals (see Q 35:26). [I.R.C. § 402(g)(7)] IRS has ruled that ministers' housing allowances could not serve as the basis for contributions to a religious organization's 403(b) plan because the tax-free housing allowance could not be treated as compensation. [Priv. Ltr. Rul. 200135045]

Any asset of a retirement income account that is owned or used by a participant or beneficiary is treated as having been distributed to that participant or beneficiary (see Qs 35:35, 35:38). [Treas. Reg. § 1.403(b)-9(a)(3)] A retirement income account may distribute benefits in a form that includes a life annuity only if (1) the amount of the distribution form has an actuarial present value, at the annuity starting date (see Q 10:3), equal to the participant's or beneficiary's accumulated benefit, based on reasonable actuarial assumptions, including regarding interest and mortality, and (2) the plan sponsor guarantees benefits in the event that a payment is due that exceeds the participant's or beneficiary's accumulated benefit. [Treas. Reg. § 1.403(b)-9(a)(5)] For purposes of the required minimum distribution rules (see Q 35:37) relating to annuity contracts, annuity payments provided with respect to retirement income accounts do not fail to satisfy such requirements merely because the payments are not made under an annuity contract purchased from an insurance company, provided that the relationship between the annuity payments and the retirement income accounts is not inconsistent with any rules prescribed by IRS. [Treas. Reg. § 1.403(b)-6(e)(5)] A church employee is also eligible for the deferred required beginning date relating to required minimum distributions. [I.R.C. § 401(a) (9)(C)]

Self-employed ministers and ministers, such as chaplains, who are employed by organizations that are not Section 501(c)(3) organizations (see Q 35:3) may participate in church plans. Eligibility to participate in church plans has been expanded to include ministers who are self-employed in connection with the exercise of their ministry. A self-employed individual is someone who has net earnings from self-employment (see Qs 6:60, 6:61). A self-employed minister is treated as the minister's own employer that is a Section 501(c)(3) organization. The self-employed minister's includible compensation (see Q 35:24) is determined on the basis of the minister's net earnings from self-employment, instead of the amount of compensation received from an employer. In determining the number of years of service (see Q 35:25), the years and portions of years in which the minister was self-employed with respect to the ministry must be included. In addition to self-employed ministers, ministers who are employed by organizations other than Section 501(c)(3) organizations can participate in church plans. Such ministers are treated as if they were employed by churches and may, therefore, participate in church plans. To be eligible for this treatment as a church employee, the minister's employment by such an organization must be in connection with the exercise of the ministry. An employer that is not eligible to participate in a church plan may exclude a minister who participates in a church plan and who is employed in the exercise of the ministry from being treated as an employee for purposes of the employer's nondiscrimination testing for nondenominational plans. Such nondenominational plans include a qualified retirement plan, a 403(b) plan, and a retirement income account. Compensation that is taken into account for purposes of determining contributions or benefits with respect to a church plan may not also be taken into account for purposes of determining contributions or benefits under a non-church plan; the compensation may be considered only once. As discussed, eligibility to participate in retirement income accounts now includes ministers who are self-employed or are employed by entities other than Section 501(c)(3) organizations (such as chaplains). The contribution made by such a minister to a retirement income account is excludable from the income of the minister to the extent that the contribution would be excludable if the minister were an employee of a church and the contribution were made to the plan. [I.R.C. §§ 403(b)(1)(A)(iii), 404(a)(10), 414(e)(5); Treas. Reg. §§ 1.403(b)-4(e)(3)(ii), 1.403(b)-9(c); IRS Pub. 571] In the case of foreign missionaries, amounts contributed to a plan by the employer are treated as investment in the contract or basis (see Qs 13:3, 35:40), because the amounts, if paid directly to the employee, would have been excludable from gross income.

The regulations are generally applicable for taxable years beginning after December 31, 2008 (see Q 35:1). However, under a transition rule, for a 403(b) plan maintained by a church-related organization for which the authority to amend the contract is held by a church convention, the final regulations do not apply before the first day of the plan year that begins after December 31, 2009. [Treas. Reg. § 1.403(b)-11(c)(1)] In the case of a loan or other extension of credit to the employer that was entered into under a retirement income account before July 26, 2007 the plan does not fail to satisfy the exclusive benefit rule on account of the loan or other extension of credit to the employer before the applicable date or as promptly as practical thereafter (including taking steps after July 26, 2007 and before the applicable date). [Treas. Reg. § 1.403(b)-11(c)(2)]

PPA (see Q 1:33) made a number of changes affecting church plans.

Annuity payments provided with respect to any account maintained for a participant or beneficiary under a qualified church plan does not fail to meet the minimum distribution rules (see Q 35:37) merely because the payments are not made under an annuity contract purchased from an insurance company if such payments would not fail such requirements if provided with respect to a retirement income account. A qualified church plan is a money purchase pension plan (see Q 2:4) that (1) is a church plan with respect to which the election to satisfy the minimum coverage and nondiscrimination requirements has not been made and (2) was in existence on April 17, 2002. This provision is effective for years beginning after August 17, 2006, and no inference is intended from this provision with respect to the proper application of the minimum distribution rules to church plans before the effective date. [PPA § 865]

Debt-financed income of a tax-exempt entity is subject to unrelated business income tax (UBIT; see Q 1:6). Debt-financed property generally is property that is held to produce income and with respect to which there is acquisition indebtedness. There is an exception to the UBIT rules for debt-financed property held by qualifying organizations, and qualifying organizations include qualified retirement plans. PPA provides that a retirement income account of a church (or certain other organizations) is a qualified organization for purposes of the exemption from the UBIT debt-financed property rules. This provision is effective for taxable years beginning on or after August 17, 2006. [I.R.C. § 514(c)(9)(C)(iv)]

PPA provides that the 100-percent-of-compensation limit (see Q 6:11) does not apply to a defined benefit plan (see Q 2:3) maintained by a church or qualified church-controlled organization except with respect to highly compensated benefits. Highly compensated benefits are any benefits accrued for an employee in any year on or after the first year in which such employee is an HCE (see Q 3:2) of the organization. For purposes of applying the compensation limit to highly compensated benefits, all the benefits of the employee that would otherwise be taken into account in applying the limit are taken into account; that is, the limit does not apply only to those benefits accrued in or after the first year in which the employee is an HCE. This provision is effective for years beginning after December 31, 2006. [I.R.C. § 415(b)(11)]

Chapter 36

Qualified Domestic Relations Orders

The rate of divorce in the United States has increased over the years; and, in many cases, qualified retirement plan benefits represent the major marital asset. The Retirement Equity Act of 1984 established a new category of plan benefit recipients—alternate payees under qualified domestic relations orders (QDROs). This chapter analyzes the requirements for QDROs and their tax consequences.

Q 36:1 What is a qualified domestic relations order?

A QDRO is a domestic relations order (DRO; see Q 36:2) that creates or recognizes the existence of an alternate payee's (see Q 36:5) right to, or assigns to an alternate payee the right to, receive all or a portion of the benefits payable with respect to a participant under a qualified retirement plan and that complies with certain special requirements (see Q 36:2). [I.R.C. § 414(p)(1)(A); ERISA § 206(d)(3); Treas. Reg. § 1.401(a)-13(g)(1); Hawkins v. Comm'r, 86 F.3d 982 (10th Cir. 1996); Brotman, 105 T.C. 141 (1995); In re Norfleet, No. 4-92-0780 (Ill. App. Ct. 4th Dist. 1993); Brotman v. Molitch, No. 88-9876 (E.D. Pa. 1989)]

Federal courts and state courts have concurrent jurisdiction to rule on the validity of QDROs. [ERISA §§ 502(a)(1)(B), 502(e)(1); Mack v. Kuckenmeister, 2010 WL 2853881 (9th Cir. 2010); Geiger v. Foley Hoag LLP Retirement Plan, No. 07-1208 (1st Cir. 2008); Board of Trustees of the Laborers Pension Trust Fund for N. Cal. v. Levingston, 816 F. Supp. 1496 (N.D. Cal. 1993); In re Marriage of Levingston, 12 Cal. App. 4th 1303 (1993)] If the terms of a QDRO are ambiguous, the proper forum for resolving the dispute is at the trial level, not at the appellate level. [Hullett v. Towers, Perrin, Forster & Crosby, Inc., No. 94-1517 (3d Cir. 1994)]

An appellate court determined that a property settlement agreement constituted a DRO and, as such, not mentioning the QDRO in the agreement did not preclude the trial court's later entry of the QDRO to recognize and enforce the ex-wife's rights created under the agreement. The court further found that the language of the agreement neither mandated payment of benefits to the ex-wife through her former husband nor precluded the use of a QDRO to enforce distribution of the benefits and also determined that the QDRO did not modify the agreement or the terms of the agreement because the effect of the QDRO was merely to enforce the ex-wife's right to receive retirement benefits. [Hopkins v. State of Missouri, No. WD 54337 (Mo. Ct. App. 1997)] A consent decree agreed to by a husband and wife in a divorce proceeding did not rise to the level of a QDRO, concluded one court. [Winters v. Kutrip, 2002 U.S. App. LEXIS 20557 (3d Cir. 2002)] One court held that the terms of a QDRO are obligatory and, where a conflict exists, take precedence over a plan fiduciary's duty to diversify plan investments. Upon their divorce, a husband and wife entered into a QDRO that provided for 50 percent of the husband's plan account to be segregated for the benefit of his wife. The QDRO further provided that this segregated account was to accumulate interest at a rate equivalent to a one-year certificate of deposit. The plan was not required to distribute the segregated account to the wife before the husband reached retirement age. The wife claimed that this minimal interest arrangement violated the prudent person investment standard (see Q 23:81). The court upheld the terms of the QDRO and concluded that once a plan administrator (see Q 20:1) has determined that a DRO meets the criteria for a QDRO, the administrator is required to act in accordance with the QDRO. [Matassarin v. F.F. Lynch, 174 F.3d 549 (5th Cir. 1999)]

In one case, a husband received a lump-sum distribution (see Q 13:5) from a qualified retirement plan and transferred the distribution to an IRA established in his wife's name. Because the distribution and transfer were not made pursuant to a QDRO, the distribution was includible in the husband's gross income and penalties were assessed against both the husband and the wife (see Qs 13:26, 30:9). [Rodoni, 105 T.C. 29 (1995); *see also* Hackenberg, T.C. Summ. Op. 2010-135; Amarasinghe, No. 08-1226 (4th Cir. 2008); Simpson, I, 86 T.C.M. 470 (2003); Bougas III, 86 T.C.M. 9 (2003); Dorn, 86 T.C.M. 5 (2003); Jones, 80 T.C.M. 76 (2000); Bunney, 114 T.C. 259 (2000); Czepiel, 78 T.C.M. 378 (1999), *aff'd*, 00-1257 (1st Cir. 2000); Burton, 73 T.C.M. 1729 (1997)]

Courts have ruled that a QDRO with respect to the survivor annuity portion of a retirement benefit could not be created in favor of the participant's first spouse where the participant had remarried and had commenced receiving retirement benefits in the form of a qualified joint and survivor annuity (QJSA; see Q 10:8). [Carmona v. Carmona, 2008 WL 4225547 (9th Cir. 2008); Rivers v. Central & S.W. Corp., 186 F.3d 681 (5th Cir. 1999); Hopkins v. AT&T Global Info. Solutions Co, 105 F.3d 153 (4th Cir. 1997)] A former spouse was denied survivor benefits where the divorce decree was not sufficiently specific to satisfy the QDRO requirements and the decree was submitted to the plan administrator four years after the decree was issued and two years after the participant died. [Woodall v. The Southern Co. Pension Plan, 2008 WL 2397391 (M.D. Ala. 2008)] Another court concluded that the death of a participant during the process of having a DRO approved as a QDRO by the plan terminates the former spouse's rights if the participant has remarried and is survived by a current spouse. [Stahl v. Exxon Corp., 212 F. Supp. 2d 657 (S.D. Tex. 2002)] However, another court ruled that a QDRO could be created in favor of the first spouse even though the participant (1) had remarried, (2) had commenced receiving retirement benefits, and (3) had died, because it related to the marital property right of the first spouse pursuant to the state community property law. [Bailey v. New Orleans S.S. Ass'n/ILA, 100 F.3d 28 (5th Cir. 1996)] Courts have concluded that a QDRO may be obtained after the death of a participant. [IBM Savings Plan v. Price, No. 2:04-CV-187 (D. Vt. 2004); Patton v. Denver Post Corp., 326 F.3d 1148 (10th Cir. 2003); Trustees of the Dirs. Guild of Am.–Producer Pension Benefits Plans v. Tise, 234 F.3d 415 (9th Cir. 2000)] A property settlement agreement, incorporated by reference into a divorce decree, was held to be a QDRO, even though the decree and agreement were not presented to the plan administrator until after the participant had died. [Metropolitan Life Ins. Co. v. Drainville, 2009 WL 2208111 (D. R.I. 2009); Smith v. Estate of Smith, 248 F. Supp. 2d 348 (D. N.J. 2003)] When a divorce decree, awarding a portion of an employee's plan benefits to his former spouse, was received and acknowledged by an employer prior to the employee's death, it was enforceable by the former spouse although she was not named as an alternate payee until after the employee's death. The divorce decree had awarded the employee's spouse half of the employee's plan funds, but the court order naming the spouse as alternate payee was not entered until two days after the employee's death. The court opined that the employer had been put on notice that a decree had been issued that could be a QDRO, the decree designated the spouse as entitled to part of the employee's plan benefits, and the court order naming the spouse as alternate payee was filed well within the 18-month period allowed to qualify a QDRO (see Q 36:22). Taken together, the plan administrator had sufficient basis for qualifying the DRO, the court determined. [Hogan v. Raytheon Co., 302 F.3d 854 (8th Cir. 2002)] However, another ruled that under state law a QDRO could not be issued after the participant's death. [Davenport v. Davenport, D.D.S., M.S., P.A., 146 F. Supp. 2d 770 (M.D. N.C. 2001)] See Q 36:2 concerning the interim final regulation issued by DOL.

One court held that the rights of a surviving spouse to a qualified preretirement survivor annuity (QPSA; see Q 10:9) cannot be divested by the claims of children designated as beneficiaries in a marital dissolution order, because only the surviving spouse, or a former spouse properly designated in a QDRO, may be eligible for a QPSA. Without a QDRO, the children are not in a position to assert claims competing with the widow's rights as a surviving spouse, the court said. Further, the dissolution order did not qualify as a QDRO, because it did not comply with the specificity requirements for a QDRO, concluded the court. [Hamilton v. Washington State Plumbing & Pipefitting Industry Pension Plan, 433 F.3d 1091 (9th Cir. 2006)] DOL has opined that a DRO that designates a state child support enforcement agency as the party to whom payments will be made on behalf of an alternate payee may be a QDRO, even though the agency is not an alternate payee, since the agency acts as an agent for children in collecting and paying support. [DOL Op. Ltr. 2002-03A]

The rules relating to QDROs generally became effective on January 1, 1985. However, a plan administrator may treat a DRO entered before 1985 as a QDRO, whether or not it meets the above definition, but must treat it as a QDRO if, on January 1, 1985, the plan administrator was paying benefits in compliance therewith. If a plan administrator chooses not to treat a pre-1985 order as a QDRO, the alternate payee should try to have the DRO amended to satisfy the requirements for a QDRO. [*In re* Carbaugh, 278 B.R. 512 (10th Cir. 2002); Metropolitan Life Ins. Co. v. Bigelow, 2002 WL 362665 (2d Cir. 2002); *In re*

Zeitler, 1997 Bankr. LEXIS 1495 (Bankr. E.D.N.C. 1997); Layton v. TDS Healthcare Sys. Corp., No. C-93-1827-MHP (9th Cir. 1994); Reineke v. Reineke, No. 92-3333 (Fla. Dist. Ct. App. 1st Dist. 1993); *see also* Platt, T.C.M. 2008-17] One court ruled that a plan's claim in federal court that a DRO was invalid should not have been stayed pending a state court decision concerning the validity of the DRO. [Rouse v. Daimler Chrysler Corp. UAW Noncontributory Plan, 2002 WL 1836580 (6th Cir. 2002)]

Congress recognized that the rules relating to QDROs serve important purposes in protecting spousal rights to qualified retirement plan benefits but that these rules are extremely complicated. Because Congress believed it was appropriate to direct IRS to develop sample language for QDROs so that spouses could more easily comply with these important rules, SBA '96 directed IRS to develop sample language for inclusion in a form for a QDRO that satisfies the legal requirements for a QDRO and that focuses attention on the need to consider the treatment of a lump-sum payment, QJSA, or qualified preretirement survivor annuity (QPSA; see Q 10:9). [SBA '96 § 1457(a)] In compliance with this directive, IRS provided information to assist attorneys, employees, spouses and former spouses, and plan administrators in drafting and reviewing a QDRO. [IRS Notice 97-11, 1997-1 C.B. 379]

In addition, Pension Benefit Guaranty Corporation (PBGC; see Q 25:10) has published a booklet entitled "Divorce Orders & PBGC" to assist attorneys and others who prepare QDROs. The booklet sets forth guidelines for QDROs submitted to PBGC after a plan terminates and PBGC becomes trustee. [PBGC Pub. 1005 (Sept. 1996)] PBGC has requested public comments regarding its intention to make revisions to the booklet. [PBGC Notice, 70 Fed. Reg. 60,308 (Oct. 17, 2005)] In addition, PBGC has requested that the Office of Management and Budget extend its approval, with modifications, of the guidance, model language, and forms contained in the booklet, whose title will be changed to "Qualified Domestic Relations Orders & PBGC." [71 Fed. Reg. 33,778 (June 12, 2006)] In March 2007, PBGC issued an update of the booklet, now titled "Qualified Domestic Relations Orders & PBGC." The revised booklet includes an explanation of the earliest PBGC retirement date, a new model QDRO specifically for child support, and a new model QDRO providing only for a surviving spouse benefit. In addition, draft language concerning a contingent alternate payee and subsidized early retirement benefits in a separate interest QDRO is included. [PBGC News Rel. (March 14, 2007)] A more comprehensive booklet, "QDROs: The Division of Pensions Through Qualified Domestic Relations Orders," has been published by the Department of Labor (DOL). DOL has advised that it will update this booklet. PBGC issued regulations concerning the ability of its Appeals Board to refer certain categories of appeals to other PBGC departments for a written response. Among those is an initial determination regarding whether a DRO is a QDRO. [PBGC Reg. §§ 4003.1, 4003.2, 4003.58(b)]

Q 36:2   What is a domestic relations order?

A DRO is a judgment, decree, or order (including approval of a property settlement agreement) made pursuant to a state domestic relations law (including a community property law) that relates to the provision of child support, alimony payments, or marital property rights to an alternate payee (see Q 36:5). [I.R.C. § 414(p)(1)(B); ERISA § 206(d)(3)(B)(ii)]

A state authority, generally a court, must actually issue a judgment, decree, or order or otherwise formally approve a property settlement agreement before it can be a DRO. The mere fact that a property settlement is agreed to and signed by the parties will not, in and of itself, cause the agreement to be a DRO. A DRO may be issued by any state agency or instrumentality with the authority to issue judgments, decrees, or orders, or to approve property settlement agreements, pursuant to state domestic relations law (including community property law). [I.R.C. § 414(p)(1)(B); ERISA § 206(d)(3)(B)(ii)] DOL has opined that an income withholding notice issued by a state agency to enforce a child support order is a DRO and that ERISA does not require that a judgment, decree, or order be issued by a court in order to be a DRO. [DOL Op. Ltr. 2001-06A] One court ruled that a QDRO benefiting the domestic partner of a plan participant is not disqualified by the partner's non-marital status because her quasi-marital relationship with the participant gave rise, *under state law*, to marital property rights. [Owens v. Automotive Machinists Pension Trust, 551 F.3d 1138 (9th Cir. 2009)]

There is no requirement that both parties to a marital proceeding sign or otherwise endorse or approve an order. It is also not necessary that the qualified retirement plan be brought into state court or made a party to a domestic relations proceeding for an order issued in that proceeding to be a DRO or a QDRO (see Q 36:1). Because state law is generally preempted by ERISA to the extent that it relates to qualified retirement plans, it is the position of DOL that plans cannot be joined as a party in a domestic relations proceeding pursuant to state law. Moreover, plans are neither permitted nor required to follow the terms of DROs purporting to assign plan benefits unless they are QDROs. [I.R.C. § 414(p)(1)(B); ERISA §§ 206(d)(3)(B)(ii), 514(a), 514(b)(7); Taliaferro v. Goodyear Tire & Rubber Co., No. 06-40570 (5th Cir. 2008)]

A DRO must also satisfy certain special requirements. The DRO must clearly specify:

1. The name and last known mailing address (if any) of the participant and the name and mailing address of each alternate payee covered by the order;

2. The amount or percentage of the participant's benefits to be paid by the qualified retirement plan to each such alternate payee or the manner in which such amount or percentage is to be determined;

3. The number of payments or period to which the order applies; and

4. The qualified retirement plan to which the order applies.

[I.R.C. § 414(p)(2); ERISA § 206(d)(3)(C)]

In addition, a DRO may not require:

1. The qualified retirement plan to provide any type or form of benefit, or any option, not otherwise provided under the plan (see Q 36:18);

2. The qualified retirement plan to provide increased benefits (determined on the basis of actuarial value); or

3. The payment of benefits to an alternate payee that are required to be paid to another alternate payee under another order previously determined to be a QDRO (see Q 36:1).

[I.R.C. § 414(p)(3); ERISA § 206(d)(3)(D); Winters v. Kutrip, 2002 U.S. App. LEXIS 20557 (3d Cir. 2002)]

A QDRO can assign rights to benefits under more than one plan of the same or different employers as long as each plan and the assignment of benefit rights under each plan are clearly specified. [I.R.C. § 414(p)(2)(D); ERISA § 206(d)(3)(C)(iv)]

One court concluded that ERISA does not require, or even permit, a qualified retirement plan to look beneath the surface of a QDRO—compliance with a QDRO is obligatory—and that any amounts required to be paid pursuant to a DRO that satisfies the seven statutory conditions listed above must be paid. In order to ensure compliance with those seven conditions, the plan must follow certain procedures (see Q 36:21); and, if these procedures are followed and all of the conditions are satisfied, then the plan obligation to the participant and each alternate payee is discharged to the extent of any payment made. [Blue v. UAL Corp., 160 F.3d 383 (7th Cir. 1998); see also Matassarin v. F.F. Lynch, 174 F.3d 549 (5th Cir. 1999)] However, DOL has advised that a plan administrator (see Q 20:1) is required to attempt to resolve the question of the validity of a DRO when confronted with evidence that the DRO is a sham (see Q 36:21). [DOL Op. Ltr. 99-13A]

An order will not be disqualified merely because it does not specify the current mailing address of the participant and each alternate payee, as long as the plan administrator (see Q 20:1) has reason to know the addresses independently of the order (for example, the alternate payee is also a plan participant and the plan records include a current address for each participant). [Stewart v. Thorpe Holding Co. Profit Sharing Plan, 207 F.3d 1143 (9th Cir. 2000); see also Mattingly v. Hoge, 2008 WL 116392 (6th Cir. 2008); REA Sen. Comm. Rep.] Another court concluded that a plan participant's daughters, rather than his father who had been designated as beneficiary, were entitled to the plan benefits because the order designating his daughters as beneficiaries constituted a QDRO even though not all of the required information was included in the order. [Metropolitan Life Ins. Co. v. Bigelow, 2002 WL 362665 (2d Cir. 2002)] However, one court ruled that a court order was not a QDRO because, upon the death of the nonparticipant spouse, the individual who would succeed to the nonparticipant spouse's benefits might not qualify as an alternate payee. [Shelstead v. Shelstead, 78 Cal. Rptr. 2d 365 (Cal. 1998)] Another court determined that a preliminary injunction issued by a state court ordering a couple not to change ownership of marital assets during the divorce proceeding was not a QDRO because the statutory requirements were not satisfied. [Central States, Southeast & Southwest Areas Pension Fund v. Howell, 227 F.3d 672 (6th Cir. 2000). A former spouse, who was the named beneficiary of her ex-spouse's retirement benefits, was deemed to have effectively waived her right to those benefits when she signed the property settlement agreement pursuant to their divorce since the property settlement did not amount to a QDRO in that it did not satisfy all seven of the statutory conditions. [Von Haden v. Supervised Estate of Von Haden, No. 52A02-9712-CV-876 (Ind. Ct. App. 1998)] A property settlement agreement that designated the deceased participant's children as beneficiaries under a qualified retirement plan was ruled not to be a QDRO and, therefore, unenforceable under the anti-alienation rules (see Qs 4:27, 36:7) because the agreement did not clearly set forth the number of payments or period to which the order applied. Thus, the decedent's estate was entitled to the benefits. [Belfer v. Zee, Nos. 97-5725, 98-5153 (3d Cir. 1998)] One court concluded that a judgment entered into pursuant to a divorce did not constitute a QDRO because it did not contain the exact amount of the benefit the plan was to pay, the applicable payment period or number of payments, the names of the plans, or a statement that the former spouse was to be considered the surviving spouse. Consequently, the former spouse was not entitled to survivor's benefits because a QDRO was not entered before the participant's death. [Guzman v. Commonwealth Edison Co., No. 99 C 582 (N.D. Ill. 2000)] An order will not be treated as providing increased benefits unless it provides for the payment of benefits in excess of those to which the participant would be entitled in the absence of the order. One court ruled that a DRO, issued in connection with a wife's divorce from her husband, did not meet the requirements for treatment as a QDRO because the DRO would have required the plan to pay the wife benefits in an amount that would have exceeded the balance in her husband's retirement account [Alberici Corp. v. Davis, 2006 WL 1841210 (8th Cir. 2006)]

An ex-wife did not reasonably rely on a plan's miscalculation of the amount owed her under the divorce agreement because she knew that the payments she received were more than provided to her by the QDRO. Consequently, the plan could establish a schedule for the recoupment of the overpayment. [Julia v. Bridgestone/Firestone, Inc., 2004 U.S. App. LEXIS 10662 (6th Cir. 2004)]

If a DRO satisfies all of the above seven statutory conditions, then the order will satisfy the special requirements of a QDRO.

PPA (see Q 1:33) directed DOL to issue regulations to clarify the status of certain DROs. In particular, the regulations are to clarify that a DRO otherwise meeting the QDRO requirements will not fail to be treated as a QDRO solely because of the time it is issued or because it is issued after or revises another DRO or QDRO. The regulations are also to clarify that such a DRO is in all respects subject to the same requirements and protections that apply to QDROs. For example, as under present law, such DRO may not require the payment of benefits to an alternate payee that are required to be paid to another alternate payee under an earlier QDRO. In addition, the present-law rules regarding segregated amounts that apply while the status of a DRO as a QDRO is being determined continue to apply (see Q 36:22). [PPA § 1001]. DOL issued the following final regulation to comply with the PPA mandate. [DOL Reg. § 2530.206]

Any DRO described in the final regulation is subject to the same requirements and protections that apply to QDROs under ERISA Section 206(d)(3). [DOL Reg.

§ 2530.206(d)(1)] Subject to the preceding sentence, a DRO will not fail to be treated as a QDRO solely because the order is issued after, or revises, another DRO or QDRO. [DOL Reg. § 2530.206(b)(1)]

> **Example 1.** *Subsequent DRO between the same parties.* Participant and spouse divorce, and the administrator of the participant's 401(k) plan (see Q 27:1) receives a DRO. The administrator determines that the order is a QDRO. The QDRO allocates a portion of the participant's benefits to the spouse as the alternate payee. Subsequently, before benefit payments have commenced, the participant and the spouse seek and receive a second DRO. The second order reduces the portion of the participant's benefits that the spouse was to receive under the QDRO. The second order does not fail to be treated as a QDRO solely because the second order is issued after, and reduces the prior assignment contained in, the first order. The result would be the same if the order were instead to increase the prior assignment contained in the first order.

> **Example 2.** *Subsequent DRO between different parties.* Participant and spouse 1 divorce, and the administrator of the participant's 401(k) plan receives a DRO. The administrator determines that the order is a QDRO. The QDRO allocates a portion of the participant's benefits to spouse 1 as the alternate payee. The participant marries spouse 2, and then they divorce. The plan administrator subsequently receives a DRO pertaining to spouse 2. The order assigns to spouse 2 a portion of the participant's 401(k) benefits not already allocated to spouse 1. The second order does not fail to be a QDRO solely because the second order is issued after the plan administrator has determined that an earlier order pertaining to spouse 1 is a QDRO.

A DRO will not fail to be treated as a QDRO solely because of the time at which it is issued. [DOL Reg. § 2530.206(c)(1)]

> **Example 3.** *Orders issued after death.* Participant and spouse divorce, and the administrator of the plan receives a DRO; but the administrator finds the order deficient and determines that it is not a QDRO. Shortly thereafter, the participant dies while actively employed. A second DRO correcting the defects in the first order is subsequently submitted to the plan. The second order does not fail to be treated as a QDRO solely because it is issued after the death of the participant. The result would be the same even if no order had been issued before the participant's death; in other words, if the order issued after death were the only order.

> **Example 4.** *Orders issued after divorce.* Participant and spouse divorce. As a result, the spouse no longer meets the definition of "surviving spouse" under the terms of the plan. Subsequently, the plan administrator receives a DRO requiring that the spouse be treated as the participant's surviving spouse for purposes of receiving a death benefit payable under the terms of the plan only to a participant's surviving spouse. The order does not fail to be treated as a QDRO solely because, at the time it is issued, the spouse no longer meets the definition of a "surviving spouse" under the terms of the plan.

Example 5. *Orders issued after annuity starting date.* Participant retires and begins receipt of benefits in the form of a straight life annuity, equal to $1,000 per month, and with respect to which the spouse waives the surviving spousal rights (see Q 10:1). The participant and the spouse divorce after the participant's annuity starting date (see Q 10:3) and present the plan with a DRO requiring 50 percent ($500) of the participant's future monthly annuity payments under the plan to be paid instead to the spouse, as an alternate payee (so that monthly payments of $500 will be made to the spouse during the participant's lifetime). The order does not fail to be a QDRO solely because it is issued after the annuity starting date. If the order instead had required payments to the spouse for the lifetime of the spouse, this would constitute a reannuitization with a new annuity starting date, rather than merely allocating to the spouse a part of the determined annuity payments due to the participant, so that the order, while not failing to be a QDRO because of the timing of the order, would fail to meet the requirement that the DRO may not require a plan to provide any type or form of benefit, or any option, not otherwise provided under the plan (unless the plan otherwise permits such a change after the participant's annuity starting date). See example 9.

As noted previously, a DRO described in the final regulation is subject to the same requirements and protections that apply to QDROs.

Example 6. *Type or form of benefit.* Participant and spouse divorce, and their divorce decree provides that the parties will prepare a DRO assigning 50 percent of the participant's benefits under a 401(k) plan to the spouse, to be paid in monthly installments over a ten-year period. Shortly thereafter, the participant dies while actively employed. A DRO consistent with the decree is subsequently submitted to the 401(k) plan; however, the plan does not provide for ten-year installment payments of the type described in the order. The order does not fail to be treated as a QDRO solely because it is issued after the death of the participant, but the order would fail to be a QDRO because the order requires the plan to provide a type or form of benefit, or any option, not otherwise provided under the plan.

Example 7. *Segregation of payable benefits.* Participant and spouse divorce, and the administrator of the plan receives a DRO under which the spouse would begin to receive benefits immediately if the order is determined to be a QDRO. The plan administrator separately accounts for the amounts covered by the DRO as is required (see Q 36:22). The plan administrator finds the order deficient and determines that it is not a QDRO. Subsequently, after the expiration of the segregation period pertaining to that order, the plan administrator receives a second DRO relating to the same parties under which the spouse would begin to receive benefits immediately if the second order is determined to be a QDRO. Notwithstanding the expiration of the first segregation period, the amounts covered by the second order must be separately accounted for by the plan administrator for an 18-month period.

Example 8. *Previously assigned benefits.* Participant and spouse 1 divorce, and the administrator of participant's 401(k) plan receives a DRO. The administrator determines that the order is a QDRO. The QDRO assigns a portion of the participant's benefits to spouse 1 as the alternate payee. Participant marries spouse 2, and then they divorce. The plan administrator subsequently receives a DRO pertaining to spouse 2. The order assigns spouse 2 a portion of the participant's 401(k) benefits already assigned to spouse 1. The second order does not fail to be treated as a QDRO solely because the second order is issued after the plan administrator has determined that an earlier order pertaining to spouse 1 is a QDRO. The second order, however, would fail to be a QDRO because it assigns all or a portion of the participant's benefits that are already assigned to spouse 1 by the prior QDRO.

Example 9. *Type or form of benefit.* Participant retires and commences benefit payments in the form of a straight life annuity based on the life of the participant, with respect to which the spouse consents to the waiver of the surviving spousal rights provided under the plan. Participant and the spouse divorce after the annuity starting date and present the plan with a DRO that eliminates the straight life annuity based on the participant's life and provides for the spouse, as alternate payee, to receive all future benefits in the form of a straight life annuity based on the life of the spouse. The plan does not allow reannuitization with a new annuity starting date. The order does not fail to be a QDRO solely because it is issued after the annuity starting date, but the order would fail to be a QDRO because the order requires the plan to provide a type or form of benefit, or any option, not otherwise provided under the plan. However, the order would not fail to be a QDRO if instead it were to require all of the participant's future payments under the plan to be paid instead to the spouse, as an alternate payee (so that payments that would otherwise be paid to the participant during the participant's lifetime are instead to be made to the spouse during the participant's lifetime).

The final regulation states that it also applies in circumstances not described in the above examples. [DOL Reg. § 2530.206(a)]

Q 36:3   May a QDRO be part of the divorce decree or property settlement?

Yes. There is nothing in ERISA or the Code that requires that a QDRO (see Q 36:1) be issued as a separate judgment, decree, or order. Accordingly, a QDRO may be included as part of a divorce decree or court-approved property settlement, or issued as a separate order, without affecting its qualified status. The order must satisfy certain requirements to be a QDRO (see Q 36:2). [I.R.C. § 414(p)(1); ERISA § 206(d)(3)(B); Hogle v. Hogle, 732 N.E.2d 1278 (Ind. Ct. App. 2000); Ross v. Ross, 705 A.2d 784 (N.J. Super. Ct. App. Div. 1998)]

Q 36:4   Must a DRO be issued as part of a divorce proceeding to be a QDRO?

No. A DRO (see Q 36:2) that provides for child support or recognizes marital property rights may be a QDRO (see Q 36:1), without regard to the existence of a divorce proceeding. Such an order, however, must be issued pursuant to state domestic relations law and create or recognize the rights of an individual who is an alternate payee (see Q 36:5). [I.R.C. § 414(p)(1); ERISA § 206(d)(3)(B); DOL Op. Ltr. 90-46A]

An order issued in a probate proceeding begun after the death of the participant that purports to recognize an interest with respect to plan benefits arising solely under state community property law, but does not relate to the dissolution of a marriage or recognition of support obligations, is not a QDRO because the proceeding does not relate to a legal separation, marital dissolution, or family support obligation. [Boggs v. Boggs, 520 U.S. 833 (1997)] However, a QDRO for child support arrears can be obtained after the death of a participant. [Trustees of the Dirs. Guild of Am.–Producer Pension Benefits Plans v. Tise, 234 F.3d 415 (9th Cir. 2000)]

Q 36:5   Who is an alternate payee?

An alternate payee is a spouse, former spouse, child, or other dependent of a participant who is recognized by a DRO (see Q 36:2) as having a right to receive all or a portion of the benefits payable under the qualified retirement plan with respect to the participant. [I.R.C. § 414(p)(8); ERISA § 206(d)(3)(K)]

One court ruled that a QDRO benefiting the domestic partner of a plan participant is not disqualified by the partner's non-marital status because her quasi-marital relationship with the participant gave rise, *under state law*, to marital property rights. The court also addressed the plan administrator's contention that the participant's domestic partner was not an alternate payee because she was neither a former spouse, child, or other dependent. The court held, however, that, because the domestic partner essentially performed the duties of a homemaker during their relationship and because she was financially dependent upon the participant as the household's sole breadwinner, she qualified as a dependent under ERISA for purposes of the right to receive benefits under a QDRO. [Owens v. Automotive Machinists Pension Trust, 551 F.3d 1138 (9th Cir. 2009)]

If an alternate payee is a minor or is legally incompetent, the QDRO (see Q 36:1) can require payment to someone with legal responsibility for the alternate payee (such as a guardian in the case of a child or a trustee as agent for the alternate payee). DOL has opined that a DRO that designates a state child support enforcement agency as the party to whom payments will be made on behalf of an alternate payee may be a QDRO, even though the agency is not an alternate payee, since the agency acts as an agent for children in collecting and paying support. [DOL Op. Ltr. 2002-03A] Whether the alternate payee is the spouse or a former spouse of the participant, as opposed to a child or other dependent of the participant, affects the tax consequences of a distribution from the qualified retirement plan pursuant to a QDRO. See Qs 36:30 through 36:32 for details.

A person who is an alternate payee under a QDRO generally is considered a beneficiary under the plan for the purposes of ERISA. [Boggs v. Boggs, 520 U.S.

833 (1997); Nelson v. Raimetta, 322 F.3d 541 (8th Cir. 2003); *In re* Hthiy, 283 B.R. 447 (Bankr. E.D. Mich. 2002)] Accordingly, the alternate payee must be furnished, upon written request, copies of a variety of documents, including the latest summary plan description, the latest annual report, any final annual report, and the collective bargaining agreement, trust agreement, contract, or other instrument under which the plan is established or operated (see Qs 22:1, 22:13). The plan administrator (see Q 20:1) may impose a reasonable charge to cover the cost of furnishing such copies.

One court concluded that a DRO providing the nonemployee spouse with the right to name a successor-in-interest to receive her share of undistributed pension benefits was not a QDRO because of the possibility that a successor-in-interest would not fall within the definition of an alternate payee. [Shelstead v. Shelstead, 78 Cal. Rptr. 2d 365 (Cal. 1998)]

Q 36:6 Has PBGC adopted disclosure of records to alternate payees?

Pension Benefit Guaranty Corporation (PBGC; see Q 25:10) has adopted two routine uses of records for a system of records maintained pursuant to the Privacy Act of 1974, entitled PBGC-6, Plan Participant and Beneficiary Data—PBGC. This system of records is maintained for use in determining whether participants and beneficiaries are eligible for benefits under plans covered by Title IV of ERISA (see Q 25:9), the amounts of benefits to be paid, making benefit payments, and collecting benefit overpayments. Names, addresses, and telephone numbers are used to survey customers to measure their satisfaction with the PBGC's benefit payment services and to track (for follow up) those who do not respond to surveys.

The first routine use permits disclosure of certain benefit information to a participant's spouse, former spouse, child, or other dependent of the participant solely to obtain a QDRO (see Q 36:1). The second routine use permits disclosure of information from a participant's initial determination to the participant's spouse, former spouse, child, or other dependent who is an alternate payee (see Q 36:5) under a QDRO to explain how PBGC determined the benefit due the alternate payee so that the alternate payee can pursue an administrative appeal.

Routine use 12 permits PBGC to disclose the information needed to obtain a QDRO to a spouse, former spouse, child, or other dependent of a participant. PBGC will disclose the information only upon the receipt of a notarized, written request by a prospective alternate payee that describes the requester's relationship to the participant and states that the information will be used solely to obtain a QDRO under state domestic relations law.

Routine use 13 permits PBGC to disclose information from a participant's initial determination to the participant's spouse, former spouse, child, or other dependent who is an alternate payee under a QDRO. The information explains how PBGC determined the benefit due the alternate payee so that the alternate payee can pursue an administrative appeal of the benefit determination. PBGC will not disclose the participant's address, telephone number, Social Security number, and any sensitive medical information under the routine use.

PBGC will notify the participant of the information that is disclosed under the routine uses. [PBGC Notice, 65 Fed. Reg. 57,629 (Sept. 25, 2000)]

PBGC has proposed new routine use 14 that would permit PBGC to disclose to IRS and DOL the names, addresses, Social Security numbers, and dates of birth of eligible PBGC pension recipients. The new routine use became effective December 3, 2002 without further notice, unless comments result in a contrary determination and a notice is published to that effect. [PBGC Notice, 67 Fed. Reg. 66,674 (Nov. 1, 2002)]

Q 36:7 Does a QDRO violate the anti-assignment rule?

Generally, a retirement plan will not be a qualified retirement plan unless the plan provides that plan benefits may not be assigned or alienated. However, this prohibition against the assignment of plan benefits does not apply to the creation, assignment, or recognition of a right to any benefit payable with respect to a participant pursuant to a QDRO (see Qs 4:27, 36:1). [I.R.C. § 401(a)(13); Treas. Reg. § 1.401(a)-13(g); Priv. Ltr. Ruls. 200252093, 9234014] The waiver, in a divorce decree, by the former spouse of a deceased plan participant of her rights to plan benefits did not violate the anti-alienation provisions of ERISA even though no QDRO was filed, ruled the court. [Kennedy v. Plan Administrator for DuPont Savings and Investment Plan, 129 S. Ct. 865 (2009)] In another case, on October 1, 1986, the interest of a participant in a company pension plan became vested (see Q 9:1), as did the interest of his wife as his designated beneficiary. In 1988, the plan was terminated; and, in order to satisfy its obligations to the participants, the plan purchased annuity contracts from an insurance company. The annuity contracts contained a provision permitting the annuitant to change the beneficiary designation. The decedent and his wife divorced in 1994 and entered into a settlement agreement whereby each waived any right to an interest in any pension plans, retirement plans, profit sharing plans, etc. At the time of the decedent's death in 2005, he had remarried but never changed the annuity beneficiary designation. His surviving spouse, as the executor of his estate, commenced an action against the former wife and the insurance company, claiming that the former wife had waived her interest in the annuity and that all payments should be made to the estate. The former wife contended that her rights in the plan vested on the date of the decedent's retirement, at which time she was still his wife and designated beneficiary, and her interest was therefore non-assignable under ERISA. The estate contended that the annuity was a private contract governed by state law and that, under state law, the former wife had waived her interest in the annuity. The district court ruled in favor of the former wife, but the appellate court noted that ERISA permits the termination of a plan where the employer obligates itself to purchase annuities to provide the benefit the employee would have otherwise enjoyed under the plan. The court then held that the purchase of the annuities terminated the plan, and that termination severed the applicability of ERISA.

The dispute was thus to be determined pursuant to state law, and the case was remanded to the district court for adjudication of the estate's claims pursuant to state law. [Hallingby v. Hallingby, 574 F.3d 51 (2d Cir. 2009)]

A divorce decree requiring payment of the wife's attorneys' fees from the husband's qualified retirement plan account did not meet the requirements of a QDRO and was not enforced because the payment would have violated the anti-alienation rule. [Johnson v. Johnson, 727 A.2d 473 (N.J. Super. Ct. App. Div. 1999)] However, another court permitted a husband to recover attorneys' fees from his wife's plan account pursuant to a QDRO. [Silverman v. Spiro, 784 N.E.2d 1 (Mass. 2003)]

A postnuptial agreement requiring that a portion of the husband's benefits in a qualified retirement plan be segregated in a separate plan account for the wife caused the plan to be disqualified. Because the postnuptial agreement was not a QDRO, the segregation violated the anti-assignment rule. [Merchant v. Kelly, Haglund, Garnsey & Kahn, 874 F. Supp. 300 (D. Colo. 1995)] Another court ruled that a DRO providing the nonemployee spouse with the right to name a successor-in-interest to receive her share of undistributed pension benefits was an invalid alienation of benefits because of the possibility that a successor-in-interest would not fall within the definition of an alternate payee. [Shelstead v. Shelstead, 78 Cal. Rptr. 2d 365 (Cal. 1998)] The anti-alienation rule preempted California's community property law, which allows a predeceased spouse's interest in her ex-husband's qualified retirement plan to pass to her heirs, because the court order between the former spouses failed to meet the requirements of a QDRO, ruled one court. [Branco v. UFCW-N. Cal. Employers Joint Pension Plan, 2002 WL 200910 (9th Cir. 2002)]

Q 36:8   Do the QDRO rules apply to all qualified retirement plans?

Yes. The QDRO (see Q 36:1) requirements apply to all qualified retirement plans and also apply to tax-sheltered annuities (403(b) plans; see Q 35:1). [I.R.C. §§ 401(a)(13), 414(p)(9)]

The QDRO rules have also been extended to governmental plans and church plans; however, distributions from such plans are treated as made pursuant to a QDRO without the necessity of satisfying the special QDRO requirements (see Qs 36:1, 36:2). If these types of plans provide that plan benefits may not be assigned or alienated (see Q 36:7) and such a provision is enforceable under state law, it is possible that plan benefits may not be reachable even with a QDRO. [I.R.C. §§ 414(d), 414(e), 414(p)(11); In re Cason, 1997 Bankr. LEXIS 1009 (Bankr. N.D. Fla. 1997)]

Although the QDRO rules do not apply to IRAs (see Q 30:1) or Roth IRAs (see Q 31:1), the transfer of an individual's interest in an IRA or a Roth IRA to the individual's spouse or former spouse under a divorce or separation agreement is not considered a taxable transfer made by such individual; and, thereafter, the IRA or Roth IRA is treated as maintained for the benefit of the spouse or former spouse (see Qs 30:51, 31:35). It is also possible for a QDRO to require a distribution of benefits to the participant and then a transfer of a portion or all of the distribution to an IRA for the benefit of the former spouse. [I.R.C. § 408(d)(6); Priv. Ltr. Ruls. 9739044, 9016077]

An IRA may also be used to implement a QDRO if a direct transfer of the participant's interest in a retirement plan to the participant's spouse is otherwise prohibited. When a QDRO required a participant-contract holder to transfer his interest in a 403(b) plan to his spouse, but the terms of the annuity prevented a transfer to anyone other than the contract holder, the participant-contract holder could surrender the 403(b) plan for its cash surrender value, roll over the distribution to an IRA, and then transfer the IRA to his spouse. [I.R.C. § 408(d)(6); Priv. Ltr. Rul. 8916083]

The QDRO rules do not apply to nonqualified plans. [Priv. Ltr. Rul. 9340032] However, courts have ruled that life insurance benefits under an employer-sponsored nonqualified plan, an ERISA welfare benefit plan, are subject to the QDRO rules if the divorce decree specifies how the life insurance benefits must be distributed. [Metropolitan Life Ins. Co. v. Marsh, 119 F.3d 415 (6th Cir. 1997); Metropolitan Life Ins. Co. v. Wheaton, 42 F.3d 1080 (7th Cir. 1994); Kuhn v. Metropolitan Life Ins. Co., No. 5:98-cv-82 (W.D. Mich. 1999); Metropolitan Life Ins. Co. v. Fowler, 922 F. Supp. 8 (E.D. Mich. 1996); *but see* Equitable Life Assurance Soc'y of the United States v. Crysler, 66 F.3d 944 (8th Cir. 1995)] DOL has also opined that a QDRO may apply to a company-paid survivor benefit. [DOL Op. Ltr. 2000-09A]

Q 36:9 Does a QDRO affect the qualification of a retirement plan?

A qualified retirement plan will not be treated as failing to satisfy the general qualification requirements (see Q 4:1) and the restriction on distributions under a 401(k) plan (see Q 27:14) solely because of a payment to an alternate payee (see Q 36:5) pursuant to a QDRO (see Q 36:1). This is the case even if the plan provides for payments pursuant to a QDRO to an alternate payee prior to the time the plan may make payments to a participant. For example, a qualified retirement plan may pay an alternate payee even though the participant may not receive a distribution because the participant continues to be employed by the employer (see Q 36:18). [I.R.C. § 414(p)(10); Treas. Reg. § 1.401(a)-13(g)(3)]

Where there were insufficient liquid assets in a qualified retirement plan to make a payment to an alternate payee pursuant to a QDRO, DOL ruled that a loan to the plan from the participant spouse to enable the plan to comply with the QDRO was exempt from the prohibited transaction rules (see Q 24:1). [DOL Op. Ltr. 94-28A; PTCE 80-26; ERISA § 206(d)(3)]

Q 36:10 Must a qualified retirement plan include provisions regarding QDROs?

No. A qualified retirement plan need not include provisions with regard to QDROs (see Q 36:1), and this exclusion will not cause the retirement plan to fail to satisfy the general qualification requirements. [Treas. Reg. § 1.401(a)-13(g)(2)]

Q 36:11   What is the best way to divide a participant's pension benefits in a QDRO?

There is no single best way to divide qualified retirement plan benefits in a QDRO (see Q 36:1). What will be best in a specific case will depend on many factors, including the type of plan, the nature of the participant's plan benefits, and why the parties are seeking to divide those benefits. In deciding how to divide a participant's plan benefits in a QDRO, it is also important to consider two aspects of a participant's benefits: (1) the retirement benefit payable under the plan directly to the participant and (2) any benefit that is payable under the plan on behalf of the participant to someone else after the participant dies (see Q 36:27).

See Qs 36:12 through 36:17 for more details.

Q 36:12   How much can be given to an alternate payee through a QDRO?

A QDRO (see Q 36:1) can give an alternate payee (see Q 36:5) any part or all of the qualified retirement plan benefits payable with respect to a participant under the plan. However, the QDRO cannot require the plan to provide increased benefits (determined on the basis of actuarial value), nor can a QDRO require a plan to provide a type or form of benefit or any option not otherwise provided under the plan (with one exception for an alternate payee's right to receive payment at the participant's earliest retirement age; see Q 36:18). The QDRO also cannot require the payment of benefits to an alternate payee that are required to be paid to another alternate payee under another QDRO already recognized by the plan (see Q 36:2). [I.R.C. §§ 414(p)(1)(A)(i), 414(p)(3), 414(p)(4); ERISA §§ 206(d)(3)(B)(i)(I), 206(d)(3)(D), 206(d)(3)(E); Winters v. Kutrip, 2002 U.S. App. LEXIS 20557 (3d Cir. 2002)]

When a QDRO only related to lifetime benefits payable to an alternate payee but did not relate to survivor benefits after the plan participant died, courts have ruled that the surviving alternate payee was not entitled to any further benefits and that the QDRO could not be amended after the participant's death because (1) the alternate payee's entitlement had to be established as of the day the participant died and (2) a *nunc pro tunc* order (i.e., an order having retroactive effect) after the participant's death was necessarily an order that increased benefits (see Q 36:2) and thus could not become a QDRO. [Dorn v. International Bhd. of Elec. Workers, 211 F.3d 938 (5th Cir. 2000); Samaroo v. Samaroo, 193 F.3d 185 (3d Cir. 1999); Robson v. Electrical Contractors Ass'n Local 134, 727 N.E.2d 692 (Ill. App. Ct. 1st Dist. 2000); *see also* Kazel v. Estate of Kazel, No. 163 (N.Y. App., 4th Div., 2004), Cosby v. Cosby, 773 N.E.2d 516 (Ohio 2002), and Rich v. Southern Cal. IBEW-NECA Pension Plan, 2d Civil No. B127215 (Cal. Ct. App. 2d App. Dist. 1999)] Where the deceased participant had not remarried and no other person had a vested interest in the plan benefits, one court rejected these holdings and issued a *nunc pro tunc* order adding a second plan's benefits that were inadvertently omitted from the original DRO. [Patton v. Denver Post Corp., 326 F.3d 1148 (10th Cir. 2003); *see also* IBM Savings Plan v. Price, No. 2:04-CV-187 (D. Vt. 2004)] The Third Circuit distinguished its holding in

Samaroo v. Samaroo and determined that a property settlement agreement entered into prior to the participant's death, and before the entry of a QDRO, conferred plan benefits to the participant's former spouse, because the agreement provided the former spouse with a right to benefits for which the participant had been eligible prior to his death. [Files v. ExxonMobil Pension Plan, 428 F.3d 478 (3d Cir. 2005)] See Q 36:2 concerning regulations to be issued by DOL.

A former wife was not entitled to a division of dividends (see Qs 28:10–28:12) from a qualified retirement plan in which her former husband participated that were earned in the year between the entry of their divorce decree and the entry of the QDRO, because the language of the decree and the property settlement agreement only provided for division of the funds as of the date the decree and settlement agreement were entered. This was so even though the former wife had paid income taxes on the pass-through dividends the former husband had received after the decree was entered. [Oliver v. Oliver, No. CA99-862 (Ark. Ct. App. 2000)]

Q 36:13 Why are the reasons for dividing the plan benefits important?

Generally, QDROs (see Q 36:1) are used either to provide support payments (temporary or permanent) to the alternate payee (see Q 36:5) or to divide marital property in the course of dissolving a marriage. These differing goals often result in different choices in drafting a QDRO. Two common different approaches in drafting QDROs are usually used for these two different purposes.

One approach that is used in some orders is to split the actual benefit payments made with respect to a participant under the plan to give the alternate payee part of each payment. This approach to dividing retirement benefits is often called the "shared payment" approach. Under this approach, the alternate payee will not receive any payments unless the participant receives a payment or is already in pay status. This approach is often used when a support order is being drafted after a participant has already begun to receive payments from the plan.

A QDRO providing for shared payments, like any other QDRO, must also specify the amount or percentage of the participant's benefit payments that is assigned to the alternate payee (or the manner in which such amount or percentage is to be determined) and the number of payments or period to which it applies (see Q 36:2). This is particularly important to the shared payment QDRO, which must specify when the alternate payee's right to share the payments begins and ends. For example, if the purpose is to provide support to a child of a participant, a QDRO might require payments to the alternate payee to begin as soon as possible after the order is determined to be a QDRO and to continue until the alternate payee reaches maturity. Alternatively, when support is being provided to a former spouse, the QDRO might state that payments to the alternate payee will end when the former spouse remarries. If payments are to end upon the occurrence of an event, notice and reasonable substantiation that the event has occurred must be provided for the plan to be able to comply with the terms of the QDRO. One court concluded that an ex-wife's share of her former husband's pension benefits was calculated at the date of receipt and not the date of their divorce because the QDRO awarded the ex-wife a percentage of the benefits if, as, and when received by the husband. [Hurley v. Hurley, No. 01-96-00865 CV (Tex. Ct. App. 1st Dist. 1997)] Another court ruled that a former spouse was entitled to receive pension benefits calculated under the distribution formula in effect when the participant's benefits commenced and not under the formula in effect at the time of divorce. [Neal v. Neal, No. A110603 (Or. Ct. App. 2002)]

QDROs that seek to divide a plan benefit as part of the marital property upon divorce or legal separation often take a different approach to dividing the retirement benefit. These QDROs usually divide the participant's retirement benefit (rather than just the payments) into two separate portions with the intent of giving the alternate payee a separate right to receive a portion of the retirement benefit to be paid at a time and in a form different from that chosen by the participant. This approach to dividing a retirement benefit is often called the "separate interest" approach.

A QDRO that provides for a separate interest for the alternate payee must also specify the amount or percentage of the participant's retirement benefit to be assigned to the alternate payee (or the manner in which such amount or percentage is to be determined) and the number of payments or period to which it applies, and such QDROs often satisfy this requirement simply by giving the alternate payee the right that the participant would have had under the plan to elect the form of benefit payment and the time at which the separate interest will be paid.

Neither ERISA nor the Code requires the use of either approach for any specific domestic relations purpose. The shared payment approach and the separate interest approach can each be used for either defined contribution or defined benefit plans (see Qs 2:2, 2:3). Understanding the type of qualified retirement plan is important because the order cannot be a QDRO unless its assignment of rights or division of plan benefits complies with the terms of the plan (see Qs 36:14, 36:15).

[I.R.C. § 414(p)(2)(B)-(D); ERISA § 206(d)(3)(C)(ii)-(iv)]

When a QDRO only related to lifetime benefits payable to an alternate payee but did not relate to survivor benefits after the plan participant died, courts have ruled that the surviving alternate payee was not entitled to any further benefits and that the QDRO could not be amended after the participant's death. [Dorn v. International Bhd. of Elec. Workers, 211 F.3d 938 (5th Cir. 2000); Samaroo v. Samaroo, 193 F.3d 185 (3d Cir. 1999); Robson v. Electrical Contractors Ass'n Local 134, 727 N.E.2d 692 (Ill. App. Ct. 1st Dist. 2000); *see also* Kazel v. Estate of Kazel, No. 163 (N.Y. App., 4th Div., 2004), Cosby v. Cosby, 773 N.E.2d 516 (Ohio 2002), and Rich v. Southern Cal. IBEW-NECA Pension Plan, 2d Civil No. B127215 (Cal. Ct. App. 2d App. Dist. 1999); *but see* Files v. ExxonMobil Pension Plan, 428 F.3d 478 (3d Cir. 2005) and Patton v. Denver Post Corp., 326 F.3d 1148 (10th Cir. 2003)] See Q 36:2 concerning regulations to be issued by DOL.

Q 36:14   How may the participant's retirement benefit be divided if the plan is a defined contribution plan?

A DRO (see Q 36:2) dividing a retirement benefit under a defined contribution plan (see Q 2:2) may adopt either a separate interest approach or a shared payment approach or some combination of these approaches (see Q 36:13). DROs that provide the alternate payee (see Q 36:5) with a separate interest, either by assigning to the alternate payee a percentage or a dollar amount of the account balance as of a certain date, often also provide that the separate interest will be held in a separate account under the plan with respect to which the alternate payee is entitled to exercise the rights of a participant. Provided that the DRO does not assign a right or option to an alternate payee that is not otherwise available under the plan, an order that creates a separate account for the alternate payee may qualify as a QDRO (see Q 36:1).

DROs that provide for shared payments from a defined contribution plan should clearly establish the amount or percentage of the participant's payments that will be allocated to the alternate payee and the number of payments or period of time during which the allocation to the alternate payee is to be made. A QDRO can specify that any or all payments made to the participant will be shared between the participant and the alternate payee.

[I.R.C. § 414(p)(2); ERISA § 206(d)(3)(C)].

Q 36:15   How may the participant's retirement benefit be divided if the plan is a defined benefit plan?

A DRO (see Q 36:2) may adopt either the shared payment or the separate interest approach or a combination of the two in dividing plan benefits in a defined benefit plan (see Qs 2:3, 36:13).

If shared payments are desired, the DRO should specify the amount of each shared payment allocated to the alternate payee (see Q 36:5) either by percentage or by dollar amount. The DRO must also describe the number of payments or period of time during which the allocation to the alternate payee will be made. This is usually done by specifying a beginning date and an ending date (or an event that will cause the allocation to begin and/or end). If a DRO specifies a triggering event that may occur outside the plan's knowledge, notice of its occurrence must be given to the plan before the plan is required to act in accordance with the DRO. If the intent is that all payments made under the plan will be shared between the participant and the alternate payee, the DRO may so specify.

A defined benefit plan may provide for subsidies under certain circumstances and may also provide increased benefits or additional benefits either earned through additional service or provided by way of plan amendment. A QDRO (see Q 36:1) that uses the shared payment method to give the alternate payee a percentage of each payment may be structured to take into account any such future increases in the benefits paid to the participant. Such a QDRO does not need to address the treatment of future subsidies or other benefit increases because the alternate payee will automatically receive a share of any subsidy or other benefit increases that are paid to the participant. If the parties do not wish to provide for the sharing of such subsidies or increases, the DRO should so specify.

If a separate interest is desired for the alternate payee, it is important that the QDRO be based on adequate information from the plan administrator (see Q 20:1), the plan documents concerning the participant's retirement benefit, and the rights, options, and features provided under the plan. The DRO may specify whether, and to what extent, an alternate payee is to receive any subsidies or future benefit increases.

[I.R.C. §§ 414(p)(2), 414(p)(3); ERISA §§ 206(d)(3)(C), 206(d)(3)(D)]

Q 36:16   May the QDRO specify the form in which the alternate payee's benefits will be paid?

A QDRO (see Q 36:1) that provides for a separate interest (see Q 36:13) may specify the form in which the alternate payee's (see Q 36:5) benefits will be paid subject to certain limitations (see Q 36:2). In determining the form of payment for an alternate payee, a QDRO may substitute the alternate payee's life for the life of the participant to the extent that the form of payment is based on the duration of an individual's life. Alternatively, a QDRO may give the alternate payee the right that the participant would have had under the plan to elect the form of benefit payment. For example, if a participant would have the right to elect a single life annuity, the alternate payee may exercise that right and choose to have the assigned benefit paid over the alternate payee's life. However, the QDRO must permit the plan to determine the amount payable to the alternate payee under any form of payment in a manner that does not require the plan to pay increased benefits (determined on an actuarial basis).

A plan may by its own terms provide alternate payees with additional types or forms of benefit, or options, not otherwise provided to participants, such as a lump-sum payment option, but the plan cannot prevent a QDRO from assigning to an alternate payee any type or form of benefit, or option, provided generally under the plan to the participant.

[I.R.C. §§ 401(a)(9), 401(a)(13)(B), 414(p)(3), 414(p)(4)(A)(iii); ERISA §§ 206(d)(3)(A), 206(d)(3)(D), 206(d)(3)(E)(i)(III)]

For a discussion of special rules relating to required minimum distributions to an alternate payee, see Q 11:46.

Q 36:17   When can the alternate payee get the benefits assigned under a QDRO?

A QDRO (see Q 36:1) that provides for shared payments (see Q 36:13) must specify the date on which the alternate payee (see Q 36:5) will begin to share the participant's payments. Such a date, however, cannot be earlier than the date on which the plan receives the QDRO. With respect to a separate interest (see Q 36:13), a QDRO may either specify the time (after the QDRO is received by the plan) at which the alternate payee will receive the separate interest or assign to the alternate payee the same right the participant would have had under the plan with regard to the timing of payment. In either case, a QDRO cannot provide that an alternate payee will receive a benefit earlier than the date on which the participant reaches the earliest retirement age (see Qs 36:18, 36:19), unless the plan permits payments at an earlier date. The plan itself may contain provisions permitting alternate payees to receive separate interests awarded under a QDRO at an earlier time or under different circumstances than the participant could receive the benefit. For example, a plan may provide that an alternate payee may elect to receive a single-sum payment of a separate interest at any time. [I.R.C. §§ 401(a)(9), 414(p)(2), 414(p)(3), 414(p)(4); ERISA §§ 206(d)(3)(C), 206(d)(3)(D), 206(d)(3)(E); Treas. Reg. § 1.401(a)-13(g)(3)]

When a portion of a participant's plan benefits was assigned to his former wife under a QDRO but the plan distributed such benefits to the participant, the court ruled that, if the distribution by the plan was intentional, the former wife could recover interest from the plan, but if the plan acted inadvertently, she would have to recover interest from the participant. [Johnson v. Capital Accumulation Plan of the Chubb Corp., Chubb & Son, Inc., & Participating Affiliates, 2000 U.S. Dist. LEXIS 10241 (N.D. Tex. 2000); *see also* North American Coal Corp. Retirement Savings Plan v. Roth, No. 04-2213 (8th Cir. 2005)]

Q 36:18   What is the earliest retirement age rule?

A DRO may not require a qualified retirement plan to provide any type or form of benefit, or any option, not otherwise provided under the plan (see Q 36:2). [I.R.C. § 414(p)(3)(A)]

A DRO will not fail to satisfy the above requirement solely because the DRO requires that payment of benefits be made to an alternate payee (see Q 36:5):

1. In the case of any payment before the participant has separated from service, on or after the date on which the participant attains (or would have attained) the earliest retirement age (see Q 36:19);

2. As if the participant had retired on the date on which such payment is to begin under the DRO; and

3. In any form in which such benefits may be paid under the qualified retirement plan to the participant.

[I.R.C. § 414(p)(4)(A)]

A DRO will be a QDRO (see Q 36:1) even though the order provides that payments to the alternate payee may begin on or after the date on which the participant attains the earliest retirement age under the qualified retirement plan, whether or not the participant actually retires on that date. Therefore, a participant cannot delay an alternate payee's receipt of benefits by failing to take advantage of an early retirement option provided by the plan. [I.R.C. § 414(p)(4)(A)(i)] One court concluded that a participant's former spouse, who had received a QDRO that was meant to provide her with a portion of the participant's pension benefits, was nonetheless entitled to receive only preretirement surviving spouse benefits, because the participant died before the earliest age at which he would have been entitled under the plan to start receiving pension benefits. [Galenski v. Ford Motor Co. Pension Plan, 2008 WL 3929795 (6th Cir. 2008)] For an exception to the earliest retirement age rule, see Q 36:20.

Payments of benefits prior to a participant's separation from service, but after earliest retirement age, must be made as if the participant had actually retired on the date payments are to begin under the QDRO. Only benefits actually accrued on that date are taken into account, and any employer subsidy for early retirement is not taken into account. An employer subsidizes an early retirement benefit to the extent that the benefit provided is greater than the actuarial equivalent of a retirement benefit commencing at normal retirement age. For example, if a participant would be entitled to a monthly retirement benefit under a qualified retirement plan of $1,000 at age 65 and the plan permits the participant to retire at age 62 with the full $1,000 monthly retirement benefit, the employer is subsidizing the early retirement benefit. Actuarial equivalency is computed using the interest rate specified in the qualified retirement plan. If the plan does not specify an interest rate for determining actuarial equivalency (as would be the case if the employer were subsidizing the benefit), a 5 percent interest rate is used. [I.R.C. § 414(p)(4)(A)(ii); In re Marriage of Oddino, 939 P.2d 1266 (Sup. Ct. Cal. 1997)]

Benefit payments to an alternate payee after the earliest retirement age generally may be in any form allowed under the qualified retirement plan; however, benefits may not be paid in the form of a joint and survivor annuity with respect to the alternate payee and the alternate payee's subsequent spouse. [I.R.C. § 414(p)(4)(A)(iii); Treas. Reg. § 1.401(a)-13(g)(4)(iii)(B)]

The amount payable under a QDRO following the participant's earliest retirement age cannot exceed the amount that the participant would be entitled to receive at such time. For example, assume that a profit sharing plan provides that a participant may withdraw some, but not all, of the participant's account balance (see Q 9:2) before separation from service. A QDRO may provide for payment to an alternate payee up to the amount that the participant may withdraw. [REA Sen. Comm. Rep.]

Q 36:19   What does earliest retirement age mean?

Earliest retirement age means the *earlier* of:

1. The earliest date on which the participant is entitled to a distribution under the qualified retirement plan, or

2. The *later* of (a) the date on which the participant attains age 50 or (b) the earliest date on which the participant could begin receiving a distribution from the plan if the participant separated from service. [I.R.C. § 414(p)(4)(B); ERISA § 206(d)(3)(E)]

If the plan permits distributions to be made to the employee while an active participant (in-service distributions), the QDRO (see Q 36:1) can require that payments be made to the alternate payee (see Q 36:5) at any time when the participant qualifies for an in-service distribution. If the plan does not permit in-service distributions but distributions may begin at any time after separation from service, the earliest retirement age will be the earlier of age 50 or the date of separation from service. If the plan does not permit in-service distributions and does not permit distributions until the attainment of a specified age (age 65, for example), the earliest retirement age will, in this case, be age 65. One court enforced a QDRO that required a distribution to be made to an alternate payee even though, before the QDRO became final, the plan was retroactively amended to prohibit any distributions prior to age 65. [Stephen Allen Lynn, P.C. Employee Profit Sharing Plan v. Stephen Allen Lynn, P.C., No. 93-1501 (5th Cir. 1994)]

> **Example 1.** A profit sharing plan permits a participant to make withdrawals only upon attainment of age 59½ or termination from service. The earliest retirement age for a QDRO under this plan is the earlier of (1) when the participant actually terminates employment or reaches age 59½ or (2) the later of the date the participant reaches age 50 or the date the participant could receive the account balance if the participant terminated employment. Since the participant could terminate employment at any time and thereby be able to receive the account balance under the plan's terms, the later of the two dates described in (2) above is age 50. The earliest retirement age formula for this plan can be simplified to read the earlier of (1) actually reaching age 59½ or terminating employment or (2) age 50. Since age 50 is earlier than age 59½, the earliest retirement age for this plan will be the earlier of age 50 or the date the participant actually terminates from service.

> **Example 2.** A defined benefit plan permits retirement benefits to be paid beginning when the participant reaches age 65 and terminates employment. It does not permit earlier payments. The earliest retirement age for this plan is the earlier of (1) the date on which the participant actually reaches age 65 and terminates employment or (2) the later of age 50 or the date on which the participant reaches age 65 (whether the participant terminates employment or not). Because age 65 is later than age 50, the second part of the formula can be simplified to read age 65 so that the earliest retirement age is the earlier of (1) the date on which the participant reaches age 65 and actually terminates or (2) the date the participant reaches age 65. Under this plan, therefore, the earliest retirement age will be the date on which the participant reaches age 65.

One court concluded that a participant's former spouse, who had received a QDRO that was meant to provide her with a portion of the participant's pension benefits, was nonetheless entitled to receive only preretirement surviving spouse benefits, because the participant died before the earliest age at which he would have been entitled under the plan to start receiving pension benefits. [Galenski v. Ford Motor Co. Pension Plan, 2008 WL 3929795 (6th Cir. 2008)]

Q 36:20 Can a distribution to an alternate payee be made before the earliest retirement age?

Yes. If the qualified retirement plan so permits, a QDRO (see Q 36:1) may require that payments be made to the alternate payee (see Q 36:5) prior to the participant's earliest retirement age (see Q 36:19). If the plan does not contain such a provision, then to do so the plan must be amended to permit a pre-earliest retirement age distribution. [Treas. Reg. § 1.401(a)-13(g)(3); Priv. Ltr. Ruls. 8837013, 8744023]

Q 36:21 Must a qualified retirement plan establish a procedure to determine the qualified status of a DRO?

A qualified retirement plan must establish reasonable procedures to determine the qualified status of DROs (see Q 36:2) and to administer distributions made pursuant to QDROs (see Q 36:1). [I.R.C. § 414(p)(6)(B); ERISA § 206(d)(3)(G)(ii)]

Although a qualified retirement plan need not include provisions regarding QDROs (see Q 36:10), the plan procedures must:

1. Be in writing;
2. Be reasonable;
3. Provide that each person specified in a DRO received by the plan as entitled to payment of benefits under the plan will be notified (at the address specified in the DRO) of the plan's procedures for making QDRO determinations upon receipt of a DRO; and
4. Permit an alternate payee (see Q 36:5) to designate a representative for receipt of copies of notices and plan information that are sent to the alternate payee with respect to a DRO.

It is the view of DOL that a plan's QDRO procedures would not be considered reasonable if the procedures unduly inhibited or hampered the obtaining of a QDRO determination or the making of distributions under a QDRO. For example, any procedure that conditioned making a QDRO determination on the payment of a fee by a participant or alternate payee (either directly or as a charge against the participant's account) would not be considered a reasonable procedure (see Q 36:22).

Where a plan required that a "hold" be placed on a participant's account *after* receipt of a DRO, but the hold was placed *before* receipt because the plan administrator (see Q 20:1) had been informed that a DRO would be issued, the court ruled that the hold violated ERISA because it was contrary to the plan's written procedures. [Schoonmaker v. Employee Sav. Plan of Amoco Corp. & Participating Cos., 987 F.2d 410 (7th Cir. 1993)]

One court held that, if the procedures are followed and all of the conditions (see Q 36:2) are satisfied, then the plan's obligation to the participant and each alternate payee is discharged to the extent of any payment made. [Blue v. UAL Corp., 160 F.3d 383 (7th Cir. 1998)]

Q 36:22   What happens when a qualified retirement plan receives a DRO?

If a DRO (see Q 36:2) is received by a qualified retirement plan, the plan administrator (see Q 20:1) must promptly notify the participant and each alternate payee (see Q 36:5) of the receipt of the DRO and the plan's procedures (see Q 36:21) for determining its qualified status. In addition, the plan administrator must determine whether the DRO is a QDRO (see Q 36:1) and notify the participant and each alternate payee of the determination within a reasonable period after receipt of the DRO (see Q 36:23). After the DRO is issued, it is not the responsibility of the plan administrator to determine if an individual is, in fact, the spouse, former spouse, child, or other dependent of the participant. [I.R.C. § 414(p)(6)(A); Sippe v. Sippe, 101 N.C. App. 194 (1990); DOL Op. Ltr. 92-17A]

During the period in which the determination of whether a DRO is a QDRO is being made (by the plan administrator, by a court of competent jurisdiction, or otherwise), the plan administrator must separately account for the amounts (segregated amounts) that would have been payable to the alternate payee during such period if the DRO had been determined to be a QDRO. [I.R.C. § 414(p)(7)(A); ERISA §§ 206(d)(3)(H), 404(a); Board of Trustees of the Laborers Pension Trust Fund for N. Cal. v. Levingston, 816 F. Supp. 1496 (N.D. Cal. 1993)]

If, within the 18-month period beginning with the date on which the first payment under the DRO would be required, the DRO (or any modification thereof) is determined to be a QDRO, the plan administrator must pay the segregated amounts (including any interest thereon) to the alternate payee or payees. [I.R.C. §§ 414(p)(7)(B), 414(p)(7)(E); IBM Savings Plan v. Price, No. 2:04-CV-187 (D. Vt. 2004)]

If, within the 18-month period, it is determined that the DRO is not a QDRO or the determination is not made, then the plan administrator must pay the segregated amounts (including any interest thereon) to the person or persons who would have been entitled to such amounts if there had been no DRO. If a determination that a DRO is a QDRO is made after the 18-month period, it may be applied prospectively only. Therefore, the qualified retirement plan should not be liable to the alternate payee for payments for the period prior to the determination if the qualification is determined after the 18-month period. However, if a DRO is determined to be a QDRO after the 18-month period, the alternate payee may have a cause of action against the participant under state law for the amounts that were paid to the participant but that otherwise should have been paid to the alternate payee. [I.R.C. §§ 414(p)(7)(C), 414(p)(7)(D); ERISA §§ 206(d)(3)(H), 404(a); REA Sen. Comm. Rep.]

When a divorce decree, awarding a portion of an employee's plan benefits to his former spouse, was received and acknowledged by an employer prior to the employee's death, it was enforceable by the former spouse although she was not named as an alternate payee until after the employee's death. The divorce decree had awarded the employee's spouse half of the employee's plan funds, but the court order naming the spouse as alternate payee was not entered until two days after the employee's death. The court opined that the employer had been put on notice that a decree had been issued that could be a QDRO, the decree designated the spouse as entitled to part of the employee's plan benefits, and the court order naming the spouse as alternate payee was filed well within the 18-month period. Taken together, the plan administrator had sufficient basis for qualifying the DRO the court determined. [Hogan v. Raytheon Co., 302 F.3d 854 (8th Cir. 2002)]

A plan accepted and recognized a DRO presented by one of its participants as a QDRO. Subsequently, the participant presented a newer DRO, calling for a reduced payment to the alternate payee. DOL advised that a plan administrator may not fail to qualify a DRO on the basis that it would supersede or amend a pre-existing QDRO by reducing benefits previously assigned to an alternate payee. [DOL Op. Ltr. 2004-02A]

DOL believes that the 18-month period is not the measure of a reasonable period for determining the qualified status of a DRO and in most cases would be an unreasonably long period of time to review a DRO. If the plan administrator fails to notify the participant and each alternate payee promptly of the procedures for determining the qualified status of the DRO or fails to complete the determination process within a reasonable period after receipt, the plan administrator may be liable for breach of fiduciary duty. One court ruled that a state law that allowed a party to recover attorneys' fees from plan fiduciaries for their alleged unreasonable refusal to qualify a DRO was preempted by ERISA. [AT&T Mgmt. Pension Plan v. Tucker, No. CV 95-2263 (C.D. Cal. 1995)]

In 1994, DOL ruled that a plan administrator could not charge fees to a plan participant or alternate payee or against a plan account for determining and administering a QDRO. [DOL Op Ltr 94-32A] However, DOL subsequently concluded that this position was not legally compelled by ERISA. Consequently, expenses for processing a QDRO may be charged to the defined contribution plan (see Q 2:2) account of the participant or alternate payee. [DOL Field Assistance Bull. 2003-3] This DOL guidance addressed defined contribution plans and not defined benefit plans (see Q 2:3). See Q 23:34 for further details.

IRS has ruled that, in a salary-reduction-only 403(b) contract (see Qs 35:1, 35:11), it is the employee-participant who determines that a DRO is a QDRO. [Priv. Ltr. Rul. 9619040] One court held that it was an abuse of discretion for a plan administrator, who was also a divorced participant under the plan, to construe an ambiguous plan term so as to deny effect to a DRO that was issued to correct an error in calculating plan payments to his wife. [Fox v. Fox, 167 F.3d 880 (4th Cir. 1999)]

An employer requested guidance from DOL concerning the treatment of QDROs. The employer had reason to be suspicious about 16 QDROs, all issued in the same location, and all of which dealt only with an ESOP (see Q 28:1) and a 401(k) plan (see Q 27:1) but not the employer's defined benefit plan. The employer also noted that some QDROs were from the same attorney, many used similar language, some showed the alternate payee and the participant at the same address, and many contained wording similar to a pamphlet that was being distributed by an employee in the same area. The pamphlet informed individuals that they could get a distribution from their retirement plans before retirement by divorcing a spouse, assigning all benefits under the plans to the spouse, and then remarrying the same spouse. DOL opined that plan administrators are not free to ignore information indicating that a DRO is invalid; and, although plan administrators are not required to review the correctness of a determination made by a competent state authority, plan administrators are required to attempt to resolve the question of a DRO's validity when confronted with evidence that the DRO may be a sham. [DOL Op. Ltr. 99-13A]

Q 36:23 What kind of notice is required to be provided by a plan administrator following a QDRO determination?

The plan administrator (see Q 20:1) is required to notify the participant and each alternate payee (see Q 36:5) of the administrator's determination as to whether the DRO (see Q 36:2) constitutes a QDRO (see Q 36:1). This notice should be in writing and furnished promptly following a determination (see Q 36:21).

In the case of a determination that a DRO is not a QDRO, the notice should include the reasons for the rejection. DOL believes that, where a reasonable good-faith effort has been made to draft a QDRO, prudent plan administration requires the plan administrator to furnish to the parties the information, advice, and guidance that is reasonably required to understand the reasons for a rejection, either as part of the notification process or otherwise, if such information, advice, and guidance could serve to reduce multiple submissions of deficient orders and therefore the burdens and costs to plans attendant on review of such orders.

The notice of the plan administrator's determination should be written in a manner that can be understood by the parties. Multiple submissions and unnecessary expenses may be avoided by clearly communicating in the rejection notice:

1. The reasons why the order is not a QDRO;
2. References to the plan provisions on which the plan administrator's determination is based;
3. An explanation of any time limits that apply to rights available to the parties under the plan (such as the duration of any protective actions the plan administrator will take); and
4. A description of any additional material, information, or modifications necessary for the DRO to be a QDRO and an explanation of why such material, information, or modifications are necessary.

[I.R.C. § 414(p)(6)(A)(ii); ERISA §§ 206(d)(3)(G)(i)(II), 206(d)(3)(I)]

**Q 36:24   Is a plan administrator required to reject a DRO as
defective if it fails to specify certain factual identifying
information?**

No. In many cases, a DRO (see Q 36:2) that is submitted to a plan may clearly
describe the identity and rights of the parties but may be incomplete only with
respect to factual identifying information within the plan administrator's (see
Q 20:1) knowledge or easily obtained through a simple communication with the
alternate payee (see Q 36:5) or the participant. For example, a DRO may misstate
the plan's name or the name of the participant or alternate payee, and the plan
administrator can clearly determine the correct names, or a DRO may omit the
address of the participant or alternate payee, and the plan administrator's
records include this information. In such a case, the plan administrator should
supplement the order with the appropriate identifying information, rather than
rejecting the DRO as not qualified. [I.R.C. § 414(p)(2); ERISA §§ 206(d)(3)(C),
206(d)(3)(I)]

**Q 36:25   May plan administrators provide parties with a model form
or forms to assist in the preparation of a QDRO?**

Yes. Although they are not required to do so, plan administrators (see Q 20:1)
may develop and make available model QDRO forms to assist in the preparation
of a QDRO (see Q 36:1). Such model forms may make it easier for the parties to
prepare a QDRO and reduce the time and expenses associated with a plan
administrator's determination of the qualified status of an order. Plan administrators are required to honor any QDRO that satisfies the requirements to be a
QDRO. DOL believes that a plan may not condition its determinations of QDRO
status on the use of any particular form.

**Q 36:26   Can the amounts segregated for an alternate payee
under a QDRO be forfeited?**

If an alternate payee (see Q 36:5) cannot be located, the qualified retirement
plan is not permitted to provide for the forfeiture of the alternate payee's
segregated amounts (see Q 36:22) unless the plan provides for the segregated
amounts to be fully reinstated when the alternate payee is located. [REA Senate
Comm. Rep.]

The rights of an alternate payee under a QDRO (see Q 36:1) are protected in
the event of plan amendments, a plan merger, or a change in the sponsor of the
plan to the same extent that rights of participants or beneficiaries are protected
with respect to benefits accrued (see Q 9:25) as of the date of the event. A DRO
will remain qualified with respect to a successor qualified retirement plan of the
same employer or a qualified retirement plan of a successor employer. An order
will not fail to be a QDRO even if the form of the benefit does not continue to be
a form permitted under the qualified retirement plan because of a plan amendment or a change of law. In the case of a plan amendment, an alternate payee
remains entitled to receive benefits in the form specified in the order. In the case
of a law change that makes the benefit form specified in the order impermissible,

the plan must permit the alternate payee to select a form of benefit specified in the plan. In either case, the elected form cannot affect, in any way, the amount or form of benefits payable to the participant. [I.R.C. §§ 401(a)(13)(B), 411(d)(6); ERISA §§ 204(g), 206(d)(3)(A), 403(c)(1)]

If the plan is terminated, the rights granted by a QDRO must be taken into account in the termination of a plan as if the terms of the QDRO were part of the plan. To the extent that the QDRO grants the alternate payee part of the participant's benefits, the plan administrator (see Q 20:1), in terminating the plan, must provide the alternate payee with the notification, consent, payment, or other rights that it would have provided to the participant with respect to that portion of the participant's benefits. [ERISA §§ 206(d)(3)(A), 403(d)]

When a plan covered by PBGC (see Q 36:6) terminates without enough money to pay all guaranteed benefits, PBGC becomes trustee of the terminating plan and pays the plan benefits subject to certain limits on amount and form. PBGC has special rules that apply to payment of benefits under QDROs. For example, if a QDRO is issued prior to plan termination, PBGC will not modify the form of benefit payable to an alternate payee specified in the QDRO. If, in contrast, a QDRO is issued after plan termination, PBGC will generally limit the form of benefit that PBGC will pay under the QDRO to the form permitted by PBGC in other circumstances (generally a single life annuity). For details on plan termination, see chapter 25.

Q 36:27   How does a QDRO affect the qualified preretirement survivor annuity and qualified joint and survivor annuity requirements?

A QDRO (see Q 36:1) may provide that a former spouse will be treated as the participant's current spouse for some or all of the QPSA (see Q 10:9) and QJSA (see Q 10:8) requirements. [I.R.C. § 414(p)(5); Treas. Reg. §§ 1.401(a)-13(g)(4)(i)(A), 1.401(a)-13(g)(4)(ii); Prop. Treas. Reg. § 1.401(a)-13(g)(4)(ii)]

To the extent a former spouse is treated as the participant's current spouse by reason of a QDRO, the actual current spouse will not be treated as the participant's current spouse. [I.R.C. § 414(p)(5); Treas. Reg. § 1.401(a)-13(g)(4)(i)(B); Braehler v. Ford Motor Co. UAW Retirement Plan, 2007 WL 1805045 (W.D. Ken. 2007)]

Example 1. Assume Barrie is divorced from Larry, but a QDRO provides that Barrie shall be treated as Larry's current spouse with respect to all of Larry's benefits under a qualified retirement plan. Barrie will be treated as the surviving spouse under the QPSA and QJSA unless Larry obtains Barrie's consent to waive the QPSA or QJSA or both. The fact that Larry married Carrie after Larry's divorce from Barrie is disregarded. If, however, the QDRO had provided that Barrie would be treated as Larry's current spouse only with respect to benefits that accrued prior to the divorce, then Larry would need Barrie's consent to waive the QPSA or QJSA with respect to benefits accrued before the divorce, and Carrie's consent would be required with respect to the remainder of the benefits.

Example 2. Assume the same facts as in Example 1, except that the QDRO ordered that a portion of Larry's benefit must be distributed to Barrie rather than ordering that Barrie be treated as Larry's spouse. The QPSA and QJSA requirements would not apply to the part of Larry's benefit awarded Barrie. Instead, the QDRO would determine how Barrie's portion of Larry's benefit would be paid. Larry would be required to obtain Carrie's consent if Larry wanted to elect to waive either the QPSA or QJSA with respect to the remaining portion of his benefit.

Example 3. Assume the same facts as in Example 1, except that there was no QDRO and Larry died after marrying Carrie but never removed Barrie as his designated beneficiary. One court ruled that Carrie was entitled to one-half of Larry's plan benefits as his surviving spouse, but that Barrie was entitled to the other half (see Q 15:10). [McMillan v. Parrott, 913 F.2d 310 (6th Cir. 1990)] However, another court ruled that Barrie was not entitled to any benefits. [Von Haden v. Supervised Estate of Von Haden, No. 52A02-9712-CV-876 (Ind. Ct. App. 1998)]

The waiver, in a divorce decree, by the former spouse of a deceased plan participant of her rights to plan benefits did not violate the anti-alienation provisions of ERISA even though no QDRO was filed, ruled the court. The court concluded that the plan administrator was not required to change the beneficiary designation, which still named the former spouse, based upon the waiver in the divorce decree where the plan documents made no provision for such a change. [Kennedy v. Plan Administrator for DuPont Savings and Investment Plan, 129 S. Ct. 865 (2009)]

If, because of a QDRO, more than one individual is treated as the surviving spouse, the qualified retirement plan may provide that the total amount to be paid in the form of a QPSA or survivor portion of a QJSA may not exceed the amount that would be paid if there were only one surviving spouse. The QPSA or survivor portion of the QJSA payable to each surviving spouse must be paid as an annuity based on the life expectancy of each respective spouse. If the QDRO splits the participant's benefit between the participant and a former spouse (either through separate accounts or percentage of the benefit), the surviving actual current spouse of the participant would be entitled to a QPSA or QJSA based on the participant's benefit reduced by the separate account or percentage payable to the former spouse. The calculation is made as if the separate account or percentage had been distributed to the participant. [Treas. Reg. § 1.401(a)-13(g)(4)(i)(C)]

If an alternate payee is treated pursuant to a QDRO as having an interest in the plan benefit, including a separate account or percentage of the participant's benefit, then the QDRO cannot provide the alternate payee with a greater right to designate a beneficiary for the alternate payee's benefit amount than the participant's right. The QPSA or QJSA provisions do not apply to the spouse of an alternate payee. If the former spouse who is treated as a current spouse should die prior to the participant's annuity starting date (see Q 10:3), then any actual current spouse of the participant would be treated as the current spouse, except as otherwise provided in the QDRO. [Treas. Reg. § 1.401(a)-13(g)(4)(iii)]

When a QDRO only related to lifetime benefits payable to an alternate payee but did not relate to survivor benefits after the plan participant died, courts have ruled that the surviving alternate payee was not entitled to any further benefits and that the QDRO could not be amended after the participant's death. [Dorn v. International Bhd. of Elec. Workers, 211 F.3d 938 (5th Cir. 2000); Samaroo v. Samaroo, 193 F.3d 185 (3d Cir. 1999); Robson v. Electrical Contractors Ass'n Local 134, 727 N.E.2d 692 (Ill. App. Ct. 1st Dist. 2000); *see also* Kazel v. Estate of Kazel, No. 163 (N.Y. App., 4th Div., 2004), Cosby v. Cosby, 773 N.E.2d 516 (Ohio 2002), and Rich v. Southern Cal. IBEW-NECA Pension Plan, 2d Civil No. B127215 (Cal. Ct. App. 2d App. Dist. 1999); *but see* Patton v. Denver Post Corp., 326 F.3d 1148 (10th Cir. 2003)] The Third Circuit distinguished its holding in *Samaroo v. Samaroo* and determined that a property settlement agreement entered into prior to the participant's death, and before the entry of a QDRO, conferred plan benefits to the participant's former spouse, because the agreement provided the former spouse with a right to benefits for which the participant had been eligible prior to his death. [Files v. ExxonMobil Pension Plan, 428 F.3d 478 (3d Cir. 2005)] See Q 36:2 concerning the interim final regulation issued by DOL.

A decedent did not remove his ex-wife as the designated beneficiary of a life insurance policy after their divorce, even though the divorce decree designated the decedent's minor children as beneficiaries until they reached the age of majority. The ex-wife contended that she remained the designated beneficiary under the policy and that ERISA required that the policy be enforced according to its terms. The second wife countered that the divorce decree constituted a QDRO, and the court held that the decree was a QDRO since it named alternate payees of the insurance proceeds. The court also concluded that the estate of the decedent was the appropriate beneficiary since the minor children replaced the ex-wife, the minor children's beneficiary status lapsed upon their majority, and thus the estate was the proper beneficiary under the terms of the policy in the absence of a designated beneficiary. [Seaman v. Johnson, 2004 U.S. App. LEXIS 4400 (6th Cir. 2004)]

In accordance with the divorce decree, a decedent designated his ex-wife as a 50 percent beneficiary of his pension plan should he die before retirement. After he remarried, he named his new wife as the beneficiary of the remaining 50 percent. After his remarriage, the decedent, his wife, and his ex-wife entered into a QDRO assigning to the first wife a new annuity created from a lump-sum transfer of 45 percent of his pension accumulations. All parties waived all other interests in each other's estates. The decedent never changed the beneficiary designation so that when he died before retirement, his wife and ex-wife were still listed on the plan's records as 50 percent beneficiaries. The plan paid 50 percent of the funds to the decedent's widow but withheld payment of the other 50 percent. The court held that federal common law determines whether the QDRO acted as a renunciation of the ex-wife's rights to the pension plan, that under federal common law her waiver was explicit, voluntary, and made in good faith, and that therefore it was an effective waiver. Thus, the widow was also entitled to the remaining 50 percent. [Silber v. Silber, 99 N.Y.2d 395 (2003)]

Q 36:28   Must an alternate payee consent to a distribution from a qualified retirement plan?

The general rules that apply to the distribution of benefits to a participant from a qualified retirement plan also apply to the distribution of benefits to an alternate payee (see Q 36:5) pursuant to a QDRO (see Q 36:1). The plan administrator (see Q 20:1) must act in accordance with the provisions of the QDRO as if it were a part of the plan. In particular, if, under a plan, a participant has the right to elect the form in which benefits will be paid and the QDRO gives the alternate payee that right, the plan administrator must permit the alternate payee to exercise that right under the circumstances and in accordance with the terms that would apply to the participant, as if the alternate payee were the participant. (For exceptions, see Qs 36:9, 36:18, 36:27.) [I.R.C. §§ 401(a)(13)(B), 414(p)(4)(A)(iii); ERISA §§ 206(d)(3)(A), 206(d)(3)(E)(i)(III)]

If the distribution to the alternate payee does not exceed $5,000, the alternate payee's consent is not required. However, if the distribution exceeds $5,000, the alternate payee's consent is required (see Q 10:61).

In determining whether the present value of the benefit payable to the alternate payee exceeds $5,000, the present value of the participant's remaining benefit is disregarded. Similarly, for purposes of determining whether the present value of the benefit payable to the participant exceeds $5,000, the present value of the benefit payable to the alternate payee under a QDRO is disregarded.

Q 36:29   Does a QDRO affect the maximum amount of the participant's benefits under a qualified retirement plan?

Even though a participant's benefits are awarded to an alternate payee (see Q 36:5) pursuant to a QDRO (see Q 36:1), the benefits awarded to the alternate payee are still considered benefits of the participant for purposes of applying the limitations of Section 415 to the participant's benefits. [Treas. Reg. § 1.401(a)-13(g)(4)(iv)] See chapter 6 for details.

IRS representatives have opined that payments under a QDRO relating to the benefits of a restricted employee are subject to the limitation on distributions (see Q 25:8).

Q 36:30   What are the income tax consequences of a QDRO to the participant?

If the alternate payee (see Q 36:5) pursuant to a QDRO (see Q 36:1) is other than the participant's spouse or former spouse (e.g., a child), any distribution from a qualified retirement plan to such alternate payee will be included in the participant's gross income for the year of distribution. If, however, any portion of the distribution represents a recovery of the participant's investment in the contract (see Q 13:3), that portion will be excluded from the participant's gross income. [I.R.C. §§ 402(a), 402(e)(1)(A)] At the time of a married couple's divorce, the husband was entitled to receive pension benefits, but he chose to continue working. Under the state community property law, the ex-wife was entitled to one-half of his accrued benefit, and the husband was ordered to pay his ex-wife an amount equal to one-half thereof until he retired. Under the state's community property law, each spouse is taxed on one-half of both spouse's income because the earnings are the property of the community and not of the spouse providing the services that produce the income. Since the income assigned to his ex-wife did not belong to the husband, he was not liable for the taxes thereon, and he therefore was not required to include in his income the amounts he paid to his ex-wife. [Dunkin, 124 T.C. 180 (2005)] On appeal, the decision was reversed; the husband had to include in income the amount paid to his ex-wife, and the amount paid was not deductible as alimony. [United States v. Dunkin, 500 F.3d 1065 (9th Cir. 2007)]

The balance to the credit of an employee (see Q 13:6) does not include an amount payable to an alternate payee under a QDRO. So, an alternate payee's decision to receive payments in a form other than a lump sum will not affect the participant's eligibility for the special tax treatment afforded a lump-sum distribution (see Q 13:5) or the participant's eligibility to roll over a distribution from the qualified retirement plan. [I.R.C. § 402(e)(4)(D)(v); Priv. Ltr. Ruls. 8935041, 8743102]

See chapters 13 and 34 for details on taxation of distributions and rollovers.

Q 36:31 What are the income tax consequences of a QDRO to an alternate payee spouse or former spouse?

If the alternate payee (see Q 36:5) is the spouse or former spouse of the participant, any distribution from a qualified retirement plan to such alternate payee pursuant to a QDRO (see Q 36:1) will be included in the alternate payee's gross income for the year of distribution. The participant's investment in the contract (see Q 13:3) must be apportioned between the participant and such alternate payee. The investment in the contract will be allocated on a pro rata basis between the present value of the distribution to the alternate payee and the present value of all other benefits payable with respect to the participant. [I.R.C. §§ 72(m)(10), 402(e)(1)(A); Mitchell, 131 T.C. No. 15 (2008); Joubert, 94 T.C.M. 327 (2007); Kelley, T.C. Summ. Op. 2005-68; Hawkins v. Comm'r, 86 F.3d 982 (10th Cir. 1996); Brotman, 105 T.C. 141 (1995); Rudzin, 69 T.C.M. 1649 (1995); Powell, 101 T.C. 489 (1993); Priv. Ltr. Ruls. 9138004, 9013007]

If a distribution of the balance to the credit of an employee (see Q 13:6) would be treated as a lump-sum distribution (see Q 13:5), then the payment under a QDRO of the balance to the credit of an alternate payee spouse or former spouse of the participant will be treated as a lump-sum distribution. The balance to the credit of the alternate payee does not include any amount payable to the participant. [I.R.C. § 402(e)(4)(D)(vii)]

One court concluded that a distribution to an alternate payee former spouse from her former husband's qualified retirement plan pursuant to a QDRO was taxable to the alternate payee. The QDRO's provision that the former husband was liable for the tax on the distribution did not shift the tax burden to him; the

Code, not state law, determines how the parties are taxed. Although the alternate payee may have a cause of action based on the QDRO against her former husband to recover her tax payment, she remains liable for the tax on the distribution. [Clawson, 72 T.C.M. 814 (1996)] In divorce settlement negotiations, the parties, residents of a community property state, agreed on the amount of the community property interest in the husband's qualified retirement plan benefits. In a marital settlement agreement incorporating a QDRO, the parties agreed that the community property interest would be distributed from the plan and used to pay off two mortgage loans for which they were jointly liable with the remainder of the funds to be split equally between the parties. According to the court, a distribution from a plan is taxed to the distributee, ordinarily defined as the participant entitled to receive the distribution under the plan, the husband. However, a distribution received by a former spouse who is an alternate payee pursuant to a QDRO is taxable to the alternate payee, the wife, instead of the participant. The court determined that the husband had been a distributee as to half of the cost of paying off the joint loans and all cash he received beyond that amount and that the former wife was likewise a distributee as to half of the cost of paying off the joint loans and all proceeds from the distribution she received beyond that amount. [Seidel, 89 T.C.M. 972 (2005)]

If there is no QDRO, the spouse or former spouse is not an alternate payee and a distribution from the plan to the participant, who then gives the payment to such spouse, or from the plan directly to the spouse or former spouse is included in the participant's gross income (see Qs 13:1, 36:1). Pursuant to a QDRO, a participant's ex-spouse was entitled to a portion of his qualified retirement plan benefits. Subsequently, however, the participant received a distribution of the entire plan benefit, rolled over the distribution to an IRA, and designated his new spouse as beneficiary. Upon the participant's death, the new spouse received the IRA proceeds and paid income tax on the proceeds. After a lawsuit was commenced by the ex-spouse, she received a settlement payment from the new spouse. IRS concluded that the settlement payment did not constitute a taxable distribution from either a qualified retirement plan or an IRA, but did not rule on whether the payment was taxable under other Code sections. [Priv. Ltr. Rul. 9327083]

If pursuant to a QDRO a distribution is made to an alternate payee and the employee continues to participate in the qualified retirement plan, the five-year period will continue to apply for purposes of top-heavy plan testing (see Q 26:16), opined IRS representatives.

For a discussion of special rules relating to required minimum distributions to an alternate payee, see Q 11:47; and, for details on taxation of distributions, see chapter 13.

Q 36:32   Can an alternate payee roll over a distribution pursuant to a QDRO from a qualified retirement plan?

A distribution from a qualified retirement plan pursuant to a QDRO (see Q 36:1) to an alternate payee (see Q 36:5) who is not the spouse or former spouse of the participant (e.g., a child) may not be rolled over to another plan or to an IRA. Since such alternate payee pays no income tax on the distribution, the ineligibility of the alternate payee to roll over the distribution is of no importance to the alternate payee. However, because the participant remains taxable on a distribution to a nonspouse or non-former spouse alternate payee, this ineligibility to roll over will cause the participant to include the distribution in income. This remains true even if the participant receives, at the same time, a distribution from the plan eligible to be rolled over and does roll over such distribution (see Q 36:30).

If, however, the alternate payee is the spouse or former spouse of the participant and receives an eligible rollover distribution pursuant to a QDRO, the alternate payee is eligible to roll over any portion or all of the distribution to an eligible retirement plan (see Q 34:16). [I.R.C. §§ 402(c), 402(e)(1)(B); Priv. Ltr. Ruls. 9726032, 9109052, 9013007; Cogliano v Anderson, Nos. CC-05-1061, CC-05-1202 (BAP 9th Cir. 2006)]

An eligible rollover distribution made to an alternate payee spouse or former spouse may be subject to mandatory 20 percent income tax withholding (see Q 20:10). Since an alternate payee nonspouse or non-former spouse pays no income tax on the distribution, the distribution will not be subject to the automatic withholding rules. [I.R.C. § 3405(c); Priv. Ltr. Rul. 9726032]

For details on rollovers, see chapter 34.

Q 36:33   Does the 10 percent early distribution tax apply to a distribution made to an alternate payee pursuant to a QDRO?

The 10 percent tax on early distributions (see Qs 16:1, 16:13) from qualified retirement plans does not apply to any distribution to any alternate payee (see Q 36:5) pursuant to a QDRO (see Q 36:1). [I.R.C. § 72(t)(2)(C); Priv. Ltr. Ruls. 9051041, 9013007, 8935041] However, if the distribution is not made pursuant to a QDRO, the participant spouse may be subject to the 10 percent penalty tax. [Simpson I, 86 T.C.M. 470 (2003); Bougas III, 86 T.C.M. 9 (2003); Burton, 73 T.C.M. 1729 (1997); Rodoni, 105 T.C. 29 (1995)]

Because of this exception, the 10 percent early distribution tax will not be imposed on the participant if the alternate payee is a nonspouse or non-former spouse (e.g., a child)(see Q 36:30) and will not be imposed on a spouse or former spouse alternate payee (see Q 36:31).

If, for example, a spouse or former spouse alternate payee rolls over to an IRA a distribution pursuant to a QDRO from a qualified retirement plan (see Q 36:32) and commences distributions from the IRA prior to age 59½, the 10 percent tax on early distributions may apply. However, the alternate payee can commence distributions from the IRA prior to age 59½ in a series of substantially equal periodic payments and avoid the 10 percent tax on early distributions. [I.R.C. § 72(t)(2)(A)(iv); Priv. Ltr. Rul. 9109052] See chapter 16 for details.

Q 36:34 Are qualified retirement plan benefits subject to equitable distribution?

Some portion or all of a participant's benefits under a qualified retirement plan may be awarded to the participant's spouse pursuant to a divorce decree or pursuant to a QDRO (see Q 36:1). [Witcher, 84 T.C.M. 582 (2002); Hamstead v. Hamstead, No. 19529 (W. Va. 1990); Givler v. Givler, No. Ca-181 (Tenn. Ct. App. E.D. 1990)] One court ruled that benefits could be awarded to the participant's spouse even though she had executed an antenuptial agreement waiving her rights, because the waiver was ineffective (see Q 10:22). [Richards v. Richards, 232 A.D.2d 303 (1st Dept. N.Y. 1996)] Other courts have concluded that a waiver in an antenuptial agreement is invalid as it applies to a spouse's survivorship rights, but is valid as it applies to the equitable distribution of a plan benefit as marital property. Thus, in a divorce proceeding, the waiver of rights to plan benefits in an antenuptial agreement is enforceable. [Strong v. Dubin, ___ A.D.3d ___ (1st Dept. N.Y. 2010); Savage-Keough v. Keough, 861 A.2d 131 (N.J. Super., App. Div. 2004); Edmonds v. Edmonds, 710 N.Y.S.2d 765 (N.Y. Sup. Ct. 2000)]

At least one court has ruled that qualified retirement plan benefits accrued prior to the marriage are not subject to an equitable distribution of marital assets absent evidence of a gift or conveyance. [Zaborowski v. Zaborowski, No. 88-1802 (Fla. Dist. Ct. App. 5th Dist. 1989)] However, another court ruled that plan benefits accrued during the time a couple lived together before marriage were subject to division upon divorce. [Bays v. Bays, No. 5-3635 (Alaska 1991)]

In a matter in which a couple separated and, during the separation but prior to the divorce, one spouse became covered under a new plan, the court ruled that the new retirement benefits were separate property and not community property and therefore the nonparticipant spouse had no entitlement to the benefits. [*In re* Marriage of Manry, 60 Wash. App. 146 (1991); *see also* Lipsey v. Lipsey, No. 2-98-090 CV (Tex. Ct. App. 2d Dist. 1998)] In another case, to accomplish a division of marital property, the court ruled that the value of the spouse's pension benefits should be based on present value and not the projected value at age 65. [*In re* Marriage of Keedy, No. 90-598 (Mont. 1991)]

An enhanced pension benefit elected by an employee as part of an early retirement incentive program that occurred after divorce was held to be marital property subject to equitable distribution because it was a modification of a marital asset and not the creation of a new asset. [Olivo v. Olivo, 82 N.Y.2d 202 (1993)] Another court ruled that benefit increases not attributable to the employee's efforts between the marital separation date and the benefit commencement date would be shared by the spouse, but increases resulting from the employee's efforts (e.g., salary increases) would not be shared. [Berrington v. Berrington, No. 20 W.D. App. Dkt. (Pa. 1993)]

The portion of distributions from an employee's qualified retirement plan representing compensation for postdivorce employment could be treated as income available for maintenance of a former spouse even though the plan had been considered an asset in an earlier property settlement agreement, one court has ruled. The court rejected the employee's argument that this constituted "double-counting." [*In re* Marriage of Olski, No. 93-3332 (Wis. 1995)]

One court determined that a qualified retirement plan benefit earned during marriage is treated as any other divisible marital property, enabling the nonparticipant spouse to make a testamentary disposition of her share of the benefit. [Brosick v. Brosick, No. 94-CI-562 (Ky. Ct. App. 1998); *but see* Shelstead v. Shelstead, 78 Cal. Rptr. 2d 365 (Cal. 1998); Qs 36:2, 36:5–36:7]

Q 36:35 Can a QDRO be enforced by an attachment of the participant's monthly retirement benefits?

One court has held that an order made pursuant to the state domestic relations law that relates to alimony payments is a QDRO (see Q 36:1), which may be enforced by attachment of the participant's (husband's) qualified retirement plan benefits. The court determined that, since the state domestic law allowed attachment of the husband's income in any form, the attachment order against his qualified retirement plan benefits was a QDRO, which allowed the wife to recover amounts for alimony. [Taylor v. Taylor, 541 N.E.2d 55 (Ohio 1989)] Another court ruled that a garnishment judgment against a plan participant for failure to make required alimony and child support payments must satisfy the QDRO requirements [Arizona Laborers, etc. Local 385 Pension Fund v. Nevarez, 8 Employee Benefits Cas. (BNA) 2227 (D. Ariz. 1987)]; and, consistent with that holding, courts have determined that the entry of a QDRO directing the payment of maintenance arrearages owed to an ex-wife from the retirement benefits of her ex-husband was appropriate because a QDRO is a proper method for enforcing an earlier support judgment and collecting delinquent maintenance from the husband's pension plan. [Hogle v. Hogle, 732 N.E.2d 1278 (Ind. Ct. App. 2000); *In re* Marriage of LeBlanc, No. 96CA0881 (Colo. Ct. App. 1997); *see also* Trustees of the Dirs. Guild of Am.–Producer Pension Benefits Plans v. Tise, 234 F.3d 415 (9th Cir. 2000)]

Even though an award of attorneys' fees incurred by a spouse to obtain a QDRO for spousal support was not itself a QDRO, a court ruled that qualified retirement plan benefits could be used to satisfy the award. [*In re* Marriage of Olivarez, 8 Employee Benefits Cas. (BNA) 1263 (Cal. Ct. App. 1986); *but see* Johnson v. Johnson, 727 A.2d 473 (N.J. Super. Ct. App. Div. 1999)] Another court permitted a husband to recover attorneys' fees from his wife's plan account pursuant to a QDRO. [Silverman v. Spiro, 784 N.E.2d 1 (Mass. 2003)]

Q 36:36 Can a QDRO be discharged in bankruptcy?

One court has held that a participant's obligation to pay one-half of his qualified retirement plan benefits to his former spouse as part of a divorce decree's property settlement was a "debt" under the U.S. Bankruptcy Code that was dischargeable in bankruptcy. The property settlement awarded the former spouse one-half of the participant's qualified retirement plan benefits as he received them. The participant filed a Chapter 7 bankruptcy petition and listed that obligation as a dischargeable debt. The Bankruptcy Code defines a debt as a liability on a claim and a claim as a right to payment, whether or not such right is contingent or unmatured. The court held that the former spouse had a claim for a share of future qualified retirement plan payments, however contingent or unmatured that claim might be. Although a debt for alimony, maintenance, or support is not dischargeable under the Bankruptcy Code, the obligation in this case was a property settlement and, therefore, a debt that was dischargeable in bankruptcy. [Bush v. Taylor, No. 88-2145 (8th Cir. 1990); *see also In re* Ellis, 1995 U.S. App. LEXIS 35337 (8th Cir. 1995); Anderson v. Lifeline Healthcare Group, Ltd., No. 92-5076 (10th Cir. 1993)] One court concluded that, since the divorce decree was not a valid QDRO (see Qs 36:1, 36:35), the divorced spouse's claim was dischargeable in bankruptcy. [*In re* Zeitler, 1997 Bankr. LEXIS 1495 (Bankr. E.D.N.C. 1997); *but see In re* Carbaugh, 278 B.R. 512 (10th Cir. 2002)]

However, other courts have ruled that since the wife had been awarded a part of the husband's pension fund, it had become her property and was not a dischargeable debt of the participant-husband when he filed a bankruptcy petition. [Hines v. Hines, 2006 WL 1792705 (6th Cir. 2006);] *In re* Grossman, 2001 WL 277690 (Bankr. D.N.D. 2001); Lowenschuss v. Selnick, 170 F.3d 923 (9th Cir. 1999); Gendreau v. Gendreau, 122 F.3d 815 (9th Cir. 1997); Hopkins v. State, No. W.D. 54337 (Mo. Ct. App. 1997); McCaferty v. McCaferty, No. 95-3919 (6th Cir. 1996); Erb v. Erb, 75 Ohio St. 3d 18 (1996); *In re* Bennett, 1994 Bankr. LEXIS 1942 (Bankr. E.D. Pa. 1994); *In re* Zick, No. 89-02388 (Bankr. E.D. Wis. 1990)] Another court concluded that an ex-husband's bankruptcy filing did not discharge an obligation, created in a QDRO, to transfer his interest in a pension plan to his ex-wife for two reasons. One, the obligation to transfer the pension interest was not his personal debt, because the QDRO required the plan administrator, not the husband, to pay the ex-wife her interest in the plan. Second, because her interest in the pension account vested before he filed for bankruptcy, her interest in the pension plan became her separate property right and was not the ex-husband's debt obligation that could have been discharged in bankruptcy. [*In re* Nouri, 2003 WL 23192668 (Bankr. M.D. Pa. 2003)]

One court concluded that a participant's community property interest in his plan benefits was subject to a federal tax lien, even though his former wife also had a claim to the benefits, because the lien attached prior to the entry of a QDRO transferring the benefits to her. [Agents Pension Plan of Allstate Ins. Co. v. Weeks, 1999 WL 261700 (N.D. Ill. 1999)] However, another court concluded that a QDRO has priority over a prior federal tax lien where the plan determined within the requisite 18-month qualification period (see Q 36:22) that a DRO qualified as a QDRO and the DRO preceded the notice of tax lien. [United States v. Taylor, 2003 U.S. App. LEXIS 15276 (8th Cir. 2003)]

The anti-alienation rule (see Q 4:27) did not protect from claims of creditors an alternate payee's (see Q 36:5) interest in plan benefits under a QDRO, concluded a court, because the alternate payee was neither a plan participant nor a plan beneficiary. [*In re* Johnston, 218 B.R. 813 (Bankr. E.D. Va. 1998)] Another court concluded that a debtor's interest in her former husband's qualified retirement plan that she received pursuant to their divorce was not exempt from her bankruptcy estate under state exemption statutes and that the exclusion for interests in ERISA qualified plans (see Q 4:28) did not apply, because her interest was based upon a QDRO rather than on the plan. [*In re* Hageman, 260 B.R. 852 (Bankr. S.D. Ohio 2001)] To the contrary, an increasing number of courts has determined that an alternate payee is a plan beneficiary; and, as such, the portion of the plan benefit awarded to the alternate payee pursuant to a QDRO was excludable from the bankruptcy estate. [Nelson v. Raimetta, 322 F.3d 541 (8th Cir. 2003); *In re* Quinn, No. HL-005810 (Bankr. W.D. Mich. 2003); *In re* Farmer, No. 02-16039-7 (Bankr. W.D. Wis. 2003); *In re* Hthiy, 283 B.R. 447 (Bankr. E.D. Mich. 2002); *see also* Cogliano v. Anderson, Nos. CC-05-1061, CC-05-1202 (BAP 9th Cir. 2006)]

See Q 1:27 for a discussion of the Bankruptcy Abuse Prevention and Consumer Protection Act of 2005, which protects retirement plan benefits from claims of creditors during bankruptcy proceedings.

Appendix A

Joint and Last Survivor Table

Joint and Last Survivor Table

[NOTE: The following table has been reformatted from the regulation as published, to enhance readability]

Ages	0	1	2	3	4	5	6	7	8	9
0	90.0	89.5	89.0	88.6	88.2	87.8	87.4	87.1	86.8	86.5
1	89.5	89.0	88.5	88.1	87.6	87.2	86.8	86.5	86.1	85.8
2	89.0	88.5	88.0	87.5	87.1	86.6	86.2	85.8	85.5	85.1
3	88.6	88.1	87.5	87.0	86.5	86.1	85.6	85.2	84.8	84.5
4	88.2	87.6	87.1	86.5	86.0	85.5	85.1	84.6	84.2	83.8
5	87.8	87.2	86.6	86.1	85.5	85.0	84.5	84.1	83.6	83.2
6	87.4	86.8	86.2	85.6	85.1	84.5	84.0	83.5	83.1	82.6
7	87.1	86.5	85.8	85.2	84.6	84.1	83.5	83.0	82.5	82.1
8	86.8	86.1	85.5	84.8	84.2	83.6	83.1	82.5	82.0	81.6
9	86.5	85.8	85.1	84.5	83.8	83.2	82.6	82.1	81.6	81.0
10	86.2	85.5	84.8	84.1	83.5	82.8	82.2	81.6	81.1	80.6
11	85.9	85.2	84.5	83.8	83.1	82.5	81.8	81.2	80.7	80.1
12	85.7	84.9	84.2	83.5	82.8	82.1	81.5	80.8	80.2	79.7
13	85.4	84.7	84.0	83.2	82.5	81.8	81.1	80.5	79.9	79.2
14	85.2	84.5	83.7	83.0	82.2	81.5	80.8	80.1	79.5	78.9
15	85.0	84.3	83.5	82.7	82.0	81.2	80.5	79.8	79.1	78.5
16	84.9	84.1	83.3	82.5	81.7	81.0	80.2	79.5	78.8	78.1
17	84.7	83.9	83.1	82.3	81.5	80.7	80.0	79.2	78.5	77.8
18	84.5	83.7	82.9	82.1	81.3	80.5	79.7	79.0	78.2	77.5
19	84.4	83.6	82.7	81.9	81.1	80.3	79.5	78.7	78.0	77.3
20	84.3	83.4	82.6	81.8	80.9	80.1	79.3	78.5	77.7	77.0
21	84.1	83.3	82.4	81.6	80.8	79.9	79.1	78.3	77.5	76.8
22	84.0	83.2	82.3	81.5	80.6	79.8	78.9	78.1	77.3	76.5
23	83.9	83.1	82.2	81.3	80.5	79.6	78.8	77.9	77.1	76.3
24	83.8	83.0	82.1	81.2	80.3	79.5	78.6	77.8	76.9	76.1
25	83.7	82.9	82.0	81.1	80.2	79.3	78.5	77.6	76.8	75.9
26	83.6	82.8	81.9	81.0	80.1	79.2	78.3	77.5	76.6	75.8
27	83.6	82.7	81.8	80.9	80.0	79.1	78.2	77.4	76.5	75.6
28	83.5	82.6	81.7	80.8	79.9	79.0	78.1	77.2	76.4	75.5
29	83.4	82.6	81.6	80.7	79.8	78.9	78.0	77.1	76.2	75.4
30	83.4	82.5	81.6	80.7	79.7	78.8	77.9	77.0	76.1	75.2
31	83.3	82.4	81.5	80.6	79.7	78.8	77.8	76.9	76.0	75.1
32	83.3	82.4	81.5	80.5	79.6	78.7	77.8	76.8	75.9	75.0
33	83.2	82.3	81.4	80.5	79.5	78.6	77.7	76.8	75.9	74.9
34	83.2	82.3	81.3	80.4	79.5	78.5	77.6	76.7	75.8	74.9

Ages	0	1	2	3	4	5	6	7	8	9
35	83.1	82.2	81.3	80.4	79.4	78.5	77.6	76.6	75.7	74.8
36	83.1	82.2	81.3	80.3	79.4	78.4	77.5	76.6	75.6	74.7
37	83.0	82.2	81.2	80.3	79.3	78.4	77.4	76.5	75.6	74.6
38	83.0	82.1	81.2	80.2	79.3	78.3	77.4	76.4	75.5	74.6
39	83.0	82.1	81.1	80.2	79.2	78.3	77.3	76.4	75.5	74.5
40	82.9	82.1	81.1	80.2	79.2	78.3	77.3	76.4	75.4	74.5
41	82.9	82.0	81.1	80.1	79.2	78.2	77.3	76.3	75.4	74.4
42	82.9	82.0	81.1	80.1	79.1	78.2	77.2	76.3	75.3	74.4
43	82.9	82.0	81.0	80.1	79.1	78.2	77.2	76.2	75.3	74.3
44	82.8	81.9	81.0	80.0	79.1	78.1	77.2	76.2	75.2	74.3
45	82.8	81.9	81.0	80.0	79.1	78.1	77.1	76.2	75.2	74.3
46	82.8	81.9	81.0	80.0	79.0	78.1	77.1	76.1	75.2	74.2
47	82.8	81.9	80.9	80.0	79.0	78.0	77.1	76.1	75.2	74.2
48	82.8	81.9	80.9	80.0	79.0	78.0	77.1	76.1	75.1	74.2
49	82.7	81.8	80.9	79.9	79.0	78.0	77.0	76.1	75.1	74.1
50	82.7	81.8	80.9	79.9	79.0	78.0	77.0	76.0	75.1	74.1
51	82.7	81.8	80.9	79.9	78.9	78.0	77.0	76.0	75.1	74.1
52	82.7	81.8	80.9	79.9	78.9	78.0	77.0	76.0	75.0	74.1
53	82.7	81.8	80.8	79.9	78.9	77.9	77.0	76.0	75.0	74.0
54	82.7	81.8	80.8	79.9	78.9	77.9	76.9	76.0	75.0	74.0
55	82.6	81.8	80.8	79.8	78.9	77.9	76.9	76.0	75.0	74.0
56	82.6	81.7	80.8	79.8	78.9	77.9	76.9	75.9	75.0	74.0
57	82.6	81.7	80.8	79.8	78.9	77.9	76.9	75.9	75.0	74.0
58	82.6	81.7	80.8	79.8	78.8	77.9	76.9	75.9	74.9	74.0
59	82.6	81.7	80.8	79.8	78.8	77.9	76.9	75.9	74.9	74.0
60	82.6	81.7	80.8	79.8	78.8	77.8	76.9	75.9	74.9	73.9
61	82.6	81.7	80.8	79.8	78.8	77.8	76.9	75.9	74.9	73.9
62	82.6	81.7	80.7	79.8	78.8	77.8	76.9	75.9	74.9	73.9
63	82.6	81.7	80.7	79.8	78.8	77.8	76.8	75.9	74.9	73.9
64	82.5	81.7	80.7	79.8	78.8	77.8	76.8	75.9	74.9	73.9
65	82.5	81.7	80.7	79.8	78.8	77.8	76.8	75.8	74.9	73.9
66	82.5	81.7	80.7	79.7	78.8	77.8	76.8	75.8	74.9	73.9
67	82.5	81.7	80.7	79.7	78.8	77.8	76.8	75.8	74.9	73.9
68	82.5	81.6	80.7	79.7	78.8	77.8	76.8	75.8	74.8	73.9
69	82.5	81.6	80.7	79.7	78.8	77.8	76.8	75.8	74.8	73.9
70	82.5	81.6	80.7	79.7	78.8	77.8	76.8	75.8	74.8	73.9
71	82.5	81.6	80.7	79.7	78.7	77.8	76.8	75.8	74.8	73.8
72	82.5	81.6	80.7	79.7	78.7	77.8	76.8	75.8	74.8	73.8
73	82.5	81.6	80.7	79.7	78.7	77.8	76.8	75.8	74.8	73.8

Ages	0	1	2	3	4	5	6	7	8	9
74	82.5	81.6	80.7	79.7	78.7	77.8	76.8	75.8	74.8	73.8
75	82.5	81.6	80.7	79.7	78.7	77.8	76.8	75.8	74.8	73.8
76	82.5	81.6	80.7	79.7	78.7	77.8	76.8	75.8	74.8	73.8
77	82.5	81.6	80.7	79.7	78.7	77.7	76.8	75.8	74.8	73.8
78	82.5	81.6	80.7	79.7	78.7	77.7	76.8	75.8	74.8	73.8
79	82.5	81.6	80.7	79.7	78.7	77.7	76.8	75.8	74.8	73.8
80	82.5	81.6	80.7	79.7	78.7	77.7	76.8	75.8	74.8	73.8
81	82.4	81.6	80.7	79.7	78.7	77.7	76.8	75.8	74.8	73.8
82	82.4	81.6	80.7	79.7	78.7	77.7	76.8	75.8	74.8	73.8
83	82.4	81.6	80.7	79.7	78.7	77.7	76.8	75.8	74.8	73.8
84	82.4	81.6	80.7	79.7	78.7	77.7	76.8	75.8	74.8	73.8
85	82.4	81.6	80.6	79.7	78.7	77.7	76.8	75.8	74.8	73.8
86	82.4	81.6	80.6	79.7	78.7	77.7	76.7	75.8	74.8	73.8
87	82.4	81.6	80.6	79.7	78.7	77.7	76.7	75.8	74.8	73.8
88	82.4	81.6	80.6	79.7	78.7	77.7	76.7	75.8	74.8	73.8
89	82.4	81.6	80.6	79.7	78.7	77.7	76.7	75.8	74.8	73.8
90	82.4	81.6	80.6	79.7	78.7	77.7	76.7	75.8	74.8	73.8
91	82.4	81.6	80.6	79.7	78.7	77.7	76.7	75.8	74.8	73.8
92	82.4	81.6	80.6	79.7	78.7	77.7	76.7	75.8	74.8	73.8
93	82.4	81.6	80.6	79.7	78.7	77.7	76.7	75.8	74.8	73.8
94	82.4	81.6	80.6	79.7	78.7	77.7	76.7	75.8	74.8	73.8
95	82.4	81.6	80.6	79.7	78.7	77.7	76.7	75.8	74.8	73.8
96	82.4	81.6	80.6	79.7	78.7	77.7	76.7	75.8	74.8	73.8
97	82.4	81.6	80.6	79.7	78.7	77.7	76.7	75.8	74.8	73.8
98	82.4	81.6	80.6	79.7	78.7	77.7	76.7	75.8	74.8	73.8
99	82.4	81.6	80.6	79.7	78.7	77.7	76.7	75.8	74.8	73.8
100	82.4	81.6	80.6	79.7	78.7	77.7	76.7	75.8	74.8	73.8
101	82.4	81.6	80.6	79.7	78.7	77.7	76.7	75.8	74.8	73.8
102	82.4	81.6	80.6	79.7	78.7	77.7	76.7	75.8	74.8	73.8
103	82.4	81.6	80.6	79.7	78.7	77.7	76.7	75.8	74.8	73.8
104	82.4	81.6	80.6	79.7	78.7	77.7	76.7	75.8	74.8	73.8
105	82.4	81.6	80.6	79.7	78.7	77.7	76.7	75.8	74.8	73.8
106	82.4	81.6	80.6	79.7	78.7	77.7	76.7	75.8	74.8	73.8
107	82.4	81.6	80.6	79.7	78.7	77.7	76.7	75.8	74.8	73.8
108	82.4	81.6	80.6	79.7	78.7	77.7	76.7	75.8	74.8	73.8
109	82.4	81.6	80.6	79.7	78.7	77.7	76.7	75.8	74.8	73.8
110	82.4	81.6	80.6	79.7	78.7	77.7	76.7	75.8	74.8	73.8
111	82.4	81.6	80.6	79.7	78.7	77.7	76.7	75.8	74.8	73.8
112	82.4	81.6	80.6	79.7	78.7	77.7	76.7	75.8	74.8	73.8

Ages	0	1	2	3	4	5	6	7	8	9
113	82.4	81.6	80.6	79.7	78.7	77.7	76.7	75.8	74.8	73.8
114	82.4	81.6	80.6	79.7	78.7	77.7	76.7	75.8	74.8	73.8
115	82.4	81.6	80.6	79.7	78.7	77.7	76.7	75.8	74.8	73.8

Ages	10	11	12	13	14	15	16	17	18	19
10	80.0	79.6	79.1	78.7	78.2	77.9	77.5	77.2	76.8	76.5
11	79.6	79.0	78.6	78.1	77.7	77.3	76.9	76.5	76.2	75.8
12	79.1	78.6	78.1	77.6	77.1	76.7	76.3	75.9	75.5	75.2
13	78.7	78.1	77.6	77.1	76.6	76.1	75.7	75.3	74.9	74.5
14	78.2	77.7	77.1	76.6	76.1	75.6	75.1	74.7	74.3	73.9
15	77.9	77.3	76.7	76.1	75.6	75.1	74.6	74.1	73.7	73.3
16	77.5	76.9	76.3	75.7	75.1	74.6	74.1	73.6	73.1	72.7
17	77.2	76.5	75.9	75.3	74.7	74.1	73.6	73.1	72.6	72.1
18	76.8	76.2	75.5	74.9	74.3	73.7	73.1	72.6	72.1	71.6
19	76.5	75.8	75.2	74.5	73.9	73.3	72.7	72.1	71.6	71.1
20	76.3	75.5	74.8	74.2	73.5	72.9	72.3	71.7	71.1	70.6
21	76.0	75.3	74.5	73.8	73.2	72.5	71.9	71.3	70.7	70.1
22	75.8	75.0	74.3	73.5	72.9	72.2	71.5	70.9	70.3	69.7
23	75.5	74.8	74.0	73.3	72.6	71.9	71.2	70.5	69.9	69.3
24	75.3	74.5	73.8	73.0	72.3	71.6	70.9	70.2	69.5	68.9
25	75.1	74.3	73.5	72.8	72.0	71.3	70.6	69.9	69.2	68.5
26	75.0	74.1	73.3	72.5	71.8	71.0	70.3	69.6	68.9	68.2
27	74.8	74.0	73.1	72.3	71.6	70.8	70.0	69.3	68.6	67.9
28	74.6	73.8	73.0	72.2	71.3	70.6	69.8	69.0	68.3	67.6
29	74.5	73.6	72.8	72.0	71.2	70.4	69.6	68.8	68.0	67.3
30	74.4	73.5	72.7	71.8	71.0	70.2	69.4	68.6	67.8	67.1
31	74.3	73.4	72.5	71.7	70.8	70.0	69.2	68.4	67.6	66.8
32	74.1	73.3	72.4	71.5	70.7	69.8	69.0	68.2	67.4	66.6
33	74.0	73.2	72.3	71.4	70.5	69.7	68.8	68.0	67.2	66.4
34	73.9	73.0	72.2	71.3	70.4	69.5	68.7	67.8	67.0	66.2
35	73.9	73.0	72.1	71.2	70.3	69.4	68.5	67.7	66.8	66.0
36	73.8	72.9	72.0	71.1	70.2	69.3	68.4	67.6	66.7	65.9
37	73.7	72.8	71.9	71.0	70.1	69.2	68.3	67.4	66.6	65.7
38	73.6	72.7	71.8	70.9	70.0	69.1	68.2	67.3	66.4	65.6
39	73.6	72.7	71.7	70.8	69.9	69.0	68.1	67.2	66.3	65.4
40	73.5	72.6	71.7	70.7	69.8	68.9	68.0	67.1	66.2	65.3
41	73.5	72.5	71.6	70.7	69.7	68.8	67.9	67.0	66.1	65.2
42	73.4	72.5	71.5	70.6	69.7	68.8	67.8	66.9	66.0	65.1

Ages	10	11	12	13	14	15	16	17	18	19
43	73.4	72.4	71.5	70.6	69.6	68.7	67.8	66.8	65.9	65.0
44	73.3	72.4	71.4	70.5	69.6	68.6	67.7	66.8	65.9	64.9
45	73.3	72.3	71.4	70.5	69.5	68.6	67.6	66.7	65.8	64.9
46	73.3	72.3	71.4	70.4	69.5	68.5	67.6	66.6	65.7	64.8
47	73.2	72.3	71.3	70.4	69.4	68.5	67.5	66.6	65.7	64.7
48	73.2	72.2	71.3	70.3	69.4	68.4	67.5	66.5	65.6	64.7
49	73.2	72.2	71.2	70.3	69.3	68.4	67.4	66.5	65.6	64.6
50	73.1	72.2	71.2	70.3	69.3	68.4	67.4	66.5	65.5	64.6
51	73.1	72.2	71.2	70.2	69.3	68.3	67.4	66.4	65.5	64.5
52	73.1	72.1	71.2	70.2	69.2	68.3	67.3	66.4	65.4	64.5
53	73.1	72.1	71.1	70.2	69.2	68.3	67.3	66.3	65.4	64.4
54	73.1	72.1	71.1	70.2	69.2	68.2	67.3	66.3	65.4	64.4
55	73.0	72.1	71.1	70.1	69.2	68.2	67.2	66.3	65.3	64.4
56	73.0	72.1	71.1	70.1	69.1	68.2	67.2	66.3	65.3	64.3
57	73.0	72.0	71.1	70.1	69.1	68.2	67.2	66.2	65.3	64.3
58	73.0	72.0	71.0	70.1	69.1	68.1	67.2	66.2	65.2	64.3
59	73.0	72.0	71.0	70.1	69.1	68.1	67.2	66.2	65.2	64.3
60	73.0	72.0	71.0	70.0	69.1	68.1	67.1	66.2	65.2	64.2
61	73.0	72.0	71.0	70.0	69.1	68.1	67.1	66.2	65.2	64.2
62	72.9	72.0	71.0	70.0	69.0	68.1	67.1	66.1	65.2	64.2
63	72.9	72.0	71.0	70.0	69.0	68.1	67.1	66.1	65.2	64.2
64	72.9	71.9	71.0	70.0	69.0	68.0	67.1	66.1	65.1	64.2
65	72.9	71.9	71.0	70.0	69.0	68.0	67.1	66.1	65.1	64.2
66	72.9	71.9	70.9	70.0	69.0	68.0	67.1	66.1	65.1	64.1
67	72.9	71.9	70.9	70.0	69.0	68.0	67.0	66.1	65.1	64.1
68	72.9	71.9	70.9	70.0	69.0	68.0	67.0	66.1	65.1	64.1
69	72.9	71.9	70.9	69.9	69.0	68.0	67.0	66.1	65.1	64.1
70	72.9	71.9	70.9	69.9	69.0	68.0	67.0	66.0	65.1	64.1
71	72.9	71.9	70.9	69.9	69.0	68.0	67.0	66.0	65.1	64.1
72	72.9	71.9	70.9	69.9	69.0	68.0	67.0	66.0	65.1	64.1
73	72.9	71.9	70.9	69.9	68.9	68.0	67.0	66.0	65.0	64.1
74	72.9	71.9	70.9	69.9	68.9	68.0	67.0	66.0	65.0	64.1
75	72.8	71.9	70.9	69.9	68.9	68.0	67.0	66.0	65.0	64.1
76	72.8	71.9	70.9	69.9	68.9	68.0	67.0	66.0	65.0	64.1
77	72.8	71.9	70.9	69.9	68.9	68.0	67.0	66.0	65.0	64.1
78	72.8	71.9	70.9	69.9	68.9	67.9	67.0	66.0	65.0	64.0
79	72.8	71.9	70.9	69.9	68.9	67.9	67.0	66.0	65.0	64.0
80	72.8	71.9	70.9	69.9	68.9	67.9	67.0	66.0	65.0	64.0
81	72.8	71.8	70.9	69.9	68.9	67.9	67.0	66.0	65.0	64.0

Ages	10	11	12	13	14	15	16	17	18	19
82	72.8	71.8	70.9	69.9	68.9	67.9	67.0	66.0	65.0	64.0
83	72.8	71.8	70.9	69.9	68.9	67.9	67.0	66.0	65.0	64.0
84	72.8	71.8	70.9	69.9	68.9	67.9	67.0	66.0	65.0	64.0
85	72.8	71.8	70.9	69.9	68.9	67.9	66.9	66.0	65.0	64.0
86	72.8	71.8	70.9	69.9	68.9	67.9	66.9	66.0	65.0	64.0
87	72.8	71.8	70.9	69.9	68.9	67.9	66.9	66.0	65.0	64.0
88	72.8	71.8	70.9	69.9	68.9	67.9	66.9	66.0	65.0	64.0
89	72.8	71.8	70.9	69.9	68.9	67.9	66.9	66.0	65.0	64.0
90	72.8	71.8	70.9	69.9	68.9	67.9	66.9	66.0	65.0	64.0
91	72.8	71.8	70.9	69.9	68.9	67.9	66.9	66.0	65.0	64.0
92	72.8	71.8	70.9	69.9	68.9	67.9	66.9	66.0	65.0	64.0
93	72.8	71.8	70.9	69.9	68.9	67.9	66.9	66.0	65.0	64.0
94	72.8	71.8	70.8	69.9	68.9	67.9	66.9	66.0	65.0	64.0
95	72.8	71.8	70.8	69.9	68.9	67.9	66.9	66.0	65.0	64.0
96	72.8	71.8	70.8	69.9	68.9	67.9	66.9	66.0	65.0	64.0
97	72.8	71.8	70.8	69.9	68.9	67.9	66.9	66.0	65.0	64.0
98	72.8	71.8	70.8	69.9	68.9	67.9	66.9	66.0	65.0	64.0
99	72.8	71.8	70.8	69.9	68.9	67.9	66.9	66.0	65.0	64.0
100	72.8	71.8	70.8	69.9	68.9	67.9	66.9	66.0	65.0	64.0
101	72.8	71.8	70.8	69.9	68.9	67.9	66.9	66.0	65.0	64.0
102	72.8	71.8	70.8	69.9	68.9	67.9	66.9	66.0	65.0	64.0
103	72.8	71.8	70.8	69.9	68.9	67.9	66.9	66.0	65.0	64.0
104	72.8	71.8	70.8	69.9	68.9	67.9	66.9	66.0	65.0	64.0
105	72.8	71.8	70.8	69.9	68.9	67.9	66.9	66.0	65.0	64.0
106	72.8	71.8	70.8	69.9	68.9	67.9	66.9	66.0	65.0	64.0
107	72.8	71.8	70.8	69.9	68.9	67.9	66.9	66.0	65.0	64.0
108	72.8	71.8	70.8	69.9	68.9	67.9	66.9	66.0	65.0	64.0
109	72.8	71.8	70.8	69.9	68.9	67.9	66.9	66.0	65.0	64.0
110	72.8	71.8	70.8	69.9	68.9	67.9	66.9	66.0	65.0	64.0
111	72.8	71.8	70.8	69.9	68.9	67.9	66.9	66.0	65.0	64.0
112	72.8	71.8	70.8	69.9	68.9	67.9	66.9	66.0	65.0	64.0
113	72.8	71.8	70.8	69.9	68.9	67.9	66.9	66.0	65.0	64.0
114	72.8	71.8	70.8	69.9	68.9	67.9	66.9	66.0	65.0	64.0
115	72.8	71.8	70.8	69.9	68.9	67.9	66.9	66.0	65.0	64.0

Ages	20	21	22	23	24	25	26	27	28	29
20	70.1	69.6	69.1	68.7	68.3	67.9	67.5	67.2	66.9	66.6
21	69.6	69.1	68.6	68.2	67.7	67.3	66.9	66.6	66.2	65.9

Ages	20	21	22	23	24	25	26	27	28	29
22	69.1	68.6	68.1	67.6	67.2	66.7	66.3	65.9	65.6	65.2
23	68.7	68.2	67.6	67.1	66.6	66.2	65.7	65.3	64.9	64.6
24	68.3	67.7	67.2	66.6	66.1	65.6	65.2	64.7	64.3	63.9
25	67.9	67.3	66.7	66.2	65.6	65.1	64.6	64.2	63.7	63.3
26	67.5	66.9	66.3	65.7	65.2	64.6	64.1	63.6	63.2	62.8
27	67.2	66.6	65.9	65.3	64.7	64.2	63.6	63.1	62.7	62.2
28	66.9	66.2	65.6	64.9	64.3	63.7	63.2	62.7	62.1	61.7
29	66.6	65.9	65.2	64.6	63.9	63.3	62.8	62.2	61.7	61.2
30	66.3	65.6	64.9	64.2	63.6	62.9	62.3	61.8	61.2	60.7
31	66.1	65.3	64.6	63.9	63.2	62.6	62.0	61.4	60.8	60.2
32	65.8	65.1	64.3	63.6	62.9	62.2	61.6	61.0	60.4	59.8
33	65.6	64.8	64.1	63.3	62.6	61.9	61.3	60.6	60.0	59.4
34	65.4	64.6	63.8	63.1	62.3	61.6	60.9	60.3	59.6	59.0
35	65.2	64.4	63.6	62.8	62.1	61.4	60.6	59.9	59.3	58.6
36	65.0	64.2	63.4	62.6	61.9	61.1	60.4	59.6	59.0	58.3
37	64.9	64.0	63.2	62.4	61.6	60.9	60.1	59.4	58.7	58.0
38	64.7	63.9	63.0	62.2	61.4	60.6	59.9	59.1	58.4	57.7
39	64.6	63.7	62.9	62.1	61.2	60.4	59.6	58.9	58.1	57.4
40	64.4	63.6	62.7	61.9	61.1	60.2	59.4	58.7	57.9	57.1
41	64.3	63.5	62.6	61.7	60.9	60.1	59.3	58.5	57.7	56.9
42	64.2	63.3	62.5	61.6	60.8	59.9	59.1	58.3	57.5	56.7
43	64.1	63.2	62.4	61.5	60.6	59.8	58.9	58.1	57.3	56.5
44	64.0	63.1	62.2	61.4	60.5	59.6	58.8	57.9	57.1	56.3
45	64.0	63.0	62.2	61.3	60.4	59.5	58.6	57.8	56.9	56.1
46	63.9	63.0	62.1	61.2	60.3	59.4	58.5	57.7	56.8	56.0
47	63.8	62.9	62.0	61.1	60.2	59.3	58.4	57.5	56.7	55.8
48	63.7	62.8	61.9	61.0	60.1	59.2	58.3	57.4	56.5	55.7
49	63.7	62.8	61.8	60.9	60.0	59.1	58.2	57.3	56.4	55.6
50	63.6	62.7	61.8	60.8	59.9	59.0	58.1	57.2	56.3	55.4
51	63.6	62.6	61.7	60.8	59.9	58.9	58.0	57.1	56.2	55.3
52	63.5	62.6	61.7	60.7	59.8	58.9	58.0	57.1	56.1	55.2
53	63.5	62.5	61.6	60.7	59.7	58.8	57.9	57.0	56.1	55.2
54	63.5	62.5	61.6	60.6	59.7	58.8	57.8	56.9	56.0	55.1
55	63.4	62.5	61.5	60.6	59.6	58.7	57.8	56.8	55.9	55.0
56	63.4	62.4	61.5	60.5	59.6	58.7	57.7	56.8	55.9	54.9
57	63.4	62.4	61.5	60.5	59.6	58.6	57.7	56.7	55.8	54.9
58	63.3	62.4	61.4	60.5	59.5	58.6	57.6	56.7	55.8	54.8
59	63.3	62.3	61.4	60.4	59.5	58.5	57.6	56.7	55.7	54.8
60	63.3	62.3	61.4	60.4	59.5	58.5	57.6	56.6	55.7	54.7

Ages	20	21	22	23	24	25	26	27	28	29
61	63.3	62.3	61.3	60.4	59.4	58.5	57.5	56.6	55.6	54.7
62	63.2	62.3	61.3	60.4	59.4	58.4	57.5	56.5	55.6	54.7
63	63.2	62.3	61.3	60.3	59.4	58.4	57.5	56.5	55.6	54.6
64	63.2	62.2	61.3	60.3	59.4	58.4	57.4	56.5	55.5	54.6
65	63.2	62.2	61.3	60.3	59.3	58.4	57.4	56.5	55.5	54.6
66	63.2	62.2	61.2	60.3	59.3	58.4	57.4	56.4	55.5	54.5
67	63.2	62.2	61.2	60.3	59.3	58.3	57.4	56.4	55.5	54.5
68	63.1	62.2	61.2	60.2	59.3	58.3	57.4	56.4	55.4	54.5
69	63.1	62.2	61.2	60.2	59.3	58.3	57.3	56.4	55.4	54.5
70	63.1	62.2	61.2	60.2	59.3	58.3	57.3	56.4	55.4	54.4
71	63.1	62.1	61.2	60.2	59.2	58.3	57.3	56.4	55.4	54.4
72	63.1	62.1	61.2	60.2	59.2	58.3	57.3	56.3	55.4	54.4
73	63.1	62.1	61.2	60.2	59.2	58.3	57.3	56.3	55.4	54.4
74	63.1	62.1	61.2	60.2	59.2	58.2	57.3	56.3	55.4	54.4
75	63.1	62.1	61.1	60.2	59.2	58.2	57.3	56.3	55.3	54.4
76	63.1	62.1	61.1	60.2	59.2	58.2	57.3	56.3	55.3	54.4
77	63.1	62.1	61.1	60.2	59.2	58.2	57.3	56.3	55.3	54.4
78	63.1	62.1	61.1	60.2	59.2	58.2	57.3	56.3	55.3	54.4
79	63.1	62.1	61.1	60.2	59.2	58.2	57.2	56.3	55.3	54.3
80	63.1	62.1	61.1	60.1	59.2	58.2	57.2	56.3	55.3	54.3
81	63.1	62.1	61.1	60.1	59.2	58.2	57.2	56.3	55.3	54.3
82	63.1	62.1	61.1	60.1	59.2	58.2	57.2	56.3	55.3	54.3
83	63.1	62.1	61.1	60.1	59.2	58.2	57.2	56.3	55.3	54.3
84	63.0	62.1	61.1	60.1	59.2	58.2	57.2	56.3	55.3	54.3
85	63.0	62.1	61.1	60.1	59.2	58.2	57.2	56.3	55.3	54.3
86	63.0	62.1	61.1	60.1	59.2	58.2	57.2	56.2	55.3	54.3
87	63.0	62.1	61.1	60.1	59.2	58.2	57.2	56.2	55.3	54.3
88	63.0	62.1	61.1	60.1	59.2	58.2	57.2	56.2	55.3	54.3
89	63.0	62.1	61.1	60.1	59.1	58.2	57.2	56.2	55.3	54.3
90	63.0	62.1	61.1	60.1	59.1	58.2	57.2	56.2	55.3	54.3
91	63.0	62.1	61.1	60.1	59.1	58.2	57.2	56.2	55.3	54.3
92	63.0	62.1	61.1	60.1	59.1	58.2	57.2	56.2	55.3	54.3
93	63.0	62.1	61.1	60.1	59.1	58.2	57.2	56.2	55.3	54.3
94	63.0	62.1	61.1	60.1	59.1	58.2	57.2	56.2	55.3	54.3
95	63.0	62.1	61.1	60.1	59.1	58.2	57.2	56.2	55.3	54.3
96	63.0	62.1	61.1	60.1	59.1	58.2	57.2	56.2	55.3	54.3
97	63.0	62.1	61.1	60.1	59.1	58.2	57.2	56.2	55.3	54.3
98	63.0	62.1	61.1	60.1	59.1	58.2	57.2	56.2	55.3	54.3
99	63.0	62.1	61.1	60.1	59.1	58.2	57.2	56.2	55.3	54.3

Ages	20	21	22	23	24	25	26	27	28	29
100	63.0	62.1	61.1	60.1	59.1	58.2	57.2	56.2	55.3	54.3
101	63.0	62.1	61.1	60.1	59.1	58.2	57.2	56.2	55.3	54.3
102	63.0	62.1	61.1	60.1	59.1	58.2	57.2	56.2	55.3	54.3
103	63.0	62.1	61.1	60.1	59.1	58.2	57.2	56.2	55.3	54.3
104	63.0	62.1	61.1	60.1	59.1	58.2	57.2	56.2	55.3	54.3
105	63.0	62.1	61.1	60.1	59.1	58.2	57.2	56.2	55.3	54.3
106	63.0	62.1	61.1	60.1	59.1	58.2	57.2	56.2	55.3	54.3
107	63.0	62.1	61.1	60.1	59.1	58.2	57.2	56.2	55.3	54.3
108	63.0	62.1	61.1	60.1	59.1	58.2	57.2	56.2	55.3	54.3
109	63.0	62.1	61.1	60.1	59.1	58.2	57.2	56.2	55.3	54.3
110	63.0	62.1	61.1	60.1	59.1	58.2	57.2	56.2	55.3	54.3
111	63.0	62.1	61.1	60.1	59.1	58.2	57.2	56.2	55.3	54.3
112	63.0	62.1	61.1	60.1	59.1	58.2	57.2	56.2	55.3	54.3
113	63.0	62.1	61.1	60.1	59.1	58.2	57.2	56.2	55.3	54.3
114	63.0	62.1	61.1	60.1	59.1	58.2	57.2	56.2	55.3	54.3
115	63.0	62.1	61.1	60.1	59.1	58.2	57.2	56.2	55.3	54.3

Ages	30	31	32	33	34	35	36	37	38	39
30	60.2	59.7	59.2	58.8	58.4	58.0	57.6	57.3	57.0	56.7
31	59.7	59.2	58.7	58.2	57.8	57.4	57.0	56.6	56.3	56.0
32	59.2	58.7	58.2	57.7	57.2	56.8	56.4	56.0	55.6	55.3
33	58.8	58.2	57.7	57.2	56.7	56.2	55.8	55.4	55.0	54.7
34	58.4	57.8	57.2	56.7	56.2	55.7	55.3	54.8	54.4	54.0
35	58.0	57.4	56.8	56.2	55.7	55.2	54.7	54.3	53.8	53.4
36	57.6	57.0	56.4	55.8	55.3	54.7	54.2	53.7	53.3	52.8
37	57.3	56.6	56.0	55.4	54.8	54.3	53.7	53.2	52.7	52.3
38	57.0	56.3	55.6	55.0	54.4	53.8	53.3	52.7	52.2	51.7
39	56.7	56.0	55.3	54.7	54.0	53.4	52.8	52.3	51.7	51.2
40	56.4	55.7	55.0	54.3	53.7	53.0	52.4	51.8	51.3	50.8
41	56.1	55.4	54.7	54.0	53.3	52.7	52.0	51.4	50.9	50.3
42	55.9	55.2	54.4	53.7	53.0	52.3	51.7	51.1	50.4	49.9
43	55.7	54.9	54.2	53.4	52.7	52.0	51.3	50.7	50.1	49.5
44	55.5	54.7	53.9	53.2	52.4	51.7	51.0	50.4	49.7	49.1
45	55.3	54.5	53.7	52.9	52.2	51.5	50.7	50.0	49.4	48.7
46	55.1	54.3	53.5	52.7	52.0	51.2	50.5	49.8	49.1	48.4
47	55.0	54.1	53.3	52.5	51.7	51.0	50.2	49.5	48.8	48.1
48	54.8	54.0	53.2	52.3	51.5	50.8	50.0	49.2	48.5	47.8
49	54.7	53.8	53.0	52.2	51.4	50.6	49.8	49.0	48.2	47.5

Ages	30	31	32	33	34	35	36	37	38	39
50	54.6	53.7	52.9	52.0	51.2	50.4	49.6	48.8	48.0	47.3
51	54.5	53.6	52.7	51.9	51.0	50.2	49.4	48.6	47.8	47.0
52	54.4	53.5	52.6	51.7	50.9	50.0	49.2	48.4	47.6	46.8
53	54.3	53.4	52.5	51.6	50.8	49.9	49.1	48.2	47.4	46.6
54	54.2	53.3	52.4	51.5	50.6	49.8	48.9	48.1	47.2	46.4
55	54.1	53.2	52.3	51.4	50.5	49.7	48.8	47.9	47.1	46.3
56	54.0	53.1	52.2	51.3	50.4	49.5	48.7	47.8	47.0	46.1
57	54.0	53.0	52.1	51.2	50.3	49.4	48.6	47.7	46.8	46.0
58	53.9	53.0	52.1	51.2	50.3	49.4	48.5	47.6	46.7	45.8
59	53.8	52.9	52.0	51.1	50.2	49.3	48.4	47.5	46.6	45.7
60	53.8	52.9	51.9	51.0	50.1	49.2	48.3	47.4	46.5	45.6
61	53.8	52.8	51.9	51.0	50.0	49.1	48.2	47.3	46.4	45.5
62	53.7	52.8	51.8	50.9	50.0	49.1	48.1	47.2	46.3	45.4
63	53.7	52.7	51.8	50.9	49.9	49.0	48.1	47.2	46.3	45.3
64	53.6	52.7	51.8	50.8	49.9	48.9	48.0	47.1	46.2	45.3
65	53.6	52.7	51.7	50.8	49.8	48.9	48.0	47.0	46.1	45.2
66	53.6	52.6	51.7	50.7	49.8	48.9	47.9	47.0	46.1	45.1
67	53.6	52.6	51.7	50.7	49.8	48.8	47.9	46.9	46.0	45.1
68	53.5	52.6	51.6	50.7	49.7	48.8	47.8	46.9	46.0	45.0
69	53.5	52.6	51.6	50.6	49.7	48.7	47.8	46.9	45.9	45.0
70	53.5	52.5	51.6	50.6	49.7	48.7	47.8	46.8	45.9	44.9
71	53.5	52.5	51.6	50.6	49.6	48.7	47.7	46.8	45.9	44.9
72	53.5	52.5	51.5	50.6	49.6	48.7	47.7	46.8	45.8	44.9
73	53.4	52.5	51.5	50.6	49.6	48.6	47.7	46.7	45.8	44.8
74	53.4	52.5	51.5	50.5	49.6	48.6	47.7	46.7	45.8	44.8
75	53.4	52.5	51.5	50.5	49.6	48.6	47.7	46.7	45.7	44.8
76	53.4	52.4	51.5	50.5	49.6	48.6	47.6	46.7	45.7	44.8
77	53.4	52.4	51.5	50.5	49.5	48.6	47.6	46.7	45.7	44.8
78	53.4	52.4	51.5	50.5	49.5	48.6	47.6	46.6	45.7	44.7
79	53.4	52.4	51.5	50.5	49.5	48.6	47.6	46.6	45.7	44.7
80	53.4	52.4	51.4	50.5	49.5	48.5	47.6	46.6	45.7	44.7
81	53.4	52.4	51.4	50.5	49.5	48.5	47.6	46.6	45.7	44.7
82	53.4	52.4	51.4	50.5	49.5	48.5	47.6	46.6	45.6	44.7
83	53.4	52.4	51.4	50.5	49.5	48.5	47.6	46.6	45.6	44.7
84	53.4	52.4	51.4	50.5	49.5	48.5	47.6	46.6	45.6	44.7
85	53.3	52.4	51.4	50.4	49.5	48.5	47.5	46.6	45.6	44.7
86	53.3	52.4	51.4	50.4	49.5	48.5	47.5	46.6	45.6	44.6
87	53.3	52.4	51.4	50.4	49.5	48.5	47.5	46.6	45.6	44.6
88	53.3	52.4	51.4	50.4	49.5	48.5	47.5	46.6	45.6	44.6

Ages	30	31	32	33	34	35	36	37	38	39
89	53.3	52.4	51.4	50.4	49.5	48.5	47.5	46.6	45.6	44.6
90	53.3	52.4	51.4	50.4	49.5	48.5	47.5	46.6	45.6	44.6
91	53.3	52.4	51.4	50.4	49.5	48.5	47.5	46.6	45.6	44.6
92	53.3	52.4	51.4	50.4	49.5	48.5	47.5	46.6	45.6	44.6
93	53.3	52.4	51.4	50.4	49.5	48.5	47.5	46.6	45.6	44.6
94	53.3	52.4	51.4	50.4	49.5	48.5	47.5	46.6	45.6	44.6
95	53.3	52.4	51.4	50.4	49.5	48.5	47.5	46.5	45.6	44.6
96	53.3	52.4	51.4	50.4	49.5	48.5	47.5	46.5	45.6	44.6
97	53.3	52.4	51.4	50.4	49.5	48.5	47.5	46.5	45.6	44.6
98	53.3	52.4	51.4	50.4	49.5	48.5	47.5	46.5	45.6	44.6
99	53.3	52.4	51.4	50.4	49.5	48.5	47.5	46.5	45.6	44.6
100	53.3	52.4	51.4	50.4	49.5	48.5	47.5	46.5	45.6	44.6
101	53.3	52.4	51.4	50.4	49.5	48.5	47.5	46.5	45.6	44.6
102	53.3	52.4	51.4	50.4	49.5	48.5	47.5	46.5	45.6	44.6
103	53.3	52.4	51.4	50.4	49.5	48.5	47.5	46.5	45.6	44.6
104	53.3	52.4	51.4	50.4	49.5	48.5	47.5	46.5	45.6	44.6
105	53.3	52.4	51.4	50.4	49.4	48.5	47.5	46.5	45.6	44.6
106	53.3	52.4	51.4	50.4	49.4	48.5	47.5	46.5	45.6	44.6
107	53.3	52.4	51.4	50.4	49.4	48.5	47.5	46.5	45.6	44.6
108	53.3	52.4	51.4	50.4	49.4	48.5	47.5	46.5	45.6	44.6
109	53.3	52.4	51.4	50.4	49.4	48.5	47.5	46.5	45.6	44.6
110	53.3	52.4	51.4	50.4	49.4	48.5	47.5	46.5	45.6	44.6
111	53.3	52.4	51.4	50.4	49.4	48.5	47.5	46.5	45.6	44.6
112	53.3	52.4	51.4	50.4	49.4	48.5	47.5	46.5	45.6	44.6
113	53.3	52.4	51.4	50.4	49.4	48.5	47.5	46.5	45.6	44.6
114	53.3	52.4	51.4	50.4	49.4	48.5	47.5	46.5	45.6	44.6
115	53.3	52.4	51.4	50.4	49.4	48.5	47.5	46.5	45.6	44.6

Ages	40	41	42	43	44	45	46	47	48	49
40	50.2	49.8	49.3	48.9	48.5	48.1	47.7	47.4	47.1	46.8
41	49.8	49.3	48.8	48.3	47.9	47.5	47.1	46.7	46.4	46.1
42	49.3	48.8	48.3	47.8	47.3	46.9	46.5	46.1	45.8	45.4
43	48.9	48.3	47.8	47.3	46.8	46.3	45.9	45.5	45.1	44.8
44	48.5	47.9	47.3	46.8	46.3	45.8	45.4	44.9	44.5	44.2
45	48.1	47.5	46.9	46.3	45.8	45.3	44.8	44.4	44.0	43.6
46	47.7	47.1	46.5	45.9	45.4	44.8	44.3	43.9	43.4	43.0
47	47.4	46.7	46.1	45.5	44.9	44.4	43.9	43.4	42.9	42.4
48	47.1	46.4	45.8	45.1	44.5	44.0	43.4	42.9	42.4	41.9

Ages	40	41	42	43	44	45	46	47	48	49
49	46.8	46.1	45.4	44.8	44.2	43.6	43.0	42.4	41.9	41.4
50	46.5	45.8	45.1	44.4	43.8	43.2	42.6	42.0	41.5	40.9
51	46.3	45.5	44.8	44.1	43.5	42.8	42.2	41.6	41.0	40.5
52	46.0	45.3	44.6	43.8	43.2	42.5	41.8	41.2	40.6	40.1
53	45.8	45.1	44.3	43.6	42.9	42.2	41.5	40.9	40.3	39.7
54	45.6	44.8	44.1	43.3	42.6	41.9	41.2	40.5	39.9	39.3
55	45.5	44.7	43.9	43.1	42.4	41.6	40.9	40.2	39.6	38.9
56	45.3	44.5	43.7	42.9	42.1	41.4	40.7	40.0	39.3	38.6
57	45.1	44.3	43.5	42.7	41.9	41.2	40.4	39.7	39.0	38.3
58	45.0	44.2	43.3	42.5	41.7	40.9	40.2	39.4	38.7	38.0
59	44.9	44.0	43.2	42.4	41.5	40.7	40.0	39.2	38.5	37.8
60	44.7	43.9	43.0	42.2	41.4	40.6	39.8	39.0	38.2	37.5
61	44.6	43.8	42.9	42.1	41.2	40.4	39.6	38.8	38.0	37.3
62	44.5	43.7	42.8	41.9	41.1	40.3	39.4	38.6	37.8	37.1
63	44.5	43.6	42.7	41.8	41.0	40.1	39.3	38.5	37.7	36.9
64	44.4	43.5	42.6	41.7	40.8	40.0	39.2	38.3	37.5	36.7
65	44.3	43.4	42.5	41.6	40.7	39.9	39.0	38.2	37.4	36.6
66	44.2	43.3	42.4	41.5	40.6	39.8	38.9	38.1	37.2	36.4
67	44.2	43.3	42.3	41.4	40.6	39.7	38.8	38.0	37.1	36.3
68	44.1	43.2	42.3	41.4	40.5	39.6	38.7	37.9	37.0	36.2
69	44.1	43.1	42.2	41.3	40.4	39.5	38.6	37.8	36.9	36.0
70	44.0	43.1	42.2	41.3	40.3	39.4	38.6	37.7	36.8	35.9
71	44.0	43.0	42.1	41.2	40.3	39.4	38.5	37.6	36.7	35.9
72	43.9	43.0	42.1	41.1	40.2	39.3	38.4	37.5	36.6	35.8
73	43.9	43.0	42.0	41.1	40.2	39.3	38.4	37.5	36.6	35.7
74	43.9	42.9	42.0	41.1	40.1	39.2	38.3	37.4	36.5	35.6
75	43.8	42.9	42.0	41.0	40.1	39.2	38.3	37.4	36.5	35.6
76	43.8	42.9	41.9	41.0	40.1	39.1	38.2	37.3	36.4	35.5
77	43.8	42.9	41.9	41.0	40.0	39.1	38.2	37.3	36.4	35.5
78	43.8	42.8	41.9	40.9	40.0	39.1	38.2	37.2	36.3	35.4
79	43.8	42.8	41.9	40.9	40.0	39.1	38.1	37.2	36.3	35.4
80	43.7	42.8	41.8	40.9	40.0	39.0	38.1	37.2	36.3	35.4
81	43.7	42.8	41.8	40.9	39.9	39.0	38.1	37.2	36.2	35.3
82	43.7	42.8	41.8	40.9	39.9	39.0	38.1	37.1	36.2	35.3
83	43.7	42.8	41.8	40.9	39.9	39.0	38.0	37.1	36.2	35.3
84	43.7	42.7	41.8	40.8	39.9	39.0	38.0	37.1	36.2	35.3
85	43.7	42.7	41.8	40.8	39.9	38.9	38.0	37.1	36.2	35.2
86	43.7	42.7	41.8	40.8	39.9	38.9	38.0	37.1	36.1	35.2
87	43.7	42.7	41.8	40.8	39.9	38.9	38.0	37.0	36.1	35.2

Ages	40	41	42	43	44	45	46	47	48	49
88	43.7	42.7	41.8	40.8	39.9	38.9	38.0	37.0	36.1	35.2
89	43.7	42.7	41.7	40.8	39.8	38.9	38.0	37.0	36.1	35.2
90	43.7	42.7	41.7	40.8	39.8	38.9	38.0	37.0	36.1	35.2
91	43.7	42.7	41.7	40.8	39.8	38.9	37.9	37.0	36.1	35.2
92	43.7	42.7	41.7	40.8	39.8	38.9	37.9	37.0	36.1	35.1
93	43.7	42.7	41.7	40.8	39.8	38.9	37.9	37.0	36.1	35.1
94	43.7	42.7	41.7	40.8	39.8	38.9	37.9	37.0	36.1	35.1
95	43.6	42.7	41.7	40.8	39.8	38.9	37.9	37.0	36.1	35.1
96	43.6	42.7	41.7	40.8	39.8	38.9	37.9	37.0	36.1	35.1
97	43.6	42.7	41.7	40.8	39.8	38.9	37.9	37.0	36.1	35.1
98	43.6	42.7	41.7	40.8	39.8	38.9	37.9	37.0	36.0	35.1
99	43.6	42.7	41.7	40.8	39.8	38.9	37.9	37.0	36.0	35.1
100	43.6	42.7	41.7	40.8	39.8	38.9	37.9	37.0	36.0	35.1
101	43.6	42.7	41.7	40.8	39.8	38.9	37.9	37.0	36.0	35.1
102	43.6	42.7	41.7	40.8	39.8	38.9	37.9	37.0	36.0	35.1
103	43.6	42.7	41.7	40.8	39.8	38.9	37.9	37.0	36.0	35.1
104	43.6	42.7	41.7	40.8	39.8	38.8	37.9	37.0	36.0	35.1
105	43.6	42.7	41.7	40.8	39.8	38.8	37.9	37.0	36.0	35.1
106	43.6	42.7	41.7	40.8	39.8	38.8	37.9	37.0	36.0	35.1
107	43.6	42.7	41.7	40.8	39.8	38.8	37.9	37.0	36.0	35.1
108	43.6	42.7	41.7	40.8	39.8	38.8	37.9	37.0	36.0	35.1
109	43.6	42.7	41.7	40.7	39.8	38.8	37.9	37.0	36.0	35.1
110	43.6	42.7	41.7	40.7	39.8	38.8	37.9	37.0	36.0	35.1
111	43.6	42.7	41.7	40.7	39.8	38.8	37.9	37.0	36.0	35.1
112	43.6	42.7	41.7	40.7	39.8	38.8	37.9	37.0	36.0	35.1
113	43.6	42.7	41.7	40.7	39.8	38.8	37.9	37.0	36.0	35.1
114	43.6	42.7	41.7	40.7	39.8	38.8	37.9	37.0	36.0	35.1
115	43.6	42.7	41.7	40.7	39.8	38.8	37.9	37.0	36.0	35.1

Ages	50	51	52	53	54	55	56	57	58	59
50	40.4	40.0	39.5	39.1	38.7	38.3	38.0	37.6	37.3	37.1
51	40.0	39.5	39.0	38.5	38.1	37.7	37.4	37.0	36.7	36.4
52	39.5	39.0	38.5	38.0	37.6	37.2	36.8	36.4	36.0	35.7
53	39.1	38.5	38.0	37.5	37.1	36.6	36.2	35.8	35.4	35.1
54	38.7	38.1	37.6	37.1	36.6	36.1	35.7	35.2	34.8	34.5
55	38.3	37.7	37.2	36.6	36.1	35.6	35.1	34.7	34.3	33.9
56	38.0	37.4	36.8	36.2	35.7	35.1	34.7	34.2	33.7	33.3
57	37.6	37.0	36.4	35.8	35.2	34.7	34.2	33.7	33.2	32.8

Ages	50	51	52	53	54	55	56	57	58	59
58	37.3	36.7	36.0	35.4	34.8	34.3	33.7	33.2	32.8	32.3
59	37.1	36.4	35.7	35.1	34.5	33.9	33.3	32.8	32.3	31.8
60	36.8	36.1	35.4	34.8	34.1	33.5	32.9	32.4	31.9	31.3
61	36.6	35.8	35.1	34.5	33.8	33.2	32.6	32.0	31.4	30.9
62	36.3	35.6	34.9	34.2	33.5	32.9	32.2	31.6	31.1	30.5
63	36.1	35.4	34.6	33.9	33.2	32.6	31.9	31.3	30.7	30.1
64	35.9	35.2	34.4	33.7	33.0	32.3	31.6	31.0	30.4	29.8
65	35.8	35.0	34.2	33.5	32.7	32.0	31.4	30.7	30.0	29.4
66	35.6	34.8	34.0	33.3	32.5	31.8	31.1	30.4	29.8	29.1
67	35.5	34.7	33.9	33.1	32.3	31.6	30.9	30.2	29.5	28.8
68	35.3	34.5	33.7	32.9	32.1	31.4	30.7	29.9	29.2	28.6
69	35.2	34.4	33.6	32.8	32.0	31.2	30.5	29.7	29.0	28.3
70	35.1	34.3	33.4	32.6	31.8	31.1	30.3	29.5	28.8	28.1
71	35.0	34.2	33.3	32.5	31.7	30.9	30.1	29.4	28.6	27.9
72	34.9	34.1	33.2	32.4	31.6	30.8	30.0	29.2	28.4	27.7
73	34.8	34.0	33.1	32.3	31.5	30.6	29.8	29.1	28.3	27.5
74	34.8	33.9	33.0	32.2	31.4	30.5	29.7	28.9	28.1	27.4
75	34.7	33.8	33.0	32.1	31.3	30.4	29.6	28.8	28.0	27.2
76	34.6	33.8	32.9	32.0	31.2	30.3	29.5	28.7	27.9	27.1
77	34.6	33.7	32.8	32.0	31.1	30.3	29.4	28.6	27.8	27.0
78	34.5	33.6	32.8	31.9	31.0	30.2	29.3	28.5	27.7	26.9
79	34.5	33.6	32.7	31.8	31.0	30.1	29.3	28.4	27.6	26.8
80	34.5	33.6	32.7	31.8	30.9	30.1	29.2	28.4	27.5	26.7
81	34.4	33.5	32.6	31.8	30.9	30.0	29.2	28.3	27.5	26.6
82	34.4	33.5	32.6	31.7	30.8	30.0	29.1	28.3	27.4	26.6
83	34.4	33.5	32.6	31.7	30.8	29.9	29.1	28.2	27.4	26.5
84	34.3	33.4	32.5	31.7	30.8	29.9	29.0	28.2	27.3	26.5
85	34.3	33.4	32.5	31.6	30.7	29.9	29.0	28.1	27.3	26.4
86	34.3	33.4	32.5	31.6	30.7	29.8	29.0	28.1	27.2	26.4
87	34.3	33.4	32.5	31.6	30.7	29.8	28.9	28.1	27.2	26.4
88	34.3	33.4	32.5	31.6	30.7	29.8	28.9	28.0	27.2	26.3
89	34.3	33.3	32.4	31.5	30.7	29.8	28.9	28.0	27.2	26.3
90	34.2	33.3	32.4	31.5	30.6	29.8	28.9	28.0	27.1	26.3
91	34.2	33.3	32.4	31.5	30.6	29.7	28.9	28.0	27.1	26.3
92	34.2	33.3	32.4	31.5	30.6	29.7	28.8	28.0	27.1	26.2
93	34.2	33.3	32.4	31.5	30.6	29.7	28.8	28.0	27.1	26.2
94	34.2	33.3	32.4	31.5	30.6	29.7	28.8	27.9	27.1	26.2
95	34.2	33.3	32.4	31.5	30.6	29.7	28.8	27.9	27.1	26.2
96	34.2	33.3	32.4	31.5	30.6	29.7	28.8	27.9	27.0	26.2

Ages	50	51	52	53	54	55	56	57	58	59
97	34.2	33.3	32.4	31.5	30.6	29.7	28.8	27.9	27.0	26.2
98	34.2	33.3	32.4	31.5	30.6	29.7	28.8	27.9	27.0	26.2
99	34.2	33.3	32.4	31.5	30.6	29.7	28.8	27.9	27.0	26.2
100	34.2	33.3	32.4	31.5	30.6	29.7	28.8	27.9	27.0	26.1
101	34.2	33.3	32.4	31.5	30.6	29.7	28.8	27.9	27.0	26.1
102	34.2	33.3	32.4	31.4	30.5	29.7	28.8	27.9	27.0	26.1
103	34.2	33.3	32.4	31.4	30.5	29.7	28.8	27.9	27.0	26.1
104	34.2	33.3	32.4	31.4	30.5	29.6	28.8	27.9	27.0	26.1
105	34.2	33.3	32.3	31.4	30.5	29.6	28.8	27.9	27.0	26.1
106	34.2	33.3	32.3	31.4	30.5	29.6	28.8	27.9	27.0	26.1
107	34.2	33.3	32.3	31.4	30.5	29.6	28.8	27.9	27.0	26.1
108	34.2	33.3	32.3	31.4	30.5	29.6	28.8	27.9	27.0	26.1
109	34.2	33.3	32.3	31.4	30.5	29.6	28.7	27.9	27.0	26.1
110	34.2	33.3	32.3	31.4	30.5	29.6	28.7	27.9	27.0	26.1
111	34.2	33.3	32.3	31.4	30.5	29.6	28.7	27.9	27.0	26.1
112	34.2	33.3	32.3	31.4	30.5	29.6	28.7	27.9	27.0	26.1
113	34.2	33.3	32.3	31.4	30.5	29.6	28.7	27.9	27.0	26.1
114	34.2	33.3	32.3	31.4	30.5	29.6	28.7	27.9	27.0	26.1
115	34.2	33.3	32.3	31.4	30.5	29.6	28.7	27.9	27.0	26.1

Ages	60	61	62	63	64	65	66	67	68	69
60	30.9	30.4	30.0	29.6	29.2	28.8	28.5	28.2	27.9	27.6
61	30.4	29.9	29.5	29.0	28.6	28.3	27.9	27.6	27.3	27.0
62	30.0	29.5	29.0	28.5	28.1	27.7	27.3	27.0	26.7	26.4
63	29.6	29.0	28.5	28.1	27.6	27.2	26.8	26.4	26.1	25.7
64	29.2	28.6	28.1	27.6	27.1	26.7	26.3	25.9	25.5	25.2
65	28.8	28.3	27.7	27.2	26.7	26.2	25.8	25.4	25.0	24.6
66	28.5	27.9	27.3	26.8	26.3	25.8	25.3	24.9	24.5	24.1
67	28.2	27.6	27.0	26.4	25.9	25.4	24.9	24.4	24.0	23.6
68	27.9	27.3	26.7	26.1	25.5	25.0	24.5	24.0	23.5	23.1
69	27.6	27.0	26.4	25.7	25.2	24.6	24.1	23.6	23.1	22.6
70	27.4	26.7	26.1	25.4	24.8	24.3	23.7	23.2	22.7	22.2
71	27.2	26.5	25.8	25.2	24.5	23.9	23.4	22.8	22.3	21.8
72	27.0	26.3	25.6	24.9	24.3	23.7	23.1	22.5	22.0	21.4
73	26.8	26.1	25.4	24.7	24.0	23.4	22.8	22.2	21.6	21.1
74	26.6	25.9	25.2	24.5	23.8	23.1	22.5	21.9	21.3	20.8
75	26.5	25.7	25.0	24.3	23.6	22.9	22.3	21.6	21.0	20.5
76	26.3	25.6	24.8	24.1	23.4	22.7	22.0	21.4	20.8	20.2

Ages	60	61	62	63	64	65	66	67	68	69
77	26.2	25.4	24.7	23.9	23.2	22.5	21.8	21.2	20.6	19.9
78	26.1	25.3	24.6	23.8	23.1	22.4	21.7	21.0	20.3	19.7
79	26.0	25.2	24.4	23.7	22.9	22.2	21.5	20.8	20.1	19.5
80	25.9	25.1	24.3	23.6	22.8	22.1	21.3	20.6	20.0	19.3
81	25.8	25.0	24.2	23.4	22.7	21.9	21.2	20.5	19.8	19.1
82	25.8	24.9	24.1	23.4	22.6	21.8	21.1	20.4	19.7	19.0
83	25.7	24.9	24.1	23.3	22.5	21.7	21.0	20.2	19.5	18.8
84	25.6	24.8	24.0	23.2	22.4	21.6	20.9	20.1	19.4	18.7
85	25.6	24.8	23.9	23.1	22.3	21.6	20.8	20.1	19.3	18.6
86	25.5	24.7	23.9	23.1	22.3	21.5	20.7	20.0	19.2	18.5
87	25.5	24.7	23.8	23.0	22.2	21.4	20.7	19.9	19.2	18.4
88	25.5	24.6	23.8	23.0	22.2	21.4	20.6	19.8	19.1	18.3
89	25.4	24.6	23.8	22.9	22.1	21.3	20.5	19.8	19.0	18.3
90	25.4	24.6	23.7	22.9	22.1	21.3	20.5	19.7	19.0	18.2
91	25.4	24.5	23.7	22.9	22.1	21.3	20.5	19.7	18.9	18.2
92	25.4	24.5	23.7	22.9	22.0	21.2	20.4	19.6	18.9	18.1
93	25.4	24.5	23.7	22.8	22.0	21.2	20.4	19.6	18.8	18.1
94	25.3	24.5	23.6	22.8	22.0	21.2	20.4	19.6	18.8	18.0
95	25.3	24.5	23.6	22.8	22.0	21.1	20.3	19.6	18.8	18.0
96	25.3	24.5	23.6	22.8	21.9	21.1	20.3	19.5	18.8	18.0
97	25.3	24.5	23.6	22.8	21.9	21.1	20.3	19.5	18.7	18.0
98	25.3	24.4	23.6	22.8	21.9	21.1	20.3	19.5	18.7	17.9
99	25.3	24.4	23.6	22.7	21.9	21.1	20.3	19.5	18.7	17.9
100	25.3	24.4	23.6	22.7	21.9	21.1	20.3	19.5	18.7	17.9
101	25.3	24.4	23.6	22.7	21.9	21.1	20.2	19.4	18.7	17.9
102	25.3	24.4	23.6	22.7	21.9	21.1	20.2	19.4	18.6	17.9
103	25.3	24.4	23.6	22.7	21.9	21.0	20.2	19.4	18.6	17.9
104	25.3	24.4	23.5	22.7	21.9	21.0	20.2	19.4	18.6	17.8
105	25.3	24.4	23.5	22.7	21.9	21.0	20.2	19.4	18.6	17.8
106	25.3	24.4	23.5	22.7	21.9	21.0	20.2	19.4	18.6	17.8
107	25.2	24.4	23.5	22.7	21.8	21.0	20.2	19.4	18.6	17.8
108	25.2	24.4	23.5	22.7	21.8	21.0	20.2	19.4	18.6	17.8
109	25.2	24.4	23.5	22.7	21.8	21.0	20.2	19.4	18.6	17.8
110	25.2	24.4	23.5	22.7	21.8	21.0	20.2	19.4	18.6	17.8
111	25.2	24.4	23.5	22.7	21.8	21.0	20.2	19.4	18.6	17.8
112	25.2	24.4	23.5	22.7	21.8	21.0	20.2	19.4	18.6	17.8
113	25.2	24.4	23.5	22.7	21.8	21.0	20.2	19.4	18.6	17.8
114	25.2	24.4	23.5	22.7	21.8	21.0	20.2	19.4	18.6	17.8
115	25.2	24.4	23.5	22.7	21.8	21.0	20.2	19.4	18.6	17.8

Ages	70	71	72	73	74	75	76	77	78	79
70	21.8	21.3	20.9	20.6	20.2	19.9	19.6	19.4	19.1	18.9
71	21.3	20.9	20.5	20.1	19.7	19.4	19.1	18.8	18.5	18.3
72	20.9	20.5	20.0	19.6	19.3	18.9	18.6	18.3	18.0	17.7
73	20.6	20.1	19.6	19.2	18.8	18.4	18.1	17.8	17.5	17.2
74	20.2	19.7	19.3	18.8	18.4	18.0	17.6	17.3	17.0	16.7
75	19.9	19.4	18.9	18.4	18.0	17.6	17.2	16.8	16.5	16.2
76	19.6	19.1	18.6	18.1	17.6	17.2	16.8	16.4	16.0	15.7
77	19.4	18.8	18.3	17.8	17.3	16.8	16.4	16.0	15.6	15.3
78	19.1	18.5	18.0	17.5	17.0	16.5	16.0	15.6	15.2	14.9
79	18.9	18.3	17.7	17.2	16.7	16.2	15.7	15.3	14.9	14.5
80	18.7	18.1	17.5	16.9	16.4	15.9	15.4	15.0	14.5	14.1
81	18.5	17.9	17.3	16.7	16.2	15.6	15.1	14.7	14.2	13.8
82	18.3	17.7	17.1	16.5	15.9	15.4	14.9	14.4	13.9	13.5
83	18.2	17.5	16.9	16.3	15.7	15.2	14.7	14.2	13.7	13.2
84	18.0	17.4	16.7	16.1	15.5	15.0	14.4	13.9	13.4	13.0
85	17.9	17.3	16.6	16.0	15.4	14.8	14.3	13.7	13.2	12.8
86	17.8	17.1	16.5	15.8	15.2	14.6	14.1	13.5	13.0	12.5
87	17.7	17.0	16.4	15.7	15.1	14.5	13.9	13.4	12.9	12.4
88	17.6	16.9	16.3	15.6	15.0	14.4	13.8	13.2	12.7	12.2
89	17.6	16.9	16.2	15.5	14.9	14.3	13.7	13.1	12.6	12.0
90	17.5	16.8	16.1	15.4	14.8	14.2	13.6	13.0	12.4	11.9
91	17.4	16.7	16.0	15.4	14.7	14.1	13.5	12.9	12.3	11.8
92	17.4	16.7	16.0	15.3	14.6	14.0	13.4	12.8	12.2	11.7
93	17.3	16.6	15.9	15.2	14.6	13.9	13.3	12.7	12.1	11.6
94	17.3	16.6	15.9	15.2	14.5	13.9	13.2	12.6	12.0	11.5
95	17.3	16.5	15.8	15.1	14.5	13.8	13.2	12.6	12.0	11.4
96	17.2	16.5	15.8	15.1	14.4	13.8	13.1	12.5	11.9	11.3
97	17.2	16.5	15.8	15.1	14.4	13.7	13.1	12.5	11.9	11.3
98	17.2	16.4	15.7	15.0	14.3	13.7	13.0	12.4	11.8	11.2
99	17.2	16.4	15.7	15.0	14.3	13.6	13.0	12.4	11.8	11.2
100	17.1	16.4	15.7	15.0	14.3	13.6	12.9	12.3	11.7	11.1
101	17.1	16.4	15.6	14.9	14.2	13.6	12.9	12.3	11.7	11.1
102	17.1	16.4	15.6	14.9	14.2	13.5	12.9	12.2	11.6	11.0
103	17.1	16.3	15.6	14.9	14.2	13.5	12.9	12.2	11.6	11.0
104	17.1	16.3	15.6	14.9	14.2	13.5	12.8	12.2	11.6	11.0
105	17.1	16.3	15.6	14.9	14.2	13.5	12.8	12.2	11.5	10.9
106	17.1	16.3	15.6	14.8	14.1	13.5	12.8	12.2	11.5	10.9
107	17.0	16.3	15.6	14.8	14.1	13.4	12.8	12.1	11.5	10.9
108	17.0	16.3	15.5	14.8	14.1	13.4	12.8	12.1	11.5	10.9

Ages	70	71	72	73	74	75	76	77	78	79
109	17.0	16.3	15.5	14.8	14.1	13.4	12.8	12.1	11.5	10.9
110	17.0	16.3	15.5	14.8	14.1	13.4	12.7	12.1	11.5	10.9
111	17.0	16.3	15.5	14.8	14.1	13.4	12.7	12.1	11.5	10.8
112	17.0	16.3	15.5	14.8	14.1	13.4	12.7	12.1	11.5	10.8
113	17.0	16.3	15.5	14.8	14.1	13.4	12.7	12.1	11.4	10.8
114	17.0	16.3	15.5	14.8	14.1	13.4	12.7	12.1	11.4	10.8
115	17.0	16.3	15.5	14.8	14.1	13.4	12.7	12.1	11.4	10.8

Ages	80	81	82	83	84	85	86	87	88	89
80	13.8	13.4	13.1	12.8	12.6	12.3	12.1	11.9	11.7	11.5
81	13.4	13.1	12.7	12.4	12.2	11.9	11.7	11.4	11.3	11.1
82	13.1	12.7	12.4	12.1	11.8	11.5	11.3	11.0	10.8	10.6
83	12.8	12.4	12.1	11.7	11.4	11.1	10.9	10.6	10.4	10.2
84	12.6	12.2	11.8	11.4	11.1	10.8	10.5	10.3	10.1	9.9
85	12.3	11.9	11.5	11.1	10.8	10.5	10.2	9.9	9.7	9.5
86	12.1	11.7	11.3	10.9	10.5	10.2	9.9	9.6	9.4	9.2
87	11.9	11.4	11.0	10.6	10.3	9.9	9.6	9.4	9.1	8.9
88	11.7	11.3	10.8	10.4	10.1	9.7	9.4	9.1	8.8	8.6
89	11.5	11.1	10.6	10.2	9.9	9.5	9.2	8.9	8.6	8.3
90	11.4	10.9	10.5	10.1	9.7	9.3	9.0	8.6	8.3	8.1
91	11.3	10.8	10.3	9.9	9.5	9.1	8.8	8.4	8.1	7.9
92	11.2	10.7	10.2	9.8	9.3	9.0	8.6	8.3	8.0	7.7
93	11.1	10.6	10.1	9.6	9.2	8.8	8.5	8.1	7.8	7.5
94	11.0	10.5	10.0	9.5	9.1	8.7	8.3	8.0	7.6	7.3
95	10.9	10.4	9.9	9.4	9.0	8.6	8.2	7.8	7.5	7.2
96	10.8	10.3	9.8	9.3	8.9	8.5	8.1	7.7	7.4	7.1
97	10.7	10.2	9.7	9.2	8.8	8.4	8.0	7.6	7.3	6.9
98	10.7	10.1	9.6	9.2	8.7	8.3	7.9	7.5	7.1	6.8
99	10.6	10.1	9.6	9.1	8.6	8.2	7.8	7.4	7.0	6.7
100	10.6	10.0	9.5	9.0	8.5	8.1	7.7	7.3	6.9	6.6
101	10.5	10.0	9.4	9.0	8.5	8.0	7.6	7.2	6.9	6.5
102	10.5	9.9	9.4	8.9	8.4	8.0	7.5	7.1	6.8	6.4
103	10.4	9.9	9.4	8.8	8.4	7.9	7.5	7.1	6.7	6.3
104	10.4	9.8	9.3	8.8	8.3	7.9	7.4	7.0	6.6	6.3
105	10.4	9.8	9.3	8.8	8.3	7.8	7.4	7.0	6.6	6.2
106	10.3	9.8	9.2	8.7	8.2	7.8	7.3	6.9	6.5	6.2
107	10.3	9.8	9.2	8.7	8.2	7.7	7.3	6.9	6.5	6.1
108	10.3	9.7	9.2	8.7	8.2	7.7	7.3	6.8	6.4	6.1

Ages	80	81	82	83	84	85	86	87	88	89
109	10.3	9.7	9.2	8.7	8.2	7.7	7.2	6.8	6.4	6.0
110	10.3	9.7	9.2	8.6	8.1	7.7	7.2	6.8	6.4	6.0
111	10.3	9.7	9.1	8.6	8.1	7.6	7.2	6.8	6.3	6.0
112	10.2	9.7	9.1	8.6	8.1	7.6	7.2	6.7	6.3	5.9
113	10.2	9.7	9.1	8.6	8.1	7.6	7.2	6.7	6.3	5.9
114	10.2	9.7	9.1	8.6	8.1	7.6	7.1	6.7	6.3	5.9
115	10.2	9.7	9.1	8.6	8.1	7.6	7.1	6.7	6.3	5.9

Ages	90	91	92	93	94	95	96	97	98	99
90	7.8	7.6	7.4	7.2	7.1	6.9	6.8	6.6	6.5	6.4
91	7.6	7.4	7.2	7.0	6.8	6.7	6.5	6.4	6.3	6.1
92	7.4	7.2	7.0	6.8	6.6	6.4	6.3	6.1	6.0	5.9
93	7.2	7.0	6.8	6.6	6.4	6.2	6.1	5.9	5.8	5.6
94	7.1	6.8	6.6	6.4	6.2	6.0	5.9	5.7	5.6	5.4
95	6.9	6.7	6.4	6.2	6.0	5.8	5.7	5.5	5.4	5.2
96	6.8	6.5	6.3	6.1	5.9	5.7	5.5	5.3	5.2	5.0
97	6.6	6.4	6.1	5.9	5.7	5.5	5.3	5.2	5.0	4.9
98	6.5	6.3	6.0	5.8	5.6	5.4	5.2	5.0	4.8	4.7
99	6.4	6.1	5.9	5.6	5.4	5.2	5.0	4.9	4.7	4.5
100	6.3	6.0	5.8	5.5	5.3	5.1	4.9	4.7	4.5	4.4
101	6.2	5.9	5.6	5.4	5.2	5.0	4.8	4.6	4.4	4.2
102	6.1	5.8	5.5	5.3	5.1	4.8	4.6	4.4	4.3	4.1
103	6.0	5.7	5.4	5.2	5.0	4.7	4.5	4.3	4.1	4.0
104	5.9	5.6	5.4	5.1	4.9	4.6	4.4	4.2	4.0	3.8
105	5.9	5.6	5.3	5.0	4.8	4.5	4.3	4.1	3.9	3.7
106	5.8	5.5	5.2	4.9	4.7	4.5	4.2	4.0	3.8	3.6
107	5.8	5.4	5.1	4.9	4.6	4.4	4.2	3.9	3.7	3.5
108	5.7	5.4	5.1	4.8	4.6	4.3	4.1	3.9	3.7	3.5
109	5.7	5.3	5.0	4.8	4.5	4.3	4.0	3.8	3.6	3.4
110	5.6	5.3	5.0	4.7	4.5	4.2	4.0	3.8	3.5	3.3
111	5.6	5.3	5.0	4.7	4.4	4.2	3.9	3.7	3.5	3.3
112	5.6	5.3	4.9	4.7	4.4	4.1	3.9	3.7	3.5	3.2
113	5.6	5.2	4.9	4.6	4.4	4.1	3.9	3.6	3.4	3.2
114	5.6	5.2	4.9	4.6	4.3	4.1	3.9	3.6	3.4	3.2
115	5.5	5.2	4.9	4.6	4.3	4.1	3.8	3.6	3.4	3.1

Ages	100	101	102	103	104	105	106	107	108	109
100	4.2	4.1	3.9	3.8	3.7	3.5	3.4	3.3	3.3	3.2
101	4.1	3.9	3.7	3.6	3.5	3.4	3.2	3.1	3.1	3.0
102	3.9	3.7	3.6	3.4	3.3	3.2	3.1	3.0	2.9	2.8
103	3.8	3.6	3.4	3.3	3.2	3.0	2.9	2.8	2.7	2.6
104	3.7	3.5	3.3	3.2	3.0	2.9	2.7	2.6	2.5	2.4
105	3.5	3.4	3.2	3.0	2.9	2.7	2.6	2.5	2.4	2.3
106	3.4	3.2	3.1	2.9	2.7	2.6	2.4	2.3	2.2	2.1
107	3.3	3.1	3.0	2.8	2.6	2.5	2.3	2.2	2.1	2.0
108	3.3	3.1	2.9	2.7	2.5	2.4	2.2	2.1	1.9	1.8
109	3.2	3.0	2.8	2.6	2.4	2.3	2.1	2.0	1.8	1.7
110	3.1	2.9	2.7	2.5	2.3	2.2	2.0	1.9	1.7	1.6
111	3.1	2.9	2.7	2.5	2.3	2.1	1.9	1.8	1.6	1.5
112	3.0	2.8	2.6	2.4	2.2	2.0	1.9	1.7	1.5	1.4
113	3.0	2.8	2.6	2.4	2.2	2.0	1.8	1.6	1.5	1.3
114	3.0	2.7	2.5	2.3	2.1	1.9	1.8	1.6	1.4	1.3
115	2.9	2.7	2.5	2.3	2.1	1.9	1.7	1.5	1.4	1.2

Ages	110	111	112	113	114	115
110	1.5	1.4	1.3	1.2	1.1	1.1
111	1.4	1.2	1.1	1.1	1.0	1.0
112	1.3	1.1	1.0	1.0	1.0	1.0
113	1.2	1.1	1.0	1.0	1.0	1.0
114	1.1	1.0	1.0	1.0	1.0	1.0
115	1.1	1.0	1.0	1.0	1.0	1.0

Internal Revenue Code Sections

[References are to question numbers.]

IRC §

IRC §

Table of Treasury Regulations

[References are to question numbers.]

Treas. Reg. §

Table of ERISA Sections

[References are to question numbers.]

Table of DOL Regulations, Letters, Releases, etc.

[References are to question numbers.]

DOL Proposed Regulations

DOL Prop. Reg. §

DOL Prop. Reg. §

DOL Advisory Opinions

DOL Adv. Op.

Table of Revenue Rulings

[References are to question numbers.]

Table of Revenue Procedures

[References are to question numbers.]

Table of Private Letter Rulings

[References are to question numbers.]

Priv. Ltr. Rul.

Table of Notices and Announcements

[References are to question numbers.]

Notice

Notice

Table of Notices and Announcements

Notice

Announcements

Ann.

Table of PBGC Regulations, News Releases, Opinion Letters, etc.

[References are to question numbers.]

PBGC Regulations

PBGC Reg. §

PBGC Reg. §

Pension Protection Act of 2006

[References are to question numbers.]

Table of Cases

[References are to question numbers.]

D

Table of Cases

M

Table of Cases

N

S

Table of Cases

Glossary

The following is a list of terms (arranged in alphabetical order) that is intended to provide the reader with additional guidance in understanding the complex concepts that apply to qualified pension and profit sharing plans.

Accrued Benefit: A benefit that an employee has earned (or accrued) through participation in the plan. In a defined contribution plan (e.g., a profit sharing plan), the accrued benefit of a participant is the balance in his or her individual account at a given time. In a defined benefit plan, the accrued benefit is determined by reference to the benefit that will be provided to a participant when he or she reaches normal retirement age as specified by the plan. The accrued benefit should not be confused, however, with the benefit (or portion thereof) that a participant has a right (nonforfeitable) to receive if he or she leaves prior to retirement. This benefit is determined by reference to the plan's vesting schedule and the years of service credited to a participant.

Accumulated Funding Deficiency: With respect to a multiemployer plan for any plan year, the excess of the total charges to the funding standard account over the total credits to such account.

ACP Test: See **Actual Contribution Percentage Test.**

Actual Contribution Percentage (ACP) Test: A special nondiscrimination test applied to employer matching contributions and employee contributions.

Actual Deferral Percentage (ADP) Test: A special test designed to limit the extent to which elective contributions made on behalf of highly compensated employees may exceed the elective contributions made on behalf of non-highly compensated employees under a 401(k) plan.

Actuarial Assumptions: Contributions to a defined benefit plan depend upon certain assumptions made by the plan's actuary, which may include mortality, investment return, employee turnover, retirement age, and salary scale.

Actuarial Equivalence: Two different sets of values are in an actuarial equivalence when they have an equal present value under a given set of actuarial assumptions.

Adjusted Funding Target: The funding target for the plan year increased by the aggregate amount of purchases of annuities that were added to assets for purposes of determining the plan's adjusted plan assets.

Adjusted Funding Target Attainment Percentage (AFTAP): A fraction (expressed as a percentage), the numerator of which is the adjusted plan assets for the plan year and the denominator of which is the adjusted funding target for the plan year.

Adjusted Gross Income (AGI): In the case of an individual, gross income minus various permissible deductions.

Adjusted Plan Assets: An amount determined by subtracting the plan's funding standard carryover balance and prefunding balance as of the valuation date from the value of plan assets for the plan year and increasing the resulting value by the aggregate amount of purchases of annuities for participants and beneficiaries (other than HCEs) that were made by the plan during the preceding two plan years.

ADP Test: See **Actual Deferral Percentage Test.**

Affiliated Service Group: Generally, an affiliated service group consists of two or more related service or management organizations, whether or not incorporated. Employees of the members of an affiliated service group are treated as employed by a single employer for plan qualification purposes.

AFTAP: See **Adjusted Funding Target Attainment Percentage**.

Age-Based Profit Sharing Plan: A profit sharing plan that uses both age and compensation as a basis for allocating employer contributions among plan participants.

AGI: See **Adjusted Gross Income.**

Alternate Payee: A spouse, former spouse, child, or other dependent of a participant who is recognized by a domestic relations order as having a right to receive all or a portion of the benefits payable under the qualified retirement plan with respect to the participant.

Annual Addition: Term used in connection with the limitation on the contributions that may be made for a participant under a defined contribution plan.

Annual Retirement Benefit: Term used in connection with the limitation on the benefit that may be paid to a participant under a defined benefit plan.

Annuity: A series of periodic payments, usually level in amount or adjusted according to some index (e.g., cost-of-living), that typically continue for the lifetime of the recipient. In contrast, an installment payment is one of a specific number of payments that will be paid whether or not the recipient lives to receive them.

Annuity Contract: For 403(b) plans, except where a custodial account is treated as an annuity contract, an annuity contract is a contract that is issued by an insurance company qualified to issue annuities in a state and that includes payments in the form of an annuity. The contract is referred as a "403(b) contract".

Annuity Starting Date: The first day of the first period for which a benefit is payable as an annuity. For benefits payable in any other form, it is the first day on which all events have occurred that entitle the participant to the benefit.

Anonymous Submission Procedure: An IRS procedure that permits a qualified plan, 403(b) plan, SEP, or SIMPLE IRA to correct qualification failures without initially identifying the plan or plan sponsor.

Anti-Alienation Rule: As a general rule, benefits provided under a qualified retirement plan may not be assigned or alienated. There are, however, exceptions to this rule.

Anti-Cutback Rule: A qualified retirement plan may not be amended to eliminate or reduce a Section 411(d)(6) protected benefit that has already accrued, unless IRS approves a request to amend the plan or the elimination or reduction satisfies certain requirements.

Audit CAP: See **Correction on Audit.**

Automatic Contribution Arrangements: Under a 401(k) plan, an employee is deemed to have elected to have the employer contribute a percentage of the employee's compensation to the plan under a cash-or-deferred election unless the employee specifically elects in writing not to defer compensation. In other words, the employee does not make an affirmative election to contribute.

Bankruptcy Abuse Prevention and Consumer Protection Act of 2005: Enacted on April 20, 2005. This act, which took effect on October 17, 2005, protects all retirement plan assets from creditors during bankruptcy proceedings by exempting those assets from the debtor's bankruptcy estate. An individual's bankruptcy estate will not include retirement funds to the extent that those funds are in a qualified retirement plan, SEP, SIMPLE plan, TSA, IRA, Roth IRA, or Section 457 plan. Generally, the amount of IRA assets that is protected during bankruptcy proceedings is limited to $1 million, but amounts attributable to rollovers from protected plans do not count toward the $1 million limit.

Beneficiary: A person designated by a participant or one who, by the terms of the plan, is or may be eligible for benefits under the plan if the participant dies.

C Corporation: See **S Corporation.**

Cash Balance Plan: A defined benefit plan that exhibits features of both defined benefit and defined contribution plans. The most recognizable feature of the cash balance plan is its use of a separate account for each participant. A cash balance account is established for each employee upon the employee's becoming a member of the plan. See also **Hybrid Defined Benefit Plan.**

Cash-or-Deferred Plan: A qualified profit sharing or stock bonus plan that gives a participant an option to take cash or to have the employer contribute the money to a qualified profit sharing plan as an "employer" contribution to the plan (i.e., an "elective deferral"). These arrangements are often called "401(k) plans." See **Chapter 27.**

Catch-Up IRA Contributions: An individual who has attained age 50 by the close of the taxable year may make additional catch-up contributions to an IRA and/or a Roth IRA.

CB: Cumulative Bulletin. A government publication in which revenue rulings and other pertinent IRS pronouncements are published. The Cumulative Bulletin is published semiannually and incorporates the materials that were published weekly by IRS in its Internal Revenue Bulletins (IRBs).

CBA: A collective bargaining agreement. See **Collectively Bargained Plans.**

Closely Held Corporation: A nonpublic corporation that is owned by a small number of shareholders.

Code: The Internal Revenue Code of 1986, as amended.

Collectively Bargained Plans: Plans that provide retirement benefits under a collective bargaining agreement. Generally speaking, if more than one employer is required to contribute to the collectively bargained plan, the plan is treated as a multiemployer plan, subject to special rules. If only one employer (including affiliates) is required to contribute to the plan, however, the plan is treated in the same way that other plans that do not cover union employees are treated.

Combination Plans: Plans using two or more plans in combination to provide retirement benefits for employees and their beneficiaries. A defined contribution plan may be combined with a defined benefit pension plan or with another defined contribution plan.

Common-Law Employee: A person who performs service(s) for an employer, if the employer has the right to direct both the objective of the services and the manner in which they are performed.

Commonly Controlled Businesses: All employees of corporations that are members of a "controlled group of corporations" are treated as employed by a single employer for purposes of plan qualification. A comparable requirement applies to partnerships, sole proprietorships, and other businesses under common control. See also **Controlled Group of Corporations.**

Comparability Plan: Generally, a profit sharing plan in which the contribution percentage formula for one category of participants is greater than the contribution percentage formula for other categories of participants. To satisfy the nondiscrimination requirements, a comparability plan is tested under the cross-testing rules.

Contributory Plan: A pension plan under which employee contributions are required as a condition of participation.

Controlled Group of Corporations: There are three types of controlled groups: (1) the parent-subsidiary controlled group, (2) the brother-sister controlled group, and (3) the combined group. Two tests must be met to have a "parent-subsidiary" controlled group: (1) stock equal to 80 percent of the combined voting power of each corporation, or at least 80 percent of the value of all outstanding stock of each corporation, is owned by one or more of the corporations of the group, and (2) the common parent corporation owns at least 80 percent of the voting power or value of at least one of the corporations in the group. Two tests must be met to have a "brother-sister" controlled group: (1) five or fewer persons (individuals, estates, or trusts) own at least 80 percent of the combined voting power or value of two or more corporations, and (2) taking into account the ownership of each stockholder only to the extent that it is identical in each of the corporations involved, the five or fewer persons own more than 50 percent of the combined voting power or value of the corporations involved. A "combined group" is a group of two or more corporations if: (1) each corporation is a member of either a parent-subsidiary group or a brother-sister group, and (2) at least one of the corporations is the common parent of a parent-subsidiary group and also is a member of a brother-sister controlled group. All employees of corporations that are members of a controlled group of corporations are treated as employed by a single employer for plan qualification purposes.

Correction on Audit (Audit CAP): An IRS program that enables a plan sponsor to negotiate a monetary sanction if a qualification failure is identified during an examination and corrected, without plan disqualification.

Cross-Testing: A qualified retirement plan may not discriminate in favor of highly compensated employees with respect to the amount of contributions or benefits. Whether a defined contribution plan satisfies this requirement is generally determined with respect to the amount of contributions. As an alternative, however, a defined contribution plan (other than an ESOP) may be tested with respect to the equivalent amount of benefits. Similarly, whether a defined benefit plan satisfies this requirement is generally determined with respect to the amount of benefits. As an alternative, however, a defined benefit plan may be tested with respect to the equivalent amount of contributions.

Cumulative List: The annual list of changes required by IRS to be reflected in the following year's opinion, advisory, or determination letter submissions. No reliance can be provided for changes in a plan that are not included in the applicable Cumulative List.

Curtailments: The reduction of benefits or the augmenting of eligibility requirements so as to amount to a partial or a complete termination of the plan.

Custodial Account: Treated as an annuity contract for purposes of the 403(b) plan rules. A custodial account is a plan, or a separate account under a plan, in which an amount attributable to 403(b) plan contributions is invested in stock of a regulated investment account (i.e., mutual funds).

Death Benefits: Payments to a beneficiary of a deceased participant that may be provided under a qualified retirement plan, but they must be incidental to the retirement benefits, which are the major purpose of the plan.

Deemed IRA: A qualified retirement plan or 403(b) plan may permit employees to make voluntary employee contributions to a separate account or annuity that (1) is established under the plan and (2) meets the requirements applicable to either IRAs or Roth IRAs. In such event, the separate account or annuity will be deemed an IRA or a Roth IRA, as applicable, for all purposes of the Code.

Deficit Reduction Act of 2005: Enacted on February 8, 2006. This act increased the single-employer flat rate premium to $30 per participant and the multiemployer plan flat-rate premium to $8. For each plan year beginning in a calendar year after 2006, the flat rate premiums are indexed to the national average wage index. This act also contained a new premium for certain single-employer plans that are terminated (generally, situations where PBGC takes over as trustee of the terminated plan).

Defined Benefit Plan: A plan that is designed to provide participants with a definite benefit at retirement (e.g., a monthly benefit of 20 percent of compensation upon reaching age 65). Contributions under the plan are determined by reference to the benefits provided, not on the basis of a percentage of compensation.

Defined Benefit Excess Plan: A defined benefit plan under which the rate at which benefits are determined with respect to compensation above a specified level is greater than the rate with respect to compensation at or below the specified level. See also Permitted Disparity.

Defined Benefit Offset Plan: A defined benefit plan that provides that each participant's benefit is reduced by a specified percentage of the participant's compensation up to the offset level. See also **Permitted Disparity.**

Defined Contribution Plan: A plan that provides an individual account for each participant and in which benefits are based solely upon the amount contributed to the account (plus or minus any income, expenses, gain, losses, and forfeitures allocated to the account).

Defined Contribution Excess Plan: A defined contribution plan under which the rate at which contributions are allocated with respect to compensation above a specified level is greater than the rate at which contributions are allocated with respect to compensation at or below the specified level. See also **Permitted Disparity.**

Delinquent Filer Voluntary Compliance Program (DFVC): A program established by DOL to encourage, through the assessment of reduced civil penalties, delinquent plan administrators to comply with the annual reporting requirements.

Designated Beneficiary: For required minimum distribution purposes, an individual who is designated as a beneficiary under the plan. An individual may be designated as a beneficiary under the plan either by the terms of the plan or, if the plan provides, by an affirmative election by the employee (or the employee's surviving spouse) specifying the beneficiary.

Designated Roth Contribution: A 401(k) plan and a 403(b) plan are permitted to include provisions that enable an employee to elect to have all or a portion of the employee's elective deferrals under the plan treated as designated Roth contributions. Designated Roth contributions are elective deferrals that the employee designates as not excludable from the employee's gross income.

Determination Letter: Letter issued by the IRS District Director's office determining that a plan submitted to it either meets or does not meet the requirements for qualification.

DFVC: See **Delinquent Filer Voluntary Compliance Program.**

Direct Rollover: A distribution to an employee made in the form of a direct trustee-to-trustee transfer from a qualified retirement plan to an eligible retirement plan.

Discretionary Formula Plan: A profit sharing plan that provides that the amount of each year's contribution will be determined by the board of directors (or the responsible official(s)) of the sponsoring employer, in its discretion. (Contributions must be "recurring and substantial" to keep the plan in a qualified status.)

Discrimination: A situation in which a plan, through its provisions or through its operations, favors officers, shareholders, or highly compensated employees to the detriment of other employees.

Disqualification: Loss of qualified (tax-favored) status by a plan, generally resulting from operation of the plan in a manner that is contrary to the provisions of the plan or that discriminates against rank-and-file employees. See also **Discrimination.**

Disqualified Persons: See **Party in Interest.**

Distress Termination: The termination of a single-employer defined benefit plan covered by PBGC that is unable to pay all its benefit liabilities.

DOL: Department of Labor. Administers the nontax (regulatory and administrative) provisions of ERISA. The Department issues opinion letters and other pronouncements, and requires certain information forms to be filed.

Domestic Relations Order (DRO): A judgment, decree, or order (including approval of a property settlement agreement) made pursuant to a state domestic relations law (including a community property law) that relates to the provision of child support, alimony payments, or marital property rights to an alternate payee.

DRO: See **Domestic Relations Order.**

EACA: See **Eligible Automatic Contribution Arrangement.**

Earned Income: The net earnings from self-employment in a trade or business in which personal services of the taxpayer are a material income-producing factor. Earned income is the criterion for contributions to a qualified retirement plan on behalf of a self-employed individual.

Economic Growth and Tax Relief Reconciliation Act of 2001 (EGTRRA 2001): Enacted on June 7, 2001. This act raised contribution limits on IRAs and qualified retirement plans, liberalized portability and vesting rules, and made a host of changes affecting qualified retirement plans.

EFAST: See **ERISA Filing Acceptance System.**

EFAST2: See **ERISA Filing Acceptance System 2.**

EGTRRA 2001: See **Economic Growth and Tax Relief Reconciliation Act of 2001.**

Elective Contribution: A contribution made to a 401(k) plan or a 403(b) plan by the employer on an employee's behalf pursuant to the employee's cash-or-deferred election.

Elective Deferral: See **Elective Contribution.**

Elective Deferral Catch-Up Contributions: An individual who participates in a 401(k) plan or in a 403(b) plan, who has attained age 50 by the end of the year, and for whom no other elective deferrals may otherwise be made for the year because of the application of any other limitation may be able to make additional elective deferrals (i.e., catch-up contributions) for that year.

Eligible Automatic Contribution Arrangement (EACA): An automatic contribution arrangement under which participants may make permissible withdrawals of elective deferrals.

Eligible Retirement Plan: An IRA, a qualified retirement plan, a 403(b) plan, and/or a governmental Section 457 plan.

Eligible Rollover Distribution: A distribution from a qualified retirement plan that may be rolled over to an eligible retirement plan.

Employee: An individual who provides services for compensation to an employer and whose duties are under the control of the employer.

Employee Contributions: See **Mandatory Employee Contributions and Voluntary Contributions.**

Employee Plans Compliance Resolution System (EPCRS): A comprehensive system of correction programs implemented by IRS that are intended to correct qualification failures with respect to qualified plans, 403(b) plans, SEPs, and SIMPLE IRAs without plan disqualification. See also **Anonymous Submission Procedure, Audit CAP, Group Submissions, SCP,** and **VCP.**

Employee Stock Ownership Plan (ESOP): A profit sharing, stock bonus, or money purchase pension plan, the funds of which must be invested primarily in employer company stock. Unlike other plans, an ESOP may borrow from the employer or use the employer's credit to acquire company stock. See also **Stock Bonus Plan.**

Employer Securities: For an ESOP, common stock issued by the employer that is readily tradable on an established securities market. If the employer has no readily tradable common stock, employer securities include employer-issued common stock that has a combination of voting power and dividend rights at least the equal of the class of common stock with the greatest voting power and the class of common stock with the greatest dividend rights. Noncallable preferred stock that is convertible into common stock that meets the requirements of employer securities also qualifies if the conversion price is reasonable.

Employer-Sponsored IRA: An IRA that is sponsored by the employer for purposes of helping its employees make a tax-deductible contribution to an IRA and to invest the funds in a particular type of investment. The employer-sponsored IRA should be distinguished from a simplified employee pension plan (SEP), which requires employer contributions and must meet certain requirements with respect to participation, discrimination, withdrawals, and contributions.

Enrolled Actuary: A person who performs actuarial services for a defined benefit plan. His or her services include making a determination of how much has to be contributed to the plan each year to provide the stated benefits at retirement, and the preparation of a statement that has to be filed with the plan's annual return to IRS. Actuaries who perform these services are enrolled with the Joint Board for the Enrollment of Actuaries.

EPCRS: See **Employee Plans Compliance Resolution System.**

ERISA: Employee Retirement Income Security Act of 1974. The basic law covering qualified retirement plans and incorporates both the pertinent Internal Revenue Code provisions and labor law provisions. ERISA is designed to protect the rights of beneficiaries of employee benefit plans offered by employers, unions, and the like. Additionally, ERISA imposes various qualification standards and fiduciary responsibilities on both welfare benefit and retirement plans, and provides enforcement procedures as well. In the retirement area, it also provides standards for tax qualification.

ERISA Filing Acceptance System: DOL's computerized system designed to process the annual Form 5500 series return/report.

ERISA Filing Acceptance System 2: DOL's all-electronic system designed to receive and process the annual Form 5500 series return/report required to be filed electronically.

ESOP: See **Employee Stock Ownership Plan.**

Excess Aggregate Contributions: The excess of the aggregate amount of employee contributions and matching contributions made on behalf of highly compensated employees for a plan year over the maximum amount of such contributions permitted under the ACP test.

Excess Contribution: The excess of the elective contributions (including qualified nonelective and matching contributions that are treated as elective contributions) made to a 401(k) plan on behalf of highly compensated employees for the plan year over the maximum amount of such contributions permitted under the ADP test for such plan year.

Excess Deferral: An employee's elective contributions for the taxable year in excess of $15,000 (increased for inflation).

Exclusive Benefit Rule: A qualified retirement plan must prohibit the use or diversion of funds for purposes other than the exclusive benefit of employees or their beneficiaries. Plan fiduciaries must discharge their duties solely in the interest of participants and beneficiaries for the exclusive purpose of providing benefits to participants and beneficiaries and paying administration expenses. See also **Fiduciary.**

FASB: Financial Accounting Standards Board. The body that sets uniform standards for treatment of accounting items. In the employee benefits context, FASB has prepared an exposure draft concerning disclosure of unfunded benefit liabilities.

FASB 87: The statement issued by FASB regarding employers' accounting for pensions.

Fiduciary: Any person who exercises discretionary authority or control over the management or disposition of plan assets or who gives investment advice to the plan for a fee or other compensation.

Field Service Advice (FSA): Advice issued by IRS Office of Chief Counsel or Office of Associate Chief Counsel. Field Service Advice is not binding on IRS examination or appeals officers and is not a final case determination. Field Service Advice issued to IRS examination or appeals officers is advisory only and does not resolve an IRS position on an issue or provide the final basis for closing a case and is not to be relied upon or otherwise cited as precedent.

First-Time Homebuyer: Individuals (and spouses) who did not own an interest in a principal residence during the two years prior to the purchase of a home and who were not in an extended period for filing with respect to the gain from the sale of a principal residence.

Fiscal year: A 12-month period used for accounting purposes.

5 Percent Owner: Any person who owns, directly or indirectly, more than 5 percent of the stock of the employer. If the employer is not a corporation, the ownership test is applied to the person's capital or profits interest in the employer. See also Key Employee and Top-Heavy Plan.

Forfeitures: The benefits that a participant loses if he or she terminates employment before becoming eligible for full retirement benefits under the plan. For example, a participant who leaves the service of an employer at a time when he or she will receive only 60 percent of benefits forfeits the remaining 40 percent.

401(k) Plan: An arrangement (defined by Section 401(k)) under which a covered employee can elect to defer income by making pretax contributions to a profit sharing or stock bonus plan. A cafeteria plan may provide a 401(k) plan as a qualified benefit option. See **Chapter 27.**

402(f) Notice: A written explanation of the tax effects of a distribution from a qualified retirement plan that must be provided to a recipient.

403(b) Plan: A special type of deferred compensation arrangement that is available only to employees of tax-exempt organizations described in Section 501(c)(3) or employees of public schools.

Frozen Plan: A qualified pension or profit sharing plan that continues to exist even though employer contributions have been discontinued and benefits are no longer accrued by participants. The plan is "frozen" for purposes of distribution of benefits under the terms of the plan.

FSA: See **Field Service Advice.**

Funding Shortfall: The excess of the funding target of the plan over the value of plan assets for a plan year.

Funding Standard Account: Each multiemployer pension plan subject to the minimum funding standards must maintain a funding standard account, which is a device used to ease the administration of the funding rules by keeping track of the plan's charges and credits.

Funding Standard Carryover Balance: An amount initially established as the balance in the funding standard account as of the last day of plan year before 2008.

Funding Target: The present value of all benefits accrued or earned under the plan as of the beginning of the plan year.

Group Submission: A special procedure that permits an eligible organization to voluntarily correct a failure in a qualified plan, 403(b) plan, SEP, or SIMPLE IRA resulting from a systemic error that affects at least 20 plans.

Gulf Opportunity Zone Act of 2005: Enacted on December 21, 2005. This act codified and expanded the pension-related relief provided by KETRA to include victims of Hurricanes Rita and Wilma.

HCE: See **Highly Compensated Employee.**

Health Insurance Portability and Accountability Act of 1996 (HIPAA '96): Enacted on August 21, 1996. This act provided that distributions from IRAs made after 1996 will not be subject to the 10 percent penalty tax on early withdrawals if the amounts are used to pay medical expenses in excess of $7\frac{1}{2}$ percent of adjusted gross income. In addition, the 10 percent penalty tax will not apply to IRA distributions that are used by certain unemployed, formerly unemployed, or self-employed individuals to pay health insurance premiums.

HERO: See **Heroes Earned Retirement Opportunities Act.**

Heroes Earned Retirement Opportunities Act (HERO): Enacted on May 29, 2006. For taxable years beginning on or after January 1, 2004, members of the armed forces may treat combat pay as compensation for purposes of the IRA contribution and deduction rules.

Highly Compensated Employee (HCE): An employee who: (1) during the year or the preceding year is (or was) a 5 percent owner or (2) during the preceding year received compensation in excess of $80,000 (adjusted for cost-of-living increases) and was a member of the top-paid group of employees (if the employer elects).

H.R. 10 Plan: See **Keogh Plan.**

Hybrid Defined Benefit Plan: A plan that is either a lump-sum based plan or a plan that has a similar effect to a lump sum based plan. A lump-sum based plan is a defined benefit plan under the terms of which the accumulated benefit of a participant is expressed as the balance of a hypothetical account balance or accumulated percentage. See also **Cash Balance Plan.**

Includible Compensation: For the purpose of calculating the overall limitation for the limitation year for a 403(b) plan, the amount of compensation received that is includible in gross income for the most recent period that may be counted as one year of service.

Individual Account Plan: A plan that provides for an individual account for each participant and in which benefits are based solely on the amount contributed to an account and any income, expenses, gains, losses, and forfeitures allocated to the account.

Inherited IRA: An IRA becomes an inherited IRA after the death of the IRA owner unless the sole beneficiary is the IRA owner's surviving spouse. The nonspouse beneficiary cannot make a tax-deductible contribution to an inherited IRA, and distributions from an inherited IRA do not qualify for rollover treatment.

Insured Plan: A plan funded exclusively by insurance contracts.

Integrated Plan: See **Permitted Disparity.**

Interested Parties: Generally, all employees of the employer at the time the employer applies for a determination letter. IRS requires that interested parties be notified when the application is made.

IRA: Individual retirement account or individual retirement annuity. Any working person and certain divorced spouses receiving alimony may establish IRAs and gain deductions for contributions to the IRAs and tax deferrals on the earnings.

IRB: Internal Revenue Bulletin. A weekly collection of materials published by IRS. See also **CB.**

IRC: Internal Revenue Code of 1986 as amended. The basic federal tax law.

IRS: Internal Revenue Service. An agency of the Treasury Department, headed by the Commissioner of Internal Revenue, charged with primary responsibility for administering, interpreting, and enforcing the Code. (Note, however, that the Secretary of the Treasury, not IRS, issues regulations under the Code.)

IRS Coordinated Issue Papers: IRS releases coordinated issue papers, which are reviewed by the Office of Chief Counsel, to achieve uniformity in application of the law and to provide guidance to IRS examiners. Although issue papers are not official pronouncements on the issues, they do set forth the current views of IRS.

JCWAA 2002: See **Job Creation and Worker Assistance Act of 2002.**

Job Creation and Worker Assistance Act of 2002 (JCWAA 2002): Enacted on March 9, 2002. This act contains changes to the funding rules for defined benefit plans and makes a number of technical corrections to provisions relating to qualified retirement plans that were enacted by EGTRRA 2001.

Katrina Emergency Tax Relief Act of 2005 (KETRA): On September 23, 2005, the Katrina Emergency Tax Relief Act of 2005 was signed into law. KETRA modified existing rules governing retirement plan withdrawals and loans in order to free up additional funds for Hurricane Katrina victims.

Keogh Plan: A qualified retirement plan, either a defined contribution plan or a defined benefit plan, that covers a self-employed person. (Other employees might also be covered.)

KETRA: See **Katrina Emergency Tax Relief Act of 2005.**

Key Employee: A participant who, at any time during the plan year is (1) an officer having annual compensation greater than $130,000 (subject to cost-of-living adjustments), (2) a more-than-5-percent owner of the employer, or (3) a more-than-1-percent owner whose annual compensation exceeds $150,000. See also **5 Percent Owner, Officer, 1 Percent Owner,** and **Top-Heavy Plan.**

Leased Employee: An individual who performs services for another person (the recipient) under an arrangement between the recipient and a third person (the leasing organization) who is otherwise treated as the individual's employer. The services performed by an individual for the recipient must be under the primary direction or control of the recipient.

Leveraged ESOP: An employee stock ownership plan that borrows to acquire employer company stock. See also **Employee Stock Ownership Plan.**

Limitation Year: With respect to any qualified retirement plan maintained by an employer, the calendar year. However, instead of using the calendar year, an employer may elect to use any other consecutive 12-month period as the limitation year.

Lump-Sum Distribution: A type of distribution that is required for purposes of using the forward averaging method in computing the income tax that is due and to defer income tax relating to net unrealized appreciation on employer securities. The basic requirements to qualify as a lump-sum distribution are (1) the distribution must be made within one taxable year of the recipient; (2) it must include the entire balance credited to an employee's account; and (3) it must be made on account of an employee's death, separation from service (except in the case of a self-employed person), or attainment of age $59\frac{1}{2}$ (or, in the case of a self-employed person only, on account of disability).

Mandatory Employee Contributions: Contributions made by an employee in order to become eligible to participate under a plan.

Master Plan: A retirement plan that is sponsored by a financial institution such as an insurance company, bank, mutual fund, or stock brokerage firm, and that may be adopted by an employer merely by executing a participation agreement.

Matching Contribution: Any (1) employer contribution (including a contribution made at the employer's discretion) to a defined contribution plan on account of an employee contribution to a plan maintained by the employer; (2) employer contribution (including a contribution made at the employer's discretion) to a defined contribution plan on account of an elective deferral; and (3) forfeiture allocated on the basis of employee contributions, matching contributions, or elective deferrals. It is sometime referred to as a "qualified matching contribution" or "QMAC".

Minimum Coverage Requirement: A retirement plan must satisfy one of two coverage tests in order to qualify for favorable tax treatment: (1) the ratio percentage test or (2) the average benefit test.

Minimum Funding Standards: To ensure that sufficient money will be available to pay promised retirement benefits, minimum funding standards have been established for defined benefit plans, money purchase pension plans, and target benefit plans. A plan will be treated as satisfying the minimum funding standard for a plan year if: (1) in the case of a defined benefit plan that is not a multiemployer plan, the employer makes contributions to the plan not less than the minimum required contribution for the plan year; (2) in the case of a money purchase pension plan that is not a multiemployer plan, the employer makes contributions to the plan for the plan year required under the terms of the plan; and (3) in the case of a multiemployer plan, the employers make contributions to the plan sufficient to ensure that the plan does not have an accumulated funding deficiency as of the end of the plan year.

Minimum Required Contribution: With respect to any plan year of a defined benefit plan that is not a multiemployer plan: (1) in any case in which the value of assets of the plan is less than the funding target of the plan, the sum of: (a) the target normal cost for the plan year, (b) the shortfall amortization charge if any for the plan year, and (c) the waiver amortization charge if any for the plan year, and (2) in any case in which the value of assets of the plan equals or exceeds the funding target of the plan, the target normal cost of the plan for the plan year reduced by such excess.

Minimum Participation Requirement: In addition to the minimum coverage requirement, a minimum participation requirement must be met by defined benefit plans in order to be qualified.

Money Purchase Pension Plan: A defined contribution plan under which the employer's contributions are mandatory and are usually based on each participant's compensation. Retirement benefits under the plan are based on the amount in the participant's individual account at retirement.

Multiemployer Plan: A pension plan, maintained under a collective bargaining agreement, that covers the employees of more than one employer. Generally, the various employers are not financially related but rather are engaged in the same industry.

Named Fiduciary: A fiduciary who is named in the plan instrument or identified through a procedure set forth in the plan. One of the distinguishing features of the named fiduciary is that he or she has the authority to designate others to carry out fiduciary responsibilities (e.g., invest the plan funds).

Negative Election 401(k) Plan: Now referred to as automatic contribution arrangements. An employee is deemed to have elected to have the employer contribute a percentage of the employee's compensation to the plan under a cash-or-deferred election unless the employee specifically elects in writing not to defer compensation. In other words, the employee does not make an affirmative election to contribute. See **401(k) Plan**.

Net Unrealized Appreciation (NUA): Special rules apply to appreciated stock and other securities of the employer that are included in a lump-sum distribution. These rules apply to employer securities distributed from an ESOP or from any other type of qualified retirement plan. The gain on the securities while they were held by the qualified retirement plan (the net unrealized appreciation) is not subject to tax until the securities are sold by the recipient, at which time the gain is eligible for capital gains treatment.

NHCE: See **Non-Highly Compensated Employee.**

Noncontributory Plan: A pension plan under which employees are eligible to participate and receive accrued benefits without contributing to the plan.

Nondiscrimination Requirements: A retirement plan is a qualified plan only if the contributions or the benefits provided under the plan do not discriminate in favor of HCEs. A plan will satisfy this nondiscrimination rule only if it complies *both* in form and in operation with the requirements promulgated by IRS.

Nonelective Contribution: A contribution to a cash-or-deferred arrangement other than an elective deferral. (An elective deferral is a participant-elected contribution that the participant could have chosen to receive instead as cash.) It is sometimes referred as a "qualified nonelective contribution" or "QNEC". If the amount of the nonelective contribution depends on the amount of a participant's elective deferral, it is an "employer matching contribution."

Nonforfeitable Benefits: Benefits that cannot be lost by a participant even if he or she terminates service with the employer before qualifying for full retirement benefits. The nonforfeitable benefits are determined by applying the years of credited service to the vesting schedule used by the plan. See also **Vested Benefits.**

Non-Highly Compensated Employee (NHCE): An employee who is not a highly compensated employee.

Normal Retirement Age: The earlier of (1) the time specified in the plan as the normal retirement age or (2) the later of the time a participant attains age 65 or the fifth anniversary of the participant's date of initial plan participation. A qualified retirement plan must provide that an employee's right to benefits is nonforfeitable once the employee reaches the plan's normal retirement age.

Notice of Intent to Terminate (NOIT): The 60-day advance notice to affected parties advising them of a proposed standard termination of a defined benefit plan covered by PBGC.

Notice of Plan Benefits: The notice to participants and beneficiaries to advise them of their benefits under a terminated defined benefit plan covered by PBGC.

Officer: An administrative executive of a corporate employer who is in regular and continued service. One employed for a special and single transaction or one who has only nominal administrative duties is excluded.

Old Age, Survivors, and Disability Insurance (OASDI): Payroll tax imposed on employers that is equal to a set percentage of the wages paid to employees. The OASDI tax rate is used for purposes of providing for permitted disparity in a defined contribution plan and a simplified employee pension (SEP). Social Security payroll taxes also include Medicare taxes. See also **Permitted Disparity.**

1 Percent Owner: Any person who owns, directly or indirectly, more than 1 percent of the stock of the employer. If the employer is not a corporation, the ownership test is applied to the person's capital or profits interest in the employer. A 1 percent owner is a key employee only if his or her annual compensation from the employer is more than $150,000. See also **Key Employee** and **Top-Heavy Plan.**

One-Year Break in Service: A calendar year, a plan year, or any other consecutive 12-month period designated in the plan during which an employee does not complete more than 500 hours of service. An employee's one-year break in service has significance in terms of eligibility and vesting of benefits.

Owner-Employee: A sole proprietor or a partner who owns more than 10 percent of either the capital interest or the profits interest in a partnership.

Partial Termination: Reducing benefits or making participation requirements less liberal, although not amounting to a complete termination of the plan, may be considered a partial termination, resulting in the vesting of accrued benefits for at least part of the plan. The typical types of partial terminations include: the employer closing a plant and thereby substantially reducing the percentage of employees participating under the plan, the reduction of benefits for participating employees, the substantial reduction of contributions to the plan, and the exclusion of a group of employees from participation after they were included in the plan.

Party in Interest: A party which, because of his or her or its relationship with the plan (e.g., as a fiduciary, provider of services, or the plan sponsor), is prohibited from entering into certain transactions with the plan. See also **Prohibited Transactions.**

Pension Annuitants Protection Act (PPA '94): Enacted on October 22, 1994. This act permits a participant, beneficiary, or fiduciary to bring an action if the purchase of an insurance or annuity contract in connection with the termination of a person's status as a plan participant would violate fiduciary standards.

Pension Benefit Guaranty Corporation (PBGC): A nonprofit corporation, functioning under the jurisdiction of the Department of Labor, that is responsible for insuring pension benefits.

Pension Funding Equity Act of 2004 (PFEA): Enacted on April 10, 2004. This Act makes significant changes to the way in which a defined benefit plan computes its funding obligations. Specifically, the Act replaces use of the 30-year Treasury bond interest rate used in determining required plan funding contributions. In its place, defined benefit plans may now use a rate based on long-term investment grade corporate bonds, as specified by IRS.

Pension Plan: A retirement plan that provides retirement income to employees.

Pension Protection Act of 2006 (PPA): Signed into law on August 17, 2006. The most comprehensive pension legislation since ERISA. Among its many provisions, the changes contained in EGTRRA 2001 have been made permanent. Other changes affect minimum funding rules, reporting and disclosure, PBGC, investment of plan assets, prohibited transactions, fiduciary rules, plan contributions and benefits, plan distributions, rollovers, plan qualification, plan administration, and IRAs and Roth IRAs.

Permitted Disparity: The use of Social Security to determine contributions in a defined contribution plan and benefits in a defined benefit plan. Prior to TRA '86, this was referred to as integration.

Phased Retirement Program: A written, employer-adopted program pursuant to which employees may reduce the number of hours they customarily work beginning on or after a retirement date specified under the program and receive phased retirement benefits.

Plan Administrator: The person or persons responsible for administering a qualified retirement plan. Generally, the plan administrator is a person specifically designated by the qualified retirement plan as the administrator. If no person or group is designated, the employer is the administrator; and, if a plan administrator cannot be determined, the plan administrator is the person or persons actually responsible for control, disposition, or management of the property received by the qualified retirement plan.

Plan Year: Any 12-consecutive-month period that has been chosen by the plan for keeping its records. The 12-month period may be the calendar year, a fiscal year, or a policy year (if insurance is used to fund all plan benefits). The plan year does not have to coincide with the employer's taxable year or begin on the first day of the month. Change of a plan year usually requires the consent of IRS.

PPA: See **Pension Protection Act of 2006**.

Prefunding Balance: An amount maintained for a plan consisting of a beginning balance of zero and increased by the amount of excess contributions.

Private Letter Ruling (Priv Ltr Rul): A private ruling issued by IRS in response to a request from a taxpayer as to the tax consequences of a proposed or completed transaction. Private letter rulings are published informally by several publishers. They are not considered as precedents for use by taxpayers other than the one that requested the ruling, but they do give an indication of IRS's current attitude as to a particular type of transaction.

Profit Sharing Plan: A defined contribution plan under which the employer agrees to make discretionary contributions (usually out of profits). A participant's retirement benefits are based on the amount in his or her individual account at retirement.

Prohibited Transactions: Specified transactions that may not be entered into (directly or indirectly) by a party in interest with the plan. Those include, for example, sales or exchanges, leases, and loans between the parties. The Department of Labor may exempt a specific transaction or grant a class exemption from the prohibited transactions restriction. See also **Party in Interest.**

Prototype Plans: See **Master Plan.**

Prudent-Person Rule: The standard under which a fiduciary must act. The fiduciary is required to act "with the care, skill, prudence, and diligence under the circumstances then prevailing that a prudent person acting in a like capacity and familiar with such matters would use in the conduct of an enterprise of a like character and with like aims."

QACA: See **Qualified Automatic Contribution Arrangement.**

QDRO: See **Qualified Domestic Relations Order.**

Qualified Automatic Contribution Arrangement (QACA): An automatic contribution arrangement that satisfies certain requirements is treated as meeting the ADP test with respect to elective deferrals and the ACP test with respect to matching contributions.

Qualified Cash-or-Deferred Arrangement: See **401(k) Plan.**

Qualified Default Investment Alternative: An investment alternative available to participants and beneficiaries in a self-directed account plan.

Qualified Distributions: A distribution from a designated Roth account or Roth IRA that is not includible in the recipient's gross income.

Qualified Domestic Relations Order (QDRO): A court order issued under state domestic relations law that relates to the payment of child support or alimony or to marital property rights. A QDRO creates or recognizes an alternate payee's right, or assigns to an alternate payee the right, to receive plan benefits payable to a participant. The alternate payee may be the participant's spouse, former spouse, or dependent.

Qualified Election Period: The six-plan-year period beginning with the plan year after the first plan year beginning after 1986 in which the employee is a qualified participant and during which the employee can make a diversification election.

Qualified Joint and Survivor Annuity (QJSA): An immediate annuity for the life of the participant, with a survivor annuity for the life of the participant's spouse. The amount of the survivor annuity may not be less than 50 percent, nor more than 100 percent, of the amount of the annuity payable during the time that the participant and spouse are both alive.

Qualified Optional Survivor Annuity: An annuity for the life of the participant with a survivor annuity for the life of the spouse that is equal to the applicable percentage of the amount of the annuity that is payable during the joint lives of the participant and the spouse and that is the actuarial equivalent of a single annuity for the life of the participant. For example, if the survivor annuity provided by the QJSA under the plan is less than 75 percent of the annuity payable during the joint lives of the participant and spouse, the applicable percentage is 75 percent.

Qualified Participant: An employee who has completed at least ten years of participation in an ESOP and has attained age 55.

Qualified Preretirement Survivor Annuity (QPSA): An immediate annuity for the life of the surviving spouse of a participant who dies before the annuity starting date.

Qualified Retirement Plan (Qualified Plan): A plan that meets the requirements of the Internal Revenue Code (generally Section 401(a)). The advantage of qualification is that the plan is eligible for special tax considerations. For example, employers are permitted to deduct contributions to the plan even though the benefits provided under the plan are deferred to a later date.

Qualified Replacement Plan: A plan into which at least 25 percent of the reversion from a terminated defined benefit plan is transferred in order to reduce the excise tax on reversions from 50 percent to 20 percent.

Qualified Replacement Property: Any security issued by a domestic operating corporation that did not have passive investment income (e.g., rents, royalties, dividends, or interest) that exceeded 25 percent of its gross receipts in its taxable year preceding the purchase.

Qualified Rollover Contribution: No rollover contribution may be made to a Roth IRA unless it is a qualified rollover contribution. A qualified rollover contribution is a rollover contribution to a Roth IRA from another Roth IRA or from an IRA, provided that certain requirements are satisfied. For distributions made after December 31, 2007, a Roth IRA can accept rollovers from other eligible retirement plans.

Qualified Securities: Employer securities that (1) are issued by a domestic corporation that for one year before and immediately after the sale has no readily tradable stock outstanding, and (2) have not been received by the seller as a distribution from a qualified retirement plan or pursuant to an option or other right to acquire stock granted by the employer.

Quality Assurance Bulletin (QAB): IRS issues QABs on topics of interest to ensure the consistent processing of case files. QABs are a resource intended for IRS use and may not be relied upon. They are updated periodically to reflect changes in position or procedures.

REA: Retirement Equity Act of 1984. This act, among other things, reduced the age requirement for participation in a plan; increased the period of service considered for vesting purposes; broadened the survivor-benefit requirements; and allowed the assignment or alienation of benefits in divorce proceedings.

Replacement Period: The period beginning three months before the date of sale of employer securities to an ESOP and ending 12 months after the sale. The qualified replacement property must be purchased during this period.

Reportable Event: An event that may indicate that the plan is in danger of being terminated. ERISA requires plan administrators and sponsors of certain defined benefit plans to notify the PBGC of the occurrence of such event so as to give the PBGC enough time to protect the benefits of participants and beneficiaries. The notice must usually be given within 30 days of the occurrence of the reportable event unless the PBGC waives notice.

Required Beginning Date: The date on which plan or IRA distributions must commence to be paid.

Required Minimum Distribution: The minimum amount that must be paid each year commencing with the required beginning date.

Retirement Income Account: A defined contribution program established or maintained by a church-related organization to provide 403(b) plan benefits for its employees or their beneficiaries. A retirement income account is treated as a 403(b) contract, and amounts paid by an employer to a retirement income account are treated as amounts contributed by the employer for a 403(b) contract for the employee on whose behalf the account is maintained.

Retirement Protection Act of 1994 (RPA '94): Part of GATT enacted on December 8, 1994. The primary purpose of this act was to strengthen PBGC. Among its provisions: removed impediments to funding certain plans; phased out the PBGC variable-rate premium cap; rounded down cost-of-living adjustments; and extended IRS user fee program.

Rev Proc: A revenue procedure issued by IRS. It is somewhat similar to a revenue ruling, but deals with procedural matters or details the requirements to be followed in connection with various dealings with IRS. Also sets forth (at times) guidelines that IRS follows in handling certain tax matters.

Rev Rul: A public revenue ruling issued by IRS. These rulings express IRS's views as to the tax results that apply to a specific problem.

Reversion of Employer Contributions: A qualified plan (or trust) is prohibited from diverting corpus or income for purposes other than the exclusive benefit of employees. However, this prohibition does not preclude the return of a contribution made by an employer if the contribution was made, for example, by reason of a mistake of fact or conditioned on the qualification of the plan or the deductibility of the contribution.

Rollover: A tax-free transfer of cash or other assets from one retirement plan to another. An IRA account owner may shift assets from his or her present IRA to another. Certain payouts from a qualified retirement plan may also be rolled over to an IRA or to another employer's plan.

Rollover IRA Account: An individual retirement account that is established for the purpose of receiving a distribution from a qualified retirement plan.

Roth IRA: An IRA to which contributions are nondeductible and from which all distributions may be nontaxable.

S Corporation: A corporation whose shareholders have elected not to be taxed as a regular (or "C") corporation, but like a partnership, with profits and losses passing through directly to the shareholders, rather than at the corporate level. Subject to a number of requirements, an ESOP may be a shareholder of an S corporation.

Salary-Reduction Arrangement: Under this type of cash-or-deferred arrangement, each eligible employee may elect to reduce his or her current compensation or to forgo a salary increase and have these amounts instead contributed to the plan on his or her behalf on a pre-tax basis. See also **Cash-or-Deferred Plan.**

Salary Reduction Catch-Up Contributions: An individual who participates in a 401(k) plan or 403(b) plan, who will attain age 50 by the end of the plan year and for whom no other elective contributions may otherwise be made for the plan year because of the application of any limitation contained in the IRC or in the plan, will be able to make additional elective contributions to the plan for that plan year.

Sarbanes-Oxley Act of 2002: This act (the Public Company Accounting Reform and Investor Protection Act of 2002) was signed into law on July 30, 2002. The act bars company directors and executive officers from trading in employer securities during a blackout period imposed on participants in individual account plans of the employer, requires plan administrators to provide at least 30 days advance notice of blackout periods to participants and beneficiaries under individual account plans, and increases criminal penalties for willful violations of ERISA's requirements. In addition, the act contains a prohibition on loans to company officers, which may be interpreted as preventing company officers from taking loans from 401(k) plans maintained by the company.

Saver's Credit: An eligible individual may be allowed a nonrefundable tax credit for the taxable year in an amount equal to the applicable percentage of the individual's qualified retirement savings contributions for the year up to $2,000.

Savings Incentive Match Plan for Employees (SIMPLE): A simplified retirement plan structured as an IRA plan or a 401(k) plan that allows employees to make elective contributions and requires employers to make matching or nonelective contributions.

Savings Plan: See **Thrift Plan.**

SBA '96: See **Small Business Job Protection Act of 1996.**

SCP: See **Self-Correction Program.**

Section 204(h) Notice: A written notice concerning a plan amendment that provides for a significant reduction in the rate of future benefit accrual, including any elimination or significant reduction of an early retirement benefit or retirement-type subsidy. The plan administrator is required to provide in this notice, in a manner calculated to be understood by the average plan participant, sufficient information to allow participants to understand the effect of the amendment.

Section 411(d)(6) Protected Benefits: Benefits, early retirement benefits, retirement-type subsidies, and optional forms of benefit are Section 411(d)(6) protected benefits to the extent they have accrued and cannot, therefore, be eliminated, reduced, or made subject to employer discretion except to the extent permitted by regulations.

Section 415 Limitations: A retirement plan will not be qualified if: (1) in the case of a defined benefit plan, the annual benefit with respect to any participant for any limitation year exceeds certain limitations, or (2) in the case of a defined contribution plan, the annual additions credited with respect to any participant for any limitation year exceed certain limitations. See also **Annual Addition** and **Annual Retirement Benefit**.

Section 417(a)(3) Explanation: The written explanation required to be provided a participant with respect to a QJSA or a QPSA.

Self-Correction Program (SCP): IRS program designed to allow plan sponsors to correct insigificant operational failures at any time and to correct significant operational failures within a two-year period.

Self-Directed Account Plan: An individual account plan that permits a participant to make an independent choice from a broad range of investment alternatives regarding the manner in which any portion of the assets in the participant's individual account is invested.

Self-Employed Person: A sole proprietor or a partner in a partnership.

SEP: See **Simplified Employee Pension**.

Separate Line of Business: All employees of a single employer are taken into account for purposes of applying the minimum coverage requirement and, if applicable, the minimum participation requirement. However, if an employer is treated as operating qualified separate lines of business, the employer is permitted to apply the minimum coverage requirement separately with respect to the employees of each qualified separate line of business. A similar exception (but only with IRS consent) is provided for purposes of applying the minimum participation requirement.

Shortfall Amortization Base: For a plan year, the funding shortfall minus the present value of the aggregate total of the shortfall amortization installments and waiver amortization installments.

Shortfall Amortization Charge: The aggregate total of the shortfall amortization installments for a plan year with respect to the shortfall amortization bases.

Shortfall Amortization Installments: The amounts necessary to amortize the shortfall amortization base of the plan for any plan year in level annual installments.

SIMPLE: See **Savings Incentive Match Plan for Employees.**

Simplified Employee Pension (SEP): A retirement program that takes the form of individual retirement accounts for all eligible employees (subject to special rules on contributions and eligibility).

Single Employer Pension Plan Amendments Act (SEPPAA): The Act that changed the single-employer defined benefit plan termination rules of Title IV of ERISA.

Small Business Job Protection Act of 1996 (SBA '96): Enacted on August 20, 1996. This act adopted many pension simplification provisions.

SMM: See **Summary Description of Material Modifications**.

Social Security Retirement Age (SSRA): For purposes of calculating adjustments with respect to formulas in defined benefit plans using permitted disparity, the age used as the retirement age under the Social Security Act (rounded to the next lower whole number) that depends on the calendar year of birth.

SPD: See **Summary Plan Description.**

Split-Funded Plan: A plan that is funded in part by insurance contracts and in part by funds accumulated in a separate trusteed fund.

Spousal IRA: An IRA that is established for the nonworking spouse of an employee who qualifies for an IRA. The total amount of allowable annual contributions to the working spouse's IRA and to the spousal IRA is double the dollar amount in effect for the taxable year (or 100 percent of the working spouse's earnings if less). The contributions to both IRAs need not be split equally between the spouses. However, the maximum IRA contribution on behalf of either spouse is the dollar amount in effect for the taxable year. A spousal Roth IRA is also permitted.

SSRA: See **Social Security Retirement Age.**

Standard Termination: The termination of a single-employer defined benefit plan covered by PBGC that is able to pay all its benefit liabilities.

State Income Taxation of Pension Income Act of 1995: Enacted on January 10, 1996. This act prohibits states from taxing the retirement income payments of their former residents.

Stock Bonus Plan: A defined contribution plan that is similar to a profit sharing plan except that benefit payments generally must be made in employer company stock. See also **Profit Sharing Plan** and **Employee Stock Ownership Plan.**

Subchapter S Corporation: See **S Corporation.**

Summary Description of Material Modifications (SMM): Any change in the provisions of the plan or in the administration of the plan that constitutes a material modification must be disclosed to participants and beneficiaries. See **Summary Plan Description**.

Summary Plan Description (SPD): A detailed, but easily understood, summary describing a retirement plan's provisions that must be provided to participants and beneficiaries.

Table 2001: Costs applied to current life insurance protection provided under the plan for purposes of determining the amount of the participant's tax liability for the coverage.

TAMRA: Technical and Miscellaneous Revenue Act of 1988. Contained many corrections to and clarification of OBRA '87 and TRA '86.

Target Benefit Plan: A cross between a defined benefit plan and a money purchase plan. Similar to a defined benefit plan, the annual contribution is determined by the amount needed each year to accumulate a fund sufficient to pay a targeted retirement benefit to each participant on reaching retirement. Similar to a money purchase plan, contributions are allocated to separate accounts maintained for each participant.

Target Normal Cost: The present value of all benefits that are expected to accrue or to be earned under the plan during the plan year.

Tax Increase Prevention and Reconciliation Act of 2005 (TIPRA): Enacted on May 17, 2006. This act contains a provision repealing the income limits on conversions of traditional IRAs to Roth IRAs, starting in 2010. TIPRA also imposes an excise tax on any entity manager of a tax-exempt entity who knowingly approves a prohibited tax-shelter transaction.

Tax Reform Act of 1984 (TRA '84): Enacted on July 18, 1984. This act, among other things, delayed, until 1988, cost-of-living increases in contributions and benefits; repealed the estate tax exclusion for death benefits from a pension plan or an IRA; allowed partial distributions from a pension plan to be rolled over to an IRA; and applied restrictive distribution rules to 5 percent owners only.

Tax Reform Act of 1986 (TRA '86): Enacted on October 22, 1986. This act made such major changes to the Code that it resulted in the Code being renamed the "Internal Revenue Code of 1986."

Tax-Sheltered Annuity (TSA): See **403(b) Plan**.

Tax Technical Corrections Act of 1998 (TTC '98): Enacted on July 22, 1998 as Title IV of the Internal Revenue Service Restructuring and Reform Act of 1998. This act made significant changes to the Roth IRA.

Taxable Year: The 12-month period used by an employer to report income for income tax purposes. The employer's taxable year does not have to coincide with the year used by the plan to keep its records.

Taxpayer Relief Act of 1997 (TRA '97): Enacted on August 5, 1997. This act contained many provisions affecting qualified retirement plans and IRAs and also created the Roth IRA.

TEFRA: Tax Equity and Fiscal Responsibility Act of 1982. Lowered limits on contributions and benefits for corporate plans; certain loans from plans to be treated as distributions; reduced estate tax exclusion for retirement plan death benefits to maximum of $100,000; repealed special Keogh plan and S corporation restrictions; added "top-heavy" plan requirements.

10 Percent Tax on Early Distributions: If an individual receives a distribution from a qualified plan, including an IRA and a 403(b) plan, prior to age 59 $\frac{1}{2}$, the individual's tax for the taxable year in which the distribution is received is increased by an amount equal to 10 percent of the portion of the distribution includible in gross income, unless an exception applies.

Thrift Plan: A defined contribution plan that is contributory in the sense that employer contributions are geared to mandatory contributions by the employee. Employer contributions are made on a matching basis—for example, 50 percent of the total contribution made by the employee.

TIPRA: See **Tax Increase Prevention and Reconciliation Act of 2005.**

Top-Heavy Plan: A plan that primarily benefits key employees is considered top-heavy and qualifies for favorable tax treatment only if, in addition to the regular qualification requirements, it meets several special requirements. See also **Key Employee.**

TRA '97: See **Taxpayer Relief Act of 1997.**

Treasury Regulations: Regulations promulgated by the Treasury Department. IRS is a part of the Treasury Department, and regulations interpreting the Internal Revenue Code are technically Treasury regulations.

Trust: A fund established under local trust law to hold and administer the assets of a plan.

Trustees: The parties named in the trust instrument or plan that are authorized to hold the assets of the plan for the benefit of the participants. The trustees may function merely in the capacity of a custodian of the assets or may also be given authority over the investment of the assets. Their function is determined by the trust instrument or, if no separate trust agreement is executed, under the trust provisions of the plan.

TSA: See **403(b) plan.**

TTC '98: See **Tax Technical Corrections Act of 1998.**

Unemployment Compensation Amendments of 1992 (UC '92): Enacted on July 3, 1992. The tax measure expanded rollover rules and introduced mandatory income tax withholding on certain plan distributions.

Uniformed Services Employment and Reemployment Rights Act of 1994 (USERRA): Enacted on October 13, 1994. This act prohibits discrimination against employees because of membership in the uniformed services.

Unit Benefit Plan: A type of defined benefit pension plan that calculates benefits on the basis of units earned by the employee during his or her employment, taking into consideration length of service as well as compensation.

User Fee: The fee charged by IRS for each request for a determination letter, letter ruling, opinion letter, and other similar rulings or determinations.

VCP: See **Voluntary Correction Program with Service Approval.**

Vested Benefits: Accrued benefits of a participant that have become nonforfeitable under the vesting schedule adopted by the plan. Thus, for example, if the schedule provides for vesting at the rate of 20 percent per year, a participant who has been credited with three years of service has a right to 60 percent of the accrued benefit. If he or she terminates service without being credited with any additional years of service, he or she is entitled to receive 60 percent of the accrued benefit.

VFC Program: See **Voluntary Fiduciary Correction Program.**

Volume Submitter Plan: Under the volume submitter program, a practitioner who qualifies may request IRS to issue an advisory letter regarding a volume submitter specimen plan. A specimen plan is a sample plan of a practitioner (rather than the actual plan of an employer) that contains provisions that are identical or substantially similar to the provisions in plans that such practitioner's clients have adopted or are expected to adopt.

Voluntary Contributions: Amounts that a participant voluntarily contributes to a plan in addition to the contributions made by the employer. Voluntary contributions, unlike employer contributions, are not deductible on the employee's tax return.

Voluntary Correction Program with Service Approval (VCP): A program that permits plan sponsors to voluntarily correct qualification failures in a qualified plan, 403(b) plan, SEP, or SIMPLE IRA and to obtain a compliance statement that provides that the corrections are acceptable and that IRS will not pursue disqualification of the plan.

Voluntary Fiduciary Correction Program: A program designed to encourage the voluntary and timely correction of possible fiduciary breaches by allowing the avoidance of potential ERISA civil actions initiated by DOL and assessment of civil penalties.

Waiver Amortization Base: The amount of the waived funding deficiency for a plan year.

Waiver Amortization Charge: The aggregate total of the waiver amortization installments with respect to the waiver amortization bases for a plan year.

Waiver Amortization Installments: The amounts necessary to amortize the waiver amortization base of the plan for any plan year in level annual installments.

Withdrawal Liabilities: An employer that withdraws from a multiemployer plan is liable for its proportionate share of unfunded vested benefits, determined as of the date of withdrawal. The liability is imposed upon withdrawal without reference to the plan's termination.

Worker, Retiree, and Employer Recovery Act of 2008 (WRERA 2008): Signed into law on December 23, 2008. This act suspended required minimum distributions for 2009, mandated nonspouse beneficiary rollovers, and provided funding relief for defined benefit plans, among other provisions.

Working Families Tax Relief Act of 2004: Enacted on October 4, 2004. Among other changes and technical corrections affecting qualified retirement plans, the act reflected the modified treatment of elective deferrals for purposes of the employer deduction limits, by removing elective deferrals from consideration in the application of the exception to the 10 percent excise tax on nondeductible contributions.

WRERA 2008: See **Worker, Retiree, and Employer Recovery Act of 2008.**

Year of Service: A 12-month period during which an employee is credited with at least 1,000 hours of service. For 403(b) plan purposes, a different calculation is made.

Index

[*References are to question numbers.*]

A

Abandoned plans, termination of, 25:64

Abusive transactions
anti-abuse provisions, 27:76
Roth IRAs, 31:4
tax avoidance transactions, EPCRS and, 19:4
vesting, 9:6

Accelerated benefit distributions
limitations on, 8:6
pension benefits, younger participants, 4:1

Accountants
fiduciaries, as, 23:10
operation of plan, role of, 20:31

Accrued benefits
amendment to reduce or stop benefit accruals, 25:60
defined, 9:2
defined benefit plans
cash balance formula, conversion of defined benefit plan with traditional formula to, 9:3
contingent accruals, 2:3
exceeding TRA '86 requirements, 6:33
freezing of accruals, partial terminations, 25:5
statutory hybrid plans, 2:24
failure of employee to accrue, 5:20
freezing of accruals, defined benefit plans, 9:11, 25:5
funding limits on benefits and benefit accruals, 8:6
future benefit accruals
optional form of benefit, elimination of, 10:39
limits on benefits and benefit accruals, funding-based, 8:6

termination of plan, effect on, 25:4
top-heavy plans, 26:2
vesting
amendment to reduce accrued benefits, 9:25, 9:52
amendment to reduce future accruals, 9:36
cost-of-living adjustments, 9:25
decrease because of increasing age or service, 9:26
definition, 9:2
disregarding of accrued benefits, 9:24
elimination or reduction of accrued benefits, 9:35
freezing of accruals, defined benefit plans, 9:11, 25:5
future accruals of benefits, amendment of plan to reduce, 9:36
minimum vesting standards (*See* Minimum vesting standards)
reduction of benefits, 9:25

Accumulated funding deficiencies, 8:8, 8:22

ACH. *See* Automated clearing house (ACH)

ACP test. *See* Actual contribution percentage (ACP) test

Acquisitions. *See also* Mergers and acquisitions
ESOPs, use of to finance, 28:29
property for resale, 12:22

Actions against fiduciaries. *See* Fiduciaries

Active participants. *See specific topic*

Actual contribution percentage (ACP) test
acquisition or disposition, effect of, 4:19
applicability of, 6:37
employer matching contributions, 3:1
failure to satisfy, 5:19
correction methods, 19:32
VCS program and, 19:31, 19:32

Benefit and contribution limitations (*cont'd*)
qualified joint and survivor annuities
(QJSAs), 6:18
qualified retirement plans, generally (*See also
lines throughout this topic*)
ACP test, 6:37
annual compensation limit, 6:45-6:50
deductible employee contributions, 6:40
disqualification of plan, 6:57
employee contributions, 6:37-6:38
nonqualified retirement plans compared,
1:12
self-employed individuals, amount of
contribution, 6:63
12-month period other than plan year, use
of, 6:47
voluntary contributions, limitations on,
6:38
rehired employees, 6:12
restorative payments, 6:34
rollovers
annual benefit attributable to rollover
contributions from annual benefit, 6:15
Section 415 regulations
effective date, 6:1
incorporation by reference, 6:4–6:5
qualification requirements, effect on, 6:10
self-employed individuals, 6:59-6:63
both self-employed and employee of
another employer, 6:62
compensation, defined, 6:71
defined, 6:60
earned income, defined, 6:61
generally, 6:41, 6:59
qualifications to claim deductions, 6:59
special rules for, 6:71
severance from employment, 6:43
defined, 6:8
dollar and compensation limits, increase,
6:12
and high three-years of service, 6:13
simplified employee pensions (SEPs)
annual addition limitation, contributions
treated as compensation, 6:41
disqualification of plan, 6:57
stock bonus plans, provisions, 6:3
straight-life annuity, 6:14
paid in form other than, 6:18
successor employers, aggregation of plans,
6:52
tax deduction rules, 12:25
$10,000 exception, application to, 6:21
terminated plan, benefits provided under,
6:17
12-month period other than plan year, use
of, 6:47
$200,000 cap on compensation, 6:46, 6:50
$245,000 cap on compensation, 6:46

voluntary contributions, 6:15
tax advantages of, 6:39
Benefiting under plan, employee treated as,
5:20
Benefit limitations. *See* Benefit and
contribution limitations
Benefit plan investors
defined, 23:30
level of participation, 23:29
Benefits, rights, and features
corrective amendments, 4:20
nondiscrimination requirements, 4:10, 4:20
life insurance, 15:16
**Bernard L. Madoff Investment Securities
LLC,** 2:3
Black Lung Law, 25:55
Blackout periods
Sarbanes-Oxley Act of 2002, 1:24
notice for, 20:22
self-directed account plans, 23:14
**Block trading, prohibited transaction
exemption,** 24:9, 24:14
Board of directors
termination of plan, 25:2
Bonding of plan officials
ERISA fidelity bonds, losses covered by,
20:33
fiduciaries, exemption, 20:37
funds or other property, defined, 20:35
generally, 20:32
handling of funds, defined, 20:36
increase of funds handled during plan year,
20:43
losses covered by ERISA fidelity bond,
20:33
more than one plan, bond insuring, 20:41
omnibus clause, 20:42
only one participant in plan, 20:39
parties in interest, 20:38
SIMPLE IRAs, 20:40
simplified employee pensions (SEPs), 20:40
who must be bonded, 20:34
Bonds
funding and corporate bond performance,
8:2
long-term investment grade corporate
bond, 2:24
Bonuses
closely held corporation, working owner of,
1:2
Break in service
maternity or paternity period of absence,
5:14
one-year, 5:10

Defined contribution plans. (*cont'd*)
money purchase pension plans (*See* Money purchase pension plans)
multiemployer plans
offset of benefit, 2:22
mutual funds, investment in
prohibited transactions, 24:1
nondiscrimination requirements, 4:20
contribution amounts, 4:12
cross-testing, 4:22-4:24
normal retirement age, 10:55
overall limitation, amount of, 35:29
professional employer organizations (PEOs), 4:1
profit sharing plans (*See* Profit sharing plans)
prohibited transactions
mutual funds, investment in, 24:1
pro rata share of administrative expenses charged, 23:34
QDROs, 36:14
QPSAs, 10:9
required minimum distributions (RMDs), 11:20-11:27
amount used for determining, 11:21
applicable distribution period, 11:22
calendar year, for, 11:20
death, applicable distribution period for RMDs after, 11:23
distribution period, 11:22, 11:23
distributions taken into account, 11:27
excise taxes, 11:69
individual account, amount used for determining, 11:21
life expectancies used to determine, 11:24
lifetime of employee, applicable distribution period, 11:22
more than one designated beneficiary, 11:25
rollovers, 34:1
segregated share rule, 11:43
separate account rule, 11:43
sole designated beneficiary, distribution period, 11:22
suspension of, 11:41, 34:11, 34:29
vesting, effect of, 11:26
withholding, 34:8
reversions
qualified replacement plans, 25:53
rollovers
account balances, payments from, 34:10
reasonable actuarial assumptions, 34:9
self-employed individuals, 12:14
SEPs (*See* Simplified employee pensions (SEPs))
SIMPLE plans (*See* SIMPLE plans (Savings incentive match plans for employees))
split into defined benefit plan and defined

contribution plan
vesting, 9:56
stock bonus plans (*See* Stock bonus plans)
summary plan descriptions (SPDs) and, 22:4
survivor benefits
automatic survivor benefit requirements, 10:18
transferee plans, 10:13
target benefit plans (*See* Target benefit plans)
tax deduction rules
definition of compensation, 12:15
excess assets transferred from defined benefit plan, 12:23
limitation on contributions, 12:8, 12:17
restorative payments, 12:2
Section 415 limits, deductions to provide benefits in excess of, 12:25
self-employed individuals, limitations on contributions, 12:14
termination of plan, 25:1
defined benefit plan, conversion from, 25:6
factors causing, 25:3
underfunded plans, 25:63
thrift or savings plans (*See* Thrift or savings plans)
top-heavy plans (*See also* Top-heavy plans)
defined, 26:3
defined benefit plans *also* maintained by employer, 26:48
minimum contribution requirements, 26:41, 26:44
transfer of benefits between defined benefit plans and defined contribution plans, 9:32
25 percent of compensation limitation, 12:17
underfunded plans
determination letters, 18:18
termination of, 25:63
uniform allocation formula, 4:12
VCS, 19:32
vesting
amendment to reduce accrued benefits, 9:25
anti-cutback rule and, 9:28
employee contributions, 9:9
in-kind distributions, 9:31
mergers and acquisitions, 9:56
one-year break in service, 9:17
separate accounts, 9:2
spinoffs, 9:56
split into defined benefit plan and defined contribution plan, 9:56
transfer of benefits between defined benefit plans and defined contribution plans, 9:32

balance, effect on value of plan assets, 8:5
bankruptcy
  limits on benefits and benefit accruals,
    funding-based, 8:6
benefits and benefit accruals, funding
  limits, 8:6
change in plan's funding method, approval by
  IRS, 8:15
collective bargaining agreements
  limits on benefits and benefit accruals,
    funding-based, 8:6
conditional funding waivers, 8:24
controlled groups
  funding standard accounts, separate, 8:21
and corporate bonds, performance, 8:2
defined benefit plans
  assets, valuation, 8:19
  costs, 2:19, 2:20, 8:14
  limits on benefits and benefit accruals,
    funding-based, 8:6
  minimum required contribution, 8:2
  quarterly contributions, 8:32
80 percent, percentage less than, 8:6
elections, 8:5
endangered status, plan in, 8:8
and excess contributions, 8:5
frozen plans
  limits on benefits and benefit accruals,
    funding-based, 8:6
funding-based limits on benefits and benefit
  accruals, 8:6
funding standard account
  defined, 8:20
  separate accounts, maintenance of, 8:21
funding standard carryover balance
  limits on benefits and benefit accruals,
    funding-based, 8:6
funding target attainment percentage
  (FTAP)
  defined, 8:2
funding target, defined, 8:2
insurance contract plans
  defined, 8:11
  pension plans, conversion to, 8:12
investment earnings, effect of, 8:18
IRS approval of change in method, 8:15
and mandatory employer contributions, 8:2
minimum funding standards (See Minimum
  funding standards)
minimum required contributions
  defined, 8:2
  funding balances reducing, 8:5
money purchase pension plans
  minimum required contribution, 8:2
multiemployer plans

additional rules, 8:8
annual notice, 8:7
enrolled actuary, change in, 8:8
method, changes to, 8:8
penalties, 8:8
standard account, 8:8
waivers, 8:24
multiple employer plans, 8:5
  special rules, 8:9
notice requirements
  annual notice, 8:7
overstatement of pension liabilities,
  penalty, 8:16
pension plans
  funding standard account, defined,
    8:20
  investment earnings, 8:18
  normal retirement age, effect of, 8:17
plan amendments
  limits on benefits and benefit accruals,
    funding-based, 8:6
plan assets, effect of balance on value of,
  8:5
prefunding balance, 8:5
  limits on benefits and benefit accruals,
    funding-based, 8:6
prohibited payments, 8:6
quarterly contributions, 8:32
reduction of balances, 8:5
segmented interest rate, 8:2
shortfall amortization charge, 8:2
  defined, 8:3
single-employer plans, 8:19
  annual notice, 8:7
  costs, 8:14
60 percent, percentage more than, 8:6
software, valuation, changes in, 8:15
target benefit plans
  minimum required contribution, 8:2
target normal cost, defined, 8:2
termination of plan
  limits on benefits and benefit accruals,
    funding-based, 8:6
unconditional funding waivers, 8:24
waiver amortization charge, 8:2, 8:4
waivers, 8:24
yield curve, 8:2

**Funding target attainment percentage
(FTAP),** 8:6
defined, 8:2

FUTA. *See* Federal Unemployment Taxes Act
(FUTA)

Future benefit accruals. *See* Accrued
benefits

G

Gains and losses
ESOPs, sale of securities, deferral of gain, 28:34-28:48

Garnishments
IRAs, 30:51
qualified retirement plans, 4:29, 4:30

Geographic location, classification by
qualified retirement plans, 1:46

Gifts, Roth IRAs, 31:31

Gift tax
and life insurance, 15:15

Government agencies, reporting to,
21:1-21:36
automated clearing house (ACH), 21:27
bankruptcy, 21:30
counting of participants for premium filing, 21:28
criminal penalties, ERISA, 21:12
distress terminations, 21:23, 21:30
DOL, 21:11, 21:12, 21:21
due date for premium filings, 21:24
filing of forms with PBGC, 21:36
IRS, 21:1-21:10, 21:13-21:19 (See also Internal Revenue Service (IRS))
large plans, 21:24, 21:33
mid-sized plans, 21:24, 21:33
newly covered plans, 21:25
new plans, 21:25
PBGC, 21:22-21:36
    automated clearing house (ACH), 21:27
    completion of filing, 21:27
    due date for premium filings, 21:24
    large plans, 21:24, 21:33
    mid-sized plans, 21:24, 21:33
    small plans, 21:24
    who must file with, 21:23
"plans without employees," 21:21
premium filing
    counting of participants for, 21:28
    participant, defined, 21:28
    PBGC Comprehensive Premium Filing, 21:27, 21:31
small plans, 21:24
termination of plan, 21:23
    distress terminations, 21:23, 21:30
unfunded vested benefits, 21:29, 21:30

Governmental employees and plans
determination letters, 18:7
401(k) plans, nondiscrimination and coverage requirements, 27:12
403(b) plans, 35:1
QDROs, 36:8
Railroad Retirement Acts, 25:12

required minimum distributions (RMDs)
    generally, 11:1
state or local government plans, 35:40
termination of plan, 25:12

GO Zone. See Gulf Opportunity Zone Act of 2005 (GO Zone)

Grantor attained annuity trusts
structured as grantor trust, transfers to, 28:42

Green cards
foreign country, contributions to pension scheme for aliens not green card holders, 27:1

Gross income exclusion
403(b) plans, 35:12

Gross income inclusion
direct rollovers, 34:21
403(b) plans, employee contributions, 35:23-35:24
pure life insurance, costs included in, 15:8
unused PTO, dollar equivalent, 27:4

Group term life insurance
annual addition limitation, contributions treated as compensation, 6:41

Guaranteed annuity contracts (GACs)
Rollovers as Business Start-ups (ROBS), 4:2

Guaranteed benefits
phase-in rules, 25:20
termination of plan, 25:16-25:21

Guaranteed investment contracts (GICs)
Rollovers as Business Start-ups (ROBS), 4:2

Gulf Opportunity Zone Act of 2005 (GO Zone), 1:29

GUST
remedial amendment period for changes, 19:27

H

Handling of funds, defined
bonding of plan officials, 20:36

Hardship. See also Hardship distributions
minimum funding standards, waivers of alternatives if IRS will not waive standards, 8:29
rollovers, waiver of 60-day rollover period, 34:36
temporary substantial business hardship, 8:24

Hardship distributions
allocation of basis, 35:42
amendment of standards, elimination or

M

O

W

Withdrawal liability of employer
multiemployer plans (*See* Multiemployer
plans)

Withholding
automatic withholding rules
effective date, 20:19
20 percent automatic withholding,
20:10–20:12
defined contribution plans
required minimum distributions (RMDs),
34:8
direct rollovers
generally, 20:10
20 percent automatic withholding, 20:10
distributions, 20:10–20:19
employer securities, 20:16
failure to withhold, liabilities, 20:13
generally, 20:10
property other than cash distributed,
20:15
20 percent automatic withholding,
20:10–20:12
types of retirement plans subject to rules,
20:14
eligible rollover distributions
automatic withholding rules, 20:11, 20:19
employer securities, exception from
withholding, 20:16
generally, 20:10
loans from qualified retirement plans,
20:18
more than 20 percent withheld, 20:12
required minimum distributions (RMDs),
11:41
20 percent automatic withholding, 20:10,
20:11
200, amount less than, 20:17
failure to withhold, liabilities, 20:13
loans from qualified retirement plans,
14:11, 20:18
property other than cash distributed, 20:15
required minimum distributions (RMDs),
20:10
mandatory 20 percent income tax
withholding, 11:41
saver's credit and, 17:12

**Worker Adjustment and Retraining
Notification Act of 1988 (WARN),** 2:3

**Worker, Retiree, and Employer Recovery Act
of 2008 (WRERA 2008),** 1:36
defined benefit plans
tax deduction rules, 12:18
defined benefit plans and defined contribution
plans, employee participating in both,
12:21
multiemployer plans, underfunded plans,
29:1

reporting requirements, 21:6
required minimum distributions (RMDs)
defined contribution plans, 11:20
and modification of procedures, 11:1
rollovers
one rollover per year rule, 34:1
unemployment compensation and, 34:1
Roth IRAs, rollovers, 31:40
unemployment compensation
rollovers and, 34:1

Working Families Tax Relief Act of 2004,
1:26

Wrap fees
IRAs, 30:31

WRERA 2008. *See* Worker, Retiree, and
Employer Recovery Act of 2008 (WRERA
2008)

Written explanation
eligible rollover distributions, 34:29
ESOPs
sale of securities, deferral of gain, 28:39
403(b) plans
extension of, 35:9
safe harbors, 35:51
QJSAs and QPSAs, 10:20, 10:31
Section 417(a)(3) Explanation, 10:33

Y

Years of service
allocation rates, cross-testing, 4:23
benefit and contribution limitations
maximum annual retirement benefit and,
6:22
controlled group of corporations, 5:11
defined, 5:8
disregarding
accrual purposes, 9:24
eligibility purposes, 5:12
vesting, 9:12, 9:21
eligibility, years taken into account, 5:11
controlled group of corporations, 5:11
past service with former employer, 5:13
predecessor of employer, 5:11
403(b) plans, exclusion allowance, 35:24,
35:25
hours of service
calculation of, 5:9
crediting, 5:9
defined, 5:9
elapsed time method of calculating, 5:9,
9:10
maternity or paternity period of absence,
5:14